PREFACE

We at AMG Publishers are doing our best to make every word of the Bible understandable to the English reader by reference to the original manuscripts. *The Complete Word Study Old Testament* is one more result of the desire of our president, Dr. Spiros Zodhiates, to see this accomplished.

Our first effort was to provide the *Hebrew Greek Key Study Bible*, available in the King James Version or the New American Standard, thus making it possible for all to benefit by referring to the original Hebrew and Greek words. This Bible, however, contains only the explanations of certain key words, with grammatical codes being used only in the New Testament.

The second step was to provide *The Complete Word Study New Testament* in the King James Version. This work gives every word in the New Testament a grammatical code which explains its structure as it is used in the Greek text. In addition, a number over each word identifies it according to the numbering system of James Strong's *Exhaustive Concordance of the Bible*. This New Testament also contains a Greek concordance and has a section indicating all the Greek words which an English word represents in translation. Word studies expound upon key words, and footnotes explain key passages.

With that basic word and grammar identification, the next step was the creation of a companion volume, a lexicon of the Greek New Testament. *The Complete Word Study Dictionary: New Testament* is a complete dictionary of every word in the Greek New Testament. In addition to a complete definition for each word, the dictionary includes a discussion of the theological importance of some words, as well as derivatives, synonyms, and antonyms of words when such exist.

We now present the ultimate tool for the study of the Old Testament. Each word in the Hebrew Old Testament is represented by a number and a grammatical code that are printed above the English text. The number corresponds to the original Hebrew word in Strong's *Dictionary of the Hebrew Bible* and the Lexical Aids (both of which appear in the Study Helps section at the back). The grammatical codes identify the forms and parts of speech of the Hebrew and Aramaic words and are explained in the Grammatical Notations section of the Study Helps.

Included in the Study Helps is a Translational Reference Index. This index makes it possible to find, by Strong's number, all the Hebrew words that a particular English word represents in the King James Version of the Old Testament.

Although we have labored to make this work free from error, we are not infallible. If you should find a mistake, please let us know.

Warren Baker
AMG Publishers

EXPLANATION OF GENERAL FORMAT

PLACEMENT OF NOTATIONS AND NUMBERS

In most cases, grammatical notations associated with a word are placed directly before the Strong's number representing that word. However, certain grammatical particles are not assigned numbers in Strong's dictionary and therefore have only notations. The opposite also occurs, as is the case with *eth* (853, the sign of the object), which was not assigned a grammatical notation because it is not technically assigned a part of speech, is not translatable, and is the only word that serves the function. Notations and numbers are placed above the word they designate (whenever possible) or are placed as close as possible above the word(s) with which they are associated.

When two English words placed next to each other represent a single Hebrew word, the grammatical notation and number of that Hebrew word are placed above and between the two English words. (For procedures adopted when three or more adjacent English words are used to translate a single Hebrew word, see WORD CLUSTERS, below.)

When two or more Hebrew words are represented by a single English word, a virgule (slash) is used to separate the respective notations and numbers (e.g., "prison" [Gen. 39:20], which is coded cs,nn1004/df,nn5470).

On occasion, words which appear in the Hebrew text are not translated into English. Such words are depicted by having their corresponding notations and/or numbers placed in parentheses above the text in the position that the English translation best allows. If a word represented by a Strong's number is not translated, but some of the grammatically coded preformatives and/or sufformatives attached to it are, the notations for those preformatives and sufformatives will be placed before the parentheses that enclose the Strong's number of the word to which they are attached.

The less common stems of the Hebrew and Aramaic languages, some of which it can be debated are not separate stems at all, but are actually morphemic variants of the traditional stems, have not been given separate codes within the work. Instead, they have been coded with the codes of the stems from which they are derived, but with an asterisk added to the end of the code. Hence, a participle in the hithpalpel stem, which is derived from and has the same meaning as a participle in the hithpael stem, would have the code htpt*. Two less common stems, however, because they constitute compounded stems with separate meaning, have been coded separately. These are the hothpael and nithpael stems. (For a list of the irregular stems and how each is coded, see the "List of Irregular Verb Forms" in the Study Helps section of the book.)

Words in the original text that are neither Hebrew nor Aramaic, such as the Egyptian word *'avrēkh* (86), have not been given grammatical codes.

WORD CLUSTERS are groups of three or more adjacent English words which are connected with each other. These have been set off by asterisks between each word in that cluster. Asterisks have been placed after the first word in the cluster, before the last word in the cluster, and between intervening words. Word clusters have been used in the following instances:

WORD STUDY OLD TESTAMENT

pl,nn,pnx6862   qpf**1961**   pp,nn**7218**   pl,qpta,pnx341   qpf7951   cj3588   nn**3068**
5 Her adversaries are the chief, her enemies prosper; for the LORD hath
hipf,pnx3013   pr5921   cs,nn7230   pl,nn,pnx**6588**   pl,nn,pnx5768   qpf**1980**
afflicted her for the multitude of her transgressions: her children are gone into
nn**7628**   pp,pl,cs,nn**6440**   cc6862
captivity before the enemy.

pr4480   nn1323   nn6726 cs,nn3605   nn,pnx**1926**   wcs,qmf3318   pl,nn,pnx**8269**
6 And from the daughter of Zion all her beauty is departed: her princes are
qpf**1961**   pp,pl,nn354   qpf4672 ptn**3808**   nn4829   wcs,qmf**1980** pp,ptn**3808**   nn3581
become like harts (*that*) find no pasture, and they are gone without strength
pp,pl,cs,nn**6440**   qpta7291
before the pursuer.

nn3389   qpf**2142**   pl,cs,nn**3117**   nn,pnx6040   wcj,pl,nn,pnx4788
7 Jerusalem remembered in the days of her affliction and of her miseries
cs,nn3605   pl,nn,pnx4262   pnl834   qpf**1961** pr4480/pl,cs,nn**3117**   nn**6924**   nn,pnx5971 pp,qnc**5307**
all her pleasant things that she had in*the*days of old, when her people fell
pp,cs,nn**3027**   nn6862   wcj,ptn369   qpta5826 pp,pnx   pl,nn6862   qpf,pnx**7200**
into the hand of the enemy, and none did help her: the adversaries saw her,
qpf7832 pr5921   pl,nn,pnx4868
and did mock at her sabbaths.

nn3389   qpf**2398**/nn**2399**   pr5921/ad**3651**   qpf**1961**   pp,nn5206   cs,nn3605
8 Jerusalem hath grievously sinned; therefore she is removed: all that
pl,pipt,pnx**3513**   hipf,pnx2151   cj3588   qpf**7200**   nn,pnx**6172**   ad1571 pnp1931   nipf584
honored her despise her, because they have seen her nakedness: yea, she sigheth,
wcs,qmf**7725**   nn268
and turneth backward.

nn,pnx**2932**   pp,pl,nn,pnx7757   qpf**2142**   ptn**3808**   nn,pnx319
9 Her filthiness *is* in her skirts; she remembereth not her last end; therefore
wcs,qmf3381   pl,nn**6382**   pp,pnx   ptn369   nn3068   qmv**7200**   (853)
she came down wonderfully: she had no comforter. O LORD, behold my
nn,pnx6040 cj3588   qpta341   hipf1431
affliction: for the enemy hath magnified *himself*.

nn6862   qpf6566   nn,pnx**3027**   pr5921 cs,nn3605   pl,nn,pnx4261
10 The adversary hath spread out his hand upon all her pleasant things:
cj3588   qpf**7200**   pl,nn1471   qpf935   nn,pnx**4720**   pnl834
for she hath seen *that* the heathen entered into her sanctuary, whom thou didst
pipf**6680**   ptn**3808** qpf935   pp,pnx   dfp,nn**6951**
command *that* they should not enter into thy congregation.

cs,nn3605   nn,pnx**5971**   pl,nipt584   pl,pipt1245   nn3899   qpf**5414**
11 All her people sigh, they seek bread; they have given their
pl,nn,pnx4262   pp,nn400   pp,hinc**7725**   nn**5315** qmv**7200**   nn**3068**   wcj,himv5027 cj3588
pleasant things for meat to relieve the soul: see, O LORD, and consider; for I am
qpf**1961**   qpta2151
become vile.

ptn**3808**   pr,pnx413   cs,nn3605   pl,cs,qpta**5674**/nn**1870**   himv5027   wcj,qmv**7200** cj518
☞12 *Is it* nothing to you, all ye that pass by? behold, and see if
pta3426   nn4341   pp,nn,pnx4341 pnl834   (pupf***5953**)   pp,pnx   pnl834
there be any sorrow like unto my sorrow, which is done unto me, wherewith the
nn**3068**   hipf3013   pp,cs,nn**3117**   cs,nn2740 nn,pnx**639**
LORD hath afflicted *me* in the day of his fierce anger.

☞ 1:12 Some have compared this verse to Jesus' sorrow when he looked at Jerusalem and saw the impending destruction of the city, even as Jeremiah had seen in his day (Matt. 23:37–39; Luke 13:34, 35). Others suggest that this verse refers to Christ's agony on the cross of Calvary, as he cried for those who are separated from God as a result of sin. The true sorrow is seen in that it has been inflicted on Christ by God Himself (Luke 23:26–38).

ITALICS are used in the text to indicate words which are not found in the Hebrew but are implied by it.

PARENTHESES around a notation and/or a number indicate that the corresponding Hebrew word has not been translated into English.

KEYS indicate explanatory notes at the bottom of the page.

ASTERISKS in the codes indicate verb forms that are irregular, which are discussed in the List of Irregular Verb Forms.

ABBREVIATIONS

abs. (absolute)
acc. (accusative)
act. (active)
adj. (adjective, adjectival)
adv. (adverb, adverbial, adverbially)
ant. (antonym)
Aram. (Aramaic)
art. (article)
ASV (American Standard Version)
attrib. (attributive)
cf. (compare, comparison)
chap. (chapter)
class. (classify, classified, classification)
coll. (collective)
com. (common)
comp. (compound, compounds)
conj. (conjunction, conjunctive)
const. (construct)
def. (definite)
deriv. (derivative[s], derivation)
E. (East)
e.g. (for example)
emph. (emphatic)
Eng. (English)
etc. (and so forth)
f. (following)
ff. (following in the plural)
fem. (feminine)
fut. (future)
hith. (hithpael)
ibid. (in the same place)
i.e. (that is)
imper. (imperative)
imperf. (imperfect)
indef. (indefinite, indefinitely)
inf. (infinitive)
intens. (intensive)
interj. (interjection)
intrans. (intransitive)
KJV (King James Version)
loc. (location)
masc. (masculine)

mid. (middle)
MS (manuscript)
MSS (manuscripts)
MT (Masoretic text
N. (North)
NEB (New English Bible)
N.E. (Northeast)
N.W. (Northwest)
NASB (New American Standard Bible)
NIV (New International Version)
NKJV (New King James Version)
NT (New Testament)
neg. (negative)
neut. (neuter)
nom. (nominative)
obj. (object, objective[ly])
OT (Old Testament)
p. (page), pp. (pages)
part. (participle, participial)
pass. (passive)
perf. (perfect)
pl. (plural)
poss. (possessive)
prep. (preposition)
pres. (present)
priv. (privative)
pron. (pronoun)
RSV (Revised Standard Version)
S. (South)
S.E. (Southeast)
S.W. (Southwest)
Sept. (Septuagint)
sing. (singular)
subst. (substantive)
subj. (subject, subjective)
s.v. (under the word)
syn. (synonym, synonymous)
trans. (transitive, transitively)
v. (verse), vv. (verses)
voc. (vocative)
vol. (volume)
W. (West)

THE BOOKS OF THE BIBLE

THE OLD TESTAMENT

Book	Abbrev.	Book	Abbrev.
Genesis	Gen.	Ecclesiastes	Eccl.
Exodus	Ex.	Song of Solomon	Song
Leviticus	Lev.	Isaiah	Is.
Numbers	Num.	Jeremiah	Jer.
Deuteronomy	Deut.	Lamentations	Lam.
Joshua	Josh.	Ezekiel	Ezek.
Judges	Judg.	Daniel	Dan.
Ruth	Ruth	Hosea	Hos.
1 Samuel	1 Sam.	Joel	Joel
2 Samuel	2 Sam.	Amos	Amos
1 Kings	1 Kgs.	Obadiah	Obad.
2 Kings	2 Kgs.	Jonah	Jon.
1 Chronicles	1 Chr.	Micah	Mic.
2 Chronicles	2 Chr.	Nahum	Nah.
Ezra	Ezra	Habakkuk	Hab.
Nehemiah	Neh.	Zephaniah	Zeph.
Esther	Esth.	Haggai	Hag.
Job	Job	Zechariah	Zech.
Psalms	Ps.	Malachi	Mal.
Proverbs	Prov.		

THE NEW TESTAMENT

Book	Abbrev.	Book	Abbrev.
The Gospel According to:		Thessalonians	2 Thess.
Matthew	Matt.	1 Timothy	1 Tim.
Mark	Mark	2 Timothy	2 Tim.
Luke	Luke	Titus	Titus
John	John	Philemon	Phile.
Acts	Acts	Hebrews	Heb.
Romans	Rom.	James	James
1 Corinthians	1 Cor.	1 Peter	1 Pet.
2 Corinthians	2 Cor.	2 Peter	2 Pet.
Galatians	Gal.	1 John	1 John
Ephesians	Eph.	2 John	2 John
Philippians	Phil.	3 John	3 John
Colossians	Col.	Jude	Jude
1 Thessalonians	1 Thess.	Revelation	Rev.

CONTRIBUTORS

Dr. Warren Baker, former seminary professor, is the general editor of this work. Dr. Baker is the director of the Special Projects department, AMG Publishers' department for research and development.

The staff of the Special Projects department: Jeff and Patricia Ferrell, Amy Huber, David Kemp, Mark Oshman, Tim Rake, Sam Wallace, and Tim Wehse. These people are responsible for the research and preparation of this project.

Rev. George A. Hadjiantoniou, Ph.D., who has taught theology, Greek grammar, and exegesis in seminaries and universities in Europe and Canada. Dr. Hadjiantoniou carefully read over the grammatical codes used in the work and helped to code some of the books.

Typist who prepared the manuscripts: Lynda Greeley.

Volunteers who assisted in proofreading, checking the correctness of the Strong's numbers, Scripture references, and English grammar: Miss Dorothy Boyse, Mr. and Mrs. Jim Gee, and Alma Stewart.

CONTENTS

THE OLD TESTAMENT

STUDY HELPS

Old Testament

The Book of
GENESIS

The name "Genesis" comes from a Greek word meaning "beginning." This word was the title of the book in the Septuagint, the ancient Greek translation of the Old Testament. The Hebrew name for Genesis is $b^e r\bar{e}'sh\bar{\imath}th$, "in the beginning." The Hebrews often identified the books of the Old Testament by the first word of the text. In this way when a scroll was unrolled they were able to tell immediately which book it contained.

Aside from Genesis, there are no other writings that inform us of the major events which predated Moses. The first part of the book describes the key events in the early history of man. The remainder of the book records the history of the patriarchs.

Genesis was written in a prescientific age and was not meant to be a scientific document. Consequently, only divine inspiration can account for the perfect accuracy of its technical information. In Genesis, it is made clear that all things were designed and created by God and continue to operate within the boundaries of His purpose. Although the human race departed from God's original plan, God has lovingly provided a way for men to be reconciled to Him.

Though the Book of Genesis contains no express record as to who wrote the book, there are no compelling reasons for denying that Moses is the author, not only of Genesis, but of all five books of the Pentateuch. The unity of the Pentateuch is attested to in various portions of the Old Testament, as well as in portions of the New Testament. Even the opening phrase of the Book of Exodus, "Now these are the names," provides clear evidence to that unity. The Hebrew prefix that is translated "now" is the common form of the conjunction in Hebrew (most often translated "and" or "but") and indicates that there was some other book which preceded the Book of Exodus. Jesus refers to Moses as an author of Scripture in Luke 16:31; 24:44; and John 5:46, 47. And in John 7:23, the New Testament refers to circumcision as a part of the Law of Moses (see Gen. 17:12; Ex. 12:48; Lev. 12:3).

It has also been suggested that Moses made use of certain documents and oral traditions to write the book. Certain terms have been cited as proof of the previous authorship of certain portions. For instance, the term $t\bar{o}l^e d\bar{o}th$ (pl. of $t\bar{o}l^e d\bar{a}h$ [8435]), "generations," is said to be used to identify the author or the possessor of certain portions (Gen. 6:9; 11:27). The "looking over" or "familiarity with" other writings is not unheard of among the biblical writers, nor is it contrary to biblical inspiration (see Luke 1:1–4). However, it must be remembered that the actual writing of the Book of Genesis was done by Moses, under the inspiration of the Holy Spirit.

The Book of Genesis is an appropriate introduction to the entire Bible. It provides answers for the universal questions of the origin of all living things, the universe, sin, and evil in the world. More than half of human history is covered in its fifty chapters. However, the Book of Genesis is not merely the introductory book of the Pentateuch, but rather the foundation of it, of the whole Old Testament, of the whole of the Scriptures. Without the Book of Genesis, what would be known of the creation of the universe, the fall of man, the judgment of God, or the promise of redemption? Since God is invisible, man may know of Him only through His works, which are seen in nature, revealed in Scripture, and accomplished in the life of the believer. And how deficient would our knowledge of God be without this book! Are not "His eternal power and Godhead" displayed in His creation (Ps. 19:1; Rom. 1:20)?

Yet the creation, in all that it portrays of the divine Creator, is not sufficient in its instruction to provide man with the knowledge necessary to attain salvation. At this point as well, however, the Book of Genesis lays the foundation of all the Scripture. For the book is not limited to the account of creation, but rather emphasizes the fact that the world was founded by God, that man was created in righteousness and true holiness, but that man fell by his own disobedience, and therefore was cursed by God. Furthermore, the first promise of a Redeemer, by whom the curse of death would be vanquished, is found in this book (Gen. 3:15, 16). The remainder of the Book of Genesis is in fact the first chapter of the history of redemption, in which God chose the seed of Abraham to be the line of the Messiah and the heirs of the promise (Gen. 12:1–3; Matt. 1:17; Gal. 3:6–9, 29).

Creation

1

pp,cs,nn**7225**   pl,nn**430**   qpf**1254**   (853)   df,du,nn**8064**   wcj(853)   df,nn**776**

In the beginning God created   the heaven and   the earth.

wcj,df,nn**776** qpf**1961**   nn**8414**   wcj,nn**922**   wcj,nn**2822**   pr**5921**

2 And the earth was without form, and void; and darkness *was* upon

pl,cs,nn**6440**   nn**8415**   wcj,cs,nn**7307**   pl,nn**430**   pipt**7363**   pr**5921**   pl,cs,nn**6440**

the face of the deep. And the Spirit of God moved upon the face of the

df,pl,nn**4325**

waters.

1:1 – 2:4   The chronology which one often finds in the marginal notes of many of the older Bibles, notably in the Authorized Version of King James, is *not* a part of the Bible itself by any means! Archbishop Usher arrived at the date of 4004 B.C. by using his calculations of the years in the patriarchal genealogies (Gen. 5; 11). A comparison of these genealogies with those in the Gospels will reveal that biblical genealogies are not necessarily complete by design nor were they given to allow us to calculate the span of time between various events in the early history of man. They present certain significant names and omit others. Therefore, they cannot be used to establish the date of creation. The earliest time from which we can calculate calendar years with approximate accuracy is the time of Abraham. The age which one prescribes for the earth is extremely dependant on one's view of creation.

There are five major theories on the interpretation of the six days of creation. The pictorial day theory claims that the six days mentioned in Genesis are the six days during which God revealed the events of creation. But the Bible relates the creation as clearly, simply, and historically as it does any other event. To interpret the text in this manner requires the abandonment of all exegetical principles.

The gap view claims that Genesis 1:1 describes an original creation which was followed by the fall of Satan and great judgment. Genesis 1:2 is then supposed to be a description of the re-creation or restoration that took place (see the note on Genesis 1:2). Exodus 20:11 teaches that all the universe, including the heavens and the earth (Gen. 1:1), was created in the six day period mentioned in the first chapter of Genesis.

The intermittent day view claims that the days mentioned are literal days, but that they are separated by

pl,nn430 wcs,qmf559   qcj1961 nn216   wcs,qmf1961 nn216
3 And God said, Let there be light: and there was light.

pl,nn430 wcs,qmf7200 (853)   df,nn216 cj3588   aj2896   pl,nn430 wcs,himf914/pr996   df,nn216
4 And God saw the light, that *it was* good: and God divided the light
wcj,pr996   df,nn2822
from the darkness.

pl,nn430 wcs,qmf7121   pp,nn216 nn3117   wcj,pp,nn2822 qpf7121 nn3915
5 And God called the light Day, and the darkness he called Night. And
wcs(qmf1961)   nn6153   nn1242 wcs,qmf1961 nu259 nn3117
the evening and the morning were the first day.

pl,nn430 wcs,qmf559   qcj1961 nn7549   pp,cs,nn8432 dfp,pl,nn4325
6 And God said, Let there be a firmament in the midst of the waters, and
wcj,qcj1961 hipt914/pr996 pl,nn4325   pp,pl,nn4325
let it divide the waters from the waters.

pl,nn430 wcs,qmf6213 (853)   df,nn7549   wcs,himf914/pr996 df,pl,nn4325 pnl834
7 And God made the firmament, and divided the waters which *were*
pr4480/pr8478 dfp,nn7549 wcj,pr996 df,pl,nn4325 pnl834   pr4480/pr5921   dfp,nn7549
under the firmament from the waters which *were* above the firmament: and it
wcs,qmf1961 ad3651
was so.

pl,nn430 wcs,qmf7121 dfp,nn7549 du,nn8064   wcs(qmf1961)   nn6153
8 And God called the firmament Heaven. And the evening and the
nn1242 wcs,qmf1961 nuor8145 nn3117
morning were the second day.

pl,nn430 wcs,qmf559   df,pl,nn4325 pr4480/pr8478 df,du,nn8064   nimf6960   pr413
9 And God said, Let the waters under the heaven be*gathered*together unto
nu259 nn4725   df,nn3004 wcj,nimf7200   wcs,qmf1961 ad3651
one place, and let the dry *land* appear: and it was so.

pl,nn430 wcs,qmf7121 dfp,nn3004   nn776   wcj,pp,cs,nn4723
10 And God called the dry *land* Earth; and the gathering together of the
df,pl,nn4325 qpf7121 pl,nn3220 pl,nn430 wcs,qmf7200 cj3588   aj2896
waters called he Seas: and God saw that *it was* good.

pl,nn430 wcs,qmf559   df,nn776 hicj1876 nn1877 nn6212 hipt2232 nn2233
11 And God said, Let the earth bring forth grass, the herb yielding seed, *and*

---

long periods of time. However, unless all the creative activity is limited to the literal days, this view is in direct contradiction to Exodus 20:11.

The day–age theory claims that the word *yōm* (3117), which is the Hebrew word for "day," is used to refer to periods of indefinite length, not to literal days. While this is a viable meaning of the word (Lev. 14:2, 9, 10) it is not the common meaning, nor is it the meaning of the word sufficient foundation for the theory.

The literal day theory accepts the clear meaning of the text: the universe was created in six literal days. The various attempts to join together the biblical account of creation and evolution are not supportable even by the various gap theories because the order of creation is in direct opposition to the views of modern science (e.g., the creation of trees before light). The phrase "evening and morning" indicates literal days (cf. Dan. 8:14 where the same phrase in the Hebrew is translated "day").

☞ 1:1 God of His own free will and by His absolute power called the universe into being, creating it out of nothing (see Ex. 20:11; Ps. 33:6, 9; 102:25; Is. 45:12; Jer. 10:12; John 1:3; Acts 14:15; 17:24; Rom. 4:17; Col. 1:15–17; Heb. 3:4; 11:3; Rev. 4:11). When one acknowledges the absolute power of God, he must accept His power to create and destroy as stated in the Scriptures. There are many concepts such as this in Scripture which the finite mind cannot completely grasp. The believer must accept those things by faith (Heb. 11:3).

☞ 1:2 The Old Scofield Bible maintains that the condition of the earth in verse two is the result of judgment, and therefore interprets the verb *hāyāh* (1961) as "became." However, the Hebrew construction of verse two is disjunctive, describing the result of the creation described in verse one. The phrase "without form and void" is often misunderstood because of this rendering. These words are found only in a few other places (Is. 34:11; 45:18; Jer. 4:23). They do not describe chaos, but rather emptiness. A better translation would be "unformed and unfilled." See the note on Genesis 1:1–2:4.

nn6529 cs,nn6086 qpta**6213** nn6529 pp,nn,pnx4327 pnl834 nn,pnx**2233** pp,pnx pr5921

the fruit tree yielding fruit after his kind, whose seed *is* in itself, upon the

df,nn776 wcs,qmf**1961** ad3651

earth: and it was so.

df,nn776 wcs,himf3318 nn1877 nn6212 hipt2232 nn2233 pp,nn,pnx4327

12 And the earth brought forth grass, *and* herb yielding seed after his kind,

wcj,nn6086 qpta**6213** nn6529 pnl834 nn,pnx**2233** pp,pnx pp,nn,pnx4327 pl,nn430

and the tree yielding fruit, whose seed *was* in itself, after his kind: and God

wcs,qmf7200 cj3588 aj2896

saw that *it was* good.

wcs(qmf**1961**) nn6153 nn1242 wcs,qmf**1961** nuor7992 nn3117

13 And the evening and the morning were the third day.

pl,nn**430** wcs,qmf559 qcj1961 pl,nn3974 pp,cs,nn7549 df,du,nn**8064**

14 And God said, Let there be lights in the firmament of the heaven to

pp,hinc**914**/pr996 df,nn3117 wcj,pr996 df,nn3915 wcs,qpf**1961** pp,pl,nn226 wcj,pp,pl,nn4150

divide the day from the night; and let them be for signs, and for seasons,

wcj,pp,pl,nn**3117** wcj,pl,nn8141

and for days, and years:

wcs,qpf**1961** pp,pl,nn3974 pp,cs,nn7549 df,du,nn**8064** pp,hinc215

15 And let them be for lights in the firmament of the heaven to give light

pr5921 df,nn776 wcs,qmf**1961** ad3651

upon the earth: and it was so.

pl,nn**430** wcs,qmf**6213** (853) du,cs,nu8147 df,aj1419 df,pl,nn**3974** (853) df,aj1419 df,nn3974 pp,cs,nn4475

16 And God made two great lights; the greater light to rule the

df,nn3117 wcj(853) df,aj6996 df,nn3974 pp,cs,nn4475 df,nn3915 wcj(853) df,pl,nn3556

day, and the lesser light to rule the night: *he made* the stars also.

pl,nn**430** wcs,qmf**5414** pnx(853) pp,cs,nn7549 df,du,nn**8064** pp,hinc215

17 And God set them in the firmament of the heaven to give light

pr5921 df,nn776

upon the earth,

wcj,pp,qnc**4910** dfp,nn3117 wcj,dfp,nn3915 wcj,pp,hinc**914**/pr996

18 And to rule over the day and over the night, and to divide the

df,nn216 wcj,pr996 df,nn2822 pl,nn**430** wcs,qmf7200 cj3588 aj2896

light from the darkness: and God saw that *it was* good.

wcs(qmf**1961**) nn6153 nn1242 wcs,qmf**1961** nuor7243 nn3117

19 And the evening and the morning were the fourth day.

pl,nn**430** wcs,qmf559 df,pl,nn4325 qmf8317 nn8318

20 And God said, Let the waters bring*forth*abundantly the moving creature

nn5315/aj2416 wcj,nn5775 pimf*5774 pr5921 df,nn776 pr5921 pl,cs,nn**6440**

that hath life, and fowl *that* may fly above the earth in the open

cs,nn7549 df,du,nn**8064**

firmament of heaven.

pl,nn**430** wcs,qmf1254 (853) df,aj1419 df,pl,nn**8577** wcj(853) cs,nn3605 df,aj2416 cs,nn5315

21 And God created great whales, and every living creature that

df,qpta7430 pnl834 df,pl,nn4325 qpf8317 pp,nn,pnx4327 wcj(853)

moveth, which the waters brought*forth*abundantly, after their kind, and

cs,nn3605 nn3671 cs,nn5775 pp,nn,pnx4327 pl,nn**430** wcs,qmf7200 cj3588 aj2896

every winged fowl after his kind: and God saw that *it was* good.

pl,nn**430** wcs,pimf1288 pnx(853) pp,qnc559 qmv6509 wcj,qmv7235 wcj,qmv4390

22 And God blessed them, saying, Be fruitful, and multiply, and fill

(853) df,pl,nn4325 dfp,pl,nn3220 wcj,df,nn5775 qcj7235 dfp,nn776

the waters in the seas, and let fowl multiply in the earth.

wcs,qmf**1961**) nn6153 nn1242 wcs,qmf**1961** nuor2549 nn3117

23 And the evening and the morning were the fifth day.

pl,nn**430** wcs,qmf559 df,nn776 hicj3318 aj2416 nn5315

24 And God said, Let the earth bring forth the living creature after his

pp,nn,pnx4327   nn929   wcj,nn7431   wcj,cs,nn**2416**   nn776   pp,nn,pnx4327

kind, cattle, and creeping thing, and beast of the earth after his   kind: and it

wcs,qmf**1961** ad**3651**

was   so.

pl,nn**430** wcs,qmf**6213** (853)   cs,nn**2416**   df,nn776   pp,nn,pnx4327   wcj(853) df,nn929

25 And God made   the beast of the earth after his   kind,   and   cattle

pp,nn,pnx4327   wcj(853)   cs,nn3605   cs,nn7431   df,nn127

after their   kind,   and   every thing that creepeth upon the earth after his

pp,nn,pnx4327   pl,nn**430** wcs,qmf**7200** cj3588   aj**2896**

kind: and God   saw   that *it was* good.

pl,nn**430** wcs,qmf559   qmf6213   nn120   pp,nn,pnx6754   pp,nn,pnx1823

☞ 26 And God said, Let us make man in our image, after our likeness: and let

wcj,qmf**7287**   pp,cs,nn1710   df,nn3220   wcj,pp,cs,nn5775

them have dominion over the   fish of the sea, and over the   fowl   of the

df,du,nn**8064**   wcj,dfp,nn929   wcj,pp,cs,nn3605   df,nn776   wcj,pp,cs,nn3605

air,   and over the cattle, and over   all   the earth, and over   every

df,nn7431   df,qpta7430   pr5921   df,nn776

creeping thing that creepeth upon the earth.

pl,nn**430** wcs,qmf**1254** (853) df,nn**120**   pp,nn,pnx6754   pp,cs,nn6754   pl,nn**430** qpf**1254**

27 So God created   man in his *own* image, in the image of God created he

pnx(853)   nn2145   wcj,nn**5347**   qpf**1254**   pnx(853)

him; male and female created he   them.

pl,nn**430** wcs,pimf**1288** pnx(853)   pl,nn**430** wcs,qmf559   pp,pnx   qmv6509

28 And God blessed   them, and God   said unto them, Be fruitful, and

wcj,qmv7235   wcj,qmv**4390**   (853)   df,nn776   wcj,qmv,pnx3533   wcj,qmv**7287**

multiply, and replenish   the earth, and subdue it: and have dominion over the

pp,cs,nn1710   df,nn3220   wcj,pp,cs,nn5775   df,du,nn**8064**   wcj,pp,cs,nn3605

fish of the sea, and over the   fowl   of the   air,   and over   every

nn**2416**   df,qpta7430   pr5921   df,nn776

living thing that moveth upon the earth.

pl,nn**430** wcs,qmf559   ptdm2009   qpf5414   pp,pnx (853) cs,nn3605 nn6212 qpta2232   nn**2233**

29 And God   said, Behold, I have given you   every herb bearing seed,

pnl834   pr5921   pl,cs,nn**6440**   cs,nn3605   df,nn776   wcj(853) cs,nn3605 df,nn6086   pnl834/pp,pnx

which *is* upon the face   of all   the earth, and   every tree, in the which *is*

cs,nn6529   nn6086   qpta2232   nn**2233**   pp,pnx   qmf**1961**   pp,nn402

the fruit of a tree yielding seed; to you it shall   be   for meat.

☞ **1:26, 27** Is God a singular entity (Deut. 6:4; 32:39; Is. 45:5, 6; John 17:3; 1 Cor. 8:6) or a plural entity (Gen. 3:22; 11:4; 18:1–3; Is. 6:8; 48:16; John 10:30, 34–38)? The Hebrew word for God is *'elōhīm* (430), a plural noun. In Genesis 1:1 it is used in grammatical agreement with a singular verb *bārā'* (1254), "created." When plural pronouns are used, "Let us make man in our image after our likeness," does it denote a plural of number or the concept of excellence or majesty which may be indicated in such a way in Hebrew? Could God be speaking to the angels, the earth, or nature, thus denoting Himself in relation to one of these? Or is this a germinal hint of a distinction in the divine personality? One cannot be certain. Until Jesus came, the essential (internal) unity of the Godhead was not understood to a great extent, though it was intimated (Is. 48:16).

God is essentially Spirit (John 4:24). Therefore, man, who is similar to God, possesses an immortal spirit. Men resemble God in certain respects (Gen. 1:26) without being equal with Him (Is. 40:25). Man's likeness to God is what truly distinguishes him from the rest of creation. Man is a personal being with the power to think, feel, and decide. He has the ability to make moral choices and the capacity for spiritual growth or decline. In the beginning, man loved God and was a holy creature. The Fall changed this. Man's spirit was so altered by sin that he fled from God and now loves evil more than righteousness (John 3:19, 20). After Abraham's time, only those who lived uprightly before God were considered to be his offspring (see Matt. 3:7–10; 13:38; John 12:36; Acts 13:10; Col. 3:6). Man is no longer in the perfect state of innocence as he was at the time of his creation. Therefore, he does not have the same spiritual, God-like attributes and qualities of that original state. Jesus, the last Adam (1 Cor. 15:45), came to undo Satan's works (1 John 3:8) and to restore in man a spiritual likeness to God (2 Cor. 3:18; Eph. 4:24; Col. 3:10)

_{wcj,pp,cs,nn3605 cs,nn2416   df,nn776   wcj,pp,cs,nn3605 cs,nn5775   df,du,nn8064}

30 And to   every   beast of the earth, and to   every   fowl of the   air,

_{wcj,pp,cs,nn3605   qpta7430   pr5921   df,nn776 pnl834/pp,pnx   nn5315/nn2416}

and to every thing that creepeth upon the earth, wherein *there is*   life,   *I have*

_{(853) cs,nn3605 cs,nn3418 nn6212   pp,nn402   wcs,qmf1961 ad3651}

given   every green herb for meat: and it   was   so.

_{pl,nn430 wcs,qmf7200 (853)   cs,nn3605 pnl834   qpf6213   wcj,ptdm2009   ad3966}

31 And God   saw   every thing that he had made, and, behold, *it was* very

_{aj2896   wcs(qmf1961)   nn6153   nn1242   wcs,qmf1961 df,nuor8345 nn3117}

good. And   the evening and the morning   were   the   sixth   day.

_{df,du,nn8064   wcj,df,nn776   wcs,pumf3615   wcj,cs,nn3605   nn,pnx6635}

2 Thus the heavens and the   earth   were finished, and   all   the   host of

them.

_{df,nuor7637 dfp,nn3117 pl,nn430 wcs,pimf3615   nn,pnx4399   pnl834   qpf6213}

2 And on the seventh   day   God   ended   his   work   which   he had made; and he

_{wcs,qmf7673   df,nuor7637 dfp,nn3117 pr4480/cs,nn3605   nn,pnx4399   pnl834   qpf6213}

rested on the seventh   day   from all   his   work   which   he had made.

_{pl,nn430 wcs,pimf1288 (853)   df,nuor7637 cs,nn3117   wcs,pimf6942 pnx(853)   cj3588}

3 And God blessed   the seventh   day, and sanctified   it: because that

_{pp,pnx   qpf7673   pr4480/cs,nn3605   nn,pnx4399 pnl834 pl,nn430 qpf1254   pp,qnc6213}

in it he had rested   from all   his   work   which God created and made.

Adam and Eve in the Garden

_{pndm428   pl,cs,nn8435   df,du,nn8064   wcj,df,nn776}

☞ 4 These *are* the generations of the heavens and of the   earth   when they were

_{pp,ninc,pnx1254   pp,cs,nn3117   nn3068 pl,nn430 qnc6213   nn776   wcj,du,nn8064}

created, in the   day   that the Lord God made the earth and the heavens,

_{wcj,cs,nn3605 cs,nn7880   df,nn7704 ad2962   qmf1961   dfp,nn776   wcj,cs,nn3605 cs,nn6212}

5 And every   plant of the field before it was in the earth, and   every   herb

_{df,nn7704 ad2962   qmf6779 cj3588   nn3068 pl,nn430   ptn3808   hipf4305   pr5921}

of the field before it grew: for the Lord God had   not   caused*it*to*rain upon the

_{df,nn776   ptn369 wcj,nn120   pp,qnc5647 (853)   df,nn127}

earth, and *there was* not   a   man   to   till   the ground.

_{qmf5927   wcj,nn108 pr4480   df,nn776   wcs,hipf8248 (853)   cs,nn3605 pl,cs,nn6440}

6 But there went up a   mist   from the earth, and watered   the whole   face

_{df,nn127}

of the ground.

_{nn3068 pl,nn430 wcs,qmf3335 (853) df,nn120   nn6083 pr4480   df,nn127   wcs,qmf5301}

☞ 7 And the Lord God formed   man *of* the dust   of   the   ground, and breathed

_{pp,du,nn,pnx639   cs,nn5397   pl,nn2416   df,nn120 wcs,qmf1961 aj2416 pp,nn5315}

into his   nostrils   the breath of life; and man became a living soul.

☞ **2:4** It is well known that there seem to be two different accounts of creation in the first two chapters of Genesis, but this need not cause us to conclude that they are incompatible, as some have suggested. The two sections actually complement each other. Genesis 1:1—2:4a presents a wide-angle view of all seven days of creation and deals with the creation of man and woman as a single act. Then in 2:4b–24 the author focuses on the sixth day, giving details which were not mentioned in the overview in chapter one. The separate origins of man and woman are brought into sharp focus. Therefore, chapters one and two are not in chronological sequence, but Genesis 2:4b–24 presents in greater detail some of what Genesis 1:11, 12, 24–31 merely summarizes.

☞ **2:7** The term "soul" has been used in a variety of senses by different writers in the Bible. The Old Testament Hebrew word is *nephesh* (5315) which means "that which breathes." It corresponds to the Greek word *psuché* in the New Testament, which is usually translated "soul" or "life" (see the Lexical Aids section

nn3068   pl,nn430   wcs,qmf5193   nn1588   pr4480/nn6924   pp,nn5731   ad8033   wcs,qmf7760

8 And the LORD God planted a garden eastward in Eden; and there he put

(853)   df,nn120   pnl834   qpf3335

the man whom he had formed.

pr4480   df,nn127   nn3068   pl,nn430   wcs,himf6779   cs,nn3605   nn6086

9 And out of the ground made the LORD God to grow every tree

nipt2530   pp,nn4758   wcj,aj2896   pp,nn3978   wcj,cs,nn6086   df,pl,nn2416

that*is*pleasant to the sight, and good for food; the tree of life also in the

pp,cs,nn8432   df,nn1588   wcj,cs,nn6086   df,nn1847   aj2896   wcj,aj7451

midst of the garden, and the tree of knowledge of good and evil.

wcj,nn5104   qpta3318   pr4480/nn5731   pp,hinc8248   (853)   df,nn1588   wcj,pr4480/ad8033

10 And a river went out of Eden to water the garden; and from thence it

nimf6504   wcs,qpf1961   pp,nu702   pl,nn7218

was parted, and became into four heads.

cs,nn8034   df,nu259   nn6376   pnp1931   df,qpta5437   (853)   cs,nn3605

11 The name of the first is Pison: that is it which compasseth the whole

cs,nn776   df,nn2341   pnl834/ad8033   df,nn2091

land of Havilah, where there is gold;

wcj,cs,nn2091   df,pndm1931   df,nn776   aj2896   ad8033   df,nn916   df,nn7718

12 And the gold of that land is good: there is bdellium and the onyx

wcj,cs,nn68

stone.

wcj,cs,nn8034   df,nuor8145   df,nn5104   nn1521   pnp1931   df,qpta5437

13 And the name of the second river is Gihon: the same is it that compasseth

(853)   cs,nn3605   cs,nn776   nn3568

the whole land of Ethiopia.

wcj,cs,nn8034   df,nuor7992   df,nn5104   nn2313   pnp1931   df,qpta1980

14 And the name of the third river is Hiddekel: that is it which goeth

cs,nn6926   nn804   df,nuor7243   wcj,df,nn5104   (pnp1931)   nn6578

toward the east of Assyria. And the fourth river is Euphrates.

nn3068   pl,nn430   wcs,qmf3947   (853)   df,nn120   wcs,himf,pnx5117   pp,cs,nn1588

15 And the LORD God took the man, and put him into the garden

nn5731   pp,qnc,pnx5647   wcj,pp,qnc,pnx8104

of Eden to dress it and to keep it.

---

for a more complete definition). The term "living soul" does not refer to Adam's spirit as immortal, but simply to the fact that he was a living, physical being. The same term is used in Genesis 1:20, 21 with reference to flying and swimming creatures. It merely signifies that Adam became alive; it denies the possibility of theistic evolution (the soul being breathed into a living animal form). The immortality of the human spirit is taught, however, in Genesis 1:26, 27.

2:8, 9   Although there may have been other purposes for the tree of the knowledge of good and evil which are not mentioned in Scripture, it functioned as a test of obedience. Adam and Eve had to choose whether to obey God or break His commandment. There is conjecture as to what would have become of the tree and what other purpose it may have served if Adam and Eve had not fallen, but these views should be recognized as conjecture. When they actually ate the forbidden fruit, the consequences of their actions became self-evident. They found themselves in a different relationship to God because of sin. Access to the tree of life was based upon a proper relationship with God. The real questions which faced Adam and Eve are the same ones that face people today: Which path should be chosen? What kind of relationship does one want with God?

2:15-17   Man was always meant to work, but God intended for man to enjoy it. Work only became drudgery after the Fall (Gen. 3:17-19). Is it possible for anyone to live sinlessly as Adam did prior to the Fall? The Bible explicitly states that all human beings are sinners (Ps. 14:1-3; Rom. 3:9-23; 5:12-15), and cites the origin of their sin in Adam. Because of Adam's disobedience, all men are made sinners. But how is the sin of Adam imputed to the rest of mankind? Some people say that Adam's state of corruption and guilt is transmitted to his descendants. Others feel that Adam acted as the federal representative of the human race (Rom. 5:12-20; 10:5). The fact remains that all humans are now hopelessly lost and in need of a Savior. That is why Jesus came (Luke 19:10).

nn3068   pl,nn430   wcs,pimf6680/pr5921   df,nn120   pp,qnc559   pr4480/cs,nn3605   cs,nn6086

16 And the LORD God commanded the man, saying, Of every tree of the

df,nn1588   qna398/qmf398

garden thou mayest freely eat:

wcj,pr4480/cs,nn6086   df,nn1847   aj2896   wcj,aj7451   ptn3808 qmf398

17 But of*the*tree of the knowledge of good and evil, thou shalt not eat

pr,pnx4480   cj3588   pp,cs,nn3117   qnc,pnx398 pr,pnx4480   qna4191/qmf4191

of it: for in the day that thou eatest thereof thou shalt surely die.

nn3068   pl,nn430 wcs,qmf559   ptn3808 aj2896   df,nn120   qnc1961 pp,nn,pnx905

18 And the LORD God said, It is not good that the man should be alone; I

qmf6213 pp,pnx   nn5828   pp,pr,pnx5048

will make him a help meet*for*him.

pr4480   df,nn127   nn3068   pl,nn430 wcs,qmf3335 cs,nn3605 cs,nn2416   df,nn7704

19 And out of the ground the LORD God formed every beast of the field, and

wcj(853)   cs,nn3605 cs,nn5775   df,du,nn8064   wcs,himf935   pr413   df,nn121   pp,qnc7200 pnid4100

every fowl of the air; and brought them unto Adam to see what he

qmf7121   pp,pnx   wcj,cs,nn3605/pnl834 df,nn121 qmf7121/pp,pnx   aj2416   nn5315   pndm1931

would call them: and whatsoever Adam called every living creature, that was

nn,pnx8034

the name thereof.

df,nn121   wcs,qmf7121   pl,nn8034   pp,cs,nn3605 df,nn929   wcj,pp,cs,nn5775

20 And Adam gave names to all cattle, and to the fowl of the

df,du,nn8064   wcj,pp,cs,nn3605 cs,nn2416   df,nn7704   wcj,pp,nn121   ptn3808 qpf4672

air, and to every beast of the field; but for Adam there was not found a

nn5828   pp,pr,pnx5048

help meet*for*him.

nn3068   pl,nn430   nn8639   wcs,himf5307 pr5921   df,nn121

○⇥ 21 And the LORD God caused a deep sleep to fall upon Adam, and he

wcs,qmf3462   wcs,qmf3947 nu259 pr4480/pl,nn,pnx6763   wcs,qmf5462   nn1320 pr,pnx8478

slept: and he took one of*his*ribs, and closed up the flesh instead thereof;

(853)   df,nn6763   pnl834   nn3068   pl,nn430   qpf3947   pr4480 df,nn120 wcs,qmf1129

22 And the rib, which the LORD God had taken from man, made he a

pp,nn802   wcs,himf,pnx935   pr413   df,nn120

woman, and brought her unto the man.

df,nn121   wcs,qmf559   pndm2063   df,nn6471   nn6106   pr4480/pl,nn,pnx6106   wcj,nn1320

23 And Adam said, This is now bone of*my*bones, and flesh

pr4480/nn,pnx1320   pp,pndm2063   nimf7121   nn802   cj3588   pndm2063   pupf3947   pr4480/nn376

of*my*flesh: she shall be called Woman, because she was taken out*of*Man.

pr5921/ad3651   nn376   qmf5800 (853)   nn,pnx1   wcj(853)   nn,pnx517

24 Therefore shall a man leave his father and his mother, and shall

wcs,qpf1692   pp,nn,pnx802   wcs,qpf1961 nu259 pp,nn1320

cleave unto his wife: and they shall be one flesh.

wcs,qmf1961 du,nu,pnx8147   aj6174   df,nn120   wcj,nn,pnx802   wcj,ptn3808

○⇥ 25 And they were both naked, the man and his wife, and were not

htmf*954

ashamed.

○⇥ **2:21–24** Monogamy for a lifetime was and is God's original plan. The Lord Jesus reemphasized this principle in Matthew 19:3–9.

○⇥ **2:25** There was no shame before sin entered into the world. Only after Adam and Eve sinned did they become self-conscious of their naked bodies (Gen. 3:7, 10, 21). God intends for intimate, sexual joys to be fulfilled only within the bonds of marriage, and there without shame (Heb. 13:4).

Man Falls

3 wcj,df,nn**5175** qpf**1961**   aj**6175** pr4480/cs,nn**3605** cs,nn**2416**   df,nn**7704** pnl834
⊙ Now the serpent was more subtle than any beast of the field which the

nn**3068** pl,nn**430**   qpf**6213**   wcs,qmf**559** pr413   df,nn**802** cj637/cj3588   pl,nn**430**
Lord God had made. And he said unto the woman, Yea, hath God

qpf**559**   ptn**3808** qmf**398** pr4480/cs,nn**3605** cs,nn**6086**   df,nn**1588**
said, Ye shall not eat of every tree of the garden?

df,nn**802** wcs,qmf**559** pr413   df,nn**5175**   qmf**398** pr4480/cs,nn**6529**
2 And the woman said unto the serpent, We may eat of*the*fruit of the

cs,nn**6086** df,nn**1588**
trees of the garden:

wcj,pr4480/cs,nn**6529**   df,nn**6086** pnl834   pp,cs,nn**8432**   df,nn**1588** pl,nn**430**
3 But of*the*fruit of the tree which *is* in the midst of the garden, God hath

qpf**559**   ptn**3808** qmf**398** pr,pnx4480   wcj,ptn**3808**   qmf**5060** pp,pnx cj6435   qmf**4191**
said, Ye shall not eat of it, neither shall ye touch it, lest ye die.

df,nn**5175** wcs,qmf**559** pr413   df,nn**802**   ptn**3808** qna**4191**/qmf**4191**
4 And the serpent said unto the woman, Ye shall not surely die:

cj3588 pl,nn**430**   qpta**3045** cj3588   pp,cs,nn**3117**   qnc,pnx398 pr,pnx4480   du,nn,pnx**5869**
5 For God doth know that in the day ye eat thereof, then your eyes

wcs,nipf**6491**   wcs,qpf**1961** pp,pl,nn**430** pl,cs,qpta**3045** nn**2896** wcj,nn**7451**
shall be opened, and ye shall be as gods, knowing good and evil.

df,nn**802** wcs,qmf**7200** cj3588   df,nn**6086** aj**2896** pp,nn**3978** wcj,cj3588
6 And when the woman saw that the tree *was* good for food, and that

pnp1931 nn**8378** dfp,du,nn**5869** df,nn**6086** wcj,nipt**2530** pp,hinc**7919**
it *was* pleasant to the eyes, and a tree to be desired to make*one*wise, she

wcs,qmf**3947** pr4480/nn,pnx**6529** wcs,qmf398 wcs,qmf**5414** ad1571 pp,nn,pnx**376** pr,pnx**5973**
took of*the*fruit thereof, and did eat, and gave also unto her husband with

wcs,qmf**398**
her; and he did eat.

du,cs,nn**5869** du,nu,pnx**8147** wcs,nimf**6491** wcs,qmf**3045** cj3588 pnp1992
7 And the eyes of them both were opened, and they knew that they

aj**5903** wcs,qmf**8609** nn**8384** cs,nn**5929** wcs,qmf**6213** pp,pnx pl,nn**2290**
were naked; and they sewed fig leaves together, and made themselves aprons.

wcs,qmf**8085** (853) cs,nn**6963** nn**3068** pl,nn**430** htpt**1980** dfp,nn**1588**
⊙ 8 And they heard the voice of the Lord God walking in the garden in the

---

⊙ **3:1–7** The idea that the fruit mentioned in this passage was an apple could have come from the similarity of the Latin words *malam* (apple) and *malum* (evil). Whatever the fruit was, eating it was a clear violation of the divine prohibition. The seriousness of the offense lies in Adam and Eve's deliberate, willful rejection of God's explicit command.

Satan's temptation of Eve begins by planting the seed of doubt, "Yea, hath God said . . . ?" Notice how Satan negatively restates the prohibition that God made in Genesis 2:16, 17. And Eve belies her desire for the fruit and her hatred of God's command by adding the phrase "neither shall ye touch it" to God's prohibition.

Satan did not attempt to explain why "Ye shall not surely die;" he merely said it! He said it so convincingly that Eve believed it. Then the serpent went on to slander God's motives, claiming that God was keeping something from them. Once Eve "accepted" these assumptions, her desire for the fruit grew until she took of the tree and ate.

⊙ **3:8** God is omnipresent (2 Chr. 16:9; Ps. 34:15; 139:7–10; Jer. 23:23, 24; Amos 9:2, 3; Zech. 4:10). In this instance the presence of God from which Adam and Eve fled was the visible and special manifestation to them at that time. These manifestations are called "theophanies," appearances of God in human form. They are instances where God appeared in the form of man to relate to human weaknesses so that He might communicate with man in a more personal way. However, God is not a man, and He does not look like man or think like man (Is. 55:8, 9). But God is a personal being who seeks to fellowship with man, like a loving father.

pp,cs,nn**7307**   df,nn**3117**   df,nn121   wcj,nn,pnx**802**   wcs,htmf**2244**   pr4480/pl,cs,nn**6440**

cool of the day: and Adam and his   wife   hid themselves from*the*presence of

nn**3068**   pl,nn**430**   pp,cs,nn**8432**   cs,nn**6086**   df,nn1588

the LORD God amongst the trees of the garden.

nn**3068**   pl,nn**430**   wcs,qmf**7121**   pr413   df,nn121   wcs,qmf**559**   pp,pnx   pnit,pnx335

9 And the LORD God called   unto Adam, and   said   unto him, Where *art*

thou?

wcs,qmf**559**   qpf**8085**   (853)   nn,pnx6963   dfp,nn1588   wcs,qmf**3372**

10 And he   said, I heard   thy voice in the garden, and I was afraid,

cj3588   pnp595   aj**5903**   wcs,nimf**2244**

because I *was* naked; and I hid myself.

wcs,qmf**559**   pnit4310 hipf**5046** pp,pnx   cj3588 pnp859   aj**5903**   qpf398   he,pr4480

11 And he said, Who told thee that thou *wast* naked? Hast thou eaten   of

df,nn**6086** pnl834/pr,pnx4880   pipf,pnx**6680**   pp,ptn1115 qnc398

the tree,   whereof I commanded thee that thou shouldest not eat?

df,nn**120** wcs,qmf**559**   df,nn**802**   pnl834   qpf**5414**   pr,pnx**5973**   pnp**1931**

12 And the man said, The woman whom thou gavest *to be* with me, she

qpf**5414** pp,pnx pr4480   df,nn**6086**   wcs,qmf398

gave me of the tree, and I did eat.

nn**3068**   pl,nn**430** wcs,qmf**559**   dfp,nn**802**   pnit4100   pndm2063

13 And the LORD God   said unto the woman, What *is* this   *that* thou hast

qpf**6213**   df,nn**802** wcs,qmf**559**   df,nn**5175**   hipf,pnx**5377**   wcs,qmf398

done? And the woman said, The serpent beguiled me, and I did   eat.

God's Judgment

nn**3068**   pl,nn**430** wcs,qmf**559** pr413   df,nn**5175**   cj3588   qpf**6213** pndm2063

14 And the LORD God   said unto the serpent, Because thou hast done this,

pnp859   qptp**779**   pr4480/cs,nn3605 df,nn**929**   wcj,pr4480/cs,nn3605 cs,nn**2416**   df,nn**7704** pr5921   nn,pnx1512

thou *art* cursed above all cattle, and above every beast of the field; upon thy belly

qmf**1980**   wcj,nn**6083**   qmf398 cs,nn3605   pl,cs,nn**3117**   pl,nn,pnx**2416**

shalt thou go, and dust shalt thou eat   all   the days of thy   life:

qmf**7896** wcj,nn**342**   pr,pnx996   wcj(pr996)   df,nn**802**   wcj,pr996

15 And I will put enmity between thee and   the woman, and between thy

nn,pnx**2233**   wcj(pr996)   nn,pnx**2233** pnp**1931**   qmf,pnx**7779**   nn**7218**   wcj,pnp859   qmf,pnx**7779**

seed and   her seed;   it   shall bruise thy head, and thou shalt bruise his

nn**6119**

heel.

pr413   df,nn**802**   qpf**559**   hina**7235**   himf**7235**   nn,pnx**6093**

16 Unto the woman he said, I will greatly multiply thy sorrow and thy

wcj,nn,pnx**2032**   pp,nn**6089**   qmf**3205**   pl,nn**1121**   nn,pnx**8669**   wcj,pr413

conception; in sorrow thou shalt bring forth children; and thy desire *shall be*   to

nn,pnx**376**   wcj,pnp**1931**   qmf**4910**   pp,pnx

thy husband, and   he   shall rule over thee.

wcj,pp,nn121   qpf**559**   cj3588   qpf**8085**   pp,cs,nn6963

17 And unto Adam he said, Because thou hast hearkened unto the voice of

nn,pnx**802**   wcs,qmf398 pr4480   df,nn**6086**   pnl834   pipf,pnx**6680**   pp,qnc**559**

thy wife, and hast eaten   of the tree, of which I commanded thee, saying, Thou

ptn**3808** qmf398 pr,pnx4480   qptp**779**   df,nn**127**   pp,pr,pnx5668   pp,nn**6093**

shalt not eat   of   it: cursed *is* the ground for*thy*sake; in sorrow shalt thou

qmf,pnx398   cs,nn3605   pl,cs,nn**3117**   pl,nn,pnx**2416**

eat *of* it all the days of thy   life;

wcj,nn6975   wcj,nn1863   himf6779   pp,pnx   wcs,qpf398 (853)
18 Thorns also and thistles shall it bring forth to thee; and thou shalt   eat
cs,nn6212   df,nn**7704**
the herb of the field;

pp,cs,nn2188   du,nn,pnx**639**   qmf398 nn3899 cj5704   qnc,pnx**7725** pr413
19 In the sweat of thy face shalt thou eat bread, till thou return unto the
df,nn**127** cj3588 pr,pnx4480   pupf3947 cj3588 nn**6083** pnp859   wcj,pr413 nn**6083**
ground; for out of it wast thou taken: for dust thou *art*, and unto dust shalt thou
qmf**7725**
return.

df,nn121   wcs,qmf**7121**   nn,pnx**802** cs,nn8034 nn2332   cj3588   pnp1931 qpf**1961**   cs,nn**517**
⊙☞ 20 And Adam called his wife's name Eve; because she   was the mother of
cs,nn3605   aj**2416**
all   living.

pp,nn121   wcj,pp,nn,pnx**802**   nn3068   pl,nn**430** wcs,qmf**6213** pl,cs,nn3801
21 Unto Adam also and to his   wife   did the Lord God   make   coats of
nn**5785**   wcs,himf,pnx3847
skins, and   clothed   them.

Adam and Eve Leave Eden

nn3068   pl,nn**430** wcs,qmf**559** ptdm2005   df,nn**120**   qpf**1961**   pp,cs,nu259 pr,pnx4480
22 And the Lord God said, Behold, the man is become as   one   of   us,
pp,qnc3045   aj**2896**   wcj,aj**7451**   wcj,ad6258 cj6435   qmf7971   nn,pnx**3027**   wcs,qpf3947 ad1571
to know good and evil: and now, lest he put forth his hand, and   take   also
pr4480/cs,nn6086   df,pl,nn**2416**   wcs,qpf398   wcs,qpf**2425** pp,nn**5769**
of*the*tree of life,   and, eat,   and   live   forever:
nn3068   pl,nn**430**   wcs,pimf,pnx7971   pr4480/cs,nn1588   nn5731   pp,qnc**5647**
23 Therefore the Lord God sent*him*forth from*the*garden of Eden, to   till
(853)   df,nn**127**   pr4480/ad8033/pnl834   pupf3947
the ground from whence he was taken.

wcs,pimf1644   (853)   df,nn**120**   wcs,himf**7931**   pr4480/nn**6924**   pp,cs,nn1588
24 So he drove out   the man; and he placed at*the*east of the garden of
nn5731 (853)   df,pl,nn**3742**   wcj(853)   cs,nn**3858** df,nn**2719**   df,htpt**2015**   pp,qnc**8104**
Eden   Cherubims, and   a flaming sword which turned*every*way, to keep
(853)   cs,nn**1870**   cs,nn6086   df,pl,nn**2416**
the way of the tree of life.

Cain and Abel

wcj,df,nn121 qpf**3045** (853) nn2332   nn,pnx**802**   wcs,qmf2029   wcs,qmf3205 (853)
⊙☞ And Adam knew   Eve his wife; and she conceived, and   bore
nn7014   wcs,qmf**559**   qpf7069   nn376 pr854   nn3068
Cain, and said, I have gotten a man from the Lord.

wcs,himf3254 pp,qnc3205 (853)   nn,pnx**251** (853) nn1893   nn1893 wcs,qmf**1961**   qpta7462
2 And she again   bore   his brother   Abel. And Abel was   a keeper of
nn6629   wcj,nn7014 qpf**1961** qpta**5647**   nn**127**
sheep, but Cain   was a tiller of the ground.

⊙☞ **3:20** The name "Eve" (Hebrew *chawwāh*, [2332]) means "life." The fact that "Eve" is a Hebrew name does not mean that Hebrew was the original language. As thoughts were conveyed from one language to another, proper nouns were adjusted to carry their original meaning.

⊙☞ **4:1, 2** The Hebrew word *yāda'* (3045) indicates the most intimate relationship between a man and a woman, the sexual bond. Its basic meaning is "to know," but it could be translated "and Adam experienced Eve." Cain and Abel may have been twins, since conception is mentioned only once.

pr4480/cs,nn7093   pl,nn**3117**   wcs,qmf**1961**   nn7014   wcs,himf935   pr4480/cs,nn6529

⊙̅ᵣ 3 And in process of time it*came*to*pass, that Cain brought of*the*fruit of
df,nn**127**   nn**4503**   pp,nn**3068**

the ground an offering unto the Lᴏʀᴅ.

wcj,nn1893   pnp1931   ad1571   hipf935   pr4480/pl,cs,nn1062   nn,pnx6629

4 And   Abel,   he   also   brought   of*the*firstlings   of   his   flock   and
wcj,pr4480/pl,nn,pnx2459   nn3068   wcs,qmf8159 pr413 nn1893   wcj,pr413   nn,pnx**4503**

of*the*fat   thereof. And the Lᴏʀᴅ had respect unto Abel and   to   his offering:
wcj,pr413   nn7014   wcj,pr413   nn,pnx**4503**   qpf8159/ptn**3808**   pp,nn7014

5 But unto Cain and   to   his offering he had*not*respect. And Cain was
ad3966 wcs,qmf**2734**   pl,nn,pnx**6440**   wcs,qmf**5307**

very wroth, and his countenance   fell.

nn3068   wcs,qmf559   pr413   nn7014   pnit4100   pp,pnx   qpf**2734**   wcj,pnit4100

6 And the Lᴏʀᴅ   said   unto Cain, Why art thou wroth? and   why   is thy
pl,nn,pnx**6440**   qpf**5307**

countenance fallen?

cj518   himf3190   he,ptn**3808**   nn7613   wcj,cj518   ptn**3808**

7 If thou doest well, shalt thou   not   be accepted? and   if   thou doest not
himf3190   nn**2403**   qpta7257   dfp,nn6607   wcj,pr,pnx413   nn,pnx**8669**   wcj,pnp859

well, sin lieth at the door. And   unto   thee *shall be* his desire, and   thou   shalt
qmf**4910**   pp,pnx

rule over him.

nn7014   wcs,qmf**559**   pr413   nn1893   nn,pnx**251**   wcs,qmf**1961**

⊙̅ᵣ 8 And Cain talked with Abel his brother: and it*came*to*pass, when they
pp,qnc,pnx**1961**   dfp,nn**7704**   nn7014 wcs,qmf**6965**   pr413   nn1893   nn,pnx**251**   wcs,qmf,pnx**2026**

were   in the field, that Cain rose up against Abel his brother, and   slew   him.

nn3068   wcs,qmf**559** pr413   nn7014   pnit335   nn1893   nn,pnx**251**   wcs,qmf**559**

9 And the Lᴏʀᴅ   said   unto Cain, Where *is* Abel thy brother? And he   said,   I
qpf3045   ptn**3808**   pnp595   nn,pnx**251**   he,qpta8104

know not: *Am* I my brother's keeper?

wcs,qmf**559** pnit4100   qpf**6213**   cs,nn6963   nn,pnx**251**   pl,cs,nn**1818** pl,qpta6817

10 And he   said,   What hast thou done? the voice of thy brother's blood crieth
pr,pnx413   pr4480   df,nn**127**

unto me from the ground.

wcj,ad6258   pnp859   qptp779   pr4480   df,nn**127**   pnl834   qpf**6475**   (853)   nn,pnx**6310**

11 And   now   *art* thou cursed from the earth, which hath opened   her mouth
pp,qnc3947   nn,pnx**251**   (853) pl,cs,nn**1818**   pr4480/nn,pnx**3027**

to receive thy brother's   blood from*thy*hand;

⊙̅ᵣ **4:3–7** Is God a respecter of persons (Ex. 2:25; Lev. 26:9; 2 Kgs. 13:23; Ps. 138:6), or is He completely impartial (2 Chr. 19:7; Acts 10:34; Rom. 2:11; Gal. 2:6; Eph. 6:9; 1 Pet. 1:17)? In the first series of texts, the word "respect" is used in the sense of acknowledging or paying attention to something. In the second set of references, "respect" refers to granting special favors to someone because of some meritorious quality within that person. Although God, according to this second group of verses, is "no respecter of persons" (i.e., no one has a higher standing in God's eyes because of their position in life or of something they themselves have done), He does, according to His sovereign will, pay specific attention to certain individuals and situations.

In this particular passage, the fact that God accepted Abel's sacrifice and rejected Cain's was not based on the fact that Cain's sacrifice was bloodless. Many of the required Old Testament offerings were bloodless (as meal and meat offerings). The difference was in the hearts of the two men. Abel offered in faith (Heb. 11:4), while Cain did not. Thus, God was not showing special favor to Abel over Cain because of something inherent in their outward deeds, but refused Cain's offering because of his improper attitude. Only when they are offered in faith do the sacrifices and service of men please God (Is. 1:11–17; Eph. 6:5–7).

⊙̅ᵣ **4:8** The Septuagint, the Samaritan Pentateuch, and the Syriac Version add the phrase, "Let us go out to the field," after the phrase "and Cain talked with Abel his brother."

nn3929   wcs,qmf**2421**   ad310   hinc,pnx3205 (853)   nn5146   wcj,nu2568   pl,nu3967   (nn8141)   wcj,nu8673

30 And Lamech lived after he begot   Noah five hundred   ninety

nu2568   nn8141   wcs,himf3205 pl,nn**1121**   wcj,pl,nn1323

and five years, and begot sons and daughters:

cs,nn3605   pl,cs,nn**3117**   nn3929   wcs,qmf**1961**   wcj,cs,nu7651   pl,nu3967   (nn8141)   wcj,pl,nu7657

31 And all the days of Lamech were seven hundred   seventy and

nu7651   nn8141   wcs,qmf**4191**

seven years: and he died.

nn5146   wcs,qmf**1961**   cs,nu2568   pl,nu3967   nn8141   cs,nn**1121**   nn5146   wcs,himf3205 (853)   nn8035   (853)

32 And Noah was   five hundred years old: and Noah begot   Shem,

nn2526   wcj(853)   nn3315

Ham, and   Japheth.

Evil Rules Over Mankind

6

         wcs,qmf**1961**   cj3588   df,nn**120**   hipf**2490**   pp,qnc7231   pr5921   pl,cs,nn**6440**

☞ And it*came*to*pass, when men began to multiply on the face of

df,nn**127**   wcj,pl,nn1323   pupf3205   pp,pnx

the earth, and daughters were born unto them,

pl,cs,nn**1121**   df,pl,nn**430**   wcs,qmf**7200** (853)   pl,cs,nn1323   df,nn**120**   cj3588   pnp2007   aj**2896**

2 That the sons of God saw   the daughters of men that they *were* fair;

wcs,qmf3947   pp,pnx   pl,nn**802**   pr4480/nn3605   pnl834   qpf**977**

and they took them wives of all which they chose.

☞ **6:1–4** The identity of the "sons of God" is uncertain. Three main theories are advanced to identify the "sons of God" and the "daughters of men." The first theory is that the "sons of God" are fallen angels and the "daughters of men" are mortals. The wickedness for which they are condemned is the unlawful marriage between those who are supernatural and those who are mortal. This ancient viewpoint hinges in part on the assumption that Jude 1:6, 7 refer to these angels. The proponents of this view insist, perhaps with some Scriptural backing, that the term "sons of God" refers only to angels (Job 1:6–12). However, there is no precedent at this point from which this conclusion can be made. And if this sin is, at least to a large extent, the fault of the angels, why is man punished by the Flood? When the proponents of this theory are reminded of the fact that Christ, in Matthew 22:30, says that angels do not marry, they answer that He only said that they do not, not that they could not or did not. Besides the mythological quality which this viewpoint brings to the text, there is considerable theological difficulty with the existence of human beings who are, at least in part, not descended from Adam (Acts 17:26).

The second theory as to their identity is the one most often held to within conservative scholarship. The "sons of God" are reckoned to be the godly line of Seth while the "daughters of men" are of the line of Cain. Thus the sin with which they are charged is one which is common to the whole of Scripture, and especially to the Pentateuch: the intermarriage of the chosen people of God (the believers) with those who are unholy. How can these men be considered holy when the Bible states that only Noah was holy (Gen. 6:8, 9)? And why is the term "sons of God" not used with this meaning in any other place? Other people also question why only sons and not daughters are associated with the line of Seth.

The last theory is one that is gaining popularity among conservatives. Recent archaeological evidence has suggested that the phrase "sons of God" was sometimes used to describe kings (Ex. 21:6; 22:8; Ps. 82:6, 7). Therefore the "sons of God" are immoral human kings who used their power to take as many women and whatever women they chose. It must be noted that the Scripture never describes human rulers as deities. This theory rests upon the conjecture that the "giants" of verse four are the children of the union described in the preceding verses. The word "giant" comes from the Septuagint rendering of the Hebrew Nephilīm (5303), "the fallen ones," which comes from nāphal (5307), "to fall." It is often associated with violence, and so translated "overthrow, fall upon." The term emphasizes their violence and lack of respect for others. However, neither the text nor the fact that they were "giants" supports the idea that they are the result of a union between angels and human beings. No one believes that because the children of Anak, Goliath and his brothers, were giants that they were necessarily the offspring of some supernatural union.

nn3068 wcs,qmf559 nn,pnx7307 ptn3808 pp,nn5769 qmf1777 dfp,nn120
3 And the LORD said, My spirit shall not always strive with man, for that
pnp1931 pp,pnl7945/ad1571 nn1320 pl,nn,pnx3117 wcs,qpf1961 nu3967 wcj,pl,nu6242 nn8141
he also *is* flesh: yet his days shall be a hundred and twenty years.
qpf1961 df,pl,nn5303 dfp,nn776 df,pndm1992 dfp,pl,nn3117 wcj,ad1571 ad310 ad3651 pnl834
4 There were giants in the earth in those days; and also after that, when
pl,cs,nn1121 df,pl,nn430 qmf935 pr413 pl,cs,nn1323 df,nn120 wcs,qpf3205
the sons of God came in unto the daughters of men, and they bore *children*
pp,pnx pndm1992 df,pl,nn1368 pnl834 pr4480/nn5769 pl,cs,nn376 df,nn8034
to them, the same *became* mighty men which *were* of old, men of renown.
nn3068 wcs,qmf7200 cj3588 cs,nn7451 df,nn120 aj7227 dfp,nn776
5 And GOD saw that the wickedness of man *was* great in the earth, and *that*
wcj,cs,nn3605 cs,nn3336 pl,cs,nn4284 nn,pnx3820 ad7535 aj7451 cs,nn3605/df,nn3117
every imagination of the thoughts of his heart *was* only evil continually.
wcs,nimf5162 nn3068 cj3588 qpf6213 (853) df,nn120 dfp,nn776
6 And it repented the LORD that he had made man on the earth, and it
wcs,htmf6087 pr413 nn,pnx3820
grieved him at his heart.
nn3068 wcs,qmf559 qmf4229 (853) df,nn120 pnl834 qpf1254 pr4480/pr5921
7 And the LORD said, I will destroy man whom I have created from the
pl,cs,nn6440 df,nn127 pr4480/nn120 pr5704 nn929 pr5704 nn7431 wcj,pr5704 cs,nn5775
face of the earth; both man, and beast, and the creeping thing, and the fowls
df,du,nn8064 cj3588 nipf5162 cj3588 qpf,pnx6213
of the air; for it repenteth me that I have made them.
wcj,nn5146 qpf4672 nn2580 pp,du,cs,nn5869 nn3068
8 But Noah found grace in the eyes of the LORD.

Noah

pndm428 pl,cs,nn8435 nn5146 nn5146 qpf1961 aj6662 nn376 aj8549
9 These *are* the generations of Noah: Noah was a just man *and* perfect in his
pp,pl,nn,pnx1755 nn5146 htpf1980 pr854 df,pl,nn430
generations, *and* Noah walked with God.
nn5146 wcs,himf3205 nu7969 pl,nn1121 (853) nn8035 (853) nn2526 wcj(853) nn3315
10 And Noah begot three sons, Shem, Ham, and Japheth.
df,nn776 wcs,nimf7843 pp,pl,cs,nn6440 df,pl,nn430 df,nn776 wcs,nimf4390
11 The earth also was corrupt before God, and the earth was filled with
nn2555
violence.
pl,nn430 wcs,qmf7200 (853) df,nn776 wcj,ptdm2009 nipf7843 cj3588 cs,nn3605
12 And God looked upon the earth, and, behold, it was corrupt; for all
nn1320 hipf7843 (853) nn,pnx1870 pr5921 df,nn776
flesh had corrupted his way upon the earth.

6:6 This verse has puzzled students of the Bible for many years. The phrase "it repented the LORD" does not mean that God changed (Num. 23:19; 1 Sam. 15:29; Mal. 3:6; James 1:17), or that He is affected by sorrow or other feelings which are common to humanity. However, it was necessary for the inspired biblical writers to use terms which were comprehensible to the minds of human beings. A person cannot conceive of God except in human terms and concepts.

6:9 How could Noah be called "perfect" (blameless) when no one is perfect (1 Kgs. 8:46; Ps. 14:1–3; Prov. 20:9; Eccl. 7:20; Mark 10:18; Rom. 3:23; 1 John 1:8)? In both the Old and New Testaments, the words translated "perfect" refer to completeness and maturity rather than to sinlessness. Some have suggested that "perfect in his generations" (lit. "blameless in his time") refers to Noah's having an ancestry from the line of Seth, free from the mixing with the worldly line of Cain which ruined the rest of the race (see the note on Gen. 6:1–4). It is also possible that Noah is called "blameless" by comparison to the wicked mass of humanity. Noah is recorded in the list of the heroes of faith (Heb. 11:7) as one who stood alone for righteousness.

pl,nn**430** wcs,qmf**559**   pp,nn5146   cs,nn7093   cs,nn3605 nn**1320**   qpta935 pp,pl,nn,pnx**6440**

13 And God said unto Noah, The end of all flesh is come before me;

cj3588   df,nn776   qpf**4390**   nn2555   pr4480/pl,nn,pnx**6440**   wcj,ptdm,pnx2009   hipt,pnx**7843**

for the earth is filled with violence through them; and, behold, I will destroy

pr854   df,nn776

them with the earth.

qmv**6213** pp,pnx   cs,nn8392   nn1613 pl,cs,nn6086 pl,nn7064   qmf**6213** (853)   df,nn8392

14 Make thee an ark of gopher wood; rooms shalt thou make in the ark,

wcs,qpf**3722** pnx(853)   pr4480/nn**1004**   wcj,pr4480/nn2351   dfp,nn**3724**

and shalt pitch it within and without with pitch.

wcj,pndm2088   pnl834   qmf**6213** pnx(853)   cs,nn**753**

○ 15 And this *is the fashion* which thou shalt make it *of:* The length of

df,nn8392   cs,nu7969 pl,nu3967 nn520   nn,pnx7341   pl,nu2572 nn520

the ark *shall be* three hundred cubits, the breadth of it fifty cubits, and the

nn,pnx6967   wcj,nu7970 nn520

height of it thirty cubits.

nn6672   qmf**6213**   dfp,nn8392   wcj,pr413 nn520   pimf,pnx**3615**

16 A window shalt thou make to the ark, and in a cubit shalt thou finish

pr4480/pp,ad,lh4605   wcj,cs,nn6607   df,nn8392   qmf**7760**   pp,nn,pnx6654

it above; and the door of the ark shalt thou set in the side thereof;

aj8482   pl,nuor8145   wcj,pl,nuor7992   qmf,pnx**6213**

with lower, second, and third *stories* shalt thou make it.

ptdm,pnx2009   wcj,pnp589 hipt935 (853) df,nn3999 pl,nn4325 pr5921   df,nn**776**

17 And, behold, I, even I, do bring a flood of waters upon the earth,

pp,pinc**7843** cs,nn3605   nn**1320** pnl834/pp,pnx   cs,nn7307   pl,nn2416   pr4480/pr8478   df,du,nn**8064**

to destroy all flesh, wherein *is* the breath of life, from under heaven; *and*

cs,nn3605   pnl834   dfp,nn776   qmf**1478**

every thing that *is* in the earth shall die.

pr,pnx854   wcs,hipf**6965** (853)   nn,pnx**1285**   wcs,qpf935 pr413

18 But with thee will I establish my covenant; and thou shalt come into

df,nn8392   pnp859   wcj,pl,nn,pnx**1121**   wcj,nn,pnx**802**   pl,nn,pnx**1121** wcj,pl,cs,nn**802** pr,pnx854

the ark, thou, and thy sons, and thy wife, and thy sons' wives with

thee.

wcj,pr4480/cs,nn3605   df,nn**2416**   pr4480/cs,nn3605   nn**1320** du,nu8147 pr4480/nn3605

19 And of every living thing of all flesh, two of every *sort* shalt thou

himf935 pr413   df,nn8392   pp,hinc**2421**   pr,pnx854   qmf**1961** nn2145   wcj,nn**5347**

bring into the ark, to keep*them*alive with thee; they shall be male and female.

pr4480/df,nn5775   pp,nn,pnx4327   wcj,pr4480 df,nn929   pp,nn,pnx4327 pr4480/cs,nn3605

20 Of fowls after their kind, and of cattle after their kind, of every

cs,nn7431   df,nn**127**   pp,nn,pnx4327 du,nu8147 pr4480/nn3605   qmf935 pr,pnx413

creeping thing of the earth after his kind, two of every *sort* shall come unto

pp,hinc**2421**

thee, to keep*them*alive.

qmv3947 wcj,pnp859   pp,pnx   pr4480/cs,nn3605 nn3978 pnl834   nimf398

21 And take thou unto thee of all food that is eaten, and thou shalt

wcs,qpf**622**   pr,pnx413   wcs,qpf**1961** pp,nn402 pp,pnx   wcj,pp,pnx

gather *it* to thee; and it shall be for food for thee, and for them.

○ **6:15** The dimensions of the ark present an interesting contrast when set beside the Sumerian account of the flood. In the longest and most famous of these accounts, the Akkadian Epic of Gilgamesh, the base of the ark was a perfect square, 200 feet long on each side. Such an ark would have hardly been seaworthy unless completely enclosed, in which case it would have spun around and around in the current of the flood waters. On the other hand, the relative dimensions of Noah's ark are not only seaworthy, but that of modern ships are very similar.

wcs,qmf**6213**   nn5146   pp,cs,nn3605 pnl834 pl,nn**430**   pipf**6680**   pnx(853)

22 Thus   did   Noah; according to   all   that God commanded   him,

ad**3651** qpf**6213**

so   did   he.

The Flood

nn3068   wcs,qmf**559**   pp,nn5146   qmv935   pnp859   wcj,cs,nn3605   nn,pnx**1004**   pr413

7 And the LORD said unto Noah, Come thou and   all   thy house into the

df,nn8392   cj3588   pnx(853)   qpf**7200**   aj**6662**   pp,pl,nn,pnx**6440**   df,pndm2088

ark;   for   thee have I seen righteous   before   me in   this

dfp,nn**1755**

generation.

pr4480/cs,nn3605 df,aj**2889**   df,nn929   qmf3947   pp,pnx   nu7651/nu7651   nn**376**

2 Of every clean beast thou shalt take to thee by sevens, the male and his

wcj,nn,pnx**802**   wcj,pr4480   df,nn929 pnl834   ptn3808   aj**2889**   (pnp1931)   du,nu8147   nn**376**

female: and   of   beasts that *are* not clean   by two, the male and his

wcj,nn,pnx**802**

female.

pr4480/cs,nn5775 ad1571   df,du,nn**8064**   nu7651/nu7651   nn2145   wcj,nn**5347**

3 Of fowls also of the   air   by sevens, the male and the female; to keep

nn2233 pp,pinc**2421** pr5921   pl,cs,nn**6440**   cs,nn3605   df,nn776

seed alive upon the face of all the earth.

cj3588 ad5750 nu7651 pp,pl,nn**3117**   pnp595   hipt4305 pr5921   df,nn776 pl,nn705 nn**3117**

4 For yet seven days, and I   will cause it to rain upon the earth forty days

wcj,pl,nn705   nn**3915**   (853) cs,nn3605   df,nn3351   pnl834   qpf**6213**   wcs,qpf**4229**

and forty nights; and   every living substance that I have made will I destroy

pr4480/pr5921   pl,cs,nn**6440**   df,nn**127**

from off the face of the earth.

nn5146 wcs,qmf**6213**   pp,cs,nn3605 pnl834   nn3068   pipf,pnx**6680**

5 And Noah   did   according unto   all   that the LORD commanded him.

wcj,nn5146   nu8337   pl,nu3967   nn8141 cs,nn**1121**   wcj,df,nn3999   pl,nn4325   qpf**1961**

6 And Noah *was* six hundred years old when the flood of waters was

pr5921   df,nn776

upon the earth.

nn5146   wcs,qmf935   wcj,pl,nn,pnx**1121**   wcj,nn,pnx**802**   pl,nn,pnx**1121**

7 And Noah went in, and his   sons,   and his   wife,   and his   sons'

wcj,pl,cs,nn**802** pr,pnx854   pr413   df,nn8392 pr4480/pl,cs,nn**6440**   pl,cs,nn4325   df,nn3999

wives with him, into the ark,   because of the waters of the flood.

pr4480 df,aj**2889**   df,nn929   wcj,pr4480 df,nn929 pnl834   ptn,pnx369   aj**2889**   wcj,pr4480 df,nn5775

8 Of clean beasts, and   of   beasts that *are* not clean, and   of   fowls,

wcj,cs,nn3605   pnl834 qpta7430   pr5921   df,nn**127**

and of every thing that creepeth upon the earth,

qpf935   du,nu8147   du,nu8147 pr413   nn5146 pr413   df,nn8392   nn2145

9 There went in two and two unto Noah into the ark, the male and the

wcj,nn**5347** pp,pnl834 pl,nn**430**   pipf**6680**   (853)   nn5146

female, as   God had commanded   Noah.

wcs,qmf**1961**   pp,cs,nu7651 df,pl,nn**3117**   wcj,pl,cs,nn4325   df,nn3999

10 And it*came*to*pass after seven days, that the waters of the flood

qpf**1961** pr5921   df,nn776

were upon the earth.

(nn8141) nu8337   pl,nu3967   pp,cs,nn8141   nn5146 pp,pl,cs,nn**2416**   df,nuor8145 dfp,nn2320

11 In the   six hundredth year of Noah's life, in the second month,

pp,nu7651/nu6240 nn**3117**   dfp,nn2320   df,pndm2320 dfp,nn**3117**   cs,nn3605   pl,cs,nn4599

the seventeenth day of the month, the same day were all the fountains of the

aj7227 nn8415 nipf1234   wcj,pl,cs,nn699   df,du,nn**8064**   nipf6605

great deep broken up, and the windows of heaven were opened.

df,nn1653 wcs,qmf**1961** pr5921   df,nn776 pl,nu705 nn**3117**   wcj,pl,nu705   nn**3915**

◎₌ 12 And the rain was upon the earth forty days and forty nights.

pp,cs,nn**6106**/df,pndm2088 df,nn**3117**   qpf935   nn5146   wcj,nn8035   wcj,nn2526

13 In the selfsame day entered Noah, and Shem, and Ham, and

wcj,nn3315   pl,cs,nn**1121**   nn5146   nn5146 wcj,cs,nn**802**   wcj,nu7969 pl,cs,nn**802**

Japheth, the sons of Noah, and Noah's wife, and the three wives of his

pl,nn,pnx**1121** pr,pnx854   pr413   df,nn8392

sons with them, into the ark;

pnp1992   wcj,cs,nn3605 df,nn**2416**   pp,nn,pnx4327   wcj,cs,nn3605   df,nn929

14 They, and every beast after his kind, and all the cattle after their

pp,nn,pnx4327   wcj,cs,nn3605   df,nn7431   df,qpta7430 pr5921   df,nn**776**   pp,nn,pnx4327

kind, and every creeping thing that creepeth upon the earth after his kind,

wcj,cs,nn3605 df,nn5775   pp,nn,pnx4327 cs,nn3605 nn6833   cs,nn3605 nn3671

and every fowl after his kind, every bird of every sort.

wcs,qmf935   pr413   nn5146   pr413   df,nn8392 du,nu8147   du,nu8147 pr4480/cs,nn3605 df,nn**1320**

15 And they went in unto Noah into the ark, two and two of all flesh,

pnl834/pp,pnx   cs,nn**7307**   pl,nn**2416**

wherein *is* the breath of life.

wcj,df,pl,qpta935   qpf935   nn2145   wcj,nn**5347** pr4480/cs,nn3605 nn**1320** pp,pnl834

16 And they that went in, went in male and female of all flesh, as

pl,nn**430**   pipf**6680**   pnx(853)   nn3068 wcs,qmf5462/pr,pnx1157

God had commanded him: and the Lᴏʀᴅ shut*him*in.

df,nn3999 wcs,qmf**1961** pl,nu705 nn**3117** pr5921   df,nn**776**   df,pl,nn4325 wcs,qmf7235

17 And the flood was forty days upon the earth; and the waters increased,

wcs,qmf**5375** (853)   df,nn8392   wcs,qmf7311 pr4480/pr5921   df,nn**776**

and bore up the ark, and it was lifted up above the earth.

df,pl,nn4325 wcs,qmf1396   wcs,qmf7235 ad3966 pr5921   df,nn**776**

18 And the waters prevailed, and were increased greatly upon the earth; and the

df,nn8392 wcs,qmf**1980** pr5921   pl,cs,nn**6440**   df,pl,nn4325

ark went upon the face of the waters.

wcj,df,pl,nn4325 qpf1396   ad3966/ad3966 pr5921   df,nn**776**   cs,nn3605   df,aj1364

19 And the waters prevailed exceedingly upon the earth; and all the high

df,pl,nn2022 pnl834   pr8478   cs,nn3605 df,du,nn**8064**   wcs,pumf**3680**

hills, that *were* under the whole heaven, were covered.

cs,nu2568/nu6240 nn520 pr4480/pp,ad,lh4605   df,pl,nn4325 qpf1396   df,pl,nn2022

20 Fifteen cubits upward did the waters prevail; and the mountains were

wcs,pumf**3680**

covered.

cs,nn3605 nn**1320** wcs,qmf**1478**   df,qpta7430 pr5921   df,nn**776**   dfp,nn5775

21 And all flesh died that moved upon the earth, both of fowl, and of

wcj,dfp,nn929   wcj,dfp,nn**2416**   wcj,pp,cs,nn3605 df,nn8318   df,qpta8317 pr5921

cattle, and of beast, and of every creeping thing that creepeth upon the

df,nn**776**   wcj,cs,nn3605 df,nn**120**

earth, and every man:

◎₌ **7:12** The number forty is not merely an arbitrary period nor a rounded figure of the period during which it rained. The number forty is used repeatedly in Scripture to signify periods of testing, sometimes of judgmental testing. Other prominent references involving the number forty are: Noah's waiting after the tops of the mountains appeared (Gen. 8:6); Moses' forty days on Mt. Sinai (Ex. 24:18; Deut. 19:9); the spies' forty days searching out Canaan (Num. 13:25); the forty years in the wilderness (Num. 14:33); the forty days Nineveh was given until judgment (Jon. 3:4); the forty days Jesus spent in the wilderness being tempted by Satan (Luke 4:1, 2).

cs,nn3605 (pnl834)   pp,du,nn,pnx639   cs,nn5397/cs,nn7307   pl,nn2416 pr4480/cs,nn3605 pnl834
22 All   in whose nostrils *was* the   breath   of life,   of all   that

dfp,nn2724   qpf4191
was in the   dry   *land*, died.

(853) cs,nn3605   df,nn3351   wcs,qmf4229   pnl834   pr5921   pl,cs,nn6440
23 And   every living substance was destroyed which was upon the   face   of

df,nn127   pr4480/nn120   pr5704   nn929   pr5704   nn7431   wcj,pr5704   cs,nn5775
the ground, both man, and cattle, and the creeping things,   and   the fowl of the

df,du,nn8064   wcs,nimf4229   pr4480   df,nn776   nn5146   ad389   wcs,nimf7604
heaven; and they were destroyed from the earth: and Noah only remained *alive*, and

wcj,pnl834   pr,pnx854   dfp,nn8392
they that   *were* with him in the   ark.

df,pl,nn4325 wcs,qmf1396   pr5921   df,nn776   wcj,cs,nu3967   pl,nu2572 nn3117
24 And the waters prevailed upon the earth a hundred and   fifty   days.

The Flood Ends

pl,nn430   wcs,qmf2142   (853)   nn5146   wcj(853) cs,nn3605   df,nn2416   wcj(853)
8 And God remembered   Noah, and   every living thing, and

cs,nn3605   df,nn929 pnl834   pr,pnx854   dfp,nn8392   pl,nn430   nn7307
all   the cattle that *was* with him in the   ark: and God made a wind to

wcs,himf5674 pr5921   df,nn776   df,pl,nn4325   wcs,qmf7918
pass   over the earth, and the waters assuaged;

pl,cs,nn4599   nn8415   wcj,pl,cs,nn699   df,du,nn8064   wcs,nimf5534
2 The fountains also of the deep and the windows of heaven were stopped, and

df,nn1653   pr4480 df,du,nn8064   wcs,nimf3607
the   rain   from heaven was restrained;

df,pl,nn4325   wcs,qmf7725   pr4480/pr5921   df,nn776   qna1980/wcj,qna7725   pr4480/cs,nn7097
3 And the waters returned from off the earth continually: and after*the*end of

wcj,cs,nu3967   pl,nu2572 nn3117   df,pl,nn4325   wcs,qmf2637
the hundred and   fifty days the waters were abated.

df,nn8392 wcs,qmf5117   df,nuor7637   dfp,nn2320   pp,nu7651/nu6240   nn3117
4 And the   ark   rested in the seventh month, on the seventeenth day of the

dfp,nn2320   pr5921   pl,cs,nn2022   nn780
month, upon the mountains of Ararat.

wcj,df,pl,nn4325   wcj,qna2637   qpf1961/qna1980   pr5704   df,nuor6224 df,nn2320   dfp,nuor6224
5 And the   waters   decreased continually until the   tenth   month: in the   tenth

pp,nu259   dfp,nn2320   pl,cs,nn7218   df,pl,nn2022   nipf7200
month, on the first *day* of the month, were the   tops   of the mountains seen.

wcs,qmf1961   pr4480/cs,nn7093   pl,nu705   nn3117   nn5146   wcs,qmf6605   (853)
6 And it*came*to*pass at*the*end of forty days, that Noah opened   the

cs,nn2474   df,nn8392 pnl834   qpf6213
window of the   ark   which he had made:

wcs,pimf7971   (853)   df,nn6158   wcs,qmf3318   qna3318/wcj,qna7725 pr5704   df,pl,nn4325
7 And he sent forth   a raven, which went forth to*and*fro, until the waters

qnc3001   pr4480/pr5921   df,nn776
were dried up from off the earth.

wcs,pimf7971   (853)   df,nn3123 pr4480/pr,pnx854   pp,qnc7200   df,pl,nn4325
8 Also he sent forth   a dove   from   him, to   see   if the waters were

he,qpf7043   pr4480/pr5921   pl,cs,nn6440   df,nn127
abated from off the   face   of the ground;

df,nn3123   qpf4672 wcj,ptn3808 nn4494   pp,cs,nn3709   nn,pnx7272   wcs,qmf7725
9 But the dove found   no   rest for the   sole   of her foot, and she returned

pr,pnx413   pr413   df,nn8392 cj3588   pl,nn4325   pr5921   pl,cs,nn6440   cs,nn3605 df,nn776
unto him into the ark, for the waters *were* on   the   face   of the whole earth:

wcs,qmf7971   nn,pnx**3027**   wcs,qmf,pnx3947   wcs,himf935/pnx(853)   pr,pnx413   pr413

then he put forth his hand, and   took   her, and pulled*her*in unto him into the

df,nn8392

ark.

wcs,qmf**2342** ad5750 aj312 cs,nu7651 pl,nn**3117**   wcs,himf3254   pinc7971   (853)   df,nn3123

10 And he stayed yet other seven days; and again he sent forth   the dove

pr4480   df,nn8392

out of the ark;

df,nn3123 wcs,qmf935 pr,pnx413   pp,cs,nn**6256**   nn6153   wcj,ptdm2009

11 And the dove came in to him in the evening; and, lo, in her

pp,nn,pnx**6310**   nn2132 cs,nn5929   aj2965   nn5146 wcs,qmf**3045** cj3588   df,pl,nn4325

mouth *was* an olive leaf plucked off: so Noah knew that the waters were

qpf**7043** pr4480/pr5921   df,nn**776**

abated from off the earth.

wcs,nimf**3176** ad5750 aj312 cs,nu7651 pl,nn**3117**   wcs,pimf7971 (853)   df,nn3123

12 And he stayed yet other seven days; and sent forth   the dove; which

qnc**7725** wcj,ptn**3808** qpf3254 pr,pnx413   ad5750

returned not again unto him any more.

wcs,qmf**1961**   wcj,nu8337   pl,nu3967   pp,nu259 nn8141   dfp,aj**7223**

13 And it*came*to*pass in the six hundredth and first year, in the first

pp,nu259   dfp,nn2320   df,pl,nn4325   qpf**2717** pr4480/pr5921   df,nn**776**

month, the first *day* of the month, the waters were dried up from off the earth:

nn5146   wcs,himf**5493** (853)   cs,nn4372   df,nn8392   wcs,qmf**7200**   wcj,ptdm2009

and Noah removed   the covering of the ark, and looked, and, behold, the

pl,cs,nn**6440**   df,nn**127**   qpf**2717**

face of the ground was dry.

df,nuor8145 wcj,dfp,nn2320   pp,nu7651   wcj,pl,nu6242 nn3117   dfp,nn2320

14 And in the second month, on the seven and twentieth day of the month,

df,nn**776** qpf**3001**

was the earth dried.

pl,nn**430** wcs,pimf**1696** pr413   nn5146 pp,qnc**559**

15 And God spoke unto Noah, saying,

qmv3318   pr4480   df,nn8392 pnp859   wcj,nn,pnx**802**   wcj,pl,nn,pnx**1121**

16 Go forth of the ark, thou, and thy wife, and thy   sons, and thy

pl,nn,pnx**1121** wcj,pl,cs,nn**802** pr,pnx854

sons' wives with thee.

himv3318   pr,pnx854   cs,nn3605   df,nn**2416**   pnl834   pr,pnx854   pr4480/cs,nn3605   nn**1320**

17 Bring forth with thee every living thing that *is* with thee, of all flesh,

dfp,nn5775   wcj,dfp,nn929   wcj,pp,cs,nn3605   df,nn7431   df,qpta7430   pr5921

both of fowl, and of cattle, and of every creeping thing that creepeth upon the

df,nn**776**   wcj,qpf8317   dfp,nn**776**   wcj,qpf6509   wcj,qpf7235

earth; that they may breed abundantly in the earth, and be fruitful, and multiply

pr5921   df,nn**776**

upon the earth.

nn5146   wcs,qmf3318   wcj,pl,nn,pnx**1121**   wcj,nn,pnx**802**   pl,nn,pnx**1121**

18 And Noah went forth, and his sons, and his wife, and his sons'

wcj,pl,cs,nn**802** pr,pnx854

wives with him:

cs,nn3605   df,nn**2416** cs,nn3605   df,nn7431   wcj,cs,nn3605 df,nn5775   nn3605

19 Every beast, every creeping thing, and every fowl, *and* whatsoever

qpta7430   pr5921   df,nn**776**   pp,pl,nn,pnx**4940** qpf3318   pr4480   df,nn8392

creepeth upon the earth, after their kinds, went forth out of the ark.

nn5146 wcs,qmf1129   nn**4196**   pp,nn**3068**   wcs,qmf3947 pr4480/cs,nn3605 df,aj**2889** df,nn929

20 And Noah built an altar unto the LORD; and took of every clean beast,

wcj,pr4480/cs,nn3605 df,aj**2889** df,nn5775   wcs,himf**5927**   pl,nn**5930**   dfp,nn**4196**

and of every clean fowl, and offered burnt offerings on the altar.

nn3068　wcs,himf7306　df,nn5207　(853)　cs,nn7381　　　nn3068　wcs,qmf559　pr413　nn,pnx3820

☞ 21 And the LORD smelled a sweet　　savor; and the LORD said　in his heart,

ptn3808　himf3254　pp,pinc7043　(853)　　df,nn127　ad5750　pp,pr5668/df,nn120　cj3588

I will　not　again　curse　　the　ground　any more for*man's*sake;　for the

cs,nn3336　df,nn120　cs,nn3820　aj7451　pr4480/pl,nn,pnx5271　wcj,ptn3808　himf3254　pp,hinc5221

imagination of man's heart *is* evil from*his*youth; neither will I again smite

ad5750　(853)　cs,nn3605　aj2416　pp,pnl834　qpf6213

any more　　every thing living,　as　I have done.

ad5750　df,nn776　cs,nn3605/pl,cs,nn3117　nn2233　　wcj,nn7105　　wcj,nn7120　　wcj,nn2527

22 While the earth　remaineth,　seedtime and harvest, and　cold　and heat,

wcj,nn7019　　wcj,nn2779　　wcj,nn3117　　wcj,nn3915　　ptn3808　qmf7673

and summer and winter, and　day　and night shall not cease.

Noahic Covenant

pl,nn430　wcs,pimf1288　(853)　nn5146　　wcj(853)　pl,nn,pnx1121　　wcs,qmf559　　pp,pnx

9 And God blessed　　Noah and　　his　sons, and　said　unto them,

qmv6509　　wcj,qmv7235　　wcj,qmv4390　(853)　df,nn776

Be fruitful, and multiply, and replenish　　the earth.

wcj,nn,pnx4172　　　wcj,nn,pnx2844　　qmf1961　pr5921　cs,nn3605　cs,nn2416

2 And the　fear　of you and the　dread　of you shall be　upon every beast

df,nn776　　wcj,pr5921　cs,nn3605　cs,nn5775　　df,du,nn8064　　pp,cs,nn3605　pnl834　qmf7430

of the earth, and upon every fowl of the　air,　upon　all　that moveth *upon*

df,nn127　　wcj,pp,cs,nn3605　pl,cs,nn1709　df,nn3220　　pp,nn,pnx3027

the earth, and upon　all　the fishes of the sea; into your hand are they

nipf5414

delivered.

cs,nn3605　nn7431　pnl834 (pndm1931)　aj2416　qmf1961 pp,nn402　pp,pnx

3 Every moving thing that　　liveth shall be　meat for you; even as the

pp,nn3418 nn6212　qpf5414 pp,pnx (853)　nn3605

green herb have I given you　all things.

ad389 nn1320　pp,nn,pnx5315　nn,pnx1818　ptn3808

4 But flesh with the　life　thereof, *which is* the blood thereof, shall ye not

qmf398

eat.

wcj,ad389 (853)　nn,pnx1818　pp,pl,nn,pnx5315　qmf1875　pr4480/cs,nn3027

5 And surely　your blood of your　lives　will I require; at*the*hand of

cs,nn3605 nn2416　qmf,pnx1875　wcj,pr4480/cs,nn3027　df,nn120　pr4480/cs,nn3027　nn376

every beast will I require it, and at*the*hand of man; at*the*hand of every man's

nn,pnx251　qmf1875 (853)　cs,nn5315　df,nn120

brother will I require　the　life　of man.

qpta8210　df,nn120　cs,nn1818　dfp,nn120　nn,pnx1818　nimf8210 cj3588

6 Whoso sheddeth man's blood, by　man　shall his blood be shed: for in the

pp,cs,nn6754　pl,nn430 qpf6213　(853) df,nn120

image of God made he　man.

wcj,pnp859　qmv6509　wcj,qmv7235　qmv8317　dfp,nn776

7 And you, be*ye*fruitful, and multiply; bring*forth*abundantly in the earth,

wcj,qmv7235　pp,pnx

and multiply therein.

☞ **8:21, 22** Contained in this promise is a stipulation that is easy to miss. Day, night, and the seasons will continue as seen in the phrase "while the earth remaineth." The earth was not intended by God to be eternal. Its final destruction is described in Psalm 102:26 (quoted in Heb. 1:11, 12). The most graphic account of the end of the world, indeed of the entire physical universe, is found in 2 Peter 3:10.

_{pl,nn**430** wcs,qmf**559** pr413   nn5146   wcj,pr413   pl,nn,pnx1121 pr,pnx854   pp,qnc**559**}

☞ 8 And God spoke unto Noah, and   to his sons   with him, saying,

_{wcj,pnp589 ptdm,pnx2009   hipt**6965**   (853)   nn,pnx1285   pr,pnx854   wcj,pr854}

9 And   I,   behold, I establish   my covenant with you, and with your

_{nn,pnx**2233** pr,pnx310}

seed   after you;

_{wcj,pr854 cs,nn3605 df,aj**2416**   cs,nn**5315** pnl834   pr,pnx854   dfp,nn5775   dfp,nn929}

10 And with every living creature that *is* with you, of the fowl, of the cattle,

_{wcj,pp,cs,nn3605 cs,nn**2416**   df,nn776 pr,pnx854   pr4480/nn3605   pl,cs,qpta3318   df,nn8392}

and of every   beast of the earth with you; from all that go out of the ark, to

_{pp,nn3605 cs,nn**2416**   df,nn776}

every beast of the earth.

_{wcj.hipf**6965** (853)   nn,pnx1285   pr,pnx854   wcj,ptn**3808**   cs,nn3605 nn**1320**}

11 And I will establish   my covenant with you; neither shall   all   flesh be

_{nimf**3772**   ad5750   pr4480/pl,cs,nn4325   df,nn3999 wcj,ptn**3808**   ad5750   qmf**1961**}

cut off any more by*the*waters of a flood; neither shall there any more   be a

_{nn3999   pp,pinc**7843**   df,nn776}

flood to destroy the earth.

_{pl,nn**430** wcs,qmf**559** pndm2063   cs,nn226   df,nn**1285** pnl834   pnp589 qpta**5414**}

12 And God said,   This *is* the token of the covenant which   I   make

_{pr,pnx996   wcj,pnx(pr996)   wcj(pr996) cs,nn3605 aj**2416**   nn5315 pnl834   pr,pnx854}

between me and   you and   every living creature that *is* with you, for

_{nn5769   pp,pl,cs,nn**1755**}

perpetual generations:

_{qpf**5414** (853)   nn,pnx7198   dfp,nn**6051**   wcj,qpf**1961**   pp,cs,nn226}

13 I do set   my bow in the cloud, and it shall   be   for a token of a

_{nn**1285**   pr,pnx996   wcj(pr996)   df,nn776}

covenant between me and   the earth.

_{wcj,qpf**1961**   pp,pinc,pnx**6049**   nn**6051**   pr5921   df,nn776}

14 And it*shall*come*to*pass, when I   bring   a cloud over the earth, that the

_{df,nn7198   wcj,nipf**7200**   dfp,nn**6051**}

bow shall be   seen   in the cloud:

_{wcj,qpf**2142**   (853)   nn,pnx1285   pnl834   pr,pnx996   wcj,pnx(pr996)}

15 And I will remember   my covenant, which *is* between me and

_{wcj(pr996) cs,nn3605   aj**2416**   nn**5315**   pp,cs,nn3605   nn**1320**   df,pl,nn4325   wcj,ptn**3808**}

you and   every living creature of   all   flesh; and the waters shall   no

_{ad5750   qmf**1961**   pp,nn3999   pp,pinc**7843** cs,nn3605 nn**1320**}

more become a flood to destroy all   flesh.

_{df,nn7198   wcs,qpf**1961**   dfp,nn**6051**   wcs,qpf,pnx**7200**}

16 And the bow shall   be   in the cloud; and I will look upon it, that I may

_{pp,qnc**2142**   nn5769   nn**1285**   pr996   pl,nn**430**   wcj(pr996) cs,nn3605 aj**2416**   nn**5315**}

remember the everlasting covenant between God and   every living creature of

_{pp,cs,nn3605 nn**1320** pnl834   pr5921   df,nn776}

all   flesh that *is* upon the earth.

☞ **9:8–17** Throughout history God has dealt with man through covenants or agreements. Later, the Jews regarded this covenant between God and Noah as the basis of the relationship between God and all mankind, but the covenants with Abraham (chap. 15) and with Moses at Mount Sinai were seen as forming the basis of God's special relationship with Israel. Some believe that the stipulations laid on the Gentiles in Acts 15:20, 29 find validity here in the covenant between God and Noah. In spite of the fact that the distinction between clean and unclean animals existed (Gen. 7:2), God allowed the eating of any plant or animal. The only restriction was the eating of animal blood, for that is where the life of the animal resided (Gen. 9:4). Later, Israel was forbidden to eat not only blood but also the flesh of certain animals. The Lord removed the clean–unclean distinction from food altogether under the New Covenant (Mark 7:15; Acts 10:15; 1 Tim. 4:4, 5; Titus 1:15).

pl,nn**430** wcs,qmf**559** pr413   nn5146   pndm2063   cs,nn**226**   df,nn**1285**   pnl834

17 And God said   unto Noah, This *is* the token of the covenant, which I

hipf**6965**   pr,pnx996   wcj(pr996) cs,nn3605 nn**1320**   pr5921   df,nn**776**

have established between me and   all flesh that *is* upon the earth.

pl,cs,nn**1121**   nn5146   df,pl,qpta3318   pr4480   df,nn8392 wcs,qmf**1961**   nn8035

18 And the sons of Noah, that went forth of the ark, were Shem, and

wcj,nn2526   wcj,nn3315   wcj,nn2526 (pnp1931)   cs,nn1   nn3667

Ham, and Japheth: and Ham   *is* the father of Canaan.

pndm428   nu7969   pl,cs,nn**1121**   nn5146   wcj,pr4480/pndm428   cs,nn3605 df,nn**776**

19 These *are* the three sons of Noah: and of them   was the whole earth

qpf5310

overspread.

nn5146 wcs,himf**2490**   cs,nn**376**/df,nn**127**   wcs,qmf5193   nn3754

☜ 20 And Noah began *to be* an husbandman, and he planted a vineyard:

wcs,qmf8354 pr4480   df,nn3196   wcs,qmf7937   wcs,htmf**1540**

21 And he drank   of the wine, and was drunken; and he was uncovered

pp,cs,nn**8432**   nn,pnx**168**

within his tent.

nn2526   cs,nn1   nn3667 wcs,qmf**7200** (853)   cs,nn**6172**   nn,pnx1

22 And Ham, the father of Canaan, saw   the nakedness of his father, and

wcs,himf**5046**   pp,du,cs,nu8147   pl,nn,pnx**251**   dfp,nn2351

told his   two   brethren without.

nn8035   wcj,nn3315 wcs,qmf3947 (853)   df,nn8071   wcs,qmf**7760**   pr5921   du,nu,pnx8147

23 And Shem and Japheth took   a garment, and laid *it* upon both

cs,nn7926   wcs,qmf**1980**   ad322   wcs,pimf**3680** (853)   cs,nn**6172**   nn,pnx1

their shoulders, and went backward, and covered   the nakedness of their father;

wcj,pl,nn,pnx**6440**   ad322   qpf**7200** ptn3808   nn,pnx1   wcj,cs,nn**6172**

and their   faces   *were* backward, and they saw not their father's nakedness.

nn5146 wcs,qmf3364   pr4480/nn,pnx3196   wcs,qmf3045 (853) pnl834   df,aj6996   nn,pnx**1121**

24 And Noah awoke from*his*wine, and knew   what his younger   son

qpf**6213**   pp,pnx

had done unto him.

wcs,qmf559   qptp779   nn3667   cs,nn**5650**   pl,nn**5650**   qmf**1961**

25 And he said, Cursed *be* Canaan; a servant of servants shall he be unto

pp,pl,nn,pnx**251**

his brethren.

wcs,qmf**559** qptp**1288**   nn3068 pl,cs,nn**430**   nn8035   nn3667   wcj,qcj**1961**

26 And he said, Blessed *be* the Lord God of Shem; and Canaan shall   be

pp,pnx   nn**5650**

his servant.

pl,nn**430**   hicj6601   pp,nn3315   wcj,qmf**7931**   pp,pl,cs,nn**168**   nn8035

27 God shall enlarge Japheth, and he shall dwell in the tents of Shem; and

nn3667   wcj,qcj**1961** pp,pnx   nn**5650**

Canaan shall   be   his servant.

nn5146 wcs,qmf**2421** pr310   df,nn3999 cs,nu7969 pl,nu3967   (nn8141)   wcj,pl,nu2572 nn8141

28 And Noah lived after the flood three hundred   and fifty years.

☜ **9:20–27**   The Hebrew word used here for "nakedness" ('*erwāh* [6172]) actually means "shameful naked-ness" and is often used to describe immoral behavior. A different word ('*ērōm* [5903]) is used to describe simple nakedness or bareness.

The statement in verse twenty–two that Ham was the father of Canaan, and the fact that Noah's curse is directed against Canaan (v. 25), indicate that Canaan was somehow involved in immoral and indecent behavior with his drunken grandfather. Ham was indirectly to blame because he had allowed Canaan to grow up with this character and because he evidently did not treat Noah with respect when he found him.

The prophecy of Noah was to a large extent fulfilled when the Canaanites became "hewers of wood and drawers of water" for the Israelites (v. 25, cf. Josh. 9:23).

cs,nn3605   pl,cs,nn**3117**   nn5146   wcs,qmf**1961**   cs,nu8672   pl,nu3967   (nn8141)   wcj,pl,nu2572

29 And   all   the   days   of Noah   were   nine   hundred   and   fifty

nn8141   wcs,qmf**4191**

years: and he died.

Noah's Family Record

10

wcj,pndm428   pl,cs,nn**8435**   pl,cs,nn**1121**   nn5146   nn8035   nn2526

Now   these   *are* the generations of the   sons   of Noah, Shem, Ham,

wcj,nn3315   pp,pnx   pl,nn1121   wcs,nimf3205   pr310   df,nn3999

and Japheth: and unto them were sons   born   after the flood.

pl,cs,nn**1121**   nn3315   nn1586   wcj,nn4031   wcj,nn4074   wcj,nn3120

2 The   sons   of Japheth; Gomer, and Magog, and Madai, and Javan, and

wcj,nn8422   wcj,nn4902   wcj,nn8494

Tubal, and Meshech, and Tiras.

wcj,pl,cs,nn**1121**   nn1586   nn813   wcj,nn7384   wcj,nn8425

3 And the   sons   of Gomer; Ashkenaz, and Riphath, and Togarmah.

wcj,pl,cs,nn**1121**   nn3120   nn473   wcj,nn8659   nn3794   wcj,nn1721

4 And the   sons   of Javan; Elishah, and Tarshish, Kittim, and Dodanim.

pr4480/pndm428   pl,cs,nn339   df,pl,nn**1471**   nipf6504   pp,pl,nn,pnx776   nn376

5 By these were the   isles   of the Gentiles divided in their   lands;   every one

pp,nn,pnx3956   pp,pl,nn,pnx**4940**   pp,pl,nn,pnx**1471**

after his tongue, after their families, in their nations.

wcj,pl,cs,nn**1121**   nn2526   nn3568   wcj,nn4714   wcj,nn6316   wcj,nn3667

6 And the   sons   of Ham; Cush, and Mizraim, and Phut, and Canaan.

wcj,pl,cs,nn**1121**   nn3568   nn5434   wcj,nn2341   wcj,nn5454   wcj,nn7484

7 And the   sons   of Cush; Seba, and Havilah, and Sabtah, and Raamah, and

wcj,nn5455   wcj,pl,cs,nn**1121**   nn7484   nn7614   wcj,nn1719

Sabtecha: and the   sons   of Raamah; Sheba, and Dedan.

wcj,nn3568   qpf3205   (853)   nn5248   pnp1931   hipf**2490**   pp,qnc**1961**   nn1368

8 And Cush begot   Nimrod: he   began to   be   a mighty one in the

dfp,nn**776**

earth.

pnp1931   qpf**1961**   cs,aj1368   nn6718   pp,pl,cs,nn**6440**   nn3068   pr5921/ad**3651**   nimf**559**

9 He   was   a mighty hunter   before   the Lᴏʀᴅ: wherefore it is said, Even as

pp,nn5248   cs,aj1368   nn6718   pp,pl,cs,nn**6440**   nn3068

Nimrod the mighty hunter   before   the Lᴏʀᴅ.

cs,nn**7225**   nn,pnx**4467**   wcs,qmf**1961**   nn894   wcj,nn751   wcj,nn390

10 And the beginning of his kingdom   was   Babel, and Erech, and Accad, and

wcj,nn3641   pp,cs,nn**776**   nn8152

Calneh, in the   land   of Shinar.

pr4480   df,pndm1931   df,nn**776**   qpf3318   nn804   wcs,qmf1129   (853)   nn5210   wcj(853)

11 Out of   that   land went forth Asshur, and   built   Nineveh, and

nn5892   nn7344   wcj(853)   nn3625

the city Rehoboth, and   Calah,

wcj(853)   nn7449   pr996   nn5210   wcj(pr996)   nn3625   pnp1931   df,aj1419

12 And   Resen between Nineveh and   Calah: the same *is* a great

df,nn**5892**

city.

wcj,nn4714   qpf3205   (853)   nn3866   wcj(853)   nn6047   wcj(853)   nn3853

13 And Mizraim begot   Ludim, and   Anamim, and   Lehabim, and

wcj(853)   nn5320

Naphtuhim,

^{wcj(853)}   ⁿⁿ⁶⁶²⁵   ^{wcj(853)}   ⁿⁿ³⁶⁹⁵   ^{pr4480/ad8033/pnl834}   ^{qpf3318}   ⁿⁿ⁶⁴³⁰

14 And   Pathrusim, and   Casluhim, (out*of*whom came Philistim,)

^{wcj(853)}   ⁿⁿ³⁷³²

and   Caphtorim.

^{wcj,nn3667}   ^{qpf3205}   ⁽⁸⁵³⁾   ⁿⁿ⁶⁷²¹   ^{nn,pnx1060}   ^{wcj(853)}   ⁿⁿ²⁸⁴⁵

15 And Canaan begot   Sidon his firstborn, and   Heth,

^{wcj(853)}   ^{df,nn2983}   ^{wcj(853)}   ^{df,nn567}   ^{wcj(853)}   ^{df,nn1622}

16 And   the Jebusite, and   the Amorite, and   the Girgasite,

^{wcj(853)}   ^{df,nn2340}   ^{wcj(853)}   ^{df,nn6208}   ^{wcj(853)}   ^{df,nn5513}

17 And   the Hivite, and   the Arkite, and   the Sinite,

^{wcj(853)}   ^{df,nn721}   ^{wcj(853)}   ^{df,nn6786}   ^{wcj(853)}   ^{df,nn2577}

18 And   the Arvadite, and   the Zemarite, and   the Hamathite: and

^{wcj,ad310}   ^{pl,cs,nn4940}   ^{df,nn3669}   ^{nipf6327}

afterward were the families of the Canaanites spread abroad.

^{cs,nn1366}   ^{df,nn3669}   ^{wcs,qmf1961}   ^{pr4480/nn6721}   ^{qnc,pnx935}

19 And the border of the Canaanites was   from Sidon, as thou comest to

^{nn,lh1642}   ^{pr5704}   ⁿⁿ⁵⁸⁰⁴   ^{qnc,pnx935}   ^{nn,lh5467}   ^{wcj,nn6017}   ^{wcj,nn126}

Gerar, unto Gaza; as thou goest, unto Sodom, and Gomorrah, and Admah, and

^{wcj,nn6636}   ^{pr5704}   ⁿⁿ³⁹⁶²

Zeboim, even unto Lasha.

^{pndm428}   ^{pl,cs,nn1121}   ⁿⁿ²⁵²⁶   ^{pp,pl,nn,pnx4940}   ^{pp,pl,nn,pnx3956}

20 These *are* the   sons   of Ham, after their families, after their tongues, in

^{pp,pl,nn,pnx776}   ^{pp,pl,nn,pnx1471}

their countries, *and* in their nations.

^{wcj,pp,nn8035}   ^{cs,nn1}   ^{cs,nn3605}   ^{pl,cs,nn1121}   ⁿⁿ⁵⁶⁷⁷   ^{cs,nn251}

21 Unto Shem also the father of all the children of Eber, the brother of

ⁿⁿ³³¹⁵   ^{df,aj1419}   ^{ad1571}   ^{pnp1931}   ^{pupf3205}

Japheth the elder, even to him were *children* born.

^{pl,cs,nn1121}   ⁿⁿ⁸⁰³⁵   ⁿⁿ⁵⁸⁶⁷   ^{wcj,nn804}   ^{wcj,nn775}   ^{wcj,nn3865}

22 The children of Shem; Elam, and Asshur, and Arphaxad, and Lud, and

^{wcj,nn758}

Aram.

^{wcj,pl,cs,nn1121}   ⁿⁿ⁷⁵⁸   ⁿⁿ⁵⁷⁸⁰   ^{wcj,nn2343}   ^{wcj,nn1666}   ^{wcj,nn4851}

23 And the children of Aram; Uz, and Hul, and Gether, and Mash.

^{wcj,nn775}   ^{qpf3205}   ⁽⁸⁵³⁾   ⁿⁿ⁷⁹⁷⁴   ^{wcj,nn7974}   ^{qpf3205}   ⁽⁸⁵³⁾   ⁿⁿ⁵⁶⁷⁷

24 And Arphaxad begot   Salah; and Salah begot   Eber.

^{wcj,pp,nn5677}   ^{pupf3205}   ^{du,cs,nu8147}   ^{pl,nn1121}   ^{cs,nn8034}   ^{df,nu259}   ⁿⁿ⁶³⁸⁹   ^{cj3588}

25 And unto Eber were born two   sons: the name of one *was* Peleg; for

^{pp,pl,nn,pnx3117}   ^{df,nn776}   ^{nipf6385}   ^{nn,pnx251}   ^{wcj,cs,nn8034}   ⁿⁿ³³⁵⁵

in his days   was the earth divided; and his brother's name *was* Joktan.

^{wcj,nn3355}   ^{qpf3205}   ⁽⁸⁵³⁾   ⁿⁿ⁴⁸⁶   ^{wcj(853)}   ⁿⁿ⁸⁰²⁶   ^{wcj(853)}   ⁿⁿ²⁷⁰⁰

26 And Joktan begot   Almodad, and   Sheleph, and   Hazarmaveth,

^{wcj(853)}   ⁿⁿ³³⁹²

and   Jerah,

^{wcj(853)}   ⁿⁿ¹⁹¹³   ^{wcj(853)}   ⁿⁿ¹⁸⁷   ^{wcj(853)}   ⁿⁿ¹⁸⁵³

27 And   Hadoram, and   Uzal, and   Diklah,

^{wcj(853)}   ⁿⁿ⁵⁷⁴⁵   ^{wcj(853)}   ⁿⁿ³⁹   ^{wcj(853)}   ⁿⁿ⁷⁶¹⁴

28 And   Obal, and   Abimael, and   Sheba,

10:15–17 The Hivites were one of the seven nations descended from Canaan (Gen. 10:17; Deut. 7:1). They were present in Shechem, Gibeon, and Lebanon (Gen. 34:2; Josh. 9:3–7; Judg. 3:3). Israel was commanded to destroy them, but they failed to obey, and some were still present in Solomon's day (1 Kgs. 9:20, 21).

wcj(853)   nn211   wcj(853)   nn2341   wcj(853)   nn3103   cs,nn3605   pndm428

29 And   Ophir, and   Havilah, and   Jobab: all   these *were* the

pl,cs,nn1121   nn3355

sons of Joktan.

nn,pnx4186   wcs,qmf1961   pr4480/nn4852   qnc,pnx935   nn,lh5611   cs,nn2022

30 And their dwelling was   from Mesha, as thou goest unto Sephar a mount

df,nn6924

of the east.

pndm428   pl,cs,nn1121   nn8035   pp,pl,nn,pnx4940   pp,pl,nn,pnx3956

31 These *are* the sons of Shem, after their families, after their tongues, in

pp,pl,nn,pnx776   pp,pl,nn,pnx1471

their lands, after their nations.

pndm428   pl,cs,nn4940   pl,cs,nn1121   nn5146   pp,pl,nn,pnx8435

32 These *are* the families of the sons of Noah, after their generations, in their

pp,pl,nn,pnx1471   wcj,pr4480/pndm428   df,pl,nn1471   nipf6504   dfp,nn776   pr310   df,nn3999

nations: and by these   were the nations divided in the earth after the flood.

The Tower of Babel

cs,nn3605   df,nn776   wcs,qmf1961   nu259   nn8193   pl,nu259   wcj,pl,nn1697

11

And the whole earth was of one language, and of one speech.

wcs,qmf1961   pp,qnc,pnx5265   pr4480/nn6924

2 And it*came*to*pass, as they journeyed from*the*east, that

wcs,qmf4672   nn1237   pp,cs,nn776   nn8152   wcs,qmf3427   ad8033

they found a plain in the land of Shinar; and they dwelt there.

wcs,qmf559   nn376   pr413   nn,pnx7453   qmf3051   qcj3835   pl,nn3843   wcj,qcj8313

3 And they said one to another, Go to, let us make brick, and burn them

pp,nn8316   pp,pnx wcs,qmf1961 df,nn3843   pp,nn68   wcj,df,nn2564 qpf1961 pp,pnx   dfp,nn2563

throughly. And they had brick for stone, and slime had they for mortar.

wcs,qmf559   qmf3051   qmf1129 pp,pnx   nn5892   wcj,nn4026   wcj,nn,pnx7218

4 And they said, Go to, let us build us a city and a tower, whose top

dfp,du,nn8064   wcj,qmf6213 pp,pnx   nn8034   cj6435   qmf6327

may reach unto heaven; and let us make us a name, lest we be scattered abroad

pr5921   pl,cs,nn6440   cs,nn3605   df,nn776

upon the face of the whole earth.

nn3068   wcs,qmf3381   pp,qnc7200   (853)   df,nn5892   wcj(853)   df,nn4026   pnl834

5 And the LORD came down to see   the city and   the tower, which

pl,cs,nn1121   df,nn120   qpf1129

the children of men built.

nn3068   wcs,qmf559   ptdm2005   nn5971   nu259   pp,nn,pnx3605 nu259

6 And the LORD said, Behold, the people *is* one, and they have all one

wcj,nn8193   wcj,pndm2088   hinc,pnx2490   pp,qnc6213   wcj,ad6258 ptn3808/nn3605   nimf1219

language; and this they begin to do: and now nothing will be restrained

pr,pnx4480   pnl834   qmf2161   pp,qnc6213

from them, which they have imagined to do.

qmv3051   qcj3381   ad8033   wcj,qcj1101   nn,pnx8193   pnl834   ptn3808

7 Go to, let us go down, and there confound their language, that they may not

qmf8085   nn376   nn,pnx7453   cs,nn8193

understand one another's speech.

☞ **11:1–9** Josephus, the Jewish historian, places Babel in the days of Nimrod. Babel was a pointed rejection of God's instruction to "replenish the earth" (Gen. 9:1). It was a flagrant example of the corporate pride and willfulness of man. The intent of the tower may not have been to reach heaven; the expression can refer to a tower with an idolatrous "temple of heaven" on its top.

nn**3068**   wcs,himf6327/pnx(853)   pr4480/ad8033   pr5921   pl,cs,nn**6440**   cs,nn3605

8 So the LORD scattered*them*abroad from thence upon the face of all the

df,nn**776**   wcs,qmf2308   pp,qnc1129   df,nn5892

earth: and they left off to build the city.

pr5921/ad**3651**   nn,pnx8034   qpf7121   nn894   cj3588   nn**3068**   ad8033

9 Therefore is the name of it called Babel; because the LORD did there

qpf**1101**   cs,nn**8193**   cs,nn3605   df,nn**776**   wcj,pr4480/ad8033   nn**3068**

confound the language of all the earth: and from thence did the LORD

hipf,pnx6327   pr5921   pl,cs,nn**6440**   cs,nn3605   df,nn**776**

scatter*them*abroad upon the face of all the earth.

Shem's Family Record

pndm428   pl,cs,nn**8435**   nn8035   nn8035   cs,nu3967   nn8141   cs,nn**1121**

☞ 10 These *are* the generations of Shem: Shem *was* a hundred years old, and

wcs,himf3205 (853)   nn775   du,nn8141 pr310   df,nn3999

begot   Arphaxad two years after the flood:

nn8035   wcs,qmf**2421**   ad310   hinc,pnx3205 (853)   nn775   cs,nu2568   pl,nu3967   nn8141

11 And Shem lived after he begot   Arphaxad five hundred years, and

wcs,himf3205 pl,nn**1121**   wcj,pl,nn1323

begot sons and daughters.

wcj,nn775   qpf**2425** nu2568   wcj,nu7970   nn8141   wcs,himf3205 (853)   nn7974

12 And Arphaxad lived five and thirty years, and begot   Salah:

nn775   wcs,qmf**2421**   ad310   hinc,pnx3205 (853)   nn7974 wcj,nu702   pl,nu3967   (nn8141)

13 And Arphaxad lived after he begot   Salah four hundred   and

nu7969   pl,nn8141   wcs,himf3205 pl,nn**1121**   wcj,pl,nn1323

three years, and begot sons and daughters.

wcj,nn7974 qpf**2425**   nu7970   nn8141   wcs,himf3205 (853)   nn5677

14 And Salah lived thirty years, and begot   Eber:

nn7974   wcs,qmf**2421**   ad310   hinc,pnx3205 (853)   nn5677 wcj,nu702   pl,nu3967   (nn8141)   nu7969

15 And Salah lived after he begot   Eber four hundred   and three

pl,nn8141   wcs,himf3205 pl,nn**1121**   wcj,pl,nn1323

years, and begot sons and daughters.

nn5677   wcs,qmf**2421** nu702   wcj,nu7970   nn8141   wcs,himf3205 (853)   nn6389

16 And Eber lived four and thirty years, and begot   Peleg:

nn5677   wcs,qmf**2421**   ad310   hinc,pnx3205 (853)   nn6389 wcj,nu702   pl,nu3967   (nn8141)   nu7970

17 And Eber lived after he begot   Peleg four hundred   and thirty

nn8141   wcs,himf3205 pl,nn**1121**   wcj,pl,nn1323

years, and begot sons and daughters.

nn6389   wcs,qmf**2421** nu7970   nn8141   wcs,himf3205 (853)   nn7466

18 And Peleg lived thirty years, and begot   Reu:

nn6389   wcs,qmf**2421**   ad310   hinc,pnx3205 (853)   nn7466   wcj,du,nu3967   (nn8141)   nu8672

19 And Peleg lived after he begot   Reu two hundred   and nine

pl,nn8141   wcs,himf3205 pl,nn**1121**   wcj,pl,nn1323

years, and begot sons and daughters.

nn7466 wcs,qmf**2421** du,nu8147   wcj,nu7970   nn8141   wcs,himf3205 (853)   nn8286

20 And Reu lived two and thirty years, and begot   Serug:

nn7466   wcs,qmf**2421**   ad310   hinc,pnx3205 (853)   nn8286   wcj,du,nu3967   (nn8141)   nu7651

21 And Reu lived after he begot   Serug two hundred   and seven

pl,nn8141   wcs,himf3205 pl,nn**1121**   wcj,pl,nn1323

years, and begot sons and daughters.

nn8286   wcs,qmf**2421**   nu7970   nn8141   wcs,himf3205 (853)   nn5152

22 And Serug lived thirty years, and begot   Nahor:

☞ **11:10–27**   Note the steadily decreasing lifespan (Gen. 5:1–32).

nn8286 wcs,qmf**2421** ad310 hinc,pnx3205 (853) nn5152 du,nu3967 nn8141

23 And Serug lived after he begot Nahor two hundred years, and

wcs,himf3205 pl,nn**1121** wcj,pl,nn1323

begot sons and daughters.

nn5152 wcs,qmf**2421** nu8672 wcj,pl,nu6242 nn8141 wcs,himf3205 (853) nn8646

24 And Nahor lived nine and twenty years, and begot Terah:

nn5152 wcs,qmf**2421** ad310 hinc,pnx3205 (853) nn8646 wcj,cs,nu3967 (nn8141) cs,nu8672/nu6240

25 And Nahor lived after he begot Terah a hundred and nineteen

nn8141 wcs,himf3205 pl,nn**1121** wcj,pl,nn1323

years, and begot sons and daughters.

nn8646 wcs,qmf**2421** pl,nu7657 nn8141 wcs,himf3205 (853) nn87 (853) nn5152

26 And Terah lived seventy years, and begot Abram, Nahor, and

wcj(853) nn2039

Haran.

wcj,pndm428 pl,cs,nn**8435** nn8646 nn8646 hipf3205 (853) nn87 (853)

27 Now these *are* the generations of Terah: Terah begot Abram,

nn5152 wcj(853) nn2039 wcj,nn2039 hipf3205 (853) nn3876

Nahor, and Haran; and Haran begot Lot.

nn2039 wcs,qmf**4191** pr5921/pl,cs,nn**6440** nn,pnx1 nn8646 pp,cs,nn**776** nn,pnx4138

28 And Haran died before his father Terah in the land of his nativity,

pp,nn218 nn3778

in Ur of the Chaldees.

nn87 wcj,nn5152 wcs,qmf3947 pp,pnx pl,nn**802** cs,nn8034 nn87 cs,nn**802**

29 And Abram and Nahor took them wives: the name of Abram's wife *was*

nn8297 wcj,cs,nn8034 nn5152 cs,nn**802** nn4435 cs,nn1323 nn2039 cs,nn1

Sarai; and the name of Nahor's wife, Milcah, the daughter of Haran, the father of

nn4435 wcj,cs,nn1 nn3252

Milcah, and the father of Iscah.

nn8297 wcs,qmf**1961** aj6135 pp,pnx ptn369 nn2056

30 But Sarai was barren; she *had* no child.

nn8646 wcs,qmf3947 (853) nn87 nn,pnx1121 wcj(853) nn3876 cs,nn1121 nn2039

⌖ 31 And Terah took Abram his son, and Lot the son of Haran

nn,pnx1121 cs,nn1121 wcj(853) nn8297 nn,pnx3618 nn,pnx1121 nn87 cs,nn**802**

his son's son, and Sarai his daughter-in-law, his son Abram's wife; and

wcs,qmf3318 pr,pnx854 pr4480/nn218 nn3778 pp,qnc**1980** nn,lh**776**

they went forth with them from Ur of the Chaldees, to go into the land of

nn3667 wcs,qmf935 pr5704 nn2771 wcs,qmf**3427** ad8033

Canaan; and they came unto Haran, and dwelt there.

pl,cs,nn**3117** nn8646 wcs,qmf**1961** wcj,du,nu3967 (nn8141) nu2568 pl,nn8141

32 And the days of Terah were two hundred and five years: and

nn8646 wcs,qmf**4191** pp,nn2771

Terah died in Haran.

⌖ **11:31** The statement that "Terah took Abram" is worded in that way because of Oriental propriety. Even though Abram was the practical leader of the family (Gen. 12:4, 5), his old and probably infirm father still occupied the place of honor. When Abram took this step, he was motivated by faith in the promise of God and did not even know his ultimate destination (Heb. 11:31; Gal. 3:6–9). The phrase "to go into the land of Canaan" in Gen. 11:31 is an infinitive of result, not of purpose.

God Calls Abram

12 ☞ Now the LORD had said unto Abram, Get*thee*out of*thy*country, and from*thy*kindred, and from*thy*father's*house, unto a land that I will show thee:

2 And I will make of thee a great nation, and I will bless thee, and make*thy*name*great; and thou shalt be a blessing:

3 And I will bless them that bless thee, and curse him that curseth thee: and in thee shall all families of the earth be blessed.

4 So Abram departed, as the LORD had spoken unto him; and Lot went with him: and Abram *was* seventy and five years old when he departed out*of*Haran.

5 And Abram took Sarai his wife, and Lot his brother's son, and all their substance that they had gathered, and the souls that they had gotten in Haran; and they went forth to go into the land of Canaan; and into the land of Canaan they came.

6 And Abram passed through the land unto the place of Sichem, unto the plain of Moreh. And the Canaanite *was* then in the land.

7 And the LORD appeared unto Abram, and said, Unto thy seed will I give this land: and there built he an altar unto the LORD, who appeared unto him.

8 And he removed from thence unto a mountain on*the*east of Bethel, and pitched his tent, *having* Bethel on*the*west, and Hai on*the*east: and there he built an altar unto the LORD, and called upon the name of the LORD.

☞ **12:1–3** This promise to Abraham is one of the most significant passages in the entire Bible. It points ultimately to the redemption of the whole world. Abraham's family became a divinely appointed channel through which blessing would come to all men. This promise was formalized in a covenant (Gen. 15:18–21), and was repeated four additional times: twice to Abraham (Gen. 17:6–8; 22:16–18); once to Isaac (Gen. 26:3, 4); and once to Jacob (Gen. 28:13, 14). Note the circumstances of the family in each case. This promise is emphasized in the New Testament in Acts 3:35, Romans 4:13, Galatians 3:8, 29, and Ephesians 2:12. Galatians calls it "the Gospel." Its importance to the Gentiles is stressed in Galatians as well as Ephesians where it is clearly stated that Gentiles who were "far off" and "strangers to the covenant of promise" have been brought to it by the blood of Christ.

nn87   wcs,qmf5265   qna**1980**   wcj,qna5265   df,nn,lh5045

9 And Abram journeyed, going on still toward the south.

Abram Goes to Egypt

wcs,qmf**1961**   nn7458   dfp,nn776   nn87   wcs,qmf3381   nn,lh4714

10 And there was a famine in the land: and Abram went down into Egypt to

pp,qnc1481 ad8033 cj3588   df,nn7458   aj3515   dfp,nn**776**

sojourn there; for the famine *was* grievous in the land.

wcs,qmf**1961**   pp,pnl834   hipf**7126**   pp,qnc935   nn,lh4714

11 And it*came*to*pass, when he was come near to enter into Egypt, that he

wcs,qmf559   pr413   nn8297   nn,pnx**802** ptdm2009 pte**4994**   qpf**3045** cj3588 pnp859   cs,aj3303   nn**802**

said unto Sarai his wife, Behold now, I know that thou *art* a fair woman to

nn**4758**

look upon:

wcs,qpf**1961**   cj3588   df,nn4713   qmf**7200** pnx(853)

12 Therefore it*shall*come*to*pass, when the Egyptians shall see   thee,

wcs,qpf559   pndm2063   nn,pnx**802**   wcs,qpf2026 pnx(853)

that they shall say, This *is* his wife: and they will   kill   me, but they

wcj,pnx(853)   pimf**2421**

will save*thee*alive.

qmv559   pte**4994**   pnp859   nn,pnx**269** pp,cj4616   qmf**3190**   pp,pnx

13 Say, I*pray*thee, thou *art* my sister: that it may be well with me

pp,pr,pnx5668   nn,pnx**5315**   wcs,qpf**2421** pp,nn,pnx1558

for*thy*sake; and my soul shall live because of thee.

wcs,qmf**1961**   nn87   pp,qnc935   nn,lh4714

14 And it*came*to*pass, that, when Abram was come into Egypt, the

df,nn4713   wcs,qmf**7200** (853)   df,nn**802** cj3588 pnp1931   ad3966 aj3303

Egyptians beheld   the woman that she *was* very fair.

pl,cs,nn**8269**   nn6547   wcs,qmf**7200** pnx(853)   wcs,pimf**1984**   pnx(853)

15 The princes also of Pharaoh saw   her, and commended   her

pr413   nn6547   df,nn**802**   wcs,homf3947   nn6547   cs,nn**1004**

before Pharaoh: and the woman was taken into Pharaoh's house.

hipf**3190**/wcj,pp,nn87   pp,pr,pnx5668   pp,pnx wcs,qmf**1961**   nn6629

16 And he entreated*Abram*well for*her*sake: and he   had   sheep, and

wcj,nn1241   wcj,pl,nn2543   wcj,pl,nn**5650**   wcj,pl,nn8198   wcj,pl,nn860

oxen, and he asses, and menservants, and maidservants, and she asses, and

wcj,pl,nn1581

camels.

nn**3068**   wcs,pimf**5060** (853)   nn6547   wcj(853)   nn,pnx**1004**   aj1419 pl,nn**5061**

17 And the Lord plagued   Pharaoh and   his house with great plagues

pr5921/cs,nn**1697**   nn8297   nn87   cs,nn**802**

because of Sarai Abram's wife.

nn6547   wcs,qmf**7121** pp,nn87   wcs,qmf559 pnit4100 pndm2063   qpf**6213**

18 And Pharaoh called Abram, and said, What *is* this *that* thou hast done

pp,pnx   pp,pnit4100   ptn3808 hipf5046 pp,pnx cj3588 pnp1931   nn,pnx**802**

unto me? why didst thou not tell me that she *was* thy wife?

pp,pnit4100 qpf**559**   pnp1931   nn,pnx**269**   wcs,qmf3947 pnx(853)

19 Why saidst thou, She *is* my sister? so I might have taken   her

pp,pnx   pp,nn**802**   wcj,ad6258 ptdm2009 nn,pnx**802** qmv3947   wcj,qmv**1980**

to me to wife: now therefore behold thy wife, take *her*, and go*thy*way.

12:11–20 See the note on Genesis 20:2–18.

nn6547   wcs,pimf**6680**   pl,nn**376**   pr,pnx5921   wcs,pimf7971/pnx(853)

20 And Pharaoh commanded *his* men concerning him: and they sent*him*away,

wcj(853)   nn,pnx**802**   wcj(853) cs,nn3605 pnl834 pp,pnx

and   his wife, and   all   that he had.

Abram and Lot Separate

nn87   wcs,qmf**5927**   pr4480/nn4714   pnp1931   wcj,nn,pnx**802**   wcj,cs,nn3605

13 And Abram went up out*of*Egypt, he, and his wife, and all

pnl834 pp,pnx   wcj,nn3876 pr,pnx5973   df,nn,lh5045

that he had, and Lot with him, into the south.

wcj,nn87   ad3966 aj3515   dfp,nn4735   dfp,nn3701   wcj,dfp,nn2091

2 And Abram *was* very rich in cattle, in silver, and in gold.

wcs,qmf**1980**   pp,pl,nn,pnx4550   pr4480/nn5045   wcj,pr5704   nn1008   pr5704

3 And he went on his journeys from*the*south even to Bethel, unto the

df,nn4725 pnl834/ad8033   nn,pnx**168**   qpf**1961**   dfp,nn8462   pr996   nn1008   wcj(pr996) df,nn5857

place where his tent had been at the beginning, between Bethel and Hai;

pr413   cs,nn4725   df,nn**4196** pnl834   qpf**6213** ad8033   dfp,aj**7223**   ad8033

4 Unto the place of the altar, which he had made there at the first: and there

nn87   wcs,qmf**7121**   pp,cs,nn8034   nn**3068**

Abram called on the name of the LORD.

pp,nn3876 wcj,ad1571   df,qpta**1980** pr854   nn87   qpf**1961**   nn6629   wcj,nn1241

5 And Lot also, which went with Abram, had flocks, and herds, and

wcj,pl,nn**168**

tents.

df,nn**776**   wcj,ptn**3808**   qpf**5375**   pnx(853)   pp,qnc**3427**

6 And the land was not able*to*bear them, that they might dwell

ad3162   cj3588   nn,pnx7399   qpf**1961**   aj7227   qpf3201 wcj,ptn**3808** pp,qnc**3427**   ad3162

together: for their substance was great, so that they could not dwell together.

wcs,qmf**1961**   nn7379   pr996   pl,cs,qpta7462   nn87   cs,nn4735   wcj(pr996)

7 And there was a strife between the herdsmen of Abram's cattle and

pl,cs,qpta7462   nn3876 cs,nn4735   wcj,df,nn3669   wcj,df,nn6522   qpta**3427**   ad227

the herdsmen of Lot's cattle: and the Canaanite and the Perizzite dwelled then in the

dfp,nn**776**

land.

nn87   wcs,qmf**559** pr413 nn3876   qcj**1961** ptn408 nn4808   pte**4994**   pr,pnx996

8 And Abram said unto Lot, Let there be no strife, I*pray*thee, between

wcj,pnx(pr996)   wcj,pr996   pl,qpta,pnx7462   wcj(pr996)   pl,qpta,pnx7462 cj3588 pnp587

me and   thee, and between my herdsmen and   thy herdsmen; for we

(pl,nn**376**)   pl,nn**251**

be brethren.

he,ptn**3808**   cs,nn3605 df,nn**776**   pp,pl,nn,pnx**6440**   nimv6504   pte**4994**

9 *Is* not the whole land before thee? separate thyself, I*pray*thee,

pr4480/pr,pnx5921   cj518   df,nn8040   wcj,hicj3231   wcj,cj518

from me: if *thou wilt take* the left hand, then I will go*to*the*right; or if

df,nn3225   wcj,hicj8041

thou depart to the right hand, then I will go*to*the*left.

nn3876 wcs,qmf**5375** (853)   du,nn,pnx**5869**   wcs,qmf**7200** (853) cs,nn3605   cs,nn3603 df,nn3383

10 And Lot lifted up his eyes, and beheld all the plain of Jordan,

cj3588   nn4945   nn,pnx3605   pp,pl,cs,nn**6440**   nn**3068**   pinc**7843**   (853) nn5467

that it *was* well watered every where, before the LORD destroyed Sodom and

wcj(853)   nn6017   pp,cs,nn1588   nn**3068**   pp,cs,nn**776**   nn4714

Gomorrah, *even* as the garden of the LORD, like the land of Egypt, as thou

qnc,pnx935   nn6820

comest unto Zoar.

qmf,pnx**3423**　cj3588/cj518　pnl834　qmf3318　pr4480/pl,nn,pnx**4578**　(pnp1931)

be thine　heir;　　but　　he that shall come forth out*of*thine*own*bowels

qmf,pnx**3423**

shall be thine　heir.

wcs,himf3318/pnx(853)　df,nn,lh2351　wcs,qmf**559** himv5027 pte**4994**　df,du,nn,lh**8064**

　5 And he brought*him*forth abroad, and said, Look now toward heaven, and

wcj,qmv**5608**　df,pl,nn3556 cj518　qmf3201　pp,qnc**5608**　pnx(853)　wcs,qmf**559**　pp,pnx

tell　the stars,　if　thou be able to number　　them: and he　said　unto him,

ad3541　nn,pnx**2233** qmf**1961**

So shall thy seed be.

wcj,hipf**539**　pp,nn**3068**　wcs,qmf,pnx**2803**　pp,pnx　nn**6666**

☞ 6 And he believed in the LORD; and he counted it to him for righteousness.

wcs,qmf**559** pr,pnx413　pnp589　nn**3068** pnl834 hipf,pnx3318　pr4480/nn218

　7 And he said　unto him,　I　*am* the LORD that brought thee out*of*Ur of

nn3778　pp,qnc**5414** pp,pnx (853) df,pndm2063 df,nn**776**　pp,qnc,pnx**3423**

the Chaldees, to give thee　　this　land to inherit it.

wcs,qmf**559** nn**136**　nn3069　dfp,pnit4100　qmf3045 cj3588　qmf,pnx**3423**

　8 And he said, Lord GOD, whereby shall I know that I shall inherit it?

wcs,qmf**559**　pr,pnx413　qmv3947 pp,pnx　nn5697　pupt8027

　9 And he said　unto him, Take me an heifer of three*years*old, and a

wcj,nn5795　pupt8027　wcj,nn352　pupt8027　wcj,nn8449

she goat of three*years*old, and a　ram　of three*years*old, and a turtledove, and a

wcj,nn1469

young pigeon.

wcs,qmf3947　pp,pnx　(853) cs,nn3605 pndm428　wcs,pimf1334 pnx(853)

　10 And he took　unto him　　all　these, and divided　　them in the

dfp,nn**8432**　wcs,qmf**5414** nn**376** nn,pnx1335　pp,qnc7125 nn,pnx**7453**　wcj(853)　df,nn6833 qpf1334

midst, and　laid　each piece one against another: but　　the birds divided he

ptn**3808**

not.

df,nn5861　wcs,qmf3381　pr5921　df,pl,nn**6297**　nn87

　11 And　when　the　fowls　came down　upon　the　carcasses,　Abram

wcs,himf5380/pnx(853)

drove*them*away.

wcs(qmf**1961**)　df,nn8121　pp,qnc935　wcj,nn8639　qpf**5307** pr5921

　12 And　　　　when the　sun　was going down, a deep sleep fell upon

nn87　wcj,ptdm2009　nn367　aj1419　nn2825　qpta**5307** pr,pnx5921

Abram; and,　lo,　a horror of great darkness fell　upon him.

wcs,qmf**559**　pp,nn87　qna**3045**/qmf**3045**　cj3588　nn,pnx**2233**　qmf**1961**

☞ 13 And he　said　unto Abram, Know*of*a*surety that thy seed shall be a

---

☞ **15:6** This verse is believed by some to be the key verse of the entire Old Testament. It is an important witness to the doctrine of justification by faith and to the doctrine of the unity of believers in both dispensations. Abraham's faith was accounted to him for righteousness before he was circumcised and more than four hundred years before the law was given to his descendants. Therefore, neither circumcision nor the law had a part in Abraham's righteousness. Paul proves that Abraham's faith was not merely a general confidence in God nor simple obedience to God's command, but that it was indeed faith in the promise of redemption through Christ (Rom. 3:21, 22; 4:18–25; Gal. 3:14).

☞ **15:13–16** God gave Abraham a preview of events in his family's future up to the point of their possession of the land which He had promised. They would first be temporary residents in a strange land for 400 years and become slaves. Their bondage in Egypt was certainly a part of God's overall plan. Four hundred years is a round figure. There is no conflict with the 430 years mentioned in Exodus 12:40, 41. The four generations of their sojourn should be understood as four lifetimes. One hundred years would have been a conservative estimate for one lifetime in patriarchal times.

nn**1616**   pp,nn**776**   ptn**3808**   pp,pnx   wcs,qpf,pnx**5647**   wcs,pipf6031
stranger in a land *that is* not theirs, and shall   serve   them; and they shall afflict

pnx(853)   nu702   pl,nu3967   nn8141
them four hundred years;

wcj,ad1571   (853)   df,nn**1471**   pnl834   qmf**5647**   pnp595   qpta**1777**
14 And   also   that nation, whom they shall serve, will   I   judge: and

wcj,ad310/ad**3651**   qmf3318   aj1419   pp,nn7399
afterward shall they come out with great substance.

wcj,pnp859   qmf935 pr413   pl,nn,pnx1   pp,nn**7965**   nimf**6912**   aj**2896**
15 And thou shalt go   to thy fathers in peace; thou shalt be buried in a good

pp,nn**7872**
old age.

nuor7243   wcj,nn**1755**   qmf**7725**/ad2008   cj3588   cs,nn**5771**
⚬ᵣₐ 16 But in the fourth generation they shall come*hither*again: for the iniquity of

df,nn567   ptn**3808** pr5704/ad2008   aj**8003**
the Amorites *is* not   yet   full.

wcs,qmf**1961**   df,nn8121   qpf935   qpf**1961** wcj,nn5939
17 And it*came*to*pass, that, when the   sun   went down, and it was dark,

wcj,ptdm2009   nn6227   cs,nn8574   nn784   wcj,cs,nn3940 pnl834   qpf**5674**   pr996   df,pndm428
behold a smoking furnace, and a burning   lamp   that passed between those

df,pl,nn**1506**
pieces.

df,pndm1931 dfp,nn**3117**   nn**3068** qpf**3772**   nn**1285**   pr854   nn87   pp,qnc**559**
18 In the   same   day the LORD made a covenant with Abram, saying, Unto

pp,nn,pnx**2233**   qpf**5414** df,pndm2063 (853) df,nn**776**   pr4480/cs,nn5104   nn4714   pr5704   df,aj1419
thy seed   have I given this   land, from*the*river of Egypt unto the great

df,nn5104   cs,nn5104   nn6578
river, the river Euphrates:

(853)   df,nn7017   wcj(853)   df,nn7074   wcj(853)   df,nn6935
19   The Kenites, and   the Kenizzites, and   the Kadmonites,

wcj(853)   df,nn2850   wcj(853)   df,nn6522   wcj(853)   df,nn**7497**
20 And   the Hittites, and   the Perizzites, and   the Rephaims,

wcj(853)   df,nn567   wcj(853)   df,nn3669   wcj(853)   df,nn1622
21 And   the Amorites, and   the Canaanites, and   the Girgashites,

wcj(853)   df,nn2983
and   the Jebusites.

Hagar and Ishmael

wcj,nn8297   nn87   cs,nn**802**   qpf3205/pp,pnx/ptn**3808**   wcj,pp,pnx
16 Now Sarai Abram's wife bore*him*no*children: and   she   had an

nn8198   nn4713   wcj,nn,pnx8034   nn1904
handmaid, an Egyptian, whose   name *was* Hagar.

nn8297 wcs,qmf**559** pr413   nn87   ptdm2009 pte**4994**   nn**3068**   qpf,pnx6113
2 And Sarai   said   unto Abram, Behold now, the LORD hath restrained me

pr4480/qnc3205   pte**4994**   qmv935   pr413   nn,pnx8198   ad194
from bearing: I*pray*thee, go in unto my   maid; it*may*be that I may

nimf1129   pr,pnx4480   nn87   wcs,qmf**8085**   pp,cs,nn6963   nn8297
obtain children   by   her. And Abram hearkened to the voice of Sarai.

⚬ᵣₐ **15:16** The Amorite nation was one of the seven nations of Canaan and was governed by many independent kings (Josh. 5:1; 9:10). Originally they inhabited a mountain district in the south (Num. 13:29), but later they acquired an extensive tract of land from Moab, east of Jordan (Num. 21:26). They had many strong cities (Num. 32:17, 33). They were profane, wicked, and idolatrous (Josh. 24:15). They interfered with Israel at times (Num. 21:24), again were peaceful, but were finally brought into bondage by Solomon (1 Kgs. 9:20, 21).

nn8297   nn87   cs,nn**802** wcs,qmf3947 (853) nn1904   nn,pnx8198   df,nn4713 pr4480/cs,nn7093

3 And Sarai Abram's wife took Hagar her maid the Egyptian, after

nn87   pp,qnc**3427** nu6235 pl,nn8141   pp,cs,nn**776**   nn3667   wcs,qmf**5414** pnx(853)

Abram had dwelt ten years in the land of Canaan, and gave her to her

nn,pnx**376** pp,nn87   pp,pnx pp,nn**802**

husband Abram to be his wife.

wcs,qmf935   pr413   nn1904   wcs,qmf2029   wcs,qmf**7200** cj3588

4 And he went in unto Hagar, and she conceived: and when she saw that she

qpf2029   nn,pnx**1404**   wcs,qmf**7043**   pp,du,nn,pnx**5869**

had conceived, her mistress was despised in her eyes.

nn8297 wcs,qmf**559** pr413   nn87   nn,pnx**2555** pr,pnx**5921**   pnp595   qpf**5414**

5 And Sarai said unto Abram, My wrong *be* upon thee: I have given my

nn,pnx8198   pp,nn,pnx2436   wcs,qmf**7200** cj3588   qpf2029

maid into thy bosom; and when she saw that she had conceived, I was

wcs,qmf**7043**   pp,du,nn,pnx**5869**   nn3068   qmf**8199** pr,pnx996   wcj,pnx(pr996)

despised in her eyes: the LORD judge between me and thee.

nn87   wcs,qmf**559** pr413   nn8297   ptdm2009   nn,pnx8198   pp,nn,pnx**3027** qmv**6213**

6 But Abram said unto Sarai, Behold, thy maid *is* in thy hand; do

pp,pnx   df,nn**2896**/pp,du,nn,pnx**5869**   nn8297   wcs,pimf,pnx6031   wcs,qmf1272

to her as*it*pleaseth thee. And when Sarai dealt hardly with her, she fled

pr4480/pl,nn,pnx**6440**

from*her*face.

cs,nn**4397**   nn3068 wcs,qmf,pnx4672   pr5921   cs,nn**5869**   df,pl,nn4325

7 And the angel of the LORD found her by a fountain of water in the

dfp,nn4057 pr5921   df,nn**5869**   pp,cs,nn**1870** nn7793

wilderness, by the fountain in the way to Shur.

wcs,qmf**559**   nn1904   nn8297   cs,nn8198 pnit335/pr4480/pndm2088   qpf935   wcj,ad,lh575

8 And he said, Hagar, Sarai's maid, whence camest thou? and whither

qmf1980   wcs,qmf**559** pnp595   qpta1272   pr4480/pl,cs,nn**6440**   nn,pnx**1404**   nn8297

wilt thou go? And she said, I flee from*the*face of my mistress Sarai.

cs,nn**4397**   nn3068 wcs,qmf**559**   pp,pnx   qmv**7725** pr413   nn,pnx**1404**

9 And the angel of the LORD said unto her, Return to thy mistress, and

wcj,htmv6031   pr8478   du,nn,pnx**3027**

submit thyself under her hands.

cs,nn**4397**   nn3068 wcs,qmf**559**   pp,pnx

10 And the angel of the LORD said unto her, I will

hina7235/himf7235/(853)/nn,pnx**2233**   wcj,ptn**3808**   nimf**5608**   pr4480/nn7230

multiply*thy*seed*exceedingly, that it shall not be numbered for multitude.

cs,nn**4397**   nn3068 wcs,qmf**559**   pp,pnx   ptdm,pnx2009   aj2030

11 And the angel of the LORD said unto her, Behold, thou *art* with child,

wcs,qpf3205   nn1121   wcs,qpf**7121**   nn,pnx8034 nn3458   cj3588   nn**3068**

and shalt bear a son, and shalt call his name Ishmael; because the LORD hath

qpf**8085**/pr413   nn,pnx6040

heard thy affliction.

wcj,pnp1931   qmf**1961** cs,nn6501 nn**120**   nn,pnx**3027**   dfp,nn3605

12 And he will be a wild man; his hand *will be* against every man,

nn3605   wcj,cs,nn**3027** pp,pnx   qmf**7931** wcj,pr5921/pl,cs,nn**6440**   cs,nn3605

and every man's hand against him; and he shall dwell in*the*presence of all

pl,nn,pnx**251**

his brethren.

wcs,qmf**7121**   cs,nn8034   nn3068 df,qpta**1696** pr,pnx413   pnp859 nn**410** nn**7210**

13 And she called the name of the LORD that spoke unto her, Thou God seest

cj3588   qpf**559**   he,ad1571 ad1988 qpf**7200** pr310   qpta,pnx**7200**

me: for she said, Have I also here looked after him*that*seeth me?

pr5921/ad**3651**   dfp,nn875   qpf**7121**   nn883   ptdm2009   pr996   nn6946

14 Wherefore the well was called Beer-lahai-roi; behold, *it is* between Kadesh

wcj(pr996)   nn1260

and   Bered.

nn1904   wcs,qmf3205   pp,nn87   nn**1121**   nn87   wcs,qmf**7121**   nn,pnx**1121**   cs,nn8034   pnl834

☞ 15 And Hagar bore Abram a son: and Abram called his son's name, which

nn1904   qpf3205   nn3458

Hagar bore, Ishmael.

wcj,nn87   pl,nu8084   (nn8141)   wcj,nu8337   pl,nn8141   cs,nn**1121**   nn1904   pp,qnc3205

16 And Abram *was* fourscore   and six years old, when Hagar bore

(853)   nn3458   pp,nn87

Ishmael to Abram.

Circumcision Is The Sign Of The Covenant

nn87   wcs,qmf**1961**   nu8673   nn8141   cs,nn**1121**   wcj,nu8672   (pl,nn8141)

17 And when Abram was ninety years old and nine,   the

nn**3068**   wcs,nimf**7200**   pr413   nn87   wcs,qmf**559**   pr,pnx413   pnp589

Lord appeared to Abram, and said unto him, I *am* the

nn**7706**   nn410   htmv**1980**   pp,pl,nn,pnx**6440**   wcj,qmv**1961**   aj8549

Almighty God; walk before me, and be thou perfect.

wcj,qcj**5414**   nn,pnx**1285**   pr,pnx996   wcj,pnx(pr996)

2 And I will make my covenant between me and   thee, and will

wcj,himf7235   pnx(853)   pp,ad3966/ad3966

multiply   thee exceedingly.

nn87   wcs,qmf**5307**   pr5921   pl,nn,pnx**6440**   pl,nn**430**   wcs,pimf**1696**   pr,pnx854   pp,qnc**559**

3 And Abram fell on his face: and God talked with him, saying,

pnp589   ptdm2009   nn,pnx**1285**   pr,pnx854   wcs,qpf**1961**   pp,cs,nn1

4 As*for*me, behold, my covenant *is* with thee, and thou shalt   be   a father

cs,nn1995   pl,nn**1471**

of many nations.

wcj,ptn**3808**   (853)   nn,pnx8034   ad5750   nimf**7121**   nn87   nn,pnx8034

☞ 5 Neither shall   thy name any more be called Abram, but thy name shall

wcs,qpf**1961**   nn85   cj3588   cs,nn1   cs,nn1995   pl,nn**1471**   qpf,pnx**5414**

be   Abraham; for a father of many nations have I made thee.

pnx(853)   pp,ad3966/ad3966   wcj,hipf6509   wcj,qpf,pnx**5414**   pp,pl,nn**1471**

6 And I will make   thee exceeding fruitful, and I will   make   nations of

wcj,pl,nn**4428**   qmf3318   pr,pnx4480

thee, and kings shall come out of thee.

wcs,hipf**6965**   (853)   nn,pnx**1285**   pr,pnx996   wcj,pnx(pr996)   wcj(pr996)

7 And I will establish   my covenant between me and   thee and

nn,pnx2233   pr,pnx310   pp,pl,nn,pnx**1755**   nn5769   pp,cs,nn**1285**   pp,qnc**1961**

thy seed after thee in their generations for an everlasting covenant, to   be   a

pp,pl,nn**430**   pp,pnx   wcj,pp,nn,pnx2233   pr,pnx310

God unto thee, and to thy   seed   after thee.

☞ **16:15, 16** The Ishmaelites were the descendants of Ishmael and were divided into twelve tribes (Gen. 25:16). They were also called Hagarites, Hagarenes, and Arabians (1 Chr. 5:10; Ps. 83:6; Is. 13:20). They lived in tents and traveled around in large caravans (Gen. 37:25; Is. 13:20; Jer. 25:24). They were rich in cattle, but a great portion of their wealth may have been gained by lawless activity (1 Chr. 5:21; Jer. 3:2). After harassing Israel for a time, they were overcome by Gideon (Judg. 8:10–21). During the reign of the more powerful kings they became more peacefully inclined to the Israelites; they even sent presents to King Solomon and King Jehoshaphat (1 Kgs. 10:15; 2 Chr. 17:11). However, these peaceful inclinations did not endure for long, for some Midianite tribes fought against King Uzziah (2 Chr. 26:7).

☞ **17:5, 6** In Hebrew, the name Abram means "exalted father" (87), and the name Abraham means "father of a multitude" (85).

wcs,qpf**5414**   pp,pnx   wcj,pp,nn,pnx**2233**   pr,pnx310   (853)   cs,nn**776**

8 And I will give unto thee, and to thy seed after thee, the land

pl,nn,pnx**4033**   (853)   cs,nn3605   cs,nn**776**   nn3667   nn**5769**

wherein thou art a stranger,   all   the land of Canaan, for an everlasting

pp,cs,nn**272**   wcs,qpf**1961**   pp,pnx   pp,pl,nn**430**

possession; and I will be their God.

pl,nn**430**   wcs,qmf**559**   pr413   nn85   wcj,pnp859   qmf**8104**   (853)   nn,pnx**1285**

9 And God said unto Abraham, Thou shalt keep   my covenant therefore,

pnp859   wcj,nn,pnx**2233**   pr,pnx310   pp,pl,nn,pnx**1755**

thou, and thy   seed   after thee in their generations.

pndm2063   nn,pnx**1285**   pnl834   qmf**8104**   pr,pnx996   wcj,pnx(pr996)

10 This *is* my covenant, which ye shall keep, between me and   you

wcj(pr996)   nn,pnx**2233**   pr,pnx310   cs,nn3605   nn2145   pp,pnx   nina**4135**

and   thy seed after thee; Every man child among you shall be circumcised.

wcs,nipf**4135**   (853)   cs,nn**1320**   nn,pnx**6190**   wcs,qpf**1961**

11 And ye shall circumcise   the flesh of your foreskin; and it shall   be   a

pp,cs,nn**226**   nn**1285**   pr,pnx996   wcj,pnx(pr996)

token of the covenant between me and   you.

cs,nu8083   pl,nn**3117**   wcj,cs,nn**1121**   nimf**4135**   pp,pnx   cs,nn3605

12 And he that is eight days   old   shall be circumcised among you, every

nn2145   pp,pl,nn,pnx**1755**   cs,aj3211   nn**1004**   wcj,cs,nn4736   nn3701

man child in your generations, he that is born in the house, or bought with money

pr4480/nn3605 cs,nn1121/nn**5236**   (pnp1931)   pnl834   ptn**3808**   pr4480/nn,pnx**2233**

of any stranger,   which *is* not of*thy*seed.

cs,aj3211   nn,pnx**1004**   wcj,cs,nn4736   nn,pnx3701

13 He that is born in thy house, and he that is bought with thy money, must

nina**4135**/nimf**4135**   nn,pnx**1285**   wcs,qpf**1961**   pp,pnx,pnx**1320**

needs*be*circumcised: and my covenant shall   be   in your   flesh   for an

nn**5769**   pp,cs,nn**1285**

everlasting covenant.

wcj,aj**6189**   nn2145   pnl834   (853) cs,nn**1320**   nn,pnx**6190**   ptn**3808**

14 And the uncircumcised man child whose   flesh of his foreskin is not

nimf**4135**   df,pndm1931   df,nn**5315**   wcs,nipf**3772**   pr4480/pl,nn,pnx**5971**   hipf**6565**   (853)

circumcised,   that   soul shall be cut off from*his*people; he hath broken   my

nn,pnx**1285**

covenant.

pl,nn**430**   wcs,qmf**559**   pr413   nn85   nn8297   nn,pnx**802**   ptn**3808** qmf**7121**

15 And God said   unto Abraham, As for Sarai thy wife, thou shalt not call

(853)   nn,pnx8034   nn8297   cj3588   nn8283   nn,pnx8034

her name Sarai, but Sarah *shall* her name *be*.

wcs,pipf**1288**   pnx(853)   qpf**5414**   pp,pnx   nn1121   wcj,ad1571   pr,pnx4480

16 And I will bless   her, and give thee a son   also   of   her: yea, I

wcs,pipf,pnx**1288**   wcs,qpf**1961**   pp,pl,nn**1471**   pl,cs,nn**4428**   pl,nn**5971**

will bless her, and she shall   be   *a mother* of nations; kings of people shall

qmf**1961**   pr,pnx4480

be   of   her.

nn85   wcs,qmf**5307**   pr5921   pl,nn,pnx**6440**   wcs,qmf**6711**   wcs,qmf**559**

17 Then Abraham   fell   upon his   face,   and laughed, and   said   in his

pp,nn,pnx**3820**   nimf3205   nu3967   nn8141   he,pp,cs,nn**1121**   wcj(cj518)

heart, Shall *a child* be born unto him that is a hundred years   old?   and

nn8283   nu8673   nn8141   he,cs,nn1323 qmf3205

shall Sarah, that is ninety years   old,   bear?

nn85   wcs,qmf**559**   pr413   df,pl,nn**430**   ptx3863   nn3458   qmf**2421** pp,pl,nn,pnx**6440**

18 And Abraham said   unto God, O that Ishmael might live   before   thee!

pl,nn**430** wcs,qmf**559**   nn8283   nn,pnx**802**   qpta3205 pp,pnx   nn**1121**   ad61

19 And God said, Sarah thy wife shall bear thee a son indeed; and thou

wcj,qpf**7121** (853)   nn,pnx8034 nn3327   wcs,hipf**6965** (853)   nn,pnx**1285** pr,pnx854

shalt call   his name Isaac: and I will establish   my covenant with him for

nn**5769**   pp,cs,nn**1285**   pp,nn,pnx**2233** pr,pnx310

an everlasting covenant, *and* with his   seed   after him.

wcj,pp,nn3458   qpf,pnx**8085**   ptdm2009   pipf**1288**   pnx(853)

20 And as for Ishmael, I have heard thee: Behold, I have blessed   him,

wcj,hipf6509/pnx(853)   wcj,hipf7235   pnx(853)   pp,ad3966/ad3966   du,nu8147/nu6240

and will make*him*fruitful, and will multiply   him exceedingly;   twelve

pl,nn**5387**   himf3205   wcs,qpf,pnx**5414**   aj1419   pp,nn**1471**

princes shall he beget, and I will   make   him a great nation.

wcj(853)   nn,pnx**1285**   himf**6965**   pr854   nn3327   pnl834   nn8283   qmf3205

21 But   my covenant will I establish with Isaac, which Sarah shall bear

pp,pnx   df,pndm2088   dfp,nn**4150**   df,aj312 dfp,nn8141

unto thee at   this   set time in the next year.

wcs,pimf**3615** pp,pinc**1696** pr,pnx854   pl,nn**430** wcs,qmf**5927** pr4480/pr5921   nn85

22 And he left off talking with him, and God went up   from   Abraham.

nn85   wcs,qmf3947 (853)   nn3458   nn,pnx**1121**   wcj(853) cs,nn3605   cs,aj3211

23 And Abraham took   Ishmael his son, and   all   that were born

nn,pnx**1004**   wcj(853) cs,nn3605   cs,nn4736   nn,pnx3701 cs,nn3605 nn2145

in his house, and   all   that were bought with his money, every male among

pp,pl,cs,nn**376**   nn85   cs,nn**1004**   wcs,qmf**4135**   (853)   cs,nn**1320**   nn,pnx**6190**

the   men   of Abraham's house; and circumcised   the flesh of their foreskin in

pp,cs,nn**6106**/df,pndm2088 df,nn3117 pp,pnl834 pl,nn**430**   pipf**1696** pr,pnx854

the   selfsame   day,   as   God had said unto him.

wcj,nn**85**   nu8673   nn8141 cs,nn**1121**   wcj,nu8672   pp,ninc,pnx**4135**

24 And Abraham *was* ninety years old and nine, when he was circumcised

cs,nn**1320**   nn,pnx**6190**

in the flesh of his foreskin.

wcj,nn3458   nn,pnx**1121**   cs,nu7969/nu6240 nn8141 cs,nn**1121**   pp,ninc,pnx**4135**

25 And Ishmael his son *was* thirteen years old, when he was circumcised

(853)   cs,nn**1320**   nn,pnx**6190**

in the flesh of his foreskin.

pp,cs,nn**6106**/df,pndm2088 df,nn3117   nn85   nipf**4135**   wcj,nn3458

26 In the   selfsame   day   was Abraham circumcised, and Ishmael his

nn,pnx**1121**

son.

wcj,cs,nn3605   pl,cs,nn**376**   nn,pnx**1004** cs,aj3211   nn**1004**   wcj,cs,nn4736

27 And   all   the men of his house, born in the house, and bought with

nn3701   pr4480/pr854   cs,nn**1121**/nn**5236**   nipf**4135**   pr,pnx854

money   of   the stranger, were circumcised with him.

The Promise Of A Son

nn3068   wcs,nimf**7200** pr,pnx413   pp,pl,cs,nn**436**   nn4471

18 And the LORD appeared unto him in the plains of Mamre: and

wcj,pnp1931 qpta3427   df,nn**168** cs,nn6607   pp,cs,nn2527   df,nn3117

he   sat in the tent door in the heat of the day;

wcs,qmf**5375**   du,nn,pnx**5869**   wcs,qmf**7200**   wcj,ptdm2009 nu7969 pl,nn**376** pl,nipt**5324**

2 And he lifted up his   eyes   and looked, and,   lo,   three men stood

---

17:19 In Hebrew, the name Isaac means "laughter" (3327). Both Abraham and Sarah laughed when they thought of the apparent impossibility of this birth (Gen. 17:17; 21:6).

18:1–33 Did Abraham actually see and talk with God? Does this contradict John 1:18, "No man hath seen

pr,pnx5921   wcs,qmf7200   wcs,qmf7323   pp,qnc,pnx7125

by   him: and   when   he   saw   *them*,   he   ran   to   meet   them

pr4480/cs,nn6607/df,nn168   wcs,htmf*7812   nn,lh776

from*the*tent*door, and bowed   himself toward the ground,

wcs,qmf559   nn136   cj518   pte4994   qpf4672   nn2580   pp,du,nn,pnx5869

3 And   said,   My   Lord,   if   now   I   have   found   favor   in   thy   sight,

qmf5674/ptn408   pte4994   pr4480/pr5921   nn,pnx5650

pass*not*away, I*pray*thee,   from   thy servant:

cs,nn4592   pl,nn4325   pte4994   homf3947   wcj,qmv7364   du,nn,pnx7272

4 Let a   little   water, I*pray*you, be fetched, and   wash   your   feet,   and

wcj,nimv8172   pr8478   df,nn6086

rest   yourselves under the tree:

wcj,qcj3947   cs,nn6595   nn3899   wcj,qmf5582   nn,pnx3820   ad310

5 And I will   fetch   a morsel of bread, and comfort ye your hearts; after that ye

qmf5674   cj3588   pr5921/ad3651   qpf5674   pr5921   nn,pnx5650   wcs,qmf559   ad3651

shall pass on: for therefore are ye come   to   your servant. And they said,   So

qmf6213 pp,pnl834   pipf1696

do,   as   thou hast said.

nn85   wcs,pimf4116   df,nn,lh168   pr413   nn8283   wcs,qmf559

6 And   Abraham   hastened   into   the   tent   unto   Sarah,   and   said,

pimv4116   cs,nu7969   pl,nn5429   nn5560   nn7058   qmv3888   wcj,qmf6213

Make*ready*quickly   three   measures   of   fine   meal,   knead   *it*,   and   make

pl,nn5692

cakes*upon*the*hearth.

nn85   qpf7323 wcj,pr413   df,nn1241   wcs,qmf3947   cs,nn1121/nn1241   aj7390   wcj,aj2896

7 And Abraham ran   unto   the herd, and fetched a   calf   tender and good,

wcs,qmf5414   pr413   df,nn5288   wcs,pimf4116   pp,qnc6213 pnx(853)

and   gave   *it* unto a young man; and he hasted to dress   it.

wcs,qmf3947   nn2529   wcj,nn2461   wcj,cs,nn1121/df,nn1241   pnl834   qpf6213

8 And he   took   butter, and   milk,   and   the   calf   which he had dressed,

wcs,qmf5414   pp,pl,nn,pnx6440   wcj,pnp1931   qpta5975   pr,pnx5921   pr8478   df,nn6086

and   set   *it*   before   them; and   he   stood   by   them under the tree,   and

wcs,qmf398

they did   eat.

wcs,qmf559 pr,pnx413   pnit346   nn8283   nn,pnx802   wcs,qmf559   ptdm2009

9 And they   said   unto   him, Where *is* Sarah thy wife? And he   said,   Behold,

dfp,nn168

in the   tent.

wcs,qmf559   qna7725/qmf7725   pr,pnx413   dfp,nn6256

10 And he   said,   I will certainly return   unto   thee according to the   time   of

aj2416   wcj,ptdm2009 pp,nn8283   nn,pnx802   nn1121   wcj,nn8283 cs,qpta8085   df,nn168

life; and,   lo,   Sarah thy wife shall have a son. And Sarah heard *it* in the tent

cs,nn6607 wcj,pnp1931   pr,pnx310

door,   which *was* behind him.

wcj,nn85   wcj,nn8283   aj2205   pl,qpta935   dfp,pl,nn3117

11 Now Abraham and   Sarah   *were* old *and* well stricken in   age;   *and* it

qpf2308   pp,qnc1961   pp,nn8283   nn734   dfp,pl,nn802

ceased to   be   with Sarah after the manner of women.

God at any time"? This theophany (an appearance of God to man) in the Old Testament is believed to have been Christ. The New Testament teaches that Christ existed co-eternally with God the Father (John 1:1; 8:56–58; 10:30; 17:5; Col. 1:15–17), and it is not inconceivable that He would at times take the appearance of humanity prior to His incarnation. For verily, Jesus Christ is the personal manifestation of God to man (John 14:9).

nn8283   wcs,qmf6711   pp,nn,pnx**7130**   pp,qnc**559**   ad310   qnc,pnx1086

☞ 12 Therefore Sarah laughed within herself, saying, After I am waxed old shall

qpf**1961**/pp,pnx   nn5730   wcj,nn,pnx113   qpf**2204**

I have pleasure, my lord being old also?

nn**3068**   wcs,qmf**559**   pr413   nn85   pp,pnit4100/pndm2088   nn8283   qpf6711   pp,qnc**559**

13 And the Lord said unto Abraham, Wherefore did Sarah laugh, saying,

he,cj637/ad**552**   qmf3205   wcj,pnp589   qpf**2204**

Shall I of*a*surety bear*a*child, which am old?

nn**1697**   he,nimf**6381**   pr4480/nn**3068**   dfp,nn**4150**   qmf**7725**

14 Is any thing too hard for*the*Lord? At the time appointed I will return

pr,pnx413   dfp,nn**6256**   aj2416   wcj,pp,nn8283   nn**1121**

unto thee, according to the time of life, and Sarah shall have a son.

nn8283   wcs,pimf3584   pp,qnc**559**   qpf6711   ptn**3808**   cj3588   qpf**3372**

15 Then Sarah denied, saying, I laughed not; for she was afraid. And he

wcs,qmf**559**   ptn**3808**   cj3588   qpf6711

said, Nay; but thou didst laugh.

Abraham Begs For Sodom

df,pl,nn**376**   wcs,qmf**6965**   pr4480/ad8033   wcs,himf8259   pr5921/pl,cs,nn**6440**   nn5467

☞ 16 And the men rose up from thence, and looked toward Sodom: and

wcj,nn85   qpta1980   pr,pnx5973   pp,pinc,pnx7971

Abraham went with them to bring*them*on*the*way.

wcj,nn**3068**   qpf559   pnp589   he,pipt**3680**   pr4480/nn85   pnl834   pnp589

17 And the Lord said, Shall I hide from Abraham that thing which I

qpta**6213**

do;

wcj,nn85   qna**1961**/qmf**1961**   aj1419   wcj,aj6099   pp,nn**1471**

18 Seeing that Abraham shall surely become a great and mighty nation, and

cs,nn3605   pl,cs,nn**1471**   df,nn**776**   wcs,nipf**1288**   pp,pnx

all the nations of the earth shall be blessed in him?

cj3588   qpf,pnx**3045**   pp,cj4616/pnl834   pimf**6680**   (853)   pl,nn,pnx**1121**   wcj(853)

19 For I know him, that he will command his children and his

nn,pnx**1004**   pr,pnx310   wcs,qpf**8104**   cs,nn**1870**   nn**3068**   pp,qnc**6213**   nn**6666**

household after him, and they shall keep the way of the Lord, to do justice

wcj,nn**4941**   pp,cj4616   nn**3068**   hinc935   pr5921   nn85   (853)   pnl834

and judgment; that the Lord may bring upon Abraham that which he hath

pipf**1696**   pr,pnx5921

spoken of him.

nn**3068**   wcs,qmf**559**   cj3588   cs,nn2201   nn5467   wcj,nn6017   qpf7231

20 And the Lord said, Because the cry of Sodom and Gomorrah is great,

cj3588   wcj,nn,pnx**2403**   ad3966   qpf**3513**

and because their sin is very grievous;

qcj3381   pte**4994**   wcj,qmf**7200**   qpf**6213**   ad**3617**

21 I will go down now, and see whether they have done altogether

---

☞ **18:12** There are several different kinds of laughter in the Bible: (1) the laughter of incredulity (Gen. 17:17; 18:12); (2) the laughter of joyful wonder (Gen. 21:6); (3) the laughter of defiance (Job 5:22); (4) the laughter of approbation (Job 29:24); (5) hollow laughter with undertones of sorrow (Prov. 14:13); (6) the laughter of scorn (Ps. 2:4); (7) the laughter of rapturous delight (Ps. 126:2).

☞ **18:16–33** Abraham's intercession for Sodom, and in reality for Lot, was based on the principle in verse twenty-five, "Shall not the Judge of all the earth do right?" He succeeded in postponing the judgment for the sake of a few righteous persons: 50, 45, 40, 30, 20, and finally only 10. But Lot had been an even poorer missionary than Abraham supposed, failing even to witness to his own family (Gen. 19:14, 26, 30–36); the ten righteous persons could not be found. Yet the Lord spared Lot and his family on Abraham's behalf (see the note on Gen. 19:26).

he,pp,nn,pnx6818 df,qpf935 pr,pnx413 wcj,cj518 ptn3808
according to the cry of it, which is come unto me; and if not, I will

qcj3045
know.

df,pl,nn376 wcs,qmf6437 pr4480/ad8033 wcs,qmf1980 nn,lh5467
22 And the men turned*their*faces from thence, and went toward Sodom:

wcj,nn85 qpta5975 ad,pnx5750 pp,pl,cs,nn6440 nn3068
but Abraham stood yet before the LORD.

nn85 wcs,qmf5066 wcs,qmf559 he,cj637 qmf5595 aj6662
23 And Abraham drew near, and said, Wilt thou also destroy the righteous

pr5973 aj7563
with the wicked?

ad194 pta3426 pl,nu2572 aj6662 pp,cs,nn8432 df,nn5892 he,cj637
24 Peradventure there be fifty righteous within the city: wilt thou also

qmf5595 wcj,ptn3808 qmf5375 dfp,nn4725 pp,pr4616 pl,nu2572 df,aj6662 pnl834 pp,nn,pnx7130
destroy and not spare the place for the fifty righteous that *are* therein?

ptx,lh2486 pp,pnx pr4480/qnc6213 df,pndm2088 dfp,nn1697 pp,hinc4191
25 That*be*far from thee to do after this manner, to slay the

aj6662 pr5973 aj7563 dfp,aj6662 wcs,qpf1961 dfp,aj7563
righteous with the wicked: and that the righteous should be as the wicked,

ptx,lh2486 pp,pnx ptn3808 he,cs,qpta8199 cs,nn3605 df,nn776 qmf6213 nn4941
that*be*far from thee: Shall not the Judge of all the earth do right?

nn3068 wcs,qmf559 cj518 qmf4672 pp,nn5467 pl,nu2572 aj6662 pp,cs,nn8432 df,nn5892
26 And the LORD said, If I find in Sodom fifty righteous within the city,

wcs,qpf5375 pp,cs,nn3605 df,nn4725 pp,pr,pnx5668
then I will spare all the place for*their*sakes.

nn85 wcs,qmf6030 wcs,qmf559 ptdm2009 pte4994 hipf2974
27 And Abraham answered and said, Behold now, I have taken upon me to

pp,pinc1696 pr413 nn136 wcj,pnp595 nn6083 wcj,nn665
speak unto the Lord, which *am but* dust and ashes:

ad194 qmf2637 nu2568 pl,nu2572 df,aj6662 he,himf7843
28 Peradventure there shall lack five of the fifty righteous: wilt thou destroy

(853) cs,nn3605 df,nn5892 dfp,nu2568 wcs,qmf5375 cj518 qmf4672 ad8033 pl,nu705
all the city for *lack of* five? And he said, If I find there forty and

wcj,nu2568 ptn3808 himf7843
five, I will not destroy *it*.

pp,pinc1696 pr,pnx413 ad5750 wcs,himf3254 wcs,qmf559 ad194
29 And he spoke unto him yet again, and said, Peradventure there shall be

pl,nu705 nimf4672 ad8033 wcs,qmf559 ptn3808 qmf6213 pp,pr5668/df,pl,nu705
forty found there. And he said, I will not do *it* for*forty's*sake.

wcs,qmf559 pte4994 ptn408 pp,nn136 qcj2734 wcj,picj1696
30 And he said *unto him*, Oh let not the Lord be angry, and I will speak:

ad194 nu7970 nimf4672 ad8033 wcs,qmf559 ptn3808 qmf6213 cj518
Peradventure there shall thirty be found there. And he said, I will not do *it*, if

qmf4672 nu7970 ad8033
I find thirty there.

wcs,qmf559 ptdm2009 pte4994 hipf2974 pp,pinc1696 pr413 nn136
31 And he said, Behold now, I have taken upon me to speak unto the Lord:

ad194 pl,nu6242 nimf4672 ad8033 wcs,qmf559 ptn3808 himf7843
Peradventure there shall be twenty found there. And he said, I will not destroy *it*

pp,pr5668/df,pl,nu6242
for*twenty's*sake.

wcs,qmf559 pte4994 ptn408 pp,nn136 qcj2734 wcj,picj1696 ad389
32 And he said, Oh let not the Lord be angry, and I will speak yet but

df,nn6471   ad194   nu6235   nimf4672   ad8033   wcs,qmf559   ptn3808   himf7843

this once: Peradventure ten shall be found there. And he said, I will not destroy

pp,pr5668/df,nu6235

it for*ten's*sake.

nn3068   wcs,qmf1980   pp,pnl834   pipf3615   pp,pinc1696   pr413

33 And the LORD went*his*way, as*soon*as he had left communing with

nn85   wcj,nn85   qpf7725   pp,nn,pnx4725

Abraham: and Abraham returned unto his place.

God Destroys Sodom and Gomorrah

wcs,qmf935 du,cs,nu8147 df,pl,nn4397   nn,lh5467   dfp,nn6153   wcj,nn3876 qpta3427

19 And there came two   angels to Sodom at even; and Lot   sat

pp,cs,nn8179   nn5467   nn3876 wcs,qmf7200   wcs,qmf6965   pp,qnc,pnx7125

in the gate of Sodom: and Lot seeing *them* rose up to meet

wcs,himf*7812   du,nn639   nn,lh776

them; and he bowed himself with his face toward the ground;

wcs,qmf559   ptdm2009   pte4994   pl,nn,pnx113   qmv5493   pte4994   pr413

2 And he said, Behold now, my lords, turn in, I*pray*you, into your

nn,pnx5650   cs,nn1004   wcj,qmv3885   wcj,qmv7364   du,nn,pnx7272

servant's house, and tarry*all*night, and wash your feet, and ye shall

wcj,hipf7925   wcj,qpf1980   pp,nn,pnx1870   wcs,qmf559 ptn3808 cj3588

rise*up*early, and go on your ways. And they said, Nay; but we will

qmf3885/dfp,nn7339

abide*in*the*street*all*night.

wcs,qmf6484   pp,pnx   ad3966   wcs,qmf5493 pr,pnx413   wcs,qmf935

3 And he pressed upon them greatly; and they turned in unto him, and entered

pr413   nn,pnx1004   wcs,qmf6213 pp,pnx   nn4960   qpf644   wcj,pl,nn4682

into his house; and he made them a feast, and did bake unleavened bread, and

wcs,qmf398

they did eat.

ad2962   qmf7901   wcj,pl,cs,nn376   df,nn5892   pl,cs,nn376

4 But before they lay down, the men of the city, *even* the men of

nn5467   nipf5437/pr5921   df,nn1004   wcj(pr5704) aj2205   pr4480/nn5288 cs,nn3605   df,nn5971

Sodom, compassed the house round, both   old and young, all the people

pr4480/nn7097

from*every*quarter:

wcs,qmf7121 pr413 nn3876   wcs,qmf559   pp,pnx   pnit346   df,pl,nn376 pnl834

5 And they called unto Lot, and said unto him, Where *are* the men which

qpf935   pr,pnx413   df,nn3915   himv,pnx3318   pr,pnx413   wcj,qcj3045 pnx(853)

came in to   thee this night? bring*them*out unto us, that we may know

them.

nn3876   wcs,qmf3318   df,nn,lh6607 pr,pnx413   qpf5462   wcj,df,nn1817 pr,pnx310

6 And Lot went out at the door unto them, and shut the door after him,

wcs,qmf559   pte4994   pl,nn,pnx251   himf7489/ptn408

7 And said, I*pray*you, brethren, do*not*so*wickedly.

ptdm2009   pte4994 pp,pnx   du,cs,nu8147   pl,nn1323   pnl834   ptn3808 qpf3045   nn376

8 Behold now, I have two daughters which have not known man; let me,

pte4994   hicj3318/pnx(853)   pr,pnx413   wcj,qmv6213   pp,pnx   dfp,aj2896

I*pray*you, bring*them*out unto you, and   do ye to them as *is* good in your

pp,du,nn,pnx5869 ad7535   df,pndm411 dfp,pl,nn376 qmf6213 ptn408/nn1697 cj3588 pr5921/ad3651 qpf935

eyes: only unto these men do nothing; for therefore came they under the

pp,cs,nn6738   nn,pnx6982

shadow of my roof.

wcs,qmf**559**   qmv**5066**   ad1973   wcs,qmf**559**   df,nu259

9 And they said, Stand back. And they said *again*, This one *fellow*

qpf935   pp,qnc**1481**   wcs,qmf**8199**/qna**8199**   ad6258   himf**7489**

came in to sojourn, and he will needs*be*a*judge: now will we deal worse

pp,pnx   pr,pnx4480   wcs,qmf6484   ad3966   dfp,nn376   pp,nn3876

with thee, than with them. And they pressed sore upon the man, *even* Lot, and

wcs,qmf**5066**   pp,qnc**7665**   df,nn1817

came near to break the door.

df,pl,nn376   wcs,qmf7971   (853)   nn,pnx3027   wcs,himf935   (853)   nn3876   df,nn,lh**1004**

10 But the men put forth   their hand, and pulled   Lot into the house

pr,pnx413   qpf5462   wcj(853)   df,nn1817

to them, and shut to   the door.

hipf**5221**   wcj(853)   df,pl,nn376   pnl834   cs,nn6607   df,nn**1004**

11 And they smote   the men that *were* at the door of the house with

dfp,pl,nn5575   pr4480/aj6996   wcj(pr5704)   aj1419   wcs,qmf3811   pp,qnc4672

blindness, both small and   great: so that they wearied themselves to find

df,nn6607

the door.

df,pl,nn376   wcs,qmf**559**   pr413   nn3876   pp,pnx   ad6311   pnit4310   ad5750

12 And the men said unto Lot, Hast thou here any besides a

nn2860   wcj,pl,nn,pnx**1121**   wcj,pl,nn,pnx1323   wcj,nn3605/pnl834   pp,pnx

son-in-law, and thy sons,   and thy daughters? and whatsoever thou hast in the

dfp,nn5892   himv3318   pr4480   df,nn4725

city, bring *them* out of this place:

cj3588   pnp587   pl,hipf**7843**   (853)   df,pndm2088   df,nn4725   cj3588   nn,pnx6818

13 For we will destroy   this   place, because the   cry   of them is

qpf1431   (853)   pl,cs,nn**6440**   nn3068   nn3068   wcs,pimf,pnx7971

waxen great   before the face of the LORD; and the LORD hath   sent   us to

pp,pinc,pnx**7843**

destroy it.

nn3876   wcs,qmf3318   wcs,pimf**1696**   pr413   pl,nn,pnx2860   pl,cs,qpta3947

14 And Lot went out, and spoke unto his sons-in-law, which married his

pl,nn,pnx1323   wcs,qmf**559**   qmv6965   qmv3318   pr4480   df,pndm2088   df,nn4725   cj3588   nn3068

daughters, and said, Up, get*you*out of   this   place; for the LORD will

hipf**7843**   (853)   df,nn5892   wcs,qmf**1961**   pp,pipt6711   pp,du,cs,nn**5869**   pl,nn,pnx2860

destroy   this city. But he seemed as one that mocked   unto   his sons-in-law.

wcj,pp,pnx3644   df,nn7837   qpf5927   df,pl,nn**4397**   wcs,himf213   pp,nn3876   pp,qnc**559**

15 And when the morning arose, then the angels hastened Lot, saying,

qmv6965   qmv3947   (853)   nn,pnx**802**   wcj(853)   du,cs,nu8147   pl,nn,pnx1323   df,pl,nipt4672   cj6435

Arise, take   thy wife, and   thy two daughters, which are here; lest thou

nimf5595   pp,cs,nn5771   df,nn5892

be consumed in the iniquity of the city.

wcs,htmf*4102   df,pl,nn376   wcs,himf**2388**   pp,nn,pnx**3027**

16 And while he lingered, the men laid hold upon his   hand,   and upon the

wcj,pp,cs,nn**3027**   nn,pnx**802**   wcj,pp,cs,nn**3027**   du,cs,nu8147   pl,nn,pnx1323   nn3068

hand   of his wife, and upon the   hand   of his   two   daughters; the LORD

pp,cs,nn2551   pr,pnx5921   wcs,himf,pnx3318   wcs,himf,pnx5117   pr4480/nn2351

being merciful unto him: and they brought*him*forth, and   set   him without

dfp,nn5892

the city.

wcs,qmf**1961**   pp,hinc,pnx3318/pnx(853)   df,nn,lh2351

17 And it*came*to*pass, when they had brought*them*forth abroad, that he

wcs,qmf**559**   nimv**4422**   pr5921   nn,pnx5315   himf5027   ptn408   pr,pnx310   wcj,ptn408   qmf5975   pp,cs,nn3605

said, Escape for thy life; look not behind thee, neither stay thou in   all

df,nn3603   nimv**4422**   df,nn,lh2022   cj6435   nimf5595

the plain; escape to the mountain, lest thou be consumed.

nn3876 wcs,qmf**559** pr,pnx413   pte**4994** ptn408   nn**136**

18 And Lot said unto them, Oh, not so, my Lord:

ptdm2009   pte**4994**   nn,pnx**5650**   qpf4672 nn2580   pp,du,nn,pnx**5869**

19 Behold now, thy servant hath found grace in thy sight, and thou hast

wcs,himf1431   nn,pnx**2617** pnl834   qpf**6213** pr,pnx5973   pp,hinc**2421** (853)   nn,pnx**5315**

magnified thy mercy, which thou hast showed unto me in saving my life;

wcj,pnp595 ptn**3808**/qmf3201 pp,ninc**4422**   df,nn,lh2022 cj6435   df,nn**7451** qmf,pnx1692

and I cannot escape to the mountain, lest some evil take me, and I

wcs,qpf**4191**

die:

ptdm2009 pte**4994** df,pndm2063 df,nn5892   aj7138   pp,qnc5127 ad,lh8033 wcj,pnp1931   nn4705

20 Behold now, this city *is* near to flee unto, and it *is* a little one:

pte**4994**   nicj**4422** ad,lh8033 pnp1931 he,ptn**3808**   nn4705   nn,pnx**5315**   wcj,qcj**2421**

Oh, let me escape thither, (*is* it not a little one?) and my soul shall live.

wcs,qmf**559** pr,pnx413   ptdm2009   qpf**5375**/pl,nn,pnx**6440**   df,pndm2088

21 And he said unto him, See, I have accepted thee concerning this

dfp,nn**1697** ad1571   pp,ptn1115 qnc,pnx**2015** (853) df,nn5892   pnl834

thing also, that I will not overthrow this city, for the which thou hast

pipf**1696**

spoken.

pimv4116   nimv**4422** ad,lh8033 cj3588   ptn**3808**/qmf3201 pp,qnc**6213** nn**1697** pr5704

22 Haste thee, escape thither; for I cannot do any thing till thou be

qnc,pnx935 ad,lh8033 pr5921/ad**3651** cs,nn8034   df,nn5892 qpf**7121** nn6820

come thither. Therefore the name of the city was called Zoar.

df,nn8121   qpf3318 pr5921 df,nn**776**   wcj,nn3876 qpf935 nn,lh6820

23 The sun was risen upon the earth when Lot entered into Zoar.

wcj,nn**3068** hipf4305 pr5921 nn5467   wcj,pr5921 nn6017   nn1614

24 Then the LORD rained upon Sodom and upon Gomorrah brimstone and

wcj,nn784 pr4480/pr854   nn**3068** pr4480 df,du,nn**8064**

fire from the LORD out of heaven;

wcs,qmf**2015** (853) df,pndm411 df,pl,nn5892   wcj(853) cs,nn3605   df,nn3603   wcj(853)

25 And he overthrew those cities, and all the plain, and

cs,nn3605   pl,cs,qpta**3427**   df,pl,nn5892   wcj,cs,nn6780   df,nn**127**

all the inhabitants of the cities, and that which grew upon the ground.

nn,pnx802 wcs,himf5027   pr4480/pr,pnx310   wcs,qmf**1961** cs,nn5333

◎⛏ 26 But his wife looked back from behind him, and she became a pillar of

nn4417

salt.

nn85   wcs,himf7925   dfp,nn1242 pr413   df,nn4725 pnl834/ad8033 qpf5975

27 And Abraham got*up*early in the morning to the place where he stood

(853) pl,cs,nn**6440**   nn**3068**

before the LORD:

wcs,himf8259 pr5921/pl,cs,nn**6440** nn5467   wcj,nn6017   wcj,pr5921/pl,cs,nn**6440** cs,nn3605

28 And he looked toward Sodom and Gomorrah, and toward all

cs,nn776   df,nn3603   wcs,qmf**7200** wcj,ptdm2009 cs,nn7008   df,nn**776** qpf5927

the land of the plain, and beheld, and, lo, the smoke of the country went up as

pp,cs,nn7008   df,nn3536

the smoke of a furnace.

wcs,qmf**1961**   pl,nn430 pp,pinc**7843** (853) pl,cs,nn5892 pl,nn3603

29 And it*came*to*pass, when God destroyed the cities of the plain, that

---

◎⛏ **19:26** There was for centuries a peculiar formation of crumbling, crystalline rock that was associated by tradition with the story of Lot's wife. Josephus (Antiquities I.xi.4) declared that this pillar still remained in his day and that he had seen it. Clement of Rome, Irenaeus, and Benjamin of Tudela also wrote of this strange formation as visible in their day, but later writers stated that it had ceased to exist. Perhaps the existence of this pillar was used as an object lesson for the admonition of Christ to His disciples (Luke 17:32).

pl,nn**430**   wcs,qmf**2142**   (853)   nn85   wcs,pimf7971   (853)   nn3876   pr4480/cs,nn**8432**

God remembered   Abraham, and   sent   Lot out*of*the*midst of the

df,nn2018   pp,qnc**2015**   (853)   df,pl,nn5892   pp,pnp2004/pnl834 nn3876   qpf**3427**

overthrow, when he overthrew   the cities in the   which   Lot dwelt.

Lot's Daughters Commit Incest

nn3876   wcs,qmf**5927**   pr4480/nn6820   wcs,qmf**3427**   dfp,nn2022

30 And Lot went up out*of*Zoar, and   dwelt   in the mountain, and his

wcj,du,cs,nu8147   pl,nn,pnx1323   pr,pnx5973   cj3588   qpf**3372**   pp,qnc**3427**   pp,nn6820   wcs,qmf**3427**

two   daughters with him; for he feared to dwell in Zoar: and he dwelt in a

dfp,nn4631 pnp1931   wcj,du,cs,nu8147   pl,nn,pnx1323

cave, he and his   two   daughters.

df,nn1067   wcs,qmf**559**   pr413   df,aj6810   nn,pnx1   qpf**2204**

31 And the firstborn said unto the younger, Our father is old, and there is

ptn369   wcj,nn**376**   dfp,nn**776**   pp,qnc935   pr,pnx5921   pp,cs,nn**1870**   cs,nn3605   df,nn**776**

not a man in the earth to come in unto us after the manner of all the earth:

qmv**1980**   (853)   nn,pnx1   himf8248   nn3196   wcj,qcj7901   pr,pnx5973

32 Come, let us make   our father drink wine, and we will lie with him,

wcj,pimf**2421**   nn2233   pr4480/nn,pnx1

that we may preserve seed of*our*father.

(853)   nn,pnx1   wcs,himf8248   nn3196   pndm1931   dfp,nn**3915**   df,nn1067

33 And they made   their father drink wine that night: and the firstborn

wcs,qmf935   wcs,qmf7901   pr854   nn,pnx1   qpf**3045**   wcj,ptn**3808**   pp,qnc,pnx7901

went in, and   lay with her father; and he perceived   not   when she lay down,

wcj,pp,qnc,pnx**6965**

nor when she   arose.

wcs,qmf**1961**   pr4480/nn4283   df,nn1067   wcs,qmf**559**   pr413

34 And it*came*to*pass on*the*morrow, that the firstborn   said   unto the

df,aj6810   ptdm2005   qpf7901   ad570   pr854   nn,pnx1   himf,pnx8248   nn3196

younger, Behold, I lay last night with my father: let us make him   drink wine

df,nn**3915**   ad1571   wcj,qmv935   qmv7901   pr,pnx5973   wcj,pimf**2421**   nn2233

this night also; and go*thou*in, and lie   with him, that we may preserve seed

pr4480/nn,pnx1

of*our*father.

(853)   nn,pnx1   wcs,himf8248   nn3196   df,pndm1931   dfp,nn**3915**   ad1571

35 And they made   their father drink wine that   night also: and the

df,aj6810   wcs,qmf**6965**   wcs,qmf7901   pr,pnx5973   qpf**3045**   wcj,ptn**3808**

younger arose, and   lay with   him; and he perceived   not   when she

pp,qnc,pnx7901   wcj,pp,qnc,pnx**6965**

lay down, nor when she   arose.

du,cs,nu8147   pl,cs,nn1323   nn3876   wcs,qmf2029   pr4480/nn,pnx1

36 Thus were both   the daughters of Lot with child by*their*father.

df,nn1067   wcs,qmf3205   nn**1121**   wcs,qmf**7121**   nn,pnx8034   nn4124   pnp1931

☞ 37 And the firstborn bore   a son, and called his name Moab: the same is the

cs,nn1   nn4124   pr5704   df,nn**3117**

father of the Moabites unto this day.

☞ 19:37 The Moabites were the descendants of Lot and were neighbors of the Amorites on the opposite side of the Arnon River (Num. 21:13). They possessed many great cities (Num. 21:28–30; 23:7; Is. 15:1), and were prosperous, arrogant, and idolatrous. They were mighty men of war (Is. 16:6). The Amorites deprived them of a large part of their territory (Num. 21:26). The Moabites refused to let Israel pass through their country and were so greatly impressed and alarmed by the multitude of the Israelite army that, along with Midian, they sent Balaam to curse it (Num. 22–24). Subsequently, Israel was enticed into idolatry and even intermarried with them. They were always hostile to Israel until King Saul subdued them (1 Sam. 14:47). Later they became

wcj,df,aj6810   pnp1931 ad1571 qpf3205   nn**1121**   wcs,qmf**7121**   nn,pnx8034   nn1151

☞ 38 And the younger, she also bore a son, and called his name Ben-ammi:

pnp1931   cs,nn1   pl,cs,nn**1121**   nn5983   pr5704   df,nn**3117**

the same *is* the father of the children of Ammon unto this day.

Abraham and Abimelech

                    nn85   wcs,qmf5265   pr4480/ad8033   df,nn5045   nn,lh**776**

20 And Abraham journeyed from thence toward the south country, and

        wcs,qmf**3427**   pr996   nn6946   wcj(pr996) nn7793   wcs,qmf**1481**   pp,nn1642

dwelled between Kadesh and   Shur, and sojourned in Gerar.

          nn85   wcs,qmf559 pr413   nn8283   nn,pnx**802** pnp1931   nn,pnx**269**   nn40

☞ 2 And Abraham said   of Sarah his wife, She *is* my sister: and Abimelech

cs,nn**4428**   nn1642 wcs,qmf7971   wcs,qmf3947 (853)   nn8283

king of Gerar sent,   and   took   Sarah.

              pl,nn**430** wcs,qmf935 pr413   nn40   pp,nn2472   df,nn**3915**   wcs,qmf559   pp,pnx

3 But God came   to Abimelech in a dream by night, and   said   to him,

ptdm,pnx2009   qpta**4191**   pr5921   df,nn**802** pnl834   qpf3947   wcj,pnp1931

Behold, thou *art but* a dead man, for the woman which thou hast taken; for   she

nn1167   cs,qptp1166

is a man's wife.

              wcj,nn40   ptn3808 qpf**7126**/pr,pnx413   wcs,qmf559   nn136   qmf2026

4 But Abimelech had not come near her: and he said, Lord, wilt thou slay

ad1571   aj**6662**   he,nn**1471**

also a righteous nation?

          qpf559 pnp1931 he,ptn**3808**   pp,pnx   pnp1931   nn,pnx**269**   wcj,pnp1931 ad1571   pnp1931

5 Said he   not unto me, She *is* my sister? and   she, even she herself

qpf559   pnp1931   nn,pnx251   pp,cs,nn**8537**   nn,pnx3824   wcj,pp,cs,nn**5356**   du,nn,pnx**3709**

said, He *is* my brother: in the integrity of my heart and innocency of my hands

          qpf**6213** pndm2063

have I done this.

              df,pl,nn**430** wcs,qmf559 pr,pnx413   dfp,nn2472   ad1571 pnp595 qpf**3045** cj3588   qpf**6213**

6 And God said unto him in a dream, Yea, I   know that thou didst

pndm2063   pp,cs,nn**8537**   nn,pnx3824   pnp595 ad1571 wcs,qmf2820   pnx(853)   pr4480/qnc**2398**

this in the integrity of thy heart; for I   also withheld   thee from sinning

pp,pnx   pr5921/ad**3651** qpf,pnx**5414**   ptn3808 pp,qnc**5060**/pr,pnx413

against me: therefore suffered I thee not to   touch   her.

          wcj,ad6258   himv**7725**   df,nn**376**   cs,nn**802** cj3588 pnp1931   nn5030

7 Now therefore restore the man *his* wife; for he *is* a prophet, and he shall

---

tributary to David and succeeding Jewish kings (2 Sam. 8:2, 12; 2 Kgs. 3:4), but they finally joined Babylon against Judah (2 Kgs. 24:2). On several occasions, God pronounced judgments against Moab (Is. 15:1 – 16:14; Jer. 48:1–47; Amos 2:1–3).

☞ **19:38** The Ammonites were the children of Lot (Deut. 2:19). They were a cruel, covetous, proud, vindictive, and idolatrous nation (see Judg. 10:6; Ezek. 25:3, 6; Amos 1:13; Zeph. 2:10). Their chief city was Rabbah (2 Sam. 12:26, 27), from which they were governed by hereditary kings (Jer. 27:3). They had various encounters with Israel. With the Philistines they oppressed Israel for eighteen years (Judg. 10:7–9). King Saul succeeded against them (1 Sam. 11:11). David and Joab also overcame them (2 Sam. 10:7–14), but Solomon intermarried with their women and introduced their idols into Israel (1 Kgs. 11:1–5).

☞ **20:2–18** How does this section relate to Gen. 12:11–20? Similar events are not necessarily identical. For example, there were two American Presidents named Roosevelt who were in office within a few years of one another. Likewise, the cases of Pharaoh and Abimelech were distinctly different but similar circumstances. In the first instance, Pharaoh was quite taken with the beautiful sixty–five–year–old princess. Abimelech merely wanted a political alliance with a rich, nomadic chieftain. The text does not say that this ninety–year–old woman was beautiful to Abimelech. The case of Isaac in Genesis 26:6–11 is only similar in the use of Abimelech, a mere title of the kings of Gerar.

wcj,htmf6419 pr,pnx1157   wcj,qmv2421   wcj,cj518   hipt7725   ptn,pnx369 qmv3045

pray   for   thee, and thou shalt live: and   if   thou restore *her* not,   know

cj3588   qna4191/qmf4191   pnp859   wcj,cs,nn3605 pnl834   pp,pnx

thou that thou shalt surely die, thou, and   all   that *are* thine.

nn40   wcs,himf7925   dfp,nn1242   wcs,qmf7121   pp,cs,nn3605

8 Therefore Abimelech rose early in the morning, and called   all   his

pl,nn,pnx5650   wcs,pimf1696   (853) cs,nn3605 df,pndm428 df,pl,nn1697   pp,du,nn,pnx241   df,pl,nn376

servants, and   told   all   these   things in their   ears: and the   men

wcs,qmf3372/ad3966

were*sore*afraid.

nn40   wcs,qmf7121   pp,nn85   wcs,qmf559   pp,pnx   pnit4100   qpf6213

9 Then Abimelech called Abraham, and   said   unto him, What hast thou done

pp,pnx   wcj,pnit4100   qpf2398   pp,pnx   cj3588   hipf935   pr,pnx5921

unto us? and   what   have I offended thee, that thou hast brought   on   me and

wcj,pr5921   nn,pnx4467   aj1419   nn2401   qpf6213 pl,nn4639 pr,pnx5973   pnl834   ptn3808

on   my kingdom a great sin? thou hast done deeds   unto   me that ought not to

nimf6213

be done.

nn40   wcs,qmf559 pr413   nn85   pnit4100 qpf7200   cj3588   qpf6213

10 And Abimelech   said   unto Abraham, What sawest thou, that thou hast done

(853) df,pndm2088   df,nn1697

this   thing?

nn85   wcs,qmf559   cj3588   qpf559   ad7535   cs,nn3374   pl,nn430   ptn369

11 And Abraham said, Because I thought, Surely the fear of God *is* not in

df,pndm2088 dfp,nn4725   wcj,qpf,pnx2026   pr5921   nn,pnx802 cs,nn1697

this   place; and they will   slay   me for my wife's sake.

wcj,ad1571   ad546   nn,pnx269 pnp1931   cs,nn1323   nn,pnx1   ad389

☞ 12 And   yet   indeed *she is* my sister; she   *is* the daughter of my father, but

ptn3808   cs,nn1323   nn,pnx517   wcs,qmf1961 pp,pnx pp,nn802

not the daughter of my mother; and she became my wife.

wcs,qmf1961   pp,pnl834   pl,nn430   pnx(853)   hipf8582

13 And   it*came*to*pass, when   God   caused   me   to   wander

pr4480/cs,nn1004/nn,pnx1   wcs,qmf559   pp,pnx   pndm2088   nn,pnx2617 pnl834

from*my*father's*house, that I   said   unto her, This   *is* thy kindness which thou

qmf6213 pr,pnx5973   pr413 cs,nn3605 df,nn4725 pnl834/ad,lh8033   qmf935 qmv559   pp,pnx   pnp1931

shalt show   unto me; at every place   whither   we shall come, say of me, He   *is*

nn,pnx251

my brother.

nn40   wcs,qmf3947   nn6629   wcj,nn1241   wcj,pl,nn5650

14 And   Abimelech   took   sheep,   and   oxen,   and   menservants,   and

wcj,pl,nn8198   wcs,qmf5414   pp,nn85   wcs,himf7725 pp,pnx   (853)   nn8283

womenservants, and   gave   *them* unto Abraham, and restored him   Sarah his

nn,pnx802

wife.

nn40   wcs,qmf559   ptdm2009   nn,pnx776   pp,pl,nn,pnx6440   qmv3427

15 And Abimelech   said,   Behold, my   land   *is*   before   thee: dwell where it

dfp,nn2896/pp,du,nn,pnx5869

pleaseth   thee.

wcj,pp,nn8283   qpf559   ptdm2009   qpf5414   pp,nn,pnx251   cs,nu505

16 And unto   Sarah   he said, Behold, I have given thy   brother a thousand

---

☞ **20:12** Abraham speaks of Sarah as his half-sister. The common Jewish tradition referred to by Josephus (Antiquities I.vi.6) and also by Jerome is that Sarah was identical with Iscah (see Gen. 11:29), daughter of Haran and sister of Lot, who is called Abraham's "brother" (Gen. 13:8).

ⁿⁿ³⁷⁰¹ ^{ptdm2009} ^{pnp1931}   ^{pp,pnx}   ^{cs,nn3682}   ^{du,nn5869}   ^{pp,nn3605} ^{pnl834}

pieces of silver: behold,   he   *is* to thee a covering of the eyes, unto   all   that *are*

^{pr,pnx854}   ^{wcj,pr854} ⁿⁿ³⁶⁰⁵   ^{wcj,nipt3198}

with thee, and with   all   *other*: thus she was reproved.

ⁿⁿ⁸⁵   ^{wcs,htmf6419} ^{pr413} ^{df,pl,nn430}   ^{pl,nn430} ^{wcs,qmf7495} (853)   ⁿⁿ⁴⁰   ^{wcj(853)}

17 So Abraham prayed unto God: and God healed   Abimelech, and

^{nn,pnx802}   ^{wcj,pl,nn,pnx519}   ^{wcs,qmf3205}

his wife, and his maidservants; and they   bore *children*.

^{cj3588}   ⁿⁿ³⁰⁶⁸   ^{qna6113/qpf6113/pr1157} ^{cs,nn3605}   ⁿⁿ⁷³⁵⁸   ^{pp,cs,nn1004}

18 For the LORD had fast*closed*up   all   the wombs of the house of

ⁿⁿ⁴⁰   ^{pr5921/cs,nn1697}   ⁿⁿ⁸²⁸³   ⁿⁿ⁸⁵   ^{cs,nn802}

Abimelech, because of Sarah Abraham's wife.

Isaac Is Born

^{wcj,nn3068}   ^{qpf6485}   (853)   ⁿⁿ⁸²⁸³ ^{pp,pnl834}   ^{qpf559}   ⁿⁿ³⁰⁶⁸

21 And the LORD visited   Sarah   as   he had said, and the LORD

^{wcs,qmf6213}   ^{pp,nn8283} ^{pp,pnl834}   ^{pipf1696}

did   unto Sarah   as   he had spoken.

ⁿⁿ⁸²⁸³   ^{wcs,qmf2029}   ^{wcs,qmf3205} ^{pp,nn85}   ⁿⁿ¹¹²¹   ^{pp,pl,nn,pnx2208}

2 For Sarah conceived, and   bore   Abraham a son in his old age, at the

^{dfp,nn4150}   ^{pnl834} ^{pl,nn430}   ^{pipf1696}   ^{pnx(853)}

set time of which God had spoken   to him.

ⁿⁿ⁸⁵   ^{wcs,qmf7121} (853)   ^{cs,nn8034}   ^{nn,pnx1121}   ^{df,nipt3205}   ^{pp,pnx}

3 And Abraham called   the name of his   son   that was   born unto him,

^{pnl834}   ⁿⁿ⁸²⁸³ ^{qpf3205} ^{pp,pnx}   ⁿⁿ³³²⁷

whom Sarah bore to him, Isaac.

ⁿⁿ⁸⁵   ^{wcs,qmf4135}   ^{nn,pnx1121} ⁿⁿ³³²⁷   ^{cs,nu8083} ^{pl,nn3117} ^{cs,nn1121} ^{pp,pnl834} ^{pl,nn430}

4 And Abraham circumcised his   son   Isaac being eight days old,   as   God

^{pipf6680}   ^{pnx(853)}

had commanded   him.

^{wcj,nn85}   ^{cs,nu3967}   ⁿⁿ⁸¹⁴¹ ^{cs,nn1121}   ^{nn,pnx1121} ⁿⁿ³³²⁷

5 And Abraham was a hundred years   old,   when   his   son Isaac was

^{pp,ninc3205}   ^{pp,pnx}

born unto him.

ⁿⁿ⁸²⁸³ ^{wcs,qmf559} ^{pl,nn430}   ^{qpf6213} ^{pp,pnx}   ⁿⁿ⁶⁷¹²   ^{cs,nn3605}   ^{df,qpta8085}

6 And Sarah said, God hath made me to laugh, *so that*   all   that hear will

^{qmf6711}   ^{pp,pnx}

laugh with me.

^{wcs,qmf559} ^{pnit4310}   ^{pipf4448}   ^{pp,nn85}   ⁿⁿ⁸²⁸³

7 And she said, Who would have said unto Abraham, that Sarah should

^{hipf3243/pl,nn1121}   ^{cj3588}   ^{qpf3205}   ⁿⁿ¹¹²¹   ^{pp,pl,nn,pnx2208}

have*given*children*suck? for I have born *him* a son in his old age.

Hagar and Ishmael Are Sent Away

^{df,nn3206} ^{wcs,qmf1431}   ^{wcs,nimf1580}   ⁿⁿ⁸⁵   ^{wcs,qmf6213}   ^{aj1419}   ⁿⁿ⁴⁹⁶⁰

8 And the child grew, and was weaned: and Abraham made a great feast the

^{pp,cs,nn3117}   (853) ⁿⁿ³³²⁷   ^{ninc1580}

same day   that   Isaac was weaned.

ⁿⁿ⁸²⁸³ ^{wcs,qmf7200} (853)   ^{cs,nn1121}   ⁿⁿ¹⁹⁰⁴   ^{df,nn4713} ^{pnl834}   ^{qpf3205}

9 And Sarah saw   the son of Hagar the Egyptian, which she had born

^{pp,nn85}   ^{pipt6711}

unto Abraham, mocking.

wcs,qmf**559**   pp,nn85   pimv1644   df,pndm2063   df,nn519   wcj(853)

10 Wherefore she said unto Abraham, Cast out this bondwoman and

nn,pnx1121   cj3588   cs,nn1121   df,pndm2063   df,nn519   ptn3808   qmf3423   pr5973   nn,pnx1121

her son: for the son of this bondwoman shall not be heir with my son,

pr5973   nn3327

even with Isaac.

df,nn**1697**   wcs,qmf**7489**/ad3966   nn85   pp,du,cs,nn**5869**   pr5921/pl,cs,nn182

11 And the thing was*very*grievous in Abraham's sight because of his

nn,pnx1121

son.

pl,nn**430**   wcs,qmf559   pr413   nn85   ptn408   qmf**7489**   pp,du,nn,pnx**5869**

12 And God said unto Abraham, Let it not be grievous in thy sight

pr5921   df,nn5288   wcj,pr5921   nn,pnx519   nn3605 pnl834 nn8283   qmf**559**

because of the lad, and because of thy bondwoman; in all that Sarah hath said

pr,pnx413   qmv**8085**   pp,nn,pnx6963 cj3588   pp,nn3327   pp,pnx nn**2233**   nimf7121

unto thee, hearken unto her voice; for in Isaac shall thy seed be called.

wcj,ad1571   (853)   cs,nn1121   df,nn519   qmf,pnx**7760**   pp,nn**1471**

13 And also of the son of the bondwoman will I make a nation,

cj3588   pnp1931   nn,pnx**2233**

because he is thy seed.

nn85   wcs,himf7925   dfp,nn1242   wcs,qmf3947   nn3899

14 And Abraham rose*up*early in the morning, and took bread, and a

wcj,cs,nn2573   pl,nn4325   wcs,qmf**5414**   pr413   nn1904   qpta**7760**   pr5921   nn,pnx7926   wcj(853)

bottle of water, and gave it unto Hagar, putting it on her shoulder, and

df,nn3206   wcs,pimf,pnx7971   wcs,qmf**1980**   wcs,qmf**8582**   pp,cs,nn4057

the child, and sent*her*away: and she departed, and wandered in the wilderness of

nn884

Beer-sheba.

df,pl,nn4325   wcs,qmf**3615** pr4480   df,nn2573   wcs,himf**7993** (853)   df,nn3206

15 And the water was spent in the bottle, and she cast the child

pr8478   cs,nu259   df,pl,nn**7880**

under one of the shrubs.

wcs,qmf**1980**   wcs,qmf**3427**/pp,pnx   pr4480/pr5048   hina7368

16 And she went, and sat*her*down over against him a good*way*off, as it

pp,pl,cs,pipt*2909/nn7198 cj3588   qpf559   ptn408 qmf**7200**   pp,cs,nn**4194**   df,nn3206

were a bowshot: for she said, Let me not see the death of the child. And

wcs,qmf**3427**   pr4480/pr5048   wcs,qmf**5375** (853)   nn,pnx6963   wcs,qmf1058

she sat over against him, and lifted up her voice, and wept.

pl,nn**430** wcs,qmf**8085** (853)   cs,nn6963   df,nn5288   cs,nn**4397**   pl,nn**430** wcs,qmf**7121** pr413

17 And God heard the voice of the lad; and the angel of God called to

nn1904   pr4480   df,du,nn**8064**   wcs,qmf559   pp,pnx   pnit4100   pp,pnx   nn1904   qmf3372 ptn408 cj3588

Hagar out of heaven, and said unto her, What aileth thee, Hagar? fear not; for

pl,nn**430**   qpf**8085**/pr413   cs,nn6963   df,nn5288 pp,pnl834/ad8033 pnp1931

God hath heard the voice of the lad where he is.

qmv6965   qmv**5375** (853)   df,nn**5288**   wcj,himv**2388** pp,pnx pr854   nn,pnx**3027** cj3588

18 Arise, lift up the lad, and hold him in thine hand; for I will

qmf,pnx**7760**   aj1419   pp,nn**1471**

make him a great nation.

pl,nn**430**   wcs,qmf6491 (853)   du,nn,pnx**5869**   wcs,qmf**7200**   cs,nn875   pl,nn4325

19 And God opened her eyes, and she saw a well of water; and she

wcs,qmf**1980**   wcs,pimf**4390** (853)   df,nn2573   pl,nn4325   (853)   df,nn5288 wcs,himf8248

went, and filled the bottle with water, and gave the lad drink.

pl,nn**430**   wcs,qmf**1961**   pr854   df,nn5288   wcs,qmf1431   wcs,qmf**3427**

20 And God was with the lad; and he grew, and dwelt in the

dfp,nn4057   wcs,qmf**1961**   qpta7235/nn7199

wilderness, and became an archer.

^{wcs,qmf3427} ^{pp,cs,nn4057} ⁿⁿ⁶²⁹⁰ ^{nn,pnx517} ^{wcs,qmf3947} ^{pp,pnx} ⁿⁿ⁸⁰²
21 And he dwelt in the wilderness of Paran: and his mother took him a wife
^{pr4480/cs,nn776} ⁿⁿ⁴⁷¹⁴
out*of*the*land of Egypt.

Abraham Makes an Agreement with Abimelech

^{wcs,qmf1961} ^{df,pndm1931} ^{dfp,nn6256} ⁿⁿ⁴⁰ ^{wcj,nn6369}
22 And it*came*to*pass at that time, that Abimelech and Phichol the
^{cs,nn8269} ^{nn,pnx6635} ^{wcs,qmf559} ^{pr413} ⁿⁿ⁸⁵ ^{pp,qnc559} ^{pl,nn430} ^{pr,pnx5973}
chief captain of his host spoke unto Abraham, saying, God is with thee in
^{pp,nn3605} ^{pnl834} ^{pnp859} ^{qpta6213}
all that thou doest:

^{wcj,ad6258} ^{nimv7650} ^{pp,pnx} ^{ad2008} ^{pp,pl,nn430} ^(cj518)
23 Now therefore swear unto me here by God that thou wilt not
^{qmf8266} ^{pp,pnx} ^{wcj,pp,nn,pnx5209} ^{wcj,pp,nn,pnx5220}
deal falsely with me, nor with my son, nor with my son's son: but according
^{dfp,nn2617} ^{pnl834} ^{qpf6213} ^{pr,pnx5973} ^{qmf6213} ^{pr,pnx5978} ^{wcj,pr5973}
to the kindness that I have done unto thee, thou shalt do unto me, and to
^{df,nn776} ^{pnl834/pp,pnx} ^{qpf1481}
the land wherein thou hast sojourned.

ⁿⁿ⁸⁵ ^{wcs,qmf559} ^{pnp595} ^{nimf7650}
24 And Abraham said, I will swear.

ⁿⁿ⁸⁵ ^{wcs,hipf3198} ⁽⁸⁵³⁾ ⁿⁿ⁴⁰ ^{pr5921/pl,cs,nn182} ^{cs,nn875} ^{df,pl,nn4325} ^{pnl834}
25 And Abraham reproved Abimelech because of a well of water, which
ⁿⁿ⁴⁰ ^{pl,cs,nn5650} ^{qpf1497}
Abimelech's servants had violently*taken*away.

ⁿⁿ⁴⁰ ^{wcs,qmf559} ^{qpf3045} ^{ptn3808} ^{pnit4310} ^{qpf6213} ⁽⁸⁵³⁾ ^{df,pndm2088} ^{df,nn1697} ^{ptn3808}
26 And Abimelech said, I know not who hath done this thing: neither
^(wcj,ad1571) ^{pnp859} ^{hipf5046} ^{pp,pnx} ^{ptn3808} ^{wcj,ad1571} ^{qpf8085} ^{pnp595} ^{ptn1115} ^{df,nn3117}
didst thou tell me, neither yet heard I of it, but today.

ⁿⁿ⁸⁵ ^{wcs,qmf3947} ⁿⁿ⁶⁶²⁹ ^{wcj,nn1241} ^{wcs,qmf5414} ^{pp,nn40}
27 And Abraham took sheep and oxen, and gave them unto Abimelech;
^{du,nu,pnx8147} ^{wcs,qmf3772} ⁿⁿ¹²⁸⁵
and both of them made a covenant.

ⁿⁿ⁸⁵ ^{wcs,himf5324} ⁽⁸⁵³⁾ ^{nu7651} ^{pl,cs,nn3535} ^{df,nn6629} ^{pp,nn,pnx905}
28 And Abraham set seven ewe lambs of the flock by themselves.

ⁿⁿ⁴⁰ ^{wcs,qmf559} ^{pr413} ⁿⁿ⁸⁵ ^{pnit4100} ^(pndm2007) ^{df,pndm428} ^{nu7651}
29 And Abimelech said unto Abraham, What mean these seven
^{pl,nn3535} ^{pnl834} ^{hipf5324} ^{pp,nn,pnx905}
ewe lambs which thou hast set by themselves?

^{wcs,qmf559} ^{cj3588} ⁽⁸⁵³⁾ ^{nu7651} ^{pl,nn3535} ^{qmf3947} ^{pr4480/nn,pnx3027}
30 And he said, For these seven ewe lambs shalt thou take of*my*hand,
^{pp,cj5668} ^{qmf1961} ^{pp,nn5713} ^{pp,pnx} ^{cj3588} ^{qpf2658} ⁽⁸⁵³⁾ ^{df,pndm2088} ^{df,nn875}
that they may be a witness unto me, that I have digged this well.

^{pr5921/ad3651} ^{qpf7121} ^{df,pndm1931} ^{dfp,nn4725} ⁿⁿ⁸⁸⁴ ^{cj3588} ^{ad8033} ^{nipf7650}
31 Wherefore he called that place Beer-sheba; because there they swore
^{du,nu,pnx8147}
both of them.

^{wcs,qmf3772} ⁿⁿ¹²⁸⁵ ^{pp,nn884} ⁿⁿ⁴⁰ ^{wcs,qmf6965}
32 Thus they made a covenant at Beer-sheba: then Abimelech rose up, and
^{wcj,nn6369} ^{cs,nn8269} ^{nn,pnx6635} ^{wcs,qmf7725} ^{pr413} ^{cs,nn776}
Phichol the chief captain of his host, and they returned into the land of the
ⁿⁿ⁶⁴³⁰
Philistines.

wcs,qmf5193   nn**815**   pp,nn884   wcs,qmf**7121** ad8033

33 And *Abraham* planted a grove in Beer-sheba, and called there on the

pp,cs,nn8034   nn**3068**   nn**5769**   nn**410**

name of the LORD, the everlasting God.

nn85   wcs,qmf**1481**   nn6430   pp,cs,nn**776** aj7227 pl,nn**3117**

34 And Abraham sojourned in the Philistines' land many days.

God Tests Abraham

wcs,qmf**1961**   pr310 df,pndm428 df,pl,nn**1697**   wcj,df,pl,nn**430**   pipf**5254**

22 ☞ And it*came*to*pass after these things, that God did tempt

(853)   nn85   wcs,qmf559 pr,pnx413   nn85   wcs,qmf559 ptdm,pnx2009

Abraham, and said unto him, Abraham: and he said, Behold,

here I *am.*

wcs,qmf559 qmv3947 pte**4994** (853)   nn,pnx**1121** (853)   aj,pnx**3173**   (853) nn3327   pnl834

2 And he said, Take now   thy son,   thine only *son*   Isaac, whom

qpf**157**   wcj,qmv**1980**/pp,pnx   pr413   cs,nn**776**   df,nn4179   wcj,himv,pnx**5927**   ad8033

thou lovest, and   get   thee into the land of Moriah; and   offer   him there

pp,nn**5930**   pr5921 cs,nu259   df,pl,nn2022   pnl834   qmf559   pr,pnx413

for a burnt offering upon one of the mountains which I will tell thee of.

nn85   wcs,himf7925   dfp,nn1242   wcs,qmf**2280** (853)   nn,pnx2543

3 And Abraham rose*up*early in the morning, and saddled   his   ass,   and

wcs,qmf3947 (853) du,cs,nu8147   pl,nn,pnx5288   pr,pnx854   wcj(853) nn3327   nn,pnx**1121**

took   two   of his young men with him, and   Isaac his son,   and

wcs,pimf1234   pl,cs,nn6086   nn**5930**   wcs,qmf6965   wcs,qmf1980 pr413   df,nn4725

cleaved the wood for the burnt offering, and rose up, and went unto the place

pnl834   df,pl,nn**430**   qpf559 pp,pnx

of which God had told him.

df,nuor7992 dfp,nn**3117**   nn85   wcs,qmf5375   (853)   du,nn,pnx**5869**   wcs,qmf**7200** (853)

4 Then on the third   day Abraham lifted up   his   eyes,   and saw

df,nn4725 pr4480/nn7350

the place afar off.

nn85   wcs,qmf559 pr413   pl,nn,pnx5288   qmv**3427** pp,pnx ad6311 pr5973   df,nn2543

5 And Abraham said unto his young men, Abide ye here with the ass; and

wcj,pnp589   wcj,df,nn5288   qcj**1980** pr5704/ad3541   wcj,htcj***7812**   wcj,qcj**7725**   pr,pnx413

I   and the   lad   will go yonder and worship, and come again   to   you.

nn85   wcs,qmf3947 (853)   pl,cs,nn6086   df,nn**5930**   wcs,qmf**7760**   pr5921

6 And Abraham took   the wood of the burnt offering, and laid *it* upon

nn3327   nn,pnx**1121**   wcs,qmf3947 (853)   df,nn784   pp,nn,pnx**3027**   wcj(853)   df,nn3979

Isaac his son; and he took   the fire in his hand,   and   a knife; and

wcs,qmf**1980** du,nu,pnx8147   ad3162

they went   both   of them together.

nn3327 wcs,qmf559 pr413   nn85   nn,pnx1   wcs,qmf559   nn,pnx1

7 And Isaac spoke unto Abraham his father, and said, My father: and he

wcs,qmf559 ptdm,pnx2009   nn,pnx**1121**   wcs,qmf559 ptdm2009   df,nn784   wcj,df,pl,nn6086

said,   Here *am* I, my son. And he said, Behold the fire and the   wood:

wcj,pnit346   df,nn7716   pp,nn**5930**

but where *is* the lamb for a burnt offering?

☞ **22:1** Some versions translate Genesis 22:1 as God "tempting" Abraham. The Hebrew word in question
is *nāsāh* (5254), which means to "put to the test." (See the Lexical Aids section for a more detailed definition.)
God may allow us to be tested, but He will never place inducements before us to lead us into temptation which
is more than we can bear (1 Cor. 10:13). Abraham proved faithful to the test for he believed that God would
bring Isaac back to life to keep His promise even if Abraham had killed him (Heb. 11:17–19).

nn85   wcs,qmf**559**   nn,pnx**1121**   pl,nn**430**   qmf**7200**   pp,pnx   df,nn**7716**

8 And Abraham said, My son, God will provide himself a lamb for a

pp,nn**5930**   wcs,qmf**1980**   du,nu,pnx**8147**   ad**3162**

burnt offering: so they went   both   of them together.

wcs,qmf**935**   pr**413**   df,nn**4725**   pnl**834**   df,pl,nn**430**   qpf**559**   pp,pnx   nn85

9 And they came to the place which God had told him of; and Abraham

wcs,qmf**1129**   (853)   df,nn**4196**   ad**8033**   wcs,qmf**6186**/(853)/df,pl,nn**6086**   wcs,qmf**6123**   (853)   nn**3327**

built   an altar there, and laid*the*wood*in*order, and bound   Isaac his

nn,pnx**1121**   wcs,qmf**7760** pnx(853)   pr**5921**   df,nn**4196** pr**4480**/ad**4605**   dfp,pl,nn**6086**

son, and laid   him on the altar   upon   the wood.

nn85   wcs,qmf**7971**   (853)   nn,pnx**3027**   wcs,qmf**3947**   (853)   df,nn**3979**

10 And Abraham stretched forth   his hand, and   took   the knife to

pp,qnc**7819**   (853)   nn,pnx**1121**

slay   his son.

cs,nn**4397**   nn**3068**   wcs,qmf**7121**   pr,pnx**413**   pr**4480**   df,du,nn**8064**   wcs,qmf**559**

11 And the angel of the Lᴏʀᴅ called   unto him out of heaven, and   said,

nn85   nn85   wcs,qmf**559** ptdm,pnx**2009**

Abraham, Abraham: and he said,   Here   *am* I.

wcs,qmf**559**   qmf**7971**   ptn**408**   nn,pnx**3027**   pr**413**   df,nn**5288**   wcj,ptn**408**   qcj**6213**

☞ 12 And he said, Lay not thine hand upon the lad, neither do thou

pnid**3972**   pp,pnx   cj**3588** ad**6258**   qpf**3045**   cj**3588** pnp**859**   cs,aj**3373**   pl,nn**430**   wcj,ptn**3808**

any thing unto him: for now I know that thou fearest God, seeing thou hast   not

qpf**2820**   (853)   nn,pnx**1121** (853)   aj,pnx**3173**   pr,pnx**4480**

withheld   thy son,   thine only *son* from me.

nn85   wcs,qmf**5375**   (853)   du,nn,pnx**5869**   wcs,qmf**7200**   wcj,ptdm**2009**   pr**310**

13 And Abraham lifted up   his eyes,   and looked, and   behold behind *him*

nn**352**   nipf**270**   pp,nn**5442**   pp,du,nn,pnx**7161**   nn85   wcs,qmf**1980**   wcs,qmf**3947** (853)

a ram caught in a thicket by his   horns: and Abraham went and took   the

df,nn**352**   wcs,himf,pnx**5927**   pp,nn**5930**   pr**8478**   nn,pnx**1121**

ram, and offered*him*up for a burnt offering in*the*stead*of his   son.

nn85   wcs,qmf**7121**   cs,nn**8034**   df,pndm**1931** df,nn**4725** nn**3070** [nn**3068**/qmf**7200**] pnl**834**   nimf**559**

14 And Abraham called the name of   that   place Jehovah-jireh: as   it is said

df,nn**3117**   pp,cs,nn**2022**   nn**3068**   nimf**7200**

to this day, In the mount of the Lᴏʀᴅ it shall be seen.

cs,nn**4397**   nn**3068** wcs,qmf**7121**   pr**413**   nn85   pr**4480**   df,du,nn**8064**

15 And the angel of the Lᴏʀᴅ called   unto Abraham out of heaven the

nuor**8145**

second time,

wcs,qmf**559**   pp,pnx   nipf**7650**   cs,nn**5002**   nn**3068**   cj**3588** cj**3282**/pnl**834**

16 And said, By myself have I sworn, saith the Lᴏʀᴅ, for because thou hast

qpf**6213**   (853)   df,pndm**2088**   df,nn**1697**   wcj,ptn**3808**   qpf**2820**   (853)   nn,pnx**1121** (853)   aj,pnx**3173**

done   this   thing, and hast   not   withheld   thy son,   thine only *son*:

cj**3588**   pina**1288**   pimf,pnx**1288**   wcj,hina**7235**   himf**7235**   (853)

17 That in blessing I will   bless   thee, and in multiplying I will multiply   thy

---

☞ **22:12** Since God is all-knowing, some question how He could say, "For now I know that you fear God." One cannot profitably discuss God's foreknowledge, because it is clearly a part of God's thoughts that are higher than man's (Is. 55:9). In one sense, this use of "know" may parallel the use suggested in the note on Genesis 4:1, God "experienced" Abraham's fear of Him. The test of Abraham's faith was a valid one, truly reflecting his absolute trust in God. Abraham was not imitating idolatrous neighbors who practiced child sacrifice (Lev. 18:21; Deut. 18:10). On the contrary, God commanded Abraham to sacrifice his son. Abraham did not have to give up his beloved son, but he was fully prepared to kill Isaac when God's angel suddenly intervened. God's provision of a substitute animal showed that He did not want human sacrifices. The only human sacrifice approved by God was that of His Son, the sinless Lamb of God (John 1:29).

nn,pnx**2233**   pp,pl,cs,nn3556   df,du,nn**8064**   wcj,dfp,nn2344   pnl834   pr5921   df,nn3220

seed   as   the   stars   of the heaven, and as the   sand   which *is* upon the   sea

cs,nn**8193**   nn,pnx**2233**   wcj,qmf**3423**   (853)   cs,nn8179   pl,qpta,pnx341

shore; and thy   seed   shall possess   the gate of his enemies;

pp,nn,pnx**2233**   cs,nn3605   pl,cs,nn**1471**   df,nn776   wcs,htpf**1288**   ad6118/pnl834

18 And in thy   seed   shall   all   the nations of the earth be blessed; because

qpf**8085**   pp,nn,pnx6963

thou hast obeyed my   voice.

nn85   wcs,qmf**7725**   pr413   pl,nn,pnx5288   wcs,qmf**6965**   wcs,qmf**1980**

19 So Abraham returned unto his young men, and they rose up and   went

ad3162   pr413   nn884   nn85   wcs,qmf**3427**   pp,nn884

together to Beer-sheba; and Abraham dwelt at Beer-sheba.

Nahor's Family

wcs,qmf**1961**   pr310   df,pndm428   df,pl,nn**1697**   wcs,homf**5046**   pp,nn85

20 And it*came*to*pass after these   things, that it was   told   Abraham,

pp,qnc**559**   ptdm2009   nn4435   pnp1931   ad1571   qpf3205   pl,nn**1121**   nn,pnx**251**   pp,nn5152

saying, Behold, Milcah,   she   hath also born children unto thy brother Nahor;

(853)   nn5780   nn,pnx1060   wcj(853)   nn938   nn,pnx**251**   wcj(853)   nn7055   cs,nn**1**

21   Huz his firstborn, and   Buz his brother, and   Kemuel the father

nn758

of Aram,

wcj(853)   nn3777   wcj(853)   nn2375   wcj(853)   nn6394   wcj(853)   nn3044

22 And   Chesed, and   Hazo, and   Pildash, and   Jidlaph, and

wcj(853)   nn1328

Bethuel.

wcj,nn1328   qpf3205   (853)   nn7259   pndm428   nu8083   nn4435   qpf3205   pp,nn5152

23 And Bethuel begot   Rebekah: these eight Milcah did bear to Nahor,

nn85   cs,nn**251**

Abraham's brother.

wcj,nn,pnx**6370**   wcj,nn,pnx8034   nn7208   pnp1931   wcs,qmf3205   ad1571   (853)

24 And his concubine, whose   name *was* Reumah,   she   bore   also

nn2875   wcj(853)   nn1514   wcj(853)   nn8477   wcj(853)   nn4601

Tebah, and   Gaham, and   Thahash, and   Maachah.

Sarah Dies

nn8283   wcs,qmf**1961**   nu3967   (nn8141)   wcj,nu7651   (pl,nn8141)   wcj,pl,nu6242   nn8141

23 And Sarah   was   a hundred   and seven   and twenty years

pl,cs,nn**2416**   pl,cs,nn8141   pl,cs,nn**2416**   nn8283

old: *these were* the years of the   life   of Sarah.

nn8283   wcs,qmf**4191**   pp,nn7153   pndm1931   nn2275   pp,cs,nn776

2 And Sarah   died   in Kirjath-arba; the same   *is* Hebron in the   land   of

nn3667   nn85   wcs,qmf935   pp,qnc5594   pp,nn8283   wcj,pp,qnc,pnx1058

Canaan: and Abraham came   to mourn for Sarah, and to   weep   for her.

23:2, 3, 19 The Hittites were descendants of Canaan's son, Heth, and one of the seven Canaanite nations. They dwelt in Hebron (Deut. 7:1; 1 Kgs. 10:29). Their land was promised to Israel and the Israelites were commanded to destroy them, but Israel did not destroy them entirely (Deut. 7:1, 2, 24; Judg. 3:5). Among their prominent leaders were Ephron, Ahimelech, and Uriah (Gen. 49:30; 1 Sam. 26:6; 2 Sam. 11:6, 21). Esau, Solomon, and many other Israelites intermarried with the Hittites. They were warlike people and made many conquests.

nn85   wcs,qmf**6965**   pr4480/pr5921/pl,cs,nn**6440**   qpta,pnx**4191**   wcs,pimf**1696**   pr413

3 And Abraham stood up from before his dead, and spoke unto the

pl,cs,nn**1121**   nn2845   pp,qnc**559**

sons of Heth, saying,

pnp595   nn**1616**   wcj,nn**8453**   pr,pnx5973   qmv**5414**   pp,pnx   cs,nn**272**

4 I *am* a stranger and a sojourner with you: give me a possession of a

nn**6913**   pr,pnx5973   wcj,qcj**6912**   qpta,pnx**4191**   pr4480/pp,pl,nn,pnx**6440**

burial place with you, that I may bury my dead out*of*my*sight.

pl,cs,nn**1121**   nn2845   wcs,qmf6030   (853)   nn85   pp,qnc**559**   pp,pnx

5 And the children of Heth answered Abraham, saying unto him,

qmv,pnx**8085**   nn,pnx113   pnp859   pl,nn**430**   cs,nn**5387**   pp,nn,pnx**8432**   pp,cs,nn4005

6 Hear us, my lord: thou *art* a mighty prince among us: in the choice of

pl,nn,pnx**6913**   qmv**6912**   (853)   qpta,pnx**4191**   nn376/ptn**3808**   pr,pnx4480   qmf3607   pr,pnx4480   (853)

our sepulchers bury thy dead; none of us shall withhold from thee

nn,pnx**6913**   pr4480/qnc**6912**   qpta,pnx**4191**

his sepulcher, but that*thou*mayest*bury thy dead.

nn85   wcs,qmf**6965**   wcs,htmf**7812**   pp,cs,nn**5971**   df,nn**776**

7 And Abraham stood up, and bowed himself to the people of the land, *even*

pp,pl,cs,nn**1121**   nn2845

to the children of Heth.

wcs,pimf**1696**   pr,pnx854   pp,qnc**559**   cj518   pta3426   (853)   nn,pnx**5315**

8 And he communed with them, saying, If it be your mind that I should

pp,qnc**6912**   (853)   qpta,pnx**4191**   pr4480/pp,pl,nn,pnx**6440**   qmv,pnx**8085**   wcj,qmv**6293**   pp,pnx   pp,nn6085

bury my dead out*of*my*sight; hear me, and entreat for me to Ephron

cs,nn**1121**   nn6714

the son of Zohar,

wcj,qcj**5414**   pp,pnx   (853)   cs,nn4631   df,nn4375   pnl834   pp,pnx   pnl834

9 That he may give me the cave of Machpelah, which he hath, which

pp,cs,nn7097   nn,pnx**7704**   pp,nn3701   aj4392   qmf,pnx**5414**

is in the end of his field; for as much money as it is worth he shall give it

pp,pnx   pp,cs,nn**272**   nn**6913**   pp,nn,pnx**8432**

me for a possession of a burial place amongst you.

wcj,nn6085   qpta3427   pp,cs,nn**8432**   pl,cs,nn**1121**   nn2845   nn6085   df,nn2850

10 And Ephron dwelt among the children of Heth: and Ephron the Hittite

wcs,qmf6030   (853)   nn85   pp,du,cs,nn**241**   pl,cs,nn**1121**   nn2845   pp,cs,nn3605

answered Abraham in the audience of the children of Heth, *even* of all that

pl,cs,qpta935   cs,nn8179   nn,pnx5892   pp,qnc**559**

went in at the gate of his city, saying,

ptn**3808**   nn,pnx113   qmv,pnx**8085**   df,nn**7704**   qpf**5414**   pp,pnx   wcj,df,nn4631   pnl834

11 Nay, my lord, hear me: the field give I thee, and the cave that *is*

pp,pnx   qpf,pnx**5414**   pp,pnx   pp,du,cs,nn**5869**   pl,cs,nn**1121**   nn,pnx**5971**   qpf,pnx**5414**   pp,pnx

therein, I give it thee; in the presence of the sons of my people give I it thee:

qmv**6912**   qpta,pnx**4191**

bury thy dead.

nn85   wcs,htmf**7812**   pp,pl,cs,nn**6440**   cs,nn**5971**   df,nn**776**

12 And Abraham bowed*down*himself before the people of the land.

wcs,pimf**1696**   pr413   nn6085   pp,du,cs,nn**241**   cs,nn**5971**   df,nn**776**

13 And he spoke unto Ephron in the audience of the people of the land,

pp,qnc**559**   ad389   cj518   pnp859   pte3863   qmv,pnx**8085**   qpf**5414**   cs,nn3701

saying, But if thou *wilt give it*, I*pray*thee, hear me: I will give thee money for

df,nn**7704**   qmv3947   pr,pnx4480   wcj,qcj**6912**   (853)   qpta,pnx**4191**   ad,lh8033

the field; take *it* of me, and I will bury my dead there.

nn6085   wcs,qmf6030   (853)   nn85   pp,qnc**559**   pp,pnx

14 And Ephron answered Abraham, saying unto him,

nn,pnx113   qmv,pnx**8085**   nn**776**   nu702   pl,nu3967   cs,nn8255   nn3701

15 My lord, hearken unto me: the land *is worth* four hundred shekels of silver;

pnit4100   pndm1931   pr,pnx996   wcj,pnx(pr996)   qmv**6912**   wcj(853)   qpta,pnx**4191**

what *is* that between me and   thee? bury therefore   thy dead.

           nn85   wcs,qmf**8085**   pr413   nn6085   nn85   wcs,qmf8254   pp,nn6085   (853)

16 And Abraham hearkened unto Ephron; and Abraham weighed to Ephron

df,nn3701   pnl834   pipf**1696**   pp,du,cs,nn**241**   pl,cs,nn**1121**   nn2845   nu702   pl,cs,nu3967

the silver, which he had named in the audience of the   sons   of Heth, four hundred

cs,nn8255   nn3701   qpta**5674**   dfp,qpta5503

shekels of silver, current *money* with the merchant.

         cs,nn**7704**   nn6085   pnl834   dfp,nn4375   pnl834   pp,pl,cs,nn**6440**

17 And the field of Ephron, which *was* in Machpelah, which *was* before

nn4471   df,nn**7704**   wcj,df,nn4631   pnl834   pp,pnx   wcj,cs,nn3605   df,nn6086   pnl834

Mamre, the field, and the   cave   which *was* therein, and   all   the trees that

dfp,nn**7704**   pnl834   pp,cs,nn3605   nn,pnx1366   ad5439   wcs,qmf**6965**

were in the field, that *were* in   all   the borders round about, were made sure

       pp,nn85   pp,nn4736   pp,du,cs,nn**5869**   pl,cs,nn**1121**   nn2845

18 Unto Abraham for a possession in the presence of the children of Heth,

pp,cs,nn3605   pl,cs,qpta935   cs,nn8179   nn,pnx5892

before   all   that went in at the gate of his city.

         wcj,ad310   ad**3651**   nn85   qpf**6912**   (853)   nn8283   nn,pnx**802**   pr413   cs,nn4631

19 And after this, Abraham buried   Sarah his   wife   in   the cave of the

cs,nn**7704**   df,nn4375   pr5921/pl,cs,nn**6440**   nn4471   pndm1931   nn2275   pp,cs,nn**776**

field of Machpelah   before   Mamre: the same *is* Hebron in the   land   of

nn3667

Canaan.

           df,nn**7704**   wcj,df,nn4631   pnl834   pp,pnx   wcs,qmf**6965**   pp,nn85

20 And the field, and the   cave   that *is* therein, were made sure unto Abraham

      pp,cs,nn**272**   nn**6913**   pr4480/pr854   pl,cs,nn**1121**   nn2845

for a possession of a burial place   by   the   sons of Heth.

Isaac Marries Rebekah

           wcj,nn85   qpf**2204**   qpf935   dfp,pl,nn**3117**   wcj,nn**3068**

24 And Abraham was old, *and* well stricken in   age: and the LORD

           pipf**1288**   (853)   nn85   dfp,nn3605

had blessed   Abraham in all things.

         nn85   wcs,qmf**559**   pr413   cs,aj**2205**   nn,pnx**5650**   nn,pnx**1004**   df,qpta**4910**

2 And Abraham   said   unto his eldest servant of his house, that ruled over

pp,cs,nn3605   pnl834   pp,pnx   qmv**7760**   pte**4994**   nn,pnx**3027**   pr8478   nn,pnx**3409**

all   that he had, Put, I*pray*thee, thy hand under my thigh:

            wcj,himf,pnx**7650**   pp,nn**3068**   pl,cs,nn**430**   df,du,nn**8064**

3 And I will make thee   swear   by the LORD, the   God   of heaven, and the

wcj,pl,cs,nn**430**   df,nn**776**   pnl834   ptn3808   qmf3947   nn**802**   pp,nn,pnx**1121**

God   of the earth, that thou shalt not   take   a   wife unto my   son

pr4480/pl,cs,nn1323   df,nn3669   pp,nn,pnx**7130**   pnl834   pnp595   qpta**3427**

of*the*daughters of the Canaanites, among whom   I   dwell:

       cj3588   qmf**1980**   pr413   nn,pnx**776**   wcj,pr413   nn,pnx4138   wcs,qpf3947

4 But thou shalt   go   unto my country, and   to   my kindred, and   take   a

nn**802**   pp,nn,pnx1121   pp,nn3327

wife unto my   son   Isaac.

          df,nn**5650**   wcs,qmf**559**   pr,pnx413   ad194   df,nn**802**   ptn3808

5 And the servant   said   unto   him, Peradventure the woman will   not

qmf14   pp,qnc**1980**/pr,pnx310   pr413   df,pndm2063   df,nn**776**   he,hina**7725**/himf**7725**   (853)   nn,pnx**1121**

be willing to   follow   me unto   this   land: must*I*needs*bring   thy son

      pr413   df,nn**776**   pnl834/pr4480/ad8033   qpf3318

again unto the land from   whence thou camest?

nn85   wcs,qmf559   pr,pnx413   nimv8104   pp,pnx   cj6435   himf7725   (853)

6 And Abraham said unto him, Beware thou that thou bring not   my

nn,pnx1121 ad,lh8033

son thither again.

nn3068   pl,cs,nn430   df,du,nn8064 pnl834 qpf,pnx3947   pr4480/cs,nn1004/nn,pnx1

7 The Lord God of heaven, which took me from*my*father's*house, and

wcj,pr4480/cs,nn776   nn,pnx4138   wcj,pnl834 pipf1696 pp,pnx   wcj,pnl834 nipf7650

from*the*land of my kindred, and which spoke unto me, and that swore

pp,pnx   pp,qnc559   pp,nn,pnx2233   qmf5414 (853) df,pndm2063 df,nn776 pnp1931   qmf7971

unto me, saying, Unto thy seed will I give   this land; he shall send his

nn,pnx4397 pp,pl,nn,pnx6440   wcs,qpf3947   nn802   pp,nn,pnx1121 pr4480/ad8033

angel before thee, and thou shalt take a wife unto my son from thence.

wcj,cj518   df,nn802   ptn3808 qmf14   pp,qnc1980/pr,pnx310

8 And if the woman will not be willing to   follow   thee, then thou

wcs,nipf5352   pr4480/nn,pnx7621/pndm2063 ad7535 hicj7725 ptn3808 (853)   nn,pnx1121 ad,lh8033

shalt be clear from*this*my*oath: only bring not   my son thither again.

df,nn5650 wcs,qmf7760 (853)   nn,pnx3027 pr8478   cs,nn3409   nn85   pl,nn,pnx113

9 And the servant put   his hand under the thigh of Abraham his master,

wcs,nimf7650 pp,pnx   pr5921   df,pndm2088 df,nn1697

and swore to him concerning that matter.

df,nn5650 wcs,qmf3947 nu6235 pl,nn1581 pr4480/pl,cs,nn1581 pl,nn,pnx113

10 And the servant took   ten camels of*the*camels of his master, and

wcs,qmf1980 wcj,cs,nn3605   cs,nn2898   pl,nn,pnx113   pp,nn,pnx3027   wcs,qmf6965

departed; for all   the goods of his master *were* in his hand: and he arose,

wcs,qmf1980 pr413   nn763   pr413   cs,nn5892   nn5152

and went to Mesopotamia, unto the city of Nahor.

df,pl,nn1581   wcs,himf1288   pr4480/nn2351   dfp,nn5892 pr413 cs,nn875

11 And he made his camels to kneel down without the city by a well of

df,pl,nn4325   pp,cs,nn6256   nn6153   pp,cs,nn6256   qnc3318 df,pl,qpta7579

water at the time of the evening, *even* the time that women go out to   draw

water.

wcs,qmf559   nn3068   pl,cs,nn430   nn,pnx113   nn85   pte4994

12 And he said, O Lord God of my master Abraham, I*pray*thee,

himv7136/pp,pl,nn,pnx6440   df,nn3117 wcj,qmv6213 nn2617 pr5973   nn,pnx113   nn85

send*me*good*speed this day, and show kindness unto my master Abraham.

ptdm2009   pnp595 nipt5324   pr5921   cs,nn5869   df,pl,nn4325   wcj,pl,cs,nn1323

13 Behold, I stand *here* by the well of water; and the daughters of the

pl,cs,nn376   df,nn5892   pl,qpta3318   pp,qnc7579 pl,nn4325

men of the city come out to draw water:

wcj,qpf1961   df,nn5291   pnl834   qmf559/pr,pnx413

14 And let it come*to*pass, that the damsel to whom I shall   say,

himv5186   nn,pnx3537   pte4994   wcj,qmf8354   wcs,qpf559 qmv8354

Let down thy pitcher, I*pray*thee, that I may drink; and she shall say, Drink,

pl,nn,pnx1581   himf8248 wcj,ad1571   pnx(853)

and I will give*thy*camels drink also: *let the same be*   she *that* thou hast

hipf3198   pp,nn,pnx5650 pp,nn3327   wcj,pp,pnx   qmf3045 cj3588   qpf6213

appointed for thy servant Isaac; and thereby shall I know that thou hast showed

nn2617   pr5973   nn,pnx113

kindness unto my master.

wcs,qmf1961   ad2962 pnp1931 pipf3615 pp,pinc1696   wcj,ptdm2009 nn7259

15 And it*came*to*pass, before he had done speaking, that, behold, Rebekah

qpta3318   pnl834   pupf3205   pp,nn1328   cs,nn1121   nn4435   cs,nn802   nn5152

came out, who was born to Bethuel, son of Milcah, the wife of Nahor,

nn85   cs,nn251   wcj,nn,pnx3537 pr5921   nn,pnx7926

Abraham's brother, with her pitcher upon her shoulder.

^{wcj,df,nn5291} ^{ad3966} ^{cs,aj2896} ⁿⁿ⁴⁷⁵⁸ ⁿⁿ¹³³⁰ ^{ptn3808}

16 And the damsel *was* very fair to*look*upon, a virgin, neither had any

^{wcj,nn376} ^{qpf,pnx3045} ^{wcs,qmf3381} ^{df,nn,lh5869} ^{wcs,pimf4390} ^{nn,pnx3537}

man known her: and she went down to the well, and filled her pitcher, and

^{wcs,qmf5927}

came up.

^{df,nn5650} ^{wcs,qmf7323} ^{pp,qnc,pnx7125} ^{wcs,qmf559} ^{pte4994}

17 And the servant ran to meet her, and said, Let me, I*pray*thee,

^{himv,pnx1572} ^{cs,nn4592} ^{pl,nn4325} ^{pr4480/nn,pnx3537}

drink a little water of*thy*pitcher.

^{wcs,qmf559} ^{qmv8354} ^{nn,pnx113} ^{wcs,pimf4116} ^{wcs,himf3381} ^{nn,pnx3537}

18 And she said, Drink, my lord: and she hasted, and let down her pitcher

^{pr5921} ^{nn,pnx3027} ^{wcs,himf,pnx8248}

upon her hand, and gave him drink.

^{wcs,pimf3615} ^{pp,hinc,pnx8248} ^{wcs,qmf559} ^{qmf7579}

19 And when she had done giving him drink, she said, I will draw *water*

^{pp,pl,nn,pnx1581} ^{ad1571} ^{cj5704/cj518} ^{pipf3615} ^{pp,qnc8354}

for thy camels also, until they have done drinking.

^{wcs,pimf4116} ^{wcs,pimf6168} ^{nn,pnx3537} ^{pr413} ^{df,nn8268} ^{wcs,qmf7323} ^{ad5750}

20 And she hasted, and emptied her pitcher into the trough, and ran again

^{pr413} ^{df,nn875} ^{pp,qnc7579} ^{wcs,qmf7579} ^{pp,cs,nn3605} ^{pl,nn,pnx1581}

unto the well to draw *water*, and drew for all his camels.

^{wcj,df,nn376} ^{htpt*7583} ^{pp,pnx} ^{hipt2790} ^{pp,qnc3045}

21 And the man wondering at her held*his*peace, to know whether the

ⁿⁿ³⁰⁶⁸ ^{nn,pnx1870} ^{he,hipf6743} ^{cj518} ^{ptn3808}

LORD had made his journey prosperous or not.

^{wcs,qmf1961} ^{pp,pnl834} ^{df,pl,nn1581} ^{pipf3615} ^{pp,qnc8354} ^{df,nn376}

22 And it*came*to*pass, as the camels had done drinking, that the man

^{wcs,qmf3947} ⁿⁿ²⁰⁹¹ ^{cs,nn5141} ^{cs,nn1235} ^{nn,pnx4948} ^{wcj,du,cs,nu8147} ^{pl,nn6781} ^{pr5921}

took a golden earring of half*a*shekel weight, and two bracelets for her

^{du,nn,pnx3027} ^{nu6235} ^{nn,pnx4948} ⁿⁿ²⁰⁹¹

hands of ten *shekels* weight of gold;

^{wcs,qmf559} ^{pnit4310} ^{cs,nn1323} ^{pnp859} ^{himv5046} ^{pp,pnx} ^{pte4994} ^{he,pta3426} ⁿⁿ⁴⁷²⁵

23 And said, Whose daughter *art* thou? tell me, I*pray*thee: is there room

^{nn,pnx1} ^{cs,nn1004} ^{pp,pnx} ^{pp,qnc3885}

in thy father's house for us to lodge in?

^{wcs,qmf559} ^{pr,pnx413} ^{pnp595} ^{cs,nn1323} ⁿⁿ¹³²⁸ ^{cs,nn1121}

24 And she said unto him, I *am* the daughter of Bethuel the son of

ⁿⁿ⁴⁴³⁵ ^{pnl834} ^{qpf3205} ^{pp,nn5152}

Milcah, which she bore unto Nahor.

^{wcs,qmf559} ^{pr,pnx413} ^{pnx(pr5973)} ^{ad1571} ⁿⁿ⁸⁴⁰¹ ^{ad1571} ⁿⁿ⁴⁵⁵⁴

25 She said moreover unto him, We have both straw and provender

^{aj7227} ^{ad1571} ⁿⁿ⁴⁷²⁵ ^{pp,qnc3885}

enough, and room to lodge in.

^{df,nn376} ^{wcs,qmf6915} ^{wcs,himf*7812} ^{pp,nn3068}

26 And the man bowed*down*his*head, and worshiped the LORD.

^{wcs,qmf559} ^{qptp1288} ⁿⁿ³⁰⁶⁸ ^{pl,cs,nn430} ^{nn,pnx113} ⁿⁿ⁸⁵ ^{pnl834}

27 And he said, Blessed *be* the LORD God of my master Abraham, who hath

^{ptn3808} ^{qpf5800/pr4480/pr5973} ^{nn,pnx113} ^{nn,pnx2617} ^{wcj,nn,pnx571} ^{pnp595}

not left destitute my master of his mercy and his truth: I *being* in

^{dfp,nn1870} ⁿⁿ³⁰⁶⁸ ^{qpf,pnx5148} ^{cs,nn1004} ^{nn,pnx113} ^{pl,cs,nn251}

the way, the LORD led me to the house of my master's brethren.

^{df,nn5291} ^{wcs,qmf7323} ^{wcs,himf5046} ^{nn,pnx517} ^{pp,cs,nn1004} ^{df,pndm428}

28 And the damsel ran, and told *them of* her mother's house these

^{dfp,pl,nn1697}

things.

wcj,pp,nn7259   nn251   wcj,nn,pnx8034   nn3837   nn3837   wcs,qmf7323
29 And Rebekah had a brother, and his   name   *was* Laban: and Laban   ran

df,nn,lh2351   pr413   df,nn376   pr413   df,nn5869
out   unto the man, unto the well.

wcs,qmf1961   pp,qnc7200   (853)   df,nn5141   wcj(853) df,pl,nn6781
30 And it*came*to*pass, when he   saw   the earring and   bracelets

pr5921   nn,pnx269 du,cs,nn3027   wcj,pp,qnc,pnx8085 (853)   pl,cs,nn1697   nn7259
upon his sister's hands, and when he   heard   the words of Rebekah his

nn,pnx269   pp,qnc559   ad3541   pipf1696   df,nn376   pr,pnx413   wcs,qmf935   pr413   df,nn376
sister, saying, Thus spoke the man   unto me; that he   came unto the man; and,

wcj,ptdm2009   qpta5975 pr5921   df,pl,nn1581 pr5921   df,nn5869
behold, he stood by the camels at the well.

wcs,qmf559   qmv935   cs,qptp1288   nn3068   pp,pnit4100   qmf5975
31 And he said, Come in, thou blessed of the LORD; wherefore standest thou

dfp,nn2351   wcj,pnp595   pipf6437   df,nn1004   wcj,nn4725   dfp,pl,nn1581
without? for   I   have prepared the house, and   room for the camels.

df,nn376 wcs,qmf935   df,nn,lh1004   wcs,pimf6605   df,pl,nn1581   wcs,qmf5414
32 And the man came into the house: and he ungirded his camels, and   gave

nn8401   wcj,nn4554   dfp,pl,nn1581   wcj,pl,nn4325   pp,qnc7364   du,nn,pnx7272
straw and provender for the camels, and   water to wash his   feet,   and the

df,pl,nn376 wcj,du,cs,nn7272 pnl834   pr,pnx854
men's   feet   that *were* with him.

wcs,homf7760   pp,pl,nn,pnx6440   pp,qnc398   wcs,qmf559   ptn3808
33 And there was set *meat* before him to eat: but he said, I will not

qmf398   cj5704/cj518   pipf1696   pl,nn,pnx1697   wcs,qmf559   pimv1696
eat,   until   I have told mine errand. And he said, Speak on.

wcs,qmf559 pnp595   nn85   cs,nn5650
34 And he said,   I *am* Abraham's servant.

wcj,nn3068   pipf1288   (853)   nn,pnx113   ad3966   wcs,qmf1431
35 And the LORD hath blessed   my master greatly; and he is become great:

wcs,qmf5414 pp,pnx   nn6629   wcj,nn1241   wcj,nn3701   wcj,nn2091   wcj,pl,nn5650
and he hath given him flocks, and herds, and silver, and gold, and menservants,

wcj,pl,nn8198   wcj,pl,nn1581   wcj,pl,nn2543
and maidservants, and camels, and asses.

nn8283   nn,pnx113   cs,nn802 wcs,qmf3205   nn1121   pp,nn,pnx113 pr310
36 And Sarah my master's wife   bore a son to my master when she was

nn,pnx2209   pp,pnx   wcs,qmf5414 (853) cs,nn3605 pnl834 pp,pnx
old: and unto him hath he given   all that he hath.

nn,pnx113   wcs,himf,pnx7650 pp,qnc559   ptn3808 qmf3947   nn802
37 And my master made me swear,   saying, Thou shalt not take a wife to

pp,nn,pnx1121   pr4480/pl,cs,nn1323   df,nn3669   pnl834 pp,nn,pnx776 pnp595 qpta3427
my   son   of*the*daughters of the Canaanites, in whose land   I dwell:

cj518/ptn3808   qmf1980 pr413   nn,pnx1   cs,nn1004   wcj,pr413   nn,pnx4940
38   But   thou shalt go unto my father's house, and to   my kindred, and

wcs,qpf3947 nn802   pp,nn,pnx1121
take a wife unto my   son.

wcs,qmf559   pr413   nn,pnx113   ad194   df,nn802   ptn3808 qmf1980/pr,pnx310
39 And I   said   unto my master, Peradventure the woman will not   follow

me.

wcs,qmf559 pr,pnx413   nn3068   pp,pl,nn,pnx6440 pnl834 htpf1980   qmf7971
40 And he said unto me, The LORD,   before whom I walk, will send his

nn,pnx4397 pr,pnx854   wcs,hipf6743   nn,pnx1870   wcs,qpf3947   nn802
angel with thee, and prosper thy way; and thou shalt take a wife for my

pp,nn,pnx1121   pr4480/nn,pnx4940   wcj,pr4480/cs,nn1004/nn,pnx1
son   of*my*kindred, and of*my*father's*house:

ad227   nimf5352   pr4480/nn,pnx423   cj3588   qmf935   pr413

41 Then shalt thou be clear from*_this_*my*oath, when thou comest to my

nn,pnx4940   wcj,cj518   qmf5414 ptn3808 pp,pnx   wcs,qpf1961 aj5355   pr4480/nn,pnx423

kindred; and if they give not thee _one_, thou shalt be clear from*my*oath.

wcs,qmf935   df,nn3117 pr413   df,nn5869   wcs,qmf559   nn3068   pl,cs,nn430

42 And I came this day unto the well, and said, O LORD God of my

nn,pnx113   nn85   cj518 pte4994   pta,pnx3426 hipt6743   nn,pnx1870 pnl834/pr,pnx5921 pnp595 qpta1980

master Abraham, if now thou do prosper my way which I go:

ptdm2009   pnp595 nipt5324 pr5921   cs,nn5869   df,pl,nn4325   wcj,qpf1961

43 Behold, I stand by the well of water; and it*shall*come*to*pass, that

df,nn5959   df,qpta3318   pp,qnc7579   wcj,qpf559 pr,pnx413

when the virgin cometh forth to draw _water_, and I say to her, Give me,

pte4994   cs,nn4592 pl,nn4325   pr4480/nn,pnx3537   himv,pnx8248

I*pray*thee, a little water of*thy*pitcher to drink;

wcj,qpf559 pr,pnx413   ad1571 qmv8354 pnp859   wcj,ad1571 qmf7579

44 And she say to me, Both drink thou, and I will also draw for thy

pp,pl,nn,pnx1581   pnp1931   df,nn802 pnl834   nn3068   hipf3198

camels: _let_ the same _be_ the woman whom the LORD hath appointed out for my

nn,pnx113   pp,cs,nn1121

master's son.

ad2962   pnp589 pimf3615   pp,pinc1696   pr413   nn,pnx3820 wcj,ptdm2009   nn7259

45 And before I had done speaking in mine heart, behold, Rebekah

qpta3318   wcj,nn,pnx3537 pr5921   nn,pnx7926   wcs,qmf3381   df,nn,lh5869

came forth with her pitcher on her shoulder; and she went down unto the well,

wcs,qmf7579   wcs,qmf559 pr,pnx413   himv,pnx8248   pte4994

and drew _water_: and I said unto her, Let me drink, I*pray*thee.

wcs,pimf4116   wcs,himf3381   nn,pnx3537 pr4480/pr,pnx5921

46 And she made haste, and let down her pitcher from her _shoulder_, and

wcs,qmf559 qmv8354   pl,nn,pnx1581 himf8248 wcj,ad1571   wcs,qmf8354

said, Drink, and I will give thy camels drink also: so I drank, and she made the

df,pl,nn1581 hipf8354 wcj,ad1571

camels drink also.

wcs,qmf7592 pnx(853)   wcs,qmf559 pnit4310   cs,nn1323   pnp859   wcs,qmf559

47 And I asked her, and said, Whose daughter _art_ thou? And she said,

cs,nn1323   nn1328   nn5152   cs,nn1121 pnl834   nn4435 qpf3205   pp,pnx   wcs,qmf7760

The daughter of Bethuel, Nahor's son, whom Milcah bore unto him: and I put

df,nn5141 pr5921   nn,pnx639   wcj,df,pl,nn6781 pr5921   du,nn,pnx3027

the earring upon her face, and the bracelets upon her hands.

wcs,qmf6915   htmf*7812   pp,nn3068   wcs,pimf1288 (853)

48 And I bowed*down*my*head, and worshiped the LORD, and blessed the

nn3068   pl,cs,nn430   nn,pnx113   nn85   pnl834   hipf,pnx5148   nn571 pp,cs,nn1870

LORD God of my master Abraham, which had led me in the right way to

pp,qnc3947 (853)   nn,pnx113   cs,nn251   cs,nn1323   pp,nn,pnx1121

take my master's brother's daughter unto his son.

wcj,ad6258 cj518   pta,pnx3426 pl,qpta6213   nn2617   wcj,nn571 pr854   nn,pnx113 himv5046 pp,pnx

49 And now if ye will deal kindly and truly with my master, tell me:

wcj,cj518 ptn3808 himv5046 pp,pnx   wcj,qmf6437 pr5921   nn3225   cj176 pr5921   nn8040

and if not, tell me; that I may turn to the right hand, or to the left.

nn3837   wcj,nn1328   wcs,qmf6030   wcs,qmf559   df,nn1697 qpf3318

50 Then Laban and Bethuel answered and said, The thing proceedeth

pr4480/nn3068   qmf3201/ptn3808 pinc1696 pr,pnx413   nn7451 cj176 nn2896

from*the*LORD: we cannot speak unto thee bad or good.

ptdm2009   nn7259   pp,pl,nn,pnx6440   qmv3947   wcj,qmv1980   wcj,qcj1961

51 Behold, Rebekah _is_ before thee, take _her_, and go, and let her be

pl,nn,pnx113   pp,cs,nn1121 nn802 pp,pnl834   nn3068   pipf1696

thy master's son's wife, as the LORD hath spoken.

52 And it*came*to*pass, that, when Abraham's servant heard   their words, he worshiped the LORD, *bowing himself* to the earth.

53 And the servant brought forth jewels of silver, and   jewels   of gold, and raiment,   and   gave   *them*   to Rebekah: he gave also to her brother and to her mother   precious things.

54 And they did   eat   and drink,   he   and the   men   that *were* with him, and tarried*all*night;   and   they   rose up   in   the   morning,   and   he   said, Send*me*away unto my master.

55 And her brother and her mother   said,   Let the damsel abide with us *a few* days, at*the*least ten; after that she shall go.

56 And he   said   unto   them, Hinder   me   not,   seeing   the LORD hath prospered my   way; send*me*away that I may   go   to my master.

57 And they   said, We will   call   the damsel, and inquire at   her mouth.

58 And they called Rebekah, and   said   unto   her, Wilt thou   go   with this   man? And she said,   I will go.

59 And they sent away   Rebekah their sister, and   her nurse, and Abraham's servant, and   his men.

60 And they blessed   Rebekah, and   said   unto her, Thou *art* our sister, be   thou *the mother* of thousands of millions, and let thy seed possess   the gate of those*which*hate them.

61 And Rebekah arose, and her   damsels,   and they   rode   upon the camels, and   followed   the man: and the servant took   Rebekah, and went*his*way.

62 And Isaac came from*the*way of the well Lahai-roi; for   he   dwelt in the south country.

63 And Isaac went out to meditate in the   field   at the eventide: and he lifted up his eyes,   and saw,   and, behold, the camels *were* coming.

64 And Rebekah lifted up   her eyes,   and when she saw   Isaac, she lighted   off   the camel.

65 For she *had* said unto the servant, What man *is* this that walketh in the field to meet us? And the servant *had* said, It *is* my master: therefore she took a veil, and covered herself.

66 And the servant told Isaac all things that he had done.

67 And Isaac brought her into his mother Sarah's tent, and took Rebekah, and she became his wife; and he loved her: and Isaac was comforted after his mother's *death*.

Abraham's Other Family

25 Then again Abraham took a wife, and her name *was* Keturah.

2 And she bore him Zimran, and Jokshan, and Medan, and Midian, and Ishbak, and Shuah.

3 And Jokshan begot Sheba, and Dedan. And the sons of Dedan were Asshurim, and Letushim, and Leummim.

4 And the sons of Midian; Ephah, and Epher, and Hanoch, and Abida, and Eldaah. All these *were* the children of Keturah.

5 And Abraham gave all that he had unto Isaac.

6 But unto the sons of the concubines, which Abraham had, Abraham gave gifts, and sent*them*away from Isaac his son, while he yet lived, eastward, unto the east country.

Abraham Dies

7 And these *are* the days of the years of Abraham's life which he lived, a hundred threescore*and*fifteen years.

25:1, 2 How can this fact be reconciled with Genesis 17:17 and Hebrews 11:12? These verses speak of Abraham's condition before the miracle of God that allowed the birth of Isaac. The great age of Abraham at death suggests that the miraculous quickening of his virile powers, by which he was enabled to become the father of Isaac, continued for some years.

nn85   wcs,qmf**1478**   wcs,qmf**4191**   aj**2896**   pp,nn**7872**

8 Then Abraham gave*up*the*ghost, and died in a good old age, an

aj**2205**   wcj,aj7649   wcs,nimf622   pr413   pl,nn,pnx**5971**

old man, and full *of years*; and was gathered to his people.

pl,nn,pnx**1121** nn3327   wcj,nn3458 wcs,qmf**6912** pnx(853)   pr413   cs,nn4631

9 And his sons Isaac and Ishmael buried him in the cave of

df,nn4375   pr413   cs,nn**7704**   nn6085   cs,nn**1121**   nn6714   df,nn2850   pnl834

Machpelah, in the field of Ephron the son of Zohar the Hittite, which *is*

pr5921/pl,cs,nn**6440** nn4471

before Mamre;

df,nn**7704** pnl834   nn85   qpf7069   pr4480/pr854 pl,cs,nn**1121** nn2845 ad,lh8033

10 The field which Abraham purchased of the sons of Heth: there was

nn85   pupf**6912**   wcj,nn8283   nn,pnx**802**

Abraham buried, and Sarah his wife.

wcs,qmf**1961**   pr310   cs,nn**4194**   nn85   pl,nn**430** wcs,pimf**1288**

11 And it*came*to*pass after the death of Abraham, that God blessed his

nn,pnx**1121** (853)   nn3327   nn3327 wcs,qmf**3427** pr5973   nn883 [cs,nn875/pp,aj**2416**/nn**7203**]

son Isaac; and Isaac dwelt by the well Lahai-roi.

Ishmael's Family

wcj,pndm428   pl,cs,nn**8435**   nn3458   nn85   cs,nn**1121** pnl834 nn1904

12 Now these *are* the generations of Ishmael, Abraham's son, whom Hagar

df,nn4713   nn8283   cs,nn8198 qpf3205   pp,nn85

the Egyptian, Sarah's handmaid, bore unto Abraham:

wcj,pndm428   pl,cs,nn**8034**   pl,cs,nn**1121**   nn3458   pp,pl,nn,pnx8034

13 And these *are* the names of the sons of Ishmael, by their names,

pp,pl,nn,pnx**8435**   cs,nn1060   nn3458   nn5032   wcj,nn6938

according to their generations: the firstborn of Ishmael, Nebajoth; and Kedar, and

wcj,nn110   wcj,nn4017

Adbeel, and Mibsam,

wcj,nn4927   wcj,nn1746   wcj,nn4854

14 And Mishma, and Dumah, and Massa,

nn2301   wcj,nn8485 nn3195   nn5305   wcj,nn6929

15 Hadar, and Tema, Jetur, Naphish, and Kedemah:

pndm428 (pnp1992)   pl,cs,nn**1121**   nn3458   wcj,pndm428   pl,nn,pnx8034

16 These *are* the sons of Ishmael, and these *are* their names, by

pp,pl,nn,pnx2691   wcj,pp,pl,nn,pnx2918 du,nu8147/nu6240   pl,nn**5387**

their towns, and by their castles; twelve princes according to their

pp,pl,nn,pnx**523**

nations.

wcj,pndm428   pl,cs,nn8141   cs,aj**2416**   nn3458   cs,nu3967 (nn8141)

17 And these *are* the years of the life of Ishmael, a hundred and

wcj,nu7970 (nn8141)   wcj,nu7651 pl,nn8141   wcs,qmf**1478**   wcs,qmf**4191**

thirty and seven years: and he gave*up*the*ghost and died; and was

wcs,nimf**622** pr413   pl,nn,pnx**5971**

gathered unto his people.

wcs,qmf**7931**   pr4480/nn2341   pr5704 nn7793 pnl834 pr5921/pl,cs,nn**6440** nn4714

18 And they dwelt from Havilah unto Shur, that *is* before Egypt, as thou

qnc,pnx935   nn,lh804   qpf**5307** pr5921 pl,cs,nn**6440** cs,nn3605 pl,nn,pnx**251**

goest toward Assyria: *and* he died in the presence of all his brethren.

Isaac's Twin Boys

wcj,pndm428   pl,cs,nn**8435**   nn3327   nn85   cs,nn**1121**   nn85   hipf3205
19 And these *are* the generations of Isaac, Abraham's son: Abraham begot

(853)   nn3327
Isaac:

nn3327   wcs,qmf**1961**   pl,nn705   nn8141   cs,nn**1121**   pp,qnc,pnx3947 (853)   nn7259   (pp,pnx)
20 And Isaac was forty years old when he took Rebekah to

pp,nn**802**   cs,nn1323   nn1328   df,nn761   pr4480/nn6307   cs,nn**269**   nn3837
wife, the daughter of Bethuel the Syrian of Padan-aram, the sister to Laban the

df,nn761
Syrian.

nn3327   wcs,qmf**6279**   pp,nn**3068** pp,pr5227   nn,pnx**802**   cj3588   pnp1931   aj6135
21 And Isaac entreated the LORD for his wife, because she *was* barren: and

nn**3068**   wcs,nimf**6279**   pp,pnx   nn7259   nn,pnx**802**   wcs,qmf2029
the LORD was entreated of him, and Rebekah his wife conceived.

df,pl,nn**1121**   wcs,htmf*7533   pp,nn,pnx7130   wcs,qmf559 cj518
22 And the children struggled together within her; and she said, If *it be*

ad3651 pp,pnit4100   pnp595 pndm2088   wcs,qmf**1980**   pp,qnc1875   (853)   nn**3068**
so, why *am* I thus? And she went to inquire of the LORD.

nn**3068**   wcs,qmf559   pp,pnx   du,cs,nu8147   pl,nn**1471**   pp,nn,pnx**990**
23 And the LORD said unto her, Two nations *are* in thy womb, and

wcj,du,cs,nu8147   pl,nn**3816**   nimf6504   pr4480/pl,nn,pnx**4578**   wcj,nn**3816**
two manner of people shall be separated from*thy*bowels; and *the one* people

qmf553   pr4480/nn**3816**   wcj,aj7227   qmf**5647**   aj6810
shall be stronger than*the*other*people; and the elder shall serve the younger.

pl,nn,pnx**3117**   pp,qnc3205   wcs,qmf**4390**   wcj,ptdm2009
24 And when her days to be delivered were fulfilled, behold, *there were*

pl,nn8380   pp,nn,pnx**990**
twins in her womb.

df,aj**7223**   wcs,qmf3318   aj132   nn,pnx3605   nn8181   pp,cs,nn155   wcs,qmf**7121**
25 And the first came out red, all over like an hairy garment; and they called

nn,pnx8034   nn6215
his name Esau.

wcj,ad310/ad**3651**   qpf3318   nn,pnx**251**   wcj,nn,pnx**3027**   qpta270   nn6215
26 And after that came his brother out, and his hand took hold on Esau's

pp,cs,nn**6119**   nn,pnx8034   wcs,qmf**7121**   nn3290   wcj,nn3327   pl,nu8346   nn8141   cs,nn**1121**
heel; and his name was called Jacob: and Isaac *was* threescore years old

pp,qnc3205   pnx(853)
when she bore them.

df,pl,nn**5288**   wcs,qmf1431   nn6215   wcs,qmf**1961** (nn**376**)   qpta**3045**   nn6718   cs,nn**376**
⌖ **27** And the boys grew: and Esau was a cunning hunter, a man of

nn**7704**   wcj,nn3290   aj**8535** cs,nn**376** qpta3427   pl,nn168
the field; and Jacob *was* a plain man, dwelling in tents.

nn3327   wcs,qmf**157** (853)   nn6215   cj3588   pp,nn,pnx**6310**   nn6718
28 And Isaac loved Esau, because he did eat of *his* venison: but

wcj,nn7259   qpta**157** (853)   nn3290
Rebekah loved Jacob.

⌖ **25:27** The strife between Rebekah's twin sons Jacob and Esau began even before their birth (vv. 22, 23) and continued not only throughout their lives but between their descendants. Much of the suffering of the Israelites (Jacob) came at the hands of the Edomites (Esau) as is noted throughout the Old Testament (Num. 20:20, 21; 2 Sam. 8:13, 14; Ps. 137:7; Joel 3:19).

nn3290   wcs,himf2102   nn5138   nn6215 wcs,qmf935 pr4480   df,nn**7704**   wcj,pnp1931
🕮 29 And Jacob   sod   pottage: and Esau came from the field, and   he   *was*
aj5889
faint:

nn6215   wcs,qmf**559** pr413   nn3290   himv,pnx3938   pte**4994**   pr4480 (df,aj122)   df,pndm2088
30 And Esau   said   to Jacob,   Feed   me, I*pray*thee, with   that same
df,aj122   cj3588 pnp595   aj5889   pr5921/ad**3651**   nn,pnx8034 qpf**7121**   nn123
red *pottage*; for   I   *am* faint: therefore was his   name   called Edom.

nn3290   wcs,qmf559   qmv4376 pp,pnx   dfp,nn**3117** (853)   nn,pnx1062
31 And Jacob said,   Sell me this   day   thy birthright.

nn6215   wcs,qmf**559** ptdm2009   pnp595   qpta**1980**   pp,qnc**4191**   wcj,pp,pnit4100
32 And Esau   said,   Behold,   I   *am* at*the*point to   die: and what profit
pndm2088   nn1062   pp,pnx
shall this   birthright do to me?

nn3290   wcs,qmf559 nimv**7650**   pp,pnx   dfp,nn**3117**   wcs,nimf**7650**   pp,pnx
33 And Jacob said,   Swear to me this   day;   and he   swore   unto him: and he
wcs,qmf4376 (853)   nn,pnx1062   pp,nn3290
sold   his birthright unto Jacob.

wcj,nn3290 qpf**5414** pp,nn6215 nn3899   wcj,cs,nn5138   pl,nn5742   wcs,qmf398
34 Then Jacob gave Esau bread and pottage of lentiles; and he did   eat   and
wcs,qmf8354   wcs,qmf**6965**   wcs,qmf**1980**   nn6215 wcs,qmf959   (853)   df,nn1062
drink, and rose up, and went*his*way: thus Esau despised   *his* birthright.

Isaac Moves to Gerar

wcs,qmf**1961**   nn7458   dfp,nn776 pr4480/pp,nn905   df,aj**7223** df,nn7458 pnl834
26 And there   was   a famine in the land,   beside   the first famine that
qpf**1961**   pp,pl,cs,nn**3117**   nn85   nn3327 wcs,qmf**1980** pr413   nn40
was in the   days   of Abraham. And Isaac   went   unto Abimelech
cs,nn**4428**   nn6430   nn,lh1642
king of the Philistines unto Gerar.

nn3068   wcs,nimf**7200** pr,pnx413   wcs,qmf559   qmf3381/ptn408   nn,lh4714
2 And the Lord appeared unto   him, and   said,   Go*not*down into Egypt;
qmv7931   dfp,nn776 pnl834   qmf559   pr,pnx413
dwell in the land   which I shall tell thee   of:

qmv**1481**   df,pndm2063 dfp,nn776   wcj,qmf**1961** pr,pnx5973   wcj,pimf,pnx**1288**
3 Sojourn in   this   land, and I will   be   with thee, and will   bless
cj3588   pp,pnx   wcj,pp,nn,pnx**2233**   qmf**5414** (853) cs,nn3605 df,pndm411   df,pl,nn776
thee; for unto thee, and unto thy   seed,   I will give   all   these countries,
wcs,hipf**6965** (853)   df,nn7621 pnl834   nipf**7650**   pp,nn85   nn,pnx1
and I will perform   the oath   which I swore unto Abraham thy father;

(853)   nn,pnx**2233**   wcj,hipf7235   pp,pl,cs,nn3556   df,du,nn**8064**
4 And I will make   thy seed   to multiply as the   stars   of heaven, and will
wcj,qpf**5414**   pp,nn,pnx**2233** (853) cs,nn3605 df,pndm411   df,pl,nn776   pp,nn,pnx**2233**   cs,nn3605
give unto thy   seed   all   these countries; and in thy   seed   shall   all
pl,cs,nn**1471**   df,nn776   wcj,htpf**1288**
the nations of the earth be blessed;

ad6118   pnl834   nn85   qpf**8085**   pp,nn,pnx6963   wcs,qmf**8104**   nn,pnx**4931**
5 Because that Abraham obeyed my   voice,   and   kept   my charge,   my
pl,nn,pnx**4687**   pl,nn,pnx**2708**   wcj,pl,nn,pnx8451
commandments, my statutes, and my   laws.

nn3327 wcs,qmf**3427**   pp,nn1642
6 And Isaac dwelt in Gerar:

🕮 25:29–34   See the note on Genesis 27:1–38.

pl,cs,nn**376**   df,nn**4725** wcs,qmf**7592**   pp,nn,pnx**802**   wcs,qmf**559** pnp**1931**

7 And the men of the place asked *him* of his wife; and he said, She *is*

nn,pnx**269** cj**3588**   qpf**3372**   pp,qnc**559**   nn,pnx**802** cj**6435**   pl,cs,nn**376**

my sister: for he feared to say, *She is* my wife; lest, *said he*, the men of the

df,nn**4725**   qmf,pnx**2026** pr**5921** nn**7259** cj**3588** pnp**1931** cs,aj**2896**   nn**4758**

place should kill me for Rebekah; because she *was* fair to look upon.

wcs,qmf**1961**   cj**3588** pp,pnx   ad**8033** qpf**748** df,pl,nn**3117**   nn**40**

8 And it*came*to*pass, when he had been there a long time, that Abimelech

cs,nn**4428**   nn**6430** wcs,himf**8259** pr**1157** df,nn**2474** wcs,qmf**7200** wcj,ptdm**2009** nn**3327**

king of the Philistines looked out at a window, and saw, and, behold, Isaac

pipt**6711** (853) nn**7259** nn,pnx**802**

was sporting with Rebekah his wife.

nn**40** wcs,qmf**7121** pp,nn**3327** wcs,qmf**559** ptdm**2009** ad**389** pnp**1931**

9 And Abimelech called Isaac, and said, Behold, of*a*surety she *is* thy

nn,pnx**802** wcj,ptx**349** qpf**559** pnp**1931** nn,pnx**269** nn**3327** wcs,qmf**559** pr,pnx**413**

wife: and how saidst thou, She *is* my sister? And Isaac said unto him,

cj**3588** qpf**559** cj**6435** qmf**4191** pr,pnx**5921**

Because I said, Lest I die for her.

nn**40** wcs,qmf**559** pnit**4100** pndm**2063** qpf**6213** pp,pnx cs,nu**259**

10 And Abimelech said, What *is* this thou hast done unto us? one of the

df,nn**5971** pp,nn**4592** qpf**7901** pr**854** nn,pnx**802** wcj,hipf**935**

people might lightly have lain with thy wife, and thou shouldest have brought

nn**817** pr,pnx**5921**

guiltiness upon us.

nn**40** wcs,pimf**6680** (853) cs,nn**3605** df,nn**5971** pp,qnc**559** df,qpta**5060**

11 And Abimelech charged all *his* people, saying, He that toucheth

df,pndm**2088** dfp,nn**376** wcj,pp,nn,pnx**802** qna**4191**/homf**4191**

this man or his wife shall surely*be*put*to*death.

nn**3327** wcs,qmf**2232** df,pndm**1931** dfp,nn**776** wcs,qmf**4672** df,pndm**1931** dfp,nn**8141**

12 Then Isaac sowed in that land, and received in the same year a

nu**3967**/pl,nn**8180** nn**3068** wcs,pimf,pnx**1288**

hundredfold: and the Lᴏʀᴅ blessed him.

df,nn**376** wcs,qmf**1431** wcs,qmf**1980** qna**1980** wcj,aj**1432** cj**5704**/cj**3588**

13 And the man waxed great, and went forward, and grew until he

qpf**1431**/ad**3966**

became*very*great:

pp,pnx wcs,qmf**1961** cs,nn**4735** nn**6629** wcj,cs,nn**4735** nn**1241**

14 For he had possession of flocks, and possession of herds, and

aj**7227** wcj,nn**5657** nn**6430** wcs,pimf**7065** pnx(853)

great store of servants: and the Philistines envied him.

wcj,cs,nn**3605** df,pl,nn**875** pnl**834** nn,pnx**1** pl,cs,nn**5650** qpf**2658** pp,pl,cs,nn**3117**

15 For all the wells which his father's servants had digged in the days

nn**85** nn,pnx**1** nn**6430** pipf,pnx**5640** wcs,pimf,pnx**4390**

of Abraham his father, the Philistines had stopped them, and filled them with

nn**6083**

earth.

nn**40** wcs,qmf**559** pr**413** nn**3327** qmv**1980** pr**4480**/pr,pnx**5973** cj**3588**

16 And Abimelech said unto Isaac, Go from us; for thou

qpf**6105**/ad**3966** pr,pnx**4480**

art*much*mightier than we.

nn**3327** wcs,qmf**1980** pr**4480**/ad**8033** wcs,qmf**2583** pp,cs,nn**5158** nn**1642**

17 And Isaac departed thence, and pitched*his*tent in the valley of Gerar,

wcs,qmf**3427** ad**8033**

and dwelt there.

nn**3327** wcs,qmf**2658** wcs,qmf**7725** (853) pl,cs,nn**875** df,pl,nn**4325** pnl**834** qpf**2658**

18 And Isaac digged again the wells of water, which they had digged in

pp,pl,cs,nn**3117**   nn85   nn,pnx1   nn6430   wcs,pimf,pnx5640   pr310

the   days   of Abraham his father; for the Philistines had   stopped   them after the

cs,nn**4194**   nn85   wcs,qmf**7121**   pp,pnx   pl,nn8034   dfp,pl,nn8034   pnl834   nn,pnx1

death of Abraham: and he called their names after the   names   by which his father

qpf**7121**   pp,pnx

had called them.

nn3327   pl,cs,nn**5650**   wcs,qmf2658   dfp,nn5158   wcs,qmf4672   ad8033   cs,nn875

19 And Isaac's servants   digged   in the valley, and   found   there   a   well of

aj**2416**   pl,nn4325

springing water.

pl,cs,qpta7462   nn1642   wcs,qmf**7378**   pr5973   nn3327   pl,cs,qpta7462   pp,qnc**559**

20 And the herdsmen of Gerar did   strive   with Isaac's herdsmen, saying, The

df,pl,nn4325   pp,pnx   wcs,qmf**7121**   cs,nn8034   df,nn875   nn6230   cj3588   htpf6229

water   is ours: and he called the name of the well Esek; because they strove

pr,pnx5973

with   him.

wcs,qmf2658   aj312   nn875   wcs,qmf**7378**   pr,pnx5921   ad1571   wcs,qmf**7121**

21 And they digged   another well, and   strove   for   that also: and he called

nn,pnx8034   nn7856

the   name of it Sitnah.

wcs,himf6275   pr4480/ad8033   wcs,qmf2658   aj312   nn875   pr,pnx5921

22 And he removed from thence, and digged another well; and   for   that they

qpf**7378**   wcj,ptn**3808**   wcs,qmf**7121**   nn,pnx8034   nn7344   wcs,qmf**559** cj3588 ad6258

strove   not: and he called the name of it Rehoboth; and he   said,   For now the

nn**3068**   hipf7337   pp,pnx   wcj,qpf6509   dfp,nn776

LORD hath made room for us, and we shall be fruitful in the land.

wcs,qmf**5927**   pr4480/ad8033   nn884

23 And he went   up from thence to Beer-sheba.

nn**3068**   wcs,nimf**7200**   pr,pnx413   df,pndm1931   dfp,nn**3915**   wcs,qmf**559** pnp595

24 And the LORD appeared unto him the   same   night, and   said,   I   am the

pl,cs,nn**430**   nn85   nn,pnx1   qmf**3372** ptn408 cj3588 pnp595   pr,pnx854   wcs,pipf,pnx**1288**

God   of Abraham thy father: fear not, for   I   am with thee, and will   bless

wcs,hipf7235   (853)   nn,pnx**2233** pp,pr5668   nn,pnx**5650**   nn85

thee, and multiply   thy   seed   for   my servant Abraham's sake.

wcs,qmf1129   nn**4196**   ad8033   wcs,qmf**7121**   pp,cs,nn8034   nn**3068**

25 And he   built   an altar there, and   called   upon the   name   of the LORD, and

wcs,qmf5186   nn,pnx168   ad8033   ad8033   nn3327   pl,cs,nn**5650** wcs,qmf3738   nn875

pitched his   tent   there: and there Isaac's servants digged a well.

Isaac Makes an Agreement with Abimelech

wcj,nn40   qpf**1980** pr,pnx413   pr4480/nn1642   wcj,nn276

26 Then Abimelech went   to   him from Gerar,   and   Ahuzzath one of his

nn,pnx4828   wcj,nn6369   cs,nn**8269**   nn,pnx**6635**

friends, and Phichol the chief captain of his army.

nn3327   wcs,qmf**559** pr,pnx413   ad4069   qpf935   pr,pnx413   wcj,pnp859

27 And Isaac   said   unto them, Wherefore come ye   to   me, seeing   ye

qpf**8130** pnx(853)   wcs,pimf,pnx7971   pr4480 pnx(pr854)

hate   me, and have sent*me*away from   you?

wcs,qmf**559**   qna**7200**/qpf**7200**   cj3588   nn**3068** qpf**1961** pr,pnx5973

28 And they   said,   We saw certainly that the LORD was   with   thee: and we

wcs,qmf**559**   qcj**1961** pte**4994**   nn423   pr,pnx996   pr,pnx996   wcj,pnx(pr996)

said, Let there   be   now an oath between us, even between us and   thee,

wcj,qcj**3772**   nn**1285**   pr,pnx5973

and let us make a covenant with thee;

cj518   qmf6213 pnx(pr5973)   nn7451 pp,pnl834   ptn3808 qpf,pnx5060

29 That thou wilt do   us no hurt,   as   we have not touched thee, and

wcj,pp,pnl834   qpf6213 pr,pnx5973   ad7535   aj2896   wcs,pimf,pnx7971

as   we have done unto   thee nothing but good, and have sent*thee*away in

pp,nn7965 pnp859   ad6258   cs,qptp1288   nn3068

peace: thou *art* now the blessed of the LORD.

wcs,qmf6213 pp,pnx   nn4960   wcs,qmf398   wcs,qmf8354

30 And he made them a feast, and they did   eat   and drink.

wcs,himf7925   dfp,nn1242   wcs,nimf7650 nn376   pp,nn,pnx251

31 And they rose*up*quickly in the morning, and   swore one to another: and

nn3327   wcs,pimf,pnx7971   wcs,qmf1980 pr4480/pr,pnx854   pp,nn7965

Isaac sent*them*away, and they departed   from   him in peace.

wcs,qmf1961   df,pndm1931 dfp,nn3117   nn3327   pl,cs,nn5650 wcs,qmf935

32 And it*came*to*pass the   same   day, that Isaac's servants came, and

wcs,himf5046 pp,pnx pr5921/pl,cs,nn182   df,nn875 pnl834   qpf2658   wcs,qmf559 pp,pnx

told   him concerning the well which they had digged, and   said   unto him, We

qpf4672   pl,nn4325

have found water.

wcs,qmf7121   pnx(853)   nn7656   pr5921/ad3651   cs,nn8034   df,nn5892

33 And he called   it Shebah: therefore the   name of the   city   *is*

nn884   pr5704 df,pndm2088 df,nn3117

Beer-sheba unto   this   day.

nn6215 wcs,qmf1961 pl,nn8141 cs,nn1121   wcs,qmf3947   nn802 (853)   nn3067

34 And Esau   was   forty years old when he   took   to wife   Judith the

cs,nn1323   nn882   df,nn2850   wcj(853)   nn1315   cs,nn1323   nn356   df,nn2850

daughter of Beeri the Hittite, and   Bashemath the daughter of Elon the Hittite:

wcs,qmf1961   cs,nn4786   nn7307   pp,nn3327   wcj,pp,nn7259

35 Which were   a grief of mind unto Isaac and to Rebekah.

Jacob Steals Isaac's Blessing

wcs,qmf1961   cj3588   nn3327   qpf2204   du,nn,pnx5869

27 ☙ And it*came*to*pass, that when Isaac was old, and his   eyes

wcs,qmf3543   pr4480/qnc7200   wcs,qmf7121 (853) nn6215   df,aj1419

were dim, so*that*he*could*not*see, he called   Esau his eldest

nn,pnx1121   wcs,qmf559 pr,pnx413   nn,pnx1121   wcs,qmf559 pr,pnx413   ptdm,pnx2009

son,   and   said   unto him, My son: and he   said   unto him, Behold, *here*

am I.

☙ **27:1-38** There is often confusion about the difference between the birthright and the blessing in the narrative about Jacob and Esau. The birthright is related to the order of birth of sons. The firstborn son was given the title to the family name and a double portion of his father's inheritance. In this case Esau foolishly gave in to Jacob's extortion and sold his birthright to Jacob. Yet despite Jacob's wickedness and Esau's foolishness, the agreement over the birthright was binding. The regulation was later given that the father could not alter the birthright nor give it to another (Deut. 21:17).

None of this had anything to do with the blessing of Isaac upon Esau. As Esau himself recognized, a father could bless his son in any way he saw fit (Gen. 27:36). Therefore, when Jacob deceived his father and got Esau's blessing, he stole something from his brother to which he had no right.

Esau had already sold his birthright to Jacob. Jacob was now seeking to secure Isaac's final blessing as well, which would additionally constitute an acknowledgement of Jacob's possession of the birthright. Jacob realized that once the blessing had been given, it could not be withdrawn (27:33). In this act, Jacob revealed the true meaning of his name, "one who supplants." While God had previously recognized Jacob to be in the line of promise, He did not approve of Jacob's conduct. Jacob's scheming bore terrible fruits throughout his life. He was banished from home never to see his mother again, he was tricked by his uncle Laban repeatedly (chaps. 29—30), and he lived in fear of Esau for years (chap. 31). His dishonesty also affected his children, who not

wcs,qmf559 ptdm2009   pte4994   qpf2204   qpf3045 ptn3808   cs,nn3117   nn,pnx4194

2 And he said, Behold now, I am old, I know not the day of my death:

wcj,ad6258   qmv5375   pte4994   pl,nn,pnx3627   nn,pnx8522   wcj,nn,pnx7198

3 Now therefore take, I*pray*thee, thy weapons, thy quiver and thy bow,

wcj,qmv3318   df,nn7704   wcj,qmv6679 pp,pnx   nn6718

and go out to the field, and take me *some* venison;

wcj,qmv6213 pp,pnx   pl,nn4303   pp,pnl834   qpf157   wcj,himv935   pp,pnx

4 And make me savory meat, such as I love, and bring *it* to me, that I

wcj,qcj398 pp,cj5668   nn,pnx5315   pimf,pnx1288   pp,ad2962   qmf4191

may eat; that my soul may bless thee before I die.

wcj,nn7259   qpta8085   nn3327 pp,pinc1696 pr413 nn6215   nn,pnx1121   nn6215 wcs,qmf1980

5 And Rebekah heard when Isaac spoke to Esau his son. And Esau went

df,nn7704   pp,qnc6679   nn6718   pp,hinc935

to the field to hunt *for* venison, *and* to bring *it*.

wcj,nn7259   qpf559   pr413   nn3290   nn,pnx1121 pp,qnc559   ptdm2009   qpf8085   (853)

6 And Rebekah spoke unto Jacob her son, saying, Behold, I heard thy

nn,pnx1 pipt1696 pr413   nn6215   nn,pnx251   pp,qnc559

father speak unto Esau thy brother, saying,

himv935 pp,pnx   nn6718   wcj,qmv6213 pp,pnx   pl,nn4303   wcj,qcj398

7 Bring me venison, and make me savory meat, that I may eat, and

wcj,pimf,pnx1288   pp,pl,cs,nn6440   nn3068 pp,pl,cs,nn6440   nn,pnx4194

bless thee before the Lord before my death.

wcj,ad6258   nn,pnx1121 qmv8085   pp,nn,pnx6963   pp,pnl834   pnp589

8 Now therefore, my son, obey my voice according to that which I

pipt6680   pnx(853)

command thee.

qmv1980 pte4994 pr413   df,nn6629   wcj,qmv3947 pp,pnx   pr4480/ad8033 du,cs,nu8147 aj2896 pl,cs,nn1423

9 Go now to the flock, and fetch me from thence two good kids of

pl,nn5795   wcj,qmf6213 pnx(853)   pl,nn4303   pp,nn,pnx1 pp,pnl834

the goats; and I will make them savory meat for thy father, such as he

qpf157

loveth:

wcj,hipf935   pp,nn,pnx1   wcj,qpf398   pp,cj5668/pnl834

10 And thou shalt bring *it* to thy father, that he may eat, and that he

pimf,pnx1288   pp,pl,cs,nn6440   nn,pnx4194

may bless thee before his death.

nn3290 wcs,qmf559 pr413   nn7259   nn,pnx517 ptdm2005   nn6215   nn,pnx251

11 And Jacob said to Rebekah his mother, Behold, Esau my brother *is* a

aj8163   nn376   wcj,pnp595   aj2509   nn376

hairy man, and I *am* a smooth man:

nn,pnx1   ad194   qmf,pnx4959   wcs,qpf1961 pp,du,nn,pnx5869

12 My father peradventure will feel me, and I shall seem to him as a

pp,pipt*8591   wcs,hipf935   nn7045 pr,pnx5921   wcj,ptn3808   nn1293

deceiver; and I shall bring a curse upon me, and not a blessing.

nn,pnx517 wcs,qmf559   pp,pnx   pr,pnx5921   nn,pnx7045   nn,pnx1121 ad389

13 And his mother said unto him, Upon me *be* thy curse, my son: only

qmv8085   pp,nn,pnx6963   wcj,qmv1980 qmv3947 pp,pnx

obey my voice, and go fetch me *them*.

---

only dealt treacherously with the Shechemites (chap. 34), but also deceived their own father regarding the alleged death of his favorite son, Joseph (chap. 37). These results show not only God's disapproval, but also the bitter harvest that sin can bring in one's life. Jacob ultimately repented of his conduct and finished his years as a changed man (chap. 32). In spite of his weaknesses, God chose to confirm the blessing of Abraham to him (Gen. 28:12–15).

14 And he went, and fetched, and brought *them* to his mother: and his mother made savory meat, such as his father loved.

15 And Rebekah took goodly raiment of her eldest son Esau, which *were* with her in the house, and put*them*upon Jacob her younger son:

16 And she put the skins of the kids of the goats upon his hands, and upon the smooth of his neck:

17 And she gave the savory meat and the bread, which she had prepared, into the hand of her son Jacob.

18 And he came unto his father, and said, My father: and he said, Here *am* I; who *art* thou, my son?

19 And Jacob said unto his father, I *am* Esau thy firstborn; I have done according as thou biddest me: arise, I*pray*thee, sit and eat of*my*venison, that thy soul may bless me.

20 And Isaac said unto his son, How *is* it that thou hast found *it* so quickly, my son? And he said, Because the LORD thy God brought *it* to me.

21 And Isaac said unto Jacob, Come near, I*pray*thee, that I may feel thee, my son, whether thou *be* my very son Esau or not.

22 And Jacob went near unto Isaac his father; and he felt him, and said, The voice *is* Jacob's voice, but the hands *are* the hands of Esau.

23 And he discerned him not, because his hands were hairy, as his brother Esau's hands: so he blessed him.

24 And he said, *Art* thou my very son Esau? And he said, I *am*.

25 And he said, Bring*it*near to me, and I will eat of my son's venison, that my soul may bless thee. And he brought*it*near to him, and he did eat: and he brought him wine, and he drank.

26 And his father Isaac said unto him, Come near now, and kiss me, my son.

wcs,qmf**5066**　　　wcs,qmf**5401**　pp,pnx　　　　wcs,himf**7306**　(853)　　cs,nn**7381**

27 And he came near, and kissed him: and he smelled　　the smell of his

pl,nn,pnx**899**　　wcs,pimf,pnx**1288**　　wcs,qmf**559**　qmv**7200**　cs,nn**7381**　　nn,pnx**1121**

raiment, and blessed him, and said, See, the smell of my son *is* as the

pp,cs,nn**7381**　　nn**7704**　pnl**834**　　nn**3068**　pipf,pnx**1288**

smell of a field which the LORD hath blessed:

df,pl,nn**430** wcj,qmf**5414** pp,pnx　pr4480/cs,nn**2919**　df,du,nn**8064**　wcj(pr4480)　pl,cs,nn**4924**

28 Therefore God give thee of*the*dew of heaven, and　　the fatness

df,nn**776**　wcj,cs,nn**7230**　nn**1715**　wcj,nn**8492**

of the earth, and plenty of corn and wine:

pl,nn**5971** qmf,pnx**5647**　pl,nn**3816** wcj,htmf***7812** pp,pnx　qmv**1933** nn**1376**

29 Let people serve thee, and nations bow down to thee: be lord over thy

pp,pl,nn,pnx**251**　　nn,pnx**517** pl,cs,nn**1121** wcj,htmf***7812** pp,pnx　qptp**779**

brethren, and let thy mother's sons bow down to thee: cursed *be* every one that

pl,qpta,pnx**779**　　qptp**1288**　　wcj,pl,pipt,pnx**1288**

curseth thee, and blessed *be* he that blesseth thee.

wcs,qmf**1961**　　pp,pnl**834**　nn**3327**　　pipf**3615**　　pp,pinc**1288**　(853)

30 And it*came*to*pass, as*soon*as Isaac had made*an*end of blessing

nn**3290**　　nn**3290** wcs,qmf**1961** ad**389**　qna**3318**/qpf**3318**　pr4480/pr**854**　pl,cs,nn**6440**　nn**3327**

Jacob, and Jacob was yet scarce*gone*out from the presence of Isaac his

nn,pnx**1**　wcj,nn**6215**　nn,pnx**251**　qpf**935**　　pr4480/nn,pnx**6718**

father, that Esau his brother came in from*his*hunting.

pnp**1931** ad**1571**　　wcs,qmf**6213**　pl,nn**4303**　　wcs,himf**935**　　pp,nn,pnx**1**

31 And he also had made savory meat, and brought it unto his father, and

wcs,qmf**559**　　　pp,nn,pnx**1**　　nn,pnx**1** qmf**6965**　wcj,qmf**398**　　nn,pnx**1121** pr4480/cs,nn**6718** pp,cj**5668**

said unto his father, Let my father arise, and eat of his son's venison, that

nn,pnx**5315**　pimf,pnx**1288**

thy soul may bless me.

nn**3327**　　nn,pnx**1** wcs,qmf**559**　pp,pnx　　pnit**4310**　　pnp**859**　　wcs,qmf**559** pnp**589**

32 And Isaac his father said unto him, Who *art* thou? And he said, I *am*

nn,pnx**1121**　　nn,pnx**1060**　nn**6215**

thy son, thy firstborn Esau.

nn**3327**　wcs,qmf**2729**　nn**2731**/aj**1419**/pr**5704**/ad**3966**　　wcs,qmf**559** pnit**4310**　pnit**645**　pnp**1931**

33 And Isaac trembled very exceedingly, and said, Who? where *is* he that

df,qpta**6679**　nn**6718**　　wcs,himf**935**　pp,pnx　　wcs,qmf**398** pr4480/nn**3605** pp,ad**2962**

hath taken venison, and brought *it* me, and I have eaten of all before thou

qmf**935**　　wcs,pimf,pnx**1288**　ad**1571**　　qmf**1961** qptp**1288**

camest, and have blessed him? yea, *and* he shall be blessed.

nn**6215** pp,qnc**8085** (853)　pl,cs,nn**1697**　nn,pnx**1**　wcs,qmf**6817**　aj**1419**

34 And when Esau heard the words of his father, he cried with a great

cj**5704**　ad**3966**　wcj,aj**4751** nn**6818**　wcs,qmf**559**　　pp,nn,pnx**1** pimv,pnx**1288**　pnp**589** ad**1571**

and exceeding bitter cry, and said unto his father, Bless me, *even* me also, O

nn,pnx**1**

my father.

wcs,qmf**559**　　nn,pnx**251**　qpf**935**　　pp,nn**4820**　　wcs,qmf**3947**

35 And he said, Thy brother came with subtlety, and hath taken away thy

nn,pnx**1293**

blessing.

wcs,qmf**559**　　he,cj**3588** qpf**7121**/nn,pnx**8034**　nn**3290**　　wcs,qmf,pnx**6117**

36 And he said, Is not he rightly named Jacob? for he hath supplanted me

pndm**2088**　du,nn**6471**　　qpf**3947**　(853)　　nn,pnx**1062**　wcj,ptdm**2009** ad**6258**

these two times: he took away my birthright; and, behold, now he hath

qpf**3947**　　nn,pnx**1293**　　wcs,qmf**559**　he,ptn**3808**　qpf**680**　　nn**1293**

taken away my blessing. And he said, Hast thou not reserved a blessing

pp,pnx

for me?

nn3327 wcs,qmf6030   wcs,qmf559   pp,nn6215   ptdm2005   qpf,pnx7760   pp,pnx

37 And Isaac answered and said unto Esau, Behold, I have made him thy

nn1376   wcj(853) cs,nn3605   pl,nn,pnx251   qpf5414   pp,pnx   pp,pl,nn5650   wcj,nn1715

lord, and   all his brethren have I given to him for servants; and with corn

wcj,nn8492   qpf,pnx5564   pnit4100   qmf6213 pnit645   wcj,pp,pnx   nn,pnx1121

and wine have I sustained him: and what shall I do now unto thee, my son?

nn6215   wcs,qmf559 pr413   nn,pnx1   pp,pnx   nu259   he,nn1293   (pndm1931)

38 And Esau said unto his father, Hast thou but one blessing,   my

nn,pnx1   pimv,pnx1288   pnp589 ad1571   nn,pnx1   nn6215   wcs,qmf5375   nn,pnx6963

father? bless me, *even* me also, O my father. And Esau lifted up his voice, and

wcs,qmf1058

wept.

nn3327   nn,pnx1   wcs,qmf6030   wcs,qmf559 pr,pnx413   ptdm2009   nn,pnx4186

39 And Isaac his father answered and said unto him, Behold, thy dwelling

qmf1961   pr4480/pl,cs,nn4924   df,nn776   wcj,pr4480/cs,nn2919   df,du,nn8064   pr4480/nn5920

shall be the   fatness of the earth, and of*the*dew of heaven from above;

wcj,pr5921   nn,pnx2719   qmf2421   qmf5647 wcj(853)   nn,pnx251

40 And   by   thy sword shalt thou live, and shalt serve   thy brother; and

wcs,qpf1961   pp,pnl834   himf7300   wcs,qpf6561

it*shall*come*to*pass when thou shalt have*the*dominion, that thou shalt break

nn,pnx5923 pr4480/pr5921   nn,pnx6677

his yoke from off thy neck.

Jacob Runs Away From Esau

nn6215   wcs,qmf7852 (853)   nn3290   pr5921   df,nn1293   pnl834   nn,pnx1

41 And Esau hated   Jacob because of the blessing wherewith his father

pipf,pnx1288   nn6215 wcs,qmf559   pp,nn,pnx3820   pl,cs,nn3117   cs,nn60   nn,pnx1

blessed him: and Esau said in his heart, The days of mourning for my father

qmf7126   wcj,qcj2026 (853)   nn,pnx251   nn3290

are*at*hand; then will I slay   my brother Jacob.

(853)   pl,cs,nn1697   nn6215   df,aj1419 nn,pnx1121   wcs,homf5046   pp,nn7259

42 And   these words of Esau her elder son were told to Rebekah: and

wcs,qmf7971   wcs,qmf7121 pp,nn3290   df,aj6996   nn,pnx1121   wcs,qmf559 pr,pnx413   ptdm2009

she sent and called Jacob her younger son, and said unto him, Behold, thy

nn,pnx251   nn6215   pp,pnx   htpt5162   pp,qnc,pnx2026

brother Esau, as*touching*thee, doth comfort himself, *purposing* to   kill   thee.

wcj,ad6258   nn,pnx1121 qmv8085   pp,nn,pnx6963   wcj,qmv6965 qmv1272 pp,pnx pr413

43 Now therefore, my son, obey my voice; and arise, flee thou to

nn3837   nn,pnx251   nn,lh2771

Laban my brother to Haran;

wcs,qpf3427 pr,pnx5973   pl,nu259 pl,nn3117 pr5704/pnl834   nn,pnx251   cs,nn2534   qmf7725

44 And tarry with him a few days, until thy brother's fury turn away;

pr5704   nn,pnx251   cs,nn639   qnc7725   pr,pnx4480   wcs,qpf7911 (853)

45 Until thy brother's anger turn away from thee, and he forget   *that*

27:39, 40 The Edomites were the descendants of Esau. They inhabited a rich, fertile country which was given especially to them (Deut. 2:5). Their country was traversed by roads, though it was mountainous and rocky (Num. 20:17; Jer. 49:16). In character they are said to have been shrewd, proud and self–confident, strong, cruel, and idolatrous (Jer. 27:3; 49:7, 16, 19; Ezek. 25:12; 2 Chr. 25:14, 20). They inhabited the cities of Avith, Pau, Bozrah, and Teman and were implacable enemies of Israel. It was forbidden to hate them and they could be received into the congregation (Deut. 23:7, 8). King Saul made war against them and David conquered them (1 Sam. 14:47; 2 Sam. 8:14). They took refuge in Egypt and returned after David's death (1 Kgs. 11:17–22). They were again overthrown by Israel (2 Chr. 20:22, 23) but finally aided Babylon against Judah (Ps. 137:7; Obad. 1:11). God pronounced special judgment against Edom (Ezek. 35).

pnl834   qpf**6213**   pp,pnx   wcj,qpf**7971**   wcj,qpf,pnx3947   pr4480/ad8033

which thou hast done to him: then I will send, and   fetch   thee from thence:

pp,pnit4100   qmf7921   ad1571   du,nu,pnx8147   nu259 nn**3117**

why should I be deprived also of you   both   in one day?

nn7259   wcs,qmf**559** pr413 nn3327   qpf**6973**   pp,aj,pnx**2416** pr4480/pl,cs,nn**6440**

46 And Rebekah said   to Isaac, I am weary of my   life   because of the

pl,cs,nn1323   nn2845 cj518 nn3290 qpta3947   nn**802**   pr4480/pl,cs,nn1323   nn2845   dfp,pndm428

daughters of Heth: if Jacob take a wife of*the*daughters of Heth, such as these

pr4480/pl,cs,nn1323   df,nn776   pp,pnit4100   aj**2416**   pp,pnx

which are of*the*daughters of the land, what good shall my life do me?

nn3327 wcs,qmf**7121**/pr413 nn3290   wcs,pimf**1288** pnx(853)   wcs,pimf,pnx**6680**

28 And Isaac called   Jacob, and blessed   him, and charged him,

wcs,qmf**559**   pp,pnx   ptn3808 qmf3947   nn**802**   pr4480/pl,cs,nn1323

and said unto him, Thou shalt not take a wife of*the*daughters of

nn3667

Canaan.

qmv**6965** qmv**1980**   nn,lh6307   cs,nn,lh**1004**   nn1328   nn,pnx517   cs,nn1

2 Arise, go to Padan-aram, to the house of Bethuel thy mother's father; and

wcj,qmv3947 pp,pnx   nn**802**   pr4480/ad8033   pr4480/pl,cs,nn1323   nn3837   nn,pnx517   cs,nn251

take   thee a wife from thence of*the*daughters of Laban thy mother's brother.

wcj,nn**410**   nn**7706**   pimf**1288** pnx(853)   wcj,himf,pnx6509   wcj,himf,pnx7235

3 And God Almighty bless   thee, and make*thee*fruitful, and multiply

wcs,qpf**1961**   pp,cs,nn**6951**   pl,nn**5971**

thee, that thou mayest be   a multitude of people;

wcj,qmf**5414** pp,pnx (853)   cs,nn**1293**   nn85   pp,pnx   wcj,pp,nn,pnx**2233**

4 And give   thee   the blessing of Abraham, to thee, and to thy   seed

pr,pnx854   pp,qnc,pnx**3423** (853)   cs,nn776   pl,nn,pnx**4033** pnl834

with thee; that thou mayest inherit   the land wherein thou art a stranger, which

pl,nn**430** qpf**5414**   pp,nn85

God gave unto Abraham.

nn3327 wcs,qmf7971   (853) nn3290   wcs,qmf**1980**   nn,lh6307   pr413   nn3837

5 And Isaac sent away   Jacob: and he   went   to Padan-aram unto Laban,

cs,nn**1121**   nn1328   df,nn761   cs,nn251   nn7259   nn3290   wcj,nn6215 cs,nn517

son of Bethuel the Syrian, the brother of Rebekah, Jacob's and Esau's mother.

nn6215 wcs,qmf**7200** cj3588 nn3327   pipf**1288** (853) nn3290   wcj,pipf7971/pnx(853)

6 When Esau   saw   that Isaac had blessed   Jacob, and sent*him*away to

nn,lh6307   pp,qnc3947 pp,pnx   nn**802**   pr4480/ad8033   pp,pinc,pnx**1288** pnx(853)

Padan-aram, to take him a wife from thence; and that as he blessed   him he

wcs,pimf**6680**/pr,pnx5921   pp,qnc559   ptn3808 qmf3947   nn**802**   pr4480/pl,cs,nn1323

gave*him*a*charge, saying, Thou shalt not   take   a wife of*the*daughters of

nn3667

Canaan;

nn3290 wcs,qmf**8085**/pr413   nn,pnx1   wcj(pr413)   nn,pnx517   wcs,qmf**1980**

7 And that Jacob obeyed   his father and   his mother, and was gone to

nn,lh6307

Padan-aram;

nn6215 wcs,qmf**7200** cj3588   pl,cs,nn1323   nn3667 aj**7451**/pp,du,cs,nn**5869** nn3327   nn,pnx1

8 And Esau seeing that the daughters of Canaan pleased not Isaac his father;

wcs,qmf**1980** nn6215 pr413   nn3458   wcs,qmf3947 pr5921   pl,nn,pnx**802**   pp,pnx

9 Then went Esau unto Ishmael, and took unto the wives which he had

(853)   nn4258   cs,nn1323   nn3458   nn85   cs,nn1121   cs,nn269   nn5032
Mahalath the daughter of Ishmael Abraham's son, the sister of Nebajoth, to be
pp,nn802
his wife.

Jacob Has a Dream at Bethel

         nn3290   wcs,qmf3318   pr4480/nn884   wcs,qmf1980   nn,lh2771
⌖ 10 And Jacob went out from Beer-sheba, and went toward Haran.
        wcs,qmf6293   dfp,nn4725   wcs,qmf3885/ad8033   cj3588
11 And he lighted upon a certain place, and tarried*there*all*night, because the
df,nn8121   qpf935   wcs,qmf3947   pr4480/pl,cs,nn68   df,nn4725   wcs,qmf7760
sun was set; and he took of*the*stones of that place, and put *them for* his
pl,nn,pnx4763   wcs,qmf7901   df,pndm1931 dfp,nn4725
pillows, and lay down in that place to sleep.
         wcs,qmf2492   wcj,ptdm2009   nn5551   hopt5324   nn,lh776   wcj,nn,pnx7218
12 And he dreamed, and behold a ladder set up on the earth, and the top
     hipt5060   df,du,nn,lh8064   wcj,ptdm2009   pl,cs,nn4397   pl,nn430   pl,qpta5927   wcj,pl,qpta3381
of it reached to heaven: and behold the angels of God ascending and descending
pp,pnx
on it.
       wcj,ptdm2009   nn3068   nipt5324   pr,pnx5921   wcs,qmf559 pnp589   nn3068   pl,cs,nn430
13 And, behold, the LORD stood above it, and said, I *am* the LORD God
   nn85   nn,pnx1   wcj,pl,cs,nn430   nn3327   df,nn776   pnl834/pr,pnx5921   pnp859   qpta7901
of Abraham thy father, and the   God   of Isaac: the land whereon thou liest,
pp,pnx   qmf,pnx5414   wcj,pp,nn,pnx2233
to thee will I give it, and to thy   seed;
         nn,pnx2233   wcs,qpf1961   pp,cs,nn6083   df,nn776
14 And thy seed shall be as the dust of the earth, and thou shalt
wcs,qpf6555   nn,lh3220   wcj,ad,lh6924   wcj,nn,lh6828   wcj,nn,lh5045
spread abroad to the west, and to the east, and to the north, and to the south:
pp,pnx   wcj,pp,nn,pnx2233   cs,nn3605   pl,cs,nn4940   df,nn127   wcs,nipf1288
and in thee and in thy   seed shall all the families of the earth be blessed.
       wcj,ptdm2009 pnp595   pr,pnx5973   wcs,qpf,pnx8104   pp,nn3605
15 And, behold, I *am* with thee, and will keep thee in all *places*
pnl834   qmf1980   wcs,hipf,pnx7725   pr413 df,pndm2063 df,nn127 cj3588   ptn3808
whither thou goest, and will bring*thee*again into this land; for I will not
qmf,pnx5800   pr5704/pnl834/cj518   qpf6213   (853)   pnl834   pipf1696   pp,pnx
leave thee, until I have done *that* which I have spoken to thee of.
       nn3290   wcs,qmf3364   pr4480/nn,pnx8142   wcs,qmf559   ad403   nn3068   pta3426
16 And Jacob awaked out*of*his*sleep, and he said, Surely the LORD is in
df,pndm2088 dfp,nn4725   wcj,pnp595 qpf3045   ptn3808
this place; and I knew *it* not.
       wcs,qmf3372   wcs,qmf559 pnid4100   nipt3372   df,pndm2088 df,nn4725 pndm2088   ptn369
17 And he was afraid, and said, How dreadful *is* this place! this *is* none
cj3588/cj518   cs,nn1004   pl,nn430   wcj,pndm2088   cs,nn8179   df,du,nn8064
other but the house of God, and this *is* the gate of heaven.
       nn3290   wcs,himf7925   dfp,nn1242   wcs,qmf3947 (853)   df,nn68 pnl834
18 And Jacob rose*up*early in the morning, and took   the stone that he

---

⌖ **28:10–22** God promised Jacob two things: He assured Jacob that he was the promised carrier of both the seed and the covenant of Abraham, and He assured him of his personal safety and blessing. Jacob accepted these promises by faith and desired to commune with and to serve God. Many look upon this passage as the time of Jacob's conversion.

<small>qpf7760   pl,nn,pnx4763   wcs,qmf7760/pnx(853)   nn4676   wcs,qmf3332 nn8081   pr5921</small>
had put *for* his pillows, and set*it*up *for* a pillar, and poured oil upon the

<small>nn,pnx7218</small>
top   of it.

<small>   wcs,qmf7121 (853)   cs,nn8034   df,pndm1931 df,nn4725   nn1008   wcj,cj199   cs,nn8034</small>
19 And he called   the name of that   place Bethel: but the name of that

<small>df,nn5892   nn3870   dfp,aj7223</small>
city *was called* Luz at the first.

<small>   nn3290   wcs,qmf5087   nn5088   pp,qnc559   cj518 pl,nn430   qmf1961 pr,pnx5973</small>
20 And Jacob vowed a vow, saying, If God will be   with me, and will

<small>wcs,qpf,pnx8104   df,pndm2088 dfp,nn1870 pnl834 pnp595 qpta1980   wcs,qpf5414 pp,pnx   nn3899   pp,qnc398</small>
keep me in this   way that I   go, and will give me bread to eat, and

<small>wcj,nn899   pp,qnc3847</small>
raiment to put on,

<small>   wcs,qpf7725   pr413   nn,pnx1   cs,nn1004   pp,nn7965   nn3068</small>
21 So that I come again to my father's house in peace; then shall the Lᴏʀᴅ

<small>wcs,qpf1961 pp,pnx pp,pl,nn430</small>
be   my God:

<small>   df,pndm2063 wcj,df,nn68 pnl834   qpf7760   nn4676   qmf1961   pl,nn430 cs,nn1004</small>
22 And this   stone, which I have set *for* a pillar, shall be God's house:

<small>wcj,nn3605 pnl834   qmf5414 pp,pnx   pina6237/pimf,pnx6237   pp,pnx</small>
and of   all   that thou shalt give me I will surely*give*the*tenth unto thee.

Jacob Arrives at Laban's House

<small>   nn3290   wcs,qmf5375/du,nn,pnx7272   wcs,qmf1980   nn,lh776</small>
29 Then Jacob went*on*his*journey, and came into the land of the

<small>pl,cs,nn1121   nn6924</small>
people of the east.

<small>   wcs,qmf7200   wcj,ptdm2009   nn875   dfp,nn7704   wcj,ptdm2009 ad8033   nu7969</small>
2 And he looked, and behold a well in the field, and,   lo,   there *were* three

<small>pl,cs,nn5739   nn6629 pl,qpta7257 pr,pnx5921   cj3588   pr4480 df,pndm1931 df,nn875   himf8248   df,pl,nn5739</small>
flocks of sheep lying by it; for out of that well they watered the flocks:

<small>aj1419 wcj,df,nn68   pr5921   df,nn875   cs,nn6310</small>
and a great stone *was* upon the well's mouth.

<small>   ad,lh8033   cs,nn3605   df,pl,nn5739   wcs,nipf622   wcs,qpf1556 (853)   df,nn68</small>
3 And thither were   all   the flocks gathered: and they rolled   the stone

<small>pr4480/pr5921   df,nn875 cs,nn6310   wcs,hipf8248 (853)   df,nn6629   wcs,hipf7725 (853)   df,nn68</small>
from   the well's mouth, and watered   the sheep, and   put   the stone again

<small>pr5921   df,nn875 cs,nn6310   pp,nn,pnx4725</small>
upon the well's mouth in his place.

<small>   nn3290 wcs,qmf559   pp,pnx   pl,nn,pnx251 pr4480/ad370   pnp859   wcs,qmf559</small>
4 And Jacob said unto them, My brethren, whence *be* ye? And they said,

<small>pr4480/nn2771   pnp587</small>
Of Haran *are* we.

<small>   wcs,qmf559   pp,pnx   he,qpf3045   (853)   nn3837   cs,nn1121   nn5152</small>
5 And he said unto them, Know ye   Laban the son of Nahor? And they

<small>wcs,qmf559   qpf3045</small>
said, We know *him*.

<small>   wcs,qmf559   pp,pnx   pp,pnx he,nn7965   wcs,qmf559   nn7965</small>
6 And he   said unto them, *Is* he well? And they said, *He is* well: and,

<small>wcj,ptdm2009   nn7354   nn,pnx1323   qpta935   pr5973   df,nn6629</small>
behold, Rachel his daughter cometh with the sheep.

<small>   wcs,qmf559 ptdm2005   ad5750 aj1419 df,nn3117   ptn3808   cs,nn6256   df,nn4735</small>
7 And he said, Lo, *it is* yet high day, neither *is it* time that the cattle

ninc622   himv8248   df,nn6629   wcj,qmv1980   qmv7462
should be gathered together: water ye the sheep, and   go *and* feed *them.*

                    wcs,qmf559   ptn3808/qmf3201 pr5704/pnl834 cs,nn3605   df,pl,nn5739
8 And   they   said,   We   cannot,   until   all   the   flocks   be

nimf622   wcs,qpf1556 (853) df,nn68 pr4480/pr5921 df,nn875 cs,nn6310
gathered together, and *till* they   roll   the stone from   the well's mouth; then

wcs,hipf8248   df,nn6629
we water the sheep.

                ad,pnx5750 pipt1696 pr,pnx5973   wcj,nn7354   qpf935 pr5973 (pnl834)   pp,nn,pnx1
9 And while he   yet   spoke with them, Rachel came with   her father's

df,nn6629 cj3588 pnp1931 qpta7462
sheep: for she kept them.

                wcs,qmf1961   pp,pnl834 nn3290 qpf7200 (853) nn7354   cs,nn1323   nn3837
10 And it*came*to*pass, when Jacob saw   Rachel the daughter of Laban his

nn,pnx517 cs,nn251   wcj(853)   cs,nn6629   nn3837   nn,pnx517 cs,nn251   nn3290
mother's brother, and   the sheep of Laban his mother's brother, that Jacob

wcs,qmf5066   wcs,himf1556 (853) df,nn68 pr4480/pr5921 df,nn875 cs,nn6310   wcs,himf8248 (853)
went near, and rolled   the stone from   the well's mouth, and watered   the

cs,nn6629   nn3837   nn,pnx517 cs,nn251
flock of Laban his mother's brother.

            nn3290 wcs,qmf5401 pp,nn7354   wcs,qmf5375 (853)   nn,pnx6963   wcs,qmf1058
11 And Jacob kissed Rachel, and lifted up   his voice, and wept.

            nn3290   wcs,himf5046 pp,nn7354 cj3588 pnp1931   nn,pnx1   cs,nn251   wcj,cj3588
12 And Jacob told   Rachel that he *was* her father's brother, and   that

pnp1931   nn7259   cs,nn1121   wcs,qmf7323   wcs,himf5046   pp,nn,pnx1
he *was* Rebekah's son: and she   ran   and told   her father.

                wcs,qmf1961   nn3837 pp,qnc8085 (853)   cs,nn8088   nn3290   nn,pnx269
13 And it*came*to*pass, when Laban heard   the tidings of Jacob his sister's

cs,nn1121   wcs,qmf7323   pp,qnc,pnx7125   wcs,pimf2263   pp,pnx   wcs,pimf5401 pp,pnx
son, that he   ran   to   meet   him, and embraced him, and kissed him, and

wcs,himf,pnx935   pr413   nn,pnx1004   wcs,pimf5608 pp,pnx3837 (853) cs,nn3605 df,pndm428 df,pl,nn1697
brought him to his house. And he told   Laban   all   these things.

            nn3837   wcs,qmf559 pp,pnx   ad389 pnp859   nn,pnx6106   wcj,nn,pnx1320
14 And Laban said to him, Surely thou *art* my bone and my flesh.   And

wcs,qmf3427 pr,pnx5973   pl,nn3117   cs,nn2320
he abode with him the space of a month.

Jacob Works to Pay For Two Wives

            nn3837   wcs,qmf559   pp,nn3290 he,cj3588   pnp859   nn,pnx251
15 And Laban said   unto Jacob, Because thou *art* my brother, shouldest thou

wcj,qpf,pnx5647   ad2600   himv5046 pp,pnx pnit4100   nn,pnx4909
therefore serve   me for naught? tell me, what *shall* thy wages *be?*

            wcj,pp,nn3837   du,cs,nu8147   pl,nn1323   cs,nn8034   df,aj1419   nn3812
16 And Laban had   two   daughters: the name of the elder *was* Leah, and

wcj,cs,nn8034   df,aj6996   nn7354
the name of the younger *was* Rachel.

            nn3812   aj7390 wcj,du,cs,nn5869   wcj,nn7354 qpf1961 cs,aj3303/nn8389 wcj,cs,aj3303   nn4758
17 Leah *was* tender   eyed;   but Rachel was beautiful and   well favored.

            nn3290 wcs,qmf157 (853)   nn7354   wcs,qmf559   qmf,pnx5647   nu7651 pl,nn8141
18 And Jacob loved   Rachel; and said, I will serve thee seven years for

pp,nn7354   df,aj6996 nn,pnx1323
Rachel thy younger daughter.

nn3837 wcs,qmf559 aj2896 qnc,pnx5414 pnx(853) pp,pnx

19 And Laban said, *It is* better that I give her to thee,

pr4480/qnc,pnx5414 pnx(853) aj312 pp,nn376 qmv3427 pr,pnx5973

than*that*I*should*give her to another man: abide with me.

nn3290 wcs,qmf5647 nu7651 pl,nn8141 pp,nn7354 wcs,qmf1961/pp,du,nn,pnx5869

20 And Jacob served seven years for Rachel; and they seemed unto

pl,nu259 pp,pl,nn3117 pp,nn,pnx160 pnx(853)

him *but* a few days, for the love he had to her.

nn3290 wcs,qmf559 pr413 nn3837 qmv3051 (853) nn,pnx802 cj3588 pl,nn,pnx3117

21 And Jacob said unto Laban, Give *me* my wife, for my days are

qpf4390 wcj,qcj935 pr,pnx413

fulfilled, that I may go in unto her.

nn3837 wcs,qmf622 (853) cs,nn3605 pl,cs,nn376 df,nn4725 wcs,qmf6213

22 And Laban gathered together all the men of the place, and made a

nn4960

feast.

wcs,qmf1961 dfp,nn6153 wcs,qmf3947 (853) nn3812 nn,pnx1323

23 And it*came*to*pass in the evening, that he took Leah his daughter,

wcs,himf935 pnx(853) pr,pnx413 wcs,qmf935 pr,pnx413

and brought her to him; and he went in unto her.

nn3837 wcs,qmf5414 pp,pnx nn,pnx1323 pp,nn3812 (853) nn2153 nn,pnx8198

24 And Laban gave unto his daughter Leah Zilpah his maid *for* a

nn8198

handmaid.

wcs,qmf1961 dfp,nn1242 wcj,ptdm2009 pnp1931 nn3812

25 And it*came*to*pass, that in the morning, behold, it *was* Leah: and he

wcs,qmf559 pr413 nn3837 pnit4100 pndm2063 qpf6213 pp,pnx he,ptn3808 qpf5647 pr,pnx5973

said to Laban, What *is* this thou hast done unto me? did not I serve with

pp,nn7354 wcj,pp,pnit4100 pipf,pnx7411

thee for Rachel? wherefore then hast thou beguiled me?

nn3837 wcs,qmf559 ptn3808 ad3651 nimf6213 pp,nn,pnx4725 pp,qnc5414

26 And Laban said, It must not be so done in our country, to give the

df,aj6810 pp,pl,cs,nn6440 df,nn1067

younger before the firstborn.

pimv4390 pndm2063 cs,nn7620 wcj,qcj5414 pp,pnx (853) pndm2063 ad1571 dfp,nn5656

27 Fulfill her week, and we will give thee this also for the service

pnl834 qmf5647 pr,pnx5973 ad5750 nu7651 aj312 pl,nn8141

which thou shalt serve with me yet seven other years.

nn3290 wcs,qmf6213 ad3651 wcs,pimf4390 pndm2063 cs,nn7620 wcs,qmf5414 pp,pnx (853)

28 And Jacob did so, and fulfilled her week: and he gave him

nn7354 nn,pnx1323 (pp,pnx) pp,nn802

Rachel his daughter to wife also.

nn3837 wcs,qmf5414 pp,nn7354 nn,pnx1323 (853) nn1090 nn,pnx8198 pp,pnx

29 And Laban gave to Rachel his daughter Bilhah his handmaid to be her

pp,nn8198

maid.

wcs,qmf935 ad1571 pr413 nn7354 wcs,qmf157 ad1571 (853) nn7354

30 And he went in also unto Rachel, and he loved also Rachel

pr4480/nn3812 wcs,qmf5647 pr,pnx5973 ad5750 nu7651 aj312 pl,nn8141

more*than*Leah, and served with him yet seven other years.

Jacob's Family Record

nn3068   wcs,qmf7200 cj3588   nn3812   qptp8130   wcs,qmf6605 (853)   nn,pnx7358
31 And when the LORD saw that Leah *was* hated, he opened   her womb:

wcj,nn7354   aj6135
but Rachel *was* barren.

nn3812   wcs,qmf2029   wcs,qmf3205   nn1121   wcs,qmf7121   nn,pnx8034   nn7205
32 And Leah conceived, and bore a son, and she called his name Reuben:

cj3588   qpf559   cj3588   nn3068   qpf7200   pp,nn,pnx6040 ad6258   cj3588
for she said, Surely the LORD hath looked upon my affliction; now therefore my

nn,pnx376   qmf,pnx157
husband will love me.

wcs,qmf2029   ad5750   wcs,qmf3205   nn1121   wcs,qmf559   cj3588   nn3068
33 And she conceived again, and bore a son; and said, Because the LORD

qpf8085   cj3588 pnp595   qptp8130   wcs,qmf5414 pp,pnx (853) pndm2088   ad1571
hath heard that I *was* hated, he hath therefore given me   this *son* also: and

wcs,qmf7121   nn,pnx8034   nn8095
she called his name Simeon.

wcs,qmf2029   ad5750   wcs,qmf3205   nn1121   wcs,qmf559   ad6258   df,nn6471
34 And she conceived again, and bore a son; and said, Now this time will

nn,pnx376   nimf3867 pr,pnx413   cj3588   qpf3205 pp,pnx nu7969 pl,nn1121 pr5921/ad3651
my husband be joined unto me, because I have born him three sons: therefore was

nn,pnx8034 qpf7121   nn3878
his name called Levi.

wcs,qmf2029   ad5750   wcs,qmf3205   nn1121   wcs,qmf559 df,nn6471
35 And she conceived again, and bore a son: and she said, Now will I

himf3034 (853)   nn3068 pr5921/ad3651   qpf7121   nn,pnx8034 nn3063   wcs,qmf5975 pr4480/qnc3205
praise   the LORD: therefore she called his name Judah; and left   bearing.

nn7354   wcs,qmf7200 cj3588   qpf3205/ptn3808/pp,nn3290   nn7354
And when Rachel saw   that she bore*Jacob*no*children, Rachel

wcs,pimf7065   pp,nn,pnx269   wcs,qmf559 pr413 nn3290   qmv3051 pp,pnx pl,nn1121 wcj,cj518
envied her sister; and said unto Jacob, Give me children,   or

ptn369 pnp595 qpta4191
else I die.

nn3290   cs,nn639   wcs,qmf2734   pp,nn7354   wcs,qmf559   pnp595
2 And Jacob's anger was kindled against Rachel: and he said, *Am* I in

pl,nn430 he,pr8478 pnl834   qpf4513 pr,pnx4480   cs,nn6529   nn990
God's stead, who hath withheld from thee the fruit of the womb?

wcs,qmf559   ptdm2009   nn,pnx519   nn1090   qmv935 pr,pnx413
3 And she said, Behold my maid Bilhah, go in unto her; and she shall

wcj,qmf3205 pr5921   du,nn,pnx1290   pnp595   ad1571   wcj,nimf1129 pr,pnx4480
bear upon my knees, that I may also have children by   her.

wcs,qmf5414 pp,pnx (853)   nn1090   nn,pnx8198   pp,nn802   nn3290 wcs,qmf935
4 And she gave him   Bilhah her handmaid to wife: and Jacob went in

pr,pnx413
unto her.

nn1090   wcs,qmf2029   wcs,qmf3205 pp,nn3290 nn1121
5 And Bilhah conceived, and bore Jacob a son.

nn7354   wcs,qmf559 pl,nn430   qpf,pnx1777   wcj,ad1571 qpf8085   pp,nn,pnx6963
6 And Rachel said, God hath judged me, and hath also heard my voice,

wcs,qmf5414 pp,pnx   nn1121 pr5921/ad3651   qpf7121   nn,pnx8034 nn1835
and hath given me a son: therefore called she his name Dan.

nn1090   nn7354   cs,nn8198   wcs,qmf2029   ad5750   wcs,qmf3205 pp,nn3290   nuor8145   nn1121
7 And Bilhah Rachel's maid conceived again, and bore Jacob a second son.

    nn7354   wcs,qmf**559**   pl,nn**430**   pl,cs,nn5319   nipf6617   pr5973   nn,pnx**269** ad1571

8 And Rachel said, With great wrestlings have I wrestled with my sister, and

      qpf3201   wcs,qmf**7121**   nn,pnx8034   nn5321

I have prevailed: and she called his name Naphtali.

      nn3812 wcs,qmf**7200** cj3588   qpf5975 pr4480/qnc3205   wcs,qmf3947 (853)   nn2153

9 When Leah saw that she had left bearing, she took Zilpah her

nn,pnx8198   wcs,qmf**5414** pnx(853)   pp,nn3290   pp,nn**802**

maid, and gave her Jacob to wife.

      nn2153   nn3812   cs,nn8198 wcs,qmf3205 pp,nn3290   nn**1121**

10 And Zilpah Leah's maid bore Jacob a son.

     nn3812 wcs,qmf**559**   qpf**1413**   wcs,qmf**7121** (853)   nn,pnx8034 nn**1410**

11 And Leah said, A troop cometh: and she called his name Gad.

     nn2153   nn3812   cs,nn8198 wcs,qmf3205 pp,nn3290 nuor8145 nn**1121**

12 And Zilpah Leah's maid bore Jacob a second son.

     nn3812   wcs,qmf**559** pp,nn,pnx**837**   cj3588   pl,nn1323   pipf,pnx**833**

13 And Leah said, Happy am I, for the daughters will call*me*blessed: and

wcs,qmf**7121** (853)   nn,pnx8034   nn836

she called his name Asher.

     nn7205   wcs,qmf**1980**   pp,pl,cs,nn**3117**   pl,nn2406 cs,nn7105   wcs,qmf4672   pl,nn**1736**

14 And Reuben went in the days of wheat harvest, and found mandrakes

dfp,nn**7704** wcs,himf935 pnx(853)   pr413   nn,pnx517   nn3812   nn7354 wcs,qmf**559** pr413

in the field, and brought them unto his mother Leah. Then Rachel said to

nn3812 qmv**5414** pp,pnx   pte4994   nn,pnx**1121** pr4480/pl,cs,nn**1736**

Leah, Give me, I*pray*thee, of thy son's mandrakes.

         wcs,qmf**559**   pp,pnx   he,nn4592   qnc,pnx3947 (853)

15 And she said unto her, Is it a small matter that thou hast taken my

nn,pnx**376**   wcj,pp,qnc3947 (853)   nn,pnx**1121** pl,cs,nn**1736**   ad1571   nn7354

husband? and wouldest thou take away my son's mandrakes also? And Rachel

wcs,qmf**559** pp,ad**3651**   qmf7901 pr,pnx5973   df,nn**3915** pr8478   nn,pnx**1121** pl,cs,nn**1736**

said, Therefore he shall lie with thee tonight for thy son's mandrakes.

     nn3290 wcs,qmf935 pr4480   df,nn**7704** dfp,nn6153   nn3812 wcs,qmf3318

16 And Jacob came out of the field in the evening, and Leah went out to

pp,qnc,pnx7125   wcs,qmf**559**   qmf935 pr,pnx413 cj3588   qna7936/qpf,pnx7936

meet him, and said, Thou must come in unto me; for surely*I*have*hired

nn,pnx**1121** pp,pl,cs,nn**1736**   wcs,qmf7901 pr,pnx5973 pndm1931 dfp,nn**3915**

thee with my son's mandrakes. And he lay with her that night.

      pl,nn**430** wcs,qmf**8085**   pr413 nn3812   wcs,qmf2029   wcs,qmf3205 pp,nn3290

17 And God hearkened unto Leah, and she conceived, and bore Jacob the

nuor2549 nn**1121**

fifth son.

     nn3812 wcs,qmf**559** pl,nn**430**   qpf**5414**   nn,pnx7939 pnl834   qpf**5414**

18 And Leah said, God hath given me my hire, because I have given my

nn,pnx8198 pp,nn,pnx**376**   wcs,qmf**7121** nn,pnx8034   nn3485

maiden to my husband: and she called his name Issachar.

     nn3812   wcs,qmf2029   ad5750   wcs,qmf3205 pp,nn3290 nuor8345 nn**1121**

19 And Leah conceived again, and bore Jacob the sixth son.

     nn3812   wcs,qmf**559** pl,nn**430**   qpf,pnx2064   pnx(853)   aj**2896** nn2065 df,nn6471

20 And Leah said, God hath endued me with a good dowry; now will

 nn,pnx**376**   qmf,pnx2082   cj3588   qpf3205 pp,pnx nu8337 pl,nn**1121**   wcs,qmf**7121** (853)

my husband dwell with me, because I have born him six sons: and she called

nn,pnx8034   nn2074

his name Zebulun.

     wcj,ad310   qpf3205   nn1323   wcs,qmf**7121** (853)   nn,pnx8034 nn1783

21 And afterwards she bore a daughter, and called her name Dinah.

pl,nn**430** wcs,qmf**2142** (853) nn7354 pl,nn**430** wcs,qmf**8085** pr,pnx413

22 And God remembered Rachel, and God hearkened to her, and

wcs,qmf6605 (853) nn,pnx7358

opened her womb.

wcs,qmf2029 wcs,qmf3205 nn1121 wcs,qmf559 pl,nn**430** qpf**622** (853)

23 And she conceived, and bore a son; and said, God hath taken away

nn,pnx**2781**

my reproach:

wcs,qmf**7121** (853) nn,pnx8034 nn3130 pp,qnc559 nn**3068** hicj3254

24 And she called his name Joseph; and said, The LORD shall add

pp,pnx aj312 nn**1121**

to me another son.

Jacob's Bargain

wcs,qmf**1961** pp,pnl834 nn7354 qpf3205 (853) nn3130 nn3290 wcs,qmf**559**

25 And it*came*to*pass, when Rachel had born Joseph, that Jacob said

pr413 nn3837 pimv,pnx7971 wcj,qcj**1980** pr413 nn,pnx4725

unto Laban, Send*me*away, that I may go unto mine own place, and to my

wcj,pp,nn,pnx**776**

country.

qmv**5414** (853) pl,nn,pnx**802** wcj(853) pl,nn,pnx3206 pnl834/pp,pnp2004 qpf**5647**

26 Give me my wives and my children, for whom I have served

pnx(853) wcj,qcj**1980** cj3588 pnp859 qpf**3045** (853) nn,pnx**5656** pnl834 qpf,pnx**5647**

thee, and let me go: for thou knowest my service which I have done

thee.

nn3837 wcs,qmf**559** pr,pnx413 pte**4994** cj518 qpf4672 nn2580

27 And Laban said unto him, I*pray*thee, if I have found favor in thine

pp,du,nn,pnx**5869** pipf**5172** nn**3068** wcs,pimf,pnx**1288**

eyes, tarry: for I have learned*by*experience that the LORD hath blessed me

pp,nn,pnx1558

for*thy*sake.

wcs,qmf**559** qmv**5344**/pr,pnx5921 nn,pnx7939 wcj,qcj**5414**

28 And he said, Appoint me thy wages, and I will give it.

wcs,qmf**559** pr,pnx413 pnp859 qpf**3045** (853) pnl834 qpf,pnx**5647**

29 And he said unto him, Thou knowest how I have served thee, and

wcj(853) pnl834 nn,pnx4735 qpf**1961** pr,pnx854

how thy cattle was with me.

cj3588 nn4592 pnl834 pp,pnx qpf**1961** pp,pl,nn,pnx**6440** wcs,qmf6555

30 For it was little which thou hadst before I came, and it is now increased

pp,nn7230 nn**3068** wcs,pimf**1288** pnx(853) pp,nn,pnx7272 wcj,ad6258

unto a multitude; and the LORD hath blessed thee since my coming: and now

pnit4970 pnp595 qmf**6213** pp,nn,pnx1004 ad1571

when shall I provide for mine own house also?

wcs,qmf**559** pnit4100 qmf**5414** pp,pnx nn3290 wcs,qmf**559** ptn3808

31 And he said, What shall I give thee? And Jacob said, Thou shalt not

qmf**5414** pp,pnx pnid3972 cj518 qmf**6213** df,pndm2088 df,nn**1697** pp,pnx qcj**7725** qmf7462

give me any thing: if thou wilt do this thing for me, I will again feed and

qmf**8104** nn,pnx6629

keep thy flock:

qmf**5674** pp,cs,nn3605 nn,pnx6629 df,nn**3117** hina**5493** pr4480/ad8033 cs,nn3605

32 I will pass through all thy flock today, removing from thence all

aj5348 wcj,qptp2921 nn7716 wcj,cs,nn3605 aj2345 nn7716 dfp,pl,nn3775

the speckled and spotted cattle, and all the brown cattle among the sheep, and

wcj,qptp2921   wcj,aj5348   dfp,pl,nn5795   wcs,qpf**1961**   nn,pnx7939

the spotted and speckled among the goats: and *of such* shall be my hire.

                                    nn,pnx**6666**   wcs,qpf6030   pp,pnx   pp,nn3117   ad4279   cj3588

33 So shall my righteousness answer for me in time to come, when it shall

qmf935   pr5921   nn,pnx7939   pp,pl,nn,pnx**6440**   nn3605   pnl834   ptn,pnx369   aj5348

come for my hire before thy face: every one that *is* not speckled and

wcj,qptp2921   dfp,pl,nn5795   wcj,aj2345   dfp,pl,nn3775   pnp1931

spotted among the goats, and brown among the sheep, that shall be counted

qptp1589   pr,pnx854

stolen with me.

              nn3837   wcs,qmf**559**   ptdm2005   ptx3863   qcj**1961**   pp,nn,pnx**1697**

34 And Laban said, Behold, I would it might be according to thy word.

                  wcs,himf**5493**   df,pndm1931   dfp,nn3117   (853)   df,pl,nn8495   df,aj6124

35 And he removed that day the he goats that were ringstreaked and

wcj,df,pl,qptp2921   wcj(853)   cs,nn3605   df,pl,nn5795   df,aj5348   wcj,df,pl,qptp2921

spotted, and all the she goats that were speckled and spotted, *and*

cs,nn3605   pnl834   aj3836   pp,pnx   wcj,cs,nn3605   aj2345   dfp,pl,nn3775

every one that had *some* white in it, and all the brown among the sheep, and

wcs,qmf**5414**   pp,cs,nn**3027**   pl,nn,pnx**1121**

gave *them* into the hand of his sons.

              wcs,qmf**7760**   cs,nu7969   pl,nn3117   cs,nn**1870**   pr,pnx996   wcj(pr996)   nn3290

36 And he set three days' journey between himself and Jacob: and

wcj,nn3290   qpta7462   (853)   df,pl,nipt**3498**   nn3837   cs,nn6629

Jacob fed the rest of Laban's flocks.

                  nn3290   wcs,qmf3947   pp,pnx   cs,nn4731   aj3892   nn3839   wcj,nn3869

37 And Jacob took him rods of green poplar, and of the hazel and

wcj,nn6196   wcs,pimf6478   aj3836   pl,nn6479   pp,pnp2004   df,aj3836   cs,nn4286   pnl834

chestnut tree; and peeled white streaks in them, and made the white appear which

pr5921   df,pl,nn4731

was in the rods.

              wcs,himf3322   (853)   df,pl,nn4731   pnl834   pipf6478   pp,pr5227   df,nn6629

38 And he set the rods which he had peeled before the flocks in the

dfp,pl,nn7298   df,pl,nn4325   pp,pl,cs,nn8268   pnl834   df,nn6629   qmf935   pp,qnc8354

gutters in the watering troughs when the flocks came to drink, that they should

wcs,qmf3179   pp,qnc,pnx935   pp,qnc8354

conceive when they came to drink.

                  df,nn6629   wcs,qmf3179   pr413   df,pl,nn4731   wcs,qmf3205   df,nn6629

39 And the flocks conceived before the rods, and brought forth cattle

aj6124   aj5348   wcj,pl,qptp2921

ringstreaked, speckled, and spotted.

              nn3290   hipf6504   wcj,df,pl,nn3775   wcs,qmf**5414**   pl,cs,nn**6440**   df,nn6629

40 And Jacob did separate the lambs, and set the faces of the flocks

pr413   aj6124   wcj,cs,nn3605   aj2345   pp,cs,nn6629   nn3837

toward the ringstreaked, and all the brown in the flock of Laban; and he

wcs,qmf7896   pp,pnx   pl,nn5739   pp,nn,pnx905   qpf,pnx7896   wcj,ptn**3808**   pr5921   nn3837   cs,nn6629

put his own flocks by themselves, and put them not unto Laban's cattle.

                  wcj,qpf**1961**   pp,cs,nn3605   df,pl,pupt7194   df,nn6629   pinc3179

41 And it*came*to*pass, whensoever the stronger cattle did conceive, that

nn3290   wcj,qpf**7760**   (853)   df,pl,nn4731   pp,du,cs,nn**5869**   df,nn6629   dfp,pl,nn7298

Jacob laid the rods before the eyes of the cattle in the gutters, that they

          pp,pinc,pnx3179   dfp,pl,nn4731

might conceive among the rods.

                  df,nn6629   wcj,pp,hinc5848   qmf**7760**   ptn**3808**   df,pl,qptp5848

42 But when the cattle were feeble, he put *them* not in: so the feebler

wcs,qpf**1961**   pp,nn3837   wcj,df,pl,qptp7194   pp,nn3290

were Laban's, and the stronger Jacob's.

df,nn**376**   wcs,qmf**6555**   ad3966/ad3966   wcs,qmf**1961**/pp,pnx   aj7227   cs,nn6629

43 And the man increased exceedingly, and had much cattle, and

wcj,pl,nn8198   wcj,pl,nn**5650**   wcj,pl,nn1581   wcj,pl,nn2543

maidservants, and menservants, and camels, and asses.

Jacob Runs Away From His Uncle

wcs,qmf**8085**   (853)   pl,cs,nn**1697**   nn3837   pl,cs,nn1121   pp,qnc559   nn3290

31 And he heard the words of Laban's sons, saying, Jacob hath

qpf3947   (853) cs,nn3605 pnl834   pp,nn,pnx1   wcj,pr4480/pnl834

taken away all that *was* our father's; and of*that*which *was* our

pp,nn,pnx1   qpf**6213** (853) cs,nn3605 df,pndm2088 df,nn**3519**

father's hath he gotten all this glory.

nn3290 wcs,qmf**7200** (853)   pl,cs,nn**6440**   nn3837   wcj,ptdm2009   ptn,pnx369

2 And Jacob beheld the countenance of Laban, and, behold, it *was* not

pr,pnx5973   pp,ad8543/ad8032

toward him as before.

nn3068 wcs,qmf559 pr413   nn3290   qmv7725   pr413   cs,nn776   pl,nn,pnx1

3 And the LORD said unto Jacob, Return unto the land of thy fathers, and to

wcj,pp,nn,pnx4138   wcj,qmf**1961** pr,pnx5973

thy kindred; and I will be with thee.

nn3290 wcs,qmf7971   wcs,qmf7121 pp,nn7354   wcj,pp,nn3812   df,nn**7704** pr413

4 And Jacob sent and called Rachel and Leah to the field unto his

nn,pnx6629

flock,

wcs,qmf**559**   pp,pnx   pnp595 qpta**7200** (853)   nn,pnx1   pl,cs,nn**6440**   cj3588

5 And said unto them, I see your father's countenance, that it *is*

ptn,pnx369 pr,pnx413   pp,ad8543/ad8032   wcj,pl,cs,nn**430**   nn,pnx1   qpf**1961** pr,pnx5973

not toward me as before; but the God of my father hath been with me.

wcj,pnp859 qpf3045 cj3588   pp,cs,nn3605   nn,pnx3581   qpf5647 (853)   nn,pnx1

6 And ye know that with all my power I have served your father.

wcj,nn,pnx1   hipf2048   pp,pnx   wcj,hipf2498 (853)   nn,pnx4909 cs,nu6235 pl,nn4489

7 And your father hath deceived me, and changed my wages ten times;

pl,nn**430** qpf**5414**   wcj,ptn**3808**   pp,hinc**7489**/pr,pnx5978

but God suffered him not to hurt me.

cj518   nmf559   ad3541   aj5348   qmf**1961**   nn,pnx7939   cs,nn3605   df,nn6629

8 If he said thus, The speckled shall be thy wages; then all the cattle

wcs,qpf3205   aj5348   wcj,cj518   qmf**559** ad3541   aj6124   qmf**1961**   nn,pnx7939

bore speckled: and if he said thus, The ringstreaked shall be thy hire; then

wcs,qpf3205 cs,nn3605   df,nn6629   aj6124

bare all the cattle ringstreaked.

pl,nn**430**   wcs,him**5337**   (853)   cs,nn4735   nn,pnx1   wcs,qmf**5414**

9 Thus God hath taken away the cattle of your father, and given *them*

pp,pnx

to me.

wcs,qmf**1961**   pp,cs,nn**6256**   df,nn6629   pinc3179   wcs,qmf**5375**

10 And it*came*to*pass at the time that the cattle conceived, that I lifted up

du,nn,pnx**5869**   wcs,qmf**7200**   pp,nn2472   wcj,ptdm2009   df,pl,nn6260   df,pl,qpta**5927** pr5921

mine eyes, and saw in a dream, and, behold, the rams which leaped upon

df,nn6629   aj6124   aj5348   wcj,aj1261

the cattle *were* ringstreaked, speckled, and grizzled.

cs,nn**4397**   df,pl,nn**430** wcs,qmf**559** pr,pnx413   pp,nn2472   nn3290

11 And the angel of God spoke unto me in a dream, *saying*, Jacob: And I

wcs,qmf**559** ptdm,pnx2009

said, Here *am* I.

12 And he said, Lift up now thine eyes, and see, all the rams which leap upon the cattle *are* ringstreaked, speckled, and grizzled: for I have seen all that Laban doeth unto thee.

13 I *am* the God of Bethel, where thou anointedst the pillar, *and* where thou vowedst a vow unto me: now arise, get*thee*out from this land, and return unto the land of thy kindred.

14 And Rachel and Leah answered and said unto him, *Is there* yet any portion or inheritance for us in our father's house?

15 Are we not counted of him strangers? for he hath sold us, and hath quite devoured also our money.

16 For all the riches which God hath taken from*our*father, that *is* ours, and our children's: now then, whatsoever God hath said unto thee, do.

17 Then Jacob rose up, and set his sons and his wives upon camels;

18 And he carried away all his cattle, and all his goods which he had gotten, the cattle of his getting, which he had gotten in Padan-aram, for to go to Isaac his father in the land of Canaan.

19 And Laban went to shear his sheep: and Rachel had stolen the images that *were* her father's.

20 And Jacob stole away unawares to Laban the Syrian, in that he told him not that he fled.

21 So he fled with all that he had; and he rose up, and passed over the river, and set his face *toward* the mount Gilead.

Laban Pursues Jacob

22 And it was told Laban on the third day that Jacob was fled.

23 And he took his brethren with him, and pursued after him seven days' journey; and they overtook him in the mount Gilead.

pl,nn**430**   wcs,qmf**935**   pr413   nn3837   df,nn761   pp,cs,nn2472   df,nn**3915**   wcs,qmf**559**

24 And God came to Laban the Syrian in a dream by night, and said

pp,pnx   nimv**8104**/pp,pnx   cj6435   pimf**1696**   pr5973 nn3290   pr4480/nn**2896**   pr5704 nn**7451**

unto him, Take heed that thou speak not to Jacob either good or bad.

nn3837   wcs,himf5381   (853)   nn3290   wcj,nn3290   qpf**8628**   (853)   nn,pnx168

25 Then Laban overtook   Jacob. Now Jacob had pitched   his tent in the

dfp,nn2022   wcj,nn3837   pr854   pl,nn,pnx**251**   qpf**8628**   pp,cs,nn2022   df,nn**1568**

mount: and Laban with his brethren pitched in the mount of Gilead.

nn3837   wcs,qmf**559**   pp,nn3290 pnit4100   qpf**6213**   wcs,qmf1589

26 And Laban said to Jacob, What hast thou done, that thou hast stolen away

(853)   nn,pnx3824   wcs,pimf5090   (853)   pl,nn,pnx1323   pp,pl,cs,qptp**7617**

unawares to me, and carried away   my daughters, as captives *taken* with the

nn**2719**

sword?

pp,pnit4100   nipf2244   pp,qnc1272   wcs,qmf1589   pnx(853)

27 Wherefore didst thou flee away secretly, and steal away   from me; and

wcj,ptn**3808**   hipf**5046**   pp,pnx   wcs,pimf,pnx7971   pp,nn8057

didst not tell me, that I might have sent*thee*away with mirth, and with

wcj,pp,pl,nn**7892**   pp,nn8596   wcj,pp,nn3658

songs, with tabret, and with harp?

wcj,ptn**3808**   qpf,pnx**5203**   pp,pinc**5401**   pp,pl,nn,pnx**1121**   wcj,pp,pl,nn,pnx**1323**

28 And hast not suffered me to kiss my sons and my daughters?

ad6258   hipf5528   qnc**6213**

thou hast now done foolishly in *so* doing.

pta3426   pp,cs,nn**410**   nn,pnx3027   pp,qnc**6213** pnx(pr5973)   nn7451   wcj,pl,cs,nn**430**

29 It is in the power of my hand to do   you hurt: but the   God   of

nn,pnx1   qpf**559**   pr,pnx413   ad570   pp,qnc559   nimv**8104**/pp,pnx   pr4480/pinc**1696**

your father spoke unto me last night, saying, Take*thou*heed that*thou*speak not

pr5973 nn3290   pr4480/nn**2896**   pr5704 nn**7451**

to Jacob either good or bad.

wcj,ad6258   qna1980/qpf1980   cj3588

30 And   now,   *though*   thou   wouldest   needs*be*gone,   because   thou

nina3700/nipf3700   nn,pnx1   pp,cs,nn**1004**   pp,pnit4100   qpf1589 (853)   pl,nn,pnx**430**

sore longedst after thy father's house, *yet* wherefore hast thou stolen   my gods?

nn3290   wcs,qmf6030   wcs,qmf**559**   pp,nn3837   cj3588   qpf3372   cj3588   qpf559

31 And Jacob answered and said to Laban, Because I was afraid: for I said,

cj6435   qmf1497   (853)   pl,nn,pnx1323   pr4480/pr,pnx5973

Peradventure thou wouldest take*by*force   thy daughters   from   me.

pr5973   pnl834   qmf4672   (853)   pl,nn,pnx**430**   ptn**3808** qmf2421   pr5048

32 With whomsoever thou findest   thy gods, let him not live: before our

pl,nn,pnx**251**   himv**5234**   pnid4100   pp,pnx   pr,pnx5973   wcj,qmv3947   pp,pnx   nn3290

brethren discern thou what *is* thine with me, and   take   *it* to thee. For Jacob

qpf3045   wcj,ptn**3808** cj3588   nn7354   qpf,pnx1589

knew   not   that Rachel had stolen them.

nn3837   wcs,qmf935   nn3290   pp,cs,nn**168**   nn3812   wcj,pp,cs,nn**168**

33 And Laban went into Jacob's tent, and into Leah's   tent,   and into the

du,cs,nu8147   df,pl,nn519   wcj,pp,cs,nn**168**   qpf4672   wcj,ptn**3808**   wcs,qmf3318

two   maidservants'   tents;   but he found *them* not. Then went he

pr4480/cs,nn**168**/nn3812   wcs,qmf935   nn7354   pp,cs,nn**168**

out*of*Leah's*tent, and entered into Rachel's tent.

wcj,nn7354   qpf3947   (853)   df,pl,nn**8655**   wcs,qmf,pnx7760   df,nn**1581**

34 Now Rachel had taken   the images, and   put   them in the camel's

pp,cs,nn**3733**   wcs,qmf3427 pr,pnx5921   nn3837   wcs,pimf4959 (853) cs,nn3605   df,nn**168**   qpf4672

furniture, and   sat   upon them. And Laban searched   all   the tent, but found

wcj,ptn**3808**

them not.

wcs,qmf**559**　pr413　　　　　nn,pnx1　　　　　ptn408　qcj**2734**/pp,du,cs,nn**5869**　　　nn,pnx113　cj3588

35 And she said to her father, Let it not displease my lord that I

ptn**3808**/qmf3201　pp,qnc**6965**　pr4480/pl,nn,pnx**6440**　cj3588　　cs,nn**1870**　　pl,nn**802**　　pp,pnx

cannot rise up before thee; for the custom of women is upon me. And he

wcs,pimf2664　　　qpf4672　wcj,ptn**3808**　(853)　　df,pl,nn**8655**

searched, but found not the images.

pp,nn3290　wcs,qmf**2734**　　wcs,qmf**7378**　　pp,nn3837　　nn3290　wcs,qmf6030

36 And Jacob was wroth, and chided with Laban: and Jacob answered and

wcs,qmf**559**　　pp,nn3837　pnit4100　　　nn,pnx**6588**　pnit4100　　　nn,pnx**2403**　cj3588

said to Laban, What is my trespass? what is my sin, that thou hast so

qpf1814　　pr,pnx310

hotly pursued after me?

cj3588　　　　　　pipf4959　(853)　cs,nn3605　　pl,nn,pnx3627　pnit4100　　　　qpf4672

37 Whereas thou hast searched all my stuff, what hast thou found

pr4480/cs,nn3605　　nn,pnx1004　pl,cs,nn3627　qmv**7760**　ad3541　pr5048　　pl,nn,pnx**251**　　wcj,pl,nn,pnx**251**

of all thy household stuff? set it here before my brethren and thy brethren,

wcj,himf**3198**　pr996　du,nu,pnx8147

that they may judge between us both.

pndm2088　pl,nu6242　nn8141　pnp595　　pr,pnx5973　　　pl,nn,pnx7353

38 This twenty years have I been with thee; thy ewes and thy

wcj,pl,nn,pnx5795　ptn**3808**　pipf7921　　　wcj,pl,cs,nn352　　nn,pnx6629　ptn**3808**

she goats have not cast*their*young, and the rams of thy flock have I not

qpf398

eaten.

nn2966　　　　hipf935　ptn**3808**　pr,pnx413　　pnp595　pimf,pnx**2398**

39 That which was torn of beasts I brought not unto thee; I bore*the*loss

pr4480/nn,pnx**3027**　pimf,pnx1245　　　　cs,qptp1589　　nn3117　　wcj,cs,qptp1589

of it; of*my*hand didst thou require it, whether stolen by day, or stolen by

nn**3915**

night.

qpf**1961**　dfp,nn3117　nn2721　qpf,pnx398　　　wcj,nn7140　dfp,nn**3915**

40 Thus I was; in the day the drought consumed me, and the frost by night;

nn,pnx8142　wcs,qmf5074　pr4480/du,nn,pnx**5869**

and my sleep departed from*mine*eyes.

pndm2088　pp,pnx　pl,nu6242　nn8141　　pp,nn,pnx1004　qpf,pnx5647　nu702/nu6240

41 Thus have I been twenty years in thy house; I served thee fourteen

nn8141　　pp,du,cs,nu8147　pl,nn,pnx1323　wcj,nu8337　pl,nn8141　pp,nn,pnx6629

years for thy two daughters, and six years for thy cattle: and thou hast

wcs,himf2498　(853)　nn,pnx4909　nu6235　pl,nn4489

changed my wages ten times.

cj3884　　pl,cs,nn**430**　nn,pnx1　pl,cs,nn**430**　nn85　　wcj,cs,nn**6343**

42 Except the God of my father, the God of Abraham, and the fear of

nn3327　qpf**1961**　pp,pnx　cj3588　　pipf,pnx7971　ad6258　ad7387　pl,nn**430**

Isaac, had been with me, surely thou hadst sent*me*away now empty. God hath

qpf**7200**　(853)　　nn,pnx6040　wcj(853)　cs,nn3018　du,nn,pnx3709　wcs,himf**3198**

seen mine affliction and the labor of my hands, and rebuked thee

ad570

last night.

Jacob's New Agreement With Laban

nn3837　wcs,qmf6030　pr413　nn3290　df,pl,nn1323

43 And Laban answered and said unto Jacob, These daughters are my

pl,nn,pnx1323　　wcj,df,pl,nn**1121**　　pl,nn,pnx**1121**　　wcj,df,nn6629　　nn,pnx6629

daughters, and these children are my children, and these cattle are my cattle,

wcj,nn3605 pnl834 pnp859 qpta7200 (pnp1931)   pp,pnx   pnit4100   qmf6213   df,nn3117   dfp,pndm428

and all that thou seest *is* mine: and what can I do this day unto these

wcj,pp,pl,nn,pnx1323 cj176   pp,pl,nn,pnx1121 pnl834   qpf3205

my daughters, or unto their children which they have born?

wcj,ad6258   qmv1980   qcj3772   nn1285   pnp589   wcj,pnp859

44 Now therefore come thou, let us make a covenant, I and thou; and let

wcs,qpf1961   pp,nn5707   pr,pnx996   wcj,pnx(pr996)

it be for a witness between me and thee.

nn3290 wcs,qmf3947   nn68   wcs,himf,pnx7311   nn4676

45 And Jacob took a stone, and set*it*up *for* a pillar.

nn3290   wcs,qmf559   pp,pl,nn,pnx251 qmv3950   pl,nn68   wcs,qmf3947 pl,nn68

46 And Jacob said unto his brethren, Gather stones; and they took stones,

wcs,qmf6213   nn1530   wcs,qmf398 ad8033 pr5921   df,nn1530

and made an heap: and they did eat there upon the heap.

nn3837   wcs,qmf7121 pp,pnx   nn3026   wcj,nn3290 qpf7121 pp,pnx   nn1567

47 And Laban called it Jegar-sahadutha: but Jacob called it Galeed.

nn3837   wcs,qmf559 df,pndm2088 df,nn1530   nn5707   pr,pnx996   wcj,pnx(pr996)

48 And Laban said, This heap *is* a witness between me and thee

df,nn3117 pr5921/ad3651   nn,pnx8034   qpf7121   nn1567

this day. Therefore was the name of it called Galeed;

wcj,df,nn4709 pnl834   qpf559   nn3068 qcj6822 pr,pnx996   wcj,pnx(pr996)

49 And Mizpah; for he said, The LORD watch between me and thee,

cj3588   nimf5641   nn376   pr4480/nn,pnx7453

when we are absent one from another.

cj518   pimf6031 (853)   pl,nn,pnx1323   wcj,cj518   qmf3947   pl,nn802

50 If thou shalt afflict my daughters, or if thou shalt take *other* wives

pr5921   pl,nn,pnx1323 ptn369 nn376   pr,pnx5973 qmv7200 pl,nn430   nn5707   pr,pnx996

beside my daughters, no man *is* with us; see, God *is* witness between me and

wcj,pnx(pr996)

thee.

nn3837   wcs,qmf559   pp,nn3290 ptdm2009 df,pndm2088 df,nn1530   wcj,ptdm2009   df,nn4676

51 And Laban said to Jacob, Behold this heap, and behold *this* pillar,

pnl834   qpf3384   pr,pnx996   wcj,pnx(pr996)

which I have cast between me and thee;

df,pndm2088 df,nn1530   nn5707   df,nn4676   wcj,nn5713   cj518 pnp589   ptn3808

52 This heap *be* witness, and *this* pillar *be* witness, that I will not

qmf5674   (853) df,pndm2088 df,nn1530 pr,pnx413   wcj,cj518 pnp859   ptn3808   qmf5674   (853)

pass over this heap to thee, and that thou shalt not pass over

df,pndm2088 df,nn1530   wcj(853) df,pndm2063 df,nn4676 pr,pnx413   pp,nn7451

this heap and this pillar unto me, for harm.

pl,cs,nn430   nn85   wcj,pl,cs,nn430   nn5152   pl,cs,nn430   nn,pnx1

53 The God of Abraham, and the God of Nahor, the God of their father,

qmf8199   pr,pnx996   nn3290 wcs,nimf7650   pp,cs,nn6343   nn,pnx1 nn3327

judge between us. And Jacob swore by the fear of his father Isaac.

nn3290 wcs,qmf2076   nn2077   dfp,nn2022   wcs,qmf7121   pp,pl,nn,pnx251

54 Then Jacob offered sacrifice upon the mount, and called his brethren to

pp,qnc398   nn3899   wcs,qmf398 nn3899   wcs,qmf3885   dfp,nn2022

eat bread: and they did eat bread, and tarried*all*night in the mount.

dfp,nn1242   nn3837   wcs,himf7925   wcs,pimf5401   pp,pl,nn,pnx1121

55 And early in the morning Laban rose up, and kissed his sons and his

wcj,pp,pl,nn,pnx1323   wcs,pimf1288   pnx(853)   nn3837   wcs,qmf1980   wcs,qmf7725

daughters, and blessed them: and Laban departed, and returned unto his

pp,nn,pnx4725

place.

Jacob Prepares To Meet Esau

32

wcj,nn3290 qpf**1980**   pp,nn,pnx**1870**   pl,cs,nn**4397**   pl,nn**430** wcs,qmf**6293** pp,pnx
And Jacob went on his way, and the angels of God met him.

pp,pnl834   nn3290   qpf,pnx**7200**   wcs,qmf559 pndm2088   pl,nn430   cs,nn**4264**
2 And when Jacob saw them, he said, This *is* God's host:

wcs,qmf**7121**   cs,nn8034   df,pndm1931 df,nn**4725**   nn4266
and he called the name of that place Mahanaim.

nn3290   wcs,qmf7971   pl,nn**4397**   pp,pl,nn,pnx**6440**   pr413   nn6215   nn,pnx**251**
3 And Jacob sent messengers before him to Esau his brother unto the

cs,nn,lh776   nn8165   cs,nn**7704**   nn123
land of Seir, the country of Edom.

wcs,pimf**6680**   pnx(853)   pp,qnc559   ad3541   qmf559   pp,nn,pnx113
4 And he commanded them, saying, Thus shall ye speak unto my lord

pp,nn6215   nn,pnx**5650**   nn3290   qpf**559**   ad3541   qpf**1481**   pr5973   nn3837   wcs,qmf309
Esau; Thy servant Jacob saith thus, I have sojourned with Laban, and stayed there

pr5704 ad6258
until now:

pp,pnx   wcs,qmf**1961**   nn7794   wcj,nn2543   nn6629   wcj,nn**5650**
5 And I have oxen, and asses, flocks, and menservants, and

wcj,nn8198   wcs,qmf7971   pp,hinc**5046**   pp,nn,pnx113   pp,qnc4672   nn2580
womenservants: and I have sent to tell my lord, that I may find grace in

pp,du,nn,pnx**5869**
thy sight.

df,pl,nn**4397**   wcs,qmf**7725** pr413   nn3290   pp,qnc**559**   qpf935 pr413   nn,pnx**251**   (pr413)
6 And the messengers returned to Jacob, saying, We came to thy brother

nn6215   wcj,ad1571   qpta**1980**   pp,qnc,pnx7125   wcj,nu702   pl,nu3967   nn376   pr,pnx5973
Esau, and also he cometh to meet thee, and four hundred men with him.

nn3290   wcs,qmf**3372**/ad3966   wcs,qmf3334/pp,pnx   wcs,qmf2673   (853)   df,nn**5971**
7 Then Jacob was*greatly*afraid and distressed: and he divided the people

pnl834   pr,pnx854   wcj(853)   df,nn6629   wcj(853)   df,nn1241   wcj,df,pl,nn1581
that *was* with him, and the flocks, and herds, and the camels, into

pp,du,cs,nu8147   pl,nn**4264**
two bands;

wcs,qmf**559**   cj518   nn6215   qmf935   pr413   df,nu259   df,nn**4264**   wcs,hipf,pnx**5221**
8 And said, If Esau come to the one company, and smite it, then

wcs(qpf**1961**)   df,nn**4264**   df,nipf**7604**   pp,nn**6413**
the other company which is left shall escape.

nn3290   wcs,qmf**559**   pl,cs,nn**430**   nn,pnx1   nn85   wcj,pl,cs,nn**430**   nn,pnx1
9 And Jacob said, O God of my father Abraham, and God of my father

nn3327   nn**3068**   df,qpta559 pr,pnx413   qmv**7725**   pp,nn,pnx776
Isaac, the LORD which saidst unto me, Return unto thy country, and to thy

wcj,pp,nn,pnx4138   wcj,hicj**3190**   pr,pnx5973
kindred, and I will deal well with thee:

qpf6994   pr4480/cs,nn3605   df,pl,nn**2617**   wcj,pr4480/cs,nn3605
10 I am not worthy of the least of all the mercies, and of all the

df,nn**571**   pnl834   qpf**6213**   (853)   nn,pnx**5650**   cj3588   pp,nn,pnx4731
truth, which thou hast showed unto thy servant; for with my staff I

qpf**5674**   (853) df,pndm2088   df,nn3383   wcj,ad6258   qpf**1961**   pp,du,cs,nu8147   pl,nn**4264**
passed over this Jordan; and now I am become two bands.

himv,pnx**5337**   pte**4994**   pr4480/cs,nn**3027**   nn,pnx**251**   pr4480/cs,nn**3027**
11 Deliver me, I*pray*thee, from*the*hand of my brother, from*the*hand of

nn6215   cj3588   pnp595   qpta**3372** pnx(853)   cj6435   qmf935   wcs,hipf,pnx**5221**   nn517
Esau: for I fear him, lest he will come and smite me, *and* the mother

pr5921   pl,nn1121
with the children.

wcj,pnp859 qpf559   hina3190/himf3190/pr,pnx5973   wcs,qpf7760 (853)   nn,pnx2233

12 And thou saidst, I will surely*do*thee*good, and make thy seed as

pp,cs,nn2344   df,nn3220 pnl834 ptn3808   nimf5608   pr4480/nn7230

the sand of the sea, which cannot be numbered for multitude.

wcs,qmf3885 ad8033   df,pndm1931 dfp,nn3915   wcs,qmf3947 pr4480   df,qpta935

13 And he lodged there that same night; and took of that which came to

pp,nn,pnx3027   nn4503   pp,nn6215   nn,pnx251

his hand a present for Esau his brother;

du,nu3967   pl,nn5795   pl,nu6242 wcj,pl,nn8495   du,nu3967   pl,nn7353

14 Two hundred she goats, and twenty he goats, two hundred ewes, and

pl,nu6242 wcj,pl,nn352

twenty rams,

nu7970   pl,hipt3243   pl,nn1581   wcj,pl,nn,pnx1121 pl,nu705 pl,nn6510   nu6235 wcj,pl,nn6499

15 Thirty milch camels with their colts, forty kine, and ten bulls,

pl,nu6242   pl,nn860   nu6235 wcj,pl,nn5895

twenty she asses, and ten foals.

wcs,qmf5414

16 And he delivered *them* into the hand of his servants, every drove

pp,nn,pnx905   wcs,qmf559 pr413   pl,nn,pnx5650 qmf5674 pp,pl,nn,pnx6440   qmf7760

by themselves; and said unto his servants, Pass over before me, and put a

wcj,nn7305   pr996   nn5739   wcj(pr996)   nn5739

space between drove and drove.

wcs,pimf6680 (853)   df,aj7223   pp,qnc559 cj3588   nn6215   nn,pnx251

17 And he commanded the foremost, saying, When Esau my brother

qmf,pnx6298   wcs,qpf,pnx7592   pp,qnc559 pp,pnit4310   pnp859   wcj,ad,lh575   qmf1980

meeteth thee, and asketh thee, saying, Whose *art* thou? and whither goest thou?

wcj,pp,pnit4310   pndm428 pp,pl,nn,pnx6440

and whose *are* these before thee?

wcs,qpf559   pp,nn,pnx5650   pp,nn3290 pnp1931   nn4503   qptp7971

18 Then thou shalt say, *They be* thy servant Jacob's; it *is* a present sent

pp,nn,pnx113 pp,nn6215   wcj,ptdm2009 ad1571 pnp1931   pr,pnx310

unto my lord Esau: and, behold, also he *is* behind us.

ad1571   wcs,pimf6680   (853)   df,nuor8145 ad1571 (853)   df,nuor7992 ad1571 (853) cs,nn3605

19 And so commanded he the second, and the third, and all

df,pl,qpta1980/pr310   df,pl,nn5739 pp,qnc559   df,pndm2088 dfp,nn1697   pimf1696 pr413 nn6215

that followed the droves, saying, On this manner shall ye speak unto Esau,

pp,qnc,pnx4672 pnx(853)

when ye find him.

wcs,qpf559   ad1571 ptdm2009   nn,pnx5650 nn3290 *is* pr,pnx310   cj3588

20 And say ye moreover, Behold, thy servant Jacob *is* behind us. For he

qpf559   picj3722/pl,nn,pnx6440   dfp,nn4503   df,qpta1980 pp,pl,nn,pnx6440

said, I will appease him with the present that goeth before me, and

wcj,ad310/ad3651   qmf7200   pl,nn,pnx6440   ad194   qmf5375/pl,nn,pnx6440

afterward I will see his face; peradventure he will accept of me.

wcs,qmf5674   df,nn4503   pr5921/pl,nn,pnx6440   wcj,pnp1931 qpf3885 df,pndm1931

21 So went the present over before him: and himself lodged that

dfp,nn3915   dfp,nn4264

night in the company.

Jacob Wrestles With God

wcs,qmf6965 pndm1931 dfp,nn3915   wcs,qmf3947 (853)   du,cs,nu8147 pl,nn,pnx802   wcj(853)

22 And he rose up that night, and took his two wives, and his

32:22–32 The events at the ford Jabbok represent a climactic point in Jacob's spiritual growth. He proved that he could persevere and overcome without cheating. He saw that his own strength was futile and he humbly

du,cs,nu8147   pl,nn,pnx8198   wcj(853)   nu259/nu6240 pl,nn,pnx3206   wcs,qmf5674   (853)   cs,nn4569

two   womenservants, and   his eleven   sons,   and passed over   the ford

nn2999

Jabbok.

wcs,qmf,pnx3947   wcs,himf,pnx5674   (853)   df,nn5158   wcs,himf5674   (853)

23 And he   took   them, and sent*them*over   the brook, and sent over

pnl834 pp,pnx

that he had.

nn3290   wcs,nimf3498 pp,nn,pnx905   wcs,nimf79   nn376 pr,pnx5973   pr5704

24 And Jacob was   left   alone; and there wrestled a man   with him until the

qnc5927   df,nn7837

breaking of the day.

wcs,qmf7200 cj3588   qpf3201   ptn3808   pp,pnx   wcs,qmf5060

25 And when he   saw   that he prevailed not against him, he touched the

pp,cs,nn3709   nn,pnx3409   cs,nn3709   nn3290 cs,nn3409   wcs,qmf3363

hollow of his thigh; and the hollow of Jacob's thigh was out*of*joint, as he

pp,ninc,pnx79 pr,pnx5973

wrestled with him.

wcs,qmf559   pimv,pnx7971   cj3588   df,nn7837   qpf5927   wcs,qmf559   ptn3808

26 And he said, Let*me*go, for the day breaketh. And he said, I will not

pimf,pnx7971   cj3588/cj518   pipf,pnx1288

let*thee*go, except thou bless me.

wcs,qmf559 pr,pnx413   pnit4100   nn,pnx8034   wcs,qmf559 nn3290

27 And he said unto him, What is thy name? And he said, Jacob.

wcs,qmf559   nn,pnx8034   nimf559 ptn3808 ad5750   nn3290 cj3588/cj518   nn3478

28 And he said, Thy name shall be called no more Jacob,   but   Israel:

cj3588   qpf8280   pr5973 pl,nn430   wcj,pr5973 pl,nn376   wcs,qmf3201

for as*a*prince*hast*thou*power with God and with men, and hast prevailed.

nn3290 wcs,qmf7592   wcs,qmf559 himv5046   pte4994   nn,pnx8034

29 And Jacob asked him, and said,   Tell me, I*pray*thee, thy name. And he

wcs,qmf559   pp,pnit4100   pndm2088   qmf7592   pp,nn,pnx8034   wcs,pimf1288

said, Wherefore is   it   that thou dost ask after my name? And he blessed

pnx(853)   ad8033

him there.

nn3290 wcs,qmf7121   cs,nn8034   df,nn4725   nn6439   cj3588   qpf7200 pl,nn430 pl,nn6440

30 And Jacob called the name of the place Peniel: for I have seen God face

pr413 pl,nn6440   nn,pnx5315   wcs,nimf5337

to face, and my life is preserved.

pp,pnl834   qpf5674   (853)   nn6439   df,nn8121 wcs,qmf2224   pp,pnx

31 And   as   he passed over   Penuel the   sun   rose   upon him, and

wcj,pnp1931 qpta6760 pr5921   nn,pnx3409

he   halted upon his thigh.

pr5921/ad3651   pl,cs,nn1121   nn3478 qmf398 ptn3808   (853)   cs,nn1517   df,nn5384

32 Therefore the children of Israel eat not of   the sinew which shrank,

pnl834   pr5921   cs,nn3709   df,nn3409 pr5704 df,pndm2088 df,nn3117 cj3588   qpf5060

which is upon the hollow of the thigh, unto   this   day: because he touched the

pp,cs,nn3709   nn3290 cs,nn3409   pp,cs,nn1517   df,nn5384

hollow of Jacob's thigh in the sinew that shrank.

---

sought help from God. From his salvation at Bethel (see the note on Genesis 28:10–22) to this point, Jacob had undergone tremendous spiritual growth. He was a different man than the one who had supplanted his brother through deceit. Therefore, God gave to him a new name, Israel ("he who strives with God").

Jacob Meets Esau

33

nn3290 wcs,qmf5375 du,nn,pnx5869 wcs,qmf7200 wcj,ptdm2009 nn6215 qpta935
And Jacob lifted up his eyes, and looked, and, behold, Esau came,

wcj,pr,pnx5973 nu702 pl,nu3967 nn376 wcs,qmf2673 (853) df,pl,nn3206
and with him four hundred men. And he divided the children

pr5921 nn3812 wcj,pr5921 nn7354 wcj,pr5921 du,cs,nu8147 df,pl,nn8198
unto Leah, and unto Rachel, and unto the two handmaids.

wcs,qmf7760 (853) df,pl,nn8198 wcj(853) pl,nn,pnx3206 aj7223 wcj(853)
2 And he put the handmaids and their children foremost, and

nn3812 wcj,pl,nn,pnx3206 aj314 wcj(853) nn7354 wcj(853) nn3130 aj314
Leah and her children after, and Rachel and Joseph hindmost.

wcj,pnp1931 qpf5674 pp,pl,nn,pnx6440 wcs,htmf*7812 nn,lh776
3 And he passed over before them, and bowed himself to the ground

nu7651 pl,nn6471 cj5704 qnc,pnx5066 pr5704 nn,pnx251
seven times, until he came near to his brother.

nn6215 wcs,qmf7323 pp,qnc,pnx7125 wcs,pimf,pnx2263 wcs,qmf5307 pr5921
4 And Esau ran to meet him, and embraced him, and fell on his

nn,pnx6677 wcs,qmf,pnx5401 wcs,qmf1058
neck, and kissed him: and they wept.

wcs,qmf5375 (853) du,nn,pnx5869 wcs,qmf7200 (853) df,pl,nn802 wcj(853) the
5 And he lifted up his eyes, and saw the women and the

df,pl,nn3206 wcs,qmf559 pnit4310 pndm428 pp,pnx wcs,qmf559 df,pl,nn3206 pnl834
children; and said, Who are those with thee? And he said, The children which

pl,nn430 qpf2603 (853) nn,pnx5650
God hath graciously given thy servant.

df,pl,nn8198 wcs,qmf5066 pnp2007 wcj,pl,nn,pnx3206
6 Then the handmaidens came near, they and their children, and they

wcs,htmf*7812
bowed themselves.

nn3812 ad1571 wcj,pl,nn,pnx3206 wcs,qmf5066 wcs,htmf*7812
7 And Leah also with her children came near, and bowed themselves: and

wcj,ad310 nipf5066/nn3130 wcj,nn7354 wcs,htmf*7812
after came*Joseph*near and Rachel, and they bowed themselves.

wcs,qmf559 pnit4310 pp,pnx cs,nn3605 df,pndm2088 df,nn4264 pnl834 qpf6298
8 And he said, What meanest thou by all this drove which I met? And

wcs,qmf559 pp,qnc4672 nn2580 pp,du,cs,nn5869 nn,pnx113
he said, These are to find grace in the sight of my lord.

nn6215 wcs,qmf559 pp,pnx pta3426 aj7227 nn,pnx251 qmf1961 pnl834 pp,pnx
9 And Esau said, I have enough, my brother; keep that thou hast

pp,pnx
unto thyself.

nn3290 wcs,qmf559 ptn408 pte4994 cj518 pte4994 qpf4672 nn2580
10 And Jacob said, Nay, I*pray*thee, if now I have found grace in thy

pp,du,nn,pnx5869 wcj,qpf3947 nn,pnx4503 pr4480/nn,pnx3027 cj3588 pr5921/ad3651 qpf7200
sight, then receive my present at*my*hand: for therefore I have seen thy

pl,nn,pnx6440 pp,qnc7200 pl,cs,nn6440 pl,nn430 wcs,qmf,pnx7521
face, as though I had seen the face of God, and thou wast pleased with me.

qmv3947 pte4994 (853) nn,pnx1293 pnl834 hopf935 pp,pnx cj3588 pl,nn430
11 Take, I*pray*thee, my blessing that is brought to thee; because God

qpf,pnx2603 wcj,cj3588 pp,pnx pta3426 nn3605 wcs,qmf6484 pp,pnx
hath dealt graciously with me, and because I have enough. And he urged him,

wcs,qmf3947
and he took it.

^{wcs,qmf559}   ^{qcj5265}   ^{wcj,qcj1980}   ^{wcj,qcj1980}

12 And he said, Let us take*our*journey, and let us go, and I will go

^{pp,pr,pnx5048}

before thee.

^{wcs,qmf559} ^{pr,pnx413}   ^{nn,pnx113} ^{qpta3045}   ^{cj3588}   ^{df,pl,nn3206}   ^{aj7390}

13 And he said unto him, My lord knoweth that the children *are* tender,

^{wcj,df,nn6629}   ^{wcj,df,nn1241}   ^{pl,qpta5763}   ^{pr,pnx5921}   ^{wcj,qpf,pnx1849}

and the flocks and herds with young *are* with me: and if men should overdrive

^{nu259 nn3117} ^{cs,nn3605}   ^{df,nn6629}   ^{wcs,qpf4191}

them one day, all the flock will die.

^{nn,pnx113}   ^{pte4994}   ^{qmf5674}   ^{pp,pl,cs,nn6440}   ^{nn,pnx5650}   ^{wcj,pnp589}

14 Let my lord, I*pray*thee, pass over before his servant: and I will

^{htcj5095}   ^{pp,nn,pnx328}   ^{pp,cs,nn7272}   ^{df,nn4399} ^{pnl834}   ^{pp,pl,nn,pnx6440}   ^{df,pl,nn3206}

lead on softly, according as the cattle that goeth before me and the children be

^{wcj,pp,cs,nn7272} ^{pr5704/pnl834}   ^{qmf935} ^{pr413}   ^{nn,pnx113}   ^{nn,lh8165}

able to endure, until I come unto my lord unto Seir.

ⁿⁿ⁶²¹⁵ ^{wcs,qmf559}   ^{pte4994} ^{hicj3322} ^{pr,pnx5973}   ^{pr4480}   ^{df,nn5971} ^{pnl834}

15 And Esau said, Let me now leave with thee *some* of the folk that *are*

^{pr,pnx854}   ^{wcs,qmf559} ^{pp,pnit4100}   ^{pndm2088}   ^{qmf4672} ⁿⁿ²⁵⁸⁰   ^{pp,du,cs,nn5869}

with me. And he said, What needeth it? let me find grace in the sight of

^{nn,pnx113}

my lord.

ⁿⁿ⁶²¹⁵   ^{wcs,qmf7725} ^{df,pndm1931} ^{dfp,nn3117}   ^{pp,nn,pnx1870}   ^{nn,lh8165}

16 So Esau returned that day on his way unto Seir.

^{wcj,nn3290}   ^{qpf5265}   ^{nn,lh5523}   ^{wcs,qmf1129} ^{pp,pnx}   ⁿⁿ¹⁰⁰⁴   ^{qpf6213} ^{pl,nn5521}

17 And Jacob journeyed to Succoth, and built him a house, and made booths

^{wcj,pp,nn,pnx4735} ^{pr5921/ad3651}   ^{cs,nn8034}   ^{df,nn4725} ^{qpf7121}   ⁿⁿ⁵⁵²³

for his cattle: therefore the name of the place is called Succoth.

ⁿⁿ³²⁹⁰ ^{wcs,qmf935}   ^{aj8003}   ^{cs,nn5892}   ⁿⁿ⁷⁹²⁷   ^{pnl834}   ^{pp,cs,nn776}

18 And Jacob came to Shalem, a city of Shechem, which *is* in the land of

ⁿⁿ³⁶⁶⁷   ^{pp,qnc,pnx935}   ^{pr4480/nn6307}   ^{wcs,qmf2583}   ⁽⁸⁵³⁾ ^{pl,cs,nn6440}

Canaan, when he came from Padan-aram; and pitched*his*tent before the

^{df,nn5892}

city.

^{wcs,qmf7069} ⁽⁸⁵³⁾   ^{cs,nn2513}   ^{df,nn7704} ^{pnl834/ad8033}   ^{qpf5186}   ^{nn,pnx168}

19 And he bought a parcel of a field, where he had spread his tent,

^{pr4480/cs,nn3027}   ^{pl,cs,nn1121}   ⁿⁿ²⁵⁴⁴   ⁿⁿ⁷⁹²⁷   ^{cs,nn1}   ^{pp,nu3967}

at*the*hand of the children of Hamor, Shechem's father, for a hundred

ⁿⁿ⁷¹⁹²

pieces*of*money.

^{wcs,himf5324} ^{ad8033}   ⁿⁿ⁴¹⁹⁶   ^{wcs,qmf7121} ^{pp,pnx} ⁿⁿ⁴¹⁵ [^{nn410/pl,cs,nn430/nn3478}]

20 And he erected there an altar, and called it El-elohe-Israel.

Dinah Is Raped

ⁿⁿ¹⁷⁸³   ^{cs,nn1323}   ⁿⁿ³⁸¹² ^{pnl834}   ^{qpf3205}   ^{pp,nn3290}

34 And Dinah the daughter of Leah, which she bore unto Jacob,

^{wcs,qmf3318}   ^{pp,qnc7200}   ^{pp,pl,cs,nn1323}   ^{df,nn776}

went out to see the daughters of the land.

ⁿⁿ⁷⁹²⁷   ^{cs,nn1121}   ⁿⁿ²⁵⁴⁴   ^{df,nn2340} ^{cs,nn5387}   ^{df,nn776}

2 And when Shechem the son of Hamor the Hivite, prince of the country,

^{wcs,qmf7200} ^{pnx(853)}   ^{wcs,qmf3947} ^{pnx(853)}   ^{wcs,qmf7901} ^{pnx(853)}   ^{wcs,pimf,pnx6031}

saw her, he took her, and lay with her, and defiled her.

nn,pnx5315 wcs,qmf1692 pp,nn1783 cs,nn1323 nn3290 wcs,qmf157 (853)

3 And his soul cleaved unto Dinah the daughter of Jacob, and he loved

df,nn5291 wcs,pimf1696 pr5921/cs,nn3820 df,nn5291

the damsel, and spoke kindly unto the damsel.

nn7927 wcs,qmf559 pr413 nn,pnx1 nn2544 pp,qnc559 qmv3947 pp,pnx (853) df,pndm2063

4 And Shechem spoke unto his father Hamor, saying, Get me this

df,nn3207 pp,nn802

damsel to wife.

wcj,nn3290 qpf8085 cj3588 pipf2930 (853) nn1783 nn,pnx1323

5 And Jacob heard that he had defiled Dinah his daughter: now his

wcj,pl,nn,pnx1121 qpf1961 pr854 nn,pnx4735 dfp,nn7704 nn3290 wcj,hipf2790 pr5704

sons were with his cattle in the field: and Jacob held*his*peace until they

qnc,pnx935

were come.

nn2544 cs,nn1 nn7927 wcs,qmf3318 pr413 nn3290 pp,pinc1696 pr,pnx854

6 And Hamor the father of Shechem went out unto Jacob to commune with

him.

wcj,pl,cs,nn1121 nn3290 qpf935 pr4480 df,nn7704 pp,qnc,pnx8085

7 And the sons of Jacob came out of the field when they heard it: and

df,pl,nn376 wcs,htmf6087 pp,pnx wcs,qmf2734/ad3966 cj3588 qpf6213 nn5039

the men were grieved, and they were*very*wroth, because he had wrought folly in

pp,nn3478 pp,qnc7901 (853) nn3290 cs,nn1323 wcj,ad3651 ptn3808 nimf6213

Israel in lying with Jacob's daughter; which thing ought not to be done.

nn2544 wcs,pimf1696 pr,pnx854 pp,qnc559 nn,pnx5315 nn,pnx1121 nn7927

8 And Hamor communed with them, saying, The soul of my son Shechem

qpf2836 pp,nn,pnx1323 pte4994 qmv5414 pnx(853) pp,pnx pp,nn802

longeth for your daughter: I*pray*you give her him to wife.

wcj,htmv2859 pr,pnx854 qmf5414 pl,nn,pnx1323 pp,pnx qmf3947

9 And make*ye*marriages with us, and give your daughters unto us, and take

wcj(853) pl,nn,pnx1323 pp,pnx

our daughters unto you.

qmf3427 wcj,pr,pnx854 wcj,df,nn776 qmf1961 pp,pl,nn,pnx6440

10 And ye shall dwell with us: and the land shall be before you;

qmv3427 wcj,qmv,pnx5503 wcj,nimv270 pp,pnx

dwell and trade ye therein, and get*you*possessions therein.

nn7927 wcs,qmf559 pr413 nn,pnx1 wcj,pr413 pl,nn,pnx251 qmf4672

11 And Shechem said unto her father and unto her brethren, Let me find

nn2580 pp,du,nn,pnx5869 wcj,pnl834 qmf559 pr,pnx413 qmf5414

grace in your eyes, and what ye shall say unto me I will give.

himv7235/pr,pnx5921 ad3966 nn4119 wcj,nn4976 wcj,qcj5414

12 Ask me never*so*much dowry and gift, and I will give

pp,pnl834 qmf559 pr,pnx413 wcj,qmv5414 pp,pnx (853) df,nn5291 pp,nn802

according as ye shall say unto me: but give me the damsel to wife.

pl,cs,nn1121 nn3290 wcs,qmf6030 (853) nn7927 wcj(853) nn2544 nn,pnx1

13 And the sons of Jacob answered Shechem and Hamor his father

pp,nn4820 wcs,pimf1696 pnl834 pipf2930 (853) nn1783 nn,pnx269

deceitfully, and said, because he had defiled Dinah their sister:

wcs,qmf559 pr,pnx413 ptn3808/qmf3201 pp,qnc6213 df,pndm2088 df,nn1697 pp,qnc5414 (853)

14 And they said unto them, We cannot do this thing, to give

nn,pnx269 pp,nn376 pnl834 pp,pnx/nn6190 cj3588 pndm1931 nn2781 pp,pnx

our sister to one that is uncircumcised; for that were a reproach unto us:

ad389 pp,pndm2063 nimf225 pp,pnx cj518 qmf1961 pp,pnx

15 But in this will we consent unto you: If ye will be as we be, that

cs,nn3605 nn2145 pp,pnx pp,ninc4135

every male of you be circumcised;

_{wcs,qpf**5414** (853)   pl,nn,pnx1323   pp,pnx   qmf3947 wcj(853)}
16 Then will we   give   our daughters unto you, and we will take

_{pl,nn,pnx1323   pp,pnx   wcs,qpf**3427** pr,pnx854   wcs,qpf**1961**   nu259}
your daughters to us, and we will dwell with you, and we will become one

_{pp,nn5971}
people.

_{wcj,cj518   ptn**3808**   qmf**8085**   pr,pnx413   pp,ninc**4135**}
17 But   if   ye will not hearken unto us, to be circumcised; then will we

_{wcs,qpf3947 (853)   nn,pnx1323   wcs,qpf**1980**}
take   our daughter, and we will be gone.

_{pl,nn,pnx**1697** wcs,qmf**3190**/pp,du,cs,nn**5869**   nn2544   wcj(pp,du,cs,nn**5869**)   nn7927   nn2544}
18 And their words   pleased   Hamor, and   Shechem Hamor's

_{cs,nn1121}
son.

_{df,nn5288   pipf309   wcj,ptn**3808**   pp,qnc**6213**   df,nn**1697**   cj3588}
19 And the young man deferred   not   to   do   the thing, because he

_{qpf**2654**   nn3290   pp,cs,nn1323   wcj,pnp1931   nipt**3513**   pr4480/cs,nn**3605**}
had delight in Jacob's daughter: and   he   *was* more honorable than all the

_{cs,nn**1004**   nn,pnx1}
house of his father.

_{nn2544   wcj,nn7927   nn,pnx**1121** wcs,qmf935   pr413   cs,nn8179   nn,pnx5892}
20 And Hamor and Shechem his   son   came unto the gate of their city,

_{wcs,pimf**1696**   pr413   pl,cs,nn**376**   nn,pnx5892   pp,qnc559}
and commoned with the men of their city, saying,

_{df,pndm428 df,pl,nn**376** (pnp1992)   aj**8003**   pr,pnx854   wcj,qmf**3427**}
21 These men   *are* peaceable with us; therefore let them dwell in the

_{dfp,nn776   wcj,qmf5503 pnx(853)   wcj,df,nn**776**   ptdm2009   cs,aj**7342**/du,nn**3027** pp,pl,nn,pnx**6440**}
land, and   trade   therein; for the land, behold, *it is* large enough   for

_{qmf3947 (853)   pl,nn,pnx1323   pp,pnx   pp,pl,nn**802**   qmf**5414** pp,pnx wcj(853)}
them; let us take   their daughters to us for wives, and let us give them   our

_{pl,nn,pnx1323}
daughters.

_{ad389 pp,pndm2063   df,pl,nn**376**   nimf225   pp,pnx   pp,qnc**3427** pr,pnx854   pp,qnc**1961**}
22 Only herein will the men   consent unto us for to dwell with us, to   be

_{nu259 pp,nn**5971**   cs,nn3605 nn2145   pp,pnx   pp,ninc**4135**   pp,pnl834 pnp1992   pl,nipt**4135**}
one people, if every male among us be circumcised,   as   they *are* circumcised.

_{he,ptn**3808**   pl,nn,pnx4735   wcj,nn,pnx7075   wcj,cs,nn3605   nn,pnx929}
23 *Shall* not their cattle and their substance and every   beast of theirs

_{(pnp1992)   pp,pnx   ad389   nicj225   pp,pnx   wcj,qmf**3427** pr,pnx854}
be ours? only let us consent unto them, and they will dwell with us.

_{pr413   nn2544   wcj,pr413   nn7927   nn,pnx**1121**   wcs,qmf**8085** cs,nn3605}
24 And unto Hamor and unto Shechem his   son   hearkened all   that

_{pl,cs,qpta3318   cs,nn8179   nn,pnx5892   cs,nn3605 nn2145   wcs,nimf**4135**   cs,nn3605}
went out of the gate of his city; and every male was circumcised,   all   that

_{pl,cs,qpta3318   cs,nn8179   nn,pnx5892}
went out of the gate of his city.

_{wcs,qmf**1961**   df,nuor7992   dfp,nn3117   pp,qnc,pnx**1961** pl,qpta3510}
25 And it*came*to*pass on the third day, when they were   sore, that

_{du,cs,nu8147   pl,cs,nn**1121**   nn3290   nn8095   wcj,nn3878   nn1783   pl,cs,nn**251** wcs,qmf3947}
two of the sons of Jacob, Simeon and Levi, Dinah's brethren,   took

_{nn376   nn,pnx**2719**   wcs,qmf935 pr5921   df,nn5892   nn983   wcs,qmf**2026** cs,nn3605   nn2145}
each man his sword, and came upon the city boldly, and slew   all the males.

_{qpf**2026** wcj(853)   nn2544   wcj(853)   nn7927   nn,pnx**1121**   pp,cs,nn**6310**}
26 And they slew   Hamor and   Shechem his son with the edge of

_{nn**2719**   wcs,qmf3947 (853)   nn1783   nn7927   pr4480/cs,nn**1004**   wcs,qmf3318}
the sword, and took   Dinah out of Shechem's house, and went out.

pl,cs,nn**1121**   nn3290   qpf935   pr5921   df,pl,nn2491   wcs,qmf962   df,nn5892   pnl834

27 The sons of Jacob came upon the slain, and spoiled the city, because

pipf**2930**   nn,pnx**269**

they had defiled their sister.

qpf3947 (853)   nn,pnx6629   wcj(853)   nn,pnx1241   wcj(853)   pl,nn,pnx2543

28 They took their sheep, and their oxen, and their asses, and

wcj(853)   pnl834   dfp,nn5892   wcj(853)   pnl834   dfp,nn**7704**

that which *was* in the city, and that which *was* in the field,

wcj(853)   cs,nn3605   nn,pnx**2428**   wcj(853)   cs,nn3605   nn,pnx**2945**   wcj(853)

29 And all their wealth, and all their little ones, and their

pl,nn,pnx**802**   qpf**7617**   wcs,qmf962   wcj(853)   cs,nn3605 pnl834   dfp,nn**1004**

wives took*they*captive, and spoiled even all that *was* in the house.

nn3290   wcs,qmf**559**   pr413   nn8095   wcj(pr413)   nn3878   qpf5916   pnx(853)

30 And Jacob said to Simeon and Levi, Ye have troubled me to

pp,hinc,pnx**887**   pp,cs,qpta**3427**   df,nn776   dfp,nn3669

make me to stink among the inhabitants of the land, among the Canaanites and

wcj,dfp,nn6522   wcj,pnp589   pl,cs,nn4962   nn4557

the Perizzites: and I *being* few in number, they shall

wcj,nipf**622**   pr,pnx5921   wcj,hipf,pnx**5221**   wcj,nipf**8045**

gather*themselves*together against me, and slay me; and I shall be destroyed,

pnp589   wcj,nn,pnx**1004**

I and my house.

wcs,qmf**559**   qmf**6213**   (853)   nn,pnx**269**   he,pp,qpta**2181**

31 And they said, Should he deal with our sister as with an harlot?

Jacob Returns to Bethel

pl,nn**430**   wcs,qmf**559**   pr413   nn3290   qmv**6965**   qmv**5927**   nn1008   wcj,qmv**3427**

35 And God said unto Jacob, Arise, go up to Bethel, and dwell

ad8033   wcj,qmv**6213**   ad8033   nn4196   dfp,nn**410**   df,nipt**7200**   pr,pnx413

there: and make there an altar unto God, that appeared unto thee

pp,qnc,pnx1272   pr4480/pl,cs,nn**6440**   nn6215   nn,pnx**251**

when thou fleddest from*the*face of Esau thy brother.

nn3290   wcs,qmf**559**   pr413   nn,pnx**1004**   wcj,pr413 cs,nn3605 pnl834   pr,pnx5973

2 Then Jacob said unto his household, and to all that *were* with him,

himv**5493**   (853)   df,nn**5236**   pl,cs,nn**430** pnl834   pp,nn,pnx**8432**   wcj,htmv**2891**   wcj,himv2498

Put away the strange gods that *are* among you, and be clean, and change

pl,nn,pnx8071

your garments:

wcj,qcj**6965**   wcj,qcj**5927**   nn1008   wcj,qmf**6213**   ad8033   nn4196

3 And let us arise, and go up to Bethel; and I will make there an altar unto

dfp,nn**410**   df,qpta6030   pnx(853)   pp,cs,nn3117   nn,pnx6869   wcs,qmf1961 pr,pnx5973

God, who answered me in the day of my distress, and was with me in

dfp,nn**1870** pnl834   qpf**1980**

the way which I went.

wcs,qmf**5414**   pr413   nn3290   (853) cs,nn3605   df,nn**5236**   pl,cs,nn**430**   pnl834

4 And they gave unto Jacob all the strange gods which *were* in their

pp,nn,pnx**3027**   wcj(853) df,pl,nn5141   pnl834   pp,du,nn,pnx**241**   nn3290   wcs,qmf2934

hand, and *all their* earrings which *were* in their ears; and Jacob hid

pnx(853)   pr8478   df,nn424   pnl834   pr5973   nn7927

them under the oak which *was* by Shechem.

wcs,qmf5265   cs,nn**2847**   pl,nn**430** wcs,qmf1961   pr5921   df,pl,nn5892 pnl834

5 And they journeyed: and the terror of God was upon the cities that *were*

pr,pnx5439   wcj,ptn**3808**   qpf7291   pr310   pl,cs,nn**1121**   nn3290

round about them, and they did not pursue after the sons of Jacob.

nn3290   wcs,qmf935   nn,lh3870   pnl834   pp,cs,nn**776**   nn3667   pnp1931   nn1008

6 So Jacob came to Luz, which *is* in the land of Canaan, that *is*, Bethel,

pnp1931   wcj,cs,nn3605   df,nn**5971**   pnl834   pr,pnx5973

he and all the people that *were* with him.

       wcs,qmf1129   ad8033   nn**4196**   wcs,qmf**7121**   dfp,nn4725   nn416 [nn**410**/nn1008]   cj3588

7 And he built there an altar, and called the place El-bethel: because

ad8033   df,pl,nn**430**   nipf**1540**   pr,pnx413   pp,qnc,pnx1272   pr4480/pl,cs,nn**6440**   nn,pnx**251**

there God appeared unto him, when he fled from*the*face of his brother.

      nn1683   nn7259   cs,hipt3243   wcs,qmf**4191**   wcs,nimf**6912**   pr4480/pr8478   pp,nn1008

8 But Deborah Rebekah's nurse died, and she was buried beneath Bethel

pr8478   df,nn437   nn,pnx8034   wcs,qmf**7121**   nn439

under an oak: and the name of it was called Allon-bachuth.

       pl,nn**430**   wcs,nimf**7200**   pr413   nn3290   ad5750   pp,qnc,pnx935   pr4480/nn6307

9 And God appeared unto Jacob again, when he came out*of*Padan-aram,

wcs,pimf**1288** pnx(853)

and blessed   him.

       pl,nn**430**   wcs,qmf**559**   pp,pnx   nn,pnx8034   nn3290   nn,pnx8034   ptn**3808**

10 And God said unto him, Thy name *is* Jacob: thy name shall not be

nimf**7121**   ad5750   nn3290   cj3588/cj518   nn3478   qmf**1961**   nn,pnx8034   wcs,qmf**7121**   (853)

called any more Jacob, but Israel shall be thy name: and he called   his

nn,pnx8034   nn3478

name Israel.

       pl,nn**430**   wcs,qmf**559**   pp,pnx   pnp589   nn**410**   nn**7706**   qmv6509   wcj,qmv7235

11 And God said unto him, I *am* God Almighty: be fruitful and multiply;

nn**1471**   wcj,cs,nn**6951**   pl,nn**1471**   qmf**1961**   pr,pnx4480   wcj,pl,nn**4428**

a nation and a company of nations shall be of thee, and kings shall

qmf3318   pr4480/du,nn,pnx2504

come out of*thy*loins;

       wcj(853)   df,nn**776**   pnl834   qpf**5414**   pp,nn85   wcj,pp,nn3327   pp,pnx   qmf,pnx**5414**

12 And   the land which I gave Abraham and Isaac, to thee I will give

        wcj,pp,nn,pnx**2233** pr,pnx310   qmf**5414** (853)   df,nn**776**

it, and to thy seed after thee will I give the land.

       pl,nn**430**   wcs,qmf**5927**   pr4480/pr,pnx5921   dfp,nn4725   pnl834   pipf**1696**   pr,pnx854

13 And God went up from him in the place where he talked with him.

       nn3290   wcs,himf**5324**   nn**4676**   dfp,nn4725   pnl834   pipf**1696**   pr,pnx854

14 And Jacob set up a pillar in the place where he talked with him, *even* a

cs,nn**4678**   nn68   wcs,himf**5258**   nn**5262**   pr,pnx5921   wcs,qmf3332   nn**8081**   pr,pnx5921

pillar of stone: and he poured a drink offering thereon, and he poured oil thereon.

       nn3290   wcs,qmf**7121**   (853)   cs,nn8034   df,nn4725   pnl834   pl,nn**430**   pipf**1696**   pr,pnx854

15 And Jacob called   the name of the place where God spoke with him,

(ad8033)   nn1008

Bethel.

Rachel Dies

        wcs,qmf5265   pr4480/nn1008   wcs,qmf**1961**   ad5750   cs,nn3530/df,nn**776**

16 And they journeyed from Bethel; and there was but a little way to

pp,qnc935   nn,lh672   nn7354   wcs,qmf3205   wcs,pimf7185   pp,qnc,pnx3205

come to Ephrath: and Rachel travailed, and she had hard labor.

         wcs,qmf**1961**   pp,hinc,pnx7185   pp,qnc,pnx3205   df,pipt3205

17 And it*came*to*pass, when she was*in*hard labor, that the midwife

wcs,qmf**559**   pp,pnx   qmf**3372** ptn408 (cj3588)   pp,pnx   pndm2088 nn**1121** ad1571

said unto her, Fear not; thou shalt have this son also.

wcs,qmf**1961**   nn,pnx**5315**   pp,qnc3318   cj3588   qpf**4191**

18 And it*came*to*pass, as her soul was in departing, (for she died) that she

wcs,qmf**7121**   nn,pnx**8034**   nn1126   wcj,nn,pnx1   qpf**7121**   pp,pnx   nn1144

called his name Ben-oni: but his father called him Benjamin.

nn7354   wcs,qmf**4191**   wcs,nimf**6912**   pp,nn**1870**   nn,lh672   pnp1931

19 And Rachel died, and was buried in the way to Ephrath, which *is*

nn1035

Bethlehem.

nn3290   wcs,himf**5324**   nn4676   pr5921   nn,pnx**6900**   pnp1931   cs,nn**4678**   nn7354

20 And Jacob set a pillar upon her grave: that *is* the pillar of Rachel's

cs,nn**6900**   pr5704   df,nn**3117**

grave unto this day.

nn3478   wcs,qmf5265   wcs,qmf5186   nn,pnx168   pr4480/ad1973   pp,cs,nn4026   nn4029

21 And Israel journeyed, and spread his tent beyond the tower of Edar.

Jacob's Sons

wcs,qmf**1961**   nn3478   pp,qnc**7931**   df,pndm1931   dfp,nn**776**   nn7205

22 And it*came*to*pass, when Israel dwelt in that land, that Reuben

wcs,qmf**1980**   wcs,qmf7901   (853)   nn1090   nn,pnx1   cs,nn**6370**   nn3478   wcs,qmf**8085**

went and lay with Bilhah his father's concubine: and Israel heard *it*. Now the

pl,cs,nn**1121**   nn3290   wcs,qmf**1961**   du,nu8147/nu6240

sons of Jacob were twelve:

pl,cs,nn**1121**   nn3812   nn7205   nn3290   cs,nn1060   wcj,nn8095   wcj,nn3878

23 The sons of Leah; Reuben, Jacob's firstborn, and Simeon, and Levi, and

wcj,nn3063   wcj,nn3485   wcj,nn2074

Judah, and Issachar, and Zebulun:

pl,cs,nn**1121**   nn7354   nn3130   wcj,nn1144

24 The sons of Rachel; Joseph, and Benjamin:

wcj,pl,cs,nn**1121**   nn1090   nn7354   cs,nn8198   nn1835   wcj,nn5321

25 And the sons of Bilhah, Rachel's handmaid; Dan, and Naphtali:

wcj,pl,cs,nn**1121**   nn2153   nn3812   cs,nn8198   nn1410   wcj,nn836   pndm428

26 And the sons of Zilpah, Leah's handmaid; Gad, and Asher: these *are* the

pl,cs,nn**1121**   nn3290   pnl834   pupf3205   pp,pnx   pp,nn6307

sons of Jacob, which were born to him in Padan-aram.

Isaac Dies

nn3290   wcs,qmf935   pr413   nn3327   nn,pnx1   nn4471

27 And Jacob came unto Isaac his father unto Mamre, unto the

nn7153 [cs,nn7151/df,nn704]   pnp1931   nn2275   pnl834/ad8033   nn85   wcj,nn3327   qpf**1481**

city*of*Arbah, which *is* Hebron, where Abraham and Isaac sojourned.

pl,cs,nn**3117**   nn3327   wcs,qmf**1961**   cs,nu3967   (nn8141)   wcj,pl,nu8084   nn8141

28 And the days of Isaac were a hundred and fourscore years.

35:23–26 This brief listing of Jacob's twelve sons and their mothers follows a longer account of the circumstances of their births. Although later there would be twelve tribes of Israel, Jacob's sons and the heads of those twelve tribes are not the same in every case. Ten of the sons, excluding Levi and Joseph, were the heads of tribes named for them. God later claimed the tribe of Levi as an exchange for the firstborn sons to which He had right because of the Passover in Egypt. Therefore, they had no portion of the inheritance of Israel. Joseph was Jacob's favorite son and was afforded the honor of having two tribes come from him. Jacob formally adopted his two grandsons, Ephraim and Manasseh, as his own sons. Through them Joseph received a double portion of his father's inheritance. With the double portion of Joseph there remained twelve tribes to share the inheritance which God promised to Israel.

29 And Isaac gave*up*the*ghost, and died, and was gathered unto his people,

being old and full of days: and his sons Esau and Jacob buried him.

Esau's Family Record

36 Now these *are* the generations of Esau, who *is* Edom.

2 Esau took his wives of*the*daughters of Canaan; Adah the daughter of Elon the Hittite, and Aholibamah the daughter of Anah the daughter of Zibeon the Hivite;

3 And Bashemath Ishmael's daughter, sister of Nebajoth.

4 And Adah bore to Esau Eliphaz; and Bashemath bore Reuel;

5 And Aholibamah bore Jeush, and Jaalam, and Korah: these *are* the sons of Esau, which were born unto him in the land of Canaan.

6 And Esau took his wives, and his sons, and his daughters, and all the persons of his house, and his cattle, and all his beasts, and all his substance, which he had got in the land of Canaan; and went into the country from*the*face of his brother Jacob.

7 For their riches were more than that*they*might*dwell together; and the land wherein they were strangers could not bear them because of their cattle.

8 Thus dwelt Esau in mount Seir: Esau *is* Edom.

9 And these *are* the generations of Esau the father of the Edomites in mount Seir:

10 These *are* the names of Esau's sons; Eliphaz the son of Adah the wife of Esau, Reuel the son of Bashemath the wife of Esau.

11 And the sons of Eliphaz were Teman, Omar, Zepho, and Gatam, and Kenaz.

12 And Timna was concubine to Eliphaz Esau's son; and she bore to Eliphaz Amalek: these *were* the sons of Adah Esau's wife.

^{wcj,pndm428} ^{pl,cs,nn1121} ⁿⁿ⁷⁴⁶⁷ ⁿⁿ⁵¹⁸⁴ ^{wcj,nn2226} ⁿⁿ⁸⁰⁴⁸
13 And these *are* the sons of Reuel; Nahath, and Zerah, Shammah, and

^{wcj,nn4199} ^{pndm428} ^{qpf1961} ^{pl,cs,nn1121} ⁿⁿ¹³¹⁵ ⁿⁿ⁶²¹⁵ ^{cs,nn802}
Mizzah: these were the sons of Bashemath Esau's wife.

^{wcj,pndm428} ^{qpf1961} ^{pl,cs,nn1121} ⁿⁿ¹⁷³ ^{cs,nn1323} ⁿⁿ⁶⁰³⁴
14 And these were the sons of Aholibamah, the daughter of Anah the

^{cs,nn1323} ⁿⁿ⁶⁶⁴⁹ ⁿⁿ⁶²¹⁵ ^{cs,nn802} ^{wcs,qmf3205} ^{pp,nn6215} ⁽⁸⁵³⁾ ⁿⁿ³²⁶⁶ ^{wcj(853)}
daughter of Zibeon, Esau's wife: and she bore to Esau Jeush, and

ⁿⁿ³²⁸¹ ^{wcj(853)} ⁿⁿ⁷¹⁴¹
Jaalam, and Korah.

^{pndm428} ^{pl,cs,nn441} ^{pl,cs,nn1121} ⁿⁿ⁶²¹⁵ ^{pl,cs,nn1121} ⁿⁿ⁴⁶⁴ ^{cs,nn1060}
15 These *were* dukes of the sons of Esau: the sons of Eliphaz the firstborn

ⁿⁿ⁶²¹⁵ ⁿⁿ⁴⁴¹ ⁿⁿ⁸⁴⁸⁷ ⁿⁿ⁴⁴¹ ⁿⁿ²⁰¹ ⁿⁿ⁴⁴¹ ⁿⁿ⁶⁸²⁵ ⁿⁿ⁴⁴¹ ⁿⁿ⁷⁰⁷³
son of Esau; duke Teman, duke Omar, duke Zepho, duke Kenaz,

ⁿⁿ⁴⁴¹ ⁿⁿ⁷¹⁴¹ ⁿⁿ⁴⁴¹ ⁿⁿ¹⁶⁰⁹ ⁿⁿ⁴⁴¹ ⁿⁿ⁶⁰⁰² ^{pndm428} ^{pl,cs,nn441}
16 Duke Korah, duke Gatam, *and* duke Amalek: these *are* the dukes *that came*

ⁿⁿ⁴⁶⁴ ^{pp,cs,nn776} ⁿⁿ¹²³ ^{pndm428} ^{pl,cs,nn1121} ⁿⁿ⁵⁷¹¹
of Eliphaz in the land of Edom; these *were* the sons of Adah.

^{wcj,pndm428} ^{pl,cs,nn1121} ⁿⁿ⁷⁴⁶⁷ ⁿⁿ⁶²¹⁵ ^{cs,nn1121} ⁿⁿ⁴⁴¹ ⁿⁿ⁵¹⁸⁴ ⁿⁿ⁴⁴¹ ⁿⁿ²²²⁶
17 And these *are* the sons of Reuel Esau's son; duke Nahath, duke Zerah,

ⁿⁿ⁴⁴¹ ⁿⁿ⁸⁰⁴⁸ ⁿⁿ⁴⁴¹ ⁿⁿ⁴¹⁹⁹ ^{pndm428} ^{pl,cs,nn441} ⁿⁿ⁷⁴⁶⁷ ^{pp,cs,nn776}
duke Shammah, duke Mizzah: these *are* the dukes *that came* of Reuel in the land

ⁿⁿ¹²³ ^{pndm428} ^{pl,cs,nn1121} ⁿⁿ¹³¹⁵ ⁿⁿ⁶²¹⁵ ^{cs,nn802}
of Edom; these *are* the sons of Bashemath Esau's wife.

^{wcj,pndm428} ^{pl,cs,nn1121} ⁿⁿ¹⁷³ ⁿⁿ⁶²¹⁵ ^{cs,nn802} ⁿⁿ⁴⁴¹ ⁿⁿ³²⁶⁶ ⁿⁿ⁴⁴¹
18 And these *are* the sons of Aholibamah Esau's wife; duke Jeush, duke

ⁿⁿ³²⁸¹ ⁿⁿ⁴⁴¹ ⁿⁿ⁷¹⁴¹ ^{pndm428} ^{pl,cs,nn441} ⁿⁿ¹⁷³ ^{cs,nn1323}
Jaalam, duke Korah: these *were* the dukes *that came* of Aholibamah the daughter of

ⁿⁿ⁶⁰³⁴ ⁿⁿ⁶²¹⁵ ^{cs,nn802}
Anah, Esau's wife.

^{pndm428} ^{pl,cs,nn1121} ⁿⁿ⁶²¹⁵ ^{pnp1931} ⁿⁿ¹²³ ^{wcj,pndm428} ^{pl,nn,pnx441}
19 These *are* the sons of Esau, who *is* Edom, and these *are* their dukes.

^{pndm428} ^{pl,cs,nn1121} ⁿⁿ⁸¹⁶⁵ ^{df,nn2752} ^{pl,cs,qpta3427} ^{df,nn776} ⁿⁿ³⁸⁷⁷
20 These *are* the sons of Seir the Horite, who inhabited the land; Lotan, and

^{wcj,nn7732} ^{wcj,nn6649} ^{wcj,nn6034}
Shobal, and Zibeon, and Anah,

^{wcj,nn1787} ^{wcj,nn687} ^{wcj,nn1789} ^{pndm428} ^{pl,cs,nn441} ^{df,nn2752}
21 And Dishon, and Ezer, and Dishan: these *are* the dukes of the Horites, the

^{pl,cs,nn1121} ⁿⁿ⁸¹⁶⁵ ^{pp,cs,nn776} ⁿⁿ¹²³
children of Seir in the land of Edom.

^{pl,cs,nn1121} ⁿⁿ³⁸⁷⁷ ^{wcs,qmf1961} ⁿⁿ²⁷⁵³ ^{wcj,nn1967} ⁿⁿ³⁸⁷⁷ ^{wcj,cs,nn269}
22 And the children of Lotan were Hori and Hemam; and Lotan's sister *was*

ⁿⁿ⁸⁵⁵⁵
Timna.

^{pl,cs,nn1121} ⁿⁿ⁷⁷³² ^{wcj,pndm428} ⁿⁿ⁵⁹³⁵ ^{wcj,nn4506} ^{wcj,nn5858}
23 And the children of Shobal *were* these; Alvan, and Manahath, and Ebal,

ⁿⁿ⁸¹⁹⁵ ^{wcj,nn208}
Shepho, and Onam.

^{wcj,pndm428} ^{pl,cs,nn1121} ⁿⁿ⁶⁶⁴⁹ ^{wcj,nn345} ^{wcj,nn6034} ^{pnp1931}
24 And these *are* the children of Zibeon; both Ajah, and Anah: this *was that*

ⁿⁿ⁶⁰³⁴ ^{pnl834} ^{qpf4672} ⁽⁸⁵³⁾ ^{df,pl,nn3222} ^{dfp,nn4057} ^{pp,qnc,pnx7462} ⁽⁸⁵³⁾ ^{df,pl,nn2543}
Anah that found the mules in the wilderness, as he fed the asses of

^{pp,nn6649} ^{nn,pnx1}
Zibeon his father.

25 And the children of Anah *were* these; Dishon, and Aholibamah the

daughter of Anah.

26 And these *are* the children of Dishon; Hemdan, and Esh-ban, and Ithran,

and Cheran.

27 The children of Ezer *are* these; Bilhan, and Zaavan, and Akan.

28 The children of Dishan *are* these; Uz, and Aran.

29 These *are* the dukes *that came* of the Horites; duke Lotan, duke Shobal,

duke Zibeon, duke Anah,

30 Duke Dishon, duke Ezer, duke Dishan: these *are* the dukes *that came* of

Hori, among their dukes in the land of Seir.

31 And these *are* the kings that reigned in the land of Edom, before

there reigned any king over the children of Israel.

32 And Bela the son of Beor reigned in Edom: and the name of his city

was Dinhabah.

33 And Bela died, and Jobab the son of Zerah of Bozrah reigned

in*his*stead.

34 And Jobab died, and Husham of*the*land of Temani reigned in*his*stead.

35 And Husham died, and Hadad the son of Bedad, who smote Midian

in the field of Moab, reigned in*his*stead: and the name of his city *was*

Avith.

36 And Hadad died, and Samlah of Masrekah reigned in*his*stead.

37 And Samlah died, and Saul of Rehoboth *by* the river reigned in*his*stead.

38 And Saul died, and Baalhanan the son of Achbor reigned in*his*stead.

39 And Baalhanan the son of Achbor died, and Hadar reigned in*his*stead:

and the name of his city *was* Pau; and his wife's name *was* Mehetabel, the

daughter of Matred, the daughter of Mezahab.

40 And these *are* the names of the dukes *that came* of Esau, according to

pp,pl,nn,pnx**4940**　　　pp,pl,nn,pnx4725　　　pp,pl,nn,pnx8034　nn**441**　nn8555　nn**441**　nn5933

their families, after their places, by their names; duke Timnah, duke Alvah,

nn**441**　nn3509

duke Jetheth,

　　nn**441**　nn173　nn**441**　nn425　nn**441**　nn6373

41 Duke Aholibamah, duke Elah, duke Pinon,

　　nn**441**　nn7073　nn**441**　nn8487　nn**441**　nn4014

42 Duke Kenaz, duke Teman, duke Mibzar,

　　nn**441**　nn4025　nn**441**　nn5902　pndm428　　　pl,cs,nn**441**　nn123

43 Duke Magdiel, duke Iram: these *be* the dukes of Edom, according to their

pp,pl,nn,pnx**4186**　　pp,cs,nn**776**　　　nn,pnx**272**　pnp1931　nn6215　cs,nn**1**　　nn123

habitations in the land of their possession: he *is* Esau the father of the Edomites.

Joseph Has a Dream

　　　　　　　　nn3290　wcs,qmf**3427**　pp,cs,nn**776**　　　nn,pnx1　　　pl,cs,nn**4033**

37 ☞ And Jacob dwelt in the land wherein his father was a stranger,

　　　　pp,cs,nn**776**　nn3667

in the land of Canaan.

pndm428　　　pl,cs,nn**8435**　　nn3290　nn3130　cs,nu7651/nu6240　nn8141　cs,nn**1121** qpf**1961**

2 These *are* the generations of Jacob. Joseph, *being* seventeen years old, was

qpta7462　dfp,nn6629　pr854　pl,nn,pnx**251**　wcj(pnp1931)　nn5288　pr854　pl,cs,nn**1121**

feeding the flock with his brethren; and the lad *was* with the sons of

nn1090　wcj,pr854　pl,cs,nn**1121**　nn2153　nn,pnx1　pl,cs,nn**802**　nn3130　wcs,himf935　pr413

Bilhah, and with the sons of Zilpah, his father's wives: and Joseph brought unto

nn,pnx1　（853）aj**7451** nn,pnx1681

his father their evil report.

　　wcj,nn3478　qpf**157**　（853）　nn3130　pr4480/cs,nn3605　pl,nn,pnx**1121**　cj3588　pnp1931

3 Now Israel loved Joseph more*than*all his children, because he *was*

cs,nn**1121**　pp,pnx　pl,nn**2208**　wcj,qpf**6213** pp,pnx　cs,nn3801　pl,nn6446

the son of his old age: and he made him a coat of *many* colors.

　　pl,nn,pnx**251**　wcs,qmf**7200** cj3588　nn,pnx1　qpf**157**　pnx(853)　pr4480/cs,nn3605

4 And when his brethren saw that their father loved him more*than*all

pl,nn,pnx**251**　wcs,qmf**8130** pnx(853)　qpf3201　wcj,ptn**3808** pinc,pnx**1696**　pp,nn**7965**

his brethren, they hated him, and could not speak peaceably unto him.

　　nn3130　wcs,qmf2492　nn2472　wcs,himf**5046**　pp,pl,nn,pnx**251**　qnc**8130**

5 And Joseph dreamed a dream, and he told *it* his brethren: and they hated

pnx(853)　ad5750　wcs,himf3254

him yet the more.

　　wcs,qmf**559** pr,pnx413　qmv**8085**　pte**4994**　df,pndm2088　df,nn2472　pnl834

6 And he said unto them, Hear, I*pray*you, this dream which I have

qpf2492

dreamed:

　　wcj,ptdm2009 pnp587　pl,pipt481　pl,nn485　pp,cs,nn**8432**　df,nn**7704**　wcj,ptdm2009

7 For, behold, we *were* binding sheaves in the field, and, lo, my

---

☞ **37:1–11** Joseph was singled out by God from his conception. His very birth was an answer to his mother Rachel's prayers. His father's preferential treatment of him, his special coat being an emblem of this, caused his brothers to envy him and Joseph's prophetic dreams only intensified their feelings. Yet these dreams, and Joseph's ability to interpret them, were a sign of God's special blessing on Joseph. They would be the means of his advancement in Egypt and the preservation of God's people. Joseph's personal faith and obedience never wavered, whether he was in a prison or a palace. His clever suggestions to Pharaoh would provide a place for Jacob's family to grow into a nation. They would also usher in a time of prosperity for Egypt—God is willing to bless others so that His people may prosper.

nn,pnx485   qpf**6965**   wcj,ad1571   nipf**5324**   wcj,ptdm2009   pl,nn,pnx485
sheaf   arose,   and   also   stood upright;   and,   behold,   your   sheaves

qmf5437   wcs,htmf***7812**   pp,nn,pnx485
stood*round*about, and made obeisance to my sheaf.

pl,nn,pnx**251**   wcs,qmf**559**   pp,pnx   he,qna**4427**/qmf**4427**   pr,pnx5921   cj518
8 And his brethren   said   to him, Shalt thou indeed reign   over   us? or shalt

qna**4910**/qmf**4910**   pp,pnx   qnc**8130** pnx(853)   ad5750   wcs,himf3254 pr5921
thou indeed*have*dominion over   us? And they hated   him yet the   more   for

pl,nn,pnx2472   wcj,pr5921   pl,nn,pnx**1697**
his dreams, and   for his words.

wcs,qmf2492   ad5750   aj312   nn2472   wcs,pimf**5608** pnx(853)   pp,pl,nn,pnx251
9 And he dreamed yet another dream, and told   it his brethren, and

wcs,qmf**559**   ptdm2009   qpf2492   nn2472   ad5750   wcj,ptdm2009   df,nn8121
said,   Behold, I have dreamed a dream more; and, behold, the   sun   and the

wcj,df,nn3394   wcj,nu259/nu6240 pl,nn3556   pl,htpt*7812   pp,pnx
moon and the   eleven   stars made obeisance to me.

wcs,pimf**5608**   pr413   nn,pnx1   wcj,pr413   pl,nn,pnx**251**   nn,pnx1
10 And he   told   *it* to his father, and   to   his brethren: and his father

wcs,qmf**1605** pp,pnx   wcs,qmf**559**   pp,pnx   pnit4100   df,pndm2088 df,nn2472 pnl834   qpf2492
rebuked him, and   said unto him, What *is*   this   dream that thou hast dreamed?

pnp589   wcj,nn,pnx**517**   wcj,pl,nn,pnx**251**   he,qna935/qmf935   pp,htnc*7812
Shall   I   and thy mother and thy brethren indeed come to bow*down*ourselves

pp,pnx   nn,lh776
to thee to the earth?

pl,nn,pnx251 wcs,pimf**7065** pp,pnx   wcj,nn,pnx1 qpf**8104**   (853)   df,nn**1697**
11 And his brethren envied him; but his father observed   the saying.

Joseph Becomes a Slave

pl,nn,pnx251   wcs,qmf**1980**   pp,qnc7462 (853)   nn,pnx1   cs,nn6629   pp,nn7927
12 And his brethren went to feed   their father's flock in Shechem.

nn3478   wcs,qmf**559**   pr413   nn3130   he,ptn**3808**   pl,nn,pnx**251** pl,qpta7462
13 And Israel said unto Joseph, Do   not   thy brethren feed *the flock* in

pp,nn7927   qmv**1980**   wcj,qmf,pnx7971   pr,pnx413   wcs,qmf**559**   pp,pnx
Shechem? come, and I will   send   thee unto   them. And he   said to him,

ptdm,pnx2009
Here   *am I.*

wcs,qmf**559**   pp,pnx   qmv**1980**   pte**4994**   qmv**7200**   (853)   cs,nn**7965**
14 And he   said to him, Go, I*pray*thee, see whether   it be well with

pl,nn,pnx**251**   wcj(853) cs,nn**7965**   df,nn6629   wcj,himv,pnx**7725**   nn**1697**
thy brethren, and   well with the flocks; and   bring   me word again. So he

wcs,qmf,pnx7971   pr4480/cs,nn6010   nn2275   wcs,qmf935   nn,lh7927
sent   him out*of*the*vale of Hebron, and he came to Shechem.

nn376   wcs,qmf,pnx4672   wcj,ptdm2009   qpta**8582**
15 And a certain man   found   him, and, behold, *he was* wandering in the

dfp,nn**7704**   df,nn376 wcs,qmf,pnx**7592**   pp,qnc559 pnit4100   pimf1245
field: and the man   asked   him, saying, What seekest thou?

wcs,qmf**559** pnp595 pipt1245 (853)   pl,nn,pnx**251** himv**5046** pp,pnx   pte**4994**   pnit375 pnp1992
16 And he said,   I seek   my brethren: tell me, I*pray*thee, where they

pl,qpta7462
feed *their flocks.*

df,nn**376** wcs,qmf**559**   qpf5265   pr4480/pndm2088 cj3588   qpf**8085**   pl,qpta559
17 And the man said,   They are departed   hence;   for I heard them say,

qcj1980   nn,lh1886   nn3130   wcs,qmf1980   pr310   pl,nn,pnx251   wcs,qmf,pnx4672

Let us go to Dothan. And Joseph went after his brethren, and found them in

pp,nn1886

Dothan.

wcs,qmf7200 pnx(853)   pr4480/nn7350   wcj,pp,ad2962   qmf7126   pr,pnx413

18 And when they saw him afar off, even before he came near unto

wcs,htmf5230 pnx(853)   pp,hinc,pnx4191

them, they conspired against him to slay him.

wcs,qmf559 nn376 pr413   nn,pnx251   ptdm2009   pndm1976   cs,nn1167/df,pl,nn2472   qpta935

19 And they said one to another, Behold, this dreamer cometh.

qmv1980   wcj,ad6258   wcj,qmf,pnx2026   wcj,himf,pnx7993

20 Come now therefore, and let us slay him, and cast him into

pp,nu259 df,pl,nn953   wcj,qpf559   aj7451 nn2416   qpf398

some pit, and we will say, Some evil beast hath devoured him: and we shall

wcj,qmf7200 pnit4100   qmf1961   pl,nn,pnx2472

see what will become of his dreams.

nn7205   wcs,qmf8085   wcs,himf5337   pr4480/nn,pnx3027   wcs,qmf559

21 And Reuben heard *it*, and he delivered him out*of*their*hands; and said,

ptn3808 himf,pnx5221 (nn5315)

Let us not kill him.

nn7205   wcs,qmf559 pr,pnx413   qmf8210 ptn408   nn1818   himv7993 pnx(853)   pr413

22 And Reuben said unto them, Shed no blood, *but* cast him into

df,pndm2088 df,nn953 pnl834   dfp,nn4057   qmf7971 ptn408 wcj,nn3027   pp,pnx   pr4616

this pit that *is* in the wilderness, and lay no hand upon him; that he might

hinc5337 pnx(853)   pr4480/nn,pnx3027   pp,hinc,pnx7725   pr413   nn,pnx1

rid him out*of*their*hands, to deliver him to his father again.

wcs,qmf1961   pp,pnl834 nn3130   qpf935 pr413   pl,nn,pnx251

23 And it*came*to*pass, when Joseph was come unto his brethren, that they

wcs,himf6584 (853)   nn3130   (853)   nn,pnx3801   (853)   cs,nn3801   df,pl,nn6446 pnl834

stripped Joseph out of his coat, *his* coat of *many* colors that *was*

pr,pnx5921

on him;

wcs,qmf,pnx3947   wcs,himf7993 pnx(853)   df,nn,lh953   wcj,df,nn953

24 And they took him, and cast him into a pit: and the pit

aj7386   ptn369 pl,nn4325 pp,pnx

was empty, *there was* no water in it.

wcs,qmf3427   pp,qnc398   nn3899   wcs,qmf5375   wcs,qmf5869

⊙ 25 And they sat down to eat bread: and they lifted up their eyes and

wcs,qmf7200   wcj,ptdm2009   cs,nn736   nn3459   qpta935   pr4480/nn1568

looked, and, behold, a company of Ishmaelites came from Gilead with their

wcj,pl,nn,pnx1581   pl,qpta5375   nn5219   wcj,nn6875   wcj,nn3910 pl,qpta1980   pp,hinc3381   nn,lh4714

camels bearing spicery and balm and myrrh, going to carry*it*down to Egypt.

nn3063   wcs,qmf559   pr413   pl,nn,pnx251   pnit4100   nn1215   cj3588   qmf2026 (853)

26 And Judah said unto his brethren, What profit *is it* if we slay our

nn,pnx251   wcs,pipf3680 (853)   nn,pnx1818

brother, and conceal his blood?

qmv1980   wcj,qmf4376   dfp,nn3459   ptn408   wcj,nn,pnx3027

27 Come, and let us sell him to the Ishmaelites, and let not our hand

qcj1961   pp,pnx   cj3588   pnp1931   nn,pnx251   nn,pnx1320   pl,nn,pnx251

be upon him; for he *is* our brother *and* our flesh. And his brethren were

wcs,qmf8085

content.

⊙ **37:25, 28, 36** It is possible that the Ishmaelites may have been the owners of the caravan, which was made up of other peoples. Another possibility is the term "Midianites" is only given as a geographical reference. However, it is most likely that several different groups traveled together in the caravan to help ward off robbers.

_{wcs,qmf5674}   _{pl,nn376/nn4084}   _{pl,qpta5503}   _{wcs,qmf4900}
○⊣ 28 Then there passed by Midianites merchantmen; and they drew and

_{wcs,himf5927}   (853)   _{nn3130}   _{pr4480}   _{df,nn953}   _{wcs,qmf4376} (853)   _{nn3130}   _{dfp,nn3459}
lifted up   Joseph out of the pit, and sold   Joseph to the Ishmaelites for

_{pp,pl,nu6242}   _{nn3701}   _{wcs,himf935} (853)   _{nn3130}   _{nn,lh4714}
twenty *pieces* of silver: and they brought   Joseph into Egypt.

_{nn7205}   _{wcs,qmf7725}   _{pr413}   _{df,nn953}   _{wcj,ptdm2009}   _{nn3130}   _{ptn369}
29 And Reuben returned unto the pit; and, behold, Joseph *was* not in the

_{dfp,nn953}   _{wcs,qmf7167} (853)   _{pl,nn,pnx899}
pit; and he rent   his clothes.

_{wcs,qmf7725}   _{pr413}   _{pl,nn,pnx251}   _{wcs,qmf559}   _{df,nn3206}   _{ptn,pnx369}   _{wcj,pnp589}
30 And he returned unto his brethren, and said, The child *is* not; and I,

_{ad,lh575}   _{pnp589} _{qpta935}
whither shall I go?

_{wcs,qmf3947} (853)   _{nn3130}   _{cs,nn3801}   _{wcs,qmf7819}   _{cs,nn8163}   _{pl,nn5795}
31 And they took   Joseph's coat, and killed a kid of the goats, and

_{wcs,qmf2881} (853)   _{df,nn3801}   _{dfp,nn1818}
dipped   the coat in the blood;

_{wcs,pimf7971} (853)   _{cs,nn3801}   _{df,pl,nn6446}   _{wcs,himf935}   _{pr413}
32 And they sent   the coat of *many* colors, and they brought *it* to their

_{nn,pnx1}   _{wcs,qmf559} _{pndm2063}   _{qpf4672}   _{himv5234} _{pte4994}   _{pnp1931}   _{nn,pnx1121}
father; and said, This have we found: know now whether it *be* thy son's

_{df,nn3801} _{cj518} _{ptn3808}
coat or no.

_{wcs,himf,pnx5234}   _{wcs,qmf559}   _{nn,pnx1121} _{cs,nn3801}   _{aj7451} _{nn2416}
33 And he knew it, and said, It *is* my son's coat; an evil beast hath

_{qpf,pnx398}   _{nn3130}   _{qna2963/pupf2963}
devoured him; Joseph is without*doubt*rent*in*pieces.

_{nn3290} _{wcs,qmf7167}   _{pl,nn,pnx8071}   _{wcs,qmf7760}   _{nn8242}   _{pp,du,nn,pnx4975}
34 And Jacob rent his clothes, and put sackcloth upon his loins, and

_{wcs,htmf56}   _{pr5921}   _{nn,pnx1121} _{aj7227}   _{pl,nn3117}
mourned for his son many days.

_{cs,nn3605}   _{pl,nn,pnx1121}   _{wcj,cs,nn3605}   _{pl,nn,pnx1323}   _{wcs,qmf6965}   _{pp,pinc,pnx5162}
35 And all his sons and all his daughters rose up to comfort him;

_{wcs,pimf3985}   _{pp,htnc5162}   _{wcs,qmf559} _{cj3588}   _{qmf3381}   _{nn,lh7585}
but he refused to be comforted; and he said, For I will go down into the grave

_{pr413}   _{nn,pnx1121}   _{aj57}   _{nn,pnx1} _{wcs,qmf1058} _{pnx(853)}
unto my son mourning. Thus his father wept   for him.

_{wcj,df,nn4092}   _{qpf4376} _{pnx(853)}   _{pr413}   _{nn4714}   _{pp,nn6318}   _{cs,nn5631}
○⊣ 36 And the Midianites sold   him into Egypt unto Potiphar, an officer of

_{nn6547}   _{cs,nn8269}   _{df,pl,nn2876}
Pharaoh's, *and* captain of the guard.

Judah and Tamar

_{wcs,qmf1961}   _{df,pndm1931} _{dfp,nn6256}   _{nn3063}   _{wcs,qmf3381}   _{pr4480/pr854}
38 And it*came*to*pass at that time, that Judah went down from

_{pl,nn,pnx251}   _{wcs,qmf5186}   _{pr5704}   _{nn376}   _{nn5726}   _{wcj,nn,pnx8034}
his brethren, and turned in to a certain Adullamite, whose name

_{nn2437}
was Hirah.

_{nn3063}   _{wcs,qmf7200}   _{ad8033}   _{cs,nn1323}   _{nn376}   _{nn3669}   _{wcj,nn,pnx8034}
2 And Judah saw there a daughter of a certain Canaanite, whose name

_{nn7770}   _{wcs,qmf,pnx3947}   _{wcs,qmf935} _{pr,pnx413}
was Shuah; and he took her, and went in unto her.

wcs,qmf2029   wcs,qmf3205   nn1121   wcs,qmf7121 (853)   nn,pnx8034 nn6147

3 And she conceived, and   bore   a son; and he called   his name Er.

wcs,qmf2029   ad5750   wcs,qmf3205   nn1121   wcs,qmf7121 (853)   nn,pnx8034

4 And she conceived again, and   bore   a son; and she called   his name

nn209

Onan.

ad5750   wcs,himf3254   wcs,qmf3205 nn1121   wcs,qmf7121 (853)   nn,pnx8034

5 And she yet again conceived, and   bore   a son; and called   his name

nn7956   wcj,qpf1961   pp,nn3580   pp,qnc,pnx3205 pnx(853)

Shelah: and he was at Chezib, when she   bore   him.

nn3063 wcs,qmf3947   nn802   pp,nn6147   nn,pnx1060   wcj,nn,pnx8034   nn8559

6 And Judah took   a wife for   Er his firstborn, whose   name   *was* Tamar.

nn6147   nn3063   cs,nn1060   wcs,qmf1961 aj7451   pp,du,cs,nn5869   nn3068

7 And Er, Judah's firstborn, was wicked in the   sight of the LORD; and

nn3068   wcs,himf,pnx4191

the LORD slew   him.

nn3063   wcs,qmf559   pp,nn209 qmv935   pr413   nn,pnx251 cs,nn802   wcj,pimv2992

☙ 8 And Judah said   unto Onan, Go in unto thy brother's wife, and   marry

pnx(853)   wcj,himv6965 nn2233   pp,nn,pnx251

her, and raise up seed to thy brother.

nn209   wcs,qmf3045 cj3588   df,nn2233   ptn3808 qmf1961 pp,pnx   wcs,qpf1961

9 And Onan knew that the seed should not be his; and it*came*to*pass,

cj518   qpf935   pr413   nn,pnx251 cs,nn802   wcj,pipf7843   nn,lh776   pp,ptn1115

when he went in unto his brother's wife, that he spilled *it* on the ground, lest

qnc5414 nn2233   pp,nn,pnx251

that he should give seed to his brother.

pnl834   qpf6213 wcs,qmf7489/pp,du,cs,nn5869   nn3068   wcs,himf4191

10 And the thing which he did   displeased   the LORD: wherefore he   slew

pnx(853)   ad1571

him also.

wcs,qmf559   nn3063   pp,nn8559   nn,pnx3618   qmv3427   nn490

11 Then said   Judah to Tamar his daughter-in-law, Remain a widow at thy

nn,pnx1   cs,nn1004 cj5704   nn7956   nn,pnx1121 qmf1431   cj3588   qpf559   cj6435

father's house, till Shelah my   son be grown: for he said, Lest peradventure

pnp1931 qmf4191 ad1571   pp,pl,nn,pnx251   nn8559 wcs,qmf1980   wcs,qmf3427   nn,pnx1

he   die also, as his brethren *did.* And Tamar went and dwelt in her father's

cs,nn1004

house.

wcs,qmf7235/df,pl,nn3117   cs,nn1323   nn7770   nn3063   cs,nn802 wcs,qmf4191

12 And in*process*of*time the daughter of Shuah Judah's wife died; and

nn3063   wcs,nimf5162   wcs,qmf5927 pr5921   pl,cs,qpta1494/nn,pnx6629   nn,lh8553 pnp1931

Judah was comforted, and went up unto his sheepshearers to Timnath, he and his

nn,pnx7453 wcj,nn2437   df,nn5726

friend Hirah the Adullamite.

wcs,homf5046   pp,nn8559   pp,qnc559   ptdm2009   nn,pnx2524   qpta5927

13 And it was   told   Tamar, saying, Behold thy father-in-law goeth up to

nn,lh8553   pp,qnc1494   nn,pnx6629

Timnath to shear his sheep.

wcs,himf5493   nn,pnx491   pl,cs,nn899 pr4480/pr,pnx5921   wcs,pimf3680

14 And she put   her widow's garments off from her, and covered her with

dfp,nn6809   wcs,htmf5968   wcs,qmf3427   nn5879 pp,cs,nn6607 pnl834   pr5921   cs,nn1870

a veil, and wrapped herself, and   sat   in an open place, which *is* by the way

---

☙ **38:8** See the note on Ruth 4:1–8, on kinsman redeemer.

nn,lh8553   cj3588   qpf7200   cj3588   nn7956   qpf1431   wcj,pnp1931   ptn3808   nipf5414

to Timnath; for she saw that Shelah was grown, and   she   was not given

pp,pnx   pp,nn802

unto him to wife.

nn3063   wcs,qmf,pnx7200   wcs,qmf,pnx2803   pp,qpta2181   cj3588

15 When Judah   saw   her, he thought her *to be* a harlot; because she had

pipf3680   pl,nn,pnx6440

covered her face.

wcs,qmf5186 pr,pnx413   pr413   df,nn1870   wcs,qmf559   qmv3051   pte4994

16 And he turned unto her by the way, and said, Go to, I*pray*thee, let

qmf935   pr,pnx413   cj3588   qpf3045 ptn3808 cj3588 pnp1931   nn,pnx3618

me come in unto thee; (for he knew not that she *was* his daughter-in-law.) And

wcs,qmf559 pnit4100   qmf5414 pp,pnx cj3588   qmf935   pr,pnx413

she said, What wilt thou give me, that thou mayest come in unto me?

wcs,qmf559 pnp1931   pimf7971   cs,nn1423/pl,nn5795 pr4480   df,nn6629

17 And he said,   I   will send *thee* a   kid   from the flock. And she

wcs,qmf559 (cj518)   qmf5414   nn6162   pr5704   qnc,pnx7971

said,   Wilt thou give *me* a pledge, till thou send *it*?

wcs,qmf559 pnit4100 df,nn6162   (pnl834)   qmf5414 pp,pnx   wcs,qmf559

18 And he said, What pledge   shall I give thee? And she said, Thy

nn,pnx2368   wcj,nn,pnx6616   wcj,nn,pnx4294 pnl834   pp,nn,pnx3027   wcs,qmf5414

signet, and thy bracelets, and thy staff that *is* in thine hand. And he gave *it*

pp,pnx   wcs,qmf935   pr,pnx413   wcs,qmf2029   pp,pnx

her, and came in unto her, and she conceived by him.

wcs,qmf6965   wcs,qmf1980   wcs,himf5493   nn,pnx6809 pr4480/pr,pnx5921

19 And she arose, and went away, and laid by her veil   from   her, and

wcs,qmf3847   pl,cs,nn899   nn,pnx491

put on the garments of her widowhood.

nn3063   wcs,qmf7971   (853)   cs,nn1423/df,pl,nn5795   pp,cs,nn3027   nn,pnx7453

20 And Judah sent   the   kid   by the hand of his friend the

df,nn5726   pp,qnc3947   df,nn6162   df,nn802 pr4480/cs,nn3027   qpf,pnx4672

Adullamite, to receive *his* pledge from the woman's   hand: but he found her

wcj,ptn3808

not.

wcs,qmf7592 (853)   pl,cs,nn376   nn,pnx4725 pp,qnc559 pnit346   df,nn6948

21 Then he asked   the men of that place, saying, Where *is* the harlot,

pnp1931   dfp,nn5879 pr5921   df,nn1870   wcs,qmf559   qpf1961 ptn3808 nn6948

that *was* openly by the way side? And they said, There was no harlot in

pp,pndm2088

this *place.*

wcs,qmf7725 pr413 nn3063   wcs,qmf559 ptn3808 qpf,pnx4672   wcj,ad1571

22 And he returned to Judah, and said, I cannot find her; and also the

pl,cs,nn376   df,nn4725 qpf559   qpf1961 ptn3808 nn6948   pp,pndm2088

men of the place said, *that* there was no harlot in this *place.*

nn3063   wcs,qmf559   qmf3947   pp,pnx   cj6435   qmf1961 dfp,nn937   ptdm2009

23 And Judah said, Let her take *it* to her, lest we be shamed: behold, I

qpf7971 df,pndm2088 df,nn1423   wcj,pnp859   ptn3808 qpf,pnx4672

sent this   kid, and thou hast not found her.

wcs,qmf1961   pp,pr4480/cs,nu7969 pl,nn2320   wcs,homf5046 pp,nn3063

24 And it*came*to*pass about three months after, that it was told   Judah,

pp,qnc559   nn8559   nn,pnx3618   qpf2181   wcj,ad1571 ptdm2009

saying, Tamar thy daughter-in-law hath played*the*harlot; and also, behold, she *is*

aj2030   pp,pl,nn2183   nn3063 wcs,qmf559   himv,pnx3318   wcj,nimf8313

with child by whoredom. And Judah said, Bring*her*forth, and let her be burnt.

pnp1931   hopt3318   wcj,pnp1931 qpf7971 pr413   nn,pnx2524   pp,qnc559

25 When she *was* brought forth, she sent to her father-in-law, saying, By

^{pp,nn376} ^{pnl834/pp,pnx} ^{pndm428}   ^{pnp595}   ^{aj2030}   ^{wcs,qmf559}   ^{himv5234}
the man,   whose   these   *are, am*   I   with child: and she   said,   Discern,

^{pte4994}   ^{pp,pnit4310} ^{df,pndm428} ^{df,nn2858}   ^{wcj,df,pl,nn6616}   ^{wcj,df,nn4294}
I*pray*thee, whose *are* these, the signet, and bracelets, and   staff.

                ⁿⁿ³⁰⁶³   ^{wcs,himf5234}   ^{wcs,qmf559}   ^{qpf6663}
26 And Judah acknowledged *them*, and   said,   She hath been more righteous

^{pr,pnx4480}   ^{cj3588}   ^{pr5921/ad3651} ^{qpf,pnx5414} ^{ptn3808} ^{pp,nn7956}   ^{nn,pnx1121}   ^{pp,qnc,pnx3045}
than   I; because   that   I gave her not to Shelah my son.   And he   knew   her

^{qpf3254} ^{wcj,ptn3808} ^{ad5750}
again   no   more.

                ^{wcs,qmf1961}   ^{pp,cs,nn6256}   ^{qnc,pnx3205}   ^{wcj,ptdm2009} ^{pl,nn8380}
27 And it*came*to*pass in the   time   of her travail, that, behold, twins *were*

^{pp,nn,pnx990}
in her womb.

                ^{wcs,qmf1961}   ^{pp,qnc,pnx3205}   ^{wcs,qmf5414}   ⁿⁿ³⁰²⁷
28 And it*came*to*pass, when she travailed, that *the one* put out *his* hand: and

^{df,pipt3205} ^{wcs,qmf3947}   ^{wcs,qmf7194} ^{pr5921}   ^{nn,pnx3027}   ⁿⁿ⁸¹⁴⁴   ^{pp,qnc559} ^{pndm2088}
the midwife   took   and bound upon his   hand   a scarlet thread, saying, This

^{qpf3318}   ^{aj7223}
came out first.

                ^{wcs,qmf1961}   ^{pp,hipt7725}   ^{nn,pnx3027}   ^{wcj,ptdm2009}   ^{nn,pnx251}
29 And it*came*to*pass, as he drew back his hand, that, behold, his brother

^{qpf3318}   ^{wcs,qmf559} ^{pnit4100}   ^{qpf6555}   ⁿⁿ⁶⁵⁵⁶   ^{pr,pnx5921}
came out: and she   said,   How hast thou broken forth? *this* breach *be* upon thee:

            ^{nn,pnx8034}   ^{wcs,qmf7121} ⁿⁿ⁶⁵⁵⁷
therefore his name was called Pharez.

            ^{wcj,ad310}   ^{qpf3318}   ^{nn,pnx251} ^{pnl834}   ^{df,nn8144}   ^{pr5921}
30 And afterward came out his brother, that had the scarlet thread upon his

^{nn,pnx3027}   ^{nn,pnx8034}   ^{wcs,qmf7121} ⁿⁿ²²²⁶
hand: and his name was called Zarah.

Joseph and Potiphar's Wife

^{wcj,nn3130}   ^{hopf3381}   ^{nn,lh4714}   ⁿⁿ⁶³¹⁸   ^{cs,nn5631}
39
And Joseph was brought down to Egypt; and Potiphar, an officer of

ⁿⁿ⁶⁵⁴⁷   ^{cs,nn8269}   ^{df,pl,nn2876}   ^{cs,nn376/nn4713} ^{wcs,qmf,pnx7069}
Pharaoh,   captain   of   the   guard,   an   Egyptian,   bought   him

^{pr4480/cs,nn3027}   ^{df,nn3459}   ^{pnl834}   ^{hipf,pnx3381}   ^{ad,lh8033}
of*the*hands of the Ishmaelites, which had brought*him*down thither.

                ⁿⁿ³⁰⁶⁸ ^{wcs,qmf1961} ^{pr854}   ⁿⁿ³¹³⁰   ^{wcs,qmf1961}   ^{hipt6743}   ⁿⁿ³⁷⁶
2 And the LORD   was   with Joseph, and he   was   a prosperous man; and he

^{wcs,qmf1961}   ^{pp,cs,nn1004}   ^{pl,nn,pnx113}   ^{df,nn4713}
was   in the house of his master the Egyptian.

                ^{pl,nn,pnx113} ^{wcs,qmf7200} ^{cj3588}   ⁿⁿ³⁰⁶⁸   ^{pr,pnx854}   ⁿⁿ³⁰⁶⁸
3 And his master   saw   that the LORD *was*   with him, and that the LORD made

^{wcj,cs,nn3605} ^{pnl834} ^{pnp1931} ^{qpta6213} ^{hipt6743}   ^{pp,nn,pnx3027}
all   that he   did to prosper in his   hand.

                ⁿⁿ³¹³⁰   ^{wcs,qmf4672} ⁿⁿ²⁵⁸⁰   ^{pp,du,nn,pnx5869}   ^{wcs,pimf8334} ^{pnx(853)}
4 And Joseph found   grace in his   sight,   and he served   him: and he

^{wcs,himf,pnx6485}   ^{pr5921}   ^{nn,pnx1004}   ^{wcj,nn3605}   ^{pp,pnx} ^{pta3426}   ^{qpf5414}
made*him*overseer over his house, and   all   *that* he   had   he   put   into his

^{pp,nn,pnx3027}
hand.

                ^{wcs,qmf1961}   ^{pr4480/ad227}   ^{hipf6485/pnx(853)}
5 And it*came*to*pass from*the*time *that* he had made*him*overseer in his

pp,nn,pnx**1004**   wcj,pr5921 cs,nn3605 pnl834 pp,pnx pta3426   nn**3068** wcs,pimf**1288** (853)   df,nn4713
house, and over all that he had, that the LORD blessed   the Egyptian's

cs,nn**1004**   pp,cs,nn1558/nn3130   cs,nn**1293**   nn**3068** wcs,qmf**1961**   pp,cs,nn3605 pnl834 pp,pnx
house for*Joseph's*sake; and the blessing of the LORD   was   upon   all   that he

pta3426   dfp,nn**1004**   wcj,dfp,nn**7704**
had in the house, and in the   field.

wcs,qmf**5800** cs,nn3605 pnl834 pp,pnx   nn3130   pp,cs,nn**3027**   qpf3045 wcj,ptn**3808**
6 And he   left   all   that he had in Joseph's hand; and he knew   not

pnid3972   pr,pnx854 cj3588/cj518   df,nn3899 pnl834 pnp1931   qpta398   nn3130   wcs,qmf**1961**
aught he had,   save   the bread which he   did eat. And Joseph was a

cs,aj3303/nn8389   wcj,cs,aj3303   nn**4758**
goodly *person*, and well favored.

wcs,qmf**1961**   pr310 df,pndm428 df,pl,nn**1697**   pl,nn,pnx**113** cs,nn**802** wcs,qmf**5375** (853)
7 And it*came*to*pass after these things, that his master's wife cast   her

du,nn,pnx**5869** pr413   nn3130   wcs,qmf559 qmv7901 pr,pnx5973
eyes   upon Joseph; and she said, Lie with me.

wcs,pimf**3985**   wcs,qmf559 pr413   pl,nn,pnx**113** cs,nn**802** ptdm2005   nn,pnx**113**
8 But he refused, and said unto his master's wife, Behold, my master

qpf3045   ptn**3808** pnit4100   pr,pnx854   dfp,nn**1004**   qpf**5414** wcj,nn3605 pnl834
knoweth not what *is* with me in the house, and he hath committed all that

pp,pnx pta3426   pp,nn,pnx**3027**
he hath to my hand;

ptn,pnx369   aj1419   df,pndm2088 dfp,nn**1004** pr,pnx4480   wcj,ptn**3808**   qpf2820
9 *There is* none greater in this house than I; neither hath he kept back

pnid3972   pr,pnx4480   cj3588/cj518 pnx(853)   pp,pnl834 pnp859   nn,pnx**802** wcj,pnit349
any thing from me   but   thee, because thou *art* his wife: how then can I

qmf6213 df,pndm2063 df,aj1419   df,nn**7451**   wcs,qpf**2398**   pp,pl,nn**430**
do this great wickedness, and sin against God?

wcs,qmf**1961**   pp,pinc,pnx**1696** pr413   nn3130   nn**3117**   nn**3117**
10 And it*came*to*pass, as she   spoke   to Joseph day by day, that he

qpf**8085**   wcj,ptn**3808** pr,pnx413   pp,qnc7901 pr,pnx681   pp,qnc**1961** pr,pnx5973
hearkened not unto her, to lie by her, *or* to be with her.

wcs,qmf**1961**   df,pndm2088 dfp,nn**3117**   wcs,qmf935   df,nn,lh**1004**
11 And it*came*to*pass about this time, that *Joseph* went into the house

pp,qnc**6213**   nn,nn,pnx**4399**   wcj,ptn369/nn**376** pr4480/pl,cs,nn**376**   df,nn**1004** ad8033
to do his business; and *there was* none of*the*men of the house there

dfp,nn**1004**
within.

wcs,qmf,pnx8610   pp,nn,pnx899 pp,qnc559 qmv7901 pr,pnx5973
12 And she caught him by his garment, saying, Lie with me: and he

wcs,qmf**5800**   nn,pnx899   pp,nn,pnx**3027** wcs,qmf5127   wcs,qmf3318   df,nn,lh2351
left   his garment in her hand, and fled, and got him out.

wcs,qmf**1961**   pp,qnc,pnx**7200** cj3588   qpf**5800**   nn,pnx899
13 And it*came*to*pass, when she   saw   that he had left his garment in her

pp,nn,pnx**3027**   wcs,qmf5127 df,nn,lh2351
hand, and was fled forth,

wcs,qmf7121   pp,pl,cs,nn**376**   nn,pnx**1004**   wcs,qmf559   pp,pnx
14 That she called unto the   men   of her house, and spoke unto them,

pp,qnc559   qmv**7200**   hipf935   cs,nn**376**/nn5680   pp,pnx   pp,pinc6711 pp,pnx   qpf935
saying, See, he hath brought in   a Hebrew unto us to mock us; he came in

pr,pnx413   pp,qnc7901 pr,pnx5973   wcs,qmf7121   aj1419 pp,nn6963
unto me to lie with me, and I cried with a loud voice:

wcs,qmf**1961**   pp,qnc,pnx**8085** cj3588   hipf7311   nn,pnx6963
15 And it*came*to*pass, when he   heard   that I lifted up my voice and

wcs,qmf7121   wcs,qmf**5800**   nn,pnx899 pr,pnx681   wcs,qmf5127   wcs,qmf3318   df,nn,lh2351
cried, that he   left   his garment with me, and fled, and got him out.

wcj,ad1571 qpf6213 ptn3808/pnid3972 cj3588 qpf7760 pnx(853) dfp,nn953
also have I done nothing that they should put me into the dungeon.

    cs,nn8269 df,pl,qpta644 wcs,qmf7200 cj3588 qpf6622 aj2896 wcs,qmf559
16 When the chief baker saw that the interpretation was good, he said

pr413 nn3130 pnp589 cj637 pp,nn,pnx2472 wcj,ptdm2009 cs,nu7969 nn2751 pl,cs,nn5536
unto Joseph, I also *was* in my dream, and, behold, *I had* three white baskets

pr5921 nn,pnx7218
on my head:

    df,aj5945 wcj,dfp,nn5536 pr4480/cs,nn3605 cs,nn3978/cs,nn4639/qpta644
17 And in the uppermost basket *there was* of*all*manner of bakedmeats

nn6547 wcj,df,nn5775 qpta398 pnx(853) pr4480 df,nn5536 pr4480/pr5921
for Pharaoh; and the birds did eat them out of the basket upon my

nn,pnx7218
head.

   nn3130 wcs,qmf6030 wcs,qmf559 pndm2088 nn,pnx6623
18 And Joseph answered and said, This *is* the interpretation thereof: The

cs,nu7969 df,pl,nn5536 (pnp1992) cs,nu7969 pl,nn3117
three baskets *are* three days:

pp,ad5750 cs,nu7969 pl,nn3117 nn6547 qmf5375 (853) nn,pnx7218 pr4480/pr,pnx5921
19 Yet within three days shall Pharaoh lift up thy head from off thee,

  wcs,qpf8518 pnx(853) pr5921 nn6086 df,nn5775 wcs,qpf398 (853) nn,pnx1320
and shall hang thee on a tree; and the birds shall eat thy flesh

pr4480/pr,pnx5921
from off thee.

  wcs,qmf1961 df,nuor7992 dfp,nn3117 (853) nn6547 cs,nn3117/honc3205
20 And it*came*to*pass the third day, *which was* Pharaoh's birthday,

 wcs,qmf6213 nn4960 pp,cs,nn3605 pl,nn,pnx5650 wcs,qmf5375 (853) cs,nn7218
that he made a feast unto all his servants: and he lifted up the head of the

cs,nn8269 df,pl,nn4945 wcj(853) (cs,nn7218) cs,nn8269 df,pl,qpta644 pp,cs,nn8432 pl,nn,pnx5650
chief butler and of the chief baker among his servants.

  wcs,himf7725 (853) cs,nn8269 df,pl,nn4945 pr5921 nn,pnx4945
21 And he restored the chief butler unto his butlership again; and he

wcs,qmf5414 df,nn3563 pr5921 nn6547 cs,nn3709
gave the cup into Pharaoh's hand:

  qpf8518 wcj(853) cs,nn8269 df,pl,qpta644 pp,pnl834 nn3130 qpf6622 pp,pnx
22 But he hanged the chief baker: as Joseph had interpreted to them.

  wcj,ptn3808 cs,nn8269 df,pl,nn4945 qpf2142 (853) nn3130 wcs,qmf,pnx7911
23 Yet did not the chief butler remember Joseph, but forgot him.

Joseph Explains Pharaoh's Dream

  wcs,qmf1961 pr4480/cs,nn7093 du,nn8141/pl,nn3117 wcj,nn6547
41 And it*came*to*pass at*the*end of two*full*years, that Pharaoh

qpta2492 wcj,ptdm2009 qpta5975 pr5921 df,nn2975
dreamed: and, behold, he stood by the river.

wcj,ptdm2009 pl,qpta5927 pr4480 df,nn2975 nu7651 cs,aj3303 nn4758 pl,nn6510
2 And, behold, there came up out of the river seven well favored kine and

wcj,cs,aj1277/nn1320 wcs,qmf7462 dfp,nn260
fatfleshed; and they fed in a meadow.

  wcj,ptdm2009 nu7651 aj312 pl,nn6510 pl,qpta5927 pr,pnx310 pr4480 df,nn2975 cs,aj7451
3 And, behold, seven other kine came up after them out of the river, ill

nn4758 wcj,cs,aj1851/nn1320 wcs,qmf5975 pr681 df,pl,nn6510 pr5921 cs,nn8193
favored and leanfleshed; and stood by the *other* kine upon the brink of the

df,nn2975
river.

cs,aj**7451** df,nn**4758**   wcj,cs,aj1851/df,nn**1320** df,pl,nn6510   wcs,qmf398 (853)   nu7651 cs,aj3303

4 And the ill favored and leanfleshed kine did eat up   the seven well

df,nn**4758**   wcj,df,aj1277 df,pl,nn6510   nn6547   wcs,qmf3364

favored and   fat   kine. So Pharaoh awoke.

wcs,qmf3462   wcs,qmf2492   nuor8145   wcj,ptdm2009   nu7651

5 And he slept   and dreamed the second time: and, behold, seven

pl,nn7641   pl,qpta**5927**   nu259 pp,nn7070 aj1277   wcj,aj**2896**

ears*of*corn came up upon one stalk, rank and good.

wcj,ptdm2009   nu7651   aj1851   pl,nn7641   wcj,pl,cs,qptp7710   nn6921   pl,qpta6779

6 And, behold, seven thin ears and   blasted with the east wind sprung up

pr,pnx310

after them.

df,aj1851 df,pl,nn7641   wcs,qmf**1104**   (853)   nu7651 df,aj1277   wcj,df,aj4392 df,pl,nn7641

7 And the seven thin   ears devoured   the seven rank and   full   ears.

nn6547   wcs,qmf3364   wcj,ptdm2009   nn2472

And Pharaoh awoke, and, behold, *it was* a dream.

wcs,qmf**1961**   dfp,nn1242   nn,pnx**7307**   wcs,nimf6470

8 And it*came*to*pass in the morning that his spirit was troubled; and he

wcs,qmf7971   wcs,qmf**7121**   (853) cs,nn3605   pl,cs,nn**2748**   nn4714   wcj(853) cs,nn3605

sent and called for   all   the magicians of Egypt, and   all   the

aj,pnx**2450**   nn6547 wcs,pimf**5608** pp,pnx (853)   nn,pnx2472   wcj,ptn369

wise men thereof: and Pharaoh told   them   his dream; but *there was* none that

qpta6622 pnx(853)   pp,nn6547

could interpret   them unto Pharaoh.

wcs,pimf**1696**   cs,nn**8269** df,pl,nn**4945** (853)   nn6547 pp,qnc559 pnp589   hipt**2142**   (853)

9 Then spoke the chief butler   unto Pharaoh, saying, I do remember

pl,nn,pnx**2399**   df,nn**3117**

my faults this day:

nn6547   qpf**7107**   pr5921   pl,nn,pnx**5650**   wcs,qmf**5414** pnx(853)   pp,cs,nn4929

10 Pharaoh was wroth with his servants, and   put   me in ward in the

cs,nn**8269**   df,pl,nn2876 cs,nn**1004**   pnx(853)   wcj(853)   cs,nn**8269** df,pl,qpta644

captain of the guard's house, *both*   me and   the chief baker:

wcs,qmf2492   nn2472   nu259 pp,nn**3915** pnp589   wcj,pnp1931   qpf2492

11 And we dreamed a dream in one night, I   and   he; we dreamed each

nn376   pp,cs,nn6623   nn,pnx2472

man according to the interpretation of his dream.

wcj,ad8033 pr,pnx854   nn5288   nn5680   nn**5650**

12 And *there was* there with us a young man, a Hebrew, servant to the

pp,cs,nn**8269**   df,pl,nn2876   wcs,pimf**5608** pp,pnx   wcs,qmf6622   pp,pnx (853)   pl,nn,pnx2472

captain of the guard; and we   told   him, and he interpreted to us   our dreams;

nn376   pp,nn,pnx2472   qpf6622

to each man according to his dream he did interpret.

wcs,qmf**1961**   pp,pnl834   qpf6622   pp,pnx   ad**3651**   qpf**1961** pnx(853)

13 And it*came*to*pass,   as   he interpreted to us, so it was;   me he

hip**7725**   pr5921   nn,pnx3653   wcj,pnx(853)   qpf8518

restored unto mine office, and   him he hanged.

nn6547   wcs,qmf7971   wcs,qmf**7121** (853) nn3130   wcs,himf,pnx7323

14 Then Pharaoh sent   and called   Joseph, and they brought*him*hastily

pr4480 df,nn**953**   wcs,pimf1548   wcs,pimf2498   pl,nn,pnx8071   wcs,qmf935

out of the dungeon: and he shaved *himself*, and changed his raiment, and came in

pr413   nn6547

unto Pharaoh.

nn6547   wcs,qmf559 pr413   nn3130   qpf2492   nn2472   ptn369

15 And Pharaoh said unto Joseph, I have dreamed a dream, and *there is* none

wcj,qpta6622 pnx(853)   wcj,pnp589   qpf8085 pp,qnc559 pr,pnx5921
that can interpret   it: and   I   have heard say   of   thee, *that* thou canst

qmf8085   nn2472   pp,qnc6622 pnx(853)
understand a dream to interpret   it.

nn3130   wcs,qmf6030   (853)   nn6547 pp,qnc559   ptn,pnx1107   pl,nn430
16 And Joseph answered   Pharaoh, saying, *It is* not in me: God shall

qmf6030/nn6547   (853) cs,nn7965
give*Pharaoh*an*answer of   peace.

nn6547   wcs,pimf1696 pr413   nn3130   pp,nn,pnx2472 ptdm,pnx2009 qpta5975 pr5921
17 And Pharaoh   said   unto Joseph, In my dream, behold, I stood upon the

cs,nn8193 df,nn2975
bank of the river:

wcj,ptdm2009   pl,qpta5927   pr4480   df,nn2975 nu7651 pl,nn6510 cs,aj1277/nn1320
18 And, behold, there came up out of the river seven kine, fatfleshed and

wcj,cs,aj3303   nn8389   wcs,qmf7462   dfp,nn260
well favored; and they   fed   in a meadow:

wcj,ptdm2009 nu7651 aj312 pl,nn6510 pl,qpta5927 pr,pnx310   cs,aj1800   ad3966 wcj,cs,aj7451
19 And, behold, seven other kine came up after them, poor and very   ill

nn8389   wcj,cs,aj7534/nn1320 pp,pnp2007   ptn3808 qpf7200 pp,cs,nn3605 cs,nn776   nn4714
favored and leanfleshed, such as I never saw in   all   the land of Egypt for

dfp,nn7455
badness:

df,aj7534   wcj,df,aj7451 df,pl,nn6510   wcs,qmf398 (853)   df,aj7223 nu7651 df,aj1277
20 And the lean and the ill favored kine did eat up   the first seven fat

df,pl,nn6510
kine:

wcs,qmf935/pr413/nn,pnx7130   wcj,ptn3808   nipf3045   cj3588
21 And when they had eaten*them*up, it could not be known that they had

qpf935/pr413/nn,pnx7130   wcj,pl,nn,pnx4758/aj7451 pp,pnl834   dfp,nn8462
eaten   them; but they *were* still ill favored,   as at the beginning. So I

wcs,qmf3364
awoke.

wcs,qmf7200   pp,nn,pnx2472   wcj,ptdm2009 nu7651 pl,nn7641 pl,qpta5927   nu259
22 And I   saw   in my dream, and, behold, seven ears   came up in one

pp,nn7070 aj4392   wcj,aj2896
stalk, full and good:

wcj,ptdm2009 nu7651 pl,nn7641 pl,qptp6798 aj1851   pl,cs,qptp7710   nn6921
23 And, behold, seven ears, withered, thin, *and* blasted with the east wind,

pl,qpta6779 pr,pnx310
sprung up after them:

df,aj1851 df,pl,nn7641 wcs,qmf1104 (853)   nu7651 df,aj2896 df,pl,nn7641   wcs,qmf559
24 And the thin   ears devoured   the seven good ears: and I told *this*

pr413   df,pl,nn2748   wcj,ptn369   hipt5046   pp,pnx
unto the magicians; but *there was* none that could declare *it* to me.

nn3130   wcs,qmf559 pr413   nn6547   cs,nn2472   nn6547 (pnp1931)   nu259 df,pl,nn430
25 And Joseph said   unto Pharaoh, The dream of Pharaoh   *is* one: God

hipf5046   pp,nn6547 (853) pnl834   qpta6213
hath showed Pharaoh   what he *is* about to do.

nu7651 df,aj2896 pl,nn6510 (pnp2007)   nu7651 pl,nn8141   wcj,nu7651 df,aj2896 df,pl,nn7641
26 The seven good kine   *are* seven years; and the seven good ears

(pnp2007)   nu7651 pl,nn8141   nn2472 (pnp1931)   nu259
are seven years: the dream   *is* one.

wcj,nu7651 df,aj7534   wcj,df,aj7451 df,pl,nn6510   df,pl,qpta5927 pr,pnx310   (pnp2007)
27 And the seven thin and ill favored kine that came up after them

nu7651   pl,nn8141   wcj,nu7651 df,aj7386   df,pl,nn7641 pl,cs,qptp7710   df,nn6921   qmf1961
are seven years; and the seven empty ears   blasted with the east wind shall be
nu7651   pl,cs,nn8141   nn7458
seven years of famine.

pndm1931   df,nn1697   pnl834   pipf1696   pr413   nn6547   pnl834 df,pl,nn430
28 This *is* the thing which I have spoken unto Pharaoh: What God *is* about
qpta6213   hipf7200   (853)   nn6547
to do he showeth   unto Pharaoh.

ptdm2009   pl,qpta935 nu7651   pl,nn8141   aj1419   nn7647   pp,cs,nn3605   cs,nn776
29 Behold, there come seven years of great plenty throughout   all   the land
nn4714
of Egypt:

wcj,qpf6965 pr,pnx310   cs,nu7651 pl,cs,nn8141   nn7458   cs,nn3605
30 And there shall   arise   after them seven   years of famine; and   all   the
df,nn7647   wcj,nipf7911   pp,cs,nn776   nn4714   df,nn7458   wcj,pipf3615 (853)
plenty shall be forgotten in the   land   of Egypt; and the famine shall consume
df,nn776
the land;

df,nn7647   wcj,ptn3808   nimf3045   dfp,776   pr4480/pl,cs,nn6440 df,pndm1931
31 And the plenty shall   not   be known in the land by*reason*of   that
df,nn7458   pr310/ad3651   cj3588 pnp1931   ad3966   aj3515
famine following; for   it   *shall be* very grievous.

wcj,pr5921   df,nn2472   ninc8138   pr413   nn6547 du,nn6471   cj3588
32 And   for   that the dream was doubled unto Pharaoh twice; *it is* because the
df,nn1697   nipt3559   pr4480/pr5973 df,pl,nn430   df,pl,nn430   wcj,pipt4116   pp,qnc,pnx6213
thing *is* established   by   God, and God will shortly bring*it*to*pass.
wcj,ad6258   nn6547   qci7200   nn376   nipt995   wcj,aj2450   wcj,qmf,pnx7896
33 Now   therefore let Pharaoh look out a man discreet and wise, and   set
pr5921   cs,nn776   nn4714
him over the land of Egypt.

nn6547   qmf6213   wcj,hici6485   pl,nn6496   pr5921   df,nn776
34 Let Pharaoh do *this*, and let him appoint officers over the land, and
wcs,pipf2567   (853)   cs,nn776   nn4714   pp,nu7651   df,nn7647   pl,cs,nn8141
take*up*the*fifth*part of   the land of Egypt in the seven plenteous years.
wcj,qmf6908 (853) cs,nn3605   cs,nn400   df,pndm428 df,aj2896 df,pl,nn8141   df,pl,qpta935
35 And let them gather   all   the food of those good   years that come,
wcj,qmf6651 nn1250 pr8478   cs,nn3027   nn6547   wcs,qpf8104   nn400
and lay up corn under the   hand of Pharaoh, and let them   keep   food in the
dfp,pl,nn5892
cities.

df,nn400   wcs,qpf1961   pp,nn6487   dfp,nn776   pp,cs,nu7651 pl,cs,nn8141
36 And that food shall   be   for store to the land against the   seven   years
df,nn7458   pnl834   qmf1961   pp,cs,nn776   nn4714   df,nn776 nimf3772 wcj,ptn3808
of famine, which shall be   in the land   of Egypt; that the land perish   not
dfp,nn7458
through the famine.

Pharaoh Makes Joseph A Ruler

df,nn1697   wcs,qmf3190   pp,du,cs,nn5869   nn6547   wcj,pp,du,cs,nn5869
37 And the thing was good in the   eyes   of Pharaoh, and in the   eyes
cs,nn3605   pl,nn,pnx5650
of   all   his servants.

nn6547   wcs,qmf559 pr413   pl,nn,pnx5650   he,qmf4672   pp,pndm2088

38 And Pharaoh said unto his servants, Can we find *such a one* as this

nn376 pp,pnx pnl834   cs,nn7307   pl,nn430

is, a man in whom the Spirit of God *is*?

nn6547   wcs,qmf559 pr413   nn3130   ad310   pl,nn430   hinc3045 pnx(853)

39 And Pharaoh said unto Joseph, Forasmuch as God hath showed thee

(853) cs,nn3605 pndm2063   ptn369   nipt995   wcj,aj2450 pp,pnx3644

all this, *there is* none so discreet and wise as thou *art*:

pnp859   qmf1961 pr5921   nn,pnx1004   wcj,pr5921   nn,pnx6310   cs,nn3605

40 Thou shalt be over my house, and according unto thy word shall all

nn,pnx5971   qmf5401 ad7535   df,nn3678   qmf1431   pr,pnx4480

my people be ruled: only in the throne will I be greater than thou.

nn6547   wcs,qmf559 pr413   nn3130   qmv7200   qpf5414 pnx(853)   pr5921 cs,nn3605

41 And Pharaoh said unto Joseph, See, I have set thee over all the

cs,nn776   nn4714

land of Egypt.

nn6547   wcs,himf5493 (853)   nn,pnx2885 pr4480/pr5921   nn,pnx3027   wcs,qmf5414 pnx(853)

42 And Pharaoh took off his ring from his hand, and put it

pr5921   nn3130 cs,nn3027   wcs,himf3847 pnx(853)   pl,cs,nn899   nn8336   wcs,qmf7760

upon Joseph's hand, and arrayed him in vestures of fine linen, and put a

df,nn2091 cs,nn7242 pr5921   nn,pnx6677

gold chain about his neck;

pnx(853)   wcs,himf7392   df,nn4932 pp,cs,nn4818 pnl834 pp,pnx

43 And he made him to ride in the second chariot which he had; and

wcs,qmf7121 pp,pl,nn,pnx6440   86   wcj,qna5414 pnx(853)   pr5921 cs,nn3605

they cried before him, Bow*the*knee: and he made him *ruler* over all

cs,nn776   nn4714

the land of Egypt.

nn6547   wcs,qmf559 pr413   nn3130   pnp589   nn6547   wcj,ptn,pnx1107

44 And Pharaoh said unto Joseph, I *am* Pharaoh, and without thee shall

ptn3808 nn376 himf7311 (853)   nn,pnx3027   wcj(853) nn,pnx7272 pp,cs,nn3605 cs,nn776   nn4714

no man lift up his hand or foot in all the land of Egypt.

nn6547   wcs,qmf7121   nn3130 cs,nn8034   nn6847   wcs,qmf5414 pp,pnx

45 And Pharaoh called Joseph's name Zaphnath-paaneah; and he gave him to

pp,nn802 (853)   nn621   cs,nn1323   nn6319   cs,nn3548   nn204   nn3130   wcs,qmf3318

wife Asenath the daughter of Poti-pherah priest of On. And Joseph went out

pr5921   cs,nn776   nn4714

over *all* the land of Egypt.

wcj,nn3130   nu7970 nn8141 cs,nn1121   pp,qnc,pnx5975 pp,pl,cs,nn6440 nn6547 cs,nn4428

46 And Joseph *was* thirty years old when he stood before Pharaoh king

nn4714   nn3130   wcs,qmf3318   pr4480/pp,pl,cs,nn6440   nn6547   wcs,qmf5674

of Egypt. And Joseph went out from*the*presence of Pharaoh, and went

pp,cs,nn3605   cs,nn776   nn4714

throughout all the land of Egypt.

pp,nu7651   df,nn7647   pl,cs,nn8141   df,nn776   wcs,qmf6213   pp,pl,nn7062

47 And in the seven plenteous years the earth brought forth by handfuls.

wcs,qmf6908   (853) cs,nn3605   cs,nn400   nu7651 pl,nn8141 pnl834   qpf1961

48 And he gathered up all the food of the seven years, which were in

---

41:42-49 Joseph was at the summit of political power. The ring and necklace were symbols of his office; riding in the second chariot suggests that Joseph was second in command over the whole kingdom. Joseph's service in the house of Potiphar and in the prison was divinely ordained preparation for directing the most populous nation in the ancient world. His scheme of gathering grain directly under Pharaoh's control (41:35, 48) undermined the power of the provincial nobles, and gives us reason to believe that he served under Pharaoh Sesostris III.

^{pp,cs,nn776} ⁿⁿ⁴⁷¹⁴ ^{wcs,qmf5414} ⁿⁿ⁴⁰⁰ ^{dfp,pl,nn5892} ^{cs,nn400} ^{cs,nn7704}
the land of Egypt, and laid up the food in the cities: the food of the field,
^{pnl834} ^{pr,pnx5439} ^{df,nn5892} ^{qpf5414} ^{pp,nn,pnx8432}
which *was* round about every city, laid*he*up in the same.

ⁿⁿ³¹³⁰ ^{wcs,qmf6651} ⁿⁿ¹²⁵⁰ ^{pp,cs,nn2344} ^{df,nn3220} ^{ad3966} ^{hina7235} ^{pr5704} ^(cj3588)
49 And Joseph gathered corn as the sand of the sea, very much, until
^{qpf2308} ^{pp,qnc5608} ^{cj3588} ^{ptn369} ⁿⁿ⁴⁵⁵⁷
he left numbering; for *it was* without number.

^{wcj,pp,nn3130} ^{pupf3205} ^{du,cs,nu8147} ^{pl,nn1121} ^{pp,ad2962} ^{cs,nn8141} ^{df,nn7458} ^{qmf935}
50 And unto Joseph were born two sons before the years of famine came,
^{pnl834} ⁿⁿ⁶²¹ ^{cs,nn1323} ⁿⁿ⁶³¹⁹ ^{cs,nn3548} ⁿⁿ²⁰⁴ ^{qpf3205} ^{pp,pnx}
which Asenath the daughter of Poti-pherah priest of On bore unto him.

ⁿⁿ³¹³⁰ ^{wcs,qmf7121} ⁽⁸⁵³⁾ ^{cs,nn8034} ^{df,nn1060} ⁿⁿ⁴⁵¹⁹ ^{cj3588} ^{pl,nn430}
51 And Joseph called the name of the firstborn Manasseh: For God, *said*
^{pipf,pnx5382} ⁽⁸⁵³⁾ ^{cs,nn3605} ^{nn,pnx5999} ^{wcj(853)} ^{cs,nn3605} ^{nn,pnx1} ^{cs,nn1004}
he, hath made me forget all my toil, and all my father's house.

^{wcj(853)} ^{cs,nn8034} ^{df,nuor8145} ^{qpf7121} ⁿⁿ⁶⁶⁹ ^{cj3588} ^{pl,nn430}
52 And the name of the second called he Ephraim: For God hath caused
^{hipf,pnx6509} ^{pp,cs,nn776} ^{nn,pnx6040}
me to be fruitful in the land of my affliction.

^{cs,nu7651} ^{pl,cs,nn8141} ^{df,nn7647} ^{pnl834} ^{qpf1961} ^{pp,cs,nn776} ⁿⁿ⁴⁷¹⁴
53 And the seven years of plenteousness, that was in the land of Egypt,
^{wcs,qmf3615}
were ended.

^{cs,nu7651} ^{pl,cs,nn8141} ^{df,nn7458} ^{wcs,himf2490} ^{pp,qnc935} ^{pp,pnl834} ⁿⁿ³¹³⁰
54 And the seven years of dearth began to come, according as Joseph had
^{qpf559} ⁿⁿ⁷⁴⁵⁸ ^{wcs,qmf1961} ^{pp,cs,nn3605} ^{df,pl,nn776} ^{wcj,pp,cs,nn3605} ^{cs,nn776} ⁿⁿ⁴⁷¹⁴
said: and the dearth was in all lands; but in all the land of Egypt
^{qpf1961} ⁿⁿ³⁸⁹⁹
there was bread.

^{cs,nn3605} ^{cs,nn776} ⁿⁿ⁴⁷¹⁴ ^{wcs,qmf7456} ^{df,nn5971} ^{wcs,qmf6817} ^{pr413}
55 And when all the land of Egypt was famished, the people cried to
ⁿⁿ⁶⁵⁴⁷ ^{dfp,nn3899} ⁿⁿ⁶⁵⁴⁷ ^{wcs,qmf559} ^{pp,cs,nn3605} ⁿⁿ⁴⁷¹⁴ ^{qmv1980} ^{pr413}
Pharaoh for bread: and Pharaoh said unto all the Egyptians, Go unto
ⁿⁿ³¹³⁰ ^{pnl834} ^{qmf559} ^{pp,pnx} ^{qmf6213}
Joseph; what he saith to you, do.

^{wcj,df,nn7458} ^{qpf1961} ^{pr5921} ^{cs,nn3605} ^{pl,cs,nn6440} ^{df,nn776} ⁿⁿ³¹³⁰ ^{wcs,qmf6605}
56 And the famine was over all the face of the earth: And Joseph opened
⁽⁸⁵³⁾ ^{cs,nn3605} ^{pnl834/pp,pnx} ^{wcs,qmf7666} ^{pp,nn4714} ^{df,nn7458}
all the storehouses, and sold unto the Egyptians; and the famine
^{wcs,qmf2388} ^{pp,cs,nn776} ⁿⁿ⁴⁷¹⁴
waxed sore in the land of Egypt.

^{wcj,cs,nn3605} ^{df,nn776} ^{qpf935} ^{nn,lh4714} ^{pr413} ⁿⁿ³¹³⁰ ^{pp,qnc7666}
57 And all countries came into Egypt to Joseph for to buy *corn*;
^{cj3588} ^{df,nn7458} ^{qpf2388} ^{pp,cs,nn3605} ^{df,nn776}
because that the famine was*so*sore in all lands.

Joseph's Brothers Come to Buy Food

ⁿⁿ³²⁹⁰ ^{wcs,qmf7200} ^{cj3588} ^{pta3426} ⁿⁿ⁷⁶⁶⁸ ^{pp,nn4714} ⁿⁿ³²⁹⁰ ^{wcs,qmf559}
42 Now when Jacob saw that there was corn in Egypt, Jacob said
^{pp,pl,nn,pnx1121} ^{pp,pnit4100} ^{htmf7200}
unto his sons, Why do ye look*one*upon*another?

^{wcs,qmf559} ^{ptdm2009} ^{qpf8085} ^{cj3588} ^{pta3426} ⁿⁿ⁷⁶⁶⁸ ^{pp,nn4714}
2 And he said, Behold, I have heard that there is corn in Egypt:

qmv3381　　ad,lh8033　　wcj,qmv7666　pp,pnx　　pr4480/ad8033　　　　　　wcj,qmf2421

get*you*down thither, and　buy　for us from thence; that we may　live,　and

wcj,ptn3808　qmf4191

not　die.

nn3130　nu6235　pl,cs,nn251　wcs,qmf3381　　pp,qnc7666　nn1250　pr4480/nn4714

3 And Joseph's ten brethren went down to　buy　corn in Egypt.

wcj(853)　　nn1144　　nn3130　cs,nn251　　nn3290　qpf7971 ptn3808　pr854　　pl,nn,pnx251　cj3588

4 But　　　Benjamin, Joseph's brother, Jacob sent　not　with his brethren; for

qpf559　　cj6435　　　nn611　qmf,pnx7122

he said, Lest peradventure mischief befall　him.

pl,cs,nn1121　　nn3478　wcs,qmf935　pp,qnc7666　　pp,cs,nn8432　　　df,pl,qpta935　cj3588

5 And the　sons　of Israel came to　buy　corn among those that came: for

df,nn7458　qpf1961　pp,cs,nn776　　nn3667

the famine was in the　land　of Canaan.

wcj,nn3130　(pnp1931)　　df,aj7989　pr5921　df,nn776　pnp1931　　　　df,hipt7666

6 And Joseph　　was the governor over the land, and　he　it was that sold

pp,cs,nn3605　　cs,nn5971　　　df,nn776　　　nn3130　pl,cs,nn251　wcs,qmf935

to　all　the　people　of the　land: and　Joseph's　brethren　came,　and

wcs,htmf*7812　　　pp,pnx　　　　du,nn639　　nn,lh776

bowed*down*themselves before　him with their faces to the earth.

nn3130　wcs,qmf7200　(853)　　pl,nn,pnx251　　　　　wcs,himf,pnx5234

7 And　Joseph　saw　　his　brethren,　and　he　knew　them,　but

wcs,htmf5234　　pr,pnx413　　　wcs,pimf1696　aj7186　pr,pnx854　　　wcs,qmf559

made*himself*strange unto　them, and　spoke　roughly　unto　them; and he　said

pr,pnx413　　pr4480/ad370　qpf935　　　wcs,qmf559　pr4480/cs,nn776　　nn3667　pp,qnc7666

unto　them, Whence come ye? And they　said, From*the*land of Canaan to　buy

nn400

food.

nn3130　wcs,himf5234 (853)　　pl,nn,pnx251　wcj,pnp1992 hipf,pnx5234 ptn3808

8 And Joseph knew　　his brethren, but　they　knew　not him.

nn3130　wcs,qmf2142　(853)　df,pl,nn2472　pnl834　　qpf2492　　pp,pnx

9 And Joseph remembered　the　dreams　which　he　dreamed of them, and

wcs,qmf559 pr,pnx413　　pnp859　pl,pipt7270　pp,qnc7200 (853)　cs,nn6172　　df,nn776

said　unto them, Ye are spies; to　see　the nakedness of the land ye are

qpf935

come.

wcs,qmf559　pr,pnx413　ptn3808　nn,pnx113　　pp,qnc7666　nn400

10 And they　said　unto　him, Nay, my　lord,　but to　buy　food are thy

wcj,pl,nn,pnx5650　qpf935

servants come.

pnp5168　nn,pnx3605 nu259　nn376　pl,cs,nn1121 pnp587　aj3651　　　pl,nn,pnx5650 qpf1961 ptn3808

11 We are　all　one　man's　sons;　we are true men, thy servants are　no

pl,pipt7270

spies.

wcs,qmf559 pr,pnx413　　ptn3808 cj3588　pp,qnc7200　cs,nn6172　　df,nn776

12 And he　said　unto　them, Nay, but to　see　the nakedness of the land ye

qpf935

are come.

42:8 Why did Joseph's brothers not recognize him? To begin with, Joseph had been a teenager when he was sold into slavery. Almost twenty years had elapsed since that time. His brothers had never expected to see him again; as far as they were concerned, he was dead. In fact, both because of regret and because Jacob had most likely lamented over the loss of Joseph for all these years, his brothers had likely done all they could to forget Joseph. As an Egyptian leader, he would have been clean-shaven and well-dressed. And lastly, Joseph, whose voice was probably much different now, spoke to them through an interpreter. They would never have dreamed that it could be Joseph.

13 And they said, Thy servants *are* twelve brethren, the sons of one man in the land of Canaan; and, behold, the youngest *is* this day with our father, and one *is* not.

14 And Joseph said unto them, That *is it* that I spoke unto you, saying, Ye *are* spies:

15 Hereby ye shall be proved: By the life of Pharaoh ye shall not go forth hence, except your youngest brother come hither.

16 Send one of you, and let him fetch your brother, and ye shall be kept in prison, that your words may be proved, whether *there be any* truth in you: or else by the life of Pharaoh surely ye *are* spies.

17 And he put*them*all*together into ward three days.

18 And Joseph said unto them the third day, This do, and live; *for* I fear God:

19 If ye *be* true *men*, let one of your brethren be bound in the house of your prison: go ye, carry corn for the famine of your houses:

20 But bring your youngest brother unto me; so shall your words be verified, and ye shall not die. And they did so.

21 And they said one to another, We *are* verily guilty concerning our brother, in that we saw the anguish of his soul, when he besought us, and we would not hear; therefore is this distress come upon us.

22 And Reuben answered them, saying, Spoke I not unto you, saying, Do not sin against the child; and ye would not hear? therefore, behold, also his blood is required.

23 And they knew not that Joseph understood *them*; for he spoke unto them by an interpreter.

24 And he turned*himself*about from them, and wept; and returned to them again, and communed with them, and took from them Simeon, and bound him before their eyes.

ptn3808 pr,pnx413   wcj,hipf,pnx3322   pp,pl,nn,pnx6440   pp,pnx   wcj,qpf2398

him not unto thee, and   set   him before thee, then let me bear*the*blame

cs,nn3605/df,pl,nn3117

forever:

cj3588   cj3884   htpf*4102   cj3588   ad6258   qpf7725   pndm2088   du,nn6471

10 For except we had lingered, surely now we had returned this second time.

nn,pnx1   nn3478   wcs,qmf559   pr,pnx413   cj518   ad3651   pnit645   qmv6213

11 And their father Israel said unto them, If *it must be* so now, do

pndm2063   qmv3947   pr4480/cs,nn2173   df,nn776   pp,pl,nn,pnx3627   wcj,himv3381

this; take of*the*best*fruits in the land in your vessels, and carry down the

dfp,nn376   nn4503   cs,nn4592   nn6875   wcj,cs,nn4592   nn1706   nn5219   wcj,nn3910   pl,nn992

man a present, a little balm, and a little honey, spices, and myrrh, nuts, and

wcj,pl,nn8247

almonds:

qmv3947   nn4932   wcj,nn3701   pp,nn,pnx3027   wcj(853)   df,nn3701

12 And take double money in your hand; and   the money that was

df,hopf7725   pp,cs,nn6310   pl,nn,pnx572   himf7725   pp,nn,pnx3027

brought again in the mouth of your sacks, carry*it*again in your hand;

ad194   pnp1931   nn4870

peradventure it *was* an oversight:

qmv3947   wcj(853)   nn,pnx251   wcj,qmv6965   qmf7725   pr413   df,nn376

13 Take also   your brother, and arise, go again unto the man:

wcj,nn410   nn7706   qmf5414   pp,pnx   pl,nn7356   pp,pl,cs,nn6440   df,nn376

14 And God Almighty give you mercy before the man, that he may

wcs,pipf7971   (853)   pp,pnx   aj312   nn,pnx251   wcj(853)   nn1144   pp,pnl834 wcj,pnp589   qpf7921

send away   your other brother, and   Benjamin. If I be bereaved *of*

qpf7921

my children, I am bereaved.

df,pl,nn376   wcs,qmf3947   (853)   df,pndm2063   df,nn4503   qpf3947   wcj,nn4932   nn3701

15 And the men took   that present, and they took double money in

pp,nn,pnx3027   wcj(853)   nn1144   wcs,qmf6965   wcs,qmf3381   nn4714

their hand, and   Benjamin; and rose up, and went down to Egypt, and

wcs,qmf5975 pp,pl,cs,nn6440   nn3130

stood before Joseph.

nn3130   wcs,qmf7200   (853)   nn1144   pr,pnx854   wcs,qmf559

16 And when Joseph saw   Benjamin with them, he said to the

dpf,pnl834/pr5921   nn,pnx1004   himv935   (853)   df,pl,nn376 df,nn,lh1004   wcj,qmv2873/nn2874   wcj,himv3559

ruler of his house, Bring *these* men home, and slay, and make ready;

cj3588   df,pl,nn376   qmf398 pr,pnx854   dfp,pl,nn6672

for *these* men shall dine with me at noon.

df,nn376   wcs,qmf6213 pp,pnl834   nn3130   qpf559   df,nn376 wcs,himf935 (853)   df,pl,nn376

17 And the man did as Joseph bade; and the man brought the men

nn3130   cs,nn,lh1004

into Joseph's house.

df,pl,nn376   wcs,qmf3372   cj3588   hopf935   nn3130   cs,nn1004

18 And the men were afraid, because they were brought into Joseph's house;

wcs,qmf559   pr5921/cs,nn1697   df,nn3701   df,qpta7725   pp,pl,nn,pnx572

and they said, Because of the money that was returned in our sacks at the

dfp,nn8462   pnp587   pl,hopf935   pp,htnc*1556   pr,pnx5921   wcj,pp,htnc5307

first time are we brought in; that he may seek occasion against us, and fall

pr,pnx5921   wcj,pp,qnc3947 pnx(853)   pp,pl,nn5650   wcj(853)   pl,nn,pnx2543

upon us, and take   us for bondmen, and   our asses.

wcs,qmf5066   pr413   df,nn376/pnl834/pr5921   nn3130   cs,nn1004

19 And they came near to the steward of Joseph's house, and they

wcs,pimf1696   pr,pnx413

communed with him at the door of the house,

cs,nn6607   df,nn1004

wcs,qmf**559** pte994 nn,pnx**113**   qna3381/qpf3381   dfp,nn8462   pp,qnc7666

20 And said,   O   sir,   we came*indeed*down at the first time to buy

nn**400**

food:

wcs,qmf**1961**   cj3588   qpf935 pr413   df,nn4411   wcs,qmf6605 (853)

21 And it*came*to*pass, when we came to the inn, that we opened   our

pl,nn,pnx572 wcj,ptdm2009   nn376 cs,nn3701   pp,cs,nn**6310**   nn,pnx572 nn,pnx3701

sacks, and, behold, *every* man's money *was* in the mouth of his sack, our money

pp,nn,pnx4948   wcs,himf**7725**/pnx(853)   pp,nn,pnx**3027**

in full weight: and we have brought*it*again in our hand.

aj312 wcj,nn3701   hipf3381   pp,nn,pnx**3027** pp,qnc7666 nn**400**

22 And other money have we brought down in our hands to buy food: we

ptn**3808** qpf3045 pnit4310 qpf**7760**   nn,pnx3701   pp,pl,nn,pnx572

cannot tell who put our money in our sacks.

wcs,qmf559 nn**7965**   pp,pnx qmf**3372** ptn408   pl,nn,pnx**430**   wcj,pl,cs,nn**430**

23 And he said, Peace *be* to you, fear not: your God, and the God of

nn,pnx1   qpf**5414** pp,pnx nn4301   pp,pl,nn,pnx572 pnx(pr413) qpf935   nn,pnx3701

your father, hath given you treasure in your sacks: I had your money. And

wcs,himf3318/(853)/nn8095   pr,pnx413

he brought*Simeon*out unto them.

df,nn**376** wcs,himf935 (853)   df,pl,nn**376**   nn3130 cs,nn,lh**1004**   wcs,qmf**5414**

24 And the man brought   the men into Joseph's house, and gave *them*

pl,nn**4325**   wcs,qmf**7364** du,nn,pnx**7272**   wcs,qmf**5414**   pp,pl,nn,pnx2543 nn4554

water, and they washed their feet; and he gave their asses provender.

wcs,himf**3559**   (853)   df,nn**4503** pr5704   nn3130 qnc935   dfp,pl,nn6672 cj3588

25 And they made ready   the present against Joseph came at noon: for

qpf**8085** cj3588   qmf398 nn3899 ad8033

they heard that they should eat bread there.

nn3130 wcs,qmf935 df,nn,lh**1004**   wcs,himf935 pp,pnx (853)   df,nn**4503** pnl834

26 And when Joseph came home, they brought him   the present which *was*

pp,nn,pnx**3027**   df,nn,lh**1004**   wcs,htmf**7812**   pp,pnx   nn,lh776

in their hand into the house, and bowed themselves to him to the earth.

wcs,qmf**7592** pp,pnx   pp,nn7965   wcs,qmf**559**   nn,pnx1 he,nn**7965**

27 And he asked them of *their* welfare, and said, *Is* your father well, the

df,aj**2205**   pnl834   qpf**559**   he,ad,pnx5750 aj**2416**

old man of whom ye spoke? *Is* he   yet   alive?

wcs,qmf**559**   pp,nn,pnx**5650**   pp,nn,pnx1   nn**7965**   ad,pnx5750

28 And they answered, Thy servant our father *is* in good health, he *is*   yet

aj**2416**   wcs,qmf6915   wcs,htmf*7812**

alive. And they bowed*down*their*heads, and made obeisance.

wcs,qmf**5375**   du,nn,pnx**5869**   wcs,qmf**7200**   nn,pnx251 (853)   nn1144

29 And he lifted up his eyes,   and saw his brother   Benjamin, his

nn,pnx517 cs,nn**1121**   wcs,qmf**559** he,pndm2088   df,aj6996 nn,pnx251   pnl834   qpf**559** pr,pnx413

mother's son, and said, *Is* this your younger brother, of whom ye spoke unto

wcs,qmf**559** pl,nn**430** qmf,pnx**2603**   nn,pnx**1121**

me? And he said, God be gracious unto thee, my son.

nn3130   wcs,pimf4116   cj3588   pl,nn,pnx**7356**   nipf3648 pr413   nn,pnx**251**

30 And Joseph made haste; for his bowels did yearn upon his brother: and he

wcs,pimf**1245**   pp,qnc1058   wcs,qmf935   df,nn,lh**2315**   wcs,qmf1058 ad,lh8033

sought *where* to weep; and he entered into *his* chamber, and wept there.

wcs,qmf**7364**   pl,nn,pnx**6440**   wcs,qmf3318   wcs,htmf662   wcs,qmf**559**

31 And he washed his face,   and went out, and refrained himself, and said,

qmv**7760** nn3899

Set on bread.

wcs,qmf**7760** pp,pnx   pp,nn,pnx905   wcj,pp,pnx   pp,nn,pnx905

32 And they set on for him by himself, and for them by themselves, and for

wcj,dfp,pl,nn4713   df,pl,qpta398   pr,pnx854   pp,nn,pnx905   cj3588   df,pl,nn4713
the Egyptians, which did   eat   with him, by themselves: because the Egyptians

qmf3201 ptn3808 pp,qnc398   nn3899 pr854   df,pl,nn5680 cj3588 pndm1931   nn8441
might not   eat   bread with the Hebrews; for   that   is an abomination unto the

pp,pl,nn4714
Egyptians.

            wcs,qmf3427 pp,pl,nn,pnx6440   df,nn1060   pp,nn,pnx1062
33 And they   sat   before   him, the firstborn according to his birthright, and

wcj,df,aj6810   pp,nn,pnx6812   df,pl,nn376 wcs,qmf8539 nn376 pr413 nn,pnx7453
the youngest according to his youth: and the men marveled one at another.

            wcs,qmf5375   pl,nn4864   pr,pnx413   pr4480/pr854 pl,nn,pnx6440
34 And he   took   and sent messes unto them from   before   him: but

nn1144 cs,nn4864   wcs,qmf7235/pr4480/pl,cs,nn4864/nu2568/pl,nn3027   nn,pnx3605
Benjamin's mess was   five*times*so*much*as   any of theirs. And they

wcs,qmf8354   wcs,qmf7937   pr,pnx5973
drank, and were merry with him.

Joseph's Silver Cup is Missing

                wcs,pimf6680   (853)   pnl834/pr5921   nn,pnx1004 pp,qnc559 pimv4390 (853)
44 And he commanded   the steward of his house, saying, Fill   the

df,pl,nn376 pl,cs,nn572   nn400   pp,pnl834   qmf3201 qnc5375   wcj,qmv7760
men's   sacks with food, as*much*as they can carry, and   put

nn376   cs,nn3701   nn,pnx572 pp,cs,nn6310
every man's money in his sack's mouth.

            qmf7760   wcj(853)   nn,pnx1375   df,nn3701 cs,nn1375   cs,nn572   pp,cs,nn6310
2 And put   my cup, the silver cup, in the sack's mouth of the

df,aj6996   nn,pnx7668 wcj(853) cs,nn3701   wcs,qmf6213   pp,cs,nn1697 pnl834
youngest, and his corn   money. And he did according to the word that

nn3130   pipf1696
Joseph had spoken.

            df,nn1242   qpf215   wcj,df,pl,nn376   pupf7971   pnp1992
3 As soon as the morning was light, the   men   were sent away, they and

wcj,pl,nn,pnx2543
their   asses.

            pnp1992   qpf3318   (853)   df,nn5892   ptn3808   hipf7368 wcj,nn3130
4 And when they were gone*out*of   the city, and not yet far off, Joseph

qpf559   dfp,pnl834/pr5921/nn,pnx1004 qmv6965 qmv7291 pr310   df,pl,nn376
said unto his   steward,   Up, follow after the men; and when thou dost

wcj,hipf,pnx5381   wcj,qpf559 pr,pnx413   pp,pnit4100   pipf7999   nn7451 pr8478 nn2896
overtake them,   say unto them, Wherefore have ye rewarded evil for good?

    he,ptn3808 pndm2088 pp,pnx   pnl834   nn,pnx113 qmf8354   pp,pnx
5 Is   not   this   it   in which my lord drinketh, and whereby

wcj,pnp1931/pina5172/pimf5172   hipf7489   pnl834 qpf6213
indeed*he*divineth? ye have done evil in so doing.

            wcs,himf,pnx5381   wcs,pimf1696 pr,pnx413   (853) df,pndm428 df,pl,nn1697
6 And he overtook them, and he spoke unto them   these same words.

            wcs,qmf559 pr,pnx413   pp,pnit4100   pimf1696   nn,pnx113 df,pndm428 dfp,pl,nn1697
7 And they said unto him, Wherefore saith my lord these words?

ptx2486   pp,pl,nn,pnx5650   pr4480/qnc6213   df,pndm2088 dfp,nn1697
God forbid that thy servants   should do according to this thing:

        ptdm2005   nn3701   pnl834   qpf4672   pl,nn,pnx572 pp,cs,nn6310   hipf7725
8 Behold, the money, which we found in our sacks' mouths, we brought again

pr,pnx413   pr4480/cs,nn776   nn3667   wcj,pnit349   qmf1589

unto   thee   out*of*the*land   of   Canaan: how   then   should   we   steal

pr4480/cs,nn1004/pl,nn,pnx113   nn3701   cj176   nn2091

out*of*thy*lord's*house   silver   or   gold?

pr,pnx854   pnl834   pr4480/pl,nn,pnx5650   nimf4672   wcs,qpf4191   pnp587

9 With   whomsoever   of*thy*servants   it be found,   both let him   die,   and we

wcj,ad1571   qmf1961   pp,nn,pnx113   pp,pl,nn5650

also   will   be   my   lord's   bondmen.

wcs,qmf559   ad6258   ad1571/ad3651   pnp1931   pp,pl,nn,pnx1697

10 And he said,   Now   also   let   it   be according unto your   words: he

pr,pnx854   pnl834   nimf4672   qmf1961 pp,pnx   nn5650   wcj,pnp859   qmf1961   aj5355

with whom it is found shall   be   my servant; and   ye   shall   be   blameless.

wcs,pimf4116   wcs,himf3381   nn376   (853)   nn,pnx572   nn,lh776

11 Then they speedily   took down every man   his   sack   to the ground,   and

wcs,qmf6605   nn376   nn,pnx572

opened every man his sack.

wcs,pimf2664   hipf2490   dfp,aj1419   pipf3615   wcj,dfp,aj6996

12 And he searched,   and began at the eldest,   and   left   at the youngest: and the

df,nn1375   wcs,nimf4672   nn1144   pp,cs,nn572

cup   was   found   in Benjamin's sack.

wcs,qmf7167   pl,nn,pnx8071   wcs,qmf6006   nn376   (pr5921)   nn,pnx2543

13 Then they   rent   their clothes, and   laded   every man   his   ass,   and

wcs,qmf7725   df,nn,lh5892

returned to the   city.

nn3063   wcj,pl,nn,pnx251 wcs,qmf935   nn3130   cs,nn,lh1004   wcj,pnp1931

14 And Judah and his   brethren   came   to Joseph's house;   for   he   was

ad,pnx5750   ad8033   wcs,qmf5307 pp,pl,nn,pnx6440   nn,lh776

yet   there: and they   fell   before   him on the ground.

nn3130   wcs,qmf559   pp,pnx   pnit4100 df,nn4639   df,pndm2088 pnl834   qpf6213

15 And Joseph   said   unto them,   What   deed   is   this   that ye have done?

qpf3045   he,ptn3808 cj3588   nn376   (pnl834) pp,pnx3644   pina5172/pimf5172

know ye   not   that such a man   as I   can certainly divine?

nn3063   wcs,qmf559 pnit4100   qmf559   pp,nn,pnx113 pnit4100   pimf1696

16 And Judah said,   What shall we say unto my   lord?   what shall we speak?

wcj,pnit4100   htmf6663   df,pl,nn430   qpf4672   (853)   cs,nn5771

or   how   shall we clear ourselves?   God   hath found out   the iniquity of thy

pl,nn,pnx5650   ptdm,pnx2009   pp,nn,pnx113   pl,nn5650   ad1571 pnp587   ad1571

servants: behold,   we   are my   lord's   servants,   both   we,   and   he   also   with

pnl834/pp,nn,pnx3027   df,nn1375   nipf4672

whom   the   cup   is found.

wcs,qmf559   ptx2486/pp,pnx   pr4480/qnc6213   pndm2063   df,nn376   pnl834

17 And he   said,   God forbid that*I*should*do   so: but the   man   in whose

pp,nn,pnx3027   df,nn1375   nipf4672 pnp1931   qmf1961 pp,pnx   nn5650   wcj,pnp859

hand   the   cup   is found,   he   shall   be   my   servant; and as for   you,

qmv5927   pp,nn7965 pr413   nn,pnx1

get*you*up in peace unto your father.

nn3063   wcs,qmf5066   pr,pnx413   wcs,qmf559 pte994   nn,pnx113   nn,pnx5650

18 Then Judah came near unto him, and said,   Oh my lord,   let thy servant,

pte4994   pimf1696   nn1697   nn,pnx113 pp,du,cs,nn241   wcj,ptn408   nn,pnx639 qmf2734

I*pray*thee,   speak a word in my lord's   ears,   and let   not   thine anger burn

pp,nn,pnx5650 cj3588   pp,pnx3644   nn6547

against thy servant: for thou art even as Pharaoh.

---

15 Divination, or foretelling the future, was a common practice in ancient Egypt. Joseph here is speaking in his role as an Egyptian. Joseph did receive information from God concerning the future, but he did not practice the idolatrous divinations of the Egyptians.

nn,pnx113 qpf7592 (853)   pl,nn,pnx5650   pp,qnc559 he,pta3426 pp,pnx   nn1   cj176   nn251
19 My lord asked   his servants, saying, Have ye a father, or a brother?

wcs,qmf559 pr413   nn,pnx113 pp,pnx pta3426   nn1   aj2205   wcj,cs,nn3206
20 And we said unto my lord, We have a father, an old man, and a   child

pl,nn2208   aj6996   wcj,nn,pnx251   qpf4191   pnp1931 pp,nn,pnx905   wcs,nimf3498
of his old age, a little one; and his brother is dead, and he   alone is left of

pp,nn,pnx517   wcj,nn,pnx1 qpf,pnx157
his mother, and his father loveth him.

wcs,qmf559 pr413   pl,nn,pnx5650   himv,pnx3381   pr,pnx413
21 And thou saidst unto thy servants, Bring*him*down unto me, that I may

wcj,qcj7760   nn,pnx5869 pr,pnx5921
set mine eyes upon him.

wcs,qmf559 pr413   nn,pnx113   df,nn5288 ptn3808/qmf3201 pp,qnc5800 (853)   nn,pnx1
22 And we said unto my lord, The lad   cannot leave   his father: for

wcs,qpf5800 (853)   nn,pnx1   wcs,qpf4191
if he should leave   his father, *his father* would die.

wcs,qmf559 pr413   pl,nn,pnx5650 cj518/ptn3808   df,aj6996   nn,pnx251
23 And thou saidst unto thy servants, Except your youngest brother

qmf3381   pr,pnx854   pp,qnc7200 pl,nn,pnx6440 ptn3808 himf3254
come down with you, ye shall see my face   no more.

wcs,qmf1961   cj3588   qpf5927   pr413   nn,pnx5650   nn,pnx1
24 And it*came*to*pass when we came up unto thy servant my father, we

wcs,himf5046 pp,pnx (853)   pl,cs,nn1697   nn,pnx113
told him   the words of my lord.

nn,pnx1 wcs,qmf559   qmv7725   qmv7666 pp,pnx cs,nn4592 nn400
25 And our father said, Go again, *and* buy us a little food.

wcs,qmf559   ptn3808/qmf3201   pp,qnc3381 cj518   df,aj6996   nn,pnx251 pta3426 pr,pnx854
26 And we said, We cannot go down: if our youngest brother be   with

wcs,qpf3381   cj3588   qmf3201 ptn3808 pp,qnc7200   df,nn376 pl,cs,nn6440 ptn,pnx369
us, then will we go down: for we may not   see   the man's face, except our

df,aj6996 wcj,nn,pnx251   pr,pnx854
youngest brother *be* with us.

nn,pnx5650   nn,pnx1 wcs,qmf559 pr,pnx413   pnp859 qpf3045 cj3588   nn,pnx802 qpf3205
27 And thy servant my father said   unto us, Ye know that my wife bore

pp,pnx du,nu8147
me two *sons*:

df,nu259   wcs,qmf3318   pr4480/pr,pnx854   wcs,qmf559 ad389
28 And the one   went out   from   me, and I said, Surely he

qna2963/pupf2963   qpf,pnx7200   wcj,ptn3808   pr5704/ad,lh2008
is*torn*in*pieces; and I saw him not   since:

wcj,qpf3947 (853) pndm2088 ad1571 pr4480/pr5973 pl,nn,pnx6440   nn611   wcj,qpf,pnx7136
29 And if ye take   this also from me, and mischief befall him,

wcj,hipf3381   (853)   nn,pnx7872   pp,nn7451   nn,lh7585
ye shall bring down   my gray hairs with sorrow to the grave.

wcj,ad6258   pp,qnc,pnx935 pr413   nn,pnx5650   nn,pnx1   wcj,df,nn5288
30 Now therefore when I come   to thy servant my father, and the   lad

ptn369 pr,pnx854   wcj,nn,pnx5315   qptp7194   pp,nn,pnx5315
be not with us; seeing that his life is bound up in the lad's life;

wcj,qpf1961   pp,qnc,pnx7200 cj3588   df,nn5288 ptn369
31 It*shall*come*to*pass, when he seeth that the lad *is* not *with us*, that

wcj,qpf4191   pl,nn,pnx5650   wcj,hipf3381 (853)   cs,nn7872   nn,pnx5650
he will die: and thy servants shall bring down   the gray hairs of thy servant

nn,pnx1   pp,nn3015   nn,lh7585
our father with sorrow to the grave.

cj3588   nn,pnx5650   qpf6148   (853)   df,nn5288 pr4480/pr5973   nn,pnx1 pp,qnc559
32 For thy servant became surety for   the lad   unto my father, saying,

cj518   himf,pnx935   ptn**3808** pr,pnx413   wcs,qpf**2398**   pp,nn,pnx1

If I bring him not unto thee, then I shall bear*the*blame to my father

cs,nn3605/df,pl,nn**3117**

forever.

wcj,ad6258   pte**4994**   nn,pnx**5650** qcj**3427**   pr8478   df,nn5288

33 Now therefore, I*pray*thee, let thy servant abide instead of the lad a

nn**5650**   pp,nn,pnx113   wcj,df,nn5288 qcj**5927** pr5973   pl,nn,pnx**251**

bondman to my lord; and let the   lad   go up with his brethren.

cj3588 pnit349   qmf**5927** pr413   nn,pnx1   wcj,df,nn5288   ptn,pnx369 pr,pnx854

34 For how shall I go up to my father, and the   lad *be* not   with me?

cj6435   qmf**7200**   dfp,nn**7451** pnl834   qmf4672   (853)   nn,pnx1

lest peradventure I see the evil that shall come on   my father.

Joseph Reveals Himself to His Brothers

nn3130   qpf**3201** wcj,ptn**3808**   pp,htnc662   pp,cs,nn3605

45 *Then Joseph could not refrain himself before all   them that

df,pl,nipt**5324** pr,pnx5921   wcs,qmf**7121**   cs,nn3605 nn**376**   himv3318

stood   by   him; and he cried, Cause every man to go out

pr4480/pr,pnx5921   qpf5975 wcj,ptn**3808** nn**376** pr,pnx854   nn3130

from   me. And there stood   no   man with him, while Joseph

pp,htnc**3045**   pr413   pl,nn,pnx**251**

made*himself*known unto his brethren.

wcs,qmf**5414**/(853)/nn,pnx6963/pp,nn1065   pl,nn4714 wcs(qmf**8085**)   cs,nn**1004**

2 And he   wept aloud: and the Egyptians   and the house of

nn6547 wcs,qmf**8085**

Pharaoh heard.

nn3130   wcs,qmf**559** pr413   pl,nn,pnx**251** pnp589   nn3130   nn,pnx1 he,ad5750

3 And Joseph said unto his brethren, I *am* Joseph; doth my father yet

aj**2416**   pl,nn,pnx**251** qpf3201 wcj,ptn**3808** pp,qnc6030 pnx(853)   cj3588   nipf**926**

live? And his brethren could not answer   him; for they were troubled

pr4480/pl,nn,pnx**6440**

at*his*presence.

nn3130   wcs,qmf**559** pr413   pl,nn,pnx**251** qmv**5066** pr,pnx413   pte**4994**

4 And Joseph said unto his brethren, Come near to me, I*pray*you. And

wcs,qmf**5066**   wcs,qmf**559** pnp589   nn3130   nn,pnx251 pnl834 qpf4376 pnx(853)

they came near. And he said,   I *am* Joseph your brother, whom ye sold

nn,lh4714

into Egypt.

wcj,ad6258   ptn408 nimf**6087** wcj,ptn408 qcj**2734**   pp,du,nn,pnx**5869** cj3588   qpf4376

5 Now therefore be not grieved, nor angry with yourselves, that ye sold

pnx(853)   ad2008 cj3588 pl,nn**430** qpf,pnx7971   pp,pl,nn,pnx**6440**   pp,nn**4241**

me hither: for God did send me before you to preserve life.

cj3588 pndm2088   du,nn8141   df,nn7458   pp,cs,nn**7130** df,nn776   wcj,ad5750

6 For these two years *hath* the famine *been* in the land: and yet *there*

nu2568 pl,nn8141   pnl834   ptn369   nn2758   wcj,nn7105

are five years, in the which *there shall* neither *be* earing nor harvest.

pl,nn**430** wcs,qmf,pnx7971   pp,pl,nn,pnx**6440**   pp,qnc**7760** pp,pnx   nn**7611**   dfp,nn776

7 And God sent   me before you to preserve you a posterity in the earth,

wcj,pp,hinc**2421**/pp,pnx   aj1419   pp,nn**6413**

and to save*your*lives by a great deliverance.

wcj,ad6258   ptn**3808** pnp859   qpf7971 pnx(853)   ad2008 cj3588 df,pl,nn**430**

8 So now *it was* not you *that* sent   me hither, but God: and he hath

wcs,qmf,pnx**7760**   pp,nn1   pp,nn6547   wcj,pp,nn113   pp,cs,nn3605   nn,pnx**1004**   wcj,qpta**4910**

made   me a father to Pharaoh, and   lord   of   all   his house, and a   ruler

         pp,cs,nn3605   cs,nn776   nn4714

throughout   all   the land of Egypt.

    pimv4116   wcj,qmv5927   pr413   nn,pnx1   wcj,qpf559   pr,pnx413   ad3541   qpf**559**

9 Haste ye, and go up   to   my   father, and   say   unto   him, Thus saith thy

nn,pnx1121   nn3130   pl,nn**430**   qpf,pnx**7760**   pp,nn113   pp,cs,nn3605   nn4714   qmv3381   pr,pnx413

son   Joseph, God hath made me lord of   all   Egypt: come down unto me,

qmf5975   ptn408

tarry not:

        wcs,qpf3427   pp,cs,nn**776**   nn1657   wcs,qpf**1961**   aj7138

10 And thou shalt dwell in the   land   of Goshen, and thou shalt   be   near

pr,pnx413   pnp859   wcj,pl,nn,pnx**1121**   pl,nn,pnx1121   wcj,pl,cs,nn1121   wcj,nn,pnx6629

unto me, thou, and thy children,   and thy children's children, and thy   flocks,   and

wcj,nn,pnx1241   wcj,cs,nn3605   pnl834   pp,pnx

thy herds, and   all   that thou hast:

    ad8033   wcj,pipf*3557 pnx(853)   cj3588 ad5750   nu2568   pl,nn8141   nn7458

11 And there will I nourish   thee; for yet *there are* five years of famine;

cj6435   pnp859   wcj,nn,pnx**1004**   wcj,cs,nn3605 pnl834   pp,pnx   nimf**3423**

lest thou, and thy household, and   all   that thou hast, come*to*poverty.

     wcj,ptdm2009   du,nn,pnx**5869**   pl,qpta7200   wcj,du,cs,nn5869   nn,pnx251   nn1144

12 And, behold, your   eyes   see,   and the   eyes   of my brother Benjamin,

cj3588   nn,pnx**6310**   df,pipt**1696**   pr,pnx413

that *it is* my mouth that speaketh unto you.

     wcs,hipf**5046**   pp,nn,pnx**1**   (853)   cs,nn3605   nn,pnx**3519**   pp,nn4714   wcj(853)

13 And ye shall   tell   my father of   all   my glory in Egypt, and   of

cs,nn3605 pnl834   qpf7200   wcs,pipf4116   wcs,hipf3381   (853)   nn,pnx1   ad2008

all   that ye have seen; and ye shall   haste   and bring down   my father hither.

       wcs,qmf**5307**   pr5921   nn,pnx251   nn1144   pl,cs,nn6677   wcs,qmf1058

14 And he   fell   upon his brother   Benjamin's   neck,   and   wept;   and

wcj,nn1144   qpf1058   pr5921   pl,nn,pnx6677

Benjamin wept upon his   neck.

       wcs,pimf**5401**   pp,cs,nn3605   pl,nn,pnx251   wcs,qmf1058   pr,pnx5921

15 Moreover he   kissed   all   his brethren, and   wept   upon   them: and

wcj,ad310 ad**3651**   pl,nn,pnx251   pipf**1696**   pr,pnx854

after   that his brethren talked   with   him.

        wcj,df,nn6963   nipf**8085**   nn6547   cs,nn**1004**   pp,qnc559   nn3130

16 And the   fame   thereof was heard in Pharaoh's   house,   saying,   Joseph's

pl,cs,nn**251**   qpf935   wcs,qmf3190/pp,du,cs,nn**5869**/nn6547   wcj(pp,du,cs,nn**5869**)   pl,nn,pnx**5650**

brethren are come: and it pleased*Pharaoh*well, and   his servants.

       nn6547   wcs,qmf559   pr413   nn3130   qmv559   pr413   pl,nn,pnx251   pndm2063   qmv**6213**

17 And Pharaoh   said   unto Joseph, Say unto thy brethren, This   do   ye;

qmv2943 (853)   nn,pnx1165   wcj,qmv**1980**   qmv935   cs,nn,lh776   nn3667

lade   your beasts, and   go,   get you unto the land of Canaan;

     wcj,qmv3947 (853)   nn,pnx1   wcj(853)   pl,nn,pnx**1004**   wcj,qmv935   pr,pnx413

18 And   take   your father and   your households, and   come   unto me:

     wcj,qcj**5414** pp,pnx (853)   cs,nn2898   cs,nn776   nn4714   wcj,qmv398 (853)

and I will   give   you   the good of the land of Egypt, and ye shall   eat   the

cs,nn2459   cs,nn776

fat   of the land.

      wcj,pnp859   pupf**6680**   pndm2063   qmv**6213**   qmv3947   pp,pnx   pl,nn5699

19 Now   thou   art   commanded,   this   do   ye;   take   you   wagons

   pr4480/cs,nn**776**   nn4714   pp,nn,pnx2945   wcj,pp,pl,nn,pnx**802**   wcj,qpf**5375**

out*of*the*land of Egypt for your little ones, and for your   wives,   and   bring

(853)   nn,pnx1   wcj,qpf935

your father, and come.

wcj,nn,pnx**5869**/qcj2347 ptn408 (pr5921)   pl,nn,pnx3627 cj3588   cs,nn**2898**   cs,nn3605   cs,nn776

20 Also   regard   not   your stuff;   for the good of   all   the land of

nn4714 (pnp1931)   pp,pnx

Egypt   *is* yours.

pl,cs,nn**1121**   nn3478   wcs,qmf**6213** ad3651   nn3130   wcs,qmf**5414** pp,pnx   pl,nn5699

21 And the children of Israel   did   so: and Joseph   gave   them wagons,

pr5921   cs,nn**6310**   nn6547   wcs,qmf**5414** pp,pnx   nn6720

according to the commandment of Pharaoh, and   gave   them provision for the

dfp,nn**1870**

way.

pp,nn,pnx3605   qpf**5414**   dfp,nn**376** pl,cs,nn2487   pl,nn8071   wcj,pp,nn1144

22 To   all   of them he gave each man changes of raiment; but to Benjamin

qpf**5414** cs,nu**7969** pl,cs,nu**3967**   nn3701   wcj,nu2568 pl,cs,nn2487   pl,nn8071

he gave three hundred *pieces* of silver, and   five   changes of raiment.

wcj,pp,nn,pnx1   qpf**7971**   pp,pndm2063   nu6235   pl,nn860   pl,qpta**5375**

23 And to his   father   he sent after   this   *manner*; ten   asses   laden

pr4480/cs,nn**2898**   nn4714   wcj,nu6235   pl,nn2543   pl,qpta**5375**   nn1250   wcj,nn3899

with*the*good*things of Egypt, and   ten   she asses   laden with corn and bread

wcj,nn4202   pp,nn,pnx1   dfp,nn**1870**

and meat for his father by the way.

wcs,pimf7971 (853)   pl,nn,pnx251   wcs,qmf**1980**   wcs,qmf559 pr,pnx413

24 So he   sent   his brethren away, and they departed: and he   said   unto

qmf**7264**/ptn408   dfp,nn**1870**

them, See that ye fall*not*out by the way.

wcs,qmf**5927**   pr4480/nn4714   wcs,qmf935   cs,nn776   nn3667   pr413

25 And they went up out*of*Egypt, and came into the land of Canaan unto

nn3290   nn,pnx1

Jacob their father,

wcs,himf**5046** pp,pnx   pp,qnc559   nn3130   ad5750   aj**2416**   wcj(cj3588) pnp1931   qpta**4910**

26 And   told   him, saying, Joseph *is* yet alive, and   he *is* governor

pp,cs,nn3605   cs,nn776   nn4714   nn,pnx3820 wcs,qmf6313 cj3588   hipf539   pp,pnx

over   all   the land of Egypt. And Jacob's heart fainted, for he believed them

ptn3808

not.

wcs,pimf**1696**/pr,pnx413   (853) cs,nn3605   pl,cs,nn**1697**   nn3130   pnl834

27 And they   told   him   all   the words of Joseph, which he had

pipf1696 pr,pnx413   wcs,qmf**7200** (853)   df,pl,nn5699   pnl834   nn3130   qpf7971

said unto them: and when he   saw   the wagons which Joseph had sent to

pp,qnc**5375** pnx(853)   cs,nn**7307**   nn3290   nn,pnx1   wcs,qmf**2421**

carry   him, the spirit of Jacob their father revived:

nn3478 wcs,qmf559   aj**7227**   nn3130   nn,pnx1121   ad5750   aj**2416**   qcj**1980**

28 And Israel said, *It is* enough; Joseph my   son   *is* yet alive: I will   go

wcj,qmf,pnx**7200**   pp,ad2962   qmf**4191**

and   see   him before I die.

Jacob and His Family Move to Egypt

nn3478   wcs,qmf**5265**   wcj,cs,nn3605 pnl834 pp,pnx   wcs,qmf935

46 And Israel took*his*journey with   all   that he had, and came to

nn,lh884   wcs,qmf**2076** pl,nn**2077**   pp,pl,cs,nn**430**   nn,pnx1   nn3327

Beer-sheba, and offered sacrifices unto the   God   of his father Isaac.

pl,nn**430** wcs,qmf559   pp,nn3478   pp,pl,cs,nn4759   df,nn**3915**   wcs,qmf559   nn3290

2 And God spoke unto Israel in the   visions   of the night, and   said,   Jacob,

nn3290   wcs,qmf**559** ptdm,pnx2009

Jacob. And he said,   Here   *am* I.

wcs,qmf**559** pnp595   df,nn**410**   pl,cs,nn**430**   nn,pnx1 qmf**3372** ptn408   pr4480/qnc,lh3381

3 And he said, I *am* God, the God of thy father: fear not to go down

nn,lh4714 cj3588   ad8033 qmf,pnx**7760**   aj1419 pp,nn**1471**

into Egypt; for I will there make of thee a great nation:

pnp595   qmf3381   pr,pnx5973   nn,lh4714   wcj,pnp595   ad1571

4 I will go down with thee into Egypt; and I will also

himf,pnx**5927**/qna**5927**   wcj,nn3130   qmf7896   nn,pnx**3027** pr5921   du,nn,pnx**5869**

surely*bring*thee*up *again*: and Joseph shall put his hand upon thine eyes.

nn3290   wcs,qmf**6965**   pr4480/nn884   pl,cs,nn**1121**   nn3478   wcs,qmf**5375** (853)

5 And Jacob rose up from Beer-sheba: and the sons of Israel carried

nn3290   nn,pnx1   wcj(853)   nn,pnx**2945**   wcj(853)   pl,nn,pnx**802**   dfp,pl,nn5699

Jacob their father, and   their little ones, and   their wives, in the wagons

pnl834   nn6547   qpf7971   pp,qnc**5375** pnx(853)

which Pharaoh had sent to carry him.

wcs,qmf3947 (853)   pl,nn,pnx4735   wcj(853)   nn,pnx7399 pnl834

6 And they took   their cattle, and   their goods, which they had

qpf7408   pp,cs,nn**776**   nn3667   wcs,qmf935   nn,lh4714   nn3290   wcj,cs,nn3605

gotten in the land of Canaan, and came into Egypt, Jacob, and all his

nn,pnx**2233** pr,pnx854

seed with him:

pl,nn,pnx**1121**   pl,nn,pnx1121 wcj,pl,cs,nn**1121** pr,pnx854   pl,nn,pnx1323

7 His sons, and his sons' sons with him, his daughters, and his

pl,nn,pnx1121 wcj,pl,cs,nn1323   wcj,cs,nn3605   nn,pnx**2233** hipf935   pr,pnx854   nn,lh4714

sons' daughters, and all his seed brought he with him into Egypt.

wcj,pndm428   pl,cs,nn8034   pl,cs,nn**1121**   nn3478   df,pl,qpta935

8 And these *are* the names of the children of Israel, which came into

nn,lh4714   nn3290   wcj,pl,nn,pnx**1121**   nn7205   nn3290   cs,nn1060

Egypt, Jacob and his sons: Reuben, Jacob's firstborn.

wcj,pl,cs,nn**1121**   nn7205   nn2585   wcj,nn6396   wcj,nn2696   wcj,nn3756

9 And the sons of Reuben; Hanoch, and Phallu, and Hezron, and Carmi.

wcj,pl,cs,nn**1121**   nn8095   nn3223   wcj,nn3226   wcj,nn161   wcj,nn3199

10 And the sons of Simeon; Jemuel, and Jamin, and Ohad, and Jachin, and

wcj,nn6714   wcj,nn7586   cs,nn**1121**   df,nn3669

Zohar, and Shaul the son of a Canaanitish woman.

wcj,pl,cs,nn**1121**   nn3878   nn1648   nn6955   wcj,nn4847

11 And the sons of Levi; Gershon, Kohath, and Merari.

wcj,pl,cs,nn**1121**   nn3063   nn6147   wcj,nn209   wcj,nn7956   wcj,nn6557

12 And the sons of Judah; Er, and Onan, and Shelah, and Pharez, and

wcj,nn2226   nn6147   wcj,nn209 wcs,qmf**4191**   pp,cs,nn**776**   nn3667   pl,cs,nn**1121**   nn6557

Zerah: but Er and Onan died in the land of Canaan. And the sons of Pharez

wcs,qmf**1961** nn2696   wcj,nn2538

were Hezron and Hamul.

wcj,pl,cs,nn**1121**   nn3485   nn8439   wcj,nn6312   wcj,nn3102   wcj,nn8110

13 And the sons of Issachar; Tola, and Phuvah, and Job, and Shimron.

wcj,pl,cs,nn**1121**   nn2074   nn5624   wcj,nn356   wcj,nn3177

14 And the sons of Zebulun; Sered, and Elon, and Jahleel.

pndm428   pl,cs,nn**1121**   nn3812   pnl834   qpf3205   pp,nn3290   pp,nn6307

15 These *be* the sons of Leah, which she bore unto Jacob in Padan-aram,

wcj,pr854   nn,pnx1323   nn1783   cs,nn3605   cs,nn**5315**   pl,nn,pnx**1121**   wcj,pl,nn,pnx1323

with his daughter Dinah: all the souls of his sons and his daughters *were*

nu7970   wcj,nu7969

thirty and three.

wcj,pl,cs,nn**1121**   nn1410   nn6837   wcj,nn2291   nn7764   wcj,nn675   nn6179

16 And the sons of Gad; Ziphion, and Haggi, Shuni, and Ezbon, Eri, and

wcj,nn722   wcj,nn692

Arodi, and Areli.

wcj,pl,cs,nn**1121**   nn836   nn3232   wcj,nn3438   wcj,nn3440   wcj,nn1283

17 And the   sons   of Asher; Jimnah, and Ishuah, and Isui, and Beriah, and

wcj,nn8294   nn,pnx**269**   wcj,pl,cs,nn**1121**   nn1283   nn2268   wcj,nn4439

Serah their sister: and the   sons   of Beriah; Heber, and Malchiel.

pndm428   pl,cs,nn**1121**   nn2153   pnl834   nn3837   qpf**5414**   pp,nn3812   nn,pnx1323

18 These *are* the sons of Zilpah, whom Laban gave to Leah his daughter,

(853) pndm428   wcs,qmf3205   pp,nn3290   nu8337/nu6240   nn**5315**

and   these she   bore   unto Jacob, *even* sixteen souls.

pl,cs,nn**1121**   nn7354   nn3290   cs,nn**802**   nn3130   wcj,nn1144

19 The sons of Rachel Jacob's wife; Joseph, and Benjamin.

pp,nn3130   pp,cs,nn**776**   nn4714   wcs,nimf3205 (853)   nn4519   wcj(853)

20 And unto Joseph in the land of Egypt were born   Manasseh and

nn669   pnl834   nn621   cs,nn1323   nn6319   cs,nn**3548**   nn204 qpf3205   pp,pnx

Ephraim, which Asenath the daughter of Poti-pherah priest of On bore unto him.

wcj,pl,cs,nn**1121**   nn1144   nn1106   wcj,nn1071   wcj,nn788   nn1617

21 And the   sons   of Benjamin *were* Belah, and Becher, and Ashbel, Gera,

wcj,nn5283   nn278   wcj,nn7220   nn4649   wcj,nn2650   wcj,nn714

and Naaman, Ehi, and Rosh, Muppim, and Huppim, and Ard.

pndm428   pl,cs,nn**1121**   nn7354   pnl834   pupf3205   pp,nn3290 cs,nn3605   nn**5315**

22 These *are* the sons of Rachel, which were born to Jacob: all   the souls

nu702/nu6240

were fourteen.

wcj,pl,cs,nn**1121**   nn1835   nn2366

23 And the   sons   of Dan; Hushim.

wcj,pl,cs,nn**1121**   nn5321   nn3183   wcj,nn1476   wcj,nn3337   wcj,nn8006

24 And the   sons   of Naphtali; Jahzeel, and Guni, and Jezer, and Shillem.

pndm428   pl,cs,nn**1121**   nn1090   pnl834   nn3837   qpf**5414**   pp,nn7354   nn,pnx1323

25 These *are* the sons of Bilhah, which Laban gave unto Rachel his daughter,

wcs,qmf3205 (853) pndm428   pp,nn3290 cs,nn3605   nn**5315**   nu7651

and she   bore   these unto Jacob: all   the souls *were* seven.

cs,nn3605   df,nn**5315**   df,qpta935   pp,nn3290   nn,lh4714   pl,cs,qpta3318

☞ 26 All   the souls that came with Jacob into Egypt, which came out of his

nn,pnx**3409** pr4480/pp,nn905   nn3290   pl,cs,nn**1121** pl,cs,nn**802** cs,nn3605   nn**5315**   pl,nu8346   wcj,nu8337

loins, besides Jacob's sons' wives, all   the souls *were* threescore and six;

wcj,pl,cs,nn**1121**   nn3130   pnl834   pupf3205 pp,pnx   pp,nn4714   du,nu8147

27 And the   sons   of Joseph, which were born him in Egypt, *were* two

nn**5315** cs,nn3605   df,nn**5315**   pp,cs,nn**1004**   nn3290   df,qpta935   nn,lh4714

souls: all   the souls of the house of Jacob, which came into Egypt, *were*

pl,nu7657

threescore*and*ten.

☞ **46:26, 27** The differences between this and other passages (Ex. 1:1–5; Acts 7:14) as to the number who migrated to Egypt are due to the point of reference and method of calculation, not to contradiction or error. Jacob's direct descendants in Canaan, his children, grandchildren, and great-grandchildren, amounted to sixty-six persons (Gen. 46:8–26). The seventy souls of the house of Jacob mentioned in verse twenty-seven and in Exodus 1:5 adds to the sixty-six above Jacob himself, Joseph, and Joseph's two sons. In Acts 7:14 Stephen states that the number of Joseph's kindred who came to Egypt was seventy-five. Jacob, who is mentioned separately, and Joseph and his family who were already in Egypt, were not a part of this number. But remember that the sixty-six persons mentioned elsewhere included only the direct descendants of Jacob. The number mentioned in Acts also includes those who came with Jacob, but who were not his direct descendants; in other words, his son's wives. Since Judah's wives and Simeon's wives were dead, there were only nine of the wives who made the trip with Jacob. These nine, plus his sixty-six direct descendants made up the seventy-five persons who traveled with Jacob from Egypt.

qpf7971 wcj(853)   nn3063   pp,pl,nn,pnx6440   pr413   nn3130   pp,hinc3384   pp,pl,nn,pnx6440

28 And he sent   Judah   before   him unto Joseph, to direct his   face

nn,lh1657   wcs,qmf935   cs,nn,lh776   nn1657

unto Goshen; and they came into the land of Goshen.

nn3130   wcs,qmf631   nn,pnx4818   wcs,qmf5927   pp,qnc7125 nn3478   nn,pnx1

29 And Joseph made ready his chariot, and went up to meet Israel his father,

nn,lh1657   wcs,nimf7200   pr,pnx413   wcs,qmf5307 pr5921   pl,nn,pnx6677

to Goshen, and presented himself unto him; and he   fell   on his neck, and

wcs,qmf1058 pr5921   pl,nn,pnx6677   ad5750

wept   on his   neck   a good while.

nn3478   wcs,qmf559   pr413   nn3130   df,nn6471   qcj4191   ad310   qnc,pnx7200 (853)

30 And Israel said unto Joseph, Now let me die, since I have seen   thy

pl,nn,pnx6440   cj3588   ad,pnx5750   aj2416

face,   because thou *art* yet alive.

nn3130   wcs,qmf559   pr413   pl,nn,pnx251   wcj,pr413   nn,pnx1   cs,nn1004

31 And Joseph said unto his brethren, and unto his father's house, I will

qmf5927   wcj,hicj5046   pp,nn6547   wcj,qcj559 pr,pnx413   pl,nn,pnx251   nn,pnx1

go up, and show Pharaoh, and say   unto him, My brethren, and my father's

wcj,cs,nn1004 pnl834   pp,cs,nn776   nn3667   qpf935 pr,pnx413

house, which *were* in the land of Canaan, are come unto me;

wcj,df,pl,nn376   pl,cs,qpta7462/nn6629 cj3588   pl,cs,nn376   qpf1961   nn4735

32 And the men   *are* shepherds, for their trade hath been to feed cattle;

hipf935   wcj,nn,pnx6629   wcj,nn,pnx1241   wcj,cs,nn3605 pnl834 pp,pnx

and they have brought their flocks,   and their herds,   and   all   that they have.

wcj,qpf1961   cj3588   nn6547   qmf7121 pp,pnx   wcs,qpf559

33 And it*shall*come*to*pass, when Pharaoh shall call you, and shall say,

pnit4100   pl,nn,pnx4639

What *is* your occupation?

wcs,qpf559   pl,nn,pnx5650   pl,cs,nn376   qpf1961   nn4735

34 That ye shall say, Thy servants' trade hath been about cattle

pr4480/pl,nn,pnx5271   wcj,pr5704 ad6258 ad1571 pnp587   ad1571   pl,nn,pnx1 pp,cj5668

from*our*youth even until now, both we, *and* also our fathers: that ye may

qmf3427   pp,cs,nn776   nn1657   cj3588 cs,nn3605 qpta7462/nn6629   cs,nn8441

dwell in the land of Goshen; for every shepherd *is* an abomination unto the

nn4714

Egyptians.

46:34 Throughout its history, Egypt had a hatred for foreign things. Their very language depicts foreigners as a lower class of humans. In addition, the particular manners and customs of the Jews were totally disgusting to the Egyptians. The Jews had hair and beards, while the Egyptians, both men and women, shaved all their body hair off (41:14). This attitude of superiority is reflected in Pharaoh's instructions to basically "leave everything behind because we will give you good Egyptian stuff" (45:20). God had carefully chosen Egypt as the one place where Israel could grow into a nation. The Egyptian abhorrence for the Jews would limit the danger of intermingling, either racially or religiously (a problem which would lead to much trouble in Canaan). The size and prosperity of Egypt would allow the Hebrew people to become numerous while still being a minority in the country. The later invasion of the Hyksos, an eastern people, led to the enslavement of the Jews, which served to make them physically strong.

47

nn3130　　　wcs,qmf935　　　　wcs,himf5046　pp,nn6547　　　wcs,qmf559　　nn,pnx1

Then Joseph came and told Pharaoh, and said, My father and

wcj,pl,nn,pnx251　　　　wcj,nn,pnx6629　　　wcj,nn,pnx1241　wcj,cs,nn3605 pnl834

my brethren, and their flocks, and their herds, and all that

pp,pnx　　　qpf935　　　　pr4480/cs,nn776　　　nn3667　　wcj,ptdm,pnx2009

they have, are come out*of*the*land of Canaan; and, behold, they *are* in the

pp,cs,nn776　　nn1657

land of Goshen.

qpf3947　wcj,pr4480/cs,nn7097　　pl,nn,pnx251　　　nu2568　pl,nn376　　wcs,himf,pnx3322

2 And he took some of his brethren, *even* five men, and presented them

pp,pl,cs,nn6440　　nn6547

unto Pharaoh.

nn6547　　wcs,qmf559　pr413　　　pl,nn,pnx251　　pnit4100　　　　pl,nn,pnx4639

3 And Pharaoh said unto his brethren, What *is* your occupation? And they

wcs,qmf559　pr413　　nn6547　　pl,nn,pnx5650　cs,qpta7462/nn6629 ad1571 pnp587　ad1571　　pl,nn,pnx1

said unto Pharaoh, Thy servants *are* shepherds, both we, *and* also our fathers.

wcs,qmf559　　　　pr413　　nn6547　　　pp,qnc1481　　　dfp,nn776　　　qpf935

4 They said moreover unto Pharaoh, For to sojourn in the land are we come;

cj3588/pnl834　pp,pl,nn,pnx5650　　ptn369　nn4829　　dfp,nn6629 cj3588　df,nn7458　aj3515

for thy servants have no pasture for their flocks; for the famine *is* sore in the

pp,cs,nn776　　nn3667　wcj,ad6258　　　pte4994　　　　　pl,nn,pnx5650　qmf3427

land of Canaan: now therefore, we*pray*thee, let thy servants dwell in the

pp,cs,nn776　　nn1657

land of Goshen.

nn6547　　wcs,qmf559　pr413　　nn3130　pp,qnc559　　　nn,pnx1　　　wcj,pl,nn,pnx251

5 And Pharaoh spoke unto Joseph, saying, Thy father and thy brethren are

qpf935　pr,pnx413

come unto thee:

cs,nn776　　　nn4714　(pndm1934)　pp,pl,nn,pnx6440　　　pp,cs,nn4315　　　df,nn776

6 The land of Egypt *is* before thee; in the best of the land make

(853)　　nn,pnx1　　wcj(853)　pl,nn,pnx251　himv3427　　pp,cs,nn776　　nn1657　　qmf3427

thy father and brethren to dwell; in the land of Goshen let them dwell:

wcj,cj518　　qpf3045　　pl,cs,nn376　　nn2428　(wcj,pta3426)　pp,pnx　　　wcj,qpf,pnx7760

and if thou knowest *any* men of activity among them, then make

pl,cs,nn8269　pr5921/pnl834/pp,pnx　nn4735

them rulers over my cattle.

nn3130　　wcs,himf935　(853)　nn3290　his　nn,pnx1　　wcs,himf,pnx5975　　pp,pl,cs,nn6440

7 And Joseph brought in Jacob his father, and set him before

nn6547　　　nn3290　wcs,pimf1288　(853)　　nn6547

Pharaoh: and Jacob blessed Pharaoh.

nn6547　　wcs,qmf559　pr413　　nn3290　dfp,pnit4100 pl,cs,nn3117/pl,cs,nn8141/aj,pnx2416

8 And Pharaoh said unto Jacob, How old *art* thou?

nn3290　wcs,qmf559　pr413　　nn6547　　pl,cs,nn3117　　pl,cs,nn8141　　pl,nn,pnx4033

9 And Jacob said unto Pharaoh, The days of the years of my pilgrimage

wcj,cs,nu3967　nu7970　nn8141　nn4592　wcj,aj7451　pl,cs,nn3117　pl,cs,nn8141

are a hundred and thirty years: few and evil have the days of the years of my

aj,pnx2416　qpf1961　　　wcj,ptn3808　hipf5381　(853)　pl,cs,nn3117　pl,cs,nn8141　cs,aj2416

life been, and have not attained unto the days of the years of the life

pl,nn,pnx1　　pp,pl,cs,nn3117　　pl,nn,pnx4033

of my fathers in the days of their pilgrimage.

nn3290　wcs,pimf1288　(853)　　nn6547　　　wcs,qmf3318　pr4480/pp,pl,cs,nn6440　nn6547

10 And Jacob blessed Pharaoh, and went out from before Pharaoh.

nn3130　wcs,himf3427　(853)　nn,pnx1　　wcj(853)　pl,nn,pnx251　wcs,qmf5414　pp,pnx

11 And Joseph placed his father and his brethren, and gave them a

nn272   pp,cs,nn776   nn4714   pp,cs,nn4315   df,nn776   pp,cs,nn776

possession in the land of Egypt, in the best of the land, in the land of

nn7486   pp,pnl834   nn6547   pipf6680

Rameses, as Pharaoh had commanded.

nn3130   wcs,pimf*3557   (853)   nn,pnx1   wcj(853)   pl,nn,pnx251   wcj(853)   cs,nn3605

12 And Joseph nourished his father, and his brethren, and all

nn,pnx1   cs,nn1004   nn3899   pp,cs,nn6310   df,nn2945

his father's household, with bread, according to *their* families.

The Seven Years of Famine

ptn369   wcj,nn3899   pp,cs,nn3605   df,nn776   cj3588   df,nn7458   ad3966   aj3515

13 And *there was* no bread in all the land; for the famine *was* very sore,

cs,nn776   nn4714   wcj,cs,nn776   nn3667   wcs,qmf3856   pr4480/pl,cs,nn6440

so that the land of Egypt and *all* the land of Canaan fainted by*reason*of the

df,nn7458

famine.

nn3130   wcs,pimf3950   (853) cs,nn3605   df,nn3701   df,nipf4672   pp,cs,nn776

14 And Joseph gathered up all the money that was found in the land of

nn4714   wcj,pp,cs,nn776   nn3667   dfp,nn7668   pnl834   pnp1992   pl,qpta7666   nn3130

Egypt, and in the land of Canaan, for the corn which they bought: and Joseph

wcs,himf935   (853)   df,nn3701   nn6547   cs,nn,lh1004

brought the money into Pharaoh's house.

df,nn3701   wcs,qmf8552   pr4480/cs,nn776   nn4714   wcj,pr4480/cs,nn776   nn3667

15 And when money failed in*the*land of Egypt, and in*the*land of Canaan,

cs,nn3605   nn4714   wcs,qmf935   pr413   nn3130   pp,qnc559   qmv3051   pp,pnx   nn3899   wcj,pp,pnit4100

all the Egyptians came unto Joseph, and said, Give us bread: for why

qmf4191   pr,pnx5048   cj3588   nn3701   qpf656

should we die in thy presence? for the money faileth.

nn3130   wcs,qmf559   qmv3051   pl,nn,pnx4735   wcj,qcj5414   pp,pnx

16 And Joseph said, Give your cattle; and I will give you for your

pp,pl,nn,pnx4735   cj518   nn3701   qpf656

cattle, if money fail.

wcs,himf935   (853)   pl,nn,pnx4735   pr413   nn3130   nn3130   wcs,qmf5414   pp,pnx

17 And they brought their cattle unto Joseph: and Joseph gave them

nn3899   dfp,pl,nn5483   wcj,pp,cs,nn4735/df,nn6629   wcj,pp,cs,nn4735

bread *in exchange* for horses, and for the flocks, and for the cattle of

df,nn1241   wcj,dfp,pl,nn2543   wcs,pimf,pnx5095   dfp,nn3899   pp,cs,nn3605

the herds, and for the asses: and he fed them with bread for all their

nn,pnx4735   df,pndm1931   dfp,nn8141

cattle for that year.

df,pndm1931   df,nn8141   wcs,qmf8552   wcs,qmf935   pr,pnx413   df,nuor8145   dfp,nn8141

18 When that year was ended, they came unto him the second year, and

wcs,qmf559   pp,pnx   ptn3808   pimf3582   pr4480   nn,pnx113   cj3588/cj518   df,nn3701

said unto him, We will not hide *it* from my lord, how that our money is

qpf8552   nn,pnx113   pr413   wcj,cs,nn4735   df,nn929   ptn3808   nipf7604

spent; my lord also hath our herds of cattle; there is not aught left in the

pp,pl,cs,nn6440   nn,pnx113   ptn1115/cj518   nn,pnx1472   wcj,nn,pnx127

sight of my lord, but our bodies, and our lands:

pp,pnit4100   qmf4191   pp,du,nn,pnx5869   ad1571   pnp587   ad1571   nn,pnx127

19 Wherefore shall we die before thine eyes, both we and our land?

qmv7069   pnx(853)   wcj(853)   nn,pnx127   dfp,nn3899   pnp587   wcj,nn,pnx127   wcj,qmf1961

buy us and our land for bread, and we and our land will be

pl,nn**5650**   pp,nn6547   wcj,qmv**5414**   nn2233   wcj,qmf**2421**   wcj,ptn**3808** qmf**4191**

servants unto Pharaoh: and give *us* seed, that we may live, and not die, that

wcj,df,nn**127**   qmf**3456**/ptn**3808**

the land be*not*desolate.

nn3130   wcs,qmf7069   (853)   cs,nn3605   cs,nn**127**   nn4714   pp,nn6547   cj3588

20 And Joseph bought   all   the land of Egypt for Pharaoh; for the

nn4714   qpf4376   nn**376**   nn,pnx7704   cj3588   df,nn7458   qpf**2388**   pr,pnx5921

Egyptians sold every man his field, because the famine prevailed over them: so

df,nn776 wcs,qmf**1961**   pp,nn6547

the land became Pharaoh's.

wcj(853)   df,nn**5971**   hipf**5674**   pnx(853)   dfp,pl,nn5892   pr4480/cs,nn7097

21 And as for   the people, he removed   them to cities from*one*end

cs,nn1366   nn4714   wcj,pr5704   nn,pnx7097

of the borders of Egypt even to the *other* end thereof.

ad7535   cs,nn**127**   df,pl,nn3548   qpf7069   ptn**3808** cj3588   dfp,pl,nn3548   nn**2706**

22 Only the land of the priests bought he not; for the priests had a portion

pr4480/pr854   nn6547   wcj,qpf398 (853)   nn,pnx**2706** pnl834   nn6547   qpf**5414**

assigned them   of   Pharaoh, and did eat   their portion which Pharaoh gave

pp,pnx   pr5921/ad**3651**   qpf4376 ptn**3808** (853)   nn,pnx**127**

them: wherefore they sold not   their lands.

nn3130   wcs,qmf**559** pr413   df,nn**5971**   ptdm2005   qpf7069   pnx(853)

23 Then Joseph said unto the people, Behold, I have bought   you this

df,nn**3117**   wcj(853)   nn,pnx**127**   pp,nn6547   ptx1887   nn2233   pp,pnx

day and   your land for Pharaoh: lo, *here is* seed for you, and ye shall

wcj,qpf2232 (853)   df,nn**127**

sow   the land.

wcj,qpf**1961**   dfp,pl,nn8393   wcj,qpf**5414**   nuor2549

24 And it*shall*come*to*pass in the increase, that ye shall give the fifth

pp,nn6547   wcj,nu702 df,pl,nn**3027**   qmf**1961**   pp,pnx   pp,cs,nn2233   df,nn**7704**

part unto Pharaoh, and four parts shall be your own, for seed of the field,

wcj,pp,nn,pnx400   wcj,pp,pnl834   pp,pl,nn,pnx**1004**   wcj,pp,qnc398

and for your food, and for them of your households, and for food for

pp,nn,pnx**2945**

your little ones.

wcs,qmf**559**   hipf,pnx**2421**   qmf4672   nn2580   pp,du,cs,nn**5869**

25 And they said, Thou hast saved*our*lives: let us find grace in the   sight

nn,pnx113   wcs,qpf**1961**   pp,nn6547   pl,nn**5650**

of my lord, and we will be   Pharaoh's servants.

nn3130   wcs,qmf**7760** pnx(853)   pp,nn**2706** pr5921   cs,nn**127**   nn4714   pr5704 df,pndm2088

26 And Joseph made   it a law over the land of Egypt unto this

df,nn**3117**   pp,nn6547   dfp,nn2569   ad7535   cs,nn**127**   df,pl,nn**3548**

day, *that* Pharaoh should have the fifth *part*; except the land of the priests

pp,nn,pnx905   qpf**1961** ptn**3808**   pp,nn6547

only, *which* became not Pharaoh's.

Jacob's Last Wish

nn3478 wcs,qmf**3427**   pp,cs,nn776   nn4714   pp,cs,nn776   nn1657

27 And Israel dwelt in the land of Egypt, in the country of Goshen; and they

wcs,nimf270   pp,pnx   wcs,qmf6509   wcs,qmf7235   ad3966

had possessions therein, and grew, and multiplied exceedingly.

nn3290   wcs,qmf**2421**   pp,cs,nn776   nn4714   nu7651/nu6240   nn8141

28 And Jacob lived in the land of Egypt seventeen years: so the

pl,cs,nn**3117**/pl,cs,nn8141/aj,pnx**2416**   nn3290   wcs,qmf**1961**   wcj,cs,nu3967 wcj,pl,nu705 (nn8141)   nu7651   pl,nn8141

whole age   of Jacob was a hundred forty   and seven years.

pl,cs,nn3117   wcs,qmf7126   nn3478   pp,qnc4191   wcs,qmf7121   pp,nn,pnx1121

29 And the time drew nigh that Israel must die: and he called his   son

pp,nn3130   wcs,qmf559   pp,pnx   cj518 pte4994   qpf4672   nn2580   pp,du,nn,pnx5869 qmv7760

Joseph, and said unto him, If now I have found grace in thy   sight,   put,

pte4994   nn,pnx3027 pr8478   nn,pnx3409 wcj,qpf6213 nn2617   wcj,nn571 pr,pnx5973

I*pray*thee, thy hand under my thigh, and deal kindly and truly with me;

qmf,pnx6912   ptn408   pte4994   pp,nn4714

bury me not, I*pray*thee, in Egypt:

wcs,qpf7901 pr5973   pl,nn,pnx1   wcs,qpf,pnx5375   pr4480/nn4714

30 But I will lie with my fathers, and thou shalt carry   me out*of*Egypt,

wcs,qpf,pnx6912   pp,nn,pnx6900   wcs,qmf559 pnp595   qmf6213

and bury me in their burial place. And he said,   I will do as thou hast

pp,nn,pnx1697

said.

wcs,qmf559   nimv7650   pp,pnx   wcs,nimf7650   pp,pnx   nn3478

🔑 31 And he said, Swear unto me. And he swore unto him. And Israel

wcs,htmf*7812   pr5921   df,nn4296 cs,nn7218

bowed himself upon the bed's head.

Jacob Gives His Blessing to Joseph's Two Sons

wcs,qmf1961   pr310   df,pndm428 df,pl,nn1697   wcs,qmf559   pp,nn3130

48 And it*came*to*pass after these things, that *one* told Joseph,

ptdm2009   nn,pnx1   qpta2470   wcs,qmf3947 pr,pnx5973   (853)   du,cs,nu8147

Behold, thy father *is* sick: and he took with him   his two

pl,nn,pnx1121 (853)   nn4519   wcj(853)   nn669

sons,   Manasseh and   Ephraim.

wcs,himf5046 pp,nn3290   wcs,qmf559   ptdm2009   nn,pnx1121 nn3130   qpf935   pr,pnx413

2 And *one* told Jacob, and said, Behold, thy son Joseph cometh unto

nn3478   wcs,htmf2388   wcs,qmf3427 pr5921   df,nn4296

thee: and Israel strengthened himself, and sat upon the bed.

nn3290 wcs,qmf559 pr413   nn3130   nn410   nn7706   nipf7200   pr,pnx413   pp,nn3870

3 And Jacob said unto Joseph, God Almighty appeared unto me at Luz in

pp,cs,nn776   nn3667   wcs,pimf1288 pnx(853)

the land of Canaan, and blessed   me,

wcs,qmf559 pr,pnx413   ptdm,pnx2009   hipt,pnx6509   wcj,hipt,pnx7235

4 And said unto me, Behold, I will make*thee*fruitful, and multiply thee,

wcj,qpf,pnx5414   pp,cs,nn6951   pl,nn5971   wcj,qpf5414 (853) df,pndm2063 df,nn776

and I will make of thee a multitude of people; and will give   this land to

pp,nn,pnx2233 pr,pnx310   nn5769   cs,nn272

thy seed after thee *for* an everlasting possession.

wcj,ad6258   du,cs,nu8147 pl,nn,pnx1121   nn669   wcj,nn4519   df,pl,nipf3205

🔑 5 And now thy two sons, Ephraim and Manasseh, which were born

pp,pnx   pp,cs,nn776   nn4714   pr5704   qnc,pnx935 pr,pnx413   nn,lh4714 (pnp1992)

unto thee in the land of Egypt before I came unto thee into Egypt,   *are*

pp,pnx   pp,nn7205   wcj,nn8095   qmf1961 pp,pnx

mine; as Reuben and Simeon, they shall be mine.

🔑 **47:31** Did Jacob support himself on the head of his bed or did he support himself by his staff (Heb. 11:21)? The present Hebrew vocalization (*mittāh* [4296]) is translated as "bed," while the Septuagint and the Epistle to the Hebrews use a different vocalization (*matteh* [4294]), which is translated as "staff." Since the Hebrew vowels were not inserted into the Hebrew consonantal text until much later, one cannot be sure which vocalization is correct. However, the meaning and context of the passage are unaffected regardless of which is chosen. In addition, there is the possibility that the two passages may not be referring to the same incident.

🔑 **48:5** See the note on Genesis 35:23–26.

wcj,nn,pnx4138   pnl834   hipf3205   pr,pnx310   qmf1961   pp,pnx

6 And thy issue, which thou begettest after them, shall be thine, *and* shall

nimf7121   pr5921   cs,nn8034   pl,nn,pnx251   pp,nn,pnx5159

be called after the name of their brethren in their inheritance.

wcj,pnp589   pp,qnc,pnx935   pr4480/nn6307   nn7354   qpf4191 pr,pnx5921

7 And as for me, when I came from Padan, Rachel died by me in the

pp,cs,nn776   nn3667   dfp,nn1870   pp,ad5750   cs,nn3530 nn776   ' pp,qnc935

land of Canaan in the way, when yet *there was* but a little way to come unto

nn,lh672   wcs,qmf7200   ad8033   pp,cs,nn1870   nn672   pnp1931   nn1035

Ephrath: and I buried her there in the way of Ephrath; the same *is* Bethlehem.

nn3478   wcs,qmf7200   nn3130   (853) pl,cs,nn1121   wcs,qmf559 pnit4310   pndm428

8 And Israel beheld Joseph's   sons, and said, Who *are* these?

nn3130   wcs,qmf559   pr413   nn,pnx1   pnp1992   pl,nn,pnx1121 pnl834   pl,nn430

9 And Joseph said unto his father, They *are* my sons, whom God hath

qpf5414   pp,pnx   pp,pndm2088   wcs,qmf559 qmv,pnx3947   pte4994   pr,pnx413

given me in this *place*. And he said, Bring them, I*pray*thee, unto me,

wcj,pimf,pnx1288

and I will bless them.

wcj,du,cs,nn5869   nn3478   qpf3513   pr4480/nn2207   qmf3201 ptn3808 pp,qnc7200

10 Now the eyes   of Israel were dim for age, *so that* he could not see.

wcs,himf5066/pnx(853)   pr,pnx413   wcs,qmf5401 pp,pnx   wcs,pimf2263 pp,pnx

And he brought*them*near unto him; and he kissed them, and embraced them.

nn3478   wcs,qmf559   pr413   nn3130   ptn3808   pipf6419   qnc7200   pl,nn,pnx6440

11 And Israel said unto Joseph, I had not thought to see thy face: and,

wcj,ptdm2009 pl,nn430   hipf7200   pnx(853)   ad1571 (853)   nn,pnx2233

lo,   God hath showed me also   thy seed.

nn3130   wcs,himf3318/pnx(853)   pr4480/pr5973   du,nn,pnx1290

12 And Joseph brought*them*out from between his knees, and he

wcs,himf*7812   pp,du,nn,pnx639   nn,lh776

bowed himself with his face to the earth.

nn3130   wcs,qmf3947 (853)   du,nu,pnx8147 (853)   nn669   pp,nn,pnx3225

13 And Joseph took   them both,   Ephraim in his right hand toward

nn3478   pr4480/cs,nn8040   wcj(853)   nn4519   pp,nn,pnx8040   nn3478   pr4480/cs,nn3225

Israel's left hand, and   Manasseh in his left hand toward Israel's right hand,

wcs,himf5066   pr,pnx413

and brought*them*near unto him.

nn3478   wcs,qmf7971   (853)   nn,pnx3225   wcs,qmf7896   pr5921   nn669

14 And Israel stretched out   his right hand, and laid *it* upon Ephraim's

cs,nn7218 wcj,pnp1931   df,aj6810   wcj(853)   nn,pnx8040   pr5921   nn4519   cs,nn7218

head, who *was* the younger, and   his left hand upon Manasseh's head,

pipf7919/(853)/du,nn,pnx3027   cj3588   nn4519   df,nn1060

guiding*his*hands*wittingly; for Manasseh *was* the firstborn.

wcs,pimf1288   (853)   nn3130   wcs,qmf559 df,pl,nn430 pp,pl,nn,pnx6440 pnl834   pl,nn,pnx1

15 And he blessed   Joseph, and said, God,   before whom my fathers

nn85   wcj,nn3327   htpf1980   df,pl,nn430   df,qpta7462 pnx(853)   pr4480/ad,pnx5750

Abraham and Isaac did walk, the God which fed   me all*my*life*long

pr5704 df,pndm2088 df,nn3117

unto this day,

df,nn4397   df,qpta1350   pnx(853)   pr4480/cs,nn3605 nn7451 pimf1288 (853)   df,pl,nn5288

16 The Angel which redeemed   me from all evil, bless   the lads; and

nn,pnx8034   wcj,nimf7121   pp,pnx   wcj,cs,nn8034   pl,nn,pnx1   nn85

let my name be named on them, and the name of my fathers Abraham and

wcj,nn3327   wcj,qmf1711   pp,aj7230   pp,cs,nn7130   df,nn776

Isaac; and let them grow into a multitude in the midst of the earth.

nn3130   wcs,qmf7200 cj3588   nn,pnx1 qmf7896   nn,pnx3225 cs,nn3027 pr5921   cs,nn7218

17 And when Joseph saw that his father laid his right hand upon the head

nn669   wcs,qmf**7489**/pp,du,nn,pnx**5869**   wcs,qmf**8551**   nn,pnx**1**   cs,nn**3027**   pp,hinc**5493**

of Ephraim, it   displeased   him: and he held up his father's hand, to remove

pnx(**853**)   pr**4480**/pr**5921**   nn669   cs,nn**7218**   pr**5921**   nn**4519**   cs,nn**7218**

it   from   Ephraim's head unto Manasseh's head.

nn**3130**   wcs,qmf**559**   pr**413**   nn,pnx**1**   ptn**3808**   ad**3651**   nn,pnx**1**   cj**3588**   pndm**2088**

18 And Joseph   said   unto his father, Not so, my father: for this   *is* the

df,nn**1060**   qmv**7760**   nn,pnx**3225**   pr**5921**   nn,pnx**7218**

firstborn; put thy right hand upon his head.

nn,pnx**1**   wcs,pimf**3985**   wcs,qmf**559**   qpf**3045**   nn,pnx**1121**   qpf**3045**   pnp**1931**   ad**1571**

19 And his father refused, and   said, I know *it*, my son, I know *it*: he   also

qmf**1961**   pp,nn**5971**   pnp**1931**   wcj,ad**1571**   qmf**1431**   wcj,ad**199**   df,aj**6996**

shall become a people, and   he   also   shall be great: but truly   his younger

nn,pnx**251**   qmf**1431**   pr,pnx**4480**   wcj,nn,pnx**2233**   qmf**1961**   cs,nn**4393**

brother shall be greater   than   he   and his   seed   shall become a multitude of

df,pl,nn**1471**

nations.

wcs,pimf,pnx**1288**   df,pndm**1931**   dfp,nn**3117**   pp,qnc**559**   pp,pnx   nn**3478**   pimf**1288**

   20 And he   blessed   them   that   day,   saying, In thee shall Israel bless,

pp,qnc**559**   pl,nn**430**   qmf,pnx**7760**   pp,nn**669**   wcj,pp,nn**4519**   wcs,qmf**7760**   (**853**)   nn669

saying, God make   thee as Ephraim and as Manasseh: and he   set   Ephraim

pp,pl,cs,nn**6440**   nn**4519**

before   Manasseh.

nn**3478**   wcs,qmf**559**   pr**413**   nn**3130**   ptdm**2009**   pnp**595**   qpta**4191**   pl,nn**430**   wcj,qpf**1961**

21 And Israel   said   unto Joseph, Behold,   I   die: but God shall   be

pr,pnx**5973**   wcj,hipf**7725**/pnx(**853**)   pr**413**   cs,nn**776**   pl,nn,pnx**1**

with   you, and bring*you*again unto the land of your fathers.

wcj,pnp**589**   qpf**5414**   pp,pnx   nu**259**   nn**7926**   pr**5921**   pl,nn,pnx**251**   pnl**834**

22 Moreover   I   have given to thee one portion above thy brethren, which I

qpf**3947**   pr**4480**/cs,nn**3027**   df,nn**567**   pp,nn,pnx**2719**   wcj,pp,nn,pnx**7198**

took out*of*the*hand of the Amorite with my   sword   and with my   bow.

Jacob Gives a Blessing to All His Sons

nn**3290**   wcs,qmf**7121**   pr**413**   pl,nn,pnx**1121**   wcs,qmf**559**

49

And   Jacob   called   unto   his   sons,   and   said,

nimv**622**   wcj,hicj**5046** pp,pnx   (**853**)   pnl**834**

Gather*yourselves*together, that I may   tell   you *that*   which shall

qmf**7122**   pnx(**853**)   pp,cs,nn**319**   df,pl,nn**3117**

befall   you in the   last   days.

nimv**6908**   wcj,qmv**8085**   pl,cs,nn**1121**   nn**3290**   wcj,qmv**8085**   pr**413**

2 Gather*yourselves*together, and   hear, ye   sons   of Jacob; and hearken unto

nn**3478**   nn,pnx**1**

Israel your father.

nn**7205**   pnp**859**   nn,pnx**1060**   nn,pnx**3581**   wcj,cs,nn**7225**   nn,pnx**202**

3 Reuben, thou *art* my firstborn, my might, and the beginning of my strength,

cs,nn**3499**   nn**7613**   wcj,cs,nn**3499**   aj**5794**

the excellency of dignity, and the excellency of power:

nn**6349**   dfp,pl,nn**4325**   ptn**408**   hicj**3498**   cj**3588**   qpf**5927**

4 Unstable as   water,   thou shalt   not   excel; because thou wentest up to thy

nn,pnx**1**   pl,cs,nn**4904**   ad**227**   pipf**2490**   qpf**5927**   nn,pnx**3326**

father's   bed;   then defiledst thou *it*: he went up to my couch.

nn**8095**   wcj,nn**3878**   pl,nn**251**   pl,cs,nn**3627**   nn**2555**

5 Simeon   and   Levi   *are* brethren; instruments of cruelty *are* *in* their

pl,nn,pnx**4380**

habitations.

nn,pnx5315   qmf935   ptn408   pp,nn,pnx5475   pp,nn,pnx6951

6 O my soul, come not thou into their secret; unto their assembly, mine

nn,pnx3519   ptn408   qmf3161   cj3588   pp,nn,pnx639   qpf2026   nn376

honor, be not thou united: for in their anger they slew a man, and in their

wcj,pp,nn,pnx7522   pipf6131   nn7791

self-will they digged down a wall.

qptp779   nn,pnx639   cj3588   aj5794   wcj,nn,pnx5678 cj3588   qpf7185

7 Cursed *be* their anger, for *it was* fierce; and their wrath, for it was cruel: I

pimf,pnx2505   pp,nn3290   wcj,himf,pnx6327   pp,nn3478

will divide them in Jacob, and scatter them in Israel.

nn3063   pnp859   pl,nn,pnx251   himf,pnx3034   nn,pnx3027

8 Judah, thou *art he* whom thy brethren shall praise: thy hand *shall be* in the

pp,cs,nn6203   pl,qpta,pnx341   nn,pnx1   pl,cs,nn1121   htmf7812   pp,pnx

neck of thine enemies; thy father's children shall bow down before thee.

nn3063   nn738   cs,nn1482   pr4480/nn2964   nn,pnx1121   qpf5927

9 Judah *is* a lion's whelp: from*the*prey, my son, thou art gone up: he

qpf3766   qpf7257   pp,nn738   wcj,pp,nn3833   pnit4310   himf,pnx6965

stooped down, he couched as a lion, and as an old lion; who shall rouse*him*up?

nn7626   ptn3808   qmf5493   pr4480/nn3063   wcj,pipt*2710   pr4480/pr996

10 The scepter shall not depart from Judah, nor a lawgiver from between his

du,nn,pnx7272 pr5704/cj3588   nn7886   qmf935   wcj,pp,pnx   cs,nn3349   pl,nn5971

feet, until Shiloh come; and unto him *shall* the gathering of the people *be*.

cs,qpta631   nn,pnx5895   dfp,nn1612   nn,pnx860 cs,nn1121   wcj,dfp,nn8321

11 Binding his foal unto the vine, and his ass's colt unto the choice vine;

pipf3526   nn,pnx3830   dfp,nn3196   nn,pnx5497   wcj,pp,cs,nn1818   pl,nn6025

he washed his garments in wine, and his clothes in the blood of grapes:

du,nn5869   aj2447   pr4480/nn3196   du,nn8127 wcj,cs,aj3836   pr4480/nn2461

12 His eyes *shall be* red with wine, and his teeth white with milk.

nn2074   qmf7931   pp,cs,nn2348   pl,nn3220   wcj,pnp1931

13 Zebulun shall dwell at the haven of the sea; and he *shall be* for a

pp,cs,nn2348   pl,nn591   wcj,nn,pnx3411   pr5921   nn6721

haven of ships; and his border *shall be* unto Zidon.

nn3485   nn1634   nn2543   qpta7257   pr996   df,du,nn4942

14 Issachar *is* a strong ass couching down between two burdens:

wcs,qmf7200   cj3588   nn4496   aj2896   wcj(853)   df,nn776 cj3588   qpf5276

15 And he saw that rest *was* good, and the land that *it was* pleasant;

wcs,qmf5186   nn,pnx7926   pp,qnc5445   wcs,qmf1961   qpta5647   pp,cs,nn4522

and bowed his shoulder to bear, and became a servant unto tribute.

nn1835   qmf1777   nn,pnx5971   pp,cs,nu259   pl,cs,nn7626   nn3478

16 Dan shall judge his people, as one of the tribes of Israel.

nn1835   qmf1961   nn5175   pr5921   nn1870   nn8207 pr5921   nn734   df,qpta5391

17 Dan shall be a serpent by the way, an adder in the path, that biteth the

nn5483   pl,cs,nn6119   qpta,pnx7392   wcs,qmf5307   nn268

horse heels, so that his rider shall fall backward.

pipf6960   pp,nn,pnx3444   nn3068

18 I have waited for thy salvation, O LORD.

nn1410   nn1416   qmf,pnx1464   wcj,pnp1931   qmf1464   nn6119

19 Gad, a troop shall overcome him: but he shall overcome at the last.

pr4480/nn836   nn,pnx3899   aj8082   wcj,pnp1931   qmf5414   nn4428   pl,cs,nn4574

20 Out*of*Asher his bread *shall be* fat, and he shall yield royal dainties.

nn5321   nn355   qptp7971   df,qpta5414   nn8233   pl,cs,nn561

21 Naphtali *is* a hind let loose: he giveth goodly words.

49:10 This does not mean that there will be a continuous sovereignty by the descendants of Judah, but merely that their line will retain a permanent right to rule. Note that the scepter and staff represent only the right to rule. This verse is normally regarded as a messianic prophecy.

nn3130   qpta6509   cs,nn**1121**   qpta6509   cs,nn**1121** pr5921   nn**5869**   pl,nn1323

22 Joseph *is* a fruitful bough, *even* a fruitful bough by a well; *whose* branches

qpf6805 pr5921   nn7791

run over the wall:

pl,cs,nn**1167**/pl,nn2671   wcs,pimf,pnx4843   wcj,qpf7232   wcs,qmf,pnx7852

23 The   archers   have sorely grieved him, and   shot   *at him*, and   hated

him:

nn,pnx7198 wcs,qmf**3427**   pp,aj386   pl,cs,nn2220   du,nn,pnx**3027**

24 But his bow   abode in strength, and the   arms of his hands   were

wcs,qmf6339   pr4480/du,cs,nn**3027**   cs,nn46   nn3290   pr4480/ad8033

made strong by*the*hands of the mighty *God* of Jacob; (from thence *is* the

qpta7462   cs,nn68   nn3478

shepherd, the stone of Israel:)

pr4480/cs,nn**410**   nn,pnx1   wcj,qmf,pnx5826   wcj(853)

25 *Even* by*the*God of thy father, who shall   help   thee; and   by the

nn**7706**   wcj,pimf,pnx**1288**   pl,cs,nn**1293**   du,nn**8064** pr4480/nn5920 pl,cs,nn**1293**

Almighty, who shall   bless   thee with blessings of heaven above, blessings of

nn8415   qpta7257   ad8478   pl,cs,nn**1293**   du,nn7699   wcj,nn**7356**

the deep that lieth under, blessings of the breasts, and of the womb:

pl,cs,nn**1293**   nn,pnx1   qpf1396   pr5921   pl,cs,nn**1293**

26 The blessings of thy father have prevailed above the blessings of my

pl,qpta,pnx2029   pr5704   cs,nn8379   nn**5769**   pl,cs,nn1389   qmf**1961**

progenitors unto the utmost bound of the everlasting hills: they shall be on the

pp,cs,nn**7218**   nn3130   wcj,pp,cs,nn6936   cs,nn**5139**

head of Joseph, and on the crown*of*the*head of him*that*was*separate*from his

pl,nn,pnx**251**

brethren.

nn1144   qmf2963   nn2061   dfp,nn1242   qmf398   nn5706

27 Benjamin shall raven *as* a wolf: in the morning he shall devour the prey, and

wcj,dfp,nn6153   pimf2505   nn7998

at night   he shall divide the spoil.

cs,nn3605 pndm428   du,nu8147/nu6240 pl,cs,nn**7626**   nn3478   wcj,pndm2063   pnl834

28 All these *are* the   twelve   tribes of Israel: and   this   *is it* that their

nn,pnx1 pipf**1696**   pp,pnx   wcs,pimf**1288** pnx(853)   nn376/pnl834   pp,nn,pnx1293

father spoke unto them, and blessed   them; every one according to his blessing

pipf**1288**   pnx(853)

he blessed   them.

Jacob Dies

wcs,pimf**6680** pnx(853)   wcs,qmf559 pr,pnx413   pnp589   nipt622

29 And he charged   them, and said   unto them,   I   am to be gathered

pr413   nn,pnx**5971** qmv**6912** pnx(853)   pr413   pl,nn,pnx1 pr413   df,nn4631 pnl834   pp,cs,nn**7704**

unto my people: bury   me with my fathers in the cave that *is* in the field

nn6085   df,nn2850

of Ephron the Hittite,

dfp,nn4631 pnl834   pp,cs,nn**7704**   df,nn4375   pnl834   pr5921/pl,cs,nn**6440**

30 In the cave   that *is* in the field of Machpelah, which *is*   before

nn4471   pp,cs,nn**776**   nn3667   pnl834   nn85   qpf7069   pr854   df,nn**7704** pr4480/pr854

Mamre, in the land of Canaan, which Abraham bought with the field   of

nn6085   df,nn2850   pp,cs,nn**272**   nn6913

Ephron the Hittite for a possession of a burial place.

ad,lh8033   qpf6912   (853)   nn85   wcj(853)   nn8283   nn,pnx802   ad,lh8033   qpf6912

31 There they buried   Abraham and   Sarah his wife; there they buried

(853)   nn3327   wcj(853)   nn7259   nn,pnx802   wcj,ad,lh8033   qpf6912   (853)   nn3812

Isaac and   Rebekah his wife; and   there   I buried   Leah.

cs,nn4735   df,nn7704   wcj,df,nn4631 pnl834   pp,pnx   pr4480/pr854

32 The purchase of the field and of the   cave   that is therein was   from   the

pl,cs,nn1121   nn2845

children of Heth.

nn3290   wcs,pimf3615   pp,pinc6680   (853)   pl,nn,pnx1121

33 And when Jacob had made*an*end of commanding   his   sons,   he

wcs,qmf622   du,nn,pnx7272 pr413   df,nn4296   wcs,qmf1478   wcs,nimf622

gathered up his   feet   into the bed, and yielded*up*the*ghost, and was gathered

pr413   pl,nn,pnx5971

unto his people.

Joseph Comforts His Brothers

nn3130   wcs,qmf5307   pr5921   nn,pnx1   pl,cs,nn6440   wcs,qmf1058 pr,pnx5921

50 And Joseph   fell   upon his father's   face,   and   wept   upon   him,

wcs,qmf5401   pp,pnx

and kissed him.

nn3130   wcs,pimf6680   (853)   pl,nn,pnx5650 (853)   df,pl,qpta7495   pp,qnc2590   (853)

2 And Joseph commanded   his servants   the physicians to embalm   his

nn,pnx1   df,pl,qpta7495   wcs,qmf2590   (853)   nn3478

father: and the physicians embalmed   Israel.

pl,nu705   nn3117   wcs,qmf4390   pp,pnx   cj3588   ad3651   qmf4390   pl,cs,nn3117

3 And forty days were fulfilled for him; for   so   are fulfilled the   days   of

df,pl,nn2590   nn4714   wcs,qmf1058   pnx(853)

those*which*are*embalmed: and   the   Egyptians   mourned   for   him

pl,nu7657   nn3117

threescore*and*ten days.

pl,cs,nn3117   nn,pnx1068   wcs,qmf5674   nn3130   wcs,pimf1696   pr413

4 And when the   days   of his mourning were   past,   Joseph   spoke   unto the

cs,nn1004   nn6547   pp,qnc559   cj518   pte4994   qpf4672   nn2580   pp,du,nn,pnx5869   pimv1696

house of Pharaoh, saying, If now I have found grace in your   eyes,   speak,

pte4994   pp,du,cs,nn241   nn6547   pp,qnc559

I*pray*you, in the   ears   of Pharaoh, saying,

nn,pnx1   hipf,pnx7650   pp,qnc559   ptdm2009 pnp595 qpta4191   pp,nn,pnx6913   pnl834

5 My father made me swear, saying, Lo,   I   die: in my   grave   which I

qpf3738   pp,pnx   pp,cs,nn776   nn3667   ad,lh8033   qmf,pnx6912   wcj,ad6258

have digged for me in the   land   of Canaan, there shalt thou   bury   me.   Now

qmf5927   pte4994   wcj,qcj6912   (853)   nn,pnx1

therefore let me go up, I*pray*thee,   and   bury   my father,   and   I will

wcj,qcj7725

come again.

nn6547   wcs,qmf559   qmv5927   wcj,qmv6912   (853)   nn,pnx1   pp,pnl834

6 And Pharaoh said, Go up, and   bury   thy father, according as he made

hipf,pnx7650

thee swear.

nn3130   wcs,qmf5927   pp,qnc6912   (853)   nn,pnx1   pr,pnx854   wcs,qmf5927   cs,nn3605

7 And Joseph went up to bury   his father: and   with   him went up   all

pl,cs,nn5650   nn6547   cs,aj2205   nn,pnx1004   wcj,cs,nn3605   cs,aj2205   cs,nn776

the servants of Pharaoh, the elders of his house, and   all   the elders of the land

nn4714

of Egypt,

8 And all the house of Joseph, and his brethren, and his father's house: only their little ones, and their flocks, and their herds, they left in the land of Goshen.

9 And there went up with him both chariots and horsemen: and it was a very great company.

10 And they came to the threshingfloor of Atad, which is beyond Jordan, and there they mourned with a great and very sore lamentation: and he made a mourning for his father seven days.

11 And when the inhabitants of the land, the Canaanites, saw the mourning in the floor of Atad, they said, This is a grievous mourning to the Egyptians: wherefore the name of it was called Abel-mizraim, which is beyond Jordan.

12 And his sons did unto him according as he commanded them:

13 For his sons carried him into the land of Canaan, and buried him in the cave of the field of Machpelah, which Abraham bought with the field for a possession of a buryingplace of Ephron the Hittite, before Mamre.

14 And Joseph returned into Egypt, he, and his brethren, and all that went up with him to bury his father, after he had buried his father.

Joseph Dies

15 And when Joseph's brethren saw that their father was dead, they said, Joseph will peradventure hate us, and will certainly requite us all the evil which we did unto him.

16 And they sent*a*messenger unto Joseph, saying, Thy father did command before he died, saying,

17 So shall ye say unto Joseph, Forgive, I*pray*thee now, the trespass of thy brethren, and their sin; for they did unto thee evil: and now,

pte**4994**   qmv**5375**   pp,cs,nn**6588**   pl,cs,nn**5650**   pl,cs,nn**430**   nn,pnx**1**

we*pray*thee, forgive the trespass of the servants of the God of thy father. And

nn**3130**   wcs,qmf**1058**   pp,pinc,pnx**1696**   pr,pnx**413**

Joseph wept when they spoke unto him.

pp,nn,pnx**251**   ad**1571**   wcs,qmf**1980**   wcs,qmf**5307**   pp,pl,nn,pnx**6440**

18 And his brethren also went and fell down before his face; and they

wcs,qmf**559**   ptdm,pnx**2009**   pp,pnx   pp,pl,nn**5650**

said, Behold, we *be* thy servants.

nn**3130**   wcs,qmf**559**   pr,pnx**413**   qmf**3372**   ptn**408**   cj**3588**   pnp**589**   he,pr**8478**   pl,nn**430**

19 And Joseph said unto them, Fear not: for *am* I in*the*place of God?

wcj,pnp**859**   qpf**2803**   nn**7451**   pr,pnx**5921**   pl,nn**430**   qpf,pnx**2803**   pp,nn**2896**

20 But as for you, ye thought evil against me; *but* God meant it unto good,

pr**4616**   qnc**6213**   df,pndm**2088**   dfp,nn**3117**   pp,hinc**2421**/nn**5971**/aj**7227**

to bring*to*pass, as *it is* this day, to save*much*people*alive.

wcj,ad**6258**   qmf**3372**   ptn**408**   pnp**595**   pimf*3557**   pnx(**853**)   wcj(**853**)

21 Now therefore fear ye not: I will nourish you, and your

nn,pnx**2945**   wcs,pimf**5162**   pnx(**853**)   wcs,pimf**1696**   pr**5921**/nn,pnx**3820**

little ones. And he comforted them, and spoke kindly unto them.

nn**3130**   wcs,qmf**3427**   pp,nn**4714**   pnp**1931**   nn,pnx**1**   wcj,cs,nn**1004**   nn**3130**

22 And Joseph dwelt in Egypt, he, and his father's house: and Joseph

wcs,qmf**2421**   nu**3967**   wcj,nu**6235**   pl,nn**8141**

lived a hundred and ten years.

nn**3130**   wcs,qmf**7200**   pp,nn**669**   pl,cs,nn**1121**   aj**8029**   pl,cs,nn**1121**

23 And Joseph saw Ephraim's children of the third *generation*: the children

ad**1571**   nn**4353**   cs,nn**1121**   nn**4519**   pupf**3205**   pr**5921**   nn**3130**   du,cs,nn**1290**

also of Machir the son of Manasseh were brought up upon Joseph's knees.

nn**3130**   wcs,qmf**559**   pr**413**   pl,nn,pnx**251**   pnp**595**   qpta**4191**   wcj,pl,nn**430**   qna**6485**/qmf**6485**

24 And Joseph said unto his brethren, I die: and God will surely visit

pnx(**853**)   wcs,hipf**5927** pnx(**853**)   pr**4480**   df,pndm**2063**   df,nn**776**   pr**413**   df,nn**776**   pnl**834**   nipf**7650**

you, and bring you out of this land unto the land which he swore

pp,nn**85**   pp,nn**3327**   wcj,pp,nn**3290**

to Abraham, to Isaac, and to Jacob.

nn**3130**   wcs,himf**7650**   (**853**)   pl,cs,nn**1121**   nn**3478**   pp,qnc**559**   pl,nn**430**

25 And Joseph took*an*oath of the children of Israel, saying, God will

qna**6485**/qmf**6485**   pnx(**853**)   wcs,hipf**5927**   (**853**)   pl,nn,pnx**6106**   pr**4480**/pndm**2088**

surely visit you, and ye shall carry up my bones from hence.

nn**3130**   wcs,qmf**4191**   nu**3967**   wcj,nu**6235**   pl,nn**8141**   cs,nn**1121**

26 So Joseph died, *being* a hundred and ten years old: and they

wcs,qmf**2590**   pnx(**853**)   wcs,qmf**3455**   dfp,nn**727**   pp,nn**4714**

embalmed him, and he was put in a coffin in Egypt.

The Book of
EXODUS

Exodus is a Greek word which means "departure" and is derived from *ek*, "out of," and *hodós*, "road." The Hebrew title (the first words of the Hebrew text) means "and these are the names of."

The book of Exodus describes the deliverance of the Israelites from Egypt, their journey to Mount Sinai, and the events that occurred during their sojourn there.

The patriarch Jacob had brought his family to Egypt to avoid starvation (see Gen. 46:1–27). When the Hyksos invaded Egypt in the early seventeenth century B.C. and gained political power, the descendants of Jacob were forced into slavery (Ex. 1:8, 10). Despite the bitterness of their bondage, Jacob's descendants grew from a family of seventy (see the note on Gen. 46:26, 27) into a nation of about two million (based on the figure of six hundred thousand men over twenty years of age, Ex. 12:37). The primary emphasis in Genesis was on the family of Abraham, but the Book of Exodus focuses on the developing nation of Israel.

The main theme of Exodus is redemption. The deliverance of the children of Israel from bondage in Egypt is a type of all redemption, and Moses who led them is a type of Christ.

A New King in Egypt

1
^{wcj,pndm428   pl,cs,nn8034   pl,cs,nn1121   nn3478   df,pl,qpta935}
☞ Now these *are* the names of the children of Israel, which came into
^{nn,lh4714   nn376   wcj,nn,pnx1004   qpf935   pr854   nn3290}
Egypt; every man and his household came with Jacob.

^{nn7205   nn8095   nn3878   wcj,nn3063}
2 Reuben, Simeon, Levi, and Judah,

^{nn3485   nn2074   wcj,nn1144}
3 Issachar, Zebulun, and Benjamin,

^{nn1835   wcj,nn5321   nn1410   wcj,nn836}
4 Dan, and Naphtali, Gad, and Asher.

^{cs,nn3605   cs,nn5315   pl,cs,qpta3318   cs,nn3409   nn3290   wcs,qmf1961   pl,nu7657}
5 And all the souls that came out of the loins of Jacob were seventy
^{nn5315   wcj,nn3130   qpf1961   pp,nn4714}
souls: for Joseph was in Egypt *already*.

^{nn3130   wcs,qmf4191   wcj,cs,nn3605   pl,nn,pnx251   wcj,cs,nn3605   df,pndm1931   df,nn1755}
☞ 6 And Joseph died, and all his brethren, and all that generation.

^{wcj,pl,cs,nn1121   nn3478   qpf6509   wcs,qmf8317}
7 And the children of Israel were fruitful, and increased abundantly, and

---

☞ **1:1–5** See the note on Genesis 46:26, 27.

☞ **1:6** The word "generation" is used in a variety of ways in the Scriptures. In some cases it refers to an unspecified period of time (Ps. 102:24), while at other times it is used as a simple reference to the past (Is. 51:8) or the future (Ps. 100:5). It is also used to designate men who belonged to a certain class in society. In this verse it refers to all those in a particular class living at a designated time.

wcs,qmf7235   wcs,qmf6105/pp,ad3966/ad3966   df,nn776   wcs,nimf4390 pr,pnx854

multiplied, and waxed*exceeding*mighty; and the land was filled with them.

                wcs,qmf6965   aj2319 nn4428 cs,pr5921 nn4714 pnl834 qpf3045 ptn3808 (853) nn3130

☞ 8 Now there arose up a new king over Egypt, which knew not   Joseph.

              wcs,qmf559 pr413   nn,pnx5971 ptdm2009   cs,nn5971   pl,cs,nn1121   nn3478

9 And he said unto his people, Behold, the people of the children of Israel

aj7227   wcj,aj6099   pr,pnx4480

are more and mightier than we:

      qmv3051   htcj2449   pp,pnx   cj6435   qmf7235

10 Come on, let us deal wisely with them; lest they multiply, and it

wcs,qpf1961   cj3588   qmf7122   nn4421 pnp1931 wcs,nipf3254 ad1571 pr5921

come*to*pass, that, when there falleth out any war, they join also unto our

pl,qpta,pnx8130   wcs,nipf3898   pp,pnx   wcs,qpf5927   pr4480   df,nn776

enemies, and fight against us, and *so* get*them*up out of the land.

          wcs,qmf7760 pr,pnx5921   pl,cs,nn8269/pl,nn4522 pp,pr4616 pinc,pnx6031

11 Therefore they did set over them taskmasters to afflict them with

pp,pl,nn,pnx5450   wcs,qmf1129   pp,nn6547   pl,nn4543 pl,cs,nn5892 (853) nn6619   wcj(853)

their burdens. And they built for Pharaoh treasure cities,   Pithom and

nn7486

Rameses.

       wcj,pp,pnl834   pimf6031   pnx(853)   ad3651   qmf7235

12 But the more they afflicted   them, the more they multiplied and

wcj,ad3651/qmf6555   wcs,qmf6973 pr4480/pl,cs,nn6440   pl,cs,nn1121   nn3478

grew. And they were grieved because of the children of Israel.

       nn4714   (853)   pl,cs,nn1121   nn3478 wcs,himf5647   pp,nn6531

13 And the Egyptians made   the children of Israel to serve with rigor:

       (853)   pl,nn,pnx2416 wcs,pimf4843   aj7186   pp,nn5656   pp,nn2563

14 And they made their lives bitter with hard bondage, in mortar, and

wcj,pp,pl,nn3843   wcj,pp,cs,nn3605   nn5656   dfp,nn7704 (853) cs,nn3605   nn,pnx5656

in brick, and in all manner of service in the field: all their service,

pnl834   qpf5647/pp,pnx   pp,nn6531

wherein they made*them*serve, *was* with rigor.

       cs,nn4428   nn4714 wcs,qmf559   df,nn5680 dfp,pl,pipt3205   pnl834   cs,nn8034

15 And the king of Egypt spoke to the Hebrew midwives, of which the name

df,nu259   nn8236   wcj,cs,nn8034   df,nuor8145 nn6326

of the one *was* Shiphrah, and the name of the other Puah:

       wcs,qmf559   pp,pinc,pnx3205   (853)

16 And he said, When ye do*the*office*of*a*midwife to   the

df,pl,nn5680   wcj,qpf7200   pr5921   df,du,nn70 cj518 pnp1931   nn1121

Hebrew women, and see *them* upon the stools; if it *be* a son, then ye shall

wcj,hipf4191 pnx(853)   wcj,cj518 pnp1931   nn1323   wcj,qpf2425

kill him: but if it *be* a daughter, then she shall live.

       df,pl,pipt3205 wcs,qmf3372 (853) df,pl,nn430   qpf6213 wcj,ptn3808 pp,pnl834   cs,nn4428   nn4714

☞ 17 But the midwives feared   God, and did not as the king of Egypt

pipf1696/pr,pnx413   wcs,pimf2421 (853)   df,pl,nn3206

commanded them, but saved   the men children alive.

☞ **1:8** The expression "arose over Egypt" could better be translated "arose against Egypt." This probably refers to the invasion of the Hyksos, a people related to the Hebrews, who conquered Egypt. The Hyksos were never numerous, so the growing nation of Israel posed a threat to them (Ex. 1:9). This threat ultimately led the Hyksos rulers to enslave the Jews. When the Hyksos were later driven out, all of the hatred which the native Egyptians had for foreigners was focused on the Hebrews. Because the native Egyptians also feared they would become too numerous, they made the Israelite servitude more harsh (Ex. 1:13) and attempted to control the population by killing the male babies (see the note on Ex. 1:17–20).

☞ **1:17–20** God has instituted civil government for the good of all people (Rom. 13:1–5). Throughout Scripture, He instructs His people to be in submission to the powers of government (Eccl. 8:2; 1 Pet. 2:13, 14).

18 And the king of Egypt called for the midwives, and said unto them, Why have ye done this thing, and have saved the men children alive?

19 And the midwives said unto Pharaoh, Because the Hebrew women *are* not as the Egyptian women; for they *are* lively, and are delivered ere the midwives come in unto them.

20 Therefore God dealt well with the midwives: and the people multiplied, and waxed*very*mighty.

21 And it*came*to*pass, because the midwives feared God, that he made them houses.

22 And Pharaoh charged all his people, saying, Every son that is born ye shall cast into the river, and every daughter ye shall save alive.

Moses Is Born

2 And there went a man of*the*house of Levi, and took *to wife* a daughter of Levi.

2 And the woman conceived, and bore a son: and when she saw him that he *was a* goodly *child,* she hid him three months.

3 And when she could not longer hide him, she took for him an ark of bulrushes, and daubed it with slime and with pitch, and put the child therein; and she laid *it* in the flags by the river's brink.

4 And his sister stood afar off, to know what would be done to him.

5 And the daughter of Pharaoh came down to wash *herself* at the river; and her maidens walked along by the river's side; and when she saw the ark among the flags, she sent her maid to fetch it.

6 And when she had opened *it,* she saw the child: and, behold, the

---

However, the governments were not granted the right to compel men to do things which are contrary to God's law (Dan. 3:16, 18; Acts 4:19; 5:29). The question arises here whether the midwives were blessed for lying and refusing obedience to the king. The fact was that God blessed the midwives, not for their lying, but for their obedience to God. See the note on Joshua 2:1.

nn5288   qpta1058   wcs,qmf2550   pr,pnx5921   wcs,qmf**559**   pndm2088

babe wept. And she had compassion on him, and said, This *is one*

pr4480/pl,cs,nn3206/df,pl,nn5680

of*the*Hebrews'*children.

wcs,qmf**559**   nn,pnx**269**   pr413   nn6547   cs,nn1323   he,qmf**1980**   wcs,qpf7121

7 Then said his sister to Pharaoh's daughter, Shall I go and call

pp,pnx   nn**802**/hipt3243   pr4480   wcj,himf3243   (853)   df,nn3206

to thee a nurse of the Hebrew women, that she may nurse the child

pp,pnx

for thee?

nn6547   cs,nn1323   wcs,qmf**559**   pp,pnx   qmv**1980**   df,nn**5959** wcs,qmf**1980**   wcs,qmf7121

8 And Pharaoh's daughter said to her, Go. And the maid went and called

df,nn3206   (853)   cs,nn**517**

the child's   mother.

nn6547   cs,nn1323   wcs,qmf**559**   pp,pnx   himv**1980**/(853)/df,pndm2088/df,nn3206

9 And Pharaoh's daughter said unto her, Take*this*child*away, and

wcj,himv,pnx3243   pp,pnx   wcj,pnp589   qmf**5414**   (853)   nn,pnx7939   df,nn**802**

nurse it for me, and I will give *thee* thy wages. And the woman

wcs,qmf3947   df,nn3206   wcs,himf,pnx5134

took the child, and nursed it.

df,nn3206 wcs,qmf1431   wcs,himf,pnx935   nn6547   pp,cs,nn1323

☞ 10 And the child grew, and she brought him unto Pharaoh's daughter, and

wcs,qmf**1961** pp,pnx pp,nn**1121**   wcs,qmf7121   nn,pnx8034   nn4872   wcs,qmf**559**   cj3588

he became her son. And she called his name Moses: and she said, Because I

qpf,pnx4871   pr4480   df,pl,nn4325

drew him out of the water.

Moses Runs Away

wcs,qmf**1961**   df,pndm1992 dfp,pl,nn**3117**   nn4872   wcs,qmf1431

11 And it*came*to*pass in those days, when Moses was grown, that he

wcs,qmf3318   pr413   pl,nn,pnx**251**   wcs,qmf**7200**   pp,pl,nn,pnx5450   wcs,qmf**7200**

went out unto his brethren, and looked on their burdens: and he spied an

cs,nn**376**/nn4713   hipt**5221**   cs,nn**376**/nn5680   pr4480/pl,nn,pnx**251**

Egyptian smiting a Hebrew, one of*his*brethren.

wcs,qmf6437   ad3541   wcj,ad3541   wcs,qmf**7200** cj3588

12 And he looked this way and that way, and when he saw that *there was*

ptn369   nn**376**   wcs,himf**5221** (853)   df,nn4713   wcs,qmf,pnx2934   dfp,nn2344

no man, he slew the Egyptian, and hid him in the sand.

wcs,qmf3318   df,nuor8145 dfp,nn**3117** wcj,ptdm2009   du,cs,nu**8147** pl,nn**376**

13 And when he went out the second day, behold, two men of the

pl,nn5680   pl,nipt5327   wcs,qmf**559**   dfp,aj7563   pnit4100

Hebrews strove together: and he said to him*that*did*the*wrong, Wherefore

himf**5221**   nn,pnx**7453**

smitest thou thy fellow?

wcs,qmf**559** pnit4310 qpf,pnx**7760**   (pp,nn**376**)   nn8269   wcj,qpta**8199** pr,pnx5921

14 And he said, Who made thee a prince and a judge over us?

☞ **2:10** It is likely that the name given him by the Egyptian princess was a compound of an Egyptian river–god's name (such as Hapi or Osiris) and the Egyptian word *mos* meaning "child" (i.e. Hapimos). To the Egyptian princess, drawing Moses out of the water meant that a river–god had given birth to him. Moses may have thereafter dropped the false god's name and used the Hebrew name *Mōsheh* (4872), "Moses," from the Hebrew word *māshāh* (4871), "to draw out." The text here could also mean that Moses' mother named him since the Hebrew does not specify which "she," Pharaoh's daughter or Moses' mother, actually named him.

qpta**559** pnp859 he,pp,qnc,pnx**2026** pp,pnl834 qpf**2026** (853) df,nn4713 nn**4872**

intendest thou to kill me, as thou killedst the Egyptian? And Moses

wcs,qmf**3372** wcs,qmf**559** ad403 df,nn**1697** nipf**3045**

feared, and said, Surely this thing is known.

nn6547 wcs,qmf**8085** df,pndm2088 (853) df,nn**1697** wcs,pimf1245 pp,qnc2026 (853) nn**4872**

15 Now when Pharaoh heard this thing, he sought to slay Moses.

nn**4872** wcs,qmf1272 pr4480/pl,cs,nn**6440** nn6547 wcs,qmf**3427** pp,cs,nn776 nn4080

But Moses fled from*the*face of Pharaoh, and dwelt in the land of Midian:

wcs,qmf**3427** pr5921 df,nn875

and he sat down by a well.

wcj,pp,cs,nn**3548** nn4080 nu7651 pl,nn1323 wcs,qmf935

16 Now the priest of Midian had seven daughters: and they came and

wcs,qmf1802 wcs,pimf**4390** (853) df,pl,nn7298 pp,hinc8248 nn,pnx1 cs,nn6629

drew *water*, and filled the troughs to water their father's flock.

df,pl,qpta7462 wcs,qmf935 wcs,pimf,pnx1644 nn4872 wcs,qmf**6965**

17 And the shepherds came and drove*them*away: but Moses stood up and

wcs,himf,pnx**3467** wcs,himf8248 (853) nn,pnx6629

helped them, and watered their flock.

wcs,qmf935 pr413 nn7467 nn,pnx1 wcs,qmf**559** ad4069

18 And when they came to Reuel their father, he said, How *is it that* ye are

qnc935 pipf4116 df,nn**3117**

come so soon today?

wcs,qmf**559** cs,nn**376**/nn4713 hipf,pnx**5337** pr4480/cs,nn**3027** df,pl,qpta7462

19 And they said, An Egyptian delivered us out*of*the*hand of the shepherds,

wcj,ad1571 qna1802/qpf1802 pp,pnx wcs,himf8248 (853) df,nn6629

and also drew*water*enough for us, and watered the flock.

wcs,qmf**559** pr413 pl,nn,pnx1323 wcj,pnit,pnx346 pp,pnit4100 pndm2088

20 And he said unto his daughters, And where *is* he? why *is* it *that*

qpf**5800** (853) df,nn**376** qmv7121 pp,pnx wcj,qmf398 nn3899

ye have left the man? call him, that he may eat bread.

nn**4872** wcs,himf**2974** pp,qnc**3427** pr854 df,nn**376** wcs,qmf**5414** pp,nn4872 (853)

21 And Moses was content to dwell with the man: and he gave Moses

nn6855 nn,pnx1323

Zipporah his daughter.

wcs,qmf3205 nn**1121** wcs,qmf**7121** (853) nn,pnx8034 nn1648 cj3588

22 And she bore *him* a son, and he called his name Gershom: for he

qpf559 qpf**1961** nn**1616** aj**5237** pp,nn776

said, I have been a stranger in a strange land.

wcs,qmf**1961** dfp,pl,nn**3117**/df,aj7227/df,pndm1992 cs,nn**4428** nn4714 wcs,qmf**4191**

23 And it*came*to*pass in process*of*time, that the king of Egypt died:

pl,cs,nn**1121** nn3478 wcs,nimf584 pr4480 df,nn**5656** wcs,qmf**2199**

and the children of Israel sighed by*reason*of the bondage, and they cried, and

nn,pnx**7775** wcs,qmf**5927** pr413 df,pl,nn**430** pr4480 df,nn**5656**

their cry came up unto God by*reason*of the bondage.

2:15 The Midianites were descendants of Abraham by another wife, Keturah, whom he married after Sarah died (Gen. 25:1).

2:16, 21 In Numbers 12:1, Moses' wife is said to be an Ethiopian. Since Ethiopia was settled by descendants of Cush, they can be referred to as both. It can also be seen from Habakkuk 3:7 that "Cushan" and "Midian" are either interchangeable names or that Midian is the place where these people lived. Therefore, Zipporah was most likely the Ethiopian wife. Another possibility is that, at the point of Numbers 12:1, Moses' first wife Zipporah had died, and he married an Ethiopian woman (just as Abraham had married Keturah after the death of Sarah; see the note on Gen. 2:15–17).

2:22 In Hebrew the name "Gershom" suggests a foreigner who was banished into exile. Moses second son, Eliezer ("God is a Helper"), is mentioned in Exodus 18:4.

pl,nn**430** wcs,qmf**8085** (853)   nn,pnx5009   pl,nn**430**   wcs,qmf**2142**   (853)   nn,pnx**1285**

24 And God heard   their groaning, and God remembered   his covenant

pr854   nn85   pr854   nn3327   wcj,pr854   nn3290

with Abraham, with Isaac, and with Jacob.

pl,nn**430**   wcs,qmf**7200**   (853)   pl,cs,nn**1121**   nn3478   pl,nn**430**   wcs,qmf**3045**

25 And God looked upon   the children of Israel, and God had respect unto

them.

God Sends Moses to Egypt

wcj,nn4872   qpf**1961**/qpta7462   (853)   cs,nn6629   nn3503   nn,pnx2859   cs,nn**3548**

3 Now Moses kept   the flock of Jethro his father-in-law, the priest of

nn4080   wcs,qmf5090 (853)   df,nn6629   pr310   df,nn4057

Midian: and he led   the flock to the backside of the desert, and

wcs,qmf935 pr413   cs,nn2022   df,pl,nn**430**   nn,lh2722

came to the mountain of God, *even* to Horeb.

cs,nn**4397**   nn3068   wcs,nimf**7200**   pr,pnx413   pp,cs,nn3827   nn784

⟨⟩ 2 And the angel of the Lᴏʀᴅ appeared unto him in a flame of fire

pr4480/cs,nn**8432**   df,nn5572   wcs,qmf**7200**   wcj,ptdm2009   df,nn5572   qpta1197

out*of*the*midst of a bush: and he looked, and, behold, the bush burned with

dfp,nn784   wcj,df,nn5572   ptn,pnx369   pupt398

fire, and the bush *was* not consumed.

nn4872   wcs,qmf**559**   pte4994   qcj**5493**   wcj,qmf**7200** df,pndm2088 df,aj1419 (853) df,nn**4758**

3 And Moses said, I will now turn aside, and   see   this   great   sight,

ad4069   df,nn5572   ptn**3808**   qmf1197

why the bush is not burnt.

nn3068   wcs,qmf**7200**   cj3588   qpf**5493**   pp,qnc**7200** pl,nn**430** wcs,qmf**7121** pr,pnx413

4 And when the Lᴏʀᴅ saw that he turned aside to see, God called unto

pr4480/cs,nn**8432**   df,nn5572   wcs,qmf**559**   nn4872   nn4872   wcs,qmf**559** ptdm,pnx2009

him out*of*the*midst of the bush, and said, Moses, Moses. And he said,   Here

am I.

wcs,qmf**559**   qmf**7126**/ptn408   ad1988   qmv5394   pl,nn,pnx5275   pr4480/pr5921

5 And he said, Draw*not*nigh hither: put off thy   shoes   from off thy

du,nn,pnx7272 cj3588   df,nn4725 pnl834/pr,pnx5921 pnp859   qpta5975   (pnp1931)   nn**6944**   cs,nn**127**

feet, for the place whereon thou standest   *is* holy ground.

wcs,qmf**559** pnp595   pl,cs,nn**430**   nn,pnx1   pl,cs,nn**430**   nn85

6 Moreover he said,   I *am* the God of thy father, the God of Abraham,

pl,cs,nn**430**   nn3327   wcj,pl,cs,nn**430**   nn3290   nn4872   wcs,himf5641   pl,nn,pnx**6440** cj3588

the God of Isaac, and the   God   of Jacob. And Moses hid   his   face;   for

qpf3372   pr4480/hinc5027   pr413   df,pl,nn**430**

he was afraid to look upon God.

nn3068   wcs,qmf**559**   qna7200/qpf**7200**   (853)   cs,nn6040   nn,pnx**5971** pnl834

7 And the Lᴏʀᴅ said, I have surely seen   the affliction of my people which

pp,nn4714   qpf**8085** wcj(853)   nn,pnx6818   pr4480/pl,cs,nn**6440**   pl,qpta,pnx5065   cj3588

are in Egypt, and have heard   their   cry   by*reason*of their taskmasters; for I

qpf**3045**   (853)   pl,nn,pnx4341

know   their sorrows;

wcs,qmf3381   pp,hinc,pnx**5337**   pr4480/cs,nn**3027**   nn4714

8 And I am come down to deliver them out*of*the*hand of the Egyptians,

wcj,pp,hinc,pnx**5927**   pr4480   df,pndm1931 df,nn776 pr413   aj2896   nn776   wcj,aj7342   pr413   nn776

and to bring*them*up out of   that   land unto a good land and a large, unto a land

---

⟨⟩ 3:2–6   See the note on Exodus 23:20–23.

cs,qpta2100   nn2461   wcj,nn1706 pr413   cs,nn4725   df,nn3669   wcj,df,nn2850
flowing with milk and honey; unto the place of the Canaanites, and the Hittites, and
wcj,df,nn567   wcj,df,nn6522   wcj,df,nn2340   wcj,df,nn2983
the Amorites, and the Perizzites, and the Hivites, and the Jebusites.

wcj,ad6258   ptdm2009   cs,nn6818   pl,cs,nn1121   nn3478   qpf935   pr,pnx413
9 Now therefore, behold, the cry of the children of Israel is come unto me:
wcj,ad1571 qpf7200 (853)   df,nn3906   pnl834   nn4714   pl,qpta3905 pnx(853)
and I have also seen the oppression wherewith the Egyptians oppress

them.

qmv1980 wcj,ad6258   wcj,qmf,pnx7971   pr413   nn6547
10 Come now therefore, and I will send thee unto Pharaoh, that thou
wcj,himv3318   (853)   nn,pnx5971   pl,cs,nn1121   nn3478   pr4480/nn4714
mayest bring forth my people the children of Israel out*of*Egypt.

nn4872   wcs,qmf559   pr413   df,pl,nn430   pnit4310   pnp595 wcj,cj3588   qmf1980   pr413
11 And Moses said unto God, Who am I, that I should go unto
nn6547   cj3588   himf3318   (853)   pl,cs,nn1121   nn3478   pr4480/nn4714
Pharaoh, and that I should bring forth the children of Israel out*of*Egypt?

wcs,qmf559   cj3588   qmf1961 pr,pnx5973   wcj,pndm2088
12 And he said, Certainly I will be with thee; and this *shall be* a
df,nn226   pp,pnx   cj3588 pnp595 qpf,pnx7971   pp,hinc,pnx3318   (853)
token unto thee, that I have sent thee: When thou hast brought forth the
df,nn5971   pr4480/nn4714   qmf5647 (853) df,pl,nn430 pr5921 df,pndm2088   df,nn2022
people out*of*Egypt, ye shall serve God upon this mountain.

nn4872   wcs,qmf559 pr413 df,pl,nn430 ptdm2009   pnp595 qpta935 pr413   pl,cs,nn1121
13 And Moses said unto God, Behold, *when* I come unto the children of
nn3478   wcj,qpf559   pp,pnx   pl,cs,nn430   pl,nn,pnx1   qpf,pnx7971 pr,pnx413
Israel, and shall say unto them, The God of your fathers hath sent me unto
wcj,qpf559   pp,pnx   pnit4100   nn,pnx8034 pnit4100   qmf559 pr,pnx413
you; and they shall say to me, What *is* his name? what shall I say unto them?

pl,nn430 wcs,qmf559 pr413 nn4872   qmf1961 pnl834   qmf1961   wcs,qmf559 ad3541
14 And God said unto Moses, I AM THAT I AM: and he said, Thus shalt
qmf559   pp,pl,cs,nn1121   nn3478 qmf1961   qpf,pnx7971   pr,pnx413
thou say unto the children of Israel, I AM hath sent me unto you.

pl,nn430 wcs,qmf559   ad5750   pr413   nn4872   ad3541   qmf559   pr413
15 And God said moreover unto Moses, Thus shalt thou say unto the
pl,cs,nn1121   nn3478   nn3068   pl,cs,nn430   pl,nn,pnx1   pl,cs,nn430   nn85
children of Israel, The LORD God of your fathers, the God of Abraham, the
pl,cs,nn430   nn3327   wcj,pl,cs,nn430   nn3290   qpf,pnx7971   pr,pnx413   pndm2088
God of Isaac, and the God of Jacob, hath sent me unto you: this *is* my
nn,pnx8034 pp,nn5769   wcj,pndm2088   nn,pnx2143   pp,nn1755/nn1755
name forever, and this *is* my memorial unto all generations.

qmv1980   wcj,qpf622 (853)   cs,aj2205   nn3478   wcj,qpf559 pr,pnx413
16 Go, and gather the elders of Israel together, and say unto them, The
nn3068   pl,cs,nn430   pl,nn,pnx1   pl,cs,nn430   nn85   nn3327   wcj,nn3290
LORD God of your fathers, the God of Abraham, of Isaac, and of Jacob,

---

3:14 The phrase "I AM" in Hebrew appears to be closely related to God's personal name of Jehovah (Ex. 6:3; or Yahweh or YHWH) which occurs more than 6,000 times in the Old Testament. However, the abbreviated form of Yahweh is *Yāh* ([3050] Ps. 68:4; and in the word *hallelujah*). Hence, the meaning of Jehovah is not completely clear to biblical scholars, though it seems to suggest the timelessness of God, who is the very foundation of all existence. Perhaps there is a hint of this understanding of the name in Revelation 1:4 where it is said of Christ, "Him which is, and which was, and which is to come" (see also Heb. 13:8). Jesus probably alluded to this name of God in John 8:58, "Before Abraham was, I AM."

nipf7200   pr,pnx413   pp,qnc559   qna6485/qpf6485   pnx(853)   wcj(853)

appeared unto me, saying, I have surely visited   you, and *seen*   that

df,qptp6213   pp,pnx   pp,nn4714

which is done to you in Egypt:

wcs,qmf559   himf5927/pnx(853)   pr4480/cs,nn6040   nn4714   pr413

17 And I have said, I will bring*you*up out*of*the*affliction of Egypt unto

cs,nn776   df,nn3669   wcj,df,nn2850   wcj,df,nn567   wcj,df,nn6522

the land of the Canaanites, and the Hittites, and the Amorites, and the Perizzites,

wcj,df,nn2340   wcj,df,nn2983   pr413   nn776   cs,qpta2100   nn2461   wcj,nn1706

and the Hivites, and the Jebusites, unto a land flowing with milk and honey.

wcs,qpf8085   pp,nn,pnx6963   wcs,qpf935 pnp859

18 And they shall hearken to thy voice: and thou shalt come, thou and the

wcj,cs,aj2205   nn3478   pr413   cs,nn4428   nn4714   wcs,qpf559 pr,pnx413   nn3068

elders of Israel, unto the king of Egypt, and ye shall say unto him, The Lord

pl,cs,nn430   df,pl,nn5680   nipf7136 pr,pnx5921   wcj,ad6258   qcj1980   pte4994

God of the Hebrews hath met with us: and now let us go, we*beseech*thee,

cs,nu7969 pl,nn3117 cs,nn1870   dfp,nn4057   wcj,qcj2076   pp,nn3068

three days' journey into the wilderness, that we may sacrifice to the Lord our

pl,nn,pnx430

God.

wcj,pnp589   qpf3045 cj3588   cs,nn4428   nn4714   ptn3808 qmf5414 pnx(853)   pp,qnc1980

19 And I am sure that the king of Egypt will not let   you go,

wcj,ptn3808   aj2389   pp,nn3027

no, not by a mighty hand.

wcs,qpf7971   (853)   nn,pnx3027   wcs,hipf5221 (853) nn4714   pp,cs,nn3605

20 And I will stretch out   my hand, and smite   Egypt with all my

pl,nipt,pnx6381   pnl834   qmf6213   pp,nn,pnx7130   wcj,ad310 ad3651   pnx(853)

wonders which I will do in the midst thereof: and after that he will let

pimf7971

you go.

wcs,qpf5414 df,pndm2088 df,nn5971 (853) nn2580   pp,du,cs,nn5869   nn4714

21 And I will give this people favor in the sight of the Egyptians:

wcs,qpf1961   cj3588   qmf1980   ptn3808 qmf1980 ad7387

and it*shall*come*to*pass, that, when ye go, ye shall not go empty:

nn802   wcs,qpf7592   pr4480/nn,pnx7934   wcj,pr4480/cs,qpta1481

22 But every woman shall borrow of*her*neighbor, and of*her*that*sojourneth

nn,pnx1004 pl,cs,nn3627   nn3701   wcj,pl,cs,nn3627   nn2091   wcj,pl,nn8071

in her house, jewels of silver, and jewels of gold, and raiment: and ye shall

wcs,qpf7760   pr5921   pl,nn,pnx1121   wcj,pr5921   pl,nn,pnx1323   wcs,pipf5337 (853)

put *them* upon your sons, and upon your daughters; and ye shall spoil

nn4714

the Egyptians.

God Gives Power to Moses

nn4872   wcs,qmf6030   wcs,qmf559   wcj,ptdm2005   ptn3808   himf539   pp,pnx

4 And Moses answered and said, But, behold, they will not believe me,

wcj,ptn3808   qmf8085   pp,nn,pnx6963 cj3588   qmf559   nn3068   ptn3808

nor hearken unto my voice: for they will say, The Lord hath not

nipf7200   pr,pnx413

appeared unto thee.

nn3068   wcs,qmf559 pr,pnx413   pnit4100/pndm2088   pp,nn,pnx3027   wcs,qmf559

2 And the Lord said unto him, What*is*that in thine hand? And he said,

nn4294

A rod.

wcs,qmf**559** himv,pnx**7993**   nn,lh**776**   wcs,himf,pnx**7993**   nn,lh**776**

3 And he said, Cast it on the ground. And he cast it on the ground,

wcs,qmf**1961**   pp,nn**5175**   nn**4872** wcs,qmf**5127** pr**4480**/pl,nn,pnx**6440**

and it became a serpent; and Moses fled from before it.

nn**3068** wcs,qmf**559** pr**413**   nn**4872**   qmv**7971**   nn,pnx**3027**   wcj,qmv**270**

4 And the LORD said unto Moses, Put forth thine hand, and take it by the

pp,nn,pnx**2180**   wcs,qmf**7971**   nn,pnx**3027**   wcs,himf**2388** pp,pnx   wcs,qmf**1961**   pp,nn**4294**

tail. And he put forth his hand, and caught it, and it became a rod in his

pp,nn,pnx**3709**

hand:

pp,cj**4616**   himf**539**   cj**3588**   nn**3068** pl,cs,nn**430**   pl,nn,pnx**1**   pl,cs,nn**430**

5 That they may believe that the LORD God of their fathers, the God of

nn**85**   pl,cs,nn**430**   nn**3327**   wcj,pl,cs,nn**430**   nn**3290**   nipf**7200**   pr,pnx**413**

Abraham, the God of Isaac, and the God of Jacob, hath appeared unto thee.

nn**3068** wcs,qmf**559**   ad**5750**   pp,pnx   himv**935** pte**4994**   nn,pnx**3027**

6 And the LORD said furthermore unto him, Put now thine hand into thy

pp,nn,pnx**2436**   wcs,himf**935**   nn,pnx**3027**   pp,nn,pnx**2436**   wcs,himf,pnx**3318**

bosom. And he put his hand into his bosom: and when he took*it*out,

wcj,ptdm**2009**   nn,pnx**3027**   pupt**6879**   dfp,nn**7950**

behold, his hand *was* leprous as snow.

wcs,qmf**559** himv**7725**   nn,pnx**3027** pr**413**   nn,pnx**2436**   wcs,himf**7725**

7 And he said, Put thine hand into thy bosom again. And he put his

nn,pnx**3027** pr**413**   nn,pnx**2436**   wcs,himf,pnx**3318**   pr**4480**/nn,pnx**2436**   wcj,ptdm**2009**

hand into his bosom again; and plucked*it*out of*his*bosom, and, behold, it was

qpf**7725**   pp,nn,pnx**1320**

turned again as his *other* flesh.

wcj,qpf**1961**   cj**518**   ptn**3808** himf**539**   pp,pnx   wcj,ptn**3808**   qmf**8085**

8 And it*shall*come*to*pass, if they will not believe thee, neither hearken to

pp,nn,pnx**6963**   df,aj**7223** df,nn**226**   wcs,hipf**539**   pp,cs,nn**6963**   df,aj**314** df,nn**226**

the voice of the first sign, that they will believe the voice of the latter sign.

wcs,qpf**1961**   cj**518**   ptn**3808** himf**539**   ad**1571** df,pndm**428** pp,du,cs,nu**8147**

9 And it*shall*come*to*pass, if they will not believe also these two

df,pl,nn**226** wcj,ptn**3808**   qmf**8085**   pp,nn,pnx**6963**   wcs,qpf**3947** pr**4480**/pl,cs,nn**4325**

signs, neither hearken unto thy voice, that thou shalt take of*the*water of the

df,nn**2975**   wcs,qpf**8210**   df,nn**3004**   wcj(qpf**1961**)   df,pl,nn**4325** pnl**834**   qmf**3947**

river, and pour *it* upon the dry *land*: and the water which thou takest

pr**4480**   df,nn**2975**   wcs,qpf**1961** pp,nn**1818**   dfp,nn**3006**

out of the river shall become blood upon the dry *land*.

nn**4872** wcs,qmf**559** pr**413**   nn**3068** pte**994**   nn**136** pnp**595**   ptn**3808** cs,nn**376**/pl,nn**1697**

10 And Moses said unto the LORD, O my Lord, I *am* not eloquent,

ad**1571** pr**4480**/ad**8543**/ad**1571**/pr**4480**/ad**8032** ad**1571** pr**4480**/ad**227**   pinc,pnx**1696** pr**413**   nn,pnx**5650** cj**3588**

neither heretofore, nor since thou hast spoken unto thy servant: but

pnp**595**   cs,aj**3515**   nn**6310**   wcj,cs,aj**3515**   nn**3956**

I *am* slow of speech, and of a slow tongue.

nn**3068** wcs,qmf**559** pr,pnx**413**   pnit**4310**   qpf**7760**   dfp,nn**120**   nn**6310**   cj**176** pnit**4310**

11 And the LORD said unto him, Who hath made man's mouth? or who

qmf**7760**   aj**483**   cj**176** aj**2795**   cj**176**   aj**6493**   cj**176**   aj**5787**   he,ptn**3808** pnp**595**

maketh the dumb, or deaf, or the seeing, or the blind? have not I the

nn**3068**

LORD?

wcj,ad**6258**   qmv**1980**   wcj,pnp**595**   qmf**1961** pr**5973**   nn,pnx**6310**   wcs,hipf,pnx**3384**

12 Now therefore go, and I will be with thy mouth, and teach

pnl**834**   pimf**1696**

thee what thou shalt say.

wcs,qmf**559** pte994   nn**136**   qmv7971   pte**4994**   pp,cs,nn**3027**

⚷ 13 And he said, O my Lord, send, I*pray*thee, by the hand *of him whom*

qmf7971

thou wilt send.

cs,nn**639**   nn**3068**   wcs,qmf**2734**   pp,nn**4872**   wcs,qmf**559**

14 And the anger of the Lᴏʀᴅ was kindled against Moses, and he said, *Is*

he,ptn**3808** nn175   df,nn**3881**   nn,pnx**251**   qpf**3045** cj3588 pnp1931   pina**1696**/pimf**1696**   wcj,ad1571

not Aaron the Levite thy brother? I know that he can speak well. And also,

ptdm2009   pnp1931   qpta3318   pp,qnc,pnx7125   wcs,qpf,pnx**7200**

behold, he cometh forth to   meet   thee: and when he   seeth   thee, he will

wcs,qpf8055   pp,nn,pnx**3820**

be glad in his heart.

wcs,pipf**1696** pr,pnx413   wcs,qpf**7760** (853) df,pl,nn**1697**   pp,nn,pnx**6310**

15 And thou shalt speak unto him, and   put   words in his mouth: and

wcj,pnp595   qmf**1961** pr5973   nn,pnx**6310**   wcj,pr5973   pp,nn,pnx**6310**   wcs,hipf**3384** pnx(853)

I will be with thy mouth, and with his mouth, and will teach   you

(853) pnl834   qmf**6213**

what ye shall do.

pnp1931   wcs,pipf**1696**/pp,pnx   pr413   df,nn**5971**   wcs,qmf**1961**

16 And he   shall be*thy*spokesman unto the people: and he shall   be,   *even*

pnp1931   qmf**1961** pp,pnx   pp,nn**6310**   wcj,pnp859   qmf**1961** pp,pnx

he shall be to thee instead of a mouth, and thou shalt be to him instead of

pp,pl,nn**430**

God.

qmf3947   wcj(853) df,pndm2088 df,nn**4294**   pp,nn,pnx**3027**   pnl834/pp,pnx

17 And thou shalt take   this   rod in thine hand,   wherewith thou

qmf**6213** (853) df,pl,nn**226**

shalt do   signs.

Moses Returns to Egypt

nn4872   wcs,qmf**1980**   wcs,qmf**7725** pr413   nn3503   nn,pnx2859   wcs,qmf**559**

18 And Moses went and returned to Jethro his father-in-law, and said

pp,pnx   qcj**1980**   pte**4994**   wcj,qcj**7725** pr413   pl,nn,pnx**251** pnl834

unto him, Let me go, I*pray*thee, and return unto my brethren which *are* in

pp,nn4714   wcj,qmf**7200**   he,ad,pnx5750   aj**2416**   nn3503 wcs,qmf**559**   pp,nn4872 qmv**1980**

Egypt, and see whether*they*be*yet alive. And Jethro said to Moses, Go in

pp,nn**7965**

peace.

nn**3068** wcs,qmf**559** pr413   nn**4872**   pp,nn4080   qmv**1980** qmv**7725**   nn4714 cj3588

19 And the Lᴏʀᴅ said   unto Moses in Midian, Go, return into Egypt: for

cs,nn3605   df,pl,nn**376**   qpf**4191**   df,pl,pipt1245 (853)   nn,pnx**5315**

all the men are dead which sought   thy life.

nn4872   wcs,qmf3947 (853)   nn,pnx**802**   wcj(853)   pl,nn,pnx**1121**   wcs,himf,pnx7392

20 And Moses took   his wife and   his sons, and   set   them

pr5921   df,nn2543   wcs,qmf**7725**   nn,lh776   nn4714   nn4872 wcs,qmf3947 (853) cs,nn**4294**

upon an ass, and he returned to the land of Egypt: and Moses took   the rod

df,pl,nn**430**   pp,nn,pnx**3027**

of God in his hand.

nn**3068** wcs,qmf**559** pr413   nn4872   pp,qnc,pnx**1980**   pp,qnc**7725**   nn,lh4714

21 And the Lᴏʀᴅ said unto Moses, When thou   goest   to return into Egypt,

---

qmv7200   wcj,qpf,pnx6213   cs,nn3605   df,pl,nn4159   pp,pl,cs,nn6440   nn6547   pnl834   qpf7760

see that thou   do   all   those wonders before Pharaoh, which I have put in

pp,nn,pnx3027   wcj,pnp589   pimf2388   (853)   nn,pnx3820   wcj,ptn3808   (853)

thine hand: but   I   will harden   his heart, that he shall   not   let   the

df,nn5971   pimf7971

people go.

wcs,qpf559   pr413   nn6547   ad3541   qpf559   nn3068   nn3478   nn,pnx1121

22 And thou shalt   say   unto Pharaoh, Thus saith the Lord, Israel *is* my son,

nn,pnx1060

even my firstborn:

wcs,qmf559   pr,pnx413   (853)   nn,pnx1121 pimv7971   wcj,qmf,pnx5647

23 And I say   unto thee, Let   my   son   go, that he may   serve   me:

wcs,pimf3985   pp,pinc,pnx7971 ptdm2009   pnp595   qpta2026 (853)   nn,pnx1121

and if thou refuse to let him   go,   behold, I   will slay   thy son, *even*

nn,pnx1060

thy firstborn.

wcs,qmf1961   dfp,nn1870   dfp,nn4411   nn3068   wcs,qmf,pnx6298

24 And it*came*to*pass by the   way   in the   inn,   that the Lord   met

wcs,pimf1245   hinc,pnx4191

him, and sought to   kill   him.

nn6855   wcs,qmf3947   nn6864   wcs,qmf3772 (853)   cs,nn6190

25 Then Zipporah   took   a sharp stone, and cut off   the foreskin of her

nn,pnx1121   wcs,himf5060   pp,du,nn,pnx7272   wcs,qmf559   cj3588   pl,nn1818   cs,nn2860   pnp859

son, and   cast   *it* at his   feet,   and said, Surely a bloody husband *art* thou

pp,pnx

to me.

wcs,qmf7503/pr,pnx4480   ad227   qpf559   pl,nn1818   cs,nn2860

26 So he let*him*go: then she said, A bloody husband *thou art*, because of

dfp,pl,nn4139

the circumcision.

nn3068   wcs,qmf559   pr413   nn175   qmv1980   df,nn,lh4057   pp,qnc7125   nn4872

27 And the Lord   said   to Aaron, Go into the wilderness to meet Moses.

wcs,qmf1980   wcs,qmf,pnx6298   pp,cs,nn2022   df,pl,nn430   wcs,qmf5401   pp,pnx

And he went, and   met   him in the mount of God, and kissed him.

nn4872   wcs,himf5046   pp,nn175 (853)   cs,nn3605   pl,cs,nn1697   nn3068   pnl834   qpf,pnx7971

28 And Moses   told   Aaron   all   the words of the Lord who had   sent

wcj(853)   cs,nn3605   df,pl,nn226   pnl834   pipf6680

him, and   all   the signs which he had commanded him.

nn4872   wcj,nn175   wcs,qmf1980   wcs,qmf622   (853)   cs,nn3605   cs,aj2205

29 And Moses and Aaron went   and gathered together   all   the elders of

pl,cs,nn1121   nn3478

the children of Israel:

nn175   wcs,pimf1696   (853)   cs,nn3605   df,pl,nn1697   pnl834   nn3068   pipf1696   pr413

30 And Aaron spoke   all   the words which the Lord had spoken unto

nn4872   wcs,qmf6213   df,pl,nn226   pp,du,cs,nn5869   df,nn5971

Moses, and   did   the signs in the   sight   of the people.

df,nn5971   wcs,himf539   wcs,qmf8085 cj3588   nn3068   qpf6485   (853)

31 And the people believed: and when they   heard that the Lord had visited

pl,cs,nn1121   nn3478   wcj,cj3588   qpf7200   (853)   nn,pnx6040

the children of Israel, and   that   he had looked upon   their affliction, then they

wcs,qmf6915   wcs,himf*7812

bowed*their*heads and worshiped.

Moses and Aaron Meet Pharaoh

5 wcj,ad310   nn4872   wcj,nn175   qpf935   wcs,qmf559/pr413   nn6547   ad3541   qpf559
And afterward Moses and Aaron went in, and   told   Pharaoh, Thus saith

nn3068   pl,cs,nn430   nn3478   (853)   nn,pnx5971   pimv7971
the LORD God of Israel, Let   my people   go,   that they may

wcj,qmf2287   pp,pnx   dfp,nn4057
hold*a*feast unto me in the wilderness.

nn6547   wcs,qmf559   pnit4310   nn3068   pnl834   qmf8085   pp,nn,pnx6963
2 And Pharaoh said, Who is the LORD, that I should obey his voice to let

(853) nn3478   pp,pinc7971   qpf3045   ptn3808 (853)   nn3068   wcj,ad1571/ptn3808   (853)   nn3478   pimf7971
Israel go? I know not the LORD, neither will I let Israel go.

wcs,qmf559   pl,cs,nn430   df,pl,nn5680   nipf7122   pr,pnx5921   qcj1980
3 And they said, The God of the Hebrews hath met with us: let us go,

pte4994   cs,nu7969 pl,nn3117   cs,nn1870   dfp,nn4057   wcj,qcj2076   pp,nn3068
we*pray*thee, three days' journey into the desert, and sacrifice unto the LORD our

pl,nn,pnx430 cj6435   qmf,pnx6293   dfp,nn1698   cj176   dfp,nn2719
God; lest he fall upon us with pestilence, or with the sword.

cs,nn4428   nn4714   wcs,qmf559   pr,pnx413   pp,pnit4100   nn4872
4 And the king of Egypt said unto them, Wherefore do ye, Moses and

wcj,nn175   himf6544 (853)   df,nn5971   pr4480/pl,nn,pnx4639   qmv1980   pp,pl,nn,pnx5450
Aaron, let the people from*their*works? get you unto your burdens.

nn6547   wcs,qmf559   ptdm2005   cs,nn5971   df,nn776   ad6258   aj7227
5 And Pharaoh said, Behold, the people of the land now are many, and ye

wcj,hipf7673/pnx(853)   pr4480/pl,nn,pnx5450
make*them*rest from*their*burdens.

nn6547   wcs,pimf6680   df,pndm1931 dfp,nn3117 (853)   df,pl,qpta5065   dfp,nn5971
6 And Pharaoh commanded the same day   the taskmasters of the people,

wcj(853)   pl,nn,pnx7860   pp,qnc559
and   their officers, saying,

ptn3808 himf3254 pp,qnc5414   dfp,nn5971   nn8401   pp,qnc3835 df,pl,nn3843   pp,ad8543/ad8032
7 Ye shall no more give the people straw to make brick, as heretofore: let

pnp1992   qmf1980   wcs,pipf*7197   nn8401   pp,pnx
them go and gather straw for themselves.

wcj(853)   cs,nn4971   df,pl,nn3843   pnl834   pnp1992   pl,qpta6213   ad8543/ad8032
8 And   the tale of the bricks, which they did make heretofore, ye shall

qmf7760   pr,pnx5921   ptn3808   qmf1639   pr,pnx4480 cj3588 pnp1992   pl,nipt7503 pr5921/ad3651
lay upon them; ye shall not diminish aught thereof: for they be idle; therefore

pnp1992 pl,qpta6817   pp,qnc559   qcj1980   qcj2076   pp,pl,nn,pnx430
they cry, saying, Let us go and sacrifice to our God.

qmf3513/df,nn5656   pr5921   df,pl,nn376   wcj,qmf6213   pp,pnx
9 Let there more*work*be*laid upon the men, that they may labor therein;

wcj,ptn408   qmf8159   nn8267 pp,pl,cs,nn1697
and let them not regard vain words.

pl,cs,qpta5065   df,nn5971   wcs,qmf3318   wcj,pl,nn,pnx7860
10 And the taskmasters of the people went out, and their officers, and they

wcs,qmf559 pr413   df,nn5971   pp,qnc559   ad3541   qpf559   nn6547   ptn,pnx369 qpta5414 pp,pnx   nn8401
spoke to the people, saying, Thus saith Pharaoh, I will not give you straw.

qmv1980   pnp859   qmv3947   pp,pnx   nn8401   pr4480/pnl834   qmf4672   cj3588   ptn369   nn1697
11 Go ye, get you straw where ye can find it: yet not aught

pr4480/nn,pnx5656   nipt1639
of*your*work shall be diminished.

df,nn5971   wcs,himf6327   pp,cs,nn3605 cs,nn776   nn4714
12 So the people were scattered abroad throughout all the land of Egypt to

pp,pinc*7197   nn7179   dfp,nn8401
gather stubble instead of straw.

wcj,df,pl,qpta5065   pl,qpta213   pp,qnc559   pimv3615   pl,nn,pnx4639
13 And the taskmasters hasted *them*, saying, Fulfill your works, *your*

nn3117/pp,nn,pnx3117 cs,nn1697   pp,pnl834   pp,qnc1961 df,nn8401
daily   tasks, as when there was straw.

pl,cs,nn7860   pl,cs,nn1121   nn3478   pnl834   nn6547   pl,cs,qpta5065
14 And the officers of the children of Israel, which Pharaoh's taskmasters had

qpf7760 pr,pnx5921   wcs,homf5221   pp,qnc559   ad4069   ptn3808 pipf3615
set over them, were beaten, *and* demanded, Wherefore have ye not fulfilled

nn,pnx2706   pp,qnc3835   ad1571   ad8543   ad1571 df,nn3117   pp,ad8543/ad8032
your task in making brick both yesterday and today, as heretofore?

pl,cs,nn7860   pl,cs,nn1121   nn3478 wcs,qmf935   wcs,qmf6817 pr413   nn6547
15 Then the officers of the children of Israel came and cried unto Pharaoh,

pp,qnc559   pnit4100   qmf6213   ad3541   pp,pl,nn,pnx5650
saying, Wherefore dealest thou thus with thy servants?

ptn369   nn8401   nipt5414   pp,pl,nn,pnx5650   pl,qpta559 pp,pnx   qmv6213
16 There is no straw given unto thy servants, and they say to us, Make

wcj,pl,nn3843   wcj,ptdm2009   pl,nn,pnx5650   pl,hopt5221   wcj,qpf2398   nn,pnx5971
brick: and, behold, thy servants *are* beaten; but the fault *is* in thine own people.

wcs,qmf559 pnp859   pl,nipt7503   pl,nipt7503 pr5921/ad3651 pnp859 pl,qpta559   qcj1980
17 But he said, Ye *are* idle, *ye are* idle: therefore ye say, Let us go

qcj2076   pp,nn3068
and do sacrifice to the LORD.

qmv1980   wcj,ad6258   qmv5647   ptn3808 wcj,nn8401   nimf5414 pp,pnx
18 Go therefore now, *and* work; for there shall no straw be given you, yet

qmf5414   wcj,cs,nn8506   pl,nn3843
shall ye deliver the tale of bricks.

pl,cs,nn7860   pl,cs,nn1121   nn3478   wcs,qmf7200   pnx(853)
19 And the officers of the children of Israel did see *that* they *were* in

pp,nn7451   pp,qnc559   ptn3808 qmf1639   pr4480/pl,nn,pnx3843
evil *case*, after it was said, Ye shall not minish *aught* from*your*bricks of your

nn3117/pp,nn,pnx3117 cs,nn1697
daily   task.

wcs,qmf6293 (853)   nn4872   wcj(853)   nn175   pl,nipt5324 pp,qnc,pnx7125
20 And they met   Moses and   Aaron, who stood in*the*way, as they

pp,qnc,pnx3318   pr4480/pr854   nn6547
came forth from Pharaoh:

wcs,qmf559 pr,pnx413   nn3068 qcj7200 pr,pnx5921   wcj,qmf8199 pnl834
21 And they said unto them, The LORD look upon you, and judge; because

(853)   nn,pnx7381   hipf887   pp,du,cs,nn5869   nn6547
ye have made   our savor to be abhorred in the eyes of Pharaoh, and in the

wcj,pp,du,cs,nn5869   pl,nn,pnx5650   pp,qnc5414   nn2719   pp,nn,pnx3027 pp,qnc,pnx2026
eyes of his servants, to put a sword in their hand to slay us.

God Promises to Deliver Israel

nn4872   wcs,qmf7725   pr413   nn3068   wcs,qmf559 nn136   pp,pnit4100
22 And Moses returned unto the LORD, and said, Lord, wherefore hast thou *so*

hipf7489   df,pndm2088 dfp,nn5971 pp,pnit4100   pndm2088   qpf,pnx7971
evil entreated this people? why *is* it *that* thou hast sent me?

wcj,pr4480/ad227   qpf935 pr413   nn6547   pp,pinc1696   pp,nn,pnx8034   hipf7489
23 For since I came to Pharaoh to speak in thy name, he hath done evil to

df,pndm2088 dfp,nn5971   ptn3808   wcj,hina5337 (853)   nn,pnx5971 hipf5337
this people; neither hast thou delivered thy people at all.

6

nn3068　wcs,qmf559　pr413　nn4872　ad6258　qmf7200　pnl834　qmf6213
Then the LORD said unto Moses, Now shalt thou see what I will do to

pp,nn6547　cj3588　aj2389　pp,nn3027　pimf,pnx7971　aj2389
Pharaoh: for with a strong hand shall he let them go, and with a strong

wcj,pp,nn3027　pimf,pnx1644　pr4480/nn,pnx776
hand shall he drive*them*out of*his*land.

pl,nn430　wcs,pimf1696　pr413　nn4872　wcs,qmf559　pr,pnx413　pnp589　nn3068
2 And God spoke unto Moses, and said unto him, I *am* the LORD:

wcs,nimf7200　pr413　nn85　pr413　nn3327　wcj,pr413　nn3290
☞ 3 And I appeared unto Abraham, unto Isaac, and unto Jacob, by *the name of*

pp,nn410　nn7706　wcj,nn,pnx8034　nn3068　ptn3808　nipf3045　pp,pnx
God Almighty, but by my name JEHOVAH was I not known to them.

wcj,ad1571　hipf6965　(853)　nn,pnx1285　pr,pnx854　pp,qnc5414　pp,pnx　(853)
4 And I have also established my covenant with them, to give them

cs,nn776　nn3667　(853)　cs,nn776　pl,nn,pnx4033　pnl834/pp,pnx　qpf1481
the land of Canaan, the land of their pilgrimage, wherein they were strangers.

pnp589　wcj,ad1571　qpf8085　(853)　cs,nn5009　pl,cs,nn1121　nn3478
5 And I have also heard the groaning of the children of Israel,

pnl834/pnx(853)　nn4714　pl,hipt5647　wcs,qmf2142　(853)　nn,pnx1285
whom the Egyptians keep*in*bondage; and I have remembered my covenant.

pp,ad3651　qmv559　pp,pl,cs,nn1121　nn3478　pnp589　nn3068
6 Wherefore say unto the children of Israel, I *am* the LORD, and I will

wcj,hipf3318/pnx(853)　pr4480/pr8478　pl,cs,nn5450　nn4714　wcj,hipf5337　pnx(853)
bring*you*out from under the burdens of the Egyptians, and I will rid you

pr4480/pr,pnx5656　wcj,qpf1350　pnx(853)　qptp5186　pp,nn2220
out*of*their*bondage, and I will redeem you with a stretched out arm, and

aj1419　wcj,pp,pl,nn8201
with great judgments:

wcj,qpf3947　pnx(853)　pp,pnx　pp,nn5971　wcj,qpf1961　pp,pnx
7 And I will take you to me for a people, and I will be to you a

pp,pl,nn430　wcj,qpf3045　cj3588　pnp589　nn3068　pl,nn,pnx430
God: and ye shall know that I *am* the LORD your God, which

df,hipt3318/pnx(853)　pr4480/pr8478　pl,cs,nn5450　nn4714
bringeth*you*out from under the burdens of the Egyptians.

wcj,hipf935/pnx(853)　pr413　df,nn776　pnl834
8 And I will bring*you*in unto the land, concerning the which I did

qpf5375/(853)/nn,pnx3027　pp,qnc5414　pnx(853)　pp,nn85　pp,nn3327　wcj,pp,nn3290
swear to give it to Abraham, to Isaac, and to Jacob; and I will

wcj,qpf5414　pnx(853)　pp,pnx　nn4181　pnp589　nn3068
give it you for a heritage: I *am* the LORD.

nn4872　wcs,pimf1696　ad3651　pr413　pl,cs,nn1121　nn3478　qpf8085　wcj,ptn3808
9 And Moses spoke so unto the children of Israel: but they hearkened not

pr413　nn4872　pr4480/cs,nn7115　nn7307　wcj,pr4480/nn5656/aj7186
unto Moses for anguish of spirit, and for*cruel*bondage.

☞ **6:3** In light of such passages as Genesis 12:8 and 14:18, 22 in which LORD is equivalent to JEHOVAH in this verse, this name of God was evidently known among the patriarchs. Some scholars have suggested that Moses, because of his personal knowledge of the Lord at this time, inserted the name in the passages in Genesis when he wrote it at a later time. However, the key to this problem probably lies in a proper understanding of the Hebrew word *yādhāh* (3034), "known." One meaning of this word is "to know by instruction or experience." Israel was about to witness the events of their exodus from Egypt, a more graphic demonstration of God's power than their forefathers had ever seen. It was by this name, Jehovah, that God's powerful works of salvation would be done. Israel would know by experience the full meaning of His name. Though they knew He was called "LORD," the patriarchs had not seen such a demonstration of power. Therefore, they had not known all the implications of that name.

nn3068　wcs,pimf1696　pr413　　nn4872　　pp,qnc559
10 And the LORD spoke unto Moses, saying,

qmv935　pimv1696　pr413　nn6547　cs,nn4428　nn4714　　(853)　pl,cs,nn1121
11 Go in, speak unto Pharaoh king of Egypt, that he let　the children of

nn3478　wcj,pimf7971　pr4480/nn,pnx776
Israel　go　out*of*his*land.

nn4872　wcs,pimf1696　pp,pl,cs,nn6440　nn3068　pp,qnc559　ptdm2005　pl,cs,nn1121　nn3478
12 And Moses spoke before the LORD, saying, Behold, the children of Israel

ptn3808　qpf8085　pr,pnx413　wcj,pnit349　nn6547　qmf,pnx8085　wcj,pnp589
have not hearkened unto me; how then shall Pharaoh hear me, who am of

cs,aj6189　du,nn8193
uncircumcised lips?

nn3068　wcs,pimf1696　pr413　nn4872　wcj,pr413　nn175
13 And the LORD spoke unto Moses and unto Aaron, and

wcs,pimf,pnx6680　pr413　pl,cs,nn1121　nn3478　wcj,pr413　nn6547　cs,nn4428　nn4714
gave*them*a*charge unto the children of Israel, and unto Pharaoh king of Egypt,

pp,hinc3318　(853)　pl,cs,nn1121　nn3478　pr4480/cs,nn776　nn4714
to bring　the children of Israel out of*the*land of Egypt.

Moses and Aaron's Family Records

pndm428　pl,cs,nn7218　pl,nn,pnx1　cs,nn1004　pl,cs,nn1121　nn7205
14 These be the heads of their fathers' houses: The sons of Reuben the

cs,nn1060　nn3478　nn2585　wcj,nn6396　nn2696　wcj,nn3756　pndm428　pl,cs,nn4940
firstborn of Israel; Hanoch, and Pallu, Hezron, and Carmi: these be the families of

nn7205
Reuben.

wcj,pl,cs,nn1121　nn8095　nn3223　wcj,nn3226　wcj,nn161　wcj,nn3199
15 And the sons of Simeon; Jemuel, and Jamin, and Ohad, and Jachin, and

wcj,nn6714　wcj,nn7586　cs,nn1121　df,nn3669　pndm428　pl,cs,nn4940
Zohar, and Shaul the son of a Canaanitish woman: these are the families of

nn8095
Simeon.

wcj,pndm428　pl,cs,nn8034　pl,cs,nn1121　nn3878
16 And these are the names of the sons of Levi according to their

pp,pl,nn,pnx8435　nn1648　wcj,nn6955　wcj,nn4847　wcj,pl,cs,nn8141　pl,cs,nn2416
generations; Gershon, and Kohath, and Merari: and the years of the life of

nn3878　wcj,cs,nu3967　wcj,nu7970　nu7651　nn8141
Levi were a hundred thirty and seven years.

pl,cs,nn1121　nn1648　nn3845　wcj,nn8096　pp,pl,nn,pnx4940
17 The sons of Gershon; Libni, and Shimi, according to their families.

wcj,pl,cs,nn1121　nn6955　nn6019　wcj,nn3324　wcj,nn2275　wcj,nn5816
18 And the sons of Kohath; Amram, and Izhar, and Hebron, and Uzziel:

wcj,pl,cs,nn8141　pl,cs,nn2416　nn6955　wcj,cs,nu3967　wcj,nu7970　nu7969　nn8141
and the years of the life of Kohath were a hundred thirty and three years.

wcj,pl,cs,nn1121　nn4847　nn4249　wcj,nn4187　pndm428　pl,cs,nn4940
19 And the sons of Merari; Mahali and Mushi: these are the families of

df,nn3878　pp,pl,nn,pnx8435
Levi according to their generations.

nn6019　wcs,qmf3947　pp,pnx　(853)　nn3115　nn,pnx1733　pp,nn802
☞ 20 And Amram took him　Jochebed his father's sister to wife; and she

---

☞ 6:20 Variant readings in the Septuagint, the Syriac, and the Latin Vulgate indicate that Jochebed was actually Amram's paternal cousin.

wcs,qmf3205 pp,pnx (853)   nn175   wcj(853)   nn4872   wcj,pl,cs,nn8141   pl,cs,nn2416   nn6019

bore   him   Aaron and   Moses: and the   years   of the   life   of Amram

         wcj,cs,nu3967   wcj,nu7970   nu7651   nn8141

were a hundred and thirty and seven years.

              wcj,pl,cs,nn1121   nn3324   nn7141   wcj,nn5298   wcj,nn2147

21 And the   sons   of Izhar; Korah, and Nepheg, and Zichri.

             wcj,pl,cs,nn1121   nn5816   nn4332   wcj,nn469   wcj,nn5644

22 And the   sons   of Uzziel; Mishael, and Elzaphan, and Zithri.

      nn175   wcs,qmf3947 pp,pnx (853)   nn472   cs,nn1323   nn5992   cs,nn269

23 And Aaron   took   him   Elisheba, daughter of Amminadab, sister of

nn5177   pp,nn802   wcs,qmf3205 pp,pnx (853)   nn5070   wcj(853)   nn30   (853)   nn499

Naashon, to wife; and she bore   him   Nadab, and   Abihu,   Eleazar, and

wcj(853)   nn385

Ithamar.

          wcj,pl,cs,nn1121   nn7141   nn617   wcj,nn511   wcj,nn23   pndm428

24 And the   sons   of Korah; Assir, and Elkanah, and Abiasaph: these *are* the

pl,cs,nn4940   df,nn7145

families of the Korhites.

          wcj,nn499   nn175   cs,nn1121 qpf3947 pp,pnx   pr4480/pl,cs,nn1323   nn6317   pp,pnx/pp,nn802

25 And Eleazar Aaron's son   took him *one* of*the*daughters of Putiel to wife;

        wcs,qmf3205 pp,pnx (853)   nn6372   pndm428   pl,cs,nn7218   pl,cs,nn1   df,pl,nn3881

and she bore   him   Phinehas: these *are* the heads of the fathers of the Levites

             pp,pl,nn,pnx4940

according to their families.

     pnp1931   nn175   wcj,nn4872 pp,pnx pnl834   nn3068   qpf559   himv3318   (853)

26 These *are* that Aaron and Moses, to whom the Lord said, Bring out

   pl,cs,nn1121   nn3478   pr4480/cs,nn776   nn4714   pr5921   pl,nn,pnx6635

the children of Israel from*the*land of Egypt according to their armies.

    pndm1992   df,pl,pipt1696 pr413   nn6547   cs,nn4428   nn4714   pp,hinc3318   (853)

27 These *are* they which spoke to Pharaoh king of Egypt, to bring out

   pl,cs,nn1121   nn3478   pr4480/nn4714   pndm1931   nn4872   wcj,nn175

the children of Israel from Egypt: these *are* that Moses and Aaron.

Moses and Aaron Return to Pharaoh

           wcs,qmf1961   pp,cs,nn3117   nn3068   pipf1696 pr413 nn4872

28 And it*came*to*pass on the   day   *when* the Lord spoke unto Moses in the

pp,cs,nn776   nn4714

land of Egypt,

          nn3068   wcs,pimf1696 pr413   nn4872   pp,qnc559 pnp589   nn3068   pimv1696

29 That the Lord spoke unto Moses, saying, I *am* the Lord: speak thou

pr413   nn6547 cs,nn4428   nn4714 (853) cs,nn3605 pnl834 pnp589 qpta1696 pr,pnx413

unto Pharaoh king of Egypt   all   that I   say unto thee.

          nn4872 wcs,qmf559 pp,pl,cs,nn6440   nn3068   ptdm2005 pnp589   cs,aj6189

30 And Moses said   before the Lord, Behold, I   *am* of uncircumcised

du,nn8193   wcj,pnit349   nn6547   qmf8085 pr,pnx413

lips, and how shall Pharaoh hearken unto me?

          nn3068 wcs,qmf559 pr413   nn4872   qmv7200   qpf,pnx5414   pl,nn430

7 And the Lord said unto Moses, See, I have made thee a god to

pp,nn6547   wcj,nn175   nn,pnx251   qmf1961   nn,pnx5030

Pharaoh: and Aaron thy brother shall be thy prophet.

      pnp859   pimf1696 (853) cs,nn3605 pnl834   pimf,pnx6680   wcj,nn175   nn,pnx251

2 Thou shalt speak   all   that I command thee: and Aaron thy brother shall

pimf**1696**   pr413   nn6547   wcs,pipf7971 (853)   pl,cs,nn**1121**   nn3478   pr4480/nn,pnx**776**

speak unto Pharaoh, that he   send   the children of Israel out*of*his*land.

wcj,pnp589   himf7185   (853)   nn6547   cs,nn**3820**   wcs,hipf7235 (853)   pl,nn,pnx**226**

✍ 3 And   I   will harden   Pharaoh's heart, and multiply   my   signs   and

wcj(853)   pl,nn,pnx**4159**   pp,cs,nn776   nn4714

my wonders in the   land   of Egypt.

nn6547   wcj,ptn**3808**   qmf8085   pr,pnx413   wcs,qpf5414 (853)   nn,pnx**3027**

4 But Pharaoh shall   not   hearken unto you, that I may   lay   my   hand

pp,nn4714   wcs,hipf3318   (853)   pl,nn,pnx**6635**   (853)   nn,pnx**5971**   pl,cs,nn**1121**

upon Egypt, and bring forth   mine armies, *and*   my people the children of

nn3478   pr4480/nn**776**   nn4714   aj1419   pp,pl,nn**8201**

Israel, out*of*the*land of Egypt by great judgments.

nn4714   wcs,qpf**3045** cj3588 pnp589   nn**3068**   pp,qnc,pnx5186

5 And the Egyptians shall   know   that   I   *am* the Lᴄɢɢ when I stretch forth

(853)   nn,pnx**3027**   pr5921   nn4714   wcs,hipf3318   (853)   pl,cs,nn**1121**   nn3478   pr4480/nn,pnx**8432**

mine   hand   upon Egypt, and bring out   the children of Israel from among

them.

nn4872   wcj,nn175   wcs,qmf**6213** pp,pnl834   nn**3068**   pipf**6680**   pnx(853)   ad**3651**

6 And Moses and Aaron   did   as   the Lᴄɢɢ commanded   them, so

qpf**6213**

did they.

wcj,nn4872   pl,nu8084   nn8141   cs,nn**1121**   wcj,nn175   wcj,pl,nu8084   nu7969   nn8141

7 And Moses *was* fourscore years   old,   and Aaron fourscore and three years

cs,nn**1121**   pp,pinc,pnx**1696** pr413   nn6547

old, when they   spoke   unto Pharaoh.

nn**3068**   wcs,qmf559   pr413   nn4872   wcj,pr413   nn175   pp,qnc559

8 And the Lᴄɢɢ spoke unto Moses and unto Aaron, saying,

cj3588   nn6547   pimf**1696** pr,pnx413   pp,qnc559   qmv**5414**   nn4159   pp,pnx

9 When Pharaoh shall speak   unto   you, saying, Show a miracle for you: then

wcs,qpf559   pr413   nn175   qmv3947 (853)   nn,pnx**4294**   wcj,himv**7993**   pp,pl,cs,nn**6440**   nn6547

thou shalt   say   unto Aaron, Take   thy   rod,   and   cast   *it* before   Pharaoh,

qcj**1961**   pp,nn**8577**

and it shall become a serpent.

nn4872   wcj,nn175   wcs,qmf935   pr413   nn6547   wcs,qmf**6213** ad**3651** pp,pnl834

10 And Moses and Aaron went in unto Pharaoh, and they   did   so   as   the

nn**3068**   pipf**6680**   nn175   wcs,himf**7993**   (853)   nn,pnx**4294**   pp,pl,cs,nn**6440**   nn6547

Lᴄɢɢ had commanded: and Aaron cast down   his   rod   before   Pharaoh, and

wcj,pp,pl,cs,nn**6440**   pl,nn,pnx**5650**   wcs,qmf**1961**   pp,nn**8577**

before   his servants, and it became a serpent.

nn6547   ad1571   wcs,qmf**7121**   dfp,pl,nn**2450**   wcj,dfp,pl,pipt3784

11 Then Pharaoh also   called   the   wise men   and   the   sorcerers: now   the

pl,cs,nn**2748**   nn4714   pnp1992 ad1571 wcs,qmf**6213**   ad**3651**   pp,pl,nn,pnx**3858**

magicians of Egypt, they also   did   in*like*manner with their enchantments.

wcs,himf**7993**   nn376   nn,pnx**4294**   wcs,qmf**1961**   pp,pl,nn**8577**

12 For they cast down every man his   rod,   and they became   serpents: but

nn175   cs,nn**4294**   wcs,qmf**1104**   (853)   pl,nn,pnx**4294**

Aaron's rod   swallowed up   their   rods.

✍ **7:3**   Compare this verse to Exodus 8:15, where Pharaoh is said to have hardened his own heart. Scripture indicates that the natural inclination of man is to oppose God (Rom. 3:9–23; 5:10). Furthermore, Romans 1:24 reveals that God, in certain cases, allows men to follow the evil desires of their own hearts. God may have simply allowed Pharaoh, in his pride and sinfulness, to do as he desired. This would account for God "hardening" his heart in that God could have softened Pharaoh's heart had He chosen to intervene.

wcs,qmf**2388**   nn6547   cs,nn**3820**   qpf**8085**   wcj,ptn**3808** pr,pnx413

13 And he hardened Pharaoh's heart, that he hearkened not unto them;

pp,pnl834   nn**3068**   pipf**1696**

as the LORD had said.

The Waters Turned to Blood

nn**3068** wcs,qmf**559** pr413   nn4872   nn6547   cs,nn**3820**   aj3515   pipf**3985**

14 And the LORD said unto Moses, Pharaoh's heart *is* hardened, he refuseth

df,nn**5971** pp,pinc7971

to let the people go.

qmv**1980**   pr413   nn6547   dfp,nn**1242** ptdm2009   qpta3318   df,pl,nn,lh4325

15 Get thee unto Pharaoh in the morning; lo, he goeth out unto the water;

wcj,nipf**5324** pr5921   df,nn2975 cs,nn**8193** pp,qnc,pnx7125   wcj,df,nn**4294** pnl834

and thou shalt stand by the river's brink against*he*come; and the rod which

nipf**2015**   pp,nn**5175**   qmf3947   pp,nn,pnx**3027**

was turned to a serpent shalt thou take in thine hand.

wcs,qpf**559** pr,pnx413   nn**3068** pl,cs,nn**430**   df,nn**5680**

16 And thou shalt say unto him, The LORD God of the Hebrews hath

qpf,pnx**7971**   pr,pnx413   pp,qnc**559**   (853)   nn,pnx**5971** pimv7971   wcj,qmf,pnx**5647**

sent me unto thee, saying, Let my people go, that they may serve me

dfp,nn**4057**   wcj,ptdm2009 pr5704/ad3541   ptn**3808** qpf**8085**

in the wilderness: and, behold, hitherto thou wouldest not hear.

ad3541   qpf**559**   nn**3068**   pp,pndm2063   qmf**3045** cj3588 pnp589   nn**3068**

17 Thus saith the LORD, In this thou shalt know that I *am* the LORD:

ptdm2009 pnp595   hipt**5221**   dfp,nn**4294** pnl834   pp,nn,pnx**3027** pr5921   df,pl,nn4325

behold, I will smite with the rod that *is* in mine hand upon the waters

pnl834   dfp,nn2975   wcs,nipf**2015** pp,nn**1818**

which *are* in the river, and they shall be turned to blood.

wcj,df,nn1710 pnl834   df,nn2975   qmf**4191**   dfp,nn2975   wcs,qpf**887**

18 And the fish that *is* in the river shall die, and the river shall stink;

nn4714   wcs,nipf**3811** pp,qnc**8354** pl,nn4325 pr4480   df,nn2975

and the Egyptians shall loathe to drink of the water of the river.

nn**3068** wcs,qmf**559** pr413   nn4872 qmv559 pr413   nn175 qmv3947   nn,pnx**4294**

19 And the LORD spoke unto Moses, Say unto Aaron, Take thy rod, and

wcj,qmv5186   nn,pnx**3027** pr5921   pl,cs,nn**4325**   nn4714   pr5921   pl,nn,pnx5104   pr5921

stretch out thine hand upon the waters of Egypt, upon their streams, upon their

pl,nn,pnx2975   wcj,pr5921   pl,nn,pnx98   wcj,pr5921 cs,nn3605   cs,nn**4723**   pl,nn,pnx4325

rivers, and upon their ponds, and upon all their pools of water, that they

wcj,qmf**1961** nn**1818**   wcj,qpf**1961** nn**1818**   pp,cs,nn3605   cs,nn**776**

may become blood; and *that* there may be blood throughout all the land of

nn4714   wcj,dfp,pl,nn6086   wcj,dfp,pl,nn68

Egypt, both in *vessels of* wood, and in *vessels of* stone.

nn4872   wcj,nn175 wcs,qmf**6213** ad3651 pp,pnl834   nn**3068**   pipf**6680**

20 And Moses and Aaron did so, as the LORD commanded; and he

wcs,himf7311   dfp,nn**4294**   wcs,himf**5221** (853)   df,pl,nn4325 pnl834   dfp,nn2975

lifted up the rod, and smote the waters that *were* in the river, in the

pp,du,cs,nn**5869**   nn6547   wcj,pp,du,cs,nn**5869**   pl,nn,pnx5650 cs,nn3605 df,pl,nn4325

sight of Pharaoh, and in the sight of his servants; and all the waters

pnl834   dfp,nn2975   wcs,nimf**2015** pp,nn**1818**

that *were* in the river were turned to blood.

wcj,df,nn1710 pnl834   dfp,nn2975 qpf**4191**   df,nn2975 wcs,qmf**887**

21 And the fish that *was* in the river died; and the river stank, and the

nn4714   qpf3201   wcj,ptn3808   pp,qnc8354   pl,nn4325   pr4480   df,nn2975   wcs,qmf1961   df,nn1818

Egyptians could not drink of the water of the river; and there was blood

pp,cs,nn3605   cs,nn776   nn4714

throughout all the land of Egypt.

pl,cs,nn2748   nn4714   wcs,qmf6213   ad3651   pp,pl,nn,pnx3909

22 And the magicians of Egypt did so with their enchantments: and

nn6547   cs,nn3820   wcs,qmf2388   wcj,ptn3808   qpf8085   pr,pnx413   pp,pnl834   nn3068

Pharaoh's heart was hardened, neither did he hearken unto them; as the LORD

pipf1696

had said.

nn6547   wcs,qmf6437   wcs,qmf935   pr413   nn,pnx1004   wcj,ptn3808   qpf7896

23 And Pharaoh turned and went into his house, neither did he set his

nn,pnx3820   dfp,pndm2063   ad1571

heart to this also.

cs,nn3605   nn4714   wcs,qmf2658   ad5439   df,nn2975   pl,nn4325   pp,qnc8354

24 And all the Egyptians digged round about the river for water to drink;

cj3588   qpf3201   ptn3808   pp,qnc8354   pr4480/pl,cs,nn4325   df,nn2975

for they could not drink of*the*water of the river.

cs,nu7651   pl,nn3117   wcs,nimf4390   ad310   nn3068   hinc5221   (853)   df,nn2975

25 And seven days were fulfilled, after that the LORD had smitten the river.

The Plague of Frogs

nn3068   wcs,qmf559   pr413   nn4872   qmv935   pr413   nn6547   wcj,qpf559   pr,pnx413

And the LORD spoke unto Moses, Go unto Pharaoh, and say unto him,

ad3541   qpf559   nn3068   (853)   nn,pnx5971   pimv7971   wcj,qmf5647

Thus saith the LORD, Let my people go, that they may serve me.

wcj,cj518   pnp859   aj3986   pp,pinc7971   ptdm2009   pnp595   qpta5062   (853)   cs,nn3605

2 And if thou refuse to let *them* go, behold, I will smite all thy

nn,pnx1366   dfp,pl,nn6854

borders with frogs:

df,nn2975   wcj,qpf8317/pl,nn6854   wcj,qpf5927

3 And the river shall bring*forth*frogs*abundantly, which shall go up and

wcj,qpf935   pp,nn,pnx1004   wcj,pp,cs,nn2315/nn,pnx4904   wcj,pr5921   nn,pnx4296

come into thine house, and into thy bedchamber, and upon thy bed, and

wcj,pp,cs,nn1004   pl,nn,pnx5650   wcj,pp,nn,pnx5971

into the house of thy servants, and upon thy people, and into thine

wcj,pp,pl,pnx8574   wcj,pp,pl,nn,pnx4863

ovens, and into thy kneading troughs:

df,pl,nn6854   qmf5927   wcj,pp,pnx   wcj,pp,nn,pnx5971

4 And the frogs shall come up both on thee, and upon thy people, and

wcj,pp,cs,nn3605   pl,nn,pnx5650

upon all thy servants.

nn3068   wcs,qmf559   pr413   nn4872   qmv559   pr413   nn175   qmv5186   (853)

5 And the LORD spoke unto Moses, Say unto Aaron, Stretch forth thine

nn,pnx3027   pp,nn,pnx4294   pr5921   df,pl,nn5104   pr5921   df,pl,nn2975   wcj,pr5921   df,pl,nn98

hand with thy rod over the streams, over the rivers, and over the ponds, and

(853)   df,pl,nn6854   wcj,himv5927   pr5921   cs,nn776   nn4714

cause frogs to come up upon the land of Egypt.

nn175   wcs,qmf5186   (853)   nn,pnx3027   pr5921   pl,cs,nn4325   nn4714

6 And Aaron stretched out his hand over the waters of Egypt; and the

df,nn6854   wcs,qmf5927   wcs,pimf3680   (853)   cs,nn776   nn4714

frogs came up, and covered the land of Egypt.

df,pl,nn2748   wcs,qmf6213   ad3651   pp,pl,nn,pnx3909   wcs,himf5927   (853)

7 And the magicians   did   so   with their enchantments, and brought up

df,pl,nn6854   pr5921   cs,nn776   nn4714

frogs   upon the land of Egypt.

nn6547   wcs,qmf7121   pp,nn4872   wcj,pp,nn175   wcs,qmf559   himf6279/pr413   nn3068

8 Then Pharaoh called for Moses and Aaron, and said, Entreat the LORD,

wcj,hicj5493   df,pl,nn6854   pr,pnx4480   wcj,pr4480/nn,pnx5971

that he may take away the frogs   from   me, and from*my*people; and I will let

(853)   df,nn5971   wcj,picj7971   wcj,qmf2076   pp,nn3068

the people   go,   that they may do sacrifice unto the LORD.

nn4872   wcs,qmf559   pp,nn6547   htmv6286   pr,pnx5921   pp,pnit4970   himf6279

9 And Moses   said   unto Pharaoh, Glory   over   me: when   shall I entreat

pp,pnx   wcj,pp,pl,nn,pnx5650   wcj,pp,nn,pnx5971   pp,hinc3772   df,pl,nn6854   pr,pnx4480

for thee, and for thy   servants,   and for thy   people,   to destroy the frogs   from

wcj(pr4480)/pl,nn,pnx1004   nimf7604   dfp,nn2975   ad7535

thee and thy   houses,   *that* they may remain in the   river   only?

wcs,qmf559   pp,ad4279   wcs,qmf559   pp,nn,pnx1697

10 And he   said, Tomorrow. And he   said,   *Be it* according to thy   word:

pp,cj4616   qmf3045   cj3588   ptn369   pp,nn3068   pl,nn,pnx430

that   thou mayest know that *there is* none like unto the LORD our   God.

df,pl,nn6854   wcs,qpf5493   pr,pnx4480   wcj,pr4480/pl,nn,pnx1004

11 And the   frogs   shall depart   from   thee   and from*thy*houses,   and

wcj,pr4480/pl,nn,pnx5650   wcj,pr4480/nn,pnx5971   nimf7604   dfp,nn2975   ad7535

from*thy*servants, and from*thy*people; they shall remain in the   river   only.

nn4872   wcj,nn175   wcs,qmf3318   pr4480/pr5973   nn6547   nn4872   wcs,qmf6817   pr413

12 And Moses and Aaron went out   from   Pharaoh: and Moses   cried   unto

nn3068   pr5921/cs,nn1697   df,pl,nn6854   pnl834   qpf7760   pp,nn6547

the LORD because of the   frogs   which   he had brought against Pharaoh.

nn3068   wcs,qmf6213   pp,cs,nn1697   nn4872   df,pl,nn6854

13 And the LORD   did   according to the   word   of Moses; and the   frogs

wcs,qmf4191   pr4480   df,pl,nn1004   pr4480   df,pl,nn2691   wcj,pr4480   df,pl,nn7704

died   out of the houses, out of the villages, and out of the fields.

wcs,qmf6651/pnx(853)   pl,nn2563/pl,nn2563   df,nn776   wcs,qmf887

14 And they gathered*them*together upon heaps: and the land stank.

nn6547   wcs,qmf7200   cj3588   qpf1961   df,nn7309   wcj,hina3513   (853)   nn,pnx3820

15 But when Pharaoh   saw   that there was respite, he hardened   his heart,

qpf8085   wcj,ptn3808   pr,pnx413   pp,pnl834   nn3068   pipf1696

and hearkened   not   unto them;   as   the LORD had said.

The Plague of Lice

nn3068   wcs,qmf559   pr413   nn4872   qmv559   pr413   nn175   qmv5186   (853)

16 And the LORD   said   unto Moses, Say unto Aaron, Stretch out   thy

nn,pnx4294   wcj,himv5221 (853)   cs,nn6083   df,nn776   wcj,qpf1961   nn3654

rod,   and smite   the dust of the land, that it may become lice throughout

pp,cs,nn3605   cs,nn776   nn4714

all   the land of Egypt.

wcs,qmf6213   ad3651   nn175   wcs,qmf5186   (853)   nn,pnx3027   pp,nn,pnx4294

17 And they   did   so; for Aaron stretched out   his hand with his   rod,

wcs,himf5221 (853)   cs,nn6083   df,nn776   wcs,qmf1961   df,nn3654   dfp,nn120   wcj,dfp,nn929

and smote   the dust of the earth, and it became   lice   in man, and in beast;

cs,nn3605   cs,nn6083   df,nn776   qpf1961   pl,nn3654   pp,cs,nn3605   cs,nn776   nn4714

all   the dust of the land became   lice   throughout   all   the land of Egypt.

df,pl,nn2748   wcs,qmf6213   ad3651   pp,pl,nn,pnx3909   pp,hinc3318   (853)

18 And the magicians   did   so   with their enchantments to bring forth

df,pl,nn3654   qpf3201   wcj,ptn3808   wcs,qmf1961 df,nn3654   dfp,nn120   wcj,dfp,nn929

lice, but they could not: so there were lice upon man, and upon beast.

df,pl,nn2748   wcs,qmf559   pr413   nn6547   pndm1931   cs,nn676   pl,nn430

19 Then the magicians said unto Pharaoh, This *is* the finger of God: and

nn6547   cs,nn3820   wcs,qmf2388   qpf8085   wcj,ptn3808 pr,pnx413   pp,pnl834   nn3068

Pharaoh's heart was hardened, and he hearkened not unto them; as the LORD

pipf1696

had said.

Swarms of Flies

nn3068   wcs,qmf559   pr413   nn4872   himv7925   dfp,nn1242

20 And the LORD said unto Moses, Rise*up*early in the morning, and

wcj,htmv3320 pp,pl,cs,nn6440   nn6547   ptdm2009   qpta3318   df,pl,nn,lh4325   wcj,qpf559 pr,pnx413

stand before Pharaoh; lo, he cometh forth to the water; and say unto

ad3541   qpf559   nn3068   nn,pnx5971 pimv7971   wcj,qmf,pnx5647

him, Thus saith the LORD, Let my people go, that they may serve me.

cj3588   cj518   ptn,pnx369   (853)   nn,pnx5971 pipt7971 ptdm,pnx2009   hipt7971 (853)

21 Else, if thou wilt not let my people go, behold, I will send

df,nn6157   pp,pnx   wcj,pp,pl,nn,pnx5650   wcj,pp,nn,pnx5971

swarms *of flies* upon thee, and upon thy servants, and upon thy people, and

wcj,pp,pl,nn,pnx1004   pl,cs,nn1004   nn4714   wcj,qpf4390   (853) df,nn6157

into thy houses: and the houses of the Egyptians shall be full of swarms *of*

wcj,ad1571   df,nn127 pnl834/pr,pnx5921 pnp1992

flies, and also the ground whereon they *are*.

wcj,hipf6395   df,pndm1931 dfp,nn3117 (853)   cs,nn776   nn1657   pr,pnx5921 pnl834

22 And I will sever in that day the land of Goshen, in which my

nn,pnx5971   qpta5975   pp,ptn1115   nn6157   qnc1961   ad8033   pp,cj4616

people dwell, that no swarms *of flies* shall be there; to*the*end thou mayest

qmf3045 cj3588 pnp589   nn3068   pp,cs,nn7130   df,nn776

know that I *am* the LORD in the midst of the earth.

wcs,qpf7760   nn6304   pr996   nn,pnx5971   wcj(pr996)   nn,pnx5971

23 And I will put a division between my people and thy people:

pp,nn4279   df,pndm2088 df,nn226 qmf1961

tomorrow shall this sign be.

nn3068   wcs,qmf6213 ad3651   wcs,qmf935   aj3515   nn6157

24 And the LORD did so; and there came a grievous swarm *of flies* into

cs,nn,lh1004   nn6547   pl,nn,pnx5650 wcj,cs,nn1004   wcj,pp,cs,nn3605   cs,nn776

the house of Pharaoh, and *into* his servants' houses, and into all the land of

nn4714   df,nn776   nimf7843   pr4480/pl,cs,nn6440   df,nn6157

Egypt: the land was corrupted by*reason*of the swarm *of flies*.

nn6547   wcs,qmf7121 pr413   nn4872   wcj,pp,nn175   wcs,qmf559 qmv1980   qmv2076

25 And Pharaoh called for Moses and for Aaron, and said, Go ye, sacrifice

pp,pl,nn,pnx430   dfp,nn776

to your God in the land.

nn4872   wcs,qmf559   ptn3808 nipt3559 ad3651   pp,qnc6213 cj3588   qmf2076

26 And Moses said, It is not meet so to do; for we shall sacrifice the

cs,nn8441   nn4714   pp,nn3068   pl,nn,pnx430 ptdm2005   qmf2076   (853)

abomination of the Egyptians to the LORD our God: lo, shall we sacrifice the

cs,nn8441   nn4714   pp,du,nn,pnx5869   wcj,ptn3808 qmf,pnx5619

abomination of the Egyptians before their eyes, and will they not stone us?

qmf1980 cs,nu7969 pl,nn3117 cs,nn1870   dfp,nn4057   wcs,qpf2076

27 We will go three days' journey into the wilderness, and sacrifice to the

pp,nn3068   pl,nn,pnx430 pp,pnl834   qmf559/pr,pnx413

LORD our God, as he shall command us.

nn6547　wcs,qmf559　pnp595　　　　pnx(853)　　pimf7971　　　　　　　wcs,qpf2076

28 And Pharaoh said,　I　will let　　　　you　go,　that ye may sacrifice to the

pp,nn3068　　pl,nn,pnx430　　　　dfp,nn4057　ad7535　　ptn3808　pp,qnc1980　hina7368/himf7368

LORD your　God　in the wilderness; only ye shall　not　　go　very*far*away:

himv6279　pr,pnx1157

entreat　for　me.

nn4872　wcs,qmf559　ptdm2009　pnp595　qpta3318　pr4480/pr,pnx5973　　　　　wcj,hipf6279/pr413

29 And Moses said, Behold,　I　go out　from　thee, and I will　entreat

nn3068　　　df,nn6157　　　　wcj,qpf5493　pr4480/nn6547　　pr4480/pl,nn,pnx5650

the LORD that the swarms of flies may depart from Pharaoh, from*his*servants, and

wcj,pr4480/nn,pnx5971　　ad4279　　ad7535　　ptn408　　nn6547　　hinc2048　　hicj3254

from*his*people, tomorrow: but let　not　Pharaoh deal deceitfully any more in

pp,ptn1115　　(853)　　df,nn5971　pinc7971　pp,qnc2076　　pp,nn3068

not letting　　the people　go　to sacrifice to the LORD.

nn4872　wcs,qmf3318　pr4480/pr,pnx5973　nn6547　　wcs,qmf6279/pr413　　nn3068

30 And Moses went out　from　Pharaoh, and entreated the LORD.

nn3068　wcs,qmf6213　　　　pp,cs,nn1697　nn4872　　wcs,qmf5493

31 And the LORD　did　according to the　word　of Moses; and he removed the

df,nn6157　　　pr4480/nn6547　　pr4480/pl,nn,pnx5650　　　wcj,pr4480/nn,pnx5971

swarms　of flies　from Pharaoh,　from*his*servants,　and　from*his*people; there

nipf7604　　ptn3808　nu259

remained　not　one.

nn6547　wcs,himf3513　(853)　　nn,pnx3820　df,pndm2063　dfp,nn6471　ad1571　wcj,ptn3808

32 And Pharaoh hardened　　his heart at　this　　time also, neither would he

(853)　　df,nn5971　pipf7971

let　the people　go.

The Animals Die

nn3068　wcs,qmf559　pr413　　nn4872　qmv935　pr413　　nn6547　　wcj,pipf1696/pr,pnx413

9 Then the LORD　said　unto Moses, Go in unto Pharaoh, and　　tell

ad3541　qpf559　　nn3068　pl,cs,nn430　df,pl,nn5680　　(853)　　nn,pnx5971　pimv7971

him, Thus saith the LORD God　of the Hebrews, Let　　my people　go,

wcj,qmf,pnx5647

that they may　serve　me.

cj3588　cj518　pnp859　aj3986　　　　　pp,pinc7971　　　　hipt2388　pp,pnx　wcj,ad,pnx5750

2 For if thou refuse to let them　go,　and wilt hold them　still,

ptdm2009　cs,nn3027　　nn3068　qpta1961　　pp,nn,pnx4735　pnl834　　　　dfp,nn7704

3 Behold, the hand of the LORD　is　upon thy　cattle　which is in the field,

dfp,pl,nn5483　　dfp,pl,nn2543　　dfp,pl,nn1581　　dfp,nn1241

upon the horses, upon the　asses, upon the camels, upon the oxen, and upon the

wcj,dfp,nn6629　　ad3966　aj3515　nn1698

sheep: there shall be a very grievous murrain.

nn3068　wcj,hipf6395　pr996　　cs,nn4735　nn3478　wcj(pr996)　cs,nn4735

4 And the LORD shall　sever　between the cattle of Israel and　　the cattle

nn4714　　wcj,ptn3808/nn1697　qmf4191　pr4480/cs,nn3605　pp,pl,cs,nn1121　nn3478

of Egypt: and there shall　nothing　die　of all　that is the children's of Israel.

nn3068　wcs,qmf7760　nn4150　pp,qnc559　ad4279　　nn3068　　qmf6213

5 And the LORD appointed a set time, saying, Tomorrow the LORD shall　do

df,pndm2088 df,nn1697　dfp,nn776

this　thing in the land.

nn3068　wcs,qmf6213　(853)　df,pndm2088　df,nn1697　pr4480/nn4283　cs,nn3605　cs,nn4735

6 And the LORD　did　　that　thing on*the*morrow, and　all　the cattle

nn4714　wcs,qmf4191　wcj,pr4480/cs,nn4735　pl,cs,nn1121　nn3478　qpf4191 ptn3808　nu259

of Egypt　died: but of*the*cattle of the children of Israel died not one.

_{nn6547}   _{wcs,qmf7971}   _{wcj,ptdm2009}   _{ptn3808} _(or5704) _{nu259}   _{pr4480/cs,nn4735}

7 And Pharaoh sent, and, behold, there was not   one of*the*cattle of

_{nn3478}   _{qpf4191}   _{cs,nn3820}   _{nn6547}   _{wcs,qmf3513}   _{wcj,ptn3808}

the Israelites dead. And the heart of Pharaoh was hardened, and he did   not   let

₍₈₅₃₎   _{df,nn5971}   _{pipf7971}

the people go.

The Boils

       _{nn3068}   _{wcs,qmf559}   _{pr413}   _{nn4872}   _{wcj,pr413}   _{nn175}   _{qmv3947}   _{pp,pnx}

8 And the Lᴏʀᴅ said   unto   Moses and   unto   Aaron, Take   to you

_{cs,nn4393/du,nn,pnx2651}   _{cs,nn6368}   _{nn3536}   _{nn4872} _{wcj,qpf,pnx2236}   _{df,du,nn,lh8064}

handfuls   of ashes of the furnace, and let Moses sprinkle it toward the heaven

_{pp,du,cs,nn5869}   _{nn6547}

in the   sight   of Pharaoh.

       _{wcj,qpf1961}   _{pp,nn80}   _{pr5921} _{cs,nn3605}   _{cs,nn776}   _{nn4714}   _{wcj,qpf1961}

9 And it shall become small dust in   all   the land of Egypt, and shall   be

_{pp,nn7822}   _{qpta6524}   _{pl,nn76}   _{pr5921}   _{df,nn120}   _{wcj,pr5921}   _{df,nn929}   _{pp,cs,nn3605}

a boil breaking forth *with* blains upon man, and upon beast, throughout   all

_{cs,nn776}   _{nn4714}

the land of Egypt.

     _{wcs,qmf3947} ₍₈₅₃₎ _{cs,nn6368}   _{df,nn3536}   _{wcs,qmf5975} _{pp,pl,cs,nn6440}   _{nn6547}

10 And they   took   ashes of the furnace, and   stood   before   Pharaoh; and

_{nn4872}   _{wcs,qmf2236}   _{pnx(853)}   _{df,du,nn,lh8064}   _{wcs,qmf1961}   _{nn7822}   _{qpta6524}

Moses sprinkled   it up toward heaven; and it became a boil breaking forth *with*

_{pl,nn76}   _{dfp,nn120}   _{wcj,dfp,nn929}

blains upon man, and upon   beast.

       _{df,pl,nn2748}   _{qpf3201} _{wcj,ptn3808} _{pp,qnc5975} _{pp,pl,cs,nn6440}   _{nn4872}   _{pr4480/pl,cs,nn6440}   _{df,nn7822}

11 And the magicians could   not   stand   before   Moses because of the boils;

_{cj3588}   _{df,nn7822} _{qpf1961}   _{dfp,pl,nn2748}   _{wcj,pp,cs,nn3605}   _{nn4714}

for the boil   was upon the magicians, and upon   all   the Egyptians.

       _{nn3068}   _{wcs,pimf2388}   ₍₈₅₃₎   _{cs,nn3820}   _{nn6547}   _{qpf8085}   _{wcj,ptn3808}

12 And the Lᴏʀᴅ hardened   the heart of Pharaoh, and he hearkened   not

_{pr,pnx413}   _{pp,pnl834}   _{nn3068}   _{pipf1696}   _{pr413}   _{nn4872}

unto them; as   the Lᴏʀᴅ had spoken unto Moses.

The Plague of Hail

       _{nn3068}   _{wcs,qmf559}   _{pr413}   _{nn4872}   _{himv7925}   _{dfp,nn1242}

13 And the Lᴏʀᴅ said   unto   Moses, Rise*up*early in the   morning, and

_{wcj,htmv3320} _{pp,pl,cs,nn6440}   _{nn6547}   _{wcj,qpf559}   _{pr,pnx413}   _{ad3541}   _{qpf559}   _{nn3068}   _{pl,cs,nn430}

stand   before   Pharaoh, and   say   unto   him, Thus saith the Lᴏʀᴅ God   of the

_{df,nn5680}   ₍₈₅₃₎   _{nn,pnx5971}   _{pimv7971}   _{wcj,qmf,pnx5647}

Hebrews, Let   my people go, that they may   serve   me.

       _{cj3588} _{pnp589}   _{df,pndm2063} _{dfp,nn6471} _{qpta7971} ₍₈₅₃₎ _{cs,nn3605}   _{pl,nn,pnx4046}   _{pr413}   _{nn,pnx3820}

14 For I will at   this   time   send   all   my plagues upon thine heart,

       _{wcj,pp,pl,nn,pnx5650}   _{wcj,pp,nn,pnx5971} _{pp,cj5668}   _{qmf3045} _{cj3588}

and upon thy   servants, and upon thy   people;   that   thou mayest know that *there*

_{ptn369}   _{pp,pnx3644}   _{pp,cs,nn3605}   _{df,nn776}

is none like me in   all   the earth.

       _{cj3588} _{ad6258}   _{qpf7971}   ₍₈₅₃₎   _{nn,pnx3027}   _{wcs,himf5221} _{pnx(853)}

15 For now I will stretch out   my hand, that I may   smite   thee and

_{wcj(853)}   _{nn,pnx5971}   _{dfp,nn1698}   _{wcs,nimf3582} _{pr4480}   _{df,nn776}

thy people with pestilence; and thou shalt be cut off from the earth.

^{wcj,ad199} ^{pp,pr5668} ^{pndm2063}   ^{hipf,pnx5975}   ^{pp,pr5668}   ^{hinc,pnx7200}

16 And in*very*deed for this *cause* have I raised*thee*up, for to show

⁽⁸⁵³⁾   ^{nn,pnx3581}   ^{wcj,pp,cj4616}   ^{nn,pnx8034}   ^{pinc5608}   ^{pp,cs,nn3605}

in thee   my power; and that my name may be declared throughout all

^{df,nn776}

the earth.

^{ad,pnx5750}   ^{htpt5549}   ^{pp,nn,pnx5971}   ^{pp,ptn1115}

17 As yet exaltest*thou*thyself against my people, that thou wilt not

^{pinc,pnx7971}

let*them*go?

^{ptdm,pnx2009}   ^{ad4279}   ^{dfp,nn6256}   ^{hipt4305}   ^{ad3966}   ^{aj3515}

18 Behold, tomorrow about this time I will cause it to rain a very grievous

ⁿⁿ¹²⁵⁹ ^{pnl834} ^{pp,pnx3644}   ^{ptn3808} ^{qpf1961}   ^{pp,nn4714} ^{pp,pr4480/df,nn3117}   ^{ninc,pnx3245}

hail, such as hath not been in Egypt since the foundation thereof even

^{wcj,pr5704} ^{ad6258}

until now.

^{qmv7971}   ^{wcj,ad6258}   ^{himv5756} ⁽⁸⁵³⁾   ^{nn,pnx4735}   ^{wcj(853)} ^{cs,nn3605} ^{pnl834} ^{pp,pnx}

19 Send therefore now, *and* gather thy cattle, and all that thou

^{dfp,nn7704}   ^{cs,nn3605} ^{df,nn120}   ^{wcj,df,nn929} ^{pnl834}   ^{nimf4672}   ^{dfp,nn7704}

hast in the field; *for upon* every man and beast which shall be found in the field,

^{wcj,ptn3808}   ^{nimf622}   ^{df,nn,lh1004}   ^{df,nn1259}   ^{wcs,qpf3381}   ^{pr,pnx5921}

and shall not be brought home, the hail shall come down upon them, and

^{wcs,qpf4191}

they shall die.

^{df,qpta3372} ⁽⁸⁵³⁾   ^{cs,nn1697}   ⁿⁿ³⁰⁶⁸   ^{pr4480/pl,cs,nn5650}   ⁿⁿ⁶⁵⁴⁷

20 He that feared the word of the Lord among*the*servants of Pharaoh

⁽⁸⁵³⁾   ^{pl,nn,pnx5650}   ^{wcj(853)}   ^{nn,pnx4735} ^{hipf5127} ^{pr413}   ^{df,pl,nn1004}

made his servants and his cattle flee into the houses:

^{wcj,pnl834} ^{qpf7760/nn,pnx3820} ^{ptn3808} ^(pr413)   ^{cs,nn1697}   ⁿⁿ³⁰⁶⁸   ^{wcs,qmf5800} ⁽⁸⁵³⁾

21 And he that regarded not the word of the Lord left his

^{pl,nn,pnx5650}   ^{wcj(853)}   ^{nn,pnx4735}   ^{dfp,nn7704}

servants and his cattle in the field.

ⁿⁿ³⁰⁶⁸   ^{wcs,qmf559}   ^{pr413}   ⁿⁿ⁴⁸⁷²   ^{qmv5186}   ⁽⁸⁵³⁾   ^{nn,pnx3027}   ^{pr5921}

22 And the Lord said unto Moses, Stretch forth thine hand toward

^{df,du,nn8064}   ^{wcj,qcj1961} ⁿⁿ¹²⁵⁹   ^{pp,cs,nn3605}   ^{cs,nn776}   ⁿⁿ⁴⁷¹⁴   ^{pr5921} ^{df,nn120}

heaven, that there may be hail in all the land of Egypt, upon man, and

^{wcj,pr5921} ^{df,nn929}   ^{wcj,pr5921} ^{wcj,cs,nn3605} ^{cs,nn6212}   ^{df,nn7704}   ^{pp,cs,nn776}   ⁿⁿ⁴⁷¹⁴

upon beast, and upon every herb of the field, throughout the land of Egypt.

ⁿⁿ⁴⁸⁷²   ^{wcs,qmf5186}   ⁽⁸⁵³⁾   ^{nn,pnx4294}   ^{pr5921}   ^{df,du,nn8064}   ^{wcj,nn3068} ^{qpf5414}

23 And Moses stretched forth his rod toward heaven: and the Lord sent

^{pl,nn6963}   ^{wcj,nn1259}   ⁿⁿ⁷⁸⁴   ^{wcs,qmf1980}   ^{nn,lh776}   ⁿⁿ³⁰⁶⁸   ^{wcs,himf4305}

thunder and hail, and the fire ran along upon the ground; and the Lord rained

ⁿⁿ¹²⁵⁹ ^{pr5921}   ^{cs,nn776}   ⁿⁿ⁴⁷¹⁴

hail upon the land of Egypt.

^{wcs,qmf1961} ⁿⁿ¹²⁵⁹   ^{wcj,nn784}   ^{htpt3947}   ^{pp,cs,nn8432}   ^{df,nn1259} ^{ad3966}   ^{aj3515}

24 So there was hail, and fire mingled with the hail, very grievous,

^{pnl834}   ^{qpf1961} ^{ptn3808} ^{pp,pnx3644}   ^{pp,cs,nn3605}   ^{cs,nn776}   ⁿⁿ⁴⁷¹⁴   ^{pr4480/ad227}   ^{qpf1961}

such as there was none like it in all the land of Egypt since it became a

^{pp,nn1471}

nation.

^{df,nn1259} ^{wcs,himf5221}   ^{pp,cs,nn3605}   ^{cs,nn776}   ⁿⁿ⁴⁷¹⁴   ⁽⁸⁵³⁾ ^{cs,nn3605} ^{pnl834}

25 And the hail smote throughout all the land of Egypt all that

^{dfp,nn7704}   ^{pr4480/nn120}   ^{wcj(pr5704)}   ⁿⁿ⁹²⁹   ^{df,nn1259} ^{hipf5221} ^{wcj(853)} ^{cs,nn3605} ^{cs,nn6212}

was in the field, both man and beast; and the hail smote every herb

^{df,nn7704}   ^{pipf7665} ^{wcj(853)} ^{cs,nn3605} ^{cs,nn6086}   ^{df,nn7704}

of the field, and broke every tree of the field.

ad7535   pp,cs,nn776   nn1657   pnl834/ad8033   pl,cs,nn1121   nn3478   qpf1961
26 Only in the land of Goshen, where the children of Israel *were*, was there

ptn3808 nn1259
no hail.

nn6547   wcs,qmf7971   wcs,qmf7121   pp,nn4872   wcj,pp,nn175   wcs,qmf559 pr,pnx413
27 And Pharaoh sent, and called for Moses and Aaron, and said unto

qpf2398   df,nn6471   nn3068   df,aj6662   wcj,pnp589   wcj,nn,pnx5971
them, I have sinned this time: the L<small>ORD</small> *is* righteous, and I and my people

df,aj7563
are wicked.

himv6279/pr413   nn3068   wcj,aj7227   pr4480/qnc1961   pl,nn430
28 Entreat the L<small>ORD</small> (for *it is* enough) that*there*be*no *more* mighty

pl,cs,nn6963   wcj,nn1259   pnx(853)   wcs,picj7971   pp,qnc5975 wcj,ptn3808
thunderings and hail; and I will let   you   go,   and ye shall stay   no

himf3254
longer.

nn4872   wcs,qmf559 pr,pnx413   pp,qnc,pnx3318   (853)   df,nn5892
29 And Moses said unto him, As soon as I am gone out of   the city, I

qmf6566   (853)   du,nn,pnx3709 pr413   nn3068   df,pl,nn6963   qmf2308
will spread abroad   my hands unto the L<small>ORD</small>; *and* the thunder shall cease,

ptn3808   qmf1961   ad5750   wcj,df,nn1259 pp,cj4616   qmf3045   cj3588
neither shall there be any more hail;   that thou mayest know how that the

df,nn776   pp,nn3068
earth *is* the L<small>ORD</small>'s.

wcj,pnp859   wcj,pl,nn,pnx5650 qpf3045 cj3588   ad2962
30 But as for thee and thy servants, I know that ye will not yet

qmf3372/pr4480/pl,cs,nn6440   nn3068 pl,nn430
fear   the L<small>ORD</small> God.

wcj,df,nn6594   wcj,df,nn8184   pupf5221 cj3588 df,nn8184   nn24
31 And the flax and the barley was smitten: for the barley *was* in the ear,

wcj,df,nn6594   nn1392
and the flax *was* bolled.

wcj,df,nn2406   wcj,df,nn3698   ptn3808   pupf5221 cj3588 pnp2007
○<small>ᾱ</small> 32 But the wheat and the   rye   were not smitten: for they *were*

aj648
not*grown*up.

nn4872   wcs,qmf3318   (853)   df,nn5892 pr4480/pr5973 nn6547   wcs,qmf6566
33 And Moses went out of   the city from   Pharaoh, and spread abroad

du,nn,pnx3709 pr413   nn3068   df,pl,nn6963 wcj,df,nn1259 wcs,qmf2308   wcj,nn4306
his hands unto the L<small>ORD</small>: and the thunders and hail ceased, and the rain was

ptn3808 nipf5413   nn,lh776
not poured upon the earth.

nn6547   wcs,qmf7200 cj3588 df,nn4306   wcj,df,nn1259   wcj,df,pl,nn6963
34 And when Pharaoh saw that the rain and the hail and the thunders

qpf2308   pp,qnc2398   wcs,himf3254   wcs,himf3513   nn,pnx3820 pnp1931   wcj,pl,nn,pnx5650
were ceased, he sinned yet more, and hardened his heart, he and his servants.

cs,nn3820   nn6547   wcs,qmf2388 wcj,ptn3808   (853)   pl,cs,nn1121
35 And the heart of Pharaoh was hardened, neither would he let   the children

nn3478   pipf7971 pp,pnl834   nn3068   pipf1696 pp,cs,nn3027 nn4872
of Israel go;   as the L<small>ORD</small> had spoken by   Moses.

○<small>ᾱ</small> **9:32** Rye or spelt was a wild wheat which was more edible than barley, but it was not as good as wheat. It was harvested later than barley and was difficult to separate from its chaff. The Egyptians used it to make their basic bread.

Locusts

10

nn3068 wcs,qmf559 pr413 nn4872 qmv935 pr413 nn6547 cj3588 pnp589
☞ And the LORD said unto Moses, Go in unto Pharaoh: for I

hipf3513 (853) nn,pnx3820 wcj(853) cs,nn3820 pl,nn,pnx5650 pp,pr4616
have hardened   his heart, and   the heart of his servants, that

qnc,pnx7896 pndm428 pl,nn,pnx226 pp,nn,pnx7130
I might show these my signs before him:

wcj,pp,cj4616 pimf5608 pp,du,cs,nn241 nn,pnx1121 nn,pnx1121
2 And that thou mayest tell in the ears of thy son, and of thy son's

wcj,cs,nn1121 (853) pnl834 htpf5953 pp,nn4714 wcj(853) pl,nn,pnx226 pnl834
son, what things I have wrought in Egypt, and   my signs which I have

qpf7760 pp,pnx wcj,qpf3045 cj3588 pnp589 nn3068
done among them; that ye may know how that I *am* the LORD.

nn4872 wcj,nn175 wcs,qmf935 pr413 nn6547 wcs,qmf559 pr,pnx413 ad3541
3 And Moses and Aaron came in unto Pharaoh, and said unto him, Thus

qpf559 nn3068 pl,cs,nn430 df,nn5680 pr5704/pnit4970 pipf3985 pp,ninc6031
saith the LORD God of the Hebrews, How long wilt thou refuse to humble thyself

pr4480/pl,nn,pnx6440 nn,pnx5971 pimv7971 wcj,qmf,pnx5647
before me? let my people go, that they may serve me.

cj3588 cj518 pnp859 aj3986 (853) nn,pnx5971 pp,pinc7971 ptdm,pnx2009 ad4279
4 Else, if thou refuse to let   my people go, behold, tomorrow will I

hipt935 nn697 pp,nn,pnx1366
bring the locusts into thy coast:

wcj,pipf3680 (853) cs,nn5869 df,nn776 wcj,ptn3808 qmf3201
5 And they shall cover   the face of the earth, that one cannot be able to

pp,qnc7200 (853) df,nn776 wcs,qpf398 (853) cs,nn3499 df,nn6413
see   the earth: and they shall eat   the residue of that*which*is*escaped,

df,nipt7604 pp,pnx pr4480 df,nn1259 wcs,qpf398 (853) cs,nn3605 df,nn6086
which remaineth unto you from the hail, and shall eat   every tree which

df,qpta6779 pp,pnx pr4480 df,nn7704
groweth for you out of the field:

wcs,qpf4390 pl,nn,pnx1004 wcj,pl,cs,nn1004 cs,nn3605 pl,nn,pnx5650
6 And they shall fill thy houses, and the houses of all thy servants, and

wcj,pl,cs,nn1004 cs,nn3605 nn4714 pnl834 ptn3808 pl,nn,pnx1 pl,nn,pnx1
the houses of all the Egyptians; which neither thy fathers, nor thy fathers'

wcj,pl,cs,nn1 qpf7200 pr4480/cs,nn3117 qnc,pnx1961 pr5921 df,nn127 pr5704 df,pndm2088 df,nn3117
fathers have seen, since*the*day that they were upon the earth unto this day.

wcs,qmf6437 wcs,qmf3318 pr4480/pr5973 nn6547
And he turned himself, and went out from Pharaoh.

nn6547 pl,cs,nn5650 wcs,qmf559 pr,pnx413 pr5704/pnit4970 pndm2088 qmf1961
7 And Pharaoh's servants said unto him, How long shall this man be a

pp,nn4170 pp,pnx (853) df,pl,nn376 pimv7971 wcj,qmf5647 (853) nn3068
snare unto us? let   the men go, that they may serve   the LORD their

pl,nn,pnx430 qmf3045 he,ad2962 cj3588 nn4714 qpf6
God: knowest thou not yet that Egypt is destroyed?

(853) nn4872 wcj(853) nn175 wcs,homf7725 pr413 nn6547
8 And   Moses and   Aaron were brought again unto Pharaoh: and he

wcs,qmf559 pr,pnx413 qmv1980 qmv5647 (853) nn3068 pl,nn,pnx430 pnit4310/wcj,pnit4310
said unto them, Go, serve   the LORD your God: *but* who   *are* they

df,pl,qpta1980
that shall go?

nn4872 wcs,qmf559 qmf1980 pp,pl,nn,pnx5288 wcj,pp,ad,pnx2205
9 And Moses said, We will go with our young and with our old,

---

☞ **10:1–20** See the note on Joel 1:4 regarding locusts.

pp,pl,nn,pnx**1121**   wcj,pp,pl,nn,pnx1323   pp,nn,pnx6629

with our   sons   and with our daughters, with our flocks and with our

wcj,pp,nn,pnx1241   qmf**1980** cj**3588** pp,pnx   cs,nn**2282**   nn**3068**

herds   will we go; for we *must hold* a feast unto the Lᴏʀᴅ.

wcs,qmf**559** pr,pnx413   nn**3068** qcj**1961** ad**3651** pr,pnx5973   pp,pnl834

10 And he said unto them, Let the Lᴏʀᴅ be so with you, as I will

pnx(853)   pimf7971   wcj(853)   nn,pnx**2945** qmv**7200**   cj**3588** nn**7451**   pr5048/pl,nn,pnx**6440**

let   you go, and   your little ones: look *to it;* for evil *is* before   you.

ptn**3808** ad**3651** qmv**1980** pte**4994**   df,pl,nn**1397**   wcj,qmv**5647** (853)   nn**3068** cj**3588** pnx(853)

11 Not so: go now ye *that are* men, and serve   the Lᴏʀᴅ; for

pnp859   pl,pipt1245   pnx(853)   wcs,pimf1644 pr4480/pr854 nn6547   pl,cs,nn**6440**

that ye did desire. And   they were driven out from Pharaoh's presence.

nn**3068** wcs,qmf**559** pr413 nn4872   qmv5186   nn,pnx**3027** pr5921   cs,nn**776**

12 And the Lᴏʀᴅ said unto Moses, Stretch out thine hand over the land of

nn4714   dfp,nn697   wcj,qcj**5927** pr5921 cs,nn**776**   nn4714   wcj,qmf398

Egypt for the locusts, that they may come up upon the land of Egypt, and eat

(853) cs,nn3605 cs,nn**6212** df,nn**776**   (853) cs,nn3605 pnl834   df,nn1259   hipf**7604**

every herb of the land, *even*   all that the hail hath left.

nn4872   wcs,qmf5186   (853)   nn,pnx**4294** pr5921 cs,nn**776**   nn4714

13 And Moses stretched forth   his rod over the land of Egypt, and the

wcj,nn**3068** pipf5090   nn6921 cs,nn**7307**   dfp,nn**776** cs,nn3605 df,pndm1931 df,nn**3117**   wcj,cs,nn3605

Lᴏʀᴅ brought an east wind upon the land all   that day, and all *that*

df,nn**3915**   qpf**1961** df,nn1242   df,nn6921 wcj,cs,nn**7307** qpf**5375** (853)   df,nn697

night; *and* when it was morning, the east wind brought the locusts.

df,nn697   wcs,qmf**5927** pr5921 cs,nn3605   cs,nn**776**   nn4714   wcs,qmf5117

14 And the locusts went up over all   the land of Egypt, and rested in

pp,cs,nn3605   cs,nn1366   nn4714 ad3966 aj3515   pp,pl,nn,pnx**6440**   qpf**1961** ptn**3808**

all   the coasts of Egypt: very grievous *were they;* before them there were no

ad**3651** nn697   pp,pnx   ptn**3808** wcj,pr,pnx310   qmf**1961** ad**3651**

such locusts as they, neither after them shall be such.

wcs,pimf**3680** (853)   cs,nn**5869**   cs,nn3605 df,nn**776**   df,nn**776**

15 For they covered   the face of the whole earth, so that the land was

wcs,qmf**2821**   wcs,qmf398 (853) cs,nn3605 cs,nn**6212**   df,nn**776** wcj(853) cs,nn3605   cs,nn**6529**

darkened; and they did eat   every herb of the land, and   all the fruit

df,nn6086 pnl834   df,nn1259   hipf**3498**   nipf**3498** wcj,ptn**3808** cs,nn3605   nn3418

of the trees which the hail had left: and there remained not   any green thing

dfp,nn6086   wcj,pp,cs,nn**6212**   df,nn**7704**   pp,cs,nn3605 cs,nn**776** nn4714

in the trees, or in the   herbs of the field, through all   the land of Egypt.

nn6547 pp,qnc**7121**   pp,nn4872   wcj,pp,nn175 wcs,pimf4116   wcs,qmf**559**

16 Then Pharaoh called for Moses and Aaron in haste; and he said, I have

qpf**2398**   pp,nn**3068**   pl,nn,pnx**430**   wcj,pp,pnx

sinned against the Lᴏʀᴅ your God, and against you.

wcj,ad6258   qmv**5375** pte**4994**   nn,pnx**2403** ad389 df,nn**6471**   wcj,himv**6279**

17 Now therefore forgive, I*pray*thee, my sin only this once, and entreat

pp,nn**3068** pl,nn,pnx**430**   wcj,hicj**5493** pr4480/pr,pnx5921 df,pndm2088 (853) df,nn**4194** ad7535

the Lᴏʀᴅ your God, that he may take away   from me this   death only.

wcs,qmf3318 pr4480/pr5973 nn6547   wcs,qmf**6279**/pr413   nn**3068**

18 And he went out from   Pharaoh, and entreated the Lᴏʀᴅ.

nn**3068** wcs,qmf**2015** ad3966 aj**2389** nn3220 cs,nn**7307**   wcs,qmf**5375** (853)

19 And the Lᴏʀᴅ turned a mighty strong west wind, which took away   the

df,nn697   wcs,qmf,pnx**8628**   nn5488 nn,lh3220   nipf**7604** ptn**3808** nu259 nn697

locusts, and   cast   them into the Red sea; there remained not one locust in

pp,cs,nn3605   cs,nn1366   nn4714

all   the coasts of Egypt.

nn3068   wcs,pimf2388 (853)   nn6547   cs,nn3820   wcj,ptn3808   (853)

20 But the LORD hardened   Pharaoh's heart, so that he would   not   let

pl,cs,nn1121   nn3478 pipf7971

the children of Israel go.

Three Days of Darkness

nn3068   wcs,qmf559 pr413   nn4872   qmv5186   nn,pnx3027 pr5921   df,du,nn8064

21 And the LORD said unto Moses, Stretch out thine hand toward heaven,

wcj,qcj1961   nn2822   pr5921   cs,nn776   nn4714   nn2822

that there may   be   darkness over the land of Egypt, even darkness *which* may be

wcj,himf4959

felt.

nn4872   wcs,qmf5186 (853)   nn,pnx3027 pr5921 df,du,nn8064   wcs,qmf1961

22 And Moses stretched forth   his hand toward heaven; and there was a

cs,nn653   nn2822   pp,cs,nn3605   cs,nn776   nn4714 cs,nu7969 pl,nn3117

thick darkness in   all   the land of Egypt three days:

qpf7200 ptn3808 nn376 (853) nn,pnx251   wcj,ptn3808 qpf6965 nn376   pr4480/pr,pnx8478   cs,nu7969

23 They saw not one   another, neither rose any from*his*place for three

pl,nn3117   wcj,pp,cs,nn3605   pl,cs,nn1121   nn3478 qpf1961 nn216   pp,pl,nn,pnx4186

days: but   all   the children of Israel had light in their dwellings.

nn6547   wcs,qmf7121 pr413   nn4872   wcs,qmf559 qmv1980   qmv5647 (853)   nn3068

24 And Pharaoh called unto Moses, and said,   Go ye, serve   the LORD;

ad7535   nn,pnx6629   wcj,nn,pnx1241   homf3322   nn,pnx2945   ad1571 qmf1980

only let your flocks and your   herds   be stayed: let your little ones also   go

pr,pnx5973

with you.

nn4872   wcs,qmf559 pnp859   qmf5414 pp,nn,pnx3027 ad1571   pl,nn2077

25 And   Moses   said, Thou must give   us   also sacrifices and

wcj,pl,nn5930   wcs,qpf6213   pp,nn3068   pl,nn,pnx430

burnt offerings, that we may sacrifice unto the LORD our God.

nn,pnx4735 wcj,ad1571   qmf1980 pr,pnx5973   ptn3808   nn6541

26 Our cattle also shall go with us; there shall not a hoof be

nimf7604   cj3588 pr,pnx4480   qmf3947 pp,qnc5647 (853)   nn3068   pl,nn,pnx430 wcj,pnp587

left behind; for thereof must we take to serve   the LORD our God; and we

qmf3045 ptn3808   pnid4100   qmf5647 (853)   nn3068 pr5704 qnc,pnx935 ad,lh8033

know not with what we must serve   the LORD, until we come thither.

nn3068   wcs,pimf2388 (853)   nn6547   cs,nn3820   qpf14   wcj,ptn3808

27 But the LORD hardened   Pharaoh's heart, and he would   not   let them

pp,pinc,pnx7971

go.

nn6547   wcs,qmf559   pp,pnx   qmv1980   pr4480/pr,pnx5921   nimv8104

28 And Pharaoh said unto him, Get thee   from   me, take heed

pp,pnx   qnc7200 pl,nn,pnx6440 ptn408 hicj3254 cj3588   pp,cs,nn3117 qnc,pnx7200 pl,nn,pnx6440

to thyself, see my face no more; for in *that* day thou seest my face

qmf4191

thou shalt die.

nn4872   wcs,qmf559   pipf1696 ad3651   qnc7200   nn,pnx6440 himf3254 ptn3808

29 And Moses said, Thou hast spoken well, I will see thy face again no

ad5750

more.

All Firstborn Must Die

11 ⁿⁿ³⁰⁶⁸ ^{wcs,qmf559} ^{pr413} ⁿⁿ⁴⁸⁷² ^{ad5750} ^{himf935} ^{nu259} ⁿⁿ⁵⁰⁶¹
And the LORD said unto Moses, Yet will I bring one plague *more*
^{pr5921} ⁿⁿ⁶⁵⁴⁷ ^{wcj,pr5921} ⁿⁿ⁴⁷¹⁴ ^{ad310/ad3651} ^{pnx(853)} ^{pimf7971}
upon Pharaoh, and upon Egypt; afterwards he will let you go
^{pr4480/pndm2088} ^{pp,pinc,pnx7971} ^{pina1644/pimf1644/pnx(853)} ^{pr4480/pndm2088}
hence: when he shall let *you* go, he shall surely*thrust*you*out hence
^{ad3617}
altogether.

^{pimv1696} ^{pte4994} ^{pp,du,cs,nn241} ^{df,nn5971} ⁿⁿ³⁷⁶ ^{wcj,qmf7592} ^{pr4480/pr854}
2 Speak now in the ears of the people, and let every man borrow of
^{nn,pnx7453} ^{wcj,nn802} ^{pr4480/pr854} ^{nn,pnx7468} ^{pl,cs,nn3627} ⁿⁿ³⁷⁰¹ ^{wcj,pl,cs,nn3627}
his neighbor, and every woman of her neighbor, jewels of silver, and jewels
ⁿⁿ²⁰⁹¹
of gold.

ⁿⁿ³⁰⁶⁸ ^{wcs,qmf5414} ^{df,nn5971} ⁽⁸⁵³⁾ ^{cs,nn2580} ^{pp,du,cs,nn5869} ⁿⁿ⁴⁷¹⁴
3 And the LORD gave the people favor in the sight of the Egyptians.
^{ad1571} ^{df,nn376} ⁿⁿ⁴⁸⁷² ^{ad3966} ^{aj1419} ^{pp,cs,nn776} ⁿⁿ⁴⁷¹⁴ ^{pp,du,cs,nn5869}
Moreover the man Moses *was* very great in the land of Egypt, in the sight of
ⁿⁿ⁶⁵⁴⁷ ^{pl,cs,nn5650} ^{wcj,pp,du,cs,nn5869} ^{df,nn5971}
Pharaoh's servants, and in the sight of the people.

ⁿⁿ⁴⁸⁷² ^{wcs,qmf559} ^{ad3541} ^{qpf559} ⁿⁿ³⁰⁶⁸ ^{pp,cs,nn2676/df,nn3915} ^{pnp589} ^{qpta3318}
4 And Moses said, Thus saith the LORD, About midnight will I go out
^{pp,cs,nn8432} ⁿⁿ⁴⁷¹⁴
into the midst of Egypt:

^{cs,nn3605} ⁿⁿ¹⁰⁶⁰ ^{pp,cs,nn776} ⁿⁿ⁴⁷¹⁴ ^{wcj,qpf4191} ^{pr4480/cs,nn1060}
5 And all the firstborn in the land of Egypt shall die, from*the*firstborn
ⁿⁿ⁶⁵⁴⁷ ^{df,qpta3427} ^{pr5921} ^{nn,pnx3678} ^{pr5704} ^{cs,nn1060} ^{df,nn8198}
of Pharaoh that sitteth upon his throne, even unto the firstborn of the maidservant
^{pnl834} ^{pr310} ^{df,du,nn7347} ^{wcj,cs,nn3605} ^{cs,nn1060} ⁿⁿ⁹²⁹
that *is* behind the mill; and all the firstborn of beasts.

^{wcj,qpf1961} ^{aj1419} ⁿⁿ⁶⁸¹⁸ ^{pp,cs,nn3605} ^{cs,nn776} ⁿⁿ⁴⁷¹⁴
6 And there shall be a great cry throughout all the land of Egypt,
^{pnl834} ^{nipf1961} ^{ptn3808} ^{pp,pnx3644} ^{ptn3808} ^{wcj,pp,pnx3644} ^{himf3254}
such as there was none like it, nor shall be like it any more.

^{wcj,pp,cs,nn3605} ^{pl,cs,nn1121} ⁿⁿ³⁴⁷⁸ ^{ptn3808} ⁿⁿ³⁶¹¹ ^{qmf2782}
7 But against any of the children of Israel shall not a dog move his
^{nn,pnx3956} ^{pp,pr4480/nn376} ^{wcj,cj5704} ⁿⁿ⁹²⁹ ^{pp,pr4616} ^{qmf3045} ^{pnl834} ⁿⁿ³⁰⁶⁸
tongue, against man or beast: that ye may know how that the LORD doth
^{himf6395} ^{pr996} ⁿⁿ⁴⁷¹⁴ ^{wcj(pr996)} ⁿⁿ³⁴⁷⁸
put*a*difference between the Egyptians and Israel.

^{cs,nn3605} ^{pndm428} ^{pl,nn,pnx5650} ^{wcs,qpf3381} ^{pr,pnx413}
8 And all these thy servants shall come down unto me, and
^{wcs,htpf*7812} ^{pp,pnx} ^{pp,qnc559} ^{qmv3318/pnp859} ^{wcj,cs,nn3605} ^{df,nn5971} ^{pnl834}
bow*down*themselves unto me, saying, Get*thee*out, and all the people that
^{pp,du,nn,pnx7272} ^{wcj,ad310} ^{ad3651} ^{qmf3318} ^{wcs,qmf3318} ^{pr4480/pr5973} ⁿⁿ⁶⁵⁴⁷
follow thee: and after that I will go out. And he went out from Pharaoh in a
^{pp,cs,nn2750} ⁿⁿ⁶³⁹
great anger.

ⁿⁿ³⁰⁶⁸ ^{wcs,qmf559} ^{pr413} ⁿⁿ⁴⁸⁷² ⁿⁿ⁶⁵⁴⁷ ^{ptn3808} ^{qmf8085} ^{pr,pnx413}
9 And the LORD said unto Moses, Pharaoh shall not hearken unto you;
^{pp,pr4616} ^{pl,nn,pnx4159} ^{qnc7235} ^{pp,cs,nn776} ⁿⁿ⁴⁷¹⁴
that my wonders may be multiplied in the land of Egypt.

^{wcj,nn4872} ^{wcj,nn175} ^{qpf6213} ⁽⁸⁵³⁾ ^{cs,nn3605} ^{df,pndm428} ^{df,pl,nn4159} ^{pp,pl,cs,nn6440} ⁿⁿ⁶⁵⁴⁷
10 And Moses and Aaron did all these wonders before Pharaoh: and

nn3068   wcs,pimf**2388**   (853)   nn6547   cs,nn**3820**   wcj,ptn**3808**   (853)   pl,cs,nn**1121**

the LORD hardened   Pharaoh's heart, so that he would   not   let   the children

nn3478   pipf7971   pr4480/nn,pnx**776**

of Israel   go   out*of*his*land.

The Passover

nn3068   wcs,qmf**559**   pr413   nn4872   wcj(pr413)   nn175   pp,cs,nn**776**

12 And the LORD spoke unto Moses and   Aaron in the   land   of

nn4714   pp,qnc**559**

Egypt, saying,

df,pndm2088   df,nn2320   pp,pnx   cs,nn**7218**   pl,nn2320   pnp1931

2 This   month *shall be* unto you the beginning of months: it   *shall be* the

aj**7223**   pp,pl,cs,nn2320   df,nn8141   pp,pnx

first   month   of the   year   to you.

pimv**1696**   pr413   cs,nn3605   cs,nn**5712**   nn3478   pp,qnc**559**   dfp,nn6218

3 Speak ye unto   all   the congregation of Israel, saying, In the   tenth   *day* of

df,pndm2088   dfp,nn2320   wcj,qmf3947   pp,pnx   nn**376**   nn7716

this   month they shall   take   to them every man a lamb, according to the

pp,cs,nn**1004**   pl,nn1   nn7716   dfp,nn**1004**

house of *their* fathers, a lamb for a house:

wcj,cj518   df,nn**1004**   qmf4591   pr4480/qnc**1961**/pr4480/nn7716   pnp1931

4 And   if   the household be*too*little   for*the*lamb,   let   him   and   his

wcj,aj,pnx**7934**   df,aj7138   pr413   nn,pnx**1004**   wcs,qpf3947   pp,cs,nn**4373**   pl,nn**5315**

neighbor next unto his house   take   *it* according to the number of the souls;

nn**376**   pp,cs,nn**6310**   nn,pnx400   qmf3699   pr5921   df,nn**7716**

every man according to his eating shall make your count for the lamb.

pp,pnx   nn7716   qmf**1961**   aj**8549**   nn2145   cs,nn**1121** nn8141

5 Your lamb shall   be   without blemish, a male of the   first   year: ye shall

qmf3947   pr4480   df,pl,nn3532   wcj,pr4480   df,pl,nn5795

take*it*out from the sheep, or from the goats:

pp,pnx   wcs,qpf**1961**/pp,nn**4931**   pr5704   nu702/nu6240   nn**3117**   df,pndm2088

6 And ye shall   keep   it up until the fourteenth day of the   same

dfp,nn2320   cs,nn3605   cs,nn**6951**   cs,nn**5712**   nn3478   wcs,qpf**7819** pnx(853)   pr996

month: and the whole assembly of the congregation of Israel shall   kill   it in

df,du,nn6153

the evening.

wcs,qpf3947   pr4480   df,nn**1818**   wcs,qpf**5414**   pr5921   du,cs,nu8147   df,pl,nn4201

7 And they shall   take   of the blood, and strike *it* on the   two   side posts

wcj,pr5921   df,nn4947   pr5921   df,pl,nn**1004**   pnl834/pp,pnx   qmf398 pnx(853)

and   on   the upper*door*post of the houses, wherein they shall eat   it.

wcs,qpf398   (853)   df,nn**1320**   df,pndm2088   dfp,nn**3915**   cs,nn6748   nn784

8 And they shall   eat   the flesh in   that   night, roast with fire, and

wcj,pl,nn**4682**   pr5921   pl,nn4844   qmf,pnx398

unleavened bread; *and* with bitter *herbs* they shall   eat   it.

qmf398   ptn408   pr,pnx4480   aj4995   wcj,aj1311/pupt1310   dfp,nn**4325** cj3588/cj518   cs,nn6748   nn784

9 Eat not   of   it raw, nor sodden*at*all with   water,   but   roast *with* fire;

nn,pnx**7218**   pr5921   du,nn,pnx3767   wcj,pr5921   nn,pnx**7130**

his head with his   legs,   and with the purtenance thereof.

12:2 The Jewish calendar, which is based on lunar months, had its beginning at this time. The first month was called Abib (Ex. 13:4) up until the Babylonian Captivity. After that time it was called Nisan (see Neh. 2:1; Esth. 3:7). On modern calendars it corresponds to the latter part of March and the first part of April.

wcj,ptn**3808**   pr,pnx4480   himf**3498**   pr5704   nn1242

10 And ye shall let nothing   of   it remain until the morning; and that which

wcj,df,nipt**3498**   pr,pnx4480   pr5704   nn1242   qmf**8313**   dfp,nn784

remaineth   of   it until the morning ye shall burn with fire.

wcj,ad3602   qmf398 pnx(853)   du,nn,pnx4975   pl,qptp2296   pl,nn,pnx5275

11 And thus shall ye eat   it; *with* your loins girded, your shoes on

pp,du,nn,pnx7272   wcj,nn,pnx4731   pp,nn,pnx**3027**   wcs,qpf398 pnx(853)

your feet,   and your   staff   in your hand; and ye shall   eat   it in

pp,nn2649 pnp1931   pp,nn**3068**   nn**6453**

haste: it *is* the LORD's passover.

wcs,qpf**5674**   pp,cs,nn776   nn4714   df,pndm2088 dfp,nn**3915**   wcs,hipf**5221**

12 For I will pass through the land of Egypt this   night, and will smite

cs,nn3605   nn1060   pp,cs,nn776   nn4714   pr4480/nn**120**   wcj(pr5704)   nn929

all   the firstborn in the   land of Egypt, both man and   beast; and against

wcj,pp,cs,nn3605   pl,cs,nn**430**   nn4714   qmf**6213**   pl,nn**8201**   pnp589   nn**3068**

all   the gods of Egypt I will execute judgment: I *am* the LORD.

df,nn1818   wcs,qpf**1961**   pp,pnx   pp,nn226   pr5921   df,pl,nn**1004**   pnl834   pnp859

13 And the blood shall   be   to you for a token upon the houses where ye

(ad8033)   wcs,qpf**7200** (853)   df,nn**1818**   wcs,qpf**6452** pr,pnx5921   nn5063

are: and when I   see   the blood, I will   pass   over you, and the plague

wcj,ptn**3808** qmf**1961**   pp,pnx   pp,nn**4889**   pp,hinc,pnx**5221**   pp,cs,nn776   nn4714

shall not   be upon you to destroy *you*, when I   smite   the land of Egypt.

df,pndm2088 df,nn**3117**   wcs,qpf**1961**   pp,pnx   pp,pl,nn,pnx**1755**   qmf,pnx2287

14 And   this   day shall   be   unto you for a memorial; and ye shall   keep

pnx(853)   nn2282   pp,nn**3068**   pp,pl,nn,pnx**1755**   qmf,pnx2287

it a feast to the LORD throughout your generations; ye shall keep*it*a*feast by

cs,nn2708   nn**5769**

an ordinance forever.

cs,nu7651   pl,nn**3117**   qmf398   pl,nn**4682**   ad389   df,aj**7223** dfp,nn**3117**

15 Seven days shall ye eat unleavened bread; even the first   day   ye shall

himf**7673**   nn7603   pr4480/pl,nn,pnx**1004**   cj3588   cs,nn3605   qpta398   nn**2557**

put away   leaven out*of*your*houses: for   whosoever eateth leavened bread

pr4480/df,aj**7223**/cs,nn3117   pr5704   df,nuor7637 cs,nn**3117** df,pndm1931 df,nn**5315**   wcs,nipf**3772**   pr4480/nn3478

from*the*first*day until the seventh day,   that   soul shall be cut off from Israel.

df,aj**7223** wcj,dfp,nn**3117**   nn**6944**   nn**4744**

16 And in the first   day   *there shall be* a holy convocation, and in the

df,nuor7637   wcj,dfp,nn**3117**   qmf**1961**   nn**6944**   nn**4744**   pp,pnx   ptn**3808** cs,nn3605   nn**4399**

seventh   day there shall be   a holy convocation to you; no manner of work

nimf**6213**   pp,pnx   ad389   pnl834 pp,cs,nn3605 nn5315   nimf398 pndm1931 pp,nn,pnx905

shall be done in them, save *that* which every man must eat, that   only   may

nimf**6213**   pp,pnx

be done of you.

wcs,qpf**8104**   (853)   df,pl,nn**4682**   cj3588   df,pndm2088

17 And ye shall observe   *the feast of* unleavened bread; for in   this

pp,cs,nn**6106**   df,nn**3117**   hipf3318/(853)/pl,nn,pnx**6635**   pr4480/cs,nn776   nn4714

selfsame   day have I brought*your*armies*out of*the*land of Egypt: therefore shall

wcs,qpf**8104** (853) df,pndm2088 df,nn**3117**   pp,pl,nn,pnx**1755**   cs,nn**2708**   nn**5769**

ye observe   this   day in your generations by an ordinance forever.

dfp,aj**7223**   pp,nu702/nu6240 nn**3117**   dfp,nn2320   dfp,nn6153

18 In the first *month*, on the fourteenth day of the month at even, ye shall

qmf398   pl,nn**4682**   pr5704   df,nu259   wcj,pl,nu6242 cs,nn**3117**   dfp,nn2320   dfp,nn6153

eat unleavened bread, until the one and twentieth day of the month at even.

cs,nu7651   pl,nn**3117**   ptn3808   nn7603   nimf4672   pp,pl,nn,pnx**1004** cj3588

19 Seven days shall there be   no   leaven found in your   houses: for

cs,nn3605   qpta398   nn**2557**   df,pndm1931 df,nn**5315**   wcs,nipf**3772**

whosoever eateth that which is leavened, even   that   soul shall be cut off pr4480/cs,nn**5712**   nn**3478**   dfp,nn**1616**   wcj,pp,cs,nn**249**   df,nn**776**

from*the*congregation of Israel, whether he be a stranger, or born in the land.

qmf**398**   cs,nn3605/ptn**3808**   nn**2557**   pp,nn**3605**   pl,nn,pnx**4186**   qmf**398**

20 Ye shall eat nothing leavened; in all your habitations shall ye eat

pl,nn**4682**

unleavened bread.

nn**4872**   wcs,qmf**7121**   pp,cs,nn**3605**   cs,aj**2205**   nn**3478**   wcs,qmf**559**   pr,pnx**413**

21 Then Moses called for all the elders of Israel, and said unto them,

qmv**4900**   wcj,qmv**3947**   pp,pnx   nn**6629**   pp,pl,nn,pnx**4940**   wcj,qmv**7819**

Draw out and take you a lamb according to your families, and kill the

df,nn**6453**

passover.

wcj,qpf**3947**   cs,nn**92**   nn**231**   wcj,qpf**2881**   dfp,nn**1818**   pnl**834**

☞ 22 And ye shall take a bunch of hyssop, and dip it in the blood that is in

dfp,nn**5592**   wcj,hipf**5060**/pr**413**   df,nn**4947**   wcj(pr**413**)   du,cs,nu**8147**   df,pl,nn**4201**   pr**4480**   df,nn**1818**

the basin, and strike the lintel and the two side posts with the blood

pnl**834**   dfp,nn**5592**   ptn**3808**/nn**376**   wcj,pnp**859**   qmf**3318**   pr**4480**/cs,nn**6607**   nn,pnx**1004**

that is in the basin; and none of you shall go out at*the*door of his house

pr**5704**   nn**1242**

until the morning.

nn**3068**   wcs,qpf**5674**   pp,qnc**5062** (853)   nn**4714**

23 For the LORD will pass through to smite the Egyptians; and when he

wcs,qpf**7200** (853)   df,nn**1818**   pr**5921**   df,nn**4947**   wcj,pr**5921**   du,cs,nu**8147**   df,pl,nn**4201**   nn**3068**

seeth the blood upon the lintel, and on the two side posts, the LORD will

wcs,qpf**6452**   pr**5921**   df,nn**6607**   wcj,ptn**3808**   qmf**5414**   df,hipf**7843**   pp,qnc**935**   pr**413**

pass over the door, and will not suffer the destroyer to come in unto your

pl,nn,pnx**1004**   pp,qnc**5062**

houses to smite you.

wcs,qpf**8104**   (853) df,pndm**2088** df,nn**1697**   pp,nn**2706**   pp,pnx

24 And ye shall observe this thing for an ordinance to thee and to thy

wcj,pp,pl,nn,pnx**1121** pr**5704**/nn**5769**

sons forever.

wcs,qpf**1961**   cj**3588**   qmf**935**   pr**413**   df,nn**776**   pnl**834**   nn**3068**

25 And it*shall*come*to*pass, when ye be come to the land which the LORD

qmf**5414**   pp,pnx   pp,pnl**834**   pipf**1696**   wcj,qpf**8104** (853) df,pndm**2063**

will give you, according as he hath promised, that ye shall keep this

df,nn**5656**

service.

wcj,qpf**1961**   cj**3588**   pl,nn,pnx**1121**   qmf**559**   pr,pnx**413**   pnit**4100**

26 And it*shall*come*to*pass, when your children shall say unto you, What

pp,pnx   df,pndm**2063**   df,nn**5656**

mean ye by this service?

wcs,qpf**559** pnp**1931**   cs,nn**2077**   pp,nn**3068**   nn**6453**   pnl**834**   qpf**6452**

27 That ye shall say, It is the sacrifice of the LORD's passover, who passed

pr**5921**   pl,cs,nn**1004**   pl,cs,nn**1121**   nn**3478**   pp,nn**4714**   pp,qnc,pnx**5062** (853)

over the houses of the children of Israel in Egypt, when he smote the

nn**4714**   hipf**5337**   wcj(853)   pl,nn,pnx**1004**   df,nn**5971**   wcs,qmf**6915**

Egyptians, and delivered our houses. And the people bowed*the*head and

wcs,himf*7812

worshiped.

☞ **12:22** Hyssop most likely refers to a group of plants such as Egyptian marjoram and thyme. The hairy stems of these plants would serve well as a brush.

pl,cs,nn1121 nn3478 wcs,qmf1980 wcs,qmf6213 pp,pnl834 nn3068

28 And the children of Israel went away, and did as the LORD had

pipf6680 (853) nn4872 wcj,nn175 ad3651 qpf6213

commanded Moses and Aaron, so did they.

The Death of the Firstborn

wcs,qmf1961   pp,cs,nn2677/df,nn3915 wcj,nn3068 hipf5221 cs,nn3605

29 And it*came*to*pass, that at midnight the LORD smote all the

nn1060 pp,cs,nn776 nn4714 pr4480/cs,nn1060 nn6547 df,qpta3427 pr5921

firstborn in the land of Egypt, from*the*firstborn of Pharaoh that sat on his

nn,pnx3678 pr5704 cs,nn1060 df,nn7628 pnl834 pp,cs,nn1004/df,nn953 wcj,cs,nn3605

throne unto the firstborn of the captive that *was* in the dungeon; and all the

cs,nn1060 nn929

firstborn of cattle.

nn6547 wcs,qmf6965 nn3915 pnp1931 wcj,cs,nn3605 pl,nn,pnx5650

30 And Pharaoh rose up in the night, he, and all his servants, and

wcj,cs,nn3605 nn4714 wcs,qmf1961 aj1419 nn6818 pp,nn4714 cj3588 ptn369

all the Egyptians; and there was a great cry in Egypt; for *there was* not a

nn1004 pnl834/ad8033 ptn369 qpta4191

house where *there was* not one dead.

wcs,qmf7121 pp,nn4872 wcj,pp,nn175 nn3915 wcs,qmf559 qmv6965

31 And he called for Moses and Aaron by night, and said, Rise up, *and*

qmv3318 pr4480/cs,nn8432 nn,pnx5971 ad1571 pnp859 ad1571 pl,cs,nn1121 nn3478

get*you*forth from among my people, both ye and the children of Israel; and

wcj,qmv1980 qmv5647 (853) nn3068 pp,pinc,pnx1696

go, serve the LORD, as ye have said.

ad1571 qmv3947 nn,pnx6629 ad1571 nn,pnx1241 pp,pnl834 pipf1696 wcj,qmv1980

32 Also take your flocks and your herds, as ye have said, and be gone;

wcj,pipf1288 pnx(853) ad1571

and bless me also.

nn4714 wcs,qmf2388 pr5921 df,nn5971

33 And the Egyptians were urgent upon the people, that they might

pp,pinc,pnx7971 pr4480 df,nn776 pp,pinc4116 cj3588 qpf559 nn,pnx3605 pl,qpta4191

send*them*out of the land in haste; for they said, We *be* all dead *men.*

df,nn5971 wcs,qmf5375 (853) nn,pnx1217 ad2962 qmf2556

34 And the people took their dough before it was leavened, their

pl,nn,pnx4863 pl,qptp6887 pp,pl,nn,pnx8071 pr5921 nn,pnx7926

kneading troughs being bound up in their clothes upon their shoulders.

wcj,pl,cs,nn1121 nn3478 qpf6213 pp,cs,nn1697 nn4872

35 And the children of Israel did according to the word of Moses; and they

wcs,qmf7592 pr4480/nn4714 pl,cs,nn3627 nn3701 wcj,pl,cs,nn3627 nn2091 wcj,pl,nn8071

borrowed of*the*Egyptians jewels of silver, and jewels of gold, and raiment:

wcj,nn3068 qpf5414 df,nn5971 (853) nn2580 pp,du,cs,nn5869 nn4714

36 And the LORD gave the people favor in the sight of the Egyptians, so

wcs,himf,pnx7592 wcs,pimf5337 (853)

that they lent unto them *such things as they required.* And they spoiled the

nn4714

Egyptians.

The Long Trip Begins

<pre>
        pl,cs,nn1121   nn3478   wcs,qmf5265   pr4480/nn7486   nn,lh5523   pp,nu8337
</pre>
37 And the children of Israel journeyed from Rameses to Succoth, about   six

<pre>
pl,nu3967   nu505   aj7273   df,pl,nn1397 pp,nn905 pr4480/nn2945
</pre>
hundred thousand on foot *that were* men, beside children.

<pre>
              nn6154   aj7227   qpf5927   wcj,ad1571 pr,pnx854   wcj,nn6629   wcj,nn1241
</pre>
38 And a mixed multitude went up   also   with them; and flocks, and herds,

<pre>
   ad3966   aj3515   nn4735
</pre>
even very much cattle.

<pre>
           wcs,qmf644   pl,nn4682   pl,cs,nn5692   (853)   df,nn1217   pnl834
</pre>
39 And they baked unleavened cakes of   the   dough which they

<pre>
hipf3318   pr4480/nn4714   cj3588   ptn3808/qpf2556   cj3588   pupf1644
</pre>
brought forth out*of*Egypt, for it was*not*leavened; because they were thrust out

<pre>
pr4480/nn4714   qpf3201   wcj,ptn3808 pp,htnc*4102 wcj,ad1571/ptn3808   qpf6213   pp,pnx
</pre>
of Egypt, and could not   tarry,   neither   had they prepared for themselves

<pre>
   nn6720
</pre>
any victual.

<pre>
           wcj,cs,nn4186   pl,cs,nn1121   nn3478 pnl834 qpf3427   pp,nn4714   wcj,nu702
</pre>
☙ 40 Now the sojourning of the children of Israel, who dwelt in Egypt, *was* four

<pre>
pl,cs,nu3967 (nn8141)   nu7970   nn8141
</pre>
hundred   and thirty years.

<pre>
            wcs,qmf1961   pr4480/cs,nn7093   wcj,nu702 pl,cs,nu3967 (nn8141)   nu7970   nn8141
</pre>
41 And it*came*to*pass at*the*end of the four hundred   and thirty years,

<pre>
       df,pndm2088/pp,cs,nn6106 df,nn3117   wcs,qmf1961   cs,nn3605   pl,cs,nn6635   nn3068
</pre>
even the   selfsame   day it*came*to*pass, that all   the hosts of the LORD

<pre>
qpf3318   pr4480/cs,nn776   nn4714
</pre>
went out from*the*land of Egypt.

<pre>
      pnp1931   cs,nn3915   pl,nn8107   pp,nn3068   pp,hinc,pnx3318
</pre>
42 It *is* a night to be*much*observed unto the LORD for bringing*them*out

<pre>
pr4480/cs,nn776   nn4714   df,pndm2088   pnp1931   df,nn3915   pp,nn3068   pl,nn8107
</pre>
from*the*land of Egypt: this   *is* that night of the LORD to be observed of

<pre>
pp,cs,nn3605   pl,cs,nn1121   nn3478   pp,pl,nn,pnx1755
</pre>
all   the children of Israel in their generations.

<pre>
             nn3068 wcs,qmf559 pr413   nn4872   wcj,nn175 pndm2063   cs,nn2708
</pre>
43 And the LORD said unto Moses and Aaron, This *is* the ordinance of the

<pre>
df,nn6453   ptn3808/cs,nn3605 cs,nn1121/nn5236 qmf398   pp,pnx
</pre>
passover: There shall   no   stranger eat thereof:

<pre>
wcj,cs,nn3605   nn376   nn5650   cs,nn4736   nn3701
</pre>
44 But every man's servant that is bought for money, when thou hast

<pre>
wcs,qpf4135   pnx(853)   ad227   qmf398   pp,pnx
</pre>
circumcised   him, then shall he eat thereof.

<pre>
      nn8453   wcj,aj7916   ptn3808 qmf398   pp,pnx
</pre>
45 A foreigner and a hired servant shall not eat thereof.

<pre>
   nu259 pp,nn1004   nimf398   ptn3808   himf3318   pr4480   df,nn1320
</pre>
☙ 46 In one house shall it be eaten; thou shalt not carry forth aught of the flesh

<pre>
nn,lh2351   pr4480   df,nn1004 ptn3808   qmf7665   wcj,nn6106 pp,pnx
</pre>
abroad out of the house; neither shall ye break a bone thereof.

<pre>
     cs,nn3605   cs,nn5712   nn3478   qmf6213 pnx(853)
</pre>
47 All the congregation of Israel shall keep   it.

☙ **12:40** The Samaritan Pentateuch and the Septuagint add the words "and in the land of Canaan" after "Egypt." See the note on Genesis 15:13–16.

☙ **12:46** In this verse and in Numbers 9:12, the breaking of the lamb's bones is forbidden. This passage, not Psalm 34:20, is the reference that is fulfilled in John 19:36, where Jesus' legs were not broken. In a passage reminiscent of Exodus chapter twelve, Paul refers to Jesus as the Christians' Passover Lamb (1 Cor. 5:7).

wcj,qmv,pnx1234   pl,cs,nn1121   nn3478   wcj,qmf935   dfp,nn3004
and   divide   it: and the children of Israel shall   go   on   dry   *ground* through the

pp,cs,nn8432   df,nn3220
midst of the sea.

wcj,pnp589 ptdm,pnx2009   pipt2388   (853)   cs,nn3820   nn4714
17 And   I,   behold, I will harden   the hearts of the Egyptians, and they

wcj,qmf935/pr,pnx310   wcj,nicj3513   pp,nn6547   wcj,pp,cs,nn3605
shall   follow   them: and I will get*me*honor upon Pharaoh, and upon   all

nn,pnx2428   pp,nn,pnx7393   wcj,pp,pl,nn,pnx6571
his host, upon his chariots, and upon his   horsemen.

nn4714   wcs,qpf3045   cj3588 pnp589   nn3068
18 And the Egyptians shall   know   that   I   *am* the LORD, when I have

pp,ninc,pnx3513   pp,nn6547   pp,nn,pnx7393   wcj,pp,pl,nn,pnx6571
gotten*me*honor upon Pharaoh, upon his chariots, and upon his horsemen.

cs,nn4397   df,pl,nn430   df,qpta1980 pp,pl,cs,nn6440   cs,nn4264   nn3478   wcs,qmf5265
19 And the angel of God, which went   before   the camp of Israel, removed

wcs,qmf1980   pr4480/pr,pnx310   cs,nn5982   df,nn6051   wcs,qmf5265
and   went   behind   them;   and   the   pillar   of   the   cloud   went

pr4480/pl,nn,pnx6440   wcs,qmf5975 pr4480/pr,pnx310
from*before*their*face, and   stood   behind   them:

wcs,qmf935   pr996   cs,nn4264   nn4714   wcj(pr996)   cs,nn4264
20 And it came between the camp of the Egyptians and   the camp of

nn3478   wcs,qmf1961   df,nn6051   wcj,df,nn2822   wcs,himf215   (853)   df,nn3915
Israel; and it   was   a cloud and darkness *to them*, but it gave light   by night *to*

pndm2088 qpf7126/wcj,ptn3808   (pr413)   pndm2088 cs,nn3605   df,nn3915
these: so that the   one   came*not*near   the other   all   the night.

nn4872   wcs,qmf5186   (853)   nn,pnx3027 pr5921   df,nn3220   nn3068
21 And Moses stretched out   his   hand over the sea; and the LORD caused

(853)   df,nn3220   wcs,himf1980   aj5794 nn6921 pp,cs,nn7307 cs,nn3605   df,nn3915   wcs,qmf7760
the sea to   go   *back* by a strong east wind   all   that night, and   made

(853)   df,nn3220 dfp,nn2724   df,pl,nn4325   wcs,nimf1234
the sea   dry *land*, and the waters were divided.

pl,cs,nn1121   nn3478 wcs,qmf935   pp,cs,nn8432   df,nn3220
22 And the children of Israel   went   into the   midst   of the   sea   upon the

dfp,nn3004   wcj,df,pl,nn4325   nn2346   pp,pnx   pr4480/nn,pnx3225
dry *ground*: and the   waters   *were* a wall unto them on*their*right*hand, and

wcj,pr4480/nn,pnx8040
on*their*left.

nn4714   wcs,qmf7291   wcs,qmf935   pr,pnx310   pr413   cs,nn8432
23 And the Egyptians pursued, and went in after them to the midst of the

df,nn3220   cs,nn3605   nn6547   cs,nn5483   nn,pnx7393   wcj,pl,nn,pnx6571
sea, *even* all   Pharaoh's horses, his chariots, and his horsemen.

wcs,qmf1961   df,nn1242   pp,cs,nn821   nn3068   wcs,himf8259 pr413
24 And it*came*to*pass, that in the morning watch the LORD looked unto the

cs,nn4264   nn4714   pp,cs,nn5982   nn784   wcj,nn6051   wcs,qmf2000 (853)
host of the Egyptians through the   pillar   of fire and of the cloud, and troubled

cs,nn4264   nn4714
the host of the Egyptians,

wcs,himf5493 (853)   pl,nn,pnx4818 cs,nn212   wcs,pimf,pnx5090   pp,nn3517
25 And took off   their chariot wheels, that they   drove   them heavily: so

nn4714   wcs,qmf559   qcj5127   pr4480/pl,cs,nn6440   nn3478 cj3588   nn3068   nipt3898
that the Egyptians said, Let us flee from*the*face of Israel; for the LORD fighteth

pp,pnx   pp,nn4714
for them against the Egyptians.

nn3068 wcs,qmf559 pr413   nn4872   qmv5186   (853)   nn,pnx3027 pr5921   df,nn3220
26 And the LORD said unto Moses, Stretch out   thine hand over the sea,

df,pl,nn4325   wcj,qmf7725   pr5921   nn4714   pr5921   nn,pnx7393   wcj,pr5921
that the waters may come again upon the Egyptians, upon their chariots, and upon

pl,nn,pnx6571
their horsemen.

nn4872   wcs,qmf5186   (853)   nn,pnx3027   pr5921   df,nn3220   df,nn3220
27 And Moses stretched forth   his hand over the   sea,   and the   sea
wcs,qmf7725   pp,aj,pnx386   nn1242   pp,qnc6437   wcj,nn4714   pl,qpta5127
returned to his strength when the morning appeared; and the Egyptians   fled
pp,qnc,pnx7125   nn3068   wcs,pimf5287   (853)   nn4714   pp,cs,nn8432   df,nn3220
against it; and the LORD overthrew   the Egyptians in the midst of the sea.

df,pl,nn4325   wcs,qmf7725   wcs,pimf3680   (853)   df,nn7393   wcj(853)
28 And the waters returned, and covered   the chariots, and   the
df,pl,nn6571   pp,cs,nn3605   cs,nn2428   nn6547   df,pl,qpta935   dfp,nn3220 pr,pnx310
horsemen, and   all   the host of Pharaoh that came into the   sea   after them;
nipf7604   ptn3808   pr5704   nu259   pp,pnx
there remained not so*much*as one of them.

wcj,pl,cs,nn1121   nn3478   qpf1980   dfp,nn3004   pp,cs,nn8432
29 But the children of Israel walked upon   dry   land in the midst of the
df,nn3220   wcj,df,pl,nn4325   nn2346   pp,pnx   pr4480/nn,pnx3225
sea;   and the   waters   were a wall unto them on*their*right*hand, and
wcj,pr4480/nn,pnx8040
on*their*left.

nn3068   wcs,himf3467   (853)   nn3478   df,pndm1931 dfp,nn3117   pr4480/cs,nn3027
30 Thus the LORD saved   Israel   that   day out*of*the*hand of the
nn4714   nn3478 wcs,qmf7200 (853)   nn4714   qpta4191 pr5921   df,nn3220 cs,nn8193
Egyptians; and Israel saw   the Egyptians dead upon the sea shore.

nn3478   wcs,qmf7200   (853)   df,aj1419 df,nn3027   pnl834   nn3068   qpf6213
31 And Israel   saw   (853)   that great work which the LORD did upon the
pp,nn4714   df,nn5971 wcs,qmf3372 (853)   nn3068   wcs,himf539   pp,nn3068
Egyptians: and the people feared   the LORD, and believed the LORD, and his
nn,pnx5650   wcj,pp,nn4872
servant Moses.

Moses' Song

ad227   qmf7891   nn4872   wcj,pl,cs,nn1121   nn3478   (853) df,pndm2063 df,nn7892
15 Then sang Moses and the children of Israel   this   song unto the
pp,nn3068   wcs,qmf559   pp,qnc559   qcj7891   pp,nn3068   cj3588
LORD, and spoke, saying, I will sing unto the LORD, for he hath
qna1342/qpf1342   nn5483   wcj,qpta,pnx7392   qpf7411   dfp,nn3220
triumphed gloriously: the horse and his   rider   hath he thrown into the sea.

nn3050   nn,pnx5797   wcj,nn2176   wcs,qmf1961 pp,pnx   pp,nn3444   pndm2088
2 The LORD is my strength and song, and he is become my salvation: he   is

---

14:30, 31 Moses had commanded Israel in verse thirteen to "stand still, and see the salvation of the Lord." The confirmation is now made that on the day that God saved them, they saw His great work and believed. He had led them into a position in which they were not able to save themselves, and they could only depend upon Him for that salvation. The deliverance of the Israelites from Egypt is a central theme throughout the Old Testament. Throughout their history the descendants of these Israelites remembered the events of that day (2 Kgs. 17:7; 2 Chr. 6:4, 5). In times of apostasy, the Lord called upon Israel to remember that work of salvation (Jer. 11:3, 4; Hos. 12:13). The story of that deliverance went before them. Forty years later, as they marched forward to possess Canaan, their adversaries remembered the demonstration of the power of their God in their flight from Egypt (Josh. 2:10).

nn,pnx**410** wcj,himf,pnx5115 nn,pnx1 pl,cs,nn**430**

my God, and I will prepare*him*a*habitation; my father's God, and I will

wcj,pimf*,pnx7311

exalt him.

nn**3068** cs,nn**376** nn4421 nn**3068** nn,pnx8034

3 The LORD *is* a man of war: the LORD *is* his name.

nn6547 pl,cs,nn4818 wcj,nn,pnx**2428** qpf**3384** dfp,nn3220 wcj,cs,nn4005

4 Pharaoh's chariots and his host hath he cast into the sea: his chosen

pl,nn,pnx**7991** pupf2883 nn5488 pp,cs,nn**3220**

captains also are drowned in the Red sea.

pl,nn**8415** pimf,pnx**3680** qpf3381 pp,pl,nn4688 pp3644 nn68

5 The depths have covered them: they sank into the bottom as a stone.

nn,pnx**3225** nn**3068** cs,nipt**142** dfp,nn3581 nn,pnx**3225**

6 Thy right hand, O LORD, is become glorious in power: thy right hand, O

nn**3068** qmf7492 qpta341

LORD, hath dashed*in*pieces the enemy.

wcj,pp,cs,nn**7230** nn,pnx1347 qmf**2040**

7 And in the greatness of thine excellency thou hast overthrown them that

pl,qpta,pnx**6965** pimf7971 nn,pnx2740 qmf,pnx398 dfp,nn7179

rose*up*against thee: thou sentest forth thy wrath, *which* consumed them as stubble.

wcj,pp,cs,nn**7307** du,nn,pnx**639** pl,nn4325 nipf**6192**

8 And with the blast of thy nostrils the waters were gathered together, the

pl,qpta5140 nipf**5324** pp3644 nn5067 pl,nn**8415** qpf7087 pp,cs,nn**3820**

floods stood upright as a heap, *and* the depths were congealed in the heart of

nn3220

the sea.

qpta341 qpf**559** qmf7291 himf5381 pimf2505 nn7998

9 The enemy said, I will pursue, I will overtake, I will divide the spoil; my

nn,pnx**5315** qmf,pnx**4390** himf7324 nn,pnx**2719** nn,pnx**3027** himf,pnx**3423**

lust shall be satisfied upon them; I will draw my sword, my hand shall destroy

them.

qpf5398 pp,nn,pnx**7307** nn3220 pipf,pnx**3680** qpf6749 dfp,nn5777

10 Thou didst blow with thy wind, the sea covered them: they sank as lead

aj**117** pp,pl,nn4325

in the mighty waters.

pnit4310 pp,pnx3644 nn**3068** dfp,pl,nn**410** pnit4310 pp,pnx3644

11 Who *is* like*unto*thee, O LORD, among the gods? who *is* like thee,

nipt**142** dfp,nn**6944** nipt**3372** pl,nn**8416** cs,qpta**6213** nn6382

glorious in holiness, fearful *in* praises, doing wonders?

qpf5186 nn,pnx3225 nn**776** qmf,pnx**1104**

12 Thou stretchedst out thy right hand, the earth swallowed them.

pp,nn,pnx**2617** qpf5148 nn5971 pnl2098 qpf**1350**

13 Thou in thy mercy hast led forth the people which thou hast redeemed:

pipf5095 pp,nn,pnx5797 pr413 nn,pnx**6944** cs,nn5116

thou hast guided *them* in thy strength unto thy holy habitation.

pl,nn**5971** qpf**8085** qmf**7264** nn2427 qpf**270**

14 The people shall hear, *and* be afraid: sorrow shall take hold on the

pl,cs,qpta**3427** nn6429

inhabitants of Philistia.

ad**227** pl,cs,nn**441** nn123 nipf**926** pl,cs,nn352 nn4124

15 Then the dukes of Edom shall be amazed; the mighty men of Moab,

nn**7461** qmf,pnx270 cs,nn3605 pl,cs,qpta**3427** nn3667

trembling shall take*hold*upon them; all the inhabitants of Canaan shall

nipf4127

melt away.

nn367   wcj,nn6343   qmf5307   pr,pnx5921   pp,cs,aj1419   nn,pnx2220

16 Fear and dread shall fall upon them; by the greatness of thine arm they

qmf1826   dfp,nn68 cj5704   nn,pnx5971   qmf5674   nn3068   cj5704   nn5971

shall be*as*still as a stone; till thy people pass over, O LORD, till the people

qmf5674   pnl2098   qpf7069

pass over, which thou hast purchased.

himf,pnx935   wcj,qmf,pnx5193   pp,cs,nn2022

17 Thou shalt bring*them*in, and plant them in the mountain of thine

nn,pnx5159   nn4349   nn3068   qpf6466   pp,qnc,pnx3427

inheritance, in the place, O LORD, which thou hast made for thee to dwell in, in the

nn4720   nn136   du,nn,pnx3027   pipf*3559

Sanctuary, O Lord, which thy hands have established.

nn3068   qmf4427 pp,nn5769   wcj,nn5703

18 The LORD shall reign forever and ever.

Miriam's Song

cj3588   cs,nn5483   nn6547   qpf935   pp,nn,pnx7393   wcj,pp,nn,pnx6571

19 For the horse of Pharaoh went in with his chariots and with his horsemen

dfp,nn3220   nn3068   wcs,himf7725   (853)   pl,cs,nn4325   df,nn3220 pr,pnx5921

into the sea, and the LORD brought again the waters of the sea upon them;

wcj,pl,cs,nn1121   nn3478 qpf1980   dfp,nn3004   pp,cs,nn8432   df,nn3220

but the children of Israel went on dry land in the midst of the sea.

nn4813   df,nn5031   cs,nn269   nn175 wcs,qmf3947 (853)   df,nn8596

20 And Miriam the prophetess, the sister of Aaron, took a timbrel in her

pp,nn,pnx3027   cs,nn3605   df,pl,nn802 wcs,qmf3318 pr,pnx310   pp,pl,nn8596   wcj,pp,pl,nn4246

hand; and all the women went out after her with timbrels and with dances.

nn4813   wcs,qmf6030   pp,pnx   qmv7891   pp,nn3068 cj3588

21 And Miriam answered them, Sing ye to the LORD, for he hath

qna1342/qpf1342   nn5483   wcj,qpta,pnx7392   qpf7411   dfp,nn3220

triumphed gloriously; the horse and his rider hath he thrown into the sea.

The Bitter Water at Marah

nn4872   wcs,himf5265 (853) nn3478   pr4480/cs,nn3220/nn5488   wcs,qmf3318   pr413

22 So Moses brought Israel from*the*Red*sea, and they went out into the

cs,nn4057   nn7793   wcs,qmf1980 cs,nu7969 pl,nn3117   dfp,nn4057   qpf4672 wcj,ptn3808

wilderness of Shur; and they went three days in the wilderness, and found no

pl,nn4325

water.

wcs,qmf935   nn,lh4785   qpf3201 wcj,ptn3808 pp,qnc8354   pl,nn4325

☙ 23 And when they came to Marah, they could not drink of the waters

pr4480/nn4785   cj3588 pnp1992   aj4751 pr5921/ad3651   nn,pnx8034   qpf7121   nn4785

of Marah, for they were bitter: therefore the name of it was called Marah.

df,nn5971   wcs,nimf3885   pr5921   nn4872   pp,qnc559 pnit4100   qmf8354

24 And the people murmured against Moses, saying, What shall we drink?

wcs,qmf6817 pr413   nn3068   nn3068 wcs,himf,pnx3384   nn6086

25 And he cried unto the LORD; and the LORD showed him a tree, which

---

☙ **15:23–25**   The Lord did not take Israel to Canaan by the most direct route. The people needed not only to observe the mighty works of His power, but also to depend upon Him in a practical way for the necessities of life. Ultimately, they needed to understand that all would be accomplished by God's own power and not by their own ability (cf. Deut. 8:2). At Marah they needed water, but that which was available was not fit for drinking until God acted. Thus, God was instructing them that even though they had been brought out of bondage and had witnessed the defeat of the Egyptian army, they must still depend on Him.

wcs,himf**7993** pr413   df,pl,nn**4325**   df,pl,nn**4325**   wcs,qmf**4985**   ad**8033**   qpf**7760**
when he had   cast   into the waters, the waters were made sweet: there he made

pp,pnx   nn**2706**   wcj,nn**4941**   wcj,ad**8033**   pipf,pnx**5254**
for them a statute and an ordinance, and there he proved them,

wcs,qmf**559** cj518   qna**8085**/qmf**8085**   pp,cs,nn**6963**   nn**3068**
26 And said, If thou wilt diligently hearken to the voice of the LORD thy

pl,nn,pnx**430**   qmf**6213**   wcj,df,aj**3477**   pp,du,nn,pnx**5869**   wcs,hipf**238**
God, and wilt do that*which*is*right in his sight, and wilt give ear to his

pp,pl,nn,pnx**4687**   wcs,qpf**8104** cs,nn**3605**   pl,nn,pnx**2706**   qpf**7760** ptn**3808**/cs,nn**3605**
commandments, and keep all his statutes, I will put none of these

df,nn**4245** pr,pnx**5921**   pnl834   qmf**7760**   pp,nn**4714** cj**3588** (pnp589)
diseases upon thee, which I have brought upon the Egyptians: for am the

nn**3068**   qpta,pnx**7495**
LORD that healeth thee.

wcs,qmf**935**   nn,lh362 wcj,ad**8033**   du,nu**8147**/nu**6240** pl,cs,nn**5869**   pl,nn**4325**
27 And they came to Elim, where were twelve wells of water, and

wcj,pl,nu**7657**   pl,nn**8558**   wcs,qmf**2583** ad**8033** pr**5921**   df,pl,nn**4325**
threescore*and*ten palm trees: and they encamped there by the waters.

Manna and Quail

wcs,qmf**5265**   pr4480/nn362   cs,nn**3605**   cs,nn**5712**
16 And they took*their*journey from Elim, and all the congregation

pl,cs,nn**1121**   nn**3478** wcs,qmf**935** pr413   cs,nn**4057**   nn**5512** pnl834
of the children of Israel came unto the wilderness of Sin, which is

pr996   nn362   wcj(pr996)   nn**5514**   dfp,nu**2508**/nu**6240** nn**3117**   df,nuor**8145** dfp,nn**2320**
between Elim and   Sinai, on the fifteenth day of the second month after

pp,qnc,pnx**3318**   pr4480/cs,nn**776**   nn**4714**
their departing out of*the*land of Egypt.

cs,nn**3605**   cs,nn**5712**   pl,cs,nn**1121**   nn**3478** wcs,nimf**3885** pr**5921**   nn**4872**
2 And the whole congregation of the children of Israel murmured against Moses

wcj(pr**5921**)   nn175   dfp,nn**4057**
and   Aaron in the wilderness:

pl,cs,nn**1121**   nn**3478** wcs,qmf**559** pr,pnx413   pnit**4310**/qmf**5414**   qnc,pnx**4191**
3 And the children of Israel said unto them, Would*to*God we had died

pp,cs,nn**3027**   nn**3068**   pp,cs,nn**776**   nn**4714**   pp,qnc,pnx**3427** pr**5921**   df,nn**1320**
by the hand of the LORD in the land of Egypt, when we sat by the flesh

cs,nn**5518**   pp,qnc,pnx398 nn**3899**   dfp,nn**7648** cj**3588**   hipf3318/pnx(853)
pots, and when we did eat bread to the full; for ye have brought*us*forth

pr413 df,pndm2088   df,nn**4057**   pp,hinc**4191** (853) df,pndm2088 cs,nn**3605**   df,nn**6951**   dfp,nn**7458**
into this wilderness, to kill this whole assembly with hunger.

wcs,qmf**559**   nn**3068** pr413   nn**4872**   ptdm,pnx2009   hipt**4305** nn**3899** pr4480 df,du,nn**8064**
4 Then said the LORD unto Moses, Behold, I will rain bread from heaven

pp,pnx   df,nn**5971**   wcj,qpf3318   wcj,qpf**3950**   cs,nn**1697**/nn**3117**/pp,nn,pnx**3117**   pp,pr4616
for you; and the people shall go out and gather a certain*rate*every*day, that I

pimf,pnx**5254**   he,qmf**1980**   pp,nn,pnx**8451** cj518 ptn**3808**
may prove them, whether they will walk in my law, or no.

wcs,qpf**1961**   df,nuor**8345** dfp,nn**3117**   wcs,hipf**3559** (853)
5 And it*shall*come*to*pass, that on the sixth day they shall prepare

pnl834   himf935   wcs,qpf**1961** nn**4932**   pr**5921**/pnl834   qmf**3950** nn**3117**/nn**3117**
that which they bring in; and it shall be twice as*much*as they gather daily.

nn**4872**   wcj,nn175 wcs,qmf**559** pr413 cs,nn**3605**   pl,cs,nn**1121**   nn**3478**   nn**6153**
6 And Moses and Aaron said unto all the children of Israel, At even, then

wcj,qpf**3045** cj**3588**   nn**3068**   hipf3318/pnx(853)   pr4480/cs,nn**776**   nn**4714**
ye shall know that the LORD hath brought*you*out from*the*land of Egypt:

wcj,nn1242   wcj,qpf7200 (853)   cs,nn3519   nn3068

7 And in the morning, then ye shall   see   the glory of the LORD; for that

pp,qnc,pnx8085 (853)   pl,nn,pnx8519   pr5921   nn3068   pnit4100   wcj,pnp5168 cj3588

he heareth   your murmurings against the LORD: and what *are*   we,   that ye

himf3885   pr,pnx5921

murmur against us?

nn4872   wcs,qmf559   nn3068   pp,qnc5414 pp,pnx

8 And Moses said,   *This shall be*, when the LORD shall   give   you in the

dfp,nn6153   nn1320   pp,qnc398   dfp,nn1242 wcj,nn3899   pp,qnc7646   nn3068

evening flesh to eat,   and in the morning bread to the full; for that the LORD

pp,qnc8085   (853)   pl,nn,pnx8519   pnl834 pnp859 pl,hipt3885   pr,pnx5921   pnit4100   wcj,pnp5168

heareth   your murmurings which   ye   murmur against him: and what *are*   we?

pl,nn,pnx8519   ptn3808 pr,pnx5921   cj3588   pr5921   nn3068

your murmurings *are* not against us, but against the LORD.

nn4872   wcs,qmf559 pr413   nn175   qmv559   pr413 cs,nn3605   cs,nn5712

9 And Moses spoke unto Aaron, Say unto   all   the congregation of the

pl,cs,nn1121   nn3478   qmv7126   pp,pl,cs,nn6440   nn3068   cj3588   qpf8085   (853)

children of Israel, Come near before   the LORD: for he hath heard   your

pl,nn,pnx8519

murmurings.

wcs,qmf1961   nn175   pp,pinc1696 pr413   cs,nn3605   cs,nn5712

10 And it*came*to*pass, as Aaron spoke unto the whole congregation of the

pl,cs,nn1121   nn3478   wcs,qmf6437   pr413   df,nn4057   wcj,ptdm2009   cs,nn3519

children of Israel, that they looked toward the wilderness, and, behold, the glory of

nn3068   nipf7200   dfp,nn6051

the LORD appeared in the cloud.

nn3068   wcs,pimf1696 pr413   nn4872   pp,qnc559

11 And the LORD spoke unto Moses, saying,

qpf8085   (853)   pl,cs,nn8519   pl,cs,nn1121   nn3478   pimv1696 pr,pnx413

12 I have heard   the murmurings of the children of Israel: speak unto them,

pp,qnc559   pr996 df,du,nn6153   qmf398   nn1320   wcj,dfp,nn1242   qmf7646

saying, At   even   ye shall eat flesh, and in the morning ye shall be filled with

nn3899   wcs,qpf3045 cj3588 pnp589   nn3068   pl,nn,pnx430

bread; and ye shall know that   I   *am* the LORD your God.

wcs,qmf1961   dfp,nn6153   df,nn7958   wcs,qmf5927   wcs,pimf3680 (853)

☞ 13 And it*came*to*pass, that at even the quails came up, and covered   the

df,nn4264   wcj,dfp,nn1242   df,nn2919 qpf1961/cs,nn7902   ad5439   dfp,nn4264

camp: and in the morning the dew   lay   round about the host.

df,nn2919   cs,nn7902   wcs,qmf5927 wcj,ptdm2009 pr5921   pl,cs,nn6440

14 And when the dew that lay was gone up, behold, upon the face of the

df,nn4057   aj1851   pupt2636   aj1851   dfp,nn3713 pr5921   df,nn776

wilderness *there lay* a small round thing, *as* small as the hoar frost on the ground.

pl,cs,nn1121   nn3478 wcs,qmf7200   wcs,qmf559 nn376 pr413   nn,pnx251 pnp1931

15 And when the children of Israel saw *it*, they said one to another, It

---

☞ **16:13-15** The events of this passage were another of the steps in building the faith of Israel. There were no resources in the Sinai wilderness to feed several million people, let alone their herds and flocks. God had provided water; He would now provide food. The provision of quail was miraculous—the birds were native to the region, but normally they could only be found in small and scattered numbers. God brought multitudes of quail, though the text does not tell how frequently this occurred. Manna differed in that it was God's daily provision from this time until Israel entered the promised land and was able to eat its crops (Josh. 5:12). Gathering the manna each day would increase Israel's dependence upon God. The amount gathered would be just sufficient (Ex. 16:18), confirming God's personal care. There is no natural way to explain the nature of manna; it was truly "bread from heaven." Manna was a type of Jesus, who is "Bread of life" (John 6:32-35).

nn**4478**   cj3588   qpf**3045**   ptn**3808** pnid4100 pnp1931   nn4872   wcs,qmf**559** pr,pnx413   pnp1931
is manna: for they knew not what   it   *was*. And Moses   said   unto them, This

df,nn3899   pnl834   nn**3068**   qpf**5414**   pp,pnx   pp,nn402
is the bread which the LORD hath given you to eat.

pndm2088   df,nn**1697**   pnl834   nn**3068**   pipf**6680**   qmf3950   pr,pnx4480
16 This   *is* the thing which the LORD hath commanded, Gather   of   it

nn376   pp,cs,nn**6310**   nn,pnx400   nn6016   dfp,nn**1538**
every man according to his eating, an omer for every man, *according to* the

cs,nn4557   pl,nn,pnx**5315** qmf3947   nn376   pp,pnl834   pp,nn,pnx**168**
number of your persons; take ye every man for *them* which *are* in his tents.

pl,cs,nn**1121**   nn3478   wcs,qmf**6213** ad3651   wcs,qmf**3950**   df,hipt7235
17 And the children of Israel   did   so, and gathered, some more, some

wcj,df,hipt4591
less.

wcs,qmf4058   dfp,nn6016   df,hipt7235
18 And when they did   mete   *it* with an omer, he that gathered much

hipf5736/wcj,ptn**3808**   wcj,df,hipt4591   ptn3808   hipf2637   qpf3950
had*nothing*over, and he that gathered   little   had   no   lack; they gathered

nn376   pp,cs,nn**6310**   nn,pnx400
every man according to his eating.

nn4872   wcs,qmf**559** (pr,pnx413)   ptn408   nn376   hicj3498 pr,pnx4480   pr5704   nn1242
19 And Moses said,   Let no man leave   of   it till the morning.

qpf**8085**   wcj,ptn**3808**   pr413   nn4872   pl,nn376
20 Notwithstanding they hearkened   not   unto Moses; but some of them

wcs,himf3498 pr,pnx4480   pr5704   nn1242   wcs,qmf7311 pl,nn8438   wcs,qmf**887**   nn4872
left   of   it until the morning, and it   bred   worms, and stank: and Moses

wcs,qmf**7107**   pr,pnx5921
was wroth with them.

wcs,qmf**3950**   pnx(853)   dfp,nn1242/dfp,nn1242   nn376   pp,cs,nn**6310**
21 And they gathered   it every morning, every man according to his

nn,pnx400   df,nn8121   wcj,qpf2552   wcj,nipf4549
eating: and when the   sun   waxed hot, it melted.

wcs,qmf**1961**   df,nuor8345 dfp,nn3117   qpf3950   nn4932
22 And it*came*to*pass, *that* on the sixth   day they gathered twice*as*much

nn3899   du,cs,nu8147 df,nn6016   dfp,nu259   cs,nn3605   pl,cs,nn**5387**   df,nn**5712**
bread, two   omers for one *man*: and   all   the rulers of the congregation

wcs,qmf935   wcs,himf**5046** pp,nn4872
came and told Moses.

wcs,qmf**559** pr,pnx413   pndm1931   pnl834   nn**3068**   pipf**1696**
23 And he said   unto them, This *is that* which the LORD hath said,

nn4279   nn7677   nn**6944** cs,nn**7676**   pp,nn3068 qmv644   (853)   pnl834
Tomorrow *is* the rest of the holy sabbath unto the LORD: bake *that*   which ye will

qmf644   pimv1310 wcj(853) pnl834   pimf1310   wcj(853)   cs,nn3605   df,qpta5736
bake *today*, and seethe   that ye will seethe; and   that which remaineth over

himv5117   pp,pnx   pp,nn4931 pr5704   df,nn1242
lay up for you to be kept until the morning.

himf5117/pnx(853) pr5704   df,nn1242   pp,pnl834   nn4872   pipf**6680**   wcj,ptn**3808**
24 And they laid*it*up till the morning,   as   Moses bade: and it did   not

hipf**887**   ptn**3808** qpf**1961**   wcj,nn7415   pp,pnx
stink, neither was there any worm therein.

nn4872   wcs,qmf**559** qmv,pnx398   df,nn3117 cj3588 df,nn3117   nn7676   pp,nn3068
25 And Moses said,   Eat   that today; for today *is* a sabbath unto the LORD:

df,nn3117   ptn**3808** qmf,pnx4672   dfp,nn**7704**
today ye shall not   find   it in the field.

^{cs,nu8337 pl,nn3117}   ^{qmf,pnx3950}   ^{df,nuor7637 wcj,dfp,nn3117}

26 Six   days ye shall   gather it; but on the   seventh   day, *which is* the

ⁿⁿ⁷⁶⁷⁶   ^{pp,pnx}   ^{qmf1961}   ^{ptn3808}

sabbath, in it there shall be none.

^{wcs,qmf1961}   ^{qpf3318}   ^{pr4480}   ^{df,nn5971}

27 And it*came*to*pass, *that* there went out *some* of the people on the

^{df,nuor7637 dfp,nn3117}   ^{pp,qnc3950}   ^{qpf4672 wcj,ptn3808}

seventh day for to gather, and they found none.

ⁿⁿ³⁰⁶⁸   ^{wcs,qmf559} ^{pr413}   ⁿⁿ⁴⁸⁷²   ^{pr5704/ad,lh575} ^{pipf3985}   ^{pp,qnc8104}

28 And the LORD   said   unto Moses, How long refuse ye to keep my

^{pl,nn,pnx4687}   ^{wcj,pl,nn,pnx8451}

commandments and my   laws?

^{qmv7200 cj3588}   ⁿⁿ³⁰⁶⁸   ^{qpf5414} ^{pp,pnx}   ^{df,nn7676} ^{pr5921/ad3651} ^{pnp1931} ^{qpta5414}

29 See, for that the LORD hath given you the sabbath, therefore he   giveth

^{pp,pnx}   ^{df,nuor8345 dfp,nn3117}   ^{cs,nn3899}   ^{du,nn3117}   ^{qmv3427}   ⁿⁿ³⁷⁶   ^{pr,pnx8478}

you on the sixth   day   the bread of two days; abide ye every man in his place,

^{ptn408 nn376}   ^{qmf3318}   ^{pr4480/nn,pnx4725}   ^{df,nuor7637 dfp,nn3117}

let no man go out of*his*place on the seventh day.

^{df,nn5971 wcs,qmf7673}   ^{df,nuor7637 dfp,nn3117}

30 So the people rested on the seventh day.

^{cs,nn1004}   ⁿⁿ³⁴⁷⁸ ^{wcs,qmf7121} ⁽⁸⁵³⁾   ^{nn,pnx8034}   ⁿⁿ⁴⁴⁷⁸   ^{wcj,pnp1931}

31 And the house of Israel called   the name thereof Manna: and   it

ⁿⁿ¹⁴⁰⁷   ^{pp,cs,nn2233} ^{aj3836}   ^{wcj,nn,pnx2940}   ^{pp,nn6838}

was like coriander seed, white; and the   taste   of it *was* like wafers *made* with

^{pp,nn1706}

honey.

ⁿⁿ⁴⁸⁷² ^{wcs,qmf559} ^{pndm2088}   ^{df,nn1697} ^{pnl834}   ⁿⁿ³⁰⁶⁸   ^{pipf6680}   ^{cs,nn4393}

32 And Moses said,   This *is* the thing which the LORD commandeth, Fill an

^{df,nn6016 pr,pnx4480}   ^{pp,nn4931}   ^{pp,pl,nn,pnx1755} ^{pp,pr4616}   ^{qmf7200 (853)}   ^{df,nn3899}

omer   of   it to be kept for your generations; that they may see   the bread

^{pnl834}   ^{hipf398 pnx(853)}   ^{dfp,nn4057}   ^{pp,hinc,pnx3318/pnx(853)}

wherewith I have fed   you in the wilderness, when I brought*you*forth

^{pr4480/cs,nn776}   ⁿⁿ⁴⁷¹⁴

from*the*land of Egypt.

ⁿⁿ⁴⁸⁷² ^{wcs,qmf559} ^{pr413}   ⁿⁿ¹⁷⁵ ^{qmv3947} ^{nu259 nn6803}   ^{wcj,qmv5414}   ^{df,nn6016 cs,nn4393}

33 And Moses said unto Aaron, Take a   pot, and   put   an omer full of

ⁿⁿ⁴⁴⁷⁸   ^{ad,lh8033}   ^{wcj,himv5117/pnx(853)} ^{pp,pl,cs,nn6440}   ⁿⁿ³⁰⁶⁸   ^{pp,nn4931}

manna therein, and   lay*it*up   before   the LORD, to be kept for your

^{pp,pl,nn,pnx1755}

generations.

^{pp,pnl834}   ⁿⁿ³⁰⁶⁸   ^{pipf6680/pr413}   ⁿⁿ⁴⁸⁷²   ⁿⁿ¹⁷⁵ ^{wcs,himf,pnx5117} ^{pp,pl,cs,nn6440}

34 As   the LORD commanded Moses, so Aaron laid*it*up   before the

^{df,nn5715}   ^{pp,nn4931}

Testimony, to be kept.

^{wcj,pl,cs,nn1121}   ⁿⁿ³⁴⁷⁸   ^{qpf398 (853)} ^{df,nn4478} ^{pl,nu705 nn8141} ^{pr5704}   ^{qnc,pnx935}

35 And the children of Israel did eat   manna forty years, until they came

^{pr413}   ^{cs,nn776}   ^{nipt3427}   ^{qpf398 (853)} ^{df,nn4478} ^{pr5704}   ^{qnc,pnx935 pr413}   ^{cs,nn7097}

to a land inhabited; they did eat   manna, until they came unto the borders of

^{cs,nn776}   ⁿⁿ³⁶⁶⁷

the land of Canaan.

^{wcj,df,nn6016 (pnp1931)}   ^{cs,nuor6224}   ^{df,nn374}

36 Now an omer   *is* the tenth *part* of an ephah.

nn3503 nn4872 cs,nn2859 wcs,qmf3947 (853) nn6855 nn4872 cs,nn802 ad310

2 Then Jethro, Moses' father-in-law, took Zipporah, Moses' wife, after he

pl,nn,pnx7964

had sent*her*back,

wcj(853) du,cs,nu8147 pl,nn,pnx1121 pnl834 cs,nn8034 df,nu259 nn1648

3 And her two sons; of which the name of the one *was* Gershom;

cj3588 qpf559 qpf1961 nn1616 aj5237 pp,nn776

for he said, I have been an alien in a strange land:

wcj,cs,nn8034 df,nu259 nn461 cj3588 pl,cs,nn430 nn,pnx1

4 And the name of the other *was* Eliezer; for the God of my father, *said*

pp,nn,pnx5828 wcs,himf,pnx5337 pr4480/cs,nn2719 nn6547

he, was mine help, and delivered me from*the*sword of Pharaoh:

nn3503 nn4872 cs,nn2859 wcs,qmf935 wcj,pl,nn,pnx1121 wcj,nn,pnx802

5 And Jethro, Moses' father-in-law, came with his sons and his wife

pr413 nn4872 pr413 df,nn4057 pnl834/ad8033 pnp1931 qpta2583 cs,nn2022 df,pl,nn430

unto Moses into the wilderness, where he encamped at the mount of God:

wcs,qmf559 pr413 nn4872 pnp589 nn,pnx2859 nn3503 qpta935 pr,pnx413

6 And he said unto Moses, I thy father-in-law Jethro am come unto thee,

wcj,nn,pnx802 wcj,du,cs,nu8147 pl,nn,pnx1121 pr,pnx5973

and thy wife, and her two sons with her.

nn4872 wcs,qmf3318 pp,qnc7125 nn,pnx2859 wcs,htmf7812

7 And Moses went out to meet his father-in-law, and did obeisance, and

wcs,qmf5401 pp,pnx wcs,qmf7592 nn376 pp,nn,pnx7453 pp,nn7965 wcs,qmf935

kissed him; and they asked each other of *their* welfare; and they came into the

df,nn,lh168

tent.

nn4872 wcs,pimf5608 pp,nn,pnx2859 (853) cs,nn3605 pnl834 nn3068 qpf6213

8 And Moses told his father-in-law all that the Lord had done unto

pp,nn6547 wcj,pp,nn4714 pr5921 nn3478 pl,cs,nn182 (853) cs,nn3605 df,nn8513 pnl834

Pharaoh and to the Egyptians for Israel's sake, *and* all the travail that had

qpf,pnx4672 dfp,nn1870 nn3068 wcs,himf,pnx5337

come upon them by the way, and *how* the Lord delivered them.

nn3503 wcs,qmf2302 pr5921 cs,nn3605 df,nn2896 pnl834 nn3068 qpf6213

9 And Jethro rejoiced for all the goodness which the Lord had done to

pp,nn3478 pnl834 hipf,pnx5337 pr4480/cs,nn3027 nn4714

Israel, whom he had delivered out*of*the*hand of the Egyptians.

nn3503 wcs,qmf559 qptp1288 nn3068 pnl834 hipf5337 pnx(853)

10 And Jethro said, Blessed *be* the Lord, who hath delivered you

wcj,pr4480/cs,nn3027 nn4714 pr4480/cs,nn3027 nn6547 pnl834

out*of*the*hand of the Egyptians, and out*of*the*hand of Pharaoh, who hath

hipf5337 (853) df,nn5971 pr4480/pr8478 cs,nn3027 nn4714

delivered the people from under the hand of the Egyptians.

ad6258 qpf3045 cj3588 nn3068 aj1419 pr4480/cs,nn3605 df,pl,nn430 cj3588 dfp,nn1697

11 Now I know that the Lord *is* greater than all gods: for in the thing

pnl834 qpf2102 pr,pnx5921

wherein they dealt proudly *he was* above them.

nn3503 nn4872 cs,nn2859 wcs,qmf3947 nn5930 wcj,pl,nn2077

12 And Jethro, Moses' father-in-law, took a burnt offering and sacrifices for

pp,pl,nn430 nn175 wcs,qmf935 wcj,cs,nn3605 cs,aj2205 nn3478 pp,qnc398 nn3899 pr5973

God: and Aaron came, and all the elders of Israel, to eat bread with

nn4872 cs,nn2859 pp,pl,cs,nn6440 df,pl,nn430

Moses' father-in-law before God.

wcs,qmf1961 pr4480/nn4283 nn4872 wcs,qmf3427 pp,qnc8199 (853)

13 And it*came*to*pass on*the*morrow, that Moses sat to judge the

df,nn5971 df,nn5971 wcs,qmf5975 pr5921 nn4872 pr4480 df,nn1242 pr5704 df,nn6153

people: and the people stood by Moses from the morning unto the evening.

nn4872   cs,nn2859   wcs,qmf7200   (853)   cs,nn3605   pnl834   pnp1931   qpta6213
14 And when Moses' father-in-law saw   all   that   he   did   to the

dfp,nn5971   wcs,qmf559   pnit4100   df,pndm2088   df,nn1697   pnl834   pnp859   qpta6213   dfp,nn5971   pnit4069   qpta3427
people, he said, What is this   thing that thou doest to the people? why sittest

pnp859   pp,nn,pnx905   wcj,cs,nn3605   df,nn5971   nipt5324   pr,pnx5921   pr4480   nn1242   pr5704
thou thyself alone, and   all   the people stand   by   thee from morning unto

nn6153
even?

nn4872   wcs,qmf559   pp,nn,pnx2859   cj3588   df,nn5971   qmf935   pr,pnx413
15 And Moses said unto his father-in-law, Because the people come unto me

pp,qnc1875   pl,nn430
to inquire of God:

cj3588   pp,pnx   qmf1961   nn1697   qpf935   pr,pnx413   wcj,qpf8199   pr996   nn376
16 When they have a matter, they come unto me; and I judge between one

wcj(pr996)   nn,pnx7453   wcj,hipf3045   (853)   pl,cs,nn2706   df,pl,nn430   wcj(853)
and   another, and I do make*them*known   the statutes of God, and

pl,nn,pnx8451
his laws.

nn4872   cs,nn2859   wcs,qmf559   pr,pnx413   df,nn1697   pnl834   pnp859   qpta6213   ptn3808
17 And Moses' father-in-law said   unto him, The thing that thou doest is not

aj2896
good.

qna5034/qmf5034   ad1571   pnp859   ad1571   df,pndm2088   df,nn5971   pnl834   pr,pnx5973
18 Thou wilt surely*wear*away, both thou, and   this   people that is with

cj3588   df,nn1697   aj3515   pr,pnx4480   ptn3808   qmf3201   qnc,pnx6213
thee: for this thing is too heavy   for   thee; thou art not able to perform it thyself

pp,nn,pnx905
alone.

qmv8085   ad6258   pp,nn,pnx6963   qmf,pnx3289   pl,nn430
19 Hearken now unto my   voice,   I will give*thee*counsel, and God shall

wcj,qcj1961   pr,pnx5973   qmv1961   pnp859   dfp,nn5971   pr4136/df,pl,nn430   pnp859   wcs,hipf935
be   with thee: Be thou for the people to Godward, that thou mayest bring

(853)   df,pl,nn1697   pr413   df,pl,nn430
the causes unto God:

wcs,hipf2094   pnx(853)   (853)   df,pl,nn2706   wcj(853)   df,pl,nn8451
20 And thou shalt teach   them   ordinances and   laws, and shalt

wcs,hipf3045   pp,pnx   (853)   df,nn1870   pp,pnx   qmf1980   wcj(853)   df,nn4640   pnl834
show them   the way wherein they must walk, and   the work that they

qmf6213
must do.

wcj,pnp859   qmf2372   pr4480/cs,nn3605   df,nn5971   nn2428   pl,cs,nn376   cs,aj3373
21 Moreover thou shalt provide out*of*all the people able men, such as fear

pl,nn430   pl,cs,nn376   nn571   pl,cs,qpta8130   nn1215   wcs,qpf7760   pr,pnx5921
God, men of truth, hating covetousness; and place such over them, to be

pl,cs,nn8269   pl,nu505   pl,cs,nn8269   pl,nu3967   pl,cs,nn8269   pl,nu2572   wcj,pl,cs,nn8269
rulers of thousands, and rulers of hundreds, rulers of fifties, and rulers of

pl,nu6235
tens:

wcs,qpf8199   (853)   df,nn5971   pp,cs,nn3605   nn6256   wcs,qpf1961
22 And let them judge   the people at   all   seasons: and it*shall*be, that

cs,nn3605   df,aj1419   df,nn1697   himf935   pr,pnx413   wcj,cs,nn3605   df,aj6996   df,nn1697   pnp1992
every great matter they shall bring unto thee, but every small matter they shall

qmf8199   wcj,himv7043   pr4480/pr,pnx5921   wcs,qpf5375
judge: so shall it be easier   for   thyself, and they shall bear the burden

pr,pnx854
with thee.

cj518   qmf**6213** (853) df,pndm2088 df,nn**1697**   pl,nn**430** wcs,pipf,pnx**6680**

23 If thou shalt do   this thing, and God command thee *so*, then thou

wcs,qpf3201   qnc5975   cs,nn3605 df,pndm2088 df,nn**5971**   wcj,ad1571 qmf935 pr5921   nn,pnx4725

shalt be able to endure, and all   this people shall also   go   to their place

pp,nn**7965**

in peace.

           nn4872   wcs,qmf**8085**   pp,cs,nn6963   nn,pnx2859   wcs,qmf**6213** cs,nn3605

24 So Moses hearkened to the voice of his father-in-law, and did   all

pnl834   qpf559

that he had said.

          nn4872 wcs,qmf**977** nn2428 pl,cs,nn**376** pr4480/cs,nn3605 nn3478   wcs,qmf**5414** pnx(853)   pl,nn**7218**

25 And Moses chose able men out*of*all Israel, and made   them heads

pr5921   df,nn**5971** pl,cs,nn**8269**   pl,nu505   pl,cs,nn**8269**   pl,nu3967 pl,cs,nn**8269**   pl,nu2572

over the people, rulers of thousands, rulers of hundreds, rulers of fifties, and

wcj,pl,cs,nn**8269**   pl,nu6235

rulers of tens.

          wcj,qpf**8199** (853)   df,nn**5971** pp,cs,nn3605 nn6256   df,aj**7186** (853) df,nn**1697**

26 And they judged   the people at   all   seasons: the hard   causes they

himf935   pr413   nn4872 wcj,cs,nn3605 df,aj6996 df,nn**1697**   qmf**8199**   pnp1992

brought unto Moses, but every small matter they judged themselves.

          nn4872   (853)   nn,pnx2859 wcs,pimf7971   wcs,qmf**1980**/pp,pnx   pr413

27 And Moses let   his father-in-law depart; and he went*his*way into his

nn,pnx**776**

own land.

Mount Sinai

          df,nuor7992 dfp,nn2320   pl,cs,nn**1121**   nn3478   pp,qnc3318

19 ☞ In the third month, when the children of Israel were gone forth

pr4480/cs,nn**776**   nn4714   df,pndm2088 dfp,nn**3117** qpf935

out*of*the*land of Egypt, the same   day came they *into* the

cs,nn4057   nn5514

wilderness of Sinai.

          wcs,qmf5265   pr4480/nn7508   wcs,qmf935   cs,nn4057

2 For they were departed from Rephidim, and were come *to* the desert of

nn5514   wcs,qmf2583   dfp,nn4057   ad8033 nn3478 wcs,qmf2583 pr5048   df,nn2022

Sinai, and had pitched in the wilderness; and there Israel camped before the mount.

          wcj,nn4872   qpf**5927** pr413 df,pl,nn**430**   nn3068 wcs,qmf7121 pr,pnx413   pr4480

3 And Moses went up unto God, and the L ORD called   unto him out of the

df,nn2022   pp,qnc559 ad3541   qmf559   pp,cs,nn**1004**   nn3290   wcj,himf**5046**

mountain, saying, Thus shalt thou say to the house of Jacob, and   tell   the

pp,pl,cs,nn**1121**   nn3478

children of Israel;

          pnp859   qpf**7200** pnl834 qpf**6213**   pp,nn4714   wcs,qmf5375 pnx(853)

4 Ye have seen what I did unto the Egyptians, and *how* I bore   you

pr5921 pl,nn5404 pl,cs,nn3671 wcs,himf935 pnx(853)   pr,pnx413

on eagles' wings, and brought   you unto myself.

          wcj,ad6258   cj518   qna**8085**/qmf**8085**/pp,nn,pnx6963   wcs,qpf**8104** (853)

☞ 5 Now therefore, if   ye will obey*my*voice*indeed, and keep   my

---

☞ **19:1** Israel had now arrived at Mount Sinai where they would remain for almost a year (Ex. 19:1, cf. Num. 10:11). Some of the high points and low points of their history occurred here. At Sinai, they rebelled against God and made an idol of gold (Ex. 32), but also at this holy mountain they received and ratified the Ten Commandments and most of the Law of Moses (Ex. 19 – 24).

☞ **19:5, 6** God here makes a conditional promise to Israel that if they would obey Him and keep His covenant, He would regard and treat them in a special way. The people chose instead to make a golden calf

nn,pnx**1285**   wcs,qpf**1961**   nn**5459**   pp,pnx   pr4480/cs,nn3605   df,pl,nn**5971**   cj3588
covenant, then ye shall   be   a peculiar treasure unto me above all people: for

cs,nn3605   df,nn**776**   pp,pnx
all   the earth *is* mine:

wcj,pnp859   qmf**1961**   pp,pnx   cs,nn**4467**   pl,nn**3548**   aj6918   wcj,nn**1471**
6 And   ye   shall   be   unto me a kingdom of priests, and a holy nation.

pndm428   df,pl,nn**1697**   pnl834   pimf**1696**   pr413   pl,cs,nn**1121**   nn3478
These *are* the words which thou shalt speak unto the children of Israel.

nn4872   wcs,qmf935   wcs,qmf**7121**   pp,cs,aj**2205**   df,nn**5971**   wcs,qmf**7760**
7 And Moses came and called for the elders of the people, and laid before

pp,pl,nn,pnx**6440** (853) cs,nn3605 df,pndm428 df,nn**1697**   pnl834   nn3068   pipf,pnx**6680**
their faces   all   these words which the Lord commanded him.

cs,nn3605   df,nn**5971**   wcs,qmf6030   ad3162   wcs,qmf**559** cs,nn3605 pnl834   nn3068
8 And all   the people answered together, and said,   All that the Lord hath

pipf**1696**   qmf**6213**   nn4872   wcs,himf**7725** (853)   pl,cs,nn**1697**   df,nn**5971**   pr413
spoken we will do. And Moses returned   the words of the people unto the

nn3068
Lord.

nn3068   wcs,qmf**559** pr413   nn4872   ptdm2009 pnp595 qpta935 pr,pnx413   pp,cs,nn5645
9 And the Lord said unto Moses, Lo,   I   come unto thee in a   thick

df,nn**6051** pp,cj5668   df,nn**5971**   qmf**8085**   pp,pinc,pnx1696 pr,pnx5973   wcj(ad1571)   himf**539**
cloud, that the people may hear when I speak   with thee, and   believe

pp,pnx   pp,nn**5769**   nn4872 wcs,himf**5046** (853)   pl,cs,nn**1697**   df,nn**5971** pr413   nn3068
thee forever. And Moses   told   the words of the people unto the Lord.

nn3068   wcs,qmf**559** pr413   nn4872   qmv**1980** pr413   df,nn**5971**   wcj,pipf,pnx**6942**
10 And the Lord said unto Moses, Go unto the people, and sanctify them

df,nn**3117**   wcj,ad4279   wcj,pipf**3526**   pl,nn,pnx8071
today and tomorrow, and let them wash their clothes,

wcj,qpf**1961** pl,nipt**3559**   df,nuor7992 dfp,nn**3117** cj3588   df,nuor7992 dfp,nn**3117**   nn3068
11 And   be   ready against the   third   day: for the third   day the Lord

qmf**3381**   pp,du,cs,nn**5869**   cs,nn3605   df,nn**5971**   pr5921 cs,nn2022 nn5514
will come down in the   sight   of all the people upon mount Sinai.

wcs,hipf**1379**   (853)   df,nn**5971**   nn5439   pp,qnc559
12 And thou shalt set bounds   unto the people round about, saying,

nimv**8104**   pp,pnx   qnc**5927**   dfp,nn2022   wcj,qnc**5060**   pp,nn,pnx7097
Take heed to yourselves, *that ye* go*not*up into the mount, or touch the border

cs,nn3605   df,qpta**5060**   dfp,nn2022   qna**4191**/homf**4191**
of it: whosoever toucheth the mount shall be surely*put*to*death:

ptn**3808**   nn**3027**   qmf**5060** pp,pnx cj3588   qna**5619**/nimf**5619**   cj176
13 There shall not a hand touch it, but he shall surely*be*stoned, or

qna**3384**/nimf**3384**   cj518   nn929 cj518 nn376   ptn**3808** qmf**2421**   df,nn3104
shot through; whether *it be* beast or man, it shall not live: when the trumpet

pp,qnc4900   pnp1992   qmf**5927**   dfp,nn2022
soundeth long, they shall come up to the mount.

nn4872   wcs,qmf**3381**   pr4480   df,nn2022 pr413   df,nn**5971**   wcs,pimf**6942** (853)
14 And Moses went down from the mount unto the people, and sanctified

df,nn**5971**   wcs,pimf**3526**   pl,nn,pnx8071
the people; and they washed their clothes.

---

and forsake the God who had rescued them from Egyptian slavery (Ex. 32). This event, as well as persistent infidelity throughout most of their history, greatly limited the extent to which Israel could realize these promises. This passage is applied to Christians in 1 Peter 2:9, 10, showing how a believer's obedience will benefit him (see also Is. 43:20, 21).

wcs,qmf559 pr413 df,nn5971 qmv1961 pl,nipt3559   pp,cs,nu7969 pl,nn3117 qmf5066

15 And he said unto the people, Be ready against the third day: come

ptn408 pr413 nn802

not at *your* wives.

wcs,qmf1961   df,nuor7992 dfp,nn3117 (pp,qnc1961) df,nn1242

16 And it*came*to*pass on the third day in the morning, that there

wcs,qmf1961 pl,nn6963 wcj,pl,nn1300 aj3515 wcj,nn6051 pr5921 df,nn2022 wcj,cs,nn6963

were thunders and lightnings, and a thick cloud upon the mount, and the voice

nn7782 ad3966 aj2389 cs,nn3605 df,nn5971 pnl834 dfp,nn4264

of the trumpet exceeding loud; so that all the people that *was* in the camp

wcs,qmf2729

trembled.

nn4872 wcs,himf3318 (853) df,nn5971 pr4480 df,nn4264 pp,qnc7125

17 And Moses brought forth the people out of the camp to meet with

df,pl,nn430 wcs,htmf3320 pp,cs,nn8482 df,nn2022

God; and they stood at the nether part of the mount.

wcj,cs,nn2022 nn5514 nn,pnx3605 qpf6225 pr4480/pl,cs,nn6440/pnl834 nn3068

18 And mount Sinai was altogether on*a*smoke, because the LORD

qpf3381 pr,pnx5921 dfp,nn784 nn,pnx6227 wcs,qmf5927 pp,cs,nn6227

descended upon it in fire: and the smoke thereof ascended as the smoke of a

df,nn3536 cs,nn3605 df,nn2022 wcs,qmf2729 ad3966

furnace, and the whole mount quaked greatly.

wcs,qmf1961 cs,nn6963 df,nn7782 qpta1980

19 And when the voice of the trumpet sounded long, and

wcj,qpta2388/ad3966 nn4872 pimf1696 wcj,df,pl,nn430 qmf,pnx6030 pp,nn6963

waxed*louder*and*louder, Moses spoke, and God answered him by a voice.

nn3068 wcs,qmf3381 pr5921 cs,nn2022 nn5514 pr413 cs,nn7218 df,nn2022

20 And the LORD came down upon mount Sinai, on the top of the mount:

nn3068 wcs,qmf7121 pp,nn4872 pr413 cs,nn7218 df,nn2022 nn4872 wcs,qmf5927

and the LORD called Moses *up* to the top of the mount; and Moses went up.

nn3068 wcs,qmf559 pr413 nn4872 qmv3381 himv5749 dfp,nn5971 cj6435

21 And the LORD said unto Moses, Go down, charge the people, lest they

qmf2040 pr413 nn3068 pp,qnc7200 aj7227 pr,pnx4480 wcs,qpf5307

break through unto the LORD to gaze, and many of them perish.

df,pl,nn3548 wcj,ad1571 df,pl,nipt5066 pr413 nn3068

22 And let the priests also, which come near to the LORD,

htmf6942 cj6435 nn3068 qmf6555 pp,pnx

sanctify themselves, lest the LORD break forth upon them.

nn4872 wcs,qmf559 pr413 nn3068 df,nn5971 ptn3808/qmf3201 pp,qnc5927 pr413 cs,nn2022

23 And Moses said unto the LORD, The people cannot come up to mount

nn5514 cj3588 pnp859 hipf5749 pp,pnx pp,qnc559 himv1379 (853) df,nn2022 wcj,pipf,pnx6942

Sinai: for thou chargedst us, saying, Set bounds about the mount, and sanctify

it.

nn3068 wcs,qmf559 pr,pnx413 qmv1980 qmv3381

24 And the LORD said unto him, Away, get*thee*down, and thou shalt

wcj,qpf5927 pnp859 wcj,nn175 pr,pnx5973 ptn408 wcj,df,pl,nn3548 wcj,df,nn5971

come up, thou, and Aaron with thee: but let not the priests and the people

qmf2040 pp,qnc5927 pr413 nn3068 cj6435 qmf6555 pp,pnx

break through to come up unto the LORD, lest he break forth upon them.

nn4872 wcs,qmf3381 pr413 df,nn5971 wcs,qmf559 pr,pnx413

25 So Moses went down unto the people, and spoke unto them.

The Ten Commandments

pl,nn**430** wcs,pimf**1696** (853) cs,nn3605 df,pndm428 df,pl,nn**1697** pp,qnc**559**

20 ☞ And God spoke   all   these words, saying,

pnp595   nn**3068**   pl,nn,pnx**430**   pnl834   hipf,pnx3318

2 I *am* the LORD thy God, which have brought*thee*out

pr4480/cs,nn**776** nn4714   pr4480/cs,nn**1004**   pl,nn**5650**

of*the*land of Egypt, out*of*the*house of bondage.

pp,pnx   qmf**1961** ptn**3808** aj312 pl,nn**430** pr5921/pl,nn,pnx**6440**

3 Thou shalt have no other gods   before   me.

ptn**3808** qmf**6213**   pp,pnx   nn**6459**   wcj,cs,nn3605 nn**8544**

4 Thou shalt not make unto thee any graven image, or   any   likeness *of any*

pnl834   dfp,du,nn**8064** pr4480/ad4605   wcj,pnl834   dfp,nn**776** pr4480/ad8478   wcj,pnl834

thing that *is* in heaven above, or that *is* in the earth beneath, or that *is* in the

dfp,pl,nn4325 pr4480/ad8478   dfp,nn**776**

water   under the earth:

ptn**3808**   htmf**7812**   pp,pnx   wcj,ptn**3808** homf,pnx**5647**   cj3588 pnp595

5 Thou shalt not bow*down*thyself to them, nor   serve them: for I

nn**3068**   pl,nn,pnx**430**   aj**7067**   nn**410** qpta**6485**   cs,nn**5771**   pl,nn1   pr5921

the LORD thy God *am* a jealous God, visiting the iniquity of the fathers upon the

pl,nn**1121** pr5921   aj8029   wcj(pr5921) aj7256   pp,pl,qpta,pnx**8130**

children unto the third and   fourth *generation* of them that   hate   me;

wcj,qpta**6213**   nn**2617**   pp,pl,nu505   pp,pl,qpta,pnx**157**

6 And showing mercy unto thousands of them that   love   me, and

wcj,pp,pl,cs,qpta**8104**   pl,nn,pnx**4687**

keep   my commandments.

ptn**3808** qmf**5375** (853)   cs,nn**8034**   nn**3068**   pl,nn,pnx**430** dfp,nn**7723** cj3588

7 Thou shalt not take   the name of the LORD thy God in vain; for the

nn**3068**   ptn**3808**   pimf**5352**   (853) pnl834 qmf**5375** (853)   nn,pnx8034   dfp,nn**7723**

LORD will not hold*him*guiltless   that taketh   his name in vain.

qna**2142**   (853) df,nn**7676** cs,nn**3117**   pp,pinc,pnx**6942**

8 Remember the   sabbath day, to keep*it*holy.

cs,nu8337 pl,nn**3117**   qmf**5647**   wcs,qpf**6213** cs,nn3605   nn,pnx**4399**

9 Six days shalt thou labor, and do   all thy work:

df,nuor7637 wcj,cs,nn**3117**   nn**7676**   pp,nn**3068**   pl,nn,pnx**430**

10 But the seventh day *is* the sabbath of the LORD thy God: *in it* thou

ptn**3808** qmf**6213** cs,nn3605   nn**4399**   pnp859   wcj,nn,pnx**1121**   wcj,nn,pnx1323

shalt not do any work, thou, nor thy son,   nor thy daughter, thy

nn,pnx**5650**   wcj,nn,pnx519   wcj,nn,pnx929   wcj,nn,pnx**1616** pnl834

manservant, nor thy maidservant, nor thy cattle, nor thy stranger that *is* within thy

pp,pl,nn,pnx8179

gates:

cj3588   cs,nu8337 pl,nn**3117**   nn**3068** qpf**6213** (853) df,du,nn**8064**   wcj(853) df,nn**776** (853)   df,nn3220

11 For *in* six days the LORD made   heaven and   earth,   the sea,

---

☞ **20:1–17** With these Ten Commandments the covenant with Israel begins. The ancient rabbis isolated 613 separate commandments in the entire Law of Moses, but these ten are the principles upon which the rest are based. By themselves they are called "the words of the covenant" (Ex. 34:28). The first four commandments deal directly with man's relationship with and especially his reverence toward God, while the latter six have to do with man's relationship with other human beings. The first four have as their theme total love for God, as expressed in Deuteronomy 6:5. The last six are summarized in the statement in Leviticus 19:18: "You shall love your neighbor as yourself." Therefore, Jesus took 613 commandments which had been condensed to ten in the Law of Moses and reduced them to two (see Matt. 22:35–40). All of God's commandments in the Old Testament dealing with how His people should live may be abbreviated simply to have love for God and for man.

wcj(853) cs,nn3605 pnl834   pp,pnx   wcs,qmf5117   df,nuor7637 dfp,nn3117 pr5921/ad3651   nn3068
and   all   that in them *is*, and rested the seventh day: wherefore the LORD

pipf1288   (853)   df,nn7676 cs,nn3117   wcs,pimf,pnx6942
blessed the   sabbath day, and hallowed it.

pimv3513   (853)   nn,pnx1   wcj(853)   nn,pnx517 pp,pr4616   pl,nn,pnx3117   himf748
12 Honor   thy father and   thy mother: that thy days   may be long

pr5921   df,nn127 pnl834   nn3068   pl,nn,pnx430 qpta5414 pp,pnx
upon the land which the LORD thy God   giveth thee.

ptn3808 qmf7523
13 Thou shalt not kill.

ptn3808   qmf5003
14 Thou shalt not commit adultery.

ptn3808 qmf1589
15 Thou shalt not steal.

ptn3808 qmf6030 nn8267 cs,nn5707   pp,nn,pnx7453
16 Thou shalt not bear false witness against thy neighbor.

ptn3808   qmf2530   nn,pnx7453   cs,nn1004   ptn3808 qmf2530
17 Thou shalt not covet thy neighbor's house, thou shalt not covet thy

nn,pnx7453   cs,nn802   wcj,nn,pnx5650   wcj,nn,pnx519   wcj,nn,pnx7794
neighbor's wife, nor his manservant, nor his maidservant, nor his ox, nor his

wcj,nn,pnx2543   wcj,nn,pnx3605 pnl834   pp,nn,pnx7453
ass, nor any thing that *is* thy neighbor's.

wcj,cs,nn3605   df,nn5971 pl,qpta7200 (853)   df,pl,nn6963   wcj(853)   df,pl,nn3940
18 And   all   the people saw   the thunderings, and   the lightnings,

wcj(853)   cs,nn6963   df,nn7782   wcj(853)   df,nn2022   aj6226
and   the noise of the trumpet, and   the mountain smoking: and when the

df,nn5971 wcs,qmf7200   wcs,qmf5128   wcs,qmf5975 pr4480/nn7350
people   saw   *it*, they removed, and stood afar off.

wcs,qmf559 pr413   nn4872 pimv1696 pnp859 pr,pnx5973   wcj,qcj8085
19 And they said unto Moses, Speak thou with us, and we will hear: but

wcj,ptn408 pl,nn430 pimf1696 pr,pnx5973   cj6435   qmf4191
let not God speak with us, lest we die.

nn4872 wcs,qmf559 pr413   df,nn5971 qmf3372 ptn408 cj3588 df,pl,nn430   qpf935 pp,pp,cj5668
20 And Moses said unto the people, Fear not: for God is come   to

pinc5254 pnx(853)   wcj,pp,cj5668   nn,pnx3374   qmf1961 pr5921   pl,nn,pnx6440   qmf2398
prove   you, and   that   his fear may be before your faces, that ye sin

pp,ptn1115
not.

df,nn5971   wcs,qmf5975   pr4480/nn7350   wcj,nn4872   nipf5066   pr413
21 And the people   stood   afar off, and Moses drew near unto the

df,nn6205   pnl834/ad8033 df,pl,nn430
thick darkness where God *was*.

Instructions for Building an Altar

nn3068 wcs,qmf559 pr413   nn4872   ad3541   qmf559 pr413   pl,cs,nn1121
22 And the LORD   said   unto Moses, Thus thou shalt say unto the children of

nn3478 pnp859   qpf7200 cj3588   pipf1696 pr,pnx5973   pr4480 df,du,nn8064
Israel, Ye have seen that I have talked with you from heaven.

ptn3808   qmf6213 pr,pnx854   pl,cs,nn430   nn3701 ptn3808   qmf6213
23 Ye shall not make with me gods of silver, neither shall ye make

pp,pnx   wcj,pl,cs,nn430   nn2091
unto you gods of gold.

cs,nn4196   nn127   qmf6213   pp,pnx   wcs,qpf2076 pr,pnx5921 (853)
24 An altar of earth thou shalt make unto me, and shalt sacrifice thereon

pl,nn,pnx**5930**   wcj(853)   pl,nn,pnx**8002**   (853)   nn,pnx6629   wcj(853)

thy burnt offerings, and   thy peace offerings,   thy sheep, and   thine

nn,pnx1241   pp,cs,nn3605   df,nn4725   pnl834   himf2142   (853)   nn,pnx8034   qmf935   pr,pnx413

oxen: in   all   places where I record   my name I will come unto thee, and I

wcs,pipf,pnx**1288**

will   bless   thee.

wcj,cj518   qmf6213   pp,pnx   cs,nn4196   pl,nn68   ptn**3808** qmf1129   pnx(853)

25 And   if   thou wilt make me an altar of stone, thou shalt not build

nn1496   cj3588   hipf5130   nn,pnx2719   pr,pnx5921   wcs,pimf**2490**

it of hewn stone: for if thou lift up thy   tool   upon it, thou hast polluted it.

wcj,ptn**3808**   qmf5927   pp,pl,nn4609   pr5921   nn,pnx4196   pnl834   nn,pnx**6172**

26 Neither shalt thou go up by   steps   unto mine altar, that thy nakedness be

ptn**3808**   nimf**1540**   pr,pnx5921

not discovered thereon.

The Treatment of Servants

wcj,pndm428   df,pl,nn**4941**   pnl834   qmf**7760** pp,pl,nn,pnx**6440**

21 Now these *are* the judgments which thou shalt set   before   them.

cj3588   qmf7069   nn5680   nn5650   nu8337 pl,nn8141   qmf5647

2 If   thou buy a Hebrew servant,   six   years he shall serve: and

wcj,dfp,nuor7637   qmf3318   dfp,aj2670   ad**2600**

in the   seventh   he shall go out free for nothing.

cj518   qmf935   pp,nn,pnx1610   qmf3318   pp,nn,pnx1610   cj518   pnp1931

3 If   he came in by   himself, he   shall go out by   himself: if   he   were

cs,nn1167/nn802   nn,pnx802   wcs,qpf3318 pr,pnx5973

married, then his   wife   shall go out   with   him.

cj518   pl,nn,pnx113   qmf5414   pp,pnx   nn802   wcs,qpf3205 pp,pnx   pl,nn1121   cj176

4 If   his   master have given him a wife, and she have   born   him   sons   or

pl,nn1323   df,nn802   wcj,pl,nn,pnx3206   qmf1961   pp,pl,nn,pnx113   wcj,pnp1931

daughters; the wife and her   children   shall   be   her master's, and   he   shall

qmf3318   pp,nn,pnx1610

go out by himself.

wcj,cj518   df,nn5650   qna559/qmf559   qpf157   (853)   nn,pnx113   (853)   nn,pnx802

5 And   if   the servant shall plainly say, I love   my master,   my wife,

wcj(853)   pl,nn,pnx1121   ptn3808   qmf3318   aj2670

and   my children; I will not go out free:

pl,nn,pnx113   wcs,hipf,pnx5066   pr413   df,pl,nn430   wcs,hipf,pnx5066

6 Then his master shall   bring   him unto the judges; he shall also   bring

pr413   df,nn1817 cj176   pr413   dfp,nn4201   pl,nn,pnx113   wcs,qpf7527/(853)/nn,pnx241

him to the door, or unto the door post; and his master shall bore*his*ear*through

dfp,nn4836   wcs,qpf,pnx5647   pp,nn5769

with an awl; and he shall   serve   him forever.

wcj,cj3588   nn376   qmf4376   (853)   nn,pnx1323   pp,nn519   ptn**3808**

7 And   if   a man   sell   his daughter to be a maidservant, she shall   not

qmf3318   df,pl,nn**5650**   pp,qnc3318

go out as the menservants   do.

cj518   aj7451/pp,du,cs,nn**5869**   pl,nn,pnx113   pnl834   (ptn3808)/qpf,pnx3259   pp,pnx

8 If   she   please   not   her   master, who hath   betrothed   her to himself, then

wcj,hipf,pnx**6299**   pp,qnc,pnx4376   aj5237   pp,nn5971

shall he let her be redeemed: to   sell   her unto a strange nation he shall have

ptn**3808**   qmf**4910**   pp,qnc,pnx898   pp,pnx

no power, seeing he hath dealt deceitfully with her.

                wcj,cj518   qmf,pnx3259   pp,nn,pnx1121   qmf6213   pp,pnx
9 And   if   he have betrothed her unto his   son,   he shall deal with her after
pp,cs,nn4941   df,pl,nn1323
the manner of daughters.

        cj518   qmf3947   pp,pnx   aj312   nn,pnx7607   nn,pnx3682
10 If   he   take   him   another *wife*;   her   food,   her   raiment,   and   her
wcj,nn,pnx5772   ptn3808   qmf1639
duty*of*marriage, shall he not diminish.

            wcj,cj518   qmf6213 ptn3808 pndm428 cs,nu7969   pp,pnx   wcs,qpf3318 ad2600
11 And   if   he   do   not these three unto her, then shall she go out free
ptn369   nn3701
without money.

Laws Against Violence

            cs,hipt5221   nn376   wcs,qpf4191   qna4191/homf4191
12 He that smiteth a man, so that he   die,   shall be surely*put*to*death.

        wcj,pnl834   qpf6658/ptn3808   wcj,df,pl,nn430   pipf579   pp,nn,pnx3027
13 And   if   a man lie*not*in*wait, but   God   deliver *him* into his   hand;
            wcj,qpf7760   pp,pnx   nn4725   pnl834/ad,lh8033   qmf5127
then I will appoint thee a place   whither   he shall flee.

        wcj,cj3588   nn376   himf2102   pr5921   nn,pnx7453   pp,qnc,pnx2026
14 But   if   a man come presumptuously upon his neighbor, to   slay   him
pp,nn6195   qmf,pnx3947   pr4480/pr5973   nn,pnx4196   pp,qnc4191
with guile; thou shalt   take   him   from   mine altar, that he may   die.

            wcj,cs,hipt5221   nn,pnx1   wcj,nn,pnx517   qna4191/homf4191
15 And he that   smiteth   his father, or his mother, shall be surely*put*to*death.

            wcj,cs,qpta1589   nn376   wcs,qpf,pnx4376   wcs,nipf4672
16 And he that   stealeth   a man, and   selleth   him, or if he be   found   in his
pp,nn,pnx3027   qna4191/homf4191
    hand,   he shall surely*be*put*to*death.

            wcj,cs,pipt7043   nn,pnx1   wcj,nn,pnx517   qna4191/homf4191
17 And he that   curseth   his father, or his mother, shall   surely*be*put*to*death.

            wcj,cj3588 pl,nn376   qmf7378   nn376 wcs,hipf5221 (853) nn,pnx7453   pp,nn68 cj176
18 And   if   men strive together, and one   smite   another with a stone, or
        pp,nn106   qmf4191 wcj,ptn3808   wcs,qpf5307   pp,nn4904
with *his* fist, and he die   not,   but keepeth *his* bed:

        cj518   qmf6965   wcs,htpf1980 dfp,nn2351   pr5921   nn,pnx4938
19 If   he rise again, and   walk   abroad upon his   staff, then shall he that
df,hipt5221   wcs,nipf5352 ad7535   qmf5414   nn,pnx7674
smote *him* be quit: only he shall   pay   *for* the loss*of*his*time, and shall cause *him*
            wcj,pina7495/pimf7495
to be thoroughly healed.

        wcj,cj3588   nn376 himf5221 (853)   nn,pnx5650 cj176 (853)   nn,pnx519   dfp,nn7626
20 And   if   a man smite   his servant, or   his maid, with a rod, and
wcs,qpf4191 pr8478   nn,pnx3027   qna5358/nimf5358
he   die   under his hand; he shall be surely   punished.

        ad389   cj518   qmf5975   nn3117 cj176 du,nn3117   ptn3808   homf5358
21 Notwithstanding, if he continue a day or   two,   he shall not be punished:
cj3588 pnp1931   nn,pnx3701
for   he   *is* his money.

        wcj,cj3588 pl,nn376 nimf5327   wcs,qpf5062   nn802   aj2030   pl,nn,pnx3206
22   If   men strive, and   hurt   a woman with child, so that her   fruit
wcs,qpf3318   wcj,ptn3808   nn611   qmf1961   qna6064/nimf6064
depart *from her*, and yet   no   mischief follow: he shall be surely punished,

pp,pnl834   df,nn**802**   cs,nn**1167**   qmf7896 pr,pnx5921   wcs,qpf**5414**

according as the woman's husband will lay upon him; and he shall pay as the

pp,pl,nn**6414**

judges *determine*.

          wcj,cj518   nn611   qpf**1961**   wcs,qpf**5414** nn5315 pr8478 nn5315

23 And if *any* mischief follow, then thou shalt give life for life,

     nn**5869** pr8478 nn**5869**   nn8127 pr8478   nn8127   nn**3027** pr8478   nn**3027**   nn7272 pr8478 nn7272

24 Eye for eye, tooth for tooth, hand for hand, foot for foot,

        nn3555   pr8478   nn3555   nn6482 pr8478   nn6482   nn2250 pr8478 nn2250

25 Burning for burning, wound for wound, stripe for stripe.

       wcj,cj3588   nn376   himf**5221** (853)   cs,nn**5869**   nn,pnx5650 cj176 (853)   cs,nn**5869**

26 And if a man smite   the eye of his servant, or   the eye of his

nn,pnx519   wcs,pipf,pnx**7843**   pimf,pnx7971 dfp,aj2670   pr8478/nn,pnx**5869**

maid, that it perish; he shall let him   go   free for*his*eye's*sake.

        wcj,cj518   himf**5307**   nn,pnx5650   cs,nn8127 cj176   nn,pnx519   cs,nn8127

27 And if he smite out his manservant's tooth, or his maidservant's tooth;

          pimf,pnx7971 dfp,aj2670   pr8478/nn,pnx8127

he shall let him   go   free for*his*tooth's*sake.

        wcj,cj3588   nn7794 qmf5055 (853)   nn376 cj176 (853)   nn802   wcs,qpf**4191**

28 If an ox gore   a man or   a woman, that they die: then the

df,nn7794   qna5619/nimf5619   (853)   nn,pnx1320   wcj,ptn**3808**   nimf398

ox   shall be surely stoned, and   his flesh shall   not   be eaten; but the

wcj,cs,nn**1167**   df,nn7794   aj**5355**

owner of the ox *shall be* quit.

       wcj,cj518   nn7794 (pnp1931)   aj5056   pr4480/ad8543/ad8032

29 But if   the ox   were wont*to*push*with*his*horn in*time*past,

                 wcs,hopf**5749**   pp,pl,nn,pnx**1167**   wcj,ptn**3808**   qmf,pnx**8104**

and it hath been testified to his   owner,   and he hath   not   kept*him*in, but that

      wcs,hipf**4191**   nn376 cj176   nn**802**   df,nn7794   nimf5619   pl,nn,pnx**1167**

he hath killed a man or a woman; the   ox   shall be stoned, and his owner

wcj,ad1571   homf**4191**

also   shall be put*to*death.

           cj518   homf7896 pr,pnx5921   nn3724   wcs,qpf**5414**

30 If there be laid   on   him a sum*of*money, then he shall give   for the

cs,nn**6306**   nn,pnx**5315** pp,nn3605/pnl834 homf7896 pr,pnx5921

ransom of his life   whatsoever is laid upon him.

        cj176   qmf5055   nn**1121** cj176   qmf5055   nn1323

31 Whether he have gored a son, or have gored a daughter, according to

df,pndm2088   dfp,nn**4941**   nimf**6213**   pp,pnx

this   judgment shall it be done unto him.

        cj518   df,nn7794   qmf5055   nn**5650**   cj176   nn519   qmf**5414**

32 If the ox   shall push a manservant or a maidservant; he shall give unto

pp,pl,nn,pnx**113**   nu7970   pl,nn8255   cs,nn3701   wcj,df,nn7794   nimf5619

their master thirty shekels of silver, and the   ox   shall be stoned.

       wcj,cj3588   nn376   qmf6605   nn953 cj176 cj3588   nn376   qmf3738   nn953

33 And   if a man shall open a pit, or if a man shall dig a pit, and

wcj,ptn**3808** pimf,pnx**3680**   nn7794 cj176   nn2543 wcs,qpf5307 ad,lh8033

not   cover it, and an ox or an ass fall therein;

        cs,nn**1167**   df,nn**953**   pimf**7999**   himf**7725**   nn3701

34 The owner of the pit   shall make*it*good, *and* give money unto the

pp,pl,nn,pnx**1167**   wcj,df,qpta**4191**   qmf**1961** pp,pnx

owner of them; and the   dead *beast* shall be his.

        wcj,cj3588   nn376   cs,nn7794 qmf**5062** (853) cs,nn7794/nn,nn**7453**   wcs,qpf**4191**

35 And if   one man's   ox hurt   another's, that he die; then they

wcs,qpf4376 (853)   df,aj2416 df,nn7794   wcs,qpf2673 (853)   nn,pnx3701   (853)   df,qpta4191

shall sell   the live ox, and divide   the money of it; and   the dead *ox*

wcj,ad1571   qmf2673

also they shall divide.

cj176   nipf**3045**   cj3588   nn7794   aj5056   (pnp1931) pr4480/ad8543/ad8032

36 Or if it be known that the ox hath used*to*push   in*time*past, and

pl,nn,pnx**1167**   wcj,ptn**3808** qmf,pnx**8104**   pina**7999**/pimf**7999** nn7794 pr8478 df,nn7794

his owner hath   not kept*him*in; he shall surely pay ox for ox; and the

wcj,df,qpta**4191**   qmf**1961**   pp,pnx

dead   shall be his own.

Laws About Repayment

cj3588   nn**376**   qmf1589   nn7794 cj176   nn7716   wcs,qpf,pnx**2873**   cj176 qpf,pnx4376

22 If a man shall steal an ox, or a sheep, and   kill   it, or   sell

pimf**7999** nu2568 nn1241 pr8478   df,nn7794   wcj,nu702 nn6629 pr8478

it; he shall restore five oxen for an ox, and four sheep for a

df,nn7716

sheep.

cj518   df,nn1590   nimf4672   dfp,nn4290   wcs,hopf**5221**   wcs,qpf**4191**

2 If a thief be found breaking up, and be smitten that he   die,   *there shall*

ptn369 pl,nn**1818**   pp,pnx

no blood *be shed* for him.

cj518   df,nn8121   qpf2224 pr,pnx5921   pl,nn**1818**   pp,pnx

3 If the sun be risen upon him, *there shall be* blood *shed* for him; *for* he

pina**7999**/pimf**7999**   cj518 pp,pnx   ptn369   wcs,nipf4376

should make*full*restitution; if he have nothing, then he shall be   sold   for his

pp,nn,pnx1591

theft.

cj518   df,nn1591   nina4672/nimf4672   pp,nn,pnx**3027** aj2416   pr4480/nn7794   pr5704

4 If the theft be certainly found in his   hand   alive, whether*it*be*ox, or

nn2543 pr5704 nn7716   pimf**7999**   du,nu8147

ass, or sheep; he shall restore double.

cj3588   nn**376**   nn7704 cj176   nn3754   hicj1197   wcs,pipf7971 (853)

5 If a man shall cause a field or vineyard to be eaten, and shall put in

nn,pnx1165   wcs,pipf1197   aj312   pp,cs,nn**7704**   cs,nn4315   nn,pnx**7704**

his beast, and shall   feed   in another man's field; of the best of his own field,

wcj,cs,nn4315   nn,pnx3754   pimf**7999**

and of the best   of his own vineyard, shall he make restitution.

cj3588 nn784   qmf3318   wcs,qpf4672   pl,nn6975   nn1430   cj176

6 If fire break out, and catch in thorns, so that the stacks*of*corn, or the

df,nn7054   cj176   df,nn**7704**   wcs,nipf398   df,hipt1197 (853)   df,nn**1200**

standing corn, or the field, be consumed *therewith*; he that kindled   the fire

pina**7999**/pimf**7999**

shall surely*make*restitution.

cj3588   nn**376**   qmf**5414**   pr413   nn,pnx**7453**   nn3701 cj176 pl,nn3627   pp,qnc**8104**

7 If a man shall deliver unto his neighbor money or stuff to keep, and it be

wcs,pupf1589   pr4480/cs,nn**1004**/df,nn**376**   cj518   df,nn1590   nimf4672   pimf**7999** du,nu8147

stolen out*of*the*man's*house; if the thief be found, let him pay double.

cj518   df,nn1590   ptn**3808** nimf4672   cs,nn**1167**   df,nn**1004**   wcs,nipf7126

8 If the thief be not found, then the master of the house shall be brought

pr413   df,pl,nn**430**   cj518/ptn**3808**   qpf7971   nn,pnx**3027**   nn,pnx**7453** pp,cs,nn**4399**

unto the judges, *to see* whether he have put his hand unto his neighbor's goods.

pr5921 cs,nn3605 cs,nn**1697**   nn6588   pr5921 nn7794 pr5921 nn2543 pr5921   nn7716

9 For   all   manner of trespass, *whether it be* for ox, for ass, for sheep,

pr5921   nn8008   pr5921   cs,nn3605   nn9   pnl834   qmf559
for raiment, *or* for any manner of lost thing, which *another* challengeth

cj3588/pnp1931/pndm2088   cs,nn1697   du,nu,pnx8147   qmf935   pr5704   df,pl,nn430   pnl834
to*be*his,   the cause of both parties shall come before the judges; *and* whom

pl,nn430   himf7561   pimf7999   du,nu8147   pp,nn,pnx7453
the judges shall condemn, he shall pay double unto his neighbor.

        cj3588   nn376   qmf5414   pr413   nn,pnx7453   nn2543 cj176   nn7794 cj176   nn7716
10 If a man deliver unto his neighbor an ass, or an ox, or a sheep, or

wcj,cs,nn3605   nn929   pp,qnc8104   wcs,qpf4191 cj176   nipf7665   cj176   nipf7617   ptn369   qpta7200
any   beast, to keep; and it die,   or be hurt, or driven away, no man seeing

it:

                    cs,nn7621   nn3068   qmf1961   pr996   du,nu,pnx8147 cj518
11 *Then* shall an oath of the LORD be between them both,   that he hath

ptn3808 qpf7971   nn,pnx3027   nn,pnx7453   pp,cs,nn4399   pl,nn,pnx1167   wcj,qpf3947
not put his hand unto his neighbor's goods; and the owner of it shall accept

                    wcj,ptn3808   pimf7999
thereof, and he shall   not   make*it*good.

            wcj,cj518   qna1589/nimf1589 pr4480/pr,pnx5973   pimf7999
12 And if it be stolen   from   him, he shall make restitution unto the

pp,pl,nn,pnx1167
owner   thereof.

            cj518   qna2963/nimf2963   himf,pnx935   nn5707   ptn3808
13 If it be torn*in*pieces, *then* let him bring it *for* witness, *and* he shall not

pimf7999   df,nn2966
make good that*which*was*torn.

            wcj,cj3588   nn376   qmf7592   pr4480/pr5973   nn,pnx7453   wcs,nipf7665   cj176
14 And   if   a man borrow *aught*   of   his neighbor, and it be hurt, or

qpf4191   pl,nn,pnx1167   ptn369 pr,pnx5973   pina7999/pimf7999
die, the owner thereof *being* not   with   it, he shall surely*make*it*good.

            cj518   pl,nn,pnx1167   pr,pnx5973   ptn3808   pimf7999   cj518
15 *But* if the owner thereof *be* with it, he shall not make*it*good: if

pnp1931   aj7916   qpf935   pp,nn,pnx7939
it   *be* a hired *thing*, it came for his   hire.

Laws of Human Relations

        wcj,cj3588   nn376   pimf6601   nn1330   pnl834   ptn3808   pupf781   wcj,qpf7901 pr,pnx5973
16 And   if   a man entice a maid that is   not   betrothed, and   lie   with

qna4117/qmf,pnx4117   pp,pnx pp,nn802
her, he shall surely endow her to be his wife.

        cj518   nn,pnx1   pina3985/pimf3985   pp,qnc,pnx5414   pp,pnx   qmf8254   nn3701
17 If her father utterly refuse to   give   her unto him, he shall pay money

                    pp,cs,nn4119   df,pl,nn1330
according to the dowry of virgins.

                    ptn3808   pimf2421/pipt3784
18 Thou shalt not suffer*a*witch*to*live.

            cs,nn3605   qpta7901 pr5973   nn929   qna4191/homf4191
19 Whosoever lieth with a beast shall surely*be*put*to*death.

            qpta2076   dfp,pl,nn430 ptn1115   pp,nn3068 pp,nn,pnx905
20 He that sacrificeth unto *any* god,   save unto the LORD only,   he shall be

homf2763
utterly destroyed.

ptn3808   himf3238   wcj,nn1616   wcj,ptn3808   qmf,pnx3905   cj3588   qpf1961

21 Thou shalt neither vex a stranger, nor oppress him: for ye were

pl,nn1616   pp,cs,nn776   nn4714

strangers in the land of Egypt.

ptn3808   pimf6031   cs,nn3605   nn490   wcj,nn3490

22 Ye shall not afflict any widow, or fatherless child.

cj518   pina6031/pimf6031/pnx(853)   cj3588 (cj518)   qna6817/qmf6817 pr,pnx413

23 If thou afflict*them*in*any*wise, and they cry*at*all unto me, I will

qna8085/qmf8085   nn,pnx6818

surely hear their cry;

nn,pnx639   wcs,qpf2734   wcs,qpf2026 pnx(853)   dfp,nn2719

24 And my wrath shall wax hot, and I will kill you with the sword;

pl,nn,pnx802   wcs,qpf1961   pl,nn490   wcj,pl,nn,pnx1121   pl,nn3490

and your wives shall be widows, and your children fatherless.

cj518   himf3867   nn3701   (853)   nn,pnx5971   (853) df,aj6041 pr,pnx5973

25 If thou lend money to *any of* my people *that is* poor by thee,

ptn3808 qmf1961   pp,pnx   pp,qpta5383   ptn3808   qmf7760 pr,pnx5921   nn5392

thou shalt not be to him as a usurer, neither shalt thou lay upon him usury.

cj518   qna2254/qmf2254/nn,pnx7453/cs,nn8008   himf,pnx7725

26 If thou at*all*take*thy*neighbor's*raiment*to*pledge, thou shalt deliver it

pp,pnx   pr5704   df,nn8121   qnc935

unto him by that the sun goeth down:

cj3588 pnp1931   nn,pnx3682   pp,nn,pnx905 pnp1931   nn,pnx8071   pp,nn,pnx5785 dfp,pnit4100

27 For that *is* his covering only, it *is* his raiment for his skin: wherein

qmf7901   wcs,qpf1961   cj3588   qmf6817   pr,pnx413

shall he sleep? and it*shall*come*to*pass, when he crieth unto me, that I will

wcs,qpf8085 cj3588 pnp589   aj2587

hear; for I *am* gracious.

ptn3808   pimf7043   pl,nn430 ptn3808   qmf779   wcj,nn5387   pp,nn,pnx5971

28 Thou shalt not revile the gods, nor curse the ruler of thy people.

ptn3808   pimf309   nn,pnx4395

29 Thou shalt not delay *to offer* the first*of*thy*ripe*fruits, and of thy

wcj,nn,pnx1831   cs,nn1060   pl,nn,pnx1121   qmf5414   pp,pnx

liquors: the firstborn of thy sons shalt thou give unto me.

ad3651   qmf6213   pp,nn,pnx7794   pp,nn,pnx6629 cs,nu7651

30 Likewise shalt thou do with thine oxen, *and* with thy sheep: seven

pl,nn3117   qmf1961 pr5973   nn,pnx517   df,nuor8066 dfp,nn3117   qmf,pnx5414   pp,pnx

days it shall be with his dam; on the eighth day thou shalt give it me.

qmf1961   nn6944 wcj,pl,cs,nn376   pp,pnx   ptn3808   qmf398   wcj,nn1320

31 And ye shall be holy men unto me: neither shall ye eat *any* flesh

nn2966   dfp,nn7704   himf7993 pnx(853)   dfp,nn3611

that is torn*of*beasts in the field; ye shall cast it to the dogs.

ptn3808 qmf5375   nn7723   cs,nn8088   qmf7896 ptn408   nn,pnx3027 pr5973

23 Thou shalt not raise a false report: put not thine hand with the

aj7563   pp,qnc1961   nn2555   cs,nn5707

wicked to be an unrighteous witness.

ptn3808 qmf1961/pr310   aj7227   pp,pl,nn7451 wcj,ptn3808   qmf6030 pr5921

2 Thou shalt not follow a multitude to *do* evil; neither shalt thou speak in

nn7379   pp,qnc5186   pr310   aj7227   pp,hinc5186

a cause to decline after many to wrest *judgment*:

ptn3808   qmf1921   wcj,aj1800   pp,nn,pnx7379

3 Neither shalt thou countenance a poor man in his cause.

cj3588   qmf6293   qpta,pnx341 cs,nn7794 cj176   nn,pnx2543   qpta8582

4 If thou meet thine enemy's   ox   or his   ass   going astray, thou shalt

hina7725/himf,pnx7725/pp,pnx

surely*bring*it*back*to*him*again.

cj3588   qmf7200   cs,nn2543   qpta,pnx8130   qpta7257 pr8478   nn,pnx4853

5 If thou see the ass of him that hateth thee lying under his burden, and

wcs,qpf2308 pr4480/qnc5800 pp,pnx   qna5800/qmf5800 pr,pnx5973

wouldest forbear to help him, thou shalt surely help with him.

ptn3808 himf5186   cs,nn4941   nn,pnx34   pp,nn,pnx7379

6 Thou shalt not wrest the judgment of thy poor in his cause.

qmf7368   pr4480/cs,nn1697/nn8267   wcj,aj5355   wcj,aj6662   qmf2026

7 Keep*thee*far from*a*false*matter; and the innocent and righteous slay thou

ptn408 cj3588   ptn3808 himf6663   aj7563

not: for I will not justify the wicked.

qmf3947 ptn3808 wcj,nn7810 cj3588   df,nn7810   pimf5786   aj6493

8 And thou shalt take   no   gift: for the gift blindeth the wise, and

wcj,pimf5557   pl,cs,nn1697   aj6662

perverteth the words of the righteous.

ptn3808 qmf3905   wcj,nn1616   wcj,pnp859 qpf3045 (853)   cs,nn5315

9 Also thou shalt not oppress a stranger: for   ye   know   the heart of a

df,nn1616   cj3588   qpf1961   pl,nn1616   pp,cs,nn776   nn4714

stranger, seeing ye were strangers in the   land   of Egypt.

The Seventh Year

wcj,nu8337 pl,nn8141   qmf2232 (853)   nn,pnx776   wcs,qpf622 (853)

10 And   six   years thou shalt sow   thy land, and shalt gather in   the

nn,pnx8393

fruits thereof:

wcj,df,nuor7637   qmf,pnx8058   wcs,qpf,pnx5203   cs,nn34

🔊 11 But the seventh year thou shalt let*it*rest and lie still; that the poor of thy

nn,pnx5971   wcs,qpf398   wcj,nn,pnx3499   cs,nn2416   df,nn7704   qmf398

people may eat: and what*they*leave the beasts of the field shall eat.

ad3651   qmf6213   pp,nn,pnx3754   pp,nn,pnx2132

In*like*manner thou shalt deal with thy vineyard, and with thy oliveyard.

cs,nu8337 pl,nn3117   qmf6213   pl,nn,pnx4639   df,nuor7637 wcj,dfp,nn3117

12 Six   days thou shalt do thy work, and on the seventh day thou

qmf7673 pp,pr4616 nn,pnx7794   wcj,nn,pnx2543   qmf5117   cs,nn1121

shalt rest: that thine ox and thine   ass   may rest, and the son of thy

nn,pnx519   wcj,df,nn1616   wcj,nimf5314

handmaid, and the stranger, may be refreshed.

wcj,pp,nn3605   pnl834   qpf559 pr,pnx413   nimf8104

13 And in   all   things that I have said unto you be circumspect: and

himf2142/ptn3808   wcj,cs,nn8034   aj312   pl,nn430 ptn3808   nimf8085   pr5921

make*no*mention of the   name   of other gods, neither let it be heard out of thy

nn,pnx6310

mouth.

🔊 **23:11** This was a sabbath rest for the land. A fuller form of this law of the sabbatical year is found in Leviticus 25:1–7. Though it followed sound agricultural principles (restoring fertility to the soil), this was not the purpose stated for its observance. The natural uncultivated growth of the grain and fruit would be a much needed resource for the poor and even provide food for the wild animals.

Three Festivals Each Year

^{nu7969　pl,nn7272　　　qmf2287　　pp,pnx　　　dfp,nn8141}
14 Three times thou shalt keep*a*feast unto me in the year.

^{qmf8104　(853)　　　cs,nn2282　　df,pl,nn4682　　　qmf398}
15 Thou shalt keep　　　the feast of unleavened bread: (thou shalt eat

^{pl,nn4682　　cs,nu7651　pl,nn3117　pp,pnl834　　pipf,pnx6680　　　pp,nn4150}
unleavened bread seven days, as I commanded thee, in the time appointed of the

^{cs,nn2320　df,nn24　cj3588　pp,pnx　　qpf3318　　pr4480/nn4714　　wcj,ptn3808　　nimf7200　pl,nn,pnx6440}
month Abib; for in it thou camest out from Egypt: and none shall appear before

^{ad7387}
me empty:)

^{wcj,cs,nn2282　　df,nn7105　　pl,cs,nn1061　　　pl,nn,pnx4639　pnl834}
16 And the feast of harvest, the firstfruits of thy labors, which thou hast

^{qmf2232　　dfp,nn7704　　wcj,cs,nn2282　　df,nn614　　　pp,qnc3318}
sown in the field: and the feast of ingathering, *which is* in the end of the

^{df,nn8141　　　pp,qnc,pnx622　(853)　pl,nn,pnx4639　pr4480　df,nn7704}
year, when thou hast gathered in　thy labors out of the field.

^{nu7969　pl,nn6471　dfp,nn8141　cs,nn3605　nn,pnx2138　nimf7200　pr413/pl,cs,nn6440　df,nn113}
17 Three times in the year all thy males shall appear before the Lord

ⁿⁿ³⁰⁶⁸
God.

^{ptn3808 qmf2076　cs,nn1818　　nn,pnx2077　pr5921　　nn2557　　wcj,ptn3808}
18 Thou shalt not offer the blood of my sacrifice with leavened bread; neither

^{cs,nn2459　　nn,pnx2282　qmf3885　pr5704　　nn1242}
shall the fat of my sacrifice remain until the morning.

^{cs,nn7225　　pl,cs,nn1061　　nn,pnx127　　himf935　　cs,nn1004}
19 The first of the firstfruits of thy land thou shalt bring into the house of the

^{nn3068　　pl,nn,pnx430　　ptn3808 pimf1310　nn1423　　nn,pnx517　pp,cs,nn2461}
LORD thy God. Thou shalt not seethe a kid in his mother's milk.

God's Angel

^{ptdm2009　pnp595　qpta7971　　nn4397　pp,pl,nn,pnx6440　　pp,qnc,pnx8104　　　dfp,nn1870}
20 Behold, I send an Angel before thee, to keep thee in the way,

^{wcj,pp,hinc,pnx935　pr413　df,nn4725　pnl834　　hipf3559}
and to bring thee into the place which I have prepared.

23:14–17 These three appearances before God by the people were three of the seven annual feasts of the Jews (see Lev. 23:16, 17, 33–36). They are listed as the Feast of Unleavened Bread (which was closely associated with the Passover; see Ex. 12:1–11, 14–20; Lev. 23:4–8; Deut. 16:1–8), the Feast of Harvest or Firstfruits (later called the Feast of Weeks and in New Testament times known as Pentecost [see Lev. 23:9–14; Deut. 16:9–12]), and the Feast of Ingathering (later called the Feast of Tabernacles; see Lev. 23:33–36, 39–43; Deut. 16:13–15). At the time of each of these feasts, all males were to make a pilgrimage to the sanctuary, which was at this time the Tabernacle and later became the Temple in Jerusalem.

23:20–23 There is strong evidence that the appearances of the "angel of the LORD" are in fact preincarnate appearances of Christ, the Son of God. Things are said of the angel of the LORD that go beyond the category of angels, and are applicable only to Christ. Hagar called Him by the name of God (Gen. 16:13). When the angel of the LORD appeared to Moses from within the burning bush, the text of the Scripture, the angel Himself, and Moses all affirm that the angel is God (Ex. 3:2–6). Here in Exodus chapter twenty–three it is said of the angel of the LORD that He has the power to forgive sins and that He has the name of God in Him (cf. Luke 7:49; Mark 2:7). No man could see God and live, but the Son of God, who is the fullness of the Godhead bodily, has declared Him (Ex. 33:20; John 1:18; Col. 2:9).

21 Beware   of   him, and obey his voice, provoke him not; for he
will not pardon your transgressions: for my name *is*   in   him.

22 But if thou shalt indeed obey his voice, and   do   all that I speak;
then I will be*an*enemy   unto thine enemies, and an adversary   unto thine
adversaries.

23 For mine Angel shall go   before   thee, and bring*thee*in unto the
Amorites, and the Hittites, and the Perizzites, and the Canaanites, the Hivites, and
the Jebusites: and I will cut*them*off.

24 Thou shalt not bow down to their gods,   nor   serve them, nor
do after their works: but thou shalt utterly overthrow them, and
quite*break*down their images.

25 And ye shall serve   the LORD your God, and he shall bless   thy
bread, and   thy water; and I will take*sickness*away from*the*midst of thee.

26 There shall nothing cast*their*young, nor be barren, in thy land: the
number of thy days I will fulfill.

27 I will send   my fear   before thee, and will destroy   all   the
people to whom thou shalt come, and I will make   all thine enemies
turn*their*backs unto thee.

28 And I will send   hornets before thee, which shall drive out   the
Hivite,   the Canaanite, and   the Hittite, from before thee.

29 I will not drive*them*out from before thee in one year; lest the land
become desolate, and the beast of the field multiply against thee.

30 By little and little I will drive*them*out from before thee,   until thou
be increased, and inherit   the land.

31 And I will   set   thy bounds from*the*Red*sea even unto the sea of
the Philistines, and from*the*desert unto the river: for I will deliver   the
inhabitants of the land into your hand; and thou shalt drive*them*out before
thee.

qmf**3772** ptn**3808**   nn**1285**   pp,pnx   wcj,pp,pl,nn,pnx**430**

32 Thou shalt make no covenant with them, nor with their   gods.

ptn**3808** qmf**3427**   pp,nn,pnx776 cj6435   himf**2398**/pnx(853)   pp,pnx

33 They shall not dwell in thy   land,   lest they make*thee*sin against me:

cj3588   qmf**5647** (853)   pl,nn,pnx**430**   cj3588 qmf**1961**   pp,nn**4170**   pp,pnx

for if thou serve   their gods, it will surely be a snare unto thee.

The Covenant is Signed

qpf**559** wcj,pr413   nn**4872**   qmv**5927**   pr413   nn**3068**   pnp859   wcj,nn**175**

24

And he said unto Moses, Come up unto the LORD, thou, and Aaron,

nn**5070**   wcj,nn30   wcj,pl,nu7657   pr4480/cs,aj**2205**   nn3478   wcj,hipf***7812**

Nadab, and Abihu, and seventy of*the*elders of Israel; and worship

pr4480/nn**7350**

ye afar off.

nn**4872**   pp,nn,pnx905   wcj,nipf**5066**/pr413   nn**3068**   wcj,pnp1992   ptn**3808**

2 And Moses alone   shall come near the LORD: but   they   shall not

qmf**5066**   ptn**3808**   wcj,df,nn**5971** qmf**5927** pr,pnx5973

come nigh; neither shall the people go up with him.

nn**4872**   wcs,qmf935   wcs,pimf**5608**   df,nn**5971**   (853) cs,nn**3605**   pl,cs,nn**1697**   nn**3068**

3 And Moses came and told   the people   all   the words of the LORD,

wcj(853) cs,nn**3605**   df,pl,nn**4941**   cs,nn**3605**   dfp,nn**5971**   wcs,qmf6030   nu259   nn6963

and   all   the judgments: and all   the people answered with one voice, and

wcs,qmf**559** cs,nn**3605**   df,pl,nn**1697** pnl834   nn**3068**   pipf**1696**   qmf**6213**

said,   All the words which the LORD hath said will we do.

nn**4872**   wcs,qmf**3789** (853) cs,nn**3605**   pl,cs,nn**1697**   nn**3068**   wcs,himf**7925**

4 And Moses wrote   all   the words of the LORD, and rose*up*early in

dfp,nn**1242**   wcs,qmf**1129**   nn**4196** pr8478   df,nn**2022** wcj,du,nu8147/nu**6240**   nn**4676**

the morning, and built an altar under the hill, and   twelve   pillars, according

wcj,du,nu8147/nu**6240** pl,cs,nn**7626**   nn3478

to the   twelve   tribes of Israel.

wcs,qmf**7971** (853)   pl,cs,nn**5288**   pl,cs,nn**1121**   nn3478   wcs,himf**5927**

5 And he   sent   young men of the children of Israel, which offered

pl,nn**5930**   wcs,qmf**2076** pl,nn**8002** pl,nn**2077**   pl,nn**6499**   pp,nn**3068**

burnt offerings, and sacrificed peace offerings of oxen unto the LORD.

nn**4872**   wcs,qmf**3947** cs,nn**2677**   df,nn**1818**   wcs,qmf**7760**   dfp,pl,nn101   wcj,cs,nn**2677**

6 And Moses took   half of the blood, and put it in basins; and   half

df,nn**1818**   qpf**2236**   pr5921   df,nn**4196**

of the blood he sprinkled on the altar.

wcs,qmf**3947**   cs,nn**5612**   df,nn**1285**   wcs,qmf**7121**   pp,du,cs,nn**241**

7 And he   took   the book of the covenant, and   read in the audience of the

df,nn**5971**   wcs,qmf**559** cs,nn**3605** pnl834   nn**3068**   pipf**1696**   qmf**6213**

people: and they said,   All that the LORD hath said will we do, and

wcj,qmf**8085**

be obedient.

nn**4872** wcs,qmf**3947** (853)   df,nn**1818**   wcs,qmf**2236**   pr5921   df,nn**5971**   wcs,qmf**559**

8 And Moses took   the blood, and sprinkled it on the people, and said,

ptdm2009   cs,nn**1818**   df,nn**1285** pnl834   nn**3068**   qpf**3772** pr,pnx5973   pr5921

Behold the blood of the covenant, which the LORD hath made with you concerning

cs,nn**3605** df,pndm428 df,pl,nn**1697**

all   these words.

wcs,qmf**5927**   nn**4872**   wcj,nn**175**   nn**5070**   wcj,nn30   wcj,pl,nu7657

9 Then went up Moses, and Aaron, Nadab, and Abihu, and seventy

pr4480/cs,aj**2205**   nn3478

of*the*elders of Israel:

wcs,qmf**7200** (853)   pl,cs,nn**430**   nn3478   wcj,pr8478   du,nn,pnx7272

10 And they   saw   the God of Israel: and *there was* under his   feet   as

cs,nn3840 pp,cs,nn4639   df,nn5601   wcj,pp,cs,nn**6106**   df,du,nn**8064**

it were a paved   work of a sapphire stone, and as it were the   body   of heaven

dfp,nn**2892**

in *his* clearness.

wcj,pr413   pl,cs,nn**678**   pl,cs,nn**1121**   nn3478   qpf7971   ptn**3808**   nn,pnx**3027**

11 And upon the nobles of the children of Israel he laid   not his hand: also

wcs,qmf**2372** (853) df,pl,nn**430**   wcs,qmf398   wcs,qmf**8354**

they saw   God, and did   eat   and drink.

The Tablets of Stone

nn**3068**   wcs,qmf**559**   pr413   nn4872   qmv**5927**   pr,pnx413   df,nn,lh2022

12 And the LORD   said   unto Moses, Come up   to   me into the mount, and

wcj,qmf**1961**   ad8033   wcj,qcj**5414** pp,pnx   (853)   pl,cs,nn3871   df,nn68   wcj,df,nn**8451**

be   there: and I will   give   thee   tables of stone, and a   law,   and

wcj,df,nn**4687**   pnl834   qpf3789   pp,hinc,pnx**3384**

commandments which I have written; that thou mayest   teach   them.

nn4872   wcs,qmf**6965**   pipt,pnx**8334** wcj,nn3091   nn4872   wcs,qmf**5927**   pr413

⌾☞ 13 And Moses rose up, and his minister Joshua: and Moses went up into the

cs,nn2022   df,pl,nn**430**

mount of God.

qpf**559**   wcj,pr413   df,aj**2205**   qmv**3427**   pp,pndm2088   pp,pnx   pr5704/pnl834

14 And he said   unto   the elders, Tarry ye   here   for us,   until   we

qmf**7725**   pr,pnx413   wcj,ptdm2009   nn175   wcj,nn2354   pr,pnx5973   pnit4310 cs,nn**1167**

come again unto you: and, behold, Aaron and Hur *are* with you: if any man

pl,nn**1697**   qmf**5066** pr,pnx413

have any matters to do, let him come unto them.

nn4872   wcs,qmf**5927**   pr413   df,nn2022   df,nn**6051** wcs,pimf**3680** (853)   df,nn2022

15 And Moses went up into the mount, and a cloud covered   the mount.

cs,nn3519   nn3068   wcs,qmf**7931**   pr5921 cs,nn2022   nn5514   df,nn**6051**

16 And the glory of the LORD   abode upon mount Sinai, and the cloud

wcs,pimf,pnx**3680**   cs,nu8337   pl,nn3117   df,nuor7637   dfp,nn3117   wcs,qmf7121   pr413   nn4872

covered it   six days: and the seventh day   he called unto Moses

pr4480/cs,nn**8432**   df,nn**6051**

out*of*the*midst of the cloud.

wcj,cs,nn**4758**   cs,nn3519   nn**3068**   qpta398   pp,nn784

17 And the sight of the glory of the LORD *was* like devouring fire on the

pp,cs,nn**7218**   df,nn2022   pp,du,cs,nn**5869**   pl,cs,nn**1121**   nn3478

top   of the mount in the   eyes   of the children of Israel.

nn4872   wcs,qmf935   pp,cs,nn**8432**   df,nn**6051**   wcs,qmf**5927**   pr413

18 And Moses went into the midst of the cloud, and got*him*up into the

df,nn2022   nn4872   wcs,qmf**1961**   dfp,nn2022 pl,nu705 nn3117   wcj,pl,nu705   nn3915

mount: and Moses   was   in the mount forty days and forty nights.

⌾☞ **24:13** See the note on Numbers 27:18–23, concerning Joshua, Moses' "minister."

Gifts for the Tent

25
nn3068 wcs,pimf1696 pr413 nn4872 pp,qnc559
And the LORD spoke unto Moses, saying,

pimv1696 pr413 pl,cs,nn1121 nn3478 wcj,qmf3947 pp,pnx
2 Speak unto the children of Israel, that they bring me an

nn8641 pr4480/pr854 cs,nn3605 nn376 pnl834 qmf,pnx5068 nn,pnx3820 qmf3947 (853)
offering: of every man that giveth*it*willingly with his heart ye shall take

nn,pnx8641
my offering.

wcj,pndm2063 df,nn8641 pnl834 qmf3947 pr4480/pr,pnx854 nn2091
3 And this *is* the offering which ye shall take of them; gold, and

wcj,nn3701 wcj,nn5178
silver, and brass,

wcj,nn8504 wcj,nn713 wcj,cs,nn8438/nn8144 wcj,nn8336 wcj,pl,nn5795
4 And blue, and purple, and scarlet, and fine linen, and goats' *hair*,

pl,nn352 wcj,pl,cs,nn5785 pl,pupt119 pl,nn8476 wcj,cs,nn5785 pl,nn7848 wcj,pl,cs,nn6086
5 And rams' skins dyed red, and badgers' skins, and shittim wood,

nn8081 dfp,nn3974 pl,nn1314 df,nn4888 pp,cs,nn8081 df,pl,nn5561 wcj,pp,cs,nn7004
6 Oil for the light, spices for anointing oil, and for sweet incense,

nn7718 pl,cs,nn68 wcj,pl,cs,nn68 pl,nn4394 dfp,nn646 wcj,dfp,nn2833
7 Onyx stones, and stones to be set in the ephod, and in the breastplate.

wcs,qpf6213 pp,pnx nn4720 wcs,qpf7931 pp,nn,pnx8432
8 And let them make me a sanctuary; that I may dwell among them.

pp,nn3605 pnl834 pnp589 hipt7200 pnx(853) (853) cs,nn8403
9 According to all that I show thee, *after* the pattern of the

df,nn4908 wcj(853) cs,nn8403 cs,nn3605 pl,nn,pnx3627 wcj,ad3651
tabernacle, and the pattern of all the instruments thereof, even so shall ye

qmf6213
make *it*.

The Ark of the Covenant

wcs,qpf6213 cs,nn727 pl,nn7848 pl,cs,nn6086 du,nn520 wcj,nn2677
10 And they shall make an ark *of* shittim wood: two cubits and a half

nn,pnx753 wcj,nn520 wcj,nn2677 nn,pnx7341
shall be the length thereof, and a cubit and a half the breadth thereof, and a

wcj,nn520 wcj,nn2677 nn,pnx6967
cubit and a half the height thereof.

25:7 The word "ephod" (646) is a Hebrew name for the sacred upper garment of the priest, of plain linen for the regular priest. It was multi-colored and embroidered especially for the high priest. The breastplate, which was worn only by the high priest alone, went on top of the ephod or upper garment. It was square and contained twelve precious stones, one for each tribe, inset. It extended from the waist to the shoulders and was connected at the shoulders by a gem. The robe was sleeveless under the ephod and came down to the ankles.

25:8, 9 The Lord commanded Moses to build a sanctuary. It was to be a tabernacle or moveable tent which would be suitable for Israel's nomadic lifestyle. The Levites would have responsibility for it (Num. 18:2-4). It was to be a dwelling place for the Lord among His people (v. 8) and a depository for the tables of the law or testimony, hence it was called "the tabernacle of testimony" (Ex. 38:21). Also, it was known as the "tent of meeting" (Ex. 40:34), because the Lord met His people there. Its general designation was "the house of the LORD" (Ex. 34:26), and it was to be filled with "the glory of the LORD" (Ex. 40:36-38) and by His presence. From there He would lead the children of Israel on their journey.

wcs,pipf6823   pnx(853)   aj**2889**   nn2091   pr4480/nn**1004**   wcj,pr4480/nn2351

11 And thou shalt overlay   it with pure gold, within and   without shalt

pimf,pnx6823   wcs,qpf**6213**   pr,pnx5921   cs,nn2213   nn2091   ad5439

thou overlay it, and shalt make   upon it a crown of gold round about.

wcs,qpf3332   nu702   pl,cs,nn2885   nn2091   pp,pnx   wcs,qpf**5414**   pr5921

12 And thou shalt   cast four rings of gold for it, and   put   *them* in the

nu702   pl,nn,pnx6471   wcj,du,cs,nu8147 pl,nn2885   pr5921   df,nu259 nn,pnx6763

four corners thereof; and   two   rings *shall be* in the one   side   of it, and

wcj,du,cs,nu8147 pl,nn2885 pr5921   df,nuor8145 nn,pnx6763

two   rings   in the other   side   of it.

wcs,qpf**6213**   pl,cs,nn905   pl,nn7848   pl,cs,nn6086   wcs,pipf6823   pnx(853)

13 And thou shalt make   staves *of* shittim wood, and overlay   them with

nn2091

gold.

wcs,hipf935 (853)   df,pl,nn905   dfp,pl,nn2885 pr5921   pl,cs,nn6763

14 And thou shalt   put   the staves into the   rings   by the sides of the

df,nn**727**   (853)   df,nn**727**   pp,qnc5375   pp,pnx

ark, that   the ark may be borne with them.

df,pl,nn905   qmf1961   pp,pl,cs,nn2885   df,nn**727**   ptn**3808**   qmf**5493**

15 The staves shall be   in the   rings   of the ark: they shall not be taken

pr,pnx4480

from it.

wcs,qpf**5414**   pr413   df,nn**727** (853)   df,nn**5715**   pnl834

16 And thou shalt   put   into the ark   the testimony which I shall

qmf**5414**/pr,pnx413

give   thee.

wcs,qpf**6213**   cs,nn3727   aj**2889** nn2091 du,nn520   wcj,nn2677

17 And thou shalt make a mercy seat *of* pure gold: two cubits and a   half

nn,pnx753   wcj,nn520   wcj,nn2677   nn,pnx7341

shall be the length thereof, and a cubit and a   half   the breadth thereof.

wcs,qpf**6213**   du,nu8147   pl,nn3742   nn2091   nn4749

18 And thou shalt make   two   cherubims *of* gold, *of* beaten work shalt thou

qmf**6213** pnx(853)   pr4480/du,cs,nu8147 pl,cs,nn7098   df,nn3727

make   them, in*the*two   ends   of the mercy seat.

wcj,qmv**6213**   nu259   nn3742   pr4480/pndm2088/pr4480/nn7098   nu259 wcj,nn3742

19 And   make   one   cherub on*the*one*end,   and the other cherub

pr4480/pndm2088/pr4480/nn7098   pr4480   df,nn3727   qmf**6213** (853)   df,pl,nn3742 pr5921

on*the*other*end: *even* of the mercy seat shall ye make   the cherubims on the

du,cs,nu8147 pl,nn,pnx7098

two   ends   thereof.

df,pl,nn**3742**   wcs,qpf1961   pl,cs,qpta6566   du,nn3671 pp,ad,lh4605   pl,qpta5526/pr5921

20 And the cherubims shall   stretch forth *their* wings on high, covering the

df,nn3727   pp,du,nn,pnx3671   wcj,pl,nn,pnx6440   nn376 pr413   nn,pnx251

mercy seat with their wings, and their   faces *shall look* one to another;

pr413   df,nn3727   pl,cs,nn6440   df,pl,nn3742   qmf1961

toward the mercy seat shall the faces of the cherubims be.

wcs,qpf**5414** (853)   df,nn3727   pr4480/pp,ad,lh4605 pr5921   df,nn727

21 And thou shalt put   the mercy seat   above   upon the ark; and

wcj,pr413   df,nn**727**   qmf**5414** (853)   df,nn**5715** pnl834   qmf**5414**/pr,pnx413

in the ark thou shalt put   the testimony that I shall   give   thee.

ad8033   wcs,nipf**3259**   pp,pnx   wcs,pipf**1696**   pr,pnx854

22 And there I will   meet   with thee, and I will commune with thee

pr4480/pr5921   df,nn**3727**   pr4480/pr996   du,cs,nu8147   df,pl,nn**3742**   pnl834   pr5921

from above the mercy seat, from between the   two   cherubims which *are* upon cs,nn**727**   df,nn**5715**   (853)   cs,nn3605   pnl834

the   ark   of   the   testimony,   of   all   *things*   which   I   will

pimf**6680**/pnx(853)   pr413   pl,cs,nn**1121**   nn3478

give*thee*in*commandment   unto the children of Israel.

The Table for the Shewbread

wcs,qpf**6213**   cs,nn7979   pl,nn7848   pl,cs,nn6086   du,nn520

23 Thou shalt also make   a table *of* shittim wood: two cubits *shall be* the

nn,pnx**753**   wcj,nn520   nn,pnx7341   wcj,nn520   wcj,nn2677   nn,pnx6967

length thereof, and a cubit the breadth thereof, and a cubit and a   half the height

thereof.

wcs,pipf6823 pnx(853)   aj**2889**   nn2091   wcs,qpf**6213**   pp,pnx   cs,nn2213

24 And thou shalt overlay   it with pure gold, and make thereto a crown of

nn2091   ad5439

gold round about.

wcs,qpf**6213**   pp,pnx   cs,nn4526   nn2948   ad5439

25 And thou shalt make unto it a border of a handbreadth round about, and

wcs,qpf**6213**   nn2091   cs,nn2213   pp,nn,pnx4526   ad5439

thou shalt make a golden crown to the border thereof round about.

wcs,qpf**6213**   pp,pnx   nu702 pl,cs,nn2885   nn2091   wcs,qpf**5414** (853)   df,pl,nn2885

26 And thou shalt make for it four rings of gold, and   put   the rings

pr5921   nu702   df,pl,nn6285 pnl834   pp,cs,nu702 du,nn,pnx7272

in the four corners that *are* on the   four   feet   thereof.

pp,pr5980   df,nn4526   df,pl,nn2885 qmf**1961**   pp,pl,nn**1004**   pp,pl,nn905

27 Over against the border shall the   rings   be for places of the staves to

pp,qnc**5375** (853)   df,nn7979

bear   the table.

wcs,qpf**6213** (853)   df,pl,nn905   pl,nn7848   pl,cs,nn6086   wcs,pipf6823 pnx(853)

28 And thou shalt make   the staves *of* shittim wood, and overlay   them

nn2091   (853)   df,nn7979   wcs,nipf**5375**   pp,pnx

with gold, that   the table may be borne with them.

wcs,qpf**6213**   pl,nn,pnx7086   wcj,pl,nn,pnx**3709**

29 And thou shalt make the   dishes   thereof, and   spoons   thereof, and

wcj,pl,nn,pnx7184   wcj,pl,nn,pnx4518   homf5258   pnl834/pp,pnp2004   aj**2889**   nn2091

covers   thereof, and   bowls   thereof, to cover   withal: *of* pure gold shalt

qmf**6213** pnx(853)

thou make   them.

wcs,qpf**5414** pr5921   df,nn7979 cs,nn3899/pl,nn**6440** pp,pl,nn,pnx**6440**   nn8548

30 And thou shalt set   upon the table shewbread before me always.

wcs,qpf**6213**   cs,nn4501   aj**2889** nn2091   nn4749

31 And thou shalt make a candlestick *of* pure gold: *of* beaten work shall the

df,nn4501   nimf**6213**   nn,pnx**3409**   wcj,nn,pnx7070   pl,nn,pnx1375   pl,nn,pnx3730

candlestick be made: his shaft, and his branches, his bowls, his knops, and his

wcj,pl,nn,pnx6525   qmf**1961** pr,pnx4480

flowers, shall be   of   the same.

wcj,nu8337   pl,nn7070   pl,qpta3318   pr4480/pl,nn,pnx6654   nu7969 pl,cs,nn7070

32 And   six   branches shall come out*of*the*sides of it; three branches of the

nn4501   pr4480/nn,pnx6654/df,nu259   wcj,nu7969   pl,cs,nn7070   nn4501

candlestick out*of*the*one*side,   and   three   branches   of   the   candlestick

pr4480/nn,pnx6654/df,nuor8145

out*of*the*other*side:

nu7969   pl,nn1375   pl,pupt8246   nn3730   wcj,nn6525   df,nu259

33 Three bowls made*like*unto*almonds, *with* a knop and a flower in one

dfp,nn7070 wcj,nu7969 pl,nn1375 pl,pupt8246 df,nu259 dfp,nn7070 nn3730
branch; and three bowls made*like*almonds in the other branch, *with* a knop and a

wcj,nn6525 ad3651 pp,cs,nu8337 df,pl,nn7070 df,pl,qpta3318 pr4480 df,nn4501
flower: so in the six branches that come out of the candlestick.

wcj,dfp,nn4501 nu702 pl,nn1375 pl,pupt8246
34 And in the candlestick *shall be* four bowls made*like*unto*almonds, *with*

pl,nn,pnx3730 wcj,pl,nn,pnx6525
their knops and their flowers.

wcj,nn3730 pr8478 du,cs,nu8147 df,pl,nn7070 pr,pnx4480
35 And *there shall be* a knop under two branches of the same, and a

wcj,nn3730 pr8478 du,cs,nu8147 df,pl,nn7070 pr,pnx4480 wcj,nn3730 pr8478 du,cs,nu8147 df,pl,nn7070
knop under two branches of the same, and a knop under two branches

pr,pnx4480 pp,cs,nu8337 df,pl,nn7070 df,pl,qpta3318 pr4480
of the same, according to the six branches that proceed out of the

df,nn4501
candlestick.

pl,nn,pnx3730 wcj,pl,nn,pnx7070 qmf1961 pr,pnx4480 nn,pnx3605
36 Their knops and their branches shall be of the same: all it *shall*

nu259 nn4749 aj2889 nn2091
be one beaten work *of* pure gold.

wcs,qpf6213 (853) nu7651 pl,nn,pnx5216 wcs,hipf5927
37 And thou shalt make the seven lamps thereof: and they shall light

(853) pl,nn,pnx5216 wcs,hipf215 pr5921/cs,nn5676/pl,nn,pnx6440
the lamps thereof, that they may give light over against it.

wcj,du,nn,pnx4457 wcj,pl,nn,pnx4289 aj2889 nn2091
38 And the tongs thereof, and the censers thereof, *shall be of* pure gold.

nn3603 aj2889 nn2091 qmf6213 pnx(853) pr854 cs,nn3605 df,pndm428 df,pl,nn3627
39 *Of* a talent of pure gold shall he make it, with all these vessels.

wcj,qmv7200 wcj,qmv6213 pp,nn,pnx8403 pnl834 hopt7200
40 And look that thou make *them* after their pattern, which was showed

pnp859 dfp,nn2022
thee in the mount.

The Tabernacle

qmf6213 wcj(853) df,nn4908 cs,nu6235 pl,nn3407
26 Moreover thou shalt make the tabernacle *with* ten curtains *of*

nn8336/hopt7806 wcj,nn8504 wcj,nn713 wcj,cs,nn8438/nn8144
fine*twined*linen, and blue, and purple, and scarlet: *with*

pl,nn3742 qpta2803 cs,nn4639 qmf6213 pnx(853)
cherubims of cunning work shalt thou make them.

cs,nn753 df,nu259 df,nn3407 nu8083 wcj,pl,nu6242 dfp,nn520 wcj,nn7341
2 The length of one curtain *shall be* eight and twenty cubits, and the breadth

df,nu259 df,nn3407 nu702 dfp,nn520 pp,cs,nn3605 df,pl,nn3407 nu259 nn4060
of one curtain four cubits: and every one of the curtains shall have one measure.

cs,nu2568 df,pl,nn3407 qmf1961 pl,qpta2266 nn802 pr413 nn,pnx269
3 The five curtains shall be coupled together one to another; and *other*

wcj,nu2568 pl,nn3407 pl,qpta2266 nn802 pr413 nn,pnx269
five curtains *shall be* coupled one to another.

wcs,qpf6213 pl,cs,nn3924 nn8504 pr5921 cs,nn8193 df,nu259 df,nn3407
4 And thou shalt make loops of blue upon the edge of the one curtain

pr4480/nn7098 dfp,nn2279 wcj,ad3651 qmf6213 df,aj7020
from*the*selvage in the coupling; and likewise shalt thou make in the uttermost

pp,cs,nn8193 df,nn3407 dfp,nn4225 df,nuor8145
edge of *another* curtain, in the coupling of the second.

pl,nu2572 pl,nn3924   qmf**6213**   df,nn259 dfp,nn3407   wcj,pl,nu2572 pl,nn3924

5 Fifty loops shalt thou make in the one curtain, and fifty loops shalt thou

qmf**6213**   pp,cs,nn7097   df,nn3407 pnl834   dfp,nn4225   df,nuor8145

make in the edge of the curtain that is in the coupling of the second; that the

df,pl,nn3924   pl,cs,hipt6901   nn802 pr413 nn,pnx**269**

loops may take hold one of another.

wcs,qpf**6213** pl,nu2572 pl,cs,nn7165   nn2091   wcs,pipf2266 (853)   df,pl,nn3407

6 And thou shalt make fifty tacks of gold, and couple the curtains

nn802/pr413/nn,pnx**269**   dfp,pl,nn7165   wcs,qpf**1961** nu259 df,nn**4908**

together with the tacks: and it shall be one tabernacle.

wcs,qpf**6213** pl,cs,nn3407   pl,nn5795   pp,nn**168**   pr5921

7 And thou shalt make curtains of goats' hair to be a covering upon the

df,nn**4908**   nu6249/nu6240 pl,nn3407   qmf**6213**   (pnx853)

tabernacle: eleven curtains shalt thou make.

cs,nn753   df,nu259 df,nn3407   nu7970 dfp,nn520   wcj,nn7341   df,nu259

8 The length of one curtain *shall be* thirty cubits, and the breadth of one

df,nn3407 nu702 dfp,nn520   pp,nu6249/nu6240 pl,nn3407   nu259 nn4060

curtain four cubits: and the eleven curtains *shall be all* of one measure.

wcs,pipf2266 (853) cs,nn2568 df,pl,nn3407   pp,nn905   wcj(853) cs,nu8337

9 And thou shalt couple five curtains by themselves, and six

df,pl,nn3407   pp,nn905   wcs,qpf3717   df,nuor8345 (853) df,nn3407   pr413/pr4136/pl,cs,nn**6440**

curtains by themselves, and shalt double the sixth curtain in*the*forefront of

df,nn**168**

the tabernacle.

wcs,qpf**6213** pl,nu2572 pl,nn3924 pr5921   cs,nn**8193**   df,nu259 df,nn3407

10 And thou shalt make fifty loops on the edge of the one curtain *that is*

df,aj7020   dfp,nn2279   wcj,pl,nu2572 pl,nn3924 pr5921   cs,nn**8193**   df,nn3407

outermost in the coupling, and fifty loops in the edge of the curtain which

df,nn2279   df,nuor8145

coupleth the second.

wcs,qpf**6213** pl,nu2572 pl,cs,nn7165   nn5178   wcs,hipf935 (853)   df,pl,nn7165

11 And thou shalt make fifty tacks of brass, and put the tacks into

dfp,pl,nn3924   wcs,pipf2266/(853)/df,nn**168**   wcs,qpf**1961** nu259

the loops, and couple*the*tent*together, that it may be one.

wcj,cs,nn**5629**   df,qpta5736   pp,pl,cs,nn3407   df,nn**168**   cs,nn2677 df,nn3407

12 And the remnant that remaineth of the curtains of the tent, the half curtain

df,qpta5736   qmf5628 pr5921   pl,cs,nn268   df,nn**4908**

that remaineth, shall hang over the backside of the tabernacle.

wcj,df,nn520   pr4480/pndm2088   wcj,df,nn520   pr4480/pndm2088

13 And a cubit on*the*one*side, and a cubit on*the*other*side of that

dfp,qpta5736   pp,cs,nn753   pl,cs,nn3407   df,nn**168** qmf**1961** qptp5628 pr5921

which remaineth in the length of the curtains of the tent, it shall hang over the

pl,cs,nn6654   df,nn**4908**   pr4480/pndm2088   wcj,pr4480/pndm2088   pp,pinc,pnx**3680**

sides of the tabernacle on*this*side and on*that*side, to cover it.

wcs,qpf**6213**   nn4372   dfp,nn**168**   pl,nn352 pl,cs,nn5785   pl,pupt119

14 And thou shalt make a covering for the tent of rams' skins dyed red,

wcj,cs,nn4372 pr4480/pp,nn,lh4605   pl,nn8476 pl,cs,nn5785

and a covering above of badgers' skins.

wcs,qpf**6213** (853) df,pl,nn7175   dfp,nn**4908**   pl,nn7848 pl,cs,nn6086

15 And thou shalt make boards for the tabernacle of shittim wood

pl,qpta5975

standing up.

nu6235 pl,nn520   cs,nn753   df,nn7175   wcj,nn520   wcj,cs,nn2677 (df,nn520)

16 Ten cubits *shall be* the length of a board, and a cubit and a half

cs,nn7341   df,nu259 df,nn7175

shall be the breadth of one board.

du,cs,nu8147   pl,nn3027   df,nu259   dfp,nn7175   pl,pupt7947   nn802   pr413

17 Two   tenons   *shall* *there* *be* in   one   board,   set*in*order   one   against

nn,pnx269   ad3651   qmf6213   pp,cs,nn3605   pl,cs,nn7175   df,nn4908

another: thus shalt thou make for   all   the boards of the tabernacle.

wcs,qpf6213   (853)   df,pl,nn7175   dfp,nn4908   pl,nu6242   nn7175

18 And thou shalt make   the boards for the tabernacle, twenty boards on the

nn,lh5045   pp,cs,nn6285   nn,lh8486

south   side   southward.

qmf6213   wcj,pl,nu705   pl,cs,nn134   nn3701   pr8478   pl,nu6242   df,nn7175

19 And thou shalt make   forty   sockets of silver under the   twenty boards;

du,cs,nu8147   pl,nn134   pr8478   df,nu259   df,nn7175   pp,du,cs,nu8147   pl,nn,pnx3027   wcj,du,cs,nu8147   pl,nn134

two   sockets under   one   board for his   two   tenons, and   two   sockets

pr8478   df,nu259   df,nn7175   pp,du,cs,nu8147   pl,nn,pnx3027

under another board for his   two   tenons.

df,nuor8145   wcj,pp,cs,nn6763   df,nn4908   nn6828   pp,cs,nn6285

20 And for the second   side   of the tabernacle on the north   side   *there*

pl,nu6242   nn7175

shall *be* twenty boards:

wcj,pl,nu705   pl,nn,pnx134   nn3701   du,cs,nu8147   pl,nn134   pr8478   df,nu259   df,nn7175

21 And their   forty   sockets *of* silver;   two   sockets under   one   board, and

wcj,du,cs,nu8147   pl,nn134   pr8478   df,nu259   df,nn7175

two   sockets under another board.

wcj,pp,du,cs,nn3411   df,nn4908   nn,lh3220   qmf6213   nu8337

22 And for the   sides   of the tabernacle westward thou shalt make   six

pl,nn7175

boards.

wcj,du,cs,nu8147   pl,nn7175   qmf6213   pp,pl,cs,nn4742   df,nn4908

23 And   two   boards shalt thou make for the   corners of the tabernacle in

dfp,du,nn3411

the two sides.

wcj,qmf1961   pl,qpta8382   pr4480/pp,ad4295   qmf1961

24 And they shall   be   coupled together   beneath,   and they shall   be

pl,qpta8382   wcj,ad3162/pr5921   nn,pnx7218   pr413   df,nu259   df,nn2885   ad3651   qmf1961

coupled together   above   the   head   of it unto   one   ring: thus shall it   be   for

pp,du,nu,pnx8147   qmf1961   pp,du,cs,nu8147   df,pl,nn4740

them   both;   they shall   be   for the   two   corners.

wcs,qpf1961   nu8083   pl,nn7175   wcj,pl,nn,pnx134   nn3701   nu8337/nu6240

25 And they shall   be   eight boards, and their   sockets *of* silver,   sixteen

pl,nn134   du,cs,nu8147   pl,nn134   pr8478   df,nu259   df,nn7175   wcj,du,cs,nu8147   pl,nn134   pr8478   df,nu259

sockets;   two   sockets under   one   board, and   two   sockets under another

df,nn7175

board.

wcs,qpf6213   pl,nn1280   pl,nn7848   pl,cs,nn6086   nu2568   pp,pl,cs,nn7175

26 And thou shalt   make   bars *of* shittim   wood; five for the   boards   of the

df,nu259   cs,nn6763   df,nn4908

one   side of the tabernacle,

wcj,nu2568   pl,nn1280   pp,pl,cs,nn7175   df,nuor8145   cs,nn6763   df,nn4908

27 And   five   bars for the   boards   of the   other   side   of the tabernacle, and

wcj,nu2568   pl,nn1280   pp,pl,cs,nn7175   cs,nn6763   df,nn4908   dfp,du,nn3411

five   bars for the   boards   of the   side   of the tabernacle, for the two sides

nn,lh3220

westward.

df,aj8484   wcj,df,nn1280   pp,cs,nn8432   df,pl,nn7175   hipt1272   pr4480   df,nn7097

28 And the middle   bar   in the   midst   of the boards shall reach from   end

pr413   df,nn7097

to   end.

<small>pimf6823   wcj(853)   df,pl,nn7175   nn2091   qmf6213   wcj(853)</small>

29 And thou shalt overlay   the boards with gold, and make   their

<small>pl,nn,pnx2885   nn2091   pl,nn1004   dfp,pl,nn1280   wcs,pipf6823 (853)   df,pl,nn1280</small>

rings *of* gold *for* places for the bars: and thou shalt overlay   the bars with

<small>nn2091</small>

gold.

<small>wcs,hipf6965   (853)   df,nn4908   pp,nn,pnx4941</small>

30 And thou shalt rear up   the tabernacle according to the fashion thereof

<small>pnl834   hopf7200   dfp,nn2022</small>

which was showed thee in the mount.

<small>wcj,qpf6213   nn6532   nn8504   wcj,nn713   wcj,cs,nn8438/nn8144</small>

☙ 31 And thou shalt make a veil *of* blue, and purple, and   scarlet,   and

<small>wcj,nn8336/hopt7806   qpta2803   cs,nn4639   pl,nn3742   pnx(853)   qmf6213</small>

fine*twined*linen of cunning work: with cherubims shall   it be made:

<small>wcs,qpf5414 pnx(853)   pr5921 nu702 pl,cs,nn5982   pl,nn7848   pl,pupt6823</small>

32 And thou shalt hang   it upon four pillars of shittim *wood* overlaid

<small>nn2091   pl,nn,pnx2053   nn2091   pr5921   nu702 pl,cs,nn134   nn3701</small>

with gold: their hooks *shall be of* gold, upon the four sockets of silver.

<small>wcs,qpf5414   (853)   df,nn6532   pr8478   df,pl,nn7165</small>

33 And thou shalt hang up   the veil under the tacks, that thou mayest

<small>wcs,hipf935   ad,lh8033   pr4480/cs,nn1004   dfp,nn6532 (853)   cs,nn727   df,nn5715   df,nn6532</small>

bring in thither   within   the veil   the ark of the testimony: and the veil

<small>wcs,hipf914   pp,pnx   pr996   df,nn6944   wcj(pr996)   cs,nn6944/df,pl,nn6944</small>

shall divide unto you between the holy *place* and   the most holy.

<small>wcs,qpf5414 (853)   df,nn3727   pr5921   cs,nn727   df,nn5715</small>

34 And thou shalt   put   the mercy seat upon the ark of the testimony in

<small>pp,cs,nn6944/df,pl,nn6944</small>

the most holy *place*.

<small>wcs,qpf7760   (853)   df,nn7979 pr4480/nn2351   dfp,nn6532   wcj(853)</small>

35 And thou shalt   set   the table without the veil, and   the

<small>df,nn4501   pr5227   df,nn7979 pr5921   cs,nn6763   df,nn4908   nn,lh8486</small>

candlestick over against the table on the side of the tabernacle toward the south:

<small>qmf5414   wcj,df,nn7979 pr5921   nn6828 cs,nn6763</small>

and thou shalt put the table   on the north side.

<small>wcs,qpf6213   nn4539   pp,cs,nn6607   df,nn168   nn8504</small>

36 And thou shalt make a hanging for the door of the tent, *of* blue, and

<small>wcj,nn713   wcj,cs,nn8438/nn8144   wcj,nn8336/hopt7806   cs,nn4639/qpta7551</small>

purple, and   scarlet,   and fine*twined*linen, wrought with needlework.

<small>wcs,qpf6213   dfp,nn4539 nu2568 pl,cs,nn5982   pl,nn7848</small>

37 And thou shalt make for the hanging five pillars *of* shittim *wood*, and

<small>wcs,pipf6823 pnx(853)   nn2091   wcj,pl,nn,pnx2053   nn2091</small>

overlay   them with gold, *and* their   hooks *shall be of* gold: and thou shalt

<small>wcs,qpf3332 nu2568 pl,cs,nn134   nn5178   pp,pnx</small>

cast   five sockets of brass for them.

☙ **26:31–35** The veil, literally "a separation," was hung between the Holy of Holies and the Holy Place. Its function was to separate all men, even the priests, from the presence of God. Only one man, the high priest, went beyond that veil and he was permitted to do so only once a year, on the Day of Atonement (Lev. 16:1–19). His duty was to take the blood of a bull as an offering for his sins and the sins of the priests, and the blood of a goat as an offering for the sins of the people. The meaning was clear: man was separated from God by reason of sin and could approach Him only through blood which was presented by a priest, who prior to the sin-offerings had to offer incense that he might find mercy and not die (Lev. 16:13). When Jesus died on the cross, the veil hanging in the temple was torn in two (Matt. 27:51). Jesus went beyond that veil (Heb. 9:12, 24) as high priest (Heb. 9:11; 7:23–28), taking His own blood (Heb. 9:12), and making full atonement (Heb. 10:10, 12).

The Altar of Burnt Offering

27 And thou shalt make an altar *of* shittim wood, five cubits long,
wcs,qpf**6213** (853)   df,nn**4196**   pl,nn7848   pl,cs,nn6086   nu2568   pl,cs,nn520   nn**753**

and five cubits broad; the altar shall be foursquare: and the
wcj,nu2568   pl,cs,nn520   nn7341   df,nn**4196**   qmf**1961**   qptp7251

height thereof *shall be* three cubits.
nn,pnx6967   wcj,nu7969   pl,cs,nn520

2 And thou shalt make the horns of it upon the four corners thereof: his
wcs,qpf**6213**   pl,nn,pnx7161   pr5921   cs,nu702   pl,nn,pnx6438

horns shall be of the same: and thou shalt overlay it with brass.
pl,nn,pnx7161   qmf**1961** pr,pnx4480   wcs,pipf6823 pnx(853)   nn5178

3 And thou shalt make his pans to receive*his*ashes, and his shovels, and
wcs,qpf**6213**   pl,nn,pnx5518   pp,pinc,pnx**1878**   wcj,pl,nn,pnx3257

his basins, and his fleshhooks, and his firepans: all the vessels thereof thou
wcj,pl,nn,pnx4219   wcj,pl,nn,pnx4207   wcj,pl,nn,pnx4289 pp,cs,nn3605   pl,nn,pnx3627

shalt make *of* brass.
qmf**6213**   nn5178

4 And thou shalt make for it a grate of network *of* brass; and upon the
wcs,qpf**6213**   pp,pnx   nn4345   cs,nn4639/cs,nn7568   nn5178   pr5921

net shalt thou make four brazen rings in the four corners thereof.
df,nn7568   wcs,qpf**6213** nu702   nn5178   pl,cs,nn2885 pr5921   nu702   pl,nn,pnx7098

5 And thou shalt put it under the compass of the altar beneath, that
wcs,qpf**5414** pnx(853)   pr8478   cs,nn3749   df,nn**4196** pr4480/pp,ad4295

the net may be even to the midst of the altar.
df,nn7568   wcs,qpf**1961**   pr5704   cs,nn2677   df,nn**4196**

6 And thou shalt make staves for the altar, staves *of* shittim wood, and
wcs,qpf**6213**   pl,nn905   dfp,nn**4196**   pl,cs,nn905   pl,nn7848   pl,cs,nn6086

overlay them with brass.
wcs,pipf6823 pnx(853)   nn5178

7 And the staves shall be put into the rings, and the staves shall
(853)   pl,nn,pnx905   wcs,hopf935   dfp,pl,nn2885   df,pl,nn905

be upon the two sides of the altar, to bear it.
wcs,qpf**1961** pr5921   du,cs,nu8147   pl,cs,nn6763   df,nn**4196**   pp,qnc**5375** pnx(853)

8 Hollow with boards shalt thou make it: as it was showed thee in
cs,qptp5014   pl,nn3871   qmf**6213** pnx(853)   pp,pnl834   hipf**7200**   pnx(853)

the mount, so shall they make *it*.
dfp,nn2022 ad**3651**   qmf**6213**

The Enclosure of the Tabernacle

9 And thou shalt make the court of the tabernacle: for the south side
wcs,qpf**6213** (853)   cs,nn2691   df,nn**4908**   cs,nn5045 pp,cs,nn6285

southward *there shall be* hangings for the court *of* fine*twined*linen of a hundred
nn,lh8486   pl,nn7050   dfp,nn2691   nn8336/hopt7806   nu3967

cubits long for one side:
dfp,nn520 nn**753**   df,nu259 dfp,nn6285

10 And the twenty pillars thereof and their twenty sockets *shall be of*
pl,nu6242   wcj,pl,nn,pnx5982   pl,nu6242   wcj,pl,nn,pnx134

brass; the hooks of the pillars and their fillets *shall be of* silver.
nn5178   pl,cs,nn2053   df,pl,nn5982   wcj,pl,nn,pnx2838   nn3701

11 And likewise for the north side in length *there shall be* hangings of a
wcj,ad**3651**   nn6828 pp,cs,nn6285   dfp,nn**753**   pl,nn7050

nu3967   nn**753**   pl,nu6242   wcj,pl,nn,pnx5982   pl,nu6242 wcj,pl,nn,pnx134   nn5178
hundred *cubits* long, and his twenty   pillars   and their twenty   sockets *of* brass;

pl,cs,nn2053   df,pl,nn5982   wcj,pl,nn,pnx2838   nn3701
the hooks of the pillars and their   fillets *of* silver.

                    wcj,cs,nn7341   df,nn2691   nn3220 pp,cs,nn6285   pl,nn7050
12 And *for* the breadth of the court on the west   side   *shall be* hangings of

pl,nu2572   nn520   pl,nn,pnx5982 nu6235   wcj,pl,nn,pnx134 nu6235
fifty cubits: their pillars ten, and their sockets ten.

                    wcj,cs,nn7341   df,nn2691   ad,lh**6924** pp,cs,nn6285 nn,lh4217   pl,nu2572
13 And the breadth of the court on the east   side   eastward *shall be* fifty

nn520
cubits.

              pl,nn7050   dfp,nn3802   wcj,nu2568/nu6240   nn520
14 The hangings of one side *of the gate shall be*   fifteen   cubits: their

pl,nn,pnx5982   nu7969   wcj,pl,nn,pnx134   nu7969
pillars three, and their sockets three.

              df,nuor8145 wcj,dfp,nn3802   pl,nn7050 cs,nu2568/nu6240   pl,nn,pnx5982
15 And on the other   side   *shall be* hangings fifteen *cubits*: their pillars

nu7969   wcj,pl,nn,pnx134 nu7969
three, and their sockets three.

              wcj,pp,cs,nn8179   df,nn2691   nn4539   pl,nu6242 nn520
16 And for the   gate   of the court *shall be* a hanging of twenty cubits, *of*

nn8504   wcj,nn713   wcj,cs,nn8438/nn8144   wcj,nn8336/hopt7806   cs,nn4639/qpta7551
blue, and purple, and   scarlet,   and fine*twined*linen, wrought with needlework:

pl,nn,pnx5982   nu702   wcj,pl,nn,pnx134   nu702
and their pillars *shall be* four, and their sockets four.

cs,nn3605   pl,cs,nn5982   ad5439   df,nn2691   pl,pupt**2836**   nn3701
17 All   the pillars round about the court *shall be* filleted with silver; their

pl,nn,pnx2053   nn3701   wcj,pl,nn,pnx134   nn5178
hooks *shall be of* silver, and their sockets *of* brass.

            cs,nn**753**   df,nn2691   nu3967 dfp,nn520   wcj,nn7341
18 The length of the court *shall be* a hundred cubits, and the breadth

pl,nu2572/dfp,pl,nu2572   wcj,nn6967   nu2568 pl,nn520   nn8336/hopt7806
fifty*every*where,   and the height five cubits *of* fine*twined*linen, and their

wcj,pl,nn,pnx134   nn5178
sockets *of* brass.

              pp,cs,nn3605   pl,cs,nn3627   df,nn**4908**   pp,cs,nn3605   nn,pnx**5656**
19 All   the vessels of the tabernacle in   all   the service thereof, and

wcj,cs,nn3605   pl,nn,pnx3489   wcj,cs,nn3605   pl,cs,nn3489   df,nn2691   nn5178
all   the pins   thereof, and   all   the pins of the court, *shall be of* brass.

Taking Care of the Lamp

            wcj,pnp859   pimf**6680**   (853)   pl,cs,nn**1121**   nn3478   wcj,qmf3947/pr,pnx413
20 And thou shalt command   the children of Israel, that they   bring

aj2134 cs,nn**8081** nn2132 aj3795   dfp,nn3974   nn5216   pp,hinc5927   nn8548
thee pure oil olive beaten for the light, to cause the lamp to burn always.

                    pp,cs,nn168   nn4150   pr4480/nn2351   dfp,nn6532 pnl834   pr5921
21 In the tabernacle of the congregation without the veil, which *is* before the

df,nn5715   nn175   wcj,pl,nn,pnx1121   qmf6186 pnx(853)   pr4480/nn6153   pr5704   nn1242
testimony, Aaron and his   sons   shall order   it from evening to morning

pp,pl,cs,nn**6440**   nn3068   cs,nn2708   nn5769   pp,pl,nn,pnx**1755**   pr4480/pr854
before the LORD: *it shall be* a statute forever unto their generations on*the*behalf

pl,cs,nn**1121**   nn3478
of the children of Israel.

The Priest's Clothes

28 ☉ And take thou unto thee Aaron thy brother, and his
sons with him, from among the children of Israel, that he may
minister*unto*me*in*the*priest's*office, *even* Aaron, Nadab and Abihu, Eleazar and
Ithamar, Aaron's sons.

2 And thou shalt make holy garments for Aaron thy brother for glory and for
beauty.

3 And thou shalt speak unto all *that are* wise hearted, whom I have
filled with the spirit of wisdom, that they may make Aaron's garments to
consecrate him, that he may minister*unto*me*in*the*priest's*office.

4 And these *are* the garments which they shall make; a breastplate, and an
ephod, and a robe, and an embroidered coat, a miter, and a girdle: and they
shall make holy garments for Aaron thy brother, and his sons, that he may
minister*unto*me*in*the*priest's*office.

5 And they shall take gold, and blue, and purple, and
scarlet, and fine linen.

6 And they shall make the ephod *of* gold, *of* blue, and *of* purple, *of*
scarlet, and fine*twined*linen, with cunning work.

7 It shall have the two shoulder pieces thereof joined at the two
edges thereof; and *so* it shall be joined together.

8 And the curious girdle of the ephod, which *is* upon it, shall be of the
same, according to the work thereof; *even of* gold, *of* blue, and purple, and
scarlet, and fine*twined*linen.

9 And thou shalt take two onyx stones, and grave on them the
names of the children of Israel:

10 Six of*their*names on one stone, and *the other* six names of the
rest on the other stone, according to their birth.

☉ **28:1–5** See the note on Exodus 32:25–29, concerning the priesthood.

cs,nn4639   cs,nn2796   nn68   pl,cs,nn6603   nn2368

11 With the work of an engraver in stone, *like* the engravings of a signet, shalt

pimf6605   (853)   du,cs,nu8147 df,pl,nn68   pr5921   pl,cs,nn8034   pl,cs,nn1121   nn3478

thou engrave   the   two   stones with the names of the children of Israel: thou

qmf6213   pnx(853)   pl,hopt4142   pl,cs,nn4865   nn2091

shalt make   them to be   set   in ouches of gold.

wcs,qpf7760 (853)   du,cs,nu8147 df,pl,nn68 pr5921   pl,cs,nn3802   df,nn646

12 And thou shalt   put   the   two   stones upon the shoulders of the ephod

pl,cs,nn68   nn2146   pp,pl,cs,nn1121   nn3478   nn175   wcs,qpf5375 (853)

for stones of memorial unto the children of Israel: and Aaron shall   bear   their

pl,nn,pnx8034 pp,pl,cs,nn6440   nn3068   pr5921   du,cs,nu8147 pl,nn,pnx3802   pp,nn2146

names   before the Lord upon his   two   shoulders for a memorial.

wcs,qpf6213   pl,cs,nn4865   nn2091

13 And thou shalt make ouches *of* gold;

wcj,du,cs,nu8147 pl,cs,nn8333   aj2889   nn2091   pl,nn4020   nn5688   cs,nn4639

14 And   two   chains *of* pure gold at the ends; *of* wreathen work shalt thou

qmf6213 pnx(853)   wcs,qpf5414 (853)   df,pl,nn5688   pl,cs,nn8333 pr5921   df,pl,nn4865

make   them, and fasten   the wreathen chains to the ouches.

wcs,qpf6213   cs,nn2833   nn4941   qpta2803   cs,nn4639

15 And thou shalt make the breastplate of judgment with cunning work; after

pp,cs,nn4639   nn646   qmf,pnx6213   nn2091   nn8504   wcj,nn713

the work of the ephod thou shalt make it; *of* gold, *of* blue, and *of* purple, and *of*

wcj,cs,nn8438/nn8144   wcj,nn8336/hopt7806   qmf6213 pnx(853)

scarlet,   and *of* fine*twined*linen, shalt thou make   it.

qptp7251   qmf1961   qptp3717   nn2239   nn,pnx753

16 Foursquare it shall   be   *being* doubled; a span *shall be* the length thereof,

wcj,nn2239   nn,pnx7341

and a span *shall be* the breadth thereof.

wcs,pipf4390 pp,pnx   cs,nn4396   nn68   nu702 pl,nn2905   nn68

17 And thou shalt set   in it settings of stones, *even* four rows of stones: *the*

cs,nn2905   nn124   nn6357   wcj,nn1304   df,nu259 df,nn2905

first row *shall be* a sardius, a topaz, and a carbuncle: *this shall be* the first row.

df,nuor8145 wcj,df,nn2905   nn5306   nn5601   wcj,nn3095

18 And the second   row   *shall be* an emerald, a sapphire, and a diamond.

df,nuor7992 wcj,df,nn2905   nn3958   nn7618   wcj,nn306

19 And the third   row   a ligure, an agate, and an amethyst.

df,nuor7243 wcj,df,nn2905   nn8658   wcj,nn7718   wcj,nn3471   qmf1961

20 And the fourth   row   a beryl, and an onyx, and a jasper: they shall   be

pl,pupt7660   nn2091   pp,pl,nn,pnx4396

set   in gold in their enclosings.

wcj,df,pl,nn68   qmf1961 pr5921   pl,cs,nn8034   pl,cs,nn1121   nn3478

21 And the stones shall be with the names of the children of Israel,

du,nu8147/nu6240   pr5921   pl,nn,pnx8034   pl,cs,nn6603   nn2368   nn376   pr5921

twelve, according to their names, *like* the engravings of a signet; every one with

nn,pnx8034   qmf1961   pp,du,cs,nu8147/nu6240   nn7626

his name shall they be according to the   twelve   tribes.

wcs,qpf6213 pr5921   df,nn2833   pl,cs,nn8331   nn1383   nn5688

22 And thou shalt make upon the breastplate chains at the ends *of* wreathen

cs,nn4639   aj2889   nn2091

work *of* pure gold.

wcs,qpf6213 pr5921   df,nn2833   du,cs,nu8147 pl,cs,nn2885   nn2091

23 And thou shalt make upon the breastplate two   rings of gold, and shalt

wcs,qpf5414 (853)   du,cs,nu8147 df,pl,nn2885 pr5921   du,cs,nu8147 pl,cs,nn7098   df,nn2833

put   the   two   rings on the two   ends of the breastplate.

_{wcs,qpf**5414** (853)}   _{du,cs,nu8147}   _{pl,cs,nn5688}   _{df,nn2091 pr5921}

24 And thou shalt   put   the   two   wreathen *chains* of gold   in   the
_{du,cs,nu8147 df,pl,nn2885}   _{pr413}   _{pl,cs,nn7098}   _{df,nn2833}

two   rings *which are* on the   ends   of the breastplate.

_{wcj(853)}   _{du,cs,nu8147 pl,cs,nn7098}   _{du,cs,nu8147 df,pl,nn5688}

25 And   *the other* two   ends of the   two   wreathen *chains* thou shalt
_{qmf5414 pr5921}   _{du,cs,nu8147 df,pl,nn4865}   _{wcs,qpf5414}   _{pr5921}   _{pl,cs,nn3802}

fasten   in   the   two   ouches, and   put   *them* on   the shoulder pieces of the
_{df,nn646   pr413/pr4136/pl,nn,pnx**6440**}

ephod   before   it.

_{wcs,qpf**6213** du,cs,nu8147 pl,cs,nn2885}   _{nn2091}   _{wcs,qpf7760 pnx(853)}

26 And thou shalt make   two   rings of gold, and thou shalt   put
_{pr5921}   _{du,cs,nu8147 pl,cs,nn7098}   _{df,nn2833   pr5921}   _{nn,pnx**8193**}   _{pnl834}   _{pr413}

them upon the   two   ends of the breastplate in the border thereof, which *is* in
_{cs,nn5676}   _{df,nn646   nn,lh**1004**}

the side of the ephod inward.

_{du,cs,nu8147}   _{pl,cs,nn2885}   _{nn2091}   _{wcs,qpf**6213**}   _{wcs,qpf5414 pnx(853)}

27 And   two   *other* rings of gold thou shalt make, and shalt   put
_{pr5921}   _{du,cs,nu8147 pl,cs,nn3802}   _{df,nn646   pr4480/pp,ad4295 pr4480/pr4136}   _{pl,nn,pnx**6440**}

them on the   two   sides of the ephod underneath, toward the forepart thereof,
_{pp,pr5980}   _{nn,pnx4225}   _{pr4480/ad4605 pp,cs,nn2805}   _{df,nn646}

over against the *other* coupling thereof, above   the curious girdle of the ephod.

_{wcj,qmf7405   (853)}   _{df,nn2833}   _{pr4480/pl,nn,pnx2885}   _{pr413}

28 And they shall   bind   the breastplate by*the*rings thereof unto the
_{pl,cs,nn2885}   _{df,nn646}   _{pp,cs,nn6616}   _{nn8504}   _{pp,qnc**1961** pr5921}

rings   of the ephod with a   lace   of blue, that *it* may   be   above the
_{cs,nn2805}   _{df,nn646}   _{df,nn2833}   _{wcj,ptn3808 nimf2118 pr4480/pr5921}

curious girdle of the ephod, and that the breastplate be   not   loosed from   the
_{df,nn646}

ephod.

_{nn175}   _{wcs,qpf5375 (853)}   _{pl,cs,nn8034}   _{pl,cs,nn1121}   _{nn3478}

29 And Aaron shall   bear   the names of the children of Israel in the
_{pp,cs,nn2833}   _{df,nn4941}   _{pr5921}   _{nn,pnx**3820**}   _{pp,qnc,pnx935 pr413}   _{df,nn6944}

breastplate of judgment upon his heart, when he goeth in unto the holy *place*, for a
_{pp,nn2146}   _{pp,pl,cs,nn**6440**}   _{nn3068}   _{nn8548}

memorial before the Lord continually.

_{wcs,qpf5414 pr413}   _{cs,nn2833}   _{df,nn4941 (853)}   _{df,pl,nn217}   _{wcj(853)}

30 And thou shalt   put   in the breastplate of judgment   the Urim and
_{df,pl,nn8550}   _{wcs,qpf**1961** pr5921}   _{nn175}   _{cs,nn**3820**}   _{pp,qnc,pnx935 pp,pl,cs,nn**6440**}

the Thummim; and they shall   be   upon Aaron's heart, when he goeth in before
_{nn3068}   _{nn175}   _{wcs,qpf5375 (853)}   _{cs,nn4941}   _{pl,cs,nn1121}   _{nn3478 pr5921}

the Lord: and Aaron shall   bear   the judgment of the children of Israel upon his
_{nn,pnx**3820** pp,pl,cs,nn**6440**}   _{nn3068}   _{nn8548}

heart   before the Lord continually.

28:30 This is the first Old Testament mention of these sacred objects called the "Urim and Thummim." They were used by the priests to receive divine messages and were kept in the high priest's breastplate. The mention of the ephod in connection with simple oracles (1 Sam. 23:6, 9–12) suggests that at times these objects may have been associated with the priest's ephod. No one knows what the Urim and Thummim looked like or how they worked, but it appears that they provided only yes or no answers. Sometimes there was no answer given at all. This would help explain King Saul's inability to get an answer from God on two different occasions (1 Sam. 14:36, 37; 28:6). The Urim and Thummim are not mentioned in the Old Testament between the early monarchy and post–exilic times. This was the period of the prophets, when God revealed Himself much more fully than in the simple answers to questions posed by priests. Quite possibly the lack of description of the Urim and Thummim is deliberate, in order to prevent copies from being made.

<small>wcs,qpf2280</small>   <small>pl,nn4021</small>   <small>pp,pnx</small>   <small>nn3550</small>   <small>wcs,qpf1961</small>   <small>pp,pnx</small>

put   the bonnets on them: and the priest's office shall   be   theirs for a

<small>nn5769</small>   <small>pp,cs,nn2708</small>   <small>wcs,pipf4390/cs,nn3027</small>   <small>nn175</small>   <small>wcj(cs,nn3027)</small>   <small>pl,nn,pnx1121</small>

perpetual statute: and thou shalt consecrate Aaron and   his sons.

                              <small>(853)</small>   <small>df,nn6499</small>   <small>wcs,hipf7126</small>   <small>pp,pl,cs,nn6440</small>   <small>cs,nn168</small>

10 And thou shalt cause   a bullock to be brought before the tabernacle of

          <small>nn4150</small>   <small>nn175</small>   <small>wcj,pl,nn,pnx1121</small>   <small>wcs,qpf5564</small> <small>(853)</small>   <small>du,nn,pnx3027</small> <small>pr5921</small>

the congregation: and Aaron and his   sons   shall put   their hands upon

      <small>cs,nn7218</small>   <small>df,nn6499</small>

the head of the bullock.

                <small>wcs,qpf7819</small> <small>(853)</small>   <small>df,nn6499</small>   <small>pp,pl,cs,nn6440</small>   <small>nn3068</small>   <small>cs,nn6607</small>

11 And thou shalt   kill   the bullock before the LORD, *by* the door of the

      <small>cs,nn168</small>   <small>nn4150</small>

tabernacle of the congregation.

                <small>wcs,qpf3947</small>   <small>pr4480/cs,nn1818</small>   <small>df,nn6499</small>   <small>wcs,qpf5414</small>   <small>pr5921</small>

12 And thou shalt take   of*the*blood of the bullock, and   put   *it* upon the

<small>pl,cs,nn7161</small>   <small>df,nn4196</small>   <small>pp,nn,pnx676</small>   <small>qmf8210</small> <small>wcj(853)</small> <small>cs,nn3605</small>   <small>df,nn1818</small>   <small>pr413</small>

horns of the altar with thy finger, and pour   all   the blood beside the

<small>cs,nn3247</small>   <small>df,nn4196</small>

bottom of the altar.

                <small>wcs,qpf3947</small> <small>(853)</small> <small>cs,nn3605</small>   <small>df,nn2459</small>   <small>df,pipt3680</small>   <small>(853)</small>   <small>df,nn7130</small>

13 And thou shalt take   all   the   fat   that covereth   the inwards, and

<small>wcj(853)</small>   <small>df,nn3508</small>   <small>pr5921</small>   <small>df,nn3516</small>   <small>wcj(853)</small>   <small>du,cs,nu8147</small> <small>df,pl,nn3629</small>   <small>wcj(853)</small>

      the caul *that is* above the liver, and   the two   kidneys, and   the

<small>df,nn2459</small> <small>pnl834</small>   <small>pr,pnx5921</small>   <small>wcs,hipf6999</small>   <small>df,nn,lh4196</small>

fat that *is* upon them, and burn *them* upon the altar.

                <small>wcj(853)</small>   <small>cs,nn1320</small>   <small>df,nn6499</small>   <small>wcj(853)</small>   <small>nn,pnx5785</small>   <small>wcj(853)</small>   <small>nn,pnx6569</small>

14 But   the flesh of the bullock, and   his skin, and   his dung,

                <small>qmf8313</small>   <small>dfp,nn784</small> <small>pr4480/cs,nn2351</small>   <small>dfp,nn4264</small> <small>pnp1931</small>   <small>nn2403</small>

shalt thou burn with fire   without the camp: it *is* a sin offering.

                <small>qmf3947</small> <small>wcj(853)</small> <small>df,nu259</small> <small>df,nn352</small>   <small>nn175</small>   <small>wcj,pl,nn,pnx1121</small>

15 Thou shalt also take   one   ram; and Aaron and his   sons   shall

<small>wcs,qpf5564</small> <small>(853)</small>   <small>du,nn,pnx3027</small> <small>pr5921</small>   <small>cs,nn7218</small>   <small>df,nn352</small>

put   their hands upon the head of the ram.

                <small>wcs,qpf7819</small> <small>(853)</small>   <small>df,nn352</small>   <small>wcs,qpf3947</small> <small>(853)</small>   <small>nn,pnx1818</small>

16 And thou shalt   slay   the ram, and thou shalt   take   his blood, and

<small>wcs,qpf2236</small>   <small>ad5439</small>   <small>pr5921</small>   <small>df,nn4196</small>

sprinkle *it* round about upon the altar.

                <small>pimf5408</small> <small>wcj(853)</small>   <small>df,nn352</small>   <small>pp,pl,nn,pnx5409</small>   <small>wcs,qpf7364</small>   <small>nn,pnx7130</small>

17 And thou shalt cut   the ram in pieces,   and wash the inwards of

          <small>wcj,pl,nn,pnx3767</small>   <small>wcs,qpf5414</small>   <small>pr5921</small>   <small>pl,nn,pnx5409</small>   <small>wcj,pr5921</small>   <small>nn,pnx7218</small>

him, and his   legs,   and put *them* unto his pieces, and unto his head.

                <small>wcs,hipf6999</small> <small>(853)</small>   <small>cs,nn3605</small> <small>df,nn352</small>   <small>df,nn,lh4196</small> <small>pnp1931</small>

18 And thou shalt burn   the whole ram upon the altar: it   *is* a

      <small>nn5930</small>   <small>pp,nn3068</small>   <small>nn5207</small> <small>cs,nn7381</small> <small>(pnp1931)</small>   <small>nn801</small>

burnt offering unto the LORD: it *is* a sweet savor,   an offering*made*by*fire

          <small>pp,nn3068</small>

unto the LORD.

                <small>wcs,qpf3947</small> <small>(853)</small>   <small>df,nuor8145</small> <small>df,nn352</small>   <small>nn175</small>   <small>wcj,pl,nn,pnx1121</small>

19 And thou shalt take   the other ram; and Aaron and his   sons   shall

<small>wcs,qpf5564</small> <small>(853)</small>   <small>du,nn,pnx3027</small> <small>pr5921</small>   <small>cs,nn7218</small>   <small>df,nn352</small>

put   their hands upon the head of the ram.

                <small>wcs,qpf7819</small> <small>(853)</small>   <small>df,nn352</small>   <small>wcs,qpf3947</small>   <small>pr4480/nn,pnx1818</small>   <small>wcs,qpf5414</small>

20 Then shalt thou kill   the ram, and take   of*his*blood, and   put   *it*

<small>pr5921</small>   <small>cs,nn8571</small>   <small>cs,nn241</small>   <small>nn175</small>   <small>wcj,pr5921</small>   <small>cs,nn8571</small>   <small>df,aj3233</small> <small>cs,nn241</small>

upon the tip of the right ear of Aaron, and upon the tip of the right ear of

pl,nn,pnx**1121**   wcj,pr5921   cs,nn931   df,aj3233   nn,pnx**3027**   wcj,pr5921   cs,nn931

his sons, and upon the thumb of their right hand, and upon the great toe of

df,aj3233 nn,pnx7272   wcs,qpf**2236**   (853)   df,nn1818 pr5921   df,nn**4196**   ad5439

their right foot, and sprinkle   the blood upon the altar round about.

wcs,qpf3947   pr4480   df,nn1818   pnl834   pr5921   df,nn**4196**

21 And thou shalt take   of the blood that *is* upon the altar, and

wcj,pr4480/cs,nn**8081**/df,nn**4888**   wcs,hipf**5137**   pr5921   nn175   wcj,pr5921   pl,nn,pnx899

of*the*anointing*oil, and sprinkle *it* upon Aaron, and upon his garments, and

wcj,pr5921   pl,nn,pnx**1121**   wcj,pr5921   pl,cs,nn899   pl,nn,pnx1121 pr,pnx854   pnp1931

upon his sons, and upon the garments of his   sons   with him: and he shall

wcs,qpf**6942**   wcj,pl,nn,pnx899   wcj,pl,nn,pnx**1121**   pl,nn,pnx1121 wcj,pl,cs,nn899 pr,pnx854

be hallowed, and his garments, and his   sons,   and his sons' garments with

him.

wcs,qpf3947 pr4480   df,nn352   df,nn2459   wcj,df,nn451   wcj(853)

22 Also thou shalt take   of the ram the fat   and the rump, and   the

df,nn2459   df,pipt**3680**   (853)   df,nn**7130**   wcj(853)   cs,nn3508   df,nn3516   wcj(853)

fat that covereth   the inwards, and   the caul *above* the liver, and

du,cs,nu8147   df,pl,nn3629   wcj(853)   df,nn2459 pnl834   pr,pnx5921   wcj(853)   df,nn3225

the two kidneys, and   the fat that *is* upon them, and   the right

cs,nn7785 cj3588 pnp1931   cs,nn352   pl,nn4394

shoulder; for it *is* a ram of consecration:

nu259 wcj,cs,nn3603   nn3899   nu259 wcj,cs,nn2471   nn**8081**   nn3899   nu259 wcj,nn7550

23 And one   loaf of bread, and one   cake   of oiled bread, and one wafer

pr4480/cs,nn5536   df,pl,nn**4682**   pnl834   pp,pl,cs,nn**6440**   nn3068

out*of*the*basket of the unleavened bread that *is* before the LORD:

wcs,qpf**7760** df,nn3605 pr5921   du,cs,nn**3709**   nn175   wcj,pr5921   du,cs,nn**3709**

24 And thou shalt put   all   in the hands of Aaron, and   in   the hands

pl,nn,pnx**1121**   wcs,hipf**5130** pnx(853)   nn8573   pp,pl,cs,nn**6440**   nn3068

of his   sons; and shalt wave   them *for* a wave offering before the LORD.

wcs,qpf3947 pnx(853)   pr4480/nn,pnx**3027**   wcs,hipf**6999**

25 And thou shalt receive   them of*their*hands, and burn *them* upon the

df,nn,lh**4196** pr5921   df,nn**5930**   nn5207 pp,cs,nn7381 pp,pl,cs,nn**6440**   nn3068 pnp1931

altar   for a burnt offering, for a sweet savor   before the LORD: it *is* an

nn**801**   pp,nn**3068**

offering*made*by*fire unto the LORD.

wcs,qpf3947   (853)   df,nn2373   pr4480/cs,nn352   (pnl834)   pp,nn175

26 And thou shalt take   the breast of*the*ram   of Aaron's

df,pl,nn4394   wcs,hipf**5130** pnx(853)   nn8573   pp,pl,cs,nn**6440**   nn3068

consecration, and wave   it *for* a wave offering before the LORD: and it shall

wcs,qpf**1961** pp,pnx pp,nn4490

be   thy part.

wcs,pipf**6942**   (853)   cs,nn2373   df,nn**8573**   wcj(853)

27 And thou shalt sanctify   the breast of the wave offering, and   the

cs,nn7785   df,nn**8641**   pnl834   hopf**5130**   wcj,pnl834   hopf7311

shoulder of the heave offering, which is waved, and which is heaved up,

pr4480/cs,nn352   df,pl,nn4394   pr4480/pnl834   pp,nn175   wcj,pr4480/pnl834

of*the*ram of the consecration, *even* of*that*which *is* for Aaron, and of*that*which

pp,pl,nn,pnx**1121**

is for his   sons:

wcj,qpf**1961**   pp,nn175   wcj,pp,pl,nn,pnx**1121**   pp,cs,nn2706 nn5769 pr4480/pr854

28 And it shall be   Aaron's and his   sons'   by a statute forever from

pl,cs,nn**1121**   nn3478   cj3588 pnp1931   nn**8641**   qmf**1961**

the children of Israel: for   it   *is* a heave offering: and it shall be a wcj,nn**8641**   pr4480/pr854   pl,cs,nn**1121**   nn3478   pr4480/pl,cs,nn**2077**

heave offering   from   the   children   of   Israel   of*the*sacrifice   of   their

pl,nn,pnx**8002**   nn,pnx**8641**   pp,nn**3068**

peace offerings, *even* their heave offering unto the LORD.

df,nn**6944** wcj,pl,cs,nn899 (pnl834)   pp,nn175   qmf**1961**   pp,pl,nn,pnx**1121** pr,pnx310

29 And the holy   garments   of Aaron shall   be   his   sons'   after him, to

pp,qnc**4886**   pp,pnx   wcj,pp,pinc**4390**/(853)/nn,pnx**3027**   pp,pnx

be anointed therein, and to be   consecrated   in them.

pr4480/pl,nn,pnx**1121**   df,nn**3548**   pr,pnx8478   qmf,pnx3847   cs,nu7651   pl,nn**3117**

30 *And*   that son   that is priest in*his*stead shall put*them*on seven days,

pnl834   qmf935   pr413   cs,nn**168**   nn**4150**   pp,pinc**8334**   dfp,nn**6944**

when he cometh into the tabernacle of the congregation to minister in the   holy

place.

qmf3947 wcj(853)   cs,nn352   df,pl,nn**4394**   wcs,pipf1310   (853)

31 And thou shalt take   the ram of the consecration, and   seethe   his

nn,pnx**1320**   aj6918   pp,nn**4725**

flesh in the holy place.

nn175   wcj,pl,nn,pnx**1121**   wcs,qpf398   (853)   cs,nn**1320**   df,nn352   wcj(853)

32 And Aaron and his   sons   shall   eat   the flesh of the ram, and

df,nn3899 pnl834   dfp,nn5536   cs,nn6607   cs,nn**168**   nn**4150**

the bread that *is* in the basket, *by* the   door of the tabernacle of the congregation.

wcs,qpf398 pnx(853)   pnl834/pp,pnx   pupf3722

33 And they shall   eat   those things wherewith the atonement*was*made,

pp,pinc**4390**/(853)/nn,pnx**3027**   pp,pinc**6942** pnx(853)   wcj,qpta2114   ptn3808 qmf398

to   consecrate   *and* to sanctify   them: but a stranger shall not   eat *thereof*,

cj3588   pnp1992   nn**6944**

because they *are* holy.

wcj,cj518   pr4480/cs,nn**1320**   df,pl,nn**4394**   wcj,pr4480   df,nn3899

34 And   if   aught*of*the*flesh of the consecrations, or   of   the   bread,

nimf3498   pr5704   df,nn1242   wcs,qpf8313 (853)   df,nipt3498   dfp,nn784

remain unto the morning, then thou shalt burn   the remainder with fire: it shall

ptn3808   nimf398   cj3588   pnp1931   nn**6944**

not be eaten, because   it   *is* holy.

ad3602   wcs,qpf**6213**   pp,nn175   wcj,pp,pl,nn,pnx**1121**

35 And thus shalt thou   do   unto Aaron, and to his   sons,   according to

pp,nn3605   pnl834   pipf**6680**   pnx(853)   cs,nu7651 pl,nn**3117**   pimf**4390**/nn,pnx**3027**

all   *things* which I have commanded   thee: seven days shalt thou consecrate

them.

qmf**6213**   dfp,nn**3117**   wcj,cs,nn6499   nn2403   pr5921

36 And thou shalt offer every   day   a   bullock *for* a   sin offering   for

df,pl,nn**3725**   wcs,pipf2398/pr5921   df,nn**4196**   pp,pinc,pnx3722

atonement: and thou shalt   cleanse   the altar, when thou hast made*an*atonement

pr,pnx5921   wcs,qpf**4886** pnx(853)   pp,pinc,pnx**6942**

for   it, and thou shalt anoint   it, to   sanctify it.

cs,nu7651   pl,nn**3117**   pimf3722   pr5921   df,nn**4196**   wcs,pipf**6942** pnx(853)

37 Seven days thou shalt make*an*atonement for   the altar, and sanctify

wcs,qpf**1961**   df,nn**4196** cs,nn**6944**/pl,nn**6944**   cs,nn3605   df,qpta5060   dfp,nn**4196**

it; and it shall   be   an altar most holy: whatsoever toucheth the altar shall

qmf**6942**

be holy.

Two Lambs Every Day

wcj,pndm2088 pnl834 qmf6213 pr5921 df,nn4196 du,nu8147 pl,nn3532

38 Now this *is that* which thou shalt offer upon the altar; two lambs of

pl,cs,nn1121 nn8141 dfp,nn3117 nn8548

the first year day*by*day continually.

(853) df,nu259 df,nn3532 qmf6213 dfp,nn1242 wcj(853) df,nuor8145

39 The one lamb thou shalt offer in the morning; and the other

df,nn3532 qmf6213 pr996 df,du,nn6153

lamb thou shalt offer at even:

df,nu259 dfp,nn3532 wcj,nn6241 nn5560 qptp1101 cs,nu7253

40 And with the one lamb a tenth deal of flour mingled with the fourth part

df,nn1969 aj3795 pp,nn8081 cs,nuor7243 df,nn1969 nn3196

of a hin of beaten oil; and the fourth part of a hin of wine *for* a

wcj,nn5262

drink offering.

wcj(853) df,nuor8145 df,nn3532 qmf6213 pr996 df,du,nn6153 qmf6213 pp,pnx

41 And the other lamb thou shalt offer at even, and shalt do thereto

pp,cs,nn4503 df,nn1242 wcj,pp,nn,pnx5262

according to the meat offering of the morning, and according to the drink offering

nn5207 pp,cs,nn7381 nn801 pp,nn3068

thereof, for a sweet savor, an offering*made*by*fire unto the LORD.

nn8548 cs,nn5930 pp,pl,nn,pnx1755

42 *This shall be* a continual burnt offering throughout your generations *at* the

cs,nn6607 cs,nn168 nn4150 pp,pl,cs,nn6440 nn3068 pnl834/ad,lh8033 nimf3259

door of the tabernacle of the congregation before the LORD: where I will meet

pp,pnx pp,pinc1696 ad8033 pr,pnx413

you, to speak there unto thee.

ad,lh8033 wcs,nipf3259 pp,pl,cs,nn1121 nn3478

43 And there I will meet with the children of Israel, and *the tabernacle* shall

wcj,nipf6942 pp,nn,pnx3519

be sanctified by my glory.

wcs,pipf6942 (853) cs,nn168 nn4150 wcj(853) df,nn4196

44 And I will sanctify the tabernacle of the congregation, and the altar:

pimf6942 wcj(853) nn175 wcj(853) pl,nn,pnx1121

I will sanctify also both Aaron and his sons, to

pp,pinc3547/pp,pnx

minister*to*me*in*the*priest's*office.

wcs,qpf7931 pp,cs,nn8432 pl,cs,nn1121 nn3478 wcs,qpf1961 pp,pnx pp,pl,nn430

45 And I will dwell among the children of Israel, and will be their God.

wcs,qpf3045 cj3588 pnp589 nn3068 pl,nn,pnx430 pnl834

46 And they shall know that I *am* the LORD their God, that

hipf3318/pnx(853) pr4480/cs,nn776 nn4714 pp,qnc,pnx7931 pp,nn,pnx8432

brought*them*forth out*of*the*land of Egypt, that I may dwell among them:

pnp589 nn3068 pl,nn,pnx430

I *am* the LORD their God.

The Incense Altar

wcj,qpf6213 nn4196 cs,nn4729 nn7004 pl,nn7848

30 And thou shalt make an altar to burn incense upon: *of* shittim

pl,cs,nn6086 qmf6213 pnx(853)

wood shalt thou make it.

nn520 nn,pnx753 wcj,nn520 nn,pnx7341

2 A cubit *shall be* the length thereof, and a cubit the breadth thereof;

qptp7251   qmf**1961**   wcj,du,nn520   nn,pnx6967   pl,nn,pnx7161
foursquare shall it be: and two cubits *shall be* the height thereof: the   horns

pr,pnx4480
thereof *shall be* of   the same.

wcs,pipf6823   pnx(853)   aj**2889**   nn2091   (853)   nn,pnx1406
3 And thou shalt overlay   it with pure gold,   the   top   thereof, and

wcj(853)   pl,nn,pnx**7023**   ad5439   wcj(853)   pl,nn,pnx7161
the sides   thereof round about, and   the   horns   thereof; and thou shalt

wcs,qpf**6213**   pp,pnx   cs,nn2213   nn2091   ad5439
make unto it a crown of gold round about.

wcj,du,cs,nu8147   nn2091   pl,cs,nn2885   qmf**6213**   pp,pnx   pr4480/pr8478   pp,nn,pnx2213
4 And   two   golden   rings shalt thou make to it   under   the   crown   of it,

pr5921   du,cs,nu8147   pl,nn,pnx6763   pr5921   du,cs,nu8147   pl,nn,pnx6654   qmf**6213**
by the   two   corners thereof, upon the   two   sides   of it shalt thou make *it*;

wcs,qpf**1961**   pp,pl,nn**1004**   pp,pl,nn905   pp,qnc**5375** pnx(853)   pp,pnp1992
and they shall   be   for places for the staves to bear   it withal.

wcs,qpf**6213**   (853)   df,pl,nn905   pl,nn7848   pl,cs,nn6086   wcs,pipf6823 pnx(853)
5 And thou shalt make   the staves *of* shittim wood, and overlay   them

nn2091
with gold.

wcs,qpf**5414** pnx(853)   pp,pl,cs,nn**6440**   df,nn6532 pnl834   pr5921   cs,nn**727**
6 And thou shalt put   it before the veil that *is* by the ark of the

df,nn**5715**   pp,pl,cs,nn**6440**   df,nn3727   pnl834   pr5921   df,nn**5715**   pnl834/ad,lh8033   nimf3259
testimony,   before   the mercy seat that *is* over the testimony,   where   I will meet

pp,pnx
with thee.

nn175   wcs,hipf**6999**   pr,pnx5921   pl,nn5561   cs,nn**7004**   dfp,nn1242/dfp,nn1242
7 And Aaron shall   burn   thereon sweet incense every morning: when he

pp,hinc,pnx**3190** (853)   df,pl,nn**5216**   himf,pnx**6999**
dresseth   the lamps, he shall burn incense upon it.

nn175   wcj,pp,hinc**5927** (853)   df,pl,nn**5216** pr996 df,du,nn6153   himf,pnx**6999**
8 And when Aaron lighteth   the lamps at   even, he shall burn incense

nn8548   cs,nn**7004** pp,pl,cs,nn**6440**   nn3068   pp,pl,nn,pnx**1755**
upon it, a perpetual incense   before   the LORD throughout your generations.

himf**5927** ptn**3808** qpta**2114**   cs,nn**7004** pr,pnx5921   wcj,nn**5930**
9 Ye   shall   offer   no   strange incense thereon,   nor   burnt sacrifice,   nor

wcj,nn**4503**   ptn**3808**   qmf**5258**   wcj,nn**5262**   pr,pnx5921
meat offering; neither shall ye pour drink offering thereon.

nn175   wcs,pipf**3722**   pr5921   pl,nn,pnx7161   nu259   dfp,nn**8141**
10 And Aaron shall make*an*atonement upon the   horns   of it once in a   year

pr4480/cs,nn**1818**   cs,nn**2403**   df,pl,nn**3725**   nu259   dfp,nn**8141**
with*the*blood of the sin offering of atonements: once in the   year   shall he

pimf**3722**   pr,pnx5921   pp,pl,nn,pnx**1755** pnp1931   cs,nn**6944**/pl,cs,nn**6944**
make atonement upon it throughout your generations: it   *is* most holy   unto the

pp,nn**3068**
LORD.

A Tax for the Tent

nn**3068**   wcs,pimf**1696** pr413   nn4872   pp,qnc**559**
11 And the LORD spoke unto Moses, saying,

cj3588   qmf**5375** (853)   cs,nn**7218**   pl,cs,nn**1121**   nn3478   pp,pl,qptp,pnx**6485**
12 When thou takest   the sum of the children of Israel after their   number,

wcs,qpf**5414**   nn376   nn3724   nn,pnx5315   pp,nn3068
then shall they   give   every man a ransom for his   soul   unto the LORD, when thou

pp,qnc**6485**   pnx(853)   qmf**1961**   wcj,ptn**3808**   nn**5063**   pp,pnx

numberest   them; that there   be   no   plague among them, when *thou*

pp,qnc**6485**   pnx(853)

numberest   them.

pndm2088   qmf**5414**   cs,nn3605   df,qpta**5674**   pr5921

13 This   they   shall   give, every one   that   passeth   among   them   that   are

df,pl,qptp**6485**   cs,nn4276   df,nn8255   pp,cs,nn8255   df,nn**6944**   df,nn8255   pl,nu6242

numbered,   half   a shekel after   the   shekel   of the sanctuary: (a shekel *is* twenty

nn1626   cs,nn4276   df,nn8255   nn**8641**   pp,nn**3068**

gerahs:) a   half   shekel *shall be* the offering of the Lord.

cs,nn3605   df,qpta**5674**   pr5921   df,pl,qptp**6485**   pl,nu6242   nn8141

14 Every one that passeth among them that are numbered, from twenty years

pr4480/cs,nn1121   wcj,ad,lh4605   qmf**5414**   cs,nn**8641**   nn**3068**

old   and above, shall give an offering unto the Lord.

df,nn6223   ptn**3808**   himf7235   wcj,df,aj1800   ptn**3808**   himf4591

15 The   rich   shall   not   give more,   and the   poor   shall   not   give less

pr4480/cs,nn4276   df,nn8255   pp,qnc**5414**   (853)   cs,nn**8641**   nn**3068**

than half   a shekel, when *they*   give   an offering unto the Lord, to

pp,pinc**3722**   pr5921   pl,nn,pnx**5315**

make*an*atonement for your souls.

wcs,qpf3947   (853)   df,pl,nn**3725**   cs,nn3701   pr4480/pr854   pl,cs,nn1121

16 And thou shalt take   the atonement money   of   the children of

nn3478   wcs,qpf**5414**   pnx(853)   pr5921   cs,nn**5656**   cs,nn168

Israel,   and shalt appoint   it   for   the   service   of the   tabernacle of the

nn4150   wcs,qpf**1961**   pp,nn2146   pp,pl,cs,nn1121   nn3478 pp,pl,cs,nn**6440**

congregation; that it may   be   a memorial unto the children of Israel before the

nn**3068**   pp,pinc**3722**   pr5921   pl,nn,pnx**5315**

Lord, to make*an*atonement for your souls.

The Brass Basin

nn**3068**   wcs,pimf**1696**   pr413   nn4872   pp,qnc559

17 And the Lord spoke unto Moses, saying,

wcj,qpf**6213**   cs,nn3595   nn5178   wcj,nn,pnx3653   nn5178

18 Thou shalt also make a laver *of* brass, and his   foot   *also of* brass, to

pp,qnc7364   wcj,qpf**5414** pnx(853)   pr996   cs,nn168

wash *withal*: and thou shalt   put   it between the tabernacle of the

nn4150   wcj(pr996)   df,nn4196   wcj,qpf**5414** pl,nn4325   ad,lh8033

congregation and   the altar, and thou shalt   put   water therein.

nn175   wcj,pl,nn,pnx1121   wcj,qpf7364   (853)   wcj(853)

19 For Aaron and his   sons   shall   wash   their   hands   and   their

du,nn,pnx7272   pr,pnx4480

feet   thereat:

pp,qnc,pnx935 pr413   cs,nn168   nn4150   qmf7364

20 When they   go   into the tabernacle of the congregation, they shall wash

pl,nn4325   qmf4191 wcj,ptn**3808** cj176   pp,qnc,pnx5066   pr413   df,nn4196

with water, that they   die   not;   or   when they come near   to   the altar to

pp,pinc8334   pp,hinc6999   nn801   pp,nn**3068**

minister, to   burn   offering*made*by*fire unto the Lord:

wcs,qpf7364   du,nn,pnx3027   wcj,du,nn,pnx7272   qmf4191 wcj,ptn**3808**

21 So they shall wash their hands and their   feet,   that they   die   not:

wcs,qpf**1961**   cs,nn2706   nn5769   pp,pnx   pp,pnx   wcj,pp,nn,pnx2233

and it shall   be   a statute forever to them, *even* to him and to his   seed

pp,pl,nn,pnx1755

throughout their generations.

How to Make the Oil

nn3068   wcs,pimf1696   pr413   nn4872   pp,qnc559
22 Moreover the LORD spoke unto Moses, saying,

qmv3947   wcj,pnp859   pp,pnx   nn7218   pl,nn1314   nn1865   cs,nn4753   cs,nu2568   pl,nu3967
23 Take thou also unto thee principal spices, of pure myrrh five hundred

nn1314   wcj,cs,nn7076   nn,pnx4276   wcj,du,nu3967   pl,nu2572
shekels, and of sweet cinnamon half*so*much, *even* two hundred and fifty *shekels*,

nn1314   wcj,cs,nn7070   wcj,du,nu3967   pl,nu2572
and of sweet calamus two hundred and fifty *shekels*,

wcj,nn6916   cs,nu2568   pl,nu3967   pp,cs,nn8255   df,nn6944
24 And of cassia five hundred *shekels*, after the shekel of the sanctuary, and

wcj,cs,nn8081   nn2132   nn1969
of oil olive a hin:

wcj,qpf6213   pnx(853)   cs,nn8081   cs,nn6944   cs,nn4888   nn7545
25 And thou shalt make it an oil of holy ointment, an ointment

cs,nn4842   cs,nn4639   qpta7543   qmf1961   nn6944   cs,nn4888   cs,nn8081
compound after the art of the apothecary: it shall be a holy anointing oil.

wcs,qpf4886   (853)   cs,nn168   nn4150   pp,pnx
26 And thou shalt anoint the tabernacle of the congregation therewith, and

wcj(853)   cs,nn727   df,nn5715
the ark of the testimony,

wcj(853)   df,nn7979   wcj(853) cs,nn3605   pl,nn,pnx3627   wcj(853)   df,nn4501
27 And the table and all his vessels, and the candlestick and

wcj(853)   pl,nn,pnx3627   wcj(853)   cs,nn4196   df,nn7004
his vessels, and the altar of incense,

wcj(853)   cs,nn4196   df,nn5930   wcj(853) cs,nn3605   pl,nn,pnx3627   wcj(853)
28 And the altar of burnt offering with all his vessels, and

df,nn3595   wcj(853)   nn,pnx3653
the laver and his foot.

wcs,pipf6942   pnx(853)   wcs,qpf1961   cs,nn6944/pl,nn6944
29 And thou shalt sanctify them, that they may be most holy:

cs,nn3605   df,qpta5060   pp,pnx   qmf6942
whatsoever toucheth them shall be holy.

qmf4886   wcj(853)   nn175   wcj(853)   pl,nn,pnx1121   wcs,pipf6942   pnx(853)
30 And thou shalt anoint Aaron and his sons, and consecrate

pp,pinc3547/pp,pnx
them, that *they* may minister*unto*me*in*the*priest's*office.

pimf1696   wcj,pr413   pl,cs,nn1121   nn3478   pp,qnc559   pndm2088   qmf1961
31 And thou shalt speak unto the children of Israel, saying, This shall be a

nn6944   cs,nn4888   cs,nn8081   pp,pnx   pp,pl,nn,pnx1755
holy anointing oil unto me throughout your generations.

pr5921   nn120   cs,nn1320   ptn3808   pumf3251   ptn3808   qmf6213
32 Upon man's flesh shall it not be poured, neither shall ye make *any other*

pp,pnx3644   wcj,pp,nn,pnx4971   pnp1931   nn6944   qmf1961 nn6944   pp,pnx
like it, after the composition of it: it *is* holy, *and* it shall be holy unto you.

nn376/pnl834   qmf7543   pp,pnx3644   wcj,pnl834   qmf5414   pr,pnx4480
33 Whosoever compoundeth *any* like it, or whosoever putteth *any* of it

pr5921   qpta2114   wcs,nipf3772   pr4480/pl,nn,pnx5971
upon a stranger, shall even be cut off from*his*people.

How to Make the Incense

nn3068   wcs,qmf559   pr413   nn4872   qmv3947   pp,pnx   pl,nn5561   nn5198
34 And the LORD said unto Moses, Take unto thee sweet spices, stacte, and

wcj,nn7827   wcj,nn2464   pl,nn5561   aj2134   wcj,nn3828   pp,nn905

onycha, and galbanum; *these* sweet spices with pure frankincense: of each shall

qmf1961   nn905

there be a like *weight*:

wcs,qpf6213   pnx(853)   nn7004   cs,nn7545   cs,nn4639

35 And thou shalt make   it a perfume, a confection after the art of the

qpta7543   pupt4414   aj2889   nn6944

apothecary, tempered together, pure *and* holy:

wcs,qpf7833   pr,pnx4480   hina1854   wcs,qpf5414   pr,pnx4480

36 And thou shalt beat *some* of it very small, and put of it

pp,pl,cs,nn6440   df,nn5715   pp,cs,nn168   nn4150   pnl834/ad,lh8033   nimf3259

before the testimony in the tabernacle of the congregation, where I will meet

pp,pnx   qmf1961   pp,pnx   cs,nn6944/pl,nn6944

with thee: it shall be unto you most holy.

wcj,df,nn7004   pnl834   qmf6213   ptn3808   qmf6213

37 And *as for* the perfume which thou shalt make, ye shall not make

pp,pnx   pp,nn,pnx4971   qmf1961   pp,pnx   nn6944

to yourselves according to the composition thereof: it shall be unto thee holy for

pp,nn3068

the LORD.

nn376/pnl834   qmf6213   pp,pnx3644   pp,hinc7306   pp,pnx

38 Whosoever shall make like*unto*that, to smell thereto, shall even be

wcs,nipf3772   pr4480/pl,nn,pnx5971

cut off from*his*people.

God Appoints the Builders

nn3068   wcs,pimf1696   pr413   nn4872   pp,qnc559

31

And the LORD spoke unto Moses, saying,

qmv7200   qpf7121   pp,nn8034   nn1212   cs,nn1121   nn221   cs,nn1121

2 See, I have called by name Bezaleel the son of Uri, the son

nn2354   pp,cs,nn4294   nn3063

of Hur, of the tribe of Judah:

wcs,pimf4390   pnx(853)   cs,nn7307   pl,nn430   pp,nn2451

3 And I have filled   him with the spirit of God, in wisdom, and in

wcj,pp,nn8394   wcj,pp,nn1847   wcj,pp,cs,nn3605   nn4399

understanding, and in knowledge, and in all manner of workmanship,

pp,qnc2803   pl,nn4284   pp,qnc6213   dfp,nn2091   wcj,dfp,nn3701   wcj,dfp,nn5178

4 To devise cunning works, to work in gold, and in silver, and in brass,

wcj,pp,cs,nn2799   nn68   pp,pinc4390   wcj,pp,cs,nn2799   nn6086

5 And in cutting of stones, to set *them*, and in carving of timber, to

pp,qnc6213   pp,cs,nn3605   nn4399

work in all manner of workmanship.

wcj,pnp589   ptdm2009   qpf5414   pr,pnx854   (853)   nn171   cs,nn1121

6 And I, behold, I have given with him   Aholiab, the son of

nn294   pp,cs,nn4294   nn1835   wcj,pp,cs,nn3820   cs,nn3605   cs,aj2450

Ahisamach, of the tribe of Dan: and in the hearts of all that are wise

nn3820   qpf5414   nn2451   wcj,qpf6213 (853) cs,nn3605 pnl834   pipf,pnx6680

hearted I have put wisdom, that they may make   all that I have commanded

thee;

(853)   cs,nn168   nn4150   wcj(853)   df,nn727   dfp,nn5715

7 The tabernacle of the congregation, and   the ark of the testimony,

wcj(853)   df,nn**3727**   pnl834   pr,pnx5921   wcj(853) cs,nn3605   pl,cs,nn3627

and   the mercy seat that *is* thereupon, and   all   the furniture of the

df,nn**168**

tabernacle,

wcj(853)   df,nn**7979**   wcj(853)   pl,nn,pnx3627   wcj(853)   df,aj**2889**   df,nn4501

8 And   the table and   his furniture, and   the pure candlestick with

wcj(853) cs,nn3605   pl,nn,pnx3627   wcj(853)   cs,nn**4196**   df,nn**7004**

all   his furniture, and   the altar of incense,

wcj(853)   cs,nn**4196**   df,nn**5930**   wcj(853) cs,nn3605   pl,nn,pnx3627   wcj(853)

9 And   the altar of burnt offering with   all   his furniture, and

df,nn3595   wcj(853)   nn,pnx3653

the laver and   his foot,

wcj(853)   pl,cs,nn899   df,nn8278   wcj(853)   df,nn**6944**   pl,cs,nn899   pp,nn175

10 And   the cloths of service, and   the holy garments for Aaron the

df,nn**3548**   wcj(853)   pl,cs,nn899   pl,nn,pnx**1121**   pp,pinc**3547**

priest, and   the garments of his sons, to minister*in*the*priest's*office,

wcj(853)   df,nn**4888**   cs,nn**8081**   wcj(853) df,pl,nn5561   cs,nn**7004**   dfp,nn**6944**

11 And   the anointing oil, and   sweet incense for the holy *place*:

pp,nn3605 pnl834   pipf,pnx**6680**   qmf6213

according to   all   that I have commanded thee shall they do.

Rest on the Seventh Day

nn**3068** wcs,qmf559 pr413   nn4872   pp,qnc559

12 And the LORD spoke unto Moses, saying,

pimv**1696** wcj,pnp859   pr413   pl,cs,nn**1121**   nn3478   pp,qnc559   ad389   (853)   pl,nn,pnx**7676**

13 Speak   thou also unto the children of Israel, saying, Verily   my sabbaths

qmf**8104**   cj3588 pnp1931   nn226   pr,pnx996   wcj,pnx(pr996)

ye shall keep: for   it   *is* a sign between me and   you throughout your

pp,pl,nn,pnx1755   pp,qnc3045 cj3588 pnp589   nn3068   pipt,pnx**6942**

generations; that *ye* may know that I *am* the LORD that doth sanctify you.

wcs,qpf**8104** (853)   df,nn**7676**   cj3588 pnp1931   nn**6944**   pp,pnx

14 Ye shall keep   the sabbath therefore; for   it   *is* holy unto you:

pl,pipt,pnx**2490**   qna**4191**/homf**4191**   cj3588 cs,nn3605   df,qpta**6213**

every*one*that*defileth it shall surely*be*put*to*death: for whosoever doeth *any*

nn**4399**   pp,pnx   df,pndm1931 df,nn**5315**   wcs,nipf3772   pr4480/cs,nn7130   pl,nn,pnx5971

work therein,   that   soul shall be cut off from among his people.

cs,nu8337 pl,nn**3117**   nn**4399**   nimf**6213**   wcj,dfp(nn3117) df,nuor7637   cs,nn**7676**

15 Six   days may work be done; but in the   seventh *is* the sabbath of

nn**7677** nn**6944**   pp,nn**3068** cs,nn3605   df,qpta**6213**   nn**4399**   df,nn**7676** pp,cs,nn**3117**

rest, holy to the LORD: whosoever doeth *any* work in the sabbath   day,   he shall

qna**4191**/homf**4191**

surely*be*put*to*death.

pl,cs,nn**1121**   nn3478   wcs,qpf**8104** (853)   df,nn**7676**   pp,qnc**6213** (853)

16 Wherefore the children of Israel shall keep   the sabbath, to observe

df,nn**7676**   pp,pl,nn,pnx**1755**   nn5769   cs,nn**1285**

the sabbath throughout their generations, *for* a perpetual covenant.

pnp1931   nn226 pr,pnx996   wcj(pr996)   pl,cs,nn**1121**   nn3478   pp,nn**5769** cj3588

17 It *is* a sign between me and   the children of Israel forever: for *in*

cs,nu8337 pl,nn**3117**   nn**3068** qpf**6213** (853) df,du,nn**8064**   wcj(853) df,nn**776**   df,nuor7637 wcj,dfp,nn**3117**

six days the LORD made   heaven and   earth, and on the seventh   day

qpf**7673**   wcs,nimf5314

he rested, and was refreshed.

wcs,qmf**5414** pr413   nn4872   pp,pinc,pnx**3615**   pp,pinc**1696** pr,pnx854

18 And he gave unto Moses, when he had made*an*end of communing with

pp,cs,nn2022   nn5514   du,cs,nu8147 pl,cs,nn3871   df,nn5715   pl,cs,nn3871   nn68   pl,qptp3789
him upon mount Sinai,   two   tables of testimony, tables of stone, written with

pp,cs,nn676   pl,nn430
the finger of God.

The Golden Calf

df,nn5971   wcs,qmf7200 cj3588   nn4872   pipf*954   pp,qnc3381
32 And when the people   saw   that Moses delayed to come down

pr4480   df,nn2022   df,nn5971   wcs,nimf6950   pr5921
out of the mount, the people gathered*themselves*together unto

nn175   wcs,qmf559 pr,pnx413   qmv6965 qmv6213 pp,pnx pl,nn430 pnl834   qmf1980 pp,pl,nn,pnx6440
Aaron, and said   unto him, Up, make us gods, which shall go   before   us;

cj3588   pndm2088   nn4872   df,nn376 pnl834   hipf,pnx5927   pr4480/cs,nn776   nn4714
for *as for* this Moses, the man that brought*us*up out*of*the*land of Egypt, we

qpf3045   ptn3808 pnid4100   qpf1961   pp,pnx
know not what is become of him.

nn175   wcs,qmf559 pr,pnx413   pimv6561   df,nn2091   pl,cs,nn5141 pnl834
2 And Aaron   said   unto them, Break off the golden earrings, which *are* in

pp,du,cs,nn241   pl,nn,pnx802   pl,nn,pnx1121   wcj,pl,nn,pnx1323   wcj,himv935
the   ears   of your wives, of your sons,   and of your daughters, and bring *them*

pr,pnx413
unto me.

cs,nn3605   df,nn5971   wcs,htmf6561   (853)   df,nn2091   pl,cs,nn5141   pnl834
3 And   all   the people broke off   the golden earrings which *were* in their

pp,du,nn,pnx241   wcs,himf935   pr413   nn175
ears,   and brought *them* unto Aaron.

wcs,qmf3947   pr4480/nn,pnx3027   wcs,qmf6696   pnx(853)
4 And he received *them* at*their*hand, and fashioned   it with a

dfp,nn2747   wcs,qmf,pnx6213   nn4541   cs,nn5695   wcs,qmf559   pndm428
graving tool, after he had   made   it a molten calf: and they said, These *be* thy

pl,nn,pnx430   nn3478   pnl834   hipf,pnx5927   pr4480/cs,nn776   nn4714
gods, O Israel, which brought*thee*up out*of*the*land of Egypt.

nn175   wcs,qmf7200   wcs,qmf1129   nn4196 pp,pl,nn,pnx6440   nn175
5 And when Aaron   saw   *it,* he   built   an altar before   it; and Aaron

wcs,qmf7121   wcs,qmf559   ad4279   nn2282   pp,nn3068
made proclamation, and said, Tomorrow *is* a feast to the LORD.

wcs,himf7925   pr4480/nn4283   wcs,himf5927   pl,nn5930
6 And they rose*up*early on*the*morrow, and offered burnt offerings, and

wcs,himf5066   pl,nn8002   df,nn5971   wcs,qmf3427   pp,qnc398   wcj,qna8354
brought peace offerings; and the people sat down to eat   and to drink, and

wcs,qmf6965   pp,pinc6711
rose up to play.

nn3068   wcs,pimf1696   pr413   nn4872   qmv1980   qmv3381   cj3588   nn,pnx5971
7 And the LORD   said   unto Moses, Go, get*thee*down; for thy people,

pnl834   hipf5927   pr4480/cs,nn776   nn4714   pipf7843
which thou broughtest out*of*the*land of Egypt, have corrupted *themselves*:

qpf5493   ad4118   pr4480   df,nn1870 pnl834   pipf,pnx6680
8 They have turned aside quickly out of the way which I commanded them:

qpf6213   pp,pnx   nn4541   cs,nn5695   wcs,htmf7812   pp,pnx   wcs,qmf2076
they have made them a molten calf, and have worshiped it, and have sacrificed

pp,pnx   wcs,qmf559   pndm428   pl,nn,pnx430   nn3478   pnl834   hipf,pnx5927
thereunto, and said, These *be* thy gods, O Israel, which have brought*thee*up

pr4480/cs,nn776   nn4714
out*of*the*land of Egypt.

nn3068   wcs,qmf559   pr413   nn4872   qpf7200 (853) df,pndm2088 df,nn5971

9 And the LORD said unto Moses, I have seen this people, and,

wcj,ptdm2009 pnp1931   cs,aj7186/nn6203   cs,nn5971

behold, it *is* a stiffnecked people:

wcj,ad6258   himv5117/pp,pnx   nn,pnx639   wcj,qcj2734   pp,pnx

10 Now therefore let*me*alone, that my wrath may wax hot against them,

wcs,pimf,pnx3615   wcj,qmf6213 pnx(853)   aj1419   pp,nn1471

and that I may consume them: and I will make of thee a great nation.

nn4872   wcs,pimf2470 (853) (pl,cs,nn6440)   nn3068   pl,nn,pnx430   wcs,qmf559 nn3068 pnit4100

11 And Moses besought the LORD his God, and said, LORD, why

nn,pnx639   qmf2734   pp,nn,pnx5971 pnl834   hipf3318

doth thy wrath wax hot against thy people, which thou hast brought forth

pr4480/cs,nn776   nn4714   aj1419   pp,nn3581   aj2389 wcj,pp,nn3027

out*of*the*land of Egypt with great power, and with a mighty hand?

pp,pnit4100   nn4714   qmf559   pp,qnc559   pp,nn7451

12 Wherefore should the Egyptians speak, and say, For mischief did he

hipf,pnx3318   pp,qnc2026 pnx(853)   dfp,pl,nn2022   wcj,pp,pinc,pnx3615

bring*them*out, to slay them in the mountains, and to consume them

pr4480/pr5921   pl,cs,nn6440   df,nn127 qmv7725   pr4480/cs,nn2740/nn,pnx639 wcj,nimv5162 pr5921

from the face of the earth? Turn from*thy*fierce*wrath, and repent of this

df,nn7451   pp,nn,pnx5971

evil against thy people.

qmv2142   pp,nn85   pp,nn3327   wcj,pp,nn3478   pl,nn,pnx5650   pnl834 pp,pnx   nipf7650

13 Remember Abraham, Isaac, and Israel, thy servants, to whom thou sworest

pp,pnx   wcs,pimf1696 pr,pnx413   him7235 (853)   nn,pnx2233

by*thine*own*self, and saidst unto them, I will multiply your seed as the

pp,pl,cs,nn3556   df,du,nn8064   wcj,cs,nn3605 df,pndm2063 df,nn776 pnl834   qpf559   qmf5414

stars of heaven, and all this land that I have spoken of will I give unto

pp,nn,pnx2233   wcs,qpf5157   pp,nn5769

your seed, and they shall inherit *it* forever.

nn3068   wcs,nimf5162 pr5921   df,nn7451 pnl834   pipf1696   pp,qnc6213

14 And the LORD repented of the evil which he thought to do unto his

pp,nn,pnx5971

people.

nn4872   wcs,qmf6437   wcs,qmf3381   pr4480   df,nn2022   wcj,du,cs,nu8147

15 And Moses turned, and went down from the mount, and the two

pl,cs,nn3871   df,nn5715   pp,nn,pnx3027   pl,nn3871   pl,qptp3789 pr4480/du,cs,nu8147

tables of the testimony *were* in his hand: the tables *were* written on both their

pl,nn,pnx5676   pr4480/pndm2088   wcj,pr4480/pndm2088   pnp1992 pl,qptp3789

sides; on*the*one*side and on*the*other *were* they written.

wcj,df,pl,nn3871 (pnp1992)   cs,nn4639   pl,nn430   wcj,df,nn4385 (pnp1931)

16 And the tables *were* the work of God, and the writing *was*

cs,nn4385   pl,nn430 qptp2801 pr5921   df,pl,nn3871

the writing of God, graven upon the tables.

nn3091   wcs,qmf8085 (853)   cs,nn6963   df,nn5971   pp,nn,pnx7452

17 And when Joshua heard the noise of the people as they shouted, he

wcs,qmf559 pr413   nn4872   cs,nn6963   nn4421   dfp,nn4264

said unto Moses, *There is* a noise of war in the camp.

wcs,qmf559   ptn369   cs,nn6963   qnc6030   nn1369   wcj,ptn369

18 And he said, *It is* not the voice of *them that* shout for mastery, neither *is*

cs,nn6963   qnc6030   nn2476   cs,nn6963   pinc6031

it the voice of *them that* cry for being overcome: but the noise of *them that* sing

pnp595 qpta8085

do I hear.

wcs,qmf1961   pp,pnl834   qpf7126   pr413   df,nn4264

19 And it*came*to*pass, as*soon*as he came nigh unto the camp, that he

_{wcs,qmf**7200**} (853)   _{df,nn5695}   _{wcj,pl,nn4246}   _{nn4872}   _{cs,nn**639**}   _{wcs,qmf**2734**}   _{wcs,himf**7993**}

saw   the calf, and the dancing: and Moses' anger waxed hot, and he   cast

₍₈₅₃₎   _{df,pl,nn3871}   _{pr4480/du,nn,pnx**3027**}   _{wcs,pimf**7665**} _{pnx(853)}   _{pr8478}   _{df,nn2022}

the tables out*of*his*hands, and broke   them beneath the mount.

_{wcs,qmf3947} (853)   _{df,nn5695}   _{pnl834}   _{qpf6213}   _{wcs,qmf**8313**}

20 And he   took   the calf which they had made, and burnt *it* in the

_{dfp,nn784}   _{wcs,qmf2912}   _{pr5704} _{pnl834/qpf1854}   _{wcs,qmf2219}   _{pr5921/pl,cs,nn6440}   _{df,pl,nn4325}

fire, and ground *it* to powder, and strewed *it*   upon   the water, and made

₍₈₅₃₎   _{pl,cs,nn**1121**}   _{nn3478} _{wcs,himf8248}

the children of Israel drink *of it*.

_{nn4872}   _{wcs,qmf559} _{pr413}   _{nn175}   _{pnit4100} _{qpf**6213**} _{df,pndm2088}   _{df,nn**5971**}   _{pp,pnx}   _{cj3588}

21 And Moses said unto Aaron, What did   this   people unto thee, that

_{hipf935}   _{aj1419}   _{nn**2401**} _{pr,pnx5921}

thou hast brought so great a sin upon them?

_{nn175} _{wcs,qmf559} _{ptn408}   _{cs,nn**639**}   _{nn,pnx113} _{qcj**2734**} _{pnp859} _{qpf**3045**}   ₍₈₅₃₎

22 And Aaron said, Let not the anger of my lord wax hot: thou knowest

_{df,nn**5971**} _{cj3588} _{pnp1931}   _{pp,nn**7451**}

the people, that they *are set* on mischief.

_{wcs,qmf559}   _{pp,pnx}   _{qmv**6213**} _{pp,pnx} _{pl,nn**430**} _{pnl834}   _{qmf**1980**} _{pp,pl,nn,pnx**6440**}

23 For they said unto me, Make us gods, which shall go   before us:

_{cj3588}   _{pndm2088} _{nn4872}   _{df,nn**376**} _{pnl834}   _{hipf,pnx**5927**}   _{pr4480/cs,nn**776**}   _{nn4714}

for *as for* this Moses, the man that brought*us*up out*of*the*land of Egypt, we

_{qpf**3045**} _{ptn**3808**} _{pnid4100}   _{qpf**1961**}   _{pp,pnx}

know not what is become of him.

_{wcs,qmf559}   _{pp,pnx}   _{pp,pnit4310}   _{nn2091}   _{htmv6561}

24 And I said unto them, Whosoever hath any gold, let them break*it*off.

_{wcs,qmf**5414**}   _{pp,pnx}   _{wcs,himf,pnx**7993**}   _{dfp,nn784}   _{wcs,qmf3318} _{df,pndm2088}

So they gave *it* me: then I   cast   it into the fire, and there came out this

_{df,nn5695}

calf.

_{nn4872}   _{wcs,qmf**7200**} _{cj3588} ₍₈₅₃₎   _{df,nn**5971**}   _(pnp1931)   _{qptp6544} _{cj3588}   _{nn175}

◎☞ 25 And when Moses saw   that   the people   *were* naked; (for Aaron

_{qpf,pnx**6544**}   _{pp,nn8103}   _{pp,pl,qpta,pnx**6965**}

had made*them*naked unto *their* shame among their enemies:)

_{nn4872}   _{wcs,qmf5975}   _{pp,cs,nn8179}   _{df,nn**4264**}   _{wcs,qmf559} _{pnit4310}

◎☞ 26 Then Moses stood in the   gate of the camp, and said, Who *is* on the

_{pp,nn**3068**}   _{pr,pnx413}   _{cs,nn3605}   _{pl,cs,nn**1121**}   _{nn3878}

LORD's side? *let* *him* *come* unto me. And all   the   sons   of Levi

_{wcs,nimf**622**}   _{pr,pnx413}

gathered*themselves*together unto him.

◎☞ **32:25–29** This passage describes how the Levites won the privilege of serving the Lord in the Tabernacle. Apparently some of the people were still rebellious. The Levites responded immediately when Moses asked the question, "Who is on the LORD's side?" They were then commissioned by Moses to go throughout the camp executing the rebels. For their loyalty to God, they became His special ministers.

The priests were a special class within the tribe of Levi whose ministry included the more sacred functions, which functions other members of the tribe were not permitted to perform. For even though, in a general sense, God wanted all Israel to be a "kingdom of priests" (Ex. 19:6), a special priesthood already existed (Ex. 19:22, 24). Only Aaron and his sons could be priests (Ex. 28:1; Num. 3:10). The choice of Aaron's line was made a hereditary appointment after Phinehas' act of zealous loyalty to God (Num. 25:6–13).

◎☞ **32:26, 27** The Law had just been given to Moses by God and it strictly forbade both the worship of false gods and murder. In this passage, God commanded that the people who were guilty of breaking the Law were to be put to death. Even though the Israelites had promised earlier, "All the words which the Lord hath said will we do" (Ex. 24:3), these had forsaken God. In His sovereignty, God required that this sin be judged. The children of Israel were merely the means that God chose to carry out His judgment.

^{wcs,qmf559} ^{pp,pnx} ^{ad3541} ^{qpf559} ⁿⁿ³⁰⁶⁸ ^{pl,cs,nn430} ⁿⁿ³⁴⁷⁸ ^{qmv7760}
27 And he said unto them, Thus saith the LORD God of Israel, Put

ⁿⁿ³⁷⁶ ^{nn,pnx2719} ^{pr5921} ^{nn,pnx3409} ^{qmv5674} ^{wcj,qmv7725} ^{pr4480/nn8179} ^{pp,nn8179}
every man his sword by his side, *and* go in and out from gate to gate

^{dfp,nn4264} ^{wcj,qmv2026} ⁿⁿ³⁷⁶ ⁽⁸⁵³⁾ ^{nn,pnx251} ^{wcj,nn376} ⁽⁸⁵³⁾
throughout the camp, and slay every man his brother, and every man his

^{nn,pnx7453} ^{wcj,nn376} ⁽⁸⁵³⁾ ^{aj,pnx7138}
companion, and every man his neighbor.

^{pl,cs,nn1121} ⁿⁿ³⁸⁷⁸ ^{wcs,qmf6213} ^{pp,cs,nn1697} ⁿⁿ⁴⁸⁷²
28 And the children of Levi did according to the word of Moses: and there

^{wcs,qmf5307} ^{pr4480} ^{df,nn5971} ^{df,pndm1931} ^{dfp,nn3117} ^{pp,cs,nu7969} ^{pl,cs,nu505} ⁿⁿ³⁷⁶
fell of the people that day about three thousand men.

ⁿⁿ⁴⁸⁷² ^{wcs,qmf559} ^{qmv4390/nn,pnx3027} ^{df,nn3117} ^{pp,nn3068} ^{cj3588}
29 For Moses had said, Consecrate yourselves today to the LORD, even

ⁿⁿ³⁷⁶ ^{pp,nn,pnx1121} ^{wcj,pp,nn,pnx251} ^{wcj,pp,qnc5414} ^{pr,pnx5921}
every man upon his son, and upon his brother; that he may bestow upon

ⁿⁿ¹²⁹³ ^{df,nn3117}
you a blessing this day.

^{wcs,qmf1961} ^{pr4480/nn4283} ⁿⁿ⁴⁸⁷² ^{wcs,qmf559} ^{pr413} ^{df,nn5971}
30 And it*came*to*pass on*the*morrow, that Moses said unto the people,

^{pnp859} ^{qpf2398} ^{aj1419} ⁿⁿ²⁴⁰¹ ^{wcj,ad6258} ^{qmf5927} ^{pr413} ⁿⁿ³⁰⁶⁸ ^{ad194}
Ye have sinned a great sin: and now I will go up unto the LORD; peradventure I

^{picj3722} ^{pr1157} ^{nn,pnx2403}
shall make*an*atonement for your sin.

ⁿⁿ⁴⁸⁷² ^{wcs,qmf7725} ^{pr413} ⁿⁿ³⁰⁶⁸ ^{wcs,qmf559} ^{pte577} ^{df,pndm2088} ^{df,nn5971}
31 And Moses returned unto the LORD, and said, Oh, this people have

^{qpf2398} ^{aj1419} ⁿⁿ²⁴⁰¹ ^{wcs,qmf6213} ^{pp,pnx} ^{pl,cs,nn430} ⁿⁿ²⁰⁹¹
sinned a great sin, and have made them gods of gold.

^{wcj,ad6258} ^{cj518} ^{qmf5375} ^{nn,pnx2403} ^{wcj,cj518} ^{ptn369} ^{qmv,pnx4229}
32 Yet now, if thou wilt forgive their sin; and if not, blot me,

^{pte4994} ^{pr4480/nn,pnx5612} ^{pnl834} ^{qpf3789}
I*pray*thee, out*of*thy*book which thou hast written.

ⁿⁿ³⁰⁶⁸ ^{wcs,qmf559} ^{pr413} ⁿⁿ⁴⁸⁷² ^{pnit4310/pnl834} ^{qpf2398} ^{pp,pnx}
33 And the LORD said unto Moses, Whosoever hath sinned against me, him

^{qmf,pnx4229} ^{pr4480/nn,pnx5612}
will I blot out of*my*book.

^{wcj,ad6258} ^{qmv1980} ^{qmv5148} ⁽⁸⁵³⁾ ^{df,nn5971} ^{pr413} ^{pnl834}
34 Therefore now go, lead the people unto *the place* of which I have

^{pipf1696} ^{pp,pnx} ^{ptdm2009} ^{nn,pnx4397} ^{qmf1980} ^{pp,pl,nn,pnx6440}
spoken unto thee: behold, mine Angel shall go before thee: nevertheless in the

^{wcj,pp,cs,nn3117} ^{qnc,pnx6485} ^{wcs,qpf6485} ^{nn,pnx2403} ^{pr,pnx5921}
day when I visit I will visit their sin upon them.

ⁿⁿ³⁰⁶⁸ ^{wcs,qmf5062} ⁽⁸⁵³⁾ ^{df,nn5971} ^{pr5921/pnl834} ^{qpf6213} ⁽⁸⁵³⁾ ^{df,nn5695}
35 And the LORD plagued the people, because they made the calf,

^{pnl834} ⁿⁿ¹⁷⁵ ^{qpf6213}
which Aaron made.

God Gives the Orders to March

33 And the LORD said unto Moses, Depart, *and* go up hence, thou
and the people which thou hast brought up out*of*the*land of Egypt,
unto the land which I swore unto Abraham, to Isaac, and to Jacob, saying, Unto
thy seed will I give it:

2 And I will send an angel before thee; and I will drive out the
Canaanite, the Amorite, and the Hittite, and the Perizzite, the Hivite, and the
Jebusite:

3 Unto a land flowing with milk and honey: for I will not go up in the
midst of thee; for thou *art* a stiffnecked people: lest I consume thee in the way.

4 And when the people heard these evil tidings, they mourned: and
no man did put on him his ornaments.

5 For the LORD had said unto Moses, Say unto the children of Israel, Ye
are a stiffnecked people: I will come up into the midst of thee in a moment,
and consume thee: therefore now put off thy ornaments from thee, that I
may know what to do unto thee.

6 And the children of Israel stripped themselves of their ornaments
by*the*mount Horeb.

7 And Moses took the tabernacle, and pitched it without the camp,
afar off from the camp, and called it the Tabernacle of the congregation. And
it*came*to*pass, *that* every one which sought the LORD went out unto the
tabernacle of the congregation, which *was* without the camp.

8 And it*came*to*pass, when Moses went out unto the tabernacle, *that* all
the people rose up, and stood every man *at* his tent door, and looked after
Moses, until he was gone into the tabernacle.

9 And it*came*to*pass, as Moses entered into the tabernacle, the cloudy pillar
descended, and stood *at* the door of the tabernacle, and *the* LORD talked with
Moses.

        cs,nn3605   df,nn5971 wcs,qpf7200 (853)   df,nn6051 cs,nn5982 qpta5975   df,nn168

10 And all the people saw   the cloudy pillar stand *at* the tabernacle

cs,nn6607 cs,nn3605 df,nn5971 wcs,qpf6965   wcs,htpf*7812   nn376   nn,pnx168 cs,nn6607

door: and all the people rose up and worshiped, every man *in* his tent door.

        nn3068 wcs,pipf1696 pr413   nn4872 pl,nn6440 pr413 pl,nn6440 pp,pnl834   nn376 pimf1696   pr413

11 And the LORD spoke unto Moses face to face, as a man speaketh unto

nn,pnx7453   wcs,qpf7725 pr413 df,nn4264   wcj,pipt,pnx8334 nn3091   cs,nn1121

his friend. And he turned again into the camp: but his servant Joshua, the son of

nn5126   nn5288   himf4185 ptn3808 pr4480/cs,nn8432   df,nn168

Nun, a young man, departed not   out of the tabernacle.

        nn4872 wcs,qmf559 pr413   nn3068 qmv7200 pnp859 qpta559 pr,pnx413   himv5927   (853)

12 And Moses said unto the LORD, See, thou sayest unto me, Bring up

df,pndm2088 df,nn5971   wcj,pnp859 ptn3808   hipf,pnx3045 (853) pnl834   qmf7971 pr,pnx5973

this people: and thou hast not let me know   whom thou wilt send with

wcj,pnp859   qpf559   qpf,pnx3045   pp,nn8034   wcj,ad1571 qpf4672 nn2580

me. Yet thou hast said, I know thee by name, and thou hast also found grace

      pp,du,nn,pnx5869

in my sight.

      wcj,ad6258   pte4994   cj518   qpf4672 nn2580   pp,du,nn,pnx5869

13 Now therefore, I*pray*thee, if I have found grace in thy sight,

himv,pnx3045   pte4994 (853)   nn,pnx1870 pr4616   wcj,qmf,pnx3045   qmf4672 nn2580

show me now   thy way, that I may know   thee, that I may find grace in

pp,du,nn,pnx5869   wcj,qmv7200 cj3588 df,pndm2088 df,nn1471   nn,pnx5971

thy sight: and consider that this nation *is* thy people.

        wcs,qmf559   pl,nn,pnx6440   qmf1980   wcj,hipf5117/pp,pnx

14 And he said, My presence shall go *with thee*, and I will give*thee*rest.

        wcs,qmf559   pr,pnx413   cj518   pl,nn,pnx6440 pl,qpta1980 ptn369

15 And he   said   unto him, If thy presence go   not *with me*,

himf,pnx5927/ptn408   pr4480/pndm2088

carry*us*not*up hence.

        wcj,dfp,pnit4100   nimf3045 cj645 cj3588 pnp589   wcj,nn,pnx5971   qpf4672

16 For wherein shall it be known here that I and thy people have found

nn2580   pp,du,nn,pnx5869   he,ptn3808   pp,qnc,pnx1980 pr,pnx5973

grace in thy sight? *is it* not in that thou goest with us? so shall we be

wcj,nipf6395 pnp589   wcj,nn,pnx5971 pr4480/cs,nn3605 df,nn5971 pnl834   pr5921   pl,cs,nn6440

separated, I and thy people, from all the people that *are* upon the face of

df,nn127

the earth.

       nn3068 wcs,qmf559 pr413   nn4872   qmf6213 (853) df,pndm2088 df,nn1697 ad1571 pnl834

17 And the LORD said unto Moses, I will do   this thing also that thou

   pipf1696   cj3588   qpf4672 nn2580   pp,du,nn,pnx5869   wcs,qmf,pnx3045

hast spoken: for thou hast found grace in my sight, and I know thee by

pp,nn8034

name.

        wcs,qmf559   pte4994   himv,pnx7200   (853)   nn,pnx3519

18 And he said, I*beseech*thee, show me   thy glory.

        wcs,qmf559 pnp589   cs,nn3605   nn,pnx2898 himf5674 pr5921/pl,nn,pnx6440

19 And he said, I will make all my goodness pass before   thee, and

wcs,qpf7121   pp,cs,nn8034   nn3068 pp,pl,nn,pnx6440   wcs,qpf2603 (853)

I will proclaim the name of the LORD before thee; and will be gracious   to

pnl834   qmf2603   wcs,pipf7355 (853)   pnl834   pimf7355

whom I will be gracious, and will show mercy   on whom I will show mercy.

33:11 See the note on Num. 27:18–23, on Joshua.

      wcs,qmf**559**   qmf3201   ptn**3808**   pp,qnc**7200**   (853)   pl,nn,pnx**6440**   cj3588   ptn3808

20 And he said, Thou canst not see my face: for there shall no

df,nn**120**   qmf,pnx**7200**   wcs,qpf**2425**

man see me, and live.

         nn**3068**   wcs,qmf**559**   ptdm2009   nn4725   pr,pnx854

21 And the LORD said, Behold, *there is* a place by me, and thou shalt

wcj,nipf**5324**   pr5921   df,nn**6697**

stand upon a rock:

       wcj,qpf**1961**   nn,pnx**3519**   pp,qnc**5674**   wcj,qpf,pnx**7760**

22 And it*shall*come*to*pass, while my glory passeth by, that I will put

pp,cs,nn**5366**   df,nn**6697**   wcs,qpf5526/pr,pnx**5921**   nn,pnx**3709**   cj5704

thee in a cleft of the rock, and will cover thee with my hand while I

qnc,pnx**5674**

pass by:

       wcj,hipf**5493**   (853)   nn,pnx**3709**   wcj,qpf**7200**   (853)

23 And I will take away mine hand, and thou shalt see my

pl,nn,pnx268   wcj,pl,nn,pnx**6440**   ptn**3808**   nimf**7200**

back parts: but my face shall not be seen.

The New Tablets

         nn**3068**   wcs,qmf**559**   pr413   nn4872   qmv**6458**   pp,pnx   du,cs,nu8147   pl,cs,nn3871   pl,nn68

34 And the LORD said unto Moses, Hew thee two tables of stone

         dfp,aj**7223**   wcj,qpf3789 pr5921   df,pl,nn3871 (853)   df,pl,nn**1697**

like unto the first: and I will write upon *these* tables the words

pnl834 qpf**1961** pr5921   df,aj**7223** df,pl,nn3871 pnl834   pipf**7665**

that were in the first tables, which thou didst break.

      wcj,qmv**1961**   nipt**3559**   dfp,nn1242   wcj,qpf**5927**   dfp,nn1242   pr413   cs,nn2022

2 And be ready in the morning, and come up in the morning unto mount

nn5514   wcj,nipf**5324**   ad8033   pp,pnx   pr5921   cs,nn7218   df,nn2022

Sinai, and present thyself there to me in the top of the mount.

      ptn**3808** wcj,nn**376**   qmf**5927**   pr,pnx5973   ptn408/wcj,ad1571   nn**376**   nimf**7200**

3 And no man shall come up with thee, neither let any man be seen

      pp,cs,nn3605   df,nn2022   ptn408/ad1571   df,nn6629   wcj,df,nn1241   qmf7462   pr413/pr4136

throughout all the mount; neither let the flocks nor herds feed before

df,pndm1931   df,nn2022

that mount.

      wcs,qmf**6458**   du,cs,nu8147   pl,cs,nn3871   pl,nn68   dfp,aj**7223**   nn4872

4 And he hewed two tables of stone like unto the first; and Moses

wcs,himf7925   dfp,nn1242   wcs,qmf**5927**   pr413   cs,nn2022   nn5514   pp,pnl834   nn**3068**

rose*up*early in the morning, and went up unto mount Sinai, as the LORD had

pipf**6680**   pnx(853)   wcs,qmf3947   pp,nn,pnx3027   du,cs,nu8147   pl,cs,nn3871   pl,nn68

commanded him, and took in his hand the two tables of stone.

       nn**3068**   wcs,qmf**3381**   dfp,nn**6051**   wcs,htmf3320   pr,pnx5973   ad8033

5 And the LORD descended in the cloud, and stood with him there, and

wcs,qmf**7121**   pp,cs,nn8034   nn**3068**

proclaimed the name of the LORD.

      nn**3068**   wcs,qmf**5674**   pr5921/pl,nn,pnx**6440**   wcs,qmf**7121**   nn**3068**

6 And the LORD passed by before him, and proclaimed, The LORD, The

nn**3068**   nn410   aj7349   wcj,aj**2587**   cs,aj750/du,nn639   wcj,cs,aj7227   nn**2617**

LORD God, merciful and gracious, longsuffering, and abundant in goodness and

wcj,nn571

truth,

    qpta**5341**   nn**2617**   dfp,pl,nu505   qpta**5375**   nn5771   wcj,nn6588   wcj,nn**2403**

7 Keeping mercy for thousands, forgiving iniquity and transgression and sin,

ptn3808/wcj,pina5352/pimf5352   qpta6485   cs,nn5771   pl,nn1   pr5921

and that will by*no*means*clear *the guilty*; visiting the iniquity of the fathers upon

pl,nn1121   wcj,pr5921   pl,nn1121   pl,cs,nn1121   pr5921   aj8029   wcj,pr5921   aj7256

the children, and   upon   the children's children, unto the third and   to   the fourth

generation.
nn4872   wcs,pimf4116   wcs,qmf6915   nn,lh776

8 And   Moses   made haste,   and   bowed*his*head   toward   the   earth,   and

wcs,htmf*7812
worshiped.

wcs,qmf559 cj518 pte4994   qpf4672   nn2580   pp,du,nn,pnx5869   nn136

9 And he   said,   If   now   I have found grace in thy   sight,   O Lord, let my

nn136   pte4994   qmf1980   pp,nn,pnx7130   cj3588   pnp1931   cs,aj7186/nn6203   cs,nn5971   wcs,qpf5545

Lord, I*pray*thee,   go   among   us;   for   it   *is* a stiffnecked people; and pardon

pp,nn,pnx5771   wcj,pp,nn,pnx2403   wcs,qpf,pnx5157

our iniquity and our   sin,   and take*us*for*thine*inheritance.

God's Covenant

wcs,qmf559   ptdm2009   pnp595 qpta3772   nn1285   pr5048   cs,nn3605   nn,pnx5971

10 And he   said,   Behold,   I   make a covenant: before   all   thy people I will

qmf6213   pl,nipt6381   pnl834   ptn3808   nipf1254   pp,cs,nn3605   df,nn776   wcj,pp,cs,nn3605

do   marvels, such as have   not   been done in   all   the earth, nor in   any

df,pl,nn1471   cs,nn3605   df,nn5971   pp,nn,pnx7130   pnl834   pnp859   wcj,qpf7200 (853)   cs,nn4639

nation: and   all   the people among   which thou *art* shall   see   the work of the

nn3068   cj3588 pnp1931   nipt3372   pnl834 pnp589   qpta6213 pr,pnx5973

Lord: for   it   *is* a terrible thing that   I   will   do   with thee.

qmv8104   pp,pnx   (853)   pnl834   pnp595   pipt,pnx6680   df,nn3117   ptdm,pnx2009

11 Observe thou   that which   I   command thee this   day: behold,   I

qpta1644   pr4480/pl,nn,pnx6440   (853)   df,nn567   wcj,df,nn3669   wcj,df,nn2850

drive out   before   thee   the Amorite, and the Canaanite, and the Hittite, and

wcj,df,nn6522   wcj,df,nn2340   wcj,df,nn2983

the Perizzite, and the Hivite, and the Jebusite.

nimv8104   pp,pnx   cj6435   qmf3772   nn1285   pp,qpta3427

12 Take heed to thyself, lest thou make a covenant with the inhabitants of the

df,nn776 pnl834/pr,pnx5921 pnp859 qpta935 cj6435   qmf1961   pp,nn4170   pp,nn,pnx7130

land   whither   thou goest, lest it   be   for a snare in the   midst   of thee:

cj3588   qmf5422   (853)   pl,nn,pnx4196 pimf7665 wcj(853)   pl,nn,pnx4676   qmf3772

13 But ye shall destroy   their altars, break   their images, and cut down

wcj(853)   pl,nn,pnx842

their groves:

cj3588   htmf*7812   ptn3808 aj312   pp,nn410 cj3588   nn3068   nn,pnx8034

14 For thou shalt worship   no   other   god: for   the Lord,   whose   name   *is*

aj7067   (pnp1931)   aj7067   nn410

Jealous,   *is* a jealous God:

cj6435   qmf3772   nn1285   pp,cs,qpta3427   df,nn776

15 Lest thou make   a covenant with the   inhabitants   of the land,   and they

wcs,qpf2181   pr310   pl,nn,pnx430   wcs,qpf2076   pp,pl,nn,pnx430   wcs,qpf7121

go*a*whoring after their   gods,   and do sacrifice unto their   gods,   and *one*   call

pp,pnx   wcs,qpf398   pr4480/nn,pnx2077

thee, and thou   eat   of*his*sacrifice;

wcs,qpf3947   pr4480/pl,nn,pnx1323   pp,pl,nn,pnx1121   pl,nn,pnx1323

◯ⷬ 16 And thou   take   of*their*daughters unto thy   sons,   and their daughters

---

◯ⷬ **34:16** In much of the Old Testament Israel is referred to as the bride of the Lord (see Is. 54:5, 6; 62:5; Jer. 31:33). Idolatry was equivalent to adultery (see Jer. 3:8, 9, 20; Ezek. 16:20-34; 23:37).

^{wcs,qpf2181}   ^{pr310}   ^{pl,nn,pnx430}   (853)   ^{pl,nn,pnx1121}   ^{wcs,hipf2181}   ^{pr310}

go*a*whoring after their gods, and make   thy sons go*a*whoring after their

^{pl,nn,pnx430}

gods.

^{qmf6213}   ^{pp,pnx}   ^{ptn3808}   ⁿⁿ⁴⁵⁴¹   ^{pl,cs,nn430}

17 Thou shalt make thee no molten gods.

(853)   ^{cs,nn2282}   ^{df,pl,nn4682}   ^{qmf8104}   ^{cs,nu7651}   ^{pl,nn3117}

18   The feast of unleavened bread shalt thou keep. Seven days thou shalt

^{qmf398}   ^{pl,nn4682}   ^{pnl834}   ^{pipf,pnx6680}   ^{pp,nn4150}   ^{cs,nn2320} ^{df,nn24} ^{cj3588}

eat unleavened bread, as I commanded thee, in the time of the month Abib: for

^{pp,cs,nn2320} ^{df,nn24}   ^{qpf3318}   ^{pr4480/nn4714}

in the month Abib thou camest out from Egypt.

^{cs,nn3605}   ^{cs,nn6363}   ⁿⁿ⁷³⁵⁸   ^{pp,pnx}   ^{wcj,cs,nn3605}   ^{cs,nn6363}

19 All that openeth the matrix is mine; and every firstling among thy

^{nn,pnx4735}   ⁿⁿ⁷⁷⁹⁴   ^{wcj,nn7716}   ^{df,nn2145}

cattle, *whether* ox or sheep, *that is* male.

^{wcj,cs,nn6363}   ⁿⁿ²⁵⁴³   ^{qmf6299}   ^{pp,nn7716}   ^{wcj,cj518}

20 But the firstling of an ass thou shalt redeem with a lamb: and if thou

^{qmf6299}   ^{ptn3808}   ^{wcs,qpf,pnx6202}   ^{cs,nn3605}   ^{cs,nn1060}   ^{pl,nn,pnx1121}

redeem *him* not, then shalt thou break*his*neck. All the firstborn of thy sons

^{qmf6299}   ^{wcj,ptn3808}   ^{nimf7200}   ^{pl,nn,pnx6440}   ^{ad7387}

thou shalt redeem. And none shall appear before me empty.

^{cs,nu8337}   ^{pl,nn3117}   ^{qmf5647}   ^{df,nuor7637}   ^{wcj,dfp,nn3117}   ^{qmf7673}

21 Six days thou shalt work, but on the seventh day thou shalt rest: in

^{dfp,nn2758}   ^{wcj,dfp,nn7105}   ^{qmf7673}

earing time and in harvest thou shalt rest.

^{pp,pnx}   ^{qmf6213}   ^{wcj,cs,nn2282}   ^{pl,nn7620}   ^{pl,cs,nn1061}   ^{pl,nn2406}

22 And thou shalt observe the feast of weeks, of the firstfruits of wheat

^{cs,nn7105}   ^{wcj,cs,nn2282}   ^{df,nn614}   ^{df,nn8141} ^{cs,nn8622}

harvest, and the feast of ingathering at the year's end.

^{nu7969/pl,nn6471}   ^{dfp,nn8141}   ^{cs,nn3605}   ^{nn,pnx2138}   ^{nimf7200}   (853) ^{pl,cs,nn6440}

23 Thrice in the year shall all your men children appear   before the

^{df,nn113} ⁿⁿ³⁰⁶⁸   ^{pl,cs,nn430}   ⁿⁿ³⁴⁷⁸

Lord Gᴏᴅ, the God of Israel.

^{cj3588}   ^{himf3423}   ^{pl,nn1471}   ^{pr4480/pl,nn,pnx6440}   ^{wcs,hipf7337} (853)   ^{nn,pnx1366}

24 For I will cast out the nations before thee, and enlarge thy borders:

^{wcj,ptn3808}   ⁿⁿ³⁷⁶   ^{qmf2530}   (853)   ^{nn,pnx776}   ^{pp,qnc,pnx5927}   ^{pp,ninc7200} (853)

neither shall any man desire thy land, when thou shalt go up to appear

^{pl,cs,nn6440}   ⁿⁿ³⁰⁶⁸   ^{pl,nn,pnx430} ^{nu7969/pl,nn6471}   ^{dfp,nn8141}

before the Lᴏʀᴅ thy God thrice in the year.

^{ptn3808} ^{qmf7819}   ^{cs,nn1818}   ^{nn,pnx2077}   ^{pr5921}   ⁿⁿ²⁵⁵⁷   ^{wcj,ptn3808}

25 Thou shalt not offer the blood of my sacrifice with leaven; neither shall the

^{cs,nn2077}   ^{cs,nn2282}   ^{df,nn6453}   ^{qmf3885}   ^{dfp,nn1242}

sacrifice of the feast of the passover be left unto the morning.

^{cs,nn7225}   ^{pl,cs,nn1061}   ^{nn,pnx127}   ^{himf935}   ^{cs,nn1004}

26 The first of the firstfruits of thy land thou shalt bring unto the house of

ⁿⁿ³⁰⁶⁸   ^{pl,nn,pnx430}   ^{ptn3808} ^{pimf1310}   ⁿⁿ¹⁴²³   ^{nn,pnx517}   ^{pp,cs,nn2461}

the Lᴏʀᴅ thy God. Thou shalt not seethe a kid in his mother's milk.

ⁿⁿ³⁰⁶⁸   ^{wcs,qmf559}   ^{pr413}   ⁿⁿ⁴⁸⁷²   ^{qmv3789} ^{pp,pnx} (853) ^{df,pndm428} ^{df,pl,nn1697} ^{cj3588}   ^{pr5921}

27 And the Lᴏʀᴅ said unto Moses, Write thou   these words: for after the

^{cs,nn6310}   ^{df,pndm428} ^{df,pl,nn1697}   ^{qpf3772}   ⁿⁿ¹²⁸⁵   ^{pr,pnx854}   ^{wcj,pr854}   ⁿⁿ³⁴⁷⁸

tenor of these words I have made a covenant with thee and with Israel.

wcs,qmf**1961** ad8033 pr5973 nn**3068** pl,nu705 nn**3117** wcj,pl,nu705 nn**3915**

28 And he was there with the LORD forty days and forty nights; he did

ptn**3808** qpf398 nn3899 ptn**3808** qpf8354 wcj,pl,nn4325 wcs,qmf3789 pr5921 df,pl,nn3871 (853) pl,cs,nn**1697**

neither eat bread, nor drink water. And he wrote upon the tables the words

df,nn**1285** cs,nu6235 df,pl,nn**1697**

of the covenant, the ten commandments.

wcs,qmf**1961** nn4872 pp,qnc3381 pr4480/cs,nn2022 nn5514

29 And it*came*to*pass, when Moses came down from mount Sinai with the

wcj,du,cs,nu8147 pl,cs,nn3871 df,nn**5715** nn4872 pp,cs,nn**3027** pp,qnc,pnx3381 pr4480

two tables of testimony in Moses' hand, when he came down from the

df,nn2022 wcj,nn4872 qpf3045 ptn3808 cj3588 cs,nn5785 pl,nn,pnx**6440** qpf7160 pp,pinc,pnx1696

mount, that Moses knew not that the skin of his face shone while he talked

pr,pnx854

with him.

nn175 wcj,cs,nn3605 pl,cs,nn1121 nn3478 wcs,qmf**7200** (853) nn4872

30 And when Aaron and all the children of Israel saw Moses,

wcj,ptdm2009 cs,nn**5785** pl,nn,pnx**6440** qpf7160 wcs,qmf3372 pr4480/qnc5066/pr,pnx413

behold, the skin of his face shone; and they were afraid to*come*nigh him.

nn4872 wcs,qmf**7121** pr,pnx413 nn175 wcj,cs,nn3605 df,pl,nn**5387**

31 And Moses called unto them; and Aaron and all the rulers of the

dfp,nn**5712** wcs,qmf**7725** pr,pnx413 nn4872 wcs,pimf**1696** pr,pnx413

congregation returned unto him: and Moses talked with them.

wcj,ad310/ad**3651** cs,nn3605 pl,cs,nn**1121** nn3478 nipf5066

32 And afterward all the children of Israel came nigh: and he

wcs,pimf,pnx**6680** (853) cs,nn3605 pnl834 nn**3068** pipf1696 pr,pnx854

gave*them*in*commandment all that the LORD had spoken with him in

pp,cs,nn2022 nn5514

mount Sinai.

nn4872 wcs,pimf**3615** pr4480/pinc**1696** pr,pnx854 wcs,qmf**5414** nn4533 pr5921

33 And *till* Moses had done speaking with them, he put a veil on his

pl,nn,pnx**6440**

face.

nn4872 wcj,pp,qnc935 pp,pl,cs,nn**6440** nn**3068** pp,pinc1696 pp,pnx854

34 But when Moses went in before the LORD to speak with him, he

himf**5493**/pnx(853)/df,nn4533 pr5704 qnc,pnx3318 wcs,qpf3318 wcs,pipf**1696** pr413

took*the*veil*off, until he came out. And he came out, and spoke unto the

pl,cs,nn**1121** nn3478 (853) pnl834 pumf**6680**

children of Israel *that* which he was commanded.

pl,cs,nn**1121** nn3478 wcs,qpf**7200** (853) pl,cs,nn**6440** nn4872 cj3588 cs,nn**5785**

35 And the children of Israel saw the face of Moses, that the skin of

nn4872 pl,cs,nn**6440** qpf7160 nn4872 wcj,hipf**7725** (853) df,nn4533 pr5921 pl,nn,pnx**6440** pr5704

Moses' face shone: and Moses put the veil upon his face again, until

qnc,pnx935 pp,pinc**1696** pr,pnx854

he went in to speak with him.

Regulations for the Sabbath

nn4872 wcs,himf**6950** (853) cs,nn3605 cs,nn**5712** pl,cs,nn**1121**

35
And Moses gathered all the congregation of the children of

nn3478 wcs,qmf559 pr,pnx413 pndm428 df,pl,nn**1697** pnl834

Israel together, and said unto them, These *are* the words which the

nn**3068** pipf**6680** pp,qnc6213 pnx(853)

LORD hath commanded, that *ye* should do them.

cs,nu8337 pl,nn3117 nn**4399** nimf6213 df,nuor7637 wcj,dfp,nn3117 qmf**1961**

2 Six days shall work be done, but on the seventh day there shall be

_{pp,pnx} _{cs,nn**6944**}   _{cs,nn**7676**}   _{nn**7677**}   _{pp,nn**3068**}   _{cs,nn3605}   _{df,qpta**6213**} _{nn**4399**}   _{pp,pnx}

to you a holy day, a sabbath of rest to the LORD: whosoever doeth work therein

_{homf**4191**}

shall be put*to*death.

_{pimf1197} _{ptn**3808**} _{nn**784**}   _{pp,cs,nn3605}   _{pl,nn,pnx**4186**}   _{df,nn**7676**} _{pp,cs,nn**3117**}

3 Ye shall kindle no fire throughout your habitations upon the sabbath day.

Collecting the Building Materials

_{nn**4872**} _{wcs,qmf559} _{pr413} _{cs,nn3605}   _{cs,nn**5712**}   _{pl,cs,nn**1121**}   _{nn3478}

4 And Moses spoke unto all the congregation of the children of Israel,

_{pp,qnc559} _{pndm2088}   _{df,nn**1697**} _{pnl834}   _{nn3068}   _{pipf**6680**}   _{pp,qnc559}

saying, This *is* the thing which the LORD commanded, saying,

_{qmv3947}   _{pr4480/pr,pnx854}   _{nn**8641**}   _{pp,nn**3068**}   _{cs,nn3605}

5 Take ye from among you an offering unto the LORD: whosoever *is* of a

_{cs,aj**5081**} _{nn,pnx**3820**}   _{himf,pnx935}   ₍₈₅₃₎   _{cs,nn**8641**}   _{nn**3068**} _{nn2091}   _{wcj,nn3701}

willing heart, let him bring it,   an offering of the LORD; gold, and silver, and

_{wcj,nn5178}

brass,

_{wcj,nn**8504**}   _{wcj,nn713}   _{wcj,cs,nn8438/nn8144}   _{wcj,nn**8336**}   _{wcj,pl,nn**5795**}

6 And blue, and purple, and   scarlet,   and fine linen, and goats' *hair*,

_{pl,nn352} _{wcj,pl,cs,nn**5785**}   _{pl,pupt119}   _{pl,nn8476}   _{wcj,pl,cs,nn**5785**}   _{pl,nn7848} _{wcj,pl,cs,nn6086}

7 And rams'   skins   dyed red, and badgers'   skins,   and shittim   wood,

_{wcj,nn**8081**}   _{dfp,nn**3974**}   _{wcj,pl,nn1314}   _{df,nn**4888**}   _{pp,cs,nn8081}   _{df,pl,nn5561}

8 And oil for the light, and spices for anointing oil, and for the sweet

_{wcj,pp,cs,nn**7004**}

incense,

_{nn7718}   _{wcj,pl,cs,nn68}   _{wcj,pl,cs,nn68}   _{pl,nn4394}   _{dfp,nn646}

9 And onyx stones, and stones to be set for the ephod, and for the

_{wcj,dfp,nn2833}

breastplate.

_{wcj,cs,nn3605} _{cs,aj**2450**}   _{nn**3820**}   _{pp,pnx}   _{qmf935}   _{wcj,qmf**6213**} ₍₈₅₃₎ _{cs,nn3605} _{pnl834}

10 And every wise hearted among you shall come, and make   all   that

_{nn3068}   _{pipf**6680**}

the LORD hath commanded;

₍₈₅₃₎   _{df,nn**4908**}   ₍₈₅₃₎   _{nn,pnx**168**}   _{wcj(853)}   _{nn,pnx4372}   ₍₈₅₃₎   _{pl,nn,pnx7165}

11   The tabernacle,   his tent, and   his covering,   his tacks, and

_{wcj(853)}   _{pl,nn,pnx7175} ₍₈₅₃₎   _{pl,nn,pnx1280} ₍₈₅₃₎   _{pl,nn,pnx5982}   _{wcj(853)}   _{pl,nn,pnx134}

his boards,   his bars,   his pillars, and   his sockets,

₍₈₅₃₎   _{df,nn**727**}   _{wcj(853)}   _{pl,nn,pnx905}   ₍₈₅₃₎   _{df,nn**3727**}   _{wcj(853)}

12   The ark, and   the staves thereof, *with*   the mercy seat, and

_{cs,nn6532}   _{df,nn4539}

the veil of the covering,

₍₈₅₃₎   _{df,nn7979}   _{wcj(853)}   _{pl,nn,pnx905}   _{wcj(853)} _{cs,nn3605}   _{pl,nn,pnx3627}   _{wcj(853)}

13   The table, and   his staves, and   all his vessels, and   the

_{cs,nn3899/df,pl,nn**6440**}

shewbread,

_{wcj(853)}   _{cs,nn4501}   _{df,nn**3974**}   _{wcj(853)}   _{pl,nn,pnx3627}   _{wcj(853)}

14   The candlestick also for the light, and   his furniture, and   his

_{pl,nn,pnx**5216**}   _{wcj(853)}   _{cs,nn**8081**}   _{df,nn**3974**}

lamps, with   the oil for the light,

_{wcj(853)}   _{df,nn**7004**} _{cs,nn4196}   _{wcj(853)}   _{pl,nn,pnx905}   _{wcj(853)}   _{df,nn**4888**}

15 And   the incense altar, and   his staves, and   the anointing

cs,nn**8081**   wcj(853)   df,pl,nn5561   cs,nn**7004**   wcj(853)   cs,nn4539   df,nn6607

oil, and   the sweet incense, and   the hanging for the door at the

pp,cs,nn6607   df,nn**4908**

entering in of the tabernacle,

(853)   cs,nn**4196**   df,nn**5930**   wcj(853)   pnl834/pp,pnx   df,nn5178   cs,nn4345   (853)

16   The altar of burnt offering, with   his   brazen grate,   his

pl,nn,pnx905   wcj(853) cs,nn3605   pl,nn,pnx3627 (853)   df,nn3595   wcj(853)   nn,pnx3653

staves, and   all   his vessels,   the laver and   his foot,

(853)   pl,cs,nn7050   df,nn2691   (853)   pl,nn,pnx5982   wcj(853)   pl,nn,pnx134

17   The hangings of the court,   his pillars, and   their sockets, and

wcj(853)   cs,nn4539   cs,nn8179   df,nn2691

the hanging for the door of the court,

(853)   pl,cs,nn3489   df,nn**4908**   wcj(853)   pl,cs,nn3489   df,nn2691   wcj(853)

18   The pins of the tabernacle, and   the pins of the court, and

pl,nn,pnx4340

their cords,

(853)   pl,cs,nn899   df,nn8278   pp,pinc**8334**   dfp,nn**6944**   (853)   df,nn**6944**

19   The cloths of service, to do service in the holy *place*,   the holy

pl,cs,nn899   pp,nn175   df,nn3548   wcj(853)   pl,cs,nn899   pl,nn,pnx1121

garments for Aaron the priest, and   the garments of his   sons,   to

pp,pinc**3547**

minister*in*the*priest's*office.

cs,nn3605   cs,nn5712   pl,cs,nn1121   nn3478   wcs,qmf3318

20 And   all   the congregation of the children of Israel departed

pr4480/pp,pl,cs,nn**6440**   nn4872

from*the*presence of Moses.

wcs,qmf935   cs,nn3605   nn376   pnl834   nn,pnx3820   qpf,pnx5375   wcj,nn3605

21 And they came, every one whose heart stirred*him*up, and every one

pnl834/pnx(853)   nn,pnx7307   qpf5068   hipf935   (853)   nn3068   cs,nn8641

whom   his spirit made willing, *and* they brought   the LORD's offering to the

pp,cs,nn4399   cs,nn168   nn4150   wcj,pp,cs,nn3605   nn,pnx5656

work of the tabernacle of the congregation, and for   all   his service, and for

df,nn**6944** wcj,pp,pl,cs,nn899

the holy garments.

wcs,qmf935   df,pl,nn**376**   (pr5921)   df,pl,nn**802**   cs,nn3605   cs,aj**5081**

22 And they came, both   men   and   women, as*many*as were willing

nn3820   hipf935   nn2397   wcj,nn5141   wcj,nn2885   wcj,nn3558 cs,nn3605 cs,nn3627

hearted, *and* brought bracelets, and earrings, and rings, and tablets,   all   jewels of

nn2091   wcj,cs,nn3605   nn376   pnl834   hipf**5130**   cs,nn8573   nn2091   pp,nn**3068**

gold: and   every   man that offered *offered* an offering of gold unto the LORD.

wcj,cs,nn3605   nn376   pr,pnx854   pnl834   nipf4672   nn8504   wcj,nn713   wcj,cs,nn8438/nn8144

23 And   every   man, with whom was found blue, and purple, and   scarlet,

wcj,nn8336   wcj,pl,nn5795   pl,pupt119   wcj,pl,cs,nn5785   pl,nn352   pl,nn8476

and fine linen, and goats' *hair*, and   red   skins   of rams, and badgers'

wcj,pl,cs,nn**5785**   hipf935

skins, brought *them*.

cs,nn3605   hipt7311   cs,nn**8641**   nn3701   wcj,nn5178   hipf935   (853)

24 Every one that did offer an offering of silver and brass brought   the

nn3068   cs,nn**8641**   wcj,nn3605   nn376   pr,pnx854   pnl834   nipf4672   pl,nn7848   pl,cs,nn6086   pp,cs,nn3605

LORD's offering: and every man, with whom was found shittim wood for   any

cs,nn**4399**   df,nn**5656**   hipf935

work of the service, brought *it*.

wcj,cs,nn3605   nn802   cs,aj**2450**   nn3820   qpf2901   pp,du,nn,pnx**3027**

25 And   all   the women that were wise hearted did spin with their   hands,

wcs,himf935   nn4299   (853)   df,nn8504   wcj(853)   df,nn713   (853)

and brought that which they had spun, *both*   of blue, and   of purple, *and*

cs,nn8438/df,nn8144   wcj(853)   df,nn8336

of scarlet, and   of fine linen.

    wcj,cs,nn3605   df,pl,nn802   pnl834   nn,pnx3820   qpf5375/pnx(853)   pp,nn2451   qpf2901   (853)

26 And   all   the women whose heart stirred*them*up in wisdom spun

df,pl,nn5795

goats' *hair.*

    wcj,df,pl,nn5387   hipf935   (853)   df,nn7718   pl,cs,nn68   wcj(853)   pl,cs,nn68   df,pl,nn4394

27 And the   rulers   brought   onyx stones, and   stones to be set, for

dfp,nn646   wcj,dfp,nn2833

the ephod, and for the breastplate;

    wcj(853)   df,nn1314   wcj(853)   df,nn8081   pp,nn3974   df,nn4888   wcj,pp,cs,nn8081

28 And   spice, and   oil for the light, and for the anointing   oil,

    df,pl,nn5561 wcj,pp,cs,nn7004

and for the sweet incense.

    pl,cs,nn1121   nn3478   pp,hinc935   nn5071   pp,nn3068   cs,nn3605   nn376

29 The children of Israel brought a willing offering unto the LORD, every man

   wcj,nn802   pnl834   nn,pnx3820   qpf5068/pnx(853)   pp,hinc935   pp,cs,nn3605   df,nn4399

and woman, whose heart made*them*willing to bring for all manner of work,

pnl834   nn3068   pipf6680   pp,qnc6213   pp,cs,nn3027   nn4872

which the LORD had commanded to be made by the hand of Moses.

    nn4872   wcs,qmf559   pr413   pl,cs,nn1121   nn3478   qmv7200   nn3068   qpf7121

30 And Moses   said   unto the children of Israel, See, the LORD hath called by

pp,nn8034   nn1212   cs,nn1121   nn221   cs,nn1121   nn2354   pp,cs,nn4294   nn3063

name Bezaleel the   son   of Uri, the   son   of Hur, of the   tribe   of Judah;

    wcs,pimf4390   pnx(853)   cs,nn7307   pl,nn430   pp,nn2451

31 And he hath   filled   him with the spirit of God, in wisdom, in

pp,nn8394   wcj,pp,nn1847   wcj,pp,cs,nn3605   nn4399

understanding, and in knowledge, and in all manner of workmanship;

    wcj,pp,qnc2803   pl,nn4284   pp,qnc6213   dfp,nn2091   wcj,dfp,nn3701

32 And to   devise   curious works, to work in gold, and in   silver,   and in

wcj,dfp,nn5178

brass,

       wcj,pp,cs,nn2799   nn68   pp,pinc4390   wcj,pp,cs,nn2799   nn6086

33 And in the   cutting   of stones, to   set   *them*, and in   carving   of wood, to

pp,qnc6213   pp,cs,nn3605   nn4284   cs,nn4399

make any manner of cunning work.

     qpf5414   pp,nn,pnx3820   wcj,pp,hinc3384   pnp1931

34 And he hath put in his   heart   that he may   teach,   *both* he,   and

wcj,nn171   cs,nn1121   nn294   pp,cs,nn4294   nn1835

Aholiab, the   son   of Ahisamach, of the   tribe   of Dan.

   pnx(853)   pipf4390   cs,nn2451   nn3820   pp,qnc6213   cs,nn3605

35   Them hath he filled with wisdom of heart, to   work   all manner of

cs,nn4399   nn2796   wcj,qpta2803   wcj,qpta7551

work, of the engraver, and of the cunning workman, and of the embroiderer, in

dfp,nn8504   wcj,dfp,nn713   pp,cs,nn8438/df,nn8144   wcj,dfp,nn8336   wcj,qpta707

blue, and in purple, in   scarlet,   and in fine linen, and of the weaver, *even* of

pl,cs,qpta6213   cs,nn3605   nn4399   wcj,pl,cs,qpta2803   pl,nn4284

them*that*do   any   work, and of those*that*devise cunning work.

wcj,qpf**6213**   nn**1212**   wcj,nn**171**   wcj,cs,nn**3605** cs,aj**2450**   nn**3820**   nn**376**

36
Then wrought Bezaleel and Aholiab, and every wise hearted man,

pnl834/pp,pnp1992   nn**3068** qpf**5414**   nn**2451**   wcj,nn**8394**   pp,qnc**3045**

in whom the Lord put wisdom and understanding to know how

pp,qnc**6213** (853)   cs,nn**3605**   cs,nn**4399**   cs,nn**5656**   df,nn**6944**   pp,nn**3605**

to work all manner of work for the service of the sanctuary, according to all

pnl834   nn**3068**   pipf**6680**

that the Lord had commanded.

nn**4872** wcs,qmf**7121**/pr413   nn**1212**   wcj(pr413)   nn**171**   wcj(pr413) cs,nn**3605** cs,aj**2450**

2 And Moses called Bezaleel and Aholiab, and every wise

nn**3820**   nn**376**   pnl834 pp,nn,pnx**3820**   nn**3068**   qpf**5414** nn**2451**   nn**3605**   pnl834

hearted man, in whose heart the Lord had put wisdom, *even* every one whose

nn,pnx**3820**   qpf,pnx**5375**   pp,qnc**7126** pr413 df,nn**4399**   pp,qnc**6213** pnx(853)

heart stirred*him*up to come unto the work to do it:

wcs,qmf**3947** pr4480/pp,pl,cs,nn**6440**   nn**4872** (853) cs,nn**3605**   df,nn**8641** pnl834

3 And they received of Moses all the offering, which the

pl,cs,nn**1121**   nn**3478**   hipf**935**   pp,cs,nn**4399**   cs,nn**5656**   df,nn**6944**

children of Israel had brought for the work of the service of the sanctuary, to

pp,qnc**6213** pnx(853)   wcj,pnp1992   hipf**935**   ad5750 pr,pnx413   nn**5071**

make it *withal*. And they brought yet unto him free offerings

dfp,nn**1242**/dfp,nn**1242**

every morning.

cs,nn**3605**   df,aj**2450**   df,pl,qpta**6213** (853) cs,nn**3605**   cs,nn**4399**   df,nn**6944**

4 And all the wise men, that wrought all the work of the sanctuary,

wcs,qmf**935**   nn**376**/nn**376**   pr4480/nn,pnx**4399**   pnl834 pnp1992 pl,qpta**6213**

came every man from*his*work which they made;

wcs,qmf**559**   pr413   nn**4872**   pp,qnc**559**   df,nn**5971** pp,hinc**935**   pl,hipt**7235**

5 And they spoke unto Moses, saying, The people bring much more

pr4480/cs,nn**1767**   df,nn**5656**   dfp,nn**4399** pnl834/pnx(853)   nn**3068**   pipf**6680**   pp,qnc**6213**

than enough for the service of the work, which the Lord commanded to make.

nn**4872**   wcs,pimf**6680**   wcs,himf**5674**/nn**6963**

6 And Moses gave commandment, and they caused*it*to*be*proclaimed

dfp,nn**4264** pp,qnc**559**   ptn408   nn**376**   wcj,nn**802** qmf**6213** ad5750   nn**4399**

throughout the camp, saying, Let neither man nor woman make any more work for

pp,cs,nn**8641**   df,nn**6944**   df,nn**5971**   wcs,nimf**3607**   pr4480/hinc**935**

the offering of the sanctuary. So the people were restrained from bringing.

wcj,df,nn**4399**   qpf**1961**   nn,pnx**1767**   pp,cs,nn**3605**   df,nn**4399**   pp,qnc**6213** pnx(853)

7 For the stuff they had was sufficient for all the work to make

wcj,hina**3498**

it, and too much.

The Making of the Tabernacle

cs,nn**3605** cs,aj**2450**   nn**3820**   pp,pl,cs,qpta**6213**   df,nn**4399**   (853)

8 And every wise hearted man among them that wrought the work of the

df,nn**4908**   wcs,qmf**6213** nu6235 pl,nn**3407**   nn8336/hopt**7806**   wcj,nn**8504**   wcj,nn**713**

tabernacle made ten curtains *of* fine*twined*linen, and blue, and purple, and

wcj,cs,nn**8438**/nn**8144**   pl,nn**3742**   qpta**2803** cs,nn**4639** qpf**6213**   pnx(853)

scarlet: *with* cherubims of cunning work made he them.

cs,nn**753**   df,nu259 df,nn**3407** wcj,pl,nu6242   nu8083 dfp,nn**520**   wcj,nn**7341**

9 The length of one curtain *was* twenty and eight cubits, and the breadth of

df,nu259 df,nn**3407** nu702 dfp,nn**520**   df,nn**3407**   pp,cs,nn**3605**   nu259 nn**4060**

one curtain four cubits: the curtains *were* all of one size.

wcs,pimf2266 (853)   cs,nu2568 df,pl,nn3407 nu259 pr413   nu259   wcj,nu2568

10 And he coupled   the five   curtains one unto another: and *the other*   five

pl,nn3407   pipf2266   nu259 pr413   nu259

curtains he coupled one unto another.

wcs,qmf**6213**   pl,cs,nn3924   nn8504 pr5921   cs,nn**8193** df,nu259 df,nn3407

11 And he   made   loops   of blue   on   the   edge   of one   curtain

pr4480/nn7098   dfp,nn4225   ad**3651**   qpf**6213**   df,aj7020   pp,cs,nn**8193**

from*the*selvage in the coupling: likewise he made in the uttermost   side   of

df,nn3407   dfp,nn4225   df,nuor8145

another curtain, in the coupling of the second.

pl,nu2572 pl,nn3924 qpf**6213**   df,nu259 dfp,nn3407   wcj,pl,nu2572 pl,nn3924 qpf**6213**

12 Fifty   loops made he in one curtain, and   fifty   loops made he in the

pp,cs,nn7097   df,nn3407   pnl834   dfp,nn4225   df,nuor8145   df,pl,nn3924 pl,hipt6901

edge   of the curtain which *was* in the coupling of the second: the loops   held

nu259   pr413   nu259

one *curtain* to another.

wcs,qmf**6213** pl,nu2572 pl,cs,nn7165   nn2091   wcs,pimf2266 (853)   df,pl,nn3407 nu259 pr413

13 And he   made   fifty   tacks of gold, and coupled   the curtains one unto

nu259   dfp,pl,nn7165   wcs,qmf**1961** nu259   df,nn**4908**

another with the tacks: so it became one tabernacle.

wcs,qmf**6213**   pl,cs,nn3407   pl,nn5795   pp,nn**168** pr5921   df,nn**4908**

14 And he   made   curtains *of* goats' *hair* for the   tent   over the tabernacle:

nu6249/nu6240   pl,nn3407   qpf**6213** pnx(853)

eleven curtains he made   them.

cs,nn**753**   df,nu259 df,nn3407   nu7970 dfp,nn520   wcj,nu702 pl,nn520

15 The length of one   curtain *was* thirty cubits, and four   cubits *was* the

cs,nn7341   df,nu259 df,nn3407   pp,nu6249/nu6240 pl,nn3407   nu259 nn4060

breadth of one curtain: the   eleven   curtains *were* of one size.

wcs,pimf2266 (853) cs,nu2568 df,pl,nn3407   pp,nn905   wcj(853) cs,nu8337 df,pl,nn3407

16 And he coupled   five curtains by themselves, and   six   curtains by

pp,nn905

themselves.

wcs,qmf**6213** pl,nu2572 pl,nn3924 pr5921   df,aj7020   cs,nn**8193**   df,nn3407

17 And he   made   fifty loops upon the uttermost edge of the curtain in the

dfp,nn4225   wcj,pl,nu2572 pl,nn3924 qpf**6213**   pr5921   cs,nn**8193**   df,nn3407   df,nn2279

coupling, and   fifty   loops made he upon the edge of the curtain which coupleth

df,nuor8145

the second.

wcs,qmf**6213** pl,nu2572 pl,cs,nn7165   nn5178   pp,pinc2266/(853)/df,nn**168**

18 And he   made   fifty   tacks *of* brass to couple*the*tent*together, that it

pp,qnc**1961** nu259

might   be   one.

wcs,qmf**6213**   nn4372   dfp,nn**168**   pl,nn352 pl,cs,nn**5785**   pl,pupt119

19 And he   made   a covering for the   tent   *of* rams' skins dyed red, and a

wcj,cs,nn4372   pl,nn8476 pl,cs,nn**5785** pr4480/pp,ad,lh4605

covering *of* badgers' skins   above   *that*.

wcs,qmf**6213** (853) df,pl,nn7175   dfp,nn**4908**   pl,nn7848 pl,cs,nn6086   pl,qpta5975

20 And he   made   boards for the tabernacle *of* shittim wood, standing up.

cs,nn**753**   df,nn7175   nu6235 pl,nn520   cs,nn7341   df,nu259 df,nn7175

21 The length of a board *was* ten cubits, and the breadth of a   board one

wcj,nn520   wcj,cs,nn2677 (df,nn520)

cubit and a half.

df,nu259 dfp,nn7175   du,cs,nu8147 pl,nn**3027**   pl,pupt7947   nu259 pr413   nu259   ad**3651**

22 One board had   two   tenons, equally distant one from another: thus did

qpf**6213**   pp,cs,nn3605   pl,cs,nn7175   df,nn**4908**

he make for   all   the boards of the tabernacle.

wcs,qmf**6213** (853) df,pl,nn7175   dfp,nn**4908**   pl,nu6242   pl,nn7175   nn5045

23 And he made   boards for the tabernacle; twenty boards for the south

pp,cs,nn6285   nn,lh8486

side   southward:

wcj,pl,nu705   pl,cs,nn134   nn3701   qpf**6213**   pr8478   pl,nu6242 df,pl,nn7175   du,cs,nu8147

24 And   forty   sockets of silver he made under the twenty boards;   two

pl,nn134   pr8478 df,nu259 df,nn7175   pp,du,cs,nu8147   pl,nn,pnx**3027**   wcj,du,cs,nu8147   pl,nn134   pr8478

sockets under one board for his   two   tenons, and   two   sockets under

df,nu259   df,nn7175   pp,du,cs,nu8147   pl,nn,pnx**3027**

another board for his   two   tenons.

df,nuor8145 wcj,pp,cs,nn6763   df,nn**4908**   nn6828

25 And for the other   side   of the tabernacle, *which is* toward the north

pp,cs,nn6285   qpf**6213**   pl,nu6242   pl,nn7175

corner, he made twenty boards,

wcj,pl,nu705 df,nn,pnx134   nn3701   du,cs,nu8147   pl,nn134   pr8478 df,nu259   df,nn7175

26 And their   forty   sockets of silver;   two   sockets under   one   board, and

wcj,du,cs,nu8147   pl,nn134   pr8478   df,nu259   df,nn7175

two   sockets under another board.

wcj,pp,du,cs,nn3411   df,nn**4908**   nn,lh3220   qpf**6213**   nu8337   pl,nn7175

27 And for the   sides   of the tabernacle westward he made   six   boards.

wcj,du,cs,nu8147   pl,nn7175   qpf**6213**   pp,pl,cs,nn4742   df,nn**4908**

28 And   two   boards made he for the   corners   of the tabernacle in the

dfp,du,nn3411

two sides.

wcj,qpf**1961**   pl,qpta**8382**   pr4480/pp,ad4295   qmf**1961**/pl,qpta**8382**   wcj,ad3162   pr413   nn,pnx**7218**

29 And they   were   coupled   beneath,   and   coupled   together   at   the   head

pr413 df,nu259 df,nn2885 ad**3651**   qpf**6213**   pp,du,nu,pnx8147   pp,du,cs,nu8147   df,pl,nn4740

thereof, to   one   ring: thus he did to   both   of them in   both   the corners.

wcj,qpf**1961**   nu8083   pl,nn7175   wcj,pl,nn,pnx134   nu8337/nu6240   pl,nn134

30 And there   were   eight boards; and their   sockets   *were* sixteen sockets of

nn3701   (du,cs,nu8147)   (pl,nn134)   pr8478   df,nu259   df,nn7175   du,cs,nu8147   pl,nn134

silver,   under every board   two   sockets.

wcs,qmf**6213**   pl,cs,nn1280   pl,nn7848   pl,cs,nn6086   nu2568   pp,pl,cs,nn7175   df,nu259

31 And he made   bars   of shittim wood; five for the   boards   of the   one

cs,nn6763   df,nn**4908**

side   of the tabernacle,

wcj,nu2568   pl,nn1280   pp,pl,cs,nn7175   df,nuor8145 cs,nn6763   df,nn**4908**

32 And   five   bars for the   boards   of the   other   side   of the tabernacle, and

wcj,nu2568   pl,nn1280   pp,pl,cs,nn7175   df,nn**4908**   dfp,du,nn3411   nn,lh3220

five   bars for the   boards   of the tabernacle for the   sides   westward.

wcs,qmf**6213** (853)   df,aj8484 df,nn1280   pp,qnc1272   pp,cs,nn**8432**   df,pl,nn7175   pr4480

33 And he made   the middle   bar   to   shoot   through the boards from the

df,nn7097   pr413   df,nn7097

one end to the other.

pipf6823   wcj(853)   df,pl,nn7175   nn2091   qpf**6213**   wcj(853)   pl,nn,pnx2885

34 And he overlaid   the boards with gold, and made   their   rings   *of*

nn2091   pl,nn**1004**   dfp,pl,nn1280   wcs,pimf6823 (853)   df,pl,nn1280   nn2091

gold *to be* places for the   bars,   and overlaid   the   bars   with gold.

wcs,qmf**6213**   (853)   df,nn6532   nn8504   wcj,nn713   wcj,cs,nn8438/nn8144

35 And he made   a   veil   *of* blue, and purple,   and   scarlet,   and

wcj,nn8336/hopt7806   pl,nn3742   qpf**6213**   pnx(853)   qpta**2803**   cs,nn4639

fine*twined*linen: *with* cherubims made he   it of cunning work.

wcs,qmf**6213**   pp,pnx   nu702   pl,cs,nn5982   pl,nn7848   wcs,pimf,pnx6823

36 And he made thereunto four pillars *of* shittim *wood*, and   overlaid   them

nn2091   wcj,pl,nn,pnx2053   nn2091   wcs,qmf3332   pp,pnx   nu702   pl,cs,nn134

with gold: their   hooks   *were of* gold; and he   cast   for them four sockets of

nn3701

silver.

wcs,qmf**6213**   nn4539   df,nn**168**   pp,cs,nn6607   nn8504   wcj,nn713

37 And he made a hanging for the tabernacle door *of* blue, and purple, and

wcj,cs,nn8438/nn8144   wcj,nn8336/hopt7806   cs,nn4639/qpta7551

scarlet,   and fine*twined*linen, of needlework;

wcj(853)   nu2568 pl,nn,pnx5982   wcj(853)   pl,nn,pnx2053   wcj,pipf6823

38 And   the five pillars of it with   their hooks: and he overlaid their

pl,nn,pnx**7218**   wcj,pl,nn,pnx2838   nn2091   nu2568 wcj,pl,nn,nn134   nn5178

chapiters and their   fillets   with gold: but their five sockets *were of* brass.

Making the Ark of God

37
nn1212   wcs,qmf**6213**   (853)   df,nn**727**   pl,nn7848 pl,cs,nn6086   du,nn520

And Bezaleel made   the ark *of* shittim wood: two cubits and a

wcj,nn2677   nn,pnx**753**   wcj,nn520   wcj,nn2677   nn,pnx7341

half *was* the length of it, and a cubit and a half the breadth of it,

wcj,nn520   wcj,nn2677   nn,pnx6967

and a cubit and a half the height of it:

wcs,pimf,pnx6823   aj**2889**   nn2091   pr4480/nn**1004**   wcj,pr4480/nn2351   wcs,qmf**6213**

2 And he overlaid it with pure gold within and without, and made a

nn2213   cs,nn2091 pp,pnx   ad5439

crown of gold to it round about.

wcs,qmf3332   pp,pnx   nu702 pl,cs,nn2885   nn2091   pr5921   nu702 pl,nn,pnx6471

3 And he   cast   for it four rings of gold, *to be set* by the four corners of

wcj,du,cs,nu8147 pl,nn2885 pr5921   df,nu259 nn,pnx6763   wcj,du,cs,nu8147 pl,nn2885 pr5921

it; even   two   rings upon the one   side of it, and   two   rings upon the

df,nuor8145 nn,pnx6763

other   side   of it.

wcs,qmf**6213** pl,cs,nn905   pl,nn7848 pl,cs,nn6086   wcs,pimf6823 pnx(853)   nn2091

4 And he made staves *of* shittim wood, and overlaid   them with gold.

wcs,himf935 (853)   df,pl,nn905   dfp,pl,nn2885 pr5921   pl,cs,nn6763   df,nn**727**

5 And he   put   the staves into the rings   by the sides of the ark, to

pp,qnc**5375** (853)   df,nn**727**

bear   the ark.

wcs,qmf**6213**   nn3727   aj**2889** nn2091   du,nn520   wcj,nn2677

6 And he made the mercy seat *of* pure gold: two cubits and a half *was* the

nn,pnx**753**   wcj,nn520   wcj,nn2677   nn,pnx7341

length thereof, and one cubit and a half the breadth thereof.

wcs,qmf**6213** du,cs,nu8147   pl,nn3742   nn2091   nn4749   qpf**6213**

7 And he made   two   cherubims *of* gold, beaten*out*of*one*piece made he

pnx(853)   pr4480/du,cs,nu8147 pl,cs,nn7098   df,nn**3727**

them, on*the*two ends of the mercy seat;

nu259   nn**3742**   pr4480/nn7098   pr4480/pndm2088   nu259   wcj,nn**3742**   pr4480/nn7098

8 One cherub on*the*end on*this*side, and another cherub on*the**other**end

pr4480/pndm2088   pr4480   df,nn**3727**   qpf**6213** (853)   df,pl,nn**3742**   pr4480/du,cs,nu8147 pl,nn,pnx7098

on*that*side: out of the mercy seat made he   the cherubims on*the*two   ends

thereof.

df,pl,nn**3742**   wcs(qmf**1961**)   pl,cs,qpta6566   du,nn3671   pp,ad,lh4605   pl,qpta5526

9 And the cherubims   spread out *their* wings on high, *and* covered

<small>pp,du,nn,pnx3671   pr5921   df,nn3727   wcj,pl,nn,pnx**6440**   nn**376**   pr413   nn,pnx**251**</small>

with their   wings   over the mercy seat, with their   faces   one to another; *even*

<small>pr413   df,nn**3727**   qpf**1961**   pl,cs,nn**6440**   df,pl,nn**3742**</small>

to the mercy seatward were the faces of the cherubims.

<small>wcs,qmf**6213**   (853)   df,nn7979   pl,nn7848   pl,cs,nn6086   du,nn520   nn,pnx**753**</small>

10 And he   made   the table *of* shittim   wood: two cubits *was* the length

<small>wcj,nn520   nn,pnx7341   wcj,nn520   wcj,nn2677   nn,pnx6967</small>

thereof, and a   cubit   the breadth thereof, and a   cubit   and a   half   the height

thereof:

<small>wcs,pimf6823   pnx(853)   aj2889   nn2091   wcs,qmf6213   pp,pnx   cs,nn2213</small>

11 And he overlaid   it with pure gold, and   made   thereunto a crown of

<small>nn2091   ad5439</small>

gold round about.

<small>wcs,qmf**6213**   pp,pnx   cs,nn4526   nn2948   ad5439   wcs,qmf**6213**</small>

12 Also he   made   thereunto a border of a handbreadth round about; and   made

<small>cs,nn2213   nn2091   cs,nn,pnx4526   ad5439</small>

a crown of gold for the   border   thereof round about.

<small>wcs,qmf3332   pp,pnx   nu702   pl,cs,nn2885   nn2091   wcs,qmf**5414**   (853)   df,pl,nn2885   pr5921</small>

13 And he   cast   for it four   rings   of gold, and   put   the   rings   upon

<small>cs,nu702   df,pl,nn6285   pnl834   pp,cs,nu702   du,nn,pnx7272</small>

the four corners that *were* in the   four   feet   thereof.

<small>pp,pr5980   df,nn4526   qpf**1961**   df,pl,nn2885   pl,nn**1004**   dfp,pl,nn905   pp,qnc**5375**</small>

14 Over against the border were the   rings,   the places for the staves to   bear

<small>(853)   df,nn7979</small>

the table.

<small>wcs,qmf**6213** (853)   df,pl,nn905   pl,nn7848   pl,cs,nn6086   wcs,pimf6823   pnx(853)</small>

15 And he   made   the staves *of* shittim wood, and overlaid   them with

<small>nn2091   pp,qnc**5375** (853)   df,nn7979</small>

gold, to bear   the table.

<small>wcs,qmf**6213** (853)   df,pl,nn3627   pnl834   pr5921   df,nn7979 (853)   pl,nn,pnx7086</small>

16 And he   made   the vessels which *were* upon the table,   his   dishes,

<small>wcj(853)   pl,nn,pnx**3709**   wcj(853)   pl,nn,pnx4518   wcj(853)   df,pl,nn7184   (pnl834)   homf**5258**</small>

and   his   spoons, and   his   bowls,   and   his   covers   to cover

<small>pp,pnp2004   aj**2889**   nn2091</small>

withal, *of* pure gold.

Making the Lampstand

<small>wcs,qmf**6213**   (853)   df,nn4501   aj**2889**   nn2091   nn4749   qpf**6213**   (853)</small>

17 And he   made   the candlestick *of* pure gold: *of* beaten work made he

<small>df,nn4501   nn,pnx**3409**   wcj,nn,pnx7070   pl,nn,pnx1375   pl,nn,pnx3730</small>

the candlestick; his shaft, and his branch, his bowls, his knops, and his

<small>wcj,pl,nn,pnx6525   qpf**1961**   pr,pnx4480</small>

flowers, were   of   the same:

<small>wcj,nu8337   pl,nn7070   pl,qpta3318   pr4480/pl,nn,pnx6654   nu7969   pl,cs,nn7070</small>

18 And   six   branches going out of*the*sides thereof; three branches of the

<small>nn4501   pr4480/nn,pnx6654/df,nu259   wcj,nu7969   pl,cs,nn7070   nn4501</small>

candlestick out*of*the*one*side thereof, and   three   branches of the candlestick

<small>pr4480/nn,pnx6654/df,nuor8145</small>

out*of*the*other*side thereof:

<small>nu7969   pl,nn1375   pl,pupt8246   df,nu259   dfp,nn7070   nn3730</small>

19 Three bowls made*after*the*fashion*of*almonds in one branch, a knop and

wcj,nn6525   wcj,nu7969 pl,nn1375   pl,pupt8246   nu259   pp,nn7070   nn3730

a flower; and three bowls made*like*almonds in another branch, a knop and a

wcj,nn6525 ad**3651**   pp,cs,nu8337 df,pl,nn7070   df,pl,qpta3318 pr4480   df,nn4501

flower: so throughout the six branches going out of the candlestick.

           wcj,dfp,nn4501   nu702 pl,nn1375   pl,pupt8246   pl,nn,pnx3730

20 And in the candlestick *were* four bowls made*like*almonds, his knops, and

wcj,pl,nn,pnx6525

his flowers:

         wcj,nn3730   pr8478 du,cs,nu8147 df,pl,nn7070 pr,pnx4480   wcj,nn3730   pr8478

21 And a knop under two branches of the same, and a knop under

du,cs,nu8147 df,pl,nn7070 pr,pnx4480   wcj,nn3730 pr8478 du,cs,nu8147 df,pl,nn7070 pr,pnx4480

two branches of the same, and a knop under two branches of the

          pp,cs,nu8337 df,pl,nn7070   df,pl,qpta3318 pr,pnx4480

same, according to the six branches going out of it.

         pl,nn,pnx3730   wcj,pl,nn,pnx7070 qpf**1961** pr,pnx4480   nn,pnx3605

22 Their knops and their branches were of the same: all of it *was*

nu259   nn4749   aj**2889** nn2091

one beaten work *of* pure gold.

        wcs,qmf**6213** (853)   nu7651 pl,nn,pnx**5216**   wcj,du,nn,pnx4457   wcj,pl,nn,pnx4289

23 And he made his seven lamps, and his snuffers, and his censers, *of*

aj**2889** nn2091

pure gold.

       nn3603   aj**2889** nn2091 qpf**6213**   pnx(853)   wcj(853) cs,nn3605   pl,nn,pnx3627

24 *Of* a talent of pure gold made he it, and all the vessels

thereof.

Making the Incense Altar

        wcs,qmf**6213** (853)   df,nn**7004** cs,nn4196   pl,nn7848 pl,cs,nn6086   nn,pnx**753**

25 And he made the incense altar *of* shittim wood: the length of it *was* a

nn520   nn,pnx7341   wcj,nn520   qptp7251   wcj,du,nn520   nn,pnx6967

cubit, and the breadth of it a cubit; *it was* foursquare; and two cubits *was* the height

      pl,nn,pnx7161   qpf**1961** pr,pnx4480

of it; the horns thereof were of the same.

        wcs,pimf6823 pnx(853)   aj**2889** nn2091 (853)   nn,pnx1406   wcj(853)

26 And he overlaid it with pure gold, *both* the top of it, and

pl,nn,pnx**7023**   ad5439   wcj(853)   pl,nn,pnx7161   wcs,qmf**6213** pp,pnx

the sides thereof round about, and the horns of it: also he made unto it

cs,nn2213   nn2091   ad5439

a crown of gold round about.

       qpf**6213** wcj,du,cs,nu8147 pl,cs,nn2885   nn2091 pp,pnx   pr4480/pr8478   pp,nn,pnx2213

27 And he made two rings of gold for it under the crown thereof,

pr5921   du,cs,nu8147 pl,nn,pnx6763   pr5921   du,cs,nu8147 pl,nn,pnx6654   pp,pl,nn**1004**

by the two corners of it, upon the two sides thereof, to be places for the

pp,pl,nn905 pp,qnc**5375** pnx(853)   pp,pnx

staves to bear it withal.

        wcs,qmf**6213** (853)   df,pl,nn905   pl,nn7848 pl,cs,nn6086   wcs,pimf6823 pnx(853)

28 And he made the staves *of* shittim wood, and overlaid them with

nn2091

gold.

        wcs,qmf**6213** (853)   nn6944   df,nn**4888** cs,nn**8081**   wcj(853)   aj**2889** cs,nn**7004**

29 And he made the holy anointing oil, and the pure incense of

df,pl,nn5561   cs,nn4639   qpta7543

sweet spices, according to the work of the apothecary.

Making the Altar and the Basin

38 And he made the altar of burnt offering *of* shittim wood: five cubits *was* the length thereof, and five cubits the breadth thereof; *it was* foursquare; and three cubits the height thereof.

2 And he made the horns thereof on the four corners of it; the horns thereof were of the same: and he overlaid it with brass.

3 And he made all the vessels of the altar, the pots, and the shovels, and the basins, *and* the fleshhooks, and the firepans: all the vessels thereof made he *of* brass.

4 And he made for the altar a brazen grate of network under the compass thereof beneath unto the midst of it.

5 And he cast four rings for the four ends of the grate of brass, *to be* places for the staves.

6 And he made the staves *of* shittim wood, and overlaid them with brass.

7 And he put the staves into the rings on the sides of the altar, to bear it withal; he made the altar hollow with boards.

8 And he made the laver *of* brass, and the foot of it *of* brass, of the looking glasses of *the women* assembling, which assembled *at* the door of the tabernacle of the congregation.

Making the Enclosure

9 And he made the court: on the south side southward the hangings of the court *were of* fine*twined*linen, a hundred cubits:

10 Their pillars *were* twenty, and their brazen sockets twenty; the hooks of the pillars and their fillets *were of* silver.

11 And for the north side *the hangings were* a hundred cubits, their

pl,nn,pnx5982   pl,nu6242   wcj,pl,nn,pnx134   nn5178   pl,nu6242   pl,cs,nn2053   df,pl,nn5982

pillars *were* twenty, and their sockets of brass twenty; the hooks of the pillars

wcj,pl,nn,pnx2838   nn3701

and their fillets *of* silver.

nn3220 wcj,pp,cs,nn6285   pl,nn7050   pl,nu2572 dfp,nn520   pl,nn,pnx5982 nu6235

12 And for the west side *were* hangings of fifty cubits, their pillars ten,

wcj,pl,nn,pnx134 nu6235   pl,cs,nn2053   df,pl,nn5982   wcj,pl,nn,pnx2838   nn3701

and their sockets ten; the hooks of the pillars and their fillets *of* silver.

ad,lh**6924** wcj,pp,cs,nn6285 cs,nn,lh4217 pl,nu2572   nn520

13 And for the east side eastward fifty cubits.

pl,nn7050   pr413   df,nn3802   cs,nu2568/nu6240   nn520

14 The hangings of the one side *of the gate were* fifteen cubits; their

pl,nn,pnx5982 nu7969   wcj,pl,nn,pnx134 nu7969

pillars three, and their sockets three.

df,nuor8145 wcj,dfp,nn3802   df,nn2691 pp,cs,nn8179   pr4480/pndm2088

15 And for the other side of the court gate, on*this*hand and

wcj(pr4480)/pndm2088   pl,nn7050   cs,nu2568/nu6240   nn520   pl,nn,pnx5982   nu7969

that hand, *were* hangings of fifteen cubits; their pillars three, and their

wcj,pl,nn,pnx134 nu7969

sockets three.

cs,nn3605   pl,cs,nn7050   df,nn2691   ad5439   nn8336/hopt7806

16 All the hangings of the court round about *were* of fine*twined*linen.

wcj,df,pl,nn134   dfp,pl,nn5982   nn5178   pl,cs,nn2053   df,pl,nn5982

17 And the sockets for the pillars *were of* brass; the hooks of the pillars and

wcj,pl,nn,pnx2838   nn3701   wcj,cs,nn6826   pl,nn,pnx**7218**   nn3701   cs,nn3605

their fillets *of* silver; and the overlaying of their chapiters *of* silver; and all

pl,cs,nn5982   df,nn2691 wcj(pnp1992)   pl,pupt**2836**   nn3701

the pillars of the court *were* filleted with silver.

wcj,cs,nn4539   cs,nn8179   df,nn2691   cs,nn4639/qpta7551   nn8504

18 And the hanging for the gate of the court *was* needlework, *of* blue, and

wcj,nn713   wcj,cs,nn8438/nn8144   wcj,nn8336/hopt7806   wcj,pl,nu6242   nn520   nn**753**

purple, and scarlet, and fine*twined*linen: and twenty cubits *was* the length,

wcj,nn6967   pp,nn7341   nu2568 pl,nn520   pp,pr5980   pl,cs,nn7050

and the height in the breadth *was* five cubits, answerable to the hangings of the

df,nn2691

court.

wcj,pl,nn,pnx5982   nu702   wcj,pl,nn,pnx134   nn5178   nu702

19 And their pillars *were* four, and their sockets *of* brass four; their

pl,nn,pnx2053   nn3701   wcj,cs,nn6826   pl,nn,pnx**7218**   wcj,pl,nn,pnx2838   nn3701

hooks *of* silver, and the overlaying of their chapiters and their fillets *of* silver.

wcj,cs,nn3605   df,pl,nn3489   dfp,nn**4908**   wcj,dfp,nn2691   ad5439

20 And all the pins of the tabernacle, and of the court round about,

nn5178

were of brass.

The Sum of the Tabernacle

pndm428   pl,cs,qptp**6485**   df,nn**4908**   cs,nn**4908**   df,nn5715

21 This is the sum of the tabernacle, *even* of the tabernacle of testimony,

pnl834   pupf**6485**   pr5921   cs,nn**6310**   nn4872   cs,nn**5656**

as it was counted, according to the commandment of Moses, *for* the service of the

df,pl,nn3881   pp,cs,nn**3027**   nn385   cs,nn**1121**   nn175   df,nn3548

Levites, by the hand of Ithamar, son to Aaron the priest.

wcj,nn1212   cs,nn1121   nn221   cs,nn1121   nn2354   pp,cs,nn4294   nn3063

22 And Bezaleel the son of Uri, the son of Hur, of the tribe of Judah,

qpf6213 (853) cs,nn3605 pnl834   nn3068   pipf6680   (853)   nn4872

made all that the LORD commanded Moses.

wcj,pr,pnx854   nn171   cs,nn1121   nn294   pp,cs,nn4294   nn1835

23 And with him *was* Aholiab, son of Ahisamach, of the tribe of Dan,

nn2796   wcj,qpta2803   wcj,qpta7551   dfp,nn8504   wcj,dfp,nn713

an engraver, and a cunning workman, and an embroiderer in blue, and in purple,

wcj,pp,cs,nn8438/df,nn8144   wcj,dfp,nn8336

and in scarlet, and fine linen.

cs,nn3605   df,nn2091   df,pl,qptp6213   dfp,nn4399   pp,cs,nn3605   cs,nn4399

24 All the gold that was occupied for the work in all the work of the

df,nn6944   cs,nn2091   df,nn8573   wcs,qmf1961   wcj,pl,nu6242   nu8672   nn3603

holy *place*, even the gold of the offering, was twenty and nine talents, and

wcj,cs,nu7651   pl,nu3967   wcj,nu7970   nn8255   pp,cs,nn8255   df,nn6944

seven hundred and thirty shekels, after the shekel of the sanctuary.

wcj,cs,nn3701   pl,cs,qptp6485   df,nn5712

25 And the silver of them that were*numbered of the congregation *was* a

cs,nu3967   nn3603   wcj,nu505   wcj,cs,nu7651   pl,nu3967   wcj,pl,nu7657/wcj,nu2568   nn8255

hundred talents, and a thousand seven hundred and threescore*and*fifteen shekels,

pp,cs,nn8255   df,nn6944

after the shekel of the sanctuary:

nn1235   dfp,nn1538   cs,nn4276   df,nn8255   pp,cs,nn8255

26 A bekah for every man, *that is,* half a shekel, after the shekel of the

df,nn6944   pp,cs,nn3605   df,qpta5674 pr5921   df,pl,qptp6485   pr4480/cs,nn1121/pl,nu6242/nn8141

sanctuary, for every one that went to be numbered, from*twenty*years*old and

wcj,ad,lh4605   pp,nu8337 pl,cs,nu3967   nu505   wcj,nu7969   pl,nu505   wcj,cs,nu2568   pl,nu3967

upward, for six hundred thousand and three thousand and five hundred and

wcj,pl,nu2572

fifty *men*.

cs,nu3967   cs,nn3603   df,nn3701 wcs,qmf1961 pp,qnc3332 (853)   pl,cs,nn134

27 And of the hundred talents of silver were cast the sockets of the

df,nn6944   wcj(853)   pl,cs,nn134   df,nn6532   cs,nu3967   pl,nn134   pp,cs,nn3967

sanctuary, and the sockets of the veil; a hundred sockets of the hundred

df,nn3603   nn3603   dfp,nn134

talents, a talent for a socket.

wcj(853)   df,nu505   wcj,cs,nu7651   df,pl,nu3967   wcj,pl,nu7657   wcj,nu2568

28 And of the thousand seven hundred seventy and five shekels he

qpf6213 pl,nn2053   dfp,pl,nn5982   wcj,pipf6823   pl,nn,pnx7218   wcj,pipf2836 pnx(853)

made hooks for the pillars, and overlaid their chapiters, and filleted them.

wcj,cs,nn5178   df,nn8573   pl,nu7657   nn3603   wcj,du,nu505

29 And the brass of the offering *was* seventy talents, and two thousand and

wcj,nu702   pl,nu3967   nn8255

four hundred shekels.

pp,pnx   wcs,qmf6213 (853)   pl,cs,nn134   cs,nn6607   cs,nn168

30 And therewith he made the sockets to the door of the tabernacle of the

nn4150   wcj(853)   df,nn5178 cs,nn4196   wcj(853) df,nn5178 cs,nn4345 (pnl834)   pp,pnx

congregation, and the brazen altar, and the brazen grate for it, and

wcj(853) cs,nn3605   pl,cs,nn3627   df,nn4196

all the vessels of the altar,

wcj(853)   pl,cs,nn134   df,nn2691   ad5439   wcj(853)   pl,cs,nn134

31 And the sockets of the court round about, and the sockets of the

df,nn2691 cs,nn8179   wcj(853) cs,nn3605   pl,cs,nn3489   df,nn4908   wcj(853) cs,nn3605   pl,cs,nn3489

court gate, and all the pins of the tabernacle, and all the pins

df,nn2691   ad5439

of the court round about.

The Making of the Priest's Clothes

39 ^{wcj,pr4480} ^{df,nn8504} ^{wcj,df,nn713} ^{wcj,cs,nn8438/df,nn8144} ^{qpf6213} ^{pl,cs,nn899}
And of the blue, and purple, and scarlet, they made cloths
ⁿⁿ⁸²⁷⁸ ^{pp,pinc8334} ^{dfp,nn6944} ^{wcs,qmf6213} (853) ^{df,nn6944}
of service, to do service in the holy *place*, and made the holy
^{pl,cs,nn899} (pnl834) ^{pp,nn175} ^{pp,pnl834} ⁿⁿ³⁰⁶⁸ ^{pipf6680} (853) ⁿⁿ⁴⁸⁷²
garments for Aaron; as the Lord commanded Moses.

^{wcs,qmf6213} (853) ^{df,nn646} ⁿⁿ²⁰⁹¹ ⁿⁿ⁸⁵⁰⁴ ^{wcj,nn713} ^{wcj,cs,nn8438/nn8144}
2 And he made the ephod *of* gold, blue, and purple, and scarlet, and
^{wcj,nn8336/hopt7806}
fine*twined*linen.

^{wcs,pimf7554} (853) ^{df,nn2091} ^{pl,cs,nn6341} ^{wcj,pipf7112} ^{pl,nn6616}
3 And they did beat the gold into thin plates, and cut *it into* wires,
^{pp,qnc6213} ^{pp,cs,nn8432} ^{df,nn8504} ^{wcj,pp,cs,nn8432} ^{df,nn713} ^{wcj,pp,cs,nn8432} ^{cs,nn8438/df,nn8144}
to work *it* in the blue, and in the purple, and in the scarlet,
^{wcj,pp,cs,nn8432} ^{df,nn8336} ^{qpta2803} ^{cs,nn4639}
and in the fine linen, *with* cunning work.

^{qpf6213} ^{pl,nn3802} ^{pp,pnx} ^{pl,qpta2266} ^{pr5921} ^{du,cs,nu8147}
4 They made shoulder pieces for it, to couple*it*together: by the two
^{pl,nn,pnx7098} ^{pupf2266}
edges was it coupled together.

^{wcj,cs,nn2805} ^{nn,pnx642} ^{pnl834} ^{pr,pnx5921} ^{pr,pnx4480} ^{pnp1931}
5 And the curious girdle of his ephod, that *was* upon it, *was* of the same,
^{pp,nn,pnx4639} ⁿⁿ²⁰⁹¹ ⁿⁿ⁸⁵⁰⁴ ^{wcj,nn713} ^{wcj,cs,nn8438/nn8144}
according to the work thereof; *of* gold, blue, and purple, and scarlet, and
^{wcj,nn8336/hopt7806} ^{pp,pnl834} ⁿⁿ³⁰⁶⁸ ^{pipf6680} (853) ⁿⁿ⁴⁸⁷²
fine*twined*linen; as the Lord commanded Moses.

^{wcs,qmf6213} (853) ^{df,nn7718} ^{pl,cs,nn68} ^{pl,cs,hopt4142} ^{pl,cs,nn4865} ⁿⁿ²⁰⁹¹ ^{pl,pupf6605}
6 And they wrought onyx stones enclosed in ouches of gold, graven, as
ⁿⁿ²³⁶⁸ ^{pl,cs,nn6603} ^{pr5921} ^{pl,cs,nn8034} ^{pl,cs,nn1121} ⁿⁿ³⁴⁷⁸
signets are graven, with the names of the children of Israel.

^{wcs,qmf7760} ^{pnx(853)} ^{pr5921} ^{pl,cs,nn3802} ^{df,nn646}
7 And he put them on the shoulders of the ephod, *that they should be*
^{pl,cs,nn68} ⁿⁿ²¹⁴⁶ ^{pp,pl,cs,nn1121} ⁿⁿ³⁴⁷⁸ ^{pp,pnl834} ⁿⁿ³⁰⁶⁸ ^{pipf6680} (853)
stones for a memorial to the children of Israel; as the Lord commanded
ⁿⁿ⁴⁸⁷²
Moses.

^{wcs,qmf6213} (853) ^{df,nn2833} ^{qpta2803} ^{cs,nn4639} ^{pp,cs,nn4639}
8 And he made the breastplate *of* cunning work, like the work of the
ⁿⁿ⁶⁴⁶ ⁿⁿ²⁰⁹¹ ⁿⁿ⁸⁵⁰⁴ ^{wcj,nn713} ^{wcj,cs,nn8438/nn8144} ^{wcj,nn8336/hopt7806}
ephod; *of* gold, blue, and purple, and scarlet, and fine*twined*linen.

^{qpf1961} ^{qptp7251} ^{qpf6213} (853) ^{df,nn2833} ^{qptp3717} ⁿⁿ²²³⁹ ^{nn,pnx753}
9 It was foursquare; they made the breastplate double: a span *was* the length
^{wcj,nn2239} ^{nn,pnx7341} ^{qptp3717}
thereof, and a span the breadth thereof, *being* doubled.

^{wcs,pimf4390} ^{pp,pnx} ^{nu702} ^{pl,cs,nn2905} ⁿⁿ⁶⁸ ^{cs,nn2905} ⁿⁿ¹²⁴
10 And they set in it four rows of stones: *the first* row *was* a sardius, a
ⁿⁿ⁶³⁵⁷ ^{wcj,nn1304} ^{df,nu259 df,nn2905}
topaz, and a carbuncle: this *was* the first row.

^{df,nuor8145 wcj,df,nn2905} ⁿⁿ⁵³⁰⁶ ⁿⁿ⁵⁶⁰¹ ^{wcj,nn3095}
11 And the second row, an emerald, a sapphire, and a diamond.

^{df,nuor7992 wcj,df,nn2905} ⁿⁿ³⁹⁵⁸ ⁿⁿ⁷⁶¹⁸ ^{wcj,nn306}
12 And the third row, a ligure, an agate, and an amethyst.

df,nuor7243 wcj,df,nn2905 nn8658 nn7718 wcj,nn3471 pl,cs,hopt4142

13 And the fourth row, a beryl, an onyx, and a jasper: *they were* enclosed in

pl,cs,nn4865 nn2091 pp,pl,pnx4396

ouches of gold in their enclosings.

wcj,df,pl,nn68 pr5921 pl,cs,nn8034 pl,cs,nn1121 nn3478

14 And the stones *were* according to the names of the children of Israel,

(pnp2007) du,nu8147/nu6240 pr5921 pl,nn,pnx8034 pl,cs,nn6603 nn2368

twelve, according to their names, *like* the engravings of a signet,

nn376 pr5921 nn,pnx8034 pp,du,nu8147/nu6240 nn7626

every one with his name, according to the twelve tribes.

wcs,qmf6213 pr5921 df,nn2833 pl,cs,nn8333 nn1383 nn5688 cs,nn4639

15 And they made upon the breastplate chains at the ends, *of* wreathen work

aj2889 nn2091

of pure gold.

wcs,qmf6213 du,cs,nu8147 pl,cs,nn4865 nn2091 wcj,du,cs,nu8147 nn2091 pl,cs,nn2885

16 And they made two ouches *of* gold, and two gold rings; and

wcs,qmf5414 (853) du,cs,nu8147 df,pl,nn2885 pr5921 du,cs,nu8147 pl,cs,nn7098 df,nn2833

put the two rings in the two ends of the breastplate.

wcs,qmf5414 du,cs,nu8147 df,pl,nn5688 df,nn2091 pr5921 du,cs,nu8147

17 And they put the two wreathen chains of gold in the two

df,pl,nn2885 pr5921 pl,cs,nn7098 df,nn2833

rings on the ends of the breastplate.

wcj(853) du,cs,nu8147 pl,cs,nn7098 du,cs,nu8147 df,pl,nn5688 qpf5414

18 And the two ends of the two wreathen chains they fastened

pr5921 du,cs,nu8147 df,pl,nn4865 wcs,qmf,pnx5414 pr5921 pl,cs,nn3802 df,nn646

in the two ouches, and put them on the shoulder pieces of the ephod,

pr413/pr4136/pl,nn,pnx6440

before it.

wcs,qmf6213 du,cs,nu8147 pl,cs,nn2885 nn2091 wcs,qmf7760 pr5921 du,cs,nu8147

19 And they made two rings of gold, and put *them* on the two

pl,cs,nn7098 df,nn2833 pr5921 nn,pnx8193 pnl834 pr413 cs,nn5676

ends of the breastplate, upon the border of it, which *was* on the side of the

df,nn646 nn,lh1004

ephod inward.

wcs,qmf6213 du,cs,nu8147 nn2091 pl,cs,nn2885 wcs,qmf,pnx5414 pr5921

20 And they made two *other* golden rings, and put them on the

du,cs,nu8147 pl,cs,nn3802 df,nn646 pr4480/pp,ad4295 pr4480/pr4136 pl,nn,pnx6440 pp,pr5980

two sides of the ephod underneath, toward the forepart of it, over against the

nn,pnx4225 pr4480/ad4605 pp,cs,nn2805 df,nn646

other coupling thereof, above the curious girdle of the ephod.

wcs,qmf7405 (853) df,nn2833 pr4480/pl,nn,pnx2885 pr413 pl,cs,nn2885

21 And they did bind the breastplate by*his*rings unto the rings of the

df,nn646 pp,cs,nn6616 nn8504 pp,qnc1961 pr5921 cs,nn2805

ephod with a lace of blue, that it might be above the curious girdle of the

df,nn646 df,nn2833 wcj,ptn3808 nimf2118 pr4480/pr5921 df,nn646 pp,pnl834

ephod, and that the breastplate might not be loosed from the ephod; as the

nn3068 pipf6680 (853) nn4872

LORD commanded Moses.

wcs,qmf6213 (853) cs,nn4598 df,nn646 qpta707 cs,nn4639 cs,aj3632 nn8504

22 And he made the robe of the ephod *of* woven work, all *of* blue.

wcj,cs,nn6310 pp,nn,pnx8432 df,nn4598 pp,cs,nn6310

23 And *there was* a hole in the midst of the robe, as the hole of a

nn8473 nn8193 ad5439 pp,nn,pnx6310 ptn3808 nimf7167

habergeon, *with* a band round about the hole, that it should not rend.

wcs,qmf6213   pr5921   pl,cs,nn7757   df,nn4598   pl,cs,nn7416   nn8504
24 And they made upon the hems of the robe pomegranates *of* blue, and
wcj,nn713   wcj,cs,nn8438/nn8144   hopt7806
purple, and   scarlet,   *and* twined *linen.*

wcs,qmf6213 pl,cs,nn6472   aj2889   nn2091   wcs,qmf5414 (853)   df,pl,nn6472 pp,cs,nn8432
25 And they made bells *of* pure gold, and   put   the bells between the
df,pl,nn7416   pr5921   pl,cs,nn7757   df,nn4598   ad5439   pp,cs,nn8432   df,pl,nn7416
pomegranates upon the   hem   of the robe, round about between the pomegranates;

nn6472   wcj,nn7416   nn6472   wcj,nn7416   ad5439/pr5921
26 A bell and a pomegranate, a bell and a pomegranate, round about the
pl,cs,nn7757   df,nn4598   pp,pinc8334   pp,pnl8334   nn3068   pipf6680   (853)   nn4872
hem of the robe to minister *in*;   as   the Lord commanded   Moses.

wcs,qmf6213 (853) df,pl,nn3801   nn8336   qpta707 cs,nn4639   pp,nn175
27 And they made   coats *of* fine linen *of* woven work for Aaron, and for
wcj,pp,pl,nn,pnx1121
his   sons,

wcj(853)   df,nn4701   nn8336   wcj(853) pl,cs,nn6287 df,pl,nn4021   nn8336
28 And   a miter *of* fine linen, and   goodly bonnets *of* fine linen, and
wcj(853) df,nn906 du,cs,nn4370   nn8336/hopt7806
linen breeches *of* fine*twined*linen,

wcj(853)   df,nn73   nn8336/hopt7806   wcj,nn8504   wcj,nn713
29 And   a girdle *of* fine*twined*linen, and   blue,   and purple, and
wcj,cs,nn8438/nn8144   cs,nn4639/qpta7551 pp,pnl834   nn3068   pipf6680   (853)   nn4872
scarlet,   *of* needlework;   as   the Lord commanded   Moses.

wcs,qmf6213 (853)   cs,nn6731   df,nn6944 cs,nn5145   aj2889   nn2091   wcs,qmf3789
30 And they made   the plate of the holy crown *of* pure gold, and wrote
pr,pnx5921   cs,nn4385   pl,cs,nn6603   nn2368   nn6944   pp,nn3068
upon it a writing, *like to* the engravings of a signet, HOLINESS TO THE LORD.

wcs,qmf5414 pr,pnx5921   cs,nn6616   nn8504   pp,qnc5414   pr4480/pp,ad,lh4605 pr5921
31 And they tied   unto it a lace of blue, to fasten *it*   on high upon the
df,nn4701 pp,pnl834   nn3068   pipf6680   (853)   nn4872
miter;   as   the Lord commanded   Moses.

The Tabernacle is Completed

cs,nn3605   cs,nn5656   cs,nn4908   cs,nn168   nn4150
32 Thus was   all   the work of the tabernacle of the tent of the congregation
wcs,qmf3615   pl,cs,nn1121   nn3478 wcs,qmf6213   pp,nn3605 pnl834   nn3068
finished: and the children of Israel   did   according to   all   that the Lord
pipf6680   (853)   nn4872   ad3651 qpf6213
commanded   Moses, so did they.

wcs,himf935 (853)   df,nn4908   pr413   nn4872   (853)   df,nn168   wcj(853) cs,nn3605
33 And they brought   the tabernacle unto Moses,   the tent, and   all
pl,nn,pnx3627   pl,nn,pnx7165   pl,nn,pnx7175   pl,nn,pnx1280   wcj,pl,nn,pnx5982
his furniture, his   tacks,   his boards, his   bars,   and his   pillars,   and his
wcj,pl,nn,pnx134
sockets,

wcj(853)   cs,nn4372   df,pl,nn352 pl,cs,nn5785   df,pl,pupt119   wcj(853)   cs,nn4372
34 And   the covering of rams' skins dyed red, and   the covering of
df,pl,nn8476   pl,cs,nn5785   wcj(853)   cs,nn6532   df,nn4539
badgers' skins, and   the veil of the covering,

(853)   cs,nn727   df,nn5715   wcj(853)   pl,nn,pnx905   wcj(853)
35   The ark of the testimony, and   the staves thereof, and   the
df,nn3727
mercy seat,

36   The table, *and*   all the vessels thereof, and   the shewbread,

37   The pure candlestick, *with*   the lamps thereof, *even with* the lamps to be set*in*order, and   all the vessels thereof, and   the oil for light,

38   And the golden altar, and   the anointing oil, and   the sweet incense, and   the hanging for the tabernacle door,

39   The brazen altar, and   his   grate of brass,   his staves, and all his vessels,   the laver and   his foot,

40   The hangings of the court,   his pillars, and   his sockets, and the hanging for the court gate,   his cords, and his   pins,   and   all the vessels of the service of the tabernacle, for the   tent   of the congregation,

41   The cloths of service to do service in the   holy *place*, and   the holy garments   for   Aaron   the   priest,   and   his   sons'   garments,   to minister*in*the*priest's*office.

42 According to   all   that the LORD commanded   Moses,   so   the children of Israel made   all   the work.

43 And Moses did look upon   all   the work, and, behold, they had done it   as   the LORD had commanded, even so had they done it: and Moses blessed   them.

Setting Up the Tabernacle

40   And the LORD spoke unto Moses, saying,

2 On the   first day   of the first month shalt thou set up the tabernacle of the tent of the congregation.

3 And thou shalt   put   therein   the ark of the testimony, and   cover the ark with the veil.

4 And   thou   shalt   bring in   the   table,   and   set*in*order   the things*that*are*to*be*set*in*order upon it; and   thou   shalt   bring in   the candlestick, and   light   the lamps thereof.

wcs,qpf**5414** (853)   cs,nn**4196**   df,nn**2091**   pp,nn**7004** pp,pl,cs,nn**6440**   cs,nn**727**

5 And thou shalt set   the altar of gold for the incense before the ark

df,nn**5715**   wcs,qpf**7760** (853)   cs,nn**4539**   df,nn**6607**   dfp,nn**4908**

of the testimony, and   put   the hanging of the door to the tabernacle.

wcs,qpf**5414** (853)   cs,nn**4196**   df,nn**5930**   pp,pl,cs,nn**6440**   cs,nn**6607**

6 And thou shalt set   the altar of the burnt offering before the door of

cs,nn**4908**   cs,nn**168**   nn**4150**

the tabernacle of the tent of the congregation.

wcs,qpf**5414** (853)   df,nn**3595**   pr**996**   cs,nn**168**   nn**4150**

7 And thou shalt set   the laver between the tent of the congregation and

wcj(pr996)   df,nn**4196**   wcs,qpf**5414** pl,nn**4325** ad**8033**

the altar, and shalt   put   water therein.

wcs,qpf**7760** (853)   df,nn**2691**   ad**5439**   wcs,qpf**5414** (853)   cs,nn**4539**

8 And thou shalt set up   the court round about, and hang up   the hanging

df,nn**2691** cs,nn**8179**

at the court gate.

wcs,qpf**3947** (853)   df,nn**4888**   cs,nn**8081**   wcs,qpf**4886** (853)   df,nn**4908**

9 And thou shalt take   the anointing oil, and anoint   the tabernacle,

wcj(853) cs,nn**3605** pnl834   pp,pnx   wcs,pipf**6942** pnx(853)   wcj(853) cs,nn**3605**   pl,nn,pnx**3627**

and   all that is therein, and shalt hallow   it, and   all the vessels

wcs,qpf**1961** nn**6944**

thereof: and it shall be   holy.

wcs,qpf**4886** (853)   cs,nn**4196**   df,nn**5930**   wcj(853) cs,nn**3605**

10 And thou shalt anoint   the altar of the burnt offering, and   all his

pl,nn,pnx**3627**   wcs,pipf**6942** (853)   df,nn**4196**   wcs,qpf**1961**   df,nn**4196** cs,nn**6944**/pl,nn**6944**

vessels, and sanctify   the altar: and it shall   be   an altar most holy.

wcs,qpf**4886** (853)   df,nn**3595**   wcj(853)   nn,pnx**3653**   wcs,pipf**6942** pnx(853)

11 And thou shalt anoint   the laver and   his foot, and sanctify   it.

wcs,hipf**7126** (853)   nn**175**   wcj(853)   pl,nn,pnx**1121** pr**413**   cs,nn**6607**

12 And thou shalt bring   Aaron and   his sons unto the door of the

cs,nn**168**   nn**4150**   wcs,qpf**7364** pnx(853)   dfp,pl,nn**4325**

tabernacle of the congregation, and wash   them with water.

wcs,hipf**3847** (853)   nn**175**   (853) df,nn**6944**   pl,cs,nn**899**   wcs,qpf**4886** pnx(853)

13 And thou shalt put upon   Aaron the   holy garments, and anoint

wcs,pipf**6942** pnx(853)   wcs,pipf**3547**/pp,pnx

him, and sanctify   him; that he may minister*unto*me*in*the*priest's*office.

himf**7126** wcj(853)   pl,nn,pnx**1121**   wcs,hipf**3847** pnx(853)   pl,nn**3801**

14 And thou shalt bring   his sons, and clothe   them with coats:

wcs,qpf**4886** pnx(853)   pp,pnl834   qpf**4886**   (853)   nn,pnx**1**

15 And thou shalt anoint   them,   as   thou didst anoint   their father,

wcs,pipf**3547**/pp,pnx   qnc,pnx**4886**

that they may minister*unto*me*in*the*priest's*office: for their anointing shall

wcj,qpf**1961**/pp,qnc**1961** (pp,pnx)   nn**5769**   pp,cs,nn**3550**   pp,pl,nn,pnx**1755**

surely be   an everlasting priesthood throughout their generations.

wcs,qmf**6213**   nn**4872**   pp,nn**3605** pnl834   nn**3068**   pipf**6680**   pnx(853)

16 Thus   did   Moses: according to   all   that the LORD commanded

ad**3651** qpf**6213**

him, so did he.

wcs,qmf**1961**   df,aj**7223** dfp,nn**2320**   df,nuor**8145** dfp,nn**8141**   pp,nu**259**

17 And it*came*to*pass in the first month in the second year, on the first

dfp,nn**2320**   df,nn**4908**   hopf**6965**

day of the month, that the tabernacle was reared up.

nn**4872** wcs,himf**6965**   (853)   df,nn**4908**   wcs,qmf**5414** (853)   pl,nn,pnx**134**

18 And Moses reared up   the tabernacle, and fastened   his sockets, and

wcs,qmf7760 (853)   pl,nn,pnx7175   wcs,qmf5414 (853)   pl,nn,pnx1280   wcs,himf6965

set up   the boards thereof, and put in   the bars   thereof, and reared up

(853)   pl,nn,pnx5982

his pillars.

     wcs,qmf6566   (853)   df,nn168   pr5921   df,nn4908   wcs,qmf7760 (853)

19 And he spread abroad   the tent over the tabernacle, and   put   the

cs,nn4372   df,nn168 pr4480/pp,ad,lh4605 pr,pnx5921   pp,pnl834   df,nn3068   pipf6680   (853)   nn4872

covering of the tent   above   upon it;   as   the LORD commanded   Moses.

     wcs,qmf3947   wcs,qmf5414 (853)   df,nn5715   pr413   df,nn727   wcs,qmf7760 (853)

20 And he took   and   put   the testimony into the ark, and   set

df,pl,nn905 pr5921   df,nn727   wcs,qmf5414 (853)   df,nn3727   pr4480/pp,ad,lh4605 pr5921   df,nn727

the staves on the ark, and   put   the mercy seat   above   upon the ark:

     wcs,himf935 (853)   df,nn727   pr413   df,nn4908   wcs,qmf7760 (853)   cs,nn6532

21 And he brought   the ark into the tabernacle, and set up   the veil of

df,nn4539   wcs,himf5526/pr5921   cs,nn727   df,nn5715   pp,pnl834   nn3068

the covering, and   covered   the ark of the testimony;   as   the LORD

pipf6680   (853)   nn4872

commanded   Moses.

     wcs,qmf5414 (853)   df,nn7979   pp,cs,nn168   nn4150   pr5921

22 And he   put   the table in the   tent   of the congregation, upon the

cs,nn3409   df,nn4908   nn,lh6828   pr4480/nn2351   dfp,nn6532

side of the tabernacle northward, without the veil.

     wcs,qmf6186   nn3899   nn6187   pr,pnx5921   pp,pl,cs,nn6440   nn3068   pp,pnl834

23 And he   set   the bread in order   upon   it   before   the LORD;   as   the

nn3068   pipf6680   (853)   nn4872

LORD had commanded   Moses.

     wcs,qmf7760 (853)   df,nn4501   pp,cs,nn168   nn4150

24 And he   put   the candlestick in the   tent   of the congregation,

pr5227   df,nn7979 pr5921   cs,nn3409   df,nn4908   nn,lh5045

over against the table, on   the   side of the tabernacle southward.

     wcs,himf5927   df,pl,nn5216   pp,pl,cs,nn6440   nn3068   pp,pnl834   nn3068   pipf6680

25 And he lighted the lamps   before   the LORD;   as   the LORD commanded

(853)   nn4872

Moses.

     wcs,qmf7760 (853)   df,nn2091   cs,nn4196   pp,cs,nn168   nn4150

26 And he   put   the golden altar in the   tent   of the congregation

pp,pl,cs,nn6440   df,nn6532

before the veil:

     wcs,himf6999   pl,nn5561   cs,nn7004   pr,pnx5921   pp,pnl834   nn3068   pipf6680   (853)

27 And he   burnt   sweet incense thereon;   as   the LORD commanded

nn4872

Moses.

     wcs,qmf7760 (853)   cs,nn4539   df,nn6607   dfp,nn4908

28 And he set up   the hanging *at* the door of the tabernacle.

     qpf7760 wcj(853)   cs,nn4196   df,nn5930   cs,nn6607   cs,nn4908

29 And he put   the altar of burnt offering *by* the door of the tabernacle

cs,nn168   nn4150   wcs,himf5927 pr,pnx5921   (853)   df,nn5930

of the tent of the congregation, and offered   upon   it   the burnt offering and

wcj(853)   df,nn4503   pp,pnl834   nn3068   pipf6680   (853)   nn4872

the meat offering;   as   the LORD commanded   Moses.

     wcs,qmf7760 (853)   df,nn3595   pr996   cs,nn168   nn4150   wcj(pr996)

30 And he   set   the laver between the tent of the congregation and

df,nn4196   wcs,qmf5414 pl,nn4325 ad,lh8033   pp,qnc7364

the altar, and   put   water there, to wash *withal.*

nn4872   wcj,nn175   wcj,pl,nn,pnx1121   wcj,qpf7364 (853)   du,nn,pnx3027   wcj(853)

31 And Moses and Aaron and his   sons   washed   their hands and

du,nn,pnx7272   pr,pnx4480

their feet   thereat:

pp,qnc,pnx935   pr413   cs,nn168   nn4150

32 When they   went   into the tent of the congregation, and when they

wcj,pp,qnc,pnx7126 pr413   df,nn4196   qmf7364   pp,pnl834   nn3068   pipf6680   (853)   nn4872

came near unto the altar, they washed; as the LORD commanded   Moses.

wcs,himf6965   (853)   df,nn2691   ad5439   dfp,nn4908   wcj,dfp,nn4196

33 And he reared up   the court round about the tabernacle and the   altar,

wcs,qmf5414 (853)   cs,nn4539   df,nn2691 cs,nn8179   nn4872   wcs,pimf3615 (853)   df,nn4399

and set up   the hanging of the court gate. So Moses finished   the work.

The Glory of the LORD Fills the Tabernacle

df,nn6051   wcs,pimf3680   (853)   cs,nn168   nn4150   wcj,cs,nn3519

🕮 34 Then a cloud covered   the tent of the congregation, and the   glory of

nn3068   qpf4390 (853)   df,nn4908

the LORD filled   the tabernacle.

nn4872   wcj,ptn3808 qpf3201   pp,qnc935 pr413   cs,nn168   nn4150

35 And Moses was   not able to enter into the tent of the congregation,

cj3588   df,nn6051   qpf7931   pr,pnx5921   wcj,cs,nn3519   nn3068   qpf4390 (853)

because the cloud abode thereon, and the   glory of the LORD filled   the

df,nn4908

tabernacle.

df,nn6051   wcj,pp,ninc5927   pr4480/pr5921   df,nn4908   pl,cs,nn1121

36 And when the cloud was taken up from over the tabernacle, the children of

nn3478   qmf5265   pp,cs,nn3605   pl,nn,pnx4550

Israel went onward in   all   their journeys:

wcj,cj518   df,nn6051   ptn3808   nimf5927   qmf5265   wcj,ptn3808 pr5704

37 But   if   the cloud were not taken up, then they journeyed   not   till the

cs,nn3117   ninc,pnx5927

day that it was taken up.

cj3588   cs,nn6051   nn3068   pr5921   df,nn4908   ad3119   wcj,nn784 qmf1961

38 For the cloud of the LORD was upon the tabernacle by day, and fire   was

pp,pnx   nn3915   pp,du,cs,nn5869   cs,nn3605   cs,nn1004   nn3478   pp,cs,nn3605

on it by night, in the   sight   of   all   the house of Israel, throughout   all   their

pl,nn,pnx4550

journeys.

🕮 **40:34** The phrase "the glory of the Lord filled the tabernacle," indicated that He approved of their work. Evidently, this glory appeared before Israel in the form of a cloud, the same cloud by which the Lord Himself went before the people when they came out of Egypt. At night it took the form of a pillar of fire (Ex. 13:21, 22). In these forms, He led them throughout their journey (Ex. 40:38). When Solomon had completed building the temple (2 Chr. 5:13, 14) it was also filled with the glory of the Lord in the form of a cloud. During the time of Zedekiah that glory departed (Ezek. 11:22, 23) and will not return again until it fills the millennial Temple (Ezek. 43:1–9). When this Temple is built, God promises that the "latter glory of this house shall be greater than the former . . . and in this place I shall give peace" (see the note on Hag. 2:6–9).

The Book of
LEVITICUS

The title "Leviticus" is a transliteration of the title in the Septuagint, the ancient Greek translation of the Old Testament. It is so named because it records the duties of the Levites. The Hebrew name for the book (the first word of the Hebrew text) means "and He called." This title is representative of the content and purpose of the book, namely the calling of God's people, and in particular the calling of the Levites to minister before Him.

This third book of Moses is a primer for the moral and ethical instruction of the chosen people of God. As such, it contains civil, sanitary, ceremonial, moral, and religious regulations for the nation of Israel. All the offerings, as well as the ceremonies and laws, served to constantly remind Israel that God was eminently holy. God could be approached only by the priests, and then only in strict obedience to the detailed instructions for purification. God required the sacrifice of innocent animals for the covering of man's sin. These sacrifices were symbolic of the ultimate sacrifice which would take away the sin of the whole world (John 1:29).

Burnt Offerings

1

nn3068   wcs,qmf7121   pr413   nn4872   wcs,pimf1696   pr,pnx413
⊙₮ And the LORD called unto Moses, and spoke unto him

pr4480/cs,nn168   nn4150   pp,qnc559
out*of*the*tabernacle of the congregation, saying,

pimv1696   pr413   pl,cs,nn1121   nn3478   wcj,qpf559 pr,pnx413   cj3588   nn120   pr,pnx4480
2 Speak unto the children of Israel, and say unto them, If any man of

himf7126   nn7133   pp,nn3068   himf7126 (853)   nn,pnx7133   pr4480   df,nn929
you bring an offering unto the LORD, ye shall bring your offering of the cattle,

pr4480   df,nn1241   wcj,pr4480   df,nn6629
even of the herd, and of the flock.

cj518   nn,pnx7133   nn5930   pr4480   df,nn1241   himf,pnx7126   nn2145
3 If his offering *be* a burnt sacrifice of the herd, let him offer a male

aj8549   himf7126 pnx(853)   pp,nn,pnx7522   pr413   cs,nn6607
without blemish: he shall offer it of his own voluntary will at the door of

cs,nn168   nn4150   pp,pl,cs,nn6440   nn3068
the tabernacle of the congregation before the LORD.

wcs,qpf5564   nn,pnx3027 pr5921   cs,nn7218   df,nn5930
4 And he shall put his hand upon the head of the burnt offering; and it

wcs,nipf7521   pp,pnx   pp,pinc3722   pr,pnx5921
shall be accepted for him to make atonement for him.

⊙₮ **1:1** The Book of Leviticus emphasizes the fact that God was speaking directly to Moses. In fact, this is recorded no less than fifty times in the book. In this verse He speaks to Moses from the Holy of Holies above the ark of the covenant. This speaking face–to–face with God distinguished Moses even from the prophets who followed him (Deut. 34:10).

wcs,qpf**7819** (853)   cs,nn**1121**/df,nn1241   pp,pl,cs,nn**6440**   nn**3068**   df,pl,nn**3548**

5 And he shall   kill   the   bullock   before   the LORD: and the priests,

nn**175**   pl,cs,nn**1121**   wcs,hipf**7126** (853)   df,nn**1818**   wcs,qpf**2236** (853)   df,nn**1818**   ad**5439**

Aaron's sons, shall bring   the blood, and sprinkle   the blood round about

pr**5921**   df,nn**4196** pnl834   cs,nn**6607**   cs,nn**168**   nn**4150**

upon the altar that *is by* the door of the tabernacle of the congregation.

wcs,hipf**6584** (853)   df,nn**5930**   wcs,pipf**5408** pnx(853)

6 And he shall   flay   the burnt offering, and   cut   it into his

pp,pl,nn,pnx**5409**

pieces.

pl,cs,nn**1121**   nn**175**   df,nn**3548**   wcs,qpf**5414** nn**784** pr**5921**   df,nn**4196**

7 And the   sons   of Aaron the priest shall   put   fire upon the altar, and

wcs,qpf**6186**/pl,nn**6086**   pr**5921**   df,nn**784**

lay*the*wood*in*order upon the fire:

df,pl,nn**3548**   nn**175**   pl,cs,nn**1121**   wcj,qpf**6186** (853)   df,pl,nn**5409** (853)   df,nn**7218**

8 And the priests, Aaron's sons, shall   lay   the parts,   the head, and

wcj(853)   df,nn**6309**   pr**5921**   df,pl,nn**6086** pnl834   pr**5921**   df,nn**784** pnl834   pr**5921**

the fat, in order upon the wood that *is* on the fire which *is* upon the

df,nn**4196**

altar:

wcj,nn,pnx**7130**   wcj,du,nn,pnx3767   qmf**7364**   dfp,pl,nn**4325**   df,nn**3548**

9 But his inwards and his   legs   shall he wash in water: and the priest

wcs,qpf**6999** (853)   df,nn3605   df,nn,lh**4196**   nn**5930**

shall   burn   all   on   the   altar,   *to be* a   burnt sacrifice,   an

cs,nn**801**   nn5207 cs,nn7381   pp,nn**3068**

offering*made*by*fire, of a sweet savor unto the LORD.

wcj,cj518   nn,pnx**7133**   pr4480   df,nn**6629**   pr4480   df,pl,nn3775 cj176 pr4480

10 And   if   his offering *be* of the flocks, *namely*, of the sheep, or of

df,pl,nn**5795**   pp,nn**5930**   himf,pnx**7126**   nn2145   aj**8549**

the goats, for a burnt sacrifice; he shall   bring   it a male without blemish.

wcs,qpf**7819** pnx(853)   pr**5921**   cs,nn**3409**   df,nn**4196**   nn,lh6828   pp,pl,cs,nn**6440**

11 And he shall   kill   it on the side of the altar northward   before

nn**3068**   df,pl,nn**3548**   nn**175**   pl,cs,nn**1121**   wcs,qpf**2236** (853)   nn,pnx**1818**   ad**5439**

the LORD: and the priests, Aaron's sons, shall sprinkle   his blood round about

pr**5921**   df,nn**4196**

upon the altar.

wcs,pipf**5408** pnx(853)   pp,pl,nn,pnx5409 wcj,pr854   nn,pnx**7218**   wcj(pr854)

12 And he shall   cut   it into his   pieces,   with his   head and

nn,pnx6309   df,nn**3548**   wcs,qpf**6186**/pnx(853)   pr5921   df,pl,nn**6086** pnl834   pr5921

his   fat: and the priest shall lay*them*in*order on   the   wood that *is* on the

df,nn**784** pnl834   pr5921   df,nn**4196**

fire which *is* upon the altar:

qmf**7364**   wcj,df,nn**7130**   wcj,df,du,nn3767   dfp,pl,nn**4325**   df,nn**3548**

13 But he shall wash the inwards and the   legs   with   water: and the priest

wcs,hipf**7126** (853) df,nn3605   wcs,hipf**6999**   df,nn,lh**4196** pnp1931   nn**5930**

shall   bring   *it*   all,   and   burn   *it* upon the altar: it   *is* a burnt sacrifice, an

cs,nn**801**   nn5207 cs,nn7381   pp,nn**3068**

offering*made*by*fire, of a sweet savor unto the LORD.

wcj,cj518   nn**5930**   nn,pnx**7133**   pp,nn**3068** pr4480 df,nn**5775**

14 And   if   the burnt sacrifice for his offering to the LORD *be* of   fowls, then

wcs,himf**7126** (853)   nn,pnx**7133** pr4480   df,pl,nn**8449**   cj176 pr4480 pl,cs,nn**1121**   df,nn**3123**

he shall bring   his offering of turtledoves, or   of   young   pigeons.

df,nn**3548**   wcs,hipf,pnx**7126**   pr413   df,nn**4196**   wcs,qpf**4454** (853)   nn,pnx**7218**

15 And the priest shall   bring   it unto the altar, and wring off   his head,

wcs,hipf**6999**   df,nn,lh**4196**   nn,pnx**1818**   wcs,nipf**4680**   pr**5921**   cs,nn**7023**

and burn *it* on the altar; and the blood thereof shall be wrung out at the side

df,nn**4196**

of the altar:

wcj,hipf**5493**   (853)   nn,pnx**4760**   pp,nn,pnx**5133**   wcj,hipf**7993** pnx(853)

16 And he shall pluck away   his   crop with his feathers, and   cast   it

pr**681**   df,nn**4196**   nn,lh**6924**   pr**413**   cs,nn**4725**   df,nn**1880**

beside the altar on the east part, by the place of the ashes:

wcs,pipf**8156** pnx(853)   pp,pl,nn,pnx**3671**   ptn**3808**

17 And he shall cleave   it with the   wings   thereof, *but* shall not

himf**914**   df,nn**3548**   wcs,himf**6999** pnx(853)   df,nn,lh**4196** pr**5921**

divide*it*asunder: and the priest shall   burn   it upon the altar, upon the

df,pl,nn**6086** pnl**834**   pr**5921**   df,nn**784** pnp**1931**   nn**5930**   cs,nn**801**

wood that *is* upon the fire: it *is* a burnt sacrifice, an offering*made*by*fire, of

nn**5207**   nn**7381**   pp,nn**3068**

a sweet savor unto the LORD.

Meat Offerings

cj**3588**   wcj,nn**5315**   himf**7126**   nn**4503**   cs,nn**7133**   pp,nn**3068**   nn,pnx**7133**

2 And when any will offer a meat offering unto the LORD, his offering shall

qmf**1961**   nn**5560**   wcs,qpf**3332** nn**8081** pr,pnx**5921**   wcs,qpf**5414**

be *of* fine flour; and he shall   pour   oil   upon it, and   put

nn**3828**   pr,pnx**5921**

frankincense thereon:

wcs,hipf,pnx**935** pr**413**   nn**175** pl,cs,nn**1121**   df,pl,nn**3548**   wcs,qpf**7061**

2 And he shall   bring   it to Aaron's sons the priests: and he shall take

pr**4480**/ad**8033**   cs,nn**4393**/nn,pnx**7062** pr**4480**/nn,nn**5560**   wcj,pr**4480**/nn,pnx**8081**   pr**5921** cs,nn**3605**

therefrom his   handful of*the*flour thereof, and of*the*oil thereof, with all

nn,pnx**3828**   df,nn**3548**   wcs,hipf**6999** (853)   nn,pnx**234**

the frankincense thereof; and the priest shall   burn   the memorial of it upon the

df,nn,lh**4196**   cs,nn**801**   nn**5207** cs,nn**7381**   pp,nn**3068**

altar, *to be* an offering*made*by*fire, of a sweet savor unto the LORD:

wcj,df,nipt**3498** pr**4480**   df,nn**4503**   pp,nn**175**   wcj,pp,pl,nn,pnx**1121**

3 And the remnant of the meat offering *shall be* Aaron's and his   sons':

cs,nn**6944**/pl,nn**6944**   pr**4480**/pl,cs,nn**801**/nn**3068**

it is a thing*most*holy of*the*offerings*of*the*LORD*made*by*fire.

wcj,cj**3588**   himf**7126**   cs,nn**7133**   nn**4503**   cs,nn**3989**   nn**8574**

4 And   if   thou bring an oblation of a meat offering baked in the oven, *it*

pl,nn**4682**   pl,nn**2471**   nn**5560**   pl,qptp**1101**   dfp,nn**8081**   pl,nn**4682** wcj,pl,cs,nn**7550**

shall be unleavened cakes of fine flour mingled with oil, or unleavened wafers

pl,qptp**4886**   dfp,nn**8081**

anointed with oil.

wcj,cj**518**   nn,pnx**7133**   nn**4503**   pr**5921** df,nn**4227**   qmf**1961**

5 And if thy oblation *be* a meat offering *baked* in a pan, it shall be *of*

nn**5560**   nn**4682**   qptp**1101**   dfp,nn**8081**

fine flour unleavened, mingled with oil.

qna**6626** pnx(853)   pl,nn**6595**   wcs,qpf**3332** nn**8081** pr,pnx**5921** pnp**1931**

6 Thou shalt part   it in pieces, and   pour   oil thereon: it   *is* a

nn**4503**

meat offering.

wcj,cj**518**   nn,pnx**7133**   cs,nn**4503**   nn**4802**

7 And   if   thy oblation *be* a meat offering *baked* in the frying pan, it shall be

nimf**6213**   nn**5560**   dfp,nn**8081**

made *of* fine flour with oil.

8 And thou shalt bring the meat offering that is made of*these*things unto the LORD: and when it is presented unto the priest, he shall bring it unto the altar.

9 And the priest shall take from the meat offering a memorial thereof, and shall burn *it* upon the altar: *it is* an offering*made*by*fire, of a sweet savor unto the LORD.

10 And that which*is*left of the meat offering *shall be* Aaron's and his sons': *it is* a thing*most*holy of*the*offerings*of*the*LORD*made*by*fire.

11 No meat offering, which ye shall bring unto the LORD, shall be made with leaven: for ye shall burn no leaven, nor any honey, in any offering*of*the*LORD*made*by*fire.

12 As for the oblation of the firstfruits, ye shall offer them unto the LORD: but they shall not be burnt on the altar for a sweet savor.

13 And every oblation of thy meat offering shalt thou season with salt; neither shalt thou suffer the salt of the covenant of thy God to be lacking from thy meat offering: with all thine offerings thou shalt offer salt.

14 And if thou offer a meat offering of thy firstfruits unto the LORD, thou shalt offer for the meat offering of thy firstfruits green*ears*of*corn dried by the fire, *even* corn beaten out of full ears.

15 And thou shalt put oil upon it, and lay frankincense thereon: it *is* a meat offering.

16 And the priest shall burn the memorial of it, *part* of*the*beaten*corn thereof, and *part* of*the*oil thereof, with all the frankincense thereof: *it is* an offering*made*by*fire unto the LORD.

Peace Offerings

3 And if his oblation *be* a sacrifice of peace offering, if he offer *it* of the herd; whether *it be* a male or female, he shall offer it without blemish before the LORD.

2 And he shall lay his hand upon the head of his offering, and kill it *at* the door of the tabernacle of the congregation: and Aaron's sons the priests shall sprinkle the blood upon the altar round about.

3 And he shall offer of*the*sacrifice of the peace offering an offering*made*by*fire unto the LORD; the fat that covereth the inwards, and all the fat that *is* upon the inwards,

4 And the two kidneys, and the fat that *is* on them, which *is* by the flanks, and the caul above the liver, with the kidneys, it shall he take away.

5 And Aaron's sons shall burn it on the altar upon the burnt sacrifice, which *is* upon the wood that *is* on the fire: *it is* an offering*made*by*fire, of a sweet savor unto the LORD.

6 And if his offering for a sacrifice of peace offering unto the LORD *be* of the flock; male or female, he shall offer it without blemish.

7 If he offer a lamb for his offering, then shall he offer it before the LORD.

8 And he shall lay his hand upon the head of his offering, and kill it before the tabernacle of the congregation: and Aaron's sons shall sprinkle the blood thereof round about upon the altar.

9 And he shall offer of*the*sacrifice of the peace offering an offering*made*by*fire unto the LORD; the fat thereof, *and* the whole rump, it shall he take off hard by the backbone; and the fat that covereth the inwards, and all the fat that *is* upon the inwards,

10 And the two kidneys, and the fat that *is* upon them, which

pr5921   df,pl,nn**3689**   wcj(853)   df,nn3508   pr5921   df,nn3516   pr5921   df,pl,nn**3629**

is by the flanks, and   the caul above the liver, with the kidneys, it shall he

himf,pnx**5493**

take away.

       df,nn**3548**   wcs,hipf,pnx**6999**   df,nn,lh**4196**   cs,nn3899

11 And the priest shall   burn   it upon the altar: *it is* the food of the

nn**801**   pp,nn**3068**

offering*made*by*fire unto the Lord.

      wcj,cj518   nn,pnx**7133**   nn5795   wcs,hipf,pnx**7126**   pp,pl,cs,nn**6440**

12 And   if   his offering *be* a goat, then he shall   offer   it before   the

nn**3068**

Lord.

      wcs,qpf5564 (853)   nn,pnx**3027** pr5921   nn,pnx**7218**   wcs,qpf**7819** pnx(853)

13 And he shall   lay   his hand upon the head of it, and   kill   it

pp,pl,cs,nn**6440**   cs,nn**168**   nn4150   pl,cs,nn**1121**   nn175   wcs,qpf**2236**

before   the tabernacle of the congregation: and the sons of Aaron shall sprinkle

(853)   nn,pnx**1818**   pr5921   df,nn**4196**   ad5439

the blood thereof upon the altar round about.

      wcs,hipf**7126**   pr,pnx4480   nn,pnx**7133**   nn**801**

14 And he shall   offer   thereof his offering, *even* an offering*made*by*fire

    pp,nn**3068** (853)   df,nn**2459**   df,pipt**3680** (853)   df,nn**7130**   wcj(853) cs,nn3605   df,nn**2459**

unto the Lord;   the fat that covereth   the inwards, and   all   the fat

pnl834   pr5921   df,nn**7130**

that *is* upon the inwards,

      wcj(853)   du,cs,nu8147 df,pl,nn3629   wcj(853)   df,nn2459 pnl834   pr,pnx5921   pnl834

15 And   the   two   kidneys, and   the   fat that *is* upon them, which

pr5921   df,pl,nn**3689**   wcj(853)   df,nn3508   pr5921   df,nn3516   pr5921   df,pl,nn3629

is by the flanks, and   the caul above the liver, with the kidneys, it shall he

himf,pnx**5493**

take away.

       df,nn**3548**   wcs,hipf,pnx**6999**   df,nn,lh**4196**   cs,nn3899

16 And the priest shall   burn   them upon the altar: *it is* the food of the

nn**801**   nn5207   pp,cs,nn7381 cs,nn3605   nn2459   pp,nn**3068**

offering*made*by*fire for a sweet savor: all   the fat *is* the Lord's.

       nn5769   cs,nn**2708**   pp,pl,nn,pnx**1755**   pp,cs,nn3605

17 *It shall be* a perpetual statute for your generations throughout   all   your

pl,nn,pnx**4186**   qmf398 ptn**3808**/cs,nn3605 nn2459   wcj(cs,nn3605)   nn**1818**

dwellings, that ye eat   neither   fat nor   blood.

Sin Offerings

        nn**3068**   wcs,pimf**1696**   pr413   nn4872   pp,qnc**559**

4 And the Lord spoke unto Moses, saying,

       pimv**1696**   pr413   pl,cs,nn**1121**   nn3478   pp,qnc**559**   cj3588   nn5315   qmf2398

2 Speak unto the children of Israel, saying, If   a soul shall sin

    pp,nn**7684**   pr4480/cs,nn3605   pl,cs,nn**4687**   nn**3068**

through ignorance against any of the commandments of the Lord *concerning things*

pnl834   ptn**3808**   nimf**6213**   wcj,qpf**6213**   pr4480/nu259   pr4480/pnp2007

which ought not to be done, and shall   do   against any of them:

    cj518   df,nn**3548**   df,nn**4899**   qmf**2398**   pp,cs,nn**819**   df,nn**5971**

3 If the priest that is anointed do   sin   according to the   sin   of the people;

      wcs,hipf**7126**   pr5921   nn,pnx**2403**   pnl834   qpf2398   cs,nn**1121**/nn**1241**   nn6499

then let him bring for his   sin,   which he hath sinned, a   young   bullock

   aj**8549**   pp,nn**3068**   pp,nn**2403**

without blemish unto the Lord for a sin offering.

^{wcj,hipf935} (853)   ^{df,nn6499}   ^{pr413}   ^{cs,nn6607}   ^{cs,nn168}

4 And he shall bring   the bullock unto the door of the tabernacle of the

ⁿⁿ⁴¹⁵⁰   ^{pp,pl,cs,nn6440}   ⁿⁿ³⁰⁶⁸   ^{wcj,qpf5564} (853)   ^{nn,pnx3027} ^{pr5921}   ^{df,nn6499}

congregation before the LORD; and shall lay   his hand upon the bullock's

^{cs,nn7218}   ^{wcj,qpf7819} (853)   ^{df,nn6499} ^{pp,pl,cs,nn6440}   ⁿⁿ³⁰⁶⁸

head, and kill   the bullock before the LORD.

^{df,nn3548}   ^{df,nn4899}   ^{wcj,qpf3947}   ^{pr4480/cs,nn1818/df,nn6499}

5 And the priest that is anointed shall take of*the*bullock's*blood, and

^{wcj,hipf935 pnx(853)}   ^{pr413}   ^{cs,nn168}   ⁿⁿ⁴¹⁵⁰

bring   it to the tabernacle of the congregation:

^{df,nn3548}   ^{wcj,qpf2881} (853)   ^{nn,pnx676}   ^{df,nn1818}   ^{wcj,hipf5137} ^{pr4480}

6 And the priest shall dip   his finger in the blood, and sprinkle of the

^{df,nn1818}   ^{nu7651}   ^{pl,nn6471} ^{pp,pl,cs,nn6440}   ⁿⁿ³⁰⁶⁸   (853) ^{pl,cs,nn6440}   ^{cs,nn6532}   ^{df,nn6944}

blood seven times before the LORD,   before the veil of the sanctuary.

^{df,nn3548}   ^{wcj,qpf5414}   ^{pr4480}   ^{df,nn1818} ^{pr5921}   ^{pl,cs,nn7161}   ^{cs,nn4196}

7 And the priest shall put *some* of the blood upon the horns of the altar

^{df,pl,nn5561} ^{cs,nn7004} ^{pp,pl,cs,nn6440}   ⁿⁿ³⁰⁶⁸   ^{pnl834}   ^{pp,cs,nn168}   ⁿⁿ⁴¹⁵⁰

of sweet incense before the LORD, which *is* in the tabernacle of the congregation;

^{qmf8210} ^{wcj(853)} ^{cs,nn3605}   ^{cs,nn1818}   ^{df,nn6499} ^{pr413}   ^{cs,nn3247}   ^{cs,nn4196}

and shall pour   all   the blood of the bullock at the bottom of the altar of

^{df,nn5930}   ^{pnl834}   ^{cs,nn6607}   ^{cs,nn168}   ⁿⁿ⁴¹⁵⁰

the burnt offering, which *is at* the door of the tabernacle of the congregation.

^{himf7311}   ^{pr,pnx4480}   ^{wcj(853)} ^{cs,nn3605}   ^{cs,nn2459}   ^{cs,nn6499}

8 And he shall take off from it   all   the fat of the bullock for the

^{df,nn2403}   (853)   ^{df,nn2459}   ^{df,pipt3680/pr5921}   ^{df,nn7130}   ^{wcj(853)} ^{cs,nn3605}   ^{df,nn2459} ^{pnl834}

sin offering;   the fat that covereth the inwards, and   all   the fat that

^{pr5921}   ^{df,nn7130}

is upon the inwards,

^{wcj(853)}   ^{du,cs,nu8147} ^{df,pl,nn3629}   ^{wcj(853)}   ^{df,nn2459} ^{pnl834}   ^{pr,pnx5921}   ^{pnl834}

9 And   the two kidneys, and   the fat that *is* upon them, which

^{pr5921}   ^{df,pl,nn3689}   ^{wcj(853)}   ^{df,nn3508} ^{pr5921}   ^{df,nn3516} ^{pr5921}   ^{df,pl,nn3629}

is by the flanks, and   the caul above the liver, with the kidneys, it shall he

^{himf,pnx5493}

take away,

^{pp,pnl834}   ^{homf7311}   ^{pr4480/cs,nn7794}   ^{cs,nn2077}   ^{df,pl,nn8002}

10 As   it was taken off from*the*bullock of the sacrifice of peace offerings:

^{df,nn3548}   ^{wcs,hipf,pnx6999}   ^{pr5921}   ^{cs,nn4196}   ^{df,nn5930}

and the priest shall burn them upon the altar of the burnt offering.

^{wcj(853)}   ^{cs,nn5785}   ^{df,nn6499}   ^{wcj(853)} ^{cs,nn3605}   ^{nn,pnx1320} ^{pr5921}   ^{nn,pnx7218}

11 And   the skin of the bullock, and   all   his flesh, with his head,

^{wcj,pr5921}   ^{du,nn,pnx3767}   ^{wcj,nn,pnx7130}   ^{wcj,nn,pnx6569}

and with his legs, and his inwards, and his dung,

(853)   ^{cs,nn3605}   ^{df,nn6499}   ^{wcs,hipf3318}   ^{pr413/pr4480/nn2351}   ^{dfp,nn4264}   ^{pr413}

12 Even   the whole bullock shall he carry forth without   the camp unto a

^{aj2889}   ⁿⁿ⁴⁷²⁵   (pr413)   ^{df,nn1880}   ^{cs,nn8211}   ^{wcs,qpf8313} ^{pnx(853)}   ^{pr5921}

clean place,   where the ashes are poured out, and burn   him on the

^{pl,nn6086}   ^{dfp,nn784} ^{pr5921}   ^{df,nn1880}   ^{cs,nn8211}   ^{nimf8313}

wood with fire: where the ashes are poured out shall he be burnt.

^{wcj,cj518}   ^{cs,nn3605}   ^{cs,nn5712}   ⁿⁿ³⁴⁷⁸   ^{qmf7686}

13 And if   the whole congregation of Israel sin*through*ignorance, and the

ⁿⁿ¹⁶⁹⁷   ^{wcs,nipf5956}   ^{pr4480/du,cs,nn5869}   ^{df,nn6951}   ^{wcs,qpf6213}

thing be hid   from*the*eyes of the assembly, and they have done *somewhat*

^{nu259/pr4480/cs,nn3605}   ^{pl,cs,nn4687}   ⁿⁿ³⁰⁶⁸   ^{pnl834}

against any of   the commandments of the LORD *concerning things* which

^{ptn3808}   ^{nimf6213}   ^{wcs,qpf816}

should not be done, and are guilty;

14 When the sin, which they have sinned against it, is known, then the congregation shall offer a young bullock for the sin, and bring him before the tabernacle of the congregation.

15 And the elders of the congregation shall lay their hands upon the head of the bullock before the LORD: and the bullock shall be killed before the LORD.

16 And the priest that is anointed shall bring of*the*bullock's*blood to the tabernacle of the congregation:

17 And the priest shall dip his finger in some of the blood, and sprinkle it seven times before the LORD, even before the veil.

18 And he shall put some of the blood upon the horns of the altar which is before the LORD, that is in the tabernacle of the congregation, and shall pour out all the blood at the bottom of the altar of the burnt offering, which is at the door of the tabernacle of the congregation.

19 And he shall take all his fat from him, and burn it upon the altar.

20 And he shall do with the bullock as he did with the bullock for a sin offering, so shall he do with this: and the priest shall make*an*atonement for them, and it shall be forgiven them.

21 And he shall carry forth the bullock without the camp, and burn him as he burned the first bullock: it is a sin offering for the congregation.

22 When a ruler hath sinned, and done somewhat through ignorance against any of the commandments of the LORD his God concerning things which should not be done, and is guilty;

23 Or if his sin, wherein he hath sinned, come*to*his*knowledge; he shall bring his offering, a kid of the goats, a male without blemish:

24 And he shall lay his hand upon the head of the goat, and kill

pp,cs,nn4725   pnl834   qmf7819 (853)   df,nn5930   pp,pl,cs,nn6440   nn3068   pnp1931

it in the place where they kill   the burnt offering before the LORD: it *is* a

nn2403

sin offering.

     df,nn3548   wcs,qpf3947   pr4480   cs,nn1818   df,nn2403

25 And the priest shall   take   of   the blood of the sin offering with his

pp,nn,pnx676   wcs,qpf5414   pr5921   pl,cs,nn7161   cs,nn4196   df,nn5930

finger, and   put   *it* upon the horns of the altar of burnt offering, and shall

qmf8210   wcj(853)   nn,pnx1818 pr413   cs,nn3247   cs,nn4196   df,nn5930

pour out   his blood at the bottom of the altar of burnt offering.

     himf6999   wcj(853)   cs,nn3605   nn,pnx2459   df,nn,lh4196   pp,cs,nn2459

⛏ 26 And he shall burn   all   his   fat   upon the altar, as the   fat   of

cs,nn2077   df,pl,nn8002   df,nn3548   wcs,pipf3722   pr,pnx5921

the sacrifice of peace offerings: and the priest shall make*an*atonement   for   him

pr4480/nn,pnx2403   wcs,nipf5545   pp,pnx

as*concerning*his*sin, and it shall be forgiven him.

    wcj,cj518   nu259   nn5315   pr4480/cs,nn5971/df,nn776   qmf2398   pp,nn7684

27 And   if   any one of*the*common*people   sin   through ignorance, while he

pp,qnc.pnx6213   nu259   pr4480/pl,cs,nn4687   nn3068

doeth   *somewhat against* any of*the*commandments of the LORD *concerning*

pnl834   ptn3808   nimf6213   wcs,qpf816

things which ought not to be done, and be guilty;

    cj176   nn,pnx2403   pnl834   qpf2398   hopf3045/pr,pnx413

28 Or if his   sin,   which he hath sinned, come*to*his*knowledge: then he

wcj,hipf935   nn,pnx7133   cs,nn8166   pl,nn5795   nn5347   aj8549   pr5921

shall bring his offering, a   kid   of the goats, a female without blemish, for his

nn,pnx2403   pnl834   qpf2398

sin   which he hath sinned.

     wcj,qpf5564   (853)   nn,pnx3027   pr5921   cs,nn7218   df,nn2403

29 And he shall   lay   his   hand   upon the head of the sin offering, and

wcj,qpf7819 (853)   df,nn2403   pp,cs,nn4725   df,nn5930

slay   the sin offering in the   place   of the burnt offering.

     df,nn3548   wcj,qpf3947   pr4480/nn,pnx1818   pp,nn,pnx676   wcj,qpf5414

30 And the priest shall   take   of*the*blood thereof with his   finger, and   put

pr5921   pl,cs,nn7161   cs,nn4196   df,nn5930   qmf8210   wcj(853) cs,nn3605

it upon the   horns   of the altar of burnt offering, and shall pour out   all   the

nn,pnx1818   pr413   cs,nn3247   df,nn4196

blood thereof at the bottom of the altar.

     himf5493   wcj(853) cs,nn3605   nn,pnx2459   pp,pnl834   nn2459

31 And he shall take away   all   the   fat   thereof,   as   the   fat   is

hopf5493   pr4480   pr5921   cs,nn2077   df,pl,nn8002   df,nn3548   wcj,hipf6999

taken away from off the sacrifice of peace offerings; and the priest shall   burn   *it*

df,nn,lh4196   nn5207   pp,cs,nn7381   pp,nn3068   df,nn3548

upon the   altar   for a   sweet   savor   unto the LORD; and   the   priest shall

wcj,pipf3722   pr,pnx5921   wcj,nipf5545   pp,pnx

make*an*atonement   for   him, and it shall be forgiven him.

⛏ **4:26** This passage might seem to suggest that forgiveness and atonement came about through the act of the sacrifice. However, the Scriptures deny that animal sacrifices can take away sin (Heb. 10:4, 11). Transgressions were not forgiven under the Law through the shedding of the blood of animals, because their blood could offer no real atonement. The sacrifices made under the Old Testament Law were symbolical and typical of the atonement of Christ. Therefore, forgiveness in the Old Testament was granted in anticipation of and by faith in Jesus' final offering (Heb. 9:15).

32 And   if   he bring a lamb for a   sin   offering, he shall bring it a female
without blemish.

33 And he shall   lay   his hand upon the head of the sin offering, and
slay   it for a sin offering in the   place   where they   kill   the
burnt offering.

34 And the priest shall   take   of*the*blood of the sin offering with his finger,
and   put   it upon the   horns of the altar of burnt offering, and shall pour out
all   the blood thereof at the bottom of the altar:

35 And he shall take away   all   the   fat   thereof, as   the   fat   of
the lamb is taken away from*the*sacrifice of the peace offerings; and the priest
shall burn   them upon the altar, according to the offerings*made*by*fire
unto the LORD: and the priest shall make*an*atonement   for his   sin   that
he hath committed, and it shall be forgiven him.

Trespass Offerings

5 And if a soul sin, and hear the voice of swearing, and   is a
witness, whether he hath seen or known *of it*; if he do not utter *it*, then
he shall bear his iniquity.

2 Or if a soul   touch any   unclean thing, whether *it be* a carcass of an
unclean beast, or a carcass of unclean cattle, or the carcass of unclean
creeping things, and *if* it be hidden from him;   he   also shall be unclean, and
guilty.

3 Or if he touch the uncleanness of man, whatsoever uncleanness *it be* that a
man shall be defiled withal, and it be   hid   from him; when   he   knoweth *of*
it, then he shall be guilty.

4 Or if a soul swear, pronouncing with *his* lips to do evil, or to
do good, whatsoever *it be* that a man shall pronounce with an oath, and it be

wcs,nipf5956 pr,pnx4480   wcj,pnp1931   qpf3045   wcj,qpf816   pp,nu259
hid   from him; when   he   knoweth *of it*, then he shall be guilty in   one

pr4480/pndm428
of these.

                                   wcj,qpf1961   cj3588   qmf816   pp,nu259 pr4480/pndm428
5 And it shall   be,   when he shall be guilty in   one   of these *things*, that he

        wcs,htpf3034 pnl834   qpf2398   pr,pnx5921
shall confess that he hath sinned   in   that *thing*:

                        wcj,hipf935 (853)   nn,pnx817   pp,nn3068 pr5921   nn,pnx2403
6 And he shall bring   his trespass offering unto the LORD for his   sin

     pnl834   qpf2398   nn5347   pr4480   df,nn6629   nn3776 cj176 cs,nn8166   pl,nn5795
which he hath sinned, a female from the flock, a lamb or a   kid of the goats, for

      pp,nn2403   df,nn3548   wcj,pipf3722   pr,pnx5921
a   sin offering;   and   the   priest   shall   make*an*atonement   for   him

pr4480/nn,pnx2403
concerning*his*sin.

              wcj,cj518   ptn3808 himf5060/nn,pnx3027/cs,nn1767   nn7716   wcs,hipf935 (853)
7 And   if   he be not   able*to*bring   a lamb, then he shall bring   for

nn,pnx817   pnl834   qpf2398   du,cs,nn8147   pl,nn8449   cj176 du,cs,nu8147 pl,cs,nn1121
his trespass, which he hath committed,   two   turtledoves,   or   two   young

nn3123   pp,nn3068 nu259   pp,nn2403   wcj,nu259   pp,nn5930
pigeons, unto the LORD; one for a sin offering, and the other for a burnt offering.

            wcj,hipf935 pnx(853)   pr413   df,nn3548   wcj,hipf7126 (853)
8 And he shall bring   them unto the priest, who shall offer   *that*

pnl834   dfp,nn2403   aj7223   wcj,qpf4454   (853)   nn,pnx7218 pr4480/pr4136   nn,pnx6203
which *is* for the sin offering first, and wring off   his head   from   his   neck,

        wcj,ptn3808   himf914
but shall   not   divide*it*asunder:

                        wcj,hipf5137   pr4480/cs,nn1818   df,nn2403   pr5921   cs,nn7023
9 And he shall sprinkle of*the*blood of the sin offering upon the side of the

df,nn4196   wcj,df,nipt7604   dfp,nn1818   qmf4680   pr413   cs,nn3247   df,nn4196
altar; and the   rest   of the blood shall be wrung out at the bottom of the altar:

pnp1931   nn2403
it   *is* a sin offering.

         qmf6213 wcj(853)   df,nuor8145   nn5930
10 And he shall offer   the second *for* a burnt offering, according to the

dfp,nn4941   df,nn3548   wcs,pipf3722   pr,pnx5921   pr4480/nn,pnx2403   pnl834
manner: and the priest shall make*an*atonement   for   him for*his*sin which he

     qpf2398   wcj,nipf5545 pp,pnx
hath sinned, and it shall be forgiven him.

            wcj,cj518   ptn3808 himf5381/nn,pnx3027 pp,du,nu8147   pl,nn8449   cj176 pp,du,nu8147 pl,cs,nn1121
11 But   if   he be not able*to*bring   two   turtledoves, or   two   young

nn3123   pnl834 qpf2398   wcs,hipf935 (853)   nn,pnx7133   cs,nuor6224
pigeons, then he that sinned shall bring   for his offering the tenth part of an

df,nn374   nn5560   pp,nn2403   qmf7760 ptn3808 nn8081 pr,pnx5921   wcj,ptn3808
ephah of fine flour for a sin offering; he shall put no   oil   upon it, neither shall

   qmf5414   nn3828   pr,pnx5921 cj3588 pnp1931   nn2403
he put *any* frankincense thereon: for   it   *is* a sin offering.

            wcj,hipf,qpf935   pr413   df,nn3548   df,nn3548   wcs,qpf7061
12 Then shall he   bring   it to the priest, and the priest shall   take   his

cs,nn4393/nn,pnx7062 pr,pnx4480   (853)   nn,pnx234   wcs,hipf6999   df,nn,lh4196
handful   of   it, *even*   a memorial thereof, and   burn *it* on the altar,

    pr5921   pl,cs,nn801   nn3068 pnp1931   nn2403
according to the offerings*made*by*fire unto the LORD: it *is* a sin offering.

         df,nn3548   wcs,pipf3722   pr,pnx5921   pr5921   nn,pnx2403
13 And the priest shall make*an*atonement for   him as touching his   sin

pnl834   qpf2398   pr4480/nu259 pr4480/pndm428   wcj,nipf5545   pp,pnx
that he hath sinned in one of these, and it shall be forgiven him: and *the remnant*

wcj,qpf1961   dfp,nn3548   dfp,nn4503
shall   be   the priest's, as a meat offering.

nn3068   wcs,pimf1696 pr413   nn4872   pp,qnc559
14 And the LORD spoke unto Moses, saying,

cj3588   nn5315   qmf4603   nn4604   wcs,qpf2398   pp,nn7684   pr4480
15 If   a soul commit a trespass, and   sin   through ignorance, in   the

pl,cs,nn6944   nn3068   wcs,hipf935 (853)   nn,pnx817   pp,nn3068
holy things of the LORD; then he shall bring   for his trespass unto the LORD a

nn352   aj8549   pr4480   df,nn6629   pp,nn,pnx6187   pl,nn8255   cs,nn3701
ram without blemish out of the flocks, with thy estimation by shekels of silver,

pp,cs,nn8255   df,nn6944   pp,nn817
after the shekel of the sanctuary, for a trespass offering:

pimf7999   wcj(853)   pnl834/qpf2398   pr4480
16 And he shall make amends   for the harm*that*he*hath*done in the

df,nn6944   hicj3254 wcj(853)   nuor,pnx2549 pr,pnx5921   wcs,qpf5414 pnx(853)
holy thing, and shall add   the fifth part thereto, and   give   it unto the

dfp,nn3548   wcj,df,nn3548   pimf3722   pr,pnx5921   pp,cs,nn352
priest: and the priest shall make*an*atonement for him with the   ram of the

df,nn817   wcs,nipf5545 pp,pnx
trespass offering, and it shall be forgiven him.

wcj,cj518   nn5315 (cj3588) qmf2398   wcs,qpf6213 cs,nu259   pr4480/cs,nn3605   pnl834
17 And   if   a soul   sin, and commit any of*these*things which are

ptn3808   nimf6213   pl,cs,nn4687   nn3068   qpf3045 wcj,ptn3808
forbidden to be done by the commandments of the LORD; though he knew *it* not,

wcj,qpf816   wcj,qpf5375   nn,pnx5771
yet is*he*guilty, and shall bear his iniquity.

wcs,hipf935   nn352   aj8549   pr4480   df,nn6629
18 And he shall bring a ram without blemish out of the flock, with thy

pp,nn,pnx6187   pp,nn817   pr413   df,nn3548   df,nn3548
estimation, for a trespass offering, unto the priest: and the priest shall

wcs,pipf3722   pr,pnx5921   pr5921   nn,pnx7684   pnl834   qpf7683
make*an*atonement for   him concerning his ignorance wherein he erred and

wcj(pnp1931) qpf3045 ptn3808   wcs,nipf5545 pp,pnx
knew *it* not, and it shall be forgiven him.

pnp1931   nn817   qna816/qpf816   pp,nn3068
19   It *is* a trespass offering: he hath certainly trespassed against the LORD.

The Guilty Must Make Restitution

nn3068   wcs,pimf1696 pr413   nn4872   pp,qnc559
6 And the LORD spoke unto Moses, saying,

cj3588   nn5315 qmf2398   wcs,qpf4603   nn4604   pp,nn3068   wcs,pimf3584
2 If a soul sin, and commit a trespass against the LORD, and   lie

nn,pnx5997   pp,nn6487   cj176   pp,cs,nn8667/nn3027 cj176
unto his neighbor in that*which*was*delivered*him*to*keep, or in fellowship, or

pp,nn1498   cj176   qpf6231   (853)   nn,pnx5997
in a thing*taken*away*by*violence, or hath deceived   his neighbor;

cj176   qpf4672   nn9   wcj,pipf3584   pp,pnx   wcj,nipf7650
3 Or have found that*which*was*lost, and   lieth concerning it, and sweareth

pr5921/nn8267 pr5921 nu259 pr4480/nn3605   pnl834 df,nn120 qmf6213 pp,qnc2398 pp,pnp2007
falsely; in any of all these that a man doeth, sinning therein:

nn8641   pp,nn3068   pp,pnx/qmf1961   dfp,nn3548   df,qpta2236   (853)

heave offering unto the LORD, *and* it shall   be   the priest's that sprinkleth

cs,nn1818   df,pl,nn8002

the blood of the peace offerings.

         wcj,cs,nn1320   cs,nn2077   pl,nn,pnx8002   cs,nn8426

15 And the   flesh   of the sacrifice of his peace offerings for thanksgiving shall

nimf398   pp,cs,nn3117   nn,pnx7133   ptn3808   himf5117   pr,pnx4480   pr5704

be eaten the same   day   that it is offered; he shall   not   leave any of it until the

nn1242

morning.

        wcj,cj518   cs,nn2077   nn,pnx7133   nn5088   cj176   nn5071

16 But   if   the sacrifice of his offering *be* a vow, or a voluntary offering, it

      nimf398   pp,cs,nn3117   hinc,pnx7126   (853)   nn,pnx2077   wcj,pr4480/nn4283

shall be eaten the same   day   that he offereth   his sacrifice: and on*the*morrow

         wcj,df,nipt3498   pr,pnx4480   nimf398

also the remainder   of   it shall be eaten:

         wcj,df,nipt3498   pr4480/cs,nn1320   df,nn2077   df,nuor7992 dfp,nn3117

17 But the remainder of*the*flesh of the sacrifice on the   third   day   shall be

nimf8313   dfp,nn784

burnt with fire.

        wcj,cj518   pr4480/cs,nn1320   cs,nn2077   pl,nn,pnx8002

18 And   if   *any* of*the*flesh of the   sacrifice   of his peace offerings be

nina398/nimf398   df,nuor7992 dfp,nn3117   ptn3808   nimf7521   ptn3808   nimf2803

eaten*at*all on the   third   day, it shall   not   be accepted, neither shall it be imputed

pp,pnx   df,hipt7126   pnx(853)   qmf1961   nn6292   wcj,df,nn5315

unto him that offereth   it: it shall   be   an abomination, and the   soul   that

df,qpta398 pr,pnx4480   qmf5375   nn,pnx5771

eateth   of   it shall bear his iniquity.

         wcj,df,nn1320 pnl834   qmf5060   pp,cs,nn3605   aj2931   ptn3808   nimf398

19 And the   flesh   that toucheth   any   unclean *thing* shall   not   be eaten; it

nimf8313   dfp,nn784   wcj,df,nn1320   cs,nn3605   aj2889   qmf398

shall be burnt with fire: and as for the   flesh,   all   that be clean shall eat

nn1320

thereof.

        wcj,df,nn5315 pnl834   qmf398   nn1320   pr4480/cs,nn2077   df,pl,nn8002

20 But the   soul   that eateth *of* the flesh of*the*sacrifice of peace offerings,

pnl834   pp,nn3068   wcj,nn,pnx2932   pr,pnx5921   df,pndm1931 df,nn5315

that *pertain* unto the LORD, having his uncleanness upon   him,   even   that   soul

     wcs,nipf3772   pr4480/pl,nn,pnx5971

shall be cut off from*his*people.

        wcj,nn5315   cj3588   qmf5060   pp,cs,nn3605   aj2931

21 Moreover the   soul   that shall touch   any   unclean *thing*, *as* the

pp,cs,nn2932   nn120   cj176   aj2931   pp,nn929   cj176 pp,cs,nn3605   nn8263   aj2931

uncleanness of man, or *any* unclean beast, or   any   abominable unclean *thing*,

wcs,qpf398   pr4480/cs,nn1320   cs,nn2077   df,pl,nn8002   pnl834

and   eat   of*the*flesh of the sacrifice of peace offerings, which *pertain* unto the

pp,nn3068   df,pndm1931 df,nn5315   wcs,nipf3772   pr4480/pl,nn,pnx5971

LORD, even   that   soul shall be cut off from*his*people.

        nn3068   wcs,pimf1696   pr413   nn4872   pp,qnc559

22 And the LORD spoke   unto Moses, saying,

        pimv1696   pr413   pl,cs,nn1121   nn3478   pp,qnc559   qmf398 ptn3808/cs,nn3605   nn2459

23 Speak unto the children of Israel, saying, Ye shall   eat   no manner of fat, of

nn7794   wcj,nn3775   wcj,nn5795

ox, or of sheep, or of goat.

        wcj,cs,nn2459   nn5038   wcj,cs,nn2459

24 And the   fat   of   the beast*that*dieth*of*itself, and the   fat   of

ⁿⁿ²⁹⁶⁶   ^{nimf6213}   ^{pp,cs,nn3605}   ⁿⁿ⁴³⁹⁹

that*which*is*torn*with*beasts,   may   be   used   in   any   other   use: but   ye

^{ptn3808/wcj,qna398/qmf,pnx398}

shall*in*no*wise*eat of it.

^{cj3588}   ^{cs,nn3605}   ^{qpta398}   ⁿⁿ²⁴⁵⁹   ^{pr4480}   ^{df,nn929}   ^{pnl834/pr,pnx4480}   ^{himf7126}

25 For   whosoever   eateth   the   fat   of   the   beast,   of   which   men   offer   an

ⁿⁿ⁸⁰¹   ^{pp,nn3068}   ^{df,nn5315}   ^{df,qpta398}   ^{wcs,nipf3772}

offering*made*by*fire unto the LORD, even the   soul   that eateth *it* shall be cut off

^{pr4480/pl,nn,pnx5971}

from*his*people.

^{qmf398}   ^{ptn3808/wcj,cs,nn3605}   ⁿⁿ¹⁸¹⁸   ^{dfp,nn5775}

26 Moreover ye shall   eat   no manner of blood, *whether it be* of fowl   or of

^{wcj,dfp,nn929}   ^{pp,cs,nn3605}   ^{pl,nn,pnx4186}

beast,   in   any   of your dwellings.

^{cs,nn3605}   ⁿⁿ⁵³¹⁵   ^{pnl834}   ^{qmf398}   ^{cs,nn3605}   ⁿⁿ¹⁸¹⁸   ^{df,pndm1931} ^{df,nn5315}

27 Whatsoever soul *it be* that eateth any manner of blood, even   that   soul

^{wcs,nipf3772}   ^{pr4480/pl,nn,pnx5971}

shall be cut off from*his*people.

ⁿⁿ³⁰⁶⁸   ^{wcs,pimf1696}   ^{pr413}   ⁿⁿ⁴⁸⁷²   ^{pp,qnc559}

28 And the LORD spoke   unto Moses, saying,

^{pimv1696}   ^{pr413}   ^{pl,cs,nn1121}   ⁿⁿ³⁴⁷⁸   ^{pp,qnc559}   ^{df,hipf7126}   (853)   ^{cs,nn2077}

29 Speak unto the children of Israel, saying, He that offereth   the sacrifice of

^{pl,nn,pnx8002}   ^{pp,nn3068}   ^{himf935} (853)   ^{nn,pnx7133}   ^{pp,nn3068}

his peace offerings unto the LORD shall bring   his oblation unto the LORD

^{pr4480/cs,nn2077}   ^{pl,nn,pnx8002}

of*the*sacrifice of his peace offerings.

^{du,nn,pnx3027}   ^{himf935} (853)   ^{pl,cs,nn801/nn3068}

30 His   own   hands   shall   bring   the offerings*of*the*LORD*made*by*fire,

(853)   ^{df,nn2459}   ^{pr5921}   ^{df,nn2373}   ^{himf,pnx935} (853)   ^{df,nn2373}

the   fat   with the breast, it shall he bring,   that the breast may be

^{pp,hinc5130/(pnx853)}   ⁿⁿ⁸⁵⁷³   ^{pp,pl,cs,nn6440}   ⁿⁿ³⁰⁶⁸

waved   *for* a wave offering before   the LORD.

^{df,nn3548}   ^{wcs,hipf6999} (853)   ^{df,nn2459}   ^{df,nn,lh4196}   ^{df,nn2373}

31 And the priest shall burn   the   fat   upon the altar: but the breast shall

^{wcs,qpf1961}   ^{pp,nn175}   ^{wcj,pp,pl,nn,pnx1121}

be   Aaron's and his   sons'.

^{wcj(853)}   ^{df,nn3225}   ^{cs,nn7785}   ^{qmf5414}   ^{dfp,nn3548}

32 And   the   right   shoulder   shall   ye   give   unto   the   priest   *for*   a

ⁿⁿ⁸⁶⁴¹   ^{pr4480/pl,cs,nn2077}   ^{pl,nn,pnx8002}

heave offering of*the*sacrifices of your peace offerings.

^{pr4480/pl,cs,nn1121}   ⁿⁿ¹⁷⁵   ^{df,hipf7126}   (853)   ^{cs,nn1818}

33 He   among*the*sons   of   Aaron,   that   offereth   the   blood   of   the

^{df,pl,nn8002}   ^{wcj(853)}   ^{df,nn2459}   ^{qmf1961/pp,pnx}   ^{df,nn3225}   ^{cs,nn7785}   ^{pp,nn4440}

peace offerings, and   the fat,   shall   have   the right shoulder for *his* part.

^{cj3588}   (853)   ^{df,nn8573} ^{cs,nn2373}   ^{wcj(853)}   ^{df,nn8641}   ^{cs,nn7785}   ^{qpf3947}   ^{pr4480/pr854}

34 For   the wave breast and   the heave shoulder have I taken   of   the

^{pl,cs,nn1121}   ⁿⁿ³⁴⁷⁸   ^{pr4480/pl,cs,nn2077}   ^{pl,nn,pnx8002}   ^{wcs,qmf5414}

children of Israel from*off*the*sacrifices of their peace offerings, and have   given

^{pnx(853)}   ^{pp,nn175}   ^{df,nn3548}   ^{wcj,pp,pl,nn,pnx1121}   ^{pp,cs,nn2706}   ⁿⁿ⁵⁷⁶⁹

   them unto Aaron the priest and unto his   sons   by   a   statute   forever

^{pr4480/pr854}   ^{pl,cs,nn1121}   ⁿⁿ³⁴⁷⁸

from among the children of Israel.

^{pndm2063}   ^{cs,nn4888}   ⁿⁿ¹⁷⁵   ^{wcj,cs,nn4888}

35 This   *is the portion* of the anointing of Aaron, and of the anointing of his

pl,nn,pnx**1121**   pr4480/pl,cs,nn801/nn**3068**   pp,cs,nn**3117**

sons,   out*of*the*offerings*of*the*Lord*made*by*fire,   in   the   day   *when* he

hipf**7126**   pnx(853)   pp,pinc**3547**/pp,nn**3068**

presented   them to minister*unto*the*Lord*in*the*priest's*office;

pnl**834**   nn**3068**   pipf**6680**   pp,qnc**5414**   pp,pnx   pr4480/pr854   pl,cs,nn**1121**

36 Which the Lord commanded to be given them   of   the children of

nn**3478**   pp,cs,nn**3117**   qnc,pnx**4886**   pnx(853)   cs,nn**2708**   nn**5769**

Israel, in the   day   that he anointed   them, *by* a statute forever throughout

pp,pl,nn,pnx**1755**

their generations.

pndm2063   df,nn**8451**   dfp,nn**5930**   dfp,nn**4503**

37 This *is* the   law   of the burnt offering, of the meat offering, and of the

wcj,dfp,nn**2403**   wcj,dfp,nn**817**   wcj,dfp,pl,nn**4394**

sin offering, and of the trespass offering, and of the consecrations, and of the

wcj,pp,cs,nn**2077**   df,pl,nn**8002**

sacrifice of the peace offerings;

pnl**834**   nn**3068**   pipf**6680**   (853)   nn**4872**   pp,cs,nn**2022**   nn**5514**   pp,cs,nn**3117**

38 Which the Lord commanded   Moses in mount Sinai, in the   day   that

pinc,pnx**6680**   (853)   pl,cs,nn**1121**   nn**3478**   pp,hinc**7126** (853)   pl,nn,pnx**7133**   pp,nn**3068**

he commanded   the children of Israel to offer   their oblations unto the Lord,

pp,cs,nn**4057**   nn**5514**

in the wilderness of Sinai.

Aaron and His Sons Are Ordained

nn**3068**   wcs,pimf**1696**   pr413   nn**4872**   pp,qnc**559**

8 And the Lord spoke   unto Moses, saying,

qmv**3947** (853)   nn**175**   wcj(853)   pl,nn,pnx**1121**   pr,pnx854   wcj(853)

2 Take   Aaron and   his   sons   with   him,   and   the

df,pl,nn**899**   wcj(853)   df,nn**4888**   cs,nn**8081**   wcj(853)   cs,nn**6499**   df,nn**2403**

garments, and   the anointing oil, and   a bullock for the sin offering, and

wcj(853)   du,cs,nu**8147** df,pl,nn**352**   wcj(853)   cs,nn**5536**   df,pl,nn**4682**

   two   rams, and   a basket of unleavened bread;

himv**6950**   wcj(853) cs,nn**3605**   df,nn**5712**   pr413   cs,nn**6607**

3 And gather thou   all   the congregation together unto the   door of the

cs,nn**168**   nn**4150**

tabernacle of the congregation.

nn**4872**   wcs,qmf**6213** pp,pnl**834**   nn**3068**   pipf**6680**   pnx(853)   df,nn**5712**

4 And Moses   did   as   the Lord commanded   him; and the assembly

wcs,nimf**6950**   pr413   cs,nn**6607**   cs,nn**168**   nn**4150**

was gathered together unto the door of the tabernacle of the congregation.

nn**4872**   wcs,qmf**559**   pr413   df,nn**5712**   pndm2088   df,nn**1697**   pnl**834**   nn**3068**

5 And Moses said   unto the congregation, This *is* the thing which the Lord

pipf**6680**   pp,qnc**6213**

commanded to be done.

nn**4872**   wcs,himf**7126** (853)   nn**175**   wcj(853)   pl,nn,pnx**1121**   wcs,qmf**7364** pnx(853)

6 And Moses brought   Aaron and   his   sons,   and washed   them

dfp,pl,nn**4325**

with water.

wcs,qmf**5414**   pr,pnx**5921**   (853)   df,nn**3801**   wcs,qmf**2296** pnx(853)   dfp,nn**73**

7 And he   put   upon   him   the coat, and girded   him with the girdle,

wcs,himf**3847** pnx(853)   pr854   df,nn**4598**   wcs,qmf**5414** (853)   df,nn**646**   pr,pnx**5921**

and clothed   him with the robe, and   put   the ephod upon him, and he wcs,qmf2296　pnx(853)　　　　　　　　　　　pp,cs,nn2805　　　　　df,nn646　　wcs,qmf640　　　pp,pnx

girded　　　　him with the curious girdle of the ephod, and bound *it* unto him

pp,pnx

therewith.

　　　　　　　wcs,qmf7760　(853)　　　df,nn2833　pr,pnx5921　　　　　　wcs,qmf5414　pr413

8 And he　put　　the breastplate upon him: also he　put　　in　the

df,nn2833　(853)　df,pl,nn224　wcj(853)　　df,pl,nn8550

breastplate　the Urim and　　the Thummim.

　　　　　wcs,qmf7760　(853)　　df,nn4701　pr5921　nn,pnx7218　pr5921　df,nn4701　　pr413

9 And he　put　　the miter upon his head; also upon the miter, *even* upon

pr4136/pl/nn,pnx6440　wcs,qmf7760　(853)　df,nn2091　cs,nn6731　df,nn6944　cs,nn5145　pp,pnl834　nn3068

his forefront, did he　put　　the golden plate, the holy crown; as　the LORD

pipf6680　(853)　nn4872

commanded　Moses.

　　　nn4872　wcs,qmf3947　(853)　df,nn4888　cs,nn8081　wcs,qmf4886　(853)　df,nn4908

10 And Moses took　　the anointing oil, and anointed　　the tabernacle

wcj(853)　cs,nn3605　pnl834　pp,pnx　　wcs,pimf6942　pnx(853)

and　　all that *was* therein, and sanctified　　them.

　　　wcs,himf5137　pr,pnx4480　pr5921　df,nn4196　nu7651　pl,nn6471　wcs,qmf4886　(853)

11 And he sprinkled thereof upon the altar seven times, and anointed　　the

df,nn4196　wcj(853)　df,cs,nn3605　pl,nn,pnx3627　wcj(853)　df,nn3595　wcj(853)　nn,pnx3653

altar and　　all　his vessels, both　　the laver and　　his foot, to

pp,pinc,pnx6942

sanctify them.

　　　wcs,qmf3332　pr4480/cs,nn8081/df,nn4888　pr5921　nn175　cs,nn7218　wcs,qmf4886　pnx(853)

12 And he poured of*the*anointing*oil upon Aaron's head, and anointed

pp,pinc,pnx6942

him, to sanctify him.

　　　nn4872　wcs,himf7126　(853)　nn175　pl,cs,nn1121　wcs,himf,pnx3847/pl,nn3801

13 And Moses brought　　Aaron's sons, and put*coats*upon them, and

wcs,qmf2296　pnx(853)　　　nn73　wcs,qmf2280　pl,nn4021　pp,pnx　pp,pnl834　nn3068

girded　　them with girdles, and　put　bonnets upon them; as　the LORD

pipf6680　(853)　nn4872

commanded　Moses.

　　　wcs,himf5066　(853)　cs,nn6499　　df,nn2403　nn175

14 And he brought　　the bullock for the sin offering: and Aaron and his

wcj,pl,nn,pnx1121　wcs,qmf5564　(853)　du,nn,pnx3027　pr5921　cs,nn7218　cs,nn6499

sons　　laid　　their hands upon the head of the bullock for the

df,nn2403

sin offering.

　　　wcs,qmf7819　nn4872　wcs,qmf3947　(853)　df,nn1818　wcs,qmf5414　pr5921

15 And he slew *it*; and Moses took　　the blood, and　put　*it* upon the

pl,cs,nn7161　df,nn4196　ad5439　pp,nn,pnx676　wcs,pimf2398　(853)　df,nn4196

horns of the altar round about with his finger, and purified　　the altar, and

qpf3332　wcj(853)　df,nn1818　pr413　cs,nn3247　df,nn4196　wcs,pimf,pnx6942

poured　　the blood at the bottom of the altar, and sanctified it, to

pp,pinc3722　pr,pnx5921

make reconciliation upon it.

　　　wcs,qmf3947　(853)　cs,nn3605　df,nn2459　pnl834　pr5921　df,nn7130　wcj(853)

16 And he took　　all the fat that *was* upon the inwards, and　　the

cs,nn3508　df,nn3516　wcj(853)　du,cs,nu8147　df,pl,nn3629　wcj(853)　nn,pnx2459

caul *above* the liver, and　　the two kidneys, and　　their fat, and

nn4872　wcs,himf6999　df,nn,lh4196

Moses burned *it* upon the altar.

　　　wcj(853)　df,nn6499　wcj(853)　nn,pnx5785　(wcj853)　nn,pnx1320　wcj(853)

17 But　　the bullock, and　　his hide,　　his flesh, and　　his

nn,pnx6569   qpf8313   dfp,nn784 pr4480/nn2351   dfp,nn4264 pp,pnl834   nn3068   pipf6680   (853)

dung, he burnt with fire without the camp; as the LORD commanded

nn4872

Moses.

wcs,himf7126 (853)   cs,nn352   df,nn5930   nn175

18 And he brought   the ram for the burnt offering: and Aaron and his

wcj,pl,nn,pnx1121 wcs,qmf5564 (853)   du,nn,pnx3027 pr5921   cs,nn7218   df,nn352

sons   laid   their hands upon the head of the ram.

wcs,qmf7819   nn4872   wcs,qmf2236   (853)   df,nn1818 pr5921   df,nn4196

19 And he killed it; and Moses sprinkled   the blood upon the altar

ad5439

round about.

pipf5408 wcj(853)   df,nn352   pp,pl,nn,pnx5409   nn4872 wcs,himf6999 (853)   df,nn7218

20 And he cut   the ram into pieces; and Moses burnt   the head,

wcj(853)   df,pl,nn5409   wcj(853)   df,nn6309

and   the pieces, and   the fat.

qpf7364   wcj(853)   df,nn7130   wcj(853)   df,du,nn3767   dfp,pl,nn4325   nn4872

21 And he washed   the inwards and   the legs in water; and Moses

wcs,himf6999 (853)   cs,nn3605 df,nn352   df,nn,lh4196 pnp1931   nn5930   nn5207

burnt   the whole ram upon the altar: it was a burnt sacrifice for a sweet

pp,cs,nn7381   (pnp1931)   nn801   pp,nn3068 pp,pnl834   nn3068

savor, and   an offering*made*by*fire unto the LORD; as   the LORD

pipf6680   (853)   nn4872

commanded   Moses.

wcs,himf7126 (853)   df,nuor8145 df,nn352 cs,nn352   df,pl,nn4394   nn175

22 And he brought   the other ram, the ram of consecration: and Aaron and

wcj,pl,nn,pnx1121 wcs,qmf5564 (853)   du,nn,pnx3027 pr5921   cs,nn7218   df,nn352

his sons laid   their hands upon the head of the ram.

wcs,qmf7819   nn4872 wcs,qmf3947 pr4480/nn,pnx1818   wcs,qmf5414 pr5921

23 And he slew it; and Moses took of*the*blood of it, and put it upon

cs,nn8571   nn175   df,aj3233 cs,nn241   wcj,pr5921   cs,nn931   df,aj3233 nn,pnx3027   wcj,pr5921

the tip of Aaron's right ear, and upon the thumb of his right hand, and upon

cs,nn931   df,aj3233 nn,pnx7272

the great toe of his right foot.

wcs,himf7126 (853)   nn175   pl,cs,nn1121   nn4872 wcs,qmf5414 pr4480   df,nn1818 pr5921

24 And he brought   Aaron's sons, and Moses put   of the blood upon

cs,nn8571   df,aj3233 nn,pnx241   wcj,pr5921   cs,nn931   df,aj3233 nn,pnx3027   wcj,pr5921

the tip of their right ear, and upon the thumbs of their right hands, and upon

cs,nn931   df,aj3233 nn,pnx7272   nn4872 wcs,qmf2236 (853)   df,nn1818 pr5921   df,nn4196

the great toes of their right feet: and Moses sprinkled   the blood upon the altar

ad5439

round about.

wcs,qmf3947 (853)   df,nn2459   wcj(853)   df,nn451   wcj(853) cs,nn3605   df,nn2459

25 And he took   the fat, and   the rump, and   all   the fat

pnl834   pr5921   df,nn7130   wcj(853)   cs,nn3508   df,nn3516   wcj(853)   du,cs,nu8147

that was upon the inwards, and   the caul above the liver, and   the two

df,pl,nn3629   wcj(853)   nn,pnx2459   wcj(853)   df,nn3225 cs,nn7785

kidneys, and   their fat, and   the right shoulder:

wcj,pr4480/cs,nn5536   df,pl,nn4682   pnl834   pp,pl,cs,nn6440   nn3068

26 And out*of*the*basket of unleavened bread, that was before the LORD, he

qpf3947 nu259   nn4682   cs,nn2471   nu259 wcj,cs,nn2471   nn8081 nn3899   nu259 wcj,nn7550

took one unleavened cake, and a   cake of oiled bread, and one wafer, and

wcs,qmf7760   pr5921   df,pl,nn2459   wcj,pr5921   df,nn3225 cs,nn7785

put them on the fat, and upon the right shoulder:

27 And he put all upon Aaron's hands, and upon his sons' hands, and waved them *for* a wave offering before the LORD.

28 And Moses took them from off their hands, and burnt *them* on the altar upon the burnt offering: they *were* consecrations for a sweet savor: it *is* an offering*made*by*fire unto the LORD.

29 And Moses took the breast, and waved it *for* a wave offering before the LORD: *for* of*the*ram of consecration it was Moses' part; as the LORD commanded Moses.

30 And Moses took of*the*anointing*oil, and of the blood which *was* upon the altar, and sprinkled *it* upon Aaron, *and* upon his garments, and upon his sons, and upon his sons' garments with him; and sanctified Aaron, *and* his garments, and his sons, and his sons' garments with him.

31 And Moses said unto Aaron and to his sons, Boil the flesh *at* the door of the tabernacle of the congregation: and there eat it with the bread that *is* in the basket of consecrations, as I commanded, saying, Aaron and his sons shall eat it.

32 And that which remaineth of the flesh and of the bread shall ye burn with fire.

33 And ye shall not go out of*the*door of the tabernacle of the congregation *in* seven days, until the days of your consecration be*at*an*end: for seven days shall he consecrate you.

34 As he hath done this day, *so* the LORD hath commanded to do, to make*an*atonement for you.

35 Therefore shall ye abide *at* the door of the tabernacle of the congregation day and night seven days, and keep the charge of the LORD, that ye die not: for so I am commanded.

36 So Aaron and his sons did all things which the LORD commanded by the hand of Moses.

Aaron Offers Sacrifices

9 wcs,qmf1961   df,nuor8066 dfp,nn3117   nn4872   qpf7121   pp,nn175
And it*came*to*pass on the eighth day, *that* Moses called Aaron and his

wcj,pp,pl,nn,pnx1121   wcj,pp,cs,aj2205   nn3478
sons,   and the elders of Israel;

wcs,qmf559 pr413   nn175   qmv3947 pp,pnx   cs,nn1121/nn1241 nn5695   pp,nn2403
2 And he said unto Aaron, Take thee a   young   calf for a sin offering, and

wcj,nn352   pp,nn5930   aj8549   wcj,himv7126   pp,pl,cs,nn6440   nn3068
a ram for a burnt offering, without blemish, and offer *them* before the LORD.

wcj,pr413   pl,cs,nn1121   nn3478   pimf1696   pp,qnc559 qmv3947   cs,nn8163
3 And unto the children of Israel thou shalt speak, saying, Take ye a kid of

pl,nn5795   pp,nn2403   wcj,nn5695   wcj,nn3532   pl,cs,nn1121 nn8141
the goats for a sin offering; and a calf and a lamb, *both* of the first year,

aj8549   pp,nn5930
without blemish, for a burnt offering;

wcj,nn7794   wcj,nn352   pp,pl,nn8002   pp,qnc2076 pp,pl,cs,nn6440
4 Also a bullock and a ram for peace offerings, to sacrifice before the

nn3068   wcj,nn4503   qptp1101   dfp,nn8081 cj3588 df,nn3117   nn3068   nipf7200
LORD; and a meat offering mingled with oil: for today the LORD will appear

pr,pnx413
unto you.

wcs,qmf3947 (853)   pnl834   nn4872   pipf6680   pr413/pl,cs,nn6440   cs,nn168
5 And they brought   *that* which Moses commanded before   the tabernacle

nn4150   cs,nn3605   df,nn5712   wcs,qmf7126   wcs,qmf5975 pp,pl,cs,nn6440
of the congregation: and all the congregation drew near and stood before the

nn3068
LORD.

nn4872 wcs,qmf559 pndm2088   df,nn1697 pnl834   nn3068   pipf6680
6 And Moses said, This *is* the thing which the LORD commanded that ye

qmf6213   cs,nn3519   nn3068   wcj,nicj7200 pr,pnx413
should do: and the glory of the LORD shall appear unto you.

nn4872 wcs,qmf559 pr413   nn175   qmv7126 pr413   df,nn4196   wcj,qmv6213 (853)
7 And Moses said unto Aaron, Go unto the altar, and offer   thy

nn,pnx2403   wcj(853)   nn,pnx5930   wcj,pimv3722   pr,pnx1157
sin offering, and   thy burnt offering, and make*an*atonement for thyself,

wcj,pr1157   df,nn5971   wcj,qmv6213 (853)   cs,nn7133   df,nn5971
and for the people: and offer   the offering of the people, and

wcj,pimv3722   pr,pnx1157   pp,pnl834   nn3068   pipf6680
make*an*atonement for them; as the LORD commanded.

nn175   wcs,qmf7126 pr413   df,nn4196   wcs,qmf7819 (853)   cs,nn5695
8 Aaron therefore went unto the altar, and slew   the calf of the

df,nn2403   pnl834   pp,pnx
sin offering, which *was* for himself.

pl,cs,nn1121   nn175 wcs,himf7126 (853)   df,nn1818 pr,pnx413   wcs,qmf2881
9 And the sons of Aaron brought   the blood unto him: and he dipped his

nn,pnx676   dfp,nn1818   wcs,qmf5414   pr5921   pl,cs,nn7161   df,nn4196   qpf3332   wcj(853)
finger in the blood, and   put *it* upon the horns of the altar, and poured out

df,nn1818 pr413   cs,nn3247   df,nn4196
the blood at the bottom of the altar:

wcj(853)   df,nn2459   wcj(853)   df,pl,nn3629   wcj(853)   df,nn3508   pr4480
10 But   the fat, and   the kidneys, and   the caul above the

df,nn3516 pr4480   df,nn2403   hipf6999   df,nn,lh4196 pp,pnl834   nn3068   pipf6680
liver of the sin offering, he burnt upon the altar; as the LORD commanded

(853)   nn4872
Moses.

wcj(853)   df,nn1320   wcj(853)   df,nn5785   qpf8313   dfp,nn784 pr4480/nn2351

11 And the flesh and the hide he burnt with fire without the

dfp,nn4264

camp.

wcs,qmf7819 (853)   df,nn5930   nn175 pl,cs,nn1121 wcs,himf4672 pr,pnx413

12 And he slew the burnt offering; and Aaron's sons presented unto

(853) df,nn1818   wcs,qmf,pnx2236 ad5439 pr5921 df,nn4196

him the blood, which he sprinkled round about upon the altar.

hipf4672 wcj(853)   df,nn5930   pr,pnx413   pp,pl,nn,pnx5409

13 And they presented the burnt offering unto him, with the pieces

wcj(853) df,nn7218 wcs,himf6999 pr5921 df,nn4196

thereof, and the head: and he burnt *them* upon the altar.

wcs,qmf7364 (853) df,nn7130 wcj(853) df,du,nn3767 wcs,himf6999

14 And he did wash the inwards and the legs, and burnt *them*

pr5921   df,nn5930   df,nn,lh4196

upon the burnt offering on the altar.

wcs,himf7126 (853) df,nn5971 cs,nn7133 wcs,qmf3947 (853) cs,nn8163 pnl834

15 And he brought the people's offering, and took the goat, which

df,nn2403 dfp,nn5971 wcs,qmf,pnx7819 wcs,pimf,pnx2398

was the sin offering for the people, and slew it, and offered*it*for*sin, as the

dfp,aj7223

first.

wcs,himf7126 (853) df,nn5930 wcs,qmf,pnx6213

16 And he brought the burnt offering, and offered it according to the

dfp,nn4941

manner.

wcs,himf7126 (853) df,nn4503 wcs,pimf4390/nn,pnx3709 pr,pnx4480

17 And he brought the meat offering, and took*a*handful thereof, and

wcs,himf6999 pr5921 df,nn4196 pr4480/pp,cs,nn905 cs,nn5930 df,nn1242

burnt *it* upon the altar, beside the burnt sacrifice of the morning.

wcs,qmf7819 (853) df,nn7794 wcj(853) df,nn352 cs,nn2077

18 He slew also the bullock and the ram *for* a sacrifice of

df,pl,nn8002 pnl834 dfp,nn5971 nn175 pl,cs,nn1121 wcs,himf4672 pr,pnx413

peace offerings, which *was* for the people: and Aaron's sons presented unto him

df,nn1818 wcs,qmf,pnx2236 pr5921 df,nn4196 ad5439

the blood, which he sprinkled upon the altar round about,

wcj(853) df,pl,nn2459 pr4480 df,nn7794 wcj,pr4480 df,nn352 df,nn451

19 And the fat of the bullock and of the ram, the rump, and

wcj,df,nn4374 wcj,df,pl,nn3629 wcj,cs,nn3508 df,nn3516

that*which*covereth *the inwards*, and the kidneys, and the caul *above* the liver:

wcs,qmf7760 (853) df,pl,nn2459 pr5921 df,pl,nn2373 wcs,himf6999 df,pl,nn2459

20 And they put the fat upon the breasts, and he burnt the fat

df,lh4196

upon the altar:

wcj(853) df,pl,nn2373 wcj(853) df,nn3225 cs,nn7785 nn175 hipf5130

21 And the breasts and the right shoulder Aaron waved *for* a

nn8573 pp,pl,cs,nn6440 nn3068 pp,pnl834 nn4872 pipf6680

wave offering before the LORD; as Moses commanded.

nn175 wcs,qmf5375 (853) du,nn,pnx3027 pr413 df,nn5971 wcs,pimf,pnx1288

22 And Aaron lifted up his hand toward the people, and blessed them,

wcs,qmf3381 pr4480/qnc6213 df,nn2403 wcj,df,nn5930

and came down from offering of the sin offering, and the burnt offering, and

wcj,df,pl,nn8002

peace offerings.

nn4872 wcj,nn175 wcs,qmf935 pr413 cs,nn168 nn4150

23 And Moses and Aaron went into the tabernacle of the congregation, and

wcs,qmf3318   wcs,pimf**1288** (853)   df,nn**5971**   cs,nn**3519**   nn**3068**   wcs,nimf**7200**   pr413

came out, and blessed   the people: and the glory of the LORD appeared unto

cs,nn**3605**   df,nn**5971**

all   the people.

wcs,qmf3318/nn784   pr4480/pp,pl,cs,nn**6440**   nn**3068**   wcs,qmf398   pr5921

24 And there came*a*fire*out from before the LORD, and consumed upon the

df,nn**4196** (853)   df,nn**5930**   wcj(853)   df,pl,nn**2459**   cs,nn**3605**   df,nn**5971**

altar   the burnt offering and   the   fat: *which* when   all   the people

wcs,qmf**7200**   wcs,qmf7442   wcs,qmf**5307** pr5921   pl,nn,pnx**6440**

saw,   they shouted, and   fell   on   their faces.

Nadab and Abihu Sin

     nn5070   wcj,nn30   pl,cs,nn**1121**   nn175   wcs,qmf3947   nn**376**

10 🗝 And Nadab and Abihu, the sons of Aaron, took either of

     nn,pnx4289   wcs,qmf5414 nn784   pp,pnp2004   wcs,qmf**7760**   nn**7004**   pr,pnx**5921**

them his censer, and   put   fire therein, and   put   incense thereon,

wcs,himf**7126**   qpta2114   nn784 pp,pl,cs,nn**6440**   nn**3068**   pnl834   pipf**6680**   pnx(853)   ptn**3808**

and offered strange fire before the LORD, which he commanded   them not.

     wcs,qmf3318   nn784   pr4480/pp,pl,cs,nn**6440**   nn**3068**   wcs,qmf398   pnx(853)

2 And there went out fire   from   the LORD, and devoured   them, and

     wcs,qmf**4191** pp,pl,cs,nn**6440**   nn**3068**

they died   before the LORD.

     nn4872   wcs,qmf**559**   pr413   nn175   pndm1931   pnl834   nn**3068**   pipf**1696**   pp,qnc**559**

3 Then Moses said unto Aaron, This *is it* that the LORD spoke, saying, I

nimf**6942**   pp,aj,pnx7138   wcj,pr5921/pl,cs,nn**6440** cs,nn**3605**   df,nn**5971**

will be sanctified in them*that*come*nigh me, and   before   all   the people I

nimf**3513**   nn175   wcs,qmf1826

will be glorified. And Aaron held*his*peace.

     nn4872   wcs,qmf**7121**/pr413   nn4332   wcj(pr413)   nn469   pl,cs,nn**1121**   nn5816

4 And Moses called Mishael and   Elzaphan, the sons of Uzziel the

cs,nn**1730**   nn175   wcs,qmf**559** pr,pnx413   qmv**7126**   qmv**5375** (853)   pl,nn,pnx251   pr4480/pr854

uncle of Aaron, and   said   unto them, Come near, carry   your brethren from

pl,cs,nn**6440**   df,nn**6944**   pr413/pr4480/nn2351   dfp,nn**4264**

before the sanctuary   out of   the camp.

     wcs,qmf**7126**   wcs,qmf,pnx**5375**   pp,pl,nn,pnx3801   pr413/pr4480/nn2351

5 So they went near, and   carried them in their   coats   out of   the

dfp,nn**4264** pp,pnl834   nn4872   pipf**1696**

camp;   as   Moses had said.

     nn4872   wcs,qmf**559**   pr413   nn175   wcj,pp,nn499   wcj,pp,nn385

6 And Moses said   unto Aaron, and unto Eleazar and unto Ithamar, his

pl,nn,pnx**1121**   qmf**6544**   ptn408   pl,nn,pnx**7218**   ptn**3808**   qmf6533   wcj,pl,nn,pnx899 wcj,ptn**3808**   qmf**4191**

sons, Uncover not your heads, neither rend your clothes;   lest ye die, and

---

🗝 **10:1–3**   Nadab and Abihu's sin in offering "strange fire" to Yahweh is not defined in the text. It is most likely that they performed some ceremony in a forbidden manner. Some have suggested that these newly consecrated priests were anxious to begin the more honorable portion of their duty, and so they proceeded to offer incense when they had not been commanded to do so. Special incense had been prepared for such an offering (Ex. 39:38). However, this incense was likely kept in the custody of Moses or Aaron, requiring Nadab and Abihu to use common incense. Hence, they were guilty of offering strange incense (Ex. 30:9). They may also have been drunk (see Lev. 10:9). Whatever their sinful action may have been, the punishment for it was swift and complete; another fire came forth from God and consumed them. There is a similar instance of judgment in the New Testament where Ananias and Sapphira died immediately after lying to God, and it had a beneficial sobering effect upon all who heard about it (Acts 5:1–11).

_{qmf7107}   _{wcj,pr5921}   _{cs,nn3605}   _{df,nn5712}   _{wcj,pl,nn,pnx251}   _{cs,nn3605}   _{cs,nn1004}

lest wrath come upon all the people: but let your brethren, the whole house of

_{nn3478}   _{qmf1058}   ₍₈₅₃₎   _{df,nn8316}   _{pnl834}   _{nn3068}   _{qpf8313}

Israel, bewail   the burning which the LORD hath kindled.

_{ptn3808}   _{qmf3318}   _{wcj,pr4480/cs,nn6607}   _{cs,nn168}   _{nn4150}

7 And ye shall not go out from*the*door of the tabernacle of the congregation,

_{cj6435}   _{qmf4191}   _{cj3588}   _{cs,nn4888}   _{cs,nn8081}   _{nn3068}   _{pr,pnx5921}   _{wcs,qmf6213}

lest ye die: for the anointing oil of the LORD *is* upon you. And they did

_{pp,cs,nn1697}   _{nn4872}

according to the word of Moses.

Rules for Priests

_{nn3068}   _{wcs,pimf1696}   _{pr413}   _{nn175}   _{pp,qnc559}

8 And the LORD spoke unto Aaron, saying,

_{ptn408}   _{qcj8354}   _{nn3196}   _{wcj,nn7941}   _{pnp859}   _{wcj,pl,nn,pnx1121}   _{pr,pnx854}

9 Do not drink wine nor strong drink, thou, nor thy sons with thee,

_{pp,qnc,pnx935}   _{pr413}   _{cs,nn168}   _{nn4150}   _{wcj,ptn3808}   _{qmf4191}

when ye go into the tabernacle of the congregation, lest ye die: *it shall be*

_{cs,nn2708}   _{nn5769}   _{pp,pl,nn,pnx1755}

a statute forever throughout your generations:

_{wcj,pp,hinc914}   _{pr996}   _{df,nn6944}   _{wcj(pr996)}   _{df,nn2455}

10 And that ye may put difference between holy and unholy, and

_{wcj,pr996}   _{df,aj2931}   _{wcj(pr996)}   _{df,aj2889}

between unclean and clean;

_{wcj,pp,hinc3384}   ₍₈₅₃₎   _{pl,cs,nn1121}   _{nn3478}   ₍₈₅₃₎   _{cs,nn3605}   _{df,pl,nn2706}

11 And that ye may teach the children of Israel all the statutes

_{pnl834}   _{nn3068}   _{pipf1696}   _{pr,pnx413}   _{pp,cs,nn3027}   _{nn4872}

which the LORD hath spoken unto them by the hand of Moses.

_{nn4872}   _{wcs,pimf1696}   _{pr413}   _{nn175}   _{wcj,pr413}   _{nn499}   _{wcj,pr413}   _{nn385}

12 And Moses spoke unto Aaron, and unto Eleazar and unto Ithamar, his

_{pl,nn,pnx1121}   _{df,pl,nipt3498}   _{qmv3947}   ₍₈₅₃₎   _{df,nn4503}   _{df,nipt3498}

sons that were left, Take the meat offering that remaineth

_{pr4480/pl,cs,nn801/nn3068}   _{wcj,qmv,pnx398}   _{pl,nn4682}   _{pr681}

of*the*offerings*of*the*LORD*made*by*fire, and eat it without leaven beside

_{df,nn4196}   _{cj3588}   _{pnp1931}   _{cs,nn6944/pl,nn6944}

the altar: for it *is* most holy:

_{wcj,qpf398}   _{pnx(853)}   _{aj6918}   _{pp,nn4725}   _{cj3588}   _{nn,pnx2706}

13 And ye shall eat it in the holy place, because it *is* thy due, and

_(pnp1931)   _{pl,nn,pnx1121}   _{wcj,cs,nn2706}   _{pr4480/pl,cs,nn801/nn3068}   _{cj3588}   _{ad3651}

thy sons' due, of*the*sacrifices*of*the*LORD*made*by*fire: for so I

_{pupf6680}

am commanded.

_{wcj(853)}   _{df,nn8573}   _{cs,nn2373}   _{wcj(853)}   _{df,nn8641}   _{cs,nn7785}   _{qmf398}   _{aj2889}

14 And the wave breast and heave shoulder shall ye eat in a clean

_{pp,nn4725}   _{pnp859}   _{wcj,pl,nn,pnx1121}   _{wcj,pl,nn,pnx1323}   _{pr,pnx854}   _{cj3588}   _{nn,pnx2706}

place; thou, and thy sons, and thy daughters with thee: for *they be* thy due,

_{pl,nn,pnx1121}   _{wcj,cs,nn2706}   _{pipf5414}   _{pr4480/pl,cs,nn2077}   _{pl,cs,nn8002}

and thy sons' due, *which* are given out*of*the*sacrifices of peace offerings of

_{pl,cs,nn1121}   _{nn3478}

the children of Israel.

_{df,nn8641}   _{cs,nn7785}   _{df,nn8573}   _{wcj,cs,nn2373}   _{himf935}   _{pr5921}

15 The heave shoulder and the wave breast shall they bring with the

_{pl,cs,nn801}   _{df,pl,nn2459}   _{pp,hinc5130}   _{nn8573}   _{pp,pl,cs,nn6440}

offerings*made*by*fire of the fat, to wave *it for* a wave offering before the

ptn408   pimf**8262**/(853)/pl,nn,pnx**5315**   pp,cs,nn3605   df,nn8318

43 Ye shall not make*yourselves*abominable with any creeping thing that

df,qpta8317   wcj,ptn**3808**   htmf**2930**   pp,pnx

creepeth, neither shall ye make*yourselves*unclean with them, that ye should be

wcs,nipf**2930**   pp,pnx

defiled thereby.

cj3588 pnp589   nn**3068**   pl,nn,pnx**430**   wcs,hipf**6942**

44 For I *am* the LORD your God: ye shall therefore sanctify yourselves,

wcs,qpf**1961**   aj**6918**   cj3588 pnp589   aj**6918**   wcj,ptn**3808**   pimf**2930**   (853)   pl,nn,pnx**5315**

and ye shall be holy; for I *am* holy: neither shall ye defile yourselves

pp,cs,nn3605   df,nn8318   df,qpta7430   pr5921   df,nn**776**

with any manner of creeping thing that creepeth upon the earth.

cj3588 pnp589   nn**3068**   df,hipt**5927**/pnx(853)   pr4480/cs,nn**776**   nn4714

45 For I *am* the LORD that bringeth*you*up out*of*the*land of Egypt, to

pp,qnc**1961** pp,pnx pp,pl,nn**430**   wcs,qpf**1961**   aj**6918**   cj3588 pnp589   aj**6918**

be your God: ye shall therefore be holy, for I *am* holy.

pndm2063   cs,nn**8451**   df,nn929   wcj,df,nn5775   wcj,cs,nn3605 df,aj**2416**

46 This *is* the law of the beasts, and of the fowl, and of every living

cs,nn**5315**   df,qpta7430   dfp,pl,nn**4325**   wcj,pp,cs,nn3605   nn**5315**   df,qpta8317   pr5921

creature that moveth in the waters, and of every creature that creepeth upon the

df,nn**776**

earth:

pp,hinc**914**   pr996   df,aj**2931**   wcj(pr996)   df,aj**2889**   wcj,pr996

47 To make*a*difference between the unclean and the clean, and between

df,nn**2416**   df,nipt398   wcj(pr996)   df,nn**2416** pnl834   ptn**3808**   nimf398

the beast that may be eaten and the beast that may not be eaten.

The Purification of Women After Childbirth

nn**3068**   wcs,pimf**1696**   pr413   nn4872   pp,qnc**559**

12 And the LORD spoke unto Moses, saying,

pimv**1696**   pr413   pl,cs,nn**1121**   nn3478   pp,qnc**559**   cj3588   nn**802**

2 Speak unto the children of Israel, saying, If a woman have

himf2232   wcs,qpf**3205**   nn2145   wcs,qpf**2930**   cs,nu7651 pl,nn**3117**

conceived seed, and borne a man child: then she shall be unclean seven days;

pp,pl,cs,nn**3117**   cs,nn5079   qnc,pnx1738   qmf**2930**

according to the days of the separation for her infirmity shall she be unclean.

df,nuor8066 wcj,dfp,nn**3117**   cs,nn**1320**   nn,pnx**6190**   nimf**4135**

3 And in the eighth day the flesh of his foreskin shall be circumcised.

qmf**3427**   pp,pl,cs,nn**1818**   nn2893   wcj,cs,nu7969   (pl,nn**3117**)

4 And she shall then continue in the blood of her purifying three

wcj,nu7970   nn**3117**   qmf**5060** ptn**3808**/pp,cs,nn3605   nn**6944**   ptn**3808** qmf935   wcj,pr413

and thirty days; she shall touch no hallowed thing, nor come into the

df,nn**4720**   pr5704   pl,cs,nn**3117**   nn,pnx**2892**   qnc4390

sanctuary, until the days of her purifying be fulfilled.

wcj,cj518   qmf3205   nn**5347**   wcs,qpf**2930**   du,nn7620

5 But if she bear a maid child, then she shall be unclean two weeks, as in

---

11:44, 45 The holiness of God is a major theme throughout the whole Old Testament, and particularly in the Book of Leviticus. God commands His people to reflect His holiness in their lives. Peter quotes these verses (see also Lev. 19:2; 20:26) to challenge his readers to live pure lives (1 Pet. 1:15, 16). God's people are to live holy lives because they have been separated from the world unto God (2 Cor. 6:17, quoted from Is. 52:11).

pp,nn,pnx5079   qmf3427   pr5921   pl,cs,nn1818   nn2893   wcj,pl,nu8346

her separation: and she shall continue in the blood of her purifying threescore
(nn3117)   wcj,cs,nu8337 pl,nn3117

and   six   days.

pl,cs,nn3117   nn,pnx2892   wcj,pp,qnc4390   pp,nn1121 cj176

6 And when the days of her purifying are fulfilled, for a son, or for a
pp,nn1323   himf935   nn3532   cs,nn1121 nn,pnx8141   pp,nn5930

daughter, she shall bring a lamb of the first year for a burnt offering, and a
wcj,cs,nn1121   nn3123   cj176   nn8449   pp,nn2403   pr413   cs,nn6607   cs,nn168

young pigeon, or a turtledove, for a sin offering, unto the door of the tabernacle
nn4150   pr413   df,nn3548

of the congregation, unto the priest:

wcs,hipf,pnx7126   pp,pl,cs,nn6440   nn3068   wcs,pipf3722   pr,pnx5921

7 Who shall offer   it before the LORD, and make*an*atonement for her;
wcs,qpf2891   pr4480/cs,nn4726   pl,nn,pnx1818 pndm2063   cs,nn8451

and she shall be cleansed from*the*issue of her blood. This is the law for her
df,qpta3205   dfp,nn2145 cj176   dfp,nn5347

that hath born a male or a female.

wcj,cj518   ptn3808 qmf4672/nn,pnx3027/cs,nn1767   nn7716   wcs,qpf3947 du,cs,nu8147

8 And if she be not able*to*bring a lamb, then she shall bring two
pl,nn8449   cj176 du,cs,nu8147 pl,cs,nn1121   nn3123   nu259   pp,nn5930   wcj,nu259

turtles, or two young pigeons; the one for the burnt offering, and the other for
pp,nn2403   df,nn3548   wcs,pipf3722   pr,pnx5921

a sin offering: and the priest shall make*an*atonement for her, and she shall
wcs,qpf2891

be clean.

Laws About Leprosy

nn3068 wcs,pimf1696 pr413   nn4872   wcj(pr413)   nn175   pp,qnc559

13 And the LORD spoke unto Moses and   Aaron, saying,
cj3588   nn120   qmf1961   pp,cs,nn5785   nn,pnx1320   nn7613   (cj176)

2 When a man shall have in the skin of his flesh a rising,
nn5597 cj176   nn934   wcs,qpf1961   pp,cs,nn5785   nn,pnx1320   pp,cs,nn5061

a scab, or bright spot, and it be in the skin of his flesh like the plague of
nn6883   wcs,hopf935 pr413   nn175   df,nn3548 cj176 pr413 nu259 pr4480/pl,nn,pnx1121

leprosy; then he shall be brought unto Aaron the priest, or unto one of*his*sons the
df,pl,nn3548

priests:

df,nn3548   wcs,qpf7200   (853)   df,nn5061   pp,cs,nn5785   df,nn1320

3 And the priest shall look on   the plague in the skin of the flesh: and
wcj,nn8181   dfp,nn5061   qpf2015   aj3836   df,nn5061   wcj,cs,nn4758   aj6013

when the hair in the plague is turned white, and the plague in sight be deeper
pr4480/cs,nn5785   nn,pnx1320 pnp1931   cs,nn5061   nn6883   df,nn3548   wcj,qpf,pnx7200

than*the*skin of his flesh, it is a plague of leprosy: and the priest shall look on
wcj,pipf2930/pnx(853)

him, and pronounce*him*unclean.
wcj,cj518   nn934   (pnp1931)   aj3836   pp,cs,nn5785   nn,pnx1320   nn,pnx4758

4 If the bright spot   be white in the skin of his flesh, and in sight

---

12:6–8 Compare the offering brought by Mary and Joseph to the temple soon after Jesus was born (Luke 2:24).

ptn369 wcj,aj6013 pr4480   df,nn**5785**   wcj,nn,pnx8181   ptn**3808** qpf**2015** aj3836
be not deeper than the skin, and the   hair   thereof be not turned white; then the

df,nn**3548**   wcj,hipf5462   (853)   df,nn**5061** cs,nu7651 pl,nn**3117**
priest shall shut up *him that hath*   the plague seven days:

df,nn**3548**   wcj,qpf,pnx**7200**   df,nuor7637 dfp,nn**3117**   wcj,ptdm2009
5 And the priest shall look on him the seventh day: and, behold, *if* the

df,nn**5061** pp,du,nn,pnx**5869**   qpf5975   df,nn**5061** qpf6581 ptn**3808**   dfp,nn**5785**
plague in his   sight   be*at*a*stay, *and* the plague spread not in the skin; then

df,nn**3548**   wcj,hipf,pnx5462   cs,nu7651 pl,nn**3117** nuor8145
the priest shall shut*him*up seven days more:

df,nn**3548**   wcj,qpf**7200**   pnx(853)   nuor8145   df,nuor7637 dfp,nn**3117**   wcj,ptdm2009
6 And the priest shall look on   him again the seventh day: and, behold, *if*

df,nn**5061**   aj3544   df,nn**5061** qpf6581 wcj,ptn**3808**   dfp,nn**5785**   df,nn**3548**
the plague *be* somewhat dark, *and* the plague spread   not   in the skin, the priest

wcj,pipf,pnx**2891**   pnp1931   nn4556   wcj,pipf3526   pl,nn,pnx899
shall pronounce*him*clean: it   *is but* a scab: and he shall wash his clothes, and

wcj,qpf**2891**
be clean.

wcj,cj518   df,nn4556   qna6581/qmf6581   dfp,nn**5785**   ad310
7 But   if   the scab spread*much*abroad in the skin, after that he hath been

ninc,pnx**7200** pr413   df,nn**3548**   pp,nn,pnx**2893**   wcs,nipf**7200** pr413   df,nn**3548** nuor8145
seen   of the priest for his cleansing, he shall be   seen   of the priest again:

df,nn**3548** wcs,qpf**7200**   wcj,ptdm2009   df,nn4556   qpf6581   dfp,nn**5785**
8 And *if* the priest   see   that, behold, the scab spreadeth in the skin, then

df,nn**3548**   wcj,pipf,pnx**2930**   pnp1931   nn6883
the priest shall pronounce*him*unclean: it   *is* a leprosy.

cj3588   cs,nn**5061**   nn6883 qmf**1961**   pp,nn120   wcs,hopf935 pr413
9 When the plague of leprosy   is   in a man, then he shall be brought unto the

df,nn**3548**
priest;

df,nn**3548**   wcs,qpf**7200**   wcj,ptdm2009   nn7613   aj3836
10 And the priest shall   see   *him*: and, behold, *if* the rising *be* white in the

dfp,nn**5785**   wcj,pnp1931   qpf**2015**   nn8181 aj3836   wcj,cs,nn4241 aj2416 nn1320
skin, and   it   have turned the hair white, and *there be* quick raw flesh in the

pp,nn7613
rising;

pnp1931   nipt3462   nn6883   pp,nn**5785**   nn,pnx1320   df,nn**3548**
11 It   *is* an   old   leprosy in the   skin   of his flesh, and the priest shall

wcj,pipf,pnx**2930**   ptn**3808** himf,pnx5462   cj3588 pnp1931   aj2931
pronounce*him*unclean, and shall not shut*him*up: for   he   *is* unclean.

wcj,cj518   df,nn6883   qna6524/qmf6524   dfp,nn**5785**   df,nn6883 wcs,pipf3680
12 And   if   a leprosy break*out*abroad in the skin, and the leprosy cover

(853) cs,nn3605   cs,nn**5785**   df,nn**5061**   pr4480/nn,pnx7218   wcj,pr5704
    all   the skin of *him that hath* the plague from*his*head even   to   his

du,nn,pnx7272   pp,cs,nn3605   df,nn**3548** cs,nn4758/du,cs,nn**5869**
foot,   wheresoever the priest   looketh;

df,nn**3548**   wcs,qpf**7200**   wcj,ptdm2009   df,nn6883   pipf3680   (853)
13 Then the priest shall consider: and, behold, *if* the leprosy have covered

cs,nn3605   nn,pnx1320   wcj,pipf**2891**   (853)   df,nn**5061**   nn,pnx3605
all   his flesh, he shall pronounce*him*clean *that hath*   the plague: it is   all

qpf**2015**   aj3836 pnp1931   aj2889
turned white: he   *is* clean.

wcj,pp,cs,nn**3117** aj2416 nn1320   ninc**7200**   pp,pnx   qmf**2930**
14 But   when   raw flesh appeareth in him, he shall be unclean.

df,nn**3548**   wcs,qpf**7200**   (853)   df,aj2416   df,nn1320
15 And   the   priest   shall   see   the   raw   flesh,   and

^{wcs,pipf,pnx2930}   ^{df,aj2416} ^{df,nn1320} ^(pnp1931)   ^{aj2931}   ^{pnp1931}
pronounce*him*to*be*unclean: *for* the raw flesh   *is* unclean: it *is* a
ⁿⁿ⁶⁸⁸³
leprosy.

^{cj176} ^{cj3588}   ^{df,aj2416} ^{df,nn1320} ^{qmf7725}   ^{wcs,nipf2015}   ^{pp,aj3836}
16 Or if the raw flesh turn again, and be changed unto white, he shall
^{wcs,qpf935} ^{pr413}   ^{df,nn3548}
come unto the priest;

^{df,nn3548}   ^{wcs,qpf,pnx7200}   ^{wcj,ptdm2009}   ^{df,nn5061}   ^{nipf2015}
17 And the priest shall   see   him: and, behold, *if* the plague be turned into
^{pp,aj3836}   ^{df,nn3548}   ^{wcj,pipf2891}   ⁽⁸⁵³⁾   ^{df,nn5061} ^{pnp1931}
white; then the priest shall pronounce*him*clean *that hath*   the plague: he *is*
^{aj2889}
clean.

^{wcj,nn1320}   ^{pp,pnx}   ^{pp,nn,pnx5785}   ^{cj3588/qmf1961} ⁿⁿ⁷⁸²²
18 The flesh also, in which, *even* in the skin thereof, was a boil, and
^{wcs,nipf7495}
is healed,

^{pp,cs,nn4725}   ^{df,nn7822}   ^{wcs,qpf1961} ^{aj3836}   ⁿⁿ⁷⁶¹³ ^{cj176}
19 And in the place of the boil there be a white rising, or a
ⁿⁿ⁹³⁴   ^{aj3836}   ^{aj125}   ^{wcs,nipf7200} ^{pr413}   ^{df,nn3548}
bright spot, white, and somewhat reddish, and it be showed to the priest;

^{df,nn3548} ^{wcs,qpf7200}   ^{wcj,ptdm2009}   ^{nn,pnx4758} ^{aj8217} ^{pr4480}
20 And if, when the priest seeth it, behold, it *be* in sight lower than the
^{df,nn5785}   ^{wcj,nn,pnx8181}   ^{qpf2015}   ^{aj3836}   ^{df,nn3548}
skin, and the   hair   thereof be turned white; the priest shall
^{wcj,pipf,pnx2930}   ^{pnp1931} ^{cs,nn5061}   ⁿⁿ⁶⁸⁸³ ^{qpf6524}   ^{dfp,nn7822}
pronounce*him*unclean: it *is* a plague of leprosy broken out of the boil.

^{wcj,cj518}   ^{df,nn3548} ^{qmf,pnx7200}   ^{wcj,ptdm2009}   ^{ptn369} ^{aj3836} ⁿⁿ⁸¹⁸¹
21 But if the priest look on it, and, behold, *there be* no white hairs
^{pp,pnx}   ^{ptn369} ^{wcj,aj8217} ^{pr4480}   ^{df,nn5785}   ^{wcj(pnp1931)}   ^{aj3544}
therein, and *if* it *be* not lower than the skin, but   *be* somewhat dark; then
^{df,nn3548}   ^{wcs,hipf,pnx5462} ^{cs,nu7651} ^{pl,nn3117}
the priest shall shut*him*up seven days:

^{wcj,cj518}   ^{qna6581/qmf6581}   ^{dfp,nn5785}   ^{df,nn3548}
22 And if it spread*much*abroad in the skin, then the priest shall
^{wcs,pipf2930/pnx(853)}   ^{pnp1931}   ⁿⁿ⁵⁰⁶¹
pronounce*him*unclean: it *is* a plague.

^{wcj,cj518}   ^{df,nn934} ^{qmf5975}   ^{pr,pnx8478}   ^{qpf6581} ^{ptn3808} ^{pnp1931}
23 But if the bright spot stay in his place, *and* spread not, it *is* a
^{cs,nn6867} ^{df,nn7822}   ^{df,nn3548}   ^{wcj,pipf,pnx2891}
burning boil; and the priest shall pronounce*him*clean.

^{cj176} ^{cj3588}   ^{qmf1961}   ⁿⁿ¹³²⁰   ^{pp,nn,pnx5785}   ⁿⁿ⁷⁸⁴ ^{cs,nn4348}
24 Or if there be *any* flesh, in the skin whereof *there is* a hot burning,
^{cs,nn4241}   ^{df,nn4348} ^{wcs,qpf1961} ^{aj3836}   ⁿⁿ⁹³⁴   ^{aj125}   ^{cj176}
and the quick *flesh* that burneth have a white bright spot, somewhat reddish, or
^{aj3836}
white;

^{df,nn3548}   ^{wcs,qpf7200}   ^{pnx(853)}   ^{wcj,ptdm2009}   ⁿⁿ⁸¹⁸¹
25 Then the priest shall look upon   it: and, behold, *if* the hair in the
^{dfp,nn934}   ^{nipf2015} ^{aj3836}   ^{wcj,nn,pnx4758} ^{aj6013} ^{pr4480} ^{df,nn5785} ^{pnp1931}
bright spot be turned white, and it *be in* sight deeper than the skin; it *is* a
ⁿⁿ⁶⁸⁸³   ^{qpf6524}   ^{dfp,nn4348}   ^{df,nn3548}
leprosy broken out of the burning: wherefore the priest shall
^{wcj,pipf2930/pnx(853)}   ^{pnp1931}   ^{cs,nn5061}   ⁿⁿ⁶⁸⁸³
pronounce*him*unclean: it *is* the plague of leprosy.

wcj,cj518 df,nn3548 qmf,pnx7200 wcj,ptdm2009 ptn369 aj3836 nn8181

26 But if the priest look on it, and, behold, *there be* no white hair in the

df,nn934   ptn,pnx369 wcj,aj8217 pr4480   df,nn5785 wcj(pnp1931)

bright spot, and it *be* no lower than the *other* skin, but *be*

aj3544 df,nn3548 wcs,hipf,pnx5462 cs,nu7651 pl,nn3117

somewhat dark; then the priest shall shut*him*up seven days:

df,nn3548 wcs,qpf,pnx7200 df,nuor7637 dfp,nn3117 cj518

27 And the priest shall look upon him the seventh day: *and* if it be

qna6581/qmf6581 dfp,nn5785   df,nn3548 wcs,pipf2930/pnx(853) pnp1931

spread*much*abroad in the skin, then the priest shall pronounce*him*unclean: it

cs,nn5061 nn6883

is the plague of leprosy.

wcj,cj518 df,nn934 qmf5975 pr,pnx8478 qpf6581 ptn3808 dfp,nn5785

28 And if the bright spot stay in his place, *and* spread not in the skin,

wcj,pnp1931 aj3544 pnp1931 cs,nn7613 df,nn4348 df,nn3548

but it *be* somewhat dark; it *is* a rising of the burning, and the priest shall

wcj,pipf,pnx2891 cj3588 pnp1931 cs,nn6867 df,nn4348

pronounce*him*clean: for it *is* an inflammation of the burning.

cj3588 wcj,nn376 cj176 nn802 pp,pnx/qmf1961 nn5061   pp,nn7218 cj176 pp,nn2206

29 If a man or woman have a plague upon the head or the beard;

df,nn3548 wcs,qpf7200 (853) df,nn5061 wcj,ptdm2009 nn,pnx4758

30 Then the priest shall see the plague: and, behold, if it *be* in sight

aj6013 pr4480 df,nn5785 wcj,pp,pnx aj6669 aj1851 nn8181 df,nn3548

deeper than the skin; *and there be* in it a yellow thin hair; then the priest shall

wcs,pipf2930/pnx(853) pnp1931 nn5424 (pnp1931) cs,nn6883 df,nn7218

pronounce*him*unclean: it *is* a dry scurf, *even* a leprosy upon the head

cj176 df,nn2206

or beard.

wcj,cj3588 df,nn3548 qmf7200 (853) cs,nn5061 df,nn5424 wcj,ptdm2009

31 And if the priest look on the plague of the scurf, and, behold, it *be*

ptn369 nn,pnx4758 aj6013 pr4480 df,nn5785   ptn369 aj7838 wcj,nn8181 pp,pnx

not in sight deeper than the skin, and *that there is* no black hair in it; then the

df,nn3548 wcs,hipf5462 (853) cs,nn5061 df,nn5424 cs,nu7651 pl,nn3117

priest shall shut up *him that hath* the plague of the scurf seven days:

df,nuor7637 dfp,nn3117 df,nn3548 wcs,qpf7200 (853) df,nn5061

32 And in the seventh day the priest shall look on the plague: and,

wcj,ptdm2009 df,nn5424 qpf6581 ptn3808 qpf1961 pp,pnx wcj,ptn3808 aj6669 nn8181

behold, *if* the scurf spread not, and there be in it no yellow hair, and the

df,nn5424 ptn369 wcj,cs,nn4758 aj6013 pr4480 df,nn5785

scurf *be* not in sight deeper than the skin;

wcj,htpf1548 wcj(853) df,nn5424 ptn3808 pimf1548 df,nn3548

33 He shall be shaven, but the scurf shall he not shave; and the priest

wcs,hipf5462 (853) df,nn5424 cs,nu7651 pl,nn3117 nuor8145

shall shut up *him that hath* the scurf seven days more:

df,nuor7637 dfp,nn3117 df,nn3548 wcs,qpf7200 (853) df,nn5424 wcj,ptdm2009

34 And in the seventh day the priest shall look on the scurf: and, behold,

df,nn5424 ptn3808 qpf6581 dfp,nn5785 ptn,pnx369 wcj,nn,pnx4758 aj6013 pr4480 df,nn5785

if the scurf be not spread in the skin, nor *be* in sight deeper than the skin;

df,nn3548 wcj,pipf2891/pnx(853)   wcj,pipf3526 pl,nn,pnx899

then the priest shall pronounce*him*clean: and he shall wash his clothes, and

wcj,qpf2891

be clean.

wcj,cj518 df,nn5424 qna6581/qmf6581 dfp,nn5785 pr310 nn,pnx2893

35 But if the scurf spread much in the skin after his cleansing;

^{df,nn3548}   ^{wcs,qpf,pnx7200}   ^{wcj,ptdm2009}   ^{df,nn5424}   ^{qpf6581}

36 Then the priest shall look on him: and, behold, if the scurf be spread in

^{dfp,nn5785}   ^{df,nn3548}   ^{ptn3808} ^{pimf1239}   ^{df,aj6669} ^{dfp,nn8181} ^{pnp1931}   ^{aj2931}

the skin, the priest shall not seek for yellow hair; he is unclean.

^{wcj,cj518}   ^{df,nn5424}   ^{pp,du,nn,pnx5869}   ^{qpf5975}   ^{aj7838}

37 But if the scurf be in his   sight at*a*stay, and that there is black

^{wcj,nn8181}   ^{qpf6779}   ^{pp,pnx}   ^{df,nn5424} ^{nipf7495} ^{pnp1931}   ^{aj2889}   ^{df,nn3548}

hair grown up therein; the scurf is healed, he is clean: and the priest shall

^{wcj,pipf,pnx2891}

pronounce*him*clean.

^{cj3588}   ^{wcj,nn376}   ^{cj176}   ⁿⁿ⁸⁰²   ^{qmf1961}   ^{pp,cs,nn5785}   ^{nn,pnx1320}

38 If a man also or a woman have in the   skin   of their flesh

^{pl,nn934}   ^{aj3836}   ^{pl,nn934}

bright spots, even white bright spots;

^{df,nn3548}   ^{wcs,qpf7200}   ^{wcj,ptdm2009}   ^{pl,nn934}   ^{pp,cs,nn5785}

39 Then the priest shall look: and, behold, if the bright spots in the skin of

^{nn,pnx1320}   ^{aj3544}   ^{aj3836}   ^{pnp1931}   ⁿⁿ⁹³³   ^{qpf6524}   ^{dfp,nn5785} ^{pnp1931}

their flesh be darkish white; it is a freckled spot that groweth in the skin; he

^{aj2889}

is clean.

^{wcj,nn376}   ^{cj3588}   ^{nimf4803}   ^{nn,pnx7218} ^{pnp1931}   ^{aj7142}   ^{pnp1931}

40 And the man whose hair*is*fallen*off his head, he is bald; yet is he

^{aj2889}

clean.

^{wcj(cj518)}   ^{nimf4803}   ^{pr4480/cs,nn6285}   ^{nn,pnx7218}

41 And   he that hath*his*hair*fallen*off from*the*part of his head

^{pl,nn,pnx6440} ^{pnp1931}   ^{aj1371}   ^{pnp1931} ^{aj2889}

toward his face, he is forehead bald: yet is he clean.

^{wcj,cj3588}   ^{qmf1961}   ^{dfp,nn7146} ^{cj176}   ^{dfp,nn1372}   ^{aj3836}   ^{aj125}

42 And if there be in the bald head, or bald forehead, a white reddish

ⁿⁿ⁵⁰⁶¹ ^{pnp1931}   ⁿⁿ⁶⁸⁸³   ^{qpta6524}   ^{pp,nn,pnx7146} ^{cj176}   ^{pp,nn,pnx1372}

sore; it is a leprosy sprung up in his bald head, or his bald forehead.

^{df,nn3548}   ^{wcs,qpf7200} ^{pnx(853)}   ^{wcj,ptdm2009}   ^{cs,nn7613}

43 Then the priest shall look upon   it: and, behold, if the rising of the

^{df,nn5061} ^{aj3836}   ^{aj125}   ^{pp,nn,pnx7146} ^{cj176}   ^{pp,nn,pnx1372}   ^{cs,nn6883}

sore be white reddish in his bald head, or in his bald forehead, as the leprosy

^{pp,cs,nn4758}   ^{cs,nn5785}   ⁿⁿ¹³²⁰

appeareth in the skin of the flesh;

^{pnp1931}   ^{qptp6879}   ⁿⁿ³⁷⁶   ^{pnp1931}   ^{aj2931}   ^{df,nn3548}

44 He is a leprous man,   he is unclean: the priest shall

^{pina2930/pimf,pnx2930}   ^{nn,pnx5061}   ^{pp,nn,pnx7218}

pronounce*him*utterly*unclean; his plague is in his head.

^{wcj,df,qptp6879} ^{pp,pnx} ^{pnl834}   ^{df,nn5061}   ^{pl,nn,pnx899}   ^{qmf1961} ^{pl,qptp6533}

45 And the leper in whom the plague is, his clothes shall be rent, and

^{wcj,nn,pnx7218} ^(qmf1961) ^{qptp6544}   ^{qmf5844}   ^{wcj,pr5921}   ⁿⁿ⁸²²²

his head   bare, and he shall put*a*covering upon his upper lip, and shall

^{qmf7121} ^{wcj,aj2931}   ^{aj2931}

cry, Unclean, unclean.

^{cs,nn3605}   ^{pl,cs,nn3117}   ^{pnl834}   ^{df,nn5061}   ^{pp,pnx}   ^{qmf2930}

46 All the days wherein the plague shall be in him he shall be defiled;

^{pnp1931}   ^{aj2931}   ^{qmf3427}   ⁿⁿ⁹¹⁰ ^{pr4480/nn2351}   ^{dfp,nn4264}   ^{nn,pnx4186}

he is unclean: he shall dwell alone; without the camp shall his habitation be.

Cleansing a Leper's Garment

^{wcj,df,nn899}   ^{cj3588}   ^{cs,nn5061}   ⁿⁿ⁶⁸⁸³   ^{qmf1961} ^{pp,pnx}   ⁿⁿ⁶⁷⁸⁵

47 The garment also that the plague of leprosy   is   in, *whether it be* a woolen

^{pp,cs,nn899}   ^{cj176}   ^{pl,nn6593}   ^{pp,cs,nn899}

garment, or a linen garment;

^{cj176}   ^{pp,nn8359} ^{cj176} ^{pp,nn6154}   ^{dfp,pl,nn6593}   ^{wcj,dfp,nn6785}   ^{cj176}

48 Whether *it be* in the warp, or woof; of linen, or of woolen; whether in a

^{pp,nn5785} ^{cj176}   ^{pp,cs,nn3605}   ^{cs,nn4399}   ⁿⁿ⁵⁷⁸⁵

skin, or in   any   thing made of skin;

^{df,nn5061}   ^{wcs,qpf1961}   ^{aj3422}   ^{cj176}   ^{aj125}   ^{dfp,nn899}   ^{cj176}

49 And if the plague   be   greenish or reddish in the garment, or in the

^{dfp,nn5785}   ^{cj176}   ^{dfp,nn8359} ^{cj176}   ^{dfp,nn6154} ^{cj176}   ^{pp,cs,nn3605} ^{cs,nn3627}   ⁿⁿ⁵⁷⁸⁵ ^{pnp1931}

skin, either in the warp, or in the woof, or in   any   thing of skin;   it   *is* a

^{cs,nn5061}   ⁿⁿ⁶⁸⁸³   ^{wcs,hopf7200} ⁽⁸⁵³⁾   ^{df,nn3548}

plague of leprosy, and shall be showed   unto the priest:

^{df,nn3548}   ^{wcs,qpf7200}   ⁽⁸⁵³⁾   ^{df,nn5061}   ^{wcs,hipf5462}   ⁽⁸⁵³⁾

50 And the priest shall look upon   the plague, and shut up *it that hath*

^{df,nn5061} ^{cs,nu7651} ^{pl,nn3117}

the plague seven days:

^{wcs,qpf7200}   ⁽⁸⁵³⁾   ^{df,nn5061}   ^{df,nuor7637} ^{dfp,nn3117} ^{cj3588}   ^{df,nn5061}

51 And he shall look on   the plague on the seventh day: if the plague be

^{qpf6581}   ^{dfp,nn899}   ^{cj176}   ^{dfp,nn8359} ^{cj176}   ^{dfp,nn6154} ^{cj176}   ^{dfp,nn5785}

spread in the garment, either in the warp, or in the woof, or in a skin, *or* in

^{pp,nn3605} ^{pp,nn4399} ^{pnl834}   ^{nimf6213}   ^{df,nn5785}   ^{df,nn5061}   ^{hipt3992}   ⁿⁿ⁶⁸⁸³   ^{pnp1931}   ^{aj2931}

any   work that is made of skin; the plague *is* a fretting leprosy;   it   *is* unclean.

^{wcs,qpf8313 (853)}   ^{df,nn899}   ^{cj176}   ⁽⁸⁵³⁾ ^{df,nn8359} ^{cj176} ⁽⁸⁵³⁾ ^{df,nn6154}

52 He shall therefore burn   that garment, whether   warp   or   woof, in

^{dfp,nn6785} ^{cj176}   ^{dfp,pl,nn6593} ^{cj176} ⁽⁸⁵³⁾ ^{cs,nn3605} ^{cs,nn3627}   ^{df,nn5785} ^{pnl834/pp,pnx}   ^{df,nn5061} ^{qmf1961} ^{cj3588}

woolen or in linen, or   any   thing of skin, wherein the plague   is: for

^{pnp1931}   ^{hipt3992}   ⁿⁿ⁶⁸⁸³   ^{nimf8313}   ^{dfp,nn784}

it   *is* a fretting leprosy; it shall be burnt in the fire.

^{wcj,cj518}   ^{df,nn3548}   ^{qmf7200}   ^{wcj,ptdm2009}   ^{df,nn5061}   ^{ptn3808}   ^{qpf6581}

53 And   if   the priest shall look, and, behold, the plague be   not   spread in

^{dfp,nn899}   ^{cj176}   ^{dfp,nn8359} ^{cj176}   ^{dfp,nn6154} ^{cj176}   ^{pp,cs,nn3605} ^{cs,nn3627}   ⁿⁿ⁵⁷⁸⁵

the garment, either in the warp, or in the woof, or in   any   thing of skin;

^{df,nn3548}   ^{wcj,pipf6680}   ^{wcj,pipf3526}   ⁽⁸⁵³⁾ ^{pnl834/pp,pnx}

54 Then the priest shall command that they wash *the thing*   wherein the

^{df,nn5061}   ^{wcj,hipf,pnx5462} ^{cs,nu7651} ^{pl,nn3117} ^{nuor8145}

plague *is*, and he shall shut*it*up seven days more:

^{df,nn3548}   ^{wcj,qpf7200}   ⁽⁸⁵³⁾   ^{df,nn5061}   ^{ad310}   ^{hotnc*3526}

55 And the priest shall look on   the plague, after that it is washed: and,

^{wcj,ptdm2009}   ^{df,nn5061}   ^{ptn3808}   ^{qpf2015}   ⁽⁸⁵³⁾   ^{nn,pnx5869}   ^{wcj,df,nn5061}   ^{ptn3808}

behold, *if* the plague have   not   changed   his color, and the plague be   not

^{qpf6581}   ^{pnp1931}   ^{aj2931}   ^{qmf,pnx8313}   ^{dfp,nn784} ^{pnp1931}   ⁿⁿ⁶³⁵⁶

spread;   it   *is* unclean; thou shalt   burn   it in the fire;   it   *is* fret inward,

^{pp,nn,pnx7146}   ^{cj176} ^{pp,nn,pnx1372}

whether it *be* bare within or without.

^{wcj,cj518}   ^{df,nn3548} ^{qpf7200}   ^{wcj,ptdm2009}   ^{df,nn5061}   ^{aj3544}   ^{ad310}

56 And   if   the priest look, and, behold, the plague *be* somewhat dark after

^{hotnc3526}   ^{pnx(853)}   ^{wcj,qpf7167} ^{pnx(853)}   ^{pr4480}   ^{df,nn899} ^{cj176}   ^{pr4480}

the washing   of it; then he shall   rend   it out of the garment, or out of

^{df,nn5785} ^{cj176}   ^{pr4480}   ^{df,nn8359} ^{cj176}   ^{pr4480}   ^{df,nn6154}

the skin, or out of the warp, or out of the woof:

^{wcj,cj518}   ^{nimf7200} ^{ad5750}   ^{dfp,nn899}   ^{cj176}   ^{dfp,nn8359} ^{cj176}   ^{dfp,nn6154}

57 And   if   it appear still in the garment, either in the warp, or in the woof,

cj176   pp,cs,nn3605 cs,nn3627   nn5785 pnp1931   qpta6524   qmf,pnx8313 (853)

or in   any   thing of skin;   it   *is* a spreading *plague*: thou shalt   burn   that

pnl834/pp,pnx   df,nn5061   dfp,nn784

wherein the plague *is* with fire.

wcj,df,nn899   cj176   df,nn8359 cj176 df,nn6154 cj176   cs,nn3605   cs,nn3627   df,nn5785

58 And the garment, either warp,   or   woof,   or   whatsoever thing of skin *it be*,

pnl834   pimf3526   df,nn5061   wcs,qpf5493   pr,pnx4480

which thou shalt   wash,   if the plague be departed   from   them, then it shall be

wcs,pupf3526   nuor8145   wcs,qpf2891

washed the second time,   and shall be clean.

pndm2063   cs,nn8451   cs,nn5061   nn6883   cs,nn899   df,nn6785 cj176

59 This *is* the   law   of the plague of leprosy in a garment of woolen or

df,pl,nn6593   cj176   df,nn8359   cj176   df,nn6154   cj176   cs,nn3605   cs,nn3627   nn5785

linen,   either   in   the   warp,   or   woof,   or   any   thing   of   skins,   to

pp,pinc,pnx2891   cj176   pp,pinc,pnx2930

pronounce*it*clean,   or to pronounce*it*unclean.

Purification of a Leper

nn3068   wcs,pimf1696   pr413   nn4872   pp,qnc559

14

And the LORD spoke unto Moses, saying,

pndm2063   qmf1961   cs,nn8451   df,pupt6879   pp,cs,nn3117

2 This shall   be   the   law   of the   leper   in the   day   of his

nn,pnx2893   wcs,hopf935   pr413   df,nn3548

cleansing: He shall be brought unto the priest:

df,nn3548   wcs,qpf3318   pr413/pr4480/nn2351   dfp,nn4264   df,nn3548   wcs,qpf7200

3 And the priest shall go forth   out of   the camp; and the priest shall   look,

wcj,ptdm2009   cs,nn5061   df,nn6883   nipf7495   pr4480   df,qptp6879

and, behold, *if* the plague of leprosy be healed   in   the leper;

df,nn3548   wcj,pipf6680   wcj,qpf3947   dfp,htpt2891

4 Then shall the priest command to   take   for him that is to be cleansed

du,cs,nu8147 pl,nn6833 aj2416   aj2889   nn730 wcj,cs,nn6086   wcj,cs,nn8144/nn8438   wcj,nn231

two   birds alive *and* clean, and cedar   wood,   and   scarlet,   and hyssop:

df,nn3548   wcj,pipf6680   (853)   df,nu259   df,nn6833   wcj,qpf7819 pr413

5 And the priest shall command   that one of the birds be killed   in   an

nn2789   cs,nn3627 pr5921   aj2416   pl,nn4325

earthen vessel over running water:

(853)   df,aj2416 df,nn6833   qmf3947 pnx(853)   wcj(853)   df,nn730 cs,nn6086

6 As for   the living bird, he shall take   it, and   the cedar wood,

wcj(853)   cs,nn8144/df,nn8438   wcj(853)   df,nn231   wcs,qpf2881 pnx(853)   wcj(853)

and   the   scarlet,   and   the hyssop, and shall   dip   them and

df,aj2416 df,nn6833   pp,cs,nn1818   df,nn6883   df,qptp7819 pr5921   df,aj2416 df,pl,nn4325

the living bird in the blood of the bird *that was* killed over the running water:

wcs,hipf5137   pr5921   df,htpt2891   pr4480   df,nn6883 nu7651

7 And he shall sprinkle upon him that is to be cleansed from the leprosy seven

pl,nn6471   wcs,pipf,pnx2891   (853)   df,aj2416 df,nn6833 wcs,pipf7971 pr5921

times, and shall pronounce*him*clean, and shall let   the living bird   loose into

pl,cs,nn6440 df,nn7704

the open   field.

df,htpt2891   wcs,pipf3526 (853)   pl,nn,pnx899   wcs,pipf1548   (853)

8 And he that is to be cleansed shall   wash   his clothes, and shave off

cs,nn3605   nn,pnx8181   wcs,qpf7364   dfp,pl,nn4325   wcs,qpf2891   wcj,ad310

all   his hair,   and   wash himself in water, that he may be clean: and after that

qmf935   pr413   df,nn4264   wcs,qpf3427 pr4480/nn2351   pp,nn,pnx168 cs,nu7651
he shall come into the camp, and shall tarry abroad out of his tent seven

pl,nn3117
days.

                wcs,qpf1961   df,nuor7637   dfp,nn3117   pimf1548/(853)/cs,nn3605/nn,pnx8181
    9 But it shall be on the seventh day, that he shall shave*all*his*hair*off

(853)   nn,pnx7218   wcj(853)   nn,pnx2206   wcj(853)   pl,cs,nn1354/du,nn,pnx5869   wcj(853) cs,nn3605
his head and   his beard and   his   eyebrows,   even   all his

nn,pnx8181   pimf1548   wcs,pipf3526 (853)   pl,nn,pnx899   wcs,qpf7364
hair   he shall shave off: and he shall wash   his clothes, also he shall wash

(853)   nn,pnx1320   dfp,pl,nn4325   wcs,qpf2891
his flesh in water, and he shall be clean.

             df,nuor8066 wcj,dfp,nn3117   qmf3947   du,cs,nu8147   pl,nn3532   aj8549
    10 And on the eighth day he shall take two he lambs without blemish,

    nu259 wcj,nn3535   cs,nn1323 nn,pnx8141   aj8549   wcj,nu7969   pl,nn6241
and one ewe lamb of the first year without blemish, and three tenth deals of

nn5560   nn4503   qptp1101   dfp,nn8081   nu259 wcj,nn3849   nn8081
fine flour *for* a meat offering, mingled with oil, and one log of oil.

             df,nn3548   df,pipt2891   wcs,hipf5975 (853)   df,nn376
    11 And the priest that maketh*him*clean shall present   the man that is to be

df,htpt2891   wcj,pnx(853)   pp,pl,cs,nn6440   nn3068   cs,nn6607
made clean, and   those things, before the LORD, *at* the door of the

cs,nn168   nn4150
tabernacle of the congregation:

             df,nn3548   wcs,qpf3947 (853) df,nu259 df,nn3532   wcs,hipf7126 pnx(853)
    12 And the priest shall take   one he lamb, and offer   him for a

pp,nn817   wcj(853)   cs,nn3849   df,nn8081   wcs,hipf5130 pnx(853)
trespass offering, and   the log of oil, and wave   them *for* a

nn8573   pp,pl,cs,nn6440   nn3068
wave offering before the LORD:

             wcs,qpf7819 (853)   df,nn3532   pp,cs,nn4725 pnl834   qmf7819 (853)
    13 And he shall slay   the lamb in the place where he shall kill   the

df,nn2403   wcj(853)   df,nn5930   df,nn6944 pp,cs,nn4725 cj3588   dfp,nn2403
sin offering and   the burnt offering, in the holy place: for as the sin offering

(pnp1931)   dfp,nn3548   df,nn817   pnp1931 cs,nn6944/pl,nn6944
is the priest's, *so is* the trespass offering: it *is* most holy:

             df,nn3548   wcs,qpf3947   pr4480/cs,nn1818   df,nn817
    14 And the priest shall take *some* of*the*blood of the trespass offering, and

df,nn3548   wcs,qpf5414   pr5921   cs,nn8571   df,aj3233 cs,nn241
the priest shall put *it* upon the tip of the right ear of him that is to be

df,htpt2891   wcj,pr5921   cs,nn931   df,aj3233 nn,pnx3027   wcj,pr5921   cs,nn931
cleansed, and upon the thumb of his right hand, and upon the great toe of his

df,aj3233 nn,pnx7272
right foot:

             df,nn3548   wcs,qpf3947   pr4480/cs,nn3849   df,nn8081   wcs,qpf3332   pr5921
    15 And the priest shall take *some* of*the*log of oil, and pour *it* into the

cs,nn3709   df,nn3548   df,aj8042
palm of his own left hand:

             df,nn3548   wcs,qpf2881 (853)   df,aj3233 nn,pnx676 pr4480   df,nn8081 pnl834   pr5921
    16 And the priest shall dip   his right finger in the oil that *is* in his

df,aj8042 nn,pnx3709   wcs,hipf5137 pr4480   df,nn8081   pp,nn,pnx676 nu7651 pl,nn6471 pp,pl,cs,nn6440
left hand, and shall sprinkle of the oil with his finger seven times before

nn3068
the LORD:

             wcj,pr4480/cs,nn3499   df,nn8081 pnl834   pr5921   nn,pnx3709   df,nn3548 qmf5414 pr5921
    17 And of*the*rest of the oil that *is* in his hand shall the priest put upon

cs,nn8571   df,aj3233 cs,nn241   df,htpt2891   wcj,pr5921   cs,nn931
the tip of the right ear of him that is to be cleansed, and upon the thumb of

df,aj3233 nn,pnx3027   wcj,pr5921   cs,nn931   df,aj3233 nn,pnx7272 pr5921   cs,nn1818
his right hand, and upon the great toe of his right   foot, upon the blood of the

df,nn817
trespass offering:

wcj,df,nipt3498   dfp,nn8081 pnl834   pr5921   df,nn3548 cs,nn3709   qmf5414
18 And the remnant of the   oil   that *is* in the priest's hand he shall pour

pr5921   cs,nn7218   df,htpt2891   df,nn3548   wcs,pipf3722
upon the head of him that is to be cleansed: and the priest shall make*an*atonement

pr,pnx5921   pp,pl,cs,nn6440   nn3068
for him before the LORD.

df,nn3548   wcs,qpf6213 (853)   df,nn2403   wcs,pipf3722   pr5921
19 And the priest shall offer   the sin offering, and make*an*atonement for

df,htpt2891   pr4480/nn,pnx2932   wcj,ad310   qmf7819 (853)
him that is to be cleansed from*his*uncleanness; and afterward he shall kill   the

df,nn5930
burnt offering:

df,nn3548   wcs,hipf5927 (853)   df,nn5930   wcj(853)   df,nn4503
20 And the priest shall offer   the burnt offering and   the meat offering

df,nn,lh4196   df,nn3548   wcs,pipf3722   pr,pnx5921
upon the altar: and the priest shall make*an*atonement   for   him, and he shall

wcs,qpf2891
be clean.

wcj,cj518 pnp1931   aj1800   wcj,ptn369/nn,pnx3027/hipt5381   wcs,qpf3947 nu259
21 And if   he *be* poor, and cannot*get*so*much; then he shall take   one

nn3532   nn817   pp,nn8573   pp,pinc3722   pr,pnx5921
lamb *for* a trespass offering to be waved, to make*an*atonement   for   him, and

nu259 wcj,nn6241   nn5560   qptp1101   dfp,nn8081   pp,nn4503   wcj,cs,nn3849
one tenth deal of fine flour mingled with   oil   for a meat offering, and a   log

nn8081
of oil;

wcj,du,cs,nu8147   pl,nn8449   cj176 du,cs,nu8147 pl,cs,nn1121   nn3123   pnl834
22 And   two   turtledoves,   or   two   young pigeons, such as he is

himf5381/nn,pnx3027   nu259   wcs,qpf1961   nn2403   wcj,df,nu259
able*to*get; and the one shall   be   a sin offering, and the   other   a

nn5930
burnt offering.

wcs,hipf935 pnx(853)   df,nuor8066 dfp,nn3117   pp,nn,pnx2893 pr413
23 And he shall bring   them on the eighth   day for his cleansing unto

df,nn3548 pr413   cs,nn6607   cs,nn168   nn4150   pp,pl,cs,nn6440   nn3068
the priest, unto the door of the tabernacle of the congregation, before the LORD.

df,nn3548   wcs,qpf3947 (853)   cs,nn3532   df,nn817   wcj(853)
24 And the priest shall take   the lamb of the trespass offering, and

cs,nn3849   df,nn8081   df,nn3548   wcs,hipf5130 pnx(853)   nn8573
the log of oil, and the priest shall wave   them *for* a wave offering

pp,pl,cs,nn6440   nn3068
before the LORD:

wcs,qpf7819 (853)   cs,nn3532   df,nn817   df,nn3548
25 And he shall kill   the lamb of the trespass offering, and the priest

wcs,qpf3947   pr4480/cs,nn1818   df,nn817   wcs,qpf5414   pr5921
shall take *some* of*the*blood of the trespass offering, and put *it* upon the

cs,nn8571   df,aj3233 cs,nn241   df,htpt2891   wcj,pr5921   cs,nn931
tip of the right ear of him that is to be cleansed, and upon the thumb of his

df,aj3233 nn,pnx3027   wcj,pr5921   cs,nn931   df,aj3233 nn,pnx7272
right hand, and upon the great toe of his right foot:

26 And the priest shall pour of the oil into the palm of his own left hand:

27 And the priest shall sprinkle with his right finger *some* of the oil that *is* in his left hand seven times before the LORD:

28 And the priest shall put of the oil that *is* in his hand upon the tip of the right ear of him that is to be cleansed, and upon the thumb of his right hand, and upon the great toe of his right foot, upon the place of the blood of the trespass offering:

29 And the rest of the oil that *is* in the priest's hand he shall put upon the head of him that is to be cleansed, to make*an*atonement for him before the LORD.

30 And he shall offer the one of the turtledoves, or of the young pigeons, such as he can get;

31 *Even* such as he is able*to*get, the one *for* a sin offering, and the other *for* a burnt offering, with the meat offering: and the priest shall make*an*atonement for him that is to be cleansed before the LORD.

32 This *is* the law *of him* in whom *is* the plague of leprosy, whose hand is not able*to*get that *which pertaineth* to his cleansing.

Cleansing Infected Houses

33 And the LORD spoke unto Moses and unto Aaron, saying,

34 When ye be come into the land of Canaan, which I give to you for a possession, and I put the plague of leprosy in a house of the land of your possession;

35 And he*that*owneth the house shall come and tell the priest, saying, It seemeth to me *there is* as it were a plague in the house:

36 Then the priest shall command that they empty the house, before the

df,nn3548 qmf935   pp,qnc7200 (853)   df,nn5061   cs,nn3605 pnl834   dfp,nn1004   wcj,ptn3808
priest go *into it* to   see   the plague, that all   that *is* in the house be   not

qmf2930   wcj,pr310/ad3651   df,nn3548   qmf935   pp,qnc7200 (853)   df,nn1004
made unclean: and afterward the priest shall go in to   see   the house:

                          wcs,qpf7200   (853)   df,nn5061   wcj,ptdm2009   df,nn5061
37 And he shall look on   the plague, and, behold, *if* the plague *be* in the

pp,pl,cs,nn7023   df,nn1004   pl,nn8258   aj3422 cj176   aj125   wcj,nn,pnx4758
walls   of the house with hollow streaks, greenish or reddish, which in   sight

        aj8217   pr4480   df,nn7023
are lower than the wall;

                  df,nn3548   wcs,qpf3318 pr4480   df,nn1004 pr413   cs,nn6607   df,nn1004
38 Then the priest shall go out of the house to the door of the house, and

wcs,hipf5462 (853)   df,nn1004 cs,nu7651 pl,nn3117
shut up   the house seven days:

                  df,nn3548   wcs,qpf7725   df,nuor7637 dfp,nn3117   wcs,qpf7200
39 And the priest shall come again the seventh day, and shall look: and,

wcj,ptdm2009   df,nn5061   qpf6581   pp,pl,cs,nn7023   df,nn1004
behold, *if* the plague be spread in the   walls   of the house;

                  df,nn3548   wcj,pipf6680   wcj,pipf2502   (853)   df,pl,nn68 pnl834/pp,pnp2004
40 Then the priest shall command that they take away   the stones in which

df,nn5061   wcj,hipf7993 pnx(853)   pr413   aj2931   nn4725 pr4480/nn2351/pr413
the plague *is*, and they shall   cast   them into an unclean place   without the

dfp,nn5892
city:

                      wcj(853)   df,nn1004   himf7106 pr4480/nn1004   ad5439
41 And he shall cause   the house to be scraped within round about, and

            wcs,qpf8210   (853)   df,nn6083 pnl834   hipf7096   pr413/pr4480/nn2351   dfp,nn5892 pr413
they shall pour out   the dust that they scrape off   without   the   city into an

aj2931   nn4725
unclean place:

                  wcj,qpf3947 aj312   pl,nn68   wcj,hipf935   pr413   pr8478
42 And they shall   take   other stones, and   put   *them* in the place of those

df,pl,nn68   qmf3947 aj312 wcj,nn6083   wcs,qpf2902 (853)   df,nn1004
stones; and he shall take other mortar, and shall plaster   the house.

            wcj,cj518   df,nn5061   qmf7725   wcs,qpf6524   dfp,nn1004   ad310
43 And   if   the plague come again, and break out in the house, after that he

pipf2502   (853)   df,pl,nn68   wcj,ad310   hinc7096   (853)   df,nn1004   wcj,ad310
hath taken away   the stones, and after he hath scraped   the house, and after

ninc2902
it is plastered;

                  df,nn3548   wcj,qpf935   wcj,qpf7200   wcj,ptdm2009   df,nn5061   qpf6581
44 Then the priest shall come and look, and, behold, *if* the plague be spread

dfp,nn1004 pnp1931   hipt3992   nn6883   dfp,nn1004 pnp1931   aj2931
in the house, it *is* a fretting leprosy in the house: it *is* unclean.

                  wcj,qpf5422   (853)   df,nn1004 (853)   pl,nn,pnx68   wcj(853)
45 And he shall break down   the house,   the stones of it, and   the

pl,nn,pnx6086   wcj(853) cs,nn3605   cs,nn6083   df,nn1004
timber   thereof, and   all   the mortar of the house; and he shall

wcj,hipf3318   pr413/pr4480/nn2351   dfp,nn5892 pr413   aj2931   nn4725
carry**them**forth   out of   the city into an unclean place.

                  wcj,df,qpta935 pr413   df,nn1004 cs,nn3605   pl,cs,nn3117   pnx(853)
46 Moreover he that   goeth into the house all   the while that   it is

hipf5462   qmf2930   pr5704   df,nn6153
shut up shall be unclean until the even.

wcj,df,qpta7901   dfp,nn1004   pimf3526 (853)   pl,nn,pnx899
47 And he that   lieth   in the house shall wash   his clothes; and he that
wcj,df,qpta398   dfp,nn1004   pimf3526 (853)   pl,nn,pnx899
eateth in the house shall wash   his clothes.

wcj,cj518   df,nn3548   qna935/qmf935   wcs,qpf7200   wcj,ptdm2009
48 And if the priest shall come in, and look upon it, and, behold, the
df,nn5061   ptn3808   qpf6581   dfp,nn1004   ad310 (853)   df,nn1004   ninc2902
plague hath not spread in the house, after   the house was plastered: then the
df,nn3548   wcj,pipf2891/(853)/df,nn1004   cj3588   df,nn5061   nipf7495
priest shall pronounce*the*house*clean, because the plague is healed.

wcj,qpf3947   pp,pinc2398   (853)   df,nn1004 du,cs,nu8147 pl,nn6833   nn730
49 And he shall take to cleanse   the house two birds, and cedar
wcj,cs,nn6086   wcj,cs,nn8144/nn8438   wcj,nn231
wood, and   scarlet,   and hyssop:

wcj,qpf7819 (853)   df,nu259   df,nn6833 pr413   nn2789 cs,nn3627 pr5921
50 And he shall kill   the one of the birds in an earthen vessel over
aj2416   pl,nn4325
running water:

wcj,qpf3947 (853)   df,nn730 cs,nn6086   wcj(853)   df,nn231   wcj(853)
51 And he shall take   the cedar wood, and   the hyssop, and   the
cs,nn8144/df,nn8438   wcj(853)   df,aj2416 df,nn6833   wcj,qpf2881 pnx(853)   pp,cs,nn1818
scarlet, and   the living bird, and dip   them in the blood of the
df,qptp7819 df,nn6833   df,aj2416 wcj,dfp,pl,nn4325   wcj,hipf5137/pr413   df,nn1004 nu7651 pl,nn6471
slain bird, and in the running   water, and sprinkle the house seven times:

wcj,pipf2398 (853)   df,nn1004   pp,cs,nn1818   df,nn6833
52 And he shall cleanse   the house with the blood of the bird, and with the
df,aj2416 wcj,dfp,pl,nn4325   df,aj2416 wcj,dfp,nn6833   df,nn730 wcj,pp,cs,nn6086
running   water,   and with the living   bird,   and with the cedar   wood,   and
wcj,dfp,nn231   wcj,pp,cs,nn8144/df,nn8438
with the hyssop, and with the   scarlet:

wcj,pipf7971 (853)   df,aj2416 df,nn6833 pr413/pr4480/nn2351   dfp,nn5892 pr413
53 But he shall let go   the living bird out of the city into the
pl,cs,nn6440 df,nn7704   wcj,pipf3722   pr5921   df,nn1004   wcj,qpf2891
open fields, and make*an*atonement for the house: and it shall be clean.

pndm2063   df,nn8451   pp,cs,nn3605   cs,nn5061   df,nn6883   wcj,dfp,nn5424
54 This is the law for all manner of plague of leprosy, and   scurf,

wcj,pp,cs,nn6883   df,nn899   wcj,dfp,nn1004
55 And for the leprosy of a garment, and of a house,

wcj,dfp,nn7613   wcj,dfp,nn5597   wcj,dfp,nn934
56 And for a rising, and for a   scab,   and for a bright spot:

pp,hinc3384 pp,cs,nn3117   df,aj2931   wcj,pp,cs,nn3117   df,aj2889 pndm2063   cs,nn8451
57 To teach when it is unclean, and   when   it is clean: this is the law
df,nn6883
of leprosy.

Unclean Discharges From the Body

nn3068 wcs,pimf1696 pr413   nn4872   wcj,pr413   nn175   pp,qnc559
15 And the LORD spoke unto Moses and   to   Aaron, saying,
pimv1696   pr413   pl,cs,nn1121   nn3478   wcj,qpf559 pr,pnx413   cj3588
2 Speak unto the children of Israel, and say   unto them, When
nn376/nn376 qmf1961   qpta2100   pr4480/nn,pnx1320   nn,pnx2101 pnp1931
any man hath a running issue out*of*his*flesh, because of his issue   he is
aj2931
unclean.

wcj,pndm2063   qmf1961   nn,pnx2932   pp,nn,pnx2101   nn,pnx1320

3 And this shall be his uncleanness in his issue: whether his flesh

qpf7325   pr854   nn,pnx2101   cj176   nn,pnx1320   hipf2856   pr4480/nn,pnx2101   pnp1931

run with his issue, or his flesh be stopped from*his*issue, it *is* his

nn,pnx2932

uncleanness.

cs,nn3605   df,nn4904   pnl834/pr,pnx5921   qmf7901   df,qpta2100   qmf2930   wcj,cs,nn3605

4 Every bed, whereon he lieth that*hath*the*issue, is unclean: and every

df,nn3627   pnl834/pr,pnx5921   qmf3427   qmf2930

thing, whereon he sitteth, shall be unclean.

wcj,nn376/pnl834   qmf5060   pp,nn,pnx4904   pimf3526   pl,nn,pnx899   wcs,qpf7364

5 And whosoever toucheth his bed shall wash his clothes, and bathe

dfp,pl,nn4325   wcs,qpf2930   pr5704   df,nn6153

himself in water, and be unclean until the even.

wcj,df,qpta3427   pr5921   df,nn3627   pnl834/pr,pnx5921   qmf3427   df,qpta2100

6 And he*that*sitteth on *any* thing whereon he sat that*hath*the*issue

pimf3526   pl,nn,pnx899   wcs,qpf7364   dfp,pl,nn4325   wcs,qpf2930   pr5704   df,nn6153

shall wash his clothes, and bathe *himself* in water, and be unclean until the even.

wcj,df,qpta5060   pp,cs,nn1320   df,qpta2100   pimf3526

7 And he that toucheth the flesh of him that*hath*the*issue shall wash his

pl,nn,pnx899   wcs,qpf7364   dfp,pl,nn4325   wcs,qpf2930   pr5704   df,nn6153

clothes, and bathe *himself* in water, and be unclean until the even.

wcj,cj3588   df,qpta2100   qmf7556   dfp,aj2889

8 And if he*that*hath*the*issue spit upon him that*is*clean; then he shall

wcs,pipf3526   pl,nn,pnx899   wcs,qpf7364   dfp,pl,nn4325   wcs,qpf2930   pr5704   df,nn6153

wash his clothes, and bathe *himself* in water, and be unclean until the even.

wcj,cs,nn3605/df,nn4817/pnl834   qmf7392   pr,pnx5921   df,qpta2100   qmf2930

9 And what*saddle*soever he rideth upon that hath*the*issue shall be unclean.

wcj,cs,nn3605   df,qpta5060   pp,nn3605   pnl834   qmf1961   pr,pnx8478   qmf2930

10 And whosoever toucheth any thing that was under him shall be unclean

pr5704   df,nn6153   wcj,df,qpta5375   pnx(853)   pimf3526   pl,nn,pnx899

until the even: and he that beareth *any of* those things shall wash his clothes,

wcs,qpf7364   dfp,pl,nn4325   wcs,qpf2930   pr5704   df,nn6153

and bathe *himself* in water, and be unclean until the even.

wcj,nn3605/pnl834   qmf5060/pp,pnx   df,qpta2100   ptn3808   qpf7857

11 And whomsoever he toucheth that hath*the*issue, and hath not rinsed his

wcj,du,nn,pnx3027   dfp,pl,nn4325   wcj,pipf3526   pl,nn,pnx899   wcj,qpf7364   dfp,pl,nn4325

hands in water, he shall wash his clothes, and bathe *himself* in water, and

wcj,qpf2930   pr5704   df,nn6153

be unclean until the even.

wcj,cs,nn3627   nn2789   pnl834/pp,pnx   qmf5060   df,qpta2100

12 And the vessel of earth, that he toucheth which*hath*the*issue, shall

nimf7665   wcj,cs,nn3605   cs,nn3627   nn6086   nimf7857   dfp,pl,nn4325

be broken: and every vessel of wood shall be rinsed in water.

wcj,cj3588   df,qpta2100   qmf2891   pr4480/nn,pnx2101

13 And when he that*hath*an*issue is cleansed of*his*issue; then he shall

wcs,qpf5608   pp,pnx   cs,nu7651 pl,nn3117   pp,nn,pnx2893   wcs,pipf3526   pl,nn,pnx899   wcs,qpf7364

number to himself seven days for his cleansing, and wash his clothes, and bathe

nn,pnx1320   aj2416   pp,pl,nn4325   wcs,qpf2891

his flesh in running water, and shall be clean.

df,nuor8066   wcj,dfp,nn3117   qmf3947   pp,pnx   du,cs,nu8147   pl,nn8449   cj176

14 And on the eighth day he shall take to him two turtledoves, or

du,cs,nu8147   pl,cs,nn1121   nn3123   wcs,qpf935   pp,pl,cs,nn6440   nn3068   pr413   cs,nn6607

two young pigeons, and come before the LORD unto the door of the

cs,nn168   nn4150   wcs,qpf,pnx5414   pr413   df,nn3548

tabernacle of the congregation, and give them unto the priest:

df,nn3548   wcs,qpf6213 pnx(853)   nu259   nn2403
15 And the priest shall offer   them, the one *for* a sin offering, and the

wcj,df,nu259   nn5930   df,nn3548   wcs,pipf3722   pr,pnx5921
other *for* a burnt offering; and the priest shall make*an*atonement   for   him

pp,pl,cs,nn6440   nn3068   pr4480/nn,pnx2101
before the LORD for*his*issue.

cj3588   wcj,nn376   nn2233   cs,nn7902   qmf3318 pr,pnx4480
16 And if any man's seed of copulation go out from him, then he shall

wcs,qpf7364 (853) cs,nn3605   nn,pnx1320   dfp,pl,nn4325   wcs,qpf2930   pr5704   df,nn6153
wash   all his flesh in water, and be unclean until the even.

wcj,cs,nn3605   nn899   wcj,cs,nn3605   nn5785 pnl834/pr,pnx5921 qmf1961   nn2233
17 And every garment, and every skin, whereon   is   the seed of

cs,nn7902   wcs,pupf3526   dfp,pl,nn4325 wcs,qpf2930 pr5704 df,nn6153
copulation, shall be washed with water, and be unclean until the even.

wcj,nn802   pnl834/pnx(853) nn376   qmf7901   nn2233   cs,nn7902
18 The woman also with whom man shall lie *with* seed of copulation, they

wcs,qpf7364   dfp,pl,nn4325   wcs,qpf2930 pr5704   df,nn6153
shall *both* bathe *themselves* in water, and be unclean until the even.

cj3588   wcj,nn802 qmf1961   qpta2100   nn,pnx2101   pp,nn,pnx1320 qmf1961   nn1818
19 And if a woman have an issue, *and* her issue in her flesh   be blood,

qmf1961 pp,nn,pnx5079 cs,nu7651 pl,nn3117   wcj,cs,nn3605 df,qpta5060 pp,pnx   qmf2930
she shall be put apart seven days: and whosoever toucheth her shall be unclean

pr5704   df,nn6153
until the even.

wcj,nn3605   pnl834   qmf7901 pr,pnx5921   pp,nn,pnx5079   qmf2930
20 And every thing that she lieth upon in her separation shall be unclean:

wcj,nn3605   pnl834   qmf3427 pr,pnx5921   qmf2930
every thing also that she sitteth upon shall be unclean.

wcj,cs,nn3605   df,qpta5060   pp,nn,pnx4904   pimf3526   pl,nn,pnx899 wcs,qpf7364
21 And whosoever toucheth her   bed   shall wash his clothes, and bathe

dfp,pl,nn4325   wcs,qpf2930 pr5704   df,nn6153
himself in water, and be unclean until the even.

wcj,cs,nn3605   df,qpta5060 pp,cs,nn3605 nn3627 pnl834   qmf3427 pr,pnx5921   pimf3526
22 And whosoever toucheth   any   thing that she sat   upon shall wash his

pl,nn,pnx899   wcs,qpf7364   dfp,pl,nn4325 wcs,qpf2930 pr5704 df,nn6153
clothes, and bathe *himself* in water, and be unclean until the even.

wcj,cj518 pnp1931   pr5921   df,nn4904 cj176 pr5921   df,nn3627 pnl834/pr,pnx5921 pnp1931 qpta3427
23 And if it *be* on *her* bed, or on any thing whereon   she sitteth,

pp,qnc,pnx5060 pp,pnx   qmf2930   pr5704 df,nn6153
when he toucheth it, he shall be unclean until the even.

wcj,cj518   nn376   qna7901/qmf7901/pnx(853)   nn,pnx5079 wcj,qcj1961 pr,pnx5921
24 And if any man lie*with*her*at*all, and her flowers   be   upon him,

wcs,qpf2930   cs,nu7651 pl,nn3117   wcj,cs,nn3605 df,nn4904 pnl834/pr,pnx5921   qmf7901
he shall be unclean seven days; and   all   the bed   whereon   he lieth shall

qmf2930
be unclean.

cj3588   wcj,nn802   qmf2100/cs,nn2101   nn,pnx1818 aj7227 pl,nn3117 pp,ptn3808   cs,nn6256
25 And if a woman have*an*issue of her blood many days out of the time

nn,pnx5079   cj176 cj3588   qmf2100   pr5921   nn,pnx5079 cs,nn3605
of her separation, or if it run beyond the time of her separation; all the

pl,cs,nn3117   nn2101   nn,pnx2932   qmf1961   pp,pl,cs,nn3117   nn,pnx5079
days of the issue of her uncleanness shall be as the   days of her separation:

pnp1931   aj2931
she *shall be* unclean.

cs,nn3605 df,nn4904 pnl834/pr,pnx5921 qmf7901 cs,nn3605 pl,cs,nn3117   nn,pnx2101   qmf1961
26 Every bed whereon she lieth all the days of her issue shall be

pp,pnx   pp,cs,nn4904   nn,pnx5079   wcj,cs,nn3605/df,nn3627   qmf3427   pnl834/pr,pnx5921

unto her as the   bed   of her separation: and   whatsoever   she sitteth   upon

qmf1961   aj2931   pp,cs,nn2932   nn,pnx5079

shall   be   unclean, as the uncleanness of her separation.

       wcj,cs,nn3605   df,qpta5060   pp,pnx   qmf2930   wcs,pipf3526

27 And whosoever toucheth those things shall be unclean, and shall   wash   his

pl,nn,pnx899   wcs,qpf7364   dfp,pl,nn4325   wcs,qpf2930   pr5704   df,nn6153

clothes, and bathe *himself* in water, and be unclean until the even.

     wcj,cj518   qpf2891   pr4480/nn,pnx2101   wcj,qpf5608   pp,pnx

28 But   if   she be cleansed of*her*issue, then she shall number to herself

cs,nu7651   pl,nn3117   wcj,ad310   qmf2891

seven days, and after that she shall be clean.

       df,nuor8066   wcj,dfp,nn3117   qmf3947   pp,pnx   du,cs,nu8147   pl,nn8449   cj176

29 And on the eighth   day   she shall take   unto her   two   turtles,   or

du,cs,nu8147   pl,cs,nn1121   nn3123   wcs,hipf935   pnx(853)   pr413   df,nn3548   pr413   cs,nn6607

two   young   pigeons, and   bring   them unto the priest,   to   the   door   of the

cs,nn168   nn4150

tabernacle of the congregation.

       df,nn3548   wcs,qpf6213   (853)   df,nu259   nn2403   wcj(853)

30 And the priest shall   offer   the   one   *for* a sin offering, and   the

df,nu259   nn5930   df,nn3548   wcs,pipf3722   pr,pnx5921

other *for* a burnt offering; and the priest shall make*an*atonement   for   her

pp,pl,cs,nn6440   nn3068   pr4480/cs,nn2101   nn,pnx2932

before   the LORD for*the*issue of her uncleanness.

       wcs,hipf5144   (853)   pl,cs,nn1121   nn3478   pr4480/nn,pnx2932

31 Thus shall ye separate   the children of Israel from*their*uncleanness; that

qmf4191   wcj,ptn3808   pp,nn,pnx2932   pp,pinc,pnx2930   (853)   nn,pnx4908   pnl834

they die   not   in their uncleanness, when they   defile   my tabernacle that *is*

pp,nn,pnx8432

among   them.

       pndm2063   cs,nn8451   df,qpta2100   wcj,pnl834   cs,nn7902/nn2233

32 This   *is* the   law   of him that*hath*an*issue, and *of him* whose   seed

qmf3318   pr,pnx4480   pp,qnc2930   pp,pnx

goeth   from   him, and is defiled therewith;

       wcj,df,aj1739   pp,nn,pnx5079   wcj,df,qpta2100/(853)/nn,pnx2101

33 And of her that*is*sick of her flowers, and of him that*hath*an*issue, of the

dfp,nn2145   wcj,dfp,nn5347   wcj,pp,nn376   pnl834   qmf7901   pr5973   aj2931

man,   and of the woman, and of   him   that lieth with her*that*is*unclean.

The Day of Atonement

16
        nn3068   wcs,pimf1696   pr413   nn4872   pr310   cs,nn4194   du,cs,nu8147

And the LORD   spoke   unto Moses after the death of the   two

pl,cs,nn1121   nn175   pp,qnc,pnx7126   pp,pl,cs,nn6440   nn3068   wcs,qmf4191

sons   of Aaron, when they   offered   before   the LORD, and   died;

       nn3068   wcs,qmf559   pr413   nn4872   pimv1696   pr413   nn175   nn,pnx251

2 And the LORD   said   unto Moses, Speak   unto Aaron thy   brother, that he

qmf935   wcj,ptn408   pp,cs,nn3605   nn6256   pr413   df,nn6944   pr4480/cs,nn1004   dfp,nn6532   pr413/pl,cs,nn6440

come   not   at   all   times into the holy *place* within   the   veil   before   the

---

16:2, 14   See the note on Exodus 26:31–35 concerning the "veil" and "most holy place."

df,nn**3727**   pnl834   pr5921   df,nn**727**   qmf**4191** wcj,ptn**3808** cj3588   nimf**7200**

mercy seat, which *is* upon the ark; that he die not: for I will appear in the

dfp,nn**6051** pr5921   df,nn**3727**

cloud upon the mercy seat.

pp,pndm2063   nn175 qmf935 pr413   df,nn**6944**   cs,nn**1121**/nn1241 pp,cs,nn6499

3 Thus shall Aaron come into the holy *place*: with a young bullock for a

pp,nn**2403**   wcj,nn352   pp,nn**5930**

sin offering, and a ram for a burnt offering.

qmf3847   nn**6944** cs,nn906 cs,nn3801   qmf**1961**   nn906 wcj,du,cs,nn4370

4 He shall put on the holy linen coat, and he shall have the linen breeches

pr5921   nn,pnx**1320**   qmf2296   nn906 wcj,pp,cs,nn73   nn906

upon his flesh, and shall be girded with a linen girdle, and with the linen

wcj,pp,cs,nn4701   qmf6801 pndm1992   nn**6944** pl,cs,nn899   wcs,qpf**7364** (853)

miter shall he be attired: these *are* holy garments; therefore shall he wash

nn,pnx**1320** dfp,pl,nn4325   wcs,qpf,pnx3847

his flesh in water, and *so* put*them*on.

qmf3947 wcj,pr4480/pr854   cs,nn**5712**   pl,cs,nn**1121**   nn3478 du,cs,nu8147

5 And he shall take of the congregation of the children of Israel two

pl,cs,nn**8163**   pl,nn5795   pp,nn**2403**   nu259 wcj,nn352   pp,nn**5930**

kids of the goats for a sin offering, and one ram for a burnt offering.

nn175   wcs,hipf**7126** (853)   cs,nn6499   df,nn**2403**   pnl834

6 And Aaron shall offer his bullock of the sin offering, which *is*

pp,pnx   wcs,pipf**3722**   pr,pnx1157   wcj,pr1157   nn,pnx**1004**

for himself, and make*an*atonement for himself, and for his house.

wcs,qpf3947 (853)   du,cs,nu8147 df,pl,nn**8163**   wcs,hipf5975 pnx(853)   pp,pl,cs,nn**6440**

7 And he shall take the two goats, and present them before the

nn3068   cs,nn6607   cs,nn168   cs,nn**4150**

LORD *at* the door of the tabernacle of the congregation.

nn175   wcs,qpf5414 pl,nn1486 pr5921   du,cs,nu8147 df,pl,nn**8163** nu259 nn1486   pp,nn**3068**

8 And Aaron shall cast lots upon the two goats; one lot for the LORD,

nu259 wcj,nn1486   pp,nn5799

and the other lot for the scapegoat.

nn175   wcs,hipf**7126** (853)   df,nn**8163** pr,pnx5921 pnl834   pp,nn**3068** df,nn1486 qpf**5927**

9 And Aaron shall bring the goat upon which the LORD's lot fell, and

wcj,qpf,pnx**6213**   nn**2403**

offer him *for* a sin offering.

wcj,df,nn**8163** pr,pnx5921   pnl834   df,nn1486 qpf**5927**   pp,nn5799

10 But the goat, on which the lot fell to be the scapegoat, shall be

homf5975   aj**2416** pp,pl,cs,nn**6440**   nn3068   pp,pinc**3722**   pr,pnx5921

presented alive before the LORD, to make*an*atonement with him, *and* to

pp,pinc7971/pnx(853)   pp,nn5799   df,nn,lh4057

let*him*go for a scapegoat into the wilderness.

nn175   wcs,hipf**7126** (853)   cs,nn6499   df,nn**2403**   pnl834

11 And Aaron shall bring the bullock of the sin offering, which *is*

pp,pnx   wcs,pipf**3722**   pr,pnx1157   wcj,pr1157   nn,pnx**1004**

for himself, and shall make*an*atonement for himself, and for his house, and

wcs,qpf**7819** (853)   cs,nn6499   df,nn**2403**   pnl834   pp,pnx

shall kill the bullock of the sin offering which *is* for himself:

wcs,qpf3947   df,nn4289 cs,nn4393   pl,cs,nn1513   nn784 pr4480/pr5921

12 And he shall take a censer full of burning coals of fire from off the

df,nn**4196**   pr4480/pp,pl,cs,nn**6440**   nn3068   du,nn,pnx2651 wcj,cs,nn4393   pl,nn5561 cs,nn**7004**

altar before the LORD, and his hands full of sweet incense

aj1851   wcs,hipf935 pr4480/cs,nn**1004**   dfp,nn6532

beaten small, and bring *it* within the veil:

wcs,qpf5414 (853)   df,nn**7004** pr5921   df,nn784 pp,pl,cs,nn**6440**   nn3068

13 And he shall put the incense upon the fire before the LORD, that

^{cs,nn6051}   ^{df,nn7004}   ^{wcs,pipf3680} (853)   ^{df,nn3727}   ^{pnl834}   ^{pr5921}   ^{df,nn5715}

the cloud of the incense may cover   the mercy seat that *is* upon the testimony,

^{qmf4191} ^{wcj,ptn3808}

that he die not:

^{wcs,qpf3947}   ^{pr4480/cs,nn1818}   ^{df,nn6499}   ^{wcs,hipf5137}

⊙⚲ 14 And he shall take of*the*blood of the bullock, and sprinkle *it* with his

^{pp,nn,pnx676} ^{pr5921/pl,cs,nn6440}   ^{df,nn3727}   ^{ad,lh6924}   ^{wcj,pp,pl,cs,nn6440}   ^{df,nn3727}

finger   upon   the mercy seat eastward; and   before   the mercy seat shall he

^{himf5137}   ^{pr4480}   ^{df,nn1818}   ^{pp,nn,pnx676} ^{cs,nu7651}   ^{pl,nn6471}

sprinkle of the blood with his finger seven times.

^{wcs,qpf7819}   (853)   ^{cs,nn8163}   ^{df,nn2403}   ^{pnl834}   ^{dfp,nn5971}

   15 Then shall he kill   the goat of the sin offering, that *is* for the people,

^{wcs,hipf935} (853)   ^{nn,pnx1818} ^{pr413/pr4480/cs,nn1004}   ^{dfp,nn6532}   ^{wcs,qpf6213}   ^{pr854}   ^{nn,pnx1818} ^{pp,pnl834}

and bring   his blood within   the veil, and   do   with that blood   as

^{qpf6213}   ^{pp,cs,nn1818}   ^{df,nn6499}   ^{wcj,hipf5137}   ^{pnx(853)}   ^{pr5921}   ^{df,nn3727}

he did with the blood of the bullock, and sprinkle   it upon the mercy seat,

^{wcj,pp,pl,cs,nn6440}   ^{df,nn3727}

and   before   the mercy seat:

^{wcj,pipf3722}   ^{pr5921}   ^{df,nn6944}

   16 And   he   shall   make*an*atonement   for   the   holy   *place*,

^{pr4480/pl,cs,nn2932}   ^{pl,cs,nn1121}   ⁿⁿ³⁴⁷⁸

because*of*the*uncleanness of   the   children   of   Israel,   and

^{wcj,pr4480/pl,nn,pnx6588}   ^{pp,cs,nn3605}   ^{pl,nn,pnx2403}   ^{wcj,ad3651}   ^{qmf6213}

because*of*their*transgressions in   all   their   sins: and   so   shall he do   for

^{pp,cs,nn168}   ⁿⁿ⁴¹⁵⁰   ^{df,qpta7931}   ^{pr,pnx854}   ^{pp,cs,nn8432}

the tabernacle of the congregation, that remaineth among them in the midst of their

^{pl,nn,pnx2932}

uncleanness.

^{qmf1961}   ^{ptn3808/wcj,cs,nn3605} ⁿⁿ¹²⁰   ^{pp,cs,nn168}   ⁿⁿ⁴¹⁵⁰

   17 And there shall be   no   man in the tabernacle of the congregation

^{pp,qnc,pnx935}   ^{pp,pinc3722}   ^{dfp,nn6944}   ^{pr5704}   ^{qnc,pnx3318}

when he goeth in to make*an*atonement in the holy *place*, until he come out, and

^{wcs,pipf3722}   ^{pr,pnx1157}   ^{wcj,pr1157}   ^{nn,pnx1004}   ^{wcj,pr1157} ^{cs,nn3605}

have made*an*atonement for himself, and for his household, and for   all

^{cs,nn6951}   ⁿⁿ³⁴⁷⁸

the congregation of Israel.

^{wcs,qpf3318}   ^{pr413}   ^{df,nn4196} ^{pnl834}   ^{pp,pl,cs,nn6440}   ⁿⁿ³⁰⁶⁸

  18 And he shall go out unto the altar that *is* before   the LORD, and

^{wcs,pipf3722}   ^{pr,pnx5921}   ^{wcs,qpf3947}   ^{pr4480/cs,nn1818}   ^{df,nn6499}

make*an*atonement   for   it; and shall   take   of*the*blood of the bullock, and

^{wcj,pr4480/cs,nn1818}   ^{df,nn8163}   ^{wcs,qpf5414}   ^{pr5921}   ^{pl,cs,nn7161}   ^{df,nn4196}   ^{ad5439}

of*the*blood of the goat, and   put   *it* upon the horns of the altar round about.

^{wcs,hipf5137} ^{pr4480}   ^{df,nn1818} ^{pr,pnx5921}   ^{pp,nn,pnx676} ^{cs,nu7651} ^{pl,nn6471}

   19 And he shall sprinkle of the blood upon it with his finger seven times,

^{wcs,pipf,pnx2891}   ^{wcs,pipf,pnx6942}   ^{pr4480/pl,cs,nn2932}   ^{pl,cs,nn1121}   ⁿⁿ³⁴⁷⁸

and cleanse it, and   hallow   it from*the*uncleanness of the children of Israel.

The Scapegoat

^{wcs,pipf3615}   ^{pr4480/pinc3722}   (853)   ^{df,nn6944}   ^{wcj(853)}

   20 And when he hath made*an*end of reconciling   the holy *place*, and

^{cs,nn168}   ⁿⁿ⁴¹⁵⁰   ^{wcj(853)}   ^{df,nn4196}   ^{wcs,hipf7126} (853)   ^{df,aj2416}

the tabernacle of the congregation, and   the altar, he shall bring   the live

^{df,nn8163}

goat:

nn175 wcs,qpf5564 (853) du,cs,nu8147 du,nn,pnx3027 pr5921 cs,nn7218 df,aj2416

21 And Aaron shall lay both his hands upon the head of the live

df,nn8163 wcs,htpf3034 pr,pnx5921 (853) cs,nn3605 pl,cs,nn5771 pl,cs,nn1121 nn3478

goat, and confess over him all the iniquities of the children of Israel, and

wcj(853) cs,nn3605 pl,nn,pnx6588 pp,cs,nn3605 pl,nn,pnx2403 wcs,qpf5414 pnx(853) pr5921

all their transgressions in all their sins, putting them upon the

cs,nn7218 df,nn8163 wcs,pipf7971 pp,cs,nn3027 aj6261 nn376

head of the goat, and shall send*him*away by the hand of a fit man into the

df,nn,lh4057

wilderness:

df,nn8163 wcs,qpf5375 pr,pnx5921 (853) cs,nn3605 pl,nn,pnx5771 pr413 cs,nn776

22 And the goat shall bear upon him all their iniquities unto a land

nn1509 wcs,pipf7971 (853) df,nn8163 dfp,nn4057

not inhabited: and he shall let go the goat in the wilderness.

nn175 wcs,qpf935 pr413 cs,nn168 nn4150

23 And Aaron shall come into the tabernacle of the congregation, and shall

wcs,qpf6584 (853) df,nn906 pl,cs,nn899 pnl834 qpf3847 pp,qnc,pnx935 pr413 df,nn6944

put off the linen garments, which he put on when he went into the holy

wcj,hipf,pnx5117 ad8033

place, and shall leave them there:

wcj,qpf7364 (853) nn,pnx1320 dfp,pl,nn4325 aj6918 pp,nn4725 wcj,qpf3847

24 And he shall wash his flesh with water in the holy place, and put on

(853) pl,nn,pnx899 wcj,qpf3318 wcj,qpf6213 (853) nn,pnx5930 wcj(853)

his garments, and come forth, and offer his burnt offering, and the

cs,nn5930 df,nn5971 wcj,pipf3722 pr,pnx1157 wcj,pr1157

burnt offering of the people, and make*an*atonement for himself, and for the

df,nn5971

people.

wcj(853) cs,nn2459 df,nn2403 himf6999 df,nn,lh4196

25 And the fat of the sin offering shall he burn upon the altar.

wcj,df,pipt7971 (853) df,nn8163 pp,nn5799 pimf3526 pl,nn,pnx899

26 And he that*let*go the goat for the scapegoat shall wash his clothes, and

wcs,qpf7364 (853) nn,pnx1320 dfp,pl,nn4325 wcj,ad310/ad3651 qmf935 pr413 df,nn4264

bathe his flesh in water, and afterward come into the camp.

wcj(853) cs,nn6499 df,nn2403 wcj(853) cs,nn8163

27 And the bullock *for* the sin offering, and the goat *for* the

df,nn2403 (853) pnl834 nn,pnx1818 hopf935 pp,pinc3722 dfp,nn6944

sin offering, whose blood was brought in to make atonement in the holy

himf3318 pr413/pr4480/nn2351 dfp,nn4264 wcs,qpf8313 dfp,nn784

place, shall *one* carry forth without the camp; and they shall burn in the fire

(853) pl,nn,pnx5785 wcj(853) nn,pnx1320 wcj(853) nn,pnx6569

their skins, and their flesh, and their dung.

wcj,df,qpta8313 pnx(853) pimf3526 pl,nn,pnx899 wcs,qpf7364 (853)

28 And he*that*burneth them shall wash his clothes, and bathe his

nn,pnx1320 dfp,pl,nn4325 wcj,ad310/ad3651 qmf935 pr413 df,nn4264

flesh in water, and afterward he shall come into the camp.

Regulations for the Day of Atonement

wcs,qpf1961 pp,cs,nn2708 nn5769 pp,pnx df,nuor7637 dfp,nn2320

☞ 29 And *this* shall be a statute forever unto you: *that* in the seventh month,

---

☞ **16:29** Here the Day of Atonement is said to be on the tenth day of the seventh month, whereas Leviticus 23:32 specifies the ninth day of the month. The latter passage provides the solution to this apparent discrepancy.

dfp,nn6218   dfp,nn2320   pimf6031 (853)   pl,nn,pnx5315   qmf6213 ptn3808   nn4399
on the tenth *day* of the month, ye shall afflict   your souls, and do   no   work
wcj,cs,nn3605   df,nn249   wcj,df,nn1616   df,qpta1481
at   all,   *whether it be* one*of*your*own*country, or a stranger that sojourneth
pp,nn,pnx8432
among you:

cj3588   df,pndm2088 dfp,nn3117   pimf3722   pr,pnx5921
   30 For on   that   day shall *the priest* make*an*atonement for   you, to
pp,pinc2891 pnx(853)   qmf2891   pr4480/cs,nn3605   pl,nn,pnx2403 pp,pl,cs,nn6440   nn3068
cleanse   you, *that* ye may be clean from all your   sins   before the LORD.

pnp1931   cs,nn7676   nn7677   pp,pnx   wcs,pipf6031 (853)
   31 It *shall be* a sabbath of rest unto you, and ye shall afflict   your
pl,nn,pnx5315   cs,nn2708   nn5769
souls, by a statute forever.

df,nn3548   pnl834   qmf4886   (pnx853)   wcj,pnl834
   32 And the priest, whom he shall anoint,   and whom he shall
pimf4390/(853)/nn,pnx3027   pp,pinc3547   pr8478/nn,pnx1
consecrate   to   minister*in*the*priest's*office   in*his*father's*stead,   shall
wcs,pipf3722   wcj,qpf3847   (853)   df,nn906   pl,cs,nn899   df,nn6944
make*the*atonement, and shall put on   the linen clothes, *even* the holy
pl,cs,nn899
garments:

wcs,pipf3722   (853)   df,nn6944   cs,nn4720
   33 And he shall make*an*atonement for   the holy sanctuary, and he shall
pimf3722   wcj(853)   cs,nn168   cs,nn4150   wcj(853)
make*an*atonement   for the tabernacle of the congregation, and   for the
df,nn4196   pimf3722   wcj,pr5921   df,pl,nn3548   wcj,pr5921 cs,nn3605
altar, and he shall make*an*atonement for   the priests, and   for   all the
cs,nn5971   df,nn6951
people of the congregation.

pndm2063   wcs,qpf1961   nn5769   pp,cs,nn2708   pp,pnx
   34 And   this   shall   be   an everlasting statute unto you,   to
pp,pinc3722   pr5921   pl,cs,nn1121   nn3478 pr4480/cs,nn3605   pl,nn,pnx2403 nu259   dfp,nn8141
make*an*atonement for the children of Israel for all their sins once a year.
wcs,qmf6213 pp,pnl834   nn3068   pipf6680   (853)   nn4872
And he   did   as   the LORD commanded   Moses.

Blood is Sacred

nn3068   wcs,pimf1696   pr413   nn4872   pp,qnc559
And the LORD spoke unto Moses, saying,
pimv1696   pr413   nn175   wcj,pr413   pl,nn,pnx1121   wcj,pr413 cs,nn3605
   2 Speak unto Aaron, and unto his   sons, and unto   all   the
pl,cs,nn1121   nn3478   wcj,qpf559 pr,pnx413   pndm2088   df,nn1697 pnl834   nn3068
children of Israel, and say   unto them; This *is* the thing which the LORD hath
pipf6680   pp,qnc559
commanded, saying,

nn376/nn376   pr4480/cs,nn1004   nn3478 pnl834 qmf7819   nn7794 cj176
   3 What*man*soever *there be* of*the*house of Israel, that killeth an ox, or
nn3775 cj176 nn5795   dfp,nn4264 cj176 pnl834 qmf7819   pr4480/nn2351   dfp,nn4264
lamb, or goat, in the camp, or that killeth *it* out of the camp,

---

It says that the rest is to begin on the ninth day of the month "at evening." For the Hebrews, the tenth day
began on the evening of the ninth day.

^{hipf,pnx935} ^{ptn3808} ^{wcj,pr413} ^{cs,nn6607} ^{cs,nn168} ⁿⁿ⁴¹⁵⁰

4 And bringeth it not unto the door of the tabernacle of the congregation, to

^{pp,hinc7126} ⁿⁿ⁷¹³³ ^{pp,nn3068} ^{pp,pl,cs,nn6440} ^{cs,nn4908} ⁿⁿ³⁰⁶⁸ ⁿⁿ¹⁸¹⁸

offer an offering unto the LORD before the tabernacle of the LORD; blood shall be

^{nimf2803} ^{df,pndm1931} ^{dfp,nn376} ^{qpf8210} ⁿⁿ¹⁸¹⁸ ^{df,pndm1931} ^{df,nn376} ^{wcj,nipf3772}

imputed unto that man; he hath shed blood; and that man shall be cut off

^{pr4480/cs,nn7130} ^{nn,pnx5971}

from among his people:

^{pp,cj4616} ^{pnl834} ^{pl,cs,nn1121} ⁿⁿ³⁴⁷⁸ ^{himf935} ⁽⁸⁵³⁾ ^{pl,nn,pnx2077} ^{pnl834}

5 To*the*end that the children of Israel may bring their sacrifices, which

^{pnp1992} ^{pl,qpta2076} ^{pr5921} ^{pl,cs,nn6440} ^{df,nn7704} ^{wcs,hipf,pnx935} ^{pp,nn3068}

they offer in the open field, even that they may bring them unto the LORD,

^{pr413} ^{cs,nn6607} ^{cs,nn168} ⁿⁿ⁴¹⁵⁰ ^{pr413} ^{df,nn3548} ^{wcs,qpf2076}

unto the door of the tabernacle of the congregation, unto the priest, and offer

^{pnx(853)} ^{pl,nn8002} ^{pl,cs,nn2077} ^{pp,nn3068}

them *for* peace offerings unto the LORD.

^{df,nn3548} ^{wcs,qpf2236} ⁽⁸⁵³⁾ ^{df,nn1818} ^{pr5921} ^{cs,nn4196} ⁿⁿ³⁰⁶⁸

6 And the priest shall sprinkle the blood upon the altar of the LORD *at* the

^{cs,nn6607} ^{cs,nn168} ⁿⁿ⁴¹⁵⁰ ^{wcs,hipf6999} ^{df,nn2459} ⁿⁿ⁵²⁰⁷

door of the tabernacle of the congregation, and burn the fat for a sweet

^{pp,cs,nn7381} ^{pp,nn3068}

savor unto the LORD.

^{wcj,ptn3808} ^{ad5750} ^{qmf2076} ⁽⁸⁵³⁾ ^{pl,nn,pnx2077} ^{dfp,pl,nn8163} ^{pr,pnx310} ^{pnl834}

7 And they shall no more offer their sacrifices unto devils, after whom

^{pnp1992} ^{pl,qpta2181} ^{pndm2063} ^{qmf1961} ^{cs,nn2708} ⁿⁿ⁵⁷⁶⁹ ^{pp,pnx}

they have gone*a*whoring. This shall be a statute forever unto them throughout

^{pp,pl,nn,pnx1755}

their generations.

^{qmf559} ^{wcj,pr,pnx413} ^{nn376/nn376} ^{pr4480/cs,nn1004}

8 And thou shalt say unto them, Whatsoever man *there be* of*the*house of

ⁿⁿ³⁴⁷⁸ ^{wcj,pr4480} ^{df,nn1616} ^{pnl834} ^{qmf1481} ^{pp,nn,pnx8432} ^{pnl834} ^{himf5927}

Israel, or of the strangers which sojourn among you, that offereth a

ⁿⁿ⁵⁹³⁰ ^{cj176} ⁿⁿ²⁰⁷⁷

burnt offering or sacrifice,

^{himf,pnx935} ^{ptn3808} ^{wcj,pr413} ^{cs,nn6607} ^{cs,nn168} ⁿⁿ⁴¹⁵⁰

9 And bringeth it not unto the door of the tabernacle of the congregation, to

^{pp,qnc6213} ^{pnx(853)} ^{pp,nn3068} ^{df,pndm1931} ^{df,nn376} ^{wcs,nipf3772}

offer it unto the LORD; even that man shall be cut off

^{pr4480/pl,nn,pnx5971}

from*among*his*people.

^{wcj,nn376/nn376} ^{pr4480/cs,nn1004} ⁿⁿ³⁴⁷⁸ ^{wcj,pr4480} ^{df,nn1616}

10 And whatsoever man *there be* of*the*house of Israel, or of the strangers

^{df,qpta1481} ^{pp,nn,pnx8432} ^{pnl834} ^{qmf398} ^{cs,nn3605} ⁿⁿ¹⁸¹⁸ ^{wcs,qpf5414}

that sojourn among you, that eateth any manner of blood; I will even set my

^{pl,nn,pnx6440} ^{dfp,nn5315} ^{df,qpta398} ⁽⁸⁵³⁾ ^{df,nn1818} ^{wcs,hipf3772/pnx(853)} ^{pr4480/cs,nn7130}

face against that soul that eateth blood, and will cut*him*off from among

^{nn,pnx5971}

his people.

^{cj3588} ^{cs,nn5315} ^{df,nn1320} ^(pnp1931) ^{dfp,nn1818} ^{wcj,pnp589} ^{qpf,pnx5414}

11 For the life of the flesh *is* in the blood: and I have given it

^{pp,pnx} ^{pr5921} ^{df,nn4196} ^{pp,pinc3722} ^{pr5921} ^{pl,nn,pnx5315} ^{cj3588} ^{pnp1931}

to you upon the altar to make*an*atonement for your souls: for it *is* the

^{df,nn1818} ^{pimf3722} ^{dfp,nn5315}

blood *that* maketh*an*atonement for the soul.

^{pr5921/ad3651} ^{qpf559} ^{pp,pl,cs,nn1121} ⁿⁿ³⁴⁷⁸ ^{ptn3808/cs,nn3605} ⁿⁿ⁵³¹⁵ ^{pr,pnx4480}

12 Therefore I said unto the children of Israel, No soul of you shall

qmf398   nn1818   ptn3808   wcj,df,nn1616   df,qpta1481   pp,nn,pnx8432   qmf398   nn1818

eat blood, neither shall any stranger that sojourneth among you eat blood.

             wcj,nn376/nn376   pr4480/pl,cs,nn1121   nn3478   wcj,pr4480

13 And whatsoever man *there be* of*the*children of Israel, or of the

df,nn1616   df,qpta1481   pp,nn,pnx8432   pnl834   qmf6679   cs,nn6718   nn2416 cj176 nn5775

strangers that sojourn among you, which hunteth and catcheth any beast or fowl

pnl834   nimf398   wcs,qpf8210   (853)   nn,pnx1818   wcs,pipf,pnx3680

that may be eaten; he shall even pour out   the blood thereof, and cover it

     dfp,nn6083

with dust.

       cj3588   cs,nn5315   cs,nn3605   nn1320   nn,pnx1818   (pndm1931)   pp,nn,pnx5315

14 For *it is* the life of all flesh; the blood of it *is* for the life

             wcs,qmf559   pp,pl,cs,nn1121   nn3478   qmf398   cs,nn1818

thereof: therefore I said unto the children of Israel, Ye shall eat the blood of

ptn3808/cs,nn3605   nn1320   cj3588   cs,nn5315   cs,nn3605 nn1320 (pndm1931)   nn,pnx1818

no manner of flesh: for the life of all flesh *is* the blood thereof:

cs,nn3605   pl,qpta,pnx398   nimf3772

whosoever eateth it shall be cut off.

        wcj,cs,nn3605   nn5315   pnl834   qmf398   nn5038

15 And every soul that eateth that*which*died *of itself,* or

       wcj,nn2966   dfp,nn249

that*which*was*torn *with beasts, whether it be* one*of*your*own*country, or a

wcj,df,dfp,nn1616   wcs,pipf3526   pl,nn,pnx899   wcs,qpf7364   dfp,pl,nn4325

stranger, he shall both wash his clothes, and bathe *himself* in water, and

wcs,qpf2930   pr5704   df,nn6153   wcs,qpf2891

be unclean until the even: then shall he be clean.

      wcj,cj518   pimf3526   ptn3808 ptn3808 qmf7364   wcj,nn,pnx1320   wcs,qpf5375

16 But if he wash *them* not, nor bathe his flesh; then he shall bear his

nn,pnx5771

iniquity.

Forbidden Sexual Practices

                nn3068   wcs,pimf1696 pr413   nn4872   pp,qnc559

18 And the Lord spoke unto Moses, saying,

            pimv1696   pr413   pl,cs,nn1121   nn3478   wcj,qpf559 pr,pnx413   pnp589

2 Speak unto the children of Israel, and say unto them, I

nn3068   pl,nn,pnx430

am the Lord your God.

           pp,cs,nn4639   cs,nn776   nn4714   pnl834/pp,pnx   qpf3427   ptn3808 qmf6213

3 After the doings of the land of Egypt, wherein ye dwelt, shall ye not do:

        wcj,pp,cs,nn4639   cs,nn776   nn3667   pnl834/ad,lh8033 pnp589 hipt935 pnx(853)

and after the doings of the land of Canaan, whither I bring you, shall

ptn3808 qmf6213 ptn3808   qmf1980   wcj,pp,pl,nn,pnx2708

ye not do: neither shall ye walk in their ordinances.

          qmf6213 (853)   pl,nn,pnx4941   qmf8104 wcj(853)   pl,nn,pnx2708   pp,qnc1980

4 Ye shall do my judgments, and keep mine ordinances, to walk

pp,pnx   pnp589   nn3068   pl,nn,pnx430

therein: I *am* the Lord your God.

         wcs,qpf8104 (853)   pl,nn,pnx2708   wcj(853)   pl,nn,pnx4941 pnl834

5 Ye shall therefore keep my statutes, and my judgments: which if a

df,nn120 qmf6213 pnx(853)   wcs,qpf2425   pp,pnx   pnp589   nn3068

man do, he shall live in them: I *am* the Lord.

ptn3808/nn376/nn376   qmf7126   pr413   cs,nn3605   cs,nn7607   nn,pnx1320

6   None   of you shall approach to   any that is near of   kin   to him, to

pp,pinc1540   nn6172   pnp589   nn3068

uncover *their* nakedness: I   *am* the LORD.

cs,nn6172   nn,pnx1   wcj,cs,nn6172   nn,pnx517   ptn3808

7 The nakedness of thy father, or the nakedness of thy mother, shalt thou not

pimf1540   pnp1931   nn,pnx517   ptn3808   pimf1540   nn,pnx6172

uncover: she *is* thy mother; thou shalt not uncover her nakedness.

cs,nn6172   nn,pnx1   cs,nn802   ptn3808   pimf1540   pnp1931

8 The nakedness of thy father's wife shalt thou not uncover: it   *is* thy

nn,pnx1   cs,nn6172

father's nakedness.

cs,nn6172   nn,pnx269   cs,nn1323   nn,pnx1   cj176   cs,nn1323

9 The nakedness of thy sister, the daughter of thy father, or daughter of thy

nn,pnx517   cs,nn4138   nn1004   cj176 cs,nn4138   nn2351   nn,pnx6172

mother, *whether she be* born at home, or born abroad, *even* their nakedness thou

ptn3808   pimf1540

shalt not uncover.

cs,nn6172   nn,pnx1121   cs,nn1323   cj176   cs,nn1323   nn,pnx1323

10 The nakedness of thy son's daughter, or of thy daughter's daughter, *even*

nn,pnx6172   ptn3808   pimf1540   cj3588 pnp2007   nn,pnx6172

their nakedness thou shalt not uncover: for theirs *is* thine own nakedness.

cs,nn6172   nn,pnx1   cs,nn802   cs,nn1323   cs,nn4138   nn,pnx1   pnp1931

11 The nakedness of thy father's wife's daughter, begotten of thy father, she *is*

nn,pnx269   ptn3808   pimf1540   nn,pnx6172

thy sister, thou shalt not uncover her nakedness.

ptn3808   pimf1540   cs,nn6172   nn,pnx1   cs,nn269   pnp1931

12 Thou shalt not uncover the nakedness of thy father's sister: she   *is* thy

nn,pnx1   cs,nn7607

father's near kinswoman.

ptn3808   pimf1540   cs,nn6172   nn,pnx517   cs,nn269   cj3588 pnp1931

13 Thou shalt not uncover the nakedness of thy mother's sister: for   she   *is*

nn,pnx517   cs,nn7607

thy mother's near kinswoman.

ptn3808   pimf1540   cs,nn6172   nn,pnx1   cs,nn251   ptn3808

14 Thou shalt not uncover the nakedness of thy father's brother, thou shalt not

qmf7126   pr413   nn,pnx802 pnp1931   nn,pnx1733

approach to his wife: she *is* thine aunt.

ptn3808   pimf1540   cs,nn6172   nn,pnx3618   pnp1931

15 Thou shalt not uncover the nakedness of thy daughter-in-law: she *is* thy

nn,pnx1121 cs,nn802   ptn3808   pimf1540   nn,pnx6172

son's wife; thou shalt not uncover her nakedness.

ptn3808   pimf1540   cs,nn6172   nn,pnx251   cs,nn802   pnp1931

16 Thou shalt not uncover the nakedness of thy brother's wife: it   *is* thy

nn,pnx251   cs,nn6172

brother's nakedness.

ptn3808   pimf1540   cs,nn6172   nn802   wcj,nn,pnx1323   ptn3808

17 Thou shalt not uncover the nakedness of a woman and her daughter, neither

qmf3947 (853)   nn,pnx1121   cs,nn1323   wcj(853)   nn,pnx1323   cs,nn1323   pp,pinc1540

shalt thou take   her son's daughter, or   her daughter's daughter, to uncover

nn,pnx6172   pnp2007   nn,pnx7608   pnp1931   nn2154

her nakedness; *for* they *are* her near kinswomen: it *is* wickedness.

ptn3808   qmf3947   wcj,nn802 pr413   nn,pnx269   pp,qnc6887   pp,pinc1540

18 Neither shalt thou take a wife to her sister, to   vex   *her*, to uncover her

nn,pnx6172   pr,pnx5921   pp,pl,nn,pnx2416

nakedness, beside the other in her   life   *time*.

ptn3808 qmf7126 wcj,pr413 nn802 pp,pinc1540 nn,pnx6172

19 Also thou shalt not approach unto a woman to uncover her nakedness, as

pp,cs,nn5079 nn,pnx2932

long as she is put apart for her uncleanness.

ptn3808 qmf5414/nn,pnx7903/pp,nn2233 wcj,pr413 nn,pnx5997 cs,nn802

20 Moreover thou shalt not lie carnally with thy neighbor's wife, to

pp,qnc2930 pp,pnx

defile thyself with her.

ptn3808 qmf5414 wcj,pr4480/nn,pnx2233 pp,hinc5674 dfp,nn4432

☙ 21 And thou shalt not let any of*thy*seed pass through *the fire* to Molech,

wcj,ptn3808 pimf2490 (853) cs,nn8034 pl,nn,pnx430 pnp589 nn3068

neither shalt thou profane the name of thy God: I *am* the LORD.

ptn3808 qmf7901 wcj,pr854 nn2145 pl,cs,nn4904 nn802 pnp1931

22 Thou shalt not lie with mankind, as with womankind: it *is*

nn8441

abomination.

ptn3808 qmf5414/nn,pnx7903 wcj,pp,cs,nn3605 nn929 pp,qnc2930

23 Neither shalt thou lie with any beast to defile thyself

pp,pnx ptn3808 wcj,nn802 qmf5975 pp,pl,cs,nn6440 nn929 pp,qnc,pnx7250 pnp1931

therewith: neither shall any woman stand before a beast to lie down thereto: it

nn8397

is confusion.

htmf2930/ptn408 pp,cs,nn3605 pndm428 cj3588 pp,cs,nn3605 pndm428

24 Defile*not*ye*yourselves in any of these things: for in all these the

df,pl,nn1471 nipf2930 pnl834 pnp589 pipt7971 pr4480/pl,nn,pnx6440

nations are defiled which I cast out before you:

df,nn776 wcs,qmf2930 wcs,qmf6485 nn,pnx5771 pr,pnx5921

25 And the land is defiled: therefore I do visit the iniquity thereof upon it,

df,nn776 wcs,himf6958 (853) pl,qpta,pnx3427

and the land itself vomiteth out her inhabitants.

pnp859 wcj,qpf8104 (853) pl,nn,pnx2708 wcj(853) pl,nn,pnx4941

26 Ye shall therefore keep my statutes and my judgments, and shall

wcj,ptn3808 qmf6213 pr4480/cs,nn3605/df,pndm428 df,pl,nn8441 df,nn249

not commit *any* of these abominations; *neither* any*of*your*own*nation,

wcj,df,nn1616 df,qpta1481 pp,nn,pnx8432

nor any stranger that sojourneth among you:

cj3588 (853) cs,nn3605 df,pndm411 df,pl,nn8441 pl,cs,nn376 df,nn776 qpf6213 pnl834

27 (For all these abominations have the men of the land done, which

pp,pl,nn,pnx6440 df,nn776 wcs,qmf2930

were before you, and the land is defiled;)

df,nn776 himf6958/wcj,ptn3808/pnx(853) pp,pinc,pnx2930 pnx(853) pp,pnl834

28 That the land spew*not*you*out also, when ye defile it, as it

qpf6958 (853) df,nn1471 pnl834 pp,pl,nn,pnx6440

spewed out the nations that *were* before you.

cj3588 cs,nn3605/pnl834 qmf6213 pr4480/cs,nn3605 df,pndm428 df,pl,nn8441

29 For whosoever shall commit any of these abominations, even the

df,pl,nn5315 df,pl,qpta6213 wcs,nipf3772 pr4480/cs,nn7130 nn,pnx5971

souls that commit *them* shall be cut off from among their people.

☙ **18:21** Perhaps one of the most atrocious elements of the religion of Israel's neighbors in Canaan was the practice of human sacrifice. This passage and others (Lev. 20:2; Deut. 18:10) show how God hates this practice. Yet, some of the kings of Judah sacrificed their sons to Molech, the Ammonite national deity (2 Kgs. 16:3; 21:6; see the note on 2 Kgs 23:10). The people of Judah even built a special high place where they could sacrifice their sons and daughters (Jer. 7:31). All of this was done in the worship of foreign gods, which only served to intensify God's hatred of it.

wcs,qpf**8104** (853)   nn,pnx**4931**   qnc**6213**/pp,ptn1115

30 Therefore shall ye keep   mine ordinance, that**ye*commit*not *any one*

pr4480/pl,cs,nn**2708**/df,pl,nn**8441**   pnl834   nipf**6213**   pp,pl,nn**6440**

of*these*abominable*customs, which were committed before you, and that ye

htmf**2930**/wcj,ptn**3808**   pp,pnx   pnp589   nn**3068**   pl,nn,pnx**430**

defile*not*yourselves therein: I *am* the LORD your God.

Laws of Holiness and Justice

nn**3068** wcs,pimf**1696** pr413   nn4872   pp,qnc559

19

And the LORD spoke unto Moses, saying,

pimv**1696**   pr413 cs,nn3605   cs,nn**5712**   pl,cs,nn**1121**   nn3478

2 Speak unto   all the congregation of the children of Israel, and

wcj,qpf**559** pr,pnx413   qmf**1961** aj**6918** cj3588 pnp589   nn**3068**   pl,nn,pnx**430**   aj**6918**

say unto them, Ye shall be holy: for I the LORD your God *am* holy.

qmf**3372**   nn**376**   nn,pnx**517**   wcj,nn,pnx**1**   qmf**8104** wcj(853)

3 Ye shall fear every man his mother, and his father, and keep   my

pl,nn,pnx**7676** pnp589   nn**3068**   pl,nn,pnx**430**

sabbaths: I *am* the LORD your God.

qmf**6437**   ptn408 pr413 df,pl,nn**457** ptn**3808** qmf**6213**   pp,pnx   nn**4541** wcj,pl,cs,nn**430** pnp589

4 Turn ye not unto idols, nor make to yourselves molten gods: I *am* the

nn**3068**   pl,nn,pnx**430**

LORD your God.

wcj,cj3588   qmf**2076**   cs,nn**2077**   pl,nn**8002**   pp,nn**3068**

5 And if   ye offer a sacrifice of peace offerings unto the LORD, ye shall

qmf,pnx**2076**   pp,nn,pnx**7522**

offer it at your own   will.

nimf398   pp,cs,nn**3117**   nn,pnx**2077**   wcj,pr4480/nn**4283**

6 It shall be eaten the same day ye offer it, and on*the*morrow: and if

wcj,df,nipt**3498** pr5704 df,nuor7992 cs,nn**3117**   nimf**8313**   dfp,nn784

aught remain until the third day, it shall be burnt in the fire.

wcj,cj518   nina398/nimf398   df,nuor7992 dfp,nn**3117** pnp1931   nn**6292**

7 And if it be eaten*at*all on the third day, it *is* abominable; it shall

ptn**3808**   nimf**7521**

not be accepted.

wcj,pl,qpta,pnx398   qmf**5375**   nn,pnx**5771**   cj3588

8 Therefore *every one* that   eateth   it shall bear his iniquity, because he hath

pipf**2490**   (853)   cs,nn**6944**   nn**3068**   df,pndm1931 df,nn**5315**   wcj,nipf**3772**

profaned   the hallowed thing of the LORD: and   that   soul shall be cut off

pr4480/pl,nn,pnx**5971**

from*among*his*people.

wcj,pp,qnc,pnx**7114** (853)   cs,nn**7105**   nn,pnx**776**   ptn**3808**

9 And when ye   reap   the harvest of your land, thou shalt not

pimf**3615**/pp,qnc**7114**   cs,nn**6285**   nn,pnx**7704** ptn**3808**   pimf**3950**   wcj,cs,nn3951

wholly reap the corners of thy field, neither shalt thou gather the gleanings of thy

nn,pnx**7105**

harvest.

ptn**3808** pimf***5953**   wcj,nn,pnx3754 ptn**3808**   pimf**3950**

10 And thou shalt not glean thy vineyard, neither shalt thou gather *every*

19:9, 10 The Law of Moses contains numerous laws that protect poor people and foreigners. These
verses, along with Leviticus 23:22, put restrictions on how closely crops could be harvested, so the poor would
have something to glean. That the law was being followed during the period of the judges is evident from the
fact that Ruth gleaned in the field of Boaz, her future husband (Ruth 2:2–7).

wcj,cs,nn6528   nn,pnx3754   qmf5800 pnx(853)   dfp,aj6041   wcj,dfp,nn1616 pnp589

grape of thy vineyard; thou shalt leave   them for the poor and stranger: I

nn3068   pl,nn,pnx430

am the LORD your God.

ptn3808 qmf1589 wcj,ptn3808   pimf3584   wcj,ptn3808 pimf8266 nn376   pp,nn,pnx5997

11 Ye shall not steal, neither deal falsely, neither lie one to another.

wcj,ptn3808 nimf7650   pp,nn,pnx8034 dfp,nn8267   wcs,pipf2490

12 And ye shall   not   swear by my   name   falsely, neither shalt thou profane

(853)   cs,nn8034   pl,nn,pnx430 pnp589   nn3068

the name of thy God: I *am* the LORD.

ptn3808 qmf6231   (853)   nn,pnx7453 wcj,ptn3808 qmf1497   cs,nn6468

13 Thou shalt not defraud   thy neighbor, neither rob *him*: the wages of

aj7916   ptn3808   qmf3885/pr,pnx854   pr5704   nn1242

him*that*is*hired shall not abide*with*thee*all*night until the morning.

ptn3808 pimf7043   aj2795 ptn3808 qmf5414   nn4383   wcj,pp,pl,cs,nn6440

14 Thou shalt not curse the deaf, nor put a stumblingblock   before   the

aj5787   wcs,qpf3372/pr4480/pl,nn,pnx430 pnp589   nn3068

blind, but shalt   fear*thy*God: I *am* the LORD.

qmf6213 ptn3808   nn5766   dfp,nn4941   ptn3808 qmf5375

15 Ye shall do   no unrighteousness in judgment: thou shalt not respect the

pl,cs,nn6440   aj1800 wcj,ptn3808 qmf1921   pl,cs,nn6440   aj1419   pp,nn6664

person of the poor,   nor   honor the person of the mighty: *but* in righteousness shalt

qmf8199   nn,pnx5997

thou judge thy neighbor.

ptn3808   qmf1980   nn7400   pp,pl,nn,pnx5971 ptn3808

16 Thou shalt not go*up*and*down *as* a talebearer among thy people: neither

qmf5975 pr5921   cs,nn1818   nn,pnx7453 pnp589   nn3068

shalt thou stand against the blood of thy neighbor: I *am* the LORD.

ptn3808   qmf8130 (853)   nn,pnx251   pp,nn,pnx3824

17 Thou shalt not hate   thy brother in thine   heart: thou shalt

hina3198/himf3198   (853)   nn,pnx5997   wcj,ptn3808 qmf5375 nn2399 pr,pnx5921

in*any*wise*rebuke   thy neighbor, and   not suffer sin upon him.

ptn3808   qmf5358 wcj,ptn3808   qmf5201   (853)   pl,cs,nn1121

☞ 18 Thou shalt not avenge,   nor   bear*any*grudge against   the children of

nn,pnx5971   wcs,qpf157   pp,nn,pnx7453 pp,pnx3644 pnp589   nn3068

thy people, but thou shalt love thy neighbor as thyself: I *am* the LORD.

qmf8104 (853)   pl,nn,pnx2708   ptn3808   nn,pnx929 himf7250

19 Ye shall keep   my statutes. Thou shalt not let thy cattle engender with a

du,nn3610   ptn3808 qmf2232   nn,pnx7704   du,nn3610   ptn3808

diverse kind: thou shalt not sow thy field with mingled seed: neither shall a

wcj,cs,nn899 du,nn3610   nn8162   qmf5927 pr,pnx5921

garment mingled of linen*and*woolen come upon thee.

wcj,nn376/cj3588 qmf7901 cs,nn7902/nn2233 pr854   nn802   wcj,pnp1931   nn8198

20 And whosoever lieth carnally with a woman,   that   *is* a bondmaid,

nipt2778   pp,nn376   ptn3808 wcj,hona6299/nipf6299 cj176/ptn3808   nn2668   nipf5414 pp,pnx

betrothed to a husband, and not at*all*redeemed,   nor   freedom given her; she

qmf1961   nn1244   ptn3808   homf4191   cj3588   pupf2666/ptn3808

shall be scourged; they shall not be put*to*death, because she was*not*free.

wcs,hipf935 (853)   nn,pnx817   pp,nn3068 pr413   cs,nn6607

21 And he shall bring   his trespass offering unto the LORD, unto the door

cs,nn168   nn4150   cs,nn352   nn817

of the tabernacle of the congregation, *even* a ram for a trespass offering.

☞ **19:18** See the note on Exodus 20:1–17.

df,nn3548　　　　wcs,pipf3722　　　　pr,pnx5921　　　　pp,cs,nn352

22 And the priest shall make*an*atonement for him with the ram of the

df,nn817　　　pp,pl,cs,nn6440　　　nn3068　　pr5921　　nn,pnx2403　　pnl834　　　　qpf2398

trespass offering before the LORD for his sin which he hath done: and the

pr4480/nn,pnx2403　pnl834　　　　qpf2398　　　　wcj,nipf5545　　pp,pnx

sin which he hath done shall be forgiven him.

wcj,cj3588　　　qmf935　pr413　　df,nn776　　　　wcs,qpf5193　　cs,nn3605

23 And when ye shall come into the land, and shall have planted all manner of

cs,nn6086　　nn3978　　　wcs,qpf6188 (853)　　nn,pnx6529　　　　aj,pnx6189　　nu7969

trees for food, then ye shall count the fruit thereof as uncircumcised: three

pl,nn8141　　qmf1961　　aj6189　　pp,pnx　　ptn3808　　nimf398

years shall it be as uncircumcised unto you: it shall not be eaten of.

df,nuor7243　wcj,dfp,nn8141　cs,nn3605　　nn,pnx6529　　　qmf1961　nn6944　pl,nn1974

24 But in the fourth year all the fruit thereof shall be holy to praise

pp,nn3068

the LORD *withal*.

df,nuor2549　wcj,dfp,nn8141　　qmf398 (853)　　nn,pnx6529

25 And in the fifth year shall ye eat of the fruit thereof, that it

pp,hinc3254　　pp,pnx　　nn,pnx8393　　pnp589　　nn3068　　pl,nn,pnx430

may yield unto you the increase thereof: I *am* the LORD your God.

ptn3808　qmf398　　　　pr5921　df,nn1818　ptn3808

26 Ye shall not eat *any thing* with the blood: neither shall ye

pimf5172　　wcj,ptn3808　pimf*6049

use enchantment, nor observe times.

ptn3808　himf5362　　cs,nn6285　　nn,pnx7218　wcj,ptn3808　　himf7843 (853)

27 Ye shall not round the corners of your heads, neither shalt thou mar the

cs,nn6285　　nn,pnx2206

corners of thy beard.

ptn3808　qmf5414　　wcj,nn8296　　pp,nn,pnx1320　　dfp,nn5315 ptn3808 qmf5414

28 Ye shall not make any cuttings in your flesh for the dead, nor print

wcj,cs,nn3793/nn7085　pp,pnx　pnp589　　nn3068

any marks upon you: I *am* the LORD.

ptn408　pimf2490　(853)　　nn,pnx1323　　pp,hinc,pnx2181　wcj,ptn3808

29 Do not prostitute thy daughter, to cause her to be*a*whore; lest the

df,nn776　　qmf2181　　df,nn776　wcs,qpf4390　　nn2154

land fall*to*whoredom, and the land become full of wickedness.

qmf8104 (853)　　pl,nn,pnx7676　　qmf3372　　wcj,nn,pnx4720 pnp589

30 Ye shall keep my sabbaths, and reverence my sanctuary: I *am* the

nn3068

LORD.

qmf6437　ptn408　(pr413)　　　df,pl,nn178　　ptn408　pimf1245　wcj,pr413

31 Regard not them*that*have*familiar*spirits, neither seek after

df,pl,nn3049　　pp,qnc2930　pp,pnx　pnp589　　nn3068　pl,nn,pnx430

wizards, to be defiled by them: I *am* the LORD your God.

qmf6965　pr4480/pl,cs,nn6440　　nn7872　　wcs,qpf1921　pl,cs,nn6440

32 Thou shalt rise up before the hoary head, and honor the face of the

aj2205　wcs,qpf3372/pr4480/pl,nn,pnx430 pnp589　　nn3068

old man, and fear*thy*God: I *am* the LORD.

wcj,cj3588　　nn1616　qmf1481　pr,pnx854　　pp,nn,pnx776　　ptn3808 himf3238

☉⚥ 33 And if a stranger sojourn with thee in your land, ye shall not vex

pnx(853)

him.

☉⚥ **19:33, 34** This did not eliminate all the distinctions between the Israelites and the foreigners living among them. In certain contexts, especially in the lending of money, the foreigners were to be treated differently. The

df,nn1616   df,qpta1481   pr,pnx854   qmf1961   pp,pnx

34 *But* the stranger that dwelleth with you shall be unto you as

pp,nn249/pr,pnx4480   wcs,qpf157 pp,pnx   pp,pnx3644   cj3588   qpf1961   pl,nn1616

one*born*among you, and thou shalt love him as thyself; for ye were strangers in

pp,cs,nn776   nn4714   pnp589   nn3068   pl,nn,pnx430

the land of Egypt: I *am* the LORD your God.

qmf6213 ptn3808   nn5766   dfp,nn4941   dfp,nn4060   dfp,nn4948

35 Ye shall do no unrighteousness in judgment, in meteyard, in weight, or

wcj,dfp,nn4884

in measure.

nn6664   du,cs,nn3976   nn6664   pl,cs,nn68   nn6664 cs,nn374   nn6664 wcj,cs,nn1969   pp,pnx qmf1961

36 Just balances, just weights, a just ephah, and a just hin, shall ye have:

pnp589   nn3068   pl,nn,pnx430   pnl834   hipf3318/pnx(853)   pr4480/cs,nn776   nn4714

I *am* the LORD your God, which brought*you*out of*the*land of Egypt.

wcj,qpf8104   (853)   cs,nn3605   pl,nn,pnx2708   wcj(853) cs,nn3605

37 Therefore shall ye observe all my statutes, and all my

pl,nn,pnx4941   wcj,qpf6213 pnx(853)   pnp589   nn3068

judgments, and do them: I *am* the LORD.

The Penalties for Sin

nn3068 wcs,pimf1696 pr413   nn4872   pp,qnc559

20 And the LORD spoke unto Moses, saying,

qmf559 wcj,pr413   pl,cs,nn1121   nn3478   nn376/nn376

2 Again, thou shalt say to the children of Israel, Whosoever

pr4480/pl,cs,nn1121   nn3478   wcj,pr4480   df,nn1616   df,qpta1481   pp,nn3478 pnl834

he be of*the*children of Israel, or of the strangers that sojourn in Israel, that

qmf5414   pr4480/nn,pnx2233   dfp,nn4432   qna4191/homf4191   cs,nn5971

giveth *any* of*his*seed unto Molech; he shall surely*be*put*to*death: the people of

df,nn776   qmf,pnx7275   dfp,nn68

the land shall stone him with stones.

wcj,pnp589   qmf5414   (853)   pl,nn,pnx6440   df,pndm1931 dfp,nn376

3 And I will set my face against that man, and will

wcs,hipf3772/pnx(853)   pr4480/cs,nn7130   nn,pnx5971   cj3588   qpf5414   pr4480/nn,pnx2233

cut*him*off from among his people; because he hath given of*his*seed unto

dfp,nn4432   pp,pr4616 pinc2930 (853)   nn,pnx4720   wcj,pp,pinc2490 (853)   nn,pnx6944 cs,nn8034

Molech, to defile my sanctuary, and to profane my holy name.

wcj,cj518   cs,nn5971   df,nn776   hina5956/himf5956   (853)   du,nn,pnx5869

4 And if the people of the land do any*ways*hide their eyes

pr4480/df,nn376/df,pndm1931   pp,qnc,pnx5414   pr4480/nn,pnx2233   dfp,nn4432   hinc4191 pnx(853)

from*the*man, when he giveth of*his*seed unto Molech, and kill him

pp,ptn1115

not:

pnp589   wcs,qpf7760 (853)   pl,nn,pnx6440   df,pndm1931 dfp,nn376

5 Then I will set my face against that man, and against his

---

usual reason to lend to a fellow countryman was to help a poor man get back on his feet, and no interest was to be exacted (Lev. 25:35–38). The case was different for foreigners, who could be charged interest (Deut. 23:20) and whose debts were not cancelled on the Sabbatical Year (Deut. 15:1–3). Nevertheless, Leviticus 19:33, 34 expresses the overriding ethical concern, and it is based on the fact that they themselves had been foreigners in Egypt.

wcj,pp,nn,pnx**4940**   wcs,hipf**3772**/pnx(853)   wcj(853)   cs,nn3605   df,pl,qpta**2181**   pr,pnx310

family, and will cut*him*off, and all that go*a*whoring after him, to

pp,qnc**2181**   pr310   df,nn4432   pr4480/cs,nn**7130**   nn,pnx**5971**

commit whoredom with Molech, from among their people.

         wcj,df,nn**5315**   pnl834   qmf6437   pr413   df,pl,nn**178**   wcj,pr413

6 And the soul that turneth after such*as*have*familiar*spirits, and after

df,pl,nn**3049**   pp,qnc**2181**   pr,pnx310   wcs,qpf**5414** (853)   pl,nn,pnx**6440**

wizards, to go*a*whoring after them, I will even set my face against

df,pndm1931   dfp,nn**5315**   wcs,hipf**3772**/pnx(853)   pr4480/cs,nn**7130**   nn,pnx**5971**

that soul, and will cut*him*off from among his people.

        wcs,htpf**6942**   wcs,qpf**1961**   aj6918   cj3588   pnp589   nn**3068**

7 Sanctify yourselves therefore, and be ye holy: for I *am* the LORD your

pl,nn,pnx**430**

God.

         wcs,qpf**8104** (853)   pl,nn,pnx**2708**   wcs,qpf**6213** pnx(853)   pnp589   nn**3068**

8 And ye shall keep my statutes, and do them: I *am* the LORD

pipt,pnx**6942**

which sanctify you.

    cj3588   nn**376**/nn**376**   pnl834   pimf**7043** (853)   nn,pnx1   wcj(853)   nn,pnx**517**

9 For every one that curseth his father or his mother shall be

qna4191/homf**4191**   pipf**7043**   nn,pnx1   wcj,nn,pnx**517**   pl,nn,pnx**1818**

surely*put*to*death: he hath cursed his father or his mother; his blood *shall be*

pp,pnx

upon him.

      pnl834   nn**376**   pnl834   qmf5003   pr854   nn**376**   cs,nn**802**

10 And the man that committeth adultery with *another* man's wife, *even he*

pnl834   qmf5003   pr854   nn,pnx**7453**   cs,nn**802**   df,qpta5003   wcj,df,qpta5003

that committeth adultery with his neighbor's wife, the adulterer and the adulteress

         qna4191/homf**4191**

shall surely*be*put*to*death.

       wcj,nn**376**   pnl834   qmf7901   pr854   nn,pnx1   cs,nn**802**   pipf**1540**   nn,pnx1

11 And the man that lieth with his father's wife hath uncovered his father's

cs,nn**6172**   du,nu,pnx**8147**   qna4191/homf**4191**   pl,nn,pnx**1818**

nakedness: both of them shall surely*be*put*to*death; their blood *shall be*

pp,pnx

upon them.

       pnl834   wcj,nn**376**   qmf7901   pr854   nn,pnx3618   du,nu,pnx8147

12 And if a man lie with his daughter-in-law, both of them shall

qna4191/homf**4191**   qpf**6213**   nn8397   pl,nn,pnx**1818**

surely*be*put*to*death: they have wrought confusion; their blood *shall be*

pp,pnx

upon them.

       pnl834   wcj,nn**376**   qmf7901   pr854   nn2145   pl,cs,nn4904   nn**802**   du,nu,pnx8147

13 If a man also lie with mankind, as he lieth with a woman, both

         qpf**6213**   nn**8441**   qna4191/homf**4191**

of them have committed an abomination: they shall surely*be*put*to*death; their

pl,nn,pnx**1818**   pp,pnx

blood *shall be* upon them.

       pnl834   wcj,nn**376**   qmf3947 (853)   nn**802**   wcj(853)   nn,pnx**517**   pnp1931   nn**2154**

14 And if a man take a wife and her mother, it *is* wickedness:

         qmf**8313**   dfp,nn784   pnx(853)   wcj,pnx(853)   qmf1961   wcj,ptn3808

they shall be burnt with fire, both he and they; that there be no

nn**2154**   pp,nn,pnx**8432**

wickedness among you.

15 And if a man lie with a beast, he shall surely*be*put*to*death:
and ye shall slay the beast.

16 And if a woman approach unto any beast, and lie down thereto,
thou shalt kill the woman, and the beast: they shall
surely*be*put*to*death; their blood *shall be* upon them.

17 And if a man shall take his sister, his father's daughter, or his
mother's daughter, and see her nakedness, and she see his nakedness;
it *is* a wicked thing; and they shall be cut off in the sight of their
people: he hath uncovered his sister's nakedness; he shall bear his iniquity.

18 And if a man shall lie with a woman having*her*sickness, and shall
uncover her nakedness; he hath discovered her fountain, and she hath
uncovered the fountain of her blood: and both of them shall be cut off
from among their people.

19 And thou shalt not uncover the nakedness of thy mother's sister, nor of thy
father's sister: for he uncovereth his near kin: they shall bear their iniquity.

20 And if a man shall lie with his uncle's wife, he hath uncovered his
uncle's nakedness: they shall bear their sin; they shall die childless.

21 And if a man shall take his brother's wife, it *is* an unclean thing:
he hath uncovered his brother's nakedness; they shall be childless.

22 Ye shall therefore keep all my statutes, and all my
judgments, and do them: that the land, whither I bring you to
dwell therein, spew*you*not*out.

23 And ye shall not walk in the manners of the nation, which I cast out
before you: for they committed all these things, and therefore I
abhorred them.

24 But I have said unto you, Ye shall inherit their land, and I will
give it unto you to possess it, a land that floweth with milk and honey: I
am the LORD your God, which have separated you from *other* people.

_{wcj,hipf914   pr996   df,aj2889 df,nn929   dfp,aj2931}
25 Ye shall therefore put difference between clean beasts and unclean, and

_{wcj,pr996   df,aj2931 df,nn5775   dfp,aj2889   wcj,ptn3808   pimf8262/(853)/pl,nn,pnx5315}
between unclean fowls and clean: and ye shall   not   make*your*souls*abominable

_{dfp,nn929   wcj,dfp,nn5775   wcj,pp,nn3605   qmf7430/pnl834}
by beast, or by   fowl,   or by any manner of living*thing*that*creepeth on the

_{df,nn127   pnl834   hipf914   pp,pnx   pp,pinc2930}
ground, which I have separated from you as unclean.

_{wcj,qpf1961 aj6918   pp,pnx   cj3588 pnp589   nn3068   aj6918}
 26 And ye shall   be   holy unto me: for   I   the LORD *am* holy, and have

_{wcs,himf914 pnx(853)   pr4480   df,pl,nn5971   pp,qnc1961 pp,pnx}
severed   you from *other* people, that ye should   be   mine.

_{wcj,nn376   cj176   nn802   cj3588 pp,pnx/qmf1961   nn178   cj176   nn3049}
27 A man also or woman that   hath   a familiar spirit, or that is a wizard,

_{qna4191/homf4191   qmf7275 pnx(853)   dfp,nn68   pl,nn,pnx1818}
shall surely*be*put*to*death: they shall stone   them with stones: their blood

_{pp,pnx}
shall be upon them.

The Holiness of the Priests

_{nn3068   wcs,qmf559 pr413   nn4872   qmv559   pr413   df,pl,nn3548   pl,cs,nn1121}
2 And the LORD said unto Moses, Speak unto the priests the   sons of

_{nn175   wcj,qpf559 pr,pnx413   ptn3808   htmf2930}
1 Aaron, and   say   unto them, There shall none be defiled for the

_{pp,nn5315   pp,pl,nn,pnx5971}
dead among his people:

_{cj3588/cj518   pp,nn,pnx7607   df,aj7138 pr,pnx413   pp,nn,pnx517}
2   But   for his   kin,   that is near unto him, *that is,* for his mother, and for

_{wcj,pp,nn,pnx1   wcj,pp,nn,pnx1121   wcj,pp,nn,pnx1323   wcj,pp,nn,pnx251}
his father, and for his   son,   and for his daughter, and for his brother,

_{wcj,pp,nn,pnx269 df,nn1330   df,aj7138 pr,pnx413   pnl834   qpf1961 ptn3808}
3 And for his   sister   a virgin, that is nigh unto him, which hath had   no

_{pp,nn376   pp,pnx   htmf2930}
husband; for her may he be defiled.

_{ptn3808   htmf2930   nn1167   pp,pl,nn,pnx5971}
4 *But* he shall   not defile himself, *being* a chief man among his people,   to

_{pp,ninc,pnx2490}
profane himself.

_{ptn3808 qmf7139   nn7144   pp,nn,pnx7218 ptn3808   pimf1548}
5 They shall not make baldness upon their head, neither shall they shave off

_{wcj,cs,nn6285   nn,pnx2206 ptn3808 qmf8295   nn8296   wcj,pp,nn,pnx1320}
the corner of their beard, nor make any cuttings in their   flesh.

_{qmf1961   aj6918   pp,pl,nn,pnx430   wcj,ptn3808   pimf2490   cs,nn8034}
6 They shall be holy unto their God,   and   not   profane the name of their

_{pl,nn,pnx430 cj3588   (853)   pl,cs,nn801/nn3068   cs,nn3899}
God: for   the offerings*of*the*LORD*made*by*fire, *and* the bread of their

_{pl,nn,pnx430 pnp1992   pl,hipt7126   wcs,qpf1961 nn6944}
God, they do offer: therefore they shall   be   holy.

_{ptn3808 qmf3947   nn802   qpta2181   wcj,aj2491   ptn3808}
7 They shall not take a wife *that is* a whore, or profane; neither shall they

qmf3947   wcj,nn802   qptp1644   pr4480/nn,pnx376   cj3588 pnp1931   aj6918   pp,pl,nn,pnx430
take a woman put away from*her*husband: for he *is* holy unto his   God.

             wcs,pipf,pnx6942   cj3588 pnp1931   hipt7126   (853)   cs,nn3899
8 Thou shalt sanctify him therefore; for he offereth   the bread of thy

pl,nn,pnx430   qmf1961 aj6918   pp,pnx   cj3588 pnp589   nn3068   pipt,pnx6942
God: he shall be holy unto thee: for I   the LORD, which sanctify you, *am*

aj6918
holy.

          wcj,cs,nn1323   nn376   nn3548   cj3588   nimf2490
9 And the daughter of any priest, if   she profane herself by

pp,qnc2181   pnp1931   pipt2490   (853)   nn,pnx1   nimf8313   dfp,nn784
playing*the*whore, she profaneth   her father: she shall be burnt with fire.

          df,aj1419 wcj,df,nn3548   pr4480/pl,nn,pnx251   pr5921 pnl834   nn,pnx7218
10 And *he that is* the high priest among*his*brethren, upon whose head the

df,nn4888   cs,nn8081   homf3332   wcs,pipf4390/(853)/nn,pnx3027   pp,qnc3847 (853)   df,pl,nn899
anointing oil was poured, and that is   consecrated   to put on   the garments,

ptn3808   qmf6544   (853)   nn,pnx7218 ptn3808 qmf6533   wcj,pl,nn,pnx899
shall not uncover   his head, nor rend his clothes;

     ptn3808   qmf935 wcj,pr5921 cs,nn3605 qpta4191 pl,cs,nn5315 ptn3808   htmf2930
11 Neither shall he go in to   any dead body, nor defile himself for his

pp,nn,pnx1   wcj,pp,nn,pnx517
father, or for his   mother;

     ptn3808   qmf3318 wcj,pr4480   df,nn4720   wcj,ptn3808 pimf2490   (853)   cs,nn4720
12 Neither shall he go out of   the sanctuary, nor profane   the sanctuary

pl,nn,pnx430 cj3588   cs,nn5145   cs,nn4888   cs,nn8081   pl,nn,pnx430 pr,pnx5921   pnp589
of his God; for the crown of the anointing oil of his God *is* upon him: I

nn3068
am the LORD.

     wcj,pnp1931   qmf3947   nn802   pp,pl,nn,pnx1331
13 And he   shall take a wife in her virginity.

     nn490   wcj,qptp1644   wcj,aj2491   qpta2181 (853) pndm428
14 A widow, or a divorced woman, or profane, *or* a harlot,   these shall he

ptn3808 qmf3947 cj3588/cj518   qmf3947   nn1330   pr4480/pl,nn,pnx5971   nn802
not take: but he shall take a virgin of*his*own*people to wife.

     wcj,ptn3808   pimf2490   nn,pnx2233   pp,pl,nn,pnx5971 cj3588 pnp589   nn3068
15 Neither shall he profane his seed among his people: for I   the LORD

pipt,pnx6942
do sanctify him.

     nn3068 wcs,pimf1696 pr413   nn4872   pp,qnc559
16 And the LORD spoke unto Moses, saying,

     pimv1696   pr413   nn175   pp,qnc559   nn376/pnl834   pr4480/nn,pnx2233   pp,pl,nn,pnx1755
17 Speak unto Aaron, saying, Whosoever *he be* of*thy*seed in their generations

qmf1961/pp,pnx   nn3971   ptn3808   qmf7126   pp,hinc7126   cs,nn3899   pl,nn,pnx430
that hath *any* blemish, let him not approach to offer the bread of his God.

cj3588   cs,nn3605   nn376   pnl834/pp,pnx   nn3971   ptn3808 qmf7126
18 For whatsoever man *he be*   that   hath a blemish, he shall not approach: a

aj5787   nn376 aj176   aj6455 cj176   qptp2763   cj176   qptp8311
blind man, or a lame, or he*that*hath*a*flat*nose, or any*thing*superfluous,

cj176   nn376 pnl834 qmf1961/pp,pnx   cs,nn7667/nn7272 cj176   cs,nn7667/nn3027
19 Or a man that is   broken-footed, or broken-handed,

cj176   aj1384   cj176   aj1851 cj176   nn8400   pp,nn,pnx5869 cj176
20 Or crookbacked, or a dwarf, or that hath a blemish in his eye,   or be

nn1618   cj176   nn3217 cj176   nn810   cs,aj4790
scurvy, or scabbed, or hath his stones broken;

     ptn3808/cs,nn3605 nn376 pnl834/pp,pnx   nn3971   pr4480/cs,nn2233   nn175   df,nn3548
21   No   man that   hath a blemish of*the*seed of Aaron the priest shall

^{qmf5066}   ^{pp,hinc7126}   (853)   ^{pl,cs,nn801/nn3068}   ^{pp,pnx}

come nigh to offer   the offerings*of*the*LORD*made*by*fire: he hath a

ⁿⁿ³⁹⁷¹   ^{ptn3808}   ^{qmf5066}   ^{pp,hinc7126} (853)   ^{cs,nn3899}   ^{pl,nn,pnx430}

blemish; he shall not come nigh to offer   the bread of his God.

^{qmf398}   ^{cs,nn3899}   ^{pl,nn,pnx430}   ^{pr4480/pl,cs,nn6944/df,pl,nn6944}   ^{wcj,pr4480}

22 He shall eat the bread of his God, *both* of*the*most*holy, and of the

^{df,pl,nn6944}

holy.

^{ad389}   ^{ptn3808} ^{qmf935}   ^{pr413}   ^{df,nn6532} ^{ptn3808}   ^{qmf5066}   ^{wcj,pr413}   ^{df,nn4196}

23 Only he shall not go in unto the veil, nor come nigh unto the altar,

^{cj3588}   ^{pp,pnx}   ⁿⁿ³⁹⁷¹   ^{pimf2490} ^{wcj,ptn3808} (853)   ^{pl,nn,pnx4720} ^{cj3588} ^{pnp589}

because he hath a blemish; that he profane not   my sanctuaries: for I   the

ⁿⁿ³⁰⁶⁸   ^{pipt,pnx6942}

LORD do sanctify them.

ⁿⁿ⁴⁸⁷²   ^{wcs,pimf1696} ^{pr413}   ⁿⁿ¹⁷⁵   ^{wcj,pr413}   ^{pl,nn,pnx1121}   ^{wcj,pr413} ^{cs,nn3605}

24 And Moses told *it* unto Aaron, and to his sons, and unto all the

^{pl,cs,nn1121}   ⁿⁿ³⁴⁷⁸

children of Israel.

The Holiness of the Offerings

ⁿⁿ³⁰⁶⁸ ^{wcs,pimf1696} ^{pr413}   ⁿⁿ⁴⁸⁷²   ^{pp,qnc559}

And the LORD spoke unto Moses, saying,

^{pimv1696}   ^{pr413}   ⁿⁿ¹⁷⁵   ^{wcj,pr413}   ^{pl,nn,pnx1121}

2 Speak unto Aaron and to his sons, that they

^{wcj,nimf5144}   ^{pr4480/pl,cs,nn6944}   ^{pl,cs,nn1121}   ⁿⁿ³⁴⁷⁸

separate themselves from*the*holy*things of the children of Israel, and that they

^{pimf2490} ^{wcj,ptn3808} (853)   ^{nn,pnx6944} ^{cs,nn8034}   ^{pnl834} ^{pnp1992} ^{pl,hipt6942} ^{pp,pnx}   ^{pnp589}

profane not   my holy name *in those things* which they hallow unto me: I

ⁿⁿ³⁰⁶⁸

am the LORD.

^{qmv559} ^{pr,pnx413}   ^{cs,nn3605/nn376}   ^{pr4480/cs,nn3605}   ^{nn,pnx2233}

3 Say unto them, Whosoever *he be* of all   your seed among your

^{pp,pl,nn,pnx1755}   ^{pnl834} ^{qmf7126} ^{pr413}   ^{df,pl,nn6944}   ^{pnl834}   ^{pl,cs,nn1121}   ⁿⁿ³⁴⁷⁸   ^{himf6942}

generations, that goeth unto the holy things, which the children of Israel hallow

^{pp,nn3068}   ^{wcj,nn,pnx2932} ^{pr,pnx5921}   ^{df,pndm1931} ^{df,nn5315}   ^{wcs,nipf3772}

unto the LORD, having his uncleanness upon him, that soul shall be cut off

^{pr4480/pp,pl,nn,pnx6440} ^{pnp589}   ⁿⁿ³⁰⁶⁸

from*my*presence: I *am* the LORD.

^{nn376/nn376}   ^{pr4480/cs,nn2233}   ⁿⁿ¹⁷⁵ (wcj,pnp1931)   ^{qptp6879} ^{cj176}

4 What*man*soever of*the*seed of Aaron   *is* a leper, or

^{qpta2100}   ^{ptn3808} ^{qmf398}   ^{dfp,pl,nn6944} ^{cj5704/pnl834}   ^{qmf2891}

hath*a*running*issue; he shall not eat of the holy things, until he be clean.

^{wcj,df,qpta5060}   ^{pp,cs,nn3605}   ^{cs,aj2931}   ⁿⁿ⁵³¹⁵ ^{cj176}   ⁿⁿ³⁷⁶   ^{pnl834}

And whoso toucheth any thing *that is* unclean by the dead, or a man whose

^{cs,nn7902/nn2233} ^{qmf3318} ^{pr,pnx4480}

seed goeth from him;

^{cj176}   ^{nn376/pnl834}   ^{qmf5060}   ^{pp,cs,nn3605}   ⁿⁿ⁸³¹⁸   ^{pnl834}   ^{pp,pnx}

5 Or whosoever toucheth any   creeping thing, whereby he may be

^{qmf2930}   ^{cj176}   ^{pp,nn120}   ^{pnl834} ^{pp,pnx}   ^{qmf2930}   ^{pp,cs,nn3605}

made unclean, or a man of whom he may take uncleanness, whatsoever

^{nn,pnx2932}

uncleanness he hath;

nn5315 pnl834   qmf5060   pp,pnx   wcs,qpf2930   pr5704 df,nn6153

6 The soul which hath touched any such shall be unclean until even, and shall

wcj,ptn3808 qmf398 pr4480   df,pl,nn6944   cj3588/cj518   qpf7364   nn,pnx1320   dfp,pl,nn4325

not   eat of the holy things, unless he wash his flesh with water.

df,nn8121 wcj,qpf935   wcj,qpf2891   wcj,ad310   qmf398 pr4480

7 And when the sun is down, he shall be clean, and shall afterward eat of

df,pl,nn6944   cj3588 pnp1931   nn,pnx3899

the holy things; because it is his food.

nn5038   wcj,nn2966   ptn3808 qmf398   pp,qnc2930

8 That*which*dieth*of*itself, or is torn with beasts, he shall not eat to defile

pp,pnx   pnp589   nn3068

himself therewith: I am the LORD.

wcs,qpf8104 (853)   nn,pnx4931 wcj,ptn3808   qmf5375 nn2399 pr,pnx5921

9 They shall therefore keep   mine ordinance, lest they bear sin   for

wcs,qpf4191   pp,pnx   cj3588   pimf,pnx2490   pnp589   nn3068   pipt,pnx6942

it, and die therefore, if they profane it: I the LORD do sanctify them.

ptn3808/wcj,cs,nn3605 qpta2114 qmf398   nn6944   cs,nn8453

10 There shall   no   stranger eat of the holy thing: a sojourner of the

nn3548   wcj,aj7916   ptn3808 qmf398   nn6944

priest, or a hired servant, shall not eat of the holy thing.

cj3588   wcj,nn3548 qmf7069   nn5315 cs,nn7075/nn,pnx3701 pnp1931   qmf398 pp,pnx

11 But if the priest buy any soul with*his*money, he shall eat of it, and

wcj,cs,aj3211   nn,pnx1004 pnp1992   qmf398   pp,nn,pnx3899

he*that*is*born in his house: they shall eat of his   meat.

cj3588   nn3548 wcj,cs,nn1323   qmf1961   pp,nn376/qpta2114 pnp1931   ptn3808

12 If the priest's daughter also be married unto a stranger, she may not

qmf398   pp,cs,nn8641   df,pl,nn6944

eat of an offering of the holy things.

cj3588   nn3548 wcj,cs,nn1323 qmf1961   nn490   wcj,qptp1644   (pp,pnx) ptn369

13 But if the priest's daughter be a widow, or divorced, and have   no

wcj,nn2233   wcs,qpf7725   pr413   nn,pnx1   cs,nn1004   pp,pl,nn,pnx5271   qmf398

child, and is returned unto her father's house, as in her   youth,   she shall eat

pr4480/cs,nn3899/nn,pnx1   wcj,cs,nn3605/ptn3808   qpta2114   qmf398   pp,pnx

of*her*father's*meat: but there shall   no   stranger eat thereof.

cj3588   wcj,nn376 qmf398   nn6944   pp,nn7684   wcs,qpf3254

14 And if a man eat of the holy thing unwittingly, then he shall   put   the

nuor,pnx2549   pr,pnx5921   wcs,qpf5414   dfp,nn3548 (853)

fifth   part thereof unto it, and shall give it unto the priest   with the

df,nn6944

holy thing.

wcj,ptn3808 pimf2490   (853)   pl,cs,nn6944   pl,cs,nn1121   nn3478

15 And they shall   not profane   the holy things of the children of Israel,

(853) pnl834   himf7311   pp,nn3068

which they offer unto the LORD;

pnx(853)   wcs,hipf5375   cs,nn5771   nn819   pp,qnc,pnx398

16 Or suffer   them to bear the iniquity of trespass, when they   eat

(853)   pl,nn,pnx6944   cj3588 pnp589   nn3068   pipt,pnx6942

their holy things: for I the LORD do sanctify them.

nn3068 wcs,pimf1696 pr413   nn4872   pp,qnc559

17 And the LORD spoke unto Moses, saying,

pimv1696   pr413   nn175   wcj,pr413   pl,nn,pnx1121   wcj,pr413 cs,nn3605   pl,cs,nn1121

18 Speak unto Aaron, and   to   his sons,   and unto all   the children of

nn3478   wcj,qpf559 pr,pnx413   nn376/nn376   pr4480/cs,nn1004   nn3478   wcj,pr4480

Israel, and say   unto them, Whatsoever he be of*the*house of Israel, or of

df,nn1616   pp,nn3478 pnl834   himf7126   nn,pnx7133   pp,cs,nn3605   pl,nn,pnx5088

the strangers in Israel, that will offer his oblation for   all   his vows, and for

df,nuor7637   wcj,dfp,nn8141   qmf1961   cs,nn7676   nn7677   dfp,nn776

4 But in the seventh year shall be a sabbath of rest unto the land, a

nn7676   pp,nn3068   ptn3808   qmf2232   nn,pnx7704 ptn3808 qmf2168   wcj,nn,pnx3754

sabbath for the LORD: thou shalt neither sow thy field, nor prune thy vineyard.

(853)   cs,nn5599   nn,pnx7105   ptn3808

5 That*which*groweth*of*its*own*accord of thy harvest thou shalt not

qmf7114   ptn3808   qmf1219   wcj(853)   pl,cs,nn6025   nn,pnx5139   qmf1961   cs,nn8141

reap, neither gather   the grapes of thy vine undressed: *for* it is a year of

nn7677   dfp,nn776

rest unto the land.

cs,nn7676   df,nn776   wcs,qpf1961 pp,nn402   pp,pnx   pp,pnx

6 And the sabbath of the land shall be meat for you; for thee, and for thy

wcj,pp,nn,pnx5650   wcj,pp,nn,pnx519   wcj,pp,aj,pnx7916   wcj,pp,nn,pnx8453

servant, and for thy maid, and for thy hired servant, and for thy stranger

df,pl,qpta1481   pr,pnx5973

that sojourneth with thee,

wcj,pp,nn,pnx929   wcj,dfp,nn2416 pnl834   pp,nn,pnx776   cs,nn3605

7 And for thy cattle, and for the beast that *are* in thy land, shall all

nn,pnx8393   qmf1961 pp,qnc398

the increase thereof be meat.

wcs,qpf5608 cs,nu7651 pl,cs,nn7676   pl,nn8141   pp,pnx   cs,nu7651 pl,nn6471 cs,nu7651

8 And thou shalt number seven sabbaths of years unto thee, seven times seven

pl,nn8141   pl,cs,nn3117   cs,nu7651 pl,cs,nn7676   df,pl,nn8141   wcs,qpf1961   pp,pnx   wcj,pl,nu705

years; and the space of the seven sabbaths of years shall be unto thee forty

nu8672   nn8141

and nine years.

cs,nn7782   nn8643   wcs,hipf5674   dfp,nn6218

9 Then shalt thou cause the trumpet of the jubilee to sound on the tenth *day*

(dfp,nn2320)   df,nuor7637   dfp,nn2320   pp,cs,nn3117   df,pl,nn3725   nn7782

of the seventh month, in the day of atonement shall ye make the trumpet

himf5674   pp,cs,nn3605   nn,pnx776

sound throughout all your land.

wcs,pipf6942   (853)   (cs,nn8141)   df,pl,nu2572   nn8141   wcs,qpf7121   nn1865

10 And ye shall hallow   the fiftieth year, and proclaim liberty

dfp,nn776   pp,cs,nn3605   pl,qpta,pnx3427   pnp1931   qmf1961

throughout *all* the land unto all the inhabitants thereof: it shall be a

nn3104   pp,pnx   wcs,qpf7725   nn376   pr413   nn,pnx272

jubilee unto you; and ye shall return every man unto his possession, and ye shall

qmf7725   wcj,nn376   pr413   nn,pnx4940

return every man unto his family.

nn3104   pndm1931 (cs,nn8141) df,pl,nu2572 nn8141 qmf1961   pp,pnx   ptn3808 qmf2232

11 A jubilee shall that   fiftieth year be unto you: ye shall not sow,

wcj,ptn3808 qmf7114 (853)   pl,nn,pnx5599   wcj,ptn3808   qmf1219   (853)

neither reap that*which*groweth*of*itself in it, nor gather *the grapes* in it

pl,nn,pnx5139

of thy vine undressed.

cj3588   pnp1931   nn3104   qmf1961 nn6944   pp,pnx   qmf398 (853)

12 For it *is* the jubilee; it shall be holy unto you: ye shall eat the

nn,pnx8393   pr4480   df,nn7704

increase thereof out of the field.

pp,cs,nn8141   df,pndm2063   df,nn3104   qmf7725   nn376   pr413

13 In the year of this jubilee ye shall return every man unto his

nn,pnx272

possession.

wcj,cj3588   qmf4376   nn4465   pp,nn,pnx5997   cj176   qna7069

14 And   if   thou   sell   aught unto thy neighbor,   or   buyest *aught*

pr4480/cs,nn**3027**/nn,pnx5997   ptn408 himf**3238** nn376 (853) nn,pnx**251**

of*thy*neighbor's*hand, ye shall not oppress one   another:

              pp,cs,nn4557 pl,nn8141 pr310   df,nn3104   qmf7069 pr4480/pr854

15 According to the number of years after the jubilee thou shalt buy   of

nn,pnx5997   pp,cs,nn4557 pl,cs,nn8141   pl,nn8393   qmf4376

thy neighbor, *and* according unto the number of years of the fruits he shall sell

pp,pnx

unto thee:

       pp,cs,nn**6310**   cs,nn7230   df,pl,nn8141   himf7235   nn,pnx4736

16 According to the multitude of years thou shalt increase the price thereof,

wcj,pp,cs,nn**6310**   qnc4591 df,pl,nn8141   himf4591   nn,pnx4736   cj3588

and according to the fewness of years thou shalt diminish the price of it: for

cs,nn4557   pl,nn8393   pnp1931 qpta4376   pp,pnx

according to the number *of the years* of the fruits doth he   sell unto thee.

         wcj,ptn**3808**   himf**3238** (853) nn376 nn,pnx5997

17 Ye shall   not   therefore oppress   one another; but thou shalt

wcs,qpf**3372**/pr4480/pl,nn,pnx**430** cj3588 pnp589   nn**3068**   pl,nn,pnx**430**

fear*thy*God: for   I   *am* the LORD your God.

                wcs,qpf**6213** (853)   pl,nn,pnx**2708**   qmf**8104** wcj(853)   pl,nn,pnx**4941**

18 Wherefore ye shall   do   my statutes, and keep   my judgments, and

wcs,qpf**6213** pnx(853)   wcs,qpf**3427** pr5921 df,nn776   pp,nn**983**

do   them; and ye shall dwell in the land in safety.

df,nn**776**   wcs,qpf**5414**   nn,pnx6529   wcs,qpf398   pp,nn7648

19 And the land shall   yield   her fruit, and ye shall   eat   your   fill,   and

wcs,qpf**3427** pr,pnx5921 pp,nn**983**

dwell therein in safety.

       wcj,cj3588   qmf559 pnit4100   qmf398   df,nuor7637 dfp,nn8141 ptdm2005

20 And   if ye shall say, What shall we eat the seventh year? behold, we

ptn**3808** qmf2232 wcj,ptn**3808**   qmf622   (853)   nn,pnx8393

shall not sow, nor   gather in   our increase:

                 wcs,pipf**6680** (853)   nn,pnx**1293**   pp,pnx   df,nuor8345 dfp,nn8141

21 Then I will command   my blessing upon you in the sixth   year, and it

wcs,qpf**6213** (853) df,nn8393   pp,cs,nu7969 df,pl,nn8141

shall bring forth   fruit for three   years.

         wcs,qpf2232   (853) df,nuor8066 df,nn8141   wcs,qpf398   pr4480 aj3465 df,nn8393 pr5704

22 And ye shall   sow   the   eighth year, and eat *yet* of old fruit until

df,nuor8671 df,nn8141 pr5704   nn,pnx8393 qnc935   qmf398   aj3465

the ninth year; until her fruits come in ye shall eat *of* the old *store*.

       wcj,df,nn**776**   ptn**3808** nimf4376 pp,nn**6783** cj3588 df,nn**776**   pp,pnx cj3588 pnp859

23 The land   shall not be sold forever: for the land *is* mine; for ye *are*

pl,nn**1616**   wcj,pl,nn**8453** pr,pnx5973

strangers and sojourners with me.

       wcj,pp,cs,nn3605   cs,nn776   nn,pnx272   qmf**5414**   nn1353

24 And in   all   the land of your possession ye shall grant a redemption for

dfp,nn**776**

the land.

    cj3588   nn,pnx**251**   qmf4134   wcs,qpf**4376**

25 If   thy   brother be*waxen*poor,   and   hath sold away *some*

pr4480/nn,pnx**272**   df,aj7138/pr,pnx413 wcs,qpf935 qpta,pnx**1350**   wcs,qpf**1350**

of*his*possession, and if any*of*his*kin come to redeem it, then shall he redeem

(853)   cs,nn4465/nn,pnx**251**

that*which*his*brother*sold.

cj3588   wcj,nn376   qmf1961   ptn3808/qpta1350   pp,pnx   wcs,hipf5381/nn,pnx3027
26 And   if   the   man   have   none*to*redeem   it,   and   himself

wcs,qpf4672/pp,cs,nn1767   nn,pnx1353
be able   to redeem it;

wcs,pipf2803 (853)   pl,cs,nn8141   nn,pnx4465   wcs,hipf7725 (853)
27 Then let him count   the years of the sale thereof, and restore   the

df,qpta5736   dfp,nn376   pnl834   qpf4376 pp,pnx   wcj,qpf7725   pp,nn,pnx272
surplus unto the man to whom he sold it; that he may return unto his possession.

wcj,cj518   nn,pnx3027 ptn3808/qpf4672/cs,nn1767   hinc7725   pp,pnx   nn,pnx4465
28 But   if   he   be*not*able   to restore it to him, then that*which*is*sold

wcj,qpf1961   pp,cs,nn3027   df,qpta7069   pnx(853)   pr5704   cs,nn8141
shall remain in the   hand   of him that*hath*bought   it until the   year   of

df,nn3104   dfp,nn3104   wcj,qpf3318   wcj,qpf7725   pp,nn,pnx272
jubilee: and in the jubilee it shall go out, and he shall return unto his possession.

cj3588   wcj,nn376   qmf4376   cs,nn4186   cs,nn1004   nn2346   nn5892
29 And   if   a man   sell   a dwelling house in a walled city, then he may

wcs,qpf1961/nn,pnx1353   pr5704   qnc8552   cs,nn8141   nn,pnx4465   pl,nn3117
redeem   it within a whole   year   after it is   sold; within a full year may he

qmf1961/nn,pnx1353
redeem   it.

wcj,cj518   ptn3808   nimf1350   pr5704   qnc4390/pp,pnx   aj8549   nn8141
30 And   if   it be   not   redeemed within the   space   of a full year, then the

df,nn1004   pnl834   pnl834/pp,pnx/nn2346   dfp,nn5892   wcs,qpf6965   dfp,nn6783
house   that   is   in   the   walled   city   shall   be   established   forever   to

dfp,qpta7069   pnx(853)   pp,pl,nn,nn1755   ptn3808   qmf3318
him*that*bought   it throughout his generations: it shall   not   go out in the

dfp,nn3104
jubilee.

wcj,pl,cs,nn1004   df,pl,nn2691   pnl834/pp,pnx   ptn369 nn2346   ad5439
31 But the   houses   of the villages   which   have   no   wall round about them

nimf2803   pr5921   cs,nn7704   df,nn776   qmf1961   nn1353/pp,pnx
shall be counted   as   the fields of the country: they may   be   redeemed, and they

qmf3318   wcj,dfp,nn3104
shall go out in the jubilee.

wcj,pl,cs,nn5892   df,pl,nn3881   pl,cs,nn1004   pl,cs,nn5892
32 Notwithstanding the   cities   of the Levites, and the houses of the   cities

nn,pnx272   pp,pl,nn3881 qmf1961/cs,nn1353   nn5769
of their possession, may the Levites   redeem   at*any*time.

wcj,pnl834   qmf1350   pr4480   df,pl,nn3881   nn1004   cs,nn4465
33 And if a man   purchase   of   the Levites, then the house that was sold, and

wcj,cs,nn5892   nn,pnx272   wcs,qpf3318   dfp,nn3104 cj3588   pl,cs,nn1004
the   city   of his possession, shall go out in the year of jubilee: for the houses of

pl,cs,nn5892   df,pl,nn3881 (pnp1931)   nn,pnx272   pp,cs,nn8432   pl,cs,nn1121   nn3478
the cities of the Levites   are their possession among the children of Israel.

wcj,cs,nn7704   cs,nn4054   pl,nn,pnx5892   ptn3808   nimf4376 cj3588 pnp1931
34 But the   field   of the suburbs of their   cities   may not be sold; for   it

pp,pnx   nn5769   cs,nn272
is their perpetual possession.

wcj,cj3588   nn,pnx251   qmf4134   wcs,qpf4131/nn,pnx3027   pr,pnx5973
☿ 35 And   if   thy brother be*waxen*poor, and fallen*in*decay   with thee; then

---

☿ **25:35–38**   See the note on Leviticus 19:33, 34.

<small>wcs,hipf2388   pp,pnx   nn1616   wcj,nn8453</small>
thou shalt relieve him: *yea, though he be* a stranger, or a sojourner; that he may
<small>wcs,qpf2421   pr,pnx5973</small>
live   with thee.

<small>qmf3947   ptn408 nn5392 pr4480/pr,pnx854   wcj,nn8636   wcs,qpf3372/pr4480/pl,nn,pnx430</small>
36 Take thou no usury   of   him, or increase: but   fear*thy*God;   that
<small>nn,pnx251   wcs,qpf2421 pr,pnx5973</small>
thy brother may live   with thee.

<small>ptn3808 qmf5414 pp,pnx (853)   nn,pnx3701   pp,nn5392 ptn3808 qmf5414</small>
37 Thou shalt not give him   thy money upon usury, nor lend him thy
<small>nn,pnx400   wcj,pp,nn4768</small>
victuals for increase.

<small>pnp589   nn3068   pl,nn,pnx430 pnl834   hipf3318/pnx(853)   pr4480/cs,nn776</small>
38 I *am* the Lord your God, which brought*you*forth out*of*the*land of
<small>nn4714   pp,qnc5414 pp,pnx (853)   cs,nn776   nn3667   pp,qnc1961 pp,pnx pp,pl,nn430</small>
Egypt, to give you   the land of Canaan, *and* to be   your God.

<small>wcj,cj3588   nn,pnx251   pr,pnx5973   qmf4134</small>
39 And   if   thy brother *that dwelleth* by   thee be*waxen*poor, and be
<small>wcs,nipf4376   pp,pnx   ptn3808   qmf5647/pp,pnx   cs,nn5656/nn5650</small>
sold   unto thee; thou shalt not compel*him*to*serve as a bondservant:

<small>pp,aj7916   pp,nn8453   qmf1961 pr,pnx5973</small>
40 *But* as a hired servant, *and* as a sojourner, he shall be   with thee, *and*
<small>qmf5647/pr,pnx5973   pr5704   cs,nn8141   df,nn3104</small>
shall   serve   thee unto the year of jubilee:

<small>wcs,qpf3318 pr4480/pr,pnx5973   pnp1931   wcj,pl,nn,pnx1121</small>
41 And *then* shall he depart   from   thee, *both* he   and his children
<small>pr,pnx5973   wcs,qpf7725 pr413   nn,pnx4940   wcj,pr413   cs,nn272</small>
with him, and shall return unto his own family, and unto the possession of his
<small>pl,nn,pnx1   qmf7725</small>
fathers shall he return.

<small>cj3588 pnp1992   pl,nn,pnx5650 pnl834   hipf3318   pnx(853)   pr4480/cs,nn776</small>
42 For they *are* my servants, which I brought forth   out*of*the*land of
<small>nn4714   ptn3808   nimf4376   cs,nn4466/nn5650</small>
Egypt: they shall not be sold as bondmen.

<small>ptn3808 qmf7287   pp,pnx   pp,nn6531   wcs,qpf3372/pr4480/pl,nn,pnx430</small>
43 Thou shalt not rule over him with rigor; but shalt   fear*thy*God.

<small>wcj,nn,pnx5650   wcj,nn,pnx519   pnl834   pp,pnx   qmf1961</small>
44 Both thy bondmen, and thy bondmaids, which thou shalt have, *shall be*
<small>pr4480/pr854   df,pl,nn1471 pnl834   pr,pnx5439   pr,pnx4480   qmf7069   nn5650</small>
of   the heathen that are round about you;   of   them shall ye buy bondmen
<small>wcj,nn519</small>
and bondmaids.

<small>wcj,ad1571   pr4480/pl,cs,nn1121   df,pl,nn8453   df,pl,qpta1481 pr,pnx5973   pr,pnx4480</small>
45 Moreover of*the*children of the strangers that do sojourn among you,   of
<small>qmf7069   wcj,pr4480/nn,pnx4940 pnl834   pr,pnx5973   pnl834   hipf3205</small>
them shall ye buy, and of*their*families that *are* with you, which they begot in
<small>pp,nn,pnx776   wcj,qpf1961 pp,pnx   pp,nn272</small>
your land: and they shall   be   your possession.

<small>wcj,htpf5157/pnx(853)   pp,pl,nn,pnx1121 pr,pnx310</small>
46 And ye shall take*them*as*an*inheritance for your children after you, to
<small>pp,qnc3423   nn272   qmf5647/pp,pnx   pp,nn5769</small>
inherit *them for* a possession; they shall be*your*bondmen forever: but over your
<small>wcj,pp,pl,nn,pnx251   pl,cs,nn1121   nn3478   ptn3808 qmf7287/pp,pnx pr376   pp,nn,pnx251   pp,nn6531</small>
brethren   the children of Israel, ye shall not   rule   one over another with rigor.

<small>wcj,cj3588   cs,nn3027/nn1616   wcj,nn8453   himf5381 pr,pnx5973   nn,pnx251</small>
47 And   if   a sojourner or stranger wax rich   by   thee, and thy brother *that*

pr,pnx5973   wcs,qpf4134   wcs,nipf4376   pp,nn**1616**   nn**8453**   pr,pnx5973

dwelleth by him wax poor, and sell himself unto the stranger *or* sojourner by

cj176   pp,cs,nn6133   nn**1616**   cs,nn**4940**

thee, or to the stock of the stranger's family:

ad310   nipf4376   qmf**1961**   nn1353/pp,pnx   nu259   pr4480/pl,nn,pnx**251**

48 After that he is sold he may be redeemed again; one of*his*brethren may

qmf,pnx**1350**

redeem him:

cj176   nn,pnx**1730**   cj176   nn,pnx**1730**   cs,nn**1121**   qmf,pnx**1350**   cj176   pr4480/cs,nn**7607**

49 Either his uncle, or his uncle's son, may redeem him, or *any* that*is*nigh

nn,pnx**1320**   pr4480/nn,pnx**4940**   qmf,pnx**1350**   cj176   hipf5381/nn,pnx**3027**

of kin unto him of*his*family may redeem him; or if he be able, he may

wcj,nipf**1350**

redeem himself.

wcj,pipf**2803**   pr5973   qpta,pnx**7069**   pr4480/cs,nn8141

50 And he shall reckon with him*that*bought him from*the*year that he was

ninc,pnx4376   pp,pnx   pr5704   cs,nn8141   df,nn3104   cs,nn3701   nn,pnx4465   wcj,qpf**1961**

sold to him unto the year of jubilee: and the price of his sale shall be

pp,cs,nn4557   pl,nn8141   pp,pl,cs,nn**3117**   aj7916

according unto the number of years, according to the time of a hired servant

qmf**1961** pr,pnx5973

shall it be with him.

cj518   ad5750   aj7227   dfp,pl,nn8141   pp,nn,pnx**6310**

51 If *there be* yet many years *behind*, according unto them he shall

himf**7725**   nn,pnx**1353**   pr4480/cs,nn3701   nn,pnx4736

give again the price*of*his*redemption out*of*the*money that he was bought for.

wcj,cj518   nipf**7604**   nn4592 dfp,pl,nn8141 pr5704   cs,nn8141   df,nn3104

52 And if there remain but few years unto the year of jubilee, then he

wcj,pipf**2803**   pp,pnx   pp,cs,nn**6310**   pl,nn,pnx8141   himf**7725**   (853)

shall count with him, *and* according unto his years shall he give*him*again

nn,pnx**1353**

the price*of*his*redemption.

nn8141/pp,nn8141   pp,cs,aj7916   qmf**1961** pr,pnx5973

53 *And* as a yearly hired servant shall he be with him: *and the other*

ptn**3808**   qmf,pnx**7287**/pp,nn6531   pp,du,nn,pnx**5869**

shall not rule*with*rigor*over him in thy sight.

wcj,cj518   ptn**3808**   nimf**1350**   pp,pndm428   wcs,qpf3318

54 And if he be not redeemed in these *years*, then he shall go out in the

pp,cs,nn8141   df,nn3104   pnp1931   wcj,pl,nn,pnx**1121** pr,pnx5973

year of jubilee, *both* he, and his children with him.

cj3588   pp,pnx   pl,cs,nn**1121**   nn3478   pl,nn**5650**   pnp1992   pl,nn,pnx**5650**

55 For unto me the children of Israel *are* servants; they *are* my servants

pnl834/pnx(853)   hipf3318   pr4480/cs,nn**776**   nn4714   pnp589   nn**3068**   pl,nn,pnx**430**

whom I brought forth out*of*the*land of Egypt: I *am* the LORD your God.

Blessings for Obedience

qmf**6213** pp,pnx ptn**3808** pl,nn**457**   wcj,nn**6459**   ptn**3808**   himf**6965**/pp,pnx

26 Ye shall make you no idols nor graven image, neither rear*you*up a

wcj,nn**4676**   ptn**3808**   qmf**5414**   nn**4906**   wcj,cs,nn68

standing image, neither shall ye set up *any* image of stone in your

pp,nn,pnx**776**   pp,htnc***7812**   pr,pnx5921   cj3588 pnp589   nn**3068**   pl,nn,pnx**430**

land, to bow down unto it: for I *am* the LORD your God.

_{qmf8104} (853)   _{pl,nn,pnx7676}   _{qmf3372}   _{wcj,nn,pnx4720}   _{pnp589}

2 Ye shall keep   my sabbaths, and reverence my sanctuary: I *am* the
_{nn3068}
LORD.

_{cj518}   _{qmf1980}   _{pp,pl,nn,pnx2708}   _{qmf8104} _{wcj(853)}   _{pl,nn,pnx4687}   _{wcs,qpf6213}

3 If ye walk in my statutes, and keep   my commandments, and   do
_{pnx(853)}
   them;

_{wcs,qpf5414}   _{pl,nn,pnx1653}   _{pp,nn,pnx6256}   _{df,nn776}   _{wcs,qpf5414}

4 Then I will give you   rain in due season, and the land shall yield her
_{nn,pnx2981}   _{wcj,cs,nn6086}   _{df,nn7704}   _{qmf5414}   _{nn,pnx6529}

increase, and the   trees of the field shall yield their fruit.

_{pp,pnx}   _{nn1786}   _{wcs,hipf5381} (853)   _{nn1210}   _{wcj,nn1210}

5 And your threshing shall reach   unto the vintage, and the vintage shall
_{himf5381} (853)   _{nn2233}   _{wcs,qpf398}   _{nn,pnx3899}   _{dfp,nn7648}

reach   unto the sowing time: and ye shall   eat   your bread to the full, and
_{wcs,qpf3427}   _{pp,nn,pnx776} _{pp,nn983}

dwell in your   land safely.

_{wcs,qpf5414} _{nn7965}   _{dfp,nn776}   _{wcs,qpf7901}   _{wcj,ptn369}

6 And I will   give peace in the land, and ye shall lie down, and none shall
_{hipt2729}   _{wcs,hipf7673} _{aj7451} _{nn2416}   _{pr4480}   _{df,nn776}   _{ptn3808}

make*you*afraid: and I will   rid   evil beasts out of the land, neither shall the
_{wcj,nn2719} _{qmf5674}   _{pp,nn,pnx776}

sword go through your land.

_{wcs,qpf7291} (853)   _{pl,qpta,pnx341}   _{wcs,qpf5307} _{pp,pl,nn,pnx6440}

7 And ye shall chase   your enemies, and they shall   fall   before you by
_{dfp,nn2719}

the sword.

_{nu2568} _{pr,pnx4480}   _{wcs,qpf7291}   _{nu3967}   _{wcj,nu3967} _{pr,pnx4480}

8 And five   of   you shall chase a hundred, and a hundred   of   you shall
_{qmf7291/nn7233}   _{pl,qpta,pnx341}   _{wcs,qpf5307} _{pp,pl,nn,pnx6440}

put*ten*thousand*to*flight: and your enemies shall   fall   before you by the
_{dfp,nn2719}

sword.

_{wcs,qpf6437}   _{pr,pnx413}   _{wcs,hipf6509/pnx(853)}   _{wcs,hipf7235} _{pnx(853)}

☞ 9 For I will have respect unto you, and make*you*fruitful, and multiply
_{wcs,hipf6965} (853)   _{nn,pnx1285}   _{pr,pnx854}

you, and establish   my covenant with you.

_{wcs,qpf398} _{aj3465/nipt3462}   _{himf3318}   _{wcj,aj3465} _{pr4480/pl,cs,nn6440}

10 And ye shall   eat   old store, and bring forth the   old   because   of the
_{aj2319}

new.

_{wcs,qpf5414}   _{nn,pnx4908}   _{pp,nn,pnx8432}   _{nn,pnx5315}   _{wcj,ptn3808}

11 And I will   set   my tabernacle among you: and my soul shall   not
_{qmf1602} _{pnx(853)}

abhor   you.

_{wcs,htpf1980} _{pp,nn,pnx8432}   _{wcs,qpf1961} _{pp,pnx} _{pp,pl,nn430}   _{wcj,pnp859}

12 And I will walk   among you, and will   be   your God, and ye   shall
_{qmf1961} _{pp,pnx} _{pp,nn5971}

be my people.

_{pnp589}   _{nn3068}   _{pl,nn,pnx430} _{pnl834}   _{hipf3318/pnx(853)}   _{pr4480/cs,nn776}

13 I *am* the LORD your God, which brought*you*forth out*of*the*land of

---

☞ **26:9** This conditional statement is built upon the promises to Abraham (Gen. 12:1–3; 13:16; 15:5; 17:5, 6; 18:18; 22:17, 18), but it does not change those unconditional promises (Gal. 3:17).

nn4714   pr4480/qnc**1961**   pp,pnx   pl,nn**5650**   wcs,qmf**7665**   pl,cs,nn4133

Egypt, that*ye*should*not*be their bondmen; and I have broken the bands of your

nn,pnx5923   wcs,himf**1980**/pnx(853)   ad6968

yoke, and made*you*go upright.

Punishment for Disobedience

wcj,cj518   ptn**3808**   qmf**8085**   pp,pnx   wcj,ptn**3808**   qmf**6213**   (853)   cs,nn3605

14 But   if   ye will   not   hearken unto me, and will   not   do   all

df,pndm428   df,pl,nn**4687**

these commandments;

wcj,cj518   qmf**3988**   pp,pl,nn,pnx**2708**   wcj,cj518   nn,pnx**5315**   qmf**1602**   (853)

15 And   if   ye shall despise my statutes, or   if   your soul abhor   my

pl,nn,pnx**4941**   pp,ptn1115   qnc**6213**   (853)   cs,nn3605   pl,nn,pnx**4687**

judgments, so that ye will   not   do   all   my commandments, *but* that ye

pp,hinc,pnx**6565** (853)   nn,pnx**1285**

break   my covenant:

pnp589   cj637   qmf**6213** pndm2063   pp,pnx   wcs,hipf**6485** pr,pnx5921   nn**928**   (853)

16 I   also will do   this   unto you; I will even appoint over   you terror,

df,nn7829   wcj(853)   df,nn6920   pl,pipt**3615**   du,nn**5869**

consumption, and   the burning ague, that shall consume the eyes, and

wcj,pl,hipt1727   nn**5315**   wcs,qpf2232   nn,pnx**2233**   dfp,nn7385   pl,qpta,pnx341

cause sorrow of heart: and ye shall   sow   your   seed   in vain, for your enemies

wcs,qpf,pnx398

shall   eat   it.

wcs,qpf**5414**   pl,nn,pnx**6440**   pp,pnx   wcs,nipf**5062** pp,pl,cs,nn**6440**

17 And I will   set   my   face   against you, and ye shall be   slain   before

pl,qpta,pnx341   pl,qpta,pnx**8130**   wcs,qpf**7287**   pp,pnx   wcs,qpf5127

your enemies: they*that*hate you shall   reign   over you; and ye shall   flee   when

wcj,ptn369   qpta7291   pnx(853)

none   pursueth   you.

wcj,cj518   ptn**3808**   cj5704   pndm428   qmf**8085**   pp,pnx   pp,pinc**3256**

18 And   if   ye will   not yet for   all   this   hearken unto me, then I will punish

pnx(853)   nu7651   wcs,qpf3254 pr5921   pl,nn,pnx**2403**

you seven times more   for   your   sins.

wcs,qpf**7665** (853)   cs,nn1347   nn,pnx5797   wcs,qpf**5414** (853)

19 And I will break   the pride of your power; and I will make   your

du,nn,pnx**8064**   dfp,nn1270   wcj(853)   nn,pnx776   dfp,nn5154

heaven as iron, and   your earth as brass:

nn,pnx3581   wcs,qpf**8552**   dfp,nn7385 .   nn,pnx**776**   wcj,ptn**3808** qmf**5414**

20 And your strength shall be spent in vain: for your   land   shall   not   yield

(853)   nn,pnx2981   ptn**3808**   wcj,cs,nn6086   df,nn776 qmf**5414**   nn,pnx6529

her increase, neither shall the   trees   of the land yield their fruits.

wcj,cj518   qmf**1980**   nn7147   pr,pnx5973   qmf14 wcj,ptn**3808** pp,qnc**8085**   pp,pnx

21 And   if   ye walk contrary unto   me, and will   not   hearken unto me; I

wcs,qpf3254/nu7651   nn**4347**   pr,pnx5921   pp,pl,nn,pnx**2403**

will bring*seven*times*more plagues upon   you according to your   sins.

wcs,hipf7971   (853)   df,nn**7704**   cs,nn2416   pp,pnx

22 I   will   also   send   wild   beasts   among you,   which   shall

wcs,pipf7921/pnx(853)   wcs,hipf3772   (853)   nn,pnx929

rob*you*of*your*children,   and   destroy   your   cattle,   and

wcs,hipf4591/pnx(853)   pl,nn,pnx**1870**   wcs,nipf**8074**

make*you*few*in*number; and your *high*   ways   shall be desolate.

23 And   if   ye will   not   be reformed   by me   by these things,   but will   walk

contrary unto me;

24 Then will   I   also   walk contrary unto you, and   will punish

you yet seven times for your sins.

25 And I will   bring   a sword   upon   you, that shall avenge the quarrel of *my*

covenant: and when ye are gathered together within your cities, I will   send   the

pestilence among you; and ye shall be delivered into the   hand   of the enemy.

26 *And* when I have   broken   the staff of your bread, ten women shall bake

your bread in one oven, and they shall deliver*you*your*bread*again by weight:

and ye shall eat, and   not   be satisfied.

27 And   if   ye will not for all this hearken unto me, but   walk   contrary

unto me;

28 Then I will   walk contrary unto you also in   fury;   and I, even   I,   will

chastise   you seven times for your   sins.

29 And ye shall   eat   the flesh of your   sons,   and the   flesh   of your

daughters shall ye eat.

30 And I will destroy   your high places, and cut down   your images, and

cast   your carcasses upon the carcasses of your   idols,   and my   soul   shall

abhor   you.

31 And   I   will   make   your   cities   waste,   and

bring*your*sanctuaries*unto*desolation, and I will   not   smell the   savor   of your

sweet odors.

32 And   I   will   bring*the*land*into*desolation: and your enemies which

dwell   therein shall be astonished   at   it.

33 And I will scatter   you among the heathen, and will draw out a sword

after you: and your land shall   be   desolate, and your   cities   waste.

34 Then shall the land enjoy   her sabbaths, as*long*as   it lieth desolate,

wcj,pnp859   pl,qpta,pnx341   pp,cs,nn776   ad227   df,nn776 qmf7673   wcs,hipf7521 (853)

and   ye   *be* in your enemies' land;   *even* then shall the land rest, and   enjoy

pl,nn,pnx7676

her sabbaths.

cs,nn3605/pl,cs,nn3117   honc,pnx8074   qmf7673 (853)   pnl834   ptn3808 qpf7673

35 As*long*as it lieth desolate it shall rest;   because it did not rest in your

pp,pl,nn,pnx7676   pp,qnc,pnx3427 pr,pnx5921

sabbaths, when ye   dwelt   upon it.

wcj,df,pl,nipt7604   pp,pnx   wcj,hipf935   nn4816

36 And upon them that*are*left *alive* of you I will   send   a faintness into their

pp,nn,pnx3824   pp,pl,cs,nn776   pl,qpta,pnx341   cs,nn6963   nipt5086   nn5929   wcj,qpf7291

hearts in the lands of their enemies; and the sound of a shaken leaf shall chase

pnx(853)   wcj,qpf5127   cs,nn4499   nn2719   wcj,qpf5307

them; and they shall flee,   as fleeing from a sword; and they shall   fall

wcj,ptn369   qpta7291

when none pursueth.

wcj,qpf3782   nn376   pp,nn,pnx251   pp,pr4480/pl,cs,nn6440   nn2719

37 And they shall   fall   one upon another, as it were   before   a sword,

ptn369   wcj,qpta7291   pp,pnx   qmf1961 wcj,ptn3808   nn8617   pp,pl,cs,nn6440

when none pursueth: and   ye   shall have   no   power*to*stand before   your

pl,qpta,pnx341

enemies.

wcs,qpf6   dfp,pl,nn1471   cs,nn776   pl,qpta,pnx341

38 And ye shall perish among the heathen, and the land of your enemies shall

wcs,qpf398/pnx(853)

eat*you*up.

wcj,df,pl,nipt7604   pp,pnx   nimf4743   pp,nn,pnx5771

39 And they that*are*left of you shall pine away in their iniquity in your

pl,qpta,pnx341 pp,pl,cs,nn776   wcj,cj637   pp,pl,cs,nn5771   pl,nn,pnx1   nimf4743

enemies' lands; and also in the iniquities of their fathers shall they pine away

pr,pnx854

with them.

wcs,htpf3034 (853)   nn,pnx5771   wcj(853)   cs,nn5771   pl,nn,pnx1

40 If they shall confess   their iniquity, and   the iniquity of their fathers,

pp,nn,pnx4604   pnl834   qpf4603   pp,pnx   pnl834 wcj,cj637

with their trespass which they trespassed against me, and that also   they have

qpf1980   pp,nn7147 pr,pnx5973

walked contrary unto me;

pnp589 cj637   qmf1980   pp,nn7147 pr,pnx5973   wcs,hipf935 pnx(853)

41 And *that* I   also have walked contrary unto them, and have brought

pp,cs,nn776   pl,qpta,pnx341 cj176 ad227   df,aj6189   nn,pnx3824

them into the land of their enemies; if then their uncircumcised hearts be

nimf3665   wcj,ad227 qmf7521   (853)   nn,pnx5771

humbled, and they then accept of   the punishment*of*their*iniquity:

wcs,qpf2142   (853)   nn,pnx1285   nn3290   wcj,cj637 (853)

42 Then will I remember   my covenant with Jacob, and also   my

nn,pnx1285   nn3327   wcj,cj637 (853)   nn,pnx1285   nn85   qmf2142

covenant with Isaac, and also   my covenant with Abraham will I remember; and

qmf2142   wcj,df,nn776

I will remember the land.

wcj,df,nn776   nimf5800 pr,pnx4480   wcj,qmf7521 (853)

43 The   land   also shall be left   of   them, and shall enjoy   her

pl,nn,pnx7676   pp,honc8074   pr,pnx4480   wcj,pnp1992   qmf7521 (853)

sabbaths, while she lieth desolate without them: and   they shall accept   of the nn,pnx5771   cj3282   wcj,pp,cj3282   qpf3988   pp,pl,nn,pnx4941

punishment*of*their*iniquity: because, even because they despised my judgments,

nn,pnx5315   qpf1602   wcj(853)   pl,nn,pnx2708

and because their soul abhorred   my statutes.

wcj,cj637   ad1571/pndm2063   pp,qnc,pnx1961   pp,cs,nn776   pl,qpta,pnx341

44 And yet for*all*that, when they   be   in the land of their enemies, I

ptn3808   qpf,pnx3988   wcj,ptn3808   qpf,pnx1602   pp,pinc,pnx3615

will not cast*them*away, neither will I abhor them, to destroy*them*utterly, and

pp,hinc6565   nn,pnx1285   pr,pnx854   cj3588 pnp589   nn3068   pl,nn,pnx430

to break my covenant with them: for   I   *am* the LORD their God.

pp,pnx   wcj,qpf2142   cs,nn1285   aj7223   pnl834/pnx(853)

45 But I will for*their*sakes remember the covenant of their ancestors,   whom

hipf3318   pr4480/cs,nn776   nn4714   pp,du,cs,nn5869   df,pl,nn1471

I brought forth out*of*the*land of Egypt in the   sight   of the heathen, that I

pp,qnc1961   pp,pnx   pp,pl,nn430   pnp589   nn3068

might   be   their God: I   *am* the LORD.

pndm428   df,pl,nn2706   wcj,df,pl,nn4941   wcj,df,pl,nn8451   pnl834   nn3068   qpf5414

46 These *are* the statutes and judgments and   laws,   which the LORD made

pr,pnx996   wcj(pr996)   pl,cs,nn1121   nn3478   pp,cs,nn2022   nn5514   pp,cs,nn3027

between him and   the children of Israel in mount Sinai by the   hand   of

nn4872

Moses.

Laws About Dedications

nn3068   wcs,pimf1696   pr413   nn4872   pp,qnc559

27 And the LORD spoke unto Moses, saying,

pimv1696   pr413   pl,cs,nn1121   nn3478   wcj,qpf559   pr,pnx413   cj3588

2 Speak unto the children of Israel, and   say   unto them, When

nn376   himf6381   nn5088   pl,nn5315   pp,nn3068

a man shall make*a*singular vow, the persons *shall be* for the LORD by thy

pp,nn,pnx6187

estimation.

nn,pnx6187   wcs,qpf1961   df,nn2145   pr4480/cs,nn1121/pl,nu6242/nn8141

3 And thy estimation shall   be   of the male from*twenty*years*old even

wcj,pr5704   pl,nu8346   nn8141   cs,nn1121   nn,pnx6187   wcs,qpf1961   pl,nu2572   nn8255   nn3701

unto sixty years old, even thy estimation shall   be   fifty shekels of silver,

pp,cs,nn8255   df,nn6944

after the shekel of the sanctuary.

wcj,cj518   pnp1931   nn5347   nn,pnx6187   wcs,qpf1961   nu7970   nn8255

4 And if   it *be* a female, then thy estimation shall   be   thirty shekels.

wcj,cj518   pr4480/cs,nn1121/nu2568/pl,nn8141   wcj,pr5704   pl,nu6242   nn8141   cs,nn1121

5 And if   *it be* from*five*years*old even unto twenty years old, then thy

nn,pnx6187   wcs,qpf1961   df,nn2145   pl,nu6242   pl,nn8255   wcj,dfp,nn5347   cs,nu6235

estimation shall   be   of the male twenty shekels, and for the   female   ten

pl,nn8255

shekels.

wcj,cj518   pr4480/cs,nn1121/nn2320   wcj,pr5704   nu2568   pl,nn8141   cs,nn1121

6 And if   *it be* from*a*month*old even   unto   five years old, then thy

nn,pnx6187   wcs,qpf1961   df,nn2145 nu2568   pl,nn8255   nn3701   wcj,dfp,nn5347

estimation shall   be   of the male five shekels of silver, and for the female thy

nn,pnx6187   cs,nu7969   pl,nn8255   nn3701

estimation *shall be* three shekels of silver.

wcj,cj518   pr4480/cs,nn1121/pl,nu8346/nn8141   wcj,ad,lh4605 cj518   nn2145

7 And   if   *it be* from*sixty*years*old and above; if *it be* a male, then thy

nn,pnx6187   wcs,qpf1961 nu2568/nu6240   nn8255   wcj,dfp,nn5347 nu6235   pl,nn8255

estimation shall   be   fifteen shekels, and for the female ten shekels.

wcj,cj518 pnp1931   qpta4134   pr4480/nn,pnx6187   wcs,hipf,pnx5975

8 But   if   he be poorer than*thy*estimation, then he shall present himself

pp,pl,cs,nn6440   df,nn3548   df,nn3548   wcs,hipf6186   pnx(853)   pr5921/cs,nn6310/pnl834

before   the priest, and the priest shall value   him; according to his

himf5381/cs,nn3027   df,qpta5087   df,nn3548 himf,pnx6186

ability   that vowed shall the priest value him.

wcj,cj518   nn929   pnl834/pr,pnx4480   himf7126   nn7133   pp,nn3068 nn3605

9 And   if *it be* a beast, whereof men bring an offering unto the LORD, all

pnl834   qmf5414   pr,pnx4480   pp,nn3068   qmf1961   nn6944

that *any man* giveth   of   such unto the LORD shall be holy.

ptn3808 himf,pnx2498   wcj,ptn3808 himf4171 pnx(853)   aj2896   pp,aj7451 cj176   aj7451

10 He shall not   alter it, nor change   it, a good for a bad, or a bad

pp,aj2896   wcj,cj518   hina4171/himf4171   nn929   pp,nn929   wcj(qpf1961) pnp1931

for a good: and   if   he shall at*all*change beast for beast, then   it   and

wcj,nn,pnx8545   qmf1961   nn6944

the exchange thereof shall be holy.

wcj,cj518   cs,nn3605 aj2931   nn929 pnl834/pr,pnx4480   ptn3808 himf7126   nn7133

11 And if *it be* any unclean beast, of which they do not offer a sacrifice

pp,nn3068   wcs,hipf5975 (853)   df,nn929 pp,pl,cs,nn6440   df,nn3548

unto the LORD, then he shall present   the beast before the priest:

df,nn3548   wcs,hipf6186 pnx(853)   pr996   aj2896   wcj(pr996) aj7451

12 And the priest shall value   it, whether it be good or   bad: as

pp,nn,pnx6187   df,nn3548 ad3651   qmf1961

thou valuest it, *who art* the priest, so shall it be.

wcj,cj518   qna1350/qmf,pnx1350   wcs,qpf3254   nuor,pnx2549

13 But   if   he will at*all*redeem it, then he shall   add   a   fifth *part*

pr5921   nn,pnx6187

thereof unto thy estimation.

cj3588   wcj,nn376   himf6942 (853)   nn,pnx1004   nn6944   pp,nn3068

14 And when a man shall sanctify   his house *to be* holy unto the LORD,

df,nn3548   wcs,hipf,pnx6186   pr996   aj2896   wcj(pr996) aj7451 pp,pnl834 df,nn3548

then the priest shall estimate it, whether it be good or   bad: as   the priest

himf6186 pnx(853)   ad3651   qmf6965

shall estimate   it, so shall it stand.

wcj,cj518   df,hipf6942   qmf1350   (853)   nn,pnx1004

15 And   if   he that sanctified it will redeem   his house, then he shall

wcs,qpf3254 cs,nuor2549   cs,nn3701   nn,pnx6187 pr,pnx5921   wcs,qpf1961

add the fifth *part* of the money of thy estimation unto it, and it shall   be

pp,pnx

his.

wcj,cj518   nn376   himf6942   pp,nn3068   pr4480/cs,nn7704

16 And   if   a man shall sanctify unto the LORD *some part* of*a*field of his

nn,pnx272   nn,pnx6187   wcs,qpf1961   pp,cs,nn6310   nn,pnx2233   cs,nn2563

possession, then thy estimation shall   be   according to the seed thereof: a homer

pl,nn8184 cs,nn2233   pp,pl,nu2572 cs,nn8255   nn3701

of barley seed *shall be valued* at fifty shekels of silver.

cj518   himf6942   nn,pnx7704   pr4480/cs,nn8141   df,nn3104

17 If he sanctify his field from*the*year of jubilee, according to thy

pp,nn,pnx6187   qmf6965

estimation it shall stand.

wcj,cj518   himf6942   nn,pnx7704 pr310   df,nn3104   df,nn3548   wcs,pipf2803

18 But   if   he sanctify his field after the jubilee, then the priest shall reckon

pp,pnx   (853)   df,nn3701   pr5921/cs,nn**6310**   df,pl,nn8141   df,pl,nipt**3498**   pr5704   cs,nn8141

unto him   the money according to the   years   that remain, even unto the   year

df,nn3104   wcs,nipf1639   pr4480/nn,pnx6187

of the jubilee, and it shall be abated from*thy*estimation.

wcj,cj518   df,hipt**6942**   (853)   df,nn7704   qna**1350**/qmf**1350**   pnx(853)

19 And   if   he that sanctified   the   field will in*any*wise*redeem   it,

wcs,qpf3254   cs,nuor2549   cs,nn3701   nn,pnx6187   pr,pnx5921

then he shall   add   the   fifth   *part* of the money of thy estimation   unto it, and it

wcs,qpf**6965**   pp,pnx

shall be assured to him.

wcj,cj518   ptn**3808**   qmf**1350**   (853)   df,nn7704   wcj,cj518   qpf4376 (853)

20 And   if   he will   not redeem   the field, or   if   he have sold   the

df,nn7704   aj312   pp,nn376   ptn**3808**   nimf**1350**   ad5750

field to another man, it shall   not   be redeemed any   more.

df,nn7704   pp,qnc,pnx3318   dfp,nn3104   wcs,qpf**1961**   nn**6944**

21 But the field, when it goeth out in the jubilee, shall   be   holy unto the

pp,nn3068   pp,cs,nn7704   df,nn2764   nn,pnx272   qmf**1961**   dfp,nn**3548**

LORD, as a   field   devoted; the possession thereof shall   be   the priest's.

wcj,cj518   himf**6942**   pp,nn**3068** (853)   cs,nn7704   nn,pnx4736

22 And   if   *a man* sanctify unto the LORD   a   field which he hath bought,

pnl834   ptn**3808**   pr4480/cs,nn7704   nn,pnx272

which *is* not of*the*fields of his possession;

df,nn**3548**   wcs,pipf**2803**   pp,pnx   (853)   cs,nn4373   df,nn,pnx6187

23 Then the priest shall reckon unto him   the worth of thy estimation, *even*

pr5704   cs,nn8141   df,nn3104   wcs,qpf**5414** (853)   nn,pnx6187   df,pndm1931

unto the   year   of the jubilee: and he shall   give   thine estimation in   that

dfp,nn3117   nn**6944**   pp,nn3068

day, *as* a holy thing unto the LORD.

pp,cs,nn8141   df,nn3104   df,nn7704   qmf**7725**   pp,pnl834 pr4480/pr,pnx854

24 In the   year   of the jubilee the   field shall return unto   him   of whom it

qpf,pnx7069   pp,pnx   pp,pnl834   cs,nn272   df,nn776

was bought, *even* to him to whom the possession of the land *did belong*.

wcj,cs,nn3605   nn,pnx6187   qmf**1961**   pp,cs,nn8255

25 And   all   thy estimations shall   be   according to the   shekel   of the

df,nn**6944**   pl,nu6242   nn1626   qmf**1961**   df,nn8255

sanctuary: twenty gerahs shall   be   the shekel.

ad389   nn1060   pp,nn929   pnl834   pp,nn3068   pumf1069   ptn**3808**

26 Only the firstling of the beasts, which should be the LORD's firstling,   no

nn376   him:f**6942**   pnx(853)   cj518   nn7794 cj518   nn7716   pnp1931   pp,nn3068

man shall sanctify   it; whether *it be* ox, or sheep: it   *is* the LORD's.

wcj,cj518   df,aj**2931**   dfp,nn929   wcs,qpf**6299**

27 And   if   *it be* of an unclean beast, then he shall redeem *it* according to

pp,nn,pnx6187   wcs,qpf3254   nuor,pnx2549   pr,pnx5921   wcj,cj518   ptn**3808**

thine estimation, and shall   add   a   fifth   *part* of it thereto: or   if   it be not

nimf**1350**   wcs,nipf4376   pp,nn,pnx6187

redeemed, then it shall be   sold   according to thy estimation.

ad389   ptn**3808**/cs,nn3605   nn2764   pnl834   nn376   him**2763**

28 Notwithstanding   no   devoted thing, that a man shall devote unto the

pp,nn3068   pr4480/cs,nn3605 pnl834 pp,pnx   pr4480/nn120   wcj,nn929   wcj,pr4480/cs,nn7704

LORD   of all   that he hath, *both* of man and beast, and of*the*field of his

nn,pnx272   nimf4376   wcj(ptn**3808**)   nimf**1350**   cs,nn3605   nn2764   (pnp1931)

possession, shall be sold   or   redeemed: every   devoted thing   *is*

cs,nn**6944**/pl,nn**6944**   pp,nn3068

most holy unto the LORD.

ptn3808/cs,nn3605   nn2764   pnl834   homf2763   pr4480   df,nn120   r:::f6299

29 None   devoted, which shall be devoted of men, shall be redeemed; *but*

qna4191/homf4191

shall surely*be*put*to*death.

wcj,cs,nn3605   cs,nn4643   df,nn776   pr4480/cs,nn2233   df,nn776

30 And   all   the tithe of the land, *whether* of*the*seed of the land, *or*

pr4480/cs,nn6529   df,nn6086 (pnp1931)   pp,nn3068   nn6944   pp,nn3068

of*the*fruit of the tree,   *is* the LORD's: *it is* holy unto the LORD.

wcj,cj518   nn376   qna1350/qmf1350   pr4480/nn,pnx4643   himf3254

31 And   if   a man will at*all*redeem *aught* of*his*tithes, he shall   add

pr,pnx5921   nuor,pnx2549

thereto the   fifth   *part* thereof.

wcj,cs,nn3605   cs,nn4643   nn1241   wcj,nn6629   nn3605/pnl834

32 And concerning the tithe of the herd, or of the flock, *even* of whatsoever

qmf5674   pr8478   df,nn7626   df,nuor6224   qmf1961 nn6944   pp,nn3068

passeth under the rod, the tenth shall be   holy unto the LORD.

ptn3808 pimf1239   pr996   aj2896   dfp,aj7451 wcj,ptn3808   himf,pnx4171

33 He shall not search whether it be good or bad, neither shall he change it:

wcj,cj518   hina4171/himf,pnx4171   wcs(qpf1961)   pnp1931   v:cj,nn,pnx8545

and if he change*it*at*all, then   both   it   and the change thereof shall

qmf1961 nn6944   ptn3808   nimf1350

be holy; it shall not be redeemed.

pndm428   df,pl,nn4687   pnl834   nn3068   pinf6680   (853)   nn4872   pr413

34 These *are* the commandments, which the LORD commanded   Moses for

pl,cs,nn1121   nn3478   pp,cs,nn2022   nn5514

the children of Israel in mount Sinai.

The Book of
NUMBERS

The book of Numbers is so named because it records several occasions when the people were counted or numbered (chaps. 1; 3; 4; 26). The Hebrew title (the first word in the Hebrew text) means "in the wilderness," and appropriately gives the setting for the events in this book. The Book of Numbers relates the earliest experiences of Israel under the theocracy. When the people were obedient to God, they enjoyed His blessing and protection (Num. 21:21–35), but their disobedience brought His judgment (Num. 21:4–9). Despite the wonders that God performed on Israel's behalf, the people were ready to return to Egypt on several occasions (Num. 11:4–6; 14:2–4; 20:4, 5; 21:5) because of their unbelief—it was easier to get Israel out of Egypt than to get Egypt out of the Israelites!

A large portion of the forty years that Israel spent in the wilderness is covered in this book. During this time God removed the generation that failed to trust Him (all but Joshua and Caleb, Num. 14:30) and molded the new generation into a unified nation, prepared to conquer the land He had promised them.

Census of Israel at Sinai

1 nn3068 wcs,pimf1696 pr413 nn4872 pp,cs,nn4057 nn5514
⚷ And the LORD spoke unto Moses in the wilderness of Sinai, in the
pp,cs,nn168 nn4150 pp,nu259 df,nuor8145 dfp,nn2320
tabernacle of the congregation, on the first *day* of the second month, in the
df,nuor8145 dfp,nn8141 pp,qnc,pnx3318 pr4480/cs,nn776 nn4714 pp,qnc559
second year after they were come out of*the*land of Egypt, saying,

qmv5375 (853) cs,nn7218 cs,nn3605 cs,nn5712 pl,cs,nn1121 nn3478
⚷ 2 Take ye the sum of all the congregation of the children of Israel, after
pp,pl,nn,pnx4940 pp,cs,nn1004 pl,nn,pnx1 pp,cs,nn4557 pl,nn8034 cs,nn3605
their families, by the house of their fathers, with the number of *their* names, every
nn2145 pp,pl,nn,pnx1538
male by their polls;

pl,nu6242 nn8141 pr4480/cs,nn1121 wcj,ad,lh4605 cs,nn3605 qpta3318
3 From twenty years old and upward, all that are*able*to*go*forth to
nn6635 pp,nn3478 pnp859 wcj,nn175 qmf6485 pnx(853) pp,pl,nn,pnx6635
war in Israel: thou and Aaron shall number them by their armies.

wcj,pr,pnx854 qmf1961 nn376 nn376 dfp,nn4294 nn376 nn7218
4 And with you there shall be a man of every tribe; every one head of the
pp,cs,nn1004 pl,nn,pnx1 (pnp1931)
house of his fathers.

⚷ **1:1** God speaks with Moses one month after the construction of the Tabernacle was completed (Ex. 40:17) and one year and fifteen days after the original Passover, when Israel began its journey from Egypt (Ex. 12:6; Num. 33:3).

⚷ **1:2** The Book of Numbers, as its name suggests, records the taking of two censuses (numberings) of Israel. The first census was taken just before Israel left Mount Sinai, because their intention was to conquer Canaan immediately. Unfortunately, the people sinned at Kadesh–barnea, and had to spend a total of forty years in the wilderness, until all the men who rebelled against God had died. This was a military census, counting only the males at the military age of twenty years old and older. For a discussion of the procedure used for counting the tribe of Levi, see the note on Numbers 3:39.

pp,pl,cs,nn**1121**　　　nn3130　　　　　　pp,pl,cs,nn**1121**　　　nn669
32 Of the children of Joseph, *namely*, of the children of Ephraim, by their

pl,nn,pnx**8435**　　　　pp,pl,nn,pnx**4940**　　　pp,cs,nn**1004**　　　pl,nn,pnx1
generations, after their families, by the house of their fathers, according to the

pp,cs,nn4557　　　pl,nn8034　　　pl,nu6242　　nn8141　　pr4480/cs,nn**1121**　　wcj,ad,lh4605　　nn3605
number of the names, from twenty years old and upward, all that

qpta3318　　　　nn**6635**
were*able*to*go*forth to war;

pl,qptp,pnx**6485**　　　　　　　pp,cs,nn**4294**　　　nn669
33 Those that were numbered of them, *even* of the tribe of Ephraim, *were*

pl,nu705　　nu505　　　wcj,cs,nu2568　　pl,nu3967
forty thousand and five hundred.

pp,pl,cs,nn**1121**　　　nn4519　　　　　pl,nn,pnx**8435**　　　　　pp,pl,nn,pnx**4940**
34 Of the children of Manasseh, by their generations, after their families, by

pp,cs,nn**1004**　　　　pl,nn,pnx1　　　　　pp,cs,nn4557　　　pl,nn8034　　　pl,nu6242
the house of their fathers, according to the number of the names, from twenty

nn8141　pr4480/cs,nn**1121**　　wcj,ad,lh4605　nn3605　　　qpta3318　　　　nn**6635**
years old and upward, all that were*able*to*go*forth to war;

pl,qptp,pnx**6485**　　　　　　pp,cs,nn**4294**　　　nn4519
35 Those that were numbered of them, *even* of the tribe of Manasseh, *were*

wcj,nu7970　　du,nu8147　　nu505　　　wcj,du,nu3967
thirty and two thousand and two hundred.

pp,pl,cs,nn**1121**　　　nn1144　　　　　pl,nn,pnx**8435**　　　　　pp,pl,nn,pnx**4940**
36 Of the children of Benjamin, by their generations, after their families, by

pp,cs,nn**1004**　　　　pl,nn,pnx1　　　　　pp,cs,nn4557　　　pl,nn8034　　　pl,nu6242
the house of their fathers, according to the number of the names, from twenty

nn8141　pr4480/cs,nn**1121**　　wcj,ad,lh4605　nn3605　　　qpta3318　　　　nn**6635**
years old and upward, all that were*able*to*go*forth to war;

pl,qptp,pnx**6485**　　　　　　pp,cs,nn**4294**　　　nn1144
37 Those that were numbered of them, *even* of the tribe of Benjamin, *were*

wcj,nu7970　　nu2568　　nu505　　　wcj,nu702　pl,nu3967
thirty and five thousand and four hundred.

pp,pl,cs,nn**1121**　　　nn1835　　　　　pl,nn,pnx**8435**　　　　　pp,pl,nn,pnx**4940**
38 Of the children of Dan, by their generations, after their families, by the

pp,cs,nn**1004**　　　　pl,nn,pnx1　　　　　pp,cs,nn4557　　　pl,nn8034　　　pl,nu6242　　nn8141
house of their fathers, according to the number of the names, from twenty years

pr4480/cs,nn**1121**　　wcj,ad,lh4605　nn3605　　　qpta3318　　　　nn**6635**
old and upward, all that were*able*to*go*forth to war;

pl,qptp,pnx**6485**　　　　　pp,cs,nn**4294**　　　nn1835
39 Those that were numbered of them, *even* of the tribe of Dan, *were*

wcj,pl,nu8346　　du,nu8147　　nu505　　　wcj,cs,nu7651　pl,nu3967
threescore and two thousand and seven hundred.

pp,pl,cs,nn**1121**　　　nn836　　　　　pl,nn,pnx**8435**　　　　　pp,pl,nn,pnx**4940**
40 Of the children of Asher, by their generations, after their families, by the

pp,cs,nn**1004**　　　　pl,nn,pnx1　　　　　pp,cs,nn4557　　　pl,nn8034　　　pl,nu6242　　nn8141
house of their fathers, according to the number of the names, from twenty years

pr4480/cs,nn**1121**　　wcj,ad,lh4605　nn3605　　　qpta3318　　　　nn**6635**
old and upward, all that were*able*to*go*forth to war;

pl,qptp,pnx**6485**　　　　　pp,cs,nn**4294**　　　nn836
41 Those that were numbered of them, *even* of the tribe of Asher, *were*

wcj,pl,nu705　　nu259　　nu505　　　wcj,cs,nu2568　pl,nu3967
forty and one thousand and five hundred.

pl,cs,nn**1121**　　　nn5321　　　　　pl,nn,pnx**8435**
42 Of the children of Naphtali, throughout their generations, after their

pp,pl,nn,pnx**4940**   pp,cs,nn**1004**   pl,nn,pnx**1**   pp,cs,nn**4557**   pl,nn**8034**

families, by the house of their fathers, according to the number of the names, from

pl,nu6242   nn8141   pr4480/cs,nn**1121**   wcj,ad,lh4605   nn3605   qpta3318   nn**6635**

twenty years   old   and upward, all that were*able*to*go*forth to war;

                  pl,qptp,pnx**6485**   pp,cs,nn**4294**   nn5321

      43 Those that were numbered of them, *even* of the   tribe   of Naphtali, *were*

wcj,pl,nu2572   nu7969   nu**505**   wcj,nu702   pl,nu3967

    fifty   and three thousand and   four   hundred.

        pndm428   df,pl,qptp**6485**   pnl834   nn4872   wcj,nn175   qpf**6485**

      44 These *are* those that were numbered, which Moses and Aaron numbered,

wcj,pl,cs,nn**5387**   nn3478   du,nu8147/nu6240   nn**376**   nn**376**   nu259   qpf**1961**   pp,cs,nn**1004**

and the   princes   of Israel, *being*   twelve   men: each one was for the   house of

pl,nn,pnx**1**

his fathers.

            wcs,qmf**1961**   cs,nn3605   pl,cs,qptp**6485**   pl,cs,nn**1121**   nn3478

      45 So   were   all   those that were numbered of the children of Israel, by the

pp,cs,nn**1004**   pl,nn,pnx**1**   pl,nu6242   nn8141   pr4480/cs,nn**1121**   wcj,ad,lh4605   cs,nn3605

house   of their fathers, from twenty years   old   and upward,   all   that

         qpta3318   nn**6635**   pp,nn3478

were*able*to*go*forth to war in Israel;

            cs,nn3605   df,pl,qptp**6485**   wcs,qmf**1961**   nu8337   pl,nu3967   nu**505**

      46 Even   all   they that were numbered were   six   hundred thousand and

wcj,cs,nu7969   pl,nu**505**   wcj,cs,nu2568   pl,nu3967   wcj,pl,nu2572

three   thousand and   five   hundred and   fifty.

The Levites are Exempted

             wcj,df,pl,nn**3881**   pp,cs,nn**4294**   pl,nn,pnx**1**   ptn3808   hotpf**6485**

      47 But the   Levites   after the   tribe   of their fathers were   not   numbered

pp,nn,pnx**8432**

among them.

           nn**3068**   wcs,pimf**1696**   pr413   nn4872   pp,qnc**559**

      48 For the Lord had spoken unto Moses, saying,

       ad389   ptn**3808**   qmf**6485**   (853)   cs,nn**4294**   nn3878   ptn**3808**   qmf**5375**   wcj(853)

      49 Only thou shalt not number   the   tribe   of Levi, neither take   the

nn,pnx7218   pp,cs,nn**8432**   pl,cs,nn**1121**   nn3478

sum   of them among the children of Israel:

       wcj,pnp859   himv**6485**   (853)   df,pl,nn**3881**   pr5921   cs,nn**4908**   df,nn**5715**

      50 But thou shalt appoint   the Levites over the tabernacle of testimony, and

wcj,pr5921 cs,nn3605   pl,nn,pnx3627   wcj,pr5921   cs,nn3605   pnl834   pp,pnx   pnp1992

over   all   the vessels thereof, and   over   all things that *belong* to it: they shall

qmf5375   (853)   df,nn**4908**   wcj(853)   cs,nn3605   pl,nn,pnx3627   wcj,pnp1992

bear   the tabernacle, and   all   the   vessels thereof; and   they   shall

pimf,pnx**8334**   qmf2583   wcj,ad5439   dfp,nn**4908**

minister unto it, and shall encamp round about the tabernacle.

           df,nn**4908**   wcj,pp,qnc5265   df,pl,nn**3881**   himf3381/pnx(853)

      51 And when the tabernacle setteth forward, the Levites shall take*it*down: and

          df,nn**4908**   wcj,pp,qnc2583   df,pl,nn**3881**   himf**6965**/pnx(853)   wcj,df,qpta2114

when the tabernacle is to be pitched, the Levites shall set*it*up: and the stranger

       df,aj7131   homf**4191**

that cometh nigh shall be put*to*death.

          pl,cs,nn**1121**   nn3478   wcs,qpf2583   nn**376**   pr5921

      52 And the children of Israel shall pitch*their*tents, every man by   his   own

nn,pnx**4264**   wcj,nn**376**   pr5921   nn,pnx1714   pp,pl,nn,pnx**6635**

camp, and every man by   his own standard, throughout their   hosts.

_{wcj,cs,nn**4294**}   _{nn1144}   _{wcj,nn**5387**}   _{pp,pl,cs,nn**1121**}   _{nn1144}

22 Then the   tribe   of Benjamin: and the captain of the   sons   of Benjamin

_{nn27}   _{cs,nn**1121**}   _{nn1441}

shall be Abidan the   son   of Gideoni.

_{wcj,nn,pnx**6635**}   _{wcj,pl,qptp,pnx**6485**}   _{wcj,nu7970}

23 And his   host,   and those that were numbered of them,   *were*   thirty and

_{nu2568}   _{nu**505**}   _{wcj,nu702}   _{pl,nu3967}

five thousand and   four   hundred.

_{cs,nn3605}   _{df,pl,qptp**6485**}   _{pp,cs,nn**4264**}   _{nn669}   _{cs,nu3967}

24   All   that were numbered of the   camp   of Ephraim *were* a hundred

_{nu**505**}   _{wcj,cs,nu8083}   _{pl,nu**505**}   _{wcj,nu3967}   _{pp,pl,nn,pnx**6635**}

thousand and   eight   thousand and a hundred, throughout their   armies.   And they

_{qmf5265}   _{wcj,nuor7992}

shall go forward in the   third   rank.

_{cs,nn1714}   _{cs,nn**4264**}   _{nn1835}   _{nn,lh6828}

25 The   standard   of the camp of Dan *shall be* on the north side by their

_{pp,pl,nn,pnx**6635**}   _{wcj,nn**5387**}   _{pp,pl,cs,nn**1121**}   _{nn1835}   _{nn295}   _{cs,nn**1121**}

armies: and the captain of the children of Dan *shall be* Ahiezer the   son   of

_{nn5996}

Ammishaddai.

_{wcj,nn,pnx**6635**}   _{wcj,pl,qptp,pnx**6485**}   _{wcj,pl,nu8346}

26 And his   host,   and those that were   numbered of them,   *were* threescore

_{du,nu8147}   _{nu**505**}   _{wcj,cs,nu7651}   _{pl,nu3967}

and   two   thousand and   seven   hundred.

_{wcj,df,pl,qpta2583}   _{pr,pnx5921}   _{cs,nn**4294**}   _{nn836}

27 And those that encamp   by   him *shall be* the   tribe   of Asher: and the

_{wcj,nn**5387**}   _{pp,pl,cs,nn**1121**}   _{nn836}   _{nn6295}   _{cs,nn**1121**}   _{nn5918}

captain of the children of Asher *shall be* Pagiel the   son   of Ocran.

_{wcj,nn,pnx**6635**}   _{wcj,pl,qptp,pnx**6485**}   _{wcj,pl,nu705}

28 And his   host,   and those that were numbered of them,   *were*   forty   and

_{nu259}   _{nu**505**}   _{wcj,cs,nu2568}   _{pl,nu3967}

one thousand and   five   hundred.

_{wcj,cs,nn**4294**}   _{nn5321}   _{wcj,nn**5387**}   _{pp,pl,cs,nn**1121**}   _{nn5321}

29 Then the   tribe   of Naphtali: and the captain of the children of Naphtali

_{nn299}   _{cs,nn**1121**}   _{nn5881}

shall be Ahira the   son   of Enan.

_{wcj,nn,pnx**6635**}   _{wcj,pl,qptp,pnx**6485**}   _{wcj,pl,nu2572}

30 And his   host,   and those that were numbered of them,   *were*   fifty   and

_{nu7969}   _{nu**505**}   _{wcj,nu702}   _{pl,nu3967}

three thousand and   four   hundred.

_{cs,nn3605}   _{df,pl,qptp**6485**}   _{pp,cs,nn**4264**}   _{nn1835}   _{cs,nu3967}

31   All   they that were numbered in the   camp   of Dan *were* a hundred

_{nu**505**}   _{wcj,pl,nu2572}   _{wcj,nu7651}   _{nu**505**}   _{wcj,nu8337}   _{pl,nu3967}   _{qmf5265}

thousand and   fifty   and seven thousand and   six   hundred. They shall   go

_{dfp,aj314}   _{pp,pl,nn,pnx1714}

hindmost with their standards.

_{pndm428}   _{pl,cs,qptp**6485**}   _{pl,cs,nn**1121**}   _{nn3478}   _{pp,cs,nn**1004**}

32 These *are* those which were numbered of the children of Israel by the   house

_{pl,nn,pnx1}   _{cs,nn3605}   _{pl,cs,qptp**6485**}   _{df,pl,nn**4264**}

of their fathers: all   those that were numbered of the camps throughout their

_{pp,pl,nn,pnx**6635**}   _{nu8337}   _{pl,nu3967}   _{nu**505**}   _{wcj,cs,nu7969}   _{pl,nu**505**}   _{wcj,cs,nu2568}   _{pl,nu3967}

hosts   *were* six hundred thousand and   three   thousand and   five   hundred

_{wcj,pl,nu2572}

and   fifty.

wcj,df,pl,nn3881   ptn3808   hotpf6485   pp,cs,nn8432   pl,cs,nn1121   nn3478   pp,pnl834

33 But the Levites were not numbered among the children of Israel; as

nn3068   pipf6680   (853)   nn4872

the LORD commanded Moses.

pl,cs,nn1121   nn3478   wcs,qmf6213   pp,nn3605   pnl834   nn3068

34 And the children of Israel did according to all that the LORD

pipf6680   (853)   nn4872   ad3651   qpf2583   pp,pl,nn,pnx1714   wcj,ad3651

commanded Moses: so they pitched by their standards, and so they

qpf5265   nn376   pp,pl,nn,pnx4940   pr5921   cs,nn1004   pl,nn,pnx1

set forward, every one after their families, according to the house of their fathers.

The Levites are Set Apart

wcj,pndm428   pl,cs,nn8435   nn175   wcj,nn4872   pp,nn3117

3 These also *are* the generations of Aaron and Moses in the day *that* the

nn3068   pipf1696   pr854   nn4872   pp,cs,nn2022   nn5514

LORD spoke with Moses in mount Sinai.

wcj,pndm428   pl,cs,nn8034   pl,cs,nn1121   nn175   nn5070   df,nn1060

2 And these *are* the names of the sons of Aaron; Nadab the firstborn, and

wcj,nn30   nn499   wcj,nn385

Abihu, Eleazar, and Ithamar.

pndm428   pl,cs,nn8034   pl,cs,nn1121   nn175   df,pl,nn3548

3 These *are* the names of the sons of Aaron, the priests which were

df,pl,qptp4886   pnl834   pipf4390/nn,pnx3027   pp,pinc3547

anointed, whom he consecrated to minister*in*the*priest's*office.

nn5070   wcj,nn30   wcs,qmf4191 pp,pl,cs,nn6440   nn3068   pp,hinc,pnx7126   qpta2114

4 And Nadab and Abihu died before the LORD, when they offered strange

nn784 pp,pl,cs,nn6440   nn3068   pp,cs,nn4057   nn5514   qpf1961/pp,pnx ptn3808 wcj,pl,nn1121

fire before the LORD, in the wilderness of Sinai, and they had no children:

nn499   wcj,nn385   wcs,pimf3547   pr5921   pl,cs,nn6440   nn175

and Eleazar and Ithamar ministered*in*the*priest's*office in the sight of Aaron

nn,pnx1

their father.

nn3068   wcs,pimf1696 pr413   nn4872   pp,qnc559

5 And the LORD spoke unto Moses, saying,

himv7126/(853)/cs,nn4294/nn3878   wcj,hipf5975 pnx(853)   pp,pl,cs,nn6440   nn175

6 Bring*the*tribe*of*Levi*near, and present them before Aaron the

df,nn3548   wcj,pipf8334   pnx(853)

priest, that they may minister unto him.

wcj,qpf8104 (853)   nn,pnx4931   wcj(853)   cs,nn4931   cs,nn3605

7 And they shall keep his charge, and the charge of the whole

df,nn5712   pp,pl,cs,nn6440   cs,nn168   nn4150   pp,qnc5647 (853)   cs,nn5656

congregation before the tabernacle of the congregation, to do the service of

df,nn4908

the tabernacle.

wcj,qpf8104 (853) cs,nn3605   pl,cs,nn3627   cs,nn168

8 And they shall keep all the instruments of the tabernacle of the

nn4150   wcj(853)   cs,nn4931   pl,cs,nn1121   nn3478   pp,qnc5647 (853)   cs,nn5656

congregation, and the charge of the children of Israel, to do the service

nn4908

of the tabernacle.

wcj,qpf5414 (853)   df,pl,nn3881   pp,nn175   wcj,pp,pl,nn,pnx1121 pnp1992

9 And thou shalt give the Levites unto Aaron and to his sons: they

pl,qptp5414/pl,qptp5414   pp,pnx   pr4480/pr854   pl,cs,nn1121   nn3478

are wholly given unto him out of the children of Israel.

qmf6485 wcj(853) nn175 wcj(853) pl,nn,pnx1121

10 And thou shalt appoint Aaron and his sons, and they shall

wcs,qpf8104 (853) nn,pnx3550 wcj,df,qpta2114 df,aj7131

wait on their priest's office: and the stranger that cometh nigh shall be

homf4191

put*to*death.

The Redemption of the Firstborn

nn3068 wcs,pimf1696 pr413 nn4872 pp,qnc559

11 And the LORD spoke unto Moses, saying,

wcj,pnp589 ptdm2009 qpf3947 (853) df,pl,nn3881 pr4480/cs,nn8432 pl,cs,nn1121

12 And I, behold, I have taken the Levites from among the children of

nn3478 pr8478 cs,nn3605 cs,nn1060 cs,nn6363 nn7358 pr4480/pl,cs,nn1121

Israel instead of all the firstborn that openeth the matrix among*the*children of

nn3478 df,pl,nn3881 wcj,qpf1961 pp,pnx

Israel: therefore the Levites shall be mine;

cj3588 cs,nn3605 nn1060 pp,pnx pp,cs,nn3117 hinc5221 cs,nn3605

13 Because all the firstborn are mine; for on the day that I smote all

nn1060 pp,cs,nn776 nn4714 hipf6942 pp,pnx cs,nn3605 nn1060 pp,nn3478

the firstborn in the land of Egypt I hallowed unto me all the firstborn in Israel,

pr4480/nn120 pr5704 nn929 pp,pnx qmf1961 pnp589 nn3068

both man and beast: mine shall they be: I am the LORD.

nn3068 wcs,pimf1696 pr413 nn4872 pp,cs,nn4057 nn5514 pp,qnc559

14 And the LORD spoke unto Moses in the wilderness of Sinai, saying,

qmv6485 (853) pl,cs,nn1121 nn3878 pp,cs,nn1004 pl,nn,pnx1

15 Number the children of Levi after the house of their fathers, by their

pp,pl,nn,pnx4940 cs,nn3605 nn2145 nn2320 pr4480/cs,nn1121 wcj,ad,lh4605 qmf,pnx6485

families: every male from a month old and upward shalt thou number them.

nn4872 wcs,qmf6485 pnx(853) pr5921 cs,nn6310 nn3068 pp,pnl834

16 And Moses numbered them according to the word of the LORD, as

pupf6680

he was commanded.

pndm428 wcs,qmf1961 pl,cs,nn1121 nn3878 pp,pl,nn,pnx8034 nn1648

17 And these were the sons of Levi by their names; Gershon, and

wcj,nn6955 wcj,nn4847

Kohath, and Merari.

Duties of the Gershonites

wcj,pndm428 pl,cs,nn8034 pl,cs,nn1121 nn1648 pp,pl,nn,pnx4940

18 And these are the names of the sons of Gershon by their families;

nn3845 wcj,nn8096

Libni, and Shimei.

☞ **3:10** See the note on Exodus 32:25–29.

☞ **3:12, 13** In the time of the patriarchs, the firstborn son had a position of special honor and responsibility in the family structure. God proclaimed Israel to be His firstborn (Ex. 4:22). With the death of the Egyptians' firstborn sons, all the firstborn sons of Israel who had been saved on the night of the Passover were to be sanctified unto the Lord (Ex. 11:4, 5; 12:21–29; 13:2, 11–16). These were set apart for the Lord and it was necessary to make a sacrifice for their redemption (Ex. 22:29). Now all the male members of the tribe of Levi, from one month old and above, were substituted for the firstborn males of the rest of the tribes of Israel (see vv. 41, 45). Thus, the Levites were to be consecrated for the Lord's service. See the note on Num. 3:46–51.

^{wcj,pl,cs,nn1121} ⁿⁿ⁶⁹⁵⁵ ^{pp,pl,nn,pnx4940} ⁿⁿ⁶⁰¹⁹ ^{wcj,nn3324} ⁿⁿ²²⁷⁵

19 And the   sons   of Kohath by their families; Amram, and Izehar, Hebron,

^{wcj,nn5816}

and Uzziel.

^{wcj,pl,cs,nn1121} ⁿⁿ⁴⁸⁴⁷ ^{pp,pl,nn,pnx4940} ⁿⁿ⁴²⁴⁹ ^{wcj,nn4187} ^{pndm428}

20 And the   sons   of Merari by their families; Mahli, and Mushi. These

^(pnp1992) ^{pl,cs,nn4940} ^{df,pl,nn3881} ^{pp,cs,nn1004} ^{pl,nn,pnx1}

are the families of the Levites according to the house of their fathers.

^{pp,nn1648} ^{cs,nn4940} ^{df,nn3846} ^{wcj,cs,nn4940} ^{df,nn8097}

21 Of Gershon *was* the family of the Libnites, and the family of the Shimites:

^{pndm428 (pnp1992)} ^{pl,cs,nn4940} ^{df,nn1649}

these   *are* the families of the Gershonites.

^{pl,qptp,pnx6485} ^{pp,cs,nn4557} ^{cs,nn3605}

22 Those that were numbered of them, according to the number of   all   the

ⁿⁿ²¹⁴⁵ ⁿⁿ²³²⁰ ^{pr4480/cs,nn1121} ^{wcj,ad,lh4605} ^{pl,qptp,pnx6485}

males, from a month   old   and upward, *even* those that were numbered of

^{cs,nu7651} ^{pl,nu505} ^{wcj,cs,nu2568} ^{pl,nu3967}

them *were* seven thousand and   five   hundred.

^{pl,cs,nn4940} ^{df,nn1649} ^{qmf2583} ^{pr310} ^{df,nn4908} ^{nn,lh3220}

23 The families of the Gershonites shall pitch behind the tabernacle westward.

^{wcj,cs,nn5387} ^{cs,nn1004} ⁿⁿ¹ ^{dfp,nn1649}

24 And the   chief   of the house of the father of the Gershonites *shall be*

ⁿⁿ⁴⁶⁰ ^{cs,nn1121} ⁿⁿ³⁸¹⁵

Eliasaph the son of Lael.

^{wcj,cs,nn4931} ^{pl,cs,nn1121} ⁿⁿ¹⁶⁴⁷ ^{pp,cs,nn168}

25 And the charge of the   sons   of Gershon in the tabernacle of the

ⁿⁿ⁴¹⁵⁰ ^{df,nn4908} ^{wcj,df,nn168} ^{nn,pnx4372}

congregation *shall be* the tabernacle, and the tent,   the covering thereof, and the

^{wcj,cs,nn4539} ^{cs,nn6607} ^{cs,nn168} ⁿⁿ⁴¹⁵⁰

hanging for the door of the tabernacle of the congregation,

^{wcj,pl,cs,nn7050} ^{df,nn2691} ^{wcj(853)} ^{cs,nn4539} ^{cs,nn6607}

26 And the hangings of the court, and   the curtain for the door of the

^{df,nn2691} ^{pnl834} ^{pr5921} ^{df,nn4908} ^{wcj,pr5921} ^{df,nn4196} ^{ad5439} ^{wcj(853)}

court, which *is* by the tabernacle, and by   the altar round about, and   the

^{pl,nn,pnx4340} ^{pp,cs,nn3605} ^{nn,pnx5656}

cords of it for   all   the service thereof.

Duties of the Kohathites

^{wcj,pp,nn6955} ^{cs,nn4940} ^{df,nn6020} ^{wcj,cs,nn4940}

27 And of Kohath *was* the family of the Amramites, and the family of the

^{df,nn3325} ^{wcj,cs,nn4940} ^{df,nn2276} ^{wcj,cs,nn4940} ^{df,nn5817}

Izeharites, and the family of the Hebronites, and the family of the Uzzielites:

^{pndm428 (pnp1992)} ^{pl,cs,nn4940} ^{df,nn6956}

these   *are* the families of the Kohathites.

^{pp,cs,nn4557} ^{cs,nn3605} ⁿⁿ²¹⁴⁵ ⁿⁿ²³²⁰ ^{pr4480/cs,nn1121} ^{wcj,ad,lh4605}

28 In the number of all the males, from a month   old   and upward, *were*

^{cs,nu8083} ^{pl,nu505} ^{wcj,cs,nu8337} ^{pl,nu3967} ^{pl,cs,qpta8104} ^{cs,nn4931} ^{cs,nn6944}

eight thousand and   six   hundred, keeping the charge of the sanctuary.

^{pl,cs,nn4940} ^{pl,cs,nn1121} ⁿⁿ⁶⁹⁵⁵ ^{qmf2583} ^{pr5921} ^{cs,nn3409}

29 The families of the   sons   of Kohath shall pitch on the side of the

^{df,nn4908} ^{nn,lh8486}

tabernacle southward.

wcj,cs,nn**5387**   cs,nn**1004**   nn1   pp,pl,cs,nn**4940**   df,nn6956

30 And the   chief   of the house of the father of the families of the Kohathites

nn469   cs,nn**1121**   nn5816

shall be Elizaphan the   son   of Uzziel.

wcj,nn,pnx**4931**   df,nn727   wcj,df,nn7979   wcj,df,nn4501

31 And their   charge   *shall be* the   ark, and the   table,   and the   candlestick,

wcj,df,pl,nn**4196**   wcj,pl,cs,nn3627   df,nn**6944**   pnl834   pimf**8334**

and the   altars,   and the   vessels   of the sanctuary wherewith they minister, and the

wcj,df,nn4539   wcj,cs,nn3605   nn,pnx**5656**

hanging, and   all   the service thereof.

nn499   cs,nn**1121**   nn175   df,nn**3548**   wcj,cs,nn**5387**   pl,cs,nn**5387**

32 And Eleazar the   son   of Aaron the priest *shall be*   chief   over the   chief

df,pl,nn3881   cs,nn**6486**   pl,cs,qpta**8104**   cs,nn**4931**

of the Levites, *and have* the   oversight of them that   keep   the charge of the

df,nn**6944**

sanctuary.

Duties of the Sons of Merari

pp,nn4847   cs,nn**4940**   df,nn4250   wcj,cs,nn**4940**   df,nn4188

33 Of Merari *was* the family of the Mahlites, and the   family   of the Mushites:

pndm428 (pnp1992)   pl,cs,nn**4940**   nn4847

these   *are* the families of Merari.

wcj,pl,qptp,pnx**6485**   pp,cs,nn4557   cs,nn3605

34 And those that were   numbered   of them, according to the number of   all

nn2145   nn2320   pr4480/cs,nn**1121**   wcj,ad,lh4605   cs,nu8337   pl,nu505

the   males,   from a   month   old   and   upward, *were*   six   thousand and

wcj,du,nu3967

two   hundred.

wcj,cs,nn**5387**   cs,nn**1004**   nn1   pp,pl,cs,nn**4940**   nn4847

35 And the   chief   of the house of the father of the families of Merari *was*

nn6700   cs,nn**1121**   nn32   qmf2583   pr5921   cs,nn**3409**   df,nn**4908**

Zuriel the   son   of Abihail: *these* shall pitch   on   the   side   of the tabernacle

nn,lh6828

northward.

wcj,cs,nn**6486**   cs,nn**4931**   pl,cs,nn**1121**   nn4847

36 And *under* the custody and charge of the   sons   of Merari *shall be* the

pl,cs,nn7175   df,nn**4908**   wcj,pl,nn,pnx1280   wcj,pl,nn,pnx5982

boards of the tabernacle, and the   bars   thereof, and the   pillars   thereof, and

wcj,pl,nn,pnx134   wcj,cs,nn3605   pl,nn,pnx3627   wcj,cs,nn3605   nn,pnx**5656**

the   sockets   thereof, and   all   the   vessels thereof, and   all   that serveth

thereto,

wcj,pl,cs,nn**5982**   df,nn2691   ad5439   wcj,pl,nn,pnx134

37 And the   pillars   of the   court round about, and their   sockets,   and their

wcj,pl,nn,pnx3489   wcj,pl,nn,pnx4340

pins,   and their   cords.

wcj,df,pl,qpta2583 pp,pl,cs,nn**6440**   df,nn**4908**   nn,lh6924

38 But those that   encamp   before   the tabernacle toward the east, *even*

pp,pl,cs,nn**6440**   cs,nn168   nn4150   nn,lh4217   nn4872   wcj,nn175

before   the tabernacle of the congregation eastward, *shall be* Moses, and Aaron and

wcj,pl,nn,pnx1121   pl,qpta**8104**   cs,nn**4931**   df,nn**4720**   pp,cs,nn**4931**   pl,cs,nn**1121**

his   sons,   keeping the charge of the sanctuary for the charge of the children of

nn3478   wcj,df,qpta**2114**   df,aj7131   homf**4191**

Israel; and the   stranger that cometh   nigh shall be put*to*death.

cs,nn3605   pl,cs,qptp6485   df,pl,nn3881   pnl834   nn4872   wcj,nn175   qpf6485

⊙ᵣ 39   All   that were numbered of the Levites, which Moses and Aaron numbered

pr5921   cs,nn6310   nn3068   pp,pl,nn,pnx4940 cs,nn3605   nn2145

at the commandment of the LORD, throughout their families,   all   the males from

nn2320   pr4480/cs,nn1121   wcj,ad,lh4605   wcj,pl,nu6242   du,nu8147   nu505

a month   old   and upward, *were* twenty and two   thousand.

nn3068   wcs,qmf559 pr413   nn4872   qmv6485   cs,nn3605   cs,nn1060   nn2145

40 And the LORD   said unto Moses, Number all   the firstborn of the males

pp,pl,cs,nn1121   nn3478   nn2320   pr4480/cs,nn1121   wcj,ad,lh4605   wcj,qmv5375 (853)

of the children of Israel from a month   old   and upward, and   take   the

cs,nn4557   pl,nn,pnx8034

number of their names.

wcj,qpf3947 (853)   df,pl,nn3881   pp,pnx   pnp589   nn3068   pr8478

41 And thou shalt take   the Levites for me   (I *am* the LORD) instead of

cs,nn3605   nn1060   pp,pl,cs,nn1121   nn3478   wcj(853)   cs,nn929   df,pl,nn3881

all   the firstborn among the children of Israel; and   the cattle of the Levites

pr8478   cs,nn3605   nn1060   pp,cs,nn929   pl,cs,nn1121   nn3478

instead of all the firstlings among the cattle of the children of Israel.

nn4872   wcs,qmf6485   pp,pnl834   nn3068   pipf6680   pnx(853)   (853) cs,nn3605

42 And Moses numbered,   as   the LORD commanded   him,   all   the

nn1060   pp,pl,cs,nn1121   nn3478

firstborn among the children of Israel.

cs,nn3605   cs,nn1060   nn2145   pp,cs,nn4557   pl,nn8034   nn2320

43 And   all   the firstborn males by the number of names, from a month

pr4480/cs,nn1121   wcj,ad,lh4605   pp,pl,qptp,pnx6485   wcs,qmf1961 wcj,pl,nu6242

old   and upward, of those that were numbered of them,   were   twenty and

du,nu8147   nu505   wcj,du,nu3967   nu7969/wcj,pl,nu7657

two thousand two hundred and threescore*and*thirteen.

nn3068   wcs,pimf1696 pr413   nn4872   pp,qnc559

44 And the LORD spoke unto Moses, saying,

qmv3947 (853)   df,pl,nn3881   pr8478   cs,nn3605   nn1060   pp,pl,cs,nn1121

45 Take   the Levites instead of   all   the firstborn among the children of

nn3478   wcj(853)   cs,nn929   df,pl,nn3881   pr8478   nn,pnx929   df,pl,nn3881

Israel, and   the cattle of the Levites instead of their cattle; and the Levites shall

wcj,qpf1961 pp,pnx pnp589   nn3068

be   mine: I *am* the LORD.

wcj(853)   pl,cs,qptp6299   wcj,df,du,nu3967

⊙ᵣ 46 And   for those that are to be redeemed of the two hundred and

df,nu7969/wcj,df,pl,nu7657   pr4480/cs,nn1060   pl,cs,nn1121   nn3478   df,pl,qpta5736

threescore*and*thirteen of*the*firstborn of the children of Israel, which are more

pr5921   df,pl,nn3881

than the Levites;

⊙ᵣ **3:39** A different method was used to number those of the tribe of Levi than was used to number the rest of Israel. All males as old as one month were counted, and the total for the census before Israel left Mount Sinai was 22,000. Using the same method, 23,000 were recorded at the second census, about thirty–seven years later (Num. 26:26). Since Levi was not to be given a separate tribal territory, the figures were kept separate from the number of the rest of Israel.

⊙ᵣ **3:46–51** The firstborn of Israel were numbered at 22,273 and the Levites at 22,000 (v. 39), a difference of 273. In the substitution of the Levites for the firstborn these 273 extra among the firstborn were to be redeemed by a contribution of five shekels of silver apiece which were to be given to Aaron and his sons, the priestly family. The shekel of silver was to weigh 20 gerahs (Ex. 30:12–16). A gerah has been estimated to have been slightly less than six–tenths of a gram. Therefore, the shekel would have weighed approximately eleven and one–half grams or four–tenths of an ounce. Hence, the redemption price for each of the 273 extra among the firstborn was two ounces of silver.

^{df,nn**4888**}   ^{wcj,cs,nn**8081**}   ^{cs,nn**6486**}   ^{cs,nn3605}   ^{df,nn**4908**}   ^{wcj,cs,nn3605}   ^{pnl834}

anointing   oil,   *and* the oversight of   all   the tabernacle, and of   all   that

^{pp,pnx}   ^{pp,nn**6944**}   ^{wcj,pp,pl,nn,pnx3627}

therein *is*, in the sanctuary, and in the   vessels   thereof.

^{nn**3068**}   ^{wcs,pimf**1696**}   ^{pr413}   ⁿⁿ⁴⁸⁷²   ^{wcj,pr413}   ⁿⁿ¹⁷⁵   ^{pp,qnc**559**}

17 And the L<small>ORD</small> spoke   unto Moses and unto Aaron, saying,

^{himf**3772**/ptn408}   ⁽⁸⁵³⁾   ^{cs,nn**7626**}   ^{pl,cs,nn**4940**}   ^{df,nn6956}   ^{pr4480/cs,nn**8432**}

18 Cut*ye*not*off   the tribe of the families of the Kohathites from among

^{df,pl,nn**3881**}

the Levites:

^{wcj,pndm2063}   ^{qmv**6213**}   ^{pp,pnx}   ^{wcs,qpf**2421**}   ^{wcj,ptn**3808**}   ^{qmf**4191**}

19 But   thus   do   unto them, that they may   live,   and   not   die,   when

^{pp,qnc,pnx**5066**}   ⁽⁸⁵³⁾   ^{cs,nn**6944**/df,pl,nn**6944**}   ⁿⁿ¹⁷⁵   ^{wcj,pl,nn,pnx**1121**}   ^{qmf935}

they approach   unto the most*holy*things: Aaron and his   sons   shall go in,

^{wcs,qpf**7760**}   ^{pnx(853)}   ^{nn376/nn376}   ^{pr5921}   ^{nn,pnx**5656**}   ^{wcj,pr413}   ^{nn,pnx**4853**}

and appoint   them every one to his service and   to   his burden:

^{wcj,ptn**3808**}   ^{qmf935}   ^{pp,qnc**7200**}   ⁽⁸⁵³⁾   ^{df,nn**6944**}   ^{pp,pinc**1104**}

20 But they shall   not   go in to   see   when   the holy things are covered,

^{wcs,qpf**4191**}

lest they   die.

^{nn**3068**}   ^{wcs,pimf**1696**}   ^{pr413}   ⁿⁿ⁴⁸⁷²   ^{pp,qnc**559**}

21 And the L<small>ORD</small> spoke   unto Moses, saying,

^{qna**5375**}   ^(pnp1992)   ^{ad1571}   ⁽⁸⁵³⁾   ^{cs,nn**7218**}   ^{pl,cs,nn**1121**}   ⁿⁿ¹⁶⁴⁸

22 Take   also   the sum of the   sons   of Gershon, throughout the

^{pp,cs,nn**1004**}   ^{pl,nn,pnx1}   ^{pp,pl,nn,pnx**4940**}

houses of their fathers, by their families;

^{nu7970}   ⁿⁿ⁸¹⁴¹   ^{pr4480/cs,nn**1121**}   ^{wcj,ad,lh4605}   ^{pr5704}   ^{pl,nu2572}   ⁿⁿ⁸¹⁴¹   ^{cs,nn**1121**}

23 From thirty years   old   and upward until fifty   years   old   shalt thou

^{qmf**6485**}   ^{pnx(853)}   ^{cs,nn3605}   ^{df,qpta935}   ^{pp,qnc**6633**}   ^{nn**5656**}   ^{pp,qnc**5647**}   ^{nn**5656**}

number   them;   all   that enter in to perform the service, to   do   the work in

^{pp,cs,nn**168**}   ^{nn**4150**}

the tabernacle of the congregation.

^{pndm2063}   ^{cs,nn**5656**}   ^{pl,cs,nn**4940**}   ^{df,nn1649}   ^{pp,qnc**5647**}

24 This   *is* the service of the families of the Gershonites, to serve, and for

^{wcj,pp,nn**4853**}

burdens:

^{wcs,qpf**5375**}   ⁽⁸⁵³⁾   ^{pl,cs,nn**3407**}   ^{df,nn**4908**}   ^{wcj(853)}

25 And they shall   bear   the curtains of the tabernacle, and   the

^{cs,nn**168**}   ^{nn**4150**}   ^{nn,pnx4372}   ^{wcj,cs,nn4372}   ^{df,nn8476}

tabernacle of the congregation, his covering, and the covering of the badgers' skins

^{pnl834}   ^{pr4480/pp,ad,lh4605}   ^{pr,pnx5921}   ^{wcj(853)}   ^{cs,nn4539}   ^{cs,nn6607}   ^{cs,nn**168**}

that *is*   above   upon it, and   the hanging for the   door of the tabernacle of

^{nn**4150**}

the congregation,

^{wcj(853)}   ^{pl,cs,nn7050}   ^{df,nn2691}   ^{wcj(853)}   ^{cs,nn4539}   ^{cs,nn6607}

26 And   the hangings of the court, and   the hanging for the   door of

^{cs,nn8179}   ^{df,nn2691}   ^{pnl834}   ^{pr5921}   ^{df,nn**4908**}   ^{wcj,pr5921}   ^{df,nn**4196**}

the   gate   of the court, which *is*   by   the tabernacle and   by   the altar

^{ad5439}   ^{wcj(853)}   ^{pl,nn,pnx4340}   ^{wcj(853)} ^{cs,nn3605}   ^{pl,cs,nn3627}   ^{nn,pnx**5656**}

round about, and   their cords, and   all   the instruments of their service,

^{wcj(853)} ^{cs,nn3605} ^{pnl834}   ^{nimf**6213**}   ^{pp,pnx}   ^{wcj,qpf**5647**}

and   all   that is made for them: so shall they serve.

^{pr5921}   ^{cs,nn**6310**}   ⁿⁿ¹⁷⁵   ^{wcj,pl,nn,pnx**1121**}   ^{qmf**1961**} ^{cs,nn3605}   ^{cs,nn**5656**}

27 At the appointment of Aaron and his   sons   shall   be   all   the service

pl,cs,nn1121   df,nn1649   pp,cs,nn3605   nn,pnx**4853**   wcj,pp,cs,nn3605

of the   sons   of the Gershonites, in   all   their burdens, and in   all   their

nn,pnx**5656**   wcs,qpf**6485**   pr,pnx5921   pp,nn**4931**   (853) cs,nn3605   nn,pnx**4853**

service: and ye shall appoint unto   them in charge   all   their burdens.

pndm2063   cs,nn**5656**   pl,cs,nn**4940**   pl,cs,nn**1121**   df,nn1649

28 This   *is* the service of the families of the   sons   of Gershon in the

pp,cs,nn**168**   nn4150   wcj,nn,pnx**4931**   pp,cs,nn**3027**

tabernacle of the congregation: and their   charge   *shall be* under the   hand   of

nn385   cs,nn**1121**   nn175   df,nn**3548**

Ithamar the   son   of Aaron the priest.

pl,cs,nn**1121**   nn4847   qmf**6485**   pnx(853)

29 As for the   sons   of Merari, thou shalt number   them after their

pp,pl,nn,pnx**4940**   pp,cs,nn**1004**   pl,nn,pnx**1**

families, by the   house   of their fathers;

nu7970   nn8141   pr4480/cs,nn**1121**   wcj,ad,lh4605   wcj,pr5704   pl,nu2572   nn8141   cs,nn**1121**

30 From thirty years   old   and upward even   unto   fifty years   old   shalt

qmf,pnx**6485**   cs,nn3605   df,qpta935   dfp,nn**6635**   pp,qnc**5647**   (853)   cs,nn**5656**

thou number them, every one that entereth into the service, to   do   the work

cs,nn**168**   nn4150

of the tabernacle of the congregation.

wcj,pndm2063   cs,nn**4931**   nn,pnx**4853**   pp,cs,nn3605   nn,pnx**5656**

31 And   this   *is* the charge of their burden, according to   all   their service

pp,cs,nn**168**   nn4150   pl,cs,nn7175   df,nn**4908**

in the   tabernacle of the congregation; the boards of the tabernacle, and the

wcj,pl,nn,pnx1280   wcj,pl,nn,pnx5982   wcj,pl,nn,pnx134

bars   thereof, and the   pillars   thereof, and sockets thereof,

wcj,pl,cs,nn5982   df,nn2691   ad5439   wcj,pl,nn,pnx134

32 And the   pillars   of the court round about, and their   sockets,   and their

wcj,pl,nn,pnx3489   wcj,pl,nn,pnx4340   pp,cs,nn3605   pl,nn,pnx3627   wcj,pp,cs,nn3605

pins,   and their   cords,   with   all   their instruments, and with   all

nn,pnx**5656**   wcj,pp,pl,nn8034   qmf**6485**   (853)   pl,cs,nn3627   cs,nn**4931**

their service: and by   name   ye shall reckon   the instruments of the charge of

nn,pnx**4853**

their burden.

pndm2063   cs,nn**5656**   pl,cs,nn**4940**   pl,cs,nn**1121**   nn4847

33 This   *is* the service of the families of the   sons   of Merari, according to

pp,cs,nn3605   nn,pnx**5656**   pp,cs,nn**168**   nn4150   pp,cs,nn**3027**

all   their service, in the tabernacle of the congregation, under the   hand   of

nn385   cs,nn**1121**   nn175   df,nn**3548**

Ithamar the   son   of Aaron the priest.

The Number of Eligible Levites for Service

nn4872   wcj,nn175   wcj,pl,cs,nn**5387**   df,nn**5712**   wcs,qmf**6485**   (853)

34 And Moses and Aaron and the   chief   of the congregation numbered

pl,cs,nn**1121**   df,aj6956   pp,pl,nn,pnx**4940**   wcj,pp,cs,nn**1004**

the   sons   of the Kohathites after their families, and after the   house   of their

pl,nn,pnx**1**

fathers,

nu7970   nn8141   pr4480/cs,nn**1121**   wcj,ad,lh4605   wcj,pr5704   pl,nu2572   nn8141   cs,nn**1121**

35 From thirty years   old   and upward even   unto   fifty years   old,

cs,nn3605   df,qpta935   dfp,nn**6635**   pp,nn5656   pp,cs,nn**168**

every one that entereth into the service, for the   work   in the tabernacle of the

nn**4150**

congregation:

pl,qptp,pnx**6485**   pp,pl,nn,pnx**4940**   wcs,qmf**1961**

36 And those that were numbered of them by their families were

du,nu**505**   cs,nu7651   pl,nu3967   wcj,pl,nu2572

two thousand seven hundred and fifty.

pndm428   pl,cs,qptp**6485**   pl,cs,nn**4940**   df,nn6956   cs,nn3605

37 These *were* they that were numbered of the families of the Kohathites, all

df,qpta5647   pp,cs,nn**168**   nn4150   pnl834   nn4872   wcj,nn175

that might do service in the tabernacle of the congregation, which Moses and Aaron

qpf**6485**   pr5921   cs,nn**6310**   nn3068   pp,cs,nn**3027**   nn4872

did number according to the commandment of the Lord by the hand of Moses.

wcj,pl,cs,qptp**6485**   pl,cs,nn**1121**   nn1648

38 And those that were numbered of the sons of Gershon, throughout their

pp,pl,nn,pnx**4940**   wcj,pp,cs,nn**1004**   pl,nn,pnx1

families, and by the house of their fathers,

nu7970   nn8141   pr4480/cs,nn**1121**   wcj,ad,lh4605   wcj,pr5704   pl,nu2572   nn8141   cs,nn**1121**

39 From thirty years old and upward even unto fifty years old,

cs,nn3605   df,qpta935   dfp,nn**6635**   pp,nn**5656**   pp,cs,nn**168**

every one that entereth into the service, for the work in the tabernacle of the

nn**4150**

congregation,

pl,qptp,pnx**6485**   pp,pl,nn,pnx**4940**

40 Even those that were numbered of them, throughout their families, by the

pp,cs,nn**1004**   pl,nn,pnx1   wcs,qmf**1961**   du,nu**505**   wcj,cs,nu8337   pl,nu3967   wcj,nu7970

house of their fathers, were two thousand and six hundred and thirty.

pndm428   pl,cs,qptp**6485**   pl,cs,nn**4940**   pl,cs,nn**1121**   nn1648

41 These *are* they that were numbered of the families of the sons of Gershon,

cs,nn3605   df,qpta5647   pp,cs,nn**168**   nn4150   pnl834   nn4872

of all that might do service in the tabernacle of the congregation, whom Moses

wcj,nn175   qpf**6485**   pr5921   cs,nn**6310**   nn3068

and Aaron did number according to the commandment of the Lord.

wcj,pl,cs,qptp**6485**   pl,cs,nn**4940**   pl,cs,nn**1121**   nn4847

42 And those that were numbered of the families of the sons of Merari,

pp,pl,nn,pnx**4940**   pp,cs,nn**1004**   pl,nn,pnx1

throughout their families, by the house of their fathers,

nu7970   nn8141   pr4480/cs,nn**1121**   wcj,ad,lh4605   wcj,pr5704   pl,nu2572   nn8141   cs,nn**1121**

43 From thirty years old and upward even unto fifty years old,

cs,nn3605   df,qpta935   dfp,nn**6635**   dfp,nn**5656**   pp,cs,nn**168**

every one that entereth into the service, for the work in the tabernacle of the

nn**4150**

congregation,

pl,qptp,pnx**6485**   pp,pl,nn,pnx**4940**   wcs,qmf**1961**   cs,nu7969

44 Even those that were numbered of them after their families, were three

pl,nu**505**   wcj,du,nu3967

thousand and two hundred.

pndm428   pl,cs,qptp**6485**   pl,cs,nn**4940**   pl,cs,nn**1121**   nn4847

45 These *be* those that were numbered of the families of the sons of Merari,

pnl834   nn4872   wcj,nn175   qpf**6485**   pr5921   cs,nn**6310**   nn3068

whom Moses and Aaron numbered according to the word of the Lord by the

pp,cs,nn**3027**   nn4872

hand of Moses.

cs,nn3605   df,pl,qptp**6485**   (853)   df,pl,nn3881   pnl834   nn4872   wcj,nn175

46 All those that were numbered of the Levites, whom Moses and Aaron

wcj,pl,cs,nn**5387**   nn3478   qpf**6485**   pp,pl,nn,pnx**4940**   wcj,pp,cs,nn**1004**

and the chief of Israel numbered, after their families, and after the house of

pl,nn,pnx1

their fathers,

nu7970   nn8141   pr4480/cs,nn1121   wcj,ad,lh4605   wcj,pr5704 pl,nu2572   nn8141   cs,nn1121

47 From thirty years   old   and upward even unto fifty years old,

cs,nn3605   df,qpta935   pp,qnc5647   cs,nn5656   nn5656   wcj,cs,nn5656

every one that came to   do   the service of the ministry, and the service of the

nn4853   pp,cs,nn168   nn4150

burden in the tabernacle of the congregation,

pl,qptp,pnx6485   wcs,qmf1961 cs,nu8083   pl,nu505   wcj,cs,nu2568

48 Even those that were numbered of them, were eight thousand and   five

pl,nu3967   wcj,pl,nu8084

hundred and fourscore.

pr5921   cs,nn6310   nn3068 pnx(853)   qpf6485

49 According to the commandment of the LORD   they were numbered by

pp,cs,nn3027   nn4872   nn376/nn376   pr5921   nn,pnx5656   wcj,pr5921

the hand of Moses, every one according to his service, and according to his

nn,pnx4853   wcj,pl,qptp,pnx6485   pnl834   nn3068   pipf6680   (853)   nn4872

burden: thus were they numbered of him, as the LORD commanded   Moses.

Unclean People

5

nn3068 wcs,pimf1696 pr413   nn4872   pp,qnc559

☉ And the LORD spoke unto Moses, saying,

pimv6680   (853)   pl,cs,nn1121   nn3478   wcj,pimf7971 pr4480   df,nn4264

2 Command   the children of Israel, that they put out of the camp

cs,nn3605   qptp6879   wcj,cs,nn3605   qpta2100   wcj,cs,nn3605   aj2931

every leper, and every one that hath*an*issue, and whosoever is defiled by the

dfp,nn5315

dead:

pr4480/nn2145 pr5704   nn5347   pimf7971 pr413/pr4480/nn2351   dfp,nn4264

3 Both   male   and female shall ye put out,   without   the camp shall ye

pimf,pnx7971   pimf2930 wcj,ptn3808 (853)   pl,nn,pnx4264   pp,nn,pnx8432 pnl834   pnp589

put   them; that they defile not   their camps, in the midst whereof I

qpta7931

dwell.

pl,cs,nn1121   nn3478 wcs,qmf6213 ad3651   wcs,pimf7971/pnx(853)   pr413/pr4480/nn2351

4 And the children of Israel   did   so, and put*them*out   without   the

dfp,nn4264 pp,pnl834   nn3068 pipf1696 pr413   nn4872   ad3651 qpf6213   pl,cs,nn1121   nn3478

camp: as the LORD spoke unto Moses, so did the children of Israel.

Restitution for Wrongs

nn3068 wcs,pimf1696 pr413   nn4872   pp,qnc559

5 And the LORD spoke unto Moses, saying,

pimv1696   pr413   pl,cs,nn1121   nn3478 cj3588   nn376 cj176   nn802   qmf6213

6 Speak unto the children of Israel, When a man or woman shall commit

pr4480/cs,nn3605 pl,nn2403   df,nn120   pp,qnc4603   nn4604   pp,nn3068

any   sin   that men commit, to   do   a trespass against the LORD, and

df,pndm1931   df,nn5315   wcs,qpf816

that person be guilty;

wcs,htpf3034 (853)   nn,pnx2403 pnl834   qpf6213

7 Then they shall confess   their sin which they have done: and he shall

---

☉ 5:1–4   This is an application of some of the laws which appear in Leviticus chapters fourteen and fifteen.

wcj,hipf7725   (853)   nn,pnx817   pp,nn,pnx7218   himf3254 pr,pnx5921
recompense his   trespass with the principal thereof, and add   unto   it the
wcj,nuor,pnx2549   wcs,qpf5414   pp,pnx   pp,pnl834   qpf816
fifth   *part* thereof, and give *it* unto *him* against whom he hath trespassed.

           wcj,cj518   dfp,nn376   ptn369   qpta1350   pp,hinc7725   df,nn817   pr,pnx413
8 But   if   the man   have no kinsman to recompense the trespass unto, let the
df,nn817   df,hopt7725   pp,nn3068   dfp,nn3548 pr4480/pp,nn905 cs,nn352
trespass be recompensed unto the LORD, *even* to the priest; beside   the ram of the
df,pl,nn3725   pnl834/pp,pnx   pimf3722   pr,pnx5921
atonement, whereby an atonement*shall*be*made   for   him.

          wcj,cs,nn3605   nn8641   pp,cs,nn3605   pl,cs,nn6944   pl,cs,nn1121   nn3478
9 And   every   offering of   all   the holy things of the children of Israel,
pnl834   himf7126   dfp,nn3548   qmf1961 pp,pnx
which they bring unto the priest, shall   be   his.

             wcj,nn376   (853)   pl,nn,pnx6944   qmf1961 pp,pnx   pnl834   nn376
10 And every man's   hallowed things shall   be   his: whatsoever any man
qmf5414   dfp,nn3548   qmf1961 pp,pnx
giveth the priest, it shall   be   his.

Wives Suspected of Adultery

         nn3068 wcs,pimf1696 pr413   nn4872   pp,qnc559
⚷ 11 And the LORD spoke unto Moses, saying,
       pimv1696   pr413   pl,cs,nn1121   nn3478   wcj,qpf559 pr,pnx413   cj3588   nn376/nn376
12 Speak unto the children of Israel, and   say   unto them, If   any man's
nn,pnx802   qmf7847   wcs,qpf4603   nn4604   pp,pnx
wife go aside, and commit a trespass against him,

           nn376   wcs,qpf7901 pr,pnx854   cs,nn7902/nn2233   wcs,nipf5956   pr4480/du,cs,nn5869
13 And a man   lie   with her carnally, and it be   hid   from*the*eyes of
nn,pnx376   wcs,nipf5641   wcj,pnp1931   nipf2930   ptn369 wcj,nn5707
her husband, and be kept close, and   she   be defiled, and *there be* no witness
pp,pnx   ptn3808 wcj,pnp1931   nipf8610
against her, neither   she   be taken *with the manner*;

           cs,nn7307   nn7068   wcj,qpf5674 pr,pnx5921   wcj,pipf7065   (853)
14 And the spirit of jealousy come upon him, and he be jealous   of his
nn,pnx802   wcj,pnp1931   nipf2930   cj176   cs,nn7307   nn7068   qpf5674 pr,pnx5921
wife, and   she   be defiled: or if the spirit of jealousy come upon him, and he
wcj,pipf7065   (853)   nn,pnx802   wcj,pnp1931   ptn3808 nipf2930
be jealous   of his wife, and   she   be not defiled:

           df,nn376 wcj,hipf935 (853)   nn,pnx802 pr413   df,nn3548   wcj,hipf935
15 Then shall the man bring   his wife unto the priest, and he shall bring
(853)   nn,pnx7133 pr,pnx5921   cs,nuor6224   df,nn374   pl,nn8184 cs,nn7058
her offering   for   her, the tenth *part* of an ephah of barley meal; he shall
qmf3332 ptn3808 nn8081 pr,pnx5921   wcj,ptn3808 qmf5414   nn3828   pr,pnx5921 cj3588 pnp1931   cs,nn4503
pour no oil upon it, nor put frankincense thereon; for   it *is* an offering
pl,nn7068   cs,nn4503   nn2146   cs,hipt2142/nn5771
of jealousy, an offering of memorial, bringing*iniquity*to*remembrance.

         df,nn3548   wcs,hipf7126/pnx(853)   wcs,hipf,pnx5975   pp,pl,cs,nn6440   nn3068
16 And the priest shall bring*her*near, and   set   her before the LORD:
         df,nn3548   wcs,qpf3947 aj6918 pl,nn4325   nn2789   pp,cs,nn3627   wcj,pr4480
17 And the priest shall take   holy water in an earthen vessel; and   of   the

---

⚷ **5:11–31** When a married woman was suspected of sexual infidelity, God's personal judgment was to be sought in the matter. The punishment for such unfaithfulness was death (Lev. 20:10). Sometimes called the "law of jealousy," this passage contains the prescribed ritual by which the priest was to ask God to reveal whether this woman was guilty or innocent.

df,nn6083 pnl834 qmf1961　　pp,cs,nn7172　　df,nn4908　　df,nn3548　　qmf3947　　wcs,qpf5414

dust that is in the floor of the tabernacle the priest shall take, and put *it*

pr413　　df,pl,nn4325

into the water:

df,nn3548　　wcs,himf5975 (853)　　df,nn802 pp,pl,cs,nn6440　　nn3068　　wcs,qpf6544

18 And the priest shall set the woman before the LORD, and uncover

(853)　　df,nn802　　cs,nn7218　　wcs,qpf5414 (853)　　cs,nn4503　　df,nn2146 pr5921　　du,nn,pnx3709

the woman's head, and put the offering of memorial in her hands,

pnp1931　　pl,nn7068　　cs,nn4503　　df,nn3548　　qmf1961　　wcj,pp,cs,nn3027　　df,aj4751

which *is* the jealousy offering: and the priest shall have in his hand the bitter

pl,cs,nn4325　　df,pl,pipt779

water that causeth*the*curse:

df,nn3548　　wcs,hipf7650/pnx(853)　　wcs,qpf559 pr413　　df,nn802 cj518

19 And the priest shall charge*her*by*an*oath, and say unto the woman, If

ptn3808 nn376　　qpf7901 pr,pnx854　　wcj,cj518　　ptn3808　　qpf7847　　nn2932

no man have lain with thee, and if thou hast not gone aside to uncleanness

pr8478　　nn,pnx376　　nimv5352　　df,pndm428 df,aj4751 pr4480/pl,cs,nn4325

with another instead of thy husband, be*thou*free from this bitter water

df,pl,pipt779

that causeth*the*curse:

cj3588 wcj,pnp859　　qpf7847　　pr8478　　nn,pnx376

20 But if thou hast gone aside *to another* instead of thy husband, and

wcj,cj3588　　nipf2930　　nn376　　wcs,qmf5414/(853)/nn,pnx7903　　pp,pnx　　pr4480/ptn1107

if thou be defiled, and some man have lain with thee beside

nn,pnx376

thine husband:

df,nn3548　　wcj,hipf7650 (853)　　df,nn802　　pp,cs,nn7621　　df,nn423

21 Then the priest shall charge the woman with an oath of cursing, and

df,nn3548　　wcj,qpf559　　dfp,nn802　　nn3068 qmf5414 pnx(853)　　pp,nn423

the priest shall say unto the woman, The LORD make thee a curse and an

wcj,pp,nn7621 pp,cs,nn8432　　nn,pnx5971　　nn3068　　pp,qnc5414 (853)　　nn,pnx3409　　qpta5307

oath among thy people, when the LORD doth make thy thigh to rot, and

wcj(853)　　nn,pnx990　　aj6639

thy belly to swell;

df,pndm428 df,pl,nn4325　　df,pl,pipt779　　wcj,qpf935　　pp,pl,nn,pnx4578

22 And this water that causeth*the*curse shall go into thy bowels, to

nn990　　pp,hinc6638　　nn3409　　wcj,pp,hinc5307　　df,nn802　　wcj,qpf559

make *thy* belly to swell, and *thy* thigh to rot: And the woman shall say,

ad543　　ad543

Amen, amen.

df,nn3548　　wcj,qpf3789 df,pndm428 (853) df,pl,nn423　　dfp,nn5612

23 And the priest shall write these curses in a book, and he shall

wcj,qpf4229　　pr413　　df,aj4751 pl,cs,nn4325

blot*them*out with the bitter water:

(853)　　df,nn802　　wcj,hipf8248 (853)　　df,aj4751 pl,cs,nn4325

24 And he shall cause the woman to drink the bitter water that

df,pl,pipt779　　df,pl,nn4325　　df,pl,pipt779　　wcj,qpf935 pp,pnx

causeth*the*curse: and the water that causeth*the*curse shall enter into her, *and*

pp,aj4751

become bitter.

df,nn3548　　wcj,qpf3947 (853)　　df,pl,nn7068　　cs,nn4503　　df,nn802

25 Then the priest shall take the jealousy offering out of the woman's

pr4480/cs,nn3027　　wcj,hipf5130 (853)　　df,nn4503　　pp,pl,cs,nn6440　　nn3068　　wcj,hipf7126 pnx(853)

hand, and shall wave the offering before the LORD, and offer it

pr413　　df,nn4196

upon the altar:

df,nn3548   wcj,qpf7061   pr4480   df,nn4503   (853)   nn,pnx234
26 And the priest shall take*a*handful of the offering, *even*   the memorial

wcj,hipf6999   df,nn,lh4196   wcj,ad310   (853)   df,nn802
thereof, and burn *it* upon the altar, and afterward shall cause   the woman to

himf8248 (853)   df,pl,nn4325
drink   the water.

wcj,hipf,pnx8248   (853)   df,pl,nn4325
27 And   when   he   hath   made*her*to*drink   the   water,   then

wcj,qpf1961   cj518   nipf2930   wcs,qmf4603   nn4604
it*shall*come*to*pass, *that*, if she be defiled, and have   done   trespass against her

pp,nn,pnx376   df,pl,nn4325   df,pl,pipt779   wcj,qpf935   pp,pnx
husband, that the water that causeth*the*curse shall enter into her, *and become*

pp,aj4751   nn,pnx990   wcj,qpf6638   nn,pnx3409   wcj,qpf5307   df,nn802
bitter, and her belly shall swell, and her thigh shall rot: and the woman shall

wcj,qpf1961   pp,nn423 pp,cs,nn7130   nn,pnx5971
be   a curse among her people.

wcj,cj518   df,nn802   ptn3808   nipf2930   (pnp1931)   wcj,aj2889
28 And   if   the woman be not defiled, but   be clean; then she shall

wcj,nipf5352   wcj,nipf2232   nn2233
be free, and shall conceive seed.

pndm2063   cs,nn8451   df,pl,nn7068   pnl834   nn802   qmf7847
29 This *is* the   law   of jealousies, when a wife goeth aside *to another*

pr8478   nn,pnx376   wcs,nipf2930
instead of her husband, and is defiled;

cj176 (nn376) pnl834   cs,nn7307   nn7068   qmf5674   pr,pnx5921   wcs,pipf7065 (853)
30 Or   when the spirit of jealousy cometh upon him, and he be jealous

nn,pnx802   wcs,hipf5975 (853)   df,nn802 pp,pl,cs,nn6440   nn3068   df,nn3548
over his wife, and shall   set   the woman before the LORD, and the priest

wcs,qpf6213   pp,pnx   (853) cs,nn3605 df,pndm2063 df,nn8451
shall execute upon her   all   this   law.

df,nn376   wcs,nipf5352   pr4480/nn5771   df,pndm1931 wcj,df,nn802   qmf5375
31 Then shall the man be guiltless from iniquity, and this   woman shall bear

(853)   nn,pnx5771
her iniquity.

The Nazarite Vow

nn3068   wcs,pimf1696 pr413   nn4872   pp,qnc559
6 And the LORD spoke unto Moses, saying,

pimv1696   pr413   pl,cs,nn1121   nn3478   wcj,qpf559 pr,pnx413   cj3588
2 Speak unto the children of Israel, and say   unto them, When either

nn376 cj176   nn802   himf6381   pp,qnc5087 cs,nn5088   nn5139   pp,hinc5144
man or woman shall separate *themselves* to vow a vow of a Nazarite, to separate

pp,nn3068
themselves unto the LORD:

himf5144   pr4480/nn3196   wcj,nn7941   qmf8354 ptn3808
3 He shall separate *himself* from wine and strong drink, and shall drink no

---

6:2–21 The word Nazarite, not to be confused with Nazarene, means "separated," and in this context means specifically "one who was separated unto the Lord." It was probably similar to a vow which existed among the Hebrews prior to Mount Sinai, but in this passage, it is brought under the regulation of the law. By the terms of the vow, men or women could voluntarily separate themselves unto the Lord for a specific period of time, even for life. They did not, however, become hermits, separating themselves from society. Samson (Judg. 13:5) and Samuel (1 Sam. 1:11, 28) are two of the Nazarites mentioned in the Bible. It is also thought that John the Baptist may have been a Nazarite (Luke 1:15) and that perhaps this is the vow associated with the Apostle Paul (Acts 21:23–26).

cs,nn2558　　nn3196　　wcj,cs,nn2558　　　nn7941　　ptn**3808**　　　　qmf8354　wcj,cs,nn3605　cs,nn4952

vinegar of wine, or vinegar of strong drink, neither shall he drink　any　liquor of

pl,nn6025　ptn**3808** qmf398　aj3892　wcj,pl,nn6025　wcj,aj**3002**

grapes, nor　eat moist grapes, or dried.

cs,nn3605　　pl,cs,nn**3117**　　　nn,pnx**5145**　　　　qmf398 ptn**3808**/pr4480/nn3605 pnl834　nimf**6213**

4　All　the　days　of his separation shall he eat　　nothing　that is made of

df,nn3196 pr4480/cs,nn1612　pr4480/pl,nn2785　wcj,pr5704　nn2085

of the vine　tree,　from*the*kernels even　to　the husk.

cs,nn3605　　pl,cs,nn**3117**　　cs,nn**5088**　　nn,pnx**5145**　　　ptn**3808** nn8593　qmf**5674**

5　All　the　days　of the vow　of his separation there shall　no　razor come

pr5921　　nn,pnx**7218** pr5704　df,pl,nn**3117**　qnc4390　　pnl834　　himf**5144**

upon his　head: until the　days　be fulfilled, in the which he separateth *himself* unto

pp,nn**3068**　　qmf**1961** aj**6918**　　　cs,nn6545　　cs,nn8181　　nn,pnx**7218**

the LORD, he shall　be　holy, *and* shall let the locks of the　hair　of his　head

pinc1431

grow.

cs,nn3605　　pl,cs,nn**3117**　　　hinc,pnx**5144**　　　　pp,nn**3068**　　qmf935 pr5921

6　All　the　days　that he separateth *himself* unto the LORD he shall come　at

ptn**3808** qpta4191　nn**5315**

no　dead body.

ptn**3808**　　htmf2930　　(pp,pnx)　　pp,nn,pnx1　　wcj,pp,nn,pnx517

7 He shall　not　make*himself*unclean　　for his father, or for his　mother,

pp,nn,pnx251　　wcj,pp,nn,pnx269　　pp,qnc,pnx4191　cj3588　　cs,nn**5145**

for his brother, or for his　sister,　when they　die:　because the consecration of

pl,nn,pnx430　pr5921　　nn,pnx**7218**

his　God　*is* upon his head.

cs,nn3605　　pl,cs,nn**3117**　　nn,pnx**5145**　pnp1931　aj**6918**　　pp,nn**3068**

8　All　the　days of his separation　he　*is* holy unto the LORD.

wcj,cj3588　qpta4191　qmf4191 pp,nn6621　ad6597　pr,pnx5921　　　　wcs,pipf**2930**

9 And　if　any man　die　very suddenly　by　him, and he hath defiled the

cs,nn**7218**　　nn,pnx**5145**　　wcs,pipf1548　nn,pnx**7218**　　pp,cs,nn**3117**

head　of his consecration; then he shall　shave　his　head　in the　day　of his

nn,pnx2893　　　df,nuor7637 dfp,nn**3117**　　pimf,pnx1548

cleansing, on the seventh　day　shall he shave it.

df,nuor8066 wcj,dfp,nn**3117**　　himf935 du,cs,nu8147　pl,nn8449 cj176 du,cs,nu8147 pl,cs,nn1121

10 And on the eighth　day　he shall bring　two　turtles, or　two　young

nn3123　pr413　df,nn**3548** pr413　cs,nn6607　　cs,nn**168**　　nn4150

pigeons,　to the priest,　to　the door of the tabernacle of the congregation:

df,nn**3548**　　wcs,qpf**6213**　nu259　　pp,nn**2403**　　wcj,nu259

11 And the priest shall　offer　the one for a sin offering, and the other for a

pp,nn**5930**　　wcs,pipf**3722**　pr,pnx5921　　pr4480/pnl834　qpf2398　pr5921

burnt offering, and make*an*atonement　for　him, for that he sinned by the

df,nn**5315**　　wcj,pipf**6942** (853)　nn,pnx**7218** df,pndm1931 dfp,nn**3117**

dead, and shall hallow　his head that　same　day.

wcj,hipf**5144**　　pp,nn**3068** (853)　pl,cs,nn**3117**　　nn,pnx**5145**

12 And he shall consecrate unto the LORD　the　days　of his separation, and

wcj,hipf935　nn3532　cs,nn1121 nn,pnx8141　　pp,nn**817**　　wcj,df,pl,nn**3117**

shall　bring a lamb of the first　year　for a trespass offering: but the　days

df,aj**7223**　　qmf5307　cj3588　nn,pnx**5145**　qpf**2930**

that*were*before shall be lost, because his separation was defiled.

wcj,pndm2063　cs,nn**8451**　df,nn**5139** pp,cs,nn**3117**　pl,cs,nn**3117**　　nn,pnx**5145**

13 And　this　*is* the law of the Nazarite, when the　days　of his separation

qnc**4390**　pnx(853)　　himf935 pr413　cs,nn6607　　cs,nn**168**

are fulfilled:　　he shall be brought unto the　door　of the tabernacle of the

nn4150

congregation:

pr4480/ad370/pp,pnx   nn1320   pp,qnc5414   pp,cs,nn3605 df,pndm2088   df,nn5971   cj3588
13   Whence   should I have flesh to give unto   all   this people? for

qmf1058 pr,pnx5921   pp,qnc559 qmv5414 pp,pnx   nn1320   wcj,qmf398
they weep unto me, saying, Give us flesh, that we may eat.

pnp595   qmf3201/ptn3808   pp,qnc5375 (853) cs,nn3605 df,pndm2088   df,nn5971 pp,nn,pnx905 cj3588
14   I am*not*able to bear   all   this people alone, because it is

aj3515   pr,pnx4480
too heavy   for me.

wcj,cj518 pnp859 qpta6213 ad3602   pp,pnx qmv,pnx2026   pte4994   qna2026
15 And if thou deal thus with me, kill me, I*pray*thee, out*of*hand,

cj518   qpf4672 nn2580   pp,du,nn,pnx5869   wcj,ptn408 qmf7200   pp,nn,pnx7451
if I have found favor in thy   sight; and let me not see my wretchedness.

nn3068   wcs,qmf559   pr413   nn4872   qmv622   pp,pnx   pl,nu7657   nn376
16 And the LORD said unto Moses, Gather unto me seventy men

pr4480/cs,aj2205   nn3478   pnl834   qpf3045   (cj3588) (pnp1992)   pp,cs,aj2205
of*the*elders of Israel, whom thou knowest   to be the elders of the

df,nn5971   wcj,pl,nn,pnx7860   wcj,qpf3947 pnx(853)   pr413   cs,nn168
people, and officers over them; and bring   them unto the tabernacle of the

nn4150   wcj,htpf3320 ad8033 pr,pnx5973
congregation, that they may stand there with thee.

wcj,qpf3381   wcj,pipf1696 pr,pnx5973   ad8033   wcj,qpf680 pr4480
17 And I will come down and talk   with thee there: and I will take of

df,nn7307 pnl834 pr,pnx5921   wcj,qpf7760   pr,pnx5921   wcj,qpf5375
the spirit which is upon thee, and will put it upon them; and they shall bear

pp,cs,nn4853   df,nn5971 pr,pnx854   pnp859 qmf5375 wcj,ptn3808   pp,nn,pnx905
the burden of the people with thee, that thou bear it not thyself alone.

qmf559   wcj,pr413   df,nn5971   htmv6942   pp,ad4279
18 And say thou unto the people, Sanctify yourselves against tomorrow, and

wcs,qpf398 nn1320 cj3588   qpf1058   pp,du,cs,nn241   nn3068 pp,qnc559 pnit4310
ye shall eat flesh: for ye have wept in the ears of the LORD, saying, Who

nn1320   himf,pnx398 cj3588   qpf2895   pp,pnx   pp,nn4714   nn3068
shall give us flesh to eat? for it was well with us in Egypt: therefore the LORD

wcj,qpf5414 pp,pnx   nn1320   wcj,qpf398
will give you flesh, and ye shall eat.

ptn3808 qmf398 nu259 nn3117 wcj,ptn3808   du,nn3117   wcj,ptn3808 nu2568 pl,nn3117 wcj,ptn3808 nu6235
19 Ye shall not eat one day, nor two days, nor five days, neither ten

pl,nn3117 wcj,ptn3808 pl,nu6242 nn3117
days, nor twenty days;

pr5704   pl,nn3117 cs,nn2320 ad5704/pnl834   qmf3318   pr4480/nn,pnx639   wcs,qpf1961
20 But even a whole month,   until it come out at*your*nostrils, and it be

pp,nn2214   pp,pnx cj3282   cj3588   qpf3988   (853)   nn3068 pnl834   pp,nn,pnx7130
loathsome unto you: because that ye have despised   the LORD which is among

wcs,qmf1058 pp,pl,nn,pnx6440   pp,qnc559 pnit4100/pndm2088   qpf3318
you, and have wept   before   him, saying,   Why   came*we*forth

pr4480/nn4714
out*of*Egypt?

nn4872   wcs,qmf559   df,nn5971 pp,nn,pnx7130 pnl834 pnp595   nu8337 pl,cs,nu3967
21 And Moses said, The people, among whom I am, are six hundred

nu505   aj7273   wcj,pnp859   qpf559   qmf5414   nn1320   wcs,qpf398
thousand footmen; and thou hast said, I will give them flesh, that they may eat

pl,nn3117 cs,nn2320
a whole month.

11:20   God will hold people accountable for the words which they speak, just as He did here (Prov. 5:21; Matt. 12:36, 37; Heb. 4:13).

_{he,nn6629}   _{wcj,nn1241}   _{nimf7819}   _{pp,pnx}   _{wcs,qpf4672} _{pp,pnx}   _{cj518} (853)

22 Shall the flocks and the herds be slain for them, to suffice them? or

_{cs,nn3605}   _{pl,cs,nn1709}   _{df,nn3220}   _{nimf622}   _{pp,pnx}   _{wcs,qpf4672} _{pp,pnx}

shall all the fish of the sea be gathered together for them, to suffice them?

_{nn3068} _{wcs,qmf559} _{pr413}   _{nn4872}   _{nn3068}   _{he,cs,nn3027}   _{qmf7114}

23 And the Lord said unto Moses, Is the Lord's hand waxed short? thou

_{qmf7200} _{ad6258}   _{nn,pnx1697}   _{he,qmf,pnx7136}   _{cj518} _{ptn3808}

shalt see now whether my word shall come*to*pass unto thee or not.

_{nn4872}   _{wcs,qmf3318}   _{wcs,pimf1696/pr413}   _{df,nn5971} (853)   _{pl,cs,nn1697}   _{nn3068}

24 And Moses went out, and   told   the people   the words of the Lord,

_{wcs,qmf622}   _{pl,nu7657}   _{nn376}   _{pr4480/cs,aj2205}   _{df,nn5971}   _{wcs,himf5975} _{pnx(853)}

and gathered the seventy men of*the*elders of the people, and   set   them

_{ad5439}   _{df,nn168}

round about the tabernacle.

_{nn3068}   _{wcs,qmf3381}   _{dfp,nn6051}   _{wcs,pimf1696} _{pr,pnx413}   _{wcs,himf680}

25 And the Lord came down in a cloud, and spoke   unto him, and   took

_{pr4480}   _{df,nn7307} _{pnl834}   _{pr,pnx5921}   _{wcs,qmf5414}   _{pr5921}   _{pl,nu7657}   _{nn376/df,aj2205}

of the spirit that *was* upon him, and gave *it* unto the seventy elders: and

_{wcs,qmf1961}   _{df,nn7307} _{pp,qnc5117} _{pr,pnx5921}   _{wcs,htmf5012}

it*came*to*pass, *that*, when the spirit rested upon them, they prophesied, and did

_{wcj,ptn3808}   _{qpf3254}

 not   cease.

_{wcs,nimf7604}   _{du,cs,nu8147}   _{pl,nn376}   _{dfp,nn4264} _{cs,nn8034}   _{df,nu259}

26 But there remained   two *of the* men in the camp, the name of the one

_{nn419}   _{wcj,cs,nn8034}   _{df,nuor8145}   _{nn4312}   _{df,nn7307} _{wcs,qmf5117} _{pr,pnx5921}

was Eldad, and the name of the other Medad: and the spirit rested upon them;

_{wcj,pnp1992}   _{dfp,pl,qptp3789}   _{qpf3318/wcj,ptn3808}   _{df,nn,lh168}

and   they *were* of them that were written, but went*not*out unto the tabernacle:

_{wcs,htmf5012}   _{dfp,nn4264}

and they prophesied in the camp.

_{wcs,qmf7323}   _{df,nn5288}   _{wcs,himf5046} _{pp,nn4872}   _{wcs,qmf559}   _{nn419}

27 And there   ran   a young man, and   told   Moses, and said, Eldad and

_{wcj,nn4312}   _{pl,htpt5012}   _{dfp,nn4264}

Medad do prophesy in the camp.

_{nn3091}   _{cs,nn1121}   _{nn5126}   _{cs,pipt8334}   _{nn4872}   _{pr4480/pl,nn,pnx979}

28 And Joshua the son of Nun, the servant of Moses, *one* of*his*young*men,

_{wcs,qmf6030}   _{wcs,qmf559}   _{nn,pnx113}   _{nn4872}   _{qmv,pnx3607}

answered and said, My lord Moses, forbid them.

_{nn4872}   _{wcs,qmf559}   _{pp,pnx}   _{he,pipt7065} _{pnp859}   _{pp,pnx}   _{wcj,pnit4310/qmf5414}

29 And Moses said unto him, Enviest thou for*my*sake? would God that

_{cs,nn3605}   _{nn3068}   _{cs,nn5971}   _{pl,nn5030}   _{cj3588}   _{nn3068}   _{qmf5414} (853)   _{nn,pnx7307}

all the Lord's people were prophets, *and* that the Lord would put   his spirit

_{pr,pnx5921}

upon them!

_{nn4872}   _{wcs,nimf622}   _{pr413}   _{df,nn4264} _{pnp1931}   _{wcj,pl,cs,nn2205}   _{nn3478}

30 And Moses got   him into the camp, he and the elders of Israel.

_{qpf5265}   _{wcj,nn7307} _{pr4480/pr854}   _{nn3068}   _{wcs,qmf1468} _{pl,nn7958} _{pr4480}

31 And there went forth a wind from the Lord, and brought quails from the

_{df,nn3220}   _{wcs,qmf5203}   _{pr5921}   _{df,nn4264}   _{nn3117} _{pp,cs,nn1870}   _{ad3541}

sea, and let*them*fall by the camp, as it were a day's journey on this side, and

_{nn3117} _{wcj,pp,cs,nn1870}   _{ad3541}   _{pr5439}   _{df,nn4264}

as it were a day's journey on the other side, round about the camp, and as it were

_{wcj,pp,du,nn520}   _{pr5921}   _{pl,cs,nn6440}   _{df,nn776}

two cubits *high* upon the face of the earth.

_{df,nn5971}   _{wcs,qmf6965} _{cs,nn3605} _{df,pndm1931} _{df,nn3117}   _{wcj,cs,nn3605}   _{df,nn3915}

32 And the people stood up all   that   day, and   all   *that* night, and

wcj,cs,nn3605   df,nn4283   cs,nn3117   wcs,qmf622   (853)   df,nn7958   df,hipt4591
all   the next day, and they gathered   the quails: he that gathered least

qpf622   nu6235   pl,nn2563   wcs,qmf7849/qna7849   pp,pnx   ad5439
gathered ten homers: and they spread*_them_*all*abroad for themselves round about

df,nn4264
the camp.

                      df,nn1320   ad,pnx5750   pr996   du,nn,pnx8127 ad2962   nimf3772
33 And while the flesh _was_ yet between their teeth, ere it was chewed,

wcj,cs,nn639   nn3068   qpf2734   dfp,nn5971   nn3068 wcs,himf5221
the wrath of the LORD was kindled against the people, and the LORD smote the

dfp,nn5971   ad3966 aj7227   nn4347
people with a very great plague.

                      wcs,qmf7121 (853)   cs,nn8034   df,pndm1931 df,nn4725   nn6914   cj3588
34 And he called   the name of that   place Kibroth-hattaavah: because

ad8033   qpf6912 (853)   df,nn5971   df,pl,htpt183
there they buried   the people that lusted.

                df,nn5971   qpf5265   pr4480/nn6914   nn2698   wcs,qmf1961
35 _And_ the people journeyed from Kibroth-hattaavah unto Hazeroth; and abode

pp,nn2698
at Hazeroth.

Miriam Is Punished

                nn4813   wcj,nn175   wcs,pimf1696   pp,nn4872   pr5921/pl,cs,nn182
And Miriam and Aaron   spoke   against Moses   because   of the

                df,nn3569   df,nn802   pnl834   qpf3947   cj3588   qpf3947
Ethiopian woman whom he had married: for he had married an

df,nn3569   nn802
Ethiopian woman.

                wcs,qmf559   nn3068   ad389   pipf1696   he,ad7535   pp,nn4872
2 And they said, Hath the LORD indeed spoken only by Moses? hath he

he,ptn3808   pipf1696 ad1571 pp,pnx   nn3068 wcs,qmf8085
not spoken also by us? And the LORD heard _it_.

                wcj,df,nn376   nn4872   ad3966   nn6035 pr4480/cs,nn3605   df,nn120 pnl834   pr5921
3 (Now the   man Moses _was_ very meek, above all the men which _were_ upon

pl,cs,nn6440   df,nn127
the face of the earth.)

                nn3068   wcs,qmf559   ad6597   pr413   nn4872   wcj,pr413   nn175   wcj,pr413
4 And the LORD spoke suddenly unto Moses, and unto Aaron, and unto

nn4813   qmv3318   nu,pnx7969 pr413   cs,nn168   nn4150
Miriam, Come out ye three unto the tabernacle of the congregation. And they

nu,pnx7969   wcs,qmf3318
three came out.

                nn3068   wcs,qmf3381   pp,cs,nn5982   nn6051   wcs,qmf5975
5 And the LORD came down in the pillar of the cloud, and stood _in_ the

cs,nn6607   df,nn168   wcs,qmf7121   nn175   wcj,nn4813   du,nu,pnx8147
door of the tabernacle, and called Aaron and Miriam: and they   both

wcs,qmf3318
came forth.

12:3 Some scholars have thought it necessary to consider this verse a later insertion in the text, possibly by Joshua, as it did not seem proper for Moses (the author) to glorify himself. However, the purpose of the statement was not to glorify Moses but to explain why he took no steps to justify himself when Miriam and Aaron questioned his authority as God's spokesman. The book was written by Moses under the inspiration of the Holy Spirit. The same objectivity that allowed him to record his spiritual successes also allowed for the recording of his own faults and sins.

6 And he said, Hear now my words: If there be a prophet among you, *I* the LORD will make*myself*known unto him in a vision, *and* will speak unto him in a dream.

☞ 7 My servant Moses *is* not so, who *is* faithful in all mine house.

8 With him will I speak mouth to mouth, even apparently, and not in dark speeches; and the similitude of the LORD shall he behold: wherefore then were*ye*not*afraid to speak against my servant Moses?

9 And the anger of the LORD was kindled against them; and he departed.

☞ 10 And the cloud departed from off the tabernacle; and, behold, Miriam *became* leprous, *white* as snow: and Aaron looked upon Miriam, and, behold, *she was* leprous.

11 And Aaron said unto Moses, Alas, my lord, I*beseech*thee, lay not the sin upon us, wherein we have done foolishly, and wherein we have sinned.

12 Let her not be as*one*dead, of whom the flesh is half consumed when he cometh out of his mother's womb.

13 And Moses cried unto the LORD, saying, Heal her now, O God, I*beseech*thee.

14 And the LORD said unto Moses, If her father had*but*spit in her face, should she not be ashamed seven days? let her be shut out from the camp seven days, and after that let her be received in *again*.

15 And Miriam was shut out from the camp seven days: and the people journeyed not till Miriam was brought in *again*.

☞ **12:7** Moses was more than just the leader of Israel or a well-known prophet. The writer of Hebrews describes him as a type of Christ (Heb. 3:2-6). He was chosen by God to be a deliverer (Ex. 3:1-10) and was designated as a prophet (Deut. 18:15). As a servant in God's house, he was considered faithful and trustworthy (Heb. 3:5, 6). Moses was a mediator between Jehovah and Israel (Ex. 17:1-7; 32:30-35) as Christ is for His church (see 1 John 2:1, 2).

☞ **12:10** Miriam had apparently initiated this insurrection against Moses (v. 1), and was therefore punished. Aaron was again showing his lack of spiritual backbone, just as he did in the incident of the golden calf (Ex. 32:1-6; 21-24).

wcj,ad310   df,nn5971   qpf5265   pr4480/nn2698   wcs,qmf2583

16 And afterward the people removed from Hazeroth, and pitched in the

pp,cs,nn4057   nn6290

wilderness of Paran.

The Spies Explore Canaan

nn3068   wcs,pimf1696   pr413   nn4872   pp,qnc559

13 And the LORD spoke unto Moses, saying,

qmv7971   pp,pnx   pl,nn376   wcj,qmf8446 (853)   cs,nn776   nn3667

2 Send thou men, that they may search   the land of Canaan,

pnl834   pnp589   qpta5414   pp,pl,cs,nn1121   nn3478   pp,cs,nn4294   pl,nn,pnx1

which I give unto the children of Israel: of every tribe of their fathers shall ye

qmf7971 (nu259) (nn376) nu259   nn376   cs,nn3605   nn5387   pp,pnx

send   a man, every one a ruler among them.

nn4872   pr5921   cs,nn6310   nn3068   wcs,qmf7971   pnx(853)

3 And Moses by the commandment of the LORD sent   them

pr4480/cs,nn4057   nn6290   nn,pnx3605   pndm1992   pl,nn376   pl,cs,nn7218   pl,cs,nn1121

from*the*wilderness of Paran: all those men *were* heads of the children of

nn3478

Israel.

wcj,pndm428   pl,nn,pnx8034   pp,cs,nn4294   nn7205   nn8051   cs,nn1121

4 And these *were* their names: of the tribe of Reuben, Shammua the son

nn2139

of Zaccur.

pp,cs,nn4294   nn8095   nn8202   cs,nn1121   nn2753

5 Of the tribe of Simeon, Shaphat the son of Hori.

pp,cs,nn4294   nn3063   nn3612   cs,nn1121   nn3312

6 Of the tribe of Judah, Caleb the son of Jephunneh.

pp,cs,nn4294   nn3485   nn3008   cs,nn1121   nn3130

7 Of the tribe of Issachar, Igal the son of Joseph.

pp,cs,nn4294   nn669   nn1954   cs,nn1121   nn5126

8 Of the tribe of Ephraim, Joshua the son of Nun.

pp,cs,nn4294   nn1144   nn6406   cs,nn1121   nn7505

9 Of the tribe of Benjamin, Palti the son of Raphu.

pp,cs,nn4294   nn2074   nn1427   cs,nn1121   nn5476

10 Of the tribe of Zebulun, Gaddiel the son of Sodi.

pp,cs,nn4294   nn3130   pp,cs,nn4294   nn4519   nn1426

11 Of the tribe of Joseph, *namely*, of the tribe of Manasseh, Gaddi the

cs,nn1121   nn5485

son of Susi.

pp,cs,nn4294   nn1835   nn5988   cs,nn1121   nn1582

12 Of the tribe of Dan, Ammiel the son of Gemalli.

pp,cs,nn4294   nn836   nn5639   cs,nn1121   nn4317

13 Of the tribe of Asher, Sethur the son of Michael.

pp,cs,nn4294   nn5321   nn5147   cs,nn1121   nn2058

14 Of the tribe of Naphtali, Nahbi the son of Vophsi.

pp,cs,nn4294   nn1410   nn1345   cs,nn1121   nn4352

15 Of the tribe of Gad, Geuel the son of Machi.

pndm428   pl,cs,nn8034   df,pl,nn376   pnl834   nn4872   qpf7971   pp,qnc8446   (853)

☞ 16 These *are* the names of the men which Moses sent to spy out   the

df,nn776   nn4872   wcs,qmf7121   pp,nn1954   cs,nn1121   nn5126   nn3091

land. And Moses called Joshua the son of Nun Jehoshua.

☞ **13:16** See the note on Numbers 27:18–23.

nn4872   wcs,qmf7971   pnx(853)   pp,qnc8446   (853)   cs,nn776   nn3667   wcs,qmf559

⊙ 17 And Moses   sent   them to spy out   the land of Canaan, and   said

pr,pnx413   qmv5927   pndm2088   dfp,nn5045   wcj,qpf5927 pr854   df,nn2022

unto them, Get*you*up   this *way* southward, and go up into the mountain:

wcj,qpf7200 (853)   df,nn776 pnid4100 pnp1931   wcj(853)   df,nn5971   df,qpta3427

18 And   see   the land, what   it   *is*; and   the people that dwelleth

pr,pnx5921   pnp1931   he,aj2389   he,aj7504 (pnp1931) he,nn4592 cj518 aj7227

therein, whether they *be* strong or weak,   few   or many;

wcj,pnid4100   df,nn776   pnl834 pnp1931 qpta3427 pp,pnx   pnp1931   he,aj2896 cj518 aj7451

19 And what the land *is* that they dwell in whether it *be* good or bad;

wcj,pnid4100 df,pl,nn5892   pnl834 pnp1931 qpta3427 pp,pnp2007   he,pp,pl,nn4264 cj518

and what cities *they be* that they dwell   in,   whether in tents,   or in

pp,pl,nn4013

strongholds;

wcj,pnid4100   df,nn776   pnp1931   he,aj8082 cj518 aj7330   he,pta3426

20 And what the land *is*, whether it *be* fat or lean, whether there be

nn6086   pp,pnx   cj518 ptn369   wcj,htpf2388   wcj,qpf3947 pr4480/cs,nn6529

wood therein, or not. And be*ye*of*good*courage, and bring of*the*fruit of the

df,nn776   wcj,df,pl,nn3117   pl,cs,nn3117   pl,cs,nn1061 pl,nn6025

land. Now the time *was* the time of the firstripe grapes.

wcs,qmf5927   wcs,qmf8446 (853)   df,nn776   pr4480/cs,nn4057   nn6790

21 So they went up, and searched   the land from*the*wilderness of Zin

pr5704   nn7340   pp,qnc935   nn2574

unto Rehob, as men come to Hamath.

wcs,qmf5927   dfp,nn5045   wcs,qmf935 pr5704   nn2275   wcj,ad8033   nn289

⊙ 22 And they ascended by the south, and came unto Hebron; where Ahiman,

nn8344   wcj,nn8526   cs,aj3211 df,nn6061   wcj,nn2275   nipf1129   nu7651

Sheshai, and Talmai, the children of Anak, *were*. (Now Hebron was built seven

pl,nn8141 pp,pl,cs,nn6440 nn6814   nn4714

years before Zoan in Egypt.)

wcs,qmf935 pr5704   cs,nn5158   nn812   wcs,qmf3772   pr4480/ad8033

23 And they came unto the brook of Eshcol, and cut down from thence a

nn2156   nu259 wcj,cs,nn811   pl,nn6025   wcs,qmf,pnx5375   pp,du,nu8147

branch with one cluster of grapes, and they   bore   it between two   upon a

dfp,nn4132   wcj,pr4480   df,pl,nn7416   wcj,pr4480   df,pl,nn8384

staff; and *they brought* of the pomegranates, and of the figs.

dfp,nn4725   (df,pndm1931)   qpf7121   cs,nn5158   nn812   pr5921/pl,cs,nn182

24 The place   was called the brook Eshcol, because   of the

df,nn811   pnl834   pl,cs,nn1121   nn3478 qpf3772   pr4480/ad8033

cluster*of*grapes which the children of Israel cut down from thence.

wcs,qmf7725   pr4480/qnc8446   df,nn776 pr4480/cs,nn7093 pl,nu705 nn3117

25 And they returned from searching of the land   after   forty days.

_____

⊙ **13:17** The word *Neghev* (5045), translated "southward," is better translated "south country." The south country was a well-defined territory forming the southernmost and least fertile part of Canaan and was subsequently a part of Judah's inheritance. It extended northward from Kadesh to within a few miles of Hebron and from the Dead Sea westward to the Mediterranean.

The word *har* (2022), translated "mountain," may also be used to refer to a range of hills or mountains. This was a description of the country of southern and central Canaan, mostly within the borders of the inheritance of Judah and Ephraim. It began a few miles south of Hebron and extended northward to the plain of Jezreel, continuing northwest to the sea just above Mount Carmel.

⊙ **13:22** Until recently, Zoan was identified with Tanis and Avaris, later Egyptian cities. More recent archaeological evidence has again confirmed the biblical account, suggesting that a city in the area of modern Qantir is Zoan. Moreover, this city is doubtless the site of "Rameses," mentioned in Exodus 1:11. This would seem to confirm that the Hyksos rulers began the oppression of Israel in Egypt. It was near Hebron that the Hebrew patriarchs had been buried (Gen. 23:19; 49:31).

wcs,qmf**1980**   wcs,qmf**935**   pr413   nn4872   wcj,pr413   nn175   wcj,pr413   cs,nn3605

26 And they went and came to Moses, and to Aaron, and to all

cs,nn**5712**   pl,cs,nn**1121**   nn3478   pr413   cs,nn4057   nn6290   du,nn,lh6946

the congregation of the children of Israel, unto the wilderness of Paran, to Kadesh;

wcs,himf**7725**   nn**1697**   pnx(853)   wcj(853)   cs,nn3605   df,nn**5712**

and brought back word   unto them, and   unto all the congregation, and

wcs,himf,pnx**7200**   (853)   cs,nn6529   df,nn776

showed them   the fruit of the land.

wcs,pimf**5608**   pp,pnx   wcs,qmf**559**   qpf935   pr413   df,nn**776**   pnl834

27 And they told him, and said, We came unto the land whither thou

qpf,pnx7971   wcj,ad1571   pnp1931   cs,qpta2100   nn2461   wcj,nn1706   wcj,pndm2088   nn,pnx6529

sentest us, and surely it floweth with milk and honey; and this *is* the fruit

of it.

ptn657/cj3588   df,nn**5971**   aj5794   df,qpta**3427**   dfp,nn**776**   wcj,df,pl,nn5892

28 Nevertheless the people *be* strong that dwell in the land, and the cities

pl,qptp1219   ad3966   aj1419   wcj,ad1571   qpf**7200**   cs,aj3211   df,nn6061   ad8033

are walled, *and* very great: and moreover we saw the children of Anak there.

nn6003   qpta**3427**   pp,cs,nn**776**   df,nn5045   wcj,df,nn2850

29 The Amalekites dwell in the land of the south: and the Hittites, and the

wcj,df,nn2983   wcj,df,nn567   qpta**3427**   dfp,nn2022   wcj,df,nn3669   qpta**3427**   pr5921

Jebusites, and the Amorites, dwell in the mountains: and the Canaanites dwell by

df,nn3220   wcj,pr5921   cs,nn**3027**   df,nn3383

the sea, and by the coast of Jordan.

nn3612   wcs,himf2013   (853)   df,nn**5971**   pr413   nn4872   wcs,qmf**559**

30 And Caleb stilled   the people before Moses, and said, Let us

qna**5927**/qmf**5927**   wcs,qpf**3423**   pnx(853)   cj3588   qna3201   qmf3201   pp,pnx

go*up*at*once, and possess   it; for we are*well*able to overcome it.

🔑 **13:26** Kadesh, also known as Kadesh–Barnea, was an oasis in the wilderness just south of Canaan proper. It was often a place of defeat, failure, and death for the nation of Israel during their years of wandering. The people rebelled when the twelve spies returned to Kadesh (Num. 14:1–10); they were repulsed in their rash attack from Kadesh (Num. 14:40–45); Miriam, Moses' sister, died and was buried at Kadesh (Num. 20:1); and the great sin of Moses in smiting the rock occurred at Kadesh (Num. 20:11, 12). Aaron died shortly afterwards on Mount Hor (Num. 20:23–29), and Moses died on Mount Nebo (Deut. 34:1–5).

The rebellion at Kadesh is expounded upon in Psalm 95:7b–11. The psalmist attributed Israel's loss of God's "rest" to this rebellion. In addition, the Book of Hebrews affirms that the loss was only temporary, and that God's "rest" was still available if God's people in the New Testament did not "fall after the same example of unbelief" (Heb. 4:9, 11).

🔑 **13:28** Regarding the cities that were "walled and very great," modern archaeologists have found that there were indeed numerous walled fortresses throughout Canaan even in 1440 B.C. These cities made invasion by foreign armies difficult for some time, until the science of siege warfare was as well developed as the techniques of fortification.

🔑 **13:30–33** The spies reported that the people of the land were large: "men of great stature" and "giants." The Hebrew word for "giant" is *nephilim* (5303), which appears elsewhere only in Genesis 6:4 (see the note on this passage). Obviously these people have no connection to those in Genesis chapter six, since those events occurred before the flood. The emphasis of this passage may be that these sons of Anak were not only large, but violent and evil as well (see Deut. 2:10, 11 where "giant" is a translation of *rephā'īm* [7497]).

Caleb and Joshua were the spies who brought back the faithful report that, with the Lord's help, Canaan could easily be taken (Num. 14:6–9). For their faithfulness, God allowed them to survive the wilderness experience and enter Canaan (Num. 14:30). When the second census was taken as preparations were being made to move into Canaan (see the note on Num. 26:52–56), Caleb and Joshua were the only ones from the original group that were still alive. After the major campaigns of the conquest were completed, Joshua divided the land of Canaan by lot. In keeping with God's promise forty–five years earlier, Caleb was the first to be given his land (Num. 14:24; Josh. 14:6–15). He was allotted Hebron, near the cave of Machpelah, where the patriarchs had been buried.

^{wcj,df,pl,nn376} ^{pnl834}   ^{qpf5927}   ^{pr,pnx5973}   ^{qpf559}   ^{qmf3201/ptn3808}   ^{pp,qnc5927}

31 But the   men   that went up   with   him said, We be*not*able to go up

^{pr413}   ^{df,nn5971}   ^{cj3588} ^{pnp1931}   ^{aj2389}   ^{pr,pnx4480}

against the people; for they *are* stronger than we.

^{wcs,himf3318}   ^{cs,nn1681}   ^{df,nn776}   ^{pnl834}   ^{qpf8446}

32 And they brought up an evil report of the land which they had searched

^(pnx853) ^{pr413}   ^{pl,cs,nn1121}   ⁿⁿ³⁴⁷⁸   ^{pp,qnc559}   ^{df,nn776}   ^{pnl834/pp,pnx}   ^{qpf5674}

unto the children of Israel, saying, The land, through   which   we have gone to

^{pp,qnc8446} ^{pnx(853)}   ⁿⁿ⁷⁷⁶ ^{pnp1931}   ^{qpta398}   ^{pl,qpta,pnx3427}   ^{wcj,cs,nn3605}

search   it, *is* a land that eateth up the inhabitants thereof; and   all   the

^{df,nn5971} ^{pnl834}   ^{qpf7200} ^{pp,nn,pnx8432}   ^{pl,cs,nn376}   ^{pl,nn4060}

people that we saw   in   it *are* men of a great stature.

^{wcj,ad8033}   ^{qpf7200} ⁽⁸⁵³⁾   ^{df,pl,nn5303}   ^{pl,cs,nn1121}   ⁿⁿ⁶⁰⁶¹   ^{pr4480}

33 And there we saw   the giants, the   sons   of Anak, *which come* of the

^{df,pl,nn5303}   ^{wcs,qmf1961}   ^{pp,du,nn,pnx5869}   ^{dfp,pl,nn2284}   ^{wcj,ad3651}   ^{qpf1961}

giants: and we   were   in our own   sight   as grasshoppers, and   so   we were in

^{pp,du,nn,pnx5869}

their   sight.

The People Rebel

14 ^{cs,nn3605}   ^{df,nn5712}   ^{wcs,qmf5375} ⁽⁸⁵³⁾   ^{nn,pnx6963}   ^{wcs,qmf5414}

     🗝 And   all   the congregation lifted up   their voice, and   cried;

^{df,nn5971}   ^{wcs,qmf1058} ^{df,pndm1931} ^{dfp,nn3915}

and the people wept   that   night.

^{cs,nn3605}   ^{pl,cs,nn1121}   ⁿⁿ³⁴⁷⁸   ^{wcs,nimf3885}   ^{pr5921}   ⁿⁿ⁴⁸⁷²   ^{wcj,pr5921}   ⁿⁿ¹⁷⁵

2 And   all   the children of Israel murmured against Moses and against Aaron:

^{cs,nn3605}   ^{df,nn5712}   ^{wcs,qmf559} ^{pr,pnx413}   ^{ptx3863}   ^{qpf4191}

and the whole congregation   said   unto them, Would*God*that we had died in the

^{pp,cs,nn776}   ⁿⁿ⁴⁷¹⁴   ^{cj176}   ^{ptx3863}   ^{qpf4191}   ^{df,pndm2088}   ^{dfp,nn4057}

land of Egypt! or would God we had died in   this   wilderness!

^{wcj,pnit4100}   ⁿⁿ³⁰⁶⁸   ^{hipt935}   ^{pnx(853)}   ^{pr413} ^{df,pndm2063} ^{df,nn776}   ^{pp,qnc5307}

3 And wherefore hath the Lᴏʀᴅ brought   us unto   this   land, to   fall   by

^{dfp,nn2719}   ^{pl,nn,pnx802}   ^{wcj,nn,pnx2945}   ^{qmf1961}   ^{pp,nn957}   ^{he,ptn3808}

the sword, that our   wives   and our   children   should   be   a prey? were it   not

^{aj2896}   ^{pp,pnx}   ^{qnc7725}   ^{nn,lh4714}

better for us to return into Egypt?

^{wcs,qmf559} ⁿⁿ³⁷⁶ ^{pr413}   ^{nn,pnx251}   ^{qmf5414}   ⁿⁿ⁷²¹⁸   ^{wcj,qmf7725}

4 And they   said   one   to   another, Let us make a captain, and let us return

^{nn,lh4714}

into Egypt.

ⁿⁿ⁴⁸⁷²   ^{wcj,nn175} ^{wcs,qmf5307} ^{pr5921}   ^{pl,nn,pnx6440} ^{pp,pl,cs,nn6440} ^{cs,nn3605}   ^{cs,nn6951}

5 Then Moses and Aaron   fell   on their   faces   before   all   the assembly

^{cs,nn5712}   ^{pl,cs,nn1121}   ⁿⁿ³⁴⁷⁸

of the congregation of the children of Israel.

^{wcj,nn3091}   ^{cs,nn1121}   ⁿⁿ⁵¹²⁶   ^{wcj,nn3612}   ^{cs,nn1121}   ⁿⁿ³³¹²

🗝 6 And Joshua the   son   of Nun, and Caleb the   son   of Jephunneh, *which were*

^{pr4480}   ^{df,pl,qpta8446} ⁽⁸⁵³⁾   ^{df,nn776} ^{qpf7167}   ^{pl,nn,pnx899}

of them that searched   the land, rent their clothes:

^{wcs,qmf559} ^{pr413} ^{cs,nn3605}   ^{cs,nn5712}   ^{pl,cs,nn1121}   ⁿⁿ³⁴⁷⁸   ^{pp,qnc559}

7 And they spoke unto   all   the company of the children of Israel, saying, The

---

🗝 **14:1–10**   See the note on Numbers 13:26.
🗝 **14:6–9**   See the note on Numbers 13:30–33.

df,nn776 pnl834/pp,pnx qpf5674 pp,qnc8446 pnx(853) ad3966/ad3966 aj2896 df,nn776

land, which we passed through to search it, *is* an exceeding good land.

cj518 nn3068 qpf2654 pp,pnx wcj,hipf935 pnx(853) pr413 df,pndm2063 df,nn776

8 If the Lord delight in us, then he will bring us into this land, and

wcj,qpf,pnx5414 pp,pnx nn776 pnl834 (pnp1931) cs,qpta2100 nn2461 wcj,nn1706

give it us; a land which floweth with milk and honey.

ad389 qmf4775 ptn408 pp,nn3068 ptn408 qmf3372 wcj,pnp859 (853) cs,nn5971

9 Only rebel not ye against the Lord, neither fear ye the people of the

df,nn776 cj3588 pnp1992 nn,pnx3899 nn,pnx6738 qpf5493 pr4480/pr,pnx5921

land; for they *are* bread for us: their defense is departed from them, and the

wcj,nn3068 pr,pnx854 qmf,pnx3372 ptn408

Lord *is* with us: fear them not.

cs,nn3605 df,nn5712 wcs,qmf559 pp,qnc7275 pnx(853) dfp,pl,nn68

10 But all the congregation bade stone them with stones. And the

wcj,cs,nn3519 nn3068 nipf7200 pp,cs,nn168 nn4150 pr413 cs,nn3605

glory of the Lord appeared in the tabernacle of the congregation before all the

pl,cs,nn1121 nn3478

children of Israel.

nn3068 wcs,qmf559 pr413 nn4872 pr5704/ad575 df,pndm2088 df,nn5971 pimf,pnx5006

11 And the Lord said unto Moses, How long will this people provoke

wcj,pr5704/ad575 ptn3808 himf539 pp,pnx pp,cs,nn3605 df,nn226 pnl834

me? and how long will it be ere they believe me, for all the signs which I

qpf6213 pp,nn,pnx7130

have showed among them?

himf,pnx5221 dfp,nn1698 wcj,himf,pnx3423 wcj,qmf6213

12 I will smite them with the pestilence, and disinherit them, and will make

pnx(853) aj1419 pp,nn1471 wcj,aj6099 pr,pnx4480

of thee a greater nation and mightier than they.

nn4872 wcs,qmf559 pr413 nn3068 nn4714 wcj,qpf8085 cj3588

13 And Moses said unto the Lord, Then the Egyptians shall hear *it*, (for

hipf5927 (853) df,pndm2088 df,nn5971 pp,nn,pnx3581 pr4480/nn,pnx7130

thou broughtest up this people in thy might from among them;)

wcj,qpf559 pr413 cs,qpta3427 df,pndm2063 df,nn776

14 And they will tell *it* to the inhabitants of this land: *for* they have

qpf8085 cj3588 pnp859 nn3068 pp,cs,nn7130 df,pndm2088 df,nn5971 pnl834 pnp859 nn3068 nipf7200 nn5869

heard that thou Lord *art* among this people, that thou Lord art seen face to

pp,nn5869 wcj,nn,pnx6051 qpta5975 pr,pnx5921 pnp859 qpta1980 pp,pl,nn,pnx6440

face, and *that* thy cloud standeth over them, and *that* thou goest before

ad3119 wcj,pp,cs,nn5982 nn6051 wcj,pp,cs,nn5982 nn784 ad3915

them, by*day*time in a pillar of a cloud, and in a pillar of fire by night.

wcj,hipf4191 (853) df,pndm2088 df,nn5971 nu259 pp,nn376 df,pl,nn1471

15 Now if thou shalt kill *all* this people as one man, then the nations

pnl834 qpf8085 (853) nn,pnx8088 wcj,qpf559 pp,qnc559

which have heard the fame of thee will speak, saying,

pr4480/ptn1115 nn3068 qnc3201 pp,hinc935 (853) df,pndm2088 df,nn5971 pr413 df,nn776

16 Because the Lord was not able to bring this people into the land

pnl834 nipf7650 pp,pnx wcs,qmf,pnx7819 dfp,nn4057

which he sware unto them therefore he hath slain them in the wilderness.

wcj,ad6258 pte4994 cs,nn3581 nn136 qmf1431 pp,pnl834

17 And now, I*beseech*thee, let the power of my Lord be great, according as

pipf1696 pp,qnc559

thou hast spoken, saying,

nn3068 cs,aj750/du,nn639 wcj,cs,aj7227 nn2617 qpta5375 nn5771

18 The Lord *is* longsuffering, and of great mercy, forgiving iniquity and

transgression, and by*no*means*clearing *the guilty*, visiting the iniquity of the
fathers upon the children unto the third and   fourth *generation*.

19 Pardon, I*beseech*thee, the iniquity of   this   people according unto the
greatness of thy mercy, and   as   thou hast forgiven this   people, from Egypt
even until now.

God Punishes Israel

20 And the LORD said, I have pardoned according to thy   word:

21 But *as* truly *as*   I   live,   all   the earth shall be   filled   with the glory
of the LORD.

22 Because   all   those   men   which have   seen   my glory, and   my
miracles, which I   did   in Egypt and in the wilderness, and have tempted   me
now these   ten   times, and have   not   hearkened to my   voice;

23 Surely they shall not   see   the   land   which   I   swore   unto   their   fathers,
neither shall   any   of them that provoked me   see   it:

24 But my   servant   Caleb, because he   had another   spirit   with   him, and hath
followed*me*fully, him will I   bring   into the   land   whereinto   he   went; and his
seed   shall   possess it.

25 (Now the   Amalekites   and the   Canaanites   dwelt   in the   valley.)   Tomorrow
turn   you,   and   get   you into the wilderness by the   way   of the   Red   sea.

26 And the LORD   spoke   unto   Moses   and   unto   Aaron   saying,

27 How   long   *shall I bear with*   this   evil   congregation,   which   murmur

---

14:22 There are two views concerning Israel's having tempted God "ten times." Some scholars hold that there are actually ten instances recorded in Scripture which involve Israel and their exodus from Egypt. They were the two temptations at the Red Sea (Ex. 14:11; Ps. 106:7); demanding water twice (Ex. 15:23; 17:2); demanding food twice (Ex. 16:20, 27); demanding flesh twice (Ex. 16:3; Num. 11:4); the incident with the golden calf (Ex. 32); and the incident with the twelve spies (Ex. 13). Others say that the number "ten" times that Israel tempted God is not to be taken literally. They say it is symbolic of completeness. In either case it refers to Israel's frequent acts of rebellion, of which the Lord had grown weary.

14:24, 30 See the note on Numbers 13:30–33 regarding Joshua and Caleb.

14:25 This verse notes the beginning of the wilderness wanderings. Unbelief had cost a whole generation the blessings of the Promised Land that God desired to give them.

pr,pnx5921   qpf**8085**   (853)   pl,cs,nn8519   pl,cs,nn**1121**   nn3478   pnl834   pnp1992

against me? I have heard   the murmurings of the children of Israel, which they

pl,hipt3885   pr,pnx5921

murmur against me.

qmv559   pr,pnx413   pnp589   aj2416   cs,nn5002   nn**3068**   (cj518)/(ptn**3808**) pp,pnl834

28 Say unto them, *As truly as* I live, saith the Lᴏʀᴅ,   as   ye

pipf**1696**   pp,du,nn,pnx241 ad3651   qmf**6213**   pp,pnx

have spoken in mine   ears,   so will I do to you:

pl,nn,pnx**6297**   qmf5307   df,pndm2088   dfp,nn4057   wcj,cs,nn3605

29 Your carcasses shall fall in   this   wilderness; and   all   that were

pl,qptp,pnx**6485**   wcj,cs,nn3605   nn,pnx4557   pl,nu6242   nn8141   pr4480/cs,nn**1121**

numbered of you, according to your whole number, from twenty years   old

wcj,ad,lh4605   pnl834   hipf3885   pr,pnx5921

and upward, which have murmured against me,

cj518   pnp859   qmf935   pr413   df,nn776   pnl834

☞ 30 Doubtless ye   shall not   come into the land, *concerning* which I

qpf5375/(853)/nn,pnx**3027**   pnx(853)   pp,pinc**7931**   pp,pnx   cj3588/cj518   nn3612   cs,nn**1121**

swore   to make   you dwell therein,   save   Caleb the   son of

nn3312   wcj,nn3091   cs,nn**1121**   nn5126

Jephunneh, and Joshua the son of Nun.

wcj,nn,pnx**2945** pnl834   qpf559   qmf**1961**   dfp,nn957 pnx(853)

31 But your little ones, which ye said should be   a   prey,   them will I

wcs,hipf935   wcs,qpf3045 (853)   df,nn776   pnl834   pp,pnx   qpf**3988**

bring in, and they shall know   the land which ye have despised.

pnp859   wcj,pl,nn,pnx**6297**   qmf5307 df,pndm2088   dfp,nn4057

32 But *as for* you, your carcasses, they shall fall in   this   wilderness.

wcj,pl,nn,pnx**1121**   qmf**1961**/pl,qpta7462   dfp,nn4057   pl,nu705   nn8141

33 And your children shall   wander   in the wilderness forty years, and

wcs,qpf5375 (853)   pl,nn,pnx2184   pr5704   pl,nn,pnx**6297**   qnc8552   dfp,nn4057

bear   your whoredoms, until your carcasses be wasted in the wilderness.

pp,cs,nn4557   df,pl,nn3117   pnl834   qpf8446   (853)   df,nn776   pl,nu705

34 After the number of the days in which ye searched   the land, *even* forty

nn3117   nn3117/dfp,nn8141/nn3117/dfp,nn8141   qmf5375 (853)   pl,nn,pnx5771   pl,nu705   nn8141

days, each*day*for*a*year, shall ye bear   your iniquities, *even* forty years, and

wcs,qpf3045 (853)   nn,pnx8569

ye shall know   my breach*of*promise.

pnp589   nn**3068**   pipf**1696**   cj518/ptn**3808** qmf**6213** pndm2063   pp,cs,nn3605 df,pndm2063 df,aj**7451**

35 I the Lᴏʀᴅ have said, I will surely do   it   unto all   this   evil

df,nn**5712**   df,pl,nipt3259   pr,pnx5921   df,pndm2088   dfp,nn4057

congregation, that are gathered together against me: in this   wilderness they shall

qmf**8552**   wcj,ad8033   qmf**4191**

be consumed, and there they shall die.

wcj,df,pl,nn**376** pnl834   nn4872 qpf7971   pp,qnc8446 (853)   df,nn776   wcs,qmf**7725**

36 And the   men,   which Moses sent to search   the land, who returned,

(853) cs,nn3605   df,nn**5712**   wcs,himf3885 pr,pnx5921   pp,hinc3318

and made   all   the congregation to murmur against him, by bringing up a

nn1681   pr5921   df,nn**776**

slander upon the land,

df,pl,nn**376**   pl,cs,hipt3318   aj**7451** cs,nn1681   df,nn776 wcs,qmf**4191**

37 Even those men that did bring up the evil report upon the land,   died by

dfp,nn4046 pp,pl,cs,nn**6440**   nn**3068**

the plague before the Lᴏʀᴅ.

wcj,nn3091   cs,nn**1121**   nn5126   wcj,nn3612   cs,nn**1121**   nn3312

38 But Joshua the son of Nun, and Caleb the son of Jephunneh, *which were*

pr4480 (df,pnp1992) df,pl,nn**376** df,pl,qpta**1980** pp,qnc8446 (853)   df,nn776 qpf**2421**

of   the men that went to search   the land, lived *still*.

nn4872   wcs,pimf1696 (853) df,pndm428 df,pl,nn1697   pr413 cs,nn3605   pl,cs,nn1121   nn3478

39 And Moses   told   these sayings unto all the children of Israel: and

df,nn5971   wcs,htmf56   ad3966

the people mourned greatly.

wcs,himf7925   dfp,nn1242   wcs,qmf5927   pr413   cs,nn7218

40 And they rose*up*early in the morning, and got*them*up into the top of

df,nn2022   pp,qnc559 ptdm,pnx2009   wcj,qpf5927 pr413 df,nn4725 pnl834

the mountain, saying,   Lo,   we *be here*, and will go up unto the place which the

nn3068   qpf559   cj3588   qpf2398

LORD hath promised: for we have sinned.

nn4872   wcs,qmf559   pp,pnit4100 pndm2088   pnp859 pl,qpta5674   (853)   cs,nn6310

41 And Moses said, Wherefore now do ye transgress   the commandment

nn3068   wcj,pnp1931   ptn3808 qmf6743

of the LORD? but   it   shall not prosper.

qmf5927/ptn408 cj3588   nn3068   ptn369 pp,nn,pnx7130   wcj,ptn3808 nimf5062

42 Go*not*up, for the LORD *is* not among you; that ye be not smitten

pp,pl,cs,nn6440   pl,qpta,pnx341

before your enemies.

cj3588   df,nn6003   wcj,df,nn3669   ad8033 pp,pl,nn,pnx6440

43 For the Amalekites and the Canaanites *are* there before you, and ye shall

wcs,qpf5307   dfp,nn2719 cj3588/pr5921/ad3651   qpf7725   pr4480/pr310   nn3068

fall   by the sword: because   ye are turned away   from the LORD, therefore

nn3068   wcj,ptn3808 qmf1961 pr,pnx5973

the LORD will   not   be   with you.

wcs,himf6075   pp,qnc5927 pr413   df,nn2022 cs,nn7218   wcj,cs,nn727

⌖ 44 But they presumed to go up unto the hill   top: nevertheless the   ark   of

cs,nn1285   nn3068   wcj,nn4872   qpf4185   ptn3808 pr4480/cs,nn7130   df,nn4264

the covenant of the LORD, and Moses, departed not   out of   the camp.

df,nn6003   wcs,qmf3381   wcj,df,nn3669   df,qpta3427 df,pndm1931

45 Then the Amalekites came down, and the Canaanites which dwelt in   that

dfp,nn2022 wcs,himf,pnx5221   wcs,himf,pnx3807   pr5704 df,nn2767

hill, and   smote   them, and discomfited them, *even* unto Hormah.

Laws About Offerings

nn3068   wcs,pimf1696 pr413   nn4872   pp,qnc559

And the LORD spoke unto Moses, saying,

pimv1696   pr413   pl,cs,nn1121   nn3478   wcj,qpf559 pr,pnx413   cj3588

2 Speak unto the children of Israel, and say   unto them, When

qmf935 pr413   cs,nn776   pl,nn,pnx4186 pnl834 pnp589 qpta5414   pp,pnx

ye be come into the land of your habitations, which I   give unto you,

wcs,qpf6213   nn801   pp,nn3068   nn5930   cj176

3 And will make   an offering*by*fire unto the LORD, a burnt offering, or a

nn2077   pp,pinc6381   nn5088 cj176   pp,nn5071   cj176   pp,pl,nn,pnx4150

sacrifice in performing a vow, or in a freewill offering, or in your solemn feasts,

pp,qnc6213   nn5207 cs,nn7381   pp,nn3068 pr4480 df,nn1241 cj176 pr4480 df,nn6629

to make a sweet savor unto the LORD, of the herd, or of the flock:

df,hipf7126   nn,pnx7133   pp,nn3068 wcs,hipf7126   nn4503

4 Then shall he*that*offereth his offering unto the LORD bring a meat offering

nn6241   nn5560   qptp1101   pp,cs,nuor7243   df,nn1969 nn8081

of a tenth deal of flour mingled with the fourth *part* of a hin of oil.

⌖ **14:44** The children of Israel were adding the sin of presumptuous self-confidence to their sin of unbelief (vv. 1–4).

cs,nuor7243   df,nn1969   wcj,nn3196   dfp,nn5262

5 And the fourth *part* of a hin of wine for a drink offering shalt thou

qmf6213   pr5921   df,nn5930   cj176   dfp,nn2077   df,nu259 dfp,nn3532

prepare with the burnt offering or sacrifice, for one lamb.

cj176   dfp,nn352   qmf6213   nn4503   du,cs,nu8147   pl,nn6241

6 Or for a ram, thou shalt prepare *for* a meat offering   two   tenth deals of

nn5560   qptp1101   cs,nuor7992   df,nn1969   dfp,nn8081

flour mingled with the third *part* of a hin of oil.

dfp,nn5262   himf7126   cs,nuor7992   df,nn1969   wcj,nn3196

7 And for a drink offering thou shalt offer the third *part* of a hin of wine,

nn5207   cs,nn7381   pp,nn3068

for a sweet savor unto the LORD.

wcj,cj3588   qmf6213   cs,nn1121/nn1241   nn5930   cj176   nn2077

8 And when thou preparest a bullock *for* a burnt offering, or *for* a sacrifice

pp,pinc6381   nn5088   cj176   pl,nn8002   pp,nn3068

in performing a vow, or peace offerings unto the LORD:

wcs,hipf7126   pr5921   cs,nn1121/df,nn1241   nn4503   nu7969   pl,nn6241

9 Then shall he bring with a   bullock   a meat offering of three tenth deals

nn5560   qptp1101   cs,nn2677   df,nn1969   dfp,nn8081

of flour mingled with half a hin of oil.

himf7126   dfp,nn5262   cs,nn2677   df,nn1969   wcj,nn3196

10 And thou shalt bring for a drink offering half a   hin   of wine, *for* an

cs,nn801   nn5207   cs,nn7381   pp,nn3068

offering*made*by*fire, of a sweet savor unto the LORD.

ad3602   nimf6213   df,nu259   dfp,nn7794   cj176   df,nu259 dfp,nn352 cj176

11 Thus shall it be done for one bullock, or for one ram, or for a

dfp,nn7716/dfp,pl,nn3532   cj176   dfp,pl,nn5795

lamb,   or a kid.

dfp,nn4557   pnl834   qmf6213   ad3602   qmf6213

12 According to the number that ye shall prepare,   so   shall ye   do   to

dfp,nu259   pp,nn,pnx4557

every one according to their number.

cs,nn3605   df,nn249   qmf6213   (853)   pndm428

13 All   that   are born*of*the*country   shall   do   these things

ad3602   pp,hinc7126   cs,nn801   nn5207   cs,nn7381

after*this*manner, in offering an offering*made*by*fire, of a sweet savor

pp,nn3068

unto the LORD.

wcj,cj3588   nn1616   qmf1481   pr,pnx854   cj176   pnl834   pp,nn,pnx8432

14 And   if   a stranger sojourn with you, or whosoever *be* among you in

pp,pl,nn,pnx1755   wcs,qpf6213   cs,nn801   nn5207   cs,nn7381

your generations, and will offer an offering*made*by*fire, of a sweet savor unto

pp,nn3068 pp,pnl834   qmf6213 ad3651   qmf6213

the LORD; as ye do, so he shall do.

nu259   nn2708   pp,pnx   df,nn6951

15 One ordinance *shall be both* for you of the congregation, and also for the

wcj,dfp,nn1616   df,qpta1481   cs,nn2708   nn5769   pp,pl,nn,pnx1755   pp,pnx

stranger that sojourneth *with you*, an ordinance forever in your generations: as ye

dfp,nn1616   qmf1961   pp,pl,cs,nn6440   nn3068

are, so shall the stranger be   before the LORD.

nu259   nn8451   nu259   wcj,nn4941   qmf1961   pp,pnx   wcj,dfp,nn1616

16 One law and one manner shall   be   for you, and for the stranger that

df,qpta1481   pr,pnx854

sojourneth with you.

nn3068   wcs,pimf1696   pr413   nn4872   pp,qnc559

17 And the LORD spoke unto Moses, saying,

^{pimv**1696**} ^{pr413} ^{pl,cs,nn**1121**} ⁿⁿ³⁴⁷⁸ ^{wcj,qpf**559**} ^{pr,pnx413} ^{pp,qnc,pnx935}

18 Speak unto the children of Israel, and say unto them, When ye come

^{pr413} ^{df,nn**776** pnl834/ad,lh8033 pnp589 hipt935 pnx(853)}

into the land whither I bring you,

^{wcj,qpf**1961**} ^{pp,qnc,pnx398} ^{pr4480/cs,nn3899} ^{df,nn**776**}

19 Then it shall be, that, when ye eat of*the*bread of the land, ye shall

^{himf7311} ^{nn**8641**} ^{pp,nn**3068**}

offer up a heave offering unto the LORD.

^{himf7311} ⁿⁿ²⁴⁷¹ ^{cs,nn**7225**} ^{pl,nn,pnx6182} ^{nn**8641**}

20 Ye shall offer up a cake of the first of your dough *for* a heave offering:

^{pp,cs,nn**8641**} ⁿⁿ¹⁶³⁷ ^{ad**3651**} ^{himf7311 pnx(853)}

as *ye do* the heave offering of the threshingfloor, so shall ye heave it.

^{pr4480/cs,nn**7225**} ^{pl,nn,pnx6182} ^{qmf5414} ^{pp,nn**3068**} ^{nn**8641**}

21 Of*the*first of your dough ye shall give unto the LORD a heave offering in

^{pp,pl,nn,pnx**1755**}

your generations.

^{wcj,cj3588} ^{qmf7686} ^{wcj,ptn3808} ^{qmf6213} ⁽⁸⁵³⁾ ^{cs,nn3605} ^{df,pndm428}

22 And if ye have erred, and not observed all these

^{df,pl,nn**4687**} ^{pnl834} ^{nn**3068**} ^{pipf**1696** pr413} ⁿⁿ⁴⁸⁷²

commandments, which the LORD hath spoken unto Moses,

^{(853) cs,nn3605 pnl834} ^{nn**3068**} ^{pipf**6680**/pr,pnx413} ^{pp,cs,nn3027} ⁿⁿ⁴⁸⁷²

23 *Even* all that the LORD hath commanded you by the hand of Moses,

^{pr4480} ^{df,nn3117 pnl834} ^{nn**3068**} ^{pipf**6680**} ^{wcj,ad1973}

from the day that the LORD commanded *Moses*, and henceforward among your

^{pp,pl,nn,pnx**1755**}

generations;

^{wcj,qpf**1961**} ^{cj518} ^{nipf6213} ^{pp,nn**7684**}

24 Then it shall be, if *aught* be committed by ignorance

^{pr4480/pl,cs,nn**5869**} ^{df,nn5712} ^{cs,nn3605} ^{df,nn5712} ^{wcj,qpf6213}

without*the*knowledge of the congregation, that all the congregation shall offer

^{nu259 cs,nn**1121**/nn1241} ⁿⁿ⁶⁴⁹⁹ ^{pp,nn5930} ^{nn5207 pp,cs,nn7381} ^{pp,nn**3068**}

one young bullock for a burnt offering, for a sweet savor unto the LORD, with

^{wcj,nn,pnx**4503**} ^{wcj,nn,pnx5262} ^{dfp,nn**4941**} ^{nu259 wcj,cs,nn**8163**}

his meat offering, and his drink offering, according to the manner, and one kid

^{pl,nn**5795**} ^{pp,nn**2403**}

of the goats for a sin offering.

^{df,nn3548} ^{wcj,pipf**3722**} ^{pr5921 cs,nn3605} ^{cs,nn5712}

25 And the priest shall make*an*atonement for all the congregation of the

^{pl,cs,nn**1121**} ⁿⁿ³⁴⁷⁸ ^{wcj,nipf**5545**} ^{pp,pnx} ^{cj3588 pnp1931} ^{nn**7684**} ^{wcj,pnp1992}

children of Israel, and it shall be forgiven them; for it *is* ignorance: and they

^{hipf935} ⁽⁸⁵³⁾ ^{nn,pnx**7133**} ⁿⁿ⁸⁰¹ ^{pp,nn**3068**}

shall bring their offering, a sacrifice*made*by*fire unto the LORD, and their

^{wcj,nn,pnx**2403**} ^{pp,pl,cs,nn**6440**} ⁿⁿ³⁰⁶⁸ ^{pr5921} ^{nn,pnx**7684**}

sin offering before the LORD, for their ignorance:

^{wcj,nipf**5545**} ^{pp,cs,nn3605} ^{cs,nn5712} ^{pl,cs,nn**1121**} ⁿⁿ³⁴⁷⁸

26 And it shall be forgiven all the congregation of the children of Israel,

^{wcj,dfp,nn**1616**} ^{df,qpta1481} ^{pp,nn,pnx**8432**} ^{cj3588} ^{pp,cs,nn3605} ^{df,nn5971}

and the stranger that sojourneth among them; seeing all the people *were* in

^{pp,nn**7684**}

ignorance.

^{wcj,cj518 nu259 nn5315 qmf2398} ^{pp,nn**7684**} ^{wcs,hipf7126} ⁿⁿ⁵⁷⁹⁵

27 And if any soul sin through ignorance, then he shall bring a she goat

^{cs,nn1323 nn,pnx8141} ^{pp,nn**2403**}

of the first year for a sin offering.

^{df,nn3548} ^{wcs,pipf**3722**} ^{pr5921} ^{df,nn5315}

28 And the priest shall make*an*atonement for the soul that

cj518 pndm428   qmf**4191**   pp,cs,nn**4194**   cs,nn3605 df,nn**120**   nimf**6485**

29 If these men die the common death of all men, or if they be visited

pr,pnx5921 wcj,cs,nn**6486** cs,nn3605 df,nn**120**   nn**3068**   ptn**3808** qpf,pnx7971

after the visitation of all men; *then* the LORD hath not sent me.

          wcj,cj518   nn**3068** qmf**1254**   nn1278   df,nn**127** wcs,qpf6475 (853)   nn,pnx**6310**

30 But if the LORD make a new thing, and the earth open her mouth,

wcs,qpf**1104**/pnx(853)   wcj(853) cs,nn3605 pnl834   pp,pnx

and swallow*them*up, with all that *appertain* unto them, and they

wcs,qpf3381   aj**2416**   nn,lh7585   wcs,qpf3045   cj3588 df,pndm428 df,pl,nn**376**

go down quick into the pit; then ye shall understand that these men have

pipf**5006**   (853)   nn**3068**

provoked the LORD.

          wcs,qmf**1961**   pp,pinc,pnx**3615**   pp,pinc**1696**   (853) cs,nn3605 df,pndm428

31 And it*came*to*pass, as he had made*an*end of speaking all these

df,pl,nn**1697**   df,nn**127**   wcs,nimf1234   pnl834   pr,pnx8478

words, that the ground cleaved asunder that *was* under them:

         df,nn776 wcs,qmf6605 (853)   nn,pnx**6310**   wcs,qmf**1104**/pnx(853)   wcj(853)

☞ 32 And the earth opened her mouth, and swallowed*them*up, and their

pl,nn,pnx**1004**   wcj(853) cs,nn3605   df,nn**120** pnl834   pp,nn7141   wcj(853) cs,nn3605

houses, and all the men that *appertained* unto Korah, and all *their*

df,nn**7399**

goods.

pnp1992   wcj,cs,nn3605 pnl834   pp,pnx   wcs,qmf3381   aj**2416**   nn,lh7585

33 They, and all that *appertained* to them, went down alive into the pit,

df,nn776 wcs,pimf**3680** pr,pnx5921   wcs,qmf6   pr4480/cs,nn**8432**   df,nn**6951**

and the earth closed upon them: and they perished from among the congregation.

wcj,cs,nn3605 nn3478 pnl834   pr,pnx5439   qpf5127   pp,nn,pnx6963

34 And all Israel that *were* round about them fled at the cry of them:

cj3588   qpf**559** cj6435   df,nn**776**   qmf,pnx**1104**

for they said, Lest the earth swallow*us*up *also*.

         qpf3318   wcj,nn784 pr4480/pr854   nn**3068**   wcs,qmf398   (853)

35 And there came out a fire from the LORD, and consumed the

wcj,du,nu**3967**   df,pl,nu2572 nn**376**   pl,cs,hipt**7126** df,nn**7004**

two hundred and fifty men that offered incense.

        nn**3068** wcs,pimf**1696** pr413   nn4872   pp,qnc**559**

36 And the LORD spoke unto Moses, saying,

qmv**559**   pr413   nn499   cs,nn**1121**   nn175   df,nn**3548**   wcj,himf7311 (853)

37 Speak unto Eleazar the son of Aaron the priest, that he take up the

df,pl,nn**4289** pr4480/pr996 df,nn**8316**   qmv2219   wcj(853)   df,nn784 ad1973 cj3588

censers out of the burning, and scatter thou the fire yonder; for they are

qpf**6942**

hallowed.

  (853)   pl,cs,nn**4289** df,pndm428 df,pl,nn**2400**   pp,pl,nn,pnx**5315**

38 The censers of these sinners against their own souls, let them

wcj,qpf**6213**/pnx(853)   pl,cs,nn**7555** pl,nn**6341**   nn6826   dfp,nn**4196** cj3588   hipf,pnx**7126**

make them broad plates *for* a covering of the altar: for they offered them

pp,pl,cs,nn**6440**   nn**3068**   wcs,qmf**6942**   wcs,qmf**1961** pp,nn226

before the LORD, therefore they are hallowed: and they shall be a sign unto

pp,pl,cs,nn**1121**   nn3478

the children of Israel.

☞ **16:32** The phrase "and all that appertained unto them" does not refer to their possessions nor to the children of Korah, but to all those (whether of Korah's house or not) who had taken part in the crime. Korah's children did not perish as a result of his sin (Numbers 26:11). Some of his descendants are mentioned in Numbers 26:58; 1 Chronicles 9:19; and in the titles of Psalms 84; 85; 87; 88.

nn499   df,nn3548   wcs,qmf3947   (853)   df,nn5178   pl,cs,nn4289   pnl834

39 And Eleazar the priest took   the brazen censers, wherewith they that

df,pl,qptp8313   hipf7126   wcs,pimf,pnx7554   nn6826

were burnt had offered; and they were made broad *plates for* a covering of the

dfp,nn4196

altar:

nn2146   pp,pl,cs,nn1121   nn3478   pp,pr4616/pnl834   ptn3808   nn376/qpta2114   pnp1931

40 *To be* a memorial unto the children of Israel,   that   no stranger, which

ptn3808   pr4480/cs,nn2233   nn175   qmf7126   pp,hinc6999   nn7004   pp,pl,cs,nn6440   nn3068

is not of*the*seed of Aaron, come near to offer incense before the LORD; that

qmf1961 wcj,ptn3808   pp,nn7141   wcj,pp,nn,pnx5712 pp,pnl834   nn3068   pipf1696   pp,pnx

he be   not as Korah, and as his company: as the LORD said to him by the

pp,cs,nn3027   nn4872

hand of Moses.

Others Complain and Die

pr4480/nn4283   cs,nn3605   cs,nn5712   pl,cs,nn1121   nn3478

41 But on*the*morrow   all   the congregation of the children of Israel

wcs,nimf3885   pr5921   nn4872   wcj,pr5921   nn175   pp,qnc559   pnp859   hipf4191   (853)   cs,nn5971

murmured against Moses and against Aaron, saying, Ye have killed   the people

nn3068

of the LORD.

wcs,qmf1961   df,nn5712   pp,ninc6950   pr5921   nn4872

42 And it*came*to*pass, when the congregation was gathered against Moses

wcj,pr5921   nn175   wcs,qmf6437   pr413   cs,nn168   nn4150

and against Aaron, that they looked toward the tabernacle of the congregation: and,

wcj,ptdm2009   df,nn6051   pipf,pnx3680   cs,nn3519   nn3068   wcs,nimf7200

behold, the cloud covered it, and the glory of the LORD appeared.

nn4872   wcj,nn175 wcs,qmf935 pr413/pl,cs,nn6440   cs,nn168   nn4150

43 And Moses and Aaron came   before the tabernacle of the congregation.

nn3068   wcs,pimf1696   pr413   nn4872   pp,qnc559

44 And the LORD spoke unto Moses, saying,

nimv7426   pr4480/cs,nn8432   df,pndm2063   df,nn5712   wcs,pimf3615   pnx(853)

45 Get*you*up from among   this   congregation, that I may consume

pp,nn7281   wcs,qmf5307   pr5921   pl,nn,pnx6440

them as in a moment. And they   fell upon their faces.

nn4872   wcs,qmf559   pr413   nn175   qmv3947   (853)   df,nn4289   wcj,qmv5414   nn784   pr,pnx5921

46 And Moses said unto Aaron, Take   a censer, and   put   fire therein

pr4480/pr5921   df,nn4196   wcj,qmv7760   nn7004   wcj,himv1980   nn4120   pr413   df,nn5712

from off the altar, and put on incense, and   go   quickly unto the congregation,

wcj,pimv3722   pr,pnx5921   cj3588   df,nn7110   qpf3318   pr4480/pp,pl,cs,nn6440

and make*an*atonement for   them: for there is wrath gone out   from   the

nn3068   df,nn5063   hipf2490

LORD; the plague is begun.

nn175   wcs,qmf3947 pp,pnl834   nn4872   pipf1696   wcs,qmf7323   pr413   cs,nn8432

47 And Aaron took   as   Moses commanded, and   ran   into the midst of

df,nn6951   wcj,ptdm2009   df,nn5063   hipf2490   dfp,nn5971

the congregation; and, behold, the plague was begun among the people: and he

wcs,qmf5414 (853)   df,nn7004   wcs,pimf3722   pr5921   df,nn5971

put on   incense, and made*an*atonement for the people.

wcs,qmf5975   pr996   df,pl,qpta4191   wcj(pr996)   df,aj2416   df,nn4046

48 And he stood between the   dead   and   the living; and the plague

wcs,nimf6113

was stayed.

ptdm2009   qpf**5414** wcj,pp,pl,cs,nn**1121** nn3878 cs,nn3605 nn**4643** pp,nn3478

21 And, behold, I have given the children of Levi all the tenth in Israel

pp,nn**5159** cs,nn2500   nn,pnx**5656** pnl834 pnp1992 pl,qpta**5647** (853) cs,nn**5656**

for an inheritance, for their service which they serve, *even* the service of the

cs,nn**168**   nn**4150**

tabernacle of the congregation.

wcj,ptn**3808**   pl,cs,nn**1121** nn3478 ad5750 qmf**7126**/pr413   cs,nn**168**

22 Neither must the children of Israel henceforth come nigh the tabernacle of

nn**4150**   pp,qnc**5375** nn2399 pp,qnc**4191**

the congregation, lest they bear sin, and die.

df,pl,nn3881 (pnp1931) wcs,qpf**5647** (853) cs,nn**5656**   cs,nn**168**

23 But the Levites shall do the service of the tabernacle of the

nn**4150** wcj,pnp1992 qmf**5375** nn,pnx**5771**   cs,nn**2708** nn**5769**

congregation, and they shall bear their iniquity: *it shall be* a statute forever

pp,pl,nn,pnx**1755** wcj,pp,cs,nn**8432** pl,cs,nn**1121** nn3478 qmf**5157** ptn**3808**

throughout your generations, that among the children of Israel they have no

nn**5159**

inheritance.

cj3588 (853) cs,nn**4643** pl,cs,nn**1121** nn3478 pnl834 himf**7311**

24 But the tithes of the children of Israel, which they offer *as* a

nn**8641**   pp,nn3068 qpf**5414** pp,pl,nn3881 pp,nn**5159** pr5921/ad**3651**

heave offering unto the LORD, I have given to the Levites to inherit: therefore I

qpf**559** pp,pnx pp,cs,nn**8432** pl,cs,nn**1121** nn3478   qmf**5157** ptn**3808** nn**5159**

have said unto them, Among the children of Israel they shall have no inheritance.

nn3068 wcs,pimf**1696** pr413 nn4872 pp,qnc**559**

25 And the LORD spoke unto Moses, saying,

pimf**1696** wcj,pr413 df,pl,nn3881 wcs,qpf**559** pr,pnx413   cj3588 qmf3947 pr4480/pr854

26 Thus speak unto the Levites, and say unto them, When ye take of

pl,cs,nn**1121** nn3478 (853) df,nn**4643** pnl834 qpf**5414** pp,pnx pr4480/pr,pnx854

the children of Israel the tithes which I have given you from them for your

pp,nn,pnx**5159**   wcj,hipf**7311** cs,nn**8641** pr,pnx4480   nn3068

inheritance, then ye shall offer up a heave offering of it for the LORD, *even* a

nn**4643** pr4480 df,nn**4643**

tenth *part* of the tithe.

nn,pnx**8641**   wcj,nipf**2803** pp,pnx

27 And *this* your heave offering shall be reckoned unto you, as though *it were*

dfp,nn**1715** pr4480   df,nn**1637**   wcj,pp,nn4395 pr4480 df,nn3342

the corn of the threshingfloor, and as the fullness of the winepress.

ad**3651** pnp859 ad1571 himf**7311** cs,nn**8641**   nn3068 pr4480/cs,nn3605

28 Thus ye also shall offer a heave offering unto the LORD of all your

pl,nn,pnx**4643** pnl834 qmf3947 pr4480/pr854 pl,cs,nn**1121** nn3478   wcs,qpf**5414** pr,pnx4480

tithes, which ye receive of the children of Israel; and ye shall give thereof

(853) nn3068 cs,nn**8641** pp,nn175 df,nn**3548**

the LORD's heave offering to Aaron the priest.

pr4480/cs,nn3605 pl,nn,pnx**4979** himf**7311** (853) cs,nn3605 cs,nn**8641**   nn3068

29 Out*of*all your gifts ye shall offer every heave offering of the LORD,

pr4480/cs,nn3605 nn,pnx2459 (853) nn,pnx**4720** pr,pnx4480

of all the best thereof, *even* the hallowed part thereof out of it.

wcs,qpf**559** pr,pnx413

30 Therefore thou shalt say unto them, When ye have heaved   the

nn,pnx2459 pr,pnx4480   wcs,nipf**2803** pp,pl,nn3881 pp,cs,nn**8393**

best thereof from it, then it shall be counted unto the Levites as the increase of

nn1637   wcj,pp,cs,nn**8393** nn3342

the threshingfloor, and as the increase of the winepress.

wcs,qpf398 pnx(853) pp,pp,cs,nn3605 nn4725 pnp859   wcj,nn,pnx**1004** cj3588

31 And ye shall eat   it in every place, ye and your households: for

pnp1931　pp,pnx　nn7939　cs,nn2500　　nn,pnx5656　　pp,cs,nn168　　　nn4150

it *is* your reward for your service in the tabernacle of the congregation.

　　　qmf5375　wcj,ptn3808　nn2399　pr,pnx5921　　　　pp,hinc,pnx7311

32 And ye shall bear no sin by*reason*of it, when ye have heaved from

(853)　　'nn,pnx2459　pr,pnx4480　　ptn3808　　　pimf2490　wcj(853)　　pl,cs,nn6944

it the best of it: neither shall ye pollute the holy things of the

pl,cs,nn1121　　nn3478　wcj,ptn3808　qmf4191

children of Israel, lest ye die.

Purifying an Unclean Person

　　　　　　　nn3068　wcs,pimf1696　pr413　nn4872　　wcj,pr413　nn175　pp,qnc559

19 And the LORD spoke unto Moses and unto Aaron, saying,

　　　　　　pndm2063　　cs,nn2708　　df,nn8451　pnl834　　　nn3068

2 This *is* the ordinance of the law which the LORD hath

pipf6680　pp,qnc559　pimv1696　pr413　pl,cs,nn1121　nn3478　　wcj,qmf3947/pr,pnx413

commanded, saying, Speak unto the children of Israel, that they bring thee a

aj122　nn6510　aj8549　pnl834/pp,pnx　ptn369　nn3971　pr,pnx5921　pnl834　ptn3808　qpf5927

red heifer without spot, wherein *is* no blemish, *and* upon which never came

nn5923

yoke:

　　　　　　wcj,qpf5414　pnx(853)　　　pr413　　nn499　　df,nn3548

3 And ye shall give her unto Eleazar the priest, that he may

wcj,hipf3318/pnx(853)　pr413/pr4480/nn2351　dfp,nn4264　　wcj,qpf7819　pnx(853)　pp,pl,nn,pnx6440

bring*her*forth without the camp, and *one* shall slay her before his

face:

　　　　　nn499　　df,nn3548　wcj,qpf3947　pr4480/nn,pnx1818　　pp,nn,pnx676　wcj,hipf5137

4 And Eleazar the priest shall take of*her*blood with his finger, and sprinkle

pr4480/nn,pnx1818　pr413/cs,nn5227　pl,cs,nn6440　cs,nn168　　nn4150　nu7651　pl,nn6471

of*her*blood directly before the tabernacle of the congregation seven times:

　　　wcj,qpf8313　(853)　df,nn6510　pp,du,nn,pnx5869　(853)　nn,pnx5785　wcj(853)

5 And *one* shall burn the heifer in his sight; her skin, and

nn,pnx1320　wcj(853)　nn,pnx1818　pr5921　nn,pnx6569　qmf8313

her flesh, and her blood, with her dung, shall he burn:

　　　　df,nn3548　wcs,qpf3947　nn730　cs,nn6086　wcj,nn231　wcj,cs,nn8144/nn8438

6 And the priest shall take cedar wood, and hyssop, and scarlet, and

wcs,hipf7993　pr413　cs,nn8432　cs,nn8316　df,nn6510

cast *it* into the midst of the burning of the heifer.

　　　　df,nn3548　wcs,pipf3526　pl,nn,pnx899　　wcs,qpf7364　nn,pnx1320

7 Then the priest shall wash his clothes, and he shall bathe his flesh in

dfp,pl,nn4325　wcj,ad310　qmf935　pr413　df,nn4264　　df,nn3548　wcs,qpf2930

water, and afterward he shall come into the camp, and the priest shall be unclean

pr5704　df,nn6153

until the even.

　　　wcj,df,qpta8313　pnx(853)　pimf3526　pl,nn,pnx899　dfp,pl,nn4325　wcs,qpf7364

8 And he that burneth her shall wash his clothes in water, and bathe

nn,pnx1320　dfp,pl,nn4325　wcs,qpf2930　pr5704　df,nn6153

his flesh in water, and shall be unclean until the even.

　　　nn376　aj2889　wcs,qpf622　(853)　cs,nn665　df,nn6510

9 And a man *that is* clean shall gather up the ashes of the heifer, and

wcs,hipf5117　pr4480/nn2351　dfp,nn4264　aj2889　pp,nn4725　wcs,qpf1961　pp,nn4931

lay*them*up without the camp in a clean place, and it shall be kept for the

pp,cs,nn**5712**　　　pl,cs,nn**1121**　　nn3478　　　pp,pl,cs,nn**4325**　　nn5079　　pnp1931
congregation of the children of Israel for a　water　of separation:　it　*is* a

nn**2403**
purification*for*sin.

df,qpta**622**　(853)　cs,nn665　　df,nn6510　　wcs,pipf**3526** (853)　pl,nn,pnx899
10 And he that gathereth　　the ashes of the heifer shall　wash　　his clothes,

wcs,qpf**2930**　pr5704　df,nn6153　　　wcs,qpf**1961**　　pp,pl,cs,nn**1121**　　nn3478
and be unclean until the even: and it shall　be　unto the children of Israel, and

wcj,dfp,nn**1616**　　df,qpta**1481**　pp,nn,pnx**8432**　　pp,cs,nn**2708**　nn5769
unto the stranger that sojourneth among them, for a statute forever.

df,qpta**5060**　　pp,qpta**4191**　nn5315　　pp,cs,nn3605　nn120　　　wcs,qpf**2930**　cs,nu7651
11 He that toucheth the　dead　body of　any　man shall be unclean seven

pl,nn**3117**
days.

pnp1931　　htmf**2398**　pp,pnx　　df,nuor7992　dfp,nn**3117**　　df,nuor7637
12 He　shall purify himself with it on the　third　day,　and on the seventh

wcj,dfp,nn**3117**　qmf**2891**　wcj,cj518　htmf**2398**/ptn**3808**　df,nuor7992 dfp,nn**3117**
day　he shall be clean: but　if　he purify*not*himself the　third　day,　then

df,nuor7637 wcj,dfp,nn**3117**　ptn**3808**　qmf**2891**
the seventh　day　he shall not be clean.

cs,nn3605　df,qpta**5060**　　pp,qpta**4191** pp,cs,nn5315　df,nn120 pnl834　qmf**4191**
13 Whosoever toucheth the　dead　body　of any man that is dead,　and

htmf**2398**/wcj,ptn**3808**　pipf**2930**　(853)　cs,nn**4908**　nn3068　df,pndm1931 df,nn5315
purifieth*not*himself, defileth　　the tabernacle of the LORD; and　that　soul shall

wcj,nipf**3772**　pr4480/nn3478　cj3588　pl,cs,nn**4325**　nn5079　ptn**3808** pupf**2236**　pr,pnx5921
be cut off from Israel: because the　water　of separation was　not sprinkled upon

qmf**1961**　aj**2931**　nn,pnx**2932**　ad5750　pp,pnx
him, he shall　be　unclean; his uncleanness *is*　yet　upon him.

pndm2063　df,nn**8451** cj3588　nn120　qmf**4191**　pp,nn168 cs,nn3605　df,qpta935　pr413
14 This　*is* the law, when a man dieth in a tent:　all　that come　into the

df,nn**168**　wcj,cs,nn3605 pnl834　dfp,nn**168**　qmf**2930**　cs,nu7651 pl,nn**3117**
tent, and　all　that *is* in the tent, shall be unclean seven days.

wcj,cs,nn3605 qptp6605　cs,nn3627　pnl834　ptn369　nn6781　nn6616　pr,pnx5921 pnp1931
15 And　every　open vessel, which hath　no　covering bound upon　it,　*is*

aj**2931**
unclean.

wcj,nn3605/pnl834　qmf**5060**　pp,cs,nn2491　　nn2719　pr5921　pl,cs,nn**6440**
16 And whosoever toucheth one*that*is*slain with　a sword　in　the　open

df,nn**7704** cj176　pp,qpta**4191**　cj176　pp,cs,nn**6106**　nn120　cj176　pp,nn**6913**　qmf**2930**　cs,nu7651
fields,　or a dead body,　or　a bone　of a man, or a grave, shall be unclean seven

pl,nn**3117**
days.

dfp,aj**2931**　　wcs,qpf3947　pr4480/cs,nn**6083**　　cs,nn**8316**
17 And for an unclean *person* they shall　take　of*the*ashes of the burnt heifer

df,nn**2403**　　aj**2416**　pl,nn**4325**　wcs,qpf**5414** pr,pnx5921 pr413　nn3627
of purification*for*sin, and running water shall be　put　thereto　in a vessel:

aj**2889**　nn376　wcs,qpf3947　nn231　　wcs,qpf**2881**　dfp,pl,nn**4325**
18 And a clean person shall　take　hyssop, and　dip　*it* in the　water,　and

wcs,hipf**5137**　pr5921　df,nn**168**　wcj,pr5921 cs,nn3605　df,pl,nn**3627**　wcj,pr5921　df,pl,nn**5315** pnl834
sprinkle *it* upon the tent, and upon　all　the vessels, and upon the persons that

qpf**1961**　ad8033　wcj,pr5921　df,qpta**5060**　dfp,nn**6106** cj176　dfp,nn2491 cj176　dfp,qpta**4191** cj176
were there, and　upon him that touched a bone,　or one slain,　or one dead,　or a

dfp,nn**6913**
grave:

df,aj**2889**　　wcj,hipf**5137**　pr5921　df,aj**2931**　df,nuor7992 dfp,nn**3117**
19 And the clean *person* shall sprinkle upon the unclean on the　third　day,

and on the seventh   day: and on the seventh   day   he shall   purify   himself, and
wash   his clothes, and bathe   himself in   water, and shall   be clean at even.

20 But the man that shall be unclean, and shall   not   purify   himself,   that
soul shall be cut off from among the congregation, because he hath defiled   the
sanctuary of the LORD: the water of separation hath not been sprinkled upon him;
he *is* unclean.

21 And it shall   be   a perpetual statute unto them, that he that sprinkleth the
water of separation shall wash his clothes; and he that toucheth the water of
separation shall be unclean until even.

22 And whatsoever the unclean *person* toucheth shall be unclean; and the
soul   that toucheth *it* shall be unclean until even.

Moses and Aaron Sin

20 Then came the children of Israel, *even* the whole congregation, into
the desert of Zin in the first month: and the people   abode in
Kadesh; and Miriam   died   there, and was buried there.

2 And   there   was   no   water   for   the   congregation: and   they
gathered*themselves*together against Moses and against Aaron.

3 And the people chided with Moses, and spoke, saying, Would God that we
had died when our brethren died   before the LORD!

4 And   why   have ye brought up   the congregation of the Lord into
this   wilderness, that we and our cattle   should die   there?

5 And wherefore have ye made us to come up out*of*Egypt, to bring*us*in
unto   this   evil place? it *is* no place of seed, or of figs, or of vines, or of
pomegranates; neither *is* there any water to drink.

6 And Moses and Aaron went from*the*presence of the assembly unto the
door of the tabernacle of the congregation, and they   fell upon their faces: and
the glory of the LORD appeared unto them.

wcj,cs,nn793   df,pl,nn5158 pnl834   qpf5186   pp,cs,nn7675   nn6144

15 And at the stream of the brooks that goeth down to the dwelling of Ar, and

wcj,nipf**8172**   pp,cs,nn1366   nn4124

lieth upon the border of Moab.

pr4480/ad8033   nn,lh876 df,pndm1931   df,nn875 pnl834   nn**3068**

16 And from thence *they went* to Beer: that *is* the well whereof the LORD

qpf559   pp,nn4872   qmv622/(853)/df,nn**5971**   wcj,qcj**5414** pp,pnx pl,nn4325

spoke unto Moses, Gather*the*people*together, and I will give them water.

ad**227**   nn3478 qmf**7891** (853) df,pndm2063 df,nn**7892**   qmv5927   nn875 qmv6030   pp,pnx

17 Then Israel sang this song, Spring up, O well; sing ye unto it:

pl,nn**8269** qpf,pnx2658   nn875   pl,cs,nn**5081**   df,nn**5971** qpf,pnx3738

18 The princes digged the well, the nobles of the people digged it, by *the*

pp,pipt***2710**   pp,pl,nn,pnx4938   wcj,pr4480/nn4057

direction of the lawgiver, with their staves. And from*the*wilderness *they went* to

nn4980

Mattanah:

wcj,pr4480/nn4980   nn5160   wcj,pr4480/nn5160   nn1120

19 And from Mattanah to Nahaliel: and from Nahaliel to Bamoth:

wcj,pr4480/nn1120   df,nn1516 pnl834   pp,cs,nn**7704**   nn4124   cs,nn**7218**

20 And from Bamoth *in* the valley, that *is* in the country of Moab, to the top

df,nn6449   wcj,nipf8259 pr5921/pl,cs,nn**6440**   df,nn3452

of Pisgah, which looketh toward Jeshimon.

nn3478 wcs,qmf7971   pl,nn**4397**   pr413   nn5511 cs,nn**4428**   df,nn567 pp,qnc**559**

21 And Israel sent messengers unto Sihon king of the Amorites, saying,

qcj**5674**   pp,nn,pnx776   ptn**3808** qmf5186   pp,nn**7704**

22 Let me pass through thy land: we will not turn into the fields, or into the

wcj,pp,nn3754   ptn**3808** qmf8354   pl,cs,nn4325   nn875   qmf**1980**

vineyards; we will not drink *of* the waters of the well: *but* we will go along by the

df,nn**4428**   pp,cs,nn**1870** ad5704/pnl834   qmf**5674**   nn,pnx1366

king's *high* way, until we be past thy borders.

nn5511   wcj,ptn**3808** qpf**5414** (853)   nn3478   qnc**5674**   pp,nn,pnx1366

23 And Sihon would not suffer Israel to pass through his border: but

nn5511   wcs,qmf622/(853)/cs,nn3605/nn,pnx**5971**   wcs,qmf3318 pp,qnc7125   nn3478

Sihon gathered*all*his*people*together, and went out against Israel into the

df,nn,lh4057   wcs,qmf935 nn,lh3096   wcs,nimf3898   pp,nn3478

wilderness: and he came to Jahaz, and fought against Israel.

nn3478 wcs,himf,pnx**5221**   pp,cs,nn**6310**   nn2719   wcs,qmf**3423** (853)

24 And Israel smote him with the edge of the sword, and possessed

nn,pnx776   pr4480/nn769   pr5704   nn2999   pr5704   pl,cs,nn**1121**   nn5983 cj3588

his land from Arnon unto Jabbok, even unto the children of Ammon: for the

cs,nn1366   pl,cs,nn**1121**   nn5983   aj5794

border of the children of Ammon *was* strong.

nn3478   wcs,qmf3947 (853) cs,nn3605 df,pndm428 df,pl,nn5892   nn3478 wcs,qmf**3427**   pp,cs,nn3605

25 And Israel took all these cities: and Israel dwelt in all the

pl,cs,nn5892   df,nn567   pp,nn2809   wcj,pp,cs,nn3605   pl,nn,pnx1323

cities of the Amorites, in Heshbon, and in all the villages thereof.

cj3588   nn2809   (pndm1931)   cs,nn5892   nn5511   cs,nn**4428**   df,nn567

26 For Heshbon *was* the city of Sihon the king of the Amorites,

wcj,pnp1931   nipf3898   df,aj**7223** pp,cs,nn**4428**   nn4124   wcs,qmf3947 (853) cs,nn3605

who had fought against the former king of Moab, and taken all his

nn,pnx776   pr4480/nn,pnx**3027**   pr5704   nn769

land out*of*his*hand, even unto Arnon.

pr5921/ad**3651**   df,pl,qpta4911   qmf559   qmv935   nn2809

27 Wherefore they that speak*in*proverbs say, Come into Heshbon, let the

cs,nn5892   nn5511   nimf1129   wcj,htmf***3559**

city of Sihon be built and prepared:

28 For there is a fire gone out of Heshbon, a flame from*the*city of Sihon: it hath consumed Ar of Moab, *and* the lords of the high places of Arnon.

29 Woe to thee, Moab! thou art undone, O people of Chemosh: he hath given his sons that escaped, and his daughters, into captivity unto Sihon king of the Amorites.

30 We have shot at them; Heshbon is perished even unto Dibon, and we have laid*them*waste even unto Nophah, which *reacheth* unto Medeba.

31 Thus Israel dwelt in the land of the Amorites.

32 And Moses sent to spy out Jaazer, and they took the villages thereof, and drove out the Amorites that *were* there.

33 And they turned and went up by the way of Bashan: and Og the king of Bashan went out against them, he, and all his people, to the battle at Edrei.

34 And the LORD said unto Moses, Fear him not: for I have delivered him into thy hand, and all his people, and his land; and thou shalt do to him as thou didst unto Sihon king of the Amorites, which dwelt at Heshbon.

35 So they smote him, and his sons, and all his people, until there was none left him alive: and they possessed his land.

Balak Sends For Balaam

22 And the children of Israel set forward, and pitched in the plains of Moab on*this*side Jordan *by* Jericho.

2 And Balak the son of Zippor saw all that Israel had done to the Amorites.

3 And Moab was*sore*afraid of the people, because they *were* many: and Moab was distressed because of the children of Israel.

4 And Moab said unto the elders of Midian, Now shall this company lick up

(853) cs,nn3605　　pr,pnx5439　　df,nn7794　pp,qnc3897　(853)　cs,nn3418　df,nn**7704**

all *that are* round about us, as the　ox　licketh up　the grass of the field.

wcj,nn1111　cs,nn**1121**　nn6834　nn**4428**　pp,nn4124　df,pndm1931 dfp,nn**6256**

And Balak the　son　of Zippor *was* king of the Moabites at　that　time.

wcs,qmf7971　pl,nn**4397**　pr413　nn1109　cs,nn**1121**　nn1160　nn,lh6604

☞ 5 He　sent　messengers therefore unto Balaam the　son　of Beor to Pethor,

pnl834　pr5921　df,nn5104　cs,nn776　pl,cs,nn**1121**　nn,pnx5971　pp,qnc7121 pp,pnx

which *is* by　the river of the land of the children of his people, to　call　him,

pp,qnc559　ptdm2009　nn5971　qpf3318　pr4480/nn4714　ptdm2009　pipf**3680** (853)

saying, Behold, there is a people come out from Egypt: behold, they cover　　　the

cs,nn**5869**　df,nn776　wcj,pnp1931 qpta**3427**　pr4480/pr,pnx4136

face　of the earth, and　they　abide over against me:

qmv1980　wcj,ad6258　pte**4994**　qmv779　pp,pnx (853) df,pndm2088　df,nn5971　cj3588 pnp1931

6 Come　now　therefore, I*pray*thee, curse me　　　this　people; for they

aj6099/pr,pnx4480　ad194　qmf3201　him**f5221** pp,pnx

are too*mighty*for me: peradventure I shall prevail, *that* we may smite them, and

wcj,pimf,pnx1644　pr4480　df,nn776　cj3588　qpf**3045** (853)　pnl834　pimf**1288**

that I may drive*them*out of　the　land: for I know　　that he whom thou blessest

pupt**1288**　wcj,pnl834　qmf779　homf779

is blessed, and he whom thou cursest is cursed.

cs,aj**2205**　nn4124　wcj,cs,aj**2205**　nn4080　wcs,qmf1980

7 And the elders of Moab and the　elders　of Midian departed with the

wcj,pl,nn**7081**　pp,nn,pnx3027　wcs,qmf935　pr413　nn1109　wcs,pimf**1696**

rewards*of*divination in their　hand; and they　came　unto Balaam, and　spoke

pr,pnx413　pl,cs,nn**1697**　nn1111

unto　him the words of Balak.

wcs,qmf**559** pr,pnx413　qmv3885　ad6311　df,nn3915　wcj,hipf**7725** pnx(853)

8 And he　said　unto them, Lodge here this night, and I will　bring　　　you

nn**1697**　pp,pnl834　nn**3068**　pimf**1696** pr,pnx413　pl,cs,nn**8269**　nn4124 wcs,qmf**3427**

word again,　as　the Lord shall speak unto me: and the princes of Moab abode

pr5973　nn1109

with Balaam.

pl,nn**430** wcs,qmf935　pr413　nn1109　wcs,qmf**559**　pnit4310 df,pl,nn**376**　df,pndm428 pr,pnx5973

9 And God　came　unto Balaam, and　said, What　men　*are*　these　with

thee?

nn1109　wcs,qmf**559** pr413 df,pl,nn**430**　nn1111　cs,nn**1121**　nn6834　cs,nn**4428**　nn4124

10 And Balaam　said　unto God, Balak the　son　of Zippor, king of Moab,

qpf7971 pr,pnx413

hath sent　unto me, *saying,*

ptdm2009　df,nn**5971**　df,qpta3318　pr4480/nn4714　wcs,pimf**3680** (853)　cs,nn**5869**

11 Behold, *there is* a people come out of Egypt, which covereth　　the　face

---

☞ **22:5 – 24:25** Balaam lived a long distance away from Moab, yet he must have been quite famous for Balak to have known of him and sent for him. Balak was motivated by his fear of Israel (22:5, 6). Balaam refers to his activity as divination (Num. 22:7; 23:23; 24:1), but in this he may have been reflecting on a foreign custom, as did Joseph (Gen. 44:15). Certainly Balaam's response to Balak was done in accordance with the Lord's instructions. However, a comparison of 22:20 and 22:22 suggests that Balaam may have been motivated by something other than the fear of God. Certainly Balaam's later suggestions to the Midianites were opposed to God's plans, and brought about his own death, judgment on Israel, and the destruction of Midian (Num. 25:1–9; 31:2, 8, 15–17). Balaam's prophecies of blessing on Israel and judgment on Israel's enemies, especially the messianic reference (Num. 24:17), are indeed remarkable.

Archaeological evidence from Deir Alla indicates that Balaam was highly regarded by pagans 500 years after his death. Two New Testament writers tell us that Balaam is an example of those who sin for personal gain (2 Pet. 2:15; Jude 11). John uses Balaam as an example of one who taught others how to sin (Rev. 2:14).

<small>df,nn776   qmv1980   ad6258   qmv6895   pp,pnx   pnx(853)   ad194   qmf3201</small>
of the earth: come now, curse me   them; peradventure I shall be able to
<small>pp,ninc3898   pp,pnx   wcs,pipf,pnx1644</small>
overcome them, and drive*them*out.

<small>pl,nn430   wcs,qmf559   pr413   nn1109   ptn3808   qmf1980   pr,pnx5973</small>
12 And God said unto Balaam, Thou shalt not go with them; thou shalt
<small>ptn3808   qmf779   (853)   df,nn5971   cj3588   pnp1931   qptp1288</small>
not curse the people: for they *are* blessed.

<small>nn1109   wcs,qmf6965   dfp,nn1242   wcs,qmf559   pr413   pl,cs,nn8269   nn1111</small>
13 And Balaam rose up in the morning, and said unto the princes of Balak,
<small>qmv1980   pr413   nn,pnx776   cj3588   nn3068   pipf3985   pp,qnc,pnx5414   pp,qnc1980   pr,pnx5973</small>
Get you into your land: for the LORD refuseth to give*me*leave to go with
you.

<small>pl,cs,nn8269   nn4124   wcs,qmf6965   wcs,qmf935   pr413   nn1111   wcs,qmf559</small>
14 And the princes of Moab rose up, and they went unto Balak, and said,
<small>nn1109   pipf3985   qnc1980   pr,pnx5973</small>
Balaam refuseth to come with us.

<small>nn1111   qnc7971   ad5750   wcs,himf3254   pl,nn8269   aj7227   wcj,pl,nipt3513   pr4480/pndm428</small>
15 And Balak sent yet again princes, more, and more honorable than they.
<small>wcs,qmf935   pr413   nn1109   wcs,qmf559   pp,pnx   ad3541   qpf559   nn1111   cs,nn1121</small>
16 And they came to Balaam, and said to him, Thus saith Balak the son
<small>nn6834   ptn408   pte4994   nimf4513   pr4480/qnc1980   pr,pnx413</small>
of Zippor, Let nothing, I*pray*thee, hinder thee from coming unto me:
<small>cj3588   pinc3513/pimf,pnx3513/ad3966   qmf6213   wcj,nn3605/pnl834</small>
17 For I will promote*thee*unto*very*great*honor, and I will do whatsoever
<small>qmf559   pr,pnx413   wcj,qmv1980   pte4994   qmv6895   pp,pnx   (853)   df,pndm2088   df,nn5971</small>
thou sayest unto me: come therefore, I*pray*thee, curse me this people.

<small>nn1109   wcs,qmf6030   wcs,qmf559   pr413   pl,cs,nn5650   nn1111   cj518   nn1111</small>
18 And Balaam answered and said unto the servants of Balak, If Balak
<small>qmf5414   pp,pnx   nn,pnx1004   cs,nn4393   nn3701   wcj,nn2091   qmf3201/ptn3808   pp,qnc5674   (853)</small>
would give me his house full of silver and gold, I cannot go beyond the
<small>cs,nn6310   nn3068   pl,nn,pnx430   pp,qnc6213   aj6996   cj176   aj1419</small>
word of the LORD my God, to do less or more.

<small>wcj,ad6258   pte4994   qmv3427   pnp859   ad1571   pp,pndm2088   df,nn3915</small>
19 Now therefore, I*pray*you, tarry ye also here this night, that I may
<small>wcj,qcj3045   pnid4100   nn3068   pinc1696   pr,pnx5973   himf3254</small>
know what the LORD will say unto me more.

<small>pl,nn430   wcs,qmf935   pr413   nn1109   nn3915   wcs,qmf559   pp,pnx   cj518   df,pl,nn376</small>
20 And God came unto Balaam at night, and said unto him, If the men
<small>qpf935   pp,qnc7121   pr,pnx   qmv6965   qmv1980   pr,pnx854   wcj,ad389   (853)   df,nn1697   pnl834</small>
come to call thee, rise up, *and* go with them; but yet the word which I
<small>pimf1696   pr,pnx413   pnx(853)   qmf6213</small>
shall say unto thee, that shalt thou do.

Balaam Meets the Angel of the LORD

<small>nn1109   wcs,qmf6965   dfp,nn1242   wcs,qmf2280   (853)   nn,pnx860   wcs,qmf1980</small>
21 And Balaam rose up in the morning, and saddled his ass, and went
<small>pr5973   pl,cs,nn8269   nn4124</small>
with the princes of Moab.

<small>pl,nn430   cs,nn639   wcs,qmf2734   cj3588   pnp1931   qpta1980   cs,nn4397   nn3068</small>
22 And God's anger was kindled because he went: and the angel of the LORD

wcs,htmf3320   dfp,nn**1870**   pp,nn**7854**   pp,pnx   wcj,pnp1931   qpta7392   pr5921
stood in the way for an adversary against him. Now   he   was riding upon his

nn,pnx860   wcj,du,cs,nu8147 pl,nn,pnx5288   pr,pnx5973
ass, and his   two   servants *were* with him.

df,nn860   wcs,qmf**7200** (853)   cs,nn**4397**   nn**3068**   nipt5324   dfp,nn**1870**
23 And the ass   saw   the angel of the LORD standing in the way, and his

wcj,nn,pnx**2719** qptp8025   pp,nn,pnx**3027**   df,nn860   wcs,qmf5186   pr4480   df,nn**1870**
sword   drawn in his   hand: and the ass turned aside out of the way, and

wcs,qmf**1980**   dfp,nn**7704**   nn1109   wcs,himf5221 (853)   df,nn860   pp,hinc,pnx5186
went into the field: and Balaam smote   the ass, to   turn   her into the

df,nn**1870**
way.

cs,nn**4397**   nn**3068** wcs,qmf5975   pp,cs,nn4934   df,pl,nn3754   wcj,nn1447
24 But the angel of the LORD stood in a   path of the vineyards, a   wall

pr4480/pndm2088   nn1447   pr4480/pndm2088
being on*this*side, and a wall on*that*side.

df,nn860 wcs,qmf**7200** (853)   cs,nn**4397**   nn**3068**   wcs,nimf3905   pr413
25 And when the ass   saw   the angel of the LORD, she thrust herself unto

df,nn**7023**   wcs,qmf3905 (853)   nn1109   cs,nn7272   pr413   df,nn**7023**   pp,hinc,pnx**5221**
the wall, and crushed   Balaam's foot against the wall: and he   smote   her

wcs,himf3254
again.

cs,nn**4397**   nn**3068** qnc5674 wcs,himf3254   wcs,qmf5975   aj6862   pp,nn4725
26 And the angel of the LORD went further, and   stood in a narrow place,

pnl834   ptn369 nn**1870**   pp,qnc5186   nn3225   wcj,nn8040
where *was* no way to turn either to the right hand or to the left.

df,nn860 wcs,qmf**7200** (853)   cs,nn**4397**   nn**3068**   wcs,qmf7257   pr8478
27 And when the ass   saw   the angel of the LORD, she fell down under

nn1109   nn1109   nn639   wcs,qmf2734   wcs,himf5221 (853)   df,nn860   dfp,nn4731
Balaam: and Balaam's anger was kindled, and he smote   the ass with a staff.

nn**3068**   wcs,qmf6605 (853)   cs,nn6310   df,nn860   wcs,qmf**559**
28 And the LORD opened   the mouth of the ass, and she   said   unto

pp,nn1109   pnit4100   qpf**6213**   pp,pnx   cj3588   hipf,pnx5221   pndm2088 nu7969 pl,nn7272
Balaam, What have I done unto thee, that thou hast smitten me these three times?

nn1109   wcs,qmf**559**   dfp,nn860   cj3588   htpf5953 pp,pnx   ptx3863
29 And Balaam said   unto the ass, Because thou hast mocked me: I would

pta3426   nn**2719**   pp,nn,pnx**3027** cj3588 ad6258   qpf,pnx**2026**
there were a sword in mine hand, for now would I   kill   thee.

df,nn860 wcs,qmf**559**   pr413   nn1109   he,ptn3808 pnp595   nn,pnx860 pr,pnx5921   pnl834
30 And the ass   said unto Balaam, *Am* not   I   thine ass, upon which

qpf7392   pr4480/ad,pnx5750   pr5704 df,pndm2088 df,nn3117   he,hina5532/hipf5532
thou hast ridden ever since *I* was thine unto   this   day? was I   ever wont to

pp,qnc**6213** ad3541   pp,pnx   wcs,qmf**559** ptn3808
do   so unto thee? And he said, Nay.

nn**3068**   wcs,pimf1540 (853)   du,cs,nn5869   nn1109   wcs,qmf**7200** (853)
31 Then the LORD opened   the eyes   of Balaam, and he   saw   the

cs,nn**4397**   nn**3068** nipt5324   dfp,nn**1870**   wcj,nn,pnx**2719** qptp8025   pp,nn,pnx**3027**
angel of the LORD standing in the way, and his   sword   drawn in his hand: and

wcs,qmf6915   wcs,htmf7812   pp,du,nn,pnx639
he bowed*down*his*head, and fell flat on his   face.

cs,nn**4397**   nn**3068** wcs,qmf**559** pr,pnx413   pr5921/pnit4100   hipf5221
32 And the angel of the LORD   said   unto him, Wherefore hast thou smitten

(853)   nn,pnx860 pndm2088 nu7969 pl,nn7272 ptdm2009 pnp595   qpf3318   pp,nn**7854**   cj3588
thine ass these three times? behold, I   went out to withstand thee, because

df,nn**1870**   qpf3399   pp,pr,pnx5048
thy way is perverse before me:

df,nn860   wcs,qmf,pnx**7200**   wcs,qmf5186   pp,pl,nn,pnx**6440**   pndm2088   nu7969   pl,nn7272

33 And the ass   saw   me, and turned   from   me these three times:

ad194   qpf5186   pr4480/pl,nn,pnx**6440**   cj3588   ad6258   ad1571   qpf**2026** pnx(853)

unless she had turned   from   me, surely now also I had slain   thee, and

hipf**2421**/wcj,pnx(853)

saved*her*alive.

nn1109   wcs,qmf559   pr413   cs,nn4397   nn3068   qpf2398   cj3588   qpf**3045**

34 And Balaam   said unto the angel of the LORD, I have sinned; for I knew

ptn3808   cj3588   pnp859   nipt5324   dfp,nn1870   pp,qnc,pnx7125   wcj,ad6258   cj518

not that thou stoodest in the way   against me: now therefore, if it

qpf7489/pp,du,nn,pnx**5869**   qcj**7725**/pp,pnx

displease   thee, I will get*me*back*again.

cs,nn4397   nn3068   wcs,qmf559   pr413   nn1109   qmv**1980** pr5973   df,pl,nn376

35 And the angel of the LORD said unto Balaam, Go with the men: but

wcj,ad657 (853)   df,nn1697 pnl834   pimf1696   pr,pnx413   pnx(853)   pimf1696

only   the word that I shall speak unto thee,   that thou shalt speak. So

nn1109   wcs,qmf1980 pr5973   pl,cs,nn**8269**   nn1111

Balaam went with the princes of Balak.

Balaam Arrives and Blesses Israel

nn1111   wcs,qmf**8085** cj3588   nn1109   qpf935   wcs,qmf3318   pp,qnc,pnx7125

36 And when Balak heard that Balaam was come, he went out to   meet

pr413   cs,nn5892   nn4124   pnl834   pr5921   cs,nn1366   nn769   pnl834

him unto a city of Moab, which *is* in the border of Arnon, which *is* in the

pp,cs,nn7097 df,nn1366

utmost coast.

nn1111   wcs,qmf559   pr413   nn1109   he,ptn3808   qna7971/qpf7971   pr,pnx413

37 And Balak said unto Balaam, Did I not earnestly send unto thee to

pp,qnc7121   pp,pnx   pnit4100   qpf**1980**   ptn3808   pr,pnx413   qmf3201/ptn3808   he,ad552

call   thee? wherefore camest thou not unto me? am*I*not*able indeed to

pinc,pnx**3513**

promote*thee*to*honor?

nn1109   wcs,qmf559   pr413   nn1111   ptdm2009   qpf935   pr,pnx413   ad6258

38 And Balaam said unto Balak, Lo, I am come unto thee: have I now

he,qna3201/qmf3201   pinc1696   pnid3972   df,nn1697 pnl834 pl,nn430 qmf**7760**   pp,nn,pnx6310 pnx(853)

any*power*at*all to say any thing? the word that God putteth in my mouth,

pimf1696

that shall I speak.

nn1109   wcs,qmf**1980** pr5973   nn1111   wcs,qmf935   nn7155

39 And Balaam went with Balak, and they came unto Kirjath-huzoth.

nn1111   wcs,qmf**2076** nn1241   wcj,nn6629   wcs,pimf7971   pp,nn1109

40 And Balak offered oxen and sheep, and sent to Balaam, and to the

wcj,dfp,pl,nn**8269** pnl834   pr,pnx854

princes that *were* with him.

wcs,qmf**1961**   dfp,nn1242   nn1111   wcs,qmf3947 (853)   nn1109

41 And it*came*to*pass on the morrow, that Balak took   Balaam, and

wcs,himf,pnx**5927**   pl,cs,nn**1116**   nn1168   pr4480/ad8033   wcs,qmf**7200**

brought*him*up into the high places of Baal, that thence he might see   the

cs,nn7097   df,nn**5971**

utmost *part* of the people.

23 And Balaam said unto Balak, Build me here seven altars, and prepare me here seven oxen and seven rams.

2 And Balak did as Balaam had spoken; and Balak and Balaam offered on *every* altar a bullock and a ram.

3 And Balaam said unto Balak, Stand by thy burnt offering, and I will go: peradventure the LORD will come to meet me: and whatsoever he showeth me I will tell thee. And he went to a high place.

4 And God met Balaam: and he said unto him, I have prepared seven altars, and I have offered upon *every* altar a bullock and a ram.

5 And the LORD put a word in Balaam's mouth, and said, Return unto Balak, and thus thou shalt speak.

6 And he returned unto him, and, lo, he stood by his burnt sacrifice, he, and all the princes of Moab.

7 And he took up his parable, and said, Balak the king of Moab hath brought me from Aram, out*of*the*mountains of the east, *saying*, Come, curse me Jacob, and come, defy Israel.

8 How shall I curse, whom God hath not cursed? or how shall I defy, *whom* the LORD hath not defied?

9 For from*the*top of the rocks I see him, and from*the*hills I behold him: lo, the people shall dwell alone, and shall not be reckoned among the nations.

10 Who can count the dust of Jacob, and the number of the fourth *part* of Israel? Let me die the death of the righteous, and let my last end be like his!

11 And Balak said unto Balaam, What hast thou done unto me? I took thee to curse mine enemies, and, behold, thou hast blessed*them*altogether.

12 And he answered and said, Must I not take heed to speak that which the LORD hath put in my mouth?

13 And Balak said unto him, Come, I*pray*thee, with me unto another

nn4725　pnl834/pr4480/ad8033　　　　　　　　qmf,pnx7200　　　　　　　qmf7200　ad657　　　nn,pnx7097

place, from whence thou mayest　see　them: thou shalt see　but the utmost part

　　　　　　　　　　　　ptn3808　qmf7200　wcj,nn,pnx3605　wcj,qmv,pnx6895　pp,pnx　　pr4480/ad8033

of them, and shalt not　see　them　all:　and　curse　me them from thence.

　　　　　　　　wcs,qmf,pnx3947　　　cs,nn7704　pl,nn6839　pr413　cs,nn7218　df,nn6449

14 And he　brought　him into the field of Zophim, to the　top　of Pisgah, and

wcs,qmf1129　nu7651　pl,nn4196　wcs,himf5927　nn6499　wcj,nn352　dfp,nn4196

built　seven altars, and offered a bullock and a　ram　on *every* altar.

　　　　　wcs,qmf559　pr413　nn1111　htmv3320　ad3541　pr5921　　nn,pnx5930　　wcj,pnp595

15 And he　said　unto Balak, Stand here　by　thy burnt offering, while　　I

nimf7136　　　ad3541

meet *the Lord* yonder.

　　　　　　　nn3068　wcs,nimf7136/pr413　nn1109　wcs,qmf7760　nn1697　pp,nn,pnx6310

16 And the Lord　　met　Balaam, and　put　a word in his　mouth, and

wcs,qmf559　qmv7725　pr413　nn1111　pimf1696 wcj,ad3541

said,　Go again unto Balak, and　say　thus.

　　　　　　　wcs,qmf935　pr,pnx413　wcj,ptdm,pnx2009　nipt5324　pr5921　　nn,pnx5930

17 And when he came　to　him,　behold,　he stood　by　his burnt offering,

wcj,pl,cs,nn8269　nn4124　pr,pnx854　　　nn1111　wcs,qmf559　pp,pnx　pnit4100

and the　princes　of Moab with him. And Balak　said　unto him, What hath the

nn3068　pipf1696

Lord spoken?

　　　　wcs,qmf5375　　nn,pnx4912　wcs,qmf559　qmv6965　nn1111　　wcj,qmv8085　himv238

18 And he took up his parable, and　said, Rise up, Balak, and　hear; hearken

pr,pnx5704　nn,pnx1121　nn6834

unto　me, thou　son　of Zippor:

　　nn410　ptn3808　nn376　　　　　wcj,pimf3576　　wcj,cs,nn1121　nn120

19 God *is* not a man, that he should　lie;　neither the　son　of man, that he

wcj,htmf5162　he,pnp1931　qpf559　　wcj,ptn3808　qmf6213　　wcj,pipf1696

should repent: hath　he　said, and shall he　not　do *it*? or hath he spoken, and

wcj,ptn3808　himf,pnx6965

shall he　not　make*it*good?

　　ptdm2009　　　qpf3947　　　　　　　pinc1288　　wcj,pipf1288

20 Behold, I have received *commandment* to bless: and he hath blessed; and I

wcj,ptn3808　himf,pnx7725

cannot reverse it.

　　ptn3808　hipf5027　nn205　pp,nn3290　wcj,ptn3808　　qpf7200　nn5999

21 He hath　not　beheld iniquity in Jacob, neither hath he seen perverseness in

pp,nn3478　nn3068　pl,nn,pnx430　pr,pnx5973　wcj,cs,nn8643　nn4428　pp,pnx

Israel: the Lord his　God　*is* with him, and the　shout　of a king *is* among them.

　　nn410　hipt,pnx3318　pr4480/nn4714　　　　　pp,pl,cs,nn8443

22 God brought*them*out of Egypt; he hath as it were the　strength　of a

nn7214

unicorn.

　　cj3588　ptn3808　nn5173　　pp,nn3290　wcj,ptn3808

23 Surely *there is*　no　enchantment against Jacob,　neither *is there* any

nn7081　pp,nn3478　dfp,nn6256　nimf559　pp,nn3290

divination against Israel: according to this　time　it shall be said of Jacob and of

wcj,pp,nn3478　pnid4100　nn410　qpf6466

Israel,　What hath God wrought!

　　ptdm2005　nn5971　qmf6965　pp,nn3833　htmf5375

24 Behold, the people shall rise up as a great lion, and lift*up*himself as a

wcj,pp,nn738　ptn3808　qmf7901　cj5704　qmf398　nn2964　qmf8354　wcj,cs,nn1818

young lion: he shall not lie down until he eat *of* the prey, and drink the　blood

pl,nn2491

of the slain.

nn1111   wcs,qmf559   pr413   nn1109   ad1571/ptn3808   qna6895/qmf,pnx6895   ad1571/ptn3808

25 And Balak said unto Balaam, Neither curse*them*at*all, nor

pinc1288/pimf,pnx1288

bless*them*at*all.

nn1109   wcs,qmf6030   wcs,qmf559   pr413   nn1111   pipf1696/pr,pnx413   he,ptn3808

26 But Balaam answered and said unto Balak, Told not I thee,

pp,qnc559   nn3605   pnl834   nn3068   pimf1696   pnx(853)   qmf6213

saying, All that the LORD speaketh, that I must do?

nn1111   wcs,qmf559   pr413   nn1109   qmv1980   pte4994   qmf,pnx3947   pr413

27 And Balak said unto Balaam, Come, I*pray*thee, I will bring thee unto

aj312   nn4725   ad194   qmf3474/pp,du,cs,nn5869   df,pl,nn430   wcs,qpf,pnx6895

another place; peradventure it will please God that thou mayest curse

pp,pnx   pr4480/ad8033

me them from thence.

nn1111   wcs,qmf3947   (853)   nn1109   cs,nn7218   df,nn6465   df,nipt8259

28 And Balak brought Balaam unto the top of Peor, that looketh

pr5921/pl,cs,nn6440   df,nn3452

toward Jeshimon.

nn1109   wcs,qmf559   pr413   nn1111   qmv1129   pp,pnx   pp,pndm2088   nu7651   pl,nn4196   wcj,himv3559

29 And Balaam said unto Balak, Build me here seven altars, and prepare

pp,pnx   pp,pndm2088   nu7651   pl,nn6499   wcj,nu7651   pl,nn352

me here seven bullocks and seven rams.

nn1111   wcs,qmf6213   pp,pnl834   nn1109   qpf559   wcs,himf5927   nn6499   wcj,nn352

30 And Balak did as Balaam had said, and offered a bullock and a ram

dfp,nn4196

on *every* altar.

nn1109   wcs,qmf7200   cj3588   qpf2895/pp,du,cs,nn5869   nn3068   pp,pinc1288   (853)

24 And when Balaam saw that it pleased the LORD to bless

nn3478   qpf1980   wcj,ptn3808   pp,nn6471/pp,nn6471   pp,qnc7125   pl,nn5173

Israel, he went not, as at other times, to seek for enchantments,

wcs,qmf7896   pl,nn,pnx6440   pr413   df,nn4057

but he set his face toward the wilderness.

nn1109   wcs,qmf5375   (853)   du,nn,pnx5869   wcs,qmf7200   (853)   nn3478   qpta7931

2 And Balaam lifted up his eyes, and he saw Israel abiding *in his*

pp,pl,nn,pnx7626   cs,nn7307   pl,nn430   wcs,qmf1961   pr,pnx5921

tents according to their tribes; and the spirit of God came upon him.

wcs,qmf5375   nn,pnx4912   wcs,qmf559   nn1109   nn,pnx1121   nn1160   cs,nn5002

3 And he took up his parable, and said, Balaam the son of Beor hath said,

df,nn1397   df,nn5869   cs,qptp8365   wcj,cs,nn5002

and the man whose eyes are open hath said:

cs,nn5002   qpta8085   pl,cs,nn561   nn410   pnl834   qmf2372   cs,nn4236

4 He hath said, which heard the words of God, which saw the vision of the

nn7706   qpta5307   du,nn5869   wcj,cs,qptp1540

Almighty, falling *into a trance*, but having his eyes open:

pnid4100   qpf2895   pl,nn,pnx168   nn3290   pl,nn,pnx4908   nn3478

5 How goodly are thy tents, O Jacob, *and* thy tabernacles, O Israel!

pp,pl,nn5158   nipf5186   pp,pl,nn1593   pr5921   nn5104

6 As the valleys are they spread forth, as gardens by the river's side, as the

dfp,pl,nn174   nn3068   qpf5193   dfp,pl,nn730   pr5921

trees*of*lign*aloes which the LORD hath planted, *and* as cedar trees beside the

pl,nn4325

waters.

_{qmf5140}   _{pl,nn4325}   _{pr4480/du,nn,pnx1805}   _{wcj,nn,pnx2233}

7 He shall pour the water out*of*his*buckets, and his   seed   *shall be* in

_{aj7227}   _{pp,pl,nn4325}   _{nn,pnx4428}   _{wcj,qcj7311}   _{pr4480/nn90}   _{nn,pnx4438}

many waters, and his   king   shall be higher than Agag, and his kingdom shall be

_{wcj,htmf5375}

exalted.

_{nn410}   _{hipt,pnx3318}   _{pr4480/nn4714}   _{pp,pnx}   _{pp,pl,cs,nn8443}

8 God brought*him*forth out*of*Egypt; he hath as it were the strength of a

_{nn7214}   _{qmf398}   _{pl,nn1471}   _{pl,nn,pnx6862}   _{pimf1633}   _{wcj,pl,nn,pnx6106}

unicorn: he shall eat up the nations his enemies, and shall break their   bones,   and

_{qmf4272}   _{wcj,pl,nn,pnx2671}

pierce*them*through with his   arrows.

_{qpf3766}   _{qpf7901}   _{dfp,nn738}   _{wcj,pp,nn3833}   _{pnit4310}

9 He couched, he lay down as a lion,   and as a great lion: who shall

_{himf,pnx6965}   _{pl,pipt,pnx1288}   _{qptp1288}   _{wcj,pl,qpta,pnx779}   _{qptp779}

stir*him*up? Blessed *is* he that blesseth thee, and   cursed   *is* he that curseth thee.

Balaam's Prophecy

_{nn1111}   _{cs,nn639}   _{wcs,qmf2734}   _{pr413}   _{nn1109}

10 And   Balak's   anger   was   kindled   against   Balaam,   and   he

_{wcs,qmf5606/(853)/du,nn,pnx3709}   _{nn1111}   _{wcs,qmf559}   _{pr413}   _{nn1109}   _{qpf,pnx7121}   _{pp,qnc6895}

smote*his*hands*together: and Balak   said   unto Balaam, I called thee to curse

_{pl,qpta,pnx341}   _{wcj,ptdm2009}   _{pipf1288/pina1288}   _{pndm2088}   _{nu7969}   _{pl,nn6471}

mine enemies, and, behold, thou hast altogether blessed *them* these three times.

_{wcj,ad6258}   _{qmv1272}   _{pp,pnx}   _{pr413}   _{nn,pnx4725}   _{qpf559}

11 Therefore   now   flee   thou   to   thy   place: I   thought   to

_{pina3513/pimf,pnx3513}   _{wcj,ptdm2009}   _{nn3068}   _{qpf,pnx4513}

promote*thee*unto*great*honor; but,   lo,   the L<small>ORD</small> hath kept*thee*back

_{pr4480/nn3519}

from honor.

_{nn1109}   _{wcs,qmf559}   _{pr413}   _{nn1111}   _{pipf1696}   _{he,ptn3808}   _{ad1571}   _{pr413}   _{pl,nn,pnx4397}

12 And Balaam   said   unto Balak, Spoke I   not   also   to   thy messengers

_{pnl834}   _{qpf7971}   _{pr,pnx413}   _{pp,qnc559}

which thou sentest unto me, saying,

_{cj518}   _{nn1111}   _{qmf5414}   _{pp,pnx}   _{nn,pnx1004}   _{cs,nn4393}   _{nn3701}   _{wcj,nn2091}   _{ptn3808/qmf3201}

13 If Balak would give me his house   full   of silver and gold, I   cannot

_{pp,qnc5674}   ₍₈₅₃₎   _{cs,nn6310}   _{nn3068}   _{pp,qnc6213}   _{nn2896}   _{cj176}   _{nn7451}

go beyond   the commandment of the L<small>ORD</small>, to   do   *either* good or bad

_{pr4480/nn,pnx3820}   _{pnl834}   _{nn3068}   _{pimf1696}   _{pnx(853)}   _{pimf1696}

of*mine*own*mind; *but* what the L<small>ORD</small> saith,   that will I speak?

_{wcj,ad6258}   _{ptdm,pnx2009}   _{qpta1980}   _{pp,nn,pnx5971}   _{qmf1980}

14 And   now,   behold, I   go   unto my people: come *therefore, and* I will

_{qmf,pnx3289}   _{pnl834}   _{df,pndm2088}   _{df,nn5971}   _{qmf6213}   _{pp,nn,pnx5971}   _{pp,cs,nn319}   _{df,pl,nn3117}

advertise thee what   this   people shall   do   to thy people in the latter   days.

_{wcs,qmf5375}   _{nn,pnx4912}   _{wcs,qmf559}   _{nn1109}   _{nn,pnx1121}   _{nn1160}

15 And he took up his parable, and   said,   Balaam the   son   of Beor hath

_{cs,nn5002}   _{df,nn1397}   _{df,nn5869}   _{cs,qptp8365}   _{wcj,cs,nn5002}

said, and the man whose eyes are open hath   said:

_{cs,nn5002}   _{qpta8085}   _{pl,cs,nn561}   _{nn410}   _{wcj,qpta3045}   _{cs,nn1847}

16 He hath said, which heard the words of God, and   knew the knowledge of

---

24:7   Perhaps Agag was a general title given to the Amalekite kings, just as Pharaoh was the general title for the kings of Egypt.

nn5945　qmf2372　cs,nn4236　nn7706　qpta5307

the most High, *which* saw the vision of the Almighty, falling *into a trance*, but

du,nn5869　wcj,cs,qptp1540

having his eyes   open:

qmf,pnx7200　wcj,ptn3808　ad6258　qmf,pnx7789　wcj,ptn3808　aj7138

17 I shall   see   him, but   not   now: I shall behold him, but   not   nigh:

qpf1869　nn3556　pr4480/nn3290　nn7626　wcs,qpf6965　pr4480/nn3478

there shall come a Star out*of*Jacob, and a Scepter shall rise out*of*Israel, and

wcs,qpf4272　du,cs,nn6285　nn4124　wcs,qpf4272　cs,nn3605　pl,cs,nn1121　nn8352

shall smite the corners of Moab, and destroy all the children of Sheth.

nn123　wcj,qpf1961　nn3424　nn8165　wcj,qpf1961　nn3424

18 And Edom shall   be   a possession, Seir also shall   be   a possession for

pl,qpta,pnx341　wcj,nn3478　qpta6213　nn2428

his enemies; and Israel shall do valiantly.

pr4480/nn3290　wcj,qcj7287　wcj,hipf6

19 Out*of*Jacob shall come he that shall have dominion, and shall destroy him

nn8300　pr4480/nn5892

that remaineth of*the*city.

wcs,qmf7200　(853)　nn6002　wcs,qmf5375　nn,pnx4912　wcs,qmf559

20 And when he looked on   Amalek, he took up his parable, and said,

nn6002　cs,nu7225　pl,nn1471　wcj,nn,pnx319　nn8

Amalek *was* the first of the nations; but his latter end *shall be* that he perish

nn5703

forever.

wcs,qmf7200　(853)　df,nn7017　wcs,qmf5375　nn,pnx4912　wcs,qmf559

21 And he looked on   the Kenites, and took up his parable, and said,

aj386　nn,pnx4186　wcj,qptp7760　nn,pnx7064　dfp,nn5553

Strong is thy dwelling place, and thou puttest thy nest in a rock.

cj3588/cj518　nn7014　qmf1961　pp,pinc1197　pr5704/pnid4100　nn804

22 Nevertheless the Kenite shall   be   wasted,   until   Asshur   shall

qmf,pnx7617

carry*thee*away*captive.

wcs,qmf5375　nn,pnx4912　wcs,qmf559　ptx188　pnid4310　qmf2421　nn410

23 And he took up his parable, and said, Alas, who shall live when God

pr4480/qnc,pnx7760

doeth   this!

wcj,pl,nn6716　pr4480/cs,nn3027　nn3794　wcs,pipf6031

24 And ships *shall come* from*the*coast of Chittim, and shall   afflict

nn804　wcs,pipf6031　nn5677　pnp1931　wcj,ad1571　nn8　nn5703

Asshur, and shall afflict Eber, and he   also shall perish forever.

nn1109　wcs,qmf6965　wcs,qmf1980　wcs,qmf7725　pp,nn,pnx4725　nn1111

25 And Balaam rose up, and went and returned to his place: and Balak

wcj,ad1571　qpf1980　pp,nn,pnx1870

also went his way.

Moabite Women Seduce Israel

nn3478　wcs,qmf3427　dfp,nn7851　df,nn5971　wcs,himf2490

25 And   Israel abode in Shittim, and the people began to

pp,qnc2181　pr413　pl,cs,nn1323　nn4124

commit whoredom with the daughters of Moab.

wcs,qmf7121　dfp,nn5971　pp,pl,cs,nn2077　pl,nn,pnx430　df,nn5971

2 And they called the people unto the sacrifices of their gods: and the people

wcs,qmf398　wcs,htmf7812　pp,pl,nn,pnx430

did eat, and bowed down to their gods.

nn3478   wcs,nimf6775   pp,nn1187   cs,nn639   nn3068

3 And Israel joined himself unto Baal-peor: and the anger of the LORD was

wcs,qmf2734   pp,nn3478

kindled against Israel.

nn3068   wcs,qmf559   pr413   nn4872   qmv3947   (853)   cs,nn3605   pl,cs,nn7218   df,nn5971

4 And the LORD said unto Moses, Take   all   the heads of the people,

wcj,himv3363/pnx(853)   pp,nn3068   pr5048   df,nn8121   cs,nn2740   cs,nn639

and hang*them*up before the LORD against the sun, that the fierce anger of the

nn3068   wcj,qcj7725   pr4480/nn3478

LORD may be turned away from Israel.

nn4872   wcs,qmf559   pr413   pl,cs,qpta8199   nn3478   qmv2026   nn376   pl,nn,pnx582

5 And Moses said unto the judges of Israel, Slay ye every one his   men

df,pl,nipt6775   pp,nn1187

that were joined unto Baal-peor.

wcj,ptdm2009   nn376   pr4480/pl,cs,nn1121   nn3478   qpf935   wcs,himf7126   pr413

🗝 6 And, behold, one of*the*children of Israel came and brought unto his

pl,nn,pnx251   (853)   df,nn4084   pp,du,cs,nn5869   nn4872   wcj,pp,du,cs,nn5869

brethren   a Midianitish woman in the   sight   of Moses, and in the   sight

cs,nn3605   cs,nn5712   pl,cs,nn1121   nn3478   wcj,pnp1992   pl,qpta1058

of all the congregation of the children of Israel, who were weeping before the

cs,nn6607   cs,nn168   nn4150

door of the tabernacle of the congregation.

nn6372   cs,nn1121   nn499   cs,nn1121   nn175   df,nn3548

7 And when Phinehas, the son of Eleazar, the son of Aaron the priest,

wcs,qmf7200   wcs,qmf6965   pr4480/cs,nn8432   df,nn5712   wcs,qmf3947   nn7420

saw   it, he rose up from among the congregation, and took   a javelin in his

pp,nn,pnx3027

hand;

wcs,qmf935   pr310   cs,nn376   nn3478   pr413   df,nn6898   wcs,qmf1856 (853) du,nu,pnx8147

8 And he went after the man of Israel into the tent, and thrust   both

(853)   cs,nn376   nn3478   wcj(853)   df,nn802   pr413   nn,pnx6897

of them through,   the man of Israel, and   the woman through her belly. So

df,nn4046   wcs,nimf6113 pr4480/pr5921   pl,cs,nn1121   nn3478

the plague was stayed   from   the children of Israel.

df,pl,qpta4191   dfp,nn4046 wcs,qmf1961 wcj,pl,nu6242   nu702   nu505

9 And those that died in the plague were   twenty and four thousand.

nn3068   wcs,pimf1696 pr413   nn4872   pp,qnc559

10 And the LORD spoke unto Moses, saying,

nn6372   cs,nn1121   nn499   cs,nn1121   nn175   df,nn3548

11 Phinehas, the   son   of Eleazar, the   son   of Aaron the priest, hath

hipf7725/(853)/nn,pnx2534   pr4480/pr5921   pl,cs,nn1121   nn3478   pp,pinc,pnx7065

turned*my*wrath*away   from   the children of Israel, while he was zealous

pr854/nn,pnx7068   pp,nn,pnx8432   pipf3615   wcj,ptn3808 (853)   pl,cs,nn1121   nn3478

for*my*sake among them, that I consumed   not   the children of Israel in my

pp,nn,pnx7068

jealousy.

pp,ad3651   qmv559 ptdm,pnx2009   qpta5414   pp,pnx   (853)   nn,pnx1285   nn7965

12 Wherefore say, Behold, I give unto him   my covenant of peace:

wcj,qpf1961 pp,pnx   wcj,pp,nn,pnx2233 pr,pnx310   cs,nn1285

13 And he shall have it, and his   seed   after him, even the covenant of

nn5769   cs,nn3550   pr8478/pnl834   pipf7065   pp,pl,nn,pnx430

an everlasting priesthood; because he was zealous for his   God,   and

wcs,pimf3722   pr5921   pl,cs,nn1121   nn3478

made*an*atonement for the children of Israel.

🗝 25:6–13   See the note on Exodus 32:25–29.

wcj,cs,nn8034   cs,nn**376**/nn3478   df,hopt**5221**   pnl834   hopf**5221**   pr854

14 Now the   name   of the Israelite that was slain *even* that was slain with

df,nn4084   nn2174   cs,nn**1121**   nn5543   cs,nn**5387**   nn1   cs,nn**1004**

the Midianitish woman, *was* Zimri, the   son   of Salu, a prince of a chief house

dfp,nn8099

among the Simeonites.

wcj,cs,nn8034   df,nn4084   df,nn**802**   df,hopt**5221**   nn3579

15 And the   name   of the Midianitish woman that was   slain *was* Cozbi, the

cs,nn1323   nn6698 pp,pnp1931   cs,nn**7218**   pl,cs,nn**523**   (pnp1931)   nn1   cs,nn**1004**

daughter of Zur;   he   *was* head over a people, *and*   of a chief house in

pp,nn4080

Midian.

nn3068   wcs,pimf**1696** pr413   nn4872   pp,qnc**559**

16 And the LORD spoke unto Moses, saying,

qna6887 (853)   df,nn4084   wcj,hipf**5221**   pnx(853)

17 Vex   the Midianites, and smite   them:

cj3588 pnp1992 pl,qpta6887 pp,pnx   pp,pl,nn,pnx5231   pnl834   pipf5230   pp,pnx

18 For they   vex   you with their   wiles,   wherewith they have beguiled you

pr5921   cs,nn**1697**   nn6465   wcj,pr5921   cs,nn**1697**   nn3579   cs,nn1323   cs,nn**5387**

in the matter of Peor, and   in   the matter of Cozbi, the daughter of a prince of

nn4080   nn,pnx**269**   df,hopt**5221**   pp,cs,nn**3117**   df,nn4046   pr5921/cs,nn**1697**/nn6465

Midian, their sister, which was slain in the   day   of the plague for*Peor's*sake.

The Second Census

wcs,qmf**1961**   pr310   df,nn4046   nn3068 wcs,qmf**559** pr413   nn4872

26 And it*came*to*pass after the plague, that the Lord spoke unto Moses

wcj,pr413   nn499   cs,nn**1121**   nn175   df,nn**3548**   pp,qnc**559**

and unto Eleazar the   son   of Aaron the priest, saying,

qmv**5375**   (853)   cs,nn**7218**   cs,nn3605   cs,nn**5712**   pl,cs,nn**1121**   nn3478

2 Take   the sum of   all   the congregation of the children of Israel, from

pl,nu6242   nn8141   pr4480/cs,nn**1121**   wcj,ad,lh4605   pl,nn,pnx1   pp,cs,nn**1004** cs,nn3605

twenty years   old   and upward, throughout their fathers' house,   all   that

qpta3318   nn6635   pp,nn3478

are*able*to*go to war in Israel.

nn4872   wcj,nn499   df,nn**3548** wcs,pimf**1696** pr,pnx854   pp,pl,cs,nn**6160**   nn4124

3 And Moses and Eleazar the priest spoke with them in the   plains   of Moab

pr5921   nn3383   nn3405   pp,qnc**559**

by Jordan *near* Jericho, saying,

pl,nu6242   nn8141   pr4480/cs,nn**1121**   wcj,ad,lh4605 pp,pnl834

4 *Take the sum of the people*, from twenty years   old   and upward;   as

nn3068   pipf**6680**   (853)   nn4872   wcj,pl,cs,nn**1121**   nn3478   df,pl,qpta3318

the LORD commanded   Moses and the   children   of Israel, which went forth

pr4480/cs,nn**776**   nn4714

out*of*the*land of Egypt.

nn7205   cs,nn1060   nn3478   pl,cs,nn**1121**   nn7205   nn2585

5 Reuben, the eldest son of Israel: the children of Reuben; Hanoch, *of whom*

cs,nn**4940**   df,nn2599   pp,nn6396   cs,nn**4940**   df,nn6384

cometh the family of the Hanochites: of Pallu, the family of the Palluites:

pp,nn2696   cs,nn**4940**   df,nn2697   pp,nn3756   cs,nn**4940**

6 Of Hezron, the family of the Hezronites: of Carmi, the family of the

df,nn3757

Carmites.

pndm428   pl,cs,nn**4940**   df,nn7206   pl,qptp,pnx**6485**

7 These *are* the families of the Reubenites: and they that were numbered of

wcs,qmf**1961** wcj,pl,nu705   nu7969   nu**505**   wcj,cs,nu7651   pl,nu3967   wcj,nu7970

them were forty and three thousand and seven hundred and thirty.

wcj,pl,cs,nn**1121**   nn6396   nn446

8 And the sons of Pallu; Eliab.

wcj,pl,cs,nn**1121**   nn446   nn5241   wcj,nn1885   wcj,nn48   pndm1931

9 And the sons of Eliab; Nemuel, and Dathan, and Abiram. This *is that*

nn1885   wcj,nn48   cs,aj7148   df,nn**5712**   pnl834 hipf5327 pr5921

Dathan and Abiram, *which were* famous in the congregation, who strove against

nn4872   wcj,pr5921   nn175   pp,cs,nn**5712**   nn7141   pp,hinc,pnx5327 pr5921

Moses and against Aaron in the company of Korah, when they strove against the

nn**3068**

LORD:

df,nn776   wcs,qmf6605 (853)   nn,pnx**6310**   wcs,qmf**1104**/pnx(853)

10 And the earth opened her mouth, and swallowed*them*up*together

wcj,pnx854 nn7141   df,nn**5712**   pp,qnc**4191**   df,nn784 pp,qnc398   wcj,du,nu3967

with Korah, when that company died, what time the fire devoured two hundred

(853) pl,nu2572 nn376   wcs,qmf**1961**   pp,nn5251

and fifty men: and they became a sign.

wcj,pl,cs,nn**1121**   nn7141   qpf**4191** ptn**3808**

11 Notwithstanding the children of Korah died not.

pl,cs,nn**1121**   nn8095   pp,pl,nn,pnx**4940**   pp,nn5241   cs,nn**4940**

12 The sons of Simeon after their families: of Nemuel, the family of the

df,nn5242   pp,nn3226   cs,nn**4940**   df,nn3228   pp,nn3199   cs,nn**4940**

Nemuelites: of Jamin, the family of the Jaminites: of Jachin, the family of the

df,nn3200

Jachinites:

pp,nn2226   cs,nn**4940**   df,nn2227   pp,nn7586   cs,nn**4940**   df,nn7587

13 Of Zerah, the family of the Zarhites: of Shaul, the family of the Shaulites.

pndm428   pl,cs,nn**4940**   df,nn8099 wcj,pl,nu6242 du,nu8147 nu**505**

14 These *are* the families of the Simeonites, twenty and two thousand and

wcj,du,nu3967

two hundred.

pl,cs,nn**1121**   nn1410   pp,pl,nn,pnx**4940**   pp,nn6827   cs,nn**4940**

15 The children of Gad after their families: of Zephon, the family of the

df,nn3831   pp,nn2291   cs,nn**4940**   df,nn2291   pp,nn7764   cs,nn**4940**

Zephonites: of Haggi, the family of the Haggites: of Shuni, the family of the

df,nn7765

Shunites:

pp,nn244   cs,nn**4940**   df,nn244   pp,nn6179   cs,nn**4940**   df,nn6180

16 Of Ozni, the family of the Oznites: of Eri, the family of the Erites:

pp,nn720   cs,nn**4940**   df,nn722   pp,nn692   cs,nn**4940**   df,nn692

17 Of Arod, the family of the Arodites: of Areli, the family of the Arelites.

pndm428   pl,cs,nn**4940**   pl,cs,nn**1121**   nn1410

18 These *are* the families of the children of Gad according to those that were

pp,pl,qptp,pnx**6485**   pl,nu705   nu**505**   wcj,cs,nu2568   pl,nu3967

numbered of them, forty thousand and five hundred.

pl,cs,nn**1121**   nn3063   nn6147   wcj,nn209   nn6147   wcj,nn209 wcs,qmf**4191**

19 The sons of Judah *were* Er and Onan: and Er and Onan died in the

pp,cs,nn776   nn3667

land of Canaan.

pl,cs,nn**1121**   nn3063   pp,pl,nn,pnx**4940** wcs,qmf**1961**   pp,nn7956   cs,nn**4940**

20 And the sons of Judah after their families were; of Shelah, the family of

df,nn8024   pp,nn6557   cs,nn4940   df,nn6558   pp,nn2226   cs,nn4940

the Shelanites: of Pharez, the family of the Pharzites: of Zerah, the family of the

df,nn2227

Zarhites.

pl,cs,nn1121   nn6557   wcs,qmf1961   pp,nn2696   cs,nn4940   df,nn2697

21 And the sons of Pharez were; of Hezron, the family of the Hezronites: of

pp,nn2538   cs,nn4940   df,nn2539

Hamul, the family of the Hamulites.

pndm428   pl,cs,nn4940   nn3063   pp,pl,qptp,pnx6485

22 These *are* the families of Judah according to those that were numbered of

nu8337/wcj,pl,nu7657   nu505   wcj,cs,nu2568   pl,nu3967

them, threescore*and*sixteen thousand and five hundred.

pl,cs,nn1121   nn3485   pp,pl,nn,pnx4940   nn8439   cs,nn4940

23 *Of* the sons of Issachar after their families: *of* Tola, the family of the

df,nn8440   pp,nn6312   cs,nn4940   df,nn6324

Tolaites: of Pua, the family of the Punites:

pp,nn3437   cs,nn4940   df,nn3432   pp,nn8110   cs,nn4940

24 Of Jashub, the family of the Jashubites: of Shimron, the family of the

df,nn8117

Shimronites.

pndm428   pl,cs,nn4940   nn3485   pp,pl,qptp,pnx6485

25 These *are* the families of Issachar according to those that were numbered of

wcj,pl,nu8346   nu702   nu505   wcj,cs,nu7969   pl,nu3967

them, threescore and four thousand and three hundred.

pl,cs,nn1121   nn2074   pp,pl,nn,pnx4940   pp,nn5624   cs,nn4940

26 *Of* the sons of Zebulun after their families: of Sered, the family of the

df,nn5625   pp,nn356   cs,nn4940   df,nn440   pp,nn3177   cs,nn4940   df,nn3178

Sardites: of Elon, the family of the Elonites: of Jahleel, the family of the Jahleelites.

pndm428   pl,cs,nn4940   df,nn2075

27 These *are* the families of the Zebulunites according to those that were

pp,pl,qptp,pnx6485   pl,nu8346   nu505   wcj,cs,nu2568   pl,nu3967

numbered of them, threescore thousand and five hundred.

pl,cs,nn1121   nn3130   pp,pl,nn,pnx4940   nn4519   wcj,nn669

28 The sons of Joseph after their families *were* Manasseh and Ephraim.

pl,cs,nn1121   nn4519   pp,nn4353   cs,nn4940   df,nn4354

29 Of the sons of Manasseh: of Machir, the family of the Machirites: and

wcj,nn4353   hipf3205 (853)   nn1568   pp,nn1568   cs,nn4940   df,nn1569

Machir begot Gilead: of Gilead *come* the family of the Gileadites.

pndm428   pl,cs,nn1121   nn1568   nn372   cs,nn4940   df,nn373

30 These *are* the sons of Gilead: *of* Jeezer, the family of the Jeezerites: of

pp,nn2507   cs,nn4940   df,nn2516

Helek, the family of the Helekites:

wcj,nn844   cs,nn4940   df,nn845   wcj,nn7928   cs,nn4940

31 And *of* Asriel, the family of the Asrielites: and *of* Shechem, the family of

df,nn7930

the Shechemites:

wcj,nn8061   cs,nn4940   df,nn8062   wcj,nn2660   cs,nn4940

32 And *of* Shemida, the family of the Shemidaites: and *of* Hepher, the family of

df,nn2662

the Hepherites.

wcj,nn6765   cs,nn1121   nn2660   qpf1961/pp,pnx   ptn3808   pl,nn1121   cj3588/cj518   pl,nn1323

33 And Zelophehad the son of Hepher had no sons, but daughters:

wcj,cs,nn8034   pl,cs,nn1323   nn6765   nn4244   wcj,nn5270   nn2295

and the names of the daughters of Zelophehad *were* Mahlah, and Noah, Hoglah,

nn4435   wcj,nn8656

Milcah, and Tirzah.

pndm428   pl,cs,nn**4940**   nn4519   wcj,pl,qptp,pnx**6485**

34 These *are* the families of Manasseh, and those that were numbered of them,

wcj,pl,nu2572   du,nu8147   nu**505**   wcj,cs,nu7651   pl,nu3967

fifty and two thousand and seven hundred.

pndm428   pl,cs,nn**1121**   nn669   pp,pl,nn,pnx**4940**   pp,nn7803

35 These *are* the sons of Ephraim after their families: of Shuthelah, the

cs,nn**4940**   df,nn8364   pp,nn1071   cs,nn**4940**   df,nn1076   pp,nn8465

family of the Shuthalhites: of Becher, the family of the Bachrites: of Tahan, the

cs,nn**4940**   df,nn8470

family of the Tahanites.

wcj,pndm428   pl,cs,nn**1121**   nn7803   pp,nn6197   cs,nn**4940**

36 And these *are* the sons of Shuthelah: of Eran, the family of the

df,nn6198

Eranites.

pndm428   pl,cs,nn**4940**   pl,cs,nn**1121**   nn669

37 These *are* the families of the sons of Ephraim according to those that were

pp,pl,qptp,pnx**6485**   wcj,nu7970   du,nu8147   nu**505**   wcj,cs,nu2568   pl,nu3967   pndm428

numbered of them, thirty and two thousand and five hundred. These *are* the

pl,cs,nn**1121**   nn3130   pp,pl,nn,pnx**4940**

sons of Joseph after their families.

pl,cs,nn**1121**   nn1144   pp,pl,nn,pnx**4940**   pp,nn1106   cs,nn**4940**

38 The sons of Benjamin after their families: of Bela, the family of the

df,nn1108   pp,nn788   cs,nn**4940**   df,nn789   pp,nn297   cs,nn**4940**

Belaites: of Ashbel, the family of the Ashbelites: of Ahiram, the family of the

df,nn298

Ahiramites:

pp,nn8197   cs,nn**4940**   df,nn7781   pp,nn2349   cs,nn**4940**

39 Of Shupham, the family of the Shuphamites: of Hupham, the family of the

df,nn2350

Huphamites.

pl,cs,nn**1121**   nn1106   wcs,qmf**1961**   nn714   wcj,nn5283   cs,nn**4940**

40 And the sons of Bela were Ard and Naaman: *of Ard*, the family of the

df,nn716   pp,nn5283   cs,nn**4940**   df,nn5280

Ardites: *and* of Naaman, the family of the Naamites.

pndm428   pl,cs,nn**1121**   nn1144   pp,pl,nn,pnx**4940**

41 These *are* the sons of Benjamin after their families: and they that were

wcj,pl,qptp,pnx**6485**   wcj,pl,nu705   nu2568   nu**505**   wcj,cs,nu8337   pl,nu3967

numbered of them *were* forty and five thousand and six hundred.

pndm428   pl,cs,nn**1121**   nn1835   pp,pl,nn,pnx**4940**   pp,nn7748   cs,nn**4940**

42 These *are* the sons of Dan after their families: of Shuham, the family of

df,nn7749   pndm428   pl,cs,nn**4940**   nn1835   pp,pl,nn,pnx**4940**

the Shuhamites. These *are* the families of Dan after their families.

cs,nn3605   pl,cs,nn**4940**   df,nn7749   pp,pl,qptp,pnx**6485**

43 All the families of the Shuhamites, according to those that were numbered

wcj,pl,nu8346   nu702   nu**505**   wcj,cs,nu702   pl,nu3967

of them, *were* threescore and four thousand and four hundred.

pl,cs,nn**1121**   nn836   pp,pl,nn,pnx**4940**   pp,nn3232   cs,nn**4940**

44 *Of* the children of Asher after their families: of Jimna, the family of the

df,nn3232   pp,nn3440   cs,nn**4940**   df,nn3441   pp,nn1283   cs,nn**4940**   df,nn1284

Jimnites: of Jesui, the family of the Jesuites: of Beriah, the family of the Beriites.

pp,pl,cs,nn**1121**   nn1283   pp,nn2268   cs,nn**4940**   df,nn2277

45 Of the sons of Beriah: of Heber, the family of the Heberites: of

pp,nn4439   cs,nn**4940**   df,nn4440

Malchiel, the family of the Malchielites.

wcj,cs,nn8034   cs,nn1323   nn836   nn8294

46 And the name of the daughter of Asher *was* Sarah.

47 These *are* the families of the sons of Asher according to those that were numbered of them; *who were* fifty and three thousand and four hundred.

48 *Of* the sons of Naphtali after their families: of Jahzeel, the family of the Jahzeelites: of Guni, the family of the Gunites:

49 Of Jezer, the family of the Jezerites: of Shillem, the family of the Shillemites.

50 These *are* the families of Naphtali according to their families: and they that were numbered of them *were* forty and five thousand and four hundred.

51 These *were* the numbered of the children of Israel, six hundred thousand and a thousand seven hundred and thirty.

☞ 52 And the LORD spoke unto Moses, saying,

53 Unto these the land shall be divided for an inheritance according to the number of names.

54 To many thou shalt give*the*more inheritance, and to few thou shalt give*the*less inheritance: to every one shall his inheritance be given according to those that were numbered of him.

55 Notwithstanding the land shall be divided by lot: according to the names of the tribes of their fathers they shall inherit.

56 According to the lot shall the possession thereof be divided between many and few.

57 And these *are* they that were numbered of the Levites after their families: of Gershon, the family of the Gershonites: of Kohath, the family of the Kohathites: of Merari, the family of the Merarites.

☞ **26:52–56** Approximately thirty–seven years after the first census, a second one was taken following the same procedure (Num. 26:1–51). These figures were to be used in determining the size of the territory allotted to each tribe (Num. 26:52–56). When the figures from the two censuses are compared, some interesting facts emerge. Only two men, Joshua and Caleb, who had not rebelled at Kadesh–barnea, were counted in both censuses. The first numbering found 603,550 fighting men in the twelve tribes (Num. 1:46), a remarkable number for Moses to have led through the wilderness. The totals for the second census were 601,730 (Num. 26:51), which reflects almost no change in thirty–seven years. The composition of the two groups was, however, totally different. Had the 24,000 who were killed just before the second census because of their sin at Baal–peor (Num. 25:9) still been alive, the adult male population would have shown a modest increase. See the note on Numbers 1:2.

^{pndm428}   ^{pl,cs,nn4940}   ^{pl,nn3881}   ^{cs,nn4940}   ^{df,nn3864}   ^{cs,nn4940}

58 These *are* the families of the Levites: the family of the Libnites, the family

^{df,nn2276}   ^{cs,nn4940}   ^{df,nn4250}   ^{cs,nn4940}   ^{df,nn4188}   ^{cs,nn4940}

of the Hebronites, the family of the Mahlites, the family of the Mushites, the family

^{df,nn7145}   ^{wcj,nn6955 hipf3205 (853)}   ⁿⁿ⁶⁰¹⁹

of the Korathites. And Kohath begot   Amram.

^{wcj,cs,nn8034}   ⁿⁿ⁶⁰¹⁹   ^{cs,nn802}   ⁿⁿ³¹¹⁵   ^{cs,nn1323}   ⁿⁿ³⁸⁷⁸

59 And the name of Amram's wife *was* Jochebed, the daughter of Levi,

^{pnl834}   ^{qpf3205 (pnx853)}   ^{pp,nn3878}   ^{pp,nn4714}   ^{wcs,qmf3205}   ^{pp,nn6019 (853)}

whom *her mother* bore   to Levi in Egypt: and she bore unto Amram

ⁿⁿ¹⁷⁵   ^{wcj(853)}   ⁿⁿ⁴⁸⁷²   ^{wcj(853)}   ⁿⁿ⁴⁸¹³   ^{nn,pnx269}

Aaron and   Moses, and   Miriam their sister.

^{pp,nn175}   ^{wcs,nimf3205 (853)}   ⁿⁿ⁵⁰⁷⁰   ^{wcj(853)}   ⁿⁿ³⁰   ⁽⁸⁵³⁾   ⁿⁿ⁴⁹⁹

60 And unto Aaron was born   Nadab, and   Abihu,   Eleazar, and

^{wcj(853)}   ⁿⁿ³⁸⁵

Ithamar.

ⁿⁿ⁵⁰⁷⁰   ^{wcj,nn30}   ^{wcs,qmf4191}   ^{pp,hinc,pnx7126} ^{qpta2114} ^{nn784 pp,pl,cs,nn6440}

61 And Nadab and Abihu died, when they offered strange fire before the

ⁿⁿ³⁰⁶⁸

LORD.

^{pl,qptp,pnx6485}   ^{wcs,qmf1961 wcj,pl,nu6242}   ^{nu7969}   ^{nu505}

62 And those that were numbered of them were   twenty and three thousand,

^{cs,nn3605}   ^{aj2145}   ⁿⁿ²³²⁰   ^{pr4480/cs,nn1121}   ^{wcj,ad,lh4605 cj3588}   ^{ptn3808}   ^{hotpf6485}

all males from a month old and upward: for they were not numbered

^{pp,cs,nn8432}   ^{pl,cs,nn1121}   ⁿⁿ³⁴⁷⁸   ^{cj3588}   ^{ptn3808}   ⁿⁿ⁵¹⁵⁹   ^{nipf5414} ^{pp,pnx} ^{pp,cs,nn8432}

among the children of Israel, because there was no inheritance given them among

^{pl,cs,nn1121}   ⁿⁿ³⁴⁷⁸

the children of Israel.

^{pndm428}   ^{pl,cs,qptp6485}   ⁿⁿ⁴⁸⁷²   ^{wcj,nn499}   ^{df,nn3548} ^{pnl834}

63 These *are* they that were numbered by Moses and Eleazar the priest, who

^{qpf6485}   ⁽⁸⁵³⁾   ^{pl,cs,nn1121}   ⁿⁿ³⁴⁷⁸   ^{pp,pl,cs,nn6160}   ⁿⁿ⁴¹²⁴ ^{pr5921} ⁿⁿ³³⁸³

numbered   the children of Israel in the plains of Moab by Jordan *near*

ⁿⁿ³⁴⁰⁵

Jericho.

^{wcj,pp,pndm428}   ^{qpf1961 ptn3808}   ⁿⁿ³⁷⁶   ⁿⁿ⁴⁸⁷²   ^{wcj,nn175}

64 But among these   there was not a man of them whom Moses and Aaron

^{df,nn3548}   ^{pr4480/pl,cs,qptp6485} ^{pnl834}   ^{qpf6485}   ⁽⁸⁵³⁾   ^{pl,cs,nn1121}   ⁿⁿ³⁴⁷⁸

the priest numbered, when they numbered   the children of Israel in the

^{pp,cs,nn4057}   ⁿⁿ⁵⁵¹⁴

wilderness of Sinai.

^{cj3588}   ⁿⁿ³⁰⁶⁸   ^{qpf559} ^{pp,pnx}   ^{qna4191/qmf4191}   ^{dfp,nn4057}

65 For the LORD had said of them, They shall surely die in the wilderness.

^{wcj,ptn3808} ^{nipf3498}   ⁿⁿ³⁷⁶ ^{pr,pnx4480}   ^{cj3588/cj518} ⁿⁿ³⁶¹²   ^{cs,nn1121}

And there was not left a man of them, save Caleb the son of

ⁿⁿ³³¹²   ^{wcj,nn3091}   ^{cs,nn1121}   ⁿⁿ⁵¹²⁶

Jephunneh, and Joshua the son of Nun.

26:64, 65 See the note on Numbers 13:30-33.

The Law of Inheritance

27 Then came the daughters of Zelophehad, the son of Hepher, the son of Gilead, the son of Machir, the son of Manasseh, of the families of Manasseh the son of Joseph: and these *are* the names of his daughters; Mahlah, Noah, and Hoglah, and Milcah, and Tirzah.

2 And they stood before Moses, and before Eleazar the priest, and before the princes and all the congregation, *by* the door of the tabernacle of the congregation, saying,

3 Our father died in the wilderness, and he was not in the company of them that gathered*themselves*together against the LORD in the company of Korah; but died in his own sin, and had no sons.

4 Why should the name of our father be done away from among his family, because he hath no son? Give unto us *therefore* a possession among the brethren of our father.

5 And Moses brought their cause before the LORD.

6 And the LORD spoke unto Moses, saying,

7 The daughters of Zelophehad speak right: thou shalt surely give them a possession of an inheritance among their father's brethren; and thou shalt cause the inheritance of their father to pass unto them.

8 And thou shalt speak unto the children of Israel, saying, If a man die, and have no son, then ye shall cause his inheritance to pass unto his daughter.

9 And if he have no daughter, then ye shall give his inheritance unto his brethren.

10 And if he have no brethren, then ye shall give his inheritance unto his father's brethren.

11 And if his father have no brethren, then ye shall give his inheritance unto his kinsman that is next to him of*his*family, and he shall

wcs,qpf**3423**   pnx(853)   wcs,qpf**1961**   pp,pl,cs,nn**1121**   nn**3478**   pp,cs,nn**2708**   nn**4941**

possess   it: and it shall   be   unto the children of Israel a statute of judgment,

pp,pnl834   nn**3068**   pipf**6680**   (853)   nn**4872**

as   the LORD commanded   Moses.

Joshua Named to Succeed Moses

nn**3068**   wcs,qmf**559**   pr413   nn**4872**   qmv**5927**   pr413   df,pndm2088   cs,nn2022   df,nn**5682**

12 And the LORD   said   unto Moses, Get*thee*up into   this   mount Abarim,

wcj,qmv**7200** (853)   df,nn**776**   pnl834   qpf**5414**   pp,pl,cs,nn**1121**   nn**3478**

and   see   the land which I have given unto the children of Israel.

wcj,qpf**7200**   pnx(853)   pnp859   ad1571   wcj,nipf**622**   pr413

13 And when thou hast   seen   it, thou also shalt be gathered unto thy

pl,nn,pnx**5971** pp,pnl834   nn**175**   nn,pnx**251**   nipf**622**

people,   as   Aaron thy brother was gathered.

pp,pnl834   qpf**4784**   nn,pnx**6310**   pp,cs,nn**4057**   nn**6790**

14 For ye rebelled against my commandment in the   desert   of Zin, in the

pp,cs,nn**4808**   df,nn**5712**   pp,hinc,pnx**6942**   dfp,pl,nn**4325**   pp,du,nn,pnx**5869**

strife of the congregation, to sanctify me at the water before their   eyes:

pnp,1992   pl,cs,nn**4325**   cs,nn**4809**   nn**6946**   cs,nn**4057**   nn**6790**

that *is* the water of Meribah in Kadesh in the wilderness of Zin.

nn**4872**   wcs,pimf**1696** pr413   nn**3068**   pp,qnc**559**

15 And Moses spoke unto the LORD, saying,

nn**3068**   pl,cs,nn**430**   df,pl,nn**7307**   pp,cs,nn**3605** nn**1320** qmf**6485**   nn**376** pr5921

16 Let the LORD, the God of the spirits of   all   flesh, set a man over the

df,nn**5712**

congregation,

pnl834   qmf3318   pp,pl,nn,pnx**6440**   wcj,pnl834   qmf935   pp,pl,nn,pnx**6440**

17 Which may go out   before   them, and which may go in   before   them,

wcj,pnl834   himf,pnx3318   wcj,pnl834   himf,pnx935   cs,nn**5712**

and which may lead*them*out, and which may bring*them*in; that the congregation

nn**3068** qmf**1961** wcj,ptn**3808**   dfp,nn**6629** pnl834/pp,pnx   ptn369 (pp,pnx)   qpta7462

of the LORD be   not   as sheep which have no   shepherd.

nn**3068** wcs,qmf**559** pr413   nn**4872**   qmv3947 pp,pnx (853)   nn3091   cs,nn**1121**   nn5126

☞ 18 And the LORD   said   unto Moses, Take thee   Joshua the son of Nun, a

nn**376** pnl834/pp,pnx   nn**7307**   wcj,qpf**5564** (853)   nn,pnx3027 pr,pnx5921

man in whom *is* the spirit, and   lay   thine hand upon him;

wcj,hipf5975 pnx(853)   pp,pl,cs,nn**6440**   nn499   df,nn**3548**   wcj,pp,pl,cs,nn**6440** cs,nn3605

19 And   set   him before Eleazar the priest, and   before   all   the

df,nn**5712**   wcj,pipf**6680**/pnx(853)   pp,du,nn,pnx**5869**

congregation; and give*him*a*charge in their   sight.

wcj,qpf**5414**   pr4480/nn,pnx**1935**   pr,pnx5921   pp,pr4616 cs,nn3605

20 And thou shalt   put   *some* of*thine*honor upon   him,   that   all   the

cs,nn**5712**   pl,cs,nn**1121**   nn**3478**   qmf**8085**

congregation of the children of Israel may be obedient.

qmf5975 wcj,pp,pl,cs,nn**6440**   nn499   df,nn**3548**   wcs,qpf**7592**

21 And he shall stand   before   Eleazar the priest, who shall   ask   *counsel*

pp,pnx   pp,cs,nn**4941**   df,pl,nn**224** pp,pl,cs,nn**6440**   nn**3068** pr5921   nn,pnx**6310**

for him after the judgment of Urim   before   the LORD: at his word shall they

---

☞ **27:18–23** Knowing that it would not be long before he would die, Moses asked God to choose a successor to lead Israel in his place (v. 16). God selected Joshua, a man who had been Moses' close associate and servant since the time when Israel was still at Mount Sinai (Ex. 24:13; 32:17; 33:11). Even before their arrival at Sinai, Moses had appointed Joshua to be the leader of the army against Amalek (Ex. 17:8–13). His public commissioning involved more than the role of military leader, but it was in this area that he was to make his greatest contribution. Joshua is mentioned twice in the New Testament (Acts 7:45; Heb. 4:8).

qmf3318   wcj,pr5921   nn,pnx6310   qmf935   pnp1931   wcj,cs,nn3605
go out, and   at   his   word   they shall come in, *both*   he,   and   all   the

pl,cs,nn1121   nn3478   pr,pnx854   wcj,cs,nn3605   df,nn5712
children of Israel with him, even   all   the congregation.

          nn4872   wcs,qmf6213 pp,pnl834   nn3068   pipf6680   pnx(853)   wcs,qmf3947 (853)
22 And Moses   did   as   the LORD commanded   him: and he   took

nn3091   wcs,himf,pnx5975   pp,pl,cs,nn6440   nn499   df,nn3548   wcj,pp,pl,cs,nn6440 cs,nn3605
Joshua, and   set   him   before Eleazar the priest, and   before   all   the

df,nn5712
congregation:

          wcs,qmf5564   (853)   du,nn,pnx3027 pr,pnx5921   wcs,pimf,pnx6680   pp,pnl834
23 And he   laid   his hands   upon him, and gave*him*a*charge,   as

nn3068   pipf1696   pp,cs,nn3027   nn4872
the LORD commanded by the   hand   of Moses.

Laws for Offerings

                    nn3068   wcs,pimf1696 pr413   nn4872   pp,qnc559
28 And the LORD spoke unto Moses, saying,

              pimv6680   (853)   pl,cs,nn1121   nn3478   wcj,qpf559 pr,pnx413   (853)
2 Command   the children of Israel, and   say   unto them,

nn,pnx7133   nn,pnx3899   pp,pl,nn,pnx801   nn,pnx5207 cs,nn7381
My offering, *and* my bread for my sacrifices*made*by*fire, *for* a sweet savor

               qmf8104   pp,hinc7126   pp,pnx   pp,nn,pnx4150
unto me, shall ye observe to offer unto me in their due season.

              wcs,qpf559   pp,pnx   pndm2088   df,nn801   pnl834
3 And thou shalt   say   unto them, This *is* the offering*made*by*fire which

him f7126   pp,nn3068   du,nu8147   pl,nn3532   pl,cs,nn1121   nn8141   aj8549
ye shall offer unto the LORD; two   lambs of the   first   year without spot

dfp,nn3117   nn8548   nn5930
day*by*day, *for* a continual burnt offering.

   (853)   nu259 df,nn3532   qmf6213   dfp,nn1242   wcj(853)   df,nuor8145 df,nn3532
4   The one lamb shalt thou offer in the morning, and   the other lamb

          qmf6213 pr996 df,du,nn6153
shalt thou offer at   even;

         wcj,cs,nuor6224   df,nn374   nn5560   pp,nn4503   qptp1101
5 And a   tenth   *part* of an ephah of flour for a meat offering, mingled with

cs,nuor7243   df,nn1969   aj3795   pp,nn8081
the fourth *part* of a hin of beaten oil.

          nn8548   cs,nn5930   df,qptp6213   pp,cs,nn2022 nn5514
6 *It is* a continual burnt offering, which was ordained in mount Sinai for a

nn5207 pp,cs,nn7381   nn801   pp,nn3068
sweet savor, a sacrifice*made*by*fire unto the LORD.

          wcj,nn,pnx5262   cs,nuor7243   df,nn1969
7 And the drink offering thereof *shall be* the fourth *part* of a hin   for the

df,nu259 dfp,nn3532   dfp,nn6944   nn7941   himv5258
one lamb: in the holy *place* shalt thou cause the strong wine to be poured unto

pp,nn3068   cs,nn5262
the LORD *for* a drink offering.

          wcj(853) df,nuor8145 df,nn3532   qmf6213 pr996 df,du,nn6153   pp,cs,nn4503
8 And the   other lamb shalt thou offer at   even: as the meat offering of

---

28:5, 7 The "ephah" and "hin" are Egyptian measures, which reveal the influence of Israel's sojourn in Egypt.

df,nn1242 wcj,pp,nn,pnx5262 qmf6213
the morning, and as the drink offering thereof, thou shalt offer it, a

cs,nn801 nn5207 cs,nn7381 pp,nn3068
sacrifice*made*by*fire, of a sweet savor unto the LORD.

df,nn7676 wcj,pp,cs,nn3117 du,cs,nu8147 pl,nn3532 pl,cs,nn1121 nn8141 aj8549
9 And on the sabbath day two lambs of the first year without spot,

wcj,du,cs,nu8147 pl,nn6241 nn5560 nn4503 qptp1101 dfp,nn8081
and two tenth deals of flour for a meat offering, mingled with oil, and the

wcj,nn,pnx5262
drink offering thereof:

cs,nn5930 cs,nn7676/pp,nn,pnx7676 pr5921 df,nn8548
10 This is the burnt offering of every sabbath, beside the continual

cs,nn5930 wcj,nn,pnx5262
burnt offering, and his drink offering.

wcj,pp,pl,cs,nn7218 pl,nn,pnx2320 himf7126 nn5930
☞ 11 And in the beginnings of your months ye shall offer a burnt offering unto

pp,nn3068 du,nu8147 pl,cs,nn1121/nn1241 pl,nn6499 nu259 wcj,nn352 nu7651 pl,nn3532 pl,cs,nn1121 nn8141
the LORD; two young bullocks, and one ram, seven lambs of the first year

aj8549
without spot;

wcj,nu7969 pl,nn6241 nn5560 nn4503 qptp1101 dfp,nn8081
12 And three tenth deals of flour for a meat offering, mingled with oil, for

df,nu259 dfp,nn6499 wcj,du,cs,nu8147 pl,nn6241 nn5560 nn4503 qptp1101
one bullock; and two tenth deals of flour for a meat offering, mingled with

dfp,nn8081 df,nu259 dfp,nn352
oil, for one ram;

wcj,nn6241/nn6241 nn5560 qptp1101 dfp,nn8081 nn4503
13 And a several*tenth*deal of flour mingled with oil for a meat offering

df,nu259 dfp,nn3532 nn5930 nn5207 cs,nn7381 nn801
unto one lamb; for a burnt offering of a sweet savor, a sacrifice*made*by*fire

pp,nn3068
unto the LORD.

wcj,pl,nn,pnx5262 qmf1961 cs,nn2677 df,nn1969 nn3196 dfp,nn6499
14 And their drink offerings shall be half a hin of wine unto a bullock,

wcj,cs,nuor7992 df,nn1969 dfp,nn352 wcj,cs,nuor7243 df,nn1969
and the third part of a hin unto a ram, and a fourth part of a hin unto a

dfp,nn3532 pndm2063 cs,nn5930 nn2320/pp,nn,pnx2320 pp,pl,cs,nn2320
lamb: this is the burnt offering of*every*month throughout the months of the

df,nn8141
year.

nu259 wcj,cs,nn8163 pl,nn5795 pp,nn2403 pp,nn3068
15 And one kid of the goats for a sin offering unto the LORD shall be

nimf6213 pr5921 df,nn8548 cs,nn5930 wcj,nn,pnx5262
offered, beside the continual burnt offering, and his drink offering.

☞ **28:11–15** The phrase "beginnings of your months" refers to the observance of the new moon (1 Chr. 23:31; Ezra 3:5). Though it was characterized by the blowing of trumpets, it is not to be confused with the Feast of Trumpets (Num. 29:1–6). The Feast of Trumpets was celebrated at the beginning of the seventh month, not the first day of every month as is the case with these observances. Special sacrifices were offered, and it was a time of inquiring of God's messengers and worshiping at God's house, as well as a time for fellowship (1 Sam. 20:5, 18; 2 Kgs. 4:23). The observance was one of great solemnity; all business and work was to cease. When Israel began to approach it with insincerity and treated it as a mere ritual, God condemned its observance (Is. 1:13, 14).

Offerings at the Annual Assemblies

pp,nu702/nu6240 nn3117 (dfp,nn2320) df,aj7223 wcj,dfp,nn2320 nn6453

16 And in the fourteenth day of the first month *is* the passover of the

pp,nn3068

LORD.

wcj,pp,nu2568/nu6240 nn3117 df,pndm2088 dfp,nn2320 nn2282 cs,nu7651 pl,nn3117

17 And in the fifteenth day of this month *is* the feast: seven days shall

pl,nn4682 nimf398

unleavened bread be eaten.

df,aj7223 dfp,nn3117 nn6944 cs,nn4744 qmf6213 ptn3808/cs,nn3605

18 In the first day *shall be* a holy convocation; ye shall do no manner of

nn5656 cs,nn4399

servile work *therein*:

wcs,hipf7126 nn801 nn5930

19 But ye shall offer a sacrifice*made*by*fire *for* a burnt offering unto the

pp,nn3068 du,nu8147 pl,cs,nn1121/nn1241 pl,nn6499 nu259 wcj,nn352 wcj,nu7651 pl,nn3532 pl,cs,nn1121

LORD; two young bullocks, and one ram, and seven lambs of the first

nn8141 qmf1961 pp,pnx aj8549

year: they shall be unto you without blemish:

wcj,nn,pnx4503 nn5560 qptp1101 dfp,nn8081 nu7969

20 And their meat offering *shall be of* flour mingled with oil: three

pl,nn6241 qmf6213 dfp,nn6499 wcj,du,cs,nu8147 pl,nn6241 dfp,nn352

tenth deals shall ye offer for a bullock, and two tenth deals for a ram;

nn6241/nn6241 qmf6213 df,nu259 dfp,nn3532 pp,cs,nu7651

21 A several*tenth*deal shalt thou offer for every lamb, throughout the seven

df,pl,nn3532

lambs:

nu259 wcj,cs,nn8163 nn2403 pp,pinc3722 pr,pnx5921

22 And one goat *for* a sin offering, to make*an*atonement for you.

qmf6213 (853) pndm428 pr4480/pp,nn905 cs,nn5930 df,nn1242 pnl834

23 Ye shall offer these beside the burnt offering in the morning, which *is*

df,nn8548 pp,cs,nn5930

for a continual burnt offering.

dfp,pndm428 qmf6213 dfp,nn3117 cs,nu7651 pl,nn3117 cs,nn3899

24 After this manner ye shall offer daily, throughout the seven days, the meat

cs,nn801 nn5207 cs,nn7381 pp,nn3068 nimf6213

of the sacrifice*made*by*fire, of a sweet savor unto the LORD: it shall be offered

pr5921 df,nn8548 cs,nn5930 wcj,nn,pnx5262

beside the continual burnt offering, and his drink offering.

df,nuor7637 wcj,dfp,nn3117 pp,pnx qmf1961 nn6944 cs,nn4744 qmf6213

25 And on the seventh day ye shall have a holy convocation; ye shall do

ptn3808/cs,nn3605 nn5656 cs,nn4399

no servile work.

wcj,pp,cs,nn3117 df,pl,nn1061 pp,hinc,pnx7126 aj2319

26 Also in the day of the firstfruits, when ye bring a new

nn4503 pp,nn3068 pp,pl,nn,pnx7620 pp,pnx qmf1961 nn6944

meat offering unto the LORD, after your weeks *be out*, ye shall have a holy

cs,nn4744 qmf6213 ptn3808/cs,nn3605 nn5656 cs,nn4399

convocation; ye shall do no servile work:

wcs,hipf7126 nn5930 nn5207 pp,cs,nn7381 pp,nn3068

27 But ye shall offer the burnt offering for a sweet savor unto the LORD;

du,cs,nu8147 pl,cs,nn1121/nn1241 pl,nn6499 nu259 nn352 nu7651 pl,nn3532 pl,cs,nn1121 nn8141

two young bullocks, one ram, seven lambs of the first year;

wcj,nn,pnx4503　　　　nn5560　　qptp1101　　　　　dfp,nn8081　nu7969　　　pl,nn6241

28 And their meat offering of flour mingled with oil, three tenth deals unto

df,nu259　dfp,nn6499　cs,nu8147　　pl,nn6241　　　　df,nu259　dfp,nn352

one bullock, two tenth deals unto one ram,

nn6241/nn6241　　　df,nu259　dfp,nn3532　　　　　pp,cs,nu7651　df,pl,nn3532

29 A several*tenth*deal unto one lamb, throughout the seven lambs;

nu259　cs,nn8163　　　pl,nn5795　　　pp,pinc3722　　pr,pnx5921

30 *And* one kid of the goats, to make*an*atonement for you.

qmf6213　　　pr4480/pp,nn905　　　df,nn8548　　　cs,nn5930

31 Ye shall offer *them* beside the continual burnt offering, and his

wcj,nn,pnx4503　　　qmf1961　　pp,pnx　　　aj8549　　　　wcj,pl,nn,pnx5262

meat offering, (they shall be unto you without blemish) and their drink offerings.

df,nuor7637　wcj,dfp,nn2320　　　pp,nu259　　　　dfp,nn2320　pp,pnx

29 And in the seventh month, on the first *day* of the month, ye shall

qmf1961　　nn6944　　cs,nn4744　　　qmf6213 ptn3808/cs,nn3605　　nn5656　cs,nn4399　qmf1961

have a holy convocation; ye shall do no servile work: it is

cs,nn3117　　　　nn8643　　　　pp,pnx

a day of blowing*the*trumpets unto you.

wcs,qpf6213　　nn5930　　　nn5207　pp,cs,nn7381　　　pp,nn3068　nu259

2 And ye shall offer a burnt offering for a sweet savor unto the LORD; one

cs,nn1121/nn1241　nn6499　nu259　nn352　　nu7651　pl,cs,nn3532　　pl,cs,nn1121　nn8141　　aj8549

young bullock, one ram, *and* seven lambs of the first year without blemish:

wcj,nn,pnx4503　　　nn5560　　qptp1101　　　dfp,nn8081　nu7969

3 And their meat offering *shall be of* flour mingled with oil, three tenth

pl,nn6241 for a　dfp,nn6499　　du,cs,nu8147　pl,nn6241　　dfp,nn352

deals bullock, *and* two tenth deals for a ram,

nu259　wcj,nn6241　　df,nu259　dfp,nn3532　　　pp,cs,nu7651　df,pl,nn3532

4 And one tenth deal for one lamb, throughout the seven lambs:

nu259　wcj,cs,nn8163　　　pl,nn5795　　　nn2403　　　　pp,pinc3722

5 And one kid of the goats *for* a sin offering, to make*an*atonement

pr,pnx5921

for you:

pr4480/pp,nn905　　　cs,nn5930　　　df,nn2320　　　wcj,nn,pnx4503

6 Beside the burnt offering of the month, and his meat offering, and the

df,nn8548　wcj,cs,nn5930　　　wcj,nn,pnx4503　　　wcj,pl,nn,pnx5262

daily burnt offering, and his meat offering, and their drink offerings, according

pp,nn,pnx4941　　nn5207　pp,cs,nn7381　　　nn801　　　　pp,nn3068

unto their manner, for a sweet savor, a sacrifice*made*by*fire unto the LORD.

pp,pnx　　　qmf1961　　　wcj,dfp,nn6218　　df,pndm2088　df,nuor7637　dfp,nn2320　　nn6944

7 And ye shall have on the tenth *day* of this seventh month a holy

cs,nn4744　　　　wcs,pipf6031　(853)　　pl,nn,pnx5315　　ptn3808　qmf6213　cs,nn3605　nn4399

convocation; and ye shall afflict your souls: ye shall not do any work

therein:

wcs,hipf7126　　　nn5930　　　pp,nn3068　　nn5207　cs,nn7381　nu259

8 But ye shall offer a burnt offering unto the LORD *for* a sweet savor; one

cs,nn1121/nn1241　nn6499　nu259　nn352　　nu7651　pl,nn3532　　pl,cs,nn1121　nn8141　　qmf1961

young bullock, one ram, *and* seven lambs of the first year; they shall be

pp,pnx　　　aj8549

unto you without blemish:

wcj,nn,pnx**4503**   nn5560   qptp**1101**   dfp,nn**8081** nu7969   pl,nn**6241**

9 And their meat offering *shall be of* flour mingled with oil,   three tenth deals

dfp,nn**6499**   du,cs,nu8147   pl,nn**6241**   df,nu259 dfp,nn352

to a bullock, *and* two   tenth deals to one ram,

nn6241/nn**6241**   df,nu259 dfp,nn3532   pp,cs,nu7651 df,pl,nn3532

10 A several*tenth*deal for one lamb, throughout the seven lambs:

nu259   cs,nn**8163**   pl,nn5795   nn**2403**   pr4480/pp,nn905   cs,nn**2403**

11 One   kid of the goats *for* a sin offering;   beside   the sin offering of

df,pl,nn**3725**   df,nn**8548**   wcj,cs,nn**5930**   wcj,nn,pnx**4503**

atonement, and the continual burnt offering, and the meat offering of it, and their

wcj,pl,nn,pnx**5262**

drink offerings.

wcj,pp,nu2568/nu6240 nn**3117**   df,nuor7637 dfp,nn2320 pp,pnx   qmf**1961**   nn**6944**

12 And on the   fifteenth   day of the seventh month ye shall have a holy

cs,nn**6944**   qmf6213 ptn**3808**/cs,nn3605   nn5656   cs,nn**4399**   wcs,qpf2287   nn**2282**

convocation; ye shall   do   no   servile work, and ye shall keep a feast unto

pp,nn**3068** cs,nu7651 pl,nn**3117**

the LORD seven days:

wcs,hipf**7126**   nn**5930**   cs,nn**801**   nn5207

13 And ye shall offer a burnt offering, a sacrifice*made*by*fire, of a sweet

cs,nn7381   pp,nn**3068** nu7969/nu6240 cs,nn**1121**/nn1241   pl,nn6499   du,nu8147 pl,nn352   nu702/nu6240 pl,nn3532

savor unto the LORD; thirteen   young   bullocks, two rams, *and* fourteen lambs

pl,cs,nn**1121** nn8141   qmf**1961**   aj**8549**

of the first year; they shall be   without blemish:

wcj,nn,pnx**4503**   nn5560   qptp**1101**   dfp,nn**8081** nu7969

14 And their meat offering *shall be of* flour mingled with   oil,   three

pl,nn**6241**   df,nu259 dfp,nn**6499**   pp,nu7969/nu6240   pl,nn6499   du,cs,nu8147   pl,nn**6241**

tenth deals unto every bullock of the thirteen   bullocks,   two   tenth deals to

df,nu259 dfp,nn352   pp,du,nu8147 df,pl,nn352

each ram of the   two   rams,

wcj,nn6241/nn**6241**   df,nu259 dfp,nn3532   pp,nu702/nu6240 pl,nn3532

15 And a several*tenth*deal to each lamb of the fourteen lambs:

nu259 wcj,cs,nn**8163**   pl,nn5795   nn**2403**   pr4480/pp,nn905   df,nn**8548**

16 And one   kid   of the goats *for* a sin offering;   beside   the continual

cs,nn**5930**   nn,pnx**4503**   wcj,nn,pnx**5262**

burnt offering, his meat offering, and his drink offering.

df,nuor8145 wcj,dfp,nn**3117**   du,nu8147/nu6240 pl,cs,nn**1121**/nn1241   pl,nn6499

17 And on the second   day *ye shall offer* twelve   young   bullocks,

du,nu8147 pl,nn352 nu702/nu6240 pl,nn3532   pl,cs,nn**1121** nn8141   aj**8549**

two rams, fourteen lambs of the   first   year without spot:

wcj,nn,pnx**4503**   wcj,pl,nn,pnx**5262**   dfp,pl,nn6499

18 And their meat offering and their drink offerings for the bullocks, for the

dfp,pl,nn352   wcj,dfp,pl,nn3532   pp,nn,pnx4557   dfp,nn**4941**

rams, and for the lambs, *shall be* according to their number, after the manner:

nu259 wcj,cs,nn**8163**   pl,nn5795   nn**2403**   pr4480/pp,nn905   df,nn**8548**

19 And one   kid   of the goats *for* a sin offering;   beside   the continual

cs,nn**5930**   wcj,nn,pnx**4503**   wcj,pl,nn,pnx**5262**

burnt offering, and the meat offering thereof, and their drink offerings.

df,nuor7992 wcj,dfp,nn**3117** nu6249/nu6240   pl,nn6499   du,nu8147 pl,nn352 nu702/nu6240 pl,nn3532

20 And on the third   day   eleven bullocks, two rams, fourteen lambs of

pl,cs,nn**1121** nn8141   aj**8549**

the first year without blemish;

wcj,nn,pnx**4503**   wcj,pl,nn,pnx**5262**   dfp,pl,nn6499

21 And their meat offering and their drink offerings for the bullocks, for the

dfp,pl,nn352   wcj,pp,pl,nn3532   pp,nn,pnx4557   dfp,nn**4941**

rams, and for the lambs, *shall be* according to their number, after the manner:

nu259 wcj,cs,nn**8163** nn**2403** pr4480/pp,nn905 df,nn**8548** cs,nn**5930**

22 And one goat *for* a sin offering; beside the continual burnt offering,

wcj,nn,pnx**4503** wcj,nn,pnx**5262**

and his meat offering, and his drink offering.

df,nuor7243 wcj,dfp,nn**3117** nu6235 pl,nn6499 du,nu8147 pl,nn352 nu702/nu6240 pl,nn3532

23 And on the fourth day ten bullocks, two rams, *and* fourteen lambs of

pl,cs,nn**1121** nn8141 aj8549

the first year without blemish:

nn,pnx**4503** wcj,pl,nn,pnx**5262** dfp,pl,nn6499 dfp,pl,nn352

24 Their meat offering and their drink offerings for the bullocks, for the rams,

wcj,dfp,pl,nn3532 pp,nn,pnx4557 dfp,nn**4941**

and for the lambs, *shall be* according to their number, after the manner:

nu259 wcj,cs,nn**8163** pl,nn5795 nn**2403** pr4480/pp,nn905 df,nn**8548**

25 And one kid of the goats *for* a sin offering; beside the continual

cs,nn**5930** nn,pnx**4503** wcj,nn,pnx**5262**

burnt offering, his meat offering, and his drink offering.

df,nuor2549 wcj,dfp,nn**3117** nu8672 pl,nn6499 du,nu8147 pl,nn352 nu702/nu6240 pl,nn3532

26 And on the fifth day nine bullocks, two rams, *and* fourteen lambs

pl,cs,nn**1121** nn8141 aj8549

of the first year without spot:

wcj,nn,pnx**4503** wcj,pl,nn,pnx**5262** dfp,pl,nn6499

27 And their meat offering and their drink offerings for the bullocks, for the

dfp,pl,nn352 wcj,dfp,pl,nn3532 pp,nn,pnx4557 dfp,nn**4941**

rams, and for the lambs, *shall be* according to their number, after the manner:

nu259 wcj,cs,nn**8163** nn**2403** pr4480/pp,nn905 df,nn**8548** cs,nn**5930**

28 And one goat *for* a sin offering; beside the continual burnt offering,

wcj,nn,pnx**4503** wcj,nn,pnx**5262**

and his meat offering, and his drink offering.

df,nuor8345 wcj,dfp,nn**3117** nu8083 pl,nn6499 du,nu8147 pl,nn352 nu702/nu6240 pl,nn3532

29 And on the sixth day eight bullocks, two rams, *and* fourteen lambs

pl,cs,nn**1121** nn8141 aj8549

of the first year without blemish:

wcj,nn,pnx**4503** wcj,pl,nn,pnx**5262** dfp,pl,nn6499

30 And their meat offering and their drink offerings for the bullocks, for the

dfp,pl,nn352 wcj,dfp,pl,nn3532 pp,nn,pnx4557 dfp,nn**4941**

rams, and for the lambs, *shall be* according to their number, after the manner:

nu259 wcj,cs,nn**8163** nn**2403** pr4480/pp,nn905 df,nn**8548** cs,nn**5930**

31 And one goat *for* a sin offering; beside the continual burnt offering,

nn,pnx**4503** wcj,pl,nn,pnx**5262**

his meat offering, and his drink offering.

df,nuor7637 wcj,dfp,nn**3117** nu7651 pl,nn6499 du,nu8147 pl,nn352 nu702/nu6240 pl,nn3532

32 And on the seventh day seven bullocks, two rams, *and* fourteen lambs

pl,cs,nn**1121** nn8141 aj8549

of the first year without blemish:

wcj,nn,pnx**4503** wcj,pl,nn,pnx**5262** dfp,pl,nn6499

33 And their meat offering and their drink offerings for the bullocks, for the

dfp,pl,nn352 wcj,dfp,pl,nn3532 pp,nn,pnx4557 pp,nn,pnx**4941**

rams, and for the lambs, *shall be* according to their number, after the manner:

nu259 wcj,cs,nn**8163** nn**2403** pr4480/pp,nn905 df,nn**8548** cs,nn**5930**

34 And one goat *for* a sin offering; beside the continual burnt offering,

nn,pnx**4503** wcj,nn,pnx**5262**

his meat offering, and his drink offering.

df,nuor8066 dfp,nn**3117** pp,pnx qmf**1961** nn6116 qmf**6213**

35 On the eighth day ye shall have a solemn assembly: ye shall do

ptn**3808**/cs,nn3605 nn5656 cs,nn**4399**

no servile work *therein:*

36 But ye shall offer a burnt offering, a sacrifice*made*by*fire, of a sweet
savor unto the LORD: one bullock, one ram, seven lambs of the first year
without blemish:

37 Their meat offering and their drink offerings for the bullock, for the ram,
and for the lambs, *shall be* according to their number, after the manner:

38 And one goat *for* a sin offering; beside the continual burnt offering,
and his meat offering, and his drink offering.

39 These *things* ye shall do unto the LORD in your set feasts, beside your
vows, and your freewill offerings, for your burnt offerings, and for your
meat offerings, and for your drink offerings, and for your peace offerings.

40 And Moses told the children of Israel according to all that the
LORD commanded Moses.

Women's Vows

30 And Moses spoke unto the heads of the tribes concerning the
children of Israel, saying, This *is* the thing which the LORD hath
commanded.

2 If a man vow a vow unto the LORD, or swear an oath to bind his
soul with a bond; he shall not break his word, he shall do according to all
that proceedeth out of*his*mouth.

3 If a woman also vow a vow unto the LORD, and bind herself by a bond,
being in her father's house in her youth;

4 And her father hear her vow, and her bond wherewith she hath
bound her soul, and her father shall hold*his*peace at her: then all her
vows shall stand, and every bond wherewith she hath bound her soul shall
stand.

5 But if her father disallow her in the day that he heareth; not
any of her vows, or of her bonds wherewith she hath bound her soul, shall

qmf6965   wcj,nn3068   qmf5545   pp,pnx   cj3588   nn,pnx1   hipf5106   pnx(853)

stand: and the LORD shall forgive her, because her father disallowed   her.

              wcj,cj518   qna1961/qmf1961   pp,nn376   wcj,pl,nn,pnx5088/pr,pnx5921 cj176   cs,nn4008

6 And   if   she had*at*all a husband, when she   vowed,   or uttered

              du,nn,pnx8193   pnl834   qpf631/pr5921   nn,pnx5315

aught out of her   lips,   wherewith she bound her soul;

              nn,pnx376   wcj,qpf8085   wcj,hipf2790   pp,pnx   pp,cs,nn3117

7 And her husband heard it, and held*his*peace at her in the   day   that he

qnc,pnx8085   pl,nn,pnx5088   wcj,qpf6965   wcj,pl,nn,pnx632   pnl834   qpf631/pr5921

heard it: then her   vows shall stand, and her   bonds   wherewith she bound her

nn,pnx5315   qmf6965

soul shall stand.

              wcj,cj518   nn,pnx376   himf5106   pnx(853)   pp,cs,nn3117   qnc8085

8 But   if   her husband disallowed   her on the   day   that he heard it;

                    (853)   nn,pnx5088   pnl834/pr,pnx5921   wcj(853)

then   he   shall   make   her   vow   which*she*vowed,   and

              cs,nn4008   du,nn,pnx8193   pnl834   qpf631/pr5921   nn,pnx5315

that*which*she*uttered with her   lips,   wherewith she bound   her   soul,

wcs,hipf6565   wcj,nn3068   qmf5545   pp,pnx

of*none*effect: and the LORD shall forgive her.

              nn3605   wcj,cs,nn5088   nn490   wcj,qptp1644   pnl834

9 But every   vow   of a widow, and of her that is divorced, wherewith they

qpf631/pr5921   nn,pnx5315   qmf6965   pr,pnx5921

have bound their souls, shall stand against her.

              wcj,cj518   qpf5087   nn,pnx376   cs,nn1004 cj176 qpf631/pr5921   nn,pnx5315

10 And   if   she vowed in her husband's house, or   bound her soul by a

nn632   pp,nn7621

bond with an oath;

              nn,pnx376   wcj,qpf8085   wcj,hipf2790   pp,pnx   hipf5106   pnx(853)

11 And her husband heard it, and held*his*peace at her, and disallowed

ptn3808   cs,nn3605   pl,nn,pnx5088   wcj,qpf6965   wcj,cs,nn3605   nn632   pnl834

her not: then   all   her vows shall stand, and every   bond wherewith she

qpf631/pr5921   nn,pnx5315   qmf6965

bound her soul shall stand.

              wcj,cj518   nn,pnx376   hina6565/himf6565/pnx(853)   pp,cs,nn3117   qnc,pnx8085

12 But   if   her husband hath utterly*made*them*void on the   day   he heard

              cs,nn3605   cs,nn4161   du,nn,pnx8193   pp,pl,nn,pnx5088

them; then whatsoever proceeded out of her   lips   concerning her   vows,   or

              wcj,pp,cs,nn632   nn,pnx5315   ptn3808   qmf6965   nn,pnx376

concerning the   bond of her soul,   shall not   stand: her husband

              hipf,pnx6565   wcj,nn3068   qmf5545 pp,pnx

hath*made*them*void; and the LORD shall forgive her.

              cs,nn3605   nn5088   wcj,cs,nn3605   nn632   cs,nn7621   pp,pinc6031   nn5315   nn,pnx376

13 Every vow, and every binding oath to afflict the soul, her husband may

himf,pnx6965   wcj,nn,pnx376   himf,pnx6565

establish it, or her husband may make*it*void.

              wcj,cj518   nn,pnx376   hina2790/himf2790   pp,pnx   pr4480/nn3117   pr413   nn3117

14 But   if   her husband altogether*hold*his*peace at her from day to day;

wcs,hipf6965   (853) cs,nn3605   pl,nn,pnx5088 cj176 (853) cs,nn3605   pl,nn,pnx632 pnl834   pr,pnx5921

then he establisheth   all   her vows,   or   all her bonds, which are upon

hipf6965   pnx(853)   cj3588   hipf2790   pp,pnx   pp,cs,nn3117

her: he confirmeth   them, because he held*his*peace at her in the   day   that

qnc,pnx8085

he heard them.

wcj,cj518   hina6565/himf6565/pnx(853)   ad310   qnc,pnx8085

15 But   if   he shall any*ways*make*them*void after that he hath heard

wcs,qpf5375 (853)   nn,pnx5771

them; then he shall bear   her iniquity.

pndm428   df,pl,nn2706   pnl834   nn3068   pipf6680   (853)   nn4872   pr996

16 These are the statutes, which the LORD commanded   Moses, between a

nn376   pp,nn,pnx802   pr996   nn1   pp,nn,pnx1323   pp,pl,nn,pnx5271

man and his   wife,   between the father and his daughter, being yet in her   youth

nn,pnx1   cs,nn1004

in her father's house.

War Against Midian

nn3068   wcs,pimf1696   pr413   nn4872   pp,qnc559

31

2 And the LORD spoke unto Moses, saying,

qmv5358/cs,nn5360   pl,cs,nn1121   nn3478   pr4480/pr854   df,nn4084

2 Avenge   the   children of Israel   of   the   Midianites:

ad310   nimf622   pr413   pl,nn,pnx5971

afterward shalt thou be gathered unto thy people.

nn4872   wcs,pimf1696   pr413   df,nn5971   pp,qnc559   nimv2502   pl,nn376   pr4480/pr,pnx854

3 And Moses spoke unto the people, saying, Arm some of yourselves unto

dfp,nn6635   wcj,qmf1961   pr5921   nn4080   pp,qnc5414/cs,nn5360   nn3068

the war, and let them   go   against the Midianites, and   avenge   the LORD of

pp,nn4080

Midian.

dfp,nn4294/nu505/dfp,nn4294/nu505   pp,cs,nn3605   pl,cs,nn4294   nn3478

4 Of every*tribe*a*thousand, throughout   all   the tribes of Israel, shall ye

qmf7971   dfp,nn6635

send to the war.

wcs,nimf4560   pr4480/pl,cs,nu505   nn3478   nu505

5 So there were delivered out*of*the*thousands of Israel, a thousand of every

dfp,nn4294   du,nu8147/nu6240   nu505   pl,cs,qptp2502   nn6635

tribe,   twelve   thousand armed for war.

nn4872   wcs,qmf7971   pnx(853)   dfp,nn6635   nu505   dfp,nn4294   pnx(853)

6 And Moses   sent   them to the war, a thousand of every   tribe

wcj(853)   nn6372   cs,nn1121   nn499   df,nn3548   dfp,nn6635   df,nn6944

them, and   Phinehas the   son   of Eleazar the priest, to the   war,   with the holy

wcj,pl,cs,nn3627   wcj,pl,nn2689   df,nn8643   pp,nn,pnx3027

instruments, and the trumpets to blow in his   hand.

wcs,qmf6633   pr5921   nn4080   pp,pnl834   nn3068   pipf6680   (853)

7 And they warred against the Midianites,   as   the LORD commanded

nn4872   wcs,qmf2026 cs,nn3605   nn2145

Moses; and they slew   all   the males.

qpf2026   wcj(853)   pl,cs,nn4428   nn4080   pr5921

8 And   they   slew   the   kings   of   Midian,   beside   the

pl,nn,pnx2491   (853)   nn189   wcj(853)   nn7552   wcj(853)   nn6698

rest*of*them*that*were*slain; namely,   Evi, and   Rekem, and   Zur, and

wcj(853)   nn2354   wcj(853)   nn7254   cs,nu2568   pl,cs,nn4428   nn4080   wcj(853)   nn1109   cs,nn1121

Hur, and   Reba, five   kings of Midian: Balaam also the   son   of

nn1160   qpf2026   dfp,nn2719

Beor they slew with the sword.

pl,cs,nn1121   nn3478   (853)   pl,cs,nn802   nn4080   wcs,qmf7617

9 And the children of Israel took all   the women of Midian captives, and

wcj(853)   nn,pnx**2945**   qpf962   wcj(853)   cs,nn3605   nn,pnx929   wcj(853) cs,nn3605

their little ones, and took*the*spoil   of   all   their cattle, and   all

pl,nn,pnx4735   wcj(853) cs,nn3605   nn,pnx**2428**

their flocks, and   all   their goods.

qpf**8313**   wcj(853) cs,nn3605   pl,nn,pnx5892   pp,pl,nn,pnx**4186**   wcj(853)

10 And they burnt   all   their   cities wherein they   dwelt,   and

cs,nn3605   pl,nn,pnx2918   dfp,nn784

all   their goodly castles, with fire.

wcs,qmf3947 (853) cs,nn3605   df,nn7998   wcj(853) cs,nn3605   df,nn4455   dfp,nn**120**

11 And they   took   all   the spoil, and   all   the prey, *both* of men

wcj,dfp,nn929

and of beasts.

wcs,himf935 (853)   df,nn**7628**   wcj(853)   df,nn4455   wcj(853)   df,nn7998

12 And they brought   the captives, and   the prey, and   the spoil,

pr413   nn4872   wcj(pr413)   nn499   df,nn**3548**   wcj,pr413   cs,nn**5712**   pl,cs,nn**1121**

unto Moses, and   Eleazar the priest, and unto the congregation of the children

nn3478   pr413   df,nn**4264** pr413   pl,cs,nn**6160**   nn4124   pnl834   pr5921   nn3383

of Israel, unto the camp   at   the plains of Moab, which *are* by   Jordan *near*

nn3405

Jericho.

nn4872   wcj,nn499   df,nn**3548**   wcj,cs,nn3605   pl,cs,nn**5387**

13 And Moses, and Eleazar the   priest, and   all   the princes of the

df,nn**5712**   wcs,qmf3318   pp,qnc,pnx7125   pr413/pr4480/nn2351   dfp,nn**4264**

congregation, went forth to   meet   them   without   the camp.

nn4872   wcs,qmf**7107**   pr5921   pl,cs,qptp**6485**   df,nn**2428**   pl,cs,nn**8269**

14 And Moses was wroth with the officers of the host, *with* the captains over

df,pl,nu**505**   wcj,pl,cs,nn**8269**   df,pl,nu3967   df,pl,qpta935   pr4480/cs,nn**6635**/df,nn4421

thousands, and captains over hundreds, which came from*the*battle.

nn4872   wcs,qmf559 pr,pnx413   he,pipf**2421**/cs,nn3605/nn**5347**

15 And Moses   said   unto them, Have*ye*saved*all*the*women*alive?

ptdm2005   pndm2007   qpf**1961**   pp,pl,cs,nn**1121**   nn3478   pp,cs,nn**1697**   nn1109

16 Behold, these caused the children of Israel, through the counsel of Balaam,

pp,qnc4560   nn**4604**   pp,nn**3068** pr5921   cs,nn**1697**   nn6465   wcs,qmf**1961**

to commit trespass against the LORD   in   the matter of Peor, and there   was   a

df,nn4046   pp,cs,nn**5712**   nn**3068**

plague among the congregation of the LORD.

wcj,ad6258   qmv**2026** cs,nn3605 nn2145   dfp,nn**2945**   qmv**2026** wcj,cs,nn3605

17 Now therefore kill   every male among the little ones, and   kill   every

nn**802**   cs,qpta**3045** nn376   pp,cs,nn4904   nn2145

woman that hath known man by   lying   with him.

wcj,cs,nn3605   dfp,pl,nn**802** df,nn**2945** pnl834   ptn**3808** qpf**3045**   nn2145   cs,nn4904

18 But   all   the women children, that have not known a man by lying with

himv**2421**   pp,pnx

him, keep alive for yourselves.

wcj,pnp859 qmv2583 pr4480/nn2351   dfp,nn**4264** cs,nu7651 pl,nn**3117**   cs,nn3605   qpta**2026**

19 And do   ye   abide without the camp seven days: whosoever hath killed

nn**5315**   wcj,cs,nn3605   qpta**5060**   dfp,nn2491 htmf**2398**   pnp859

any person, and whosoever hath touched any slain, purify *both* yourselves and your

wcj,nn,pnx**7628**   df,nuor7992 dfp,nn**3117**   df,nuor7637 wcj,dfp,nn**3117**

captives on the third day, and on the seventh day.

htmf**2398** wcj,cs,nn3605   nn899   wcj,cs,nn3605 cs,nn3627   nn**5785**

20 And purify   all   *your* raiment, and   all   that*is*made of skins, and

wcj,cs,nn3605 cs,nn4639   pl,nn**5795**   wcj,cs,nn3605 cs,nn3627   nn6086

all   work of goats' *hair*, and all things made of wood.

Division of the Booty

nn499   df,nn3548 wcs,qmf559 pr413   pl,cs,nn376   df,nn6635   df,pl,qpta935
21 And Eleazar the priest said unto the men of war which went to the

dfp,nn4421 pndm2063   cs,nn2708   df,nn8451 pnl834   nn3068   pipf6680   (853)   nn4872
battle, This is the ordinance of the law which the LORD commanded   Moses;

ad389   (853)   df,nn2091   wcj(853)   df,nn3701 (853)   df,nn5178 (853)   df,nn1270 (853)
22 Only   the gold, and   the silver,   the brass,   the iron,   the

df,nn913   wcj(853)   df,nn5777
tin, and   the lead,

cs,nn3605   nn1697 pnl834   qmf935   dfp,nn784   himf5674   dfp,nn784
23 Every thing that may abide the fire, ye shall make*it*go through the fire,

wcs,qpf2891   ad389   htmf2398   pp,pl,cs,nn4325
and it shall be clean: nevertheless it shall be purified with the   water   of

nn5079   wcj,nn3605 pnl834   qmf935   ptn3808   dfp,nn784   himf5674
separation: and   all   that abideth not the fire ye shall make go through the

dfp,pl,nn4325
water.

wcs,pipf3526   pl,nn,pnx899   df,nuor7637 dfp,nn3117
24 And ye shall wash your clothes on the seventh day, and ye shall

wcs,qpf2891   wcj,ad310   qmf935 pr413   df,nn4264
be clean, and afterward ye shall come into the camp.

nn3068 wcs,qmf559 pr413   nn4872   pp,qnc559
25 And the LORD spoke unto Moses, saying,

qmv5375 (853)   cs,nn7218   cs,nn4455   df,nn7628   dfp,nn120   wcj,dfp,nn929
26 Take   the sum of the prey that was taken, both of man and of beast,

pnp859   wcj,nn499   df,nn3548   wcj,pl,cs,nn7218 pl,cs,nn1   df,nn5712
thou, and Eleazar the priest, and the   chief   fathers of the congregation:

wcj,qpf2673 (853)   df,nn4455   pr996   pl,cs,qpta8610
27 And divide   the prey into two parts; between them that   took   the

df,nn4421   df,pl,qpta3318   dfp,nn6635   wcj,pr996 cs,nn3605   df,nn5712
war upon them, who went out to battle, and between all the congregation:

wcj,hipf7311   nn4371   pp,nn3068 pr4480/pr854 pl,cs,nn376 df,nn4421
28 And   levy a tribute unto the LORD of   the men of war which

df,pl,qpta3318 dfp,nn6635 nu259 nn5315 pr4480/cs,nn2568 df,pl,nu3967   pr4480   df,nn120   wcj,pr4480
went out to battle: one soul of five hundred, both of the persons, and   of   the

df,nn1241   wcj,pr4480   df,pl,nn2543   wcj,pr4480   df,nn6629
beefs, and   of   the asses, and   of   the sheep:

qmf3947   pr4480/nn,pnx4276   wcs,qpf5414   pp,nn499   df,nn3548
29 Take it of*their*half, and   give it unto Eleazar the priest, for a

cs,nn8641   nn3068
heave offering of the LORD.

pl,cs,nn1121   nn3478 wcj,pr4480/cs,nn4276   qmf3947 nu259 qptp270 pr4480
30 And of the children of Israel's   half,   thou shalt take one portion of

df,pl,nu2572 pr4480   df,nn120   pr4480   df,nn1241 pr4480   df,pl,nn2543 wcj,pr4480   df,nn6629
fifty,   of the persons, of the beefs, of the asses, and of the flocks,

pr4480/cs,nn3605   df,nn929   wcs,qpf5414 pnx(853)   pp,pl,nn3881   pl,cs,qpta8104
of*all*manner of beasts, and give   them unto the Levites, which keep   the

cs,nn4931   cs,nn4908   nn3068
charge of the tabernacle of the LORD.

nn4872   wcj,nn499   df,nn3548 wcs,qmf6213 pp,pnl834   nn3068   pipf6680   (853)
31 And Moses and Eleazar the priest did   as   the LORD commanded

nn4872
Moses.

df,nn4455   cs,nn3499   df,nn957 pnl834   cs,nn5971 df,nn6635
32 And the booty, being the rest of the prey which the men of war had

qpf962　wcs,qmf**1961**　nu8337　pl,nu3967　nu**505**　wcj,pl,nu7657　nu**505**　wcj,cs,nu2568　pl,nu**505**

caught, was six hundred thousand and seventy thousand and five thousand

nn6629

sheep,

du,nu8147/wcj,pl,nu7657　nu**505**　wcj,nn1241

33 And threescore*and*twelve thousand beefs,

wcj,pl,nu8346　nu259　nu**505**　wcj,pl,nn2543

34 And threescore and one thousand asses,

wcj,nu7970　du,nu8147　nu**505**　wcj,cs,nn5315/nn120　cs,nn3605/cs,nn5315　pr4480　df,pl,nn802　pnl834

35 And thirty and two thousand persons in all, of women that

ptn**3808**　qpf**3045**　cs,nn4904　nn2145

had not known man by lying with him.

df,nn4275　cs,nn2506　df,pl,qpta3318　dfp,nn6635　wcs,qmf**1961**

36 And the half, *which was* the portion of them that went out to war, was

cs,nn4557　cs,nu7969　pl,nu3967　nu**505**　wcj,cs,nu7651　(pl,nu**505**)　wcj,nu7970　nu**505**

in number three hundred thousand and seven and thirty thousand and

wcj,cs,nu2568　pl,nu3967　df,nn6629

five hundred sheep:

pp,nn**3068**　df,nn4371　pr4480　df,nn6629　wcs,qmf**1961**　cs,nu8337　pl,nu3967

37 And the LORD's tribute of the sheep was six hundred and

nu2568/wcj,pl,nu7657

threescore*and*fifteen.

wcj,df,nn1241　wcj,nu7970　nu8337　nu**505**　pp,nn**3068**

38 And the beefs *were* thirty and six thousand; of which the LORD's

wcj,nn,pnx4371　du,nu8147/wcj,pl,nu7657

tribute *was* threescore*and*twelve.

wcj,pl,nn2543　nu7970　nu**505**　wcj,cs,nu2568　pl,nu3967

39 And the asses *were* thirty thousand and five hundred; of which the

pp,nn**3068**　wcj,nn,pnx4371　wcj,pl,nu8346　nu259

LORD's tribute *was* threescore and one.

wcj,cs,nn5315/nn120　nu8337/nu6240　nu**505**　pp,nn**3068**　wcj,nn,pnx4371

40 And the persons *were* sixteen thousand; of which the LORD's tribute

wcj,nu7970　du,nu8147　nn5315

was thirty and two persons.

nn4872　wcs,qmf**5414**　(853)　nn4371　nn**3068**　cs,nn**8641**

41 And Moses gave the tribute, *which was* the LORD's heave offering,

pp,nn499　df,nn**3548**　pp,pnl834　nn**3068**　pipf**6680**　(853)　nn4872

unto Eleazar the priest, as the LORD commanded Moses.

pl,cs,nn**1121**　nn3478　wcj,pr4480/nn4276　pnl834　nn4872　qpf2673　pr4480

42 And of the children of Israel's half, which Moses divided from the

df,pl,nn376　df,pl,qpta**6633**

men that warred,

cs,nn4275　df,nn**5712**　wcs,qmf**1961**　cs,nu7969　pl,nu3967

43 (Now the half *that pertained unto* the congregation was three hundred

nu**505**　wcj,nu7970　nu**505**　cs,nu7651　pl,nu**505**　wcj,cs,nu2568　pl,nu3967　(pr4480)　df,nn6629

thousand and thirty thousand *and* seven thousand and five hundred sheep,

wcj,nu7970　nu8337　nu**505**　wcj,nn1241

44 And thirty and six thousand beefs,

nu7970　nu**505**　wcj,pl,nn2543　wcj,cs,nu2568　pl,nu3967

45 And thirty thousand asses and five hundred,

nu8337/nu6240　nu**505**　wcj,cs,nn5315/nn120

46 And sixteen thousand persons;)

pl,cs,nn**1121**　nn3478　pr4480/cs,nn4276　nn4872　wcs,qmf3947　nu259　(853)　df,qptp270　pr4480

47 Even of the children of Israel's half, Moses took one portion of

df,pl,nu2572　pr4480　df,nn120　wcj,pr4480　df,nn929　wcs,qmf**5414**　pnx(853)　pp,pl,nn3881

fifty, *both* of man and of beast, and gave them unto the Levites, pl,cs,qpta8104   cs,nn4931   cs,nn4908   nn3068   pp,pnl834   nn3068   pipf6680

which   kept   the charge of the tabernacle of the LORD;   as   the LORD commanded

(853)   nn4872

Moses.

df,pl,qptp6485   pnl834   pp,pl,cs,nu505   df,nn6635   pl,cs,nn8269

48 And the officers which *were* over thousands of the host, the captains of

df,pl,nu505   wcj,pl,cs,nn8269   df,pl,nu3967   wcs,qmf7126   pr413   nn4872

thousands, and captains of hundreds, came near unto Moses:

wcs,qmf559   pr413   nn4872   pl,nn,pnx5650   qpf5375   (853)   cs,nn7218

49 And they   said   unto Moses, Thy servants have taken   the   sum of the

pl,cs,nn376   df,nn4421   pnl834   pp,nn,pnx3027   nipf6485   wcj,ptn3808   nn376

men   of   war   which *are* under our charge, and there lacketh   not   one man

pr,pnx4480

of   us.

wcs,himf7126   (853)   cs,nn7133   nn3068   pnl834   nn376

50 We have therefore brought   an oblation for the LORD, what every man

qpf4672   cs,nn3627   nn2091   nn685   wcj,nn6781   nn2885   nn5694   wcj,nn3558

hath gotten, of jewels of gold, chains, and bracelets, rings, earrings, and tablets, to

pp,pinc3722   pr5921   pl,nn,pnx5315   pp,pl,cs,nn6440   nn3068

make*an*atonement for our   souls   before   the LORD.

nn4872   wcj,nn499   df,nn3548   wcs,qmf3947 (853)   df,nn2091   pr4480/pr,pnx854

51 And Moses and Eleazar the priest took   the gold   of   them, *even*

cs,nn3605   cs,nn4639   nn3627

all   wrought jewels.

cs,nn3605   cs,nn2091   df,nn8641   pnl834   hipf7311   pp,nn3068

52 And   all   the   gold   of the offering that they offered up to the LORD,

pr4480/pr854   pl,cs,nn8269   df,pl,nu505   wcj,pr4480/pr854   pl,cs,nn8269   df,pl,nu3967   wcs,qmf1961

of   the captains of thousands, and   of   the captains of hundreds,   was

nu8337/nu6240   nu505   cs,nu7651   pl,nu3967   wcj,pl,nu2572   nn8255

sixteen thousand seven hundred and   fifty   shekels.

pl,cs,nn376   df,nn6635   qpf962   nn376   pp,pnx

53 (*For* the   men   of   war   had taken spoil, every   man   for   himself.)

nn4872   wcj,nn499   df,nn3548   wcs,qmf3947 (853)   df,nn2091   pr4480/pr854   pl,cs,nn8269

54 And Moses and Eleazar the priest   took   the gold   of   the captains

df,pl,nu505   wcj,df,pl,nu3967   wcs,himf935   pnx(853)   pr413   cs,nn168

of thousands and of hundreds, and brought   it into the tabernacle of the

nn4150   nn2146   pp,pl,cs,nn1121   nn3478   pp,pl,cs,nn6440   nn3068

congregation, *for* a memorial for the children of Israel before the LORD.

Three Tribes Settle East of the Jordan

pp,pl,cs,nn1121   nn7205   wcj,pp,pl,cs,nn1121   nn1410   qpf1961   ad3966

32 Now the children of Reuben and the   children   of Gad had a very

aj6099   aj7227   wcj,nn4735   wcs,qmf7200   (853)   cs,nn776   nn3270

great multitude of cattle: and when they   saw   the land of Jazer,

wcj(853)   cs,nn776   nn1568   wcj,ptdm2009   df,nn4725   cs,nn4725   nn4735

and   the land of Gilead, that, behold, the place *was* a place for cattle;

pl,cs,nn1121   nn1410   wcj,pl,cs,nn1121   nn7205   wcs,qmf935   wcs,qmf559   pr413

2 The children of Gad and the   children   of   Reuben came   and spoke unto

nn4872   wcj,pr413   nn499   df,nn3548   wcj,pr413   pl,cs,nn5387   df,nn5712

Moses, and   to   Eleazar the priest, and   unto   the princes of the congregation,

pp,qnc559

saying,

nn5852　　　wcj,nn1769　　　wcj,nn3270　　　wcj,nn5247　　　wcj,nn2809　　　wcj,nn500

3 Ataroth, and Dibon, and Jazer, and Nimrah, and Heshbon, and Elealeh, and

wcj,nn7643　　wcj,nn5015　　wcj,nn1194

Shebam, and Nebo, and Beon,

df,nn776　　pnl834　　　nn3068　hipf5221　pp,pl,cs,nn6440　　cs,nn5712　　　nn3478

4 *Even* the country which the LORD smote before the congregation of Israel,

(pnp1931)　cs,nn776　　nn4735　　wcj,pp,pl,nn,pnx5650　　nn4735

is a land for cattle, and thy　servants　have cattle:

wcs,qmf559　　　cj518　　　qpf4672　nn2580　　pp,du,nn,pnx5869　　(853)

5 Wherefore,　said　they,　if　we have found grace in thy　sight,　let

df,pndm2063　df,nn776　　homf5414　　pp,pl,nn,pnx5650　　pp,nn272　　himf,pnx5674/ptn408

this　land be given unto thy　servants　for a possession, *and* bring*us*not*over

(853)　df,nn3383

Jordan.

nn4872　wcs,qmf559　　pp,pl,cs,nn1121　　nn1410　　wcj,pp,pl,cs,nn1121　　nn7205

6 And Moses　said　unto the children of Gad and to the　children　of Reuben,

he,pl,nn,pnx251 qmf935　dfp,nn4421　　wcj,pnp859 qmf3427　ad6311

Shall your brethren go　to　war,　and shall　ye　sit here?

wcj,pp,pnit4100　　himf5106　　(853)　　cs,nn3820　　pl,cs,nn1121　　nn3478

7 And　wherefore discourage ye　　　the　heart　of　the children of　Israel

pr4480/qnc5674　　pr413　df,nn776　pnl834　　nn3068　　qpf5414　pp,pnx

from*going*over into the land which the LORD hath given them?

ad3541　qpf6213　　pl,nn,pnx1　　　pp,qnc7971 pnx(853)　　　pr4480/nn6947

8 Thus　did　your fathers, when I　sent　　them from Kadesh-barnea to

pp,qnc7200 (853)　　df,nn776

see　　the land.

wcs,qmf5927　pr5704　cs,nn5158　　nn812　　wcs,qmf7200 (853)　df,nn776

9 For when they went up unto the valley of Eshcol, and　saw　　the land,

wcs,himf5106　(853)　cs,nn3820　pl,cs,nn1121　nn3478　　pp,ptn1115 qnc935

they discouraged　the heart of the children of Israel, that they should　not　go

pr413　df,nn776　pnl834　　nn3068　　qpf5414　pp,pnx

into the land which the LORD had given them.

nn3068　cs,nn639　wcs,qmf2734　df,pndm1931 dfp,nn3117　wcs,nimf7650　pp,qnc559

10 And the LORD's anger was kindled the　same　time, and he swore, saying,

cj518　　　df,pl,nn376　　df,pl,qpta5927　pr4480/nn4714　　pl,nu6242　nn8141

11 Surely none of the　men　that came up out*of*Egypt, from twenty years

pr4480/cs,nn1121　wcj,ad,lh4605　qmf7200 (853)　df,nn127　pnl834　nipf7650　　pp,nn85

old　and upward, shall see　　the land which I swore unto Abraham, unto

pp,nn3327　wcj,pp,nn3290　cj3588　　ptn3808 pipf4390　pr,pnx310

Isaac, and unto Jacob; because they have not wholly followed me:

ptn1115　nn3612　cs,nn1121　　nn3312　　df,nn7074　wcj,nn3091　cs,nn1121

12 Save Caleb the　son　of Jephunneh the　Kenezite, and Joshua the　son　of

nn5126 cj3588　　pipf4390　pr310　　nn3068

Nun: for they have wholly followed the LORD.

nn3068　cs,nn639　wcs,qmf2734　　pp,nn3478

13 And the LORD's anger was kindled against Israel, and he made them

wcs,himf,pnx5128　dfp,nn4057　pl,nu705　nn8141　pr5704 cs,nn3605　df,nn1755　df,qpta6213

wander in the wilderness forty years, until　all　the generation, that had done

df,aj7451　pp,du,cs,nn5869　nn3068　qnc8552

evil in the　sight　of the LORD, was consumed.

wcj,pndm2009　qpf6965　pr8478/pl,nn,pnx1　cs,nn8635　aj2400

14 And, behold, ye are risen up in*your*fathers'*stead, an increase of sinful

pl,nn376　pp,qnc5595/pr5921 ad5750　cs,nn2740 cs,nn639　nn3068　pr413　nn3478

men, to augment　yet the fierce anger of the LORD toward Israel.

cj3588   qmf7725   pr4480/pr,pnx310   ad5750 wcs,qpf3254 pp,hinc,pnx5117
15 For if ye turn away from after him, he will yet again leave them in

dfp,nn4057   wcs,pipf7843 pp,cs,nn3605 df,pndm2088 df,nn5971
the wilderness; and ye shall destroy all this people.

        wcs,qmf5066   pr,pnx413   wcs,qmf559   qmf1129 pl,cs,nn1488/nn6629 ad6311
16 And they came near unto him, and said, We will build sheepfolds here

pp,nn,pnx4735   wcj,pl,nn5892   pp,nn,pnx2945
for our cattle, and cities for our little ones:

        wcj,pnp587   nimf2502/pl,qptp2363   pp,pl,cs,nn6440   pl,cs,nn1121   nn3478
17 But we ourselves will go*ready*armed before the children of Israel,

pr5704/pnl834/cj518   hipf,pnx935   pr413   nn,pnx4725   nn,pnx2945   wcj,qpf3427
until we have brought them unto their place: and our little ones shall dwell

df,nn4013 pp,pl,cs,nn5892 pr4480/pl,cs,nn6440   pl,cs,qpta3427   df,nn776
in the fenced cities because of the inhabitants of the land.

      ptn3808   qmf7725   pr413   pl,nn,pnx1004   pr5704   pl,cs,nn1121   nn3478
18 We will not return unto our houses, until the children of Israel have

htnc5157   nn376   nn,pnx5159
inherited every man his inheritance.

      cj3588   ptn3808 qmf5157 pr,pnx854   pr4480/nn5676   dfp,nn3383   wcj,ad1973
19 For we will not inherit with them on*yonder*side Jordan, or forward;

cj3588   nn,pnx5159   qpf935 pr,pnx413   pr4480/cs,nn5676 df,nn3383 nn,lh4217
because our inheritance is fallen to us on*this*side Jordan eastward.

      nn4872   wcs,qmf559 pr,pnx413   cj518   qmf6213 (853) df,pndm2088 df,nn1697 cj518
20 And Moses said unto them, If ye will do this thing, if ye will

nimf2502 pp,pl,cs,nn6440   nn3068   dfp,nn4421
go armed before the LORD to war,

        wcs,qpf5674 cs,nn3605 pp,pnx   qptp2502   (853) df,nn3383 pp,pl,cs,nn6440   nn3068
21 And will go all of you armed over Jordan before the LORD,

pr5704   hinc,pnx3423 (853) pl,qptp,pnx341 pr4480/pl,nn,pnx6440
until he hath driven out his enemies from before him,

        df,nn776   wcs,nipf3533 pp,pl,cs,nn6440   nn3068   wcj,ad310   qmf7725
22 And the land be subdued before the LORD: then afterward ye shall return,

wcs,qpf1961 aj5355   pr4480/nn3068   wcj,pr4480/nn3478   df,pndm2063 df,nn776
and be guiltless before*the*LORD, and before Israel; and this land shall

wcs,qpf1961 pp,pnx   pp,nn272   pp,pl,cs,nn6440   nn3068
be your possession before the LORD.

      wcj,cj518   ptn3808 qmf6213 ad3651 ptdm2009   qpf2398   pp,nn3068
23 But if ye will not do so, behold, ye have sinned against the LORD:

wcj,qmv3045   nn,pnx2403 (pnl834)   qmf4672/pnx(853)
and be sure your sin will find*you*out.

      qmv1129 pp,pnx pl,nn,pnx5892   pp,nn,pnx2945   wcj,pl,nn1448   pp,nn,pnx6792   qmf6213
24 Build you cities for your little ones, and folds for your sheep; and do

      wcj,df,qpta3318   pr4480/nn,pnx6310
that which hath proceeded out of*your*mouth.

      pl,cs,nn1121   nn1410   wcj,pl,cs,nn1121   nn7205   wcs,qmf559 pr413   nn4872
25 And the children of Gad and the children of Reuben spoke unto Moses,

pp,qnc559   pl,nn,pnx5650   qmf6213 pp,pnl834   nn,pnx113   pipt6680
saying, Thy servants will do as my lord commandeth.

      nn,pnx2945   pl,nn,pnx802   pl,nn,pnx4735 wcj,cs,nn3605   nn,pnx929   qmf1961
26 Our little ones, our wives, our flocks, and all our cattle, shall be

ad8033   pp,pl,cs,nn5892   df,nn1568
there in the cities of Gilead:

      wcj,pl,nn,pnx5650   qmf5674   cs,nn3605 cs,qptp2502   nn6635 pp,pl,cs,nn6440
27 But thy servants will pass over, every man armed for war, before the

nn3068   dfp,nn4421 pp,pnl834   nn,pnx113 qpta1696
LORD to battle, as my lord saith.

28 So concerning them Moses commanded Eleazar the priest, and
Joshua the son of Nun, and the chief fathers of the tribes of the children
of Israel:

29 And Moses said unto them, If the children of Gad and the children of
Reuben will pass*with*you*over Jordan, every man armed to battle, before
the LORD, and the land shall be subdued before you; then ye shall give them
the land of Gilead for a possession:

30 But if they will not pass over with you armed, they shall
have possessions among you in the land of Canaan.

31 And the children of Gad and the children of Reuben answered, saying,
As the LORD hath said unto thy servants, so will we do.

32 We will pass over armed before the LORD into the land of Canaan, that
the possession of our inheritance on*this*side Jordan *may be* ours.

33 And Moses gave unto them, *even* to the children of Gad, and to the
children of Reuben, and unto half the tribe of Manasseh the son of
Joseph, the kingdom of Sihon king of the Amorites, and the kingdom of
Og king of Bashan, the land, with the cities thereof in the coasts, *even* the
cities of the country round about.

34 And the children of Gad built Dibon, and Ataroth, and
Aroer,

35 And Atroth, Shophan, and Jaazer, and Jogbehah,

36 And Beth-nimrah, and Beth-haran, fenced cities: and folds
for sheep.

37 And the children of Reuben built Heshbon, and Elealeh, and
Kirjathaim,

38 And Nebo, and Baal-meon, (their names being changed), and
Shibmah: and gave*other*names unto the cities which they built.

pl,cs,nn**1121**   nn4353   cs,nn**1121**   nn4519   wcs,qmf**1980**   nn,lh1568

39 And the children of Machir the son of Manasseh went to Gilead, and

wcs,qmf,pnx3920   wcs,himf**3423**   (853)   df,nn567   pnl834   pp,pnx

took it, and dispossessed the Amorite which *was* in it.

nn4872   wcs,qpf**5414**   (853)   df,nn1568   pp,nn4353   cs,nn**1121**   nn4519

40 And Moses gave Gilead unto Machir the son of Manasseh; and he

wcs,qmf**3427**   pp,pnx

dwelt therein.

wcj,nn2971   cs,nn**1121**   nn4519   qpf**1980**   wcs,qmf3920   (853)   pl,nn,pnx2333

41 And Jair the son of Manasseh went and took the small towns

wcs,qmf**7121** pnx(853)   nn2334

thereof, and called them Havoth-jair.

wcj,nn5025   qpf**1980**   wcs,qmf3920 (853)   nn7079   wcj(853)   pl,nn,pnx1323

42 And Nobah went and took Kenath, and the villages thereof, and

wcs,qmf**7121**   nn5025   pp,nn,pnx8034

called it Nobah, after his own name.

Israel's Wilderness Itinerary

pndm428   pl,cs,nn**4550**   pl,cs,nn**1121**   nn3478   pnl834   qpf3318

33 These *are* the journeys of the children of Israel, which went forth

pr4480/cs,nn**776**   nn4714   pp,pl,nn,pnx**6635**   pp,cs,nn**3027**

out*of*the*land of Egypt with their armies under the hand of

nn4872   wcj,nn175

Moses and Aaron.

nn4872   wcs,qmf3789   (853)   pl,nn,pnx4161   pp,pl,nn,pnx4550   pr5921

2 And Moses wrote their goings out according to their journeys by the

cs,nn**6310**   nn3068   wcj,pndm428   pp,pl,nn,pnx4550

commandment of the LORD: and these *are* their journeys according to their

pp,pl,nn,pnx4161

goings out.

wcs,qmf5265   pr4480/nn7486   df,aj**7223** dfp,nn2320   pp,nu2568/nu6240 nn**3117**

3 And they departed from Rameses in the first month, on the fifteenth day of

df,aj**7223** dfp,nn2320   pr4480/cs,nn4283   df,nn**6453**   pl,cs,nn**1121**   nn3478   qpf3318

the first month; on*the*morrow after the passover the children of Israel went out

qpta7311 pp,nn**3027**   pp,du,cs,nn**5869**   cs,nn3605   nn4714

with a high hand in the sight of all the Egyptians.

wcj,nn4714   pl,pipt**6912** cs,nn3605   nn1060   (853)   pnl834   nn**3068**   hipf**5221**

4 For the Egyptians buried all *their* firstborn, which the LORD had smitten

pp,pnx   wcj,pp,pl,nn,pnx**430**   nn**3068**   qpf**6213**   pl,nn**8201**

among them: upon their gods also the LORD executed judgments.

pl,cs,nn**1121**   nn3478   wcs,qmf5265   pr4480/nn7486   wcs,qmf2583   pp,nn5523

5 And the children of Israel removed from Rameses, and pitched in Succoth.

wcs,qmf5265   pr4480/nn5523   wcs,qmf2583   pp,nn864   pnl834

6 And they departed from Succoth, and pitched in Etham, which *is* in the

pp,cs,nn7097   df,nn4057

edge of the wilderness.

wcs,qmf5265   pr4480/nn864   wcs,qmf**7725**   pr5921   nn6367   pnl834

7 And they removed from Etham, and turned again unto Pi-hahiroth, which *is*

pr5921/pl,cs,nn**6440**   nn1189   wcs,qmf2583 pp,pl,cs,nn**6440**   nn4024

before Baal-zephon: and they pitched before Migdol.

wcs,qmf5265   pr4480/pl,cs,nn**6440**   nn6367   wcs,qmf**5674**   pp,cs,nn**8432**

8 And they departed from before Pi-hahiroth, and passed through the midst of

df,nn3220 df,nn,lh4057 wcs,qmf1980 nu7969 pl,nn3117 cs,nn1870 pp,cs,nn4057

the sea into the wilderness, and went three days' journey in the wilderness of

nn864 wcs,qmf2583 pp,nn4785

Etham, and pitched in Marah.

wcs,qmf5265 pr4480/nn4785 wcs,qmf935 nn,lh362 wcj,pp,nn362

9 And they removed from Marah, and came unto Elim: and in Elim *were*

du,nu8147/nu6240 pl,cs,nn5869 pl,nn4325 wcj,pl,nu7657 pl,nn8558 wcs,qmf2583

twelve fountains of water, and threescore*and*ten palm trees; and they pitched

ad8033

there.

wcs,qmf5265 pr4480/nn362 wcs,qmf2583 pr5921 nn5488 cs,nn3220

10 And they removed from Elim, and encamped by the Red sea.

wcs,qmf5265 nn5488 pr4480/cs,nn3220 wcs,qmf2583 pp,cs,nn4057

11 And they removed from the Red sea, and encamped in the wilderness

nn5512

of Sin.

wcs,qmf5265 pr4480/cs,nn4057 nn5512 wcs,qmf2583

12 And they took*their*journey out*of*the*wilderness of Sin, and encamped in

pp,nn1850

Dophkah.

wcs,qmf5265 pr4480/nn1850 wcs,qmf2583 pp,nn442

13 And they departed from Dophkah, and encamped in Alush.

wcs,qmf5265 pr4480/nn442 wcs,qmf2583 pp,nn7508 ad8033 qpf1961

14 And they removed from Alush, and encamped at Rephidim, where was

wcj,ptn3808 pl,nn4325 dfp,nn5971 pp,qnc8354

no water for the people to drink.

wcs,qmf5265 pr4480/nn7508 wcs,qmf2583 pp,cs,nn4057 nn5514

15 And they departed from Rephidim, and pitched in the wilderness of Sinai.

wcs,qmf5265 pr4480/cs,nn4057 nn5514 wcs,qmf2583

16 And they removed from*the*desert of Sinai, and pitched at

pp,nn6914

Kibroth-hattaavah.

wcs,qmf5265 pr4480/nn6914 wcs,qmf2583 pp,nn2698

17 And they departed from Kibroth-hattaavah, and encamped at Hazeroth.

wcs,qmf5265 pr4480/nn2698 wcs,qmf2583 pp,nn7575

18 And they departed from Hazeroth, and pitched in Rithmah.

wcs,qmf5265 pr4480/nn7575 wcs,qmf2583 pp,nn7428

19 And they departed from Rithmah, and pitched at Rimmon-parez.

wcs,qmf5265 pr4480/nn7428 wcs,qmf2583 pp,nn3841

20 And they departed from Rimmon-parez, and pitched in Libnah.

wcs,qmf5265 pr4480/nn3841 wcs,qmf2583 pp,nn7446

21 And they removed from Libnah, and pitched at Rissah.

wcs,qmf5265 pr4480/nn7446 wcs,qmf2583 pp,nn6954

22 And they journeyed from Rissah, and pitched in Kehelathah.

wcs,qmf5265 pr4480/nn6954 wcs,qmf2583 pp,cs,nn2022 nn8234

23 And they went from Kehelathah, and pitched in mount Shapher.

wcs,qmf5265 pr4480/cs,nn2022 nn8234 wcs,qmf2583 pp,nn2732

24 And they removed from mount Shapher, and encamped in Haradah.

wcs,qmf5265 pr4480/nn2732 wcs,qmf2583 pp,nn4722

25 And they removed from Haradah, and pitched in Makheloth.

wcs,qmf5265 pr4480/nn4722 wcs,qmf2583 pp,nn8480

26 And they removed from Makheloth, and encamped at Tahath.

wcs,qmf5265 pr4480/nn8480 wcs,qmf2583 pp,nn8646

27 And they departed from Tahath, and pitched at Tarah.

wcs,qmf5265 pr4480/nn8646 wcs,qmf2583 pp,nn4989

28 And they removed from Tarah, and pitched in Mithcah.

wcs,qmf5265   pr4480/nn4989   wcs,qmf2583   pp,nn2832
29 And they went from Mithcah, and pitched in Hashmonah.

wcs,qmf5265   pr4480/nn2832   wcs,qmf2583   pp,nn4149
30 And they departed from Hashmonah, and encamped at Moseroth.

wcs,qmf5265   pr4480/nn4149   wcs,qmf2583   pp,nn1142
31 And they departed from Moseroth, and pitched in Bene-jaakan.

wcs,qmf5265   pr4480/nn1142   wcs,qmf2583   pp,nn2735
32 And they removed from Bene-jaakan, and encamped at Horhagidgad.

wcs,qmf5265   pr4480/nn2735   wcs,qmf2583   pp,nn3193
33 And they went from Horhagidgad, and pitched in Jotbathah.

wcs,qmf5265   pr4480/nn3193   wcs,qmf2583   pp,nn5684
34 And they removed from Jotbathah, and encamped at Ebronah.

wcs,qmf5265   pr4480/nn5684   wcs,qmf2583   pp,nn6100
35 And they departed from Ebronah, and encamped at Ezion-gaber.

wcs,qmf5265   pr4480/nn6100   wcs,qmf2583   pp,cs,nn4057   nn6790
36 And they removed from Ezion-gaber, and pitched in the wilderness of Zin,

pnp1931   nn6946
which is Kadesh.

wcs,qmf5265   pr4480/nn6946   wcs,qmf2583   df,nn2022 pp,nn2023   pp,cs,nn7097
37 And they removed from Kadesh, and pitched in mount Hor, in the edge

cs,nn776   nn123
of the land of Edom.

nn175   df,nn3548 wcs,qmf5927 pr413 df,nn2022 nn2023 pr5921   cs,nn6310
38 And Aaron the priest went up into mount Hor at the commandment of the

nn3068   wcs,qmf4191   ad8033   df,pl,nu705 pp,cs,nn8141   pl,cs,nn1121   nn3478
LORD, and died   there, in the fortieth year   after the children of Israel were

pp,qnc3318   pr4480/cs,nn776   nn4714   pp,nu259   (dfp,nn2320)   df,nuor2549 dfp,nn2320
come out of*the*land of Egypt, in the first day   of the fifth   month.

wcj,nn175   wcj,cs,nu3967   wcj,pl,nu6242   nu7969   nn8141   cs,nn1121
39 And Aaron was a hundred and twenty and three years   old   when he

pp,nn,pnx4194   df,nn2022 pp,nn2023
died   in mount Hor.

cs,nn4428   nn6166   df,nn3669   wcj,pnp1931 qpta3427   dfp,nn5045   pp,cs,nn776
40 And king Arad the Canaanite, which dwelt in the south in the land of

nn3667   wcs,qmf8085   pp,qnc935   pl,cs,nn1121   nn3478
Canaan, heard of the coming of the children of Israel.

wcs,qmf5265   df,nn2022 pr4480/nn2023   wcs,qmf2583   pp,nn6758
41 And they departed from mount Hor,   and pitched in Zalmonah.

wcs,qmf5265   pr4480/nn6758   wcs,qmf2583   pp,nn6325
42 And they departed from Zalmonah, and pitched in Punon.

wcs,qmf5265   pr4480/nn6325   wcs,qmf2583   pp,nn88
43 And they departed from Punon, and pitched in Oboth.

wcs,qmf5265   pr4480/nn88   wcs,qmf2583   pp,nn5863   pp,cs,nn1366
44 And they departed from Oboth, and pitched in Ije-abarim, in the border of

nn4124
Moab.

wcs,qmf5265   pr4480/nn5864   wcs,qmf2583   pp,nn1769
45 And they departed from Iim, and pitched in Dibon-gad.

wcs,qmf5265   pr4480/nn1769   wcs,qmf2583   pp,nn5963
46 And they removed from Dibon-gad, and encamped in Almon-diblathaim.

wcs,qmf5265   pr4480/nn5963   wcs,qmf2583   pp,pl,cs,nn2022
47 And they removed from Almon-diblathaim, and pitched in the mountains of

df,nn5682 pp,pl,cs,nn6440 nn5015
Abarim, before Nebo.

wcs,qmf5265   pr4480/pl,cs,nn2022   df,nn5682   wcs,qmf2583

48 And they departed from*the*mountains of Abarim, and pitched in the

pp,pl,cs,nn**6160**   nn4124   pr5921   nn3383   nn3405

plains of Moab by Jordan *near* Jericho.

wcs,qmf2583 pr5921 df,nn3383   pr4480/nn1020   pr5704   nn63

49 And they pitched by Jordan, from Beth-jesimoth *even* unto Abel-shittim in

pp,pl,cs,nn**6160**   nn4124

the plains of Moab.

Instructions for Taking Over Canaan

nn**3068**   wcs,pimf**1696** pr413   nn4872   pp,pl,cs,nn**6160**   nn4124   pr5921   nn3383

50 And the LORD spoke unto Moses in the plains of Moab by Jordan *near*

nn3405   pp,qnc**559**

Jericho, saying,

pimv**1696**   pr413   pl,cs,nn**1121**   nn3478   wcj,qpf**559** pr,pnx413   cj3588   pnp859

51 Speak unto the children of Israel, and say unto them, When ye are

pl,qpta**5674**   (853) df,nn3383 pr413   cs,nn776   nn3667

passed over   Jordan into the land of Canaan;

wcj,hipf**3423**   (853) cs,nn3605   pl,cs,qpta**3427**   df,nn776 pr4480/pl,nn,pnx**6440**

52 Then ye shall drive out   all   the inhabitants of the land from before

wcj,pipf**6**   (853) cs,nn3605   pl,nn,pnx**4906**   pimf**6**   wcj(853) cs,nn3605   pl,nn,pnx**4541**

you, and destroy   all   their pictures, and destroy   all   their molten

pl,cs,nn**6754**   himf**8045**   wcj(853) cs,nn3605   pl,nn,pnx**1116**

images and quite*pluck*down   all   their high places:

wcs,hipf**3423**   (853)   df,nn776   wcs,qpf**3427**   pp,pnx

53 And ye shall dispossess *the inhabitants*   of the land, and dwell therein:

cj3588   qpf**5414** pp,pnx (853)   df,nn776   pp,qnc**3423** pnx(853)

for I have given you   the land to possess   it.

wcj,htpf**5157** (853)   df,nn776   pp,nn1486

54 And ye shall divide   the land by lot for an inheritance among your

pp,pl,nn,pnx**4940**   dfp,aj7227   himf7235   (853)   nn,pnx5159

families: *and* to the more ye shall give*the*more   inheritance, and to the

wcj,dfp,nn4592   himf4591   (853)   nn,pnx5159   pp,pnx   qmf1961

fewer ye shall give*the*less   inheritance: every*man's*inheritance shall be

pr413/pnl834/ad,lh8033   pp,pnx df,nn1486 qmf3318   pp,pl,cs,nn**4294**   pl,nn,pnx1

in*the*place*where his   lot falleth; according to the   tribes of your fathers ye

htmf**5157**

shall inherit.

wcj,cj518   ptn3808   himf**3423**   (853)   pl,cs,qpta**3427**   df,nn776 pr4480/pl,nn,pnx**6440**

55 But if   ye will not drive out   the inhabitants of the land from before

wcsqpf**1961**   pnl834   himf**3498** pr,pnx4480

you; then it*shall*come*to*pass, that those which ye let remain   of   them *shall be*

pp,pl,nn7899   pp,du,nn,pnx**5869** wcj,pp,pl,nn6976   pp,pl,nn,pnx6654   wcs,qpf6887 pnx(853)

pricks in your eyes,   and thorns in your sides,   and shall vex   you

pr5921   df,nn**776** pnl834/pp,pnx pnp859 pl,qpta**3427**

in the land wherein ye dwell.

wcs,qpf**1961**   pp,qnc**6213**   pp,pnx   pp,pnl834

56 Moreover it*shall*come*to*pass, *that* I shall   do   unto you,   as   I

pipf**1819**   qmf**6213**   pp,pnx

thought to do unto them.

34

nn3068 wcs,pimf1696 pr413 nn4872 pp,qnc559
And the LORD spoke unto Moses, saying,

pimv6680 (853) pl,cs,nn1121 nn3478 wcj,qpf559 pr,pnx413
2 Command   the children of Israel, and say unto them,

cj3588 pnp859 pl,qpta935 pr413 dfp,nn776 nn3667 pndm2063 df,nn776 pnl834 qmf5307
When ye come into the land of Canaan; (this is the land that shall fall

pp,pnx pp,nn5159 cs,nn776 nn3667 pp,pl,nn,pnx1367
unto you for an inheritance, even the land of Canaan with the coasts thereof:)

pp,pnx nn5045 cs,nn6285 wcj,qpf1961 pr4480/cs,nn4057 nn6790 pr5921
3 Then your south quarter shall be from*the*wilderness of Zin along by

du,cs,nn3027 nn123 pp,pnx nn5045 cs,nn1366 wcs,qpf1961 pr4480/cs,nn7097
the coast of Edom, and your south border shall be the outermost coast of the

df,nn4417 cs,nn3220 ad,lh6924
salt sea eastward:

pp,pnx df,nn1366 wcs,nipf5437 pr4480/nn5045 pp,cs,nn4608 nn6137
4 And your border shall turn from*the*south to the ascent of Akrabbim,

wcs,qpf5674 nn,lh6790 pl,nn,pnx8444 wcs,qpf1961 pr4480/nn5045
and pass on to Zin: and the going forth thereof shall be from*the*south to

pp,nn6947 wcs,qpf3318 nn2692 wcs,qpf5674 nn,lh6111
Kadesh-barnea, and shall go on to Hazar-addar, and pass on to Azmon:

df,nn1366 wcs,nipf5437 pr4480/nn6111 nn,lh5158 nn4714
5 And the border shall fetch*a*compass from Azmon unto the river of Egypt,

pl,nn,pnx8444 wcs,qpf1961 df,nn,lh3220
and the goings out of it shall be at the sea.

nn3220 wcj,cs,nn1366 pp,pnx wcs,qpf1961 df,aj1419 df,nn3220
6 And as for the western border, ye shall even have the great sea for a

wcj,nn1366 pndm2088 qmf1961 pp,pnx nn3220 cs,nn1366
border: this shall be your west border.

wcj,pndm2088 qmf1961 pp,pnx nn6828 cs,nn1366 pr4480 df,aj1419 df,nn3220
7 And this shall be your north border: from the great sea ye shall

pimf8376 pp,pnx df,nn2022 nn2023
point out for you mount Hor:

df,nn2022 pr4480/nn2023 pimf8376 pp,qnc935
8 From mount Hor ye shall point out your border unto the entrance of

nn2574 pl,cs,nn8444 df,nn1366 wcs,qpf1961 nn,lh6657
Hamath; and the goings forth of the border shall be to Zedad:

df,nn1366 wcs,qpf3318 nn,lh2202 pl,nn,pnx8444 wcs,qpf1961
9 And the border shall go on to Ziphron, and the goings out of it shall be

nn2704 pndm2088 qmf1961 pp,pnx nn6828 cs,nn1366
at Hazar-enan: this shall be your north border.

wcs,htpf184 pp,pnx ad,lh6924 pp,nn1366 pr4480/nn2704 nn,lh8221
10 And ye shall point out your east border from Hazar-enan to Shepham:

df,nn1366 wcs,qpf3381 pr4480/nn8221 df,nn7247 pr4480/nn6924
11 And the coast shall go down from Shepham to Riblah, on*the*east*side of

pp,nn5871 df,nn1366 wcs,qpf3381 wcs,qpf4229 pr5921 cs,nn3802 cs,nn3220
Ain; and the border shall descend, and shall reach unto the side of the sea of

nn3672 ad,lh6924
Chinnereth eastward:

df,nn1366 wcs,qpf3381 df,nn,lh3383 pl,nn,pnx8444
12 And the border shall go down to Jordan, and the goings out of it shall

wcs,qpf1961 df,nn4417 cs,nn3220 pndm2063 qmf1961 pp,pnx df,nn776 pp,pl,nn,pnx1367
be at the salt sea: this shall be your land with the coasts thereof

ad5439
round about.

nn4872 wcs,pimf6680 (853) pl,cs,nn1121 nn3478 pp,qnc559 pndm2063 df,nn776
13 And Moses commanded   the children of Israel, saying, This is the land

pnl834   htmf5157 pnx(853)   pp,nn1486 pnl834   nn3068   pipf6680   pp,qnc5414

which ye shall inherit   by lot, which the LORD commanded to give unto the

pp,cs,nu8672 df,pl,nn4294   wcj,cs,nn2677 df,nn4294

nine   tribes, and to the   half tribe:

cj3588   cs,nn4294   pl,cs,nn1121   df,nn7206   pp,cs,nn1004

14 For the tribe of the children of Reuben according to the house of their

pl,nn,pnx1   wcj,cs,nn4294   pl,cs,nn1121   df,nn1410   pp,cs,nn1004

fathers, and the tribe of the children of Gad according to the house of their

pl,nn,pnx1   qpf3947   wcj,cs,nn2677 cs,nn4294   nn4519

fathers, have received *their inheritance*; and half the tribe of Manasseh have

qpf3947   nn,pnx5159

received their inheritance:

du,cs,nu8147 df,pl,nn4294   wcj,cs,nn2677 df,nn4294   qpf3947   nn,pnx5159

15 The two   tribes and the   half   tribe have received their inheritance

pr4480/nn5676 pp,nn3383   nn3405   ad,lh6924   nn,lh4217

on*this*side Jordan *near* Jericho eastward, toward the sunrising.

nn3068 wcs,pimf1696 pr413   nn4872   pp,qnc559

16 And the LORD spoke unto Moses, saying,

pndm428   pl,cs,nn8034   df,pl,nn376 pnl834   qmf5157 (853)   df,nn776   pp,pnx

17 These *are* the names of the men which shall divide   the land unto you:

nn499   df,nn3548   wcj,nn3091   cs,nn1121   nn5126

Eleazar the priest, and Joshua the son of Nun.

qmf3947   nu259/wcj,nn5387/nu259/nn5387   pr4480/nn4294

18 And   ye   shall   take   one prince   of*every*tribe,   to

pp,qnc5157/(853)/df,nn776

divide*the*land*by*inheritance.

pl,cs,nn8034   df,pl,nn376   wcj,pndm428   pp,cs,nn4294 nn3063   nn3612

19 And the names of the men *are* these: Of the tribe of Judah, Caleb the

cs,nn1121   nn3312

son of Jephunneh.

wcj,pp,cs,nn4294   pl,cs,nn1121   nn8095   nn8050   cs,nn1121

20 And of the   tribe of the children of Simeon, Shemuel the son of

nn5989

Ammihud.

pp,cs,nn4294   nn1144   nn449   cs,nn1121   nn3692

21 Of the tribe of Benjamin, Eliad the son of Chislon.

nn5387   wcj,pp,cs,nn4294   pl,cs,nn1121   nn1835   nn1231   cs,nn1121

22 And the prince of the   tribe of the children of Dan, Bukki the son of

nn3020

Jogli.

nn5387   pp,pl,cs,nn1121   nn3130   pp,cs,nn4294   pl,cs,nn1121

23 The prince of the children of Joseph, for the tribe of the children of

nn4519   nn2592   cs,nn1121   nn641

Manasseh, Hanniel the son of Ephod.

nn5387   wcj,pp,cs,nn4294   pl,cs,nn1121   nn669   nn7055

24 And the prince of the   tribe   of the children of Ephraim, Kemuel the

cs,nn1121   nn8204

son of Shiphtan.

nn5387   wcj,pp,cs,nn4294   pl,cs,nn1121   nn2074   nn469

25 And the prince of the   tribe   of the children of Zebulun, Elizaphan the

cs,nn1121   nn6535

son of Parnach.

nn5387   wcj,pp,cs,nn4294   pl,cs,nn1121   nn3485   nn6409   cs,nn1121

26 And the prince of the   tribe   of the children of Issachar, Paltiel the son

nn5821

of Azzan.

nn5387 wcj,pp,cs,nn4294 pl,cs,nn1121 nn836 nn282 cs,nn1121

27 And the prince of the tribe of the children of Asher, Ahihud the son

nn8015

of Shelomi.

nn5387 wcj,pp,cs,nn4294 pl,cs,nn1121 nn5321 nn6300

28 And the prince of the tribe of the children of Naphtali, Pedahel the

cs,nn1121 nn5989

son of Ammihud.

pndm428 pnl834 nn3068 pipf6680 pp,pinc5157 (853)

29 These *are they* whom the LORD commanded to divide*the*inheritance

pl,cs,nn1121 nn3478 pp,cs,nn776 nn3667

unto the children of Israel in the land of Canaan.

Cities for the Levites

nn3068 wcs,pimf1696 pr413 nn4872 pp,pl,cs,nn6160 nn4124 pr5921 nn3383

35 And the LORD spoke unto Moses in the plains of Moab by Jordan

nn3405 pp,qnc559

near Jericho, saying,

pimv6680 (853) pl,cs,nn1121 nn3478 wcj,qpf5414 pp,pl,nn3881

2 Command the children of Israel, that they give unto the Levites

pr4480/cs,nn5159 nn,pnx272 pl,nn5892 pp,qnc3427 qmf5414

of*the*inheritance of their possession cities to dwell in; and ye shall give *also* unto

pp,pl,nn3881 wcj,nn4054 dfp,pl,nn5892 pr,pnx5439

the Levites suburbs for the cities round about them.

df,pl,nn5892 pp,pnx wcs,qpf1961 pp,qnc3427 wcj,pl,nn,pnx4054

3 And the cities shall they have to dwell in; and the suburbs of them shall

qmf1961 pp,nn,pnx929 wcj,pp,nn,pnx7399 wcj,pp,cs,nn3605 nn,pnx2416

be for their cattle, and for their goods, and for all their beasts.

wcj,pl,cs,nn4054 df,pl,nn5892 pnl834 qmf5414 pp,pl,nn3881

4 And the suburbs of the cities, which ye shall give unto the Levites, *shall*

pr4480/cs,nn7023 df,nn5892 wcj,nn,lh2351 nu505 nn520 ad5439

reach from*the*wall of the city and outward a thousand cubits round about.

wcs,qpf4058 pr4480/nn2351 dfp,nn5892 (853) nn,lh6924 cs,nn6285

5 And ye shall measure from without the city on the east side

du,nu505 dfp,nn520 wcj(853) nn5045 cs,nn6285 du,nu505 dfp,nn520 wcj(853)

two thousand cubits, and on the south side two thousand cubits, and on

nn3220 cs,nn6285 du,nu505 dfp,nn520 wcj(853) nn6828 cs,nn6285 du,nu505

the west side two thousand cubits, and on the north side two thousand

dfp,nn520 wcj,df,nn5892 dfp,nn8432 pndm2088 qmf1961 pp,pnx pl,cs,nn4054

cubits; and the city *shall be* in the midst: this shall be to them the suburbs

df,pl,nn5892

of the cities.

wcj,pr854 df,pl,nn5892 pnl834 qmf5414 pp,pl,nn3881 (853)

6 And among the cities which ye shall give unto the Levites *there shall be*

nu8337 pl,cs,nn5892 df,nn4733 pnl834 qmf5414 df,qpta7523 pp,qnc5127

six cities for refuge, which ye shall appoint for the manslayer, that he may flee

ad,lh8033 wcj,pr,pnx5921 qmf5414 pl,nu705 wcj,du,nu8147 nn5892

thither: and to them ye shall add forty and two cities.

cs,nn3605 df,pl,nn5892 pnl834 qmf5414 pp,pl,nn3881 pl,nu705

7 *So* all the cities which ye shall give to the Levites *shall be* forty and

wcj,nu8083 nn5892 pnx(853) pr,pnx854 pl,nn,pnx4054

eight cities: them *shall ye give* with their suburbs.

wcj,df,pl,nn5892 pnl834 qmf5414 pr4480/cs,nn272

8 And the cities which ye shall give *shall be* of*the*possession of the

pl,cs,nn1121   nn3478   pr4480/pr854   df,aj7227   himf7235   wcj,pr4480/pr854

children of Israel: from *them that have* many ye shall give many; but   from

                df,nn4592   himf4591   nn376   qmf5414   pr4480/pl,nn,pnx5892

them that have few ye shall give few: every one shall give of*his*cities unto the

pp,pl,nn3881   pp,cs,nn6310   nn,pnx5159   pnl834   qmf5157

Levites according to his inheritance which he inheriteth.

The Cities of Refuge

          nn3068   wcs,pimf1696   pr413   nn4872   pp,qnc559

9 And the LORD spoke unto Moses, saying,

       pimv1696   pr413   pl,cs,nn1121   nn3478   wcj,qpf559 pr,pnx413   cj3588   pnp859

10 Speak unto the children of Israel, and   say   unto them, When ye be

pl,qpta5674   (853) df,nn3383   nn,lh776   nn3667

come over   Jordan into the land of Canaan;

                wcs,hipf7136   pl,nn5892   qmf1961 pl,nn5892   nn4733   pp,pnx

11 Then ye shall appoint you cities to be   cities of refuge for you; that the

qpta7523   wcs,qpf5127 ad,lh8033   cs,hipt5221   nn5315   pp,nn7684

slayer may flee thither, which killeth any person at unawares.

              wcs,qpf1961   pp,pnx   df,pl,nn5892   pp,nn4733   pr4480/qpta1350

12 And they shall   be   unto you cities for refuge from*the*avenger; that the

df,qpta7523   qmf4191 wcj,ptn3808 pr5704   qnc,pnx5975 pp,pl,cs,nn6440   df,nn5712   dfp,nn4941

manslayer die   not, until he stand   before the congregation in judgment.

              wcj,df,pl,nn5892   pnl834   qmf5414 nu8337 pl,cs,nn5892   pp,pnx qmf1961

13 And of these   cities   which ye shall give six   cities shall ye have for

nn4733

refuge.

            qmf5414   (853) cs,nu7969   df,pl,nn5892   pr4480/nn5676   dfp,nn3383   wcj(853) cs,nu7969

14 Ye shall give   three   cities on*this*side Jordan, and   three

df,pl,nn,pnx5892   qmf5414   pp,cs,nn776   nn3667   qmf1961 pl,cs,nn5892   nn4733

cities   shall ye give in the land of Canaan, *which* shall be   cities of refuge.

          df,pndm428 nu8337 df,pl,nn5892   qmf1961   pp,nn4733   pp,pl,cs,nn1121   nn3478

15 These six   cities shall be a refuge, *both* for the children of Israel, and

wci,dfp,nn1616   wcj,dfp,nn8453 pp,nn,pnx8432   cs,nn3605   cs,hipt5221

for the stranger, and for the sojourner among them: that every one that killeth any

nn5315   pp,nn7684   pp,qnc5127 ad,lh8033

person unawares may   flee   thither.

          wcj,cj518   hipf,pnx5221   pp,cs,nn3627   nn1270   wcs,qmf4191 pnp1931

16 And if   he smite him with an instrument of iron, so that he die,   he

qpta7523   df,qpta7523   qna4191/homf4191

is a murderer: the murderer shall surely*be*put*to*death.

          wcj,cj518   hipf,pnx5221   nn3027   pp,cs,nn68 pnl834/pp,pnx   qmf4191

17 And if   he smite him with throwing a stone, wherewith he may die, and

wcs,qmf4191 pnp1931   qpta7523   df,qpta7523   qna4191/homf4191

he die,   he *is* a murderer: the murderer shall surely*be*put*to*death.

       cj176   hipf,pnx5221   nn3027 pp,cs,nn3627   nn6086   pnl834/pp,pnx   qmf4191

18 Or *if* he smite him with a hand weapon of wood, wherewith he may die,

wcs,qmf4191 pnp1931   qpta7523   df,qpta7523   qna4191/homf4191

and he die,   he *is* a murderer: the murderer shall surely*be*put*to*death.

          cs,qpta1350   df,nn1818 pnp1931   himf4191 (853)   df,qpta7523   pp,qnc,pnx6293

19 The revenger of blood himself shall slay   the murderer: when he meeteth

pp,pnx pnp1931   himf,pnx4191

him, he shall slay him.

nn,pnx5159   nimf1639   wcj,pr4480/cs,nn5159   cs,nn4294

so shall their inheritance be taken away from*the*inheritance of the tribe of our

pl,nn,pnx1

fathers.

nn4872   wcs,pimf6680   (853)   pl,cs,nn1121   nn3478   pr5921   cs,nn6310

5 And Moses commanded   the children of Israel according to the word of the

nn3068   pp,qnc559   cs,nn4294   pl,cs,nn1121   nn3130   pl,qpta1696   aj3651

LORD, saying, The tribe of the sons of Joseph hath said well.

pndm2088   df,nn1697   pnl834   nn3068   pipf6680   pp,pl,cs,nn1323

6 This is the thing which the LORD doth command concerning the daughters of

nn6765   pp,qnc559   qmf1961/pp,pl,nn802   dfp,aj2896/pp,du,nn,pnx5869   ad389

Zelophehad, saying, Let them marry to whom they think best; only to the

pp,cs,nn4940   cs,nn4294   nn,pnx1   qmf1961/pp,pl,nn802

family of the tribe of their father shall they marry.

wcj,ptn3808   nn5159   pp,pl,cs,nn1121   nn3478   qmf5437   pr4480/nn4294   pr413

7 So shall not the inheritance of the children of Israel remove from tribe to

nn4294   cj3588   nn376   pl,cs,nn1121   nn3478   qmf1692   pp,cs,nn5159

tribe: for every one of the children of Israel shall keep himself to the inheritance of

cs,nn4294   pl,nn,pnx1

the tribe of his fathers.

wcj,cs,nn3605   nn1323   qpta3423   nn5159   pr4480/df,pl,cs,nn4294

8 And every daughter, that possesseth an inheritance in*any*tribe of the

pl,cs,nn1121   nn3478   qmf1961   pp,nn802   pp,nu259   pr4480/cs,nn4940   cs,nn4294

children of Israel, shall be wife unto one of*the*family of the tribe of her

nn,pnx1   pp,pr4616   pl,cs,nn1121   nn3478   qmf3423   nn376   cs,nn5159

father, that the children of Israel may enjoy every man the inheritance of his

pl,nn,pnx1

fathers.

wcj,ptn3808   nn5159   qmf5437   pr4480/nn4294   aj312   pp,nn4294   cj3588

9 Neither shall the inheritance remove from*one*tribe to another tribe; but

nn376   pl,cs,nn4294   pl,cs,nn1121   nn3478   qmf1692

every one of the tribes of the children of Israel shall keep himself to his own

pp,nn,pnx5159

inheritance.

pp,pnl834   nn3068   pipf6680   (853)   nn4872   ad3651   qpf6213   pl,cs,nn1323

10 Even as the LORD commanded   Moses, so did the daughters of

nn6765

Zelophehad:

nn4244   nn8656   wcj,nn2295   wcj,nn4435   wcj,nn5270   pl,cs,nn1323

11 For Mahlah, Tirzah, and Hoglah, and Milcah, and Noah, the daughters of

nn6765   wcs,qmf1961/pp,pl,nn802   pl,nn,pnx1730   pp,pl,cs,nn1121

Zelophehad, were married unto their father's brothers' sons:

qpf1961/pp,pl,nn802   pr4480/pl,cs,nn4940   pl,cs,nn1121   nn4519

12 And they were married into*the*families of the sons of Manasseh the

cs,nn1121   nn3130   nn,pnx5159   wcs,qmf1961   pr5921   cs,nn4294   cs,nn4940

son of Joseph, and their inheritance remained in the tribe of the family of their

nn,pnx1

father.

pndm428   df,pl,nn4687   wcj,df,pl,nn4941   pnl834   nn3068

13 These are the commandments and the judgments, which the LORD

pipf6680   pp,cs,nn3027   nn4872   pr413   pl,cs,nn1121   nn3478   pp,pl,cs,nn6160

commanded by the hand of Moses unto the children of Israel in the plains of

nn4124   pr5921   nn3383   nn3405

Moab by Jordan near Jericho.

The Book of

DEUTERONOMY

"Deuteronomy" comes from the transliteration of a Greek word which means "second law." This title for the book is derived from the incorrect translation of Deuteronomy 17:18 in the Septuagint, the ancient Greek translation of the Old Testament. The Hebrew text is properly translated in the KJV, "that he shall write him a copy of this law in a book." Deuteronomy is not a "second Law," but merely a repetition and expansion of the laws contained in the first books of the Pentateuch. The Hebrew title (the first words of the text) means "these are the words."

Deuteronomy is the fifth and final book of the Pentateuch or the Law of Moses. The three final discourses of Moses which are recorded in this book (Deut. 1:6—4:43; 4:44—26:19; 27—31) were given while the Israelites were encamped in the plains of Moab. These discourses reviewed the history of the Israelites up to that time, repeated and expanded upon the laws that God had given, and listed the promised blessings for obedience and cursings for disobedience. Moses was addressing the children of Israel only two months before they would cross the Jordan into Canaan (Deut. 1:3, cf. Josh. 4:19).

The form of the Book of Deuteronomy is very similar to that of the vassal–treaties written prior to 1000 B.C. It contains a historical introduction, an enumeration of laws, and concluding threats and promises. Unfortunately, Israel did not take heed to this or subsequent warnings that they would be judged for their disobedience. They were commanded not to do that which was right in their own eyes (Deut. 12:8), but this later became a characteristic of the entire nation (Judg. 17:6; 21:25). They were also given instructions which specified what kind of king should rule over them and outlined his responsibilities, but these directives were often forgotten or ignored (Deut. 17:14–20, cf. 1 Sam. 8:7–9; 1 Kgs. 10:26; 11:1–8).

Sections of Deuteronomy are strongly prophetic in nature. For example, the discourse on the prophet who would be like Moses (Deut. 18) is a prophecy of the Messiah. Likewise, certain portions of the book have great significance to the history of Israel. Consequently, words and phrases from Deuteronomy reappear throughout the Old Testament. The prophets in particular sought to call the people back to the standards found in this book.

The New Testament writers quoted from the Book of Deuteronomy nearly two hundred times. Christ Himself quoted from it exclusively in His answers to Satan's temptations (Matt. 4:1–11, cf. Deut. 6:13, 16; 8:3).

Israel at Horeb

1 ⟐ pndm428 — These *be* the df,pl,nn**1697** words pnl834 which nn4872 Moses pipf**1696** spoke pr413 unto cs,nn3605 all nn3478 Israel pp,cs,nn5676 on*this*side

df,nn3383 Jordan in the dfp,nn4057 wilderness, in the dfp,nn**6160** plain pr4136 over against the nn5489 Red *sea*, pr996 between

nn6290 Paran, and wcj(pr996) nn8603 Tophel, and wcj,nn3837 Laban, and wcj,nn2698 Hazeroth, and wcj,nn1774 Dizahab.

2 (*There are* nu259/nu6240 eleven nn3117 days *journey* pr4480/nn2722 from Horeb by the cs,nn**1870** way of cs,nn2022 mount nn8165 Seir pr5704 unto

nn6947 Kadesh-barnea.)

3 And wcs,qmf**1961** it*came*to*pass in the pp,pl,nu705 fortieth nn8141 year, in the pp,cs,nu6249/nu6240 eleventh nn2320 month, on the

pp,nu259 first *day* dfp,nn2320 of the month, nn4872 *that* Moses pipf**1696** spoke pr413 unto the pl,cs,nn**1121** children of nn3478 Israel, according

pp,nn3605 unto all pnl834 that the nn**3068** LORD had pipf**6680**/pnx(853) given*him*in*commandment pr,pnx413 unto them;

4 ad310 After hinc,pnx**5221** he had (853) slain nn5511 Sihon the df,nn**4428** king of the Amorites, pnl834 which qpta**3427** dwelt in

pp,nn2809 Heshbon, and wcj(853) nn5747 Og the cs,nn**4428** king of df,nn1316 Bashan, pnl834 which qpta**3427** dwelt pp,nn6252 at Astaroth pp,nn154 in Edrei:

5 pp,cs,nn5676 On*this*side df,nn3383 Jordan, pp,cs,nn776 in the land nn4124 of Moab, hipf**2974** began nn4872 Moses to pipf874 declare (853)

df,pndm2063 this df,nn**8451** law, pp,qnc559 saying,

6 The nn**3068** LORD pl,nn,pnx**430** our God pipf**1696** spoke pr,pnx413 unto us pp,nn2722 in Horeb, pp,qnc559 saying, pp,pnx Ye have qnc**3427** dwelt

aj7227 long enough in df,pndm2088 this dfp,nn2022 mount:

7 qmv6437 Turn you, and wcj,qmv5265/pp,pnx take*your*journey, and wcj,qmv935 go cs,nn2022 to the mount df,nn567 of the Amorites,

wcj,pr413 and unto cs,nn3605 all pl,nn,pnx**7934** *the places* nigh dfp,nn**6160** thereunto, in the plain, dfp,nn2022 in the hills, and in the

wcj,dfp,nn8219 vale, and in the wcj,dfp,nn5045 south, df,nn3220 and by the wcj,pp,cs,nn2348 sea cs,nn**776** side, to the land of the

df,nn3669 Canaanites, and unto wcj,df,nn3844 Lebanon, pr5704 unto the df,aj1419 great df,nn5104 river, the cs,nn5104 river nn6578 Euphrates.

8 qmv**7200** Behold, I have qpf5414 set (853) the df,nn**776** land pp,pl,nn,pnx**6440** before you: qmv935 go in and wcj,qmv**3423** possess (853) the

df,nn**776** land pnl834 which the nn**3068** LORD nipf**7650** swore pp,pl,nn,pnx1 unto your fathers, pp,nn85 Abraham, pp,nn3327 Isaac, and wcj,pp,nn3290 Jacob, to

pp,qnc5414 give pp,pnx unto them and to their wcj,pp,nn,pnx**2233** seed pr,pnx310 after them.

9 And wcs,qmf559 I spoke pr,pnx413 unto you df,pndm1931 at that dfp,nn**6256** time, pp,qnc559 saying, qmf3201/ptn**3808** I am*not*able to qnc5375 bear pnx(853)

pp,nn,pnx905 you myself alone:

⟐ **1:1** The phrase "on this side Jordan" should read "beyond Jordan" as it does in Deuteronomy 3:20, 25. This was the common term used for land east of the Jordan River. Later, the land was inhabited by Greeks, who named the area Perea. The "wilderness" is a general reference to the region southeast of Jordan; the "plain over against the Red Sea" is more specifically the land along the Rift Valley from the Dead Sea to the Gulf of Aqabah.

nn3068   pl,nn,pnx430   hipf7235   pnx(853)   wcj,ptdm,pnx2009

10 The LORD your   God   hath multiplied   you, and, behold, ye *are* this

df,nn3117   pp,pl,cs,nn3556   df,du,nn8064   dfp,nn7230

day as the   stars   of heaven for multitude.

nn3068   pl,cs,nn430   pl,nn,pnx1   pnx(pr5921)   cs,nu505   pl,cs,nn6471

11 (The LORD God of your fathers make   you a thousand   times

himf3254   pp,pnx   wcj,pimf1288 pnx(853)   pp,pnl834   pipf1696   pp,pnx

so*many*more as ye *are*, and bless   you,   as he hath promised you!)

ad349   pp,nn,pnx905 qmf5375   nn,nn2960   wcj,nn,pnx4853

12 How can I myself alone   bear your encumbrance, and your burden, and

wcj,nn,pnx7379

your strife?

qmv3051 pp,pnx aj2450   pl,nn376   wcj,pl,nipt995   wcj,pl,qptp3045   pp,pl,nn,pnx7626

13 Take you wise men, and understanding, and known among your tribes,

wcs,qmf7760   pp,pl,nn,pnx7218

and I will   make   them   rulers   over you.

wcs,qmf6030   pnx(853)   wcs,qmf559   df,nn1697 pnl834   pimf1696

14 And ye answered   me, and said, The thing which thou hast spoken *is*

aj2896   pp,qnc6213

good *for us* to   do.

wcs,qmf3947   (853)   pl,cs,nn7218   pl,nn,pnx7626 aj2450   pl,nn376   wcj,pl,qptp3045

15 So I   took   the chief of your tribes, wise men, and known, and

wcs,qmf5414 pnx(853)   pl,nn7218 pr,pnx5921   pl,cs,nn8269   pl,nu505   wcj,pl,cs,nn8269

made   them heads over you, captains over thousands, and captains over

pl,nu3967   wcj,pl,cs,nn8269   pl,nu2572   wcj,pl,cs,nn8269   pl,nu6235   wcj,pl,nn7860

hundreds, and captains over fifties, and captains over tens, and officers among

pp,pl,nn,pnx7626

your tribes.

wcs,pimf6680   (853)   pl,qpta,pnx8199   df,pndm1931 dfp,nn6256   pp,qnc559   qna8085

16 And I charged   your judges at that   time, saying, Hear *the causes*

pr996   pl,nn,pnx251   wcj,qpf8199   nn6664   pr996   nn376   wcj(pr996)

between your brethren, and judge righteously between *every* man and   his

nn,pnx251   wcj(pr996)   nn,pnx1616

brother, and   the stranger *that is* with him.

ptn3808   himf5234   pl,nn6440   dfp,nn4941   qmf8085   dfp,aj6996

17 Ye shall not respect persons in judgment; *but* ye shall hear the small as

dfp,aj1419   ptn3808   qmf1481   pr4480/pl,cs,nn6440   nn376   cj3588   df,nn4941

well as the great; ye shall not be afraid of*the*face of man; for the judgment

(pnp1931)   pp,pl,nn430   wcj,df,nn1697 pnl834   qmf7185   pr,pnx4480   him7126   pr,pnx413

is God's: and the cause that is*too*hard for you, bring *it* unto me, and

wcs,qpf,pnx8085

I will hear it.

wcs,pimf6680   pnx(853)   df,pndm1931 dfp,nn6256 (853) cs,nn3605   df,pl,nn1697 pnl834

18 And I commanded   you at that   time   all the things which ye

qmf6213

should do.

___

1:16 The Hebrew word *gēr* (1616), translated "stranger," means a "sojourner," "immigrant," or "alien." These were non-Israelites who, for the most part, enjoyed equal rights under the Law of Moses while residing with their Hebrew neighbors. If they were poor, they were provided for along with the Levites, the orphans, and the widows. However, they were required to be circumcised and conform to the Law of Moses.

The Spies and God's Punishment

19 And when we departed from Horeb, we went through all that great and terrible wilderness, which ye saw by the way of the mountain of the Amorites, as the LORD our God commanded us; and we came to Kadesh-barnea.

20 And I said unto you, Ye are come unto the mountain of the Amorites, which the LORD our God doth give unto us.

21 Behold, the LORD thy God hath set the land before thee: go up and possess it, as the LORD God of thy fathers hath said unto thee; fear not, neither be discouraged.

22 And ye came near unto me every one of you, and said, We will send men before us, and they shall search*us*out the land, and bring us word again by what way we must go up, and into what cities we shall come.

23 And the saying pleased*me*well: and I took twelve men of you, one of a tribe:

24 And they turned and went up into the mountain, and came unto the valley of Eshcol, and searched*it*out.

25 And they took of*the*fruit of the land in their hands, and brought*it*down unto us, and brought us word again, and said, It is a good land which the LORD our God doth give us.

26 Notwithstanding ye would not go up, but rebelled against the commandment of the LORD your God:

27 And ye murmured in your tents, and said, Because the LORD hated us, he hath brought*us*forth out*of*the*land of Egypt, to deliver us into the hand of the Amorites, to destroy us.

28 Whither shall we go up? our brethren have discouraged our heart, saying, The people is greater and taller than we; the cities are great and

wcj,pl,qptp1219   dfp,du,nn8064   wcj,ad1571   qpf7200   pl,cs,nn1121   nn6062   ad8033

walled up to heaven; and moreover we have seen the sons of the Anakims there.

wcs,qmf559 pr,pnx413   qmf6206 ptn3808 wcj,ptn3808   qmf3372   pr,pnx4480

29 Then I said unto you, Dread not, neither be afraid of them.

nn3068   pl,nn,pnx430   df,qpta1980 pp,pl,nn,pnx6440   pnp1931   nimf3898   pp,pnx

30 The LORD your God which goeth before you, he shall fight for you,

pp,nn3605 pnl834   qpf6213 pr,pnx854   pp,nn4714   pp,du,nn,pnx5869

according to all that he did for you in Egypt before your eyes;

wcj,dfp,nn4057   pnl834   qpf7200   pnl834   nn3068   pl,nn,pnx430

31 And in the wilderness, where thou hast seen how that the LORD thy God

qpf,pnx5375   pp,pnl834   nn376   qmf5375 (853)   nn,pnx1121   pp,cs,nn3605   df,nn1870 pnl834   qpf1980

bore thee, as a man doth bear his son, in all the way that ye went,

pr5704   qnc,pnx935 pr5704 df,pndm2088 df,nn4725

until ye came into this place.

df,pndm2088 wcj,dfp,nn1697   ptn,pnx369   pl,hipt539   pp,nn3068   pl,nn,pnx430

32 Yet in this thing ye did not believe the LORD your God,

df,qpta1980   dfp,nn1870 pp,pl,nn,pnx6440   pp,qnc8446/pp,pnx   nn4725

33 Who went in the way before you, to search*you*out a place to

pp,qnc,pnx2583   dfp,nn784   nn3915   pp,hinc,pnx7200   pnl834/pp,pnx dfp,nn1870

pitch*your*tents *in*, in fire by night, to show you by what way ye should

qmf1980   wcj,dfp,nn6051   ad3119

go, and in a cloud by day.

nn3068   wcs,qmf8085 (853)   cs,nn6963   pl,nn,pnx1697   wcs,qmf7107

34 And the LORD heard the voice of your words, and was wroth, and

wcs,nimf7650   pp,qnc559

swore, saying,

cj518   nn376   df,pndm428 dfp,pl,nn376   df,pndm2088 df,aj7451   df,nn1755   qmf7200

35 Surely there shall not one of these men of this evil generation see

(853)   df,aj2896 df,nn776   pnl834   nipf7650   pp,pl,nn,pnx1

that good land, which I swore to give unto your fathers,

pr2108   nn3612   cs,nn1121   nn3312   pnp1931   qmf,pnx7200   wcj,pp,pnx

36 Save Caleb the son of Jephunneh; he shall see it, and to him will I

qmf5414 (853)   df,nn776 pnl834   qpf1869   pp,pnx   wcj,pp,pl,nn,pnx1121 cj3282/pnl834

give the land that he hath trodden upon, and to his children, because he hath

pipf4390   pr310   nn3068

wholly followed the LORD.

ad1571   nn3068   htpf599   pp,pnx   pp,nn,pnx1558   pp,qnc559   pnp859 ad1571

☞ 37 Also the LORD was angry with me for*your*sakes, saying, Thou also shalt

ptn3808 qmf935   ad8033

not go in thither.

nn3091   cs,nn1121   nn5126   df,qpta5975 pp,pl,nn,pnx6440   pnp1931   qmf935

38 *But* Joshua the son of Nun, which standeth before thee, he shall go in

ad,lh8033   pimv2388   pnx(853)   cj3588 pnp1931   (853) nn3478   himf,pnx5157

thither: encourage him: for he shall cause Israel to inherit it.

wcj,nn,pnx2945   pnl834   qpf559   qmf1961   pp,nn957

39 Moreover your little ones, which ye said should be a prey, and your

wcj,pl,nn,pnx1121   pnl834   df,nn3117   qpf3045/ptn3808   aj2896   wcj,aj7451 pnp1992

children, which in that day had*no*knowledge between good and evil, they

qmf935   ad,lh8033   wcj,pp,pnx   qmf,pnx5414   wcj,pnp1992   qmf,pnx3423

shall go in thither, and unto them will I give it, and they shall possess it.

☞ 1:37   See the note on Numbers 20:12.

wcj,pnp859 qmv6437 pp,pnx   wcj,qmv5265   df,nn,lh4057

40 But *as for* you, turn you, and take*your*journey into the wilderness by

cs,nn**1870**   nn5488 cs,nn3220

the way of the Red sea.

wcs,qmf6030   wcs,qmf**559** pr,pnx413   qpf2398   pp,nn3068

41 Then ye answered and said unto me, We have sinned against the L<small>ORD</small>,

pnp587   qmf**5927**   wcs,nipf3898   pp,nn3605 pnl834   nn**3068**   pl,nn,pnx**430**

we will go up and fight, according to all that the L<small>ORD</small> our God

pipf,pnx**6680**   wcs,qmf2296   nn**376**   (853)   pl,cs,nn3627   nn,pnx4421

commanded us. And when ye had girded on every man his weapons of war,

wcs,himf1951   pp,qnc**5927**   df,nn,lh2022

ye were ready to go up into the hill.

nn**3068**   wcs,qmf**559** pr,pnx413   qmv**559**   pp,pnx   qmf5927/ptn**3808** wcj,ptn**3808** nimf3898

42 And the L<small>ORD</small> said unto me, Say unto them, Go*not*up, neither fight;

cj3588   ptn,pnx369 pp,nn,pnx**7130**   wcj,ptn**3808**   nimf5062   pp,pl,cs,nn**6440**   pl,qpta,pnx341

for I *am* not among you; lest ye be smitten before your enemies.

wcs,pimf**1696** pr,pnx413   wcj,ptn**3808** qpf**8085**   wcs,himf**4784**   (853)

43 So I spoke unto you; and ye would not hear, but rebelled against

cs,nn**6310**   nn**3068**   wcs,himf**5927**/wcj,qmf2102   df,nn,lh2022

the commandment of the L<small>ORD</small>, and went*presumptuously*up into the hill.

df,nn567   df,qpta**3427**   df,pndm1931   dfp,nn2022   wcs,qmf3318   pp,qnc,pnx7125

44 And the Amorites, which dwelt in that mountain, came out against

wcs,qmf7291 pnx(853)   pp,pnl834 df,pl,nn1682 qmf**6213**   wcs,himf**3807** pnx(853)   pp,nn8165

you, and chased you, as bees do, and destroyed you in Seir,

pr5704   nn2767

even unto Hormah.

wcs,qmf**7725**   wcs,qmf1058 pp,pl,cs,nn**6440**   nn**3068**   nn**3068**   wcj,ptn**3808**

45 And ye returned and wept before the L<small>ORD</small>; but the L<small>ORD</small> would not

qpf**8085**   pp,nn,pnx6963 wcj,ptn**3808**   hipf**238**   pr,pnx413

hearken to your voice, nor give ear unto you.

wcs,qmf**3427**   pp,nn6946   aj7227   pl,nn**3117**   dfp,pl,nn**3117** pnl834

46 So ye abode in Kadesh many days, according unto the days that ye

qpf**3427**

abode *there*.

The Journey in the Wilderness

2

wcs,qmf6437   wcs,qmf5265   df,nn,lh4057   cs,nn**1870**

Then we turned, and took*our*journey into the wilderness by the way of

nn5488 cs,nn3220 pp,pnl834   nn**3068** pipf**1696** pr,pnx413   wcs,qmf5437   (853) cs,nn2022

the Red sea, as the L<small>ORD</small> spoke unto me: and we compassed mount

nn8165   aj7227   pl,nn**3117**

Seir many days.

nn**3068**   wcs,qmf**559** pr,pnx413   pp,qnc**559**

2 And the L<small>ORD</small> spoke unto me, saying,

pp,pnx   qnc5437   (853) df,pndm2088   df,nn2022   aj7227   qmv6437 pp,pnx   nn,lh6828

3 Ye have compassed this mountain long enough: turn you northward.

pimv**6680**   wcj(853)   df,nn**5971**   pp,qnc**559**   pnp859   pl,qpta**5674**

4 And command thou the people, saying, Ye *are* to pass through the

pp,cs,nn1366   pl,nn,pnx**251**   pl,cs,nn**1121**   nn6215   df,pl,qpta**3427**   pp,nn8165

coast of your brethren the children of Esau, which dwell in Seir; and they shall

wcj,qmf**3372**   pr,pnx4480   wcj,nipf**8104**/ad3966

be afraid of you: take*ye*good*heed*unto*yourselves*therefore:

5 Meddle not with them; for I will not give you of*their*land, no, not so much as a foot breadth; because I have given mount Seir unto Esau *for* a possession.

6 Ye shall buy meat of them for money, that ye may eat; and ye shall also buy water of them for money, that ye may drink.

7 For the LORD thy God hath blessed thee in all the works of thy hand: he knoweth thy walking through this great wilderness: these forty years the LORD thy God *hath been* with thee; thou hast lacked nothing.

8 And when we passed by from our brethren the children of Esau, which dwelt in Seir, through*the*way of the plain from Elath, and from Ezion-gaber, we turned and passed by the way of the wilderness of Moab.

9 And the LORD said unto me, Distress not the Moabites, neither contend with them in battle: for I will not give thee of*their*land *for* a possession; because I have given Ar unto the children of Lot *for* a possession.

10 The Emims dwelt therein in*times*past, a people great, and many, and tall, as the Anakims;

11 Which also were accounted giants, as the Anakims; but the Moabites call them Emims.

12 The Horims also dwelt in Seir aforetime; but the children of Esau succeeded them, when they had destroyed them from before them, and dwelt in*their*stead; as Israel did unto the land of his possession, which the LORD gave unto them.

13 Now rise up, *said I*, and get*you*over the brook Zered. And we went over the brook Zered.

14 And the space in which we came from Kadesh-barnea, until we were come over the brook Zered, *was* thirty and eight years; until all the

---

2:10, 11 See the note on Numbers 13:30–33.

df,nn1755   pl,cs,nn376   df,nn4421   qnc8552   pr4480/cs,nn7130   df,nn4264 pp,pnl834

generation of the men of war were wasted out*from*among the host, as the

nn3068 nipf7650 pp,pnx

LORD swore unto them.

wcj,ad1571   cs,nn3027   nn3068 qpf1961   pp,pnx   pp,qnc,pnx2000

15 For indeed the hand of the LORD was against them, to destroy them

pr4480/cs,nn7130   df,nn4264 pr5704   qnc,pnx8552

from among the host, until they were consumed.

wcs,qmf1961   pp,pnl834 cs,nn3605   pl,cs,nn376   df,nn4421   qpf8552

16 So it*came*to*pass, when all the men of war were consumed and

pp,qnc4191   pr4480/cs,nn7130   df,nn5971

dead from among the people,

nn3068 wcs,pimf1696 pr,pnx413   pp,qnc559

17 That the LORD spoke unto me, saying,

pnp859   qpta5674   (853) nn6144 (853)   cs,nn1366   nn4124   df,nn3117

18 Thou art to pass over through Ar the coast of Moab, this day:

wcj,qpf7126   pr4136   pl,cs,nn1121   nn5983 qmf,pnx6696

19 And *when* thou comest nigh over against the children of Ammon, distress

ptn408 wcj,ptn408 htmf1624   pp,pnx   cj3588   ptn3808 qmf5414 pp,pnx   pr4480/cs,nn776

them not, nor meddle with them: for I will not give thee of*the*land of the

pl,cs,nn1121   nn5983   nn3425   cj3588   qpf,pnx5414   pp,pl,cs,nn1121

children of Ammon *any* possession; because I have given it unto the children of

nn3876   nn3425

Lot *for* a possession.

pndm1931 cj637   nimf2803   cs,nn776   pl,nn7497   pl,nn7497 qpf3427   pp,pnx

20 (That also was accounted a land of giants: giants dwelt therein in

pp,pl,nn6440   wcj,df,nn5984 qmf7121 pp,pnx   nn2157

old time; and the Ammonites call them Zamzummims;

nn5971   aj1419   wcj,aj7227   wcj,qpta7311   dfp,nn6062   nn3068

21 A people great, and many, and tall, as the Anakims; but the LORD

wcs,himf,pnx8045   pr4480/pl,nn,pnx6440   wcs,qmf,pnx3423   wcs,qmf3427

destroyed them before them; and they succeeded them, and dwelt

pr,pnx8478

in*their*stead:

pp,pnl834   qpf6213   pp,pl,cs,nn1121   nn6215   df,pl,qpta3427   pp,nn8165 pnl834

22 As he did to the children of Esau, which dwelt in Seir, when he

hipf8045 (853)   df,nn2752   pr4480/pl,nn,pnx6440   wcs,qmf,pnx3423   wcs,qmf3427

destroyed the Horims from before them; and they succeeded them, and dwelt

pr,pnx8478   pr5704 df,pndm2088 df,nn3117

in*their*stead even unto this day:

wcj,df,nn5757   df,pl,qpta3427   pp,nn2699   pr5704   nn5804

23 And the Avims which dwelt in Hazerim, *even* unto Azzah, the

nn3732   df,pl,qpta3318   pr4480/nn3731 hipf,pnx8045   wcs,qmf3427

Caphtorims, which came forth out*of*Caphtor, destroyed them, and dwelt

pr,pnx8478

in*their*stead.)

qmv6965   qmv5265   wcj,qmv5674 (853)   cs,nn5158 nn769 qmv7200

24 Rise*ye*up, take*your*journey, and pass over the river Arnon: behold,

---

2:23 The word translated "Hazerim" is not a proper noun but a word that means "villages" or "enclosures." The Avim mentioned in this verse are called Avites in Joshua 13:3. They were the scattered remnant of a people conquered by the Caphtorim, a tribe descended from the Egyptians (Gen. 10:14; 1 Chr. 1:12). Their name means "ruins" and seems to be a statement about their fallen state. "Azzah" refers to Gaza of the New Testament and modern times.

qpf**5414**   pp,nn,pnx**3027** (853) nn5511   df,nn567 cs,nn**4428**   nn2809   wcj(853)

I have given into thine hand   Sihon the Amorite, king of Heshbon, and

nn,pnx**776** himv**2490**   qmv**3423**   wcj,htmv1624   pp,pnx   nn4421

his land: begin to possess *it*, and contend with him in battle.

df,pndm2088 df,nn**3117**   himf**2490** qnc**5414** nn,pnx**6343**   wcj,nn,pnx**3374**

25 This   day will I begin to put the dread of thee and the   fear   of thee

pr5921   (pl,cs,nn**6440**)   df,pl,nn**5971**   pr8478   cs,nn3605 df,du,nn**8064** pnl834   qmf**8085** nn,pnx**8088**

upon   the nations *that are* under the whole heaven, who shall hear report of

wcs,qpf**7264**   wcj,qpf**2342**   pr4480/pl,nn,pnx**6440**

thee, and shall tremble, and be*in*anguish   because   of thee.

Israel Defeats Sihon

wcs,qmf**7971**   pl,nn**4397**   pr4480/cs,nn4057   nn6932   pr413   nn5511

26 And I   sent   messengers out*of*the*wilderness of Kedemoth unto Sihon

cs,nn**4428**   nn2809   pl,cs,nn**1697**   nn7965   pp,qnc**559**

king of Heshbon with words of peace, saying,

qmf**5674**   pp,nn,pnx**776**   qmf**1980**   dfp,nn**1870**/dfp,nn**1870**

27 Let me pass through thy land: I will go along by the   highway, I will

ptn**3808** qmf**5493**   nn3225   wcj,nn8040

neither turn unto the right hand nor to the   left.

himf,pnx**7666**   nn400   dfp,nn**3701**   wcs,qpf398   qmf**5414** pp,pnx

28 Thou shalt   sell   me meat for money, that I may eat;   and give me

wcj,pl,nn**4325**   dfp,nn**3701**   wcs,qpf8354 ad7535   qmf**5674**   pp,du,nn,pnx**7272**

water for money, that I may drink: only I will pass through on my   feet;

pp,pnl834   pl,cs,nn**1121**   nn6215   df,pl,qpta**3427** pp,nn8165   wcj,df,nn**4125**

29 (As the children of Esau which dwell in Seir, and the Moabites which

df,pl,qpta**3427**   pp,nn6144 qpf**6213**   pp,pnx   pr5704/pnl834   qmf**5674**   (853) df,nn3383 pr413   df,nn**776**

dwell in Ar,   did unto me;)   until   I shall pass over   Jordan into the land

pnl834   nn**3068**   pl,nn,pnx**430** qpta**5414** pp,pnx

which the Lord our   God   giveth us.

nn5511 cs,nn**4428**   nn2809   qpf**14** wcj,ptn**3808**   hinc,pnx**5674**   pp,pnx   cj3588

30 But Sihon king of Heshbon would   not   let us pass by him: for the

nn**3068**   pl,nn,pnx**430** hipf**7185**   (853)   nn,pnx**7307**   wcj,pipf553/(853)/nn,pnx3824   pp,cj4616

Lord thy   God   hardened   his spirit, and made*his*heart*obstinate, that he

qnc,pnx**5414**   pp,nn,pnx**3027**   df,pndm2088 dfp,nn**3117**

might deliver him into thy hand, as *appeareth* this   day.

nn**3068** wcs,qmf**559** pr,pnx413   qmv**7200**   hipf**2490** qnc**5414** (853) nn5511

31 And the Lord said   unto me, Behold, I have begun to give   Sihon and

wcj(853)   nn,pnx**776** pp,pl,nn,pnx**6440**   himv**2490**   qmv**3423**   pp,qnc**3423** (853)

his land   before   thee: begin to possess, that thou mayest inherit   his

nn,pnx**776**

land.

nn5511   wcs,qmf**3318** pp,qnc,pnx7125   pnp1931   wcj,cs,nn3605   nn,pnx**5971** dfp,nn4421

32 Then Sihon came out against us, he and   all   his people, to fight at

nn,lh3096

Jahaz.

nn**3068**   pl,nn,pnx**430** wcs,qmf,pnx**5414**   pp,pl,nn,pnx**6440**   wcs,himf**5221** (853)

33 And the Lord our   God   delivered him before   us; and we smote

wcj(853)   pl,nn,pnx**1121**   wcj(853) cs,nn3605   nn,pnx**5971**

him, and   his sons, and   all his people.

wcs,qmf**3920** (853) cs,nn3605   pl,nn,pnx**5892** df,pndm1931 dfp,nn**6256**   wcs,himf**2763**

34 And we took   all his cities at   that   time, and utterly destroyed pl,nn4962   wcj,df,pl,nn802   wcj,df,nn2945   (853)   cs,nn3605 nn5892   hipf7604 ptn3808

the men, and the women, and the little ones,   of every city, we left none to

nn8300

remain:

ad7535   df,nn929   qpf962   pp,pnx   wcj,cs,nn7998

35 Only the cattle we took*for*a*prey unto ourselves, and the   spoil   of the

df,pl,nn5892   pnl834   qpf3920

cities   which we took.

pr4480   nn6177   pnl834   pr5921   cs,nn8193   cs,nn5158   nn769

36 From Aroer, which *is* by the brink of the river of Arnon, and *from* the

wcj,df,nn5892 pnl834   dfp,nn5158   wcj,pr5704 df,nn1568   qpf1961 ptn3808   nn7151 (pnl834)

city   that *is* by the river, even   unto   Gilead, there was   not   one   city

qpf7682   pr,pnx4480   nn3068   pl,nn,pnx430 qpf5414   (853) df,nn3605 pp,pl,nn,pnx6440

too strong   for   us: the LORD our   God   delivered   all   unto   us:

ad7535   pr413   cs,nn776   pl,cs,nn1121   nn5983   qpf7126 ptn3808

37 Only unto the land of the children of Ammon thou camest not, *nor* unto

cs,nn3605 cs,nn3027   cs,nn5158   nn2999   wcj,pl,cs,nn5892   df,nn2022

any   place of the river Jabbok, nor unto the   cities   in the mountains, nor unto

wcj,nn3605   (pnl834)   nn3068   pl,nn,pnx430   pipf6680

whatsoever   the LORD our   God   forbade us.

Israel Defeats Og

wcs,qmf6437   wcs,qmf5927   cs,nn1870   df,nn1316   nn5747   cs,nn4428

3 Then we turned, and went up the way to Bashan: and Og the king of

df,nn1316   wcs,qmf3318   pp,qnc,pnx7125   pnp1931   wcj,cs,nn3605   nn,pnx5971   dfp,nn4421

Bashan came out against us, he and   all   his people, to battle at

nn154

Edrei.

nn3068   wcs,qmf559 pr,pnx413   qmf3372 pnx(853)   ptn408 cj3588   qpf5414   pnx(853)

2 And the LORD   said   unto me, Fear   him not: for I will deliver

wcj(853) cs,nn3605   nn,pnx5971   wcj(853)   nn,pnx776   pp,nn,pnx3027

him, and   all   his people, and   his land, into thy   hand; and thou shalt

wcj,qpf6213   pp,pnx   pp,pnl834   qpf6213   pp,nn5511 cs,nn4428   df,nn567   pnl834 qpta3427

do   unto him   as   thou didst unto Sihon king of the Amorites, which dwelt at

pp,nn2809

Heshbon.

nn3068   pl,nn,pnx430   wcs,qmf5414   pp,nn,pnx3027   (853) nn5747 ad1571   cs,nn4428

3 So the LORD our   God   delivered into our   hands   Og also, the king of

df,nn1316   wcj(853)   cs,nn3605   nn,pnx5971   wcs,himf,pnx5221   pr5704 ptn1115   hipf7604

Bashan, and   all   his people: and we   smote   him until none was left

pp,pnx   nn8300

to him remaining.

wcs,qmf3920   (853) cs,nn3605   pl,nn,pnx5892   df,pndm1931 dfp,nn6256   qpf1961 ptn3808   nn7151

4 And we took   all   his cities at   that   time, there was not a city

pnl834   qpf3947 ptn3808 pr4480/pr,pnx854   pl,nu8346   nn5892   cs,nn3605   cs,nn2256   nn709

which we took not   from   them, threescore cities,   all   the region of Argob,

cs,nn4467   nn5747   dfp,nn1316

the kingdom of Og in Bashan.

cs,nn3605 pndm428 pl,nn5892   pl,cs,qptp1219   aj1364   nn2346   du,nn1817   wcj,nn1280   pp,nn905

5 All   these cities *were* fenced with high walls, gates, and bars; beside

df,nn6521   pr4480/pl,cs,nn5892   ad3966 hina7235

unwalled   towns   a great many.

6 And we utterly destroyed them, as we did unto Sihon king of Heshbon, utterly destroying the men, women, and children, of every city.

7 But all the cattle, and the spoil of the cities, we took*for*a*prey to ourselves.

8 And we took at that time out*of*the*hand of the two kings of the Amorites the land that was on this side Jordan, from*the*river of Arnon unto mount Hermon;

9 (Which Hermon the Sidonians call Sirion; and the Amorites call it Shenir;)

10 All the cities of the plain, and all Gilead, and all Bashan, unto Salchah and Edrei, cities of the kingdom of Og in Bashan.

11 For only Og king of Bashan remained of*the*remnant of giants; behold, his bedstead was a bedstead of iron; is it not in Rabbath of the children of Ammon? nine cubits was the length thereof, and four cubits the breadth of it, after the cubit of a man.

The Transjordanic Tribes

12 And this land, which we possessed at that time, from Aroer, which is by the river Arnon, and half mount Gilead, and the cities thereof, gave I unto the Reubenites and to the Gadites.

13 And the rest of Gilead, and all Bashan, being the kingdom of Og, gave I unto the half tribe of Manasseh; all the region of Argob, with all Bashan, which was called the land of giants.

14 Jair the son of Manasseh took all the country of Argob unto the coasts of Geshuri and Maachathi; and called them after his own name, Bashan-havoth-jair, unto this day.

15 And I gave Gilead unto Machir.

16 And unto the Reubenites and unto the Gadites I gave from Gilead even

wcj,pr5704   cs,nn5158   nn769   cs,nn**8432**   df,nn5158   wcj,nn1366   wcj,pr5704   cs,nn5158

unto the river Arnon half the valley, and the border even unto the river

nn2999   cs,nn1366   pl,cs,nn**1121**   nn5983

Jabbok, *which is* the border of the children of Ammon;

wcj,df,nn**6160**   wcj,df,nn3383   wcj,nn1366   pr4480/nn3672

17 The plain also, and Jordan, and the coast *thereof*, from Chinnereth even

wcj,pr5704   cs,nn3220   df,nn**6160**   df,nn4417 cs,nn3220 pr8478   pl,cs,nn798/df,nn6449   nn,lh4217

unto the sea of the plain, *even* the salt sea, under Ashdoth-pisgah eastward.

wcs,pimf**6680**   pnx(853)   df,pndm1931 dfp,nn**6256** pp,qnc559   nn3068   pl,nn,pnx**430**

18 And I commanded   you at that time, saying, The LORD your God

qpf5414 pp,pnx (853) df,pndm2063 df,nn**776**   pp,qnc,pnx**3423**   qmf5674   pl,qptp2502 pp,pl,cs,nn**6440**

hath given you   this land to possess it: ye shall pass over armed before

pl,nn,pnx**251**   pl,cs,nn**1121**   nn3478 cs,nn3605   pl,cs,nn**1121**/nn2438

your brethren the children of Israel, all *that are* meet*for*the*war.

ad7535   pl,nn,pnx**802**   wcj,nn,pnx2945   wcj,nn,pnx4735   qpf3045 cj3588

19 But your wives, and your little ones, and your cattle, (*for* I know that

pp,pnx   aj7227 nn4735   qmf3427   pp,pl,nn,pnx5892 pnl834   qpf5414 pp,pnx

ye have much cattle,) shall abide in your cities which I have given you;

cj5704/pnl834   nn3068   himf5117   pp,pl,nn,pnx**251**   pp,pnx

20 Until the LORD have given rest unto your brethren, as well as unto you,

pnp1992 ad1571 wcs,qpf**3423** (853)   df,nn**776** pnl834   nn3068   pl,nn,pnx**430**   qpta5414

and *until* they also possess the land which the LORD your God hath given

pp,pnx pp,cs,nn5676 df,nn3383   wcs,qpf7725   nn376   pp,nn,pnx**3425** pnl834

them beyond Jordan: and *then* shall ye return every man unto his possession, which

qpf**5414** pp,pnx

I have given you.

pipf**6680**   wcj(853)   nn3091   df,pndm1931 dfp,nn**6256** pp,qnc559   du,nn,pnx**5869**

21 And I commanded   Joshua at that time, saying, Thine eyes have

df,pl,qpta**7200** (853) cs,nn3605 pnl834   nn**3068**   pl,nn,pnx**430**   qpf6213   df,pndm428 df,du,cs,nu8147 df,pl,nn**4428**

seen   all that the LORD your God hath done unto these two kings:

ad3651   nn**3068** qmf**6213**   pp,cs,nn3605   df,pl,nn**4467**   pnl834/ad,lh8033 pnp859   qpta5674

so shall the LORD do unto all the kingdoms whither thou passest.

ptn3808   qmf,pnx**3372**   cj3588   nn**3068**   pl,nn,pnx**430** pnp1931   df,nipt3898

22 Ye shall not fear them: for the LORD your God he shall fight

pp,pnx

for you.

Moses Is Forbidden To Enter Canaan

wcs,htmf**2603**/pr413   nn**3068**   df,pndm1931 dfp,nn**6256** pp,qnc559

23 And I besought the LORD at that time, saying,

nn136   nn3069 pnp859   hipf**2490**   pp,hinc**7200** (853)   nn,pnx**5650** (853)   nn,pnx1433

24 O Lord GOD, thou hast begun to show   thy servant   thy greatness, and

wcj(853)   df,aj**2389**   nn,pnx**3027** pnl834 pnit4310 nn**410**   dfp,du,nn**8064**   wcj,dfp,nn**776** pnl834   qmf**6213**

thy mighty hand: for what God *is there* in heaven or in earth, that can do

pp,pl,nn,pnx4639   wcj,pp,pl,nn,pnx1369

according to thy works, and according to thy might?

pte4994   qcj**5674**   wcj,qmf**7200** (853)   df,aj**2896** df,nn**776** pnl834   pp,cs,nn5676

25 I*pray*thee, let me go over, and see   the good land that *is* beyond

df,nn3383   df,pndm2088 df,aj**2896**   df,nn2022   wcj,df,nn3844

Jordan, that goodly mountain, and Lebanon.

nn**3068**   wcs,htmf**5674**   pp,pnx   pp,pr,pnx4616   wcj,ptn**3808**

26 But the LORD was wroth with me for*your*sakes, and would not

qpf**8085**/pr,pnx413   nn**3068**   wcs,qmf**559**   pr,pnx413   ad7227   pp,pnx   pinc**1696**   ptn408

hear   me: and the LORD   said   unto   me, Let it suffice thee; speak   no

himf3254/ad5750   pr,pnx413   df,pndm2088   dfp,nn**1697**

more   unto me of   this   matter.

qmv**5927**   cs,nn**7218**   df,nn6449   wcj,qmv**5375**   du,nn,pnx**5869**   nn,lh3220

27 Get*thee*up into the   top of Pisgah, and lift up thine   eyes   westward,

wcj,nn,lh6828   wcj,nn,lh8486   wcj,nn,lh4217   wcj,qmv**7200**   pp,du,nn,pnx**5869**

and northward, and southward, and eastward, and behold it with thine   eyes:

cj3588   ptn3808   qmf**5674**   (853) df,pndm2088   df,nn3383

for thou shalt not go over   this   Jordan.

wcj,pimv**6680** (853)   nn3091   wcj,pimv,pnx**2388**   wcj,pimv,pnx553   cj3588 pnp1931

28 But charge   Joshua, and encourage him, and strengthen him: for   he

qmf**5674** pp,pl,cs,nn**6440** df,pndm2088   df,nn**5971**   wcj,pnp1931   pnx(853)   himf**5157**

shall go over   before   this people, and he   shall cause   them to inherit

(853)   df,nn776   pnl834   qmf**7200**

the land which thou shalt see.

wcs,qmf**3427**   dfp,nn1516   pr4136   nn1047

29 So we abode in the valley over against Beth-peor.

Moses Urges Obedience

wcj,ad6258   qmv**8085**   nn3478   pr413   df,pl,nn**2706**   wcj,pr413   df,pl,nn**4941**

4 Now therefore hearken, O Israel, unto the statutes and unto the judgments,

pnl834   pnp595 pipt**3925** pnx(853)   pp,qnc**6213**   pp,cj4616   qmf**2421**

which I   teach   you, for to   do   them, that ye may live, and

wcs,qpf935   wcs,qpf**3423** (853)   df,nn776 pnl834   nn3068 pl,cs,nn,pnx**430**   pl,nn,pnx1 qpta**5414** pp,pnx

go in and possess   the land which the LORD   God of your fathers giveth you.

ptn**3808** himf3254 pr5921   df,nn**1697** pnl834 pnp595 pipt**6680**   pnx(853)   wcj,ptn**3808**

2 Ye shall not   add unto the word which   I   command   you, neither

qmf1639   pr,pnx4480   pp,qnc**8104** (853)   pl,cs,nn**4687**

shall ye diminish aught from it, that ye may   keep   the commandments of the

nn3068   pl,nn,pnx**430** pnl834 pnp595 pipt**6680** pnx(853)

LORD your God which I   command   you.

du,nn,pnx**5869**   df,pl,qpta**7200** (853) pnl834   nn3068 qpf**6213**   pp,nn1187 cj3588

3 Your   eyes   have   seen   what the LORD did because of Baal-peor: for

cs,nn3605   df,nn376 pnl834 qpf**1980**/pr310   nn1187   nn3068   pl,nn,pnx**430** hipf,pnx**8045**

all   the men that followed Baal-peor, the LORD thy God   hath destroyed them

pr4480/nn,pnx**7130**

from among you.

wcj,pnp859   df,aj1695   pp,nn**3068**   pl,nn,pnx**430**   aj**2416** nn,pnx3605

4 But   ye   that did cleave unto the LORD your   God are alive every one of

df,nn**3117**

you this day.

qmv**7200**   pipf**3925** pnx(853)   pl,nn**2706** wcj,pl,nn**4941** pp,pnl834   nn3068

5 Behold, I have taught   you statutes and judgments, even as the LORD my

pl,nn,pnx**430** pipf,pnx**6680**   pp,qnc**6213** ad3651 pp,cs,nn**7130**   df,nn776 pnl834/ad,lh8033 pnp859

God commanded me, that ye should   do   so   in   the land whither ye

pl,qpta935   pp,qnc,pnx**3423**

go to possess it.

wcs,qpf**8104**   wcs,qpf**6213**   cj3588 pndm1931   nn,pnx2451

6 Keep therefore and   do   them; for   this is your wisdom and your

pp,ptn1097/nn**1847**   wcj(pnp1931)   qpta**8130**   pp,pnx   ptn**3808**   pr4480/ad8543/ad8032   wcs,qpf5127   pr413   nu259   pr4480

unawares, and   hated him not in*times*past; and that fleeing unto one of

df,pndm411   df,pl,nn5892   wcs,qpf**2425**

these   cities   he might   live:

             (853)   nn1221   dfp,nn4057   df,nn**4334**   pp,cs,nn776   dfp,nn7206

43 *Namely,*   Bezer in the wilderness, in the plain country, of the Reubenites;

wcj(853)   nn7216   dfp,nn1568   dfp,nn1425   wcj(853)   nn1474   dfp,nn1316

and   Ramoth in Gilead, of the Gadites; and   Golan in Bashan, of the

dfp,nn4520

Manassites.

Moses Reiterates the Law

         wcj,pndm2063   df,nn**8451**   pnl834   nn4872   qpf**7760**   pp,pl,cs,nn**6440**   pl,cs,nn**1121**   nn3478

44 And   this   *is* the law which Moses set   before   the children of Israel:

      pndm428   df,pl,nn5713   wcj,df,pl,nn2706   wcj,df,pl,nn**4941**   pnl834   nn4872

45 These *are* the testimonies, and the statutes, and the judgments, which Moses

pipf**1696**   pr413   pl,cs,nn**1121**   nn3478   pp,qnc,pnx3318   pr4480/nn4714

spoke unto the children of Israel, after they came forth out*of*Egypt,

          pp,cs,nn5676   df,nn3383   dfp,nn1516   pr4136   nn1047   pp,cs,nn776

46 On*this*side Jordan, in the valley over against Beth-peor, in the   land   of

nn5511   cs,nn**4428**   df,nn567   pnl834   qpta**3427**   pp,nn2809   pnl834   nn4872   wcj,pl,cs,nn**1121**

Sihon king of the Amorites, who dwelt at Heshbon, whom Moses and the children

nn3478   hipf**5221**   pp,qnc,pnx3318   pr4480/nn4714

of Israel smote, after they were come forth out*of*Egypt:

          wcs,qmf3423   (853)   nn,pnx776   wcj(853)   cs,nn776   nn5747 cs,nn**4428**   df,nn1316

47 And they possessed   his land, and   the land of Og   king of Bashan,

du,cs,nu8147   pl,cs,nn**4428**   df,nn567   pnl834   pp,cs,nn5676   df,nn3383

two   kings   of   the   Amorites,   which   *were*   on*this*side   Jordan

         cs,nn4217/nn8121

toward*the*sunrising;

       pr4480/nn6177   pnl834   pr5921   cs,nn**8193**   cs,nn5158   nn769   wcj,pr5704   cs,nn2022

48 From Aroer, which *is* by the bank of the river Arnon, even unto mount

nn7865   pnp1931   nn2768

Zion, which *is* Hermon,

        wcj,cs,nn3605   df,nn**6160**   cs,nn5676   df,nn3383   nn,lh4217   wcj,pr5704   cs,nn3220

49 And   all   the plain on*this*side Jordan eastward, even   unto   the   sea

      df,nn**6160**   pr8478   pl,cs,nn794   df,nn6449

of the plain, under the springs of Pisgah.

The Ten Commandments

5   nn4872   wcs,qmf**7121**/pr413   cs,nn3605   nn3478   wcs,qmf559   pr,pnx413   qmv**8085**   nn3478

And Moses   called   all   Israel, and   said   unto them, Hear, O Israel,

     (853)   df,pl,nn**2706**   wcj(853)   df,pl,nn**4941**   pnl834   pnp595   qpta**1696**   pp,du,nn,pnx**241**

the statutes and   judgments which   I   speak in your   ears   this

df,nn3117   wcj,qpf3925   pnx(853)   wcj,qpf**8104**   pp,qnc,pnx**6213**

day, that ye may learn   them, and keep, and   do   them.

        nn3068   pl,nn,pnx**430**   qpf3772   nn1285   pr,pnx5973   pp,nn2722

2 The LORD our   God   made a covenant   with   us in Horeb.

nn3068   qpf3772   ptn3808   (853)   df,pndm2063   df,nn1285   pr854   pl,nn,pnx1   cj3588   pr,pnx854
3 The LORD made not   this   covenant with our fathers, but   with

pnp587   pndm428   nn,pnx3605   ad6311   aj2416   df,nn3117
us, *even* us, who *are*   all   of us here alive this day.

nn3068   pipf1696   pr,pnx5973   pl,nn6440/pp,pl,nn6440   dfp,nn2022   pr4480/cs,nn8432
4 The LORD talked   with you face*to*face in the mount out*of*the*midst of

df,nn784
the fire,

pnp595   qpta5975   pr996   nn3068   wcj,pnx(pr996)   df,pndm1931 dfp,nn6256   pp,hinc5046 pp,pnx
5 (I   stood between the LORD and   you at   that   time, to show you

(853)   cs,nn1697   nn3068   cj3588   qpf3372   pr4480/pl,cs,nn6440   df,nn784
the   word   of   the   LORD: for ye   were afraid by*reason*of   the   fire,

qpf5927/wcj,ptn3808   dfp,nn2022   pp,qnc559
and went*not*up into the mount;) saying,

pnp595   nn3068   pl,nn,pnx430 pnl834 hipf,pnx3318   pr4480/nn776   nn4714
6 I *am* the LORD thy God,   which brought thee out*of*the*land of Egypt,

pr4480/cs,nn1004   pl,nn5650
from*the*house of bondage.

pp,pnx   qmf1961 ptn3808 aj312   pl,nn430 pr5921/pl,nn,pnx6440
7 Thou shalt have none other gods   before   me.

ptn3808 qmf6213 pp,pnx   nn6459   cs,nn3605   nn8544
8 Thou shalt not make thee *any* graven image, *or* any   likeness *of any thing*

pnl834   df,du,nn8064 pr4480/ad4605   wcj,pnl834   dfp,nn776 pr4480/pr8478   wcj,pnl834
that *is* in heaven above,   or   that *is* in the earth beneath, or that *is* in the

dfp,pl,nn4325 pr4480/pr8478   dfp,nn776
waters beneath the earth:

ptn3808   htmf7812   pp,pnx   wcj,ptn3808 homf,pnx5647   cj3588 pnp595
9 Thou shalt not bow*down*thyself unto them,   nor   serve   them: for   I

nn3068   pl,nn,pnx430   aj7067   nn410   qpta6485   cs,nn5771   pl,nn1   pr5921
the LORD thy God *am* a jealous God, visiting the iniquity of the fathers upon the

pl,nn1121 wcj,pr5921   pl,nu8029   wcj(pr5921) pl,aj7256   pp,pl,qpta,pnx8130
children unto the third and   fourth *generation* of them that   hate   me,

wcj,qpta6213   nn2617   pp,pl,nu505   pp,pl,qpta,pnx157
10 And showing mercy unto thousands of them that   love   me and

wcj,pp,pl,cs,qpta8104   pl,nn,pnx4687
keep   my commandments.

ptn3808 qmf5375 (853)   cs,nn8034   nn3068   pl,nn,pnx430 dfp,nn7723 cj3588
11 Thou shalt not take   the name of the LORD thy God in vain: for the

nn3068   ptn3808   pimf5352   (853) pnl834 qmf5375 (853)   nn,pnx8034   dfp,nn7723
LORD will not hold*him*guiltless   that taketh   his name in vain.

qna8104   (853)   df,nn7676   cs,nn3117   pp,pinc,pnx6942   pp,pnl834   nn3068   pl,nn,pnx430
12 Keep   the sabbath day to sanctify it,   as   the LORD thy God hath

pipf,pnx6680
commanded thee.

cs,nu8337 pl,nn3117   qmf5647   wcs,qpf6213 cs,nn3605   nn,pnx4399
13 Six   days thou shalt labor, and   do   all thy work:

df,nuor7637 wcj,cs,nn3117   nn7676   pp,nn3068   pl,nn,pnx430
14 But the seventh   day *is* the sabbath of the LORD thy God: *in it* thou

ptn3808 qmf6213 cs,nn3605   nn4399   pnp859   wcj,nn,pnx1121   wcj,nn,pnx1323
shalt not do   any work, thou, nor thy son,   nor thy daughter, nor thy

wcj,nn,pnx5650   wcj,nn,pnx519   wcj,nn,pnx7794   wcj,nn,pnx2543 wcj,cs,nn3605
manservant, nor thy maidservant, nor thine   ox,   nor thine   ass,   nor any

---

5:9 See the note on Ezekiel 18:1–32.

nn,pnx929   wcj,nn,pnx1616 pnl834   pp,pl,nn,pnx8179 pp,cj4616   nn,pnx5650

of thy cattle, nor thy stranger that *is* within thy   gates;   that thy manservant and

wcj,nn,pnx519   qmf5117   pp,pnx

thy maidservant may rest as*well*as*thou.

wcs,qpf2142   cj3588   qpf1961   nn5650   pp,cs,nn776   nn4714

15 And remember that thou wast a servant in the land of Egypt, and *that* the

nn3068   pl,nn,pnx430   wcs,himf,pnx3318   pr4480/ad8033   aj2389   pp,nn3027

LORD thy   God brought*thee*out thence   through a mighty hand and by a

qptp5186   wcj,pp,nn2220 pr5921/ad3651   nn3068   pl,nn,pnx430   pipf,pnx6680   pp,qnc6213 (853)

stretched out   arm: therefore the LORD thy   God   commanded thee to keep

df,nn7676   cs,nn3117

the sabbath day.

pina3513 (853)   nn,pnx1   wcj(853)   nn,pnx517 pp,pnl834   nn3068   pl,nn,pnx430

16 Honor   thy father and   thy mother,   as   the LORD thy   God hath

pipf,pnx6680   pp,cj4416   pl,nn,pnx3117   himf748   wcj,pp,cj4616   qmf3190

commanded thee; that thy days may be prolonged, and   that   it may go well

pp,pnx   pr5921   df,nn127 pnl834   nn3068   pl,nn,pnx430 qpta5414   pp,pnx

with thee, in the land which the LORD thy   God   giveth thee.

ptn3808 qmf7523

17 Thou shalt not kill.

wcj,ptn3808   qmf5003

18 Neither shalt thou commit adultery.

wcj,ptn3808   qmf1589

19 Neither shalt thou steal.

wcj,ptn3808   qmf6030 nn7723   nn5707   pp,nn,pnx7453

20 Neither shalt thou bear false witness against thy neighbor.

wcj,ptn3808   qmf2530   nn,pnx7453   cs,nn802 wcj,ptn3808   htmf183

21 Neither shalt thou desire thy neighbor's wife, neither shalt thou covet thy

nn,pnx7453   cs,nn1004   nn,pnx7704   wcj,nn,pnx5650   wcj,nn,pnx519   nn,pnx7794

neighbor's house, his field, or his manservant, or his maidservant, his ox, or his

wcj,nn,pnx2543   wcj,nn3605   pnl834   pp,nn,pnx7453

ass,   or any *thing* that *is* thy neighbor's.

(853) df,pndm428 df,pl,nn1697   nn3068 pipf1696   pr413 cs,nn3605   nn,pnx6951   dfp,nn2022

22   These words the LORD spoke unto   all   your assembly in the mount

pr4480/cs,nn8432   df,nn784   df,nn6051   wcj,df,nn6205   aj1419

out*of*the*midst of the fire, of the cloud, and of the thick darkness, with a great

nn6963   qpf3254/wcj,ptn3808   wcs,qmf,pnx3789   pr5921 du,cs,nu8147 pl,cs,nn3871   pl,nn68

voice: and he added*no*more. And he wrote   them in   two   tables of stone,

wcs,qmf,pnx5414   pr,pnx413

and delivered them unto me.

wcs,qmf1961   pp,qnc,pnx8085 (853)   df,nn6963   pr4480/cs,nn8432

23 And it*came*to*pass, when ye   heard   the voice out*of*the*midst of

df,nn2822   wcj,df,nn2022   qpta1197   dfp,nn784   wcs,qmf7126   pr,pnx413

the darkness, (for the mountain did burn with fire,) that ye came near unto me,

cs,nn3605   pl,cs,nn7218   pl,nn,pnx7626   wcj,aj,pnx2205

even all the heads of your tribes, and your elders;

wcs,qmf559   ptdm2005   nn3068   pl,nn,pnx430   hipf,pnx7200   (853)   nn,pnx3519

24 And ye said, Behold, the LORD our   God   hath showed us   his glory

wcj(853)   nn,pnx1433   qpf8085 wcj(853)   nn,pnx6963   pr4480/cs,nn8432

and   his greatness, and we have heard   his voice out*of*the*midst of the

df,nn784   qpf7200 df,pndm2088 df,nn3117 cj3588 pl,nn430   pimf1696 pr854 df,nn120   wcs,qpf2425

fire: we have seen   this   day that God doth talk with man, and he liveth.

wcj,ad6258   pp,pnit4100   qmf4191 cj3588 df,pndm2063 df,aj1419 df,nn784   qmf,pnx398

25 Now therefore why should we die? for   this   great fire will consume

cj518 pnp587 pp,qnc**8085** (853)   cs,nn6963   nn**3068**   pl,nn,pnx**430** pl,qpta3254/ad5750
us: if we hear   the voice of the L<small>ORD</small> our God any more, then we shall
wcs,qpf**4191**
die.

cj3588 pnit4310   cs,nn3605 nn1320 pnl834   qpf**8085**   cs,nn6963   aj2416   pl,nn**430**
26 For who *is there of* all flesh, that hath heard the voice of the living God
pipt**1696**   pr4480/cs,nn**8432**   df,nn784 pp,pnx3644   wcs,qmf**2421**
speaking out*of*the*midst of the fire, as we *have*, and lived?

qmv7126/pnp859   wcj,qmv**8085** (853) cs,nn3605 pnl834   nn**3068**   pl,nn,pnx**430**   qmf**559**
27 Go*thou*near, and hear   all that the L<small>ORD</small> our God shall say: and
pimf**1696** wcj,pnp859 pr,pnx413   (853) cs,nn3605 pnl834   nn**3068**   pl,nn,pnx**430**   pimf**1696** pr,pnx413
speak thou unto us   all that the L<small>ORD</small> our God shall speak unto thee;
wcs,qpf**8085**   wcs,qpf**6213**
and we will hear *it*, and do *it*.

nn**3068** wcs,qmf**8085** (853)   cs,nn6963   pl,nn,pnx**1697**   pp,pinc,pnx**1696** pr,pnx413
28 And the L<small>ORD</small> heard   the voice of your words, when ye spoke unto
nn**3068** wcs,qmf**559** pr,pnx413   qpf**8085** (853)   cs,nn6963   pl,cs,nn**1697**
me; and the L<small>ORD</small> said unto me, I have heard   the voice of the words of
df,pndm2088 df,nn**5971** pnl834   pipf**1696** pr,pnx413   hipf**3190** cs,nn3605 pnl834
this people, which they have spoken unto thee: they have well said all   that
pipf**1696**
they have spoken.

pnid4310/qmf**5414**   wcs,qpf**1961** pndm2088 nn,pnx3824 pp,pnx   pp,qnc**3372** pnx(853)
29 O that there were such a heart in them, that they would fear
wcj,pp,qnc**8104** (853) cs,nn3605   pl,nn,pnx**4687** cs,nn3605/df,pl,nn**3117** pp,cj4616   qmf**3190**
me, and keep   all my commandments always,   that it might be well
pp,pnx   wcj,pp,pl,nn,pnx**1121** pp,nn**5769**
with them, and with their children forever!

qmv**1980** qmv**559** pp,pnx qmv**7725** pp,pnx   pp,pl,nn,pnx**168**
30 Go say to them, Get you into your tents again.

wcj,pnp859 qmv5975 ad6311 pr,pnx5978   wcj,picj**1696** pr,pnx413   (853)
31 But as for thee, stand thou here by me, and I will speak unto thee
cs,nn3605   df,nn**4687**   wcj,df,pl,nn**2706**   wcj,df,pl,nn**4941** pnl834
all the commandments, and the statutes, and the judgments, which thou shalt
pimf,pnx**3925**   wcs,qpf**6213**   dfp,nn776 pnl834 pnp595 qpta**5414** pp,pnx
teach them, that they may do *them* in the land which I give them to
pp,qnc,pnx**3423**
possess it.

wcs,qpf**8104**   pp,qnc**6213**   pp,pnl834   nn**3068**   pl,nn,pnx**430**
32 Ye shall observe to do therefore as the L<small>ORD</small> your God hath
pipf**6680**   pnx(853)   ptn3808   qmf5493   nn3225   wcj,nn8040
commanded   you: ye shall not turn aside to the right hand or to the left.
qmf**1980**   pp,cs,nn3605   df,nn**1870** pnl834   nn**3068**   pl,nn,pnx**430**
33 Ye shall walk in   all the ways which the L<small>ORD</small> your God hath
pipf**6680**   pnx(853)   pp,cj4616   qmf**2421**   wcs,qpf**2895** pp,pnx
commanded   you, that ye may live, and *that it may be* well with you, and
wcs,hipf**748**   pl,nn3117   dfp,nn776 pnl834   qmf**3423**
that ye may prolong *your* days in the land which ye shall possess.

Remember God Every Day

6 Now these *are* the commandments, the statutes, and the judgments, which the LORD your God commanded to teach you, that ye might do *them* in the land whither ye go to possess it:

2 That thou mightest fear the LORD thy God, to keep all his statutes and his commandments, which I command thee, thou, and thy son, and thy son's son, all the days of thy life; and that thy days may be prolonged.

3 Hear therefore, O Israel, and observe to do *it*; that it may be well with thee, and that ye may increase mightily, as the LORD God of thy fathers hath promised thee, in the land that floweth with milk and honey.

4 Hear, O Israel: The LORD our God *is* one LORD:

5 And thou shalt love the LORD thy God with all thine heart, and with all thy soul, and with all thy might.

6 And these words, which I command thee this day, shall be in thine heart:

7 And thou shalt teach*them*diligently unto thy children, and shalt talk of them when thou sittest in thine house, and when thou walkest by the way, and when thou liest down, and when thou risest up.

8 And thou shalt bind them for a sign upon thine hand, and they shall be as frontlets between thine eyes.

9 And thou shalt write them upon the posts of thy house, and on thy gates.

6:4–9 To the Jew, this is the most important text in the Old Testament. Jesus Himself called the injunction in 6:5 "the first and great commandment" (Matt. 22:36–38; see the note on Ex. 20:1–17). The Jews refer to Deuteronomy 6:4 as the "Shema," naming it after the first word in the text. In this instance the word means to heed, or listen and obey. Moses is teaching not only the priority of belief in one God, but also a means to preserve that belief. As time went on, the proper understanding of the Shema with its spiritual implications was no longer grasped by the people (Zech. 7:12–14; James 1:22–25). This absence of saving knowledge became a factor in their spiritual downfall (Hos. 4:6) which ultimately led to the deportation of Israel and the exile of Judah.

wcj,qpf1961   cj3588   nn3068   pl,nn,pnx430   himf,pnx935   pr413

10 And it shall be,   when the LORD thy   God   shall have brought thee into

df,nn776   pnl834   nipf7650   pp,pl,nn,pnx1   pp,nn85   pp,nn3327   wcj,pp,nn3290

the land which he swore unto thy fathers, to Abraham, to Isaac, and to Jacob, to

pp,qnc5414 pp,pnx aj1419   wcj,aj2896 pl,nn5892 pnl834   qpf1129   ptn3808

give thee great and goodly cities, which thou buildedst not,

wcj,pl,nn1004 aj4392   cs,nn3605 nn2898   pnl834   pipf4390   ptn3808   wcj,pl,nn953

11 And houses full of   all   good *things*, which thou filledst not, and wells

pl,qptp2672   pnl834   qpf2672   ptn3808   pl,nn3754   wcj,pl,nn2132   pnl834   qpf5193

digged, which thou diggedst not, vineyards and olive trees, which thou plantedst

ptn3808   wcj,qpf398   wcj,qpf7646

not; when thou shalt have eaten and be full;

nimf8104/pp,pnx cj6435   qmf7911   (853)   nn3068   pnl834   hipf,pnx3318

12 *Then* beware lest thou forget   the LORD, which brought*thee*forth

pr4480/cs,nn776   nn4714   pr4480/cs,nn1004   pl,nn5650

out*of*the*land of Egypt, from*the*house of bondage.

qmf3372 (853)   nn3068   pl,nn,pnx430   qmf5647 wcj,pnx(853)

☞ 13 Thou shalt fear   the LORD thy God, and serve   him, and shalt

nimf7650   wcj,pp,nn,pnx8034

swear by his   name.

ptn3808   qmf1980   pr310   aj312   pl,nn430   pr4480/pl,cs,nn430   df,pl,nn5971   pnl834

14 Ye shall not   go after other gods, of*the*gods of the people which *are*

pr,pnx5439

round about you;

cj3588   nn3068   pl,nn,pnx430   aj7067   nn410 pp,nn,pnx7130   cj6435   cs,nn639

15 (For the LORD thy   God   *is* a jealous God among you) lest the anger of the

nn3068   pl,nn,pnx430   qmf2734   pp,pnx   wcs,hipf,pnx8045   pr4480/pr5921   pl,cs,nn6440

LORD thy   God   be kindled against thee, and destroy thee from off the face of

df,nn127

the earth.

ptn3808   pimf5254   (853)   nn3068   pl,nn,pnx430 pp,pnl834   pipf5254

☞ 16 Ye shall not tempt   the LORD your God,   as   ye tempted *him* in

dfp,nn4532

Massah.

qna8104/qmf8104   (853)   pl,cs,nn4687   nn3068   pl,nn,pnx430

17 Ye shall diligently keep   the commandments of the LORD your God, and

wcj,pl,nn,pnx5713   wcj,pl,nn,pnx2706 pnl834   pipf,pnx6680

his testimonies, and his statutes, which he hath commanded thee.

wcj,qpf6213   df,aj3477   wcj,df,aj2896   pp,du,cs,nn5869

18 And thou shalt do   *that which is* right and good in the   sight of the

nn3068   pp,cj4616   qmf3190   pp,pnx   wcs,qpf935   wcs,qpf3423 (853)

LORD: that it may be well with thee, and that thou mayest go in and possess

df,aj2896 df,nn776 pnl834   nn3068   nipf7650   pp,pl,nn,pnx1

the good land which the LORD swore unto thy fathers,

pp,qnc1920 (853) cs,nn3605   pl,qpta,pnx341 pr4480/pl,nn,pnx6440   pp,pnl834   nn3068

19 To cast out   all   thine enemies from before thee,   as   the LORD hath

pipf1696

spoken.

cj3588   nn,pnx1121 qmf,pnx7592   ad4279   pp,qnc559 pnit4100

20 *And* when thy   son   asketh thee in*time*to*come, saying, What *mean* the

---

☞ **6:13, 16** Jesus quoted part of verse thirteen and Deuteronomy 10:20 in response to one of Satan's temptations (Matt. 4:10; Luke 4:8). In fact, the early part of this book, which was spoken by Moses while Israel was still in the period of her wilderness wanderings, formed the basis of all three of Jesus' responses to Satan. "Thou shalt not tempt the Lord thy God" (Matt. 4:7; Luke 4:12) comes from Deuteronomy 6:16, and "Man shall not live by bread alone" (Matt. 4:4; Luke 4:4) is a quotation of Deuteronomy 8:3.

df,pl,nn**5713**   wcj,df,pl,nn**2706**   wcj,df,pl,nn**4941**   pnl834   nn**3068**   pl,nn,pnx**430**
testimonies, and the statutes, and the judgments, which the LORD our God hath

pipf**6680**   pnx(853)
commanded   you?

                  wcj,qpf**559**   pp,nn,pnx**1121**   qpf**1961**   pp,nn**6547**   pl,nn**5650**
21 Then thou shalt say unto thy son, We were Pharaoh's bondmen in

pp,nn**4714**   nn**3068**   wcs,himf,pnx**3318**   pr4480/nn**4714**   aj**2389**   pp,nn**3027**
Egypt; and the LORD brought*us*out of Egypt with a mighty hand:

              nn**3068**   wcs,qmf**5414** pl,nn**226**   wcj,df,nn**4159** aj**1419**   wcj,aj**7451**   pp,nn**4714**
22 And the LORD showed signs and wonders, great and sore, upon Egypt, upon

pp,nn**6547**   wcj,pp,cs,nn**3605**   nn,pnx**1004**   pp,du,nn,pnx**5869**
Pharaoh, and upon all   his household, before our eyes:

              hipf3318/wcj,pnx(853)   pr4480/ad8033   pp,cj4616   hinc935/pnx(853)   pp,qnc**5414**
23 And he brought*us*out from thence, that he might bring*us*in, to give

pp,pnx (853)   df,nn**776** pnl834   nipf**7650**   pp,pl,nn,pnx**1**
us   the land which he swore unto our fathers.

              nn**3068**   wcs,pimf,pnx**6680**   pp,qnc**6213** (853) cs,nn**3605** df,pndm428 df,pl,nn**2706**   pp,qnc**3372**
24 And the LORD commanded us to do   all   these statutes, to fear

(853) nn**3068**   pl,nn,pnx**430**   pp,pnx pp,nn**2896** cs,nn3605/df,pl,nn**3117**   pp,pinc,pnx**2421**
the LORD our God, for our good   always,   that he might preserve*us*alive,

              df,pndm2088 dfp,nn**3117**
as it is at this day.

              qmf**1961** pp,pnx   wcj,nn**6666**   cj3588   qmf**8104**   pp,qnc**6213** (853) cs,nn3605
25 And it shall be our righteousness, if we observe to do   all

df,pndm2063   df,nn**4687**   pp,pl,cs,nn**6440**   nn**3068**   pl,nn,pnx**430** pp,pnl834   pipf,pnx**6680**
these commandments before the LORD our God, as he hath commanded us.

Totally Destroy The Canaanite Culture

          cj3588   nn**3068**   pl,nn,pnx**430**   himf,pnx**935**   pr413   df,nn**776** pnl834/ad,lh8033 pnp859
7 When the LORD thy God shall bring thee into the land whither thou

          qpta935   pp,qnc,pnx**3423**   wcs,qpf5394   aj7227   pl,nn**1471** pr4480/pl,nn,pnx**6440**
goest to possess it, and hath cast out many nations   before   thee, the

df,nn2850   wcj,df,nn1622   wcj,df,nn567   wcj,df,nn3669
Hittites, and the Girgashites, and the Amorites, and the Canaanites, and the

wcj,df,nn6522   wcj,df,nn2340   wcj,df,nn2983   nu7651   pl,nn**1471**   aj7227   wcj,aj6099
Perizzites, and the Hivites, and the Jebusites, seven nations greater and mightier

pr,pnx4480
than thou;

              nn**3068**   pl,nn,pnx**430**   wcs,qpf,pnx**5414**   pp,pl,nn,pnx**6440**
2 And when the LORD thy God shall deliver them before thee; thou shalt

wcs,hipf,pnx**5221**   hina2763/himf2763   pnx(853)   qmf3772 ptn3808   nn1285
smite them, and utterly destroy   them; thou shalt make no covenant

pp,pnx   wcj,ptn**3808**   qmf,pnx**2603**
with them, nor show mercy unto them:

          wcj,ptn**3808**   htmf2859   pp,pnx   nn,pnx1323   ptn3808
3 Neither shalt thou make marriages with them; thy daughter thou shalt not

qmf5414   pp,nn,pnx**1121** ptn3808 wcj,nn,pnx1323   qmf3947   pp,nn,pnx**1121**
give unto his son, nor his daughter shalt thou take unto thy son.

          cj3588   himf5493   (853)   nn,pnx1121   pr4480/pr,pnx310
4 For they will turn away   thy son from following me, that they may

_{wcs,qpf5647} _{aj312} _{pl,nn430}   _{cs,nn639}   _{nn3068}   _{wcs,qpf2734}   _{pp,pnx}
serve other gods: so will the anger of the Lord be kindled against you, and

_{wcs,hipf,pnx8045}   _{ad4118}
destroy thee suddenly.

_{cj3588/cj518} _{ad3541}   _{qmf6213}   _{pp,pnx;}   _{qmf5422}   _{pl,nn,pnx4196}
5 But   thus shall ye deal with them; ye shall destroy their altars, and

_{pimf7665}   _{wcj,pl,nn,pnx4676}   _{pimf1438}   _{wcj,pl,nn,pnx842}   _{qmf8313}
break down their   images,   and cut down their groves,   and burn their

_{wcj,pl,nn,pnx6456}   _{dfp,nn784}
graven images with fire.

_{cj3588} _{pnp859}   _{aj6918} _{nn5971}   _{pp,nn3068}   _{pl,nn,pnx430}   _{nn3068}   _{pl,nn,pnx430}
6 For thou *art* a holy people unto the Lord thy God: the Lord thy   God

_{qpf977}   _{pp,pnx}   _{pp,qnc1961}   _{nn5459} _{pp,cs,nn5971}   _{pp,pnx}   _{pr4480/cs,nn3605} _{df,pl,nn5971} _{pnl834}
hath chosen thee to be a special people unto himself, above all people that *are*

_{pr5921}   _{pl,cs,nn6440}   _{df,nn127}
upon the face of the earth.

_{nn3068}   _{ptn3808}   _{qpf2836}   _{pp,pnx}   _{wcs,qmf977} _{pp,pnx}
7 The Lord did not set*his*love upon you, nor choose you, because ye were

_{pr4480/nn,pnx7230}   _{pr4480/cs,nn3605} _{df,pl,nn5971} _{cj3588} _{pnp859}   _{df,nn4592} _{pr4480/cs,nn3605} _{df,pl,nn5971}
more*in*number than any people; for ye *were* the fewest of all   people:

_{cj3588}   _{nn3068} _{pr4480/cs,nn160} _{pnx(853)}   _{wcj,pr4480/qnc,pnx8104}   ₍₈₅₃₎
8 But because the Lord   loved   you, and because*he*would*keep   the

_{df,nn7621} _{pnl834}   _{nipf7650}   _{pp,pl,nn,pnx1}   _{nn3068}   _{hipf3318/pnx(853)}
oath which he had sworn unto your fathers, hath the Lord brought*you*out with a

_{aj2389} _{pp,nn3027}   _{wcs,qmf,pnx6299}   _{pr4480/cs,nn1004}   _{pl,nn5650}   _{pr4480/cs,nn3027}
mighty hand, and redeemed you out*of*the*house of bondmen, from*the*hand of

_{nn6547}   _{cs,nn4428}   _{nn4714}
Pharaoh king of Egypt.

_{wcj,qpf3045}   _{cj3588}   _{nn3068}   _{pl,nn,pnx430} _{pnp1931}   _{df,pl,nn430}   _{df,nipt539} _{df,nn410}
9 Know therefore that the Lord thy God,   he *is* God, the faithful God,

_{qpta8104}   _{df,nn1285}   _{wcj,df,nn2617}   _{pp,pl,qpta,pnx157}   _{wcj,pp,pl,cs,qpta8104}
which keepeth covenant and mercy with them that love   him and   keep

_{pl,nn,pnx4687}   _{pp,cs,nu505}   _{nn1755}
his commandments to a thousand generations;

_{wcj,pipt7999}   _{pp,pl,qpta,pnx8130}   _{pr413}   _{pl,nn,pnx6440} _{pp,hinc,pnx6}
10 And repayeth them that   hate   him to their face, to destroy them: he

_{ptn3808}   _{pimf309}   _{pp,qpta,pnx8130}   _{pimf7999} _{pp,pnx} _{pr413}   _{pl,nn,pnx6440}
will not be slack to him that hateth him, he will repay him to his face.

_{wcs,qpf8104} ₍₈₅₃₎   _{df,nn4687}   _{wcj(853)}   _{df,pl,nn2706}
11 Thou shalt therefore keep   the commandments, and   the statutes,

_{wcj(853)}   _{df,pl,nn4941}   _{pnl834} _{pnp595}   _{pipt,pnx6680}   _{df,nn3117}   _{pp,qnc,pnx6213}
and   the judgments, which I   command thee this day, to   do   them.

_{wcs,qpf1961}   _{cj6118}   _{qmf8085} ₍₈₅₃₎ _{df,pndm428} _{df,pl,nn4941}
12 Wherefore it*shall*come*to*pass, if ye hearken   to these judgments,

_{wcs,qpf8104}   _{wcs,qpf6213} _{pnx(853)}   _{nn3068}   _{pl,nn,pnx430}   _{wcs,qpf8104} _{pp,pnx}
and keep, and   do   them, that the Lord thy God shall keep unto thee

₍₈₅₃₎   _{df,nn1285}   _{wcj(853)}   _{df,nn2617} _{pnl834}   _{nipf7650}   _{pp,pl,nn,pnx1}
the covenant and   the mercy which he swore unto thy fathers:

_{wcj,qpf,pnx157}   _{wcj,pipf,pnx1288}   _{wcj,hipf,pnx7235}
13 And he will   love   thee, and bless   thee, and multiply thee: he will

_{wcj,pipf1288}   _{cs,nn6529}   _{nn,pnx990}   _{wcj,cs,nn6529}   _{nn,pnx127}   _{nn,pnx1715}
also bless the fruit of thy womb, and the   fruit of thy land, thy corn, and thy

_{wcj,nn,pnx8492}   _{wcj,nn,pnx3323}   _{cs,nn7698}   _{pl,nn,pnx504}   _{wcj,pl,cs,nn6251}
wine, and thine oil, the increase of thy kine, and the   flocks of thy

_{nn,pnx6629} _{pr5921}   _{df,nn127} _{pnl834}   _{nipf7650}   _{pp,pl,nn,pnx1} _{pp,qnc5414} _{pp,pnx}
sheep, in the land which he swore unto thy fathers to give thee.

qmf**1961**   qptp**1288**   pr4480/cs,nn3605   df,pl,nn**5971**   ptn**3808**   qmf**1961**   aj6135

14 Thou shalt be blessed above all people: there shall not be male or

wcj,aj6135   pp,pnx   wcj,pp,nn,pnx929

female barren among you, or among your cattle.

nn3068   wcj,hipf**5493**   pr,pnx4480   cs,nn3605   nn2483   qmf,pnx**7760**

15 And the LORD will take away from thee all sickness, and will put

wcj,cs,nn3605/ptn**3808**   df,aj**7451**   pl,cs,nn4064   nn4714   pnl834   qpf3045   pp,pnx

none of the evil diseases of Egypt, which thou knowest, upon thee; but will

wcs,qpf,pnx**5414**   pp,cs,nn3605   pl,qpta,pnx130

lay them upon all *them* that hate thee.

wcs,qpf398   (853) cs,nn3605   df,pl,nn**5971**   pnl834   nn3068   pl,nn,pnx**430**

16 And thou shalt consume all the people which the LORD thy God

qpta**5414**   pp,pnx   nn,pnx**5869**   qmf2347/ptn**3808**   pr,pnx5921   wcj,ptn**3808**

shall deliver thee; thine eye shall have*no*pity upon them: neither shalt thou

qmf**5647** (853)   pl,nn,pnx**430** cj3588 pnp1931   nn**4170**   pp,pnx

serve their gods; for that *will be* a snare unto thee.

cj3588   qmf**559**   pp,nn,pnx3824 df,pndm428 df,pl,nn**1471**   aj7227   pr,pnx4480   pnit349

17 If thou shalt say in thine heart, These nations *are* more than I; how

qmf3201   pp,hinc,pnx**3423**

can I dispossess them?

ptn**3808**   qmf**3372**   pr,pnx4480   qna2142/qmf**2142**   (853) pnl834

18 Thou shalt not be afraid of them: *but* shalt well remember what the

nn3068   pl,nn,pnx**430** qpf6213   pp,nn6547   wcj,pp,cs,nn3605   nn4714

LORD thy God did unto Pharaoh, and unto all Egypt;

df,aj**1419**   df,pl,nn**4531**   pnl834   du,nn,pnx**5869** qpf**7200**   wcj,df,pl,nn**226**

19 The great temptations which thine eyes saw, and the signs, and the

wcj,df,pl,nn**4159**   df,aj**2389** wcj,df,nn**3027**   df,qptp5186   wcj,df,nn2220   pnl834   nn3068

wonders, and the mighty hand, and the stretched out arm, whereby the LORD

pl,nn,pnx**430**   hipf,pnx3318   ad3651   nn3068   pl,nn,pnx**430** qmf**6213**   pp,cs,nn3605

thy God brought*thee*out: so shall the LORD thy God do unto all the

df,pl,nn**5971**   pnl834   pnp859   qpta**3372**/pr4480/pl,nn,pnx**6440**

people of whom thou art afraid.

wcj,ad1571   nn3068   pl,nn,pnx**430**   pimf**7971** (853)   df,nn6880   pp,pnx   pr5704

20 Moreover the LORD thy God will send the hornet among them, until

df,pl,nipt**7604**   wcj,df,pl,nipt5641   pr4480/pl,nn,pnx**6440**   qnc6

they that are left, and hide themselves from thee, be destroyed.

ptn**3808**   qmf**6206**   pr4480/pl,nn,pnx**6440**   cj3588   nn3068   pl,nn,pnx**430**

21 Thou shalt not be frightened at them: for the LORD thy God *is*

pp,nn,pnx**7130**   aj1419   nn**410**   wcj,nipt**3372**

among you, a mighty God and terrible.

nn3068   pl,nn,pnx**430**   wcs,qpf5394 (853) df,pndm411 df,pl,nn**1471** pr4480/pl,nn,pnx**6440**

22 And the LORD thy God will put out those nations before thee by

nn4592   nn4592   qmf3201   ptn**3808**   pinc,pnx3615   ad4118   cj6435   cs,nn2416   df,nn**7704**

little and little: thou mayest not consume them at once, lest the beasts of the field

qmf7235   pr,pnx5921

increase upon thee.

nn3068   pl,nn,pnx**430**   wcs,qpf,pnx**5414**   pp,pl,nn,pnx**6440**

23 But the LORD thy God shall deliver them unto thee, and shall

wcs,qpf**5414**   aj1419   nn**4103**   pr5704   ninc,pnx**8045**

destroy them with a mighty destruction, until they be destroyed.

wcs,qpf**5414**   pl,nn,pnx**4428**   pp,pl,nn,pnx3027   wcs,hipf6

24 And he shall deliver their kings into thine hand, and thou shalt destroy

(853)   nn,pnx8034   pr4480/pr8478   df,du,nn**8064**   ptn**3808**   nn376   htmf3320   pp,pl,nn,pnx**6440**

their name from under heaven: there shall no man be able to stand before

pr5704   hipf,pnx**8045**   pnx(853)

thee, until thou have destroyed them.

pl,cs,nn**6456**   pl,nn,pnx**430**   qmf**8313**   dfp,nn**784**   ptn**3808**

25 The graven images of their gods shall ye burn with fire: thou shalt not

qmf**2530**   nn**3701**   wcj,nn**2091**   pr,pnx**5921**   pp,pnx   cj**6435**

desire the silver or gold *that is* on them, nor take *it* unto thee, lest thou be

nimf**3369**   pp,pnx   cj**3588** pnp**1931**   cs,nn**8441**   nn**3068**   pl,nn,pnx**430**

snared therein: for it *is* an abomination to the LORD thy God.

wcj,ptn**3808**   himf**935**   nn**8441**   pr**413**   nn,pnx**1004**   wcs,qpf**1961**

26 Neither shalt thou bring an abomination into thine house, lest thou be a

nn**2764**   pp,pnx**3644**   pina**8262**/pimf,pnx**8262**   wcj,pina**8581**/pimf,pnx**8581**

cursed thing like it: *but* thou shalt utterly detest it, and thou shalt utterly abhor it;

cj**3588** pnp**1931**   nn**2764**

for it *is* a cursed thing.

Remember God in Canaan

cs,nn**3605**   df,nn**4687**   pnl**834** pnp**595**   pipt,pnx**6680**   df,nn**3117**

8 All the commandments which I command thee this day shall ye

qmf**8104**   pp,qnc**6213** pp,cj**4616**   qmf**2421**   wcs,qpf**7235**   wcs,qpf**935**   wcs,qpf**3423**

observe to do, that ye may live, and multiply, and go in and possess

(853)   df,nn**776** pnl**834**   nn**3068**   nipf**7650**   pp,pl,nn,pnx**1**

the land which the LORD swore unto your fathers.

wcj,qpf**2142**   (853) cs,nn**3605**   df,nn**1870** pnl**834**   nn**3068**   pl,nn,pnx**430**

2 And thou shalt remember   all the way which the LORD thy God

hipf,pnx**1980**   pndm**2088** pl,nu**705** nn**8141**   dfp,nn**4057**   pp,cj**4616** pinc,pnx**6031**   pp,pinc,pnx**5254**

led thee these forty years in the wilderness, to humble thee, *and* to prove

pp,qnc**3045** (853) pnl**834**   pp,nn,pnx**3824**   he,qmf**8104**

thee, to know what *was* in thine heart, whether thou wouldest keep his

pl,nn,pnx**4687**   cj**518** ptn**3808**

commandments, or not.

wcs,pimf,pnx**6031**   wcs,himf,pnx**7456**   wcs,himf,pnx**398**   pr**854**

☉ 3 And he humbled thee, and suffered*thee*to*hunger, and fed thee with

df,nn**4478**   pnl**834**   qpf**3045** ptn**3808** wcj,ptn**3808**   pl,nn,pnx**1**   qpf**3045** pp,cj**4616**

manna, which thou knewest not, neither did thy fathers know; that he might

hinc,pnx**3045**   cj**3588** df,nn**120**   ptn**3808** qmf**2421** pr**5921** df,nn**3899** pp,nn,pnx**905** cj**3588** pr**5921** cs,nn**3605**

make*thee*know that man doth not live by bread only, but by every *word*

cs,nn**4161**   cs,nn**6310**   nn**3068**   df,nn**120** qmf**2421**

that proceedeth out of the mouth of the LORD doth man live.

nn,pnx**8071**   qpf**1086**/ptn**3808**   pr**4480**/pr,pnx**5921**   ptn**3808**   wcj,nn,pnx**7272** qpf**1216**

4 Thy raiment waxed*not*old upon thee, neither did thy foot swell,

pndm**2088** pl,nu**705** nn**8141**

these forty years.

wcj,qpf**3045**   pr**5973**   nn,pnx**3824** cj**3588** pp,pnl**834**   nn**376**   pimf**3256**   (853)

5 Thou shalt also consider in thine heart, that, as a man chasteneth his

nn,pnx**1121**   nn**3068**   pl,nn,pnx**430**   pipt,pnx**3256**

son, *so* the LORD thy God chasteneth thee.

wcs,qpf**8104** (853)   pl,cs,nn**4687**   nn**3068**   pl,nn,pnx**430**

6 Therefore thou shalt keep   the commandments of the LORD thy God, to

pp,qnc**1980**   pp,pl,nn,pnx**1870**   wcj,pp,qnc**3372** pnx(853)

walk in his ways, and to fear him.

☉ 8:3 See the note on Deuteronomy 6:13, 16.

7 For the LORD thy God bringeth thee into a good land, a land of brooks of water, of fountains and depths that spring out of valleys and hills;

8 A land of wheat, and barley, and vines, and fig trees, and pomegranates; a land of oil olive, and honey;

9 A land wherein thou shalt eat bread without scarceness, thou shalt not lack any *thing* in it; a land whose stones *are* iron, and out*of*whose*hills thou mayest dig brass.

10 When thou hast eaten and art full, then thou shalt bless the LORD thy God for the good land which he hath given thee.

11 Beware that*thou*forget*not the LORD thy God, in not keeping his commandments, and his judgments, and his statutes, which I command thee this day:

12 Lest *when* thou hast eaten and art full, and hast built goodly houses, and dwelt *therein*;

13 And *when* thy herds and thy flocks multiply, and thy silver and thy gold is multiplied, and all that thou hast is multiplied;

14 Then thine heart be lifted up, and thou forget the LORD thy God, which brought*thee*forth out*of*the*land of Egypt, from*the*house of bondage;

15 Who led thee through that great and terrible wilderness, *wherein were* fiery serpents, and scorpions, and drought, where *there was* no water; who brought*thee*forth water out*of*the*rock of flint;

16 Who fed thee in the wilderness with manna, which thy fathers knew not, that he might humble thee, and that he might prove thee, to do*thee*good at thy latter end;

17 And thou say in thine heart, My power and the might of *mine* hand hath gotten me this wealth.

18 But thou shalt remember the LORD thy God: for *it is* he that giveth

pp,pnx nn3581   pp,qnc6213   nn2428   pp,cj4616   hinc6965   (853)   nn,pnx1285   pnl834   nipf7650

thee power to   get   wealth,   that   he may establish   his covenant which he swore

pp,pl,nn,pnx1   df,pndm2088 dfp,nn3117

unto thy fathers, as *it is*   this   day.

wcj.qpf1961 cj518   qna7911/qmf7911 (853)   nn3068   pl,nn,pnx430

   19 And it shall   be,   if   thou do at*all*forget   the LORD thy   God,   and

wcs,qpf1980 pr310   aj312   pl,nn430   wcs,qpf,pnx5647   wcs,hipf7812 pp,pnx   hipf5749   pp,pnx

walk   after other gods, and   serve   them, and worship them, I testify against you

df,nn3117 cj3588   qna6/qmf6

this day that ye shall surely perish.

dfp,pl,nn1471   pnl834   nn3068   hipt6   pr4480/pl,nn,pnx6440   ad3651

   20 As the nations which the LORD destroyeth before*your*face, so shall ye

qmf6   cj6118   ptn3808   qmf8085   pp,cs,nn6963   nn3068   pl,nn,pnx430

perish; because ye would not be obedient unto the voice of the LORD your God.

God Will Destroy The Canaanites

9

qmv8085   nn3478   pnp859   qpta5674   (853) df,nn3383   df,nn3117   pp,qnc935

Hear, O Israel: Thou *art* to pass over   Jordan this day, to go in to

pp,qnc3423   pl,nn1471   aj1419   wcj,aj6099   pr,pnx4480   pl,nn5892   aj1419

possess nations greater and mightier   than   thyself, cities great and

wcj,pl,qptp1219   dfp,du,nn8064

fenced up to heaven,

nn5971   aj1419   wcj,qpta7311   pl,cs,nn1121   nn6062   pnl834 pnp859   qpf3045

   2 A people great and   tall,   the children of the Anakims, whom thou knowest,

wcj,pnp859   qpf8085   pnit4310   htmf3320 pp,pl,cs,nn6440   pl,cs,nn1121   nn6061

and *of whom* thou hast heard *say*, Who can stand before the children of Anak!

wcs,qpf3045   df,nn3117 cj3588   nn3068   pl,nn,pnx430 pnp1931

   3 Understand therefore this day, that the LORD thy   God   *is*   he   which

df,qpta5674   pp,pl,nn,pnx6440   qpta398   nn784 pnp1931   himf,pnx8045   wcj,pnp1931

goeth over   before   thee; *as* a consuming fire he   shall destroy them, and   he

himf,pnx3665   pp,pl,nn,pnx6440   wcs,hipf,pnx3423   wcs,hipf,pnx6

shall bring*them*down before*thy*face: so shalt thou drive*them*out, and destroy

ad4118   pp,pnl834   nn3068   pipf1696   pp,pnx

them quickly,   as   the LORD hath said unto thee.

qmf559   ptn408   pp,nn,pnx3824   nn3068   pl,nn,pnx430

   4 Speak not thou in thine heart, after that the LORD thy   God   hath

pp,qnc1920/pnx(853)   pr4480/pp,pl,nn,pnx6440   pp,qnc559   pp,nn,pnx6666   nn3068

cast*them*out from before   thee, saying, For my righteousness the LORD hath

hipf,pnx935   pp,qnc3423 (853) df,pndm2063 df,nn776   wcj,pp,cs,nn7564   df,pndm428 df,pl,nn1471

brought*me*in to possess   this   land: but for the wickedness of these nations

nn3068   hipt,pnx3423   pr4480/pl,nn,pnx6440

the LORD doth drive*them*out from before thee.

ptn3808   pp,nn,pnx6666   wcj,pp,cs,nn3476   nn,pnx3824   pnp859

   5 Not for thy righteousness, or for the uprightness of thine heart, dost thou

qpta935   pp,qnc3423 (853)   nn,pnx776 cj3588   pp,cs,nn7564   df,pndm428 df,pl,nn1471   nn3068

go to possess   their land: but for the wickedness of these nations the LORD

pl,nn,pnx430   hipt,pnx3423   pr4480/pl,nn,pnx6440   wcj,pp,cj4616   hinc6965 (853)

thy   God   doth drive*them*out from before thee, and   that   he may perform

df,nn1697   pnl834   nn3068   nipf7650   pp,pl,nn,pnx1   pp,nn85   pp,nn3327   wcj,pp,nn3290

the word which the LORD swore unto thy fathers, Abraham, Isaac, and Jacob.

Remember the Rebellions in the Wilderness

^{wcj,qpf**3045**} ^{cj3588} ⁿⁿ³⁰⁶⁸ ^{pl,nn,pnx430} ^{qpta5414} ^{pp,pnx} ^{ptn3808} (853) ^{df,pndm2063}
6 Understand therefore, that the LORD thy God giveth thee not   this

^{df,aj2896} ^{df,nn776} ^{pp,qnc,pnx3423} ^{pp,nn,pnx6666} ^{cj3588} ^{pnp859} ^{cs,aj7186/nn6203} ⁿⁿ⁵⁹⁷¹
good land to possess it for thy righteousness; for thou art a stiffnecked people.

^{qmv2142} ^{qmf7911} ^{ptn408} (853) ^{pnl834} ^{hipf7107} (853) ⁿⁿ³⁰⁶⁸ ^{pl,nn,pnx430}
7 Remember, and forget not,   how thou provokedst   the LORD thy God

^{dfp,nn4057} ^{pp,pr4480} ^{df,nn3117} ^{pnl834} ^{qpf3318} ^{pr4480/cs,nn776}
to wrath in the wilderness: from the day that thou didst depart out*of*the*land of

ⁿⁿ⁴⁷¹⁴ ^{pr5704} ^{qnc,pnx935} ^{pr5704} ^{df,pndm2088} ^{df,nn4725} ^{qpf1961} ^{pl,hipf4784} ^{pr5973} ⁿⁿ³⁰⁶⁸
Egypt, until ye came unto this place, ye have been rebellious against the LORD.

^{wcj,pp,nn2722} ^{hipf7107} (853) ⁿⁿ³⁰⁶⁸ ⁿⁿ³⁰⁶⁸
8 Also in Horeb ye provoked   the LORD to wrath, so that the LORD

^{wcs,htmf599} ^{pp,pnx} ^{pp,hinc8045} ^{pnx(853)}
was angry with you to have destroyed   you.

^{pp,qnc,pnx5927} ^{df,nn,lh2022} ^{pp,qnc3947} ^{pl,cs,nn3871} ^{df,pl,nn68}
9 When I was gone up into the mount to receive the tables of stone, even the

^{pl,cs,nn3871} ^{df,nn1285} ^{pnl834} ⁿⁿ³⁰⁶⁸ ^{qpf3772} ^{pr,pnx5973} ^{wcs,qmf3427}
tables of the covenant which the LORD made with you, then I abode in the

^{dfp,nn2022} ^{pl,nu705} ⁿⁿ³¹¹⁷ ^{wcj,pl,nu705} ⁿⁿ³⁹¹⁵ ^{ptn3808} ^{qpf398} ⁿⁿ³⁸⁹⁹ ^{ptn3808} ^{qpf8354} ^{wcj,pl,nn4325}
mount forty days and forty nights, I neither did eat bread nor drink water:

ⁿⁿ³⁰⁶⁸ ^{wcs,qmf5414} ^{pr,pnx413} (853) ^{du,cs,nu8147} ^{pl,cs,nn3871} ^{df,pl,nn68} ^{pl,qptp3789}
10 And the LORD delivered unto me   two tables of stone written with

^{pp,cs,nn676} ^{pl,nn430} ^{wcj,pr,pnx5921} ^{pp,cs,nn3605} ^{df,pl,nn1697}
the finger of God; and   on   them was written according to   all the words,

^{pnl834} ⁿⁿ³⁰⁶⁸ ^{pipf1696} ^{pr,pnx5973} ^{dfp,nn2022} ^{pr4480/cs,nn8432} ^{df,nn784}
which the LORD spoke with you in the mount out*of*the*midst of the fire in the

^{pp,cs,nn3117} ^{df,nn6951}
day of the assembly.

^{wcs,qmf1961} ^{pr4480/cs,nn7093} ^{pl,nu705} ⁿⁿ³¹¹⁷ ^{wcj,pl,nu705} ⁿⁿ³⁹¹⁵
11 And it*came*to*pass at*the*end of forty days and forty nights, that the

ⁿⁿ³⁰⁶⁸ ^{qpf5414/pr,pnx413} (853) ^{du,cs,nu8147} ^{pl,cs,nn3871} ^{df,pl,nn68} ^{pl,cs,nn3871}
LORD gave me   the two tables of stone, even the tables of the

^{df,nn1285}
covenant.

ⁿⁿ³⁰⁶⁸ ^{wcs,qmf559} ^{pr,pnx413} ^{qmv6965} ^{qmv3381} ^{ad4118} ^{pr4480/pndm2088}
12 And the LORD said unto me, Arise, get*thee*down quickly from hence;

^{cj3588} ^{nn,pnx5971} ^{pnl834} ^{hipf3318} ^{pr4480/nn4714} ^{pipf7843}
for thy people which thou hast brought forth out*of*Egypt have corrupted

^{ad4118} ^{qpf5493} ^{pr4480} ^{df,nn1870} ^{pnl834} ^{pipf,pnx6680}
themselves; they are quickly turned aside out of the way which I commanded

^{qpf6213} ^{pp,pnx} ⁿⁿ⁴⁵⁴¹
them; they have made them a molten image.

ⁿⁿ³⁰⁶⁸ ^{wcs,qmf559} ^{pr,pnx413} ^{pp,qnc559} ^{qpf7200} (853) ^{df,pndm2088}
13 Furthermore the LORD spoke unto me, saying, I have seen   this

^{df,nn5971} ^{wcj,ptdm2009} ^{pnp1931} ^{cs,aj7186/nn6203} ⁿⁿ⁵⁹⁷¹
people, and, behold, it is a stiffnecked people:

^{himv7503/pr,pnx4480} ^{wcj,himf8045} (853) ^{nn,pnx8034}
14 Let*me*alone, that I may destroy them, and blot out   their name

^{pr4480/pr8478} ^{df,du,nn8064} ^{wcj,qmf6213} ^{pnx(853)} ^{pp,nn1471} ^{aj6099} ^{wcj,aj7227}
from under heaven: and I will make   of thee a nation mightier and greater

^{pr,pnx4480}
than they.

^{wcs,qmf6437} ^{wcs,qmf3381} ^{pr4480} ^{df,nn2022} ^{wcj,df,nn2022} ^{qpta1197}
15 So I turned and came down from the mount, and the mount burned with

dfp,nn784   wcj,du,cs,nu8147 pl,cs,nn3871   df,nn**1285**   pr5921   du,cs,nu8147 du,nn,pnx**3027**

fire: and the   two   tables of the covenant *were* in my   two   hands.

wcs,qmf**7200**   wcj,ptdm2009   qpf**2398**   pp,nn**3068**   pl,nn,pnx**430**

16 And I looked, and, behold, ye had sinned against the Lᴏʀᴅ your God, *and*

qpf**6213** pp,pnx   nn**4541** cs,nn5695   qpf**5493**   ad4118   pr4480   df,nn**1870** pnl834

had made you a molten calf: ye had turned aside quickly out of the way which

nn**3068**   pipf**6680**   pnx(853)

the Lᴏʀᴅ had commanded   you.

wcs,qmf**8610**   pp,du,cs,nu8147 df,pl,nn3871   wcs,himf,pnx**7993**   pr4480/pr5921   du,cs,nu8147

17 And I took the   two   tables, and   cast   them out of my   two

du,nn,pnx**3027** wcs,pimf,pnx**7665**   pp,du,nn,pnx**5869**

hands, and   broke   them before your eyes.

wcs,htmf**5307**   pp,pl,cs,nn**6440**   nn**3068**   dfp,aj**7223** pl,nu705 nn**3117**   wcj,pl,nu705

18 And I fell down before the Lᴏʀᴅ, as at the first, forty days and forty

nn**3915**   ptn**3808** qpf398 nn3899 ptn**3808** qpf**8354** wcj,pl,nn4325 pr5921 cs,nn3605   nn,pnx**2403**

nights: I did neither eat bread, nor drink water, because of all your sins

pnl834   qpf**2398**   pp,qnc**6213** df,nn**7451**   pp,du,cs,nn**5869**   nn**3068**

which ye sinned, in doing   wickedly in the   sight   of the Lᴏʀᴅ, to

pp,hinc,pnx**3707**

provoke*him*to*anger.

cj3588   qpf**3025**   pr4480/pl,cs,nn**6440**   df,nn**639**   wcj,df,nn**2534**   pnl834

19 For I was afraid   of   the anger and hot displeasure, wherewith the

nn**3068**   qpf**7107**   pr,pnx5921   pp,hinc**8045** pnx(853)   nn**3068** wcs,qmf**8085** pr,pnx413

Lᴏʀᴅ was wroth against you to destroy   you. But the Lᴏʀᴅ hearkened unto

df,pndm1931 dfp,nn6471 ad1571

me at that   time also.

nn**3068**   htpf**599**/ad3966   wcj,pp,nn175   pp,hinc,pnx**8045**

20 And the Lᴏʀᴅ was*very*angry with Aaron to have destroyed him: and I

wcs,htmf**6419** pr1157 nn175 ad1571 df,pndm1931 dfp,nn**6256**

prayed for Aaron also the same   time.

qpf3947 wcj(853)   nn,pnx**2403** (853)   df,nn5695 pnl834   qpf**6213**   wcs,qmf**8313**

21 And I took   your sin,   the calf which ye had made, and burnt

pnx(853)   dfp,nn784 wcs,qmf**3807** pnx(853)   qna2912   hina3190   cj5704 pnl834

it with fire, and stamped   it, *and* ground *it* very small, *even* until it

qpf1854   pp,nn**6083**   wcs,himf**7993** (853)   nn,pnx**6083**   pr413   df,nn5158

was*as*small as dust: and I   cast   the   dust   thereof into the brook that

df,qpta3381   pr4480   df,nn2022

descended out of the mount.

wcj,pp,nn**8404**   wcj,pp,nn**4532**   wcj,pp,nn**6914**   (qpf**1961**) pl,hipt**7107**

22 And at Taberah, and at Massah, and at Kibroth-hattaavah, ye   provoked

(853)   nn**3068**

the Lᴏʀᴅ to wrath.

nn**3068** wcj,pp,qnc**7971** pnx(853)   pr4480/nn**6947**   pp,qnc**559**

23 Likewise when the Lᴏʀᴅ   sent   you from Kadesh-barnea, saying,

qmv**5927**   wcj,qmv**3423** (853)   df,nn776 pnl834   qpf**5414** pp,pnx   wcs,himf**4784**   (853)

Go up and possess   the land which I have given you; then ye rebelled against

cs,nn**6310**   nn**3068**   pl,nn,pnx**430**   hipf**539** pp,pnx wcj,ptn**3808** wcj,ptn**3808**

the commandment of the Lᴏʀᴅ your God, and ye believed him not,   nor

qpf**8085**   pp,nn,pnx**6963**

hearkened to his voice.

qpf**1961** pl,hipt**4784**   pr5973   nn**3068**   pr4480/cs,nn**3117**   qnc,pnx**3045** pnx(853)

24 Ye have been rebellious against the Lᴏʀᴅ from*the*day that I knew

you.

wcs,htmf**5307**   pp,pl,cs,nn**6440**   nn**3068**   (853) pl,nu705 df,nn**3117**   wcj(853) pl,nu705 df,nn**3915**

25 Thus I fell down before the Lᴏʀᴅ   forty days and   forty nights,

as I fell down *at the first*; because the LORD had said he would destroy you.

26 I prayed therefore unto the LORD, and said, O Lord GOD, destroy not thy people and thine inheritance, which thou hast redeemed through thy greatness, which thou hast brought forth out*of*Egypt with a mighty hand.

27 Remember thy servants, Abraham, Isaac, and Jacob; look not unto the stubbornness of this people, nor to their wickedness, nor to their sin:

28 Lest the land whence thou broughtest*us*out say, Because the LORD was*not*able to bring them into the land which he promised them, and because*he*hated them, he hath brought*them*out to slay them in the wilderness.

29 Yet they *are* thy people and thine inheritance, which thou broughtest out by thy mighty power and by thy stretched out arm.

The Second Set of Stone Tablets

10 At that time the LORD said unto me, Hew thee two tables of stone like unto the first, and come up unto me into the mount, and make thee an ark of wood.

2 And I will write on the tables the words that were in the first tables which thou didst break, and thou shalt put them in the ark.

3 And I made an ark *of* shittim wood, and hewed two tables of stone like unto the first, and went up into the mount, having the two tables in mine hand.

4 And he wrote on the tables, according to the first writing, the ten commandments, which the LORD spoke unto you in the mount out*of*the*midst of the fire in the day of the assembly: and the LORD gave them unto me.

10:1–5 God's rewriting of His Law was a demonstration of His forgiveness. The ark of the covenant, made of wood (humanity) and covered with gold (deity), is believed by some to be a symbol of Jesus, in whom full humanity and full deity were combined (Col. 2:9).

wcs,qmf6437   wcs,qmf3381   pr4480   df,nn2022   wcs,qmf7760   (853)

5 And I turned myself and came down from the mount, and   put   the

df,pl,nn3871   dfp,nn727   pnl834   qpf6213   ad8033   wcs,qmf1961 pp,pnl834   nn3068

tables in the   ark   which I had made; and there they be,   as   the LORD

pipf,pnx6680

commanded me.

wcj,pl,cs,nn1121   nn3478   qpf5265   pr4480/cs,nn881   pl,cs,nn1121

6 And the children of Israel took*their*journey from Beeroth of the children of

nn3292   nn4149   ad8033   nn175 qpf4191   ad8033   wcs,nimf6912   nn499   nn,pnx1121

Jaakan to Mosera: there Aaron died, and there he was buried; and Eleazar his   son

wcs,pimf3547   pr,pnx8478

ministered*in*the*priest's*office in*his*stead.

pr4480/ad8033   qpf5265   df,nn1412   wcj,pr4480   df,nn1412   nn3193

7 From thence they journeyed unto Gudgodah; and from Gudgodah to Jotbath,

cs,nn776   pl,cs,nn5158   pl,nn4325

a land of rivers of waters.

df,pndm1931 dfp,nn6256   nn3068   hipf914   (853)   cs,nn7626   df,nn3878   pp,qnc5375 (853)

8 At   that   time the LORD separated   the tribe of Levi, to bear   the

cs,nn727   cs,nn1285   nn3068   pp,qnc5975 pp,pl,cs,nn6440   nn3068   pp,pinc,pnx8334

ark of the covenant of the LORD, to stand   before the LORD to minister unto

wcj,pp,pinc1288   pp,nn,pnx8034 pr5704 df,pndm2088 df,nn3117

him, and to bless   in his name, unto this day.

pr5921/ad3651   pp,nn3878 qpf1961 ptn3808 nn2506   wcj,nn5159   pr5973   pl,nn,pnx251   nn3068

9 Wherefore Levi hath no part nor inheritance with his brethren; the LORD

(pnp1931)   nn,pnx5159   pp,pnl834   nn3068   pl,nn,pnx430 pipf1696   pp,pnx

is his inheritance, according as the LORD thy God   promised him.

wcj,pnp595 qpf5975   dfp,nn2022   df,aj7223 dfp,pl,nn3117 pl,nu705 nn3117

10 And   I   stayed in the mount, according to the first time, forty days

wcj,pl,nu705 nn3915   nn3068 wcs,qmf8085 pr,pnx413   df,pndm1931 dfp,nn6471 ad1571

and forty nights; and the LORD hearkened unto me at   that   time also, *and* the

nn3068   qpf14   ptn3808 hinc,pnx7843

LORD would not destroy thee.

nn3068 wcs,qmf559 pr,pnx413   qmv6965 qmv1980   pp,nn4550 pp,pl,cs,nn6440   df,nn5971

11 And the LORD said   unto me, Arise, take *thy* journey before the people,

wcj,qmf935   wcj,qmf3423 (853)   df,nn776   pnl834   nipf7650   pp,pl,nn,pnx1

that they may go in and possess   the land, which I swore unto their fathers to

pp,qnc5414   pp,pnx

give unto them.

What God Requires

wcj,ad6258   nn3478   pnit4100   nn3068   pl,nn,pnx430 qpta7592 pr4480/pr,pnx5973

12 And now, Israel, what doth the LORD thy God require   of   thee,

cj3588/cj518   pp,qnc3372 (853)   nn3068   pl,nn,pnx430 pp,qnc1980   pp,cs,nn3605   pl,nn,pnx1870

but to fear   the LORD thy God, to walk in   all   his ways, and to

wcj,pp,qnc157 pnx(853)   wcj,pp,qnc5647 (853)   nn3068   pl,nn,pnx430   pp,cs,nn3605   nn,pnx3824

love   him, and to serve   the LORD thy God with all   thy heart

wcj,pp,cs,nn3605   nn,pnx5315

and with   all   thy soul,

pp,qnc8104 (853)   pl,cs,nn4687   nn3068   wcj(853)   pl,nn,pnx2708 pnl834

13 To keep   the commandments of the LORD, and   his statutes, which

pnp595   pipt,pnx6680   df,nn3117   pp,pnx pp,nn2896

I command thee this day for thy good?

ptdm2005   df,du,nn**8064**   wcj,du,cs,nn**8064**   df,du,nn**8064**   pp,nn**3068**   pl,nn,pnx**430**

14 Behold, the heaven and the heaven of heavens *is* the LORD's thy God,

df,nn**776**   wcj,nn**3605** pnl834   pp,pnx

the earth *also*, with all that therein *is*.

ad7535   nn**3068**   qpf**2836**   pp,pl,nn,pnx**1**   pp,qnc**157** pnx(853)

15 Only the LORD had*a*delight in thy fathers to love   them, and he

wcs,qmf**977**   pp,nn,pnx**2233** pr,pnx310   pp,pnx pr4480/cs,nn**3605** df,pl,nn**5971**   df,pndm2088 dfp,nn**3117**

chose their seed after them, *even* you above all people, as *it is* this day.

wcj,qpf**4135**   (853)   cs,nn**6190**   nn,pnx3824   ptn**3808** ad5750

○⚏ 16 Circumcise therefore   the foreskin of your heart, and be no more

wcj,nn,pnx**6203**/himf7185

stiffnecked.

cj3588   nn**3068**   pl,nn,pnx**430** (pnp1931)   pl,cs,nn**430**   df,pl,nn**430**   wcj,pl,cs,nn**113**   df,pl,nn**113**

17 For the LORD your God   *is* God of gods, and Lord of lords, a

df,aj**1419** df,nn**410**   df,aj**1368**   wcj,df,nipt**3372** pnl834   qmf**5375** ptn**3808**   pl,nn**6440**   wcj,ptn**3808** qmf**3947**

great God, a mighty, and a terrible, which regardeth not persons, nor taketh

nn**7810**

reward:

qpta**6213**   cs,nn**4941**   nn**3490**   wcj,nn**490**   wcj,qpta**157**

18 He doth execute the judgment of the fatherless and widow, and loveth the

nn**1616**   pp,qnc**5414** pp,pnx nn**3899**   wcj,nn**8071**

stranger, in giving him food and raiment.

wcs,qpf**157**   (853)   df,nn**1616**   cj3588   qpf**1961**   pl,nn**1616**   pp,cs,nn**776**

19 Love ye therefore   the stranger: for ye were strangers in the land of

nn4714

Egypt.

qmf**3372** (853)   nn**3068**   pl,nn,pnx**430** pnx(853)   qmf**5647**

○⚏ 20 Thou shalt fear   the LORD thy God;   him shalt thou serve, and

wcj,pp,pnx   qmf**1692**   nimf**7650**   wcj,pp,nn,pnx**8034**

to him shalt thou cleave, and swear by his name.

pnp1931   nn,pnx**8416**   wcj,pnp1931   pl,nn,pnx**430** pnl834   qpf**6213** pr,pnx854   (853)

21 He *is* thy praise, and he *is* thy God, that hath done for thee

df,pndm428 df,aj**1419**   wcj(853)   df,pl,nipt**3372**   pnl834   du,nn,pnx**5869**   qpf**7200**

these great and   terrible things, which thine eyes have seen.

pl,nn,pnx**1**   qpf**3381**   nn,lh4714   pp,pl,nu**7657**   nn**5315**

22 Thy fathers went down into Egypt with threescore*and*ten persons; and

wcj,ad6258   nn**3068**   pl,nn,pnx**430**   qpf,pnx**7760**   pp,pl,cs,nn**3556** df,du,nn**8064**   pp,nn**7230**

now the LORD thy God hath made thee as the stars of heaven for multitude.

God's Great Acts

11

wcj,qpf**157** (853)   nn**3068**   pl,nn,pnx**430**   wcj,qpf**8104**

Therefore thou shalt love   the LORD thy God, and keep his

nn,pnx**4931**   wcj,pl,nn,pnx**2708**   wcj,pl,nn,pnx**4941**   wcj,pl,nn,pnx**4687**

charge, and his statutes, and his judgments, and his commandments,

cs,nn**3605**/df,pl,nn**3117**

always.

○⚏ **10:16** Circumcision had been instituted as an outward sign of obedience and of relationship to God (Gen. 17:9–14). The citizen of a country has certain rights because of that citizenship. Circumcision was a sign, not that one was a citizen of the nation of Israel, but that he had certain rights under the covenant. In this verse the figure of circumcision is used to call for a change of heart. The circumcision of the flesh could not create a saving relationship with God. Indeed, the circumcision of the heart (repentance unto salvation) was that by which an Israelite (male or female) was made an heir to the promise of eternal life (Gal. 3:29).

○⚏ **10:20** See the note on Deuteronomy 6:13, 16.

wcj,qpf**3045**   df,nn**3117** cj3588   ptn**3808** pr854   pl,nn,pnx**1121** pnl834   ptn**3808**

2 And know ye this day: for *I speak* not with your children which have not

qpf**3045**   wcj,pnl834   ptn**3808** qpf**7200** (853)   cs,nn**4148**   nn**3068**   pl,nn,pnx**430** (853)

known, and which have not seen   the chastisement of the LORD your God,

nn,pnx1433   (853)   df,aj**2389** nn,pnx**3027**   df,qptp5186   wcj,nn,pnx2220

his greatness,   his mighty hand, and his stretched out arm,

wcj(853)   pl,nn,pnx**226**   wcj(853)   pl,nn,pnx4639 pnl834   qpf**6213**   pp,cs,nn**8432**

3 And   his miracles, and   his acts, which he did in the midst of

nn4714   pp,nn6547   cs,nn**4428**   nn4714   wcj,pp,cs,nn3605   nn,pnx776

Egypt unto Pharaoh the king of Egypt, and unto   all   his land;

wcj,pnl834   qpf**6213**   pp,cs,nn**2428**   nn4714   pp,pl,nn,pnx5483

4 And what he did unto the army of Egypt, unto their horses, and to their

wcj,pp,nn,pnx7393 pnl834   (853)   pl,cs,nn4325   nn5488 cs,nn3220   hipf6687/pr5921/pl,nn,pnx**6440**

chariots; how he made   the water of the Red sea to   overflow   them as

pp,qnc,pnx7291 pr,pnx310   nn**3068**   wcs,pimf,pnx**6**   pr5704 df,pndm2088 df,nn**3117**

they pursued after you, and *how* the LORD hath destroyed them unto   this   day;

wcj,pnl834   qpf**6213**   pp,pnx   dfp,nn4057   pr5704   qnc,pnx935 pr5704 df,pndm2088

5 And what he did unto you in the wilderness, until ye came into   this

df,nn4725

place;

wcj,pnl834   qpf**6213**   pp,nn1885   wcj,pp,nn48   pl,cs,nn**1121**   nn446   cs,nn**1121**

6 And what he did unto Dathan and Abiram, the sons of Eliab, the son of

nn7205   pnl834   df,nn776   qpf6475   (853)   nn,pnx**6310**   wcs,qmf,pnx**1104**   wcj(853)

Reuben: how the earth opened   her mouth, and swallowed*them*up, and

pl,nn,pnx**1004**   wcj(853)   pl,nn,pnx168   wcj(853) cs,nn3605   df,nn3351   pnl834

their households, and   their tents, and   all   the substance that *was* in

pp,du,nn,pnx7272   pp,cs,nn**7130**   cs,nn3605 nn3478

their possession, in the midst of   all   Israel:

cj3588   du,nn,pnx**5869**   df,pl,qpta**7200** (853) cs,nn3605   df,aj1419 cs,nn4639   nn**3068**   pnl834

7 But your eyes have seen   all the great acts of the LORD which

qpf**6213**

he did.

New Life in the New Land

wcj,qpf**8104** (853) cs,nn3605   df,nn**4687**   pnl834   pnp595   pipt,pnx**6680**

8 Therefore shall ye keep   all the commandments which   I   command

df,nn**3117** pp,cj4616   qmf**2388**   wcs,qpf935   wcs,qpf**3423** (853)   df,nn776

you this day, that ye may be strong, and go in and possess   the land,

pnl834/ad,lh8033 pnp859 pl,qpta**5674**   pp,qnc,pnx**3423**

whither ye   go   to possess it;

wcj,pp,cj4616   himf**748**   pl,nn**3117** pr5921   df,nn**127** pnl834   nn**3068** nipf**7650**

9 And that ye may prolong *your* days in the land, which the LORD swore

pp,pl,nn,pnx1   pp,qnc**5414**   pp,pnx   wcj,pp,nn,pnx**2233** pp,nn776   cs,qpta2100

unto your fathers to give unto them and to their   seed,   a land that floweth

nn2461   wcj,nn1706

with milk and honey.

cj3588   df,nn776 pnl834/ad,lh8033 pnp859   qpta935   pp,qnc,pnx**3423**   ptn**3808**   pp,cs,nn776

10 For the land, whither thou goest in to possess it, *is* not as the land of

nn4714   (pnp1931)   pnl834/pr4480/ad8033   qpf3318   pnl834   qmf2232   (853)   nn,pnx**2233**

Egypt,   from whence ye came out, where thou sowedst   thy seed, and

wcs,hipf8248   pp,nn,pnx7272   pp,cs,nn1588   df,nn3419

wateredst *it* with thy   foot,   as a garden of herbs:

wcj,df,nn776   pnl834/ad,lh8033   pnp859   pl,qpta5674   pp,qnc,pnx3423   cs,nn776   pl,nn2022

11 But the land, whither ye go to possess it, *is* a land of hills and

wcj,pl,nn1237   qmf8354   pl,nn4325   pp,cs,nn4306   df,du,nn8064

valleys, *and* drinketh water of the rain of heaven:

nn776   pnl834   nn3068   pl,nn,pnx430   qpta1875   pnx(853)   du,cs,nn5869   nn3068

12 A land which the Lᴏʀᴅ thy God careth for the eyes of the Lᴏʀᴅ

pl,nn,pnx430   nn8548   pp,pnx   pr4480/cs,nn7225   df,nn8141   wcj,pr5704

thy God *are* always upon it, from*the*beginning of the year even unto the

cs,nn319   nn8141

end of the year.

wcs,qpf1961   cj518   qna8085/qmf8085   pr413

13 And it*shall*come*to*pass, if ye shall hearken diligently unto my

pl,nn,pnx4687   pnl834   pnp595   pipt6680   pnx(853)   df,nn3117   pp,qnc157   (853)   nn3068

commandments which I command you this day, to love the Lᴏʀᴅ your

pl,nn,pnx430   wcj,pp,qnc,pnx5647   pp,cs,nn3605   nn,pnx3824   wcj,pp,cs,nn3605

God, and to serve him with all your heart and with all your

nn,pnx5315

soul,

wcs,qpf5414   cs,nn4306   nn,pnx776   pp,nn,pnx6256

14 That I will give *you* the rain of your land in his due season, the

nn3138   wcj,nn4456   wcs,qpf622   nn,pnx1715   wcj,nn,pnx8492

first rain and the latter rain, that thou mayest gather in thy corn, and thy wine,

wcj,nn,pnx3323

and thine oil.

wcs,qpf5414   nn6212   pp,nn,pnx7704   pp,nn,pnx929

15 And I will send grass in thy fields for thy cattle, that thou mayest

wcs,qpf398   wcs,qpf7646

eat and be full.

nimv8104   pp,pnx   cj6435   nn,pnx3824   qmf6601

16 Take heed to yourselves, that your heart be not deceived, and ye

wcs,qpf5493   wcs,qpf5647   aj312   pl,nn430   wcs,htpf7812   pp,pnx

turn aside, and serve other gods, and worship them;

nn3068   cs,nn639   wcs,qpf2734   pp,pnx   wcs,qpf6113   (853)

17 And *then* the Lᴏʀᴅ's wrath be kindled against you, and he shut up the

df,du,nn8064   qmf1961   wcj,ptn3808   nn4306   wcj,df,nn127   qmf5414   ptn3808   (853)   nn,pnx2981

heaven, that there be no rain, and that the land yield not her fruit; and

wcs,qpf6   ad4120   pr4480/pr5921   df,aj2896 df,nn776   pnl834   nn3068   qpta5414   pp,pnx

lest ye perish quickly from off the good land which the Lᴏʀᴅ giveth you.

wcs,qpf7760   (853)   pndm428   pl,nn,pnx1697   pr5921   nn,pnx3824   wcj,pr5921

18 Therefore shall ye lay up these my words in your heart and in

nn,pnx5315   wcs,qpf7194   pnx(853)   pp,nn226   pr5921   nn,pnx3027   wcs,qpf1961

your soul, and bind them for a sign upon your hand, that they may be

pp,pl,nn2903   pr996   du,nn,pnx5869

as frontlets between your eyes.

wcs,pipf3925   pnx(853)   (853)   pl,nn,pnx1121   pp,pinc1696   pp,pnx

19 And ye shall teach them your children, speaking of them when

pp,qnc,pnx3427   pp,nn,pnx1004   wcj,pp,qnc,pnx1980   dfp,nn1870

thou sittest in thine house, and when thou walkest by the way, when thou

wcj,pp,qnc,pnx7901   wcj,pp,qnc,pnx6965

liest down, and when thou risest up.

wcs,qpf,pnx3789   pr5921   pl,cs,nn4201   nn,pnx1004

20 And thou shalt write them upon the door posts of thine house, and upon

wcj,pp,pl,nn,pnx8179

thy gates:

pp,cj4616   pl,nn,pnx3117   qmf7235   wcj,pl,cs,nn3117   pl,nn,pnx1121

21 That your days may be multiplied, and the days of your children, pr5921   df,nn127   pnl834   nn3068   nipf7650   pp,pl,nn,pnx1   pp,qnc5414   pp,pnx

in the land which the LORD swore unto your fathers to give them, as the

pp,pl,cs,nn3117   df,du,nn8064   pr5921   df,nn776

days of heaven upon the earth.

cj3588   cj518   qna8104/qmf8104   (853)   cs,nn3605   df,pndm2063   df,nn4687   pnl834   pnp595

22 For if ye shall diligently keep   all   these commandments which I

pipt6680   pnx(853)   pp,qnc,pnx6213   pp,qnc157   (853)   nn3068   pl,nn,pnx430   pp,qnc1980

command   you, to   do   them, to love   the LORD your God, to walk

pp,cs,nn3605   pl,nn,pnx1870   wcj,pp,qnc1692   pp,pnx

in   all   his ways, and to cleave unto him;

nn3068   wcs,hipf3423   (853)   cs,nn3605   df,pndm428   df,pl,nn1471   pr4480/pr,pl,nn,pnx6440

23 Then will the LORD drive out   all   these nations from before you,

wcs,qpf3423   aj1419   pl,nn1471   wcj,aj6099   pr,pnx4480

and ye shall possess greater nations and mightier than yourselves.

cs,nn3605   df,nn4725   pnl834/pp,pnx   cs,nn3709   nn,pnx7272   qmf1869   qmf1961   pp,pnx

24 Every place whereon the soles of your feet   shall tread shall   be   yours:

pr4480   df,nn4057   wcj,df,nn3844   pr4480   df,nn5104   cs,nn5104   nn6578   wcj,pr5704

from the wilderness and Lebanon, from the river, the river Euphrates, even unto

df,aj314   df,nn3220   nn,pnx1366   qmf1961

the uttermost sea shall your coast be.

ptn3808   nn376   htmf3320   pp,pl,nn,pnx6440   nn3068

25 There shall no man be able to stand   before   you: *for* the LORD your

pl,nn,pnx430   qmf5414   nn,pnx6343   wcj,nn,pnx4172   pr5921/pl,cs,nn6440   cs,nn3605

God shall lay the fear of you and the dread of you   upon   all   the

df,nn776   pnl834   qmf1869   pp,pnx   pp,pnl834   pipf1696   pp,pnx

land that ye shall tread upon,   as   he hath said unto you.

qmv7200   pnp595   qpta5414   pp,pl,nn,pnx6440   df,nn3117   nn1293   wcj,nn7045

26 Behold, I   set   before   you this day a blessing and a curse;

(853)   df,nn1293   pnl834   qmf8085/pr413   pl,cs,nn4687   nn3068   pl,nn,pnx430

27   A blessing, if ye obey the commandments of the LORD your God,

pnl834   pnp595   pipt6680   pnx(853)   df,nn3117

which I command   you this day:

wcj,df,nn7045   cj518   ptn3808   qmf8085/pr413   pl,cs,nn4687   nn3068

28 And a curse, if ye will not   obey   the commandments of the LORD your

pl,nn,pnx430   wcs,qpf5493   pr4480   df,nn1870   pnl834   pnp595   pipt6680   pnx(853)   df,nn3117

God, but turn aside out of the way which I   command   you this day, to

pp,qnc1980   pr310   aj312   pl,nn430   pnl834   ptn3808   qpf3045

go   after other gods, which ye have not known.

wcj,qpf1961   cj3588   nn3068   pl,nn,pnx430   himf,pnx935

29 And it*shall*come*to*pass, when the LORD thy   God   hath brought*thee*in

pr413   df,nn776   pnl834/ad,lh8033   pnp859   qpta935   pp,qnc,pnx3423   wcs,qpf5414   (853)

unto the land   whither   thou goest to possess it, that thou shalt   put   the

df,nn1293   pr5921   cs,nn2022   nn1630   wcj(853)   df,nn7045   pr5921   cs,nn2022   nn5858

blessing upon mount Gerizim, and   the curse upon mount Ebal.

pnp1992   he,ptn3808   pp,cs,nn5676   df,nn3383   pr310   cs,nn1870   df,nn8121

30 *Are* they   not   on the other side Jordan, by the way where the sun

cs,nn3996   pp,cs,nn776   df,nn3669   df,qpta3427   dfp,nn6160

goeth down, in the   land   of the Canaanites, which dwell in the champaign

pr4136   df,nn1537   pr681   pl,cs,nn436   nn4176

over against Gilgal, beside the plains of Moreh?

cj3588   pnp859   pl,qpta5674   (853)   df,nn3383   pp,qnc935   pp,qnc3423   (853)   df,nn776   pnl834

31 For ye shall pass over   Jordan to go in to possess   the land which

nn3068   pl,nn,pnx430   qpta5414   pp,pnx   wcs,qpf3423   pnx(853)   wcs,qpf3427   pp,pnx

the LORD your God giveth you, and ye shall possess   it, and dwell therein.

wcs,qpf**8104** pp,qnc**6213** (853) cs,nn3605 df,pl,nn**2706** wcj(853) df,pl,nn**4941**

32 And ye shall observe to do all the statutes and judgments

pnl834 pnp595 qpta**5414** pp,pl,nn,pnx**6440** df,nn3117

which I set before you this day.

Worship Only in the Special Place

pndm428 df,pl,nn**2706** wcj,df,pl,nn**4941** pnl834 qmf**8104** pp,qnc**6213**

12 These *are* the statutes and judgments, which ye shall observe to do

dfp,nn776 pnl834 nn**3068** pl,cs,nn**430** pl,nn,pnx1 qpf**5414** pp,pnx

in the land, which the LORD God of thy fathers giveth thee to

pp,qnc,pnx**3423** cs,nn3605 df,pl,nn**3117** pnl834 pnp859 aj**2416** pr5921 df,nn**127**

possess it, all the days that ye live upon the earth.

pina**6**/pimf**6** (853) cs,nn3605 df,pl,nn**4725** pnl834/ad,lh8033 df,pl,nn**1471** pnl834/pnx(853)

2 Ye shall utterly destroy all the places, wherein the nations which

pnp859 pl,qpta**3423** qpf**5647** (853) pl,nn,pnx**430** pr5921 df,pl,qpta7311 df,pl,nn2022 wcj,pr5921

ye shall possess served their gods, upon the high mountains, and upon

df,pl,nn**1389** wcj,pr8478 cs,nn3605 aj7488 nn6086

the hills, and under every green tree:

wcs,pipf**5422** (853) pl,nn,pnx**4196** wcs,pipf**7665** (853) pl,nn,pnx**4676**

3 And ye shall overthrow their altars, and break their pillars, and

qmf**8313** wcj,pl,nn,pnx**842** dfp,nn784 pimf1438 wcj,pl,cs,nn**6456**

burn their groves with fire; and ye shall hew down the graven images of their

pl,nn,pnx**430** wcs,pipf**6** (853) nn,pnx8034 pr4480 df,pndm1931 df,nn4725

gods, and destroy the names of them out of that place.

ptn3808 qmf**6213** ad3651 pp,nn3068 pl,nn,pnx**430**

4 Ye shall not do so unto the LORD your God.

cj3588/cj518 pr413 df,nn4725 pnl834 nn**3068** pl,nn,pnx**430** qmf977 pr4480/cs,nn3605

☞ 5 But unto the place which the LORD your God shall choose out*of*all

pl,nn,pnx**7626** pp,qnc**7760** (853) nn,pnx8034 ad8033 pp,nn,pnx7933 qmf1875

your tribes to put his name there, *even* unto his habitation shall ye seek,

ad,lh8033 wcs,qpf935

and thither thou shalt come:

ad,lh8033 wcs,hipf935 pl,nn,pnx**5930** wcj,pl,nn,pnx**2077**

6 And thither ye shall bring your burnt offerings, and your sacrifices, and

wcj(853) pl,nn,pnx**4643** (853) cs,nn**8641** nn,pnx**3027** wcj,pl,nn,pnx**5088**

your tithes, and heave offerings of your hand, and your vows, and

wcj,pl,nn,pnx**5071** wcj,pl,cs,nn1062 nn,pnx1241 wcj,nn,pnx6629

your freewill offerings, and the firstlings of your herds and of your flocks:

ad8033 wcs,qpf398 pp,pl,cs,nn**6440** nn3068 pl,nn,pnx**430** wcs,qpf8055

7 And there ye shall eat before the LORD your God, and ye shall rejoice

pp,cs,nn3605 cs,nn4916 nn,pnx**3027** pnp859 wcj,pl,nn,pnx**1004** pnl834

in all that ye put your hand unto, ye and your households, wherein the

nn**3068** pl,nn,pnx**430** pipf,pnx**1288**

LORD thy God hath blessed thee.

ptn3808 qmf**6213** pp,nn3605 pnl834 pnp587 pl,qpta**6213** ad6311 df,nn**3117**

8 Ye shall not do after all *the things* that we do here this day,

nn**376** cs,nn3605 df,aj**3477** pp,du,nn,pnx**5869**

every man whatsoever *is* right in his own eyes.

☞ **12:5** "The place . . . God shall choose" is the prophetic reference to God's selecting one place in the Promised Land for a fixed central sanctuary to which all Israel would be related. This was necessary since the people would no longer be camped around the Tabernacle, but would be dispersed into the towns of Canaan.

cj3588   ptn3808 cj5704/ad6258   qpf935   pr413   df,nn4496   wcj,pr413   df,nn5159   pnl834

9 For ye are not   as yet come to the rest and   to   the inheritance, which

nn3068   pl,nn,pnx430   qpta5414   pp,pnx

the LORD your   God   giveth you.

wcj,qpf5674   (853)   df,nn3383   wcj,qpf3427   dfp,nn776   pnl834   nn3068

10 But *when* ye go over   Jordan, and dwell in the land which the LORD

pl,nn,pnx430   hipt5157/pnx(853)   wcj,hipf5117/pp,pnx   pr4480/cs,nn3605

your   God   giveth*you*to*inherit,   and *when* he giveth*you*rest from all   your

pl,qpta.pnx341   pr4480/ad5439   wcj,qpf3427   nn983

enemies round about, so that ye dwell in safety;

wcj,qpf1961   df,nn4725   pnl834/pp,pnx   nn3068   pl,nn,pnx430   qmf977

11 Then there shall   be   a place which the LORD your   God   shall choose

nn,pnx8034   pp,pinc7931   ad8033   ad,lh8033   himf935   (853)   cs,nn3605 pnl834 pnp595

to cause his name to dwell there; thither shall ye bring   all   that   I

pipt6680   pnx(853)   pl,nn,pnx5930   wcj,pl,nn,pnx2077   pl,nn,pnx4643

command   you; your burnt offerings, and your sacrifices, your tithes, and the

wcj,cs,nn8641   nn,pnx3027   wcj,cs,nn3605   cs,nn4005 pl,nn,pnx5088   pnl834   qmf5087

heave offering of your hand, and   all   your choice vows which ye vow unto

pp,nn3068

the LORD:

wcs,qpf8055 pp,pl,cs,nn6440   nn3068   pl,nn,pnx430 pnp859   wcj,pl,nn,pnx1121

12 And ye shall rejoice before the LORD your God,   ye, and your   sons,

wcj,pl,nn,pnx1323   wcj,pl,nn,pnx5650   wcj,pl,nn,pnx519   wcj,df,nn3881

and your daughters, and your menservants, and your maidservants, and the Levite

pnl834   pp,pl,nn,pnx8179   cj3588   pp,pnx   ptn369 nn2506   wcj,nn5159   pr,pnx854

that *is* within your   gates;   forasmuch as he hath no part nor inheritance with

you.

nimv8104   pp,pnx   cj6435   himf5927   pl,nn,pnx5930   pp,cs,nn3605 nn4725

13 Take heed to thyself that thou offer not thy burnt offerings in every place

pnl834   qmf7200

that thou seest:

cj3588/cj518   dfp,nn4725   pnl834   nn3068   qmf977   pp,cs,nu259   pl,nn,pnx7626

14   But   in the place which the LORD shall choose in   one   of thy tribes,

ad8033   himf5927   pl,nn,pnx5930   wcj,ad8033   qmf6213 nn3605 pnl834 pnp595

there thou shalt offer thy burnt offerings, and there thou shalt do   all   that   I

pipt,pnx6680

command thee.

ad7535   qmf2076   wcs,qpf398   nn1320   pp,cs,nn3605   pl,nn,pnx8179

15 Notwithstanding thou mayest kill and   eat   flesh in   all   thy gates,

pp,cs,nn3605   nn,pnx5315   cs,nn185   pp,cs,nn1293   nn3068

whatsoever thy   soul lusteth after, according to the blessing of the LORD thy

pl,nn,pnx430   pnl834   qpf5414   pp,pnx   df,aj2931   wcj,df,aj2889   qmf,pnx398

God   which he hath given thee: the unclean and the clean may   eat   thereof, as

dfp,nn6643   wcj,dfp,nn354

of the roebuck, and as of the   hart.

ad7535   ptn3808 qmf398   df,nn1818   qmf,pnx8210   pr5921   df,nn776

16 Only ye shall not   eat the blood; ye shall   pour   it upon the earth as

dfp,pl,nn4325

water.

qmf3201   ptn3808 pp,qnc398   pp,pl,nn,pnx8179   cs,nn4643   nn,pnx1715

17 Thou mayest not   eat within thy   gates   the tithe of thy corn, or of

wcj,nn,pnx8492   wcj,nn,pnx3323   wcj,pl,cs,nn1062   nn,pnx1241   wcj,nn,pnx6629

thy wine, or of thy   oil,   or the firstlings of thy herds or of thy flock, nor wcj,cs,nn3605   pl,nn,pnx5088   pnl834   qmf5087   wcj,pl,nn,pnx5071

any   of   thy   vows   which   thou   vowest,   nor   thy   freewill offerings,   or

wcj,cs,nn8641   nn,pnx3027

heave offering of thine hand:

cj3588/cj518   qmf,pnx398   pp,pl,cs,nn6440   nn3068   pl,nn,pnx430   dfp,nn4725

18   But   thou must   eat   them   before   the Lord thy   God   in the place

pnl834/pp,pnx   nn3068   pl,nn,pnx430   qmf977   pnp859   wcj,nn,pnx1121   wcj,nn,pnx1323

which   the Lord thy   God   shall choose, thou, and thy   son,   and thy daughter,

wcj,nn,pnx5650   wcj,nn,pnx519   wcj,df,nn3881   pnl834

and thy   manservant,   and thy   maidservant,   and the   Levite   that is   within thy

pp,pl,nn,pnx8179   wcs,qpf8055   pp,pl,cs,nn6440   nn3068   pl,nn,pnx430   pp,cs,nn3605

gates: and thou shalt rejoice   before   the Lord thy   God   in   all   that thou

cs,nn4916   nn,pnx3027

puttest thine hands unto.

nimv8104   pp,pnx   cj6435/qmf5800   (853)   df,nn3881

19 Take heed   to thyself   that*thou*forsake*not   the   Levite

cs,nn3605/pl,nn,pnx3117   pr5921   nn,pnx127

as*long*as*thou*livest upon the earth.

cj3588   nn3068   pl,nn,pnx430   himf7337   (853)   nn,pnx1366   pp,pnl834

20 When the Lord thy   God   shall enlarge   thy border,   as   he hath

pipf1696   pp,pnx   wcj,qpf559   qcj398   nn1320   cj3588   nn,pnx5315   pimf183

promised thee, and thou shalt   say,   I will   eat flesh, because thy   soul   longeth to

pp,qnc398   nn1320   qmf398   nn1320   pp,cs,nn3605   nn,pnx5315   cs,nn185

eat   flesh; thou mayest   eat flesh, whatsoever thy   soul   lusteth after.

cj3588   df,nn4725   pnl834   nn3068   pl,nn,pnx430   qmf977   pp,qnc7760   nn,pnx8034

21 If   the place which the Lord thy   God   hath chosen to   put   his name

ad8033   qmf7368   pr,pnx4480   wcs,qpf2076   pr4480/nn,pnx1241   wcj,pr4480/nn,pnx6629

there be*too*far   from   thee, then thou shalt   kill   of*thy*herd and of*thy*flock,

pnl834   nn3068   qpf5414   pp,pnx   pp,pnl834   pipf,pnx6680   wcj,qpf398

which   the Lord hath given thee   as   I have commanded thee, and thou shalt   eat

pp,pl,nn,pnx8179   pp,cs,nn3605   nn,pnx5315   cs,nn185

in thy   gates   whatsoever thy   soul   lusteth after.

ad389   pp,pnl834 (853)   df,nn6643   wcj(853)   df,nn354   nimf398   ad3651   qmf,pnx398

22 Even   as   the roebuck and   the hart is eaten, so   thou shalt   eat

df,aj2931   wcj,df,aj2889   qmf,pnx398   ad3162

them: the unclean and the   clean   shall   eat   of them alike.

ad7535   qmv2388   qnc398   pp,ptn1115   df,nn1818   cj3588   df,nn1818   (pnp1931)

23 Only be sure that thou eat   not   the blood: for the blood   is the

df,nn5315   wcj,ptn3808 qmf398   df,nn5315   pr5973   df,nn1320

life; and thou mayest   not   eat the   life   with the flesh.

ptn3808   qmf,pnx398   qmf,pnx8210   pr5921   df,nn776   dfp,pl,nn4325

24 Thou shalt not   eat   it; thou shalt   pour   it upon the earth as   water.

ptn3808   qmf,pnx398   pp,cj4616   qmf3190   pp,pnx

25 Thou shalt not   eat   it; that   it may   go well   with thee, and with thy

wcj,pp,pl,nn,pnx1121 pr,pnx310   cj3588   qmf6213   df,aj3477   pp,du,cs,nn5869

children   after thee, when thou shalt   do   that which is right in the   sight   of

nn3068

the Lord.

ad7535   aj,pnx6944   pnl834   pp,pnx   qmf1961   wcj,pl,nn,pnx5088   qmf5375

26 Only thy holy   things which thou hast, and thy   vows,   thou shalt take, and

wcs,qmf935 pr413   df,nn4725   pnl834   nn3068   qmf977

go   unto the place which the Lord shall choose:

wcs,qpf6213   pl,nn,pnx5930   df,nn1320   wcj,df,nn1818 pr5921

27 And thou shalt   offer   thy burnt offerings, the   flesh and the   blood,   upon

cs,nn4196   nn3068   pl,nn,pnx430   wcj,cs,nn1818   pl,nn,pnx2077

the altar   of the Lord thy   God: and the   blood   of thy sacrifices shall be

nimf**8210**   pr5921   cs,nn4196   nn3068   pl,nn,pnx**430**   qmf398   wcj,df,nn**1320**
poured out upon the altar of the LORD thy God, and thou shalt eat the flesh.

qmv**8104**   wcs,qpf**8085** (853) cs,nn**3605** df,pndm428 df,pl,nn**1697** pnl834 pnp595 pipt,pnx**6680**   pp,cj4616
28 Observe and hear   all   these   words which   I   command thee,   that

qmf**3190**   pp,pnx   wcj,pp,pl,nn,pnx**1121** pr,pnx310   pr5704/nn**5769** cj3588
it may go well with thee, and with thy children   after thee forever, when thou

qmf**6213**   df,aj2896   wcj,df,aj**3477**   pp,du,cs,nn**5869**   nn3068   pl,nn,pnx**430**
doest *that which is* good and   right   in the   sight   of the LORD thy God.

   cj3588   nn3068   pl,nn,pnx**430**   himf**3772** (853)   df,pl,nn**1471** pr4480/pl,nn,pnx**6440**
29 When the LORD thy   God   shall cut off   the nations from before thee,

pnl834/ad,lh8033 pnp859 qpta935   pp,qnc**3423**   pnx(853)   wcs,qpf**3423**   pnx(853)
whither   thou goest to possess   them, and thou succeedest   them, and

wcs,qpf**3427**   pp,nn,pnx776
dwellest in their   land;

nimv**8104**   pp,pnx   cj6435   nimf**5367**   pr,pnx310   ad310
30 Take heed to thyself that thou be not snared by following them, after that

ninc,pnx**8045** pr4480/pl,nn,pnx**6440**   wcj,cj6435   qmf1875   pp,pl,nn,pnx**430**
they be destroyed from before thee; and   that   thou inquire not after their   gods,

pp,qnc559   pnit349   df,pndm428 df,pl,nn**1471** qmf**5647** (853)   pl,nn,pnx**430** ad**3651**   pnp589 wcj,qmf**6213**
saying, How did   these   nations serve   their gods? even so will I   do

ad1571
likewise.

     ptn**3808** qmf**6213** ad**3651**   pp,nn**3068**   pl,nn,pnx**430** cj3588 cs,nn**3605**   cs,nn**8441**
31 Thou shalt not   do   so   unto the LORD thy   God: for every abomination

nn3068   pnl834   qpf**8130**   qpf**6213**   pp,pl,nn,pnx**430** cj3588 ad1571 (853)
to the LORD, which he hateth, have they done unto their   gods;   for even   their

pl,nn,pnx**1121** wcj(853)   pl,nn,pnx1323   qmf**8313**   dfp,nn784   pp,pl,nn,pnx**430**
sons and   their daughters they have burnt in the   fire   to their   gods.

(853)   cs,nn**3605**/df,nn**1697**/pnl834   pnp595   pipt**6680**   pnx(853)   qmf**8104**   pp,qnc**6213** pnx(853)
32 What*thing*soever   I   command   you, observe to   do   it:

ptn**3808** himf3254 pr,pnx5921 wcj,ptn**3808** qmf1639   pr,pnx4480
thou shalt not   add thereto,   nor   diminish from it.

13

cj3588   qmf**6965** pp,nn,pnx**7130**   nn5030   cj176   cs,qpta2492   nn2472
☞ If there arise among you a prophet, or a dreamer of dreams,

wcs,qpf**5414**/pr,pnx413   nn226 cj176   nn4159
and   giveth   thee a sign or a wonder,

df,nn**226**   wcj,df,nn**4159**   wcs,qpf935   pnl834   pipf**1696**   pr,pnx413
2 And the sign or the wonder come*to*pass, whereof he spoke   unto thee,

pp,qnc559   qcj1980   pr310   aj312   pl,nn430   pnl834   ptn**3808** qpf,pnx**3045**
saying, Let us   go   after other gods,   which   thou hast   not   known, and let us

wcj,homf,pnx**5647**
serve   them;

ptn**3808**   qmf**8085**   pr413   pl,cs,nn**1697**   df,pndm1931   df,nn**5030**   cj176 (pr413) df,pndm1931
3 Thou shalt not hearken unto the words of   that   prophet, or   that

cs,qpta2492   df,nn**2472** cj3588   nn3068   pl,nn,pnx**430** pipt**5254**   pnx(853)   pp,qnc**3045** he,pta,pnx**3426**
dreamer of dreams: for the LORD your   God   proveth   you, to know whether

pl,qpta157 (853)   nn3068   pl,nn,pnx**430**   pp,cs,nn**3605**   nn,pnx3824   wcj,pp,cs,nn**3605**
ye love   the LORD your   God with   all   your heart and with   all   your

nn,pnx**5315**
soul.

qmf1980   pr310   nn3068   pl,nn,pnx**430**   qmf**3372** wcj,pnx(853)   qmf**8104**
4 Ye shall walk after the LORD your   God,   and   fear   him, and keep

---

☞ **13:1–5** See the note on Deuteronomy 18:20–22.

wcj(853)   pl,nn,pnx**4687**   qmf**8085**   wcj,pp,nn,pnx6963   qmf**5647** wcj,pnx(853)

his commandments, and obey his   voice,   and ye shall serve   him,

qmf1692   wcj,pp,pnx

and cleave unto him.

df,pndm1931 wcj,df,nn**5030** cj176 df,pndm1931 cs,qpta2492 df,nn2472   homf**4191**

5 And   that   prophet, or   that   dreamer of dreams, shall be put*to*death;

cj3588   pipf**1696**   nn**5627**   pr5921   nn3068   pl,nn,pnx**430**

because he hath spoken to turn*_you_*away from the Lord your God,   which

df,hipt3318/pnx(853)   pr4480/cs,nn776   nn4714   wcj,df,qpta,pnx**6299**   pr4480/cs,nn**1004**

brought*you*out of*the*land of Egypt, and redeemed you out*of*the*house of

pl,nn**5650**   pp,hinc,pnx5080   pr4480   df,nn**1870** pnl834   nn3068   pl,nn,pnx**430** pipf,pnx**6680**

bondage, to thrust thee out of the way which the Lord thy God commanded

pp,qnc**1980** pp,pnx   wcj,pipf1197/df,nn**7451**   pr4480/nn,pnx**7130**

thee to walk in. So shalt thou put*the*evil*away from*the*midst of thee.

cj3588   nn,pnx**251** cs,nn121   nn,pnx**517** cj176   nn,pnx**1121** cj176   nn,pnx**1323** cj176

6 If thy brother, the son of thy mother, or thy son, or thy daughter, or

cs,nn**802**   nn,pnx2436 cj176   nn,pnx**7453** pnl834   pp,nn,pnx**5315** himf,pnx**5496**

the wife of thy bosom, or thy friend, which _is_ as thine own soul,   entice thee

dfp,nn**5643**   pp,qnc559   qcj**1980**   wcj,qcj**5647** aj312 pl,nn**430** pnl834   ptn**3808** qpf**3045**

secretly, saying, Let us go and serve other gods, which thou hast not known,

pnp859   wcj,pl,nn,pnx**1**

thou, nor thy fathers;

pr4480/pl,cs,nn**430**   df,pl,nn**5971** pnl834   pr,pnx5439   df,aj7138 pr,pnx413

7 _Namely_, of*the*gods of the people which _are_ round about you, nigh unto

cj176   df,aj7350   pr,pnx4480   pr4480/cs,nn7097   df,nn**776**   wcj,pr5704

thee, or far off from thee, from*the*_one_*end of the earth even unto the _other_

cs,nn7097   df,nn**776**

end of the earth;

ptn**3808**   qmf14   pp,pnx   wcj,ptn**3808**   qmf**8085**   pr,pnx413   wcj,ptn**3808**

8 Thou shalt not consent unto him,   nor hearken unto him; neither shall

nn,pnx**5869** qmf2347/pr,pnx5921   wcj,ptn**3808**   qmf2550 wcj,ptn**3808**   pimf**3680**/pr,pnx5921

thine eye   pity   him, neither shalt thou spare, neither shalt thou   conceal

him:

cj3588   qna**2026**/qmf,pnx**2026**   nn,pnx3027   qmf**1961** dfp,aj**7223**   pp,pnx

9 But thou shalt surely kill him; thine hand shall be first upon him to

pp,hinc,pnx**4191**   dfp,aj314   wcj,cs,nn3027   cs,nn3605   df,nn**5971**

put*him*to*death, and afterwards the hand of all the people.

wcs,qpf,pnx5619   dfp,pl,nn68   wcs,qpf**4191**   cj3588

10 And thou shalt   stone   him with stones, that he   die; because he hath

pipf1245   pp,hinc,pnx5080   pr4480/pr5921   nn3068   pl,nn,pnx**430**   df,hipt,pnx3318

sought to thrust*thee*away   from   the Lord thy God,   which brought*thee*out

pr4480/cs,nn**776**   nn4714   pr4480/cs,nn**1004**   pl,nn**5650**

of*the*land of Egypt, from*the*house of bondage.

wcj,cs,nn3605   nn3478   qmf**8085**   wcj,qmf**3372**   pp,qnc**6213** wcj,ptn**3808** himf3254

11 And   all   Israel shall hear, and   fear,   and shall do   no   more

dfp,nn**1697**   df,nn**7451**   df,pndm2088   pp,nn,pnx**7130**

any such wickedness as   this   is among you.

cj3588   qmf**8085**   pp,cs,nu259   pl,nn,pnx5892 pnl834   nn3068   pl,nn,pnx**430**

12 If thou shalt hear _say_ in one of thy cities, which the Lord thy God

qpta**5414** pp,pnx   pp,qnc**3427** ad8033   pp,qnc559

hath given thee to dwell there, saying,

pl,nn**376**   pl,cs,nn**1121**   nn**1100**   qpf3318   pr4480/nn,pnx**7130**

13 _Certain_ men, the children of Belial, are gone out from among you, and

wcs,himf5080   (853)   pl,cs,qpta3427   nn,pnx5892   pp,qnc559   qcj1980   wcj,qcj5647

have withdrawn   the inhabitants of their city, saying, Let us go and serve

aj312   pl,nn430   pnl834   ptn3808   qpf3045

other gods, which ye have not known;

wcj,qpf1875   wcj,qpf2713   wcj,qpf7592   hina3190

14 Then shalt thou inquire, and make search, and   ask   diligently; and,

wcj,ptdm2009   nn571   df,nn1697   nipt3559   df,pndm2063   df,nn8441   nipf6213

behold, if it be truth, and the thing certain, that   such   abomination is wrought

pp,nn,pnx7130

among you;

hina5221/himf5221   (853)   pl,cs,qpta3427   df,pndm1931 df,nn5892   pp,cs,nn6310

15 Thou shalt surely smite   the inhabitants of that   city with the edge

nn2719   hina2763/pnx(853)   wcj(853) cs,nn3605   pnl834   pp,pnx   wcj(853)

of the sword, destroying*it*utterly, and   all   that is therein, and   the

nn,pnx929   pp,cs,nn6310   nn2719

cattle thereof, with the   edge   of the sword.

qmf6908   wcj(853) cs,nn3605   nn,pnx7998   pr413   cs,nn8432   nn,pnx7339

16 And thou shalt gather   all   the spoil of it into the midst of the street

wcs,qpf8313   dfp,nn784 (853)   df,nn5892   wcj(853) cs,nn3605   nn,pnx7998

thereof, and shalt burn with fire   the city, and   all   the spoil thereof

aj3632   pp,nn3068   pl,nn,pnx430   wcs,qpf1961   nn8510   nn5769   ptn3808

every whit, for the LORD thy God: and it shall   be   a heap forever; it shall not

nimf1129   ad5750

be built again.

qmf1692   wcj,ptn3808/pnid3972 pr4480   df,nn2764   pp,nn,pnx3027

17 And there shall cleave   naught   of the cursed thing to thine   hand:

pp,cj4616   nn3068   qmf7725   pr4480/cs,nn2740   nn,pnx639   wcs,qpf5414 pp,pnx   nn7356

that the LORD may turn from*the*fierceness of his anger, and show thee mercy,

wcs,pipf,pnx7355   wcs,hipf,pnx7235   pp,pnl834   nipf7650

and have compassion upon thee, and multiply thee,   as   he hath sworn unto thy

pp,pl,nn,pnx1

fathers;

cj3588   qmf8085   pp,cs,nn6963   nn3068   pl,nn,pnx430   pp,qnc8104 (853)

18 When thou shalt hearken to the voice of the LORD thy God, to keep

cs,nn3605   pl,nn,pnx4687   pnl834   pnp595   pipt,pnx6680   df,nn3117   pp,qnc6213

all   his commandments which   I   command thee this day, to   do   that which

df,aj3477   pp,du,cs,nn5869   nn3068   pl,nn,pnx430

is right in the   eyes   of the LORD thy God.

pnp859   pl,cs,nn1121   pp,nn3068   pl,nn,pnx430   ptn3808

14 Ye are the children of the LORD your   God: ye shall not

htmf*1413   wcj,ptn3808   qmf7760   nn7144   pr996   du,nn,pnx5869

cut yourselves,   nor   make any baldness between your eyes   for

pp,qpta4191

the dead.

cj3588   pnp859   aj6918   nn5971   pp,nn3068   pl,nn,pnx430   nn3068

2 For thou art a holy people unto the LORD thy God, and the LORD hath

qpf977   wcj,pp,pnx   pp,qnc1961   nn5459   pp,cs,nn5971   pp,pnx   pr4480/cs,nn3605   df,pl,nn5971 pnl834

chosen thee to   be   a peculiar people unto himself, above all the nations that

pr5921/pl,cs,nn6440   df,nn127

are   upon   the earth.

Clean and Unclean Food

ptn**3808** qmf398 cs,nn3605   nn**8441**
3 Thou shalt not eat any abominable thing.

pndm2063   df,nn929 pnl834   qmf398   nn7794   cs,nn7716/pl,nn3775
4 These *are* the beasts which ye shall eat: the ox, the sheep, and the

wcj,cs,nn7716/pl,nn5795
goat,

nn354   wcj,nn**6643**   wcj,nn3180   wcj,nn689
5 The hart, and the roebuck, and the fallow deer, and the wild goat, and the

wcj,nn1788   wcj,nn8377   wcj,nn2169
pygarg, and the wild ox, and the chamois.

wcj,cs,nn3605 nn929   cs,hipt6536   nn6541   wcj,cs,qpta8156   cs,nn8157   du,cs,nu8147
6 And every beast that parteth the hoof, and cleaveth the cleft into two

pl,nn6541   cs,hipt5927   nn1625   dfp,nn929 pnx(853)   qmf398
claws, *and* cheweth the cud among the beasts, that ye shall eat.

ad389   (853) pndm2088   ptn**3808** qmf398   pr4480/pl,cs,hipt**5927**   df,nn1625
7 Nevertheless these ye shall not eat of*them*that*chew the cud, or

wcj,pr4480/pl,cs,hipt6536   df,qptp8156 df,nn6541   (853)   df,nn1581   wcj(853)   df,nn768   wcj(853)
of*them*that*divide the cloven hoof; *as* the camel, and the hare, and

df,nn8227 cj3588 pnp1992 cs,hipt**5927**   nn1625   hipf6536 ptn**3808**   wcj,nn6541   pnp1992
the coney: for they chew the cud, but divide not the hoof; *therefore* they *are*

aj**2931**   pp,pnx
unclean unto you.

wcj(853)   df,nn2386   cj3588   pnp1931   hipt6536   nn6541   wcj,ptn**3808**
8 And the swine, because it divideth the hoof, yet cheweth not the

nn1625 pnp1931   aj**2931**   pp,pnx   ptn**3808** qmf398   pr4480/nn,pnx**1320**   ptn**3808** qmf**5060**
cud, it *is* unclean unto you: ye shall not eat of*their*flesh, nor touch their

wcj,pp,nn,pnx**5038**
dead carcass.

(853) pndm2088   qmf398 pr4480/nn3605 pnl834   dfp,pl,nn4325 nn3605 pnl834 pp,pnx nn5579
9 These ye shall eat of all that *are* in the waters: all that have fins and

wcj,nn7193   qmf398
scales shall ye eat:

wcj,nn3605/pnl834 pp,pnx ptn369 nn5579   wcj,nn7193   ptn**3808** qmf398 pnp1931   aj**2931**
10 And whatsoever hath not fins and scales ye may not eat; it *is* unclean

pp,pnx
unto you.

cs,nn3605 aj**2889**   nn6833   qmf398
11 *Of* all clean birds ye shall eat.

wcj,pndm2088   pnl834   ptn**3808** qmf398 (pr,pnx4480)   df,nn5404
12 But these *are they* of which ye shall not eat: the eagle, and the

wcj,df,nn6538   wcj,df,nn5822
ossifrage, and the osprey,

14:3–21 In this passage God declares certain animals to be "unclean," thereby making it unlawful for the Israelites to eat them. They were, however, free to partake of those animals which are declared to be "clean." There are three views as to why God established this system. Some believe that the "unclean" animals were designated as such for hygienic purposes. They speculate that these animals posed certain health risks for those who would eat them, even after the animals had been properly cooked and prepared. Others have suggested that since the Israelites would soon be entering the Promised Land, this system was intended to distinguish God's people from the religions and practices of their pagan neighbors. Therefore, certain pagan practices were not allowed, such as eating or drinking blood and the boiling of a calf or small animal in its mother's milk (see v. 21), since those things were part of the idolatrous rituals of the heathen people living around them. Finally, others contend that there was nothing in the animals themselves that warranted their designation as clean or unclean, but that God established the system as a test of Israel's obedience and loyalty to Him. Notice that the last two views are not necessarily mutually exclusive.

^{wcj,df,nn7201} ^{wcj(853)} ^{df,nn344} ^{wcj,df,nn1772} ^{pp,nn,pnx4327}
13 And the glede, and   the kite, and the vulture after his kind,

^{wcj(853) cs,nn3605} ⁿⁿ⁶¹⁵⁸ ^{pp,nn,pnx4327}
14 And   every raven after his kind,

^{wcj(853)} ^{cs,nn1323/df,nn3284} ^{wcj(853)} ^{df,nn8464} ^{wcj(853)} ^{df,nn7828}
15 And   the owl,   and   the night hawk, and   the cuckoo,

^{wcj(853)} ^{df,nn5322} ^{pp,nn,pnx4327}
and   the hawk after his kind,

⁽⁸⁵³⁾ ^{df,nn3563} ^{wcj(853)} ^{df,nn3244} ^{wcj,df,nn8580}
16 The little owl, and   the great owl, and the swan,

^{wcj,df,nn6893} ^{wcj(853)} ^{df,nn7360} ^{wcj(853)} ^{df,nn7994}
17 And the pelican, and   the gier-eagle, and   the cormorant,

^{wcj,df,nn2624} ^{wcj,df,nn601} ^{pp,nn,pnx4327} ^{wcj,df,nn1744}
18 And the stork, and the heron after her kind, and the lapwing, and the
^{wcj,df,nn5847}
bat.

^{wcj,cs,nn3605} ^{cs,nn8318} ^{df,nn5775 (pnp1931)} ^{aj2931} ^{pp,pnx}
19 And every creeping thing that flieth   is unclean unto you: they shall
^{ptn3808} ^{nimf398}
not be eaten.

^{cs,nn3605} ^{aj2889} ⁿⁿ⁵⁷⁷⁵ ^{qmf398}
20 But of all   clean fowls ye may eat.

^{ptn3808} ^{qmf398} ^{cs,nn3605} ⁿⁿ⁵⁰³⁸ ^{qmf,pnx5414}
21 Ye shall not eat of any thing*that*dieth*of*itself: thou shalt   give   it
^{dfp,nn1616} ^{pnl834} ^{pp,pl,nn,pnx8179} ^{wcs,qpf,pnx398} ^{cj176}
unto the stranger that is in thy gates,   that he may   eat   it; or thou mayest
^{qna4376} ^{pp,aj5237 cj3588} ^{pnp859} ^{aj6918} ⁿⁿ⁵⁹⁷¹ ^{pp,nn3068} ^{pl,nn,pnx430}
sell it unto an alien: for thou art a holy people unto the LORD thy God. Thou
^{ptn3808} ^{pimf1310} ⁿⁿ¹⁴²³ ^{nn,pnx517} ^{pp,cs,nn2461}
shalt not seethe a kid in his mother's milk.

Tithing

^{pina6237/pimf6237} ^{(853) cs,nn3605} ^{cs,nn8393} ^{nn,pnx2233} ^{df,nn7704}
22 Thou shalt truly tithe   all   the increase of thy seed, that the field
^{df,qpta3318} ⁿⁿ⁸¹⁴¹ ⁿⁿ⁸¹⁴¹
bringeth forth year by year.

^{wcs,qpf398} ^{pp,pl,cs,nn6440} ⁿⁿ³⁰⁶⁸ ^{pl,nn,pnx430} ^{dfp,nn4725} ^{pnl834}
23 And thou shalt eat   before the LORD thy God, in the place which he
^{qmf977} ^{pp,pinc7931} ^{nn,pnx8034} ^{ad8033} ^{cs,nn4643} ^{nn,pnx1715} ^{nn,pnx8492}
shall choose to place his name there, the tithe of thy corn, of thy wine, and of
^{wcj,nn,pnx3323} ^{wcj,pl,cs,nn1062} ^{nn,pnx1241} ^{wcj,nn,pnx6629 pp,cj4616}
thine oil,   and the firstlings of thy herds and of thy flocks; that thou mayest
^{qmf3925} ^{pp,qnc3372 (853)} ⁿⁿ³⁰⁶⁸ ^{pl,nn,pnx430 cs,nn3605/df,nn3117}
learn to fear   the LORD thy God   always.

^{wcj,cj3588} ^{df,nn1870} ^{qmf7235} ^{pr,pnx4480} ^{cj3588} ^{qmf3201/ptn3808}
24 And if   the way be*too*long for   thee, so that thou art*not*able to
^{qnc,pnx5375} ^{cj3588} ^{df,nn4725} ^{qmf7368} ^{pr,pnx4480} ^{pnl834} ⁿⁿ³⁰⁶⁸ ^{pl,nn,pnx430}
carry it; or if the place be*too*far from thee, which the LORD thy God shall
^{qmf977} ^{pp,qnc7760} ^{nn,pnx8034} ^{ad8033} ^{cj3588} ⁿⁿ³⁰⁶⁸ ^{pl,nn,pnx430} ^{pimf,pnx1288}
choose to set his name there, when the LORD thy God hath blessed thee:

^{wcs,qpf5414} ^{dfp,nn3701} ^{wcs,qpf6696} ^{df,nn3701}
25 Then shalt thou turn   it into money, and bind up the money in thine

pp,nn,pnx3027   wcs,qpf1980 pr413   df,nn4725 pnl834/pp,pnx   nn3068   pl,nn,pnx430   qmf977

hand, and shalt go unto the place which the LORD thy God shall choose:

wcs,qpf5414   df,nn3701   pp,nn3605/pnl834   nn,pnx5315   pimf183

26 And thou shalt bestow that money for whatsoever thy soul lusteth after,

dfp,nn1241   wcj,dfp,nn6629   wcj,dfp,nn3196   wcj,dfp,nn7941   wcj,pp,nn3605/pnl834

for oxen, or for sheep, or for wine, or for strong drink, or for whatsoever thy

nn,pnx5315 qmf7592   wcs,qpf398 ad8033 pp,pl,cs,nn6440   nn3068   pl,nn,pnx430

soul desireth: and thou shalt eat there before the LORD thy God, and thou

wcs,qpf8055 pnp859   wcj,nn,pnx1004

shalt rejoice, thou, and thine household,

wcj,df,nn3881 pnl834   pp,pl,nn,pnx8179   ptn3808 qmf,pnx5800   cj3588

27 And the Levite that *is* within thy gates; thou shalt not forsake him; for

pp,pnx   ptn369 nn2506   wcj,nn5159   pr,pnx5973

he hath no part nor inheritance with thee.

pr4480/cs,nn7097   nu7969 pl,nn8141   himf3318 (853) cs,nn3605   cs,nn4643

28 At*the*end of three years thou shalt bring forth all the tithe of thine

nn,pnx8393   df,pndm1931 dfp,nn8141   wcs,hipf5117   pp,pl,nn,pnx8179

increase the same year, and shalt lay*it*up within thy gates:

df,nn3881   cj3588   pp,pnx   ptn369 nn2506   wcj,nn5159   pr,pnx5973

29 And the Levite, (because he hath no part nor inheritance with thee,) and

wcj,df,nn1616   wcj,df,nn3490   wcj,df,nn490 pnl834   pp,pl,nn,pnx8179

the stranger, and the fatherless, and the widow, which *are* within thy gates, shall

wcs,qpf935   wcs,qpf398   wcj,qpf7646   pp,cj4616   nn3068   pl,nn,pnx430   pimf,pnx1288

come, and shall eat and be satisfied; that the LORD thy God may bless

pp,cs,nn3605   cs,nn4639   nn,pnx3027 pnl834   qmf6213

thee in all the work of thine hand which thou doest.

The Seventh Year

15

pr4480/cs,nn7093   nu7651 pl,nn8141   qmf6213   nn8059

⟳ At*the*end of *every* seven years thou shalt make a release.

wcj,pndm2088   cs,nn1697   df,nn8059   cs,nn3605

2 And this *is* the manner of the release: Every

cs,nn1167/cs,nn4874/nn,pnx3027 pnl834 himf5383   pp,nn,pnx7453   qna8058   ptn3808

creditor that lendeth *aught* unto his neighbor shall release *it*; he shall not

qmf5065 (853)   nn,pnx7453   wcj(853)   nn,pnx251   cj3588   qpf7121   pp,nn3068

exact *it* of his neighbor, or of his brother; because it is called the LORD's

nn8059

release.

(853)   df,aj5237   qmf5065   wcj,pnl834 qmf1961 pp,pnx   pr854

3 Of a foreigner thou mayest exact *it again*: but *that* which is thine with

nn,pnx251   nn,pnx3027   himf8058

thy brother thine hand shall release;

ad657   cj3588   qmf1961 ptn3808 aj34   pp,pnx   cj3588   nn3068

4 Save when there shall be no poor among you; for the LORD shall

pina1288/pimf,pnx1288   dfp,nn776 pnl834   nn3068   pl,nn,pnx430 qpta5414 pp,pnx

greatly bless thee in the land which the LORD thy God giveth thee *for* an

nn5159   pp,qnc,pnx3423

inheritance to possess it:

ad7535 cj518   qna8085/qmf8085   pp,cs,nn6963   nn3068   pl,nn,pnx430

5 Only if thou carefully hearken unto the voice of the LORD thy God, to

---

⟳ **15:1–3**   See the note on Leviticus 19:33, 34.

⟳ **15:1–18**   See the note on Leviticus 25:1–55, on the Sabbatical Year and the Year of Jubilee.

pp,qnc**8104**   pp,qnc**6213** (853) cs,nn**3605** df,pndm**2063**   df,nn**4687**   pnl**834**   pnp**595**   pipt,pnx**6680**

observe to   do   all   these commandments which   I   command thee this

df,nn**3117**

day.

cj**3588**   nn**3068**   pl,nn,pnx**430**   pipf,pnx**1288**   pp,pnl**834**   pipf**1696**   pp,pnx

6 For the LORD thy God   blesseth thee,   as   he promised thee: and thou

wcs,hipf**5670**   aj**7227**   pl,nn**1471**   wcj,pnp**859**   ptn**3808** qmf**5670**   wcs,qpf**4910**

shalt lend unto many nations, but thou shalt not borrow; and thou shalt reign

aj**7227**   pp,pl,nn**1471**   ptn**3808** qmf**4910**   wcj,pp,pnx

over many nations, but they shall not reign over thee.

cj**3588**   qmf**1961**   pp,pnx   aj**34**   pr**4480**/cs,nu**259**   pl,nn,pnx**251**

7 If there be   among you a poor man of one   of thy brethren within

pp,cs,nu**259**   pl,nn,pnx**8179**   pp,nn,pnx**776** pnl**834**   nn**3068**   pl,nn,pnx**430** qpta**5414** pp,pnx

any of thy gates in thy land which the LORD thy God giveth thee, thou

ptn**3808**   pimf**553**   (853)   nn,pnx**3824** wcj,ptn**3808** qmf**7092** (853)   nn,pnx**3027**   df,aj**34**

shalt not harden   thine heart,   nor   shut   thine hand from thy poor

pr**4480**/nn,pnx**251**

brother:

cj**3588**   qmf**6605** (853)   nn,pnx**3027** qna**6605**   pp,pnx   wcj,hina**5670**/himf,pnx**5670**

8 But thou shalt open   thine hand wide unto him, and shalt   surely lend

cs,nn**1767**   nn,pnx**4270**   pnl**834** pp,pnx   qmf**2637**

him sufficient for his need, *in that* which he wanteth.

nimv**8104**/pp,pnx cj**6435**   qmf**1961**   nn**1697** pr**5973**   nn**1100** nn,pnx**3824** pp,qnc**559**

9 Beware that there be   not a thought in thy wicked heart, saying, The

df,nu**7651** cs,nn**8141**   cs,nn**8141**   df,nn**8059**   qpf**7126**   nn,pnx**5869** wcj,qpf**7489**

seventh year, the year of release, is*at*hand; and thine eye be evil against thy

df,aj**34** pp,nn,pnx**251**   qmf**5414** pp,pnx wcj,ptn**3808**   wcs,qpf**7121** pr**413**   nn**3068** pr,pnx**5921**

poor brother, and thou givest him naught; and he   cry   unto the LORD against thee,

wcs,qpf**1961** nn**2399**   pp,pnx

and it   be   sin unto thee.

qna**5414**/qmf**5414**   pp,pnx   nn,pnx**3824**   wcj,ptn**3808**   qmf**7489**

10 Thou shalt surely give him, and thine heart shall   not   be grieved when

pp,qnc,pnx**5414**   pp,pnx   cj**3588**   pp,cs,nn**1558** df,pndm**2088** df,nn**1697**   nn**3068**   pl,nn,pnx**430**

thou givest unto him: because that for   this   thing the LORD thy God

pimf,pnx**1288**   pp,cs,nn**3605**   nn,pnx**4639**   wcj,pp,cs,nn**3605**   cs,nn**4916**

shall bless thee in all   thy works, and in   all   that thou puttest thine

nn,pnx**3027**

hand unto.

cj**3588**   aj**34**   ptn**3808** qmf**2308** pr**4480**/cs,nn**7130**   df,nn**776** pr**5921**/ad**3651** pnp**595** pipt,pnx**6680**

11 For the poor shall never cease   out of   the land: therefore   I   command

pp,qnc**559**   qmf**6605** (853)   nn,pnx**3027** qna**6605**   pp,nn,pnx**251**   pp,aj,pnx**6041**

thee, saying, Thou shalt open   thine hand wide unto thy brother, to thy poor,

wcj,pp,aj,pnx**34**   pp,nn,pnx**776**

and to thy needy, in thy land.

cj**3588**   nn,pnx**251**   df,nn**5680**   cj**176**   df,nn**5680**   nimf**4376**

12 *And* if   thy brother, a Hebrew man, or a Hebrew woman, be sold

pp,pnx   wcs,qpf,pnx**5647**   nu**8337** pl,nn**8141**   df,nuor**7637** wcj,dfp,nn**8141**

unto thee, and   serve   thee six years; then in the seventh   year   thou shalt let

pimf,pnx**7971** aj**2670** pr**4480**/pr,pnx**5973**

him   go   free   from   thee.

wcj,cj**3588**   pimf,pnx**7971**   aj**2670** pr**4480**/pr,pnx**5973**   ptn**3808**

13 And when thou sendest*him*out free   from   thee, thou shalt not let him

pimf,pnx**7971**   ad**7387**

go away empty:

hina**6059**/himf**6059**/pp,pnx   pr**4480**/nn,pnx**6629**   wcj,pr**4480**/nn,pnx**1637**

14 Thou shalt furnish*him*liberally out*of*thy*flock, and out*of*thy*floor, and

^{wcj,pr4480/nn,pnx3342} ^{pnl834} ⁿⁿ³⁰⁶⁸ ^{pl,nn,pnx430} ^{pipf,pnx1288}
out*of*thy*winepress: *of that* wherewith the LORD thy　God　hath blessed thee thou

^{qmf5414} ^{pp,pnx}
shalt give unto him.

^{wcs,qpf2142} ^{cj3588} ^{qpf1961} ⁿⁿ⁵⁶⁵⁰ ^{pp,cs,nn776} ⁿⁿ⁴⁷¹⁴
15 And thou shalt remember that thou wast a bondman in the　land　of Egypt,

ⁿⁿ³⁰⁶⁸ ^{pl,nn,pnx430} ^{wcs,qmf,pnx6299} ^{pr5921/ad3651} ^{pnp595} ^{pipt,pnx6680} ⁽⁸⁵³⁾ ^{df,pndm2088}
and the LORD thy　God　redeemed thee: therefore　I　command thee　　this

^{df,nn1697} ^{df,nn3117}
thing today.

^{wcj,qpf1961} ^{cj3588} ^{qmf559} ^{pr,pnx413} ^{ptn3808} ^{qmf3318} ^{pr4480/pr,pnx5973}
16 And it shall　be,　　if　he　say　unto thee, I will　not　go　away　　from

^{cj3588} ^{qpf,pnx157} ^{wcj(853)} ^{nn,pnx1004} ^{cj3588} ^{pp,pnx} ^{aj2896} ^{pr,pnx5973}
thee; because he loveth thee and　　thine house, because　he　is well　with　thee;

^{wcj,qpf3947} ⁽⁸⁵³⁾ ^{df,nn4836} ^{wcj,qpf5414} ^{pp,nn,pnx241}
17 Then thou shalt　take　　an awl,　and　thrust *it* through his　　ear　　unto

^{wcj,dfp,nn1817} ^{wcj,qpf1961} ^{pp,pnx} ⁿⁿ⁵⁶⁵⁰ ⁿⁿ⁵⁷⁶⁹ ^{wcj,cj637}
the　door,　and he shall　be　thy servant forever. And　also　unto　thy

^{pp,nn,pnx519} ^{qmf6213} ^{ad3651}
maidservant thou shalt　do　likewise.

^{ptn3808} ^{qmf7185/pp,nn,pnx5869} ^{pp,pinc,pnx7971/pnx(853)} ^{aj2670}
18 It　shall　not　seem*hard*unto*thee, when　thou　sendest*him*away　free

^{pr4480/pr,pnx5973} ^{cj3588} ^{cs,nn7939} ^{cs,nn4932} ^{aj7916} ^{qpf,pnx5647}
from　　thee; for he hath been worth a double hired servant *to thee*, in serving

^{nu8337} ^{pl,nn8141} ⁿⁿ³⁰⁶⁸ ^{pl,nn,pnx430} ^{wcj,pipf,pnx1288} ^{pp,nn3605} ^{pnl834}
thee　six　years: and the LORD thy　God　shall　bless　thee in　all　that thou

^{qmf6213}
doest.

Firstborn Animals

^{cs,nn3605} ^{df,nn1060} ^{df,nn2145} ^{pnl834} ^{nimf3205} ^{pp,nn,pnx1241} ^{wcj,pp,nn,pnx6629}
19　All　the firstling males that come of thy　herd　and of thy　flock　thou

^{himf6942} ^{pp,nn3068} ^{pl,nn,pnx430} ^{ptn3808} ^{qmf5647} ^{pp,cs,nn1060}
shalt sanctify unto the LORD thy　God: thou shalt do　no　work with the firstling of

^{nn,pnx7794} ^{wcj,ptn3808} ^{qmf1494} ⁿⁿ¹⁰⁶⁰ ^{nn,pnx6629}
thy bullock,　nor　shear the firstling of thy sheep.

^{qmf,pnx398} ^{pp,pl,cs,nn6440} ⁿⁿ³⁰⁶⁸ ^{pl,nn,pnx430} ⁿⁿ⁸¹⁴¹ ^{pp,nn8141}
20 Thou shalt　eat　*it* before　the LORD thy　God　year by　year　in the

^{dfp,nn4725} ^{pnl834} ⁿⁿ³⁰⁶⁸ ^{qmf977} ^{pnp859} ^{wcj,nn,pnx1004}
place which the LORD shall choose, thou and thy household.

^{wcj,cj3588} ^{qmf1961} ⁿⁿ³⁹⁷¹ ^{pp,pnx} ^{aj6455} ^{cj176} ^{aj5787}
21 And　if　there　be　*any* blemish therein, *as if it be* lame, or blind, *or*

^{cs,nn3605} ^{aj7451} ⁿⁿ³⁹⁷¹ ^{ptn3808} ^{qmf,pnx2076} ^{pp,nn3068} ^{pl,nn,pnx430}
have any　ill　blemish, thou shalt　not　sacrifice it unto the LORD thy　God.

^{qmf,pnx398} ^{pp,pl,nn,pnx8179} ^{df,aj2931} ^{wcj,df,aj2889}
22 Thou shalt　eat　it within thy　gates:　the unclean and the　clean　*person*

^{ad3162} ^{dfp,nn6643} ^{wcj,dfp,nn354}
shall eat it alike, as the roebuck, and as the　hart.

^{ad7535} ^{ptn3808} ^{qmf398} ⁽⁸⁵³⁾ ^{nn,pnx1818} ^{qmf,pnx8210} ^{pr5921}
23 Only thou shalt　not　eat　　the blood thereof; thou shalt　pour　it upon the

^{df,nn776} ^{dfp,pl,nn4325}
ground as　water.

Three Festivals Each Year

16

^{qna8104} (853) ^{cs,nn2320} ^{df,nn24} ^{wcs,qpf6213} ⁿⁿ⁶⁴⁵³
⟐ Observe　　the month of Abib, and　keep　the passover unto the
^{pp,nn3068} ^{pl,nn,pnx430} ^{cj3588} ^{pp,cs,nn2320} ^{df,nn24} ⁿⁿ³⁰⁶⁸ ^{pl,nn,pnx430}
LORD thy　God:　for　in the　month　of Abib the LORD thy　God
^{hipf,pnx3318} ^{pr4480/nn4714} ⁿⁿ³⁹¹⁵
brought*thee*forth out*of*Egypt by night.

^{wcj,qpf2076} ⁿⁿ⁶⁴⁵³ ^{pp,nn3068} ^{pl,nn,pnx430}
2 Thou shalt therefore sacrifice the passover unto the LORD thy　God,　of the
ⁿⁿ⁶⁶²⁹ ^{wcj,nn1241} ^{dfp,nn4725} ^{pnl834} ⁿⁿ³⁰⁶⁸ ^{qmf977} ^{pp,pinc7931} ^{nn,pnx8034}
flock and the herd,　in the　place　which the LORD shall choose to　place　his　name
^{ad8033}
there.

^{qmf398} ^{ptn3808} ⁿⁿ²⁵⁵⁷ ^{pr,pnx5921} ^{cs,nu7651} ^{pl,nn3117} ^{qmf398}
3 Thou shalt　eat　no　leavened bread　with　it; seven　days　shalt thou　eat
^{pl,nn4682} ^{pr,pnx5921} ^{cs,nn3899} ⁿⁿ⁶⁰⁴⁰ ^{cj3588} ^{qpf3318}
unleavened bread therewith, *even* the　bread　of affliction;　for　thou camest forth
^{pr4480/cs,nn776} ⁿⁿ⁴⁷¹⁴ ^{pp,nn2649} ^{pp,cj4616} ^{qmf2142} (853) ^{cs,nn3117}
out*of*the*land of Egypt in haste:　that　thou mayest remember　　the　day　when
^{qnc,pnx3318} ^{pr4480/cs,nn776} ⁿⁿ⁴⁷¹⁴ ^{cs,nn3605} ^{pl,cs,nn3117} ^{pl,nn,pnx2416}
thou camest forth out*of*the*land of Egypt　all　the　days　of thy　life.

^{wcj,ptn3808} ⁿⁿ⁷⁶⁰³ ^{nimf7200} ^{pp,pnx} ^{pp,cs,nn3605}
4 And there shall be　no　leavened bread　seen　with thee in　　all　　thy
^{nn,pnx1366} ^{cs,nu7651} ^{pl,nn3117} ^{wcj,ptn3808} ^{pr4480} ^{df,nn1320} ^{pnl834}
coast　seven　days; neither　shall there *any* *thing*　of　the flesh,　which thou
^{qmf2076} ^{df,aj7223} ^{dfp,nn3117} ^{dfp,nn6153} ^{qmf3885} ^{dfp,nn1242}
sacrificedst the first　day　at even, remain*all*night until the morning.

^{qmf3201} ^{ptn3808} ^{pp,qnc2076} (853) ^{df,nn6453} ^{pp,cs,nu259} ^{pl,nn,pnx8179}
5 Thou mayest　not　sacrifice　　the　passover within　any　of thy　gates,
^{pnl834} ⁿⁿ³⁰⁶⁸ ^{pl,nn,pnx430} ^{qpta5414} ^{pp,pnx}
which the LORD thy　God　giveth thee:

^{cj3588/cj518} ^{pr413} ^{df,nn4725} ^{pnl834} ⁿⁿ³⁰⁶⁸ ^{pl,nn,pnx430} ^{qmf977} ^{pp,pinc7931}
6　But　　at　the place　which the LORD thy　God　shall choose to　place　his
^{nn,pnx8034} ^{ad8033} ^{qmf2076} (853) ^{df,nn6453} ^{dfp,nn6153} ^{pp,qnc935}
name　in, there thou shalt sacrifice　　the passover at even, at the going down of
^{df,nn8121} ^{cs,nn4150} ^{qnc,pnx3318} ^{pr4480/nn4714}
the sun,　at the season that thou camest forth out*of*Egypt.

^{wcs,pipf1310} ^{wcs,qpf398} ^{dfp,nn4725} ^{pnl834/pp,pnx} ⁿⁿ³⁰⁶⁸
7 And thou shalt　roast　and　eat　*it* in the place　which　the LORD thy
^{pl,nn,pnx430} ^{qmf977} ^{wcs,qpf6437} ^{dfp,nn1242} ^{wcs,qpf1980}
God　shall choose: and thou shalt　turn　in the morning, and　go　unto thy
^{pp,pl,nn,pnx168}
tents.

^{cs,nu8337} ^{pl,nn3117} ^{qmf398} ^{pl,nn4682} ^{df,nuor7637} ^{wcj,dfp,nn3117}
8　Six　days　thou shalt　eat　unleavened bread: and on the seventh　day
ⁿⁿ⁶¹¹⁶ ^{pp,nn3068} ^{pl,nn,pnx430} ^{qmf6213} ^{ptn3808} ⁿⁿ⁴³⁹⁹
shall be a solemn assembly to the LORD thy　God: thou shalt　do　no　work
therein.

^{nu7651} ^{pl,nn7620} ^{qmf5608} ^{pp,pnx} ^{himf2490} ^{pp,qnc5608} ^{nu7651} ^{pl,nn7620}
9 Seven weeks shalt thou number unto thee: begin to number the seven weeks
^{pr4480/hinc2490} ⁿⁿ²⁷⁷⁰ ^{dfp,nn7054}
from*such*time*as*thou*beginnest *to put* the sickle to the　corn.

⟐ **16:1–12**　See the note on Exodus 23:14–17.

wcs,qpf6213   cs,nn2282   pl,nn7620   pp,nn3068   pl,nn,pnx430

10 And thou shalt keep the feast of weeks unto the LORD thy God with a

cs,nn4530   cs,nn5071   nn,pnx3027   pnl834   qmf5414

tribute of a freewill offering of thine hand, which thou shalt give *unto the LORD thy*

pp,pnl834   nn3068   pl,nn,pnx430   pimf,pnx1288

God, according as the LORD thy God hath blessed thee:

wcs,qpf8055   pp,pl,cs,nn6440   nn3068   pl,nn,pnx430   pnp859   wcj,nn,pnx1121

11 And thou shalt rejoice before the LORD thy God, thou, and thy son,

wcj,nn,pnx1323   wcj,nn,pnx5650   wcj,nn,pnx519   wcj,df,nn3881 pnl834

and thy daughter, and thy manservant, and thy maidservant, and the Levite that *is*

pp,pl,nn,pnx8179   wcj,df,nn1616   wcj,df,nn3490   wcj,df,nn490 pnl834

within thy gates, and the stranger, and the fatherless, and the widow, that *are*

pp,nn,pnx7130   dfp,nn4725   pnl834   nn3068   pl,nn,pnx430   qmf977   pp,pinc7931

among you, in the place which the LORD thy God hath chosen to place his

nn,pnx8034   ad8033

name there.

wcs,qpf2142   cj3588   qpf1961   nn5650   pp,nn4714

12 And thou shalt remember that thou wast a bondman in Egypt: and thou shalt

wcj,qpf8104   wcj,qpf6213   (853)   df,pndm428   df,pl,nn2706

observe and do these statutes.

pp,pnx   qmf6213   cs,nn2282   df,pl,nn5521   cs,nu7651 pl,nn3117

13 Thou shalt observe the feast of tabernacles seven days, after that thou hast

pp,qnc,pnx622   pr4480/nn,pnx1637   wcj,pr4480/nn,pnx3342

gathered in*thy*corn and thy wine:

wcs,qpf8055   pp,nn,pnx2282   pnp859   wcj,nn,pnx1121

14 And thou shalt rejoice in thy feast, thou, and thy son, and thy

wcj,nn,pnx1323   wcj,nn,pnx5650   wcj,nn,pnx519   wcj,df,nn3881   wcj,df,nn1616

daughter, and thy manservant, and thy maidservant, and the Levite, the stranger,

wcj,df,nn3490   wcj,df,nn490 pnl834   pp,pl,nn,pnx8179

and the fatherless, and the widow, that *are* within thy gates.

cs,nu7651   pl,nn3117   qmf2287   pp,nn3068   pl,nn,pnx430

15 Seven days shalt thou keep*a*solemn*feast unto the LORD thy God in the

dfp,nn4725   pnl834   nn3068   qmf977   cj3588   nn3068   pl,nn,pnx430   pimf,pnx1288

place which the LORD shall choose: because the LORD thy God shall bless thee

pp,cs,nn3605   nn,pnx8393   wcj,pp,cs,nn3605   cs,nn4639   du,nn,pnx3027

in all thine increase, and in all the works of thine hands, therefore thou

wcs,qpf1961   ad389   aj8056

shalt surely rejoice.

nu7969   pl,nn6471   dfp,nn8141   cs,nn3605   nn,pnx2138   nimf7200   (853) pl,cs,nn6440   nn3068

16 Three times in a year shall all thy males appear before the LORD

pl,nn,pnx430   dfp,nn4725   pnl834   qmf977   pp,cs,nn2282   df,pl,nn4682

thy God in the place which he shall choose; in the feast of unleavened bread,

wcj,pp,cs,nn2282   df,pl,nn7620   wcj,pp,cs,nn2282   df,pl,nn5521

and in the feast of weeks, and in the feast of tabernacles: and they shall

wcj,ptn3808   nimf7200   (853) pl,cs,nn6440   nn3068   ad7387

not appear before the LORD empty:

nn376   pp,cs,nn4979/nn,pnx3027   pp,cs,nn1293   nn3068

17 Every man *shall give* as*he*is*able, according to the blessing of the LORD

pl,nn,pnx430   pnl834   qpf5414   pp,pnx

thy God which he hath given thee.

The Legal System

<small>pl,qpta8199   wcj,pl,qpta7860   qmf5414   pp,pnx   pp,cs,nn3605   pl,nn,pnx8179   pnl834</small>

18 Judges and officers shalt thou make thee in   all   thy gates, which the

<small>nn3068   pl,nn,pnx430 qpta5414   pp,pnx   pp,pl,nn,pnx7626   wcs,qpf8199 (853)</small>

LORD thy God giveth thee, throughout thy   tribes: and they shall judge   the

<small>df,nn5971   nn6664   cs,nn4941</small>

people with just judgment.

<small>ptn3808   himf5186   nn4941   ptn3808   himf5234   pl,nn6440   wcj,ptn3808 qmf3947</small>

19 Thou shalt not wrest judgment; thou shalt not respect persons, neither take

<small>nn7810 cj3588   df,nn7810   pimf5786   du,cs,nn5869   aj2450   wcj,pimf5557   pl,cs,nn1697</small>

a gift: for a gift doth blind the eyes of the wise, and pervert the words of the

<small>aj6662</small>

righteous.

<small>nn6664/nn6664   qmf7291   pp,cj4616   qmf2421</small>

20 That which is altogether just shalt thou follow, that thou mayest live, and

<small>wcs,qpf3423 (853)   df,nn776 pnl834   nn3068   pl,nn,pnx430 qpta5414   pp,pnx</small>

inherit   the land which the LORD thy God giveth thee.

<small>ptn3808   qmf5193 pp,pnx   nn842   cs,nn3605 nn6086 pr681   cs,nn4196</small>

21 Thou shalt not plant thee a grove of any   trees near unto the altar of the

<small>nn3068   pl,nn,pnx430 pnl834   qmf6213 pp,pnx</small>

LORD thy God, which thou shalt make thee.

<small>wcj,ptn3808   himf6965/pp,pnx   nn4676   pnl834   nn3068   pl,nn,pnx430 qpf8130</small>

22 Neither shalt thou set*thee*up any image; which the LORD thy God   hateth.

<small>ptn3808   qmf2076   pp,nn3068   pl,nn,pnx430   nn7794</small>

17

Thou shalt not sacrifice unto the LORD thy God any bullock, or

<small>wcj,nn7716 pnl834/pp,pnx qmf1961   nn3971   cs,nn3605   nn1697/aj7451   cj3588 pnp1931</small>

sheep, wherein is blemish, or any evilfavoredness: for that is an

<small>cs,nn8441   nn3068   pl,nn,pnx430</small>

abomination unto the LORD thy God.

<small>cj3588   nimf4672   pp,nn,pnx7130   pp,cs,nu259   pl,nn,pnx8179 pnl834</small>

2 If there be found among you, within any of thy gates which the

<small>nn3068   pl,nn,pnx430 qpta5414   pp,pnx nn376 cj176   nn802   pnl834   qmf6213 (853)   df,aj7451</small>

LORD thy God giveth thee, man or woman, that hath wrought   wickedness in

<small>pp,du,cs,nn5869   nn3068   pl,nn,pnx430   pp,qnc5674   nn,pnx1285</small>

the sight of the LORD thy God, in transgressing his covenant,

<small>wcs,qmf1980   wcs,qmf5647 aj312   pl,nn430   wcs,htmf7812   pp,pnx</small>

3 And hath gone and served other gods, and worshiped them, either the

<small>wcj,dfp,nn8121 cj176 dfp,nn3394 cj176 pp,cs,nn3605   cs,nn6635   df,du,nn8064 pnl834   ptn3808</small>

sun, or moon, or any of the host of heaven, which I have not

<small>pipf6680</small>

commanded;

<small>wcj,hopf5046 pp,pnx   wcj,qpf8085   wcj,qpf1875   hina3190</small>

4 And it be told   thee, and thou hast heard of it, and inquired diligently,

<small>wcj,ptdm2009   nn571   df,nn1697 nipt3559   df,pndm2063   df,nn8441   nipf6213</small>

and, behold, it be true, and the thing certain, that such abomination is wrought in

<small>pp,nn3478</small>

Israel:

<small>wcj,hipf3318   (853) df,pndm1931 df,nn376 cj176 df,pndm1931   df,nn802   pnl834</small>

5 Then shalt thou bring forth   that man or that woman, which have

<small>qpf6213   (853) df,pndm2088 df,aj7451 df,nn1697 pr413   pl,nn,pnx8179   (853)   df,nn376 cj176 (853)</small>

committed   that wicked thing, unto thy gates, even   that man or   that

<small>df,nn802   wcj,qpf,pnx5619   dfp,pl,nn68   wcj,qpf4191</small>

woman, and shalt stone them with stones, till they die.

6 At the mouth of two witnesses, or three witnesses, shall he that is*worthy*of*death be put*to*death; *but* at the mouth of one witness he shall not be put*to*death.

7 The hands of the witnesses shall be first upon him to put*him*to*death, and afterward the hands of all the people. So thou shalt put*the*evil*away from among you.

8 If there arise*a*matter*too*hard for thee in judgment, between blood and blood, between plea and plea, and between stroke and stroke, *being* matters of controversy within thy gates: then shalt thou arise, and get*thee*up into the place which the LORD thy God shall choose;

9 And thou shalt come unto the priests the Levites, and unto the judge that shall be in those days, and inquire; and they shall show thee the sentence of judgment:

10 And thou shalt do according to the sentence, which they of that place which the LORD shall choose shall show thee; and thou shalt observe to do according to all that they inform thee:

11 According to the sentence of the law which they shall teach thee, and according to the judgment which they shall tell thee, thou shalt do: thou shalt not decline from the sentence which they shall show thee, *to* the right hand, nor *to* the left.

12 And the man that will do presumptuously, and will not hearken unto the priest that standeth to minister there before the LORD thy God, or unto the judge, even that man shall die: and thou shalt put away the evil from Israel.

13 And all the people shall hear, and fear, and do no more presumptuously.

The Future King

cj3588　qmf935　pr413　df,nn776　pnl834　　nn3068　pl,nn,pnx430　qpta5414　pp,pnx

14 When thou art come unto the land which the LORD thy　God　giveth thee,

wcs,qpf,pnx3423　　　wcs,qpf3427　pp,pnx　　wcs,qpf559　　qcj7760　　nn4428

and shalt　possess　it, and shalt dwell therein, and shalt　say,　I will　set a king

pr,pnx5921　　pp,cs,nn3605　df,pl,nn1471 pnl834　pr,pnx5439

over me, like as　all　the nations that *are* about me;

qna7760/qmf7760　　　　nn4428　pr,pnx5921　　pnl834/pp,pnx　　　nn3068

15 Thou shalt in*any*wise*set *him*　king　over　thee,　whom　the LORD thy

pl,nn,pnx430　qmf977　　pr4480/cs,nn7130　pl,nn,pnx251　　qmf7760 nn4428 pr,pnx5921

God　shall choose: *one* from among thy brethren shalt thou　set　king　over　thee:

qmf3201 ptn3808 pp,qnc5414　nn376/aj5237 pr,pnx5921　pnl834 (pnp1931)　ptn3808　nn,pnx251

thou mayest not　set　a stranger　over　thee, which　　*is* not thy brother.

ad7535　ptn3808　himf7235　pl,nn5483　pp,pnx　wcj,ptn3808　(853)　df,nn5971

16 But he shall　not　multiply horses to himself,　nor　cause　the people to

himf7725　nn,lh4714　pp,cj4616　　hinc7235　nn5483　　wcj,nn3068

return to Egypt, to*the*end*that he should multiply horses: forasmuch as the LORD

qpf559　pp,pnx　　himf3254　pp,qnc7725 ptn3808 ad5750 df,pndm2088 dfp,nn1870

hath said unto you, Ye shall henceforth return　no　more　that　way.

wcj,ptn3808　　himf7235　pl,nn802　pp,pnx　　nn,pnx3824　qmf5493/wcj,ptn3808

17 Neither shall he multiply wives to himself, that his　heart　turn*not*away:

ptn3808　ad3966　himf7235　pp,pnx　wcj,nn3701　wcj,nn2091

neither shall he greatly multiply to himself silver and gold.

wcs,qpf1961　pp,qnc,pnx3427 pr5921　cs,nn3678　　nn,pnx4467

18 And it shall　be,　when he　sitteth　upon the throne of his kingdom, that

wcs,qpf3789　pp,pnx　(853)　cs,nn4932　df,pndm2063　df,nn8451　pr5921　nn5612

he　shall　write　him　a　copy　of　this　law　in　a　book

pr4480/pp,pl,cs,nn6440　df,pl,nn3548　df,pl,nn3881

out*of*that*which*is*before the priests the Levites:

wcs,qpf1961　pr,pnx5973　　wcs,qpf7121　pp,pnx　cs,nn3605　pl,cs,nn3117

19 And it shall　be　with　him, and he shall　read　therein　all　the days

pl,nn,pnx2416 pp,cj4616　　qmf3925　pp,qnc3372 (853)　nn3068　pl,nn,pnx430　pp,qnc8104 (853)

of his　life:　that　he may learn to　fear　the LORD his　God,　to　keep

cs,nn3605　pl,cs,nn1697　df,pndm2063 df,nn8451 wcj(853)　df,pndm428 df,pl,nn2706　pp,qnc,pnx6213

all　the words of　this　law　and these statutes, to　do　them:

nn,pnx3824　pp,ptn1115　qnc7311　pr4480/pl,nn,pnx251

20 That his　heart　be　not　lifted up above*his*brethren, and that he

qnc5493/wcj,pp,ptn1115　pr4480　df,nn4687　　nn3225　　wcj,nn8040

turn*not*aside from the commandment, *to* the right hand, or *to* the　left:

pp,cj4616　himf748　pl,nn3117 pr5921　nn,pnx4467 pnp1931　wcj,pl,nn,pnx1121

to*the*end*that he may prolong *his* days　in　his kingdom, he, and his children,

pp,cs,nn7130　nn3478

in the　midst　of Israel.

17:14–20　See the note on 1 Samuel 8:5–7.

17:16　The regulations mentioned in this verse, namely the multiplying of horses and wives, were set up so that the king's attention would not be turned from God to a reliance on himself, or worse yet, on idols. God specifically commanded that the children of Israel rely on Him when it came to military endeavors, not on horses or chariots (Josh. 11:4, 6). Israel's kings would be tempted to amass as much protection as they thought they needed; in doing so, however, their hearts would be turned away from God. The example of God destroying the Egyptians in the Red Sea was intended to show Israel that accumulating horses for the purpose of building military strength was unnecessary as long as they trusted exclusively in God (Ex. 15:19, 21; Deut. 11:4). When Elisha and his servant were surrounded by the armies of Aram, God opened the eyes of the servant so that he could see God's army of chariots surrounding the Aramean forces. God was providing His watchcare over his servants. God wanted Israel to depend on Him, not on what man could do (Ps. 33:17; 147:10). David and Solomon are examples of kings who disobeyed this command (2 Sam. 8:4; 1 Kgs. 4:26; 10:25).

pnl834   ptn**3808**   pipf,pnx**6680**   pp,pinc**1696**   wcj,pnl834   pimf**1696**   pp,cs,nn8034

which I have not commanded him to speak, or that shall speak in the name of

aj312   pl,nn**430**   df,pndm1931   df,nn**5030**   wcs,qpf**4191**

other gods, even that prophet shall die.

         wcj,cj3588   qmf559   pp,nn,pnx3824   pnit349   qmf**3045**   (853)   df,nn**1697**

21 And if thou say in thine heart, How shall we know   the word

pnl834   nn**3068**   ptn**3808** pipf,pnx**1696**

which the LORD hath not spoken?

     pnl834   df,nn**5030**   pimf**1696**   pp,cs,nn8034   nn**3068**   df,nn**1697** qmf**1961**

22 When a prophet speaketh in the name of the LORD, if the thing follow

wcj,ptn**3808** wcj,ptn**3808**   qmf935   pnp1931   df,nn**1697**   pnl834   nn**3068**   ptn**3808** pipf,pnx**1696**

not, nor come*to*pass, that *is* the thing which the LORD hath not spoken,

      df,nn**5030**   pipf,pnx**1696**   pp,nn2087   ptn**3808** qmf**1481**   pr,pnx4480

but the prophet hath spoken it presumptuously: thou shalt not be afraid of him.

The Cities of Refuge

           cj3588   nn**3068**   pl,nn,pnx**430**   himf**3772**   (853)   df,pl,nn**1471**   pnl834   (853)

19 When the LORD thy God hath cut off   the nations, whose

      nn,pnx776   nn**3068**   pl,nn,pnx**430**   qpta**5414**   pp,pnx   wcs,qpf,pnx**3423**

land the LORD thy God giveth thee, and thou succeedest them, and

wcs,qpf**3427**   pp,pl,nn,pnx5892   wcj,pp,pl,nn,pnx**1004**

dwellest in their cities, and in their houses;

     himf**914**   nu7969   pl,nn5892   pp,pnx   pp,cs,nn**8432**   nn,pnx776   pnl834

2 Thou shalt separate three cities for thee in the midst of thy land, which the

nn**3068**   pl,nn,pnx**430**   qpta**5414**   pp,pnx   pp,qnc,pnx**3423**

LORD thy God giveth thee to possess it.

        himf**3559**   pp,pnx   df,nn**1870**   wcs,pipf8027   (853)   cs,nn1366   nn,pnx776   pnl834

3 Thou shalt prepare thee a way, and divide   the coasts of thy land, which

---

one of which was how to distinguish between the true and false ones. Turbulent times, during which the people wanted to hear words of hope and security, produced the greatest outbreak of prophets for hire and seers with optimistic lies. Shortly after Judah started going into exile in Babylon, but before the fall of Jerusalem, Jeremiah and Ezekiel had to contend with a rash of these charlatans, upon whom they issued stern denunciations (Jer. 23:9–32; Ezek. 13:1–23). The penalty for being a false prophet was death (Deut. 13:5; 18:20; see Jer. 28:16).

In this passage in Deuteronomy chapter eighteen, Moses gave one of the tests by which the people could distinguish a true prophet from a false one. If the prophet's message did not come true as predicted, he was a false prophet (see 1 Kgs. 22:28). In his conflict with the false prophet Hananiah, Jeremiah expressed the test positively, so that if the prophecy came true, all would know that Hananiah was a true prophet (Jer. 28:9). This was only a general rule which applied to the case at hand, because it was possible for a false prophet to utter a true message, either as a guess or as a test from the Lord to see whether the people would obey (Deut. 13:1–3). Another test for a true prophet was that he had to have the ability, as a sign of God's calling, to perform miracles (Ex. 4:6). A third test, though it did not always apply, was that an easy message in hard times was often an unreliable one (Jer. 23:16, 17, 29; 28:8, 9; Ezek. 13:10–16). The most important test of a true prophet was that the content of his message had to be consistent with all prior revelation. Thus, if a prophet said that Israel should serve another god, he was obviously false (Deut. 13:1–3). Similarly, in the New Testament both Paul and John taught that the content of the message already received was the standard by which to measure any new message, even if it came from Paul himself or an angel (Gal. 1:8) or a spirit masquerading as God's Spirit (1 John 4:1–3). By this test alone the claims of the false religions of the world, and of the cults in particular, are silenced.

☞ **19:1–10** This passage outlines how the Israelites were to establish "cities of refuge" when they had entered the Promised Land. These places were designed to take in those who were accused of homicide but perhaps guilty of only manslaughter (killing someone without malice). Provision was made for their safety until their case could be judged. In the Promised Land there were six such cities established. Three were located on the east side of the Jordan River, while three others were established on the west side. For an explanation of the Levitical cities, of which the six "cities of refuge" were a part, see the note on Joshua 21:2.

nn3068   pl,nn,pnx430   himf,pnx5157   cs,nn3605   qpta7523   wcj,qpf1961

the LORD thy   God   giveth thee to inherit, into three parts, that every slayer   may

pp,qnc5127   ad,lh8033

flee thither.

            wcj,pndm2088   cs,nn1697   df,qpta7523   pnl834   qmf5127   ad,lh8033

4 And   this   *is* the case of the slayer, which shall flee thither, that he may

wcj,qpf2425   pnl834   himf5221   (853)   nn,pnx7453   pp,ptn1907/nn1947   pp,pnx   wcj,pnp1931   qpta8130   ptn3808   ad8032

live: Whoso killeth   his neighbor ignorantly, whom   he   hated not in time

pr4480/ad8657

past;

            wcj,pnl834   qmf935   dfp,nn3293   pr854   nn,pnx7453   pp,qnc2404   pl,nn6086

5 As when a   man   goeth into the wood with his neighbor to   hew   wood, and

nn,pnx3027   wcs,nipf5080   dfp,nn1631   pp,qnc3772   df,nn6086   df,nn1270

his hand fetcheth*a*stroke with the   axe   to cut down the tree, and the head

wcs,qpf5394   pr4480   df,nn6086   wcs,qpf4672   (853)   nn,pnx7453   wcs,qpf4191 pnp1931

slippeth from the helve, and lighteth upon   his neighbor, that he   die;   he

qmf5127 pr413 cs,nu259   df,pndm428 df,pl,nn5892   wcs,qpf2425

shall flee unto one of those cities, and live:

            cj6435   cs,qpta1350   df,nn1818   qmf7291/pr310   df,qpta7523   cj3588   nn,pnx3824   qmf3179

6 Lest the avenger of the blood pursue the slayer, while his heart is hot, and

wcs,hipf,pnx5381   cj3588   df,nn1870   qmf7235   wcs,hipf,pnx5221   nn5315   wcj,pp,pnx

overtake him, because the way is long, and   slay   him; whereas he   *was*

ptn369   cs,nn4941/nn4194   cj3588   pnp1931 qpta8130 pp,pnx ptn3808   ad8032 pr4480/ad8543

not worthy*of*death, inasmuch as he hated him not in time   past.

            pr5921/ad3651   pnp595   pipt,pnx6680   pp,qnc559   himf914   nu7969   pl,nn5892

7 Wherefore   I   command thee, saying, Thou shalt separate three cities

pp,pnx

for thee.

            wcj,cj518   nn3068   pl,nn,pnx430   himf7337   (853)   nn,pnx1366 pp,pnl834   nipf7650

8 And   if   the LORD thy God enlarge   thy coast,   as   he hath sworn

            pp,pl,nn,pnx1   wcj,qpf5414   pp,pnx (853) cs,nn3605   df,nn776 pnl834   pipf1696   pp,qnc5414

unto thy fathers, and   give thee   all   the land which he promised to   give

pp,pl,nn,pnx1

unto thy fathers;

            cj3588   qmf8104 (853) cs,nn3605 df,pndm2063   df,nn4687   pp,qnc,pnx6213   pnl834

9 If thou shalt keep   all   these commandments to   do   them, which

pnp595   pipt,pnx6680   df,nn3117   pp,qnc157 (853)   nn3068   pl,nn,pnx430   wcj,pp,qnc1980

I command thee this day, to love   the LORD thy God, and to   walk

cs,nn3605/df,pl,nn3117   pp,pl,nn,pnx1870   wcs,qpf3254 nu7969 pl,nn5892 ad5750   pp,pnx

ever   in his   ways;   then shalt thou add   three cities more for thee,

pr5921 df,pndm428 df,nu7969

beside these three:

            aj5355   nn1818   wcj,ptn3808 nimf8210 pp,cs,nn7130   nn,pnx776 pnl834   nn3068

10 That innocent blood be   not   shed   in   thy land, which the LORD thy

pl,nn,pnx430 qpta5414   pp,pnx   nn5159   pl,nn1818 wcs,qpf1961 pr,pnx5921

God   giveth thee *for* an inheritance, and *so* blood   be   upon thee.

            wcj,cj3588   nn376   qmf1961/qpta8130   pp,nn,pnx7453   wcs,qpf693   pp,pnx

11 But   if   any man   hate   his neighbor, and lie*in*wait for him, and

wcs,qpf6965 pr,pnx5921   wcs,hipf,pnx5221   nn5315   wcs,qpf4191   wcs,qpf5127 pr413 cs,nu259

rise up against him, and   smite   him mortally that he die, and fleeth into one

df,pndm411 df,pl,nn5892

of these cities:

            cs,aj2205   nn,pnx5892   wcs,qpf7971   wcs,qpf3947 pnx(853)   pr4480/ad8033

12 Then the elders of his city shall send and fetch   him thence, and

wcs,qpf5414 pnx(853)   pp,cs,nn3027   cs,qpta1350 df,nn1818   wcs,qpf4191

deliver   him into the hand of the avenger of blood, that he may   die.

nn,pnx**5869**   ptn**3808**   qmf2347/pr,pnx5921   wcs,pipf1197

13 Thine   eye   shall   not   pity   him,   but   thou   shalt   put   away

df,aj**5355**   cs,nn**1818**   pr4480/nn3478   wcs,qpf**2895**   pp,pnx

the guilt of innocent blood from Israel, that it may go well with thee.

ptn**3808**   himf5253   nn,pnx**7453**   cs,nn**1366**   pnl834   aj**7223**

14 Thou shalt not remove thy neighbor's landmark, which they*of*old*time

qpf1379   pp,nn,pnx**5159**   pnl834   qmf**5157**   dfp,nn776 pnl834   nn**3068**

have set in thine inheritance, which thou shalt inherit in the land that the LORD

pl,nn,pnx**430**   qpta**5414**   pp,pnx   pp,qnc,pnx**3423**

thy God giveth thee to possess it.

Witnesses

nu259   nn5707   ptn**3808**   qmf**6965**   pp,nn**376**   pp,cs,nn3605   nn**5771**

15 One witness shall not rise up against a man for any iniquity, or for

wcj,pp,cs,nn**2403** nn**2403**   pp,cs,nn3605 nn**2399** pnl834   qmf**2398**   pr5921   cs,nn**6310**   du,cs,nu8147   pl,nn5707

any sin, in any sin that he sinneth: at the mouth of two witnesses,

cj176 pr5921   cs,nn**6310**   nu7969   pl,nn5707   nn**1697**   qmf**6965**

or at the mouth of three witnesses, shall the matter be established.

cj3588   nn**2555**   nn5707   qmf**6965**   pp,nn**376**   pp,qnc6030   pp,pnx

16 If a false witness rise up against any man to testify against him *that*

nn**5627**

which is wrong;

du,cs,nu8147   df,pl,nn**376**   pnl834/pp,pnx   df,nn**7379**   wcs,qpf5975

17 Then both the men, between whom the controversy *is*, shall stand

pp,pl,cs,nn**6440**   nn**3068** pp,pl,cs,nn**6440**   df,pl,nn**3548**   wcj,df,pl,qpta**8199** pnl834   qmf**1961**   df,pnp**1992**

before the LORD, before the priests and the judges, which shall be in those

dfp,pl,nn**3117**

days;

df,pl,qpta**8199**   wcs,qpf1875/hina**3190**   wcj,ptdm2009   df,nn5707

18 And the judges shall make*diligent*inquisition: and, behold, *if* the witness

nn**8267**   nn5707   qpf6030   nn**8267**   pp,nn,pnx**251**

be a false witness, *and* hath testified falsely against his brother;

wcj,qpf**6213**   pp,pnx   pp,pnl834   qpf**2161**   pp,qnc**6213**

19 Then shall ye do unto him, as he had thought to have done unto his

pp,nn,pnx**251**   wcj,pipf1197/df,aj**7451**   pr4480/nn,pnx**7130**

brother: so shalt thou put*the*evil*away from among you.

wcj,df,pl,nipf**7604**   qmf**8085**   wcj,qmf**3372**   himf3254

20 And those which remain shall hear, and fear, and shall henceforth

pp,qnc**6213** wcj,ptn**3808** ad5750 dfp,nn**1697** df,pndm2088 df,aj**7451** pp,nn,pnx**7130**

commit no more any such evil among you.

du,nn,pnx**5869**   wcj,ptn**3808** qmf2347   nn**5315**   pp,nn**5315** nn**5869**

21 And thine eye shall not pity; *but* life *shall go* for life, eye for

pp,nn**5869** nn**8127**   pp,nn**8127** nn**3027**   pp,nn**3027** nn**7272**   pp,nn**7272**

eye, tooth for tooth, hand for hand, foot for foot.

How to Wage War

20 When thou goest out to battle against thine enemies, and seest
horses, and chariots, *and* a people more than thou, be*not*afraid
of them: for the LORD thy God *is* with thee, which brought*thee*up
out*of*the*land of Egypt.

2 And it shall be, when ye are come nigh unto the battle, that the priest
shall approach and speak unto the people,

3 And shall say unto them, Hear, O Israel, ye approach this day unto
battle against your enemies: let not your hearts faint, fear not, and do not
tremble, neither be ye terrified because of them;

4 For the LORD your God *is* he that goeth with you, to fight for you
against your enemies, to save you.

5 And the officers shall speak unto the people, saying, What man *is there* that
hath built a new house, and hath not dedicated it? let him go and return to his
house, lest he die in the battle, and another man dedicate it.

6 And what man *is he* that hath planted a vineyard, and hath not *yet*
eaten of it? let him *also* go and return unto his house, lest he die in the
battle, and another man eat of it.

7 And what man *is there* that hath betrothed a wife, and hath not taken
her? let him go and return unto his house, lest he die in the battle, and another
man take her.

8 And the officers shall speak further unto the people, and they shall say,
What man *is there that is* fearful and fainthearted? let him go and return unto his
house, lest his brethren's heart faint as well as his heart.

9 And it shall be, when the officers have made*an*end of speaking unto the
people, that they shall make captains of the armies to lead the people.

10 When thou comest nigh unto a city to fight against it, then proclaim peace
unto it.

11 And it shall be, if it make thee answer of peace, and open unto thee, then it shall be, *that* all the people *that is* found therein shall be tributaries unto thee, and they shall serve thee.

12 And if it will make*no*peace with thee, but will make war against thee, then thou shalt besiege it:

13 And when the Lord thy God hath delivered it into thine hands, thou shalt smite every male thereof with the edge of the sword:

14 But the women, and the little ones, and the cattle, and all that is in the city, *even* all the spoil thereof, shalt thou take unto thyself; and thou shalt eat the spoil of thine enemies, which the Lord thy God hath given thee.

15 Thus shalt thou do unto all the cities *which are* very far off from thee, which *are* not of*the*cities of these nations.

16 But of*the*cities of these people, which the Lord thy God doth give thee *for* an inheritance, thou shalt save alive nothing that breatheth:

17 But thou shalt utterly destroy them; *namely*, the Hittites, and the Amorites, the Canaanites, and the Perizzites, the Hivites, and the Jebusites; as the Lord thy God hath commanded thee:

18 That they teach you not to do after all their abominations, which they have done unto their gods; so should ye sin against the Lord your God.

19 When thou shalt besiege a city a long time, in making war against it to take it, thou shalt not destroy the trees thereof by forcing an axe against

---

20:16–18 This is the final statement of God's justice on the seven peoples listed in this passage. Five hundred years before, God had stated that "their iniquity was not yet full" (Gen. 15:16), but it was now full to overflowing. Archaeological evidence reveals how incredibly depraved these tribes were. They practiced human sacrifice and every sort of sexual perversion. Because of the multitude and grievous nature of their sins, it is said that the land "vomiteth out her inhabitants" (Lev. 18:21–25). The sinfulness of these tribes would present a strong temptation to Israel and must therefore be wiped out. As the incident with the Moabites revealed (Num. 25:1–3), Israel was all too prone to adopt the idolatrous and inhuman practices of her neighbors. In fact, the inhabitants of Canaan that Israel did not destroy according to God's command are described as being "snares" to Israel (Ex. 23:33; 34:12; Deut. 7:16; 12:30).

cj3588   qmf398 pr,pnx4480   ptn3808 qmf3772/wcj,pnx(853) cj3588

them: for thou mayest eat of them, and thou shalt not cut*them*down (for

cs,nn6086 df,nn7704 df,nn120   pp,qnc935/pr4480/pl,nn,pnx6440   dfp,nn4692

the tree of the field *is* man's *life*) to employ *them* in the siege:

     ad7535 nn6086 pnl834   qmf3045 cj3588 pnp1931 ptn3808 cs,nn6086   nn3978

20 Only the trees which thou knowest that they *be* not trees for meat, thou

himf7843 (pnx853)   wcs,qpf3772 nn4692 pr5921

shalt destroy and cut*them*down; and thou shalt build bulwarks against the

df,nn5892 pnl834/pnp1931 qpta6213 nn4421 pr,pnx5973 pr5704   qnc,pnx3381

city that   maketh war with thee, until it be subdued.

Expiation for Innocent Blood

21

   cj3588   nimf4672 nn2491   dfp,nn127 pnl834   nn3068   pl,nn,pnx430 qpta5414

If *one* be found slain in the land which the LORD thy God giveth

pp,pnx pp,qnc,pnx3423 qpta5307 dfp,nn7704   ptn3808 nipf3045 pnit4310

thee to possess it, lying in the field, *and* it be not known who hath

hipf,pnx5221

slain him:

    aj,pnx2205   wcj,pl,qpta,pnx8199   wcj,qpf3318   wcj,qpf4058

2 Then thy elders and thy judges shall come forth, and they shall measure

pr413 df,pl,nn5892 pnl834   pr5439   df,nn2491

unto the cities which *are* round about him that is slain:

      wcj,qpf1961   df,nn5892 df,aj7138 pr413 df,nn2491

3 And it shall be, *that* the city *which is* next unto the slain man, even the

cs,aj2205 df,pndm1931 df,nn5892 wcj,qpf3947 cs,nn5697/nn1241 pnl834 ptn3808 pupf5647 pp,pnx

elders of that city shall take a heifer, which hath not been wrought with,

    pnl834 ptn3808 qpf4900   pp,nn5923

and which hath not drawn in the yoke;

     cs,aj2205 df,pndm1931 df,nn5892   wcj,hipf3381 (853) df,nn5697 pr413   aj386

4 And the elders of that city shall bring down the heifer unto a rough

nn5158 pnl834/pp,pnx ptn3808 nimf5647 wcj,ptn3808 nimf2232   wcs,qpf6203 (853) df,nn5697

valley, which is neither eared nor sown, and shall strike off the heifer's

wcj,qpf6203 ad8033   dfp,nn5158

neck there in the valley:

     df,pl,nn3548 pl,cs,nn1121 nn3878   wcs,nipf5066 cj3588 pp,pnx   nn3068

5 And the priests the sons of Levi shall come near; for them the LORD thy

pl,nn,pnx430 qpf977 pp,pinc,pnx8334   wcj,pp,pinc1288 pp,cs,nn8034

God hath chosen to minister unto him, and to bless in the name of the

nn3068 wcj,pr5921 nn,nn,pnx6310 cs,nn3605 nn7379 wcj,cs,nn3605 nn5061 qmf1961

LORD; and by their word shall every controversy and every stroke be *tried*:

     wcj,cs,nn3605 cs,aj2205 df,pndm1931 df,nn5892   df,aj7138 pr413 df,nn2491

6 And all the elders of that city, *that are* next unto the slain *man*,

    qmf7364 (853) du,nn,pnx3027 pr5921 df,nn5697 df,qptp6202   dfp,nn5158

shall wash their hands over the heifer that is beheaded in the valley:

      wcs,qpf6030 wcs,qpf559 du,nn,pnx3027 ptn3808 qpf8210 (853) df,pndm2088

7 And they shall answer and say, Our hands have not shed   this

df,nn1818 ptn3808   wcj,du,nn,pnx5869 qpf7200

blood, neither have our eyes seen *it.*

    pimv3722   nn3068   pp,nn,pnx5971 nn3478 pnl834   qpf6299

8 Be merciful, O LORD, unto thy people Israel, whom thou hast redeemed,

^{qmf5414 wcj,ptn408 aj5355 nn1818   nn,pnx5971   nn3478   pp,cs,nn7130   df,nn1818}
and lay   not innocent blood unto thy people of Israel's charge. And the blood

^{wcj,ntpf3722   pp,pnx}
shall be forgiven them.

^{wcj,pnp859   pimf1197   df,aj5355   df,nn1818   pr4480/nn,pnx7130   cj3588}
9 So shalt thou put away the *guilt of* innocent blood from among you, when

^{qmf6213   df,aj3477   pp,du,cs,nn5869   nn3068}
thou shalt do *that which is* right in the   sight of the LORD.

Laws Pertaining to the Family

^{cj3588   qmf3318   dfp,nn4421   pr5921   pl,qpta,pnx341   nn3068}
10 When thou goest forth to war against thine enemies, and the LORD thy

^{pl,nn,pnx430   wcs,qpf,pnx5414   pp,nn,pnx3027   wcs,qpf7617   nn,pnx7628}
God hath delivered them into thine hands, and thou hast taken them captive,

^{wcs,qpf7200   dfp,nn7633   cs,aj3033/nn8389   cs,nn802   wcs,qpf2836}
11 And seest among the captives a beautiful woman, and hast*a*desire

^{pp,pnx   wcs,qpf3947   pp,pnx   pp,nn802}
unto her, that thou wouldest have her to thy wife;

^{wcs,hipf,pnx935   (pr413) cs,nn8432   nn,pnx1004   wcs,pipf1548}
12 Then thou shalt bring   her   home to thine house; and she shall shave

^{(853)   nn,pnx7218   wcs,qpf6213 (853)   pl,nn,pnx6856}
her head, and pare   her nails;

^{wcs,hipf5493 (853)   cs,nn8071   nn,pnx7628   pr4480/pr,pnx5921}
13 And she shall   put   the raiment of her captivity from off her, and

^{wcs,qpf3427   pp,nn,pnx1004   wcs,qpf1058 (853)   nn,pnx1   wcj(853)   nn,pnx517   pl,nn3117}
shall remain in thine house, and bewail   her father and   her mother a full

^{cs,nn3391   wcj,pr310 ad3651   qmf935 pr,pnx413   wcs,qpf,pnx1167}
month: and after that thou shalt go in unto her, and be*her*husband, and she shall

^{wcs,qpf1961 pp,pnx pp,nn802}
be thy wife.

^{wcs,qpf1961 cj518   qpf2654/ptn3808   pp,pnx}
14 And it shall be,   if thou have*no*delight in her, then thou shalt let her

^{wcj,pipf,pnx7971   pp,nn,pnx5315   ptn3808 wcj,qna4376/qmf,pnx4376   dfp,nn3701}
go   whither she   will; but thou shalt not sell*her*at*all for money, thou

^{ptn3808   htmf6014   pp,pnx   pr8478/pnl834   pipf,pnx6031}
shalt not make merchandise of her, because thou hast humbled her.

^{cj3588   pp,nn376 qmf1961 du,cs,nu8147 pl,nn802 df,nu259 qptp157   wcj,df,nu259 qptp8130}
15 If a man have two wives, one beloved, and another hated, and they

^{wcj,qpf3205 pp,pnx   pl,nn1121   df,qptp157   wcj,df,qptp8130   df,nn1060}
have born him children, *both* the beloved and the hated; and *if* the firstborn

^{df,nn1121 wcs,qpf1961   dfp,aj8146}
son be hers that was hated:

^{wcs,qpf1961   pp,cs,nn3117   (853)   pl,nn,pnx1121   hinc,pnx5157 (853)}
16 Then it shall be,   when he maketh   his   sons   to inherit   *that*

^{pnl834   pp,pnx qmf1961   qmf3201 ptn3808 pp,pinc1069 (853)   cs,nn1121   df,qptp157 pp,pinc1069}
which he hath, *that* he may not make   the son of the beloved firstborn

^{pr5921/pl,cs,nn6440   cs,nn1121   df,qptp8130   df,nn1060}
before   the son of the hated, *which is indeed* the firstborn:

^{cj3588   himf5234   cs,nn1121   df,qptp8130 (853)   df,nn1060}
17 But he shall acknowledge the son of the hated   *for* the firstborn, by

pp,qnc**5414** pp,pnx   du,nu8147 cs,nn**6310**   pp,nn3605 pnl834 pp,pnx nimf4672 cj3588 pnp1931   cs,nn**7225**

giving him a double portion of all that he hath: for he *is* the beginning of

nn,pnx202   cs,nn**4941**   df,nn1062   pp,pnx

his strength; the right of the firstborn *is* his.

cj3588   pp,nn**376** qmf**1961**   qpta**5637**   wcj,qpta**4784**   nn1121   pp,pnx369 qpta**8085**

18 If a man have a stubborn and rebellious son, which will not obey the

pp,cs,nn6963   nn,pnx1   wcj,pp,cs,nn6963   nn,pnx517

voice of his father, or the voice of his mother, and *that*, when they have

wcs,qmf**3256** pnx(853)   wcj,ptn3808   qmf8085   pr,pnx413

chastened   him, will not hearken unto them:

nn,pnx1   wcj,nn,pnx517 wcs,qpf8610   pp,pnx   wcs,hipf3318/pnx(853)

19 Then shall his father and his mother lay hold on him, and bring*him*out

pr413   cs,aj**2205**   nn,pnx5892   wcj,pr413   cs,nn8179   nn,pnx4725

unto the elders of his city, and unto the gate of his place;

wcs,qpf559   pr413   cs,aj**2205**   nn,pnx5892 pndm2088   nn,pnx1121

20 And they shall say unto the elders of his city, This our son *is*

qpta**5637**   wcj,qpta**4784**   ptn,pnx369 qpta**8085**   pp,nn,pnx6963   qpta2151

stubborn and rebellious, he will not obey our voice; *he is* a glutton, and a

wcj,qpta5433

drunkard.

cs,nn3605   pl,cs,nn**376**   nn,pnx5892   wcs,qpf7275   dfp,pl,nn68

21 And all the men of his city shall stone him with stones, that he

wcs,qpf**4191**   wcs,pipf1197/df,nn7451   pr4480/nn,pnx7130   wcj,cs,nn3605 nn3478   qmf8085

die: so shalt thou put*evil*away from among you; and all Israel shall hear,

wcj,qmf**3372**

and fear.

Various Laws

wcj,cj3588   pp,nn**376**   qmf**1961**   cs,nn**2399** cs,nn**4941**   nn4194

22 And if a man have committed a sin worthy of death, and he be to be

wcs,hopf**4191**   wcs,qpf8518 pnx(853)   pr5921   nn6086

put*to*death, and thou hang   him on a tree:

nn,pnx**5038**   ptn3808   qmf3885   pr5921   df,nn6086 cj3588

23 His body shall not remain*all*night upon the tree, but thou shalt

qna6912/qmf,pnx6912   df,pndm1931 dfp,nn3117 cj3588   qptp8518   cs,nn7045   pl,nn430

in*any*wise*bury him that day; (for he that is hanged *is* accursed of God;)

(853)   nn,pnx127   wcj,ptn3808 pimf2930   pnl834   nn3068   pl,nn,pnx430 qpta5414 pp,pnx

that thy land be not defiled, which the LORD thy God giveth thee *for* an

nn5159

inheritance.

ptn3808   qmf7200   (853)   nn,pnx251   cs,nn7794 cj176   (853)   nn,pnx7716

22 Thou shalt not see thy brother's ox or his sheep

pl,nipt5080   wcs,htpf5956   pr,pnx4480

go astray, and hide thyself from them: thou shalt

hina7725/himf,pnx7725   pp,nn,pnx251

in*any*case*bring*them*again unto thy brother.

wcj,cj518   nn,pnx251   ptn3808 aj7138 pr,pnx413   qpf,pnx3045   wcj,ptn3808

2 And if thy brother *be* not nigh unto thee, or if thou know him not,

wcj,qpf,pnx622   pr413/cs,nn8432   nn,pnx1004   wcj,qpf1961 pr,pnx5973

then thou shalt bring it unto thine own house, and it shall be with thee

pr5704   nn,pnx251   qnc1875   pnx(853)   wcj,hipf,pnx7725   pp,pnx

until thy brother seek after   it, and thou shalt restore it to him again.

wcj,ad**3651**   qmf**6213**   pp,nn,pnx2543   wcj,ad**3651**   qmf**6213**

3 In like manner shalt thou do with his ass; and so shalt thou do

pp,nn,pnx8071   pp,cs,nn3605   cs,nn9   nn,pnx251   pnl834   (pr,pnx4480)

with his raiment; and with all lost thing of thy brother's, which he hath

qmf6   wcs,qpf,pnx4672   qmf**6213**   wcj,ad**3651**   qmf3201   ptn**3808**   pp,htnc5956

lost, and thou hast found, shalt thou do likewise: thou mayest not hide thyself.

ptn**3808**   qmf**7200**   (853)   nn,pnx251   cs,nn2543   cj176   nn,pnx7794   pl,qpta**5307**

4 Thou shalt not see thy brother's ass or his ox fall down

dfp,nn**1870**   wcs,htpf5956   pr,pnx4480

by the way, and hide thyself from them: thou shalt

hina6965/himf**6965**/pr,pnx5973

surely*help*him*to*lift*_them_*up*again.

(pr5921)   nn**802**   ptn**3808**   qmf**1961**   cs,nn3627   nn**1397**   wcj,ptn**3808**

5 The woman shall not wear that*which*pertaineth unto a man, neither

nn**1397**   qmf3847   nn**802**   cs,nn8071   cj3588   cs,nn3605   cs,qpta**6213**   pndm428   cs,nn**8441**

shall a man put on a woman's garment: for all that do so _are_ abomination

nn**3068**   pl,nn,pnx**430**

unto the LORD thy God.

cj3588   nn6833   cs,nn7064   nimf7122   pp,pl,nn,pnx**6440**   dfp,nn**1870**   pp,cs,nn3605   nn6086

6 If a bird's nest chance*to*be before thee in the way in any tree,

cj176   pr5921   df,nn**776**   pl,nn667   cj176   pl,nn1000   wcj,df,nn**517**   qpta7257

or on the ground, _whether they be_ young ones, or eggs, and the dam sitting

pr5921   df,pl,nn667   cj176   pr5921   df,pl,nn1000   ptn**3808**   qmf3947   df,nn**517**   pr5921   df,pl,nn**1121**

upon the young, or upon the eggs, thou shalt not take the dam with the young:

pina7971   (853)   df,nn**517**   pimf7971   qmf3947   wcj(853)   df,pl,nn**1121**

7 _But_ thou shalt in*any*wise let the dam go, and take the young

pp,pnx   pp,cj4616   qmf**3190**   pp,pnx   wcs,hipf**748**   pl,nn3117

to thee; that it may be well with thee, and _that_ thou mayest prolong _thy_ days.

cj3588   qmf1129   aj2319   nn**1004**   wcs,qpf**6213**   nn4624

8 When thou buildest a new house, then thou shalt make a battlement for thy

pp,nn,pnx1406   qmf**7760**   wcj,ptn**3808**   pl,nn**1818**   pp,nn,pnx**1004**   cj3588   df,qpta**5307**   qmf**5307**   pr,pnx4480

roof, that thou bring not blood upon thine house, if any man fall from

thence.

ptn**3808**   qmf2232   nn,pnx3754   du,nn3610   cj6435   df,nn4395

9 Thou shalt not sow thy vineyard with divers seeds: lest the fruit of thy

df,nn**2233**   pnl834   qmf2232   wcj,cs,nn8393   df,nn3754   qmf**6942**

seed which thou hast sown, and the fruit of thy vineyard, be defiled.

ptn**3808**   qmf2790   pp,nn7794   wcj,pp,nn2543   ad3162

10 Thou shalt not plow with an ox and an ass together.

ptn**3808**   qmf3847   nn8162   nn6785   wcj,pl,nn6593

11 Thou shalt not wear a garment*of*divers*sorts, _as_ of woolen and linen

ad3162

together.

qmf**6213**   pp,pnx   pl,nn1434   pr5921   cs,nu702   pl,cs,nn3671   nn,pnx3682

12 Thou shalt make thee fringes upon the four quarters of thy vesture,

pnl834/pp,pnx   pimf**3680**

wherewith thou coverest _thyself._

Sexual Matters

cj3588   nn**376**   qmf3947   nn**802**   wcs,qpf935   pr,pnx413   wcs,qpf,pnx**8130**

13 If any man take a wife, and go in unto her, and hate her,

wcs,qpf**7760**   pl,cs,nn5949   pl,nn**1697**   pp,pnx   wcs,hipf3318   aj**7451**   nn8034

14 And give occasions of speech against her, and bring up an evil name

pr,pnx5921   wcs,qpf**559**   qpf3947 (853) df,pndm2063   df,nn**802**   wcs,qmf7126 pr,pnx413

upon her, and say, I took   this   woman, and when I came   to   her, I

qpf4672 pp,pnx wcj,ptn**3808**   pl,nn**1331**

found her   not   a maid:

cs,nn**1**   df,nn5291   wcj,nn,pnx**517** wcj,qmf3947   wcs,hipf3318

15 Then shall the father of the damsel, and her mother,   take and bring forth

(853)   df,nn5291   pl,cs,nn**1331**   pr413   cs,aj**2205**   df,nn5892   df,nn,lh8179

the tokens of the damsel's virginity unto the elders of the city in the gate:

df,nn5291   cs,nn**1**   wcj,qpf**559** pr413   df,aj**2205**   qpf5414 (853)   nn,pnx1323

16 And the damsel's father shall say unto the elders, I gave   my daughter

df,pndm2088 dfp,nn**376**   pp,nn**802**   wcs,qmf,pnx**8130**

unto this   man to wife, and he hateth   her;

wcj,ptdm2009 pnp1931   qpf**7760**   pl,cs,nn5949   pl,nn**1697**   pp,qnc**559**

17 And, lo, he   hath given occasions of speech *against her*, saying, I

qpf4672 ptn**3808**   pp,nn,pnx1323   pl,nn**1331**   wcj,pndm428   nn,pnx1323

found not thy daughter a maid; and yet these *are the tokens of* my daughter's

pl,cs,nn**1331**   wcj,qpf6566   df,nn8071 pp,pl,cs,nn**6440**   cs,aj**2205**   df,nn5892

virginity. And they shall spread the cloth before the elders of the city.

cs,aj**2205**   df,pndm1931 df,nn5892   wcj,qpf3947 (853)   df,nn**376**   wcj,pipf3256 pnx(853)

18 And the elders of that   city shall take   that man and chastise

him;

wcj,qpf**6064**   pnx(853)   nu3967   nn3701   wcj,qpf**5414**

19 And they shall amerce   him in a hundred *shekels* of silver, and give

pp,cs,nn**1**   df,nn5291   cj3588   hipf3318   aj**7451** nn8034 pr5921

them unto the father of the damsel, because he hath brought up an evil name upon a

cs,nn**1330**   nn3478   qmf**1961** wcj,pp,pnx pp,nn**802**   qmf3201 ptn**3808**   pp,pinc,pnx7971   cs,nn3605

virgin of Israel: and she shall be   his   wife; he may not put*her*away   all   his

pl,nn,pnx**3117**

days.

wcj,cj518 df,pndm2088 df,nn**1697** qpf**1961**   nn571   pl,nn**1331**   ptn**3808** nipf4672

20 But if   this thing be true, *and the tokens of* virginity be not found

dfp,nn5291

for the damsel:

wcj,hipf3318   (853)   df,nn5291 pr413   cs,nn6607   nn,pnx1   cs,nn**1004**

21 Then they shall bring out   the damsel to the door of her father's house,

pl,cs,nn**376**   nn,pnx5892   wcj,qpf,pnx5619   dfp,pl,nn68   wcj,qpf**4191** cj3588

and the men of her city shall   stone   her with stones that she die: because

qpf**6213**   nn5039   pp,nn3478   pp,qnc2181   nn,pnx1   cs,nn**1004**

she hath wrought folly in Israel, to play*the*whore in her father's house: so shalt

wcj,pipf1197/df,nn**7451**   pr4480/nn,pnx7130

thou put*evil*away from among you.

cj3588   nn**376**   nimf4672 qpta7901 pr5973   nn**802** cs,qptp**1166**   nn**1167**

22 If a man be found lying with a woman married to a husband, then they

ad1571/du,nu,pnx8147   wcs,qpf**4191**   df,nn**376**   df,qpta7901 pr5973   df,nn**802**

shall   both   of them die, *both* the man that lay with the woman, and the

wcj,df,nn**802**   wcs,pipf1197   df,aj**7451**   pr4480/nn3478

woman: so shalt thou put away evil from Israel.

cj3588   nn5291   nn**1330** qmf**1961** pupt781   pp,nn**376**   nn**376**

23 If a damsel *that is* a virgin be   betrothed unto a husband, and a man

wcs,qpf,pnx4672   dfp,nn5892   wcs,qpf7901 pr,pnx5973

find   her in the city, and lie   with her;

wcs,hipf3318/(853)/du,nu,pnx8147   pr413   cs,nn8179   df,pndm1931 df,nn5892

24 Then ye shall bring*them*both*out unto the gate of   that   city, and ye

wcs,qpf5619 pnx(853)   dfp,pl,nn68   wcj,qpf4191 (853)   df,pl,nn5291 pr5921/cs,nn1697/pnl834

shall stone   them with stones that they die;   the damsel,   because

qpf6817 ptn3808   dfp,nn5892   wcj(853)   df,nn376 pr5921/cs,nn1697/pnl834   pipf6031

she cried not, *being* in the city; and   the man,   because   he hath humbled

(853)   nn,pnx7453   cs,nn802   wcj,pipf1197 df,aj7451   pr4480/nn,pnx7130

his neighbor's wife: so thou shalt put away evil from among you.

wcj,cj518   df,nn376 qmf4672 (853)   df,nn5291   dfp,nn7704   df,nn376

25 But if a man find   a betrothed damsel in the field, and the man

wcs,hipf2388 pp,pnx   wcs,qpf7901 pr,pnx5973   df,nn376 pp,nn,pnx905 pnl834 qpf7901 pr,pnx5973

force her, and lie with her: then the man only that lay with her shall

wcs,qpf4191

die:

wcj,dfp,nn5291   qmf6213 ptn3808/nn1697   dfp,nn5291 ptn369

26 But unto the damsel thou shalt do nothing; *there is* in the damsel no

cs,nn2399   nn4194 cj3588 pp,pnl834   nn376 qmf6965 pr5921   nn,pnx7453

sin *worthy* of death: for as when a man riseth against his neighbor, and

wcj,qpf,pnx7523/nn5315   ad3651   df,pndm2088 df,nn1697

slayeth him, even so *is* this matter:

cj3588   qpf,pnx4672   dfp,nn7704   df,pupt781 df,nn5291 qpf6817

27 For he found her in the field, *and* the betrothed damsel cried, and *there*

wcj,ptn369   hipt3467 pp,pnx

was none to save her.

cj3588   nn376 qmf4672   nn5291   nn1330 pnl834 ptn3808 pupt781

28 If a man find a damsel *that is* a virgin, which is not betrothed, and

wcj,qpf,pnx8610   wcj,qpf7901 pr,pnx5973   wcj,nipf4672

lay hold on her, and lie with her, and they be found;

df,nn376   df,qpta7901 pr,pnx5973   wcj,qpf5414   df,nn5291 pp,cs,nn1

29 Then the man that lay with her shall give unto the damsel's father

pl,nu2572   nn3701   qmf1961 wcj,pp,pnx pp,nn802 pr8478/pnl834   pipf,pnx6031

fifty *shekels* of silver, and she shall be his wife; because he hath humbled her,

qmf3201 ptn3808   pinc,pnx7971 cs,nn3605   pl,nn,pnx3117

he may not put*her*away all his days.

nn376   ptn3808 qmf3947 (853)   nn,pnx1 cs,nn802 wcj,ptn3808 pimf1540   nn,pnx1

30 A man shall not take   his father's wife, nor discover his father's

cs,nn3671

skirt.

Persons Excluded From the Congregation

cs,qptp6481/nn1795   nn8212 wcj,cs,qptp3772

23 He that is wounded*in*the*stones, or hath his privy member cut off,

ptn3808 qmf935   pp,cs,nn6951   nn3068

shall not enter into the congregation of the LORD.

nn4464 ptn3808 qmf935   pp,cs,nn6951   nn3068 ad1571   nuor6224

2 A bastard shall not enter into the congregation of the LORD; even to his tenth

nn1755   pp,pnx ptn3808 qmf935   pp,cs,nn6951   nn3068

generation shall he not enter into the congregation of the LORD.

nn5984   wcj,nn4125 ptn3808 qmf935   pp,cs,nn6951   nn3068

3 An Ammonite or Moabite shall not enter into the congregation of the LORD;

ad1571   nuor6224 nn1755   pp,pnx ptn3808 qmf935   pp,cs,nn6951   nn3068

even to their tenth generation shall they not enter into the congregation of the LORD

pr5704/nn5769

forever:

<small>pr5921/cs,nn1697 pnl834 pipf6923 pnx(853)   ptn3808   dfp,nn3899   wcj,dfp,pl,nn4325</small>

4 Because they met   you not with bread and with   water   in the

<small>dfp,nn1870   pp,qnc3318   pr4480/nn4714   wcj,pnl834   qpf7936 pr,pnx5921   (853)</small>

way, when ye came forth out*of*Egypt; and because they hired against thee

<small>nn1109   cs,nn1121   nn1160   pr4480/nn6604   nn763   pp,pinc,pnx7043</small>

Balaam the son of Beor of Pethor of Mesopotamia, to curse thee.

<small>nn3068   pl,nn,pnx430 qpf14 wcj,ptn3808 pp,qnc8085   pr413   nn1109</small>

5 Nevertheless the LORD thy God would not hearken unto Balaam; but the

<small>nn3068   pl,nn,pnx430 wcs,qmf2015 (853)   df,nn7045   pp,nn1293   pp,pnx   cj3588   nn3068</small>

LORD thy God turned   the curse into a blessing unto thee, because the LORD

<small>pl,nn,pnx430 qpf,pnx157</small>

thy God loved thee.

<small>ptn3808 qmf1875   nn,pnx7965   wcj,nn,pnx2896 cs,nn3605   pl,nn,pnx3117</small>

6 Thou shalt not seek their peace nor their prosperity all thy days

<small>pp,nn5769</small>

forever.

<small>ptn3808 pimf8581   nn130   cj3588 pnp1931   nn,pnx251   ptn3808</small>

7 Thou shalt not abhor an Edomite; for he is thy brother: thou shalt not

<small>pimf8581   nn4713   cj3588   qpf1961   nn1616   pp,nn,pnx776</small>

abhor an Egyptian; because thou wast a stranger in his land.

<small>pl,nn1121 pnl834 nimf3205 pp,pnx   qmf935 pp,pnx   pp,cs,nn6951</small>

8 The children that are begotten of them shall enter into the congregation of the

<small>nn3068   nuor7992   nn1755</small>

LORD in their third generation.

Purity During War

<small>cj3588   nn4264   qmf3318   pr5921   pl,qpta,pnx341   wcs,nipf8104   pr4480/cs,nn3605</small>

9 When the host goeth forth against thine enemies, then keep thee from every

<small>aj7451   nn1697</small>

wicked thing.

<small>cj3588   qmf1961   pp,pnx   nn376   pnl834 qmf1961   ptn3808   aj2889</small>

10 If   there be   among you   any man,   that   is   not   clean

<small>pr4480/cs,nn7137   nn3915   wcs,qpf3318</small>

by*reason*of*uncleanness*that*chanceth him by night, then shall he go abroad

<small>pr413/pr4480/nn2351   dfp,nn4264   ptn3808 qmf935 pr413/cs,nn8432   df,nn4264</small>

out of   the camp, he shall not come   within the camp:

<small>wcs,qpf1961   nn6153   pp,qnc6437   qmf7364</small>

11 But it shall   be,   when evening cometh on, he shall wash himself with

<small>dfp,pl,nn4325   df,nn8121 wcj,pp,qnc935   qmf935 pr413/cs,nn8432   df,nn4264</small>

water: and when the sun is down, he shall come   into   the camp again.

<small>pp,pnx   qmf1961 wcj,nn3027   pr4480/nn2351   dfp,nn4264 ad,lh8033   wcs,qpf3318</small>

12 Thou shalt have a place also without the camp, whither thou shalt go forth

<small>nn2351</small>

abroad:

<small>pp,pnx   qmf1961 wcj,nn3489 pr5921   nn,pnx240   wcs,qpf1961</small>

13 And thou shalt have a paddle upon thy weapon; and it shall   be,   when

<small>pp,qnc,pnx3427   nn2351   wcs,qpf2658   pp,pnx   wcs,qpf7725</small>

thou wilt   ease   thyself abroad, thou shalt   dig   therewith, and shalt turn back

<small>wcs,pipf3680 (853)   nn,pnx6627</small>

and cover   that*which*cometh from thee:

<small>cj3588   nn3068   pl,nn,pnx430 htpt1980   pp,cs,nn7130   nn,pnx4264 pp,hinc,pnx5337</small>

14 For the LORD thy God walketh in the midst of thy camp, to deliver

wcj,pp,qnc**5414**   pl,qpta,pnx341   pp,pl,nn,pnx**6440**   nn,pnx**4264**   wcs,qpf**1961**

thee, and to give up thine enemies   before   thee; therefore shall thy camp   be

aj**6918**   qmf**7200** wcj,ptn**3808**   cs,nn**6172**   nn**1697**   pp,pnx   wcs,qpf**7725**   pr4480/pr,pnx310

holy: that he see   no   unclean thing in thee, and turn away   from   thee.

Various Laws

ptn**3808** himf**5462**   pr413   pl,nn,pnx**113**   nn**5650**   pnl834   nimf**5337**   pr4480/pr**5973**

15 Thou shalt not deliver unto his master the servant which is escaped   from

pl,nn,pnx**113** pr,pnx413

his master unto thee:

qmf**3427** pr,pnx5973   pp,nn,pnx**7130**   dfp,nn4725   pnl834

16 He shall dwell with   thee, *even* among you, in that place   which he shall

qmf**977**   pp,cs,nu259   pl,nn,pnx8179   dfp,aj**2896**/pp,pnx   ptn**3808** himf,pnx**3238**

choose in   one   of thy gates, where it liketh*him*best: thou shalt not oppress

him.

qmf**1961**   ptn**3808**   nn**6948**   pr4480/pl,cs,nn1323   nn3478   wcj,ptn**3808**   (qmf**1961**)

17 There shall   be   no   whore of*the*daughters of Israel,   nor   a

nn**6945**   pr4480/pl,cs,nn**1121**   nn3478

sodomite of*the*sons of Israel.

ptn**3808** himf**935**   cs,nn868   qpta**2181**   wcj,cs,nn**4242**   nn3611

◎꜔ 18 Thou shalt not bring the hire of a whore, or the   price   of a dog, into the

cs,nn**1004**   nn**3068**   pl,nn,pnx**430**   pp,cs,nn3605   nn**5088**   cj3588   ad1571   du,nu,pnx8147

house of the LORD thy God   for   any   vow: for even   both   these *are*

cs,nn**8441**   nn**3068**   pl,nn,pnx**430**

abomination unto the LORD thy God.

ptn**3808**   himf**5391**   pp,nn,pnx**251** cs,nn**5392**   nn3701   cs,nn**5392**

◎꜔ 19 Thou shalt not lend*upon*usury to thy brother; usury of money, usury of

nn400   cs,nn**5392**   cs,nn3605   nn**1697** pnl834   qmf**5391**

victuals, usury of any thing that is lent*upon*usury:

dfp,aj**5237**   himf**5391**   wcj,pp,nn,pnx**251**

20 Unto a stranger thou mayest lend*upon*usury; but unto thy   brother   thou

ptn**3808**   himf**5391**   pp,cj4616   nn**3068**   pl,nn,pnx**430**   pimf,pnx**1288**   pp,cs,nn3605

shalt not lend*upon*usury: that the LORD thy God may bless thee in   all

cs,nn**4916**   nn,pnx**3027**   pr5921   df,nn**776** pnl834/ad,lh8033 pnp859 qpta935   pp,qnc,pnx**3423**

that thou settest thine hand to in the land whither thou goest to possess it.

cj3588   qmf**5087**   nn**5088**   pp,nn**3068**   pl,nn,pnx**430**   ptn**3808** pimf309

21 When thou shalt vow a vow unto the LORD thy God, thou shalt not slack

pp,pinc,pnx**7999**   cj3588   nn**3068**   pl,nn,pnx**430**   qna1875/qmf,pnx1875   pr4480/pr,pnx5973

to pay   it: for the LORD thy God will surely require it   of   thee; and it

wcs,qpf**1961** nn**2399**   pp,pnx

would be   sin in thee.

wcj,cj3588   qmf**2308**   pp,qnc**5087**   qmf**1961** ptn**3808** nn**2399**   pp,pnx

22 But if   thou shalt forbear to vow, it shall be   no   sin in thee.

cs,nn**4161**   du,nn,pnx**8193**   qmf**8104**   wcs,qpf**6213**

23 That which is gone out of thy   lips   thou shalt keep and perform; *even* a

nn**5071**   pp,pnl834   qpf**5087**   pp,nn**3068**   pl,nn,pnx**430** pnl834

freewill offering, according   as   thou hast vowed unto the LORD thy God, which

pipf**1696**   pp,nn,pnx**6310**

thou hast promised with thy mouth.

◎꜔ **23:18** The word "dog" here means a male prostitute (see v. 17).

◎꜔ **23:19, 20** See the note on Leviticus 19:33, 34.

24 When thou comest into thy neighbor's vineyard, then thou mayest eat grapes thy fill at thine own pleasure; but thou shalt not put *any* in thy vessel.

25 When thou comest into the standing corn of thy neighbor, then thou mayest pluck the ears with thine hand; but thou shalt not move a sickle unto thy neighbor's standing corn.

24 When a man hath taken a wife, and married her, and it*come*to*pass that she find no favor in his eyes, because he hath found some uncleanness in her: then let him write her a bill of divorcement, and give *it* in her hand, and send her out*of*his*house.

2 And when she is departed out*of*his*house, she may go and be another man's *wife*.

3 And *if* the latter husband hate her, and write her a bill of divorcement, and giveth *it* in her hand, and sendeth her out*of*his*house; or if the latter husband die, which took her *to be* his wife;

4 Her former husband, which sent*her*away, may not take her again to be his wife, after that she is defiled; for that *is* abomination before the LORD: and thou shalt not cause the land to sin, which the LORD thy God giveth thee *for* an inheritance.

5 When a man hath taken a new wife, he shall not go out to war, neither shall he be charged with any business: *but* he shall be free at home one year, and shall cheer up his wife which he hath taken.

6 No man shall take the nether or the upper millstone to pledge: for he taketh *a man's* life to pledge.

7 If a man be found stealing any of*his*brethren of*the*children of Israel, and maketh merchandise of him, or selleth him; then that thief shall die; and thou shalt put*evil*away from among you.

nimv**8104**   pp,cs,nn**5061**   df,nn**6883**   pp,qnc**8104**   ad3966   wcj,pp,qnc**6213**

8 Take heed in the plague of leprosy, that thou observe diligently, and   do

pp,nn3605   pnl834   df,pl,nn**3548**   df,pl,nn**3881**   himf**3384** pnx(853)   pp,pnl834

according to   all   that the priests the Levites shall teach   you: as   I

pipf,pnx**6680**   qmf**8104**   pp,qnc**6213**

commanded them, *so* ye shall observe to do.

qna**2142**   (853) pnl834   nn**3068**   pl,nn,pnx**430** qpf**6213**   pp,nn4813   dfp,nn**1870**

9 Remember   what the LORD thy God   did unto Miriam by the way, after

pp,qnc,pnx3318   pr4480/nn4714

that ye were come forth out*of*Egypt.

cj3588   himf**5383**   pp,nn,pnx**7453** pnid3972 cs,nn**4859**   ptn**3808** qmf935 pr413

10 When thou dost lend thy brother   any thing, thou shalt not   go into his

nn,pnx**1004**   pp,qnc**5670**   nn,pnx**5667**

house to fetch his pledge.

qmf**5975**   dfp,nn**2351**   wcj,df,nn**376**   pnl834/pp,pnx pnp859   qpta**5383**

11 Thou shalt stand abroad, and the   man   to whom thou dost lend shall

himf**3318**   (853)   df,nn**5667** df,nn,lh**2351** pr,pnx413

bring out   the pledge abroad unto thee.

wcj,cj518   nn**376** (pnp1931) aj**6041**   ptn**3808** qmf**7901**   pp,nn,pnx**5667**

12 And   if   the man   *be* poor, thou shalt not sleep with his pledge:

hina**7725**/himf**7725**   pp,pnx (853)   df,nn**5667**   df,nn**8121**

13 In*any*case*thou*shalt*deliver him   the pledge again when the sun

pp,qnc935   wcs,qpf**7901**   pp,nn,pnx**8008**   wcs,pipf,pnx**1288**

goeth down, that he may sleep in his own raiment, and   bless   thee: and it shall

qmf**1961**   nn**6666**   wcj,pp,pnx   pp,pl,cs,nn**6440**   nn**3068**   pl,nn,pnx**430**

be righteousness unto thee before the LORD thy God.

ptn**3808**   qmf**6231**   aj**7916**   aj**6041**   wcj,aj34

14 Thou shalt not oppress a hired servant *that is* poor and needy, *whether he*

pr4480/pl,nn,pnx**251**   cj176   pr4480/nn,pnx**1616**   pnl834   pp,nn,pnx**776**   pp,pl,nn,pnx**8179**

be of*thy*brethren, or of*thy*strangers that *are* in thy   land   within thy   gates:

pp,nn,pnx**3117**   qmf**5414**   nn,pnx**7939** wcj,ptn**3808**   df,nn**8121**

15 At his   day   thou shalt give *him* his hire, neither shall the sun

qmf935   pr,pnx**5921**   cj3588 pnp1931   aj**6041**   (pnp1931) qpta**5375** (853)   nn,pnx**5315** wcj,pr,pnx413

go down upon it; for   he *is* poor, and   setteth   his heart   upon   it:

wcj,ptn**3808**   qmf**7121** pr,pnx**5921**   pr413   nn**3068**   wcs,qpf**1961** nn**2399**   pp,pnx

lest he cry against thee unto the LORD, and it   be   sin unto thee.

pl,nn**1**   ptn**3808**   homf**4191**   pr5921   pl,nn**1121**   ptn**3808**

16 The fathers shall not be put*to*death for the children, neither shall the

wcj,pl,nn**1121**   homf**4191**   pr5921   pl,nn**1**   nn**376**   homf**4191**

children be put*to*death for the fathers: every man shall be put*to*death for his

pp,nn,pnx**2399**

own sin.

ptn**3808**   himf**5186**   cs,nn**4941**   nn**1616**   nn**3490**

17 Thou shalt not pervert the judgment of the stranger, *nor* of the fatherless;

wcj,ptn**3808** qmf**2254**   nn**490**   cs,nn**899**   qmf**2254**

nor   take a widow's raiment to pledge:

wcs,qpf**2142**   cj3588   qpf**1961**   nn**5650**   pp,nn4714   nn**3068**

18 But thou shalt remember that thou wast a bondman in Egypt, and the LORD

pl,nn,pnx**430** wcs,qmf,pnx**6299**   pr4480/ad8033 pr5921/ad**3651** pnp595 pipt,pnx**6680**   pp,qnc**6213** (853) df,pndm2088

thy God redeemed thee thence: therefore I   command thee to   do   this

df,nn**1697**

thing.

24:16 See the note on Ezekiel 18:1–32.

cj3588 qmf7114 nn,pnx7105 pp,nn,pnx7704 wcs,qpf7911 nn6016

19 When thou cuttest down thine harvest in thy   field,   and hast forgot a sheaf

dfp,nn7704 ptn3808 qmf7725 pp,qnc,pnx3947 qmf1961 dfp,nn1616

in the field, thou shalt not go again to   fetch   it: it shall be   for the stranger,

dfp,nn3490 wcj,dfp,nn490 pp,cj4616 nn3068 pl,nn,pnx430 pimf,pnx1288

for the fatherless, and for the widow: that the LORD thy God   may   bless thee

pp,cs,nn3605 cs,nn4639 du,nn,pnx3027

in   all   the work of thine hands.

cj3588 qmf2251 nn,pnx2132 ptn3808 pimf6286

20 When thou beatest thine olive tree, thou shalt not go*over*the*boughs

pr,pnx310 qmf1961 dfp,nn1616 dfp,nn3490 wcj,dfp,nn490

again: it shall be for the stranger, for the fatherless, and for the widow.

cj3588 qmf1219 nn,pnx3754 ptn3808 pimf*5953

21 When thou gatherest*the*grapes of thy vineyard, thou shalt not glean *it*

pr,pnx310 qmf1961 dfp,nn1616 dfp,nn3490 wcj,dfp,nn490

afterward: it shall be for the stranger, for the fatherless, and for the widow.

wcs,qpf2142 cj3588 qpf1961 nn5650 pp,cs,nn776 nn4714

22 And thou shalt remember that thou wast a bondman in the   land of Egypt:

pr5921/ad3651 pnp595 pipt,pnx6680 pp,qnc6213 (853) df,pndm2088 df,nn1697

therefore   I   command thee to   do   this   thing.

25

cj3588 qmf1961 nn7379 pr996 pl,nn376 wcs,nipf5066 pr413

If there be   a controversy between men, and they come unto

df,nn4941   wcs,qpf,pnx8199   wcs,hipf6663

judgment, that *the judges* may   judge   them; then they shall justify

(853) df,aj6662 wcs,hipf7561 (853) df,aj7563

the righteous, and condemn   the wicked.

wcs,qpf1961 cj518 df,aj7563   cs,nn1121/hinc5221

2 And it shall   be,   if the wicked man *be* worthy*to*be*beaten, that the

df,qpta8199   wcs,hipf,pnx5307 wcs,hipf,pnx5221 pp,pl,nn,pnx6440

judge shall cause him to lie down, and to be beaten before his   face,

pp,cs,nn1767 nn,pnx7564 pp,nn4557

according to his fault, by a certain number.

pl,nu705 himf,pnx5221 ptn3808 himf3254 cj6435 himf3254

3 Forty stripes*he*may*give him, *and* not exceed: lest, *if* he should exceed,

pp,hinc,pnx5221 pr5921 pndm428 aj7227 nn4347 nn,pnx251 wcs,nipf7034

and beat   him above these with many stripes, then thy brother should seem vile

pp,du,nn,pnx5869

unto   thee.

ptn3808 qmf2629 nn7794 pp,qnc,pnx1758

4 Thou shalt not muzzle the ox when he treadeth out *the corn.*

cj3588 pl,nn251 qmf3427 ad3162 nu259 pr,pnx4480 wcs,qpf4191 (pp,pnx) ptn369

⚷ 5 If brethren dwell together, and one of   them   die,   and   have no

wcj,nn1121 cs,nn802 df,qpta4191 ptn3808 qmf1961 df,nn,lh2351 pp,nn376/aj2114

child, the wife of the dead shall not marry without unto a stranger: her

nn,pnx2993 qmf935 pr,pnx5921 wcs,qpf,pnx3947 pp,pnx pp,nn802

husband's brother shall go in unto her, and   take   her to him to wife, and

wcs,pipf,pnx2992

perform*the*duty*of*a*husband's*brother unto her.

wcs,qpf1961 df,nn1060 pnl834 qmf3205 qmf6965 pr5921

6 And it shall   be,   *that* the firstborn which she beareth shall succeed in the

cs,nn8034 nn,pnx251 df,qpta4191 nn,pnx8034 wcj,ptn3808 nimf4229 pr4480/nn3478

name of his brother *which is* dead, that his name be   not put out of Israel.

⚷ **25:5–10**   For an application of these regulations, see the note on Ruth 4:1–8.

wcj,cj518   df,nn376 qmf2654 ptn3808   pp,qnc3947 (853)   nn,pnx2994
7 And   if   the man like not to take   his brother's wife, then let his

nn,pnx2994   wcs,qpf5927   df,nn,lh8179 pr413   df,aj2205   wcs,qpf559
brother's wife   go up   to   the   gate   unto   the   elders,   and   say,   My

nn,pnx2993   pipf3985   pp,hinc6965   pp,nn,pnx251   nn8034   pp,nn3478   qpf14
husband's brother refuseth to raise up unto his brother a name in Israel, he will

ptn3808   pinc,pnx2992
not perform*the*duty*of*my*husband's*brother.

cs,aj2205   nn,pnx5892   wcj,qpf7121 pp,pnx   wcj,pipf1696 pr,pnx413
8 Then the elders of his   city   shall   call   him, and   speak   unto him: and if

wcj,qpf5975   wcj,qpf559 qpf2654 ptn3808   pp,qnc,pnx3947
he stand to it, and say, I like not to   take   her;

nn,pnx2994   wcj,nipf5066 pr,pnx413   pp,du,cs,nn5869   df,aj2205
9 Then shall his brother's wife   come   unto   him in the presence of the elders,

wcj,qpf2502   nn,pnx5275 pr4480/pr5921   nn,pnx7272   wcj,qpf3417   pp,pl,nn,pnx6440
and loose his shoe   from off his   foot,   and   spit   in his   face,   and shall

wcj,qpf6030   wcj,qpf559 ad3602   nimf6213   dfp,nn376 pnl834   ptn3808   qmf1129   (853)
answer and say,   So shall it be done unto that man that will not build up

nn,pnx251   cs,nn1004
his brother's house.

nn,pnx8034   wcs,nipf7121   pp,nn3478   cs,nn1004
10 And his name   shall be   called   in Israel, The house of him that hath his

df,nn5275 cs,qptp2502
shoe loosed.

cj3588   pl,nn376 nimf5327   ad3162   nn376   wcj,nn,pnx251   cs,nn802   df,nu259
11 When men strive together one with another, and the wife of the   one

wcs,qpf7126   pp,hinc5337 (853)   nn,pnx376   pr4480/cs,nn3027   hipt,pnx5221
draweth near for to deliver   her husband out*of*the*hand of him that smiteth

wcs,qpf7971   nn,pnx3027   wcs,hipf2388   pp,pl,nn,pnx4016
him, and putteth forth her hand, and taketh him by the   secrets:

wcs,qpf7112 (853)   nn,pnx3709   nn,pnx5869   ptn3808 qmf2347
12 Then thou shalt cut off   her hand, thine   eye   shall not pity her.

pp,pnx   ptn3808 qmf1961   pp,nn,pnx3599   nn68/wcj,nn68   aj1419   wcj,aj6996
13 Thou shalt not have in thy   bag   divers weights, a great and a small.

pp,pnx   ptn3808 qmf1961   pp,nn,pnx1004   nn374/wcj,nn374   aj1419   wcj,aj6996
14 Thou shalt not have in thine   house   divers measures, a great and a small.

pp,pnx   qmf1961   aj8003   wcj,nn6664   nn68   aj8003   wcj,nn6664   nn374
15 But thou shalt have a perfect and   just   weight, a perfect and   just   measure

pp,pnx qmf1961 pp,cj4616   pl,nn,pnx3117   himf748   pr5921   df,nn127 pnl834   nn3068
shalt thou have: that thy   days   may be lengthened   in   the   land which the LORD

pl,nn,pnx430   qpta5414 pp,pnx
thy God   giveth thee.

cj3588 cs,nn3605   qpta6213   pndm428   cs,nn3605   qpta6213   nn5766
16 For   all   that   do   such things, and   all   that   do   unrighteously, are an

cs,nn8441   nn3068   pl,nn,pnx430
abomination unto the LORD thy   God.

Destroy Amalek

qna2142   (853)   pnl834   nn6002   qpf6213   pp,pnx   dfp,nn1870
17 Remember   what Amalek did   unto thee by the   way,   when ye were

pp,qnc,pnx3318   pr4480/nn4714
come forth out*of*Egypt;

pnl834   qpf,pnx7136   dfp,nn**1870**   wcs,pimf2179   pp,pnx

18 How he met thee by the way, and smote*the*hindmost of thee, *even*

cs,nn3605   df,pl,nipt2826 pr,pnx310   wcj,pnp859   aj5889   wcj,aj3023

all   *that were* feeble behind thee, when thou *wast* faint and weary; and he

qpf3372   wcj,ptn3808 pl,nn430

feared   not God.

                      wcj,qpf1961   nn3068   pl,nn,pnx430   pp,hinc5117/pp,pnx

19 Therefore it shall be,   when the LORD thy   God hath given*thee*rest

pr4480/cs,nn3605   pl,qpta,pnx341   pr4480/nn5439   dfp,nn776   pnl834   nn3068   pl,nn,pnx430

from all thine enemies round about, in the   land which the LORD thy   God

qpta5414   pp,pnx   nn5159   pp,qnc,pnx3423   qmf4229   (853)

giveth thee *for* an inheritance to possess it, *that* thou shalt blot out   the

     cs,nn2143   nn6002   pr4480/pr8478 df,du,nn8064   ptn3808 qmf7911

remembrance of Amalek from under heaven; thou shalt not forget *it*.

Harvest Offerings

               wcs,qpf1961   cj3588   qmf935   pr413   df,nn776   pnl834

26 And it shall be,   when thou *art* come in unto the land which the

              nn3068   pl,nn,pnx430 qpta5414 pp,pnx   nn5159   wcs,qpf,pnx3423

LORD thy   God giveth thee *for* an inheritance, and possessest it, and

wcs,qpf3427   pp,pnx

dwellest therein;

             wcs,qpf3947 pr4480/cs,nn7225   cs,nn3605   cs,nn6529   df,nn127   pnl834

2 That thou shalt take of*the*first of all   the fruit of the earth, which thou

     himf935   pr4480/nn,pnx776 pnl834   nn3068   pl,nn,pnx430 qpta5414 pp,pnx   wcs,qpf7760

shalt bring of*thy*land that the LORD thy   God giveth thee, and shalt put   *it* in

dfp,nn2935   wcs,qpf1980 pr413   df,nn4725 pnl834   nn3068   pl,nn,pnx430   qmf977

a basket, and shalt go   unto the place which the LORD thy   God shall choose to

pp,pinc7931   nn,pnx8034 ad8033

place his name there.

            wcs,qpf935 pr413   df,nn3548 pnl834   qmf1961   dfp,pnp1992 dfp,pl,nn3117

3 And thou shalt go   unto the priest that shall be in those days, and

wcs,qpf559 pr,pnx413   hipf5046   df,nn3117   pp,nn3068   pl,nn,pnx430 cj3588   qpf935   pr413

say   unto him, I profess this day unto the LORD thy   God, that I am come unto

df,nn776   pnl834   nn3068   nipf7650   pp,pl,nn,pnx1   pp,qnc5414 pp,pnx

the country which the LORD swore unto our fathers for to give us.

            df,nn3548   wcs,qpf3947 df,nn2935   pr4480/nn,pnx3027   wcj,hipf,pnx5117

4 And the priest shall take   the basket out*of*thine*hand, and set*it*down

pp,pl,cs,nn6440   cs,nn4196   nn3068   pl,nn,pnx430

before the altar of the LORD thy God.

           wcs,qpf6030   wcs,qpf559 pp,pl,cs,nn6440   nn3068   pl,nn,pnx430   nn761

5 And thou shalt speak and say   before   the LORD thy God, A Syrian

    qpta6   nn,pnx1   wcs,qmf3381   nn,lh4714   wcs,qmf1481   ad8033

ready to perish *was* my father, and he went down into Egypt, and sojourned there

    pp,pl,cs,nn4692/nn4592   wcs,qmf1961 ad8033   pp,nn1471   aj1419   aj6099   wcj,aj7227

with a   few,   and became there a nation, great, mighty, and populous:

             df,nn4713   wcs,himf7489   pnx(853)   wcs,pimf,pnx6031   wcs,qmf5414

6 And the Egyptians evil entreated   us, and afflicted us, and laid

pr,pnx5921   aj7186   nn5656

upon us hard bondage:

           wcs,qmf6817 pr413   nn3068 pl,cs,nn430   pl,nn,pnx1   nn3068 wcs,qmf8085

7 And when we cried unto the LORD God of our fathers, the LORD heard

(853)   nn,pnx6963   wcs,qmf7200   (853)   nn,pnx6040   wcj(853)   nn,pnx5999   wcj(853)

our voice, and looked on   our affliction, and   our labor, and   our

nn,pnx3906

oppression:

nn3068   wcs,himf,pnx3318   pr4480/nn4714   aj2389   pp,nn3027

8 And the LORD brought*us*forth out*of*Egypt with a mighty hand, and with

qptp5186   wcj,pp,nn2220   aj1419   wcj,pp,nn4172   wcj,pp,pl,nn226

an outstretched   arm,   and with great terribleness, and with   signs,   and with

wcj,pp,pl,nn4159

wonders:

wcs,himf,pnx935   pr413   df,pndm2088   df,nn4725   wcs,qmf5414   pp,pnx   (853)   df,pndm2063

9 And he hath brought us into   this   place, and hath given   us   this

df,nn776   nn776   cs,qpta2100   nn2461   wcj,nn1706

land, *even* a land that floweth with milk and honey.

wcj,ad6258   ptdm2009   hipf935   (853)   cs,nn7225/cs,nn6529   df,nn127   pnl834

10 And now, behold, I have brought   the firstfruits of the land, which

nn3068   qpf5414   pp,pnx   wcj,hipf,pnx5117   pp,pl,cs,nn6440   nn3068

thou, O LORD, hast given me. And thou shalt   set   it before   the LORD thy

pl,nn,pnx430   wcj,htpf7812   pp,pl,cs,nn6440   nn3068   pl,nn,pnx430

God, and worship before the LORD thy God:

wcj,qpf8055   pp,cs,nn3605   df,nn2896   pnl834   nn3068   pl,nn,pnx430

11 And thou shalt rejoice in every good *thing* which the LORD thy God

qpf5414   pp,pnx   wcj,pp,nn,pnx1004   pnp859   wcj,df,nn3881

hath given unto thee, and unto thine   house,   thou, and the Levite, and the

wcj,df,nn1616   pnl834   pp,nn,pnx7130

stranger that *is* among you.

cj3588   pimf3615   pp,hinc6237   (853)   cs,nn3605   cs,nn4643   nn,pnx8393

12 When thou hast made*an*end of tithing   all   the tithes of thine increase

df,nuor7992   dfp,nn8141   cs,nn8141   df,nn4643   wcs,qpf5414   pp,nn3881

the third year, *which is* the year of tithing, and hast given *it* unto the Levite,

dfp,nn1616   dfp,nn3490   wcj,dfp,nn490   wcs,qpf398

the stranger, the fatherless, and the widow, that they may   eat   within thy

pp,pl,nn,pnx8179   wcs,qpf7646

gates,   and be filled;

wcs,qpf559   pp,pl,cs,nn6440   nn3068   pl,nn,pnx430   pipf1197

13 Then thou shalt say   before the LORD thy God, I have brought away

df,nn6944   pr4480   df,nn1004   wcj,ad1571   qpf,pnx5414

the hallowed things out of *mine* house, and   also   have given them unto the

pp,nn3881   wcj,dfp,nn1616   dfp,nn3490   wcj,dfp,nn490

Levite, and unto the stranger, to the fatherless, and to the widow, according to

pp,cs,nn3605   nn,pnx4687   pnl834   pipf,pnx6680   ptn3808

all   thy commandments which thou hast commanded me: I have not

qpf5674   pr4480/pl,nn,pnx4687   wcj,ptn3808   qpf7911

transgressed thy commandments, neither have I forgotten *them*:

ptn3808   qpf398   pr,pnx4480   pp,nn,pnx205   wcj,ptn3808   pipf1197

14 I have not eaten thereof in my mourning, neither have I taken away *aught*

pr,pnx4480   pp,aj2931   wcj,ptn3808   qpf5414   pr,pnx4480   pp,qpta4191

thereof for *any* unclean *use*,   nor   given *aught* thereof for the dead: *but* I have

qpf8085   pp,cs,nn6963   nn3068   pl,nn,pnx430   qpf6213   pp,nn3605

hearkened to the voice of the LORD my God, *and* have done according to   all

pnl834   pipf,pnx6680

that thou hast commanded me.

himv8259   nn,pnx6944   pr4480/cs,nn4583   pr4480   df,du,nn8064   wcj,pimv1288   (853)

15 Look down from thy holy habitation, from heaven, and bless   thy

nn,pnx5971 (853) nn3478   wcj(853) df,nn127 pnl834   qpf5414 pp,pnx pp,pnl834   nipf7650

people   Israel, and   the land which thou hast given us, as   thou sworest

pp,pl,nn,pnx1 cs,nn776 cs,qpta2100 nn2461 wcj,nn1706

unto our fathers, a land that floweth with milk and honey.

Concluding Charge

df,pndm2088 df,nn3117   nn3068   pl,nn,pnx430   pipt,pnx6680   pp,qnc6213 (853) df,pndm428

16 This day the LORD thy God hath commanded thee to do   these

df,pl,nn2706   wcj(853)   df,pl,nn4941   wcj,qpf8104   wcj,qpf6213 pnx(853)

statutes and   judgments: thou shalt therefore keep and do   them with

pp,cs,nn3605   nn,pnx3824   wcj,pp,cs,nn3605   nn,pnx5315

all   thine heart, and with   all   thy soul.

hipf559   (853)   nn3068   df,nn3117   pp,qnc1961 pp,pnx pp,pl,nn430

17 Thou hast avouched   the LORD this day to be   thy God, and to

wcj,pp,qnc1980   pp,pl,nn,pnx1870   wcj,pp,qnc8104 pl,nn,pnx2706   wcj,pl,nn,pnx4687

walk in his ways, and to keep his statutes, and his commandments, and

wcj,pl,nn,pnx4941   wcj,pp,qnc8085   pp,nn,pnx6963

his judgments, and to hearken unto his voice:

wcj,nn3068   hipf,pnx559   df,nn3117 pp,qnc1961 pp,pnx nn5459 pp,cs,nn5971

18 And the LORD hath avouched thee this day to be   his peculiar people,

pp,pnl834   pipf1696   pp,pnx   wcj,pp,qnc8104 cs,nn3605

as   he hath promised thee, and that *thou* shouldest keep all his

pl,nn,pnx4687

commandments;

wcj,pp,qnc,pnx5414   aj5945 pr5921 cs,nn3605 df,pl,nn1471 pnl834   qpf6213

19 And to   make   thee high above all   nations which he hath made, in

pp,nn8416   wcj,pp,nn8034   wcj,pp,nn8597   wcj,pp,qnc,pnx1961 aj6918 nn5971

praise, and in name, and in honor; and that thou mayest be   a holy people

pp,nn3068   pl,nn,pnx430 pp,pnl834   pipf1696

unto the LORD thy God,   as he hath spoken.

The Law at Mount Ebal

nn4872   wcj,cs,aj2205   nn3478   wcs,pimf6680 (853)   df,nn5971

27 And Moses with the elders of Israel commanded   the people,

pp,qnc559 qna8104 (853) cs,nn3605   df,nn4687   pnl834 pnp595 pipt6680   pnx(853)

saying, Keep   all   the commandments which I   command

df,nn3117

you this day.

wcj,qpf1961   dfp,nn3117 pnl834   qmf5674 (853) df,nn3383 pr413

2 And it shall be on the day when ye shall pass over   Jordan unto the

df,nn776 pnl834   nn3068   pl,nn,pnx430 qpta5414 pp,pnx   wcs,hipf6965/pp,pnx aj1419

land which the LORD thy God giveth thee, that thou shalt set*thee*up great

pl,nn68   wcs,qpf7874 pnx(853)   dfp,nn7875

stones, and plaster   them with plaster:

wcs,qpf3789 pr,pnx5921 (853) cs,nn3605 pl,cs,nn1697 df,pndm2063 df,nn8451

3 And thou shalt write upon them   all the words of this law, when

pp,qnc,pnx5674 pp,cj4616/pnl834   qmf935 pr413 df,nn776 pnl834   nn3068

thou art passed over,   that   thou mayest go in unto the land which the LORD pl,nn,pnx**430** qpta**5414** pp,pnx nn**776** cs,qpta**2100** nn**2461** wcj,nn**1706** pp,pnl**834** nn**3068**

thy God giveth thee, a land that floweth with milk and honey; as the LORD

pl,cs,nn**430** pl,nn,pnx**1** pipf**1696** pp,pnx

God of thy fathers hath promised thee.

wcj,qpf**1961** pp,qnc,pnx**5674** (853) df,nn**3383**

4 Therefore it shall be when ye be gone over Jordan, *that* ye shall

himf**6965** (853) df,pl,nn**68** pnl**834** pnp**595** pipt**6680** pnx(853) df,nn**3117** pp,cs,nn**2022** nn**5858**

set up these stones, which I command you this day, in mount Ebal,

wcs,qpf**7874** pnx(853) dfp,nn**7875**

and thou shalt plaster them with plaster.

ad**8033** wcs,qpf**1129** nn**4196** pp,nn**3068** pl,nn,pnx**430** cs,nn**4196**

5 And there shalt thou build an altar unto the LORD thy God, an altar of

pl,nn**68** ptn**3808** himf**5130** nn**1270** pr,pnx**5921**

stones: thou shalt not lift up *any* iron *tool* upon them.

qmf**1129** (853) cs,nn**4196** nn**3068** pl,nn,pnx**430** aj**8003** pl,nn**68**

6 Thou shalt build the altar of the LORD thy God of whole stones: and

wcs,hipf**5927** pl,nn**5930** pr,pnx**5921** pp,nn**3068** pl,nn,pnx**430**

thou shalt offer burnt offerings thereon unto the LORD thy God:

wcs,qpf**2076** pl,nn**8002** wcs,qpf**398** ad**8033** wcs,qpf**8055**

7 And thou shalt offer peace offerings, and shalt eat there, and rejoice

pp,pl,cs,nn**6440** nn**3068** pl,nn,pnx**430**

before the LORD thy God.

wcs,qpf**3789** pr**5921** df,pl,nn**68** (853) cs,nn**3605** pl,cs,nn**1697** df,pndm**2063** df,nn**8451**

8 And thou shalt write upon the stones all the words of this law

pina**874**/hina**3190**

very plainly.

nn**4872** wcj,df,pl,nn**3548** df,pl,nn**3881** wcs,pimf**1696** pr**413** cs,nn**3605** nn**3478** pp,qnc**559**

9 And Moses and the priests the Levites spoke unto all Israel, saying,

himv**5535** wcj,qmv**8085** nn**3478** df,pndm**2088** df,nn**3117** nipf**1961** pp,nn**5971**

Take heed, and hearken, O Israel; this day thou art become the people of the

pp,nn**3068** pl,nn,pnx**430**

LORD thy God.

wcj,qpf**8085** pp,cs,nn**6963** nn**3068** pl,nn,pnx**430** wcj,qpf**6213**

10 Thou shalt therefore obey the voice of the LORD thy God, and do

(853) pl,nn,pnx**4687** wcj(853) pl,nn,pnx**2706** pnl**834** pnp**595** pipt,pnx**6680** df,nn**3117**

his commandments and his statutes, which I command thee this day.

The Curses at Mount Ebal

nn**4872** wcs,pimf**6680** (853) df,nn**5971** df,pndm**1931** dfp,nn**3117** pp,qnc**559**

11 And Moses charged the people the same day, saying,

pndm**428** qmf**5975** pr**5921** cs,nn**2022** nn**1630** pp,pinc**1288** (853) df,nn**5971**

12 These shall stand upon mount Gerizim to bless the people, when ye are

pp,qnc,pnx**5674** (853) df,nn**3383** nn**8095** wcj,nn**3878** wcj,nn**3063** wcj,nn**3485** wcj,nn**3130**

come over Jordan; Simeon, and Levi, and Judah, and Issachar, and Joseph, and

wcj,nn**1144**

Benjamin:

wcj,pndm**428** qmf**5975** pp,cs,nn**2022** nn**5858** pr**5921** df,nn**7045** nn**7205** nn**1410**

13 And these shall stand upon mount Ebal to curse; Reuben, Gad, and

wcj,nn**836** wcj,nn**2074** nn**1835** wcj,nn**5321**

Asher, and Zebulun, Dan, and Naphtali.

_{df,pl,nn3881   wcs,qpf6030   wcs,qpf559   pr413   cs,nn3605   cs,nn376   nn3478}
14 And the Levites shall speak, and say unto all   the men of Israel with a

_{qpta7311   nn6963}
loud voice,

_{qptp779   df,nn376 pnl834   qmf6213   nn6459   wcj,nn4541   cs,nn8441}
15 Cursed *be* the man that maketh *any* graven or molten image, an abomination

_{nn3068   cs,nn4639   du,cs,nn3027   nn2796   wcs,qpf7760   dfp,nn5643}
unto the LORD, the work of the hands of the craftsman, and putteth *it* in *a* secret

_{cs,nn3605   df,nn5971   wcs,qpf6030   wcs,qpf559   ad543}
place. And all   the people shall answer and say, Amen.

_{qptp779   hipt7034   nn,pnx1   wcj,nn,pnx517   cs,nn3605}
16 Cursed *be* he that setteth light by his father or his mother. And   all   the

_{df,nn5971   wcs,qpf559   ad543}
people shall say, Amen.

_{qptp779   hipt5253   nn,pnx7453   cs,nn1366   cs,nn3605   df,nn5971}
17 Cursed *be* he that removeth his neighbor's landmark. And   all   the people

_{wcs,qmf559   ad543}
shall say, Amen.

_{qptp779   aj5787   hipt7686   dfp,nn1870   cs,nn3605}
18 Cursed *be* he that maketh the blind to wander out*of*the*way. And   all

_{df,nn5971   wcs,qpf559   ad543}
the people shall say, Amen.

_{qptp779   hipt5186   cs,nn4941   nn1616   nn3490}
19 Cursed *be* he that perverteth the judgment of the stranger, fatherless, and

_{wcj,nn490   cs,nn3605   df,nn5971   wcs,qpf559   ad543}
widow. And   all   the people shall say, Amen.

_{qptp779   qpta7901   pr5973   nn,pnx1   cs,nn802   cj3588   pipf1540}
20 Cursed *be* he that lieth with his father's wife; because he uncovereth

_{nn,pnx1   cs,nn3671   cs,nn3605   df,nn5971   wcs,qpf559   ad543}
his father's skirt. And   all   the people shall say, Amen.

_{qptp779   qpta7901   pr5973   cs,nn3605   nn929   cs,nn3605   df,nn5971}
21 Cursed *be* he that lieth with any manner of beast. And   all   the people

_{wcs,qpf559   ad543}
shall say, Amen.

_{qptp779   qpta7901   pr5973   nn,pnx269   cs,nn1323   nn,pnx1   cj176}
22 Cursed *be* he that lieth with his sister, the daughter of his father, or the

_{cs,nn1323   nn,pnx517   cs,nn3605   df,nn5971   wcs,qpf559   ad543}
daughter of his mother. And   all   the people shall say, Amen.

_{qptp779   qpta7901   pr5973   nn,pnx2859   cs,nn3605   df,nn5971}
23 Cursed *be* he that lieth with his mother-in-law. And   all   the people shall

_{wcs,qpf559   ad543}
say, Amen.

_{qptp779   hipt5221   nn,pnx7453   dfp,nn5643   cs,nn3605   df,nn5971}
24 Cursed *be* he that smiteth his neighbor secretly. And   all   the people shall

_{wcs,qpf559   ad543}
say, Amen.

_{qptp779   qpta3947   nn7810   pp,hinc5221   aj5355   (nn1818) cs,nn5315}
25 Cursed *be* he that taketh reward to slay an innocent   person. And

_{cs,nn3605   df,nn5971   wcs,qpf559   ad543}
all   the people shall say, Amen.

_{qptp779   pnl834   himf6965   ptn3808   (853)   pl,cs,nn1697   df,pndm2063   df,nn8451}
26 Cursed *be* he that confirmeth not *all*   the words of this   law to

_{pp,qnc6213 pnx(853)   cs,nn3605   df,nn5971   wcs,qpf559   ad543}
do   them. And all   the people shall say, Amen.

The Blessings for Obedience

28
wcs,qpf**1961**   cj518   qna**8085**/qmf**8085**
And it*shall*come*to*pass, if thou shalt hearken diligently unto the

pp,cs,nn**6963**   nn**3068**   pl,nn,pnx**430**   pp,qnc**8104**   (853) cs,nn3605
voice of the LORD thy God, to observe *and* to do all his

pl,nn,pnx**4687**   pnl834   pnp595   pipt,pnx**6680**   df,nn3117   nn**3068**   pl,nn,pnx**430**
commandments which I command thee this day, that the LORD thy God will

wcs,qpf,pnx**5414**   aj5945   pr5921   cs,nn3605   pl,cs,nn**1471**   df,nn**776**
set thee on high above all nations of the earth:

cs,nn3605   df,pndm428   df,pl,nn**1293**   wcs,qpf935   pr,pnx5921   wcs,hipf,pnx5381   cj3588
2 And all these blessings shall come on thee, and overtake thee, if

qmf**8085**   pp,cs,nn**6963**   nn**3068**   pl,nn,pnx**430**
thou shalt hearken unto the voice of the LORD thy God.

qptp**1288**   pnp859   dfp,nn5892   wcj,qptp**1288**   pnp859   dfp,nn**7704**
3 Blessed *shalt* thou *be* in the city, and blessed *shalt* thou *be* in the field.

qptp**1288**   cs,nn6529   nn,pnx990   wcj,cs,nn6529   nn,pnx**127**
4 Blessed *shall be* the fruit of thy body, and the fruit of thy ground, and

wcj,cs,nn6529   nn,pnx929   cs,nn7698   pl,nn,pnx504   wcj,pl,cs,nn6251   nn,pnx6629
the fruit of thy cattle, the increase of thy kine, and the flocks of thy sheep.

qptp**1288**   nn,pnx2935   wcj,nn,pnx4863
5 Blessed *shall be* thy basket and thy store.

qptp**1288**   pnp859   pp,qnc,pnx935   wcj,qptp**1288**   pnp859
6 Blessed *shalt* thou *be* when thou comest in, and blessed *shalt* thou *be* when

pp,qnc,pnx3318
thou goest out.

nn**3068**   qmf**5414**   (853)   pl,qpta,pnx341   df,pl,qpta**6965** pr,pnx5921   pl,nipt**5062**
7 The LORD shall cause thine enemies that rise up against thee to be smitten

pp,pl,nn,pnx**6440**   qmf3318   pr,pnx413   nu259 pp,nn**1870**   qmf5127 pp,pl,nn,pnx**6440**
before thy face: they shall come out against thee one way, and flee before

wcj,pp,nu7651   pl,nn**1870**
thee seven ways.

nn**3068**   pimf**6680**   (853)   df,nn**1293**   pr,pnx854   pp,pl,nn,pnx618
8 The LORD shall command the blessing upon thee in thy storehouses, and

wcj,pp,cs,nn3605   cs,nn4916   nn,pnx**3027**   wcs,pipf,pnx**1288**
in all that thou settest thine hand unto; and he shall bless thee in the

dfp,nn**776**   pnl834   nn**3068**   pl,nn,pnx**430**   qpta**5414**   pp,pnx
land which the LORD thy God giveth thee.

nn**3068**   himf,pnx**6965**   aj**6918**   pp,nn**5971**   pp,pnx   pp,pnl834
9 The LORD shall establish thee a holy people unto himself, as he hath

nipf**7650**   pp,pnx   cj3588   qmf**8104** (853)   pl,cs,nn**4687**   nn**3068**   pl,nn,pnx**430**
sworn unto thee, if thou shalt keep the commandments of the LORD thy God,

wcs,qpf**1980**   pp,pl,nn,pnx**1870**
and walk in his ways.

cs,nn3605   pl,cs,nn**5971**   df,nn**776**   wcs,qpf**7200** cj3588   nipf**7121** pr,pnx5921
10 And all people of the earth shall see that thou art called by the

cs,nn8034   nn**3068**   wcj,qpf**3372**   pr,pnx4480
name of the LORD; and they shall be afraid of thee.

nn**3068**   wcj,hipf,pnx**3498**   pp,nn**2896**   pp,cs,nn6529
11 And the LORD shall make*thee*plenteous in goods, in the fruit of thy

nn,pnx990   wcj,pp,cs,nn6529   nn,pnx929   wcj,pp,cs,nn6529   nn,pnx**127** pr5921
body, and in the fruit of thy cattle, and in the fruit of thy ground, in the

df,nn**127**   pnl834   nn**3068**   nipf**7650**   pp,pl,nn,pnx1   pp,qnc**5414** pp,pnx
land which the LORD swore unto thy fathers to give thee.

nn**3068**   qmf**6605**   pp,pnx   (853)   df,aj**2896**   nn,pnx214   (853)   df,du,nn**8064**
12 The LORD shall open unto thee his good treasure, the heaven to

^{pp,qnc5414}   ^{cs,nn4306}   ^{nn,pnx776}   ^{pp,nn,pnx6256}   ^{wcj,pp,pinc1288} (853) ^{cs,nn3605}   ^{cs,nn4639}

give the rain unto thy land in his season, and to bless   all the work

^{nn,pnx3027}   ^{wcj,hipf3867}   ^{aj7227}   ^{pl,nn1471}   ^{wcj,pnp859}   ^{ptn3808}

of thine hand: and thou shalt   lend   unto many nations, and thou shalt not

^{qmf3867}

borrow.

ⁿⁿ³⁰⁶⁸   ^{wcs,qpf,pnx5414}   ^{pp,nn7218}   ^{wcj,ptn3808}   ^{pp,nn2180}

13 And the LORD shall   make   thee the head, and   not the tail; and thou

^{wcs,qpf1961} ^{pp,ad,lh4605} ^{ad7535}   ^{wcj,ptn3808} ^{qmf1961} ^{pp,ad4295} ^{cj3588}   ^{qmf8085}

shalt   be   above only, and thou shalt not   be beneath; if that thou hearken

^{pr413}   ^{pl,cs,nn4687}   ⁿⁿ³⁰⁶⁸   ^{pl,nn,pnx430} ^{pnl834} ^{pnp595} ^{pipt,pnx6680}

unto the commandments of the LORD thy God, which I command thee this

^{df,nn3117}   ^{pp,qnc8104}   ^{wcj,pp,qnc6213}

day, to observe and to   do   them:

^{wcj,ptn3808}   ^{qmf5493}   ^{pr4480/cs,nn3605}   ^{df,pl,nn1697} ^{pnl834} ^{pnp595} ^{pipt6680}

14 And thou shalt   not   go aside from any of the words which I command

^{pnx(853)}   ^{df,nn3117}   ⁿⁿ³²²⁵   ^{wcj,nn8040}   ^{pp,qnc1980} ^{pr310} ^{aj312} ^{pl,nn430}

thee this day, to the right hand, or to the left, to go after other gods to

^{pp,qnc,pnx5647}

serve them.

The Punishment for Disobedience

^{wcs,qpf1961}   ^{cj518}   ^{ptn3808}   ^{qmf8085}   ^{pp,cs,nn6963}

15 But it*shall*come*to*pass, if thou wilt not hearken unto the voice of the

ⁿⁿ³⁰⁶⁸   ^{pl,nn,pnx430}   ^{pp,qnc8104}   ^{pp,qnc6213} (853) ^{cs,nn3605}   ^{pl,nn,pnx4687}

LORD thy God, to observe to   do   all   his commandments and his

^{wcj,pl,nn,pnx2708} ^{pnl834} ^{pnp595} ^{pipt,pnx6680}   ^{df,nn3117}   ^{cs,nn3605} ^{df,pndm428} ^{df,pl,nn7045}   ^{wcs,qpf935}

statutes which I command thee this day; that all   these curses shall come

^{pr,pnx5921}   ^{wcs,hipf,pnx5381}

upon thee, and overtake thee:

^{qptp779}   ^{pnp859}   ^{dfp,nn5892}   ^{wcj,qptp779}   ^{pnp859}   ^{dfp,nn7704}

16 Cursed shalt thou be in the city, and cursed shalt thou be in the field.

^{qptp779}   ^{nn,pnx2935}   ^{wcj,nn,pnx4863}

17 Cursed shall be thy basket and thy   store.

^{qptp779}   ^{cs,nn6529}   ^{nn,pnx990}   ^{wcj,cs,nn6529}   ^{nn,pnx127}

18 Cursed shall be the fruit of thy body, and the   fruit   of thy land, the

^{cs,nn7698}   ^{pl,nn,pnx504}   ^{wcj,pl,cs,nn6251}   ^{nn,pnx6629}

increase of thy kine, and the flocks of thy sheep.

^{qptp779}   ^{pnp859}   ^{pp,qnc,pnx935}   ^{wcj,qptp779}   ^{pnp859}

19 Cursed shalt thou be when thou comest in, and cursed shalt thou be when

^{pp,qnc,pnx3318}

thou goest out.

ⁿⁿ³⁰⁶⁸   ^{pimf7971}   ^{pp,pnx}   (853) ^{df,nn3994}   (853) ^{df,nn4103}   ^{wcj(853)} ^{df,nn4045}

20 The LORD shall send upon thee   cursing,   vexation, and   rebuke,

^{pp,cs,nn3605}   ^{cs,nn4916}   ^{nn,pnx3027}   ^{pnl834} ^{qmf6213} ^{pr5704}   ^{ninc,pnx8045}

in all   that thou settest thine hand unto for to do, until thou be destroyed,

^{wcj,pr5704}   ^{qnc,pnx6}   ^{ad4118}   ^{pr4480/pl,cs,nn6440}   ^{cs,nn7455}   ^{pl,nn,pnx4611}

and until thou perish quickly; because   of the wickedness of thy doings,

^{pnl834}   ^{qpf,pnx5800}

whereby thou hast forsaken me.

nn**3068**   (853)   df,nn**1698**   himf1692   pp,pnx   pr5704

21 The Lord shall make   the pestilence cleave unto thee, until he have

pinc,pnx**3615**   pnx(853)   pr4480/pr5921   df,nn**127**   pnl834/ad,lh8033   pnp859   qpta935   pp,qnc,pnx**3423**

consumed   thee from off the land, whither thou goest to possess it.

nn**3068**   himf,pnx**5221**   dfp,nn**7829**   wcj,dfp,nn**6920**

22 The Lord shall smite thee with a consumption, and with a fever, and

wcj,dfp,nn**1816**   wcj,dfp,nn**2746**   wcj,dfp,nn**2719**

with an inflammation, and with an extreme burning, and with the sword, and with

wcj,dfp,nn**7711**   wcj,dfp,nn**3420**   wcj,qpf,pnx**7291**   pr5704   qnc,pnx**6**

blasting, and with mildew; and they shall pursue thee until thou perish.

du,nn,pnx**8064**   pnl834   pr5921   nn,pnx**7218**   wcj,qpf**1961**   nn5178   wcj,df,nn**776**

23 And thy heaven that *is* over thy head shall be brass, and the earth

pnl834   pr,pnx8478   nn1270

that is under thee *shall be* iron.

nn**3068**   qmf**5414** (853)   cs,nn4306   nn,pnx**776**   nn80   wcj,nn**6083**   pr4480

24 The Lord shall make   the rain of thy land powder and dust: from

df,du,nn**8064**   qmf3381   pr,pnx5921   pr5704   ninc,pnx**8045**

heaven shall it come down upon thee, until thou be destroyed.

nn**3068**   qmf,pnx**5414**   nipt5062   pp,pl,cs,nn**6440**   pl,qpta,pnx341

25 The Lord shall cause thee to be smitten before thine enemies: thou shalt

qmf3318   nu259   pp,nn**1870**   pr,pnx413   qmf5127   wcj,pp,nu7651   pl,nn**1870**   pp,pl,nn,pnx**6440**

go out one way against them, and flee seven ways before them: and shalt

wcs,qpf**1961**   pp,nn2189   pp,cs,nn3605   pl,cs,nn**4467**   df,nn**776**

be removed into all the kingdoms of the earth.

nn,pnx**5038**   wcs,qpf**1961**   pp,nn3978   pp,cs,nn3605   cs,nn5775   df,du,nn**8064**

26 And thy carcass shall be meat unto all fowls of the air, and

wcj,pp,cs,nn929   df,nn**776**   wcj,ptn369   hipt**2729**

unto the beasts of the earth, and no man shall frighten*them*away.

nn**3068**   himf,pnx**5221**   pp,cs,nn7822   nn4714

27 The Lord will smite thee with the botch of Egypt, and with the

wcj,dfp,pl,nn2914   wcj,dfp,nn1618   wcj,dfp,nn2775   pnl834   qmf3201 ptn**3808**

emerods, and with the scab, and with the itch, whereof thou canst not be

pp,ninc7495

healed.

nn**3068**   himf,pnx**5221**   pp,nn7697   wcj,pp,nn5788   wcj,pp,cs,nn8541

28 The Lord shall smite thee with madness, and blindness, and astonishment

nn3824

of heart:

wcs,qpf**1961**   pipt4959   dfp,du,nn6672   pp,pnl834   df,aj5787   pimf4959   dfp,nn**653**

29 And thou shalt grope at noonday, as the blind gropeth in darkness, and

wcj,ptn**3808**   himf6743   (853)   pl,nn,pnx**1870**   wcs,qpf**1961**   ad389   qptp6231

thou shalt not prosper in*thy*ways: and thou shalt be only oppressed and

wcj,qptp1497   cs,nn3605/df,pl,nn**3117**   wcj,ptn369   hipt**3467**

spoiled evermore, and no man shall save *thee.*

pimf781   nn802   aj312   wcj,nn**376**   qmf,pnx7901

30 Thou shalt betroth a wife, and another man shall lie with her: thou shalt

qmf1129   nn**1004**   wcj,ptn**3808** qmf**3427**   pp,pnx   qmf5193   nn3754

build a house, and thou shalt not dwell therein: thou shalt plant a vineyard, and

wcj,ptn**3808**   pimf,pnx**2490**

shalt not gather*the*grapes thereof.

nn,pnx7794   qptp**2873**   pp,du,nn,pnx**5869**   wcj,ptn**3808** qmf398

31 Thine ox *shall be* slain before thine eyes, and thou shalt not eat

pr,pnx4480   nn,pnx2543   qptp1497   pr4480/pp,pl,nn,pnx**6440**

thereof: thine ass *shall be* violently*taken*away from*before*thy*face, and shall wcj,ptn3808   qmf7725   pp,pnx   nn,pnx6629   pl,qptp5414   pp,pl,qpta,pnx341   pp,pnx

not be restored to thee: thy sheep *shall be* given unto thine enemies, and thou

wcj,ptn369   hipt3467

shalt have none to rescue *them*.

pl,nn,pnx1121   wcj,pl,nn,pnx1323   pl,qptp5414   aj312   pp,nn5971

32 Thy   sons   and thy daughters *shall be* given unto another people, and

wcj,du,nn,pnx5869   pl,qpta7200   wcj,aj3616   pr,pnx413   cs,nn3605   df,nn3117

thine eyes   shall look, and fail *with longing* for them all the day

wcj,ptn369 pp,cs,nn410   nn,pnx3027

long: and *there shall be* no   might in thine hand.

cs,nn6529   nn,pnx127   wcj,cs,nn3605   nn,pnx3018   nn5971   pnl834

33 The fruit of thy land, and   all   thy labors, shall a nation which thou

qpf3045   ptn3808   qmf398   wcs,qpf1961 ad7535   qptp6231   wcj,qptp7533 cs,nn3605/df,pl,nn3117

knowest not eat up; and thou shalt be   only oppressed and crushed   always:

wcj,qpf1961   pupt7696   pr4480/cs,nn4758   du,nn,pnx5869   pnl834

34 So that thou shalt   be   mad for*the*sight of thine   eyes   which thou

qmf7200

shalt see.

nn3068   himf,pnx5221   pr5921   df,du,nn1290   wcj,pr5921   df,du,nn7785

35 The LORD shall smite thee in the knees, and in   the legs, with a

aj7451   pp,nn7822   pnl834   qmf3201/ptn3808   pp,ninc7495   pr4480/cs,nn3709   nn,pnx7272   wcj,pr5704

sore botch that cannot be healed, from*the*sole of thy   foot   unto

nn,pnx6936

the top*of*thy*head.

nn3068   himf1980 pnx(853)   wcj(853)   nn,pnx4428 pnl834   himf6965

36 The LORD shall bring   thee, and   thy king which thou shalt set

pr,pnx5921   pr413   nn1471   pnl834   ptn3808   pnp859   wcj,pl,nn,pnx1   qpf3045   ad8033

over thee, unto a nation which neither thou nor thy fathers have known; and there

wcj,qpf5647   aj312   pl,nn430   nn6086   wcj,nn68

shalt thou serve other gods, wood and stone.

wcj,qpf1961   pp,nn8047   pp,nn4912   wcj,pp,nn8148

37 And thou shalt become an astonishment, a proverb, and a byword, among

pp,cs,nn3605   df,pl,nn5971   pnl834/ad,lh8033   nn3068   pimf,pnx5090

all   nations whither the LORD shall lead thee.

himf3318/aj7227/nn2233   df,nn7704   qmf622/wcj,nn4592

38 Thou shalt carry*much*seed*out into the field, and shalt gather*but*little*in;

cj3588   df,nn697   qmf,pnx2628

for the locust shall consume it.

qmf5193   pl,nn3754   wcs,qpf5647   ptn3808   qmf8354

39 Thou shalt plant vineyards, and   dress *them*, but shalt neither drink *of* the

wcj,nn3196 wcj,ptn3808   qmf103   cj3588   df,nn8438   qmf,pnx398

wine,   nor   gather *the grapes*; for the worms shall eat   them.

pp,pnx   qmf1961   pl,nn2132   pp,cs,nn3605   nn,pnx1366   ptn3808

40 Thou shalt have olive trees throughout   all   thy coasts, but thou shalt not

qmf5480   wcj,nn8081 cj3588   nn,pnx2132   qmf5394

anoint *thyself* with the oil; for thine olive shall cast *his fruit*.

himf3205 pl,nn1121   wcj,pl,nn1323   pp,pnx   wcj,ptn3808 qmf1961   cj3588

41 Thou shalt beget sons and daughters, but thou shalt   not enjoy them; for

qmf1980   dfp,nn7628

they shall go into captivity.

cs,nn3605   nn,pnx6086   wcj,cs,nn6529   nn,pnx127   df,nn6767   pimf3423

42 All thy trees and fruit of thy land shall the locust consume.

df,nn1616   pnl834   pp,nn,pnx7130   qmf5927   pr,pnx5921   ad,lh4605/ad,lh4605

43 The stranger that *is* within thee shall get up above thee very high; and

wcj,pnp859   qmf3381   ad4295/ad4295

thou shalt come down very low.

pnp1931   himf,pnx3867   wcj,pnp859   ptn3808 himf,pnx3867   pnp1931

44 He shall lend to thee, and thou shalt not lend to him: he shall

qmf1961   pp,nn7218   wcj,pnp859   qmf1961   pp,nn2180

be the head, and thou shalt be the tail.

cs,nn3605 df,pndm428 df,pl,nn7045   wcs,qpf935 pr,pnx5921   wcs,qpf,pnx7291

45 Moreover all these curses shall come upon thee, and shall pursue

wcs,hipf,pnx5381   pr5704   ninc,pnx8045 cj3588   qpf8085   ptn3808

thee, and overtake thee, till thou be destroyed; because thou hearkenedst not unto

pp,cs,nn6963   nn3068   pl,nn,pnx430 pp,qnc8104   pl,nn,pnx4687   wcj,pl,nn,pnx2708

the voice of the LORD thy God, to keep his commandments and his statutes

pnl834   pipf,pnx6680

which he commanded thee:

wcj,qpf1961   pp,pnx   pp,nn226   wcj,pp,nn4159

46 And they shall be upon thee for a sign and for a wonder, and upon thy

wcj,pp,nn,pnx2233 pr5704/nn5769

seed forever.

pr8478/pnl834   qpf5647   ptn3808 (853)   nn3068   pl,nn,pnx430   pp,nn8057

47 Because thou servedst not the LORD thy God with joyfulness, and

wcj,pp,cs,nn2898   nn3824   pr4480/cs,nn7230   nn3605

with gladness of heart, for*the*abundance of all *things*;

wcs,qpf5647 (853)   pl,qpta,pnx341 pnl834   nn3068   pimf,pnx7971

48 Therefore shalt thou serve thine enemies which the LORD shall send

pp,pnx   pp,nn7458   wcj,pp,nn6772   wcj,pp,nn5903   wcj,pp,cs,nn2640   nn3605

against thee, in hunger, and in thirst, and in nakedness, and in want of all

wcs,qpf5414   cs,nn5923   nn1270 pr5921   nn,pnx6677 pr5704   hinc,pnx8045

things: and he shall put a yoke of iron upon thy neck, until he have destroyed

pnx(853)

thee.

nn3068   qmf5375   nn1471   pr,pnx5921   pr4480/nn7350   pr4480/cs,nn7097

49 The LORD shall bring a nation against thee from far, from*the*end of the

df,nn776   pp,pnl834   df,nn5404 qmf1675   nn1471   pnl834 nn,pnx3956   ptn3808

earth, *as swift* as the eagle flieth; a nation whose tongue thou shalt not

qmf8085

understand;

nn1471   cs,aj5794   pl,nn6440   pnl834   ptn3808 qmf5375   pl,nn6440

50 A nation of fierce countenance, which shall not regard the person of the

pp,aj2205 ptn3808 qmf2603   wcj,nn5288

old, nor show favor to the young:

wcs,qpf398   cs,nn6529   nn,pnx929   wcj,cs,nn6529   nn,pnx127

51 And he shall eat the fruit of thy cattle, and the fruit of thy land,

pr5704   ninc,pnx8045 pnl834   ptn3808 himf7604 pp,pnx   nn1715 nn8492   wcj,nn3323

until thou be destroyed: which *also* shall not leave thee *either* corn, wine, or oil,

cs,nn7698   pl,nn,pnx504   wcj,pl,cs,nn6251   nn,pnx6629 ad5704   hinc,pnx6

or the increase of thy kine, or flocks of thy sheep, until he have destroyed

pnx(853)

thee.

wcs,hipf6887 pp,pnx   pp,cs,nn3605   pl,nn,pnx8179 pr5704   df,aj1364

52 And he shall besiege thee in all thy gates, until thy high and

wcj,df,pl,qptp1219 pl,nn,pnx2346 qnc3381   pnl834/pp,pnx pnp859 qpta982   pp,cs,nn3605   nn,pnx776

fenced walls come down, wherein thou trustedst, throughout all thy land:

wcs,hipf6887 pp,pnx   pp,cs,nn3605   pl,nn,pnx8179   pp,cs,nn3605   nn,pnx776 pnl834

and he shall besiege thee in all thy gates throughout all thy land, which

nn3068   pl,nn,pnx430   qpf5414 pp,pnx

the LORD thy God hath given thee.

wcj,qpf398   cs,nn6529   nn,pnx990   cs,nn1320   pl,nn,pnx1121

53 And thou shalt eat the fruit of thine own body, the flesh of thy sons

wcj,pl,nn,pnx1323   pnl834   nn3068   pl,nn,pnx430   qpf5414   pp,pnx   pp,nn4692
and of thy daughters, which the LORD thy   God   hath given thee, in the siege, and

wcj,wcj,nn,nn4689   pnl834   qpta,pnx341   himf6693   pp,pnx
in the straitness, wherewith thine enemies shall distress thee:

df,nn376   df,aj7390   pp,pnx   ad3966 wcj,df,aj6028   nn,pnx5869
54 *So that* the man *that is* tender among you, and very delicate, his eye shall

qmf7489   pp,nn,pnx251   wcj,pp,cs,nn802   nn,pnx2436
be evil toward his brother, and toward the   wife   of his bosom, and toward the

wcj,pp,cs,nn3499   pl,nn,pnx1121   pnl834   himf3498
remnant of his children which he shall leave:

pr4480/qnc5414   pp,nu259 pr,pnx4480   pr4480/cs,nn1320   pl,nn,pnx1121
55 So*that*he*will*not*give to   any   of   them of*the*flesh of his children

pnl834   qmf398 pr4480/ptn1097   nn3605   hipf7604 pp,pnx   pp,nn4692
whom he shall eat: because he hath nothing left him in the siege, and in the

wcj,pp,nn4689   pnl834   qpta,pnx341   himf6693   pp,pnx   pp,cs,nn3605   pl,nn,pnx8179
straitness, wherewith thine enemies shall distress thee in   all   thy gates.

df,aj7390   wcj,df,aj6028   pp,pnx   pnl834   ptn3808   pipf5254
56 The tender and delicate woman among you, which would not adventure to

hinc3322   cs,nn3709   nn,pnx7272 pr5921   df,nn776   pr4480/htnc6026   wcj,pr4480/nn7391
set the sole of her foot upon the ground for delicateness and tenderness, her

nn,pnx5869   qmf7489   pp,cs,nn376   nn,pnx2436   wcj,pp,nn,pnx1121
eye shall be evil toward the husband of her bosom, and toward her   son,

wcj,pp,nn,pnx1323
and toward her daughter,

wcj,pp,nn,pnx7988   df,qpta3318   pr4480/pr996   du,nn,pnx7272
57 And toward her young one that cometh out from between her feet, and

wcj,pp,pl,nn,pnx1121 pnl834   qmf3205 cj3588   qmf,pnx398   pp,cs,nn2640
toward her children which she shall bear: for she shall   eat   them for want

nn3605   dfp,nn5643   pp,nn4692   wcj,pp,nn4689   pnl834   qpta,pnx341
of all *things* secretly in the siege and straitness, wherewith thine enemy shall

himf6693   pp,pnx   pp,pl,nn,pnx8179
distress thee in thy   gates.

cj518   ptn3808   qmf8104   pp,qnc6213 (853) cs,nn3605   pl,cs,nn1697   df,pndm2063 df,nn8451
58 If thou wilt not observe to   do   all the words of this   law that

df,pl,qptp3789   df,pndm2088 dfp,nn5612   pp,qnc3372 (853) df,pndm2088 df,nipt3513
are written in   this   book, that thou mayest fear   this   glorious and

wcj,df,nipt3372 df,nn8034 (853)   nn3068   pl,nn,pnx430
fearful name,   THE LORD THY GOD;

nn3068   (853)   pl,nn,pnx4347   wcs,hipf6381   wcj(853)   pl,cs,nn4347
59 Then the LORD will make   thy plagues wonderful, and   the plagues of

nn,pnx2233   aj1419   pl,nn4347   wcj,pl,nipt539   aj7451   wcj,pl,nn2483
thy seed, *even* great plagues, and of long continuance, and sore sicknesses, and of

wcj,pl,nipt539
long continuance.

wcs,hipf7725   pp,pnx   (853) cs,nn3605   cs,nn4064   nn4714   pnl834
60 Moreover he will bring upon thee   all   the diseases of Egypt, which

qpf3025   pr4480/pl,nn,pnx6440   wcj,qpf1692   pp,pnx
thou wast afraid   of;   and they shall cleave unto thee.

ad1571 cs,nn3605   nn2483   wcj,cs,nn3605   nn4347   pnl834   ptn3808 qptp3789   pp,cs,nn5612
61 Also every sickness, and every plague, which *is* not written in the book

df,pndm2063 df,nn8451   nn3068 himf,pnx5927 pr,pnx5921   pr5704   ninc,pnx8045
of this   law, them will the LORD bring upon thee, until thou be destroyed.

wcs,nipf7604 nn4592   pp,pl,cs,nn4962 pr8478/pnl834   qpf1961   pp,pl,cs,nn3556
62 And ye shall be left   few in number, whereas ye were as the   stars   of

^{df,du,nn8064}   ^{pp,nn7230}   ^{cj3588}   ^{ptn3808 qpf8085}   ^{pp,cs,nn6963}   ⁿⁿ³⁰⁶⁸

heaven for multitude; because thou wouldest not obey the voice of the LORD thy

^{pl,nn,pnx430}

God.

^{wcj,qpf1961}   ^{pp,pnl834}   ⁿⁿ³⁰⁶⁸   ^{qpf7797}   ^{pr,pnx5921}

63 And it*shall*come*to*pass, *that* as the LORD rejoiced over you to

^{pp,hinc3190/pnx(853)}   ^{wcj,pp,hinc7235 pnx(853)}   ^{ad3651}   ⁿⁿ³⁰⁶⁸   ^{qmf7797}   ^{pr,pnx5921}

do*you*good, and to multiply you; so the LORD will rejoice over you to

^{pp,hinc6}   ^{pnx(853)}   ^{wcj,pp,hinc8045/pnx(853)}   ^{wcs,nipf5255}   ^{pr4480/pr5921}

destroy you, and to bring*you*to*naught; and ye shall be plucked from off the

^{df,nn127 pnl834/ad,lh8033 pnp859 qpta935}   ^{pp,qnc,pnx3423}

land whither thou goest to possess it.

ⁿⁿ³⁰⁶⁸   ^{wcs,hipf,pnx6327}   ^{pp,cs,nn3605 df,pl,nn5971}   ^{pr4480/cs,nn7097}

64 And the LORD shall scatter thee among all people, from*the*one*end

^{df,nn776}   ^{wcj,pr5704}   ^{cs,nn7097/(df,nn776)}   ^{ad8033}   ^{wcs,qpf5647}   ^{aj312}   ^{pl,nn430}

of the earth even unto the other; and there thou shalt serve other gods,

^{pnl834}   ^{ptn3808}   ^{pnp859}   ^{wcj,pl,nn,pnx1}   ^{qpf3045}   ⁿⁿ⁶⁰⁸⁶   ^{wcj,nn68}

which neither thou nor thy fathers have known, *even* wood and stone.

^{df,pnp1992}   ^{wcj,dfp,pl,nn1471}   ^{himf7280/ptn3808}   ^{wcj,ptn3808}

65 And among these nations shalt thou find*no*ease, neither shall the

^{pp,cs,nn3709}   ^{nn,pnx7272}   ^{qmf1961 nn4494}   ⁿⁿ³⁰⁶⁸   ^{wcs,qpf5414}   ^{pp,pnx}   ^{ad8033}   ^{aj7268}

sole of thy foot have rest: but the LORD shall give thee there a trembling

ⁿⁿ³⁸²⁰   ^{wcj,cs,nn3631}   ^{du,nn5869}   ^{wcj,cs,nn1671}   ⁿⁿ⁵³¹⁵

heart, and failing of eyes, and sorrow of mind:

^{pl,nn,pnx2416}   ^{wcs,qpf1961}   ^{pl,qptp8511 pr4480/pr5048}   ^{pp,pnx}   ^{wcs,qpf6342}

66 And thy life shall hang in doubt before thee; and thou shalt fear

^{wcj,ad3119}   ⁿⁿ³⁹¹⁵   ^{himf539/wcj,ptn3808}   ^{pp,pl,nn,pnx2416}

day and night, and shalt have*none*assurance of thy life:

^{dfp,nn1242}   ^{qmf559}   ^{pnit4130/qmf5414}   ⁿⁿ⁶¹⁵³   ^{wcj,dfp,nn6153}

67 In the morning thou shalt say, Would God it were even! and at even

^{qmf559}   ^{pnit4130/qmf5414}   ⁿⁿ¹²⁴²   ^{pr4480/cs,nn6343}   ^{nn,pnx3824}   ^{pnl834}

thou shalt say, Would God it were morning! for*the*fear of thine heart wherewith

^{qmf6342}   ^{wcj,pr4480/pp,cs,nn4758}   ^{du,nn,pnx5869}   ^{pnl834}   ^{qmf7200}

thou shalt fear, and for*the*sight of thine eyes which thou shalt see.

ⁿⁿ³⁰⁶⁸   ^{wcs,himf,pnx7725}   ⁿⁿ⁴⁷¹⁴   ^{pp,pl,nn591}

🕮 68 And the LORD shall bring thee into Egypt again with ships, by the

^{dfp,nn1870}   ^{pnl834}   ^{qpf559}   ^{pp,pnx}   ^{pp,qnc,pnx7200}   ^{ptn3808 himf3254 ad5750}   ^{ad8033}

way whereof I spoke unto thee, Thou shalt see it no more again: and there

^{wcs,htpf4376}   ^{pp,pl,qpta,pnx341}   ^{pp,pl,nn5650}   ^{wcj,pp,pl,nn8198}   ^{wcj,ptn369}

ye shall be sold unto your enemies for bondmen and bondwomen, and no man

^{qpta7069}

shall buy *you.*

Covenant Renewal

^{pndm428}   ^{pl,cs,nn1697}   ^{df,nn1285}   ^{pnl834}   ⁿⁿ³⁰⁶⁸   ^{pipf6680}   ⁽⁸⁵³⁾

29 These *are* the words of the covenant, which the LORD commanded

ⁿⁿ⁴⁸⁷²   ^{pp,qnc3772}   ^{pr854}   ^{pl,cs,nn1121}   ⁿⁿ³⁴⁷⁸   ^{pp,cs,nn776}   ⁿⁿ⁴¹²⁴

Moses to make with the children of Israel in the land of Moab,

^{pr4480/pp,nn905}   ^{df,nn1285}   ^{pnl834}   ^{qpf3772}   ^{pr,pnx854}   ^{pp,nn2722}

beside the covenant which he made with them in Horeb.

🕮 **28:68**   See the note on Jeremiah 18:7–10.

nn4872   wcs,qmf7121   pr413   cs,nn3605   nn3478   wcs,qmf559   pr,pnx413   pnp859   qpf7200

2 And Moses called unto all Israel, and said unto them, Ye have seen

(853)   cs,nn3605   pnl834   nn3068   qpf6213   pp,du,nn,pnx5869   pp,cs,nn776   nn4714

all that the LORD did before your eyes in the land of Egypt unto

pp,nn6547   wcj,pp,cs,nn3605   pl,nn,pnx5650   wcj,pp,cs,nn3605   nn,nn776

Pharaoh, and unto all his servants, and unto all his land;

df,aj1419   df,pl,nn4531   pnl834   du,nn,pnx5869   qpf7200   df,pl,nn226   df,pnp1992

3 The great temptations which thine eyes have seen, the signs, and those

df,aj1419   wcj,df,pl,nn4159

great miracles:

nn3068   wcj,ptn3808   qpf5414   pp,pnx   nn3820   pp,qnc3045   wcj,du,nn5869   pp,qnc7200

4 Yet the LORD hath not given you a heart to perceive, and eyes to see,

wcj,du,nn241   pp,qnc8085   pr5704   df,pndm2088   df,nn3117

and ears to hear, unto this day.

wcs,himf1980   pnx(853)   pl,nu705   nn8141   dfp,nn4057   pl,nn,pnx8008

5 And I have led you forty years in the wilderness: your clothes are

ptn3808   qpf1086   pr4480/pr,pnx5921   wcj,nn,pnx5275   ptn3808   qpf1086   pr4480/pr5921

not waxen old upon you, and thy shoe is not waxen old upon thy

nn,pnx7272

foot.

ptn3808   qpf398   nn3899   ptn3808   qpf8354   wcj,nn3196   wcj,nn7941   pp,cj4616

6 Ye have not eaten bread, neither have ye drunk wine or strong drink: that

qmf3045   cj3588   pnp589   nn3068   pl,nn,pnx430

ye might know that I *am* the LORD your God.

wcs,qmf935   pr413   df,pndm2088   df,nn4725   nn5511   cs,nn4428   nn2809

7 And when ye came unto this place, Sihon the king of Heshbon, and

wcj,nn5747   cs,nn4428   df,nn1316   wcs,qmf3318   pp,qnc,pnx7125   dfp,nn4421   wcs,himf,pnx5221

Og the king of Bashan, came out against us unto battle, and we smote

them:

wcs,qmf3947   (853)   nn,pnx776   wcs,qmf,pnx5414   pp,nn5159

8 And we took their land, and gave it for an inheritance unto the

pp,nn7206   wcj,pp,nn1425   wcj,pp,cs,nn2677   cs,nn7626   df,nn4520

Reubenites, and to the Gadites, and to the half tribe of Manasseh.

wcj,qpf8104   (853)   pl,cs,nn1697   df,pndm2063   df,nn1285   wcj,qpf6213   pnx(853)

9 Keep therefore the words of this covenant, and do them,

pp,cj4616   himf7919   (853)   cs,nn3605   pnl834   qmf6213

that ye may prosper in all that ye do.

pnp859   pl,nipt5324   df,nn3117   nn,pnx3605   pp,pl,cs,nn6440   nn3068   pl,nn,pnx430

10 Ye stand this day all of you before the LORD your God; your

pl,nn,pnx7218   pl,nn,pnx7626   aj,pnx2205   wcj,pl,qpta,pnx7860   cs,nn3605   cs,nn376

captains of your tribes, your elders, and your officers, *with* all the men of

nn3478

Israel,

nn,pnx2945   pl,nn,pnx802   wcj,nn,pnx1616   pnl834   pp,cs,nn7130   nn,pnx4264

11 Your little ones, your wives, and thy stranger that *is* in thy camp,

pr4480/qpta2404   pl,nn,pnx6086   pr5704   qpta7579   pl,nn,pnx4325

from*the*hewer of thy wood unto the drawer of thy water:

pp,qnc,pnx5674   pp,cs,nn1285   nn3068   pl,nn,pnx430

12 That thou shouldest enter into covenant with the LORD thy God, and

wcj,pp,nn,pnx423   pnl834   nn3068   pl,nn,pnx430   qpta3772   pr,pnx5973   df,nn3117

into his oath, which the LORD thy God maketh with thee this day:

pp,cj4616   hinc6965 pnx(853) df,nn3117 pp,nn5971 pp,pnx

13 That he may establish thee today for a people unto himself, and *that*

wcj,pnp1931 qmf1961 pp,pnx pp,pl,nn430 pp,pnl834 pipf1696 pp,pnx wcj,pp,pnl834

he may be unto thee a God, as he hath said unto thee, and as he

nipf7650 pp,pl,nn,pnx1 pp,nn85 pp,nn3327 wcj,pp,nn3290

hath sworn unto thy fathers, to Abraham, to Isaac, and to Jacob.

wcj,ptn3808 pr,pnx854 pp,nn,pnx905 pnp595 qpta3772 (853) df,pndm2063 df,nn1285 wcj(853)

14 Neither with you only do I make this covenant and

df,pndm2063 df,nn423

this oath;

cj3588 pr854 pnl834 (pta,pnx3426) qpta5975 ad6311 pr,pnx5973 df,nn3117 pp,pl,cs,nn6440

15 But with *him* that standeth here with us this day before the

nn3068 pl,nn,pnx430 wcj,pr854 pnl834 ptn,pnx369 ad6311 pr,pnx5973 df,nn3117

Lord our God, and also with *him* that *is* not here with us this day:

cj3588 pnp859 qpf3045 (853) pnl834 qpf3427 pp,cs,nn776 nn4714 wcj(853) pnl834

16 (For ye know how we have dwelt in the land of Egypt; and how

qpf5674 pp,cs,nn7130 df,pl,nn1471 pnl834 qpf5674

we came through the nations which ye passed by;

wcs,qmf7200 (853) pl,nn,pnx8251 wcj(853) pl,nn,pnx1544 nn6086

17 And ye have seen their abominations, and their idols, wood and

wcj,nn68 nn3701 wcj,nn2091 pnl834 pr,pnx5973

stone, silver and gold, which *were* among them:)

cj6435 pta3426 pp,pnx nn376 cj176 nn802 cj176 nn4940 cj176 nn7626

18 Lest there should be among you man, or woman, or family, or tribe,

pnl834 nn,pnx3824 qpta6437 df,nn3117 pr4480/pr5973 nn3068 pl,nn,pnx430 pp,qnc1980

whose heart turneth away this day from the Lord our God, to go *and*

pp,qnc5647 (853) pl,cs,nn430 df,pnp1992 df,pl,nn1471 cj6435 pta3426 pp,pnx nn8328

serve the gods of these nations; lest there should be among you a root that

qpta6509 nn7219 wcj,nn3939

beareth gall and wormwood;

wcj,qpf1961 pp,qnc,pnx8085 (853) pl,cs,nn1697 df,pndm2063 df,nn423

19 And it*come*to*pass, when he heareth the words of this curse, that

wcj,htpf1288 pp,nn,pnx3824 pp,qnc559 pp,pnx qmf1961 nn7965 cj3588 qmf1980

he bless himself in his heart, saying, I shall have peace, though I walk in the

pp,cs,nn8307 nn,pnx3820 pp,cj4616 qnc5595 df,aj7302 pr854 df,aj6771

imagination of mine heart, to add drunkenness to thirst:

nn3068 qmf14 ptn3808 qnc5545 pp,pnx cj3588 ad227 cs,nn639 nn3068

20 The Lord will not spare him, but then the anger of the Lord and his

wcj,nn,pnx7068 qmf6225 df,pndm1931 dfp,nn376 cs,nn3605 df,nn423 df,qptp3789

jealousy shall smoke against that man, and all the curses that are written in

df,pndm2088 dfp,nn5612 wcs,qpf7257 pp,pnx nn3068 wcs,qpf4229 (853) nn,pnx8034

this book shall lie upon him, and the Lord shall blot out his name

pr4480/pr8478 df,du,nn8064

from under heaven.

nn3068 wcs,hipf,pnx914 pp,aj7451 pr4480/cs,nn3605 pl,cs,nn7626 nn3478

21 And the Lord shall separate him unto evil out*of*all the tribes of Israel,

pp,cs,nn3605 pl,cs,nn423 df,nn1285 df,qptp3789 df,pndm2088 pp,cs,nn5612

according to all the curses of the covenant that are written in this book of

df,nn8451

the law:

df,nn1755 df,aj314 pl,nn,pnx1121 pnl834 qmf6965 pr4480/pr,pnx310

22 So that the generation to come of your children that shall rise up after

wcj,df,aj5237 pnl834 qmf935 aj7350 pr4480/nn776 wcs,qpf559

you, and the stranger that shall come from a far land, shall say, when they

wcs,qpf**7200** (853)   pl,cs,nn**4347**   df,pndm1931 df,nn**776**   wcj(853)   pl,nn,pnx**8463**   pnl834   nn**3068**

see   the plagues of that land, and   the sicknesses which the LORD hath

pipf2470   pp,pnx

laid upon it;

cs,nn**3605** nn,pnx**776**   nn1614   wcj,nn**4417**   nn**8316**

23 *And that* the whole land thereof *is* brimstone, and salt, *and* burning, *that*

ptn**3808** nimf2232 wcj,ptn**3808** himf6779 wcj,ptn**3808** cs,nn**3605** nn6212 qmf**5927** pp,pnx

it is not sown, nor beareth, nor any grass groweth therein, like the

pp,cs,nn**4114**   nn5467   wcj,nn6017   nn126   wcj,nn6636   pnl834   nn**3068**

overthrow of Sodom, and Gomorrah, Admah, and Zeboim, which the LORD

qpf**2015**   pp,nn,pnx**639**   wcj,pp,nn,pnx**2534**

overthrew in his anger, and in his wrath:

cs,nn**3605** df,pl,nn**1471**   wcj,qpf**559** pr5921/pnit4100   nn**3068** qpf**6213** ad3602

24 Even all nations shall say, Wherefore hath the LORD done thus unto

df,pndm2063 dfp,nn**776** pnit4100   cs,nn**2750**   df,pndm2088 df,aj1419 df,nn**639**

this   land? what *meaneth* the heat of this great anger?

wcj,qpf**559** pr5921/pnl834   qpf**5800**   (853)   cs,nn**1285**

25 Then men shall say, Because they have forsaken   the covenant of the

nn**3068**   pl,cs,nn**430**   pl,nn,pnx**1**   pnl834   qpf**3772**   pr,pnx5973

LORD God of their fathers, which he made with   them when he

pp,hinc,pnx3318/pnx(853)   pr4480/cs,nn**776**   nn4714

brought*them*forth out*of*the*land of Egypt:

wcs,qmf**1980**   wcs,qmf**5647** aj312   pl,nn**430**   wcs,htmf**7812** pp,pnx pl,nn**430** pnl834

26 For they went and served other gods, and worshiped them, gods whom

qpf,pnx**3045** ptn**3808**   wcj,ptn**3808** qpf**2505**   pp,pnx

they knew not, and *whom* he had not given unto them:

cs,nn**639**   nn**3068**   wcs,qmf**2734**   df,pndm1931 dfp,nn**776** pp,hinc935 pr,pnx5921

27 And the anger of the LORD was kindled against this land, to bring upon

(853) cs,nn**3605**   df,nn**7045**   df,qptp3789   df,pndm2088 dfp,nn**5612**

it   all   the curses that are written in this book:

nn**3068**   wcs,qmf,pnx**5428**   pr4480/pr5921   nn,pnx**127**   pp,nn**639**   wcj,pp,nn**2534**

28 And the LORD rooted*them*out   of   their land in anger, and in wrath,

aj1419   wcj,pp,nn**7110**   wcs,himf,pnx**7993**   pr413 aj312   nn**776**   df,pndm2088 df,nn**3117**

and in great indignation, and   cast   them into another land, as *it is* this   day.

df,pl,nipt5641   pp,nn**3068**   pl,nn,pnx**430**

29 The secret *things belong* unto the LORD our God: but those *things which*

wcj,df,pl,nipt**1540**   pp,pnx   wcj,pp,pl,nn,pnx**1121** pr5704/nn**5769**   pp,qnc**6213** (853)

are revealed *belong* unto us and to our children forever, that *we* may do

cs,nn**3605**   pl,cs,nn**1697**   df,pndm2063 df,nn**8451**

all the words of this law.

God's Promise Remains Constant

wcj,qpf**1961**   cj3588 cs,nn3605 df,pndm428 df,pl,nn**1697**   qmf935 pr,pnx5921

30 And it*shall*come*to*pass, when all these things are come upon

df,nn**1293**   wcj,df,nn**7045** pnl834   qpf**5414** pp,pl,nn,pnx**6440**

thee, the blessing and the curse, which I have set before thee,

wcj,hipf**7725**   pr413 nn,pnx3824   pp,cs,nn**3605**   df,pl,nn**1471** pnl834/ad,lh8033

and thou shalt call *them* to mind among all   the nations, whither the

nn**3068**   pl,nn,pnx**430**   hipf,pnx5080

LORD thy God hath driven thee,

wcj,qpf**7725** pr5704   nn**3068**   pl,nn,pnx**430**   wcj,qpf**8085**   pp,nn,pnx6963

2 And shalt return unto the LORD thy God, and shalt obey his voice

pp,nn3605 pnl834 pnp595 pipt,pnx**6680** df,nn3117 pnp859 wcj,pl,nn,pnx**1121**
according to all that I command thee this day, thou and thy children, with

pp,cs,nn3605 nn,pnx3824 wcj,pp,cs,nn3605 nn,pnx**5315**
all thine heart, and with all thy soul;

nn**3068** pl,nn,pnx**430** wcj,qpf**7725** (853) nn,pnx**7622**
3 That then the LORD thy God will turn thy captivity, and

wcj,pipf,pnx**7355** wcj,qpf**7725** wcj,pipf,pnx**6908** pr4480/cs,nn3605
have compassion upon thee, and will return and gather thee from all the

df,pl,nn**5971** pnl834/ad,lh8033 nn3068 pl,nn,pnx**430** hipf,pnx6327
nations, whither the LORD thy God hath scattered thee.

cj518 qmf**1961** nipt,pnx5080 pp,cs,nn7097 df,du,nn**8064**
4 If *any* of thine be driven out unto the outermost *parts* of heaven,

pr4480/ad8033 nn3068 pl,nn,pnx430 pimf,pnx**6908** wcj,pr4480/ad8033 qmf3947
from thence will the LORD thy God gather thee, and from thence will he fetch

thee:

nn**3068** pl,nn,pnx**430** wcs,hipf,pnx935 pr413 df,nn776 pnl834 pl,nn,pnx1
5 And the LORD thy God will bring thee into the land which thy fathers

qpf**3423** wcs,qpf,pnx**3423** wcs,hipf,pnx**3190** wcs,hipf,pnx7235
possessed, and thou shalt possess it; and he will do*thee*good, and multiply thee

pr4480/pl,nn,pnx1
above*thy*fathers.

nn**3068** pl,nn,pnx**430** wcj,qpf**4135** (853) nn,pnx3824 wcj(853) cs,nn3824
6 And the LORD thy God will circumcise thine heart, and the heart

nn,pnx**2233** pp,qnc157 (853) nn3068 pl,nn,pnx**430** pp,cs,nn3605 nn,pnx3824
of thy seed, to love the LORD thy God with all thine heart, and with

wcj,pp,cs,nn3605 nn,pnx**5315** pp,cj4616 pl,nn,pnx**2416**
all thy soul, that thou mayest live.

nn**3068** pl,nn,pnx**430** wcj,qpf**5414** (853) cs,nn3605 df,pndm428 df,pl,nn**423** pr5921
7 And the LORD thy God will put all these curses upon thine

pl,qpta,pnx341 wcj,pr5921 pl,qpta,pnx**8130** pnl834 qpf,pnx7291
enemies, and on them that hate thee, which persecuted thee.

wcj,pnp859 qmf**7725** wcs,qpf**8085** pp,cs,nn6963 nn**3068** wcs,qpf**6213** (853)
8 And thou shalt return and obey the voice of the LORD, and do

cs,nn3605 pl,nn,pnx**4687** pnl834 pnp595 pipt,pnx**6680** df,nn**3117**
all his commandments which I command thee this day.

nn**3068** pl,nn,pnx**430** wcs,hipf,pnx**3498** pp,cs,nn3605 cs,nn4639
9 And the LORD thy God will make*thee*plenteous in every work of thine

nn,pnx**3027** pp,cs,nn6529 nn,pnx**990** wcj,pp,cs,nn6529 nn,pnx929
hand, in the fruit of thy body, and in the fruit of thy cattle, and in the

wcj,pp,cs,nn6529 nn,pnx**127** pp,nn2896 cj3588 nn**3068** qmf7725 pp,qnc7797 pr,pnx5921
fruit of thy land, for good: for the LORD will again rejoice over thee for

pp,nn2896 pp,pnl834 qpf7797 pr5921 pl,nn,pnx1
good, as he rejoiced over thy fathers:

cj3588 qmf**8085** pp,cs,nn6963 nn**3068** pl,nn,pnx**430** pp,qnc**8104**
10 If thou shalt hearken unto the voice of the LORD thy God, to keep his

pl,nn,pnx**4687** wcj,pl,nn,pnx**2708** df,qptp3789 df,pndm2088 pp,cs,nn**5612** df,nn**8451**
commandments and his statutes which are written in this book of the law,

cj3588 qmf**7725** pr413 nn**3068** pl,nn,pnx**430** pp,cs,nn3605 nn,pnx3824
and if thou turn unto the LORD thy God with all thine heart, and with

wcj,pp,cs,nn3605 nn,pnx**5315**
all thy soul.

cj3588 df,pndm2063 df,nn**4687** pnl834 pnp595 pipt,pnx**6680** df,nn**3117** pnp1931 ptn**3808**
11 For this commandment which I command thee this day, it *is* not

nipt**6381** pr,pnx4480 wcj,ptn**3808** pnp1931 aj7350
hidden from thee, neither *is* it far off.

pnp1931   ptn3808   dfp,du,nn8064   pp,qnc559 pnit4310   qmf5927   pp,pnx

12 It *is* not in heaven, that thou shouldest say, Who shall go up for us to

df,du,nn,lh8064   wcj,qmf,pnx3947   pp,pnx   wcj,himf,pnx8085 pnx(853)   wcj,qmf,pnx6213

heaven, and   bring   it unto us, that we may   hear   it, and   do   it?

wcj,ptn3808   pnp1931 pr4480/nn5676   df,nn3220   pp,qnc559 pnit4310   qmf5674

13 Neither *is* it   beyond the sea, that thou shouldest say, Who shall go

pr413/cs,nn5676   df,nn3220   pp,pnx   wcj,qmf,pnx3947   pp,pnx   wcj,himf,pnx8085 pnx(853)

over   the   sea for us, and   bring   it unto us, that we may   hear   it,

wcj,qmf,pnx6213

and   do   it?

cj3588   df,nn1697   ad3966 aj7138 pr,pnx413   pp,nn,pnx6310   wcj,pp,nn,pnx3824

14 But the word *is* very nigh unto thee, in thy mouth, and in thy   heart,

pp,qnc,pnx6213

that thou mayest   do   it.

Choose Life

qmv7200   qpf5414 pp,pl,nn,pnx6440   df,nn3117 (853) df,pl,nn2416   wcj(853) df,nn2896

15 See, I have   set   before thee this day   life   and   good, and

wcj(853) df,nn4194   wcj(853) df,nn7451

death and   evil;

pnl834 pnp595   pipt,pnx6680   df,nn3117   pp,qnc157 (853)   nn3068   pl,nn,pnx430

16 In that   I   command thee this day to love   the LORD thy God, to

pp,qnc1980   pp,pl,nn,pnx1870   wcj,pp,qnc8104   pl,nn,pnx4687   wcj,pl,nn,pnx2708

walk in his   ways,   and to   keep   his commandments and his   statutes and his

wcj,pl,nn,pnx4941   wcj,qpf2421   wcj,qpf7235   nn3068   pl,nn,pnx430

judgments, that thou mayest   live   and multiply: and the LORD thy   God   shall

wcj,pipf,pnx1288   dfp,nn776 pnl834/ad,lh8033 pnp859 qpta935   pp,qnc,pnx3423

bless   thee in the land   whither thou goest to possess it.

wcj,cj518   nn,pnx3824   qmf6437   wcj,ptn3808 qmf8085

17 But   if   thine heart turn away, so that thou wilt   not   hear, but shalt be

wcs,nipf5080   wcs,htpf7812 aj312 pp,pl,nn430   wcs,qpf,pnx5647

drawn away, and worship other gods, and   serve   them;

hipf5046   pp,pnx   df,nn3117 cj3588   qna6/qmf6

18 I denounce unto you this day, that ye shall surely perish, *and that* ye shall

ptn3808   himf748   pl,nn3117 pr5921   df,nn127 pnl834/ad,lh8033 pnp859   qpta5674   (853) df,nn3383

not prolong *your* days upon the land,   whither   thou passest over   Jordan to

pp,qnc935   pp,qnc,pnx3423

go to possess it.

hipf5749 (853) df,du,nn8064   wcj(853) df,nn776   df,nn3117   pp,pnx

19 I call   heaven and   earth to record this day against you, *that* I have

qpf5414 pp,pl,nn,pnx6440   df,pl,nn2416   wcj,df,nn4194   df,nn1293   wcj,df,nn7045   wcj,qpf977 dfp,pl,nn2416

set   before   you life and death, blessing and cursing: therefore choose   life,

pp,cj4616   pnp859   wcj,nn,pnx2233   qmf2421

that both thou and thy   seed   may live:

pp,qnc157 (853)   nn3068   pl,nn,pnx430   pp,qnc8085

20 That thou mayest love   the LORD thy God, *and* that thou mayest obey

pp,nn,pnx6963   wcj,pp,qnc1692   pp,pnx   cj3588 pnp1931   pl,nn,pnx2416

his voice, and that thou mayest cleave unto him: for he *is* thy life, and

wcj,cs,nn753   pl,nn,pnx3117   pp,qnc3427 pr5921   df,nn127 pnl834   nn3068

the length of thy days: that thou mayest dwell in the land which the LORD

nipf7650   pp,pl,nn,pnx1   pp,nn85   pp,nn3327   wcj,pp,nn3290   pp,qnc5414 pp,pnx

swore unto thy fathers, to Abraham, to Isaac, and to Jacob, to give them.

Joshua Is Appointed the New Leader

31

nn4872 wcs,qmf1980   wcs,pimf1696 (853) df,pndm428 df,pl,nn1697 pr413 cs,nn3605 nn3478
And Moses went and spoke   these words unto all Israel.

wcs,qmf559 pr,pnx413   pnp595   nu3967   wcj,pl,nu6242
2 And he said unto them, I *am* a hundred and twenty

nn8141 cs,nn1121 df,nn3117 qmf3201 ptn3808 ad5750 pp,qnc3318 wcj,pp,qnc935   wcj,nn3068
years old this day; I can no more go out and come in: also the LORD hath

qpf559 pr,pnx413   ptn3808   qmf5674 (853) df,pndm2088 df,nn3383
said unto me, Thou shalt not go over   this Jordan.

nn3068   pl,nn,pnx430 pnp1931   qpta5674 pp,pl,nn,pnx6440   pnp1931   himf8045
3 The LORD thy God, he will go over before thee, *and* he will destroy

(853) df,pndm428 df,pl,nn1471 pr4480/pp,pl,nn,pnx6440   wcs,qpf,pnx3423   nn3091
these nations from before thee, and thou shalt possess them: *and* Joshua,

pnp1931   qpta5674 pp,pl,nn,pnx6440 pp,pnl834   nn3068   pipf1696
he shall go over before thee, as the LORD hath said.

nn3068   wcj,qpf6213   pp,pnx   pp,pnl834   qpf6213   pp,nn5511   wcj,pp,nn5747
4 And the LORD shall do unto them as he did to Sihon and to Og,

pl,cs,nn4428 df,nn567   wcj,pp,pl,nn,pnx776   pnl834/(pnx853)   hipf8045
kings of the Amorites, and unto the land of them, whom he destroyed.

nn3068   wcj,qpf,pnx5414   pp,pl,nn,pnx6440   wcj,qpf6213
5 And the LORD shall give*them*up before your face, that ye may do

pp,pnx   pp,cs,nn3605   df,nn4687   pnl834   pipf6680
unto them according unto all the commandments which I have commanded

pnx(853)
you.

qmv2388   wcj,qmv553   qmf3372 ptn408 wcj,ptn408   qmf6206   pr4480/pl,nn,pnx6440
6 Be strong and of a good courage, fear not, nor be afraid of

cj3588   nn3068   pl,nn,pnx430 pnp1931   df,qpta1980 pr,pnx5973   ptn3808
them: for the LORD thy God, he *it is* that doth go with thee; he will not

himf,pnx7503   wcj,ptn3808 qmf,pnx5800
fail thee, nor forsake thee.

nn4872 wcs,qmf7121   pp,nn3091   wcs,qmf559 pr,pnx413   pp,du,cs,nn5869
7 And Moses called unto Joshua, and said unto him in the sight of

cs,nn3605 nn3478 qmv2388   wcj,qmv553   cj3588 pnp859   qmf935 pr854 df,pndm2088
all Israel, Be strong and of a good courage: for thou must go with this

df,nn5971 pr413   df,nn776 pnl834   nn3068   nipf7650   pp,pl,nn,pnx1   pp,qnc5414 pp,pnx
people unto the land which the LORD hath sworn unto their fathers to give them;

wcj,pnp859   pnx(853)   himf,pnx5157
and thou shalt cause them to inherit it.

wcj,nn3068 pnp1931   df,qpta1980 pp,pl,nn,pnx6440   pnp1931   qmf1961
8 And the LORD, he *it is* that doth go before thee; he will be with

pr,pnx5973   ptn3808 himf,pnx7503   wcj,ptn3808 qmf,pnx5800   qmf3372 ptn3808 wcj,ptn3808   qmf2865
thee, he will not fail thee, neither forsake thee: fear not, neither be dismayed.

nn4872 wcs,qmf3789 (853) df,pndm2063 df,nn8451   wcs,qmf,pnx5414   pr413   df,pl,nn3548
9 And Moses wrote this law, and delivered it unto the priests the

pl,cs,nn1121 nn3878   df,pl,qpta5375 (853) cs,nn727   cs,nn1285   nn3068   wcj,pr413
sons of Levi, which bore the ark of the covenant of the LORD, and unto

cs,nn3605 cs,aj2205   nn3478
all the elders of Israel.

nn4872 wcs,pimf6680 pnx(853)   pp,qnc559   pr4480/cs,nn7093   cs,nu7651
10 And Moses commanded them, saying, At*the*end of *every* seven

pl,nn8141   pp,cs,nn4150   cs,nn8141 df,nn8059   pp,cs,nn2282   df,pl,nn5521
years, in the solemnity of the year of release, in the feast of tabernacles,

cs,nn3605 nn3478   pp,qnc935   pp,ninc7200 (853) pl,cs,nn6440   nn3068   pl,nn,pnx430
11 When all Israel is come to appear before the LORD thy God in the

dfp,nn4725   pnl834   qmf977   qmf7121 (853) df,pndm2063 df,nn8451   pr5048   cs,nn3605   nn3478

place which he shall choose, thou shalt read   this   law before   all   Israel in

pp,du,nn,pnx241

their hearing.

himv6950/(853)/df,nn5971   df,pl,nn376   wcj,df,pl,nn802   wcj,df,nn2945

12 Gather*the*people*together,   men,   and women, and children, and thy

wcj,nn,pnx1616   pnl834   pp,pl,nn,pnx8179   pp,cj4616   qmf8085   wcj,pp,cj4616

stranger that is within thy   gates,   that they may hear, and   that   they may

qmf3925   wcs,qpf3372 (853)   nn3068   pl,nn,pnx430   wcs,qpf8104   pp,qnc6213 (853) cs,nn3605

learn, and   fear   the LORD your God, and observe to   do   all   the

pl,cs,nn1697   df,pndm2063 df,nn8451

words of   this   law:

wcj,pl,nn,pnx1121 pnl834   ptn3808   qpf3045   qmf8085

13 And that their children, which have not known any thing, may hear, and

wcs,qpf3925   pp,qnc3372 (853)   nn3068   pl,nn,pnx430 cs,nn3605/df,nn3117/pnl834 pnp859 aj2416 pr5921   df,nn127

learn to fear   the LORD your God,   as*long*as   ye live in the land

pnl834/ad,lh8033 pnp859   pl,qpta5674 (853) df,nn3383   pp,qnc,pnx3423

whither ye go over   Jordan to possess it.

nn3068   wcs,qmf559   pr413   nn4872   ptdm2005   pl,nn,pnx3117   qpf7126

14 And the LORD said unto Moses, Behold, thy   days   approach that thou

pp,qnc4191   qmv7121 (853)   nn3091   wcj,htmv3320   pp,cs,nn168

must die: call   Joshua, and present yourselves in the tabernacle of the

nn4150   wcs,pimf,pnx6680   nn4872   wcj,nn3091 wcs,qmf1980

congregation, that I may give*him*a*charge. And Moses and Joshua went, and

wcs,htmf3320   pp,cs,nn168   nn4150

presented themselves in the tabernacle of the congregation.

nn3068   wcs,nimf7200   dfp,nn168   pp,cs,nn5982   nn6051

15 And the LORD appeared in the tabernacle in a pillar of a cloud: and the

cs,nn5982   df,nn6051 wcs,qmf5975 pr5921   cs,nn6607   df,nn168

pillar of the cloud stood over the door of the tabernacle.

nn3068   wcs,qmf559 pr413   nn4872   ptdm,pnx2009   qpta7901 pr5973   pl,nn,pnx1

16 And the LORD said unto Moses, Behold, thou shalt sleep with thy fathers;

df,pndm2088   df,nn5971   wcs,qpf6965   wcs,qpf2181   pr310   pl,cs,nn430   cs,nn5236

and   this   people will rise up, and go*a*whoring after the gods of the strangers

df,nn776 pnl834/ad,lh8033 pnp1931 qpta935   pp,nn,pnx7130   wcj,qpf,pnx5800

of the land, whither they go to be among them, and will forsake me, and

wcj,hipf6565 (853)   nn,pnx1285   pnl834   qpf3772 pr,pnx854

break   my covenant which I have made with them.

nn,pnx639   wcj,qpf2734   pp,pnx   df,pndm1931 dfp,nn3117

17 Then my anger shall be kindled against them in   that   day, and I will

wcj,qpf,pnx5800   wcj,hipf5641   pl,nn,pnx6440   pr,pnx4480   wcj,qpf1961

forsake them, and I will hide my   face   from them, and they shall   be

pp,qnc398   aj7227   pl,nn7451   wcj,pl,nn6869   wcj,qpf,pnx4672   wcj,qpf559

devoured, and many evils and troubles shall   befall   them; so that they will say

df,pndm1931 dfp,nn3117   he,ptn3808 df,pndm428 df,pl,nn7451   qpf,pnx4672   pr5921/cj3588   pl,nn,pnx430   ptn369

in that   day, Are not these evils come upon us, because our   God   is not

pp,nn,pnx7130

among us?

wcj,pnp595   hina5641/himf5641   pl,nn,pnx6440   df,pndm1931 dfp,nn3117 pr5921 cs,nn3605   df,aj7451

18 And   I   will surely hide my face   in that   day for all the evils

pnl834   qpf6213   cj3588   qpf6437 pr413 aj312 pl,nn430

which they shall have wrought, in that they are turned unto other gods.

wcj,ad6258   qmv3789 (853)   df,pndm2063 df,nn7892   pp,pnx   wcj,pimv,pnx3925   (853)

19 Now therefore write   ye   this   song for you, and   teach   it   the

cj3588   nn,pnx1612   pr4480/cs,nn1612   nn5467   pr4480/pl,cs,nn7709   nn6017

32 For their vine *is* of*the*vine of Sodom, and of*the*fields of Gomorrah:

pl,nn,pnx6025   pl,cs,nn6025   nn7219   pp,pnx   pl,cs,nn811   pl,nn4846

their grapes *are* grapes of gall, their clusters *are* bitter:

nn,pnx3196   cs,nn2534   pl,nn8577   aj393   wcj,cs,nn7219   pl,nn6620

33 Their wine *is* the poison of dragons, and the cruel venom of asps.

he,ptn3808   pndm1931   qptp3647   pr,pnx5978   qptp2856

34 *Is* not this laid*up*in*store with me *and* sealed up among my

pp,pl,nn,pnx214

treasures?

pp,pnx   nn5359   wcj,nn8005   nn,pnx7272   qmf4131

35 To me *belongeth* vengeance, and recompense; their foot shall slide in *due*

pp,nn6256   cj3588   cs,nn3117   nn,pnx343   aj7138   aj6264

time: for the day of their calamity *is* at hand, and the things*that*shall*come

pp,pnx   wcs,qpta2363

upon them make haste.

cj3588   nn3068   qmf1777   nn,pnx5971   htmf5162   wcj,pr5921   pl,nn,pnx5650

36 For the LORD shall judge his people, and repent himself for his servants,

cj3588   qmf7200   cj3588   nn3027   qpf235   wcj,ptn657   qptp6113   wcj,qptp5800

when he seeth that *their* power is gone, and *there is* none shut up, or left.

wcj,qpf559   pnit335   pl,nn,pnx430   nn6697   pp,pnx   qpf2620

37 And he shall say, Where *are* their gods, *their* rock in whom they trusted,

pnl834   qmf398   cs,nn2459   pl,nn,pnx2077   qmf8354   cs,nn3196

38 Which did eat the fat of their sacrifices, *and* drank the wine of their

nn,pnx5257   qmf6965   wcj,qmf,pnx5826   qcj1961/pr,pnx5921   pl,nn5643

drink offerings? let them rise up and help you, *and* be your protection.

qmv7200   ad6258   cj3588   pnp589   pnp589   pnp1931   wcj,ptn369   pl,nn430   pr,pnx5978

39 See now that I, *even* I, *am* he, and *there is* no god with me:

pnp589   himf4191   wcj,pimf2421   qpf4272   wcj,pnp589   qmf7495   wcj,ptn369

I kill, and I make alive; I wound, and I heal: neither *is there any* that can

hipt5337   pr4480/nn,pnx3027

deliver out*of*my*hand.

cj3588   qmf5375   nn,pnx3027   pr413   du,nn8064   wcs,qpf559   pnp595   aj2416   pp,nn5769

40 For I lift up my hand to heaven, and say, I live forever.

cj518   qpf8150   cs,nn1300   nn,pnx2719   nn,pnx3027   wcs,qmf270   pp,nn4941

41 If I whet my glittering sword, and mine hand take hold on judgment; I

himf7725   nn5359   pp,pl,nn,pnx6862   pimf7999   wcj,pp,pl,pipt,pnx8130

will render vengeance to mine enemies, and will reward them that hate me.

pl,nn,pnx2671   himf7937   pr4480/nn1818   wcj,nn,pnx2719   qmf398

42 I will make mine arrows drunk with blood, and my sword shall devour

nn1320   pr4480/cs,nn1818   nn2491   wcj,nn7633   pr4480/cs,nn7218

flesh; *and that* with*the*blood of the slain and of the captives, from*the*beginning

pl,cs,nn6546   qpta341

of revenges upon the enemy.

himv7442   pl,nn1471   nn,pnx5971   cj3588   qmf5358   cs,nn1818

43 Rejoice, O ye nations, *with* his people: for he will avenge the blood of his

pl,nn,pnx5650   himf7725   wcj,nn5359   pp,pl,nn,pnx6862   wcs,pipf3722

servants, and will render vengeance to his adversaries, and will be merciful unto his

nn,pnx127   nn,pnx5971

land, *and* to his people.

nn4872   wcs,qmf935   wcs,pimf1696   (853)   cs,nn3605   pl,cs,nn1697   df,pndm2063   df,nn7892

44 And Moses came and spoke all the words of this song in the

pp,du,cs,nn241   df,nn5971   pnp1931   wcj,nn1954   cs,nn1121   nn5126

ears of the people, he, and Hoshea the son of Nun.

45 And Moses made*an*end of speaking   all   these   words   to   all
Israel:

46 And he   said   unto them, Set your hearts unto   all   the words which
I   testify among you this day, which ye shall command   your children to
observe to do,   all the words of this   law.

47 For   it *is* not a vain thing for you; because it *is* your   life: and
through this   thing ye shall prolong *your* days in the land, whither ye
go over   Jordan to possess it.

God Prepares Moses for His Death

48 And the LORD spoke unto Moses   that selfsame day, saying,

49 Get*thee*up into   this   mountain Abarim, *unto* mount Nebo, which *is* in
the land of Moab, that *is* over against Jericho; and behold   the land of Canaan,
which I   give unto the children of Israel for a possession:

50 And   die in the mount whither thou goest up, and be gathered unto thy
people; as   Aaron thy brother died in mount Hor, and was gathered unto his
people:

51 Because ye trespassed against me among the children of Israel at the
waters of Meribah-Kadesh, in the wilderness of Zin; because ye sanctified
me not in the midst of the children of Israel.

52 Yet thou shalt see   the land before *thee*; but thou shalt not   go
thither unto the land which I   give the children of Israel.

Moses Blesses Israel

33 And   this   *is* the blessing, wherewith Moses the man of God
blessed   the children of Israel before his death.

2 And he said, The LORD came from Sinai, and rose up from Seir unto them;

hipf3313   pr4480/cs,nn2022   nn6290   wcj,qpf857   pr4480/pl,cs,nn7233   nn6944

he shined forth from mount Paran, and he came with*ten*thousands of saints:

pr4480/nn,pnx3225   nn784 nn1881   pp,pnx

from*his*right*hand *went* a fiery law for them.

cj637   qpta2245   pl,nn5971   cs,nn3605   aj,pnx6918   pp,nn,pnx3027   wcj,pnp1992

3 Yea, he loved the people; all his saints *are* in thy hand: and they

pupf8497   pp,nn,pnx7272   qmf5375   pr4480/pl,nn,pnx1703

sat down at thy feet; *every one* shall receive of*thy*words.

nn4872   pipf6680   pp,pnx   nn8451   nn4181   cs,nn6952

4 Moses commanded us a law, *even* the inheritance of the congregation of

nn3290

Jacob.

wcs,qmf1961   nn4428   pp,nn3484   pl,cs,nn7218   nn5971

5 And he was king in Jeshurun, when the heads of the people *and* the

pl,cs,nn7626   nn3478   pp,htnc622   ad3162

tribes of Israel were gathered together.

nn7205   qcj2421   wcj,ptn408   qcj4191   pl,nn,pnx4962 wcj,qcj1961 nn4557

6 Let Reuben live, and not die; and let *not* his men be few.

wcj,pndm2063   pp,nn3063   wcs,qmf559 qmv8085   nn3068   cs,nn6963

7 And this *is the blessing* of Judah: and he said, Hear, LORD, the voice of

nn3063   himf,pnx935   wcj,pr413   nn,pnx5971   du,nn,pnx3027   qpf7227   pp,pnx

Judah, and bring him unto his people: let his hands be sufficient for him; and

qmf1961   wcj,nn5828   pr4480/pl,nn,pnx6862

be thou a help *to him* from*his*enemies.

wcj,pp,nn3878   qpf559   pl,nn,pnx8550   wcj,pl,nn,pnx224

8 And of Levi he said, *Let* thy Thummim and thy Urim *be* with thy

aj,pnx2623 pp,cs,nn376 pnl834   pipf,pnx5254   pp,nn4532   qmf,pnx7378

holy one, whom thou didst prove at Massah, *and with* whom thou didst strive

pr5921   pl,cs,nn4325   nn4809

at the waters of Meribah;

df,qpta559   pp,nn,pnx1   wcj,pp,nn,pnx517   ptn3808 qpf,pnx7200

9 Who said unto his father and to his mother, I have not seen him;

ptn3808   hipf5234   wcj(853)   pl,nn,pnx251 ptn3808 qpf3045 wcj(853)   pl,nn,pnx1121

neither did he acknowledge his brethren, nor knew his own children:

cj3588   qpf8104   nn,pnx565   qmf5341   wcj,nn,pnx1285

for they have observed thy word, and kept thy covenant.

himf3384 pp,nn3290   pl,nn,pnx4941   pp,nn3478   wcj,nn,pnx8451

10 They shall teach Jacob thy judgments, and Israel thy law: they shall

qmf7760   nn6988   pp,nn,pnx639   wcj,aj3632   pr5921   nn,pnx4196

put incense before thee, and whole*burnt*sacrifice upon thine altar.

pimv1288   nn3068   nn,pnx2428   qmf7521   wcj,cs,nn6467   du,nn,pnx3027

11 Bless, LORD, his substance, and accept the work of his hands:

qmv4272   du,nn4975   pl,qpta,pnx6965   wcj,pl,pipt,pnx8130

smite through the loins of them that rise against him, and of them that hate

pr4480   qmf6965

him, that they rise*not*again.

pp,nn1144   qpf559   cs,aj3039   nn3068   qmf7931   pp,nn983

12 *And* of Benjamin he said, The beloved of the LORD shall dwell in safety

pr,pnx5921   qpta2653/pr,pnx5921   cs,nn3605   df,nn3117

by him; *and the LORD* shall cover him all the day long, and he shall

qpf7931   wcj,pr996   pl,nn,pnx3802

dwell between his shoulders.

wcj,pp,nn3130   qpf559   pupt1288   nn3068   nn,pnx776

13 And of Joseph he said, Blessed of the LORD *be* his land,

pr4480/cs,nn4022   du,nn**8064**   pr4480/nn2919   wcj,pr4480/nn8415   qpta7257

for*the*precious*things of heaven, for*the*dew, and for*the*deep that coucheth

pr8478

beneath,

wcj,pr4480/cs,nn4022   pl,cs,nn8393   nn8121

14 And   for*the*precious   fruits   *brought   forth* by the sun, and

wcj,pr4480/cs,nn4022   cs,nn1645   pl,nn3391

for*the*precious*things put forth by the moon,

wcj,pr4480/cs,nn**7218**   nn6924   pl,cs,nn2042

15 And   for*the*chief*things   of   the   ancient   mountains,   and

wcj,pr4480/cs,nn4022   nn5769   pl,cs,nn1389

for*the*precious*things of the lasting hills,

wcj,pr4480/cs,nn4022   nn776   wcj,nn,pnx4393

16 And for*the*precious*things of the earth and fullness thereof, and *for* the

wcj,cs,nn**7522**   qpta**7931**   nn5572   qmf935   pp,cs,nn**7218**

good will of him that dwelt in the bush: let *the blessing* come upon the ˙ head of

nn3130   wcj,pp,cs,nn6936   cs,nn**5139**   pl,nn,pnx**251**

Joseph, and upon the top*of*the*head of him *that was* separated from his brethren.

pp,pnx   nn**1926**   cs,nn1060   nn,pnx7794   du,nn,pnx7161

17 His glory *is like* the firstling of his bullock, and his   horns   *are like* the

wcj,du,cs,nn7161   nn7214   pp,pnx   pimf5055   pl,nn**5971**   ad3162   pl,cs,nn657

horns   of unicorns: with them he shall push the people together to the ends of

nn776   wcj,pnp1992   pl,cs,nn7233   nn669   wcj,pnp1992

the earth: and   they   *are* the ten thousands of Ephraim, and   they   *are* the

pl,cs,nu**505**   nn4519

thousands of Manasseh.

wcj,pp,nn2074   qpf559   qmv8055   nn2074   pp,qnc,pnx3318   wcj,nn3485

18 And of Zebulun he said, Rejoice, Zebulun, in thy going out; and, Issachar,

pp,pl,nn,pnx**168**

in thy   tents.

qmf**7121**   pl,nn**5971**   nn2022   ad8033   qmf**2076**

19 They shall   call   the people unto the mountain; there they shall offer

pl,cs,nn**2077**   nn6664   cj3588   qmf3243   cs,nn8228   pl,nn3220

sacrifices of righteousness: for they shall suck *of* the abundance of the seas, and *of*

wcj,pl,cs,qptp8226 pl,cs,qptp2934   nn2344

treasures   hid   in the sand.

wcj,pp,nn1410   qpf559   qptp1288   hipt7337   nn1410   qpf**7931**

20 And of Gad   he said, Blessed *be* he that enlargeth Gad: he dwelleth as a

pp,nn3833   wcj,qpf2963   nn2220 cj637   nn6936

lion, and teareth the arm with the crown*of*the*head.

wcs,qmf**7200**   nn7225   pp,pnx   cj3588   ad8033   cs,nn2513

21 And he provided the first part for himself, because there, *in* a portion of the

pipt*2710   qptp5603   wcs,qmf857   pl,cs,nn**7218**   nn5971   qpf**6213**

lawgiver, *was he* seated; and he came with the heads of the people, he executed

cs,nn**6666**   nn3068   wcj,pl,nn,pnx**4941** pr5973 nn3478

the justice of the Lᴏʀᴅ, and his judgments with Israel.

wcj,pp,nn1835   qpf559 nn1835   nn738 cs,nn1482   pimf2187 pr4480 df,nn1316

22 And of   Dan   he said, Dan *is* a lion's whelp: he shall leap from Bashan.

wcj,pp,nn**5321**   qpf559   nn5321   cs,aj7649   nn**7522**   wcj,aj4392

23 And of Naphtali he said, O Naphtali, satisfied with favor, and   full   with

cs,nn**1293**   nn3068   qmv**3423**   nn3220   wcj,nn1864

the blessing of the Lᴏʀᴅ: possess thou the west and the south.

wcj,pp,nn836   qpf559   nn836   qptp1288   pr4480/pl,nn1121   qcj**1961**

24 And of Asher he said, *Let* Asher *be* blessed with children; let him be

cs,qptp7521   pl,nn,pnx**251**   wcj,qpta**2881**   nn,pnx7272   dfp,nn**8081**

acceptable to his brethren, and let him   dip   his foot in oil.

pl,nn,pnx4515   nn1270   wcj,nn5178   wcj,pp,pl,nn,pnx3117

25 Thy   shoes   *shall be* iron and brass; and as thy   days,   *so shall* thy

nn,pnx1679

strength *be.*

ptn369   pp,nn410   nn3484   qpta7392   du,nn8064

26 *There is* none like unto the God of Jeshurun, *who* rideth upon the heaven in

pp,nn,pnx5828   wcj,pp,nn,pnx1346   pl,nn7834

thy   help,   and in his excellency on the sky.

nn6924   pl,cs,nn430   nn4585   wcj,pr4480/pr8478   nn5769   pl,cs,nn2220

27 The eternal God *is thy* refuge, and underneath *are* the everlasting   arms:

wcs,pimf1644   qpta341   pr4480/pl,nn,pnx6440   wcs,qmf559   himv8045

and he shall thrust out the enemy from before thee; and shall   say,   Destroy *them.*

nn3478   wcs,qmf7931   nn983   nn910   cs,nn5869   nn3290   pr413

28 Israel then shall   dwell   in safety alone: the fountain of Jacob *shall be* upon a

cs,nn776   nn1715   wcj,nn8492   cj637   du,nn,pnx8064   qmf6201   nn2919

land of corn and wine; also his heavens shall drop   down dew.

ptx835   nn3478   pnit4310   pp,pnx3644   nn5971   nipf3467

29 Happy *art* thou, O Israel: who *is* like*unto*thee, O people saved by the

pp,nn3068   cs,nn4043   nn,pnx5828   wcj,pnl834   cs,nn2719   nn,pnx1346

Lᴏʀᴅ, the shield of thy help,   and   who   *is* the sword of thy excellency! and thine

pl,qpta,pnx341   wcj,nimf3584   pp,pnx   wcj,pnp859   qmf1869   pr5921

enemies   shall   be   found liars   unto thee;   and   thou   shalt   tread   upon their

pl,nn,pnx1116

high places.

Moses' Death

nn4872   wcs,qmf5927   pr4480/pl,cs,nn6160   nn4124   pr413   cs,nn2022

34 And Moses went up from*the*plains of Moab unto the mountain of

nn5015   cs,nn7218   df,nn6449   pnl834   pr5921   pl,cs,nn6440   nn3405

Nebo, to the   top   of Pisgah, that *is* over against Jericho. And the

nn3068   wcs,himf,pnx7200   (853) cs,nn3605   df,nn776   (853)   df,nn1568   pr5704   nn1835

Lᴏʀᴅ   showed   him   all   the land   of Gilead, unto Dan,

wcj(853)   cs,nn3605   nn5321   wcj(853)   cs,nn776   nn669   wcj,nn4519

2 And   all   Naphtali, and   the land of Ephraim, and Manasseh, and

wcj(853) cs,nn3605   cs,nn776   nn3063   pr5704   df,aj314   df,nn3220

all   the land of Judah, unto the utmost   sea,

wcj(853)   df,nn5045   wcj(853)   df,nn3603   cs,nn1237   nn3405   cs,nn5892

3 And   the south, and   the plain of the valley of Jericho, the   city   of

df,pl,nn8558   pr5704   nn6820

palm trees, unto Zoar.

nn3068   wcs,qmf559   pr,pnx413   pndm2063   df,nn776   pnl834   nipf7650

4 And the Lᴏʀᴅ   said   unto   him, This   *is* the   land   which   I   swore   unto

pp,nn85   pp,nn3327   wcj,pp,nn3290   pp,qnc559   qmf,pnx5414   pp,nn,pnx2233

Abraham, unto Isaac, and unto   Jacob, saying, I will   give   it unto thy   seed: I

hipf,pnx7200   pp,du,nn,pnx5869   ptn3808   qmf5674

have caused thee to   see   *it* with thine   eyes,   but thou shalt not go over

wcj,ad,lh8033

thither.

nn4872   cs,nn5650   nn3068   wcs,qmf4191   ad8033   pp,cs,nn776   nn4124

☞ 5 So Moses the servant of the Lᴏʀᴅ   died   there in the   land   of Moab,

pr5921   cs,nn6310   nn3068

according to the word of the Lᴏʀᴅ.

☞ **34:5–7**   The life of Moses may be divided into three periods of forty years each. The first forty years were spent in Egypt as a member of Pharaoh's household (Acts 7:21–23). Next, he lived a private family life in the

6 And he buried him in a valley in the land of Moab, over against Beth-peor: but no man knoweth of his sepulcher unto this day.

7 And Moses *was* a hundred and twenty years old when he died: his eye was*not*dim, nor his natural force abated.

8 And the children of Israel wept for Moses in the plains of Moab thirty days: so the days of weeping *and* mourning for Moses were ended.

9 And Joshua the son of Nun was full of the spirit of wisdom; for Moses had laid his hands upon him: and the children of Israel hearkened unto him, and did as the LORD commanded Moses.

10 And there arose not a prophet since in Israel like unto Moses, whom the LORD knew face to face,

11 In all the signs and the wonders, which the LORD sent him to do in the land of Egypt to Pharaoh, and to all his servants, and to all his land,

12 And in all that mighty hand, and in all the great terror which Moses showed in the sight of all Israel.

---

land of Midian (Acts 7:29, 30). Finally, he lived forty years from God's call at the burning bush until his death, during which time he led the children of Israel out of Egypt.

The Book of

JOSHUA

This book describes the conquest of the land of Canaan under the leadership of Joshua, the successor of Moses. His name means "Jehovah saves" or "Jehovah is salvation." The Greek transliteration of his name is "Jesus" (see Heb. 4:8).

Joshua had worked with Moses since the giving of the Ten Commandments at Mount Sinai. He continued to serve with Moses throughout the wilderness wanderings (Ex. 24:13), and became a strong leader who was full of faith and courage. Joshua and Caleb were in favor of conquering the land of Canaan in spite of the height and aggressive nature of the people there. Consequently, they were the only two of their generation that God permitted to cross the Jordan River (Num. 14:29, 30, 38; Deut. 1:35, 36).

The theme of the Book of Joshua is "victory through faith" (see Josh. 1:6–9). The land that God promised to Abraham (Gen. 15:18) was now being conquered. Joshua began by attacking a few key cities (e.g., Jericho and Ai) and breaking up dangerous coalitions among the Canaanites (Josh. 10:2–5). The conquest of the Promised Land under Joshua, however, was not complete. The Israelites continued to encounter resistance after they had settled in the land. In accordance with God's plan, it was left up to the individual tribes to slowly displace the Canaanites from their remaining strongholds (Ex. 23:27–31; Josh. 13:1–6; Judg. 3:1, 2).

God's Charge to Joshua

1
    pr310   cs,nn4194   nn4872   cs,nn5650   nn3068   wcs,qmf1961
○ᵃ Now after the death of Moses the servant of the LORD it*came*to*pass,

    nn3068 wcs,qmf559 pr413   nn3091   cs,nn1121 nn5126 nn4872 cs,pipt8334 pp,qnc559
that the LORD spoke unto Joshua the son of Nun, Moses' minister, saying,

  nn4872   nn,pnx5650 qpf4191 wcj,ad6258   qmv6965 qmv5674 (853) df,pndm2088 df,nn3383
2 Moses my servant is dead; now therefore arise, go over this Jordan,

pnp859   wcj,cs,nn3605 df,pndm2088 df,nn5971 pr413   df,nn776 pnl834 pnp595 qpta5414 pp,pnx
thou, and all this people, unto the land which I do give to them, *even*

    pp,pl,cs,nn1121   nn3478
to the children of Israel.

    cs,nn3605 nn4725 pnl834   cs,nn3709   nn,pnx7272   qmf1869 pp,pnx   qpf,pnx5414
○ᵃ 3 Every place that the sole of your foot shall tread upon, that have I given

  pp,pnx   pp,pnl834 pipf1696 pr413   nn4872
unto you, as I said unto Moses.

○ᵃ **1:1** Joshua is introduced as Moses' servant, which is seen in the Hebrew word *meshārēth* (8334) which is a participle meaning "one who ministers." Joshua's name had been changed from Oshea (Num. 13:16). He had been previously commissioned by God to be Moses' successor (Num. 27:16–23). This commission included instructions to inquire through the priests, via the Urim and Thummim, for answers from God. However, on this occasion of Joshua's charge to take command, God appeared directly to Joshua as He did with Moses (Num. 12:8) and later with the prophets.

○ᵃ **1:3–6** This passage amplifies the physical nature of the land promised to the children of Israel, as had been affirmed before (Gen. 15:7–21; 28:13, 14). Many scholars deny any unconditional promise of a physical

pr4480/df,nn4057   df,pndm2088   wcj,df,nn3844   wcj,pr5704   df,aj1419   df,nn5104

4 From*the*wilderness and   this   Lebanon even   unto   the great river, the

cs,nn5104   nn6578   cs,nn3605   cs,nn776   df,aj2850   wcj,pr5704   df,aj1419   df,nn3220

river Euphrates, all   the land of the Hittites, and unto the great sea toward

cs,nn3996   df,nn8121   qmf1961   nn,pnx1366

the going down of the sun, shall be your coast.

ptn3808   nn376   htmf3320   pp,pl,nn,pnx6440   cs,nn3605   pl,cs,nn3117

5 There shall not any man be able to stand before   thee all the days of

pl,nn,pnx2416   pp,pnl834   qpf1961   pr5973   nn4872   qmf1961   pr,pnx5973   ptn3808   himf,pnx7503

thy life: as   I was with Moses, *so* I will be   with thee: I will not   fail

wcj,ptn3808   qmf,pnx5800

thee, nor forsake thee.

qmv2388   wcj,qmv553   cj3588   (853)   df,pndm2088   df,nn5971   pnp859

6 Be strong and of a good courage: for unto   this   people shalt thou

himf5157   (853)   df,nn776   pnl834   nipf7650   pp,pl,nn,pnx1   pp,qnc5414

divide*for*an*inheritance   the land, which I swore unto their fathers to give

pp,pnx

them.

ad7535   qmv2388   ad3966   wcj,qmv553   pp,qnc8104   pp,qnc6213

☞ 7 Only be*thou*strong and very courageous, that thou mayest observe to do

pp,cs,nn3605   df,nn8451   pnl834   nn4872   nn,pnx5650   pipf,pnx6680   qmf5493 ptn408

according to   all   the law, which Moses my servant commanded thee: turn not

pr,pnx4480   nn3225   wcj,nn8040 cj4616   himf7919   pp,nn3605/pnl834

from it *to* the right hand or *to* the left, that thou mayest prosper whithersoever

qmf1980

thou goest.

df,pndm2088 cs,nn5612   df,nn8451   ptn3808 qmf4185   pr4480/nn,pnx6310

8 This   book of the law shall not depart out*of*thy*mouth; but thou shalt

wcs,qpf1897   pp,pnx   ad3119   wcj,nn3915 cj4616   qmf8104   pp,qnc6213

meditate therein day and night, that thou mayest observe to   do   according to

pp,cs,nn3605   df,qptp3789   pp,pnx   cj3588 ad227   himf6743 (853)   nn,pnx1870   himf6743

all   that is written therein: for then thou shalt make   thy way prosperous,

wcj,ad227   himf7919

and then thou shalt have*good*success.

he,ptn3808   pipf,pnx6680   qmv2388   wcj,qmv553

9 Have   not   I commanded thee? Be strong and of a good courage;

qmf6206/ptn408   wcj,ptn408   qmf2865   cj3588   nn3068   pl,nn,pnx430   pr,pnx5973

be*not*afraid, neither be*thou*dismayed: for the Lᴏʀᴅ thy   God *is* with thee

pp,nn3605/pnl834   qmf1980

whithersoever thou goest.

nn3091   wcs,pimf6680   (853)   pl,cs,qpta7860   df,nn5971   pp,qnc559

10 Then Joshua commanded   the officers of the people, saying,

qmv5674   pp,cs,nn7130   df,nn4264   wcj,pimv6680   (853)   df,nn5971   pp,qnc559   himv3559   pp,pnx

11 Pass through the host, and command   the people, saying, Prepare you

nn6720   cj3588 pp,ad5750   nu7969 pl,nn3117 pnp859   pl,qpta5674   (853) df,pndm2088   df,nn3383   pp,qnc935

victuals; for within three days ye shall pass over   this   Jordan, to go in to

pp,qnc3423 (853)   df,nn776   pnl834   nn3068   pl,nn,pnx430   qpta5414   pp,pnx   pp,qnc,pnx3423

possess   the land, which the Lᴏʀᴅ your God giveth you to possess it.

---

land to Israel; they are hard put to explain these references to places where the "sole of your foot shall tread,"
and to specific geographic features. There remains as yet an unfulfilled promise of this land to the descendants
of Israel.

☞ **1:7** The call to courage is really a call to faith. Believing God's promise would lead both to courage and
to obedience to the Law. God's promises must be appropriated in the same way today — by faith.

wcj,dfp,aj7206   wcj,dfp,aj1425   wcj,pp,cs,nn2677   cs,nn7626

12 And to the Reubenites, and to the Gadites, and to   half   the tribe of

df,nn4519   qpf559   nn3091   pp,qnc559

Manasseh, spoke Joshua, saying,

qna2142   (853)   df,nn1697   pnl834   nn4872   cs,nn5650   nn3068   pipf6680

◎⁓ 13 Remember   the word which Moses the servant of the LORD commanded

pnx(853)   pp,qnc559   nn3068   pl,nn,pnx430   hipt5117/pp,pnx   wcj,qpf5414 pp,pnx

you, saying, The LORD your God hath given*you*rest, and hath given you

(853) df,pndm2063 df,nn776

this   land.

pl,nn,pnx802   nn,pnx2945   wcj,pl,nn,pnx4735   qmf3427   dfp,nn776

14 Your wives, your little ones, and your cattle, shall remain in the land

pnl834   nn4872   qpf5414 pp,pnx   pp,cs,nn5676   df,nn3383   wcj,pnp859   qmf5674 pp,pl,cs,nn6440

which Moses gave you on*this*side Jordan; but ye   shall pass before your

pl,nn,pnx251   aj2571   cs,nn3605   pl,cs,nn1368   df,nn2428   wcs,qpf5826 pnx(853)

brethren armed,   all   the mighty men of valor, and help   them;

cj5704/pnl834   nn3068   himf5117   pp,pl,nn,pnx251 himf5117   pp,pnx

15 Until   the LORD have given your brethren rest, as*he*hath*given*you,

pnp1992 ad1571   wcj,qpf3423   (853)   df,nn776 pnl834   nn3068   pl,nn,pnx430 qpta5414   pp,pnx

and they also have possessed   the land which the LORD your God giveth them:

wcs,qpf7725   pp,cs,nn776   nn,pnx3425   wcs,qpf3423 pnx(853)   pnl834

then ye shall return unto the land of your possession, and enjoy   it, which

nn4872   nn3068   cs,nn5650 qpf5414 pp,pnx   pp,cs,nn5676   df,nn3383   cs,nn4217/df,nn8121

Moses the LORD's servant gave you on*this*side Jordan toward*the*sunrising.

wcs,qmf6030   (853)   nn3091   pp,qnc559 nn3605 pnl834   pipf,pnx6680

16 And they answered   Joshua, saying, All that thou commandest us we will

qmf6213   wcj,pr413/nn3605/pnl834   qmf,pnx7971   qmf1980

do, and whithersoever thou sendest us, we will go.

qpf8085   pr413   nn4872   pp,nn3605   pnl834   ad3651

17 According as we hearkened unto Moses in   all   things, so will we

qmf8085   pr,pnx413   ad7535   nn3068   pl,nn,pnx430 qmf1961 pr,pnx5973   pp,pnl834   qpf1961 pr5973

hearken unto thee: only the LORD thy God be with thee, as he was with

nn4872

Moses.

nn3605/nn376/pnl834   himf4784   (853)   nn,pnx6310

18 Whosoever he be that doth rebel against   thy commandment, and will

wcj,ptn3808   qmf8085   (853)   pl,nn,pnx1697   pp,nn3605 pnl834   pimf,pnx6680

not hearken unto   thy words in   all   that thou commandest him, he shall be

homf4191   ad7535   qmv2388   wcj,qmv553

put*to*death: only be strong and of a good courage.

Joshua Sends Spies

nn3091   cs,nn1121   nn5126 wcs,qmf7971   pr4480   df,nn7851   du,nu8147 pl,nn376   pl,pipt7270

2 ◎⁓ And Joshua the son of Nun sent out of Shittim two men to spy

ad2791   pp,qnc559   qmv1980 qmv7200 (853)   df,nn776   wcj(853)   nn3405   qmf1980

secretly, saying, Go view   the land, even   Jericho. And they went,

wcj,qmf935   nn802/qpta2181 cs,nn1004 wcj,nn,pnx8034   nn7343   wcs,qmf7901 ad,lh8033

and came into a harlot's house, named Rahab, and lodged there.

◎⁓ 1:13 It is important to realize that the term "rest," as used elsewhere, does not mean total peace; it is
a relative term.

◎⁓ 2:1 Some have tried to render this passage "the house of a woman" or "house of an innkeeper," but the
translation "harlot's house" is the correct one. The Hebrew term zānāh (2181) is the common word for an
"adulterer" or "prostitute" (Lev. 21:7; Jer. 5:7). Both the Old and New Testaments affirm that such a woman

wcs,nimf**559** pp,cs,nn**4428** nn3405 pp,qnc**559** ptdm2009 qpf935 pl,nn**376**

2 And it was told the king of Jericho, saying, Behold, there came men in

ad2008 df,nn**3915** pr4480/pl,cs,nn**1121** nn3478 pp,qnc2658 (853) df,nn**776**

hither tonight of*the*children of Israel to search out the country.

cs,nn**4428** nn3405 wcs,qmf7971 pr413 nn7343 pp,qnc**559** himv3318 df,pl,nn**376**

3 And the king of Jericho sent unto Rahab, saying, Bring forth the men

df,pl,qpta935 pr,pnx413 pnl834 qpf935 pp,nn,pnx**1004** cj3588 qpf935

that are come to thee, which are entered into thine house: for they be come

pp,qnc2658 (853) cs,nn3605 df,nn**776**

to search out all the country.

df,nn**802** wcs,qmf3947 (853) du,cs,nu8147 df,pl,nn**376** wcs,qmf6845 wcs,qmf**559**

4 And the woman took the two men, and hid them, and said

ad3651 qpf935 df,pl,nn**376** pr,pnx413 qpf3045 wcj,ptn**3808** pr4480/ad370 pnp1992

thus, There came men unto me, but I wist not whence they *were*:

wcs,qmf**1961** pp,qnc5462 df,nn8179

5 And it*came*to*pass *about the time* of shutting of the gate, when it was

dfp,nn**2822** wcj,df,pl,nn**376** qpf3318 ad,lh575 df,pl,nn**376** qpf**1980** qpf3045 ptn**3808** qmv7291 pr,pnx310

dark, that the men went out: whither the men went I know not: pursue after

pina4118 cj3588 himf,pnx5381

them quickly; for ye shall overtake them.

wcj,pnp1931 hipf,pnx**5927** df,nn,lh1406 wcs,qmf,pnx2934

6 But she had brought*them*up to the roof of the house, and hid

df,nn6086 pp,pl,cs,nn6593 df,pl,qptp6186/pp,pnx pr5921 df,nn1406

them with the stalks of flax, which she had laid*in*order upon the roof.

wcj,df,pl,nn**376** qpf7291 pr,pnx310 cs,nn**1870** df,nn3383 pr5921 df,pl,nn4569

7 And the men pursued after them the way to Jordan unto the fords: and

ad310/pp,pnl834 df,pl,qpta7291 pr,pnx310 qpf3318 qpf5462 wcj,df,nn8179

as*soon*as they which pursued after them were gone out, they shut the gate.

ad2962 wcj,pnp1992 qmf7901 wcj,pnp1931 qpf**5927** pr,pnx5921 pr5921

8 And before they were laid down, she came up unto them upon the

df,nn1406

roof;

wcs,qmf**559** pr413 df,pl,nn**376** qpf3045 cj3588 nn3068 qpf**5414** pp,pnx (853)

9 And she said unto the men, I know that the LORD hath given you the

df,nn**776** wcj,cj3588 nn,pnx367 qpf5307 pr,pnx5921 wcj,cj3588 cs,nn3605 pl,cs,qpta**3427**

land, and that your terror is fallen upon us, and that all the inhabitants of

df,nn**776** nipf4127 pr4480/pl,nn,pnx**6440**

the land faint because of you.

cj3588 qpf**8085** (853) pnl834 nn3068 hipf3001 (853) pl,cs,nn4325 nn5488

10 For we have heard how the LORD dried up the water of the Red

cs,nn3220 pr4480/pl,nn,pnx**6440** pp,qnc,pnx3318 pr4480/nn4714 wcj,pnl834 qpf6213

sea for you, when ye came out of Egypt; and what ye did unto the

pp,du,cs,nu8147 pl,cs,nn**4428** df,aj567 pnl834 pp,cs,nn5676 df,nn3383 pp,nn5511

two kings of the Amorites, that *were* on*the*other*side Jordan, Sihon and

wcj,pp,nn5747 pnl834 hipf**2763**/(pnx853)

Og, whom ye utterly destroyed.

---

can be pardoned (Luke 7:37). Rahab was not only pardoned, but raised to a position of honor. She married into an Israelite family, and was blessed by being the ancestor of David (Ruth 4:21, 22), thus placing her in the line of Jesus, the Messiah (Matt. 1:5). Moreover, she is enshrined in the New Testament "hall of faith" (Heb. 11:31; James 2:25). It was not unusual for strangers and foreigners to go to Rahab's house, thus the spies would not represent any unusual activity there. Also, the traffic through a harlot's house would provide information on the local situation. Rahab is another case in which God did not bless someone for lying, but for her faith in the report that the spies gave (see the note on Ex. 1:17–20). Note that in this case as well as in Exodus, the issue was the loss of human life.

wcs,qmf**8085**   nn,pnx3824   wcs,nimf4549   wcj,ptn**3808**

11 And as soon as we had heard *these things*, our hearts did melt, neither

qpf**6965**   ad5750   nn**7307**   pp,nn**376**   pr4480/pl,nn,pnx**6440**   cj3588   nn**3068**

did there remain any more courage in any man because of you: for the LORD your

pl,nn,pnx**430** pnp1931   pl,nn**430** dfp,du,nn**8064** pr4480/ad4605   wcj,pr5921 df,nn**776** pr4480/ad8478

God,   he *is* God in heaven above, and in   earth beneath.

wcj,ad6258   pte**4994**   nimv**7650**   pp,pnx   pp,nn**3068**   cj3588

12 Now therefore, I pray you, swear unto me by the LORD, since I have

qpf**6213**/pr,pnx5973/nn**2617**   pnp859   ad1571 wcj,qpf**6213**   nn**2617**   pr5973   nn,pnx1 cs,nn**1004**

showed*you*kindness, that ye will also show kindness unto my father's house,

wcj,qpf**5414** pp,pnx   nn**571** cs,nn**226**

and give me a true token:

wcj,hipf**2421**   (853)   nn,pnx1   wcj(853)   nn,pnx**517**   wcj(853)

13 And *that* ye will save alive   my father, and   my mother, and

pl,nn,pnx**251**   wcj(853)   pl,nn,pnx**269**   wcj(853) cs,nn3605 pnl834 pp,pnx   wcj,hipf**5337** (853)

my brethren, and   my sisters, and   all   that they have, and deliver   our

pl,nn,pnx**5315**   pr4480/nn**4194**

lives from death.

df,pl,nn**376** wcs,qmf**559**   pp,pnx   nn,pnx**5315** pr,pnx8478   (pp,qnc**4191**) cj518   himf**5046**

14 And the men answered her, Our life   for yours,   if ye utter

ptn**3808** (853) pndm2088   nn,pnx**1697**   wcs,qpf**1961**   nn**3068**   pp,qnc**5414** pp,pnx (853)

not   this our business. And it*shall*be, when the LORD hath given us   the

df,nn**776**   wcs,qpf**6213** nn**2617**   wcj,nn**571** pr,pnx5973

land, that we will deal kindly and truly with thee.

wcs,himf,pnx3381   dfp,nn**2256** cs,pr1157   df,nn**2474** cj3588   nn,pnx**1004**

15 Then she let*them*down by a cord through the window: for her house

df,nn**2346** pp,cs,nn**7023**   pnp1931 qpta**3427**   wcj,dfp,nn**2346**

was upon the town wall, and she dwelt upon the wall.

wcs,qmf**559**   pp,pnx   qm**1980**   df,nn,lh2022   cj6435   df,pl,qpta7291 qmf**6293**

16 And she said unto them, Get you to the mountain, lest the pursuers meet

pp,pnx   wcs,nipf2247   ad,lh8033   nu7969   pl,nn**3117** pr5704   df,pl,qpta7291   qnc**7725**

you; and hide yourselves there three days, until the pursuers be returned: and

wcj,ad310   qmf**1980**   pp,nn,pnx**1870**

afterward may ye go your way.

df,pl,nn**376** wcs,qmf**559** pr,pnx413   pnp587   aj**5355**   pr4480/nn,pnx**7621**/df,pndm2088

17 And the men   said unto her, We *will be* blameless of*this*thine*oath

pnl834   hipf,pnx**7650**

which thou hast made us swear.

ptdm2009   pnp587 pl,qpta935   dfp,nn**776**   qmf7194 (853) df,pndm2088 cs,nn8615

◎▱ 18 Behold, *when* we come into the land, thou shalt bind   this   line of

df,nn**8144** cs,nn2339   dfp,nn**2474** pnl834   hipf,pnx3381   pp,pnx   qmf**622**

scarlet thread in the window which thou didst let*us*down by: and thou shalt bring

wcj(853)   nn,pnx1   wcj(853)   nn,pnx**517**   wcj(853)   pl,nn,pnx**251**   wcj(853) cs,nn3605

thy father, and   thy mother, and   thy brethren, and   all thy

nn,pnx1   cs,nn**1004** df,nn,lh**1004** pr,pnx413

father's household, home unto thee.

wcs,qpf**1961**   nn3605/pnl834   qmf3318   pr4480/du,cs,nn1817   nn,pnx**1004**

19 And it*shall*be, *that* whosoever shall go out of*the*doors of thy house into

df,nn,lh2351   nn,pnx**1818**   pp,nn,pnx**7218** wcj,pnp587   aj**5355**

the street, his blood *shall be* upon his head,   and   we *will be* guiltless: and

---

◎▱ **2:18** Many writers have said that throughout Scripture this concept of the "scarlet thread" can be found: the line of blood atonement began in the Garden of Eden (Gen. 3:21), was exemplified in the Passover (Ex. 12:1–28), and was finally fulfilled in Christ's sacrifice on the cross (Heb. 9:22; 1 Pet. 1:19, 20). Here the thread was the means of deliverance for Rahab and her family. All who were to be delivered had to trust Rahab and stay in her house.

wcj,nn3605/pnl834   qmf**1961** pr,pnx854   dfp,nn**1004**   nn,pnx**1818**   pp,nn,pnx**7218** cj518

whosoever shall be with thee in the house, his blood *shall be* on our head, if

nn**3027** qmf**1961**   pp,pnx

any hand be upon him.

wcj,cj518   himf**5046** (853) pndm2088   nn,pnx**1697**   wcs,qpf**1961** aj**5355**

20 And if thou utter this our business, then we will be quit

pr4480/nn,pnx**7621** pnl834   hipf,pnx**7650**

of*thine*oath which thou hast made us to swear.

wcs,qmf**559**   pp,pl,nn,pnx**1697** ad**3651**   pnp1931

21 And she said, According unto your words, so *be* it. And she

wcs,pimf,pnx**7971**   wcs,qmf**1980**   wcs,qmf**7194** (853)   df,nn**8144** cs,nn**8615**

sent*them*away, and they departed: and she bound the scarlet line in the

dfp,nn**2474**

window.

wcs,qmf**1980**   wcs,qmf**935**   df,nn,lh**2022**   wcs,qmf**3427** ad**8033** nu**7969** pl,nn**3117**

22 And they went, and came unto the mountain, and abode there three days,

cj**5704**   df,pl,qpta**7291**   qpf**7725**   df,pl,qpta**7291** wcs,pimf**1245**   pp,cs,nn**3605**

until the pursuers were returned: and the pursuers sought *them* throughout all

df,nn**1870**   qpf**4672**   wcj,ptn**3808**

the way, but found *them* not.

du,cs,nu8147   df,pl,nn**376**   wcs,qmf**7725**   wcs,qmf**3381**   pr4480/df,nn2022

23 So the two men returned, and descended from*the*mountain, and

wcs,qmf**5674**   wcs,qmf**935** pr413   nn3091   cs,nn**1121**   nn5126   wcs,pimf**5608** pp,pnx (853) cs,nn**3605**

passed over, and came to Joshua the son of Nun, and told him all

df,pl,qpta**4672** pnx(853)

things that befell them:

wcs,qmf**559** pr413   nn3091   cj3588   nn**3068**   qpf**5414**   pp,nn,pnx**3027**

24 And they said unto Joshua, Truly the LORD hath delivered into our hands

(853) cs,nn**3605**   df,nn**776**   wcj,ad1571 cs,nn**3605**   pl,cs,qpta**3427**   df,nn**776**   nipf4127

all the land; for even all the inhabitants of the country do faint

pr4480/pl,nn,pnx**6440**

because of us.

Israel Crosses the Jordan

nn3091   wcs,himf**7925**   dfp,nn**1242**   wcs,qmf**5265**   pr4480/df,nn**7851**

3 And Joshua rose early in the morning; and they removed from Shittim, and

wcs,qmf**935** pr5704   df,nn**3383** pnp1931   wcj,cs,nn**3605**   pl,cs,nn**1121**   nn3478   wcs,qmf**3885**

came to Jordan, he and all the children of Israel, and lodged

ad**8033** ad2962   qmf**5674**

there before they passed over.

wcs,qmf**1961**   pr4480/cs,nn**7097** nu**7969** pl,nn**3117**   df,pl,nn**7860** wcs,qmf**5674** pp,cs,nn**7130**

2 And it*came*to*pass after three days, that the officers went through

df,nn**4264**

the host;

wcs,pimf**6680** (853)   df,nn**5971** pp,qnc559   pp,qnc,pnx**7200** (853)   cs,nn**727**

3 And they commanded the people, saying, When ye see the ark

cs,nn**1285**   nn**3068**   pl,nn,pnx**430**   wcj,df,pl,nn**3548**   df,pl,nn**3881** pl,qpta**5375** pnx(853)

of the covenant of the LORD your God, and the priests the Levites bearing

wcj,pnp859   qmf**5265**   pr4480/nn,pnx**4725**   wcs,qpf**1980** pr,pnx310

it, then ye shall remove from*your*place, and go after it.

ad389   qmf**1961**   aj7350   pr,pnx996   wcj,pnx(pr996)   pp,du,nu**505**

4 Yet there shall be a space between you and it, about two thousand

nn520   dfp,nn4060   ptn408/qmf7126   pr,pnx413   cj4616/pnl834   qmf3045 (853)   df,nn1870
cubits by measure: come*not*near unto it,   that   ye may know   the way by

pnl834   qmf1980/pp,pnx cj3588   ptn3808   qpf5674   dfp,nn1870 pr4480/ad8543/ad8032
which ye must   go: for ye have not passed *this* way   heretofore.

            nn3091   wcs,qmf559   pr413   df,nn5971   htmv6942   cj3588   ad4279
5 And Joshua   said   unto the people, Sanctify yourselves: for tomorrow the
nn3068   qmf6213   pl,nipt6381   pp,pnx7130
LORD will do   wonders among you.

            nn3091   wcs,qmf559   pr413   df,pl,nn3548   pp,qnc559   qmv5375   (853)   cs,nn727
6 And Joshua spoke unto the priests, saying, Take up   the ark of the
df,nn1285   wcj,qmv5674   pp,pl,cs,nn6440   df,nn5971   wcs,qmf5375 (853)   cs,nn727
covenant, and pass over before the people. And they took up   the ark of the
df,nn1285   wcs,qmf1980 pp,pl,cs,nn6440   df,nn5971
covenant, and went   before the people.

            nn3068   wcs,qmf559 pr413   nn3091   df,pndm2088 df,nn3117   himf2490   pinc,pnx1431
7 And the LORD said unto Joshua, This   day will I begin to magnify thee
pp,du,cs,nn5869   cs,nn3605 nn3478 pnl834   qmf3045 cj3588 pp,pnl834   qpf1961 pr5973   nn4872
in the   sight   of all Israel, that they may know that,   as   I was with Moses,
qmf1961 pr,pnx5973
so I will be   with thee.

wcj,pnp859   pimf6680   (853)   df,pl,nn3548   pl,cs,qpta5375   cs,nn727
8 And thou shalt command   the priests that   bear   the ark of the
df,nn1285   pp,qnc559   pp,qnc,pnx935 pr5704   cs,nn7097   pl,cs,nn4325   df,nn3383
covenant, saying, When ye are   come   to the brink of the water of Jordan, ye
qmf5975   dfp,nn3383
shall stand still in Jordan.

            nn3091   wcs,qmf559   pr413   pl,cs,nn1121   nn3478   qmv5066   ad2008   wcj,qmv8085 (853)
9 And Joshua   said   unto the children of Israel, Come hither, and   hear
pl,cs,nn1697   nn3068   pl,nn,pnx430
the words of the LORD your God.

            nn3091   wcs,qmf559 pp,pndm2063   qmf3045 cj3588   aj2416   nn410   pp,nn,pnx7130
10 And Joshua said, Hereby ye shall know that the living God *is* among you,
          wcj,hina3423/himf3423   pr4480/pl,nn,pnx6440   (853)   df,nn3669
and *that* he will without*fail*drive*out from before you   the Canaanites, and
wcj(853)   df,nn2850   wcj(853)   df,nn2340   wcj(853)   df,nn6522   wcj(853)
the Hittites, and   the Hivites, and   the Perizzites, and   the
df,nn1622   wcj,df,nn567   wcj,df,nn2983
Girgashites, and the Amorites, and the Jebusites.

            ptdm2009   cs,nn727   df,nn1285   cs,nn113 cs,nn3605   df,nn776   qpta5674
11 Behold, the ark of the covenant of the Lord of all   the earth passeth over
pp,pl,nn,pnx6440   dfp,nn3383
before   you into Jordan.

            wcj,ad6258   qmv3947 pp,pnx du,cs,nu8147/nu6240 nn376   pr4480/pl,cs,nn7626   nn3478
12 Now therefore take you   twelve   men out*of*the*tribes of Israel, out
nn376/nu259/nn376/nu259/dfp,nn7626
of every*tribe*a*man.

            wcs,qpf1961   df,pl,cs,nn3709   du,cs,nn7272
13 And it*shall*come*to*pass, as soon as the soles of the feet   of the
df,pl,nn3548   pl,cs,qpta5375   cs,nn727   nn3068   cs,nn113 cs,nn3605 df,nn776   pp,qnc5117
priests that bear   the ark of the LORD, the Lord of all   the earth, shall   rest
pp,pl,cs,nn4325   df,nn3383   pl,cs,nn4325   df,nn3383   nimf3772   df,pl,nn4325
in the waters of Jordan, *that* the waters of Jordan shall be cut off *from* the waters
df,pl,qpta3381   pr4480/pp,ad,lh4605   wcj,qmf5975   nu259 nn5067
that come down from above; and they shall stand upon a heap.

            wcs,qmf1961   df,nn5971   pp,qnc5265   pr4480/pl,nn,pnx168
14 And it*came*to*pass, when the people removed from*their*tents, to

pp,qnc5674 (853) df,nn3383 wcj,df,pl,nn3548 pl,cs,qpta5375 df,nn727 df,nn1285 pp,pl,cs,nn6440

pass over Jordan, and the priests bearing the ark of the covenant before the

df,nn5971

people;

pl,cs,qpta5375 df,nn727 wcj,pp,qnc935 pr5704 df,nn3383

☞ 15 And as they that bore the ark were come unto Jordan, and the

wcj,du,cs,nn7272 df,pl,nn3548 pl,cs,qpta5375 df,nn727 nipf2881 pp,cs,nn7097

feet of the priests that bore the ark were dipped in the brim of the

df,pl,nn4325 wcj,df,nn3383 qpta4390/pr5921 cs,nn3605 pl,nn,pnx1415 cs,nn3605 pl,cs,nn3117 nn7105

water, (for Jordan overfloweth all his banks all the time of harvest,)

df,pl,nn4325 df,pl,qpta3381 pr4480/pp,ad,lh4605 wcs,qmf5975 qpf6965

16 That the waters which came down from above stood *and* rose up upon

nu259 nn5067 ad3966 hina7368 df,nn5892 pr4480/nn121 pnl834 pr4480/cs,nn6654 nn6891

a heap very far from the city Adam, that *is* beside Zaretan: and those that

wcj,df,pl,qpta3381 pr5921 cs,nn3220 df,nn6160 df,nn4417 cs,nn3220 qpf8552

came down toward the sea of the plain, *even* the salt sea, failed, *and* were

nipf3772 wcj,df,nn5971 qpf5674 pr5048 nn3405

cut off: and the people passed over right against Jericho.

df,pl,nn3548 pl,cs,qpta5375 df,nn727 cs,nn1285 nn3068 wcs,qmf5975

17 And the priests that bore the ark of the covenant of the LORD stood

hina3559 dfp,nn2724 pp,cs,nn8432 df,nn3383 wcj,cs,nn3605 nn3478 pl,qpta5674

firm on dry ground in the midst of Jordan, and all the Israelites passed over

dfp,nn2724 cj5704/pnl834 cs,nn3605 df,nn1471 pp,qnc5674 qpf8552 pp,qnc5674 (853) df,nn3383

on dry ground, until all the people were passed clean over Jordan.

Stone Monument Set Up at Gilgal

wcs,qmf1961 pp,pnl834 cs,nn3605 df,nn1471 qpf8552 pp,qnc5674 (853)

4 And it*came*to*pass, when all the people were clean passed over

df,nn3383 nn3068 wcs,qmf559 pr413 nn3091 pp,qnc559

Jordan, that the LORD spoke unto Joshua, saying,

qmv3947 pp,pnx du,nu8147/nu6240 pl,nn376 pr4480 df,nn5971 nn376/nu259/nn376/nu259/pr4480/nn7626

2 Take you twelve men out of the people, out*of*every*tribe*a*man,

wcj,pimv6680 pnx(853) pp,qnc559 qmv5375 pp,pnx pr4480/pndm2088 pr4480/cs,nn8432

3 And command ye them, saying, Take you hence out*of*the*midst

df,nn3383 pr4480/cs,nn4673 df,pl,nn3548 du,cs,nn7272 hina3559 du,nu8147/nu6240 pl,nn68

of Jordan, out*of*the*place where the priests' feet stood firm, twelve stones,

wcj,hipf5674/pnx(853) pr,pnx5973 wcj,hipf5117 pnx(853)

and ye shall carry*them*over with you, and leave them in the

dfp,nn4411 pnl834/pp,pnx qmf3885 df,nn,lh3915

lodging place, where ye shall lodge this night.

nn3091 wcs,qmf7121/pr413 du,nu8147/df,nu6240 nn376 pnl834 hipf3559

4 Then Joshua called the twelve men, whom he had prepared

pr4480/pl,cs,nn1121 nn3478 nn376/nu259/nn376/nu259/pr4480/nn7626

of*the*children of Israel, out*of*every*tribe*a*man:

☞ **3:15-17** Notice that the Lord did not stop the flow of the Jordan until the priests' feet were actually in the water. They were called upon to exercise their faith first. The swollen condition of the Jordan River at that time of the year emphasizes God's miraculous provision for Israel. Since irrigation now drains off much of its water, the Jordan no longer floods as it once did. Some scholars have suggested that an earthquake or landslide stopped the flow, but the text of Scripture refutes any attempt at explaining away God's supernatural intervention. The Jordan lies in a deep valley, and so does not spread out when it is flooded. It merely goes over its normal banks, and further up the valley sides. When it is flooded, the only way to get across the water is to swim or sail, but neither of these methods would have been possible for several million Israelites with children, livestock, and household goods.

nn3091   wcs,qmf559   pp,pnx   qmv5674   pp,pl,cs,nn6440   cs,nn727   nn3068

5 And Joshua said unto them, Pass over before the ark of the LORD your

pl,nn,pnx430 pr413   cs,nn8432   df,nn3383   wcj,himv7311/pp,pnx   nn376   nu259 nn68 pr5921

God into the midst of Jordan, and take*ye*up every man of you a stone upon

nn,pnx7926   pp,cs,nn4557   pl,cs,nn7626   pl,cs,nn1121   nn3478

his shoulder, according unto the number of the tribes of the children of Israel:

pp,cj4616 pndm2063   qmf1961   nn226 pp,nn,pnx7130   cj3588   pl,nn,pnx1121 qmf7592

6 That this may be a sign among you, *that* when your children ask *their*

ad4279   pp,qnc559   pnit4100   pp,pnx   df,pndm428 df,pl,nn68

fathers in*time*to*come, saying, What *mean* ye by these stones?

wcs,qpf559   pp,pnx   pnl834   pl,cs,nn4325   df,nn3383   nipf3772

7 Then ye shall answer them, That the waters of Jordan were cut off

pr4480/pl,cs,nn6440   cs,nn727   cs,nn1285   nn3068   pp,qnc,pnx5674   dfp,nn3091

before the ark of the covenant of the LORD; when it passed over Jordan, the

pl,cs,nn4325   df,nn3383   nipf3772   df,pndm428 df,pl,nn68   wcj,qpf1961   pp,nn2146

waters of Jordan were cut off: and these stones shall be for a memorial unto

pp,pl,cs,nn1121   nn3478 pr5704/nn5769

the children of Israel forever.

pl,cs,nn1121   nn3478 wcs,qmf6213 ad3651 pp,pnl834   nn3091   pipf6680   wcs,qmf5375

8 And the children of Israel did so as Joshua commanded, and took up

du,nu8147/nu6240   pl,nn68   pr4480/cs,nn8432   df,nn3383 pp,pnl834   nn3068 pipf1696 pr413   nn3091

twelve stones out*of*the*midst of Jordan, as the LORD spoke unto Joshua,

pp,cs,nn4557   pl,cs,nn7626   pl,cs,nn1121   nn3478

according to the number of the tribes of the children of Israel, and

wcs,himf,pnx5674   pr,pnx5973   pr413   df,nn4411

carried*them*over with them unto the place*where*they*lodged, and

wcs,himf,pnx5117   ad8033

laid*them*down there.

nn3091   hipf6965 wcj,du,nu8147/nu6240   pl,nn68   pp,cs,nn8432   df,nn3383   pr8478

☉☛ 9 And Joshua set up twelve stones in the midst of Jordan, in*the*place

du,cs,nn7272   df,pl,nn3548   pl,cs,qpta5375   cs,nn727   df,nn1285   cs,nn4673

where the feet of the priests which bore the ark of the covenant stood: and

wcs,qmf1961   ad8033   pr5704 df,pndm2088 df,nn3117

they are there unto this day.

wcj,df,pl,nn3548   pl,cs,qpta5375   df,nn727 pl,qpta5975   pp,cs,nn8432   df,nn3383

☉☛ 10 For the priests which bore the ark stood in the midst of Jordan,

pr5704   cs,nn3605/df,nn1697   qnc8552   pnl834   nn3068   pipf6680   (853)   nn3091 pp,pinc1696 pr413

until every thing was finished that the LORD commanded Joshua to speak unto

df,nn5971   pp,nn3605 pnl834   nn4872   pipf6680   (853)   nn3091   df,nn5971

the people, according to all that Moses commanded Joshua: and the people

wcs,pimf4116   wcs,qmf5674

hasted and passed over.

wcs,qmf1961   pp,pnl834 cs,nn3605   df,nn5971   qpf8552   pp,qnc5674

11 And it*came*to*pass, when all the people were clean passed over, that

cs,nn727   nn3068 wcs,qmf5674   wcj,df,pl,nn3548   pp,pl,cs,nn6440   df,nn5971

the ark of the LORD passed over, and the priests, in the presence of the people.

pl,cs,nn1121   nn7205   wcj,pl,cs,nn1121   nn1410   wcj,cs,nn2677   cs,nn7626

12 And the children of Reuben, and the children of Gad, and half the tribe

---

☉☛ **4:9** The phrase "unto this day" signifies that when Joshua wrote this book at the end of his life (Josh. 24:26), these two pillars were still standing. For most of the year, the Jordan is a shallow river so the pillar of stones in the center of it would be visible as a sign.

☉☛ **4:10** Moses told Joshua that God would speak through him to the people and that God would be with him (see Deut. 31:7, 8).

df,nn4519   wcs,qmf5674   aj2571   pp,pl,cs,nn6440   pl,cs,nn1121   nn3478   pp,pnl834   nn4872   pipf1696

of Manasseh, passed over armed before the children of Israel, as Moses spoke

pr,pnx413

unto them:

pp,pl,nu705   nu505   pl,cs,qptp2502   df,nn6635   qpf5674   pp,pl,cs,nn6440   nn3068

13 About forty thousand prepared for war passed over before the LORD

dfp,nn4421 pr413   pl,cs,nn6160   nn3405

unto battle, to the plains of Jericho.

df,pndm1931 dfp,nn3117   nn3068   pipf1431   (853)   nn3091   pp,du,cs,nn5869   cs,nn3605

14 On that day the LORD magnified Joshua in the sight of all

nn3478   wcs,qmf3372 pnx(853)   pp,pnl834   qpf3372   (853)   nn4872   cs,nn3605   pl,cs,nn3117

Israel; and they feared him, as they feared Moses, all the days of

pl,nn,pnx2416

his life.

nn3068   wcs,qmf559 pr413   nn3091   pp,qnc559

15 And the LORD spoke unto Joshua, saying,

pimv6680   (853)   df,pl,nn3548   pl,cs,qpta5375   cs,nn727   df,nn5715

16 Command the priests that bear the ark of the testimony, that they

wcj,qmf5927   pr4480   df,nn3383

come up out of Jordan.

nn3091   wcs,pimf6680   (853)   df,pl,nn3548   pp,qnc559   qmv5927   pr4480

17 Joshua therefore commanded the priests, saying, Come*ye*up out of

df,nn3383

Jordan.

wcs,qmf1961   df,pl,nn3548   pl,cs,qpta5375   cs,nn727   cs,nn1285

18 And it*came*to*pass, when the priests that bore the ark of the covenant

nn3068   pp,qnc5927   pr4480/cs,nn8432   df,nn3383   pl,cs,nn3709

of the LORD were come up out*of*the*midst of Jordan, and the soles of the

df,pl,nn3548 du,cs,nn7272   nipf5423   pr413   df,nn2724   pl,cs,nn4325   df,nn3383 wcs,qmf7725

priests' feet were lifted up unto the dry land, that the waters of Jordan returned

pp,nn,pnx4725   wcs,qmf1980 pr5921 cs,nn3605   pl,nn,pnx1415 pp,ad8543   ad8032

unto their place, and flowed over all his banks, as they did before.

wcj,df,nn5971   qpf5927   pr4480   df,nn3383   dfp,nn6218   df,aj7223

☞ 19 And the people came up out of Jordan on the tenth day of the first

dfp,nn2320   wcs,qmf2583   dfp,nn1537   cs,nn4217 pp,cs,nn7097   nn3405

month, and encamped in Gilgal, in the east border of Jericho.

wcj(853)   df,pndm428   du,nu8147/nu6240   df,pl,nn68   pnl834   qpf3947   pr4480   df,nn3383

20 And those twelve stones, which they took out of Jordan, did

nn3091   hipf6965   dfp,nn1537

Joshua pitch in Gilgal.

wcs,qmf559   pr413   pl,cs,nn1121   nn3478   pp,qnc559   pnl834   pl,nn,pnx1121

21 And he spoke unto the children of Israel, saying, When your children shall

qmf7592 (853)   pl,nn,pnx1   ad4279   pp,qnc559 pnit4100   df,pndm428 df,pl,nn68

ask their fathers in*time*to*come, saying, What mean these stones?

☞ **4:19** After crossing the Jordan, Israel camped at Gilgal for a while before the conquest of Canaan began. Several things happened at Gilgal which signified that the wilderness wanderings were over and that Israel was embarking on a new phase of her national history. First, Joshua had the people set up twelve stones as a monument to the miraculous drying up of the Jordan for their crossing (Josh. 4:19–24). Next, the young males were circumcised, which reinstituted a practice that had not been kept for nearly forty years (5:2–9). With that accomplished (see Ex. 12:48), they could then observe the Passover (5:10). Finally, and probably most indicative of the end of their wanderings, on the day after the Passover, the manna stopped, and they ate from the produce of Canaan (5:11, 12).

(853)   pl,nn,pnx1121 wcs,hipf3045 pp,qnc559   nn3478   qpf5674   (853)
22 Then ye shall let   your children know, saying, Israel came over

df,pndm2088 df,nn3383   dfp,nn3004
this   Jordan on dry land.

pnl834   nn3068   pl,nn,pnx430   hipf3001   (853)   pl,cs,nn4325   df,nn3383 pr4480/pl,nn,pnx6440
23 For the LORD your   God dried up   the waters of Jordan from before

cj5704   qnc,pnx5674   pp,pnl834   nn3068   pl,nn,pnx430 qpf6213   nn5488 pp,cs,nn3220
you, until ye were passed over,   as   the LORD your   God   did to the Red   sea,

pnl834   hipf3001   pr4480/pl,nn,pnx6440   cj5704   qnc,pnx5674
which he dried up from before us, until we were gone over:

cj4616   cs,nn3605   pl,cs,nn5971   df,nn776   qnc3045 (853)   cs,nn3027   nn3068
24 That   all   the people of the earth might know   the hand of the LORD,

cj3588 pndm1931   aj2389   cj4616   qpf3372 (853)   nn3068   pl,nn,pnx430 cs,nn3605/df,pl,nn3117
that   it   is mighty: that ye might fear   the LORD your   God   forever.

Circumcision and Passover At Gilgal

wcs,qmf1961   cs,nn3605   pl,cs,nn4428   df,nn567   pnl834
5 And it*came*to*pass, when   all   the   kings of the Amorites, which *were*

pp,cs,nn5676   df,nn3383 nn,lh3220   wcj,cs,nn3605   pl,cs,nn4428
on the   side   of Jordan westward, and   all   the   kings of the

df,nn3669   pnl834   pr5921   df,nn3220 pp,qnc8085 (853) pnl834   nn3068   hipf3001   (853)
Canaanites, which *were* by   the sea,   heard   that the LORD had dried up   the

pl,cs,nn4325   df,nn3383   pr4480/pl,cs,nn6440   pl,cs,nn1121   nn3478   pr5704   qnc,pnx5674
waters of Jordan from before the children of Israel, until we were passed over, that

nn,pnx3824 wcs,nimf4549 wcj,ptn3808 qpf1961   nn7307   pp,pnx   ad5750   pr4480/pl,cs,nn6440
their heart melted, neither was there spirit in them any more,   because of the

pl,cs,nn1121   nn3478
children of Israel.

df,pndm1931 dfp,nn6256   nn3068   qpf559   pr413   nn3091   qmv6213   pp,pnx pl,nn6864 pl,cs,nn2719
2 At   that   time the LORD said unto Joshua, Make thee sharp knives, and

qmv4135   wcj,qmv7725 (853)   pl,cs,nn1121   nn3478   nuor8145
circumcise again   the children of Israel the second time.

nn3091   wcs,qmf6213 pp,pnx pl,nn6864 pl,cs,nn2719   wcs,qmf4135   (853)   pl,cs,nn1121
3 And Joshua made him sharp knives, and circumcised   the children of

nn3478   pr413   cs,nn1389   df,pl,nn6190
Israel at the hill of the foreskins.

wcj,pndm2088   df,nn1697 pnl834   nn3091   qpf4135   cs,nn3605   df,nn5971
4 And   this   is the cause why Joshua did circumcise: All the people that

df,qpta3318   pr4480/nn4714   df,aj2145   cs,nn3605   pl,cs,nn376   df,nn4421 qpf4191
came out of Egypt, *that were* males, *even* all   the men of war, died in the

dfp,nn4057   dfp,nn1870   pp,qnc,pnx3318   pr4480/nn4714
wilderness by the way, after they came out of Egypt.

cj3588 cs,nn3605   df,nn5971   df,pl,qpta3318 qpf1961   pl,qptp4135   wcj,cs,nn3605   df,nn5971
5 Now   all   the people that came out were circumcised: but   all   the people

df,aj3209   dfp,nn4057   dfp,nn1870   pp,qnc,pnx3318   pr4480/nn4714
that were born in the wilderness by the way as they came forth out*of*Egypt,

ptn3808   qpf4135
them they had not circumcised.

cj3588   pl,cs,nn1121   nn3478   qpf1980 pl,nu705 nn8141   dfp,nn4057   pr5704 cs,nn3605
6 For the children of Israel walked forty years in the wilderness, till   all   the

df,nn1471   pl,cs,nn376   df,nn4421   df,pl,qpta3318   pr4480/nn4714   qnc8552
people *that were* men   of war, which came out of Egypt, were consumed,

pnl834   qpf8085   ptn3808   pp,cs,nn6963   nn3068   pnl834/pp,pnx   nn3068 nipf7650
because they obeyed not the voice of the LORD: unto whom the LORD swore that

pp,ptn1115 hinc,pnx7200   (853)   df,nn776 pnl834   nn3068 nipf7650   pp,pl,nn,pnx1

he would   not   show   them   the land, which the LORD swore unto their fathers

pp,qnc5414 pp,pnx   nn776   cs,qpta2100   nn2461   wcj,nn1706

that he would give us, a land that floweth with milk and honey.

wcj(853)   pl,nn,pnx1121   hipf6965   pr,pnx8478 pnx(853)   nn3091

7 And   their children, *whom* he raised up in their stead,   them Joshua

qpf4135   cj3588   qpf1961   aj6189   cj3588   ptn3808 qpf4135   pnx(853)

circumcised: for they were uncircumcised, because they had not circumcised

dfp,nn1870

them by the way.

wcs,qmf1961   pp,pnl834   qpf8552   pp,ninc4135   cs,nn3605   df,nn1471

8 And it*came*to*pass, when they had done circumcising all the people, that

wcs,qmf3427   pr,pnx8478   dfp,nn4264 pr5704   qnc,pnx2421

they abode in their places in the camp, till they were whole.

nn3068   wcs,qmf559   pr413   nn3091   df,nn3117   qnc,pnx1556   (853)

9 And the LORD   said   unto Joshua, This day have I rolled away   the

cs,nn2781   nn4714 pr4480/pr,pnx5921   cs,nn8034   (df,pndm1931)   df,nn4725

reproach of Egypt from off you. Wherefore the name of   the place is

wcs,qmf7121 nn1537 pr5704 df,pndm2088 df,nn3117

called Gilgal unto   this   day.

pl,cs,nn1121   nn3478 wcs,qmf2583   dfp,nn1537   wcs,qmf6213 (853)   df,nn6453

10 And the children of Israel encamped in Gilgal, and   kept   the passover

pp,nu702/nu6240 nn3117   dfp,nn2320   dfp,nn6153   pp,pl,cs,nn6160   nn3405

on the fourteenth day of the month at even in the plains of Jericho.

wcs,qmf398   pr4480/cs,nn5669   df,nn776   pr4480/cs,nn4283

11 And they did   eat   of*the*old*corn of the land on*the*morrow*after the

df,nn6453   pl,nn4682   wcj,qptp7033   pp,cs,nn6106/df,pndm2088 df,nn3117

passover, unleavened cakes, and parched *corn* in the   selfsame   day.

df,nn4478   wcs,qmf7673   pr4480/nn4283   pp,qnc,pnx398

12 And   the   manna   ceased   on*the*morrow   after   they   had   eaten

pr4480/cs,nn5669   df,nn776 wcj,ptn3808 qpf1961   pp,pl,cs,nn1121   nn3478 nn4478   ad5750

of*the*old*corn of the land; neither had the children of Israel manna any more; but

wcs,qmf398   pr4480/cs,nn8393   nn776   nn3667   df,pndm1931 dfp,nn8141

they did   eat   of*the*fruit of the land of Canaan   that   year.

wcs,qmf1961   nn3091   pp,qnc1961   pp,nn3405   wcs,qmf5375

13 And it*came*to*pass, when Joshua   was   by Jericho, that he lifted up his

du,nn,pnx5869   wcs,qmf7200   wcj,ptdm2009   qpta5975   nn376   pp,pr,pnx5048

eyes   and looked, and, behold, there stood a man over against him with his

wcj,nn,pnx2719   qptp8025   pp,nn,pnx3027   nn3091 wcs,qmf1980   pr,pnx413   wcs,qmf559   pp,pnx

sword drawn in his   hand: and Joshua went unto him, and   said   unto him,

pnp859 he,pp,pnx   cj518   pp,pl,nn,pnx6862

Art thou for us,   or for our adversaries?

wcs,qmf559   ptn3808 cj3808   cs,nn8269   cs,nn6635   nn3068   pnp589 ad6258

14 And   he   said,   Nay; but *as* captain of the host of the LORD am   I   now

qpf935   nn3091 wcs,qmf5307 pr413   pl,nn,pnx6440   nn,lh776   wcs,htmf7812   wcs,qmf559

come. And Joshua   fell   on his   face   to the earth, and did worship, and   said

pp,pnx   pnit4100 pipt1696   nn,pnx113 pr413   nn,pnx5650

unto him, What saith my lord unto his servant?

cs,nn8269   nn3068 cs,nn6635 wcs,qmf559 pr413   nn3091   qmv5394   nn,pnx5275

15 And the captain of the LORD's host   said   unto Joshua, Loose thy   shoe

---

The man who is called "the captain of the host of the LORD" is actually the Angel of the LORD, a preincarnate appearance of Jesus Christ (Ex. 3:2–6; Judg. 6:12, 16). This is seen in the use of the phrase in verse fifteen: "Loose thy shoe from off thy foot; for the place whereon thou standest is holy." No man or angel could pronounce a place "holy." The angel of the LORD also appeared to Moses in the burning bush and used this phrase commanding Moses to take his shoes off (Ex. 3:5).

pr4480/pr5921   nn,pnx7272   cj3588   df,nn4725   pnl834/pr,pnx5921 pnp859   qpta5975   (pndm1931)   nn**6944**

from off thy foot; for the place whereon thou standest   *is* holy. And

nn3091   wcs,qmf**6213** ad**3651**

Joshua did   so.

Jericho Falls

wcj,nn3405   qpta5462/wcj,pupt5462   pr4480/pl,cs,nn**6440**   pl,cs,nn**1121**   nn3478

6 ☜ Now Jericho was straitly*shut*up because of the children of Israel:

ptn369   qpta3318   wcj,ptn369   qpta935

none went out, and none came in.

nn**3068**   wcs,qmf**559**   pr413   nn3091   qmv**7200**   qpf**5414**   pp,nn,pnx**3027** (853)

2 And the LORD said unto Joshua, See, I have given into thine hand

nn3405   wcj(853)   nn,pnx**4428**   cs,aj1368   df,nn**2428**

Jericho, and   the king thereof, *and* the mighty men*of*valor.

wcj,qpf5437   (853)   df,nn5892   cs,nn3605   pl,cs,nn**376**   df,nn4421

3 And ye shall compass   the city,   all   *ye* men   of war,   *and*

hina**5362**   (853)   df,nn5892 nu259/nn6471 ad3541   qmf**6213** cs,nu8337 pl,nn**3117**

go*round*about   the city   once. Thus shalt thou do   six days.

wcj,nu7651   pl,nn**3548**   qmf**5375** pp,pl,cs,nn**6440**   df,nn**727**   nu7651   pl,cs,nn7782

4 And   seven   priests shall bear before the ark seven trumpets of

df,pl,nn3104   df,nuor7637 wcj,dfp,nn**3117**   qmf5437 (853)   df,nn5892 nu7651 pl,nn6471

rams' horns: and the seventh   day   ye shall compass   the city seven times,

wcj,df,pl,nn**3548**   qmf**8628**   dfp,pl,nn7782

and the   priests   shall blow with the trumpets.

wcs,qpf**1961**   pp,qnc4900   df,nn3104

5 And it*shall*come*to*pass, that when they make*a*long*blast with the ram's

pp,cs,nn**7161**   pp,qnc,pnx**8085** (853)   cs,nn6963   df,nn7782   cs,nn3605   df,nn**5971**

horn, *and* when ye   hear   the sound of the trumpet, all   the people shall

him**i7321**   aj1419   nn8643   cs,nn2346   df,nn5892   wcs,qpf**5307**   pr,pnx8478

shout with a great shout; and the wall of the city shall fall down flat, and the

df,nn**5971**   wcs,qpf**5927**   nn**376**   pr,pnx5048

people shall ascend up every man straight before him.

nn3091   cs,nn**1121**   nn5126 wcs,qmf**7121**/pr413   dfp,pl,nn**3548**   wcs,qmf**559** pr,pnx413

6 And Joshua the son of Nun called   the priests, and said   unto them,

qmv**5375** (853)   cs,nn**727**   df,nn**1285**   qmf**5375** wcj,nu7651 pl,nn**3548** qmf**5375** nu7651   pl,cs,nn7782

Take up   the ark of the covenant, and let seven priests bear seven trumpets

pl,nn3104   pp,pl,cs,nn**6440**   cs,nn**727**   nn**3068**

of rams' horns before the ark of the LORD.

wcs,qmf**559** pr413   df,nn**5971**   qmv**5674**   wcj,qmv5437 (853)   df,nn5892

7 And he said unto the people, Pass on, and compass   the city, and let

wcj,df,qptp2502   qmf**5674**   pp,pl,cs,nn**6440**   cs,nn**727**   nn**3068**

him that is armed pass on before the ark of the LORD.

wcs,qmf**1961**   nn3091   pp,qnc559   pr413   df,nn**5971**

8 And it*came*to*pass, when Joshua had spoken unto the people, that the

---

☜ **6:1–7** This was not a mere military confrontation with people who were entrenched in a formidable stronghold. The implications are more spiritual than political. While God was bringing judgment upon those who had long refused Him, He was working on behalf of the people with whom He had just renewed His covenant. The fall of Jericho sent a powerful message to the Canaanites that Israel's successes were not mere human victories of man against man, but victories by the true God of Israel over their gods. This event, following closely upon the crossing of the Jordan by miraculous means, impressed upon the people that the same God who had led their fathers out of Egypt and through the Red Sea was with Joshua just as surely as He had been with Moses. The most recent archaeological research at Jericho has confirmed the Bible's account that the city was destroyed around 1400 B.C.

wcj,nu7651 df,pl,nn3548 pl,qpta5375   nu7651   pl,cs,nn7782   df,pl,nn3104   qpf5674   pp,pl,cs,nn6440

seven priests bearing the seven trumpets of rams' horns passed on   before   the

nn3068   wcj,qpf8628   dfp,pl,nn7782   wcj,cs,nn727   cs,nn1285   nn3068

LORD, and blew with the trumpets: and the   ark   of the covenant of the LORD

qpta1980/pr,pnx310

followed them.

            wcj,df,qptp2502   qpta1980 pp,pl,cs,nn6440   df,pl,nn3548   pl,cs,qpta8628   df,pl,nn7782

  9 And the armed men went before the priests that blew   with the trumpets,

        wcj,df,pipt622   qpta1980 pr310   df,nn727   qna1980   wcj,qna8628

and the rearward came after the ark, *the priests* going on, and blowing with the

dfp,pl,nn7782

trumpets.

            nn3091   pipf6680   wcj(853)   df,nn5971   pp,qnc559   ptn3808 himf7321

  10 And Joshua had commanded   the people, saying, Ye shall not shout,

wcj,ptn3808   himf8085   pr854   nn,pnx6963 wcj,ptn3808   nn1697   qmf3318

nor   make*any*noise with your voice, neither shall *any* word proceed out

pr4480/nn,pnx6310   pr5704   cs,nn3117   qnc,pnx559   himv7321   wcj,hipf7321

of*your*mouth, until the day I bid you shout; then shall ye shout.

            cs,nn727   nn3068   wcs,himf5437   (853)   df,nn5892   hina5362   nu259/nn6471

  11 So the ark of the LORD compassed   the city, going about *it* once: and

wcs,qmf935   df,nn4264   wcs,qmf3885   dfp,nn4264

they came into the camp, and lodged in the camp.

            nn3091   wcs,himf7925   dfp,nn1242   df,pl,nn3548 wcs,qmf5375   (853)   cs,nn727

  12 And Joshua rose early in the morning, and the priests took up   the ark

nn3068

of the LORD.

            wcj,nu7651 df,pl,nn3548 pl,qpta5375   nu7651   pl,cs,nn7782   df,pl,nn3104   pp,pl,cs,nn6440   cs,nn727

  13 And seven priests bearing seven trumpets of rams' horns before the ark

nn3068   pl,qpta1980/qna1980   wcj,qpf8628   dfp,pl,nn7782   wcj,df,qptp2502

of the LORD went*on*continually, and blew with the trumpets: and the armed men

qpta1980 pp,pl,nn,pnx6440   wcj,df,pipt622   qpta1980   pr310   cs,nn727   nn3068

went before   them; but the rearward came after the ark of the LORD, *the priests*

qna1980   wcj,qna8628   dfp,pl,nn7782

going on, and blowing with the trumpets.

            df,nuor8145 dfp,nn3117   wcs,qmf5437   (853)   df,nn5892 nu259/nn6471   wcs,qmf7725

  14 And the second day they compassed   the city   once,   and returned

        df,nn4264 ad3541   qpf6213 cs,nu8337 pl,nn3117

into the camp: so they did six days.

            wcs,qmf1961   df,nuor7637 dfp,nn3117   wcs,himf7925

  15 And it*came*to*pass on the seventh day,   that they rose early about the

pp,qnc5927   df,nn7837   wcs,qmf5437 (853)   df,nn5892   df,pndm2088 dfp,nn4941 nu7651

dawning of the day, and compassed   the city after the same   manner seven

pl,nn6471 ad7535   df,pndm2088 dfp,nn3117   qpf5437   (853)   df,nn5892 nu7651   pl,nn6471

times: only on   that   day they compassed   the city seven times.

            wcs,qmf1961   df,nuor7637 dfp,nn6471   df,pl,nn3548 qpf8628

  16 And it*came*to*pass at the seventh time, when the priests blew with the

dfp,pl,nn7782   nn3091 wcs,qmf559 pr413   df,nn5971   himv7321 cj3588   nn3068   qpf5414 pp,pnx (853)

trumpets, Joshua said unto the people, Shout; for the LORD hath given you   the

df,nn5892

city.

            df,nn5892   wcj,qpf1961   nn2764   pnp1931   wcj,cs,nn3605 pnl834   pp,pnx

☞ 17 And the city shall   be   accursed, *even* it, and   all   that *are* therein,

---

☞ **6:17** The order from the Lord regarding the plunder of Jericho treated it as the first fruits of Canaan, and this did not apply to other cities they would conquer (Deut. 20:10–18). Whatever they took from Jericho was "reserved" exclusively for God, because the firstfruits belonged to Him (Ex. 23:19).

pp,nn3068   ad7535   nn7343   df,qpta2181   qmf2421 pnp1931   wcj,cs,nn3605 pnl834   pr,pnx854

to the LORD: only Rahab the harlot shall live, she and   all   that *are* with her

dfp,nn1004   cj3588   hipf2244 (853)   df,pl,nn4397   pnl834   qpf7971

in the house, because she hid   the messengers that we sent.

pnp859   wcj,ad7357   qmv8104   pr4480   df,nn2764   cj6435

18 And ye, in*any*wise keep *yourselves* from the accursed thing, lest ye

himf2763   wcs,qpf3947 pr4480   df,nn2764   wcs,qpf7760 (853)

make *yourselves* accursed, when ye   take   of the accursed thing, and make

cs,nn4264   nn3478   pp,nn2764   wcs,qpf5916 pnx(853)

the camp of Israel a curse, and trouble   it.

wcj,nn3605   nn3701   wcj,nn2091   wcj,pl,cs,nn3627   nn5178   wcj,nn1270

19 But   all   the silver, and   gold,   and   vessels   of brass and   iron,   *are*

nn6944   (pnp1931)   pp,nn3068   qmf935   cs,nn214   nn3068

consecrated   unto the LORD: they shall come into the treasury of the LORD.

df,nn5971   wcs,himf7321   wcs,qmf8628   dfp,pl,nn7782

20 So the people shouted when *the priests* blew   with the trumpets: and

wcs,qmf1961   df,nn5971   pp,qnc8085 (853)   cs,nn6963   df,nn7782

it*came*to*pass, when the people heard   the sound of the trumpet, and the

df,nn5971   wcs,himf7321   aj1419   nn8643   df,nn2346   wcs,qmf5307   pr,pnx8478   df,nn5971

people shouted with a great shout, that the wall fell down   flat,   so that the people

wcs,qmf5927   df,nn,lh5892   nn376   pr,pnx5048   wcs,qmf3920 (853)

went up into the   city,   every man straight before him, and they   took   the

df,nn5892

city.

21 And they utterly destroyed   all   that *was* in the city, both man and

wcs,himf2763   (853) cs,nn3605 pnl834   dfp,nn5892   pr4480/nn376

wcj(pr5704)   nn802   pr4480/nn5288   wcj(pr5704) aj2205   wcj(pr5740) nn7794   wcj,nn7716   wcj,nn2543

woman, young and   old, and   ox, and sheep, and ass, with

pp,cs,nn6310   nn2719

the   edge   of the sword.

nn3091   qpf559   wcj,pp,du,nu8147 df,pl,nn376   df,pl,pipt7270   (853)

22 But Joshua had said unto the   two   men that had spied out   the

df,nn776   qmv935   df,nn802/df,qpta2181   cs,nn1004   wcj,himv3318   pr4480/ad8033 (853)   df,nn802

country, Go into the   harlot's   house, and bring out thence   the woman, and

wcj(853) cs,nn3605 pnl834 pp,pnx   pp,pnl834   nipf7650   pp,pnx

all   that she hath, as   ye swore unto her.

df,pl,nn5288   df,pl,pipt7270   wcs,qmf935   wcs,himf3318   (853)   nn7343

23 And the young men that were   spies   went in, and brought out   Rahab,

wcj(853)   nn,pnx1   wcj(853)   nn,pnx517   wcj(853)   pl,nn,pnx251   wcj(853) cs,nn3605

and   her father, and   her mother, and   her brethren, and   all

pnl834 pp,pnx   hipf3318   wcj(853) cs,nn3605   pl,nn,pnx4940   wcs,himf,pnx5117

that she had; and they brought out   all   her kindred, and   left   them

pr4480/nn2351   pp,cs,nn4264   nn3478

without the   camp   of Israel.

qpf8313   wcj,df,nn5892   dfp,nn784   wcj,cs,nn3605 pnl834   pp,pnx   ad7535

24 And they burnt the   city   with fire, and   all   that *was* therein: only the

df,nn3701   wcj,df,nn2091   wcj,pl,cs,nn3627   df,nn5178   wcj,df,nn1270   qpf5414

silver, and the   gold,   and the   vessels   of brass and of   iron,   they put into the

cs,nn214   cs,nn1004   nn3068

treasury of the house of the LORD.

nn3091   hipf2421   wcj(853)   nn7343   df,qpta2181   wcj(853)   nn,pnx1

25 And Joshua saved   Rahab the   harlot alive, and   her father's

6:21 This severe measure of killing every living thing was taken to prevent alien elements of Canaanite culture and worship, on the basis of their total corruption before God, from infecting Israel (see Rom. 1:18–32). Later, instructions like those given to Israel at Jericho were ignored in other campaigns (1 Sam. 15:3, 13–22).

cs,nn**1004**   wcj(853) cs,nn3605 pnl834 pp,pnx   wcs,qmf**3427**   pp,cs,nn**7130**   nn3478   pr5704

household, and   all that she had; and she dwelleth   in   Israel *even* unto

df,pndm2088 df,nn**3117**   cj3588   hipf2244 (853)   df,pl,nn**4397**   pnl834   nn3091 qpf7971   pp,pinc7270   (853)

this   day; because she hid   the messengers, which Joshua sent to spy out

nn3405

Jericho.

nn3091   wcs,himf**7650**   df,pndm1931 dfp,nn**6256**   pp,qnc**559**   qptp779   df,nn**376**

⟐ 26 And Joshua adjured *them* at   that   time, saying, Cursed *be* the man

pp,pl,cs,nn**6440**   nn**3068** pnl834   qmf**6965**   wcs,qpf1129   (853) df,pndm2063 df,nn**5892** (853)   nn3405

before the LORD, that riseth up and buildeth   this   city   Jericho: he shall

pimf,pnx**3245**   pp,nn,pnx1060   wcj,pp,aj,pnx6810   himf**5324**

lay the foundation thereof in his firstborn, and in his youngest *son* shall he set up

du,nn,pnx1817

the gates of it.

nn**3068**   wcs,qmf**1961** pr854   nn3091   nn,pnx8089   wcs,qmf**1961**

27 So the LORD was   with Joshua; and his fame   was   *noised* throughout

pp,cs,nn3605   df,nn**776**

all   the country.

Achan's Sin

pl,cs,nn**1121**   nn3478   wcs,qmf**4603**   nn**4604**   dfp,nn**2764**

7 ⟐ But the children of Israel committed a trespass in the accursed thing: for

nn5912   cs,nn**1121**   nn3756   cs,nn**1121**   nn2067   cs,nn**1121**   nn2226

Achan, the son of Carmi, the son of Zabdi, the son of Zerah, of the

pp,cs,nn**4294**   nn3063 wcs,qmf3947 pr4480   df,nn**2764**   cs,nn**639**   nn**3068**

tribe of Judah,   took   of the accursed thing: and the anger of the LORD was

wcs,qmf**2734**   pp,pl,cs,nn**1121**   nn3478

kindled against the children of Israel.

nn3091   wcs,qmf7971 pl,nn**376**   pr4480/nn3405   df,nn5857   pnl834   pr5973   nn1007

⟐ 2 And Joshua sent   men from Jericho to Ai, which *is* beside Beth-aven,

pr4480/nn**6924**   pp,nn1008   wcs,qmf559 pr,pnx413   pp,qnc**559**   qmv5927   wcj,pimv7270 (853)

on*the*east*side of Bethel, and spoke unto them, saying, Go up and   view

df,nn**776**   df,pl,nn**376** wcs,qmf**5927**   wcs,pimf7270 (853) df,nn5857

the country. And the men went up and viewed   Ai.

wcs,qmf**7725**   pr413   nn3091   wcs,qmf**559** pr,pnx413   ptn408 cs,nn3605

3 And they returned to Joshua, and   said   unto him, Let not   all   the

---

⟐ **6:26** This curse fell upon Hiel the Bethelite in the early days of King Ahab (1 Kings 16:34). It was a local custom to dedicate the gates and walls of a new city by burying children inside the foundations.

⟐ **7:1** The sin of Achan stands as a lesson to all Israel of the consequences to one who breaks faith with God. The nation as a collective whole was in a covenant relationship with God and was dealt with by Him not merely as a group of people living together under a common law for their own protection and to accomplish their own goals. Instead, He treated them as a whole. Understanding this concept is essential to understanding the words of Paul in Romans 5:12–21. Achan had defiled not only himself, but all of Israel. They were no longer acceptable to God because they, in the person of Achan, had broken the covenant. Therefore, God would no longer work for them in driving out the Canaanites. Only after Achan (and his family, because of their connection with him in the deed) had been dealt with did God release Israel from their guilt in the matter. Achan's sin was not simply one of stealing goods or even of covetousness. He clearly defied God by disobeying His command (vv. 1, 11). Achan's punishment (Josh. 22:20) was a warning to all that they should never allow their greed to cause them to forget God's will.

⟐ **7:2–5** This unsuccessful first battle at Ai illustrates the partnership between God and Israel during the conquest of Canaan. When the people presumed upon the power of God and fought without consulting Him, they were not victorious. What should have been an easy victory turned into a painful defeat, because God was not with them.

df,nn**5971** qmf**5927**   pp,du,nu**505** (nn376) cj176 pp,nu7969 pl,nu**505** nn376 qmf**5927** wcj,himf**5221**

people go up; but let about two   or three thousand men go up and smite

(853) df,nn5857   ptn408 (853) cs,nn3605   df,nn**5971** pimf3021 ad,lh8033 cj3588 pnp1992   ad4592

Ai; *and* make not   all the people to labor thither; for they *are but* few.

wcs,qmf**5927** ad,lh8033 pr4480   df,nn**5971**   pp,nu7969 pl,nu**505**   nn376

4 So there went up thither of the people about three thousand men: and they

wcs,qmf5127 pp,pl,cs,nn**6440**   pl,cs,nn**376**   df,nn5857

fled   before the men of Ai.

pl,cs,nn**376**   df,nn5857 wcs,himf**5221** pr,pnx4480   pp,nu7970   wcj,nu8337 nn**376**

5 And the men of Ai   smote   of them about thirty and   six   men: for

wcs,qmf,pnx7291   pp,pl,cs,nn**6440**   df,nn8179   pr5704 df,nn7671   wcs,himf,pnx**5221**

they chased them *from* before the gate *even* unto Shebarim, and   smote

dfp,nn4174   cs,nn3824   df,nn**5971** wcs,nimf4549   wcs,qmf**1961**

them in the going down: wherefore the hearts of the people melted, and became as

pp,pl,nn4325

water.

nn3091   wcs,qmf7167   pl,nn,pnx8071   wcs,qmf**5307**   nn,lh776 pr5921   pl,nn,pnx**6440**

6 And Joshua   rent   his clothes, and fell to the earth upon his   face

pp,pl,cs,nn**6440**   cs,nn727   nn**3068** pr5704 df,nn6153 pnp1931   wcj,cs,aj**2205**   nn3478

before the ark of the LORD until the eventide, he and the elders of Israel, and

wcs,qmf**5927** nn**6083** pr5921   nn,pnx**7218**

put   dust upon their heads.

nn3091   wcs,qmf**559** ptx162   nn**136** nn3069 pp,pnit4100   hina**5674**/hipf**5674**   (853)

7 And Joshua said, Alas, O Lord GOD, wherefore hast thou at*all*brought

df,pndm2088 df,nn**5971** hipf**5674** (853) df,nn3383   pp,qnc5414 pnx(853)   pp,cs,nn**3027**   df,nn567

this people over   Jordan, to deliver   us into the hand of the Amorites,

pp,hinc,pnx**6**   wcj,ptx3863   hipf**2974** wcs,qmf**3427**   pp,cs,nn5676

to destroy us? would*to*God we had been content, and dwelt on the other side

df,nn3383

Jordan!

pte994   nn**136** pnid4100   qmf**559** ad310/pnl834 nn3478 qpf**2015**   nn6203 pp,pl,cs,nn**6440**

8 O Lord, what shall I say, when Israel turneth their backs before their

pl,qpta,pnx341

enemies!

df,nn3669   wcj,cs,nn3605   pl,cs,qpta**3427**   df,nn776   wcj,qmf**8085**

9 For the Canaanites and   all   the inhabitants of the land shall hear *of it,*

wcj,nipf5437/pr,pnx5921   wcj,hipf3772 (853)   nn,pnx8034 pr4480   df,nn776   wcj,pnit4100

and shall environ*us*round, and cut off   our name from the earth: and what

qmf**6213**   df,aj1419 pp,nn,pnx8034

wilt thou do unto thy great name?

nn**3068** wcs,qmf**559** pr413   nn3091   qmv**6965**/pp,pnx   pp,pnit4100 qpta**5307** pnp859 pndm2088

10 And the LORD said unto Joshua, Get*thee*up; wherefore liest thou thus

pr5921   pl,nn,pnx**6440**

upon thy face?

nn3478   qpf**2398**   wcj,ad1571 qpf**5674**   (853)   nn,pnx**1285**   pnl834

11 Israel hath sinned, and they have also transgressed   my covenant which

pipf**6680**   pnx(853)   wcj,ad1571 qpf3947 pr4480   df,nn**2764**

I commanded   them: for they have even taken of the accursed thing, and

wcj,ad1571 qpf1589   pipf3584 wcj,ad1571   qpf**7760** wcj,ad1571

have also stolen, and dissembled also, and they have put *it* even among their

pp,pl,nn,pnx3627

own   stuff.

pl,cs,nn**1121**   nn3478 qmf3201 wcj,ptn**3808** pp,qnc6965 pp,pl,cs,nn**6440**   pl,cs,qpta,pnx341

12 Therefore the children of Israel could   not   stand before their enemies,

qmf6437   nn6203 pp,pl,cs,nn**6440**   pl,cs,qpta,pnx341 cj3588   qpf**1961** pp,nn**2764** ptn**3808**

but turned *their* backs before their enemies, because they were accursed: neither pp,qnc**1961** pr,pnx**5973**   himf**3254**   cj518/ptn**3808**   himf**8045**   df,nn**2764**   pr4480/nn,pnx**7130**

will I be   with you any more, except ye destroy the accursed from among

you.

qmv**6965**   pimv**6942**   (853)   df,nn**5971**   wcs,qpf**559**   htmv**6942**

13 Up, sanctify   the people, and say, Sanctify yourselves against

pp,nn**4279**   cj**3588** ad**3541** qpf**559**   nn**3068** pl,cs,nn**430**   nn**3478**   nn**2764**

tomorrow: for thus saith the Lord God of Israel. *There is* an accursed thing in the

pp,nn,pnx**7130**   nn**3478**   qmf**3201** ptn**3808** pp,qnc**6965** pp,pl,cs,nn**6440**   pl,qpta,pnx341 pr5704

midst of thee, O Israel: thou canst not stand before thine enemies, until ye

hinc,pnx**5493**   df,nn**2764**   pr4480/nn,pnx**7130**

take away the accursed thing from among you.

dfp,nn**1242**   wcs,nipf**7126**   pp,pl,nn,pnx**7626**

14 In the morning therefore ye shall be brought according to your tribes: and

wcs,qpf**1961**   df,nn**7626** pnl834   nn**3068** qmf,pnx**3920**   qmf**7126**

it shall be, *that* the tribe which the Lord taketh shall come according to the

dfp,pl,nn**4940**   wcj,df,nn**4940** pnl834   nn**3068**   qmf,pnx3920   qmf**7126**

families *thereof*; and the family which the Lord shall take shall come by

dfp,pl,nn**1004**   wcj,df,nn**1004** pnl834   nn**3068** qmf,pnx3920   qmf**7126**

households; and the household which the Lord shall take shall come

dfp,pl,nn**1397**

man*by*man.

wcs,qpf**1961**   df,nipf3920   dfp,nn**2764**

15 And it shall be, *that* he that is taken with the accursed thing shall be

nimf**8313**   dfp,nn784 pnx(853)   wcj(853) cs,nn3605 pnl834 pp,pnx   cj3588   qpf**5674**

burnt with fire, he and   all that he hath: because he hath transgressed

(853)   cs,nn**1285**   nn**3068** wcj,cj3588   qpf**6213** nn5039   pp,nn**3478**

the covenant of the Lord, and because he hath wrought folly in Israel.

nn3091   wcs,himf**7925**   dfp,nn**1242**   wcs,himf**7126** (853)   nn**3478**

16 So Joshua rose*up*early in the morning, and brought   Israel by their

pp,pl,nn,pnx**7626**   cs,nn**7626**   nn3063   wcs,nimf3920

tribes; and the tribe of Judah was taken:

wcs,himf**7126** (853)   cs,nn**4940**   nn3063   wcs,qmf3920 (853)   cs,nn**4940**

17 And he brought   the family of Judah; and he took   the family of the

df,nn**2227**   wcs,qmf**7126** (853)   cs,nn**4940**   df,nn**2227** dfp,pl,nn**1397**   nn**2067**

Zarhites: and he brought   the family of the Zarhites man*by*man; and Zabdi was

wcs,nimf3920

taken:

wcs,himf**7126** (853)   nn,pnx**1004**   dfp,pl,nn**1397**   nn**5912**   cs,nn**1121**

18 And he brought   his household man*by*man; and Achan, the son of

nn3756   cs,nn**1121**   nn**2067**   cs,nn**1121**   nn**2226**   pp,cs,nn**4294**   nn3063   wcs,nimf3920

Carmi, the son of Zabdi, the son of Zerah, of the tribe of Judah, was taken.

nn3091   wcs,qmf**559**   pr413   nn**5912**   nn,pnx**1121** qmv**7760**   pte**4994**   nn**3519**

19 And Joshua said unto Achan, My son, give, I*pray*thee, glory to the

pp,nn**3068** pl,cs,nn**430**   nn**3478**   wcj,qmv**5414**   nn**8426**   pp,pnx   wcj,himv**5046** pp,pnx pte**4994** pnid4100

Lord God of Israel, and make confession unto him; and tell me now what

qpf**6213** pimf**3582**   ptn408 pr,pnx**4480**

thou hast done; hide *it* not from me.

nn**5912**   wcs,qmf**6030**   (853)   nn3091   wcs,qmf**559**   ad**546** pnp595   qpf**2398**

20 And Achan answered   Joshua, and said, Indeed I have sinned against

pp,nn**3068** pl,cs,nn**430**   nn**3478**   wcj,pp,pndm2063   wcj,pp,pndm2063   qpf**6213**

the Lord God of Israel, and   thus   and   thus   have I done:

wcs,qmf**7200**   dfp,nn**7998**   nu259   aj**2896**   nn**8152**   nn**155**

21 When I saw   among the spoils a goodly Babylonish garment, and

wcj,du,nu**3967**   pl,nn**8255**   nn**3701**   nu259 wcj,cs,nn**3956**   nn2091   pl,nu**2572**   pl,nn**8255** nn,pnx**4948**

two hundred shekels of silver, and a wedge of gold of fifty shekels weight,

wcs,qmf,pnx**2530**   wcs,qmf,pnx3947   wcj,ptdm,pnx2009   pl,qptp2934

then I coveted them, and   took   them; and, behold, they *are* hid in the

dfp,nn776   pp,cs,nn**8432**   nn,pnx**168**   wcj,df,nn3701 pr,pnx8478

earth in the midst of my tent, and the silver under it.

nn3091   wcs,qmf7971   pl,nn**4397**   wcs,qmf7323   df,nn,lh**168**   wcj,ptdm2009

22 So Joshua sent messengers, and they ran unto the tent; and, behold,

qptp2934   pp,nn,pnx**168**   wcj,df,nn3701 pr,pnx8478

it was hid in his tent, and the silver under it.

wcs,qmf,pnx3947   pr4480/cs,nn**8432**   df,nn**168**   wcs,himf,pnx935

23 And they took them out*of*the*midst of the tent, and brought them

pr413   nn3091   wcj,pr413 cs,nn**3605**   pl,cs,nn**1121**   nn3478   wcs,himf,pnx3332   pp,pl,cs,nn**6440**

unto Joshua, and unto all the children of Israel, and laid*them*out before the

nn**3068**

LORD.

nn3091   wcj,cs,nn**3605** nn3478 pr,pnx5973   wcs,qmf3947 (853) nn5912   cs,nn**1121**

24 And Joshua, and all Israel with him, took Achan the son of

nn2226   wcj(853)   df,nn3701   wcj(853)   df,nn155   wcj(853)   cs,nn3956   df,nn2091

Zerah, and the silver, and the garment, and the wedge of gold, and

wcj(853)   pl,nn,pnx**1121**   wcj(853)   pl,nn,pnx1323   wcj(853)   nn,pnx7794   wcj(853)   nn,pnx2543

his sons, and his daughters, and his oxen, and his asses,

wcj(853)   nn,pnx6629   wcj(853)   nn,pnx**168**   wcj(853) cs,nn**3605** pnl834 pp,pnx

and his sheep, and his tent, and all that he had: and they

wcs,himf**5927** pnx(853)   cs,nn6010   nn5911

brought them unto the valley of Achor.

nn3091   wcs,qmf**559** pnit4100   qpf,pnx5916   nn**3068**   qmf,pnx5916

25 And Joshua said, Why hast thou troubled us? the LORD shall trouble thee

df,pndm2088 dfp,nn**3117**   cs,nn**3605** nn3478 wcs,qmf5619 pnx(853)   nn68   wcs,qmf**8313** pnx(853)

this day. And all Israel stoned him with stones, and burned them

dfp,nn784   wcs,qmf7275 pnx(853)   dfp,pl,nn68

with fire, after they had stoned them with stones.

wcs,himf**6965** pr,pnx5921   aj1419 cs,nn1530   pl,nn68   pr5704 df,pndm2088 df,nn**3117**

26 And they raised over him a great heap of stones unto this day. So

nn**3068** wcs,qmf**7725**   pr4480/cs,nn2740   nn,pnx639   pr5921/ad**3651**   cs,nn8034   df,pndm1931

the LORD turned from*the*fierceness of his anger. Wherefore the name of that

df,nn4725   qpf**7121**   cs,nn6010   nn5911   pr5704 df,pndm2088 df,nn**3117**

place was called, The valley of Achor, unto this day.

Ai Destroyed

nn**3068** wcs,qmf**559** pr413   nn3091   qmf**3372** ptn408 wcj,ptn408   qmf**2865**   qmv3947

8 And the LORD said unto Joshua, Fear not, neither be thou dismayed: take

(853) cs,nn**3605**   cs,nn**5971**   df,nn4421 pr,pnx5973   wcj,qmv**6965** qmv**5927**   df,nn5857 qmv**7200**

all the people of war with thee, and arise, go up to Ai: see, I

qpf**5414**   pp,nn,pnx**3027** (853)   cs,nn**4428**   df,nn5857   wcj(853)   nn,pnx**5971**   wcj(853)

have given into thy hand the king of Ai, and his people, and his

nn,pnx5892   wcj(853)   nn,pnx776

city, and his land:

wcj,qpf**6213**   pp,nn5857   wcj,pp,nn,pnx**4428** pp,pnl834   qpf**6213**

2 And thou shalt do to Ai and her king as thou didst unto

pp,nn3405   wcj,pp,nn,pnx**4428** ad7535   nn,pnx7998   wcj,pp,nn,pnx929

Jericho and her king: only the spoil thereof, and the cattle thereof, shall

---

7:25 Since Deuteronomy 24:16 prohibited the execution of children for the sins of their fathers, it is evident that Achan's children must have condoned or assisted him in what he did.

^{qmf962}   ^{pp,pnx}   ^{qmv7760} ^{pp,pnx}   ^{qpta693}   ^{dfp,nn5892} ^{pr4480/pr,pnx310}

ye take*for*a*prey unto yourselves: lay thee an ambush for the city   behind

it.

ⁿⁿ³⁰⁹¹ ^{wcs,qmf6965}   ^{wcj,cs,nn3605}   ^{cs,nn5971} ^{df,nn4421} ^{pp,qnc5927}   ^{df,nn5857}

3 So Joshua arose, and   all   the people of war, to go up against Ai: and

ⁿⁿ³⁰⁹¹   ^{wcs,qmf977}   ^{nu7970}   ^{nu505}   ^{cs,aj1368}   ⁿⁿ³⁷⁶   ^{df,nn2428}   ^{wcs,qmf,pnx7971}

Joshua chose out thirty thousand mighty men of valor, and sent*them*away by

ⁿⁿ³⁹¹⁵

night.

^{wcs,pimf6680}   ^{pnx(853)}   ^{pp,qnc559} ^{qmv7200} ^{pnp859}   ^{pl,qpta693}

4 And he commanded   them, saying, Behold, ye shall lie*in*wait against

^{dfp,nn5892}   ^{pr4480/pr310} ^{df,nn5892} ^{himf7368} ^{ptn408} ^{ad3966}   ^{pr4480} ^{df,nn5892} ^{wcs,qpf1961}

the city, *even* behind the city: go not very far from the city, but be ye

^{nn,pnx3605} ^{pl,nipt3559}

all ready:

^{wcj,pnp589}   ^{wcj,cs,nn3605}   ^{df,nn5971} ^{pnl834} ^{pr,pnx854}   ^{qmf7126}   ^{pr413}

5 And I,   and all   the people that *are* with me, will approach unto the

^{df,nn5892}   ^{wcs,qpf1961}   ^{cj3588}   ^{qmf3318} ^{pp,qnc,pnx7125} ^{pp,pnl834}

city: and it*shall*come*to*pass, when they come out against us, as   at the

^{dfp,aj7223}   ^{wcs,qpf5127} ^{pp,pl,nn,pnx6440}

first, that we will flee   before them,

^{wcs,qpf3318} ^{pr,pnx310}   ^{pr5704}   ^{hinc,pnx5423} ^{pnx(853)}   ^{pr4480}

6 (For they will come out after us) till we have drawn   them from the

^{df,nn5892} ^{cj3588}   ^{qmf559}   ^{pl,qpta5127} ^{pp,pl,nn,pnx6440} ^{pp,pnl834}   ^{dfp,aj7223}

city; for they will say, They flee   before us,   as at the first: therefore we

^{wcs,qpf5127} ^{pp,pl,nn,pnx6440}

will flee   before them.

^{wcj,pnp859}   ^{qmf6965}   ^{pr4480/df,qpta693}   ^{wcs,hipf3423} ⁽⁸⁵³⁾   ^{df,nn5892}

7 Then   ye   shall rise up from*the*ambush, and seize upon   the city: for

ⁿⁿ³⁰⁶⁸   ^{pl,nn,pnx430} ^{wcs,qpf,pnx5414}   ^{pp,nn,pnx3027}

the LORD your God will deliver it into your hand.

^{wcs,qpf1961}   ^{pp,qnc,pnx8610} ⁽⁸⁵³⁾   ^{df,nn5892}   ^{himf3341}

8 And it shall be,   when ye have   taken   the city, *that* ye shall set

⁽⁸⁵³⁾   ^{df,nn5892}   ^{dfp,nn784}   ^{pp,cs,nn1697}   ⁿⁿ³⁰⁶⁸   ^{qmf6213}

the city on fire: according to the commandment of the LORD shall ye do.

^{qmv7200}   ^{pipf6680}   ^{pnx(853)}

See, I have commanded   you.

ⁿⁿ³⁰⁹¹   ^{wcs,qmf,pnx7971}   ^{wcs,qmf1980} ^{pr413}   ^{df,nn3993}

9 Joshua therefore sent*them*forth: and they went   to lie in ambush, and

^{wcs,qmf3427} ^{pr996}   ⁿⁿ¹⁰⁰⁸   ^{wcj(pr996)} ^{df,nn5857}   ^{pr4480/nn3220}   ^{dfp,nn5857}   ⁿⁿ³⁰⁹¹

abode between Bethel and   Ai, on*the*west*side of Ai: but Joshua

^{wcs,qmf3885} ^{df,pndm1931} ^{dfp,nn3915} ^{pp,cs,nn8432}   ^{df,nn5971}

lodged   that   night among the people.

ⁿⁿ³⁰⁹¹   ^{wcs,himf7925}   ^{dfp,nn1242}   ^{wcs,qmf6485} ⁽⁸⁵³⁾   ^{df,nn5971}

10 And Joshua rose*up*early in the morning, and numbered   the people, and

^{wcs,qmf5927} ^{pnp1931}   ^{wcj,cs,aj2205}   ⁿⁿ³⁴⁷⁸ ^{pp,pl,cs,nn6440}   ^{df,nn5971} ^{df,nn5857}

went up, he and the elders of Israel, before the people to Ai.

^{wcj,cs,nn3605}   ^{df,nn5971}   ^{df,nn4421} ^{pnl834}   ^{pr,pnx854}

11 And all   the people, *even the people* of war that *were* with him,

^{qpf5927}   ^{wcs,qmf5066}   ^{wcs,qmf935} ^{pr5048}   ^{df,nn5892} ^{wcs,qmf2583}   ^{pr4480/cs,nn6828}

went up, and drew nigh, and came before the city, and pitched on*the*north*side

^{dfp,nn5857}   ^{wcj,df,nn1516} ^{pr,pnx996}   ^{wcj(pr996)} ^{df,nn5857}

of Ai: now *there was* a valley between them and   Ai.

^{wcs,qmf3947}   ^{pp,cs,nu2568}   ^{pl,nu505} ⁿⁿ³⁷⁶   ^{wcs,qmf7760} ^{pnx(853)}

12 And he took about five thousand men, and set   them to

qpta693   pr996   nn1008   wcj(pr996) df,nn5857   pr4480/nn3220   dfp,nn5892
lie*in*ambush between Bethel and   Ai,   on*the*west*side of the   city.

              wcs,qmf**7760**   df,nn**5971**   (853)   cs,nn3605   df,nn**4264** pnl834
13 And when they had   set   the people, *even*   all   the host that *was*

pr4480/cs,nn6828   dfp,nn5892   wcj(853)   nn,pnx**6119**   pr4480/nn3220   dfp,nn5892
on*the*north of the   city,   and   their liers*in*wait on*the*west of the   city,

nn3091   wcs,qmf**1980** df,pndm1931 dfp,nn**3915**   pp,cs,nn**8432**   df,nn6010
Joshua went   that   night into the   midst of the   valley.

                 wcs,qmf**1961**   cs,nn**4428**   df,nn5857 pp,qnc**7200**   wcs,pimf4116
14 And it*came*to*pass, when the king of   Ai   saw   *it*, that they hasted

     wcs,himf7925   pl,cs,nn**376**   df,nn5892 wcs,qmf3318   pp,qnc7125   nn3478   dfp,nn4421
and rose*up*early, and the   men   of the   city   went out against Israel to battle,

pnp1931   wcj,cs,nn3605   nn,pnx**5971**   df,nn**4150**   pp,pl,cs,nn**6440**   df,nn**6160**   wcj,pnp1931
he   and   all   his people, at a time appointed,   before   the plain; but   he

qpf3045 ptn**3808** cj3588   qpta693   pp,pnx   pr4480/pr310   df,nn5892
wist not that *there were* liers*in*ambush against him behind the   city.

          nn3091   wcj,cs,nn3605   nn3478   wcs,nimf**5060** pp,pl,nn,pnx**6440**
15 And Joshua and   all   Israel made as if they were beaten   before   them,

wcs,qmf5127   cs,nn**1870**   df,nn4057
and fled   by the way of the wilderness.

      cs,nn3605   df,nn**5971** pnl834   dfp,nn5857   wcs,nimf**2199**   pp,qnc7291
16 And   all   the people that *were* in   Ai   were called together to pursue

pr,pnx310   wcs,qmf7291 pr310   nn3091   wcs,nimf5423   pr4480   df,nn5892
after them: and they pursued after Joshua, and were drawn away from the   city.

         wcj,ptn**3808**   nn376   nipf**7604**   dfp,nn5857   wcj,nn1008 pnl834   qpf3318/ptn**3808**
17 And there was   not   a man left in   Ai   or Bethel, that went*not*out

ad310   nn3478   wcs,qmf**5800** (853)   df,nn5892 qptp6605   wcs,qmf7291   pr310   nn3478
after Israel: and they   left   the   city open, and pursued after Israel.

          nn**3068**   wcs,qmf559   pr413   nn3091   qmv5186   dfp,nn3591 pnl834
18 And the LORD   said   unto Joshua, Stretch out the   spear that *is* in thy

pp,nn,pnx**3027**   pr413   df,nn5857   cj3588   qmf,pnx**5414**   pp,nn,pnx**3027**   nn3091
hand   toward   Ai;   for   I will   give   it into thine   hand.   And   Joshua

wcs,qmf5186   dfp,nn3591 pnl834   pp,nn,pnx**3027**   pr413   df,nn5892
stretched out the spear that *he had* in his   hand   toward the city.

         wcj,df,qpta693   qpf**6965**   nn4120   pr4480/nn,pnx4725   wcs,qmf7323
19 And the ambush arose quickly out*of*their*place, and they   ran   as soon

          pp,qnc5186   nn,pnx**3027**   wcs,qmf935   df,nn5892   wcs,qmf,pnx3920
as he had stretched out his hand: and they entered into the   city,   and   took   it,

wcs,pimf4116   wcs,himf3341 (853)   df,nn5892   dfp,nn784
and hasted and   set   the   city on fire.

          pl,cs,nn**376**   df,nn5857 wcs,qmf6437   pr,pnx310   wcs,qmf**7200**   wcj,ptdm2009
20 And when the   men   of   Ai   looked behind them,   they   saw,   and, behold,

cs,nn6227   df,nn5892   qpf**5927**   df,du,nn,lh**8064**   pp,pnx   qpf**1961** wcj,ptn**3808**   du,nn**3027**
the smoke of the   city   ascended up to heaven,   and   they   had   no   power to

pp,qnc5127   ad2008   wcj,ad2008   wcj,df,nn**5971**   df,qpta5127   df,nn4057
flee   this way   or   that way: and the   people   that   fled   to the wilderness

nipf**2015**   pr413   df,qpta7291
turned back upon the pursuers.

         wcj,nn3091   wcj,cs,nn3605   nn3478   qpf**7200** cj3588   df,qpta693   qpf3920 (853)
21 And when Joshua and   all   Israel saw that the ambush had taken   the

df,nn5892   wcj,cj3588   cs,nn6227   df,nn5892   qpf**5927**   wcs,qmf**7725**
city,   and   that the smoke of the   city   ascended, then they turned again, and

wcs,himf**5221** (853)   pl,cs,nn**376**   df,nn5857
slew   the men of Ai.

         wcj,pndm428   qpf3318   pr4480   df,nn5892 pp,qnc,pnx7125   wcs,qmf**1961**
22 And the   other   issued out of   the   city   against them; so they   were   in

dfp,nn**8432**   pp,nn3478   pndm428   pr4480/pndm2088   wcj,pndm428   pr4480/pndm2088   wcs,himf**5221**

the midst of Israel, some on*this*side, and some on*that*side: and they smote

pnx(853)   cj5704   ptn1115   pp,pnx   hipf**7604**   (nn**8300**)   wcj,nn6412

them, so that they let none of them remain   or escape.

wcj(853)   cs,nn**4428**   df,nn5857   qpf8610   aj**2416**   wcs,himf**7126**   pnx(853)   pr413

23 And   the king of Ai they took alive, and brought   him to

nn3091

Joshua.

wcs,qmf**1961**   nn3478   pp,pinc**3615**   pp,qnc**2026**   (853) cs,nn**3605**

24 And it*came*to*pass, when Israel had made*an*end of slaying   all   the

pl,cs,qpta**3427**   df,nn5857   dfp,nn**7704**   dfp,nn4057   pnl834/pp,pnx   qpf,pnx7291

inhabitants of Ai in the field, in the wilderness wherein they chased them, and

nn,pnx3605   wcs,qmf**5307**   pp,cs,nn**6310**   nn**2719**   pr5704

when they were   all   fallen on the   edge   of the sword, until they were

qnc,pnx**8552**   cs,nn**3605**   nn3478   qmf**7725**   df,nn5857   wcs,himf**5221** pnx(853)

consumed, that   all   the Israelites returned unto Ai, and smote   it with the

pp,cs,nn**6310**   nn**2719**

edge of the sword.

wcs,qmf**1961**   cs,nn**3605**   df,pl,qpta**5307**   df,pndm1931   dfp,nn**3117**   pr4480/nn**376**

25 And so it was, that all that fell   that   day, both of men and

wcj(pr5704)   nn**802**   du,nu**8147**/nu**6240**   nu**505**   cs,nn**3605**   pl,cs,nn**376**   df,nn5857

women, were twelve thousand, even all the men of Ai.

wcj,nn3091 hipf**7725** ptn**3808**   nn,pnx**3027**   pnl834   qpf5186   dfp,nn3591

26 For Joshua drew not his hand back, wherewith he stretched out the spear,

cj5704/pnl834   hipf**2763**   (853) cs,nn**3605**   pl,cs,qpta**3427**   df,nn5857

until he had utterly destroyed   all   the inhabitants of Ai.

ad7535   df,nn929   wcj,cs,nn**7998**   df,pndm1931 df,nn5892   nn3478   qpf962

27 Only the cattle and the   spoil   of   that   city   Israel took*for*a*prey

pp,pnx   pp,cs,nn**1697**   nn3068   pnl834   pipf**6680**   (853)

unto themselves, according unto the   word   of the LORD which he commanded

nn3091

Joshua.

nn3091   wcs,qmf**8313** (853) df,nn5857   wcs,qmf,pnx**7760**   cs,nn8510   nn5769

28 And Joshua burnt   Ai, and   made   it a heap forever, even a

nn**8077**   pr5704 df,pndm2088 df,nn**3117**

desolation unto   this   day.

wcj(853)   cs,nn**4428**   df,nn5857   qpf8518   pr5921   df,nn6086 pr5704 cs,nn**6256**/df,nn6153

29 And   the king of Ai he hanged on a tree until eventide: and as

df,nn8121   wcj,pp,qnc935   nn3091   pipf**6680**

soon as the   sun   was down, Joshua   commanded   that   they   should

wcs,himf3381/(853)/nn,pnx**5038**   pr4480   df,nn6086   wcs,himf**7993** pnx(853)   pr413   cs,nn**6607**

take*his*carcass*down from the tree, and   cast   it at the entering of the

cs,nn**8179**   df,nn5892   wcs,himf**6965** pr,pnx5921   aj1419 cs,nn1530   pl,nn68   pr5704

gate of the city, and   raise   thereon a great heap of stones, that remaineth unto

df,pndm2088 df,nn**3117**

this   day.

The Ceremony at Mount Ebal

ad**227**   nn3091   qmf1129   nn**4196**   pp,nn3068 pl,cs,nn**430**   nn3478   pp,cs,nn2022   nn5858

30 Then Joshua built an altar unto the LORD   God   of Israel in mount Ebal,

pp,pnl834   nn4872   cs,nn**5650**   nn3068   pipf**6680**   (853)   pl,cs,nn**1121**   nn3478

31 As Moses the servant of the Lord commanded   the children of Israel, as

dfp,qptp3789   pp,cs,nn**5612**   cs,nn**8451**   nn4872   cs,nn**4196**   aj**8003**   pl,nn68   pr,pnx5921

it is written in the   book   of the   law   of Moses, an altar of whole stones, over

pnl834   ptn**3808**   hipf**5130**   nn1270   wcs,himf**5927** pr,pnx5921   pl,nn**5930**
which no man hath lifted up *any* iron: and they offered thereon burnt offerings

pp,nn**3068**   wcs,qmf**2076**   pl,nn**8002**
unto the LORD, and sacrificed peace offerings.

wcs,qmf**3789** ad8033 pr5921   df,pl,nn68 (853)   cs,nn4932   cs,nn**8451**   nn4872
32 And he wrote there upon the stones   a copy of the law of Moses,

pnl834   qpf**3789**   pp,pl,cs,nn**6440**   pl,cs,nn**1121**   nn3478
which he wrote in the presence of the children of Israel.

wcj,cs,nn**3605**   nn3478   wcj,aj,pnx**2205**   wcj,pl,nn**7860**   wcj,pl,qpta,pnx**8199**
33 And   all   Israel, and their elders, and officers, and their judges,

pl,qpta5975   pr4480/pndm2088   dfp,nn**727**   wcj,pr4480/pndm2088   pr5048   df,pl,nn**3548**   df,pl,nn**3881**
stood on*this*side the ark and on*that*side before the priests the Levites, which

pl,cs,qpta**5375**   cs,nn**727**   cs,nn**1285**   nn**3068**   dfp,nn**1616**
bore   the ark of the covenant of the LORD, as well the stranger, as he that was

dfp,nn**249**   nn,pnx2677   pr413   pr4136 cs,nn2022   nn1630   wcj,nn,pnx2677
born*among*them; half of them over against mount Gerizim, and   half   of

pr413   pr4136   cs,nn2022   nn5858 pp,pnl834   nn4872   cs,nn**5650**   nn**3068**   pipf**6680**
them over against mount Ebal; as   Moses the servant of the Lord had commanded

dfp,aj**7223**   pp,pinc**1288** (853)   df,nn**5971**   nn3478
before, that they should bless   the people of Israel.

wcj,ad310/ad**3651**   qpf**7121** (853) cs,nn**3605**   pl,cs,nn**1697**   df,nn**8451**   df,nn**1293**
34 And afterward he read   all   the words of the law, the blessings and

wcj,df,nn**7045**   pp,cs,nn3605   df,qptp**3789**   pp,cs,nn**5612**   df,nn**8451**
cursings, according to   all   that is written in the book of the law.

qpf**1961** ptn**3808**   nn**1697** pr4480/nn3605 pnl834   nn4872   pipf**6680**   pnl834   nn3091   qpf**7121**
35 There was not a word of all   that Moses commanded, which Joshua read

ptn**3808**   pr5048   cs,nn**3605**   cs,nn**6951**   nn3478   wcj,df,pl,nn**802**   wcj,df,nn**2945**
not before all   the congregation of Israel, with the women, and the little ones,

wcj,df,nn**1616**   df,qpta**1980**   pp,nn,pnx**7130**
and the strangers that were conversant among them.

The Gibeonites Deceive Joshua

wcs,qmf**1961**   cs,nn**3605**   df,pl,nn**4428** pnl834   pp,cs,nn**5676**
9 And it*came*to*pass, when all   the kings which *were* on this side

df,nn**3383**   dfp,nn2022   wcj,dfp,nn8219   wcj,pp,cs,nn**3605**   cs,nn2348
Jordan, in the hills, and in the valleys, and in   all   the coasts of the

df,aj1419 df,nn3220 pr413   pr4136   df,nn3844   df,nn2850   wcj,df,nn567   df,nn3669
great sea over against Lebanon, the Hittite, and the Amorite, the Canaanite, the

df,nn6522   df,nn2340   wcj,df,nn2983 pp,qnc**8085**
Perizzite, the Hivite, and the Jebusite, heard *thereof*;

wcs,htmf**6908**   ad3162   pp,ninc3898 pr5973   nn3091   wcj,pr5973
2 That they gathered themselves together, to fight with Joshua and with

nn3478   nu259   nn**6310**
Israel, with one accord.

wcj,pl,cs,qpta**3427**   nn1391   qpf**8085** (853) pnl834   nn3091   qpf**6213**
3 And when the inhabitants of Gibeon heard   what Joshua had done unto

pp,nn3405   wcj,dfp,nn5857
Jericho and to   Ai,

pnp1992   (ad1571)   wcs,qmf**6213**   pp,nn**6195**   wcs,qmf**1980**
4 They   did work wilily, and went and made as if they had been

wcs,htmf**6737**   wcs,qmf**3947** aj1087 pl,nn8242   pp,pl,nn,pnx2543   nn3196 wcj,pl,cs,nn**4997** aj1087
ambassadors, and took old sacks upon their asses, and wine bottles, old,

wcj,pl,pupt1234   wcj,pl,pupt**6887**
and rent, and bound up;

aj1087 wcj,pl,nn5275   wcj,pl,pupt2921   pp,du,nn,pnx7272   aj1087   wcj,pl,nn8008   pr,pnx5921

5 And old   shoes   and clouted upon their   feet,   and old garments upon

wcj,cs,nn3605   cs,nn3899   nn,pnx6718   qpf3001   (qpf1961) pl,nn5350

them; and   all   the bread of their provision was dry *and*   moldy.

wcs,qmf1980 pr413 nn3091 pr413   df,nn4264   df,nn1537   wcs,qmf559 pr,pnx413

6 And they went   to Joshua unto the camp at Gilgal, and said   unto him,

wcj,pr413   cs,nn376   nn3478   qpf935   pr4480/nn776/aj7350 wcj,cj6258   qmv3772

and to the men of Israel, We be come from*a*far*country: now therefore make

nn1285   pp,pnx

ye a league with us.

cs,nn376   nn3478 wcs,qmf559 pr413   df,nn2340   ad194   pnp859 qpta3427

7 And the men of Israel   said   unto the Hivites, Peradventure ye dwell

pp,nn,pnx7130   wcj,ad349   qmf3772   nn1285   pp,pnx

among us; and how shall we make a league with you?

wcs,qmf559 pr413   nn3091 pnp587   pl,nn,pnx5650   nn3091 wcs,qmf559 pr,pnx413

8 And they said unto Joshua, We *are* thy servants. And Joshua said   unto

pnit4310   pnp859   wcj,pr4480/ad370   qmf935

them, Who *are* ye? and from whence come ye?

wcs,qmf559 pr,pnx413   pr4480/nn776/ad3966/aj7350   pl,nn,pnx5650   qpf935

9 And they said   unto him, From*a*very*far*country thy servants are come

pp,cs,nn8034   nn3068   pl,nn,pnx430 cj3588   qpf8085   nn,pnx8089

because of the   name of the LORD thy God: for we have heard the fame of

wcj(853) cs,nn3605 pnl834   qpf6213   pp,nn4714

him, and   all that he did in Egypt,

wcj(853) cs,nn3605 pnl834   qpf6213   pp,du,cs,nu8147 pl,cs,nn4428   df,nn567   pnl834

10 And   all that he did to the   two   kings of the Amorites, that

pp,cs,nn5676 df,nn3383   pp,nn5511 cs,nn4428   nn2809   wcj,pp,nn5747 cs,nn4428   df,nn1316

were beyond Jordan, to Sihon king of Heshbon, and to   Og   king of Bashan,

pnl834   pp,nn6252

which *was* at Ashtaroth.

aj,pnx2205   wcj,cs,nn3605   pl,cs,qpta3427   nn,pnx776 wcs,qmf559 pr,pnx413

11 Wherefore our elders and   all   the inhabitants of our country spoke   to

pp,qnc559   qmv3947   nn6720   pp,nn,pnx3027   dfp,nn1870   wcj,qmv1980   pp,qnc,pnx7125

us, saying, Take victuals with you for the journey, and   go   to meet   them,

wcj,qpf559 pr,pnx413   pnp587   pl,nn,pnx5650   wcj,ad6258 qmv3772   nn1285

and say   unto them, We *are* your servants: therefore now   make ye a league

pp,pnx

with us.

pndm2088   nn,pnx3899   aj2525   htpf6679   (pnx853)   pr4480/pl,nn,pnx1004

12 This our bread we took hot *for* our provision   out*of*our*houses on

pp,cs,nn3117   qnc,pnx3318   pp,qnc1980 pr,pnx413   wcj,ad6258 ptdm2009   qpf3001

the   day   we came forth to   go   unto you; but now, behold, it is dry, and it

wcj,qpf1961   pl,nn5350

is   moldy:

wcj,pndm428 pl,cs,nn4997 df,nn3196 pnl834   pipf4390   aj2319   wcj,ptdm2009

13 And these bottles of wine, which we filled, *were* new; and, behold, they

htpf1234   wcj,pndm428   pl,nn,pnx8008   wcj,pl,nn,pnx5275   qpf1086

be rent: and these our garments and our   shoes   are become old by reason of

ad3966 pr4480/cs,aj7230   df,nn1870

the very   long   journey.

df,pl,nn376 wcs,qmf3947 pr4480/nn,pnx6718   qpf7592 ptn3808   wcj(853)

14 And the men   took of*their*victuals, and asked not *counsel*   at the

cs,nn6310   nn3068

mouth of the LORD.

nn3091 wcs,qmf6213 nn7965   pp,pnx   wcs,qmf6213   nn1285   pp,pnx

15 And Joshua made peace with them, and made a league with them, to let

pp,pinc,pnx2421   pl,cs,nn5387   df,nn5712 wcs,nimf7650 pp,pnx

them live: and the princes of the congregation swore unto them.

wcs,qmf1961   pr4480/cs,nn7097 cs,nu7969 pl,nn3117 ad310/pnl834   qpf3772

16 And it*came*to*pass at*the*end of three days after they had made a

nn1285   pp,pnx   wcs,qmf8085 cj3588 pnp1992   pr,pnx413   aj7138   pnp1992

league with them, that they heard that they *were* their neighbors, and *that* they

pl,qpta3427 wcj,pp,nn,pnx7130

dwelt among them.

pl,cs,nn1121   nn3478   wcs,qmf5265   wcs,qmf935 pr413   pl,nn,pnx5892

17 And the children of Israel journeyed, and came unto their cities on the

df,nuor7992 dfp,nn3117   wcj,pl,nn,pnx5892   nn1391   wcj,df,nn3716   wcj,nn881

third day. Now their cities *were* Gibeon, and Chephirah, and Beeroth, and

wcj,nn7157

Kirjath-jearim.

pl,cs,nn1121   nn3478   hipf,pnx5221   wcj,ptn3808   cj3588   pl,cs,nn5387

18 And the children of Israel smote them not, because the princes of the

df,nn5712   nipf7650   pp,pnx   pp,nn3068 pl,cs,nn430   nn3478   cs,nn3605

congregation had sworn unto them by the LORD God of Israel. And all the

df,nn5712   wcs,qmf3885   pr5921   df,pl,nn5387

congregation murmured against the princes.

cs,nn3605   df,pl,nn5387 wcs,qmf559 pr413 cs,nn3605   df,nn5712   pnp587   nipf7650

19 But all the princes said unto all the congregation, We have sworn

pp,pnx   pp,nn3068 pl,cs,nn430   nn3478 wcj,ad6258   qmf3201 ptn3808 pp,qnc5060 pp,pnx

unto them by the LORD God of Israel: now therefore we may not touch them.

pndm2063   qmf6213   pp,pnx   wcj,hina2421/pnx(853) wcj,ptn3808 nn7110 qmf1961

20 This we will do to them; we will even let*them*live, lest wrath be

pr,pnx5921   pr5921   df,nn7621 pnl834   nipf7650   pp,pnx

upon us, because of the oath which we swore unto them.

df,pl,nn5387 wcs,qmf559 pr,pnx413   qmf2421   wcs,qmf1961

21 And the princes said unto them, Let them live; but let them be

pl,cs,qpta2404   pl,nn6086   wcj,pl,cs,qpta7579   pl,nn4325   pp,cs,nn3605   df,nn5712   pp,pnl834

hewers of wood and drawers of water unto all the congregation; as the

df,pl,nn5387   pipf1696   pp,pnx

princes had promised them.

nn3091 wcs,qmf7121   pp,pnx   wcs,pimf1696 pr,pnx413   pp,qnc559   pp,pnid4100

22 And Joshua called for them, and he spoke unto them, saying, Wherefore

pipf7411   pnx(853)   pp,qnc559 pnp587   ad3966 aj7350 pr,pnx4480   wcj,pnp859 pl,qpta3427

have ye beguiled   us, saying, We *are* very far from you; when ye dwell

pp,nn,pnx7130

among us?

wcj,ad6258   pnp859   pl,qptp779   wcj,ptn3808 pr,pnx4480   nimf3772

23 Now therefore ye *are* cursed, and there shall none of you be freed

nn5650   wcj,pl,cs,qpta2404   pl,nn6086   wcj,pl,cs,qpta7579   pl,nn4325   pp,cs,nn1004

from being bondmen, and hewers of wood and drawers of water for the house

pl,nn,pnx430

of my God.

wcs,qmf6030   (853)   nn3091   wcs,qmf559 cj3588   hona5046/hopf5046

24 And they answered   Joshua, and said, Because it was certainly told thy

pp,pl,nn,pnx5650 (853)   pnl834   nn3068   pl,nn,pnx430 pipf6680   nn,pnx5650 (853) nn4872

servants,   how that the LORD thy God commanded his servant Moses to

pp,qnc5414 pp,pnx cs,nn3605   df,nn776   wcj,pp,hinc8045 (853) cs,nn3605   pl,cs,qpta3427   df,nn776

give you all the land, and to destroy   all the inhabitants of the land

pr4480/pl,nn,pnx**6440**　　　　　　　ad3966　wcs,qmf**3372**　　　　pp,pl,nn,pnx**5315**　pr4480/pl,nn,pnx**6440**

from before you, therefore we were sore afraid of our lives because of you,

wcs,qmf**6213** (853) df,pndm2088 df,nn**1697**

and have done this thing.

wcj,ad6258 ptdm,pnx2009　　　　　　pp,nn,pnx**3027**　　　dfp,aj**2896**　　　wcj,dfp,aj**3477**

25 And now, behold, we *are* in thine hand: as it seemeth good and right

pp,du,nn,pnx**5869**　　pp,qnc**6213**　　pp,pnx　　qmv**6213**

unto thee to do unto us, do.

ad**3651** wcs,qmf**6213**　　　　pp,pnx　　　　wcs,himf**5337** pnx(853)　　　　pr4480/cs,nn**3027**

26 And so did he unto them, and delivered them out*of*the*hand of

pl,cs,nn**1121**　　　nn3478　　qpf,pnx**2026**　wcj,ptn**3808**

the children of Israel, that they slew them not.

nn3091　wcs,qmf,pnx**5414**　　df,pndm1931 dfp,nn**3117** pl,cs,qpta2404　　pl,nn6086　　wcj,pl,cs,qpta7579

☞ 27 And Joshua made them that day hewers of wood and drawers of

pl,nn4325　　dfp,nn**5712**　　　　　　wcj,pp,cs,nn**4196**　　　nn**3068**　　pr5704 df,pndm2088

water for the congregation, and for the altar of the LORD, even unto this

df,nn**3117** pr413　df,nn4725 pnl834　　　　qmf**977**

day, in the place which he should choose.

The Amorites are Defeated

wcs,qmf**1961**　　　　　　　nn139　　　cs,nn**4428**　　　nn3389

10 Now it*came*to*pass, when Adoni-zedek king of Jerusalem had

pp,qnc**8085**　cj3588　　nn3091　　qpf3920　(853) df,nn5857　　　　wcs,himf,pnx**2763**

heard how Joshua had taken Ai, and had utterly destroyed it;

pp,pnl834　　qpf**6213**　　pp,nn**3405**　　wcj,pp,nn,pnx**4428** ad**3651**　　qpf**6213**　　pp,nn5857

as he had done to Jericho and her king, so he had done to Ai and her

wcj,pp,nn,pnx**4428**　wcj,cj3588　　pl,cs,qpta**3427**　　nn1391　　hipf,pnx**7999**　pr854　nn3478

king; and how the inhabitants of Gibeon had made peace with Israel, and

wcs,qmf**1961** pp,nn,pnx**7130**

were among them;

wcs,qmf**3372**　ad3966　　cj3588　　nn1391　　　　aj1419　nn5892　pp,cs,nu259

2 That they feared greatly, because Gibeon *was* a great city, as one of the

df,nn**4467** pl,cs,nn5892　　wcj,cj3588　pnp1931　　aj1419　pr4480 df,nn5857　wcj,cs,nn3605　pl,nn**376**

royal cities, and because it *was* greater than Ai, and all the men thereof

aj1368

were mighty.

nn139　　　cs,nn**4428**　　　nn3389　wcs,qmf7971　pr413　nn1944　cs,nn**4428**

3 Wherefore Adoni-zedek king of Jerusalem sent unto Hoham king of

nn2275　　wcj,pr413　nn6502　cs,nn**4428**　　nn3412　　wcj,pr413　nn3309　cs,nn**4428**　　nn3923

Hebron, and unto Piram king of Jarmuth, and unto Japhia king of Lachish, and

wcj,pr413　nn1688 cs,nn**4428**　　nn5700　pp,qnc559

unto Debir king of Eglon, saying,

qmv**5927**　　pr,pnx413　　wcj,qmv,pnx5826　　　wcj,himf**5221** (853)　nn1391　cj3588

4 Come up unto me, and help me, that we may smite Gibeon: for

hipf**7999**　pr854　nn3091　　wcj,pr854　　pl,cs,nn**1121**　　nn3478

it hath made peace with Joshua and with the children of Israel.

cs,nu2568 pl,cs,nn**4428**　　df,nn567　　cs,nn**4428**　　nn3389　　cs,nn**4428**

5 Therefore the five kings of the Amorites, the king of Jerusalem, the king

nn2275　　cs,nn**4428**　　　nn3412　　cs,nn**4428**　　nn3923　　cs,nn**4428**　　nn5700

of Hebron, the king of Jarmuth, the king of Lachish, the king of Eglon,

---

☞ **9:27** The Gibeonites were among those who rebuilt the walls of Jerusalem after the return of Israel from exile (Neh. 7:25). The irony is seen in that Solomon received a message from God in a dream at Gibeon (1 Kgs. 3:5–15).

wcs,nimf**622**   wcs,qmf**5927**   pnp1992   wcj,cs,nn3605   pl,nn,pnx**4264**

gathered*themselves*together, and went up, they and all their hosts, and

wcs,qmf2583   pr5921   nn1391   wcs,nimf3898   pr,pnx5921

encamped before Gibeon, and made war against it.

pl,cs,nn**376**   nn1391   wcs,qmf7971   pr413   nn3091   pr413   df,nn**4264**   df,nn,lh1537   pp,qnc**559**

6 And the men of Gibeon sent unto Joshua to the camp to Gilgal, saying,

qmf7503   ptn408   du,nn,pnx**3027**   pr4480/pl,nn,pnx**5650**   qmv**5927**   pr,pnx413   nn4120   wcj,himv**3467**

Slack not thy hand from*thy*servants; come up to us quickly, and save

pp,pnx   wcj,qmv,pnx5826   cj3588   cs,nn3605   pl,cs,nn**4428**   df,nn567   pl,cs,qpta**3427**

us, and help us: for all the kings of the Amorites that dwell in the

df,nn2022   nipf**6908**   pr,pnx413

mountains are gathered together against us.

nn3091   wcs,qmf**5927**   pr4480   df,nn1537   pnp1931   wcj,cs,nn3605   cs,nn**5971**   df,nn4421   pr,pnx5973

7 So Joshua ascended from Gilgal, he, and all the people of war with

wcj,cs,nn3605   pl,cs,nn1368   df,nn**2428**

him, and all the mighty men of valor.

nn3068   wcs,qmf559   pr413   nn3091   qmf**3372**   ptn408   cj3588   qpf,pnx**5414**

8 And the LORD said unto Joshua, Fear them not: for I have delivered them

pp,nn,pnx**3027**   ptn**3808**   nn**376**   pr,pnx4480   qmf5975   pp,pl,nn,pnx**6440**

into thine hand; there shall not a man of them stand before thee.

nn3091   wcs,qmf935   pr,pnx413   ad6597   qpf**5927**   pr4480   df,nn1537   cs,nn3605

9 Joshua therefore came unto them suddenly, *and* went up from Gilgal all

df,nn**3915**

night.

nn3068   wcs,qmf,pnx**2000**   pp,pl,cs,nn**6440**   nn3478   wcs,himf,pnx**5221**

10 And the LORD discomfited them before Israel, and slew them with a

aj1419   nn**4347**   pp,nn1391   wcs,qmf,pnx7291   cs,nn**1870**   cs,nn4608

great slaughter at Gibeon, and chased them along the way that goeth up to

nn1032   wcs,himf,pnx**5221**   pr5704   nn5825   wcj,pr5704   nn4719

Beth-horon, and smote them to Azekah, and unto Makkedah.

wcs,qmf**1961**   pp,qnc,pnx5127   pr4480/pl,cs,nn**6440**   nn3478   (pnp1992)

11 And it*came*to*pass, as they fled from before Israel, *and* were

pp,cs,nn4174   nn1032   wcj,nn**3068**   hipf**7993**   aj1419   pl,nn68   pr4480

in the going down to Beth-horon, that the LORD cast down great stones from

df,du,nn**8064**   pr,pnx5921   pr5704   nn5825   wcs,qmf**4191**   aj7227   pnl834   qpf**4191**

heaven upon them unto Azekah, and they died: *they were* more which died with

df,nn1259/pp,pl,cs,nn68   pr4480/pnl834   pl,cs,nn**1121**   nn3478   qpf**2026**   dfp,nn**2719**

hailstones than*they*whom the children of Israel slew with the sword.

ad227   pimf**1696**   nn3091   pp,nn**3068**   pp,cs,nn**3117**   nn**3068**   qnc**5414**

☞ 12 Then spoke Joshua to the LORD in the day when the LORD delivered up

(853)   df,nn567   pp,pl,cs,nn**6440**   pl,cs,nn**1121**   nn3478   wcs,qmf559   pp,du,cs,nn**5869**

the Amorites before the children of Israel, and he said in the sight of

nn3478   nn8121   qmv1826   pp,nn1391   wcj,nn3394   pp,cs,nn6010   nn357

Israel, Sun, stand*thou*still upon Gibeon; and thou, Moon, in the valley of Ajalon.

df,nn8121   wcs,qmf1826   wcj,nn3394   qpf5975   cj5704   nn**1471**

13 And the sun stood still, and the moon stayed, until the people had

qmf5358   pl,qpta,pnx341   he,ptn**3808**   pnp1931   qptp3789   pr5921   cs,nn**5612**

avenged themselves upon their enemies. *Is* not this written in the book of

---

☞ **10:12–14** At Joshua's request, God caused the sun to stand still for 12 or 24 hours so that Israel could achieve a greater victory. This is one of the two times recorded in the Old Testament when God interrupted time as a favor or a sign to a man. The other occasion was the turning back of the sundial ten points for the benefit of Hezekiah (Is. 38:7, 8).

df,nn3477　　　df,nn8121　wcs,qmf5975　　　dfp,cs,nn2677　　df,du,nn8064　　qpf213　wcj,ptn3808

Jasher? So the sun stood still in the midst of heaven, and hasted not to

pp,qnc935　　　　aj8549　pp,nn3117

go down about a whole day.

qpf1961　wcj,ptn3808　dfp,nn3117　　df,pndm1931　pp,pl,nn,pnx6440　　wcj,pr,pnx310

14 And there was no day like that before it or after it, that the

nn3068　pp,qnc8085　　　pp,cs,nn6963　　nn376　cj3588　　nn3068　nipt3898　　pp,nn3478

LORD hearkened unto the voice of a man: for the LORD fought for Israel.

nn3091　wcs,qmf7725　wcj,cs,nn3605　nn3478　pr,pnx5973　　pr413　　df,nn4264

15 And Joshua returned, and all Israel with him, unto the camp to

df,nn,lh1537

Gilgal.

df,pndm428　cs,nu2568　df,pl,nn4428　wcs,qmf5127　　　wcs,nimf2244　　　　dfp,nn4631

16 But these five kings fled, and hid themselves in a cave at

pp,nn4719

Makkedah.

wcs,homf5046　pp,nn3091　pp,qnc559　cs,nu2568　df,pl,nn4428　nipf4672　pl,nipt2244

17 And it was told Joshua, saying, The five kings are found hid in a

dfp,nn4631　　pp,nn4719

cave at Makkedah.

nn3091　wcs,qmf559　qmv1556　aj1419　pl,nn68　pr413　　cs,nn6310　　df,nn4631

18 And Joshua said, Roll great stones upon the mouth of the cave, and

wcj,himv6485　pl,nn376　pr,pnx5921　　pp,qnc,pnx8104

set men by it for to keep them:

qmf5975　wcj,pnp859　ptn408　qmv7291　pr310　　pl,qpta,pnx341　　　wcs,pipf2179

19 And stay ye not, *but* pursue after your enemies, and smite*the*hindmost

pnx(853)　　　qmf,pnx5414　　ptn408　pp,qnc935　pr413　pl,nn,pnx5892　cj3588　　nn3068

of them; suffer them not to enter into their cities: for the LORD your

pl,nn,pnx430　qpf,pnx5414　　pp,nn,pnx3027

God hath delivered them into your hand.

wcs,qmf1961　　　nn3091　　wcj,pl,cs,nn1121　　nn3478

20 And it*came*to*pass, when Joshua and the children of Israel had

pp,pinc3615　　pp,hinc,pnx5221　　ad3966　aj1419　nn4347　　pr5704

made*an*end of slaying them with a very great slaughter, till they were

nn,pnx8552　　wcj,df,pl,nn8300　qpf8277　pr,pnx4480　wcs,qmf935　pr413　df,nn4013　pl,cs,nn5892

consumed, that the rest *which* remained of them entered into fenced cities.

cs,nn3605　df,nn5971　wcs,qmf7725　pr413　　df,nn4264　pr413　nn3091　　nn4719

21 And all the people returned to the camp to Joshua at Makkedah in

pp,nn7965　ptn3808　qpf2782　(853)　nn,pnx3956　　pp,nn376　pp,pl,cs,nn1121　nn3478

peace: none moved his tongue against any of the children of Israel.

wcs,qmf559　nn3091　qmv6605　(853)　cs,nn6310　　df,nn4631　wcj,himv3318　(853)

22 Then said Joshua, Open the mouth of the cave, and bring out

df,pndm428　cs,nu2568　df,pl,nn4428　pr,pnx413　　pr4480　df,nn4631

those five kings unto me out of the cave.

wcs,qmf6213　ad3651　wcs,himf3318　(853)　df,pndm428　cs,nu2568　df,pl,nn4428　pr,pnx413

23 And they did so, and brought forth those five kings unto him

pr4480　df,nn4631　(853)　cs,nn4428　nn3389　(853)　cs,nn4428　nn2275　(853)　cs,nn4428

out of the cave, the king of Jerusalem, the king of Hebron, the king of

nn3412　(853)　cs,nn4428　nn3923　(853)　cs,nn4428　nn5700

Jarmuth, the king of Lachish, *and* the king of Eglon.

wcs,qmf1961　　　pp,hinc,pnx3318　(853)　df,pndm428　df,pl,nn4428　pr413　nn3091

24 And it*came*to*pass, when they brought out those kings unto Joshua,

nn3091　wcs,qmf7121　pr413　cs,nn3605　cs,nn376　　nn3478　wcs,qmf559　pr413　pl,cs,nn7101

that Joshua called for all the men of Israel, and said unto the captains of the

pl,cs,nn376　　df,nn4421　df,qpf1980　pr,pnx854　　qmv7126　qmv7760　(853)　du,nn,pnx7272　pr5921

men of war which went with him, Come near, put your feet upon the

pl,cs,nn6677   df,pndm428 df,pl,nn**4428**   wcs,qmf**7126**   wcs,qmf**7760** (853)   du,nn,pnx7272 pr5921

necks of these kings. And they came near, and   put   their feet   upon the

pl,nn,pnx6677

necks of them.

nn3091   wcs,qmf**559** pr,pnx413   qmf**3372** ptn408 wcj,ptn408   qmf**2865**   qmv**2388**

25 And Joshua said   unto them, Fear not,   nor be dismayed, be strong and

wcj,qmv553   cj3588 ad3602   nn**3068** qmf**6213**   pp,cs,nn3605   pl,qpta341

of good courage: for thus shall the Lord do to   all   your enemies against

pnl834/pnx(853) pnp859 pl,nipt3898

whom ye fight.

ad310/ad**3651**   nn3091   wcs,himf,pnx**5221**   wcs,himf,pnx**4191**   wcs,qmf,pnx8518

26 And afterward Joshua   smote   them, and   slew   them, and hanged

pr5921 nu2568 pl,nn6086   wcs,qmf**1961** pl,qptp8518 pr5704   df,pl,nn6086 pr5704   df,nn6153

them on five trees: and they were hanging upon the trees until the evening.

wcs,qmf**1961**   pp,nn**6256**   qnc935   df,nn8121

27 And it*came*to*pass at the time of the going down of the sun, *that*

nn3091   pipf**6680**   wcs,himf,pnx3381   pr4480/pr5921/df,pl,nn6086   wcs,himf,pnx**7993**

Joshua commanded, and they took*them*down off*the*trees, and   cast   them

pr413   df,nn4631 pnl834/ad8033   nipf2244   wcs,qmf**7760** aj1419   pl,nn68 pr5921   df,nn4631

into the cave wherein they had been hid, and laid great stones in the cave's

cs,nn**6310**   pr5704 df,pndm2088 cs,nn**6106** df,nn**3117**

mouth, *which remain* until this   very day.

Joshua Smites the Southern Cities

df,pndm1931 dfp,nn**3117**   nn3091   qpf3920 wcj(853)   nn4719   wcs,himf,pnx**5221**

28 And   that   day Joshua took   Makkedah, and smote   it with the

pp,cs,nn**6310**   nn**2719**   wcj(853)   nn,pnx**4428**   hipf**2763**   pnx(853)

edge of the sword, and   the king thereof he utterly destroyed   them,

wcj(853) cs,nn3605   df,nn**5315** pnl834   pp,pnx   hipf**7604** ptn3808   nn**8300**   wcs,qmf**6213**

and   all   the souls that *were* therein; he let none remain: and he   did   to

pp,cs,nn**4428**   nn4719 pp,pnl834   qpf**6213**   pp,cs,nn**4428**   nn3405

the king of Makkedah as he did unto the king of Jericho.

nn3091   wcs,qmf**5674**   pr4480/nn4719   wcj,cs,nn3605 nn3478 pr,pnx5973

29 Then Joshua passed from Makkedah, and   all   Israel with him, unto

pp,nn3841   wcs,nimf3898   pr5973   nn3841

Libnah, and fought against Libnah:

nn**3068** wcs,qmf**5414** ad1571   wcj(853)   nn,pnx**4428**   pp,cs,nn**3027**

30 And the Lord delivered it also, and   the king thereof, into the hand

nn3478   wcs,himf,pnx**5221**   pp,cs,nn**6310**   nn**2719**   wcj(853) cs,nn3605   df,nn**5315**

of Israel; and he smote it with the edge of the sword, and   all the souls

pnl834   pp,pnx   hipf**7604** ptn3808   nn**8300**   wcs,qmf**6213**   pp,nn,pnx**4428**

that *were* therein; he let none remain in it; but did unto the king thereof

pp,pnl834   qpf**6213**   pp,cs,nn**4428**   nn3405

as he did unto the king of Jericho.

nn3091   wcs,qmf**5674**   pr4480/nn3841   wcj,cs,nn3605 nn3478 pr,pnx5973

31 And Joshua passed from Libnah, and   all   Israel with him, unto

nn,lh3923   wcs,qmf2583   pr,pnx5921   wcs,nimf3898   pp,pnx

Lachish, and encamped against it, and fought against it:

nn**3068** wcs,qmf**5414**   (853)   nn3923   pp,cs,nn**3027**   nn3478

32 And the Lord delivered   Lachish into the hand of Israel, which

wcs,qmf,pnx3920   df,nuor8145 dfp,nn**3117** wcs,himf,pnx**5221**   pp,cs,nn**6310**   nn**2719**

took   it on the second day, and smote it with the edge of the sword, and wcj(853) cs,nn3605   df,nn5315 pnl834   pp,pnx   pp,nn3605 pnl834   qpf6213

all the souls that *were* therein, according to all that he had done to

pp,nn3841

Libnah.

ad227   nn2036   cs,nn4428   nn1507   qpf5927   pp,qnc5826 (853)   nn3923   nn3091

33 Then Horam king of Gezer came up to help Lachish; and Joshua

wcs,himf,pnx5221   wcj(853)   nn,pnx5971   pr5704   hipf7604 pp,pnx ptn1115   nn8300

smote him and his people, until he had left him none remaining.

pr4480/nn3923   nn3091 wcs,qmf5674   nn,lh5700   wcj,cs,nn3605 nn3478 pr,pnx5973

34 And from Lachish Joshua passed unto Eglon, and all Israel with him;

wcs,qmf2583 pr,pnx5921   wcs,nimf3898 pr,pnx5921

and they encamped against it, and fought against it:

wcs,qmf,pnx3920   df,pndm1931 dfp,nn3117   wcs,himf,pnx5221   pp,cs,nn6310

35 And they took it on that day, and smote it with the edge of

nn2719   wcj(853) cs,nn3605   df,nn5315 pnl834   pp,pnx   hipf2763 df,pndm1931

the sword, and all the souls that *were* therein he utterly destroyed that

dfp,nn3117   pp,nn3605 pnl834   qpf6213   pp,nn3923

day, according to all that he had done to Lachish.

nn3091   wcs,qmf5927   pr4480/nn,lh5700   wcj,cs,nn3605 nn3478 pr,pnx5973

36 And Joshua went up from Eglon, and all Israel with him, unto

nn,lh2275   wcs,nimf3898 pr,pnx5921

Hebron; and they fought against it:

wcs,qmf,pnx3920   wcs,himf,pnx5221   pp,cs,nn6310   nn2719

37 And they took it, and smote it with the edge of the sword, and

wcj(853)   nn,pnx4428   wcj(853) cs,nn3605   pl,nn,pnx5892   wcj(853) cs,nn3605

the king thereof, and all the cities thereof, and all the

df,nn5315 pnl834   pp,pnx   hipf7604 ptn3808   nn8300   pp,nn3605 pnl834

souls that *were* therein; he left none remaining, according to all that he had

qpf6213   pp,nn5700   wcs,himf2763 pnx(853)   wcj(853) cs,nn3605   df,nn5315 pnl834

done to Eglon; but destroyed it utterly, and all the souls that *were*

pp,pnx

therein.

nn3091   wcs,qmf7725   wcj,cs,nn3605 nn3478 pr,pnx5973   nn,lh1688   wcs,nimf3898

38 And Joshua returned, and all Israel with him, to Debir; and fought

pr,pnx5921

against it:

wcs,qmf,pnx3920   wcj(853)   nn,pnx4428   wcj(853) cs,nn3605   pl,nn,pnx5892

39 And he took it, and the king thereof, and all the cities

wcs,himf,pnx5221   pp,cs,nn6310   nn2719   wcs,himf2763

thereof; and they smote them with the edge of the sword, and utterly destroyed

(853) cs,nn3605   nn5315 pnl834   pp,pnx   hipf7604 ptn3808   nn8300   pp,pnl834   qpf6213

all the souls that *were* therein; he left none remaining: as he had done to

pp,nn2275 ad3651   qpf6213   pp,nn,lh1688   wcj,pp,nn,pnx4428   wcj,pp,pnl834   qpf6213

Hebron, so he did to Debir, and to the king thereof; as he had done

pp,nn3841   wcj,pp,nn,pnx4428

also to Libnah, and to her king.

nn3091   wcs,himf5221 (853) cs,nn3605   df,nn776   df,nn2022   wcj,df,nn5045

40 So Joshua smote all the country of the hills, and of the south, and

wcj,df,nn8219   wcj,df,pl,nn794   wcj(853) cs,nn3605   pl,nn,pnx4428   hipf7604 ptn3808

of the vale, and of the springs, and all their kings: he left none

---

🕮 **10:33** Because Gezer remained a Canaanite stronghold long after Joshua's time (Josh. 16:10; Judg. 1:29), one can assume that Joshua probably did not attempt to destroy it.

nn**8300**   hipf**2763**   wcj(853) cs,nn3605   df,nn**5397**   pp,pnl834   nn**3068**   pl,cs,nn**430**

remaining, but utterly destroyed   all   that breathed,   as   the LORD God of
nn3478   pipf**6680**

Israel commanded.

nn3091   wcs,himf,pnx**5221**   pr4480/nn6947   wcj,pr5704   nn5804   wcj(853)

41 And Joshua   smote   them from Kadesh-barnea even   unto Gaza, and
cs,nn3605   cs,nn776   nn1657   wcj,pr5704   nn1391

all   the country of Goshen, even unto Gibeon.

wcj(853) cs,nn3605 df,pndm428 df,pl,nn**4428**   wcj(853)   nn,pnx776   nn3091   qpf3920   nu259

42 And   all   these kings and   their land did Joshua take at one
nn6471   cj3588   nn**3068**   pl,cs,nn**430**   nn3478   nipf3898   pp,nn3478

time, because the LORD God of Israel fought for Israel.

nn3091   wcs,qmf**7725**   wcj,cs,nn3605   nn3478   pr,pnx5973   pr413   df,nn**4264**

43 And Joshua returned, and   all   Israel with him, unto the camp to
df,nn,lh1537

Gilgal.

Northern Kings are Defeated

wcs,qmf**1961**   nn2985   cs,nn**4428**   nn2674   pp,qnc**8085**

11
And it*came*to*pass, when Jabin king of Hazor had heard *those*
wcs,qmf7971 pr413 nn3103 cs,nn**4428**   nn4068   wcj,pr413   cs,nn**4428**

things, that he   sent   to Jobab king of Madon, and   to   the king
nn8110   wcj,pr413   cs,nn**4428**   nn407

of Shimron, and   to   the king of Achshaph,

wcj,pr413   df,pl,nn**4428** pnl834   pr4480/cs,nn6828   dfp,nn2022

2 And   to   the kings that *were* on*the*north of the mountains, and of the
wcj,dfp,nn**6160** cs,nn5045   nn3672   wcj,dfp,nn8219   wcj,pp,pl,cs,nn5299   nn1756

plains   south of Chinneroth, and in the   valley, and in the   borders of Dor
pr4480/nn3220

on*the*west,

df,nn3669   pr4480/nn4217   wcj,pr4480/nn3220   wcj,df,nn567

3 *And to* the Canaanite on*the*east and on*the*west, and *to* the Amorite, and
wcj,df,nn2850   wcj,df,nn6522   wcj,df,nn2983   dfp,nn2022   wcj,df,nn2340

the Hittite, and the Perizzite, and the Jebusite in the mountains, and *to* the Hivite
pr8478   nn2768   pp,cs,nn**776**   df,nn4709

under Hermon in the   land of Mizpeh.

wcs,qmf3318   pnp1992   wcj,cs,nn3605   pl,nn,pnx**4264**   pr,pnx5973   aj7227

4 And they went out, they and   all   their   hosts   with   them, much
nn**5971**   dfp,nn2344 pnl834   pr5921   df,nn3220 cs,nn**8193**   dfp,nn7230   wcj,nn5483

people, even as the sand that *is* upon the sea shore in multitude, with horses and
wcj,nn7393 ad3966 aj7227

chariots very many.

cs,nn3605 df,pndm428 df,pl,nn**4428**   wcs,nimf**3259**   wcs,qmf935   wcs,qmf2583

5 And when all   these kings were met together, they came and pitched
ad3162   pr413   pl,cs,nn4325   nn4792   pp,ninc3898 pr5973   nn3478

together at the waters of Merom, to fight against Israel.
nn**3068**   wcs,qmf**559** pr413   nn3091   ptn408   qmf3372 pr4480/pl,nn,pnx**6440**   cj3588

🔒 6 And the LORD   said   unto Joshua, Be not afraid because of them: for
ad4279   df,pndm2063 dfp,nn**6256**   pnp595   qpta**5414**   (853) nn,pnx3605 pl,nn2491 pp,pl,cs,nn**6440**

tomorrow about this   time will I deliver*them*up   all   slain before

---

🔒 **11:6** Cutting the tendons of the legs rendered the horses unfit for military service. This is illustrated in
the word translated "hamstring." Israel herself was forbidden by God to develop a cavalry (Deut. 17:16) because
God wanted them to depend upon Him, not the strength of horses (Is. 31:1, 3).

nn3478   pimf6131   (853)   pl,nn,pnx5483   qmf8313 wcj(853)   pl,nn,pnx4818   dfp,nn784
Israel: thou shalt hamstring   their horses, and burn   their chariots with fire.

             nn3091   wcs,qmf935   wcj,cs,nn3605   cs,nn5971   df,nn4421 pr,pnx5973   pr,pnx5921
    7 So Joshua came, and   all   the people of war   with him, against them
pr5921   pl,cs,nn4325   nn4792   ad6597   wcs,qmf5307   pp,pnx
by the waters of Merom suddenly; and they   fell   upon them.

                  nn3068   wcs,qmf,pnx5414   pp,cs,nn3027   nn3478   wcs,himf,pnx5221
    8 And the Lord delivered them into the   hand of Israel, who   smote   them,
wcs,qmf,pnx7291   pr5704 aj7227   nn6721   wcj,pr5704   nn4956   wcj,pr5704
and   chased   them unto great Zidon, and   unto Misrephoth-maim, and   unto the
cs,nn1237   nn4708   nn,lh4217   wcs,himf,pnx5221   pr5704   hipf7604 pp,pnx ptn1115
valley of Mizpeh eastward; and they   smote   them, until they left them none
nn8300
remaining.

                 nn3091   wcs,qmf6213   pp,pnx   pp,pnl834   nn3068   qpf559 pp,pnx   pipf6131   (853)
    9 And Joshua   did   unto them   as   the Lord bade him: he hamstrung
pl,nn,pnx5483   qpf8313   wcj(853)   pl,nn,pnx4818   dfp,nn784
their horses, and burnt   their chariots with fire.

                 nn3091   df,pndm1931 dfp,nn6256   wcs,qmf7725   wcs,qmf3920 (853)   nn2674   hipf5221
    10 And Joshua at that   time turned back, and   took   Hazor, and smote
wcj(853)   nn,nn4428   dfp,nn2719 cj3588   nn2674   pp,pl,nn6440   (pnp1931)   cs,nn7218
    the king thereof with the sword: for Hazor formerly   was the head of
cs,nn3605 df,pndm428   df,pl,nn4467
all   those kingdoms.

              wcs,himf5221 (853) cs,nn3605   df,nn5315 pnl834   pp,pnx   pp,cs,nn6310
    11 And they smote   all   the souls that were therein with the   edge of the
nn2719   hina2763   ptn3808 cs,nn3605 nipf3498   nn5397   qpf8313
sword, utterly destroying them: there was   not   any   left to breathe: and he burnt
wcj(853)   nn2674   dfp,nn784
    Hazor with fire.

              wcj(853) cs,nn3605   pl,cs,nn5892   df,pndm428 df,pl,nn4428   wcj(853) cs,nn3605   pl,nn,pnx4428
    12 And   all the cities of those kings, and   all   the kings of
          nn3091 qpf3920   wcs,himf,pnx5221   pp,cs,nn6310   nn2719
them, did Joshua take, and   smote   them with the   edge   of the sword, and he
   hipf2763   pnx(853)   pp,pnl834 nn4872   cs,nn5650   nn3068   pipf6680
utterly destroyed   them,   as   Moses the servant of the Lord commanded.

         ad7535   (cs,nn3605)   df,pl,nn5892   df,pl,qpta5975 pr5921   nn,pnx8510   nn3478 qpf,pnx8313
    13 But as for   the cities that stood still   in their strength, Israel burned
ptn3808   pr2108 (853) nn2674   pp,nn,pnx905   nn3091   qpf8313
none of them, save   Hazor   only;   that did Joshua burn.

              wcj,cs,nn3605   cs,nn7998   df,pndm428 df,pl,nn5892   wcj,df,nn929   pl,cs,nn1121
    14 And   all   the spoil of these cities, and the cattle, the children of
nn3478   qpf962   pp,pnx   ad7535 (853) cs,nn3605 df,nn120   hipf5221
Israel took*for*a*prey unto themselves; but   every man they smote with the
pp,cs,nn6310   nn2719   pr5704   hipf,pnx8045 pnx(853)   ptn3808 hipf7604   cs,nn3605
edge of the sword, until they had destroyed   them, neither left they any to
nn5397
breathe.

              pp,pnl834   nn3068   pipf6680   (853) nn4872   nn,pnx5650 ad3651   nn4872   pipf6680
    15 As   the Lord commanded   Moses his servant, so did Moses command
(853) nn3091   wcj,ad3651 qpf6213   nn3091   ptn3808/hipf5493/nn1697   pr4480/nn3605 pnl834   nn3068
Joshua, and so   did Joshua; he left*nothing*undone of all   that the Lord
pipf6680   (853)   nn4872
commanded   Moses.

Summary of Joshua's Victories

nn3091 wcs,qmf3947 (853) cs,nn3605 df,pndm2063 df,nn776 df,nn2022 wcj(853) cs,nn3605

16 So Joshua took all that land, the hills, and all the

df,nn5045 wcj(853) cs,nn3605 cs,nn776 df,nn1657 wcj(853) df,nn8219 wcj(853)

south country, and all the land of Goshen, and the valley, and

df,nn6160 wcj(853) cs,nn2022 nn3478 wcj,pl,nn,pnx8219

the plain, and the mountain of Israel, and the valley of the same;

pr4480 df,nn2022 df,nn2510 df,qpta5927 nn8165 wcj,pr5704 nn1171

17 *Even* from the mount Halak, that goeth up to Seir, even unto Baal-gad in

pp,cs,nn1237 df,nn3844 pr8478 cs,nn2022 nn2768 wcj(853) cs,nn3605 pl,nn,pnx4428 qpf3920

the valley of Lebanon under mount Hermon: and all their kings he took,

wcs,himf,pnx5221 wcs,himf,pnx4191

and smote them, and slew them.

nn3091 qpf6213 nn4421 aj7227 pl,nn3117 pr854 cs,nn3605 df,pndm428 df,pl,nn4428

18 Joshua made war a long time with all those kings.

qpf1961 ptn3808 nn5892 pnl834 hipf7999 pr413 pl,cs,nn1121 nn3478 ptn1115

19 There was not a city that made peace with the children of Israel, save the

df,nn2340 pl,cs,qpta3427 nn1391 (853) df,nn3605 qpf3947 dfp,nn4421

Hivites the inhabitants of Gibeon: all *other* they took in battle.

cj3588 qpf1961 pr4480 (853) nn3068 pp,pinc2388 (853) nn,pnx3820

20 For it was of the LORD to harden their hearts, that they should

pp,qnc7125 (853) nn3478 df,nn4421 pr4616 hinc,pnx2763 pp,pnx

come against Israel in battle, that he might destroy them utterly, *and* that they

qnc1961 pp,ptn1115 nn8467 cj3588 pr4616 hinc,pnx8045 pp,pnl834 nn3068

might have no favor, but that he might destroy them, as the LORD

pipf6680 (853) nn4872

commanded Moses.

df,pndm1931 dfp,nn6256 wcs,qmf935 nn3091 wcs,himf3772 (853) pl,nn6062 pr4480

21 And at that time came Joshua, and cut off the Anakims from the

df,nn2022 pr4480 nn2275 pr4480 nn1688 pr4480 nn6024 wcj,pr4480/cs,nn3605 cs,nn2022

mountains, from Hebron, from Debir, from Anab, and from all the mountains of

nn3063 wcj,pr4480/cs,nn3605 cs,nn2022 nn3478 nn3091 hipf,pnx2763 pr5973

Judah, and from all the mountains of Israel: Joshua destroyed them utterly with

pl,nn,pnx5892

their cities.

ptn3808 pl,nn6062 nipf3498 pp,cs,nn776 pl,cs,nn1121 nn3478

22 There was none of the Anakims left in the land of the children of Israel:

ad7535 pp,nn5804 pp,nn1661 wcj,pp,nn795 nipf7604

only in Gaza, in Gath, and in Ashdod, there remained.

nn3091 wcs,qmf3947 (853) cs,nn3605 df,nn776 pp,nn3605 pnl834 nn3068 pipf1696

23 So Joshua took the whole land, according to all that the LORD said

pr413 nn4872 nn3091 wcs,qmf,pnx5414 pp,nn5159 pp,nn3478

unto Moses; and Joshua gave it for an inheritance unto Israel according to their

pp,pl,nn,pnx4256 pp,pl,nn,pnx7626 wcj,df,nn776 qpf8252 pr4480/nn4421

divisions by their tribes. And the land rested from war.

11:21 The Anakim were the giants of whom the ten spies were so afraid (Num. 13:33). Caleb conquered them (Josh. 15:14). Caleb's action is probably in view here under Joshua's name as part of the larger campaign.

11:23 See the introduction to the Book of Joshua.

The Kings Defeated Under Moses

12 <small>wcj,pndm428</small> Now these *are* the <small>pl,cs,nn4428</small> kings of the <small>df,nn776</small> land, <small>pnl834</small> which the <small>pl,cs,nn1121</small> children of <small>nn3478</small> Israel <small>hipf5221</small> smote, <small>wcs,qmf3423</small> and possessed <small>(853)</small> their <small>nn,pnx776</small> land on the <small>pp,cs,nn5676</small> other side <small>df,nn3383</small> Jordan <small>nn,lh4217</small> toward the rising <small>df,nn8121</small> of the sun, <small>pr4480/cs,nn5158</small> from*the*river <small>nn769</small> Arnon <small>pr5704</small> unto <small>cs,nn2022</small> mount <small>nn2768</small> Hermon, and <small>wcj,cs,nn3605</small> all <small>df,nn6160</small> the plain <small>nn,lh4217</small> on the east:

2 <small>nn5511</small> Sihon <small>cs,nn4428</small> king of the Amorites, <small>df,nn567</small> who <small>df,qpta3427</small> dwelt in <small>pp,nn2809</small> Heshbon, *and* <small>qpta4910</small> ruled <small>pr4480/nn6177</small> from Aroer, <small>pnl834</small> which *is* <small>pr5921</small> upon the bank <small>cs,nn8193</small> of the river <small>cs,nn5158</small> Arnon, <small>nn769</small> and from the <small>wcj,cs,nn8432</small> middle <small>df,nn5158</small> of the river, and <small>wcj,cs,nn2677</small> from half <small>df,nn1568</small> Gilead, even <small>wcj,pr5704</small> unto the <small>df,nn5158</small> river <small>nn2999</small> Jabbok, *which is* the <small>cs,nn1366</small> border of the <small>pl,cs,nn1121</small> children of <small>nn5983</small> Ammon;

3 And from the <small>wcj,df,nn6160</small> plain <small>pr5704</small> to the <small>cs,nn3220</small> sea of <small>nn3672</small> Chinneroth on the <small>nn,lh4217</small> east, and <small>wcj,pr5704</small> unto the <small>cs,nn3220</small> sea of the <small>df,nn6160</small> plain, *even* the <small>df,nn4417</small> salt <small>cs,nn3220</small> sea on the <small>nn,lh4217</small> east, the <small>cs,nn1870</small> way to <small>df,nn1020 [cs,nn1004/df,pl,nn3451]</small> Beth-jeshimoth; <small>wcj,pr4480/nn8486</small> and from*the*south, <small>pr8478</small> under <small>nn798 [pl,cs,nn794/df,nn6449]</small> Ashdoth-pisgah:

4 And the <small>wcj,cs,nn1366</small> coast <small>nn5747</small> of Og <small>cs,nn4428</small> king of <small>df,nn1316</small> Bashan, *which was* of*the*remnant <small>pr4480/cs,nn3499</small> of the <small>df,nn7497</small> giants, <small>df,qpta3427</small> that dwelt at <small>pp,nn6252</small> Ashtaroth and at <small>wcj,pp,nn154</small> Edrei,

5 And reigned <small>wcj,qpta4910</small> in mount <small>pp,cs,nn2022</small> Hermon, <small>nn2768</small> and in Salcah, <small>wcj,pp,nn5548</small> and in all <small>wcj,pp,cs,nn3605</small> Bashan, <small>df,nn1316</small> unto <small>pr5704</small> the border <small>cs,nn1366</small> of the Geshurites <small>df,nn1651</small> and the Maachathites, <small>wcj,df,nn4602</small> and half <small>wcj,cs,nn2677</small> Gilead, <small>df,nn1568</small> the border <small>cs,nn1366</small> of Sihon <small>nn5511</small> king <small>cs,nn4428</small> of Heshbon. <small>nn2809</small>

6 Them did Moses <small>nn4872</small> the servant <small>cs,nn5650</small> of the LORD <small>nn3068</small> and the children <small>wcj,pl,cs,nn1121</small> of Israel <small>nn3478</small> smite: <small>hipf,pnx5221</small> and Moses <small>nn4872</small> the servant <small>cs,nn5650</small> of the LORD <small>nn3068</small> gave <small>wcs,qmf,pnx5414</small> it *for* a possession <small>nn3425</small> unto the Reubenites, <small>dfp,nn7206</small> and the Gadites, <small>wcj,dfp,nn1425</small> and the <small>wcj,dfp,cs,nn2677</small> half <small>cs,nn7626</small> tribe of Manasseh. <small>df,nn4519</small>

The Kings Defeated Under Joshua

7 And these <small>wcj,pndm428</small> *are* the kings <small>pl,cs,nn4428</small> of the country <small>df,nn776</small> which <small>pnl834</small> Joshua <small>nn3091</small> and the children of <small>wcj,pl,cs,nn1121</small> Israel <small>nn3478</small> smote <small>hipf5221</small> on this <small>pp,cs,nn5676</small> side Jordan <small>df,nn3383</small> on the west, <small>nn,lh3220</small> from Baal-gad <small>pr4480/nn1171</small> in the valley of <small>pp,cs,nn1237</small> Lebanon <small>df,nn3844</small> even unto <small>wcj,pr5704</small> the mount <small>df,nn2022</small> Halak, <small>df,nn2510</small> that goeth up <small>df,qpta5927</small> to Seir; <small>nn,lh8165</small> which <small>nn3091</small> Joshua

---

☞ **12:1** The extent of the conquest under Joshua's leadership was vast, but the task was too large to have been completed in his life time (Deut 7:22; Josh. 13:1–6). During the nearly seven–year military campaign (see Josh. 14:7–10), the borders of Israel were expanded from Kadesh–barnea in the south (Josh. 10:41) to the foothills of Mount Hermon in the north (Josh. 11:17). Joshua's task now was to distribute the land among the tribes and leave the further conquest to God (Josh. 13:6, 7). The details of that distribution are given in chapters 13–21.

_{wcs,qmf,pnx**5414**}   _{pp,pl,cs,nn**7626**}   _{nn3478}   _{nn**3425**}   _{pp,pl,nn,pnx4256}

gave   unto the   tribes   of Israel *for* a possession according to their divisions;

_{dfp,nn2022}   _{wcj,dfp,nn8219}   _{wcj,dfp,nn**6160**}   _{wcj,dfp,pl,nn794}

8 In the mountains, and in the valleys, and in the plains, and in the springs,

_{wcj,dfp,nn4057}   _{wcj,dfp,nn5045}   _{df,nn2850}   _{df,nn567}

and in the wilderness, and in the   south   country; the Hittites, the Amorites, and

_{wcj,df,nn3669}   _{df,nn6522}   _{df,nn2340}   _{wcj,df,nn2983}

the Canaanites, the Perizzites, the Hivites, and the Jebusites:

_{cs,nn**4428**}   _{nn3405}   _{nu259}   _{cs,nn**4428**}   _{df,nn5857} _{pnl834}   _{pr4480/cs,nn6654}   _{nn1008}   _{nu259}

9 The king of Jericho, one; the king of Ai,   which *is*   beside   Bethel, one;

_{cs,nn**4428**}   _{nn3389}   _{nu259}   _{cs,nn**4428**}   _{nn2275}   _{nu259}

10 The king of Jerusalem, one; the king of Hebron, one;

_{cs,nn**4428**}   _{nn3412}   _{nu259}   _{cs,nn**4428**}   _{nn3923}   _{nu259}

11 The king of Jarmuth, one; the king of Lachish, one;

_{cs,nn**4428**}   _{nn5700}   _{nu259}   _{cs,nn**4428**}   _{nn1507}   _{nu259}

12 The king of Eglon, one; the king of Gezer, one;

_{cs,nn**4428**}   _{nn1688}   _{nu259}   _{cs,nn**4428**}   _{nn1445}   _{nu259}

13 The king of Debir, one; the king of Geder, one;

_{cs,nn**4428**}   _{nn2767}   _{nu259}   _{cs,nn**4428**}   _{nn6166}   _{nu259}

14 The king of Hormah, one; the king of Arad, one;

_{cs,nn**4428**}   _{nn3841}   _{nu259}   _{cs,nn**4428**}   _{nn5725}   _{nu259}

15 The king of Libnah, one; the king of Adullam, one;

_{cs,nn**4428**}   _{nn4719}   _{nu259}   _{cs,nn**4428**}   _{nn1008}   _{nu259}

16 The king of Makkedah, one; the king of Bethel, one;

_{cs,nn**4428**}   _{nn8599}   _{nu259}   _{cs,nn**4428**}   _{nn2660}   _{nu259}

17 The king of Tappuah, one; the king of Hepher, one;

_{cs,nn**4428**}   _{nn663}   _{nu259}   _{cs,nn**4428**}   _{nn8289}   _{nu259}

18 The king of Aphek, one; the king of Lasharon, one;

_{cs,nn**4428**}   _{nn4068}   _{nu259}   _{cs,nn**4428**}   _{nn2674}   _{nu259}

19 The king of Madon, one; the king of Hazor, one;

_{cs,nn**4428**}   _{nn8112}   _{nu259}   _{cs,nn**4428**}   _{nn407}   _{nu259}

20 The king of Shimron-meron, one; the king of Achshaph, one;

_{cs,nn**4428**}   _{nn8590}   _{nu259}   _{cs,nn**4428**}   _{nn4023}   _{nu259}

21 The king of Taanach, one; the king of Megiddo, one;

_{cs,nn**4428**}   _{nn6943}   _{nu259}   _{cs,nn**4428**}   _{nn3362}   _{dfp,nn3760}   _{nu259}

22 The king of Kedesh, one; the king of Jokneam of Carmel, one;

_{cs,nn**4428**}   _{nn1756}   _{pp,cs,nn5299}   _{nn1756}   _{nu259}   _{cs,nn**4428**}   _{pl,nn**1471**}

☞ 23 The king of Dor in the   coast   of Dor, one; the king of the nations of

_{pp,nn1537} _{nu259}

Gilgal, one;

_{cs,nn**4428**}   _{nn8656}   _{nu259} _{cs,nn3605}   _{pl,nn**4428**} _{nu7970}   _{wcj,nu259}

24 The king of Tirzah, one: all the kings thirty and one.

The Unconquered Territory

13

_{wcj,nn3091}   _{qpf**2204**}   _{qpf935}   _{dfp,pl,nn**3117**}   _{nn3068} _{wcs,qmf**559**}

☞ Now Joshua was old *and* stricken in years; and the L<small>ORD</small>   said

_{pr,pnx413}   _{pnp859} _{qpf**2204**}   _{qpf935}   _{dfp,pl,nn**3117**}   _{nipf**7604**}

unto him, Thou art old *and* stricken in years, and there remaineth

_{ad3966} _{hina7235} _{wcj,df,nn776}   _{pp,qnc,pnx**3423**}

yet very much   land   to be possessed.

☞ **12:23** This is not the same Gilgal which is mentioned as being near Jericho or the one which was near Bethel. This Gilgal was probably located about 42 miles north of Jerusalem, just south of Carmel.

☞ **13:1–7** See the note on Joshua 12:1, on the territories that remained unconquered.

pndm2063   df,nn776   df,nipt7604   cs,nn3605   pl,cs,nn1552   df,nn6430

2 This *is* the land that yet remaineth: all   the borders of the Philistines, and

wcj,cs,nn3605   df,nn1651

all   Geshuri,

pr4480   df,nn7883   pnl834   pr5921/pl,cs,nn**6440**   nn4714   wcj,pr5704   cs,nn1366   nn6138

3 From Sihor, which *is*   before   Egypt, even   unto   the borders of Ekron

nn,lh6828   nimf**2803**   dfp,nn3669   cs,nu2568   pl,cs,nn**5633**   pl,nn6430

northward, *which* is counted to the Canaanite: five   lords   of the Philistines; the

df,nn5841   wcj,df,nn796   df,nn832   df,nn1663   wcj,df,nn6139

Gazathites, and the Ashdothites, the Eshkalonites, the Gittites, and the Ekronites;

wcj,df,nn5757

also the Avites:

pr4480/nn8486   cs,nn3605   cs,nn776   df,nn3669   wcj,nn4632 pnl834

4 From*the*south,   all   the land of the Canaanites, and Mearah that *is* beside

dfp,pl,nn6722   pr5704   nn663   pr5704   cs,nn1366   df,nn567

the Sidonians, unto Aphek,   to   the borders of the Amorites:

wcj,df,nn776   df,nn1382   wcj,cs,nn3605   df,nn3844   cs,nn4217/df,nn8121

5 And the   land   of the Giblites, and   all   Lebanon, toward*the*sunrising,

pr4480/nn1171   pr8478 cs,nn2022   nn2768   pr5704   pp,qnc935   nn2574

from Baal-gad under mount Hermon unto the entering into Hamath.

cs,nn3605   pl,cs,qpta**3427**   df,nn2022   pr4480   df,nn3844   pr5704   nn4956

6   All   the inhabitants of the hill country from Lebanon unto Misrephoth-maim,

cs,nn3605   pl,nnaj6722   pnp595   himf,pnx**3423**   pr4480/pl,cs,nn**6440**   pl,cs,nn**1121**   nn3478

and all   the Sidonians, them will I   drive out from before the children of Israel:

ad7535   himv,pnx**5307**   pp,nn3478   pp,nn5159   pp,pnl834

only divide*thou*it*by*lot unto the Israelites for an inheritance,   as   I have

pipf,pnx**6680**

commanded thee.

Division of the Land East of the Jordan

wcj,ad6258   pimv2505   (853) df,pndm2063 df,nn776   pp,nn5159   pp,cs,nu8672

7 Now   therefore divide   this   land for an inheritance unto the   nine

df,pl,nn7626   wcj,cs,nn2677 df,nn7626   df,nn4519

tribes, and the   half   tribe of Manasseh,

pr,pnx5973   df,nn7206   wcj,df,nn1425   qpf3947   nn,pnx5159

8 With whom the Reubenites and the Gadites have received their inheritance,

pnl834   nn4872   qpf**5414** pp,pnx   pp,cs,nn5676 df,nn3383   nn,lh4217   pp,pnl834   nn4872   cs,nn**5650**

which Moses gave them, beyond Jordan eastward, *even*   as   Moses the servant of

nn**3068**   qpf**5414** pp,pnx

the LORD gave them;

pr4480/nn6177   pnl834   pr5921   cs,nn**8193**   cs,nn5158   nn769   wcj,df,nn5892 pnl834

9 From Aroer, that *is* upon the bank of the river Arnon, and the   city   that

pp,cs,nn**8432**   df,nn5158   wcj,cs,nn3605   df,nn**4334**   nn4311   pr5704   nn1769

is in the midst of the river, and   all   the plain of Medeba unto Dibon;

wcj,cs,nn3605   pl,cs,nn5892   nn5511   cs,nn**4428**   df,nn567   pnl834   qpf**4427**

10 And   all   the cities of Sihon king of the Amorites, which reigned in

pp,nn2809   pr5704   cs,nn1366   pl,cs,nn**1121**   nn5983

Heshbon, unto the border of the children of Ammon;

13:3 See the note on Deuteronomy 2:23.

13:7 Although the conquest of Canaan was still incomplete, God intended that each tribe should complete the occupation of their allotment as their numbers increased to fill it.

^{wcj,df,nn1568}   ^{wcj,cs,nn1366}   ^{df,nn1651}   ^{wcj,df,nn4602}

11 And Gilead, and the border of the Geshurites and Maachathites, and

^{wcj,cs,nn3605 cs,nn2022   nn2768}   ^{wcj,cs,nn3605 df,nn1316 pr5704   nn5548}

all   mount Hermon, and   all   Bashan unto Salcah;

^{cs,nn3605   cs,nn4468   nn5747   dfp,nn1316 pnl834 qpf4427}   ^{pp,nn6252}

12 All the kingdom of Og in Bashan, which reigned in Ashtaroth and in

^{wcj,pp,nn154 pnp1931   nipf7604   pr4480/cs,nn3499   df,nn7497}   ^{nn4872   wcs,himf,pnx5221}

Edrei, who remained of*the*remnant of the giants: for these did Moses   smite,

^{wcs,himf,pnx3423}

and cast*them*out.

^{pl,cs,nn1121   nn3478   himf3423   wcj,ptn3808   (853)   df,nn1651}

13 Nevertheless the children of Israel expelled   not   the Geshurites, nor

^{wcj(853)   df,nn4602   nn1650   wcj,nn4601   wcs,qmf3427 pp,cs,nn7130}

the Maachathites: but the Geshurites and the Maachathites dwell   among the

^{nn3478   pr5704 df,pndm2088 df,nn3117}

Israelites until   this   day.

^{ad7535   pp,cs,nn7626   df,nn3878   qpf5414   ptn3808   nn5159}

14 Only   unto   the   tribe   of Levi   he   gave   none   inheritance;   the

^{pl,cs,nn801/nn3068/pl,cs,nn430/nn3478   (pnp1931)   nn,pnx5159}

sacrifices*of*the*LORD*God*of*Israel*made*by*fire   are   their   inheritance,

^{pp,pnl834   pipf1696   pp,pnx}

as   he   said unto them.

^{nn4872   wcs,qmf5414   pp,cs,nn4294   pl,cs,nn1121   nn7205}

15 And Moses   gave   unto the   tribe   of the children of Reuben *inheritance*

^{pp,pl,nn,pnx4940}

according to their families.

^{pp,pnx   df,nn1366 wcs,qmf1961   pr4480/nn6177   pnl834   pr5921   cs,nn8193   cs,nn5158}

16 And their coast   was   from Aroer, that *is* on   the bank of the river

^{nn769   wcj,df,nn5892 pnl834   pp,cs,nn8432   df,nn5158   wcj,cs,nn3605   df,nn4334 pr5921}

Arnon, and the   city   that *is* in the   midst of the river, and   all   the plain by

ⁿⁿ⁴³¹¹

Medeba;

^{nn2809   wcj,cs,nn3605   pl,nn,pnx5892 pnl834   dfp,nn4334   nn1769}

17 Heshbon, and   all   her   cities   that *are* in the   plain; Dibon, and

^{wcj,nn1120   wcj,nn1010 [wcj,cs,nn1004/nn1168/nn4583]}

Bamoth-baal, and   Beth-baal-meon,

^{wcj,nn3096   wcj,nn6932   wcj,nn4158}

18 And Jahazah, and Kedemoth, and Mephaath,

^{wcj,nn7156   wcj,nn7643   wcj,nn6890   pp,cs,nn2022   df,nn6010}

19 And Kirjathaim, and Sibmah, and Zareth-shahar in the mount of the valley,

^{wcj,nn1047   wcj,nn798 [wcj,pl,cs,nn794/df,nn6449]   wcj,nn1020}

20 And Beth-peor, and   Ashdoth-pisgah,   and Beth-jeshimoth,

^{wcj,cs,nn3605   pl,cs,nn5892   df,nn4334   wcj,cs,nn3605   cs,nn4468   nn5511}

21 And   all   the cities of the plain, and   all   the kingdom of Sihon

^{cs,nn4428   df,nn567   pnl834   qpf4427   pp,nn2809   pnl834   nn4872   hipf5221 pr,pnx854 (wcj853)}

king of the Amorites, which reigned in Heshbon, whom Moses smote with

^{pl,cs,nn5387   nn4080   (853) nn189   wcj(853)   nn7552   wcj(853) nn6698   wcj(853) nn2354}

the princes of Midian,   Evi, and   Rekem, and   Zur, and   Hur, and

^{wcj(853)   nn7254   pl,cs,nn5257   nn5511 pl,cs,qpta3427   df,nn776}

Reba, *which were* dukes of Sihon, dwelling in the country.

^{wcj(853)   nn1109   cs,nn1121   nn1160   df,qpta7080   pl,cs,nn1121}

22   Balaam also the   son   of Beor, the soothsayer, did the children of

^{nn3478 qpf2026   dfp,nn2719   pr413   pl,nn,pnx2491}

Israel slay with the sword among them that were   slain   by them.

^{cs,nn1366   pl,cs,nn1121   nn7205   wcs,qmf1961 df,nn3383   wcj,nn1366}

23 And the border of the children of Reuben   was   Jordan, and the border

<small>pndm2063   cs,nn**5159**   pl,cs,nn**1121**   nn7205   pp,pl,nn,pnx**4940**</small>

thereof. This *was* the inheritance of the children of Reuben after their families, the

<small>df,pl,nn5892   wcj,pl,nn,pnx2691</small>

cities and the villages thereof.

<small>   nn4872   wcs,qmf**5414**   pp,cs,nn**4294**   nn1410</small>

24 And Moses gave *inheritance* unto the tribe of Gad, *even* unto the

<small>pp,pl,cs,nn**1121**   nn1410   pp,pl,nn,pnx**4940**</small>

children of Gad according to their families.

<small>   pp,pnx   df,nn1366 wcs,qmf**1961**   nn3270   wcj,cs,nn3605   pl,cs,nn5892   df,nn1568</small>

25 And their coast was Jazer, and all the cities of Gilead, and

<small>wcj,cs,nn2677   cs,nn**776**   pl,cs,nn**1121**   nn5983   pr5704   nn6177 pnl834   pr5921/pl,cs,nn**6440**   nn7237</small>

half the land of the children of Ammon, unto Aroer that *is* before Rabbah;

<small>   wcj,pr4480/nn2809   pr5704 nn7434 [cs,nn7413/df,nn4707]   wcj,nn993   wcj,pr4480/nn4266</small>

26 And from Heshbon unto Ramath-mizpeh, and Betonim; and from Mahanaim

<small>pr5704   nn1366   pp,nn1688</small>

unto the border of Debir;

<small>   wcj,dfp,nn6010   nn1027   wcj,nn1039   wcj,nn5523   wcj,nn6829</small>

27 And in the valley, Beth-aram, and Beth-nimrah, and Succoth, and Zaphon,

<small>cs,nn**3499**   pr4480/cs,nn**4468**   nn5511 cs,nn**4428**   nn2809   df,nn3383   wcj,nn1366</small>

the rest of*the*kingdom of Sihon king of Heshbon, Jordan and *his* border, *even*

<small>pr5704   cs,nn7097   nn3220   nn3672   cs,nn5676   df,nn3383   nn,lh4217</small>

unto the edge of the sea of Chinnereth on the other side Jordan eastward.

<small>   pndm2063   cs,nn**5159**   pl,cs,nn**1121**   nn1410   pp,pl,nn,pnx**4940**</small>

28 This *is* the inheritance of the children of Gad after their families, the

<small>df,pl,nn5892   wcj,pl,nn,pnx2691</small>

cities, and their villages.

<small>   nn4872   wcs,qmf**5414**   dfp,cs,nn2677 cs,nn**7626**   nn4519</small>

29 And Moses gave *inheritance* unto the half tribe of Manasseh: and *this*

<small>wcs,qmf**1961**   dfp,cs,nn2677   cs,nn**4294**   pl,cs,nn**1121**   nn4519</small>

was *the possession* of the half tribe of the children of Manasseh by their

<small>pp,pl,nn,pnx**4940**</small>

families.

<small>   nn,pnx1366 wcs,qmf**1961**   pr4480/nn4266   cs,nn3605 df,nn1316 cs,nn3605   cs,nn**4468**</small>

30 And their coast was from Mahanaim, all Bashan, all the kingdom

<small>nn5747   cs,nn**4428**   df,nn1316   wcj,cs,nn3605   pl,cs,nn2333   nn2971 pnl834   dfp,nn1316</small>

of Og king of Bashan, and all the towns of Jair, which *are* in Bashan,

<small>pl,nu8346   nn5892</small>

threescore cities:

<small>   wcj,cs,nn2677   df,nn1568   wcj,nn6252   wcj,nn154 pl,cs,nn5892   cs,nn**4468**</small>

31 And half Gilead, and Ashtaroth, and Edrei, cities of the kingdom of

<small>nn5747   dfp,nn1316   pp,pl,cs,nn**1121**   nn4353   cs,nn**1121**   nn4519</small>

Og in Bashan, *were pertaining* unto the children of Machir the son of Manasseh,

<small>   dfp,cs,nn2677   pl,cs,nn**1121**   nn4353   pp,pl,nn,pnx**4940**</small>

even to the one half of the children of Machir by their families.

<small>   pndm428   pnl834   nn4872   pipf**5157**</small>

32 These *are the countries* which Moses did distribute*for*inheritance in the

<small>pp,pl,cs,nn**6160**   nn4124   pr4480/nn5676   pp,nn3383   nn3405   nn,lh4217</small>

plains of Moab, on*the*other*side Jordan, by Jericho, eastward.

<small>   wcj,pp,cs,nn**7626**   df,nn3878   nn4872   qpf**5414** ptn3808   nn5159   nn3068</small>

33 But unto the tribe of Levi Moses gave not *any* inheritance: the LORD

<small>pl,cs,nn**430**   nn3478 (pnp1931)   nn,pnx5159   pp,pnl834   pipf**1696**   pp,pnx</small>

God of Israel *was* their inheritance, as he said unto them.

Division of Canaan

14

^{wcj,pndm428} ^{pnl834} ^{pl,cs,nn1121} ⁿⁿ³⁴⁷⁸ ^{qpf5157}
And these *are the countries* which the children of Israel inherited in

^{pp,cs,nn776} ⁿⁿ³⁶⁶⁷ ^{pnl834} ⁿⁿ⁴⁹⁹ ^{df,nn3548} ^{wcj,nn3091} ^{cs,nn1121}
the land of Canaan, which Eleazar the priest, and Joshua the son

ⁿⁿ⁵¹²⁶ ^{wcj,pl,cs,nn7218} ^{pl,cs,nn1} ^{df,pl,nn4294} ^{pp,pl,cs,nn1121} ⁿⁿ³⁴⁷⁸
of Nun, and the heads of the fathers of the tribes of the children of Israel,

^{pipf5157} ^{pnx(853)}
distributed*for*inheritance   to them.

^{pp,cs,nn1486} ^{nn,pnx5159} ^{pp,pnl834} ⁿⁿ³⁰⁶⁸ ^{pipf6680} ^{pp,cs,nn3027}
2 By lot *was* their inheritance, as the LORD commanded by the hand

ⁿⁿ⁴⁸⁷² ^{pp,cs,nu8672} ^{df,pl,nn4294} ^{wcj,cs,nn2677} ^{df,nn4294}
of Moses, for the nine tribes, and *for* the half tribe.

^{cj3588} ⁿⁿ⁴⁸⁷² ^{qpf5414} ^{cs,nn5159} ^{du,cs,nu8147} ^{df,pl,nn4294} ^{wcj,cs,nn2677} ^{df,nn4294}
3 For Moses had given the inheritance of two tribes and a half tribe

^{pr4480/nn5676} ^{dfp,nn3383} ^{wcj,dfp,pl,nn3881} ^{qpf5414} ^{ptn3808} ⁿⁿ⁵¹⁵⁹ ^{pp,nn,pnx8432}
on*the*other*side Jordan: but unto the Levites he gave none inheritance among

them.

^{cj3588} ^{pl,cs,nn1121} ⁿⁿ³¹³⁰ ^{qpf1961} ^{du,cs,nu8147} ^{pl,nn4294} ⁿⁿ⁴⁵¹⁹ ^{wcj,nn669}
4 For the children of Joseph were two tribes, Manasseh and Ephraim:

^{qpf5414} ^{wcj,ptn3808} ⁿⁿ²⁵⁰⁶ ^{pp,pl,nn3881} ^{dfp,nn776} ^{cj3588/cj518} ^{pl,nn5892} ^{pp,qnc3427}
therefore they gave no part unto the Levites in the land, save cities to dwell

^{wcj,pl,nn,pnx4054} ^{pp,pl,nn,pnx4735} ^{wcj,pp,nn,pnx7075}
in, with their suburbs for their cattle and for their substance.

^{pp,pnl834} ⁿⁿ³⁰⁶⁸ ^{pipf6680} ⁽⁸⁵³⁾ ⁿⁿ⁴⁸⁷² ^{ad3651} ^{pl,cs,nn1121} ⁿⁿ³⁴⁷⁸ ^{qpf6213}
5 As the LORD commanded Moses, so the children of Israel did, and

^{wcs,qmf2505} ⁽⁸⁵³⁾ ^{df,nn776}
they divided the land.

Caleb's Inheritance

^{pl,cs,nn1121} ⁿⁿ³⁰⁶³ ^{wcs,qmf5066} ^{pr413} ⁿⁿ³⁰⁹¹ ^{dfp,nn1537} ⁿⁿ³⁶¹² ^{cs,nn1121}
☞ 6 Then the children of Judah came unto Joshua in Gilgal: and Caleb the son

ⁿⁿ³³¹² ^{df,nn7074} ^{wcs,qmf559} ^{pr,pnx413} ^{pnp859} ^{qpf3045} ⁽⁸⁵³⁾ ^{df,nn1697} ^{pnl834}
of Jephunneh the Kenezite said unto him, Thou knowest   the thing that the

ⁿⁿ³⁰⁶⁸ ^{pipf1696} ^{pr413} ⁿⁿ⁴⁸⁷² ^{cs,nn376} ^{df,pl,nn430} ^{pr5921/pl,nn,pnx182} ^{wcj(pr5921)/pnx(pl,nn182)}
LORD said unto Moses the man of God concerning me and   thee in

^{pp,nn6947}
Kadesh-barnea.

^{pl,nu705} ⁿⁿ⁸¹⁴¹ ^{cs,nn1121} ^{pnp595} ⁿⁿ⁴⁸⁷² ^{cs,nn5650} ⁿⁿ³⁰⁶⁸ ^{pp,qnc7971} ^{pnx(853)}
7 Forty years old *was* I when Moses the servant of the LORD sent

^{pr4480/nn6947} ^{pp,pinc7270} ⁽⁸⁵³⁾ ^{df,nn776} ^{wcs,himf7725} ^{pnx(853)} ⁿⁿ¹⁶⁹⁷
me from Kadesh-barnea to espy out   the land; and I brought   him word

^{pp,pnl834} ^{pr5973} ^{nn,pnx3824}
again as *it was* in mine heart.

^{wcj,pl,nn,pnx251} ^{pnl834} ^{qpf5927} ^{pr,pnx5973} ⁽⁸⁵³⁾ ^{cs,nn3820}
8 Nevertheless my brethren that went up with me made   the heart of the

^{df,nn5971} ^{hipf4529} ^{wcj,pnp595} ^{pipf4390} ^{pr310} ⁿⁿ³⁰⁶⁸ ^{pl,nn,pnx430}
people melt: but I wholly followed the LORD my God.

☞ **14:6** Kenaz was an Edomite tribe. Caleb was of the tribe of Judah (Num. 13:6; 34:19). This was a result of the Kenizzite and Judahite lineages being blended by marriage (cf. 1 Chr. 2:4, 5, 18, 19; 4:13–15).
☞ **14:6–15** See the note on Numbers 13:30–33, concerning Caleb's allotment.

nn4872　wcs,nimf**7650**　　df,pndm1931　dfp,nn**3117**　pp,qnc559　cj518/ptn**3808**　　df,nn776　pnl834/pp,pnx

⊙ 9 And Moses swore on that day, saying, Surely the land whereon thy

nn,pnx7272　　qpf1869　　qmf**1961**　pp,pnx　　pp,nn**5159**　　wcj,pp,pl,nn,pnx**1121**　pr5704/nn**5769**

feet have trodden shall be thine inheritance, and thy children's forever,

cj3588　　pipf**4390**　pr310　　nn**3068**　pl,nn,pnx**430**

because thou hast wholly followed the LORD my God.

wcj,ad6258　ptdm2009　　nn**3068**　hipf**2421**/pnx(853)　pp,pnl834　pipf**1696** pndm2088 pl,nu705

10 And now, behold, the LORD hath kept*me*alive, as he said, these forty

wcj,nu2568　nn8141　pr4480/ad**227**　nn**3068**　pipf**1696**　(853) df,pndm2088 df,nn**1697** pr413　nn4872　pnl834

and five years, even since the LORD spoke this word unto Moses, while

nn3478　qpf**1980**　　dfp,nn4057　　wcj,ad6258　ptdm2009　pnp595

the children of Israel wandered in the wilderness: and now, lo, I *am* this

df,nn**3117** wcj,pl,nu8084　nu2568　nn8141 cs,nn**1121**

day fourscore and five years old.

ad5750　　aj**2389**　df,nn**3117** pp,pnl834　　pp,cs,nn**3117**　nn4872 qnc7971

11 As yet I *am as* strong this day as *I was* in the day that Moses sent

pnx(853)　　pp,nn,pnx3581　　ad**227**　　　wcj,pp,nn,pnx3581 ad6258　dfp,nn4421

me: as my strength *was* then, even so *is* my strength now, for war, both to

wcj,pp,qnc3318　　wcj,pp,qnc935

go out, and to come in.

wcj,ad6258　　qmv**5414** pp,pnx (853) df,pndm2088　df,nn2022　pnl834　　nn**3068** pipf**1696**

12 Now therefore give me this mountain, whereof the LORD spoke in

df,pndm1931 dfp,nn**3117** cj3588 pnp859　qpf**8085**　df,pndm1931 dfp,nn**3117** cj3588　pl,nn6062　　ad8033

that day; for thou heardest in that day how the Anakims *were* there, and

wcj,pl,nn5892　　aj1419　pl,qptp1219 ad194　　nn**3068**　pr,pnx854

that the cities *were* great *and* fenced: if so be the LORD *will be* with me, then I

wcj,hipf,pnx**3423**　pp,pnl834　nn**3068** pipf**1696**

shall be able to drive*them*out, as the LORD said.

nn3091　wcs,pimf,pnx**1288**　　wcs,qmf**5414**　pp,nn3612　cs,nn**1121**　　nn3312

13 And Joshua blessed him, and gave unto Caleb the son of Jephunneh

(853)　nn2275　　pp,nn**5159**

Hebron for an inheritance.

nn2275　pr5921/ad**3651**　qpf**1961**　　pp,nn**5159**　　pp,nn3612　cs,nn**1121**　　nn3312

14 Hebron therefore became the inheritance of Caleb the son of Jephunneh the

df,nn7074　pr5704 df,pndm2088 df,nn**3117**　cj3282　pnl834　　pipf**4390**　pr310　　nn**3068** pl,cs,nn**430**

Kenezite unto this day, because that he wholly followed the LORD God of

nn3478

Israel.

wcj,cs,nn8034　　nn2275　pp,pl,nn**6440**　　nn7153　　df,aj1419

15 And the name of Hebron before *was* Kirjath-arba; *which Arba was* a great

df,nn**120**　dfp,pl,nn6062　(pnp1931)　wcj,df,nn776　qpf**8252** pr4480/nn4421

man among the Anakims. And the land had rest from war.

Judah's Portion

wcs,qmf**1961**　df,nn1486　　pp,cs,nn**4294**　　pl,cs,nn**1121**　nn3063

15 *This* then was the lot of the tribe of the children of Judah by

pp,pl,nn,pnx**4940**　pr413　cs,nn1366　nn123　cs,nn4057　nn6790

their families; *even* to the border of Edom the wilderness of Zin

nn,lh5045　　pr4480/cs,nn7097　　nn8486

southward *was* the uttermost part of the south coast.

⊙ **14:9** When Caleb explored the land of Canaan as one of the twelve spies, he visited the people known as Anakim (Deut. 1:28). Moses promised him this same region for a possession (Deut. 1:36).

pp,pnx　nn5045　cs,nn1366　wcs,qmf**1961**　pr4480/cs,nn7097　　df,nn4417　cs,nn3220　pr4480

2 And their south border　was　from*the*shore of the　salt　sea,　from the

df,nn3956　　df,qpta6437　nn,lh5045

bay　that looketh southward:

wcj,qpf3318　pr413　　pr4480/nn5045　pp,nn4610 [pp,cs,nn4608/pl,nn6137]　　wcj,qpf**5674**

3 And it went out　to　the south side to　Maaleh-acrabbim,　and passed along

nn,lh6790　wcj,qpf**5927**　pr4480/nn5045　　pp,nn6947　　　wcj,qpf**5674**

to Zin,　and ascended up on*the*south*side unto Kadesh-barnea, and passed along

nn2696　wcj,qpf**5927**　nn,lh146　wcj,nipf5437　df,nn,lh7173

to Hezron, and went up to Adar, and fetched*a*compass to Karkaa:

wcj,qpf**5674**　nn,lh6111　wcj,qpf3318　cs,nn5158　nn4714

4 *From thence* it passed toward Azmon, and went out unto the river of Egypt;

pl,cs,nn8444　df,nn1366 wcj,qpf**1961**　nn,lh3220 pndm2088　qmf**1961** pp,pnx　nn5045

and the goings out of that coast　were　at the　sea:　this　shall　be　your south

cs,nn1366

coast.

ad**6924** wcj,nn1366　df,nn4417 cs,nn3220　pr5704　cs,nn7097　df,nn3383

5 And the east border *was* the　salt　sea,　*even* unto the　end　of Jordan. And

wcj,nn1366　nn6828　pp,cs,nn6285　pr4480/cs,nn3956　df,nn3220

their　border　in　the　north　quarter　*was* from*the*bay　of　the　sea

pr4480/cs,nn7097　df,nn3383

at*the*uttermost*part of Jordan:

df,nn1366　wcs,qpf**5927**　nn1031　wcs,qpf**5674**　pr4480/nn6828

6 And the border went up to Beth-hogla, and passed along by*the*north of

pp,nn1026　df,nn1366 wcs,qpf**5927**　cs,nn68　nn932　cs,nn**1121**　nn7205

Beth-arabah; and the border went up to the stone of Bohan the　son　of Reuben:

df,nn1366　wcs,qpf**5927**　nn,lh1688　pr4480/cs,nn6010　nn5911

☞ 7 And the border went up toward Debir from*the*valley of Achor, and so

wcj,nn,lh6828　qpta6437　pr413　df,nn1537 pnl834　pr5227　pp,cs,nn4608　nn131　pnl834

northward, looking toward Gilgal, that *is* before the going up to Adummim, which

pr4480/nn5045　dfp,nn5158　df,nn1366　wcs,qpf**5674**　pr413　pl,cs,nn4325

is on*the*south*side of the　river: and the border passed toward the waters of

nn5885　pl,nn,pnx8444　wcs,qpf**1961** pr413　nn5883

En-shemesh, and the goings out thereof were　at En-rogel:

df,nn1366　wcs,qpf**5927**　cs,nn1516　cs,nn**1121**　nn2011　pr413

☞ 8 And the border went up by the　valley of the　son　of Hinnom unto the

pr4480/nn5045 cs,nn3802　df,nn2983　pnp1931　nn3389　df,nn1366 wcs,qpf**5927**　pr413

south　side　of the Jebusite; the same *is* Jerusalem: and the border went up　to

cs,nn**7218**　df,nn2022　pnl834　pr5921　cs,nn1516　nn2011　nn,lh3220　pnl834

the　top　of the mountain that *lieth* before the valley of Hinnom westward, which *is*

pp,cs,nn7097　cs,nn6010　pl,nn**7497**　nn,lh6828

at the　end　of the valley of the giants northward:

df,nn1366　wcs,qpf**8388**　pr4480/cs,nn**7218**　df,nn2022 pr413　cs,nn4599

9 And the border was drawn from*the*top of the　hill　unto the fountain of the

pl,cs,nn4325　nn5318　wcs,qpf3318　pr413　pl,cs,nn5892　cs,nn2022　nn6085　df,nn1366

water of Nephtoah, and went out　to　the　cities　of mount Ephron; and the border

wcs,qpf**8388**　nn1173　pnp1931　nn7157

was　drawn to Baalah, which *is* Kirjath-jearim:

☞ **15:7** This was not the Gilgal which was Israel's first campsite (Josh. 4:19). It is the Geliloth mentioned in Joshua 18:17.

☞ **15:8** Later, the valley of Hinnom was the site for human sacrifices in the worship of Molech (see the note on 2 Kgs. 23:10 for a further discussion of this pagan practice). The Hebrew phrase *gē ben hinnōm* ([2011] or "valley of Tophet") was transliterated to the Greek word, *Géenna*, which is the word for "hell" in the New Testament (Matt. 5:29, 30).

df,nn1366   wcs,nipf5437   pr4480/nn1173   nn,lh3220   pr413   cs,nn2022   nn8165
10 And the border compassed from Baalah westward unto mount Seir, and

wcs,qpf**5674**   pr413   cs,nn3802   cs,nn2022   nn3297   pnp1931   nn3693
passed along   unto   the   side   of   mount   Jearim,   which   *is*   Chesalon,

pr4480/nn,lh6828   wcs,qpf3381   nn1053 [cs,nn**1004**/nn8121]   wcs,qpf**5674**   nn8553
on*the*north*side, and went down to Beth-shemesh, and passed on to Timnah:

df,nn1366   wcs,qpf3318   pr413   cs,nn3802   nn6138   nn,lh6828   df,nn1366
11 And the border went out unto the side of Ekron northward: and the border

wcs,qpf8388   nn,lh7942   wcs,qpf**5674**   cs,nn2022   nn1173   wcs,qpf3318
was drawn to Shicron, and passed along to mount Baalah, and went out unto

nn2995   pl,cs,nn8444   df,nn1366   wcs,qpf1931   nn,lh3220
Jabneel; and the goings out of the border   were   at the   sea.

nn3220 wcj,nn1366   df,aj1419 df,nn3220   wcj,nn1366   pndm2088
12 And the west border *was* to the great   sea, and the coast *thereof*. This *is*

nn1366   pl,cs,nn**1121**   nn3063   ad5439   pp,pl,nn,pnx**4940**
the coast of the children of Judah round about according to their families.

wcj,pp,nn3612   cs,nn**1121**   nn3312   qpf**5414**   nn2506 pp,cs,nn**8432**   pl,cs,nn**1121**
13 And unto   Caleb   the   son of Jephunneh he gave a part among the children

nn3063   pr413   cs,nn**6310**   nn**3068**   pp,nn3091   (853)   cs,nn7151
of Judah, according to the commandment of the Lord to Joshua, *even*   the   city

nn704   cs,nn**1**   df,nn6061   pnp1931   nn2275
of Arba the father of Anak, which *city is* Hebron.

nn3612   wcs,himf**3423**   pr4480/ad8033   (853)   nu7969   pl,cs,nn**1121**   df,nn6061   (853)   nn8344
14 And Caleb drove   thence   the three   sons   of Anak,   Sheshai, and

wcj(853)   nn289   wcj(853)   nn8526   cs,aj3211   df,nn6061
Ahiman, and   Talmai, the children of Anak.

wcs,qmf**5927**   pr4480/ad8033 pr413   pl,cs,qpta**3427**   nn1688   wcj,cs,nn8034
15 And he went up thence   to   the inhabitants of Debir: and the   name   of

nn1688   pp,pl,nn**6440**   nn7158
Debir before *was* Kirjath-sepher.

nn3612   wcs,qmf**559**   pnl834   himf**5221**   (853)   nn7158   wcs,qpf,pnx3920   pp,pnx
16 And Caleb said, He that smiteth   Kirjath-sepher, and   taketh   it, to him

wcs,qpf**5414** (853)   nn5915   nn,pnx1323   pp,nn**802**
will I   give   Achsah my daughter to wife.

nn6274   cs,nn**1121**   nn7073   cs,nn**251**   nn3612   wcs,qmf,pnx3920
17 And Othniel the   son   of Kenaz, the brother of Caleb,   took   it: and he

wcs,qmf**5414** pp,pnx   (853)   nn5915   nn,pnx1323   pp,nn**802**
gave   him   Achsah his daughter to wife.

wcs,qmf**1961**   pp,qnc,pnx935   wcs,himf,pnx5496
18 And it*came*to*pass, as she   came   *unto him*, that she   moved   him to

pp,qnc7592 pr4480/pr854   nn,pnx1   nn**7704**   wcs,qmf6795 pr4480/pr5921   df,nn2543   nn3612 wcs,qmf559
ask   of   her father a field: and she lighted   off   *her* ass; and Caleb said

pp,pnx   pnit4100   pp,pnx
unto her, What wouldest thou?

wcs,qmf**559**   qmv**5414** pp,pnx   nn1293   cj3588   qpf,pnx**5414** pp,pnx   df,nn5045 cs,nn776
19 Who answered, Give me a blessing; for thou hast given   me   a south land;

wcj,qpf**5414** pp,pnx   pl,cs,nn1543   pl,nn4325   wcs,qmf**5414** pp,pnx (853)   aj5942   pl,cs,nn1543
give   me also springs of water. And he   gave   her   the upper springs, and

wcj(853)   aj8482   pl,cs,nn1543
the nether springs.

pndm2063   cs,nn**5159**   cs,nn**4294**   pl,cs,nn**1121**   nn3063
20 This *is* the inheritance of the tribe of the children of Judah according to

pp,pl,nn,pnx**4940**
their families.

pr4480/cs,nn7097 df,pl,nn5892   pp,cs,nn**4294**   pl,cs,nn**1121**   nn3063   pr413

21 And the uttermost cities of the tribe of the children of Judah toward the

cs,nn1366   nn123   dfp,nn,lh5045 wcs,qmf**1961**   nn6909   wcj,nn5740   wcj,nn3017

coast of Edom southward were Kabzeel, and Eder, and Jagur,

wcj,nn7016   wcj,nn1776   wcj,nn5735

22 And Kinah, and Dimonah, and Adadah,

wcj,nn6943   wcj,nn2674   wcj,nn3497

23 And Kedesh, and Hazor, and Ithnan,

nn2128   wcj,nn2928   wcj,nn1175

24 Ziph, and Telem, and Bealoth,

wcj,nn2674   nn2675   wcj,nn7152   nn2696   pnp1931   nn2674

25 And Hazor, Hadattah, and Kerioth, *and* Hezron, which *is* Hazor,

nn538   wcj,nn8090   wcj,nn4137

26 Amam, and Shema, and Moladah,

wcj,nn2693   wcj,nn2829   wcj,nn1046 [wcj,cs,nn**1004**/nn6404]

27 And Hazar-gaddah, and Heshmon, and   Beth-palet,

wcj,nn2705   wcj,nn884   wcj,nn964

28 And Hazarshual, and Beer-sheba, and Bizjothjah,

nn1173   wcj,nn5864   wcj,nn6107

29 Baalah, and Iim, and Azem,

wcj,nn513   wcj,nn3686   wcj,nn2767

30 And Eltolad, and Chesil, and Hormah,

wcj,nn6860   wcj,nn4089   wcj,nn5578

31 And Ziklag, and Madmannah, and Sansannah,

wcj,nn3822   wcj,nn7978   wcj,nn5871   wcj,nn7417   cs,nn3605   pl,nn5892

32 And Lebaoth, and Shilhim, and Ain, and Rimmon: all the cities *are*

pl,nu6242   wcj,nu8672   wcj,pl,nn,pnx2691

twenty and nine, with their villages:

dfp,nn8219   nn847   wcj,nn6881   wcj,nn823

33 *And* in the valley, Eshtaol, and Zoreah, and Ashnah,

wcj,nn2182   wcj,nn5873   nn8599   wcj,df,nn5879

34 And Zanoah, and En-gannim, Tappuah, and Enam,

nn3412   wcj,nn5725   nn7755   wcj,nn5825

35 Jarmuth, and Adullam, Socoh, and Azekah,

wcj,nn8189   wcj,nn5723   wcj,df,nn1449   wcj,nn1453   nu702/nu6240 pl,nn5892

36 And Sharaim, and Adithaim, and Gederah, and Gederothaim; fourteen cities

wcj,pl,nn,pnx2691

with their villages:

nn6799   wcj,nn2322   wcj,nn4028 [cs,nn4026/nn1410]

37 Zenan, and Hadashah, and   Migdal-gad,

wcj,nn1810   wcj,df,nn4708   wcj,nn3371

38 And Dilean, and Mizpeh, and Joktheel,

nn3923   wcj,nn1218   wcj,nn5700

39 Lachish, and Bozkath, and Eglon,

wcj,nn3522   wcj,nn3903   wcj,nn3798

40 And Cabbon, and Lahmam, and Kithlish,

wcj,nn1450   nn1016 [cs,nn**1004**/nn1712]   wcj,nn5279   wcj,nn4719   nu8337/nu6240 pl,nn5892

41 And Gederoth, Beth-dagon, and Naamah, and Makkedah; sixteen cities

wcj,pl,nn,pnx2691

with their villages:

nn3841   wcj,nn6281   wcj,nn6228

42 Libnah, and Ether, and Ashan,

wcj,nn3316   wcj,nn823   wcj,nn5334

43 And Jiphtah, and Ashnah, and Nezib,

wcj,nn7084   wcj,nn392   wcj,nn4762   nu8672 pl,nn5892   wcj,pl,nn,pnx2691

44 And Keilah, and Achzib, and Mareshah; nine cities with their villages:

nn6138   wcj,pl,nn,pnx1323   wcj,pl,nn,pnx2691

45 Ekron, with her   towns   and her villages:

pr4480/nn6138   wcj,nn,lh3220 nn3605 pnl834   pr5921/cs,nn**3027**   nn795

46 From Ekron even unto the   sea,   all that *lay*   near   Ashdod, with

wcj,pl,nn,pnx2691

their villages:

nn795   pl,nn,pnx1323   wcj,pl,nn,pnx2691 nn5804   pl,nn,pnx1323

47 Ashdod with her towns and her villages, Gaza with her towns and her

wcj,pl,nn,pnx2691 pr5704   cs,nn5158   nn4714   df,aj1419 wcj,df,nn3220   wcj,nn1366

villages, unto the river of Egypt, and the great sea,   and the border *thereof*:

wcj,dfp,nn2022   nn8069   wcj,nn3492   wcj,nn7755

48 And in the mountains, Shamir, and Jattir, and Socoh,

wcj,nn1837   wcj,nn7158   pnp1931   nn1688

49 And Dannah, and Kirjath-sannah, which *is* Debir,

wcj,nn6024   wcj,nn851   wcj,nn6044

50 And Anab, and Eshtemoh, and Anim,

wcj,nn1657   wcj,nn2473   wcj,nn1542 nu259/nu6240 pl,nn5892   wcj,pl,nn,pnx2691

51 And Goshen, and Holon, and Giloh; eleven cities with their villages:

nn694   wcj,nn1746   wcj,nn824

52 Arab, and Dumah, and Eshean,

wcj,nn3241   wcj,nn1054 [cs,nn**1004**/nn8598]   wcj,nn664

53 And Janum, and   Beth-tappuah, and Aphekah,

wcj,nn2547   wcj,nn7153   pnp1931   nn2275   wcj,nn6730 nu8672 pl,nn5892

54 And Humtah, and Kirjath-arba, which *is* Hebron, and Zior; nine cities with

wcj,pl,nn,pnx2691

their villages:

nn4584   nn3760   wcj,nn2128   wcj,nn3194

55 Maon, Carmel, and Ziph, and Juttah,

wcj,nn3157   wcj,nn3347   wcj,nn2182

56 And Jezreel, and Jokdeam, and Zanoah,

df,nn7014   nn1390   wcj,nn8553 nu6235 pl,nn5892   wcj,pl,nn,pnx2691

57 Cain, Gibeah, and Timnah; ten cities with their villages:

nn2478   nn1049 [cs,nn**1004**/nn6697]   wcj,nn1446

58 Halhul,   Beth-zur,   and Gedor,

wcj,nn4638   wcj,nn1042   wcj,nn515 nu8337 pl,nn5892   wcj,pl,nn,pnx2691

59 And Maarath, and Beth-anoth, and Eltekon; six cities with their villages:

nn7154   pnp1931   nn7157   wcj,df,nn7237 du,nu8147 pl,nn5892

60 Kirjath-baal, which *is* Kirjath-jearim, and Rabbah; two   cities with their

wcj,pl,nn,pnx2691

villages:

dfp,nn4057   nn1026 [cs,nn**1004**/df,nn**6160**]   nn4081   wcj,nn5527

61 In the wilderness,   Beth-arabah,   Middin, and Secacah,

wcj,df,nn5044   wcj,cs,nn5892   df,nn5898   wcj,nn5872 nu8337 pl,nn5892

62 And Nibshan, and the   city   of Salt, and En-gedi; six cities with their

wcj,pl,nn,pnx2691

villages.

wcj(853)   df,nn2983   pl,cs,qpta**3427**   nn3389   pl,cs,nn**1121**   nn3063

☚ 63 As for   the Jebusites the inhabitants of Jerusalem, the children of Judah

---

☚ **15:63** Jerusalem was located along the borders of the land that was allotted to both the tribe of Judah and the tribe of Benjamin (cf. Josh. 18:28). Both tribes attempted to drive out the Jebusites who inhabited the city, but they were unsuccessful on two consecutive campaigns (Judg. 1:8, 21). The city remained occupied by the Jebusites until David conquered them (2 Sam. 5:6–10).

qmf3201 ptn**3808**   pp,hinc,pnx**3423**   df,nn2983   wcs,qmf**3427** pr584   pl,cs,nn**1121**   nn3063

could not drive*them*out: but the Jebusites dwell with the children of Judah at

pp,nn3389 pr5704 df,pndm2088 df,nn**3117**

Jerusalem unto this day.

Ephraim and Manasseh's Portions

df,nn1486   pp,pl,cs,nn**1121**   nn3130   wcs,qmf3318   pr4480/nn3383

16 And the lot of the children of Joseph fell from Jordan by

nn3405   pp,pl,cs,nn4325   nn3405   nn,lh4217   df,nn4057

Jericho, unto the water of Jericho on the east, to the wilderness

qpta**5927**   pr4480/nn3405   dfp,nn2022   nn1008

that goeth up from Jericho throughout mount Bethel,

wcj,qpf3318   pr4480/nn1008   nn,lh3870   wcj,qpf**5674**   pr413   cs,nn1366

2 And goeth out from Bethel to Luz, and passeth along unto the borders of

df,nn757   nn5852

Archi to Ataroth,

wcj,qpf3381   nn,lh3220   pr413   cs,nn1366   df,nn3311   pr5704   cs,nn1366

3 And goeth down westward to the coast of Japhleti, unto the coast of

nn1032   aj8481   wcj,pr5704   nn1507   pl,nn,pnx8444   wcj,qpf**1961**

Beth-horon the nether, and to Gezer: and the goings out thereof are at the

nn,lh3220

sea.

pl,cs,nn**1121**   nn3130   nn4519   wcj,nn669   wcs,qmf**5157**

4 So the children of Joseph, Manasseh and Ephraim, took their inheritance.

cs,nn1366   pl,cs,nn**1121**   nn669   pp,pl,nn,pnx**4940** wcs,qmf**1961**

5 And the border of the children of Ephraim according to their families was

cs,nn1366   nn,pnx5159   nn,lh4217   wcs,qmf**1961**   nn5853

thus: even the border of their inheritance on the east side was Ataroth-addar,

pr5704   nn1032   aj**5945**

unto Beth-horon the upper;

df,nn1366   wcj,qpf3318   df,nn,lh3220   df,nn4366

6 And the border went out toward the sea to Michmethah

pr4480/nn6828   df,nn1366   wcj,nipf5437   nn,lh4217   nn8387

on*the*north*side; and the border went about eastward unto Taanath-shiloh, and

wcj,qpf**5674**   pnx(853)   pr4480/nn4217   nn3239

passed by it on*the*east to Janohah;

wcj,qpf3381   pr4480/nn3239   nn5852   wcj,nn,lh5292   wcj,qpf**6293**

7 And it went down from Janohah to Ataroth, and to Naarath, and came to

pp,nn3405   wcj,qpf3318   df,nn3383

Jericho, and went out at Jordan.

df,nn1366   qmf**1980**   pr4480/nn8599   nn,lh3220   cs,nn5158   nn7071

8 The border went out from Tappuah westward unto the river Kanah; and the

pl,nn,pnx8444   wcs,qpf**1961**   df,nn,lh3220 pndm2063   cs,nn**5159**   cs,nn**4294**

goings out thereof were at the sea. This *is* the inheritance of the tribe of the

pl,cs,nn**1121**   nn669   pp,pl,nn,pnx**4940**

children of Ephraim by their families.

df,pl,nn3995 wcj,df,pl,nn5892   pl,cs,nn**1121**   nn669   pp,cs,nn**8432**

9 And the separate cities for the children of Ephraim *were* among the

cs,nn**5159**   pp,pl,cs,nn**1121**   nn4519   cs,nn3605   df,pl,nn5892   wcj,pl,nn,pnx2691

inheritance of the children of Manasseh, all the cities with their villages.

16:2 The city of Bethel was formerly known as Luz (Gen. 28:19; Josh. 18:13; Judg. 1:23).

hipf**3423**/wcj,ptn**3808**   (853)   df,nn3669   df,qpta**3427**   pp,nn1507

✒ 10 And they drove*not*out   the Canaanites that dwelt in Gezer: but the

df,nn3669   wcs,qmf**3427**   pp,cs,nn**7130**   nn669   pr5704   df,pndm2088   df,nn**3117**   wcs(qmf**1961**)   qpta**5647**

Canaanites dwell among the Ephraimites unto this day, and   serve

pp,cs,nn4522

under tribute.

wcs,qmf**1961**   df,nn1486   pp,cs,nn**4294**   nn4519   cj3588 pnp1931

17 There was also a lot for the tribe of Manasseh; for he *was*

cs,nn1060   nn3130   pp,nn4353   cs,nn1060   nn4519

the firstborn of Joseph; *to wit*, for Machir the firstborn of Manasseh,

cs,nn**1**   df,nn1568   cj3588   pnp1931 qpf**1961**   cs,nn376   nn4421   wcs,qmf**1961**   df,nn1568

the father of Gilead: because he was a man of war, therefore he   had   Gilead

wcj,df,nn1316

and Bashan.

wcs,qmf**1961**   df,pl,nipt**3498**   pp,pl,cs,nn**1121**   nn4519

2 There was also *a lot* for the   rest   of the children of Manasseh by their

pp,pl,nn,pnx**4940**   pp,pl,cs,nn**1121**   nn44   wcj,pp,pl,cs,nn**1121**   nn2507

families; for the children of Abiezer, and for the   children of Helek, and for the

wcj,pp,pl,cs,nn**1121**   nn844   wcj,pp,pl,cs,nn**1121**   nn7928   wcj,pp,pl,cs,nn**1121**

children of Asriel, and for the   children of Shechem, and for the   children of

nn2660   wcj,pp,pl,cs,nn**1121**   nn8061   pndm428   df,aj2145   pl,cs,nn**1121**

Hepher, and for the   children of Shemida: these *were* the male children of

nn4519   cs,nn**1121**   nn3130   pp,pl,nn,pnx**4940**

Manasseh the   son of Joseph by their families.

wcj,pp,nn6765   cs,nn**1121**   nn2660   cs,nn**1121**   nn1568   cs,nn**1121**

✒ 3 But Zelophehad, the   son of Hepher, the   son of Gilead, the   son of

nn4353   cs,nn**1121**   nn4519   qpf**1961** ptn**3808** (pp,pnx) pl,nn**1121** cj3588/cj518   pl,nn1323   wcj,pndm428

Machir, the   son of Manasseh, had no   sons,   but   daughters: and these

pl,cs,nn8034   pl,nn,pnx1323   nn4244   wcj,nn5270   nn2295   nn4435   wcj,nn8656

are the names of his daughters, Mahlah, and Noah, Hoglah, Milcah, and Tirzah.

wcs,qmf**7126**   pp,pl,cs,nn**6440**   nn499   df,nn3548   wcj,pp,pl,cs,nn**6440**   nn3091

4 And they came near before Eleazar the priest, and   before   Joshua the

cs,nn**1121**   nn5126   wcj,pp,pl,cs,nn**6440**   df,pl,nn**5387**   pp,qnc559   nn3068   pipf**6680**   (853)   nn4872

son of Nun, and   before   the princes, saying, The Lᴏʀᴅ commanded   Moses

pp,qnc**5414**   pp,pnx   nn5159   pp,cs,nn**8432**   pl,nn,pnx251   pr413

to   give   us   an inheritance among our brethren. Therefore according to the

cs,nn**6310**   nn3068   wcs,qmf**5414**   pp,pnx   nn5159   pp,cs,nn**8432**   pp,pl,cs,nn**251**

commandment of the Lᴏʀᴅ he   gave   them an inheritance among the brethren of

nn,pnx1

their father.

wcs,qmf**5307** nu6235   pl,cs,nn**2256**   nn4519   pp,nn905   pr4480/cs,nn**776**   df,nn1568

5 And there   fell   ten portions to Manasseh, beside the   land   of Gilead

wcj,df,nn1316   pnl834   pp,nn5676   dfp,nn3383

and Bashan, which *were* on the other side Jordan;

cj3588   pl,cs,nn1323   nn4519   qpf**5157**/nn**5159**   pp,cs,nn**8432**   pl,nn,pnx**1121**

6 Because the daughters of Manasseh had an inheritance among his   sons: and

df,pl,nipt**3498**   nn4519   pp,pl,cs,nn**1121** qpf**1961**   wcj,cs,nn**776**   df,nn1568

the   rest of Manasseh's   sons   had the   land   of Gilead.

cs,nn1366   nn4519   wcs,qmf**1961**   pr4480/nn836   df,nn4366   pnl834

7 And the coast of Manasseh   was   from Asher to Michmethah, that *lieth*

---

pr5921/pl,cs,nn**6440**   nn7927   df,nn1366   wcj,qpf**1980**   pr413   df,nn3225   pr413

before   Shechem; and the border went along on the right hand unto the

pl,cs,qpta**3427**   nn5887

inhabitants of En-tappuah.

pp,nn4519   qpf**1961**   cs,nn776   nn8599   wcj,nn8599   pr413   cs,nn1366

8 *Now* Manasseh had the land of Tappuah: but Tappuah on the border of

nn4519   pp,pl,cs,nn**1121**   nn669

Manasseh *belonged* to the children of Ephraim;

df,nn1366   wcj,qpf3381   cs,nn5158   nn7071   nn,lh5045   dfp,nn5158

9 And the coast descended unto the river Kanah, southward of the river:

df,pndm428   pl,nn5892   pp,nn669   pp,cs,nn**8432**   pl,cs,nn5892   nn4519   wcj,cs,nn1366

these cities of Ephraim *are* among the cities of Manasseh: the coast of

nn4519   pr4480/nn6828   dfp,nn5158   pl,nn,pnx8444   wcs,qmf**1961**

Manasseh also *was* on*the*north*side of the river, and the outgoings of it were at

df,nn,lh3220

the sea:

nn,lh5045   pp,nn669   wcj,nn,lh6828   pp,nn4519

10 Southward *it was* Ephraim's, and northward *it was* Manasseh's, and the

df,nn3220   wcs,qmf**1961**   nn,pnx1366   qmf**6293**   wcj,pp,nn836   pr4480/nn6828

sea is his border; and they met together in Asher on*the*north, and in

wcj,pp,nn3485   pr4480/nn4217

Issachar on*the*east.

pp,nn4519   wcs,qmf**1961**   pp,nn3485   wcj,pp,nn836   nn1052

11 And Manasseh had in Issachar and in Asher Beth-shean and her

wcj,pl,nn,pnx1323   wcj,nn2991   wcj,pl,nn,pnx1323   wcj(853)   pl,cs,qpta**3427**   nn1756

towns, and Ibleam and her towns, and the inhabitants of Dor and her

wcj,pl,nn,pnx1323   wcj,pl,cs,qpta**3427**   nn5874   wcj,pl,nn,pnx1323   wcj,pl,cs,qpta**3427**

towns, and the inhabitants of Endor and her towns, and the inhabitants of

nn8590   wcj,pl,nn,pnx1323   wcj,pl,cs,qpta**3427**   nn4023   wcj,pl,nn,pnx1323

Taanach and her towns, and the inhabitants of Megiddo and her towns, *even*

nu7969   df,nn5316

three countries.

pl,cs,nn**1121**   nn4519   qpf3201 wcj,ptn**3808**   pp,hinc**3423**   (853)

12 Yet the children of Manasseh could not drive out *the inhabitants of*

df,pndm428 df,pl,nn5892   df,nn3669 wcs,himf**2974** pp,qnc**3427**   df,pndm2088 dfp,nn776

those cities; but the Canaanites would dwell in that land.

wcs,qmf**1961**   cj3588   pl,cs,nn**1121**   nn3478   qpf**2388**

13 Yet it*came*to*pass, when the children of Israel were waxen strong, that

wcs,qmf**5414** (853)   df,nn3669   dfp,nn4522   ptn**3808**   wcj,hina**3423**/hipf,pnx**3423**

they put the Canaanites to tribute; but did not utterly*drive*them*out.

pl,cs,nn**1121**   nn3130   wcs,pimf**1696** pr854 (853)   nn3091   pp,qnc559   ad4069

14 And the children of Joseph spoke unto Joshua, saying, Why hast thou

qpf**5414**   pp,pnx   nu259 nn1486   nu259 wcj,nn**2256**   nn5159   wcj,pnp589   aj7227   nn**5971**

given me *but* one lot and one portion to inherit, seeing I *am* a great people,

pr5704   nn**3068**   pipf,pnx**1288**   pnl834/pr5704/ad3541

forasmuch as the LORD hath blessed me hitherto?

nn3091   wcs,qmf**559**/pr,pnx413   cj518 pnp859   aj7227   nn**5971**   wcj,qmv**5927**/pp,pnx

15 And Joshua answered them, If thou *be* a great people, *then* get*thee*up

df,nn,lh3293   wcj,pipf**1254**   pp,pnx   ad8033   pp,cs,nn776   df,nn6522

to the wood *country*, and cut down for thyself there in the land of the Perizzites

wcj,df,nn**7497** cj3588 cs,nn2022   nn669   qpf213   pp,pnx

and of the giants, if mount Ephraim be too narrow for thee.

pl,cs,nn**1121**   nn3130   wcs,qmf**559**   df,nn2022   ptn**3808**   nimf4672   pp,pnx

16 And the children of Joseph said, The hill is not enough for us: and

pp,cs,nn3605   df,nn3669   df,qpta**3427**   pp,cs,nn776   df,nn6010   wcj,cs,nn7393   nn1270

all the Canaanites that dwell in the land of the valley have chariots of iron, pp,pnl834   pp,nn1052   wcj,pl,nn,pnx1323   wcj,pp,pnl834

both they who *are* of Beth-shean and her   towns,   and *they*   who   *are* of the

pp,cs,nn6010   nn3157

valley of Jezreel.

nn3091   wcs,qmf559   pr413   cs,nn**1004**   nn3130   pp,nn669

17 And Joshua spoke unto the house of Joseph, *even* to Ephraim and to

wcj,pp,nn4519   pp,qnc559   pnp859   aj7227   nn**5971**   (pp,pnx)   aj1419   wcj,nn3581   pp,pnx

Manasseh, saying, Thou *art* a great people, and hast   great power: thou shalt

ptn**3808** qmf**1961**   nu259 nn1486

not have one lot *only*:

cj3588   nn2022   qmf**1961**   pp,pnx   cj3588   pnp1931   nn3293

18 But the mountain shall   be   thine; for   it   *is* a wood, and thou shalt

wcs,pipf,pnx**1254**   pl,nn,pnx8444   wcs,qpf1931   pp,pnx   cj3588   himf**3423**   (853)

cut*it*down: and the outgoings of it shall   be   thine: for thou shalt drive out

df,nn3669   cj3588   pp,pnx   nn1270   cs,nn7393   cj3588   pnp1931   aj**2389**

the Canaanites, though they have iron chariots, *and* though they *be* strong.

The Remaining Land Is Divided

cs,nn3605   cs,nn**5712**   pl,cs,nn**1121**   nn3478

18 ⌖ And the whole congregation of the children of Israel

wcs,nimf**6950**   nn7887   wcs,himf**7931** (853)   cs,nn**168**

assembled together at Shiloh, and set up   the tabernacle of the

nn4150   ad8033   wcj,df,nn776   nipf3533   pp,pl,nn,pnx**6440**

congregation there. And the   land   was subdued   before   them.

wcs,nimf**3498**   pp,pl,cs,nn**1121**   nn3478   nu7651   pl,nn**7626**   pnl834   ptn**3808**

2 And there remained among the children of Israel seven tribes, which had not

qpf2505   (853)   nn,pnx**5159**

yet received   their inheritance.

nn3091   wcs,qmf559   pr413   pl,cs,nn**1121**   nn3478   pr5704/ad,lh575   pnp859   pl,htpf**7503**

3 And Joshua   said   unto the children of Israel, How long *are* ye   slack to

pp,qnc935   pp,qnc**3423**   (853)   df,nn776   pnl834   nn3068   pl,cs,nn**430**   pl,nn,pnx1   qpf5414   pp,pnx

go   to possess   the land, which the Lᴏʀᴅ   God   of your fathers hath given you?

qmv3051   pp,pnx   nu7969   pl,nn**376**   dfp,nn**7626**   wcj,qmf,pnx7971

4 Give out from*among*you three men for *each*   tribe: and I will   send

wcj,qmf**6965**   wcj,htmf**1980**   dfp,nn776   wcj,qmf3789   pnx(853)

them, and they shall   rise,   and   go   through the land, and describe   it

pp,cs,nn**6310**   nn,pnx**5159**   wcj,qmf935   pr,pnx413

according to the inheritance of them; and they shall come *again*   to   me.

wcj,htpf2505   pnx(853)   pp,nu7651   pl,nn2506   nn3063   qmf5975   pr5921

5 And they shall divide   it into seven parts: Judah shall abide   in   their

nn,pnx1366   pr4480/nn5045   wcj,cs,nn**1004**   nn3130   qmf5975   pr5921   nn,pnx1366

coast   on*the*south, and the   house   of Joseph shall abide   in   their coasts

pr4480/nn6828

on*the*north.

wcj,pnp859   qmf3789   (853)   df,nn776   nu7651   pl,nn2506   wcs,hipf935

6 Ye   shall therefore describe   the land *into* seven parts, and bring *the*

⌖ **18:1** The Tabernacle (tent) had been standing at Gilgal. Shiloh was a strategic site in the hill country which could be defended better, and it was more centrally located for all the tribes. Israel was a large, religious congregation, not just a nation. This holy tent was of importance to them because it was where they met with God (Ex. 29:42–46).

wcj,df,nn4708   wcj,df,nn3716   wcj,df,nn4681
26 And Mizpeh, and Chephirah, and Mozah,

wcj,nn7552   wcj,nn3416   wcj,nn8634
27 And Rekem, and Irpeel, and Taralah,

wcj,nn6762   df,nn507   wcj,df,nn2983 pnp1931   nn3389   nn1390   nn7157
28 And Zelah, Eleph, and Jebusi, which is Jerusalem, Gibeath, and Kirjath;

nu702/nu6240 pl,nn5892   wcj,pl,nn,pnx2691 pndm2063   cs,nn5159   pl,cs,nn1121
fourteen cities with their villages. This is the inheritance of the children of

nn1144   pp,pl,nn,pnx4940
Benjamin according to their families.

Simeon's Portion

df,nuor8145 df,nn1486   wcs,qmf3318   pp,nn8095   pp,cs,nn4294
19 ☉ And the second lot came forth to Simeon, even for the tribe

pl,cs,nn1121   nn8095   pp,pl,nn,pnx4940
of the children of Simeon according to their families: and their

nn,pnx5159   wcj,qmf1961 pp,cs,nn8432   cs,nn5159   pl,cs,nn1121   nn3063
inheritance was within the inheritance of the children of Judah.

pp,pnx wcs,qmf1961   pp,nn,pnx5159   nn884   wcj,nn7652   wcj,nn4137
2 And they had in their inheritance Beer-sheba, or Sheba, and Moladah,

wcj,nn2705   wcj,nn1088   wcj,nn6107
3 And Hazarshual, and Balah, and Azem,

wcj,nn513   wcj,nn1329   wcj,nn2767
4 And Eltolad, and Bethul, and Hormah,

wcj,nn6860   wcj,nn1024   wcj,nn2701
5 And Ziklag, and Beth-marcaboth, and Hazar-susah,

wcj,nn1034   wcj,nn8287   nu7969/nu6240 pl,nn5892   wcj,pl,nn,pnx2691
6 And Beth-lebaoth, and Sharuhen; thirteen cities and their villages:

nn5871   nn7417   wcj,nn6281   wcj,nn6228 nu702 pl,nn5892   wcj,pl,nn,pnx2691
7 Ain, Remmon, and Ether, and Ashan; four cities and their villages:

wcj,cs,nn3605   df,pl,nn2691   pnl834   ad5439   df,pndm428 df,pl,nn5892   pr5704
8 And all the villages that were round about these cities to

nn1192   cs,nn7418   nn5045   pndm2063   cs,nn5159   cs,nn4294
Baalath-beer, Ramath of the south. This is the inheritance of the tribe of the

pl,cs,nn1121   nn8095   pp,pl,nn,pnx4940
children of Simeon according to their families.

pr4480/cs,nn2256   pl,cs,nn1121   nn3063   cs,nn5159
9 Out*of*the*portion of the children of Judah was the inheritance of the

pl,cs,nn1121   nn8095   cj3588   cs,nn2506   pl,cs,nn1121   nn3063 qpf1961   aj7227 pr,pnx4480
children of Simeon: for the part of the children of Judah was too much for them:

pl,cs,nn1121   nn8095   wcs,qmf5157   pp,cs,nn8432   nn,pnx5159
therefore the children of Simeon had*their*inheritance within the inheritance of

them.

☉ **19:1–9**   Simeon's allotment was in the extreme south in the territory which was already given to Judah, because Judah was not large enough to fill all of her land. This had consequences for later times. During the period of the divided monarchy, although the tribe of Simeon was politically a part of the ten tribes of Israel, the tribe's proximity to Judah led to its eventual assimilation into Judah.

Zebulun's Portion

df,nuor7992   df,nn1486   wcs,qmf**5927**   pp,pl,cs,nn**1121**   nn2074

10 And the third   lot   came up for the children of Zebulun according to their

pp,pl,nn,pnx**4940**   cs,nn1366   nn,pnx5159   wcs,qmf**1961**   pr5704   nn8301

families: and the border of their inheritance   was   unto Sarid:

nn,pnx1366   wcj,qpf**5927**   dfp,nn,lh3220   wcj,nn4831   wcj,qpf**6293**

11 And their border went up toward the   sea,   and Maralah, and reached to

pp,nn1708   wcs,qmf**6293**   pr413   df,nn5158   pnl834   pr5921/pl,cs,nn**6440**   nn3362

Dabbasheth, and reached to the river that *is*   before   Jokneam;

wcj,qpf**7725**   pr4480/nn8301   ad,lh**6924**   cs,nn4217/df,nn8121   pr5921   cs,nn1366

12 And turned from Sarid eastward toward the   sunrising   unto the border of

nn3696   wcj,qpf3318   pr413   df,nn1705   wcj,qpf**5927**   nn3309

Chisloth-tabor, and then goeth out to Daberath, and goeth up to Japhia,

wcj,pr4480/ad8033   qpf**5674**   ad,lh**6924**   (nn,lh4217)   nn,lh1662

13 And from thence passeth*on*along on the east   to Gittah-hepher, to

nn,lh6278   wcj,qpf3318   nn7417   df,nn5269

Ittah-kazin, and goeth out to Remmon-methoar to Neah;

df,nn1366   wcj,nipf5437   pnx(853)   pr4480/cs,nn6828   nn2615

14 And the border compasseth   it on*the*north*side to Hannathon: and the

pl,nn,pnx8444   wcj,qpf**1961**   cs,nn1516   nn3317

outgoings thereof   are   in the valley of Jipthah-el:

wcj,nn7005   wcj,nn5096   wcj,nn8110   wcj,nn3030   wcj,nn1035

15 And Kattath, and Nahallal, and Shimron, and Idalah, and Bethlehem:

du,nu8147/nu6240   pl,nn5892   wcj,pl,nn,pnx2691

twelve   cities with their villages.

pndm2063   cs,nn**5159**   pl,cs,nn**1121**   nn2074

16 This   *is* the inheritance of the children of Zebulun according to their

pp,pl,nn,pnx**4940** df,pndm428   df,pl,nn5892   wcj,pl,nn,pnx2691

families, these   cities with their villages.

Issachar's Portion

df,nuor7243   df,nn1486   qpf3318   pp,nn3485   pp,pl,cs,nn**1121**   nn3485

17 *And* the fourth   lot   came out to Issachar, for the children of Issachar

pp,pl,nn,pnx**4940**

according to their families.

nn,pnx1366   wcs,qmf**1961**   nn3157   wcj,df,nn3694   wcj,nn7766

18 And their border   was   toward Jezreel, and Chesulloth, and Shunem,

wcj,nn2663   wcj,nn7866   wcj,nn588

19 And Hapharaim, and Shion, and Anaharath,

wcj,df,nn7245   wcj,nn7191   wcj,nn77

20 And Rabbith, and Kishion, and Abez,

wcj,nn7432   wcj,nn5873   wcj,nn5876   wcj,nn1048

21 And Remeth, and En-gannim, and En-haddah, and Beth-pazzez;

df,nn1366   wcj,qpf**6293**   pp,nn8396   wcj,nn7831   wcj,nn1053

22 And the coast reacheth to Tabor, and Shahazimah, and Beth-shemesh; and

pl,cs,nn8444   nn,pnx1366 wcj,qpf**1961**   df,nn3383   nu8337/nu6240   pl,nn5892   wcj,pl,nn,pnx2691

the outgoings of their border   were   at Jordan: sixteen   cities with their villages.

pndm2063   cs,nn**5159**   cs,nn**4294**   pl,cs,nn**1121**   nn3485

23 This   *is* the inheritance of the tribe of the children of Issachar according to

pp,pl,nn,pnx**4940**   df,pl,nn5892   wcj,pl,nn,pnx2691

their families, the cities and their villages.

Asher's Portion

24 And the   fifth   lot   came out for the   tribe   of the   children   of Asher
according to their families.

25 And their border   was   Helkath, and Hali,   and Beten,   and Achshaph,

26 And   Alammelech,   and   Amad,   and   Misheal;   and   reacheth to   Carmel
westward, and to Shihor-libnath;

27 And turneth toward the   sunrising   to Beth-dagon, and reacheth to Zebulun,
and to the   valley   of Jipthah-el toward the north side of Beth-emek, and Neiel,
and goeth out to Cabul on*the*left*hand,

28 And Hebron, and Rehob, and Hammon, and Kanah, *even* unto great Zidon;

29 And *then* the coast turneth to Ramah, and   to   the strong city Tyre; and
the   coast   turneth to Hosah; and the   outgoings   thereof   are   at the   sea
from*the*coast to Achzib:

30 Ummah also, and Aphek, and Rehob: twenty and   two   cities with their
villages.

31 This *is* the inheritance of the   tribe   of the   children   of Asher according to
their families,   these   cities   with their   villages.

Naphtali's Portion

32 The   sixth   lot   came out to the children of Naphtali, *even* for the children
of Naphtali according to their families.

33 And their   coast   was   from Heleph,   from Allon to   Zaanannim,   and
Adami,   Nekeb,   and Jabneel,   unto Lakum; and   the outgoings thereof   were   at
Jordan:

34 And *then* the   coast   turneth   westward   to Aznoth-tabor,   and   goeth out
from thence to Hukkok, and reacheth to Zebulun on*the*south*side, and reacheth to
Asher on*the*west*side, and to   Judah   upon Jordan toward the   sunrising.

nn4013   wcj,pl,cs,nn5892   df,nn6661   nn6863   wcj,nn2575   nn7557
35 And the fenced   cities   *are* Ziddim, Zer, and Hammath, Rakkath, and
wcj,nn3672
Chinnereth,

wcj,nn128   wcj,df,nn7414   wcj,nn2674
36 And Adamah, and Ramah, and Hazor,

wcj,nn6943   wcj,nn154   wcj,nn5877
37 And Kedesh, and Edrei, and En-hazor,

wcj,nn3375   wcj,nn4027   nn2765   wcj,nn1043   wcj,nn1053
38 And Iron, and Migdal-el, Horem, and Beth-anath, and Beth-shemesh;
nu8672/nu6240 pl,nn5892   wcj,pl,nn,pnx2691
nineteen cities with their villages.

pndm2063   cs,nn5159   cs,nn4294   pl,cs,nn1121   nn5321
39 This *is* the inheritance of the tribe of the children of Naphtali according to
pp,pl,nn,pnx4940   df,pl,nn5892   wcj,pl,nn,pnx2691
their families, the cities and their villages.

Dan's Portion

df,nuor7637   df,nn1486   qpf3318   pp,cs,nn4294   pl,cs,nn1121   nn1835
40 *And* the seventh   lot   came out for the   tribe   of the children of Dan
pp,pl,nn,pnx4940
according to their families.

cs,nn1366   nn,pnx5159   wcs,qmf1961   nn6881   wcj,nn847
41 And the coast of their inheritance   was   Zorah, and Eshtaol, and
wcj,nn5905
Ir-shemesh,

wcj,nn8169   wcj,nn357   wcj,nn3494
42 And Shaalabbin, and Ajalon, and Jethlah,

wcj,nn356   wcj,nn8553   wcj,nn6138
43 And Elon, and Thimnathah, and Ekron,

wcj,nn514   wcj,nn1405   wcj,nn1191
44 And Eltekeh, and Gibbethon, and Baalath,

wcj,nn3055   wcj,nn1139   wcj,nn1667
45 And Jehud, and Bene-berak, and Gath-rimmon,

wcj,nn4313   wcj,df,nn7542   pr5973   df,nn1366   pr4136   nn3305
46 And Me-jarkon, and Rakkon, with the border before Japho.

cs,nn1366   pl,cs,nn1121   nn1835   wcs,qmf3318   pr,pnx4480
47 And the coast of the children of Dan went out *too little* for them: therefore
pl,cs,nn1121   nn1835   wcs,qmf5927   wcs,nimf3898   pr5973   nn3959   wcs,qmf3920 pnx(853)
the children of Dan went up to   fight   against Leshem, and   took   it, and
wcs,himf5221 pnx(853)   pp,cs,nn6310   nn2719   wcs,qmf3423   pnx(853)   wcs,qmf3427
smote   it with the   edge   of the sword, and possessed   it, and dwelt
pp,pnx   wcs,qmf7121 pp,nn3959   nn1835   pp,cs,nn8034   nn1835   nn,pnx1
therein, and called Leshem, Dan, after the   name   of Dan their father.

pndm2063   cs,nn5159   cs,nn4294   pl,cs,nn1121   nn1835
48 This *is* the inheritance of the tribe of the children of Dan according to their
pp,pl,nn,pnx4940 df,pndm428 df,pl,nn5892   wcj,pl,nn,pnx2691
families, these   cities with their villages.

19:40–48 Dan's inheritance was on the coastal plain south of the territory given to Ephraim, but she was unable to possess it. Therefore, the tribe took the city of Leshem above the Sea of Galilee in the extreme north and settled it and the surrounding territory (Judg. 18:27–29). The tribe renamed the city "Dan," and it became a popular designation of the northern extremity of Israel (note the phrase "from Dan to Beersheba" in Judg. 20:1).

Joshua's Portion

_{wcs,pimf**3615**} _{pp,qnc**5157**/(853)/df,nn**776**}
49 When they had made an end of dividing*the*land*for*inheritance by

_{pp,pl,nn,pnx1367} _{pl,cs,nn**1121**} _{nn3478} _{wcs,qmf**5414**} _{nn5159} _{pp,nn3091} _{cs,nn**1121**}
their coasts, the children of Israel gave an inheritance to Joshua the son of

_{nn5126 pp,nn,pnx**8432**}
Nun among them:

_{pr5921} _{cs,nn**6310**} _{nn**3068**} _{qpf**5414** pp,pnx (853)} _{df,nn5892} _{pnl834}
50 According to the word of the LORD they gave him the city which he

_{qpf**7592**} ₍₈₅₃₎ _{nn8556} _{pp,cs,nn2022} _{nn669} _{wcs,qmf1129 (853)} _{df,nn5892}
asked, *even* Timnathserah in mount Ephraim: and he built the city, and

_{wcs,qmf**3427**} _{pp,pnx}
dwelt therein.

_{pndm428} _{df,pl,nn5159} _{pnl834} _{nn499} _{df,nn**3548**} _{wcj,nn3091} _{cs,nn**1121**}
51 These *are* the inheritances, which Eleazar the priest, and Joshua the son of

_{nn5126} _{wcj,pl,cs,nn**7218**} _{df,pl,nn1} _{pp,pl,cs,nn**4294**} _{pl,cs,nn**1121**} _{nn3478}
Nun, and the heads of the fathers of the tribes of the children of Israel,

_{pipf**5157**} _{pp,nn1486} _{pp,nn7887} _{pp,pl,cs,nn**6440**} _{nn**3068**} _{cs,nn**6607**}
divided*for*an*inheritance by lot in Shiloh before the LORD, at the door of

_{cs,nn**168**} _{nn4150} _{wcs,pimf**3615**} _{pr4480/pinc2505} ₍₈₅₃₎
the tabernacle of the congregation. So they made*an*end of dividing the

_{df,nn**776**}
country.

The Cities of Refuge

_{nn**3068**} _{wcs,pimf**1696** pr413} _{nn3091} _{pp,qnc559}

20 The LORD also spoke unto Joshua, saying,

_{pimv**1696**} _{pp,pl,cs,nn**1121**} _{nn3478} _{pp,qnc559} _{qmv**5414**} _{pp,pnx} ₍₈₅₃₎
2 Speak to the children of Israel, saying, Appoint out for you

_{pl,cs,nn5892} _{df,nn4733} _{pnl834} _{pipf**1696**} _{pr,pnx413} _{pp,cs,nn**3027**} _{nn4872}
cities of refuge, whereof I spoke unto you by the hand of Moses:

_{qpta**7523**} _{cs,hipt**5221**} _{nn5315} _{pp,nn**7684**} _{pp,ptn1097/nn**1847**} _{pp,qnc5127}
3 That the slayer that killeth *any* person unawares *and* unwittingly may flee

_{ad,lh8033} _{wcj,qpf**1961**} _{pp,nn4733} _{pr4480/qpta1350} _{df,nn**1818**}
thither: and they shall be your refuge from*the*avenger of blood.

_{wcj,qpf**5127**} _{pr413} _{nu259} _{df,pndm428 pr4480/df,pl,nn**5892**} _{wcj,qpf**5975**}
4 And when he that doth flee unto one of those cities shall stand at

_{cs,nn**6607**} _{cs,nn**8179**} _{df,nn5892} _{wcj,pipf**1696**} ₍₈₅₃₎ _{pl,nn,pnx**1697**}
the entering of the gate of the city, and shall declare his cause in the

_{pp,du,cs,nn**241**} _{cs,aj**2205**} _{df,pndm1931 df,nn5892} _{wcj,qpf622 pnx(853)} _{df,nn,lh**5892**}
ears of the elders of that city, they shall take him into the city

_{pp,pnx} _{wcj,qpf**5414**/pr,pnx413} _{nn4725} _{wcj,qpf**3427** pr,pnx5973}
unto them, and give him a place, that he may dwell among them.

_{wcj,cj3588} _{cs,qpta**1350**} _{df,nn**1818**} _{qmf7291} _{pr,pnx310} _{wcj,ptn**3808**}
5 And if the avenger of blood pursue after him, then they shall not

---

⚙ **19:49, 50** There is no information in the Book of Numbers regarding a special allotment for Joshua, as is done for Caleb (Num. 14:6–9, 24; Josh. 14:6–15). The name of the city given Joshua was Timnath–serah which means "abundant or extra portion." In Judges 2:9 the Septuagint and the KJV call it Timnath–heres which means "portion of the sun" (Judg. 2:9). Ancient tradition says this new name was given to commemorate Joshua's calling on God to make the sun to stand still (Josh. 10:12–14). Others believe that "heres" is a scribal error, "serah" written backwards.

⚙ **20:2–4** See the note on Deuteronomy 19:1–10, on the "cities of refuge."

^{himf5462} (853)   ^{df,qpta7523}   ^{pp,nn,pnx3027}   ^{cj3588}   ^{hipf5221} (853)   ^{nn,pnx7453}

deliver   the slayer up into his   hand; because he smote   his neighbor

^{pp,ptn1097/nn1847}   ^{qpta8130} ^{pp,pnx} ^{wcj,ptn3808} ^{pr,ad8543/ad8032}

unwittingly, and hated him   not   formerly.

^{wcj,qpf3427}   ^{df,pndm1931} ^{dfp,nn5892} ^{pr5704}   ^{qnc,pnx5975} ^{pp,pl,cs,nn6440}

6 And he shall dwell in   that   city,   until he   stand   before   the

^{df,nn5712}   ^{dfp,nn4941}   ^{pr5704}   ^{qnc4194}   ^{df,aj1419} ^{df,nn3548} ^{pnl834}   ^{qmf1961}

congregation for judgment, *and* until the death of the high priest that shall be in

^{df,pnp1992 dfp,pl,nn3117} ^{ad227}   ^{df,qpta7523} ^{qmf7725}   ^{wcs,qpf935} ^{pr413}   ^{nn,pnx5892}   ^{wcj,pr413}

those   days: then shall the slayer return, and come unto his own city, and unto

^{nn,pnx1004} ^{pr413}   ^{df,nn5892} ^{pnl834/pr4480/ad8033}   ^{qpf5127}

his own house, unto the city from whence he fled.

^{wcs,himf6942}   (853)   ⁿⁿ⁶⁹⁴³   ^{dfp,nn1551}   ^{pp,cs,nn2022}   ⁿⁿ⁵³²¹   ^{wcj(853)}

7 And they appointed   Kedesh in Galilee in mount Naphtali, and

ⁿⁿ⁷⁹²⁷   ^{pp,cs,nn2022}   ⁿⁿ⁶⁶⁹   ^{wcj(853)}   ⁿⁿ⁷¹⁵³   ^{pndm1931}   ⁿⁿ²²⁷⁵

Shechem in   mount Ephraim, and   Kirjath-arba, which *is* Hebron, in the

^{pp,cs,nn2022}   ⁿⁿ³⁰⁶³

mountain of Judah.

^{wcj,pr4480/cs,nn5676} ^{pp,nn3383}   ⁿⁿ³⁴⁰⁵   ^{nn,lh4217}   ^{qpf5414}   (853) ⁿⁿ¹²²¹

8 And on the other side Jordan by Jericho eastward, they assigned   Bezer

^{dfp,nn4057}   ^{dfp,nn4334}   ^{pr4480/cs,nn4294}   ⁿⁿ⁷²⁰⁵   ^{wcj(853)} ⁿⁿ⁷²¹⁶

in the wilderness upon the plain out*of*the*tribe of Reuben, and   Ramoth in

^{dfp,nn1568}   ^{pr4480/cs,nn4294}   ⁿⁿ¹⁴¹⁰   ^{wcj(853)}   ⁿⁿ¹⁴⁷⁴   ^{dfp,nn1316}   ^{pr4480/cs,nn4294}

Gilead out*of*the*tribe of Gad, and   Golan in Bashan out*of*the*tribe of

ⁿⁿ⁴⁵¹⁹

Manasseh.

^{pndm428} ^{qpf1961}   ^{pl,cs,nn5892}   ^{df,nn4152}   ^{pp,cs,nn3605}   ^{pl,cs,nn1121}   ⁿⁿ³⁴⁷⁸

9 These were the cities appointed for all   the children of Israel, and for the

^{wcj,dfp,nn1616}   ^{df,qpta1481}   ^{pp,nn,pnx8432}   ^{cs,nn3605}   ^{cs,hipt5221}   ⁿⁿ⁵³¹⁵

stranger that sojourneth among   them, that whosoever killeth *any* person at

^{pp,nn7684}   ^{pp,qnc5127}   ^{ad,lh8033}   ^{wcj,ptn3808} ^{qmf4191}   ^{pp,cs,nn3027}   ^{qpta1350}

unawares might flee thither, and   not die by the hand of the avenger of

^{df,nn1818} ^{pr5704}   ^{qnc,pnx5975} ^{pp,pl,cs,nn6440}   ^{df,nn5712}

blood, until he stood   before the congregation.

The Levite Cities

^{wcs,qmf5066}   ^{pl,cs,nn7218}   ^{pl,cs,nn1}   ^{df,pl,nn3881} ^{pr413}   ⁿⁿ⁴⁹⁹

21 Then came near the heads of the fathers of the Levites unto Eleazar

^{df,nn3548}   ^{wcj,pr413}   ⁿⁿ³⁰⁹¹   ^{cs,nn1121}   ⁿⁿ⁵¹²⁶   ^{wcj,pr413}   ^{pl,cs,nn7218}

the priest, and unto Joshua the son of Nun, and unto the heads of

^{pl,cs,nn1}   ^{df,pl,nn4294}   ^{pp,pl,cs,nn1121}   ⁿⁿ³⁴⁷⁸

the fathers of the tribes of the children of Israel;

^{wcs,pimf1696} ^{pr,pnx413}   ^{pp,nn7887}   ^{pp,cs,nn776}   ⁿⁿ³⁶⁶⁷   ^{pp,qnc559}

2 And they spoke unto them at Shiloh in the land of Canaan, saying, The

ⁿⁿ³⁰⁶⁸   ^{pipf6680}   ^{pp,cs,nn3027}   ⁿⁿ⁴⁸⁷²   ^{pp,qnc5414 pp,pnx} ^{pl,nn5892}   ^{pp,qnc3427}

LORD commanded by the hand of Moses to give   us cities to dwell in, with the

^{wcj,pl,nn,pnx4054}   ^{pp,nn,pnx929}

suburbs thereof for our cattle.

^{pl,cs,nn1121}   ⁿⁿ³⁴⁷⁸ ^{wcs,qmf5414}   ^{pp,nn3881}   ^{pr4480/nn,pnx5159}

3 And the children of Israel gave unto the Levites out*of*their*inheritance,

---

21:2 These were cities that the children of Israel gave to the Levites so they would have places to live and raise cattle (v. 3). There was a total of forty-eight cities which were given to the tribe of Levi and distributed throughout the land so there would be four cities for each tribe of Israel.

at the commandment of the LORD, these cities and their suburbs.

4 And the lot came out for the families of the Kohathites: and the children of Aaron the priest, *which were* of the Levites, had by lot out*of*the*tribe of Judah, and out*of*the*tribe of Simeon, and out*of*the*tribe of Benjamin, thirteen cities.

5 And the rest of the children of Kohath *had* by lot out*of*the*families of the tribe of Ephraim, and out*of*the*tribe of Dan, and out*of*the*half tribe of Manasseh, ten cities.

6 And the children of Gershon *had* by lot out*of*the*families of the tribe of Issachar, and out*of*the*tribe of Asher, and out*of*the*tribe of Naphtali, and out*of*the*half tribe of Manasseh in Bashan, thirteen cities.

7 The children of Merari by their families *had* out*of*the*tribe of Reuben, and out*of*the*tribe of Gad, and out*of*the*tribe of Zebulun, twelve cities.

8 And the children of Israel gave by lot unto the Levites these cities with their suburbs, as the LORD commanded by the hand of Moses.

9 And they gave out*of*the*tribe of the children of Judah, and out*of*the*tribe of the children of Simeon, these cities which are *here* mentioned by name,

10 Which the children of Aaron, *being* of*the*families of the Kohathites, *who* were of*the*children of Levi, had: for theirs was the first lot.

11 And they gave them the city of Arba the father of Anak, which *city* is Hebron, in the hill *country* of Judah, with the suburbs thereof round about it.

12 But the fields of the city, and the villages thereof, gave they to Caleb the son of Jephunneh for his possession.

13 Thus they gave to the children of Aaron the priest Hebron with her suburbs, *to be* a city of refuge for the slayer; and Libnah with her suburbs,

14 And   Jattir with her suburbs, and   Eshtemoa with her suburbs,

15 And   Holon with her suburbs, and   Debir with her suburbs,

16 And   Ain with her suburbs, and   Juttah with her suburbs, *and*

Beth-shemesh with her suburbs; nine cities out of those   two   tribes.

17 And out*of*the*tribe of Benjamin,   Gibeon with her suburbs,   Geba

with her suburbs,

☞ 18   Anathoth with her suburbs, and   Almon with her suburbs; four

cities.

19 All the cities of the children of Aaron, the priests, *were* thirteen cities

with their suburbs.

20 And the   families   of the children of Kohath, the Levites which remained

of*the*children of Kohath, even they   had   the   cities of their   lot

out*of*the*tribe of Ephraim.

21 For they gave them   Shechem with her suburbs in mount Ephraim, *to*

be   a city of refuge for the slayer; and   Gezer with her suburbs,

22 And   Kibzaim with her suburbs, and   Beth-horon with her

suburbs; four cities.

23 And out*of*the*tribe of Dan,   Eltekeh with her suburbs,   Gibbethon

with her suburbs,

24   Aijalon with her suburbs,   Gath-rimmon with her suburbs; four

cities.

25 And out*of*the*half tribe of Manasseh,   Tanach with her suburbs, and

Gath-rimmon with her suburbs; two cities.

26 All the cities *were* ten with their   suburbs for the families of the

children of Kohath that remained.

27 And unto the   children   of Gershon, of*the*families of the Levites,

---

☞ 21:18 See the note on Jeremiah 1:1, regarding Anathoth.

pr4480/cs,nn2677　　　cs,nn**4294**　　　nn4519　　　(853)　nn1474　　dfp,nn1316　wcj,pr854

out*of*the*other*half tribe of Manasseh *they gave*　Golan in Bashan with her

pl,nn,pnx4054　　(853)　cs,nn5892　　cs,nn4733　　df,qpta**7523**　wcj(853)　nn1203　wcj,pr854

suburbs, *to be*　a city of refuge for the slayer; and　Beesh-terah with her

pl,nn,pnx4054　du,nu8147　pl,nn5892

suburbs; two cities.

wcj,pr4480/cs,nn**4294**　　nn3485　(853)　nn7191　wcj,pr854　pl,nn,pnx4054　(853)　nn1705

28 And out*of*the*tribe of Issachar,　Kishon with her suburbs,　Daberath

wcj,pr854　　pl,nn,pnx4054

with her suburbs,

nn3412　wcj,pr854　pl,nn,pnx4054　nn5873　wcj,pr854　pl,nn,pnx4054　nu702　pl,nn5892

29 Jarmuth with her suburbs, En-gannim with her suburbs; four cities.

wcj,pr4480/cs,nn**4294**　　nn836　(853)　nn4861　wcj,pr854　pl,nn,pnx4054　(853)　nn5658

30 And out*of*the*tribe of Asher,　Mishal with her suburbs,　Abdon

wcj,pr854　　pl,nn,pnx4054

with her suburbs,

(853)　nn2520　wcj,pr854　pl,nn,pnx4054　wcj(853)　nn7340　wcj,pr854　pl,nn,pnx4054　nu702

31　Helkath with her suburbs, and　Rehob with her suburbs; four

pl,nn5892

cities.

wcj,pr4480/cs,nn**4294**　　nn5321　(853)　nn6943　dfp,nn1551　wcj,pr854　pl,nn,pnx4054

32 And out*of*the*tribe of Naphtali,　Kedesh in Galilee with her suburbs,

(853)　cs,nn5892　cs,nn4733　df,qpta**7523**　wcj(853)　nn2576　wcj,pr854　pl,nn,pnx4054

to be　a city of refuge for the slayer; and　Hammoth-dor with her suburbs,

wcj(853)　nn7178　pl,nn,pnx4054　nu7969　pl,nn5892

and　Kartan with her suburbs; three cities.

cs,nn3605　pl,cs,nn5892　df,nn1649　pp,pl,nn,pnx**4940**

33　All the cities of the Gershonites according to their families *were*

nu7969/nu6240　nn5892　wcj,pl,nn,pnx4054

thirteen cities with their suburbs.

wcj,pp,pl,cs,nn**4940**　pl,cs,nn1121　nn4847　df,pl,nipt**3498**

34 And unto the families of the children of Merari, the rest of the

df,pl,nn3881　pr4480/pr854　cs,nn**4294**　nn2074　(853)　nn3362　wcj,pr854　pl,nn,pnx4054　(853)

Levites, out of the tribe of Zebulun,　Jokneam with her suburbs, and

nn7177　wcj,pr854　pl,nn,pnx4054

Kartah with her suburbs,

(853)　nn1829　wcj,pr854　pl,nn,pnx4054　(853)　nn5096　wcj,pr854　pl,nn,pnx4054　nu702　pl,nn5892

35　Dimnah with her suburbs,　Nahalal with her suburbs; four cities.

wcj,pr4480/cs,nn**4294**　nn7205　(853)　nn1221　wcj,pr854　pl,nn,pnx4054　wcj(853)

36 And out*of*the*tribe of Reuben,　Bezer with her suburbs, and

nn3096　wcj,pr854　pl,nn,pnx4054

Jahazah with her suburbs,

(853)　nn6932　wcj,pr854　pl,nn,pnx4054　wcj(853)　nn4158　wcj,pr854　pl,nn,pnx4054　nu702

37　Kedemoth with her suburbs, and　Mephaath with her suburbs; four

pl,nn5892

cities.

wcj,pr4480/cs,nn**4294**　nn1410　(853)　nn7216　dfp,nn1568　wcj,pr854　pl,nn,pnx4054

38 And out*of*the*tribe of Gad,　Ramoth in Gilead with her suburbs, *to be*

(853)　cs,nn5892　cs,nn4733　df,qpta**7523**　wcj(853)　nn4266　wcj,pr854　pl,nn,pnx4054

a city of refuge for the slayer; and　Mahanaim with her suburbs,

(853)　nn2809　wcj,pr854　pl,nn,pnx4054　(853)　nn3270　wcj,pr854　pl,nn,pnx4054　nu702　pl,nn5892

39　Heshbon with her suburbs,　Jazer with her suburbs; four cities in

cs,nn3605

all.

cs,nn3605　df,pl,nn5892　pp,pl,cs,nn**1121**　nn4847　pp,pl,nn,pnx**4940**

40 So all the cities for the children of Merari by their families, which were

df,pl,nipt**3498**   pr4480/pl,cs,nn**4940**   df,pl,nn3881 wcs,qmf**1961**   nn,pnx1486 du,nu8147/nu6240 pl,nn5892

remaining of*the*families of the Levites, were *by* their lot twelve cities.

cs,nn3605   pl,cs,nn5892   df,pl,nn3881 pp,cs,nn**8432**   cs,nn**272**   pl,cs,nn1121

41 All the cities of the Levites within the possession of the children of

nn3478   pl,nu705   wcj,nu8083 pl,nn5892   wcj,pl,nn,pnx4054

Israel *were* forty and eight cities with their suburbs.

df,pndm428 df,pl,nn5892 qmf**1961**   nn5892/nn5892   wcj,pl,nn,pnx4054   pr,pnx5439   ad**3651**

42 These cities were every one with their suburbs round about them: thus

pp,cs,nn3605 df,pndm428 df,pl,nn5892

were all these cities.

Israel Settles the Land

nn3068   wcs,qmf**5414**   pp,nn3478 (853) cs,nn3605   df,nn776   pnl834   nipf**7650**

43 And the LORD gave unto Israel all the land which he swore to

pp,qnc**5414**   pp,pl,nn,pnx1   wcs,qmf,pnx**3423**   wcs,qmf**3427**   pp,pnx

give unto their fathers; and they possessed it, and dwelt therein.

nn3068   wcs5117/pp,pnx   pr4480/ad5439   pp,nn3605   pnl834   nipf**7650**

44 And the LORD gave*them*rest round about, according*to*all that he swore

pp,pl,nn,pnx1   qpf5975 wcj,ptn**3808**   nn376 pr4480/cs,nn3605   pl,qpta,pnx341 pp,pl,nn,pnx**6440**

unto their fathers: and there stood not a man of all their enemies before

nn3068   qpf**5414** (853) cs,nn3605   pl,qpta,pnx341   pp,nn,pnx**3027**

them; the LORD delivered all their enemies into their hand.

qpf**5307**   ptn**3808**   nn1697 pr4480/cs,nn3605 df,aj**2896** df,nn1697   pnl834   nn3068   pipf**1696**

45 There failed not aught of any good thing which the LORD had spoken

pr413   cs,nn**1004**   nn3478 df,nn3605   qpf935

unto the house of Israel; all came*to*pass.

The Eastern Tribes are Sent Home

ad**227**   nn3091   qmf**7121**   df,nn7206   wcj,dfp,nn1425   wcj,dfp,cs,nn2677

22 Then Joshua called the Reubenites, and the Gadites, and the half

cs,nn**4294**   nn4519

tribe of Manasseh,

wcs,qmf**559** pr,pnx413   pnp859   qpf**8104** (853) cs,nn3605 pnl834   nn4872   cs,nn**5650**

2 And said unto them, Ye have kept all that Moses the servant of the

nn3068   pipf**6680**   pnx(853)   wcs,qmf**8085**   pp,nn,pnx6963   pp,nn3605 pnl834

LORD commanded you, and have obeyed my voice in all that I

pipf**6680**   pnx(853)

commanded you:

ptn**3808** qpf**5800** (853)   pl,nn,pnx251 pndm2088 aj7227   pl,nn3117 pr5704 df,pndm2088 df,nn3117

3 Ye have not left your brethren these many days unto this day, but

wcj,qpf**8104** (853)   cs,nn4931   nn3068   pl,nn,pnx430

have kept the charge of the commandment of the LORD your God.

wcj,ad6258   nn3068   pl,nn,pnx**430**   hipf5117   pp,pl,nn,pnx251 pp,pnl834

4 And now the LORD your God hath given rest unto your brethren, as

pipf**1696**   pp,pnx   wcj,ad6258 qmv6437   wcj,qmv1980 pp,pnx   pp,pl,nn,pnx168

he promised them: therefore now return ye, and get you unto your tents,

pr413   cs,nn776   nn,pnx272   pnl834   nn4872   cs,nn5650   nn3068 qpf**5414**

and unto the land of your possession, which Moses the servant of the LORD gave

pp,pnx   pp,cs,nn5676   df,nn3383

you on the other side Jordan.

ad7535   ad3966   qmv**8104**   pp,qnc**6213** (853)   df,nn**4687**   wcj(853)   df,nn**8451**

5 But take diligent heed to do the commandment and the law,

pnl834　nn4872　cs,nn5650　nn3068　pipf6680　pnx(853)　pp,qnc157　(853)　nn3068
which Moses the servant of the LORD charged   you, to love   the LORD your

pl,nn,pnx430　wcj,pp,qnc1980　pp,cs,nn3605　pl,nn,pnx1870　wcj,pp,qnc8104　pl,nn,pnx4687
God, and to walk in all his ways, and to keep his commandments,

wcj,pp,qnc1692　pp,pnx　wcj,pp,qnc,pnx5647　pp,cs,nn3605　nn,pnx3824
and to cleave unto him, and to serve him with all your heart and with

wcj,pp,cs,nn3605　nn,pnx5315
all your soul.

nn3091　wcs,pimf,pnx1288　wcs,pimf,pnx7971　wcs,qmf1980　pr413
6 So Joshua blessed them, and sent*them*away: and they went unto their

pl,nn,pnx168
tents.

wcj,dfp,cs,nn2677　cs,nn7626　df,nn4519　nn4872　qpf5414
7 Now to the *one* half of the tribe of Manasseh Moses had given

dfp,nn1316　wcj,pp,nn,pnx2677　qpf5414　nn3091　pr5973
possession in Bashan: but unto the *other* half thereof gave Joshua among their

pl,nn,pnx251　pp,cs,nn5676　df,nn3383　nn,lh3220　wcj,ad3588　nn3091　pipf,pnx7971　ad1571
brethren on this side Jordan westward. And when Joshua sent*them*away also

pr413　pl,nn,pnx168　wcs,pimf,pnx1288
unto their tents, then he blessed them,

wcs,qmf559　pr,pnx413　pp,qnc559　qmv7725　aj7227　pp,pl,nn5233　pr413
8 And he spoke unto them, saying, Return with much riches unto your

pl,nn,pnx168　ad3966　aj7227　wcj,pp,nn4735　pp,nn3701　wcj,pp,nn2091　wcj,pp,nn5178
tents, and with very much cattle, with silver, and with gold, and with brass,

wcj,pp,nn1270　ad3966　hina7235　wcj,pp,pl,nn8008　qmv2505　cs,nn7998　pl,qpta,pnx341
and with iron, and with very much raiment: divide the spoil of your enemies

pr5973　pl,nn,pnx251
with your brethren.

pl,cs,nn1121　nn7205　wcj,pl,cs,nn1121　nn1410　wcj,cs,nn2677　cs,nn7626
9 And the children of Reuben and the children of Gad and the half tribe of

df,nn4519　wcs,qmf7725　wcs,qmf1980　pr4480/pr854　pl,cs,nn1121　nn3478　pr4480/nn7887　pnl834
Manasseh returned, and departed from the children of Israel out*of*Shiloh, which

pp,cs,nn776　nn3667　pp,qnc1980　pr413　cs,nn776　df,nn1568　pr413　cs,nn776
is in the land of Canaan, to go unto the country of Gilead, to the land of

nn,pnx272　pnl834　pp,pnx　nipf270　pr5921　cs,nn6310　nn3068
their possession, whereof they were possessed, according to the word of the LORD

pp,cs,nn3027　nn4872
by the hand of Moses.

wcs,qmf935　pr413　pl,cs,nn1552　df,nn3383　pnl834　pp,cs,nn776
10 And when they came unto the borders of Jordan, that *are* in the land of

nn3667　pl,cs,nn1121　nn7205　wcj,pl,cs,nn1121　nn1410　wcj,cs,nn2677　cs,nn7626
Canaan, the children of Reuben and the children of Gad and the half tribe of

df,nn4519　wcs,qmf1129　ad8033　nn4196　pr5921　df,nn3383　aj1419　nn4196　pp,nn4758
Manasseh built there an altar by Jordan, a great altar to see to.

pl,cs,nn1121　nn3478　wcs,qmf8085　pp,qnc559　ptdm2009　pl,cs,nn1121　nn7205
11 And the children of Israel heard say, Behold, the children of Reuben and

wcj,pl,cs,nn1121　nn1410　wcj,cs,nn2677　cs,nn7626　df,nn4519　qpf1129　(853)　df,nn4196
the children of Gad and the half tribe of Manasseh have built an altar

pr413/pr4136　cs,nn776　nn3667　pr413　pl,cs,nn1552　df,nn3383　pr413　cs,nn1552
over against the land of Canaan, in the borders of Jordan, at the passage of the

pl,cs,nn1121　nn3478
children of Israel.

◎🔊 **22:10, 16** The word that is translated "altar" in these verses should have been rendered "monument." When the tribes of Reuben, Gad and the half–tribe of Manasseh returned to the east side of the Jordan River, they built a monument for a testimony to God of all that He had done for them (see vv. 21–29).

_{pl,cs,nn1121   nn3478   wcs,qmf8085   cs,nn3605   cs,nn5712}

12 And when the children of Israel heard *of it*, the whole congregation of the

_{pl,cs,nn1121   nn3478   wcs,nimf6950   nn7887   pp,qnc5927   dfp,nn6635}

children of Israel gathered*themselves*together at Shiloh, to go up to war

_{pr,pnx5921}

against them.

_{pl,cs,nn1121   nn3478   wcs,qmf7971   pr413   pl,cs,nn1121   nn7205   wcj,pr413}

13 And the children of Israel sent unto the children of Reuben, and to the

_{pl,cs,nn1121   nn1410   wcj,pr413   cs,nn2677 cs,nn7626   nn4519   pr413   cs,nn776   df,nn1568}

children of Gad, and to the half tribe of Manasseh, into the land of Gilead,

_{(853)   nn6372   cs,nn1121   nn499   df,nn3548}

Phinehas the son of Eleazar the priest,

_{pr,pnx5973   wcj,nu6235   pl,nn5387   nn5387/nu259/nn5387/nu259   pp,cs,nn1004   nn1}

14 And with him ten princes, of each chief house a prince

_{pp,cs,nn3605   pl,cs,nn4294   nn3478   wcj,nn376   cs,nn7218   cs,nn1004}

throughout all the tribes of Israel; and each one *was* a head of the house of

_{nn,pnx1   pp,pl,cs,nu505   nn3478}

their fathers among the thousands of Israel.

_{wcs,qmf935   pr413   pl,cs,nn1121   nn7205   wcj,pr413   pl,cs,nn1121   nn1410}

15 And they came unto the children of Reuben, and to the children of Gad,

_{wcj,pr413   cs,nn2677 cs,nn7626   nn4519   pr413   cs,nn776   df,nn1568   wcs,pimf1696}

and to the half tribe of Manasseh, unto the land of Gilead, and they spoke

_{pr,pnx854   pp,qnc559}

with them, saying,

_{ad3541   qpf559   cs,nn3605   cs,nn5712   nn3068   pnit4100 df,nn4604   df,pndm2088 pnl834}

🔑 16 Thus saith the whole congregation of the LORD, What trespass *is* this that

_{qpf4603   pp,pl,cs,nn430   nn3478   pp,qnc7725   df,nn3117}

ye have committed against the God of Israel, to turn away this day

_{pr4480/pr310   nn3068   pp,qnc1129 pp,pnx   nn4196}

from following the LORD, in that ye have built you an altar, that ye might

_{pp,qnc,pnx4775   df,nn3117   pp,nn3068}

rebel this day against the LORD?

_{(853)   cs,nn5771   nn6465   he,ad4592   pp,pnx   pr,pnx4480   pnl834   ptn3808}

17 *Is* the iniquity of Peor too little for us, from which we are not

_{htpf2891   pr5704 df,pndm2088 df,nn3117   wcs,qmf1961   df,nn5063   pp,cs,nn5712}

cleansed until this day, although there was a plague in the congregation of

_{nn3068}

the LORD,

_{wcj,pnp859   qmf7725   df,nn3117   pr4480/pr310   nn3068}

18 But that ye must turn away this day from following the LORD? and it

_{wcs,qpf1961   pnp859   qmf4775   df,nn3117   pp,nn3068   wcj,ad4279}

will be, *seeing* ye rebel today against the LORD, that tomorrow he will be

_{qmf7107   pr413   cs,nn3605   cs,nn5712   nn3478}

wroth with the whole congregation of Israel.

_{wcj,ad389   cj518   cs,nn776   nn,pnx272   aj2931}

19 Notwithstanding, if the land of your possession *be* unclean, *then*

_{qmv5674/pp,pnx   pr413   cs,nn776   cs,nn272   nn3068   pnl834   nn3068}

pass*ye*over unto the land of the possession of the LORD, wherein the LORD's

_{cs,nn4908   qpf7931/ad8033   wcj,nimv270   pp,nn,pnx8432   qmf4775   ptn408}

tabernacle dwelleth, and take possession among us: but rebel not against the

_{wcj,pp,nn3068 ptn408 qmf4775   wcj,pnx(853)   pp,qnc,pnx1129 pp,pnx   nn4196 pr4480/pr1107   cs,nn4196}

LORD, nor rebel against us, in building you an altar beside the altar of

_{nn3068   pl,nn,pnx430}

the LORD our God.

_{he,ptn3808   nn5912   cs,nn1121   nn2226   qpf4603   nn4604}

20 Did not Achan the son of Zerah commit a trespass in the

dfp,nn2764   nn7110   qpf1961 wcj,pr5921 cs,nn3605   cs,nn5712   nn3478   wcj,pndm1931
accursed thing, and wrath fell   on   all the congregation of Israel? and   that

nn376   qpf1478   ptn3808 nu259   pp,nn,pnx5771
man perished not alone in his iniquity.

pl,cs,nn1121   nn7205   wcj,pl,cs,nn1121   nn1410   wcj,cs,nn2677 cs,nn7626
21 Then the children of Reuben and the children of Gad and the   half   tribe

df,nn4519   wcs,qmf6030   wcs,pimf1696   (853)   pl,cs,nn7218   pl,cs,nu505   nn3478
of Manasseh answered, and   said   unto   the heads of the thousands of Israel,

nn3068 nn410   pl,nn430   nn3068 nn410   pl,nn430 pnp1931 qpta3045   wcj,nn3478
22 The LORD God of gods, the LORD God of gods, he knoweth, and Israel

pnp1931   qmf3045 cj518   pp,nn4777   wcj,cj518   pp,nn4604   pp,nn3068
he   shall know; if it be in rebellion, or   if in transgression against the LORD,

himf,pnx3467   ptn408 df,pndm2088 df,nn3117
(save us not   this   day,)

pp,qnc1129 pp,pnx   nn4196   pp,qnc7725   pr4480/pr310   nn3068
23 That we have built   us an altar to   turn from following the LORD, or

wcj,cj518   pp,hinc5927 pr,pnx5921   nn5930   wcj,nn4503   wcj,cj518   pp,qnc6213 pl,nn8002
if   to offer thereon burnt offering or meat offering, or   if   to offer peace

pl,cs,nn2077 pr,pnx5921   nn3068 pnp1931 pimf1245
offerings thereon, let the LORD himself require it;

wcj,cj518   ptn3808   qpf6213 (853) pndm2063 pr4480/nn1674   pr4480/nn1697
24 And if   we have not rather done   it   for fear of*this*thing,

pp,qnc559   ad4279   pl,nn,pnx1121   qmf559   pp,pl,nn,pnx1121 pp,qnc559 pnit4100
saying, In*time*to*come your children might speak unto our children, saying, What

pp,pnx   wcj,pp,nn3068 pl,cs,nn430   nn3478
have ye to do with the LORD   God of Israel?

nn3068   qpf5414 (853) df,nn3383   wcj,nn1366   pr,pnx996   wcj,pnx(pr996)
25 For the LORD hath made   Jordan a border between us and   you, ye

pl,cs,nn1121   nn7205   wcj,pl,cs,nn1121   nn1410 pp,pnx   ptn369 nn2506   pp,nn3068
children of Reuben and children of Gad; ye have no part in the LORD: so shall

pl,nn,pnx1121   (853)   pl,nn,pnx1121 wcj,hipf7673   (pp,ptn1115) qnc3372 (853)   nn3068
your children make   our children cease from   fearing   the LORD.

wcs,qmf559   pte4994 qmf6213   pp,qnc1129 pp,pnx (853)   df,nn4196 ptn3808
26 Therefore we said, Let us now prepare to build us   an altar, not for

pp,nn5930   wcj,ptn3808   pp,nn2077
burnt offering, nor   for sacrifice:

cj3588   pnp1931   nn5707   pr,pnx996   wcj,pnx(pr996)   wcj(pr996)
27 But that   it   may be a witness between us, and   you, and   our

pl,nn,pnx1755 pr,pnx310   pp,qnc5647 (853)   cs,nn5656   nn3068 pp,pl,nn,pnx6440
generations after us, that we might   do   the service of the LORD before him

pp,pl,nn,pnx5930   wcj,pp,pl,nn,pnx2077   wcj,pp,pl,nn,pnx8002
with our burnt offerings, and with our sacrifices, and with our peace offerings;

pl,nn,pnx1121   wcj,ptn3808 qmf559   pp,pl,nn,pnx1121   ad4279   pp,pnx   ptn369
that your children may   not   say to our children in*time*to*come, Ye have no

nn2506   pp,nn3068
part in the LORD.

wcs,qmf559   wcj,qpf1961 cj3588   qmf559 pr,pnx413
28 Therefore said we, that it shall be, when they should so say   to us

wcj,pr413   pl,nn,pnx1755   ad4279   wcs,qpf559   qmv7200 (853)
or to   our generations in*time*to*come, that we may say again, Behold   the

cs,nn8403   cs,nn4196   nn3068 pnl834   pl,nn,pnx1 qpf6213 ptn3808   pp,nn5930
pattern of the altar of the LORD, which our fathers made, not for burnt offerings,

wcj,ptn3808   pp,nn2077   cj3588 pnp1931   nn5707 pr,pnx996   wcj,pnx(pr996)
nor for sacrifices; but   it   is a witness between us and   you.

ptx2486/pp,pnx   pr,pnx4480   pp,qnc4775   pp,nn3068 wcj,pp,qnc7725
29 God forbid that   we   should rebel against the LORD, and   turn   this

df,nn3117   pr4480/pr310   nn3068   pp,qnc1129   nn4196   pp,nn5930

day   from following   the LORD,   to   build   an   altar   for   burnt   offerings,   for

pp,nn4503   wcj,pp,nn2077   pr4480/pp,pr905   cs,nn4196   nn3068   pl,nn,pnx430 pnl834

meat offerings, or for sacrifices,   beside the altar of the LORD our   God   that *is*

pp,pl,cs,nn6440   nn,pnx4908

before   his tabernacle.

nn6372   df,nn3548   wcj,pl,cs,nn5387   df,nn5712

30 And when Phinehas the priest, and the   princes of the congregation and

wcj,pl,cs,nn7218   pl,cs,nu505   nn3478   pnl834   pr,pnx854   wcs,qmf8085 (853)   df,pl,nn1697

heads   of the thousands of Israel which *were* with him, heard   the words

pnl834   pl,cs,nn1121   nn7205   wcj,pl,cs,nn1121   nn1410   wcj,pl,cs,nn1121   nn4519

that the children of Reuben and the children of Gad and the children of Manasseh

pipf1696   wcs,qmf3190/pp,du,nn,pnx5869

spoke, it   pleased   them.

nn6372   cs,nn1121   nn499   df,nn3548   wcs,qmf559   pr413   pl,cs,nn1121

31 And Phinehas the   son   of Eleazar the priest   said   unto the children of

nn7205   wcj,pr413   pl,cs,nn1121   nn1410   wcj,pr413   pl,cs,nn1121   nn4519

Reuben, and   to   the children of Gad, and   to   the children of Manasseh, This

df,nn3117   qpf3045   cj3588   nn3068   pp,nn,pnx8432   pnl834   ptn3808   qpf4603

day we perceive that the LORD *is* among us, because ye have not committed

df,pndm2088   df,nn4604   pp,nn3068   ad227   hipf5337   (853)   pl,cs,nn1121   nn3478

this   trespass against the LORD: now ye have delivered   the children of Israel

pr4480/cs,nn3027   nn3068

out*of*the*hand of the LORD.

nn6372   cs,nn1121   nn499   df,nn3548   wcj,df,pl,nn5387   wcs,qmf7725

32 And Phinehas the   son   of Eleazar the priest, and the princes, returned

pr4480/pr854   pl,cs,nn1121   nn7205   wcj,pr4480/pr854   pl,cs,nn1121   nn1410   pr4480/cs,nn776

from the children of Reuben, and   from   the children of Gad, out*of*the*land

df,nn1568   pr413   cs,nn776   nn3667   pr413   pl,cs,nn1121   nn3478

of Gilead, unto the   land   of Canaan, to   the   children of Israel,   and

wcs,himf7725/pnx(853)/nn1697

brought*them*word*again.

df,nn1697   wcs,qmf3190/pp,du,nn,nn5869   pl,cs,nn1121   nn3478   pl,cs,nn1121

33 And the thing   pleased   the children of Israel; and the children of

nn3478   wcs,pimf1288   pl,nn430   wcj,ptn3808   qpf559   pp,qnc5927   pr,pnx5921   dfp,nn6635   pp,pinc7843

Israel blessed God, and did   not   intend to go up against them in battle, to destroy

(853)   df,nn776   pnl834   pl,cs,nn1121   nn7205   wcj(pl,cs,nn1121) nn1410 pl,qpta3427/pp,pnx

the land wherein the children of Reuben and   Gad   dwelt.

pl,cs,nn1121   nn7205   wcj,pl,cs,nn1121   nn1410 wcs,qmf7121   dfp,nn4196

34 And the children of Reuben and the children of Gad called the altar *Ed*:

cj3588 pnp1931   nn5707   pr,pnx996   cj3588   nn3068   df,pl,nn430

for   it   *shall be* a witness between us that the LORD *is* God.

Joshua's Charge to the People

wcs,qmf1961   aj7227   pr4480/pl,nn3117   ad310   pnl834   nn3068

23 And it*came*to*pass a long   time   after that the LORD had

hipf5117   pp,nn3478   pr4480/cs,nn3605   pl,qpta,pnx341   pr4480/nn5439

given rest unto Israel from all   their enemies round about, that

wcj,nn3091   ad2204   qpf935   dfp,pl,nn3117

Joshua waxed old *and* stricken in   age.

nn3091   wcs,qmf7121   pp,cs,nn3605   nn3478   pp,aj,pnx2205

2 And Joshua called for   all   Israel, *and* for their elders, and for their

wcj,pp,pl,nn,pnx**7218**   wcj,pp,pl,qpta,pnx**8199**   wcj,pp,pl,nn,pnx**7860**   wcs,qmf**559** pr,pnx413

heads,   and for their   judges,   and for their   officers,   and   said   unto

pnp589   qpf**2204**   qpf935   dfp,pl,nn**3117**

them,   I   am old *and* stricken in   age:

wcj,pnp859   qpf**7200** (853) cs,nn3605 pnl834   nn**3068**   pl,nn,pnx**430**   qpf**6213**

3 And   ye   have   seen   all   that the Lᴏʀᴅ your   God   hath done unto

pp,cs,nn3605 df,pndm428 df,pl,nn**1471**   pr4480/pl,nn,pnx**6440**   cj3588   nn**3068**   pl,nn,pnx**430**   pnp1931

all   these   nations   because   of you; for the Lᴏʀᴅ your   God   *is*   he   that

df,nipt3898   pp,pnx

hath fought for   you.

qmv**7200**   hipf**5307**/pp,pnx   (853) df,pndm428 df,pl,nn**1471**   df,pl,nipt**7604**

4 Behold, I have divided*unto*you*by*lot   these   nations that remain, to be

pp,nn**5159**   pp,pl,nn,pnx**7626** pr4480   df,nn3383   wcj,cs,nn3605   df,pl,nn**1471** pnl834

an inheritance for your   tribes,   from Jordan, with   all   the nations that I have

hipf**3772**   df,aj1419 wcj,df,nn3220 cs,nn3996/df,nn8121

cut off, even unto the great   sea   westward.

wcj,nn**3068**   pl,nn,pnx**430** pnp1931   qmf,pnx1920   pr4480/pl,nn,pnx**6440**

5 And the Lᴏʀᴅ your   God,   he   shall   expel   them from before you, and

wcs,hipf**3423** pnx(853)   pr4480/pl,nn,pnx**6440**   wcs,qpf**3423** (853)   nn,pnx776 pp,pnl834

drive   them from*out*of*your*sight; and ye shall possess   their land,   as

nn**3068**   pl,nn,pnx**430**   pipf**1696**   pp,pnx

the Lᴏʀᴅ your   God   hath promised unto you.

ad3966   wcj,qpf**2388**   pp,qnc**8104**   wcj,pp,qnc**6213** (853) cs,nn3605

6 Be ye therefore very courageous to   keep   and to   do   all   that is

df,qpta3789   pp,cs,nn**5612**   cs,nn**8451**   nn4872   qnc**5493** pp,ptn1115 qnc**5493** pr,pnx4480

written in   book   of the   law   of Moses, that ye turn   not   aside therefrom *to*

nn3225   wcj,nn8040

the right hand or *to* the   left;

qnc935   pp,ptn1115   df,pndm428 dfp,pl,nn**1471** df,pndm428   df,pl,nipt**7604**   pp,pnx

7 That ye come   not   among these   nations,   these   that remain among you;

ptn**3808**   himf2142   wcj,pp,cs,nn8034   pl,nn,pnx**430** wcj,ptn**3808**   himf**7650**

neither make mention of the   name   of their   gods,   nor   cause to swear *by*

wcj,ptn**3808** qmf,pnx**5647**   wcj,ptn**3808**   htmf**7812**   pp,pnx

them, neither serve them,   nor   bow yourselves unto them:

cj3588/cj518   qmf**1692**   pp,nn**3068**   pl,nn,pnx**430** pp,pnl834   qpf**6213** pr5704 df,pndm2088

8   But   cleave unto the Lᴏʀᴅ your   God,   as   ye have done unto   this

df,nn**3117**

day.

nn**3068**   wcs,himf**3423**   pr4480/pl,nn,pnx**6440**   aj1419   pl,nn**1471**   wcj,aj6099

9 For the Lᴏʀᴅ hath driven out from before you great nations and strong: but

wcj,pnp859 ptn**3808** nn**376**   qpf5975   pp,pl,nn,pnx**6440**   pr5704 df,pndm2088 df,nn**3117**

as for you,   no   man hath been able*to*stand   before   you unto   this   day.

nu259   nn**376** pr,pnx4480   qmf7291   nu505   cj3588   nn**3068**   pl,nn,pnx**430** pnp1931

10 One man   of   you shall chase a thousand: for the Lᴏʀᴅ your   God,   he

df,nipt3898   pp,pnx   pp,pnl834   pipf**1696**   pp,pnx

it is that fighteth for you,   as   he hath promised you.

ad3966   wcj,nipf**8104**   pp,pl,nn,pnx**5315**   pp,qnc157 (853)   nn**3068**

11 Take good   heed   therefore unto yourselves, that ye   love   the Lᴏʀᴅ your

pl,nn,pnx**430**

God.

cj3588   cj518   qna**7725**/qmf**7725**   wcs,qpf**1692**   pp,cs,nn**3499**   df,pndm428

☾ 12 Else   if   ye   do in*any*wise*go*back,   and cleave unto the remnant of   these

---

☾ **23:12–16** In the last two chapters of the book, Joshua addressed Israel twice. One of the features of this first speech was a stern warning about the consequences of apostasy. Although God intended to drive out the remaining Canaanites (Josh. 13:2–6), He would not do it if Israel was unfaithful to Him. The Book of Judges reveals the tragic story of Israel's infidelity and the consequences that followed.

nations, *even* these that remain among you, and shall make marriages with them, and go in unto them, and they to you:

13 Know*for*a*certainty that the LORD your God will no more drive out *any of* these nations from before you; but they shall be snares and traps unto you, and scourges in your sides, and thorns in your eyes, until ye perish from off this good land which the LORD your God hath given you.

14 And, behold, this day I *am* going the way of all the earth: and ye know in all your hearts and in all your souls, that not one thing hath failed of all the good things which the LORD your God spoke concerning you; all are come*to*pass unto you, *and* not one thing hath failed thereof.

15 Therefore it*shall*come*to*pass, *that* as all good things are come upon you, which the LORD your God promised you; so shall the LORD bring upon you all evil things, until he have destroyed you from off this good land which the LORD your God hath given you.

16 When ye have transgressed the covenant of the LORD your God, which he commanded you, and have gone and served other gods, and bowed yourselves to them; then shall the anger of the LORD be kindled against you, and ye shall perish quickly from off the good land which he hath given unto you.

Joshua's Farewell Address at Shechem

24 ☞ And Joshua gathered all the tribes of Israel to Shechem, and called for the elders of Israel, and for their heads, and for their judges, and for their officers; and they presented themselves before God.

☞ 2 And Joshua said unto all the people, Thus saith the LORD God of

---

☞ **24:1** Shechem was a historic site for the people of Israel. It was there that the Lord first promised the land of Canaan to Abram (Gen. 12:6, 7), and where Jacob destroyed the idols which had been brought from Mesopotamia (Gen. 35:2–5).

☞ **24:2** Actually, Terah had three sons (Gen. 11:27), but only Abraham and Nahor were mentioned because

nn3478   pl,nn,pnx1 qpf3427   pp,cs,nn5676   df,nn5104   pr4480/nn5769   nn8646
Israel, Your fathers dwelt on the other side of the flood in old time, *even* Terah,

cs,nn1   nn85   wcj,cs,nn1   nn5152   wcs,qmf5647 aj312 pl,nn430
the father of Abraham, and the father of Nachor: and they served other gods.

              wcs,qmf3947 (853)   nn,pnx1 (853)   nn85   pr4480/cs,nn5676   df,nn5104
3 And I   took   your father   Abraham from*the*other*side of the flood,

wcs,qmf1980 pnx(853)   pp,cs,nn3605 cs,nn776   nn3667   wcs,himf7235 (853)
and led   him throughout all   the land of Canaan, and multiplied   his

nn,pnx2233   wcs,qmf5414 pp,pnx (853) nn3327
seed, and gave him   Isaac.

              wcs,qmf5414   pp,nn3327 (853) nn3290   wcj(853)   nn6215   wcs,qmf5414   pp,nn6215
4 And I gave unto Isaac   Jacob and   Esau: and I gave   unto Esau

(853) cs,nn2022 nn8165   pp,qnc3423 pnx(853)   wcj,nn3290   wcj,pl,nn,pnx1121   qpf3381
mount Seir, to possess   it; but Jacob and his   children   went down into

nn4714
Egypt.

          wcs,qmf7971 (853) nn4872   wcj(853)   nn175   wcs,qmf5062 (853)   nn4714
5 I sent   Moses also and   Aaron, and I plagued   Egypt, according

pp,pnl834   qpf6213 pp,nn,pnx7130   wcj,ad310   hipf3318/pnx(853)
to that which I did among them: and afterward I brought*you*out.

          wcs,himf3318/(853)/pl,nn,pnx1   pr4480/nn4714   wcs,qmf935   df,nn,lh3220
6 And I brought*your*fathers*out of Egypt: and ye came unto the   sea; and

nn4714   wcs,qmf7291 pr310   pl,nn,pnx1   pp,nn7393   wcj,pp,nn6571   nn5488
the Egyptians pursued after your fathers with chariots and horsemen unto the Red

cs,nn3220
sea.

              wcs,qmf6817 pr413   nn3068   wcs,qmf7760   nn3990   pr,pnx996
7 And when they cried unto the LORD, he   put   darkness between you and

wcj(pr996)   df,nn4713   wcs,himf935 (853)   df,nn3220 pr,pnx5921   wcs,pimf,pnx3680
the Egyptians, and brought   the   sea upon them, and covered them;

du,nn,pnx5869   wcs,qmf7200 (853) pnl834   qpf6213   pp,nn4714   wcs,qmf3427
and your   eyes   have seen   what I have done in Egypt: and ye dwelt in the

dfp,nn4057   aj7227   pl,nn3117
wilderness a long season.

              wcs,himf935 pnx(853)   pr413   cs,nn776   df,nn567   df,qpta3427
8 And I brought   you into the land of the Amorites, which dwelt on the

pp,cs,nn5676   df,nn3383   wcs,nimf3898 pr,pnx854   wcs,qmf5414 pnx(853)
other side Jordan; and they fought with you: and I gave   them into your

pp,nn,pnx3027   wcs,qmf3423 (853)   nn,pnx776   wcs,himf,pnx8045   pr4480/pl,nn,pnx6440
hand, that ye might possess   their land; and I destroyed them from before you.

          nn1111   cs,nn1121   nn6834 cs,nn4428   nn4124 wcs,qmf6965   wcs,nimf3898
9 Then Balak the son of Zippor, king of Moab, arose and warred against

pp,nn3478   wcs,qmf7971   wcs,qmf7121 pp,nn1109   cs,nn1121   nn1160   pp,pinc7043 pnx(853)
Israel, and sent   and called Balaam the son of Beor to curse   you:

          qpf14   wcj,ptn3808 pp,qnc8085   pp,nn1109   wcs,pimf1288/qna1288 pnx(853)
10 But I would not hearken unto Balaam; therefore he blessed   you

wcs,himf5337 pnx(853)   pr4480/nn,pnx3027
still: so I delivered   you out*of*his*hand.

          wcs,qmf5674 (853) df,nn3383   wcs,qmf935 pr413   nn3405   pl,cs,nn1167
11 And ye went over   Jordan, and came unto Jericho: and the men of

nn3405   wcs,nimf3898   pp,pnx   df,nn567   wcj,df,nn6522   wcj,df,nn3669
Jericho fought against you, the Amorites, and the Perizzites, and the Canaanites,

they were direct ancestors of Israel. Nahor was the grandfather of Rebekah, Isaac's wife (Gen. 22:20–23) and
the great-grandfather of Rachel and Leah, who were Jacob's wives (Gen. 29:10, 16).

wcj,df,nn2850   wcj,df,nn1622   df,nn2340   wcj,df,nn2983   wcs,qmf**5414**
and the Hittites, and the Girgashites, the Hivites, and the Jebusites; and I delivered
pnx(853)   pp,nn,pnx**3027**
them into your hand.

wcs,qmf7971   (853)   df,nn6880   pp,pl,nn,pnx**6440**   wcs,pimf1644/pnx(853)
12 And I sent   the hornet   before you, which   drove*them*out
pr4480/pl,nn,pnx**6440**   du,cs,nu8147 pl,cs,nn**4428**   df,nn567   ptn**3808**   pp,nn,pnx**2719**
from before you, *even* the   two   kings of the Amorites; *but* not with thy sword,
wcj,ptn**3808**   pp,nn,pnx7198
nor   with thy bow.

wcs,qmf**5414** pp,pnx   nn776   pnl834/pp,pnx   ptn**3808**   qpf3021   wcj,pl,nn5892
13 And I have given you a land for which   ye did not labor, and   cities
pnl834   qpf1129 ptn**3808**   wcs,qmf**3427**   pp,pnx   pl,nn3754   wcj,pl,nn2132   pnl834
which ye built not, and ye dwell in them; of the vineyards and oliveyards which
qpf5193   ptn**3808**   pnp859 pl,qpta398
ye planted not do ye   eat.

wcj,ad6258   qmv**3372** (853)   nn**3068**   wcj,qmv**5647** pnx(853)   pp,aj**8549**
14 Now therefore fear   the Lord, and   serve   him in sincerity and in
wcj,pp,nn571   wcj,himv**5493**   (853)   pl,nn**430** pnl834   pl,nn,pnx1 qpf**5647**   pp,cs,nn5676
truth: and put away   the gods which your fathers served on the other side of
df,nn5104   wcj,pp,nn4714   wcj,qmv**5647**   (853)   nn**3068**
the flood, and in Egypt; and serve ye   the Lord.

wcj,cj518   qpf7489 pp,du,nn,pnx**5869**   pp,qnc**5647** (853)   nn**3068**   qmv977   pp,pnx
15 And if   it seem evil unto you to serve   the Lord, choose you this
df,nn3117 (853)   pnit4310   qmf**5647**   cj518   (853)   pl,nn**430** pnl834   pl,nn,pnx1   qpf**5647** pnl834
day   whom ye will serve; whether   the gods which your fathers served that
pp,cs,nn5676   df,nn5104 wcj,cj518 (853)   pl,cs,nn**430**   df,nn567
were on the other side of the flood,   or   the gods of the Amorites, in whose
pp,nn,pnx776 (pnl834) pnp859 pl,qpta**3427**   wcj,pnp595   wcj,nn,pnx**1004**   qmf**5647** (853)
land   ye dwell: but as for me   and my house, we will serve   the
nn**3068**
Lord.

df,nn**5971**   wcs,qmf**6030**   wcs,qmf**559**   ptx2486/pp,pnx   pr4480/qnc**5800** (853)
16 And the people answered and said, God forbid that we should forsake
nn**3068**   pp,qnc**5647** aj312   pl,nn**430**
the Lord, to serve other gods;

cj3588   nn**3068**   pl,nn,pnx**430** pnp1931   df,hipt**5927** pnx(853)   wcj(853)
17 For the Lord our God,   he *it is* that brought   us up and   our
pl,nn,pnx1   pr4480/cs,nn776   nn4714   pr4480/cs,nn**1004**   pl,nn5650   wcj,pnl834 qpf6213
fathers out*of*the*land of Egypt, from*the*house of bondage, and which did
df,pndm428 df,aj1419 (853) df,pl,nn226   pp,du,nn,pnx**5869**   wcs,qmf,pnx**8104**   pp,cs,nn3605   df,nn1870
those   great   signs in our   sight,   and preserved us in   all   the way

---

☞ **24:15, 16** This invitation of Joshua is similar to that extended by Moses to Israel on the other side of the Jordan (Deut. 30:15–20). He recognized that one can only serve God in sincerity and truth if he has freely and willingly pledged in his heart to do so. He summarizes the options that are open to Israel: (1) They could return to serve the gods of their ancestors. "On the other side of the flood" would be better translated "on the other side of the river," that is, the river Euphrates (the same meaning is true of vv. 2, 14). "The gods which your fathers served" is a reference to the ones that Terah, Abraham's father worshiped (see v. 2). These were similar to the "images" or "teraphim" which Laban called "his gods" (Gen. 31:19, 30, 34). Perhaps there were some people who secretly worshiped these gods among the children of Israel (see vv. 14–23). (2) They could serve the gods of the Amorites. Although the term "Amorites" referred to a specific people, it was also used in a generic sense for all people living in Canaan. Hence, the reference is made to Baalim and Ashteroth in Judges 10:6. (3) They could follow the example of Joshua and his family, that is, to serve the Lord. This statement of Joshua's stands as one of the greatest affirmations of faith in all the Bible.

pnl834/pp,pnx   qpf**1980**   wcj,pp,cs,nn**3605**   df,pl,nn**5971** (pnl834) pp,nn,pnx**7130**   qpf**5674**
wherein we went, and among   all   the people   through whom we passed:

         nn**3068**   wcs,pimf1644   pr4480/pl,nn,pnx**6440**   (853) cs,nn**3605**   df,pl,nn**5971**   wcj(853)
18 And the LORD drove out from before us   all   the people, even   the

df,nn**567**   qpta**3427**   df,nn**776**   pnp587 ad1571 qmf**5647** (853)   nn**3068** cj3588
Amorites which dwelt in the land: *therefore* will we also serve   the LORD; for

pnp1931   pl,nn,pnx**430**
he *is* our God.

       nn**3091**   wcs,qmf**559**   pr413   df,nn**5971**   ptn3808/qmf3201 pp,qnc**5647** (853)   nn**3068** cj3588
19 And Joshua   said   unto the people, Ye   cannot   serve   the LORD: for

pnp1931   aj6918   pl,nn**430** pnp1931   aj7072   nn**410**   ptn3808   qmf**5375**   pp,nn,pnx**6588**
he *is* a holy God; he *is* a jealous God; he will not forgive your transgressions

     wcj,pp,pl,nn,pnx**2403**
nor your sins.

    cj3588   qmf**5800**   (853)   nn**3068**   wcs,qpf**5647**   nn**5236**   pl,cs,nn**430**   wcs,qpf**7725**
20 If ye forsake   the LORD, and serve strange gods, then he will   turn

    pp,pnx wcs,hipf**7489**   wcs,pipf**3615** pnx(853)   ad310 pnl834   hipf**3190**/pp,pnx
and do you hurt, and consume   you, after that he hath done*you*good.

      df,nn**5971** wcs,qmf**559** pr413   nn3091   ptn3808 cj3588   qmf**5647** (853)   nn**3068**
21 And the people said unto Joshua, Nay; but we will serve   the LORD.

      nn3091   wcs,qmf**559**   pr413   df,nn**5971**   pnp859   pl,nn5707   pp,pnx
22 And Joshua   said   unto the people, Ye *are* witnesses against yourselves

cj3588 pnp859   qpf**977** pp,pnx (853)   nn**3068** pp,qnc**5647** pnx(853)   wcs,qmf**559**
that ye have chosen you   the LORD, to serve   him. And they said, *We*

   pl,nn5707
are witnesses.

    wcj,ad6258   himv**5493**   (853) df,nn**5236** pl,cs,nn**430** pnl834   pp,nn,pnx**7130**
23 Now therefore put away, *said he*, the   strange gods which *are* among

    wcj,himv5186 (853) nn,pnx3824 pr413   nn3068 pl,cs,nn**430**   nn3478
you, and incline   your heart unto the LORD God of Israel.

      df,nn**5971** wcs,qmf**559** pr413 nn3091 (853)   nn**3068**   pl,nn,pnx**430**   qmf**5647**
24 And the people said unto Joshua,   The LORD our   God will we serve,

   wcj,pp,nn,pnx6963   qmf**8085**
and his voice will we obey.

    nn3091   wcs,qmf**3772**   nn**1285**   dfp,nn**5971** df,pndm1931 dfp,nn**3117**   wcs,qmf**7760** pp,pnx
25 So Joshua made a covenant with the people   that   day, and   set   them

nn**2706**   wcj,nn**4941**   pp,nn**7927**
a statute and an ordinance in Shechem.

    nn3091   wcs,qmf**3789** df,pndm428 (853) df,pl,nn**1697**   pp,cs,nn**5612**   cs,nn**8451**   pl,nn**430**
26 And Joshua wrote   these   words in the book of the law of God, and

wcs,qmf**3947**   aj1419   nn68   wcs,himf,pnx**6965** ad8033   pr8478   df,nn**427** pnl834   pp,cs,nn**4720**
took a great stone, and set*it*up there under an oak, that *was* by the sanctuary

nn**3068**
of the LORD.

    nn3091   wcs,qmf**559** pr413 cs,nn**3605**   df,nn**5971** ptdm2009 df,pndm2063 df,nn68   qmf**1961**
27 And Joshua   said   unto   all   the people, Behold,   this   stone shall be a

pp,nn**5713**   pp,pnx   cj3588 pnp1931   qpf**8085** (853) cs,nn**3605**   pl,cs,nn**561**   nn**3068** pnl834
witness unto us; for   it   hath heard   all   the words of the LORD which he

pipf**1696** pr,pnx5973   wcj,qpf**1961**   pp,nn**5713** pp,pnx cj6435   pimf3584
spoke unto us: it shall   be   therefore a witness unto you, lest ye deny your

pp,pl,nn,pnx**430**
God.

    nn3091   (853)   df,nn**5971** wcs,pimf**7971**   nn**376**   pp,nn,pnx**5159**
28 So Joshua let   the people depart, every man unto his inheritance.

Joshua's Death

<small>wcs,qmf1961   pr310   df,pndm428   df,pl,nn1697   nn3091   cs,nn1121   nn5126</small>
29 And it*came*to*pass after these things, that Joshua the son of Nun, the
<small>cs,nn5650   nn3068   wcs,qmf4191   (cs,nn1121)   nu3967   wcj,nu6235   pl,nn8141</small>
servant of the LORD, died, *being*   a hundred and ten years old.
<small>wcs,qmf6912   pnx(853)   pp,cs,nn1366   nn,pnx5159</small>
30 And they buried   him in the border of his inheritance in
<small>pp,nn8556 [cs,nn8553/nn2775]   pnl834   pp,cs,nn2022   nn669   pr4480/nn6828   pp,cs,nn2022</small>
Timnathserah, which *is* in mount Ephraim, on*the*north*side of the hill of
<small>nn1608</small>
Gaash.

<small>nn3478   wcs,qmf5647 (853)   nn3068   cs,nn3605   pl,cs,nn3117   nn3091   wcj,cs,nn3605</small>
31 And Israel served   the LORD all the days of Joshua, and all the
<small>pl,cs,nn3117   df,aj2205   pnl834   hipf748/pl,nn3117/pr310   nn3091   wcj,pnl834   qpf3045   (853) cs,nn3605</small>
days of the elders that overlived Joshua, and which had known all the
<small>cs,nn4639   nn3068   pnl834   qpf6213   pp,nn3478</small>
works of the LORD, that he had done for Israel.

<small>wcj(853)   pl,cs,nn6106   nn3130   pnl834   pl,cs,nn1121   nn3478   hipf5927</small>
32 And   the bones of Joseph, which the children of Israel brought up
<small>pr4480/nn4714   qpf6912   pp,nn7927   pp,cs,nn2513   df,nn7704   pnl834   nn3290   qpf7069</small>
out*of*Egypt, buried they in Shechem, in a parcel of ground which Jacob bought
<small>pr4480/pr854   pl,cs,nn1121   nn2544   cs,nn1   nn7927   pp,nu3967   nn7192</small>
of the sons of Hamor the father of Shechem for a hundred pieces of silver:
<small>wcs,qmf1961   pp,nn5159   pp,pl,cs,nn1121   nn3130</small>
and it became the inheritance of the children of Joseph.

<small>wcj,nn499   cs,nn1121   nn175   qpf4191   wcs,qmf6912   pnx(853)   pp,cs,nn1389</small>
33 And Eleazar the son of Aaron died; and they buried   him in a hill
<small>nn6372   nn,pnx1121   pnl834   pipf5414 pp,pnx   pp,cs,nn2022   nn669</small>
that pertained to Phinehas his son, which was given him in mount Ephraim.

24:31 Moses had trained Joshua to be his successor, but Joshua and the elders of Israel failed to train their own successors, and to thoroughly ground new leaders in the faith of Israel. As a result, the next generation succumbed to Canaanite idolatry. God's people are always just one generation away from apostasy. Therefore, young people must be trained to walk in the fear of the Lord today so that they become the proper, godly leaders of tomorrow.

The Book of

JUDGES

"Judges" is the Hebrew term used to refer to those whom God raised up to lead His people during the period between the conquest of Canaan and the monarchy. There were fifteen judges during this period, but only thirteen are mentioned in the Book of Judges (the ministries of Eli and Samuel are recorded in 1 Samuel). Although these thirteen judges had a tremendous impact on the nation of Israel, none of them ruled over all of the twelve tribes. In fact, some of them were at work at the same time in different areas of the country. For this reason, the length of time that the judges ruled cannot be arrived at by simply adding the number of years that each judge ruled. The most commonly accepted figure for the time period of the judges is 350 years (see the note on Gen. 15:13–16).

The Book of Judges contains an introduction (chaps. 1; 2), narrative accounts of the judges who led the people (chaps. 3—16), and a conclusion which describes the social and spiritual state of the people (chaps. 17—21). The introduction and conclusion are not chronologically linked to the narrative accounts.

Samuel is considered the most likely one to have written the Book of Judges, and internal evidence points to its being written during his lifetime. It is inferred from the phrase, "in those days there was no king in Israel" (Judg. 17:6; 18:1; 19:1; 21:25), that at the time of the writing, there was a king. Thus, it is obvious that it was written after Saul took the throne. Also, one can be sure that this book was written before Solomon's reign because the Canaanites had not yet been driven out of Gezer (Judg. 1:29, cf. 1 Kgs. 9:16). Furthermore, it may be concluded that it was written before David conquered Jerusalem (Judg. 1:21, cf. 1 Chr. 11:4–7). That the book was written before the reign of David is also supported by the implication in the Book of Judges that Sidon, rather than Tyre, was still considered the capital of Phoenicia (Judg. 1:31; 3:3; 10:6; 18:28, cf. 2 Sam. 5:11).

The Book of Judges recounts the sad events of Israel's apostasy. It was common in Israel during the time of the judges for every man to do "that which was right in his own eyes" (Judg. 17:6; 21:25). God had to remind them again and again that He was the one true God, because they repeatedly indulged in the idolatry and immorality of the Canaanites among whom they lived. The main section of the book reflects a cycle from which Israel seemed unable to escape—Israel falls into apostasy, God sends an oppressor, Israel repents, God sends a deliverer, there is peace and prosperity, and then Israel falls away again. During the times of "rest" that Israel experienced, the Lord caused Israel's enemies to fight among themselves.

Additional Land Is Conquered

1 `pr310` `cs,nn4194` `nn3091` `wcs,qmf1961` `pl,cs,nn1121`
Now after the death of Joshua it*came*to*pass, that the children of
`nn3478` `wcs,qmf7592` `pp,nn3068` `pp,qnc559` `pnit4310` `qmf5927` `pp,pnx` `pr413`
Israel asked the LORD, saying, Who shall go up for us against the
`df,nn3669` `dfp,nn8462` `pp,ninc3898` `pp,pnx`
Canaanites first, to fight against them?

`nn3068` `wcs,qmf559` `nn3063` `qmf5927` `ptdm2009` `qpf5414` `(853)` `df,nn776`
2 And the LORD said, Judah shall go up: behold, I have delivered the land
`pp,nn,pnx3027`
into his hand.

`nn3063` `wcs,qmf559` `pp,nn8095` `nn,pnx251` `qmv5927` `pr,pnx854`
3 And Judah said unto Simeon his brother, Come up with me into my
`pp,nn,pnx1486` `wcj,nicj3898` `dfp,nn3669` `pnp589` `ad1571` `wcj,qpf1980`
lot, that we may fight against the Canaanites; and I likewise will go
`pr,pnx854` `pp,nn,pnx1486` `nn8095` `wcs,qmf1980` `pr,pnx854`
with thee into thy lot. So Simeon went with him.

`nn3063` `wcs,qmf5927` `nn3068` `wcs,qmf5414` `(853)` `df,nn3669`
4 And Judah went up; and the LORD delivered the Canaanites and the
`wcj,df,nn6522` `pp,nn,pnx3027` `wcs,himf,pnx5221` `pp,nn966` `cs,nu6235` `pl,nu505`
Perizzites into their hand: and they slew of them in Bezek ten thousand
`nn376`
men.

`wcs,qmf4672` `(853)` `nn137` `pp,nn966` `wcs,nimf3898` `pp,pnx`
5 And they found Adoni-bezek in Bezek: and they fought against him,
`wcs,himf5221` `(853)` `df,nn3669` `wcj(853)` `df,nn6522`
and they slew the Canaanites and the Perizzites.

`nn137` `wcs,qmf5127` `wcs,qmf7291` `pr,pnx310` `wcs,qmf270` `pnx(853)`
6 But Adoni-bezek fled; and they pursued after him, and caught him,
`wcs,pimf7112` `(853)` `pl,cs,nn931/du,nn,pnx3027` `wcj,du,nn,pnx/7272`
and cut off his thumbs and his great toes.

`nn137` `wcs,qmf559` `pl,nu7657` `pl,nn4428`
7 And Adoni-bezek said, Threescore*and*ten kings, having their
`pl,cs,nn931/du,nn,pnx3027` `wcj,du,nn,pnx/7272` `pl,pupt7112` `(qpf1961)` `pl,pipt3950` `pr8478`
thumbs and their great toes cut off, gathered *their meat* under my
`nn,pnx7979` `pp,pnl834` `qpf6213` `ad3651` `pl,nn430` `pipf7999` `pp,pnx` `wcs,himf,pnx935`
table: as I have done, so God hath requited me. And they brought him to
`nn3389` `ad8033` `wcs,qmf4191`
Jerusalem, and there he died.

`pl,cs,nn1121` `nn3063` `wcs,nimf3898` `pp,nn3389` `wcs,qmf3920`
8 Now the children of Judah had fought against Jerusalem, and had taken
`pnx(853)` `wcs,himf,pnx5221` `pp,cs,nn6310` `nn2719` `pipf7971` `wcj(853)` `df,nn5892`
it, and smitten it with the edge of the sword, and set the city on
`dfp,nn784`
fire.

1:1 The phrase "asked the LORD" is found only in the books of Judges and Samuel. The civil ruler of Israel had the right to ask the high priest to consult the Urim and the Thummim for him (Num. 27:21). This was the means which God set up for the judges, and later the kings, to know His judgment on any particular matter.
1:8 The early history of the city of Jerusalem is not certain, because it was known by several different names during its history. Also, it is difficult to determine which name applied at what time. This city is called Salem in Psalm 76:2. Therefore, if the Salem mentioned in Genesis 14:18 is the same site, Melchizedek was one of its early kings. It did not become the capital of Israel until David drove out the Jebusites from the fortified southern hill known as Mount Zion (see the note on 2 Sam. 5:6–10), because members of the tribe of Benjamin and the Jebusites are said to have "inhabited Jerusalem" together (Judg. 1:21).

wcj,ad310   pl,cs,nn1121   nn3063   qpf3381   pp,ninc3898

9 And afterward the children of Judah went down to fight against the

dfp,nn3669   qpta3427   df,nn2022   wcj,df,nn5045   wcj,df,nn8219

Canaanites, that dwelt in the mountain, and in the south, and in the valley.

nn3063   wcs,qmf1980   pr3413   df,nn3669   df,qpta3427   pp,nn2275

10 And Judah went against the Canaanites that dwelt in Hebron: (now the

wcj,cs,nn8034   nn2275   pp,pl,nn6440   nn7153   wcs,himf5221 (853)   nn8344   wcj(853)

name of Hebron before *was* Kirjath-arba:) and they slew Sheshai, and

nn289   wcj(853)   nn8526

Ahiman, and Talmai.

pr4480/ad8033   wcs,qmf1980   pr413   pl,cs,qpta3427   nn1688   wcj,cs,nn8034

11 And from thence he went against the inhabitants of Debir: and the name

nn1688   pp,pl,nn6440   nn7158

of Debir before *was* Kirjath-sepher:

nn3612   wcs,qmf559   pnl834   himf5221 (853)   nn7158   wcj,qpf,pnx3920   pp,pnx

12 And Caleb said, He that smiteth Kirjath-sepher, and taketh it, to him

wcj,qpf5414 (853)   nn5919   nn,pnx1323   pp,nn802

will I give Achsah my daughter to wife.

nn6274   cs,nn1121   nn7073   nn3612   df,aj6996   (pr,pnx4480)   cs,nn251   wcs,qmf,pnx3920

13 And Othniel the son of Kenaz, Caleb's younger brother, took

wcs,qmf5414 pp,pnx (853)   nn5919   nn,pnx1323   pp,nn802

it: and he gave him Achsah his daughter to wife.

wcs,qmf1961   pp,qnc,pnx935   wcs,himf,pnx5496

14 And it*came*to*pass, when she came *to him*, that she moved him to

pp,qnc7592   pr4480/pr854   nn,pnx1   df,nn7704   wcs,qmf6795   pr4480/pr5921   df,nn2543   nn3612

ask of her father a field: and she lighted from off *her* ass; and Caleb

wcs,qmf559   pp,pnx   pnit4100   pp,pnx

said unto her, What wilt thou?

wcs,qmf559   pp,pnx   qmv3051 pp,pnx   nn1293   cj3588   qpf,pnx5414

15 And she said unto him, Give me a blessing: for thou hast given me a

df,nn5045 cs,nn776 wcj,qpf5414 pp,pnx   pl,cs,nn1543   pl,nn4325   nn3612   wcs,qmf5414 pp,pnx (853)   aj5942

south land; give me also springs of water. And Caleb gave her the upper

pl,cs,nn1543   wcj(853)   aj8482   pl,cs,nn1543

springs and the nether springs.

wcj,pl,cs,nn1121   nn7017   nn4872   cs,nn2859   qpf5927

16 And the children of the Kenite, Moses' father-in-law, went up

pr4480/cs,nn5892   df,pl,nn8558   pr854   pl,cs,nn1121   nn3063   pr4480/cs,nn4057

out*of*the*city of palm trees with the children of Judah into*the*wilderness of

nn3063   pnl834   nn5045   nn6166   wcs,qmf1980   wcs,qmf3427   pr854

Judah, which *lieth* in the south of Arad; and they went and dwelt among the

df,nn5971

people.

nn3063   wcs,qmf1980   pr854   nn8095   nn,pnx251   wcs,hipf5221 (853)

17 And Judah went with Simeon his brother, and they slew the

df,nn3669   qpta3427   nn6857   wcs,himf2763   pnx(853)   (853)   cs,nn8034

Canaanites that inhabited Zephath, and utterly destroyed it. And the name

df,nn5892   wcs,qmf7121   nn2767

of the city was called Hormah.

nn3063   wcs,qmf3920 (853) nn5804 wcj(853)   nn,pnx1366   wcj(853)   nn831

18 Also Judah took Gaza with the coast thereof, and Askelon with

wcj(853)   nn,pnx1366   wcj(853)   nn6138   wcj(853)   nn,pnx1366

the coast thereof, and Ekron with the coast thereof.

nn3068   wcs,qmf1961   pr854   nn3063   wcs,himf3423 (853)

19 And the LORD was with Judah; and he drove out *the inhabitants of* the

df,nn2022   cj3588   ptn**3808**   pp,hinc**3423**   (853)   pl,cs,qpta**3427**   df,nn6010   cj3588   pp,pnx

mountain; but could not drive out   the inhabitants of the valley, because they

cs,nn7393   nn1270

had chariots of iron.

wcs,qmf**5414** (853)   nn2275   pp,nn3612 pp,pnl834   nn4872 pipf**1696**   wcs,himf**3423**

20 And they gave   Hebron unto Caleb,   as   Moses said: and he expelled

pr4480/ad8033 (853)   nu7969 pl,cs,nn**1121**   df,nn6061

thence   the three sons of Anak.

pl,cs,nn**1121**   nn1144   ptn**3808**   hipf**3423**   wcj(853)   df,nn2983

21 And the children of Benjamin did not drive out   the Jebusites that

qpta**3427**   nn3389   df,nn2983 wcs,qmf**3427** pr854   pl,cs,nn**1121**   nn1144

inhabited Jerusalem; but the Jebusites dwell with the children of Benjamin in

pp,nn3389   pr5704 df,pndm2088 df,nn**3117**

Jerusalem unto   this   day.

cs,nn**1004**   nn3130   pnp1992 ad1571 wcs,qmf**5927**   nn1008   wcj,nn**3068**

22 And the house of Joseph, they also went up against Bethel: and the LORD

pr,pnx5973

was with them.

cs,nn**1004**   nn3130   wcs,himf**8446** nn1008   wcj,cs,nn8034

23 And the house of Joseph sent to descry Bethel. (Now the   name   of the

df,nn5892 pp,pl,nn**6440**   nn3870

city   before *was* Luz.)

df,pl,qpta**8104** wcs,qmf**7200**   nn376   qpta3318   pr4480   df,nn5892   wcs,qmf**559**

24 And the spies   saw a man come forth out of the city, and they said

pp,pnx   himv**7200**   pte**4994**   (853)   cs,nn3996   df,nn5892

unto him, Show us, we*pray*thee,   the entrance into the city, and we will

wcj,qpf**6213**/pr,pnx5973   nn**2617**

show   thee mercy.

wcs,himf,pnx**7200**   (853)   cs,nn3996   df,nn5892   wcs,himf**5221** (853)

25 And when he showed them   the entrance into the city, they smote

df,nn5892   pp,cs,nn**6310**   nn2719   pipf7971 wcj(853)   df,nn376   wcj(853)

the city with the edge of the sword; but they let go   the man and

cs,nn3605   nn,pnx**4940**

all   his family.

df,nn376 wcs,qmf**1980**   cs,nn776   df,nn2850   wcs,qmf1129   nn5892

26 And the man went into the land of the Hittites, and built a city, and

wcs,qmf**7121**   nn,pnx8034   nn3870 pnp1931   nn,pnx8034   pr5704 df,pndm2088 df,nn**3117**

called the name thereof Luz: which *is* the name thereof unto   this   day.

Some Land Is Not Conquered

wcj,ptn**3808**   nn4519   hipf**3423**   (853)   nn1052   wcj(853)

27 Neither did Manasseh drive out   *the inhabitants of* Beth-shean and

pl,nn,pnx1323   wcj(853)   nn8590   wcj(853)   pl,nn,pnx1323   wcj(853)   pl,cs,qpta**3427**   nn1756

her towns, nor   Taanach and   her towns, nor   the inhabitants of Dor

wcj(853)   pl,nn,pnx1323   wcj(853)   pl,cs,qpta**3427**   nn2991   wcj(853)   pl,nn,pnx1323

and   her towns, nor   the inhabitants of Ibleam and   her towns, nor

wcj(853)   pl,cs,qpta**3427**   nn4023   wcj(853)   pl,nn,pnx1323   df,nn3669   wcs,himf**2974**

the inhabitants of Megiddo and   her towns: but the Canaanites would

pp,qnc**3427**   df,pndm2063 dfp,nn**776**

dwell in   that land.

wcs,qmf**1961**   cj3588   nn3478   qpf**2388**   wcs,qmf**7760** (853)

28 And it*came*to*pass, when Israel was strong, that they   put   the

df,nn3669   pp,nn4522   ptn**3808**   cj,hina**3423**/himf,pnx**3423**

Canaanites to tribute, and did not utterly*drive*them*out.

ptn3808　wcj,nn669　hipf3423　(853)　df,nn3669　df,qpta3427　pp,nn1507

29 Neither did Ephraim drive out the Canaanites that dwelt in Gezer; but

df,nn3669　wcs,qmf3427　pp,nn1507　pp,nn,pnx7130

the Canaanites dwelt in Gezer among them.

ptn3808　nn2074　hipf3423　(853)　pl,cs,qpta3427　nn7003　wcj(853)

30 Neither did Zebulun drive out the inhabitants of Kitron, nor the

pl,cs,qpta3427　nn5096　df,nn3669　wcs,qmf3427　pp,nn,pnx7130　wcs,qmf1961

inhabitants of Nahalol; but the Canaanites dwelt among them, and became

pp,nn4522

tributaries.

ptn3808　nn836　hipf3423　(853)　pl,cs,qpta3427　nn5910　wcj(853)

31 Neither did Asher drive out the inhabitants of Accho, nor the

pl,cs,qpta3427　nn6721　wcj(853)　nn303　wcj(853)　nn392　wcj(853)　nn2462

inhabitants of Zidon, nor of Ahlab, nor of Achzib, nor of Helbah,

wcj(853)　nn663　wcj(853)　nn7340

nor of Aphik, nor of Rehob:

df,nn843　wcs,qmf3427　pp,cs,nn7130　df,nn3669　pl,cs,qpta3427　df,nn776

32 But the Asherites dwelt among the Canaanites, the inhabitants of the land:

cj3588　ptn3808　hipf,pnx3423

for they did not drive*them*out.

ptn3808　nn5321　hipf3423　(853)　pl,cs,qpta3427　nn1053　wcj(853)

33 Neither did Naphtali drive out the inhabitants of Beth-shemesh, nor

pl,cs,qpta3427　nn1043　wcs,qmf3427　pp,cs,nn7130　df,nn3669　pl,cs,qpta3427

the inhabitants of Beth-anath; but he dwelt among the Canaanites, the inhabitants

df,nn776　wcj,pl,cs,qpta3427　nn1053　wcj,nn1043　qpf1961

of the land: nevertheless the inhabitants of Beth-shemesh and of Beth-anath became

pp,nn4522　pp,pnx

tributaries unto them.

df,nn567　wcs,qmf3905　(853)　pl,cs,nn1121　nn1835　df,nn,lh2022　cj3588

34 And the Amorites forced the children of Dan into the mountain: for

ptn3808　qpf,pnx5414　pp,qnc3381　dfp,nn6010

they would not suffer them to come down to the valley:

df,nn567　wcs,himf2974　pp,qnc3427　pp,nn2022　nn2776　pp,nn357　wcj,pp,nn8169

35 But the Amorites would dwell in mount Heres in Aijalon, and in Shaalbim:

cs,nn3027　cs,nn1004　nn3130　wcs,qmf3513　wcs,qmf1961　pp,nn4522

yet the hand of the house of Joseph prevailed, so that they became tributaries.

wcj,cs,nn1366　df,nn567　pr4480/cs,nn4608　nn6137

36 And the coast of the Amorites was from*the*going*up to Akrabbim,

pr4480/df,nn5553　wcj,ad,lh4605

from*the*rock, and upward.

God Sends His Angel

cs,nn4397　nn3068　wcs,qmf5927　pr4480　df,nn1537　pr413　df,nn1066　wcs,qmf559

2 And an angel of the LORD came up from Gilgal to Bochim, and said, I

himf5927/pnx(853)　pr4480/nn4714　wcs,himf935　pnx(853)　pr413　df,nn776

made*you*to*go*up out*of*Egypt, and have brought you unto the land

pnl834　nipf7650　pp,pl,nn,pnx1　wcs,qmf559　ptn3808/pp,nn5769　himf6565　nn,pnx1285

which I swore unto your fathers; and I said, I will never break my covenant

pr,pnx854

with you.

wcj,pnp859　qmf3772　ptn3808　nn1285　pp,pl,cs,qpta3427　df,pndm2063　df,nn776

2 And ye shall make no league with the inhabitants of this land; ye

shall throw down their altars: but ye have not obeyed my voice: why have ye done this?

3 Wherefore I also said, I will not drive*them*out from before you; but they shall be *as thorns* in your sides, and their gods shall be a snare unto you.

4 And it*came*to*pass, when the angel of the LORD spoke these words unto all the children of Israel, that the people lifted up their voice, and wept.

5 And they called the name of that place Bochim: and they sacrificed there unto the LORD.

Joshua's Death

6 And when Joshua had let the people go, the children of Israel went every man unto his inheritance to possess the land.

7 And the people served the LORD all the days of Joshua, and all the days of the elders that outlived Joshua, who had seen all the great works of the LORD, that he did for Israel.

8 And Joshua the son of Nun, the servant of the LORD, died, *being* a hundred and ten years old.

9 And they buried him in the border of his inheritance in Timnath-heres, in the mount of Ephraim, on*the*north*side of the hill Gaash.

10 And also all that generation were gathered unto their fathers: and there arose another generation after them, which knew not the LORD, nor yet the works which he had done for Israel.

Preview of Israel's Sin

11 And the children of Israel did evil in the sight of the LORD, and served Baalim:

wcs,qmf5800 (853)   nn3068   pl,cs,nn430   pl,nn,pnx1

12 And they forsook   the LORD God of their fathers, which

df,hipt3318/pnx(853)   pr4480/cs,nn776   nn4714   wcs,qmf1980/pr310 aj312 pl,nn430 pr4480/pl,cs,nn430

brought*them*out of*the*land of Egypt, and followed other gods, of*the*gods of

df,pl,nn5971 pnl834   pr,pnx5439   wcs,htmf*7812   pp,pnx

the people that *were* round about them, and bowed themselves unto them, and

wcs,himf3707 (853)   nn3068   wcs,himf3707

provoked   the LORD to anger.

wcs,qmf5800 (853)   nn3068   wcs,qmf5647 dfp,nn1168   wcj,dfp,pl,nn6252

⌖ 13 And they forsook   the LORD, and served Baal and Ashtaroth.

cs,nn639   nn3068   wcs,qmf2734   pp,nn3478   wcs,qmf,pnx5414

14 And the anger of the LORD was hot against Israel, and he delivered them

pp,cs,nn3027   pl,qpta8154   wcs,qmf8155 pnx(853)   wcs,qmf4376

into the hands of spoilers that spoiled   them, and he sold   them into the

pp,cs,nn3027   pl,qpta,pnx341 pr4480/nn5439   qpf3201 wcj,ptn3808   ad5750   pp,qnc5975

hands of their enemies round about, so that they could not any longer stand

pp,pl,cs,nn6440   pl,qpta,pnx341

before their enemies.

pp,nn3605/pnl834   qpf3318   cs,nn3027   nn3068 qpf1961   pp,pnx

15 Whithersoever they went out, the hand of the LORD was against them for

pp,aj7451 pp,pnl834   nn3068   pipf1696   wcj,pp,pnl834   nn3068   nipf7650   pp,pnx

evil, as the LORD had said, and as the LORD had sworn unto them: and

pp,pnx   ad3966   wcs,qmf3334

they were greatly distressed.

nn3068   wcs,himf6965   pl,qpta8199   wcs,himf,pnx3467

⌖ 16 Nevertheless the LORD raised up judges, which delivered them

pr4480/cs,nn3027   pl,qpta,pnx8154

out*of*the*hand of those that spoiled them.

wcj,ad1571   ptn3808   qpf8085   pr413   pl,qpta,pnx8199 cj3588

17 And yet they would not hearken unto their judges, but they

qpf2181   pr310 aj312 pl,nn430   wcs,htmf*7812   pp,pnx   qpf5493

went*a*whoring after other gods, and bowed themselves unto them: they turned

ad4118   pr4480   df,nn1870 pnl834   pl,nn,pnx1   qpf1980   pp,qnc8085   pl,cs,nn4687

quickly out of the way which their fathers walked in, obeying the commandments

nn3068   qpf6213 ptn3808 ad3651

of the LORD; *but* they did not so.

wcj,cj3588   nn3068   hipf6965/pp,pnx   pl,qpta8199   nn3068 wcj,qpf1961 pr5973

18 And when the LORD raised*them*up judges, then the LORD was with the

df,qpta8199   wcj,hipf,pnx3467   pr4480/cs,nn3027   pl,qpta,pnx341 cs,nn3605   pl,cs,nn3117

judge, and delivered them out*of*the*hand of their enemies all the days of the

---

⌖ **2:13** These Canaanite deities, Baal and Ashtaroth, remained a problem for Judah until the Babylonian Exile (two other Canaanite deities noted in Judges are Asherah [Judg. 3:7] and Dagon [Judg. 16:23]). Only the seventy years in captivity finally cured Israel of its idolatrous ways. Recent archaeological discoveries have helped to clarify the facts about the religion of Canaan in the days of the judges. Baal and Ashtaroth are the names of two individual gods in a much larger and complicated system of polytheism. Moreover, they were also community gods whose names differed from region to region. For instance, Baal was called Baal–Peor, Baal–Berith, and Baal–zebub (Num. 25:3; Judg. 8:33; 2 Kgs. 1:2). It is for this reason that Scripture describes Israel as serving "Baal" or "Baalim" ("im" is the Hebrew plural ending). Overall, the religion of the Canaanites was extremely corrupt. It was characterized by the practices of human sacrifice, ritual prostitution and homosexuality, and self mutilation. These religions taught that these practices were prevalent among their gods as well, so it is not surprising that the people became equally debased. The many gods were particularly connected with agriculture (the seasons, weather, and grain) and many of God's judgments against these people would ultimately discredit the supposed abilities of these Canaanite "gods" (1 Kgs. 18:20–40; Hos. 2:8–13; Amos 4:4–11).

⌖ **2:16** See the introduction to the Book of Judges.

^{df,qpta8199} ^{cj3588} ^{nimf5162} ⁿⁿ³⁰⁶⁸ ^{pr4480/nn,pnx5009} ^{pr4480/pl,cs,nn6440}

judge: for it repented the LORD because*of*their*groanings by*reason*of*them that

^{pl,qpta,pnx3905} ^{wcj,pl,qpta,pnx1766}

oppressed them and   vexed   them.

^{wcj,qpf1961} ^{df,qpta8199} ^{pp,qnc4191} ^{qmf7725}

19 And it*came*to*pass, when the judge was dead, *that* they returned, and

^{wcj,hipf7843} ^{pr4480/pl,nn,pnx1} ^{pp,qnc1980/pr310} ^{aj312} ^{pl,nn430} ^{pp,qnc,pnx5647}

corrupted *themselves* more*than*their*fathers, in following other gods to   serve

^{wcj,pp,htnc*7812} ^{pp,pnx} ^{hipf5307} ^{ptn3808} ^{pr4480/pl,nn,pnx4611}

them, and to bow down unto them; they ceased not from*their*own*doings, nor

^{pr4480/nn,pnx1870/df,aj7186}

from*their*stubborn*way.

^{cs,nn639} ⁿⁿ³⁰⁶⁸ ^{wcs,qmf2734} ^{pp,nn3478} ^{wcs,qmf559} ^{cj3282}

20 And the anger of the LORD was   hot   against Israel; and he said, Because

^{pnl834} ^{df,pndm2088} ^{df,nn1471} ^{qpf5674} ⁽⁸⁵³⁾ ^{nn,pnx1285} ^{pnl834} ^{pipf6680} ⁽⁸⁵³⁾

that   this   people hath transgressed   my covenant which I commanded   their

^{pl,nn,pnx1} ^{wcj,ptn3808} ^{qpf8085} ^{pp,nn,pnx6963}

fathers, and have not   hearkened unto my   voice;

^{pnp589} ^{ad1571} ^{ptn3808} ^{himf3254} ^{pp,hinc3423} ⁿⁿ³⁷⁶ ^{pr4480/pl,nn,pnx6440} ^{pr4480}

21 I   also will not henceforth drive out any from before them   of   the

^{df,pl,nn1471} ^{pnl834} ⁿⁿ³⁰⁹¹ ^{qpf5800} ^{wcs,qmf4191}

nations which Joshua left when he died:

^{pr,nn4616} ^{pp,pnx} ^{pinc5254} ⁽⁸⁵³⁾ ⁿⁿ³⁴⁷⁸ ^{pnp1992} ^{he,pl,qpta8104} ⁽⁸⁵³⁾

22 That through them I may prove   Israel, whether they will   keep

^{cs,nn1870} ⁿⁿ³⁰⁶⁸ ^{pp,qnc1980} ^{pp,pnx} ^{pp,pnl834} ^{pl,nn,pnx1} ^{qpf8104} ^{cj518} ^{ptn3808}

the way of the LORD to walk therein,   as   their fathers did keep *it*, or not.

ⁿⁿ³⁰⁶⁸ ^{wcs,himf5117} ⁽⁸⁵³⁾ ^{df,pndm428} ^{df,pl,nn1471} ^{pp,ptn1115} ^{hinc,pnx3423}

23 Therefore the LORD   left   those   nations, without driving*them*out

^{ad4118} ^{wcj,ptn3808} ^{qpf,pnx5414} ^{pp,cs,nn3027} ⁿⁿ³⁰⁹¹

hastily; neither delivered he them into the   hand   of Joshua.

The Nations Left Unconquered

3 Now these *are* the nations which the LORD left, to prove   Israel

^{wcj,pndm428} ^{df,pl,nn1471} ^{pnl834} ⁿⁿ³⁰⁶⁸ ^{hipf5117} ^{pp,pinc5254} ⁽⁸⁵³⁾ ⁿⁿ³⁴⁷⁸

^{pp,pnx} ⁽⁸⁵³⁾ ^{nn3605/pnl834} ^{ptn3808} ^{qpf3045} ⁽⁸⁵³⁾ ^{cs,nn3605} ^{pl,nn4421}

by them, *even*   as many *of Israel* as had not known   all   the wars

ⁿⁿ³⁶⁶⁷

of Canaan;

^{ad7535} ^{pp,nn4616} ^{pl,cs,nn1755} ^{pl,cs,nn1121} ⁿⁿ³⁴⁷⁸ ^{qnc3045} ^{pp,pinc,pnx3925}

2 Only that the generations of the children of Israel might know, to   teach

ⁿⁿ⁴⁴²¹ ^{ad7535} ^{pnl834} ^{pp,pl,nn6440} ^{qpf,pnx3045} ^{ptn3808}

them war, at*the*least such   as   before   knew nothing thereof;

^{nu2568} ^{pl,cs,nn5633} ^{pl,nn6430} ^{wcj,cs,nn3605} ^{df,nn3669}

3 *Namely*, five   lords   of the Philistines, and   all   the Canaanites, and the

^{wcj,df,nn6722} ^{wcj,df,nn2340} ^{qpta3427} ^{cs,nn2022} ^{df,nn3844} ^{pr4480/cs,nn2022} ⁿⁿ¹¹⁷⁹

Sidonians, and the Hivites that dwelt in mount Lebanon, from mount Baal-hermon

^{pr5704} ^{pp,qnc935} ⁿⁿ²⁵⁷⁴

unto the entering in of Hamath.

^{wcs,qmf1961} ^{pp,pinc5254} ⁽⁸⁵³⁾ ⁿⁿ³⁴⁷⁸ ^{pp,pnx} ^{pp,qnc3045}

4 And they   were to prove   Israel by them, to know whether they would

^{he,qmf8085} ⁽⁸⁵³⁾ ^{pl,cs,nn4687} ⁿⁿ³⁰⁶⁸ ^{pnl834} ^{pipf6680} ⁽⁸⁵³⁾

hearken unto   the commandments of the LORD, which he commanded   their

^{pl,nn,pnx1} ^{pp,cs,nn3027} ⁿⁿ⁴⁸⁷²

fathers by the   hand   of Moses.

wcj,pl,cs,nn**1121** nn3478 qpf**3427** pp,cs,nn**7130** df,nn3669 df,nn2850

5 And the children of Israel dwelt among the Canaanites, Hittites, and

wcj,df,nn567 wcj,df,nn6522 wcj,df,nn2340 wcj,df,nn2983

Amorites, and Perizzites, and Hivites, and Jebusites:

wcs,qmf3947 (853) pl,nn,pnx1323 pp,pnx pp,pl,nn**802** qpf**5414** wcj(853)

6 And they took their daughters to be their wives, and gave their

pl,nn,pnx1323 pp,pl,nn,pnx**1121** wcs,qmf**5647** (853) pl,nn,pnx**430**

daughters to their sons, and served their gods.

Othniel

pl,cs,nn**1121** nn3478 wcs,qmf**6213** (853) df,aj**7451** pp,du,cs,nn**5869** nn**3068**

7 And the children of Israel did evil in the sight of the LORD, and

wcs,qmf7911 (853) nn**3068** pl,nn,pnx**430** wcs,qmf**5647** (853) pl,nn1168 wcj(853) df,pl,nn**842**

forgot the LORD their God, and served Baalim and the groves.

cs,nn**639** nn**3068** wcs,qmf2734 pp,nn3478 wcs,qmf,pnx4376

8 Therefore the anger of the LORD was hot against Israel, and he sold

pp,cs,nn**3027** nn3573 cs,nn**4428** nn763 pl,cs,nn**1121**

them into the hand of Cushan-rishathaim king of Mesopotamia: and the children

nn3478 wcs,qmf**5647** (853) nn3573 nu8083 pl,nn8141

of Israel served Cushan-rishathaim eight years.

pl,cs,nn**1121** nn3478 wcs,qmf2199 pr413 nn**3068** nn**3068** wcs,himf**6965**

9 And when the children of Israel cried unto the LORD, the LORD raised up a

hipt**3467** pp,pl,cs,nn**1121** nn3478 wcs,himf,pnx**3467** (853) nn6274 cs,nn**1121**

deliverer to the children of Israel, who delivered them, *even* Othniel the son of

nn7073 nn3612 df,aj6996 (pr,pnx4480) cs,nn**251**

Kenaz, Caleb's younger brother.

cs,nn**7307** nn**3068** wcs,qmf1961 pr,pnx5921 wcs,qmf**8199** (853) nn3478

10 And the Spirit of the LORD came upon him, and he judged Israel, and

wcs,qmf3318 dfp,nn4421 nn**3068** wcs,qmf**5414** (853) nn3573 cs,nn**4428**

went out to war: and the LORD delivered Cushan-rishathaim king of

nn763 pp,nn,pnx**3027** nn,pnx**3027** wcs,qmf5810 pr5921 nn3573

Mesopotamia into his hand; and his hand prevailed against Cushan-rishathaim.

df,nn**776** wcs,qmf**8252** pl,nu705 nn8141 nn6274 cs,nn**1121** nn7073 wcs,qmf**4191**

11 And the land had rest forty years. And Othniel the son of Kenaz died.

Ehud

pl,cs,nn**1121** nn3478 pp,qnc**6213** df,aj**7451** wcs,himf3254 pp,du,cs,nn**5869** nn**3068**

12 And the children of Israel did evil again in the sight of the LORD:

nn**3068** wcs,pimf2388 (853) nn5700 cs,nn**4428** nn4124 pr5921 nn3478 pr5921/cj3588

and the LORD strengthened Eglon the king of Moab against Israel, because they

qpf**6213** (853) df,aj**7451** pp,du,cs,nn**5869** nn**3068**

had done evil in the sight of the LORD.

wcs,qmf622 pr,pnx413 (853) pl,cs,nn**1121** nn5983 wcj,nn6002

13 And he gathered unto him the children of Ammon and Amalek, and

wcs,qmf1980 wcs,himf**5221** (853) nn3478 wcs,qmf3423 (853) cs,nn5892 df,pl,nn8558

went and smote Israel, and possessed the city of palm trees.

pl,cs,nn**1121** nn3478 wcs,qmf**5647** (853) nn5700 cs,nn**4428** nn4124 nu8083/nu6240 nn8141

14 So the children of Israel served Eglon the king of Moab eighteen years.

3:7 The word translated "groves" refers to the shrines of the Canaanite goddess, Asherah. See the note on Judges 2:13.

pl,cs,nn1121   nn3478   wcs,qmf2199   pr413   nn3068   nn3068

15 But when the children of Israel cried unto the LORD, the LORD

wcj,him**f6965**/pp,pnx   hipt**3467**   (853)   nn261   cs,nn**1121**   nn1617   cs,nn**1121**/df,nn**1145**   nn**376**

raised*them*up a deliverer, Ehud the son of Gera, a Benjamite, a man

aj334/cs,nn**3027**/nn,pnx3225   pp,nn,pnx**3027**   pl,cs,nn**1121**   nn3478   wcs,qmf**7971**   nn**4503**   pp,nn5700

left-handed: and by him the children of Israel sent a present unto Eglon the

cs,nn**4428**   nn4124

king of Moab.

nn261   wcs,qmf**6213**   pp,pnx   nn2719   pp,pnx   du,cs,nu8147   pl,nn6366   nn1574   nn,pnx**753**

16 But Ehud made him a dagger which had two edges, of a cubit length;

wcs,qmf**2296**   pnx(853)   pr4480/pr**8478**   pp,pl,nn,pnx4055   pr5921   nn,pnx3225   cs,nn**3409**

and he did gird it under his raiment upon his right thigh.

wcs,him**f7126**   (853)   df,nn**4503**   pp,nn5700   cs,nn**4428**   nn4124   wcj,nn5700

17 And he brought the present unto Eglon king of Moab: and Eglon *was* a

ad3966   aj1277   nn**376**

very fat man.

wcs(qmf**1961**)   pp,pnl834   pipf**3615**   pp,hinc**7126**   (853)   df,nn**4503**

18 And when he had made*an*end to offer the present, he

wcs,pim**f7971**   (853)   df,nn**5971**   pl,cs,qpta**5375**   df,nn**4503**

sent away the people that bore the present.

wcj,pnp1931   qpf**7725**   pr4480   df,pl,nn**6456**   pnl834   pr854   nn1537

19 But he himself turned again from the quarries that *were* by Gilgal, and

wcs,qmf**559**   nn5643   cs,nn**1697**   pp,pnx   df,nn**4428**   wcs,qmf**559**   pte2013

said, I have a secret errand unto thee, O king: who said, Keep silence. And

cs,nn3605   df,pl,qpta5975   wcs,qmf3318   pr4480/pr,pnx5921

all that stood by him went out from him.

wcj,nn261   qpf935   pr,pnx413   wcj,pnp1931   qpta**3427**   df,nn**4747**   pnl**5944**

20 And Ehud came unto him; and he was sitting in a summer parlor,

834   pp,pnx   pp,nn905   nn261   wcs,qmf**559** pp,pnx   cs,nn**1697**   pl,nn**430**

which he had for himself alone. And Ehud said, I have a message from God

pr,pnx413   wcs,qmf**6965**   pr4480/pr5921   df,nn**3678**

unto thee. And he arose out of *his* seat.

nn261   wcs,qmf**7971**   (853)   nn,pnx8040   cs,nn**3027**   wcs,qmf3947   (853)   df,nn**2719**   pr4480/pr5921

21 And Ehud put forth his left hand, and took the dagger from

nn,pnx3225   cs,nn**3409**   wcs,qmf**8628**   pp,nn,pnx**990**

his right thigh, and thrust it into his belly:

df,nn**5325**   ad1571   wcs,qmf935   pr310   df,nn**3851**   df,nn2459   wcs,qmf5462   pr1157

22 And the haft also went in after the blade; and the fat closed upon the

df,nn**3851**   cj3588   ptn**3808**   qpf8025   df,nn**2719**   pr4480/nn,pnx**990**   df,nn**6574**

blade, so that he could not draw the dagger out*of*his*belly; and the dirt

wcs,qmf3318

came out.

nn261   wcs,qmf3318   df,nn,lh4528   wcs,qmf5462   pl,cs,nn**1817**

23 Then Ehud went forth through the porch, and shut the doors of the

df,nn**5944**   pr,pnx1157   wcj,qpf5274

parlor upon him, and locked *them*.

wcj,pnp1931   qpf3318   wcj,pl,nn**5650**   qpf935   wcs,qmf**7200**

24 When he was gone out, his servants came; and when they saw that,

wcj,ptdm2009   pl,cs,nn1817   df,nn**5944**   pl,qptp5274   wcs,qmf**559**   ad389   pnp1931   hipt**5526**   (853)

behold, the doors of the parlor *were* locked, they said, Surely he covereth

du,nn,pnx7272   df,nn**4747**   pp,cs,nn2315

his feet in his summer chamber.

wcs,qmf**2342**   pr5704   qna**954**   wcj,ptdm2009   qpta6605   ptn,pnx369

25 And they tarried till they were ashamed: and, behold, he opened not the

pl,cs,nn1817   df,nn5944   wcs,qmf3947 (853)   df,nn4668   wcs,qmf6605

doors of the parlor; therefore they took a key, and opened *them*: and,

wcj,ptdm2009   pl,nn,pnx113   qpta5307   qpta4191   nn,lh776

behold, their lord *was* fallen down dead on the earth.

wcj,nn261   nipf4422   pr5704   htpt*,pnx4102   wcj(pnp1931)   qpf5674   (853)

26 And Ehud escaped while they tarried, and passed beyond the

df,pl,nn6456   wcs,nimf4422   df,nn,lh8167

quarries, and escaped unto Seirath.

wcs,qmf1961   pp,qnc,pnx935   wcs,qmf8628   dfp,nn7782

27 And it*came*to*pass, when he was come, that he blew a trumpet in the

pp,cs,nn2022   nn669   pl,cs,nn1121   nn3478   wcs,qmf3381   pr,pnx5973   pr4480

mountain of Ephraim, and the children of Israel went down with him from the

df,nn2022   wcj,pnp1931   pp,pl,nn,pnx6440

mount, and he before them.

wcs,qmf559   pr,pnx413   qmv7291   pr,pnx310   cj3588   nn3068   qpf5414

28 And he said unto them, Follow after me: for the LORD hath delivered

(853)   pl,qpta,pnx341 (853)   nn4124   pp,nn,pnx3027   wcs,qmf3381   pr,pnx310

your enemies the Moabites into your hand. And they went down after

wcs,qmf3920 (853)   pl,cs,nn4569   df,nn3383   pp,nn4124   qpf5414   wcj,ptn3808   nn376

him, and took the fords of Jordan toward Moab, and suffered not a man

pp,qnc5674

to pass over.

wcs,himf5221   (853)   nn4124   df,pndm1931   dfp,nn6256   pp,nu6235   pl,nu505   nn376

29 And they slew of Moab at that time about ten thousand men,

cs,nn3605   nn8082   wcj,cs,nn3605   cs,nn376   nn2428   nipf4422   wcj,ptn3808   nn376

all lusty, and all men of valor; and there escaped not a man.

nn4124   wcs,nimf3665   df,pndm1931   dfp,nn3117   pr8478   cs,nn3027   nn3478   df,nn776

30 So Moab was subdued that day under the hand of Israel. And the land

wcs,qmf8252   pl,nu8084   nn8141

had rest fourscore years.

Shamgar

wcj,pr,pnx310   qpf1961   nn8044   cs,nn1121   nn6067   wcs,himf5221 (853)

31 And after him was Shamgar the son of Anath, which slew of the

df,pl,nn6430   nu8337   pl,nu3967   nn376   df,nn1241   pp,cs,nn4451   pnp1931   ad1571   wcs,qmf3467 (853)

Philistines six hundred men with an ox goad: and he also delivered

nn3478

Israel.

Deborah

pl,cs,nn1121   nn3478   wcs,himf3254   pp,qnc6213   df,aj7451   pp,du,nn,pnx5869   nn3068

4 And the children of Israel again did evil in the sight of the LORD,

wcj,nn261   qpf4191

when Ehud was dead.

nn3068   wcs,qmf,pnx4376   pp,cs,nn3027   nn2985   cs,nn4428   nn3667   pnl834

2 And the LORD sold them into the hand of Jabin king of Canaan, that

---

4:2 "Jabin" was probably a title for a Canaanite king (Josh. 11:1; Judg. 4:23, 24), just as Pharaoh was a title for the kings of Egypt.

qpf**4427**　　pp,nn2674　　　wcj,cs,nn**8269**　　　　nn,pnx**6635**　　　　nn5516　wcj,pnp1931　qpta**3427**

reigned in Hazor; the captain of whose host *was* Sisera, which dwelt in

pp,nn2800

Harosheth*of*the*Gentiles.

pl,cs,nn**1121**　　nn3478　wcs,qmf6817　pr413　　nn**3068**　cj3588　pp,pnx　　nu8672　pl,nu3967

3 And the children of Israel cried unto the LORD: for he had nine hundred

cs,nn7393　　nn1270　　pl,nu6242　nn8141　wcj,pnp1931　pp,nn**2393**　qpf3905　(853)　pl,cs,nn**1121**

chariots of iron; and twenty years he mightily oppressed the children of

nn3478

Israel.

wcj,nn1683　　nn**5031**/nn**802**　cs,nn**802**　nn3941　pnp1931　qpta**8199**　(853)　nn3478

⌾ 4 And Deborah, a prophetess, the wife of Lapidoth, she judged Israel at

df,pndm1931　dfp,nn**6256**

that time.

wcj,pnp1931　qpta**3427**　pr8478　　cs,nn8560　　nn1683　　pr996　df,nn7414　wcj(pr996)

5 And she dwelt under the palm tree of Deborah between Ramah and

nn1008　　pp,cs,nn2022　　nn669　　pl,cs,nn**1121**　nn3478　wcs,qmf5927　Pp,pnx413

Bethel in mount Ephraim: and the children of Israel came up to her for

dfp,nn**4941**

judgment.

wcs,qmf7971　　wcs,qmf7121　pp,nn1301　cs,nn**1121**　　nn42

⌾ 6 And she sent and called Barak the son of Abinoam

pr4480/nn6943/nn5320　wcs,qmf559　pr,pnx413　he,ptn3808　nn**3068**　pl,cs,nn**430**　nn3478

out*of*Kedesh-naphtali, and said unto him, Hath not the LORD God of Israel

pipf**6680**　　qmv1980　wcj,qpf4900　pp,cs,nn2022　nn8396　wcj,qpf3947　pr,pnx5973

commanded, *saying*, Go and draw toward mount Tabor, and take with thee

nu6235　pl,nu**505**　nn376　pr4480/pl,cs,nn**1121**　nn5321　wcj,pr4480/pl,cs,nn**1121**　nn2074

ten thousand men of*the*children of Naphtali and of*the*children of Zebulun?

wcj,qpf4900　pr,pnx413　pr413　cs,nn5158　nn7028　(853)　nn5516　cs,nn**8269**

7 And I will draw unto thee to the river Kishon Sisera, the captain of

nn2985　cs,nn**6635**　wcj(853)　nn,pnx7393　wcj(853)　nn,pnx1995　wcj,qpf,pnx**5414**

Jabin's army, with his chariots and his multitude; and I will deliver him

pp,nn,pnx**3027**

into thine hand.

nn1301　wcs,qmf559　pr,pnx413　cj518　qmf1980　pr,pnx5973　wcj,qpf**1980**

⌾ 8 And Barak said unto her, If thou wilt go with me, then I will go:

wcj,cj518　ptn3808　qmf1980　pr,pnx5973　ptn3808　qmf1980

but if thou wilt not go with me, *then* I will not go.

wcs,qmf559　qna1980/qmf1980　pr,pnx5973　ptn3808/ptn57　(pr5921)　df,nn1870

9 And she said, I will surely go with thee: notwithstanding the journey

pnl834　pnp859　qpta1980　ptn3808　qmf1961　nn,pnx8597　cj3588　nn**3068**　qmf4376　(853)　nn5516

that thou takest shall not be for thine honor; for the LORD shall sell Sisera

pp,cs,nn**3027**　nn**802**　nn1683　wcs,qmf6965　wcs,qmf1980　pr5973　nn1301

into the hand of a woman. And Deborah arose, and went with Barak to

nn,lh6943

Kedesh.

nn1301　wcs,himf**2199**　(853)　nn2074　wcj(853)　nn5321　nn,lh6943

10 And Barak called Zebulun and Naphtali to Kedesh; and he

⌾ **4:4** The name Deborah means "bee," perhaps emphasizing the organized life of that insect. She is also called a "prophetess" (Judg. 4:1) and examples of her prophetic gift are seen in verses six, nine, and fourteen. Samuel (1 Sam. 3:20) is the only other judge who was expressly called a prophet, though all of the judges received information from the Lord through some special means.

⌾ **4:6, 8** Barak wisely hesitated to lead the armies of Israel without receiving guidance from God through Deborah. He is listed as one of the "heroes of faith" (Heb. 11:32) because he trusted God and depended upon God's spokesperson.

nn7356/du,nn7356   pp,nn5516   cs,nn7998   pl,nn6648   cs,nn7998   pl,nn6648

damsel*or*two; to Sisera a prey of divers colors, a prey of divers colors of

nn7553   cs,nn6648   du,nn7553   pp,pl,cs,nn6677

needlework, of divers colors of needlework on both sides, *meet* for the necks of

nn7998

them that take the spoil?

ad3651   cs,nn3605   pl,qpta,pnx341   qmf6   nn3068   wcj,pl,qpta,pnx157

31 So let all thine enemies perish, O LORD: but *let* them that love him

df,nn8121   pp,qnc3318   pp,nn,pnx1369   df,nn776   wcs,qmf8252   pl,nu705

be as the sun when he goeth forth in his might. And the land had rest forty

nn8141

years.

Gideon's Call

pl,cs,nn1121   nn3478   wcs,qmf6213 df,aj7451   pp,du,cs,nn5869   nn3068

And the children of Israel did evil in the sight of the LORD: and the

nn3068   wcs,qmf,pnx5414   pp,cs,nn3027   nu7651 pl,nn8141

LORD delivered them into the hand of Midian seven years.

cs,nn3027   nn4080   wcs,qmf5810   pr5921   nn3478   pr4480/pl,cs,nn6440

2 And the hand of Midian prevailed against Israel: *and* because of the

nn4080   pl,cs,nn1121   nn3478   qpf6213   pp,pnx   (853)   df,pl,nn4492   pnl834

Midianites the children of Israel made them the dens which *are* in the

dfp,pl,nn2022   wcj(853) df,pl,nn4631   wcj(853)   df,pl,nn4679

mountains, and caves, and strongholds.

wcj,qpf1961   cj518   nn3478   qpf2232   nn4080   wcj,qpf5927

3 And *so* it was, when Israel had sown, that the Midianites came up, and the

wcj,nn6003   wcj,pl,cs,nn1121   nn6924   wcj,qpf5927   pr,pnx5921

Amalekites, and the children of the east, even they came up against them;

wcs,qmf2583   pr,pnx5921   wcs,himf7843 (853)   cs,nn2981   df,nn776

4 And they encamped against them, and destroyed the increase of the earth,

pr5704   qnc,pnx935   nn5804   himf7604 wcj,ptn3808   nn4241   pp,nn3478   wcj,nn7716

till thou come unto Gaza, and left no sustenance for Israel, neither sheep,

wcj,nn7794   wcj,nn2543

nor ox, nor ass.

cj3588   pnp1992   qmf5927   wcj,pl,nn,pnx4735   wcj,pl,nn,pnx168   qmf935

5 For they came up with their cattle and their tents, and they came

wcj,pp,pnp1992   nn697   pp,nn7230   wcj,pp,pnp1992   wcj,pl,nn,pnx1581

as grasshoppers for multitude; *for* both they and their camels were

ptn369   nn4557   wcs,qmf935   dfp,nn776   pp,pinc,pnx7843

without number: and they entered into the land to destroy it.

nn3478   ad3966   wcs,nimf1809   pr4480/pl,cs,nn6440   nn4080

6 And Israel was greatly impoverished because of the Midianites; and the

pl,cs,nn1121   nn3478 wcs,qmf2199 pr413   nn3068

children of Israel cried unto the LORD.

wcs,qmf1961   cj3588   pl,cs,nn1121   nn3478   qpf2199   pr413   nn3068

7 And it*came*to*pass, when the children of Israel cried unto the LORD

pr5921/pl,cs,nn182   nn4080

because of the Midianites,

nn3068   wcs,qmf7971 (nn376)   nn5030   pr413   pl,cs,nn1121   nn3478   wcs,qmf559

8 That the LORD sent a prophet unto the children of Israel, which said

pp,pnx   ad3541   qpf559   nn3068 pl,cs,nn430   nn3478   pnp595 hipf5927/pnx(853)   pr4480/nn4714

unto them, Thus saith the LORD God of Israel, I brought*you*up from Egypt,

wcs,himf3318/pnx(853)   pr4480/cs,nn1004   pl,nn5650

and brought*you*forth out*of*the*house of bondage;

wcs,himf**5337** pnx(853) pr4480/cs,nn**3027** nn4714
9 And I delivered you out*of*the*hand of the Egyptians, and

wcj,pr4480/cs,nn**3027** cs,nn3605 pl,qpta,pnx3905 wcs,pimf1644/pnx(853) pr4480/pl,nn,pnx**6440**
out*of*the*hand of all that oppressed you, and drove*them*out from before you,

wcs,qmf**5414** pp,pnx (853) nn,pnx**776**
and gave you their land;

wcj,qcj**559** pp,pnx pnp589 pl,nn,pnx**430** qmf**3372** ptn**3808** (853)
10 And I said unto you, I *am* the LORD your God; fear not the

pl,cs,nn**430** df,nn567 pnl834 pp,nn,pnx**776** pnp859 pl,qpta**3427** wcj,ptn**3808** qpf**8085**
gods of the Amorites, in whose land ye dwell: but ye have not obeyed my

pp,nn,pnx**6963**
voice.

wcs,qmf935 cs,nn**4397** nn**3068** wcs,qmf**3427** pr8478 df,nn424 pnl834
11 And there came an angel of the LORD, and sat under an oak which

pp,nn6084 pnl834 pp,nn3101 nn33 nn,pnx**1121** wcj,nn1439
was in Ophrah, that *pertained* unto Joash the Abi-ezrite: and his son Gideon

qpta2251 pl,nn2406 dfp,nn1660 pp,hinc5127 pr4480/pl,cs,nn**6440** nn4080
threshed wheat by the winepress, to hide *it* from the Midianites.

cs,nn**4397** nn**3068** wcs,nimf**7200** pr,pnx413 wcs,qmf**559** pr,pnx413
12 And the angel of the LORD appeared unto him, and said unto him, The

nn**3068** pr,pnx5973 cs,nn1368 df,nn**2428**
LORD *is* with thee, thou mighty man of valor.

nn1439 wcs,qmf**559** pr,pnx413 pte994 nn,pnx**113** nn**3068** wcj,pta3426 pr,pnx5973
13 And Gideon said unto him, Oh my Lord, if the LORD be with us,

wcj,pp,pnit4100 cs,nn3605 pndm2063 qmf,pnx4672 wcj,ad346 cs,nn3605 pl,nn,pnx**6381** pnl834
why then is all this befallen us? and where *be* all his miracles which

pl,nn,pnx**1** pipf**5608** pp,pnx pp,qnc**559** he,ptn**3808** nn**3068** hipf,pnx**5927** pr4480/nn4714
our fathers told us of, saying, Did not the LORD bring*us*up from Egypt? but

wcj,ad6258 nn**3068** qpf,pnx**5203** wcs,qmf,pnx**5414** pp,cs,nn**3709**
now the LORD hath forsaken us, and delivered us into the hands of the

nn4080
Midianites.

nn**3068** wcs,qmf6437 pr,pnx413 wcs,qmf**559** qmv**1980** pndm2088 pp,nn,pnx3581
14 And the LORD looked upon him, and said, Go in this thy might, and

wcj,hipf**3467** (853) nn3478 pr4480/cs,nn**3709** nn4080 he,ptn**3808** qpf,pnx7971
thou shalt save Israel from*the*hand of the Midianites: have not I sent

thee?

wcs,qmf**559** pr,pnx413 pte994 nn,pnx**136** dfp,pnit4100 himf**3467** (853) nn3478
15 And he said unto him, Oh my Lord, wherewith shall I save Israel?

ptdm2009 nn,pnx504 df,aj1800 pp,nn4519 wcj,pnp595 df,aj6810 nn,pnx**1**
behold, my family *is* poor in Manasseh, and I *am* the least in my father's

pp,cs,nn**1004**
house.

nn**3068** wcs,qmf**559** pr,pnx413 cj3588 qmf**1961** pr,pnx5973
16 And the LORD said unto him, Surely I will be with thee, and thou

wcj,hipf**5221** (853) nn4080 nu259 pp,nn**376**
shalt smite the Midianites as one man.

wcs,qmf**559** pr,pnx413 cj518 pte**4994** qpf4672 nn**2580** pp,du,nn,pnx**5869**
17 And he said unto him, If now I have found grace in thy sight, then

wcs,qmf**6213** pp,pnx nn**226** pnl7945/pnp859 pipt**1696** pr,pnx5973
show me a sign that thou talkest with me.

qmf4185 ptn408 pr4480/pndm2088 pte**4994** pr5704 qnc,pnx935 pr,pnx413 wcj,hipf3318
18 Depart not hence, I*pray*thee, until I come unto thee, and bring forth

₍₈₅₃₎ _{nn,pnx4503} _{wcj,hipf5117} _{pp,pl,nn,pnx6440} _{wcs,qmf559 pnp595} _{qmf3427 pr5704}
my present, and set *it* before thee. And he said, I will tarry until

_{qnc,pnx7725}
thou come again.

_{wcj,nn1439} _{qpf935} _{wcs,qmf6213} _{cs,nn1423/pl,nn5795} _{pl,nn4682}
19 And Gideon went in, and made ready a kid, and unleavened cakes

_{wcj,cs,nn374} _{nn7058} _{df,nn1320} _{qpf7760} _{dfp,nn5536} _{qpf7760} _{wcj,df,nn4839}
of an ephah of flour: the flesh he put in a basket, and he put the broth in a

_{dfp,nn6517} _{wcs,himf3318} _{pr,pnx413} _{pr413/pr8478} _{df,nn424} _{wcs,himf5066}
pot, and brought*it*out unto him under the oak, and presented *it*.

_{cs,nn4397} _{df,pl,nn430} _{wcs,qmf559} _{pr,pnx413} _{qmv3947 (853)} _{df,nn1320} _{wcj(853)}
20 And the angel of God said unto him, Take the flesh and the

_{df,pl,nn4682} _{wcj,himv5117} _{pr413} _{pndm1975 df,nn5553} _{qmv8210} _{wcj(853)} _{df,nn4839}
unleavened cakes, and lay *them* upon this rock, and pour out the broth.

_{wcs,qmf6213 ad3651}
And he did so.

_{cs,nn4397} _{nn3068} _{wcs,qmf7971 (853)} _{cs,nn7097} _{df,nn4938 pnl834}
21 Then the angel of the LORD put forth the end of the staff that *was* in

_{pp,nn,pnx3027} _{wcs,qmf5060} _{dfp,nn1320} _{wcj,dfp,pl,nn4682} _{wcs,qmf5927}
his hand, and touched the flesh and the unleavened cakes; and there rose up

_{df,nn784} _{pr4480} _{df,nn6697} _{wcs,qmf398 (853)} _{df,nn1320} _{wcj(853)} _{df,pl,nn4682}
fire out of the rock, and consumed the flesh and the unleavened cakes.

_{wcj,cs,nn4397} _{nn3068} _{qpf1980} _{pr4480/du,nn,pnx5869}
Then the angel of the LORD departed out*of*his*sight.

_{nn1439} _{wcs,qmf7200} _{cj3588 pnp1931} _{cs,nn4397} _{nn3068} _{nn1439}
22 And when Gideon perceived that he *was* an angel of the LORD, Gideon

_{wcs,qmf559} _{ptx162} _{nn136} _{nn3069} _{cj3588 cj5921/ad3651} _{qpf7200} _{cs,nn4397} _{nn3068} _{pl,nn6440 pr413}
said, Alas, O Lord GOD! for because I have seen an angel of the LORD face to

_{pl,nn6440}
face.

_{nn3068} _{wcs,qmf559} _{pp,pnx} _{nn7965} _{pp,pnx} _{qmf3372 ptn408}
23 And the LORD said unto him, Peace *be* unto thee; fear not: thou shalt

_{ptn3808 qmf4191}
not die.

_{nn1439} _{wcs,qmf1129} _{nn4196} _{ad8033} _{pp,nn3068} _{wcs,qmf7121} _{pp,pnx}
24 Then Gideon built an altar there unto the LORD, and called it

_{nn3073} _{pr5704 df,pndm2088 df,nn3117} _{ad,pnx5750} _{pp,nn6084} _{nn33}
Jehovah-shalom: unto this day it *is* yet in Ophrah of the Abi-ezrites.

Gideon Destroys Altar of Baal

_{wcs,qmf1961} _{df,pndm1931 dfp,nn3915} _{nn3068 wcs,qmf559} _{pp,pnx} _{qmv3947}
25 And it*came*to*pass the same night, that the LORD said unto him, Take

_{(853) (pnl834)} _{pp,nn,pnx1} _{cs,nn6499/df,nn7794} _{df,nuor8145 wcj,cs,nn6499} _{nu7651 pl,nn8141}
thy father's young bullock, even the second bullock of seven years old,

_{wcj,qpf2040 (853)} _{cs,nn4196} _{df,nn1168 pnl834} _{pp,nn,pnx1} _{qmf3772 wcj(853)}
and throw down the altar of Baal that thy father hath, and cut down the

_{df,nn842 pnl834} _{pr,pnx5921}
grove that *is* by it:

_{wcj,qpf1129} _{nn4196} _{pp,nn3068} _{pl,nn,pnx430} _{pr5921} _{cs,nn7218} _{df,pndm2088}
26 And build an altar unto the LORD thy God upon the top of this

_{df,nn4581} _{dfp,nn4634} _{wcj,qpf3947 (853)} _{df,nuor8145} _{df,nn6499} _{wcj,hipf5927}
rock, in the ordered place, and take the second bullock, and offer a

_{nn5930} _{pp,cs,nn6086} _{df,nn842 pnl834} _{qmf3772}
burnt sacrifice with the wood of the grove which thou shalt cut down.

nn1439   wcs,qmf3947 nu6235 pl,nn**376**   pr4480/pl,nn,pnx**5650**   wcs,qmf**6213** pp,pnl834   nn**3068**

27 Then Gideon took ten men of*his*servants, and did as the LORD

pipf**1696** pr,pnx413   wcs,qmf**1961** pp,pnl834   qpf**3372** (853)   nn,pnx1   cs,nn**1004**

had said unto him: and *so* it was, because he feared his father's household,

wcj(853)   pl,cs,nn**376**   df,nn5892   pr4480/qnc**6213** ad3119   wcs,qmf**6213**

and the men of the city, that he could not do *it* by day, that he did *it*

nn**3915**

by night.

pl,cs,nn**376**   df,nn5892 wcs,himf7925   dfp,nn1242 wcj,ptdm2009

28 And when the men of the city arose early in the morning, behold, the

cs,nn**4196**   df,nn1168   pupf**5422**   wcj,df,nn**842**   pupf**3772** pnl834   pr,pnx5921

altar of Baal was cast down, and the grove was cut down that *was* by it, and

wcj(853)   df,nuor8145 df,nn6499   hopf**5927** pr5921   df,nn**4196**   df,qptp1129

the second bullock was offered upon the altar *that was* built.

wcs,qmf559 nn**376** pr413   nn,pnx**7453** pnit4310   qpf**6213** df,pndm2088 df,nn**1697**

29 And they said one to another, Who hath done this thing? And when

wcs,qmf1875   wcs,pimf1245   wcs,qmf**559** nn1439   cs,nn**1121**   nn3101   qpf**6213** df,pndm2088

they inquired and asked, they said, Gideon the son of Joash hath done this

df,nn**1697**

thing.

pl,cs,nn**376**   df,nn5892 wcs,qmf**559** pr413   nn3101   himv3318   (853)   nn,pnx**1121**

30 Then the men of the city said unto Joash, Bring out thy son, that

wcj,qmf**4191** cj3588   qpf**5422**   (853)   cs,nn**4196** df,nn1168   wcj,cj3588

he may die: because he hath cast down the altar of Baal, and because he

qpf**3772**   df,nn**842** pnl834   pr,pnx5921

hath cut down the grove that *was* by it.

nn3101 wcs,qmf**559**   pp,nn3605 pnl834 qpf5975 pr,pnx5921   he,pnp859 qmf**7378**

31 And Joash said unto all that stood against him, Will ye plead for

dfp,nn1168 (cj518)   pnp859 himf**3467** pnx(853)   pnl834   qmf**7378**   pp,pnx

Baal? will ye save him? he that will plead for him, let him be

homf**4191**   pr5704   df,nn1242 cj518 pnp1931   pl,nn**430**   qmf**7378**   pp,pnx

put*to*death whilst *it is yet* morning: if he *be* a god, let him plead for himself,

cj3588   qpf**5422** (853)   nn,pnx**4196**

because *one* hath cast down his altar.

df,pndm1931 dfp,nn3117   wcs,qmf**7121** pp,pnx   nn3378   pp,qnc559   df,nn1168

32 Therefore on that day he called him Jerubbaal, saying, Let Baal

qmf**7378**   pp,pnx   cj3588   qpf**5422**   (853)   nn,pnx**4196**

plead against him, because he hath thrown down his altar.

Gideon Prepares for Battle

wcj,cs,nn3605   nn4080   wcj,nn6003   wcj,pl,cs,nn**1121**   nn**6924**

33 Then all the Midianites and the Amalekites and the children of the east

nipf**622** ad3162   wcs,qmf**5674**   wcs,qmf2583   pp,cs,nn6010   nn3157

were gathered together, and went over, and pitched in the valley of Jezreel.

wcj,cs,nn**7307**   nn**3068** qpf3847   (853) nn1439   wcs,qmf**8628**

34 But the Spirit of the LORD came upon Gideon, and he blew a

dfp,nn7782   nn44   wcs,nimf2199 pr,pnx310

trumpet; and Abi-ezer was gathered after him.

qpf7971   wcj,pl,nn**4397**   pp,cs,nn3605   nn4519   pnp1931 ad1571

35 And he sent messengers throughout all Manasseh; who also was

wcs,nimf2199 pr,pnx310   qpf7971   wcj,pl,nn**4397**   pp,nn836   wcj,pp,nn2074

gathered after him: and he sent messengers unto Asher, and unto Zebulun, and

wcj,pp,nn5321   wcs,qmf**5927**   pp,qnc,pnx7125

unto Naphtali; and they came up to meet them.

Gideon Pursues the Escaping Kings

8
cs,nn376   nn669   wcs,qmf559 pr,pnx413   pnit4100   qpf6213 pp,pnx
And the men of Ephraim said unto him, Why hast thou served us

df,pndm2088 (df,nn1697)   qnc7121 pp,pnx pp,ptn1115 cj3588   qpf1980   pp,ninc3898
thus, that thou calledst us not, when thou wentest to fight with

pp,nn4080   wcs,qmf7378 pr,pnx854   pp,nn2394
the Midianites? And they did chide with him sharply.

wcs,qmf559 pr,pnx413   pnit4100   qpf6213 ad6258   pp,pnx
2 And he said unto them, What have I done now in*comparison*of*you? *Is*

he,ptn3808   pl,cs,nn5955   nn669   aj2896   pr4480/cs,nn1210   nn44
not the gleaning*of*the*grapes of Ephraim better than*the*vintage of Abi-ezer?

pl,nn430   qpf5414   pp,nn,pnx3027 (853)   pl,cs,nn8269   nn4080   (853)   nn6159
3 God hath delivered into your hands the princes of Midian, Oreb and

wcj(853)   nn2062   wcj,pnit4100   qpf3201   qnc6213   pp,pnx   ad227   nn,pnx7307
Zeeb: and what was*I*able to do in*comparison*of*you? Then their anger

qpf7503   pr4480/pr,pnx5921   pp,pinc,pnx1696 df,pndm2088 (df,nn1697)
was abated toward him, when he had said that.

nn1439   wcs,qmf935   df,nn,lh3383   qpta5674   pnp1931   wcj,cs,nu7969
4 And Gideon came to Jordan, *and* passed over, he, and the three

pl,cs,nu3967 df,nn376 pnl834   pr,pnx854   aj5889   wcj,pl,qpta7291
hundred men that *were* with him, faint, yet pursuing *them*.

wcs,qmf559   pp,pl,cs,nn376   nn5523   qmv5414   pte4994   pl,cs,nn3603
5 And he said unto the men of Succoth, Give, I*pray*you, loaves of

nn3899   dfp,nn5971 pnl834 pp,du,nn,pnx7272   cj3588 pnp1992   aj5889   wcj,pnp595   qpta7291
bread unto the people that follow me; for they *be* faint, and I am pursuing

pr310   nn2078   wcj,nn6759   pl,cs,nn4428   nn4080
after Zebah and Zalmunna, kings of Midian.

pl,cs,nn8269   nn5523   wcs,qmf559   he,cs,nn3709   nn2078   wcj,nn6759
6 And the princes of Succoth said, *Are* the hands of Zebah and Zalmunna

ad6258   pp,nn,pnx3027 cj3588   qmf5414 nn3899   pp,nn,pnx6635
now in thine hand, that we should give bread unto thine army?

nn1439   wcs,qmf559   pp,ad3651   nn3068   pp,qnc5414   (853)   nn2078
7 And Gideon said, Therefore when the LORD hath delivered Zebah and

wcj(853)   nn6759   pp,nn,pnx3027   wcj,qpf1758 (853)   nn,pnx1320 pr854   pl,cs,nn6975
Zalmunna into mine hand, then I will tear your flesh with the thorns

df,nn4057   wcj,pr854 df,pl,nn1303
of the wilderness and with briers.

wcs,qmf5927   pr4480/ad8033   nn6439   wcs,pimf1696 pr,pnx413   pp,pndm2063
8 And he went up thence to Penuel, and spoke unto them likewise: and the

pl,cs,nn376   nn6439   wcs,qmf6030 pnx(853)   pp,pnl834   pl,cs,nn376   nn5523   qpf6030
men of Penuel answered him as the men of Succoth had answered *him*.

wcs,qmf559 ad1571   pp,pl,cs,nn376   nn6439   pp,qnc559   pp,qnc,pnx7725
9 And he spoke also unto the men of Penuel, saying, When I come again in

pp,nn7965   qmf5422   (853) df,pndm2088   df,nn4026
peace, I will break down this tower.

wcj,nn2078   wcj,nn6759   dfp,nn7174   wcj,pl,nn,pnx4264 pr,pnx5973
10 Now Zebah and Zalmunna *were* in Karkor, and their hosts with them,

pp,cs,nu2568/nu6240   nu505   cs,nn3605   df,pl,nipt3498 pr4480/cs,nn3605   cs,nn4264
about fifteen thousand *men*, all that were left of all the hosts of the

pl,cs,nn1121   nn6924   wcj,df,pl,qpta5307   nu3967   wcj,pl,nu6242   nu505   nn376
children of the east: for there fell a hundred and twenty thousand men that

qpta8025   nn2719
drew sword.

nn1439   wcs,qmf5927   cs,nn1870   pl,cs,qptp7931   dfp,pl,nn168
11 And Gideon went up by the way of them that dwelt in tents

pr4480/cs,nn**6924**   pp,nn5025   wcj,nn3011   wcs,himf**5221** (853)   df,nn**4264**   wcj,df,nn**4264** qpf**1961**

on*the*east of Nobah and Jogbehah, and smote   the host: for the   host   was

nn**983**

secure.

nn2078   wcj,nn6759   wcs,qmf5127   wcs,qmf7291   pr,pnx310   wcs,qmf3920

12 And when Zebah and Zalmunna fled, he pursued after them, and took

(853)   du,cs,nu8147   pl,cs,nn**4428**   nn4080   (853)   nn2078   wcj(853)   nn6759   hipf**2729**

the   two   kings of Midian,   Zebah and   Zalmunna, and discomfited

wcj,cs,nn3605   df,nn**4264**

all   the host.

nn1439   cs,nn**1121**   nn3101   wcs,qmf**7725**   pr4480   df,nn4421   pr4480/pp,cs,nn4608   df,nn2775

13 And Gideon the   son   of Joash returned from battle   before   the   sun

was up,

wcs,qmf3920   nn5288   pr4480/pl,cs,nn**376**   nn5523   wcs,qmf,pnx**7592**

14 And caught a young man of*the*men of Succoth, and inquired of him: and

wcs,qmf3789   pr,pnx413   (853)   pl,cs,nn**8269**   nn5523   wcj(853)   aj,pnx**2205**

he described unto him   the princes of Succoth, and   the elders thereof, *even*

pl,nu7657/wcj,nu7651   nn**376**

threescore*and*seventeen men.

wcs,qmf935   pr413   pl,cs,nn**376**   nn5523   wcs,qmf559   ptdm2009   nn2078

15 And he came unto the men of Succoth, and said, Behold Zebah and

wcj,nn6759   pnl834   pipf**2778**   pnx(853)   pp,qnc**559**   he,cs,nn**3709**   nn2078

Zalmunna, with whom ye did upbraid   me, saying, *Are* the hands of Zebah

wcj,nn6759   ad6258   pp,nn,pnx**3027** cj3588   qmf**5414**   nn3899   pp,pl,nn,pnx**376**

and Zalmunna now in thine   hand,   that we should give bread unto thy   men

df,aj3287

that are weary?

wcs,qmf3947 (853)   cs,aj**2205**   df,nn5892   wcj(853) pl,cs,nn6975   df,nn4057

16 And he   took   the elders of the city, and   thorns of the wilderness

wcj(853) df,pl,nn1303   pp,pnx   wcs,himf**3045** (853)   pl,cs,nn**376**   nn5523

and   briers, and with them he taught   the men of Succoth.

qpf**5422**   wcj(853)   cs,nn4026   nn6439   wcs,qmf**2026** (853)   pl,cs,nn**376**

17 And he beat down   the tower of Penuel, and   slew   the men of

df,nn5892

the city.

wcs,qmf**559**   pr413   nn2078   wcj(pr413)   nn6759   pnit375   df,pl,nn**376**

18 Then   said   he unto Zebah and   Zalmunna, What manner of   men

pnl834   qpf**2026**   pp,nn8396   wcs,qmf**559**   pp,pnx3644   pp,pnx

were they whom ye slew at Tabor? And they answered, As thou *art*, so *were* they;

nu259   pp,cs,nn8389   pl,cs,nn**1121**   df,nn**4428**

each one resembled the children of a king.

wcs,qmf**559** pnp1992   pl,nn,pnx**251**   pl,cs,nn**1121**   nn,pnx**517**

19 And he said, They *were* my brethren, *even* the   sons   of my mother: *as* the

nn3068   cs,aj**2416** cj3863   hipf**2421**/pnx(853)   ptn3808 qpf**2026** pnx(853)

LORD liveth,   if   ye had saved*them*alive, I would not slay   you.

wcs,qmf**559**   pp,nn3500   nn,pnx1060   qmv**6965**   qmv**2026** pnx(853)

20 And he   said   unto Jether his firstborn, Up, *and* slay   them. But the

df,nn5288 qpf8025 wcj,ptn**3808**   nn,pnx**2719** cj3588   qpf**3372**   cj3588   ad,pnx5750   nn5288

youth drew   not   his sword: for he feared, because he *was*   yet   a youth.

nn2078   wcj,nn6759   wcs,qmf**559** qmv**6965** pnp859   wcj,qmv**6293**   pp,pnx   cj3588

21 Then Zebah and Zalmunna said, Rise thou, and   fall   upon us: for as

dfp,nn**376**   nn,pnx1369   nn1439   wcs,qmf**6965**   wcs,qmf**2026** (853) nn2078   wcj(853)

the man *is, so is* his strength. And Gideon arose, and   slew   Zebah and

nn6759   wcs,qmf3947 (853)   df,pl,nn7720   pnl834   pl,nn,pnx1581 pp,pl,cs,nn6677

Zalmunna, and took away   the ornaments that *were* on their camels'   necks.

Gibeon's Later Years

^{cs,nn376} ⁿⁿ³⁴⁷⁸ ^{wcs,qmf559} ^{pr413} ⁿⁿ¹⁴³⁹ ^{qmv4910} ^{pp,pnx} ^{ad1571} ^{pnp859}

22 Then the men of Israel said unto Gideon, Rule thou over us, both thou,

^{ad1571} ^{nn,pnx1121} ^{nn,pnx1121 cs,nn1121} ^{ad1571 cj3588} ^{hipf,pnx3467} ^{pr4480/cs,nn3027}

and thy son, and thy son's son also: for thou hast delivered us from*the*hand

ⁿⁿ⁴⁰⁸⁰

of Midian.

ⁿⁿ¹⁴³⁹ ^{wcs,qmf559} ^{pr,pnx413} ^{pnp589} ^{ptn3808 qmf4910} ^{pp,pnx} ^{wcj,ptn3808}

23 And Gideon said unto them, I will not rule over you, neither shall

^{nn,pnx1121} ^{qmf4910} ^{pp,pnx} ⁿⁿ³⁰⁶⁸ ^{qmf4910} ^{pp,pnx}

my son rule over you: the LORD shall rule over you.

ⁿⁿ¹⁴³⁹ ^{wcs,qmf559} ^{pr,pnx413} ^{qcj7592} ⁿⁿ⁷⁵⁹⁶ ^{pr,pnx4480}

24 And Gideon said unto them, I would desire a request of you, that ye

^{wcj,qmv5414} ^{pp,pnx} ⁿⁿ³⁷⁶ ^{cs,nn5141} ^{nn,pnx7998 cj3588} ^{pp,pnx} ⁿⁿ²⁰⁹¹

would give me every man the earrings of his prey. (For they had golden

^{pl,cs,nn5141} ^{cj3588} ^{pnp1992} ⁿⁿ³⁴⁵⁹

earrings, because they *were* Ishmaelites.)

^{wcs,qmf559} ^{qna5414/qmf5414} ^{wcs,qmf6566 (853)}

25 And they answered, We will willingly*give *them*. And they spread a

^{df,nn8071} ^{wcs,himf7993} ^{ad,lh8033} ⁿⁿ³⁷⁶ ^{cs,nn5141} ^{nn,pnx7998}

garment, and did cast therein every man the earrings of his prey.

^{cs,nn4948} ^{df,nn2091} ^{pl,cs,nn5141} ^{pnl834} ^{qpf7592} ^{wcs,qmf1961} ^{nu505}

26 And the weight of the golden earrings that he requested was a thousand

^{wcj,cs,nu7651} ^{pl,nu3967} ⁿⁿ²⁰⁹¹ ^{pp,nn905/pr4480} ^{df,pl,nn7720} ^{wcj,df,pl,nn5188} ^{df,nn713}

and seven hundred *shekels* of gold; beside ornaments, and collars, and purple

^{wcj,pl,cs,nn899} ^{pnl7945/pr5921} ^{pl,cs,nn4428} ⁿⁿ⁴⁰⁸⁰ ^{wcj,pp,nn905/pr4480} ^{df,nn6060 pnl834}

raiment that *was* on the kings of Midian, and beside the chains that

^{pl,nn,pnx1581} ^{pp,pl,cs,nn6677}

were about their camels' necks.

ⁿⁿ¹⁴³⁹ ^{wcs,qmf6213} ^{pp,nn646} ^{pnx(853)} ^{wcs,himf3322 pnx(853)}

27 And Gideon made an ephod thereof, and put it in his

^{pp,nn,pnx5892} ^{pp,nn6084} ^{cs,nn3605 nn3478} ^{wcs,qmf2181/ad8033} ^{pr,pnx310}

city, *even* in Ophrah: and all Israel went*thither*a*whoring after it: which

^{wcs,qmf1961} ^{pp,nn4170} ^{pp,nn1439} ^{wcj,pp,nn,pnx1004}

thing became a snare unto Gideon, and to his house.

ⁿⁿ⁴⁰⁸⁰ ^{wcs,nimf3665} ^{pp,pl,cs,nn6440} ^{pl,cs,nn1121} ⁿⁿ³⁴⁷⁸

28 Thus was Midian subdued before the children of Israel, so that they

^{pp,qnc5375} ^{nn,pnx7218 wcj,ptn3808} ^{qpf3254} ^{df,nn776} ^{wcs,qmf8252} ^{pl,nu705 nn8141}

lifted up their heads no more. And the country was*in*quietness forty years in

^{pp,pl,cs,nn3117} ⁿⁿ¹⁴³⁹

the days of Gideon.

ⁿⁿ³³⁷⁸ ^{cs,nn1121} ^{nn3101 wcs,qmf1980} ^{wcs,qmf3427} ^{pp,nn,pnx1004}

29 And Jerubbaal the son of Joash went and dwelt in his own house.

^{wcj,pp,nn1439 qpf1961} ^{pl,nu7657} ^{pl,nn1121} ^{nn,pnx3409 pl,cs,qpta3318} ^{cj3588 pp,pnx}

30 And Gideon had threescore*and*ten sons of his body begotten: for he

^{qpf1961} ^{aj7227} ^{pl,nn802}

had many wives.

8:27 The "ephod" mentioned here may have varied from the priestly ephod (Ex. 28:5–30) or a mere copy of the breastplate of Aaron's ephod. It seems to represent man's attempt to achieve a standing with God on his own (see Judg. 17:5), and could be considered a form of their idolatry which was prevalent during this time because the objects themselves were worshiped, not God.

^{wcj,nn,pnx6370} ^{pnl834} ^{pp,nn7927} ^{pnp1931} ^{ad1571} ^{qpf3205} ^{pp,pnx} ⁿⁿ¹¹²¹ ⁽⁸⁵³⁾

31 And his concubine that *was* in Shechem, she also bore him a son,

^{nn,pnx8034} ^{wcs,qmf7760} ⁿⁿ⁴⁰

whose name he called Abimelech.

ⁿⁿ¹⁴³⁹ ^{cs,nn1121} ⁿⁿ³¹⁰¹ ^{wcs,qmf4191} ^{aj2896} ^{pp,nn7872} ^{wcs,nimf6912}

32 And Gideon the son of Joash died in a good old age, and was buried

^{pp,cs,nn6913} ⁿⁿ³¹⁰¹ ^{nn,pnx1} ^{pp,nn6084} ⁿⁿ³³

in the sepulcher of Joash his father, in Ophrah of the Abi-ezrites.

^{wcs,qmf1961} ^{pp,pnl834} ⁿⁿ¹⁴³⁹ ^{qpf4191} ^{pl,cs,nn1121}

☙ 33 And it*came*to*pass, as*soon*as Gideon was dead, that the children of

ⁿⁿ³⁴⁷⁸ ^{wcs,qmf7725} ^{wcs,qmf2181} ^{pr310} ^{df,pl,nn1168} ^{wcs,qmf7760} ⁿⁿ¹¹⁷⁰ ^{pp,pnx}

Israel turned again, and went*a*whoring after Baalim, and made Baal-berith their

^{pp,pl,nn430}

god.

^{pl,cs,nn1121} ⁿⁿ³⁴⁷⁸ ^{qpf2142} ^{wcj,ptn3808} ⁽⁸⁵³⁾ ⁿⁿ³⁰⁶⁸ ^{pl,nn,pnx430}

34 And the children of Israel remembered not the LORD their God, who

^{df,hipt5337} ⁽⁸⁵³⁾ ^{pr4480/cs,nn3027} ^{cs,nn3605} ^{pl,qpta,pnx341} ^{pr4480/nn5439}

had delivered them out*of*the*hands of all their enemies on*every*side:

^{wcj,ptn3808} ^{qpf6213} ⁿⁿ²⁶¹⁷ ^{pr5973} ^{cs,nn1004} ⁿⁿ³³⁷⁸ ⁿⁿ¹⁴³⁹

35 Neither showed they kindness to the house of Jerubbaal, *namely*, Gideon,

^{pp,cs,nn3605} ^{df,nn2896} ^{pnl834} ^{qpf6213} ^{pr5973} ⁿⁿ³⁴⁷⁸

according to all the goodness which he had showed unto Israel.

Abimelech

ⁿⁿ⁴⁰ ^{cs,nn1121} ⁿⁿ³³⁷⁸ ^{wcs,qmf1980} ^{nn,lh7927} ^{pr413} ^{nn,pnx517}

9 And Abimelech the son of Jerubbaal went to Shechem unto his mother's

^{pl,cs,nn251} ^{wcs,pimf1696} ^{pr,pnx413} ^{wcj,pr413} ^{cs,nn3605} ^{cs,nn4940}

brethren, and communed with them, and with all the family of the

^{cs,nn1004} ^{nn,pnx517} ^{cs,nn1} ^{pp,qnc559}

house of his mother's father, saying,

^{pimv1696} ^{pte4994} ^{pp,du,cs,nn241} ^{cs,nn3605} ^{pl,cs,nn1167} ⁿⁿ⁷⁹²⁷ ^{pnit4100}

2 Speak, I*pray*you, in the ears of all the men of Shechem, Whether

^{aj2896} ^{pp,pnx} ^{cs,nn3605} ^{pl,cs,nn1121} ⁿⁿ³³⁷⁸

is better for you, either that all the sons of Jerubbaal, *which are*

^{pl,nu7657} ⁿⁿ³⁷⁶ ^{he,qnc4910} ^{pp,pnx} ^{cj518} ^{nu259} ⁽ⁿⁿ³⁷⁶⁾ ^{qnc4910} ^{pp,pnx}

threescore*and*ten persons, reign over you, or that one reign over you?

^{wcj,qpf2142} ^{cj3588} ^{pnp589} ^{nn,pnx6106} ^{wcj,nn,pnx1320}

remember also that I *am* your bone and your flesh.

^{nn,pnx517} ^{pl,cs,nn251} ^{wcs,pimf1696} ^{pr,pnx5921} ^{pp,du,cs,nn241} ^{cs,nn3605}

3 And his mother's brethren spoke of him in the ears of all the

^{pl,cs,nn1167} ⁿⁿ⁷⁹²⁷ ⁽⁸⁵³⁾ ^{cs,nn3605} ^{df,pndm428} ^{df,pl,nn1697} ^{nn,pnx3820} ^{wcs,qmf5186/pr310}

men of Shechem all these words: and their hearts inclined*to*follow

ⁿⁿ⁴⁰ ^{cj3588} ^{qpf559} ^{pnp1931} ^{nn,pnx251}

Abimelech; for they said, He *is* our brother.

^{wcs,qmf5414} ^{pp,pnx} ^{pl,nu7657} ⁿⁿ³⁷⁰¹ ^{pr4480/cs,nn1004}

4 And they gave him threescore*and*ten *pieces* of silver out*of*the*house of

---

☙ **8:33** A strange contrast is made in this verse between Baal–berith, which means "Baal (the lord) of the covenant," and Jehovah, with whom Israel had made their covenant. They were in fact exchanging one covenant for the other! This apostasy was centered in Shechem, and no doubt Gideon had opened the way for this apostasy by making the ephod (see the note on Judg. 8:27).

nn1170   pp,pnx   nn40   wcs,qmf7936   aj7386   wcj,pl,qpta6348   pl,nn376
Baal-berith, wherewith Abimelech hired vain and light persons, which

wcs,qmf1980/pr,pnx310
followed him.

                    wcs,qmf935   nn,pnx1   cs,nn1004   nn,lh6084   wcs,qmf2026 (853)   pl,nn,pnx251
5 And he went unto his father's house at Ophrah, and slew his brethren

pl,cs,nn1121   nn3378   pl,nu7657   nn376   pr5921 nu259   nn68
the sons of Jerubbaal, *being* threescore*and*ten persons, upon one stone:

               nn3147   df,aj6996   cs,nn1121   nn3378   wcs,nimf3498   cj3588
notwithstanding yet Jotham the youngest son of Jerubbaal was left; for he

nipf2244
hid himself.

           cs,nn3605   pl,cs,nn1167   nn7927   wcs,nimf622   wcj,cs,nn3605
6 And all the men of Shechem gathered together, and all the

nn1037 [cs,nn1004/nn4407]   wcs,qmf1980   wcs,himf4427 (853)   nn40   pp,nn4428 pr5973   cs,nn436
house*of*Millo, and went, and made Abimelech king, by the plain of the

hopt5324 pnl834   pp,nn7927
pillar that *was* in Shechem.

           wcs,himf5046   pp,nn3147   wcs,qmf1980   wcs,qmf5975   pp,cs,nn7218
7 And when they told *it* to Jotham, he went and stood in the top of

cs,nn2022   nn1630   wcs,qmf5375   nn,pnx6963 wcs,qmf7121 wcs,qmf559 pp,pnx   qmv8085
mount Gerizim, and lifted up his voice, and cried, and said unto them, Hearken

pr,pnx413   pl,cs,nn1167   nn7927   pl,nn430   wcj,qmf8085 pr,pnx413
unto me, ye men of Shechem, that God may hearken unto you.

df,pl,nn6086   qna1980/qpf1980   pp,qnc4886   nn4428 pr,pnx5921
8 The trees went forth *on a time* to anoint a king over them; and they

wcs,qmf559   dfp,nn2132   qmv4427   pr,pnx5921
said unto the olive tree, Reign thou over us.

           df,nn2132   wcs,qmf559   pp,pnx   he,qpf2308 (853)   nn,pnx1880
9 But the olive tree said unto them, Should I leave my fatness,

pnl834   pp,pnx   pimf3513 pl,nn430   wcj,pl,nn376   wcs,qpf1980   pp,qnc5128 pr5921
wherewith by me they honor God and man, and go to be promoted over the

df,pl,nn6086
trees?

           df,pl,nn6086 wcs,qmf559   dfp,nn8384 qmv1980 pnp859   qmv4427 pr,pnx5921
10 And the trees said to the fig tree, Come thou, *and* reign over us.

           df,nn8384   wcs,qmf559   pp,pnx   he,qpf2308 (853)   nn,pnx4987
11 But the fig tree said unto them, Should I forsake my sweetness, and

wcj(853)   df,aj2896 nn,pnx8570 wcj,qpf1980   pp,qnc5128 pr5921   df,pl,nn6086
my good fruit, and go to be promoted over the trees?

           wcs,qmf559   df,pl,nn6086   dfp,nn1612 qmv1980 pnp859   qmv4427 pr,pnx5921
12 Then said the trees unto the vine, Come thou, *and* reign over us.

           df,nn1612 wcs,qmf559   pp,pnx   he,qpf2308 (853)   nn,pnx8492
13 And the vine said unto them, Should I leave my wine, which

df,pipt8055   pl,nn430   wcj,pl,nn376 wcj,qpf1980   pp,qnc5128 pr5921   df,pl,nn6086
cheereth God and man, and go to be promoted over the trees?

           wcs,qmf559 cs,nn3605   df,pl,nn6086 pr413   df,nn329   qmv1980 pnp859   qmv4427 pr,pnx5921
14 Then said all the trees unto the bramble, Come thou, *and* reign over

us.

           df,nn329 wcs,qmf559 pr413   df,pl,nn6086 cj518   pp,ad571 pnp859 pl,qpta4886 pnx(853)
15 And the bramble said unto the trees, If in truth ye anoint me

---

9:7–15   This is one of the few parables in the Old Testament.

pp,nn**4428** pr,pnx5921   qmv935   qmv**2620**   pp,nn,pnx**6738**   wcj,cj518 ptn369

king   over   you, *then* come *and* put*your*trust in my shadow: and   if   not, let

nn784   qmf3318   pr4480 df,nn329   wcj,qmf398 (853)   pl,cs,nn730   df,nn3844

fire come out of the bramble, and devour   the cedars of Lebanon.

wcj,ad6258   cj518   qpf**6213** pp,nn**571**   wcj,pp,aj**8549**

16 Now therefore, if ye have done truly and sincerely, in that ye have

wcj,himf**4427**/(853)/nn40   wcj,cj518   qpf**6213** aj**2896** pr5973   nn3378   wcj(pr5973)

made*Abimelech*king, and   if ye have dealt well with Jerubbaal and   his

nn,pnx**1004**   wcj(cj518)   qpf**6213**   pp,pnx   pp,cs,nn1576   du,nn,pnx**3027**

house, and   have done unto him according to the deserving of his hands;

pnl834   nn,pnx1   nipf3898 pr,pnx5921   wcs,himf**7993**   (853)   nn,pnx**5315** pr4480/pr5048

17 (For my father fought for   you, and adventured   his life   far,   and

wcs,himf**5337** pnx(853)   pr4480/cs,nn**3027**   nn4080

delivered   you out*of*the*hand of Midian:

wcj,pnp859   qpf**6965**   pr5921   nn,pnx1 cs,nn**1004**   df,nn3117

18 And ye   are risen up against my father's house this day, and have

wcs,qmf**2026** (853)   pl,nn,pnx**1121**   pl,nu7657   nn376   pr5921 nu259   nn68

slain   his sons, threescore*and*ten persons, upon one stone, and have made

(853)   nn40   cs,nn**1121**   nn,pnx519   wcs,himf**4427** pr5921   pl,cs,nn**1167**   nn7927

Abimelech, the son of his maidservant, king   over the men of Shechem,

cj3588   pnp1931   nn,pnx**251**

because he *is* your brother;)

wcj,cj518   qpf**6213** pp,nn**571**   wcj,pp,aj**8549** pr5973   nn3378   wcj,pr5973

19   If   ye then have dealt truly and sincerely with Jerubbaal and with his

nn,pnx**1004** df,pndm2088 df,nn**3117**   qmv8055   pp,nn40   pnp1931 ad1571 wcj,qmf8055   pp,pnx

house this day, *then* rejoice ye in Abimelech, and let him also rejoice in you:

wcj,cj518 ptn369   nn784   qmf3318   pr4480/nn40   wcj,qmf398 (853)   pl,cs,nn**1167**

20 But   if   not, let fire come out from Abimelech, and devour   the men

nn7927   wcj(853)   cs,nn**1004**   nn4407   nn784 wcj,qmf3318   pr4480/pl,cs,nn**1167**

of Shechem, and   the house of Millo; and let fire come out from*the*men of

nn7927   wcj,pr4480/cs,nn**1004**   nn4407   wcj,qmf398 (853)   nn40

Shechem, and from*the*house of Millo, and devour   Abimelech.

nn3147   wcs,qmf5127   wcs,qmf1272   wcs,qmf**1980** nn,lh876   wcs,qmf**3427** ad8033

21 And Jotham ran away, and fled, and went to Beer, and dwelt there,

pr4480/pl,cs,nn**6440**   nn40   nn,pnx**251**

for fear   of Abimelech his brother.

nn40   wcs,qmf**7786** nu7969 pl,nn8141 pr5921   nn3478

22 When Abimelech had reigned three years over Israel,

pl,nn**430** wcs,qmf7971   aj**7451** nn**7307** pr996   nn40   wcj(pr996)   pl,cs,nn**1167**

23 Then God sent an evil spirit between Abimelech and   the men of

nn7927   pl,cs,nn**1167**   nn7927   wcs,qmf**898**   pp,nn40

Shechem; and the men of Shechem dealt treacherously with Abimelech:

cs,nn**2555**   pl,nu7657   pl,cs,nn**1121**   nn3378

24 That the cruelty *done* to the threescore*and*ten sons of Jerubbaal might

pp,qnc935   wcj,nn,pnx**1818**   pp,qnc**7760** pr5921   nn40   nn,pnx**251** pnl834 qpf**2026** pnx(853)

come, and their blood be laid upon Abimelech their brother, which slew

wcj,pr5921   pl,cs,nn**1167**   nn7927   pnl834 pipf**2388**/(853)/du,nn,pnx**3027**   pp,qnc**2026**

them; and upon the men of Shechem, which   aided   him in the killing of

(853)   pl,nn,pnx**251**

his brethren.

pl,cs,nn**1167**   nn7927 wcs,qmf**7760**   pl,pipt693   pp,pnx   pr5921   pl,cs,nn**7218**

25 And the men of Shechem set   liers*in*wait for him in the   top   of

df,pl,nn2022   wcs,qmf1497 (853) nn3605 pnl834   qmf**5674**   dfp,nn**1870** pr,pnx5921

the mountains, and they robbed   all that came along that way   by them:

wcs,homf**5046**   pp,nn40

and it was   told   Abimelech.

ⁿⁿ¹⁶⁰³ ^{cs,nn1121} ⁿⁿ⁵⁶⁵¹ ^{wcs,qmf935} ^{wcj,pl,nn,pnx251} ^{wcs,qmf5674}

26 And Gaal the son of Ebed came with his brethren, and went over to

^{pp,nn7927} ^{pl,cs,nn1167} ⁿⁿ⁷⁹²⁷ ^{wcs,qmf982} ^{pp,pnx}

Shechem: and the men of Shechem put*their*confidence in him.

^{wcs,qmf3318} ^{df,nn7704} ^{wcs,qmf1219} ⁽⁸⁵³⁾ ^{pl,nn,pnx3754}

27 And they went out into the fields, and gathered their vineyards, and

^{wcs,qmf1869} ^{wcs,qmf6213} ^{pl,nn1974} ^{wcs,qmf935} ^{cs,nn1004} ^{pl,nn,pnx430}

trod *the grapes*, and made merry, and went into the house of their god, and

^{wcs,qmf398} ^{wcs,qmf8354} ^{wcs,pimf7043} ⁽⁸⁵³⁾ ⁿⁿ⁴⁰

did eat and drink, and cursed Abimelech.

ⁿⁿ¹⁶⁰³ ^{cs,nn1121} ⁿⁿ⁵⁶⁵¹ ^{wcs,qmf559} ^{pnit4310} ⁿⁿ⁴⁰ ^{wcj,pnit4310}

28 And Gaal the son of Ebed said, Who *is* Abimelech, and who *is*

ⁿⁿ⁷⁹²⁷ ^{cj3588} ^{qmf,pnx5647} ^{he,ptn3808} ^{cs,nn1121} ⁿⁿ³³⁷⁸

Shechem, that we should serve him? *is* not *he* the son of Jerubbaal? and

^{wcj,nn2083} ^{nn,pnx6496} ^{qmv5647} ⁽⁸⁵³⁾ ^{pl,cs,nn376} ⁿⁿ²⁵⁴⁴ ^{cs,nn1} ⁿⁿ⁷⁹²⁷ ^{wcj,ad4069}

Zebul his officer? serve the men of Hamor the father of Shechem: for why

^{pnp587} ^{qmf,pnx5647}

should we serve him?

^{wcj,pnit4310/qmf5414} ⁽⁸⁵³⁾ ^{df,pndm2088} ^{df,nn5971} ^{pp,nn,pnx3027}

29 And would*to*God this people were under my hand! then would I

^{wcj,hicj5493} ⁽⁸⁵³⁾ ⁿⁿ⁴⁰ ^{wcs,qmf559} ^{pp,nn40} ^{pimv7235} ^{nn,pnx6635}

remove Abimelech. And he said to Abimelech, Increase thine army, and

^{wcj,qmv3318}

come out.

ⁿⁿ²⁰⁸³ ^{cs,nn8269} ^{df,nn5892} ^{wcs,qmf8085} ⁽⁸⁵³⁾ ^{pl,cs,nn1697} ⁿⁿ¹⁶⁰³

30 And when Zebul the ruler of the city heard the words of Gaal the

^{cs,nn1121} ⁿⁿ⁵⁶⁵¹ ^{nn,pnx639} ^{wcs,qmf2734}

son of Ebed, his anger was kindled.

^{wcs,qmf7971} ^{pl,nn4397} ^{pr413} ⁿⁿ⁴⁰ ^{pp,nn8649} ^{pp,qnc559} ^{ptdm2009} ⁿⁿ¹⁶⁰³

31 And he sent messengers unto Abimelech privily, saying, Behold, Gaal the

^{cs,nn1121} ⁿⁿ⁵⁶⁵¹ ^{wcj,pl,nn,pnx251} ^{pl,qpta935} ^{nn,lh7927} ^{wcj,ptdm,pnx2009} ^{pl,qpta6696}

son of Ebed and his brethren be come to Shechem; and, behold, they fortify

⁽⁸⁵³⁾ ^{df,nn5892} ^{pr,pnx5921}

the city against thee.

^{wcj,ad6258} ^{qmv6965} ⁿⁿ³⁹¹⁵ ^{pnp859} ^{wcj,df,nn5971} ^{pnl834} ^{pr,pnx854}

32 Now therefore up by night, thou and the people that *is* with thee, and

^{wcj,qmv693} ^{dfp,nn7704}

lie*in*wait in the field:

^{wcj,qpf1961} ^{dfp,nn1242} ^{df,nn8121} ^{pp,qnc2224}

33 And it shall be, *that* in the morning, as soon as the sun is up, thou

^{himf7925} ^{wcs,qpf6584} ^{pr5921} ^{df,nn5892} ^{wcj,ptdm2009} ^{pnp1931} ^{wcj,df,nn5971}

shalt rise early, and set upon the city: and, behold, *when* he and the people

^{pnl834} ^{pr,pnx854} ^{pl,qpta3318} ^{pr,pnx413} ^{wcs,qpf6213} ^{pp,pnx} ^{pp,pnl834}

that *is* with him come out against thee, then mayest thou do to them as

^{qmf4672} ^{nn,pnx3027}

thou shalt find occasion.

ⁿⁿ⁴⁰ ^{wcs,qmf6965} ^{wcj,cs,nn3605} ^{df,nn5971} ^{pnl834} ^{pr,pnx5973}

34 And Abimelech rose up, and all the people that *were* with him, by

ⁿⁿ³⁹¹⁵ ^{wcs,qmf693} ^{pr5921} ⁿⁿ⁷⁹²⁷ ^{nu702} ^{pl,nn7218}

night, and they laid wait against Shechem in four companies.

ⁿⁿ¹⁶⁰³ ^{cs,nn1121} ⁿⁿ⁵⁶⁵¹ ^{wcs,qmf3318} ^{wcs,qmf5975} ^{cs,nn6607}

35 And Gaal the son of Ebed went out, and stood in the entering of the

^{cs,nn8179} ^{df,nn5892} ⁿⁿ⁴⁰ ^{wcs,qmf6965} ^{wcj,df,nn5971} ^{pnl834} ^{pr,pnx854}

gate of the city: and Abimelech rose up, and the people that *were* with him,

^{pr4480} ^{df,nn3993}

from lying*in*wait.

ⁿⁿ¹⁶⁰³ ^{wcs,qmf7200} (853)   ^{df,nn5971}   ^{wcs,qmf559} ^{pr413}   ⁿⁿ²⁰⁸³   ^{ptdm2009}
36 And when Gaal saw   the people, he said to Zebul, Behold, there

^{qpta3381/nn5971}   ^{pr4480/pl,cs,nn7218}   ^{df,pl,nn2022}   ⁿⁿ²⁰⁸³ ^{wcs,qmf559} ^{pr,pnx413}
come*people*down from*the*top of the mountains. And Zebul said unto him,

^{pnp859} ^{qpta7200} (853)   ^{cs,nn6738}   ^{df,pl,nn2022}   ^{dfp,pl,nn376}
Thou seest   the shadow of the mountains as *if they were* men.

ⁿⁿ¹⁶⁰³   ^{pp,pinc1696} (ad5750) ^{wcs,himf3254}   ^{wcs,qmf559} ^{ptdm2009}   ^{pl,qpta3381/nn5971}
37 And Gaal spoke   again and said,   See there come*people*down

^{pr4480/pr5973}   ^{cs,nn2872}   ^{df,nn776}   ^{nu259} ^{wcj,nn7218}   ^{qpta935}   ^{pr4480/pr5973}   ^{cs,nn436}
by the middle of the land, and another company come along by the plain of

^{pl,pipt*6049}
Meonenim.

^{wcs,qmf559}   ⁿⁿ²⁰⁸³   ^{pr,pnx413}   ^{pnit346}   ^{pnit645}   ^{nn,pnx6310}   ^{pnl834}
38 Then said Zebul unto him, Where *is* now thy mouth, wherewith thou

^{qmf559}   ^{pnit4310}   ⁿⁿ⁴⁰   ^{cj3588}   ^{qmf,pnx5647}   ^{he,ptn3808} ^{pndm2088}   ^{df,nn5971}
saidst, Who *is* Abimelech, that we should serve him? *is* not this the people

^{pnl834}   ^{qpf3988/pp,pnx} ^{qmv3318} ^{pte4994} ^{ad6258} ^{wcj,nimv3898}   ^{pp,pnx}
that thou hast despised? go out, I pray now, and fight with them.

ⁿⁿ¹⁶⁰³ ^{wcs,qmf3318} ^{pp,pl,cs,nn6440} ^{pl,cs,nn1167}   ⁿⁿ⁷⁹²⁷   ^{wcs,nimf3898}
39 And Gaal went out before the men of Shechem, and fought with

^{pp,nn40}
Abimelech.

ⁿⁿ⁴⁰   ^{wcs,qmf,pnx7291}   ^{wcs,qmf5127} ^{pr4480/pl,nn,pnx6440}   ^{aj7227}
40 And Abimelech chased him, and he fled   before   him, and many

^{wcs,qmf5307}   ^{pl,nn2491}   ^{pr5704}   ^{cs,nn6607}   ^{df,nn8179}
were overthrown *and* wounded, *even* unto the entering of the gate.

ⁿⁿ⁴⁰   ^{wcs,qmf3427}   ^{dfp,nn725}   ⁿⁿ²⁰⁸³ ^{wcs,pimf1644} (853) ⁿⁿ¹⁶⁰³   ^{wcj(853)}
41 And Abimelech dwelt at Arumah: and Zebul thrust out   Gaal and

^{pl,nn,pnx251}   ^{pr4480/qnc3427}   ^{pp,nn7927}
his brethren, that they should*not*dwell in Shechem.

^{wcs,qmf1961}   ^{pr4480/nn4283}   ^{df,nn5971} ^{wcs,qmf3318}
42 And it*came*to*pass on*the*morrow, that the people went out into the

^{df,nn7704}   ^{wcs,himf5046}   ^{pp,nn40}
field; and they told Abimelech.

^{wcs,qmf3947} (853)   ^{df,nn5971}   ^{wcs,qmf,pnx2673}   ^{pp,nu7969} ^{pl,nn7218}
43 And he took   the people, and divided them into three companies,

^{wcs,qmf693}   ^{dfp,nn7704}   ^{wcs,qmf7200} ^{wcj,ptdm2009} ^{df,nn5971}   ^{qpta3318}
and laid wait in the field, and, looked, and, behold, the people *were* come forth

^{pr4480}   ^{df,nn5892}   ^{wcs,qmf6965} ^{pr,pnx5921}   ^{wcs,himf,pnx5221}
out of the city; and he rose up against them, and smote them.

^{wcj,nn40}   ^{wcj,df,pl,nn7218} ^{pnl834}   ^{pr,pnx5973}   ^{qpf6584}
44 And Abimelech, and the company that *was* with him, rushed forward, and

^{wcs,qmf5975}   ^{cs,nn6607}   ^{cs,nn8179}   ^{df,nn5892}   ^{wcj,du,cs,nu8147}   ^{df,pl,nn7218}
stood in the entering of the gate of the city: and the two *other* companies

^{qpf6584} ^{pr5921} ⁿⁿ³⁶⁰⁵   ^{pnl834}   ^{dfp,nn7704} ^{wcs,himf,pnx5221}
ran upon all *the people* that *were* in the fields, and slew them.

^{wcj,nn40}   ^{nipt3898}   ^{dfp,nn5892} ^{cs,nn3605} ^{df,pndm1931} ^{df,nn3117}   ^{wcs,qmf3920}
45 And Abimelech fought against the city all that day; and he took

(853)   ^{df,nn5892}   ^{qpf2026} ^{wcj(853)}   ^{df,nn5971} ^{pnl834}   ^{pp,pnx}   ^{wcs,qmf5422} (853)
the city, and slew   the people that *was* therein, and beat down   the

^{df,nn5892}   ^{wcs,qmf,pnx2232}   ⁿⁿ⁴⁴¹⁷
city, and sowed it with salt.

^{cs,nn3605}   ^{pl,cs,nn1167}   ^{cs,nn4026}   ⁿⁿ⁷⁹²⁷   ^{wcs,qmf8085}
46 And when all the men of the tower of Shechem heard *that*, they

^{wcs,qmf935} ^{pr413}   ^{cs,nn6877}   ^{cs,nn1004}   ⁿⁿ⁴¹⁰ ⁿⁿ¹²⁸⁶
entered into a hold of the house of the god Berith.

_{wcs,homf5046} _{pp,nn40}   _{cj3588} _{cs,nn3605}   _{pl,cs,nn1167}   _{cs,nn4026}

47 And it was told Abimelech, that all the men of the tower of

_{nn7927}   _{htpf6908}

Shechem were gathered together.

_{nn40}   _{wcs,qmf5927}   _{cs,nn2022}   _{nn6756}   _{pnp1931}   _{wcj,cs,nn3605}   _{df,nn5971}

48 And Abimelech got*him*up to mount Zalmon, he and all the people

_{pnl834}   _{pr,pnx854}   _{nn40}   _{wcs,qmf3947} ₍₈₅₃₎   _{df,pl,nn7134}   _{pp,nn,pnx3027}

that *were* with him; and Abimelech took an axe in his hand, and

_{wcs,qmf3772}   _{cs,nn7754}   _{pl,nn6086}   _{wcs,qmf,pnx5375}   _{wcs,qmf7760}   _{pr5921}   _{nn,pnx7926}

cut down a bough from the trees, and took it, and laid *it* on his shoulder,

_{wcs,qmf559}   _{pr413}   _{df,nn5971} _{pnl834}   _{pr,pnx5973}   _{pnid4100}   _{qpf7200}   _{qpf6213}

and said unto the people that *were* with him, What ye have seen me do,

_{pimv4116}   _{qmv6213} _{pp,pnx3644}

make haste, *and* do as I *have done*.

_{cs,nn3605}   _{df,nn5971} _{ad1571}   _{wcs,qmf3772}   _{nn376}   _{nn,pnx7754}

49 And all the people likewise cut down every man his bough, and

_{wcs,qmf1980/pr310}   _{nn40}   _{wcs,qmf7760}   _{pr5921}   _{df,nn6877}   _{wcs,himf3341} ₍₈₅₃₎   _{df,nn6877}

followed Abimelech, and put *them* to the hold, and set the hold on

_{dfp,nn784} _{pr,pnx5921}   _{cs,nn3605}   _{pl,cs,nn376}   _{cs,nn4026}   _{nn7927}   _{wcs,qmf4191} _{ad1571}

fire upon them; so that all the men of the tower of Shechem died also,

_{pp,nu505}   _{nn376}   _{wcj,nn802}

about a thousand men and women.

_{wcs,qmf1980}   _{nn40}   _{pr413}   _{nn8405}   _{wcs,qmf2583}   _{pp,nn8405}

50 Then went Abimelech to Thebez, and encamped against Thebez, and

_{wcs,qmf,pnx3920}

took it.

_{qpf1961}   _{nn5797} _{wcj,cs,nn4026} _{pp,cs,nn8432}   _{df,nn5892}   _{ad,lh8033} _{wcs,qmf5127} _{cs,nn3605}

51 But there was a strong tower within the city, and thither fled all

_{df,pl,nn376}   _{wcj,df,pl,nn802} _{wcj,cs,nn3605} _{pl,cs,nn1167}   _{df,nn5892}   _{wcs,qmf5462}   _{pr,pnx1157}

the men and women, and all they of the city, and shut *it* to them,

_{wcs,qmf5927}   _{pr5921}   _{cs,nn1406}   _{df,nn4026}

and got*them*up to the top of the tower.

_{nn40}   _{wcs,qmf935}   _{pr5704}   _{df,nn4026}   _{wcs,nimf3898}   _{pp,pnx}

52 And Abimelech came unto the tower, and fought against it, and

_{wcs,qmf5066}   _{pr5704}   _{cs,nn6607}   _{df,nn4026}   _{pp,qnc,pnx8313}   _{dfp,nn784}

went hard unto the door of the tower to burn it with fire.

_{nu259}   _{nn802}   _{wcs,himf7993} _{cs,nn6400}   _{nn7393}   _{pr5921}   _{nn40}   _{cs,nn7218}

53 And a certain woman cast a piece of a millstone upon Abimelech's head,

_{wcs,himf7533} ₍₈₅₃₎   _{nn,pnx1538}

and all to broke his skull.

_{wcs,qmf7121}   _{ad4120}   _{pr413}   _{df,nn5288}   _{qpta5375/pl,nn,pnx3627}   _{wcs,qmf559}

54 Then he called hastily unto the young man his armorbearer, and said

_{pp,pnx}   _{qmv8025}   _{nn,pnx2719}   _{wcj,pimv*,pnx4191}   _{cj6435}   _{qmf559}   _{pp,pnx}   _{nn802}

unto him, Draw thy sword, and slay me, that men say not of me, A woman

_{qpf,pnx2026}   _{nn,pnx5288}   _{wcs,qmf,pnx1856}   _{wcs,qmf4191}

slew him. And his young man thrust*him*through, and he died.

_{cs,nn376}   _{nn3478} _{wcs,qmf7200} _{cj3588}   _{nn40}   _{qpf4191}   _{wcs,qmf1980}

55 And when the men of Israel saw that Abimelech was dead, they departed

_{nn376}   _{pp,nn,pnx4725}

every man unto his place.

_{pl,nn430} _{wcs,himf7725} ₍₈₅₃₎   _{cs,nn7451}   _{nn40}   _{pnl834}   _{qpf6213}

56 Thus God rendered the wickedness of Abimelech, which he did unto his

_{pp,nn,pnx1}   _{pp,qnc2026} ₍₈₅₃₎   _{pl,nu7657} _{pl,nn,pnx251}

father, in slaying his seventy brethren:

_{wcj(853)} _{cs,nn3605}   _{cs,nn7451}   _{pl,cs,nn376}   _{nn7927}   _{pl,nn430} _{hipf7725}

57 And all the evil of the men of Shechem did God render upon

pp,nn,pnx**7218**   pr,pnx413   wcs,qmf935   cs,nn**7045**   nn3147   cs,nn**1121**   nn3378

their heads: and upon them came the curse of Jotham the son of Jerubbaal.

Tola

pr310   nn40   wcs,qmf**6965**   pp,hinc**3467** (853) nn3478   nn8439   cs,nn**1121**

10

And after Abimelech there arose to defend Israel Tola the son

nn6312   cs,nn**1121**   nn1734   cs,nn**376**   nn3485   wcj,pnp1931 qpta**3427**

of Puah, the son of Dodo, a man of Issachar; and he dwelt in

pp,nn8069   pp,cs,nn2022   nn669

Shamir in mount Ephraim.

wcs,qmf**8199**   (853)   nn3478   pl,nu6242   wcj,nu7969   nn8141   wcs,qmf**4191**

2 And he judged Israel twenty and three years, and died, and was

wcs,nimf**6912**   pp,nn8069

buried in Shamir.

Jair

pr,pnx310   wcs,qmf**6965** nn2971   df,nn1569   wcs,qmf**8199** (853) nn3478   pl,nu6242

3 And after him arose Jair, a Gileadite, and judged Israel twenty and

wcj,du,nu8147   nn8141

two years.

pp,pnx wcs,qmf**1961** nu7970   pl,nn**1121**   pl,qpta7392 pr5921   nu7970   pl,nn5895   pp,pnx

4 And he had thirty sons that rode on thirty ass colts, and they had

wcj,nu7970   pl,nn5892   pp,pnx   qmf**7121**   nn2334   pr5704 df,pndm2088 df,nn**3117**   pnl834

thirty cities, which are called Havoth-jair unto this day, which *are* in the

pp,cs,nn**776**   df,nn1568

land of Gilead.

nn2971 wcs,qmf**4191**   wcs,nimf**6912**   pp,nn7056

5 And Jair died, and was buried in Camon.

pl,cs,nn**1121**   nn3478 pp,qnc**6213** df,aj**7451** wcs,himf3254   pp,du,cs,nn**5869**   nn3068

6 And the children of Israel did evil again in the sight of the LORD,

wcs,qmf**5647** (853) df,pl,nn1168   wcj(853)   df,nn6252   wcj(853)   pl,cs,nn**430**   nn758   wcj(853)

and served Baalim, and Ashtaroth, and the gods of Syria, and

pl,cs,nn**430**   nn6721   wcj(853)   pl,cs,nn**430**   nn4124   wcj(853)   pl,cs,nn**430**

the gods of Zidon, and the gods of Moab, and the gods of the

pl,cs,nn**1121**   nn5983   wcj(853)   pl,cs,nn**430**   pl,nn6430   wcs,qmf**5800** (853)

children of Ammon, and the gods of the Philistines, and forsook the

nn3068   qpf,pnx**5647** wcj,ptn**3808**

LORD, and served not him.

cs,nn**639**   nn3068   wcs,qmf**2734**   pp,nn3478   wcs,qmf,pnx4376

7 And the anger of the LORD was hot against Israel, and he sold them

pp,cs,nn**3027**   pl,nn6430   wcj,pp,cs,nn**3027**   pl,cs,nn**1121**   nn5983

into the hands of the Philistines, and into the hands of the children of Ammon.

df,pndm1931 dfp,nn8141   wcs,qmf7492   wcs,pimf*7533   (853)   pl,cs,nn**1121**   nn3478

8 And that year they vexed and oppressed the children of Israel:

nu8083/nu6240   nn8141 (853) cs,nn3605   pl,cs,nn**1121**   nn3478 pnl834   pp,cs,nn5676   df,nn3383

eighteen years, all the children of Israel that *were* on the other side Jordan in

pp,cs,nn**776**   df,nn567   pnl834   dfp,nn1568

the land of the Amorites, which *is* in Gilead.

pl,cs,nn**1121**   nn5983   wcs,qmf**5674**   (853) df,nn3383   pp,ninc3898 ad1571

9 Moreover the children of Ammon passed over Jordan to fight also

pp,nn3063   wcj,pp,nn1144   wcj,pp,cs,nn**1004**   nn669

against Judah, and against Benjamin, and against the   house   of Ephraim; so that

pp,nn3478   ad3966   wcs,qmf3334

Israel was sore distressed.

pl,cs,nn**1121**   nn3478   wcs,qmf**2199**   pr413   nn3068   pp,qnc559   qpf2398

10 And the children of Israel   cried   unto the LORD, saying, We have sinned

pp,pnx   wcj,cj3588   qpf**5800**   (853)   pl,nn,pnx**430**   wcs,qmf**5647** (853)

against thee, both because we have forsaken   our God,   and also served

df,pl,nn1168

Baalim.

nn**3068**   wcs,qmf559   pr3413   pl,cs,nn**1121**   nn3478   he,ptn**3808**

11 And the LORD   said   unto the children of Israel, *Did*   not   *I deliver you*

pr4480/nn4714   wcj,pr4480   df,nn567   wcj,pr4480   pl,cs,nn**1121**   nn5983

from*the*Egyptians, and from the Amorites, from the children of Ammon, and

wcj,pr4480   pl,nn6430

from the Philistines?

wcj,nn6722   wcj,nn6002   wcj,nn4584   qpf3905   pnx(853)

12 The Zidonians also, and the Amalekites, and the Maonites, did oppress

wcs,qmf6817   pr,pnx413   wcs,himf**3467**   pnx(853)   pr4480/nn,pnx**3027**

you; and ye cried   to   me, and I delivered   you out*of*their*hand.

pnp859   qpf**5800**   pnx(853)   wcs,qmf**5647**   aj312   pl,nn**430**   pp,ad**3651**

13 Yet   ye   have forsaken   me, and served other gods: wherefore I will

pp,hinc**3467** pnx(853)   ptn**3808** himf3254

deliver   you no more.

qmv**1980**   wcj,qmv**2199** pr413   df,pl,nn**430** pnl834   pp,pnx   qpf977   pnp1992   himf**3467**

14 Go and   cry   unto the gods which ye have chosen; let them deliver

pp,pnx   pp,cs,nn**6256**   nn,pnx6869

you in the   time   of your tribulation.

pl,cs,nn**1121**   nn3478   wcs,qmf559   pr413   nn3068   qpf2398   qmv**6213** pnp859

15 And the children of Israel   said   unto the LORD, We have sinned: do   thou

pp,pnx   pp,cs,nn3605   df,aj2896   pp,du,nn,pnx**5869**   himv,pnx**5337**   ad389   pte**4994**

unto us whatsoever seemeth good   unto   thee; deliver us only, we*pray*thee,

df,pndm2088   df,nn3117

this   day.

wcs,himf**5493**   (853)   df,nn5236   pl,cs,nn**430**   pr4480/nn,pnx**7130**   wcs,qmf**5647** (853)

16 And they put away   the strange gods from among them, and served

nn**3068**   nn,pnx**5315**   wcs,qmf7114   pp,cs,nn**5999**   nn3478

the LORD: and his   soul   was grieved for the misery of Israel.

pl,cs,nn**1121**   nn5983   wcs,nimf6817   wcs,qmf2583

17 Then the children of Ammon were gathered together, and encamped in

dfp,nn1568   pl,cs,nn**1121**   nn3478   wcs,nimf**622**   wcs,qmf2583

Gilead. And the children of Israel assembled*themselves*together, and encamped in

dfp,nn4709

Mizpeh.

df,nn**5971**   pl,cs,nn**8269**   nn1568   wcs,qmf559   nn376   pr413   nn,pnx**7453**   pnit4310   df,nn376

18 And the people *and* princes of Gilead   said   one to another, What man *is*

pnl834   himf**2490**   pp,ninc3898   pp,pl,cs,nn**1121**   nn5983   qmf**1961** pp,nn**7218**

he that will begin to   fight   against the children of Ammon? he shall   be   head

pp,cs,nn3605   pl,cs,qpta**3427**   nn1568

over   all   the inhabitants of Gilead.

Jephthah Is Asked to Lead Gilead's Army

11 Now Jephthah the Gileadite was a mighty man of valor, and he *was* the son of a harlot: and Gilead begot Jephthah.

2 And Gilead's wife bore him sons; and his wife's sons grew up, and they thrust out Jephthah, and said unto him, Thou shalt not inherit in our father's house; for thou *art* the son of a strange woman.

3 Then Jephthah fled from his brethren, and dwelt in the land of Tob: and there were gathered vain men to Jephthah, and went out with him.

4 And it*came*to*pass in*process*of*time, that the children of Ammon made war against Israel.

5 And it was so, that when the children of Ammon made war against Israel, the elders of Gilead went to fetch Jephthah out*of*the*land of Tob:

6 And they said unto Jephthah, Come, and be our captain, that we may fight with the children of Ammon.

7 And Jephthah said unto the elders of Gilead, Did not ye hate me, and expel me out of my father's house? and why are ye come unto me now when ye are in distress?

8 And the elders of Gilead said unto Jephthah, Therefore we turn again to thee now, that thou mayest go with us, and fight against the children of Ammon, and be our head over all the inhabitants of Gilead.

9 And Jephthah said unto the elders of Gilead, If ye bring*me*home*again to fight against the children of Ammon, and the LORD deliver them before me, shall I be your head?

10 And the elders of Gilead said unto Jephthah, The LORD be witness between us, if we do not so according to thy words.

11 Then Jephthah went with the elders of Gilead, and the people made him head and captain over them: and Jephthah uttered all his words before the LORD in Mizpeh.

nn3316　wcs,qmf7971　pl,nn**4397**　pr413　cs,nn**4428**　pl,cs,nn**1121**　nn5983

12 And Jephthah sent   messengers unto the king of the children of Ammon,

pp,qnc559　pnit4100　wcj,pp,pnx　pp,pnx　cj3588　qpf935　pr,pnx413　pp,ninc3898

saying, What hast thou to do with me, that thou art come against me to fight in

pp,nn,pnx**776**

my land?

cs,nn**4428**　pl,cs,nn**1121**　nn5983　wcs,qmf**559**　pr413　pl,cs,nn**4397**

13 And the king of the children of Ammon answered unto the messengers of

nn3316　cj3588　nn3478　qpf3947　(853)　nn,pnx**776**　pp,qnc,pnx**5927**　pr4480/nn4714

Jephthah, Because Israel took away   my land, when they came up out*of*Egypt,

pr4480/nn769　wcj,pr5704　df,nn2999　wcj,pr5704　df,nn3383　wcj,ad6258

from Arnon even unto   Jabbok,   and   unto   Jordan: now   therefore

himv**7725**/pnx(853)　pp,nn**7965**

restore*those*_lands_*again peaceably.

nn3316　wcs,qmf7971　pl,nn**4397**　wcs,himf3254/ad5750　pr413　cs,nn**4428**　pl,cs,nn**1121**

14 And Jephthah sent   messengers   again   unto the king of the children

nn5983

of Ammon:

wcs,qmf**559**　pp,pnx　ad3541　qpf**559**　nn3316　nn3478　qpf3947/ptn**3808**　(853)

15 And   said   unto him, Thus saith Jephthah, Israel took*not*away   the

cs,nn**776**　nn4124　wcj(853)　cs,nn**776**　pl,cs,nn**1121**　nn5983

land of Moab, nor   the land of the children of Ammon:

cj3588　nn3478　pp,qnc,pnx**5927**　pr4480/nn4714　wcs,qmf**1980**　dfp,nn4057

16 But when Israel came up from Egypt, and walked through the wilderness

pr5704　nn5488 cs,nn3220　wcs,qmf935　nn,lh6946

unto the Red sea, and came to Kadesh;

nn3478　wcs,qmf7971　pl,nn**4397**　pr413　cs,nn**4428**　nn123　pp,qnc**559**

17 Then Israel sent   messengers unto the king of Edom, saying, Let me,

pte**4994**　qcj**5674**　pp,nn,pnx**776**　cs,nn**4428**　nn123　wcj,ptn**3808**　qpf8085

I*pray*thee, pass through thy land: but the king of Edom would   not   hearken

wcj,ad1571　qpf7971　pr413　cs,nn**4428**　nn4124　qpf14　wcj,ptn**3808**

thereto. And in*like*manner they sent unto the king of Moab: but he would   not

nn3478　wcs,qmf**3427**　pp,nn6946

consent: and Israel abode in Kadesh.

wcs,qmf**1980**　dfp,nn4057　wcs,qmf5437　(853)　cs,nn**776**

18 Then they went along through the wilderness, and compassed   the land of

nn123　wcj(853)　cs,nn**776**　nn4124　wcs,qmf935　pr4480/cs,nn4217/nn8121　pp,cs,nn**776**

Edom, and   the land of Moab, and came by*the*east*side of the   land of

nn4124　wcs,qmf2583　pp,cs,nn5676　nn769　qpf935　wcj,ptn**3808**　pp,cs,nn1366

Moab, and pitched on the other side of Arnon, but came   not   within the border

nn4124　cj3588　nn769　cs,nn1366　nn4124

of Moab: for Arnon _was_ the border of Moab.

nn3478　wcs,qmf7971　pl,nn**4397**　pr413　nn5511　cs,nn**4428**　df,nn567　cs,nn**4428**

19 And Israel sent   messengers unto Sihon king of the Amorites, the king of

nn2809　nn3478　wcs,qmf**559**　pp,pnx　qcj**5674**　pte**4994**

Heshbon; and Israel   said   unto him, Let us pass, we*pray*thee, through thy

pp,nn,pnx**776** pr5704　nn,pnx4725

land   into my place.

nn5511　hipf**539**　wcj,ptn**3808**　(853)　nn3478　qnc**5674**　pp,nn,pnx1366　nn5511

20 But Sihon trusted   not   Israel to pass through his   coast: but Sihon

wcs,qmf622/(853)/cs,nn3605/nn,pnx**5971**　wcs,qmf2583　pp,nn,lh3096　wcs,nimf3898　pr5973　nn3478

gathered*all*his*people*together, and pitched in Jahaz, and fought against Israel.

nn**3068**　pl,cs,nn**430**　nn3478　wcs,qmf**5414**　(853)　nn5511　wcj(853)　cs,nn3605　nn,pnx**5971**

21 And the LORD God of Israel delivered   Sihon and   all his people

pp,cs,nn**3027**   nn3478   wcs,himf,pnx**5221**   nn3478   wcs,qmf**3423**   (853) cs,nn3605

into the   hand   of Israel, and they   smote   them: so Israel possessed   all   the

cs,nn776   df,nn567   qpta**3427**   df,pndm1931   df,nn**776**

land of the Amorites, the inhabitants of   that   country.

wcs,qmf**3423**   (853) cs,nn3605   cs,nn1366   df,nn567   pr4480/nn769

22 And they possessed   all   the coasts of the Amorites, from Arnon even

wcj,pr5704   df,nn2999   wcj,pr4480   df,nn4057   wcj,pr5704   df,nn3383

unto   Jabbok, and from the wilderness even unto Jordan.

wcj,ad6258   nn**3068**   pl,cs,nn**430**   nn3478   hipf**3423**   (853)   df,nn567

23 So   now   the LORD God of Israel hath dispossessed   the Amorites

pr4480/pl,cs,nn**6440**   nn,pnx**5971**   nn3478   wcj,pnp859 qmf,pnx**3423**

from before his people Israel, and shouldest thou   possess it?

he,ptn**3808**   qmf**3423**   (853)   pnl834   nn3645   pl,nn,pnx**430**   pnx(853)

24 Wilt   not   thou possess   that which Chemosh thy   god giveth   thee

himf,pnx**3423**   wcj(853)   nn3605/pnl834   nn**3068**   pl,nn,pnx**430**   hipf**3423**   pr4480/pl,nn,pnx**6440**

to possess? So   whomsoever the LORD our   God   shall drive out from before

pnx(853)   qmf**3423**

us,   them will we possess.

wcj,ad6258   pnp859   he,aj**2896**/aj**2896**   pr4480/nn1111   cs,nn**1121**   nn6834   cs,nn**4428**

25 And now *art* thou any*thing*better than Balak the son of Zippor, king

nn4124   he,qna**7378**/qpf**7378**   pr5973   nn3478   cj518   nina3898/nipf3898   pp,pnx

of Moab? did he ever strive against Israel, or did he ever fight against them,

nn3478   pp,qnc**3427**   pp,nn2809   wcj,pl,nn,pnx1323   wcj,pp,nn6177

26 While Israel dwelt in Heshbon and her   towns,   and in Aroer and her

wcj,pl,nn,pnx1323   wcj,pp,cs,nn3605   df,pl,nn5892 pnl834   pr5921   du,cs,nn**3027**   nn769   cs,nu7969

towns,   and in   all   the cities that *be* along by the coasts of Arnon, three

pl,cs,nu3967   nn8141   wcj,ad4069   ptn**3808** hipf**5337**   df,pndm1931 dfp,nn**6256**

hundred years? why therefore did ye not recover *them* within   that   time?

wcj,pnp595   ptn**3808**   qpf**2398**   pp,pnx   wcj,pnp859 qpta**6213** pnx(853)

27 Wherefore   I   have not sinned against thee, but thou doest   me

aj**7451**   pp,ninc3898   pp,pnx   nn**3068**   df,qpta**8199**   qmf**8199**   df,nn3117   pr996

wrong to   war   against me: the LORD the Judge be judge this day between the

pl,cs,nn**1121**   nn3478   wcj(pr996)   pl,cs,nn**1121**   nn5983

children of Israel and   the children of Ammon.

cs,nn**4428**   pl,cs,nn**1121**   nn5983   qpf**8085**   wcj,ptn**3808** pr413

28 Howbeit the king of the children of Ammon hearkened   not   unto the

pl,cs,nn**1697**   nn3316   pnl834   qpf7971/pr,pnx413

words of Jephthah which he   sent   him.

Jephthah's Vow

cs,nn**7307**   nn**3068** wcs,qmf**1961** pr5921   nn3316   wcs,qmf**5674**   (853)

☞ **29** Then the Spirit of the LORD came upon Jephthah, and he passed over

---

☞ **11:29–33** This vow of Jephthah has caused much concern for many Bible scholars. If no other consider-
ations are brought into the discussion, the language of this passage would naturally lead one to believe that
Jephthah actually did offer his daughter as a sacrifice to the Lord. Most conservative commentators, on the
contrary, hold that Jephthah did not actually put his daughter to death, but dedicated her to the service of the
Lord.

There are two major areas of discussion relative to the vow. The first deals with whether Jephthah actually
intended a human sacrifice when he made the vow. Some would attempt to prove by the choice of words used
in the vow that he did intend a human sacrifice. However, it must be pointed out that this was only one of the
possibilities according to the usage of the word "whatsoever." Otherwise, if he had intended a human sacrifice,
why would he have been so surprised and distraught when his daughter became the object of the vow (v. 35)?
Also, Jephthah knew the Law well enough that he could not have been ignorant of the fact that God did not
allow human sacrifice. Furthermore, he would have been doubly guilty since he had no other children, and

df,nn1568   wcj(853)   nn4519   wcs,qmf**5674**   (853)   cs,nn4708   nn1568

Gilead, and   Manasseh, and   passed over   Mizpeh of   Gilead, and

wcj,pr4480/cs,nn4708   nn1568   qpf**5674**   pl,cs,nn**1121**   nn5983

from Mizpeh of Gilead he passed over *unto* the children of Ammon.

     nn3316   wcs,qmf5087   nn**5088**   pp,nn3068   wcs,qmf559   cj518

30 And Jephthah vowed a vow unto the L<small>ORD</small>, and said, If thou shalt

qna**5414**/qmf**5414**   (853)   pl,cs,nn**1121**   nn5983   pp,nn,pnx**3027**

without*fail*deliver   the children of Ammon into mine hands,

    wcs,qpf**1961**   pnl834   df,qpta3318   pr4480/pl,cs,nn1817   nn,pnx**1004**

31 Then it shall   be,   that whatsoever cometh forth of*the*doors of my house

pp,qnc,pnx7125   pp,qnc,pnx**7725**   pp,nn**7965**   pr4480/pl,cs,nn**1121**   nn5983

to   meet   me, when I   return   in peace from*the*children of Ammon, shall surely

wcs,qpf**1961**   pp,nn3068   wcs,hipf,pnx5927   nn**5930**

be   the L<small>ORD</small>'s, and I will offer*it*up for a burnt offering.

    nn3316   wcs,qmf**5674**   pr413   pl,cs,nn**1121**   nn5983   pp,ninc3898

32 So Jephthah passed over unto the children of Ammon to   fight

pp,pnx   nn3068 wcs,qmf,pnx**5414**   pp,nn,pnx**3027**

against them; and the L<small>ORD</small> delivered them into his hands.

   wcs,himf,pnx**5221**   pr4480/nn6177   wcj,pr5704   qnc,pnx935   nn4511

33 And he   smote   them from Aroer, even   till   thou   come to Minnith,

pl,nu6242   nn5892   wcj,pr5704   cs,nn58   pl,nn3754   ad3966   aj1419   nn**4347**

even twenty cities, and   unto   the plain of the vineyards, with a very great slaughter.

pl,cs,nn**1121**   nn5983   wcs,nimf3665 pr4480/pl,cs,nn**6440**   pl,cs,nn**1121**   nn3478

Thus the children of Ammon were subdued   before   the children of Israel.

    nn3316   wcs,qmf935   df,nn4709   pr413   nn,pnx**1004**   wcj,ptdm2009   nn,pnx1323

34 And Jephthah came   to Mizpeh unto his house, and, behold, his daughter

qpta3318   pp,qnc,pnx7125   pp,pl,nn8596   wcj,pp,pl,nn4246   wcj(ad7535) pnp1931

came out to   meet   him with timbrels and with   dances: and   she *was his*

aj**3173**   pr,pnx4480   pp,pnx   ptn369   nn1121   cj176   nn1323

only child; beside her he had neither son nor daughter.

     wcs,qmf**1961**   pp,qnc,pnx**7200**   pnx(853)   wcs,qmf7167   (853)

35 And it*came*to*pass, when he   saw   her, that he   rent   his

pl,nn,pnx899   wcs,qmf**559**   ptx162   nn,pnx1323   hina3766/hipf,pnx3766   wcj,pnp859

clothes, and   said,   Alas, my daughter! thou hast brought*me*very*low, and   thou

qpf**1961**   pp,pl,qpta,pnx5916   wcj,pnp595   qpf6475   nn,pnx**6310**   pr413

art one of them that   trouble   me: for   I   have opened my mouth unto the

nn3068   wcj,ptn**3808**/qmf3201   pp,qnc**7725**

L<small>ORD</small>, and I   cannot   go back.

     wcs,qmf**559**   pr,pnx413   nn,pnx1   qpf6475   (853)   nn,pnx**6310**

36 And she   said   unto   him, My father, *if* thou hast opened   thy mouth

---

he knew that sacrifices to Jehovah were to be exclusively of the male gender (v. 34). Jephthah's apprehension concerning the coming battle with the children of Ammon caused him to word his vow hastily and leave open the possibility of a human sacrifice.

The second problem is whether Jephthah actually did take his own daughter's life. It would have been next to impossible for Jephthah to have found a priest who would perform such a sacrifice. The idea expressed by conservative scholars is that if this were true, Jephthah would not have been included in the "heroes of the faith" (Heb. 11:32). Furthermore, would it be proper to commend Jephthah if he had broken God's laws in such a serious matter? To say that his daughter spent her last two months of life up in the mountains with her friends rather than with her mourning father would have been peculiar. In addition to this, why is it that she bemoans her virginity rather than her short life? The phrase "and she knew no man" would be meaningless if her life had been taken. It would seem more logical to assume that she was to be wholly given to the service of the Lord where she must continue in her virginity.

The most sensible explanation of these events then would be that Jephthah did not actually perform a human sacrifice because he knew and obeyed God's laws even though, according to his original vow, this would have been the result. The phrase stating that he "did with her according to his vow" does not actually state that he took her life, but that Jephthah dedicated her to the Lord.

pr413   nn**3068**   qmv**6213**   pp,pnx   pp,pnl834   qpf**3318**

unto the LORD, do   to me according to that which hath proceeded out

pr4480/nn,pnx**6310**   ad310/pnl834   nn**3068**   qpf**6213**   pl,nn**5360**   pp,pnx

of*thy*mouth; forasmuch as the LORD hath taken vengeance for thee

pr4480/pl,qpta,pnx341   pr4480/pl,cs,nn**1121**   nn**5983**

of*thine*enemies, *even* of*the*children of Ammon.

                    wcs,qmf**559**   pr413   nn,pnx**1**   df,pndm2088   df,nn**1697**   nimf**6213**   pp,pnx

37 And she said unto her father, Let this thing be done for me:

himv**7503**/pr,pnx4480   du,nu8147   pl,nn**2320**   wcj,qcj**1980**   wcs,qpf**3381**   pr5921   df,pl,nn**2022**

let*me*alone two months, that I may go up and down upon the mountains, and

wcj,qmf1058/pr5921   pl,nn,pnx**1331**   pnp595   wcj,pl,nn,pnx**7464**

bewail my virginity, I and my fellows.

                wcs,qmf**559**   qmv**1980**   wcs,qmf**7971**/pnx(853)   du,cs,nu8147   pl,nn**2320**   pnp1931

38 And he said, Go. And he sent*her*away *for* two months: and she

wcs,qmf**1980**   wcj,pl,nn,pnx**7464**   wcs,qmf1058/pr5921   pl,nn,pnx**1331**   pr5921   df,pl,nn**2022**

went with her companions, and bewailed her virginity upon the mountains.

            wcs,qmf**1961**   pr4480/cs,nn7093   du,nu8147   pl,nn**2320**   wcs,qmf**7725**   pr413

39 And it*came*to*pass at*the*end of two months, that she returned unto her

nn,pnx**1**   wcs,qmf**6213**   pp,pnx   (853)   nn,pnx**5088**   pnl834   qpf**5087**

father, who did with her *according* to his vow which he had vowed: and

wcj,pnp1931   qpf**3045**   ptn**3808**   nn**376**   wcs,qmf**1961**   nn**2706**   pp,nn3478

she knew no man. And it was a custom in Israel,

            pl,cs,nn1323   nn3478   qmf**1980** pr4480/pl,nn3117/pl,nn,lh3117   pp,pinc8567   pp,cs,nn1323

40 *That* the daughters of Israel went   yearly   to lament the daughter of

nn3316   df,nn1569   cs,nu702 pl,nn3117   dfp,nn8141.

Jephthah the Gileadite four days in a year

Jephthah Defeats Ephraim

12

            cs,nn**376**   nn669   wcs,nimf6817   wcs,qmf**5674**

And the men of Ephraim gathered*themselves*together, and went

            nn,lh6828   wcs,qmf**559**   pp,nn3316   ad4069   qpf**5674**

northward, and said unto Jephthah, Wherefore passedst*thou*over to

pp,ninc3898   pp,pl,cs,nn**1121**   nn5983   ptn3808   qpf7121 wcj,pp,pnx   pp,qnc1980 pr,pnx5973

fight against the children of Ammon, and didst not call us to go with

            qmf**8313**   nn,pnx**1004** pr,pnx5921   dfp,nn784

thee? we will burn thine house upon thee with fire.

            nn3316   wcs,qmf**559** pr,pnx413   pnp589   wcj,nn,pnx**5971** qpf**1961** cs,nn376/nn**7379**/ad3966

2 And Jephthah said unto them, I and my people were at*great*strife

wcj,pl,cs,nn**1121**   nn5983   wcs,qmf**2199** pnx(853)   hipf**3467** pnx(853)

with the children of Ammon; and when I called   you, ye delivered   me

wcj,ptn**3808**   pr4480/nn,pnx**3027**

not out*of*their*hands.

                wcs,qmf**7200** cj3588   htpf**3467**   ptn,pnx369   wcs,qmf**7760**   nn,pnx**5315**

3 And when I saw that ye delivered *me* not, I put my life in my

pp,nn,pnx**3709**   wcs,qmf**5674**   pr413   pl,cs,nn**1121**   nn5983   nn3068 wcs,qmf,pnx**5414**

hands, and passed over against the children of Ammon, and the LORD delivered

                    pp,nn,pnx3027   wcj,pp,pnit4100   qpf5927   pr,pnx413   df,pndm2088 df,nn**3117**

them into my hand: wherefore then are ye come up unto me this day, to

pp,ninc3898   pp,pnx

fight against me?

            nn3316   wcs,qmf**6908**   (853) cs,nn3605   pl,cs,nn**376**   nn1568   wcs,nimf3898

4 Then Jephthah gathered together   all the men of Gilead, and fought

pr854   nn669   pl,cs,nn**376**   nn1568   wcs,himf**5221** (853)   nn669   cj3588   qpf559 pnp859

with Ephraim: and the men of Gilead smote   Ephraim, because they said, Ye

nn1568   pl,cs,nn6412   nn669   pp,cs,nn8432   nn669   pp,cs,nn8432
Gileadites *are* fugitives of Ephraim among the Ephraimites, *and* among the

nn4519
Manassites.

nn1568   wcs,qmf3920 (853)   pl,cs,nn4569   df,nn3383   pp,nn669
5 And the Gileadites took   the passages of Jordan before the Ephraimites:

wcj,qpf1961   cj3588   nn669   pl,cs,nn6412   qmf559
and it was *so*, that when those Ephraimites which were escaped said, Let me

qcj5674   pl,cs,nn376   nn1568   wcs,qmf559   pp,pnx   pnp859   he,aj673
go over; that the men of Gilead said unto him, *Art* thou an Ephraimite? If he

wcs,qmf559 ptn3808
said, Nay;

wcs,qmf559   pp,pnx   qmv559 pte4994   nn7641   wcs,qmf559   nn5451
6 Then said they unto him, Say now Shibboleth: and he said Sibboleth: for

wcj,ptn3808   himf3559   pp,pinc1696   aj3651   wcs,qmf270 pnx(853)
he could not frame to pronounce *it* right. Then they took   him, and

wcs,qmf,pnx7819   pr413   pl,cs,nn4569   df,nn3383   wcs,qmf5307   df,pndm1931 dfp,nn6256
slew him at the passages of Jordan: and there fell at that time

pr4480/nn669   pl,nu705   wcj,du,nu8147   nu505
of*the*Ephraimites forty and two thousand.

nn3316   wcs,qmf8199 (853)   nn3478 nu8337 pl,nn8141   wcs,qmf4191   nn3316
7 And Jephthah judged   Israel six years. Then died Jephthah the

df,nn1569   wcs,nimf6912   pp,pl,cs,nn5892   nn1568
Gileadite, and was buried in *one of* the cities of Gilead.

pr,pnx310   nn78   pr4480/nn1035   wcs,qmf8199 (853)   nn3478
8 And after him Ibzan of Bethlehem judged   Israel.

Ibzan

pp,pnx wcs,qmf1961 nu7970 pl,nn1121   wcj,nu7970   pl,nn1323   pipf7971 df,nn,lh2351
9 And he had thirty sons, and thirty daughters, *whom* he sent abroad, and

hipf935   wcj,nu7970   pl,nn1323   pr4480   df,nn2351   pp,pl,nn,pnx1121   wcs,qmf8199 (853)   nn3478
took in thirty daughters from abroad for his sons. And he judged   Israel

nu7651   pl,nn8141
seven years.

wcs,qmf4191   nn78   wcs,nimf6912   pp,nn1035
10 Then died Ibzan, and was buried at Bethlehem.

Elon

pr,pnx310   nn356   df,nn2075   wcs,qmf8199 (853)   nn3478   wcs,qmf8199 (853)
11 And after him Elon, a Zebulonite, judged   Israel; and he judged

nn3478 nu6235 pl,nn8141
Israel ten years.

nn356   df,nn2075   wcs,qmf4191   wcs,nimf6912   pp,nn357   pp,cs,nn776
12 And Elon the Zebulonite died, and was buried in Aijalon in the country of

nn2075
Zebulun.

12:6 This was a linguistic test given in order to tell whether or not a man was an Ephraimite. The word "Shibboleth" meant "a stream in flood time." However, an Ephraimite, because of the nature of his dialect, said "Sibboleth," substituting the "s" sound for the "sh" sound. Even though he denied being an Ephraimite his tongue would betray him, resulting in his certain death.

Abdon

^{pr,pnx310} ⁿⁿ⁵⁶⁵⁸ ^{cs,nn1121} ⁿⁿ¹⁹⁸⁵ ^{df,nn6553} ^{wcs,qmf8199} (853) ⁿⁿ³⁴⁷⁸
13 And after him Abdon the son of Hillel, a Pirathonite, judged Israel.

^{pp,pnx} ^{wcs,qmf1961} ^{pl,nu705} ^{pl,nn1121} ^{wcj,nu7970} ^{pl,cs,nn1121/pl,nn1121} ^{pl,qpta7392} ^{pr5921}
14 And he had forty sons and thirty nephews, that rode on

^{pl,nu7657} ^{pl,nn5895} ^{wcs,qmf8199} (853) ⁿⁿ³⁴⁷⁸ ^{nu8083} ^{pl,nn8141}
threescore*and*ten ass colts: and he judged Israel eight years.

ⁿⁿ⁵⁶⁵⁸ ^{cs,nn1121} ⁿⁿ¹⁹⁸⁵ ^{df,nn6553} ^{wcs,qmf4191} ^{wcs,nimf6912}
15 And Abdon the son of Hillel the Pirathonite died, and was buried in

^{pp,nn6552} ^{pp,cs,nn776} ⁿⁿ⁶⁶⁹ ^{pp,cs,nn2022} ^{df,nn6003}
Pirathon in the land of Ephraim, in the mount of the Amalekites.

Samson's Birth

^{pl,cs,nn1121} ⁿⁿ³⁴⁷⁸ ^{pp,qnc6213} ^{df,nn7451} ^{wcs,himf3254} ^{pp,du,cs,nn5869}
13 ☞ And the children of Israel did evil again in the sight of

ⁿⁿ³⁰⁶⁸ ⁿⁿ³⁰⁶⁸ ^{wcs,qmf,pnx5414} ^{pp,cs,nn3027}
the LORD; and the LORD delivered them into the hand of the

ⁿⁿ⁶⁴³⁰ ^{pl,nu705} ⁿⁿ⁸¹⁴¹
Philistines forty years.

^{wcs,qmf1961} ^{nu259} ⁿⁿ³⁷⁶ ^{pr4480/nn6681} ^{pr4480/cs,nn4940} ^{df,nn1839}
2 And there was a certain man of Zorah, of*the*family of the Danites,

^{wcj,nn,pnx8034} ⁿⁿ⁴⁴⁹⁵ ^{wcj,nn,pnx802} ^{aj6135} ^{qpf3205} ^{wcj,ptn3808}
whose name was Manoah; and his wife was barren, and bore not.

^{cs,nn4397} ⁿⁿ³⁰⁶⁸ ^{wcs,nimf7200} ^{pr413} ^{df,nn802} ^{wcs,qmf559} ^{pr,pnx413}
3 And the angel of the LORD appeared unto the woman, and said unto her,

^{ptdm2009} ^{pte4994} ^{pnp859} ^{aj6135} ^{qpf3205} ^{wcj,ptn3808} ^{wcj,qpf2029} ^{wcj,qpf3205}
Behold now, thou art barren, and bearest not: but thou shalt conceive, and bear

ⁿⁿ¹¹²¹
a son.

^{wcj,ad6258} ^{nimv8104} ^{pte4994} ^{qmf8354} ^{wcj,ptn408} ⁿⁿ³¹⁹⁶ ^{wcj,nn7941}
4 Now therefore beware, I*pray*thee, and drink not wine nor strong drink,

^{qmf398} ^{wcj,ptn408} ^{cs,nn3605} ^{aj2931}
and eat not any unclean thing:

^{cj3588} ^{ptdm,pnx2009} ^{aj2029} ^{wcj,cs,qpta3205} ⁿⁿ¹¹²¹ ^{ptn3808} ^{wcj,nn4177}
☞ 5 For, lo, thou shalt conceive, and bear a son; and no razor shall

^{qmf5927} ^{pr5921} ^{nn,pnx7218} ^{cj3588} ^{df,nn5288} ^{qmf1961} ^{cs,nn5139} ^{pl,nn430} ^{pr4480} ^{df,nn990}
come on his head: for the child shall be a Nazarite unto God from the womb:

^{wcj,pnp1931} ^{himf2490} ^{pp,hinc3467} (853) ⁿⁿ³⁴⁷⁸ ^{pr4480/cs,nn3027} ^{pl,nn6430}
and he shall begin to deliver Israel out*of*the*hand of the Philistines.

^{df,nn802} ^{wcs,qmf935} ^{wcs,qmf559} ^{pp,nn,pnx376} ^{pp,qnc559} ^{cs,nn376} ^{df,pl,nn430}
6 Then the woman came and told her husband, saying, A man of God

^{qpf935} ^{pr,pnx413} ^{wcj,nn,pnx4758} ^{pp,cs,nn4758} ^{cs,nn4397} ^{df,pl,nn430}
came unto me, and his countenance was like the countenance of an angel of God,

---

☞ **13:1** The Philistines were a group of people from the Aegean Sea area. Called "the sea people," they had been present in Canaan for centuries in small numbers (Gen. 20, 21, 26). In the thirteenth century B.C., a large number of these "sea people" attempted to conquer Egypt, but were defeated and afterward settled on the coast of Canaan. Even Samson's victory against them (Judg. 16:30) was not the final time that the Philistines were mentioned in regard to Israel. They were evidently still a plague to Israel even in David's day (2 Sam. 5:17–25).

☞ **13:5** See the note on Numbers 6:2–21, on the Nazarite vow.

ad3966   nipt**3372**   qpf,pnx**7592**   wcj,ptn**3808** ad335/pr4480/pndm2088 pnp1931   ptn**3808** hipf**5046**   pp,pnx

very terrible: but I asked him   not   whence   he *was*, neither told he me

wcj(853)   nn,pnx**8034**

his name:

wcs,qmf**559**   pp,pnx   ptdm,pnx2009   aj2029   wcj,cs,qpta3205   nn**1121**

7 But he   said   unto me, Behold, thou shalt conceive, and   bear   a son; and

wcj,ad6258   qmf8354 ptn408 nn3196   wcj,nn**7941**   wcj,ptn408 qmf398 cs,nn3605   nn**2932**   cj3588

now   drink no wine nor strong drink, neither eat   any   unclean *thing*: for the

df,nn5288   qmf**1961**   cs,nn**5139** pl,nn**430** pr4480 df,nn**990** pr5704   cs,nn**3117**   nn,pnx**4194**

child shall   be   a Nazarite to God from the womb to   the day of his death.

nn4495   wcs,qmf**6279**/pr413   nn**3068**   wcs,qmf**559** pte994   nn,pnx**136**   cs,nn**376**

8 Then Manoah entreated the Lᴏʀᴅ, and said,   O my Lord, let the man of

df,pl,nn**430** pnl834   qpf7971   qmf935 ad5750 (pte**4994**) pr,pnx413   wcj,himf,pnx**3384** pnid4100

God which thou didst send come again   unto us, and   teach   us what we

qmf**6213**   dfp,nn**5288**   df,pupt3205

shall do unto the child that shall be born.

df,pl,nn**430**   wcs,qmf**8085**   pp,cs,nn6963   nn4495   cs,nn**4397**   df,pl,nn**430** wcs,qmf935

9 And God hearkened to the voice of Manoah; and the angel of God   came

ad5750   pr413   df,nn**802**   wcj,pnp1931 qpta**3427**   dfp,nn**7704**   wcj,nn4495   nn,pnx**376**

again unto the woman as   she   sat in the field: but Manoah her husband

ptn369   pr,pnx5973

was not with her.

df,nn**802**   wcs,pimf4116   wcs,qmf7323   wcs,himf**5046**   pp,nn,pnx**376**

10 And the woman made haste, and   ran,   and showed her husband, and

wcs,qmf**559** pr,pnx413   ptdm2009   df,nn**376**   nipf**7200** pr,pnx413   pnl834 qpf935 pr,pnx413

said   unto him, Behold, the man hath appeared unto me, that came unto me the

dfp,nn**3117**

other day.

nn4495   wcs,qmf**6965**   wcs,qmf**1980** pr310   nn,pnx**802**   wcs,qmf935 pr413   df,nn**376**

11 And Manoah arose, and   went after his wife, and came to the man, and

wcs,qmf**559**   pp,pnx   he,pnp859   df,nn**376** pnl834 pipf**1696**   pr413   df,nn**802**   wcs,qmf**559**

said unto him, *Art* thou the man that spakest unto the woman? And he   said,

pnp589

I *am.*

nn4495   wcs,qmf**559** ad6258   pl,nn,pnx**1697**   qmf935   pnit4100

12 And Manoah said,   Now let thy   words come*to*pass. How shall we

qmf**1961**/cs,nn**4941**   df,nn**5288**   wcj,nn,pnx**4639**

order   the child, and *how* shall we   do   unto him?

cs,nn**4397**   nn**3068** wcs,qmf**559** pr413   nn4495   pr4480/cs,nn3605 pnl834   qpf559 pr413

13 And the angel of the Lᴏʀᴅ said   unto Manoah,   Of all   that I said unto

df,nn**802**   nimf**8104**

the woman let her beware.

ptn**3808** qmf398 pr4480/nn3605   pnl834   qmf3318   pr4480/cs,nn1612 (df,nn3196) ptn408

14 She may not eat of any *thing* that cometh of*the*vine,   neither let

qmf8354 wcj,nn3196   wcj,nn**7941**   ptn408 qmf398 wcj,cs,nn3605   nn**2932**   nn3605 pnl834

her drink wine or strong drink, nor   eat   any   unclean *thing*: all   that I

pipf,pnx**6680**   qmf**8104**

commanded her let her observe.

nn4495   wcs,qmf**559** pr413   cs,nn**4397**   nn**3068**   pte**4994**   qcj6113

15 And Manoah said unto the angel of the Lᴏʀᴅ, I*pray*thee, let us detain

pnx(853)   wcj,qmf**6213**   cs,nn1423/pl,nn5795 pp,pl,nn,pnx**6440**

thee, until we shall have made ready a   kid   for   thee.

cs,nn**4397**   nn**3068** wcs,qmf**559** pr413   nn4495   cj518   qmf,pnx6113

16 And the angel of the Lᴏʀᴅ said unto Manoah, Though thou detain me, I

ptn**3808** qmf398   pp,nn,pnx**3899**   wcj,cj518   qmf**6213**   nn**5930**

will not eat of thy bread: and   if   thou wilt offer a burnt offering, thou must

himf,pnx**5927**   pp,nn**3068**   cj**3588**   nn**4495**   qpf**3045** ptn**3808** cj**3588** pnp**1931**   cs,nn**4397**

offer it unto the LORD. For Manoah knew not that he *was* an angel of the

nn**3068**

LORD.

nn**4495**   wcs,qmf**559** pr**413**   cs,nn**4397**   nn**3068**   pnit**4310**   nn,pnx**8034**

17 And Manoah said unto the angel of the LORD, What *is* thy name, that

cj**3588**   nn,pnx**1697**   qmf**935**   wcs,pipf,pnx**3513**

when thy sayings come*to*pass we may do*thee*honor?

cs,nn**4397**   nn**3068** wcs,qmf**559**   pp,pnx   pp,pnit**4100**   qmf**7592**   pndm**2088**

☞ 18 And the angel of the LORD said unto him, Why askest thou thus after

pp,nn,pnx**8034**   wcj,pnp**1931**   aj**6383**

my name, seeing it *is* secret?

nn**4495**   wcs,qmf**3947** (853)   cs,nn**1423**/df,pl,nn**5795** wcj,pr**854**   df,nn**4503**   wcs,himf**5927**

19 So Manoah took a kid with a meat offering, and offered *it*

pr**5921**   df,nn**6697**   pp,nn**3068**   pp,qnc**6213**   wcj,hipt**6381**   wcj,nn**4495**

upon a rock unto the LORD: and *the angel* did wondrously; and Manoah and his

wcj,nn,pnx**802**   pl,qpta**7200**

wife looked on.

wcs,qmf**1961**   df,nn**3851**   pp,qnc**5927**   df,du,nn,lh**8064** pr**4480**/pr**5921**

20 For it*came*to*pass, when the flame went up toward heaven from off the

df,nn**4196**   cs,nn**4397**   nn**3068**   wcs,qmf**5927**   pp,cs,nn**3851**   df,nn**4196**   wcj,nn**4495**

altar, that the angel of the LORD ascended in the flame of the altar. And Manoah

wcj,nn,pnx**802**   pl,qpta**7200**   wcs,qmf**5307** pr**5921**   pl,nn,pnx**6440**   nn,lh**776**

and his wife looked on *it*, and fell on their faces to the ground.

cs,nn**4397**   nn**3068**   wcj,ptn**3808** (ad**5750**) qpf**3254** pp,ninc**7200** pr**413**   nn**4495**

21 But the angel of the LORD did no more appear to Manoah and

wcj,pr**413**   nn,pnx**802** ad**227**   nn**4495**   qpf**3045** cj**3588** pnp**1931**   cs,nn**4397**   nn**3068**

to his wife. Then Manoah knew that he *was* an angel of the LORD.

nn**4495**   wcs,qmf**559** pr**413**   nn,pnx**802**   qna**4191**/qmf**4191**   cj**3588**

☞ 22 And Manoah said unto his wife, We shall surely die, because we have

qpf**7200** pl,nn**430**

seen God.

nn,pnx**802** wcs,qmf**559**   pp,pnx   cj**3863**   nn**3068**   qpf**2654**   pp,hinc,pnx**4191**

23 But his wife said unto him, If the LORD were pleased to kill us,

ptn**3808**   qpf**3947**   nn**5930**   wcj,nn**4503**   pr**4480**/nn,pnx**3027**

he would not have received a burnt offering and a meat offering at*our*hands,

wcj,ptn**3808**   hipf,pnx**7200**   (853) cs,nn**3605** pndm**428**   ptn**3808**

neither would he have showed us all these *things*, nor would as at this

wcj,dfp,nn**6256**   hipf,pnx**8085**   pp,pndm**2063**

time have told us *such things* as these.

df,nn**802**   wcs,qmf**3205**   nn**1121**   wcs,qmf**7121** (853)   nn,pnx**8034**   nn**8123**

☞ 24 And the woman bore a son, and called his name Samson: and the

df,nn**5288** wcs,qmf**1431**   nn**3068** wcs,pimf,pnx**1288**

child grew, and the LORD blessed him.

☞ **13:18, 19** The Hebrew word translated "secret" (*pālī'* [6383]) should be translated "wonderful." This is the adjectival form of the noun *pele'* (6382) which occurs in the Messianic prophecy in Isaiah 9:6, where it is translated "Wonderful." This, plus the angel's willingness to accept offerings, indicate that this was a Christophany, an appearance of Jesus Christ before His incarnation.

☞ **13:22** See the note on Exodus 23:20–23.

☞ **13:24** Samson was a Danite, living adjacent to the Philistines. He was selected before birth as the one who would begin to deliver Israel from the Philistines (Judg. 13:5). God gave him superhuman strength to achieve this, but Samson's whole life was filled with compromise in his repeated refusal to control his sensual desires and whims. His physical blinding by the Philistines (Judg. 16:21) seemingly brought about the opening of his spiritual eyes; for he gave his life for his people, and is included with the "heroes of faith" in the New Testament (Heb. 11:32). His last act of killing the Philistines' leaders did more to defeat them than all his earlier conquests combined (Judg. 16:30).

cs,nn7307   nn3068   wcs,himf2490   pp,qnc,pnx6470   pp,cs,nn4264

25 And the Spirit of the LORD began to move him at times in the camp of

nn1835   pr996   nn6881   wcj(pr996)   nn847

Dan between Zorah and   Eshtaol.

Samson's First Wife

nn8123   wcs,qmf3381   nn,lh8553   wcs,qmf7200   nn802   pp,nn,lh8553

14 And Samson went down to Timnath, and saw a woman in Timnath

pr4480/pl,cs,nn1323   pl,nn6430

of*the*daughters of the Philistines.

wcs,qmf5927   wcs,himf5046   pp,nn,pnx1   wcj,pp,nn,pnx517   wcs,qmf559

2 And he came up, and told his father and his mother, and said, I have

qpf7200   nn802   pp,nn,lh8553   pr4480/pl,cs,nn1323   pl,nn6430   wcj,ad6258   qmv3947

seen a woman in Timnath of*the*daughters of the Philistines: now therefore get

pnx(853)   pp,pnx   pp,nn802

her for me to wife.

nn,pnx1   wcj,nn,pnx517   wcs,qmf559   pp,pnx   he,ptn369   nn802

☞ 3 Then his father and his mother said unto him, *Is there* never a woman

pp,pl,cs,nn1323   pl,nn,pnx251   wcj,pp,cs,nn3605   nn,pnx5971   cj3588   pnp859   qpta1980

among the daughters of thy brethren, or among all my people, that thou goest

pp,qnc3947   nn802   df,aj6189   pr4480/pl,nn6430   nn8123   wcs,qmf559   pr413

to take a wife of the uncircumcised Philistines? And Samson said unto his

nn,pnx1   qmv3947 pnx(853)   pp,pnx   cj3588   pnp1931   qpf3474/pp,du,nn,pnx5869

father, Get her for me; for she pleaseth*me*well.

wcj,nn,pnx1   wcj,nn,pnx517   qpf3045   ptn3808   cj3588   pnp1931   pr4480/nn3068   cj3588

4 But his father and his mother knew not that it *was* of*the*LORD, that

pnp1931   piptl245   nn8385   pr4480/pl,nn6430   df,pndm1931   wcj,dfp,nn6256

he sought an occasion against*the*Philistines: for at that time the

pl,nn6430   pl,qpta4910   pp,nn3478

Philistines had dominion over Israel.

wcs,qmf3381/nn8123   wcj,nn,pnx1   wcj,nn,pnx517   nn,lh8553

5 Then went*Samson*down, and his father and his mother, to Timnath, and

wcs,qmf935   pr5704   pl,cs,nn3754   nn,lh8553   wcj,ptdm2009   cs,nn3715   pl,nn738   qpta7580   pp,qnc,pnx7125

came to the vineyards of Timnath: and, behold, a young lion roared against

him.

cs,nn7307   nn3068   wcs,qmf6743   pr,pnx5921   wcs,pimf,pnx8156

6 And the Spirit of the LORD came mightily upon him, and he rent him

pp,pinc8156   df,nn1423   wcj,pnid3972/ptn369   pp,nn,pnx3027   hipf5046

as he would have rent a kid, and *he had* nothing in his hand: but he told

wcj,ptn3808   pp,nn,pnx1   wcj,pp,nn,pnx517   (853)   pnl834   qpf6213

not his father or his mother what he had done.

wcs,qmf3381   wcs,pimf1696   dfp,nn802

7 And he went down, and talked with the woman; and she

wcs,qmf3474/pp,du,cs,nn5869/nn8123

pleased*Samson*well.

☞ **14:3, 4** Mixed marriages by Israelites with these other races were forbidden (Deut. 7:3). Samson's parents were right to oppose his marriage to a heathen woman from the Philistine people who constantly oppressed Israel. It should not be understood here that God forced Samson into this marriage, but that he made his own decision. Though it was not right, God used it to accomplish His will in spite of the lack of wisdom on Samson's part. It proved to be the crucial link in the liberation of Israel from the Philistines (Judg. 15:1-8).

^{pr4480/pl,nn3117}　　　^{wcs,qmf7725}　　^{pp,qnc,pnx3947}　　　　　^{wcs,qmf5493}　　^{pp,qnc7200}

8 And after*a*time he returned to　　take　　her, and he turned aside to　　see

⁽⁸⁵³⁾　^{cs,nn4658}　^{df,nn738}　^{wcj,ptdm2009}　　　　^{cs,nn5712}　　^{pl,nn1682}　^{wcj,nn1706}

the carcass of the lion: and, behold, *there was* a swarm of bees and honey in

^{pp,cs,nn1472}　　　^{df,nn738}

the carcass of the lion.

^{wcs,qmf,pnx7287}　　　　^{pr413}　　^{du,nn,pnx3709}　　^{wcs,qmf1980/qna1980}　^{wcj,qna398}　　　^{wcs,qmf1980}

9 And he　　took　　thereof in his hands, and　　went on　　eating, and　came

^{pr413}　　^{nn,pnx1}　^{wcj(pr413)}　^{nn,pnx517}　　^{wcs,qmf5414}　^{pp,pnx}　　　　　^{wcs,qmf398}

to his father and　　　mother, and he　gave　them, and they did　eat:　but he

^{hipf5046} ^{wcj,ptn3808} ^{pp,pnx} ^{cj3588}　^{qpf7287}　^{df,nn1706}　^{pr4480/cs,nn1472}　^{df,nn738}

told　not　them that he had taken the honey out*of*the*carcass of the lion.

^{nn,pnx1}　^{wcs,qmf3381}　^{pr413}　　^{df,nn802}　　ⁿⁿ⁸¹²³ ^{wcs,qmf6213} ^{ad8033}　ⁿⁿ⁴⁹⁶⁰

10 So his father went down unto the woman: and Samson　made　there a feast;

^{cj3588 ad3651}　　^{df,pl,nn970}　^{qmf6213}

for　so used the young men to do.

^{wcs,qmf1961}　　　　　^{pp,qnc,pnx7200 pnx(853)}　　　　^{wcs,qmf3947 nu7970}

11 And it*came*to*pass, when they　　saw　　　him, that they brought thirty

^{pl,nn4828}　　^{wcs,qmf1961 pr,pnx854}

companions to　be　with him.

ⁿⁿ⁸¹²³　^{wcs,qmf559}　^{pp,pnx}　　　^{pte4994}　^{qmf2330}　　ⁿⁿ²⁴²⁰　^{pp,pnx}　^{cj518}

12 And Samson　said　unto them, I will now put forth a riddle unto you: if

^{hina5046/himf5046}　　^{pnx(853)}　　^{pp,pnx}　　　^{cs,nu7651 pl,cs,nn3117}　^{df,nn4960}

ye can certainly declare　　　　it　me within the　seven　days　of the feast, and

^{wcs,qpf4672}　　　　　^{wcs,qpf5414 pp,pnx} ^{nu7970}　^{pl,nn5466}　^{wcj,nu7970 pl,cs,nn2487}　^{pl,nn899}

find*it*out, then I will　give　you thirty sheets and　thirty change of garments:

^{wcj,cj518}　　^{qmf3201/ptn3808} ^{pp,hinc5046}　^{pp,pnx}　　　　^{pnp859 wcs,qpf5414 pp,pnx} ^{nu7970}　^{pl,nn5466}

13 But　if　ye　cannot　declare *it* me, then shall ye　　give　me thirty sheets

^{wcj,nu7970 pl,cs,nn2487}　^{pl,nn899}　　^{wcs,qmf559}　^{pp,pnx}　　^{qmv2330}　　^{nn,pnx2420}

and thirty change of garments. And they　said　unto him, Put forth thy riddle, that

^{wcj,qmf,pnx8085}

we may　hear　it.

^{wcs,qmf559}　　^{pp,pnx}　　　^{pr4480/df,qpta398}　　^{qpf3318}　ⁿⁿ³⁹⁷⁸

14 And　he　said　unto them, Out*of*the*eater　came forth　meat,　and

^{wcj,pr4480/aj5794}　　^{qpf3318}　　　^{aj4966}　　　^{qpf3201 wcj,ptn3808}　^{cs,nu7969 pl,nn3117}

out*of*the*strong came forth sweetness. And they could　　not　in three　days

^{pp,hinc5046}　　^{df,nn2420}

expound the riddle.

^{wcs,qmf1961}　　　^{df,nuor7637}　^{dfp,nn3117}　　^{wcs,qmf559}　　ⁿⁿ⁸¹²³

15 And it*came*to*pass on the seventh　day,　that they　said　unto Samson's

^{pp,cs,nn802} ^{pimv6601} ⁽⁸⁵³⁾　^{nn,pnx376}　　　^{wcj,himf5046}　^{pp,pnx}　⁽⁸⁵³⁾　^{df,nn2420 cj6435}

wife, Entice　thy husband, that he may declare unto us　　the riddle, lest we

^{qmf8313 pnx(853)}　　^{wcj(853)}　　^{nn,pnx1} ^{cs,nn1004}　^{dfp,nn784}　　^{qpf7121} ^{pp,pnx}

burn　　thee and　　thy father's house with　fire: have ye called　us　to

^{he,pp,qnc,pnx3423}　　^{he,ptn3808}

take*that*we*have? *is it*　not　*so?*

ⁿⁿ⁸¹²³　^{cs,nn802 wcs,qmf1058} ^{pr,pnx5921}　　　^{wcs,qmf559}　　^{ad7535 qpf,pnx8130}

16 And Samson's wife　wept　before him, and　said, Thou dost but　hate

^{qpf,pnx157}　^{wcj,ptn3808}　　　^{qpf2330}　^{df,nn2420}　　^{pp,pl,cs,nn1121}

me, and lovest me　not:　thou hast put forth a riddle unto the children of my

^{nn,pnx5971}　　^{ptn3808 hipf5046} ^{wcj,pp,pnx}　　^{wcs,qmf559}　^{pp,pnx}　^{ptdm2009}　　^{ptn3808}

people, and hast not told *it* me.　And he　said　unto her, Behold, I have　not

^{hipf5046}　　^{pp,nn,pnx1}　^{wcj,pp,nn,pnx517}　　^{himf5046} ^{wcj,pp,pnx}

told *it* my father nor my　mother, and shall I tell *it* thee?

^{wcs,qmf1058 pr,pnx5921}　　^{cs,nu7651 df,pl,nn3117} ^{pnl834}　^{pp,pnx} ^{df,nn4960} ^{qpf1961}

17 And she　wept　before him the seven　days, while their feast lasted: and

wcs,qmf**1961**   df,nuor7637 dfp,nn**3117**   wcs,himf**5046** pp,pnx   cj3588   hipf,pnx6693
it*came*to*pass on the seventh day, that he told her, because she lay sore

                wcs,himf**5046** df,nn**2420**   pp,pl,cs,nn**1121**   nn,pnx**5971**
upon him: and she told the riddle to the children of her people.

                pl,cs,nn**376**   df,nn5892 wcs,qmf559   pp,pnx   df,nuor7637 dfp,nn**3117** pp,ad2962
18 And the men of the city said unto him on the seventh day before the

df,nn,lh2775   qmf935   pnit4100   aj4966   pr4480/nn1706   wcj,pnit4100   aj5794
sun went down, What is sweeter than honey? and what is stronger

pr4480/nn738   wcs,qmf**559**   pp,pnx   cj3884   qpf2790   pp,nn,pnx5697
than*a*lion? And he said unto them, If ye had not plowed with my heifer, ye

ptn3808   qpf4672   nn,pnx**2420**
had not found out my riddle.

            cs,nn**7307**   nn3068 wcs,qmf6743 pr,pnx5921   wcs,qmf3381
19 And the Spirit of the LORD came upon him, and he went down to

nn831   wcs,himf**5221** nu7970   nn376 pr,pnx4480   wcs,qmf3947 (853)   pl,nn,pnx2488
Ashkelon, and slew thirty men of them, and took their spoil, and

wcs,qmf**5414**   df,pl,nn2487   pp,pl,cs,hipt**5046**   df,nn**2420**   nn,pnx**639**
gave change*of*garments unto them which expounded the riddle. And his anger

    wcs,qmf**2734**   wcs,qmf**5927**   nn,pnx1   cs,nn**1004**
was kindled, and he went up to his father's house.

            nn8123   cs,nn**802** wcs,qmf**1961**   pp,nn,pnx4828   pnl834   pp,pnx
20 But Samson's wife was given to his companion, whom he had

    pipf7462
used*as*his*friend.

                    wcs,qmf**1961**   pr4480/pl,nn**3117**   pp,pl,cs,nn**3117**   pl,nn2406
15 But it*came*to*pass within*a*while after, in the time of wheat

        cs,nn7105   nn8123 wcs,qmf**6485** (853)   nn,pnx**802**   pp,cs,nn1423/pl,nn5795
harvest, that Samson visited his wife with a kid; and he

wcs,qmf**559**   qcj935   pr413   nn,pnx**802**   df,nn,lh2315   nn,pnx1   wcj,ptn**3808**
said, I will go in to my wife into the chamber. But her father would not

qpf,pnx**5414**   pp,qnc935
suffer him to go in.

        nn,pnx1   wcs,qmf**559**   qna559/qpf559   cj3588   qna8130/qpf,pnx8130
2 And her father said, I verily thought that thou hadst utterly hated her;

    wcs,qmf,pnx**5414**   pp,nn,pnx4828   he,ptn**3808**   df,aj6996 nn,pnx269 aj2896 pr,pnx4480
therefore I gave her to thy companion: is not her younger sister fairer than

qmf**1961** pp,pnx   pte**4994**   pr,pnx8478
she? take her, I*pray*thee, instead of her.

        nn8123   wcs,qmf**559**   pp,pnx   df,nn6471   nipf5352
3 And Samson said concerning them, Now shall I be*more*blameless

pr4480/pl,nn6430   cj3588   pnp589 qpta6213/pr,pnx5973   aj7451
than*the*Philistines, though I do them a displeasure.

        nn8123   wcs,qmf**1980**   wcs,qmf3920 cs,nu7969 pl,cs,nu3967 pl,nn7776   wcs,qmf3947   pl,nn3940
4 And Samson went and caught three hundred foxes, and took firebrands,

wcs,himf6437 nn2180 pr413 nn2180   wcs,qmf**7760** nu259   nn3940   dfp,nn**8432** pr996   du,cs,nu8147
and turned tail to tail, and put a firebrand in the midst between two

df,pl,nn2180
tails.

        wcs,himf1197   dfp,pl,nn3940   nn784   wcs,pimf7971
5 And when he had set the brands on fire, he let them go into the

pp,pl,cs,nn7054   pl,nn6430   wcs,himf1197   pr4480/nn1430   wcj,pr5704
standing corn of the Philistines, and burnt up both*the*shocks, and also the

nn7054   wcj,pr5704   cs,nn3754   nn2132
standing corn, with the vineyards and olives.

pl,nn6430   wcs,qmf559   pnit4310   qpf6213   pndm2063   wcs,qmf559
6 Then the Philistines said, Who hath done this? And they answered,

nn8123   cs,nn2860   df,nn8554   cj3588   qpf3947   (853)   nn,pnx802
Samson, the son-in-law of the Timnite, because he had taken   his wife, and

wcs,qmf,pnx5414   pp,nn,pnx4828   pl,nn6430   wcs,qmf5927   wcs,qmf8313 pnx(853)
given   her to his companion. And the Philistines came up, and burnt   her

wcj(853)   nn,pnx1   dfp,nn784
and   her father with fire.

nn8123   wcs,qmf559   pp,pnx   cj518   qmf6213 pp,pndm2063 cj3588/cj518
7 And Samson said unto them, Though ye have done this,   yet   will I

nipf5358   pp,pnx   wcj,ad310   qmf2308
be avenged of you, and after that I will cease.

wcs,himf5221 pnx(853)   nn7785 pr5921   nn3409   aj1419   nn4347
8 And he smote   them hip and thigh with a great slaughter: and he

wcs,qmf3381   wcs,qmf3427   pp,cs,nn5585   nn5553   nn5862
went down and dwelt in the   top   of the rock Etam.

Samson Kills a Thousand Philistines

pl,nn6430   wcs,qmf5927   wcs,qmf2583   pp,nn3063   wcs,nimf5203
9 Then the Philistines went up, and pitched in Judah, and spread themselves in

dfp,nn3896
Lehi.

cs,nn376   nn3063 wcs,qmf559 pp,pnit4100   qpf5927   pr,pnx5921
10 And the men of Judah said,   Why are ye come up against us? And they

wcs,qmf559   pp,qnc631 (853)   nn8123   qpf5927   pp,qnc6213 pp,pnx pp,pnl834
answered, To bind   Samson are we come up, to do to him as he hath

qpf6213   pp,pnx
done to us.

cs,nu7969   pl,nu505   nn376 pr4480/nn3063 wcs,qmf3381 pr413 cs,nn5585   nn5553 nn5862
11 Then three thousand men of Judah went to the top of the rock Etam,

wcs,qmf559   pp,nn8123   qpf3045   he,ptn3808 cj3588   pl,nn6430   pl,qpta4910   pp,pnx
and said to Samson, Knowest thou   not   that the Philistines are rulers over us?

wcj,pnit4100   pndm2063   qpf6213   pp,pnx   wcs,qmf559   pp,pnx   pp,pnl834
what is this that thou hast done unto us? And he said unto them, As they

qpf6213   pp,pnx   ad3651   qpf6213   pp,pnx
did unto me, so have I done unto them.

wcs,qmf559   pp,pnx   qpf3381   pp,qnc,pnx631
12 And they said unto him, We are come down to   bind   thee, that we

pp,qnc,pnx5414   pp,cs,nn3027   pl,nn6430   nn8123 wcs,qmf559   pp,pnx
may deliver thee into the hand of the Philistines. And Samson said unto them,

nimv7650   pp,pnx   cj6435   qmf6293   pp,pnx   pnp859
Swear unto me, that ye will not fall upon me yourselves.

wcs,qmf559   pp,pnx   pp,qnc559 ptn3808 cj3588   qna631/qmf,pnx631
13 And they spoke unto him, saying, No; but we will bind*thee*fast, and

wcs,qpf,pnx5414   pp,nn,pnx3027   wcj,hina4191/ptn3808/himf,pnx4191
deliver   thee into their   hand: but surely*we*will*not*kill thee. And they

wcs,q,mfpnx631   pp,du,nu8147 aj2319 pl,nn5688   wcs,himf,pnx5927   pr4480   df,nn5553
bound him with two   new cords, and brought*him*up from the rock.

pnp1931 qpta935 pr5704 nn3896   wcj,pl,nn6430   hipf7321 pp,qnc,pnx7125
☞ 14 And when he   came unto Lehi, the Philistines shouted against him: and

---

☞ **15:14, 15** The great statement of these verses is that the true source of Samson's great strength was not ultimately in his long hair or in abstaining from strong drink. It was provided by God to accomplish His will. For a contrasting look at Samson's life, see the note on Judges 16:17.

cs,nn7307   nn3068   wcs,qmf6743   pr,pnx5921   df,pl,nn5688 pnl834   pr5921

the Spirit of the LORD came mightily upon him, and the cords that *were* upon his

du,nn,pnx2220   wcs,qmf1961   dfp,pl,nn6593 pnl834   qpf1197   dfp,nn784   pl,nn,pnx612 wcs,nimf4549

arms   became as   flax   that was burnt with fire, and his bands loosed

pr4480/pr5921   du,nn,pnx3027

from off his hands.

wcs,qmf4672   aj2961   cs,nn3895   nn2543   wcs,qmf7971   nn,pnx3027

15 And he found a new jawbone of an ass, and put forth his hand, and

wcs,qmf,pnx3947   wcs,himf5221   nu505   nn376   pp,pnx

took   it, and slew a thousand men therewith.

nn8123   wcs,qmf559   pp,cs,nn3895   df,nn2543   cs,nn2565/du,nn2565

16 And Samson said, With the jawbone of an ass, heaps*upon*heaps, with

pp,cs,nn3895   df,nn2543   hipf5221   nu505   nn376

the   jaw   of an ass have I slain a thousand men.

wcs,qmf1961   pp,pinc,pnx3615   pp,pinc1696

17 And it*came*to*pass, when he had made*an*end of speaking, that he

wcs,himf7993   df,nn3895   pr4480/nn,pnx3027   wcs,qmf7121 df,pndm1931 dfp,nn4725   nn7437

cast away the jawbone out*of*his*hand, and called   that   place Ramath-lehi.

wcs,qmf6770/ad3966   wcs,qmf7121 pr413   nn3068   wcs,qmf559 pnp859

18 And he was*sore*athirst, and called on the LORD, and said, Thou hast

qpf5414   (853) df,pndm2063 df,aj1419   df,nn8668   pp,cs,nn3027   nn,pnx5650   wcj,ad6258

given   this   great deliverance into the hand of thy servant: and now shall I

qmf4191   dfp,nn6772   wcs,qpf5307   pp,cs,nn3027   df,aj6189

die for thirst, and   fall   into the hand   of the uncircumcised?

pl,nn430 wcs,qmf1234 (853)   df,nn4388   pnl834   dfp,nn3895   wcs,qmf3318

19 But God cleaved   a hollow place that *was* in the jaw, and there came

pl,nn4325   pr,pnx4480   wcs,qmf8354   nn,pnx7307 wcs,qmf7725   wcs,qmf2421

water therefrom; and when he had drunk, his spirit came again, and he revived:

pr5921/ad3651   qpf7121   nn,pnx8034   nn5875   pnl834   dfp,nn3896 pr5704 df,pndm2088

wherefore he called the name thereof En-hakkore, which *is* in Lehi unto   this

df,nn3117

day.

wcs,qmf8199 (853)   nn3478   pp,pl,cs,nn3117   pl,nn6430   pl,nu6242   nn8141

20 And he judged   Israel in the   days   of the Philistines twenty years.

Samson Removes Gaza's City Gates

wcs,qmf1980   nn8123   nn,lh5804   wcs,qmf7200 ad8033   nn802/qpta2181

16 Then went Samson to Gaza, and   saw   there a   harlot,   and

wcs,qmf935 pr,pnx413

went in unto her.

dfp,pl,nn5841   pp,qnc559   nn8123   qpf935   ad2008

2 *And it was told* the Gazites, saying, Samson is come hither. And they

wcs,qmf5437   wcs,qmf693   pp,pnx   cs,nn3605 df,nn3915   pp,cs,nn8179   df,nn5892

compassed *him* in, and laid wait for him all night in the gate of the city, and

wcs,htmf2790 cs,nn3605   df,nn3915   pp,qnc559   df,nn1242   pr5704   nn216

were quiet   all   the night, saying, In the morning, when it is day, we shall

wcj,qpf,pnx2026

kill   him.

nn8123   wcs,qmf7901 pr5704 cs,nn2677/df,nn3915   wcs,qmf6965   pp,cs,nn2677/df,nn3915   wcs,qmf270

3 And Samson lay   till midnight, and arose at midnight, and took

pp,pl,cs,nn1817   cs,nn8179   df,nn5892   wcj,pp,du,cs,nu8147 df,pl,nn4201   wcs,qmf,pnx5265

the doors of the gate of the city, and the   two   posts, and went away pr5973/df,nn1280   wcs,qmf7760   pr5921   pl,nn,pnx3802   wcs,himf,pnx5927

with them, bar*and*all, and   put   *them* upon his shoulders, and carried*them*up

pr413   cs,nn7218   df,nn2022 pnl834   pr5921/pl,cs,nn6440   nn2275

to the top of a hill that *is* before Hebron.

Samson and Delilah

wcs,qmf1961   ad310/ad3651   wcs,qmf157   nn802   pp,cs,nn5158

4 And it*came*to*pass afterward, that he loved a woman in the valley of

nn7796   wcj,nn,pnx8034   nn1807

Sorek, whose name *was* Delilah.

pl,cs,nn5633   pl,nn6430   wcs,qmf5927   pr,pnx413   wcs,qmf559   pp,pnx

5 And the lords of the Philistines came up unto her, and said unto her,

pimv6601   pnx(853)   wcj,qmv7200   dfp,pnid4100   aj1419   nn,pnx3581   wcj,dfp,pnid4100

Entice   him, and   see   wherein his great strength *lieth*, and by   what

qmf3201   pp,pnx   wcs,qpf,pnx631   pp,pinc,pnx6031

means we may prevail against him, that we may   bind   him to   afflict   him: and

wcj,pnp587   qmf5414 pp,pnx   nn376   nu505/wcj,nu3967   nn3701

we   will give thee every one of us eleven hundred *pieces* of silver.

nn1807   wcs,qmf559 pr413   nn8123   himv5046 pp,pnx   pte4994   dfp,pnid4100   aj1419

6 And Delilah said   to Samson, Tell me, I*pray*thee, wherein thy great

nn,pnx3581   wcj,dfp,pnid4100   nimf631   pp,pinc,pnx6031

strength *lieth*, and wherewith thou mightest be bound to   afflict   thee.

nn8123   wcs,qmf559 pr,pnx413   cj518   qmf,pnx631   pp,nu7651 aj3892 pl,nn3499

7 And Samson said   unto her, If they bind me with seven green withes

pnl834   ptn3808   pupf2717   wcj,qpf2470   wcj,qpf1961   pp,cs,nu259 df,nn120

that were never dried, then shall I be weak, and   be   as another man.

pl,cs,nn5633   pl,nn6430   wcs,himf5927   pp,pnx   nu7651 aj3892 pl,nn3499

8 Then the   lords   of the Philistines brought up to her seven green withes

pnl834   ptn3808   pupf2717   wcs,qmf,pnx631   pp,pnx

which had not been dried, and she   bound   him with them.

wcj,df,qpta693   qpta3427   pp,pnx   dfp,nn2315

9 Now *there were* men lying*in*wait, abiding with her in the chamber. And

wcs,qmf559 pr,pnx413   pl,nn6430   pr,pnx5921   nn8123   wcs,pimf5423 (853)

she   said   unto him, The Philistines *be* upon thee, Samson. And he   broke

df,pl,nn3499   pp,pnl834   cs,nn6616   df,nn5296   nimf5423   pp,hinc,pnx7306   nn784

the withes,   as   a thread of tow is broken when it toucheth the fire. So his

nn,pnx3581   wcj,ptn3808   nipf3045

strength was   not   known.

nn1807   wcs,qmf559 pr413   nn8123   ptdm2009   hipf2048 pp,pnx

10 And Delilah   said   unto Samson, Behold, thou hast mocked me, and

wcs,pimf1696/pr,pnx413   pl,nn3577   ad6258 himv5046 pp,pnx   pte4994   dfp,pnid4100

told   me lies: now   tell   me, I*pray*thee, wherewith thou mightest be

nimf631

bound.

wcs,qmf559 pr,pnx413   cj518   qna631/qmf,pnx631   aj2319 pp,pl,nn5688 pnl834 ptn3808

11 And he   said   unto her, If they bind*me*fast with new ropes that never

nipf6213/nn4399   (pp,pnx)   wcj,qpf2470   wcj,qpf1961   pp,cs,nu259 df,nn120

were occupied,   then shall I be weak, and   be   as another man.

nn1807   wcs,qmf3947 aj2319 pl,nn5688   wcs,qmf,pnx631   pp,pnx   wcs,qmf559

12 Delilah therefore   took   new ropes, and   bound   him therewith, and   said

pr,pnx413   pl,nn6430   pr,pnx5921   nn8123   wcj,df,qpta693

unto him, The Philistines *be* upon thee, Samson. And *there were* liers*in*wait

qpta3427   dfp,nn2315   wcs,pimf,pnx5423   pr4480/pr5921   du,nn,pnx2220   dfp,nn2339

abiding in the chamber. And he   broke   them from off his   arms   like a thread.

nn1807 wcs,qmf559 pr413 nn8123 pr5704/ad2008 hipf2048 pp,pnx
13 And Delilah said unto Samson, Hitherto thou hast mocked me, and

wcs,pimf1696/pr,pnx413 pl,nn3576 himv5046 pp,pnx dfp,pnid4100 nimf631 wcs,qmf559
told me lies: tell me wherewith thou mightest be bound. And he said

pr,pnx413 cj518 qmf707 (853) cs,nu7651 pl,cs,nn4253 nn,pnx7218 pr5973 df,nn4545
unto her, If thou weavest the seven locks of my head with the web.

wcs,qmf8628 dfp,nn3489 wcs,qmf559 pr,pnx413 pl,nn6430
14 And she fastened *it* with the pin, and said unto him, The Philistines *be*

pr,pnx5921 nn8123 wcs,qmf3364 pr4480/nn,pnx8142 wcs,qmf5265 (853)
upon thee, Samson. And he awaked out*of*his*sleep, and went away with the

cs,nn3489 df,nn708 wcj(853) df,nn4545
pin of the beam, and with the web.

wcs,qmf559 pr,pnx413 pnit349 qmf559 qpf,pnx157 wcj,ptn3808
15 And she said unto him, How canst thou say, I love thee, when thine

wcj,nn,pnx3820 ptn369 pr,pnx854 hipf2048 pp,pnx nu7969 pl,nn6471 wcj,ptn3808
heart *is* not with me? thou hast mocked me these three times, and hast not

hipf5046 pp,pnx dfp,pnid4100 aj1419 nn,pnx3581
told me wherein thy great strength *lieth.*

wcs,qmf1961 cj3588 hipf6693 pp,pnx cs,nn3605/df,pl,nn3117 pp,pl,nn,pnx1697
16 And it*came*to*pass, when she pressed him daily with her words,

wcs,pimf,pnx509 nn,pnx5315 wcs,qmf7114 pp,qnc4191
and urged him, *so* that his soul was vexed unto death;

wcs,himf5046 pp,pnx (853) cs,nn3605 nn,pnx3820 wcs,qmf559 pp,pnx
17 That he told her all his heart, and said unto her, There hath

ptn3808 qpf5927 nn4177 pr5921 nn,pnx7218 cj3588 pnp589 cs,nn5139 pl,nn430
not come a razor upon mine head; for I *have been* a Nazarite unto God from

nn,pnx517 pr4480/cs,nn990 cj518 pupf1548 nn,pnx3581 wcj,qpf5493 pr,pnx4480
my mother's womb: if I be shaven, then my strength will go from me, and

wcj,qpf2470 wcj,qpf1961 pp,cs,nn3605 df,nn120
I shall become weak, and be like any *other* man.

nn1807 wcs,qmf7200 cj3588 hipf5046 pp,pnx (853) cs,nn3605 nn,pnx3820
18 And when Delilah saw that he had told her all his heart, she

wcs,qmf7971 wcs,qmf7121 pp,pl,cs,nn5633 pl,nn6430 pp,qnc559 qmv5927 df,nn6471
sent and called for the lords of the Philistines, saying, Come up this once,

cj3588 hipf5046 pp,pnx (853) cs,nn3605 nn,pnx3820 pl,cs,nn5633 pl,nn6430
for he hath showed me all his heart. Then the lords of the Philistines

wcj,qpf5927 pr,pnx413 wcs,himf5927 df,nn3701 pp,nn,pnx3027
came up unto her, and brought money in their hand.

wcs,pimf,pnx3462 pr5921 du,nn,pnx1290 wcs,qmf7121 dfp,nn376
19 And she made him sleep upon her knees; and she called for a man,

wcs,pimf1548 (853) cs,nu7651 pl,cs,nn4253 nn,pnx7218 wcs,himf2490
and she caused him to shave off the seven locks of his head; and she began

pp,pinc,pnx6031 nn,pnx3581 wcs,qmf5493 pr4480/pr,pnx5921
to afflict him, and his strength went from him.

wcs,qmf559 pl,nn6430 pr,pnx5921 nn8123 wcs,qmf3364
20 And she said, The Philistines *be* upon thee, Samson. And he awoke

pr4480/nn,pnx8142 wcs,qmf559 qmf3318 pp,nn6471/pp,nn6471
out*of*his*sleep, and said, I will go out as at other*times*before, and

---

16:13 The "web" mentioned here was undoubtedly the cloth which Delilah was weaving in a loom. The pin was the object with which the braided locks were fastened to the web. She probably wove Samson's hair into the cloth.

16:17 Samson's admission to Delilah here should be interpreted then as a denial of that trust and a breaking of his covenant, the Nazarite vow, for which God left him (Judg. 16:20). However, his strength returned one more time, allowing him to decimate the Philistine leaders. This came about only after he made a statement of repentance and admitted that God was the true source of his strength (Judg. 16:28).

wcj,nimf5287   wcj,pnp1931   qpf3045   ptn3808 cj3588   nn3068   qpf5493   pr4480/pr,pnx5921

shake myself. And   he   knew not that the LORD was departed   from   him.

pl,nn6430   wcs,qmf,pnx270   wcs,pimf5365 (853)   du,nn,pnx5869

21 But   the   Philistines   took   him, and   put out   his   eyes,   and

wcs,himf3381/pnx(853)   nn,lh5804   wcs,qmf,pnx631   wcs,qmf1961

brought*him*down to Gaza, and   bound   him with fetters*of*brass; and he   did

qpta2912   df,pl,nn615   pp,cs,nn1004

grind in the prison house.

cs,nn8181   nn,pnx7218 wcs,himf2490   pp,pinc6779   pp,pnl834   pupf1548

22 Howbeit the   hair   of his head   began   to grow   again   after he was shaven.

Samson's Death

wcj,pl,cs,nn5633   pl,nn6430   nipf622   pp,qnc2076

🗝 23 Then the   lords   of the Philistines gathered*them*together for to   offer   a

aj1419   nn2077   pp,nn1712   pl,nn,pnx430   wcj,pp,nn8057   wcs,qmf559   pl,nn,pnx430

great sacrifice unto Dagon their   god,   and to rejoice: for they said, Our   god

qpf5414   (853)   nn8123   pl,qpta,pnx341   pp,nn,pnx3027

hath delivered   Samson our   enemy   into our   hand.

df,nn5971   wcs,qmf7200 pnx(853)   wcs,pimf1984 (853)   pl,nn,pnx430 cj3588

24 And when the people   saw   him, they praised   their   god: for

qpf559   pl,nn,pnx430   qpf5414   pp,nn,pnx3027 (853)   qpta,pnx341   wcj(853)

they said, Our   god   hath delivered into our   hands   our enemy, and   the

hipt2717   nn,pnx776 wcj,pnl834 hipf7235/(853)/pl,nn,pnx2491

destroyer of our country, which   slew   many   of us.

wcs,qmf1961   cj3588   nn,pnx3820   qnc2896   wcs,qmf559 qmv7121

25 And it*came*to*pass, when their hearts were merry, that they   said,   Call

pp,nn8123   wcs,pimf7832/pp,pnx   wcs,qmf7121   pp,nn8123

for   Samson, that   he   may   make*us*sport. And   they   called   for   Samson

pr4480/cs,nn1004/df,nn615   wcs,pimf6711/pp,pl,nn,pnx6440   wcs,himf5975 pnx(853)

out*of*the*prison*house; and   he   made*them*sport: and they   set   him

pr996   df,pl,nn5982

between the pillars.

nn8123   wcs,qmf559   pr413   df,nn5288   df,hipt2388   pp,nn,pnx3027 himv5117

26 And Samson   said   unto the   lad   that   held   him by the   hand,   Suffer

pnx(853)   wcj,himv,pnx4184 (853)   df,pl,nn5982 pnl834/pr,pnx5921   df,nn1004   nipt3559

me that I may   feel   the pillars whereupon the house standeth, that I

wcj,nimf8172 pr,pnx5921

may   lean   upon them.

wcj,df,nn1004   qpf4390   df,pl,nn376   wcj,df,pl,nn802   cs,nn3605   pl,cs,nn5633

27 Now the   house   was full of   men and women; and   all   the   lords of the

pl,nn6430   wcj,ad,lh8033   wcj,pr5921   df,nn1406   pp,cs,nn7969 pl,nu505   nn376

Philistines _were_   there; and _there were_ upon the   roof about   three   thousand men

wcj,nn802   df,pl,qpta7200   nn8123   pp,qnc7832

and women, that beheld while Samson made sport.

nn8123   wcs,qmf7121 pr413   nn3068   wcs,qmf559   nn136   nn3069   qmv,pnx2142

28 And Samson called unto the LORD, and   said, O Lord GOD, remember me,

pte4994   wcj,pimv,pnx2388   pte4994   ad389 df,pndm2088 df,nn6471   df,pl,nn430

I*pray*thee, and strengthen me, I*pray*thee, only   this   once, O God, that I may

wcj,nicj5358/cs,nn5359/nu259   pr4480/pl,nn6430   pr4480/du,cs,nu8147 du,nn,pnx5869

be at*once*avenged of*the*Philistines for*my*two   eyes.

🗝 **16:23** The Philistines were a sea–faring people. Therefore, it is not surprising that one of their gods was Dagon, the fish god. See the note on Judges 2:13.

nn,pnx6310   wcj,qmv1980   pr,pnx5973   wcj,qmv1961   pp,pnx   pp,nn1   wcj,pp,nn3548   he,aj2896
mouth, and   go   with us, and   be   to us a father and a priest: *is it* better

qnc,pnx1961   nn3548   pp,cs,nn1004   nu259 nn376 cj176   qnc,pnx1961   nn3548
for thee to   be   a priest unto the house of one man, or that thou   be   a priest

pp,nn7626   wcj,pp,nn4940   pp,nn3478
unto a tribe and a family in Israel?

                df,nn3548   cs,nn3820   wcs,qmf3190   wcs,qmf3947 (853)   df,nn646   wcj(853)
20 And the priest's heart was glad, and he   took   the ephod, and

df,pl,nn8655   wcj(853)   df,nn6459   wcs,qmf935   pp,cs,nn7130   df,nn5971
the teraphim, and   the graven image, and went in the midst of the people.

            wcs,qmf6437   wcs,qmf1980   wcs,qmf7760 (853)   df,nn2945   wcj(853)
21 So they turned and departed, and   put   the little ones and   the

df,nn4735   wcj(853)   df,nn3520 pp,pl,nn,pnx6440
cattle and   the carriage before   them.

                    pnp1992   hipf7368   pr4480/cs,nn1004   nn4318   wcj,df,pl,nn376
22 *And* when they were*a*good*way from*the*house of Micah, the   men

pnl834   dfp,pl,nn1004 (pnl834) pr5973   nn4318   cs,nn1004   nipf2199
that *were* in the houses   near to Micah's house were gathered together, and

wcs,himf1692 (853)   pl,cs,nn1121   nn1835
overtook   the children of Dan.

                    wcs,qmf7121 pr413   pl,cs,nn1121   nn1835   wcs,himf5437   pl,nn,pnx6440
23 And they   cried unto the children of Dan. And they   turned   their faces,

wcs,qmf559   pp,nn4318 pnit4100   pp,pnx cj3588   nipf2199
and said unto Micah, What aileth thee, that thou comest*with*such*a*company?

                wcs,qmf559   qpf3947   (853)   pl,nn,pnx430 pnl834   qpf6213   wcj(853)
24 And he   said, Ye have taken away   my   gods which I made, and

df,nn3548   wcs,qmf1980   wcj,pnit4100   pp,pnx ad5750   wcj,pnit4100   pndm2088
the priest, and ye are gone away: and what have I   more? and what *is* this

qmf559 pr,pnx413   pnit4100   pp,pnx
that ye say unto me, What aileth thee?

            pl,cs,nn1121   nn1835 wcs,qmf559 pr,pnx413   ptn408   nn,pnx6963   himf8085
25 And the children of Dan   said   unto him, Let not thy voice be heard

pr,pnx5973   cj6435 cs,aj4751/nn5315 pl,nn376   qmf6293   pp,pnx   wcs,qpf622   nn,pnx5315
among us, lest   angry   fellows run upon thee, and thou lose thy life, with the

wcj,cs,nn5315   nn,pnx1004
lives of thy household.

            pl,cs,nn1121   nn1835 wcs,qmf1980   pp,nn,pnx1870   nn4318 wcs,qmf7200 cj3588
26 And the children of Dan   went their way: and when Micah saw   that

pnp1992   aj2389   pr,pnx4480   wcs,qmf6437   wcs,qmf7725 pr413   nn,pnx1004
they *were* too strong   for   him, he turned and went back unto his house.

            wcj,pnp1992 qpf3947 (853)   pnl834   nn4318   qpf6213   wcj(853)   df,nn3548
27 And they   took   *the things* which Micah had made, and   the priest

pnl834   pp,pnx qpf1961   wcs,qmf935 pr5921 nn3919 pr5921   nn5971   qpta8252 wcj,qpta982
which he had, and came unto Laish, unto a people *that were* at quiet and secure:

            wcs,himf5221 pnx(853)   pp,cs,nn6310   nn2719   qpf8313 wcj(853)   df,nn5892
and they smote   them with the edge of the sword, and burnt   the city

dfp,nn784
with fire.

            wcj,ptn369   hipt5337   cj3588 pnp1931   aj7350   pr4480/nn6721   pp,pnx
28 And *there was* no   deliverer, because it *was* far from Zidon, and they

ptn369 wcj,nn1697 pr5973   nn120   wcj,pnp1931   dfp,nn6010 pnl834
had no business with *any* man; and   it   was in the valley that *lieth* by

pp,nn1050   wcs,qmf1129 (853) df,nn5892   wcs,qmf3427 pp,pnx
Beth-rehob. And they built   a city, and dwelt therein.

            wcs,qmf7121   cs,nn8034   df,nn5892 nn1835   pp,cs,nn8034   nn1835
29 And they called the name of the city Dan, after the name of Dan their

nn,pnx1   pnl834   pupf3205   pp,nn3478   wcj,ad199   cs,nn8034   df,nn5892   nn3919

father, who was born unto Israel: howbeit the name of the city *was* Laish at the

dfp,aj7223

first.

pl,cs,nn1121   nn1835 wcs,himf6965/pp,pnx (853)   df,nn6459   nn3083

30 And the children of Dan   set up   the graven image: and Jonathan, the

cs,nn1121   nn1648   cs,nn1121   nn4519   pnp1931   wcj,pl,nn,pnx1121 qpf1961   pl,nn3548

son of Gershom, the son of Manasseh, he and his   sons   were priests to

pp,cs,nn7626   df,nn1839 pr5704   cs,nn3117   qnc1540   df,nn776

the tribe of Dan until the day of the captivity of the land.

wcs,qmf7760/pp,pnx   (853)   nn4318   cs,nn6459   pnl834   qpf6213 cs,nn3605

31 And they set*them*up   Micah's graven image, which he made,   all   the

pl,cs,nn3117   cs,nn1004   df,pl,nn430 qnc1961   pp,nn7887

time that the house of God   was in Shiloh.

The Levite and His Concubine

wcs,qmf1961   df,pnp1992 dfp,pl,nn3117   ptn369 wcj,nn4428

19 And it*came*to*pass in those   days, when *there was* no   king in

pp,nn3478   wcs,qmf1961   cs,nn376   nn3881   qpta1481   pp,du,cs,nn3411

Israel, that there   was   a certain Levite sojourning on the   side   of

cs,nn2022   nn669   wcs,qmf3947   pp,pnx   nn802/nn6370   pr4480/nn1035/nn3063

mount Ephraim, who   took   to him a concubine out*of*Bethlehem-judah.

nn,pnx6370   wcs,qmf2181   pr,pnx5921   wcs,qmf1980   pr4480/pr,pnx854

2 And his concubine played*the*whore against him, and went away   from

pr413   nn,pnx1   cs,nn1004   pr413   nn1035/nn3063   wcs,qmf1961   ad8033   nu702   pl,nn3117

him unto her father's house to Bethlehem-judah, and   was   there four whole

pl,nn2320

months.

nn,pnx376   wcs,qmf6965   wcs,qmf1980 pr,pnx310   pp,pinc1696 pr5921/nn,pnx3820

3 And her husband arose, and   went   after her, to speak   friendly   unto her,

pp,hinc,pnx7725   wcj,nn,pnx5288 pr,pnx5973   wcj,cs,nn6776   pl,nn2543

and to bring*her*again, having his servant   with him, and a couple of asses: and

wcs,himf,pnx935   nn,pnx1   cs,nn1004   cs,nn1   df,nn5291

she brought   him into her father's house: and when the father of the damsel

wcs,qmf,pnx7200   wcs,qmf8055   pp,qnc,pnx7125

saw   him, he rejoiced to   meet   him.

nn,pnx2859   df,nn5291   cs,nn1   wcs,qmf2388 pp,pnx   wcs,qmf3427 pr,pnx854

4 And his father-in-law, the damsel's father, retained him; and he abode with

cs,nu7969 pl,nn3117   wcs,qmf398   wcs,qmf8354   wcs,qmf3885 ad8033

him three days: so they did   eat   and drink, and lodged there.

wcs,qmf1961   df,nuor7243 dfp,nn3117   wcs,himf7925

5 And it*came*to*pass on the fourth   day, when they arose early in the

dfp,nn1242   wcs,qmf6965   pp,qnc1980   df,nn5291   cs,nn1   wcs,qmf559 pr413

morning, that he rose up to depart: and the damsel's father   said   unto his

nn,pnx2860   qmv5582   nn,pnx3820   cs,nn6595   nn3899   wcj,ad310

son-in-law, Comfort thine heart with a morsel of bread, and afterward

qmf1980

go*your*way.

wcs,qmf3427   wcs,qmf398 wcs,qmf8354 du,nu,pnx8147   ad3162

6 And they sat down, and did   eat   and drink   both   of them together: for

df,nn5291   cs,nn1   wcs,qmf559 pr413   df,nn376   himv2974   pte4994

the damsel's father had   said unto the man, Be content, I*pray*thee, and

wcj,qmv3885   nn,pnx3820   wcj,qmf3190

tarry*all*night, and let thine heart be merry.

df,nn376 wcs,qmf6965   pp,qnc1980   nn,pnx2859   wcs,qmf6484 pp,pnx

7 And when the man rose up to depart, his father-in-law urged him: therefore

wcs,qmf3885 ad8033 wcs,qmf7725

he lodged there again.

wcs,himf7925   dfp,nn1242   df,nuor2549 dfp,nn3117   pp,qnc1980

8 And he arose early in the morning on the fifth day to depart: and the

df,nn5291   cs,nn1   wcs,qmf559   qmv5582   nn,pnx3824 pte4994   wcs,htmv*4102 pr5704

damsel's father said, Comfort thine heart, I*pray*thee. And they tarried until

qnc5186/df,nn3117   wcs,qmf398 du,nu,pnx8147

afternoon, and they did eat both of them.

df,nn376 wcs,qmf6965   pp,qnc1980 pnp1931   wcj,nn,pnx6370

9 And when the man rose up to depart, he, and his concubine, and his

wcj,nn,pnx5288   nn,pnx2859   df,nn5291   cs,nn1   wcs,qmf559   pp,pnx   ptdm2009 pte4994

servant, his father-in-law, the damsel's father, said unto him, Behold, now the

df,nn3117   qpf7503   pp,qnc6150   pte4994   qmv3885   ptdm2009   df,nn3117

day draweth toward evening, I*pray*you tarry*all*night: behold, the day

qnc2583   qmv3885   ad6311   nn,pnx3824   wcj,qmf3190   ad4279

groweth*to*an*end, lodge here, that thine heart may be merry; and tomorrow

wcs,hipf7925   pp,nn,pnx1870   wcs,qpf1980 pp,nn,pnx168

get*you*early on your way, that thou mayest go home.

df,nn376   qpf14   wcj,ptn3808   pp,qnc3885   wcs,qmf6965   wcs,qmf1980

10 But the man would not tarry*that*night, but he rose up and departed,

wcs,qmf935   pr5704/nn5227   nn2982 pnp1931   nn3389   wcj,pr,pnx5973

and came over against Jebus, which is Jerusalem; and there were with him

cs,nn6776 pl,nn2543 pl,qptp2280   wcj,nn,pnx6370   pr,pnx5973

two asses saddled, his concubine also was with him.

pnp1992   pr5973 nn2982   wcj,df,nn3117   ad3966 qpf7286   df,nn5288

11 And when they were by Jebus, the day was far spent; and the servant

wcs,qmf559 pr413   pl,nn,pnx113 qmv1980   pte4994   wcj,qcj5493 pr413 df,pndm2063 cs,nn5892

said unto his master, Come, I*pray*thee, and let us turn in into this city of

df,nn2983   wcj,qmf3885 pp,pnx

the Jebusites, and lodge in it.

pl,nn,pnx113 wcs,qmf559 pr,pnx413   ptn3808   qmf5493   pr413

12 And his master said unto him, We will not turn aside hither into the

cs,nn5892   aj5237   pnl834 (pnp2007) ptn3808 pr4480/pl,cs,nn1121   nn3478   wcs,qpf5674

city of a stranger, that is not of*the*children of Israel; we will pass over

pr5704   nn1390

to Gibeah.

wcs,qmf559   pp,nn,pnx5288 qmv1980   wcj,qcj7126   pp,cs,nu259

13 And he said unto his servant, Come, and let us draw near to one of

df,pl,nn4725   wcj,qpf3885   dfp,nn1390 cj176   dfp,nn7414

these places to lodge*all*night, in Gibeah, or in Ramah.

wcs,qmf5674   wcs,qmf1980   df,nn8121   wcs,qmf935

14 And they passed on and went*their*way; and the sun went down

pp,pnx   pr681 df,nn1390 pnl834   pp,nn1144

upon them when they were by Gibeah, which belongeth to Benjamin.

wcs,qmf5493   ad8033   pp,qnc935   pp,qnc3885   dfp,nn1390

15 And they turned aside thither, to go in and to lodge in Gibeah: and when

wcs,qmf935   wcs,qmf3427   pp,cs,nn7339   df,nn5892   wcj,ptn369 nn376

he went in, he sat*him*down in a street of the city: for there was no man

pipt622 pnx(853)   df,nn,lh1004   pp,qnc3885

that took them into his house to lodging.

wcj,ptdm2009   qpta935   aj2205 nn376 pr4480   nn,pnx4639 pr4480   df,nn7704

16 And, behold, there came an old man from his work out of the field at

dfp,nn6153 wcj,df,nn3676   pr4480/cs,nn2022   nn669   wcj,pnp1931   qpta**1481**   dfp,nn1390

even,   which *was* also of mount Ephraim; and   he   sojourned in Gibeah: but the

wcj,pl,cs,nn**376**   df,nn4725   pl,nn1145

men   of the place *were* Benjamites.

wcs,qmf**5375**   du,nn,pnx5869   wcs,qmf**7200**   (853)   df,qpta732   df,nn**376**

17 And when he had lifted up his   eyes,   he   saw   a wayfaring man in

pp,cs,nn7339   df,nn5892   df,aj**2205** df,nn**376** wcs,qmf559 pr4480/ad575   qmf**1980**

the   street   of the city: and the old   man   said, Whither goest thou? and

wcj,pr4480/ad370   qmf935

whence   comest thou?

wcs,qmf**559** pr,pnx413   pnp587   pl,qpta**5674**   pr4480/nn1035/nn3063   pr5704

18 And he   said   unto him, We *are* passing from Bethlehem-judah toward the

pl,cs,nn3411   cs,nn2022   nn669   pr4480/ad8033   pnp595   wcs,qmf**1980** pr5704   nn1035/nn3063

side of mount Ephraim; from thence *am* I: and I went   to Bethlehem-judah,

pnp589   qpta**1980**   wcj(853)   cs,nn1004   nn**3068**   wcj,ptn369 nn**376**

but I *am now* going to   the house of the LORD; and there *is* no man that

pipt**622**   pnx(853)   df,nn,lh**1004**

receiveth   me to house.

pta3426 wcj,ad1571 nn8401 ad1571   nn4554   pp,pl,nn,pnx2543   pta3426   nn3899

19 Yet there is both straw and provender for our   asses; and there is bread

wcj,nn3196 wcj,ad1571   pp,pnx   wcj,pp,nn,pnx519   wcj,dfp,nn5288

and wine   also for me, and for thy handmaid, and for the young man *which is*

pr5973   pl,nn,pnx**5650**   ptn369 cs,nn4270   cs,nn3605 nn**1697**

with thy servants: *there is* no want of any thing.

df,aj**2205** df,nn**376** wcs,qmf**559**   nn7965   pp,pnx   ad7535   cs,nn3605

20 And the old   man   said, Peace *be* with thee; howsoever *let* all   thy

nn,pnx4270   pr,pnx5921   ad7535   qmf3885 ptn408   dfp,nn7339

wants *lie* upon me; only lodge not in the street.

wcs,himf,pnx935   pp,nn,pnx**1004**   wcs,qmf**1101**   dfp,pl,nn2543

21 So he   brought him into his house, and gave provender unto the   asses:

wcs,qmf**7364**   du,nn,pnx7272   wcs,qmf398   wcs,qmf8354

and they washed their   feet,   and did and drink.

pnp1992   pl,hipt**3190**/(853)/nn,nn**3820**   wcj,ptdm2009   pl,cs,nn**376**

22 *Now* as they were making*their*hearts*merry, behold, the men of the

df,nn5892 pl,cs,nn**376** pl,cs,nn1121   nn1100   nipf5437/(853)/df,nn**1004**   pl,htpt1849 pr5921

city, certain sons of Belial, beset*the*house*round*about, *and* beat at the

df,nn1817   wcs,qmf**559** pr413 (df,nn**376**)   cs,nn1167   df,nn**1004**   df,aj**2205** pp,qnc**559**

door, and spoke to   the master of the house, the old man, saying,

himv3318   (853)   df,nn**376** pnl834 qpf935 pr413   nn,pnx**1004**   wcj,qmf,pnx**3045**

Bring forth   the man that came into thine house, that we may know   him.

df,nn**376**   cs,nn1167   df,nn**1004** wcs,qmf3318 pr,pnx413   wcs,qmf**559**

23 And the man, the master of the house, went out unto them, and said

pr,pnx413   ptn408   pl,nn,pnx251   pte**4994**   himf**7489**/ptn408   ad310/pnl834

unto them, Nay, my brethren, *nay,* I*pray*you, do*not*so*wickedly; seeing that

df,pndm2088 df,nn**376**   qpf935 pr413   nn,pnx**1004** qmf**6213** ptn408 (853) df,pndm2063 df,nn5039

this   man is come into mine house, do   not   this folly.

ptdm2009   nn,pnx1323   df,nn**1330**   wcj,nn,pnx**6370**   pnx(853)

24 Behold, *here is* my daughter a maiden, and his concubine;   them I will

hicj3318   pte**4994**   wcj,qmv6031   pnx(853)   wcj,qmv**6213**   pp,pnx   pp,du,nn,pnx5869

bring out now, and humble ye   them, and do   with them what seemeth

df,aj**2896**   df,pndm2088 wcj,dfp,nn**376** qmf**6213** ptn3808 df,pndm2063 df,nn5039 cs,nn**1697**

good unto you: but unto this   man   do not   so   vile a thing.

df,pl,nn**376** qpf14 wcj,ptn**3808** pp,qnc8085   pp,pnx   df,nn**376** wcs,himf**2388**

25 But the men   would   not hearken to him: so the man   took   his

pp,nn,pnx**6370**   wcs,himf3318/df,nn2351   pr,pnx413   wcs,qmf**3045** pnx(853)

concubine, and brought*her*forth   unto them; and they knew   her, and wcs,htmf5953 pp,pnx cs,nn3605   df,nn3915 pr5704   df,nn1242   df,nn7837   pp,qnc5927

abused her all the night until the morning: and when the day began*to*spring,

wcs,pimf,pnx7971

they let her go.

wcs,qmf935   df,nn802   pp,qnc6437   df,nn1242   wcs,qmf5307

26 Then came the woman in the dawning of the day, and fell down at the

cs,nn6607   df,nn376 cs,nn1004 pnl834/ad8033   pl,nn,pnx113   pr5704   df,nn216

door of the man's house where her lord *was*, till it was light.

pl,nn,pnx113 wcs,qmf6965   dfp,nn1242   wcs,qmf6605   pl,cs,nn1817

27 And her lord rose up in the morning, and opened the doors of the

df,nn1004   wcs,qmf3318   pp,qnc1980   pp,nn,pnx1870   wcj,ptdm2009   df,nn802   nn,pnx6370

house, and went out to go his way: and, behold, the woman his concubine

qpta5307   cs,nn6607   df,nn1004   wcj,du,nn,pnx3027   pr5921

was fallen down *at* the door of the house, and her hands *were* upon the

df,nn5592

threshold.

wcs,qmf559 pr,pnx413   qmv6965   wcj,qcj1980   wcj,ptn369   qpta6030

28 And he said unto her, Up, and let us be going. But none answered.

wcs,qmf,pnx3947   pr5921   df,nn2543   df,nn376 wcs,qmf6965   wcs,qmf1980

Then the man took her *up* upon an ass, and the man rose up, and got

pp,nn,pnx4725

him unto his place.

wcs,qmf935   pr413   nn,pnx1004   wcs,qmf3947 (853)   df,nn3979

29 And when he was come into his house, he took a knife, and

wcs,himf2388   pp,nn,pnx6370   wcs,pimf,pnx5408   pp,pl,nn,pnx6106

laid hold on his concubine, and divided her, *together* with her bones, into

pp,du,nu8147/nu6240 pl,nn5409   wcs,pimf,pnx7971   pp,cs,nn3605 cs,nn1366   nn3478

twelve pieces, and sent her into all the coasts of Israel.

wcj,qpf1961   cs,nn3605   df,qpta7200 wcj,qpf559   ptn3808 pp,pndm2063

30 And it was so, that all that saw it said, There was no such deed

nipf1961 wcj,ptn3808 nipf7200   pp,pr4480/nn3117   pl,cs,nn1121   nn3478   qnc5927   pr4480/cs,nn776

done nor seen from*the*day that the children of Israel came up out*of*the*land

nn4714   pr5704 df,pndm2088 df,nn3117   qmv7760   (pp,pnx) pr,pnx5921   qmv5779   wcj,pimv1696

of Egypt unto this day: consider of it, take advice, and speak *your*

minds.

Israel Punishes Benjamin For Its Sin

cs,nn3605   pl,cs,nn1121   nn3478 wcs,qmf3318   df,nn5712

20 Then all the children of Israel went out, and the congregation

wcs,nimf6950   nu259 pp,nn376 pp,pr4480/nn1835   wcj,pr5704   nn884

was gathered together as one man, from Dan even to Beer-sheba,

wcj,cs,nn776   df,nn1568   pr413   nn3068   df,nn4709

with the land of Gilead, unto the LORD in Mizpeh.

pl,cs,nn6438   cs,nn3605   df,nn5971   cs,nn3605   pl,cs,nn7626   nn3478

2 And the chief of all the people, *even* of all the tribes of Israel,

wcs,htmf3320   pp,cs,nn6951   cs,nn5971   df,pl,nn430 nu702 pl,cs,nu3967   nu505

presented themselves in the assembly of the people of God, four hundred thousand

nn376/aj7273   qpta8025   nn2719

footmen that drew sword.

20:1 The phrase "from Dan to Beersheba" does not imply that Dan's settlement of its portion, recorded in chapter eighteen, had already been completed. It only shows that "from Dan to Beersheba" had become a proverbial expression for all the land of Israel.

^{pl,cs,nn1121} ⁿⁿ¹¹⁴⁴ ^{wcs,qmf8085} ^{cj3588} ^{pl,cs,nn1121} ⁿⁿ³⁴⁷⁸

3 (Now the children of Benjamin heard that the children of Israel were

^{qpf5927} ^{df,nn4709} ^{wcs,qmf559} ^{pl,cs,nn1121} ⁿⁿ³⁴⁷⁸ ^{pimv1696} ^{pnit349} ^{nipf1961} ^{df,pndm2063}

gone up to Mizpeh.) Then said the children of Israel, Tell *us,* how was this

^{df,aj7451}

wickedness?

^{df,nn376/df,nn3881} ^{cs,nn376} ^{df,nn802} ^{df,nipt7523} ^{wcs,qmf6030}

4 And the Levite, the husband of the woman that was slain, answered and

^{wcs,qmf559} ^{qpf935} ^{df,nn,lh1390} ^{pnl834} ^{pp,nn1144} ^{pnp589} ^{wcj,nn,pnx6370}

said, I came into Gibeah that *belongeth* to Benjamin, I and my concubine, to

^{pp,qnc3885}

lodge.

^{pl,cs,nn1167} ^{df,nn1390} ^{wcs,qmf6965} ^{pr,pnx5921}

5 And the men of Gibeah rose against me, and

^{wcs,qmf5437/(853)/df,nn1004} ^{pr,pnx5921} ⁿⁿ³⁹¹⁵ ^{pipf1819} ^{pp,qnc2026 pnx(853)}

beset*the*house*round*about upon me by night, *and* thought to have slain

^{wcj(853)} ^{nn,pnx6370} ^{pipf6031} ^{wcs,qmf4191}

me: and   my concubine have they forced, that she is dead.

^{wcs,qmf270} ^{pp,nn,pnx6370} ^{wcs,pimf,pnx5408} ^{wcs,pimf,pnx7971}

6 And I took my concubine, and cut*her*in*pieces, and sent her

^{pp,cs,nn3605} ^{cs,nn7704} ^{cs,nn5159} ⁿⁿ³⁴⁷⁸ ^{cj3588} ^{qpf6213}

throughout all the country of the inheritance of Israel: for they have committed

ⁿⁿ²¹⁵⁴ ^{wcj,nn5039} ^{pp,nn3478}

lewdness and folly in Israel.

^{ptdm2009} ^{nn,pnx3605} ^{pl,cs,nn1121} ⁿⁿ³⁴⁷⁸ ^{qmv3051} ^{ad1988} ^{pp,pnx} ⁿⁿ¹⁶⁹⁷ ^{wcj,nn6098}

7 Behold, ye *are* all children of Israel; give here your advice and counsel.

^{cs,nn3605} ^{df,nn5971} ^{wcs,qmf6965} ^{nu259} ^{pp,nn376} ^{pp,qnc559} ^{ptn3808} ⁿⁿ³⁷⁶

8 And all the people arose as one man, saying, We will not any *of us*

^{qmf1980} ^{pp,nn,pnx168} ^{wcj,ptn3808} ⁿⁿ³⁷⁶ ^{qmf5493} ^{pp,nn,pnx1004}

go to his tent, neither will we any *of us* turn into his house.

^{wcj,ad6258} ^{pndm2088} ^{df,nn1697} ^{pnl834} ^{qmf6213} ^{dfp,nn1390}

9 But now this *shall be* the thing which we will do to Gibeah; *we will go*

^{pp,nn1486} ^{pr,pnx5921}

up by lot against it;

^{wcs,qpf3947} ^{nu6235} ^{pl,nn376} ^{dfp,nu3967} ^{pp,cs,nn3605} ^{pl,cs,nn7626}

10 And we will take ten men of a hundred throughout all the tribes of

ⁿⁿ³⁴⁷⁸ ^{wcj,nu3967} ^{dfp,nu505} ^{wcj,nu505} ^{dfp,nn7233} ^{pp,qnc3947}

Israel, and a hundred of a thousand, and a thousand out of ten thousand, to fetch

ⁿⁿ⁶⁷²⁰ ^{dfp,nn5971} ^{pp,qnc6213} ^{pp,qnc,pnx935} ^{pp,nn1387}

victual for the people, that they may do, when they come to Gibeah of

ⁿⁿ¹¹⁴⁴ ^{pp,cs,nn3605} ^{df,nn5039} ^{pnl834} ^{qpf6213} ^{pp,nn3478}

Benjamin, according to all the folly that they have wrought in Israel.

^{cs,nn3605} ^{cs,nn376} ⁿⁿ³⁴⁷⁸ ^{wcs,nimf622} ^{pr413} ^{df,nn5892} ^{aj2270}

11 So all the men of Israel were gathered against the city, knit together as

^{nu259} ^{pp,nn376}

one man.

^{pl,cs,nn7626} ⁿⁿ³⁴⁷⁸ ^{wcs,qmf7971} ^{pl,nn376} ^{pp,cs,nn3605} ^{pl,cs,nn7626}

12 And the tribes of Israel sent men through all the tribe of

ⁿⁿ¹¹⁴⁴ ^{pp,qnc559} ^{pnit4100} ^{df,aj7451} ^{df,pndm2063} ^{pnl834} ^{nipf1961} ^{pp,pnx}

Benjamin, saying, What wickedness *is* this that is done among you?

^{wcj,ad6258} ^{qmv5414} ⁽⁸⁵³⁾ ^{df,pl,nn376} ^{pl,cs,nn1121} ⁿⁿ¹¹⁰⁰ ^{pnl834}

13 Now therefore deliver *us* the men, the children of Belial, which *are* in

^{dfp,nn1390} ^{wcj,himf,pnx4191} ^{wcj,picj1197} ^{aj7451} ^{pr4480/nn3478}

Gibeah, that we may put*them*to*death, and put away evil from Israel. But the pl,cs,nn1121   nn1144   qpf14   wcj,ptn3808   pp,qnc8085   pp,cs,nn6963   pl,nn,pnx251

children of Benjamin would not hearken to the voice of their brethren the

pl,cs,nn1121   nn3478

children of Israel:

pl,cs,nn1121   nn1144   wcs,nimf622   pr4480

14 But the children of Benjamin gathered*themselves*together out of the

df,pl,nn5892   df,nn,lh1390   pp,qnc3318   dfp,nn4421   pr5973   pl,cs,nn1121   nn3478

cities unto Gibeah, to go out to battle against the children of Israel.

pl,cs,nn1121   nn1144   wcs,htmf6485   df,pndm1931   dfp,nn3117

15 And the children of Benjamin were numbered at that time

pr4480/df,pl,nn5892   pl,nu6242   wcj,nu8337   nu505   nn376   qpta8025   nn2719   pp,nn905

out*of*the*cities twenty and six thousand men that drew sword, beside the

pr4480/pl,cs,qpta3427   df,nn1390   htpf6485   cs,nu7651   pl,cs,nu3967   qptp970   nn376

inhabitants of Gibeah, which were numbered seven hundred chosen men.

pr4480/cs,nn3605   df,pndm2088   df,nn5971   cs,nu7651   pl,cs,nu3967   qptp977   nn376

16 Among all this people *there were* seven hundred chosen men

aj334/cs,nn3027/nn,pnx3225   cs,nn3605/pndm2088   qpta7049   dfp,nn68   pr413   df,nn8185   wcj,ptn3808   himf2398

left-handed; every one could sling stones at a hair *breadth*, and not miss.

wcj,cs,nn376   nn3478   pp,nn905   pr4480/nn1144   htpf6485   nu702   pl,cs,nu3967

17 And the men of Israel, beside Benjamin, were numbered four hundred

nu505   nn376   qpta8025   nn2719   cs,nn3605   pndm2088   cs,nn376   nn4421

thousand men that drew sword: all these *were* men of war.

pl,cs,nn1121   nn3478   wcs,qmf6965   wcs,qmf5927   nn1008

18 And the children of Israel arose, and went up to the house*of*God, and

wcs,qmf7592   pp,pl,nn430   wcs,qmf559   pnit4310   pp,pnx   qmf5927   dfp,nn8462   dfp,nn4421

asked counsel of God, and said, Which of us shall go up first to the battle

pr5973   pl,cs,nn1121   nn1144   nn3068   wcs,qmf559   nn3063   dfp,nn8462

against the children of Benjamin? And the LORD said, Judah *shall go up* first.

pl,cs,nn1121   nn3478   wcs,qmf6965   dfp,nn1242   wcs,qmf2583   pr5921

19 And the children of Israel rose up in the morning, and encamped against

df,nn1390

Gibeah.

cs,nn376   nn3478   wcs,qmf3318   dfp,nn4421   pr5973   nn1144   cs,nn376

20 And the men of Israel went out to battle against Benjamin; and the men of

nn3478   wcs,qmf6186   nn4421   pr,pnx854   pr413   df,nn1390

Israel put*themselves*in*array to fight against them at Gibeah.

pl,cs,nn1121   nn1144   wcs,qmf3318   pr4480   df,nn1390

21 And the children of Benjamin came forth out of Gibeah, and

wcs,himf7843   nn,lh776   pp,nn3478   df,pndm1931   dfp,nn3117   wcj,pl,nu6242   du,nu8147

destroyed down to the ground of the Israelites that day twenty and two

cs,nu505   nn376

thousand men.

df,nn5971   cs,nn376   nn3478   wcs,htmf2388   pp,qnc6186

22 And the people the men of Israel encouraged themselves, and set their

nn4421   wcs,himf3254   pp,qnc6186   dfp,nn4725   pnl834/ad8033   qpf6186   df,aj7223

battle again in array in the place where they put*themselves*in*array the first

dfp,nn3117

day.

pl,cs,nn1121   nn3478   wcs,qmf5927   wcs,qmf1058   pp,pl,cs,nn6440   nn3068   pr5704

☞ 23 (And the children of Israel went up and wept before the LORD until

df,nn6153   wcs,qmf7592   pp,nn3068   pp,qnc559   pp,qnc5066   he,himf3254   dfp,nn4421   pr5973

even, and asked counsel of the LORD, saying, Shall I go up again to battle against

---

☞ **20:23** Apparently the Israelites trusted in their army and the righteousness of their cause. They did not include God in their planning. Israel needed a strong disciplinary lesson, and God used their enemies to teach it to them.

pl,cs,nn1121 nn1144 nn,pnx251 nn3068 wcs,qmf559 qmv5927 pr,pnx413
the children of Benjamin my brother? And the LORD said, Go up against him.)

pl,cs,nn1121 nn3478 wcs,qmf7126 pr413 pl,cs,nn1121 nn1144
24 And the children of Israel came near against the children of Benjamin the

df,nuor8145 dfp,nn3117
second day.

nn1144 wcs,qmf3318 pp,qnc,pnx7125 pr4480 df,nn1390 df,nuor8145 dfp,nn3117
25 And Benjamin went forth against them out of Gibeah the second day,

wcs,himf7843 nn,lh776 pp,pl,cs,nn1121 nn3478 ad5750 cs,nu8083/nu6240 nu505
and destroyed down to the ground of the children of Israel again eighteen thousand

nn376 cs,nn3605 pndm428 pl,cs,qpta8025 nn2719
men; all these drew the sword.

cs,nn3605 pl,cs,nn1121 nn3478 wcj,cs,nn3605 df,nn5971 wcs,qmf5927
26 Then all the children of Israel, and all the people, went up, and

wcs,qmf935 nn1008 wcs,qmf1058 wcs,qmf3427 ad8033 pp,pl,cs,nn6440 nn3068
came unto the house*of*God, and wept, and sat there before the LORD, and

wcs,qmf6684 df,pndm1931 dfp,nn3117 pr5704 df,nn6153 wcs,himf5927 pl,nn5930 wcj,pl,nn8002
fasted that day until even, and offered burnt offerings and peace offerings

pp,pl,cs,nn6440 nn3068
before the LORD.

pl,cs,nn1121 nn3478 wcs,qmf7592 pp,nn3068 cs,nn727
27 And the children of Israel inquired of the LORD, (for the ark of the

cs,nn1285 df,pl,nn430 wcj,ad8033 df,pnp1992 dfp,pl,nn3117
covenant of God *was* there in those days,

wcj,nn6372 cs,nn1121 nn499 cs,nn1121 nn175 qpta5975 pp,pl,nn,pnx6440
28 And Phinehas, the son of Eleazar, the son of Aaron, stood before it in

df,pnp1992 dfp,pl,nn3117 pp,qnc559 ad5750 he,himf3254 pp,qnc3318 dfp,nn4421 pr5973 pl,cs,nn1121
those days,) saying, Shall I yet again go out to battle against the children of

nn1144 nn,pnx251 cj518 qmf2308 nn3068 wcs,qmf559 qmv5927 cj3588 nn4279
Benjamin my brother, or shall I cease? And the LORD said, Go up; for tomorrow

qmf,pnx5414 pp,nn,pnx3027
I will deliver them into thine hand.

nn3478 wcs,qmf7760 pl,qpta693 ad5439/pr413 df,nn1390
29 And Israel set liers*in*wait round about Gibeah.

pl,cs,nn1121 nn3478 wcs,qmf5927 pr413 pl,cs,nn1121 nn1144
30 And the children of Israel went up against the children of Benjamin on the

df,nuor7992 dfp,nn3117 wcs,qmf6186 pr413 df,nn1390 pp,nn6471/pp,nn6471
third day, and put*themselves*in*array against Gibeah, as at other times.

pl,cs,nn1121 nn1144 wcs,qmf3318 pp,qnc7125 df,nn5971
31 And the children of Benjamin went out against the people, *and* were

hopf5423 pr4480 df,nn5892 wcs,himf2490 pp,hinc5221 pr4480/df,nn5971 pl,nn2491
drawn away from the city; and they began to smite of*the*people, *and* kill, as

pp,nn6471/pp,nn6471 dfp,pl,nn4546 pnl834 nu259 qpta5927 nn1008
at other times, in the highways, of which one goeth up to the house*of*God, and

wcj,nu259 nn,lh1390 dfp,nn7704 pp,nu7970 nn376 pp,nn3478
the other to Gibeah in the field, about thirty men of Israel.

pl,cs,nn1121 nn1144 wcs,qmf559 pnp1992 pl,nipt5062 pp,pl,nn,pnx6440
32 And the children of Benjamin said, They *are* smitten down before us, as

pp,dfp,aj7223 wcj,pl,cs,nn1121 nn3478 qpf559 qcj5127 wcs,qpf,pnx5423 pr4480
at the first. But the children of Israel said, Let us flee, and draw them from

df,nn5892 pr413 df,pl,nn4546
the city unto the highways.

wcj,cs,nn3605 cs,nn376 nn3478 qpf6965 pr4480/nn,pnx4725
33 And all the men of Israel rose up out*of*their*place, and

wcs,qmf6186   pp,nn1193   wcj,qpta693   nn3478   hipt1518
put*themselves*in*array at Baal-tamar: and the liers*in*wait of Israel came forth

pr4480/nn,pnx4725   pr4480/cs,nn4629   pr4480/nn1390
out*of*their*places, *even* out*of*the*meadows of Gibeah.

                wcs,qmf935 pr4480/pr5048 dfp,nn1390 cs,nu6235 pl,nu505   qptp977   nn376   pr4480/cs,nn3605
34 And there came against Gibeah ten thousand chosen men out*of*all

nn3478   wcj,df,nn4421   qpf3513   wcj,pnp1992 qpf3045 ptn3808 cj3588 df,aj7451   qpta5060 pnx(pr5921)
Israel, and the battle was sore: but they knew not that evil *was* near

them.

            nn3068   wcs,qmf5062 (853)   nn1144   pp,pl,cs,nn6440 nn3478   pl,cs,nn1121   nn3478
35 And the LORD smote Benjamin before Israel: and the children of Israel

wcs,himf7843   pp,nn1144   df,pndm1931 dfp,nn3117 pl,nu6242   wcj,nu2568   nu505
destroyed of the Benjamites that day twenty and five thousand and a

wcj,nu3967 nn376 cs,nn3605 pndm428 qpta8025   nn2719
hundred men: all these drew the sword.

            pl,cs,nn1121   nn1144   wcs,qmf7200 cj3588   nipf5062   cs,nn376
36 So the children of Benjamin saw that they were smitten: for the men of

nn3478 wcs,qmf5414 nn4725   pp,nn1144   cj3588   qpf982   pr413   df,qpta693
Israel gave place to the Benjamites, because they trusted unto the liers*in*wait

pnl834   qpf7760   pr413   df,nn1390
which they had set beside Gibeah.

            wcj,df,qpta693   hipf2363   wcs,qmf6584 pr413 df,nn1390   df,qpta693
37 And the liers*in*wait hasted, and rushed upon Gibeah; and the liers*in*wait

wcs,qmf4900   wcs,himf5221 (853) cs,nn3605   df,nn5892   pp,cs,nn6310
drew*themselves*along, and smote all the city with the edge of the

nn2719
sword.

            qpf1961   wcj,df,nn4150   pp,cs,nn376   nn3478   (pr5973)
38 Now there was an appointed sign between the men of Israel and the

df,qpta693   himv7235   cs,nn4864   df,nn6227 pp,hinc,pnx5927 pr4480
liers*in*wait, that they should make*a*great flame with smoke rise up out of the

df,nn5892
city.

            cs,nn376   nn3478 wcs,qmf2015   dfp,nn4421 wcj,nn1144 hipf2490   pp,hinc5221
39 And when the men of Israel retired in the battle, Benjamin began to smite

pl,nn2491   pp,cs,nn376   nn3478   pp,nu7970 nn376 cj3588   qpf559   ad389 pnp1931
and kill of the men of Israel about thirty persons: for they said, Surely they

nina5062/nipt5062 pp,pl,nn,pnx6440   df,aj7223 dfp,nn4421
are smitten down before us, as *in* the first battle.

            wcj,df,nn4864   hipf2490   pp,qnc5927   pr4480   df,nn5892   cs,nn5982
40 But when the flame began to arise up out of the city with a pillar of

nn6227   nn1144   wcs,qmf6437 pr,pnx310   wcj,ptdm2009 cs,nn3632   df,nn5892
smoke, the Benjamites looked behind them, and, behold, the flame of the city

qpf5927   df,du,nn,lh8064
ascended up to heaven.

            wcj,cs,nn376   nn3478   qpf2015   cs,nn376   nn1144
41 And when the men of Israel turned again, the men of Benjamin were

wcs,nimf926 cj3588   qpf7200 cj3588 df,aj7451   qpf5060 pr,pnx5921
amazed: for they saw that evil was come upon them.

            wcs,qmf6437   pp,pl,cs,nn6440 cs,nn376   nn3478 pr413   cs,nn1870
42 Therefore they turned *their backs* before the men of Israel unto the way

df,nn4057   wcj,df,nn4421 hipf,pnx1692   pnx(853)   wcj,pnl834
of the wilderness; but the battle overtook them; and them which *came*

pr4480/df,pl,nn5892   pl,hipt7843   pp,nn,pnx8432
out*of*the*cities they destroyed in the midst of them.

43 *Thus* they enclosed*the*Benjamites*round*about, *and* chased them, *and* trod*them*down with ease over against Gibeah toward*the*sunrising.

44 And there fell of Benjamin eighteen thousand men; all these *were* men of valor.

45 And they turned and fled toward the wilderness unto the rock of Rimmon: and they gleaned of them in the highways five thousand men; and pursued hard after them unto Gidom, and slew two thousand men of them.

46 So that all which fell that day of Benjamin were twenty and five thousand men that drew the sword; all these *were* men of valor.

47 But six hundred men turned and fled to the wilderness unto the rock Rimmon, and abode in the rock Rimmon four months.

48 And the men of Israel turned again upon the children of Benjamin, and smote them with the edge of the sword, as well the men of*every*city, as the beast, and all that came*to*hand: also they set on fire all the cities that they came to.

Wives for the Tribe of Benjamin

21 Now the men of Israel had sworn in Mizpeh, saying, There shall not any of us give his daughter unto Benjamin to wife.

2 And the people came to the house*of*God, and abode there till even before God, and lifted up their voices, and wept sore;

3 And said, O LORD God of Israel, why is this come*to*pass in Israel, that there should be today one tribe lacking in Israel?

4 And it*came*to*pass on*the*morrow, that the people rose early, and built there an altar, and offered burnt offerings and peace offerings.

5 And the children of Israel said, Who *is there* among all the tribes of Israel that came*not*up with the congregation unto the LORD? For they had made a great

df,nn**7621**   pp,pnl834   qpf**5927**/ptn**3808**   pr413   nn**3068**   df,nn**4709**   pp,qnc**559**

oath concerning him that came*not*up to the LORD to Mizpeh, saying, He shall

qna**4191**/homf**4191**

surely*be*put*to*death.

pl,cs,nn**1121**   nn**3478**   wcs,nimf**5162**   pr413   nn**1144**   nn,pnx**251**

6 And the children of Israel repented them for Benjamin their brother, and

wcs,qmf**559**   nu259 nn**7626**   nipf**1438**   pr4480/nn**3478**   df,nn**3117**

said, There is one tribe cut off from Israel this day.

pnit4100   qmf**6213**   pp,pl,nn**802**   pp,pnx   dfp,pl,nipt**3498**   wcj,pnp587   nipf**7650**

7 How shall we do for wives for them that remain, seeing we have sworn

pp,nn**3068**   pp,ptn1115 qnc**5414** pp,pnx   pr4480/pl,nn,pnx1323   pp,pl,nn**802**

by the LORD that we will not give them of*our*daughters to wives?

wcs,qmf**559** pnit4310 nu259   pr4480/cs,nn**7626**   nn**3478** pnl834   qpf**5927**/ptn**3808**

8 And they said, What one is there of*the*tribes of Israel that came*not*up to

df,nn**4709** pr413   nn**3068**   wcj,ptdm2009   qpf935   ptn**3808**/nn**376** pr413   df,nn**4264**

Mizpeh to the LORD? And, behold, there came none to the camp

pr4480/nn**3003**/nn1568   pr413   df,nn**6951**

from Jabesh-gilead to the assembly.

df,nn**5971**   wcs,htmf**6485**   wcj,ptdm2009   ptn369/nn**376**

9 For the people were numbered, and, behold, there were none

pr4480/pl,cs,qpta**3427**   nn**3003**/nn1568   ad8033

of*the*inhabitants of Jabesh-gilead there.

df,nn**5712**   wcs,qmf**7971**   ad8033   du,nu**8147**/nu**6240**   nu**505**   nn**376**

10 And the congregation sent hither twelve thousand men

pr4480/pl,cs,nn**1121**/df,nn**2428**   wcs,pimf**6680**   pnx(853)   pp,qnc**559**   qmv**1980**   wcj,hipf**5221** (853)

of*the*most*valiant, and commanded them, saying, Go and smite the

pl,cs,qpta**3427**   nn**3003**/nn1568   pp,cs,nn**6310**   nn**2719**   wcj,df,pl,nn**802**

inhabitants of Jabesh-gilead with the edge of the sword, with the women and the

wcj,df,nn**2945**

children.

wcj,pndm2088   df,nn**1697** pnl834   qmf**6213**   himf**2763**   cs,nn3605

11 And this is the thing that ye shall do, Ye shall utterly destroy every

nn2145   wcj,cs,nn**3605**   nn**802**   cs,qpta**3045**/cs,nn**4904**   nn2145

male, and every woman that hath lain by man.

wcs,qmf**4672**   pr4480/pl,cs,qpta**3427**   nn**3003**/nn1568   nu702   pl,nu**3967**   nn**5291**

12 And they found among*the*inhabitants of Jabesh-gilead four hundred young

nn**1330** pnl834   qpf**3045** ptn**3808** nn**376** pp,cs,nn**4904**   nn2145   wcs,himf935 pnx(853)

virgins, that had known no man by lying with any male: and they brought

pr413   df,nn**4264**   nn**7887** pnl834   pp,cs,nn**776**   nn3667

them unto the camp to Shiloh, which is in the land of Canaan.

cs,nn3605   df,nn**5712**   wcs,qmf**7971**   wcs,pimf**1696** pr413   pl,cs,nn**1121**

13 And the whole congregation sent some to speak to the children of

nn1144   pnl834   pp,cs,nn**5553**   nn**7417**   wcs,qmf**7121**   nn**7965**   pp,pnx

Benjamin that were in the rock Rimmon, and to call peaceably unto them.

nn1144   wcs,qmf**7725**   df,pndm1931 dfp,nn**6256**   wcs,qmf**5414** pp,pnx df,pl,nn**802**

14 And Benjamin came again at that time; and they gave them wives

pnl834   pipf**2421**   pr4480/pl,cs,nn**802**   nn**3003**/nn1568   ad**3651**

which they had saved alive of*the*women of Jabesh-gilead: and yet so they

qpf**4672** pp,pnx wcj,ptn**3808**

sufficed them not.

wcj,df,nn**5971**   nipf**5162**   pp,nn**1144**   cj3588   nn**3068**

15 And the people repented them for Benjamin, because that the LORD had

qpf**6213**   nn**6556**   pp,pl,cs,nn**7626**   nn**3478**

made a breach in the tribes of Israel.

                cs,aj2205   df,nn5712   wcs,qmf559 pnit4100   qmf6213   pp,pl,nn802
16 Then the elders of the congregation said, How shall we do for wives for

dfp,pl,nipt3498 cj3588   nn802   nipf8045   pr4480/nn1144
them that remain, seeing the women are destroyed out*of*Benjamin?

        wcs,qmf559   cs,nn3425   nn6413
17 And they said, *There must be* an inheritance for them that be escaped of

pp,nn1144   nn7626   wcj,ptn3808   nimf4229   pr4480/nn3478
Benjamin, that a tribe be   not   destroyed out*of*Israel.

            wcj,pnp587 qmf3201 ptn3808 pp,qnc5414 pp,pnx pl,nn802   pr4480/pl,nn,pnx1323 cj3588
18 Howbeit we   may   not   give   them   wives of*our*daughters: for the

pl,cs,nn1121   nn3478   nipf7650   pp,qnc559   qptp779   qpta5414   nn802   pp,nn1144
children of Israel have sworn, saying, Cursed *be* he that giveth a wife to Benjamin.

                wcs,qmf559   ptdm2009   cs,nn2282   nn3068   pp,nn7887
19 Then they said,   Behold, *there is* a feast of the LORD in Shiloh
pr4480/pl,nn3117/pl,nn,lh3117   pnl834   pr4480/nn,lh6828   pr4480/nn1008
yearly   *in a place* which *is* on*the*north*side of Bethel, on the
cs,nn,lh4217/df,nn8121   pp,nn4546   df,qpta5927   pr4480/nn1008   nn,lh7927
east side   of the highway that goeth up from Bethel to Shechem, and
wcj,pr4480/nn5045   pp,nn3829
on*the*south of Lebonah.

                wcs,pimf6680   (853)   pl,cs,nn1121   nn1144   pp,qnc559 qmv1980
20 Therefore they commanded   the children of Benjamin, saying, Go and
wcj,qpf693   dfp,pl,nn3754
lie*in*wait in the vineyards;

            wcj,qpf7200   wcj,ptdm2009 cj518   pl,cs,nn1323   nn7887   qmf3318   pp,qnc2342
21 And see, and, behold, if the daughters of Shiloh come out to dance in
dfp,pl,nn4246   wcs,qmf3318   pr4480   df,pl,nn3754   wcs,qpf2414 pp,pnx   nn376   nn,pnx802
dances, then come*ye*out of the vineyards, and catch you every man his wife
pr4480/pl,cs,nn1323   nn7887   wcs,qpf1980   cs,nn776   nn1144
of*the*daughters of Shiloh, and go   to the land of Benjamin.

            wcs,qpf1961 cj3588   pl,nn,pnx1 cj176   pl,nn,pnx251 qmf935 pr,pnx413
22 And it shall be, when their fathers or their brethren come unto us to
pp,qnc7378   wcs,qpf559 pr,pnx413   qmv,pnx2603   pnx(853)
complain, that we will say unto them, Be favorable unto   them for our
    cj3588   qpf3947   ptn3808   nn376   nn,pnx802   dfp,nn4421 cj3588 pnp859
sakes: because we reserved not to each man his wife in the war: for ye did
ptn3808 qpf5414   pp,pnx   dfp,nn6256   qmf816
not give unto them at this time, *that* ye should be guilty.

        pl,cs,nn1121   nn1144   wcs,qmf6213 ad3651   wcs,qmf5375   pl,nn802
23 And the children of Benjamin did so, and took *them* wives, according
        pp,nn,pnx4557 pr4480   df,pl,pipt*2342 pnl834   qpf1497   wcs,qmf1980
to their number, of them that danced, whom they caught: and they went and
wcs,qmf7725   pr413   nn,pnx5159   wcs,qmf1129 (853)   df,pl,nn5892   wcs,qmf3427   pp,pnx
returned unto their inheritance, and repaired   the cities, and dwelt in them.

21:16-24 The "feast" spoken of in verse nineteen probably refers to the Passover or one of the three great Jewish feasts (Ex. 23:14-17). In these unsettled times the men went up to Shiloh only once a year instead of three times (1 Sam. 1:3). Only the males kept the feasts, therefore the virgins of Shiloh would naturally be the only maidens present. The public festival would be a likely occasion for their festive dances. It is possible that this was simply a local festival which was peculiar to Shiloh, like the yearly sacrifice of David's family at Bethlehem (1 Sam. 20:29). The men of Israel had made a hasty oath in the heat of anger (Judg. 21:1). Later, when they saw the plight of Benjamin, that without wives the tribe would soon cease to exist, they felt compassion for them (Judg. 21:13, 14). However, the terms of their oath stood; though they would not give their daughters as wives to the Benjamites, they instructed them in detail how to go up to Shiloh and carry off the girls at the festival. In their minds, they would not be guilty of breaking the oath, and the Benjamites would have wives and be preserved as a tribe even though the women were gained by violent means.

^{pl,cs,nn1121}   ⁿⁿ³⁴⁷⁸   ^{wcs,htmf1980} ^{pr4480/ad8033}   ^{df,pndm1931} ^{dfp,nn6256}   ⁿⁿ³⁷⁶

24 And the children of Israel departed thence at that time, every man to

^{pp,nn,pnx7626}   ^{wcj,pp,nn,pnx4940}   ^{wcs,qmf3318}   ^{pr4480/ad8033}   ⁿⁿ³⁷⁶

his   tribe   and to his   family,   and they went out from thence every man to his

^{pp,nn,pnx5159}

inheritance.

^{df,pnp1992} ^{dfp,pl,nn3117}   ^{ptn369} ⁿⁿ⁴⁴²⁸   ^{pp,nn3478}   ⁿⁿ³⁷⁶   ^{qmf6213}

25 In those   days   *there was* no   king in Israel: every man did   *that which*

^{df,aj3477}   ^{pp,du,nn,pnx5869}

was right in his own   eyes.

The Book of

RUTH

The Book of Ruth is an inspiring love story which demonstrates God's providential care. The name of the author is not given, but traditionally the book is credited to Samuel. The Book of Ruth was originally part of the Book of Judges. However, by New Testament times it was included on a scroll with four other books that were read publicly at the feasts of Israel. These books were known as the Five Megilloth (scrolls) and were arranged in the following order: Song of Solomon, Ruth, Lamentations, Ecclesiastes, Esther. The Book of Ruth was read at the Feast of Harvest (Pentecost) because much of the story is set in the harvest fields.

The genealogy at the end of the book is very important because it shows that God chose Ruth, a woman from the heathen land of Moab, to be an ancestor of King David. Ruth is also one of the four women named in the genealogy of Jesus (Matt. 1:5).

The story of Ruth probably took place during the time of Gideon (ca. 1130 B.C.). The famine mentioned in Ruth seems to correspond to the oppression by the Midianites and Israel's subsequent deliverance (Ruth 1:1, 6, cf. Judg. 6:3, 4). Jewish tradition holds that Ruth lived at the same time as Eli the priest. Since she was at least the great–grandmother of David, she must have lived around the twelfth century B.C.

Several laws and customs were involved in the proceedings which led to the marriage of Boaz and Ruth. According to Deuteronomy 25:5, if a woman's husband died and she was left without children, her husband's brother was required to marry her so that there could be an heir to carry on the name of the man who had died. Since Ruth's deceased husband, Mahlon, had no other living brothers, she would most likely have remained unmarried. However, Naomi and Ruth decided to sell the land that belonged to Elimelech, Mahlon, and Chilion. The historian Josephus explains that in this case, the nearest kinsman would customarily have the first option to buy the land, but he would also be expected to marry Ruth (Antiquities V. 9. 4.). The nearest kinsman to Ruth refused to buy the land because in raising up heirs to Mahlon he would have marred his own children's inheritance (Ruth 4:6). In other words, any children born to him and Ruth would be the heirs to all his fortune, making it impossible for him to give an inheritance to those of his own family name. When this man refused to buy the land, Boaz, who was the next closest relative was free to marry Ruth (see the notes on Ruth 2:20; 4:1–8).

Ruth and Naomi

1
    wcs,qmf**1961**   pp,pl,cs,nn**3117**   df,pl,qpta**8199** qnc**8199**
Now it*came*to*pass in the   days when the judges ruled, that there
  wcs,qmf**1961**   nn**7458**   dfp,nn**776**   nn**376**   pr4480/nn1035/nn**3063** wcs,qmf**1980**
was a famine in the land. And a certain man of Bethlehem-judah went

pp,qnc**1481**   pp,pl,cs,nn**7704**   nn**4124** pnp1931   wcj,nn,pnx**802**   wcj,du,cs,nu8147 pl,nn,pnx**1121**
to sojourn in the country of Moab, he, and his wife, and his two   sons.

         wcj,cs,nn8034   df,nn**376**   nn458   wcj,cs,nn8034   nn,pnx**802**
2 And the name of the man _was_ Elimelech, and the name of his wife
nn5281   wcj,cs,nn8034   du,nu,pnx8147 pl,nn,pnx**1121** nn4248   wcj,nn3630 nn673
Naomi, and the name of his two   sons Mahlon and Chilion, Ephrathites
pr4480/nn1035/nn3063   wcs,qmf935   pl,cs,nn**7704**   nn4124   wcs,qmf**1961**
of Bethlehem-judah. And they came into the country of Moab, and continued
ad8033
there.

      nn458   nn5281   cs,nn**376** wcs,qmf**4191**   pnp1931   wcs,nimf**7604**
3 And Elimelech Naomi's husband died; and she was   left, and her
wcj,du,cs,nu8147 pl,nn,pnx**1121**
two   sons.

     wcs,qmf**5375** pp,pnx   pl,nn**802**   pl,nn4125   cs,nn8034   df,nu259
4 And they took them wives of the women*of*Moab; the name of the one
nn6204   wcj,cs,nn8034   df,nuor8145 nn7327   wcs,qmf**3427** ad8033   pp,nu6235
was Orpah, and the name of the other Ruth: and they dwelled there about ten
pl,nn8141
years.

       nn4248   wcj,nn3630 wcs,qmf**4191** ad1571 du,nu,pnx8147   df,nn**802**
5 And Mahlon and Chilion died also both of them; and the woman was
wcs,nimf**7604** pr4480/du,cs,nu8147/pl,nn,pnx3206 wcj,pr4480/nn,pnx**376**
left of*her*two*sons and her husband.

     pnp1931 wcs,qmf**6965**   wcj,pl,nn,pnx**3618**   wcs,qmf**7725**
6 Then she arose with her daughters-in-law, that she might   return
pr4480/pl,cs,nn**7704**   nn4124 cj3588   qpf**8085**   pp,cs,nn**7704**   nn4124   cj3588
from*the*country of Moab: for she had heard in the country of Moab how that the
nn3068   qpf**6485** (853)   nn,pnx**5971** pp,qnc**5414** pp,pnx nn3899
Lord had visited   his people in giving them bread.

        wcs,qmf3318   pr4480   df,nn**4725** pnl834/ad/lh8033   qpf**1961**
7 Wherefore she went forth out of the place   where she was, and her
wcj,du,cs,nu8147   pl,nn,pnx**3618**   pr,pnx5973   wcs,qmf**1980**   dfp,nn**1870** pp,qnc**7725** pr413
two   daughters-in-law with her; and they went on the way to return unto
cs,nn776   nn3063
the land of Judah.

       nn5281 wcs,qmf**559**   pp,du,cs,nu8147   pl,nn,pnx**3618** qmv**1980** qmv**7725** nn**802**
8 And Naomi said unto her two   daughters-in-law, Go, return each to
nn,pnx517   pp,cs,nn1004   nn3068 qmf**6213** nn2617 pr,pnx5973   pp,pnl834   qpf**6213** pr5973
her mother's house: the Lord deal kindly with you, as ye have dealt with the
df,pl,qpta**4191** wcj,pr,pnx5973
dead, and with me.

      nn3068 qmf**5414** pp,pnx   wcj,qmv4672 nn4496 nn**802**   cs,nn1004
9 The Lord grant you that ye may   find rest, each _of you_ in the house of her
nn,pnx376   wcs,qmf**5401** pp,pnx   wcs,qmf**5375**   nn,pnx6963   wcs,qmf1058
husband. Then she kissed them; and they lifted up their voice, and wept.

      wcs,qmf**559** pp,pnx   cj3588   qmf**7725** pr,pnx854   pp,nn,pnx**5971**
10 And they said unto her, Surely we will return with thee unto thy people.

      nn5281 wcs,qmf**559** qmv**7725**   pl,nn,pnx1323 pp,pnit4100   qmf**1980** pr,pnx5973
11 And Naomi said, Turn again, my daughters: why will ye go   with

he,ad5750 (pp,pnx) pl,nn1121 pp,pl,nn,pnx4578 wcs,qpf1961 pp,pnx

me? *are* there yet *any more* sons in my womb, that they may be your

dfp,pl,nn376

husbands?

qmv7725 pl,nn,pnx1323 qmv1980 cj3588 qpf2204 pr4480/qnc1961

12 Turn again, my daughters, go *your way*; for I am too old to have a

pp,nn376 cj3588 qpf559 pp,pnx pta3426 nn8615 qpf1961 pp,nn376 ad1571 df,nn3915

husband. If I should say, I have hope, *if* I should have a husband also tonight,

wcj,ad1571 qpf3205 pl,nn1121

and should also bear sons;

pimf7663 pp,pnp2004 ad5704/pnl834 qmf1431 nimf5702

13 Would ye tarry for them till they were grown? would ye stay for

pp,pnp2004 (pp,ptn1115) qnc1961 pp,nn376 ptn408 pl,nn,pnx1323 cj3588 qpf4843 pp,pnx ad3966

them from having husbands? nay, my daughters; for it grieveth me much

pr,pnx4480 cj3588 cs,nn3027 nn3068 qpf3318 pp,pnx

for your sakes that the hand of the LORD is gone out against me.

wcs,qmf5375 nn,pnx6963 wcs,qmf1058 ad5750 nn6204 wcs,qmf5401

14 And they lifted up their voice, and wept again: and Orpah kissed her

pp,nn,pnx2545 wcj,nn7327 qpf1692 pp,pnx

mother-in-law; but Ruth cleaved unto her.

wcs,qmf559 ptdm2009 nn,pnx2994 qpf7725 pr413 nn,pnx5971

15 And she said, Behold, thy sister-in-law is gone back unto her people, and

wcj,pr413 pl,nn,pnx430 qmv7725 pr310 nn,pnx2994

unto her gods: return thou after thy sister-in-law.

nn7327 wcs,qmf559 qmf6293 pp,pnx ptn408 pp,qnc,pnx5800 pp,qnc7725

16 And Ruth said, Entreat me not to leave thee, *or* to return

pr4480/pr,pnx310 cj3588 pr413/pnl834 qmf1980 qmf1980 wcj,pp,pnl834

from*following*after thee: for whither thou goest, I will go; and where thou

qmf3885 qmf3885 nn,pnx5971 nn,pnx5971 wcj,pl,nn,pnx430 pl,nn,pnx430

lodgest, I will lodge: thy people *shall be* my people, and thy God my God:

pp,pnl834 qmf4191 qmf4191 wcj,ad8033 nimf6912 nn3068 qmf6213 ad3541

17 Where thou diest, will I die, and there will I be buried: the LORD do so

pp,pnx himf3254 wcj,ad3541 cj3588 df,nn4194 himf6504 pr,pnx996 wcj,pr,pnx996

to me, and more also, *if aught* but death part thee and me.

wcs,qmf7200 cj3588 pnp1931 htpt553 pp,qnc1980 pr,pnx854

18 When she saw that she was steadfastly minded to go with her, then

wcs,qmf2308 pp,pinc1696 pr,pnx413

she left speaking unto her.

du,nu,pnx8147 wcs,qmf1980 pr5704 qnc,pnx935 nn1035

19 So they two went until they came to Bethlehem. And

wcs,qmf1961 pp,qnc,pnx935 nn1035 cs,nn3605 df,nn5892

it*came*to*pass, when they were come to Bethlehem, that all the city was

wcs,nimf1949 pr,pnx5921 wcs,qmf559 he,pndm2063 nn5281

moved about them, and they said, *Is* this Naomi?

wcs,qmf559 pr,pnx413 qmf7121 pp,pnx ptn408 nn5281 qmv7121 pp,pnx nn4755 cj3588

20 And she said unto them, Call me not Naomi, call me Mara: for the

nn7706 ad3966/hipf4843 pp,pnx

Almighty hath dealt*very*bitterly with me.

pnp589 qpf1980 aj4392 nn3068 hipf,pnx7725 wcj,ad7387

21 I went out full, and the LORD hath brought*me*home*again empty:

pp,pnit4100 qmf7121 pp,pnx nn5281 wcj,nn3068 qpf6030 pp,pnx

why *then* call ye me Naomi, seeing the LORD hath testified against me, and the

wcj,nn7706 hipf7489 pp,pnx

Almighty hath afflicted me?

nn5281 wcs,qmf7725 wcj,nn7327 df,nn4125 nn,pnx3618 pr,pnx5973

22 So Naomi returned, and Ruth the Moabitess, her daughter-in-law, with her,

df,qpta**7725**   pr4480/pl,cs,nn**7704**   nn4124   wcj,pnp1992 qpf935   nn1035

which returned out*of*the*country of Moab: and they   came to Bethlehem in the

pp,cs,nn8462   pl,nn8184   cs,nn7105

beginning of barley harvest.

Ruth Works in the Field of Boaz

wcj,pp,nn5281   nn4129   pp,nn,pnx**376**   cs,aj1368 cs,nn**376**   nn**2428**

2 ☙ And Naomi had a kinsman of her husband's, a mighty man of wealth,

pr4480/cs,nn**4940**   nn458   wcj,nn,pnx8034   nn1162

of*the*family of Elimelech; and his   name   *was* Boaz.

nn7327   df,nn4125   wcs,qmf559 pr413   nn5281   pte4994 qcj1980   df,nn**7704**

☙ 2 And Ruth the Moabitess   said unto Naomi, Let me now go to the field,

wcj,picj3950   dfp,pl,nn7641   ad310/pnl834   pp,du,nn,pnx**5869**   qmf4672   nn2580

and glean ears*of*corn after *him* in whose sight   I shall find grace. And

wcs,qmf559   pp,pnx   qmv1980   nn,pnx1323

she said unto her, Go, my daughter.

wcs,qmf1980   wcs,qmf935   wcs,pimf3950   dfp,nn**7704** pr310   df,pl,qpta7114

3 And she went, and came, and gleaned in the field after the reapers: and

nn,pnx4745   wcs,qmf7136   cs,nn2513   df,nn**7704**   pp,nn1162 pnl834

her hap was to light on a part of the field *belonging* unto Boaz, who *was*

pr4480/cs,nn**4940**   nn458

of*the*kindred of Elimelech.

wcj,ptdm2009 nn1162 qpf935   pr4480/nn1035   wcs,qmf559   dfp,pl,qpta7114

4 And, behold, Boaz came from Bethlehem, and said unto the reapers, The

nn**3068**   pr,pnx5973   wcs,qmf559 pp,pnx   nn**3068** pimf,pnx**1288**

L**ORD** *be* with you. And they answered him, The L**ORD** bless thee.

wcs,qmf559 nn1162   pp,nn,pnx5288   df,nipt5324 pr5921   dfp,pl,qpta7114 pp,pnit4310

5 Then said Boaz unto his servant that was   set over the reapers, Whose

df,nn5291   df,pndm2063

damsel *is* this?

df,nn5288   df,nipt5324 pr5921   df,pl,qpta7114 wcs,qmf6030   wcs,qmf559 pnp1931

6 And the servant that was   set   over the reapers answered and said,   It *is*

nn4125   nn5291   df,qpta**7725**   pr5973   nn5281   pr4480/cs,nn**7704**   nn4124

the Moabitish damsel that came back with Naomi out*of*the*country of Moab:

wcs,qmf559   pte4994   picj3950   wcs,qpf622 pr310   df,pl,qpta7114

7 And she said, I pray you, let me glean and gather after the reapers among

dfp,pl,nn6016   wcs,qmf935   wcs,qmf5975   pr4480/ad**227**   df,nn1242   wcj,pr5704 ad6258

the sheaves: so she came, and hath continued even from the morning until now,

pndm2088   qnc,pnx**3427**   nn4592   df,nn**1004**

that she tarried a little in the house.

wcs,qmf559 nn1162 pr413   nn7327   qpf8085   he,ptn3808   nn,pnx1323   qmf1980 ptn408

8 Then said Boaz unto Ruth, Hearest thou not, my daughter? Go not to

pp,qnc3950   aj312   pp,nn**7704** wcj,ad1571/ptn3808 qmf5674 pr4480/pndm2088 wcj,ad3541 qmf1692   pr5973

glean in another field,   neither   go from hence, but abide here fast by my

pl,nn,pnx5291

maidens:

☙ **2:1** See the note on Ruth 4:17–22, on the lineage of Boaz.

☙ **2:2, 3** The field of Boaz was near the city of Bethlehem and was the place where Ruth gleaned corn for herself and Naomi. It is also in this area that David would tend his father's sheep, and that Joseph would bring his young wife, Mary, to deliver her baby, the Lord Jesus Christ. It is possible that in the hills above these fields the shepherds were tending to their flocks on the night when Christ was born.

☙ **2:2–7** See the note on Leviticus 19:9, 10.

9 *Let* thine eyes *be* on the field that they do reap, and go thou after them: have I not charged the young men that they shall not touch thee? and when thou art athirst, go unto the vessels, and drink of*that*which the young men have drawn.

10 Then she fell on her face, and bowed herself to the ground, and said unto him, Why have I found grace in thine eyes, that thou shouldest take knowledge of me, seeing I *am* a stranger?

11 And Boaz answered and said unto her, It hath fully been showed me, all that thou hast done unto thy mother-in-law since the death of thine husband: and *how* thou hast left thy father and thy mother, and the land of thy nativity, and art come unto a people which thou knewest not heretofore.

12 The LORD recompense thy work, and a full reward be given thee of the LORD God of Israel, under whose wings thou art come to trust.

13 Then she said, Let me find favor in thy sight, my lord; for that thou hast comforted me, and for that thou hast spoken friendly unto thine handmaid, though I be not like unto one of thine handmaidens.

14 And Boaz said unto her, At mealtime come thou hither, and eat of the bread, and dip thy morsel in the vinegar. And she sat beside the reapers: and he reached her parched *corn*, and she did eat, and was sufficed, and left.

15 And when she was risen up to glean, Boaz commanded his young men, saying, Let her glean even among the sheaves, and reproach her not:

16 And let fall also *some* of the handfuls of purpose for her, and leave *them*, that she may glean *them*, and rebuke her not.

17 So she gleaned in the field until even, and beat out that she had gleaned: and it was about an ephah of barley.

18 And she took*it*up, and went into the city: and her mother-in-law saw

nn376 himf5234 (853) nn,pnx7453 wcs,qmf559 ptn408 nimf3045 cj3588 df,nn802 qpf935
one could know another. And he said, Let it not be known that a woman came

df,nn1637
into the floor.

wcs,qmf559 qmv3051 df,nn4304 pnl834 pr,pnx5921 wcj,qmv270 pp,pnx
15 Also he said, Bring the veil that *thou hast* upon thee, and hold it.

wcs,qmf270 pp,pnx wcs,qmf4058 nu8337 pl,nn8184 wcs,qmf7896
And when she held it, he measured six *measures* of barley, and laid *it*

pr,pnx5921 wcs,qmf935 df,nn5892
on her: and she went into the city.

wcs,qmf935 pr413 nn,pnx2545 wcs,qmf559 pnit4310 pnp859
16 And when she came to her mother-in-law, she said, Who *art* thou, my

nn,pnx1323 wcs,himf5046 pp,pnx (853) cs,nn3605 pnl834 df,nn376 qpf6213 pp,pnx
daughter? And she told her all that the man had done to her.

wcs,qmf559 df,pndm428 nu8337 df,pl,nn8184 qpf5414 pp,pnx cj3588 qpf559
17 And she said, These six *measures* of barley gave he me; for he said

pr,pnx413 qmf935 ptn408 ad7387 pr413 nn,pnx2545
to me, Go not empty unto thy mother-in-law.

wcs,qmf559 qmv3427 nn,pnx1323 ad5704/pnl834 qmf3045 pnit349 nn1697
18 Then said she, Sit still, my daughter, until thou know how the matter

qmf5307 cj3588 df,nn376 ptn3808 qmf8252 cj3588/cj518 pipf3615 df,nn1697
will fall: for the man will not be*in*rest, until he have finished the thing

df,nn3117
this day.

Boaz Marries Ruth

apf5927/wcj,nn1162 df,nn8179 wcs,qmf3427 ad8033 wcj,ptdm2009
4 ✡ Then went*Boaz*up to the gate, and sat*him*down there: and, behold,

df,qpta1350 nn1162 pipf1696 qpta5674 pnl834 wcs,qmf559 pnid6423
the kinsman of whom Boaz spoke came by; unto whom he said, Ho, such

aj492 qmv5493 qmv3427 ad6311 wcs,qmf5493 wcs,qmf3427
a one! turn aside, sit down here. And he turned aside, and sat down.

wcs,qmf3947 nu6235 pl,nn376 pr4480/cs,aj2205 df,nn5892 wcs,qmf559 qmv3427
2 And he took ten men of*the*elders of the city, and said, Sit*ye*down

ad6311 wcs,qmf3427
here. And they sat down.

wcs,qmf559 dfp,qpta1350 nn5281 df,qpta7725
3 And he said unto the kinsman, Naomi, that is come again

pr4480/cs,nn7704 nn4124 qpf4376 cs,nn2513 df,nn7704 pnl834 pp,nn,pnx251
out*of*the*country of Moab, selleth a parcel of land, which *was* our brother

pp,nn458
Elimelech's:

✡ **4:1-8** Boaz was willing to perform the duty of next of kin to redeem a piece of land so it could stay in the family (see Lev. 25:25), but there was a man who was a closer relative. However, the plans of the closer relative were complicated by the need to contract a "levirate marriage." Therefore, the other relative deferred to Boaz, who willingly married Ruth. The legal basis for this practice is found in Deuteronomy 25:5–10, but the obligation dates back to the patriarchs (Gen. 38:8). The legal ramifications of such cases were still being discussed in Jesus' day (Matt. 22:23–28).

It is to be noted that Ruth did not shame the relative who refused to perform his duty. According to Deuteronomy, she was supposed to take off his sandal and spit in his face, yet it appears that she was not even present with Boaz at the time. Some have suggested that Ruth was not able to do so because she was a Moabitess. Others say that because of her love for Boaz, Ruth did not want to marry the person who was the closest relative. See the introduction to the Book of Ruth.

4 **And   I   thought to advertise thee, saying, Buy** *it* **before the inhabitants, and before the elders of my people. If thou wilt redeem** *it,* **redeem** *it:* **but   if thou wilt not redeem** *it, then* **tell   me, that I may know: for** *there is* **none to redeem** *it* **beside thee; and   I** *am* **after thee. And he said,   I   will redeem** *it.*

5 **Then   said   Boaz, What   day   thou buyest the field of*the*hand of Naomi, thou must buy** *it* **also   of   Ruth the Moabitess, the wife of the   dead, to raise up the name of the   dead   upon his inheritance.**

6 **And the kinsman   said, I   cannot   redeem** *it* **for myself, lest I mar   mine own inheritance: redeem thou   my   right to thyself; for I   cannot   redeem** *it.*

7 **Now   this** *was the manner* **in former time in Israel concerning redeeming and concerning changing, for to confirm   all   things; a man plucked off his shoe, and gave** *it* **to his neighbor: and   this** *was* **a testimony in Israel.**

8 **Therefore the kinsman   said   unto Boaz, Buy** *it* **for thee. So he drew off his shoe.**

9 **And Boaz   said   unto the elders, and** *unto* **all   the people, Ye** *are* **witnesses this day, that I have bought   all   that** *was* **Elimelech's, and all   that** *was* **Chilion's and Mahlon's, of*the*hand of Naomi.**

10 **Moreover   Ruth the Moabitess, the wife of Mahlon, have I purchased to be my wife, to raise up the name of the   dead   upon his inheritance, that the name of the   dead   be   not   cut off from among his brethren, and from*the*gate of his place: ye** *are* **witnesses this day.**

11 **And   all   the people that** *were* **in the gate,   and the elders,   said,** *We are* **witnesses. The LORD make   the woman that is come into thine house like Rachel and like Leah, which   two   did build   the house of Israel: and   do   thou worthily in Ephratah, and be   famous   in Bethlehem:**

12 **And let thy house   be   like the house of Pharez, whom Tamar bore unto Judah, of   the   seed   which the LORD shall give thee of   this   young woman.**

The Genealogy of Boaz

13 So Boaz took Ruth, and she was his wife: and when he went in
unto her, the LORD gave her conception, and she bore a son.

14 And the women said unto Naomi, Blessed be the LORD, which hath not
left thee this day without a kinsman, that his name may be famous in Israel.

15 And he shall be unto thee a restorer of thy life, and a nourisher of
thine old age: for thy daughter-in-law, which loveth thee, which is better
to thee than seven sons, hath born him.

16 And Naomi took the child, and laid it in her bosom, and
became nurse unto it.

17 And the women*her*neighbors gave it a name, saying, There is a son
born to Naomi; and they called his name Obed: he is the father of Jesse, the
father of David.

18 Now these are the generations of Pharez: Pharez begot Hezron,

19 And Hezron begot Ram, and Ram begot Amminadab,

20 And Amminadab begot Nahshon, and Nahshon begot Salmon,

21 And Salmon begot Boaz, and Boaz begot Obed,

22 And Obed begot Jesse, and Jesse begot David.

4:17-22 Boaz was a descendant of Salmon who married Rahab the harlot of Jericho (Josh. 2:1-21; Matt. 1:5). Since the purpose of Hebrew genealogies was to show lineage rather than to list each particular descendant, it is possible that some generations are missing in both Ruth 4:18-22 or Matthew 1:4-6. Assuming that the generations from Ruth to David are complete, Ruth and Boaz were King David's great-grandparents.

The First Book of
SAMUEL

The books of First and Second Samuel made up one book originally. They remained so in the Hebrew text until the publishing of the Hebrew Bible in A.D. 1517 where they appeared as the separate books we know today. The Septuagint and other translations of the Old Testament that followed divided the books of Samuel and Kings into First Kings through Fourth Kings.

The Book of First Samuel presents in detail the transitional phase between the period of the judges and the period of the kings. During this time God instituted the offices of prophet and king, the latter replacing the office of the judge as Israel's political leader. It is important to note that the prophetic function did not originate at this time. Moses and Deborah are examples of those who were both political leaders over Israel and prophets (Ex. 3:11–22; Judg. 4:4, 5). These should be distinguished from Samuel and his successors, who were not rulers used in a prophetic capacity, but those who held the office of prophet. It was not until Samuel organized the "company of the prophets" (1 Sam. 19:20) that the office seems to have been formally established in Israel. Samuel bridged the gap between the periods of the judges and kings in that he was the last one to serve as a judge in all Israel (see the note on 1 Sam. 8:5–7) and that he anointed the first two kings of Israel, Saul and David.

The book, whose principal characters are Samuel, Saul, and David, is divided into two sections: the first seven chapters outline the life and ministry of Samuel, and the remainder of the book describes the events during the reign of Saul. The climax is reached when God rejects Saul as king for disobeying His command, and instructs Samuel to anoint David, the son of Jesse, as the next king (1 Sam. 15:26).

Samuel's Birth

1

wcs,qmf**1961**	nu259	nn**376**	pr4480	df,nn7436	pr4480/cs,nn2022

Now there was a certain man of Ramathaim-zophim, of mount

nn669	wcj,nn,pnx8034	nn511	cs,nn**1121**	nn3395	cs,nn**1121**

Ephraim, and his name *was* Elkanah, the son of Jeroham, the son of

nn453	cs,nn**1121**	nn8459	cs,nn**1121**	nn6689	nn6733

Elihu, the son of Tohu, the son of Zuph, an Ephrathite.

wcj,pp,pnx	du,cs,nu8147	pl,nn**802**	cs,nn8034	nu259	nn2584

2 And he had two wives; the name of the one *was* Hannah, and the

wcj,cs,nn8034	df,nuor8145	nn6444	pp,nn6444	wcs,qmf**1961**	pl,nn3206	wcj,pp,nn2584	ptn369

name of the other Peninnah: and Peninnah had children, but Hannah had no

pl,nn3206

children.

df,pndm1931	df,nn**376**	wcj,qpf**5927**	pr4480/nn,pnx5892	pr4480/pl,nn**3117**/pl,nn3117	pp,htnc*7812

3 And this man went up out*of*his*city yearly to worship and to

wcj,pp,qnc**2076**   pp,nn**3068**   pl,nn**6635**   pp,nn7887   du,cs,nu8147 pl,cs,nn**1121**   nn5941   nn2652

sacrifice unto the LORD of hosts in Shiloh. And the two sons of Eli, Hophni

       wcj,nn6372   pl,nn**3548**   pp,nn**3068**   wcj,ad8033

and Phinehas, the priests of the LORD, *were* there.

       df,nn3117 wcs,qmf**1961**   nn511   wcj,qmf**2076**   wcs,qmf**5414**   pp,nn6444

4 And when the time was that Elkanah offered, he gave to Peninnah his

nn,pnx**802**   wcj,pp,cs,nn**3605** pl,nn,pnx**1121**   wcj,pl,nn,pnx1323   pl,nn4490

wife, and to all her sons and her daughters, portions:

      wcj,pp,nn2584   qmf**5414** nu259 du,nn**639**   nn4490 cj3588   qpf157 (853)   nn2584

5 But unto Hannah he gave a worthy portion; for he loved Hannah: but

   wcj,nn**3068**   qpf5462   nn,pnx7358

the LORD had shut up her womb.

       nn,pnx6869   ad1571 wcj,pipf,pnx**3707**   nn3708 pp,pr5668   hinc,pnx7481   cj3588

6 And her adversary also provoked her sore, for to make*her*fret, because the

nn**3068**   qpf5462/pr1157   nn,pnx7358

LORD had shut up her womb.

     qmf**6213** wcj,ad**3651** nn8141 pp,nn8141 pr4480/cs,nn1767   qnc,pnx**5927**   pr4480/cs,nn**1004**

7 And *as* he did so year by year, when she went up to the house

      nn**3068** ad**3651** himf,pnx**3707**   wcs,qmf1058   wcj,ptn**3808** qmf398

of the LORD, so she provoked her; therefore she wept, and did not eat.

     wcs,qmf**559**   nn511   nn,pnx**376** pp,pnx   nn2584 wcj,pnit4100   qmf1058

8 Then said Elkanah her husband to her, Hannah, why weepest thou? and

wcj,pnit4100 qmf398   ptn**3808**   wcj,pnit4100   nn,pnx3824   qmf**7489**   he,ptn**3808** pnp595 aj**2896**

why eatest thou not? and why is thy heart grieved? *am* not I better

pp,pnx   pr4480/nu6235 pl,nn**1121**

to thee than ten sons?

     nn2584   wcs,qmf**6965** pr310   qpf398 pp,nn7887 wcj,pr310   qna8354

9 So Hannah rose up after they had eaten in Shiloh, and after they had drunk.

  wcj,nn5941   df,nn**3548** qpta**3427** pr5921 df,nn**3678** pr5921 cs,nn4201   cs,nn**1964**   nn**3068**

Now Eli the priest sat upon a seat by a post of the temple of the LORD.

      wcj,pnp1931   cs,aj**4751**   nn5315   wcs,htmf**6419** pr5921   nn**3068**

10 And she *was* in bitterness of soul, and prayed unto the LORD, and

wcj,qna1058/qmf1058

wept sore.

       wcs,qmf**5087**   nn5088   wcs,qmf**559**   nn**3068**   pl,nn**6635** cj518

🔊 11 And she vowed a vow, and said, O LORD of hosts, if thou wilt

qna**7200**/qmf**7200**   pp,cs,nn6040   nn,pnx519   wcs,qpf,pnx**2142**   wcj,ptn**3808**

indeed look on the affliction of thine handmaid, and remember me, and not

qmf7911 (853)   pp,nn,pnx519   wcs,qpf,pnx**5414**   pp,nn,pnx519 pl,nn**376** cs,nn**2233**

forget thine handmaid, but wilt give unto thine handmaid a man child, then

   wcs,qpf,pnx**5414**   pp,nn**3068** cs,nn3605   pl,cs,nn**3117**   nn,pnx**2416**

I will give him unto the LORD all the days of his life, and there shall

ptn**3808** wcj,nn4177 qmf**5927** pr5921   nn,pnx**7218**

no razor come upon his head.

      wcj,qpf**1961**   cj3588   hipf7235 pp,htnc**6419** pp,pl,cs,nn**6440**   nn**3068**

12 And it*came*to*pass, as she continued praying before the LORD, that

wcj,nn5941 qpta**8104** (853)   nn,pnx**6310**

Eli marked her mouth.

🔊 **1:11** The outward sign of not shaving Samuel's head was associated with the Nazarite vow (see the note on Num. 6:2–21). Apparently Samuel, like Samson (see Judg. 13:4, 5), was to be a Nazarite. The difference was that Samson was a Nazarite by God's instruction and Samuel's mother made the vow for her son. As a result of her faith toward God, Hannah's prayer was answered.

wcj,nn2584 pnp1931 pipt1696 pr5921   nn,pnx3820 ad7535   du,nn,pnx8193 pl,qpta5128

13 Now Hannah, she spoke in her heart; only her lips moved, but her

wcj,nn,pnx6963 ptn3808 nimf8085   nn5941 wcs,qmf2803   pp,aj7910

voice was not heard: therefore Eli thought she had been drunken.

nn5941 wcs,qmf559 pr,pnx413   pr5704 pnit4970   htmf7937 himv5493   (853)

14 And Eli said unto her, How long wilt thou be drunken? put away

nn,pnx3196 pr4480/pr,pnx5921

thy wine from thee.

nn2584   wcs,qmf6030   wcs,qmf559 ptn3808   nn,pnx113   nn802

15 And Hannah answered and said, No, my lord, I *am* a woman of a

cs,aj7186   nn7307 pnp595   qpf8354   ptn3808 wcj,nn3196   wcj,nn7941

sorrowful spirit: I have drunk neither wine nor strong drink, but have

wcs,qmf8210   (853)   nn,pnx5315 pp,pl,cs,nn6440   nn3068

poured out my soul before the Lord.

qmf5414   ptn408   (853)   nn,pnx519 pp,pl,cs,nn6440   cs,nn1323/nn1100   cj3588

16 Count not thine handmaid for a daughter*of*Belial: for

pr4480/cs,nn7230   nn,pnx7879   wcj,nn,pnx3708   pipf1696   pr5704/ad6258

out*of*the*abundance of my complaint and grief have I spoken hitherto.

nn5941 wcs,qmf6030   wcs,qmf559 qmv1980   pp,nn7965   wcj,pl,cs,nn430   nn3478

17 Then Eli answered and said, Go in peace: and the God of Israel

qmf5414   (853)   nn,pnx7596 pnl834   qpf7592 pr4480/pr,pnx5973

grant *thee* thy petition that thou hast asked of him.

wcs,qmf559   nn,pnx8198 qmf4672 nn2580   pp,du,nn,pnx5869

18 And she said, Let thine handmaid find grace in thy sight. So the

df,nn802 wcs,qmf1980   pp,nn,pnx1870   wcs,qmf398   wcj,pl,nn,pnx6440 qpf1961 (pp,pnx) ptn3808 ad5750

woman went her way, and did eat, and her countenance was no more

sad.

wcs,himf7925/dfp,nn1242   wcs,htmf7812 pp,pl,cs,nn6440   nn3068

19 And they rose*up*in*the*morning*early, and worshiped before the Lord,

wcs,qmf7725   wcs,qmf935 pr413   nn,pnx1004 df,nn,lh7414   nn511 wcs,qmf3045 (853) nn2584

and returned, and came to their house to Ramah: and Elkanah knew Hannah

nn,pnx802   nn3068 wcs,qmf,pnx2142

his wife; and the Lord remembered her.

wcs,qmf1961   df,pl,nn3117 pp,pl,cs,nn8622   nn2584

20 Wherefore it*came*to*pass, when the time was come about after Hannah

wcs,qmf2029   wcs,qmf3205 nn1121   wcs,qmf7121 (853)   nn,pnx8034 nn8050

had conceived, that she bore a son, and called his name Samuel, *saying,*

cj3588   qpf,pnx7592   pr4480/nn3068

Because I have asked him of*the*Lord.

df,nn376   nn511   wcj,cs,nn3605   nn,pnx1004 wcs,qmf5927   pp,qnc2076

21 And the man Elkanah, and all his house, went up to offer unto the

pp,nn3068 (853)   df,pl,nn3117 cs,nn2077   wcj(853)   nn,pnx5088

Lord the yearly sacrifice, and his vow.

wcj,nn2584   qpf5927/ptn3808   cj3588   qpf559   pp,nn,pnx376

22 But Hannah went*not*up; for she said unto her husband, *I will not go up*

pr5704 df,nn5288   nimf1580   wcs,hipf,pnx935   wcs,nipf7200 (853)

until the child be weaned, and *then* I will bring him, that he may appear

pl,cs,nn6440   nn3068   ad8033 wcs,qpf3427 pr5704/nn5769

before the Lord, and there abide forever.

nn511   nn,pnx376 wcs,qmf559   pp,pnx   qmv6213   pp,du,nn,pnx5869   df,aj2896

23 And Elkanah her husband said unto her, Do what seemeth thee good;

qmv3427 pr5704   qnc,pnx1580 pnx(853)   ad389   nn3068 himf6965 (853) nn,pnx1697

tarry until thou have weaned him; only the Lord establish his word. So the

df,nn802 wcs,qmf3427   wcs,qmf3243/(853)/nn,pnx1121   pr5704   qnc,pnx1580 pnx(853)

woman abode, and gave*her*son*suck until she weaned him.

pp,pnl834   qpf,pnx**1580**   wcs,qmf,pnx**5927**   pr,pnx5973   nu7969

24 And when she had weaned him, she took*him*up with her, with three

pp,pl,nn6499   nu259 wcj,nn374   nn7058   wcj,cs,nn5035   nn3196   wcs,himf935

bullocks, and one ephah of flour, and a bottle of wine, and brought him unto the

cs,nn1004   nn3068   nn7887   wcj,df,nn5288   qpf5288

house of the LORD in Shiloh: and the child *was* young.

wcs,qmf**7819** (853)   df,nn6499   wcs,himf935 (853)   df,nn5288 pr413 nn5941

25 And they slew   a bullock, and brought   the child to Eli.

wcs,qmf**559** pte994   nn,pnx113   nn,pnx5315   cs,aj2416   nn,pnx113 pnp589

26 And she said, Oh my lord, *as* thy soul liveth, my lord, I *am* the

df,nn**802**   df,nipt5324 pr,pnx5973   pp,pndm2088 pp,htnc6419   pr413   nn3068

woman that stood by thee here, praying unto the LORD.

pr413 df,pndm2088 df,nn5288   htpf**6419**   nn3068   wcs,qmf5414 pp,pnx (853)   nn,pnx7596

27 For this child I prayed; and the LORD hath given me   my petition

pnl834   qpf7592   pr4480/pr,pnx5973

which I asked   of   him:

wcj,ad1571 pnp595   hipf,pnx7592   pp,nn3068   cs,nn3605 pnl834   df,pl,nn3117

28 Therefore also   I have lent him to the LORD; as long   as he liveth

pnp1931   qpf1961 qptp7592   pp,nn3068   wcs,htmf***7812**   pp,nn3068   ad8033

he shall be lent to the LORD. And he worshiped the LORD there.

Hannah's Prayer

nn2584   wcs,htmf**6419**   wcs,qmf559   nn,pnx3820   qpf5970   pp,nn3068

2 And Hannah prayed, and said, My heart rejoiceth in the LORD, mine

nn,pnx7161   qpf7311   pp,nn3068   nn,pnx**6310**   qpf7337   pr5921   pl,qpta,pnx341

horn is exalted in the LORD: my mouth is enlarged over mine enemies;

cj3588   qpf8055   pp,nn,nn3444

because I rejoice in thy salvation.

ptn369   aj**6918**   pp,nn3068 cj3588   ptn369 ptn,pnx1115   wcj,ptn369

2 *There is* none holy as the LORD: for *there is* none beside thee: neither *is*

nn6697   pp,pl,nn,pnx**430**

there any rock like our   God.

pimf**1696**   ptn408   himf7235   aj1364/aj1364   aj6277   qmf3318

3 Talk   no   more   so   exceeding proudly; let *not* arrogance come out

pr4480/nn,pnx6310   cj3588   nn3068   cs,nn410   pl,nn**1844**   wcj,pp,pnx   pl,nn5949

of*your*mouth: for the LORD *is* a God of knowledge, and by him actions are

nipf8505

weighed.

pl,cs,nn7198   pl,nn1368   aj2844   wcj,pl,nipt**3782**   qpf247

4 The bows of the mighty men *are* broken, and they that stumbled are girded

nn**2428**

with strength.

aj7649   nipf7936   dfp,nn3899

5 *They that were* full have hired*out*themselves for bread; and *they that were*

wcj,aj7457   qpf2308   cj5704   aj6135   qpf3205   nu7651   wcj,cs,aj7227

hungry ceased: so that the barren hath born seven; and she that hath many

pl,nn**1121**   pupf535

children is waxed feeble.

nn3068   hipt**4191**   wcj,pipt**2421**   hipt3381   nn7585

6 The LORD killeth, and maketh alive: he bringeth down to the grave, and

wcs,himf**5927**

bringeth up.

nn3068   hipt3423   wcj,hipt6238   hipt8213   cj637   pipt*7311

7 The LORD maketh poor, and maketh rich: he bringeth low, and lifteth up.

^{hipt6965}   ^{aj1800}   ^{pr4480/nn6083}   ^{himf7311}   ^{aj34}

8 He raiseth up the poor out*of*the*dust, *and* lifteth up the beggar

^{pr4480/nn830}   ^{pp,hinc3427}   ^{pr5973}   ^{pl,nn5081}   ^{himf,pnx5157}

from*the*dunghill, to set *them* among princes, and to make*them*inherit the

^{wcj,cs,nn3678}   ^{aj3519}   ^{cj3588}   ^{pl,cs,nn4690}   ⁿⁿ⁷⁷⁶   ^{pp,nn3068}   ^{wcs,qmf7896}

throne of glory: for the pillars of the earth *are* the LORD's, and he hath set

ⁿⁿ⁸³⁹⁸   ^{pr,pnx5921}

the world upon them.

^{qmf8104}   ^{du,cs,nn7272}   ^{aj,pnx2623}   ^{wcj,aj7563}   ^{nimf1826}

9 He will keep the feet of his saints, and the wicked shall be silent in

^{dfp,nn2822}   ^{cj3588}   ^{pp,nn3581}   ^{ptn3808 nn376}   ^{qmf1396}

darkness; for by strength shall no man prevail.

^{pl,hipt,pnx7378}   ⁿⁿ³⁰⁶⁸   ^{qmf2865}   ^{dfp,du,nn8064}

10 The adversaries of the LORD shall be broken*to*pieces; out of heaven shall

^{himf7481}   ^{pr,pnx5921}   ⁿⁿ³⁰⁶⁸   ^{qmf1777}   ^{pl,cs,nn657}   ⁿⁿ⁷⁷⁶

he thunder upon them: the LORD shall judge the ends of the earth; and he shall

^{wcj,qmf5414}   ⁿⁿ⁵⁷⁹⁷   ^{pp,nn,pnx4428}   ^{wcj,himf7311}   ^{cs,nn7161}   ^{nn,pnx4899}

give strength unto his king, and exalt the horn of his anointed.

ⁿⁿ⁵¹¹   ^{wcs,qmf1980}   ^{df,nn,lh7414} ^{pr5921}   ^{nn,pnx1004}   ^{wcj,df,nn5288} ^{qpf1961}   ^{pipt8334}

11 And Elkanah went to Ramah to his house. And the child did minister

⁽⁸⁵³⁾   ⁿⁿ³⁰⁶⁸   ⁽⁸⁵³⁾ ^{pl,cs,nn6440} ⁿⁿ⁵⁹⁴¹   ^{df,nn3548}

unto the LORD before Eli the priest.

Eli's Corrupt Sons

^{wcj,pl,cs,nn1121}   ⁿⁿ⁵⁹⁴¹   ^{pl,cs,nn1121}   ⁿⁿ¹¹⁰⁰   ^{qpf3045} ^{ptn3808} ⁽⁸⁵³⁾

12 Now the sons of Eli *were* sons of Belial; they knew not the

ⁿⁿ³⁰⁶⁸

LORD.

^{df,pl,nn3548} ^{wcj,cs,nn4941} ^{pr854}   ^{df,nn5971}   ^{cs,nn3605} ⁿⁿ³⁷⁶   ^{qpta2076}

13 And the priests' custom with the people *was, that*, when any man offered

ⁿⁿ²⁰⁷⁷   ^{df,nn3548}   ^{cs,nn5288}   ^{wcj,qpf935}   ^{df,nn1320}   ^{pp,pinc1310}

sacrifice, the priest's servant came, while the flesh was in seething, with a

^{wcj,df,nn4207}   ^{cs,nu7969} ^{df,du,nn8127}   ^{pp,nn,pnx3027}

fleshhook of three teeth in his hand;

^{wcj,hipf5221}   ^{dfp,nn3595 cj176 dfp,nn1731 cj176}   ^{dfp,nn7037}   ^{cj176 dfp,nn6517 cs,nn3605 pnl834}

14 And he struck *it* into the pan, or kettle, or caldron, or pot; all that

^{df,nn4207}   ^{qmf5927}   ^{df,nn3548 qmf3947}   ^{pp,pnx}   ^{ad3602}   ^{qmf6213}   ^{pp,nn7887}

the fleshhook brought up the priest took for himself. So they did in Shiloh unto

^{pp,cs,nn3605}   ⁿⁿ³⁴⁷⁸   ^{df,pl,qpta935}   ^{ad8033}

all the Israelites that came thither.

^{ad1571}   ^{pp,ad2962}   ^{himf6999} ⁽⁸⁵³⁾   ^{df,nn2459}   ^{df,nn3548}   ^{cs,nn5288} ^{wcs,qpf935}   ^{wcs,qpf559}

15 Also before they burnt the fat, the priest's servant came, and said to

^{dfp,nn376}   ^{df,qpta2076}   ^{qmv5414} ⁿⁿ¹³²⁰   ^{pp,qnc6740}   ^{dfp,nn3548}   ^{wcj,ptn3808} ^{qmf3947}

the man that sacrificed, Give flesh to roast for the priest; for he will not have

^{nn1320/pupt1310}   ^{pr,pnx4480}   ^{cj3588/cj518} ^{aj2416}

sodden flesh of thee, but raw.

^{df,nn376}   ^{wcs,qmf559} ^{pr,pnx413}   ^{pina6999/himf6999}   ^{df,nn2459}

16 And *if* any man said unto him, Let*them*not*fail*to*burn the fat

^{dfp,nn3117}   ^{wcj,qmv3947} ^(pp,pnx)   ^{pp,pnl834}   ^{nn,pnx5315}   ^{pimf183}

presently, and *then* take *as much* as thy soul desireth; then he would

^{wcs,qpf559}   ^{pp,pnx}   ^{cj3588}   ^{qmf5414}   ^{ad6258}   ^{wcj,cj518} ^{ptn3808}   ^{qpf3947}

answer him, *Nay*; but thou shalt give *it me* now: and if not, I will take *it* by

^{pp,nn2394}

force.

cs,nn2403   df,pl,nn5288   wcs,qmf1961   ad3966   aj1419   (853)   pl,cs,nn6440

17 Wherefore the sin of the young men was very great   before the

nn3068 cj3588 df,pl,nn376 pipf5006 (853) cs,nn4503   nn3068

LORD: for men abhorred   the offering of the LORD.

wcj,nn8050   pipt8334   (853) pl,cs,nn6440   nn3068   nn5288   qptp2296

18 But Samuel ministered   before the LORD, *being* a child, girded with a

nn906   nn646

linen ephod.

nn,pnx517   qmf6213   pp,pnx   aj6996 wcj,nn4598   wcj,hipf5927   pp,pnx

19 Moreover his mother made him a little coat, and brought *it* to him

pr4480/pl,nn3117/pl,nn3117   pp,qnc,pnx5927 pr854   nn,pnx376   pp,qnc2076 (853)   df,pl,nn3117

from*year*to*year, when she came up with her husband to offer   the yearly

cs,nn2077

sacrifice.

nn5941 wcs,pipf1288 (853)   nn511   wcj(853)   nn,pnx802   wcs,qpf559   nn3068   cj7760

20 And Eli blessed   Elkanah and   his wife, and said, The LORD give

pp,pnx nn2233 pr4480 df,pndm2063 df,nn802 pr8478 df,nn7596 pnl834   qpf7592   pp,nn3068

thee seed of   this   woman for the loan which is lent to the LORD. And they

wcs,qpf1980   pp,nn,pnx4725

went unto their own home.

cj3588   nn3068   qpf6485 (853)   nn2584   wcs,qmf2029   wcs,qmf3205 nu7969

21 And the LORD visited   Hannah, so that she conceived, and bore three

pl,nn1121 wcj,du,cs,nu8147 pl,nn1323   df,nn5288   nn8050 wcs,qmf1431 pr5973   nn3068

sons and   two   daughters. And the child Samuel grew before the LORD.

wcj,nn5941   ad3966 aj2204   wcj,qpf8085 (853) cs,nn3605 pnl834   pl,nn,pnx1121 qmf6213

22 Now Eli was very old, and heard   all that his sons   did unto

pp,cs,nn3605 nn3478   wcj(853) pnl834   qmf7901 pr854   df,pl,nn802   df,pl,qpta6633   cs,nn6607

all   Israel; and   how they lay with the women that assembled *at* the door

cs,nn168   nn4150

of the tabernacle of the congregation.

wcs,qmf559   pp,pnx   pp,pnit4100 qmf6213   df,pndm428 dfp,pl,nn1697 pnl834 pnp595 qpta8085

23 And he said unto them, Why   do ye such things? for I hear of

(853)   aj7451 pl,nn,pnx1697 pr4480/pr854 cs,nn3605 pndm428 df,nn5971

your evil dealings by   all   this people.

ptn408   pl,nn,pnx1121 cj3588   ptn3808 aj2896 df,nn8052 pnl834 pnp595 qpta8085

24 Nay, my sons; for *it is* no good report that I hear: ye make the

nn3068 cs,nn5971   pl,hipt5674

LORD's people to transgress.

cj518   nn376 qmf2398   pp,nn376   pl,nn430   wcs,pipf,pnx6419   wcj,cj518

25 If one man sin against another, the judge shall judge him: but if   a

nn376 qmf2398   pp,nn3068 pnit4310   htmf6419   pp,pnx   wcj,ptn3808

man sin against the LORD, who shall entreat for him? Notwithstanding they

qmf8085   pp,cs,nn6963   nn,pnx1   cj3588   nn3068 qpf2654 pp,hinc,pnx4191

hearkened not unto the voice of their father, because the LORD would   slay

them.

wcj,df,nn5288   nn8050   qpta1980 wcj,aj1432   wcj,aj2896 ad1571 pr5973   nn3068

26 And the child Samuel grew on, and was in favor both with the LORD,

wcj,ad1571 pr5973 pl,nn376

and also with men.

wcs,qmf935 cs,nn376   pl,nn430 pr413 nn5941 wcs,qmf559 pr,pnx413   ad3541 qpf559

27 And there came a man of God unto Eli, and said unto him, Thus saith

nn3068   he,nina1540/nipf1540   pr413   cs,nn1004   nn,pnx1   pp,qnc,pnx1961

the LORD, Did I plainly appear unto the house of thy father, when they   were in

pp,nn4714   nn6547   pp,cs,nn1004

Egypt in Pharaoh's house?

_{wcj,qna977　pnx(853)　pr4480/cs,nn3605　pl,cs,nn7626　nn3478　pp,pnx　pp,nn3548}
28 And did I choose　　him out*of*all the tribes of Israel *to be* my priest,

_{pp,hinc5927　pr5921　nn,pnx4196　pp,hinc6999　nn7004　pp,qnc5375　nn646　pp,pl,nn,pnx6440}
to offer upon mine altar, to burn incense, to wear an ephod before me? and

_{wcs,qmf5414　pp,cs,nn1004　nn,pnx1　(853)　cs,nn3605　pl,cs,nn801}
did I give unto the house of thy father　　all the offerings*made*by*fire of

_{pl,cs,nn1121　nn3478}
the children of Israel?

_{pnit4100　qmf1163　pp,nn,pnx2077　wcj,pp,nn,pnx4503　pnl834}
29 Wherefore kick ye at my sacrifice and at mine offering, which I have

_{pipf6680　nn4583　wcs,pimf3513　(853)　pl,nn,pnx1121　pr,pnx4480}
commanded *in my* habitation; and honorest　　thy　　sons above me, to

_{pp,hinc,pnx1254　pr4480/cs,aj7225　cs,nn3605　cs,nn4503　nn3478　pp,nn,pnx5971}
make*yourselves*fat with*the*chiefest of　all　the offerings of Israel my people?

_{pp,ad3651　nn3068　pl,cs,nn430　nn3478　cs,nn5002　qna559　qpf559　nn,pnx1004}
30 Wherefore the LORD God of Israel saith, I said indeed *that* thy house, and

_{wcj,cs,nn1004　nn,pnx1　htmf1980　pp,pl,nn,pnx6440　pr5704/nn5769　wcj,ad6258　nn3068}
the house of thy father, should walk before me forever: but now the LORD

_{cs,nn5002　ptx2486　pp,pnx　cj3588　pl,pipt,pnx3513　pimf3513}
saith, Be*it*far from me; for them that honor me I will honor, and they that

_{wcj,pl,qpta,pnx959　qmf7043}
despise me shall be lightly esteemed.

_{ptdm2009　pl,nn3117　pl,qpta935　wcs,qpf1438　(853)　nn,pnx2220　wcj(853)}
☞ 31 Behold, the days come, that I will cut off　　thine arm, and　　the

_{cs,nn2220　nn,pnx1　cs,nn1004　pr4480/qnc1961　aj2205　pp,nn,pnx1004}
arm of thy father's house, that there shall not be an old man in thine house.

_{wcs,hipf5027　cs,nn6862　nn4583　pp,nn3605　pnl834}
32 And thou shalt see an enemy *in my* habitation, in　all　*the wealth* which

_{himf3190　(853)　nn3478　wcj,ptn3808　qmf1961　aj2205　pp,nn,pnx1004}
God shall give　　Israel: and there shall not　be an old man in thine house

_{cs,nn3605/df,pl,nn3117}
forever.

_{wcj,nn376　pp,pnx　ptn3808　himf3772　pr4480/pr5973　nn,pnx4196}
33 And the man of thine, *whom* I shall not cut off　from　mine altar, *shall*

_{pp,pinc3615　(853)　du,nn,pnx5869　wcj,pp,hinc109　(853)　nn,pnx5315　wcj,cs,nn3605}
be to consume　thine eyes, and to grieve　thine heart: and　all　the

_{cs,nn4768　nn,pnx1004　qmf4191　pl,nn376}
increase of thine house shall die in the flower*of*their*age.

_{wcj,pndm2088　df,nn226　pp,pnx　pnl834　qmf935　pr413　du,nn,nu8147}
34 And　this　*shall be* a sign unto thee, that shall come upon thy　two

_{pl,nn,pnx1121　pr413　nn2652　wcj,nn6372　nu259　pp,nn3117　qmf4191　du,nu,pnx8147}
sons,　on Hophni and Phinehas; in one day they shall die　both　of them.

_{wcs,hipf6965/pp,pnx　nipt539　nn3548　qmf6213}
35 And I will raise*me*up a faithful priest, *that* shall　do　according to *that*

_{pp,pnl834　pp,nn,pnx3824　wcj,pp,nn,pnx5315　wcs,qpf1129　pp,pnx　nipt539　nn1004}
which *is* in mine heart and in my　mind:　and I will build him a sure house;

_{wcs,htpf1980　pp,pl,cs,nn6440　nn,pnx4899　cs,nn3605/df,pl,nn3117}
and he shall walk before mine anointed　forever.

_{wcs,qpf1961　cs,nn3605　df,nipt3498　pp,nn,pnx1004}
36 And it*shall*come*to*pass, *that* every one that is　left　in thine house

_{qmf935　pp,htnc7812　pp,pnx　pp,cs,nn95　nn3701　wcj,cs,nn3603　nn3899}
shall come *and* crouch to him for a piece of silver and a morsel of bread, and

---

☞ **2:31–36**　See the note on 1 Kings 2:26, 27 for the fulfillment of this prophecy.

wcs,qpf559 qmv,pnx5596   pte4994   pr413 cs,nu259   df,pl,nn3550
shall say,   Put   me, I*pray*thee, into one of the priests' offices, that I may
pp,qnc398   cs,nn6595   nn3899
eat a piece of bread.

Samuel's Call

3
wcj,df,nn5288   nn8050   pipt8334   (853)   nn3068   pp,pl,cs,nn6440 nn5941
And the child Samuel ministered unto   the LORD before Eli. And the
wcj,cs,nn1697   nn3068 qpf1961   aj3368   df,pnp1992 dfp,pl,nn3117   ptn369 nipt6555
word of the LORD was precious in those days; *there was* no open
nn2377
vision.

wcs,qmf1961   dfp,nn3117 df,pndm1931 wcj,nn5941   qpta7901
2 And it*came*to*pass at that time,   when   Eli *was* laid down in his
pp,nn,pnx4725   wcj,du,nn,pnx5869 hipf2490   aj3544   qmf3201 ptn3808 pp,qnc7200
place,   and his   eyes   began to wax dim, *that* he could not   see;
ad2962   wcj,cs,nn5216   pl,nn430   qmf3518   pp,cs,nn1964   nn3068 pnl834/ad8033
3 And ere the lamp of God went out in the temple of the LORD, where
cs,nn727   pl,nn430   wcj,nn8050   qpta7901
the ark of God *was*, and Samuel was laid down *to sleep*;
nn3068   wcs,qmf7121/pr413 nn8050   wcs,qmf559 ptdm,pnx2009
4 That the LORD   called   Samuel: and he answered, Here *am* I.
wcs,qmf7323 pr413 nn5941   wcs,qmf559 ptdm,pnx2009   cj3588   qpf7121   pp,pnx
5 And he   ran   unto Eli, and said,   Here *am* I; for thou calledst me. And
wcs,qmf559   qpf7121 ptn3808 qmv7901   qmv7725   wcs,qmf1980   wcs,qmf7901
he said, I called not; lie down again. And he went and lay down.
nn3068   qnc7121 ad5750 wcs,himf3254   nn8050   nn8050   wcs,qmf6965   wcs,qmf1980
6 And the LORD called yet   again, Samuel. And Samuel arose and went
pr413 nn5941   wcs,qmf559 ptdm,pnx2009   cj3588   qpf7121 pp,pnx   wcs,qmf559
to Eli, and said,   Here *am* I; for thou didst call me. And he answered, I
qpf7121 ptn3808   nn,pnx1121 qmv7901   qmv7725
called not, my son; lie down again.
wcj,nn8050   ad2962 qpf3045 (853)   nn3068   cs,nn1697
7 Now Samuel did not yet know   the LORD, neither was the word of the
nn3068 wcj,ad2962 nimf1540 pr,pnx413
LORD yet   revealed unto him.
nn3068   qnc7121   nn8050 wcs,himf3254   dfp,nuor7992   wcs,qmf6965
8 And the LORD called Samuel again the third time. And he arose and
wcs,qmf1980 pr413 nn5941   wcs,qmf559 ptdm,pnx2009   cj3588   qpf7121 pp,pnx   nn5941
went   to Eli, and said,   Here *am* I; for thou didst call me. And Eli
wcs,qmf995   cj3588   nn3068   qpta7121   dfp,nn5288
perceived that the LORD had called the child.
nn5941 wcs,qmf559   pp,nn8050 qmv1980   qmv7901   wcj,qpf1961 cj518
9 Therefore Eli said unto Samuel, Go, lie down: and it shall be,   if he
qmf7121/pr,pnx413   wcs,qpf559 pimv1696   nn3068 cj3588   nn,pnx5650   qpta8085
call   thee, that thou shalt say, Speak, LORD; for thy servant heareth. So
nn8050 wcs,qmf1980   wcs,qmf7901   pp,nn,pnx4725
Samuel went and lay down in his place.
nn3068   wcs,qmf935   wcs,htmf3320   wcs,qmf7121   pp,nn6471/pp,nn6471
10 And the LORD came, and stood, and called as at other   times,
nn8050   nn8050   nn8050   wcs,qmf559   pimv1696 cj3588   nn,pnx5650 qpta8085
Samuel, Samuel. Then Samuel answered, Speak; for thy servant heareth.

nn3068 wcs,qmf559 pr413 nn8050 ptdm2009 pnp595 qpta6213 nn1697 pp,nn3478

11 And the LORD said to Samuel, Behold, I will do a thing in Israel, at

pnl834 du,cs,nu8147 du,nn,pnx241 cs,nn3605 qpta,pnx8085 qmf6750

which both the ears of every one that heareth it shall tingle.

df,pndm1931 dfp,nn3117 himf6965 pr413 nn5941 (853) cs,nn3605 pnl834

12 In that day I will perform against Eli all *things* which I have

pipf1696 pr413 nn,pnx1004 hina2490 wcj,pina3615

spoken concerning his house: when I begin, I will also make*an*end.

wcj,hipf5046 pp,pnx cj3588 pnp589 qpta8199 (853) nn,pnx1004 pr5704/nn5769

13 For I have told him that I will judge his house forever for the

pp,cs,nn5771 pnl834 qpf3045 cj3588 pl,nn,pnx1121 pp,pnx pl,pipt7043

iniquity which he knoweth; because his sons made themselves vile, and he

pipf3543 pp,pnx wcj,ptn3808

restrained them not.

wcj,pp,ad3651 nipf7650 pp,cs,nn1004 nn5941 cs,nn5771 nn5941

14 And therefore I have sworn unto the house of Eli, that the iniquity of Eli's

cs,nn1004 ptn518 htmf3722 pp,nn2077 wcj,pp,nn4503 pr5704/nn5769

house shall not be purged with sacrifice nor offering forever.

nn8050 wcs,qmf7901 pr5704 df,nn1242 wcs,qmf6605 (853) pl,cs,nn1817

15 And Samuel lay until the morning, and opened the doors of the

cs,nn1004 nn3068 wcj,nn8050 qpf3372 pr4480/hinc5046/pr413 nn5941 (853) df,nn4759

house of the LORD. And Samuel feared to show Eli the vision.

nn5941 wcs,qmf7121 (853) nn8050 wcs,qmf559 nn8050 nn,pnx1121

16 Then Eli called Samuel, and said, Samuel, my son. And he

wcs,qmf559 ptdm,pnx2009

answered, Here *am* I.

wcs,qmf559 pnit4100 df,nn1697 pnl834 pipf1696 pr,pnx413

17 And he said, What *is* the thing that *the* LORD hath said unto thee?

pte4994 pimf3582 ptn408 pr,pnx4480 pl,nn430 qmf6213 ad3541 pp,pnx himf3254 wcj,ad3541 cj518

I*pray*thee hide *it* not from me: God do so to thee, and more also, if

pimf3582 nn1697 pr,pnx4480 pr4480/cs,nn3605 df,nn1697 pnl834 pipf1696 pr,pnx413

thou hide *any* thing from me of all the things that he said unto thee.

nn8050 wcs,himf5046 pp,pnx (853) cs,nn3605 df,pl,nn1697 pipf3582 wcj,ptn3808 pr,pnx4480

18 And Samuel told him every whit, and hid nothing from him. And

wcs,qmf559 pnp1931 nn3068 qmf6213 pp,du,nn,pnx5869 df,nn2896

he said, It *is* the LORD: let him do what seemeth him good.

nn8050 wcs,qmf1431 wcj,nn3068 qpf1961 pr,pnx5973

19 And Samuel grew, and the LORD was with him, and did let

wcj,ptn3808/pr4480/cs,nn3605 pl,nn,nn1697 hipf5307 nn,lh776

none of his words fall to the ground.

cs,nn3605 nn3478 pr4480/nn1835 wcj,pr5704 nn884 wcs,qmf3045 cj3588 nn8050

20 And all Israel from Dan even to Beer-sheba knew that Samuel *was*

nipt539 pp,nn5030 pp,nn3068

established *to be* a prophet of the LORD.

nn3068 pp,ninc7200 wcs,himf3254 pp,nn7887 cj3588 nn3068 nipf1540

21 And the LORD appeared again in Shiloh: for the LORD revealed himself

pr413 nn8050 pp,nn7887 pp,cs,nn1697 nn3068

to Samuel in Shiloh by the word of the LORD.

3:13 Eli had probably spoken to his sons about their bad behavior, but he had failed to discipline them effectively. The proper thing would have been for him to have administered correction in love at an early stage in their lives (see Eph. 6:4; Heb. 12:5–8).

The Philistines Capture The Ark of God

4 cs,nn**1697** nn8050 wcs,qmf**1961** pp,cs,nn3605 nn3478   nn3478 wcs,qmf3318
And the word of Samuel came to all Israel. Now Israel went out

pp,qnc7125 pl,nn6430 dfp,nn4421 wcs,qmf2583 pr5921 nn72 [cs,nn68/df,nn5828]
against the Philistines to battle, and pitched beside Ebenezer: and the

wcj,pl,nn6430 qpf2583 pp,nn663
Philistines pitched in Aphek.

pl,nn6430 wcs,qmf6186 pp,qnc7125 nn3478
2 And the Philistines put*themselves*in*array against Israel: and when they

wcs,qmf5203 df,nn4421 nn3478 wcs,nimf5062 pp,pl,cs,nn**6440** pl,nn6430 wcs,himf5221
joined battle, Israel was smitten before the Philistines: and they slew of the

dfp,nn4634 dfp,nn7704 pp,cs,nu702 pl,nu505 nn376
army in the field about four thousand men.

df,nn5971 wcs,qmf935 pr413 df,nn4264 cs,aj2205 nn3478 wcs,qmf559
☙ 3 And when the people were come into the camp, the elders of Israel said,

pp,pnit4100 nn3068 qpf,pnx5062 df,nn3117 pp,pl,cs,nn**6440** pl,nn6430 qcj3947 (853)
Wherefore hath the LORD smitten us today before the Philistines? Let us fetch

cs,nn727 cs,nn1285 nn3068 pr4480/nn7887 pr,pnx413 wcj,qmf935
the ark of the covenant of the LORD out*of*Shiloh unto us, that, when it cometh

pp,nn,pnx7130 wcj,himf,pnx3467 pr4480/cs,nn3709 pl,qpta,pnx341
among us, it may save us out*of*the*hand of our enemies.

df,nn5971 wcs,qmf7971 nn7887 wcs,qmf5375 pr4480/ad8033 (853)
4 So the people sent to Shiloh, that they might bring from thence the

cs,nn727 cs,nn1285 nn3068 pl,nn6635 qpta3427 df,pl,nn3742
ark of the covenant of the LORD of hosts, which dwelleth *between* the cherubims:

du,cs,nu8147 pl,cs,nn1121 nn5941 nn2652 wcj,nn6372 wcj,ad8033 pr5973 cs,nn727
and the two sons of Eli, Hophni and Phinehas, *were* there with the ark of

cs,nn1285 df,pl,nn430
the covenant of God.

wcs(qmf**1961**) cs,nn727 cs,nn1285 nn3068 pp,qnc935 pr413 df,nn4264
5 And when the ark of the covenant of the LORD came into the camp,

cs,nn3605 nn3478 wcs,himf7321 aj1419 nn8643 df,nn776 wcs,nimf1949
all Israel shouted with a great shout, so that the earth rang again.

pl,nn6430 wcs,qmf8085 (853) cs,nn6963 df,nn8643 wcs,qmf559 pnit4100
6 And when the Philistines heard the noise of the shout, they said, What

cs,nn6963 df,pndm2063 df,aj1419 df,nn8643 pp,cs,nn4264 df,pl,nn5680
meaneth the noise of this great shout in the camp of the Hebrews? And they

wcs,qmf3045 cj3588 cs,nn727 nn3068 qpf935 pr413 df,nn4264
understood that the ark of the LORD was come into the camp.

df,pl,nn6430 wcs,qmf3372 cj3588 qpf559 pl,nn430 qpf935 pr413 df,nn4264
7 And the Philistines were afraid, for they said, God is come into the camp.

wcs,qmf559 ptx188 pp,pnx cj3588 ptn3808 qpf1961 pp,pndm2063 ad865/ad8032
And they said, Woe unto us! for there hath not been such*a*thing heretofore.

ptx188 pp,pnx pnit4310 himf,pnx5337 pr4480/cs,nn3027 df,pndm428 df,aj117 df,pl,nn430
8 Woe unto us! who shall deliver us out*of*the*hand of these mighty Gods?

pndm428 (pnp1992) df,pl,nn430 df,pl,hipt5221 (853) nn4714 pp,cs,nn3605 nn4347
these *are* the Gods that smote the Egyptians with all the plagues in

dfp,nn4057
the wilderness.

htmv2388 wcj,qmv**1961** pp,pl,nn376 pl,nn6430
9 Be strong, and quit yourselves like men, O ye Philistines,

☙ **4:3** The Israelites were treating the ark as a kind of magic charm instead of the testimony of God's power and presence. The mere presence of the ark would not bring victory in the battle.

cj3645/qmf**5647**   dfp,pl,nn5680   pp,pnl834   qpf**5647**   pp,pnx   wcj,qpf**1961**

that*ye*be*not*servants unto the Hebrews, as they have been to you: quit

pp,pl,nn**376**   wcj,nipf3898

yourselves like men, and fight.

pl,nn6430   wcs,nimf3898   nn3478   wcs,nimf**5062**   wcs,qmf5127

10 And the Philistines fought, and Israel was smitten, and they fled

nn**376**   pp,pl,nn,pnx168   wcs,qmf**1961**   ad3966   aj1419   df,nn4347

every man into his tent: and there was a very great slaughter; for there

wcs,qmf**5307** pr4480/nn3478   nu7970   nu**505**   aj7273

fell of Israel thirty thousand footmen.

wcj,cs,nn**727**   pl,nn**430**   nipf3947   wcj,du,cs,nu8147   pl,cs,nn1121   nn5941   nn2652

11 And the ark of God was taken; and the two sons of Eli, Hophni

wcj,nn6372   qpf**4191**

and Phinehas, were slain.

Eli's Death

wcs,qmf7323   cs,nn**376**   nn1144   pr4480/df,nn4634   wcs,qmf935

12 And there ran a man of Benjamin out*of*the*army, and came to

nn7887   df,pndm1931 dfp,nn**3117**   wcj,pl,nn,pnx4055 pl,qptp7167   wcj,nn**127** pr5921   nn,pnx**7218**

Shiloh the same day with his clothes rent, and with earth upon his head.

wcs,qmf935   wcj,ptdm2009   nn5941   qpta**3427**   pr5921   df,nn**3678**   cs,nn3197/nn**1870**

13 And when he came, lo, Eli sat upon a seat by the wayside

pipt6822   cj3588   nn,pnx**3820** (qpf**1961**)   aj2730   pr5921   cs,nn**727**   df,pl,nn**430**   wcj,df,nn**376**

watching: for his heart trembled for the ark of God. And when the man

qpf935   dfp,nn5892   pp,hinc**5046**   cs,nn3605   df,nn5892   wcs,qmf**2199**

came into the city, and told it, all the city cried out.

nn5941 wcs,qmf**8085** (853)   cs,nn6963   df,nn6818   wcs,qmf559   pnit4100

14 And when Eli heard the noise of the crying, he said, What *meaneth*

cs,nn6963   df,pndm2088   df,nn1995   wcj,df,nn**376** wcs,qmf935   pipf4116   wcs,himf**5046** pp,nn5941

the noise of this tumult? And the man came in hastily, and told Eli.

wcj,nn5941   nu8375   wcj,nu8083 nn8141 cs,nn1121   wcj,du,nn,pnx**5869**   qpf**6965**

15 Now Eli was ninety and eight years old; and his eyes were dim,

qpf3201 wcj,ptn**3808** pp,qnc**7200**

that he could not see.

df,nn**376** wcs,qmf559   pr413   nn5941 pnp595   df,qpta935   pr4480   df,nn4634

16 And the man said unto Eli, I *am* he that came out of the army, and

wcj,pnp589 qpf5127 df,nn**3117**   pr4480   df,nn4634   wcs,qmf559   pnit4100 qpf**1961**   df,nn1697   nn,pnx1121

I fled today out of the army. And he said, What is there done, my son?

df,pipt**1319**   wcs,qmf6030   wcs,qmf559   nn3478   qpf5127   pp,pl,cs,nn**6440**

17 And the messenger answered and said, Israel is fled before the

pl,nn6430   qpf**1961** wcj,ad1571   aj1419   nn4046   dfp,nn**5971**

Philistines, and there hath been also a great slaughter among the people, and thy

du,cs,nu8147 pl,nn,pnx1121 wcj,ad1571   nn2652   wcj,nn6372   qpf**4191**   wcj,cs,nn**727**   df,pl,nn**430**

two sons also, Hophni and Phinehas, are dead, and the ark of God is

nipf3947

taken.

wcs,qmf**1961**   pp,hinc,pnx**2142**   (853)   cs,nn**727**   df,pl,nn**430**

18 And it*came*to*pass, when he made mention of the ark of God, that

wcs,qmf**5307**   pr4480/pr5921   df,nn**3678**   ad322   pr1157   nn**3027**   df,nn8179   nn,pnx4665

he fell from off the seat backward by the side of the gate, and his neck

wcs,nimf**7665**   wcs,qmf**4191** cj3588   aj2204 df,nn**376**   wcj,aj3515   wcj,pnp1931   qpf**8199**

broke, and he died: for he was an old man, and heavy. And he had judged

(853)   nn3478   pl,nu705   nn8141

Israel forty years.

wcj,nn,pnx3618   nn6372   cs,nn**802**   aj2030

19 And his daughter-in-law, Phinehas' wife, was with child, *near* to be

pp,qnc3205   wcs,qmf**8085** (853)   df,nn8052   cs,nn**727**   df,pl,nn**430**   (pr413)

delivered: and when she heard   the tidings that the ark of God was

ninc3947   nn,pnx2524   wcj,nn,pnx**376**   wcj,qpf**4191**   wcs,qmf**3766**

taken, and that her father-in-law and her husband were dead, she bowed herself

wcs,qmf3205   cj3588   pl,nn,pnx6735 nipf**2015** pr,pnx5921

and travailed; for her pains came upon her.

wcj,pp,cs,nn**6256**   qnc,pnx**4191**   df,pl,nipt**5324**   wcs,pimf**1696**

20 And about the   time   of her death the women*that*stood by her   said

pr,pnx5921   qmf**3372** ptn408 cj3588   qpf3205   nn**1121**   qpf6030   wcj,ptn**3808** wcj,ptn**3808**

unto her, Fear not; for thou hast born a son. But she answered not,   neither did

qpf7896/nn,pnx**3820**

she   regard *it.*

wcs,qmf**7121**   dfp,nn5288   nn350   pp,qnc**559**   aj**3519**   qpf**1540**

21 And she named the   child Ichabod, saying, The glory is departed

pr4480/nn3478   pr413   cs,nn**727**   df,pl,nn**430**   ninc3947   wcj,pr413   nn,pnx2524

from Israel: because the ark of God was taken, and because of her father-in-law

wcj,nn,pnx**376**

and her husband.

wcs,qmf**559**   aj**3519**   qpf**1540**   pr4480/nn3478 cj3588   cs,nn**727**   df,pl,nn**430**

22 And she said, The glory is departed from Israel: for the ark of God is

nipf3947

taken.

God Judges the Philistines

wcj,pl,nn6430   qpf3947   (853)   cs,nn**727**   df,pl,nn**430**   wcs,himf,pnx935

5 And the Philistines took   the ark of God, and brought it

pr4480/nn72 [cs,nn68/df,nn5828]   nn,lh795

from Ebenezer unto Ashdod.

pl,nn6430   wcs,qmf3947 (853)   cs,nn**727**   df,pl,nn**430**   wcs,himf935 pnx(853)

2 When the Philistines took   the ark of God, they brought   it into

cs,nn**1004**   nn1712   wcs,himf3322 pnx(853)   pr681   nn1712

the house of Dagon, and   set   it by Dagon.

pl,nn795   wcs,himf7925   pr4480/ad4283   wcj,ptdm2009   nn1712

3 And when they of Ashdod arose early on*the*morrow, behold, Dagon *was*

qpta5307   pp,pl,nn,pnx**6440**   nn,lh776 pp,pl,cs,nn**6440**   cs,nn**727**   nn**3068**

fallen upon his   face   to the earth before   the ark of the LORD. And they

wcs,qmf3947 (853)   nn1712   wcs,himf7725 pnx(853)   pp,nn,pnx4725

took   Dagon, and   set   him in his   place again.

wcs,himf7925   pr4480/ad4283   dfp,nn1242 wcj,ptdm2009   nn1712

4 And when they arose early on*the*morrow morning, behold, Dagon *was*

qpta5307   pp,pl,nn,pnx**6440**   nn,lh776 pp,pl,cs,nn**6440**   cs,nn**727**   nn**3068**

fallen upon his   face   to the ground before the ark of the LORD; and the

wcj,cs,nn**7218**   nn1712   wcj,du,cs,nu8147   pl,cs,nn**3709**   du,nn,pnx**3027**   pl,qptp**3772**   pr413

head of Dagon and   both   the palms of his hands *were* cut off upon the

df,nn4670   ad7535   nn1712   nipf**7604** pr,pnx**5921**

threshold; only *the stump of* Dagon was left   to   him.

pr5921/ad**3651** ptn**3808**   pl,cs,nn**3548**   nn1712   wcj,cs,nn3605 df,pl,qpta935   nn1712

5 Therefore neither the priests of Dagon, nor   any   that come into Dagon's

cs,nn**1004** qmf1869 pr5921   cs,nn4670   nn1712   pp,nn795   pr5704 df,pndm2088 df,nn3117

house, tread on the threshold of Dagon in Ashdod unto   this   day.

5:2 See the note on Judges 2:13 regarding Dagon.

cs,nn**3027**   nn**3068**   wcs,qmf**3513**   pr413   df,pl,nn795

6 But the hand of the LORD was heavy upon them of Ashdod, and he

wcs,himf,pnx**8074**   wcs,himf**5221** pnx(853)   dfp,pl,nn**6076**   (853)   nn795   wcj(853)

destroyed them, and smote   them with emerods, *even*   Ashdod and   the

pl,nn,pnx1366

coasts thereof.

pl,cs,nn**376**   nn795   wcs,qmf**7200** cj3588   ad**3651**   wcj,qpf559   cs,nn**727**

7 And when the men of Ashdod saw that *it was* so, they said, The ark

pl,cs,nn**430**   nn3478   ptn3808 qmf**3427** pr,pnx5973   cj3588   nn,pnx**3027**   qpf7185 pr,pnx5921

of the God of Israel shall not abide with us: for his hand is sore upon us,

wcj,pr5921   nn1712   pl,nn,pnx**430**

and upon Dagon our god.

wcs,qmf**7971**   wcs,qmf**622**   (853) cs,nn3605   pl,cs,nn**5633**   pl,nn6430

8 They sent therefore and gathered   all the lords of the Philistines

pr,pnx413   wcs,qmf**559** pnit4100   qmf**6213**   pp,cs,nn**727**   pl,cs,nn**430**   nn3478

unto them, and said, What shall we do with the ark of the God of Israel?

wcs,qmf**559**   cs,nn**727**   pl,cs,nn**430**   nn3478   nimf5437   nn1661

And they answered, Let the ark of the God of Israel be carried about unto Gath.

wcs,himf5437 (853)   cs,nn**727**   pl,cs,nn**430**   nn3478

And they carried   the ark of the God of Israel about *thither*.

wcs,qmf**1961**   ad310   hipf5437/pnx(853)   cs,nn**3027**   nn**3068**

9 And it was *so*, that, after they had carried*it*about, the hand of the LORD

wcs,qmf**1961**   dfp,nn5892   ad3966 aj1419   nn**4103**   wcs,himf**5221** (853) pl,cs,nn**376**

was against the city with a very great destruction: and he smote   the men

df,nn5892   pr4480/aj6996   wcj(pr5704) aj1419   pl,nn**6076** pp,pnx

of the city, both small and   great, and they had emerods in their

wcs,nimf8368

secret parts.

wcs,pimf7971   (853)   cs,nn**727**   df,pl,nn**430**   nn6138

10 Therefore they sent   the ark of God to Ekron. And

wcs,qmf**1961**   cs,nn**727** df,pl,nn**430** pp,qnc935   nn6138   df,pl,nn**6139** wcs,qmf**2199**

it*came*to*pass, as the ark of God came to Ekron, that the Ekronites cried out,

pp,qnc559   hipf5437   (853)   cs,nn**727**   pl,cs,nn**430**   nn3478 pr,pnx413

saying, They have brought about   the ark of the God of Israel to us, to

pp,hinc,pnx**4191**   wcj(853)   nn,pnx**5971**

slay us and   our people.

wcs,qmf**7971**   wcs,qmf**622**   (853) cs,nn3605   pl,cs,nn**5633**   pl,nn6430

11 So they sent and gathered together   all the lords of the Philistines,

wcs,qmf**559**   pimv7971   (853)   cs,nn**727**   pl,cs,nn**430**   nn3478   wcj,qmf**7725**

and said, Send away   the ark of the God of Israel, and let it go again to his

pp,nn,pnx4725   himf4191 pnx(853)   wcj,ptn3808   wcj(853)   nn,pnx5971 cj3588   qpf1961

own place, that it slay   us not, and   our people: for there was a

nn4194   cs,nn4103   pp,cs,nn3605 df,nn5892   cs,nn**3027** df,pl,nn**430** ad3966 qpf**3513**

deadly destruction throughout   all the city; the hand of God was very heavy

ad8033

there.

wcj,df,pl,nn**376** pnl834 qpf**4191** ptn3808   hopf**5221**   dfp,pl,nn**6076**

12 And the men that died not were smitten with the emerods: and the

cs,nn7775   df,nn5892 wcs,qmf**5927**   df,du,nn**8064**

cry of the city went up to heaven.

The Philistines Return the Ark to Israel

6 And the ark of the LORD was in the country of the Philistines seven months.

2 And the Philistines called for the priests and the diviners, saying, What shall we do to the ark of the LORD? tell us wherewith we shall send it to his place.

3 And they said, If ye send away the ark of the God of Israel, send it not empty; but in*any*wise*return him a trespass offering: then ye shall be healed, and it shall be known to you why his hand is not removed from you.

4 Then said they, What *shall be* the trespass offering which we shall return to him? They answered, Five golden emerods, and five golden mice, *according to* the number of the lords of the Philistines: for one plague *was* on you all, and on your lords.

5 Wherefore ye shall make images of your emerods, and images of your mice that mar the land; and ye shall give glory unto the God of Israel: peradventure he will lighten his hand from off you, and from off your gods, and from off your land.

6 Wherefore then do ye harden your hearts, as the Egyptians and Pharaoh hardened their hearts? when he had wrought wonderfully among them, did they not let*the*people*go, and they departed?

7 Now therefore make a new cart, and take two milch kine, on which there hath come no yoke, and tie the kine to the cart, and bring their calves home from them:

8 And take the ark of the LORD, and lay it upon the cart; and

---

6:7–12 Normally, it is difficult to drive even the best trained cows straight on a road when their calves have just been taken away from them. In this case, the cows did follow a straight line, carrying the ark back to Israel, which revealed that their behavior was being controlled by God (cf. Num. 22:22–31). God is all-powerful and is able to use all facets of His creation to accomplish His will.

qmf7760 wcj(853)   pl,cs,nn3627   df,nn2091   pnl834   hipf7725 pp,pnx   nn817

put   the jewels of gold, which ye return him *for* a trespass offering, in a

dfp,nn712 pr4480/nn,pnx6654   wcs,pipf7971/pnx(853)   wcs,qpf1980

coffer by*the*side thereof; and send*it*away, that it may go.

            wcs,qpf7200 cj518   qmf5927   cs,nn1870   nn,pnx1366   nn1053

9 And see, if it goeth up by the way of his own coast to Beth-shemesh,

    pnp1931   qpf6213 pp,pnx (853) df,pndm2063 df,aj1419 df,nn7451   wcj,cj518 ptn3808   wcj,qpf3045

then he hath done us   this   great evil: but if not, then we shall know

cj3588   ptn3808   nn,pnx3027   qpf5060 pp,pnx pnp1931   nn4745   qpf1961   pp,pnx

that *it is* not his hand *that* smote us: it *was* a chance *that* happened to us.

        df,pl,nn376 wcs,qmf6213 ad3651   wcs,qmf3947 du,cs,nu8147 pl,qpta5763 pl,nn6510   wcs,qmf,pnx631

10 And the men   did   so; and took   two   milch kine, and   tied

        dfp,nn5699   qpf3607 wcj(853)   pl,nn,pnx1121 dfp,nn1004

them to the cart, and shut up   their calves at home:

        wcs,qmf7760 (853)   cs,nn727   nn3068   pr413   df,nn5699   wcj(853)

11 And they laid   the ark of the Lord upon the cart, and   the

df,nn712 wcj,pr854   pl,cs,nn5909   df,nn2091   wcj(853)   pl,cs,nn6754   pl,nn,pnx2914

coffer with the mice of gold and   the images of their emerods.

        df,pl,nn6510   wcs,pimf3474 dfp,nn1870 pr5921   cs,nn1870   nn1053

12 And the kine took*the*straight way to the way of Beth-shemesh, *and*

qpf1980   nu259   pp,nn4546 wcj,qna1600   qna1980   qpf5493/wcj,ptn3808

went along the highway, lowing as they went, and turned*not*aside *to* the

nn3225   wcj,nn8040   wcj,pl,cs,nn5633   pl,nn6430   pl,qpta1980 pr,pnx310

right hand or *to* the left; and the   lords of the Philistines went   after them

pr5704   cs,nn1366   nn1053

unto the border of Beth-shemesh.

        wcj,nn1053   pl,qpta7114   pl,nn2406 cs,nn7105   dfp,nn6010

13 And *they of* Beth-shemesh *were* reaping their wheat harvest in the valley:

    wcs,qmf5375 (853)   du,nn,pnx5869 wcs,qmf7200 (853)   df,nn727   wcs,qmf8055 pp,qnc7200

and they lifted up   their eyes, and saw   the ark, and rejoiced to see

it.

        wcj,df,nn5699   qpf935 pr413   cs,nn7704   nn3091   nn1030 [cs,nn1004/df,nn8121]

14 And the   cart   came into the field of Joshua, a Beth-shemite, and

wcs,qmf5975 ad8033 wcj,ad8033   aj1419 nn68   wcs,pimf1234 (853)   pl,cs,nn6086

stood there, where *there was* a great stone: and they cleaved   the wood of the

df,nn5699   hipf5927 wcj(853)   df,pl,nn6510   nn5930   pp,nn3068

cart, and offered   the kine a burnt offering unto the Lord.

        wcj,df,nn3881   hipf3381   (853)   cs,nn727   nn3068   wcj(853)   df,nn712

15 And the Levites took down   the ark of the Lord, and   the coffer

pnl834   pr,pnx854   pnl834/pp,pnx   pl,cs,nn3627   nn2091   wcs,qmf7760   pr413   df,aj1419

that *was* with it, wherein the jewels of gold *were*, and put   *them* on the great

df,nn68   wcj,pl,cs,nn376   nn1053   hipf5927   pl,nn5930   wcs,qmf2076

stone: and the men   of Beth-shemesh offered burnt offerings and sacrificed

pl,nn2077   df,pndm1931 dfp,nn3117   pp,nn3068

sacrifices the same day unto the Lord.

        wcj,nu2568 pl,cs,nn5633   pl,nn6430   qpf7200   wcs,qmf7725

16 And when the five   lords of the Philistines had seen *it*, they returned to

nn6138   df,pndm1931 dfp,nn3117

Ekron the same day.

        wcj,pndm428   df,nn2091 pl,cs,nn2914 pnl834   pl,nn6430   hipf7725

17 And these *are* the golden emerods which the Philistines returned *for* a

    nn817   pp,nn3068   pp,nn795 nu259   pp,nn5804 nu259   pp,nn831   nu259

trespass offering unto the Lord; for Ashdod one, for Gaza one, for Askelon one,

pp,nn1661 nu259   pp,nn6138 nu259

for Gath one, for Ekron one;

qmf3947 wcj(853)   pl,nn,pnx**7704**   wcj(853)   pl,nn,pnx3754

14 And he will take   your fields, and   your vineyards, and your

wcj,pl,nn,pnx2132   df,aj**2896**   wcs,qpf**5414**   pp,pl,nn,pnx**5650**

oliveyards, *even* the best *of them*, and give *them* to his servants.

qmf**6237**   wcj,pl,nn,pnx**2233**   wcj,pl,nn,pnx3754

15 And he will take*the*tenth of your   seed,   and of your vineyards, and

wcs,qpf**5414**   pp,pl,nn,pnx**5631**   wcj,pp,pl,nn,pnx**5650**

give to his officers, and to his   servants.

qmf3947 wcj(853)   pl,nn,pnx**5650**   wcj(853)   pl,nn,pnx8198

16 And he will take   your menservants, and   your maidservants, and

df,aj**2896**   wcj(853)   pl,nn,pnx970   wcj(853)   pl,nn,pnx2543   wcs,qpf**6213**

your goodliest   young men, and   your asses, and put *them* to his

pp,nn,pnx**4399**

work.

qmf**6237**   nn,pnx6629   wcj,pnp859   qmf**1961** pp,pnx dfp,pl,nn**5650**

17 He will take*the*tenth of your sheep: and ye   shall be   his servants.

wcs,qpf**2199**   df,pndm1931 dfp,nn3117 pr4480/pp,pl,cs,nn**6440**   nn,pnx**4428** pnl834

18 And ye shall cry out in   that   day   because of your king which ye

qpf**977**   pp,pnx   nn**3068**   wcj,ptn**3808** qmf6030 wcj(853)   df,pndm1931 dfp,nn3117

shall have chosen you; and the LORD will   not ' hear   you in ' that   day.

df,nn**5971** wcs,pimf**3985**   pp,qnc**8085**   pp,cs,nn6963   nn8050

19 Nevertheless the people refused to obey the voice of Samuel; and they

wcs,qmf**559** ptn**3808** cj3588/cj518   qmf**1961**   nn**4428** pr,pnx5921

said, Nay; but   we will have a king over us;

pnp587 ad1571   wcs,qpf**1961**   pp,cs,nn3605   df,pl,nn**1471**   nn,pnx**4428**

20 That we also may   be   like   all   the nations; and that our   king may

wcs,qpf,pnx**8199**   wcs,qpf3318 pp,pl,nn,pnx**6440**   wcs,nipf3898 (853)   pl,nn,pnx4421

judge us, and go out   before us, and fight   our battles.

nn8050   wcs,qmf**8085** (853) cs,nn3605   pl,cs,nn**1697**   df,nn**5971**   wcs,pimf,pnx**1696**

21 And Samuel heard   all   the words of the people, and he rehearsed

pp,du,cs,nn**241**   nn**3068**

them in the   ears   of the LORD.

nn**3068**   wcs,qmf**559** pr413   nn8050   qmv**8085**   pp,nn,pnx6963

22 And the LORD said   to   Samuel, Hearken unto their   voice,   and

wcs,hipf**4427**/pp,pnx/nn**4428**   nn8050   wcs,qmf**559** pr413   pl,cs,nn**376**   nn3478   qmv**1980**

make*them*a*king. And Samuel   said   unto the   men   of Israel, Go   ye

nn**376**   pp,nn,pnx5892

every man unto his   city.

Samuel Anoints Saul as King

wcs,qmf**1961**   nn**376**   pr4480/nn1144   wcj,nn,pnx8034   nn7027   cs,nn**1121**

9 Now there was   a man of Benjamin, whose   name   *was* Kish, the son

nn22   cs,nn**1121**   nn6872   cs,nn**1121**   nn1064   cs,nn**1121**   nn647

of Abiel, the son of Zeror, the son of Bechorath, the son of Aphiah, a

nn1145   cs,nn1368   nn2428

Benjamite, a mighty man of power.

wcj,pp,pnx qpf**1961**   nn1121   wcj,nn,pnx8034   nn7586   nn970

2 And   he   had a son, whose   name   *was* Saul, a choice*young*man, and a

wcj,aj**2896**   wcj,ptn369   pr4480/pl,cs,nn**1121**   nn3478   aj**2896**   nn**376**   pr4480/pnx

goodly: and *there was*   not   among*the*children of Israel a goodlier person   than

pr4480/nn,pnx7926   wcj,ad,lh4605   aj1364 pr4480/cs,nn3605   df,nn**5971**

he: from*his*shoulders and upward *he was* higher than any of the people.

df,pl,nn860   pp,nn7027   nn7586   cs,nn1   wcs,qmf6   nn7027 wcs,qmf**559** pr413 nn7586

3 And the asses of Kish Saul's father were lost. And Kish said   to Saul

nn,pnx1121 qmv3947 pte4994 (853) cs,nu259 pr4480/dfp,pl,nn5288 pr,pnx854 wcj,qmv6965 qmv1980 pimv1245 (853)

his son, Take now   one of*the*servants with thee, and arise,   go   seek

df,pl,nn860

the asses.

wcs,qmf5674 pp,cs,nn2022 nn669 wcs,qmf5674 pp,cs,nn776

4 And he passed through mount Ephraim, and passed through the land   of

nn8031 wcj,ptn4672 wcj,ptn3808 wcs,qmf5674 pp,cs,nn776

Shalisha, but they found *them* not: then they passed through the land of

nn8171 wcj,ptn369 wcs,qmf5674 pp,cs,nn776

Shalim, and *there they were* not: and he passed through the land of the

pl,nn1145 qpf4672 wcj,ptn3808

Benjamites, but they found *them* not.

pnp1992 qpf935 pp,cs,nn776 nn6689 wcj,nn7586 qpf559 pp,nn,pnx5288

5 *And* when they were come to the land of Zuph, Saul said to his servant

pnl834 pr,pnx5973 qmv1980 wcj,qcj7725 cj6435 nn,pnx1 qmf2308 pr4480

that *was* with him, Come, and let us return; lest my father leave *caring* for the

df,pl,nn860 wcs,qpf1672 pp,pnx

asses, and take thought for us.

wcs,qmf559 pp,pnx ptdm2009 pte4994 df,pndm2063 dfp,nn5892 cs,nn376

6 And he said unto him, Behold now, *there is* in   this   city a man of

pl,nn430 nipt3513 wcj,df,nn376 nn3605 pnl834 pimf1696 qna935/qmf935 ad4994

God, and *he is* an honorable man; all that he saith cometh*surely*to*pass: now

qcj1980 ad8033 cj194 himf5046 pp,pnx (853) nn,pnx1870 pnl834/pr,pnx5921

let us go thither; peradventure he can show us   our   way   that   we

qpf1980

should go.

wcs,qmf559 nn7586 pp,nn,pnx5288 wcj,ptdm2009 qmf1980 wcj,pnit4100

7 Then said Saul to his servant, But, behold, *if* we go,   what shall we

himf935 dfp,nn376 cj3588 df,nn3899 qpf235 pr4480/pl,nn,pnx3627 ptn369 wcj,nn8670

bring the man? for the bread is spent in*our*vessels, and *there is* not a present to

pp,hinc935 pp,cs,nn376 df,pl,nn430 pnit4100 pnx(pr854)

bring to the man of God: what have   we?

df,nn5288 pp,qnc6030 (853) nn7586 wcs,himf3254 wcs,qmf559 ptdm2009 nipf4672

8 And the servant answered   Saul again, and said, Behold, I*have*here at

pp,nn,pnx3027 cs,nn7253 cs,nn8255 nn3701 wcj,qpf5414 pp,cs,nn376

hand the fourth part of a shekel of silver: *that* will I give to the man of

df,pl,nn430 wcj,hipf5046 pp,pnx (853) nn,pnx1870

God, to tell   us   our way.

pp,pl,nn6440 pp,nn3478 df,nn376 pp,qnc,pnx1980 pp,qnc1875 pl,nn430 ad3541 qpf559

9 (Formerly in Israel, when a man went to inquire of God, thus he spoke,

qmv1980 wcj,qcj1980 pr5704 df,qpta7200 cj3588 df,nn3117 dfp,nn5030

Come, and let us go to the seer: for *he that is* now *called* a Prophet was

pp,pl,nn6440 nimf7121 df,qpta7200

formerly called a Seer.)

wcs,qmf559 nn7586 pp,nn,pnx5288 aj2896 nn,pnx1697 qmv1980 qcj1980

10 Then said   Saul to his servant, Well said; come, let*us*go. So they

wcs,qmf1980 pr413 df,nn5892 pnl834/ad8033 cs,nn376 df,pl,nn430

went unto the city   where the man of God *was*.

pnp1992 pl,qpta5927 pp,cs,nn4608 df,nn5892 wcj,pnp1992 qpf4672 pl,nn5291

11 *And* as they went up the   hill to the city,   they found young maidens

pl,qpta3318 pp,qnc7579 pl,nn4325 wcs,qmf559 pp,pnx he,pta3426 df,qpta7200 pp,pndm2088

going out to draw water, and said unto them, Is   the seer here?

wcs,qmf6030 pnx(853) wcs,qmf559 pta3426 ptdm2009 pp,pl,nn,pnx6440

12 And they answered   them, and said, He is; behold, *he is* before

pimv4116 ad6258 cj3588 qpf935 df,nn3117 dfp,nn5892 cj3588 cs,nn2077
you: make haste now, for he came today to the city; for *there is* a sacrifice of

dfp,nn5971 df,nn3117 dfp,nn1116
the people today in the high place:

pp,qnc,pnx935 df,nn5892 ad3651 qmf4672 pnx(853)
13 As*soon*as*ye*be*come into the city, ye shall straightway find him,

pp,ad2962 qmf5927 df,nn,lh1116 pp,qnc398 cj3588 df,nn5971 ptn3808 qmf398 pr5704
before he go up to the high place to eat: for the people will not eat until he

qnc,pnx935 cj3588 pnp1931 pimf1288 df,nn2077 pr310/ad3651 qmf398
come, because he doth bless the sacrifice; *and* afterwards they eat that be

df,pl,qptp7121 wcj,ad6258 qmv5927 cj3588 wcj,df,nn3117 qmf4672 pnx(853)
bidden. Now therefore get*you*up; for about*this*time ye shall find him.

wcs,qmf5927 df,nn5892 pnp1992 pl,qpta935 pp,cs,nn8432
14 And they went up into the city: *and* when they were come into the

df,nn5892 wcj,ptdm2009 nn8050 qpta3318 pp,qnc,pnx7125 pp,qnc5927 df,nn1116
city, behold, Samuel came out against them, for to go up to the high place.

wcj,nn3068 qpf1540 nn8050 pr854 cs,nn241 nu259 nn3117 pp,pl,cs,nn6440 nn7586 qnc935
15 Now the Lord had told Samuel in his ear a day before Saul came,

pp,qnc559
saying,

ad4279 dfp,nn6256 qmf7971 pnx(pr413) nn376 pr4480/cs,nn776
16 Tomorrow about*this*time I will send thee a man out*of*the*land of

nn1144 wcj,qpf4886 pp,nn5057 pr5921 nn,pnx5971 nn3478
Benjamin, and thou shalt anoint him *to be* captain over my people Israel, that he

wcs,hipf3467 (853) nn,pnx5971 pr4480/cs,nn3027 pl,nn6430 cj3588
may save my people out*of*the*hand of the Philistines: for I have

qpf7200 (853) nn,pnx5971 cj3588 nn,pnx6818 qpf935 pr,pnx413
looked upon my people, because their cry is come unto me.

wcj,nn8050 qpf7200 (853) nn7586 wcj,nn3068 qpf6030 ptdm2009
17 And when Samuel saw Saul, the Lord said unto him, Behold the

df,nn376 pnl834 qpf559 pr,pnx413 pndm2088 qmf6113 pp,nn,pnx5971
man whom I spoke to thee of! this same shall reign over my people.

nn7586 wcs,qmf5066 (853) nn8050 pp,cs,nn8432 df,nn8179 wcs,qmf559 himv5046 pp,pnx
18 Then Saul drew near to Samuel in the gate, and said, Tell me,

pte4994 cs,ad335/pndm2088 df,qpta7200 cs,nn1004
I*pray*thee, where the seer's house *is*.

nn8050 wcs,qmf6030 (853) nn7586 wcs,qmf559 pnp595 df,qpta7200 qmv5927
19 And Samuel answered Saul, and said, I *am* the seer: go up

pp,pl,nn,nn6440 df,nn1116 wcj,qpf398 pr,pnx5973 df,nn3117 dfp,nn1242
before me unto the high place; for ye shall eat with me today, and tomorrow

wcj,pipf,pnx7971 himf5046 pp,pnx nn,nn3605 pnl834 pp,nn,pnx3824
I will let thee go, and will tell thee all that *is* in thine heart.

pp,pnx wcj,dfp,pl,nn860 df,pl,qpta6 pr,nu7969 df,pl,nn3117 df,nn3117 qmf7760 ptn408 (853)
20 And as for thine asses that were lost three days ago, set not

nn,pnx3820 pp,pnx cj3588 nipf4672 wcj,pp,pnit4310 cs,nn3605 cs,nn2532
thy mind on them; for they are found. And on whom *is* all the desire of

nn3478 he,ptn3808 pp,pnx wcj,pp,cs,nn3605 nn,pnx1 cs,nn1004
Israel? *Is it* not on thee, and on all thy father's house?

nn7586 wcs,qmf6030 wcs,qmf559 he,ptn3808 pnp595 nn1145 pr4480/pl,cs,nn6996
21 And Saul answered and said, *Am* not I a Benjamite, of*the*smallest

---

9:21 At one point the tribe of Benjamin had been reduced to only six hundred men (Judg. 20:47).

pl,cs,nn7626   nn3478   wcj,nn,pnx4940   df,aj6810 pr4480/cs,nn3605   pl,cs,nn4940
of the tribes of Israel? and my family the least   of all   the families of the

pl,cs,nn7626   nn1144   wcj,pp,pnit4100   pipf1696   dfp,nn1697/df,pndm2088 pr,pnx413
tribe of Benjamin? wherefore then speakest thou   so   to   me?

          nn8050   wcs,qmf3947 (853) nn7586   wcj(853)   nn,pnx5288   wcs,himf,pnx935
22 And Samuel took   Saul and   his servant, and brought them into

      nn,lh3957   pp,pnx   wcs,qmf5414   pp,cs,nn7218   nn4725
the parlor,   and made them   sit   in   the chiefest place   among

      df,pl,qptp7121   wcj,pnp1992   pp,nu7970   nn376
them*that*were*bidden, which were about thirty persons.

          nn8050   wcs,qmf559   dfp,nn2876 qmv5414 (853) df,nn4490   pnl834   qpf5414   pp,pnx
23 And Samuel said unto the cook, Bring   the portion which I gave thee,

pnl834   qpf559   pr,pnx413   qmv7760 pnx(853)   pr,pnx5973
of which I said unto thee, Set   it   by thee.

          df,nn2876 wcs,himf7311 (853)   df,nn7785   wcj,df,pr,pnx5921
24 And the cook took up   the shoulder, and that which was   upon   it,

wcs,qmf7760   pp,pl,cs,nn6440 nn7586   wcs,qmf559 ptdm2009   df,nipt7604 qptp7760
and set   it before Saul. And Samuel said, Behold that which is left! set it

pp,pl,nn,pnx6440   qmv398 cj3588   dfp,nn4150   qptp8104   pp,pnx   pp,qnc559
before thee, and eat: for unto this time hath it been kept for thee since I said,

qpf7121   df,nn5971   nn7586   wcs,qmf398 pr5973   nn8050   df,pndm1931 dfp,nn3117
I have invited the people. So Saul did   eat   with Samuel that   day.

                        wcs,qmf3381   pr4480/df,nn1116   df,nn5892
25 And when they were come down from*the*high*place into the city, Samuel

wcs,pimf1696   pr5973 nn7586 pr5921   df,nn1406
communed with Saul upon the top*of*the*house.

          wcs,himf7925   wcs,qmf1961   pp,qnc5927   df,nn7837
26 And they arose early: and it*came*to*pass about the spring of the day, that

nn8050   wcs,qmf7121/pr413   nn7586   df,nn1406   pp,qnc559   qmv6965
Samuel called   Saul to the top*of*the*house, saying, Up, that I may

wcs,pimf,pnx7971   nn7586 wcs,qmf6965   wcs,qmf3318 du,nu,pnx8147   pnp1931
send*thee*away. And Saul arose, and they went out both of them, he and

wcj,nn8050 df,nn,lh2351
Samuel, abroad.

      pnp1992   pl,qpta3381   pp,cs,nn7097   df,nn5892 wcj,nn8050 qpf559 pr413
27 And as they were going down to the   end   of the city, Samuel said to

nn7586 qmv559   dfp,nn5288 wcj,qmf5674 pp,pl,nn,pnx6440   wcs,qmf5674   qmv5975/wcj,pnp859
Saul, Bid the servant pass on   before   us, (and he passed on,) but stand*thou*still

dfp,nn3117   wcj,himf,pnx8085 (853) cs,nn1697 pl,nn430
a while, that I may show   thee   the word of God.

                    nn8050   wcs,qmf3947 (853) cs,nn6378 df,nn8081   wcs,qmf3332   pr5921
10 Then Samuel took   a vial of oil, and poured it upon his

nn,pnx7218   wcs,qmf,pnx5401   wcs,qmf559   he,ptn3808   cj3588   nn3068
head, and kissed him, and said, Is it   not   because the LORD

qpf,pnx4886   pp,nn5057 pr5921   nn,pnx5159
hath anointed thee to be captain over his inheritance?

          pp,qnc,pnx1980 pr4480/pr,pnx5973   df,nn3117   wcj,qpf4672 du,cs,nu8147
2 When thou art departed   from   me today, then thou shalt find   two

pl,nn376 pr5973   nn7354   cs,nn6900   pp,cs,nn1366   nn1144   pp,nn6766
men by Rachel's sepulcher in the border of Benjamin at Zelzah; and they will

wcj,qpf559 pr,pnx413   df,pl,nn860 pnl834   qpf1980   pp,pinc1245   nipf4672   wcj,ptdm2009
say unto thee, The asses which thou wentest to seek are found: and, lo,

nn,pnx1   qpf5203 (853)   pl,cs,nn1697   df,pl,nn860   wcj,qpf1672   pp,pnx   pp,qnc559

thy father hath left   the care of the asses, and sorroweth for you, saying,

pnit4100   qmf6213   pp,nn,pnx1121

What shall I do for my son?

wcs,qpf2498 wcj,ad1973   pr4480/ad8033   wcs,qpf935 pr5704

3 Then shalt thou go on forward from thence, and thou shalt come to the

cs,nn436   nn8396   ad8033   wcs,qpf,pnx4672   nu7969 pl,nn376   pl,qpta5927   pr413 df,pl,nn430

plain of Tabor, and there shall   meet   thee three men going up to God to

nn1008 nu259 qpta5375 cs,nu7969 pl,nn1423   wcj,nu259   qpta5375   cs,nu7969 pl,cs,nn3603   nn3899

Bethel, one carrying three kids, and another carrying three loaves of bread, and

wcj,nu259   qpta5375   cs,nn5035   nn3196

another carrying a bottle of wine:

wcs,qpf7592/pp,nn7965   pp,pnx   wcs,qpf5414 pp,pnx   du,cs,nu8147   nn3899

4 And they will   salute   thee, and give thee two *loaves* of bread;

wcj,qpf3947   pr4480/nn,pnx3027

which thou shalt receive of*their*hands.

pr310/ad3651   qmf935   cs,nn1389   df,pl,nn430 pnl834/ad8033   pl,cs,nn5333

5 After that thou shalt come to the hill of God,   where *is* the garrison of

pl,nn6430   wcj,qmf1961   pp,qnc935 ad8033   df,nn5892

the Philistines: and it*shall*come*to*pass, when thou art come thither to the city,

wcs,qpf6293   cs,nn2256   pl,nn5030   pl,qpta3381   pr4480/df,nn1116

that thou shalt meet a company of prophets coming down from*the*high*place

nn5035   wcj,nn8596   wcj,nn2485   wcj,nn3658 wcj,pp,pl,nn,pnx6440

with a psaltery, and a tabret, and a pipe, and a harp,   before   them; and

wcj,pnp1992   pl,htpt5012

they shall prophesy:

cs,nn7307   nn3068   wcs,qpf6743 pr,pnx5921   wcs,htpt5012

6 And the Spirit of the LORD will come upon thee, and thou shalt prophesy

pr,pnx5973   wcs,nipf2015   aj312   pp,nn376

with them, and shalt be turned into another man.

wcs,qpf1961   cj3588   df,pndm428 df,pl,nn226   qmf935   pp,pnx   pp,pnx qmv6213

7 And let it be,   when these signs are come unto thee, *that* thou do

pnl834/qmf4672/nn,pnx3027   cj3588 df,pl,nn430   pr,pnx5973

as*occasion*serve thee; for God *is* with thee.

wcs,qpf3381   pp,pl,nn,pnx6440   df,nn1537   wcj,ptdm2009 pnp595

8 And thou shalt go down before me to Gilgal; and, behold, I will

qpta3381   pr,pnx413   pp,hinc5927   pl,nn5930   pp,qnc2076   pl,cs,nn2077

come down unto thee, to offer burnt offerings, *and* to sacrifice sacrifices of

pl,nn8002   cs,nu7651 pl,nn3117   himf3176 pr5704   qnc,pnx935 pr,pnx413   wcs,hipf3045

peace offerings: seven days shalt thou tarry, till I come to thee, and show

pp,pnx (853) pnl834   qmf6213

thee what thou shalt do.

Saul Prophesies

wcj,qpf1961

pp,hinc,pnx6437   nn,pnx7926   pp,qnc1980 pr4480/pr5973

9 And it was *so*, that when he had turned his back to go from

nn8050   pl,nn430 wcs,qmf2015 pp,pnx   aj312   nn3820   cs,nn3605 df,pndm428 df,pl,nn226   wcs,qmf935

Samuel, God gave him another heart: and all those signs came*to*pass

df,pndm1931 dfp,nn3117

that day.

wcs,qmf935   ad8033   df,nn,lh1389 wcj,ptdm2009   cs,nn2256   pl,nn5030

10 And when they came thither to the hill, behold, a company of prophets

---

10:10 See the note on 2 Kings 2:3, 5 regarding the "sons of the prophets."

pp,qnc,pnx7125   cs,nn7307   pl,nn430   wcs,qmf6743   pr,pnx5921   wcs,htmf5012   pp,nn,pnx8432

met   him; and the Spirit of God   came   upon him, and he prophesied among

them.

wcs,qmf1961   cs,nn3605   qpta,pnx3045   pr4480/ad865/ad8032 wcs,qmf7200

11 And it*came*to*pass, when all   that knew him formerly   saw that,

wcj,ptdm2009   nipf5012   pr5973   pl,nn5030   df,nn5971 wcs,qmf559 nn376 pr413   nn,pnx7453

behold, he prophesied among the prophets, then the people said one to another,

pnit4100   pndm2088   qpf1961   pp,cs,nn1121   nn7027   nn7586 he,ad1571

What is this that is come unto the   son   of Kish? Is Saul also among the

dfp,pl,nn5030

prophets?

nn376   pr4480/ad8033   wcs,qmf6030   wcs,qmf559   wcj,pnit4310   nn,pnx1

12 And one of*the*same*place answered and said, But who is their father?

pr5921/ad3651   qpf1961   pp,nn4912   nn7586 he,ad1571   dfp,pl,nn5030

Therefore it became a proverb, Is Saul also among the prophets?

wcs,pimf3615   pr4480/htnc5012   wcs,qmf935

13 And when he had made*an*end of prophesying, he   came   to   the

df,nn1116

high place.

nn7586   cs,nn1730 wcs,qmf559 pr,pnx413   wcj,pr413   nn,pnx5288   ad575   qpf1980

14 And Saul's uncle said unto him and to   his servant, Whither went ye?

wcs,qmf559   pp,pinc1245   (853)   df,pl,nn860   wcs,qmf7200 cj3588

And he said, To seek   the asses: and when we   saw   that they were

ptn369   wcs,qmf935 pr413   nn8050

no where, we came to Samuel.

nn7586   cs,nn1730 wcs,qmf559 hicj5046 pp,pnx   pte4994   pnid4100 nn8050   qpf559   pp,pnx

15 And Saul's uncle said, Tell me, I*pray*thee, what Samuel said unto you.

nn7586 wcs,qmf559 pr413   nn,pnx1730   hina5046/pp,pnx/hipf5046 cj3588   df,pl,nn860

16 And Saul said   unto his uncle, He told*us*plainly that the asses were

nipf4672   wcj(853)   cs,nn1697   df,nn4410   pnl834   nn8050   qpf559   hipf5046 pp,pnx

found. But of   the matter of the kingdom, whereof Samuel spoke, he told him

ptn3808

not.

Saul Becomes King

nn8050   wcs,himf6817/(853)/df,nn5971   pr413   nn3068   df,nn4709

17 And Samuel called*the*people*together unto the LORD to Mizpeh;

wcs,qmf559   pr413   pl,cs,nn1121   nn3478   ad3541 qpf559   nn3068 pl,cs,nn430   nn3478

18 And said unto the children of Israel, Thus saith the LORD God of Israel,

pnp595   hipf5927   (853) nn3478   pr4480/nn4714   wcs,himf5337 pnx(853)   pr4480/cs,nn3027

I brought up   Israel out*of*Egypt, and delivered   you out*of*the*hand of

nn4714   wcj,pr4480/cs,nn3027   cs,nn3605   df,pl,nn4467   df,pl,qpta3905

the Egyptians, and out*of*the*hand of all   kingdoms, and of them that oppressed

pnx(853)

you:

wcj,pnp859   df,nn3117   qpf3988   (853)   pl,nn,pnx430 pnl834   pnp1931 hipt3467 pp,pnx

19 And ye have this day rejected   your God, who himself saved you

pr4480/cs,nn3605   pl,nn,pnx7451   wcj,pl,nn,pnx6869   wcs,qmf559   pp,pnx

out*of*all your adversities and your tribulations; and ye have said unto him, Nay,

cj3588 qmf7760   nn4428   pr,pnx5921   wcj,ad6258   htmv3320   pp,pl,cs,nn6440   nn3068

but set a king over us. Now therefore present yourselves before the LORD by

pp,pl,nn,pnx7626   wcj,pp,pl,nu,pnx505

your tribes, and by your thousands.

nn8050   (853) cs,nn3605   pl,cs,nn**7626**   nn3478   wcs,himf**7126**
☞ 20 And when Samuel had caused   all   the tribes of Israel to come near,

cs,nn**7626**   nn1144   wcs,nimf3920
the tribe of Benjamin was taken.

(853)   cs,nn**7626**   nn1144   wcs,himf**7126**
21 When he had caused   the tribe of Benjamin to come near by their

pp,pl,nn,pnx**4940**   cs,nn**4940**   df,nn4309   wcs,nimf3920   nn7586   cs,nn**1121**   nn7027   wcs,nimf3920
families, the family of Matri was taken, and Saul the son of Kish was taken:

wcs,pimf,pnx1245   wcj,ptn**3808**   nipf4672
and when they sought him, he could not be found.

wcs,qmf**7592**   pp,nn**3068**   ad5750   nn376   ad5750 he,qpf935
22 Therefore they inquired of the LORD further, if the man should yet come

ad1988   nn**3068**   wcs,qmf**559**   ptdm2009   pnp1931   nipf2244   pr413   df,pl,nn3627
thither. And the LORD answered, Behold, he hath hid himself among the stuff.

wcs,qmf7323   wcs,qmf,pnx3947   pr4480/ad8033   wcs,htmf3320 pp,cs,nn**8432**
23 And they ran and fetched him thence: and when he stood among

df,nn**5971**   wcs,qmf1361 pr4480/cs,nn3605   df,nn**5971**   pr4480/nn,pnx7926   wcj,ad,lh4605
the people, he was higher than any of the people from*his*shoulders and upward.

nn8050   wcs,qmf**559** pr413 cs,nn3605   df,nn**5971** he,qpf**7200**   pp,pnx   pnl834   nn**3068**
24 And Samuel said to all the people, See ye him whom the LORD hath

qpf977   cj3588   ptn369   pp,pnx3644   pp,cs,nn3605   df,nn**5971**   cs,nn3605   df,nn**5971**
chosen, that *there is* none like him among all the people? And all the people

wcs,himf**7321**   wcs,qmf**559**   qmf2421   df,nn**4428**
shouted, and said, God save the king.

nn8050   wcs,pimf**1696**/pr413   df,nn**5971**   (853)   cs,nn**4941**   df,nn4410
25 Then Samuel told the people the manner of the kingdom, and

wcs,qmf3789   dfp,nn**5612**   wcs,himf5117   pp,pl,cs,nn**6440**   nn**3068**   nn8050   wcs,pimf7971 (853)
wrote *it* in a book, and laid*it*up before the LORD. And Samuel sent

cs,nn3605   df,nn**5971**   nn376   pp,nn,pnx1004
all the people away, every man to his house.

nn7586 wcj,ad1571 qpf**1980** pp,nn,pnx1004   nn,lh1390   wcs,qmf**1980** pr,pnx5973
26 And Saul also went home to Gibeah; and there went with him a

df,nn**2428**   pnl834   pp,nn,pnx3820 pl,nn**430**   qpf5060
band*of*men, whose hearts God had touched.

wcj,pl,cs,nn**1121**   nn1100   qpf559   pnit4100   pndm2088   himf,pnx**3467**
27 But the children of Belial said, How shall this man save us? And they

wcs,qmf,pnx959   hipf935   pp,pnx wcj,ptn**3808**   nn4503   wcs(qmf**1961**)   pp,hipt2790
despised him, and brought him no presents. But he held*his*peace.

☞ **10:20–24** That Saul was "taken" (*lākadh* [3920]) means that lots were drawn, probably out of an urn. The selection was carried out by process of elimination, beginning with the selection of the tribe of Benjamin and ending with the selection of an individual of the clan of Matri and the family of Kish. The lot fell upon Saul. The Jews understood the drawing or casting of lots to be a means of discovering God's will. As to the necessity of the procedures carried on at Mizpeh, it may be observed that neither Saul nor Samuel had informed the people of Saul's prior anointing (v. 16), making this action necessary to show the people that Saul was to be their king. It is likely that the days between the anointing and this ceremony at Mizpeh were intended for meditation and instruction (v. 8, cf. 1 Sam. 13:7, 8).

Only divine wisdom can fully understand the choice of Saul for king. Yet, it should be noted that Saul fully satisfied the desires of the people. He was a man of great stature from the most military tribe in all of Israel. Who better, they thought, to lead the people in battle against their enemies? Saul was also a man whose own spiritual life mirrored that of the majority of Israel: he was a house built upon the sand, whose lack of saving faith was made clear when the storms came. Any life or nation built upon such a foundation will surely fail.

Nevertheless, the purposes and design of God are never circumvented by the wickedness of men (Job 35:6). Soon after Saul's failure, David was chosen. Saul's reign revealed the motive of the people's demand for a king. Even if Saul had been obedient, his reign was destined to be temporary, for the tribe of Judah was the royal tribe, from which the King of Glory would come (Gen. 49:10).

Saul Rescues Jabesh-gilead

11
nn5176 · df,nn5984 · wcs,qmf**5927** · wcs,qmf2583 · pr5921
Then Nahash the Ammonite came up, and encamped against

cs,nn3003/nn1568 · cs,nn3605 · pl,cs,nn**376** · nn3003 · wcs,qmf559 · pr413 · nn5176
Jabesh-gilead: and all the men of Jabesh said unto Nahash,

qmv**3772** · nn**1285** · pp,pnx · wcj,qmf,pnx**5647**
Make a covenant with us, and we will serve thee.

nn5176 · df,nn5984 · wcs,qmf**559**/pr,pnx413 · pp,pndm2063
2 And Nahash the Ammonite answered them, On this *condition* will I

qmf**3772** · pp,pnx · pp,qnc5365 · cs,nn3605 · pp,pnx · nn3225 · cs,nn**5869**
make *a covenant* with you, that I may thrust out all your right eyes, and

wcs,qpf,pnx**7760** · nn**2781** · pr5921 · cs,nn3605 · nn3478
lay it *for* a reproach upon all Israel.

cs,aj**2205** · nn3003 · wcs,qmf559 · pr,pnx413 · pp,pnx · cs,nu7651 · pl,nn**3117** · himv**7503**
3 And the elders of Jabesh said unto him, Give us seven days' respite, that

wcj,qcj7971 · pl,nn**4397** · pp,cs,nn3605 · cs,nn1366 · nn3478 · wcj,cj518
we may send messengers unto all the coasts of Israel: and then, if *there*

ptn369 · hipt**3467** · pnx(853) · wcj,qpf3318 · pr,pnx413
be no man to save us, we will come out to thee.

wcs,qmf935 · df,pl,nn**4397** · cs,nn1390 · nn7586 · wcs,pimf**1696** · df,pl,nn**1697**
4 Then came the messengers to Gibeah of Saul, and told the tidings in the

pp,du,cs,nn**241** · df,nn5971 · cs,nn3605 · df,nn5971 · wcs,qmf5375 · (853) · nn,pnx6963 · wcs,qmf1058
ears of the people: and all the people lifted up their voices, and wept.

wcj,ptdm2009 · nn7586 · qpta935 · pr310 · df,nn1241 · pr4480 · df,nn**7704** · nn7586 · wcs,qmf559
5 And, behold, Saul came after the herd out of the field; and Saul said,

pnit4100 · dfp,nn**5971** · cj3588 · qmf1058 · wcs,pimf**5608** · pp,pnx · (853) · pl,cs,nn**1697**
What *aileth* the people that they weep? And they told him the tidings of the

pl,cs,nn**376** · nn3003
men of Jabesh.

cs,nn**7307** · pl,nn**430** · wcs,qmf6743 · pr5921 · nn7586 · pp,qnc,pnx**8085** · (853) · df,pndm428 · df,pl,nn**1697**
6 And the Spirit of God came upon Saul when he heard those tidings,

nn,pnx639 · wcs,qmf**2734** · ad3966
and his anger was kindled greatly.

wcs,qmf3947 · cs,nn6776 · nn1241 · wcs,pimf,pnx5408 · wcs,pimf**7971**
7 And he took a yoke of oxen, and hewed*them*in*pieces, and sent

pp,cs,nn3605 · cs,nn1366 · nn3478 · pp,cs,nn**3027** · df,pl,nn**4397** · pp,qnc559
them throughout all the coasts of Israel by the hands of messengers, saying,

pnl834 · ptn,pnx369/qpta3318 · pr310 · nn7586 · wcj,pr310 · nn8050 · ad3541 · nimf**6213**
Whosoever cometh*not*forth after Saul and after Samuel, so shall it be done unto

pp,nn,pnx1241 · cs,nn**6343** · nn3068 · wcs,qmf5307 · pr5921 · df,nn5971 · wcs,qmf3318
his oxen. And the fear of the LORD fell on the people, and they came out

nu259 · pp,nn**376**
with one consent.

wcs,qmf,pnx**6485** · pp,nn966 · pl,cs,nn**1121** · nn3478 · wcs,qmf**1961** · nu7969
8 And when he numbered them in Bezek, the children of Israel were three

pl,nu3967 · nu505 · wcj,cs,nn**376** · nn3063 · nu7970 · nu505
hundred thousand, and the men of Judah thirty thousand.

wcs,qmf**559** · dfp,pl,nn**4397** · df,pl,qpta935 · ad3541 · qmf**559**
9 And they said unto the messengers that came, Thus shall ye say unto the

pp,cs,nn**376** · cs,nn3003/nn1568 · nn4279 · df,nn8121 · pp,qnc2527 · pp,pnx · qmf**1961**
men of Jabesh-gilead, Tomorrow, by *that time* the sun be hot, ye shall have

nn**8668** · df,pl,nn**4397** · wcs,qmf935 · wcs,himf**5046** · pp,pl,cs,nn**376** · nn3003
help. And the messengers came and showed *it* to the men of Jabesh; and they

wcs,qmf**8055**
were glad.

cs,nn1121   nn5941   nn3068   cs,nn3548   pp,nn7887   qpta5375   nn646   wcj,df,nn5971 qpf3045

son of Eli, the Lord's priest in Shiloh, wearing an ephod. And the people knew

ptn3808 cj3588   nn3083   qpf1980

not that Jonathan was gone.

                wcj,pr996   df,pl,nn4569   pnl834   nn3083   pipf1245   pp,qnc5674 pr5921

4 And between the passages, by which Jonathan sought to go over unto the

pl,nn6430   cs,nn4673   cs,nn8127 df,nn5553 pr4480/pndm2088 pr4480/nn5676   wcj,cs,nn8127

Philistines' garrison, *there was* a sharp rock on*the*one side, and a sharp

df,nn5553   pr4480/pndm2088   pr4480/df,nn5676   wcj,cs,nn8034   df,nu259   nn949

rock on*the*other side: and the name of the one *was* Bozez, and the

wcj,cs,nn8034   df,nu259 nn5573

name of the other Seneh.

    df,nn8127   df,nu259   nn4690   pr4480/nn6828   pr4136   nn4363

5 The forefront of the one *was* situated northward over against Michmash, and

wcj,df,nu259 pr4480/nn5045   pr4136   nn1387

the other southward over against Gibeah.

      nn3083   wcs,qmf559 pr413   df,nn5288   qpta5375   nn,pnx3627 qmv1980

6 And Jonathan said to the young man that bore his armor, Come, and let

wcj,qcj5674 pr413 cs,nn4673   df,pndm428   df,pl,nn6189   cj194   nn3068

us go over unto the garrison of these uncircumcised: it may be that the Lord will

qmf6213 pp,pnx cj3588   ptn369 nn4622   pp,nn3068 pp,hinc3467 pp,aj7227 cj176   pp,nn4592

work for us: for *there is* no restraint to the Lord to save by many or by few.

     nn,pnx3627/qpta5375 wcs,qmf559 pp,pnx   qmv6213 cs,nn3605 pnl834   pp,nn,pnx3824

7 And his armorbearer said unto him, Do all that *is* in thine heart:

qmv5186 pp,pnx ptdm,pnx2009   pr,pnx5973   pp,nn,pnx3824

turn thee; behold, I *am* with thee according to thy heart.

     wcs,qmf559   nn3083   ptdm2009 pnp587   pl,qpta5674   pr413   df,pl,nn376

8 Then said Jonathan, Behold, we will pass over unto *these* men, and we

     wcj,nipf1540   pr,pnx413

will discover ourselves unto them.

    cj518   qmf559 ad3541 pr,pnx413   qmv1826 pr5704   hinc,pnx5060 pr,pnx413

9 If they say thus unto us, Tarry until we come to you; then we will

wcs,qpf5975   pr,pnx8478   wcj,ptn3808 qmf5927 pr,pnx413

stand still in*our*place, and will not go up unto them.

     wcj,cj518   qmf559 ad3541   qmv5927 pr,pnx5921   wcs,qpf5927 cj3588

10 But if they say thus, Come up unto us; then we will go up: for the

nn3068   qpf,pnx5414   pp,du,nn,pnx3027 wcj,pndm2088   df,nn226 pp,pnx

Lord hath delivered them into our hand: and this *shall be* a sign unto us.

    du,nu,pnx8147   wcs,nimf1540   pr413   cs,nn4673

11 And both of them discovered themselves unto the garrison of the

pl,nn6430   pl,nn6430 wcs,qmf559 ptdm2009   pl,nn5680   pl,qpta3318   pr4480

Philistines: and the Philistines said, Behold, the Hebrews come forth out of the

df,pl,nn2356 pnl834/ad8033   htpf2244

holes where they had hid themselves.

       pl,cs,nn376   df,nn4675 wcs,qmf6030 (853)   nn3083   wcj(853)

12 And the men of the garrison answered Jonathan and his

pl,nn,pnx3627/qpta5375 wcs,qmf559 qmv5927 pr,pnx413   wcj,hicj3045 pnx(853)   nn1697

armorbearer, and said, Come up to us, and we will show you a thing.

      nn3083   wcs,qmf559 pr413   pl,nn,pnx3627/qpta5375 qmv5927 pr,pnx310 cj3588   nn3068

And Jonathan said unto his armorbearer, Come up after me: for the Lord hath

qpf,pnx5414   pp,cs,nn3027   nn3478

delivered them into the hand of Israel.

      nn3083   wcs,qmf5927 pr5921 du,nn,pnx3027 wcj,pr5921 du,nn,pnx7272

13 And Jonathan climbed up upon his hands and upon his feet, and his

pl,nn,pnx3627/wcj,cs,qpta**5375**   pr,pnx310   wcs,qmf**5307**   pp,pl,cs,nn**6440**   nn3083

armorbearer   after   him: and   they   fell   before   Jonathan;   and   his

pl,nn,pnx3627/wcj,cs,qpta**5375**   pipt*4191   pr,pnx310

armorbearer   slew   after   him.

df,aj**7223**   df,nn**4347**   pnl834   nn3083   pl,nn,pnx3627/wcj,cs,qpta**5375**   hipf**5221**

14 And that first slaughter, which Jonathan and his   armorbearer   made,

wcs,qmf**1961**   pp,pl,nu6242   nn**376**   pp,dfp,nn2677 nn4618   nn**7704**   cs,nn6776

was   about twenty men,   within as it were a   half   acre of land, *which* a yoke

of oxen might plow.

wcs,qmf**1961**   nn**2731**   dfp,nn**4264**   dfp,nn**7704**   wcj,pp,cs,nn3605

15 And there   was   trembling in the host, in the field, and among   all

df,nn**5971**   df,nn4673   wcj,df,hipt**7843** pnp1992 ad1571   qpf**2729**   df,nn**776**   wcs,qmf**7264**

the people: the garrison, and the spoilers, they also trembled, and the earth quaked:

wcs,qmf**1961**   pl,nn**430**   pp,cs,nn**2731**

so it   was   a very great trembling.

Israel Defeats the Philistines

df,pl,qpta6822   pp,nn7586   pp,cs,nn1390   nn1144   wcs,qmf**7200**   wcj,ptdm2009

16 And the watchmen of Saul in Gibeah of Benjamin looked; and, behold, the

df,nn1995   nipf4127   wcs,qmf**1980**   wcj,qpf**1986**

multitude melted away, and they   went   on beating down *one another*.

wcs,qmf**559** nn7586   dfp,nn**5971** pnl834   pr,pnx854   pte**4994**

17 Then   said   Saul unto the people that *were* with him, Number now, and

wcj,qmv**7200** pnit4310   qpf**1980** pr4480/pr,pnx5973   wcs,qmf**6485** wcj,ptdm2009   nn3083

see   who is gone   from   us. And when they had numbered, behold, Jonathan

pl,nn,pnx3627/wcj,cs,qpta**5375**   ptn369

and his   armorbearer   *were* not *there.*

nn7586 wcs,qmf**559**   pp,nn281   himv**5066**   cs,nn**727** df,pl,nn**430** cj3588   cs,nn**727**

☞ 18 And Saul   said   unto Ahiah, Bring hither the ark of God. For the ark of

df,pl,nn**430** qpf**1961**   df,pndm1931 dfp,nn**3117**   wcj,pl,cs,nn**1121**   nn3478

God was at   that   time with the children of Israel.

wcs,qmf**1961**   cj5704   nn7586 pipf**1696**   pr413   df,nn**3548**   wcj,df,nn1995 pnl834

19 And it*came*to*pass, while Saul talked unto the priest, that the   noise   that

pp,cs,nn**4264**   pl,nn6430   wcs,qmf**1980**   qna**1980**/wcj,aj7227   nn7586 wcs,qmf**559** pr413

was in the   host   of the Philistines went on and increased: and Saul   said   unto

df,nn**3548**   qmv**622**   nn,pnx**3027**

the priest, Withdraw thine hand.

nn7586   wcj,cs,nn3605   df,nn**5971** pnl834   pr,pnx854   wcs,nimf**2199**

20 And Saul and   all   the people that *were* with him assembled themselves,

wcs,qmf935 pr5704   df,nn4421   wcj,ptdm2009   nn**376**   cs,nn**2719** qpf**1961**

and they came   to   the battle: and, behold, every man's sword was against his

pp,nn,pnx**7453**   ad3966   aj1419   nn**4103**

fellow, *and there was* a very great discomfiture.

☞ **14:18, 19** This passage states that Saul desired to know God's will by seeking the "ark of God." However, there is some controversy as to whether Saul was calling for the ark of the covenant to be brought from Kirjath–jearim (see 1 Chr. 13:5, 6), or simply asking the priest wearing the ephod to step forward. Some manuscripts have the word for "ark." There are certainly cases in Scripture where the ark of the covenant was taken along with the children of Israel when they went to battle (1 Sam. 4:3). Other Hebrew manuscripts have the word for "ephod." The Septuagint, the Greek translation of the Old Testament, also used the word "ephod." The ephod was already in Saul's camp at Gibeah (1 Sam. 14:3). It contained the Urim and Thummim and was used to receive guidance from God (1 Sam. 23:9; 30:7). Some speculate that the phrase "withdraw thy hand" is more appropriate in regard to the ephod (see 2 Sam. 6:6, 7). Still other Hebrew texts imply that Saul perhaps sought guidance through both methods.

^{wcj,df,pl,nn5680} ^{qpf1961} ^{dfp,pl,nn6430} ^{pp,ad865} ^{ad8032} ^{pnl834}
21 Moreover the Hebrews *that* were with the Philistines before that time, which

^{qpf5927} ^{pr,pnx5973} ^{dfp,nn4264} ^{ad5439} ^{pnp1992} ^{wcj,ad1571}
went up with them into the camp *from the country* round about, even they also

^{pp,qnc1961} ^{pr5973} ⁿⁿ³⁴⁷⁸ ^{pnl834} ^{pr5973} ⁿⁿ⁷⁵⁸⁶ ^{wcj,nn3083}
turned to be with the Israelites that *were* with Saul and Jonathan.

^{wcj,nn3605} ^{cs,nn376} ⁿⁿ³⁴⁷⁸ ^{df,pl,htpt2244} ^{pp,cs,nn2022}
22 Likewise all the men of Israel which had hid themselves in mount

ⁿⁿ⁶⁶⁹ ^{qpf8085} ^{cj3588} ^{pl,nn6430} ^{qpf5127} ^{pnp1992} ^{ad1571} ^{wcs,himf1692}
Ephraim, *when* they heard that the Philistines fled, even they also followed hard

^{pr,pnx310} ^{dfp,nn4421}
after them in the battle.

ⁿⁿ³⁰⁶⁸ ^{wcs,himf3467} (853) ⁿⁿ³⁴⁷⁸ ^{df,pndm1931} ^{dfp,nn3117} ^{wcj,df,nn4421} ^{qpf5674}
23 So the LORD saved Israel that day: and the battle passed over

(853) ⁿⁿ¹⁰⁰⁷
unto Beth-aven.

Jonathan and Saul's Oath

^{wcj,cs,nn376} ⁿⁿ³⁴⁷⁸ ^{nipf5065} ^{df,pndm1931} ^{dfp,nn3117} ⁿⁿ⁷⁵⁸⁶ ^{wcs,himf422}
24 And the men of Israel were distressed that day: for Saul had adjured

(853) ^{df,nn5971} ^{pp,qnc559} ^{qptp779} ^{df,nn376} ^{pnl834} ^{qmf398} ⁿⁿ³⁸⁹⁹ ^{pr5704} ^{df,nn6153}
the people, saying, Cursed *be* the man that eateth *any* food until evening, that I

^{wcs,nipf5358} ^{pr4480/pl,qpta,pnx341} ^{wcj,ptn3808/cs,nn3605} ^{df,nn5971} ^{qpf2938} ⁿⁿ³⁸⁹⁹
may be avenged on*mine*enemies. So none of the people tasted *any* food.

^{wcj,cs,nn3605} ^{df,nn776} ^{qpf935} ^{dfp,nn3293} ^{wcs,qmf1961} ⁿⁿ¹⁷⁰⁶
25 And all *they of* the land came to a wood; and there was honey

^{pr5921/pl,cs,nn6440} ^{df,nn7704}
upon the ground.

^{df,nn5971} ^{wcs,qmf935} ^{pr413} ^{df,nn3293} ^{wcj,ptdm2009} ⁿⁿ¹⁷⁰⁶
26 And when the people were come into the wood, behold, the honey

^{cs,nn1982} ^{wcj,ptn369} ^{hipt5381} ^{nn,pnx3027} ^{pr413} ^{nn,pnx6310} ^{cj3588} ^{df,nn5971} ^{qpf3372} (853)
dropped; but no man put his hand to his mouth: for the people feared the

^{df,nn7621}
oath.

^{wcj,nn3083} ^{qpf8085} ^{ptn3808} ^{nn,pnx1} ^{pp,hinc7650/(853)/df,nn5971}
27 But Jonathan heard not when his father charged*the*people*with*the*oath:

^{wcs,qmf7971} (853) ^{cs,nn7097} ^{df,nn4294} ^{pnl834} ^{pp,nn,pnx3027} ^{wcs,qmf2881}
wherefore he put forth the end of the rod that *was* in his hand, and dipped

^{pnx(853)} ^{pp,cs,nn3295/df,nn1706} ^{wcs,himf7725} ^{nn,pnx3027} ^{pr413} ^{nn,pnx6310} ^{du,nn,pnx5869}
it in a honeycomb, and put his hand to his mouth; and his eyes were

^{wcs,qmf215}
enlightened.

^{wcs,qmf6030} ⁿⁿ³⁷⁶ ^{pr4480/df,nn5971} ^{wcs,qmf559} ^{nn,pnx1}
28 Then answered one of*the*people, and said, Thy father

^{hina7650/hipf7650/(853)/df,nn5971} ^{pp,qnc559} ^{qptp779} ^{df,nn376} ^{pnl834} ^{qmf398}
straitly*charged*the*people*with*an*oath, saying, Cursed *be* the man that eateth

ⁿⁿ³⁸⁹⁹ ^{df,nn3117} ^{df,nn5971} ^{wcs,qmf5888}
any food this day. And the people were faint.

^{wcs,qmf559} ⁿⁿ³⁰⁸³ ^{nn,pnx1} ^{qpf5916} (853) ^{df,nn776} ^{qmv7200}
29 Then said Jonathan, My father hath troubled the land: see,

^{pte4994} ^{cj3588} ^{du,nn,pnx5869} ^{qpf215} ^{cj3588} ^{qpf2938} ^{cs,nn4592}
I*pray*you, how mine eyes have been enlightened, because I tasted a little of

^{df,pndm2088} ⁿⁿ¹⁷⁰⁶
this honey.

30 ^{cj637/cj3588} ^{cj3588/cj3863} ^{df,nn5971} ^{qna398/qpf398} ^{df,nn3117} ^{pr4480/cs,nn7998}
How*much*more, if haply the people had eaten freely today of*the*spoil of

^{pl,qpta,pnx341} ^{pnl834} ^{qpf4672} ^{cj3588} ^{ptn3808} ^{ad6258} ^{qpf7235}
their enemies which they found? for had there not been now a much greater

ⁿⁿ⁴³⁴⁷ ^{dfp,pl,nn6430}
slaughter among the Philistines?

31 ^{wcs,himf5221} ^{dfp,pl,nn6430} ^{df,pndm1931} ^{dfp,nn3117} ^{pr4480/nn4363} ^{nn,lh357}
And they smote the Philistines that day from Michmash to Aijalon:

^{df,nn5971} ^{ad3966} ^{wcs,qmf5888}
and the people were very faint.

32 ^{df,nn5971} ^{wcs,qmf6213} ^{pr413} ^{df,nn7998} ^{wcs,qmf3947} ⁿⁿ⁶⁶²⁹ ^{wcj,nn1241}
And the people flew upon the spoil, and took sheep, and oxen, and

^{wcj,pl,cs,nn1121/nn1241} ^{wcs,qmf7819} ^{nn,lh776} ^{df,nn5971} ^{wcs,qmf398} ^{pr5921}
calves, and slew *them* on the ground: and the people did eat *them* with

^{df,nn1818}
the blood.

33 ^{wcs,himf5046} ^{pp,nn7586} ^{pp,qnc559} ^{ptdm2009} ^{df,nn5971} ^{pl,qpta2398} ^{pp,nn3068}
Then they told Saul, saying, Behold, the people sin against the LORD,

^{pp,qnc398} ^{pr5921} ^{df,nn1818} ^{wcs,qmf559} ^{qpf898} ^{qmv1556} ^{aj1419}
in that they eat with the blood. And he said, Ye have transgressed: roll a great

ⁿⁿ⁶⁸ ^{pr,pnx413} ^{df,nn3117}
stone unto me this day.

34 ⁿⁿ⁷⁵⁸⁶ ^{wcs,qmf559} ^{qmv6327} ^{dfp,nn5971} ^{wcj,qpf559}
And Saul said, Disperse yourselves among the people, and say

^{pp,pnx} ^{himv5066/pr,pnx413} ⁿⁿ³⁷⁶ ^{nn,pnx7794} ^{wcj,nn376} ^{nn,pnx7716}
unto them, Bring*me*hither every man his ox, and every man his sheep, and

^{wcj,qpf7819} ^{pp,pndm2088} ^{wcj,qpf398} ^{qmf2398} ^{wcj,ptn3808} ^{pp,nn3068} ^{pp,qnc398} ^{pr413}
slay *them* here, and eat; and sin not against the LORD in eating with the

^{df,nn1818} ^{cs,nn3605} ^{df,nn5971} ^{wcs,himf5066} ⁿⁿ³⁷⁶ ^{nn,pnx7794} ^{pp,pnx3027} ^{df,nn3915}
blood. And all the people brought every man his ox with him that night,

^{wcs,qmf7819} ^{ad8033}
and slew *them* there.

35 ⁿⁿ⁷⁵⁸⁶ ^{wcs,qmf1129} ⁿⁿ⁴¹⁹⁶ ^{pp,nn3068} ^{pnx(853)} ^{hipf2490} ^{cs,nn4196}
And Saul built an altar unto the LORD: the same was the first altar

^{pp,qnc1129} ^{pp,nn3068}
that he built unto the LORD.

36 ⁿⁿ⁷⁵⁸⁶ ^{wcs,qmf559} ^{qcj3381} ^{pr310} ^{pl,nn6430} ⁿⁿ³⁹¹⁵ ^{wcj,qcj962}
And Saul said, Let us go down after the Philistines by night, and spoil

^{pp,pnx} ^{pr5704} ^{df,nn1242} ^{cs,nn216} ^{wcj,ptn3808} ^{himf7604} ⁿⁿ³⁷⁶ ^{pp,pnx}
them until the morning light, and let us not leave a man of them. And they

^{wcs,qmf559} ^{qmv6213} ^{cs,nn3605} ^{pp,du,nn,pnx5869} ^{df,aj2896} ^{wcs,qmf559} ^{df,nn3548}
said, Do whatsoever seemeth good unto thee. Then said the priest,

^{qcj7126} ^{ad1988} ^{pr413} ^{df,pl,nn430}
Let*us*draw*near hither unto God.

37 ⁿⁿ⁷⁵⁸⁶ ^{wcs,qmf7592} ^{pp,pl,nn430} ^{he,qmf3381} ^{pr310} ^{pl,nn6430}
And Saul asked counsel of God, Shall I go down after the Philistines? wilt

^{he,qmf,pnx5414} ^{pp,cs,nn3027} ⁿⁿ³⁴⁷⁸ ^{qpf,pnx6030} ^{wcj,ptn3808} ^{df,pndm1931}
thou deliver them into the hand of Israel? But he answered him not that

^{dfp,nn3117}
day.

14:36, 37 See the note on Exodus 28:30 concerning seeking direction from God.

nn7586 wcs,qmf**559**   qmv**5066**   ad1988   cs,nn3605   pl,cs,nn6438   df,nn**5971**

38 And Saul said, Draw*ye*near hither, all the chief of the people: and

wcj,qmv**3045**   wcj,qmv**7200** dfp,pnid4100 df,nn**2403**   qpf1961 df,pndm2063 df,nn**3117**

know and see wherein this sin hath been this day.

cj3588   nn**3068** cs,aj**2416**   df,hipt**3467** (853) nn3478 cj3588/cj518 pta,pnx3426 pp,nn3083

39 For, *as* the LORD liveth, which saveth Israel, though it be in Jonathan

nn,pnx**1121** (cj3588)   qna**4191**/qmf**4191**   wcj,ptn369   pr4480/cs,nn3605   df,nn**5971**

my son, he shall surely die. But *there was* not*a*man among all the people

qpta,pnx6030

that answered him.

wcs,qmf**559**   pr413 cs,nn3605   nn3478 qmf**1961** pnp859 nu259 pp,nn5676   wcj,pnp589

40 Then said he unto all Israel, Be ye on one side, and I and

wcj,nn3083   nn,pnx**1121**   qmf**1961**   nu259   pp,nn5676   df,nn**5971** wcs,qmf**559** pr413   nn7586

Jonathan my son will be on the other side. And the people said unto Saul,

qmv**6213**   pp,du,nn,pnx**5869** df,aj**2896**

Do what seemeth good unto thee.

nn7586 wcs,qmf**559** pr413   nn**3068** pl,cs,nn**430**   nn3478 qmf3051   aj**8549**

41 Therefore Saul said unto the LORD God of Israel, Give a perfect *lot*.

wcj,nn7586   nn3083   wcs,nimf3920   wcj,df,nn**5971** qpf3318

And Saul and Jonathan were taken: but the people escaped.

nn7586 wcs,qmf**559** himv**5307**   pr,pnx996   wcj(pr996) nn3083   nn,pnx**1121**

42 And Saul said, Cast *lots* between me and Jonathan my son. And

nn3083   wcs,nimf3920

Jonathan was taken.

nn7586 wcs,qmf**559** pr413   nn3083   himv**5046** pp,pnx pnid4100   qpf**6213**

43 Then Saul said to Jonathan, Tell me what thou hast done. And

nn3083   wcs,himf**5046** pp,pnx   wcs,qmf**559**   qna2938/qpf2938 cs,nn4592 nn1706   pp,cs,nn7097

Jonathan told him, and said, I did but taste a little honey with the end

df,nn**4294** pnl834   pp,nn,pnx**3027**   ptdm,pnx2009   qmf**4191**

of the rod that *was* in mine hand, *and*, lo, I must die.

nn7586 wcs,qmf**559** pl,nn**430** qmf**6213** ad3541 himf3254 wcj,ad3541 cj3588

44 And Saul answered, God do so and more also: for thou shalt

qna**4191**/qmf**4191**   nn3083

surely die, Jonathan.

df,nn**5971** wcs,qmf**559** pr413   nn7586   he,nn3083 qmf**4191** pnl834   qpf**6213**

45 And the people said unto Saul, Shall Jonathan die, who hath wrought

df,pndm2063 df,aj1419   df,nn**3444**   pp,nn3478   ptx2486   nn**3068** cs,aj**2416**   cj518

this great salvation in Israel? God forbid: *as* the LORD liveth, there shall not

pr4480/cs,nn8185   nn,pnx**7218** qmf**5307**   nn,lh**776** cj3588   qpf**6213**   pr5973 pl,nn**430** df,pndm2088

one hair of his head fall to the ground; for he hath wrought with God this

df,nn**3117**   df,nn**5971** wcs,qmf**6299** (853)   nn3083   qpf**4191** wcj,ptn**3808**

day. So the people rescued Jonathan, that he died not.

nn7586 wcs,qmf**5927**   pr4480/pr310   pl,nn6430   wcj,pl,nn6430   qpf**1980**

46 Then Saul went up from following the Philistines: and the Philistines went

pp,nn,pnx4725

to their own place.

Summary of Saul's Military Leadership

wcj,nn7586 qpf3920   df,nn**4410** pr5921 nn3478   wcs,nimf3898   pp,cs,nn3605

47 So Saul took the kingdom over Israel, and fought against all his

pl,qpta,pnx341   ad5439   pp,nn4124   wcj,pp,pl,cs,nn**1121**   nn5983

enemies on every side, against Moab, and against the children of Ammon, and

wcj,pp,nn123
against Edom, and against the   kings   of Zobah, and against the Philistines: and

wcj,pp,nn3605/pnl834   qmf6437   him7561
whithersoever he turned himself, he vexed *them*.

wcs,qmf6213   nn2428   wcs,himf5221 (853)   nn6002   wcs,himf5337 (853)
48 And he gathered a host, and smote   the Amalekites, and delivered

nn3478   pr4480/cs,nn3027   qpta,pnx8154
Israel out*of*the*hands of them that spoiled them.

pl,cs,nn1121   nn7586 wcs,qmf1961   nn3083   wcj,nn3440   wcj,nn4444
49 Now the sons of Saul were Jonathan, and Ishui, and Melchi-shua: and

wcj,cs,nn8034   du,cs,nu8147   pl,nn,pnx1323   cs,nn8034   df,nn1067   nn4764
the names of his   two   daughters *were these*; the name of the firstborn Merab,

wcj,cs,nn8034   df,aj6996   nn4324
and the   name   of the younger Michal:

wcj,cs,nn8034   nn7586   cs,nn802   nn293   cs,nn1323   nn290
50 And the name of Saul's wife *was* Ahinoam, the daughter of Ahimaaz: and

wcj,cs,nn8034   cs,nn8269   nn,pnx6635   nn74   cs,nn1121   nn5369 nn7586 cs,nn1730
the name of the captain of his host *was* Abner, the son of Ner, Saul's uncle.

wcj,nn7027   cs,nn1   nn7586   wcj,nn5369   cs,nn1   nn74
51 And Kish *was* the father of Saul; and Ner   the father of Abner *was* the

cs,nn1121   nn22
son of Abiel.

wcs,qmf1961 aj2389 df,nn4421 pr5921   pl,nn6430 cs,nn3605   pl,cs,nn3117   nn7586
52 And there   was   sore war against the Philistines all   the days of Saul:

nn7586 wcj,qpf7200 cs,nn3605 nn1368 cs,nn376 wcj,cs,nn3605   nn2428 cs,nn1121 wcs,qmf,pnx622
and when Saul saw   any   strong man, or   any   valiant man, he   took   him

pr,pnx413
unto him.

Saul's Second Sin at Gilgal

nn8050   wcs,qmf559   pr413   nn7586   nn3068 qpf7971 pnx(853)   pp,qnc,pnx4886
15
Samuel also said   unto Saul, The Lord sent   me to anoint

pp,nn4428 pr5921   nn,pnx5971 pr5921   nn3478 wcj,ad6258   qmv8085
thee *to be* king over his people, over Israel: now   therefore hearken

pp,cs,nn6963   pl,cs,nn1697   nn3068
thou unto the voice of the words of the Lord.

ad3541   qpf559   nn3068   pl,nn6635   qpf6485   (853)   pnl834   nn6002   qpf6213
2 Thus saith the Lord of hosts, I remember *that*   which Amalek did to

pp,nn3478 pnl834   qpf7760   pp,pnx   dfp,nn1870   pp,qnc,pnx5927   pr4480/nn4714
Israel, how he laid *wait* for him in the way, when he came up from Egypt.

ad6258   qmv1980   wcs,hipf5221 (853)   nn6002   wcs,hipf2763   (853) cs,nn3605 pnl834 pp,pnx
3 Now go   and smite   Amalek, and utterly destroy   all   that they

qmf2550/pr,pnx5921   wcj,ptn3808   wcs,hipf4191 pr4480/nn376 cj5704   nn802 (pr4480)/nn5768
have, and   spare   them not; but slay both man and woman, infant and

wcj(pr5704)   qpta3243   (pr4480)/nn7794   wcj(pr5704) nn7716 (pr4480)/nn1581 wcj(pr5704) nn2543
suckling,   ox   and   sheep, camel and   ass.

nn7586   wcs,pimf8085/(853)/df,nn5971   wcs,qmf,pnx6485   dfp,nn2923
4 And Saul gathered*the*people*together,   and numbered them in Telaim,

du,nu3967   nu505   aj7273   wcj,cs,nu6235 pl,nu505 (853) cs,nn376   nn3063
two hundred thousand footmen, and   ten   thousand   men of Judah.

nn7586 wcs,qmf935 pr5704   cs,nn5892   nn6002   wcs,qmf693   dfp,nn5158
5 And Saul came to a city of Amalek, and laid wait in the valley.

nn7586 wcs,qmf559 pr413   df,nn7017 qmv1980 qmv5493   qmv3381   pr4480/cs,nn8432
6 And Saul said unto the Kenites, Go, depart, get*you*down from among

nn6002　　cj6435　　qmf,pnx**622**　　pr,pnx5973　　　　wcj,pnp859　　qpf**6213**　　nn**2617**　　pr5973

the Amalekites, lest I destroy you with them: for ye showed kindness to

cs,nn3605　　pl,cs,nn**1121**　　nn3478　　　　　　pp,qnc,pnx**5927**　　pr4480/nn4714　　　　nn7017

all the children of Israel, when they came up out*of*Egypt. So the Kenites

wcs,qmf**5493**　　pr4480/cs,nn**8432**　　nn6003

departed from among the Amalekites.

nn7586　wcs,himf**5221**　(853)　　nn6002　　pr4480/nn2341　　　　qnc,pnx935　　nn7793

7 And Saul smote　　the Amalekites from Havilah *until* thou comest to Shur,

pnl834　　pr5921　pl,cs,nn**6440**　　nn4714

that *is* over against Egypt.

wcs,qmf8610　(853)　　nn90　　cs,nn**4428**　　　　nn6002　　aj**2416**

8 And he took　　　Agag the king of the Amalekites alive, and

hipf**2763**　　wcj(853) cs,nn3605　df,nn**5971**　　pp,cs,nn**6310**　　nn2719

utterly destroyed　　all the people with the edge of the sword.

nn7586　　wcj,df,nn**5971**　wcs,qmf2550/pr5921　nn90　　wcj(pr5921)　　cs,nn4315

9 But Saul and the people spared Agag, and　　the best of the

df,nn6629　　wcj,df,nn1241　　wcj,df,pl,nn**4932**　wcj(pr5921)　df,pl,nn**3733**　wcj(pr5921)

sheep, and of the oxen, and of the fatlings, and　　the lambs, and

cs,nn3605　　df,nn**2896**　　qpf14　wcj,ptn**3808**　hinc,pnx**2763**　　wcj,cs,nn3605　df,nn**4399**

all *that was* good, and would not utterly destroy them: but every thing *that*

nipt5240　　wcj,nipt4549 pnx(853)　　hipf**2763**

was vile and refuse,　　that they destroyed utterly.

wcs,qmf**1961**　cs,nn**1697**　nn3068　pr413　nn8050　　pp,qnc559

10 Then came the word of the LORD unto Samuel, saying,

nipf**5162**　cj3588　hipf**4427**　(853) nn7586　pp,nn**4428** cj3588　qpf**7725**

11 It repenteth me that I have set up　Saul *to be* king: for he is turned back

pr4480/pr,pnx310　　ptn**3808**　hipf**6965**　wcj(853)　　pl,nn,pnx**1697**

from following me, and hath not performed　　my commandments. And it

wcs,qmf**2734**　pp,nn8050　　wcs,qmf2199　pr413　　nn3068　cs,nn3605　df,nn**3915**

grieved Samuel; and he cried unto the LORD all night.

nn8050　wcs,himf**7925**　pp,qnc7125　nn7586　　dfp,nn1242　　wcs,homf**5046**

12 And when Samuel rose early to meet Saul in the morning, it was told

pp,nn8050　pp,qnc559　nn7586　qpf935　df,nn,lh3760　wcj,ptdm2009　hipt**5324**/pp,pnx　　nn3027

Samuel, saying, Saul came to Carmel, and, behold, he set*him*up a place, and is

wcs,nimf5437　　wcs,qmf**5674**　　wcs,qmf3381　df,nn1537

gone about, and passed on, and gone down to Gilgal.

nn8050　wcs,qmf935 pr413　nn7586　　nn7586　wcs,qmf559　pp,pnx　qptp**1288**　pnp859

13 And Samuel came to Saul: and Saul said unto him, Blessed *be* thou of

pp,nn**3068**　　hipf**6965**　(853)　cs,nn**1697**　　nn**3068**

the LORD: I have performed　　the commandment of the LORD.

nn8050　wcs,qmf559　wcj,pnit4100　　df,pndm2088　cs,nn6963　　df,nn6629

14 And Samuel said, What *meaneth* then this bleating of the sheep in

pp,du,nn,pnx**241**　wcj,cs,nn6963　df,nn1241　pnl834　pnp595 qpta**8085**

mine ears, and the lowing of the oxen which I hear?

nn7586　wcs,qmf559　　hipf,pnx935　　pr4480/nn6003　　pnl834

15 And Saul said, They have brought them from*the*Amalekites: for the

df,nn**5971**　qpf2550/pr5921　cs,nn4315　df,nn6629　wcj,df,nn1241　pp,pr4616/qnc**2076**

people spared the best of the sheep and of the oxen, to sacrifice unto the

pp,nn**3068**　pl,nn,pnx**430**　wcj(853)　df,qpta**3498**　hipf**2763**

LORD thy God; and　　the rest we have utterly destroyed.

15:8 Agag may have been a general title given to the Amalekite kings, just as Pharaoh was the general title for the King of Egypt (cf. Num. 24:7).

15:12 Carmel (which means "garden") does not refer to the famous mountain in the western part of Galilee but to a town in Judah which lay about seven miles south of Hebron.

nn8050   wcs,qmf559   pr413   nn7586   himv7503   wcj,hicj5046   pp,pnx   (853)   pnl834

16 Then Samuel said unto Saul, Stay, and I will tell thee what the

nn3068   pipf1696   pr,pnx413   df,nn3915   wcs,qmf559   pp,pnx   pimv1696

LORD hath said to me this night. And he said unto him, Say on.

nn8050   wcs,qmf559   cj518   pnp859   aj6996   pp,du,nn,pnx5869   pnp859

17 And Samuel said, When thou *wast* little in thine own sight, *wast* thou

he,ptn3808   cs,nn7218   pl,cs,nn7626   nn3478   nn3068   wcs,qmf,pnx4886   pp,nn4428

not *made* the head of the tribes of Israel, and the LORD anointed thee king

pr5921   nn3478

over Israel?

nn3068   wcs,qmf,pnx7971   pp,nn1870   wcs,qmf559   qmv1980

18 And the LORD sent thee on a journey, and said, Go and

wcj,hipf2763   (853)   df,pl,nn2400   (853)   nn6002   wcj,nipf3898   pp,pnx   pr5704

utterly destroy the sinners the Amalekites, and fight against them until

pnx(853)   pinc,pnx3615

they be consumed.

wcj,pp,pnit4100   ptn3808   qpf8085   pp,cs,nn6963   nn3068

19 Wherefore then didst thou not obey the voice of the LORD, but didst

wcs,qmf5860   pr413   df,nn7998   wcs,qmf6213   df,aj7451   pp,du,cs,nn5869   nn3068

fly upon the spoil, and didst evil in the sight of the LORD?

nn7586   wcs,qmf559   pr413   nn8050   pnl834   qpf8085   pp,cs,nn6963   nn3068

20 And Saul said unto Samuel, Yea, I have obeyed the voice of the LORD,

wcs,qmf1980   dfp,nn1870   pnl834   nn3068   qpf,pnx7971   wcs,himf935   (853)   nn90

and have gone the way which the LORD sent me, and have brought Agag

cs,nn4428   nn6002   hipf2763   wcj(853)   nn6002

the king of Amalek, and have utterly destroyed the Amalekites.

df,nn5971   wcs,qmf3947   pr4480/df,nn7998   nn6629   wcj,nn1241   cs,nn7225

21 But the people took of*the*spoil, sheep and oxen, the chief of the

df,nn2764   pp,qnc2076   pp,nn3068

things*which*should*have*been*utterly*destroyed, to sacrifice unto the LORD thy

pl,nn,pnx430   dfp,nn1537

God in Gilgal.

nn8050   wcs,qmf559   pp,nn3068   he,nn2656   pp,pl,nn5930

22 And Samuel said, Hath the LORD *as great* delight in burnt offerings and

wcj,pl,nn2077   pp,qnc8085   pp,cs,nn6963   nn3068   ptdm2009   qnc8085   aj2896

sacrifices, as in obeying the voice of the LORD? Behold, to obey *is* better

pr4480/nn2077   pp,hinc7181   pr4480/cs,nn2459   pl,nn352

than sacrifice, *and* to hearken than*the*fat of rams.

cj3588   cs,nn4805   cs,nn2403   nn7081   hina6484   wcj,nn205

23 For rebellion *is as* the sin of witchcraft, and stubbornness *is as* iniquity

wcj,pl,nn8655   cj3282   qpf3988   (853)   cs,nn1697   nn3068

and idolatry. Because thou hast rejected the word of the LORD, he hath also

wcs,qmf,pnx3988   pr4480/nn4428

rejected thee from*being*king.

nn7586   wcs,qmf559   pr413   nn8050   qpf2398   cj3588   qpf5674   (853)

24 And Saul said unto Samuel, I have sinned: for I have transgressed the

cs,nn6310   nn3068   wcj(853)   pl,nn,pnx1697   cj3588   qpf3372   (853)   df,nn5971

commandment of the LORD, and thy words: because I feared the people,

wcs,qmf8085   pp,nn,pnx6963

and obeyed their voice.

wcj,ad6258   pte4994   qmv5375   (853)   nn,pnx2403   wcj,qmv7725   pr,pnx5973

25 Now therefore, I*pray*thee, pardon my sin, and turn again with

wcj,htmf7812   pp,nn3068

me, that I may worship the LORD.

nn8050   wcs,qmf559   pr413   nn7586   ptn3808   qmf7725   pr,pnx5973   cj3588

26 And Samuel said unto Saul, I will not return with thee: for thou hast

^{qpf3988}   (853)   ^{cs,nn1697}   ⁿⁿ³⁰⁶⁸   ⁿⁿ³⁰⁶⁸   ^{wcs,qmf,pnx3988}   ^{pr4480/qnc1961}

rejected   the word of the LORD, and the LORD hath rejected thee from being
ⁿⁿ⁴⁴²⁸ ^{pr5921} ⁿⁿ³⁴⁷⁸
king over Israel.

ⁿⁿ⁸⁰⁵⁰   ^{wcs,nimf5437}   ^{pp,qnc1980}   ^{wcs,himf2388}   ^{pp,cs,nn3671}

27 And as Samuel turned about to go away, he laid hold upon the skirt of
^{nn,pnx4598}   ^{wcs,nimf7167}
his mantle, and it rent.

ⁿⁿ⁸⁰⁵⁰ ^{wcs,qmf559} ^{pr,pnx413}   ⁿⁿ³⁰⁶⁸   ^{qpf7167} (853)   ^{cs,nn4468}   ⁿⁿ³⁴⁷⁸

28 And Samuel said unto him, The LORD hath rent the kingdom of Israel
^{pr4480/pr,pnx5921}   ^{df,nn3117}   ^{wcj,qpf,pnx5414}   ^{pp,nn,pnx7453}   ^{df,aj2896}
from thee this day, and hath given it to a neighbor of thine, *that is* better
^{pr,pnx4480}
than thou.

^{wcj,ad1571}   ^{cs,nn5331}   ⁿⁿ³⁴⁷⁸   ^{ptn3808} ^{pimf8266} ^{wcj,ptn3808} ^{nimf5162} ^{cj3588}

29 And also the Strength of Israel will not lie nor repent: for he *is*
^{ptn3808}   ⁿⁿ¹²⁰   ^{pnp1931}   ^{pp,ninc5162}
not a man, that he should repent.

^{wcs,qmf559}   ^{qpf2398}   ^{pimv,pnx3513} ^{ad6258}   ^{pte4994}   ^{pr5048}

30 Then he said, I have sinned: *yet* honor me now, I*pray*thee, before the
^{cs,aj2205}   ^{nn,pnx5971}   ^{wcj,pr5048} ⁿⁿ³⁴⁷⁸   ^{wcj,qmv7725}   ^{pr,pnx5973}
elders of my people, and before Israel, and turn again with me, that I may
^{wcj,htpf7812}   ^{pp,nn3068}   ^{pl,nn,pnx430}
worship the LORD thy God.

ⁿⁿ⁸⁰⁵⁰   ^{wcs,qmf7725}   ^{pr310} ⁿⁿ⁷⁵⁸⁶   ⁿⁿ⁷⁵⁸⁶   ^{wcs,htmf7812}   ^{pp,nn3068}

31 So Samuel turned again after Saul; and Saul worshiped the LORD.

^{wcs,qmf559} ⁿⁿ⁸⁰⁵⁰   ^{himv5066}   ^{pr,pnx413} (853) ⁿⁿ⁹⁰   ^{cs,nn4428}

32 Then said Samuel, Bring*ye*hither to me Agag the king of the
ⁿⁿ⁶⁰⁰²   ⁿⁿ⁹⁰ ^{wcs,qmf1980} ^{pr,pnx413}   ^{pl,nn4574}   ⁿⁿ⁹⁰ ^{wcs,qmf559} ^{ad403}
Amalekites. And Agag came unto him delicately. And Agag said, Surely the
^{cs,nn4751}   ^{df,nn4194}   ^{qpf5493}
bitterness of death is past.

ⁿⁿ⁸⁰⁵⁰   ^{wcs,qmf559} ^{pp,pnl834}   ^{nn,pnx2719}   ^{pl,nn802} ^{pipf7921}   ^{ad3651}

33 And Samuel said, As thy sword hath made women childless, so shall
^{nn,pnx517}   ^{qmf7921}   ^{pr4480/pl,nn802}   ⁿⁿ⁸⁰⁵⁰   ^{wcs,pimf8158/(853)/nn90}
thy mother be childless among women. And Samuel hewed*Agag*in*pieces
^{pp,pl,cs,nn6440}   ⁿⁿ³⁰⁶⁸   ^{dfp,nn1537}
before the LORD in Gilgal.

ⁿⁿ⁸⁰⁵⁰   ^{wcs,qmf1980}   ^{df,nn,lh7414}   ^{wcj,nn7586}   ^{qpf5927} ^{pr413}   ^{nn,pnx1004}   ^{cs,nn1390}

34 Then Samuel went to Ramah; and Saul went up to his house to Gibeah
ⁿⁿ⁷⁵⁸⁶
of Saul.

ⁿⁿ⁸⁰⁵⁰   ^{wcj,ptn3808} ^{qpf3254}   ^{pp,qnc7200} (853) ⁿⁿ⁷⁵⁸⁶ ^{pr5704}   ^{cs,nn3117}

35 And Samuel came no more to see Saul until the day of his
^{nn,pnx4194}   ^{cj3588}   ⁿⁿ⁸⁰⁵⁰   ^{htpf56}   ^{pr413} ⁿⁿ⁷⁵⁸⁶   ^{wcj,nn3068} ^{nipf5162} ^{cj3588}
death: nevertheless Samuel mourned for Saul: and the LORD repented that he had
^{hipf4427/(853)/nn7586}   ^{pr5921}   ⁿⁿ³⁴⁷⁸
made*Saul*king over Israel.

Samuel Anoints David as King

16
nn3068　wcs,qmf559　pr413　nn8050　pr5704/pnit4100　pnp859　htpt56　pr413
And the LORD said unto Samuel, How long wilt thou mourn for

nn7586　wcj,pnp589　qpf,pnx3988　pr4480/qnc4427　pr5921　nn3478　pimv4390
Saul, seeing I have rejected him from reigning over Israel? fill

nn,pnx7161　nn8081　wcj,qmv1980　qmf,pnx7971　pr413　nn3448　df,nn1022　cj3588
thine horn with oil, and go, I will send thee to Jesse the Bethlehemite: for

qpf7200　pp,pnx　nn4428　pp,pl,nn,pnx1121
I have provided me a king among his sons.

nn8050　wcs,qmf559　ad349　qmf1980　nn7586　wcs,qpf8085　wcs,qpf,pnx2026
2 And Samuel said, How can I go? if Saul hear *it*, he will kill me.

nn3068　wcs,qmf559　qmf3947　cs,nn5697/nn1241　pp,nn,pnx3027　wcs,qpf559　qpf935
And the LORD said, Take a heifer with thee, and say, I am come to

pp,qnc2076　pp,nn3068
sacrifice to the LORD.

wcj,qpf7121　pp,nn3448　dfp,nn2077　wcj,pnp595　himf,pnx3045　(853)　pnl834
3 And call Jesse to the sacrifice, and I will show thee what thou

qmf6213　wcs,qpf4886　pp,pnx　(853)　pnl834　qmf559　pr,pnx413
shalt do: and thou shalt anoint unto me *him* whom I name unto thee.

nn8050　wcs,qmf6213　(853)　pnl834　nn3068　pipf1696　wcs,qmf935　nn1035
4 And Samuel did that which the LORD spoke, and came to Bethlehem.

cs,aj2205　df,nn5892　wcs,qmf2729　pp,qnc,pnx7122　wcs,qmf559　qnc,pnx935
And the elders of the town trembled at his coming, and said, Comest thou

nn7965
peaceably?

wcs,qmf559　nn7965　qpf935　pp,qnc2076　pp,nn3068
5 And he said, Peaceably: I am come to sacrifice unto the LORD:

htmv6942　wcj,qpf935　pr,pnx854　dfp,nn2077　wcs,pimf6942　(853)　nn3448
sanctify yourselves, and come with me to the sacrifice. And he sanctified Jesse

wcj(853)　pl,nn,pnx1121　wcs,qmf7121　pp,pnx　dfp,nn2077
and his sons, and called them to the sacrifice.

wcs,qmf1961　pp,qnc,pnx935　wcs,qmf7200　(853)　nn446
6 And it*came*to*pass, when they were come, that he looked on Eliab,

wcs,qmf559　ad389　nn3068　nn,pnx4899　pr5048
and said, Surely the LORD's anointed *is* before him.

nn3068　wcs,qmf559　pr413　nn8050　himf5027　ptn408　pr413　nn,pnx4758　wcj,pr413
7 But the LORD said unto Samuel, Look not on his countenance, or on

cs,nn1364　nn,pnx6967　cj3588　qpf,pnx3988　cj3588　ptn3808　pnl834
the height of his stature; because I have refused him: for *the* LORD *seeth* not as

df,nn120　qmf7200　cj3588　df,nn120　qmf7200　dfp,du,nn5869　wcj,nn3068　qmf7200
man seeth; for man looketh on the outward appearance, but the LORD looketh on

dfp,nn3824
the heart.

nn3448　wcs,qmf7121/pr413　nn41　wcs,himf,pnx5674　pp,pl,cs,nn6440　nn8050
8 Then Jesse called Abinadab, and made*him*pass before Samuel. And

wcs,qmf559　ad1571/ptn3808　nn3068　qpf977　pp,pndm2088
he said, Neither hath the LORD chosen this.

nn3448　nn8048　wcs,himf5674　wcs,qmf559　ad1571/ptn3808　nn3068
9 Then Jesse made Shammah to pass by. And he said, Neither hath the LORD

qpf977　pp,pndm2088
chosen this.

nn3448　cs,nu7651　pl,nn,pnx1121　wcs,himf5674　pp,pl,cs,nn6440　nn8050
10 Again, Jesse made seven of his sons to pass before Samuel. And

nn8050　wcs,qmf559　pr413　nn3448　nn3068　ptn3808　qpf977　dfp,pndm428
Samuel said unto Jesse, The LORD hath not chosen these.

11 And Samuel said unto Jesse, Are here all *thy* children? And he said,
There remaineth yet the youngest, and, behold, he keepeth the sheep. And Samuel
said unto Jesse, Send and fetch him: for we will not sit down till he
come hither.

12 And he sent, and brought him in. Now he *was* ruddy, *and* withal of
a beautiful countenance, and goodly to look to. And the LORD said, Arise, anoint
him: for this *is* he.

○⚷ 13 Then Samuel took the horn of oil, and anointed him in the
midst of his brethren: and the Spirit of the LORD came upon David
from*that*day forward. So Samuel rose up, and went to Ramah.

David Becomes Saul's Musician

14 But the Spirit of the LORD departed from Saul, and an evil spirit
from the LORD troubled him.

15 And Saul's servants said unto him, Behold now, an evil spirit from God
troubleth thee.

16 Let our lord now command thy servants, *which are* before thee, to
seek out a man, *who is* a cunning player on a harp: and it*shall*come*to*pass,
when the evil spirit from God is upon thee, that he shall play with his hand,
and thou shalt be well.

17 And Saul said unto his servants, Provide me now a man that can play
well, and bring *him* to me.

○⚷ 18 Then answered one of the servants, and said, Behold, I have seen a son of
Jesse the Bethlehemite, *that is* cunning in playing, and a mighty valiant man, and

---

○⚷ **16:13** The Jews recognized that the Messiah, the Christ, would come from David's descendants (John 7:42). One of the key titles given to Jesus during His earthly ministry was "Son of David" (Matt. 9:27; 12:23; 15:22), emphasizing His heirship of all of David's royal prerogatives, as well as His fulfillment of the messianic promises to David (2 Sam. 7:8–17, cf. Matt. 22:41–45; Luke 1:32, 69).

○⚷ **16:18** It is interesting that David is called here a "mighty valiant man, and a man of war" when he had not yet had a chance to prove himself in battle (see 1 Sam. 17:33). It seems likely that David had exhibited these qualities in his experiences as a shepherd, and they were equated with valor in war situations.

wcj,cs,nn**376**   nn4421   wcj,cs,nipf**995**   nn**1697**   nn8389   wcj,cs,nn**376**   wcj,nn**3068**

a man of war, and prudent in matters, and a comely person, and the LORD *is*

pr,pnx5973

with him.

nn7586 wcs,qmf7971   pl,nn**4397**   pr413   nn3448   wcs,qmf**559**   qmv7971   pnx(pr413)

19 Wherefore Saul   sent   messengers unto Jesse, and said, Send   me

(853)   nn1732   nn,pnx1121   pnl834   dfp,nn6629

David thy son, which *is* with the sheep.

nn3448 wcs,qmf3947 cs,nn2543   nn3899   wcj,cs,nn4997   nn3196

20 And Jesse took   an   ass *laden* with bread, and a bottle of wine, and

nu259 wcj,cs,nn1423/pl,nn5795   wcs,qmf7971   pp,cs,nn**3027** nn1732   nn,pnx1121 pr413   nn7586

a   kid,   and sent *them* by David his son unto Saul.

nn1732 wcs,qmf935 pr413 nn7586   wcs,qmf5975 pp,pl,nn,pnx**6440**   wcs,qmf,pnx**157**

21 And David came to Saul, and stood   before him: and he   loved   him

ad3966   wcs,qmf**1961** pp,pnx pl,nn3627/qpta**5375**

greatly; and he became his armorbearer.

nn7586 wcs,qmf7971 pr413 nn3448 pp,qnc**559**   nn1732   pte**4994**   qmf5975 pp,pl,nn,pnx**6440**

22 And Saul sent   to Jesse, saying, Let David, I*pray*thee, stand   before

cj3588   qpf4672 nn**2580**   pp,du,nn,pnx**5869**

me; for he hath found favor in my   sight.

wcj,qpf**1961**   pp,qnc**1961**   cs,nn7307   pl,nn**430**   pr413   nn7586

23 And it*came*to*pass, when the *evil* spirit from God was upon Saul, that

nn1732 wcj,qpf3947 (853)   df,nn3658   wcj,pipf5059   pp,nn,pnx**3027**   pp,nn7586   wcj,qpf**7304**

David took   a harp, and played with his hand: so Saul was refreshed, and

wcj,aj**2895**/(pp,pnx)   df,aj7451 cs,nn**7307**   wcj,qpf**5493**   pr4480/pr,pnx5921

was well,   and the evil spirit departed   from   him.

David and Goliath

pl,nn6430   wcs,qmf**622**   (853)   pl,nn,pnx**4264**   dfp,nn4421

17 Now the Philistines gathered together   their armies to battle, and

wcs,nimf**622**   nn7755   pnl834   pp,nn3063

were gathered together at Shochoh, which *belongeth* to Judah, and

wcs,qmf2583   pr996   nn7755   wcj(pr996)   nn5825   pp,nn658 [cs,nn657/pl,nn**1818**]

pitched between Shochoh and   Azekah, in Ephes-dammim.

wcj,nn7586   wcj,cs,nn**376**   nn3478   nipf**622**   wcs,qmf2583

2 And Saul and the men of Israel were gathered together, and pitched by

pp,cs,nn6010   df,nn425   nn4421   wcs,qmf6186 pp,qnc7125   pl,nn6430

the valley of Elah, and set the battle in array against the Philistines.

wcj,pl,nn6430   pl,qpta5975 pr413   df,nn2022   pr4480/pndm2088   wcj,nn3478 pl,qpta5975

3 And the Philistines stood on a mountain on*the*one*side, and Israel stood

pr413   df,nn2022   pr4480/pndm2088   wcj,df,nn1516 pr,pnx996

on a mountain on*the*other*side: and *there was* a valley between them.

wcs,qmf3318   cs,nn**376**/df,du,nn1143   pr4480/pl,cs,nn**4264**   pl,nn6430   nn,pnx8034

4 And there went out a champion out*of*the*camp of the Philistines, named

nn1555   pr4480/nn1661   nn,pnx1363   nu8337 pl,nn520   wcj,nn2239

Goliath, of Gath, whose height *was* six cubits and a span.

wcj,cs,nn3553   nn5178 pr5921   nn,pnx**7218**   pnp1931   qptp3847

5 And *he had* a helmet of brass upon his head, and he   *was* armed with a

wcj,cs,nn8302   pl,nn7193   wcj,cs,nn4948   df,nn8302   cs,nu2568 pl,nu**505**   pl,nn8255   nn5178

coat of mail; and the weight of the coat *was* five thousand shekels of brass.

wcj,cs,nn4697   nn5178 pr5921   du,nn,pnx7272   wcj,cs,nn3591   nn5178

6 And *he had* greaves of brass upon his legs, and a target of brass

pr996   pl,nn,pnx3802

between his shoulders.

wcj,cs,nn2671   nn,pnx2595   pl,qpta707   pp,cs,nn4500   nn,pnx2595

7 And the   staff   of his   spear *was* like a weaver's beam; and his spear's

wcj,cs,nn3852   nu8337   pl,nu3967   pl,nn8255   nn1270   wcj,qpta5375   df,nn6793   qpta1980

head   *weighed*   six   hundred   shekels of iron: and one bearing a shield went

pp,pl,nn,pnx6440

before   him.

wcs,qmf5975   wcs,qmf7121   pr413   pl,cs,nn4634   nn3478   wcs,qmf559   pp,pnx

8 And he   stood   and   cried   unto the armies of Israel, and   said   unto them,

pp,pnit4100   qmf3318   nn4421   pp,qnc6186   he,ptn3808   pnp595   df,nn6430

Why   are ye come out to set *your* battle in array? *am* not   I   a Philistine, and

wcj,pnp859   pl,nn5650   pp,nn7586   qmv1262   nn376   pp,pnx   wcj,qmf3381   pr,pnx413

ye   servants to Saul? choose you a man for you, and let him come down   to

me.

cj518   qmf3201   pp,ninc3898   pr,pnx854   wcs,hipf,pnx5221   wcj,qpf1961

9 If he be able to   fight   with me, and to   kill   me, then will we   be

pp,pnx   dfp,pl,nn5650   wcj,cj518   pnp589   qmf3201   pp,pnx   wcs,hipf,pnx5221

your servants: but   if   I   prevail against him, and   kill   him, then shall ye

wcs,qpf1961   pp,pnx   dfp,pl,nn5650   wcs,qpf5647   pnx(853)

be   our servants, and   serve   us.

df,nn6430   wcs,qmf559   pnp589   pipf2778   (853)   pl,cs,nn4634   nn3478   df,pndm2088   df,nn3117

10 And the Philistine said,   I   defy   the armies of Israel   this   day;

qmv5414   pp,pnx   nn376   wcj,nicj3898   ad3162

give me a man, that we may   fight   together.

nn7586   wcj,cs,nn3605   nn3478   wcs,qmf8085   (853)   df,pndm428   pl,cs,nn1697   df,nn6430

11 When Saul and   all   Israel heard   those   words   of the Philistine,

wcs,nimf2865   ad3966   wcs,qmf3372

they were dismayed, and greatly afraid.

wcj,nn1732   cs,nn1121   df,pndm2088   cs,nn376/nn673   pr4480/nn1035 [cs,nn1004/nn3899]/nn3063

12 Now David *was* the   son   of   that   Ephrathite   of Bethlehem-judah,

wcj,nn,pnx8034   nn3448   wcj,pp,pnx   nu8083   pl,nn1121   wcj,df,nn376   qpf935

whose   name   *was* Jesse; and   he   had eight sons: and the   man   went among

pp,pl,nn376   aj2204   pp,pl,cs,nn3117   nn7586

men *for* an old man in the   days   of Saul.

cs,nu7969   df,aj1419   pl,cs,nn1121   nn3448   wcs,qmf1980   qpf1980/pr310   nn7586   dfp,nn4421

13 And the three eldest   sons   of Jesse   went   *and* followed Saul to the battle:

wcj,cs,nn8034   nu7969   pl,nn,pnx1121   pnl834   qpf1980   dfp,nn4421   nn446   df,nn1060

and the   names   of his three   sons   that went to the battle *were* Eliab the firstborn,

wcj,nn,pnx4932   nn41   wcj,df,nuor7992   nn8048

and   next   unto him Abinadab, and the   third   Shammah.

wcj,nn1732   (pnp1931)   df,aj6996   wcj,nu7969   df,aj1419   qpf1980/pr310   nn7586

14 And David   *was* the youngest: and the   three   eldest followed Saul.

wcj,nn1732   qpta1980   wcj,qpta7725   pr4480/pr5921   nn7586   pp,qnc7462   (853)   nn,pnx1   cs,nn6629

15 But David went and returned   from   Saul to   feed   his father's sheep at

nn1035

Bethlehem.

df,nn6430   wcs,qmf5066   hina7925   wcj,hina6150   wcs,htmf3320

16 And the Philistine drew near morning and evening, and presented himself

pl,nu705   nn3117

forty days.

nn3448   wcs,qmf559   pp,nn1732   nn,pnx1121   qmv3947   pte4994   pp,pl,nn,pnx251   cs,nn374

17 And Jesse   said   unto David his   son,   Take now for thy   brethren an ephah

df,pndm2088   df,nn7039   df,pndm2088   wcj,nu6235   nn3899   wcj,himv7323   df,nn4264

of   this   parched *corn*, and   these   ten   loaves, and   run   to the camp to thy

pp,pl,nn,pnx251

brethren;

himf935 wcj(853) df,pndm428 cs,nu6235 pl,cs,nn2757/df,nn2461 pp,cs,nn**8269** df,nu505

18 And carry these ten cheeses unto the captain of *their* thousand,

qmf**6485** wcj(853) pl,nn,pnx251 pp,nn**7965** qmf3947 wcj(853) nn,pnx**6161**

and look how thy brethren fare, and take their pledge.

wcj,nn7586 wcj,pnp1992 wcj,cs,nn3605 cs,nn376 nn3478 pp,cs,nn6010

19 Now Saul, and they, and all the men of Israel, *were* in the valley

df,nn425 pl,nipt3898 pr5973 pl,nn6430

of Elah, fighting with the Philistines.

nn1732 wcs,himf7925 dfp,nn1242 wcs,qmf**5203** (853) df,nn6629 pr5921

20 And David rose*up*early in the morning, and left the sheep with a

qpta**8104** wcs,qmf5375 wcs,qmf1980 pp,pnl834 nn3448 pipf,pnx**6680** wcs,qmf935

keeper, and took, and went, as Jesse had commanded him; and he came to

df,nn,lh4570 wcj,df,nn**2428** df,qpta3318 pr413 df,nn,lh4634 wcj,hipf**7321** dfp,nn4421

the trench, as the host was going forth to the fight, and shouted for the battle.

nn3478 wcj,pl,nn6430 wcs,qmf6186 nn4634 pp,qnc7125 nn4634

21 For Israel and the Philistines had put*the*battle*in*array, army against army.

nn1732 wcs,qmf**5203** (853) (pr4480/pr,pnx5921) df,pl,nn3627 pr5921 cs,nn3027 qpta**8104**

22 And David left his carriage in the hand of the keeper of

df,pl,nn3627 wcs,qmf7323 df,nn4634 wcs,qmf935 wcs,qmf**7592**/pp,nn**7965** pp,pl,nn,pnx251

the carriage, and ran into the army, and came and saluted his brethren.

wcj,pnp1931 pipt**1696** pr,pnx5973 wcj,ptdm2009 qpta**5927** cs,nn376/df,du,nn1143

23 And as he talked with them, behold, there came up the champion,

df,nn6430 pr4480/nn1661 nn1555 nn,pnx8034 pr4480/pl,cs,nn4630 pl,nn6430

the Philistine of Gath, Goliath by name, out*of*the*armies of the Philistines, and

wcs,pimf**1696** df,pndm428 dfp,pl,nn**1697** nn1732 wcs,qmf**8085**

spoke according to the same words: and David heard *them*.

wcj,cs,nn3605 cs,nn376 nn3478 pp,qnc,pnx**7200** (853) df,nn376 wcs,qmf5127

24 And all the men of Israel, when they saw the man, fled

pr4480/pl,nn,pnx**6440** ad3966 wcs,qmf**3372**

from him, and were sore afraid.

cs,nn376 nn3478 wcs,qmf**559** he,qpf**7200** df,pndm2088 df,nn376 df,qpta**5927**

25 And the men of Israel said, Have ye seen this man that is come up?

cj3588 pp,pinc2778 (853) nn3478 qpta**5927** wcs,qpf**1961** df,nn376 pnl834 himf,pnx**5221**

surely to defy Israel is he come up: and it*shall*be, *that* the man who killeth

df,nn**4428** himf,pnx**6238** aj1419 nn6239 qmf**5414** pp,pnx wcj(853)

him, the king will enrich him with great riches, and will give him his

nn,pnx1323 qmf**6213** wcj(853) nn,pnx1 cs,nn**1004** aj2670 pp,nn3478

daughter, and make his father's house free in Israel.

nn1732 wcs,qmf**559** pr413 df,pl,nn**376** df,pl,qpta5975 pr,pnx5973 pp,qnc**559** pnit4100

26 And David spoke to the men that stood by him, saying, What shall

nimf**6213** dfp,nn376 pnl834 himf**5221** (853) pndm1975 df,nn6430 wcs,hipf**5493** nn2781

be done to the man that killeth this Philistine, and taketh away the reproach

pr4480/pr5921 nn3478 cj3588 pnit4310 df,pndm2088 df,aj**6189** df,nn6430 cj3588 pipf2778

from Israel? for who *is* this uncircumcised Philistine, that he should defy the

pl,cs,nn4634 aj**2416** pl,nn**430**

armies of the living God?

df,nn**5971** wcs,qmf**559** pp,pnx df,pndm2088 df,nn**1697** pp,qnc**559** ad3541

27 And the people answered him after this manner, saying, So shall it be

nimf**6213** dfp,nn376 pnl834 himf,pnx**5221**

done to the man that killeth him.

nn446 df,aj1419 nn,pnx251 wcs,qmf**8085** pp,pinc,pnx**1696** pr413 df,pl,nn**376**

28 And Eliab his eldest brother heard when he spoke unto the men; and

nn446 cs,nn**639** wcs,qmf**2734** pp,nn1732 wcs,qmf**559** pp,pnit4100 qpf3381

Eliab's anger was kindled against David, and he said, Why camest*thou*down

wcj,pr5921 pnit4310 qpf**5203** df,pndm2007 cs,aj4592 df,nn6629 dfp,nn4057 pnp589

hither? and with whom hast thou left those few sheep in the wilderness? I

qpf**3045**   (853)   nn,pnx**2087**   wcj(853)   cs,nn**7455**   nn,pnx3824   cj3588
know   thy pride, and   the naughtiness of thine heart; for thou art

qpf3381   pp,cj4616   qnc**7200**   df,nn4421
come down that thou mightest see the battle.

nn1732   wcs,qmf**559**   pnit4100   ad6258   qpf**6213**   (pnp1931)   he,ptn**3808**   nn**1697**
29 And David said, What have I now done? *Is there*   not a cause?

wcs,qimf5437   pr4480/nn,pnx681   pr413/nn4136/aj312   wcs,qmf**559**   df,pndm2088
30 And he turned   from   him toward another, and spoke after the same

dfp,nn**1697**   df,nn**5971**   nn**1697**   wcs,himf,pnx**7725**   df,aj**7223**   dfp,nn**1697**
manner: and the people answered him   again   after the former manner.

df,pl,nn**1697**   wcs,nimf**8085**   pnl834   nn1732   pipf**1696**   wcs,himf**5046**
31 And when the words were heard which David spoke, they rehearsed *them*

pp,pl,cs,nn**6440**   nn7586   wcs,qmf,pnx**3947**
before Saul: and he   sent   for him.

nn1732   wcs,qmf**559**   pr413   nn7586   ptn408   nn**120**   cs,nn**3820**   qmf**5307**   pr,pnx**5921**
32 And David said   to Saul, Let no man's heart fail because of him; thy

nn,pnx**5650**   qmf**1980**   wcs,nipf**3898**   pr5973   df,pndm2088   df,nn**6430**
servant will go and fight with   this   Philistine.

nn7586   wcs,qmf**559**   pr413   nn1732   ptn**3808**   qmf3201   pp,qnc**1980**   pr413   df,pndm2088
☞ 33 And Saul   said   to   David, Thou art not able to   go   against   this

df,nn**6430**   pp,ninc3898   pr,pnx5973   cj3588   pnp859   nn5288   wcj,pnp1931   cs,nn**376**   nn4421
Philistine to fight   with him: for thou *art but* a youth, and   he   a man of war

pr4480/pl,nn,pnx**5271**
from*his*youth.

nn1732   wcs,qmf**559**   pr413   nn7586   nn,pnx**5650**   qpf**1961**/qpta7462   pp,nn,pnx1   dfp,nn**6629**
34 And David said   unto Saul, Thy servant   kept   his father's sheep, and

wcj,qpf935   df,nn738   wcj(853)   df,nn1677   wcj,qpf**5375**   nn7716   pr4480/df,nn**5739**
there came a lion, and   a bear, and took a lamb out*of*the*flock:

wcs,qpf3318   pr,pnx310   wcs,hipf,pnx**5221**   wcs,hipf**5337**
35 And I went out   after   him, and   smote   him, and delivered *it*

pr4480/nn,pnx**6310**   wcs,qmf**6965**   pr,pnx5921   wcj,hipf**2388**   pp,nn,pnx**2206**
out*of*his*mouth: and when he   arose   against me, I caught *him* by his beard, and

wcj,hipf,pnx**5221**   wcj,hipf,pnx**4191**
smote   him, and   slew   him.

nn,pnx**5650**   hipf**5221**   ad1571   (853)   df,nn738   ad1571   df,nn1677   df,pndm2088   df,aj**6189**
36 Thy servant slew both   the lion and the bear: and   this   uncircumcised

df,nn**6430**   wcj,qpf**1961**   pp,nu259   pr,pnx4480   cj3588   pipf2778   pl,cs,nn**4634**
Philistine shall   be   as one   of   them, seeing he hath defied the armies of the

aj**2416**   pl,nn**430**
living God.

nn1732   wcs,qmf**559**   nn**3068**   pnl834   hipf,pnx**5337**   wcj,pr4480/cs,nn**3027**
37 David   said   moreover, The Lord that delivered me out*of*the*paw of the

df,nn738   pr4480/cs,nn**3027**   df,nn1677   pnp1931   himf,pnx**5337**   pr4480/cs,nn**3027**
lion, and out*of*the*paw of the bear,   he   will deliver me out*of*the*hand of

df,pndm2088   df,nn**6430**   nn7586   wcs,qmf**559**   pr413   nn1732   qmv**1980**   wcj,nn**3068**   qmf**1961**   pr,pnx5973
this   Philistine. And Saul   said   unto David, Go,   and the Lord   be   with

thee.

nn7586   wcs,himf3847   (853)   nn1732   pl,nn,pnx4055   wcj,qpf**5414**   cs,nn**6959**   nn5178
38 And Saul armed   David with his armor, and he   put   a helmet of brass

pr5921   nn,pnx**7218**   wcs,himf3847   pnx(853)   nn8302
upon his head; also he   armed   him with a coat*of*mail.

☞ **17:33**   See the note on 1 Samuel 16:18.

nn1732   wcs,qmf2296 (853)   nn,pnx2719   pr4480/pr5921   pp,pl,nn,pnx4055   wcs,himf**2974**

39 And David girded   his sword   upon   his   armor,   and he attempted to

pp,qnc**1980** cj3588   ptn**3808**   pipf**5254**   nn1732   wcs,qmf**559**   pr413   nn7586   qmf3201/ptn**3808**   pp,qnc**1980**

go;   for he had   not   proved   *it*.   And David   said   unto Saul,   I   cannot   go

dfp,pndm428   cj3588   ptn**3808**   pipf**5254**   nn1732   wcs,himf,pnx**5493**   pr4480/pr,pnx5921

with   these;   for I have   not   proved *them*. And David   put   them   off

him.

            wcs,qmf3947   nn,pnx4731   pp,nn,pnx**3027**   wcs,qmf**977**   pp,pnx   nu2568   pl,cs,nn2512   pl,nn68

40 And he   took   his   staff   in his   hand,   and chose him five smooth stones

pr4480   df,nn5158   wcs,qmf**7760**   pnx(853)   df,pl,qpta7462   pp,cs,nn3627   pnl834   pp,pnx

out of the brook, and   put   them in a shepherd's   bag   which   he had,

     wcj,dfp,nn3219   wcj,nn,pnx7050   pp,nn,pnx**3027**   wcs,qmf**5066**   pr413

even in a   scrip;   and his   sling   *was* in his   hand: and he drew near   to   the

df,nn6430

Philistine.

       df,nn6430   wcs,qmf**1980** qpta**1980**   wcj,aj7131   pr413   nn1732   wcj,df,nn**376**

41 And the Philistine came   on   and drew near unto David; and the   man

qpta**5375**   df,nn6793   pp,pl,nn,pnx**6440**

that bore the shield *went*   before   him.

         df,nn6430   wcs,himf5027   wcs,qmf**7200** (853)   nn1732   wcs,qmf,pnx959

42 And when the Philistine looked about, and   saw   David, he disdained

cj3588   qpf**1961**   nn5288   wcj,aj132   pr5973   cs,aj3303   nn4758

him: for he was *but* a youth, and ruddy, and   of a   fair   countenance.

        df,nn6430   wcs,qmf559   pr413   nn1732   pnp595   he,nn3611 cj3588   pnp859   qpta935

43 And the Philistine   said   unto David,   *Am*   I   a   dog,   that thou comest

pr,pnx413   dfp,pl,nn4731   df,nn6430   wcs,pimf**7043** (853)   nn1732   pp,pl,nn,pnx**430**

to   me with staves? And the Philistine cursed   David by his   gods.

       df,nn6430   wcs,qmf559 pr413   nn1732   qmv**1980**   pr,pnx413   wcj,qcj**5414** (853)

44 And the Philistine   said   to David, Come   to   me, and I will   give

nn,pnx**1320**   pp,cs,nn5775   df,du,nn**8064**   wcj,pp,cs,nn929   df,nn**7704**

thy flesh unto the fowls of the   air,   and to the   beasts   of the field.

     wcs,qmf559   nn1732   pr413   df,nn6430   pnp859   qpta935   pr,pnx413   pp,nn2719

45 Then   said   David to the Philistine, Thou comest   to   me with a sword,

   wcj,dfp,nn2595   wcj,pp,nn3591   wcj,pnp595 qpta935 pr,pnx413   pp,cs,nn8034

and with a spear,   and with a   shield: but   I   come   to   thee in the   name of

nn3068   pl,nn**6635**   pl,cs,nn**430**   pl,cs,nn4634   nn3478   pnl834   pipf2778

the LORD of hosts, the God of the armies of Israel, whom thou hast defied.

df,pndm2088   df,nn**3117**   nn3068   pimf,pnx5462   pp,nn,pnx**3027**

46 This   day   will the LORD   deliver thee into mine   hand;   and I will

wcs,hipf,pnx**5221**   wcs,hipf**5493** (853)   nn,pnx7218 pr4480/pr,pnx5921   wcs,qpf**5414**

smite   thee, and   take   thine   head   from   thee; and I will   give   the

cs,nn**6297**   cs,nn4264   pl,nn6430   df,pndm2088 df,nn**3117**   pp,cs,nn5775   df,du,nn**8064**

carcasses of the host of the Philistines   this   day unto the fowls of the   air,

      wcj,pp,cs,nn2416   df,nn776   cs,nn3605   df,nn776   wcj,qmf3045 cj3588   pta3426

and to the wild beasts of the earth; that   all   the earth may   know   that there is a

pl,nn**430**   pp,nn3478

God in Israel.

     cs,nn3605 df,pndm2088   df,nn6951   wcj,qmf3045 cj3588   nn3068   himf3467   ptn**3808**

47 And   all   this   assembly shall   know   that the LORD saveth   not   with

pp,nn2719   wcj,dfp,nn2595 cj3588   df,nn4421   pp,nn3068   wcs,qpf**5414** pnx(853)

sword and   spear: for the battle *is* the LORD's, and he will   give   you into

pp,nn,pnx**3027**

our hands.

       wcj,qpf**1961**   cj3588   df,nn6430   qpf6965   wcs,qmf**1980**   wcs,qmf7126

48 And it*came*to*pass, when the Philistine arose, and   came   and drew nigh

pp,qnc7125   nn1732   nn1732   wcs,pimf4116   wcs,qmf7323   df,nn4634   pp,qnc7125
to meet David, that David hasted, and   ran   toward the army to meet the

df,nn6430
Philistine.

            nn1732   wcs,qmf7971 (853)   nn,pnx3027 pr413   df,nn3627   wcs,qmf3947 pr4480/ad8033   nn68
49 And David   put   his hand in his bag, and   took   thence a stone,

wcs,pimf7049   wcs,himf5221 (853)   df,nn6430   pr413   nn,pnx4696   df,nn68 wcs,qmf2883
and slung it, and smote   the Philistine in his forehead, that the stone sunk

pp,nn,pnx4696   wcs,qmf5307 pr5921   pl,nn,pnx6440   nn,lh776
into his forehead; and he   fell   upon his face to the earth.

            nn1732   wcs,qmf2388 pr4480   df,nn6430   dfp,nn7050   wcj,dfp,nn68
50 So David prevailed over the Philistine with a sling and with a stone, and

wcs,himf5221 (853)   df,nn6430   wcs,himf,pnx4191   ptn369 wcj,nn2719   pp,cs,nn3027
smote   the Philistine, and   slew   him; but there was no sword in the hand

nn1732
of David.

            nn1732   wcs,qmf7323   wcs,qmf5975 pr413   df,nn6430   wcs,qmf3947 (853)
51 Therefore David   ran,   and stood upon the Philistine, and   took   his

nn,pnx2719   wcs,qmf,pnx8025   pr4480/nn,pnx8593   wcs,pimf*,pnx4191   wcs,qmf3772
sword, and   drew   it out*of*the*sheath thereof, and   slew   him, and cut off

(853)   nn,pnx7218   pp,pnx   df,pl,nn6430   wcs,qmf7200 (cj3588)   nn,pnx1368
his head therewith. And when the Philistines saw   their champion was

qpf4191   wcs,qmf5127
dead, they fled.

            pl,cs,nn376   nn3478   wcj,nn3063 wcs,qmf6965   wcs,himf7321   wcs,qmf7291 (853)
52 And the men of Israel and of Judah arose, and shouted, and pursued

df,pl,nn6430   pr5704   qnc,pnx935   nn1516   wcj,pr5704   pl,cs,nn8179   nn6138
the Philistines, until thou come to the valley, and   to   the gates of Ekron. And

pl,cs,nn2491   df,pl,nn6430   wcs,qmf5307   pp,cs,nn1870   nn8189   wcj,pr5704
the wounded of the Philistines fell down by the way   to Shaaraim, even unto

nn1661   wcj,pr5704   nn6138
Gath, and unto Ekron.

            pl,cs,nn1121   nn3478   wcs,qmf7725   pr4480/qnc1814   pr310   pl,nn6430
53 And the children of Israel returned from chasing after the Philistines, and

wcs,qmf8155 (853)   pl,nn,pnx4264
they spoiled   their tents.

            nn1732   wcs,qmf3947 (853)   cs,nn7218   df,nn6430   wcs,himf,pnx935
54 And David   took   the head of the Philistine, and   brought it to

nn3389   qpf7760 wcj(853)   pl,nn,pnx3627   pp,nn,pnx168
Jerusalem; but he put   his armor in his tent.

            nn7586   wcj,pp,qnc7200 (853) nn1732 qpta3318   pp,qnc7125   df,nn6430   qpf559
55 And when Saul   saw   David go forth against the Philistine, he said

pr413   nn74   cs,nn8269   df,nn6635   nn74   pnit4310 cs,nn1121   pndm2088 df,nn5288   nn74
unto Abner, the captain of the host, Abner, whose son is this youth? And Abner

wcs,qmf559   nn,pnx5315 cs,aj2416   df,nn4428   cj518   qpf3045
said, As thy soul liveth, O king, I cannot tell.

            df,nn4428 wcs,qmf559 qmv7592 pnp859 pnit4310 cs,nn1121   (pndm2088)   df,nn5958
56 And the king said, Inquire thou whose son the   stripling is.

            nn1732   wcj,pp,qnc7725   pr4480/hinc5221   (853)   df,nn6430   nn74
57 And as David returned from*the*slaughter of   the Philistine, Abner

---

🕮 17:55–58   It is intriguing that Saul seemingly did not recognize David here. No one knows for what length of time or how frequently David played his musical instruments for King Saul. The incident with Goliath probably happened several years after David's service in the king's court.

wcs,qmf3947 pnx(853)   wcs,himf,pnx935   pp,pl,cs,nn**6440** nn7586   wcj,cs,nn**7218**   df,nn6430

took   him, and brought him before Saul with the   head   of the Philistine

pp,nn,pnx**3027**

in his   hand.

      nn7586   wcs,qmf**559** pr,pnx413   pnit4310   cs,nn**1121**   pnp859   df,nn5288

58 And Saul   said   to   him, Whose   son   *art* thou, *thou* young man? And

nn1732   wcs,qmf**559**   cs,nn**1121**   nn,pnx**5650** nn3448   nn1022

David answered, I *am* the   son   of thy servant Jesse the Bethlehemite.

David and Jonathan Become Friends

18

wcs,qmf**1961**   pp,pinc,pnx**3615**   pp,pinc**1696**   pr413

And it*came*to*pass, when he had made*an*end of speaking unto

nn7586   wcj,cs,nn**5315**   nn3083   nipf7194   pp,cs,nn**5315**   nn1732

Saul, that the   soul   of Jonathan was knit with the   soul   of David,

nn3083   wcs,qmf,pnx**157**   pp,nn,pnx**5315**

and Jonathan   loved   him as his own   soul.

     nn7586   wcs,qmf,pnx3947   df,pndm1931   dfp,nn**3117**   qpf,pnx**5414**

2 And   Saul   took   him   that   day,   and   would   let   him

pp,qnc**7725**/wcj,ptn**3808**   nn,pnx1   cs,nn**1004**

go*no*more*home to his father's house.

     nn3083   wcj,nn1732 wcs,qmf**3772**   nn**1285**   pp,qnc,pnx**157** pnx(853)

3 Then Jonathan and David   made   a covenant, because he   loved   him as

pp,nn,pnx**5315**

his own   soul.

     nn3083   wcs,htmf6584   (853)   df,nn4598 pnl834   pr,pnx5921

4 And Jonathan stripped himself of   the robe   that *was* upon   him, and

wcs,qmf,pnx**5414**   pp,nn1732   wcj,pl,nn,pnx4055   wcj,pr5740   nn,pnx2719   wcj,pr5704

gave   it to David, and his garments, even   to   his sword, and   to   his

nn,pnx7198   wcj,pr5704   nn,pnx2290

bow, and   to   his girdle.

     nn1732   wcs,qmf3318   pnl834/pp,nn3605   nn7586   qmf,pnx7971

5 And   David   went out   whithersoever   Saul   sent   him,   *and*

himf**7919**   nn7586 wcs,qmf,pnx**7760**   pr5921   pl,cs,nn**376**   df,nn4421

behaved*himself*wisely: and Saul   set   him over the   men   of   war,   and he

wcs,qmf**3190**   pp,du,cs,nn**5869**   cs,nn3605   df,nn**5971**   wcj,ad1571   pp,du,cs,nn**5869**

was accepted in the   sight   of   all   the people, and   also   in the   sight   of

nn7586   pl,cs,nn**5650**

Saul's servants.

Saul Becomes Jealous of David

      wcs,qmf**1961**   pp,qnc,pnx935   nn1732   pp,qnc**7725**

6 And   it*came*to*pass   as   they   came,   when   David   was   returned

pr4480/hinc**5221**   (853)   df,nn6430   df,pl,nn**802**   wcs,qmf3318   pr4480/cs,nn3605 pl,cs,nn5892

from*the*slaughter of   the Philistine, that the women came out   of   all   cities

nn3478   pp,qnc**7891**   wcj,df,pl,nn4246   pp,qnc7125 df,nn**4428**   nn7586   pp,pl,nn8596   pp,nn8057

of Israel, singing and dancing, to   meet   king   Saul, with tabrets, with   joy,   and

wcj,pp,pl,nn**7991**

with instruments*of*music.

     df,pl,nn**802**   wcs,qmf6030   df,pl,pipt7832   wcs,qmf559 nn7586

7 And the women answered *one another* as they   played,   and   said,   Saul hath

hipf**5221**   pp,nu,pnx505   wcj,nn1732   pp,pl,nu,pnx7233

slain his thousands, and David his ten thousands.

pp,nn7586   ad3966   wcs,qmf**2734**   df,pndm2088   df,nn**1697**   wcs,qmf**3415**/pp,du,nn,pnx**5869**
8 And Saul was very wroth, and   the   saying   displeased   him; and he

wcs,qmf**559**   qpf**5414**   pp,nn1732   pl,nu7233   wcj,pp,pnx   qpf**5414**
said, They have ascribed unto David ten thousands, and to me they have ascribed

df,pl,nu**505**   pp,pnx   wcj,ad5750 ad389   df,nn4410
but thousands: and *what* can he have more but the kingdom?

nn7586 wcs(qmf**1961**) qpta5770 (853)   nn1732 pr4480/df,nn3117/df,pndm1931   wcj,ad1973
9 And Saul   eyed   David from*that*day and forward.

pr4480/ad4283   aj7451 cs,nn7307   pl,nn**430** wcs,qmf6743
10 And it*came*to*pass on*the*morrow, that the evil spirit from God   came

pr413 nn7586   wcs,htmf**5012**   pp,cs,nn**8432**   df,nn**1004**   wcj,nn1732 pipt5059
upon Saul, and he prophesied in the midst of the house: and David played with his

pp,nn,pnx**3027**   pp,nn3117/pp,nn3117   wcj,df,nn2595   nn7586 pp,cs,nn**3027**
hand, as at other times: and *there was* a javelin in Saul's hand.

nn7586 wcs,himf2904 (853)   df,nn2595   wcs,qmf**559**   himf**5221** pp,nn1732
11 And Saul cast   the javelin; for he said, I will smite David even to the

wcj,dfp,nn**7023**   nn1732 wcs,qmf5437   pr4480/pl,nn,pnx**6440**   du,nn6471
wall *with it.* And David avoided out*of*his*presence twice.

nn7586   wcs,qmf**3372** pr4480/pp,pl,cs,nn**6440**   nn1732   cj3588   nn**3068** qpf**1961** pr,pnx5973
12 And Saul was afraid   of   David, because the LORD was   with

qpf**5493**   wcj,pr4480/pr5973 nn7586
him, and was departed   from   Saul.

nn7586 wcs,himf,pnx**5493**   pr4480/pr,pnx5973   wcs,qmf,pnx**7760**   pp,pnx cs,nn**8269**
13 Therefore Saul removed him   from   him, and made   him his captain

nu**505**   wcs,qmf3318   wcs,qmf935 pp,pl,cs,nn**6440**   df,nn**5971**
over a thousand; and he went out and came in before the people.

nn1732 wcs(qmf**1961**)   hipt**7919**   pp,cs,nn3605   pl,nn,pnx**1870**
14 And David   behaved*himself*wisely in   all   his ways; and the

wcj,nn**3068**   pr,pnx5973
LORD *was* with him.

nn7586 wcs,qmf**7200** pnl834 pnp1931   hipt**7919**/ad3966
15 Wherefore when Saul   saw   that   he   behaved*himself*very*wisely, he

wcs,qmf**1481** pr4480/pl,cs,nn**6440**
was afraid   of   him.

wcj,cs,nn3605   nn3478   wcj,nn3063 qpta157   (853)   nn1732   cj3588   pnp1931   qpta3318
16 But   all   Israel and Judah loved   David, because he   went out and

wcj,qpta935 pp,pl,nn,pnx**6440**
came in before them.

David Marries Saul's Daughter

nn7586 wcs,qmf**559** pr413   nn1732 ptdm2009   df,aj1419   nn,pnx1323   nn4764   pnx(853)
17 And Saul said   to David, Behold my elder daughter Merab,   her will

qmf**5414** pp,pnx   pp,nn**802** ad389 qmv**1961**   pp,cs,nn**1121**/nn**2428** pp,pnx   wcj,nimv3898   nn**3068**
I give thee to wife: only be thou   valiant   for me, and fight the LORD's

pl,cs,nn4421   wcj,nn7586 qpf**559** ptn408   nn,pnx**3027** qmf**1961** pp,pnx   cs,nn**3027**
battles. For Saul said, Let not mine hand   be upon him, but let the hand of

pl,nn6430   wcs,qmf**1961** pp,pnx
the Philistines be   upon him.

nn1732 wcs,qmf**559** pr413 nn7586   pnit4310   pnp595   wcj,pnit4310   aj,pnx**2416**
18 And David said unto Saul, Who *am* I? and what *is* my life, *or* my

nn,pnx1   cs,nn**4940**   pp,nn3478 cj3588   qmf**1961**   nn2860   dfp,nn**4428**
father's family in Israel, that I should be son-in-law to the king?

wcs,qmf**1961**   pp,nn6256   (853)   nn4764   nn7586   cs,nn1323
19 But it*came*to*pass at the time when   Merab Saul's daughter should

qnc**5414** pp,nn1732 wcj,pnp1931 nipf**5414** pp,nn5741 df,nn4259
have been given to David, that she was given unto Adriel the Meholathite to
pp,nn**802**
wife.

nn4324 nn7586 cs,nn1323 wcs,qmf**157** (853) nn1732 wcs,himf**5046** pp,nn7586
20 And Michal Saul's daughter loved David: and they told Saul, and
df,nn**1697** wcs,qmf**3474**/pp,du,nn,pnx**5869**
the thing pleased him.

nn7586 wcs,qmf**559** qmf,pnx**5414** pp,pnx wcj,qmf**1961** pp,nn**4170** pp,pnx
21 And Saul said, I will give him her, that she may be a snare to him,
cs,nn**3027** pl,nn6430 wcj,qmf**1961** pp,pnx nn7586 wcs,qmf**559**
and that the hand of the Philistines may be against him. Wherefore Saul said
pr413 nn1732 df,nn**3117** pp,pnx htmf2860 pp,du,nu8147
to David, Thou shalt this day be my son-in-law in *the one of* the twain.

nn7586 wcs,pimf**6680** (853) pl,nn,pnx**5650** pimv**1696** pr413 nn1732
22 And Saul commanded his servants, *saying*, Commune with David
dfp,nn**3909** pp,qnc**559** ptdm2009 df,nn**4428** qpf**2654** pp,pnx wcj,cs,nn3605 pl,nn,pnx**5650**
secretly, and say, Behold, the king hath delight in thee, and all his servants
qpf,pnx**157** wcj,ad6258 dfp,nn**4428** htmf2860
love thee: now therefore be the king's son-in-law.

nn7586 pl,cs,nn**5650** wcs,pimf**1696** (853) df,pndm428 df,pl,nn**1697** pp,du,cs,nn**241** nn1732
23 And Saul's servants spoke those words in the ears of David. And
nn1732 wcs,qmf**559** pp,du,nn,pnx**5869** he,nipf**7043** dfp,nn**4428** htnc2860
David said, Seemeth it to you *a* light *thing* to be a king's son-in-law, seeing that
wcj,pnp595 qpta7326 nn**376** wcj,nipt7034
I *am* a poor man, and lightly esteemed?

pl,cs,nn**5650** nn7586 wcs,himf**5046** pp,pnx pp,qnc**559** df,pndm428 dfp,pl,nn**1697** pipf**1696**
24 And the servants of Saul told him, saying, On this manner spoke
nn1732
David.

nn7586 wcs,qmf**559** ad3541 qmf**559** pp,nn1732 dfp,nn**4428** nn2656 ptn369
25 And Saul said, Thus shall ye say to David, The king desireth not any
pp,nn4119 cj3588 pp,nu3967 pl,cs,nn**6190** pl,nn6430 pp,ninc5358 df,nn**4428**
dowry, but a hundred foreskins of the Philistines, to be avenged of the king's
pp,pl,cs,qpta341 wcj,nn7586 qpf**2803** (853) nn1732 pp,hinc5307 pp,cs,nn**3027**
enemies. But Saul thought to make David fall by the hand of the
pl,nn6430
Philistines.

pl,nn,pnx**5650** wcs,himf**5046** pp,nn1732 (853) df,pndm428 df,pl,nn**1697**
26 And when his servants told David these words, it
wcs,qmf**3474**/df,nn**1697**/pp,du,cs,nn**5869** nn1732 dfp,nn**4428** pp,htnc2860 df,pl,nn**3117**
pleased David well to be the king's son-in-law: and the days were
wcj,ptn3808 qpf**4390**
not expired.

nn1732 wcs,qmf**6965** wcs,qmf**1980** pnp1931 wcj,pl,nn,pnx**376** wcs,himf**5221**
27 Wherefore David arose and went, he and his men, and slew of
dfp,pl,nn6430 du,nu3967 nn**376** nn1732 wcs,himf935 (853) pl,nn,pnx**6190**
the Philistines two hundred men; and David brought their foreskins, and they
wcs,pimf,pnx**4390** dfp,nn**4428** dfp,nn**4428** pp,htnc2860
gave*them*in*full*tale to the king, that he might be the king's son-in-law. And
nn7586 wcs,qmf**5414** pp,pnx (853) nn4324 nn,pnx1323 pp,nn**802**
Saul gave him Michal his daughter to wife.

nn7586 wcs,qmf**7200** wcs,qmf**3045** cj3588 nn**3068** pr5973 nn1732 wcj,nn4324
28 And Saul saw and knew that the Lord *was* with David, and *that* Michal
cs,nn7586 nn1323 qpf,pnx**157**
Saul's daughter loved him.

nn7586   ad5750   wcs,himf3254 pp,qnc3372 pr4480/pl,cs,nn6440   nn1732   nn7586   wcs,qmf**1961** (853)

29 And Saul was yet the more afraid of David; and Saul became

nn1732   qpta341   cs,nn3605/df,pl,nn**3117**

David's enemy continually.

pl,cs,nn**8269**   pl,nn6430   wcs,qmf3318   wcs,qmf**1961**

30 Then the princes of the Philistines went forth: and it*came*to*pass,

pr4480/pl,cs,nn167   qnc,pnx3318   nn1732   qpf**7919**   pr4480/cs,nn3605

after   they went forth, *that* David behaved*himself*more*wisely than all the

pl,cs,nn**5650**   nn7586   nn,pnx8034   ad3966 wcs,qmf3365

servants of Saul; so that his name was much set by.

Saul Tries to Kill David

nn7586 wcs,pimf**1696** pr413   nn3083   nn,pnx**1121**   wcj,pr413 cs,nn3605   pl,nn,pnx**5650**

19

And Saul spoke to Jonathan his son, and to all his servants,

pp,hinc**4191** (853) nn1732

that they should kill   David.

wcj,nn3083   nn7586 cs,nn**1121**   qpf**2654**   ad3966   pp,nn1732   nn3083   wcs,himf**5046**

2 But Jonathan Saul's son delighted much in David: and Jonathan   told

pp,nn1732 pp,qnc559   nn7586   nn,pnx1   pipt1245   pp,hinc,pnx**4191**   wcj,ad6258

David, saying, Saul my father seeketh to   kill   thee: now   therefore,

pte**4994**   nimv**8104**   dfp,nn1242   wcj,qpf**3427**   dfp,nn5643

I*pray*thee, take*heed*to*thyself until the morning, and abide in a secret *place*,

wcj,nipf2244

and hide thyself:

wcj,pnp589   qmf3318   wcs,qpf5975 pp,cs,nn3027   nn,pnx1   dfp,nn**7704** pnl834/ad8033

3 And   I   will go out and stand beside my father in the field   where

pnp859   wcj,pnp589   pimf**1696** pr413 nn,pnx1 pp,pnx   pnid4100 wcs,qpf**7200**

thou *art*, and   I   will commune with my father of thee; and what I see, that I

wcs,hipf**5046** pp,pnx

will tell thee.

nn3083   wcs,pimf**1696** aj**2896**   pp,nn1732 pr413 nn7586   nn,pnx1   wcs,qmf559 pr,pnx413

4 And Jonathan spoke good of David unto Saul his father, and said unto

ptn408   df,nn**4428** qmf2398   pp,nn,pnx**5650**   pp,nn1732 cj3588   ptn**3808**

him, Let not the king sin against his servant, against David; because he hath not

qpf**2398**   pp,pnx   wcj,cj3588   pl,nn,pnx4639   pp,pnx   ad3966   aj**2896**

sinned against thee, and because his works *have been* to thee-ward very good:

wcs,qmf**7760** (853)   nn,pnx**5315**   pp,nn,pnx3709   wcs,himf**5221** (853)   nn6430

5 For he did put   his life in his hand, and slew   the Philistine,

nn3068   wcs,qmf**6213**   aj1419   nn**8668**   pp,cs,nn3605 nn3478   qpf**7200**

and the Lord wrought a great salvation for   all   Israel: thou sawest *it*, and didst

wcs,qmf8055 wcj,pp,pnit4100   qmf**2398**   aj**5355**   pp,nn1818   pp,hinc**4191** (853) nn1732

rejoice: wherefore then wilt thou sin against innocent blood, to slay   David

ad**2600**

without*a*cause?

nn7586   wcs,qmf**8085**   pp,cs,nn6963   nn3083   nn7586 wcs,nimf**7650**

6 And Saul hearkened unto the voice of Jonathan: and Saul swore, *As* the

nn3068 cs,aj**2416**   cj518   homf**4191**

Lord liveth, he shall not be slain.

nn3083   wcs,qmf**7121** pp,nn1732   nn3083   wcs,himf**5046** pp,pnx (853) cs,nn3605 df,pndm428

7 And Jonathan called David, and Jonathan showed him   all   those

df,pl,nn**1697**   nn3083   wcs,himf935 (853) nn1732 pr413 nn7586   wcs,qmf**1961**   pp,pl,nn,pnx**6440**

things. And Jonathan brought   David to Saul, and he was in his presence, as

pp,ad8032/ad865

in times past.

pp,qnc**1961** df,nn**4421** wcs,himf**3254** nn**1732** wcs,qmf**3318** wcs,nimf**3898**

8 And there was war again: and David went out, and fought with the

dfp,pl,nn**6430** wcs,himf**5221** pp,pnx aj**1419** nn**4347** wcs,qmf**5127** pr**4480**/pl,nn,pnx**6440**

Philistines, and slew them with a great slaughter; and they fled from

him.

aj**7451** cs,nn**7307** nn**3068** wcs,qmf**1961** pr**413** nn**7586** wcj,pnp**1931** qpta**3427**

9 And the evil spirit from the LORD was upon Saul, as he sat in his

pp,nn,pnx**1004** wcj,nn,pnx**2595** pp,nn,pnx**3027** wcj,nn**1732** pipt**5059** pp,nn**3027**

house with his javelin in his hand: and David played with *his* hand.

nn**7586** wcs,pimf**1245** pp,hinc**5221** pp,nn**1732** wcj,dfp,nn**7023** dfp,nn**2595**

10 And Saul sought to smite David even to the wall with the javelin; but

wcs,qmf**6362** pr**4480**/pl,cs,nn**6440**/nn**7586** wcs,himf**5221** (853) df,nn**2595**

he slipped away out*of*Saul's*presence, and he smote the javelin into the

dfp,nn**7023** wcj,nn**1732** qpf**5127** wcs,nimf**4422** pndm**1931** dfp,nn**3915**

wall: and David fled, and escaped that night.

nn**7586** wcs,qmf**7971** pl,nn**4397** pr**413** nn**1732** cs,nn**1004** pp,qnc,pnx**8104**

11 Saul also sent messengers unto David's house, to watch him, and to

wcj,pp,hinc,pnx**4191** dfp,nn**1242** nn**4324** pp,nn,pnx**802** wcs,himf**5046** pp,qnc**559** cj**518**

slay him in the morning: and Michal David's wife told him, saying, If

pipt**4422** ptn,pnx**369** (853) nn,pnx**5315** df,nn**3915** nn**4279** pnp**859** hopt**4191**

thou save not thy life tonight, tomorrow thou shalt be slain.

nn**4324** wcs,himf**3381**/(853)/nn**1732** pr**1157** df,nn**2474** wcs,qmf**1980** wcs,qmf**1272**

12 So Michal let*David*down through a window: and he went, and fled,

wcs,nimf**4422**

and escaped.

nn**4324** wcs,qmf**3947** (853) df,pl,nn**8655** wcs,qmf**7760** pr**413** df,nn**4296** qpf**7760** wcj(853)

13 And Michal took an image, and laid *it* in the bed, and put

cs,nn**3523** df,pl,nn**5795** pl,nn,pnx**4763** wcs,pimf**3680** dfp,nn**899**

a pillow of goats' *hair* for*his*bolster, and covered *it* with a cloth.

nn**7586** wcs,qmf**7971** pl,nn**4397** pp,qnc**3947** (853) nn**1732** wcs,qmf**559** pnp**1931**

14 And when Saul sent messengers to take David, she said, He *is*

qpta**2470**

sick.

nn**7586** wcs,qmf**7971** (853) df,pl,nn**4397** pp,qnc**7200** (853) nn**1732** pp,qnc**559**

15 And Saul sent the messengers *again* to see David, saying,

himv**5927**/pnx(853) pr,pnx**413** dfp,nn**4296** pp,hinc,pnx**4191**

Bring*him*up to me in the bed, that I may slay him.

df,pl,nn**4397** wcs,qmf**935** wcj,ptdm**2009** df,pl,nn**8655** pr**413**

16 And when the messengers were come in, behold, *there was* an image in

df,nn**4296** wcj,cs,nn**3523** df,pl,nn**5795** pl,nn,pnx**4763**

the bed, with a pillow of goats' *hair* for*his*bolster.

nn**7586** wcs,qmf**559** pr**413** nn**4324** pp,pnit**4100** pipf,pnx**7411** ad**3602**

17 And Saul said unto Michal, Why hast thou deceived me so, and

wcs,pimf**7971** (853) qpta,pnx**341** wcs,nimf**4422** nn**4324** wcs,qmf**559**/pr**413** nn**7586** pnp**1931**

sent away mine enemy, that he is escaped? And Michal answered Saul, He

qpf**559** pr,pnx**413** pimv,pnx**7971** pp,pnit**4100** himf,pnx**4191**

said unto me, Let me go; why should I kill thee?

wcj,nn**1732** qpf**1272** wcs,nimf**4422** wcs,qmf**935** pr**413** nn**8050** df,nn,lh**7414** wcs,himf**5046**

18 So David fled, and escaped, and came to Samuel to Ramah, and told

pp,pnx (853) cs,nn**3605** pnl**834** nn**7586** qpf**6213** pp,pnx pnp**1931** wcj,nn**8050** wcs,qmf**1980** wcs,qmf**3427**

him all that Saul had done to him. And he and Samuel went and dwelt

pp,nn**5121**

in Naioth.

wcs,homf**5046** pp,nn**7586** pp,qnc**559** ptdm**2009** nn**1732** pp,nn**5121** dfp,nn**7414**

19 And it was told Saul, saying, Behold, David *is* at Naioth in Ramah.

nn7586   wcs,qmf7971   pl,nn4397   pp,qnc3947 (853)   nn1732   wcs,qmf7200 (853)

☞ **20** And Saul sent messengers to take David: and when they saw

cs,nn3862   df,pl,nn5030   pl,nipt5012   wcj,nn8050   qpta5975   nipt5324   pr,pnx5921

the company of the prophets prophesying, and Samuel standing *as* appointed over

cs,nn7307   pl,nn430   wcs,qmf1961   pr5921   pl,cs,nn4397   nn7586   pnp1992   ad1571

them, the Spirit of God was upon the messengers of Saul, and they also

wcs,htmf5012

prophesied.

             wcs,himf5046   pp,nn7586   wcs,qmf7971   aj312   pl,nn4397   pnp1992

21 And when it was told Saul, he sent other messengers, and they

wcs,htmf5012   ad1571   nn7586 wcs,qmf7971   pl,nn4397   wcs,himf3254   nuor7992   pnp1992

prophesied likewise. And Saul sent messengers again the third time, and they

wcs,htmf5012   ad1571

prophesied also.

         wcs,qmf1980   pnp1931   ad1571   df,nn,lh7414   wcs,qmf935   pr5704   df,aj1419   nn953   pnl834

22 Then went he also to Ramah, and came to a great well that *is* in

dfp,nn7906   wcs,qmf7592   wcs,qmf559   ad375   nn8050   wcj,nn1732   wcs,qmf559

Sechu: and he asked and said, Where *are* Samuel and David? And *one* said,

ptdm2009   pp,nn5121   dfp,nn7414

Behold, *they be* at Naioth in Ramah.

        wcs,qmf1980   ad8033   pr413   nn5121   dfp,nn7414   cs,nn7307   pl,nn430   wcs,qmf1961

23 And he went thither to Naioth in Ramah: and the Spirit of God was

pr,pnx5921 pnp1931 ad1571   wcs,qmf1980/qna1980   wcs,htmf5012   pr5704   qnc,pnx935   dfp,nn5121

upon him also, and he went on, and prophesied, until he came to Naioth in

dfp,nn7414

Ramah.

       pnp1931   wcs,qmf6584   pl,nn,pnx899   ad1571   (pnp1931)   wcs,htmf5012   pp,pl,cs,nn6440

24 And he stripped off his clothes also, and prophesied before

nn8050   ad1571   wcs,qmf5307   aj6174   cs,nn3605   df,pndm1931   df,nn3117   wcj,cs,nn3605

Samuel in like manner, and lay down naked all that day and all that

df,nn3915   pr5921/ad3651   qmf559   nn7586 he,ad1571   dfp,pl,nn5030

night. Wherefore they say, *Is* Saul also among the prophets?

Jonathan Helps David Escape

               nn1732   wcs,qmf1272   pr4480/nn5121   dfp,nn7414   wcs,qmf935   wcs,qmf559

20 And David fled from Naioth in Ramah, and came and said

       pp,pl,cs,nn6440   nn3083   pnit4100   qpf6213   pnit4100   nn,pnx5771

before Jonathan, What have I done? what *is* mine iniquity? and

wcj,pnit4100   nn,pnx2403   pp,pl,cs,nn6440   nn,pnx1   cj3588   pipt1245   (853)   nn,pnx5315

what *is* my sin before thy father, that he seeketh my life?

         wcs,qmf559   pp,pnx   ptx2486   ptn3808 qmf4191   ptdm2009   nn,pnx1

2 And he said unto him, God forbid; thou shalt not die: behold, my father

qmf6213 ptn3808/nn1697   aj1419   cj176   (nn1697)   aj6996   wcj,ptn3808/qmf1540   (853)

will do nothing either great or small, but that he will show it

nn,pnx241   wcj,ad4069   nn,pnx1   himf5641   (853) df,pndm2088 df,nn1697 pr,pnx4480   pndm2063   ptn369

me: and why should my father hide this thing from me? it *is* not

so.

        nn1732   wcs,nimf7650   ad5750   wcs,qmf559   nn,pnx1   qna3045/qpf3045   cj3588

3 And David swore moreover, and said, Thy father certainly knoweth that I

qpf4672   nn2580   pp,du,nn,pnx5869   wcs,qmf559   ptn408   nn3083   qmf3045   pndm2063

have found grace in thine eyes; and he saith, Let not Jonathan know this,

---

☞ **19:20** Concerning the phrase "sons of the prophets," see the note on 2 Kings 2:3, 5.

cj6435   nimf6087   wcj,ad199   nn3068   cs,aj2416   nn,pnx5315 wcj,cs,aj2416   cj3588
lest he be grieved: but truly *as* the Lord liveth, and *as* thy soul liveth, *there is*

pp,nn6587   pr,pnx996   wcj(pr996)   df,nn4194
but a step between me and   death.

wcs,qmf559   nn3083   pr413   nn1732   pnid4100   nn,pnx5315   qmf559
4 Then said Jonathan unto David, Whatsoever thy soul desireth, I will even

wcj,qmf6213   pp,pnx
do   *it* for thee.

nn1732   wcs,qmf559   pr413   nn3083   ptdm2009   nn4279   nn2320
5 And David said   unto Jonathan, Behold, tomorrow *is* the new moon, and

wcj,pnp595   qna3427/qmf3427   pr5973   df,nn4428   pp,qnc398   wcs,pipf,pnx7971
I   should*not*fail*to*sit with the king at meat: but let me   go,   that I may

wcs,nipf5641   dfp,nn7704 pr5704   df,nuor7992   df,nn6153
hide myself in the field unto the third *day* at even.

cj518   nn,pnx1   qna6485/qmf,pnx6485   wcs,qpf559   nn1732   nina7592/nipf7592   pr,pnx4480
6 If thy father at*all*miss me, then say, David earnestly asked *leave* of

pp,qnc7323   nn1035   nn,pnx5892 cj3588   df,pl,nn3117   cs,nn2077
me that he might   run   to Bethlehem his city: for *there is* a yearly sacrifice

ad8033   pp,cs,nn3605   df,nn4940
there for   all   the family.

cj518   qmf559   ad3541   aj2896   pp,nn,pnx5650   nn7965   wcj,cj518 pp,pnx
7 If he say thus, *It is* well; thy servant shall have peace: but   if   he be

qna2734/qmf2734   qmv3045 cj3588 df,nn7451   qpf3615   pr4480/pr,pnx5973
very wroth, *then* be sure that evil is determined   by   him.

wcj,qpf6213   nn2617   pr5921   nn,pnx5650   cj3588   hipf935   (853)
8 Therefore thou shalt deal kindly with thy servant; for thou hast brought

nn,pnx5650   pp,cs,nn1285   nn3068   pr,pnx5973   wcj,cj518   pta3426
thy servant into a covenant of the Lord with thee: notwithstanding, if   there be

pp,pnx   nn5771   himv,pnx4191   pnp859   wcj,pr5704 pp,pnit4100   himf,pnx935
in me iniquity, slay me thyself; for   why shouldest thou bring me to thy

nn,pnx1
father?

nn3083   wcs,qmf559   ptx2486   pp,pnx   cj3588 cj518   qna3045/qmf3045   cj3588 df,nn7451
9 And Jonathan said, Far*be*it from thee: for if I knew certainly that evil

qpf3615   pr4480/pr5973   nn,pnx1   pp,qnc935 pr,pnx5921   wcj,ptn3808   himf5046
were determined   by   my father to come upon thee, then would   not   I tell

pnx(853)   pp,pnx
it thee?

wcs,qmf559   nn1732 pr413   nn3083   pnit4310   himf5046 pp,pnx cj176 pnit4100   nn,pnx1
10 Then said David to Jonathan, Who shall tell me? or what *if* thy father

qmf,pnx6030   aj7186
answer thee roughly?

nn3083   wcs,qmf559   pr413   nn1732   qmv1980   wcs,qmf3318   df,nn7704
11 And Jonathan said   unto David, Come, and let us go out into the field.

wcs,qmf3318   du,nu,pnx8147   df,nn7704
And they went out   both   of them into the field.

nn3083   wcs,qmf559   pr413   nn1732   nn3068 pl,cs,nn430   nn3478   cj3588
12 And Jonathan said   unto David, O Lord God of Israel, when I have

qmf2713 (853)   nn,pnx1   nn4279   dfp,nn6256   df,nuor7992   wcj,ptdm2009
sounded   my father about tomorrow any time, *or* the third *day*, and, behold, *if*

aj2896   pr413   nn1732   ad227   qmf7971 wcj,ptn3808 pr,pnx413   wcs,qpf1540/(853)/nn,pnx241
there be good toward David, and I then send   not   unto thee, and show*it*thee;

nn3068   qmf6213 ad3541   wcj,ad3541 himf3254   pp,nn3083   cj3588   himf3190/pr413
13 The Lord do   so   and much more to Jonathan: but if   it please my

nn,pnx1   pnx(pr5921)   (853) df,nn7451   wcs,qpf1540/(853)/nn,pnx241   wcs,pipf,pnx7971
father *to do*   thee   evil, then I will show*it*thee, and send*thee*away,

^{wcs,qpf**1980**}   ^{pp,nn**7965**}   ^{nn**3068**} ^{wcj,qmf**1961**} ^{pr,pnx5973}   ^{pp,pnl834}
that thou mayest   go   in peace: and the LORD   be   with thee,   as   he hath

^{qpf**1961**} ^{pr5973}   ^{nn,pnx**1**}
been with my father.

^{wcj,ptn**3808**}   ^{cj518}   ^{ad,pnx5750} ^{aj**2416**} (^{wcj,ptn**3808**}) ^{qmf**6213**/pr,pnx5973}
14 And thou shalt   not   only while   yet   I   live   show   me the

^{cs,nn**2617**}   ^{nn**3068**}   ^{qmf**4191**} ^{wcj,ptn**3808**}
kindness of the LORD, that I   die   not:

^{wcj,ptn**3808**}   ^{himf**3772**}   (853)   ^{nn,pnx**2617**}   ^{pr4480/pr5973}   ^{nn,pnx**1004**}
15 But *also* thou shalt   not   cut off   thy kindness   from   my house

^{pr5704/nn**5769**}   ^{wcj,ptn**3808**}   ^{nn**3068**}   ^{pp,hinc**3772**} (853)   ^{pl,cs,qpta341}   ⁿⁿ¹⁷³²   ^{nn**376**}
forever: no,   not when the LORD hath cut off   the enemies of David every one

^{pr4480/pr5921/pl,cs,nn**6440**}   ^{df,nn**127**}
from*the*face of the earth.

ⁿⁿ³⁰⁸³   ^{wcs,qmf**3772**}   ^{pr5973}   ^{cs,nn**1004**}   ⁿⁿ¹⁷³²
16 So Jonathan made *a covenant* with the house of David, *saying*, Let the

^{nn**3068**}   ^{wcj,pipf1245}   ^{pr4480/cs,nn**3027**}   ⁿⁿ¹⁷³²   ^{pl,cs,qpta341}
LORD even require *it* at*the*hand of David's enemies.

ⁿⁿ³⁰⁸³   (853)   ⁿⁿ¹⁷³²   ^{pp,hinc**7650**} ^{wcs,himf3254}   ^{pp,nn,pnx**160**} ^{pnx(853)}
17 And Jonathan caused   David to swear   again,   because he   loved

^{cj3588}   ^{qpf,pnx**157**}   ^{cs,nn**160**}   ^{nn,pnx**5315**}
him: for he loved him as he loved his own soul.

ⁿⁿ³⁰⁸³   ^{wcs,qmf559} ^{pp,pnx}   ⁿⁿ⁴²⁷⁹   ⁿⁿ²³²⁰
18 Then Jonathan   said   to   David, Tomorrow *is* the new moon: and thou

^{wcj,nipf**6485**}   ^{cj3588}   ^{nn,pnx**4186**}   ^{nimf**6485**}
shalt be missed, because thy   seat   will be empty.

^{wcj,pipf8027}   ^{qmf3381}   ^{ad3966}
19 And *when* thou hast stayed*three*days, *then* thou shalt go down quickly,

^{wcs,qpf935} ^{pr413}   ^{df,nn4725} ^{pnl834}   ^{nipf5641}   ^{ad8033/pp,cs,nn**3117**}   ^{df,nn4639}
and come   to the place where thou didst hide thyself   when   the business was

^{wcs,qpf**3427**} ^{pr681}   ^{df,nn68} ^{df,nn237}
in hand, and shalt remain by the stone Ezel.

^{wcj,pnp589}   ^{himf**3384**} ^{cs,nu7969} ^{df,pl,nn2671}   ⁿⁿ⁶⁶⁵⁴   ^{pp,pnx}   ^{pp,pinc7971}
20 And   I   will shoot three arrows on the side *thereof*, as*though*I   shot

^{pp,nn4307}
at a mark.

^{wcj,ptdm2009}   ^{qmf7971} (853) ^{df,nn5288}   ^{qmv**1980**}   ^{qmv4672}   (853)   ^{df,pl,nn2671}
21 And, behold, I will send   a lad, *saying*, Go, find out   the arrows.

^{cj518}   ^{qna559/qmf559}   ^{dfp,nn5288}   ^{ptdm2009}   ^{df,pl,nn2671}   ^{pr,pnx4480/wcj,ad2008}
If I expressly say unto the   lad,   Behold, the arrows *are* on*this*side of thee,

^{qmv,pnx3947}   ^{wcj,qmv935}   ^{cj3588}   ^{nn**7965**} ^{pp,pnx}   ^{wcj,ptn369} ^{nn**1697**}
take   them; then come thou: for *there is* peace to thee, and   no   hurt; *as* the

^{nn**3068**} ^{cs,aj**2416**}
LORD liveth.

^{wcj,cj518}   ^{qmf559} ^{ad3541}   ^{dfp,nn5958}   ^{ptdm2009}   ^{df,pl,nn2671}
22 But   if   I say thus unto the young man, Behold, the arrows *are*

^{pr,pnx4480/wcj,ad1973}   ^{qmv**1980**}   ^{cj3588}   ^{nn**3068**}   ^{pipf,pnx7971}
beyond   thee; go*thy*way: for the LORD hath sent*thee*away.

^{wcj,df,nn**1697**}   ^{pnl834} ^{wcj,pnp859}   ^{pnp589}   ^{pipf**1696**}   ^{ptdm2009}
23 And *as touching* the matter which thou and   I   have spoken of, behold,

^{nn**3068**}   ^{pr,pnx996}   ^{wcj,pnx(pr996)}   ^{pr5704/nn**5769**}
the LORD *be* between thee and   me forever.

ⁿⁿ¹⁷³²   ^{wcs,nimf5641}   ^{dfp,nn**7704**}   ^{df,nn2320}   ^{wcs,qmf**1961**}
24 So David hid himself in the field: and when the new moon was come, the

^{df,nn**4428**} ^{wcs,qmf**3427**}   ^{pp,qnc398} (pr5921) ^{df,nn3899}
king sat*him*down to   eat   meat.

25 And the king sat upon his seat, as at other times, *even* upon a seat by the wall: and Jonathan arose, and Abner sat by Saul's side, and David's place was empty.

26 Nevertheless Saul spoke not any thing that day: for he thought, Something*hath*befallen him, he *is* not clean; surely he *is* not clean.

27 And it*came*to*pass on*the*morrow, *which was* the second *day* of the month, that David's place was empty: and Saul said unto Jonathan his son, Wherefore cometh not the son of Jesse to meat, neither yesterday, nor today?

28 And Jonathan answered Saul, David earnestly asked *leave* of me to go to Bethlehem:

29 And he said, Let me go, I*pray*thee; for our family hath a sacrifice in the city; and my brother, he hath commanded me *to be there*: and now, if I have found favor in thine eyes, let*me*get*away, I*pray*thee, and see my brethren. Therefore he cometh not unto the king's table.

30 Then Saul's anger was kindled against Jonathan, and he said unto him, Thou son of the perverse rebellious *woman*, do not I know that thou hast chosen the son of Jesse to thine own confusion, and unto the confusion of thy mother's nakedness?

31 For as long as the son of Jesse liveth upon the ground, thou shalt not be established, nor thy kingdom. Wherefore now send and fetch him unto me, for he shall surely die.

32 And Jonathan answered Saul his father, and said unto him, Wherefore shall he be slain? what hath he done?

33 And Saul cast a javelin at him to smite him: whereby Jonathan knew that it was determined of his father to slay David.

34 So Jonathan arose from the table in fierce anger, and did eat no meat the second day of the month: for he was grieved for David, because his father had done*him*shame.

wcs,qmf**1961**   dfp,nn1242   nn3083   wcs,qmf3318   df,nn**7704**

35 And it*came*to*pass in the morning, that Jonathan went out into the field

pp,cs,nn**4150**   nn1732   aj6996 wcj,nn5288 pr,pnx5973

at the time appointed with David, and a little   lad   with him.

wcs,qmf**559**   pp,nn,pnx5288 qmv7323   qmv4672   pte**4994** (853)   df,pl,nn2671 pnl834

36 And he said unto his   lad,   Run, find out now   the arrows which

pnp595 hipt**3384**   df,nn5288 qpf7323 wcj,pnp1931 qpf**3384**   df,nn2678 pp,hinc,pnx**5674**

I   shoot. *And* as the lad ran,   he   shot an arrow beyond him.

df,nn5288   wcs,qmf935 pr5704   cs,nn4725   df,nn2678 pnl834   nn3083

37 And when the lad   was come   to the place of the arrow which Jonathan

qpf**3384**   nn3083   wcs,qmf7121 pr310   df,nn5288   wcs,qmf**559**   he,ptn**3808**   df,nn2678

had shot, Jonathan cried   after the lad,   and said, *Is* not   the arrow

pr,pnx4480/wcj,ad1973

beyond   thee?

nn3083   wcs,qmf7121 pr310   df,nn5288   qmv2363   ad4120 qmf5975 ptn408

38 And Jonathan cried   after the lad, Make speed, haste, stay not. And

nn3083   cs,nn5288 wcs,pimf**3950** (853) nn,pnx2678   wcs,qmf935 pr413   pl,nn,pnx**113**

Jonathan's lad gathered up   the arrows, and came to his master.

wcj,df,nn5288 qpf**3045** ptn**3808**   pnid3972   ad389   nn3083   wcj,nn1732 qpf**3045** (853)

39 But the lad   knew not any thing: only Jonathan and David knew   the

df,nn**1697**

matter.

nn3083   wcs,qmf**5414** (853)   pl,nn,pnx3627   pr413   pnl834/pp,pnx   df,nn5288   wcs,qmf**559**

40 And Jonathan gave   his artillery unto   his   lad,   and   said

pp,pnx   qmv**1980** himv935   df,nn5892

unto him, Go, carry *them* to the city.

df,nn5288   qpf935 wcj,nn1732   qpf**6965**   pr4480/pr681

41 *And* as soon as the lad   was gone, David arose out of *a place* toward the

df,nn5045   wcs,qmf**5307**   pp,du,nn,pnx639   nn,lh776   wcs,htmf**7812**   nu7969 pl,nn6471

south, and   fell   on his   face   to the ground, and bowed himself three times:

wcs,qmf**5401** nn376 (853)   nn,pnx7453   wcs,qmf1058 nn376 pr854   nn,pnx7453 pr5704   nn1732

and they kissed one   another, and   wept   one with another, until David

hipf1431

exceeded.

nn3083   wcs,qmf**559**   pp,nn1732 qmv**1980**   pp,nn**7965**   pnl834   nipf**7650**

42 And Jonathan said to David, Go in peace, forasmuch as we have sworn

du,nu,pnx8147   pnp587   pp,cs,nn8034   nn**3068** pp,qnc**559**   nn**3068** qmf**1961** pr,pnx996

both   of us in the name of the LORD, saying, The LORD be between me and

wcj,pnx(pr996)   wcj,pr996   nn,pnx**2233**   wcj(pr996)   nn,pnx**2233** pr5704/nn**5769**   wcs,qmf**6965**

thee, and between my seed and   thy seed forever. And he   arose

wcs,qmf**1980**   wcj,nn3083   qpf935   df,nn5892

and departed: and Jonathan went into the city.

David Gets Help From Ahimelech

wcs,qmf935   nn1732   nn,lh5011 pr413   nn288   df,nn**3548**

21 ☞ Then came David to Nob to Ahimelech the priest: and

nn288   wcs,qmf**2729**   pp,qnc7125   nn1732   wcs,qmf**559**   pp,pnx

Ahimelech was afraid at the meeting of David, and   said unto him,

pnit4069   pnp859 pp,nn,pnx905   ptn369 wcj,nn376 pr,pnx854

Why *art* thou alone, and no   man with thee?

☞ **21:1–6** According to the levitical law, the hallowed bread was only to be eaten by the priests who lived in the sanctuary (Lev. 24:9). However, there is a higher law than the levitical ordinance. It is the law of love for one's neighbor (Lev. 19:18). In the New Testament, Jesus summarized the ten commandments in what He

nn1732　wcs,qmf**559**　　pp,nn**288**　　df,nn**3548**　　df,nn**4428**　　pipf,pnx**6680**

2 And David　said　unto Ahimelech the priest, The king hath commanded me

nn**1697**　　wcs,qmf**559**　pr,pnx413　　ptn408　nn**376**　qmf**3045**　pnid3972　(853)

a business, and hath　said　unto　me, Let　no　man　know　any thing of　　the

df,nn**1697**　　pnl834　pnp595 qpta,pnx7971　　wcj,pnl834　　pipf,pnx**6680**

business whereabout　I　　send　thee, and　what I have commanded thee: and I

pipf***3045**　wcj(853)　　df,pl,nn5288　pr413 pnid6423　aj492　cs,nn4725

have appointed　　　*my* servants　to　such and such a place.

wcj,ad6258　　　　pnit4100 pta3426　pr8478　　nn,pnx**3027** qmv**5414**　nu2568　　　nn3899

3 Now therefore what　is　under thine hand? give *me* five *loaves of* bread in

pp,nn,pnx**3027** cj176　　　　df,nipt4672

mine　hand,　or what there is present.

df,nn**3548**　wcs,qmf6030　(853)　　nn1732　　wcs,qmf**559**　　ptn369　aj**2455**　nn3899

4 And the priest answered　　David, and　said, *There is* no　common bread

pr413/pr8478　　nn,pnx**3027** cj3588/cj518　pta3426　aj**6944**　nn3899　cj518　　df,pl,nn5288

under　mine　hand,　but　there is hallowed bread; if　the　young men have

nipf**8104**　　　　ad389　　pr4480/nn**802**

kept themselves at least from women.

nn1732　wcs,qmf6030　(853)　df,nn**3548**　wcs,qmf**559**　pp,pnx　cj3588/cj518

5 And David answered　　　the priest, and　said　unto him,　Of　a truth

nn**802**　　qptp6113　pp,pnx　　pp,ad8032 ad8543　pp,qnc,pnx3318

women *have been* kept from us about these three days, since I came out, and the

pl,cs,nn3627　df,pl,nn5288　aj**6944**　wcj(pnp1931)　　　　nn**1870**　aj**2455**

vessels of the young men are holy, and　　　*the bread is* in a manner common,

wcj,cj637　cj3588　　qmf**6942**　df,nn**3117**　dfp,nn3627

yea, though it were sanctified this day in the vessel.

df,nn**3548**　wcs,qmf**5414** pp,pnx　aj**6944**　　cj3588　　qpf**1961** ptn**3808**　nn3899　ad8033

6 So the priest　gave　him hallowed *bread*: for there was　no　bread there

cj3588/cj518　cs,nn3899/df,nn**6440**　df,pl,hopt5493 pr4480/pp,pl,cs,nn**6440**　nn**3068**　pp,qnc7760 aj2527 nn3899

but　the shewbread, that was　taken　from before the LORD, to　put　hot bread

pp,cs,nn**3117**　　ninc,pnx3947

in the　day　when it was taken away.

nn**376**　pr4480/pl,cs,nn**5650**　　nn7586　　wcj,ad8033 df,pndmf1931 dfp,nn**3117**　nipt6113

7 Now a certain man of*the*servants of Saul *was* there　that　day, detained

pp,pl,cs,nn**6440**　nn**3068**　　wcj,nn,pnx8034　　nn1673　　df,nn130　　cs,aj**47**

before　the LORD; and his　name　*was* Doeg, an Edomite, the chiefest of the

df,pl,qpta7462　pnl834　　　pp,nn7586

herdsmen that *belonged* to　Saul.

nn1732　wcs,qmf**559**　　pp,nn**288**　　pta3426　wcj,ptn369　ad6311　pr8478

8 And David　said　unto Ahimelech, And is there　not　here under thine

---

called the two greatest commandments: to love God with one's entire being and to love one's neighbor as oneself (Matt. 22:37–40). According to this principle, the pressing need of David and his men to obtain food warranted an overriding of the levitical law. A similar instance occurred with Christ and His disciples as they picked and ate corn on the Sabbath because they had no other food (Matt. 12:3, 4; Mark 2:25, 26; Luke 6:3, 4). When confronted by the Pharisees about this violation of the letter of the law, Christ referred back to David's actions as an example of how the Pharisees misunderstood the whole point of the laws and the Sabbath. Mercy and necessity override the letter, but not the spirit of the law (cf. Hos. 6:6), as Christ illustrated by healing on the Sabbath (Matt. 12:10–13).

The only stipulation which the priest set forth was that the men who were to eat the consecrated bread were not levitically defiled (cf. Lev. 15:18). David responded that he and his men had indeed kept themselves clean because of the mission which they were performing. He proclaimed in verse five that even though the levitical law regarding who should eat the bread was being broken, he and his men, as instruments of God, would make the bread become holy as they carried out their task for God.

nn,pnx**3027**　nn2595　cj176　nn**2719**　cj3588　　　ad1571/ptn**3808**　qpf3947　　　nn,pnx**2719**　wcj,ad1571　　　pl,nn,pnx3627

hand　spear　or　sword?　for　I have　neither　brought　my sword　nor　my weapons

pp,nn,pnx**3027**　　cj3588　　df,nn**4428**　cs,nn**1697**　qpf**1961**　qptp5169

with　me, because the king's business required haste.

df,nn**3548**　wcs,qmf559　cs,nn**2719**　nn1555　　df,nn6430　pnl834　　hipf**5221**

9 And the priest said, The sword of Goliath the Philistine, whom thou slewest

pp,cs,nn6010　df,nn425　ptdm2009　pnp1931　　qptp3874　　dfp,nn8071　pr310　　df,nn646

in the valley of Elah, behold,　it　*is here* wrapped in a cloth behind the ephod:

cj518　pp,pnx　　qmf3947　(pnx(853))　qmv3947　cj3588　　ptn369　aj312　pr,pnx2108　pp,pndm2088

if thou wilt take　　that, take *it*: for *there is*　no other　save that here.

nn1732　wcs,qmf**559**　　ptn369　pp,pnx　qmv,pnx**5414**　pp,pnx

And David said, *There is* none like that;　give it me.

David Acts Insane

nn1732　wcs,qmf**6965**　　wcs,qmf1272　df,pndm1931　dfp,nn**3117**　pr4480/pl,cs,nn**6440**　nn7586　　wcs,qmf935

10 And David arose, and　fled　that　day　for*fear*of　Saul, and went

pr413　nn397　cs,nn**4428**　nn1661

to Achish the king of Gath.

pl,cs,nn**5650**　nn397　wcs,qmf**559**　pr,pnx413　　he,ptn**3808**　pndm2088　nn1732

11 And the servants of Achish　said　unto him, *Is*　not　this　David the

cs,nn**4428**　df,nn776　he,ptn**3808**　qmf6030　　pp,pndm2088　dfp,pl,nn4246　qp,qnc**559**

king of the land? did they　not　sing*one*to*another of　him　in dances, saying,

nn7586　hipf**5221**　pp,pl,nu,pnx**505**　wcj,nn1732　pp,pl,nu,pnx7233

Saul hath slain his thousands, and David his ten thousands?

nn1732　wcs,qmf**7760**　(853) df,pndm428　df,pl,nn**1697**　　pp,nn,pnx3824　　ad3966　wcs,qmf**3372**

12 And David laid up　these　words　in his　heart,　and was sore afraid

pr4480/pl,cs,nn**6440**　nn397　cs,nn**4428**　nn1661

of　Achish the king of Gath.

wcs,pimf8138　(853)　nn,pnx**2940**　pp,du,nn,pnx**5869**　　wcs,htmf*1984

13 And he changed　his behavior　before　them, and feigned*himself*mad

pp,nn,pnx**3027**　wcs,pimf8427　pr5921　du,cs,nn1817　　df,nn8179　　nn,pnx7388

in their hands,　and scrabbled on the　doors　of the gate, and let his spittle

wcs,himf3381　pr413　nn,pnx**2206**

fall down upon his beard.

wcs,qmf**559**　nn397　pr413　pl,nn,pnx**5650**　ptdm2009　qmf**7200**　nn**376**　htpt7696

14 Then　said　Achish unto his servants, Lo,　ye　see　the man is mad:

pp,pnit4100　　himf935　pnx(853)　pr,pnx413

wherefore *then* have ye brought　him　to　me?

pnp589　cs,aj2638　pl,pupt7696　cj3588　　hipf935　(853) pndm2088

15 Have　I　need of mad men, that ye have brought　this　*fellow* to

pp,htnc7696　　pr,pnx5921　he,pndm2088　qmf935　pr413　nn,pnx**1004**

play*the*mad*man in my presence? shall　this　*fellow* come into my house?

David Raises a Small Army

nn1732　　　wcs,qmf**1980**　pr4480/ad8033　　wcs,nimf**4422**　pr413　cs,nn4631　nn5725

22 David therefore departed　thence,　and escaped　to　the cave Adullam:

pl,nn,pnx**251**　wcj,cs,nn3605　nn,pnx1　cs,nn**1004**　wcs,qmf**8085**

and when his brethren and　all　his father's house　heard　*it*, they

wcs,qmf3381　ad,lh8033　pr,pnx413

went down thither　to　him.

cs,nn3605　nn**376**　　nn4689　　wcj,cs,nn3605　nn**376**　pnl834/pp,pnx　　qpta5378

2 And every one *that was* in distress, and　every　one　that　*was* in debt, and

wcj,cs,nn3605 nn376   cs,nn4751/nn5315   wcs,htmf6908   pr,pnx413   wcs,qmf1961

every   one *that was* discontented, gathered themselves unto him; and he became a

pp,nn8269 pr,pnx5921   wcs,qmf1961 pr,pnx5973   pp,nu702 pl,nu3967 nn376

captain   over them: and there   were   with   him about   four hundred men.

nn1732 wcs,qmf1980 pr4480/ad8033   nn4708   nn4124   wcs,qmf559 pr413   cs,nn4428

3 And David went   thence to Mizpeh of Moab: and he   said   unto the king

nn4124   nn,pnx1   wcj,nn,pnx517   pte4994   qmf3318   pr,pnx854

of Moab, Let my father and my mother, I*pray*thee, come forth, *and be* with

cj5704/pnl834   qmf3045 pnit4100 pl,nn430   qmf6213 pp,pnx

you,   till   I know what God will do for me.

wcs,himf,pnx5148   (853) pl,cs,nn6440   cs,nn4428   nn4124   wcs,qmf3427 pr,pnx5973

4 And he brought them   before the king of Moab: and they dwelt   with

cs,nn3605   pl,cs,nn3117   nn1732 qnc1961   dfp,nn4686

him   all   the while that David was in the hold.

df,nn5030   nn1410 wcs,qmf559 pr413   nn1732   qmf3427 ptn3808   dfp,nn4686 qmv1980

5 And the prophet Gad   said   unto David, Abide not in the hold; depart, and

wcs,qpf935 pp,pnx   cs,nn776   nn3063   nn1732 wcs,qmf1980   wcs,qmf935   cs,nn3293

get   thee into the land of Judah. Then David departed, and came into the forest

nn2802

of Hareth.

Saul Kills the Priests Who Helped David

nn7586 wcs,qmf8085 cj3588 nn1732   nipf3045   wcj,pl,nn376 pnl834   pr,pnx854

6 When Saul heard that David was discovered, and the   men   that *were* with

wcj,nn7586 qpta3427   dfp,nn1390 pr8478   df,nn815   dfp,nn7414   wcj,nn,pnx2595

him, (now Saul abode in Gibeah under a tree in Ramah, having his   spear   in

pp,nn,pnx3027   wcj,cs,nn3605   pl,nn,pnx5650   pl,nipt5324 pr,pnx5921

his hand, and   all   his servants *were* standing about him;)

nn7586 wcs,qmf559   pp,pl,nn,pnx5650   df,pl,nipt5324 pr,pnx5921   qmv8085 pte4994

7 Then Saul said   unto his servants that stood   about him, Hear now, ye

nn1145   cs,nn1121   nn3448 qmf5414 (ad1571) pp,nn,pnx3605   pl,nn7704   wcj,pl,nn3754

Benjamites; will the son of Jesse give   every one of you fields and vineyards,

qmf7760 pp,nn,pnx3605 pl,cs,nn8269   pl,nu505   wcj,pl,cs,nn8269   pl,nu3967

and make you all   captains of thousands, and captains of hundreds;

cj3588   nn,pnx3605   qpf7194   pr,pnx5921   wcj,ptn369

8 That   all   of you have conspired against me, and *there is* none that

qpta1540/(853)/nn,pnx241   nn,pnx1121   pp,qnc3772   pr5973   cs,nn1121   nn3448

showeth   me that my   son hath made*a*league with the son of Jesse, and

wcj,ptn369 pr,pnx4480   qpta2470 pr,pnx5921   wcj,qpta1540/(853)/nn,pnx241   cj3588

there is none   of   you that is sorry   for   me, or showeth unto me that my

nn,pnx1121   hipf6965   (853)   nn,pnx5650 pr,pnx5921   pp,qpta693   df,pndm2088 dfp,nn3117

son hath stirred up   my servant against me, to lie*in*wait, as at this   day?

wcs,qmf6030   nn1673   df,nn130 wcj,pnp1931   nipt5324 pr5921   pl,cs,nn5650   nn7586

9 Then answered Doeg the Edomite, which was set over the servants of Saul,

wcs,qmf559   qpf7200 (853)   cs,nn1121   nn3448 qpta935   nn,lh5011 pr413   nn288   cs,nn1121

and said, I saw   the son of Jesse coming to Nob, to Ahimelech the son of

nn285

Ahitub.

wcs,qmf7592   pp,nn3068   pp,pnx   qpf5414 pp,pnx wcj,nn6720   qpf5414 pp,pnx

10 And he inquired of the LORD for him, and gave him victuals, and gave him

wcj(853)   cs,nn2719   nn1555   df,nn6430

the sword of Goliath the Philistine.

df,nn4428 wcs,qmf7971   pp,qnc7121 (853)   nn288   df,nn3548   cs,nn1121

11 Then the king   sent   to call   Ahimelech the priest, the son of

nn285   wcj(853) cs,nn3605   nn,pnx1   cs,nn1004   df,pl,nn3548 pnl834   pp,nn5011
Ahitub, and   all   his father's house, the priests that *were* in Nob: and they

wcs,qmf935 nn,pnx3605   pr413   df,nn4428
came   all   of them to the king.

nn7586 wcs,qmf559 qmv8085 pte4994   cs,nn1121   nn285   wcs,qmf559   ptdm,pnx2009
12 And Saul said, Hear now, thou son of Ahitub. And he answered, Here

nn,pnx113
I *am*, my lord.

nn7586 wcs,qmf559 pr,pnx413   pp,pnit4100   qpf7194   pr,pnx5921   pnp859
13 And Saul said unto him, Why have ye conspired against me, thou and

wcj,cs,nn1121   nn3448   pp,qnc,pnx5414 pp,pnx   nn3899   wcj,nn2719
the   son   of Jesse, in that thou hast given   him bread, and a sword, and hast

wcj,qna7592   pp,pl,nn430   pp,pnx   pp,qnc6965 pr,pnx413   pp,qpta693
inquired of God for him, that he should rise   against me, to lie*in*wait, as at

df,pndm2088 dfp,nn3117
this   day?

nn288   wcs,qmf6030   (853)   df,nn4428   wcs,qmf559   wcj,pnit4310   nipt539
14 Then Ahimelech answered   the king, and said, And who *is so* faithful

pp,cs,nn3605   pl,nn,pnx5650   pp,nn1732   df,nn4428   wcj,cs,nn2860   wcj,qpf5493 pr413
among all   thy servants as David, which is the king's son-in-law, and goeth at

nn,pnx4928   wcj,nipt3513   pp,nn,pnx1004
thy bidding, and is honorable in thine house?

df,nn3117   hipf2490   pp,qnc7592   pp,pl,nn430   pp,pnx   ptx2486   pp,pnx   ptn408
15 Did I then begin to inquire of God for him? be*it*far from me: let not

df,nn4428   qmf7760   nn1697   pp,nn,pnx5650   pp,cs,nn3605   cs,nn1004   nn,pnx1
the king impute *any* thing unto his servant, *nor* to   all   the house of my father:

cj3588   nn,pnx5650   qpf3045   ptn3808   pp,cs,nn3605 pndm2063 aj6996 (nn1697) cj176 aj1419
for thy servant knew nothing of   all   this,   less   or more.

df,nn4428   wcs,qmf559   qna4191/qmf4191   nn288   pnp859   wcj,cs,nn3605
16 And the king said, Thou shalt surely die, Ahimelech, thou, and   all

nn,pnx1   cs,nn1004
thy father's house.

df,nn4428   wcs,qmf559   dfp,pl,qpta7323   df,pl,nipt5324 pr,pnx5921   qmv5437
17 And the king said unto the footmen that stood   about him, Turn, and

wcj,himv4191   pl,cs,nn3548   nn3068   cj3588   nn,pnx3027 ad1571   pr5973   nn1732   wcj,cj3588
slay   the priests of the LORD; because their hand also *is* with David, and because

qpf3045   cj3588   pnp1931   qpta1272   wcj,ptn3808 qpf1540   (853)   nn,pnx241   pl,cs,nn5650
they knew when he   fled, and did not   show   it to me. But the servants of

df,nn4428   qpf14   wcj,ptn3808   pp,qnc7971   (853)   nn,pnx3027   pp,qnc6293   pp,pl,cs,nn3548
the king would not   put forth   their hand to   fall   upon the priests of the

nn3068
LORD.

df,nn4428   wcs,qmf559   pp,nn1673 qmv5437 pnp859   wcj,qmv6293   dfp,pl,nn3548
18 And the king said   to Doeg, Turn thou, and   fall   upon the priests. And

nn1673   df,nn130   wcs,qmf5437   pnp1931 wcs,qmf6293   dfp,pl,nn3548   wcs,himf4191   df,pndm1931
Doeg the Edomite turned, and he   fell   upon the priests, and slew on   that

dfp,nn3117   pl,nu8084   wcj,nn2568   nn376   qpta5375   nn906   nn646
day fourscore and five persons that did wear a linen ephod.

wcj(853)   nn5011   cs,nn5892   df,pl,nn3548   hipf5221   pp,cs,nn6310
19 And   Nob, the city of the priests, smote he with the edge of the

nn2719   pr4480/nn376   wcj(pr5704)   nn802   pr4480/nn5768   wcj(pr5704)   qpta3243   wcj,nn7794
sword, both men and   women, children and   sucklings, and oxen, and

wcj,nn2543   wcj,nn7716   pp,cs,nn6310   nn2719
asses, and sheep, with the edge of the sword.

nu259　　nn1121　　pp,nn288　　cs,nn1121　　nn285　wcj,nn,pnx8034　nn54
20 And one of the sons of Ahimelech the son of Ahitub, named Abiathar,
wcs,nimf4422　wcs,qmf1272　pr310　nn1732
escaped, and fled after David.

nn54　wcs,himf5046　pp,nn1732 cj3588　nn7586　qpf2026 (853)　nn3068　pl,cs,nn3548
21 And Abiathar showed David that Saul had slain the LORD's priests.

nn1732　wcs,qmf559　pp,nn54　qpf3045　df,pndm1931 dfp,nn3117 cj3588　nn1673
22 And David said unto Abiathar, I knew *it* that day, when Doeg the
df,nn130　ad8033　cj3588　hina5046/himf5046 pp,nn7586 pnp595　qpf5437
Edomite *was* there, that he would surely tell Saul: I have occasioned *the death*
pp,cs,nn3605　cs,nn5315　nn,pnx1　cs,nn1004
of all the persons of thy father's house.

qmv3427　pr,pnx854　qmf3372 ptn408 cj3588 pnl834 pimf1245 (853)　nn,pnx5315 pimf1245
23 Abide thou with me, fear not: for he that seeketh my life seeketh
(853)　nn,pnx5315 cj3588 pr,pnx5973　pnp859　nn4931
thy life: but with me thou *shalt be* in safeguard.

David Rescues Keilah

wcs,himf5046　pp,nn1732　pp,qnc559　ptdm2009　pl,nn6430　pl,nipt3898
23 Then they told David, saying, Behold, the Philistines fight against
pp,nn7084　wcj,pnp1992 pl,qpta8154 (853)　df,pl,nn1637
Keilah, and they rob the threshingfloors.

nn1732　wcs,qmf7592　pp,nn3068　pp,qnc559　he,qmf1980　wcj,hipf5221
2 Therefore David inquired of the LORD, saying, Shall I go and smite
df,pndm428　dfp,pl,nn6430　nn3068　wcs,qmf559　pr413　nn1732 qmv1980　wcj,hipf5221
these Philistines? And the LORD said unto David, Go, and smite the
dfp,pl,nn6430　wcj,hipf3467 (853)　nn7084
Philistines, and save Keilah.

nn1732　pl,cs,nn376 wcs,qmf559 pr,pnx413　ptdm2009　pnp587　pl,qpta3372 ad6311　pp,nn3063
3 And David's men said unto him, Behold, we be afraid here in Judah:
wcj,cj637　cj3588　qmf1980　nn7084　pr413　pl,cs,nn4634　pl,nn6430
how much more then if we come to Keilah against the armies of the Philistines?

nn1732　pp,qnc7592　pp,nn3068 ad5750 wcs,himf3254　nn3068 wcs,qmf,pnx6030
4 Then David inquired of the LORD yet again. And the LORD answered him
wcs,qmf559 qmv6965　qmv3381　nn7084 cj3588 pnp589　qpta5414 (853)　pl,nn6430
and said, Arise, go down to Keilah; for I will deliver the Philistines into
pp,nn,pnx3027
thine hand.

nn1732　wcj,pl,nn,pnx376 wcs,qmf1980　nn7084　wcs,nimf3898　dfp,pl,nn6430
5 So David and his men went to Keilah, and fought with the Philistines,
wcs,qmf5090　(853)　pl,nn,pnx4735　wcs,himf5221 pp,pnx　aj1419　nn4347
and brought away their cattle, and smote them with a great slaughter. So
nn1732　wcs,himf3467 (853)　pl,cs,qpta3427　nn7084
David saved the inhabitants of Keilah.

Saul Pursues David

wcs,qmf1961　nn54　cs,nn1121　nn288　pp,qnc1272 pr413
☞ 6 And it*came*to*pass, when Abiathar the son of Ahimelech fled to
nn1732　nn7084　qpf3381　nn646　pp,nn,pnx3027
David to Keilah, *that* he came down *with* an ephod in his hand.

☞ **23:6** See the note on Exodus 28:30 concerning the ephod.

7 And it was told Saul that David was come to Keilah. And Saul said, God hath delivered him into mine hand; for he is shut in, by entering into a town that hath gates and bars.

8 And Saul called all the people together to war, to go down to Keilah, to besiege David and his men.

9 And David knew that Saul secretly practiced mischief against him; and he said to Abiathar the priest, Bring hither the ephod.

10 Then said David, O Lord God of Israel, thy servant hath certainly heard that Saul seeketh to come to Keilah, to destroy the city for*my*sake.

11 Will the men of Keilah deliver*me*up into his hand? will Saul come down, as thy servant hath heard? O Lord God of Israel, I*beseech*thee, tell thy servant. And the Lord said, He will come down.

12 Then said David, Will the men of Keilah deliver me and my men into the hand of Saul? And the Lord said, They will deliver*thee*up.

13 Then David and his men, which were about six hundred, arose and departed out*of*Keilah, and went whithersoever they could go. And it was told Saul that David was escaped from Keilah; and he forbore to*go*forth.

14 And David abode in the wilderness in strongholds, and remained in a mountain in the wilderness of Ziph. And Saul sought him every day, but God delivered him not into his hand.

15 And David saw that Saul was come out to seek his life: and David was in the wilderness of Ziph in a wood.

16 And Jonathan Saul's son arose, and went to David into the wood, and strengthened his hand in God.

17 And he said unto him, Fear not: for the hand of Saul my father shall not find thee; and thou shalt be king over Israel, and I shall be next unto thee; and that also Saul my father knoweth.

18 And they two   made a covenant before the LORD: and David abode
in the wood, and Jonathan went to his house.

19 Then came up the Ziphites to Saul to Gibeah, saying, Doth not David
hide himself with us in strongholds in the wood, in the hill of Hachilah, which
is on*the*south of Jeshimon?

20 Now therefore, O king, come down according to all the desire of thy
soul to come down; and our part *shall be* to deliver him into the king's hand.

21 And Saul said, Blessed *be* ye of the LORD; for ye have compassion
on me.

22 Go, I*pray*you, prepare yet, and know and see his place where
his haunt is, *and* who hath seen him there: for it is told me *that* he
dealeth*very*subtlely.

23 See therefore, and take knowledge of all the lurking places where he
hideth himself, and come*ye*again to me with the certainty, and I will
go with you: and it*shall*come*to*pass, if he be in the land, that
I will search*him*out throughout all the thousands of Judah.

24 And they arose, and went to Ziph before Saul: but David and his
men *were* in the wilderness of Maon, in the plain on the south of Jeshimon.

25 Saul also and his men went to seek *him*. And they told David:
wherefore he came down into a rock, and abode in the wilderness of Maon. And
when Saul heard *that*, he pursued after David in the wilderness of Maon.

26 And Saul went on*this*side of the mountain, and David and his
men on*that*side of the mountain: and David made haste to*get*away
for*fear*of Saul; for Saul and his men compassed David and his
men round about to take them.

27 But there came a messenger unto Saul, saying, Haste thee, and come; for
the Philistines have invaded the land.

wcj,nn3068 pimf,pnx7999   aj2896   pr8478 pnl834   qpf6213   pp,pnx   df,pndm2088

wherefore the LORD reward thee good for that thou hast done unto me this

df,nn3117

day.

wcj,ad6258   ptdm2009   qpf3045   cj3588   qna4427/qmf4427

20 And now, behold, I know well that thou shalt surely*be*king, and that the

cs,nn4467   nn3478   wcs,qpf6965   pp,nn,pnx3027

kingdom of Israel shall be established in thine hand.

nimv7650 wcj,ad6258   pp,pnx   pp,nn3068 cj518   himf3772   (853)

21 Swear now therefore unto me by the LORD, that thou wilt not cut off

nn,pnx2233   pr,pnx310   wcj,cj518   himf8045   (853)   nn,pnx8034

my seed after me, and that thou wilt not destroy my name

pr4480/cs,nn1004/nn,pnx1

out*of*my*father's*house.

nn1732   wcs,nimf7650   pp,nn7586   pp,nn7586 wcs,qmf1980/pr413 nn,pnx1004   wcj,nn1732

22 And David swore unto Saul. And Saul went home; but David and

wcj,pl,nn,pnx376   qpf5927   pr5921   df,nn4686

his men got*them*up unto the hold.

Samuel's Death

nn8050   wcs,qmf4191   cs,nn3605   nn3478   wcs,nimf6908

25 And Samuel died; and all the Israelites were gathered together,

wcs,qmf5594 pp,pnx   wcs,qmf,pnx6912   pp,nn,pnx1004   pp,nn7414

and lamented him, and buried him in his house at Ramah. And

nn1732   wcs,qmf6965   wcs,qmf3381   pr413   cs,nn4057   nn6290

David arose, and went down to the wilderness of Paran.

David and Abigail

wcj,nn376   pp,nn4584   wcj,nn,pnx4639   dfp,nn3760

2 And *there was* a man in Maon, whose possessions *were* in Carmel; and the

wcj,df,nn376   ad3966   aj1419   wcj,pp,pnx   nu7969   pl,nu505   nn6629   wcj,nu505   pl,nn5795

man *was* very great, and he had three thousand sheep, and a thousand goats:

wcs,qmf1961   pp,qnc1494 (853)   nn,pnx6629   dfp,nn3760

and he was shearing his sheep in Carmel.

wcj,cs,nn8034   df,nn376   nn5037   wcj,cs,nn8034   nn,pnx802

3 Now the name of the man *was* Nabal; and the name of his wife

nn26   wcj,df,nn802   cs,aj2896   nn7922   wcj,cs,nn3303

Abigail: and *she was* a woman of good understanding, and of a beautiful

nn8389   wcj,df,nn376   aj7186   wcj,cs,aj7451   pl,nn4611   wcj,pnp1931

countenance: but the man *was* churlish and evil in his doings; and he *was*

nn3612

of*the*house*of*Caleb.

nn1732 wcs,qmf8085   dfp,nn4057   cj3588 nn5037   qpta1494 (853)   nn,pnx6629

4 And David heard in the wilderness that Nabal did shear his sheep.

nn1732   wcs,qmf7971 nu6235   pl,nn5288   nn1732 wcs,qmf559   dfp,pl,nn5288

5 And David sent out ten young men, and David said unto the young men,

qmv5927   nn,lh3760   wcj,qpf935 pr413 nn5037   wcj,qpf7592/pp,nn7965 pp,pnx   pp,nn,pnx8034

Get*you*up to Carmel, and go to Nabal, and greet him in my name:

ad3541   wcj,qpf559   dfp,aj2416   nn7965

6 And thus shall ye say to him that liveth *in prosperity*, Peace *be* both to

wcj,pnp859   nn7965   wcj,nn,pnx1004   nn7965   wcj,nn3605 pnl834 pp,pnx

thee, and peace *be* to thine house, and peace *be* unto all that thou hast.

wcj,ad6258   qpf**8085**   cj3588   pp,pnx   df,pl,qpta1494   ad6258   pl,qpta7462   pnl834/pp,pnx

7 And now I have heard that thou hast shearers: now thy shepherds which

qpf**1961**   pr,pnx5973   hipf,pnx3637   ptn3808   wcj,ptn**3808**   pnid3972   nipf**6485**   pp,pnx

were with us, we hurt them not, neither was there aught missing unto them,

cs,nn3605   pl,cs,nn**3117**   qnc,pnx**1961**   dfp,nn3760

all the while they were in Carmel.

      qmv7592   (853)   pl,nn,pnx5288   wcj,himf**5046**   pp,pnx

8 Ask thy young men, and they will show thee. Wherefore let the

df,pl,nn5288   wcj,qmf4672   nn**2580**   pp,du,nn,pnx**5869**   cj3588   qpf935   pr5921   aj**2896**   nn**3117**   qmv**5414**

young men find favor in thine eyes: for we come in a good day: give,

pte**4994**   (853)   pnl834   qmf4672   nn,pnx**3027**   pp,pl,nn,pnx**5650**

I*pray*thee, whatsoever cometh to thine hand unto thy servants, and to thy

wcj,pp,nn,pnx**1121**   pp,nn1732

son David.

      nn1732   pl,cs,nn5288   wcs,qmf935   pr413   nn5037

9 And when David's young men came, they spoke to Nabal according to

pp,cs,nn3605   df,pndm428   df,pl,nn1697   pp,cs,nn8034   nn1732   wcs,qmf5117

all those words in the name of David, and ceased.

      nn5037   wcs,qmf6030   (853)   nn1732   pl,cs,nn**5650**   wcs,qmf559   pnit4310   nn1732

10 And Nabal answered David's servants, and said, Who is David? and

wcj,pnit4310   cs,nn**1121**   nn3448   qpf7231   pl,nn**5650**   df,nn**3117**   df,pl,htpt6555

who is the son of Jesse? there be many servants now a days that break away

nn**376**   pr4480/pl,cs,nn**6440**   pl,nn,pnx113

every man from his master.

      wcj,qpf3947 (853)   nn,pnx3899   wcj(853)   pl,nn,pnx4325   wcj(853)   nn,pnx**2878**

11 Shall I then take my bread, and my water, and my flesh

pnl834   qpf**2873**   pp,pl,qpta,pnx1494   wcj,qpf**5414**   pp,pl,nn**376**   pnl834   qpf**3045**   ptn3808

that I have killed for my shearers, and give it unto men, whom I know not

ad335/pr4480/pndm2088   pnp1992

whence they be?

      nn1732   pl,cs,nn5288   wcs,qmf**2015**   pp,nn,pnx**1870**   wcs,qmf**7725**   wcs,qmf935

12 So David's young men turned their way, and went again, and came and

wcs,himf**5046**   pp,pnx   pp,cs,nn3605   df,pndm428   df,pl,nn**1697**

told him all those sayings.

      nn1732   wcs,qmf559   pp,pl,nn,pnx**376**   qmv2296   nn**376**   (853)   nn,pnx**2719**

13 And David said unto his men, Gird*ye*on every man his sword.

wcs,qmf2296   nn**376**   (853)   nn,pnx**2719**   nn1732   ad1571   wcs,qmf2296   (853)

And they girded on every man his sword; and David also girded on his

nn,pnx**2719**   wcs,qmf**5927**   pr310   nn1732   pp,nu702   pl,nu3967   nn**376**   wcj,du,nu3967

sword: and there went up after David about four hundred men; and two hundred

qpf**3427**   pr5921   df,pl,nn3627

abode by the stuff.

      nu259/nn5288   pr4480/pl,nn5288   hipf**5046**   wcj,pp,nn26   nn5037   cs,nn**802**   pp,qnc559   ptdm2009

14 But one of*the*young*men told Abigail, Nabal's wife, saying, Behold,

nn1732   qpf7971   pl,nn**4397**   pr4480/df,nn4057   pp,pinc**1288** (853)   pl,nn,pnx113

David sent messengers out*of*the*wilderness to salute our master; and he

wcs,qmf5860   pp,pnx

railed on them.

      wcj,df,pl,nn**376**   ad3966   aj**2896**   pp,pnx   wcj,ptn3808   hopf3637   wcj,ptn**3808**

15 But the men were very good unto us, and we were not hurt, neither

qpf**6485**   pnid3972   cs,nn3605/pl,cs,nn**3117**   htpf**1980**   pr,pnx854

missed we any thing, as*long*as we were conversant with them, when we

pp,qnc,pnx**1961**   dfp,nn**7704**

were in the fields:

qpf**1961**   nn2346   pr,pnx5921   ad1571   nn**3915** ad1571   ad**3119** cs,nn3605   pl,cs,nn**3117**

16 They were a wall unto us both by night and day, all the while we

qnc,pnx1961 pr,pnx5973   pl,qpta7462   df,nn6629

were with them keeping the sheep.

wcj,ad6258   qmf**3045**   wcj,qmv**7200**   pnid4100   qmf**6213** cj3588 df,nn**7451**

17 Now therefore know and consider what thou wilt do; for evil is

qpf**3615**   pr413   pl,nn,pnx**113**   wcj,pr5921 cs,nn3605   nn,pnx**1004**   wcj,pnp1931

determined against our master, and against all his household: for he *is such* a

cs,nn**1121**   nn**1100**   pr4480/pinc**1696**   pr,pnx413

son of Belial, that *a man* cannot speak to him.

nn26   wcs,pimf4116   wcs,qmf3947   du,nu3967   nn3899   wcj,du,nu8147

18 Then Abigail made haste, and took two hundred loaves, and two

pl,cs,nn**5035**   nn3196   wcj,nu2568   nn6629   pl,qptp**6213**   wcj,nu2568   pl,nn5429   nn7039

bottles of wine, and five sheep ready dressed, and five measures of parched

wcj,nu3967   pl,nn6778   wcj,du,nu3967   pl,nn1690   wcs,qmf**7760**

corn, and a hundred clusters*of*raisins, and two hundred cakes*of*figs, and laid

pr5921 df,pl,nn2543

them on asses.

wcs,qmf**559**   pp,pl,nn,pnx5288   qmv**5674**   pp,pl,nn,pnx**6440**   ptdm,pnx2005   qpta935

19 And she said unto her servants, Go on before me; behold, I come

pr,pnx310   hipf**5046** ptn3808   wcj,pp,nn,pnx**376**   nn5037

after you. But she told not her husband Nabal.

wcj,qpf**1961**   pnp1931 qpta7392 pr5921   df,nn2543   wcj,qpta3381

20 And it was *so, as* she rode on the ass, that she came down by the

pp,cs,nn5643   df,nn2022   wcj,ptdm2009   nn1732   wcj,pl,nn,pnx**376**   pl,qpta3381   pp,qnc,pnx7125

covert of the hill, and, behold, David and his men came down against her;

wcs,qmf6298 pnx(853)

and she met them.

wcj,nn1732   qpf**559**   ad389   dfp,nn**8267**   qpf**8104** (853) cs,nn3605 pnl834 pp,pndm2088

21 Now David had said, Surely in vain have I kept all that this

dfp,nn4057   wcj,ptn**3808**/pnid3972   nipf**6485**   pr4480/cs,nn3605 pnl834

fellow hath in the wilderness, so that nothing was missed of all that

pp,pnx   wcs,himf**7725** pp,pnx nn7451 pr8478 aj**2896**

pertained unto him: and he hath requited me evil for good.

ad3541   himf3254 wcj,ad3541 qmf**6213** pl,nn**430**   pp,pl,cs,qpta341   nn1732 cj518   himf**7604**

22 So and more also do God unto the enemies of David, if I leave

pr4480/cs,nn3605 pnl834   pp,pnx   pr5704   df,nn1242   hipt8366

of all that *pertain* to him by the morning light any that pisseth against the

pp,nn**7023**

wall.

nn26   wcs,qmf**7200** (853)   nn1732   wcs,pimf4116   wcs,qmf3381 pr4480/pr5921

23 And when Abigail saw David, she hasted, and lighted off the

df,nn2543   wcs,qmf**5307** pp,du,cs,nn**639**   nn1732 pr5921   pl,nn,pnx**6440**   wcs,htmf7812   nn776

ass, and fell before David on her face, and bowed herself to the ground,

wcs,qmf**5307** pr5921   du,nn,pnx7272   wcs,qmf**559** pp,pnx   pnp589   nn,pnx**113**

24 And fell at his feet, and said, Upon me, my lord, *upon* me *let*

df,nn**5771**   nn,pnx519   pte**4994**   wcj,pimf**1696**   pp,du,nn,pnx**241**

this iniquity *be*: and let thine handmaid, I*pray*thee, speak in thine audience, and

wcj,qmv**8085** (853)   pl,cs,nn**1697**   nn,pnx519

hear the words of thine handmaid.

ptn408   nn,pnx**113**   pte**4994**   qmf**7760**/(853)/nn,pnx**3820**/pr413 df,pndm2088 cs,nn**376**   df,nn**1100**

25 Let not my lord, I*pray*thee, regard this man of Belial,

(pr5921)   nn5037 cj3588   pp,nn,pnx8034   ad**3651**   pnp1931   nn5037   nn,pnx8034   wcj,nn5039

even Nabal: for as his name *is*, so *is* he; Nabal *is* his name, and folly *is* with him: but   I   thine handmaid saw   not   the young men of my lord,

whom thou didst send.

26 Now therefore, my lord, *as* the LORD liveth, and *as* thy   soul liveth,

seeing the LORD hath withheld thee from coming to *shed* blood, and from avenging

thyself with thine own hand,   now   let thine enemies, and they that   seek   evil

to my lord, be as Nabal.

27 And   now   this   blessing which thine handmaid hath brought unto my

lord,   let it even be given unto the young men   that follow   my lord.

28 I*pray*thee, forgive the trespass of thine handmaid: for the LORD will

certainly make my   lord a sure house; because my lord fighteth the battles of

the LORD, and evil hath not been found in thee *all* thy   days.

29 Yet a man is risen to pursue thee, and to   seek   thy soul: but the

soul of my lord shall   be bound in the bundle of life with the LORD thy

God; and   the souls of thine enemies, them shall he sling out, *as out* of the

middle   of a sling.

30 And it*shall*come*to*pass, when the LORD shall have done to my   lord

according to all   the good that he hath spoken concerning thee, and shall have

appointed thee ruler over Israel;

31 That this shall be   no   grief unto thee, nor offense of heart unto

my lord, either that thou hast   shed   blood causeless, or that my   lord   hath

avenged himself: but when the LORD shall have dealt well with my   lord,   then

remember   thine handmaid.

32 And David said to Abigail, Blessed *be* the LORD God of Israel, which

sent thee this   day to   meet   me:

33 And blessed *be* thy advice, and blessed *be* thou, which hast   kept   me

this   day from coming to *shed* blood, and from avenging myself with mine own

hand.

34 For in very deed, *as* the LORD God   of Israel liveth, which hath

qpf,pnx4513   pr4480/hinc7489   pnx(853)   cj3588/cj3884   pipf4116   wcs,qmf935
kept*me*back from hurting   thee,   except thou hadst hasted and come to

pp,qnc,pnx7125   cj3588   cj518   nipf3498   pp,nn5037 pr5704   df,nn1242   cs,nn216
meet   me, surely there had not been left unto Nabal by the morning light any

hipt8366   pp,nn7023
that pisseth against the wall.

nn1732   wcs,qmf3947   pr4480/nn,pnx3027   (853)   pnl834   hipf935   pp,pnx   qpf559
35 So David received of*her*hand   *that* which she had brought him, and said

wcj,pp,pnx   qmv5927   pp,nn7965   pp,nn,pnx1004 qmv7200   qpf8085   pp,nn,pnx6963
unto her, Go up in peace to thine house; see, I have hearkened to thy voice,

wcs,qmf5375   pl,nn,pnx6440
and have accepted thy person.

nn26   wcs,qmf935 pr413   nn5037   wcj,ptdm2009 pp,pnx   nn4960   pp,nn,pnx1004
36 And Abigail came to Nabal; and, behold, he held a feast in his house,

pp,cs,nn4960   df,nn4428   nn5037   wcj,cs,nn3820   aj2896   pr,pnx5921   wcj,pnp1931
like the feast of a king; and Nabal's heart *was* merry within him, for he

pr5704/ad3966   aj7910   hipf5046 pp,pnx wcj,ptn3808/nn1697 aj6996   wcj,aj1419 pr5704
was very drunken: wherefore she told him nothing, less or more, until the

df,nn1242 cs,nn216
morning light.

wcs,qmf1961   dfp,nn1242   df,nn3196   pp,qnc3318
37 But it*came*to*pass in the morning, when the wine was gone out

pr4480/nn5037   nn,pnx802   wcs,himf5046 pp,pnx (853) df,pndm428 df,pl,nn1697   nn,pnx3820 wcs,qmf4191
of Nabal, and his wife had told him   these things, that his heart died

pp,nn,pnx7130   wcj,pnp1931 qpf1961   pp,nn68
within him, and he   became *as* a stone.

wcs,qmf1961   pp,nu6235 df,pl,nn3117   nn3068   wcs,qmf5062 (853)
38 And it*came*to*pass about ten   days *after*, that the LORD smote

nn5037   wcs,qmf4191
Nabal, that he died.

nn1732   wcs,qmf8085 cj3588   nn5037   qpf4191   wcs,qmf559 qptp1288
39 And when David heard that Nabal was dead, he said, Blessed *be* the

nn3068   pnl834   qpf7378   (853)   cs,nn7379   nn,pnx2781   pr4480/cs,nn3027   nn5037
LORD, that hath pleaded   the cause of my reproach from*the*hand of Nabal, and

qpf2820 wcj(853)   nn,pnx5650   pr4480/nn7451   nn3068   hipf7725   wcj(853)
hath kept   his servant from evil: for the LORD hath returned   the

cs,nn7451   nn5037   pp,nn,pnx7218   nn1732   wcs,qmf7971   wcs,pimf1696
wickedness of Nabal upon his own head. And David sent and communed with

pp,nn26   pp,qnc,pnx3947   pp,pnx   pp,nn802
Abigail, to   take   her to him to wife.

pl,cs,nn5650   nn1732   wcs,qmf935 pr413   nn26   df,nn,lh3760
40 And when the servants of David were come to Abigail to Carmel, they

wcs,pimf1696 pr,pnx413   pp,qnc559   nn1732 qpf,pnx7971   pr,pnx413   pp,qnc,pnx3947   pp,pnx
spoke unto her, saying, David sent us unto thee, to   take   thee to him to

pp,nn802
wife.

wcs,qmf6965   wcs,htmf7812   du,nn639   nn,lh776   wcs,qmf559
41 And she arose, and bowed herself on *her* face to the earth, and said,

ptdm2009   nn,pnx519   pp,nn8198   pp,qnc7364   du,cs,nn7272   pl,cs,nn5650
Behold, *let* thine handmaid *be* a servant to wash the feet of the servants of my

nn,pnx113
lord.

nn26   wcs,pimf4116   wcs,qmf6965   wcs,qmf7392 pr5921   df,nn2543   wcj,nu2568
42 And Abigail hasted, and arose, and rode upon an ass, with five

pl,nn,pnx5291   df,pl,qpta**1980**   pp,nn,pnx7272   wcs,qmf**1980**   pr310   pl,cs,nn**4397**

damsels of hers that went   after   her; and she   went   after the messengers of

nn1732   wcs,qmf**1961**   pp,pnx   pp,nn**802**

David, and became   his   wife.

nn1732   qpf3947   wcj(853)   nn293   pr4480/nn3157   wcs,qmf**1961**   ad1571   du,nu8147

43 David also took   Ahinoam of Jezreel; and they   were   also   both

pp,pnx   pp,pl,nn**802**

of them his wives.

wcj,nn7586   qpf**5414**   (853)   nn4324   nn,pnx1323   nn1732   cs,nn**802**   pp,nn6406

☞ 44 But   Saul   had given   Michal his daughter, David's wife, to Phalti the

cs,nn**1121**   nn3919   pnl834   pr4480/nn1554

son of Laish, which *was* of Gallim.

David Spares Saul Again

df,pl,nn2130   wcs,qmf935   pr413   nn7586   df,nn,lh1390   pp,qnc**559**   he,ptn**3808**

26 And the Ziphites came unto Saul to Gibeah, saying, Doth   not

nn1732   htpt5641   pp,cs,nn1389   df,nn2444   pr5921/pl,cs,nn**6440**

David hide himself in the   hill   of Hachilah, *which is*   before

df,nn3452

Jeshimon?

nn7586   wcs,qmf**6965**   wcs,qmf3381   pr413   cs,nn4057   nn2128   nu7969

2 Then Saul arose, and went down to the wilderness of Ziph, having three

pl,nu**505**   pl,cs,nn**977**   nn**376**   nn3478   wcj,pr,pnx854   pp,pinc1245   (853)   nn1732   pp,cs,nn4057

thousand chosen men of Israel   with   him, to   seek   David in the wilderness of

nn2128

Ziph.

nn7586   wcs,qmf2583   pp,cs,nn1389   df,nn2444   pnl834   pr5921/pl,cs,nn**6440**   df,nn3452

3 And Saul pitched in the   hill   of Hachilah, which *is*   before   Jeshimon,

pr5921   df,nn**1870**   wcj,nn1732   qpta**3427**   dfp,nn4057   wcs,qmf**7200** cj3588   nn7586   qpf935

by the way. But David abode in the wilderness, and he   saw   that Saul came

pr,pnx310   df,nn,lh4057

after him into the wilderness.

nn1732   wcs,qmf7971   pl,pipt7270   wcs,qmf**3045**   cj3588   nn7586   qpf935/pr413

4 David therefore sent out spies,   and   understood that Saul   was   come in

nipt**3559**

very deed.

nn1732   wcs,qmf**6965**   wcs,qmf935   pr413   df,nn4725   pnl834/ad8033   nn7586   qpf2583

5 And David arose, and came   to   the place   where   Saul had pitched: and

nn1732   wcs,qmf**7200**   (853)   df,nn4725   pnl834/ad8033   nn7586   qpf7901   wcj,nn74   cs,nn**1121**   nn5369

David beheld   the place   where   Saul lay, and Abner the   son   of Ner, the

cs,nn**8269**   nn,pnx**6635**   wcj,nn7586   qpta7901   dfp,nn4570   wcj,df,nn**5971**   pl,qpta2583

captain of his host: and   Saul   lay   in the trench, and the people pitched

pr,pnx5439

round about him.

wcs,qmf6030   nn1732   wcs,qmf559   pr413   nn288   df,nn2850   wcj,pr413   nn52

6 Then answered David and   said   to Ahimelech the Hittite, and   to   Abishai

cs,nn**1121**   nn6870   cs,nn**251**   nn3097   pp,qnc**559**   pnit4310   qmf3381   pr,pnx854   pr413   nn7586

the son of Zeruiah, brother to Joab, saying, Who will go down with me to Saul

pr413   df,nn**4264**   nn52   wcs,qmf559   pnp589   qmf3381   pr,pnx5973

to the camp? And Abishai said,   I   will go down with thee.

☞ **25:44** Saul's second daughter, Michal, had been given in marriage to David for slaying Goliath. However, Saul, while pursuing David, decided to give her to another man. Later, David demanded her back (2 Sam. 3:14), but she no longer loved him (2 Sam. 6:16). Shortly thereafter, Michal died childless (2 Sam. 6:23).

nn1732   wcj,nn52   wcs,qmf935 pr413   df,nn**5971**   nn**3915**   wcj,ptdm2009 nn7586 qpta7901

7 So David and Abishai came to the people by night: and, behold, Saul lay

aj3463   dfp,nn4570   wcj,nn,pnx2595 qptp4600   dfp,nn776   pl,nn,pnx4763

sleeping within the trench, and his   spear   stuck in the ground at his bolster: but

wcj,nn74   wcj,df,nn**5971** pl,qpta7901   pr,pnx5439

Abner and the people   lay   round about him.

wcs,qmf559   nn52   pr413   nn1732   pl,nn**430**   pipf5462   (853)   qpta,pnx341

8 Then   said   Abishai to David, God hath delivered   thine enemy into thine

pp,nn,pnx**3027**   df,nn**3117** wcj,ad6258   himf,pnx5221   pte**4994**   dfp,nn2595

hand   this day: now therefore let me smite   him, I*pray*thee, with the spear

wcj,dfp,nn**776** nu259/nn6471   wcj,ptn**3808**   pp,pnx   qmf8138

even to the   earth   at once, and I will   not *smite* him the second time.

nn1732   wcs,qmf559 pr413   nn52   himf,pnx**7843** ptn408 cj3588 pnit4310   qpf7971

9 And David   said   to Abishai, Destroy him not: for who can stretch forth

nn,pnx**3027**   nn3068   pp,cs,nn**4899**   wcj,nipf**5352**

his hand against the LORD's anointed, and be guiltless?

nn1732   wcs,qmf559   cj3588/cj518   nn3068   aj2416   nn3068   qmf,pnx**5062**

10 David   said   furthermore, *As* the LORD liveth, the LORD shall smite him;

cj176   nn,pnx**3117**   qmf935 wcs,qpf4191 cj176   qmf3381   dfp,nn4421   wcs,nipf**5595**

or his   day   shall come to die;   or he shall descend into battle, and perish.

pr4480/nn**3068**   ptx2486   pp,pnx   pr4480/pp,qnc7971   nn,pnx**3027**

11 The LORD   forbid that   I   should stretch forth mine hand against the

nn3068   pp,cs,nn**4899**   pte**4994**   qmv3947   wcj,ad6258 (853)   df,nn2595 pnl834

LORD's anointed: but, I*pray*thee, take thou   now   the spear that *is* at his

pl,nn,pnx4763   wcj(853)   cs,nn6835   df,pl,nn4325   pp,pnx wcj,qmf,lh**1980**

bolster, and   the cruse of water, and let us   go.

nn1732   wcs,qmf3947 (853)   df,nn2595   wcj(853)   cs,nn6835   df,pl,nn4325   nn7586

12 So David   took   the spear and   the cruse of water from Saul's

pl,cs,nn4763   wcs,qmf**1980**/pp,pnx   wcj,ptn369   qpta**7200**   wcj,ptn369 qpta**3045**   wcj,ptn369

bolster; and they got*them*away, and   no   man saw *it*, nor   knew *it*, neither

hipt6974   cj3588   nn,pnx3605   aj3463   cj3588   cs,nn8639   nn3068

awaked: for they *were*   all   asleep; because a deep sleep from the LORD was

qpf5307   pr,pnx5921

fallen upon them.

nn1732   wcs,qmf5674   df,nn5676   wcs,qmf5975 pr5921   cs,nn7218

13 Then David went over to the other side, and   stood   on the top of a

df,nn2022 pr4480/aj7350   aj7227 df,nn4725   pr,pnx996

hill afar off; a great space *being* between them:

nn1732   wcs,qmf7121 pr413   df,nn**5971**   wcj,pr413   nn74   cs,nn1121   nn5369 pp,qnc559

14 And David cried to the people, and   to   Abner the son of Ner, saying,

qmf6030   he,ptn**3808**   nn74   nn74   wcs,qmf6030   wcs,qmf559 pnit4310   pnp859

Answerest thou not, Abner? Then Abner answered and said, Who *art* thou *that*

qpf7121   pr413   df,nn**4428**

criest to the king?

nn1732   wcs,qmf559 pr413   nn74   he,ptn**3808** pnp859   nn376   wcj,pnit4310

15 And David   said   to Abner, *Art* not   thou a *valiant* man? and   who *is*

pp,pnx3644   pp,nn3478 wcj,pp,pnid4100   ptn**3808** qpf**8104**/pr413   pl,nn,pnx113   df,nn**4428**

like*to*thee in Israel? wherefore then hast thou not   kept   thy lord   the king?

cj3588   qpf935 cs,nu259   df,nn**5971**   pp,hinc**7843** (853)   df,nn**4428** pl,nn,pnx113

for there came one of the people in to destroy   the king thy lord.

df,pndm2088 df,nn**1697**   ptn**3808** aj2896 pnl834   qpf6213   nn3068   aj2416 (cj3588) pnp859

16 This   thing *is* not good that thou hast done. *As* the LORD liveth,   ye

pl,cs,nn**1121**   nn**4194**   pnl834   ptn**3808** qpf**8104**/pr5921   pl,nn,pnx113 (pr5921)   nn3068

are worthy to die, because ye have not   kept   your master,   the LORD's

_{cs,nn**4899**} _{wcj,ad6258 qmv**7200**} _{ad335} _{df,nn**4428**} _{cs,nn2595} _{wcj(853)} _{cs,nn6835} _{df,pl,nn4325}
anointed. And now see where the king's spear *is*, and the cruse of water

_{pnl834} _{pl,nn,pnx4763}
that *was* at his bolster.

_{nn7586 wcs,himf**5234** (853)} _{nn1732} _{cs,nn6963} _{wcs,qmf559} _{pndm2088} _{he,nn,pnx6963}
17 And Saul knew David's voice, and said, *Is* this thy voice, my

_{nn,pnx**1121**} _{nn1732} _{nn1732 wcs,qmf**559**} _{nn,pnx6963} _{nn,pnx**113**} _{df,nn**4428**}
son David? And David said, *It is* my voice, my lord, O king.

_{wcs,qmf**559**} _{pp,pnit4100} _{nn,pnx**113** pndm2088} _{qpta7291} _{pr310} _{nn,pnx**5650**} _{cj3588}
18 And he said, Wherefore doth my lord thus pursue after his servant? for

_{pnit4100} _{qpf**6213**} _{wcj,pnit4100 nn**7451**} _{pp,nn,pnx**3027**}
what have I done? or what evil *is* in mine hand?

_{wcj,ad6258} _{pte**4994**} _{nn,pnx**113**} _{df,nn**4428** qmf**8085** (853)} _{pl,cs,nn**1697**}
19 Now therefore, I*pray*thee, let my lord the king hear the words of

_{nn,pnx**5650**} _{cj518} _{nn**3068**} _{hipf,pnx5496} _{pp,pnx} _{himf**7306**}
his servant. If the LORD have stirred*thee*up against me, let him accept an

_{nn**4503**} _{wcj,cj518} _{pl,cs,nn**1121**} _{df,nn**120** pl,qptp779} _{pnp1992 pp,pl,cs,nn**6440**} _{nn**3068**}
offering: but if *they be* the children of men, cursed *be* they before the LORD;

_{cj3588} _{pipf,pnx1644} _{df,nn**3117**} _{pr4480/htnc**5596**} _{pp,cs,nn**5159**}
for they have driven*me*out this day from abiding in the inheritance of the

_{nn**3068**} _{pp,qnc**559**} _{qmv**1980** qmv**5647**} _{aj312} _{pl,nn**430**}
LORD, saying, Go, serve other gods.

_{wcj,ad6258} _{ptn408} _{nn,pnx**1818** qmf**5307**} _{nn,lh776 pr4480/pr5048} _{pl,cs,nn**6440**}
20 Now therefore, let not my blood fall to the earth before the face of

_{nn**3068**} _{cj3588} _{cs,nn**4428**} _{nn3478} _{qpf3318} _{pp,pinc1245 (853)} _{nn6550} _{pp,pnl834} _{nu259}
the LORD: for the king of Israel is come out to seek a flea, as when one

_{qmf7291} _{df,qpta7124} _{dfp,pl,nn2022}
doth hunt a partridge in the mountains.

_{wcs,qmf**559**} _{nn7586} _{qpf**2398**} _{qmv**7725**} _{nn,pnx**1121**} _{nn1732} _{cj3588} _{ptn**3808**}
21 Then said Saul, I have sinned: return, my son David: for I will no

_{ad5750} _{himf**7489**/pp,pnx} _{pr8478/pnl834} _{nn,pnx**5315**} _{qpf3365} _{pp,du,nn,pnx**5869**} _{df,pndm2088}
more do*thee*harm, because my soul was precious in thine eyes this

_{df,nn**3117**} _{ptdm2009} _{hipf5528} _{wcs,qmf7686} _{hina7235/ad3966}
day: behold, I have played*the*fool, and have erred exceedingly.

_{nn1732} _{wcs,qmf6030} _{wcs,qmf**559**} _{ptdm2009} _{df,nn**4428**} _{df,nn2595} _{nu259}
22 And David answered and said, Behold the king's spear! and let one

_{pr4480/pl,nn5288} _{wcj,qmf**5674**} _{wcj,qmf,pnx3947}
of*the*young*men come over and fetch it.

_{wcj,nn**3068**} _{himf**7725**} _{dfp,nn376} ₍₈₅₃₎ _{nn,pnx**6666**} _{wcj(853)}
23 The LORD render to every man his righteousness and his

_{nn,pnx530} _{pnl834} _{nn**3068**} _{qpf,pnx**5414**} _{pp,nn**3027** df,nn**3117**} _{qpf14 wcj,ptn**3808**}
faithfulness: for the LORD delivered thee into *my* hand today, but I would not

_{pp,qnc7971} _{nn,pnx**3027**} _{nn**3068** pp,cs,nn**4899**}
stretch forth mine hand against the LORD's anointed.

_{wcj,ptdm2009} _{pp,pnl834} _{nn,pnx**5315**} _{qpf1431} _{df,pndm2088} _{df,nn**3117**}
24 And, behold, as thy life was much set by this day in mine

_{pp,du,nn,pnx**5869**} _{ad3651} _{nn,pnx**5315**} _{qmf1431} _{pp,du,cs,nn**5869**} _{nn**3068**}
eyes, so let my life be much set by in the eyes of the LORD, and let

_{wcj,himf,pnx**5337**} _{pr4480/cs,nn3605} _{nn6869}
him deliver me out*of*all tribulation.

_{nn7586 wcs,qmf**559**} _{pr413} _{nn1732} _{qptp**1288**} _{pnp859} _{nn,pnx**1121**} _{nn1732}
25 Then Saul said to David, Blessed *be* thou, my son David: thou shalt

_{ad1571 qna**6213**/qmf**6213**} _{wcj,ad1571} _{qna3201/qmf3201} _{nn1732 wcs,qmf**1980**} _{pp,nn,pnx**1870**}
both do great *things*, and also shalt*still*prevail. So David went on his way,

_{wcj,nn7586} _{qpf**7725**} _{pp,nn,pnx4725}
and Saul returned to his place.

David Returns to Gath

27 And David said in his heart, I shall now perish one day by the hand of Saul: *there is* nothing better for me than that I should speedily escape into the land of the Philistines; and Saul shall despair of me, to seek me any more in any coast of Israel: so shall I escape out*of*his*hand.

2 And David arose, and he passed over with the six hundred men that *were* with him unto Achish, the son of Maoch, king of Gath.

3 And David dwelt with Achish at Gath, he and his men, every man with his household, *even* David with his two wives, Ahinoam the Jezreelitess, and Abigail the Carmelitess, Nabal's wife.

4 And it was told Saul that David was fled to Gath: and he sought no more again for him.

5 And David said unto Achish, If I have now found grace in thine eyes, let them give me a place in some town in the country, that I may dwell there: for why should thy servant dwell in the royal city with thee?

6 Then Achish gave him Ziklag that day: wherefore Ziklag pertaineth unto the kings of Judah unto this day.

7 And the time that David dwelt in the country of the Philistines was a full year and four months.

8 And David and his men went up, and invaded the Geshurites, and the Gezrites, and the Amalekites: for those *nations were* of old the inhabitants of the land, as thou goest to Shur, even unto the land of Egypt.

9 And David smote the land, and left neither man nor woman alive, and took away the sheep, and the oxen, and the asses, and the camels, and the apparel, and returned, and came to Achish.

10 And Achish said, Whither have ye made*a*road today? And David said,

^{pr5921} ⁿⁿ⁵⁰⁴⁵ ⁿⁿ³⁰⁶³ ^{wcj,pr5921} ⁿⁿ⁵⁰⁴⁵ ^{df,nn3397} ^{wcj,pr413}

Against the south of Judah, and against the south of the Jerahmeelites, and against

ⁿⁿ⁵⁰⁴⁵ ^{df,nn7017}

the south of the Kenites.

ⁿⁿ¹⁷³² ^{pimf2421} ^{ptn3808} ^{wcj,nn376} ^{wcj,nn802} ^{pp,hinc935} ⁿⁿ¹⁶⁶¹

11 And David saved neither man nor woman alive, to bring *tidings* to Gath,

^{pp,qnc559} ^{cj6435} ^{himf5046} ^{pr,pnx5921} ^{pp,qnc559} ^{ad3541} ^{qpf6213} ⁿⁿ¹⁷³² ^{wcj,ad3541}

saying, Lest they should tell on us, saying, So did David, and so *will be*

^{nn,pnx4941} ^{cs,nn3605} ^{df,pl,nn3117} ^(pnl834) ^{qpf3427} ^{pp,cs,nn7704} ^{pl,nn6430}

his manner all the while he dwelleth in the country of the Philistines.

ⁿⁿ³⁹⁷ ^{wcs,himf539} ^{pp,nn1732} ^{pp,qnc559} ^{pp,nn,pnx5971} ^{pp,nn3478}

12 And Achish believed David, saying, He hath made his people Israel

^{hina887/hipf887} ^{wcj,qpf1961} ^{pp,pnx} ^{pp,nn5650} ⁿⁿ⁵⁷⁶⁹

utterly*to*abhor him; therefore he shall be my servant forever.

^{wcs,qmf1961} ^{df,pnp1992} ^{dfp,pl,nn3117} ^{pl,nn6430}

28 And it*came*to*pass in those days, that the Philistines

^{wcs,qmf6908} ⁽⁸⁵³⁾ ^{pl,nn,pnx4264} ^{dfp,nn6635} ^{pp,ninc3898} ^{pp,nn3478}

gathered together their armies for warfare, to fight with Israel.

ⁿⁿ³⁹⁷ ^{wcs,qmf559} ^{pr413} ⁿⁿ¹⁷³² ^{qna3045/qmf3045} ^{cj3588} ^{qmf3318} ^{pr,pnx854}

And Achish said unto David, Know*thou*assuredly, that thou shalt go out with

^{dfp,nn4264} ^{pnp859} ^{wcj,pl,nn,pnx376}

me to battle, thou and thy men.

ⁿⁿ¹⁷³² ^{wcs,qmf559} ^{pr413} ⁿⁿ³⁹⁷ ^{pp,ad3651} ^{pnp859} ^{qmf3045} ⁽⁸⁵³⁾ ^{pnl834} ^{nn,pnx5650}

2 And David said to Achish, Surely thou shalt know what thy servant

^{qmf6213} ⁿⁿ³⁹⁷ ^{wcs,qmf559} ^{pr413} ⁿⁿ¹⁷³² ^{pp,ad3651} ^{qmf,pnx7760} ^{qpta8104}

can do. And Achish said to David, Therefore will I make thee keeper of mine

^{pp,nn,pnx7218} ^{cs,nn3605/df,pl,nn3117}

head forever.

Saul and the Medium at Endor

^{wcj,nn8050} ^{qpf4191} ^{cs,nn3605} ⁿⁿ³⁴⁷⁸ ^{wcs,qmf5594} ^{pp,pnx} ^{wcs,qmf,pnx6912}

3 Now Samuel was dead, and all Israel had lamented him, and buried him

^{pp,nn7414} ^{wcj,pp,nn,pnx5892} ^{wcj,nn7586} ^{hipf5493}

in Ramah, even in his own city. And Saul had put away

^{df,pl,nn178} ^{wcj(853)} ^{df,pl,nn3049} ^{pr4480/df,nn776}

those*that*had*familiar*spirits, and the wizards, out*of*the*land.

^{pl,nn6430} ^{wcs,nimf6908} ^{wcs,qmf935} ^{wcs,qmf2583}

4 And the Philistines gathered*themselves*together, and came and pitched in

^{pp,nn7766} ⁿⁿ⁷⁵⁸⁶ ^{wcs,qmf6908/(853)/cs,nn3605/nn3478} ^{wcs,qmf2583} ^{dfp,nn1533}

Shunem: and Saul gathered*all*Israel*together, and they pitched in Gilboa.

ⁿⁿ⁷⁵⁸⁶ ^{wcs,qmf7200} ⁽⁸⁵³⁾ ^{cs,nn4264} ^{pl,nn6430} ^{wcs,qmf3372}

5 And when Saul saw the host of the Philistines, he was afraid, and his

^{nn,pnx3820} ^{ad3966} ^{wcs,qmf2729}

heart greatly trembled.

ⁿⁿ⁷⁵⁸⁶ ^{wcs,qmf7592} ^{pp,nn3068} ⁿⁿ³⁰⁶⁸ ^{qpf,pnx6030} ^{wcj,ptn3808} ^{ad1571}

☞ 6 And when Saul inquired of the Lord, the Lord answered him not, neither

^{pp,pl,nn2472} ^{ad1571} ^{dfp,pl,nn224} ^{ad1571} ^{dfp,pl,nn5030}

by dreams, nor by Urim, nor by prophets.

^{wcs,qmf559} ⁿⁿ⁷⁵⁸⁶ ^{pp,pl,nn,pnx5650} ^{pimv1245} ^{pp,pnx} ^{cs,nn802} ^{cs,nn1172}

7 Then said Saul unto his servants, Seek me a woman that hath a

---

☞ **28:6** See the note on Exodus 28:30 concerning the Urim and Thummim.

nn178　　　　　　　　wcj,qcj1980　pr,pnx413　　　　　wcj,qcj1875　　pp,pnx　　　　　　pl,nn,pnx5650

familiar spirit, that I may go to her, and inquire of her. And his servants

wcs,qmf559 pr,pnx413　　ptdm2009　　　　　cs,nn802　　cs,nn1172　　　nn178　　　pp,nn5874

said to him, Behold, *there is* a woman that hath a familiar spirit at Endor.

nn7586　　　　wcs,htmf2664　　　wcs,qmf3847　aj312　pl,nn899　　pnp1931 wcs,qmf1980

8 And Saul disguised himself, and put on other raiment, and he went, and

wcj,du,cs,nu8147 pl,nn376 pr,pnx5973　　wcs,qmf935 pr413　df,nn802　　nn3915　　　　wcs,qmf559

two men with him, and they came to the woman by night: and he said,

pte4994　　qmv7080　　pp,pnx　　　　dfp,nn178　　wcj,himv5927 pp,pnx　　(853)

I*pray*thee, divine unto me by the familiar spirit, and bring me *him* up,

pnl834　　　qmf559 pr,pnx413

whom I shall name unto thee.

df,nn802　wcs,qmf559 pr,pnx413　　ptdm2009 pnp859 qpf3045　(853) pnl834 nn7586

9 And the woman said unto him, Behold, thou knowest what Saul hath

qpf6213 pnl834　　　hipf3772　(853)　　df,pl,nn178　　　wcj(853)

done, how he hath cut off those*that*have*familiar*spirits, and the

df,nn3049　pr4480　df,nn776 wcj,pp,pnit4100　　pnp859　htpt5367　　pp,nn,pnx5315

wizards, out of the land: wherefore then layest thou a snare for my life, to

pp,hinc,pnx4191

cause*me*to*die?

nn7586 wcs,nimf7650　pp,pnx　　pp,nn3068 pp,qnc559　　nn3068　aj2416

10 And Saul swore to her by the LORD, saying, *As* the LORD liveth, there shall

cj518　nn5771　qmf,pnx7136　　df,pndm2088 dfp,nn1697

no punishment happen to thee for this thing.

wcs,qmf559　df,nn802　(853)　pnit4130　　himf5927　　pp,pnx

11 Then said the woman, Whom shall I bring up unto thee? And he

wcs,qmf559　himv5927/pp,pnx　(853)　nn8050

said, Bring*me*up Samuel.

df,nn802　wcs,qmf7200 (853)　nn8050　wcs,qmf2199　aj1419 pp,nn6963

12 And when the woman saw Samuel, she cried with a loud voice: and

df,nn802　wcs,qmf559 pr413 nn7586　pp,qnc559　pp,pnit4100　pipf,pnx7411　wcj,pnp859

the woman spoke to Saul, saying, Why hast thou deceived me? for thou *art*

nn7586

Saul.

df,nn4428 wcs,qmf559　pp,pnx　　ptn408 qmf3372　cj3588 pnit4100　qpf7200

13 And the king said unto her, Be not afraid: for what sawest thou? And

df,nn802　wcs,qmf559 pr413 nn7586　qpf7200 pl,nn430　pl,qpta5927　pr4480　df,nn776

the woman said unto Saul, I saw gods ascending out of the earth.

wcs,qmf559　pp,pnx　　pnit4100 nn,pnx8389　　　　wcs,qmf559　aj2205 nn376

14 And he said unto her, What form *is* he of? And she said, An old man

qpta5927　wcj,pnp1931　qpta5844　　nn4598　　nn7586 wcs,qmf3045　cj3588

cometh up; and he *is* covered with a mantle. And Saul perceived that it *was*

nn8050　　pnp1931 wcs,qmf6915　du,nn639　nn,lh776　　wcs,htmf7812

Samuel, and he stooped with *his* face to the ground, and bowed himself.

nn8050　wcs,qmf559 pr413　nn7586　pp,pnit4100　　hipf,pnx7264

15 And Samuel said to Saul, Why hast thou disquieted me, to

pp,hinc5927/pnx(853)　　nn7586 wcs,qmf559　pp,pnx　ad3966　nn6887　　　wcj,pl,nn6430

bring*me*up? And Saul answered, I am sore distressed; for the Philistines

pl,nipt3898　pp,pnx　　wcj,pl,nn430　qpf5493　pr4480/pr,pnx5921　　qpf,pnx6030

make war against me, and God is departed from me, and answereth me

wcj,ptn3808　ad5750　ad1571 pp,cs,nn3027 df,pl,nn5030　ad1571　pp,pl,nn2472　　wcs,qmf7121 pp,pnx

no more, neither by prophets, nor by dreams: therefore I have called thee,

pp,hinc,pnx3045　　pnid4100　　qmf6213

that thou mayest make known unto me what I shall do.

wcs,qmf**559**   nn8050   wcj,pp,pnit4100   qmf,pnx**7592**

16 Then said Samuel, Wherefore then dost thou ask of me, seeing the

wcj,nn**3068**   qpf**5493**   pr4480/pr,pnx**5921**   wcs,qmf**1961**   pl,nn,pnx**6145**

LORD is departed from thee, and is become thine enemy?

nn**3068**   wcs,qmf**6213**   pp,pnx   pp,pnl834   pipf**1696** pp,nn,pnx**3027**   nn**3068**

17 And the LORD hath done to him, as he spoke by me: for the LORD

wcs,qmf**7167** (853)   df,nn**4467**   pr4480/nn,pnx**3027**   wcs,qmf,pnx**5414**   pp,nn,pnx**7453**

hath rent   the kingdom out*of*thine*hand, and given it to thy neighbor,

pp,nn**1732**

even to David:

pp,pnl834   qpf**8085**   ptn**3808**   pp,cs,nn**6963**   nn**3068** wcj,ptn**3808**   qpf**6213**

18 Because thou obeyedst not the voice of the LORD, nor executedst his

cs,nn**2740** nn,pnx**639**   pp,nn**6002**   pr**5921**/ad**3651**   nn**3068** qpf**6213** df,pndm2088 df,nn**1697**   pp,pnx

fierce wrath upon Amalek, therefore hath the LORD done this thing unto thee

df,pndm2088 df,nn**3117**

this day.

ad**1571**   nn**3068**   wcj,qmf**5414** (853) nn3478 pr,pnx**5973**   pp,cs,nn**3027**

19 Moreover the LORD will also deliver Israel with thee into the hand of

pl,nn**6430**   wcj,nn**4279**   pnp859 wcj,pl,nn,pnx**1121** pr,pnx**5973**   nn**3068**

the Philistines: and tomorrow *shalt* thou and thy sons *be* with me: the LORD

ad**1571**   qmf**5414** (853)   cs,nn**4264**   nn3478   pp,cs,nn**3027**   pl,nn**6430**

also shall deliver the host of Israel into the hand of the Philistines.

nn**7586** wcs,qmf**5307**   wcs,pimf**4116**   cs,nn4393/nn,pnx**6967**   nn,lh**776**   ad**3966** wcs,qmf**3372**

20 Then Saul fell straightway all along on the earth, and was sore afraid,

pr4480/pl,cs,nn**1697**   nn8050 ad**1571**   qpf**1961** ptn**3808** nn3581   pp,pnx cj3588

because*of*the*words of Samuel: and there was no strength in him; for he had

qpf398 ptn**3808** nn3899 cs,nn3605 df,nn**3117**   wcj,cs,nn3605   df,nn**3915**

eaten no bread all the day, nor all the night.

df,nn**802**   wcs,qmf935 pr413 nn7586   wcs,qmf**7200** cj3588   ad3966   nipf**926**

21 And the woman came unto Saul, and saw that he was sore troubled, and

wcs,qmf**559** pr,pnx413   ptdm2009   nn,pnx8198   qpf**8085**   pp,nn,pnx**6963**

said unto him, Behold, thine handmaid hath obeyed thy voice, and I have

wcs,qmf**7760**   nn,pnx**5315**   pp,nn,pnx**3709**   wcs,qmf**8085**   (853)   pl,nn,pnx**1697** pnl834

put my life in my hand, and have hearkened unto thy words which

pipf**1696** pr,pnx413

thou spokest unto me.

wcj,ad6258   pte**4994**   qmv**8085** pnp859 ad**1571**   pp,cs,nn**6963**

22 Now therefore, I*pray*thee, hearken thou also unto the voice of thine

nn,pnx8198   wcj,qcj**7760**   cs,nn6595   nn3899 pp,pl,nn,pnx**6440**   wcj,qmv398   pp,pnx

handmaid, and let me set a morsel of bread before thee; and eat, that thou

wcj,qcj**1961**   nn3581 cj3588   qmf**1980**   dfp,nn**1870**

mayest have strength, when thou goest on thy way.

wcs,pimf**3985**   wcs,qmf**559**   ptn**3808** qmf398   pl,nn,pnx**5650**   wcj,ad**1571**

23 But he refused, and said, I will not eat. But his servants, together with

df,nn**802**   wcs,qmf**6555** pp,pnx   wcs,qmf**8085**   pp,nn,pnx6963   wcs,qmf**6965**

the woman, compelled him; and he hearkened unto their voice. So he arose

pr4480/df,nn**776**   wcs,qmf**3427** pr413   df,nn4296

from*the*earth, and sat upon the bed.

wcj,dfp,nn**802**   nn4770 cs,nn5695   dfp,nn**1004**   wcs,pimf**4116**

24 And the woman had a fat calf in the house; and she hasted, and

wcs,qmf,pnx**2076**   wcs,qmf**3947** nn7058   wcs,qmf**3888**   wcs,qmf,pnx644   pl,nn**4682**

killed it, and took flour, and kneaded *it*, and did bake unleavened bread

thereof:

wcs,himf**5066**   pp,pl,cs,nn**6440** nn7586   wcj,pp,pl,cs,nn**6440**   pl,nn,pnx**5650**

25 And she brought *it* before Saul, and before his servants; and they did

wcs,qmf398   wcs,qmf**6965**   wcs,qmf**1980**   df,pndm1931 dfp,nn**3915**

eat. Then they rose up, and went away that night.

The Philistines Question David's Loyalty

pl,nn6430   wcs,qmf**6908**   (853) cs,nn3605   pl,nn,pnx**4264**

29 Now the Philistines gathered together all their armies to

nn,lh663   wcj,nn3478   pl,qpta2583   dfp,nn**5869** pnl834   pp,nn3157

Aphek: and the Israelites pitched by a fountain which *is* in Jezreel.

wcj,pl,cs,nn**5633**   pl,nn6430   pl,qpta**5674**   pp,pl,nu3967   wcj,pp,pl,nu**505**

2 And the lords of the Philistines passed on by hundreds, and by thousands:

wcj,nn1732   wcj,pl,nn,pnx**376**   pl,qpta**5674**   dfp,aj314   pr5973   nn397

but David and his men passed on in the rearward with Achish.

wcs,qmf**559**   pl,cs,nn**8269**   pl,nn6430   pnit4100   df,pndm428   df,pl,nn**5680**

3 Then said the princes of the Philistines, What *do* these Hebrews *here*?

nn397   wcs,qmf**559**   pr413   pl,cs,nn**8269**   pl,nn6430   he,ptn**3808** pndm2088   nn1732

And Achish said unto the princes of the Philistines, *Is* not this David, the

cs,nn**5650**   nn7586   cs,nn**4428**   nn3478 pnl834   qpf**1961**   pr,pnx854   pndm2088 pl,nn**3117** cj176 pndm2088

servant of Saul the king of Israel, which hath been with me these days, or these

pl,nn8141   qpf4672 wcj,ptn**3808**   pnid3972   pp,pnx   pr4480/nn**3117**   qnc,pnx**5307**   pr5704

years, and I have found no fault in him since he fell *unto me* unto

df,pndm2088 df,nn**3117**

this day?

pl,cs,nn**8269**   pl,nn6430   wcs,qmf**7107** pr,pnx5973   pl,cs,nn**8269**

4 And the princes of the Philistines were wroth with him; and the princes of

pl,nn6430   wcs,qmf**559**   pp,pnx   himv**7725**/(853)/df,nn**376**   wcj,qmf**7725**   pr413

the Philistines said unto him, Make*this*fellow*return, that he may go again to

nn,pnx4725 pnl834/ad8033   hipf,pnx**6485**   wcj,ptn**3808**   qmf3381   pr,pnx5973

his place which thou hast appointed him, and let him not go down with us

dfp,nn4421 wcj,ptn**3808**   dfp,nn4421   qmf**1961**   pp,nn**7854**   pp,pnx   wcj,pp,pnit4100

to battle, lest in the battle he be an adversary to us: for wherewith should he

htmf**7521** pndm2088 pr413   pl,nn,pnx**113**   he,ptn**3808**   pp,pl,cs,nn**7218**   df,pnp1992

reconcile himself unto his master? *should it* not *be* with the heads of these

df,pl,nn**376**

men?

he,ptn**3808** pndm2088 nn1732   pnl834   qmf6030   pp,pnx   dfp,pl,nn4246 pp,qnc**559**

5 *Is* not this David, of whom they sang one*to*another in dances, saying,

nn7586 hipf**5221**   pp,pl,nu,pnx**505**   wcj,nn1732   pp,pl,nu,pnx7233

Saul slew his thousands, and David his ten thousands?

nn397   wcs,qmf**7121**/pr413   nn1732   wcs,qmf**559** pr,pnx413   nn3068

6 Then Achish called David, and said unto him, Surely, *as* the LORD

aj**2416**   (cj3588) pnp859   aj**3477**   qnc,pnx3318   wcj,qnc,pnx935 pr,pnx854

liveth, thou hast been upright, and thy going out and thy coming in with me

dfp,nn**4264** wcj,aj**2896**   pp,du,nn,pnx**5869**   cj3588   ptn**3808** qpf4672   nn**7451**   pp,pnx

in the host *is* good in my sight: for I have not found evil in thee

pr4480/cs,nn**3117**   qnc,pnx935 pr,pnx413   pr5704   df,pndm2088 df,nn**3117**

since*the*day of thy coming unto me unto this day: nevertheless the

wcj,pp,du,cs,nn**5869**/df,pl,nn**5633**   aj**2896** pnp859 ptn**3808**

lords favor thee not.

wcj,ad6258   qmv**7725**   wcj,qmv**1980**   pp,nn**7965**   qmf6213/aj**7451**/pp,du,cs,nn**5869**

7 Wherefore now return, and go in peace, that thou displease

wcj,ptn**3808**   pl,cs,nn**5633**   pl,nn6430

not the lords of the Philistines.

nn1732   wcs,qmf**559**   pr413   nn397   cj3588 pnit4100   qpf**6213**   wcj,pnit4100

8 And David said unto Achish, But what have I done? and what hast thou

qpf4672   pp,nn,pnx**5650** pr4480/nn**3117** pnl834   qpf**1961** pp,pl,nn,pnx**6440**   pr5704 df,pndm2088 df,nn**3117** cj3588

found in thy servant so long as I have been with thee unto this day, that

ptn**3808** qmf**1980** wcj,nipf3898   pp,pl,cs,qpta341   nn,pnx113   df,nn**4428**

I may not go fight against the enemies of my lord the king?

nn397   wcs,qmf6030   wcs,qmf**559** pr413   nn1732   qpf3045 cj3588 pnp859   aj**2896**

9 And Achish answered and said to David, I know that thou *art* good in my

pp,du,nn,pnx**5869**   pp,cs,nn**4397** pl,nn**430**   ad389   pl,cs,nn**8269**   pl,nn**6430**

sight, as an angel of God: notwithstanding the princes of the Philistines have

qpf**559**   ptn**3808** qmf**5927** pr,pnx5973   dfp,nn**4421**

said, He shall not go up with us to the battle.

wcj,ad6258   himv7925   dfp,nn**1242**   pl,nn,pnx113 wcj,pl,cs,nn**5650**

10 Wherefore now rise*up*early in the morning with thy master's servants

pnl834   qpf935 pr,pnx854   wcj,hipf7925   dfp,nn**1242**

that are come with thee: and as soon as ye be*up*early in the morning, and have

(pp,pnx) wcj,nn**216** wcj,qmv**1980**

light, depart.

nn1732   (pnp1931)   wcj,pl,nn,pnx**376** wcs,himf7925   pp,qnc**1980**   dfp,nn**1242**

11 So David and his men rose*up*early to depart in the morning, to

pp,qnc7725 pr413   cs,nn**776**   pl,nn**6430**   wcj,pl,nn**6430** qpf**5927**   nn3157

return into the land of the Philistines. And the Philistines went up to Jezreel.

David Defeats the Amalekites

wcs,qmf**1961**   nn1732   wcj,pl,nn,pnx**376**   pp,qnc935

30 And it*came*to*pass, when David and his men were come to

nn6860   df,nuor7992 dfp,nn**3117**   wcj,nn6003   qpf6584/pr413   nn5045

Ziklag on the third day, that the Amalekites had invaded the south,

wcj(pr413)   nn6860   wcs,himf**5221** (853)   nn6860   wcs,qmf**8313** pnx(853)   dfp,nn**784**

and Ziklag, and smitten Ziklag, and burned it with fire;

wcs,qmf**7617**/(853)/df,pl,nn**802**   pnl834   pp,pnx   hipf**4191** ptn**3808** nn**376**

2 And had taken*the*women*captives, that *were* therein: they slew not any,

wcj,pr5704 aj1419   pr4480/aj6996   wcs,qmf5090   wcs,qmf**1980**   pp,nn,pnx**1870**

either great or small, but carried*them*away, and went on their way.

nn1732   wcj,pl,nn,pnx**376** wcs,qmf935 pr413   df,nn5892   wcj,ptdm2009   qptp**8313**

3 So David and his men came to the city, and, behold, *it was* burned

dfp,nn**784**   wcj,pl,nn,pnx**802**   wcj,pl,nn,pnx**1121**   wcj,pl,nn,pnx1323

with fire; and their wives, and their sons, and their daughters, were

nipf**7617**

taken captives.

nn1732   wcj,df,nn**5971** pnl834   pr,pnx854   wcs,qmf**5375** (853)   nn,pnx6963

4 Then David and the people that *were* with him lifted up their voice and

wcs,qmf1058 cj5704/pnl834 pp,pnx   ptn369   nn3581   pp,qnc1058

wept, until they had no more power to weep.

nn1732   wcj,du,cs,nu8147 pl,cs,nn**802**   nipf**7617**   nn293   df,nn3159

5 And David's two wives were taken captives, Ahinoam the Jezreelitess,

wcj,nn26   cs,nn**802**   nn5037   df,nn3761

and Abigail the wife of Nabal the Carmelite.

pp,nn1732   ad3966   wcs,qmf3334   cj3588   df,nn**5971** qpf**559**   pp,qnc,pnx5619

6 And David was greatly distressed; for the people spoke of stoning him,

cj3588   nn**5315** cs,nn3605   df,nn**5971**   qpf4843   nn**376** pr5921   pl,nn,pnx**1121**

because the soul of all the people was grieved, every man for his sons and

wcj,pr5921   pl,nn,pnx1323   nn1732   wcs,htmf**2388**   pp,nn**3068** pl,nn,pnx**430**

for his daughters: but David encouraged himself in the LORD his God.

nn1732 wcs,qmf559 pr413   nn54   df,nn3548   nn288   cs,nn1121   pte4994

7 And David said to Abiathar the priest, Ahimelech's son, I*pray*thee,

himv5066/pp,pnx   df,nn646   nn54   wcs,himf5066   (853)   df,nn646 pr413   nn1732

bring*me*hither the ephod. And Abiathar brought thither the ephod to David.

nn1732   wcs,qmf7592   pp,nn3068   pp,qnc559   qmf7291   pr310 df,pndm2088 df,nn1416

8 And David inquired at the LORD, saying, Shall I pursue after this troop?

he,himf,pnx5381   wcs,qmf559   pp,pnx   qmv7291 cj3588

shall I overtake them? And he answered him, Pursue: for thou shalt

hina5381/himf5381   wcj,hina5337/himf5337

surely overtake *them*, and without*fail*recover *all*.

nn1732 wcs,qmf1980 pnp1931   wcj,nu8337 pl,nu3967 nn376 pnl834   pr,pnx854

9 So David went, he and the six hundred men that *were* with him, and

wcs,qmf935 pr5704 cs,nn5158 df,nn1308   wcj,df,pl,nipt3498   qpf5975

came to the brook Besor, where those*that*were*left*behind stayed.

nn1732   wcs,qmf7291 pnp1931   wcj,nu702 pl,nu3967   nn376   du,nu3967/(nn376)

10 But David pursued, he and four hundred men: for two hundred

wcs,qmf5975   pnl834   pipf6296   pr4480/qnc5674   (853)   cs,nn5158 df,nn1308

abode behind, which were so faint that they could*not*go*over the brook Besor.

wcs,qmf4672   cs,nn376/nn4713   dfp,nn7704   wcs,qmf3947 pnx(853)   pr413 nn1732

11 And they found an Egyptian in the field, and brought him to David,

wcs,qmf5414 pp,pnx nn3899   wcs,qmf398   wcs,himf,pnx8248 pl,nn4325

and gave him bread, and he did eat; and they made him drink water;

wcs,qmf5414 pp,pnx   cs,nn6400   nn1690   wcj,du,cs,nu8147

12 And they gave him a piece of a cake*of*figs, and two

pl,nn6778   wcs,qmf398   nn,pnx7307 wcs,qmf7725 pr,pnx413   cj3588

clusters*of*raisins: and when he had eaten, his spirit came again to him: for

qpf398 ptn3808 nn3899 wcj,ptn3808 qpf8354   pl,nn4325 nu7969 pl,nn3117 wcj,nu7969 pl,nn3915

he had eaten no bread, nor drunk *any* water, three days and three nights.

nn1732 wcs,qmf559   pp,pnx   pp,pnit4310   pnp859   wcj,ad335/pr4480/pndm2088

13 And David said unto him, To whom *belongest* thou? and whence

pnp859   wcs,qmf559 pnp595   cs,nn5288   nn4713   nn5650   pp,nn376/nn6003

art thou? And he said, I *am* a young man of Egypt, servant to an Amalekite;

nn,pnx113 wcs,qmf,pnx5800   cj3588 nu7969 df,nn3117   qpf2470

and my master left me, because three days ago I fell sick.

pnp587   qpf6584   cs,nn5045   df,nn3774   wcj,pr5921

14 We made*an*invasion *upon* the south of the Cherethites, and upon *the*

df,pnl834   pp,nn3063 wcj,pr5921 cs,nn5045   nn3612   qpf8313 wcj(853)

coast which *belongeth* to Judah, and upon the south of Caleb; and we burned

nn6860   dfp,nn784

Ziklag with fire.

nn1732 wcs,qmf559 pr,pnx413   he,himf,pnx3381   pr413 df,pndm2088

15 And David said to him, Canst thou bring*me*down to this

df,nn1416   wcs,qmf559 nimv7650   pp,pnx   pp,pl,nn430   cj518 qmf,pnx4191

company? And he said, Swear unto me by God, that thou wilt neither kill

wcj,cj518 himf,pnx5462   pp,cs,nn3027   nn,pnx113   wcj,himf,pnx3381   pr413

me, nor deliver me into the hands of my master, and I will bring*thee*down to

df,pndm2088   df,nn1416

this company.

wcs,himf,pnx3381   wcj,ptdm2009   pl,qptp5203

16 And when he had brought*him*down, behold, *they were* spread abroad

pr5921/pl,cs,nn6440 cs,nn3605   df,nn776 pl,qpta398 wcj,pl,qpta8354 wcj,pl,qpta2287 pp,cs,nn3605

upon all the earth, eating and drinking, and dancing, because of all the

df,aj1419   df,nn7998 pnl834   qpf3947   pr4480/cs,nn776   pl,nn6430

great spoil that they had taken out*of*the*land of the Philistines, and

wcj,pr4480/cs,nn776   nn3063

out*of*the*land of Judah.

nn1732 wcs,himf,pnx5221   pr4480/df,nn5399   wcj,pr5704   df,nn6153

17 And David   smote   them from*the*twilight even unto the evening of the

pp,nn4283   nipf4422   wcj,ptn3808   nn376   pp,pnx   cj3588/cj518 nu702 pl,nu3967   nn5288

next day: and there escaped   not a man of them,   save four hundred young

nn376   pnl834 qpf7392 pr5921 df,pl,nn1581   wcs,qmf5127

men, which rode upon camels, and fled.

nn1732   wcs,himf5337   (853) cs,nn3605 pnl834   nn6002   qpf3947

18 And David recovered   all   that the Amalekites had carried away: and

nn1732   hipf5337   wcj(853) du,cs,nu8147 pl,nn,pnx802

David rescued   his   two   wives.

wcj,ptn3808   nipf5737   pp,pnx   pr4480 df,aj6996 wcj,pr5704 df,aj1419 wcj,pr5704

19 And there was nothing lacking to them, neither small nor   great, neither

pl,nn1121   wcj,pl,nn1323   wcj,pr4480/nn7998 wcj,pr5704 cs,nn3605   pnl834   qpf3947 pp,pnx

sons nor daughters, neither spoil, nor   any thing that they had taken to them:

nn1732   hipf7725   df,nn3605

David recovered all.

nn1732 wcs,qmf3947 (853) cs,nn3605   df,nn6629   wcj,df,nn1241   qpf5090

20 And David   took   all   the flocks and the herds, which they drove

pp,pl,cs,nn6440 df,pndm1931   df,nn4735   wcs,qmf559 pndm2088   nn1732   cs,nn7998

before   those other cattle, and said, This is David's spoil.

nn1732   wcs,qmf935 pr413   du,nu3967   df,pl,nn376 pnl834   pipf6296

21 And David came to the two hundred men, which were so faint that they

pp,qnc1980/pr310   nn1732   wcs,himf,pnx3427   pp,cs,nn5158

could not follow David, whom they had made also to abide   at the brook

df,nn1308   wcs,qmf3318   pp,qnc7125   nn1732   wcj,pp,qnc7125   df,nn5971 pnl834

Besor: and they went forth to meet David, and to meet   the people that were

pr,pnx854   nn1732   wcs,qmf5066   (853)   df,nn5971   wcs,qmf7592/pp,nn7965 pp,pnx

with him: and when David came near to   the people, he   saluted   them.

wcs,qmf6030   cs,nn3605   nn7451   cs,nn376   wcj,nn1100 pr4480/df,nn376 pnl834

22 Then answered   all   the wicked men and men of Belial, of those that

qpf1980 pr5973   nn1732   wcs,qmf559 cj3282/pnl834   qpf1980 ptn3808 pr,pnx5973   ptn3808 qmf5414

went with David, and said, Because they went not with us, we will not give

pp,pnx   pr4480/df,nn7998 pnl834   hipf5337   cj3588/cj518   nn376   (853)   nn,pnx802

them aught of*the*spoil that we have recovered, save to every man   his wife

wcj(853)   pl,nn,pnx1121   wcj,qmf5090   wcj,qmf1980

and   his children, that they may lead*them*away, and depart.

wcs,qmf559   nn1732   ptn3808 qmf6213 ad3651   pl,nn,pnx251   pr854   pnl834

23 Then said David, Ye shall not do so, my brethren, with that which the

nn3068   qpf5414 pp,pnx   wcs,qmf8104 pnx(853)   wcs,qmf5414 (853)   df,nn1416

LORD hath given us, who hath preserved   us, and delivered   the company

df,qpta935 pr,pnx5921   pp,nn,pnx3027

that came against us into our hand.

wcj,pnit4310   qmf8085   pp,pnx   df,pndm2088 dfp,nn1697 cj3588   pp,cs,nn2506

24 For who will hearken unto you in this   matter? but as his   part   is

df,qpta3381   dfp,nn4421   wcj,pp,cs,nn2506   df,qpta3427 pr5921   df,pl,nn3627

that goeth down to the battle, so shall his   part   be that tarrieth by the stuff:

qmf2505   ad3162

they shall part alike.

wcs,qmf1961   pr4480/df,nn3117/df,pndm1931 wcj,ad4605   wcs,qmf,pnx7760   pp,nn2706

25 And it was so from*that*day forward, that he   made   it a statute and

wcj,pp,nn4941   pp,nn3478 pr5704 df,pndm2088 df,nn3117

an ordinance for Israel unto   this   day.

nn1732 wcs,qmf935 pr413   nn6860   wcs,pimf7971   pr4480/df,nn7998

26 And when David came to Ziklag, he   sent   of*the*spoil unto the

pp,pl,cs,nn**2205**   nn3063   pp,nn,pnx**7453**   pp,qnc**559**   ptdm2009   nn**1293**   pp,pnx
elders   of Judah, *even* to his friends, saying, Behold a present for you

pr4480/cs,nn7998   pl,cs,qpta341   nn**3068**
of*the*spoil of the enemies of the LORD;

                    pp,pnl834   pp,nn1008   wcj,pp,pnl834   nn5045   pp,nn7418
27 To *them* which *were* in Bethel, and to *them* which *were* in south Ramoth,

          wcj,pp,pnl834   pp,nn3492
and to *them* which *were* in Jattir,

                    wcj,pp,pnl834   pp,nn6177   wcj,pp,pnl834   pp,nn8224
28 And to *them* which *were* in Aroer, and to *them* which *were* in Siphmoth,

          wcj,pp,pnl834   pp,nn851
and to *them* which *were* in Eshtemoa,

                    wcj,pp,pnl834   pp,nn7403   wcj,pp,pnl834
29 And to *them* which *were* in Rachal, and to *them* which *were* in the

pp,pl,cs,nn5892   df,nn3397   wcj,pp,pnl834   pp,pl,cs,nn5892
cities   of the Jerahmeelites, and to *them* which *were* in the   cities   of the

df,nn7017
Kenites,

                    wcj,pp,pnl834   pp,nn2767   wcj,pp,pnl834
30 And to *them* which *were* in Hormah, and to *them* which *were* in

pp,nn3565   wcj,pp,pnl834   pp,nn6269
Chor-ashan, and to *them* which *were* in Athach,

                    wcj,pp,pnl834   pp,nn2275   wcj,pp,cs,nn3605   df,pl,nn4725 pnl834/ad8033
31 And to *them* which *were* in Hebron, and to   all   the places where

nn1732   pnp1931   wcj,pl,nn,pnx**376**   htpf**1980**
David himself and his   men   were wont*to*haunt.

Saul's Death

wcj,pl,nn6430   pl,nipt3898   pp,nn3478   pl,cs,nn**376**   nn3478
31 Now the Philistines fought against Israel: and the   men   of Israel

wcs,qmf5127   pr4480/pl,cs,nn**6440**   pl,nn6430   wcs,qmf**5307**   aj2491   pp,cs,nn2022
fled   from before the Philistines, and fell down slain in mount

df,nn1533
Gilboa.

                    pl,nn6430   wcs,pimf1692   (853) nn7586   wcj(853)   pl,nn,pnx**1121**
2 And the Philistines followed*hard*upon   Saul and upon   his   sons;

          pl,nn6430   wcs,himf**5221** (853)   nn3083   wcj(853)   nn41   wcj(853)   nn4444
and the Philistines slew   Jonathan, and   Abinadab, and   Malchi-shua,

nn7586   pl,cs,nn**1121**
Saul's sons.

          df,nn4421   wcs,qmf**3513**   pr413   nn7586   df,pl,hipt**3384**/pl,nn**376** wcs,qmf,pnx4672
3 And the battle went sore against Saul, and the   archers   hit   him;

(dfp,nn7198)   ad3966   wcs,qmf2342   pr4480/df,pl,hipt**3384**
and he was sore wounded of*the*archers.

          wcs,qmf**559**   nn7586   pp,qpta5375/pl,nn,pnx3627   qmv8025   nn,pnx**2719**
4 Then   said   Saul unto his   armorbearer,   Draw thy sword, and

wcj,qmv,pnx1856   pp,pnx   cj6435   df,pndm428   df,pl,nn**6189**   qmf935
thrust*me*through   therewith; lest   these   uncircumcised   come   and

wcs,qpf,pnx1856   wcs,htpf5953 pp,pnx   qpta**5375**/pl,nn,pnx3627 qpf14 wcj,ptn**3808** cj3588
thrust*me*through, and abuse me. But his armorbearer would not; for he was

ad3966   qpf**3372**   nn7586 wcs,qmf3947 (853)   df,nn**2719**   wcs,qmf**5307** pr,pnx5921
sore afraid. Therefore Saul took   a sword, and fell   upon it.

^{qpta5375/pl,nn,pnx3627   wcs,qmf7200   cj3588   nn7586   qpf4191   pnp1931   wcs,qmf5307   ad1571}

5 And when his armorbearer   saw   that Saul was dead,   he   fell   likewise

^{pr5921   nn,pnx2719   wcs,qmf4191   pr,pnx5973}

upon his sword, and   died   with   him.

^{nn7586   wcs,qmf4191   wcj,nu7969   pl,nn,pnx1121   wcj,qpta5375/pl,nn,pnx3627   ad1571   cs,nn3605}

6 So Saul died, and his three   sons,   and his   armorbearer,   and   all   his

^{pl,nn,pnx376   df,pndm1931   dfp,nn3117   ad3162}

men,   that   same   day   together.

^{pl,cs,nn376   nn3478   pnl834   pp,cs,nn5676   df,nn6010}

7 And when the   men   of Israel that *were* on the other side of the valley, and

^{wcj,pnl834   pp,cs,nn5676   df,nn3383   wcs,qmf7200   cj3588   pl,cs,nn376   nn3478   qpf5127}

they that *were* on the other side Jordan,   saw   that the   men   of Israel fled, and

^{wcj,cj3588   nn7586   wcj,pl,nn,pnx1121   qpf4191   wcs,qmf5800   (853)   df,pl,nn5892   wcs,qmf5127}

that Saul and his   sons   were dead, they forsook   the cities, and   fled;

^{pl,nn6430   wcs,qmf935   wcs,qmf3427   pp,pnp2004}

and the Philistines came and dwelt in them.

^{wcs,qmf1961   pr4480/nn4283   pl,nn6430   wcs,qmf935   pp,pinc6584}

8 And it*came*to*pass on*the*morrow, when the Philistines came to   strip

^{(853)   df,pl,nn2491   wcs,qmf4672 (853)   nn7586   wcj(853)   nu7969   pl,nn,pnx1121   pl,qpta5307   pp,cs,nn2022}

the   slain,   that they found   Saul and   his three   sons   fallen in mount

^{df,nn1533}

Gilboa.

^{wcs,qmf3772   (853)   nn,pnx7218   wcs,himf6584   (853)   pl,nn,pnx3627   wcs,pimf7971}

9 And they cut off   his head, and stripped off   his armor, and   sent

^{pp,cs,nn776   pl,nn6430   ad5439   pp,pinc1319   cs,nn1004}

into the   land   of the Philistines round about, to publish *it in* the house of their

^{pl,nn,pnx6091   wcj,pr854   df,nn5971}

idols,   and among the people.

^{wcs,qmf7760   (853)   pl,nn,pnx3627   cs,nn1004   nn6252   qpf8628}

10 And they   put   his armor in the house of Ashtaroth: and they fastened

^{wcj(853)   nn,pnx1472   pp,cs,nn2346   nn1052}

his body to the   wall   of Beth-shan.

^{pl,cs,qpta3427   cs,nn3003/nn1568   wcs,qmf8085/pr,pnx413 (853)   pnl834}

11 And when the inhabitants of Jabesh-gilead   heard   of that which the

^{pl,nn6430   qpf6213   pp,nn7586}

Philistines had done to Saul;

^{cs,nn3605   nn2428   cs,nn376   wcs,qmf6965   wcs,qmf1980   cs,nn3605   df,nn3915   wcs,qmf3947   (853)}

12 All   the valiant men arose, and   went   all   night, and   took   the

^{cs,nn1472   nn7586   wcj(853)   pl,cs,nn1472   pl,nn,pnx1121   pr4480/cs,nn2346   nn1052}

body of Saul and   the bodies of his   sons   from*the*wall of Beth-shan, and

^{wcs,qmf935   nn,lh3003   wcs,qmf8313   pnx(853)   ad8033}

came to Jabesh, and burnt   them there.

^{wcs,qmf3947   (853)   pl,nn,pnx6106   wcs,qmf6912   pr8478   df,nn815   pp,nn,lh3003}

13 And they   took   their bones, and buried *them* under a   tree at Jabesh,

^{wcs,qmf6684   cs,nu7651   pl,nn3117}

and fasted seven days.

The Second Book of

SAMUEL

The Book of Second Samuel focuses on the reign of King David. Some commentators outline the book according to the political situation, dividing it into his rule over Judah (2 Sam. 1:1—4:12) and over all Israel (2 Sam. 5:1—12:31). Others divide the book by spiritual content, making note of two particular sections: David's triumphs (2 Sam. 1:1—12:31) and David's troubles (2 Sam. 13:1—24:25).

God's reason for choosing David is clear from the statement, "the LORD hath sought him a man after his [God's] own heart" (1 Sam. 13:14). The psalms that David wrote reveal his passionate devotion to God. Despite this strong commitment, he was guilty of several great sins, the consequences of which affected not only him personally, but also the members of his family and the whole nation (2 Sam. 24:13–15).

The prophetic blessing that God gave to David includes the promise that his kingdom would be established forever (chap. 7). This blessing, called the Davidic Covenant, is an expansion of God's promises to Abraham (Gen. 12:7; 15:18; 17:8; 22:17). The promise of an all–powerful king that would reign on the throne of David is repeated many times throughout Scripture (Is. 55:3; Jer. 23:5; 30:9; 33:15–26; Ezek. 34:23, 24; 37:24, 25; Acts 15:16). The kingship of David was enhanced by the prophetic ministries of Samuel, Nathan, and Gad. For this reason, it is very possible that Nathan and Gad also wrote portions of this book (1 Chr. 29:29).

David Learns of Saul's Death

1 ☞ Now it*came*to*pass after the death of Saul, when David was returned from*the*slaughter of the Amalekites, and David had abode two days in Ziklag;

2 It*came*even*to*pass on the third day, that, behold, a man came out of the camp from Saul with his clothes rent, and earth upon his head: and *so* it was, when he came to David, that he fell to the earth, and did obeisance.

3 And David said unto him, From whence comest thou? And he said unto him, Out*of*the*camp of Israel am I escaped.

☞ **1:1–10** The story the Amalekite told was different from the actual account in 1 Samuel 31:3–5. Apparently, this man discovered Saul's dead body and looted it. Some time later he told his own version to David, hoping that he would be rewarded for his "good news" (see 2 Sam. 4:10).

nn1732 wcs,qmf559 pr,pnx413   pnit4100 qpf1961   df,nn1697   pte4994   himv5046 pp,pnx

4 And David said unto him, How went the matter? I*pray*thee, tell me.

wcj,qmf559   pnl834   df,nn5971   qpf5127 pr4480   df,nn4421   hina7235 pr4480

And he answered, That the people are fled from the battle, and many of the

df,nn5971 wcj,ad1571   qpf5307   wcs,qmf4191   nn7586   wcj,nn3083   nn,pnx1121   qpf4191

people also are fallen and dead; and Saul and Jonathan his son are dead

wcj,ad1571

also.

nn1732   wcs,qmf559   pr413   df,nn5288   df,hipt5046 pp,pnx ptx349   qpf3045

5 And David said unto the young man that told him, How knowest thou

cj3588 nn7586   wcj,nn3083   nn,pnx1121   qpf4191

that Saul and Jonathan his son be dead?

df,nn5288   df,hipt5046 pp,pnx wcs,qmf559   nipf7136   nina7122

6 And the young man that told him said, As I happened by chance upon

pp,cs,nn2022   df,nn1533   wcj,ptdm2009 nn7586 nipt8172 pr5921   nn,pnx2595   wcj,ptdm2009   df,nn7393

mount Gilboa, behold, Saul leaned upon his spear; and, lo, the chariots and

wcj,pl,cs,nn1167/df,pl,nn6571   hipf,pnx1692

horsemen   followed hard after him.

wcs,qmf6437 pr,pnx310   wcs,qmf,pnx7200   wcs,qmf7121 pr,pnx413

7 And when he looked behind him, he   saw   me, and called unto me.

wcs,qmf559   ptdm2009

And I answered, Here *am* I.

wcs,qmf559 pp,pnx   pnit4310   pnp859   wcj,qmf559   pr,pnx413 pnp595

8 And he said unto me, Who *art* thou? And I answered him, I *am* an

nn6003

Amalekite.

wcs,qmf559 pr,pnx413   qmv5975   pte4994   pr,pnx5921   wcj,pimv,pnx4191

9 He said unto me again, Stand, I*pray*thee, upon me, and   slay   me:

cj3588 df,nn7661   qpf,pnx270   cj3588   nn,pnx5315   ad5750 cs,nn3605 pp,pnx

for anguish is come upon me, because my life *is* yet whole in me.

wcs,qmf5975 pr,pnx5921   wcs,pimf,pnx4191   cj3588   qpf3045 cj3588

10 So I stood upon him, and   slew   him, because I was sure that he

ptn3808 qmf2421   ad310   qnc,pnx5307   wcs,qmf3947   df,nn5145 pnl834   pr5921

could not live after that he was fallen: and I took the crown that *was* upon his

nn,pnx7218   wcj,nn685 pnl834   pr5921   nn,pnx2220   wcs,himf,pnx935   ad2008   pr413

head, and the bracelet that *was* on his arm, and have brought them hither unto

nn,pnx113

my lord.

nn1732   wcs,himf2388   pp,pl,nn,pnx899   wcs,qmf,pnx7167   wcj,ad1571

11 Then David took hold on his clothes, and   rent   them; and likewise

cs,nn3605   pl,nn376 pnl834   pr,pnx854

all   the men that *were* with him:

wcs,qmf5594   wcs,qmf1058   wcs,qmf6684 pr5704 df,nn6153 pr5921   nn7586   wcj,pr5921

12 And they mourned, and wept, and fasted until even, for Saul, and for

nn3083   nn,pnx1121   wcj,pr5921   nn5971   nn3068   wcj,pr5921   cs,nn1004

Jonathan his son, and for the people of the LORD, and for the house of

nn3478 cj3588   qpf5307   dfp,nn2719

Israel; because they were fallen by the sword.

nn1732   wcs,qmf559 pr413   df,nn5288   df,hipt5046 pp,pnx pnit335/pr4480/pnit4100

13 And David said unto the young man that told him,   Whence   *art*

pnp859   wcs,qmf559   pnp595   cs,nn1121   nn376/nn1616   nn6003

thou? And he answered, I *am* the son of a stranger, an Amalekite.

nn1732   wcs,qmf559 pr,pnx413   ptx349   ptn3808 qpf3372   pp,qnc7971

14 And David said unto him, How wast thou not afraid to stretch forth

nn,pnx3027 pp,pinc7843 (853)   nn3068   cs,nn4899

thine hand to destroy   the LORD's anointed?

15 And David called one of*the*young*men, and said, Go near, *and* fall
upon him. And he smote him that he died.

16 And David said unto him, Thy blood *be* upon thy head; for thy mouth
hath testified against thee, saying, I have slain the LORD's anointed.

David's Lament

17 And David lamented with this lamentation over Saul and over Jonathan
his son:

18 (Also he bade them teach the children of Judah *the use of* the bow:
behold, *it is* written in the book of Jasher.)

19 The beauty of Israel is slain upon thy high places: how are the mighty
fallen!

20 Tell *it* not in Gath, publish *it* not in the streets of Askelon; lest the
daughters of the Philistines rejoice, lest the daughters of the uncircumcised triumph.

21 Ye mountains of Gilboa, *let there be* no dew, neither *let there be* rain,
upon you, nor fields of offerings: for there the shield of the mighty is
vilely*cast*away, the shield of Saul, *as though he had* not *been* anointed with
oil.

22 From*the*blood of the slain, from*the*fat of the mighty, the bow of
Jonathan turned not back, and the sword of Saul returned not empty.

23 Saul and Jonathan *were* lovely and pleasant in their lives, and in their
death they were not divided: they were swifter than eagles, they were stronger
than lions.

24 Ye daughters of Israel, weep over Saul, who clothed you in scarlet, with
other delights, who put on ornaments of gold upon your apparel.

1:18 A reference to the book of Jasher is also found in Joshua 10:13. It is apparently a historical book of military poetry, a collection of songs about heroes. It had more material added to it as the years went by, but it is now lost. Jasher is probably a name used to refer to Israel. It is seen in Deuteronomy 32:15 under the form "Jeshurun" which means "the righteous or upright one." The book printed under this name in modern times is spurious.

ptx349   aj1368   qpf**5307**   pp,cs,nn**8432**   df,nn4421   nn3083

25 How are the mighty fallen in the midst of the battle! O Jonathan, *thou wast*

nn2491 pr5921   pl,nn,pnx**1116**

slain in thine high places.

pp,pnx   qpf6887   pr,pnx5921   nn,pnx251   nn3083   ad3966   qpf5276

☞ **26** I am distressed for   thee, my brother Jonathan: very pleasant hast thou

pp,pnx   nn,pnx160 pp,pnx   nipf6381   pr4480/cs,nn160   pl,nn802

been unto me: thy love to me was wonderful, passing*the*love of women.

ptx349   aj1368   qpf**5307**   pl,cs,nn3627   nn4421   wcs,qmf6

27 How are the mighty fallen, and the weapons of war perished!

David Becomes Judah's King

wcs,qmf**1961**   pr310   ad**3651**   nn1732   wcs,qmf**7592**   pp,nn**3068**   pp,qnc559

2 And it*came*to*pass after this, that David inquired of the LORD, saying,

he,qmf**5927**   pp,nu259   pl,cs,nn5892   nn3063   nn**3068** wcs,qmf559 pr,pnx413

Shall I go up into any of the cities of Judah? And the LORD said   unto

qmv**5927**   nn1732 wcs,qmf**559**   ad575   qmf**5927**   wcs,qmf**559**   nn,lh2275

him, Go up. And David said, Whither shall I go up? And he said, Unto Hebron.

nn1732   wcs,qmf**5927**   ad8033   du,cs,nu8147 pl,nn,pnx**802** wcj,ad1571   nn293

2 So David went up thither, and his two   wives   also, Ahinoam the

df,nn3159   wcj,nn26   nn5037   cs,nn**802**   df,nn3761

Jezreelitess, and Abigail Nabal's wife the Carmelite.

wcj,pl,nn,pnx**376** pnl834   pr,pnx5973   nn1732   hipf**5927**   nn**376**

3 And his   men   that *were* with him did David bring up, every man with

wcj,nn,pnx**1004**   nn3063   wcs,qmf**3427**   pp,pl,cs,nn5892   nn2275

his household: and they dwelt in the cities   of Hebron.

pl,nn,pnx**376**   nn3063   wcs,qmf935   ad8033   wcs,qmf**4886**   (853) nn1732 pp,nn**4428** pr5921

4 And the men of Judah came, and there they anointed   David king over

cs,nn**1004**   nn3063   wcs,himf**5046**   pp,nn1732   pp,qnc559   pl,cs,nn**376**

the house of Judah. And they   told   David, saying, *That* the men of

cs,nn3003/nn1568   pnl834 qpf**6912** (853) nn7586

Jabesh-gilead *were they* that buried   Saul.

nn1732   wcs,qmf7971   pl,nn**4397**   pr413   pl,cs,nn**376**   cs,nn3003/nn1568   wcs,qmf**559**

5 And David   sent   messengers unto the men of Jabesh-gilead, and   said

pr,pnx413   pl,qptp**1288**   pnp859   pp,nn**3068** pnl834   qpf**6213** df,pndm2088   df,nn**2617**

unto them, Blessed *be* ye of the LORD, that ye have showed   this   kindness

pr5973   pl,nn,pnx**113**   pr5973 nn7586   wcs,qmf**6912** pnx(853)

unto your lord, *even* unto Saul, and have buried   him.

wcj,ad6258   nn**3068** qmf**6213**   nn**2617**   wcj,nn571 pr,pnx5973   pnp595 wcj,ad1571

6 And now the LORD show kindness and truth unto you: and I   also

qmf**6213** pnx(853)   df,pndm2063   df,nn**2896**   pnl834   qpf**6213** df,pndm2088 df,nn**1697**

will requite   you this kindness, because ye have done this   thing.

wcj,ad6258   du,nn,pnx**3027**   qmf**2388**   wcj,qmv**1961**

7 Therefore now   let   your   hands   be strengthened, and   be   ye

pp,pl,cs,nn**1121**/nn**2428** cj3588   pl,nn,pnx**113** nn7586   qpf**4191**   wcj,ad1571   cs,nn**1004**   nn3063

valiant: for your master Saul is dead, and also the house of Judah have

qpf**4886**   pnx(853)   pp,nn**4428** pr,pnx5921

anointed   me king over   them.

☞ **1:26** David and Jonathan truly loved each other, and their relationship was one of true loyalty to each other. Jonathan, the heir apparent to the throne of King Saul, was willing to take second place for the sake of David, his friend.

qpf3045   he,ptn3808 cj3588   ' qmf1961   aj4751   dfp,aj314   wcj,pr5704
knowest thou not that it will be bitterness in the latter end? how long shall it

ptn3808   qmf559   dfp,nn5971 pp,qnc7725   pr4480/pr310   pl,nn,pnx251
be then, ere thou bid the people return from following their brethren?

nn3097 wcs,qmf559   df,pl,nn430 aj2416   cj3588/cj3884   pipf1696   cj3588 ad227
27 And Joab said, As God liveth, unless thou hadst spoken, surely then in

df,nn1242   df,nn5971   nipf5927   nn376   pr4480/pr310   nn,pnx251
the morning the people had gone up every one from following his brother.

nn3097 wcs,qmf8628 dfp,nn7782 cs,nn3605   df,nn5971 wcs,qmf5975   qmf7291
28 So Joab blew a trumpet, and all the people stood still, and pursued

pr310 nn3478 wcj,ptn3808 ad5750 wcj,ptn3808 pp,ninc3898   qpf3254
after Israel no more, neither fought they any more.

wcj,nn74   wcj,pl,nn,nn376   qpf1980   nn3605 df,pndm1931 df,nn3915   dfp,nn6160
29 And Abner and his men walked all that night through the plain,

wcs,qmf5674   (853) df,nn3383   wcs,qmf1980 cs,nn3605 df,nn1338   wcs,qmf935
and passed over Jordan, and went through all Bithron, and they came to

nn4266
Mahanaim.

wcj,nn3097   qpf7725   pr4480/pr310   nn74
30 And Joab returned from following Abner: and when he had

wcs,qmf6908/(853)/cs,nn3605/df,nn5971   wcs,nimf6485   pr4480/pl,cs,nn5650/nn1732 nu8677/nu6240 nn376
gathered*all*the*people*together, there lacked of*David's*servants nineteen men

wcj,nn6214
and Asahel.

wcj,pl,cs,nn5650   nn1732   hipf5221   pr4480/nn1144   nn74
31 But the servants of David had smitten of Benjamin, and of Abner's

wcj,pr4480/pl,cs,nn376   cs,nu7969 pl,nu3967   wcj,pl,nu8346   nn376 qpf4191
men,   so that three hundred and threescore men died.

wcs,qmf5375 (853)   nn6214   wcs,qmf,pnx6912   pp,nn6913
32 And they took up Asahel, and buried him in the sepulcher of his

nn,pnx1   pnl834   nn1035   nn3097   wcj,pl,nn,pnx376 wcs,qmf1980 cs,nn3605 df,nn3915
father, which was in Bethlehem. And Joab and his men went all night,

pp,pnx   pp,nn2275   wcs,nimf215
and they came to Hebron at break*of*day.

wcs,qmf1961 aj752 df,nn4421   pr996   cs,nn1004   nn7586   wcj(pr996)   cs,nn1004
3 Now there was long war between the house of Saul and   the house

nn1732   wcj,nn1732   qpta1980/wcj,qpta2390   wcj,cs,nn1004   nn7586
of David: but David waxed*stronger*and*stronger, and the house of Saul

pl,qpta1980   wcj,aj1800
waxed weaker*and*weaker.

David's Sons Born at Hebron

pp,nn1732   pl,nn1121 wcj,nimf3205   pp,nn2275   nn,pnx1060 wcs,qmf1961
🔑 2 And unto David were sons born in Hebron: and his firstborn was

nn550   dfp,nn293   df,nn3159
Amnon, of Ahinoam the Jezreelitess;

wcj,nn,pnx4932 nn3609   pp,nn26 cs,nn802   nn5037   df,nn3761
3 And his second, Chileab, of Abigail the wife of Nabal the Carmelite; and the

wcj,df,nuor7992   nn53   cs,nn1121   nn4601   cs,nn1323   nn8526 nn4428   nn1650
third, Absalom the son of Maacah the daughter of Talmai king of Geshur;

🔑 **3:2–5**   See 1 Chronicles 3:1–9 for an additional list of David's children.

wcj,df,nuor7243   nn138   cs,nn1121   nn2294   wcj,df,nuor2549   nn8203

4 And the fourth, Adonijah the son of Haggith; and the   fifth, Shephatiah

cs,nn1121   nn37

the son of Abital;

wcj,df,nuor8345   nn3507   pp,nn5698   nn1732   cs,nn802   pndm428   pupf3205   pp,nn1732

5 And the sixth, Ithream, by Eglah David's wife. These were born to David

pp,nn2275

in Hebron.

Abner Decides to Join David

wcs,qmf1961   pp,qnc1961 df,nn4421   pr996   cs,nn1004   nn7586

6 And it*came*to*pass, while there was   war between the house of Saul and

wcj(pr996)   cs,nn1004   nn1732   wcj,nn74   (qpf1961)   htpt2388   pp,cs,nn1004

the house of David, that Abner   made*himself*strong for the house of

nn7586

Saul.

wcj,pp,nn7586   nn6370   wcj,nn,pnx8034   nn7532   nn1323

⊙̶ᴖ̶ 7 And Saul had a concubine, whose name *was* Rizpah, the daughter of

nn345   wcs,qmf559 pr413   nn74   ad4069   qpf935   pr413

Aiah: and *Ish-bosheth* said   to Abner, Wherefore hast thou gone in unto my

nn,pnx1   nn6370

father's concubine?

pp,nn74   ad3966 wcs,qmf2734 pr5921   pl,cs,nn1697   nn378   wcs,qmf559

8 Then was Abner very wroth for the words of Ish-bosheth, and said, *Am*

pnp595   nn3611 he,nn7218 pnl834   pp,nn3063   qmf6213   nn2617   df,nn3117 pr5973   cs,nn1004

I a dog's head, which against Judah do show kindness this day unto the house

nn7586   nn,pnx1   pr413   pl,nn,pnx251   wcj,pr413   nn,pnx4828   wcj,ptn3808   hipf,pnx4672

of Saul thy father, to his brethren, and to his friends, and have not delivered

pp,cs,nn3027   nn1732   wcs,qmf6485/pr,pnx5921   df,nn3117   cs,nn5771

thee into the hand of David, that thou   chargest   me today with*a*fault

df,nn802

concerning this woman?

ad3541 qmf6213 pl,nn430   pp,nn74   himf3254 wcj,ad3541 cj3588 pp,pnl834   nn3068   nipf7650

9 So do God to Abner, and more also, except, as the Lᴏʀᴅ hath sworn

pp,nn1732 cj3588 ad3651   qmf6213   pp,pnx

to David, even so I do to him;

pp,hinc5674   df,nn4467   pr4480/cs,nn1004   nn7586   wcj,pp,hinc6965   (853)

10 To translate the kingdom from*the*house of Saul, and to set up the

nn3678   nn1732 pr5921   nn3478   wcj,pr5921   nn3063   pr4480/nn1835   wcj,pr5704   nn884

throne of David over Israel and over Judah, from Dan even to   Beer-sheba.

qpf3201 wcj,ptn3808 pp,hinc7725   (853)   nn74   nn1697   ad5750   pr4480/qnc,pnx3372

11 And he could not   answer   Abner a word again, because*he*feared

pnx(853)

him.

nn74   wcs,qmf7971   pl,nn4397   pr413 nn1732   pr,pnx8478   pp,qnc559   pp,pnit4310

12 And Abner sent   messengers to David on his behalf, saying, Whose *is*

⊙̶ᴖ̶ **3:7** A concubine was much more than a mistress. In a sense, she was a secondary "wife" (Ex. 21:8–10;
Deut. 21:11–13). She was a member of the royal household, took her position by an official ceremony of
appointment, and had the rights of a married woman. Unlike a true wife, concubines were usually acquired
by purchase or were captives taken in war. She could be "divorced" summarily and then released, but never
to be a slave (Gen. 16:2, 3; 21:10; Ex. 21:7, 8; Deut. 21:10–14; Mal. 2:14–16).

Abner was a powerful, ambitious man, and he knew that possessing one of the court women was equivalent
to royal power.

nn776   pp,qnc559   qmv3772   nn,pnx1285   pr,pnx854   wcj,ptdm2009   nn,pnx3027

the land? saying *also*, Make thy league with me, and, behold, my hand *shall be*

pr,pnx5973   pp,hinc5437   (853) cs,nn3605 nn3478 pr,pnx413

with thee, to bring about   all   Israel unto thee.

         wcs,qmf559   aj2896   pnp589   qmf3772   nn1285   pr,pnx854   ad389 nu259 nn1697 pnp595

13 And he said, Well; I   will make a league with thee: but one thing   I

qpta7592   pr4480/pr,pnx854   pp,qnc559   ptn3808 qmf7200 (853)   pl,nn,pnx6440 cj3588/cj518

require   of   thee, that is, Thou shalt not see   my face,   except thou

pp,pl,cs,nn6440   hinc,pnx935 (853) nn4324   nn7586 nn1323   pp,qnc,pnx935   pp,qnc7200 (853)

first   bring   Michal Saul's daughter, when thou comest to see   my

pl,nn,pnx6440

face.

       nn1732   wcs,qmf7971   pl,nn4397 pr413   nn378   nn7586 cs,nn1121 pp,qnc559   qmv5414

14 And David   sent   messengers to Ish-bosheth Saul's son, saying, Deliver

(853)   nn,pnx802 (853)   nn4324 pnl834   pipf781   pp,pnx   pp,nu3967 pl,cs,nn6190

me   my wife   Michal, which I espoused to me for a hundred foreskins of the

pl,nn6430

Philistines.

       nn378   wcs,qmf7971   wcs,qmf,pnx3947   pr4480/pr5973   nn376

15 And Ish-bosheth sent,   and   took   her from   *her* husband, *even*

pr4480/pr5973 nn6409   cs,nn1121   nn3919

from Phaltiel the son of Laish.

       nn,pnx376   wcs,qmf1980 pr,pnx854   qna1980 wcj,qna1058 pr,pnx310   pr5704   nn980

16 And her husband went   with her along weeping behind her to Bahurim.

wcs,qmf559   nn74 pr,pnx413   qmv1980 qmv7725   wcs,qmf7725

Then said Abner unto him, Go, return. And he returned.

       nn74   qpf1961   wcj,cs,nn1697   pr5973   cs,aj2205   nn3478   pp,qnc559

17 And Abner had communication with the elders of Israel, saying, Ye

qpf1961/pl,pipt1245   (853) nn1732   ad1571/ad8543 ad1571/ad8032   pp,nn4428 pr,pnx5921

sought   for   David in times   past   *to be* king over you:

         wcj,ad6258   qmv6213   cj3588   nn3068   qpf559 pr413 nn1732 pp,qnc559

18 Now then do *it*: for the LORD hath spoken of David, saying, By the

pp,cs,nn3027   nn,pnx5650 nn1732   hinc3467 (853)   nn,pnx5971 nn3478   pr4480/cs,nn3027

hand of my servant David I will save   my people Israel out*of*the*hand of the

pl,nn6430   wcj,pr4480/cs,nn3027   cs,nn3605   pl,qpta,pnx341

Philistines, and out*of*the*hand of all   their enemies.

       nn74   ad1571 wcs,pimf1696   pp,du,cs,nn241   nn1144   nn74 wcs,qmf1980 ad1571

19 And Abner also spoke in the   ears   of Benjamin: and Abner went also

pp,pinc1696   pp,du,cs,nn241   nn1732   pp,nn2275 (853) cs,nn3605 pnl834 aj2896/pp,du,cs,nn5869   nn3478

to speak in the ears   of David in Hebron   all that seemed good to Israel,

wcj,pp,du,cs,nn5869   cs,nn3605 cs,nn1004   nn1144

and that seemed good to the whole house of Benjamin.

       nn74   wcs,qmf935 pr413 nn1732   nn2275   pl,nu6242 pl,nn376 wcj,pr,pnx854

20 So Abner came to David to Hebron, and twenty men   with him. And

nn1732 wcs,qmf6213 pp,nn74   wcj,pp,pl,nn376 pnl834   pr,pnx854   nn4960

David made Abner and the   men   that *were* with him a feast.

       nn74   wcs,qmf559 pr413   nn1732   qmf6965 wcj,qmf1980   wcj,qmf6908 (853)

21 And Abner said unto David, I will arise and go,   and will gather

cs,nn3605 nn3478 pr413   nn,pnx113   df,nn4428   wcj,qmf3772 nn1285 pr,pnx854

all Israel unto my lord the king, that they may make a league with thee, and

       wcs,qpf4427   pp,nn3605 pnl834   nn,pnx5315 pimf183   nn1732 wcs,pimf7971 (853)

that thou mayest reign over all   that thine heart desireth. And David   sent

nn74   wcs,qmf1980   pp,nn7965

Abner away; and he went in peace.

Joab Kills Abner

^{wcj,ptdm2009}   ^{pl,cs,nn5650}   ⁿⁿ¹⁷³²   ^{wcj,nn3097}   ^{qpta935}   ^{pr4480/df,nn1416}

22 And, behold, the servants of David and Joab came from*pursuing*a*troop,

^{hipf935}   ^{aj7227}   ^{wcj,nn7998}   ^{pr,pnx5973}   ^{wcj,nn74}   ^{ptn,pnx369}   ^{pr5973}   ⁿⁿ¹⁷³²

and brought in a great spoil with them: but Abner was not with David in

^{pp,nn2275}   ^{cj3588}   ^{pipf,pnx7971}   ^{wcs,qmf1980}   ^{pp,nn7965}

Hebron; for he had sent*him*away, and he was gone in peace.

^{wcj,nn3097}   ^{wcj,cs,nn3605}   ^{df,nn6635}   ^{pnl834}   ^{pr,pnx854}   ^{qpf935}

23 When Joab and all the host that was with him were come, they

^{wcs,himf5046}   ^{pp,nn3097}   ^{pp,qnc559}   ⁿⁿ⁷⁴   ^{cs,nn1121}   ⁿⁿ⁵³⁶⁹   ^{qpf935}   ^{pr413}   ^{df,nn4428}

told Joab, saying, Abner the son of Ner came to the king, and he hath

^{wcs,pimf,pnx7971}   ^{wcs,qmf1980}   ^{pp,nn7965}

sent*him*away, and he is gone in peace.

ⁿⁿ³⁰⁹⁷   ^{wcs,qmf935}   ^{pr413}   ^{df,nn4428}   ^{wcs,qmf559}   ^{pnit4100}   ^{qpf6213}   ^{ptdm2009}

24 Then Joab came to the king, and said, What hast thou done? behold,

ⁿⁿ⁷⁴   ^{qpf935}   ^{pr,pnx413}   ^{pnit4100}   ^{pipf,pnx7971}

Abner came unto thee; why is it that thou hast sent*him*away, and he is quite

^{wcs,qmf1980}

gone?

^{qpf3045}   ⁽⁸⁵³⁾   ⁿⁿ⁷⁴   ^{cs,nn1121}   ⁿⁿ⁵³⁶⁹   ^{cj3588}   ^{qpf935}   ^{pp,pinc,pnx6601}

25 Thou knowest Abner the son of Ner, that he came to deceive thee,

^{wcj,pp,qnc3045}   ⁽⁸⁵³⁾   ^{nn,pnx4161}   ^{wcj(853)}   ^{pl,nn,pnx4126}   ^{wcj,pp,qnc3045}   ⁽⁸⁵³⁾   ^{cs,nn3605}

and to know thy going out and thy coming in, and to know all

^{pnl834}   ^{pnp859}   ^{qpta6213}

that thou doest.

ⁿⁿ³⁰⁹⁷   ^{wcs,qmf3318}   ^{pr4480/pr5973}   ⁿⁿ¹⁷³²   ^{wcs,qmf7971}   ^{pl,nn4397}   ^{pr310}

26 And when Joab was come out from David, he sent messengers after

ⁿⁿ⁷⁴   ^{wcs,himf7725/pnx(853)}   ^{pr4480/cs,nn953}   ^{df,nn5626}   ^{wcj,nn1732}   ^{qpf3045}   ^{ptn3808}

Abner, which brought*him*again from*the*well of Sirah: but David knew it not.

ⁿⁿ⁷⁴   ^{wcs,qmf7725}   ⁿⁿ²²⁷⁵   ⁿⁿ³⁰⁹⁷   ^{wcs,himf,pnx5186}   ^{pr413/cs,nn8432}

27 And when Abner was returned to Hebron, Joab took*him*aside in the

^{df,nn8179}   ^{pp,pinc1696}   ^{pr,pnx854}   ^{dfp,nn7987}   ^{wcs,himf,pnx5221}   ^{ad8033}   ^{df,nn2570}

gate to speak with him quietly, and smote him there under the fifth rib, that

^{wcs,qmf4191}   ^{pp,cs,nn1818}   ⁿⁿ⁶²¹⁴   ^{nn,pnx251}

he died, for the blood of Asahel his brother.

^{pr4480/pr310/ad3651}   ⁿⁿ¹⁷³²   ^{wcs,qmf8085}   ^{wcs,qmf559}   ^{pnp595}   ^{wcj,nn,pnx4467}

28 And afterward when David heard it, he said, I and my kingdom are

^{aj5355}   ^{pr4480/pr5973}   ⁿⁿ³⁰⁶⁸   ^{pr5704/nn5769}   ^{pr4480/pl,cs,nn1818}   ⁿⁿ⁷⁴   ^{cs,nn1121}   ⁿⁿ⁵³⁶⁹

guiltless before the Lord forever from*the*blood of Abner the son of Ner:

^{qmf2342}   ^{pr5921}   ⁿⁿ⁷²¹⁸   ⁿⁿ³⁰⁹⁷   ^{wcj,pr413}   ^{cs,nn3605}   ^{nn,pnx1}   ^{cs,nn1004}

29 Let it rest on the head of Joab, and on all his father's house; and let

^{wcj,ptn408}   ^{nimf3772}   ^{pr4480/cs,nn1004}   ⁿⁿ³⁰⁹⁷   ^{qpta2100}   ^{wcj,pupt6879}

there not fail from*the*house of Joab one that hath an issue, or that is a leper,

^{wcj,hipt2388}   ^{dfp,nn6418}   ^{wcj,qpta5307}   ^{dfp,nn2719}   ^{wcj,cs,aj2638}   ⁿⁿ³⁸⁹⁹

or that leaneth on a staff, or that falleth on the sword, or that lacketh bread.

^{wcj,nn3097}   ^{wcj,nn52}   ^{nn,pnx251}   ^{qpf2026}   ^{pp,nn74}   ^{pr5921/pnl834}   ^{hipf4191}

30 So Joab and Abishai his brother slew Abner, because he had slain their

^{nn,pnx251}   ⁽⁸⁵³⁾   ⁿⁿ⁶²¹⁴   ^{pp,nn1391}   ^{dfp,nn4421}

brother Asahel at Gibeon in the battle.

ⁿⁿ¹⁷³²   ^{wcs,qmf559}   ^{pr413}   ⁿⁿ³⁰⁹⁷   ^{wcj,pr413}   ^{cs,nn3605}   ^{df,nn5971}   ^{pnl834}   ^{pr,pnx854}

31 And David said to Joab, and to all the people that were with him,

^{qmv7167}   ^{pl,nn,pnx899}   ^{wcj,qmv2296}   ^{pl,nn8242}   ^{wcj,qmv5594}   ^{pp,pl,cs,nn6440}   ⁿⁿ⁷⁴

Rend your clothes, and gird you with sackcloth, and mourn before Abner.

^{wcj,df,nn4428}   ⁿⁿ¹⁷³²   ^{pr310}   ^{df,nn4296}

And king David himself followed the bier.

wcs,qmf**6912** (853)   nn74   pp,nn2275   df,nn**4428** wcs,qmf**5375** (853)   nn,pnx6963

32 And they buried   Abner in Hebron: and the king lifted up   his voice,

wcs,qmf1058 pr413   nn**6913**   nn74   cs,nn3605   df,nn**5971** wcs,qmf1058

and wept   at the grave of Abner; and all   the people wept.

df,nn**4428** wcs,pimf6969   pr413   nn74   wcs,qmf559   qmf**4191**   nn74   aj5036

33 And the king lamented over Abner, and said, Died Abner as a fool

he,pp,cs,nn**4194**

dieth?

nn,pnx**3027**   ptn3808 pl,qpta631 ptn3808   wcj,du,nn,pnx7272 hopf**5066**   pp,du,nn5178

34 Thy hands *were* not bound, nor thy   feet   put into fetters: as a

pl,cs,nn1121 pp,qnc**5307** pp,pl,cs,nn**6440** nn5766   pl,cs,nn1121   qpf**5307**   cs,nn3605   df,nn**5971** pp,qnc1058

man falleth before wicked men, *so* fellest thou. And all the people wept

wcs,himf3254 pr,pnx5921

again over him.

cs,nn3605   df,nn**5971** wcs,qmf935   (853)   nn1732   pp,hinc1262 nn3899

35 And when all   the people came to cause   David to   eat   meat while

pp,ad5750 df,nn**3117**   nn1732 wcs,nimf**7650** pp,qnc559   ad3541 qmf**6213** pl,nn**430**   pp,pnx   himf3254 wcj,ad3541

it was   yet day, David swore, saying, So   do God to me, and more also,

cj3588/cj518   qmf2938   nn3899 cj176 cs,nn3605/pnid3972 pp,pl,cs,nn**6440**   df,nn8121   qnc935

if I taste bread, or aught else, till   the sun be down.

wcj,cs,nn3605   df,nn**5971**   hipf**5234**   wcs,qmf**3190**/pp,du,nn,pnx**5869**

36 And   all   the people took notice *of it*, and it*pleased*them: as

pp,nn3605/pnl834   df,nn**4428** qpf**6213** qpf**2895**/pp,du,cs,nn**5869** pp,cs,nn3605   df,nn**5971**

whatsoever the king did   pleased   all   the people.

cs,nn3605   df,nn**5971** wcj,cs,nn3605 nn3478 wcs,qmf**3045** df,pndm1931 dfp,nn**3117** cj3588   qpf**1961**

37 For all   the people and   all   Israel understood   that   day that it was

ptn**3808** pr4480/df,nn**4428** pp,hinc**4191**   nn74   cs,nn1121   nn5369

not of*the*king to slay Abner the son of Ner.

df,nn**4428** wcs,qmf559   pr413   pl,nn,pnx**5650** qmf**3045** he,ptn**3808** cj3588   nn**8269**

38 And the king said unto his servants, Know ye not that there is a prince

wcj,aj1419   qpf**5307** df,pndm2088 df,nn**3117**   pp,nn3478

and a great man fallen this   day in Israel?

wcj,pnp595   df,nn**3117** aj7390   wcj,qptp**4886** nn**4428**   df,pndm428 wcj,df,pl,nn**376**

39 And   I   *am* this day weak, though anointed king; and these   men

pl,cs,nn**1121**   nn6870   aj**7186** pr,pnx4480   nn**3068**   pimf**7999**   pp,cs,qpta**6213**

the sons of Zeruiah *be* too hard for   me: the LORD shall reward the doer of

df,aj**7451**   pp,nn,pnx**7451**

evil according to his wickedness.

Ish-bosheth Is Assassinated

nn7586   cs,nn1121 wcs,qmf**8085** cj3588   nn74   qpf**4191**   pp,nn2275   du,nn,pnx**3027**

4 And when Saul's son heard that Abner was dead in Hebron, his hands

wcs,qmf**7503**   wcj,cs,nn3605   nn3478   nipf**926**

were feeble, and   all   the Israelites were troubled.

nn7586   cs,nn1121 qpf**1961** wcj,du,nn,nu8147 pl,nn**376**   pl,cs,nn**8269**   pl,nn**1416**   cs,nn8034

2 And Saul's son had   two   men *that were* captains of bands: the name

df,nu259   nn1196   wcj,cs,nn8034   df,nuor8145   nn7394   pl,cs,nn1121

of the one *was* Baanah, and the   name of the other Rechab, the sons of

nn7417   df,nn886   pr4480/pl,cs,nn**1121**   nn1144   cj3588   nn881   ad1571   nimf**2803**

Rimmon a Beerothite, of*the*children of Benjamin: (for Beeroth also was reckoned

pr5921   nn1144

to Benjamin:

^{df,nn886} ^{wcs,qmf1272} ^{nn,lh1664} ^{wcs,qmf1961} ^{pl,qpta1481} ^{ad8033} ^{pr5704}
3 And the Beerothites fled to Gittaim, and were sojourners there until
^{df,pndm2088 df,nn3117}
this day.)

^{wcj,pp,nn3083} ⁿⁿ⁷⁵⁸⁶ ^{cs,nn1121} ⁿⁿ¹¹²¹ ^{cs,aj5223} ^{du,nn7272} ^{qpf1961}
4 And Jonathan, Saul's son, had a son *that was* lame of *his* feet. He was
^{nu2568} ^{pl,nn8141} ^{cs,nn1121} ^{cs,nn8052} ^{pp,qnc935} ⁿⁿ⁷⁵⁸⁶ ^{wcj,nn3083} ^{pr4480/nn3157}
five years old when the tidings came of Saul and Jonathan out*of*Jezreel, and
^{qpta,pnx539} ^{wcs,qmf,pnx5375} ^{wcs,qmf5127} ^{wcs,qmf1961} ^{pp,qnc,pnx2648}
his nurse took*him*up, and fled: and it*came*to*pass, as she made haste to
^{pp,qnc5127} ^{wcs,qmf5307} ^{wcs,nimf6452} ^{wcj,nn,pnx8034} ⁿⁿ⁴⁶⁴⁸
flee, that he fell, and became lame. And his name *was* Mephibosheth.

^{pl,cs,nn1121} ⁿⁿ⁷⁴¹⁷ ^{df,nn886} ⁿⁿ⁷³⁹⁴ ^{wcj,nn1165} ^{wcs,qmf1980}
5 And the sons of Rimmon the Beerothite, Rechab and Baanah, went, and
^{wcs,qmf935} ^{pp,nn2527} ^{df,nn3117} ^{pr413} ^{cs,nn1004} ⁿⁿ³⁷⁸ ^{wcj,pnp1931} ^{qpta7901}
came about the heat of the day to the house of Ish-bosheth, who lay on
⁽⁸⁵³⁾ ^{cs,nn4904} ^{df,pl,nn6672}
a bed at noon.

^{qpf935} ^{ad2008} ^{pr5704} ^{cs,nn8432} ^{df,nn1004}
6 And they came thither into the midst of the house, *as though* they would have
^{pl,cs,qpta3947} ^{pl,nn2406} ^{wcs,himf,pnx5221} ^{pr413} ^{df,nn2570} ^{wcj,nn7394} ^{wcj,nn1196}
fetched wheat; and they smote him under the fifth *rib*: and Rechab and Baanah
^{nn,pnx251} ^{nipf4422}
his brother escaped.

^{wcs,qmf935} ^{df,nn1004} ^{wcj,pnp1931} ^{qpta7901} ^{pr5921} ^{nn,pnx4296}
7 For when they came into the house, he lay on his bed in his
^{pp,cs,nn2315/nn,pnx4904} ^{wcs,himf,pnx5221} ^{wcs,himf,pnx4191} ^{wcs,himf5493/(853)/nn,pnx7218}
bedchamber, and they smote him, and slew him, and beheaded
^{wcs,qmf3947 (853)} ^{nn,pnx7218} ^{wcs,qmf1980} ⁿⁿ¹⁸⁷⁰ ^{df,nn6160 cs,nn3605 df,nn3915}
him, and took his head, and got*them*away through the plain all night.

^{wcj,himf935 (853)} ⁿⁿ⁷²¹⁸ ⁿⁿ³⁷⁸ ^{pr413} ⁿⁿ¹⁷³² ⁿⁿ²²⁷⁵
8 And they brought the head of Ish-bosheth unto David to Hebron, and
^{wcs,qmf559 pr413} ^{df,nn4428} ^{ptdm2009} ⁿⁿ⁷²¹⁸ ⁿⁿ³⁷⁸ ^{cs,nn1121} ⁿⁿ⁷⁵⁸⁶ ^{qpta,pnx341}
said to the king, Behold the head of Ish-bosheth the son of Saul thine enemy,
^{pnl834} ^{pipf1245 (853)} ^{nn,pnx5315} ⁿⁿ³⁰⁶⁸ ^{wcs,qmf5414/pl,nn5360} ^{pp,nn,pnx113} ^{df,nn4428}
which sought thy life; and the LORD hath avenged my lord the king
^{df,pndm2088 df,nn3117 pr4480/nn7586} ^{wcj,pr4480/nn,pnx2233}
this day of Saul, and of*his*seed.

ⁿⁿ¹⁷³² ^{wcs,qmf6030 (853)} ⁿⁿ⁷³⁹⁴ ^{wcj(853)} ⁿⁿ¹¹⁹⁶ ^{nn,pnx251} ^{pl,cs,nn1121}
9 And David answered Rechab and Baanah his brother, the sons of
ⁿⁿ⁷⁴¹⁷ ^{df,nn886} ^{wcs,qmf559} ^{pp,pnx} ⁿⁿ³⁰⁶⁸ ^{aj2416} ^{pnl834}
Rimmon the Beerothite, and said unto them, *As* the LORD liveth, who hath
^{qpf6299 (853)} ^{nn,pnx5315 pr4480/cs,nn3605} ⁿⁿ⁶⁸⁶⁹
redeemed my soul out*of*all adversity,

^{cj3588} ^{df,hipt5046 pp,pnx} ^{pp,qnc559} ^{ptdm2009} ⁿⁿ⁷⁵⁸⁶ ^{qpf4191} ^{(wcj,pnp1931) pp,du,nn,pnx5869}
10 When one told me, saying, Behold, Saul is dead, thinking to
^{qpf1961} ^{pp,pipt1319} ^{wcs,qmf270} ^{pp,pnx} ^{wcs,qmf,pnx2026} ^{pp,nn6860} ^{pnl834}
have brought*good*tidings, I took hold of him, and slew him in Ziklag, who
^{pp,qnc,pnx5414 pp,pnx} ⁿⁿ¹³⁰⁹
thought that I would have given him a reward*for*his*tidings:

^{cj637} ^{cj3588} ^{aj7563} ^{pl,nn376} ^{qpf2026 (853)} ^{aj6662} ^{pl,nn376}
11 How*much*more, when wicked men have slain a righteous person in his
^{pp,nn,pnx1004} ^{pr5921} ^{nn,pnx4904} ^{he,ptn3808} ^{wcj,ad6258} ^{pimf1245 (853)} ^{nn,pnx1818}
own house upon his bed? shall I not therefore now require his blood
^{pr4480/nn,pnx3027} ^{wcs,pipf1197/pnx(853)} ^{pr4480} ^{df,nn776}
of*your*hand, and take*you*away from the earth?

nn1732   wcs,pimf**6680**   (853)   df,pl,nn5288   wcs,qmf,pnx**2026**

12 And David commanded   his young men, and they   slew   them, and

wcs,pimf7112 (853)   du,nn,pnx**3027**   wcj(853)   du,nn,pnx7272   wcs,qmf8518   pr5921   df,nn1295

cut off   their hands and   their feet,   and hanged*them*up over the pool

pp,nn2275   qpf3947 wcj(853)   nn**7218**   nn378   wcs,qmf**6912**

in Hebron. But they took   the head of Ish-bosheth, and buried it in the

pp,nn**6913**   nn74   pp,nn2275

sepulcher of Abner in Hebron.

David Also Becomes Israel's King

wcs,qmf935 cs,nn3605   pl,cs,nn**7626**   nn3478   pr413   nn1732   nn,lh2275

5 Then came   all   the tribes of Israel to David unto Hebron, and

wcs,qmf**559** pp,qnc**559** ptdm2009 pnp587   nn,pnx**6106**   wcj,nn,pnx**1320**

spoke, saying, Behold, we are thy bone and thy flesh.

ad1571   ad865/ad8032   (ad1571)   nn7586 pp,qnc**1961** nn**4428** pr,pnx5921   pnp859 qpf**1961**

2 Also in time past,   when Saul was king over us, thou wast he that

df,hipt3318   wcj,df,hipt935   (853)   nn3478   nn**3068** wcs,qmf**559** pp,pnx   pnp859

leddest out and broughtest   in Israel: and the LORD said to thee Thou shalt

qmf7462 (853)   nn,pnx**5971** (853) nn3478   wcj,pnp859   qmf**1961**   pp,nn**5057** pr5921   nn3478

feed   my people   Israel, and thou shalt be a captain over Israel.

cs,nn3605   cs,aj**2205**   nn3478 wcj,qmf935 pr413   df,nn**4428**   nn,lh2275   df,nn**4428** nn1732

3 So all the elders of Israel came to the king to Hebron; and king David

wcs,qmf**3772**   nn1285   pp,pnx   pp,nn2275   pp,pl,cs,nn**6440**   nn**3068**   wcs,qmf**4886**   (853)

made a league with them in Hebron before the LORD: and they anointed

nn1732 pp,nn**4428** pr5921   nn3478

David king over Israel.

nn1732   nu7970   nn8141 cs,nn**1121**   pp,qnc,pnx**4427**   qpf**4427**   pl,nu705

4 David was thirty years old when he began*to*reign, and he reigned forty

nn8141

years.

pp,nn2275   qpf**4427**   pr5921   nn3063   nu7651 pl,nn8141   wcj,nu8337   pl,nn2320

5 In Hebron he reigned over Judah seven years and   six   months: and in

wcj,pp,nn3389   qpf**4427**   nu7970   wcj,nu7969 nn8141 pr5921 cs,nn3605 nn3478   wcj,nn3063

Jerusalem he reigned thirty and three years over all Israel and Judah.

David Captures Zion

df,nn**4428**   wcj,pl,nn,pnx376 wcs,qmf**1980**   nn3389   pr413   df,nn2983

6 And the king and his   men   went to Jerusalem unto the Jebusites, the

qpta3427   df,nn776   wcs,qmf**559**   pp,nn1732 pp,qnc559 cj3588/cj518   hipf,pnx**5493**

inhabitants of the land: which spoke unto David, saying, Except thou take away the

df,aj5787   wcj,df,aj6455   ptn**3808**   qmf935   ad2008   pp,qnc**559**   nn1732   ptn**3808**

blind and the   lame, thou shalt not come in hither: thinking, David cannot

qmf935   ad2008

come in hither.

5:1–5   Concerning David's rise to power over all Israel, see the note on 2 Samuel 2:8–11.
5:6–10   David's first undertaking, after being crowned king of all Israel, was to conquer the city of Jerusalem. The fortress of Zion (5:6b–7) was almost invulnerable, located as it was in the mountains of Judah. It was a strategic military site, centrally located between Judah in the south and the rest of Israel in the north. It also dominated the main trade routes in the area. Salem was an early name for the city (see the notes on Gen. 14:18–20 and Judg. 1:8). Members of the nation of Israel had been living in the area, but the central fortress remained in the hands of a group of Amorite people called "Jebusites." After David captured the fortress, he began to rebuild and expand the city, making it the seat of his kingdom.

nn1732   wcs,qmf3920 (853)   cs,nn4686   nn6726   pnp1931   nn5892
7 Nevertheless David   took   the stronghold of Zion: the same *is* the city of
nn1732
David.

nn1732   wcs,qmf559   df,pndm1931 dfp,nn3117   cs,nn3605   wcj,qmf5060   dfp,nn6794
8 And David   said   on   that   day, Whosoever getteth up to the gutter, and
hipt5221   nn2983   wcj(853)   df,aj6455   wcj(853)   df,aj5787   pl,cs,qptp8130
smiteth the Jebusites, and   the lame and   the blind, *that are* hated of
nn1732   nn5315   pr5921/ad3651   qmf559   aj5787
David's soul, *he shall be chief and captain.* Wherefore they said, The blind and the
wcj,aj6455   ptn3808 qmf935   pr413   df,nn1004
lame shall not come into the house.

nn1732   wcs,qmf3427   dfp,nn4686   wcs,qmf7121 pp,pnx   nn5892   nn1732   nn1732
9 So David dwelt in the fort, and called   it   the city of David. And David
wcs,qmf1129   ad5439   pr4480 df,nn4407   wcj,nn,lh1004
built   round about from Millo and inward.

nn1732   wcs,qmf1980/qna1980   wcj,aj1419   wcj,nn3068 pl,cs,nn430   pl,nn6635
10 And David   went on,   and grew great, and the LORD   God   of hosts *was*
pr,pnx5973
with him.

David Prospers

nn2438   cs,nn4428   nn6865 wcj,qmf7971   pl,nn4397   pr413   nn1732   pl,nn730 wcj,pl,cs,nn6086
11 And Hiram   king of Tyre   sent   messengers to David, and cedar   trees,
wcj,pl,cs,nn2796/nn6086   wcj,pl,cs,nn2796/cs,nn18/nn7023   wcs,qmf1129 pp,nn1732   nn1004
and   carpenters,   and   masons: and they   built   David a house.
nn1732   wcs,qmf3045   cj3588   nn3068   hipf,pnx3559   pp,nn4428 pr5921   nn3478
12 And David perceived that the LORD had established him   king over Israel,
wcj,cj3588   pipf5375   nn,pnx4467   nn,pnx5971   nn3478   pp,pr5668
and   that   he had exalted his kingdom for his people Israel's sake.

nn1732   wcs,qmf3947   ad5750   pl,nn6370   wcj,pl,nn802   pr4480/nn3389   pr310
13 And David   took   *him* more concubines and   wives out*of*Jerusalem, after
qnc,pnx935   pr4480/nn2275   ad5750 pl,nn1121   wcj,pl,nn1323 wcs,nimf3205
he was   come   from Hebron: and there were yet   sons and daughters   born   to
pp,nn1732
David.

wcj,pndm428   pl,cs,nn8034   df,aj3209   pp,pnx   pp,nn3389
14 And   these   *be* the names of those that were born unto him in Jerusalem;
nn8051   wcj,nn7727   wcj,nn5416   wcj,nn8010
Shammua, and Shobab, and Nathan, and Solomon,
wcj,nn2984   wcj,nn474   wcj,nn5298   wcj,nn3309
15   Ibhar also, and Elishua, and Nepheg, and Japhia,
wcj,nn476   wcj,nn450   wcj,nn467
16 And Elishama, and Eliada, and Eliphalet.

David Defeats the Philistines

pl,nn6430   wcs,qmf8085 cj3588   qpf4886   (853)   nn1732   pp,nn4428 pr5921
17 But when the Philistines   heard   that they had anointed   David   king over

---

5:8   The word "gutter" refers to a concealed passageway which was cut down through the rock under the
city.

nn3478   cs,nn3605   pl,nn6430   wcs,qmf5927   pp,pinc1245 (853)   nn1732   nn1732   wcs,qmf8085

Israel, all the Philistines came up to seek   David; and David heard *of it*,

wcs,qmf3381   pr413   df,nn4686

and went down to the hold.

wcj,pl,nn6430   qpf935   wcs,nimf5203   pp,nn6010   nn7497

18 The Philistines also came and spread themselves in the valley of Rephaim.

nn1732   wcs,qmf7592   pp,nn3068   pp,qnc559   he,qmf5927 pr413   pl,nn6430

19 And David inquired of the LORD, saying, Shall I go up to the Philistines?

he,qmf,pnx5414   pp,nn,pnx3027   nn3068 wcs,qmf559 pr413   nn1732   qmv5927

wilt thou deliver them into mine hand? And the LORD said unto David, Go up:

cj3588   qna5414/qmf5414   (853)   df,pl,nn6430   pp,nn,pnx3027

for I will doubtless deliver   the Philistines into thine hand.

nn1732   wcs,qmf935   pp,nn1188 [cs,nn1168/pl,nn6556]   nn1732 wcs,himf,pnx5221   ad8033

20 And David came to   Baal-perazim,   and David   smote   them there, and

wcs,qmf559   nn3068   qpf6555   (853)   pl,qpta,pnx6440 pp,pl,nn,pnx6440

said, The LORD hath broken*forth*upon   mine enemies   before   me, as the

pp,cs,nn6556   pl,nn4325   pr5921/ad3651   qpf7121   cs,nn8034   df,pndm1931 df,nn4725 nn1188 [cs,nn1168/pl,nn6556]

breach of waters. Therefore he called the name of   that   place   Baal-perazim.

ad8033   wcs,qmf5800 (853)   pl,nn,pnx6091   nn1732   wcj,pl,nn,pnx376

21 And there they   left   their images, and David and his   men

wcs,qmf,pnx5375

burned them.

pl,nn6430   pp,qnc5927 ad5750 wcs,himf3254   wcs,nimf5203

22 And the Philistines came up yet again, and spread themselves in the

pp,nn6010   nn7497

valley of Rephaim.

nn1732   wcs,qmf7592   pp,nn3068   wcs,qmf559   ptn3808 qmf5927

23 And when David inquired of the LORD, he said, Thou shalt not go up; *but*

himv5437/pr413   pr,pnx310   wcs,qpf935   pp,pnx   pr4480/pr4136

fetch a   compass behind them, and come upon them over against the

pl,nn1057

mulberry trees.

wcj,qmf1961   pp,qnc,pnx8085 (853)   nn6963   nn6807

24 And let it   be,   when thou hearest   the sound of a going in the

pp,pl,cs,nn7218   df,pl,nn1057   ad227   qmf2782   cj3588 ad227

tops   of the mulberry trees, that then thou shalt bestir thyself: for then shall the

nn3068   qpf3318 pp,pl,nn,pnx6440   pp,hinc5221   pp,cs,nn4264   pl,nn6430

LORD go out before thee, to smite the   host of the Philistines.

nn1732   wcs,qmf6213 ad3651 pp,pnl834   nn3068   pipf,pnx6680   wcs,himf5221 (853)

25 And David did   so, as the LORD had commanded him; and smote

pl,nn6430   pr4480/nn1387   qnc,pnx935   nn1507

the Philistines from Geba until thou come to Gazer.

David Brings the Ark to Jerusalem

ad5750   nn1732   wcs,himf622   (853) cs,nn3605   qptp977   pp,nn3478 nu7970

6 Again, David gathered together   all *the* chosen *men* of Israel, thirty

nu505

thousand.

nn1732   wcs,qmf6965   wcs,qmf1980   wcj,cs,nn3605   df,nn5971 pnl834   pr,pnx854

🔑 2 And David arose, and went with   all   the people that *were* with him

---

🔑 **6:2** The ark of the covenant had stayed in the house of Abinadab for almost a century (cf. 1 Sam. 14:18),
after its capture by the Philistines and subsequent return (1 Sam. 7:1).

pr4480/pl,cs,nn1184   nn3063   pp,hinc5927   pr4480/ad8033   (853)   cs,nn727   df,pl,nn430   pnl834   nn8034

from Baale of Judah, to bring up from thence   the ark of God, whose name is

nipf7121   cs,nn8034   nn3068   pl,nn6635   qpta3427/pr,pnx5921   df,pl,nn3742

called by the name of the LORD of hosts that   dwelleth *between* the cherubims.

wcs,himf7392 (853)   cs,nn727   df,pl,nn430   pr413   aj2319   nn5699   wcs,qmf,pnx5375

3 And they   set   the ark of God upon a new cart, and brought it

pr4480/cs,nn1004   nn41   pnl834   dfp,nn1390   wcj,nn5798   wcj,nn283   pl,cs,nn1121

out*of*the*house of Abinadab that *was* in Gibeah: and Uzzah and Ahio, the   sons

nn41   pl.qpta5090 (853)   aj2319   df,nn5699

of Abinadab, drove   the new cart.

wcs,qmf,pnx5375   pr4480/cs,nn1004   nn41   pnl834   dfp,nn1390

4 And they brought it out*of*the*house of Abinadab which *was* at Gibeah,

pr5973   cs,nn727   df,pl,nn430   wcj,nn283   qpta1980   pp,pl,cs,nn6440   df,nn727

accompanying the ark of God: and Ahio went before the ark.

wcj,nn1732   wcj,cs,nn3605   cs,nn1004   nn3478   pl,pipt7832   pp,pl,cs,nn6440   nn3068

5 And David and   all   the house of Israel played before the LORD on

pp,nn3605   pl,nn1265   pl,cs,nn6086   wcj,pp,pl,nn3658

all   manner of *instruments made of* fir   wood, even on   harps,   and on

wcj,pp,pl,nn5035   wcj,pp,pl,nn8596   wcj,pp,pl,nn4517   wcj,pp,pl,nn6767

psalteries, and on timbrels, and on   cornets, and on cymbals.

wcs,qmf935 pr5704   nn5225   cs,nn1637   nn5798   wcs,qmf7971

6 And when they came   to Nachon's threshingfloor, Uzzah put forth *his hand*

pr413   cs,nn727   df,pl,nn430   wcs,qmf270   pp,pnx   cj3588   df,nn1241   qpf8058

to the ark of God, and took hold of it; for the oxen shook *it*.

nn639   nn3068   wcs,qmf2734   pp,nn5798   df,pl,nn430 wcs,himf,pnx5221

☞ 7 And the anger of the LORD was kindled against Uzzah; and God   smote

ad8033 pr5921   df,nn7944   ad8033   wcs,qmf4191 pr5973   cs,nn727   df,pl,nn430

him there for *his* error; and there he died   by the ark of God.

pp,nn1732   wcs,qmf2734   pr5921/pnl834   nn3068   qpf6555   nn6556   pp,nn5798

8 And David was displeased, because the LORD had made a breach upon Uzzah:

wcs,qmf7121   df,pndm1931 dfp,nn4725   nn6560   pr5704 df,pndm2088 df,nn3117

and he called*the*name of   the   place Perez-uzzah to   this   day.

nn1732   wcs,qmf3372   (853)   nn3068 df,pndm1931 dfp,nn3117   wcs,qmf559 ptx349

9 And David was afraid of   the LORD that   day, and said, How shall

cs,nn727   nn3068   qmf935   pr,pnx413

the ark of the LORD come   to   me?

nn1732   qpf14   wcj,ptn3808 pp,hinc5493 (853)   cs,nn727   nn3068 pr,pnx413   pr5921

10 So David would   not   remove   the ark of the LORD unto him into the

nn5892   nn1732   nn1732   wcs,himf,pnx5186   cs,nn1004   nn5654   df,nn1663

city of David: but David carried*it*aside into the house of Obed-edom the Gittite.

cs,nn727   nn3068   wcs,qmf3427   cs,nn1004   nn5654   df,nn1663

11 And the ark of the LORD continued in the house of Obed-edom the Gittite

nu7969   pl,nn2320   nn3068 wcs,pimf1288 (853)   nn5654   wcj(853) cs,nn3605   nn,pnx1004

three months: and the LORD blessed   Obed-edom, and   all his household.

wcs,homf5046   dfp,nn4428   nn1732   pp,qnc559   nn3068   pipf1288   (853)

12 And it was   told   king David, saying, The LORD hath blessed   the

cs,nn1004   nn5654   wcj(853) cs,nn3605 pnl834   pp,pnx   pp,pr5668   cs,nn727

house of Obed-edom, and   all   that *pertaineth* unto him, because of the ark

---

☞ **6:7** God's severity toward Uzzah served notice to the people of Israel that God must be revered and obeyed. Uzzah showed disrespect for God by touching the ark (Num 4:15). Furthermore, as one of the priests, he was disobeying God by letting the ark be carried on a cart. How true it is that by disobedience of God's specific instructions, one is often led into another error! The ark was supposed to be carried by the priests upon staves or poles (Ex. 25:12–15; Josh. 3:8). However, nowhere does the text indicate that Uzzah's personal, eternal salvation was involved; his intentions were good (Matt. 7:1).

df,pl,nn**430** nn1732 wcs,qmf**1980** wcs,himf**5927** (853) cs,nn**727** df,pl,nn**430** pr4480/cs,nn**1004**
of God. So David went and brought up the ark of God from*the*house of

nn5654 nn5892 nn1732 pp,nn8057
Obed-edom into the city of David with gladness.

wcs,qmf**1961** cj3588 pl,cs,qpta**5375** cs,nn**727** nn**3068**
13 And it was so, that when they that bore the ark of the LORD had

qpf6805 nu8337 pl,nn6806 wcs,qmf**2076** nn7794 wcj,nn4806
gone six paces, he sacrificed oxen and fatlings.

wcj,nn**1732** pipt3769 pp,pl,cs,nn**6440** nn**3068** pp,cs,nn3605 nn5797 wcj,nn1732
14 And David danced before the LORD with all his might; and David

qptp2296 nn906 nn646
was girded with a linen ephod.

wcj,nn**1732** wcj,cs,nn3605 cs,nn**1004** nn3478 pl,hipt**5927** (853) cs,nn**727**
15 So David and all the house of Israel brought up the ark of the

nn**3068** pp,nn8643 wcj,pp,nn6963 nn7782
LORD with shouting, and with the sound of the trumpet.

wcj,qpf**1961** cs,nn**727** nn**3068** qpta935 nn5892 nn1732 wcj,nn4324 nn7586
16 And as the ark of the LORD came into the city of David, Michal Saul's

nn1323 nipf8259 prl157 df,nn2474 wcs,qmf**7200** (853) df,nn**4428** nn1732 pipt6339 wcj,pipt3769
daughter looked through a window, and saw king David leaping and dancing

pp,pl,cs,nn**6440** nn**3068** wcs,qmf959 pp,pnx pp,nn,pnx**3820**
before the LORD; and she despised him in her heart.

wcs,himf935 (853) cs,nn**727** nn**3068** wcs,himf3322 pnx(853)
17 And they brought in the ark of the LORD, and set it in his

pp,nn,pnx4725 pp,cs,nn**8432** df,nn168 pnl834 nn1732 qpf5186 pp,pnx nn1732
place, in the midst of the tabernacle that David had pitched for it: and David

wcs,himf**5927** pl,nn5930 wcj,pl,nn**8002** pp,pl,cs,nn**6440** nn**3068**
offered burnt offerings and peace offerings before the LORD.

nn1732 wcs,pimf3615 pr4480/hinc**5927** df,nn5930
18 And as soon as David had made*an*end of offering burnt offerings and

wcj,df,pl,nn**8002** wcs,pimf1288 (853) df,nn**5971** pp,cs,nn8034 nn**3068** pl,nn6635
peace offerings, he blessed the people in the name of the LORD of hosts.

wcs,pimf2505 pp,cs,nn3605 df,nn**5971** pp,cs,nn3605 cs,nn1995
19 And he dealt among all the people, even among the whole multitude

nn3478 wcj,pr5704 nn802 pr4480/nn376 pp,nn376 nu259 cs,nn2471 nn3899
of Israel, as well to the women as men, to every one a cake of bread, and

nu259 wcj,nn829 nu259 wcj,nn809 cs,nn3605 df,nn**5971** wcs,qmf**1980**
a good piece of flesh, and a flagon of wine. So all the people departed

nn376 pp,nn,pnx**1004**
every one to his house.

nn1732 wcs,qmf**7725** pp,pinc**1288** (853) nn,pnx**1004** nn4324 nn1323
20 Then David returned to bless his household. And Michal the daughter

nn7586 wcs,qmf3318 pp,qnc7125 nn1732 wcs,qmf559 pnit4100 nipf**3513** nn**4428** nn3478
of Saul came out to meet David, and said, How glorious was the king of Israel

df,nn3117 pnl834 nipf**1540** df,nn3117 pp,du,cs,nn5869 pl,cs,nn519
today, who uncovered himself today in the eyes of the handmaids of his

pl,nn,pnx**5650** nu259 df,aj7386 pp,ninc**1540**/ninc**1540**
servants, as one of the vain fellows shamelessly*uncovereth*himself!

nn1732 wcs,qmf**559** pr413 nn4324 pp,pl,cs,nn**6440** nn**3068** pnl834 qpf**977** pp,pnx
21 And David said unto Michal, It was before the LORD, which chose me

pr4480/nn,pnx1 wcj,pr4480/cs,nn3605 nn,pnx**1004** pp,pinc**6680** pnx(853) nn5057 pr5921
before*thy*father, and before all his house, to appoint me ruler over the

nn**5971** nn**3068** pr5921 nn3478 wcj,pipf7832 pp,pl,cs,nn**6440** nn**3068**
people of the LORD, over Israel: therefore will I play before the LORD.

ad5750 wcj,nipf**7043** pr4480/pndm2063 wcj,qpf**1961** aj8217
22 And I will yet be*more*vile than thus, and will be base in mine own

pp,du,nn,pnx5869   wcj,pr5973   df,pl,nn519   pnl834   qpf559

sight: and   of   the maidservants which thou hast spoken of, of them shall I be

nimf3513

had in honor.

wcj,pp,nn4324   nn1323   nn7586 qpf1961/pp,pnx ptn3808 nn3206 pr5704   nn3117

23 Therefore Michal the daughter of Saul   had   no child unto the day of

nn,pnx4194

her death.

God's Promise to David

wcs,qmf1961   cj3588   df,nn4428 qpf3427   pp,nn,pnx1004   wcj,nn3068

7 And it*came*to*pass, when the king sat in his house, and the LORD had

hipf5117   pr4480/ad5439   pr4480/cs,nn3605 pl,qpta,pnx341

given him rest round about from all his enemies;

df,nn4428 wcs,qmf559 pr413   nn5416   df,nn5030   qmv7200 pte4994 pnp595 qpta3427

2 That the king   said   unto Nathan the prophet, See now,   I   dwell in a

pp,cs,nn1004   pl,nn730   wcj,cs,nn727 df,pl,nn430 qpta3427 pp,cs,nn8432 df,nn3407

house of cedar, but the   ark   of God dwelleth within curtains.

nn5416 wcs,qmf559 pr413   df,nn4428 qmv1980 qmv6213 nn3605 pnl834   pp,nn,pnx3824 cj3588

3 And Nathan said   to the king, Go,   do   all that is in thine heart; for

nn3068 pr,pnx5973

the LORD is with thee.

wcs,qmf1961   df,pndm1931 dfp,nn3915   cs,nn1697   nn3068 wcj,qmf1961 pr413

☞ 4 And it*came*to*pass   that   night, that the word of the LORD came unto

nn5416   pp,qnc559

Nathan, saying,

qmv1980   wcj,qpf559/pr413   nn,pnx5650 (pr413)   nn1732 ad3541 qpf559   nn3068   df,pnp859

5 Go and   tell   my servant   David, Thus saith the LORD, Shalt thou

qmf1129 pp,pnx   nn1004   pp,qnc,pnx3427

build me a house for me to   dwell in?

cj3588   ptn3808 qpf3427   pp,nn1004   pr4480/nn3117   hinc,pnx5927 (853)

6 Whereas I have not dwelt in any house since*the*time that I brought up

pl,cs,nn1121   nn3478   pr4480/nn4714   wcj,pr5704 df,pndm2088 df,nn3117 wcs,qmf1961 htpt1980

the children of Israel out*of*Egypt, even to   this   day, but have walked in

pp,nn168   wcj,pp,nn4908

a tent and in a tabernacle.

pp,nn3605   pnl834   htpf1980   pp,cs,nn3605 pl,cs,nn1121   nn3478

7 In   all   the places wherein I have walked with   all   the children of Israel

pipf1696   he,nn1697 pr854 nu259   pl,cs,nn7626   nn3478 pnl834   pipf6680   pp,qnc7462 (853)

spoke I a word with any of the tribes of Israel, whom I commanded to   feed

nn,pnx5971 (853) nn3478 pp,qnc559 pnit4100 qpf1129 ptn3808   cs,nn1004   pl,nn730

my people   Israel, saying, Why build ye not me a house of cedar?

wcj,ad6258   ad3541   qmf559   pp,nn,pnx5650 pp,nn1732 ad3541 qpf559

8 Now therefore so shalt thou say unto my servant David, Thus saith the

---

☞ **7:4-16** David's desire to build a house for the Lord sets the stage for one of the key passages in Scripture relating to the coming Messiah (see the note on 1 Sam. 16:13). God's message through Nathan (vv. 8–16) is called the Davidic Covenant. It is both an expansion and a clarification of God's promises to Abraham. It represents an unconditional promise to David that he would be the head of an everlasting kingdom (v. 16). David is also promised that his son would reign over Israel (v. 12), and that this son (Solomon) would be the one to build a house for the Lord (v. 13). Elsewhere, God's reasons for not allowing David to build the temple are spelled out: he was a man of war and bloodshed (1 Kgs. 5:3; 1 Chr. 22:8; 28:3), whereas his son would be a man of peace. It was also too early to build the temple–the city is not yet secure (1 Kgs. 5:3, 4). David was, however, permitted to begin stockpiling the materials Solomon would use to build the temple (1 Chr. 22:2–19).

nn3068   pl,nn6635 pnp589 qpf3947   pr4480   df,nn5116   pr4480/pr310   df,nn6629
LORD of hosts, I   took   thee from the sheepcote, from following the sheep, to
pp,qnc1961 nn5057 pr5921 nn,pnx5971 pr5921 nn3478
be   ruler over my people, over Israel:

                    wcs,qmf1961 pr,pnx5973   pp,nn3605/pnl834   qpf1980   wcs,himf3772 (853)
9 And I   was   with thee whithersoever thou wentest, and have cut off
cs,nn3605   pl,qpta,pnx341   pr4480/pl,nn,pnx6440   wcj,qpf6213 pp,pnx   aj1419   nn8034
all   thine enemies out*of*thy*sight, and have made thee a great name, like unto
pp,cs,nn8034   df,aj1419   pnl834   dfp,nn776
the name of the great men that are in the earth.

                    wcj,qpf7760   nn4725   pp,nn,pnx5971 pp,nn3478   wcj,qpf,pnx5193
10 Moreover I will appoint a place for my people Israel, and will   plant
                    wcj,qpf7931   pr,pnx8478   qmf7264 wcj,ptn3808 ad5750 wcj,ptn3808
them, that they may dwell in a place of their own, and move no   more; neither
pl,cs,nn1121   nn5766   pp,pinc,pnx6031   himf3254 pp,pnl834   dfp,aj7223
shall the children of wickedness   afflict   them any more,   as   beforetime,

                    wcj,pp,pr4480   df,nn3117 pnl834   pipf6680   pl,qpta8199   pr5921   nn,pnx5971
11 And as since   the time that I commanded judges to be over my people
nn3478   pp,pnx   wcj,hipf5117 pr4480/cs,nn3605 pl,qpta,pnx341   nn3068
Israel, and have caused thee to   rest   from all thine enemies. Also the LORD
wcj,hipf5046 pp,pnx cj3588   qmf6213 pp,pnx   nn1004
telleth thee that he will make thee a house.

                    cj3588   pl,nn,pnx3117   qmf4390   wcs,qpf7901 pr854   pl,nn,pnx1
12 And when thy days be fulfilled, and thou shalt sleep with thy fathers, I
wcs,hipf6965 (853)   nn,pnx2233 pr,pnx310   pnl834   qmf3318   pr4480/pl,nn,pnx4578
will set up   thy seed after thee, which shall proceed out*of*thy*bowels, and I
wcs,hipf3559 (853)   nn,pnx4467
will establish   his kingdom.

                    pnp1931   qmf1129   nn1004   pp,nn,pnx8034   wcs,pipf3559 (853)   nn3678
☞ 13 He shall build a house for my name, and I will establish   the throne
nn,pnx4467 pr5704/nn5769
of his kingdom forever.

                    pnp589   qmf1961 pp,pnx   pp,nn1   wcj,pnp1931   qmf1961 pp,pnx pp,nn1121 pnl834
14 I   will be   his father, and   he   shall be   my   son. If he
pp,hinc,pnx5753   wcs,hipf,pnx3198   pp,cs,nn7626   pl,nn376
commit iniquity, I will chasten him with the rod   of men, and with the
wcj,pp,pl,cs,nn5061   pl,cs,nn1121   nn120
stripes   of the children of men:

                    wcj,nn,pnx2617   ptn3808   qmf5493   pr,pnx4480   pp,pnl834   hipf5493   pr4480/pr5973
15 But my mercy shall not depart away from him,   as   I took it   from
nn7586   pnl834   hipf5493   pr4480/pl,nn,pnx6440
Saul, whom I put away   before   thee.

                    nn,pnx1004   wcj,nn,pnx4467   wcj,nipf539   pr5704/nn5769 pp,pl,nn,pnx6440
16 And thine house and thy kingdom shall be established forever   before
nn,pnx3678   qmf1961   nipt3559   pr5704/nn5769
thee: thy throne shall be established forever.

                    pp,nn3605 df,pndm428 df,pl,nn1697   wcj,pp,nn3605 df,pndm2088 df,nn2384
17 According to all   these words, and according to   all   this   vision,
ad3651   nn5416   pipf1696 pr413 nn1732
so did Nathan speak unto David.

☞ 7:13 This refers initially to Solomon, but ultimately the reference is to Jesus Christ, the "Son of David" (Luke 1:31–33; Acts 2:25–35) who reigns at God's right hand (Ps. 2:7; Acts 13:33).

David's Prayer of Appreciation

wcs,qmf935   df,nn4428   nn1732   wcs,qmf3427   pp,pl,cs,nn6440   nn3069   wcs,qmf559

18 Then went king David in, and sat before the LORD, and he said,

pnit4310   pnp595   nn136   nn3069   wcj,pnit4310   nn,pnx1004   cj3588   hipf,pnx935

Who am I, O Lord GOD? and what is my house, that thou hast brought me

pr5704/ad1988

hitherto?

pndm2063   ad5750   wcs,qmf6994   pp,du,nn,pnx5869   nn136   nn3069

19 And this was yet a small thing in thy sight, O Lord GOD; but thou

wcs,pimf1696   ad1571   pr413   nn,pnx5650   cs,nn1004   pp,pr4480/aj7350

hast spoken also of thy servant's house for*a*great*while*to*come. And is

wcj,pndm2063   cs,nn8452   df,nn120   nn136   nn3069

this the manner of man, O Lord GOD?

wcj,pnit4100   nn1732   himf3254/pp,pinc1696   ad5750   pr,pnx413   wcj,pnp859   nn136   nn3069

20 And what can David   say   more unto thee? for thou, Lord GOD,

qpf3045   (853)   nn,pnx5650

knowest   thy servant.

pp,pr5668/nn,pnx1697   wcj,pp,nn,pnx3820   qpf6213

21 For*thy*word's*sake, and according to thine own heart, hast thou done

(853) cs,nn3605 df,pndm2063   df,nn1420   (853)   nn,pnx5650 pp,hinc3045

all these great things, to make thy servant know them.

pr5921/ad3651   qpf1431   nn3068   nn136   cj3588   ptn369   pp,pnx3644   wcj,ptn369

22 Wherefore thou art great, O LORD God: for there is none like thee, neither

pl,nn,pnx430   pr,pnx2108   pp,nn3605   pnl834   qpf8085

is there any God beside thee, according to all that we have heard with our

pp,du,nn,pnx241

ears.

wcj,pnit4310   nu259   nn1471   dfp,nn776   pp,nn,pnx5971   pp,nn3478

23 And what one nation in the earth is like thy people, even like Israel,

pnl834   pl,nn430 qpf1980   pp,qnc6299   pp,nn5971   pp,pnx   wcj,pp,qnc7760 pp,pnx   nn8034

whom God went to redeem for a people to himself, and to make him a name,

wcj,pp,qnc6213   pp,pnx   df,nn1420   wcj,pl,nipt3372   pp,nn,pnx776 pr4480/pl,cs,nn6440

and to do for you great things and terrible, for thy land, before thy

nn,pnx5971   pnl834   qpf6299   pp,pnx   pr4480/nn4714   pl,nn1471

people, which thou redeemedst to thee from Egypt, from the nations and their

wcj,pl,nn,pnx430

gods?

wcs,pimf3559   pp,pnx   (853)   nn,pnx5971   nn3478   pp,nn5971

☉⇌ 24 For thou hast confirmed to thyself   thy people Israel to be a people

pp,pnx   pr5704/nn5769   wcj,pnp859   nn3068   qpf1961   pp,pnx pp,pl,nn430

unto thee forever: and thou, LORD, art become their God.

wcj,ad6258   nn3068 pl,nn430   df,nn1697 pnl834   pipf1696   pr5921

25 And now, O LORD God, the word that thou hast spoken concerning thy

nn,pnx5650   wcj,pr5921   nn,pnx1004   himv6965   pr5704/nn5769   wcj,qmv6213 pp,pnl834

servant, and concerning his house, establish it, forever, and do as thou hast

pipf1696

said.

nn,pnx8034   wcj,qmf1431   pr5704/nn5769   pp,qnc559   nn3068   pl,nn6635

26 And let thy name be magnified forever, saying, The LORD of hosts is the

---

☉⇌ **7:24** These words affirm a central promise of the Scriptures to the Jewish people that He would be their God and they would be His people eternally (Gen. 17:7; Ex. 6:7; Deut. 7:6–9; Rom. 11:1–26; Rev. 21:3).

pl,nn**430** pr5921 nn3478   wcj,cs,nn**1004**   nn,pnx5650 nn1732 qmf**1961** nipt3559   pp,pl,nn,pnx**6440**
God over Israel: and let the house of thy servant David be established before

thee.

cj3588   pnp859   nn**3068**   pl,nn**6635** pl,cs,nn**430**   nn3478   qpf1540/nn**241**   nn,pnx5650
27 For thou, O LORD of hosts, God of Israel, hast revealed to thy servant,

pp,qnc559   qmf1129 pp,pnx   nn1004 pr5921/ad3651   nn,pnx5650 qpf4672   (853)   nn,pnx**3820**
saying, I will build thee a house: therefore hath thy servant found in   his heart

pp,htnc**6419** (853) df,pndm2063 df,nn**8605** pr,pnx413
to pray   this   prayer unto thee.

wcj,ad6258   nn136   nn3069 pnp859   pnp1931 df,pl,nn**430**   wcj,pl,nn,pnx1697 qmf**1961** nn571
28 And now, O Lord GOD, thou *art* that God, and thy   words   be true,

wcs,pimf**1696** (853) df,pndm2063 df,nn**2896**   pr413   nn,pnx5650
and thou hast promised   this   goodness unto thy servant:

wcj,ad6258   himv2794   wcj,pimv**1288** (853)   cs,nn**1004**   nn,pnx5650
29 Therefore now let it please thee to bless   the house of thy servant,

pp,qnc**1961**   pp,nn5769   pp,pl,nn,pnx**6440**   cj3588 pnp859   nn136   nn3069   pipf**1696**
that it may continue forever   before   thee: for thou, O Lord GOD, hast spoken *it*:

wcj,pr4480/nn,pnx1293   cs,nn**1004**   nn,pnx5650   pumf**1288**   pp,nn5769
and with*thy*blessing let the house of thy servant be blessed forever.

David's Military Success

pr310   ad**3651**   wcs,qmf**1961**   nn1732 wcs,himf5221 (853)   pl,nn**6430**
8 And after this it*came*to*pass, that David smote   the Philistines, and

wcs,himf,pnx3665   nn1732 wcs,qmf3947 (853)   nn4965   pr4480/cs,nn**3027**
subdued them: and David took   Metheg-ammah out*of*the*hand of

pl,nn**6430**
the Philistines.

wcs,himf**5221**   (853)   nn4124   wcs,pimf,pnx4058   dfp,nn**2256**
2 And he   smote   Moab, and measured them with a   line,

hina7901/pnx(853)   nn,lh776   du,cs,nu8147   pl,nn**2256**   wcs,pimf4058
casting*them*down to the ground; even with two   lines measured he to

pp,hinc**4191**   wcj,nn4393 df,nn**2256**   pp,hinc2421   nn4124   wcs,qmf**1961**
put*to*death, and with one full   line to*keep*alive. And *so* the Moabites became

pp,nn1732 dfp,pl,nn**5650**   pl,cs,qpta5375 nn4503
David's servants, *and* brought gifts.

nn1732   wcs,himf**5221**   (853)   nn1909   cs,nn**1121**   nn7340   nn**4428**   nn6678
3 David smote also   Hadadezer, the son of Rehob, king of Zobah, as he

pp,qnc,pnx**1980** pp,hinc7725   nn,pnx**3027**   pp,cs,nn5104   nn6578
went   to recover his border at the river Euphrates.

nn1732   wcs,qmf3920 pr,pnx4480   nu505   wcj,cs,nu7651   pl,nu3967
4 And David took   from him a thousand *chariots*, and   seven   hundred

pl,nn6571   wcj,pl,nu6242   nu505   nn376/aj7273   nn1732   wcs,pimf6131 (853) cs,nn3605   df,nn7393
horsemen, and twenty thousand footmen: and David hamstrung   all   the chariot

wcs,himf3498 pr,pnx4480   nu3967   nn7393
horses, but reserved of   them *for* a hundred chariots.

cs,nn758   nn1834   wcs,qmf935   pp,qnc5826   pp,nn1909   nn**4428**
5 And when the Syrians of Damascus came to succor Hadadezer king of

nn6678   nn1732 wcs,himf**5221**   pp,nn758 wcj,du,nu8147   pl,nu6242   nu505   nn376
Zobah, David slew of the Syrians   two   and twenty thousand men.

nn1732   wcs,qmf**7760**   pl,nn5333   nn758   nn1834   nn758   wcs,qmf**1961**
6 Then David   put   garrisons in Syria of Damascus: and the Syrians became

dfp,pl,nn**5650**   pp,nn1732   pl,cs,qpta**5375**   nn**4503**   nn**3068**   wcs,himf**3467**   (853)   nn1732

servants to David, *and* brought gifts. And the LORD preserved   David

pp,nn3605/pnl834   qpf**1980**

whithersoever he went.

nn1732   wcs,qmf3947   (853)   pl,cs,nn**7982**   df,nn2091 pnl834 qpf**1961** pr413   pl,cs,nn**5650**

7 And David   took   the shields of gold that were on the servants of

nn1909   wcs,himf,pnx935   nn3389

Hadadezer, and brought them to Jerusalem.

wcj,pr4480/nn984   wcj,pr4480/nn1268   pl,cs,nn5892   nn1909   df,nn**4428** nn1732 qpf3947

8 And from Betah, and from Berothai, cities of Hadadezer, king David took

ad3966   hina7235   nn5178

exceeding much brass.

nn8583   nn**4428**   nn2574   wcs,qmf**8085** cj3588 nn1732   hipf**5221**   (853) cs,nn3605   cs,nn**2428**

9 When Toi king of Hamath heard that David had smitten   all the host

nn1909

of Hadadezer,

nn8583   wcs,qmf7971   (853)   nn3141   nn,pnx1121 pr413 df,nn**4428** nn1732   pp,qnc**7592**/pp,nn**7965**

10 Then Toi   sent   Joram his   son   unto king David, to   salute

wcj,pp,pinc,pnx**1288**   pr5921/pnl834   nipf3898   pp,nn1909

him, and to   bless   him, because he had fought against Hadadezer, and

wcs,himf,pnx**5221**   cj3588   nn1909   (nn376) qpf**1961** pl,cs,nn4421   nn8583   qpf**1961**

smitten   him: for Hadadezer   had   wars with Toi. And *Joram* brought

wcj,pp,nn,pnx**3027**   pl,cs,nn3627   nn3701   wcj,pl,cs,nn3627   nn2091   wcj,pl,cs,nn3627   nn5178

with   him vessels of silver, and vessels of gold, and vessels of brass:

ad1571   df,nn**4428**   nn1732   hipf**6942**   pp,nn**3068** pr5973   df,nn3701

11 Which also king David did dedicate unto the LORD, with the silver and

wcj,df,nn2091 pnl834   hipf**6942**   pr4480/cs,nn3605 df,pl,nn**1471** pnl834   pipf3533

gold   that he had dedicated of all   nations which he subdued;

pr4480/nn758   wcj,pr4480/nn4124   wcj,pr4480/pl,cs,nn**1121**   nn5983

12 Of Syria,   and   of Moab,   and   of*the*children of   Ammon, and

wcj,pr4480/pl,nn6430   pr4480/nn6002   wcj,pr4480/cs,nn7998   nn1909   cs,nn**1121**   nn7340

of*the*Philistines, and of Amalek, and of*the*spoil of Hadadezer, son of Rehob,

cs,nn**4428**   nn6678

king of Zobah.

nn1732   wcs,qmf**6213**   nn8034   pp,qnc,pnx**7725**   pr4480/hinc,pnx**5221**   (853)

13 And David   got   *him* a name when he returned from smiting of   the

nn758   pp,cs,nn1516   nn4417   nu8083/nu6240   nu**505**

Syrians in the valley of salt, *being* eighteen thousand *men*.

wcs,qmf**7760**   pl,nn5333   pp,nn123   pp,cs,nn3605   nn123   qpf**7760**

14 And he   put   garrisons in Edom; throughout all   Edom put he

pl,nn5333   cs,nn3605   nn123   wcs,qmf**1961** pp,nn1732   pl,nn**5650**   nn**3068**

garrisons, and   all   they of Edom became David's servants. And the LORD

wcs,himf**3467** (853) nn1732   pp,nn3605/pnl834   qpf**1980**

preserved   David whithersoever he went.

David's Officials

nn1732   wcs,qmf**4427** pr5921 cs,nn3605   nn3478   wcs(qmf**1961**) nn1732   qpta**6213**   nn**4941**

15 And David reigned over   all   Israel; and   David executed judgment

wcj,nn**6666**   pp,cs,nn3605   nn,pnx**5971**

and justice unto   all   his people.

wcj,nn3097   cs,nn**1121**   nn6870   pr5921   df,nn**6635**   wcj,nn3092

16 And Joab the son of Zeruiah *was* over the host; and Jehoshaphat the

cs,nn**1121**   nn286   hipt**2142**

son of Ahilud *was* recorder;

17 And Zadok the son of Ahitub, and Ahimelech the son of Abiathar, *were* the priests; and Seraiah *was* the scribe;

18 And Benaiah the son of Jehoiada *was over* both the Cherethites and the Pelethites; and David's sons were chief rulers.

David's Kindness to Mephibosheth

9 And David said, Is there yet any that is left of the house of Saul, that I may show him kindness for Jonathan's sake?

2 And *there was* of the house of Saul a servant whose name *was* Ziba. And when they had called him unto David, the king said unto him, *Art* thou Ziba? And he said, Thy servant *is* he.

3 And the king said, *Is* there not yet any of the house of Saul, that I may show the kindness of God unto him? And Ziba said unto the king, Jonathan hath yet a son, *which is* lame on *his* feet.

4 And the king said unto him, Where *is* he? And Ziba said unto the king, Behold, he *is* in the house of Machir, the son of Ammiel, in Lo-debar.

5 Then king David sent, and fetched him out*of*the*house of Machir, the son of Ammiel, from Lo-debar.

6 Now when Mephibosheth, the son of Jonathan, the son of Saul, was come unto David, he fell on his face, and did reverence. And David said, Mephibosheth. And he answered, Behold thy servant!

7 And David said unto him, Fear not: for I will surely show thee kindness for Jonathan thy father's sake, and will restore thee (853) all the land of Saul thy father; and thou shalt eat bread at my table continually.

8 And he bowed himself, and said, What *is* thy servant, that thou shouldest look upon such a dead dog as I *am*?

9 Then the king called to Ziba, Saul's servant, and said unto him, I have

qpf**5414** pl,nn,pnx113 pp,cs,nn1121 nn3605 pnl834 qpf**1961** pp,nn7586 wcj,pp,cs,nn3605
given unto thy master's son all that pertained to Saul and to all his

nn,pnx**1004**
house.

pnp859 wcj,pl,nn,pnx**1121** wcj,pl,nn,pnx**5650** wcj,qpf**5647** (853)
10 Thou therefore, and thy sons, and thy servants, shall till the

df,nn**127** pp,pnx wcj,hipf935 pl,nn,pnx113 pp,cs,nn**1121**
land for him, and thou shalt bring in *the fruits*, that thy master's son may

wcj,qpf**1961** nn3899 wcj,qpf,pnx398 wcj,nn4648 pl,nn,pnx113 cs,nn**1121** qmf398 nn3899 nn**8548**
have food to eat: but Mephibosheth thy master's son shall eat bread always

pr5921 nn,pnx7979 wcj,pp,nn6717 nu2568/nu6240 pl,nn**1121** wcj,pl,nu6242 pl,nn**5650**
at my table. Now Ziba had fifteen sons and twenty servants.

wcs,qmf**559** nn6717 pr413 df,nn**4428** pp,nn3605 pnl834 nn,pnx113 df,nn**4428**
11 Then said Ziba unto the king, According to all that my lord the king

pimf**6680** (853) nn,pnx**5650** ad3651 nn,pnx**5650** qmf**6213** wcj,nn4648
hath commanded his servant, so shall thy servant do. As for Mephibosheth,

qpta398 pr5921 nn,pnx7979 pp,nu259 pr4480/pl,cs,nn**1121**/df,nn**4428**
said the king, he shall eat at my table, as one of*the*king's*sons.

wcj,pp,nn4648 aj6996 nn**1121** wcj,nn,pnx8034 nn4316
12 And Mephibosheth had a young son, whose name *was* Micha. And

wcj,nn3605 cs,nn**4186** cs,nn**1004** nn6717 pl,nn**5650** pp,nn4648
all that dwelt in the house of Ziba *were* servants unto Mephibosheth.

wcj,nn4648 qpta**3427** pp,nn3389 cj3588 pnp1931 qpta398 nn**8548** pr5921
13 So Mephibosheth dwelt in Jerusalem: for he did eat continually at the

df,nn**4428** cs,nn7979 wcj(pnp1931) aj6455 du,cs,nu8147 du,nn,pnx7272
king's table; and was lame on both his feet.

Israel Defeats the Ammonites And Syrians

wcs,qmf**1961** pr310 ad3651 nn**4428** pl,cs,nn**1121**
10 And it*came*to*pass after this, that the king of the children of

nn5983 wcs,qmf**4191** nn2586 nn,pnx1121 wcs,qmf**4427** pr,pnx8478
Ammon died, and Hanun his son reigned in his stead.

wcs,qmf**559** nn1732 qmf**6213** nn**2617** pr5973 nn2586 cs,nn**1121** nn5176
2 Then said David, I will show kindness unto Hanun the son of Nahash,

pp,pnl834 nn,pnx1 qpf**6213** nn**2617** pr,pnx5973 nn1732 wcs,qmf7971 pp,pinc,pnx**5162**
as his father showed kindness unto me. And David sent to comfort him by

pp,cs,nn**3027** pl,nn,pnx**5650** pr413 nn,pnx1 nn1732 pl,cs,nn**5650** wcs,qmf935 nn776
the hand of his servants for his father. And David's servants came into the land

pl,cs,nn**1121** nn5983
of the children of Ammon.

pl,cs,nn**8269** pl,cs,nn**1121** nn5983 wcs,qmf**559** pr413 nn2586 pl,nn,pnx113
3 And the princes of the children of Ammon said unto Hanun their lord,

pp,du,nn,pnx**5869** nn1732 df,pipt**3513** (853) nn,pnx1 cj3588 qpf7971 pl,pipt**5162**
Thinkest thou that David doth honor thy father, that he hath sent comforters

pp,pnx df,ptn**3808** nn1732 qpf7971 (853) pl,nn,pnx**5650** pr,pnx413 pp,pr5668 qnc2713 (853)
unto thee? hath not David *rather* sent his servants unto thee, to search

df,nn**5892** wcj,pp,pinc,pnx7270 wcj,pp,qnc,pnx**2015**
the city, and to spy*it*out, and to overthrow it?

nn2586 wcs,qmf3947 nn1732 (853) pl,cs,nn**5650** wcs,pimf1548 (853)
4 Wherefore Hanun took David's servants, and shaved off the

nn2677 nn,pnx**2206** wcs,qmf3772 (853) pl,nn,pnx4063 dfp,nn2677 pr5704
one half of their beards, and cut off their garments in the middle, *even* to their

pl,nn,pnx8357 wcs,pimf,pnx7971
buttocks, and sent*them*away.

^{wcs,himf5046}   ^{pp,nn1732}   ^{wcs,qmf7971}   ^{pp,qnc,pnx7125}   ^{cj3588}

5 When they   told   *it* unto David, he   sent   to   meet   them, because the

^{df,pl,nn376 qpf1961}   ^{ad3966}   ^{pl,nipt3637}   ^{df,nn4428 wcs,qmf559 qmv3427}   ^{pp,nn3405 pr5704}   ^{nn,pnx2206}

men were greatly ashamed: and the king   said, Tarry at Jericho until your beards

^{pimf6779}   ^{wcs,qpf7725}

be grown, and *then* return.

^{pl,cs,nn1121}   ⁿⁿ⁵⁹⁸³   ^{wcs,qmf7200 cj3588}   ^{nipf887}   ^{pp,nn1732}

6 And when the children of Ammon   saw   that they stank before David, the

^{pl,cs,nn1121}   ⁿⁿ⁵⁹⁸³   ^{wcs,qmf7971}   ^{wcs,qmf7936 (853)}   ^{cs,nn758}   ⁿⁿ¹⁰⁵⁰   ^{wcj(853)}

children of Ammon   sent   and hired   the Syrians of Beth-rehob, and   the

^{cs,nn758}   ⁿⁿ⁶⁶⁷⁸ ^{pl,nu6242} ^{nu505}   ^{aj7273}   ^{wcj(853)}   ⁿⁿ⁴⁴²⁸ ⁿⁿ⁴⁶⁰¹   ^{nu505}

Syrians of Zoba, twenty thousand footmen, and   of king Maacah a thousand

ⁿⁿ³⁷⁶   ⁿⁿ³⁸²   ^{du,nu8147/nu6240}   ^{nu505}   ⁿⁿ³⁷⁶

men, and of Ish-tob   twelve   thousand men.

^{nn1732 wcs,qmf8085}   ^{wcs,qmf7971 (853) nn3097}   ^{wcj(853) cs,nn3605}   ^{df,nn6635}

7 And when David heard of *it*, he   sent   Joab, and   all   the host

^{df,pl,nn1368}

of the mighty men.

^{pl,cs,nn1121}   ⁿⁿ⁵⁹⁸³   ^{wcs,qmf3318}   ⁿⁿ⁴⁴²¹   ^{wcs,qmf6186}

8 And the children of Ammon came out, and put the battle in array   at the

ⁿⁿ⁶⁶⁰⁷   ^{df,nn8179}   ^{wcj,cs,nn758}   ⁿⁿ⁶⁶⁷⁸   ^{wcj,nn7340}   ⁿⁿ³⁸²

entering in of the gate: and the Syrians of Zoba, and of Rehob, and Ishtob, and

^{wcj,nn4601}   ^{pp,nn,pnx905}   ^{dfp,nn7704}

Maacah, *were* by themselves in the field.

^{nn3097 wcs,qmf7200 cj3588}   ^{pl,cs,nn6440}   ^{df,nn4421 qpf1961 pr,pnx413}   ^{pr4480/pl,nn6440}

9 When Joab   saw   that the front of the battle was against him before and

^{wcj,pr4480/nn268}   ^{wcs,qmf977} ^{pr4480/cs,nn3605}   ^{pl,cs,qptp977}   ⁿⁿ³⁴⁷⁸   ^{wcj,qmf6186}

behind,   he chose   of all   the choice *men* of Israel, and put*them*in*array

^{pp,qnc7125}   ⁿⁿ⁷⁵⁸

against the Syrians:

^{wcj(853)}   ^{cs,nn3499}   ^{df,nn5971}   ^{qpf5414}   ^{pp,cs,nn3027}   ⁿⁿ⁵²

10 And   the rest of the people he delivered into the hand of Abishai his

^{nn,pnx251}   ^{wcj,qmf6186}   ^{pp,qnc7125}   ^{pl,cs,nn1121}   ⁿⁿ⁵⁹⁸³

brother, that he might put*them*in*array against the children of Ammon.

^{wcs,qmf559 cj518}   ⁿⁿ⁷⁵⁸   ^{qmf2388}   ^{pr,pnx4480}   ^{wcs,qpf1961}

11 And he said, If the Syrians be too strong   for   me, then thou shalt

^{pp,nn3444 pp,pnx}   ^{wcj,cj518}   ^{pl,cs,nn1121}   ⁿⁿ⁵⁹⁸³   ^{qmf2388} ^{pr,pnx4480}

help me: but   if the children of Ammon be too strong   for   thee, then I will

^{wcs,qpf1980}   ^{pp,hinc3467} ^{pp,pnx}

come and help thee.

^{qmv2388}   ^{wcj,htmf2388}   ^{pr1157}   ^{nn,pnx5971}   ^{pp,pr1157}

12 Be*of*good*courage, and let us play*the*men for our people, and for

^{pl,cs,nn5892}   ^{pl,nn,pnx430}   ^{wcj,nn3068 qmf6213}   ^{pp,du,nn,pnx5869}   ^{df,aj2896}

the cities of our God: and the LORD do that which seemeth him good.

ⁿⁿ³⁰⁹⁷   ^{wcs,qmf5066}   ^{wcj,df,nn5971 pnl834}   ^{pr,pnx5973}   ^{dfp,nn4421}

13 And Joab drew nigh, and the people that *were* with him, unto the battle

^{pp,nn758}   ^{wcs,qmf5127 pr4480/pl,nn,pnx6440}

against the Syrians: and they fled   before   him.

^{wcj,pl,cs,nn1121}   ⁿⁿ⁵⁹⁸³   ^{qpf7200 cj3588}   ⁿⁿ⁷⁵⁸   ^{qpf5127}

☞ 14 And when the children of Ammon saw that the Syrians were fled, then

---

☞ **10:14** After the rainy season was over, Joab commenced the siege the next spring (2 Sam. 11:1). It was too late in the year to undertake a full-scale siege.

wcs,qmf5127　　　pr4480/pl,cs,nn**6440**　　　nn52　　　　wcs,qmf935　　　df,nn5892　　　nn3097　　wcs,qmf**7725**
fled　they　also　before　Abishai,　and　entered　into　the　city.　So　Joab　returned
pr4480/pr5921　　pl,cs,nn**1121**　　　　nn5983　　　wcs,qmf935　　　nn3389
from　the　children　of　Ammon,　and　came　to　Jerusalem.

　　　　　　　　nn758　　wcs,qmf**7200**　cj3588　　　　　　　nipf**5062**　pp,pl,cs,nn**6440**　nn3478
15 And　when　the　Syrians　saw　that　they　were　smitten　before　Israel,　they
wcs,nimf**622**　　　ad3162
gathered　themselves　together.

　　　　　nn1928　　wcs,qmf7971　　　wcs,himf3318　(853)　　nn758　pnl834　　pr4480/cs,nn5676
16 And　Hadarezer　sent,　and　brought　out　　the　Syrians　that　were　beyond
df,nn5104　　wcs,qmf935　　　nn2431　　wcj,nn7731　　nn**8269**　　cs,nn**6635**
the　river:　and　they　came　to　Helam;　and　Shobach　the　captain　of　the　host　of
nn1928　　　pp,pl,nn,pnx**6440**
Hadarezer　went　before　them.

　　　　　　　wcs,homf**5046**　pp,nn1732　　　wcs,qmf**622**/(853)/cs,nn3605/nn3478
17 And　when　it　was　told　David,　he　gathered*all*Israel*together,　and
wcs,qmf**5674**　(853)　df,nn3383　wcs,qmf935　　nn,lh2431　　　　nn758
passed　over　　　Jordan,　and　came　to　Helam.　And　the　Syrians
wcs,qmf6186　　pp,qnc7125　nn1732　wcs,nimf3898　pr,pnx5973
set*themselves*in*array　against　David,　and　fought　with　him.

　　　　　　nn758　　wcs,qmf5127　pr4480/pl,cs,nn**6440**　nn3478　　　nn1732　wcs,qmf**2026**
18 And　the　Syrians　fled　before　Israel;　and　David　slew　the　men　of
cs,nu7651　pl,nu3967　nn7393　pr4480/nn758　wcj,pl,nu705　nu**505**　pl,nn6571　hipf**5221**
seven　hundred　chariots　of*the*Syrians,　and　forty　thousand　horsemen,　and　smote
wcj(853)　nn7731　nn**8269**　nn,pnx**6635**　wcs,qmf**4191**　ad8033
Shobach　the　captain　of　their　host,　who　died　there.

　　　　　cs,nn3605　df,pl,nn**4428**　　pl,cs,nn**5650**　nn1928　wcs,qmf**7200**　cj3588
19 And　when　all　the　kings　that　were　servants　to　Hadarezer　saw　that　they
nipf**5062**　pp,pl,cs,nn**6440**　nn3478　　　wcs,himf**7999**　pr854　nn3478　wcs,qmf,pnx**5647**
were　smitten　before　Israel,　they　made　peace　with　Israel,　and　served　them.　So
nn758　wcs,qmf**3372**　pp,hinc**3467**　(853)　pl,cs,nn**1121**　nn5983　ad5750
the　Syrians　feared　to　help　　the　children　of　Ammon　any　more.

David and Bath-sheba

　　　　　　wcs,qmf**1961**　　　df,nn8141　　pp,cs,nn8666　　pp,nn**6256**
11 And　it*came*to*pass,　after　the　year　was　expired,　at　the　time　when
df,pl,nn**4428**　qnc3318　　nn1732　wcs,qmf7971　(853)　nn3097　wcj(853)
kings　go　forth　to　battle,　that　David　sent　　Joab,　and　his
pl,nn,pnx**5650**　pr,pnx5973　wcj(853)　cs,nn3605　nn3478　wcs,himf**7843**　(853)　pl,cs,nn**1121**
servants　with　him,　and　all　Israel;　and　they　destroyed　the　children　of
nn5983　wcs,qmf6696/pr5921　nn7237　wcj,nn1732　qpta**3427**　pp,nn3389
Ammon,　and　besieged　Rabbah.　But　David　tarried　still　at　Jerusalem.

　　　　wcs,qmf**1961**　　　pp,cs,nn**6256**/df,nn6153　　nn1732　wcs,qmf**6965**　pr4480/pr5921
2 And　it*came*to*pass　in　an　eveningtide,　that　David　arose　from　off　his
nn,pnx4904　wcs,htmf**1980**　pr5921　cs,nn1406　df,nn**4428**　cs,nn1004　pr4480/pr5921　df,nn1406
bed,　and　walked　upon　the　roof　of　the　king's　house:　and　from　the　roof　he
wcs,qmf**7200**　nn802　qpta7364　　wcj,df,nn802　ad3966　cs,aj**2896**　nn4758
saw　a　woman　washing　herself;　and　the　woman　was　very　beautiful　to　look　upon.

　　　　nn1732　wcs,qmf7971　wcs,qmf1875　df p,nn802　　wcs,qmf559　he,ptn**3808**
3 And　David　sent　and　inquired　after　the　woman.　And　one　said,　Is　not
pndm2063　nn1339　　nn1323　　nn463　cs,nn**802**　nn223　df,nn2850
this　Bath-sheba,　the　daughter　of　Eliam,　the　wife　of　Uriah　the　Hittite?

　　　　nn1732　wcs,qmf7971　pl,nn**4397**　　wcs,qmf,pnx3947　wcs,qmf935　pr,pnx413
4 And　David　sent　messengers,　and　took　her;　and　she　came　in　unto

wcs,qmf7901   pr,pnx5973   wcj,pnp1931   htpt6942   pr4480/nn,pnx2932
him, and he   lay   with her; for   she   was purified from*her*uncleanness: and

wcs,qmf7725   pr413   nn,pnx1004
she returned unto her house.

df,nn802   wcs,qmf2029   wcs,qmf7971   wcs,himf5046   pp,nn1732   wcs,qmf559   pnp595
5 And the woman conceived, and   sent   and   told   David, and said,   I

aj2030
am with child.

nn1732   wcs,qmf7971   pr413   nn3097   qmv7971/pr,pnx413   (853)   nn223   df,nn2850
6 And David   sent   to Joab, saying,   Send   me   Uriah the Hittite. And

nn3097 wcs,qmf7971 (853)   nn223   pr413   nn1732
Joab   sent   Uriah to David.

nn223   wcs,qmf935 pr,pnx413   nn1732   wcs,qmf7592   nn3097
7 And when Uriah was   come   unto him, David demanded of him how Joab

pp,cs,nn7965   df,nn5971 wcj,pp,cs,nn7965   df,nn4421   wcj,pp,cs,nn7965
did,   and how the people   did,   and how the   war   prospered.

nn1732   wcs,qmf559   pp,nn223   qmv3381   pp,nn,pnx1004   wcj,qmv7364   du,nn,pnx7272
8 And David   said   to Uriah, Go down to thy   house,   and wash thy   feet.

nn223   wcs,qmf3318   pr4480/cs,nn1004/df,nn4428   wcs,qmf3318/pr,pnx310   cs,nn4864
And Uriah departed out*of*the*king's*house, and there   followed   him a mess of

df,nn4428
meat from the king.

nn223   wcs,qmf7901   nn6607   df,nn4428 cs,nn1004   pr854 cs,nn3605   pl,cs,nn5650
9 But Uriah   slept   at the door of the king's house with   all   the servants of

pl,nn,pnx113   qpf3381 wcj,ptn3808   pr413   nn,pnx1004
his lord, and went   not   down   to his house.

wcs,himf5046   pp,nn1732   pp,qnc559   nn223   qpf3381/ptn3808   pr413
10 And when they had   told   David, saying, Uriah went*not*down unto his

nn,pnx1004   nn1732   wcs,qmf559   pr413   nn223   qpta935   pnp859   he,ptn3808   pr4480/nn1870   ad4069
house, David   said   unto Uriah, Camest thou   not   from*thy*journey? why then

ptn3808   qpf3381   pr413   nn,pnx1004
didst thou   not   go down unto thine house?

nn223   wcs,qmf559   pr413   nn1732   df,nn727   wcj,nn3478   wcj,nn3063   pl,qpta3427
11 And Uriah   said   unto David, The ark, and Israel, and Judah, abide in

dfp,pl,nn5521   wcj,nn,pnx113   nn3097   wcj,pl,cs,nn5650   nn,pnx113   pl,qpta2583   pr5921
tents; and my   lord   Joab, and the servants of my lord, are encamped in the

pl,cs,nn6440   df,nn7704   wcj,pnp589   qmf935 pr413   nn,pnx1004   pp,qnc398   wcj,pp,qnc8354
open fields; shall   I   then go into mine house, to   eat   and to   drink,   and

wcj,pp,qnc7901 pr5973   nn,pnx802   pl,nn,pnx2416   nn,pnx5315 wcj,cs,aj2416   qmf6213
to   lie   with my wife? as thou   livest,   and as thy   soul   liveth, I will not do

(853) df,pndm2088 df,nn1697
this   thing.

nn1732   wcs,qmf559 pr413   nn223   qmv3427   pp,pndm2088 df,nn3117   ad1571   wcj,nn4279
12 And David   said   to Uriah, Tarry   here   today also, and tomorrow I will

pimf,pnx7971   nn223   wcs,qmf3427   pp,nn3389   df,pndm1931 dfp,nn3117   wcj,pr4480/nn4283
let thee depart. So Uriah abode in Jerusalem   that   day,   and the   morrow.

nn1732   wcs,qmf7121   pp,pnx   wcs,qmf398   wcs,qmf8354 pp,pl,nn,pnx6440
13 And when David had called   him, he did   eat   and   drink   before   him;

wcs,pimf,pnx7937   dfp,nn6153   wcs,qmf3318   pp,qnc7901   pp,nn,pnx4904 pr5973
and he made him   drunk: and at even he went out to   lie   on his   bed   with

pl,cs,nn5650   pl,nn,pnx113   qpf3381 ptn3808   wcj,pr413   nn,pnx1004
the servants of his   lord,   but went not down   to   his house.

wcs,qmf1961   dfp,nn1242   nn1732 wcs,qmf3789   nn5612 pr413   nn3097
14 And it*came*to*pass in the morning, that David wrote   a letter to Joab,

wcs,qmf7971   pp,cs,nn3027   nn223
and   sent   it by the   hand   of Uriah.

15 And he wrote in the letter, saying, Set ye Uriah in the forefront of the hottest battle, and retire ye from him, that he may be smitten, and die.

16 And it*came*to*pass, when Joab observed the city, that he assigned Uriah unto a place where he knew that valiant men *were*.

17 And the men of the city went out, and fought with Joab: and there fell *some* of the people of*the*servants of David; and Uriah the Hittite died also.

18 Then Joab sent and told David all the things concerning the war;

19 And charged the messenger, saying, When thou hast made*an*end of telling the matters of the war unto the king,

20 And if so be that the king's wrath arise, and he say unto thee, Wherefore approached ye so nigh unto the city when ye did fight? knew ye not that they would shoot from the wall?

21 Who smote Abimelech the son of Jerubbesheth? did not a woman cast a piece of a millstone upon him from the wall, that he died in Thebez? why went*ye*nigh the wall? then say thou, Thy servant Uriah the Hittite is dead also.

22 So the messenger went, and came and showed David all that Joab had sent him for.

23 And the messenger said unto David, Surely the men prevailed against us, and came out unto us into the field, and we were upon them even unto the entering of the gate.

24 And the shooters shot from off the wall upon thy servants; and *some* of*the*king's*servants be dead, and thy servant Uriah the Hittite is dead also.

25 Then David said unto the messenger, Thus shalt thou say unto Joab, Let not this thing displease thee, for the sword devoureth one as well

wcj,pp,pndm2090   nn,pnx4421   himv**2388**   pr413   df,nn5892   wcj,qmv,pnx**2040**

as another: make thy battle more strong against the city, and overthrow it: and

wcj,pimv,pnx**2388**

encourage thou him.

cs,nn**802**   nn223   wcs,qmf**8085** cj3588   nn223   nn,pnx**376**   qpf**4191**

26 And when the wife of Uriah heard that Uriah her husband was dead, she

wcs,qmf5594 pr5921   nn,pnx**1167**

mourned for her husband.

df,nn60   wcs,qmf5674   nn1732 wcs,qmf7971   wcs,qmf,pnx**622**   pr413

27 And when the mourning was past, David sent and fetched her to his

nn,pnx**1004**   wcs,qmf**1961** pp,pnx   pp,nn**802**   wcs,qmf3205 pp,pnx   nn**1121**   df,nn**1697** pnl834   nn1732

house, and she became his wife, and bore him a son. But the thing that David

qpf**6213**   qmf**3415**/pp,du,cs,nn**5869**   nn3068

had done displeased the Lord.

Nathan Confronts David

nn3068   wcs,qmf7971   (853)   nn5416   pr413   nn1732   wcs,qmf935

12 ☞ And the Lord sent   Nathan unto David. And he came

pr,pnx413   wcs,qmf**559**   pp,pnx   qpf**1961**   du,cs,nu8147 pl,nn**376**   nu259

unto him, and said unto him, There were two men in one

pp,nn5892   nu259   aj6223   wcj,nu259 qpta7326

city; the one rich, and the other poor.

pp,aj6223   qpf**1961**   ad3966   hina7235   nn6629   wcj,nn1241

2 The rich *man* had exceeding many flocks and herds:

wcj,dfp,qpta7326   ptn369/nn3605 cj3588/cj518 nu259   aj6996   nn3535   pnl834

3 But the poor *man* had nothing, save one little ewe lamb, which he

wcs,qmf**1961**   qpf7069   wcs,pimf,pnx**2421**   wcs,qmf1431   ad3162   pr,pnx5973   wcj,pr5973

had bought and nourished up: and it grew up together with him, and with his

pl,nn,pnx**1121**   qmf398   pr4480/nn,pnx6595   qmf8354   wcj,pr4480/nn,pnx3563   qmf7901

children; it did eat of*his*own*meat, and drank of*his*own*cup, and lay in his

wcj,pp,nn,pnx2436   wcj,qmf**1961**   pp,pnx   pp,nn1323

bosom, and was unto him as a daughter.

wcs,qmf935   nn1982   df,aj6223 pp,nn**376**   wcs,qmf2550   pp,qnc3947

4 And there came a traveler unto the rich man, and he spared to take

pr4480/nn,pnx6629   wcj,pr4480/nn,pnx1241   pp,qnc**6213**   dfp,qpta732

of*his*own*flock and of*his*own*herd, to dress for the wayfaring man that was

df,qpta935   pp,pnx   wcs,qmf3947   df,qpta7326 df,nn**376**   (853) cs,nn3535   wcs,qmf,pnx**6213**

come unto him; but took the poor man's   lamb, and dressed it for the

dfp,nn**376**   df,qpta935 pr,pnx413

man that was come to him.

nn1732   nn**639**   ad3966   wcs,qmf2734   dfp,nn**376**   wcs,qmf**559** pr413

5 And David's anger was greatly kindled against the man; and he said to

---

☞ **12:1–14**   Here the consequences of David's great sin became evident to him. Observe how skillfully Nathan used his parable (vv. 1–4) to bring David to condemn himself. David had violated four of the ten commandments in one rash sin: thou shalt not kill, thou shalt not steal, thou shalt not commit adultery, and thou shalt not covet thy neighbor's wife. Although it was about a year later, David sincerely repented of his sin (see Ps. 32:3, 4; 51:1–19). While his repentance brought about forgiveness from God, it did not prevent him from suffering the consequences of his sin. God revealed that because of David's sin, the son born from his adulterous relationship would die (2 Sam. 12:14, 18), the sword would never depart from his house (v. 10), evil would come from his own family (v. 11; see chaps. 15–18), and his wives would be publicly shamed (v. 11; see 2 Sam. 16:22). The important lesson to learn from these events is that even the best of men can sin. Also, true repentance does bring forgiveness from God, but does not eliminate the consequences of sin.

nn5416   nn3068   aj2416   df,nn376   df,qpta6213   pndm2063

Nathan, *As* the LORD liveth, the man that hath done this *thing* shall

cj3588/cs,nn1121/nn4194

surely die:

pimf7999   wcj(853)   df,nn3535   nu706   ad6118/pnl834   qpf6213   (853)   df,pndm2088

6 And he shall restore the lamb fourfold, because he did this

df,nn1697   wcj,pr5921/pnl834   ptn3808   qpf2550

thing, and because he had no pity.

nn5416   wcs,qmf559   pr413   nn1732   pnp859   df,nn376   ad3541   qpf559   nn3068   pl,cs,nn430

7 And Nathan said to David, Thou *art* the man. Thus saith the LORD God

nn3478   pnp595   qpf,pnx4886   pp,nn4428   pr5921   nn3478   wcj,pnp595   hipf,pnx5337

of Israel, I anointed thee king over Israel, and I delivered thee

pr4480/cs,nn3027   nn7586

out*of*the*hand of Saul;

wcs,qmf5414   pp,pnx   (853)   pl,nn,pnx113   cs,nn1004   wcj(853)   pl,nn,pnx113   pl,cs,nn802

8 And I gave thee thy master's house, and thy master's wives into

pp,nn,pnx2436   wcs,qmf5414   pp,pnx   (853)   cs,nn1004   nn3478   wcj,nn3063   wcj,cj518

thy bosom, and gave thee the house of Israel and of Judah; and if *that had*

nn4592   wcj,hicj3254   pp,pnx   pp,pnp2007   wcj,pp,pnp2007

been too little, I would moreover*have*given unto thee such and such things.

ad4069   qpf959   (853)   cs,nn1697   nn3068   pp,qnc6213

9 Wherefore hast thou despised the commandment of the LORD, to do

df,aj7451   pp,du,nn,pnx5869   hipf5221   (853)   nn223   df,nn2850   dfp,nn2719

evil in his sight? thou hast killed Uriah the Hittite with the sword, and hast

qpf3947   wcj(853)   nn,pnx802   pp,pnx   pp,nn802   qpf2026   wcj,pnx(853)   pp,nn2719

taken his wife *to be* thy wife, and hast slain him with the sword of

pl,cs,nn1121   nn5983

the children of Ammon.

wcj,ad6258   nn2719   ptn3808/pr5704/nn5769   qmf5493   pr4480/nn,pnx1004

10 Now therefore the sword shall never depart from*thine*house;

cj6118/cj3588   qpf,pnx959   wcs,qmf3947   (853)   cs,nn802   nn223   df,nn2850

because thou hast despised me, and hast taken the wife of Uriah the Hittite to

pp,qnc1961   pp,nn802

be thy wife.

ad3541   qpf559   nn3068   ptdm,pnx2009   hipt6965   aj7451   pr,pnx5921

11 Thus saith the LORD, Behold, I will raise up evil against thee

pr4480/nn,pnx1004   wcj,qpf3947   (853)   pl,nn,pnx802   pp,du,nn,pnx5869

out*of*thine*own*house, and I will take thy wives before thine eyes,

wcj,qpf5414   pp,nn,pnx7453   wcj,qpf7901   pr5973   pl,nn,pnx802

and give *them* unto thy neighbor, and he shall lie with thy wives in the

pp,du,cs,nn5869   df,pndm2063   df,nn8121

sight of this sun.

cj3588   pnp859   qpf6213   dfp,nn5643   wcj,pnp589   qmf6213   (853)   df,pndm2088   df,nn1697   pr5048   cs,nn3605

12 For thou didst *it* secretly: but I will do this thing before all

nn3478   wcj,pr5048   df,nn8121

Israel, and before the sun.

nn1732   wcs,qmf559   pr413   nn5416   qpf2398   pp,nn3068   nn5416

13 And David said unto Nathan, I have sinned against the LORD. And Nathan

wcs,qmf559   pr413   nn1732   nn3068   ad1571   hipf5674   nn,pnx2403   ptn3808   qmf4191

said unto David, The LORD also hath put away thy sin; thou shalt not die.

ptn657   cj3588   df,pndm2088   dfp,nn1697   pina5006   (853)

14 Howbeit, because by this deed thou hast given*great*occasion to the

pl,cs,qpta341   nn3068   pipf5006   df,nn1121   ad1571   df,aj3209   pp,pnx

enemies of the LORD to blaspheme, the child also *that is* born unto thee shall

qna4191/qmf4191

surely die.

The Child Dies

nn5416 wcs,qmf1980 pr413 nn,pnx1004   nn3068 wcs,qmf5062 (853)   df,nn3206

15 And Nathan departed unto his house. And the LORD struck   the child

pnl834 nn223 cs,nn802 qpf3205 pp,nn1732   wcs,nimf605

that Uriah's wife bore unto David, and it was very sick.

nn1732   wcs,pimf1245 (853) df,pl,nn430 pr1157 df,nn5288   nn1732 wcs,qmf6684/nn6685

16 David therefore besought   God for the child; and David   fasted,   and

wcj,qpf935   wcj,qpf7901 cs,nn3605 wcj,qpf3885   nn,lh776

went in, and lay   all night upon the earth.

cs,aj2205   nn,pnx1004 wcs,qmf6965   pr,pnx5921   pp,hinc,pnx6965

17 And the elders of his house arose, *and went* to him, to raise*him*up

pr4480 df,nn776   qpf14 wcj,ptn3808 wcj,ptn3808   qpf1262 nn3899 pr,pnx854

from the earth: but he would not, neither did he eat bread with them.

wcs,qmf1961   df,nuor7637 dfp,nn3117   df,nn3206 wcs,qmf4191

18 And it*came*to*pass on the seventh day, that the child died. And the

pl,cs,nn5650   nn1732 wcs,qmf3372 pp,hinc5046 pp,pnx cj3588 df,nn3206   qpf4191 cj3588   qpf559

servants of David feared to tell him that the child was dead: for they said,

ptdm2009   df,nn3206 pp,qnc1961 aj2416   pipf1696 pr,pnx413   wcj,ptn3808

Behold, while the child was yet alive, we spoke unto him, and he would not

qpf8085   pp,nn,pnx6963 wcj,ptx349   wcj,qpf6213/aj7451   qmf559/pr,pnx413

hearken unto our voice: how will he then   vex   himself, if we   tell

df,nn3206   qpf4191

him that the child is dead?

nn1732 wcs,qmf7200 cj3588 pl,nn,pnx5650 pl,htpt3907 nn1732 wcs,qmf995 cj3588

19 But when David saw that his servants whispered, David perceived that the

df,nn3206   qpf4191   nn1732 wcs,qmf559 pr413 pl,nn,pnx5650   df,nn3206 he,qpf4191

child was dead: therefore David said unto his servants, Is the child dead? And

wcs,qmf559   qpf4191

they said, He is dead.

nn1732 wcs,qmf6965   pr4480/df,nn776   wcs,qmf7364   wcs,qmf5480

20 Then David arose from*the*earth, and washed, and anointed *himself*, and

wcs,pimf2498   pl,nn,pnx8071 wcs,qmf935   cs,nn1004   nn3068   wcs,htmf7812

changed his apparel, and came into the house of the LORD, and worshiped: then he

wcs,qmf935 pr413   nn,pnx1004   wcs,qmf7592   wcs,qmf7760 nn3899   pp,pnx

came to his own house; and when he required, they   set   bread before him, and

wcs,qmf398

he did eat.

wcs,qmf559   pl,nn,pnx5650 pr,pnx413   pnit4100 df,nn1697 df,pndm2088 pnl834

21 Then said his servants unto him, What thing *is* this   that thou hast

qpf6213   qpf6684 wcs,qmf1058 df,nn3206 pp,pr5668   aj2416   wcj,pp,pnl834

done? thou didst fast and weep for the child, while *it was* alive; but when the

df,nn3206   qpf4191   qpf6965 wcs,qmf398 nn3899

child was dead, thou didst rise and eat bread.

wcs,qmf559   df,nn3206 pp,ad5750 aj2416 qpf6684 wcs,qmf1058 cj3588

22 And he said, While the child was yet alive, I fasted and wept: for I

qpf559 pnit4310 qpta3045   nn3068   wcs,qpf,pnx2603   df,nn3206 wcs,qpf2416

said, Who can tell *whether* GOD will be gracious to me, that the child may live?

wcj,ad6258   qpf4191 pnit4100/pndm2088 pnp589 qpta6684 he,qmf3201   pp,hinc,pnx7725

23 But now he is dead, wherefore should I fast? can I bring*him*back

ad5750 pnp589 qpta1980 pr,pnx413   wcj,pnp1931   ptn3808 qmf7725 pr,pnx413

again? I shall go   to him, but he   shall not return to me.

12:23 The phrase in this verse ". . . I shall go to him, but he shall not return to me" that David spoke after the child died should be understood to mean that David was aware previous to the death of the child of its inevitability; therefore, he no longer wept for the life of the child. In addition to this, David also realized

Solomon Is Born

nn1732   wcs,pimf**5162**   (853)   nn1339   nn,pnx**802**   wcs,qmf935   pr,pnx413

☞ 24 And David comforted   Bath-sheba his wife, and went in unto her, and

wcs,qmf7901   pr,pnx5973   wcs,qmf3205   nn**1121**   wcj,qmf7121   (853)   nn,pnx8034   nn8010

lay   with her: and she   bore   a son, and he called   his name Solomon:

wcj,nn**3068**   qpf,pnx**157**

and the LORD loved him.

wcs,qmf7971   pp,cs,nn**3027**   nn5416   df,nn**5030**   wcs,qmf7121   (853)

25 And he   sent   by the   hand   of Nathan the prophet; and he called   his

nn,pnx8034   nn3041   pp,pr5668   nn**3068**

name Jedidiah, because of the LORD.

Another Victory Over the Ammonites

nn3097   wcs,nimf3898   pp,nn7237   pl,cs,nn**1121**   nn5983   wcs,qmf3920   (853)

26 And Joab fought against Rabbah of the children of Ammon, and   took

df,nn4410   nn5892

the royal city.

nn3097   wcs,qmf7971   pl,nn**4397**   pr413   nn1732   wcs,qmf559   nipf3898

27 And Joab   sent   messengers   to David, and   said, I have fought against

pp,nn7237   ad1571   qpf3920   (853)   nn5892   df,pl,nn4325

Rabbah, and have taken   the city of waters.

wcj,ad6258   qmv**622**   (853)   cs,nn**3499**   df,nn**5971**   wcj,qmv2583

28 Now therefore gather   the   rest   of the people together, and encamp

pr5921   df,nn**5892**   wcj,qmv,pnx3920   cj6435   pnp589   qmf3920   (853)   df,nn**5892**   wcs,nipf**7121**

against the city, and   take   it: lest   I   take   the city, and it be called

pr,pnx5921   nn,pnx8034

after my name.

nn1732   wcs,qmf**622**   (853)   cs,nn3605   df,nn**5971**   wcs,qmf**1980**   nn,lh7237

29 And David gathered   all   the people together, and   went   to Rabbah,

wcs,nimf3898   pp,pnx   wcs,qmf,pnx3920

and fought against it, and   took   it.

wcs,qmf3947   (853)   nn,pnx**4428**   cs,nn5850   pr4480/pr5921   nn,pnx**7218**   wcj,nn,pnx4948

30 And he   took   their king's   crown from off his   head,   the   weight

cs,nn3603   nn2091   aj3368   wcj,nn68   wcs,qmf**1961**   pr5921   nn1732

whereof *was* a talent of gold with the precious stones: and it   was   *set* on David's

nn**7218**   hipf3318   wcj,cs,nn7998   df,nn**5892**   ad3966   hina7235

head. And he brought forth the   spoil   of the   city   in great abundance.

hipf3318   wcj(853)   df,nn**5971**   pnl834   pp,pnx   wcs,qmf**7760**

31 And he brought forth   the people that *were* therein, and   put   *them*

dfp,nn4050   wcj,pp,pl,cs,nn2757   df,nn1270   wcj,pp,pl,cs,nn4037   df,nn1270

under saws, and under   harrows   of iron, and under   axes   of iron, and

---

that there would be a time in the future when he too would die, and there he would be joined to his son who had died. While the child was alive, David's prayer was for life; after the death of the child, he no longer saw the need to mourn for him, but rather he continued living with the expectancy of someday being with his child again. This verse has been used as a source of comfort for those who have lost infants or small children to early deaths.

☞ **12:24**   Solomon's name appears fourth on the lists of Bath-sheba's sons (2 Sam. 5:14–16; 1 Chr. 3:5; 14:4), but this does not necessarily mean that he was the fourth born. This verse seems to indicate that he was the oldest of David's and Bath-sheba's sons. However, he was not David's firstborn, for it is clear from 2 Samuel 3:2–5 and 1 Chronicles 3:1–9 that he had six sons born to him in Hebron. Normally, the firstborn son would succeed the father as king; but in this case, God made Solomon his choice. In 1 Chronicles 28:4, 5, David says, ". . . he (God) hath chosen Solomon my son . . ."; and in 1 Chronicles 29:1, he says ". . . Solomon my son, whom alone God hath chosen. . . ."

wcj,hipf**5674**/pnx(853)　　　　　dfp,nn4404　　　wcj,ad**3651**　qmf**6213**　　　　pp,nn3605　　　pl,cs,nn**5892**
made*them*pass*through the brickkiln: and thus did he unto all the cities of

pl,cs,nn**1121**　　　　　nn5983　　　　nn1732　　wcj,cs,nn3605　　df,nn**5971**　wcs,qmf**7725**　　　　　nn3389
the children of Ammon. So David and　　all　　the people returned unto Jerusalem.

Amnon Rapes Tamar

　　　　　　　　　　　　wcs,qmf**1961**　　　pr310　　ad**3651**　　　wcj,pp,nn53　　cs,nn**1121**　　nn1732
13 And it*came*to*pass after this, that Absalom the　son　of David had a

　　　　aj3303　　nn**269**　　wcj,nn,pnx8034　　　nn8559　　　　nn550　　　cs,nn**1121**　　nn1732
fair sister, whose　name　*was* Tamar; and Amnon the　son　of David

wcs,qmf,pnx**157**
loved　her.

　　　pp,nn550　　　　　　wcs,qmf6887　　　　　pp,htnc2470　pr5668　　　nn,pnx**269**　　nn8559　cj3588 pnp1931
2 And Amnon was so vexed, that he fell sick for his sister Tamar; for she

nn**1330**　　　　nn550　　pp,du,cs,nn**5869**　wcs,nimf6381　　　pp,qnc**6213**　pnid3972　pp,pnx
was a virgin; and Amnon thought it　hard　for him to　do　any thing to her.

　　wcj,pp,nn550　　　　nn**7453**　　　wcj,nn,pnx8034　　　　nn3122　　cs,nn**1121**　　　nn8093
3 But Amnon had a friend, whose　name　*was* Jonadab, the　son　of Shimeah

nn1732　cs,nn**251**　　wcj,nn3122　　　ad3966　　aj**2450**　　nn**376**
David's brother: and Jonadab *was* a very subtle man.

　　　　wcs,qmf559　　pp,pnx　　ad4069　　　　pnp859　　　　　df,nn**4428**　cs,nn**1121** ad3602/aj1800
4 And he　said　unto him, Why *art* thou, *being* the king's son,　lean　from

dfp,nn1242　　dfp,nn1242　　　he,ptn**3808** himf5046 pp,pnx　　　nn550　wcs,qmf**559**　　pp,pnx　　pnp589 qpta**157**
day to day? wilt thou　not　tell me? And Amnon　said　unto him,　I　love

(853)　　nn8559　　nn,pnx**251**　wcj,nn53　cs,nn**269**
Tamar, my brother Absalom's sister.

　　　　　nn3122　　wcs,qmf**559**　pp,pnx　　　　qmv7901　　　pr5921　　　nn,pnx4904
5 And　Jonadab　said　unto him, Lay*thee*down　on　thy　bed,　and

wcj,htmv2470　　　　nn,pnx1　wcj,qpf935　　pp,qnc,pnx**7200**　　wcj,qpf**559**　pr,pnx413
make*thyself*sick: and when thy father cometh to　see　thee,　say　unto

pte**4994**　　nn,pnx**269**　nn8559　qmf935　wcj,himf,pnx1262　　nn3899　　wcs,qpf**6213**
him, I*pray*thee, let my sister Tamar come, and　give　me meat, and dress

(853)　df,nn1279　　pp,du,pnx,pnx**5869** pp,cj4616/pnl834　　qmf**7200**　　wcs,qpf398　　pr4480/nn,pnx**3027**
the meat in my　sight,　　　that　I may see *it*, and　eat　*it* at*her*hand.

　　　　　nn550　　wcs,qmf7901　　　　wcs,htmf2470　　　　　df,nn**4428**　wcs,qmf935
6 So Amnon lay down, and made*himself*sick: and when the king was come

pp,qnc,pnx**7200**　　　nn550　wcs,qmf**559**　pr413　　df,nn**4428**　pte**4994**　　　nn8559　　nn,pnx**269**
to　see　him, Amnon said unto the king, I*pray*thee, let Tamar my sister

qmf935　　wcj,pimf**3823**　　du,cs,nu8147　pl,nn3834　　pp,du,nn,pnx**5869**　　　wcj,qmf1262
come, and　make　me a couple of cakes in my　sight,　that I may　eat

pr4480/nn,pnx**3027**
at*her*hand.

　　　　　nn1732　wcs,qmf7971 df,nn,lh**1004**　pr413　　nn8559　　pp,qnc559　qmv1980 pte**4994**　　　nn,pnx**251**
7 Then David　sent　home　to　Tamar, saying,　Go　now to thy brother

nn550　　cs,nn**1004**　wcj,qmv**6213** pp,pnx df,nn1279
Amnon's house, and　dress　him meat.

　　　　nn8559　wcs,qmf**1980**　　nn,pnx**251**　　nn550　cs,nn**1004**　wcj,pnp1931　　qpta7901
8 So Tamar　went　to her brother Amnon's house; and　he　was laid down.

wcs,qmf3947 (853) df,nn1217　　wcj,qmf3888　　wcs,pimf**3823**　　　pp,du,nn,pnx**5869**
And she　took　flour, and kneaded *it*, and made cakes in his　sight,　and did

wcs,pimf1310 (853)　　df,pl,nn3834
bake　the cakes.

　　　wcs,qmf3947 (853)　df,nn4958　　wcs,qmf3332　　pp,pl,nn,pnx**6440**
9 And she　took　a pan, and poured*them*out　before　him; but he

wcs,pimf3985   pp,qnc398   nn550   wcs,qmf559   himv3318   cs,nn3605   nn376 pr4480/pr,pnx5921

refused to eat. And Amnon said, Have out all men from me. And they

wcs,qmf3318 cs,nn3605   nn376 pr4480/pr,pnx5921

went out every man from him.

                    nn550   wcs,qmf559   pr413   nn8559   himv935   df,nn1279   df,nn2315

10 And Amnon said unto Tamar, Bring the meat into the chamber, that I

wcj,qmf1262   pr4480/nn,pnx3027   nn8559 wcs,qmf3947 (853)   df,pl,nn3834   pnl834   qpf6213

may eat of*thine*hand. And Tamar took the cakes which she had made,

wcs,himf935   df,nn,lh2315   pp,nn550   nn,pnx251

and brought *them* into the chamber to Amnon her brother.

                    wcs,himf5066   pr,pnx413   pp,qnc398   wcs,himf2388   pp,pnx

11 And when she had brought *them* unto him to eat, he took hold of her,

wcs,qmf559   pp,pnx   qmv935 qmv7901 pr,pnx5973   nn,pnx269

and said unto her, Come lie with me, my sister.

                    wcs,qmf559   pp,pnx   ptn408   nn,pnx251   ptn408 pimf,pnx6031   cj3588 ptn3808

12 And she answered him, Nay, my brother, do not force me; for no

ad3651   nimf6213   pp,nn3478 qmf6213 ptn408   (853) df,pndm2063 df,nn5039

such thing ought to be done in Israel: do not thou this folly.

                wcj,pnp589   ad575   (853)   nn,pnx2781   himf1980   wcj,pnp859

13 And I, whither shall I cause my shame to go? and as for thee,

qmf1961   pp,nu259   df,pl,nn5036   pp,nn3478 wcj,ad6258   pte4994   pimv1696

thou shalt be as one of the fools in Israel. Now therefore, I*pray*thee, speak

pr413   df,nn4428 cj3588   ptn3808   qmf,pnx4513   pr,pnx4480

unto the king; for he will not withhold me from thee.

                    qpf14   wcj,ptn3808 pp,qnc8085   pp,nn,pnx6963   wcs,qmf2388

14 Howbeit he would not hearken unto her voice: but, being stronger than

wcs,pimf,pnx6031   wcs,qmf7901   pnx(853)

she, forced her, and lay with her.

                    nn550   wcs,qmf,pnx8130   nn8135/aj1419/ad3966   cj3588   df,nn8135   pnl834

☙ 15 Then Amnon hated her exceedingly; so that the hatred wherewith he

qpf,pnx8130   aj1419   pr4480/nn160   pnl834   qpf,pnx157   nn550

hated her *was* greater than*the*love wherewith he had loved her. And Amnon

wcs,qmf559   pp,pnx   qmv6965   qmv1980

said unto her, Arise, be gone.

                    wcs,qmf559   pp,pnx   ptn408 pl,nn182 df,pndm2063 df,aj7451

16 And she said unto him, *There is* no cause: this evil in

pp,pinc,pnx7971   df,aj1419   pr4480/aj312   pnl834   qpf6213 pr,pnx5973   qpf14

sending*me*away *is* greater than*the*other that thou didst unto me. But he would

wcj,ptn3808 pp,qnc8085   pp,pnx

not hearken unto her.

                    wcs,qmf7121 (853)   nn,pnx5288   pipt,pnx8334   wcs,qmf559 qmv7971

17 Then he called his servant that ministered unto him, and said, Put

pte4994 (853) pndm2063   pr4480/pr,pnx5921/df,nn,lh2351   wcj,qmv5274   df,nn1817 pr,pnx310

now this *woman* out*from*me, and bolt the door after her.

                    nn3801   pl,nn6446   wcj,pr,pnx5921   cj3588   ad3651 pl,nn4598

18 And *she had* a garment of divers colors upon her: for with such robes

df,nn4428   pl,cs,nn1323   df,pl,nn1330   qmf3847   pipt,pnx8334 wcs,himf3318

were the king's daughters *that were* virgins appareled. Then his servant brought

pnx(853)   df,nn2351   wcj,qpf5274   df,nn1817 pr,pnx310

her out, and bolted the door after her.

                    nn8559 wcs,qmf3947   nn665 pr5921   nn,pnx7218   qpf7167   wcj,cs,nn3801

19 And Tamar put ashes on her head, and rent her garment of

☙ **13:15** This verse shows how there can be consuming desire without love. Once Amnon used Tamar to satisfy his sinful lust, he was filled with a feeling of contempt.

df,pl,nn6446   pnl834   pr,pnx5921   wcs,qmf7760   nn,pnx3027   pr5921   nn,pnx7218

divers colors that *was* on her, and laid her hand on her head, and

wcs,qmf1980/qna1980   wcj,qpf2199

went on crying.

Absalom Avenges Tamar

nn53   nn,pnx251   wcs,qmf559   pr,pnx413   df,nn550   nn,pnx251   qpf1961

20 And Absalom her brother said unto her, Hath Amnon thy brother been

pr,pnx5973   himv2790   wcj,ad6258   nn,pnx269   pnp1931   nn,pnx251

with thee? but hold now thy peace, my sister: he *is* thy brother;

qmf7896/(853)/nn,pnx3820   ptn408   df,pndm2088   dfp,nn1697   nn8559   wcs,qmf3427   wcj,qpta8074   nn,pnx251

regard not this thing. So Tamar remained desolate in her brother

nn53   cs,nn1004

Absalom's house.

wcj,df,nn4428   nn1732   qpf8085   (853)   cs,nn3605   df,pndm428   df,pl,nn1697   pp,pnx   ad3966

21 But when king David heard of all these things, he was very

wcs,qmf2734

wroth.

nn53   pipf1696   pr5973   nn550   wcj,ptn3808   nn2896   wcj,pr5704   pr4480/aj7451   cj3588

22 And Absalom spoke unto his brother Amnon neither good nor bad: for

nn53   qpf8130   (853)   nn550   pr5921/cs,nn1697/pnl834   pipf6031   (853)   nn,pnx269   nn8559

Absalom hated Amnon, because he had forced his sister Tamar.

wcs,qmf1961   pp,du,nn8141/pl,nn3117   pp,nn53   wcs,pmf1961

23 And it*came*to*pass after two*full*years, that Absalom had

pl,qpta1494   pp,nn1178   pnl834   pr5973   nn669   nn53   wcs,qmf7121   pp,cs,nn3605

sheepshearers in Baal-hazor, which *is* beside Ephraim: and Absalom invited all

df,nn4428   pl,cs,nn1121

the king's sons.

nn53   wcs,qmf935   pr413   df,nn4428   wcs,qmf559   ptdm2009   pte4994   pp,nn,pnx5650

24 And Absalom came to the king, and said, Behold now, thy servant hath

pl,qpta1494   df,nn4428   pte4994   wcj,pl,nn,pnx5650   qmf1980   pr5973   nn,pnx5650

sheepshearers; let the king, I*beseech*thee, and his servants go with thy servant.

df,nn4428   wcs,qmf559   pr413   nn53   ptn408   nn,pnx1121   ptn408   nn,pnx3605   pte4994

25 And the king said to Absalom, Nay, my son, let us not all now

qmf1980   wcj,ptn3808   qmf3513   pr,pnx5921   wcs,qmf6555   pp,pnx   qpf14

go, lest we be chargeable unto thee. And he pressed him: howbeit he would

wcj,ptn3808   pp,qnc1980   wcs,pimf,pnx1288

not go, but blessed him.

wcs,qmf559   nn53   wcj,ptn3808   pte4994   nn,pnx251   nn550   qmf1980

26 Then said Absalom, If not, I*pray*thee, let my brother Amnon go

pr,pnx854   df,nn4428   wcs,qmf559   pp,pnx   pnit4100   qmf1980   pr,pnx5973

with us. And the king said unto him, Why should he go with thee?

nn53   wcs,qmf6555   pp,pnx   (853)   nn550   wcj(853)   cs,nn3605   df,nn4428

27 But Absalom pressed him, that he let Amnon and all the king's

pl,cs,nn1121   wcs,qmf7971   wcj,pr854

sons go with him.

nn53   wcs,pimf6680   (853)   pl,nn,pnx5288   pp,qnc559   qmv7200   pte4994

28 Now Absalom had commanded his servants, saying, Mark ye now when

nn550   nn3820   pp,qnc2895   dfp,nn3196   wcj,qpf559   pr,pnx413   himv5221   (853)   nn550

Amnon's heart is merry with wine, and when I say unto you, Smite Amnon;

wcj,hipf4191   pnx(853)   qmf3372   ptn408   he,ptn3808   (cj3588)   pnp595   pipf6680   pnx(853)

then kill him, fear not: have not I commanded you? be

qmv2388   wcj,qmv1961   pp,pl,cs,nn1121/nn2428

courageous, and be valiant.

pl,cs,nn5288   nn53   wcs,qmf6213   pp,nn550   pp,pnl834   nn53
29 And the servants of Absalom did unto Amnon as Absalom had
pipf6680   cs,nn3605   df,nn4428 pl,cs,nn1121 wcs,qmf6965   nn376   wcs,qmf7392   pr5921
commanded. Then all the king's sons arose, and every man got*him*up upon
nn,pnx6505   wcs,qmf5127
his mule, and fled.

wcs,qmf1961   pnp1992   dfp,nn1870   wcj,df,nn8052 qpf935   pr413
30 And it*came*to*pass, while they were in the way, that tidings came to
nn1732   pp,qnc559   nn53   hipf5221 (853) cs,nn3605   df,nn4428 pl,cs,nn1121   wcj,ptn3808
David, saying, Absalom hath slain   all the king's sons, and there is not
nu259 pr,pnx4480   nipf3498
one of them left.

df,nn4428 wcs,qmf6965   wcs,qmf7167 (853)   pl,nn,pnx899   wcs,qmf7901
31 Then the king arose, and tore   his garments, and lay on the
nn,lh776   wcj,cs,nn3605   pl,nn,pnx5650   pl,nipt5324   pl,nn899 pl,cs,qptp7167
earth; and all his servants stood by with their clothes rent.

nn3122   cs,nn1121   nn8093   nn1732 cs,nn251   wcs,qmf6030   wcs,qmf559
32 And Jonadab, the son of Shimeah David's brother, answered and said,
ptn408 nn,pnx113 qmf559   hipf4191 (853) cs,nn3605   df,pl,nn5288   df,nn4428
Let not my lord suppose *that* they have slain   all the young men the king's
pl,cs,nn1121 cj3588   nn550   pp,nn,pnx905   qpf4191 cj3588 pr5921   cs,nn6310   nn53
sons; for Amnon only is dead: for by the appointment of Absalom this hath
qpf1961   qnc7760   pr4480/nn3117   pinc,pnx6031 (853)   nn,pnx269   nn8559
been determined from*the*day that he forced   his sister Tamar.

wcj,ad6258   ptn408   nn,pnx113   df,nn4428 qmf7760   nn1697 pr413   nn,pnx3820
33 Now therefore let not my lord the king take the thing to his heart, to
pp,qnc559   cs,nn3605   df,nn4428 pl,cs,nn1121   qpf4191 cj3588/cj518   nn550   pp,nn,pnx905   qpf4191
think that all the king's sons are dead: for Amnon only is dead.

Absalom Escapes

nn53   wcs,qmf1272   df,nn5288   df,qpta6822   wcs,qmf5375 (853)
34 But Absalom fled. And the young man that kept*the*watch lifted up
du,nn,pnx5869   wcs,qmf7200   wcj,ptdm2009   pl,qpta1980   aj7227   nn5971   pr4480/nn1870
his eyes, and looked, and, behold, there came much people by*the*way
pr4480/cs,nn6654/df,nn2022   pr,pnx310
of*the*hill*side behind him.

nn3122   wcs,qmf559   pr413   df,nn4428 ptdm2009   df,nn4428 pl,cs,nn1121 qpf935
35 And Jonadab said unto the king, Behold, the king's sons come: as thy
nn,pnx5650 pp,cs,nn1697 ad3651   qpf1961
servant said, so it is.

wcs,qmf1961   pp,pinc,pnx3615   pp,pinc1696
36 And it*came*to*pass, as soon as he had made*an*end of speaking, that,
wcj,ptdm2009   df,nn4428 pl,cs,nn1121 qpf935   wcs,qmf5375   nn,pnx6963   wcs,qmf1058   df,nn4428
behold, the king's sons came, and lifted up their voice and wept: and the king
wcj,ad1571   wcj,cs,nn3605   pl,nn,pnx5650 qpf1058 ad3966 aj1419
also and all his servants wept very sore.

wcj,nn53   qpf1272   wcs,qmf1980 pr413   nn8526   cs,nn1121   nn5989   nn4428
37 But Absalom fled, and went to Talmai, the son of Ammihud, king of
nn1650   wcs,htmf56   pr5921   nn,pnx1121 cs,nn3605 df,pl,nn3117
Geshur. And *David* mourned for his son every day.

wcj,nn53   qpf1272   wcs,qmf1980   nn1650   wcs,qmf1961 ad8033 nu7969 pl,nn8141
38 So Absalom fled, and went to Geshur, and was there three years.

^{df,nn4428 nn1732 wcs,pimf3615 pp,qnc3318 pr413 nn53 cj3588}

39 And *the soul of* king David longed to go forth unto Absalom: for he was

^{nipf5162 pr5921 nn550 cj3588 qpf4191}

comforted concerning Amnon, seeing he was dead.

Joab Plots Absalom's Return

^{nn3097 cs,nn1121 nn6870 wcs,qmf3045 cj3588 df,nn4428 nn3820}

14 Now Joab the son of Zeruiah perceived that the king's heart *was*

^{pr5921 nn53}

toward Absalom.

^{nn3097 wcs,qmf7971 nn,lh8620 pr4480/ad8033 aj2450 nn802 wcs,qmf559}

2 And Joab sent to Tekoah, and fetched thence a wise woman, and said

^{pr,pnx413 pte4994 htmv56 wcj,qmv3847 pte4994 nn60}

unto her, I*pray*thee, feign*thyself*to*be*a*mourner, and put on now mourning

^{pl,cs,nn899 qmf5480 wcj,ptn408 nn8081 wcs,qpf1961 pp,nn802 pndm2088 aj7227}

apparel, and anoint not thyself with oil, but be as a woman that had a long

^{pl,nn3117 htpt56 pr5921 qpta4191}

time mourned for the dead:

^{wcs,qpf935 pr413 df,nn4428 wcs,pipf1696 pr,pnx413 df,pndm2088 dfp,nn1697 pr,pnx413}

3 And come to the king, and speak on this manner unto him. So

^{nn3097 wcs,qmf7760 (853) df,pl,nn1697 pp,nn,pnx6310}

Joab put the words in her mouth.

^{df,nn802 df,nn8621 wcj,qmf559 pr413 df,nn4428 wcs,qmf5307 pr5921}

4 And when the woman of Tekoah spoke to the king, she fell on her

^{du,nn,pnx639 nn,lh776 wcs,htmf7812 wcs,qmf559 himv3467 df,nn4428}

face to the ground, and did obeisance, and said, Help, O king.

^{df,nn4428 wcs,qmf559 pp,pnx pnit4100 pp,pnx wcs,qmf559 pnp589}

5 And the king said unto her, What aileth thee? And she answered, I *am*

^{ad61 nn490 nn802 nn,pnx376 wcs,qmf4191}

indeed a widow woman, and mine husband is dead.

^{wcj,pp,nn,pnx8198 du,cs,nu8147 pl,nn1121 du,cs,nu,pnx8147 wcs,nimf5327}

6 And thy handmaid had two sons, and they two strove together in

^{dfp,nn7704 wcj,ptn369 hipt5337/pr,pnx996 df,nu259 wcs,himf,pnx5221 (853)}

the field, and *there was* none to part them, but the one smote the

^{df,nu259 wcs,himf4191 pnx(853)}

other, and slew him.

^{wcj,ptdm2009 cs,nn3605 df,nn4940 qpf6965 pr5921 nn,pnx8198}

7 And, behold, the whole family is risen against thine handmaid, and they

^{wcs,qmf559 qmv5414 (853) hipt5221 nn,pnx251 wcj,himf,pnx4191}

said, Deliver him that smote his brother, that we may kill him, for the

^{pp,nn5315 nn,pnx251 pnl834 qpf2026 wcj,himf8045 (853) df,qpta3423 ad1571}

life of his brother whom he slew; and we will destroy the heir also: and so

^{wcj,pipf3518 (853) nn,pnx1513 pnl834 nipf7604 pp,ptn1115 qnc7604 pp,nn,pnx376}

they shall quench my coal which is left, and shall not leave to my husband

^{nn8034 wcj,nn7611 pr5921/pl,cs,nn6440 df,nn127}

neither name nor remainder upon the earth.

^{df,nn4428 wcs,qmf559 pr413 df,nn802 qmv1980 pp,nn,pnx1004 wcj,pnp589}

8 And the king said unto the woman, Go to thine house, and I will

^{pimf6680 pr,pnx5921}

give charge concerning thee.

^{df,nn802 df,nn8621 wcs,qmf559 pr413 df,nn4428 nn,pnx113 df,nn4428}

☞ 9 And the woman of Tekoah said unto the king, My lord, O king, the

---

☞ **14:9** Joab here demonstrates his shrewdness by getting Absalom restored to his position in the king's

df,nn5771   pr,pnx5921   wcj,pr5921   nn,pnx1   cs,nn1004   wcj,df,nn4428
iniquity *be* on   me, and   on   my father's house: and the   king   and his

wcj,nn,pnx3678   aj5355
throne *be* guiltless.

df,nn4428 wcs,qmf559   df,pipt1696   pr,pnx413   wcj,hipf,pnx935   pr,pnx413
10 And the king said, Whosoever saith *aught* unto thee, bring   him   to

wcj,ptn3808 pp,qnc5060 pp,pnx himf3254 ad5750
me, and he shall   not   touch thee any more.

wcs,qmf559   pte4994   df,nn4428   qmf2142   (853)   nn3068
11 Then   said   she, I*pray*thee, let the king remember   the LORD thy

pl,nn,pnx430   wcj,ptn3808   qpta1350   df,nn1818   pp,pinc7843
God,   that thou wouldest   not   suffer*the*revengers of blood to destroy

hinc7235   himf8045   (853)   nn,pnx1121   wcs,qmf559   nn3068   aj2416
any more, lest they destroy   my   son. And he said, *As* the LORD liveth,

cj518   pr4480/cs,nn8185   nn,pnx1121 qmf5307   nn,lh776
there*shall*not one hair of thy son   fall to the earth.

df,nn802   wcs,qmf559   nn,pnx8198   pte4994   pimf1696   nn1697
12 Then the woman said, Let thine handmaid, I*pray*thee, speak *one* word

pr413   nn,pnx113 df,nn4428   wcs,qmf559 pimv1696
unto my lord the king. And he said, Say on.

df,nn802   wcs,qmf559   wcj,pnit4100   qpf2803   pp,pndm2063
13 And the woman said, Wherefore then hast thou thought   such   a thing

pr5921   nn5971   pl,nn430   df,nn4428   wcj,pr4480/pinc1696 df,pndm2088 df,nn1697
against the people of God? for the king doth   speak   this   thing as

pp,aj818   df,nn4428   pp,ptn1115   hinc7725   (853)
one*which*is*faulty, in that the king doth   not fetch*home*again   his

nipt,pnx5080
banished.

cj3588   qna4191/qmf4191   wcj,dfp,pl,nn4325 df,pl,nipt5064   nn,lh776   pnl834
14 For we must*needs*die, and *are* as   water   spilt on the ground, which

ptn3808   nimf622   wcj,ptn3808   pl,nn430   qmf5375   nn5315
cannot be gathered up again; neither doth God respect *any* person: yet doth he

wcs,qpf2803 pl,nn4284   qmf5080   nipt5080 pr,pnx4480
devise means, that his banished be not expelled from him.

wcj,ad6258   pnl834   qpf935   pp,pinc1696   (853) df,pndm2088 df,nn1697 pr413   nn,pnx113
15 Now therefore that I am come to speak of   this   thing unto my lord

df,nn4428   cj3588   df,nn5971   pimf,pnx3372   nn,pnx8198 wcs,qmf559
the king, *it is* because the people have made me afraid: and thy handmaid said, I

pte4994 pimf1696 pr413 df,nn4428 ad194   df,nn4428   qmf6213   (853) cs,nn1697
will now speak unto the king; it*may*be that the king will perform   the request

nn,pnx519
of his handmaid.

cj3588   df,nn4428   qmf8085   pp,hinc5337 (853)   nn,pnx519   pr4480/nn3709
16 For the king will hear, to deliver   his handmaid out*of*the*hand of the

df,nn376   pp,hinc8045   pnx(853)   wcj(853)   nn,pnx1121   ad3162
man *that* *would* destroy   me   and   my   son   together

pr4480/cs,nn5159   pl,nn430
out*of*the*inheritance of God.

nn,pnx8198   wcs,qmf559   cs,nn1697   nn,pnx113 df,nn4428   pte4994 qmf1961
17 Then thine handmaid said, The word of my lord the king shall now be

---

family despite the fact that he murdered Amnon. Through the help of a "wise woman" (see the note on 2 Sam. 20:16), Joab induced David to pardon an intentional killing and confirm it with an oath, so that David would have no excuse for not accepting Absalom back.

pp,nn4496   cj3588   pp,cs,nn4397   df,pl,nn430 ad3651   nn,pnx113   df,nn4428   pp,qnc8085 df,nn2896
comfortable: for as an angel of God, so *is* my lord the king to discern good

df,nn7451   wcj,nn3068   pl,nn,pnx430   qmf1961 pr,pnx5973
and bad: therefore the LORD thy God will be with thee.

df,nn4428 wcs,qmf6030   wcs,qmf559 pr413   df,nn802 pimf3582 ptn408 pr,pnx4480
18 Then the king answered and said unto the woman, Hide not from me,

pte4994   nn1697 pnl834 pnp595   qpta7592 pnx(853)   df,nn802 wcs,qmf559
I*pray*thee, the thing that I shall ask thee. And the woman said, Let my

nn,pnx113   df,nn4428 pte4994 pimf1696
lord the king now speak.

df,nn4428 wcs,qmf559   he,cs,nn3027   nn3097 pr,pnx854   pp,cs,nn3605 pndm2063
19 And the king said, *Is not* the hand of Joab with thee in all this?

df,nn802   wcs,qmf6030   wcs,qmf559   nn,pnx5315 cs,aj2416   nn,pnx113   df,nn4428
And the woman answered and said, *As* thy soul liveth, my lord the king,

cj518/pta786   pp,hinc3231   wcj,pp,hinc8041   pr4480/nn3605 pnl834   nn,pnx113
none*can*turn to the right hand or to the left from aught that my lord the

df,nn4428   pipf1696 cj3588   nn,pnx5650   nn3097 pnp1931 pipf6680   wcj,pnp1931 qpf7760 (853) cs,nn3605
king hath spoken: for thy servant Joab, he bade me, and he put all

df,pndm428 df,pl,nn1697   pp,cs,nn6310   nn,pnx8198
these words in the mouth of thine handmaid:

pp,pp,pr5668   pinc5437   (853)   pl,cs,nn6440   df,nn1697   nn,pnx5650 nn3097 qpf6213 (853)
20 To fetch about this form of speech hath thy servant Joab done

df,pndm2088 df,nn1697   wcj,nn,pnx113   aj2450   pp,cs,nn2451   cs,nn4397
this thing: and my lord *is* wise, according to the wisdom of an angel of

df,pl,nn430   pp,qnc3045 (853) cs,nn3605   pnl834   dfp,nn776
God, to know all *things* that *are* in the earth.

df,nn4428 wcs,qmf559 pr413   nn3097 ptdm2009 pte4994   qpf6213 (853) df,pndm2088 df,nn1697
21 And the king said unto Joab, Behold now, I have done this thing:

wcj,qmv1980   himv7725 (853)   df,nn5288   nn53
go therefore, bring the young man Absalom again.

nn3097 wcs,qmf5307   nn,lh776 pr413   pl,nn,pnx6440   wcs,htmf7812
22 And Joab fell to the ground on his face, and bowed himself, and

wcs,pimf1288 (853)   df,nn4428   nn3097 wcs,qmf559 df,nn3117   nn,pnx5650   qpf3045 cj3588   qpf4672
thanked the king: and Joab said, Today thy servant knoweth that I have found

nn2580   pp,du,nn,pnx5869   nn,pnx113   df,nn4428 pnl834   df,nn4428   qpf6213 (853)
grace in thy sight, my lord, O king, in that the king hath fulfilled the

cs,nn1697   nn,pnx5650
request of his servant.

nn3097   wcs,qmf6965   wcs,qmf1980   nn,lh1650   wcs,himf935 (853)   nn53
23 So Joab arose and went to Geshur, and brought Absalom to

nn3389
Jerusalem.

df,nn4428 wcs,qmf559   qmf5437 pr413   nn,pnx1004   ptn3808 qmf7200
24 And the king said, Let him turn to his own house, and let him not see

wcj,pl,nn,pnx6440   nn53   wcs,qmf5437 pr413   nn,pnx1004   qpf7200 ptn3808   df,nn4428
my face. So Absalom returned to his own house, and saw not the king's

wcj,pl,cs,nn6440
face.

Absalom Returns to Jerusalem

pp,cs,nn3605   nn3478   qpf1961 ptn3808/nn376   ad3966 pp,pinc1984   wcj,pp,nn53
25 But in all Israel there was none to be so much praised as Absalom

aj3303   pr4480/nn3709   nn,pnx7272   wcj,pr5704   nn,pnx6936

for his beauty: from*the*sole of his foot even to the crown*of*his*head there

qpf1961 ptn3808   nn3971   pp,pnx

was no blemish in him.

wcj,pp,pinc,pnx1548 (853)   nn,pnx7218   wcj,qpf1961 pr4480/nn7093/pl,nn3117/dfp,pl,nn3117

26 And when he   polled   his head, (for it was   at*every*year's*end

pnl834   pimf1548   cj3588   qpf3513   pr,pnx5921   wcs,pipf,pnx1548

that he polled it: because the hair was heavy on him, therefore he polled it:)

wcs,qpf8254   (853)   cs,nn8181   nn,pnx7218   du,nu3967   pl,nn8255   df,nn4428

he weighed   the hair of his head at two hundred shekels after the king's

pp,cs,nn68

weight.

pp,nn53   wcs,nimf3205 nu7969 pl,nn1121   nu259 wcj,nn1323

27 And unto Absalom there were born three sons, and one daughter, whose

wcj,nn,pnx8034   nn8559   pnp1931 qpf1961   nn802   cs,aj3303   nn4758

name was Tamar: she was a woman of a fair countenance.

nn53   wcs,qmf3427   du,nn8141/pl,nn3117   pp,nn3389   qpf7200 ptn3808   df,nn4428

28 So Absalom dwelt two*full*years in Jerusalem, and saw not the king's

wcj,pl,cs,nn6440

face.

nn53   wcs,qmf7971 pr413   nn3097   pp,qnc7971 pnx(853)   pr413   df,nn4428

29 Therefore Absalom   sent for Joab, to have sent   him to the king;

qpf14   wcj,ptn3808 pp,qnc935 pr,pnx413   wcs,qmf7971 ad5750   nuor8145

but he would   not come   to him: and when he sent again the second time,

qpf14   wcj,ptn3808 pp,qnc935

he would   not come.

wcs,qmf559   pr413   pl,nn,pnx5650 qmv7200   nn3097   cs,nn2513   pr413 nn,pnx3027

30 Therefore he said unto his servants, See, Joab's field is near mine, and

wcj,pp,pnx   pl,nn8184 ad8033   qmv1980   wcj,himv,pnx3341   dfp,nn784   nn53   pl,cs,nn5650

he hath barley there; go and   set   it on fire. And Absalom's servants

wcs,himf3341 (853)   df,nn2513   dfp,nn784

set   the field on fire.

nn3097 wcs,qmf6965   wcs,qmf935 pr413   nn53   df,nn,lh1004   wcs,qmf559 pr,pnx413

31 Then Joab arose, and came to Absalom unto his house, and said   unto

pnit4100   pl,nn,pnx5650 hipf3341 (853)   df,nn2513 (pnl834) dfp,nn784

him, Wherefore have thy servants set   my field   on fire?

nn53   wcs,qmf559/pr413 nn3097   ptdm2009   qpf7971 pr,pnx413   pp,qnc559   qmv935

32 And Absalom answered Joab, Behold, I sent unto thee, saying, Come

ad2008   wcj,qmf7971 pnx(853)   pr413   df,nn4428   pp,qnc559 pp,pnit4100   pnp589 qpf935

hither, that I may send   thee to the king, to say, Wherefore am I come

pr4480/nn1650   aj2896 pp,pnx   ad8033 ad5750 wcj,ad6258

from Geshur? it had been good for me to have been there still: now therefore let

qmf7200   df,nn4428 pl,cs,nn6440   wcj,cj518 pta3426   nn5771   pp,pnx   wcs,hipf,pnx4191

me see the king's face; and if there be any iniquity in me, let him   kill

me.

nn3097 wcs,qmf935 pr413   df,nn4428   wcs,himf5046 pp,pnx   wcs,qmf7121 pr413

33 So Joab came to the king, and told him: and when he had called for

nn53   wcs,qmf935 pr413   df,nn4428   wcs,htmf7812 pp,pnx   pr5921   du,nn,pnx639   nn,lh776

Absalom, he came to the king, and bowed himself on his face to the ground

pp,pl,cs,nn6440   df,nn4428   df,nn4428 wcs,qmf5401   pp,nn53

before the king: and the king kissed Absalom.

Absalom Prepares For a Revolt

15 wcs,qmf1961   pr4480/pr310   ad3651   nn53   wcs,qmf6213   pp,pnx
And it*came*to*pass after this, that Absalom prepared him

nn4818   wcj,pl,nn5483   wcj,pl,nu2572   nn376   pl,qpta7323   pp,pl,nn,pnx6440
chariots and horses, and fifty men to run before him.

nn53   wcj,hipf7925   wcj,qpf5975   pr5921/cs,nn3027   nn1870   df,nn8179
2 And Absalom rose*up*early, and stood beside the way of the gate: and it

wcs,qmf1961   cs,nn3605 df,nn376 pnl834 qmf1961/pp,pnx   nn7379   pp,qnc935 pr413   df,nn4428
was *so,* that when any man that had a controversy came to the king for

dfp,nn4941   nn53   wcs,qmf7121   pr,pnx413   wcs,qmf559 pr4480/pndm2088 pnit335 nn5892
judgment, then Absalom called unto him, and said, Of what city *art*

pnp859   wcs,qmf559   nn,pnx5650   pr4480/nu259   pl,cs,nn7626   nn3478
thou? And he said, Thy servant *is* of one of the tribes of Israel.

nn53   wcs,qmf559   pr,pnx413   qmv7200   nn,pnx1697   aj2896   wcj,aj5228
3 And Absalom said unto him, See, thy matters *are* good and right; but

ptn369   df,nn4428   wcj,qpta8085
there is no man *deputed* of the king to hear thee.

nn53   wcs,qmf559   pnid4310   qmf,pnx7760 qpta8199   dfp,nn776
4 Absalom said moreover, Oh that I were made judge in the land, that

cs,nn3605 nn376 pnl834 qmf1961/pp,pnx   nn7379   wcj,nn4941   qmf935 wcj,pr,pnx5921
every man which hath any suit or cause might come unto me, and I would

wcs,hipf,pnx6663
do*him*justice!

wcs,qpf1961   nn376   pp,qnc7126   pp,htnc7812/pp,pnx
5 And it was *so,* that when any man came nigh *to him* to do*him*obeisance,

wcs,qpf7971 (853)   nn,pnx3027   wcs,hipf2388 pp,pnx   wcs,qpf5401 pp,pnx
he put forth his hand, and took him, and kissed him.

df,pndm2088 dfp,nn1697 wcs,qmf6213   nn53   pp,cs,nn3605 nn3478 pnl834 qmf935 pr413
6 And on this manner did Absalom to all Israel that came to the

df,nn4428   dfp,nn4941   nn53   wcs,pimf1589 (853)   nn3820   pl,cs,nn376   nn3478
king for judgment: so Absalom stole the hearts of the men of Israel.

wcs,qmf1961   pr4480/nn7093 pl,nn705 nn8141   nn53   wcs,qmf559 pr413   df,nn4428
7 And it*came*to*pass after forty years, that Absalom said unto the king,

pte4994   qmf1980   wcs,pimf7999 (853)   nn,pnx5088 pnl834   qpf5087
I*pray*thee, let me go and pay my vow, which I have vowed unto the

pp,nn3068   pp,nn2275
LORD, in Hebron.

cj3588   nn,pnx5650 qpf5087   nn5088   pp,qnc,pnx3427   pp,nn1650   dfp,nn758   pp,qnc559 cj518
8 For thy servant vowed a vow while I abode at Geshur in Syria, saying, If

nn3068   himf,pnx7725   nn3389   wcs,qpf5647 (853)   nn3068
the LORD shall bring*me*again indeed to Jerusalem, then I will serve the LORD.

df,nn4428 wcs,qmf559   pp,pnx   qmv1980   pp,nn7965   wcs,qmf6965   wcs,qmf1980
9 And the king said unto him, Go in peace. So he arose, and went to

nn,lh2275
Hebron.

nn53   wcs,qmf7971 pl,pipt7270   pp,cs,nn3605   pl,cs,nn7626   nn3478 pp,qnc559
10 But Absalom sent spies throughout all the tribes of Israel, saying,

pp,qnc,pnx8085 (853)   nn6963   df,nn7782   wcj,qpf559   nn53
As soon as ye hear the sound of the trumpet, then ye shall say, Absalom

qpf4427   pp,nn2275
reigneth in Hebron.

☞ **15:1–12** These verses describe the actions of Absalom by which he was attempting to assume royal power. David was showing weakness by allowing this to happen.

☞ **15:2** Judicial cases in Jewish society were decided at the city gate (Deut. 21:19; 22:15).

^{wcj,pr854} ⁿⁿ⁵³ ^{qpf1980} ^{du,nu3967} ⁿⁿ³⁷⁶ ^{pr4480/nn3389}
11 And with Absalom went two hundred men out*of*Jerusalem, *that were*

^{pl,qptp7121} ^{wcj,pl,qpta1980} ^{pp,nn,pnx8537} ^{qpf3045} ^{wcj,ptn3808} ^{cs,nn3605} ⁿⁿ¹⁶⁹⁷
called; and they went in their simplicity, and they knew not any thing.

ⁿⁿ⁵³ ^{wcs,qmf7971} ⁽⁸⁵³⁾ ⁿⁿ³⁰² ^{df,nn1526} ⁿⁿ¹⁷³² ^{qpta3289}
☞ 12 And Absalom sent for Ahithophel the Gilonite, David's counselor,

^{nn,pnx5892} ^{pr4480/nn1542} ^{pp,qnc,pnx2076} ⁽⁸⁵³⁾ ^{df,pl,nn2077}
from*his*city, *even* from Giloh, while he offered sacrifices. And the

^{df,nn7195} ^{wcs,qmf1961} ^{aj533} ^{wcj,df,nn5971} ^{wcj,aj7227} ^{qpta1980} ^{pr854} ⁿⁿ⁵³
conspiracy was strong; for the people increased continually with Absalom.

David Escapes

^{wcs,qmf935} ^{df,hipt5046} ^{pr413} ⁿⁿ¹⁷³² ^{pp,qnc559} ^{cs,nn3820} ⁿⁿ³⁷⁶
13 And there came a messenger to David, saying, The hearts of the men of

ⁿⁿ³⁴⁷⁸ ^{qpf1961} ^{pr310} ⁿⁿ⁵³
Israel are after Absalom.

ⁿⁿ¹⁷³² ^{wcs,qmf559} ^{pp,cs,nn3605} ^{pl,nn,pnx5650} ^{pnl834} ^{pr,pnx854}
14 And David said unto all his servants that *were* with him at

^{pp,nn3389} ^{qmv6965} ^{wcj,qcj1227} ^{cj3588} ^{pp,pnx} ^{qmf1961} ^{ptn3808} ⁿⁿ⁶⁴¹³ ^{pr4480/pl,cs,nn6640}
Jerusalem, Arise, and let*us*flee; for we shall not *else* escape from

ⁿⁿ⁵³ ^{pimv4116} ^{pp,qnc1980} ^{cj6435} ^{wcs,hipf,pnx5381} ^{pimf4116} ^{wcs,hipf5080} ⁽⁸⁵³⁾ ^{df,aj7451}
Absalom: make speed to depart, lest he overtake us suddenly, and bring evil

^{pr,pnx5921} ^{wcs,hipf5221} ^{df,nn5892} ^{pp,cs,nn6310} ⁿⁿ²⁷¹⁹
upon us, and smite the city with the edge of the sword.

^{df,nn4428} ^{pl,cs,nn5650} ^{wcs,qmf559} ^{pr413} ^{df,nn4428} ^{ptdm2009} ^{pl,nn,pnx5650}
15 And the king's servants said unto the king, Behold, thy servants *are ready*

^{pnl834/pp,nn3605} ^{nn,pnx113} ^{df,nn4428} ^{qmf977}
to do whatsoever my lord the king shall appoint.

^{df,nn4428} ^{wcs,qmf3318} ^{wcj,cs,nn3605} ^{nn,pnx1004} ^{pp,du,nn,pnx7272}
16 And the king went forth, and all his household after him. And

^{df,nn4428} ^{wcs,qmf5800} ⁽⁸⁵³⁾ ^{nu6235} ^{pl,nn802} ^{pl,nn6370} ^{pp,qnc8104} ^{df,nn1004}
the king left ten women, *which were* concubines, to keep the house.

^{df,nn4428} ^{wcs,qmf3318} ^{wcj,cs,nn3605} ^{df,nn5971} ^{pp,du,nn,pnx7272}
17 And the king went forth, and all the people after him, and

^{wcs,qmf5975} ^{cs,nn1004} ^{df,nn4801}
tarried in a place that was far off.

^{wcj,cs,nn3605} ^{pl,nn,pnx5650} ^{pl,qpta5674} ^{pr5921/nn,pnx3027} ^{wcj,cs,nn3605}
☞ 18 And all his servants passed on beside him; and all the

^{df,nn3774} ^{wcj,cs,nn3605} ^{df,nn6432} ^{wcj,cs,nn3605} ^{df,nn1663} ^{nu8337} ^{pl,nu3967} ⁿⁿ³⁷⁶
Cherethites, and all the Pelethites, and all the Gittites, six hundred men

^{pnl834} ^{qpf935} ^{pp,nn,pnx7272} ^{pr4480/nn1661} ^{pl,qpta5674} ^{pr5921/pl,cs,nn6440} ^{df,nn4428}
which came after him from Gath, passed on before the king.

^{wcs,qmf559} ^{df,nn4428} ^{pr413} ⁿⁿ⁸⁶³ ^{df,nn1663} ^{pnit4100} ^{qmf1980} ^{pnp859} ^{ad1571} ^{pr,pnx854}
19 Then said the king to Ittai the Gittite, Wherefore goest thou also with

---

☞ **15:12** Ahithophel had been a member of David's cabinet as well as his chief counselor. Perhaps Ahithophel turned against David because of the events surrounding the death of Uriah the Hittite, the husband of Bath–sheba. This would seem logical since Ahithophel was Bath–sheba's grandfather (2 Sam. 11:3; 23:34).
☞ **15:18** Originally, David's band of rebels that had fled with him from Saul to the Philistine city of Gath (1 Sam. 27:2) and continued with him in Ziklag, Hebron, and Jerusalem (1 Sam. 30:1; 2 Sam. 2:3; 5:6) was composed of six hundred men. Now, some thirty years later, this group of men were still together.

16

And when David was a little past the top *of the hill*, behold, Ziba the servant of Mephibosheth met him, with a couple of asses saddled, and upon them two hundred *loaves* of bread, and a hundred bunches*of*raisins, and a hundred of summer fruits, and a bottle of wine.

2 And the king said unto Ziba, What meanest thou by these? And Ziba said, The asses *be* for the king's household to ride on; and the bread and summer fruit for the young men to eat; and the wine, that such as be faint in the wilderness may drink.

3 And the king said, And where *is* thy master's son? And Ziba said unto the king, Behold, he abideth at Jerusalem: for he said, Today shall the house of Israel restore me the kingdom of my father.

☞ 4 Then said the king to Ziba, Behold, thine *are* all that *pertained* unto Mephibosheth. And Ziba said, I humbly beseech thee *that* I may find grace in thy sight, my lord, O king.

5 And when king David came to Bahurim, behold, thence came out a man of*the*family of the house of Saul, whose name *was* Shimei, the son of Gera: he came forth, and cursed still as he came.

6 And he cast stones at David, and at all the servants of king David: and all the people and all the mighty men *were* on*his*right*hand and on*his*left.

7 And thus said Shimei when he cursed, Come out, come out, thou bloody man, and thou man of Belial:

☞ 8 The LORD hath returned upon thee all the blood of the house of Saul, in whose stead thou hast reigned; and the LORD hath delivered the kingdom into

---

☞ **16:4** David's decision to trust the words of Ziba was too hasty. According to 2 Samuel 19:24–28, Ziba was lying, and Mephibosheth's loyalty to David had never changed.

☞ **16:8** In this verse Shimei was probably blaming David for the deaths of Abner (2 Sam. 3:27–39), and Ish-bosheth (2 Sam. 4:1–12) who, along with himself, were related to Saul. However, in these instances David was not guilty of any wrong. In fact, he had the men put to death that murdered Ishbosheth. It was true that David was a man of war, but he was not necessarily the one responsible for eliminating the members of Saul's family.

pp,cs,nn**3027**   nn**53**   nn,pnx**1121**   wcj,ptdm**2009**   pp,nn,pnx**7451**

the hand of Absalom thy son: and, behold, thou *art taken* in thy mischief,

cj**3588**   pnp**859**   pl,nn**1818**   nn**376**

because thou *art* a bloody man.

wcs,qmf**559**   nn**52**   cs,nn**1121**   nn**6870**   pr**413**   df,nn**4428**   pp,pnit**4100**   df,pndm**2088**

9 Then said Abishai the son of Zeruiah unto the king, Why should this

df,qpta**4191** df,nn**3611** pimf**7043** (**853**)   nn,pnx**113**   df,nn**4428**   qmf**5674**   pte**4994**   wcj,himf**5493**

dead dog curse   my lord the king? let me go over, I*pray*thee, and take off

(**853**)   nn,pnx**7218**

his head.

df,nn**4428** wcs,qmf**559** pnit**4100**   pp,pnx   wcj,pp,pnx   pl,cs,nn**1121**   nn**6870**

10 And the king said, What have I to do with you, ye sons of Zeruiah?

ad**3541**   pimf**7043**   cj**3588**   nn**3068**   qpf**559**   pp,pnx   pimv**7043** (**853**) nn**1732** wcj,pnit**4310**

so let him curse, because the Lord hath said unto him, Curse   David. Who

qmf**559**   ad**4069**   qpf**6213** ad**3651**

shall then say, Wherefore hast thou done so?

nn**1732**   wcs,qmf**559** pr**413**   nn**52**   wcj,pr**413** cs,nn**3605**   pl,nn,pnx**5650**   ptdm**2009**

11 And David said to Abishai, and to all his servants, Behold, my

nn,pnx**1121**   pnl**834**   qpf**3318**   pr**4480**/pl,nn,pnx**4578** pipt**1245** (**853**)   nn,pnx**5315**   wcj,cj**637**/cj**3588**

son, which came forth of*my*bowels, seeketh   my life: how*much*more

ad**6258**   nn**1145**   himv**5117**/pp,pnx   wcj,pimf**7043**   cj**3588**   nn**3068**

now *may this* Benjamite *do it*? let*him*alone, and let*him*curse; for the Lord hath

qpf**559**   pp,pnx

bidden him.

ad**194**   nn**3068**   qmf**7200**   pp,nn,pnx**6040**   nn**3068**

12 It*may*be that the Lord will look on mine affliction, and that the Lord will

wcs,hipf**7725** pp,pnx nn**2896** pr**8478**   nn,pnx**7045** df,pndm**2088** df,nn**3117**

requite me good for his cursing this day.

nn**1732**   wcj,pl,nn,pnx**376** wcs,qmf**1980**   dfp,nn**1870** wcj,nn**8096**   qpta**1980**

13 And as David and his men went by the way, Shimei went along on

df,nn**2022** pp,cs,nn**6763**   pp,pr,pnx**5980**   wcs,pimf**7043**   qna**1980**   wcs,pimf**5619** dfp,pl,nn**68**

the hill's side over against him, and cursed as he went, and threw stones

pp,pr,pnx**5980**   wcj,pipf**6080** dfp,nn**6083**

at   him, and cast dust.

df,nn**4428**   wcj,cs,nn**3605**   df,nn**5971** pnl**834**   pr,pnx**854**   wcs,qmf**935**   aj**5889**

○☞ 14 And the king, and all   the people that *were* with him, came weary,

wcs,nimf**5314**   ad**8033**

and refreshed themselves there.

Absalom Returns to Jerusalem

wcj,nn**53**   wcj,cs,nn**3605**   df,nn**5971**   nn**376**   nn**3478** qpf**935**   nn**3389**

15 And Absalom, and all   the people the men of Israel, came to Jerusalem,

wcj,nn**302**   pr,pnx**854**

and Ahithophel with him.

wcs,qmf**1961**   pp,pnl**834** nn**2365**   df,nn**757**   nn**1732** cs,nn**7463**   qpf**935**

16 And it*came*to*pass, when Hushai the Archite, David's friend, was come

pr**413**   nn**53**   nn**2365** wcs,qmf**559** pr**413**   nn**53**   qmf**2421**   df,nn**4428** qmf**2421**

unto Absalom, that Hushai said unto Absalom, God save the king, God save the

df,nn**4428**

king.

○☞ **16:14** He arrived at the fords of the Jordan River (2 Sam. 15:28). It is believed that David wrote Psalms 3 and 63 while fleeing through the wilderness of Judah.

                    nn53   wcs,qmf**559** pr413   nn2365   pndm2088   nn,pnx**2617**   (853)   nn,pnx**7453**
17 And Absalom said to Hushai, *Is* this thy kindness to thy friend?
pp,pnit4100   qpf**1980**   ptn**3808** pr854   nn,pnx**7453**
why wentest thou not with thy friend?

                    nn2365   wcs,qmf**559** pr413   nn53   ptn**3808** cj3588   pnl834   nn**3068**   df,pndm2088
18 And Hushai said unto Absalom, Nay; but whom the LORD, and this
wcj,df,nn**5971**   wcj,cs,nn3605   nn**376**   nn3478   qpf**977**   pp,pnx   qmf**1961**   wcj,pr,pnx854
people, and all the men of Israel, choose, his will I be, and with him will
qmf**3427**
I abide.

                    wcj,df,nuor8145 pp,pnit4310   pnp589   qmf**5647**   he,ptn**3808**   pp,pl,cs,nn**6440**
19 And again, whom should I serve? *should I* not *serve* in the presence
nn,pnx**1121** pp,pnl834   qpf**5647**   nn,pnx1   pp,pl,cs,nn**6440** ad**3651**   qmf**1961**
of his son? as I have served in thy father's presence, so will I be in thy
pp,pp,pnx**6440**
presence.

                    wcs,qmf**559**   nn53   pr413   nn302   qmv3051   nn**6098**   pp,pnx   pnid4100
20 Then said Absalom to Ahithophel, Give counsel among you what we
qmf**6213**
shall do.

                    nn302   wcs,qmf**559** pr413   nn53   qmv935   pr413   nn,pnx1   pl,cs,nn**6370**
21 And Ahithophel said unto Absalom, Go in unto thy father's concubines,
pnl834   hipf5117   pp,qnc**8104**   df,nn**1004**   cs,nn3605   nn3478   wcj,qpf**8085** cj3588
which he hath left to keep the house; and all Israel shall hear that thou art
nipf**887**   pr854   nn,pnx1   du,cs,nn**3027**   cs,nn3605 pnl834   pr,pnx854   wcj,qpf**2388**
abhorred of thy father: then shall the hands of all that *are* with thee be strong.

                    wcs,himf5186   pp,nn53   df,nn**168** pr5921   df,nn**1406**   nn53
⊙⊒ 22 So they spread Absalom a tent upon the top of the house; and Absalom
wcs,qmf935   pr413   nn,pnx1   pl,cs,nn**6370**   pp,du,cs,nn**5869**   cs,nn3605 nn3478
went in unto his father's concubines in the sight of all Israel.

                    wcj,cs,nn**6098**   nn302   pnl834   qpf**3289**   df,pnp1992 dfp,pl,nn**3117**
23 And the counsel of Ahithophel, which he counseled in those days, *was*
pp,pnl834   nn**376**   qmf**7592**   pp,cs,nn**1697**   df,pl,nn**430** ad**3651**   cs,nn3605   cs,nn**6098**
as if a man had inquired at the oracle of God: so *was* all the counsel of
nn302   ad1571   pp,nn1732 ad1571   pp,nn53
Ahithophel both with David and with Absalom.

Absalom Receives Counsel

                         nn302   wcs,qmf**559** pr413   nn53   pte**4994**   qcj**977**
17 Moreover Ahithophel said unto Absalom, Let me now choose out
                du,nu8147/nu6240   nu**505**   nn**376**   wcj,qcj**6965**   wcj,qcj**7291** pr310   nn1732
twelve thousand men, and I will arise and pursue after David this
df,nn**3915**
night:

                    wcj,qmf935   pr,pnx5921   wcj,pnp1931   aj3023   wcj,cs,aj7504   du,nn**3027**
2 And I will come upon him while he *is* weary and weak handed, and

---

⊙⊒ **16:22** This event was one of the things that Nathan predicted would happen as a result of David's sin with Bath-sheba (see the note on 2 Sam. 12:1–14). Absalom committed this evil on the counsel of Ahithophel. Besides the fact that this was forbidden by God, it made Absalom's reconciliation with David impossible and forced the people to take sides between the two of them.

wcs,hipf2729/pnx(853)   cs,nn3605   df,nn5971 pnl834   pr,pnx854   wcs,qpf5127

will make*him*afraid: and   all   the people that *are* with him shall   flee;   and I

wcs,hipf5221 (853)   df,nn4428 pp,nn,pnx905

will smite   the king   only:

wcj,himf7725   cs,nn3605   df,nn5971   pr,pnx413   df,nn376 pnl834   pnp859

3 And I will bring back   all   the people unto thee: the man   whom thou

pipt1245   df,nn3605   pp,qnc7725   cs,nn3605 df,nn5971   qmf1961   nn7965

seekest *is* as if   all   returned: *so* all   the people shall be in peace.

df,nn1697   wcs,qmf3474   nn53   pp,du,cs,nn5869   wcj(pp,du,cs,nn5869) cs,nn3605   cs,aj2205

4 And the saying pleased Absalom   well,   and   all   the elders of

nn3478

Israel.

wcs,qmf559   nn53   qmv7121 pte4994 pp,nn2365   df,nn757   ad1571   wcj,qmf8085

5 Then said Absalom, Call now Hushai the Archite also, and let us   hear

ad1571   pnid4100 pnp1931 pp,nn,pnx6310

likewise what   he   saith.

nn2365   wcs,qmf935 pr413   nn53   nn53   wcs,qmf559 pr,pnx413

6 And when Hushai was come   to   Absalom, Absalom spoke   unto him,

pp,qnc559   nn302   pipf1696   df,pndm2088 dfp,nn1697   he,qmf6213   (853)

saying, Ahithophel hath spoken after   this   manner: shall we   do   *after*   his

nn,pnx1697 cj518 ptn369 pimv1696 pnp859

saying? if not; speak thou.

nn2365   wcs,qmf559 pr413   nn53   df,nn6098 pnl834   nn302   qpf3289

7 And Hushai said   unto Absalom, The counsel that Ahithophel hath given *is*

ptn3808   aj2896   df,pndm2063 dfp,nn6471

not good at   this   time.

wcs,qmf559   nn2365   pnp859   qpf3045   (853)   nn,pnx1   wcj(853)   pl,nn,nn376 cj3588 pnp1992

8 For, said Hushai, thou knowest   thy father and   his men, that they

pl,nn1368   pnp1992   wcj,cs,aj4751   nn5315   pp,nn1677

be mighty men, and   they *be* chafed   in   their   minds,   as a   bear

aj7909   dfp,nn7704   wcj,nn,pnx1   pl,nn,pnx376   nn4421

robbed*of*her*whelps in the field: and thy father *is* a   man   of war, and will

wcj,ptn3808   qmf3885 pr854   df,nn5971

not   lodge with the people.

ptdm2009   pnp1931   nipt2244 ad6258   pp,nu259 df,pl,nn6354 cj176   pp,nu259   df,pl,nn4725

9 Behold,   he   is   hid   now in some   pit,   or in some *other* place: and

wcs,qpf1961   pp,pnx   pp,qnc5307   dfp,nn8462

it*will*come*to*pass, when some of them be overthrown at the   first,   that

wcs,qpf8085/df,qpta8085   wcs,qpf559   qpf1961   nn4046   dfp,nn5971   pnl834

whosoever heareth it will   say, There   is   a slaughter among the people that

pr310   nn53

follow Absalom.

wcj,pnp1931 ad1571   cs,nn1121/nn2428   pnl834   nn,pnx3820   pp,nn3820   df,nn738

10 And   he   also *that is* valiant, whose heart *is* as the heart of a lion,

nina4549/nimf4549   cj3588 cs,nn3605 nn3478   qpta3045 cj3588   nn,pnx1   nn1368

shall utterly melt: for   all   Israel knoweth that thy father *is* a mighty man, and

pnl834   pr,pnx854   nn2428 wcj,pl,cs,nn1121

they which *be* with him *are* valiant   men.

cj3588   qpf3289   cs,nn3605   nn3478   nina622   nimf622   pr,pnx5921

11 Therefore I counsel that   all   Israel be generally gathered   unto thee,

pr4480/nn1835   wcj,pr5704   nn884   dfp,nn2344 pnl834   pr5921   df,nn3220   dfp,nn7230

from Dan even   to   Beer-sheba, as the sand   that *is* by the   sea   for multitude;

pl,qpta1980   pp,nn7128   wcj,pl,nn,pnx6440

and that thou   go   to battle in thine own   person.

wcs,qpf935 pr,pnx413   pp,nu259 df,pl,nn4725 pnl834/ad8033   nipf4672

12 So shall we come upon him in some place   where he shall be found, and

qpf5117   pr,pnx5921   pp,pnl834   df,nn2919 qmf5307 pr5921   df,nn127   pp,pnx

we will light upon him   as   the dew falleth on the ground: and of him and of

wcj,pp,cs,nn3605   df,pl,nn376 pnl834   pr,pnx854   wcj,ptn3808   nipf3498   ad1571   nu259

all   the men that *are* with him there shall   not   be left so much as one.

wcj,cj518   nimf622   pr413   nn5892   cs,nn3605   nn3478 wcs,hipf5375

13 Moreover, if   he be gotten into a city, then shall   all   Israel bring

pl,nn2256 pr413 df,pndm1931 df,nn5892   wcs,qpf5498 pnx(853) pr5704   df,nn5158 pr5704/pnl834

ropes to   that city, and we will draw   it into the river, until   there be

ptn3808   ad1571   nn6872 nipf4672   ad8033

not one small stone found there.

nn53   wcj,cs,nn3605   cs,nn376   nn3478 wcs,qmf559   cs,nn6098   nn2365

14 And Absalom and   all   the men of Israel said, The counsel of Hushai

df,nn757   aj2896   pr4480/cs,nn6098   nn302   wcj,nn3068   pipf6680

the Archite *is* better than*the*counsel of Ahithophel. For the LORD had appointed to

pp,hinc6565 (853)   df,aj2896 cs,nn6098   nn302   pp,pr5668   nn3068   hinc935

defeat   the good counsel of Ahithophel, to the intent that the LORD might bring

df,aj7451 pr413   nn53

evil upon Absalom.

David Is Warned to Retreat

wcs,qmf559   nn2365   pr413   nn6659   wcj,pr413   nn54   df,pl,nn3548 pp,pndm2063

15 Then said Hushai unto Zadok and   to   Abiathar the priests, Thus   and

wcj,pp,pndm2063   nn302   qpf3289   (853)   nn53   wcj(853)   cs,aj2205   nn3478

thus   did Ahithophel counsel   Absalom and   the elders of Israel; and

wcj,pp,pndm2063   wcj,pp,pndm2063   pnp589   qpf3289

thus   and   thus   have I   counseled.

wcj,ad6258   qmv7971   ad4120   wcj,himv5046 pp,nn1732 pp,qnc559   qmf3885 ptn408

16 Now therefore send quickly, and   tell   David, saying, Lodge not this

df,nn3915   pp,pl,cs,nn6160   df,nn4057 wcj,ad1571   qna5674   qmf5674   cj6435   dfp,nn4428

night in the plains of the wilderness, but   speedily pass over; lest the king be

pumf1104   wcj,pp,cs,nn3605   df,nn5971 pnl834   pr,pnx854

swallowed up, and   all   the people that *are* with him.

wcj,nn3083   wcj,nn290   pl,qpta5975   pp,nn5883 cj3588   qmf3201 ptn3808

17 Now Jonathan and Ahimaaz stayed by En-rogel; for they might   not be

pp,ninc7200   pp,qnc935   df,nn,lh5892   df,nn8198 qmf1980   wcs,hipf5046 pp,pnx   wcj,pnp1992

seen to come into the   city: and a wench went and   told   them; and they

wcs,qpf1980   wcs,hipf5046 dfp,nn4428   nn1732

went and told   king David.

nn5288   wcs,qmf7200 pnx(853)   wcs,himf5046   pp,nn53

18 Nevertheless a lad   saw   them, and   told   Absalom: but they

wcs,qmf1980 du,nu,pnx8147   ad4120   wcs,qmf935 pr413   nn376   cs,nn1004   pp,nn980

went   both   of them away quickly, and came   to a man's house in Bahurim,

wcj,pp,pnx   nn875   pp,nn,pnx2691 ad8033   wcs,qmf3381

which had a well in his   court; whither they went down.

df,nn802   wcs,qmf3947   wcs,qmf6566 (853)   df,nn4539 pr5921   df,nn875   pl,cs,nn6440

19 And the woman took   and spread   a covering over the well's mouth,

wcs,qmf7849   df,pl,nn7383   pr,pnx5921   nn1697   wcj,ptn3808 nipf3045

and spread ground corn thereon; and the thing was not known.

nn53   pl,cs,nn5650 wcs,qmf935 pr413   df,nn802   df,nn,lh1004

20 And when Absalom's servants came   to the woman to the house, they

wcs,qmf559 pnit346   nn290   wcj,nn3083   df,nn802 wcs,qmf559 pp,pnx

said, Where *is* Ahimaaz and Jonathan? And the woman said unto them, They be

^{qpf5674}   ^{cs,nn4323}   ^{df,pl,nn4325}   ^{wcs,pimf1245}   ^{wcj,ptn3808} ^{qpf4672}
gone over the brook of water. And when they had sought and could not find

^{wcs,qmf7725}   ⁿⁿ³³⁸⁹
them, they returned to Jerusalem.

^{wcs,qmf1961}   ^{pr310}   ^{qnc,pnx1980}   ^{wcs,qmf5927}
21 And it*came*to*pass, after they were departed, that they came up

^{pr4480/df,nn875}   ^{wcs,qmf1980}   ^{wcs,himf5046} ^{dfp,nn4428} ⁿⁿ¹⁷³²   ^{wcs,qmf559} ^{pr413}   ⁿⁿ¹⁷³²
out*of*the*well, and went and told king David, and said unto David,

^{qmv6965}   ^{wcj,qmv5674/ad4120}   ⁽⁸⁵³⁾ ^{df,pl,nn4325} ^{cj3588} ^{ad3602}   ⁿⁿ³⁰²   ^{qpf3289}
Arise, and pass*quickly*over   the water: for thus hath Ahithophel counseled

^{pr,pnx5921}
against you.

ⁿⁿ¹⁷³²   ^{wcs,qmf6965}   ^{wcj,cs,nn3605}   ^{df,nn5971} ^{pnl834}   ^{pr,pnx854}
22 Then David arose, and all the people that were with him, and they

^{wcs,qmf5674}   ⁽⁸⁵³⁾ ^{df,nn3383} ^{pr5704}   ^{df,nn1242}   ⁿⁿ²¹⁶   ^(pr5704)   ^{nipf5737} ^{ptn3808} ^{nu259}
passed over   Jordan: by the morning light   there lacked not one of them

^{pnl834} ^{ptn3808}   ^{qpf5674}   ⁽⁸⁵³⁾ ^{df,nn3383}
that was not gone over Jordan.

^{wcj,nn302}   ^{qpf7200} ^{cj3588}   ^{nn,pnx6098}   ^{ptn3808} ^{nipf6213}   ^{wcs,qmf2280}
23 And when Ahithophel saw that his counsel was not followed, he saddled

⁽⁸⁵³⁾ ^{df,nn2543} ^{wcs,qmf6965} ^{wcs,qmf1980}   ^{pr413}   ^{nn,pnx1004} ^{pr413}   ^{nn,pnx5892}
his ass, and arose, and got him home to his house, to his city, and

^{wcs,pimf6680/pr413}   ^{nn,pnx1004}   ^{wcs,nimf2614}   ^{wcs,qmf4191}   ^{wcs,nimf6912}
put his household in order, and hanged himself, and died, and was buried

^{pp,nn6913}   ^{nn,pnx1}
in the sepulcher of his father.

^{wcj,nn1732} ^{qpf935}   ^{nn,lh4266}   ^{wcj,nn53}   ^{qpf5674}   ⁽⁸⁵³⁾ ^{df,nn3383} ^{pnp1931}
24 Then David came to Mahanaim. And Absalom passed over Jordan, he

^{wcj,cs,nn3605}   ⁿⁿ³⁷⁶   ⁿⁿ³⁴⁷⁸ ^{pr,pnx5973}
and all the men of Israel with him.

ⁿⁿ⁵³   ^{qpf7760} ^{wcj(853)}   ⁿⁿ⁶⁰²¹   ^{pr5921}   ^{df,nn6635} ^{pr8478}   ⁿⁿ³⁰⁹⁷
25 And Absalom made Amasa captain of the host instead of Joab: which

^{wcj,nn6021}   ⁿⁿ³⁷⁶   ^{cs,nn1121} ^{wcj,nn,pnx8034}   ⁿⁿ³⁵⁰¹   ^{df,nn3481} ^{pnl834} ^{qpf935}   ^{pr413}
Amasa was a man's son, whose name was Ithra an Israelite, that went in to

ⁿⁿ²⁶   ⁿⁿ¹³²³   ⁿⁿ⁵¹⁷⁶ ^{cs,nn269}   ⁿⁿ⁶⁸⁷⁰ ⁿⁿ³⁰⁹⁷   ⁿⁿ⁵¹⁷
Abigail the daughter of Nahash, sister to Zeruiah Joab's mother.

ⁿⁿ³⁴⁷⁸   ^{wcj,nn53} ^{wcs,qmf2583}   ⁿⁿ⁷⁷⁶ ^{df,nn1568}
26 So Israel and Absalom pitched in the land of Gilead.

^{wcs,qmf1961}   ⁿⁿ¹⁷³²   ^{pp,qnc935}   ^{nn,lh4266}   ^{wcj,nn7629}
27 And it*came*to*pass, when David was come to Mahanaim, that Shobi the

^{cs,nn1121}   ⁿⁿ⁵¹⁷⁶   ^{pr4480/nn7237} ^{pl,cs,nn1121}   ⁿⁿ⁵⁹⁸³   ^{wcj,nn4353}   ^{cs,nn1121}
son of Nahash of Rabbah of the children of Ammon, and Machir the son of

ⁿⁿ⁵⁹⁸⁸   ^{pr4480/nn3810}   ^{wcj,nn1271}   ^{df,nn1569}   ^{pr4480/nn7274}
Ammiel of Lo-debar, and Barzillai the Gileadite of Rogelim,

^{hipf5066}   ⁿⁿ⁴⁹⁰⁴   ^{wcj,pl,nn5592}   ^{qpta3335}   ^{wcj,nn3627}   ^{wcj,pl,nn2406}   ^{wcj,pl,nn8184}
☞ 28 Brought beds, and basins, and earthen vessels, and wheat, and barley, and

^{wcj,nn7058}   ^{wcj,nn7039}   ^{wcj,nn6321}   ^{wcj,pl,nn5742}   ^{wcj,nn7039}
flour, and parched corn, and beans, and lentils, and parched pulse,

^{wcj,nn1706}   ^{wcj,nn2529}   ^{wcj,nn6629}   ^{wcj,cs,nn8194}   ⁿⁿ¹²⁴¹   ^{pp,nn1732}
☞ 29 And honey, and butter, and sheep, and cheese of kine, for David, and for

---

☞ 17:28 The word "brought" actually occurs in verse twenty-nine in the Hebrew text.

☞ 17:29 David may have written Psalms 61 and 62 about the time the events of this verse took place.

wcj,dfp,nn**5971** pnl834   pr,pnx854   pp,qnc398 cj3588   qpf**559**   df,nn**5971**   aj7457
the people that *were* with him, to eat: for they said, The people *is* hungry, and

wcj,aj5889   wcj,aj6771   dfp,nn4057
weary, and thirsty, in the wilderness.

Absalom's Death

nn1732   wcs,qmf**6485**   (853)   df,nn**5971** pnl834   pr,pnx854   wcs,qmf**7760**
18 And David numbered   the people that *were* with him, and   set

pl,cs,nn**8269**   pl,nu505   wcj,pl,cs,nn**8269**   pl,nu3967   pr,pnx5921
captains of thousands and captains of hundreds over them.

nn1732   wcs,pimf7971   df,nuor7992   (853)   df,nn**5971**   pp,cs,nn**3027**   nn3097
2 And David sent forth a third part of   the people under the hand of Joab,

wcj,df,nuor7992   pp,cs,nn**3027**   nn52   cs,nn1121   nn6870   nn3097   cs,nn**251**
and a third part under the hand of Abishai the son of Zeruiah, Joab's brother,

wcj,df,nuor7992   pp,cs,nn**3027**   nn863   df,nn1663   df,nn**4428** wcs,qmf559 pr413
and a third part under the hand of Ittai the Gittite. And the king said unto the

df,nn**5971**   qna3318/qmf3318   pr,pnx5973   pnp589   ad1571
people, I will surely*go*forth with you myself also.

df,nn**5971**   wcs,qmf**559**   ptn3808 qmf3318 cj3588 cj518   qna5127/qmf5127
3 But the people answered, Thou shalt not go forth: for if we flee away,

ptn3808 qmf**7760**/nn**3820** pr,pnx413   ptn3808 wcj,cj518 nn,pnx2677   qmf**4191**   qmf**7760**/nn**3820**
they will not care for us; neither if half of us die, will they care

pr,pnx413   cj3588 ad6258   pp,pnx3644 nu6235 pl,nu**505**   wcj,ad6258   aj**2896**
for us: but now *thou art* worth ten thousand of us: therefore now *it is* better

cj3588   (qmf**1961**) pp,qnc5826 pp,pnx   pr4480/nn5892
that thou   succor us out*of*the*city.

df,nn**4428** wcs,qmf**559** pr,pnx413   pnl834 pp,du,nn,pnx**5869**   qmf3190   qmf6213
4 And the king said unto them, What seemeth you best I will do. And

df,nn**4428** wcs,qmf5975 pr413   df,nn8179 cs,nn**3027**   wcj,cs,nn3605   df,nn**5971** qpf3318   pp,pl,nu3967
the king stood by the gate side, and all the people came out by hundreds

wcj,dfp,pl,nu**505**
and by thousands.

df,nn**4428**   wcs,pimf**6680** (853) nn3097   wcj(853)   nn52   wcj(853)   nn863 pp,qnc**559**
5 And the king commanded Joab and   Abishai and   Ittai, saying,

pp,aj**328**   pp,pnx   dfp,nn5288   pp,nn53   wcj,cs,nn3605
Deal gently for*my*sake with the young man, *even* with Absalom. And all the

df,nn**5971**   qpf**8085**   df,nn**4428**   (853) cs,nn3605   df,pl,nn**8269** pp,pinc**6680** pr5921/cs,nn**1697**
people heard when the king gave   all the captains charge concerning

nn53
Absalom.

df,nn**5971**   wcs,qmf3318   df,nn**7704** pp,qnc7125   nn3478   df,nn4421 wcs,qmf**1961**
6 So the people went out into the field against Israel: and the battle was in

pp,nn3293   nn669
the wood of Ephraim;

ad8033   nn**5971**   nn3478   wcs,nimf**5062** pp,pl,cs,nn**6440**   pl,cs,nn**5650**   nn1732
7 Where the people of Israel were slain before the servants of David, and

wcs,qmf**1961** ad8033   aj1419   df,nn4046 df,pndm1931 dfp,nn**3117** pl,nu6242   nu**505**
there was there a great slaughter that day of twenty thousand *men*.

df,nn4421 wcs,qmf**1961** ad8033 nipt6327   pr5921   pl,cs,nn**6440** cs,nn3605   df,nn**776**
8 For the battle was there scattered over the face of all the country: and

pp,nn3293   pp,qnc398 wcs,himf7235 dfp,nn**5971** df,pndm1931 dfp,nn**3117**   df,nn**2719**   qpf398
the wood devoured more people that day than the sword devoured.

nn53   wcs,nimf7122 (pp,pl,cs,nn**6440**)   pl,cs,nn**5650**   nn1732   wcj,nn53 qpta7392
9 And Absalom met   the servants of David. And Absalom rode

pr5921　　df,nn6505　　　　df,nn6505　wcs,qmf935　pr8478　　　　cs,nn7730　　　　df,aj1419　df,nn424
upon a mule, and the mule went under the thick boughs of a great oak, and his

nn,pnx7218　wcs,qmf2388　　dfp,nn424　　　　　　　　wcs,pumf5414　　pr996　　　df,du,nn8064　　　wcj(pr996)
head caught hold of the oak, and he was taken up between the heaven and

　　df,nn776　　　df,nn6505　pnl834　　pr,pnx8478　　　qpf5674
the earth; and the mule that *was* under him went away.

　　　　　　　　nu259　　nn376　wcs,qmf7200　　　　wcs,himf5046　pp,nn3097　　　wcs,qmf559　ptdm2009　qpf7200
10 And a certain man saw *it*, and told Joab, and said, Behold, I saw

(853)　　nn53　　qptp8518　　　dfp,nn424
Absalom hanged in an oak.

　　　　　nn3097　wcs,qmf559　　　dfp,nn376　　df,hipt5046　pp,pnx　　　wcj,ptdm2009　　　qpf7200
11 And Joab said unto the man that told him, And, behold, thou sawest

wcj,ad4069　　　　ptn3808　hipf,pnx5221　　ad8033　　　nn,lh776　　wcj(pr,pnx5921)
him, and why didst thou not smite him there to the ground? and I

　　pp,qnc5414　pp,pnx　nu6235　　　　nn3701　　nu259　wcj,nn2290
would have given thee ten *shekels* of silver, and a girdle.

　　　　df,nn376　wcs,qmf559　pr413　　nn3097　wcj,cj3863　pnp595　　　qpta8254　　　nu505
12 And the man said unto Joab, Though I should receive a thousand

　　nn3701　pr5921　du,nn,pnx3709　　　ptn3808　qmf7971　nn,pnx3027　pr413
shekels of silver in mine hand, *yet* would I not put forth mine hand against

df,nn4428　cs,nn1121　cj3588　　　pp,du,nn,pnx241　df,nn4428　pipf6680　pnx(853)　　wcj(853)　nn52
the king's son: for in our hearing the king charged thee and Abishai

wcj(853)　nn863　pp,qnc559　qmv8104/pnit4130　　　　dfp,nn5288　pp,nn53
and Ittai, saying, Beware*that*none *touch* the young man Absalom.

　　cj176　　　　　qpf6213　　nn8267　　　　　　　pp,nn,pnx5315
13 Otherwise I should have wrought falsehood against mine own life: for

ptn3808/wcj,cs,nn3605/nn1697　nimf3582　pr4480　df,nn4428　　　wcj,pnp859　　htmf3320
there*is*no*matter hid from the king, and thou thyself wouldest have set thyself

pr4480/ad5048
against *me*.

　　　　　wcs,qmf559　nn3097　　ptn3808　himf3176　ad3651　pp,pl,nn,pnx6440　　wcs,qmf3947　nu7969
14 Then said Joab, I may not tarry thus with thee. And he took three

pl,nn7626　　pp,nn,pnx3709　wcs,qmf,pnx8628　　　pp,nn3820　nn53　ad5750
darts in his hand, and thrust them through the heart of Absalom, while he

　　aj2416　　pp,nn3820　df,nn424
was yet alive in the midst of the oak.

　　　　nu6235　pl,nn5288　　pl,cs,qpta5375　nn3097　pl,cs,nn3627　wcs,qmf5437
15 And ten young men that bore Joab's armor compassed about and

wcs,himf5221 (853)　　nn53　　wcs,himf,pnx4191
smote Absalom, and slew him.

　　　　nn3097　wcs,qmf8628　　dfp,nn7782　　df,nn5971　wcs,qmf7725　pr4480/qnc7291　pr310
16 And Joab blew the trumpet, and the people returned from pursuing after

nn3478　cj3588　nn3097　qpf2820　(853)　df,nn5971
Israel: for Joab held back the people.

　　　　wcs,qmf3947 (853)　　nn53　　wcs,himf7993 pnx(853)　pr413　df,aj1419　df,nn6354
17 And they took Absalom, and cast him into a great pit in

dfp,nn3293　wcs,himf5324　ad3966　aj1419　cs,nn1530　pl,nn68　pr,pnx5921　wcj,cs,nn3605　nn3478
the wood, and laid a very great heap of stones upon him: and all Israel

qpf5127　nn376　　pp,pl,nn,pnx168
fled every one to his tent.

　　　wcj,nn53　　　pp,pl,nn,pnx2416　qpf3947　wcs,himf5324　pp,pnx　(853)
18 Now Absalom in his lifetime had taken and reared up for himself a

nn4678　pnl834　　df,nn4428　pp,nn6010　cj3588　qpf559　pp,pnx　ptn369　nn1121　pr,pr5668
pillar, which *is* in the king's dale: for he said, I have no son to

hinc2142/nn,pnx8034   wcs,qmf7121   dfp,nn4678 pr5921   nn,pnx8034
keep*my*name*in*remembrance: and he called the pillar after his own name: and

pp,pnx   wcs,nimf7121 pr5704 df,pndm2088 df,nn3117   nn53   cs,nn3027
it is called unto this day, Absalom's place.

qpf559   wcj,nn290   cs,nn1121   nn6659   pte4994   qmf7323   wcs,pimf1319 (853)
19 Then said Ahimaaz the son of Zadok, Let*me*now run, and bear

df,nn4428   cj3588   nn3068   qpf,pnx8199   pl,qpta,pnx341
the king tidings, how that the LORD hath avenged him of*his*enemies.

nn3097 wcs,qmf559   pp,pnx   pnp859 ptn3808   nn376/nn1309 df,pndm2088 df,nn3117
20 And Joab said unto him, Thou shalt not bear tidings this day, but

wcj,pipf1319   aj312   pp,nn3117   df,pndm2088 wcj,df,nn3117   pimf1319/ptn3808
thou shalt bear tidings another day: but this   day thou shalt bear*no*tidings,

cj3588/pr5921   df,nn4428 cs,nn1121   qpf4191
because the king's son is dead.

wcs,qmf559 nn3097   pp,nn3569 qmv1980 himv5046   dfp,nn4428 pnl834   qpf7200
21 Then said Joab to Cushi, Go tell the king what thou hast seen. And

nn3569   wcs,htmf*7812   pp,nn3097   wcs,qmf7323
Cushi bowed himself unto Joab, and ran.

wcs,qmf559   nn290   cs,nn1121   nn6659   ad5750 wcs,himf3254 pr413   nn3097
22 Then said Ahimaaz the son of Zadok yet again to Joab, But

wcj,qmf1961/pnid4100   pnp589 pte4994   ad1571 qmf7323 pr310 df,nn3569   nn3097 wcs,qmf559
howsoever, let me, I pray thee, also run after Cushi. And Joab said,

pp,pnit4100/pndm2088   pnp859 qpta7323 nn,pnx1121   wcj,pp,pnx ptn369 nn1309 qpta4672
Wherefore wilt thou run, my son, seeing that thou hast no tidings ready?

wcj,qmf1961/pnid4100   qmf7323   wcs,qmf559 pp,pnx   qmv7323
23 But howsoever, *said he*, let me run. And he said unto him, Run. Then

nn290   wcs,qmf7323   nn1870   df,nn3603   wcs,qmf5674 (853) df,nn3569
Ahimaaz ran by the way of the plain, and overran   Cushi.

wcj,nn1732 qpta3427 pr996   du,cs,nu8147 df,pl,nn8179   df,qpta6822 wcs,qmf1980 pr413
24 And David sat between the two gates: and the watchman went up to

cs,nn1406   df,nn8179 pr413   df,nn2346   wcs,qmf5375 (853)   du,nn,pnx5869   wcs,qmf7200
the roof over the gate unto the wall, and lifted up   his eyes, and looked,

wcj,ptdm2009   nn376   qpta7323 pp,nn,pnx905
and behold a man running alone.

df,qpta6822   wcs,qmf7121   wcs,himf5046   dfp,nn4428   df,nn4428 wcs,qmf559 cj518
25 And the watchman cried, and told the king. And the king said, If he

pp,nn,pnx905   nn1309   pp,nn,pnx6310   wcs,qmf1980 qna1980   wcj,aj7131
be alone, *there is* tidings in his mouth. And he came apace, and drew near.

df,qpta6822 wcs,qmf7200 aj312   nn376   qpta7323   df,qpta6822 wcs,qmf7121
26 And the watchman saw another man running: and the watchman called

pr413   df,nn7778   wcs,qmf559 ptdm2009   nn376 qpta7323 pp,nn,pnx905   df,nn4428
unto the porter, and said, Behold *another* man running alone. And the king

wcs,qmf559 pndm2088 ad1571   pipt1319
said, He also bringeth tidings.

df,qpta6822 wcs,qmf559 pnp589 qpta7200   (853)   cs,nn4794   df,aj7223
27 And the watchman said, Me thinketh   the running of the foremost is

pp,cs,nn4794   nn290   cs,nn1121   nn6659   df,nn4428 wcs,qmf559 pndm2088
like the running of Ahimaaz the son of Zadok. And the king said, He *is* a

aj2896 nn376   qmf935   aj2896   nn1309
good man, and cometh with good tidings.

nn290   wcs,qmf7121   wcs,qmf559 pr413 df,nn4428   nn7965
28 And Ahimaaz called, and said unto the king, All is well. And he

wcs,htmf*7821   nn,lh776   pp,du,nn,pnx639   dfp,nn4428 wcs,qmf559 qptp1288
fell down to the earth upon his face before the king, and said, Blessed *be* the

nn**3068**　　pl,nn,pnx**430**　pnl834　　　　pipf5462　(853)　df,pl,nn**376**　pnl834　qpf**5375**　(853)

LORD thy God, which hath delivered up   the men that lifted up   their

nn,pnx**3027**　　　pp,nn,pnx**113**　df,nn**4428**

hand against my lord the king.

df,nn**4428**　wcs,qmf**559**　　　dfp,nn**5288**　　pp,nn53　　nn**7965**　　　nn290

29 And the king said, Is the young man Absalom safe? And Ahimaaz

wcs,qmf**559**　　　nn3097　pp,qnc7971　(853)　df,nn**4428**　nn**5650**　wcj(853)　nn,pnx**5650**　qpf**7200**

answered, When Joab sent   the king's servant, and *me*   thy servant, I saw

df,aj1419　df,nn1995　　qpf**3045**　wcj,ptn**3808**　pnid4100

a great tumult, but I knew not   what *it was*.

df,nn**4428**　wcs,qmf**559**　　　qmv5437　　htmv3320　ad3541

30 And the king said *unto him*, Turn aside, *and* stand here. And he

wcs,qmf5437　　　　wcs,qmf5975

turned aside, and stood still.

David Mourns Absalom

wcj,ptdm2009　df,nn3569　qpta935　　df,nn3569　wcs,qmf**559**　htmf**1319**　　nn,pnx**113**　df,nn**4428**　cj3588

31 And, behold, Cushi came; and Cushi said, Tidings, my lord the king: for

nn**3068**　　　qpf,pnx**8199**　　df,nn**3117**　pr4480/cs,nn**3027**　cs,nn3605　　　df,pl,qpta**6965**　pr,pnx5921

the LORD hath avenged thee this day   of   all them that rose up against

thee.

df,nn**4428**　wcs,qmf**559**　pr413　df,nn3569　　　dfp,nn**5288**　　pp,nn53　he,nn**7965**

32 And the king said unto Cushi, Is the young man Absalom safe? And

df,nn3569　wcs,qmf**559**　pl,cs,qpta341　　nn,pnx**113**　df,nn**4428**　wcj,nn3605　pnl834　qpf**6965**　pr,pnx5921

Cushi answered, The enemies of my lord the king, and all   that rise against

pp,aj**7451**　qmf**1961**　　　dfp,nn**5288**

thee to do *thee* hurt, be as *that* young man *is*.

df,nn**4428**　　wcs,qmf**7264**　　　wcs,qmf**5927**　pr5921　　cs,nn**5944**

33 And the king was much moved, and went up to the chamber over the

df,nn**8179**　wcs,qmf1058　　pp,qnc,pnx**1980**　wcj,ad3541　qpf**559**　　nn,pnx**1121**　nn53

gate, and wept: and as he went,   thus he said, O my son Absalom, my

nn,pnx**1121**　nn,pnx**1121**　nn53　　pnid4310/qmf5414　pnp589　qnc,pnx**4191**　pr,pnx8478　　　　nn53

son, my son Absalom! would God I had died for thee, O Absalom,

nn,pnx**1121**　nn,pnx**1121**

my son, my son!

wcs,homf**5046**　pp,nn3097　ptdm2009　df,nn**4428**　qpta1058　　wcs,htmf56

19 And it was told   Joab, Behold, the king weepeth and mourneth

pr5921　　nn53

for Absalom.

df,nn**8668**　wcs,qmf**1961**　dfp,nn**3117**　　　　　pp,nn60　　pp,cs,nn3605

2 And the victory that   day was *turned* into mourning unto   all   the

df,nn**5971**　cj3588　　df,nn**5971**　qpf**8085**　pp,qnc559　df,pndm1931　dfp,nn**3117**　　df,nn**4428**　nipf**6087**　pr5921

people: for the people heard say   that   day how the king was grieved for his

nn,pnx**1121**

son.

df,nn**5971**　pp,qnc935　　wcs,htmf1589　df,pndm1931　dfp,nn**3117**　　df,nn**5892**　pp,pnl834

3 And the people got them by stealth that day into the city, as

df,nn**5971**　df,pl,nipt3637　htmf**1589**　　pp,qnc,pnx**5127**　dfp,nn4421

people being ashamed steal away when they flee in battle.

wcj,df,nn4428　　qpf3813　　(853)　　　pl,nn,pnx6440　　　　df,nn4428　wcs,qmf2199　　　aj1419

4 But the king covered his face, and the king cried with a loud

nn6963　　　nn,pnx1121　　nn53　　　　nn53　　nn,pnx1121　nn,pnx1121

voice, O my son Absalom, O Absalom, my son, my son!

nn3097 wcs,qmf935　df,nn1004　pr413　　df,nn4428　　wcs,qmf559　　hipf3001

5 And Joab came into the house to the king, and said, Thou hast shamed

df,nn3117　(853)　　pl,cs,nn6440　cs,nn3605　pl,nn,pnx5650　　df,nn3117　df,pl,pipt4422 (853)

this day the faces of all thy servants, which this day have saved thy

nn,pnx5315　wcj(853)　　nn5315　pl,nn,pnx1121　wcj,pl,nn,pnx1323　wcj,nn5315

life, and the lives of thy sons and of thy daughters, and the lives of thy

pl,nn,pnx802　wcj,nn5315　pl,nn,pnx6370

wives, and the lives of thy concubines;

pp,qnc157 (853)　pl,qpta,pnx8130　wcj,pp,qnc8130 (853)　pl,qpta,pnx157 cj3588

6 In that thou lovest thine enemies, and hatest thy friends. For thou

hipf5046　df,nn3117 cj3588 pp,pnx　　ptn369　pl,nn8269　wcj,pl,nn5650 cj3588

hast declared this day, that thou regardest neither princes nor servants: for this

df,nn3117　qpf3045　cj3588 pr3863　nn53　aj2416　wcj,nn,pnx3605　pl,qpta4191　df,nn3117

day I perceive, that if Absalom had lived, and all we had died this day,

(cj3588) ad227　pp,du,nn,pnx5869/aj3477

then it had pleased*thee*well.

wcj,ad6258　　qmv6965　qmv3318　wcj,pimv1696　pr5921/nn3820　　pl,nn,pnx5650

7 Now therefore arise, go forth, and speak comfortably unto thy servants:

cj3588　nipf7650　pp,nn3068 cj3588　ptn,pnx369/qpta3318　cj518 qmf3885 nn376 pr,pnx854

for I swear by the LORD, if thou go*not*forth, there will not tarry one with thee

df,nn3915　pndm2063　wcj,qpf7489　pp,pnx　pr4480/cs,nn3605　wcj,nn7451 pnl834 qpf935/pr,pnx5921

this night: and that will be worse unto thee than all the evil that befell

pr4480/pl,nn,pnx5271　pr5704 ad6258

thee from*thy*youth until now.

df,nn4428 wcs,qmf6965　wcs,qmf3427　dfp,nn8179　hipf5046　wcj,pp,cs,nn3605

8 Then the king arose, and sat in the gate. And they told unto all

df,nn5971　pp,qnc559　ptdm2009　df,nn4428　qpta3427　dfp,nn8179 cs,nn3605　df,nn5971

the people, saying, Behold, the king doth sit in the gate. And all the people

wcs,qmf935 pp,pl,cs,nn6440　df,nn4428　wcj,nn3478　qpf5127　nn376　pp,pl,nn,pnx168

came before the king: for Israel had fled every man to his tent.

David's Kingdom is Restored

cs,nn3605　df,nn5971 wcs,qmf1961　nipt1777　pp,cs,nn3605　pl,cs,nn7626　nn3478

9 And all the people were at strife throughout all the tribes of Israel,

pp,qnc559　df,nn4428 hipf,pnx5337　pr4480/cs,nn3709　pl,qpta,pnx341　wcj,pnp1931 pipf,pnx4422

saying, The king saved us out of*the*hand of our enemies, and he delivered

pr4480/cs,nn3709　pl,nn6430　wcj,ad6258　qpf1272　pr4480　df,nn776 pr4480/pr5921

us out*of*the*hand of the Philistines; and now he is fled out of the land for

nn53

Absalom.

wcj,nn53　pnl834　qpf4886　pr,pnx5921　qpf4191　dfp,nn4421 wcj,ad6258

10 And Absalom, whom we anointed over us, is dead in battle. Now

pnit4100 pl,hipt2790 pnp859　pp,hinc7725 (853)　df,nn4428

therefore why speak ye not a word of bringing the king back?

wcj,df,nn4428　nn1732 qpf7971 pr413　nn6659　wcj,pr413　nn54　df,pl,nn3548　pp,qnc559

11 And king David sent to Zadok and to Abiathar the priests, saying,

pimv1696　pr413　cs,aj2205　nn3063　pp,qnc559　pnit4100 qmf1961　aj314　pp,hinc7725 (853)　df,nn4428

Speak unto the elders of Judah, saying, Why are ye the last to bring the king

^{pr413} ^{nn,pnx1004} ^{wcj,cs,nn1697} ^{cs,nn3605} ⁿⁿ³⁴⁷⁸ ^{qpf935} ^{pr413} ^{df,nn4428}
back to his house? seeing the speech of all Israel is come to the king, *even*

^{pr413} ^{nn,pnx1004}
to his house.

^{pnp859} ^{pl,nn,pnx251} ^{pnp859} ^{nn,pnx6106} ^{wcj,nn,pnx1320} ^{wcj,pnit4100}
12 Ye *are* my brethren, ye *are* my bones and my flesh: wherefore then

^{qmf1961} ^{aj314} ^{pp,hinc7725} ⁽⁸⁵³⁾ ^{df,nn4428}
are ye the last to*bring*back the king?

^{qmf559} ^{wcj,pp,nn6021} ^{pnp859} ^{he,ptn3808} ^{nn,pnx6106} ^{wcj,nn,pnx1320}
13 And say ye to Amasa, *Art* thou not of my bone, and of my flesh?

^{pl,nn430} ^{qmf6213} ^{ad3541} ^{pp,pnx} ^{himf3254} ^{wcj,ad3541} ^{cj518} ^{qmf1961} ^{ptn3808} ⁿⁿ⁸²⁶⁹ ⁿⁿ⁶⁶³⁵
God do so to me, and more also, if thou be not captain of the host

^{pp,pl,nn,pnx6440} ^{cs,nn3605/df,pl,nn3117} ^{pr8478} ⁿⁿ³⁰⁹⁷
before me continually in*the*room of Joab.

^{wcs,himf5186 (853)} ^{cs,nn3824} ^{cs,nn3605} ⁿⁿ³⁷⁶ ⁿⁿ³⁰⁶³
14 And he bowed the heart of all the men of Judah, even as *the heart*

^{nu259} ^{pp,nn376} ^{wcs,qmf7971} ^{pr413} ^{df,nn4428} ^{qmv7725} ^{pnp859} ^{wcj,cs,nn3605}
of one man; so that they sent *this word* unto the king, Return thou, and all

^{pl,nn,pnx5650}
thy servants.

^{df,nn4428} ^{wcs,qmf7725} ^{wcs,qmf935} ^{pr5704} ^{df,nn3383} ^{wcj,nn3063} ^{qpf935} ^{df,nn,lh1537}
15 So the king returned, and came to Jordan. And Judah came to Gilgal, to

^{pp,qnc1980} ^{pp,qnc7125} ^{df,nn4428} ^{pp,hinc5674/(853)/df,nn4428} ⁽⁸⁵³⁾ ^{df,nn3383}
go to meet the king, to conduct*the*king*over Jordan.

ⁿⁿ⁸⁰⁹⁶ ^{cs,nn1121} ⁿⁿ¹⁶¹⁷ ^{df,nn1145} ^{pnl834} ^{pr4480/nn980} ^{wcs,pimf4116}
16 And Shimei the son of Gera, a Benjamite, which *was* of Bahurim, hasted

^{wcs,qmf3381} ^{pr5973} ⁿⁿ³⁷⁶ ⁿⁿ³⁰⁶³ ^{pp,qnc7125} ^{df,nn4428} ⁿⁿ¹⁷³²
and came down with the men of Judah to meet king David.

^{wcj,nu505} ⁿⁿ³⁷⁶ ^{pr4480/nn1144} ^{pr,pnx5973} ^{wcj,nn6717}
17 And *there were* a thousand men of Benjamin with him, and Ziba the

ⁿⁿ⁵²⁸⁸ ^{cs,nn1004} ⁿⁿ⁷⁵⁸⁶ ^{wcj,cs,nn2568/nu6240} ^{pl,nn,pnx1121} ^{wcj,pl,nu6242} ^{pl,nn,pnx5650}
servant of the house of Saul, and his fifteen sons and his twenty servants

^{pr,pnx854} ^{wcj,qpf6743} ^{df,nn3383} ^{pp,pl,cs,nn6440} ^{df,nn4428}
with him; and they went over Jordan before the king.

^{wcj,qpf5674} ^{df,nn5679} ^{pp,hinc5674} ⁽⁸⁵³⁾ ^{df,nn4428} ^{cs,nn1004}
18 And there went over a ferry boat to carry over the king's household,

^{wcj,pp,qnc6213} ^{pp,du,nn,pnx5869} ^{df,aj2896} ^{wcj,nn8096} ^{cs,nn1121} ⁿⁿ¹⁶¹⁷ ^{qpf5307}
and to do what he thought good. And Shimei the son of Gera fell down

^{pp,pl,cs,nn6440} ^{df,nn4428} ^{pp,qnc,pnx5674} ^{dfp,nn3383}
before the king, as he was come over Jordan;

^{wcs,qmf559} ^{pr413} ^{df,nn4428} ^{ptn408} ^{nn,pnx113} ^{qmf2803} ⁿⁿ⁵⁷⁷¹ ^{pp,pnx}
19 And said unto the king, Let not my lord impute iniquity unto me,

^{wcj,ptn408} ^{qmf2142} ⁽⁸⁵³⁾ ^{pnl834} ^{nn,pnx5650} ^{hipf5753} ^{dfp,nn3117} ^{pnl834}
neither do thou remember that which thy servant did perversely the day that

^{nn,pnx113} ^{df,nn4428} ^{qpf3318} ^{pr4480/nn3389} ^{df,nn4428} ^{pp,qnc7760} ^{pr413}
my lord the king went out of Jerusalem, that the king should take it to his

^{nn,pnx3820}
heart.

^{cj3588} ^{nn,pnx5650} ^{qpf3045} ^{cj3588} ^{pnp589} ^{qpf2398} ^{wcj,ptdm2009}
20 For thy servant doth know that I have sinned: therefore, behold, I am

^{qpf935} ^{aj7223} ^{df,nn3117} ^{pp,cs,nn3605} ^{cs,nn1004} ⁿⁿ³¹³⁰ ^{pp,qnc3381} ^{pp,qnc7125}
come the first this day of all the house of Joseph to go down to meet my

^{nn,pnx113} ^{df,nn4428}
lord the king.

nn52 cs,nn**1121** nn6870 wcs,qmf6030 wcs,qmf**559** ptn3808 nn8096

21 But Abishai the son of Zeruiah answered and said, Shall not Shimei be

homf**4191** he,pr8478 pndm2063 cj3588 pipf**7043** (853) nn**3068** cs,nn**4899**

put*to*death for this, because he cursed the LORD's anointed?

nn1732 wcs,qmf**559** pnit4100 pp,pnx wcj,pp,pnx pl,cs,nn**1121** nn6870 cj3588

22 And David said, What have I to do with you, ye sons of Zeruiah, that

df,nn3117 qmf**1961** pp,nn**7854** pp,pnx nn376 homf**4191**

ye should this day be adversaries unto me? shall there any man be put*to*death

df,nn3117 pp,nn3478 cj3588 he,ptn**3808** qpf3045 cj3588 pnp589 df,nn3117 nn**4428** pr5921 nn3478

this day in Israel? for do not I know that I *am* this day king over Israel?

df,nn**4428** wcs,qmf**559** pr413 nn8096 ptn**3808** qmf**4191** df,nn**4428**

℀ 23 Therefore the king said unto Shimei, Thou shalt not die. And the king

wcs,nimf**7650** pp,pnx

swore unto him.

wcj,nn4648 cs,nn**1121** nn7586 qpf3381 pp,qnc7125 df,nn**4428**

℀ 24 And Mephibosheth the son of Saul came down to meet the king, and had

wcj,ptn**3808** qpf**6213** du,nn,pnx7272 wcj,ptn**3808** qpf**6213** nn,pnx8222 ptn**3808** pipf3526 wcj(853) pl,nn,pnx899

neither dressed his feet, nor trimmed his beard, nor washed his clothes,

pp,pr4480 df,nn**3117** df,nn**4428** qnc1980 pr5704 df,nn**3117** (pnl834) qpf935 pp,nn**7965**

from the day the king departed until the day he came *again* in peace.

wcs,qmf**1961** cj3588 qpf935 nn3389 pp,qnc7125 df,nn**4428**

25 And it*came*to*pass, when he was come to Jerusalem to meet the king,

df,nn**4428** wcs,qmf**559** pp,pnx pnit4100 qpf1980 ptn**3808** pr,pnx5973

that the king said unto him, Wherefore wentest not thou with me,

nn4648

Mephibosheth?

wcs,qmf**559** nn,pnx**113** df,nn**4428** nn,pnx**5650** pipf**7411** cj3588

26 And he answered, My lord, O king, my servant deceived me: for thy

nn,pnx**5650** qpf**559** qcj**2280** pp,pnx df,nn**2543** wcj,qmf7392 pr,pnx5921 wcj,qmf1980 pr854

servant said, I will saddle me an ass, that I may ride thereon, and go to

df,nn**4428** cj3588 nn,pnx**5650** aj6455

the king; because thy servant *is* lame.

wcs,pimf**7270** pp,nn,pnx**5650** pr413 nn,pnx**113** df,nn**4428** wcj,nn,pnx**113**

27 And he hath slandered thy servant unto my lord the king; but my lord

df,nn**4428** pp,cs,nn**4397** df,pl,nn**430** wcj,qmv**6213** df,aj**2896** pp,du,nn,pnx**5869**

the king *is* as an angel of God: do therefore *what is* good in thine eyes.

cj3588 cs,nn3605 nn,pnx1 cs,nn**1004** (ptn**3808**) qpf**1961** cj3588/cj518 nn**4194** pl,cs,nn**376** pp,nn,pnx**6440**

28 For all *of* my father's house were but dead men before my

pp,nn,pnx**113** df,nn**4428** wcs,qmf7896 (853) nn,pnx**5650**

lord the king: yet didst thou set thy servant among them that did

pp,pl,cs,qpta398 nn,pnx7979 wcj,pnit4100 nn**6666** pta3426 pp,pnx ad5759 wcj,pp,qnc**2199**

eat at thine own table. What right therefore have I yet to cry

ad5750 pr413 df,nn**4428**

any more unto the king?

df,nn**4428** wcs,qmf**559** pp,pnx pnit4100 pimf**1696** ad5750

29 And the king said unto him, Why speakest thou any more of thy

pl,nn,pnx**1697** qpf**559** pnp859 wcj,nn6717 qmf2505 (853) df,nn**7704**

matters? I have said, Thou and Ziba divide the land.

nn4648 wcs,qmf**559** pr413 df,nn**4428** ad1571 qmf3947 (853) df,nn3605

30 And Mephibosheth said unto the king, Yea, let him take all,

ad310/pnl834 nn,pnx**113** df,nn**4428** qpf935 pp,nn**7965** pr413 nn,pnx**1004**

forasmuch as my lord the king is come again in peace unto his own house.

℀ **19:23** David had not really forgiven Shimei; it was only intended that Shimei think he had been forgiven (cf. 1 Kgs. 2:8, 9).

℀ **19:24** In this way, Mephibosheth mourned the fact that David had to flee from Absalom (Ezek. 24:17).

31 And Barzillai the Gileadite came down from Rogelim, and went over Jordan with the king, to conduct*him*over Jordan.

32 Now Barzillai was a very aged man, *even* fourscore years old: and he had provided the king of sustenance while he lay at Mahanaim; for he *was* a very great man.

33 And the king said unto Barzillai, Come thou over with me, and I will feed thee with me in Jerusalem.

34 And Barzillai said unto the king, How long have I to live, that I should go up with the king unto Jerusalem?

35 I *am* this day fourscore years old: *and* can I discern between good and evil? can thy servant taste what I eat or what I drink? can I hear any more the voice of singing men and singing women? wherefore then should thy servant be yet a burden unto my lord the king?

36 Thy servant will go*a*little*way*over Jordan with the king: and why should the king recompense it me with such a reward?

37 Let thy servant, I*pray*thee, turn*back*again, that I may die in mine own city, *and be buried* by the grave of my father and of my mother. But behold thy servant Chimham; let him go over with my lord the king; and do to him what shall seem good unto thee.

38 And the king answered, Chimham shall go over with me, and I will do to him that which shall seem good unto thee: and whatsoever thou shalt require of me, *that* will I do for thee.

39 And all the people went over Jordan. And when the king was come over, the king kissed Barzillai, and blessed him; and he returned unto his own place.

40 Then the king went on to Gilgal, and Chimham went on with him: and all the people of Judah conducted the king, and also half the people of Israel.

wcj,nn1038   wcj,cs,nn3605   df,nn1276   wcs,nimf7035   wcs,qmf935

Beth-maachah, and   all   the Berites: and they were gathered together, and went

cj637   pr,pnx310

also after him.

wcs,qmf935   wcs,qmf6696/pr,pnx5921   pp,nn62 [pp,nn,lh59/nn1038]

15 And they came and   besieged   him in Abel*of*Beth-maachah, and they

wcs,qmf8210   nn5550   pr413   df,nn5892   wcj,qmf5975   dfp,nn2426   wcj,cs,nn3605   df,nn5971

cast up a bank against the city, and it stood in the trench: and   all   the people

pnl834   pr854   nn3097   pl,hipt7843   df,nn2346   pp,hinc5307

that *were* with Joab battered the wall, to throw*it*down.

wcs,qmf7121   aj2450   nn802   pr4480   df,nn5892   qmv8085   qmv8085   qmv559   pte4994

🔊 16 Then   cried   a wise woman out of the city, Hear, hear; say, I*pray*you,

pr413   nn3097   qmv7126   pr5704/ad2008   wcs,pimf1696 pr,pnx413

unto Joab, Come near hither, that I may speak with thee.

wcs,qmf7126   pr,pnx413   df,nn802   wcs,qmf559   df,pnp859   nn3097

17 And when he was come near unto her, the woman said, *Art* thou Joab?

wcs,qmf559   pnp589   wcs,qmf559   pp,pnx   qmv8085   pl,cs,nn1697

And he answered, I *am he.* Then she   said   unto him Hear the words of thine

nn,pnx519   wcs,qmf559   pnp595   qpta8085

handmaid. And he answered, I   do hear.

wcs,qmf559   pp,qnc559   pina1696   pimf1696   dfp,aj7223   pp,qnc559

18 Then she spoke, saying, They were wont to speak in old time, saying, They

qna7592/pimf7592   pp,nn59   wcj,ad3651   hipf8552

shall surely ask *counsel* at Abel: and   so   they ended *the matter.*

pnp595   pl,cs,qptp7999   pl,cs,qptp539   nn3478   pnp859   pipt1245

19   I   *am one of them that are* peaceable *and* faithful in Israel: thou seekest to

pp,hinc4191   nn5892   wcj,nn517   pp,nn3478 pnit4100   pimf1104   cs,nn5159

destroy a city and a mother in Israel: why wilt thou swallow up the inheritance of

nn3068

the LORD?

nn3097   wcs,qmf6030   wcs,qmf559   ptx2486   ptx2486   pp,pnx   cj518

20 And Joab answered and   said, Far*be*it, far*be*it from me, that I should

pimf1104   wcj,cj518   himf7843

swallow up   or   destroy.

df,nn1697   ptn3808 ad3651   cj3588   nn376   pr4480/nn2022   nn669   nn7652   cs,nn1121

21 The matter *is* not so: but a man of mount Ephraim, Sheba the   son   of

nn1075   nn,pnx8034   qpf5375   nn,pnx3027   dfp,nn4428   pp,nn1732

Bichri by name, hath lifted up his   hand   against the king, *even* against David:

qmv5414   pnx(853)   pp,nn,pnx905   wcj,qcj1980 pr4480/pr5921   df,nn5892   df,nn802   wcs,qmf559

deliver   him   only,   and I will depart   from   the city. And the woman   said

pr413   nn3097   ptdm2009   nn,pnx7218   hopt7993   pr,pnx413   pr1157   df,nn2346

unto Joab, Behold, his head shall be thrown   to   thee over the wall.

df,nn802   wcs,qmf935   pr413   cs,nn3605   df,nn5971   pp,nn,pnx2451

22 Then the woman   went   unto   all   the people in her wisdom. And they

wcs,qmf3772   (853)   nn7218   nn7652   cs,nn1121   nn1075   wcs,himf7993   pr413   nn3097

cut off   the head of Sheba the   son   of Bichri, and cast*it*out to Joab. And he

wcs,qmf8628   dfp,nn7782   wcs,qmf6327 pr4480/pr5921   df,nn5892   nn376   pp,pl,nn,pnx168

blew   a trumpet, and they retired   from   the city, every man to his   tent.

wcj,nn3097   qpf7725   nn3389   pr413   df,nn4428

And   Joab   returned to Jerusalem unto the king.

🔊 **20:16** The phrase "wise woman" used of the woman in this verse means that she was doing something extraordinary. The word translated "wise" is also used of Joseph when he was able to interpret the Pharaoh's dream (Gen. 41:33). In this verse, this woman is called "wise" because she did what was in the best interest of protecting her people (v. 22).

David's Officials

_{wcj,nn3097   pr413   cs,nn3605   df,nn6635   nn3478   wcj,nn1141   cs,nn1121}
23 Now Joab *was* over all the host of Israel: and Benaiah the son of
_{nn3077   pr5921   df,nn3774   wcj,pr5921   df,nn6432}
Jehoiada *was* over the Cherethites and over the Pelethites:

_{wcj,nn151   pr5921   df,nn4522   wcj,nn3092   cs,nn1121   nn286}
24 And Adoram *was* over the tribute: and Jehoshaphat the son of Ahilud *was*
_{df,hipt2142}
recorder:

_{wcj,nn7724   nn5608   wcj,nn6659   wcj,nn54   pl,nn3548}
25 And Sheva *was* scribe: and Zadok and Abiathar *were* the priests:

_{nn5896 wcj,ad1571   df,nn2972   qpf1961   nn3548   pp,nn1732}
26 And Ira   also the Jairite was a chief ruler about David.

Gibionites Are Avenged

_{wcs,qmf1961   nn7458   pp,pl,cs,nn3117   nn1732   nu7969   pl,nn8141 nn8141}
21 Then there was a famine in the days of David three years, year
_{pr310   nn8141   nn1732   wcs,pimf1245/pl,cs,nn6440   nn3068   nn3068}
after year; and David   inquired   of the LORD. And the LORD
_{wcs,qmf559   pr413   nn7586   wcj,pr413   df,pl,nn1818   cs,nn1004   pr5921/pnl834   hipf4191   (853)}
answered, *It is* for Saul, and   for *his* bloody house, because he slew   the
_{df,nn1393}
Gibeonites.

_{df,nn4428   wcs,qmf7121   dfp,nn1393   wcs,qmf559   pr,pnx413}
2 And the king called the Gibeonites, and said unto them; (now the
_{wcj,df,nn1393   (pnp1992)   ptn3808   pr4480/pl,cs,nn1121   nn3478   cj3588/cj518   pr4480/cs,nn3499}
Gibeonites   *were* not of*the*children of Israel, but of*the*remnant of the
_{df,nn567   wcj,pl,cs,nn1121   nn3478   nipf7650   pp,pnx   nn7586 wcs,pimf1245}
Amorites; and the children of Israel had sworn unto them: and Saul sought to
_{pp,hinc,pnx5221   pp,pinc,pnx7065   pp,pl,cs,nn1121   nn3478   wcj,nn3063}
slay   them in his   zeal   to the children of Israel and Judah.)
_{nn1732   wcs,qmf559   pr413   df,nn1393   pnit4100   qmf6213   pp,pnx}
3 Wherefore David said unto the Gibeonites, What shall I do for you? and
_{wcj,pp,pnit4100   pimf3722   wcj,pimv1288   (853)   cs,nn5159}
wherewith shall I make the atonement, that ye may bless   the inheritance of the
_{nn3068}
LORD?

_{df,nn1393   wcs,qmf559   pp,pnx   ptn369   nn3701   wcj,nn2091 pr5973}
4 And the Gibeonites said unto him, We will have no silver nor gold of
_{nn7586   wcj,pr5973   nn,pnx1004   wcj,ptn369   pp,pnx   pp,hinc4191   nn376   pp,nn3478}
Saul, nor of his house; neither for us shalt thou kill any man in Israel. And
_{wcs,qmf559 pnit4100 pnp859   pl,qpta559   qmf6213   pp,pnx}
he said, What ye shall say, *that* will I do for you.
_{wcs,qmf559/pr413   df,nn4428   df,nn376 pnl834   pipf,pnx3615   wcj,pnl834   pipf1819}
5 And they answered the king, The man that consumed us, and that devised
_{pp,pnx   nipf8045   pr4480/htnc3320   pp,cs,nn3605   cs,nn1366}
against us *that* we should be destroyed from remaining in any of the coasts of
_{nn3478}
Israel,

_{nu7651   pl,nn376 pr4480/pl,nn,pnx1121   homf5414   pp,pnx   wcs,hipf,pnx3363}
6 Let seven men of*his*sons be delivered unto us, and we will   hang   them

pp,nn**3068**   pp,cs,nn1390   nn7586   nn**3068**   cs,aj972   df,nn**4428**

up unto the LORD in Gibeah of Saul, *whom* the LORD did choose. And the king

wcs,qmf**559** pnp589   qmf**5414**

said,   I   will give *them.*

df,nn**4428** wcs,qmf2550/pr5921   nn4648   cs,nn**1121**   nn3083   cs,nn**1121**

7 But the king   spared   Mephibosheth, the   son of Jonathan the   son of

nn7586   pr5921   nn**3068** cs,nn**7621** pnl834   pr,pnx996   pr996   nn1732   wcj(pr996)

Saul, because of the LORD's oath that *was* between them, between David and

nn3083   cs,nn**1121**   nn7586

Jonathan the   son of Saul.

df,nn**4428** wcs,qmf3947 (853)   du,cs,nu8147 pl,cs,nn**1121**   nn7532   nn1323   nn345

8 But the king   took   the   two   sons of Rizpah the daughter of Aiah,

pnl834   qpf3205   pp,nn7586 (853)   nn764   wcj(853)   nn4648   wcj(853)   cs,nu2568

whom she bore unto Saul,   Armoni and   Mephibosheth; and   the five

pl,cs,nn**1121**   nn4324   nn1323   nn7586 pnl834   qpf3205   pp,nn5741   cs,nn**1121**

sons of Michal the daughter of Saul, whom she brought up for Adriel the son of

nn1271   df,nn4259

Barzillai the Meholathite:

wcs,qmf,pnx**5414**   pp,cs,nn**3027**   df,nn1393   wcs,himf,pnx3363

9 And he delivered them into the hands of the Gibeonites, and they hanged

dfp,nn2022 pp,pl,cs,nn**6440**   nn**3068**   wcs,qmf**5307**   nu,pnx7651 ad3162

them in the   hill   before   the LORD: and they   fell   *all* seven together, and

wcj(pnp1992)   hopf**4191**   pp,pl,cs,nn**3117**   nn7105   dfp,aj**7223**

were put*to*death in the   days   of harvest, in the first *days*, in the

pp,cs,nn8462   pl,nn8184   cs,nn7105

beginning of barley harvest.

nn7532   nn1323   nn345 wcs,qmf3947 (853)   df,nn8242   wcs,himf,pnx5186

10 And Rizpah the daughter of Aiah   took   sackcloth, and   spread   it

pp,pnx   pr413   df,nn6697   pr4480/cs,nn8462   nn7105   cj5704 pl,nn4325   nipf5413   pr,pnx5921

for her upon the rock, from*the*beginning of harvest until water dropped upon

pr4480   df,du,nn**8064**   qpf**5414**   wcj,ptn**3808**   nn5775   df,du,nn**8064**   pp,qnc5117 pr,pnx5921

them out of heaven, and suffered neither the birds of the   air   to   rest   on

ad3119   wcj(853)   cs,nn2416   df,nn**7704**   nn3915

them by day, nor   the beasts of the field by night.

wcs,homf**5046**   pp,nn1732 (853) pnl834   nn7532   nn1323   nn345

11 And it was   told   David   what Rizpah the   daughter of Aiah, the

cs,nn**6370**   nn7586   qpf**6213**

concubine of Saul, had done.

nn1732 wcs,qmf**1980**   wcs,qmf3947 (853)   pl,cs,nn**6106**   nn7586   wcj(853)   pl,cs,nn**6106**

12 And David went and   took   the bones of Saul and   the bones of

nn3083   nn,pnx1121 pr4480/pr854   pl,cs,nn**1167**   cs,nn3003/nn1568   pnl834   qpf1589   pnx(853)

Jonathan his   son   from   the   men of Jabesh-gilead, which had stolen   them

pr4480/cs,nn7339   nn1052   pnl834/ad,lh8033   pl,nn6430   qpf,pnx8511   pp,nn**3117**

from*the*street of Beth-shan,   where   the Philistines had hanged them, when the

pl,nn6430   hinc**5221** (853) nn7586   pp,nn1533

Philistines had slain   Saul in Gilboa:

wcs,himf**5927**   pr4480/ad8033   (853)   pl,cs,nn**6106**   nn7586   wcj(853)   pl,cs,nn**6106**

13 And he brought up from thence   the bones of Saul and   the bones

nn3083   nn,pnx**1121**   wcs,qmf**622** (853)   pl,cs,nn**6106**   df,pl,hopt3363

of Jonathan his   son; and they gathered   the bones of them that were hanged.

(853)   pl,cs,nn**6106**   nn7586   wcj,nn3083   nn,pnx**1121** wcs,qmf**6912**

14 And   the bones of Saul and Jonathan his   son   buried they in the

pp,nn**776**   nn1144   pp,nn6762   pp,nn**6913**   nn7027   nn,pnx1

country of Benjamin in Zelah, in the   sepulcher of Kish his   father: and they

wcs,qmf**6213**   nn3605   pnl834   df,nn**4428**   pipf**6680**   pr310/ad**3651**   pl,nn**430**   wcs,nimf**6279**

performed all that the king commanded. And after that God was entreated for the

dfp,nn**776**

land.

Philistine Giants Die in Battle

dfp,pl,nn6430   wcs,qmf**1961**   nn4421   pr854   nn3478   nn1732

15 Moreover the Philistines   had   yet war again with Israel; and David

wcs,qmf3381   wcj,pl,nn,pnx**5650** pr,pnx5973   wcs,nimf3898   (853)   pl,nn6430

went down, and his servants   with him, and fought against   the Philistines:

nn1732   wcs,qmf5774

and David waxed faint.

wcj,nn3430   pnl834   pp,pl,cs,nn3211   df,nn7498   wcj,cs,nn4948

16 And Ishbibenob, which *was* of the   sons   of the giant, the weight of

nn,pnx7013   cs,nu7969   pl,nu3967   nn5178   cs,nn4948   wcj,pnp1931

whose spear *weighed* three hundred *shekels* of brass in weight,   he   being

qptp2296   aj2319   wcs,qmf559   pp,hinc**5221** (853) nn1732

girded with a new *sword*, thought to have slain   David.

nn52   cs,nn**1121**   nn6870   wcs,qmf5826   pp,pnx   wcs,himf**5221**   (853)

17 But Abishai the   son   of Zeruiah succored him, and smote   the

df,nn**6430**   wcs,himf,pnx**4191**   ad**227**   pl,cs,nn**376**   nn1732   nipf**7650**   pp,pnx   pp,qnc**559**

Philistine, and   killed   him. Then the men of David swore unto him, saying,

qmf3318 ptn**3808** ad5750   pp,pnx   dfp,nn4421   pimf3518 wcj,ptn**3808** (853)

Thou shalt go   no more out with us to battle, that thou quench not   the

cs,nn**5216**   nn3478

light of Israel.

wcs,qmf**1961**   pr310   ad**3651**   wcs,qmf**1961**   ad5750   df,nn4421 pr5973

18 And it*came*to*pass after this, that there   was   again a battle with the

pl,nn6430   pp,nn1359 ad**227**   nn5444   df,nn2843   hipf**5221** (853)   nn5593   pnl834

Philistines at Gob: then Sibbechai the Hushathite slew   Saph, which *was* of the

pp,pl,cs,nn3211   df,nn7498

sons   of the giant.

wcs,qmf**1961**   ad5750   df,nn4421   pp,nn1359 pr5973   pl,nn6430   nn445

19 And there   was   again a battle in   Gob with the Philistines, where Elhanan

cs,nn**1121**   nn3296   nn1022   wcs,himf**5221**   (853)   nn1555

the son of Jaare-oregim, a Bethlehemite,   slew   *the brother of*   Goliath the

df,nn1663   wcj,cs,nn6086   nn,pnx2595   pl,qpta707   pp,cs,nn4500

Gittite, the   staff   of whose spear *was* like a weaver's beam.

wcs,qmf**1961**   ad5750   nn4421   pp,nn1661   wcs,qmf**1961**   nn376

20 And there   was   yet a battle in Gath, where   was   a man of *great*

pl,nn4055   du,nn,pnx**3027** nu8337 wcj,pl,cs,nn676   du,nn,pnx7272 wcj,nu8337

stature, that had on every   hand   six   fingers, and on every   foot   six

wcj,pl,cs,nn676 wcj,nu702   pl,nu6242   nn4557   pnp1931 wcj,ad1571   pupf3205   dfp,nn7498

toes,   four and twenty in number; and   he   also   was born to the giant.

wcs,pimf2778 (853)   nn3478   nn3083   cs,nn**1121**   nn8092   cs,nn**251**

21 And when he defied   Israel, Jonathan the son of Shimea the brother of

nn1732   wcs,himf,pnx**5221**

David   slew   him.

pndm428 (853) cs,nu702   pupf3205   dfp,nn7498   pp,nn1661   wcs,qmf**5307**   pp,cs,nn**3027**

22 These   four were born to the giant in Gath, and   fell   by the hand

nn1732   wcj,pp,cs,nn**3027**   pl,nn,pnx**5650**

of David, and by the   hand   of his servants.

David's Song

22 ◉ And David spoke unto the LORD the words of this song in the day *that* the LORD had delivered him out*of*the*hand of all his enemies, and out*of*the*hand of Saul:

2 And he said, The LORD *is* my rock, and my fortress, and my deliverer;

3 The God of my rock; in him will I trust: *he is* my shield, and the horn of my salvation, my high tower, and my refuge, my savior; thou savest me from violence.

4 I will call on the LORD, *who is* worthy to be praised: so shall I be saved from*mine*enemies.

5 When the waves of death compassed me, the floods of ungodly men made me afraid;

6 The sorrows of hell compassed*me*about; the snares of death prevented me;

7 In my distress I called upon the LORD, and cried to my God: and he did hear my voice out*of*his*temple, and my cry *did enter* into his ears.

8 Then the earth shook and trembled; the foundations of heaven moved and shook, because he was wroth.

9 There went up a smoke out of his nostrils, and fire out*of*his*mouth devoured: coals were kindled by it.

10 He bowed the heavens also, and came down; and darkness *was* under his feet.

11 And he rode upon a cherub, and did fly: and he was seen upon the wings of the wind.

◉ **22:1–51** This passage is a song of praise that is a personal expression of David's heart. David is praising God for deliverance, yet in his praise, he focuses strongly on the Person and omnipotence of God. David's psalms help us to understand how, with all of his failings, he was "a man after God's heart" (1 Sam. 13:14; 1 Kgs. 15:3).

wcs,qmf7896   nn2822   pl,nn5521   pr,pnx5439   cs,nn2841   pl,nn4325

12 And he made darkness pavilions round about him, dark waters, *and*

pl,cs,nn5645   pl,nn7834

thick clouds of the skies.

pr4480/nn5051   pr,pnx5048   pl,cs,nn1513   nn784   qpf1197

13 Through*the*brightness before him were coals of fire kindled.

nn3068   himf7481   pr4480   du,nn8064   wcj,aj5945   qmf5414   nn,pnx6963

14 The LORD thundered from heaven, and the most High uttered his voice.

wcs,qmf7971   pl,nn2671   wcs,himf6327   nn1300   wcj,qmf2000

15 And he sent out arrows, and scattered them; lightning, and discomfited

them.

pl,cs,nn650   nn3220   wcs,nimf7200   pl,cs,nn4146   nn8398

16 And the channels of the sea appeared, the foundations of the world were

nimf1540   pp,cs,nn1606   nn3068   pr4480/cs,nn5397   cs,nn7307   nn,pnx639

discovered, at the rebuking of the LORD, at*the*blast of the breath of his nostrils.

qmf7971   pr4480/nn4791   qmf,pnx3947   himf,pnx4871   pr4480/pl,nn4325/aj7227

17 He sent from above, he took me; he drew me out*of*many*waters;

himf,pnx5337   pr4480/qpta,pnx341/aj5794   pr4480/pl,qpta,pnx8130

18 He delivered me from*my*strong*enemy, *and* from*them*that*hated me:

cj3588   qpf553   pr,pnx4480

for they were too strong for me.

pimf,pnx6923   pp,nn3117   nn,pnx343   nn3068   wcs,qmf1961

19 They prevented me in the day of my calamity: but the LORD was my

nn4937

stay.

wcs,himf3318   dfp,nn4800/pnx(853)   pimf,pnx2502   cj3588

20 He brought*me*forth also into a large place: he delivered me, because he

qpf2654   pp,pnx

delighted in me.

nn3068   qmf,pnx1580   pp,nn,pnx6666

21 The LORD rewarded me according to my righteousness: according to the

pp,cs,nn1252   du,nn,pnx3027   himf7725   pp,pnx

cleanness of my hands hath he recompensed me.

cj3588   qpf8104   pl,cs,nn1870   nn3068   wcj,ptn3808   qpf7561

22 For I have kept the ways of the LORD, and have not wickedly departed

pr4480/pl,nn,pnx430

from*my*God.

cj3588   cs,nn3605   pl,nn,pnx4941   pp,pr,pnx5048   wcj,pl,nn,pnx2708

23 For all his judgments *were* before me: and *as for* his statutes, I did

ptn3808   qmf5493   pr,pnx4480

not depart from them.

wcs,qmf1961   aj8549   pp,pnx   wcs,htmf8104   pr4480/nn,pnx5771

24 I was also upright before him and have kept myself from*mine*iniquity.

nn3068   wcs,himf7725   pp,pnx   pp,nn,pnx6666

25 Therefore the LORD hath recompensed me according to my righteousness;

pp,nn,pnx1252   pp,pr5048   du,nn,pnx5869

according to my cleanness in his eye sight.

pr5973   aj2623   htmf2616   pr5973   aj8549   nn1368

26 With the merciful thou wilt show*thyself*merciful, *and* with the upright man

htmf8552

thou wilt show*thyself*upright.

pr5973   nipt2889   htmf1305   wcj,pr5973   aj6141

27 With the pure thou wilt show*thyself*pure; and with the froward thou wilt

htmf6617

show*thyself*unsavory.

28 And   ^{wcj(853)} ^{aj6041} ⁿⁿ⁵⁹⁷¹ the afflicted people thou wilt save: ^{himf3467} but thine ^{wcj,du,nn,pnx5869} eyes *are* ^{pr5921} upon

^{pl,qpta7311} the haughty, *that* thou mayest bring*^{himf8213}them*down.

29 For thou *art* ^{cj3588} ^{pnp859} my ^{nn,pnx5216} lamp, ⁿⁿ³⁰⁶⁸ O LORD: and the ^{wcj,nn3068} LORD will lighten ^{himf5050} my ^{nn,pnx2822} darkness.

30 For ^{cj3588} by ^{pp,pnx} thee I have run ^{qmf7323} through a troop: ⁿⁿ¹⁴¹⁶ by my ^{pp,pl,nn,pnx430} God have I leaped over ^{pimf1801}

ⁿⁿ⁷⁷⁹¹ a wall.

31 *As for* ^{df,nn410} God, his ^{nn,pnx1870} way *is* perfect; ^{aj8549} the word ^{cs,nn565} of the LORD ⁿⁿ³⁰⁶⁸ *is* tried: ^{qptp6884} he ^{pnp1931} *is* a

ⁿⁿ⁴⁰⁴³ buckler to ^{pp,nn3605} all them*that*trust ^{df,pl,qpta2620} in him. ^{pp,pnx}

32 For ^{cj3588} who ^{pnit4310} *is* God, ⁿⁿ⁴¹⁰ save ^{pr4480/pr1107} the LORD? ⁿⁿ³⁰⁶⁸ and who ^{wcj,pnit4310} *is* a rock, ⁿⁿ⁶⁶⁹⁷ save ^{pr4480/pr1107} our

^{pl,nn,pnx430} God?

33 God *is* ^{df,nn410} my strength ^{nn,pnx4581} *and* power: ⁿⁿ²⁴²⁸ and he maketh ^{wcs,himf5425} my way ^{nn,pnx1870} perfect. ^{aj8549}

34 He maketh ^{pipt7737} my feet ^{du,nn,pnx7272} like hinds' ^{dfp,pl,nn355} *feet*: and setteth ^{himf,pnx5975} me upon ^{wcj,pr5921} my

^{pl,nn,pnx1116} high places.

35 He teacheth ^{pipt3925} my hands ^{du,nn,pnx3027} to war; ^{dfp,nn4421} so that a bow ⁿⁿ⁷¹⁹⁸ of steel ⁿⁿ⁵¹⁵⁴ is broken ^{wcs,pipf5181} by mine

^{pl,nn,pnx2220} arms.

36 Thou hast also given ^{wcs,qmf5414} me the shield ^{pp,pnx} ^{cs,nn4043} of thy salvation: ^{nn,pnx3468} and thy gentleness ^{wcj,nn,pnx6038}

^{himf,pnx7235} hath*made*me*great.

37 Thou hast enlarged ^{himf7337} my steps ^{nn,pnx6806} under me; ^{pr,pnx8478} so that my feet ^{du,nn,pnx7166} did not ^{wcj,ptn3808}

^{qpf4571} slip.

38 I have pursued ^{qmf7291} mine enemies, ^{pl,qpta,pnx341} and destroyed them; ^{wcs,himf,pnx8045} and turned*not*again ^{wcj,ptn3808/qmf7725}

^{pr5704} until I had consumed them. ^{pinc,pnx3615}

39 And I have consumed them, ^{wcs,pimf,pnx3615} and wounded them, ^{wcs,qmf,pnx4272} that they could not ^{wcj,ptn3808}

^{qmf6965} arise: yea, they are fallen ^{wcs,qmf5307} under ^{pr8478} my feet. ^{du,nn,pnx7272}

40 For thou hast girded ^{wcs,pimf,pnx247} me with strength ⁿⁿ²⁴²⁸ to battle: ^{dfp,nn4421} them that rose up against ^{pl,qpta,pnx6965}

^{himf3766} me hast thou subdued under me. ^{pr,pnx8478}

41 Thou hast also given ^{qpf5414} me the necks ^{pp,pnx} ⁿⁿ⁶²⁰³ of mine enemies, ^{wcj,pl,qpta,pnx341} that I might destroy ^{wcs,himf,pnx6789}

^{pl,pipt,pnx8130} them that hate me.

42 They looked, ^{qmf8159} but *there was* none ^{wcj,ptn369} to save; ^{hipt3467} *even* unto ^{pr413} the LORD, ⁿⁿ³⁰⁶⁸ but he

^{qpf,pnx6030} answered them ^{wcj,ptn3808} not.

43 Then did I   beat   them as small as the   dust   of the earth, I did   stamp
them as the   mire   of the street, *and* did spread*them*abroad.

44 Thou also hast   delivered   me from*the*strivings of   my   people, thou hast
kept   me *to be* head of the heathen: a people *which* I knew   not   shall   serve me.

45   Strangers   shall submit themselves unto me: as soon as they   hear,   they
shall be obedient unto me.

46   Strangers   shall   fade away,   and   they   shall   be   afraid
out*of*their*close*places.

47 The LORD liveth; and blessed *be* my   rock;   and exalted be the   God   of the
rock of my salvation.

48 It *is* God that   avengeth   me, and that bringeth down the people under me,

49 And   that   bringeth*me*forth   from*mine*enemies: thou   also   hast
lifted*me*up*on*high above*them*that*rose*up against me: thou hast delivered me
from*the*violent*man.

50   Therefore I will give thanks unto thee, O LORD, among the heathen, and I
will sing praises unto thy   name.

51 *He is* the   tower of salvation for his   king: and showeth   mercy   to his
anointed, unto David, and to his   seed   forevermore.

David's Last Words

23 ☞ Now   these   *be* the   last   words of David the   son   of Jesse
said,   and the   man *who was* raised up on high, the anointed of
the   God   of Jacob, and the   sweet   psalmist of Israel,   said,

2 The Spirit of the LORD spoke by me, and his   word   *was* in my tongue.

3 The   God   of Israel said, the   Rock of Israel spoke to me, He that ruleth over
men *must be* just, ruling in the   fear   of God.

☞ **23:1–7** This song of David is a prophecy of the Messiah who would come and bring about God's new covenant of salvation.

wcj,pp,nn**216**   nn1242   nn8121   qmf2224
4 And *he shall be* as the   light of the morning, *when* the sun riseth, *even* a

nn1242   ptn**3808**   pl,nn5645   nn1877   pr4480/nn**776**
morning   without   clouds;   *as*   the   tender grass   *springing*   out*of*the*earth

pr4480/nn5051   pr4480/nn4306
by*clear*shining after rain.

cj3588   nn,pnx**1004**   ptn**3808** ad3651 pr5973 nn**410** cj3588   qpf**7760**   pp,pnx
5 Although my house *be* not   so   with God; yet he hath made   with me an

nn5769   nn1285   qptp6186   dfp,nn3605   wcj,qptp**8104** cj3588   cs,nn3605
everlasting covenant, ordered in   all   *things*, and   sure: for *this is*   all   my

nn,pnx**3468**   wcj,cs,nn3605   nn2656   cj3588   ptn**3808** himf6779
salvation, and   all   *my* desire, although he make *it* not to grow.

wcj,nn**1100**   nn,pnx3605   pp,nn6975   hopt5074   cj3588
6 But *the sons* of Belial *shall be*   all of them as thorns thrust away, because

ptn**3808** nimf3947   pp,nn**3027**
they cannot be taken with hands:

wcj,nn**376**   qmf5060   pp,pnx   nimf**4390**   nn1270   wcj,cs,nn6086
7 But the man *that* shall touch them must be fenced with iron and the   staff

nn2595   qna8313/nimf**8313** wcj,dfp,nn784   dfp,nn7675
of a spear; and they shall be utterly burned with   fire   in the *same* place.

David's Mighty Men

pndm428   pl,cs,nn8034   df,pl,nn1368   pnl834 pp,nn1732   nn8461
8 These *be* the names of the mighty men whom David had: The Tachmonite

qpta**3427**   dfp,nn7675   nn**7218**   df,pl,nn**7991**   pnp1931   nn5722   df,nn6112
that sat in the seat, chief among the captains; the same *was* Adino the Eznite: *he*

pr5921 nu8083 pl,nu3967   nn2491   nu259 pp,nn6471
lifted up his spear against eight hundred, whom he slew at one time.

wcj,pr,pnx310   nn499   cs,nn**1121**   nn1734   cs,nn**1121/nn266**
9 And   after   him *was* Eleazar the son of Dodo the Ahohite, *one* of the

pp,nu7969   df,pl,nn1368   pr5973 nn1732   pp,pinc,pnx2778   dfp,pl,nn6430   ad8033
three mighty men with David, when they   defied   the Philistines *that* were there

nipf**622**   dfp,nn4421   nn**376**   nn3478   wcs,qmf**5927**
gathered together to battle, and the men of Israel were gone away:

pnp1931 qpf**6965**   wcs,himf**5221**   dfp,pl,nn6430 cj5704/cj3588   nn,pnx**3027**   qpf3021
10 He arose, and smote the Philistines   until   his hand was weary, and his

nn,pnx**3027** wcs,qmf1692 pr413   df,nn2719   nn3068   wcs,qmf6213   aj1419   nn8668   df,pndm1931 dfp,nn3117
hand cleaved unto the sword: and the LORD wrought a great victory   that   day;

wcj,df,nn**5971** qmf**7725** pr,pnx310   ad389   pp,pinc6584
and the people returned after him only to spoil.

wcj,pr,pnx310   nn8048   cs,nn**1121**   nn89   nn2043
11 And   after   him *was* Shammah the son of Agee the Hararite. And the

pl,nn6430   wcs,nimf**622**   dfp,nn2416 ad8033 wcs,qmf1961 cs,nn2513 df,nn**7704** aj4392
Philistines were gathered together into a troop, where   was   a piece of ground full

pl,nn5742   wcj,df,nn**5971** qpf5127 pr4480/pl,cs,nn**6440**   pl,nn6430
of lentils: and the people fled   from   the Philistines.

wcs,htmf3320   pp,cs,nn**8432**   df,nn2513   wcs,himf,pnx**5337**   wcs,himf**5221** (853)
12 But he stood in the midst of the ground, and defended it, and   slew

pl,nn6430   nn3068   wcs,qmf6213   aj1419   nn8668
the Philistines: and the LORD wrought a great victory.

nu7969   df,nu7970 nn**7218**   wcs,qmf3381   wcs,qmf935 pr413   nn1732   pr413
13 And three of the thirty chief went down, and   came   to David in the

nn7105   pr413   cs,nn4631   nn5725   wcj,cs,nn2416   pl,nn6430   qpta2583

harvest time unto the cave of Adullam: and the troop of the Philistines pitched in

pp,nn6010   nn7497

the valley of Rephaim.

wcj,nn1732   ad227   dfp,nn4686   wcj,cs,nn4673   pl,nn6430   ad227

14 And David *was* then in a hold, and the garrison of the Philistines *was* then

nn1035

in Bethlehem.

nn1732   wcs,htmf183   wcs,qmf559   pnit4310   himf,pnx8248

15 And David longed, and said, Oh*that*one would give*me*drink of the

pl,nn4325   pr4480/cs,nn953   nn1035   pnl834   dfp,nn8179

water of*the*well of Bethlehem, which *is* by the gate!

cs,nu7969   df,pl,nn1368   wcs,qmf1234   pp,cs,nn4264   pl,nn6430

16 And the three mighty men broke through the host of the Philistines, and

wcs,qmf7579 pl,nn4325   pr4480/cs,nn953   nn1035   pnl834   dfp,nn8179   wcs,qmf5375

drew water out*of*the*well of Bethlehem, that *was* by the gate, and took *it*,

wcs,himf935   pr413   nn1732   qpf14   wcj,ptn3808 pp,qnc,pnx8354

and brought *it* to David: nevertheless he would not drink thereof, but

wcs,himf5258/pnx(853)   pp,nn3068

poured*it*out unto the LORD.

wcs,qmf559   ptx2486   pp,pnx   nn3068   pr4480/qnc,pnx6213 pndm2063

17 And he said, Be*it*far from me, O LORD, that*I*should*do this: *is not*

he,cs,nn1818   df,pl,nn376   df,pl,qpta1980   pp,pl,nn,pnx5315

this the blood of the men that went in jeopardy of their lives? therefore he

qpf14   wcj,ptn3808 pp,qnc,pnx8354   pndm428   qpf6213   cs,nu7969   df,pl,nn1368

would not drink it. These things did these three mighty men.

wcj,nn52   cs,nn251   nn3097   cs,nn1121   nn6870   (pnp1931)   cs,nn7218

18 And Abishai, the brother of Joab, the son of Zeruiah,   was chief

df,nuor7992   wcj,pnp1931   pipf*5782   (853)   nn,pnx2595   pr5921 df,nu7969   pl,nu3967   nn2491

among three. And he lifted up his spear against three hundred, *and* slew

wcj(pp,pnx)   nn8034   dfp,nu7969

them, and had   the name among three.

he,cj3588   pr4480   nipt3513   df,nu7969   pp,pnx wcs,qmf1961   pp,nn8269

19 Was he not most honorable of three? therefore he was their captain:

qpf935   ptn3808 wcj,pr5704   df,nu7969

howbeit he attained not unto the *first* three.

wcj,nn1141   cs,nn1121   nn3077   cs,nn1121   nn2428   nn376   pr4480/nn6909

20 And Benaiah the son of Jehoiada, the son of a valiant man, of Kabzeel,

cs,aj7227/pl,nn6467   pnp1931 hipf5221 (853) du,cs,nu8147   nn739   nn4124 wcj,pnp1931

who had done*many*acts, he slew   two lionlike men of Moab: he

qpf3381   wcj,hipf5221 (853)   df,nn738   pp,cs,nn8432   pp,cs,nn8432/df,nn953   pp,nn3117

went down also and slew   a lion in the midst of a   pit   in time of

df,nn7950

snow:

wcj,pnp1931   hipf5221 (853)   cs,nn376/nn4713   nn4758   nn376   df,nn4713

21 And he slew   an Egyptian, a goodly man: and the Egyptian had a

nn2595   wcj,pp,cs,nn3027   wcs,qmf3381   pr,pnx413   dfp,nn7626   wcs,qmf1497 (853)

spear in his hand; but he went down to him with a staff, and plucked

df,nn2595   pr4480/cs,nn3027/df,nn4713   wcs,qmf,pnx5221   pp,nn,pnx2595

the spear out*of*the*Egyptian's*hand, and slew him with his own spear.

pndm428   qpf6213   nn1141   cs,nn1121   nn3077   wcj(pp,pnx)   nn8034

22 These *things* did Benaiah the son of Jehoiada, and had   the name

pp,nu7969   df,pl,nn1368

among three mighty men.

23 He was more honorable than the thirty, but he attained not to the *first* three. And David set him over his guard.

24 Asahel the brother of Joab *was* one of the thirty; Elhanan the son of Dodo of Bethlehem,

25 Shammah the Harodite, Elika the Harodite,

26 Helez the Paltite, Ira the son of Ikkesh the Tekoite,

27 Abiezer the Anethothite, Mebunnai the Hushathite,

28 Zalmon the Ahohite, Maharai the Netophathite,

29 Heleb the son of Baanah, a Netophathite, Ittai the son of Ribai out*of*Gibeah of the children of Benjamin,

30 Benaiah the Pirathonite, Hiddai of*the*brooks of Gaash,

31 Abi-albon the Arbathite, Azmaveth the Barhumite,

32 Eliahba the Shaalbonite, of the sons of Jashen, Jonathan,

33 Shammah the Hararite, Ahiam the son of Sharar the Hararite,

34 Eliphelet the son of Ahasbai, the son of the Maachathite, Eliam the son of Ahithophel the Gilonite,

35 Hezrai the Carmelite, Paarai the Arbite,

36 Igal the son of Nathan of Zobah, Bani the Gadite,

37 Zelek the Ammonite, Naharai the Beerothite, armorbearer to Joab the son of Zeruiah,

38 Ira an Ithrite, Gareb an Ithrite,

39 Uriah the Hittite: thirty and seven in all.

David Takes a Census

24 And again the anger of the LORD was kindled against Israel, and he moved David against them to say, Go, number Israel and Judah.

⌐ **24:1–14** Opinions vary concerning the sin involved in this census. Josephus stated that David failed to

df,nn4428 wcs,qmf559 pr413 nn3097   nn8269   df,nn2428 pnl834   pr,pnx854

2 For the king said to Joab the captain of the host, which *was* with him,

qmv7751 pte4994   pp,cs,nn3605   pl,cs,nn7626   nn3478   pr4480/nn1835   wcj,pr5704   nn884

Go now through all the tribes of Israel, from Dan even to Beer-sheba,

wcj,qmv6485 (853) df,nn5971 wcj,qpf3045 (853) cs,nn4557 df,nn5971

and number ye the people, that I may know the number of the people.

nn3097 wcs,qmf559 pr413 df,nn4428   nn3068   pl,nn,pnx430 wcj,himf3254 pr413

3 And Joab said unto the king, Now the LORD thy God add unto the

df,nn5971 pp,pnp1992/wcj,pp,pnp1992 nu3967/pl,nn6471 wcj,du,cs,nn5869

people, how*many*soever*they*be a hundredfold, and that the eyes of my

nn,pnx113 df,nn4428 pl,qpta7200 pnit4100 wcj,nn,pnx113 df,nn4428 qpf2654 df,pndm2088

lord the king may see *it*: but why doth my lord the king delight in this

dfp,nn1697

thing?

df,nn4428 cs,nn1697 wcs,qmf2388 pr413 nn3097 wcj,pr5921

4 Notwithstanding the king's word prevailed against Joab, and against the

pl,cs,nn8269 df,nn2428 nn3097 wcj,pl,cs,nn8269 df,nn2428 wcs,qmf3318

captains of the host. And Joab and the captains of the host went out from the

pp,pl,cs,nn6440 df,nn4428 pp,qnc6485 (853) df,nn5971 nn3478

presence of the king, to number the people of Israel.

wcs,qmf5674 (853) df,nn3383 wcs,qmf2583 pp,nn6177 cs,nn3225

5 And they passed over Jordan, and pitched in Aroer, on the right side of

df,nn5892 pnl834 pp,cs,nn8432 df,nn5158 df,nn1410 wcj,pr413 nn3270

the city that *lieth* in the midst of the river of Gad, and toward Jazer:

wcs,qmf935 df,nn,lh1568 wcj,pr413 nn776 nn8483[pl,nn8482/nn,pnx2320]

6 Then they came to Gilead, and to the land of Tahtim-hodshi; and they

wcs,qmf935 nn,lh1842 wcj,ad5439 pr413 nn6721

came to Dan-jaan, and about to Zidon,

wcs,qmf935 cs,nn4013 nn6865 wcj,cs,nn3605 pl,cs,nn5892

7 And came to the stronghold of Tyre, and to all the cities of the

df,nn2340 wcj,df,nn3669 wcs,qmf3318 pr413 nn5045 nn3063

Hivites, and of the Canaanites: and they went out to the south of Judah, *even* to

nn884

Beer-sheba.

wcs,qmf7751 pp,cs,nn3605 df,nn776 wcs,qmf935 nn3389

8 So when they had gone through all the land, they came to Jerusalem

pr4480/cs,nn7097 nu8672 pl,nn2320 wcj,pl,nu6242 nn3117

at*the*end of nine months and twenty days.

nn3097 wcs,qmf5414 (853) cs,nn4557 cs,nn4662 df,nn5971 pr413 df,nn4428

9 And Joab gave up the sum of the number of the people unto the king:

wcs,qmf1961 nn3478 nu8083 pl,nu3967 nu505 nn2428 cs,nn376 qpta8025 nn2719

and there were in Israel eight hundred thousand valiant men that drew the sword;

wcj,nn376 nn3063 cs,nu2568 pl,nu3967 nu505 nn376

and the men of Judah *were* five hundred thousand men.

---

collect the proper offering which had been commanded in Exodus 30:12. Most scholars, however, feel that the sin was a result of David's attitude of pride and arrogance. Still others suggest that his intentions which were to maximize military strength and to tax the people further. In any event, when he repented, God gave him three options for the consequences of his sin: famine, military defeat, or pestilence. David fully trusted in God even as he chose (v. 14). There is a lesson to be learned from David's action: while one may be experiencing God's chastening, he must still rely on His ultimate grace, trust Him fully, and be committed to Him.

David's Punishment

10 And David's heart smote him after that he had numbered the people. And David said unto the LORD, I have sinned greatly in that I have done: and now, I*beseech*thee, O LORD, take away the iniquity of thy servant; for I have done very foolishly.

11 For when David was up in the morning, the word of the LORD came unto the prophet Gad, David's seer, saying,

12 Go and say unto David, Thus saith the LORD, I offer thee three *things*; choose thee one of them, that I may *do* *it* unto thee.

13 So Gad came to David, and told him, and said unto him, Shall seven years of famine come unto thee in thy land? or wilt thou flee three months before thine enemies, while they pursue thee? or that there be three days' pestilence in thy land? now advise, and see what answer I shall return to him*that*sent me.

14 And David said unto Gad, I am in a great strait: let us fall now into the hand of the LORD; for his mercies *are* great: and let me not fall into the hand of man.

15 So the LORD sent a pestilence upon Israel from*the*morning even to the time appointed: and there died of the people from Dan even to Beer-sheba seventy thousand men.

16 And when the angel stretched out his hand upon Jerusalem to destroy it, the LORD repented him of the evil, and said to the angel that destroyed the people, It*is*enough: stay now thine hand. And the angel of the LORD was by the threshingplace of Araunah the Jebusite.

17 And David spoke unto the LORD when he saw the angel that smote the people, and said, Lo, I have sinned, and I have done wickedly: but these sheep, what have they done? let thine hand, I*pray*thee, be against me, and against my father's house.

David Offers Sacrifice

18 And Gad came that day to David, and said unto him, Go up, rear an altar unto the LORD in the threshingfloor of Araunah the Jebusite.

19 And David, according to the saying of Gad, went up as the LORD commanded.

20 And Araunah looked, and saw the king and his servants coming on toward him: and Araunah went out, and bowed himself before the king on his face upon the ground.

21 And Araunah said, Wherefore is my lord the king come to his servant? And David said, To buy the threshingfloor of thee, to build an altar unto the LORD, that the plague may be stayed from the people.

22 And Araunah said unto David, Let my lord the king take and offer up what *seemeth* good unto him: behold, *here be* oxen for burnt sacrifice, and threshing instruments and *other* instruments of the oxen for wood.

23 All these *things* did Araunah, *as* a king, give unto the king. And Araunah said unto the king, The LORD thy God accept thee.

24 And the king said unto Araunah, Nay; but I will surely buy *it* of thee at a price: neither will I offer burnt offerings unto the LORD my God of that which doth cost*me*nothing. So David bought the threshingfloor and the oxen for fifty shekels of silver.

25 And David built there an altar unto the LORD, and offered burnt offerings and peace offerings. So the LORD was entreated for the land, and the plague was stayed from Israel.

The First Book of
KINGS

The books of First and Second Kings, which made up only one volume in the Hebrew Scriptures, were first divided in the edition of the Hebrew Bible that was published in A.D. 1517. The Septuagint and the translations of the Old Testament that followed divided the books of Samuel and Kings into First Kings through Fourth Kings. The books of First and Second Kings relate the history of the Jewish people from the death of David to the captivity of Judah (ca. 970 to 560 B.C.).

A recurring theme in both books involves the examples that each king chose to follow. Repeatedly, David is presented as the best example for kings (1 Kgs. 3:14; 11:4, 6; 15:3; 2 Kgs. 14:3; 16:2; 22:2) and Jeroboam as the worst (1 Kgs. 15:34; 16:2, 26, 31; 22:52; 2 Kgs. 3:3; 10:29, 31; 13:2, 6, 11).

The Talmud, the authoritative body of Jewish tradition, states that Jeremiah was the author of both books of the Kings. Nevertheless, the Holy Spirit directed him to use the records of contemporary prophets to complete the work. Some prophets who wrote during this time, but whose writings were not included in the canon of Scripture, are Jehu (1 Kgs. 16:1); Nathan, Ahijah, and Iddo (2 Chr. 9:29); and Shemaiah (2 Chr. 12:15). Even some of the prophets who wrote a portion of the Scripture did, as in the case of Isaiah, write other, non–canonical works during this period (2 Chr. 26:22).

The Book of First Kings covers the reign of Solomon, the division of the kingdom, and the reigns of the kings of Israel and Judah up through Jehoshaphat and Ahaziah respectively. The immense riches that Solomon accumulated and the tremendous advances that the nation made during his reign deteriorated under later kings. It was Solomon, however, who started the nation on this course. He brought disgrace on himself and all Israel by refusing to use discretion in his relationships with women (1 Kgs. 11:1–11). Solomon did well to ask God for wisdom to govern Israel (1 Kgs. 3:4–28), but he did not continue to act wisely. He ignored the last counsel that his father David had given him (1 Kgs. 2:2, 3) and began to trust in human means of government rather than in God. Solomon taxed the nation so heavily that the people were ready to rebel, and following his death, the nation permanently divided because his successor, Rehoboam, thought he could continue to tax the people as heavily as Solomon.

David Approaches Death

1 Now king David was old *and* stricken in years; and they covered him with clothes, but he got*no*heat.

_{wcj,df,nn4428 nn1732 qpf2204 qpf935 dfp,pl,nn3117 wcs,pimf,pnx3680}
_{dfp,pl,nn899 pp,pnx wcj,ptn3808/qmf3179}

2 Wherefore his servants said unto him, Let there be sought for my lord

_{pl,nn,pnx5650 wcs,qmf559 pp,pnx pimf1245 pp,nn,pnx113}

the king a young virgin: and let her stand before the king, and let her

cherish him, and let her lie in thy bosom, that my lord the king may

get heat.

3 So they sought for a fair damsel throughout all the coasts of Israel, and

found Abishag a Shunammite, and brought her to the king.

4 And the damsel *was* very fair, and cherished the king, and

ministered to him: but the king knew her not.

Adonijah Usurps David's Throne

5 Then Adonijah the son of Haggith exalted himself, saying, I will be

king: and he prepared him chariots and horsemen, and fifty men to run

before him.

6 And his father had not displeased him at*any*time in saying, Why hast

thou done so? and he also *was a* very goodly *man*; and *his mother* bore

him after Absalom.

7 And he conferred with Joab the son of Zeruiah, and with Abiathar

the priest: and they following Adonijah helped *him*.

8 But Zadok the priest, and Benaiah the son of Jehoiada, and Nathan the

prophet, and Shimei, and Rei, and the mighty men which *belonged* to David,

were not with Adonijah.

9 And Adonijah slew sheep and oxen and fat cattle by the stone of

Zoheleth, which *is* by En-rogel, and called all his brethren the king's sons,

and all the men of Judah the king's servants:

10 But Nathan the prophet, and Benaiah, and the mighty men, and

Solomon his brother, he called not.

1:5 According to the Jewish custom during this time, the birthright belonged to the oldest son in the family. In the case of royal families, this would include the accession to the throne. Though he was David's fourth son, Adonijah was the oldest living son, and thus he assumed he would be the next king. Although David had not informed him that this custom was not to be followed, he was wrong in seeking the throne (1 Kgs. 2:15).

11 Wherefore Nathan spoke unto Bath-sheba the mother of Solomon, saying,
Hast thou not heard that Adonijah the son of Haggith doth reign, and David our
lord knoweth *it* not?

12 Now therefore come, let me, I*pray*thee, give thee counsel, that thou
mayest save thine own life, and the life of thy son Solomon.

13 Go and get*thee*in unto king David, and say unto him, Didst not
thou, my lord, O king, swear unto thine handmaid, saying, Assuredly Solomon thy
son shall reign after me, and he shall sit upon my throne? why then
doth Adonijah reign?

14 Behold, while thou yet talkest there with the king, I also will
come in after thee, and confirm thy words.

15 And Bath-sheba went in unto the king into the chamber: and the king
was very old; and Abishag the Shunammite ministered unto the king.

16 And Bath-sheba bowed, and did obeisance unto the king. And the king
said, What wouldest thou?

17 And she said unto him, My lord, thou swarest by the LORD thy God
unto thine handmaid, *saying*, Assuredly Solomon thy son shall reign after me,
and he shall sit upon my throne.

18 And now, behold, Adonijah reigneth; and now, my lord the king, thou
knowest *it* not:

19 And he hath slain oxen and fat cattle and sheep in abundance, and hath
called all the sons of the king, and Abiathar the priest, and Joab the
captain of the host: but Solomon thy servant hath he not called.

20 And thou, my lord, O king, the eyes of all Israel *are* upon thee,
that thou shouldest tell them who shall sit on the throne of my lord the
king after him.

21 Otherwise it*shall*come*to*pass, when my lord the king shall sleep with
his fathers, that I and my son Solomon shall be counted offenders.

22 And,   lo,   while she   yet   talked with the king, Nathan the prophet also
came in.

23 And they   told   the king, saying, Behold Nathan the prophet. And when
he was   come in   before   the king, he bowed himself before the   king   with his
face   to the ground.

24 And Nathan   said,   My lord, O king, hast thou said, Adonijah shall reign
after me, and   he   shall   sit   upon my throne?

25 For he is gone down this day, and hath   slain   oxen and fat cattle and
sheep in abundance, and hath   called   all   the king's   sons, and the   captains
of the host, and Abiathar the priest; and,   behold,   they   eat   and   drink
before   him, and   say,   God save king Adonijah.

26 But   me,   *even*   me thy servant, and   Zadok   the   priest,   and Benaiah the
son   of Jehoiada, and thy servant Solomon, hath he   not   called.

27   Is   this   thing done   by   my   lord   the king, and thou hast   not
showed*it*unto   thy servant, who should   sit   on   the throne of my   lord   the
king   after him?

David Has Solomon Anointed King

28 Then   king   David answered and   said,   Call   me   Bath-sheba. And she
came into the king's presence, and   stood   before   the king.

29 And the king   swore, and   said,   *As* the LORD liveth, that hath redeemed
my   soul   out*of*all distress,

30 Even   as   I   swore unto thee by   the LORD   God   of Israel,   saying,
Assuredly Solomon thy   son   shall reign after me, and   he   shall   sit   upon my
throne in my stead; even   so   will I certainly   do   this   day.

31 Then Bath-sheba bowed with *her* face to the earth, and did reverence to the
king, and said, Let my   lord   king David live forever.

df,nn**4428** nn1732 wcs,qmf**559** qmv7121 pp,pnx pp,nn6659   df,nn**3548**   wcj,pp,nn5416   df,nn**5030**

32 And king David said, Call me Zadok the priest, and Nathan the prophet,

wcj,pp,nn1141 cs,nn**1121** nn3077   wcs,qmf935 pp,pl,cs,nn**6440** df,nn**4428**

and Benaiah the son of Jehoiada. And they came before the king.

df,nn**4428** wcs,qmf559 pp,pnx qmv3947 pr,pnx5973 (853) pl,cs,nn**5650**

33 The king also said unto them, Take with you the servants of your

pl,nn,pnx113 (853) nn8010 nn,pnx1121 wcj,hipf7392 pr5921 (pnl834) pp,pnx df,nn6506

lord, and cause Solomon my son to ride upon mine own mule, and

wcj,hipf3381/pnx(853) pr413 nn1521

bring*him*down to Gihon:

nn6659 df,nn**3548** wcj,nn5416 df,nn**5030** wcj,qpf**4886** pnx(853) ad8033 pp,nn**4428**

34 And let Zadok the priest and Nathan the prophet anoint him there king

pr5921 nn3478 wcj,qpf**8628** dfp,nn7782 wcj,qpf**559** qmf2421 df,nn**4428** nn8010

over Israel: and blow ye with the trumpet, and say, God save king Solomon.

wcs,qpf5927 pr,pnx310   wcs,qpf935 wcs,qpf3427 pr5921

35 Then ye shall come up after him, that he may come and sit upon my

nn,pnx3678 wcj,pnp1931 qmf4427 pr,pnx8478 pipf6680 wcj,pnx(853)

throne; for he shall be king in my stead: and I have appointed him to

pp,qnc1961 nn5057 pr5921 nn3478 wcj,pr5921 nn3063

be ruler over Israel and over Judah.

nn1141 cs,nn**1121** nn3077 wcs,qmf6030 (853) df,nn**4428** wcs,qmf559 ad543

36 And Benaiah the son of Jehoiada answered the king, and said, Amen:

nn3068 pl,cs,nn**430** nn,pnx113 df,nn**4428** qmf559 ad3651

the LORD God of my lord the king say so *too*.

pp,pnl834 nn3068 qpf1961 pr5973 nn,pnx113 df,nn**4428** ad3651 qmf1961 pr5973

37 As the LORD hath been with my lord the king, even so be he with

nn8010 wcj,pimf1431/(853)/nn,pnx3678 pr4480/cs,nn3678 nn,pnx113 df,nn**4428** nn1732

Solomon, and make*his*throne*greater than*the*throne of my lord king David.

nn6659 df,nn**3548** wcj,nn5416 df,nn**5030** wcj,nn1141 cs,nn**1121**

38 So Zadok the priest, and Nathan the prophet, and Benaiah the son of

nn3077 wcj,df,nn3774 wcj,df,nn6432 wcs,qmf3381 (853)

Jehoiada, and the Cherethites, and the Pelethites, went down, and caused

nn8010 wcs,himf7392 pr5921 df,nn**4428** nn1732 cs,nn6506 wcs,himf1980 pnx(853) pr5921 nn1521

Solomon to ride upon king David's mule, and brought him to Gihon.

nn6659 df,nn**3548** wcs,qmf3947 (853) cs,nn7161 df,nn**8081** pr4480 df,nn168

39 And Zadok the priest took a horn of oil out of the tabernacle, and

wcs,qmf**4886** (853) nn8010 wcs,qmf**8628** dfp,nn7782 cs,nn3605 df,nn**5971** wcs,qmf559

anointed Solomon. And they blew the trumpet; and all the people said,

qmf2421 df,nn**4428** nn8010

God save king Solomon.

cs,nn3605 df,nn**5971** wcs,qmf5927 pr,pnx310   wcj,df,nn**5971** pl,pipt2490

40 And all the people came up after him, and the people piped with

dfp,pl,nn2485 wcj,aj8056 aj1419 nn8057   df,nn776 wcs,nimf1234   pp,nn,pnx6963

pipes, and rejoiced with great joy, so that the earth rent with the sound of

them.

nn138 wcj,cs,nn3605 df,pl,qptp7121 pnl834 pr,pnx854 wcs,qmf**8085**

41 And Adonijah and all the guests that *were* with him heard *it* as

wcj,pnp1992 pipf**3615** pp,qnc398 nn3097 wcs,qmf**8085** (853) cs,nn6963

they had made*an*end of eating. And when Joab heard the sound of the

df,nn7782 wcs,qmf559 ad4069 cs,nn6963 df,nn7151 qpta1993

trumpet, he said, Wherefore *is this* noise of the city being in an uproar?

ad,pnx5750 pipt**1696** wcj,ptdm2009 nn3129 cs,nn**1121** nn54 df,nn**3548**

42 And while he yet spoke, behold, Jonathan the son of Abiathar the priest

qpf935   nn138   wcs,qmf559   qmv935   cj3588 pnp859   nn2428   nn376
came: and Adonijah said unto him, Come in; for thou *art* a valiant man, and

wcj,nn2896/pimf1319
bringest*good*tidings.

nn3129   wcs,qmf6030   wcs,qmf559   pp,nn138   ad61   pl,nn,pnx113 df,nn4428
43 And Jonathan answered and said to Adonijah, Verily our lord king

nn1732   hipf4427/(853)/nn8010
David hath made*Solomon*king.

df,nn4428   wcs,qmf7971 pr,pnx854   (853)   nn6659   df,nn3548   wcj(853)   nn5416
44 And the king hath sent with him Zadok the priest, and Nathan

df,nn5030   wcj,nn1141   cs,nn1121   nn3077   wcj,df,nn3774
the prophet, and Benaiah the son of Jehoiada, and the Cherethites, and the

wcj,df,nn6432   wcs,himf7392/pnx(853)   pr5921   df,nn4428   cs,nn6506
Pelethites, and they have caused*him*to*ride upon the king's mule:

nn6659   df,nn3548   wcj,nn5416   df,nn5030   wcs,qmf4886 pnx(853)   pp,nn4428
45 And Zadok the priest and Nathan the prophet have anointed him king

pp,nn1521   wcs,qmf5927   pr4480/ad8033   aj8056   df,nn7151 wcs,nimf1949
in Gihon: and they are come up from thence rejoicing, so that the city rang

pnp1931   df,nn6963 pnl834   qpf8085
again. This *is* the noise that ye have heard.

wcj,ad1571   nn8010   qpf3427 pr5921   cs,nn3678   df,nn4410
46 And also Solomon sitteth on the throne of the kingdom.

wcj,ad1571   df,nn4428   pl,cs,nn5650   qpf935   pp,pinc1288 (853)   pl,nn,pnx113 df,nn4428
47 And moreover the king's servants came to bless our lord king

nn1732   pp,qnc559   pl,nn430   (853)   cs,nn8034   nn8010   himf3190   pr4480/nn,pnx8034
David, saying, God make the name of Solomon better than*thy*name, and make

(853)   nn,pnx3678 wcj,pimf1431   pr4480/nn,pnx3678   df,nn4428   wcs,htmf7812   pr5921   df,nn4904
his throne greater than*thy*throne. And the king bowed himself upon the bed.

wcj,ad1571 ad3602 qpf559   df,nn4428   qptp1288   nn3068 pl,cs,nn430   nn3478   pnl834
48 And also thus said the king, Blessed *be* the LORD God of Israel, which

qpf5414   qpta3427 pr5921   nn,pnx3678 df,nn3117   wcj,du,nn,pnx5869   pl,qpta7200
hath given *one* to sit on my throne this day, mine eyes even seeing *it*.

cs,nn3605   df,pl,qptp7121 pnl834   pp,nn138   wcs,qmf2729   wcs,qmf6965
49 And all the guests that *were* with Adonijah were afraid, and rose up,

wcs,qmf1980   nn376   pp,nn,pnx1870
and went every man his way.

wcj,nn138   qpf3372   pr4480/pl,cs,nn6440   nn8010   wcs,qmf6965   wcs,qmf1980
50 And Adonijah feared because of Solomon, and arose, and went, and

wcs,himf2388   pp,pl,cs,nn7161   df,nn4196
caught hold on the horns of the altar.

wcs,homf5046   pp,nn8010   pp,qnc559   ptdm2009   nn138   qpf3372   (853) df,nn4428
51 And it was told Solomon, saying, Behold, Adonijah feareth king

nn8010   wcj,ptdm2009   qpf270   pp,pl,cs,nn7161   df,nn4196   pp,qnc559
Solomon: for, lo, he hath caught hold on the horns of the altar, saying, Let

df,nn4428   nn8010   nimf7650   pp,pnx   dfp,nn3117   cj518 himf4191 (853)   nn,pnx5650
king Solomon swear unto me today that he will not slay his servant with the

dfp,nn2719
sword.

nn8010   wcs,qmf559 cj518   qmf1961   nn2428   pp,cs,nn1121
52 And Solomon said, If he will show himself a worthy man, there shall

ptn3808   pr4480/nn,pnx8183   qmf5307   nn,lh776   wcj,cj518   aj7451   nimf4672   pp,pnx
not a hair of him fall to the earth: but if wickedness shall be found in him,

wcs,qpf4191
he shall die.

df,nn4428   nn8010   wcs,qmf7971   wcs,himf,pnx3381   pr4480/pr5921   df,nn4196
53 So king Solomon sent, and they brought*him*down from the altar.

wcs,qmf935   wcs,htmf7812   dfp,nn4428   nn8010   nn8010   wcs,qmf559
And he   came   and bowed himself to   king   Solomon: and Solomon   said

pp,pnx   qmv1980   pp,nn,pnx1004
unto him, Go to thine house.

David Gives Instructions to Solomon

pl,cs,nn3117   nn1732   wcs,qmf7126   pp,qnc4191   wcs,pimf6680
Now the days of David drew nigh that he should die; and he charged

(853)   nn8010   nn,pnx1121 pp,qnc559
Solomon his son, saying,

pnp595 qpta1980   pp,cs,nn1870   cs,nn3605   df,nn776   wcj,qpf2388   wcj,qpf1961
2 I   go the way of all   the earth: be thou strong therefore, and show

pp,nn376
thyself a man;

wcj,qpf8104 (853)   cs,nn4931   nn3068   pl,nn,pnx430 pp,qnc1980   pp,pl,nn,pnx1870
3 And keep   the charge of the LORD thy God, to walk in his ways,   to

pp,qnc8104   pl,nn,pnx2708   pl,nn,pnx4687   wcj,pl,nn,pnx4941   wcj,pl,nn,pnx5715
keep his statutes, and his commandments, and his judgments, and his testimonies,

dfp,qptp3789   (853)   pp,cs,nn8451   nn4872 pp,cj4616   himf7919   cs,nn3605 pnl834
as it is written in   the   law of Moses, that thou mayest prosper in all   that

qmf6213   wcj(853) cs,nn3605/pnl834/ad8033   qmf6437
thou doest, and   whithersoever thou turnest thyself:

pp,cj4616   nn3068   himf6965   (853)   nn,pnx1697 pnl834   pipf1696   pr,pnx5921
4 That the LORD may continue   his word which he spoke concerning me,

pp,qnc559 cj518   pl,nn,pnx1121   qmf8104   (853)   nn,pnx1870 pp,qnc1980 pp,pl,nn,pnx6440   dfp,nn571
saying, If thy children take heed to   their way, to walk   before me in truth

pp,cs,nn3605   nn,pnx3824   wcj,pp,cs,nn3605   nn,pnx5315   ptn3808 nimf3772 pp,pnx
with   all   their heart and with   all   their soul, there shall not fail thee

pp,qnc559   nn376 pr4480/pr5921   cs,nn3678   nn3478
(said he) a man   on   the throne of Israel.

wcj,ad1571 pnp859 qpf3045   (853) pnl834 nn3097   cs,nn1121   nn6870   qpf6213   pp,pnx
5 Moreover thou knowest also   what Joab the son of Zeruiah did to me,

pnl834   qpf6213   pp,du,cs,nu8147 pl,cs,nn8269   pl,cs,nn6635   nn3478   pp,nn74
and what he did to the   two   captains of the hosts of Israel, unto Abner the

cs,nn1121   nn5369   wcj,pp,nn6021   cs,nn1121   nn3500   wcs,qmf,pnx2026 wcs,qmf7760
son of Ner, and unto Amasa the son of Jether, whom he   slew,   and shed

pl,cs,nn1818   nn4421   pp,nn7965   wcs,qmf5414   pl,cs,nn1818   nn4421   pp,nn,pnx2290 pnl834
the blood of war in peace, and   put   the blood of war upon his girdle that

pp,du,nn,pnx4975   wcj,pp,nn,pnx5275 pnl834   pp,du,nn,pnx7272
was about his   loins,   and in his shoes   that were on his feet.

wcj,qpf6213   pp,nn,pnx2451   wcj,ptn3808   nn,pnx7872
6 Do   therefore according to thy wisdom, and let   not   his hoar head

himf3381   nn7585   pp,nn7965
go down to the grave in peace.

qmf6213   nn2617   wcj,pp,pl,cs,nn1121   nn1271   df,nn1569
7 But show kindness unto the   sons   of Barzillai the Gileadite, and let them

wcs,qpf1961   pp,pl,cs,qpta398   nn,pnx7979 cj3588 ad3651   qpf7126 pr,pnx413
be   of those that   eat   at thy table: for so they came   to   me when I

pp,qnc,pnx1272 pr4480/pl,cs,nn6440   nn53   nn,pnx251
fled   because of Absalom thy brother.

wcj,ptdm2009   pr,pnx5973   nn8096   cs,nn1121   nn1617   df,nn1145
8 And, behold, *thou hast* with thee Shimei the son of Gera, a Benjamite

pr4480/nn980   wcj,pnp1931 pipf,pnx7043   nipf4834   nn7045   pp,cs,nn3117   qnc,pnx1980
of Bahurim, which cursed me with a grievous curse in the day   when I went

nn4266   wcj,pnp1931   qpf3381   pp,qnc,pnx7125   df,nn3383   wcs,nimf7650

to Mahanaim: but he came down to meet me at Jordan, and I swore

pp,pnx   pp,nn3068   pp,qnc559   cj518   himf,pnx4191   dfp,nn2719

to him by the LORD, saying, I will not put*thee*to*death with the sword.

wcj,ad6258   ptn408/pimf,pnx5352   cj3588   pnp859   aj2450   nn376

9 Now therefore hold*him*not*guiltless: for thou *art* a wise man, and

wcs,qpf3045 (853)   pnl834   qmf6213   pp,pnx   (853)   nn,pnx7872

knowest what thou oughtest to do unto him; but his hoar head

wcs,hipf3381   nn7585   pp,nn1818

bring*thou*down to the grave with blood.

David's Death

nn1732   wcs,qmf7901   pr5973   pl,nn,pnx1   wcs,nimf6912   pp,cs,nn5892   nn1732

10 So David slept with his fathers, and was buried in the city of David.

wcj,df,pl,nn3117   pnl834   nn1732   qpf4427   pr5921   nn3478   pl,nu705   nn8141   nu7651

11 And the days that David reigned over Israel *were* forty years: seven

pl,nn8141   qpf4427   pp,nn2275   nu7970   wcj,nu7969 pl,nn8141   qpf4427   wcj,pp,nn3389

years reigned he in Hebron, and thirty and three years reigned he in Jerusalem.

qpf3427   wcj,nn8010   pr5921   cs,nn3678   nn1732   nn,pnx1   nn,pnx4438

12 Then sat Solomon upon the throne of David his father; and his kingdom

wcs,nimf5559   ad3966

was established greatly.

Solomon Consolidates His Rule

nn138   cs,nn1121   nn2294   wcs,qmf935 pr413   nn1339   cs,nn517

13 And Adonijah the son of Haggith came to Bath-sheba the mother of

nn8010   wcs,qmf559   qnc,pnx935   he,nn7965   wcs,qmf559   nn7965

Solomon. And she said, Comest thou peaceably? And he said, Peaceably.

wcs,qmf559   pp,pnx   nn1697   pr,pnx413   wcs,qmf559

14 He said moreover, I have somewhat*to*say unto thee. And she said,

pimv1696

Say on.

wcs,qmf559   pnp859   qpf3045   cj3588   df,nn4410   qpf1961   pp,pnx   cs,nn3605

15 And he said, Thou knowest that the kingdom was mine, and *that* all

nn3478   qpf7760   pl,nn,pnx6440   wcj,pr,pnx5921   pp,qnc4427   df,nn4410

Israel set their faces on me, that I should reign: howbeit the kingdom is

wcs,qmf5437   wcs,qmf1961   pp,nn,pnx251   cj3588   qpf1961 pp,pnx   pr4480/nn3068

turned about, and is become my brother's: for it was his from*the*LORD.

wcj,ad6258   pnp595   qpta7592   nu259   nn7596   pr4480/pr,pnx854   himf7725/(853)/pl,nn,pnx6440   ptn408

16 And now I ask one petition of thee, deny me not.

wcs,qmf559   pr,pnx413   pimv1696

And she said unto him, Say on.

wcs,qmf559   qmv559   pte4994   pp,nn8010   df,nn4428   cj3588   ptn3808

17 And he said, Speak, I*pray*thee, unto Solomon the king, (for he will not

himf7725/(853)/pl,nn,pnx6440   wcj,qmf5414 pp,pnx (853)   nn49   df,nn7767   pp,nn802

say*thee*nay,) that he give me Abishag the Shunammite to wife.

nn1339   wcs,qmf559   aj2896   pnp595   pimf1696   pr,pnx5921   df,nn4428

18 And Bath-sheba said, Well; I will speak for thee unto the king.

nn1339   wcs,qmf935   pr413 df,nn4428   nn8010   pp,pinc1696   pp,pnx   pr5921

19 Bath-sheba therefore went unto king Solomon, to speak unto him for

nn138   df,nn4428   wcs,qmf6965   pp,qnc,pnx7122   wcs,htmf7812   pp,pnx

Adonijah. And the king rose up to meet her, and bowed himself unto her, and wcs,qmf3427   pr5921   nn,pnx3678   nn3678   wcs,qmf7760   df,nn4428 pp,cs,nn517

sat down on his throne, and caused a seat to be   set   for the king's mother; and

wcs,qmf3427   pp,nn,pnx3225

she   sat   on his right hand.

wcs,qmf559 pnp595 qpta7592 nu259 aj6996   nn7596   pr4480

20 Then she   said,   I   desire one small petition of thee; *I pray thee,*

ptn408/himf7725/(853)/pl,nn,pnx6440   df,nn4428 wcs,qmf559   pp,pnx   qmv7592   nn,pnx517 cj3588

say*me*not*nay. And the king   said unto her, Ask on, my mother: for I will

ptn3808 himf7725/(853)/pl,nn,pnx6440

not   say*thee*nay.

wcs,qmf559   (853)   nn49   df,nn7767   homf5414   pp,nn138

21 And she said, Let   Abishag the Shunammite be given to Adonijah thy

nn,pnx251   pp,nn802

brother to wife.

df,nn4428   nn8010   wcs,qmf6030   wcs,qmf559   pp,nn,pnx517 wcj,pnit4100

22 And king Solomon answered and   said unto his mother, And why dost

pnp859 qpta7592 (853)   nn49   df,nn7767   pp,nn138   wcj,qmv7592 pp,pnx   (853)

thou ask   Abishag the Shunammite for Adonijah? ask for him   the

df,nn4410   cj3588 pnp1931 pr,pnx4480 df,aj1419 nn,pnx251   wcj,pp,pnx   wcj,pp,nn54

kingdom also; for he *is* mine elder brother; even for him, and for Abiathar the

df,nn3548   wcj,pp,nn3097   cs,nn1121   nn6870

priest, and for   Joab   the son of Zeruiah.

df,nn4428   nn8010   wcs,nimf7650   pp,nn3068 pp,qnc559 pl,nn430 qmf6213 ad3541   pp,pnx

23 Then king Solomon swore by the LORD, saying, God do so to me,

himf3254 wcj,ad3541 cj3588   nn138   pipf1696 (853) df,pndm2088 df,nn1697

and more also,   if Adonijah have not spoken   this   word against his own

pp,nn,pnx5315

life.

wcj,ad6258   nn3068   aj2416   pnl834   hipf,pnx3559

24 Now therefore, *as* the LORD liveth, which hath established me, and

wcs,himf,pnx3427   pr5921 cs,nn3678 nn1732 nn,pnx1 wcj,pnl834   qpf6213 pp,pnx   nn1004

set   me on the throne of David my father, and who hath made me a house,

pp,pnl834   pipf1696   nn138   homf4191   (cj3588) df,nn3117

as he promised, Adonijah shall be put*to*death   this day.

df,nn4428   nn8010 wcs,qmf7971   pp,cs,nn3027   nn1141   cs,nn1121   nn3077

25 And king Solomon sent by the hand of Benaiah the son of Jehoiada;

wcs,qmf6293   pp,pnx   wcs,qmf4191

and he   fell   upon him that he died.

wcj,pp,nn54   df,nn3548 qpf559   df,nn4428 qmv1980   nn6068   pr5921

26 And unto Abiathar the priest said the king, Get thee to Anathoth, unto thine

pl,nn,pnx7704 cj3588 pnp859 cs,nn376   nn4194   ptn3808 df,pndm2088 wcj,dfp,nn3117

own fields; for thou *art* worthy of death: but I will not at this   time

himf,pnx4191   cj3588   qpf5375   (853) cs,nn727   nn136 nn3068 pp,pl,cs,nn6440

put*thee*to*death, because thou didst bear   the ark of the Lord GOD before

nn1732   nn,pnx1   wcj,cj3588   htpf6031   pp,nn3605 pnl834   nn,pnx1

David my father, and because thou hast been afflicted in all   wherein my father

htpf6031

was afflicted.

2:22 Apparently Adonijah had not given up all aspirations of ascending to his father's throne. According to Eastern customs, marrying any of a late king's wives or concubines was recognized as an attempt to claim the former king's rights.

2:26, 27 Solomon's actions fulfilled the prophecy of 1 Samuel 2:31-36 that the priesthood would depart from the family of Eli of which Abiathar was a descendant. When Zadok was appointed priest (v. 35), the priesthood was returned to its ancient lineage since Zadok was a descendant of Eleazar the son of Aaron (1 Chr. 6:1-8). See the note on Jeremiah 1:1, with regard to Anathoth.

27 So Solomon thrust out   Abiathar from being priest unto the LORD; that he might fulfill   the word of the LORD, which he spoke concerning the house of Eli in Shiloh.

28 Then tidings came to Joab: for Joab had turned after Adonijah, though he turned not after Absalom. And Joab fled unto the tabernacle of the LORD, and caught hold on the horns of the altar.

29 And it was told king Solomon that Joab was fled unto the tabernacle of the LORD; and, behold, he is by the altar. Then Solomon sent Benaiah the son of Jehoiada, saying, Go, fall upon him.

30 And Benaiah came to the tabernacle of the LORD, and said unto him, Thus saith the king, Come forth. And he said, Nay; but I will die here. And Benaiah brought the king word again, saying, Thus said Joab, and thus he answered me.

31 And the king said unto him, Do as he hath said, and fall upon him, and bury him; that thou mayest take away the innocent blood, which Joab shed, from me, and from the house of my father.

32 And the LORD shall return his blood upon his own head, who fell upon two men more righteous and better than he, and slew them with the sword, my father David not knowing thereof, to wit, Abner the son of Ner, captain of the host of Israel, and Amasa the son of Jether, captain of the host of Judah.

33 Their blood shall therefore return upon the head of Joab, and upon the head of his seed forever: but upon David, and upon his seed, and upon his house, and upon his throne, shall there be peace forever from the LORD.

34 So Benaiah the son of Jehoiada went up, and fell upon him, and slew him: and he was buried in his own house in the wilderness.

35 And the king put Benaiah the son of Jehoiada in his room over

df,nn**6635**   wcj(853)   nn6659   df,nn**3548**   df,nn**4428** qpf**5414**   pr8478   nn54

the host: and   Zadok the priest did the king put in the room of Abiathar.

df,nn**4428** wcs,qmf**7971**   wcs,qmf**7121**   pp,nn8096   wcs,qmf**559**   pp,pnx   qmv1129

36 And the king   sent   and called for Shimei, and said unto him, Build

pp,pnx   nn**1004**   pp,nn3389   wcj,qpf**3427** ad8033   wcj,ptn**3808**/qmf3318 pr4480/ad8033 ad575 wcj,ad575

thee a house in Jerusalem, and dwell there, and go*not*forth thence any whither.

wcs,qpf**1961**   pp,cs,nn**3117**   qnc,pnx3318   wcs,qpf**5674**   (853)

37 For it shall   be, *that* on the   day   thou goest out, and passest over

cs,nn5158   nn6939   qna3045   qmf3045   cj3588   qna4191/qmf**4191**   nn,pnx**1818**

the brook Kidron, thou shalt know for certain that thou shalt surely die: thy blood

qmf**1961**   pp,nn,pnx**7218**

shall be upon thine own head.

nn8096   wcs,qmf**559**   dfp,nn**4428**   df,nn**1697**   aj2896   pp,pnl834   nn,pnx**113**

38 And Shimei said   unto the king, The saying *is* good: as   my lord the

df,nn**4428**   pipf**1696** ad**3651**   nn,pnx**5650**   qmf**6213**   nn8096 wcs,qmf**3427**   pp,nn3389   aj7227

king hath said, so will thy servant do. And Shimei dwelt in Jerusalem many

pl,nn**3117**

days.

wcs,qmf**1961**   pr4480/cs,nn**7093**   nu7969 pl,nn**8141**   du,cs,nu8147   pl,nn**5650**

39 And it*came*to*pass at*the*end of three years, that two of the servants

pp,nn8096   wcs,qmf1272   pr413   nn397   cs,nn**1121**   nn4601   cs,nn**4428**   nn1661   wcs,himf**5046**

of Shimei ran away unto Achish son of Maachah king of Gath. And they told

pp,nn8096   pp,qnc**559**   ptdm2009   pl,nn,pnx**5650**   pp,nn1661

Shimei, saying, Behold, thy servants *be* in Gath.

nn8096   wcs,qmf**6965**   wcs,qmf**2280**   (853)   nn,pnx2543   wcs,qmf**1980**   nn,lh1661 pr413

40 And Shimei arose, and saddled   his   ass,   and went to Gath to

nn397   pp,pinc1245 (853)   pl,nn,pnx**5650**   nn8096 wcs,qmf**1980**   wcs,himf935 (853)   pl,nn,pnx**5650**

Achish to   seek   his servants: and Shimei went, and brought   his servants

pr4480/nn1661

from Gath.

wcs,homf**5046**   pp,nn8010   cj3588   nn8096   qpf**1980**   pr4480/nn3389   nn1661

41 And it was   told   Solomon that Shimei had gone from Jerusalem to Gath,

wcs,qmf**7725**

and was come again.

df,nn**4428** wcs,qmf**7971**   wcs,qmf**7121**   pp,nn8096   wcs,qmf**559** pr,pnx413

42 And the king   sent and called for Shimei, and said unto him, Did I

he,ptn**3808**   hipf,pnx**7650**   pp,nn3068   wcs,himf**5749**   pp,pnx   pp,qnc**559**

not   make*thee*to*swear by the LORD, and protested unto thee, saying,

qna3045/qmf**3045**   pp,cs,nn**3117**   qnc,pnx3318   wcj,qpf**1980**   ad,lh575

Know*for*a*certain, on the   day   thou goest out, and walkest abroad any

wcj,ad,lh575 cj3588   qna4191/qmf**4191**   wcs,qmf**559** pr,pnx413   df,nn**1697**

whither, that thou shalt surely die? and thou saidst unto me, The word *that* I have

qpf**8085**   aj2896

heard *is* good.

wcj,ad4069   ptn3808 qpf**8104** (853)   cs,nn**7621**   nn3068   wcj(853)

43 Why then hast thou not kept   the oath of the LORD, and   the

df,nn**4687** pnl834   pipf**6680** pr,pnx5921

commandment that I have charged thee with?

df,nn**4428** wcs,qmf**559**   pr413   nn8096   pnp859   qpf**3045**   (853) cs,nn3605

44 The king   said moreover to Shimei, Thou knowest   all   the

df,nn**7451**   pnl834   nn,pnx3824   qpf**3045** pnl834   qpf**6213**   pp,nn1732   nn,pnx**1**

wickedness which thine heart is privy to, that thou didst to David my father:

nn3068   wcj,hipf**7725** (853)   nn,pnx**7451**   pp,nn,pnx**7218**

therefore the LORD shall return   thy wickedness upon thine own head;

wcj,df,nn4428   nn8010   qptp1288   wcj,cs,nn3678   nn1732   qmf1961
45 And   king   Solomon *shall be* blessed, and the throne of David shall   be

nipt3559   pp,pl,cs,nn6440   nn3068   pr5704/nn5769
established before   the LORD forever.

df,nn4428   wcs,pimf6680   (853)   nn1141   cs,nn1121   nn3077   wcs,qmf3318
46 So the king commanded   Benaiah the son of Jehoiada; which went out,

wcs,qmf6293   pp,pnx   wcs,qmf4191   wcj,df,nn4467   nipf3559
and   fell   upon him, that he   died.   And the kingdom was established in the

pp,cs,nn3027   nn8010
hand of Solomon.

Solomon Marries Pharaoh's Daughter

nn8010   wcs,htmf2859   pr854   nn6547   cs,nn4428   nn4714   wcs,qmf3947 (853)
3 And Solomon made affinity with Pharaoh king of Egypt, and   took

nn6547   cs,nn1323   wcs,himf,pnx935   pr413   cs,nn5892   nn1732   pr5704
Pharaoh's daughter, and brought her into the city of David, until he had

pinc,pnx3615   pp,qnc1129 (853)   nn,pnx1004   wcj(853)   cs,nn1004   nn3068
made*an*end of building   his own house, and   the house of the LORD, and

wcj(853)   cs,nn2346   nn3389   ad5439
the wall of Jerusalem round about.

ad7535   df,nn5971   pl,pipt2076   dfp,pl,nn1116   cj3588   ptn3808 nn1004 nipf1129
2 Only the people sacrificed in high places, because there was no house built

pp,cs,nn8034   nn3068   pr5704 df,pnp1992 df,pl,nn3117
unto the name of the LORD, until those days.

Solomon Asks for Wisdom

nn8010   wcs,qmf157 (853)   nn3068   pp,qnc1980   pp,pl,cs,nn2708   nn1732
3 And Solomon loved   the LORD, walking in the statutes of David his

nn,pnx1   ad7535 pnp1931   pipt2076   wcj,hipt6999   dfp,pl,nn1116
father: only he   sacrificed and burnt incense in high places.

df,nn4428   wcs,qmf1980   nn,lh1391   pp,qnc2076   ad8033 cj3588 pnp1931   df,aj1419
4 And the king   went to Gibeon to sacrifice there; for that *was* the great

df,nn1116   cs,nu505   pl,nn5930   nn8010   himf5927 pr5921 df,pndm1931 df,nn4196
high place: a thousand burnt offerings did Solomon offer upon   that altar.

pp,nn1391   nn3068   nipf7200   pr413   nn8010   dfp,nn2472   df,nn3915   pl,nn430
5 In Gibeon the LORD appeared to Solomon in a dream by night: and God

wcs,qmf559 qmv7592 pnid4100   qmf5414 pp,pnx
said, Ask what I shall give thee.

nn8010   wcs,qmf559   pnp859   qpf6213   pr5973   nn,pnx5650   nn1732   nn,pnx1
6 And Solomon said, Thou hast showed unto thy servant David my father

aj1419   nn2617   pp,pnl834   qpf1980   pp,pl,nn,pnx6440   dfp,nn571   wcj,pp,nn6666
great mercy, according as he walked   before   thee in truth, and in righteousness,

wcj,pp,cs,nn3483   nn3824   pr,pnx5973   wcs,qmf8104   pp,pnx   (853) df,pndm2088
and in uprightness of heart with thee; and thou hast kept   for him   this

df,aj1419   df,nn2617   wcs,qmf5414 pp,pnx   nn1121 qpta3427 pr5921   nn,pnx3678
great kindness, that thou hast given him a son to sit   on his throne, as *it is*

df,pndm2088 dfp,nn3117
this   day.

wcj,ad6258   nn3068   pl,nn,pnx430 pnp859   (853)   nn,pnx5650 hipf4427   pr8478
7 And now, O LORD my God, thou hast made   thy servant king instead of

nn1732   nn,pnx1   wcj,pnp595   aj6996   nn5288   qmf3045 ptn3808   qnc3318
David my father: and   I   *am but* a little child: I know not *how* to go out or

wcj,qnc935
come in.

            wcj,nn,pnx5650   pp,cs,nn8432   nn,pnx5971 pnl834   qpf977
8 And thy   servant *is* in the   midst of thy people which thou hast chosen, a

aj7227   nn5971   pnl834 ptn3808   nimf4487   wcj,ptn3808 nimf5608   pr4480/nn7230
great people, that cannot be numbered   nor   counted for multitude.

         wcs,qpf5414   pp,nn,pnx5650   qpta8085   nn3820   pp,qnc8199 (853)   nn,pnx5971
9 Give therefore thy servant an understanding heart to judge   thy people,

            pp,hinc995   pr996   nn2896   pp,aj7451 cj3588 pnit4310 qmf3201   pp,qnc8199 df,pndm2088
that I may discern between good and bad: for who is able to judge   this   thy so

df,aj3515 (853)   nn,pnx5971
great   a people?

               df,nn1697   wcs,qmf3190/pp,du,cs,nn5869   nn136   cj3588   nn8010   qpf7592   (853)
10 And the speech   pleased   the Lord, that Solomon had asked

df,pndm2088 df,nn1697
this   thing.

            pl,nn430 wcs,qmf559 pr,pnx413   cj3282/pnl834   qpf7592 (853) df,pndm2088 df,nn1697
11 And God   said   unto him, Because thou hast asked   this   thing, and

wcj,ptn3808   qpf7592   wcj,pp,pnx   aj7227 pl,nn3117 wcj,ptn3808   qpf7592 nn6239   wcj,pp,pnx wcj,ptn3808
hast   not   asked for thyself long life; neither hast asked riches for thyself,   nor

qpf7592   nn5315   pl,qpta,pnx341   wcj,qpf7592   pp,pnx   hinc995
hast asked the life of thine enemies; but hast asked for thyself understanding to

pp,qnc8085   nn4941
discern judgment;

      ptdm2009   qpf6213   pp,pl,nn,pnx1697 ptdm2009   qpf5414 pp,pnx
12 Behold, I have done according to thy   words: lo, I have given thee a

aj2450   wcj,nipt995   nn3820   pnl834   qpf1961 ptn3808 pp,pnx3644 pp,pl,nn,pnx6440
wise and an understanding heart; so that there was none like thee   before   thee,

ptn3808 wcj,pr,pnx310   qmf6965   pp,pnx3644
neither after   thee shall any arise like*unto*thee.

            wcj,ad1571 qpf5414 pp,pnx   pnl834   ptn3808 qpf7592 ad1571 nn6239
13 And I have   also   given thee that which thou hast not asked, both riches,

ad1571   nn3519   pnl834   ptn3808 qpf1961 nn376   dfp,pl,nn4428 pp,pnx3644 cs,nn3605
and honor: so that there shall not be any among the kings like*unto*thee   all

pl,nn,pnx3117
thy days.

         wcj,cj518   qmf1980   pp,pl,nn,pnx1870 pp,qnc8104   pl,nn,pnx2706
14 And   if   thou wilt walk in my   ways,   to keep my statutes and my

wcj,pl,nn,pnx4687   pp,pnl834   nn,pnx1 nn1732   qpf1980   wcj,hipf748 (853)
commandments,   as   thy father David did walk, then I will lengthen   thy

pl,nn,pnx3117
days.

         nn8010   wcs,qmf3364   wcj,ptdm2009   nn2472   wcs,qmf935
15 And Solomon awoke; and, behold, *it was* a dream. And he came to

nn3389   wcs,qmf5975 pp,pl,cs,nn6440 cs,nn727   cs,nn1285   nn136
Jerusalem, and   stood   before   the ark of the covenant of the Lord, and

wcs,himf5927   pl,nn5930   wcs,qmf6213   pl,nn8002   wcs,qmf6213   nn4960
offered up burnt offerings, and offered peace offerings, and   made   a feast to

pp,cs,nn3605   pl,nn,pnx5650
all   his servants.

An Example of Solomon's Wisdom

ad227   qmf935   du,nu8147   pl,nn802   pl,qpta2181   pr413   df,nn4428   wcs,qmf5975

16 Then came there two   women, *that were* harlots, unto the king, and stood

pp,pl,nn,pnx6440

before   him.

df,nu259   df,nn802   wcs,qmf559   pte994   nn,pnx113 pnp589   df,pndm2063 wcj,df,nn802   pl,qpta3427

17 And the one woman said,   O my lord,   I   and this   woman dwell in

nu259   pp,nn1004   wcs,qmf3205   pr,pnx5973   dfp,nn1004

one house; and I was delivered*of*a*child with her in the house.

wcs,qmf1961   df,nuor7992 dfp,nn3117   pp,qnc,pnx3205   df,pndm2063

18 And it*came*to*pass the third   day after that I was delivered, that   this

df,nn802   wcs,qmf3205   ad1571   wcj,pnp587   ad3162   ptn369   qpta2114   pr,pnx854

woman was delivered also: and   we   *were* together; *there was* no stranger with

dfp,nn1004   pr2108 pnp587 du,nu8147   dfp,nn1004

us in the house, save we   two   in the house.

df,pndm2063   df,nn802   cs,nn1121 wcs,qmf4191   nn3915   pnl834   qpf7901/pr,pnx5921

19 And   this   woman's child   died   in the night; because she   overlaid   it.

wcs,qmf6965   pp,cs,nn8432/df,nn3915   wcs,qmf3947 (853)   nn,pnx1121   pr4480/pr,pnx681

20 And she arose at midnight, and   took   my son from beside me,

wcj,nn,pnx519   aj3463   wcs,himf,pnx7901   pp,nn,pnx2436   hipf7901 wcj(853)

while thine handmaid slept, and   laid   it in her bosom, and laid   her

df,qpta4191 nn,pnx1121   pp,nn,pnx2436

dead   child in my bosom.

wcs,qmf6965   dfp,nn1242   /pp,hinc3242/(853)/nn,pnx1121   wcj,ptdm2009

21 And when I rose   in the morning to give*my*child*suck, behold, it was

qpf4191   wcs,htmf995/pr,pnx413   dfp,nn1242 wcj,ptdm2009   qpf1961 ptn3808   nn,pnx1121

dead: but when I had considered it in the morning, behold, it was not my son,

pnl834   qpf3205

which I did bear.

df,aj312   df,nn802   wcs,qmf559 ptn3808 cj3588   df,aj2416   nn,pnx1121   df,qpta4191

22 And the other woman said, Nay; but the living *is* my son, and the dead

wcj,nn,pnx1121   wcj,pndm2063 qpta559 ptn3808 cj3588   df,qpta4191   nn,pnx1121   df,aj2416

is thy son.   And   this   said, No; but the dead *is* thy son, and the living *is*

wcj,nn,pnx1121   wcs,pimf1696 pp,pl,cs,nn6440   df,nn4428

my son. Thus they spoke before the king.

wcs,qmf559   df,nn4428   pndm2063 qpta559 pndm2088   nn,pnx1121   df,aj2416

23 Then said the king, The one saith, This *is* my son that liveth, and

wcj,nn,pnx1121   df,qpta4191   wcj,pndm2063 qpta559 ptn3808 cj3588   nn,pnx1121   df,qpta4191

thy   son *is* the dead: and the   other saith, Nay; but thy   son   *is* the dead,

wcj,nn,pnx1121   df,aj2416

and my   son   *is* the living.

df,nn4428 wcs,qmf559 qmv3947 pp,pnx   nn2719   wcs,himf935   df,nn2719 pp,pl,cs,nn6440

24 And the king said, Bring me a sword. And they brought a sword before

df,nn4428

the king.

df,nn4428   wcs,qmf559   qmv1504   (853)   df,aj2416 df,nn3206   pp,du,nu8147   wcj,qmv5414 (853)

25 And the king   said, Divide   the living child in two, and give

df,nn2677   pp,nu259   wcj(853) df,nn2677   pp,nu259

half to the one, and   half to the other.

wcs,qmf559   df,nn802   pnl834   df,aj2416 nn,pnx1121   pr413   df,nn4428 cj3588

26 Then spoke the woman whose the living child *was* unto the king, for her

pl,nn,pnx7356   nipf3648   pr5921   nn,pnx1121   wcs,qmf559 pte994   nn,pnx113 qmv5414 pp,pnx (853)

bowels yearned upon her son, and she said,   O my lord, give her   the

df,aj**2416** df,qptp3205   ptn408 wcj,hina**4191**/himf,pnx4191   wcj,pndm2063 qpta**559**   qmf**1961**
living child, and in no   wise slay   it. But the   other   said, Let it be

ad1571/ptn**3808** pp,pnx ad1571 pp,pnx   qmv**1504**
neither mine nor thine, *but* divide *it.*

                    df,nn**4428** wcs,qmf6030   wcs,qmf**559** qmv**5414** pp,pnx (853)   df,aj**2416** df,qptp3205
27 Then the king answered and said, Give her   the living child, and in

ptn**3808** wcj,hina**4191**/himf,pnx**4191** pnp1931   nn,pnx**517**
no wise slay   it: she *is* the mother thereof.

            cs,nn**3605** nn3478 wcs,qmf**8085**   (853)   df,nn**4941** pnl834   df,nn**4428**   qpf**8199**
28 And all Israel heard of   the judgment which the king had judged; and

        wcs,qmf**3372**/pr4480/pl,cs,nn**6440** df,nn**4428** cj3588   qpf**7200** cj3588   cs,nn**2451**   pl,nn**430**
they   feared   the king: for they saw that the wisdom of God *was* in

pp,nn,pnx**7130** pp,qnc**6213**   nn**4941**
him, to do judgment.

Solomon's Officials

        df,nn**4428**   nn8010   wcs,qmf**1961** nn**4428** pr5921 cs,nn**3605** nn3478
4 So king Solomon was king over all Israel.

                wcj,pndm428   df,pl,nn**8269** pnl834 pp,pnx   nn5838   cs,nn**1121**
2 And these *were* the princes which he had; Azariah the son of

nn6659   df,nn**3548**
Zadok the priest,

        nn456   wcj,nn281   pl,cs,nn**1121**   nn7894   pl,nn**5608**   nn3092   cs,nn**1121**
3 Elihoreph and Ahiah, the sons of Shisha, scribes; Jehoshaphat the son of

nn286   df,hipt**2142**
Ahilud, the recorder.

        wcj,nn1141   cs,nn**1121**   nn3077   pr5921   df,nn**6635**   wcj,nn6659
4 And Benaiah the son of Jehoiada *was* over the host: and Zadok and

wcj,nn54   pl,nn**3548**
Abiathar *were* the priests:

        wcj,nn5838   cs,nn**1121**   nn5416   pr5921   df,pl,nipt**5324**   wcj,nn2071   cs,nn**1121**
5 And Azariah the son of Nathan *was* over the officers: and Zabud the son

nn5416   nn**3548**   df,nn**4428** cs,nn7463
of Nathan *was* principal officer, *and* the king's friend:

        wcj,nn301   pr5921   df,nn**1004**   wcj,nn141   cs,nn**1121**   nn5653
6 And Ahishar *was* over the household: and Adoniram the son of Abda *was*

pr5921   df,nn**4522**
over the tribute.

            wcj,pp,nn8010   du,nu8147/nu6240   pl,nipt**5324**   pr5921 cs,nn**3605**   nn3478
7 And Solomon had twelve officers over all Israel, which

wcj,pipf**3557**   (853)   df,nn**4428** wcj(853)   nn,pnx**1004** (pr5921)   df,nu259
provided victuals for   the king and   his household: each man his

nn2320   dfp,nn8141 (qmf**1961**)   pp,pinc3557
month in a year   made provision.

            wcj,pndm428   pl,nn,pnx8034   nn1133   pp,cs,nn2022   nn669
8 And these *are* their names: The son*of*Hur, in mount Ephraim:

            nn1128   pp,nn4739   wcj,pp,nn8169   wcj,nn1053
9 The son*of*Dekar, in Makaz, and in Shaalbim, and Beth-shemesh, and

wcj,nn358
Elon-beth-hanan:

            nn1136   dfp,nn700   pp,pnx   nn7755   wcj,cs,nn3605
10 The son*of*Hesed, in Aruboth; to him *pertained* Sochoh, and all the

cs,nn**776**   nn2660
land of Hepher:

nn1125   cs,nn3605   cs,nn5299   nn1756   nn2955
11 The son*of*Abinadab, in   all   the region of Dor; which had Taphath the

cs,nn1323   nn8010   (qpf1961) pp,pnx pp,nn802
daughter of Solomon   to wife:

nn1195   cs,nn1121   nn286   nn8590   wcj,nn4023
12 Baana the son of Ahilud; to him pertained Taanach and Megiddo, and

wcj,cs,nn3605   nn1052   pnl834   pr681   nn,lh6891   pr4480/pr8478 pp,nn3157   pr4480/nn1052   pr5704
all   Beth-shean, which is by Zartanah beneath Jezreel, from Beth-shean to

nn65   pr5704   pr4480/nn5676 pp,nn3361
Abel-meholah, even unto the place that is beyond Jokneam:

nn1127   pp,nn7433   pp,pnx   pl,cs,nn2333   nn2971
13 The son*of*Geber, in Ramoth-gilead; to him pertained the towns of Jair

cs,nn1121   nn4519   pnl834   dfp,nn1568 pp,pnx   cs,nn2256
the son of Manasseh, which are in Gilead; to him also pertained the region of

nn709   pnl834   dfp,nn1316   pl,nu8346 aj1419 pl,nn5892   nn2346   nn5178 wcj,cs,nn1280
Argob, which is in Bashan, threescore great cities with walls and brazen bars:

nn292   cs,nn1121   nn5714   nn,lh4266
14 Ahinadab the son of Iddo had Mahanaim:

nn290   pp,nn5321   pnp1931 ad1571 qpf3947 (853)   nn1315   cs,nn1323
15 Ahimaaz was in Naphtali; he   also took   Basmath the daughter of

nn8010   pp,nn802
Solomon to wife:

nn1195   cs,nn1121   nn2365   pp,nn836   wcj,nn1175
16 Baanah the son of Hushai was in Asher and in Aloth:

nn3092   cs,nn1121   nn6515   pp,nn3485
17 Jehoshaphat the son of Paruah, in Issachar:

nn8096   cs,nn1121   nn414   pp,nn1144
18 Shimei the son of Elah, in Benjamin:

nn1398   cs,nn1121   nn221   pp,cs,nn776   nn1568   cs,nn776   nn5511
19 Geber the son of Uri was in the country of Gilead, in the country of Sihon

cs,nn4428   df,nn567   wcj,nn5747 cs,nn4428   df,nn1316   nu259 wcj,nn5333
king of the Amorites, and of Og   king of Bashan; and he was the only officer

pnl834   dfp,nn776
which was in the land.

Solomon Prospers

nn3063   wcj,nn3478   aj7227   dfp,nn2344 pnl834   pr5921   df,nn3220
20 Judah and Israel were many, as the sand which is by the sea in

dfp,nn7230   pl,qpta398   wcj,pl,qpta8354   wcj,aj8056
multitude, eating and drinking, and making merry.

wcj,nn8010   (qpf1961) qpta4910   pp,cs,nn3605 df,pl,nn4467   pr4480   df,nn5104
21 And Solomon   reigned over   all   kingdoms from the river unto the

cs,nn776   nn6430   wcj,pr5704   cs,nn1366   nn4714   pl,hipt5066   nn4503
land of the Philistines, and unto the border of Egypt: they brought presents, and

wcj,pl,qpta5647 (853)   nn8010   cs,nn3605   pl,cs,nn3117   pl,nn,pnx2416
served   Solomon all the days of his life.

nn8010   cs,nn3899   nu259 pp,nn3117 wcs,qmf1961 nu7970   cs,nn3734   nn5560
22 And Solomon's provision for one day   was   thirty measures of fine flour,

wcj,pl,nu8346   cs,nn3734   nn7058
and threescore measures of meal,

nu6235 aj1277   nn1241   wcj,pl,nu6242 nn1241   nn7471   wcj,nu3967   nn6629
23 Ten fat oxen, and twenty oxen out of the pastures, and a hundred sheep,

pp,nn905   pr4480/nn354   wcj,nn6643   wcj,nn3180   pl,qptp75 wcj,pl,nn1257
beside harts, and roebucks, and fallow deer, and fatted fowl.

pl,cs,nn4734 pl,nn**3742** wcj,pl,nn8561 wcj,pl,cs,qptp6358 pl,nn6731 wcj,pipf6823

carvings of cherubims and palm trees and   open   flowers, and overlaid *them*

nn2091 wcs,himf7286 (853) df,nn2091 pr5921 df,pl,nn**3742** wcj,pr5921 df,pl,nn8561

with gold, and spread   gold upon the cherubims, and upon the palm trees.

 wcj,ad**3651** qpf**6213**   pp,cs,nn6607 df,nn**1964** pl,cs,nn4201 nn**8081** pl,cs,nn6086

33 So also made he for the door of the temple posts *of* olive tree, a

pr4480/pr854/nuor7243

fourth part *of the wall.*

  wcj,du,cs,nu8147 pl,cs,nn1817   pl,nn1265 pl,cs,nn6086 du,cs,nu8147 pl,nn6763

34 And the two doors *were of* fir tree: the two leaves of the

df,nu259 df,nn1817   pl,nn1550 wcj,du,cs,nu8147 pl,nn7050 df,nuor8145 df,nn1817   pl,nn1550

one door *were* folding, and the two leaves of the other door *were* folding.

  wcj,qpf7049   pl,nn**3742**   wcj,pl,nn8561 wcj,pl,cs,qptp6358 pl,nn6731

35 And he carved *thereon* cherubims and palm trees and open flowers:

wcj,pipf6823   nn2091 pupt**3474** pr5921 df,pupt2707

and covered *them* with gold fitted upon the carved work.

  wcs,qmf1129 df,aj6442 (853) df,nn2691 nu7969 pl,cs,nn2905   nn1496

36 And he built the inner court with three rows of hewed stone, and a

wcj,cs,nn2905 pl,nn730 pl,cs,qptp3773

row of cedar beams.

  df,nuor7243 dfp,nn8141   pupf**3245**   cs,nn**1004** nn**3068**

37 In the fourth year was the foundation of the house of the Lᴏʀᴅ laid, in the

pp,cs,nn3391 nn2099

month Zif:

   df,nu259/nu6240 wcj,dfp,nn8141 pp,nn3391 nn945 pnp1931 df,nuor8066 df,nn2320

38 And in the eleventh year, in the month Bul, which *is* the eighth month,

  df,nn**1004** qpf**3615**   pp,cs,nn3605 pl,nn,pnx**1697**

was the house finished throughout all the parts thereof, and according to

wcj,pp,cs,nn3605 pl,nn,pnx**4941**   nu7651 pl,nn8141 wcs,qmf,pnx1129

all the fashion of it. So was he seven years in building it.

Solomon Completes Other Building Projects

    nn8010   qpf1129 wcj(853)   nn,pnx**1004** cs,nu7969/nu6240 nn8141

7 But Solomon was building his own house thirteen years, and he

wcs,pimf**3615** (853) cs,nn3605 nn,pnx**1004**

finished all his house.

    wcs,qmf1129 (853) cs,nn**1004** cs,nn3293 df,nn3844 nn,pnx**753**

2 He built also the house of the forest of Lebanon; the length thereof *was*

nu3967 nn520   nn,pnx7341 wcj,pl,nu2572 nn520   nn,pnx6967

a hundred cubits, and the breadth thereof fifty cubits, and the height thereof

wcj,nu7970 nn520 pr5921 nu702 pl,cs,nn2905 pl,nn730 pl,cs,nn5982   pl,nn730 wcj,pl,qptp3773 pr5921

thirty cubits, upon four rows of cedar pillars, with cedar beams upon the

df,pl,nn5982

pillars.

    wcj,qptp5603   dfp,nn730 pr4480/ad4605 pr5921 df,pl,nn6763 pnl834 pr5921 pl,nu705

3 And *it was* covered with cedar above upon the beams, that *lay* on forty

wcj,nu2568 df,pl,nn5982 nu2568/nu6240 df,nn2905

five pillars, fifteen *in* a row.

    wcj,pl,nn8261 nu7969 pl,nn2905 wcj,nn4237   pr413 nn4237 nu7969

4 And *there were* windows *in* three rows, and light *was* against light *in* three

pl,nn6471

ranks.

wcj,cs,nn3605   df,pl,nn6607   wcj,df,pl,nn4201   pl,qptp7251   nn8260

5 And all the doors and posts *were* square, with the windows: and

wcj(pr4136) nn4237   pr413   nn4237   nu7969   pl,nn6471

light *was* against light *in* three ranks.

qpf**6213**   wcj(853)   cs,nn197   df,pl,nn5982   nn,pnx753   pl,nu2572   nn520

6 And he made a porch of pillars; the length thereof *was* fifty cubits, and

nn,pnx7341   wcj,nu7970   nn520   wcj,nn197   pr5921/pl,nn,pnx**6440**

the breadth thereof thirty cubits: and the porch *was* before them: and the *other*

wcj,pl,nn5982   wcj,nn5646   pr5921/pl,nn,pnx**6440**

pillars and the thick beam *were* before them.

qpf**6213**   wcj,nn197   df,nn**3678**   pnl834/ad8033   qmf**8199**   cs,nn197

7 Then he made a porch for the throne where he might judge, *even* the porch

df,nn**4941**   wcj,qptp5603   dfp,nn730   pr4480/df,nn7172   pr5704

of judgment: and *it was* covered with cedar from*one*side*of*the*floor to the

df,nn7172

other.

wcj,nn,pnx**1004**   pnl834/ad8033   qmf**3427**   df,aj312   nn2691   pr4480/cs,nn**1004**   dfp,nn197

8 And his house where he dwelt *had* another court within the porch,

qpf**1961**   df,pndm2088   dfp,nn4639   nn8010   qmf**6213**   wcj,nn**1004**   nn6547

which was of the like work. Solomon made also a house for Pharaoh's

pp,cs,nn1323   pnl834   qpf3947   df,pndm2088   dfp,nn197

daughter, whom he had taken *to wife*, like unto this porch.

cs,nn3605   pndm428   aj3368   pl,nn68   pp,pl,cs,nn4060   nn1496

9 All these *were of* costly stones, according to the measures of hewed stones,

pl,pupt**1641**   dfp,nn4050   pr4480/nn**1004**   wcj,pr4480/nn2351   wcj,pr4480/nn4527   pr5704

sawed with saws, within and without, even from*the*foundation unto the

df,pl,nn2948   wcj,pr4480/nn2351   pr5704   df,aj1419   df,nn2691

coping, and *so* on*the*outside toward the great court.

wcj,pupt**3245**   aj3368   pl,nn68   aj1419   pl,nn68   pl,cs,nn68   nu6235

10 And the foundation *was of* costly stones, even great stones, stones of ten

pl,nn520   wcj,pl,cs,nn68   nu8083   pl,nn520

cubits, and stones of eight cubits.

wcj,pr4480/pp,ad,lh4605   aj3368   pl,nn68   pp,pl,cs,nn4060   nn1496

11 And above *were* costly stones, after the measures of hewed stones,

wcj,nn730

and cedars.

df,aj1419 wcj,nn2691   ad5439   nu7969   pl,nn2905   nn1496

12 And the great court round about *was* with three rows of hewed stones,

wcj,cs,nn2905   pl,nn730   pl,qptp3773   df,aj6442 wcj,pp,cs,nn2691   cs,nn**1004**

and a row of cedar beams, both for the inner court of the house of the

nn**3068**   wcj,pp,cs,nn197   df,nn**1004**

LORD, and for the porch of the house.

df,nn**4428**   nn8010   wcs,qmf7971   wcs,qmf3947 (853)   nn2438   pr4480/nn6865

☞ 13 And king Solomon sent and fetched Hiram out*of*Tyre.

pnp1931   nn490   cs,nn1121 (nn802)   pr4480/cs,nn**4294**   nn5321   wcj,nn,pnx1

14 He *was* a widow's son of*the*tribe of Naphtali, and his father *was*

nn376   nn6876   qpta2790   nn5178   wcs,nimf**4390**   pr854   df,nn**2451**   wcj(853)

a man of Tyre, a worker in brass: and he was filled with wisdom, and

df,nn**8394**   wcj(853)   df,nn**1847**   pp,qnc**6213** cs,nn3605   nn**4399**   dfp,nn5178   wcs,qmf935 pr413

understanding, and cunning to work all works in brass. And he came to

df,nn**4428**   nn8010   wcs,qmf**6213** (853) cs,nn3605   nn,pnx**4399**

king Solomon, and wrought all his work.

☞ **7:13** This Hiram is not to be confused with King Hiram of Tyre (1 Kgs. 5:1).

df,nn**4428**   nn8010   wcs,qmf1431/pr4480/nn3605   pl,cs,nn**4428**   df,nn776   pp,nn6239

23 So king Solomon exceeded all the kings of the earth for riches and for

wcj,pp,nn**2451**

wisdom.

wcj,cs,nn3605   df,nn776 pl,pipt1245 (853) pl,cs,nn**6440**   nn8010   pp,qnc**8085** (853)   nn,pnx**2451**

24 And all the earth sought to Solomon, to hear his wisdom,

pnl834   pl,nn**430**   qpf**5414**   pp,nn,pnx**3820**

which God had put in his heart.

wcj,pnp1992   pl,hipt935   nn**376**   nn,pnx**4503** pl,cs,nn3627   nn3701   wcj,pl,cs,nn3627

25 And they brought every man his present, vessels of silver, and vessels

nn2091   wcj,pl,nn8008   wcj,nn**5402**   wcj,pl,nn1314 pl,nn5483   wcj,pl,nn6505 cs,nn**1697** nn8141

of gold, and garments, and armor, and spices, horses, and mules, a rate year by

pp,nn8141

year.

nn8010   wcs,qmf**622**   nn7393   wcj,pl,nn6571   wcs,qmf**1961**/pp,pnx

26 And Solomon gathered together chariots and horsemen: and he   had   a

nu**505**   wcj,nu702   pl,nu3967   nn7393   wcj,du,nu8147/nu6240   nu**505**   pl,nn6571

thousand and four hundred chariots, and   twelve   thousand horsemen, whom

wcs,himf,pnx**5148**   pp,pl,cs,nn5892   df,nn7393   wcj,pr5973   df,nn**4428**   pp,nn3389

he bestowed in the   cities   for chariots, and with the king at Jerusalem.

df,nn**4428** wcs,qmf**5414** (853) df,nn3701   pp,nn3389   dfp,pl,nn68   wcj(853) df,pl,nn730

27 And the king made   silver *to be* in Jerusalem as stones, and   cedars

qpf**5414**   dfp,pl,nn8256   pnl834   dfp,nn8219   dfp,nn7230

made he *to be* as the sycamore trees that *are* in the vale, for abundance.

pp,nn8010   df,pl,nn5483 (pnl834) wcj,cs,nn4161   pr4480/nn4714   wcj,pr4480/nn**4723**

28 And Solomon had horses   brought out*of*Egypt, and linen yarn: the

df,nn**4428** pl,cs,qpta5503   qmf3947   pr4480/nn**4723**   pp,nn4242

king's merchants received the linen yarn at a price.

nn4818   wcs,qmf**5927**   wcs,qmf3318   pr4480/nn4714   pp,nu8337   pl,nu3967

29 And a chariot came up and went out of Egypt for six hundred *shekels* of

nn3701   wcj,nn5483   wcj,nu3967   dfp,pl,nu2572   wcj,ad**3651**   pp,cs,nn3605   pl,cs,nn**4428**

silver, and a horse for a hundred and fifty: and so for all the kings of

df,nn2850   wcj,pp,pl,cs,nn**4428**   nn758   himf3318

the Hittites, and for the   kings   of Syria, did they bring***them***out by their

pp,nn,pnx**3027**

means.

Solomon Turns From God

wcj,df,nn**4428**   nn8010   qpf**157**   aj7227   aj**5237**   pl,nn802   wcj,pr854

But king Solomon loved many strange women, together with the

cs,nn1323   nn6547   nn4125   nn5984   nn130

daughter of Pharaoh, women of the Moabites, Ammonites, Edomites,

nn6722   nn2850

Zidonians, *and* Hittites;

pr4480   df,pl,nn**1471**   pnl834   nn3068 qpf559 pr413   pl,cs,nn**1121**   nn3478

2 Of the nations *concerning* which the LORD said unto the children of Israel,

ptn3808 qmf935   pp,pnx   ptn**3808**   wcj,pnp1992 qmf935   pp,pnx   ad403

Ye shall not go in to them, neither shall they come in unto you: *for* surely they

himf5186   (853)   nn,pnx3824 pr310   pl,nn,pnx**430**   nn8010   qpf1692   pp,pnx

will turn away   your heart after their gods: Solomon cleaved unto these in

pp,qnc**157**

love.

wcs,qmf1961/pp,pnx　　cs,nu7651　　pl,nu3967　　pl,nn802　　pl,nn8282　　cs,nu7969　　pl,nu3967

3 And he　　had　　seven hundred wives, princesses, and three hundred

wcj,pl,nn6370　　　　pl,nn,pnx802　　wcs,himf5186　　(853)　　nn,pnx3820

concubines: and his wives turned away　　his heart.

wcs,qmf1961　　pp,cs,nn6256　　nn8010　　cs,nn2209　　pl,nn,pnx802　　hipf5186

4 For it*came*to*pass, when Solomon was old, *that* his wives turned away

(853)　　nn,pnx3824　pr310　aj312　pl,nn430　　nn,pnx3824 qpf1961 wcj,ptn3808　aj8003　pr5973　　nn3068

his heart after other gods: and his heart was　not　perfect with the LORD his

pl,nn,pnx430　　　pp,cs,nn3824　　nn1732　　nn,pnx1

God, as *was* the　heart　of David his father.

nn8010　wcs,qmf1980　pr310　　nn6253　　pl,cs,nn430　　nn6722　　wcj,pr310

5 For Solomon　went　after Ashtoreth the goddess of the Zidonians, and after

nn4445　　cs,nn8251　　nn5984

Milcom the abomination of the Ammonites.

nn8010　　wcs,qmf6213　df,aj7451　　pp,du,cs,nn5869　　nn3068　　wcj,ptn3808/pipf4390

6 And Solomon　did　evil in the　sight　of the LORD, and went*not*fully

pr310　　nn3068　　pp,nn1732　　nn,pnx1

after the LORD, as *did* David his father.

ad227　　nn8010　qmf1129　　nn1116　　pp,nn3645　　cs,nn8251　　nn4124

7 Then did Solomon build a high place for Chemosh, the abomination of Moab,

dfp,nn2022 pnl834　pr5921/pl,cs,nn6440　　nn3389　　wcj,pp,nn4432　　nn8251

in the　hill　that *is*　before　Jerusalem, and for Molech, the abomination of the

pl,cs,nn1121　　nn5983

children of Ammon.

wcj,ad3651　qpf6213　　pp,cs,nn3605　　df,aj5237　pl,nn,pnx802　　pl,hipt6999

8 And likewise did he for　all　his strange wives, which burnt incense and

wcj,pl,pipt2076　　pp,pl,nn,pnx430

sacrificed unto their　gods.

The Consequences of Solomon's Sins

nn3068　　wcs,htmf599　　pp,nn8010　　cj3588　　nn,pnx3824　　qpf5186

9 And the LORD was　angry　with Solomon, because his　heart　was turned

pr4480/pr5973　　nn3068　pl,cs,nn430　　nn3478　　df,nipf7200　pr,pnx413　du,nn6471

from　the LORD God of Israel, which had appeared　unto him twice,

wcj,pipf6680/pr,pnx413　　pr5921　df,pndm2088　df,nn1697　　pp,ptn1115

10 And had commanded him concerning　this　thing, that he should　not

qnc1980　pr310　aj312　pl,nn430　　qpf8104 wcj,ptn3808 (853)　pnl834　　nn3068　　pipf6680

go　after other gods: but he kept　not　　that which the LORD commanded.

nn3068　wcs,qmf559　　pp,nn8010　　cj3282　pnl834 pndm2063 qpf1961

11 Wherefore the LORD　said　unto Solomon, Forasmuch as　this　is　done

pr,pnx5973　　wcj,ptn3808 qpf8104　nn,pnx1285　　wcj,pl,nn,pnx2708　pnl834

of　thee, and thou hast　not　kept my covenant and my　statutes,　which I have

pipf6680,pr,pnx5921　　qna7167/qmf7167　(853)　df,nn4467　pr4480/pr,pnx5921

commanded thee, I will surely rend　　the kingdom　from　thee, and will

wcs,qpf,pnx5414　　pp,nn,pnx5650

give　it to thy servant.

ad389　　　pp,pl,nn,pnx3117　　ptn3808　qmf,pnx6213

12 Notwithstanding　in　thy　days　I　will　not　do　it

pp,pr4616/nn1732/nn,pnx1　　qmf,pnx7167　pr4480/cs,nn3027　nn,pnx1121

for*David*thy*father's*sake: *but* I will　rend　it out*of*the*hand of thy　son.

ad7535　ptn3808　qmf7167　(853) cs,nn3605　df,nn4467　qmf5414　nu259

13 Howbeit I will　not　rend away　　all　the kingdom; *but* will give one

nn**7626**   pp,nn,pnx**1121**   pp,pr4616/nn1732/nn,pnx**5650**   wcj,pp,pr4616/nn3389   pnl834

tribe to thy   son   for David*my*servant's*sake, and for*Jerusalem's*sake which I

qpf**977**

have chosen.

nn**3068**   wcs,himf**6965**   nn**7854**   pp,nn8010   (853)   nn**1908**

14 And the LORD stirred up an adversary unto Solomon,   Hadad the

df,nn130   pnp1931   pr4480/cs,nn**2233**/df,nn**4428**   dfp,nn123

Edomite: he *was* of*the*king's*seed in Edom.

wcs,qmf**1961**   nn1732   pp,qnc**1961**   (853)   nn123   nn3097   cs,nn**8269**

15 For it*came*to*pass, when David was in   Edom, and Joab the captain

df,nn**6635**   pp,qnc**5927**   pp,pinc**6912** (853)   df,pl,nn2491   wcs,himf**5221** cs,nn3605 nn2145

of the host was gone up to bury   the slain, after he had smitten every male

dfp,nn123

in Edom;

cj3588   cs,nu8337   pl,nn2320   nn3097   qpf**3427**   ad8033   wcj,cs,nn3605   nn3478   pr5704

16 (For   six   months did Joab remain there with   all   Israel, until he had

hipf**3772**   cs,nn3605   nn2145   pp,nn123

cut off every male in Edom:)

nn111   wcs,qmf1272 pnp1931   wcj,pl,nn**376**   nn129   pr4480/pl,cs,nn**5650**/nn,pnx1   pr,pnx854

17 That Hadad fled,   he and certain Edomites of*his*father's*servants with

pp,qnc935   nn4714   wcj,nn1908   aj6996   nn5288

him, to   go   into Egypt; Hadad *being* yet a little child.

wcs,qmf**6965**   pr4480/nn4080   wcs,qmf935   nn6290   wcs,qmf3947   pl,nn**376**

18 And they arose out*of*Midian, and came to Paran: and they took   men

pr,pnx5973   pr4480/nn6290   wcs,qmf935   nn4714   pr413   nn6547   cs,nn**4428**   nn4714

with   them out*of*Paran, and they came to Egypt, unto Pharaoh king of Egypt;

wcs,qmf**5414** pp,pnx   nn**1004**   qpf559   pp,pnx   wcj,nn3899   qpf**5414** pp,pnx   wcj,nn**776**

which   gave   him a house, and appointed him victuals, and gave him land.

nn1908   wcs,qmf4672   ad3966   nn**2580**   pp,du,cs,nn**5869**   nn6547   wcs,qmf**5414**

19 And Hadad found great favor in the   sight   of Pharaoh, so that he   gave

pp,pnx   nn**802**   (853)   cs,nn**269**   nn,pnx**802**   cs,nn**269**   nn8472   df,nn1377

him to wife   the sister of his own wife, the sister of Tahpenes the queen.

cs,nn**269**   nn8472   wcs,qmf3205   pp,pnx   (853)   nn1592   nn,pnx**1121**

20 And the sister of Tahpenes   bare   him   Genubath his   son,   whom

nn8472   wcs,qmf,pnx**1580**   pp,cs,nn**8432**   nn6547   cs,nn**1004**   nn1592   wcs,qmf**1961**   nn6547

Tahpenes weaned   in   Pharaoh's house: and Genubath   was   in Pharaoh's

cs,nn**1004**   pp,cs,nn**8432**   pl,cs,nn**1121**   nn6547

household among the   sons   of Pharaoh.

wcj,nn1908   qpf**8085**   pp,nn4714 cj3588   nn1732   qpf7901   pr5973   pl,nn,pnx1   wcj,cj3588

21 And when Hadad heard in Egypt that David slept with his fathers, and   that

nn3097   cs,nn**8269**   df,nn**6635**   qpf**4191**   nn1908   wcs,qmf559   pr413   nn6547   pimv,pnx7971

Joab the captain of the host was dead, Hadad   said   to Pharaoh, Let me depart,

wcj,qmf**1980** pr413   nn,pnx**776**

that I may   go   to mine own country.

nn6547   wcs,qmf**559**   pp,pnx   cj3588 pnit4100   pnp859   aj2638   pr,pnx5973

22 Then Pharaoh   said   unto him, But what hast thou lacked   with   me, that,

wcj,ptdm,pnx2009   pipt1245   pp,qnc**1980** pr413   nn,pnx**776**   wcs,qmf559   ptn3808

behold,   thou seekest to   go   to thine own country? And he answered, Nothing:

cj3588   pina7971/pimf,pnx7971

howbeit let me go*in*any*wise.

pl,nn**430**   wcs,himf**6965**/pp,pnx   nn**7854**   (853)   nn7331   cs,nn**1121**   nn450

23 And God stirred*him*up *another* adversary,   Rezon the   son of Eliadah,

pnl834   qpf1272 pr4480/pr854   pl,nn,pnx**113**   nn1909   cs,nn**4428**   nn6678

which fled   from   his   lord   Hadadezer king of Zobah:

wcs,qmf**6908**   pl,nn**376**   pr,pnx5921   wcs,qmf**1961**   cs,nn**8269**   nn**1416**

24 And he gathered men   unto   him, and became captain over a band, when

nn1732 pp,qnc2026 pnx(853) wcs,qmf1980 nn1834 wcs,qmf3427

David slew them *of Zobah*: and they went to Damascus, and dwelt

pp,pnx wcs,qmf4427 pp,nn1834

therein, and reigned in Damascus.

wcs,qmf1961 nn7854 pp,nn3478 cs,nn3605 pl,cs,nn3117 nn8010 wcj,pr854

25 And he was an adversary to Israel all the days of Solomon, beside

df,aj7451 pnl834 nn1908 wcs,qmf6973 pp,nn3478 wcs,qmf4427 pr5921 nn758

the mischief that Hadad *did*: and he abhorred Israel, and reigned over Syria.

Jeroboam is Chosen to Rule Ten Tribes

wcj,nn3379 cs,nn1121 nn5028 nn673 pr4480 df,nn6868 pp,nn8010

26 And Jeroboam the son of Nebat, an Ephrathite of Zereda, Solomon's

nn5650 nn,pnx517 wcj,cs,nn8034 nn6871 nn490 nn802 wcs,himf7311

servant, whose mother's name *was* Zeruah, a widow woman, even he lifted up

nn3027 dfp,nn4428

his hand against the king.

wcj,pndm2088 df,nn1697 pnl834 hipf7311 nn3027 dfp,nn4428

27 And this *was* the cause that he lifted up *his* hand against the king:

nn8010 qpf1129 (853) df,nn4407 qpf5462 (853) cs,nn6556 cs,nn5892 nn1732

Solomon built Millo, *and* repaired the breaches of the city of David his

nn,pnx1

father.

wcj,df,nn376 nn3379 cs,aj1368 nn2428 nn8010 wcs,qmf7200

28 And the man Jeroboam *was* a mighty man*of*valor: and Solomon seeing

(853) df,nn5288 cj3588 pnp1931 qpta6213/nn4399 wcs,himf6485/pnx(853) pp,cs,nn3605

the young man that he was industrious, he made*him*ruler over all the

cs,nn5447 cs,nn1004 nn3130

charge of the house of Joseph.

wcs,qmf1961 df,pndm1931 dfp,nn6256 wcj,nn3379 qpf3318

29 And it*came*to*pass at that time when Jeroboam went out

pr4480/nn3389 df,nn5030 nn281 df,nn7888 wcs,qmf4672 pnx(853) dfp,nn1870

of Jerusalem, that the prophet Ahijah the Shilonite found him in the way;

wcj,pnp1931 htpt3680 aj2319 pp,nn8008 wcj,du,nu,pnx8147 pp,nn,pnx905

and he had clad himself with a new garment; and they two *were* alone

dfp,nn7704

in the field:

nn281 wcs,qmf8610 df,aj2319 dfp,nn8008 pnl834 pr,pnx5921 wcs,qmf,pnx7167

30 And Ahijah caught the new garment that *was* on him, and rent it

du,nu8147/nu6240 pl,nn7168

in twelve pieces:

wcs,qmf559 pp,nn3379 qmv3947 pp,pnx nu6235 pl,nn7168 cj3588 ad3541 qpf559 nn3068

31 And he said to Jeroboam, Take thee ten pieces: for thus saith the LORD,

pl,cs,nn430 nn3478 ptdm,pnx2009 qpta7167 (853) df,nn4467 pr4480/cs,nn3027

the God of Israel, Behold, I will rend the kingdom out*of*the*hand of

nn8010 wcj,qpf5414 (853) nu6235 df,pl,nn7626 pp,pnx

Solomon, and will give ten tribes to thee:

✒ **11:30–35** Only eleven of the twelve pieces of the cloak are accounted for in this passage. The most reasonable solution is that the tribe of Benjamin, which did not really have an independent existence at this time, was left out. Benjamin was still one of the twelve tribes, but one that did not figure into this prophecy concerning the division of the kingdom. The tribe of Benjamin was so small that it had all but disappeared into the tribe of Judah. In 1 Kings 12:21, the tribe of Benjamin is listed as the ally of the tribe of Judah when the latter is preparing to attack the Northern Kingdom.

pp,pnx qmf**1961** df,nu259 wcj,df,nn**7626** pp,pr4616/nn1732/nn,pnx**5650**

32 (But he shall have one tribe for*my*servant*David's*sake, and

wcj,pp,pr4616/nn**3389** df,nn**5892** pnl834 qpf**977**/pp,pnx pr4480/nn**3605** pl,cs,nn**7626**

for*Jerusalem's*sake, the city which I have chosen out*of*all the tribes of

nn3478

Israel:)

cj3282 pnl834 qpf,pnx**5800**   wcs,htmf**7812** pp,nn6253

33 Because that they have forsaken me, and have worshiped Ashtoreth the

pl,cs,nn**430** nn6721 pp,nn3645 pl,cs,nn**430** nn4124 wcj,pp,nn4445

goddess of the Zidonians, Chemosh the god of the Moabites, and Milcom the

pl,cs,nn**430** pl,cs,nn**1121** nn5983 wcj,ptn**3808** qpf**1980** pp,pl,nn,pnx**1870** pp,qnc**6213**

god of the children of Ammon, and have not walked in my ways, to do

df,aj**3477** pp,du,nn,pnx**5869** wcj,pl,nn,pnx**2708** wcj,pl,nn,pnx**4941**

that which is right in mine eyes, and *to keep* my statutes and my judgments,

pp,nn1732 nn,pnx1

as *did* David his father.

wcj,ptn**3808** qmf3947 (853) cs,nn3605 df,nn**4467** pr4480/nn,pnx**3027** cj3588

34 Howbeit I will not take the whole kingdom out*of*his*hand: but I

qmf,pnx**7896** nn**5387** cs,nn3605 pl,cs,nn**3117** pl,nn,pnx**2416**

will make him prince all the days of his life

pp,pr4616/nn1732/nn,pnx**5650** pnl834/pnx(853) qpf**977** pnl834 qpf**8104** pl,nn,pnx**4687**

for*David*my*servant's*sake, whom I chose, because he kept my commandments

wcj,pl,nn,pnx**2708**

and my statutes:

wcj,qpf3947 df,nn**4410** pr4480/cs,nn**3027**/nn,pnx**1121** wcj,qpf,pnx**5414**

35 But I will take the kingdom out*of*his*son's*hand, and will give it

pp,pnx (853) cs,nu6235 df,pl,nn**7626**

unto thee, *even* ten tribes.

wcj,pp,nn,pnx**1121** qmf**5414** nu259 nn**7626** pp,cj4616 pp,nn1732 nn,pnx**5650**

36 And unto his son will I give one tribe, that David my servant may

qnc**1961** nn5216 cs,nn3605/df,pl,nn**3117** pp,pl,nn,pnx**6440** pp,nn3389 df,nn**5892** pnl834 qpf**977**

have a light always before me in Jerusalem, the city which I have chosen

pp,pnx pp,qnc**7760** nn,pnx8034 ad8033

me to put my name there.

qmf3947 wcj,pnx(853)   wcs,qpf**4427** pp,nn3605 pnl834

37 And I will take thee, and thou shalt reign according to all that

nn,pnx**5315** pimf**183**   wcs,qpf**1961** nn**4428** pr5921 nn3478

thy soul desireth, and shalt be king over Israel.

wcs,qpf**1961** cj518   qmf**8085** (853) cs,nn3605 pnl834 pimf,pnx**6680**

38 And it shall be, if thou wilt hearken unto all that I command

wcs,qpf**1980** pp,pl,nn,pnx**1870** wcs,qpf**6213** df,aj**3477** pp,du,nn,pnx**5869**

thee, and wilt walk in my ways, and do *that is* right in my sight, to

pp,qnc**8104** pl,nn,pnx**2708** wcj,pl,nn,pnx**4687** pp,pnl834 nn1732 nn,pnx**5650** qpf**6213**

keep my statutes and my commandments, as David my servant did; that I will

wcj,qpf**1961** pr,pnx5973 wcj,qpf**1129** pp,pnx nipt**539** nn**1004** pp,pnl834 qpf**1129** pp,nn1732

be with thee, and build thee a sure house, as I built for David, and will

wcj,qpf**5414** (853) nn3478 pp,pnx

give Israel unto thee.

pp,pr4616 pndm2063 wcs,pimf6031 (853) cs,nn**2233** nn1732 ad389 ptn**3808** cs,nn3605/df,pl,nn**3117**

39 And I will for this afflict the seed of David, but not forever.

nn8010 wcs,pimf**1245** pp,hinc**4191** (853) nn3379 nn3379 wcs,qmf**6965**

40 Solomon sought therefore to kill Jeroboam. And Jeroboam arose,

wcs,qmf**1272** nn4714 pr413 nn7895 cs,nn**4428** nn4714 wcs,qmf**1961** pp,nn4714 pr5704

and fled into Egypt, unto Shishak king of Egypt, and was in Egypt until the

cs,nn**4194** nn8010

death of Solomon.

Solomon's Death

wcj,cs,nn**3499**　　　　pl,cs,nn**1697**　　　nn8010　　　　wcj,cs,nn3605　pnl834　　qpf**6213**

41 And the　rest　of　the　acts　of Solomon, and　all　that he did, and his

wcj,nn,pnx**2451**　　pnp1992　he,ptn**3808**　pl,qptp3789　pr5921　　cs,nn**5612**　　　pl,cs,nn**1697**　　nn8010

wisdom, *are* they　not　written　in　the　book　of　the　acts　of Solomon?

wcj,df,pl,nn**3117**　pnl834　　nn8010　　qpf**4427**　　　pp,nn3389　　pr5921　cs,nn3605　　nn3478

42 And the　time　that Solomon reigned in Jerusalem over　all　Israel *was*

pl,nu705　nn8141

forty years.

nn8010　　wcs,qmf7901　pr5973　　pl,nn,pnx1　　　wcs,nimf**6912**　　　　pp,cs,nn5892

43 And Solomon　slept　with his fathers, and was　buried　in　the　city　of

nn1732　　　nn,pnx1　　　nn7346　　nn,pnx1121　wcs,qmf**4427**　　pr,pnx8478

David his father: and Rehoboam his　son　reigned in his stead.

The Northern Tribes Revolt

nn7346　　　wcs,qmf**1980**　　　nn7927　cj3588　cs,nn3605　nn3478　　　qpf935

12 And Rehoboam　went　to Shechem: for　all　Israel were come to

nn7927　　　pp,hinc**4427**/pnx(853)

Shechem to make*him*king.

wcs,qmf**1961**　　　　　nn3379　　　cs,nn1121　　nn5028　wcj,pnp1931　　pr5750

2 And it*came*to*pass, when Jeroboam the　son　of Nebat,　who　was yet in

pp,nn4714　　pp,qnc**8085**　　　pnl834　　　qpf1272　　pr4480/pl,cs,nn**6440**　　df,nn**4428**　　nn8010

Egypt,　heard　*of it*, (for he was　fled　from*the*presence of　king Solomon, and

nn3379　　wcs,qmf**3427**　　pp,nn4714

Jeroboam　dwelt　in Egypt;)

wcs,qmf7971　　　wcs,qmf7121　　pp,pnx　　　　nn3379　　　　wcj,cs,nn3605

3 That　they　sent　and　called　him.　And　Jeroboam　and　all　the

cs,nn**6951**　　　nn3478　wcs,qmf935　　wcs,pimf**1696**　pr413　　nn7346　　pp,qnc559

congregation of Israel came, and　spoke　unto　Rehoboam, saying,

nn,pnx1　　　(853)　　nn,pnx5923　hipf7185　　ad6258　　　　　　wcj,pnp859

4 Thy father made　our　yoke　grievous: now therefore make　thou　the

df,aj**7186**　　pr4480/cs,nn**5656**　　　nn,pnx1　　　df,aj3515　wcj,pr4480/nn,pnx5923　pnl834　　qpf**5414** pr,pnx5921

grievous　service　of thy father, and his heavy　　yoke　　which he put　upon

himv**7043**　　　　　　wcj,qmf,pnx**5647**

us, lighter, and we will　serve　thee.

wcs,qmf**559** pr,pnx413　　qmv**1980** ad5750　nu7969 pl,nn**3117**　　wcj,qmv**7725**　pr,pnx413

5 And he　said　unto them, Depart yet *for* three days, then come again　to

df,nn**5971**　wcs,qmf**1980**

me. And the people departed.

df,nn**4428**　　nn7346　wcs,nimf**3289**　pr854　　df,aj**2205**　pnl834 (qpf**1961**) pl,qpta5975 (853) pl,cs,nn**6440**

6 And king Rehoboam consulted with the old men, that　　　stood　　　before

nn8010　　nn,pnx1 pp,qnc,pnx**1961**　　aj2416　　pp,qnc559 ptx349　　pnp859 pl,nipt**3289**

Solomon his father　while　he yet lived, and said, How do　ye　advise that I may

pp,hinc**7725**/nn**1697** (853) df,pndm2088　df,nn**5971**

answer　　　this　　people?

wcs,pimf**1696** pr,pnx413　　pp,qnc559 cj518　　qmf**1961**　　nn**5650**　　df,pndm2088

7 And they　spoke　unto him, saying, If thou wilt　be　a servant unto　this

dfp,nn**5971**　　df,nn**3117**　　wcs,qpf,pnx**5647**　　wcs,qpf,pnx6030　　wcs,pipf**1696**　aj**2896**

people this day, and wilt　serve　them, and　answer　them, and speak good

pl,nn**1697** pr,pnx413　　wcs,qpf**1961** pp,pnx　pl,nn**5650**　cs,nn3605/df,pl,nn**3117**

words　to　them, then they will　be　thy servants　forever.

wcs,qmf**5800**　(853)　cs,nn**6098**　df,aj**2205**　pnl834　　qpf,pnx**3289**

8 But he forsook　　the　counsel of the old men, which they had　given　him,

wcs,nimf**3289**   pr854   df,pl,nn3206   pnl834   qpf1431   pr,pnx854   pnl834

and consulted with the young men that were grown up with him, *and* which

df,pl,qpta5975 pp,pl,nn,pnx**6440**

stood   before   him:

wcs,qmf**559**   pr,pnx413   pnit4100   pl,nipt**3289**   pnp859   wcj,himf**7725**/nn**1697**

9 And he   said   unto them, What counsel give ye that we may   answer

(853)   df,pndm2088   df,nn**5971**   pnl834   pipf**1696**   pr,pnx413   pp,qnc**559**   df,nn**5923**   pnl834

this   people, who have spoken   to   me, saying, Make the yoke which thy

nn,pnx1   qpf**5414** pr,pnx5921   (pr4480)   himv**7043**

father did   put   upon us   lighter?

df,pl,nn3206   pnl834   qpf1431   pr,pnx854   wcs,pimf**1696** pr,pnx413

10 And the young men that were grown up with him   spoke   unto him,

pp,qnc**559**   ad3541   qmf**559**   df,pndm2088 dfp,nn**5971** pnl834 pipf**1696** pr,pnx413   pp,qnc**559**

saying, Thus shalt thou speak unto   this   people that spoke unto thee, saying,

nn,pnx1   (853)   nn,pnx5923 hipf**3513**   wcj,pnp859   himv**7043** pr4480/pr,pnx5921   ad3541

Thy father made   our yoke heavy, but make thou *it* lighter   unto   us; thus

pimf**1696** pr,pnx413   nn,pnx6995   qpf5666   nn,pnx1

shalt thou say   unto them, My little *finger* shall be thicker than my father's

pr4480/du,cs,nn4975

loins.

wcj,ad6258   nn,pnx1   hipf6006/pr,pnx5921   aj3515   nn5923 wcj,pnp589

11 And now whereas my father did   lade   you with a heavy yoke,   I

himf3254 pr5921   nn,pnx5923   nn,pnx1   pipf**3256**   pnx(853)   dfp,pl,nn7752

will add   to your yoke: my father hath chastised   you with whips, but

wcj,pnp589   pimf**3256** pnx(853)   dfp,pl,nn6137

I   will chastise   you with scorpions.

nn3379   wcj,cs,nn3605   df,nn**5971** wcs,qmf935 pr413   nn7346   df,nuor7992 dfp,nn3117

12 So Jeroboam and   all   the people came to Rehoboam the third day,

pp,pnl834   df,nn**4428**   pipf**1696**   pp,qnc**559** qmv**7725** pr,pnx413   df,nuor7992 dfp,nn**3117**

as   the king had appointed, saying, Come to me again the third day.

df,nn**4428**   wcs,qmf6030   (853)   df,nn**5971** aj7186   wcs,qmf**5800**   (853)

13 And the king answered   the people roughly, and forsook   the

df,aj2205   cs,nn**6098**   pnl834   qpf,pnx**3289**

old men's counsel that they gave him;

wcs,pimf**1696** pr,pnx413   pp,cs,nn**6098**   df,pl,nn3206   pp,qnc**559**

14 And spoke   to   them after the counsel of the young men, saying, My

nn,pnx1   (853)   nn,pnx5923 hipf**3513**   wcj,pnp589   himf3254 pr5921   nn,pnx5923   nn,pnx1

father made   your yoke heavy, and   I   will add to your yoke: my father

pipf**3256**   pnx(853)   dfp,pl,nn7752   wcj,pnp589   pimf**3256** pnx(853)

also chastised   you with whips, but   I   will chastise   you with

dfp,pl,nn6137

scorpions.

df,nn**4428**   qpf**8085**   wcj,ptn**3808** pr413   df,nn**5971** cj3588   nn5438 qpf**1961**

15 Wherefore the king hearkened not unto the people; for the cause was

pr4480/pr5973   nn**3068** pp,cj4616   hinc**6965**   (853)   nn,pnx**1697** pnl834   nn**3068** pipf**1696**

from   the LORD, that he might perform   his saying, which the LORD spoke

pp,cs,nn**3027**   nn281   df,nn7888   pr413   nn3379   cs,nn**1121**   nn5028

by   Ahijah the Shilonite unto Jeroboam the son of Nebat.

cs,nn3605 nn3478 wcs,qmf**7200** cj3588   df,nn**4428** qpf**8085** ptn**3808** pr,pnx413

16 So when all Israel saw   that the king hearkened not unto them, the

df,nn**5971** wcs,himf**7725**/nn**1697** (853)   df,nn**4428** pp,qnc**559** pnit4100   nn2506   pp,pnx   pp,nn1732 wcj,ptn**3808**

people   answered   the king, saying, What portion have we in David? neither

nn5159   pp,cs,nn**1121**   nn3448   pp,pl,nn,pnx168   nn3478 ad6258 qmv**7200**

have we inheritance in the son of Jesse: to your tents, O Israel: now see to

nn,pnx**1004** nn1732   nn3478 wcs,qmf**1980**   pp,pl,nn,pnx168

thine own house, David. So Israel departed unto their   tents.

17 But *as for* the children of Israel which dwelt in the cities of Judah, Rehoboam reigned over them.

18 Then king Rehoboam sent Adoram, who *was* over the tribute; and all Israel stoned him with stones, that he died. Therefore king Rehoboam made speed to get*him*up to his chariot, to flee to Jerusalem.

19 So Israel rebelled against the house of David unto this day.

20 And it*came*to*pass, when all Israel heard that Jeroboam was come again, that they sent and called him unto the congregation, and made*him*king over all Israel: there was none that followed the house of David, but the tribe of Judah only.

Civil War is Averted

21 And when Rehoboam was come to Jerusalem, he assembled all the house of Judah, with the tribe of Benjamin, a hundred and fourscore thousand chosen men, which were warriors, to fight against the house of Israel, to bring the kingdom again to Rehoboam the son of Solomon.

22 But the word of God came unto Shemaiah the man of God, saying,

23 Speak unto Rehoboam, the son of Solomon, king of Judah, and unto all the house of Judah and Benjamin, and to the remnant of the people, saying,

24 Thus saith the LORD, Ye shall not go up, nor fight against your brethren the children of Israel: return every man to his house; for this thing is from me. They hearkened therefore to the word of the LORD, and returned to depart, according to the word of the LORD.

Jeroboam's Apostasy

25 Then Jeroboam built Shechem in mount Ephraim, and dwelt therein; and went out from thence, and built Penuel.

nn3379   wcs,qmf**559**   pp,nn,pnx**3820** ad6258   df,nn**4467**   qmf**7725**

26 And Jeroboam said in his heart, Now shall the kingdom return to the

pp,cs,nn**1004**   nn1732

house of David:

cj518 df,pndm2088 df,nn**5971** qmf**5927**   pp,qnc**6213**   df,pndm2088 df,nn**5971**   pp,cs,nn**1004**   nn**3068**

27 If this people go up to do sacrifice in the house of the LORD at

pp,nn3389   cs,nn**3820**   df,pndm2088 df,nn**5971** wcs,qpf**7725** pr413   pl,nn,pnx113

Jerusalem, then shall the heart of this people turn again unto their lord, *even*

pr413   nn7346   nn**4428**   nn3063   wcs,qpf,pnx**2026**   wcs,qpf**7725** pr413

unto Rehoboam king of Judah, and they shall kill me, and go again to

nn7346   cs,nn**4428**   nn3063

Rehoboam king of Judah.

df,nn**4428**   wcs,nimf**3289**   wcs,qmf**6213** du,cs,nu8147 pl,cs,nn5695   nn2091

28 Whereupon the king took counsel, and made two calves *of* gold, and

wcs,qmf**559** pr,pnx413   ad7227   pp,pnx   pr4480/qnc**5927**   nn3389   ptdm2009

said unto them, It is too much for you to go up to Jerusalem: behold thy

pl,nn,pnx**430**   nn3478   pnl834 hipf,pnx**5927**   pr4480/nn**776**   nn4714

gods, O Israel, which brought thee up out*of*the*land of Egypt.

wcs,qmf**7760** (853)   df,nu259   pp,nn1008   wcj(853)   df,nu259 qpf**5414**   pp,nn1835

29 And he set the one in Bethel, and the other put he in Dan.

df,pndm2088 df,nn**1697** wcs,qmf**1961**   pp,nn**2403**   df,nn**5971** wcs,qmf**1980**   pp,pl,cs,nn**6440**

30 And this thing became a sin: for the people went *to worship* before

df,nu259   pr5704   nn1835

the one, *even* unto Dan.

wcs,qmf**6213** (853)   cs,nn**1004**   pl,nn**1116**   wcs,qmf**6213** pl,cs,nn**3548**   pr4480/pl,cs,nn7098

31 And he made a house of high places, and made priests of*the*lowest

df,nn**5971**   pnl834   qpf**1961** ptn**3808**   pr4480/pl,cs,nn**1121**   nn3878

of the people, which were not of the sons of Levi.

nn3379   wcs,qmf**6213**   nn2282   df,nuor8066 dfp,nn2320   dfp,nu2568/nu6240 nn3117

32 And Jeroboam ordained a feast in the eighth month, on the fifteenth day

dfp,nn2320   dfp,nn**2282** pnl834   pp,nn3063   wcs,himf**5927** pr5921   df,nn**4196**

of the month, like unto the feast that *is* in Judah, and he offered upon the altar.

ad**3651** qpf**6213**   pp,nn1008   pp,pinc**2076**   dfp,pl,nn5695 pnl834   qpf**6213**   wcj,hipf**5975**

So did he in Bethel, sacrificing unto the calves that he had made: and he placed

pp,nn1008 (853)   pl,cs,nn**3548**   df,pl,nn**1116**   pnl834   qpf**6213**

in Bethel the priests of the high places which he had made.

wcs,himf**5927**   pr5921   df,nn**4196** pnl834   qpf**6213**   pp,nn1008   dfp,nu2568/nu6240

33 So he offered upon the altar which he had made in Bethel the fifteenth

nn3117   df,nuor8066 dfp,nn2320   dfp,nn2320   pnl834   qpf**908**

day of the eighth month, *even* in the month which he had devised

pr4480/nn,pnx**3820**   wcs,qmf**6213**   nn2282   pp,pl,cs,nn**1121**   nn3478   wcs,himf**5927**

of*his*own*heart; and ordained a feast unto the children of Israel: and he offered

pr5921   df,nn**4196**   pp,hinc**6999**

upon the altar, and burnt incense.

12:28 "Behold thy gods, O Israel, which brought thee up out of Egypt" was the very phrase used by Aaron when he made the golden calf near Mount Sinai (Ex. 32:4). Jeroboam offered the people idolatry as an alternative to worshiping Jehovah.

A Judean Prophet Warns Jeroboam

13 And, behold, there came a man of God out*of*Judah by the word
of the LORD unto Bethel: and Jeroboam stood by the altar to
burn incense.

2 And he cried against the altar in the word of the LORD, and said, O
altar, altar, thus saith the LORD; Behold, a child shall be born unto the house of
David, Josiah by name; and upon thee shall he offer the priests of the
high places that burn incense upon thee, and men's bones shall be burnt upon
thee.

3 And he gave a sign the same day, saying, This *is* the sign which the
LORD hath spoken; Behold, the altar shall be rent, and the ashes that *are* upon it
shall be poured out.

4 And it*came*to*pass, when king Jeroboam heard the saying of the man
of God, which had cried against the altar in Bethel, that he put forth his hand
from the altar, saying, Lay hold on him. And his hand, which he put forth
against him, dried up, so that he could not pull*it*in*again to him.

5 The altar also was rent, and the ashes poured out from the altar, according
to the sign which the man of God had given by the word of the LORD.

6 And the king answered and said unto the man of God, Entreat now
the face of the LORD thy God, and pray for me, that my hand may be
restored*me*again. And the man of God besought the LORD, and the
king's hand was restored*him*again, and became as *it was* before.

7 And the king said unto the man of God, Come home with me, and
refresh thyself, and I will give thee a reward.

8 And the man of God said unto the king, If thou wilt give me half
thine house, I will not go in with thee, neither will I eat bread nor drink
water in this place:

9 For so was it charged me by the word of the LORD, saying, Eat no

nn3899   wcj,ptn3808   qmf8354   pl,nn4325   wcj,ptn3808   qmf7725   dfp,nn1870 pnl834   qpf1980

bread,   nor   drink water,   nor   turn again by the same   way   that thou camest.

wcs,qmf1980   aj312   pp,nn1870   qpf7725   wcj,ptn3808   dfp,nn1870 pnl834   qpf935

10 So he   went   another way,   and returned   not   by the   way   that he came

(pp,pnx) pr413   nn1008

to Bethel.

The Prophet Dies

qpta3427   nu259/aj2205   wcj,nn5030   pp,nn1008   nn,pnx1121 wcs,qmf935

11 Now there dwelt an   old   prophet in Bethel; and his   sons   came and

wcs,pimf5608   pp,pnx   (853) cs,nn3605   df,nn4639 pnl834   cs,nn376   df,pl,nn430   qpf6213   df,nn3117

told   him   all   the works that the man of God had done that day in

pp,nn1008 (853)   df,pl,nn1697 pnl834   pipf1696   pr413   df,nn4428   wcs,pimf,pnx5608

Bethel: the words which he had spoken unto the king, them they   told   also

pp,nn,pnx1

to their father.

nn,pnx1   wcs,pimf1696   pr,pnx413   pnit335/pndm2088 df,nn1870 qpf1980

12 And their father   said   unto   them,   What   way   went he? For his

pl,nn,pnx1121   wcs,qmf7200 (853) pnl834 df,nn1870   cs,nn376   df,pl,nn430 qpf1980   pnl834   qpf935   pr4480/nn3063

sons   had   seen   what way the man of God went, which came from Judah.

wcs,qmf559   pr413   pl,nn,pnx1121   qmv2280   pp,pnx   df,nn2543   wcs,qmf2280   pp,pnx

13 And he   said   unto his   sons,   Saddle me the ass.   So they saddled him

df,nn2543   wcs,qmf7392   pr,pnx5921

the ass: and he   rode   thereon,

wcs,qmf1980   pr310   cs,nn376   df,pl,nn430   wcs,qmf,pnx4672   qpta3427   pr8478   df,nn424

14 And   went   after the man of God,   and   found   him sitting under an oak:

wcs,qmf559   pr,pnx413   df,pnp859   cs,nn376   df,pl,nn430 pnl834   qpf935   pr4480   nn3063

and he   said   unto him, Art thou the man of God   that camest from Judah? And

wcs,qmf559 pnp589

he said,   I   am.

wcs,qmf559 pr,pnx413   qmv1980 df,nn,lh1004 pr,pnx854   wcj,qmv398   nn3899

15 Then he   said   unto him, Come home with me, and   eat   bread.

wcs,qmf559   qmf3201 ptn3808 pp,qnc7725   pr,pnx854   wcj,pp,qnc935 pr,pnx854   wcj,ptn3808

16 And he   said, I may not return with thee, nor   go in   with thee: neither

qmf398   nn3899   wcj,ptn3808 qmf8354 pl,nn4325 pr,pnx854   df,pndm2088 dfp,nn4725

will I eat bread   nor   drink water with thee in   this   place:

cj3588   nn1697 pr,pnx413   pp,cs,nn1697   nn3068   qmf398 ptn3808

17 For it was said   to   me by the   word   of the LORD, Thou shalt eat   no

nn3899   wcj,ptn3808   qmf8354 pl,nn4325 ad8033 ptn3808   qmf7725   pp,qnc1980   dfp,nn1870 pnl834

bread   nor   drink water there,   nor   turn again to   go   by the   way   that thou

qpf1980/pp,pnx

camest.

wcs,qmf559   pp,pnx   pnp589   nn5030   ad1571   pp,pnx   wcj,nn4397 pipf1696

18 He   said   unto him,   I   am a prophet also as thou art; and an angel spoke

pr,pnx413   pp,cs,nn1697   nn3068   pp,qnc559   himv,pnx7725   pr,pnx854   pr413

unto me by the   word   of the LORD, saying, Bring*him*back   with thee into thine

nn,pnx1004   wcj,qmf398   nn3899   wcj,qmf8354 pl,nn4325   pipf3584   pp,pnx

house, that he may   eat   bread and drink water. But he lied unto him.

wcs,qmf7725 pr,pnx854   wcs,qmf398 nn3899   pp,nn,pnx1004   wcs,qmf8354

19 So he went back with him, and did eat   bread in his house,   and drank

pl,nn4325

water.

_{wcs,qmf1961}   _{pnp1992}   _{pl,qpta3427} _{pr413}   _{df,nn7979}   _{cs,nn1697}

20 And it*came*to*pass, as they   sat   at the table, that the word of the

_{nn3068} _{wcs,qmf1961} _{pr413}   _{df,nn5030}   _{pnl834}   _{hipf,pnx7725}

LORD came unto the prophet that brought*him*back:

_{wcs,qmf7121}   _{pr413}   _{cs,nn376}   _{df,pl,nn430} _{pnl834} _{qpf935} _{pr4480}   _{nn3063}   _{pp,qnc559}   _{ad3541}

21 And he cried unto the man of God that came from Judah, saying, Thus

_{qpf559}   _{nn3068}   _{cj3282/cj3588}   _{qpf4784}   _{cs,nn6310}   _{nn3068}

saith the LORD, Forasmuch as thou hast disobeyed the mouth of the LORD, and hast

_{wcj,ptn3808 qpf8104} ₍₈₅₃₎   _{df,nn4687}   _{pnl834}   _{nn3068}   _{pl,nn,pnx430}   _{pipf,pnx6680}

not kept   the commandment which the LORD thy God   commanded thee,

_{wcs,qmf7725}   _{wcs,qmf398} _{nn3899}   _{wcs,qmf8354} _{pl,nn4325}   _{dfp,nn4725}

22 But camest back, and hast eaten bread and drunk water in the place, of

_{pnl834}   _{pipf1696} _{pr,pnx413}   _{qmf398 ptn408} _{nn3899}   _{qmf8354 wcj,ptn408} _{pl,nn4325}

the which the LORD did say   to thee, Eat no bread, and drink no water; thy

_{nn,pnx5038}   _{ptn3808} _{qmf935} _{pr413}   _{cs,nn6913}   _{pl,nn,pnx1}

carcass shall not come unto the sepulcher of thy fathers.

_{wcs,qmf1961}   _{pr310}   _{qnc,pnx398} _{nn3899}   _{wcj,pr310}   _{qnc,pnx8354}

23 And it*came*to*pass, after he had eaten bread, and after he had drunk,

_{wcs,qmf2280}   _{pp,pnx}   _{df,nn2543}   _{dfp,nn5030} _{pnl834}

that he saddled for him the   ass, to wit, for the prophet whom he had

_{hipf,pnx7725}

brought back.

_{wcs,qmf1980}   _{nn738} _{wcs,qmf,pnx4672}   _{dfp,nn1870}   _{wcs,himf,pnx4191}

24 And when he was gone, a lion   met   him by the way, and   slew

_{nn,pnx5038} _{wcs,qmf1961} _{hopt7993}   _{dfp,nn1870}   _{wcj,df,nn2543} _{qpta5975} _{pr,pnx681}

him: and his carcass was   cast in the way, and the   ass   stood by it, the

_{wcj,df,nn738} _{qpta5975} _{pr681}   _{df,nn5038}

lion also stood by the carcass.

_{wcj,ptdm2009} _{pl,nn376} _{pl,qpta5674}   _{wcs,qmf7200} ₍₈₅₃₎   _{df,nn5038} _{hopt7993}   _{dfp,nn1870}

25 And, behold, men passed by, and   saw   the carcass cast in the way,

_{wcj(853)}   _{df,nn738} _{qpta5975} _{pr681}   _{df,nn5038}   _{wcs,qmf935}   _{wcs,pimf1696}

and   the lion standing by the carcass: and they came and told it in the

_{dfp,nn5892} _{pnl834}   _{df,aj2205} _{df,nn5030} _{qpta3427/pp,pnx}

city   where the old prophet dwelt.

_{df,nn5030} _{pnl834}   _{hipf,pnx7725}   _{pr4480}   _{df,nn1870} _{wcs,qmf8085}

26 And when the prophet that brought*him*back from the way   heard thereof,

_{wcs,qmf559} _{pnp1931}   _{cs,nn376}   _{df,pl,nn430} _{pnl834}   _{qpf4784}   ₍₈₅₃₎   _{cs,nn6310}

he said,   It   is the man of God, who was disobedient unto   the word of the

_{nn3068}   _{nn3068}   _{wcs,qmf,pnx5414}   _{dfp,nn738}   _{wcs,qmf,pnx7665}

LORD: therefore the LORD hath delivered him unto the lion, which hath   torn

_{wcs,himf,pnx4191}   _{pp,cs,nn1697}   _{nn3068} _{pnl834}   _{pipf1696}

him, and   slain   him, according to the word of the LORD, which he spoke

_{pp,pnx}

unto him.

_{wcs,pimf1696} _{pr413}   _{pl,nn,pnx1121} _{pp,qnc559}   _{qmv2280}   _{pp,pnx} ₍₈₅₃₎   _{df,nn2543}

27 And he spoke to his sons, saying, Saddle me   the ass. And they

_{wcs,qmf2280}

saddled him.

_{wcs,qmf1980}   _{wcs,qmf4672} ₍₈₅₃₎   _{nn,pnx5038} _{hopt7993}   _{dfp,nn1870}   _{wcj,nn2543}

28 And he went and found   his carcass cast in the way, and the   ass

_{wcj,df,nn738} _{pl,qpta5975} _{pr681}   _{df,nn5038}   _{df,nn738}   _{ptn3808 qpf398} ₍₈₅₃₎   _{df,nn5038}

and the lion   standing by the carcass: the lion had not eaten   the carcass,

_{wcj,ptn3808 qpf7665} ₍₈₅₃₎   _{df,nn2543}

nor torn   the ass.

_{df,nn5030} _{wcs,qmf5375} ₍₈₅₃₎   _{cs,nn5038}   _{cs,nn376} _{df,pl,nn430} _{wcs,himf,pnx5117}

29 And the prophet took up   the carcass of the man of God, and   laid